Official
BASEBALL
REGISTER

1986 EDITION

Editor/Baseball Register
BARRY SIEGEL

Contributing Editors/Baseball Register
CRAIG CARTER
JOHN DUXBURY
BILL RABINOWITZ

President-Chief Executive Officer
RICHARD WATERS

Editor
TOM BARNIDGE

Director of Books and Periodicals
RON SMITH

Published by

The Sporting News

1212 North Lindbergh Boulevard
P.O. Box 56 — St. Louis, MO 63166

Copyright © 1986
The Sporting News Publishing Company

▼ A Times Mirror
◤ Company

ISBN 0-89204-208-7   ISSN 0067-4281

Table
of
CONTENTS

⚔☻⚔

Players included are those who played in at least one game in the major leagues in 1985, those who were part of a team's 40-man roster and selected invitees to spring training.

ON THE COVER: New York Yankee first baseman Don Mattingly, The Sporting News' Player of the Year, enjoyed an MVP 1985 season, hitting .324 with 35 home runs and a major league-high 145 runs batted in.

—Photo by John Biever/Focus West

EXPLANATION OF ABBREVIATIONS

G—Games played. Pos.—Position. AB—At Bats. R—Runs. H—Hits. 2B—Two-Base Hits. 3B—Three-Base Hits. HR—Home Runs. RBI—Runs Batted In. B.A.—Batting Average. PO—Putouts. A—Assists. E—Errors. F.A.—Fielding Average. IP—Innings Pitched. W—Won. L—Lost. Pct.—Percentage. R—Runs. ER—Earned Runs. SO—Strikeouts. BB —Bases on Balls. ERA—Earned-Run Average.

Players

*Denotes led league. ●Tied for lead. Mark before position (where more than one position is given) denotes where played as leader in department shown.

DONALD WILLIAM AASE

Name pronounced AH-see.

(Don)

Born September 8, 1954, at Orange, Calif.
Height, 6.03. Weight, 210.
Throws and bats righthanded.
Attended California State University, Fullerton, Calif.

Major League saves: 1979 (2), 1980 (2), 1981 (11), 1982 (4), 1984 (8), 1985 (14). Total—41.
Led International League pitchers in games started with 29 in 1975.
Led Carolina League pitchers in games started with 30, complete games with 18 and tied for lead in shutouts with 4 in 1974.
Named Carolina League Pitcher of the Year, 1974.

Year Club	League	G.	IP.	W.	L.	Pct.	H.	R.	ER.	SO.	BB.	ERA.
1972—Williamsport	NYP	12	62	0	*10	.000	60	48	40	40	34	5.81
1973—Winter Haven	Florida St.	29	170	12	●15	.444	153	82	68	127	73	3.60
1974—Winston-Salem	Carolina	32	*230	*17	8	.680	185	72	62	*176	84	*2.43
1975—Pawtucket	Int'national	29	186	8	13	.381	173	85	75	125	88	3.63
1976—Rhode Island†	Int'national	10	54	5	2	.714	42	23	20	40	34	3.33
1977—Pawtucket	Int'national	18	109	6	6	.500	118	67	61	64	60	5.04
1977—Boston‡	American	13	92	6	2	.750	85	36	32	49	19	3.13
1978—California	American	29	179	11	8	.579	185	88	80	93	80	4.02
1979—California	American	37	185	9	10	.474	200	104	99	96	77	4.82
1980—California	American	40	175	8	13	.381	193	83	79	74	66	4.06
1981—California	American	39	65	4	4	.500	56	17	17	38	24	2.35
1982—California§	American	24	52	3	3	.500	45	20	20	40	23	3.46
1983—California x	American					(Did not play)						
1984—Redwood y	California	4	12⅓	0	1	.000	9	9	7	10	7	5.11
1984—California z	American	23	39	4	1	.800	30	7	7	28	19	1.62
1985—Baltimore	American	54	88	10	6	.625	83	44	37	67	35	3.78
Major League Totals—8 Years		259	875	55	47	.539	877	399	371	485	343	3.82

Selected by Boston Red Sox' organization in 6th round of free-agent draft, June 6, 1972.
†On disabled list, June 23, 1976 through remainder of season.
‡Traded with cash to California Angels for Second Baseman Jerry Remy, December 8, 1977.
§On disabled list, June 3 to June 27 and July 20 to September 7, 1982.
xOn disabled list, March 30, 1983 through remainder of season.
yOn California disabled list, March 27 to June 13, 1984; included rehabilitation disability assignment to Redwood, May 10 to May 30, 1984.
zGranted free agency, November 8, 1984; signed by Baltimore Orioles, December 13, 1984.

CHAMPIONSHIP SERIES RECORD

Year Club	League	G.	IP.	W.	L.	Pct.	H.	R.	ER.	SO.	BB.	ERA.
1979—California	American	2	5	1	0	1.000	4	1	1	6	2	1.80

SHAWN WESLEY ABNER

Born June 17, 1966, at Hamilton, O.
Height, 6.01. Weight, 190.
Throws and bats righthanded.
Brother of Ben Abner, outfielder in Montreal Expos' organization.

Led Carolina League in total bases with 263, game-winning RBIs with 18 and slugging percentage with .485 in 1985.
Led Carolina League outfielders in total chances with 352 in 1985.
Named Carolina League Player of the Year, 1985.

Year Club	League	Pos.	G.	AB.	R.	H.	2B.	3B.	HR.	RBI.	B.A.	PO.	A.	E.	F.A.
1984—Kingsport	Appal.	OF	46	183	32	50	8	0	10	35	.273	87	1	1	.989
1984—Little Falls	NYP	OF	18	68	7	18	2	0	1	5	.265	40	2	1	.977
1985—Lynchburg	Carol.	OF	139	*542	71	*163	*30	*11	16	*89	.301	*332	8	12	.966

Selected by New York Mets' organization in 1st round (first player selected) of free-agent draft, June 4, 1984.

JOHNNY RAY ABREGO

Name pronounced Uh-BRAY-goh.

Born July 4, 1962, at Corpus Christi, Tex.
Height, 6.00. Weight, 185.
Throws and bats righthanded.

Pitched 1-0 no-hit victory against Nashua, August 1, 1985.
Led Northwest League in hit batsmen with 14 and tied for lead in games started by pitchers with 14 in 1983.
Tied for Eastern League lead in hit batsmen with 12 in 1985.

Year Club	League	G.	IP.	W.	L.	Pct.	H.	R.	ER.	SO.	BB.	ERA.
1981—Helena	Pioneer	12	67	3	4	.429	60	40	35	52	52	4.70
1982—Helena	Pioneer					(Did not play)						
1983—Bend†	Northwest	14	88⅓	7	5	.583	81	58	39	59	40	3.97

Year Club	League	G.	IP.	W.	L.	Pct.	H.	R.	ER.	SO.	BB.	ERA.
1984—Lodi	California	23	150⅓	9	9	.500	111	57	35	139	66	2.10
1984—Iowa	Am. Assoc.	5	26⅔	1	1	.500	28	16	15	17	9	5.06
1985—Iowa	Am. Assoc.	5	25	0	5	.000	29	24	22	12	15	7.92
1985—Pittsfield	Eastern	22	156⅓	6	6	.500	119	60	48	92	72	2.76
1985—Chicago	National	6	24	1	1	.500	32	18	17	13	12	6.38
Major League Totals—1 Year		6	24	1	1	.500	32	18	17	13	12	6.38

Selected by Philadelphia Phillies' organization in 1st round (20th player selected) of free-agent draft, June 11, 1981.
†Drafted by Chicago Cubs, December 5, 1983.

JAMES JUSTIN ACKER
(Jim)

Born September 24, 1958, at Freer, Tex.
Height, 6.02. Weight, 212.
Throws and bats righthanded.
Attended University of Texas, Austin, Tex.
Brother of Bill Acker, nose tackle with St. Louis Cardinals, Kansas City Chiefs, Cincinnati Bengals and Buffalo Bills, 1980 through 1984.
Major League saves: 1983 (1), 1984 (1), 1985 (10). Total—12.

Year Club	League	G.	IP.	W.	L.	Pct.	H.	R.	ER.	SO.	BB.	ERA.
1980—Bradenton Braves	Gulf Coast	1	5	1	0	1.000	1	0	0	5	0	0.00
1980—Savannah	Southern	13	95	5	5	.500	84	33	28	47	29	2.65
1981—Savannah	Southern	10	77	5	5	.500	57	34	23	37	34	2.69
1981—Richmond	Int'national	21	118	8	7	.533	112	63	55	72	74	4.19
1982—Savannah†‡	Southern	26	142	9	14	.391	120	96	70	96	86	4.44
1983—Toronto	American	38	97⅔	5	1	.833	103	52	47	44	38	4.33
1984—Toronto§	American	32	72	3	5	.375	79	39	35	33	25	4.38
1985—Toronto	American	61	86⅓	7	2	.778	86	35	31	42	43	3.23
Major League Totals—3 Years		131	256	15	8	.652	268	126	113	119	106	3.97

Selected by Atlanta Braves' organization in 1st round (21st player selected) of free-agent draft, June 3, 1980.
†On disabled list, April 9 to April 20, 1982.
‡Drafted by Toronto Blue Jays, December 6, 1982.
§On disabled list, August 16 to September 1, 1984.

CHAMPIONSHIP SERIES RECORD

Year Club	League	G.	IP.	W.	L.	Pct.	H.	R.	ER.	SO.	BB.	ERA.
1985—Toronto	American	2	6	0	0	.000	2	0	0	5	0	0.00

LARRY SCOTT ACKER

Born October 4, 1960, at Meadville, Pa.
Height, 6.03. Weight, 195.
Throws and bats lefthanded.

Year Club	League	G.	IP.	W.	L.	Pct.	H.	R.	ER.	SO.	BB.	ERA.
1980—Bradenton Pirates	Gulf Coast	2	4	0	0	.000	5	2	2	2	1	4.50
1980—Shelby	W. Carol.	12	43	1	3	.250	50	32	27	20	17	5.65
1981—Alexandria	Carolina	7	6	0	2	.000	11	9	5	3	5	7.50
1981—Greenwood	S. Atlantic	8	13	0	0	.000	19	11	9	11	5	6.23
1982—Greenwood†	S. Atlantic	26	181⅓	7	●15	.318	177	101	73	115	72	3.62
1983—Asheville	S. Atlantic	17	57	4	1	.800	58	22	18	38	12	2.84
1983—Columbus	Southern	1	6⅓	0	1	.000	8	3	3	1	1	4.26
1984—Columbus	Southern	28	198⅓	15	8	.652	★213	90	78	81	48	3.54
1985—Tucson	P. Coast	36	170	10	12	.455	★221	110	★103	80	68	5.45

Selected by Pittsburgh Pirates' organization in 37th round of free-agent draft, June 3, 1980.
†Released, April 5, 1983; signed by Sarasota Astros (Houston Astros' organization), June 7, 1983.

PATRICK RALPH ADAMS
(Pat)

Born June 12, 1959, at Detroit, Mich.
Height, 6.05. Weight, 205.
Throws and bats righthanded.
Received degree from University of Detroit, Detroit, Mich., in 1981.

Led Eastern League batters in strikeouts with 106, total bases with 234, game-winning RBIs with 17 and tied for lead in intentional bases on balls received with 8 in 1984.
Led Eastern League first basemen in total chances with 1,238 in 1984.
Named Eastern League Most Valuable Player, 1984.

Year Club	League	Pos.	G.	AB.	R.	H.	2B.	3B.	HR.	RBI.	B.A.	PO.	A.	E.	F.A.
1981—Sarasota W.S.	Gulf C.	1B-2B	15	45	6	13	3	0	1	9	.289	99	8	0	1.000
1981—Appleton	Midw.	1B	46	161	11	34	3	2	0	6	.211	408	21	3	.993
1982—Appleton	Midw.	1B-P	112	333	36	63	13	2	6	44	.189	859	69	9	.990
1983—Appleton	Midw.	1B	120	411	62	120	30	1	13	71	.292	897	★107	14	.986
1984—Glens Falls†	East.	1B	137	467	78	132	28	1	★24	★102	.283	1097	★131	10	.992
1985—Phoenix‡	P. C.	1B	116	401	47	105	19	1	11	63	.262	866	90	13	.987

Selected by Chicago White Sox' organization in 19th round of free-agent draft, June 8, 1981.
†Traded with Pitcher Mike Trujillo to San Francisco Giants, September 7, 1984, completing deal in which San Francisco traded Infielder Tom O'Malley to Chicago White Sox for two players to be named later, September 1, 1984.
‡On disabled list, April 11 to April 21, 1985.

PITCHING RECORD

Year Club	League	G.	IP.	W.	L.	Pct.	H.	R.	ER.	SO.	BB.	ERA.
1982—Appleton	Midwest	1	1⅓	0	0	.000	3	4	4	1	3	27.00

RICKY LEE ADAMS

Born January 21, 1959, at Upland, Calif.
Height, 6.02. Weight, 180.
Throws and bats righthanded.

Major League stolen bases: 1982 (1), 1983 (1), 1985 (1). Total—3.

Year Club	League	Pos.	G.	AB.	R.	H.	2B.	3B.	HR.	RBI.	B.A.	PO.	A.	E.	F.A.
1977—Sarasota Astros....	Gulf C.	SS	39	151	15	34	3	0	1	9	.225	54	132	19	.907
1978—Daytona Beach....	Fla. St.	SS-3B-2B	112	396	46	88	12	3	0	32	.222	181	378	45	.923
1979—Daytona Beach†..	Fla. St.	2B	107	305	31	89	12	2	0	26	.292	189	279	24	.951
1980—Salinas	Calif.	SS	15	56	5	14	2	0	0	4	.250	33	44	2	.975
1980—El Paso..................	Texas	SS-3B	92	382	68	112	16	0	12	53	.293	183	288	24	.952
1981—Holyoke.................	East.	2-S-1-O	120	446	85	117	11	3	10	48	.262	222	333	11	.981
1982—Holyoke.................	East.	2-S-1-O	60	227	37	69	9	4	4	28	.304	119	187	6	.981
1982—Spokane	P. C.	2B-SS-OF	71	248	42	77	10	3	6	33	.310	155	181	9	.974
1982—California..............	Amer.	SS	8	14	1	2	0	0	0	0	.143	6	12	1	.947
1983—California..............	Amer.	SS-3B-2B	58	112	22	28	2	0	2	6	.250	58	141	8	.961
1983—Edmonton.............	P. C.	2-3-O-S	54	208	38	65	10	4	6	38	.313	69	90	5	.970
1984—Edmonton‡...........	P. C.	S-O-3-2	105	370	67	106	24	9	6	48	.286	156	200	17	.954
1985—Phoenix	P. C.	SS-OF	42	154	22	47	8	3	4	31	.305	59	103	8	.953
1985—San Francisco	Nat.	SS-3B-2B	54	121	12	23	3	1	2	10	.190	35	101	5	.965
American League Totals—2 Years			66	126	23	30	2	0	2	6	.238	64	153	9	.960
National League Totals—1 Year..............			54	121	12	23	3	1	2	10	.190	35	101	5	.965
Major League Totals—3 Years..............			120	247	35	53	5	1	4	16	.215	99	254	14	.962

Selected by Houston Astros' organization in 1st round (14th player selected) of free-agent draft, June 7, 1977.
†Released, April 4, 1980; signed by Salinas (California Angels' organization), May 2, 1980.
‡Granted free agency, October 15, 1984; signed by Phoenix (San Francisco Giants' organization), December 25, 1984.

JAMES DAVID ADDUCI

Name pronounced Uh-DOO-see.

(Jim)

Born August 9, 1959, at Chicago, Ill.
Height, 6.04. Weight, 200.
Throws and bats lefthanded.
Attended Southern Illinois University, Carbondale, Ill.

Led American Association batters in game-winning RBIs with 14 and tied for lead in strikeouts with 103 in 1983.
Led Texas League in game-winning RBIs with 14 in 1982.
Tied for Pacific Coast League lead in errors by first basemen with 15 in 1985.

Year Club	League	Pos.	G.	AB.	R.	H.	2B.	3B.	HR.	RBI.	B.A.	PO.	A.	E.	F.A.
1980—Johnson City	Appal.	OF	17	63	15	21	4	0	5	16	.333	27	2	1	.967
1980—St. Petersburg.......	Fla. St.	OF	37	118	29	32	4	0	2	13	.271	62	3	2	.970
1981—St. Petersburg.......	Fla. St.	OF	92	321	44	87	12	7	7	45	.271	185	4	7	.964
1981—Arkansas...............	Texas	OF	40	131	16	36	8	3	5	14	.275	55	3	1	.983
1982—Arkansas...............	Texas	OF	121	392	64	117	28	5	22	92	.298	178	6	3	.984
1983—Louisville	A. A.	OF-1B	129	467	81	131	29	7	25	*101	.281	327	17	14	.961
1983—St. Louis...............	Nat.	1B-OF	10	20	0	1	0	0	0	0	.050	47	4	0	1.000
1984—Louisville†‡..........	A. A.	OF-1B	113	412	62	119	25	6	12	58	.289	252	13	5	.981
1985—Vancouver............	P. C.	1B-OF	112	393	63	109	28	2	20	77	.277	788	65	16	.982
Major League Totals—1 Year.................			10	20	0	1	0	0	0	0	.050	47	4	0	1.000

Selected by Philadelphia Phillies' organization in 28th round of free-agent draft, June 7, 1977.
Selected by St. Louis Cardinals' organization in 7th round of free-agent draft, June 3, 1980.
†On disabled list, April 25 to May 22, 1984.
‡Traded with Outfielder Paul Householder to Milwaukee Brewers for Pitchers Rich Buonantony and Jim Koontz and Infielder Ron Koenigsfeld, October 3, 1984.

MICHAEL TROY AFENIR

(Known by middle name.)

Born September 21, 1963, at Escondido, Calif.
Height, 6.04. Weight, 185.
Throws and bats righthanded.
Attended Palomar College, San Marcos, Calif.

Led South Atlantic League in passed balls with 32 in 1984.

Year Club	League	Pos.	G.	AB.	R.	H.	2B.	3B.	HR.	RBI.	B.A.	PO.	A.	E.	F.A.
1983—Sarasota Astros....	Gulf C.	C	27	89	16	26	5	1	5	24	.292	101	19	3	.976
1983—Auburn	NYP	C	7	26	2	3	0	0	0	0	.115	48	2	0	1.000
1984—Asheville...............	S. Atl.	C-1B	115	358	44	69	16	0	16	69	.193	656	61	12	.984
1985—Osceola.................	Fla. St.	*C-SS	99	323	38	80	19	1	6	41	.248	557	72	*16	.975

Selected by Chicago Cubs' organization in 1st round (second player selected) of free-agent draft, January 12, 1982.
Selected by Baltimore Orioles' organization in secondary phase of free-agent draft, June 7, 1982.
Selected by Houston Astros' organization in secondary phase of free-agent draft, January 11, 1983.

JUAN ROBERTO AGOSTO

Born February 23, 1958, at Rio Piedras, P.R.
Height, 6.02. Weight, 187.
Throws and bats lefthanded.

Major League saves: 1983 (7), 1984 (7), 1985 (1). Total—15.
Led Carolina League in balks with 4 in 1977 and 5 in 1978.

Year Club	League	G	IP	W	L	Pct.	H	R	ER	SO	BB	ERA.
1975—Winter Haven	Florida St.	6	28	0	4	.000	35	23	18	19	24	5.79
1975—Elmira	NYP	9	23	1	4	.200	27	37	22	22	34	8.61
1976—Winter Haven	Florida St.	28	107	5	11	.313	97	70	55	80	69	4.63
1977—Winston-Salem	Carolina	30	119	4	9	.308	128	106	79	98	*111	5.97
1978—Winter Haven	Florida St.	1	1	0	0	.000	5	2	2	0	0	27.00
1978—Winston-Salem†	Carolina	23	120	5	11	.313	114	76	51	74	89	3.83
1979—Puerto Rico‡	Int.-Amer.	10	31	3	2	.600	31	13	9	9	17	2.61
1980—Glens Falls	Eastern	8	22	1	0	1.000	26	18	17	8	18	6.95
1980—Appleton	Midwest	23	144	11	6	.647	118	60	43	93	52	2.69
1981—Edmonton	P. Coast	48	120	7	10	.412	128	61	52	57	49	3.90
1981—Chicago	American	2	6	0	0	.000	5	3	3	3	0	4.50
1982—Edmonton	P. Coast	50	95⅓	3	4	.429	101	63	53	39	49	5.00
1982—Chicago	American	1	2	0	0	.000	7	4	4	1	0	18.00
1983—Denver	Am. Assoc.	19	26	1	1	.800	19	8	6	19	10	2.08
1983—Chicago	American	39	41⅔	2	2	.500	41	20	19	29	11	4.10
1984—Chicago	American	49	55⅓	2	1	.667	54	20	19	26	34	3.09
1985—Chicago	American	54	60⅓	4	3	.571	45	27	24	39	23	3.58
1985—Buffalo	Am. Assoc.	6	12⅔	0	0	.000	13	3	3	11	2	2.13
Major League Totals—5 Years		145	165⅓	8	6	.571	152	74	69	98	68	3.76

Signed as free agent by Boston Red Sox' organization, August 29, 1974.
†Released, September 21, 1978; signed by Puerto Rico of Inter-American League, March 10, 1979.
‡Declared free agent when Inter-American League folded, June 15, 1979; signed by Chicago White Sox' organization, January 18, 1980.

CHAMPIONSHIP SERIES RECORD

Year Club	League	G	IP	W	L	Pct.	H	R	ER	SO	BB	ERA.
1983—Chicago	American	1	⅓	0	0	.000	0	0	0	0	0	0.00

LUIS AGUAYO (MURIEL)

Name pronounced Uh-GWY-oh.

Born March 13, 1959, at Vega Baja, P.R.
Height, 5.09. Weight, 190.
Throws and bats righthanded

Major League stolen bases: 1980 (1), 1981 (1), 1982 (1), 1985 (1). Total—4.
Led Carolina League second basemen in assists with 365, errors with 30 and fielding percentage with .953 in 1977.

Year Club	League	Pos.	G	AB	R	H	2B	3B	HR	RBI	B.A.	PO.	A	E	F.A.
1976—Spartanburg	W. Car.	2B	3	11	0	1	0	0	0	0	.091	5	2	1	.875
1976—Auburn	NYP	2B-3B-SS	51	197	27	49	9	2	0	23	.249	79	99	10	.947
1977—Peninsula	Carol.	2B-SS	130	497	73	127	28	2	9	41	.256	271	409	34	.952
1978—Reading	East.	SS-2B	115	378	49	74	19	5	4	33	.196	198	341	25	.956
1979—Oklahoma City	A. A.	SS-2B	113	370	54	101	21	1	8	46	.273	191	320	27	.950
1980—Philadelphia†	Nat.	2B-SS	20	47	7	13	1	2	1	8	.277	44	44	3	.967
1980—Oklahoma City‡	A. A.	SS	84	291	37	71	19	2	9	40	.244	154	268	*28	.938
1981—Philadelphia	Nat.	2B-SS-3B	45	84	11	18	4	0	1	7	.214	39	63	5	.953
1982—Philadelphia	Nat.	2B-SS-3B	50	56	11	15	1	2	3	7	.268	27	49	4	.950
1983—Philadelphia§	Nat.	SS	2	4	1	1	0	0	0	0	.250	3	0	0	1.000
1983—Portland	P. C.	SS-2B	71	229	38	65	14	3	5	33	.284	121	216	10	.971
1984—Philadelphia	Nat.	3B-2B-SS	58	72	15	20	4	0	3	11	.278	18	55	3	.161
1984—Portland	P. C.	SS	3	13	3	7	1	0	1	2	.538	6	7	1	.929
1985—Philadelphia	Nat.	SS-2B-3B	91	165	27	46	7	3	6	21	.279	92	158	9	.965
Major League Totals—6 Years			266	428	72	113	17	7	14	54	.264	223	369	24	.961

Signed as free agent by Philadelphia Phillies' organization, December 27, 1975.
†On disabled list, May 7 to May 22, 1980.
‡On disabled list, May 22 to August 30, 1980.
§On disabled list, March 23 to June 13, 1983.

DIVISION SERIES RECORD

Year Club	League	Pos.	G	AB	R	H	2B	3B	HR	RBI	B.A.	PO.	A	E	F.A.
1981—Philadelphia	Nat.	PR	2	0	1	0	0	0	0	0	.000	0	0	0	.000

RICHARD WARREN AGUILERA

Name pronounced Ag-ah-lair-uh.

(Rick)

Born December 31, 1961, at San Gabriel, Calif.
Height, 6.05. Weight, 195.
Throws and bats righthanded.
Attended Brigham Young University, Provo, Utah.

Tied for Carolina League lead in shutouts with 3 in 1984.
Tied for New York-Pennsylvania League lead in shutouts with 2 in 1983.

Year Club	League	G.	IP.	W.	L.	Pct.	H.	R.	ER.	SO.	BB.	ERA.
1983—Little Falls	NYP	16	104	5	6	.455	*109	55	43	84	26	3.72
1984—Lynchburg	Carolina	13	88⅓	8	3	.727	72	29	23	101	28	2.34
1984—Jackson†	Texas	11	67	4	4	.500	68	37	34	71	19	4.57
1985—Tidewater	Int'national	11	79	6	4	.600	64	24	22	55	17	2.51
1985—New York	National	21	122⅓	10	7	.588	118	49	44	74	37	3.24
Major League Totals—1 Year		21	122⅓	10	7	.588	118	49	44	74	37	3.24

Selected by St. Louis Cardinals' organization in 37th round of free-agent draft, June 3, 1980.
Selected by New York Mets' organization in 3rd round of free-agent draft, June 6, 1983.
†On disabled list, September 3 to September 15, 1985.

WILLIE MAYS AIKENS

Born October 14, 1954, at Seneca, S. C.
Height, 6.02. Weight, 225.
Throws right and bats lefthanded.
Attended South Carolina State College, Orangeburg, S.C.

Major League stolen bases: 1977 (1), 1979 (1), 1980 (1). Total—3.
Tied major league record for most consecutive games, home runs, bases filled (2), June 13 and 14, 1979.
Led American League in intentional bases on balls received with 12 in 1981.
Led Texas League in total bases with 285 in 1976.
Led Midwest League in sacrifice flies with 9 in 1975.

Year Club	League	Pos.	G.	AB.	R.	H.	2B.	3B.	HR.	RBI.	B.A.	PO.	A.	E.	F.A.
1975—Quad Cities	Midw.	1B	125	443	69	126	17	1	17	*91	.284	1038	53	*26	.977
1976—El Paso	Texas	1B	133	514	*99	163	24	4	*30	*117	.317	971	52	*20	.981
1977—Salt Lake City	P. C.	1B-C	77	295	62	99	23	2	14	73	.336	700	48	10	.987
1977—California	Amer.	1B	42	91	5	18	4	0	0	6	.198	94	8	3	.971
1978—Salt Lake City	P. C.	*1B-OF	133	470	82	153	19	0	*29	110	.326	1030	*83	*25	.978
1979—California†	Amer.	1B	116	379	59	106	18	0	21	81	.280	462	31	2	.996
1980—Kansas City	Amer.	1B	151	543	70	151	24	0	20	98	.278	1081	65	*12	.990
1981—Kansas City	Amer.	1B	101	349	45	93	16	0	17	53	.266	844	56	7	.992
1982—Kansas City‡	Amer.	1B	134	466	50	131	29	1	17	74	.281	1048	75	7	.994
1983—Kansas City §x	Amer.	1B	125	410	49	124	26	1	23	72	.302	884	64	11	.989
1984—Toronto	Amer.	1B	93	234	21	48	7	0	11	26	.205	12	1	0	1.000
1985—Toronto y	Amer.	DH	12	20	2	4	1	0	1	5	.200	0	0	0	.000
1985—Syracuse	Int.	1B	105	373	65	116	19	1	16	61	.311	200	16	3	.986
Major League Totals—8 Years			774	2492	301	675	125	2	110	415	.271	4425	300	42	.991

Selected by California Angels' organization in 1st round (second player selected) of free-agent draft, January 9, 1975.

†Traded with Shortstop Rance Mulliniks to Kansas City Royals for Outfielder Al Cowens, Shortstop Todd Cruz and a player to be named later, December 6, 1979; California Angels acquired Pitcher Craig Eaton to complete deal, April 1, 1980.

‡On disabled list, April 23 to May 8, 1982.

§On suspended list, December 15, 1983 through May 16, 1984.

xTraded to Toronto Blue Jays for Designated Hitter Jorge Orta, December 19, 1983.

yReleased, May 9, 1985; re-signed by Toronto Blue Jays' organization, May 19, 1985.

DIVISION SERIES RECORD

Year Club	League	Pos.	G.	AB.	R.	H.	2B.	3B.	HR.	RBI.	B.A.	PO.	A.	E.	F.A.
1981—Kansas City	Amer.	1B	3	9	0	3	0	0	0	0	.333	27	1	0	1.000

CHAMPIONSHIP SERIES RECORD

Year Club	League	Pos.	G.	AB.	R.	H.	2B.	3B.	HR.	RBI.	B.A.	PO.	A.	E.	F.A.
1980—Kansas City	Amer.	1B	3	11	0	4	0	0	0	2	.364	22	1	0	1.000

WORLD SERIES RECORD

Tied World Series record for most home runs, two consecutive innings (2), October 18, 1980 (first and second inning).

Year Club	League	Pos.	G.	AB.	R.	H.	2B.	3B.	HR.	RBI.	B.A.	PO.	A.	E.	F.A.
1980—Kansas City	Amer.	1B	6	20	5	8	0	1	4	8	.400	55	2	2	.966

DARREL WAYNE AKERFELDS

Born June 12, 1962, at Denver, Colo.
Height, 6.02. Weight, 210.
Throws and bats righthanded.
Attended Mesa College, Grand Junction, Colo., and
University of Arkansas, Fayetteville, Ark.

Tied for Midwest League lead in wild pitches with 19 in 1984.

Year Club	League	G.	IP.	W.	L.	Pct.	H.	R.	ER.	SO.	BB.	ERA.
1983—Bellingham†	Northwest	12	68⅓	5	3	.625	62	36	34	85	36	4.48
1984—Madison	Midwest	24	151	11	6	.647	156	86	74	137	74	4.41
1985—Huntsville‡	Southern	17	96⅓	9	6	.600	75	42	37	56	64	3.46

Selected by Atlanta Braves' organization in 9th round of free-agent draft, June 3, 1980.
Selected by Seattle Mariners' organization in 1st round (seventh player selected) of free-agent draft, June 6, 1983.
†Traded to Oakland A's, December 7, 1983, completing deal in which Seattle Mariners traded Pitcher Bill Caudill and a player to be named later to Oakland for Pitcher Dave Beard and Catcher Bob Kearney, November 21, 1983.
‡On disabled list, May 22 to June 13 and July 5 to August 20, 1985.

MICHAEL PETER ALDRETE
(Mike)

Born January 29, 1961, at Carmel, Calif.
Height, 5.11. Weight, 180.
Throws and bats lefthanded.
Received bachelor of arts degree in communication from
Stanford University, Stanford, Calif.

Led California League in total bases with 225 in 1984.

Year Club	League	Pos.	G.	AB.	R.	H.	2B.	3B.	HR.	RBI.	B.A.	PO.	A.	E.	F.A.
1983—Great Falls	Pion.	1B-OF	38	132	30	55	11	2	4	31	.417	257	17	4	.986
1983—Fresno	Calif.	1B	20	68	5	14	4	0	1	12	.206	189	9	2	.990
1984—Fresno	Calif.	1B	136	457	89	155	28	3	12	72	.339	1180	74	8	*.994
1985—Shreveport	Texas	1B-OF	127	441	80	147	32	1	15	77	.333	854	41	9	.990
1985—Phoenix	P. C.	OF	3	8	0	1	1	0	0	1	.125	3	0	0	1.000

Selected by San Francisco Giants' organization in 7th round of free-agent draft, June 6, 1983.

JAY ROBERT ALDRICH

Born April 14, 1961, at Alexandria, La.
Height, 6.03. Wight, 205.
Throws and bats righthanded.
Attended Monclair State College, Upper Montclair, N.J.

Tied for California League lead in intentional bases on balls issued with 10 in 1984.

Year Club	League	G.	IP.	W.	L.	Pct.	H.	R.	ER.	SO.	BB.	ERA.
1982—Pikeville	Ap'lachian	11	53⅔	1	2	.333	44	33	25	37	28	4.19
1983—Beloit	Midwest	28	103⅔	7	4	.636	114	59	48	96	35	4.17
1984—Stockton	California	54	105⅔	11	●14	.440	107	46	34	78	44	2.90
1985—El Paso	Texas	42	63⅓	4	1	.800	61	28	25	35	13	3.55

Selected by Milwaukee Brewers' organization in 10th round of free-agent draft, June 7, 1982.

DOYLE LAFAYETTE ALEXANDER

Born September 4, 1950, at Cordova, Ala.
Height, 6.03. Weight, 200.
Throws and bats righthanded.
Attended Jefferson State Junior College, Birmingham, Ala.

Major League saves: 1972 (2), 1975 (1). Total—3.

Year Club	League	G.	IP.	W.	L.	Pct.	H.	R.	ER.	SO.	BB.	ERA.
1968—Tri-City	Northwest	13	70	3	*9	.250	66	47	32	58	47	4.11
1969—Daytona Beach	Florida St.	30	185	13	9	.591	154	75	56	140	100	2.72
1969—Albuquerque	Texas	3	15	0	3	.000	19	10	10	3	12	6.00
1970—Albuquerque	Texas	10	80	4	3	.571	72	29	28	60	20	3.15
1970—Spokane	P. Coast	19	137	9	7	.563	137	66	55	78	26	3.61
1971—Spokane	P. Coast	15	110	6	3	.667	114	49	42	65	31	3.44
1971—Los Angeles†	National	17	92	6	6	.500	105	45	39	30	18	3.82
1972—Baltimore	American	35	106	6	8	.429	78	36	29	49	30	2.46
1973—Baltimore‡	American	29	175	12	8	.600	169	85	75	63	52	3.86
1974—Baltimore	American	30	114	6	9	.400	127	65	51	40	43	4.03
1975—Baltimore	American	32	133	8	8	.500	127	47	45	46	47	3.05
1976—Baltimore§-New York x	American	30	201	13	9	.591	172	81	75	58	63	3.36
1977—Texas	American	34	237	17	11	.607	221	103	96	82	82	3.65
1978—Texas	American	31	191	9	10	.474	198	84	82	81	71	3.86
1979—Texas y	American	23	113	5	7	.417	114	65	56	50	69	4.46
1980—Atlanta z	National	35	232	14	11	.560	227	120	108	114	74	4.19
1981—San Francisco a	National	24	152	11	7	.611	156	51	49	77	44	2.90
1982—Fort Lauderdale	Florida St.	2	11	0	1	.000	12	5	5	4	2	4.09
1982—New York bc	American	16	66⅔	1	7	.125	81	52	45	26	14	6.08
1982—Columbus	Int'national	1	3⅔	0	0	.000	5	4	4	1	2	9.82
1983—New York d-Toronto	American	25	145	7	8	.467	157	76	71	63	33	4.41
1983—Kinston	Carolina	1	6	0	0	.000	3	0	0	4	0	0.00
1984—Toronto	American	36	261⅓	17	6	*.739	238	99	91	139	59	3.13
1985—Toronto	American	36	260⅔	17	10	.630	268	105	100	142	67	3.45
National League Totals—3 Years		76	476	31	24	.564	488	216	196	221	136	3.71
American League Totals—12 Years		357	2004	118	101	.539	1950	898	816	839	630	3.66
Major League Totals—15 Years		433	2480	149	125	.544	2438	1114	1012	1060	766	3.67

Selected by Los Angeles Dodgers' organization in 44th round of free-agent draft, June 7, 1968.

†Traded with Pitcher Bob O'Brien, Catcher Sergio Robles and First Baseman-Outfielder Royle Stillman to Baltimore Orioles for Pitcher Pete Richert and Outfielder Frank Robinson, December 2, 1971.

‡On disabled list, July 10 to August 6, 1973.

§Traded with Pitchers Ken Holtzman and Grant Jackson, Catcher Elrod Hendricks and Pitcher Jimmy Freeman to New York Yankees for Pitchers Rudy May, Tippy Martinez, Dave Pagan, Scott McGregor and Catcher Rick Dempsey, June 15, 1976.

xPlayed out option year and granted free agency, November 1, 1976; signed as free agent by Texas Rangers, November 23, 1976.

yTraded with Shortstop Larvell Blanks to Atlanta Braves for Pitcher Adrian Devine, Shortstop Pepe Frias and a player to be named later, December 7, 1979; Atlanta received $50,000 to complete deal when Outfielder Jeff Burroughs exercised no-trade clause.

zTraded to San Francisco Giants for Pitcher John Montefusco and Outfielder Craig Landis, December 12, 1980.

aTraded to New York Yankees for Pitcher Andy McGaffigan and Outfielder Ted Wilborn, March 30, 1982.

bOn disabled list, May 10 to July 8, 1982; included rehabilitation disability assignment to Columbus, June 22 to July 8, 1982.
cOn disabled list, August 11 to September 10, 1982.
dReleased, May 31, 1983; signed by Toronto Blue Jays' organization, June 21, 1983.

CHAMPIONSHIP SERIES RECORD

Established American League Championship Series record for most runs and most earned runs allowed, seven-game Series (10), 1985.

Year Club	League	G.	IP.	W.	L.	Pct.	H.	R.	ER.	SO.	BB.	ERA.
1973—Baltimore	American	1	3⅔	0	1	.000	5	3	2	1	0	4.91
1985—Toronto	American	2	10⅓	0	1	.000	14	10	10	9	3	8.71
Championship Series Total—2 Years		3	14	0	2	.000	19	13	12	10	3	7.71

WORLD SERIES RECORD

Year Club	League	G.	IP.	W.	L.	Pct.	H.	R.	ER.	SO.	BB.	ERA.
1976—New York	American	1	6	0	1	.000	9	5	5	1	2	7.50

ANDREW NEAL ALLANSON
(Andy)

Born December 22, 1961, at Richmond, Va.
Height, 6.05. Weight, 220.
Throws and bats righthanded.
Attended University of Richmond, Richmond, Va.

Year Club	League	Pos.	G.	AB.	R.	H.	2B.	3B.	HR.	RBI.	B.A.	PO.	A.	E.	F.A.
1983—Waterloo	Midw.	C	17	50	4	10	0	0	0	0	.200	99	8	3	.973
1983—Batavia	NYP	C	51	145	27	38	3	0	0	6	.262	372	27	5	.988
1984—Buffalo†	East.	C	39	111	12	28	4	0	0	11	.252	154	15	3	.983
1984—Waterloo	Midw.	C	46	144	14	39	5	0	0	10	.271	68	9	1	.987
1985—Waterbury	East.	C	120	420	69	131	17	1	0	47	★.312	578	64	10	.985

Selected by Cleveland Indians' organization in 2nd round of free-agent draft, June 6, 1983.
†On disabled list, June 19 to June 29, 1984.

EDWARD ANTHONY ALLEN
(Ed)

Born June 13, 1964, at Torrance, Calif.
Height, 6.03. Weight, 190.
Throws and bats righthanded.
Led Florida State League outfielders in double plays with 6 in 1985.

Year Club	League	Pos.	G.	AB.	R.	H.	2B.	3B.	HR.	RBI.	B.A.	PO.	A.	E.	F.A.
1982—Sarasota Royals	Gulf C.	OF	37	150	32	46	0	3	0	13	.307	69	3	7	.911
1983—Charleston	S. Atl.	OF	53	153	18	21	2	0	0	10	.137	97	2	4	.961
1983—Butte	Pion.	OF	62	227	41	56	1	3	2	28	.247	98	7	4	.963
1984—Fort Myers	Fla. St.	OF	136	412	64	106	4	3	0	42	.257	298	10	5	.984
1985—Fort Myers	Fla. St.	OF	72	256	40	78	11	5	1	35	.305	171	9	3	.984
1985—Memphis	South.	OF	46	143	12	29	4	1	2	15	.203	83	4	4	.956

Selected by Kansas City Royals' organization in 3rd round of free-agent draft, June 7, 1982.

JAMES BRADLEY ALLEN
(Jamie)

Born May 29, 1958, at Yakima, Wash.
Height, 6.00. Weight, 205.
Throws and bats righthanded.
Attended Arizona State University, Tempe, Ariz.
Major League stolen bases: 1983 (6).
Led Pacific Coast League in sacrifice hits with 11 and grounding into double plays with 24 in 1982.

Year Club	League	Pos.	G.	AB.	R.	H.	2B.	3B.	HR.	RBI.	B.A.	PO.	A.	E.	F.A.
1979—Bellingham	N'west	DH	21	85	11	14	3	0	1	13	.165	0	0	0	.000
1980—Lynn	East.	3B-SS	120	446	60	128	24	7	6	56	.287	95	214	27	.920
1981—Spokane†	P. C.	3B	22	61	3	12	3	0	0	8	.197	17	20	7	.868
1982—Salt Lake City	P. C.	★3B-SS	135	496	73	139	22	5	3	65	.280	106	271	★29	.929
1983—Salt Lake City	P. C.	3B	20	65	15	22	6	1	3	13	.338	12	38	4	.926
1983—Seattle	Amer.	3B	86	273	23	61	10	0	4	21	.223	55	155	9	.959
1984—Salt Lake City	P. C.	1B-SS-3B	124	472	69	136	23	4	6	67	.288	986	107	16	.986
1985—Calgary‡	P. C.	3-1-S-2	90	315	41	77	19	0	11	50	.244	262	178	24	.948
Major League Totals—1 Year			86	273	23	61	10	0	4	21	.223	55	155	9	.959

Selected by Minnesota Twins' organization in 1st round (10th player selected) of free-agent draft, June 8, 1976.
Selected by Seattle Mariners' organization in 2nd round of free-agent draft, June 5, 1979.
†On disabled list, April 15 to May 18 and June 11, 1981 through remainder of season.
‡Granted free agency, October 15, 1985.

NEIL PATRICK ALLEN

Born January 24, 1958, at Kansas City, Kan.
Height, 6.02. Weight, 190.
Throws and bats righthanded.

Major League saves: 1979 (8), 1980 (22), 1981 (18), 1982 (19), 1983 (2), 1984 (3), 1985 (3). Total—75.
Tied for Carolina League lead in complete games with 11 in 1977.

Year	Club	League	G.	IP.	W.	L.	Pct.	H.	R.	ER.	SO.	BB.	ERA.
1976—Marion	Ap'lachian	6	33	2	0	1.000	23	8	7	29	6	1.91
1976—Wausau	Midwest	6	48	4	2	.667	51	27	20	34	20	3.75
1977—Lynchburg†	Carolina	20	142	10	2	.833	136	55	44	*126	43	2.79
1978—Jackson	Texas	16	120	5	9	.357	88	38	28	111	38	*2.10
1978—Tidewater	Int'national	10	57	2	7	.222	65	35	28	30	12	4.42
1979—New York‡	National	50	99	6	10	.375	100	46	39	65	47	3.55
1980—New York	National	59	97	7	10	.412	87	43	40	79	40	3.71
1981—New York	National	43	67	7	6	.538	64	26	22	50	26	2.96
1982—New York	National	50	64⅔	3	7	.300	65	22	22	59	30	3.06
1983—New York§-St. Louis	National	46	175⅔	12	13	.480	179	84	77	106	84	3.94
1984—St. Louis	National	57	119	9	6	.600	105	54	47	66	49	3.55
1985—St. Louis x	National	23	29	1	4	.200	32	22	18	10	17	5.59
1985—New York	American	17	29⅓	1	0	1.000	26	9	9	16	13	2.76
National League Totals—7 Years		328	651⅓	45	56	.446	632	297	265	435	293	3.66
American League Totals—1 Year		17	29⅓	1	0	1.000	26	9	9	16	13	2.76
Major League Totals—7 Years		345	680⅔	46	56	.451	658	306	274	451	306	3.62

Selected by New York Mets' organization in 11th round of free-agent draft, June 8, 1976.
†On disabled list, July 26 to September 1, 1977.
‡On disabled list, June 1 to June 25, 1979.
§Traded with Pitcher Rick Ownbey to St. Louis Cardinals for First Baseman Keith Hernandez, June 15, 1983.
xTraded to New York Yankees for a player to be named later, July 17, 1985.

GARY MARTIN ALLENSON

Born February 4, 1955, at Culver City, Calif.
Height, 5.11. Weight, 185.
Throws and bats righthanded.
Attended Arizona State University, Tempe, Ariz.

Major League stolen bases: 1979 (1), 1980 (2). Total—3.
Led International League catchers in putouts with 735 and assists with 86 in 1978.
Named International League Most Valuable Player, 1978.

Year	Club	League	Pos.	G.	AB.	R.	H.	2B.	3B.	HR.	RBI.	B.A.	PO.	A.	E.	F.A.
1976—Bristol	East.	C	50	160	18	38	7	0	1	20	.238	190	36	6	.974
1977—Winter Haven	Fla. St.	C	105	312	42	83	18	4	5	43	.266	474	*80	6	*.989
1977—Pawtucket	Int.	C-1B	3	8	1	2	0	0	1	2	.250	4	1	0	1.000
1978—Pawtucket	Int.	C-1B	133	445	82	133	31	3	20	76	.299	763	90	7	.992
1979—Boston	Amer.	C-3B	108	241	27	49	10	2	3	22	.203	410	42	9	.980
1980—Boston	Amer.	C-3B	36	70	9	25	6	0	0	10	.357	100	8	2	.982
1981—Boston†	Amer.	C	47	139	23	31	8	0	5	25	.223	235	18	8	.969
1982—Boston	Amer.	C	92	264	25	54	11	0	6	33	.205	454	39	4	.992
1983—Boston	Amer.	C	84	230	19	53	11	0	3	30	.230	393	29	7	.984
1984—Boston‡	Amer.	C	35	83	9	19	2	0	2	8	.229	135	12	2	.987
1985—Syracuse	Int.	C	62	205	21	51	10	0	6	22	.249	340	30	4	.989
1985—Toronto§	Amer.	C	14	34	2	4	1	0	0	3	.118	39	2	0	1.000
Major League Totals—7 Years		416	1061	114	235	49	2	19	131	.221	1766	150	32	.984

Selected by Boston Red Sox' organization in 9th round of free-agent draft, June 8, 1976.
†On disabled list, May 12 to June 6, 1981.
‡Granted free agency, November 8, 1984; signed by Toronto Blue Jays' organization, February 25, 1985.
§Released, August 24, 1985.

WILLIAM FRANCIS ALMON
(Bill)

Born November 21, 1952, at Providence, R. I.
Height, 6.03. Weight, 170.
Throws and bats righthanded.
Received bachelor of arts degree from Brown University, Providence, R. I., in 1979.
Brother of John Almon, outfielder in San Diego Padres' organization, 1977 through 1979.

Major League stolen bases: 1974 (1), 1976 (3), 1977 (20), 1978 (17), 1979 (6), 1980 (2), 1981 (16), 1982 (10), 1983 (26), 1984 (5), 1985 (10). Total—116.
Led National League in sacrifice hits with 20 in 1977.
Led National League shortstops in total chances with 882 in 1977.
Led Pacific Coast League shortstops in total chances with 792 in 1975.
Tied for Pacific Coast League lead in stolen bases with 33 in 1975.
Named College Player of the Year by THE SPORTING NEWS, 1974.
Received reported $100,000 bonus to sign with San Diego Padres, 1974.
Named shortstop on THE SPORTING NEWS College Baseball All-America Team, 1974.

Year	Club	League	Pos.	G.	AB.	R.	H.	2B.	3B.	HR.	RBI.	B.A.	PO.	A.	E.	F.A.
1974—Hawaii	P. C.	SS	14	36	6	8	0	0	0	3	.222	16	33	7	.875
1974—Alexandria	Texas	SS	25	97	9	18	2	2	0	5	.186	48	70	8	.937
1974—San Diego	Nat.	SS	16	38	4	12	1	0	0	3	.316	13	30	4	.915
1975—Hawaii	P. C.	SS	•144	496	76	113	22	0	1	47	.228	*288	456	*48	.939
1975—San Diego	Nat.	SS	6	10	0	4	0	0	0	0	.400	6	5	0	1.000
1976—Hawaii	P. C.	SS	129	454	67	132	16	2	3	44	.291	*248	395	*36	.947
1976—San Diego	Nat.	SS	14	57	6	14	3	0	1	6	.246	23	52	3	.962
1977—San Diego	Nat.	SS	155	613	75	160	18	11	2	43	.261	*303	538	*41	.954

Year Club	League	Pos.	G.	AB.	R.	H.	2B.	3B.	HR.	RBI.	B.A.	PO.	A.	E.	F.A.
1978—San Diego	Nat.	3B-SS-2B	138	405	39	102	19	2	0	21	.252	102	255	23	.939
1979—San Diego†	Nat.	2B-SS-OF	100	198	20	45	3	0	1	8	.227	142	193	7	.980
1980—Mtl.‡-N.Y.§	Nat.	SS-2B-3B	66	150	15	29	4	3	0	7	.193	79	134	12	.947
1981—Chicago	Amer.	SS	103	349	46	105	10	2	4	41	.301	190	340	17	.969
1982—Chicago x	Amer.	SS	111	308	40	79	10	4	4	26	.256	164	317	●26	.949
1983—Oakland	Amer.	S-3-1-O-2	143	451	45	120	29	1	4	63	.266	327	176	20	.962
1984—Oakland y	Amer.	O-1-3-S-C	106	211	24	47	11	0	7	16	.223	255	15	2	.993
1985—Pittsburgh.............	Nat.	S-O-1-3	88	244	33	66	17	0	6	29	.270	104	108	5	.977
National League Totals—8 Years............			583	1715	192	432	65	16	10	117	.252	772	1315	95	.956
American League Totals—4 Years			463	1319	155	351	60	7	19	146	.266	936	848	65	.965
Major League Totals—12 Years...............			1046	3034	347	783	125	23	29	263	.258	1708	2163	160	.960

Selected by San Diego Padres' organization in 10th round of free-agent draft, June 8, 1971.
Selected by San Diego Padres' organization in 1st round (first player selected) of free-agent draft, June 5, 1974.
†Traded with First Baseman-Outfielder Dan Briggs to Montreal Expos for Second Baseman Dave Cash, November 27, 1979.
‡Became free agent after refusing option to Denver, July 7, 1980; signed by New York Mets, July 11, 1980.
§Released, December 19, 1980; signed by Chicago White Sox' organization, February 4, 1981.
xGranted free agency, November 10, 1982; signed by Oakland A's, January 18, 1983.
yGranted free agency, November 8, 1984; signed by Pittsburgh Pirates, April 8, 1985.

EDWARD ALLEN AMELUNG
(Ed)

Born April 13, 1959, at Fullerton, Calif.
Height, 6.00. Weight, 185.
Throws and bats lefthanded.
Attended Santa Ana College, Santa Ana, Calif., and San Diego State University, San Diego, Calif.

Major League stolen bases: 1984 (3).
Led Florida State League in total bases with 224 in 1981.

Year Club	League	Pos.	G.	AB.	R.	H.	2B.	3B.	HR.	RBI.	B.A.	PO.	A.	E.	F.A.
1981—Vero Beach	Fla. St.	OF	★136	★522	84	★155	17	★14	8	75	.297	237	★22	★13	.952
1981—San Antonio..........	Texas	OF	4	15	1	2	0	0	0	1	.133	9	0	0	1.000
1982—San Antonio..........	Texas	OF	135	529	96	160	27	4	24	91	.302	301	17	7	.978
1982—Albuquerque	P. C.	OF	2	9	1	2	0	0	0	2	.222	5	0	0	1.000
1983—Albuquerque	P. C.	OF	135	534	90	157	37	8	10	85	.294	256	15	7	.975
1984—Albuquerque	P. C.	OF	107	433	89	152	35	4	15	63	.351	216	8	3	.987
1984—Los Angeles	Nat.	OF	34	46	7	10	0	0	0	4	.217	31	0	0	1.000
1985—Albuquerque	P. C.	OF	137	561	70	163	29	3	8	61	.291	288	★17	5	.984
Major League Totals—1 Year..................			34	46	7	10	0	0	0	4	.217	31	0	0	1.000

Signed as free agent by Los Angeles Dodgers' organization, August 20, 1980.

LARRY EUGENE ANDERSEN

Born May 6, 1953, at Portland, Ore.
Height, 6.03. Weight, 205.
Throws and bats righthanded.
Attended Bellevue Community College, Bellevue, Wash.

Pitched 6-0 no-hit victory against Victoria, June 1, 1974.
Major League saves: 1981 (5), 1982 (1), 1984 (4), 1985 (3). Total—13.
Led Pacific Coast League in saves with 25 in 1978 and 22 in 1983.
Led American Association in balks with 4 in 1975.

Year Club	League	G.	IP.	W.	L.	Pct.	H.	R.	ER.	SO.	BB.	ERA.
1971—Reno	California	7	24	1	0	1.000	37	20	18	10	9	6.75
1971—Sarasota Indians...........................	Gulf Coast	4	15	0	3	.000	15	7	5	10	7	3.00
1972—Reno	California	27	124	4	14	.222	166	102	90	79	57	6.53
1973—Reno	California	29	164	10	8	.556	173	91	72	115	67	3.95
1974—San Antonio...................................	Texas	25	169	10	6	.625	176	84	72	64	51	3.83
1975—Oklahoma City	Am. Assoc.	25	156	10	11	.476	179	87	73	64	52	4.21
1975—Cleveland......................................	American	3	6	0	0	.000	4	3	3	4	2	4.50
1976—Toledo	Int'national	6	23	0	2	.000	47	33	33	8	6	12.91
1976—Williamsport................................	Eastern	21	133	9	6	.600	117	47	40	74	34	2.71
1977—Toledo†	Int'national	45	65	5	6	.455	52	20	14	40	37	1.94
1977—Cleveland......................................	American	11	14	0	1	.000	10	7	5	8	9	3.21
1978—Portland..	P. Coast	57	99	10	7	.588	92	42	38	65	45	3.45
1979—Tacoma	P. Coast	27	112	10	6	.625	124	59	50	52	32	4.02
1979—Cleveland‡....................................	American	8	17	0	0	.000	25	14	14	7	4	7.41
1980—Portland§......................................	P. Coast	52	93	5	7	.417	78	24	18	65	16	1.74
1981—Seattle	American	41	68	3	3	.500	57	27	20	40	18	2.65
1982—Seattle x	American	40	79⅔	0	0	.000	100	56	53	32	23	5.99
1982—Salt Lake City y	P. Coast	5	6⅔	1	0	1.000	2	0	0	8	3	0.00
1983—Portland..	P. Coast	52	70⅓	7	8	.467	63	35	16	64	30	2.05
1983—Philadelphia	National	17	26⅓	1	0	1.000	19	7	7	14	9	2.39
1984—Philadelphia	National	64	90⅔	3	7	.300	85	32	24	54	25	2.38
1985—Philadelphia	National	57	73	3	3	.500	78	41	35	50	26	4.32
American League Totals—5 Years		103	184⅔	3	4	.429	196	107	95	91	56	4.63
National League Totals—3 Years........................		138	190	7	10	.412	182	80	66	118	60	3.13
Major League Totals—8 Years.............................		241	374⅓	10	14	.417	378	187	161	209	116	3.87

Selected by Cleveland Indians' organization in 7th round of free-agent draft, June 8, 1971.
†Appeared as first baseman with no chances.
‡Traded to Pittsburgh Pirates for Outfielder Larry Littleton and Pitcher John Burden, December 21, 1979.
§Traded to Seattle Mariners, October 29, 1980, completing deal in which Seattle traded Pitcher Odell Jones to Pittsburgh Pirates for a player to be named later, April 1, 1980.
xOn disabled list, August 11 to September 1, 1982; included rehabilitation disability assignment to Salt Lake City, August 11 to August 31, 1982.
yLoaned to Portland (Philadelphia Phillies' organization), April 1, 1983; sold to Philadelphia Phillies, July 29, 1983.

WORLD SERIES RECORD

Year Club	League	G.	IP.	W.	L.	Pct.	H.	R.	ER.	SO.	BB.	ERA.
1983—Philadelphia	National	2	4	0	0	.000	4	1	1	1	0	2.25

ALLAN LEE ANDERSON

Born January 7, 1964, at Lancaster, Ohio.
Height, 5.11. Weight, 169.
Throws and bats lefthanded.
Led California League in shutouts with 5 in 1984.

Year Club	League	G.	IP.	W.	L.	Pct.	H.	R.	ER.	SO.	BB.	ERA.
1983—Wisconsin Rapids	Midwest	7	30⅓	0	4	.000	36	28	23	46	17	6.82
1983—Elizabethton	Ap'lachian	6	12⅔	1	3	.250	17	12	12	12	7	8.53
1984—Visalia	California	26	188⅔	12	7	.632	152	80	60	151	105	2.86
1005—Toledo	Int'national	27	176	7	11	.389	176	81	67	94	79	3.43

Selected by Minnesota Twins' organization in 2nd round of free-agent draft, June 7, 1982.

DAVID CARTER ANDERSON
(Dave)

Born August 1, 1960, at Louisville, Ky.
Height, 6.02. Weight, 185.
Throws and bats righthanded.
Attended Memphis State University, Memphis, Tenn.
Major League stolen bases: 1983 (6), 1984 (15), 1985 (5). Total—26.
Led Pacific Coast League shortstops in double plays with 81 in 1982.

Year Club	League	Pos.	G.	AB.	R.	H.	2B.	3B.	HR.	RBI.	B.A.	PO.	A.	E.	F.A.
1981—Vero Beach	Fla. St.	SS	65	200	44	54	8	1	0	18	.270	109	218	23	.934
1982—Albuquerque	P. C.	SS	132	507	100	174	19	7	5	76	.343	223	397	★34	.948
1983—Albuquerque	P. C.	SS	9	27	10	11	1	1	0	3	.407	17	26	1	.977
1983—Los Angeles	Nat.	SS-3B	61	115	12	19	4	2	1	2	.165	56	100	5	.969
1984—Los Angeles	Nat.	SS-3B	121	374	51	94	16	2	3	34	.251	176	359	19	.966
1985—Los Angeles†	Nat.	3B-SS-2B	77	221	24	44	6	0	4	18	.199	61	187	9	.965
1985—Albuquerque	P. C.	SS-3B-2B	28	97	23	28	7	0	3	16	.289	29	62	11	.892
Major League Totals—3 Years			259	710	87	157	26	4	8	54	.221	293	646	33	.966

Selected by Los Angeles Dodgers' organization in 1st round (22nd player selected) of free-agent draft, June 8, 1981.
†On disabled list, April 29 to June 2 and July 31 to September 1, 1985; included rehabilitation disability assignment to Albuquerque, May 17 to June 1 and August 17 to August 31, 1985.

CHAMPIONSHIP SERIES RECORD

Year Club	League	Pos.	G.	AB.	R.	H.	2B.	3B.	HR.	RBI.	B.A.	PO.	A.	E.	F.A.
1985—Los Angeles	Nat.	PR-SS-3B	4	5	1	0	0	0	0	0	.000	3	4	0	1.000

JAMES LEA ANDERSON
(Jim)

Born February 23, 1957, at Los Angeles, Calif.
Height, 6.00. Weight, 170.
Throws and bats righthanded.
Major League stolen bases: 1979 (3), 1980 (2), 1981 (3), 1983 (1). Total—9.
Tied for American Association lead in sacrifice flies with 7 in 1985.
Led Texas League shortstops in double plays with 93 in 1977.

Year Club	League	Pos.	G.	AB.	R.	H.	2B.	3B.	HR.	RBI.	B.A.	PO.	A.	E.	F.A.
1975—Idaho Falls	Pion.	★SS-2B	71	253	42	73	3	6	0	27	.289	●94	★239	27	★.925
1976—Salinas	Calif.	SS	136	469	67	124	14	4	4	51	.264	188	★406	★40	.937
1977—El Paso	Texas	SS-2B	120	417	87	119	24	1	18	73	.285	243	381	27	.959
1978—Salt Lake City	P. C.	SS-2B	72	248	36	64	13	1	5	32	.258	124	244	22	.944
1978—California	Amer.	SS-2B	48	108	6	21	7	0	0	7	.194	72	99	8	.955
1979—California†	Amer.	SS-3-2-C	96	234	33	58	13	1	3	23	.248	141	205	17	.953
1980—Seattle	Amer.	SS-3-2-C	116	317	46	72	7	0	8	30	.227	120	255	22	.945
1981—Seattle‡	Amer.	SS-3B	70	162	12	33	7	0	2	19	.204	88	184	15	.948
1982—Denver§	A. A.	3B-SS	128	488	95	153	30	3	16	83	.314	130	296	28	.938
1983—Texas	Amer.	S-2-O-3-C	50	102	8	22	1	1	0	6	.216	46	102	5	.967
1984—Texas	Amer.	SS-3B-2B	39	47	2	5	0	0	1	1	.106	37	58	1	.990
1984—Oklahoma City x	A. A.	I-C-O-P	36	117	10	25	6	0	1	9	.214	49	55	0	1.000
1985—Oklahoma City y	A. A.	I-C-O-P	126	435	59	107	21	4	8	43	.246	285	336	11	.983
Major League Totals—6 Years			419	970	107	211	35	2	13	86	.218	504	903	68	.954

Selected by California Angels' organization in 2nd round of free-agent draft, June 4, 1975.

†Traded to Seattle Mariners, December 2, 1979, completing deal in which Seattle traded Pitcher John Montague to California Angels for a player to be named later, August 29, 1979.
‡Released, March 29, 1982; signed by Denver (Texas Rangers' organization), April 13, 1982.
§Released, December 7, 1982; signed by Texas Rangers' organization, January 25, 1983.
xReleased, April 1, 1985; re-signed by Rangers' organization, April 12, 1985.
yTraded with Pitcher Bob Sebra to Montreal Expos for Third Baseman Pete Incaviglia, November 2, 1985.

CHAMPIONSHIP SERIES RECORD

Year	Club	League	Pos.	G.	AB.	R.	H.	2B.	3B.	HR.	RBI.	B.A.	PO.	A.	E.	F.A.
1979—California		Amer.	SS	4	11	0	1	0	0	0	0	.091	4	11	0	1.000

PITCHING RECORD

Year	Club	League	G.	IP.	W.	L.	Pct.	H.	R.	ER.	SO.	BB.	ERA.
1984—Oklahoma City		Am. Assoc.	1	2⅔	0	0	.000	0	0	0	0	0	0.00
1985—Oklahoma City		Am. Assoc.	1	1	0	0	.000	0	0	0	0	0	0.00

JOAQUIN ANDUJAR

Name pronounced Wah-KEEN AHN-doo-hahr.

Born December 21, 1952, at San Pedro de Macoris, Dominican Republic.
Height, 6.00. Weight, 180.
Throws right and bats left and righthanded.

Major League saves: 1978 (1), 1979 (4), 1980 (2), 1983 (1). Total—8.
Led National League in hit batsmen with 11 in 1985 and tied for lead with 7 in 1984.
Tied for National League lead in shutouts with 4 in 1984.
Tied for National League lead in balks with 5 in 1976.
Named National League Comeback Player of the Year by THE SPORTING NEWS, 1984.
Named pitcher on THE SPORTING NEWS National League All-Star fielding team, 1984.

Year	Club	League	G.	IP.	W.	L.	Pct.	H.	R.	ER.	SO.	BB.	ERA.
1970—Bradenton Reds		Gulf Coast	12	82	3	5	.375	*86	*58	*38	88	56	4.17
1971—Sioux Falls		Northern	19	75	4	7	.364	61	67	53	82	63	6.36
1972—Three Rivers		Eastern	22	112	7	6	.538	87	59	44	101	73	3.54
1973—Indianapolis		Am. Assoc.	11	40	2	5	.286	42	45	40	23	45	9.00
1973—Three Rivers†		Eastern	10	59	5	2	.714	38	29	13	39	38	1.98
1974—Indianapolis		Am. Assoc.	33	111	8	8	.500	85	62	44	92	93	3.57
1975—Three Rivers‡§		Eastern	18	62	4	8	.333	57	36	28	44	40	4.06
1976—Houston		National	28	172	9	10	.474	163	74	69	59	75	3.61
1977—Houston		National	26	159	11	8	.579	149	80	65	69	64	3.68
1978—Houston x		National	35	111	5	7	.417	88	45	42	55	58	3.41
1979—Houston		National	46	194	12	12	.500	168	86	74	77	88	3.43
1980—Houston		National	35	122	3	8	.273	132	59	53	75	43	3.91
1981—Houston y-St. Louis z		National	20	79	8	4	.667	85	41	36	37	23	4.10
1982—St. Louis		National	38	265⅔	15	10	.600	237	85	73	137	50	2.47
1983—St. Louis		National	39	225	6	16	.273	215	112	104	125	75	4.16
1984—St. Louis		National	36	*261⅓	*20	14	.588	218	104	97	147	70	3.34
1985—St. Louis a		National	38	269⅔	21	12	.636	265	113	102	112	82	3.40
Major League Totals—10 Years			341	1858⅔	110	101	.521	1720	799	715	893	628	3.46

Signed as free agent by Cincinnati Reds' organization, November 14, 1969.
†On disabled list, August 5 to August 15, 1973.
‡On disabled list, May 11 to July 4, 1975.
§Traded to Houston Astros for two minor league players to be named later, October 24, 1975; Cincinnati Reds' organization acquired Pitchers Carlos Alfonso and Luis Sanchez to complete deal, December 12, 1975.
xOn disabled list, July 8 to July 30, 1978.
yTraded to St. Louis Cardinals for Outfielder Tony Scott, June 7, 1981.
zGranted free agency, November 13, 1981; re-signed by Cardinals, December 29, 1981.
aTraded to Oakland A's for Catcher Mike Heath and Pitcher Tim Conroy, December 10, 1985.

CHAMPIONSHIP SERIES RECORD

Established National League Championship Series record for most runs allowed (10) and most earned runs allowed (8), six-game Series, 1985.

Year	Club	League	G.	IP.	W.	L.	Pct.	H.	R.	ER.	SO.	BB.	ERA.
1980—Houston		National	1	1	0	0	.000	0	0	0	0	1	0.00
1982—St. Louis		National	1	6⅔	1	0	1.000	6	2	2	4	2	2.70
1985—St. Louis		National	2	10⅓	0	1	.000	14	10	8	9	4	6.97
Championship Series Totals—3 Years			4	18	1	1	.500	20	12	10	13	7	5.00

WORLD SERIES RECORD

Year	Club	League	G.	IP.	W.	L.	Pct.	H.	R.	ER.	SO.	BB.	ERA.
1982—St. Louis		National	2	13⅓	2	0	1.000	10	3	2	4	1	1.35
1985—St. Louis		National	2	4	0	1	.000	10	4	4	3	4	9.00
World Series Totals—2 Years			4	17⅓	2	1	.667	20	7	6	7	5	3.12

ALL-STAR GAME RECORD

Year	League	IP.	W.	L.	Pct.	H.	R.	ER.	SO.	BB.	ERA.
1979—National		2	0	0	.000	2	2	1	0	1	4.50

Named to National League All-Star Team for 1985 game; declined and replaced by Ron Darling.
Named to National League All-Star Team for 1984 game; replaced due to injury by Fernando Valenzuela.
Member of National League All-Star Team in 1977; did not play.

LUIS ANTONIO AQUINO (COLON)

Name pronounced A-Keno.

Born May 19, 1965, at Rio Piedras, Puerto Rico.
Height, 6.00. Weight, 155.
Throws and bats righthanded.

Led Southern League in saves with 20 and tied for lead in games finished in relief with 42 in 1985.
Led Carolina League in games finished in relief with 42 in 1984.

Year	Club	League	G.	IP.	W.	L.	Pct.	H.	R.	ER.	SO.	BB.	ERA.
1982—Bradenton Blue Jays	Gulf Coast	13	73⅓	4	7	.364	60	33	27	52	17	3.31
1983—Florence	S. Atlantic	29	133⅔	7	9	.438	128	91	78	104	61	5.25
1984—Kinston	Carolina	*53	70	5	6	.455	50	21	21	78	37	2.70
1984—Knoxville	Southern	3	4	0	0	.000	3	4	4	7	3	9.00
1985—Knoxville	Southern	50	83	5	7	.417	58	29	24	82	32	2.60

Signed as free agent by Toronto Blue Jays' organization, June 15, 1981.

ANTONIO RAFAEL ARMAS (MACHADO)
(Tony)

Born July 2, 1953, at Anzoatequi, Venezuela.
Height, 6.01. Weight, 200.
Throws and bats righthanded.

Established major league records for most putouts (11) and chances accepted by right fielder, game (12), June 12, 1982.
Tied major league record for fewest double plays by outfielder, season, for leader in most double plays (4), 1977.
Major League stolen bases: 1977 (1), 1978 (1), 1979 (1), 1980 (5), 1981 (5), 1982 (2), 1984 (1). Total—16.
Led American League in total bases with 339 in 1984.
Led American League batters in strikeouts with 115 in 1981 and 156 in 1984.
Tied for American League lead in grounding into double plays with 31 in 1983.
Tied for American League lead in double plays by outfielders with 4 in 1977.
Named American League Player of the Year by THE SPORTING NEWS, 1981.
Named outfielder on THE SPORTING NEWS American League All-Star Team, 1981 and 1984.
Named outfielder on THE SPORTING NEWS American League Silver Slugger team, 1984.

Year	Club	League	Pos.	G.	AB.	R.	H.	2B.	3B.	HR.	RBI.	B.A.	PO.	A.	E.	F.A.
1971—Monroe	W. Car.	OF	31	88	7	20	3	0	1	10	.227	37	3	6	.870
1971—Bradenton Pir.	Gulf C.	OF	43	169	12	39	3	3	0	17	.231	*98	5	3	.972
1972—Gastonia	W. Car.	OF	117	399	50	106	18	4	9	51	.266	165	7	8	.956
1973—Sherbrooke†	East.	OF	84	302	46	91	15	5	11	45	.301	150	6	8	.951
1974—Thetford Mines	East.	OF	*137	476	64	132	26	3	15	81	.277	*329	18	10	.972
1975—Charleston	Int.	OF	128	450	65	135	28	4	12	72	.300	220	●14	3	.987
1976—Charleston	Int.	OF-1B	114	409	62	96	24	1	21	67	.235	210	8	7	.969
1976—Pittsburgh‡	Nat.	OF	4	6	0	2	0	0	0	1	.333	3	0	0	1.000
1977—Oakland§	Amer.	OF-SS	118	363	26	87	8	2	13	53	.240	294	9	6	.981
1978—Oakland x	Amer.	OF	91	239	17	51	6	1	2	13	.213	214	3	2	.991
1979—Oakland y	Amer.	OF	80	278	29	69	9	3	11	34	.248	194	7	5	.976
1980—Oakland	Amer.	OF	158	628	87	175	18	8	35	109	.279	374	17	10	.975
1981—Oakland	Amer.	OF	●109	440	51	115	24	3	●22	76	.261	259	8	2	.993
1982—Oakland za	Amer.	OF	138	536	58	125	19	2	28	89	.233	333	9	6	.983
1983—Boston	Amer.	OF	145	574	77	125	23	2	36	107	.218	326	5	5	.985
1984—Boston	Amer.	OF	157	639	107	171	29	5	*123	*123	.268	329	4	9	.974
1985—Boston b	Amer.	OF	103	385	50	102	17	5	23	64	.265	173	3	3	.983
National League Totals—1 Year			4	6	0	2	0	0	0	1	.333	3	0	0	1.000
American League Totals—9 Years			1099	4082	502	1020	153	31	213	668	.250	2496	65	48	.982
Major League Totals—10 Years			1103	4088	502	1022	153	31	213	669	.250	2499	65	48	.982

Signed as free agent by Pittsburgh Pirates' organization, January 18, 1971.
†On disabled list, May 27 to July 12, 1973.
‡Traded with Pitchers Dave Giusti, Doc Medich, Doug Bair and Rick Langford and Outfielder Mitchell Page to Oakland A's for Infielders Tommy Helms and Phil Garner and Pitcher Chris Batton, March 15, 1977.
§On disabled list, August 5 to September 1, 1977.
xOn disabled list, April 28 to June 2, 1978.
yOn disabled list, April 15 to June 5, 1979.
zOn disabled list, May 13 to May 28, 1982.
aTraded with Catcher Jeff Newman to Boston Red Sox for Third Baseman Carney Lansford, Outfielder Garry Hancock and a player to be named later, December 6, 1982; Oakland A's acquired Pitcher Jerry King to complete deal, December 20, 1982.
bOn disabled list, June 17 to July 26, 1985.

DIVISION SERIES RECORD

Year	Club	League	Pos.	G.	AB.	R.	H.	2B.	3B.	HR.	RBI.	B.A.	PO.	A.	E.	F.A.
1981—Oakland	Amer.	OF	3	11	1	6	2	0	0	3	.545	6	0	1	.857

CHAMPIONSHIP SERIES RECORD

Year	Club	League	Pos.	G.	AB.	R.	H.	2B.	3B.	HR.	RBI.	B.A.	PO.	A.	E.	F.A.
1981—Oakland	Amer.	OF	3	12	0	2	0	0	0	0	.167	5	2	0	1.000

ALL-STAR GAME RECORD

Year	League	Pos.	AB.	R.	H.	2B.	3B.	HR.	RBI.	B.A.	PO.	A.	E.	F.A.
1981—American		OF	1	0	0	0	0	0	0	.000	0	0	0	.000

Member of American League All-Star Team in 1984; did not play.

MICHAEL DENNIS ARMSTRONG
(Mike)

Born March 7, 1954, at Glen Cove, N.Y.
Height, 6.03. Weight, 206.
Throws and bats righthanded.
Attended University of Miami, Coral Gables, Fla.

Major League saves: 1982 (6), 1983 (3), 1984 (1). Total—10.
Led Eastern League pitchers in games started with 29 in 1977.

Year Club	League	G.	IP.	W.	L.	Pct.	H.	R.	ER.	SO.	BB.	ERA.
1974—Tampa	Florida St.	6	16	0	2	.000	26	17	17	14	18	9.56
1974—Seattle	Northwest	15	102	6	7	.462	85	45	30	86	47	2.65
1975—Three Rivers	Eastern	25	150	5	10	.333	116	55	45	86	44	2.70
1976—Three Rivers	Eastern	24	146	10	10	.500	143	77	57	91	52	3.51
1977—Three Rivers	Eastern	30	184	∗16	10	.615	185	91	77	107	83	3.77
1978—Chattanooga	Southern	31	74	9	6	.600	61	34	25	54	37	3.04
1978—Indianapolis	Am. Assoc.	16	23	1	2	.333	26	18	17	17	17	6.65
1979—Nashville†	Southern	32	64	5	1	.833	58	30	24	53	29	3.38
1979—Amarillo	Texas	7	31	2	3	.400	32	15	12	34	14	3.48
1979—Hawaii	P. Coast	3	7	0	0	.000	6	2	2	4	5	2.57
1980—Hawaii	P. Coast	42	74	4	4	.500	48	18	16	67	26	1.95
1980—San Diego	National	11	14	0	0	.000	16	10	9	14	13	5.79
1981—Hawaii	P. Coast	22	36	5	2	.714	21	7	6	39	12	1.50
1981—San Diego‡	National	10	12	0	2	.000	14	9	8	9	11	6.00
1982—Omaha	Am. Assoc.	15	28	4	2	.667	19	12	10	27	20	3.21
1982—Kansas City	American	52	112⅔	5	5	.500	88	45	40	75	43	3.20
1983—Kansas City§	American	58	102⅔	10	7	.588	86	53	44	52	45	3.86
1984—Fort Lauderdale x	Florida St.	8	11⅔	1	0	1.000	9	2	1	15	5	0.77
1984—New York	American	36	54⅓	3	2	.600	47	21	21	43	26	3.48
1985—Columbus	Int'national	21	40⅔	2	2	.500	49	31	30	40	26	6.64
1985—New York	American	9	14⅔	0	0	.000	9	5	5	11	2	3.07
National League Totals—2 Years		21	26	0	2	.000	30	19	17	23	24	5.88
American League Totals—4 Years		155	284⅓	18	14	.563	230	124	110	181	116	3.48
Major League Totals—6 Years		176	310⅓	18	16	.529	260	143	127	204	140	3.68

Selected by Cleveland Indians' organization in 9th round of free-agent draft, June 6, 1972.
Selected by Cincinnati Reds' organization in 1st round (24th player selected) of free-agent draft, January 9, 1974.
†Traded to San Diego Padres' organization for Third Baseman Paul O'Neill, July 25, 1979.
‡Traded to Kansas City Royals' organization for a player to be named later, April 4, 1982; San Diego Padres' organization acquired Pitcher Walt Vanderbush to complete deal, December 8, 1982.
§Traded with Catcher Duane Dewey to New York Yankees for First Baseman Steve Balboni and Pitcher Roger Erickson, December 8, 1983.
xOn New York Yankees disabled list, March 27 to June 16, 1984; included rehabilitation disability assignment to Fort Lauderdale, May 31 to June 16, 1984.

BRADLEY JAMES ARNSBERG
(Brad)

Born August 20, 1963, at Seattle, Wash.
Height, 6.04. Weight, 205.
Throws and bats righthanded.
Attended Merced College, Merced, Calif.
Brother of Tim Arnsberg, pitcher in Houston Astros' organization.

Pitched 5-0 no-hit victory against Savannah, May 24, 1984.
Tied for South Atlantic League lead in complete games with 10 and shutouts with 4 in 1984.

Year Club	League	G.	IP.	W.	L.	Pct.	H.	R.	ER.	SO.	BB.	ERA.
1984—Greensboro	S. Atlantic	23	158⅔	12	5	.706	121	61	52	112	59	2.95
1985—Albany†	Eastern	20	141⅓	●14	2	∗.875	105	34	25	82	35	∗1.59

Selected by Cleveland Indians' organization in 19th round of free-agent draft, June 8, 1981.
Selected by St. Louis Cardinals' organization in secondary phase of free-agent draft, January 12, 1982.
Selected by Baltimore Orioles' organization in secondary phase of free-agent draft, June 7, 1982.
Selected by California Angels' organization in secondary phase of free-agent draft, January 11, 1983.
Selected by New York Yankees' organization in secondary phase of free-agent draft, June 6, 1983.
†On disabled list, May 12 to May 24 and June 23 to July 22, 1985.

RANDALL CARL ASADOOR
(Randy)

Born October 20, 1962, at Fresno, Calif.
Height, 6.01. Weight, 185.
Throws and bats righthanded.
Received degree from Fresno State University, Fresno, Calif.

Led Pacific Coast League third basemen in putouts with 90, assists with 195 and total chances with 308 in 1985.

Year Club	League	Pos.	G.	AB.	R.	H.	2B.	3B.	HR.	RBI.	B.A.	PO.	A.	E.	F.A.
1983—Tulsa	Texas	3B-SS	46	157	15	43	12	0	8	28	.274	26	65	12	.883
1984—Tulsa†	Texas	3B-SS	124	425	65	106	22	3	16	53	.249	70	208	28	.908
1985—Las Vegas	P. C.	3B-1B	126	413	57	105	27	0	17	58	.254	107	199	23	.930

Selected by Baltimore Orioles' organization in 11th round of free-agent draft, June 3, 1980.
Selected by Texas Rangers' organization in 3rd round of free-agent draft, June 6, 1983.
†Traded to San Diego Padres for Pitcher Mitch Williams, April 6, 1985.

ALAN DEAN ASHBY

Born July 8, 1951, at Long Beach, Calif.
Height, 6.02. Weight, 195.
Throws right and bats left and righthanded.
Attended Los Angeles Harbor Junior College, Wilmington, Calif.

Tied National League record for most games, switch-hit home runs, season (1), September 27, 1982.
Major League stolen bases: 1975 (3), 1978 (1), 1982 (2). Total—6.
Led National League in passed balls with 14 in 1980.
Led California League catchers in double plays with 12 in 1971.

Year Club	League	Pos.	G.	AB.	R.	H.	2B.	3B.	HR.	RBI.	B.A.	PO.	A.	E.	F.A.
1969—Sarasota Indians	Gulf C.	C	48	117	10	28	3	1	0	14	.239	219	20	2	*.992
1970—Reno†	Calif.	C	40	121	15	23	5	1	3	18	.190	321	27	7	.980
1971—Jacksonville	South.	C	13	35	4	7	2	0	0	8	.200	76	6	1	.988
1971—Reno‡	Calif.	C-3B	77	239	52	70	14	1	18	60	.293	492	59	10	.982
1972—Portland	P. C.	C	95	291	33	65	9	2	9	28	.223	601	50	8	.988
1973—Ok.C.§-Evan.	A. A.	C-OF	41	124	20	28	8	0	3	16	.226	253	26	2	.993
1973—Cleveland	Amer.	C	11	29	4	5	1	0	1	3	.172	45	0	1	.978
1974—Oklahoma City	A. A	C	66	211	26	60	19	1	2	24	.284	405	33	8	.982
1974—Cleveland	Amer.	C	10	7	1	1	0	0	0	0	.143	12	0	0	1.000
1975—Cleveland	Amer.	C-1B-3B	90	254	32	57	10	1	5	32	.224	450	43	6	.988
1976—Cleveland xy	Amer.	C-1B-3B	89	247	26	59	5	1	4	32	.239	476	52	7	.987
1977—Toronto	Amer.	C	124	396	25	83	16	3	2	29	.210	619	71	11	.984
1978—Toronto z	Amer.	C	81	264	27	69	15	0	9	29	.261	399	38	6	.986
1979—Houston a	Nat.	C	108	336	25	68	15	2	2	35	.202	548	57	8	.987
1980—Houston	Nat.	C	116	352	30	90	19	2	3	48	.256	608	60	6	.991
1981—Houston	Nat.	C	83	255	20	69	13	0	4	33	.271	434	58	9	.982
1982—Houston b	Nat.	C	100	339	40	87	14	2	12	49	.257	530	55	14	.977
1983—Houston c	Nat.	C	87	275	31	63	18	1	8	34	.229	435	56	13	.974
1984—Houston d	Nat.	C	66	191	16	50	7	0	4	27	.262	303	42	5	.986
1985—Houston e	Nat.	C	65	189	20	53	8	0	8	25	.280	312	37	8	.978
American League Totals—6 Years			405	1197	115	274	47	5	21	125	.229	2001	204	31	.986
National League Totals—7 Years			625	1937	182	480	94	7	41	251	.248	3170	365	63	.982
Major League Totals—13 Years			1030	3134	297	754	141	12	62	376	.241	5171	569	94	.984

Selected by Cleveland Indians' organization in 3rd round of free-agent draft, June 5, 1969.
†On military list, January 1 to May 23, 1970.
‡On temporary inactive list, August 27 to September 13, 1971.
§Loaned to Evansville (Milwaukee Brewers' organization), May 22, 1973; returned, July 2, 1973.
xOn disabled list, August 9, 1976 through remainder of season.
yTraded with Outfielder-First Baseman Doug Howard to Toronto Blue Jays for Pitcher Al Fitzmorris, November 5, 1976.
zTraded to Houston Astros for Pitcher Mark Lemongello, Outfielder Joe Cannon and Shortstop Pedro Hernandez, November 27, 1978.
aOn disabled list, August 30 to September 17, 1979.
bGranted free agency, November 10, 1982; re-signed by Astros, December 21, 1982.
cOn disabled list, June 27 to July 24, 1983.
dOn disabled list, April 25 to May 31, 1984.
eOn disabled list, July 29 to September 7, 1985.

DIVISION SERIES RECORD

Year Club	League	Pos.	G.	AB.	R.	H.	2B.	3B.	HR.	RBI.	B.A.	PO.	A.	E.	F.A.
1981—Houston	Nat.	C	3	9	1	1	0	0	1	2	.111	24	2	0	1.000

CHAMPIONSHIP SERIES RECORD

Year Club	League	Pos.	G.	AB.	R.	H.	2B.	3B.	HR.	RBI.	B.A.	PO.	A.	E.	F.A.
1980—Houston	Nat.	C-PH	2	8	0	1	0	0	0	1	.125	11	2	0	1.000

PAUL ANDRE ASSENMACHER

Born December 10, 1960, at Detroit, Mich.
Height, 6.03. Weight, 195.
Throws and bats lefthanded.
Attended Aquinas College, Grand Rapids, Mich.

Year Club	League	G.	IP.	W.	L.	Pct.	H.	R.	ER.	SO.	BB.	ERA.
1983—Bradenton Braves	Gulf Coast	10	36⅔	1	0	1.000	35	14	9	44	4	2.21
1984—Durham	Carolina	26	147⅓	6	11	.353	153	78	70	147	52	4.28
1985—Durham	Carolina	14	38⅓	3	2	.600	38	16	14	36	13	3.29
1985—Greenville	Southern	29	52⅔	6	0	1.000	47	16	15	59	11	2.56

Signed as free agent by Atlanta Braves' organization, July 10, 1983.

KEITH ROWE ATHERTON

Born February 19, 1959, at Mathews, Va.
Height, 6.04. Weight, 200.
Throws and bats righthanded.

Major League saves: 1983 (4), 1984 (2), 1985 (3). Total—9.
Led Eastern League in complete games with 13 in 1980.
Tied for Northwest League lead in shutouts with 2 in 1978.

Year Club	League	G.	IP.	W.	L.	Pct.	H.	R.	ER.	SO.	BB.	ERA.
1978—Bend	Northwest	12	92	7	3	.700	86	44	35	81	40	3.42
1979—Waterbury	Eastern	4	21	0	3	.000	28	23	13	7	13	5.57
1979—Modesto	California	21	146	9	8	.529	190	107	97	103	51	5.98
1980—West Haven	Eastern	27	190	11	12	.478	185	101	87	117	58	4.12
1981—West Haven	Eastern	27	175	11	13	.458	174	83	70	116	64	3.60
1982—Tacoma	P. Coast	28	★200	12	9	.571	214	108	97	128	54	4.37
1983—Tacoma	P. Coast	26	120⅓	3	8	.273	117	60	53	93	44	3.96
1983—Oakland†	American	29	68⅓	2	5	.286	53	22	21	40	23	2.77
1984—Oakland	American	57	104	7	6	.538	110	51	50	58	39	4.33
1985—Oakland‡	American	56	104⅔	4	7	.364	89	51	50	77	42	4.30
Major League Totals—3 Years		142	277	13	18	.419	252	124	121	175	104	3.93

Selected by Oakland A's organization in 2nd round of free-agent draft, June 6, 1978.
†Struck out in only at bat during season when designated hitter took the field.
‡On disabled list, July 24 to August 13, 1985.

DONALD GLENN AUGUST
(Don)

Born July 3, 1963, at Inglewood, Calif.
Height, 6.03. Weight, 190.
Throws and bats righthanded.
Attended Chapman College, Orange, Calif.

Member of 1984 U.S. Olympic baseball team.

Year Club	League	G.	IP.	W.	L.	Pct.	H.	R.	ER.	SO.	BB.	ERA.
1985—Columbus	Southern	27	176⅓	14	8	.636	183	77	58	78	49	2.96

Selected by Houston Astros' organization in 1st round (17th player selected) of free-agent draft, June 4, 1984.

BENIGNO FELIX AYALA

Name pronounced Eye-AL-uh.

(Benny)

Born February 7, 1951, at Yauco, Puerto Rico.
Height, 6.01. Weight, 195.
Throws and bats righthanded.
Attended Puerto Rico Junior College, Rio Piedras, P. R.

Major League stolen bases: 1982 (1), 1984 (1). Total—2.
Hit home run in first major league at bat, August 27, 1974.

Year Club	League	Pos.	G.	AB.	R.	H.	2B.	3B.	HR.	RBI.	B.A.	PO.	A.	E.	F.A.
1971—Visalia	Calif.	3B	21	46	3	10	0	1	1	7	.217	8	16	7	.774
1971—Pompano Beach	Fla. St.	3B-OF	63	208	38	58	7	4	8	34	.279	57	59	17	.872
1972—Visalia	Calif.	1B-OF	113	348	68	79	15	2	19	66	.227	442	38	22	.956
1973—Memphis	Texas	OF	136	462	69	119	17	6	17	68	.258	44	5	3	.942
1974—Tidewater	Int.	OF	92	288	41	79	21	1	11	40	.274	125	4	★16	.890
1974—New York	Nat.	OF	23	68	9	16	1	0	2	8	.235	37	1	3	.927
1975—Tidewater†	Int.	OF	65	177	24	49	13	0	6	28	.277	66	1	4	.944
1976—New York‡	Nat.	OF	22	26	2	3	0	0	1	2	.115	7	1	1	.889
1976—Tidewater	Int.	OF-1B	87	293	41	66	9	2	12	48	.225	47	2	3	.942
1977—New Orleans	A. A.	OF	126	450	71	134	27	5	18	73	.298	199	8	5	.976
1977—St. Louis	Nat.	OF	1	3	0	1	0	0	0	0	.333	6	1	0	1.000
1978—Springfield§	A. A.	OF	47	165	16	41	2	0	5	21	.248	70	1	3	.959
1978—Columbus xy	Int.	OF	59	203	30	69	11	4	6	35	.340	62	3	4	.942
1979—Rochester	Int.	OF	17	62	10	22	1	3	1	7	.355	37	0	2	.949
1979—Baltimore	Amer.	OF	42	86	15	22	5	0	6	13	.256	38	0	1	.974
1980—Baltimore	Amer.	OF	76	170	28	45	8	1	10	33	.265	20	2	0	1.000
1981—Baltimore	Amer.	OF	44	86	12	24	2	0	3	13	.279	3	2	0	1.000
1982—Baltimore	Amer.	OF-1B	64	128	17	39	6	0	6	24	.305	59	0	1	.983
1983—Baltimore	Amer.	OF	47	104	12	23	7	0	4	13	.221	41	0	2	.953
1984—Baltimore z	Amer.	OF	60	118	9	25	6	0	4	24	.212	10	0	0	1.000
1985—Maine	Int.	OF	14	46	2	7	1	0	1	4	.152	2	0	0	1.000
1985—Cleveland a	Amer.	OF	46	76	10	19	7	0	2	15	.250	21	1	2	.917
American League Totals—7 Years			379	768	103	197	41	1	35	135	.257	192	5	6	.970
National League Totals—3 Years			46	97	11	20	1	0	3	10	.206	50	3	4	.930
Major League Totals—10 Years			425	865	114	217	42	1	38	145	.251	242	8	10	.962

Signed as free agent by New York Mets' organization, January 28, 1971.
†On disabled list, April 22 to May 29, 1975.
‡Traded to St. Louis Cardinals' organization for Infielder Doug Clarey, March 30, 1977.
§Loaned to Columbus (Pittsburgh Pirates' organization), June 21, 1978; returned, September 5, 1978.
xOn suspended list, August 27 to September 5, 1978.
yTraded to Baltimore Orioles' organization for Outfielder Mike Dimmel, January 16, 1979.
zGranted free agency, November 8, 1984; signed by Cleveland Indians' organization, April 19, 1985.
aGranted free agency, November 12, 1985.

CHAMPIONSHIP SERIES RECORD

Year Club	League	Pos.	G.	AB.	R.	H.	2B.	3B.	HR.	RBI.	B.A.	PO.	A.	E.	F.A.
1983—Baltimore	Amer.	PH	1	0	0	0	0	0	0	1	.000	0	0	0	.000

Year	Club	League	Pos.	G.	AB.	R.	H.	2B.	3B.	HR.	RBI.	B.A.	PO.	A.	E.	F.A.
1979—Baltimore	Amer.		OF-PH	4	6	1	2	0	0	1	2	.333	4	0	0	1.000
1983—Baltimore	Amer.		PH	1	1	1	1	0	0	0	1	1.000	0	0	0	.000
World Series Totals— 2 Years				5	7	2	3	0	0	1	3	.429	4	0	0	1.000

WALTER WAYNE BACKMAN
(Wally)

Born September 22, 1959, at Hillsboro, Ore.
Height, 5.09. Weight, 160.
Throws right and bats right and lefthanded.
Major League stolen bases: 1980 (2), 1981 (1), 1982 (8), 1984 (32), 1985 (30). Total—73.
Tied for National League lead in sacrifice hits with 14 in 1985.
Led International League in bases on balls received with 87 in 1980.
Led Carolina League in caught stealing with 17 in 1978.

Year	Club	League	Pos.	G.	AB.	R.	H.	2B.	3B.	HR.	RBI.	B.A.	PO.	A.	E.	F.A.
1977—Little Falls	NYP		SS-3B	69	255	44	83	10	2	6	30	.325	96	185	19	.937
1978—Lynchburg	Carol.		SS	132	494	86	149	19	●9	3	38	.302	★202	★329	30	★.947
1979—Jackson	Texas		SS-2B	110	404	63	114	11	5	2	19	.282	184	259	31	.935
1980—Tidewater	Int.		2B-SS	125	400	53	117	15	5	1	51	.293	237	320	22	.962
1980—New York	Nat.		2B-SS	27	93	12	30	1	1	0	9	.323	62	55	1	.992
1981—New York	Nat.		2B-3B	26	36	5	10	2	0	0	0	.278	14	21	2	.946
1981—Tidewater†‡	Int.		SS-3B-2B	21	59	6	9	3	1	0	0	.150	12	38	1	.980
1982—New York§	Nat.		2B-3B-SS	96	261	37	71	13	2	3	22	.272	173	209	16	.960
1983—New York	Nat.		2B-3B	26	42	6	7	0	1	0	3	.167	16	15	2	.939
1983—Tidewater	Int.		2B-SS-3B	101	361	69	114	11	3	1	28	.316	175	278	13	.972
1984—New York	Nat.		2B-SS	128	436	68	122	19	2	1	26	.280	223	306	10	.981
1985—New York	Nat.		★2B-SS	145	520	77	142	24	5	1	38	.275	273	370	7	★.989
Major League Totals—6 Years				448	1388	205	382	59	11	5	98	.275	761	976	38	.979

Selected by New York Mets' organization in 1st round (16th player selected) of free-agent draft, June 7, 1977.
†On suspended list, June 18 to June 20, 1981.
‡On disabled list, July 9 to September 1, 1981.
§On disabled list, August 15 to September 8, 1982.

SCOTT BAILES

Born December 18, 1961, at Chillicothe, O.
Height, 6.02. Weight, 170.
Throws and bats lefthanded.
Attended St. Louis Community College at Meramec, St. Louis, Mo.

Year	Club	League	G.	IP.	W.	L.	Pct.	H.	R.	ER.	SO.	BB.	ERA.
1982—Greenwood†	S. Atlantic		3	13⅔	0	1	.000	17	12	11	8	6	7.24
1983—Alexandria	Carolina		52	75	5	2	.714	67	38	28	101	45	3.36
1984—Nashua	Eastern		54	87	6	8	.429	80	43	33	61	46	3.41
1985—Nashua‡-Waterbury	Eastern		42	126⅓	9	6	.600	123	58	38	93	43	2.71

Selected by Texas Rangers' organization in 7th round of free-agent draft, January 12, 1982.
Selected by Pittsburgh Pirates' organization in secondary phase of free-agent draft, June 7, 1982.
†On disabled list, August 12, 1982 through remainder of season.
‡Traded to Cleveland Indians' organization, July 3, 1985, completing deal in which Cleveland traded Shortstop Johnnie LeMaster to Pittsburgh Pirates for a player to be named later, May 30, 1985.

JOHN MARK BAILEY
(Known by middle name.)

Born November 4, 1961, at Springfield, Mo.
Height, 6.05. Weight, 195.
Throws right and bats right and lefthanded.
Attended Southwest Missouri State University, Springfield, Mo.
Switch-hit home runs in one game, September 16, 1984.
Led National League in passed balls with 17 in 1984 and 19 in 1985.
Led South Atlantic League catchers in fielding percentage with .989 in 1983.

Year	Club	League	Pos.	G.	AB.	R.	H.	2B.	3B.	HR.	RBI.	B.A.	PO.	A.	E.	F.A.
1982—Auburn	NYP		1B-3B-OF	65	230	46	69	10	1	11	40	.300	195	29	5	.978
1983—Asheville	S. Atl.		C-1B	122	410	68	108	23	1	19	62	.263	767	77	7	.992
1984—Columbus	South.		C-1B-OF	17	53	5	15	3	2	0	9	.283	83	11	0	1.000
1984—Houston	Nat.		C	108	344	38	73	16	1	9	34	.212	629	56	12	.983
1985—Houston	Nat.		●C-1B	114	332	47	88	14	0	10	45	.265	566	52	●13	.979
Major League Totals—2 Years				222	676	85	161	30	1	19	79	.238	1195	108	25	.981

Selected by Houston Astros' organization in 6th round of free-agent draft, June 7, 1982.

—DID YOU KNOW—

That all of the Mets' runs in a 16-4 win (first game) over Houston on July 27 were unearned? The Astros committed five errors, helping New York to score six times in both the seventh and eighth innings.

ROBERT MICHAEL BAILOR
(Bob)

Born July 10, 1951, at Connellsville, Pa.
Height, 5.10. Weight, 160.
Throws and bats righthanded.
Attended California State College, California, Pa.

Major League stolen bases: 1977 (15), 1978 (5), 1979 (14), 1980 (12), 1981 (2), 1982 (20), 1983 (18), 1984 (3), 1985 (1). Total—90.
Led American League outfielders in double plays with 7 in 1978.
Led California League in stolen bases with 63 in 1972.
Led Southern League shortstops in double plays with 85 in 1973 and tied for International League lead with 64 in 1975.
Led California League shortstops in putouts with 218 and errors with 53 in 1972.

Year	Club	League	Pos.	G.	AB.	R.	H.	2B.	3B.	HR.	RBI.	B.A.	PO.	A.	E.	F.A.
1970—Bluefield	Appal.	2-O-3-S-P	46	121	18	33	3	0	0	8	.273	53	43	6	.941
1971—Aberdeen	North.	S-3-O-2	68	268	★71	★91	11	2	2	50	★.340	92	140	32	.879
1972—Lodi	Calif.	SS-OF-2B	129	528	95	153	16	3	2	34	.290	241	330	54	.914
1973—Asheville	South.	SS	115	468	77	137	23	3	0	29	.293	★222	386	22	★.965
1973—Rochester	Int.	SS	17	47	5	13	1	0	1	4	.277	30	34	4	.941
1974—Rochester	Int.	S-O-3-2	96	330	45	76	13	3	1	25	.230	174	160	13	.963
1975—Rochester	Int.	SS	129	★501	68	147	19	6	5	39	.293	198	★386	★32	.948
1975—Baltimore	Amer.	SS-2B	5	7	0	1	0	0	0	0	.143	5	9	0	1.000
1976—Rochester†	Int.	3B-SS-OF	36	103	21	32	10	1	1	12	.311	10	24	0	1.000
1976—Baltimore‡	Amer.	SS	9	6	2	2	0	1	0	0	.333	0	0	0	.000
1977—Toronto	Amer.	OF-SS	122	496	62	154	21	5	5	32	.310	235	165	12	.971
1978—Toronto	Amer.	OF-3B-SS	154	621	74	164	29	7	1	52	.264	329	82	15	.965
1979—Toronto	Amer.	OF-3B	130	414	50	95	11	5	1	38	.229	217	32	3	.988
1980—Toronto§ x	Amer.	O-S-3-2-P	117	347	44	82	14	2	1	16	.236	233	61	2	.933
1981—New York y	Nat.	S-2-O-3	51	81	11	23	3	1	0	8	.284	43	60	4	.963
1982—New York	Nat.	SS-2-3-O	110	376	44	104	14	1	0	31	.277	166	272	11	.976
1983—New York za	Nat.	S-2-3-O	118	340	33	85	8	0	1	30	.250	171	296	16	.967
1984—Los Angeles b	Nat.	2B-3B-SS	65	131	11	36	4	0	0	8	.275	59	117	6	.967
1985—Los Angeles c	Nat.	3-2-S-O	74	118	8	29	3	1	0	7	.246	35	103	3	.979
American League Totals—6 Years			537	1891	232	498	75	20	8	138	.263	1019	349	32	.977
National League Totals—5 Years			418	1046	107	277	32	3	1	84	.265	474	848	40	.971
Major League Totals—11 Years			955	2937	339	775	107	23	9	222	.264	1493	1197	72	.974

Signed as free agent by Baltimore Orioles' organization, August 13, 1969.
†On Baltimore disabled list, April 14 to June 7; on Rochester disabled list, June 8 to June 18 and August 1 to August 16, 1976.
‡Selected by Toronto Blue Jays in American League expansion draft, November 5, 1976.
§On disabled list, June 12 to July 3, 1980.
xTraded to New York Mets for Pitcher Roy Lee Jackson, December 12, 1980.
yOn disabled list, March 31 to April 21, 1981.
zOn disabled list, May 1 to May 17, 1983.
aTraded to Los Angeles Dodgers, December 12, 1983, completing deal in which Los Angeles traded Pitcher Sid Fernandez and Infielder Ross Jones to New York Mets for Pitcher Carlos Diaz and a player to be named later, December 8, 1983.
bOn disabled list, March 22 to May 8 and August 13 to September 11, 1984.
cOn disabled list, April 4 to April 25 and June 23 to July 10, 1985.

CHAMPIONSHIP SERIES RECORD

Year	Club	League	Pos.	G.	AB.	R.	H.	2B.	3B.	HR.	RBI.	B.A.	PO.	A.	E.	F.A.
1985—Los Angeles	Nat.	PR-3B	2	1	0	0	0	0	0	0	.000	0	1	0	1.000

PITCHING RECORD

Year	Club	League	G.	IP.	W.	L.	Pct.	H.	R.	ER.	SO.	BB.	ERA.
1970—Bluefield	Ap'lachian	1	1	0	0	.000	7	8	8	1	2	72.00
1980—Toronto	American	3	2	0	0	.000	4	2	2	0	1	9.00
Major League Totals—1 Year		3	2	0	0	.000	4	2	2	0	1	9.00

HAROLD DOUGLAS BAINES

Born March 15, 1959, at St. Michaels, Md.
Height, 6.02. Weight, 195.
Throws and bats lefthanded.

Tied major league record for most plate appearances, game (12), May 8, finished May 9, 1984 (25 innings).
Established American League record for most game-winning runs batted in, season (22), 1985.
Tied American League records for longest errorless game and most innings by outfielder, game (25), May 8, finished May 9, 1984.
Major League stolen bases: 1980 (2), 1981 (6), 1982 (10), 1983 (7), 1984 (1), 1985 (1). Total—27.
Hit three home runs in a game, July 7, 1982 and September 17, 1984.
Led American League in slugging percentage with .541 in 1984.
Led American League in game-winning RBIs with 22 in 1983.
Tied for American Association lead in double plays by outfielders with 4 in 1979.
Named outfielder on THE SPORTING NEWS American League All-Star Team, 1985.

Year	Club	League	Pos.	G.	AB.	R.	H.	2B.	3B.	HR.	RBI.	B.A.	PO.	A.	E.	F.A.
1977—Appleton	Midw.	OF	69	222	37	58	11	2	5	29	.261	94	10	7	.937
1978—Knoxville	South.	OF-1B	137	502	70	138	16	6	13	72	.275	291	22	13	.960
1979—Iowa	A. A.	OF	125	466	87	139	25	8	22	87	.298	222	●16	11	.956

Year Club	League	Pos.	G.	AB.	R.	H.	2B.	3B.	HR.	RBI.	B.A.	PO.	A.	E.	F.A.
1980—Chicago	Amer.	OF	141	491	55	125	23	6	13	49	.255	229	6	9	.963
1981—Chicago	Amer.	OF	82	280	42	80	11	7	10	41	.286	120	10	2	.985
1982—Chicago	Amer.	OF	161	608	89	165	29	8	25	105	.271	326	10	7	.980
1983—Chicago	Amer.	OF	156	596	76	167	33	2	20	99	.280	312	10	9	.973
1984—Chicago	Amer.	OF	147	569	72	173	28	10	29	94	.304	307	8	6	.981
1985—Chicago	Amer.	OF	160	640	86	198	29	3	22	113	.309	318	8	2	.994
Major League Totals—6 Years			847	3184	420	908	153	36	119	501	.285	1612	52	35	.979

Selected by Chicago White Sox' organization in 1st round (first player selected) of free-agent draft, June 7, 1977.

CHAMPIONSHIP SERIES RECORD

Year Club	League	Pos.	G.	AB.	R.	H.	2B.	3B.	HR.	RBI.	B.A.	PO.	A.	E.	F.A.
1983—Chicago	Amer.	OF	4	16	0	2	0	0	0	0	.125	5	1	0	1.000

ALL-STAR GAME RECORD

Year League	Pos.	AB.	R.	H.	2B.	3B.	HR.	RBI.	B.A.	PO.	A.	E.	F.A.
1985—American	PH	1	0	1	0	0	0	0	1.000	0	0	0	.000

CHARLES DOUGLAS BAIR
(Doug)

Born August 22, 1949, at Defiance, O.
Height, 6.00, Weight, 180.
Throws and bats righthanded.
Received bachelor of science degree in industrial education from
Bowling Green State University, Bowling Green, O.

Major League saves: 1977 (8), 1978 (28), 1979 (16), 1980 (6), 1981 (1), 1982 (8), 1983 (5), 1984 (4). Total—76.
Led Carolina League in complete games with 15 in 1972.
Named Carolina League Pitcher of the Year, 1972.

Year Club	League	G.	IP.	W.	L.	Pct.	H.	R.	ER.	SO.	BB.	ERA.
1971—Salem†	Carolina	6	29	2	3	.400	35	22	19	18	26	5.90
1971—Waterbury	Eastern	1	7	1	0	1.000	5	0	0	2	0	0.00
1972—Salem	Carolina	24	180	15	7	.682	170	●86	57	186	∗95	2.85
1972—Charleston	Int'national	1	4	0	1	.000	5	3	3	5	0	6.75
1973—Charleston	Int'national	26	158	7	11	.389	173	103	77	94	87	4.39
1974—Charleston‡	Int'national	26	170	7	∗16	.304	166	87	77	117	91	4.08
1975—Charleston	Int'national	26	167	9	12	.429	157	72	56	113	58	3.02
1976—Charleston	Int'national	45	122	7	10	.412	102	48	43	108	57	3.17
1976—Pittsburgh§	National	4	6	0	0	.000	4	4	4	4	5	6.00
1977—San Jose	P. Coast	20	33	5	2	.714	24	8	8	49	17	2.18
1977—Oakland x	American	45	83	4	6	.400	78	39	32	68	57	3.47
1978—Cincinnati	National	70	100	7	6	.538	87	23	22	91	38	1.98
1979—Cincinnati	National	65	94	11	7	.611	93	47	45	86	51	4.31
1980—Cincinnati	National	61	85	3	6	.333	91	42	40	62	39	4.24
1981—Cincinnati y-St. Louis	National	35	55	4	2	.667	55	34	31	30	19	5.07
1982—St. Louis	National	63	91⅔	5	3	.625	69	27	26	68	36	2.55
1983—St. Louis z	National	26	29⅔	1	1	.500	24	11	10	21	13	3.03
1983—Detroit a	American	27	55⅔	7	3	.700	51	27	24	39	19	3.88
1984—Detroit	American	47	93⅔	5	3	.625	82	42	39	57	36	3.75
1985—Detroit b	American	21	49	2	0	1.000	54	38	34	30	25	6.24
1985—St. Louis c	National	2	2	0	0	.000	1	0	0	0	2	0.00
National League Totals—8 Years		326	463⅓	31	25	.554	424	188	178	362	203	3.46
American League Totals—4 Years		140	281⅓	18	12	.600	265	146	129	194	137	4.13
Major League Totals—10 Years		466	744⅔	49	37	.570	689	334	307	556	340	3.71

Selected by Pittsburgh Pirates' organization in 2nd round of free-agent draft, June 8, 1971.
†On temporary inactive list, June 23 to July 22, 1971.
‡Conditionally released to Detroit Tigers' organization, December 17, 1974; returned, March 28, 1975.
§Traded with Pitchers Doc Medich, Dave Giusti and Rick Langford, Outfielders Mitchell Page and Tony Armas to Oakland A's for Infielders Phil Garner and Tommy Helms, and Pitcher Chris Batton, March 15, 1977.
xTraded to Cincinnati Reds for First Baseman Dave Revering and cash, February 25, 1978.
yTraded to St. Louis Cardinals for Pitcher Joe Edelen and Second Baseman Neil Fiala, September 10, 1981.
zTraded to Detroit Tigers for a player to be named later, June 21, 1983; St. Louis Cardinals acquired Pitcher Dave Rucker to complete deal, July 5, 1983.
aGranted free agency, November 7, 1983; re-signed by Tigers, December 23, 1983.
bReleased, August 22, 1985; signed by St. Louis Cardinals, September 2, 1985.
cGranted free agency, November 12, 1985.

CHAMPIONSHIP SERIES RECORD

Year Club	League	G.	IP.	W.	L.	Pct.	H.	R.	ER.	SO.	BB.	ERA.
1979—Cincinnati	National	1	1	0	1	.000	2	1	1	0	1	9.00
1982—St. Louis	National	1	1	0	0	.000	2	0	0	0	3	0.00
Championship Series Totals—2 Years		2	2	0	1	.000	4	1	1	0	4	4.50

WORLD SERIES RECORD

Year Club	League	G.	IP.	W.	L.	Pct.	H.	R.	ER.	SO.	BB.	ERA.
1982—St. Louis	National	3	2	0	1	.000	2	2	2	3	2	9.00
1984—Detroit	American	1	⅔	0	0	.000	0	0	0	1	0	0.00
World Series Totals—2 Years		4	2⅔	0	1	.000	2	2	2	4	2	6.75

DOUGLAS LEE BAKER
(Doug)

Born April 3, 1961, at Fullerton, Calif.
Height, 5.09. Weight, 165.
Throws right and bats left and righthanded.
Attended Arizona State University, Tempe, Ariz.
Brother of Dave Baker, third baseman with Toronto Blue Jays, 1982.

Major League stolen bases: 1984 (3).
Led Southern League in sacrifice hits with 18 and being hit by pitch with 13 in 1983.
Led Southern League shortstops in total chances with 747 in 1983.

Year Club	League	Pos.	G.	AB.	R.	H.	2B.	3B.	HR.	RBI.	B.A.	PO.	A.	E.	F.A.
1982—Birmingham	South.	SS	70	213	28	48	3	4	1	21	.225	115	190	14	.956
1983—Birmingham	South.	SS	*146	452	72	109	18	3	5	51	.241	238	*482	27	.964
1984—Evansville†	A. A.	SS	77	243	34	63	21	1	8	30	.259	152	270	16	.963
1984—Detroit..................	Amer.	SS-2B	43	108	15	20	4	1	0	12	.185	56	86	5	.966
1985—Detroit..................	Amer.	SS-2B	15	27	4	5	1	0	0	1	.185	12	12	1	.960
1985—Nashville...............	A. A.	SS	107	325	42	71	9	4	2	30	.218	179	318	22	.958
Major League Totals—2 Years.................			58	135	19	25	5	1	0	13	.185	68	98	6	.965

Selected by Oakland A's organization in 9th round of free-agent draft, January 13, 1981.
Selected by Detroit Tigers' organization in 9th round of free-agent draft, June 7, 1982.
†On disabled list, June 10 to June 21, 1984.

CHAMPIONSHIP SERIES RECORD

Year Club	League	Pos.	G.	AB.	R.	H.	2B.	3B.	HR.	RBI.	B.A.	PO.	A.	E.	F.A.
1984—Detroit..................	Amer.	SS	1	0	0	0	0	0	0	0	.000	0	0	0	.000

JOHNNIE B. BAKER JR.
(Dusty)

Born June 15, 1949, at Riverside, Calif.
Height, 6.02. Weight, 200.
Throws and bats righthanded.
Attended American River Junior College, Sacramento, Calif.

Tied major league records for most plate appearances, most at bats and most times faced pitcher as batsman, inning (3), September 20, second game, 1972; most stolen bases, inning (3), June 27, 1984, third inning.
Established National League record for fewest chances accepted by outfielder, season, 150 or more games (235), 1977.
Major League stolen bases: 1972 (4), 1973 (24), 1974 (18), 1975 (12), 1976 (2), 1977 (2), 1978 (12), 1979 (11), 1980 (12), 1981 (10), 1982 (17), 1983 (7), 1984 (4), 1985 (2). Total—137.
Led National League outfielders in total chances with 407 in 1973.
Named outfielder on THE SPORTING NEWS National League All-Star Team, 1980.
Named outfielder on THE SPORTING NEWS National League All-Star fielding team, 1981.
Named outfielder on THE SPORTING NEWS National League Silver Slugger team, 1980 and 1981.

Year Club	League	Pos.	G.	AB.	R.	H.	2B.	3B.	HR.	RBI.	B.A.	PO.	A.	E.	F.A.
1967—Austin	Texas	OF	9	39	6	9	1	0	0	1	.231	17	0	1	.944
1968—W. Palm B'ch†	Fla. St.	OF	6	21	2	4	0	0	0	2	.190	6	2	0	1.000
1968—Greenwood	W. Car.	OF	52	199	45	68	11	3	6	39	.342	82	1	3	.965
1968—Atlanta	Nat.	OF	6	5	0	2	0	0	0	0	.400	0	0	0	.000
1969—Shreveport	Texas	OF	73	265	40	68	5	1	9	31	.257	135	10	3	.980
1969—Richmond..............	Int.	OF-3B	25	89	7	22	4	0	0	8	.247	40	9	4	.925
1969—Atlanta	Nat.	OF	3	7	0	0	0	0	0	0	.000	2	0	0	1.000
1970—Richmond..............	Int.	OF	118	461	97	150	29	3	11	51	.325	236	10	7	.972
1970—Atlanta	Nat.	OF	13	24	3	7	0	0	0	4	.292	11	1	3	.800
1971—Richmond..............	Int.	OF-3B	80	341	62	106	23	2	11	41	.311	136	13	4	.974
1971—Atlanta	Nat.	OF	29	62	2	14	2	0	0	4	.226	29	1	0	1.000
1972—Atlanta‡	Nat.	OF	127	446	62	143	27	2	17	76	.321	344	8	4	.989
1973—Atlanta	Nat.	OF	159	604	101	174	29	4	21	99	.288	*390	10	7	.983
1974—Atlanta	Nat.	OF	149	574	80	147	35	0	20	69	.256	359	10	7	.981
1975—Atlanta§	Nat.	OF	142	494	63	129	18	2	19	72	.261	287	10	3	.990
1976—Los Angeles	Nat.	OF	112	384	36	93	13	0	4	39	.242	254	3	1	.996
1977—Los Angeles	Nat.	OF	153	533	86	155	26	1	30	86	.291	227	8	3	.987
1978—Los Angeles	Nat.	OF	149	522	62	137	24	1	11	66	.262	250	13	4	.985
1979—Los Angeles	Nat.	OF	151	554	86	152	29	1	23	88	.274	289	14	3	.990
1980—Los Angeles	Nat.	OF	153	579	80	170	26	4	29	97	.294	308	5	3	.991
1981—Los Angeles	Nat.	OF	103	400	48	128	17	3	9	49	.320	181	8	2	.990
1982—Los Angeles	Nat.	OF	147	570	80	171	19	1	23	88	.300	226	7	6	.975
1983—Los Angeles xy.....	Nat.	OF	149	531	71	138	25	1	15	73	.260	249	4	5	.981
1984—San Francisco za.	Nat.	OF	100	243	31	71	7	2	3	32	.292	112	1	3	.974
1985—Oakland.................	Amer.	1B-OF	111	343	48	92	15	1	14	52	.268	465	29	5	.990
National League Totals—17 Years..........			1845	6532	891	1831	297	22	224	942	.280	3518	103	54	.985
American League Totals—1 Year			111	343	48	92	15	1	14	52	.268	465	29	5	.990
Major League Totals—18 Years			1956	6875	939	1923	312	23	238	994	.280	3983	132	59	.986

Selected by Atlanta Braves' organization in 26th round of free-agent draft, June 6, 1967.
†On restricted list, April 5 to June 13, 1968.
‡On military list, June 17 to July 3, 1972.
§Traded with First Baseman-Third Baseman Ed Goodson to Los Angeles Dodgers for Outfielder Jimmy Wynn, Second Baseman Lee Lacy, First Baseman-Outfielder Tom Paciorek and Infielder Jerry Royster, November 17, 1975.
xReleased on waivers, February 10, 1984; San Francisco Giants claim rejected, February 16, 1984.

yGranted free agency, February 21, 1984; signed by San Francisco Giants, April 1, 1984.
zOn restricted list, April 2 to April 11, 1984.
aTraded to Oakland A's for Pitcher Ed Puikunas and Catcher Dan Winters, March 24, 1985.

DIVISION SERIES RECORD

Year	Club	League	Pos.	G.	AB.	R.	H.	2B.	3B.	HR.	RBI.	B.A.	PO.	A.	E.	F.A.
1981—Los Angeles		Nat.	OF	5	18	2	3	1	0	0	1	.167	12	0	0	1.000

CHAMPIONSHIP SERIES RECORD

Tied Championship Series records for highest batting average, four-game Series (.467), 1978; most home runs with bases filled, game (1), October 5, 1977; most runs batted in, four-game Series (8), 1977; most runs batted in, inning (4), October 5, 1977 (fourth inning).
Tied National League Championship Series record for most hits, game (4), October 7, 1978.

Year	Club	League	Pos.	G.	AB.	R.	H.	2B.	3B.	HR.	RBI.	B.A.	PO.	A.	E.	F.A.
1977—Los Angeles		Nat.	OF	4	14	4	5	1	0	2	8	.357	3	0	0	1.000
1978—Los Angeles		Nat.	OF	4	15	1	7	2	0	0	1	.467	5	0	0	1.000
1981—Los Angeles		Nat.	OF	5	19	3	6	1	0	0	3	.316	10	0	1	.909
1983—Los Angeles		Nat.	OF	4	14	4	5	1	0	1	1	.357	9	0	0	1.000
Championship Series Totals—4 Years				17	62	12	23	5	0	3	13	.371	27	0	1	.964

WORLD SERIES RECORD

Year	Club	League	Pos.	G.	AB.	R.	H.	2B.	3B.	HR.	RBI.	B.A.	PO.	A.	E.	F.A.
1977—Los Angeles		Nat.	OF	6	24	4	7	0	0	1	5	.292	11	0	1	.917
1978—Los Angeles		Nat.	OF	6	21	2	5	0	0	1	1	.238	12	0	0	1.000
1981—Los Angeles		Nat.	OF	6	24	3	4	0	0	0	1	.167	13	0	0	1.000
World Series Totals—3 Years				18	69	9	16	0	0	2	7	.232	36	0	1	.973

ALL-STAR GAME RECORD

Year	League	Pos.	AB.	R.	H.	2B.	3B.	HR.	RBI.	B.A.	PO.	A.	E.	F.A.
1981—National		OF	2	0	1	0	0	0	0	.500	2	0	0	1.000
1982—National		OF	2	0	0	0	0	0	0	.000	0	0	0	.000
All-Star Game Totals—2 Years			4	0	1	0	0	0	0	.250	2	0	0	1.000

STEPHEN CHARLES BALBONI
(Steve)

Born January 16, 1957, at Brockton, Mass.
Height, 6.03. Weight, 225.
Throws and bats righthanded.
Attended Eckerd College, St. Petersburg, Fla.

Major League stolen bases: 1985 (1).
Led American League batters in strikeouts with 166 in 1985.
Led American League first basemen in total chances with 1,686 in 1985.
Led International League batters in strikeouts with 146 in 1981.
Led Southern League in total bases with 288 and intentional bases on balls received with 17 in 1980.
Led Florida State League batters in strikeouts with 154 in 1979.
Led Florida State League first basemen in double plays with 106 in 1979 and Southern League first basemen with 125 in 1980.
Named Southern League Most Valuable Player, 1980.
Named Florida State League Most Valuable Player, 1979.
Named designated hitter on THE SPORTING NEWS College Baseball All-America Team, 1978.

Year	Club	League	Pos.	G.	AB.	R.	H.	2B.	3B.	HR.	RBI.	B.A.	PO.	A.	E.	F.A.
1978—West Haven		East.	DH	2	2	0	0	0	0	0	0	.000	0	0	0	.000
1978—Fort Lauderdale		Fla. St.	1B	60	176	19	36	5	0	1	19	.205	475	19	4	.992
1979—Fort Lauderdale		Fla. St.	1B	★140	★504	69	127	19	2	★26	★91	.252	★1297	★97	11	★.992
1980—Nashville		South.	1B	141	521	★101	157	25	2	★34	★122	.301	★1218	76	13	★.990
1981—Columbus		Int.	1B	125	434	68	107	21	2	★33	★98	.247	631	55	★14	.980
1981—New York		Amer.	1B	4	7	2	2	1	1	0	2	.286	14	1	0	1.000
1982—Columbus		Int.	1B	83	313	57	89	17	1	★32	86	.284	426	38	8	.983
1982—New York		Amer.	1B	33	107	8	20	2	1	2	4	.187	194	13	2	.990
1983—Columbus		Int.	1B	84	317	72	87	14	0	27	81	.274	479	47	11	.980
1983—New York†		Amer.	1B	32	86	8	20	2	0	5	17	.233	178	9	3	.984
1984—Kansas City		Amer.	1B	126	438	58	107	23	2	28	77	.244	1102	79	●15	.987
1985—Kansas City		Amer.	1B	160	600	74	146	28	2	36	88	.243	★1573	101	12	.993
Major League Totals—5 Years				355	1238	150	295	56	6	71	188	.238	3061	203	32	.990

Selected by New York Yankees' organization in 4th round of free-agent draft, June 6, 1978.
†Traded with Pitcher Roger Erickson to Kansas City Royals for Pitcher Mike Armstrong and Catcher Duane Dewey, December 8, 1983.

CHAMPIONSHIP SERIES RECORD

Established American League Championship Series record for most strikeouts, seven-game Series (8), 1985.

Year	Club	League	Pos.	G.	AB.	R.	H.	2B.	3B.	HR.	RBI.	B.A.	PO.	A.	E.	F.A.
1984—Kansas City		Amer.	1B	3	11	0	1	0	0	0	0	.091	20	3	1	.958
1985—Kansas City		Amer.	1B	7	25	1	3	0	0	0	1	.120	72	7	2	.975
Championship Series Totals—2 Years				10	36	1	4	0	0	0	1	.111	92	10	3	.971

WORLD SERIES RECORD

Tied World Series record for most at-bats, inning (2), October 27, 1985 (fifth inning).

Year	Club	League	Pos.	G.	AB.	R.	H.	2B.	3B.	HR.	RBI.	B.A.	PO.	A.	E.	F.A.
1985—Kansas City		Amer.	1B	7	25	2	8	0	0	0	3	.320	70	3	0	1.000

JEFFREY SCOTT BALLARD
(Jeff)

Born August 13, 1963, at Billings, Mont.
Height, 6.03. Weight, 195.
Throws and bats lefthanded.
Attended Stanford University, Stanford, Calif.
Tied for New York-Pennsylvania League lead in shutouts with 3 in 1985.

Year	Club	League	G.	IP.	W.	L.	Pct.	H.	R.	ER.	SO.	BB.	ERA.
1985—Newark	NYP	13	96	●10	2	.833	78	20	15	91	20	1.41

Selected by Milwaukee Brewers' organization in 16th round of free-agent draft, June 8, 1981.
Selected by Baltimore Orioles' organization in 27th round of free-agent draft, June 4, 1984.
Selected by Baltimore Orioles' organizaton in 7th round of free-agent draft, June 3, 1985.

JAY SCOT BALLER

Born October 6, 1960, at Stayton, Ore.
Height, 6.06. Weight, 215.
Throws and bats righthanded.
Major League saves: 1985 (1).
Led International League in hit batsmen with 12 in 1983.
Led Eastern League in hit batsmen with 12 in 1982.
Led South Atlantic League in hit batsmen with 10 in 1980.
Led Pioneer League in home runs allowed with 9 in 1979.

Year	Club	League	G.	IP.	W.	L.	Pct.	H.	R.	ER.	SO.	BB.	ERA.
1979—Helena	Pioneer	13	67	5	6	.455	89	59	43	68	34	5.78
1980—Spartanburg	S. Atlantic	26	139	10	5	.667	132	69	55	95	72	3.56
1981—Peninsula	Carolina	27	147	9	14	.391	119	85	64	166	78	3.92
1982—Reading	Eastern	50	151⅓	9	8	.529	110	64	45	155	85	*2.68
1982—Philadelphia†	National	4	8	0	0	.000	7	4	3	7	2	3.38
1983—Charleston	Int'national	20	78⅔	4	12	.250	91	79	77	62	66	8.81
1983—Buffalo	Eastern	16	34⅔	1	2	.333	32	34	29	35	35	7.53
1984—Buffalo	Eastern	14	79½	4	5	.444	73	50	40	74	48	4.54
1984—Maine‡	Int'national	15	83⅔	9	4	.692	82	57	50	52	48	5.38
1985—Iowa	Am. Assoc.	24	149	8	9	.471	140	77	70	119	63	4.23
1985—Chicago	National	20	52	2	3	.400	52	21	20	31	17	3.46
Major League Totals—2 Years		24	60	2	3	.400	59	25	23	38	19	3.45

Selected by Philadelphia Phillies' organization in 3rd round of free-agent draft, June 5, 1979.
†Traded with Second Baseman Manny Trillo, Outfielder George Vukovich, Infielder Julio Franco and Catcher Gerry Willard to Cleveland Indians for Outfielder Von Hayes, December 9, 1982.
‡Traded to Chicago Cubs' organization for Infielder Dan Rohn, April 1, 1985.

CHRISTOPHER MICHAEL BANDO
(Chris)

Born February 4, 1956, at Cleveland, O.
Height, 6.00. Weight, 195.
Throws right and bats left and righthanded
Attended Arizona State University, Tempe, Ariz.
Brother of Sal Bando, infielder with Kansas City Athletics, Oakland A's and
Milwaukee Brewers, 1966 through 1981; Milwaukee Brewers' Special Assistant
to the General Manager since 1982; and coach with Milwaukee Brewers, 1983.
Major League stolen bases: 1984 (1).
Received reported $25,000 bonus to sign with Cleveland Indians, 1978.

Year	Club	League	Pos.	G.	AB.	R.	H.	2B.	3B.	HR.	RBI.	B.A.	PO.	A.	E.	F.A.
1978—Chattanooga	South.	C	76	241	30	55	12	0	4	21	.228	285	51	10	.971
1979—Chattanooga†	South.	C-3B	21	62	5	15	4	1	0	7	.242	61	13	0	1.000
1980—Chattanooga‡	South.	C-3B	121	404	78	141	31	3	12	73	*.349	480	97	12	.980
1981—Charleston	Int.	C-3B	96	320	47	98	16	2	11	45	.306	414	51	10	.979
1981—Cleveland	Amer.	C	21	47	3	10	3	0	0	6	.213	53	5	2	.967
1982—Cleveland§	Amer.	C-3B	66	184	13	39	6	1	3	16	.212	268	23	3	.990
1983—Cleveland	Amer.	C	48	121	15	31	3	0	4	15	.256	170	19	1	.995
1984—Maine x	Int.	C-1B	29	92	18	24	2	0	3	13	.261	138	12	5	.968
1984—Cleveland	Amer.	C-1B-3B	75	220	38	64	11	0	12	41	.291	307	30	6	.983
1985—Cleveland	Amer.	C	73	173	11	24	4	1	0	13	.139	251	28	4	.986
Major League Totals—5 Years			283	745	80	168	27	2	19	91	.226	1049	105	16	.986

Selected by Milwaukee Brewers' organization in 22nd round of free-agent draft, June 7, 1977.
Selected by Cleveland Indians' organization in 2nd round of free-agent draft, June 6, 1978.
†On disabled list, April 16 to August 9, 1979.
‡On disabled list, April 24 to May 6, 1980.
§On disabled list, May 2 to June 17, 1982.
xOn Cleveland disabled list, March 28 to April 20, 1984.

MICHAEL SCOTT BANKHEAD
(Known by middle name.)

Born July 31, 1963, at Raleigh, N.C.
Height, 5.10. Weight, 175.
Throws and bats righthanded.
Attended University of North Carolina, Chapel Hill, N.C.

Member of 1984 U.S. Olympic baseball team.

Year Club	League	G.	IP.	W.	L.	Pct.	H.	R.	ER.	SO.	BB.	ERA.
1985—Memphis	Southern	24	140⅓	8	6	.571	117	63	56	●128	56	3.59

Selected by Pittsburgh Pirates' organization in 17th round of free-agent draft, June 8, 1981.
Selected by Kansas City Royals' organization in 1st round (16th player selected) of free-agent draft, June 4, 1984.

ALAN BANNISTER

Born September 3, 1951, at Montebello, Calif.
Height, 5.11. Weight, 175.
Throws and bats righthanded.
Attended Arizona State University, Tempe, Ariz., and California State University,
Long Beach, Calif.

Major League stolen bases: 1975 (2), 1976 (12), 1977 (4), 1978 (3), 1979 (22), 1980 (14), 1981 (16), 1982 (18), 1983 (6), 1984 (3), 1985 (8). Total—108.
Tied for American League lead in sacrifice flies with 11 in 1977.
Led International League shortstops in errors with 24 in 1974.
Received reported $85,000 bonus to sign with Philadelphia Phillies, 1973.
Named shortstop on THE SPORTING NEWS College Baseball All-America Team, 1972.

Year Club	League	Pos.	G.	AB.	R.	H.	2B.	3B.	HR.	RBI.	B.A.	PO.	A.	E.	F.A.
1973—Eugene	P. C.	2-3-S-O	130	460	72	105	17	2	4	46	.228	207	342	27	.953
1974—Toledo	Int.	SS-OF	94	343	56	99	17	7	4	40	.289	164	173	27	.926
1974—Philadelphia	Nat.	OF-SS	26	25	4	3	0	0	0	1	.120	10	0	0	1.000
1975—Philadelphia†	Nat.	OF-SS-2D	24	61	10	16	3	1	0	0	.262	54	4	2	.967
1975—Toledo	Int.	OF	101	335	50	74	7	3	5	27	.221	209	3	6	.972
1976—Iowa	A. A.	SS	32	118	24	29	6	0	3	12	.246	64	106	9	.950
1976—Chicago	Amer.	O-S-2-3	73	145	19	36	6	2	0	8	.248	92	36	5	.962
1977—Chicago	Amer.	*S-2-O	139	560	87	154	20	3	3	57	.275	265	331	*40	.937
1978—Chicago‡	Amer.	OF-SS-2B	49	107	16	24	3	2	0	8	.224	34	16	2	.962
1979—Chicago	Amer.	2-O-3-1	136	506	71	144	28	8	2	55	.285	250	187	21	.954
1980—Chi.§-Clev.	Amer.	O-2-3-S	126	392	57	111	23	4	1	41	.283	189	153	14	.961
1981—Cleveland	Amer.	O-1-2-S	68	232	36	61	11	1	1	17	.263	129	76	3	.986
1982—Cleveland xy	Amer.	O-2-S-3	101	348	40	93	16	1	4	41	.267	207	124	10	.971
1983—Cleveland z	Amer.	OF-2B-1B	117	377	51	100	25	4	5	45	.265	186	66	7	.973
1984—Houston a	Nat.	SS-OF	9	20	2	4	2	0	0	0	.200	11	8	1	.950
1984—Texas b	Amer.	2-O-1-3	47	112	20	33	2	1	2	9	.295	60	30	4	.957
1985—Texas cd	Amer.	O-2-3-1	57	122	17	32	4	1	1	6	.262	46	18	1	.985
American League Totals—10 Years			913	2901	414	788	138	27	19	287	.272	1458	1037	107	.959
National League Totals—3 Years			59	106	16	23	5	1	0	1	.217	75	12	3	.967
Major League Totals—12 Years			972	3007	430	811	143	28	19	288	.270	1533	1049	110	.959

Selected by California Angels' organization in 1st round (fifth player selected) of free-agent draft, June 5, 1969.
Selected by Philadelphia Phillies' organization in 1st round (first player selected) of free-agent draft, January 10, 1973.
†Traded with Pitchers Dick Ruthven and Roy Thomas to Chicago White Sox for Pitcher Jim Kaat and Shortstop Mike Buskey, December 10, 1975.
‡On disabled list, July 29, 1978 through remainder of season.
§Traded to Cleveland Indians for Catcher-Outfielder Ron Pruitt, June 14, 1980.
xOn disabled list, July 16 to August 16, 1982.
yGranted free agency, November 10, 1982; re-signed by Indians, January 27, 1983.
zSold to Houston Astros, March 25, 1984.
aTraded to Texas Rangers for Second Baseman Mike Richardt, May 25, 1984.
bOn disabled list, June 27 to July 24, 1984.
cOn disabled list, July 22 to August 9, 1985.
dGranted free agency, November 12, 1985.

FLOYD FRANKLIN BANNISTER

Born June 10, 1955, at Pierre, S. Dakota.
Height, 6.01. Weight, 203.
Throws and bats lefthanded.
Attended Arizona State University, Tempe, Ariz.
Brother-in-law of Greg Cochran, pitcher in Oakland A's and New York Yankees'
organizations, 1975 through 1982.

Named College Player of the Year by THE SPORTING NEWS, 1976.
Named lefthanded pitcher on THE SPORTING NEWS College Baseball All-America Team, 1975 and 1976.

Year Club	League	G.	IP.	W.	L.	Pct.	H.	R.	ER.	SO.	BB.	ERA.
1976—Covington	Ap'lachian	3	13	0	0	.000	3	0	0	27	2	0.00
1976—Columbus	Southern	3	24	1	0	1.000	16	4	4	20	14	1.50
1976—Memphis	Int'national	1	6	1	0	1.000	7	1	1	6	3	1.50
1977—Houston†	National	24	143	8	9	.471	138	70	64	112	68	4.03
1978—Houston‡	National	28	110	3	9	.250	120	59	59	94	63	4.83
1979—Seattle	American	30	182	10	15	.400	185	92	82	115	68	4.05
1980—Seattle	American	32	218	9	13	.409	200	96	84	155	66	3.47
1981—Seattle§	American	21	121	9	9	.500	128	62	60	85	39	4.46
1982—Seattle x	American	35	247	12	13	.480	225	112	94	*209	77	3.43
1983—Chicago	American	34	217⅓	16	10	.615	191	88	81	193	71	3.35
1984—Chicago y	American	34	218	14	11	.560	211	127	117	152	80	4.83
1985—Chicago	American	34	210⅔	10	14	.417	211	121	114	198	100	4.87
National League Totals—2 Years		52	253	11	18	.379	258	129	123	206	131	4.38
American League Totals—7 Years		220	1414	80	85	.485	1351	698	632	1107	501	4.02
Major League Totals—9 Years		272	1667	91	103	.469	1609	827	755	1313	632	4.08

Selected by Oakland A's organization in 3rd round of free-agent draft, June 5, 1973.
Selected by Houston Astros' organization in 1st round (first player selected) of free-agent draft, June 8, 1976.
†On disabled list, July 26 to August 22, 1977.
‡Traded to Seattle Mariners for Shortstop Craig Reynolds, December 8, 1978.
§On disabled list, August 8 to August 29, 1981.
xGranted free agency, November 10, 1982; signed by Chicago White Sox, December 13, 1982.
yHad one at-bat with no hits.

CHAMPIONSHIP SERIES RECORD

Year Club	League	G.	IP.	W.	L.	Pct.	H.	R.	ER.	SO.	BB.	ERA.
1983—Chicago	American	1	6	0	1	.000	5	4	3	5	1	4.50

ALL-STAR GAME RECORD

Year League	IP.	W.	L.	Pct.	H.	R.	ER.	SO.	BB.	ERA.
1982—American	1	0	0	.000	1	0	0	0	0	0.00

JESSE LEE BARFIELD

Born October 29, 1959, at Joliet, Ill.
Height, 6.01. Weight, 200.
Throws and bats righthanded.

Major League stolen bases: 1981 (4), 1982 (1), 1983 (2), 1984 (8), 1985 (22). Total—37.
Led American League outfielders in double plays with 8 in 1985.
Led Florida State League batters in strikeouts with 125 in 1978.

Year Club	League	Pos.	G.	AB.	R.	H.	2B.	3B.	HR.	RBI.	B.A.	PO.	A.	E.	F.A.
1977—Utica	NYP	OF	70	234	37	53	9	3	5	35	.226	122	6	●13	.908
1978—Dunedin	Fla. St.	OF	133	441	40	91	12	3	2	34	.206	229	★22	★15	.944
1979—Kinston	Carol.	OF	136	477	66	126	24	5	8	71	.264	284	19	17	.947
1980—Knoxville†	South.	OF	124	433	63	104	12	8	14	65	.240	309	14	12	.964
1981—Knoxville	South.	OF	141	524	83	137	24	13	16	70	.261	270	★23	6	.980
1981—Toronto	Amer.	OF	25	95	7	22	3	2	2	9	.232	71	2	0	1.000
1982—Toronto	Amer.	OF	139	394	54	97	13	2	18	58	.246	217	15	9	.963
1983—Toronto	Amer.	OF	128	388	58	98	13	3	27	68	.253	213	16	8	.966
1984—Toronto	Amer.	OF	110	320	51	91	14	1	14	49	.284	190	9	10	.952
1985—Toronto	Amer.	OF	155	539	94	156	34	9	27	84	.289	349	★22	4	.989
Major League Totals—5 Years			557	1736	264	464	77	17	88	268	.267	1040	64	31	.973

Selected by Toronto Blue Jays' organization in 9th round of free-agent draft, June 7, 1977.
†On disabled list, August 15 to August 29, 1980.

CHAMPIONSHIP SERIES RECORD

Year Club	League	Pos.	G.	AB.	R.	H.	2B.	3B.	HR.	RBI.	B.A.	PO.	A.	E.	F.A.
1985—Toronto	Amer.	OF	7	25	3	7	1	0	1	4	.280	21	0	1	.955

GREGORY ROBERT BARGAR
(Greg)

Born January 27, 1959, at Inglewood, Calif.
Height, 6.02. Weight, 185.
Throws and bats righthanded.
Attended El Camino College, Torrance, Calif.,
and University of Arizona, Tucson, Ariz.

Tied for American Association lead in home runs allowed with 17 in 1985.
Tied for American Association lead in games started by pitchers with 29 in 1984.

Year Club	League	G.	IP.	W.	L.	Pct.	H.	R.	ER.	SO.	BB.	ERA.
1980—Memphis	Southern	14	86	5	5	.500	95	52	48	54	48	5.02
1981—Memphis	Southern	9	65	5	2	.714	58	29	26	52	27	3.60
1981—Denver	Am. Assoc.	23	91	5	6	.455	108	63	61	58	58	6.03
1982—Wichita	Am. Assoc.	9	31⅓	0	4	.000	53	45	39	18	22	11.20
1982—Memphis	Southern	16	118⅔	5	6	.455	100	61	54	124	63	4.10
1983—Memphis	Southern	8	59	4	4	.500	51	25	20	50	28	3.05
1983—Wichita	Am. Assoc.	12	73⅓	6	2	.750	78	41	38	53	32	4.66
1983—Montreal	National	8	20	2	0	1.000	23	15	15	9	8	6.75
1984—Indianapolis	Am. Assoc.	31	180⅓	9	8	.529	156	101	93	121	83	4.64
1984—Montreal	National	3	8	0	1	.000	8	7	7	2	7	7.88
1985—Indianapolis	Am. Assoc.	38	162⅔	5	★17	.227	150	97	84	119	85	4.65
Major League Totals—2 Years		11	28	2	1	.667	31	22	22	11	15	7.07

Selected by St. Louis Cardinals' organization in 10th round of free-agent draft, January 9, 1979.
Selected by Montreal Expos' organization in 3rd round of free-agent draft, June 3, 1980.

LEONARD HAROLD BARKER II
(Len)

Born July 7, 1955, at Ft. Knox, Ky.
Height, 6.04. Weight, 230.
Throws and bats righthanded.

Pitched 3-0 perfect game against Toronto Blue Jays, May 15, 1981.
Major League saves: 1977 (1), 1978 (4). Total—5.
Led American League in wild pitches with 14 in 1980.

Led Western Carolinas League in shutouts with 5 in 1974.

Year Club	League	G.	IP.	W.	L.	Pct.	H.	R.	ER.	SO.	BB.	ERA.
1973—Sarasota Rangers	Gulf Coast	11	59	*7	1	*.875	34	13	9	54	27	1.37
1974—Gastonia	W. Carol.	20	124	11	7	.611	101	57	46	140	53	3.34
1975—Pittsfield	Eastern	24	159	7	12	.368	117	72	51	133	109	2.89
1976—Sacramento	P. Coast	27	141	11	10	.524	140	103	87	92	96	5.55
1976—Texas	American	2	15	1	0	1.000	7	4	4	7	6	2.40
1977—Tucson	P. Coast	20	109	9	7	.563	114	77	69	93	77	5.70
1977—Texas	American	15	47	4	1	.800	36	15	14	51	24	2.68
1978—Tucson	P. Coast	8	26	4	0	1.000	22	8	3	16	16	1.04
1978—Texas†	American	29	52	1	5	.167	63	31	28	33	29	4.85
1979—Cleveland	American	29	137	6	6	.500	146	79	75	93	70	4.93
1980—Cleveland	American	36	246	19	12	.613	237	127	114	*187	92	4.17
1981—Cleveland	American	22	154	8	7	.533	150	72	67	*127	46	3.92
1982—Cleveland	American	33	244⅔	15	11	.577	211	117	106	187	88	3.90
1983—Cleveland‡	American	24	149⅔	8	13	.381	150	92	85	105	52	5.11
1983—Atlanta	National	6	33	1	3	.250	31	17	14	21	14	3.82
1984—Atlanta§	National	21	126⅓	7	8	.467	120	59	54	95	38	3.85
1985—Atlanta x	National	20	73⅔	2	9	.182	84	55	52	47	37	6.35
1985—Greenville	Southern	1	5	1	0	1.000	1	1	1	7	1	1.80
American League Totals—8 Years		190	1045⅓	62	55	.530	1000	537	493	790	407	4.24
National League Totals—3 Years		47	233	10	20	.333	235	131	120	163	89	4.64
Major League Totals—10 Years		237	1278¼	72	75	.490	1235	668	613	953	496	4.32

Selected by Texas Rangers' organization in 3rd round of free-agent draft, June 5, 1973.

†Traded with Outfielder Bobby Bonds to Cleveland Indians for Infielder Larvell Blanks and Pitcher Jim Kern, October 3, 1978.

‡Traded to Atlanta Braves for three players to be named later, August 28, 1983; Cleveland Indians acquired Pitcher Rick Behenna, September 2, 1983, and Outfielder Brett Butler and Infielder Brook Jacoby, October 21, 1983, to complete deal.

§On disabled list, August 4, 1984 through remainder of season.

xOn disabled list, May 29 to July 10, 1985; included rehabilitation disability assignment to Greenville, June 26 to July 10, 1985.

ALL-STAR GAME RECORD

Year League	IP.	W.	L.	Pct.	H.	R.	ER.	SO.	BB.	ERA.
1981—American	2	0	0	.000	0	0	0	1	0	0.00

JEFFREY CARVER BARKLEY

(Jeff)

Born November 21, 1959, at Hickory, N. C.
Height, 6.03. Weight, 178.
Throws right and bats right and lefthanded.
Received bachelor of arts degree in political science from
The Citadel, Charleston, S.C. in 1982.
Son of Bill Barkley, minor league pitcher, 1952 through 1955.

Major League saves: 1985 (1).
Led New York-Pennsylvania League in balks with 4 and tied for lead in complete games with 7 and shutouts with 3 in 1982.

Year Club	League	G.	IP.	W.	L.	Pct.	H.	R.	ER.	SO.	BB.	ERA.
1982—Batavia	NYP	15	90⅓	5	6	.455	81	44	41	82	34	4.08
1983—Waterloo	Midwest	24	37	5	2	.714	27	11	11	65	14	2.68
1983—Charleston	Int'national	24	58⅓	3	1	.750	64	32	30	51	23	4.63
1984—Maine	Int'national	*51	85⅓	5	6	.455	62	32	27	76	44	2.85
1984—Cleveland	American	3	4	0	0	.000	6	3	3	4	1	6.75
1985—Maine	Int'national	24	39	1	4	.200	32	12	7	34	21	1.62
1985—Cleveland	American	21	41	0	3	.000	37	26	24	30	15	5.27
Major League Totals—2 Years		24	45	0	3	.000	43	29	27	34	16	5.40

Selected by Cleveland Indians' organization in 13th round of free-agent draft, June 7, 1982.

RICKY VERNARD BARLOW

Born March 21, 1963, at Woodville, Tex.
Height, 6.02. Weight, 170.
Throws and bats righthanded.

Year Club	League	G.	IP.	W.	L.	Pct.	H.	R.	ER.	SO.	BB.	ERA.
1981—Bristol	Ap'lachian	11	58	6	3	.667	63	38	28	24	36	4.34
1982—Macon	S. Atlantic	13	64⅓	2	4	.333	64	41	39	36	49	5.46
1982—Bristol	Ap'lachian	10	57⅔	4	4	.500	46	31	24	56	37	3.75
1983—Lakeland†	Florida St.	2	3⅓	0	1	.000	9	9	9	2	6	24.30
1984—Lakeland	Florida St.	25	122	1	*17	.056	134	*116	*92	65	101	6.79
1985—Lakeland	Florida St.	9	50⅓	1	7	.125	51	34	31	35	27	5.54
1985—Birmingham	Southern	18	63⅓	1	5	.167	88	74	59	39	55	8.38

Selected by Detroit Tigers' organization in 1st round (17th player selected) of free-agent draft, June 8, 1981.

†On disabled list, April 8 to August 15, 1983.

—DID YOU KNOW—

That in the 15 years prior to 1985, the National League West team leading its division on July 4 went on to win 11 times?

WILLIAM HENRY BARNES III
(Skeeter)

Born March 7, 1957, at Cincinnati, O.
Height, 5.11. Weight, 175.
Throws and bats righthanded.
Attended University of Cincinnati, Cincinnati, O.

Major League stolen bases: 1983 (2).
Tied for Pioneer League lead in sacrifice flies with 6 in 1978.
Led Eastern League third basemen in fielding percentage with .947 in 1982 and putouts with 104 in 1981.

Year Club	League	Pos.	G.	AB.	R.	H.	2B.	3B.	HR.	RBI.	B.A.	PO.	A.	E.	F.A.
1978—Billings	Pion.	O-3-S-2-1	68	277	66	102	*22	5	3	*76	.368	56	50	16	.869
1979—Nashville	South.	3B	*145	500	54	133	19	4	12	77	.266	123	*291	*35	.922
1980—Waterbury	East.	OF	*138	533	62	156	27	6	4	64	.293	264	15	13	.955
1981—Indianapolis	A. A.	1B-OF-3B	36	118	10	31	6	1	1	11	.263	254	23	3	.989
1981—Waterbury	East.	3-O-1-2	96	363	45	93	17	0	6	49	.256	115	185	15	.952
1982—Waterbury	East.	3B-1B-SS	112	418	67	128	24	6	12	72	.306	252	192	19	.959
1982—Indianapolis	A. A.	3B-1B	18	59	8	18	5	1	1	3	.305	25	25	2	.962
1983—Indianapolis	A. A.	3-1-O-2	109	377	67	127	19	6	7	56	.337	203	140	16	.955
1983—Cincinnati	Nat.	1B-3B	15	34	5	7	0	0	1	4	.206	45	11	1	.982
1984—Wichita	A. A.	3-1-O-2	92	360	59	118	23	4	14	67	.328	143	122	13	.953
1984—Cincinnati	Nat.	3B-OF	32	42	5	5	0	0	1	3	.119	7	15	0	1.000
1985—Den.†-Ind.	A. A.	3-1-O-2	95	340	51	95	16	0	8	63	.279	308	154	10	.979
1985—Montreal	Nat.	3B-OF-1B	19	26	0	4	1	0	0	0	.154	13	6	0	1.000
Major League Totals—3 Years			66	102	10	16	1	0	2	7	.157	65	32	1	.990

Selected by Cincinnati Reds' organization in 16th round of free-agent draft, June 6, 1978.
†Traded to Montreal Expos' organization for Outfielder Max Venable, April 26, 1985.

SALOME BAROJAS (ROMERO)

Name pronounced Sahl-low-MAY BAR-oh-hass.

Born June 16, 1957, at Cordoba, Veracruz, Mex.
Height, 5.09. Weight, 188.
Throws and bats righthanded.

Major League saves: 1982 (21), 1983 (12), 1984 (2). Total—35.

Year Club	League	G.	IP.	W.	L.	Pct.	H.	R.	ER.	SO.	BB.	ERA.
1976—Cordoba	Mexican	15	43	3	1	.750	32	12	9	17	14	1.88
1977—Cordoba	Mexican	41	126	5	4	.556	109	46	28	85	45	2.00
1978—Cordoba	Mexican	40	66	8	3	.727	54	22	18	27	34	2.45
1979—Cordoba	Mexican	41	148	7	6	.538	143	49	43	64	76	2.61
1980—Reynosa	Mexican	29	126	9	5	.643	105	40	33	82	49	2.36
1981—Mexico City Reds†	Mexican	50	98	12	3	.800	81	40	33	42	41	3.04
1982—Chicago	American	61	106⅔	6	6	.500	96	43	42	56	46	3.54
1983—Chicago	American	52	87⅓	3	3	.500	70	24	24	38	32	2.47
1984—Chicago‡-Seattle	American	43	134⅔	9	7	.563	136	70	62	55	60	4.14
1984—Denver	Am. Assoc.	3	9	1	0	1.000	6	1	1	3	5	1.00
1985—Seattle§x	American	17	52⅔	0	5	.000	65	40	35	27	33	5.08
Major League Totals—4 Years		173	381⅓	18	21	.462	367	177	163	176	171	3.85

†Sold to Chicago White Sox, December 9, 1981.
‡Traded to Seattle Mariners for Pitchers Gene Nelson and Jerry Don Gleaton, June 27, 1984.
§On disabled list, June 5 to June 29, 1985.
xReleased, December 20, 1985.

CHAMPIONSHIP SERIES RECORD

Year Club	League	G.	IP.	W.	L.	Pct.	H.	R.	ER.	SO.	BB.	ERA.
1983—Chicago	American	2	1	0	0	.000	4	2	2	0	0	18.00

MARTIN GLENN BARRETT
(Marty)

Born June 23, 1958, at Arcadia, Calif.
Height, 5.10. Weight, 175.
Throws and bats righthanded.
Attended Mesa Community College, Mesa, Ariz. and Arizona State University, Tempe, Ariz.
Brother of Charlie Barrett, pitcher in Los Angeles Dodgers' organization, 1973 through 1978;
and Tom Barrett, infielder in New York Yankees' organization.

Major League stolen bases: 1984 (5), 1985 (7). Total—12.
Led American League second basemen in double plays with 110 in 1985.
Led Eastern League in sacrifice hits with 15 in 1980.
Led Florida State League in sacrifice flies with 9 in 1979.
Led International League second basemen in double plays with 99 in 1982.

Year Club	League	Pos.	G.	AB.	R.	H.	2B.	3B.	HR.	RBI.	B.A.	PO.	A.	E.	F.A.
1979—Winter Haven	Fla. St.	2B	57	178	25	53	7	0	1	28	.298	124	144	6	.978
1980—Bristol	East.	*2B-SS	128	475	72	130	17	2	1	41	.274	279	372	10	*.985
1981—Pawtucket†	Int.	2B	88	343	36	91	12	2	1	28	.265	186	254	10	.978
1982—Pawtucket	Int.	2B	131	477	72	143	27	1	5	57	.300	303	*415	11	*.985
1982—Boston	Amer.	2B	8	18	0	1	0	0	0	0	.056	11	21	0	1.000
1983—Boston	Amer.	2B	33	44	7	10	1	1	0	2	.227	32	28	1	.984
1983—Pawtucket	Int.	2B	36	119	24	41	4	2	1	18	.345	70	115	1	.995

Year Club League	Pos.	G.	AB.	R.	H.	2B.	3B.	HR.	RBI.	B.A.	PO.	A.	E.	F.A.
1984—Boston.................... Amer.	2B	139	475	56	144	23	3	3	45	.303	245	417	9	★.987
1985—Boston.................... Amer.	2B	156	534	59	142	26	0	5	56	.266	★355	479	11	.987
Major League Totals—4 Years..................		336	1071	122	297	50	4	8	103	.277	643	945	21	.987

Selected by California Angels' organization in 11th round of free-agent draft, January 11, 1977.
Selected by New York Mets' organization in 3rd round of free-agent draft, January 10, 1978.
Selected by Boston Red Sox' organization in secondary phase of free-agent draft, June 5, 1979.
†On disabled list, June 25 to July 15 and July 17 to August 4, 1981.

TIMOTHY WAYNE BARRETT
(Tim)

Born January 24, 1961, at Huntingsburg, Ind.
Height, 6.01. Weight, 185.
Throws right and bats lefthanded.
Attended Indiana State University, Terre Haute, Ind.

Year Club	League	G.	IP.	W.	L.	Pct.	H.	R.	ER.	SO.	BB.	ERA.
1984—Gastonia..........................	S. Atlantic	13	88⅓	7	2	.778	63	25	19	96	31	1.94
1984—West Palm Beach	Florida St.	11	78⅓	5	4	.556	68	25	20	64	23	2.30
1984—Jacksonville..................................	Southern	2	12⅓	1	1	.500	11	3	3	12	7	2.19
1985—Jacksonville..................................	Southern	37	145⅓	13	8	.619	145	70	65	111	63	4.03
1985—Indianapolis	Am. Assoc.	4	11⅓	0	0	.000	9	1	1	4	6	0.79

Signed as free agent by Montreal Expos' organization, October 31, 1983.

KEVIN CHARLES BASS

Born May 12, 1959, at Menlo Park, Calif.
Height, 6.00. Weight, 180.
Throws right and bats right and lefthanded.
Brother of Richard Bass, minor league outfielder, 1976 and 1977;
cousin of James Lofton, wide receiver with Green Bay Packers.

Major League stolen bases: 1983 (2), 1984 (5), 1985 (19). Total—26.
Led Midwest League in being hit by pitch with 10 in 1978.
Led Eastern League outfielders in double plays with 7 in 1980.

Year Club League	Pos.	G.	AB.	R.	H.	2B.	3B.	HR.	RBI.	B.A.	PO.	A.	E.	F.A.
1977—Newark .... NYP	OF	48	189	30	56	11	●7	1	33	.296	56	2	3	.951
1978—Burlington .... Midw.	OF	129	499	81	132	27	5	18	69	.265	★281	14	11	.964
1979—Holyoke................. East.	OF	135	490	69	129	15	4	8	54	.263	280	●16	★17	.946
1980—Holyoke................. East.	OF	136	490	79	147	★31	7	4	51	.300	305	14	★18	.947
1981—Vancouver†.......... P. C.	OF	97	339	40	87	10	5	2	30	.257	175	14	7	.964
1982—Milwaukee............ Amer.	OF	18	9	4	0	0	0	0	0	.000	7	0	0	1.000
1982—Vancouver‡.......... P. C.	OF	102	413	70	130	23	7	17	65	.315	199	15	10	.955
1982—Houston................ Nat.	OF	12	24	2	1	0	0	0	1	.042	11	0	1	.917
1983—Houston................ Nat.	OF	88	195	25	46	7	3	2	18	.236	68	1	4	.945
1984—Houston§ .... Nat.	OF	121	331	33	86	17	5	2	29	.260	149	4	4	.975
1985—Houston................ Nat.	OF	150	539	72	145	27	5	16	68	.269	328	10	1	★.997
American League Totals—1 Year		18	9	4	0	0	0	0	0	.000	7	0	0	1.000
National League Totals—4 Years............		371	1089	132	278	51	13	20	116	.255	556	15	10	.983
Major League Totals—4 Years................		389	1098	136	278	51	13	20	116	.253	563	15	10	.983

Selected by Milwaukee Brewers' organization in 2nd round of free-agent draft, June 7, 1977.
†On disabled list, July 29 to September 1, 1981.
‡Traded with Pitchers Mike Madden and Frank DiPino to Houston Astros, September 3, 1982, completing deal in which Houston traded Pitcher Don Sutton to Milwaukee Brewers for three players to be named later, August 30, 1982.
§On disabled list, March 29 to April 13, 1984.

JOSE JOAQUIN BAUTISTA

Born July 25, 1964, at Bani, Dominican Republic.
Height, 6.01. Weight, 177.
Throws and bats righthanded.

Pitched 6-0 no-hit victory against Prince William, May 26, 1985 (first game).

Year Club	League	G.	IP.	W.	L.	Pct.	H.	R.	ER.	SO.	BB.	ERA.
1981—Kingsport....................	Ap'lachian	13	66	3	6	.333	84	54	34	34	17	4.64
1982—Kingsport....................	Ap'lachian	14	38⅓	0	4	.000	61	44	38	13	19	8.92
1983—Sarasota Mets...............	Gulf Coast	13	81⅔	4	3	.571	66	31	21	44	32	2.31
1984—Columbia	S. Atlantic	19	135	13	4	.765	121	52	47	96	35	3.13
1985—Lynchburg......................	Carolina	27	169	15	8	.652	145	49	44	109	33	2.34

Signed as free agent by New York Mets' organization, April 25, 1981.

CHRISTOPHER R. BAYER
(Chris)

Born April 9, 1964, at Bay Shore, N. Y.
Height, 6.02. Weight, 195.
Throws right and bats left and righthanded.
Attended Pace University, Pace Plaza, N.Y.

Year Club	League	G.	IP.	W.	L.	Pct.	H.	R.	ER.	SO.	BB.	ERA.
1985—Elmira†	NYP	14	53⅔	1	5	.167	44	30	20	48	26	3.35

Selected by Boston Red Sox' organization in 11th round of free-agent draft, June 3, 1985.

†Traded with Pitchers Bob Ojeda, Tom McCarthy and John Mitchell to New York Mets for Pitchers Calvin Schiraldi and Wes Gardner and Outfielders John Christensen and LaSchell Tarver, November 13, 1985.

DONALD EDWARD BAYLOR
(Don)

Born June 28, 1949, at Austin, Tex.
Height, 6.01. Weight, 210.
Throws and bats righthanded.
Attended Miami-Dade Junior College, Miami, Fla., and
Blinn Junior College, Brenham, Tex.

Established major league record for most times caught stealing, inning, (2), June 15, 1974 (9th inning).

Tied major league records for most long hits, opening game of season (4), April 6, 1973 (2 doubles, 1 triple, 1 home run); most consecutive home runs, two consecutive games (4), July 1 and 2, 1975 (bases on balls included).

Tied modern major league record for most at bats, game (7), August 25, 1979.

Established American League record for most times hit by pitch, lifetime (192).

Tied American League records for most hits, two consecutive games (9), August 13 and 14, 1973; most times hit by pitch, season (24), 1985.

Major League stolen bases: 1970 (1), 1972 (24), 1973 (32), 1974 (29), 1975 (32), 1976 (52), 1977 (26), 1978 (22), 1979 (22), 1980 (6), 1981 (3), 1982 (10), 1983 (17), 1984 (1). Total—277.

Hit three home runs in a game, July 2, 1975.

Led American League in game-winning RBIs with 21 in 1982.

Led American League in sacrifice flies with 12 in 1978.

Led American League in being hit by pitch with 13 in 1973, 20 in 1976, 18 in 1978, 23 in 1984, 24 in 1985 and tied for lead with 13 in 1975.

Led International League in being hit by pitch with 19 in 1970 and 16 in 1971.

Led International League in total bases with 296 in 1970.

Led Texas League in being hit by pitch with 13 in 1969.

Led Appalachian League in stolen bases with 26, total bases with 135 and tied for lead in caught stealing with 6 in 1967.

Named American League Most Valuable Player by Baseball Writers' Association of America, 1979.

Named American League Player of the Year by THE SPORTING NEWS, 1979.

Named designated hitter on THE SPORTING NEWS American League All-Star Team, 1979 and 1985.

Named designated hitter on THE SPORTING NEWS American League Silver Slugger team, 1983 and 1985.

Named Appalachian League Player of the Year, 1967.

Named Minor League Player of the Year by THE SPORTING NEWS, 1970.

Year—Club	League	Pos.	G.	AB.	R.	H.	2B.	3B.	HR.	RBI.	B.A.	PO.	A.	E.	F.A.
1967—Bluefield	Appal.	OF	●67	246	50	★85	10	★8	8	47	★.346	106	5	5	.957
1968—Stockton	Calif.	OF	68	244	52	90	6	3	7	40	.369	135	3	7	.952
1968—Elmira	East.	OF	6	24	4	8	1	1	1	3	.333	10	1	0	1.000
1968—Rochester	Int.	OF	15	46	4	10	2	0	0	4	.217	29	1	4	.882
1969—Miami	Fla. St.	OF	17	56	13	21	5	4	3	24	.375	30	2	3	.914
1969—Dal.-Ft. Worth	Texas	OF	109	406	71	122	17	●10	11	57	.300	241	7	★13	.950
1970—Rochester	Int.	OF	●140	508	★127	166	★34	★15	22	107	.327	286	5	7	.977
1970—Baltimore	Amer.	OF	8	17	4	4	0	0	.0	4	.235	15	0	0	1.000
1971—Rochester	Int.	OF	136	492	104	154	●31	10	20	95	.313	210	4	9	.960
1971—Baltimore	Amer.	OF	1	2	0	0	0	0	0	1	.000	4	0	0	1.000
1972—Baltimore	Amer.	OF-1B	102	320	33	81	13	3	11	38	.253	206	4	5	.977
1973—Baltimore	Amer.	OF-1B	118	405	64	116	20	4	11	51	.286	228	10	6	.975
1974—Baltimore	Amer.	OF-1B	137	489	66	133	22	1	10	59	.272	260	2	5	.981
1975—Baltimore†	Amer.	OF-1B	145	524	79	148	21	6	25	76	.282	286	8	5	.983
1976—Oakland‡	Amer.	OF-1B	157	595	85	147	25	1	15	68	.247	781	45	12	.986
1977—California	Amer.	OF-1B	154	561	87	141	27	0	25	75	.251	280	16	7	.977
1978—California	Amer.	OF-1B	158	591	103	151	26	0	34	99	.255	194	9	6	.971
1979—California	Amer.	OF-1B	●162	628	★120	186	33	3	36	★139	.296	203	3	5	.976
1980—California§	Amer.	OF	90	340	39	85	12	2	5	51	.250	119	4	4	.969
1981—California	Amer.	1B-OF	103	377	52	90	18	1	17	66	.239	38	3	0	1.000
1982—California x	Amer.	DH	157	608	80	160	24	1	24	93	.263	0	0	0	.000
1983—New York	Amer.	OF-1B	144	534	82	162	33	3	21	85	.303	23	2	1	.962
1984—New York	Amer.	OF	134	493	84	129	29	1	27	89	.262	8	0	1	.889
1985—New York	Amer.	DH	142	477	70	110	24	1	23	91	.231	0	0	0	.000
Major League Totals—16 Years			1912	6961	1048	1843	327	27	284	1085	.265	2645	106	57	.980

Selected by Baltimore Orioles' organization in 2nd round of free-agent draft, June 6, 1967.

†Traded with Pitchers Mike Torrez and Paul Mitchell to Oakland Athletics for Outfielder Reggie Jackson and Pitchers Ken Holtzman and Bill Van Bommel, April 2, 1976.

‡Played out option year and granted free agency, November 1, 1976; signed as free agent by California Angels, November 16, 1976.

§On disabled list, May 11 to June 26, 1980.

xGranted free agency, November 10, 1982; signed by New York Yankees, December 1, 1982.

CHAMPIONSHIP SERIES RECORD

Established Championship Series record for most runs batted in, five-game Series (10), 1982.

Tied Championship Series records for most home runs with bases filled, game (1), October 9, 1982; most runs batted in, game (5), October 5, 1982; most runs batted in, inning (4), October 9, 1982 (eighth inning).

Tied American League Championship Series record for most times on losing club (4).

Year—Club	League	Pos.	G.	AB.	R.	H.	2B.	3B.	HR.	RBI.	B.A.	PO.	A.	E.	F.A.
1973—Baltimore	Amer.	OF-PH	4	11	3	3	0	0	0	1	.273	7	0	0	1.000
1974—Baltimore	Amer.	OF	4	15	0	4	0	0	0	0	.267	9	0	0	1.000
1979—California	Amer.	DH-OF	4	16	2	3	0	0	1	2	.188	4	0	0	1.000
1982—California	Amer.	DH	5	17	2	5	1	1	1	10	.294	0	0	0	.000
Championship Series Totals—4 Years			17	59	7	15	1	1	2	13	.254	20	0	0	1.000

Year League	Pos.	AB.	R.	H.	2B.	3B.	HR.	RBI.	B.A.	PO.	A.	E.	F.A.
1979—American	OF	4	2	2	1	0	0	1	.500	1	0	0	1.000

WILLIAM LAMAR BEANE
Name pronounced Been.
(Billy)

Born March 29, 1962, at Orlando, Fla.
Height, 6.04. Weight, 195.
Throws and bats righthanded.
Attending University of California at San Diego, La Jolla, Calif.

Led International League batters in strikeouts with 130 in 1985.
Tied for Carolina League lead in sacrifice flies with 8 in 1981.
Led Texas League outfielders in fielding percentage with .994 in 1983.

Year Club	League	Pos.	G.	AB.	R.	H.	2B.	3B.	HR.	RBI.	B.A.	PO.	A.	E.	F.A.
1980—Little Falls	NYP	OF	43	138	10	29	3	2	1	14	.210	93	5	3	.970
1981—Lynchburg	Carol.	OF	114	403	47	108	13	•9	9	59	.268	233	8	11	.956
1982—Jackson	Texas	OF	126	418	39	88	13	4	5	36	.211	200	6	10	.954
1983—Jackson	Texas	OF-1B	121	423	53	104	14	1	11	75	.246	382	24	8	.981
1984—Jackson	Texas	OF	123	455	78	128	29	3	20	72	.281	180	5	7	.964
1984—New York	Nat.	OF	5	10	0	1	0	0	0	0	.100	2	0	0	1.000
1985—Tidewater	Int.	OF	135	504	63	143	*34	4	19	77	.284	255	10	6	.978
1985—New York†	Nat.	OF	8	8	0	2	1	0	0	1	.250	1	0	0	1.000
Major League Totals—2 Years			13	18	0	3	1	0	0	1	.167	3	0	0	1.000

Selected by New York Mets' organization in 1st round (23rd player selected) of free-agent draft, June 3, 1980.
†Traded with Pitchers Bill Latham and Joe Klink to Minnesota Twins for Second Baseman Tim Teufel and Outfielder Pat Crosby, January 16, 1986.

DAVID CHARLES BEARD
(Dave)

Born October 2, 1959, at Chamblee, Ga.
Height, 6.05. Weight, 215.
Throws right and bats lefthanded

Major League saves: 1980 (1), 1981 (3), 1982 (11), 1983 (10), 1984 (5). Total—30.
Led Eastern League in complete games with 20 in 1979.
Tied for Pacific Coast League lead in balks with 3 in 1980.
Tied for Eastern League lead in intentional bases on balls issued with 9 in 1979.
Tied for California League lead in shutouts with 5 in 1978.

Year Club	League	G.	IP.	W.	L.	Pct.	H.	R.	ER.	SO.	BB.	ERA.
1977—Medicine Hat	Pioneer	11	71	4	5	.444	79	50	36	30	31	4.56
1978—Modesto	California	25	185	12	6	.667	161	94	60	142	64	2.42
1979—Waterbury	Eastern	25	*191	10	•14	.417	192	87	64	111	63	3.02
1980—Ogden†	P. Coast	16	97	7	8	.467	110	76	69	70	44	6.40
1980—Oakland	American	13	16	0	1	.000	12	6	6	12	7	3.38
1981—Tacoma	P. Coast	42	129	11	11	.500	132	67	61	114	51	4.26
1981—Oakland	American	8	13	1	1	.500	9	5	4	15	4	2.77
1982—Tacoma	P. Coast	1	1	0	0	.000	0	0	0	1	0	0.00
1982—Oakland	American	54	91⅔	10	9	.526	85	41	35	73	35	3.44
1983—Oakland‡	American	43	61	5	5	.500	55	39	38	40	36	5.61
1983—Modesto§	California	1	1	0	0	.000	0	0	0	2	0	0.00
1984—Seattle x	American	43	76	3	2	.600	88	56	49	40	33	5.80
1984—Salt Lake City y	P. Coast	2	9⅓	0	1	.000	13	7	6	0	1	5.79
1985—Maine za	Int'national	16	21⅔	1	0	1.000	21	7	6	15	11	2.49
1985—Iowa	Am. Assoc.	11	16	2	0	1.000	10	1	1	9	9	0.56
1985—Chicago b	National	9	12⅔	0	0	.000	16	9	9	4	7	6.39
American League Totals—5 Years		161	257⅔	19	18	.514	249	147	132	180	115	4.61
National League Totals—1 Year		9	12⅔	0	0	.000	16	9	9	4	7	6.39
Major League Totals—6 Years		170	270⅓	19	18	.514	265	156	141	184	122	4.69

Selected by Oakland A's organization in 6th round of free-agent draft, June 7, 1977.
†On disabled list, April 20 to May 2, 1980.
‡On disabled list, June 9 to July 1, 1983; included rehabilitation disability assignment to Modesto, June 28 to July 1, 1983.
§Traded with Catcher Bob Kearney to Seattle Mariners for Pitcher Bill Caudill and a player to be named later, November 21, 1983; Oakland A's acquired Pitcher Darrel Akerfelds to complete deal, December 7, 1983.
xOn disabled list, June 25 to July 29, 1984; included rehabilitation disability assignment to Salt Lake City, July 20 to July 29, 1984.
yReleased, April 1, 1985; signed by Maine (Cleveland Indians' organization), April 13, 1985.
zOn disabled list, May 27 to July 10, 1985.
aTraded to Iowa (Chicago Cubs' organization) for Outfielder Tom Grant, July 26, 1985.
bReleased, November 13, 1985; signed by Atlanta Braves, December 4, 1985.

DIVISION SERIES RECORD

Year Club	League	G.	IP.	W.	L.	Pct.	H.	R.	ER.	SO.	BB.	ERA.
1981—Oakland	American	1	1⅓	0	0	.000	0	0	0	2	0	0.00

CHAMPIONSHIP SERIES RECORD

Year Club	League	G.	IP.	W.	L.	Pct.	H.	R.	ER.	SO.	BB.	ERA.
1981—Oakland	American	1	⅔	0	0	.000	5	3	3	0	0	40.50

JAMES LOUIS BEATTIE
Name pronounced BEE-tee.
(Jim)

Born July 4, 1954, at Langeley AFB, Hampton, Va.
Height, 6.06. Weight, 225.
Throws and bats righthanded.
Received bachelor of arts degree in art from Dartmouth College, Hanover, N. H., in 1976.

Tied major league records for most putouts by pitcher, inning (3), September 13, 1978 (second inning); most putouts by pitcher, nine-inning game (5), September 13, 1978.

Pitched seven-inning, 2-0 no-hit victory against Spokane, July 9, 1978.

Major League saves: 1981 (1).

Year Club	League	G.	IP.	W.	L.	Pct.	H.	R.	ER.	SO.	BB.	ERA.
1975—Oneonta†	NYP	5	24	2	0	1.000	15	11	5	22	7	1.88
1975—Syracuse	Int'national	5	33	2	2	.500	25	14	12	30	21	3.27
1976—Syracuse	Int'national	17	100	5	5	.500	106	76	67	74	80	6.03
1976—West Haven	Eastern	8	60	5	2	.714	47	19	15	48	33	2.25
1977—West Haven‡	Eastern	3	27	2	0	1.000	14	5	1	22	8	0.33
1977—Fort Lauderdale	Florida St.	9	38	1	3	.250	52	27	25	28	17	5.92
1977—Syracuse	Int'national	12	80	6	5	.545	70	41	37	53	43	4.16
1978—Tacoma	P. Coast	4	23	3	0	1.000	17	5	4	15	12	1.57
1978—New York	American	25	128	6	9	.400	123	60	53	65	51	3.73
1979—Columbus	Int'national	8	53	5	1	.833	31	9	8	47	25	1.36
1979—New York§x	American	15	76	3	6	.333	85	45	44	32	41	5.21
1980—Seattle	American	33	187	5	15	.250	205	115	101	67	98	4.86
1981—Seattle	American	13	67	3	2	.600	59	24	22	36	18	2.96
1981—Spokane	P. Coast	18	120	6	9	.400	115	60	42	70	48	3.15
1982—Seattle	American	28	172⅓	8	12	.400	149	73	64	140	65	3.34
1983—Salt Lake City y	P. Coast	3	16⅔	2	1	.667	19	12	11	13	8	5.94
1983—Seattle	American	30	196⅔	10	15	.400	197	89	84	132	66	3.84
1984—Seattle	American	32	211	12	16	.429	206	86	80	119	75	3.41
1985—Seattle z	American	18	70⅓	5	6	.455	93	61	57	45	33	7.29
Major League Totals—8 Years		194	1108⅓	52	81	.391	1117	553	505	636	447	4.10

Selected by New York Yankees' organization in 4th round of free-agent draft, June 4, 1975.

†On disabled list, July 13 to July 29, 1975.

‡On disabled list, April 15 to May 2, 1977.

§On disabled list, June 25 to July 22, 1979.

xTraded with Outfielder Juan Beniquez, Catcher Jerry Narron and Pitcher Rick Anderson to Seattle Mariners for Outfielder Ruppert Jones and Pitcher Jim Lewis, November 1, 1979.

yOn Seattle disabled list, March 24 to April 27, 1983; included rehabilitation disability assignment to Salt Lake City, April 12 to April 27, 1983.

zOn disabled list, June 12 to July 26 and August 28, 1985 through remainder of season.

CHAMPIONSHIP SERIES RECORD

Year Club	League	G.	IP.	W.	L.	Pct.	H.	R.	ER.	SO.	BB.	ERA.
1978—New York	American	1	5⅓	1	0	1.000	2	1	1	3	5	1.69

WORLD SERIES RECORD

Year Club	League	G.	IP.	W.	L.	Pct.	H.	R.	ER.	SO.	BB.	ERA.
1978—New York	American	1	9	1	0	1.000	9	2	2	8	4	2.00

THOMAS JOSEPH BECKWITH
(Joe)

Born January 28, 1955, at Auburn, Ala.
Height, 6.02. Weight, 200.
Throws right and bats lefthanded.
Attended Auburn University, Auburn, Ala.

Major League saves: 1979 (2), 1982 (1), 1983 (1), 1984 (2), 1985 (1). Total—7.

Year Club	League	G.	IP.	W.	L.	Pct.	H.	R.	ER.	SO.	BB.	ERA.
1977—San Antonio	Texas	12	78	5	5	.500	88	40	29	31	20	3.35
1978—Albuquerque	P. Coast	28	150	8	9	.471	186	118	97	59	80	5.82
1979—Albuquerque	P. Coast	27	113	8	8	.500	119	74	58	64	46	4.62
1979—Los Angeles	National	17	37	1	2	.333	42	18	18	28	15	4.38
1980—Albuquerque	P. Coast	7	14	2	1	.667	15	8	4	12	5	2.57
1980—Los Angeles	National	38	60	3	3	.500	60	17	13	40	23	1.95
1981—Los Angeles†	National					(Did not play)						
1982—Albuquerque	P. Coast	26	102⅓	5	6	.455	138	90	76	80	55	6.68
1982—Los Angeles	National	19	40	2	1	.667	38	14	12	33	14	2.70
1983—Los Angeles‡	National	42	71	3	4	.429	73	40	28	50	35	3.55
1984—Kansas City	American	49	100⅔	8	4	.667	92	39	38	75	25	3.40
1985—Kansas City	American	49	95	1	5	.167	99	45	43	80	32	4.07
National League Totals—5 Years		116	208	9	10	.474	213	89	71	151	87	3.07
American League Totals—2 Years		98	195⅔	9	9	.500	191	84	81	155	57	3.73
Major League Totals—7 Years		214	403⅔	18	19	.486	404	173	152	306	144	3.39

Selected by Cleveland Indians' organization in 12th round of free-agent draft, June 8, 1976.

Selected by Los Angeles Dodgers' organization in 2nd round of free-agent draft, June 7, 1977.

†On disabled list, April 8, 1981 through remainder of season.

‡Traded to Kansas City Royals for Catcher Joe Szekely and Pitchers Jose Torres and John Serritella, December 8, 1983.

CHAMPIONSHIP SERIES RECORD

Year Club	League	G.	IP.	W.	L.	Pct.	H.	R.	ER.	SO.	BB.	ERA.
1983—Los Angeles	National	2	2⅓	0	0	.000	1	0	0	3	2	0.00

WORLD SERIES RECORD

Year Club	League	G.	IP.	W.	L.	Pct.	H.	R.	ER.	SO.	BB.	ERA.
1985—Kansas City	American	1	2	0	0	.000	1	0	0	3	0	0.00

STEPHEN WAYNE BEDROSIAN

Name pronounced Bed-ROHZ-ee-un.

(Steve)

Born December 6, 1957, at Methuen, Mass.
Height, 6.03. Weight, 195.
Throws and bats righthanded.
Attended North Essex Community College, Haverhill, Mass., and
University of New Haven, New Haven, Conn.

Established major league record for most games taken out as starting pitcher, season (37), 1985.
Major League saves: 1982 (11), 1983 (19), 1984 (11). Total—41.
Tied for Southern League lead in games started by pitchers with 29 in 1980.
Named National League Rookie Pitcher of the Year by THE SPORTING NEWS, 1982.

Year Club	League	G.	IP.	W.	L.	Pct.	H.	R.	ER.	SO.	BB.	ERA.
1978—Kingsport	Ap'lachian	6	38	2	2	.500	38	18	13	29	25	3.08
1978—Greenwood	W. Carol.	8	55	5	1	.833	45	17	13	58	34	2.13
1979—Savannah†	Southern	13	89	5	5	.500	71	36	30	58	58	3.03
1980—Savannah	Southern	29	★203	14	10	.583	167	91	72	★161	96	3.19
1981—Richmond	Int'national	26	184	10	10	.500	143	76	55	144	99	2.69
1981—Atlanta	National	15	24	1	2	.333	15	14	12	9	15	4.50
1982—Atlanta	National	64	137⅔	8	6	.571	102	39	37	123	57	2.42
1983—Atlanta	National	70	120	9	10	.474	100	50	48	114	51	3.60
1984—Atlanta‡	National	40	83⅔	9	6	.600	65	23	22	81	33	2.37
1985—Atlanta§	National	37	206⅔	7	15	.318	198	101	88	134	111	3.83
Major League Totals—5 Years		226	572	34	39	.466	480	227	207	461	267	3.26

Selected by Atlanta Braves' organization in 3rd round of free-agent draft, June 6, 1978.
†On disabled list, June 24 to September 18, 1979.
‡On disabled list, August 20 to September 4, 1984.
§Traded with Outfielder Milt Thompson to Philadelphia Phillies for Catcher Ozzie Virgil and Pitcher Pete Smith, December 10, 1985.

CHAMPIONSHIP SERIES RECORD

Year Club	League	G.	IP.	W.	L.	Pct.	H.	R.	ER.	SO.	BB.	ERA.
1982—Atlanta	National	2	1	0	0	.000	3	2	2	2	1	18.00

RICHARD KIPP BEHENNA

(Rick)

Born March 6, 1960, at Miami, Fla.
Height, 6.02. Weight, 170.
Throws and bats righthanded.

Pitched 8-0 no-hit victory against Rocky Mount, August 29, 1980.

Year Club	League	G.	IP.	W.	L.	Pct.	H.	R.	ER.	SO.	BB.	ERA.
1978—Kingsport	Ap'lachian	12	74	6	4	.600	66	37	31	37	50	3.77
1979—Greenwood	W. Carol.	8	43	0	6	.000	38	30	25	22	32	5.23
1979—Kingsport	Ap'lachian	12	83	5	3	.625	76	52	42	36	42	4.55
1980—Durham	Carolina	27	180	8	●13	.381	181	97	★83	107	81	4.15
1981—Durham	Carolina	29	★196	13	12	.520	182	92	79	162	76	3.63
1982—Savannah	Southern	28	201⅓	13	10	.565	195	97	83	153	97	3.71
1983—Atlanta	National	14	37⅓	3	3	.500	37	20	19	17	12	4.58
1983—Richmond†	Int'national	17	94⅔	6	5	.545	91	55	47	50	61	4.47
1983—Cleveland	American	5	26	0	2	.000	22	13	12	9	14	4.15
1984—Cleveland‡	American	3	9⅔	0	3	.000	17	15	15	6	8	13.97
1985—Maine§	Int'national	6	28	3	1	.750	21	8	8	10	12	2.57
1985—Cleveland	American	4	19⅔	0	2	.000	29	17	17	4	8	7.78
National League Totals—1 Year		14	37⅓	3	3	.500	37	20	19	17	12	4.58
American League Totals—3 Years		12	55⅓	0	7	.000	68	45	44	19	30	7.16
Major League Totals—3 Years		26	92⅔	3	10	.231	105	65	63	36	42	6.12

Selected by Atlanta Braves' organization in 4th round of free-agent draft, June 6, 1978.
†Traded to Cleveland Indians, September 2, 1983, as partial completion of deal in which Cleveland traded Pitcher Len Barker to Atlanta Braves for three players to be named later, August 28, 1983; Cleveland acquired Outfielder Brett Butler and Infielder Brook Jacoby to complete deal, October 21, 1983.
‡On disabled list, May 15, 1984 through remainder of season.
§On Cleveland disabled list, April 2 to May 19 and July 1, 1985 through remainder of season; included rehabilitation disability assignment to Maine, April 29 to May 19, 1985.

TIMOTHY WAYNE BELCHER
(Tim)

Born October 19, 1961, at Mount Gilead, O.
Height, 6.03. Weight, 210.
Throws and bats righthanded.
Attended Mt. Vernon Nazarene College, Mt. Vernon, O.
Named righthanded pitcher on THE SPORTING NEWS College Baseball All-America Team, 1983.

Year	Club	League	G.	IP.	W.	L.	Pct.	H.	R.	ER.	SO.	BB.	ERA.
1984—Madison		Midwest	16	98⅓	9	4	.692	80	45	39	111	48	3.57
1984—Albany		Eastern	10	54	3	4	.429	37	30	20	40	41	3.33
1985—Huntsville		Southern	29	149⅔	11	10	.524	145	99	78	90	99	4.69

Selected by Minnesota Twins' organization in 1st round (first player selected) of free-agent draft, June 6, 1983.
Selected by New York Yankees' organization in secondary phase of free-agent draft, January 17, 1984.
Selected by Oakland A's organization in player compensation pool draft, February 8, 1984. (Oakland received compensation for Baltimore Orioles' signing of free-agent Pitcher Tom Underwood, a Type A player, February 7, 1984.)

DAVID GUS BELL
(Buddy)

Born August 27, 1951, at Pittsburgh, Pa.
Height, 6.02. Weight, 185.
Throws and bats righthanded.
Attended Xavier University, Cincinnati, O., and Miami University, Oxford, O.
Son of Gus Bell, outfielder with Pittsburgh Pirates, Cincinnati Reds, New York Mets and Milwaukee Braves, 1950 through 1964; scout, Cleveland Indians, 1966, 1968 and 1969; and currently scout with Texas Rangers.

Tied major league record for most home runs, opening day of season (2), April 8, 1982.
Major League stolen bases: 1972 (5), 1973 (7), 1974 (1), 1975 (6), 1976 (3), 1977 (1), 1978 (1), 1979 (5), 1980 (3), 1981 (3), 1982 (5), 1983 (3), 1984 (2), 1985 (3). Total—48.
Led American League in sacrifice flies with 10 in 1981.
Led American League third basemen in total chances with 495 in 1978, 361 in 1981, 540 in 1982 and 523 in 1983.
Led American League third basemen in assists with 364 in 1979 and 281 in 1981.
Led American League third basemen in putouts with 144 and double plays with 44 in 1973.
Tied for American League lead in game-winning RBIs with 16 in 1979.
Tied for American League lead in double plays by third basemen with 30 in 1978.
Led Gulf Coast League second basemen in double plays with 26 in 1969.
Named third baseman on THE SPORTING NEWS American League All-Star Team, 1981 and 1984.
Named third baseman on THE SPORTING NEWS American League All-Star fielding team, 1979 through 1984.
Named third baseman on THE SPORTING NEWS American League Silver Slugger team, 1984.

Year	Club	League	Pos.	G.	AB.	R.	H.	2B.	3B.	HR.	RBI.	B.A.	PO.	A.	E.	F.A.
1969—Sarasota Ind.		Gulf C.	2B	51	170	18	39	4	●3	3	24	.229	119	108	7	★.970
1970—Sumter		W. Car.	3B-2B-SS	121	442	81	117	19	3	12	75	.265	116	189	27	.919
1971—Wichita		A. A.	★3-2-S-O	129	470	65	136	23	1	11	59	.289	★139	203	16	.955
1972—Cleveland		Amer.	OF-3B	132	466	49	119	21	1	9	36	.255	284	23	3	.990
1973—Cleveland		Amer.	3B-OF	156	631	86	169	23	7	14	59	.268	140	303	22	.959
1974—Cleveland†		Amer.	3B	116	423	51	111	15	1	7	46	.262	112	274	15	.963
1975—Cleveland		Amer.	3B	153	553	66	150	20	4	10	59	.271	★146	330	25	.950
1976—Cleveland		Amer.	3B-1B	159	604	75	170	26	2	7	60	.281	109	331	20	.957
1977—Cleveland		Amer.	3B-OF	129	479	64	140	23	4	11	64	.292	134	253	16	.960
1978—Cleveland‡		Amer.	3B	142	556	71	157	27	8	6	62	.282	★125	★355	15	.970
1979—Texas		Amer.	3B-SS	●162	★670	89	200	42	3	18	101	.299	147	429	17	.971
1980—Texas§		Amer.	★3B-SS	129	490	76	161	24	4	17	83	.329	125	282	8	★.981
1981—Texas		Amer.	3B-SS	97	360	44	106	16	1	10	64	.294	67	284	14	.962
1982—Texas		Amer.	★3B-SS	148	537	62	159	27	2	13	67	.296	★131	397	13	★.976
1983—Texas		Amer.	3B	156	618	75	171	35	3	14	66	.277	123	★383	17	.967
1984—Texas x		Amer.	3B	148	553	88	174	36	5	11	83	.315	129	323	●20	.958
1985—Texas x		Amer.	3B	84	313	33	74	13	3	4	32	.236	70	192	16	.942
1985—Cincinnati		Nat.	3B	67	247	28	54	15	2	6	36	.219	54	105	9	.946
American League Totals—14 Years				1911	7253	929	2061	348	48	151	882	.284	1843	4218	221	.965
National League Totals—1 Year				67	247	28	54	15	2	6	36	.219	54	105	9	.946
Major League Totals—14 Years				1978	7500	957	2115	363	50	157	918	.282	1897	4323	230	.964

Selected by Cleveland Indians' organization in 16th round of free-agent draft, June 5, 1969.
†On disabled list, May 27 to June 17 and August 8 to September 1, 1974.
‡Traded to Texas Rangers for Third Baseman Toby Harrah, December 8, 1978.
§On disabled list, June 9 to June 24, 1980.
xTraded to Cincinnati Reds for Outfielder Duane Walker and a player to be named later, July 19, 1985; Texas Rangers' organization acquired Pitcher Jeff Russell to complete deal, July 23, 1985.

ALL-STAR GAME RECORD

Year	League	Pos.	AB.	R.	H.	2B.	3B.	HR.	RBI.	B.A.	PO.	A.	E.	F.A.
1973—American		PH	1	0	1	0	1	0	0	1.000	0	0	0	.000
1980—American		3B	2	0	0	0	0	0	0	.000	0	2	0	1.000
1981—American		3B	1	0	0	0	0	0	1	.000	1	2	0	1.000
1982—American		PH-3B	3	0	0	0	0	0	0	.000	0	1	1	.500
1984—American		3B	1	0	0	0	0	0	0	.000	0	1	0	1.000
All-Star Game Totals—5 Years			8	0	1	0	1	0	1	.125	1	6	1	.875

ERIC ALVIN BELL

Born October 27, 1963, at Modesto, Calif.
Height, 6.00. Weight, 165.
Throws and bats lefthanded.

Tied for Carolina League lead in games started by pitchers with 26 in 1985.

Year Club	League	G.	IP.	W.	L.	Pct.	H.	R.	ER.	SO.	BB.	ERA.
1982—Bluefield	Ap'lachian	11	51⅓	4	1	.800	42	19	12	30	36	2.10
1983—Newark	NYP	18	60	3	2	.600	71	44	33	56	30	4.95
1984—Hagerstown†	Carolina	3	3⅔	0	0	.000	6	4	4	6	5	9.82
1984—Newark	NYP	15	102⅓	8	3	.727	82	40	28	114	26	2.46
1985—Hagerstown	Carolina	26	158⅓	11	6	.647	141	73	55	*162	63	3.13
1985—Baltimore	American	4	5⅔	0	0	.000	4	3	3	4	4	4.76
Major League Totals—1 Year		4	5⅔	0	0	.000	4	3	3	4	4	4.76

Selected by Baltimore Orioles' organization in 9th round of free-agent draft, June 7, 1982.
†On disabled list, May 3 to June 18, 1984.

GEORGE ANTONIO BELL (MATHY)

Born October 21, 1959, at San Pedro de Macoris, Dominican Republic.
Height, 6.01. Weight, 190.
Throws and bats righthanded.
Brother of Tito Bell, shortstop in Los Angeles Dodgers' organization.

Major League stolen bases: 1981 (3), 1983 (1), 1984 (11), 1985 (21). Total—36.
Tied for International League lead in double plays by outfielders with 4 in 1983.
Led Western Carolinas League in total bases with 270 in 1979.
Named outfielder on THE SPORTING NEWS American League Silver Slugger team, 1985.

Year Club	League	Pos.	G.	AB.	R.	H.	2B.	3B.	HR.	RBI.	B.A.	PO.	A.	E.	F.A.
1978—Helena	Pion.	OF	33	106	20	33	6	1	0	14	.311	39	4	4	.915
1979—Spartanburg	W. Car.	OF	130	491	78	150	24	*15	22	*102	.305	206	14	8	.965
1980—Reading†‡	East.	OF	22	55	11	17	5	2	0	11	.309	24	0	1	.960
1981—Toronto	Amer.	OF	60	163	19	38	2	1	5	12	.233	92	3	3	.969
1982—Syracuse§	Int.	OF	37	125	11	25	5	4	3	19	.200	72	3	1	.987
1983—Syracuse	Int.	OF	85	317	37	86	11	4	15	59	.271	135	12	6	.961
1983—Toronto	Amer.	OF	39	112	5	30	5	4	2	17	.268	61	1	3	.954
1984—Toronto	Amer.	OF-3B	159	606	85	177	39	4	26	87	.292	289	13	9	.971
1985—Toronto	Amer.	●OF-1B	157	607	87	167	28	6	28	95	.275	320	14	●11	.968
Major League Totals—4 Years			415	1488	196	412	74	15	61	211	.277	762	31	26	.968

Signed as free agent by Philadelphia Phillies' organization, June 23, 1978.
†On disabled list, June 22, 1980 through remainder of season.
‡Drafted by Toronto Blue Jays, December 8, 1980.
§On disabled list, April 20 to May 1, June 14 to June 30 and July 8, 1982 through remainder of season.

CHAMPIONSHIP SERIES RECORD

Tied American League Championship Series record for most hits, seven-game Series (9), 1985.

Year Club	League	Pos.	G.	AB.	R.	H.	2B.	3B.	HR.	RBI.	B.A.	PO.	A.	E.	F.A.
1985—Toronto	Amer.	OF	7	28	4	9	3	0	1	1	.321	13	0	0	1.000

RAFAEL LEONIDAS BELLIARD (MATIAS)

Name pronounced BELL-ee-ard.

Born October 24, 1961, at Pueblo Nuevo, Mao, D.R.
Height, 5.06. Weight, 150.
Throws and bats righthanded.

Major League stolen bases: 1982 (1), 1984 (4). Total—5.
Led Carolina League in sacrifice hits with 12 and tied for lead in caught stealing with 15 in 1981.
Tied for Eastern League lead in double plays by shortstops with 69 in 1983.

Year Club	League	Pos.	G.	AB.	R.	H.	2B.	3B.	HR.	RBI.	B.A.	PO.	A.	E.	F.A.
1980—Bradenton Pir.	Gulf C.	SS-2B-3B	12	42	6	9	1	0	0	2	.214	24	39	1	.984
1980—Shelby	S. Atl.	SS	8	24	1	3	0	0	0	2	.125	10	27	5	.881
1981—Alexandria	Carol.	SS	127	472	58	102	6	5	0	33	.216	●205	330	29	.949
1982—Buffalo†	East.	SS	40	124	14	34	1	1	0	19	.274	56	87	5	.966
1982—Pittsburgh	Nat.	SS	9	2	3	1	0	0	0	0	.500	2	2	0	1.000
1983—Lynn	East.	SS-2B	127	431	63	113	13	2	2	37	.262	203	307	26	.951
1983—Pittsburgh	Nat.	SS	4	1	1	0	0	0	0	0	.000	1	3	0	1.000
1984—Pittsburgh‡	Nat.	SS-2B	20	22	3	5	0	0	0	0	.227	12	13	3	.893
1985—Pittsburgh	Nat.	SS	17	20	1	4	0	0	0	1	.200	13	23	2	.947
1985—Hawaii	P. C.	SS-2B	100	341	35	84	12	4	1	18	.246	172	289	5	.989
Major League Totals—4 Years			50	45	8	10	0	0	0	1	.222	28	41	5	.932

Signed as free agent by Pittsburgh Pirates' organization, July 10, 1980.
†On disabled list, April 19 to July 24, 1982.
‡On disabled list, June 28 to August 28, 1984.

—DID YOU KNOW—

That in each of his first two years in the major leagues (1984 and 1985), Philadelphia's Juan Samuel reached double figures in doubles, triples, homers and stolen bases?

BRUCE EDWIN BENEDICT

Born August 18, 1955, at Birmingham, Ala.
Height, 6.01. Weight, 185.
Throws and bats righthanded.
Attended University of Nebraska, Omaha, Neb.
Son of David Benedict, pitcher in New York Yankees', Washington Senators'
and St. Louis Cardinals' organizations, 1950 through 1958.

Major League stolen bases: 1979 (1), 1980 (3), 1981 (1), 1982 (4), 1983 (1), 1984 (1). Total—11.

Year Club	League	Pos.	G.	AB.	R.	H.	2B.	3B.	HR.	RBI.	B.A.	PO.	A.	E.	F.A.
1976—Kingsport	Appal.	C	17	63	10	18	1	0	0	4	.286	98	25	3	.976
1976—Greenwood	W. Car.	C	21	54	7	13	1	0	1	10	.241	93	12	5	.955
1976—Savannah	South.	C	24	73	10	21	1	0	0	7	.288	107	12	2	.983
1977—Savannah	South.	C	124	395	55	104	15	0	7	40	.263	★770	★112	13	.985
1978—Richmond	Int.	C	111	348	41	97	13	0	2	34	.279	592	56	4	★.994
1978—Atlanta	Nat.	C	22	52	3	13	2	0	0	1	.250	81	14	1	.990
1979—Atlanta	Nat.	C	76	204	14	46	11	0	0	15	.225	344	35	6	.984
1980—Richmond	Int.	C	3	10	0	3	0	0	0	0	.300	10	5	0	1.000
1980—Atlanta	Nat.	C	120	359	18	91	14	1	2	34	.253	502	76	7	.988
1981—Atlanta	Nat.	C	90	295	26	78	12	1	5	35	.264	404	★73	7	.986
1982—Atlanta	Nat.	C	118	386	34	95	11	1	3	44	.246	602	73	5	★.993
1983—Atlanta	Nat.	C	134	423	43	126	13	1	2	43	.298	738	91	7	.992
1984—Atlanta	Nat.	C	95	300	26	67	8	1	4	25	.223	504	37	5	.991
1985—Atlanta	Nat.	C	70	208	12	42	6	0	0	20	.202	314	35	4	.989
Major League Totals—8 Years			725	2227	176	558	77	5	16	217	.251	3489	434	42	.989

Selected by Atlanta Braves' organization in 5th round of free-agent draft, June 8, 1976.

CHAMPIONSHIP SERIES RECORD

Year Club	League	Pos.	G.	AB.	R.	H.	2B.	3B.	HR.	RBI.	B.A.	PO.	A.	E.	F.A.
1982—Atlanta	Nat.	C	3	8	1	2	1	0	0	0	.250	16	2	0	1.000

ALL-STAR GAME RECORD

Year League	Pos.	AB.	R.	H.	2B.	3B.	HR.	RBI.	B.A.	PO.	A.	E.	F.A.
1981—National	C	1	0	0	0	0	0	0	.000	3	0	0	1.000
1983—National	C	1	0	1	0	0	0	0	1.000	5	0	0	1.000
All-Star Game Totals—2 Years		2	0	1	0	0	0	0	.500	8	0	0	1.000

JUAN JOSE BENIQUEZ (TORRES)

Name pronounced Be-NEE-kez.

Born May 13, 1950, at San Sebastian, Puerto Rico.
Height, 5.11. Weight, 175.
Throws and bats righthanded.

Established modern major league record for most errors, shortstop, two consecutive games (6), July 13 and 14, 1972.
Major League stolen bases: 1971 (3), 1972 (2), 1974 (19), 1975 (7), 1976 (17), 1977 (26), 1978 (10), 1979 (3), 1980 (2), 1981 (2), 1982 (3), 1983 (4), 1985 (4). Total—102.
Led American League outfielders in putouts with 410 and total chances with 434 in 1976.
Led International League in sacrifice hits with 11 in 1971.
Led Florida State League shortstops in assists with 372 and double plays with 51 in 1969.
Named outfielder on THE SPORTING NEWS American League All-Star fielding team, 1977.

Year Club	League	Pos.	G.	AB.	R.	H.	2B.	3B.	HR.	RBI.	B.A.	PO.	A.	E.	F.A.
1969—Winter Haven	Fla. St.	★SS-2B	120	426	59	111	15	★14	2	59	.261	175	373	★49	.918
1969—Winston-Salem	Carol.	SS	2	10	0	2	0	0	0	0	.200	2	6	0	1.000
1970—Winston-Salem	Carol.	SS	92	335	53	91	12	2	9	37	.272	144	275	35	.923
1970—Pawtucket	East.	SS	56	233	29	58	5	3	4	25	.249	105	167	29	.904
1971—Louisville	Int.	SS	132	534	82	149	12	★16	4	51	.279	205	364	★55	.912
1971—Boston	Amer.	SS	16	57	8	17	2	0	0	4	.298	24	27	6	.895
1972—Louisville	Int.	SS	66	277	40	82	10	7	5	32	.296	114	172	21	.932
1972—Boston	Amer.	SS	33	99	10	24	4	1	1	8	.242	38	88	14	.900
1973—Pawtucket	Int.	O-S-2-3	131	440	80	131	24	4	13	52	★.298	196	176	26	.934
1974—Boston†	Amer.	OF	106	389	60	104	14	3	5	33	.267	264	4	6	.978
1975—Boston‡§	Amer.	OF-3B	78	254	43	74	14	4	2	17	.291	110	17	1	.992
1976—Texas	Amer.	★OF-2B	145	478	49	122	14	4	0	33	.255	411	★18	7	.984
1977—Texas x	Amer.	OF	123	424	56	114	19	6	10	50	.269	311	10	4	.988
1978—Texas yz	Amer.	OF	127	473	61	123	17	3	11	50	.260	309	8	9	.972
1979—New York ab	Amer.	OF-3B	62	142	19	36	6	1	4	17	.254	100	15	2	.983
1980—Seattle cde	Amer.	OF	70	237	26	54	10	0	6	21	.228	176	3	8	.957
1981—California	Amer.	OF	58	166	18	30	5	0	3	13	.181	117	0	5	.959
1982—California	Amer.	OF	112	196	25	52	11	2	3	24	.265	113	4	2	.983
1983—California f	Amer.	OF	92	315	44	96	15	0	3	34	.305	174	8	6	.968
1984—California	Amer.	OF	110	354	60	119	17	0	8	39	.336	197	5	6	.971
1985—California g	Amer.	O-1-3-S	132	411	54	125	13	5	8	42	.304	439	26	4	.991
Major League Totals—14 Years			1264	3995	533	1090	161	29	64	385	.273	2783	233	81	.974

Signed as free agent by Boston Red Sox' organization, October 1, 1968.
†On disabled list, July 3 to July 28, 1974.
‡On disabled list, July 2 to July 18, 1975.
§Traded with Pitcher Steve Barr, a minor league player to be named later and an estimated $200,000 to Texas Rangers for Pitcher Ferguson Jenkins, November 17, 1975; Texas acquired Pitcher Craig Skok to complete deal, December 12, 1975.
xOn disabled list, July 31 to August 15, 1977.

yOn disabled list, June 13 to July 13, 1978.
zTraded with Pitchers Paul Mirabella, Mike Griffin and Dave Righetti and Outfielder Greg Jemison to New York Yankees for Pitchers Sparky Lyle, Larry McCall and Dave Rajsich, Catcher Mike Heath, Shortstop Domingo Ramos and cash, November 10, 1978.
aOn disabled list, July 9 to September 1, 1979.
bTraded with Catcher Jerry Narron and Pitchers Jim Beattie and Rick Anderson to Seattle Mariners for Outfielder Ruppert Jones and Pitcher Jim Lewis, November 1, 1979.
cOn disabled list, April 9 to June 2 and July 19 to August 8, 1980.
dOn suspended list, September 2 to September 7, 1980.
eGranted free agency, October 24, 1980; signed by California Angels, December 29, 1980.
fOn disabled list, June 20 to August 9, 1983.
gGranted free agency, November 12, 1985.

CHAMPIONSHIP SERIES RECORD

Tied American League Championship Series record for most stolen bases, three-game Series (2), 1975.

Year Club	League	Pos.	G.	AB.	R.	H.	2B.	3B.	HR.	RBI.	B.A.	PO.	A.	E.	F.A.
1975—Boston	Amer.	DH	3	12	2	3	0	0	0	1	.250	0	0	0	.000
1982—California	Amer.	OF	2	0	0	0	0	0	0	0	.000	1	0	0	1.000
Championship Series Totals—2 Years			5	12	2	3	0	0	0	1	.250	1	0	0	1.000

WORLD SERIES RECORD

Year Club	League	Pos.	G.	AB.	R.	H.	2B.	3B.	HR.	RBI.	B.A.	PO.	A.	E.	F.A.
1975—Boston	Amer.	OF PH	3	8	0	1	0	0	0	1	.125	6	1	0	1.000

ALFRED LEE BENTON
(Butch)

Born August 24, 1957, at Tampa, Fla.
Height, 6.01. Weight, 195.
Throws and bats righthanded.

Led American Association catchers in errors with 17 in 1984.
Led Texas League in passed balls with 19 in 1978.
Led Midwest League in passed balls with 36 in 1976.
Tied for International League lead in passed balls with 15 in 1979.
Tied for Carolina League lead in passed balls with 16 in 1977.

Year Club	League	Pos.	G.	AB.	R.	H.	2B.	3B.	HR.	RBI.	B.A.	PO.	A.	E.	F.A.
1975—Marion	Appal.	C	45	145	25	36	11	1	2	18	.248	284	27	12	.963
1976—Wausau	Midw.	C-1B	120	431	43	105	14	1	8	63	.244	552	70	30	.954
1977—Lynchburg	Carol.	C	59	233	40	80	18	4	3	46	.343	277	36	9	.972
1977—Jackson	Texas	C	60	181	18	52	13	0	3	18	.287	264	47	5	.984
1977—Tidewater	Int.	PH	1	1	0	0	0	0	0	0	.000	0	0	0	.000
1978—Jackson	Texas	C	106	360	49	99	31	2	6	44	.275	*672	*91	19	.976
1978—New York	Nat.	C	4	4	1	2	0	0	0	2	.500	4	0	0	1.000
1979—Tidewater†	Int.	C	94	313	39	62	9	1	3	25	.198	406	38	9	.981
1980—Tidewater	Int.	C-OF-1B	67	240	36	63	15	2	5	34	.263	259	26	7	.976
1980—New York‡	Nat.	C	12	21	0	1	0	0	0	0	.048	27	2	2	.935
1981—Iowa§	A. A.	C-3B	70	203	25	41	8	1	6	20	.202	353	40	14	.966
1982—Iowa	A. A.	*C-OF	85	291	36	96	17	4	11	57	.330	354	38	*14	.966
1982—Chicago x	Nat.	C	4	7	0	1	0	0	0	1	.143	20	1	0	1.000
1983—Wichita yz	A. A.	C-O-1-3	125	460	66	137	29	2	9	51	.298	404	44	8	.982
1984—Evansville a	A. A.	C-O-1-3-2	109	350	38	98	20	0	6	41	.280	380	60	21	.954
1985—Cleveland	Amer.	C	31	67	5	12	4	0	0	7	.179	75	13	4	.957
1985—Maine	Int.	C	48	187	16	53	10	1	2	30	.283	116	20	5	.965
National League Totals—3 Years			20	32	1	4	0	0	0	3	.125	51	3	2	.964
American League Totals—1 Year			31	67	5	12	4	0	0	7	.179	75	13	4	.957
Major League Totals—4 Years			51	99	6	16	4	0	0	10	.162	126	16	6	.959

Selected by New York Mets' organization in 1st round (sixth player selected) of free-agent draft, June 4, 1975.
†On disabled list, July 9 to August 2, 1979.
‡Sold to Iowa (Chicago Cubs' organization), April 6, 1981.
§On disabled list, June 17 to June 30, 1981.
xTraded to Montreal Expos for Infielder Jerry Manuel, February 7, 1983.
yGranted free agency, October 20, 1983; signed by Portland (Philadelphia Phillies' organization), January 30, 1984.
zReleased, March 20, 1984; signed by Evansville (Detroit Tigers' organization), March 25, 1984.
aGranted free agency, October 15, 1984; signed by Maine (Cleveland Indians' organization), January 7, 1985.

TODD ERIC BENZINGER

Born February 11, 1963, at Dayton, Ky.
Height, 6.01. Weight, 180.
Throws right and bats left and righthanded.

Year Club	League	Pos.	G.	AB.	R.	H.	2B.	3B.	HR.	RBI.	B.A.	PO.	A.	E.	F.A.
1981—Elmira	NYP	OF-1B	41	141	21	34	10	1	2	8	.241	131	9	2	.986
1982—Winston-Salem	Carol.	OF-1B	121	443	54	97	19	1	5	46	.219	438	28	8	.983
1983—Winter Haven	Fla. St.	OF-1B-3B	125	480	56	134	34	5	7	68	.279	206	10	8	.964
1984—New Britain†	East.	OF-1B	110	391	49	101	25	5	10	60	.258	465	29	14	.972
1985—Pawtucket‡	Int.	OF	70	256	31	64	13	1	11	47	.250	106	3	3	.973

Selected by Boston Red Sox' organization in 4th round of free-agent draft, June 8, 1981.
†On disabled list, August 10, 1984 through remainder of season.
‡On disabled list, April 10 to June 11, 1985.

JUAN BAUTISTA BERENGUER

Name pronounced Bare-en-GARE.

Born November 30, 1954, at Aguadulce, Panama.
Height, 5.11. Weight, 215.
Throws and bats righthanded.

Major League saves: 1983 (1).
Led Carolina League pitchers in games started with 28 and hit batsmen with 13 in 1976.
Tied for American Association lead in complete games with 9 in 1982.
Tied for Texas League pitchers lead in games started with 26 in 1977.
Tied for Midwest League lead in hit batsmen with 8 in 1975.
Named International League Pitcher of the Year, 1978.

Year Club	League	G.	IP.	W.	L.	Pct.	H.	R.	ER.	SO.	BB.	ERA.
1975—Wausau	Midwest	18	95	5	4	.556	83	41	31	58	50	2.94
1976—Lynchburg	Carolina	28	187	10	13	.435	★175	89	★75	114	★118	3.61
1977—Jackson	Texas	26	181	9	8	.529	143	89	69	★160	★126	3.43
1978—Tidewater	Int'national	24	147	10	7	.588	117	60	60	130	91	3.67
1978—New York†	National	5	13	0	2	.000	17	12	12	8	11	8.31
1979—Tacoma	P. Coast	26	166	8	8	.500	128	101	90	★220	129	4.88
1979—New York	National	5	31	1	1	.500	28	13	10	25	12	2.90
1980—Tidewater	Int'national	27	157	9	●15	.375	122	78	67	★178	76	3.84
1980—New York‡	National	6	9	0	1	.000	9	9	6	7	10	6.00
1981—Kansas City§-Toronto x	American	20	91	2	★13	.133	84	62	53	49	51	5.24
1982—Evansville	Am. Assoc.	25	156⅓	11	10	.524	152	85	80	127	80	4.61
1982—Detroit	American	2	6⅔	0	0	.000	5	5	5	8	9	6.75
1983—Detroit	American	37	157⅔	9	5	.643	110	58	55	129	71	3.14
1984—Detroit	American	31	168⅓	11	10	.524	146	75	65	118	79	3.48
1985—Detroit y	American	31	95	5	6	.455	96	67	59	82	48	5.59
National League Totals—3 Years		16	53	1	4	.200	54	34	28	40	33	4.75
American League Totals—5 Years		121	518⅔	27	34	.443	441	267	237	386	258	4.11
Major League Totals—8 Years		137	571⅔	28	38	.424	495	301	265	426	291	4.17

Signed as free agent by New York Mets' organization, February 22, 1975.
†Loaned to Tacoma (Cleveland Indians' organization), March 24, 1979; returned August 29, 1979.
‡Traded to Kansas City for Outfielder Marvell Wynne and Pitcher John Skinner, March 31, 1981.
§Sold on waivers to Toronto Blue Jays, August 8, 1981.
xReleased, March 28, 1982; signed by Evansville (Detroit Tigers' organization), April 4, 1982.
yTraded with Catcher Bob Melvin and a player to be named later to San Francisco Giants for Pitchers Dave LaPoint and Eric King and Catcher Matt Nokes, October 7, 1985; San Francisco acquired Pitcher Scott Medvin to complete deal, December 11, 1985.

BRUCE MICHAEL BERENYI

Name pronounced Buh-RENN-ee.

Born August 21, 1954, at Bryan, O.
Height, 6.03. Weight, 215.
Throws and bats righthanded.
Attended Glen Oaks Community College, Centerville, Mich. and
Northeast Missouri State University, Kirksville, Mo.
Nephew of Ned Garver, pitcher with St. Louis Browns, Detroit Tigers,
Kansas City A's and Los Angeles Angels, 1948 through 1961.

Led American Association in shutouts with 3 and wild pitches with 13 in 1979.
Named Southern League Pitcher of the Year, 1978.

Year Club	League	G.	IP.	W.	L.	Pct.	H.	R.	ER.	SO.	BB.	ERA.
1976—Eugene	Northwest	12	49	3	1	.750	50	37	26	39	55	4.78
1977—Shelby	W. Carol.	25	145	10	8	.556	102	55	37	120	75	★2.30
1978—Nashville†	Southern	23	135	10	5	.667	107	44	37	103	63	2.47
1979—Indianapolis	Am. Assoc.	25	166	9	9	.500	134	64	52	★136	98	★2.82
1980—Indianapolis	Am. Assoc.	20	123	5	8	.385	111	66	59	★121	●100	4.32
1980—Cincinnati	National	6	28	2	2	.500	34	26	24	19	23	7.71
1981—Cincinnati	National	21	126	9	6	.600	97	55	49	106	★77	3.50
1982—Cincinnati	National	34	222⅓	9	★18	.333	208	90	83	157	96	3.36
1983—Cincinnati	National	32	186⅓	9	14	.391	173	92	80	151	102	3.86
1984—Cincinnati‡-New York	National	32	166	12	13	.480	163	93	82	134	95	4.45
1985—New York§	National	3	13⅔	1	0	1.000	8	6	4	10	10	2.63
1985—Tidewater	Int'national	1	1	0	0	.000	3	1	1	1	0	9.00
Major League Totals—6 Years		128	742⅓	42	53	.442	683	362	322	577	403	3.90

Selected by Detroit Tigers' organization in 19th round of free-agent draft, June 4, 1975.
Selected by Cincinnati Reds' organization in secondary phase of free-agent draft, June 8, 1976.
†On disabled list, June 30 to July 27, 1978.
‡Traded to New York Mets for Third Baseman Eddie Williams and Pitchers Jay Tibbs and Matt Bullinger, June 15, 1984.
§On disabled list, April 24 to September 1, 1985; included rehabilitation disability assignment to Tidewater, May 18 to May 21, 1985.

—DID YOU KNOW—

That the scheduled May 20 Milwaukee-Cleveland game was the first to be rained out in 1985? Prior to that date, 458 games had been played without a postponement.

DAVID BRUCE BERGMAN
(Dave)

Born June 6, 1953, at Evanston, Ill.
Height, 6.02. Weight, 180.
Throws and bats lefthanded.
Received bachelor of arts degree in business administration
from Illinois State University, Normal, Ill., in 1974.

Major League stolen bases: 1978 (2), 1980 (1), 1981 (2), 1982 (3), 1983 (2), 1984 (3). Total—13.
Led International League in bases on balls received with 95 in 1979.
Led International League first basemen in putouts with 1,199 in 1976.
Led Eastern League first basemen in assists with 58 in 1975.
Named Eastern League Player of the Year, 1975.
Named outfielder on THE SPORTING NEWS College Baseball All-America Team, 1974.

Year Club	League	Pos.	G.	AB.	R.	H.	2B.	3B.	HR.	RBI.	B.A.	PO.	A.	E.	F.A.
1974—Oneonta	NYP	1B	56	201	60	70	6	•7	10	48	★.348	494	★29	8	★.985
1975—West Haven	East.	1B-OF	124	399	76	124	15	6	11	60	★.311	610	61	5	.993
1975—New York..............	Amer.	OF	7	17	0	0	0	0	0	0	.000	10	1	1	.917
1976—Syracuse	Int.	★1B-OF	134	455	68	134	23	2	7	65	.295	1201	82	10	★.992
1977—Syracuse	Int.	OF-1B	132	468	88	146	29	4	16	59	.312	534	39	8	.986
1977—New York†	Amer.	OF-1B	5	4	1	1	0	0	0	1	.250	8	0	0	1.000
1978—Houston	Nat.	1B-OF	104	186	15	43	5	1	0	12	.231	328	16	4	.989
1979—Charleston	Int.	1B-OF	138	461	78	129	23	3	6	58	.280	910	61	11	.989
1979—Houston	Nat.	1B	13	15	4	6	0	0	1	2	.400	8	0	0	1.000
1980—Houston	Nat.	1B-OF	90	78	12	20	6	1	0	3	.256	187	16	1	.995
1981—Hou.‡-S.F..............	Nat.	1B-OF	69	151	17	38	9	0	4	14	.252	255	25	3	.989
1982—San Francisco	Nat.	1B-OF	100	121	22	33	3	1	4	14	.273	321	20	4	.988
1983—San Francisco§	Nat.	1B-OF	90	140	16	40	4	1	6	24	.286	299	27	2	.994
1984—Detroit..................	Amer.	1B-OF	120	271	42	74	8	5	7	44	.273	658	75	8	.989
1985—Detroit x...............	Amer.	1B-OF	69	140	8	25	2	0	3	7	.179	306	25	3	.991
1985—Nashville...............	A. A.	1B	11	39	6	9	1	0	1	6	.231	87	8	1	.990
National League Totals—6 Years...........			466	691	86	180	27	4	15	69	.260	1398	104	14	.991
American League Totals—4 Years			201	432	51	100	10	5	10	52	.231	982	101	12	.989
Major League Totals—10 Years..............			667	1123	137	280	37	9	25	121	.249	2380	205	26	.990

Selected by Chicago Cubs' organization in 12th round of free-agent draft, June 8, 1971.
Selected by New York Yankees' organization in 2nd round of free-agent draft, June 5, 1974.
†Traded to Houston Astros, November 23, 1977, completing deal in which Houston traded First Baseman-Catcher Cliff Johnson to New York Yankees for Infielder Mike Fischlin, Pitcher Randy Niemann and a player to be named later, June 15, 1977.
‡Traded with Outfielder Jeff Leonard to San Francisco Giants for First Baseman Mike Ivie, April 20, 1981.
§Traded to Philadelphia Phillies for Outfielder Alejandro Sanchez, March 24, 1984; Traded by Philadelphia with Pitcher Willie Hernandez to Detroit Tigers for Outfielder Glenn Wilson and Catcher-First Baseman John Wockenfuss, March 24, 1984.
xOn disabled list, April 22 to May 29, 1985; included rehabilitation disability assignment to Nashville, May 15 to May 29, 1985.

CHAMPIONSHIP SERIES RECORD

Year Club	League	Pos.	G.	AB.	R.	H.	2B.	3B.	HR.	RBI.	B.A.	PO.	A.	E.	F.A.
1980—Houston	Nat.	PR-1B	4	3	0	1	0	1	0	2	.333	8	2	1	.909
1984—Detroit....................	Amer.	PR-1B	2	1	1	1	0	0	0	0	1.000	5	0	0	1.000
Championship Series Totals—2 Years.....			6	4	1	2	0	1	0	2	.500	13	2	1	.938

WORLD SERIES RECORD

Year Club	League	Pos.	G.	AB.	R.	H.	2B.	3B.	HR.	RBI.	B.A.	PO.	A.	E.	F.A.
1984—Detroit....................	Amer.	PR-1B	5	5	0	0	0	0	0	0	.000	22	4	0	1.000

ANTONIO BERNAZARD (GARCIA)
(Tony)

Born August 24, 1956, at Caguas, P.R.
Height, 5.09. Weight, 160.
Throws right and bats right and lefthanded.
Attended University of Florida, Gainesville, Fla., and Humacao College, Humacao, P.R.
Brother of Oscar Bernazard, outfielder in Pittsburgh Pirates'
and Montreal Expos' organizations, 1975 through 1978.

Major League stolen bases: 1979 (1), 1980 (9), 1981 (4), 1982 (11), 1983 (23), 1984 (20), 1985 (17). Total—85.
Led Eastern League in caught stealing with 20 in 1977.
Led American Association second basemen in putouts with 297, assists with 386 and double plays with 101 in 1978.
Led Eastern League second basemen in double plays with 70 in 1976.
Led Florida State League second basemen in assists with 386 in 1975.

Year Club	League	Pos.	G.	AB.	R.	H.	2B.	3B.	HR.	RBI.	B.A.	PO.	A.	E.	F.A.
1974—Kinston†................	Carol.	2B	56	225	22	45	3	1	0	16	.200	129	142	19	.934
1974—Sarasota Expos‡ ..	Gulf C.	2B	34	109	11	18	2	1	1	6	.165	95	71	7	.960
1975—W. Palm Beach....	Fla. St.	2B-SS	★134	★509	65	121	16	2	6	50	.238	282	389	28	★.960
1976—Quebec City.........	East.	2B	106	334	35	72	8	3	1	26	.216	227	257	18	.964
1977—Quebec City.........	East.	2B	125	425	68	119	11	6	1	34	.280	273	379	25	.963
1978—Denver	A. A.	★2-3-O	128	479	★107	137	30	9	9	65	.286	302	390	★32	.956
1979—Denver	A. A.	2B	82	273	58	82	15	2	3	29	.300	178	275	•19	.960
1979—Montreal	Nat.	2B	22	40	11	12	2	0	1	8	.300	22	34	1	.982

Year Club	League	Pos.	G.	AB.	R.	H.	2B.	3B.	HR.	RBI.	B.A.	PO.	A.	E.	F.A.
1980—Montreal§	Nat.	2B-SS	82	183	26	41	7	1	5	18	.224	82	151	9	.963
1981—Chicago	Amer.	2B-SS	106	384	53	106	14	4	6	34	.276	228	320	7	.987
1982—Chicago x..............	Amer.	2B	137	540	90	138	25	9	11	56	.256	353	443	12	.985
1983—Chi. y-Sea. z	Amer.	2B	139	533	65	141	34	3	8	56	.265	262	422	19	.973
1984—Cleveland..............	Amer.	2B	140	439	44	97	15	4	2	38	.221	264	397	*20	.971
1985—Cleveland a	Amer.	2B-SS	153	500	73	137	26	3	11	59	.274	313	399	16	.978
National League Totals—2 Years............			104	223	37	53	9	1	6	26	.238	104	185	10	.967
American League Totals—5 Years			675	2396	325	619	114	23	38	243	.258	1420	1981	74	.979
Major League Totals—7 Years................			779	2619	362	672	123	24	44	269	.257	1524	2166	84	.978

Signed as free agent by Montreal Expos' organization, November 13, 1973.

†On disabled list, June 10 to June 17, 1974.

‡On temporary inactive list, August 15 to September 25, 1974.

§Traded to Chicago White Sox for Pitcher Richard Wortham, December 12, 1980.

xOn disabled list, September 13, 1982 through remainder of season.

yTraded to Seattle Mariners for Second Baseman Julio Cruz, June 15, 1983.

zTraded to Cleveland Indians for Outfielder Gorman Thomas and Second Baseman Jack Perconte, December 7, 1983.

aGranted free agency, November 12, 1985; re-signed by Indians, January 8, 1986.

NEHAMES BERNSTINE JR.
(Pookie)

Born November 20, 1960, at Bryan, Tex.
Height, 5.10. Weight, 175.
Throws right and bats right and lefthanded.
Attended Lewis-Clark State College, Lewiston, Ida.

Year Club	League	Pos.	G.	AB.	R.	H.	2B.	3B.	HR.	RBI.	B.A.	PO.	A.	E.	F.A.
1982—Batavia†	NYP	OF-2B	71	263	48	82	13	2	2	18	.312	74	26	2	.980
1983—Waterloo	Midw.	OF-2B	130	455	83	106	14	8	6	29	.233	60	7	5	.931
1984—Buffalo‡	East.	OF	126	479	88	137	16	9	8	52	.286	219	7	4	.983
1985—Pittsfield	East.	OF	50	202	33	63	6	5	1	17	.312	120	5	6	.954
1985—Iowa	A. A.	OF	83	302	52	96	11	4	2	18	.318	168	6	1	.994

Selected by Cleveland Indians' organization in 5th round of free-agent draft, June 7, 1982.

†Batted righthanded.

‡Sold to Chicago Cubs' organization, April 14, 1985, after replacing Infielder-Outfielder Glenn Edwards, who was sold to Chicago organization on April 1, 1985 but was returned due to injury.

DALE ANTHONY BERRA

Born December 13, 1956, at Ridgewood, N. J.
Height, 6.00. Weight, 190.
Throws and bats righthanded.
Son of Yogi Berra, Hall of Fame catcher with New York Yankees and New York Mets, 1946 through 1963 and 1965; manager, New York Yankees, 1964, 1984 and 1985; manager, New York Mets, 1972 through 1975; coach, New York Yankees, 1976 through 1983; and currently coach with Houston Astros; Brother of Larry Berra Jr., catcher in New York Mets' organization, 1971 and 1972; and Tim Berra, wide receiver with Baltimore Colts, 1974.

Established major league record for most times awarded first base on catcher's interference, season (7), 1983.
Major League stolen bases: 1978 (3), 1980 (2), 1981 (11), 1982 (6), 1983 (8), 1984 (1), 1985 (1). Total—32.
Led National League in intentional bases on balls received with 19 in 1983.
Led New York-Pennsylvania League in sacrifice flies with 8 in 1975.
Led Western Carolinas League third basemen in double plays with 27 in 1976.
Tied for New York-Pennsylvania League lead in double plays by third basemen with 13 in 1975.

Year Club	League	Pos.	G.	AB.	R.	H.	2B.	3B.	HR.	RBI.	B.A.	PO.	A.	E.	F.A.
1975—Niagara Falls	NYP	3B	67	*269	36	69	6	4	3	*49	.257	67	*137	*24	.895
1976—Charleston	W. Car.	3B	*139	527	78	157	28	5	16	89	.298	129	*269	*41	.907
1977—Columbus..............	Int.	*3B-SS	125	438	68	127	18	7	18	54	.290	97	252	*29	.923
1977—Pittsburgh	Nat.	3B	17	40	0	7	1	0	0	3	.175	14	22	1	.973
1978—Columbus..............	Int.	SS-3B	99	361	58	101	18	5	18	63	.280	142	280	22	.950
1978—Pittsburgh	Nat.	3B-SS	56	135	16	28	2	0	6	14	.207	31	84	11	.913
1979—Portland	P. C.	SS-3B	56	210	37	68	13	2	6	32	.324	68	158	8	.966
1979—Pittsburgh	Nat.	SS-3B	44	123	11	26	5	0	3	15	.211	43	86	12	.915
1980—Pittsburgh............	Nat.	3B-SS-2B	93	245	21	54	8	2	6	31	.220	88	171	11	.959
1981—Pittsburgh............	Nat.	3B-SS-2B	81	232	21	56	12	0	2	27	.241	89	167	8	.970
1982—Pittsburgh............	Nat.	SS-3B	156	529	64	139	25	5	10	61	.263	241	505	30	.961
1983—Pittsburgh............	Nat.	SS	161	537	51	135	25	1	10	52	.251	286	505	30	.963
1984—Pittsburgh†‡........	Nat.	●SS-3B	136	450	31	100	16	0	9	52	.222	186	449	●30	.955
1985—New York.............	Amer.	3B-SS	48	109	8	25	5	1	1	8	.229	22	74	9	.914
National League Totals—8 Years............			744	2291	215	545	94	8	46	255	.238	978	1989	133	.957
American League Totals—1 Year			48	109	8	25	5	1	1	8	.229	22	74	9	.914
Major League Totals—9 Years................			792	2400	223	570	99	9	47	263	.238	1000	2063	142	.956

Selected by Pittsburgh Pirates' organization in 1st round (20th player selected) of free-agent draft, June 4, 1975.

†On disabled list, August 30 to September 14, 1984.

‡Traded with Pitcher Alfonso Pulido and Outfielder Jay Buhner to New York Yankees for Outfielder Steve Kemp, Infielder Tim Foli and $800,000, December 20, 1984.

KARL JON BEST

Born March 6, 1959, at Aberdeen, Wash.
Height, 6.04. Weight, 210.
Throws and bats righthanded.

Major League saves: 1985 (4).

Year Club	League	G.	IP.	W.	L.	Pct.	H.	R.	ER.	SO.	BB.	ERA.
1978—Stockton	California	12	40	1	5	.167	42	37	21	32	33	4.73
1978—Bellingham	Northwest	10	54	3	3	.500	58	32	30	47	32	5.00
1979—Alexandria	Carolina	24	167	8	11	.421	150	74	60	108	85	3.23
1980—Lynn	Eastern	26	154	9	14	.391	144	116	95	92	★106	5.55
1981—Lynn†	Eastern	13	71	4	4	.500	73	37	30	50	31	3.80
1982—Lynn	Eastern	21	138⅓	9	4	.692	104	63	53	125	90	3.45
1983—Salt Lake City	P. Coast	51	84	7	4	.636	86	51	45	108	64	4.82
1983—Seattle	American	4	5⅓	0	1	.000	14	9	8	3	5	13.50
1984—Salt Lake City	P. Coast	46	76	6	5	.545	69	52	44	77	55	5.21
1984—Seattle	American	5	6	1	1	.500	7	2	2	6	0	3.00
1985—Calgary	P. Coast	4	5⅓	0	0	.000	2	1	0	8	4	0.00
1985—Seattle‡	American	15	32⅓	2	1	.667	25	9	7	32	6	1.95
Major League Totals—3 Years		24	43⅔	3	3	.500	46	20	17	41	11	3.50

Selected by Seattle Mariners' organization in 12th round of free-agent draft, June 7, 1977.
†On disabled list, May 9 to July 25, 1981.
‡On disabled list, June 24, 1985 through remainder of season.

KURT ANTHONY BEVACQUA

Name pronounced Buh-VAHK-wuh.

Born January 23, 1947, at Miami Beach, Fla.
Height, 6.02. Weight, 190.
Throws and bats righthanded.
Attended Miami-Dade (North) Community College, Miami, Fla.

Major League stolen bases: 1973 (2), 1974 (1), 1975 (3), 1978 (1), 1979 (2), 1980 (1), 1982 (2). Total—12.
Led American Association third basemen in putouts with 73, assists with 168, total chances with 253, double plays with 26 and fielding percentage with .953 in 1970.
Tied for Southern League lead in double plays by third basemen with 24 in 1969.

Year Club	League	Pos.	G.	AB.	R.	H.	2B.	3B.	HR.	RBI.	B.A.	PO.	A.	E.	F.A.
1967—Tampa	Fla. St.	2B	65	217	13	48	2	1	0	11	.221	119	143	10	.963
1968—Tampa	Fla. St.	2B-1B	91	219	18	55	11	2	2	26	.251	264	74	7	.980
1969—Asheville	South.	3B	133	490	72	155	26	6	16	91	.316	★129	245	29	.928
1970—Indianapolis	A. A.	3-0-S-1-2	135	482	62	126	26	5	15	67	.261	157	216	21	.947
1971—Ind.†-Wichita	A. A.	3-S-2-O	60	235	36	71	16	1	9	38	.302	107	130	11	.956
1971—Cleveland	Amer.	2-O-3-S	55	137	9	28	3	1	3	13	.204	77	72	5	.968
1972—Portland	P. C.	3-2-O-S	145	537	57	168	27	7	9	72	.313	223	252	30	.941
1972—Cleveland‡	Amer.	OF-3B	19	35	2	4	0	0	1	1	.114	11	5	1	.941
1973—Kansas City§	Amer.	3-2-O-1	99	276	39	71	8	3	2	40	.257	120	90	9	.959
1974—Pittsburgh x	Nat.	3B-OF	18	35	1	4	1	0	0	0	.114	8	13	1	.955
1974—Kansas City y	Amer.	1-3-2-S	39	90	10	19	0	0	0	3	.211	90	29	5	.960
1975—Milwaukee	Amer.	3-2-S-1	104	258	30	59	14	0	2	24	.229	157	168	13	.962
1976—Milwaukee	Amer.	2B	12	7	3	1	0	0	0	0	.143	0	6	0	1.000
1976—Spokane z a	P. C.	3-S-2-O	95	356	70	120	24	0	12	49	.337	116	197	22	.934
1977—Tucson	P. C.	3B-SS	94	358	75	126	29	4	9	76	.352	74	231	23	.930
1977—Texas	Amer.	O-3-1-2	39	96	13	32	7	2	5	28	.333	42	31	1	.986
1978—Texas b	Amer.	3B-2B-1B	90	248	21	55	12	0	6	30	.222	62	116	18	.908
1979—San Diego	Nat.	3-2-1-O	114	297	23	75	12	4	1	34	.253	115	156	11	.961
1980—S.D.c-Pitt.	Nat.	3-O-1-2	84	114	5	26	7	1	0	16	.228	32	31	2	.969
1981—Pittsburgh	Nat.	2B-3B	29	27	2	7	1	0	1	4	.259	7	10	1	.944
1981—Portland d	P. C.	3B	14	52	6	13	1	0	0	5	.250	12	24	1	.973
1982—San Diego	Nat.	1B-OF-3B	64	123	15	31	9	0	0	24	.252	256	16	3	.989
1983—San Diego	Nat.	1B-3B-OF	74	156	17	38	7	0	2	24	.244	207	28	2	.992
1984—San Diego e	Nat.	1B-3B-OF	59	80	7	16	3	0	1	9	.200	73	15	1	.989
1985—San Diego e	Nat.	3B-1B-OF	71	138	17	33	6	0	3	25	.239	49	60	7	.940
National League Totals—8 Years			513	970	87	230	46	5	8	136	.237	747	329	28	.975
American League Totals—8 Years			457	1147	127	269	44	6	19	139	.235	559	517	52	.954
Major League Totals—15 Years			970	2117	214	499	90	11	27	275	.236	1306	846	80	.964

Selected by New York Mets' organization in 36th round of free-agent draft, June 6, 1966.
Selected by Atlanta Braves' organization in 6th round of free-agent draft, January 28, 1967.
Selected by Cincinnati Reds' organization in secondary phase of free-agent draft, June 7, 1967.
†Traded to Cleveland Indians for Outfielder Charles Bradford, May 8, 1971.
‡Traded to Kansas City Royals for Pitcher Mike Hedlund, November 2, 1972.
§Traded with Catcher-Outfielder Ed Kirkpatrick and First Baseman Winston Cole to Pittsburgh Pirates for Pitcher Nelson Briles and Infielder Fernando Gonzalez, December 4, 1973.
xTraded to Kansas City Royals for cash and Infielder Cal Meier, July 8, 1974.
ySold to Milwaukee Brewers, March 6, 1975.
zSold to Seattle Mariners, October 22, 1976.
aReleased, March 28, 1977; signed by Texas Rangers' organization, April 8, 1977.
bTraded with Catcher Bill Fahey and First Baseman Mike Hargrove to San Diego Padres for Outfielder Oscar Gamble, Catcher Dave Roberts and cash estimated at $300,000, October 25, 1978.
cTraded with a player to be named later to Pittsburgh Pirates for Outfielders Rick Lancellotti and Luis Salazar, August 5, 1980; Pittsburgh acquired Pitcher Mark Lee to complete deal, August 12, 1980.

dReleased, October 26, 1981; signed by San Diego Padres, April 2, 1982.
eGranted free agency, November 12, 1985.

CHAMPIONSHIP SERIES RECORD

Year Club League	Pos.	G.	AB.	R.	H.	2B.	3B.	HR.	RBI.	B.A.	PO.	A.	E.	F.A.
1984—San Diego .... Nat.	PH	2	2	0	0	0	0	0	0	.000	0	0	0	.000

WORLD SERIES RECORD

Year Club League	Pos.	G.	AB.	R.	H.	2B.	3B.	HR.	RBI.	B.A.	PO.	A.	E.	F.A.
1984—San Diego .... Nat.	DH	5	17	4	7	2	0	2	4	.412	0	0	0	.000

ROLAND AMERICO BIANCALANA JR.

Name pronounced Bee-AHN-ka-la-na.

(Buddy)

Born February 2, 1960, at Larkspur, Calif.
Height, 5.11. Weight, 160.
Throws right and bats right and lefthanded.
Attended College of Marin, Kentfield, Calif., and University of San Francisco, San Francisco, Calif.

Major League stolen bases: 1983 (1), 1984 (1), 1985 (1). Total—3.
Led American Association shortstops in double plays with 79 in 1982.

Year Club League	Pos.	G.	AB.	R.	H.	2B.	3B.	HR.	RBI.	B.A.	PO.	A.	E.	F.A.
1978—Sarasota Royals... Gulf C.	SS	32	76	12	13	1	1	0	2	.171	36	81	6	.951
1979—Fort Myers........... Fla. St.	SS	125	357	44	71	7	4	2	32	.199	*236	342	36	.941
1980—Fort Myers........... Fla. St.	SS	92	258	30	44	5	2	0	28	.171	189	232	23	.948
1981—Jacksonville......... South.	SS	132	385	47	81	7	2	2	27	.210	208	374	48	.924
1982—Omaha.................. A. A.	SS	130	415	56	104	16	9	2	36	.251	204	●357	18	*.969
1982—Kansas City.......... Amer.	SS	3	2	0	1	0	1	0	0	.500	2	8	0	1.000
1983—Omaha.................. A. A.	SS	113	367	41	82	13	3	5	39	.223	184	341	23	.958
1983—Kansas City.......... Amer.	SS	6	15	2	3	0	0	0	0	.200	11	21	3	.914
1984—Kansas City.......... Amer.	SS-2B	66	134	18	26	6	1	2	9	.194	62	144	8	.963
1984—Omaha.................. A. A.	2B-SS-3B	58	204	33	53	11	9	7	25	.260	78	128	2	.990
1985—Kansas City†........ Amer.	SS-2B	81	138	21	26	5	1	1	6	.188	83	169	10	.962
Major League Totals—4 Years................		156	289	41	56	11	3	3	15	.194	158	342	21	.960

Selected by Kansas City Royals' organization in 1st round (25th player selected) or free-agent draft, June 6, 1978.
†On disabled list, July 25 to August 12, 1985.

CHAMPIONSHIP SERIES RECORD

Year Club League	Pos.	G.	AB.	R.	H.	2B.	3B.	HR.	RBI.	B.A.	PO.	A.	E.	F.A.
1984—Kansas City.......... Amer.	PR-SS	2	1	0	0	0	0	0	0	.000	1	2	0	1.000
1985—Kansas City.......... Amer.	SS	7	18	2	4	1	0	0	1	.222	9	20	0	1.000
Championship Series Total—2 Years......		9	19	2	4	1	0	0	1	.211	10	22	0	1.000

WORLD SERIES RECORD

Year Club League	Pos.	G.	AB.	R.	H.	2B.	3B.	HR.	RBI.	B.A.	PO.	A.	E.	F.A.
1985—Kansas City.......... Amer.	SS	7	18	2	5	0	0	0	2	.278	6	20	0	1.000

MICHAEL JOSEPH BIELECKI

Name pronounced BY-leck-ee.

(Mike)

Born July 31, 1959, at Baltimore, Md.
Height, 6.03. Weight, 200.
Throws and bats righthanded.
Attended Loyola College, Baltimore, Md. and
Valencia Community College, Orlando, Fla.

Tied for Eastern League lead in home runs allowed with 24 in 1982.
Tied for South Atlantic League lead in games started with 28 in 1981.

Year Club League	G.	IP.	W.	L.	Pct.	H.	R.	ER.	SO.	BB.	ERA.
1979—Bradenton Pirates .... Gulf Coast	9	51	1	4	.200	48	21	13	35	21	2.29
1980—Shelby.................................... S. Atlantic	29	99	3	5	.375	106	60	50	78	58	4.55
1981—Greenwood.............................. S. Atlantic	28	192	12	11	.522	172	95	73	163	82	3.42
1982—Buffalo.................................. Eastern	25	157⅓	7	12	.368	165	96	●85	135	75	4.86
1983—Lynn.................................... Eastern	25	163⅔	●15	7	.682	126	73	58	*143	69	3.19
1984—Hawaii.................................. P. Coast	28	187⅔	*19	3	*.864	162	70	62	*162	88	2.97
1984—Pittsburgh............................. National	4	4⅓	0	0	.000	4	0	0	1	0	0.00
1985—Pittsburgh............................. National	12	45⅔	2	3	.400	45	26	23	22	31	4.53
1985—Hawaii.................................. P. Coast	20	129⅓	8	6	.571	117	58	55	111	56	3.83
Major League Totals—2 Years............................	16	50	2	3	.400	49	26	23	23	31	4.14

Selected by Kansas City Royals' organization in 6th round of free-agent draft, January 9, 1979.
Selected by Pittsburgh Pirates' organization in secondary phase of free-agent draft, June 5, 1979.

—DID YOU KNOW—

That San Diego's Dick Williams and Detroit's Sparky Anderson are only the second and third managers to pilot both leagues in All-Star play? Alvin Dark was the first.

DANN JAMES BILARDELLO
Name pronounced Bill-ar-DELL-oh.

Born May 26, 1959, at Santa Cruz, Calif.
Height, 6.00. Weight, 190.
Throws and bats righthanded.
Attended Cabrillo College, Aptos, Calif.

Major League stolen bases: 1983 (2).
Led Texas League catchers in double plays with 15 in 1982.
Led Pioneer League catchers in double plays with 5 in 1978.
Tied for Texas League lead in stealers caught with 42 in 1982.

Year	Club	League	Pos.	G.	AB.	R.	H.	2B.	3B.	HR.	RBI.	B.A.	PO.	A.	E.	F.A.
1978—Lethbridge		Pion.	C	42	133	21	33	8	1	2	20	.248	210	36	7	.972
1979—Clinton†		Midw.	C	52	142	18	34	4	0	2	15	.239	283	31	3	.991
1980—Lodi‡		Calif.	C	41	117	22	36	4	0	6	15	.308	169	30	8	.961
1981—Lodi		Calif.	C	105	352	72	108	19	2	21	80	.307	203	39	9	.964
1981—San Antonio		Texas	C	6	19	0	1	0	0	0	1	.053	34	2	1	.973
1982—San Antonio§		Texas	C	103	347	49	99	14	2	17	48	.285	546	∗80	15	.977
1983—Cincinnati		Nat.	C	109	298	27	71	18	0	9	38	.238	494	72	5	.991
1984—Cincinnati		Nat.	C	68	182	16	38	7	0	2	10	.209	323	34	3	.992
1984—Wichita		A. A.	C	49	167	21	40	9	0	5	17	.240	290	31	3	.991
1985—Cincinnati		Nat.	C	42	102	6	17	0	0	1	9	.167	198	20	3	.986
1985—Denver x		A. A.	C-1B-3B	67	236	41	57	5	3	10	37	.242	365	50	6	.986
Major League Totals—3 Years				310	582	49	126	25	0	12	57	.216	1015	126	11	.990

Selected by Seattle Mariners' organization in 3rd round of free-agent draft, January 10, 1978.
Selected by Los Angeles Dodgers' organization in secondary phase of free-agent draft, June 6, 1978.
†On disabled list, May 9 to June 14, 1979.
‡On disabled list, June 12 to August 13, 1980.
§Drafted by Cincinnati Reds, December 6, 1982.
xTraded with Pitchers Jay Tibbs, Andy McGaffigan and John Stuper to Montreal Expos for Pitcher Bill Gullickson and Catcher Sal Butera, December 19, 1985.

MICHAEL LAWRENCE BIRKBECK
(Mike)

Born March 10, 1961, at Orrville, O.
Height, 6.01. Weight, 190.
Throws and bats righthanded.
Attended University of Akron, Akron, O.

Year	Club	League	G.	IP.	W.	L.	Pct.	H.	R.	ER.	SO.	BB.	ERA.
1983—Paintsville		Ap'lachian	7	28⅔	3	1	.750	17	12	6	38	17	1.88
1983—Beloit		Midwest	7	42	2	4	.333	35	22	16	38	17	3.43
1984—Beloit		Midwest	26	177⅔	14	3	.824	134	57	43	164	64	2.18
1985—El Paso		Texas	24	155	9	9	.500	154	67	59	103	64	3.43

Selected by Chicago Cubs' organization in 11th round of free-agent draft, June 7, 1982.
Selected by Milwaukee Brewers' organization in 4th round of free-agent draft, June 8, 1983.

TIMOTHY DEAN BIRTSAS
(Tim)

Born September 5, 1960, at Clarkston, Mich.
Height, 6.07. Weight, 225.
Throws and bats lefthanded.
Received bachelor of science degree in recreation from Michigan State University, East Lansing, Mich.

Year	Club	League	G.	IP.	W.	L.	Pct.	H.	R.	ER.	SO.	BB.	ERA.
1982—Oneonta		NYP	6	16⅓	1	1	.500	19	13	7	24	17	3.86
1983—Fort Lauderdale		Florida St.	23	167⅔	12	8	.600	120	57	44	∗160	88	2.36
1984—Fort Lauderdale†		Florida St.	11	57⅔	5	1	.833	51	23	23	62	37	3.59
1985—Tacoma		P. Coast	4	26⅔	2	2	.500	21	10	9	25	14	3.04
1985—Oakland		American	29	141⅓	10	6	.625	124	72	63	94	91	4.01
Major League Totals—1 Year			29	141⅓	10	6	.625	124	72	63	94	91	4.01

Selected by New York Yankees' organization in 2nd round of free-agent draft, June 7, 1982.
†Traded with Outfielder Stan Javier and Pitchers Jay Howell, Eric Plunk and Jose Rijo to Oakland A's for Outfielder Rickey Henderson, Pitcher Bert Bradley and cash, December 5, 1984.

JEFFREY SCOTT BITTIGER
(Jeff)

Born April 13, 1962, at Jersey City, N.J.
Height, 5.10. Weight, 175.
Throws and bats righthanded.
Attended Montclair State College, Upper Montclair, N.J., and
attending Jersey City State College, Jersey City, N.J.

Tied for International League lead in games started by pitchers with 28 in 1983.
Named Texas League Pitcher of the Year, 1982.

Year	Club	League	G.	IP.	W.	L.	Pct.	H.	R.	ER.	SO.	BB.	ERA.
1980—Little Falls		NYP	7	26	0	1	.000	10	6	3	33	20	1.04
1981—Lynchburg		Carolina	24	137	11	7	.611	121	72	60	∗168	79	3.94

Year Club	League	G.	IP.	W.	L.	Pct.	H.	R.	ER.	SO.	BB.	ERA.
1981—Jackson	Texas	4	33	2	1	.667	24	4	4	27	8	1.09
1982—Jackson	Texas	25	164	12	5	.706	106	59	54	★190	94	2.96
1983—Tidewater	Int'national	28	163	12	10	.545	175	90	79	110	★111	4.36
1984—Tidewater†	Int'national	24	134⅔	8	8	.500	124	72	58	70	53	3.88
1985—Tidewater‡	Int'national	24	131⅔	11	7	.611	131	62	54	66	52	3.69

Selected by New York Mets' organization in 7th round of free-agent draft, June 3, 1980.
†On disabled list, June 13 to June 24, 1984.
‡Traded with Catcher Ronn Reynolds to Philadelphia Phillies for Pitcher Rodger Cole and First Baseman Ronnie Gideon, January 16, 1986.

RECORD AS THIRD BASEMAN

Year Club	League	Pos.	G.	AB.	R.	H.	2B.	3B.	HR.	RBI.	B.A.	PO.	A.	E.	F.A.
1980—Little Falls	NYP	3B-P	22	37	4	7	0	1	0	3	.189	11	24	8	.814

HARRY RALSTON BLACK
(Bud)

Born June 30, 1957, at San Mateo, Calif.
Height, 6.01. Weight, 180.
Throws and bats lefthanded.
Attended Lower Columbia College, Longview, Wash. and received bachelor of arts degree
in finance from San Diego State University, San Diego, Calif. in 1979.
Son of Harry Black, Sr., former minor league hockey player.

Led American League in balks with 7 in 1982.

Year Club	League	G.	IP.	W.	L.	Pct.	H.	R.	ER.	SO.	BB.	ERA.
1979—Bellingham	Northwest	2	5	0	0	.000	3	0	0	8	5	0.00
1979—San Jose	California	17	27	0	1	.000	17	11	9	24	16	3.00
1980—San Jose	California	32	86	5	3	.625	67	34	33	73	49	3.45
1981—Lynn	Eastern	22	87	2	6	.250	78	38	29	86	23	3.00
1981—Spokane	P. Coast	4	8	1	0	1.000	12	4	4	4	2	4.50
1981—Seattle†	American	2	1	0	0	.000	2	0	0	0	3	0.00
1982—Kansas City	American	22	88⅓	4	6	.400	92	48	45	40	34	4.58
1982—Omaha	Am. Assoc.	4	29	3	1	.750	23	9	8	20	10	2.48
1983—Omaha	Am. Assoc.	5	35	3	1	.750	31	13	13	32	13	3.34
1983—Kansas City	American	24	161⅓	10	7	.588	159	75	68	58	43	3.79
1984—Kansas City	American	35	257	17	12	.586	226	99	89	140	64	3.12
1985—Kansas City	American	33	205⅔	10	15	.400	216	111	99	122	59	4.33
Major League Totals—5 Years		116	713⅓	41	40	.506	695	333	301	360	203	3.80

Selected by San Francisco Giants' organization in 3rd round of free-agent draft, January 11, 1977.
Selected by New York Mets' organization in secondary phase of free-agent draft, June 7, 1977.
Selected by Seattle Mariners' organization in 17th round of free-agent draft, June 5, 1979.
†Traded to Kansas City Royals, March 2, 1982, completing deal in which Kansas City traded Infielder Manny Castillo to Seattle Mariners for a player to be named later, October 23, 1981.

CHAMPIONSHIP SERIES RECORD

Year Club	League	G.	IP.	W.	L.	Pct.	H.	R.	ER.	SO.	BB.	ERA.
1984—Kansas City	American	1	5	0	1	.000	7	4	4	3	1	7.20
1985—Kansas City	American	3	10⅔	0	0	.000	11	3	2	8	4	1.69
Championship Series Totals—2 Years		4	15⅔	0	1	.000	18	7	6	11	5	3.45

WORLD SERIES RECORD

Year Club	League	G.	IP.	W.	L.	Pct.	H.	R.	ER.	SO.	BB.	ERA.
1985—Kansas City	American	2	5⅓	0	1	.000	4	3	3	4	5	5.06

TERRY FENNELL BLOCKER

Born August 18, 1959, at Columbia, S.C.
Height, 6.02. Weight, 195.
Throws and bats lefthanded.
Received degree in health and recreation from Tennessee State University, Nashville, Tenn. in 1981.

Year Club	League	Pos.	G.	AB.	R.	H.	2B.	3B.	HR.	RBI.	B.A.	PO.	A.	E.	F.A.
1981—Little Falls	NYP	OF	36	135	28	46	8	1	7	16	.341	72	6	7	.918
1982—Jackson	Texas	OF	118	438	69	114	20	2	5	38	.260	248	7	3	★.988
1983—Jackson	Texas	OF	66	263	38	81	16	7	3	54	.308	92	5	5	.951
1983—Tidewater	Int.	OF	72	239	26	73	7	2	2	32	.305	133	4	6	.958
1984—Tidewater	Int.	OF	115	386	45	85	10	1	3	31	.220	215	2	6	.973
1985—New York†	Nat.	OF	18	15	1	1	0	0	0	0	.067	4	0	0	1.000
1985—Tidewater	Int.	OF	75	267	40	82	8	4	5	38	.307	183	5	5	.974
Major League Totals—1 Year		18	15	1	1	0	0	0	0	.067	4	0	0	1.000

Selected by New York Mets' organization in 1st round (fourth player selected) of free-agent draft, June 8, 1981.
†On disabled list, June 10 to June 25, 1985.

—DID YOU KNOW—

That Cubs' pitcher Ray Fontenot served up, on consecutive pitches, the first major league home runs to Montreal's Sal Butera and Bryn Smith on August 14, 1985?

VIDA ROCHELLE BLUE JR.

Born July 28, 1949, at Mansfield, La.
Height, 6.00. Weight, 200.
Throws left and bats left and righthanded.
Attended Southern University, Baton Rouge, La.

Tied American League record for most strikeouts by lefthanded pitcher, extra-inning game (17), July 9, 1971 (pitched 11 of 20 innings).
Pitched 6-0 no-hit victory against Minnesota Twins, September 21, 1970.
Pitched seven-inning, 4-0 no-hit victory against Appleton, June 19, 1968.
Major League saves: 1969 (1), 1975 (1). Total—2.
Led American League in shutouts with 8 in 1971.
Named National League Pitcher of the Year by THE SPORTING NEWS, 1978.
Named American League Pitcher of the Year by THE SPORTING NEWS, 1971.
Named American League Most Valuable Player by Baseball Writers' Association of America, 1971.
Won American League Cy Young Memorial Award, 1971.
Named lefthanded pitcher on THE SPORTING NEWS National League All-Star Team, 1978.
Named lefthanded pitcher on THE SPORTING NEWS American League All-Star Team, 1971.

Year Club	League	G.	IP.	W.	L.	Pct.	H.	R.	ER.	SO.	BB.	ERA.
1968—Burlington	Midwest	24	152	8	●11	.421	102	67	42	★231	80	2.49
1969—Birmingham	Southern	15	104	10	3	.769	80	40	37	112	52	3.20
1969—Oakland	American	12	42	1	1	.500	49	34	31	24	18	6.64
1970—Iowa	Am. Assoc.	17	133	12	3	★.800	88	40	32	★165	55	2.17
1970—Oakland	American	6	39	2	0	1.000	20	12	9	35	12	2.08
1971—Oakland	American	39	312	24	8	.750	209	73	63	301	88	▲1.82
1972—Oakland†	American	25	151	6	10	.375	117	55	47	111	48	2.80
1973—Oakland	American	37	264	20	9	.690	214	108	96	158	105	3.27
1974—Oakland	American	40	282	17	15	.531	246	118	102	174	98	3.26
1975—Oakland	American	39	278	22	11	.667	243	103	93	189	99	3.01
1976—Oakland	American	37	298	18	13	.581	268	90	78	166	63	2.36
1977—Oakland‡§	American	38	280	14	●19	.424	●284	138	●119	157	86	3.83
1978—San Francisco	National	35	258	18	10	.643	233	87	80	171	70	2.79
1979—San Francisco	National	34	237	14	14	.500	246	143	★132	138	111	5.01
1980—San Francisco x	National	31	224	14	10	.583	202	79	74	129	61	2.97
1981—San Francisco y	National	18	125	8	6	.571	97	40	34	63	54	2.45
1982—Kansas City	American	31	181	13	12	.520	163	80	76	103	80	3.78
1983—Kansas City z	American	19	85⅓	0	5	.000	96	62	57	53	35	6.01
1984—						(Out of Organized Baseball)						
1985—San Francisco a	National	33	131	8	8	.500	115	70	65	103	80	4.47
National League Totals—5 Years		151	975	62	48	.564	893	419	385	604	376	3.55
American League Totals—11 Years		323	2212⅓	137	103	.571	1909	873	771	1471	732	3.14
Major League Totals—16 Years		474	3187⅓	199	151	.569	2802	1292	1156	2075	1108	3.26

Selected by Kansas City A's organization in 2nd round of free-agent draft, June 6, 1967.
†On restricted list, March 30 to April 27, 1972.
‡On disqualified list, April 5 to April 16, 1977.
§Traded to San Francisco Giants for Outfielder Gary Thomasson, Catcher Gary Alexander, Pitchers Dave Heaverlo, Alan Wirth, John Johnson and Phillip Huffman, a player to be named later and cash estimated at $390,000, March 15, 1978; Oakland acquired Shortstop Mario Guerrero to to complete deal, April 7, 1978.
xOn disabled list, June 28 to August 2, 1980.
yTraded with Pitcher Bob Tufts to Kansas City Royals for Pitchers Atlee Hammaker, Craig Chamberlain and Renie Martin and a player to be named later, March 30, 1982; San Francisco Giants' organization acquired Second Baseman Brad Wellman to complete deal, April 19, 1982.
zReleased, August 5, 1983; signed by San Francisco Giants, April 6, 1985.
aGranted free agency, November 12, 1985; re-signed by Giants, December 17, 1985.

CHAMPIONSHIP SERIES RECORD

Tied Championship Series records for fewest hits allowed, game (2), October 8, 1974; most earned runs allowed, five-game Series (8), 1973.
Established American League Championship Series record for most games pitched, five game Series (4), 1972.

Year Club	League	G.	IP.	W.	L.	Pct.	H.	R.	ER.	SO.	BB.	ERA.
1971—Oakland	American	1	7	0	1	.000	7	5	5	8	2	6.43
1972—Oakland	American	4	5⅓	0	0	.000	4	0	0	5	1	0.00
1973—Oakland	American	2	7	0	1	.000	8	8	8	3	5	10.29
1974—Oakland	American	1	9	1	0	1.000	2	0	0	7	0	0.00
1975—Oakland	American	1	3	0	0	.000	6	3	3	2	0	9.00
Championship Series Totals—5 Years		9	31⅓	1	2	.333	27	16	16	25	8	4.60

WORLD SERIES RECORD

Year Club	League	G.	IP.	W.	L.	Pct.	H.	R.	ER.	SO.	BB.	ERA.
1972—Oakland	American	4	8⅔	0	1	.000	8	4	4	5	5	4.15
1973—Oakland	American	2	11	0	1	.000	10	6	6	8	3	4.91
1974—Oakland	American	2	13⅔	0	1	.000	10	5	5	9	7	3.29
World Series Totals—3 Years		8	33⅓	0	3	.000	28	15	15	22	15	4.05

ALL-STAR GAME RECORD

Only pitcher in All-Star Game history to start in each league: American League, 1971; National League, 1978.
Tied All-Star Game records for most home runs allowed, total games (4); most home runs allowed, inning (2), July 15, 1975 (second inning).

Year	League	IP.	W.	L.	Pct.	H.	R.	ER.	SO.	BB.	ERA.
1971—American		3	1	0	1.000	2	3	3	3	0	9.00
1975—American		2	0	0	.000	5	2	2	1	0	9.00
1978—National		3	0	0	.000	5	3	3	2	1	9.00
1981—National		1	1	0	1.000	0	0	0	1	0	0.00
All-Star Game Totals—4 Years		9	2	0	1.000	12	8	8	7	1	8.00

Named to American League All-Star Team in 1977; replaced due to injury.
Named to National League All-Star Team in 1980; replaced due to injury by Ed Whitson.

RIKALBERT BLYLEVEN
(Bert)

Born April 6, 1951, at Zeist, The Netherlands.
Height, 6.03. Weight, 205.
Throws and bats righthanded.

Established major league record for most putouts by pitcher, nine-inning game (6), June 24, 1984.
Tied modern major league record for most consecutive strikeouts, start of game (6), September 16, 1970.
Tied American League records for longest one-hit complete game (10 innings), June 21, 1976; most seasons, 200 or more strikeouts (7).
Pitched 6-0 no-hit victory against California Angels, September 22, 1977.
Led American League pitchers in complete games with 24 and tied for lead in games started with 37 in 1985.
Led American League in hit batsmen with 12 in 1976.
Led American League in shutouts with 9 in 1973 and 5 in 1985.
Tied for American League lead in balks with 3 in 1970.
Named American League Rookie Pitcher of the Year by THE SPORTING NEWS, 1970.

Year	Club	League	G.	IP.	W.	L.	Pct.	H.	R.	ER.	SO.	BB.	ERA.
1969—Sarasota Twins	Gulf Coast	7	32	2	2	.500	31	13	10	39	11	2.81
1969—Orlando	Florida St.	6	37	5	0	1.000	36	6	6	41	14	1.46
1970—Evansville	Am. Assoc.	8	54	4	2	.667	48	18	15	63	12	2.50
1970—Minnesota	American	27	164	10	9	.526	143	66	58	135	47	3.18
1971—Minnesota	American	38	278	16	15	.516	267	95	87	224	59	2.82
1972—Minnesota	American	39	287	17	17	.500	247	93	87	228	69	2.73
1973—Minnesota	American	40	325	20	17	.541	296	109	91	258	67	2.52
1974—Minnesota	American	37	281	17	17	.500	244	99	83	249	77	2.66
1975—Minnesota	American	35	276	15	10	.600	219	104	92	233	84	3.00
1976—Minnesota†-Texas	American	36	298	13	16	.448	283	106	95	219	81	2.87
1977—Texas†	American	30	235	14	12	.538	181	81	71	182	69	2.72
1978—Pittsburgh	National	34	244	14	10	.583	217	94	82	182	66	3.02
1979—Pittsburgh	National	37	237	12	5	.706	238	102	95	172	92	3.61
1980—Pittsburgh§	National	34	217	8	13	.381	219	102	92	168	59	3.82
1981—Cleveland	American	20	159	11	7	.611	145	52	51	107	40	2.89
1982—Cleveland x	American	4	20⅓	2	2	.500	16	14	11	19	11	4.87
1983—Cleveland	American	24	156⅓	7	10	.412	160	74	68	123	44	3.91
1984—Cleveland y	American	33	245	19	7	.731	204	86	78	170	74	2.87
1985—Cleveland z-Minnesota	American	37	★293⅔	17	16	.515	264	121	103	★206	75	3.16
National League Totals—3 Years		105	698	34	28	.548	674	298	269	522	217	3.47
American League Totals—13 Years		400	3018⅓	178	155	.535	2669	1100	975	2353	797	2.91
Major League Totals—16 Years		505	3716⅓	212	183	.537	3343	1398	1244	2875	1014	3.01

Selected by Minnesota Twins' organization in 3rd round of free-agent draft, June 5, 1969.
†Traded with Shortstop Danny Thompson to Texas Rangers for Pitcher Bill Singer, Infielders Roy Smalley and Mike Cubbage, Pitcher Jim Gideon and a reported $250,000 cash, June 1, 1976.
‡Traded with First Baseman-Outfielder John Milner to Pittsburgh Pirates for Outfielder-First Baseman Al Oliver and Infielder Nelson Norman, December 8, 1977.
§Traded with Catcher Manny Sanguillen to Cleveland Indians for Pitchers Bob Owchinko, Rafael Vasquez and Victor Cruz and Catcher Gary Alexander, December 9, 1980.
xOn disabled list, May 2, 1982 through remainder of season.
yOn disabled list, May 23 to June 10, 1984.
zTraded to Minnesota Twins for Pitcher Curt Wardle, Outfielder Jim Weaver and Infielder Jay Bell, August 1, 1985.

CHAMPIONSHIP SERIES RECORD

Year	Club	League	G.	IP.	W.	L.	Pct.	H.	R.	ER.	SO.	BB.	ERA.
1970—Minnesota	American	1	2	0	0	.000	2	1	0	2	0	0.00
1979—Pittsburgh	National	1	9	1	0	1.000	8	1	1	9	0	1.00
Championship Series Totals—2 Years		2	11	1	0	1.000	10	2	1	11	0	0.82

WORLD SERIES RECORD

Year	Club	League	G.	IP.	W.	L.	Pct.	H.	R.	ER.	SO.	BB.	ERA.
1979—Pittsburgh	National	2	10	1	0	1.000	8	2	2	4	3	1.80

ALL-STAR GAME RECORD

Year	League	IP.	W.	L.	Pct.	H.	R.	ER.	SO.	BB.	ERA.
1973—American		1	0	1	.000	2	2	2	0	2	18.00
1985—American		2	0	0	.000	3	2	2	1	1	9.00
All-Star Game Totals—2 Years		3	0	1	.000	5	4	4	1	3	12.00

BRUCE ANTON BOCHTE

Name pronounced BOCK-tee.

Born November 12, 1950, at Pasadena, Calif.
Height, 6.03. Weight, 205.
Throws and bats lefthanded.
Received bachelor of science degree in commerce from
University of Santa Clara, Santa Clara, Calif.

Major League stolen bases: 1974 (6), 1975 (3), 1976 (4), 1977 (6), 1978 (3), 1979 (2), 1980 (2), 1981 (1), 1982 (8), 1984 (2), 1985 (3). Total—40.

Led American League in grounding into double plays with 27 in 1979.

Year Club	League	Pos.	G.	AB.	R.	H.	2B.	3B.	HR.	RBI.	B.A.	PO.	A.	E.	F.A.
1972—Stockton	Calif.	1B-OF	72	266	36	87	14	2	11	42	.327	470	27	9	.982
1973—El Paso	Texas	1B-OF	122	417	57	133	32	4	10	79	.319	775	41	11	.987
1974—Salt Lake City	P. C.	OF-1B	92	332	55	118	15	2	9	56	.355	218	12	6	.975
1974—California	Amer.	OF-1B	57	196	24	53	4	1	5	26	.270	248	9	5	.981
1975—California†	Amer.	1B	107	375	41	107	19	3	3	48	.285	850	51	12	.987
1976—California	Amer.	OF-1B	146	466	53	120	17	1	2	49	.258	651	42	7	.990
1977—Calif.‡-Cleve.§	Amer.	OF-1B	137	492	64	148	23	1	7	51	.301	486	33	9	.983
1978—Seattle	Amer.	OF-1B	140	486	58	128	25	3	11	51	.263	180	7	3	.984
1979—Seattle	Amer.	1B	150	554	81	175	38	6	16	100	.316	1361	114	*14	.991
1980—Seattle	Amer.	1B	148	520	62	156	34	4	13	78	.300	1273	98	6	.996
1981—Seattle	Amer.	1B-OF	99	335	39	87	16	0	6	30	.260	766	49	4	.995
1982—Seattle x	Amer.	OF-1B	111	500	58	151	21	0	12	70	.297	428	26	3	.993
1983—					(Out of Organized Baseball)										
1984—Oakland y	Amer.	1B	148	469	58	124	23	0	5	52	.264	1048	66	8	.993
1985—Oakland z	Amer.	1B	137	424	48	125	17	1	14	60	.295	942	60	10	.990
Major League Totals—11 Years			1413	4826	586	1374	237	20	94	615	.285	8233	555	81	.991

Selected by California Angels' organization in 2nd round of free-agent draft, June 6, 1972.
†On disabled list, June 24 to August 13, 1975.
‡Traded with Pitcher Sid Monge and cash estimated at $250,000 to Cleveland Indians for Pitchers Dave Schuler and Dave LaRoche, May 11, 1977.
§Granted free agency, November 2, 1977; signed by Seattle Mariners, December 20, 1977.
xGranted free agency, November 10, 1982; signed by Oakland A's, November 14, 1983.
yGranted free agency after not being tendered a contract, December 20, 1984; re-signed by A's, December 24, 1984.
zGranted free agency, November 12, 1985; re-signed by A's, December 4, 1985.

ALL-STAR GAME RECORD

Year League	Pos.	AB.	R.	H.	2B.	3B.	HR.	RBI.	B.A.	PO.	A.	E.	F.A.
1979—American	PH-1B	1	0	1	0	0	0	1	1.000	2	0	0	1.000

BRUCE DOUGLAS BOCHY

Name pronounced BOW-chee.

Born April 16, 1955, At Landes de Bussac, France.
Height, 6.04. Weight, 229.
Throws and bats righthanded.
Attended Brevard Community College, Cocoa, Fla., and
Florida State University, Tallahassee, Fla.
Brother of Joe Bochy, catcher in Minnesota Twins' organization, 1969 through 1972.

Tied for Florida State League lead in passed balls with 12 in 1977.

Year Club	League	Pos.	G.	AB.	R.	H.	2B.	3B.	HR.	RBI.	B.A.	PO.	A.	E.	F.A.
1975—Covington	Appal.	C	37	145	31	49	9	0	4	34	.338	231	36	4	.985
1976—Columbus	South.	C	69	230	9	53	6	0	0	16	.230	266	45	6	.981
1976—Dubuque	Midw.	C-1B	30	103	9	25	4	0	1	8	.243	165	25	5	.974
1977—Cocoa	Fla. St.	C	128	430	40	109	18	2	3	35	.253	*492	67	12	.979
1978—Columbus	South.	C	79	261	25	70	10	2	7	34	.268	419	49	7	.985
1978—Houston	Nat.	C	54	154	8	41	8	0	3	15	.266	268	35	8	.974
1979—Houston	Nat.	C	56	129	11	28	4	0	1	6	.217	198	29	7	.970
1980—Houston†	Nat.	C-1B	22	22	0	4	1	0	0	0	.182	19	1	0	1.000
1981—Tidewater	Int.	C	85	269	23	61	11	2	8	38	.227	253	35	3	.990
1982—Tidewater	Int.	C	81	251	32	57	11	0	15	52	.227	427	57	5	*.990
1982—New York‡	Nat.	C-1B	17	49	4	15	4	0	2	8	.306	92	8	4	.962
1983—Las Vegas	P. C.	C	42	145	28	44	8	1	11	33	.303	157	21	3	.983
1983—San Diego	Nat.	C	23	42	2	9	1	1	0	3	.214	51	5	0	1.000
1984—Las Vegas	P. C.	C	34	121	18	32	7	0	7	22	.264	189	17	2	.990
1984—San Diego	Nat.	C	37	92	10	21	5	1	4	15	.228	147	12	2	.988
1985—San Diego	Nat.	C	48	112	16	30	2	0	6	13	.268	148	11	2	.988
Major League Totals—7 Years			257	600	51	148	25	2	16	60	.247	923	101	23	.978

Selected by Chicago White Sox' organization in 8th round of free-agent draft, January 9, 1975.
Selected by Houston Astros' organization in secondary phase of free-agent draft, June 4, 1975.
†Traded to New York Mets' organization for two players to be named later, February 11, 1981; Houston Astros acquired Infielder Randy Rogers and Catcher Stan Hough to complete deal, April 3, 1981.
‡Released, January 21, 1983; signed by Las Vegas (San Diego Padres' organization), February 23, 1983.

CHAMPIONSHIP SERIES RECORD

Year Club	League	Pos.	G.	AB.	R.	H.	2B.	3B.	HR.	RBI.	B.A.	PO.	A.	E.	F.A.
1980—Houston	Nat.	C	1	1	0	0	0	0	0	0	.000	5	1	0	1.000

Year	Club	League	Pos.	G.	AB.	R.	H.	2B.	3B.	HR.	RBI.	B.A.	PO.	A.	E.	F.A.
1984—San Diego		Nat.	PH	1	1	0	1	0	0	0	0	1.000	0	0	0	.000

RANDY WALTER BOCKUS

Born October 5, 1960, at Canton, O.
Height, 6.02. Weight, 190.
Throws right and bats lefthanded.
Attended Kent State University, Kent, O.

Led Texas League pitchers in complete games with 15 and tied for lead in games started with 27 in 1985.
Led California League pitchers in games started with 30 in 1983.
Tied for Texas League in shutouts with 3 in 1984.

Year	Club	League	G.	IP.	W.	L.	Pct.	H.	R.	ER.	SO.	BB.	ERA.
1982—Great Falls		Pioneer	18	53	2	0	1.000	60	38	27	42	22	4.58
1983—Fresno		California	30	196	14	6	.700	185	89	78	*144	78	3.58
1984—Shreveport		Texas	18	128⅓	8	5	.615	106	44	40	93	54	2.81
1985—Shreveport		Texas	28	*201	*14	11	.560	196	85	61	126	44	*2.73

Selected by San Francisco Giants' organization in 34th round of free-agent draft, June 7, 1982.

MICHAEL JAMES BODDICKER

Name pronounced BOD-dick-er

(Mike)

Born August 23, 1957, at Cedar Rapids, Iowa.
Height, 5.11. Weight, 172.
Throws and bats righthanded.
Attended University of Iowa, Iowa City, Iowa.

Tied modern major league record for most putouts by pitcher, season (49), 1984.
Led American League in shutouts with 5 in 1983.
Named American League Rookie Pitcher of the Year by THE SPORTING NEWS, 1983.
Named righthanded pitcher on THE SPORTING NEWS American League All-Star Team, 1984.

Year	Club	League	G.	IP.	W.	L.	Pct.	H.	R.	ER.	SO.	BB.	ERA.
1978—Bluefield		Ap'lachian	8	19	2	1	.667	9	2	1	28	10	0.47
1978—Charlotte		Southern	10	65	4	3	.571	42	15	14	48	17	1.94
1978—Rochester		Int'national	1	5	1	0	1.000	4	1	1	3	2	1.80
1979—Charlotte		Southern	14	102	9	3	.750	82	40	34	89	36	3.00
1979—Rochester		Int'national	15	72	4	6	.400	88	48	48	48	27	6.00
1980—Rochester		Int'national	25	190	12	9	.571	149	57	46	109	35	2.18
1980—Baltimore		American	1	7	0	1	.000	6	6	5	4	5	6.43
1981—Rochester		Int'national	30	182	10	10	.500	182	91	85	109	66	4.20
1981—Baltimore		American	2	6	0	0	.000	6	4	3	2	2	4.50
1982—Rochester		Int'national	20	133⅓	10	5	.667	121	59	53	82	36	3.58
1982—Baltimore		American	7	25⅔	1	0	1.000	25	10	10	20	12	3.51
1983—Rochester		Int'national	4	23⅔	3	1	.750	17	6	5	18	13	1.90
1983—Baltimore		American	27	179	16	8	.667	141	65	55	120	52	2.77
1984—Baltimore†		American	34	261⅓	*20	11	.645	218	95	81	128	81	*2.79
1985—Baltimore‡		American	32	203⅓	12	17	.414	227	104	92	135	89	4.07
Major League Totals—6 Years			103	682⅓	49	37	.570	623	284	246	409	241	3.24

Selected by Montreal Expos' organization in 8th round of free-agent draft, June 4, 1975.
Selected by Baltimore Orioles' organization in 6th round of free-agent draft, June 6, 1978.
†Appeared in one game as a pinch-runner.
‡Appeared in two games as a pinch-runner.

CHAMPIONSHIP SERIES RECORD

Established Championship Series record for most strikeouts, four-game Series (14), 1983.
Tied Championship Series record for most strikeouts, game (14), October 6, 1983.

Year	Club	League	G.	IP.	W.	L.	Pct.	H.	R.	ER.	SO.	BB.	ERA.
1983—Baltimore		American	1	9	1	0	1.000	5	0	0	14	3	0.00

WORLD SERIES RECORD

Year	Club	League	G.	IP.	W.	L.	Pct.	H.	R.	ER.	SO.	BB.	ERA.
1983—Baltimore		American	1	9	1	0	1.000	3	1	0	6	0	0.00

ALL-STAR GAME RECORD

Member of American League All-Star Team in 1984; did not play.

JOSEPH MARTIN BOEVER

Name rhymes with Saver.

(Joe)

Born October 4, 1960, at St. Louis, Mo.
Height, 6.01. Weight, 200.
Throws and bats righthanded.
Attended Crowder College, Neosho, Mo., St. Louis Community College at
Meramec, St. Louis, Mo., and University of Nevada, Las Vegas, Nev.

Led Florida State League in games finished in relief with 38 and tied for lead in saves with 14 in 1984.
Led Florida State League in games finished in relief with 46, saves with 26 and intentional bases on balls issued with 12 in 1983.
Tied for New York-Pennsylvania League lead in intentional bases on balls issued with 5 in 1982.

Year Club	League	G.	IP.	W.	L.	Pct.	H.	R.	ER.	SO.	BB.	ERA.
1982—Erie	NYP	19	32⅔	2	3	.400	20	8	7	63	12	1.93
1982—Springfield	Midwest	3	4	0	0	.000	3	1	1	7	2	2.25
1983—St. Petersburg	Florida St.	53	80⅓	5	6	.455	61	29	27	57	37	3.02
1984—Arkansas	Texas	8	11	0	1	.000	10	11	10	12	12	8.18
1984—St. Petersburg	Florida St.	48	77⅔	4	6	.600	52	31	26	81	45	3.01
1985—Arkansas	Texas	27	37⅔	3	1	.750	21	5	5	45	23	1.19
1985—Louisville	Am. Assoc.	21	35⅓	3	2	.600	28	11	8	37	22	2.04
1985—St. Louis	National	13	16⅓	0	0	.000	17	8	8	20	4	4.41
Major League Totals—1 Year		13	16⅓	0	0	.000	17	8	8	20	4	4.41

Signed as free agent by St. Louis Cardinals' organization, June 25, 1982.

THOMAS WINTON BOGGS
(Tommy)
Born October 25, 1955, at Poughkeepsie, N.Y.
Height, 6.02. Weight, 200.
Throws and bats righthanded.

Led International League pitchers in games started with 33, complete games with 16 and wild pitches with 18 in 1979.
Tied for Gulf Coast League lead in shutouts with 2 in 1974.

Year Club	League	G.	IP.	W.	L.	Pct.	H.	R.	ER.	SO.	BB.	ERA.
1974—Sarasota Rangers	Gulf Coast	10	64	5	2	.714	50	21	18	55	35	2.53
1975—Pittsfield	Eastern	24	162	10	11	.476	153	84	63	100	73	3.50
1976—Sacramento	P. Coast	18	115	6	11	.353	153	101	88	77	60	6.89
1976—Texas	American	13	90	1	7	.125	87	42	35	36	34	3.50
1977—Tucson	P. Coast	22	97	5	10	.333	131	107	92	70	83	8.54
1977—Texas†	American	6	27	0	3	.000	40	18	18	15	12	6.00
1978—Richmond	Int'national	8	54	5	1	.833	51	20	17	29	22	2.83
1978—Atlanta	National	16	59	2	8	.200	80	46	44	21	26	6.71
1979—Richmond	Int'national	33	⋆227	15	10	.600	⋆230	⋆108	91	⋆138	99	3.61
1979—Atlanta	National	3	13	0	2	.000	21	11	9	1	4	6.23
1980—Atlanta	National	32	192	12	9	.571	180	80	73	84	46	3.42
1981—Atlanta	National	25	143	3	13	.188	140	72	65	81	54	4.09
1982—Atlanta‡	National	10	46⅓	2	2	.500	43	22	17	29	22	3.30
1982—Richmond	Int'national	3	12	1	1	.500	9	5	2	13	3	1.50
1983—Atlanta§	National	5	6⅓	0	0	.000	8	4	4	5	1	5.68
1983—Richmond x	Int'national	4	12	0	4	.000	19	20	19	5	9	14.25
1984—Tulsa y	Texas	3	19	1	1	.500	13	5	5	12	5	2.37
1984—Oklahoma City z	Am. Assoc.	11	55	5	4	.556	67	38	33	30	24	5.40
1985—Texas	American	4	7	0	0	.000	13	9	9	6	2	11.57
1985—Oklahoma City	Am. Assoc.	13	78⅔	5	7	.417	79	39	30	31	23	3.43
National League Totals—6 Years		91	459⅔	19	34	.358	472	235	212	221	153	4.15
American League Totals—3 Years		23	124	1	10	.091	140	69	62	57	48	4.50
Major League Totals—9 Years		114	583⅔	20	44	.313	612	304	274	278	201	4.23

Selected by Texas Rangers' organization in 1st round (second player selected) of free-agent draft, June 5, 1974.
†Traded with Pitcher Adrian Devine and Outfielder Eddie Miller to Atlanta Braves for First Baseman Willie Montanez, December 8, 1977.
‡On disabled list, April 23 to August 30, 1982; included rehabilitation disability assignment to Richmond, July 28 to August 12, 1982.
§On disabled list, March 22 to September 2, 1983; included rehabilitation disability assignment to Richmond, July 7 to July 26, 1983.
xReleased, October 4, 1983; signed by Tulsa (Texas Rangers' organization), January 27, 1984.
yOn temporary inactive list, April 12 to May 29, 1984.
zOn disabled list, July 22 to August 2, 1984.

WADE ANTHONY BOGGS
Born June 15, 1958, at Omaha, Neb.
Height, 6.02. Weight, 190.
Throws right and bats lefthanded.
Attended Hillsborough Community College, Tampa, Fla.

Tied major league record for most games, one or more hits, season (135), 1985.
Established American League records for highest batting average, rookie season, 100 or more games (.349), 1982; most singles, season (187), 1985.
Major League stolen bases: 1982 (1), 1983 (3), 1984 (3), 1985 (2). Total—9.
Led American league third basemen in total chances with 486 in 1985.
Led American League third basemen in double plays with 30 in 1984.
Named third baseman on THE SPORTING NEWS American League All-Star Team, 1983 and 1985.
Named third baseman on THE SPORTING NEWS American League Silver Slugger team, 1983.

Year Club	League	Pos.	G.	AB.	R.	H.	2B.	3B.	HR.	RBI.	B.A.	PO.	A.	E.	F.A.
1976—Elmira	NYP	3B	57	179	29	47	6	0	0	15	.263	36	75	16	.874
1977—Winston-Salem	Carol.	3B-2B-SS	117	422	67	140	13	1	2	55	.332	145	223	27	.932
1978—Bristol	East.	3-S-2-O	109	354	63	110	14	2	1	32	.311	62	107	7	.960
1979—Bristol†	East.	⋆3-S-2	113	406	56	132	17	2	0	41	.325	94	213	15	⋆.953
1980—Pawtucket	Int.	3B-1B	129	418	51	128	21	0	1	45	.306	108	156	12	.957

Year Club	League	Pos.	G.	AB.	R.	H.	2B.	3B.	HR.	RBI.	B.A.	PO.	A.	E.	F.A.
1981—Pawtucket .... Int.		3B-1B	137	498	67	*167	*41	3	5	60	*.335	359	238	26	.958
1982—Boston.................... Amer.		1B-3B-OF	104	338	51	118	14	1	5	44	.349	489	168	8	.988
1983—Boston.................... Amer.		3B	153	582	100	210	44	7	5	74	*.361	118	368	*27	.947
1984—Boston.................... Amer.		3B	158	625	109	203	31	4	6	55	.325	141	330	•20	.959
1985—Boston.................... Amer.		3B	161	653	107	*240	42	3	8	78	*.368	134	335	17	.965
Major League Totals—4 Years................			576	2198	367	771	131	15	24	251	.351	882	1201	72	.967

Selected by Boston Red Sox' organization in 7th round of free-agent draft, June 8, 1976.
†On disabled list, April 20 to May 2, 1979.

ALL-STAR GAME RECORD

Year League	Pos.	AB.	R.	H.	2B.	3B.	HR.	RBI.	B.A.	PO.	A.	E.	F.A.
1985—American	3B	0	0	0	0	0	0	0	.000	0	0	0	.000

BARRY LAMAR BONDS

Born July 24, 1964, at Riverside, Calif.
Height, 6.01. Weight, 185.
Throws and bats lefthanded.
Attended Arizona State University, Tempe, Ariz.
Son of Bobby Bonds, outfielder with San Francisco, New York Yankees, California,
Chicago White Sox, Texas, Cleveland, St. Louis and Chicago Cubs,
1968 through 1981; and coach with Cleveland Indians since 1984.

Named outfielder on THE SPORTING NEWS College Baseball All-America Team, 1985.

Year Club	League	Pos.	G.	AB.	R.	H.	2B.	3B.	HR.	RBI.	B.A.	PO.	A.	E.	F.A.
1985—Prince William .... Carol.		OF	71	254	49	76	16	4	13	37	.299	202	4	5	.976

Selected by San Francisco Giants' organization in 2nd round of free-agent draft, June 7, 1982.
Selected by Pittsburgh Pirates' organization in 1st round (sixth player selected) of free-agent draft, June 3, 1985.

JUAN GUILLERMO BONILLA

Name pronounced Boh-NEE-yah.

Born February 12, 1956, at Santurce, Puerto Rico.
Height, 5.09. Weight, 170.
Throws and bats righthanded.
Attended Florida State University, Tallahassee, Fla.

Major League stolen bases: 1981 (4), 1983 (3). Total—7.
Led Midwest League in sacrifice flies with 13 in 1978.
Led Midwest League second basemen in double plays with 84 in 1978, Southern League second basemen with 104 in 1979 and Pacific Coast League second basemen with 110 in 1980.

Year Club	League	Pos.	G.	AB.	R.	H.	2B.	3B.	HR.	RBI.	B.A.	PO.	A.	E.	F.A.
1978—Waterloo............... Midw.		2B	130	470	81	137	32	1	13	78	.291	*285	*381	21	*.969
1979—Chattanooga .... South.		2B	138	550	80	150	26	0	5	59	.273	332	360	18	.975
1980—Tacoma†............... P. C.		2B	139	502	66	152	27	2	4	55	.303	*366	*422	15	.981
1981—San Diego .... Nat.		2B	99	369	30	107	13	2	1	25	.290	290	290	*13	.976
1982—San Diego‡ .... Nat.		2B	45	182	21	51	6	2	0	8	.280	99	134	6	.975
1983—San Diego§ .... Nat.		2B	152	556	55	132	17	4	4	45	.237	335	414	11	.986
1984—			(Out of Organized Baseball)												
1985—New York............. Amer.		2B	8	16	0	2	1	0	0	2	.125	7	14	1	.955
1985—Columbus x........... Int.		2B-SS-3B	102	388	60	128	22	0	1	52	*.330	155	215	15	.961
National League Totals—3 Years...........			296	1107	106	290	36	8	5	78	.262	663	838	30	.980
American League Totals—1 Year................			8	16	0	2	1	0	0	2	.125	7	14	1	.955
Major League Totals—4 Years................			304	1123	106	292	37	8	5	80	.260	670	852	31	.980

Selected by New York Yankees' organization in 24th round of free-agent draft, June 7, 1977.
Signed as free agent by Cleveland Indians' organization, January 6, 1978.
†Traded to San Diego Padres for Pitcher Bob Lacey, April 1, 1981.
‡On diabled list, May 20 to September 21, 1982.
§Released, March 26, 1984; signed by Columbus (New York Yankees' organization), February 26, 1985.
xReleased, December 11, 1985.

ROBERTO MARTIN ANTONIO BONILLA

Name pronounced Boh-NEE-yah.

(Bobby)

Born February 23, 1963, at New York, N.Y.
Height, 6.03. Weight, 210.
Throws and bats righthanded.
Attended New York Technical College, Westbury, N.Y.

Year Club	League	Pos.	G.	AB.	R.	H.	2B.	3B.	HR.	RBI.	B.A.	PO.	A.	E.	F.A.
1981—Bradenton Pir. ..... Gulf C.		1B-C-3B	22	69	6	15	5	0	0	7	.217	124	23	5	.967
1982—Bradenton Pir. ..... Gulf C.		1B	47	167	20	38	3	0	5	26	.228	318	36	*14	.962
1983—Alexandria .... Carol.		OF-1B	•136	504	88	129	19	7	11	59	.256	259	12	15	.948
1984—Nashua .... East.		*OF-1B	136	484	74	128	19	5	11	71	.264	312	8	*15	.955
1985—Prince William†‡ Carol.		1B-3B	39	130	15	34	4	1	3	11	.262	180	9	2	.990

Signed as free agent by Pittsburgh Pirates' organization, July 11, 1981.
†On disabled list, March 25 to July 19, 1985.
‡Drafted by Chicago White Sox, December 10, 1985.

ROBERT BARRY BONNELL

Name pronounced Buh-NELL.
(Known by middle name.)
Born October 27, 1953, at Cincinnati, O.
Height, 6.03. Weight, 205.
Throws and bats righthanded.
Attended Ohio State University, Columbus, O.
Brother of Glenn Bonnell, infielder in Cincinnati Reds' organization, 1976.

Major League stolen bases: 1977 (7), 1978 (12), 1979 (8), 1980 (3), 1981 (4), 1982 (14), 1983 (10), 1984 (5), 1985 (1). Total—64.

Year Club	League	Pos.	G.	AB.	R.	H.	2B.	3B.	HR.	RBI.	B.A.	PO.	A.	E.	F.A.
1975—Spart.†-Green.	W. Car.	OF	124	457	86	148	20	•6	12	80	*.324	276	19	12	.961
1976—Savannah	South.	OF	51	188	31	42	6	2	6	23	.223	117	6	5	.961
1976—Richmond	Int.	OF	66	227	36	64	13	2	5	31	.282	134	4	3	.979
1977—Richmond	Int.	OF	14	50	8	19	3	0	0	10	.380	42	2	1	.978
1977—Atlanta‡	Nat.	OF-3B	100	360	41	108	11	0	1	45	.300	203	65	8	.971
1978—Atlanta	Nat.	OF-3B	117	304	36	73	11	3	1	16	.240	187	35	6	.974
1979—Atlanta§	Nat.	OF-3B	127	375	47	97	20	3	12	45	.259	221	8	4	.983
1980—Toronto x	Amer.	OF	130	463	55	124	22	4	13	56	.268	271	15	8	.973
1981—Toronto	Amer.	OF	66	227	21	50	7	4	4	28	.220	148	5	4	.975
1982—Toronto	Amer.	OF-3B	140	437	59	128	26	3	6	49	.293	234	7	5	.980
1983—Toronto y	Amer.	OF-3B	121	377	49	120	21	3	10	54	.318	213	13	3	.987
1984—Seattle	Amer.	OF-3B-1B	110	363	42	96	15	4	8	48	.264	171	22	6	.970
1985—Seattle z	Amer.	OF-1B	48	111	9	27	8	0	1	10	.243	61	2	1	.984
National League Totals—3 Years			344	1039	124	278	42	6	14	106	.268	611	108	18	.976
American League Totals—6 Years			615	1978	235	545	99	18	42	245	.276	1098	65	27	.977
Major League Totals—9 Years			959	3017	359	823	141	24	56	351	.273	1709	173	45	.977

Selected by Chicago White Sox' organization in 8th round of free-agent draft, June 8, 1971.

Selected by Philadelphia Phillies' organization in secondary phase of free-agent draft, January 9, 1975.

†Traded with Catcher Jim Essian and cash to Atlanta Braves for First Baseman Dick Allen and Catcher Johnny Oates, May 7, 1975.

‡On disabled list, June 29 to July 21, 1977.

§Traded with Pitcher Joey McLaughlin and Shortstop Pat Rockett to Toronto Blue Jays for First Baseman Chris Chambliss and Shortstop Luis Gomez, December 5, 1979.

xOn disabled list, August 13 to September 2, 1980.

yTraded to Seattle Mariners for Pitcher Bryan Clark, December 9, 1983.

zOn disabled list, August 15 to September 14, 1985.

GREGORY SCOTT BOOKER

(Greg)

Born June 22, 1960, at Lynchburg, Va.
Height, 6.06. Weight, 233.
Throws and bats righthanded.
Attended Elon College, Elon College, N.C.
Son-in-law of Jack McKeon, minor league catcher, 1949 through 1959;
minor league manager, 1955 through 1964, 1968 through 1972 and 1976;
manager, Kansas City Royals, 1973 through 1975; manager,
Oakland A's, 1977 and 1978; and Vice-President/Baseball Operations with
San Diego Padres since 1980; related to Richard 'Buddy' Booker,
catcher with Cleveland Indians and Chicago White Sox, 1966 and 1968.

Led California League in wild pitches with 20 in 1982.

Year Club	League	G.	IP.	W.	L.	Pct.	H.	R.	ER.	SO.	BB.	ERA.
1981—Walla Walla	Northwest	11	53	2	3	.400	55	41	31	25	35	5.26
1982—Reno	California	27	161⅔	8	*13	.381	160	*133	*114	81	*157	6.35
1983—Las Vegas	P. Coast	46	102⅓	5	6	.455	120	77	63	58	68	5.54
1983—San Diego	National	6	11⅔	0	1	.000	18	10	10	5	9	7.71
1984—Las Vegas	P. Coast	9	55⅔	4	3	.571	66	39	34	23	24	5.50
1984—San Diego	National	32	57⅓	1	1	.500	67	27	21	28	27	3.30
1985—San Diego	National	17	22⅓	0	1	.000	20	17	17	7	17	6.85
1985—Las Vegas†	P. Coast	10	45	1	1	.500	46	34	27	16	34	5.40
Major League Totals—3 Years		55	91⅓	1	3	.250	105	54	48	40	53	4.73

Selected by Oakland A's organization in 32nd round of free-agent draft, June 6, 1978.

Selected by San Diego Padres' organization in 10th round of free-agent draft, June 8, 1981.

†On disabled list, July 18 to August 21, 1985.

CHAMPIONSHIP SERIES RECORD

Year Club	League	G.	IP.	W.	L.	Pct.	H.	R.	ER.	SO.	BB.	ERA.
1984—San Diego	National	1	2	0	0	.000	2	0	0	2	1	0.00

WORLD SERIES RECORD

Year Club	League	G.	IP.	W.	L.	Pct.	H.	R.	ER.	SO.	BB.	ERA.
1984—San Diego	National	1	1	0	0	.000	0	1	1	0	4	9.00

RECORD AS INFIELDER

Year Club	League	Pos.	G.	AB.	R.	H.	2B.	3B.	HR.	RBI.	B.A.	PO.	A.	E.	F.A.
1981—Walla Walla	N'west	*P-1B	31	64	8	12	0	0	4	15	.188	26	14	0	*1.000

ROBERT RAYMOND BOONE
(Bob)

Born November 19, 1947, at San Diego, Calif.
Height, 6.02. Weight, 202.
Throws and bats righthanded.
Received bachelor of arts degree in psychology from Stanford University, Palo Alto, Calif. in 1969.
Son of Ray Boone, infielder with Cleveland, Detroit, Chicago A.L., Kansas City,
Milwaukee and Boston, 1948 through 1960; and scout with Boston Red Sox since 1961;
brother of Rodney Alan Boone, catcher-outfielder in Kansas City Royals' and
Houston Astros' organization, 1972 through 1975.

Major League stolen bases: 1972 (1), 1973 (3), 1974 (3), 1975 (1), 1976 (2), 1977 (5), 1978 (2), 1979 (1), 1980 (3), 1981 (2), 1983 (4), 1984 (3), 1985 (1). Total—31.
Led American League catchers in double plays with 12 in 1983 and 15 in 1985.
Led American League catchers in total chances with 745 in 1982.
Led National League catchers in fielding percentage with .991 in 1978.
Led National League catchers in total chances with 924 in 1974.
Led Pacific Coast League catchers in passed balls with 18 and double plays with 13 in 1972.
Tied for Carolina League lead in double plays by third basemen with 18 in 1969.
Named catcher on THE SPORTING NEWS National League All-Star Team, 1976.
Named catcher on THE SPORTING NEWS American League All-Star fielding team, 1982.
Named catcher on THE SPORTING NEWS National League All-Star fielding team, 1978 and 1979.

Year	Club	League	Pos.	G.	AB.	R.	H.	2B.	3B.	HR.	RBI.	B.A.	PO.	A.	E.	F.A.
1969—Raleigh-Dur.	Carol.	3B	80	300	45	90	13	1	5	46	.300	71	160	20	.920
1970—Reading†	East.	3B	20	80	12	23	2	0	2	10	.288	28	38	7	.904
1971—Reading‡	East.	3B-C-SS	92	328	41	87	14	3	4	37	.265	206	138	17	.953
1972—Eugene	P. C.	C	138	513	77	158	32	4	17	67	.308	★699	★77	★24	.970
1972—Philadelphia	Nat.	C	16	51	4	14	1	0	1	4	.275	66	7	5	.936
1973—Philadelphia	Nat.	C	145	521	42	136	20	2	10	61	.261	868	★89	10	.990
1974—Philadelphia	Nat.	C	146	488	41	118	24	3	3	52	.242	★825	77	★22	.976
1975—Philadelphia	Nat.	C-3B	97	289	28	71	14	2	2	20	.246	459	48	5	.990
1976—Philadelphia	Nat.	C-1B	121	361	40	98	18	2	4	54	.271	587	39	6	.990
1977—Philadelphia	Nat.	C-3B	132	440	55	125	26	4	11	66	.284	654	83	8	.989
1978—Philadelphia	Nat.	C-1B-OF	132	435	48	123	18	4	12	62	.283	650	55	8	.989
1979—Philadelphia	Nat.	C-3B	119	398	38	114	21	3	9	58	.286	527	66	8	.987
1980—Philadelphia	Nat.	C	141	480	34	110	23	1	9	55	.229	741	88	★18	.979
1981—Philadelphia§	Nat.	C	76	227	19	48	7	0	4	24	.211	365	32	6	.985
1982—California	Amer.	C	143	472	42	121	17	0	7	58	.256	★650	★87	8	.989
1983—California	Amer.	C	142	468	46	120	18	0	9	52	.256	606	★83	★14	.980
1984—California	Amer.	C	139	450	33	91	16	1	3	32	.202	660	★71	12	.984
1985—California	Amer.	C	150	460	37	114	17	0	5	55	.248	670	71	10	.987
National League Totals—10 Years			1125	3690	349	957	172	21	65	456	.259	5742	584	96	.958
American League Totals—4 Years			574	1850	158	446	68	1	24	197	.241	2586	312	44	.985
Major League Totals—14 Years			1699	5540	507	1403	240	22	89	653	.253	8328	896	140	.985

Selected by Philadelphia Phillies' organization in 20th round of free-agent draft, June 5, 1969.
†On military list, May 26, 1970 through remainder of season.
‡On disabled list, April 10 to June 4, 1971.
§Sold to California Angels, December 6, 1981.

DIVISION SERIES RECORD

Year	Club	League	Pos.	G.	AB.	R.	H.	2B.	3B.	HR.	RBI.	B.A.	PO.	A.	E.	F.A.
1981—Philadelphia	Nat.	C	3	5	0	0	0	0	0	0	.000	10	2	0	1.000

CHAMPIONSHIP SERIES RECORD

Year	Club	League	Pos.	G.	AB.	R.	H.	2B.	3B.	HR.	RBI.	B.A.	PO.	A.	E.	F.A.
1976—Philadelphia	Nat.	C	3	7	0	2	0	0	0	1	.286	8	2	0	1.000
1977—Philadelphia	Nat.	C	4	10	1	4	0	0	0	0	.400	18	2	0	1.000
1978—Philadelphia	Nat.	C	3	11	0	2	0	0	0	0	.182	16	2	1	.947
1980—Philadelphia	Nat.	C	5	18	1	4	0	0	0	2	.222	22	3	0	1.000
1982—California	Amer.	C	5	16	3	4	0	0	1	4	.250	30	3	0	1.000
Championship Series Totals—5 Years			20	62	5	16	0	0	1	7	.258	94	12	1	.991

WORLD SERIES RECORD

Year	Club	League	Pos.	G.	AB.	R.	H.	2B.	3B.	HR.	RBI.	B.A.	PO.	A.	E.	F.A.
1980—Philadelphia	Nat.	C	6	17	3	7	2	0	0	4	.412	49	3	0	1.000

ALL-STAR GAME RECORD

Year	League	Pos.	AB.	R.	H.	2B.	3B.	HR.	RBI.	B.A.	PO.	A.	E.	F.A.
1976—National		C	2	0	0	0	0	0	0	.000	5	0	0	1.000
1978—National		C	1	1	1	0	0	0	2	1.000	3	1	0	1.000
1979—National		C	2	1	1	0	0	0	0	.500	0	0	0	.000
1983—American		C	0	0	0	0	0	0	0	.000	1	0	0	1.000
All-Star Game Totals—4 Years			5	2	2	0	0	0	2	.400	9	1	0	1.000

—DID YOU KNOW—

That when San Francisco's Jeff Leonard hit for the cycle on June 27, 1985, it marked the first time since April 16, 1972, that a Giant had accomplished the feat?

RICHARD ALBERT BORDI
Name pronounced BORD-ee.
(Rich)

Born April 18, 1959, at South San Francisco, Calif.
Height, 6.07. Weight, 220.
Throws and bats righthanded.
Attended Fresno State University, Fresno, Calif.

Major League saves: 1983 (1), 1984 (4), 1985 (2). Total—7.
Tied for Pacific Coast League lead in complete games with 15 in 1981.

Year Club	League	G.	IP.	W.	L.	Pct.	H.	R.	ER.	SO.	BB.	ERA.
1980—West Haven	Eastern	11	76	4	6	.400	75	42	35	49	30	4.14
1980—Oakland	American	1	2	0	0	.000	4	1	1	0	0	4.50
1981—Tacoma	P. Coast	27	191	9	11	.450	197	98	78	101	66	3.68
1981—Oakland†	American	2	2	0	0	.000	1	0	0	0	1	0.00
1982—Salt Lake City	P. Coast	25	168⅓	12	9	.571	212	105	84	118	31	4.49
1982—Seattle‡	American	7	13	0	2	.000	18	12	12	10	1	8.31
1983—Iowa§	Am. Assoc.	18	111⅓	7	2	.778	134	62	57	80	21	4.61
1983—Chicago	National	11	25⅓	0	2	.000	34	15	14	20	12	4.97
1984—Chicago xy	National	31	83⅓	5	2	.714	78	37	32	41	20	3.46
1985—New York za	American	51	98	6	8	.429	95	41	35	64	29	3.21
American League Totals—4 Years		61	115	6	10	.375	118	54	40	74	31	3.70
National League Totals—2 Years		42	108⅔	5	4	.556	112	52	46	61	32	3.81
Major League Totals—6 Years		103	223⅔	11	14	.440	230	106	94	135	63	3.78

Selected by Minnesota Twins' organization in 5th round of free-agent draft, June 7, 1977.
Selected by Oakland A's organization in 3rd round of free-agent draft, June 3, 1980.
†Traded to Seattle Mariners for Third Baseman-Outfielder Dan Meyer, December 9, 1981.
‡Traded to Chicago Cubs for Outfielder Steve Henderson, December 9, 1982.
§On disabled list, April 25 to May 10, 1983.
xOn disabled list, August 8 to August 23, 1984.
yTraded with Catcher Ron Hassey, Outfielder Henry Cotto and Pitcher Porfi Altamirano to New York Yankees for Pitcher Ray Fontenot and Outfielder Brian Dayett, December 4, 1984.
zOn disabled list, April 30 to May 15, 1985.
aTraded with Infielder Rex Hudler to Baltimore Orioles for Outfielder Gary Roenicke and a player to be named later, December 12, 1985; New York Yankees acquired Outfielder Leo Hernandez to complete deal, December 16, 1985.

CHRISTOPHER LOUIS BOSIO
Name pronounced Boz-e-o.
(Chris)

Born April 3, 1963, at Rancho Cordova, Calif.
Height, 6.03. Weight, 220.
Throws and bats righthanded.
Attended Sacramento City College, Sacramento, Calif.

Year Club	League	G.	IP.	W.	L.	Pct.	H.	R.	ER.	SO.	BB.	ERA.
1982—Pikeville	Ap'lachian	13	51⅓	3	2	.600	60	31	28	53	17	4.91
1983—Beloit	Midwest	17	107⅔	3	10	.231	125	82	67	71	41	5.60
1983—Paintsville	Ap'lachian	7	44⅓	2	2	.500	30	18	14	43	18	2.84
1984—Beloit	Midwest	26	181	*17	6	.739	159	83	55	156	56	2.73
1985—El Paso	Texas	28	181⅓	11	6	.647	186	108	77	*155	49	3.82

Selected by Pittsburgh Pirates' organization in 29th round of free-agent draft, June 8, 1981.
Selected by Milwaukee Brewers' organization in secondary phase of free-agent draft, January 12, 1982.

THADDIS BOSLEY JR.
Name pronounced BAHZ-lee.
(Thad)

Born September 17, 1956, at Oceanside, Calif.
Height, 6.03. Weight, 175.
Throws and bats lefthanded.
Attended Mira Costa Community College, Oceanside, Calif.

Major League stolen bases: 1977 (5), 1978 (12), 1979 (4), 1980 (3), 1981 (2), 1982 (3), 1983 (1), 1984 (5), 1985 (5). Total—40.
Led California League in stolen bases with 90 and caught stealing with 17 in 1976.
Led Pioneer League in bases on balls received with 71 in 1974.
Named California League Most Valuable Player, 1976.

Year Club	League	Pos.	G.	AB.	R.	H.	2B.	3B.	HR.	RBI.	B.A.	PO.	A.	E.	F.A.
1974—Idaho Falls	Pion.	OF	68	223	55	54	3	4	0	14	.242	101	4	*11	.905
1975—Quad Cities†	Midw.	OF	108	379	67	113	12	3	1	50	.298	206	2	4	*.981
1976—Salinas	Calif.	OF	134	527	105	171	26	4	2	72	*.324	285	13	7	*.977
1977—Salt Lake City	P. C.	OF	69	298	55	97	22	2	2	38	.326	169	6	5	.972
1977—California‡§	Amer.	OF	58	212	19	63	10	2	0	19	.297	130	1	5	.963
1978—Iowa	A. A.	OF	47	179	27	52	3	0	3	15	.291	77	5	2	.976
1978—Chicago x	Amer.	OF	66	219	25	59	5	1	2	13	.269	155	3	4	.975
1979—Iowa y	A. A.	OF	95	382	62	101	14	5	1	24	.264	140	6	5	.967
1979—Chicago	Amer.	OF	36	77	13	24	1	1	8	.312	57	2	2	.967
1980—Chicago za	Amer.	OF	70	147	12	33	2	0	2	14	.224	91	1	4	.958
1981—Vancouver	P. C.	OF	34	122	15	39	5	2	0	14	.320	75	0	5	.938

Year Club League	Pos.	G.	AB.	R.	H.	2B.	3B.	HR.	RBI.	B.A.	PO.	A.	E.	F.A.
1981—Milwaukee b........ Amer.	OF	42	105	11	24	2	0	0	3	.229	55	1	2	.966
1982—Seattle.................... Amer.	OF	22	46	3	8	1	0	0	2	.174	12	1	0	1.000
1982—Salt Lake C. cdef . P. C.	OF	22	84	15	25	2	2	3	9	.298	24	2	0	1.000
1983—Mexico City.......... Mex.	OF	31	107	24	35	7	3	4	18	.327	24	1	0	1.000
1983—Iowa .... A. A.	OF	39	124	22	36	11	0	7	24	.290	3	0	1	.750
1983—Chicago .... Nat.	OF	43	72	12	21	4	1	2	12	.292	27	1	0	1.000
1984—Iowa .... A. A.	OF	51	162	23	58	16	1	6	43	.358	31	4	2	.946
1984—Chicago .... Nat.	OF	55	98	17	29	2	2	2	14	.296	39	2	1	.976
1985—Chicago .... Nat.	OF	108	180	25	59	6	3	7	27	.328	84	0	1	.988
American League Totals—6 Years		294	806	83	211	21	4	5	59	.262	500	9	17	.968
National League Totals—3 Years............		206	350	54	109	12	6	11	53	.311	150	3	2	.987
Major League Totals—9 Years.................		500	1156	137	320	33	10	16	112	.277	650	12	19	.972

Selected by California Angels' organization in 4th round of free-agent draft, June 5, 1974.

†On disabled list, April 19 to May 6, 1975.

‡On disabled list, June 29 to July 10, 1977.

§Traded with Outfielder Bobby Bonds and Pitcher Dick Dotson to Chicago White Sox for Pitchers Chris Knapp and Dave Frost and Catcher Brian Downing, December 5, 1977.

xOn disabled list, June 29 to July 17, 1978.

yOn disabled list, July 15 to July 25, 1979.

zOn disabled list, August 12, 1980 through remainder of season.

aTraded to Milwaukee Brewers' organization for First Baseman-Outfielder John Poff, April 1, 1981.

bTraded to Seattle Mariners for Pitcher Mike Parrott, March 5, 1982.

cOn disabled list, June 6 to July 1 and August 3 to September 2, 1982.

dGranted free agency, September 5, 1982; signed by Tacoma (Oakland A's organization), February 14, 1983.

eSold to Iowa (Chicago Cubs' organization), March 30, 1983.

fLoaned to Mexico City Tigers, April 3, 1983; returned, May 28, 1983.

DIVISION SERIES RECORD

Year Club League	Pos.	G.	AB.	R.	H.	2B.	3B.	HR.	RBI.	B.A.	PO.	A.	E.	F.A.
1981—Milwaukee............ Amer.	PR-DH	1	0	0	0	0	0	0	0	.000	0	0	0	.000

CHAMPIONSHIP SERIES RECORD

Year Club League	Pos.	G.	AB.	R.	H.	2B.	3B.	HR.	RBI.	B.A.	PO.	A.	E.	F.A.
1984—Chicago .... Nat.	PH	2	2	0	0	0	0	0	0	.000	0	0	0	.000

DARYL LAMONT BOSTON

Born January 4, 1963, at Cincinnati, O.
Height, 6.03. Weight, 193.
Throws and bats lefthanded.

Major League stolen bases: 1984 (6), 1985 (8). Total—14.
Led Eastern League batters in strikeouts with 133 in 1983.
Led Midwest League outfielders in total chances with 312 in 1982.
Tied for American Association lead in sacrifice flies with 11 in 1984.
Tied for American Association lead in double plays by outfielders with 4 in 1984.

Year Club League	Pos.	G.	AB.	R.	H.	2B.	3B.	HR.	RBI.	B.A.	PO.	A.	E.	F.A.
1981—Sarasota W. S........ Gulf C.	OF	56	189	30	55	6	3	1	30	.291	84	9	3	.969
1982—Appleton .... Midw.	OF	★139	512	86	143	19	9	15	77	.279	★293	9	10	.968
1983—Glens Falls........... East.	OF	113	435	65	104	15	1	18	50	.239	271	8	13	.955
1983—Denver .... A. A.	OF	14	51	11	13	4	1	2	7	.255	26	1	5	.844
1984—Denver .... A. A.	OF	127	471	94	147	21	★19	15	82	.312	311	11	●10	.970
1984—Chicago .... Amer.	OF	35	83	8	14	3	1	0	3	.169	59	2	6	.910
1985—Chicago .... Amer.	OF	95	232	20	53	13	1	3	15	.228	179	7	2	.989
1985—Buffalo................... A. A.	OF	63	241	45	66	12	1	10	36	.274	151	3	3	.981
Major League Totals—2 Years.................		130	315	28	67	16	2	3	18	.213	238	9	8	.969

Selected by Chicago White Sox' organization in 1st round (seventh player selected) of free-agent draft, June 8, 1981.

DEREK WAYNE BOTELHO

Name pronounced Boh-TELL-oh.

Born August 2, 1956, at Long Beach, Calif.
Height, 6.02. Weight, 165.
Throws and bats righthanded.
Attended Miami Dade Community College (South), Miami, Fla.

Pitched seven-inning, 8-0 no-hit victory against Miami, June 17, 1981 (first game).
Tied for Eastern League lead in shutouts with 4 in 1978.

Year Club League	G.	IP.	W.	L.	Pct.	H.	R.	ER.	SO.	BB.	ERA.
1976—Spartanburg.................... W. Carol	20	134	9	9	.500	120	69	54	90	49	3.63
1977—Peninsula........................ Carolina	26	173	13	5	★.722	167	86	72	107	67	3.75
1978—Reading†........................ Eastern	27	178	15	7	.682	175	77	70	130	65	3.54
1979—Wichita‡§x .... Am. Assoc.	4	19	1	2	.333	30	20	18	18	8	8.53
1980—					(Out of Organized Baseball)						
1981—Fort Myers........................ Florida St.	8	39	2	3	.400	25	10	7	32	9	1.62
1981—Jacksonville y .... Southern	7	37	2	2	.500	27	9	8	15	4	1.95
1982—Jacksonville...................... Southern	9	65	3	4	.429	54	35	33	35	25	4.57
1982—Omaha.............................. Am. Assoc.	15	105⅓	7	5	.583	86	51	49	74	37	4.19
1982—Kansas City...................... American	8	24	2	1	.667	25	11	11	12	8	4.13

Year Club	League	G.	IP.	W.	L.	Pct.	H.	R.	ER.	SO.	BB.	ERA.
1983—Omaha z	Am. Assoc.	25	152⅔	10	★14	.417	155	105	92	101	73	5.42
1984—Iowa	Am. Assoc.	28	177⅓	10	11	.476	179	89	75	136	65	3.81
1985—Iowa	Am. Assoc.	20	125⅔	11	7	.611	117	64	60	94	53	4.30
1985—Chicago a	National	11	44	1	3	.250	52	27	26	23	23	5.32
American League Totals—1 Year		8	24	2	1	.667	25	11	11	12	8	4.13
National League Totals—1 Year		11	44	1	3	.250	52	27	26	23	23	5.32
Major League Totals—2 Years		19	68	3	4	.429	77	38	37	35	31	4.90

Selected by Philadelphia Phillies' organization in 26th round of free-agent draft, June 5, 1974.
Selected by California Angels' organization in secondary phase of free-agent draft, June 9, 1975.
Selected by Philadelphia Phillies' organization in 2nd round of free-agent draft, January 7, 1976.
†Traded with Outfielder Jerry Martin, Catcher Barry Foote, Second Baseman Ted Sizemore and Pitcher Henry Mack to Chicago Cubs for Second Baseman Manny Trillo, Outfielder Greg Gross and Catcher Dave Rader, February 23, 1979.
‡On temporary inactive list, April 11 to April 26, 1979.
§On disabled list, June 4 to August 31, 1979.
xReleased February 5,1980; signed by Jacksonville (Kansas City Royals' organization), January 6, 1981.
yOn disabled list, April 9 to May 17, 1981.
zTraded to Chicago Cubs for Pitcher Alan Hargesheimer, March 30, 1984.
aReleased, December 20, 1985; signed by Cincinnati Reds' organization, January 16, 1986.

LAWRENCE ROBERT BOWA
(Larry)

Born December 6, 1945, at Sacramento, Calif.
Height, 5.10. Weight, 155.
Throws right and bats left and righthanded.
Attended Sacramento City College, Sacramento, Calif.
Son of Paul Bowa, infielder in St. Louis Cardinals' organization, 1944 and 1946; manager,
St. Louis Cardinals' organization, 1947; nephew of Frank Bowa, minor
league infielder, 1944 through 1949.

Established major league records for highest fielding percentage by shortstop, lifetime, 1,000 or more games (.980); highest fielding percentage by shortstop, season (.991), 1979; most years leading league in fielding average by shortstop, 100 or more games (6).
Tied modern major league record for most at bats, game (7), July 12, 1975.
Established National League records for most games by shortstop, lifetime (2,222); fewest errors, season, 150 or more games, by shortstop (9), 1972; most seasons leading league in fielding percentage by shortstop, 100 or more games (6), 1971, 1972, 1974, 1978, 1979 and 1983.
Major League stolen bases: 1970 (24), 1971 (28), 1972 (17), 1973 (10), 1974 (39), 1975 (24), 1976 (30), 1977 (32), 1978 (27), 1979 (20), 1980 (21), 1981 (16), 1982 (8), 1983 (7), 1984 (10), 1985 (5). Total—318.
Led National League in sacrifice hits with 18 in 1972.
Led National League shortstops in total chances with 843 in 1971.
Tied for National League lead in double plays by shortstops with 97 in 1971.
Led Pacific Coast League in stolen bases with 48 in 1969.
Led Pacific Coast League shortstops in putouts with 468 in 1969.
Led Eastern League shortstops in double plays with 77 in 1968.
Named shortstop on THE SPORTING NEWS National League All-Star Team, 1975 and 1978.
Named shortstop on THE SPORTING NEWS National League All-Star fielding team, 1972 and 1978.

Year Club	League	Pos.	G.	AB.	R.	H.	2B.	3B.	HR.	RBI.	B.A.	PO.	A.	E.	F.A.
1966—Spartanburg	W. Car.	SS	97	429	70	134	14	4	2	36	.312	138	284	12	★.972
1966—San Diego	P. C.	SS	5	19	0	6	0	1	0	1	.316	13	20	2	.943
1967—Bakersfield†	Calif.	SS-2B	7	32	4	6	2	0	0	3	.188	15	12	1	.964
1967—Reading	East.	SS	22	89	11	25	4	0	0	9	.281	35	79	9	.927
1968—Reading	East.	SS	133	480	47	116	14	2	3	36	.242	192	●395	24	.961
1969—Eugene	P. C.	★SS-2B	135	568	80	163	11	6	1	26	.287	★215	469	18	★.974
1970—Philadelphia	Nat.	SS-2B	145	547	50	137	17	6	0	34	.250	202	418	13	.979
1971—Philadelphia	Nat.	SS	159	★650	74	162	18	5	0	25	.249	272	★560	11	★.987
1972—Philadelphia	Nat.	SS	152	579	67	145	11	★13	1	31	.250	212	494	9	★.987
1973—Philadelphia‡	Nat.	SS	122	446	42	94	11	3	0	23	.211	191	361	12	.979
1974—Philadelphia	Nat.	SS	162	669	97	184	19	10	1	36	.275	256	462	12	★.984
1975—Philadelphia§	Nat.	SS	136	583	79	178	18	9	2	38	.305	227	403	25	.962
1976—Philadelphia	Nat.	SS	156	624	71	155	15	9	0	49	.248	180	492	17	.975
1977—Philadelphia	Nat.	SS	154	624	93	175	19	3	4	41	.280	222	518	13	.983
1978—Philadelphia	Nat.	SS	156	654	78	192	31	5	3	43	.294	224	502	10	★.986
1979—Philadelphia x	Nat.	SS	147	539	74	130	17	11	0	31	.241	229	448	6	★.991
1980—Philadelphia	Nat.	SS	147	540	57	144	16	4	2	39	.267	225	449	17	.975
1981—Philadelphia y	Nat.	SS	103	360	34	102	14	3	0	31	.283	117	309	11	.975
1982—Chicago	Nat.	SS	142	499	50	123	15	7	0	29	.246	210	396	17	.973
1983—Chicago	Nat.	SS	147	499	73	133	20	5	2	43	.267	230	464	11	★.984
1984—Chicago	Nat.	SS	133	391	33	87	14	2	0	17	.223	217	378	16	.974
1985—Chi z-N.Y. a	Nat.	SS-2B	86	214	15	50	7	4	0	15	.234	109	210	11	.967
Major League Totals—16 Years			2247	8418	987	2191	262	99	15	525	.260	3323	6864	211	.980

Signed as free agent by Philadelphia Phillies' organization, October 12, 1965.
†On military list, March 7 to July 18, 1967.
‡On disabled list, July 26 to September 1, 1973.
§On disabled list, May 27 to June 23, 1975.
xOn disabled list, May 25 to June 9, 1979.
yTraded with Infielder Ryne Sandberg to Chicago Cubs for Shortstop Ivan DeJesus, January 27, 1982.
zReleased, August 13, 1985; signed by New York Mets, August 20, 1985.
aGranted free agency, November 12, 1985; named minor league manager in San Diego Padres' organization, November 14, 1985.

Year	Club	League	Pos.	G.	AB.	R.	H.	2B.	3B.	HR.	RBI.	B.A.	PO.	A.	E.	F.A.
1981—Philadelphia		Nat.	SS	5	17	0	3	1	0	0	1	.176	12	9	1	.955

CHAMPIONSHIP SERIES RECORD

Year	Club	League	Pos.	G.	AB.	R.	H.	2B.	3B.	HR.	RBI.	B.A.	PO.	A.	E.	F.A.
1976—Philadelphia		Nat.	SS	3	8	1	1	1	0	0	1	.125	2	11	0	1.000
1977—Philadelphia		Nat.	SS	4	17	2	2	0	0	0	1	.118	0	17	0	1.000
1978—Philadelphia		Nat.	SS	4	18	2	6	0	0	0	0	.333	5	16	0	1.000
1980—Philadelphia		Nat.	SS	5	19	2	6	0	0	0	0	.316	4	11	1	.938
1984—Chicago		Nat.	SS	5	15	1	3	1	0	0	1	.200	8	15	0	1.000
Championship Series Totals—5 Years				21	77	8	18	2	0	0	3	.234	19	70	1	.989

WORLD SERIES RECORD

Established World Series record for most double plays started by shortstop, six-game Series (7), 1980.
Tied World Series record for most double plays started by shortstop, nine-inning game (3), October 15, 1980.

Year	Club	League	Pos.	G.	AB.	R.	H.	2B.	3B.	HR.	RBI.	B.A.	PO.	A.	E.	F.A.
1980—Philadelphia		Nat.	SS	6	24	3	9	1	0	0	2	.375	5	18	0	1.000

ALL-STAR GAME RECORD

Year	League	Pos.	AB.	R.	H.	2B.	3B.	HR.	RBI.	B.A.	PO.	A.	E.	F.A.
1974—National		SS	2	0	0	0	0	0	0	.000	2	0	0	1.000
1975—National		SS	0	1	0	0	0	0	0	.000	2	0	0	1.000
1976—National		SS	1	0	0	0	0	0	0	.000	2	1	0	1.000
1978—National		SS	3	1	2	0	0	0	0	.667	2	4	0	1.000
1979—National		SS	2	0	0	0	0	0	0	.000	1	3	0	1.000
All-Star Game Totals—5 Years			8	2	2	0	0	0	0	.250	9	8	0	1.000

DENNIS RAY BOYD
(Oil Can)

(Given nickname from beer drinking friends in Meridian, Miss.
where beer is referred to as oil.)
Born October 6, 1959, at Meridian, Miss.
Height, 6.01. Weight, 155.
Throws and bats righthanded.
Attended Jackson State University, Jackson, Miss.
Brother of Don Boyd, outfielder in St. Louis Cardinals' organization, 1973.

Led Florida State League pitchers in games started with 28 and home runs allowed with 11 in 1981.
Tied for Eastern League lead in games started by pitchers with 27 and complete games with 13 in 1982.

Year	Club	League	G.	IP.	W.	L.	Pct.	H.	R.	ER.	SO.	BB.	ERA.
1980—Elmira		NYP	12	69	7	1	.875	54	20	19	79	30	2.48
1981—Winter Haven		Florida St.	28	186	14	8	.636	*195	90	75	154	54	3.63
1982—Bristol		Eastern	27	*205	14	8	.636	190	71	64	*191	49	2.81
1982—Boston		American	3	8⅓	0	1	.000	11	5	5	2	2	5.40
1983—Pawtucket		Int'national	20	122⅔	5	8	.385	119	69	55	129	41	4.04
1983—Boston		American	15	98⅔	4	8	.333	103	46	36	43	23	3.28
1984—Boston		American	29	197⅔	12	12	.500	207	109	96	134	53	4.37
1984—Pawtucket		Int'national	5	37⅓	3	1	.750	30	12	12	45	12	2.89
1985—Boston		American	35	272⅓	15	13	.536	*273	117	112	154	67	3.70
Major League Totals—4 Years			82	577	31	34	.477	594	277	249	333	145	3.88

Selected by Boston Red Sox' organization in 16th round of free-agent draft, June 3, 1980.

PHILIP POOLE BRADLEY
(Phil)

Born March 11, 1959, at Bloomington, Ind.
Height, 6.00. Weight, 175.
Throws and bats righthanded.
Received bachelor of science degree in personnel management from
University of Missouri, Columbia, Mo., in 1982.

Major League stolen bases: 1983 (3), 1984 (21), 1985 (22). Total—46.
Named outfielder on THE SPORTING NEWS American League All-Star Team, 1985.

Year	Club	League	Pos.	G.	AB.	R.	H.	2B.	3B.	HR.	RBI.	B.A.	PO.	A.	E.	F.A.
1981—Bellingham		N'west	OF	53	193	38	58	12	5	1	20	.301	94	3	1	*.990
1982—Bakersfield		Calif.	OF	109	405	98	134	17	10	0	37	.331	226	13	6	.976
1983—Salt Lake City		P. Coast	OF	130	458	100	148	14	4	2	41	.323	284	13	1	*.997
1983—Seattle		Amer.	OF	23	67	8	18	2	0	0	5	.269	36	1	1	.974
1984—Seattle		Amer.	OF	124	322	49	97	12	4	0	24	.301	235	3	2	.992
1985—Seattle		Amer.	OF	159	641	100	192	33	8	26	88	.300	336	10	5	.986
Major League Totals—3 Years				306	1030	157	307	47	12	26	117	.298	607	14	8	.987

Selected by Seattle Mariners' organization in 3rd round of free-agent draft, June 8, 1981.

ALL-STAR GAME RECORD

Year	League	Pos.	AB.	R.	H.	2B.	3B.	HR.	RBI.	B.A.	PO.	A.	E.	F.A.
1985—American		OF	1	0	0	0	0	0	0	.000	1	0	0	1.000

SCOTT WILLIAM BRADLEY

Born March 22, 1960, at Essex Fells, N.J.
Height, 5.11. Weight, 185.
Throws right and bats lefthanded.
Received bachelor of science degree in business administration
from University of North Carolina, Chapel Hill, N.C.

Tied for International League lead in game-winning RBIs with 14 in 1984.
Tied for Florida State League lead in game-winning RBIs with 13 in 1982.
Named International League Player of the Year, 1984.

Year Club	League	Pos.	G.	AB.	R.	H.	2B.	3B.	HR.	RBI.	B.A.	PO.	A.	E.	F.A.
1981—Oneonta	NYP	C-OF	71	276	48	85	17	4	4	54	.308	323	40	9	.976
1982—Nashville	South.	C	5	19	2	2	1	0	0	0	.105	44	2	2	.958
1982—Fort Lauderdale	Fla. St.	C-1B-3B	121	439	52	130	28	4	3	66	.296	407	57	10	.979
1983—Nashville	South.	C-3B	137	525	83	142	33	4	8	76	.270	475	88	13	.977
1984—Columbus	Int.	C-OF-3B	★138	★538	84	★180	31	2	6	●84	★.335	432	50	9	.982
1984—New York	Amer.	OF-C	9	21	3	6	1	0	0	2	.286	10	0	0	1.000
1985—New York†	Amer.	C	19	49	4	8	2	1	0	1	.163	12	0	1	.923
1985—Albany	East.	3B	6	24	2	3	1	0	0	2	.125	8	14	4	.846
1985—Columbus	Int.	C-3B	43	163	17	49	10	0	4	27	.301	118	53	4	.977
Major League Totals—2 Years			28	70	7	14	3	1	0	3	.200	22	0	1	.957

Selected by Minnesota Twins' organization in 12th round of free-agent draft, June 6, 1978.
Selected by New York Yankees' organization in 3rd round of free-agent draft, June 8, 1981.
†On disabled list, April 24 to June 17, 1985; included rehabilitation disability assignment to Sarasota, June 5 to June 8, 1985, and Albany, June 9 to June 17, 1985.

GLENN ERICK BRAGGS

Born October 17, 1962, at San Bernardino, Calif.
Height, 6.03. Weight, 210.
Throws and bats righthanded.
Attended University of Hawaii, Honolulu, Hawaii.

Led Texas League in being hit by pitch with 10 in 1985.
Led Appalachian League in total bases with 164, bases on balls received with 54 and intentional bases on balls received with 6 in 1983.
Named California League Most Valuable Player, 1984.
Named Appalachian League Player of the Year, 1983.
Received reported $50,000 bonus to sign with Milwaukee Brewers, 1983.

Year Club	League	Pos.	G.	AB.	R.	H.	2B.	3B.	HR.	RBI.	B.A.	PO.	A.	E.	F.A.
1983—Paintsville	Appal.	OF	●73	241	★65	★94	★20	1	●16	★74	★.390	115	8	6	.953
1984—Stockton	Calif.	OF	108	399	76	118	29	2	15	86	.296	158	4	6	.964
1985—El Paso	Texas	OF	117	448	105	139	26	4	20	103	.310	239	10	11	.958

Selected by New York Yankees' organization in 6th round of free-agent draft, June 3, 1980.
Selected by Milwaukee Brewers' organization in 2nd round of free-agent draft, June 6, 1983.

MICHAEL CHARLES BRANTLEY
(Mickey)

Born June 17, 1961, at Catskill, N.Y.
Height, 5.10. Weight, 180.
Throws and bats righthanded.
Attended Columbia-Greene Community College, Hudson, N.Y., and
Coastal Carolina Community College, Jacksonville, N.C.

Tied for Southern League lead in sacrifice flies with 10 in 1984.

Year Club	League	Pos.	G.	AB.	R.	H.	2B.	3B.	HR.	RBI.	B.A.	PO.	A.	E.	F.A.
1983—Bakersfield	Calif.	OF	53	185	33	55	9	3	6	29	.297	59	3	1	.984
1984—Chattanooga	South.	OF-3B	131	472	73	149	21	9	11	76	.316	211	14	8	.966
1984—Salt Lake City	P. C.	OF	4	17	2	4	0	0	0	1	.235	8	0	0	1.000
1985—Calgary	P. C.	OF	74	279	52	68	13	6	11	45	.244	165	1	3	.982

Selected by Cincinnati Reds' organization in 8th round of free-agent draft, June 7, 1982.
Selected by Seattle Mariners' organization in 2nd round of free-agent draft, June 6, 1983.

STEPHEN RUSSELL BRAUN III
(Steve)

Born May 8, 1948, at Trenton, N. J.
Height, 5.10. Weight, 180.
Throws right and bats lefthanded.

Major League stolen bases: 1971 (8), 1972 (4), 1973 (4), 1974 (4), 1976 (12), 1977 (8), 1978 (4), 1981 (1). Total—45.
Led Carolina League third basemen in fielding percentage with .925 in 1970.
Led Gulf Coast League second basemen in double plays with 47 in 1967.

Year Club	League	Pos.	G.	AB.	R.	H.	2B.	3B.	HR.	RBI.	B.A.	PO.	A.	E.	F.A.
1966—Sarasota Twins	Gulf C.	2B	45	152	23	35	5	★5	0	15	.230	70	85	★16	.906
1967—Wis. Rapids	Midw.	2B	10	9	1	2	1	0	0	2	.222	0	0	0	.000
1967—Sarasota Twins†	Gulf C.	2B	54	184	37	45	6	★8	1	13	.245	★111	★153	★14	.950
1968-69—							(In Military Service)								
1970—Lynchburg	Carol.	3B-2B	118	387	52	108	24	1	4	43	.279	109	253	29	.926
1971—Minnesota	Amer.	3-2-S-O	128	343	51	87	12	2	5	35	.254	107	193	13	.958
1972—Minnesota	Amer.	3-2-S-O	121	402	40	116	21	0	2	50	.289	110	207	13	.961

Year	Club	League	Pos.	G.	AB.	R.	H.	2B.	3B.	HR.	RBI.	B.A.	PO.	A.	E.	F.A.
1973—Minnesota	Amer.	3B-OF	115	361	46	102	28	5	6	42	.283	86	175	16	.942
1974—Minnesota	Amer.	OF-3B	129	453	53	127	12	1	8	40	.280	195	47	12	.953
1975—Minnesota	Amer.	O-1-3-2	136	453	70	137	18	3	11	45	.302	271	14	10	.966
1976—Minnesota‡	Amer.	OF-3B	122	417	73	120	12	3	3	61	.288	71	32	6	.954
1977—Seattle	Amer.	OF-3B	139	451	51	106	19	1	5	31	.235	186	11	5	.975
1978—Sea.§-Kan. City	Amer.	OF-3B	96	211	27	53	14	1	3	29	.251	68	9	4	.951
1979—Kansas City x	Amer.	OF-3B	58	116	15	31	2	0	4	10	.267	26	4	0	1.000
1980—K.C. y-Tor.	Amer.	OF-3B	51	78	4	16	2	0	1	10	.205	2	1	0	1.000
1980—Syracuse z	Int.	DH	19	61	11	20	3	1	2	11	.328	0	0	0	.000
1981—St. Louis	Nat.	OF-3B	44	46	9	9	2	1	0	2	.196	15	2	0	1.000
1982—St. Louis a	Nat.	OF-3B	58	62	6	17	4	0	0	4	.274	6	5	1	.917
1983—St. Louis	Nat.	OF-3B	78	92	8	25	2	1	3	7	.272	26	4	0	1.000
1984—St. Louis	Nat.	OF-3B	86	98	6	27	3	1	0	16	.276	10	1	0	1.000
1985—St. Louis b	Nat.	OF	64	67	7	16	4	0	1	6	.239	14	1	0	1.000
American League Totals—10 Years			1095	3285	430	895	140	16	48	353	.272	1122	693	79	.958
National League Totals—5 Years			330	365	36	94	15	3	4	35	.258	71	13	1	.988
Major League Totals—15 Years			1425	3650	466	989	155	19	52	388	.271	1193	706	80	.960

Selected by Minnesota Twins' organization in 10th round of free-agent draft, June 22, 1966.
†On military list, September 6, 1967 through September 23, 1969.
‡Selected by Seattle Mariners in American League expansion draft, November 5, 1976.
§Traded to Kansas City Royals for Pitcher Jim Colborn, June 1, 1978.
xOn disabled list, July 29 to September 1, 1979.
yReleased, June 2, 1980; signed by Toronto Blue Jays' organization, July 10, 1980.
zGranted free agency, November 5, 1980; signed by St. Louis Cardinals' organization, March 3, 1981.
aOn disabled list, June 7 to June 22, 1982.
bReleased, December 18, 1985.

CHAMPIONSHIP SERIES RECORD

Year	Club	League	Pos.	G.	AB.	R.	H.	2B.	3B.	HR.	RBI.	B.A.	PO.	A.	E.	F.A.
1978—Kansas City	Amer.	OF-PH	2	5	0	0	0	0	0	0	.000	5	0	0	1.000
1982—St. Louis	Nat.	PH	1	1	0	0	0	0	0	0	.000	0	0	0	.000
1985—St. Louis	Nat.	PH	2	2	0	0	0	0	0	0	.000	0	0	0	.000
Championship Series Totals—3 Years			5	8	0	0	0	0	0	0	.000	5	0	0	1.000

WORLD SERIES RECORD

Year	Club	League	Pos.	G.	AB.	R.	H.	2B.	3B.	HR.	RBI.	B.A.	PO.	A.	E.	F.A.
1982—St. Louis	Nat.	PH-DH	2	2	0	1	0	0	0	2	.500	0	0	0	.000
1985—St. Louis	Nat.	PH	1	1	0	0	0	0	0	0	.000	0	0	0	.000
World Series Totals—2 Years			3	3	0	1	0	0	0	2	.333	0	0	0	.000

GLEN DELL BRAXTON

Born April 17, 1967, at Idabel, Okla.
Height, 5.11. Weight, 210.
Throws and bats lefthanded.

Year	Club	League	Pos.	G.	AB.	R.	H.	2B.	3B.	HR.	RBI.	B.A.	PO.	A.	E.	F.A.
1985—Sarasota W.S.†	Gulf C.	OF	56	204	35	52	2	4	0	21	.255	72	4	4	.950

Selected by Chicago White Sox' organization in 3rd round of free-agent draft, June 3, 1985.
†Traded with Pitcher Britt Burns and Shortstop Mike Soper to New York Yankees for Catcher Ron Hassey and Pitcher Joe Cowley, December 12, 1985.

SIDNEY EUGENE BREAM

(Sid)

Born August 3, 1960, at Carlisle, Pa.
Height, 6.04. Weight, 215.
Throws and bats lefthanded.
Attended Liberty Baptist College, Lynchburg, Va.

Major League stolen bases: 1984 (1).
Led Pacific Coast League first basemen in total chances with 1,411 in 1983 and 1,200 in 1984.
Led Pacific Coast League first basemen in double plays with 106 in 1984.

Year	Club	League	Pos.	G.	AB.	R.	H.	2B.	3B.	HR.	RBI.	B.A.	PO.	A.	E.	F.A.
1981—Vero Beach	Fla. St.	1B	70	260	35	85	12	5	1	47	.327	613	45	10	.985
1982—Vero Beach	Fla. St.	1B	63	226	41	70	13	5	4	43	.310	523	40	5	.991
1982—San Antonio	Texas	1B	70	259	43	83	18	0	8	50	.320	621	40	12	.982
1982—Albuquerque	P. C.	1B	3	8	3	3	1	0	1	2	.375	11	0	0	1.000
1983—Albuquerque	P. C.	1B	138	485	115	149	23	4	●32	★118	.307	1264	★123	24	.983
1983—Los Angeles	Nat.	1B	15	11	0	2	0	0	0	2	.182	8	0	0	1.000
1984—Albuquerque	P. C.	1B	114	429	82	147	25	4	20	90	.343	1071	★112	17	.986
1984—Los Angeles	Nat.	1B	27	49	2	9	3	0	0	6	.184	95	11	0	1.000
1985—L.A.†-Pitt.	Nat.	1B	50	148	18	34	7	0	6	21	.230	367	35	3	.993
1985—Albuquerque	P. C.	1B-OF	85	297	51	110	25	3	17	57	.370	381	51	2	.995
Major League Totals—3 Years			92	208	20	45	10	0	6	29	.216	470	46	3	.994

Selected by Los Angeles Dodgers' organization in 2nd round of free-agent draft, June 8, 1981.
†Traded with Outfielder Cecil Espy, September 9, 1985, completing deal in which Los Angeles Dodgers acquired Third Baseman Bill Madlock for three players to be named later, August 31, 1985. Pittsburgh Pirates acquired Outfielder R. J. Reynolds as partial completion of deal, September 3, 1985.

ROBERT EARL BRENLY
(Bob)

Born February 25, 1954, at Coshocton, Ohio.
Height, 6.02. Weight, 210.
Throws and bats righthanded.
Received bachelor of science degree in health education from
Ohio University, Athens, Ohio in 1976.

Major League stolen bases: 1982 (6), 1983 (10), 1984 (6), 1985 (1). Total—23.
Led California League third basemen in double plays with 30 in 1978.
Led Midwest League third basemen in double plays with 21 in 1977.

Year Club	League	Pos.	G.	AB.	R.	H.	2B.	3B.	HR.	RBI.	B.A.	PO.	A.	E.	F.A.
1976—Great Falls	Pion.	3B	25	86	16	27	5	1	1	17	.314	10	16	2	.929
1976—Fresno	Calif.	3B	17	60	16	22	3	1	1	9	.367	2	6	1	.889
1977—Cedar Rapids	Midw.	*3B-OF	136	499	85	135	16	1	22	73	.271	90	*263	●31	.919
1978—Fresno	Calif.	3B	135	489	102	139	34	5	17	89	.284	*118	247	27	.931
1979—Fresno	Calif.	3B	56	212	49	65	11	2	9	37	.307	39	133	17	.910
1979—Shreveport	Texas	C-3-O-1	64	193	33	57	8	1	9	30	.295	199	55	7	.973
1980—Shreveport	Texas	3B	2	10	2	3	0	0	1	3	.300	1	2	0	1.000
1980—Phoenix	P. C.	3-C-S-O	84	287	34	74	9	6	7	45	.258	183	110	20	.936
1981—Phoenix	P. C.	C-OF-3B	76	257	42	75	11	3	7	41	.292	177	41	9	.960
1981—San Francisco	Nat.	C-3B-OF	19	43	5	15	2	1	1	4	.333	52	6	4	.935
1982—San Francisco†	Nat.	C-3B	65	180	26	51	4	1	4	15	.283	265	32	12	.961
1983—San Francisco	Nat.	C-1-OF	104	281	36	63	12	2	7	34	.224	465	73	9	.984
1984—San Francisco	Nat.	C-1-OF	145	506	74	147	28	0	20	80	.291	807	76	13	.985
1985—San Francisco	Nat.	C-3B-1B	133	440	41	97	16	1	19	56	.220	719	85	17	.979
Major League Totals—5 Years			466	1452	182	373	62	5	51	189	.257	2308	272	55	.979

Signed as free agent by San Francisco Giants' organization, June 21, 1976.
†On disabled list, March 25 to May 13, 1982.

ALL-STAR GAME RECORD

Year League	Pos.	AB.	R.	H.	2B.	3B.	HR.	RBI.	B.A.	PO.	A.	E.	F.A.
1984—National	PH	1	0	0	0	0	0	0	.000	0	0	0	.000

THOMAS MARTIN BRENNAN
(Tom)

Born October 30, 1952, at Chicago, Ill.
Height, 6.01. Weight, 180.
Throws and bats righthanded.
Received bachelor of arts degree in English from Lewis University, Lockport, Ill.

Major League saves: 1982 (2).
Led International League in shutouts with 6 and tied for lead in complete games with 11 in 1981.
Led Pacific Coast League in home runs allowed with 23 in 1978.
Named righthanded pitcher on THE SPORTING NEWS College Baseball All-America Team, 1974.

Year Club	League	G.	IP.	W.	L.	Pct.	H.	R.	ER.	SO.	BB.	ERA.
1974—Oklahoma City	Am. Assoc.	13	50	3	5	.375	46	42	38	44	56	6.79
1975—Oklahoma City	Am. Assoc.	25	122	5	14	.263	149	103	96	52	98	7.08
1976—Williamsport	Eastern	11	61	3	4	.429	63	37	30	22	40	4.43
1976—San Jose	California	16	72	3	9	.250	95	64	46	28	37	5.75
1977—Waterloo	Midwest	9	58	4	3	.571	61	35	32	30	35	4.97
1977—Jersey City	Eastern	4	28	3	1	.750	33	10	8	13	13	2.57
1977—Toledo	Int'national	11	75	1	4	.200	79	36	29	17	31	3.48
1978—Portland	P. Coast	27	172	10	8	.556	202	108	87	82	32	4.55
1979—Tacoma	P. Coast	26	176	12	7	.632	176	70	62	102	38	3.17
1980—Tacoma	P. Coast	24	152	9	3	.750	167	48	42	77	29	2.49
1981—Charleston	Int'national	25	156	11	8	.579	163	77	68	64	24	3.92
1981—Cleveland	American	7	48	2	2	.500	49	20	17	15	14	3.19
1982—Cleveland	American	30	92⅔	4	2	.667	112	51	44	46	10	4.27
1983—Charleston	Int'national	21	114⅓	9	5	.643	105	44	42	72	29	*3.31
1983—Cleveland†	American	11	39⅔	2	2	.500	45	22	17	21	8	3.86
1984—Chicago	American	4	6⅔	0	1	.000	8	5	3	3	3	4.05
1984—Denver‡	Am. Assoc.	35	105⅓	9	5	.643	86	42	38	51	32	3.25
1985—Los Angeles	National	12	31⅔	1	3	.250	41	26	26	17	11	7.39
1985—Albuquerque§	P. Coast	20	100⅔	6	5	.545	105	44	42	72	29	3.75
American League Totals—4 Years		52	187	8	7	.533	214	98	81	85	35	3.90
National League Totals—1 Year		12	31⅔	1	3	.250	41	26	26	17	11	7.39
Major League Totals—5 Years		64	218⅔	9	10	.474	255	124	107	102	46	4.40

Selected by Cleveland Indians' organization in 1st round (fourth player selected) of free-agent draft, June 5, 1974.
†Traded to Chicago White Sox for a player to be named later, January 23, 1984.
‡Granted free agency, October 15, 1984; signed by Albuquerque (Los Angeles Dodgers' organization), December 2, 1984.
§Granted free agency, October 15, 1985.

—DID YOU KNOW—

That when Houston's Nolan Ryan struck out the Mets' Danny Heep on July 11, 1985, he became the first major league pitcher to record 4,000 strikeouts?

GEORGE HOWARD BRETT

Born May 15, 1953, at Wheeling, W. Va.
Height, 6.00. Weight, 195.
Throws right and bats lefthanded.
Attended Longview Community College, Lee's Summit, Mo. and
El Camino College, Torrance, Calif.
Brother of Ken Brett, pitcher with Boston, Milwaukee, Philadelphia, Pittsburgh, New York AL,
Chicago AL, California, Minnesota, Los Angeles and Kansas City, 1967 and 1969 through 1981;
and currently manager of Utica (Co-op) in New York-Pennsylvania League;
John Brett, third baseman in Boston Red Sox' organization, 1968;
and Bob Brett, outfielder in Kansas City Royals' organization, 1972.

Established major league record for most consecutive games, three or more hits, season (6), May 8 through 13, 1976.
Tied major league records for most consecutive seasons leading major league in triples (2), 1975 and 1976; most home runs, month of October (4), 1985.
Established American League record for fewest putouts by third baseman for leader in most putouts, season (140), 1976.
Became sixth major-league player to collect 20 or more doubles, triples and home runs in one season, 1979.
Hit three home runs in a game, July 22, 1979 and April 20, 1983.
Hit for the cycle, May 28, 1979.
Major League stolen bases: 1974 (8), 1975 (13), 1976 (21), 1977 (14), 1978 (23), 1979 (17), 1980 (15), 1981 (14), 1982 (6), 1985 (9). Total—140.
Led American League in intentional bases on balls received with 31 in 1985.
Led American League in slugging percentage with .664 in 1980, .563 in 1983 and .585 in 1985.
Led American League in total bases with 298 in 1976.
Led American League third basemen in double plays with 33 in 1985.
Led American League third basemen in assists with 373, errors with 30 and total chances with 532 in 1979.
Led American League third baseman in putouts with 140 in 1976.
Led California League in sacrifice hits with 8 in 1972.
Led California League third basemen in assists with 172 in 1972.
Named Man of the Year by THE SPORTING NEWS, 1980.
Named Major League Player of the Year by THE SPORTING NEWS, 1980.
Named American League Player of the Year by THE SPORTING NEWS, 1980.
Named American League Most Valuable Player by Baseball Writers' Association of America, 1980.
Named third baseman on THE SPORTING NEWS American League All-Star Team, 1976, 1979 and 1980.
Named third baseman on THE SPORTING NEWS American League All-Star fielding team, 1985.
Named third baseman on THE SPORTING NEWS Silver Slugger team, 1980 and 1985.

Year	Club	League	Pos.	G.	AB.	R.	H.	2B.	3B.	HR.	RBI.	B.A.	PO.	A.	E.	F.A.
1971—Billings	Pion.		SS-3B	68	258	44	75	8	5	5	44	.291	87	140	28	.890
1972—San Jose†	Calif.		*3-S-2	117	431	66	118	13	5	10	68	.274	101	213	*30	.913
1973—Omaha	A. A.		3B-OF	117	405	66	115	16	4	8	64	.284	92	219	26	.923
1973—Kansas City	Amer.		3B	13	40	2	5	2	0	0	0	.125	9	28	1	.974
1974—Omaha	A. A.		3B	16	64	9	17	2	0	2	14	.266	8	31	4	.907
1974—Kansas City	Amer.		3B-SS	133	457	49	129	21	5	2	47	.282	102	279	21	.948
1975—Kansas City	Amer.		●3B-SS	159	*634	84	*195	35	●13	11	89	.308	132	356	●26	.949
1976—Kansas City	Amer.		3B-SS	159	*645	94	*215	34	*14	7	67	*.333	146	350	26	.950
1977—Kansas City	Amer.		3B-SS	139	564	105	176	32	13	22	88	.312	115	325	21	.954
1978—Kansas City‡	Amer.		3B-SS	128	510	79	150	*45	8	9	62	.294	104	289	16	.961
1979—Kansas City	Amer.		3B-1B	154	645	119	*212	42	*20	23	107	.329	176	378	31	.947
1980—Kansas City§	Amer.		3B-1B	117	449	87	175	33	9	24	118	*.390	107	256	17	.955
1981—Kansas City	Amer.		3B	89	347	42	109	27	7	6	43	.314	74	170	14	.946
1982—Kansas City	Amer.		3B-OF	144	552	101	166	32	9	21	82	.301	130	295	17	.962
1983—Kansas City x	Amer.		3B-1B-OF	123	464	90	144	38	2	25	93	.310	210	192	25	.941
1984—Kansas City y	Amer.		3B	104	377	42	107	21	3	13	69	.284	59	201	14	.949
1985—Kansas City	Amer.		3B	155	550	108	184	38	5	30	112	.335	107	*339	15	.967
Major League Totals—13 Years				1617	6234	1002	1967	400	108	193	977	.316	1471	3458	244	.953

Selected by Kansas City Royals' organization in 2nd round of free-agent draft, June 8, 1971.
†On disabled list, April 29 to May 11, 1972.
‡On disabled list, May 4 to May 19 and July 27 to August 14, 1978.
§On disabled list, June 11 to July 10, 1980.
xOn disabled list, June 8 to June 29, 1983.
yOn disabled list, April 1 to May 18, 1984.

DIVISION SERIES RECORD

Year	Club	League	Pos.	G.	AB.	R.	H.	2B.	3B.	HR.	RBI.	B.A.	PO.	A.	E.	F.A.
1981—Kansas City	Amer.		3B	3	12	0	2	0	0	0	0	.167	1	6	1	.876

CHAMPIONSHIP SERIES RECORD

Established Championship Series records for most games with one club (27); highest slugging average, total Series, 10 or more games and 30 or more at-bats (.728); most runs, total Series (22); most three-base hits, total Series (4); most runs, four-game Series (7), 1978; most home runs, total Series (9); most Series, two or more home runs (3); most total bases, total Series (75); most long hits, total Series (18).
Tied Championship Series records for most home runs, game (4), October 11, 1985; most three-base hits, Series (2), 1977; most home runs, game (3), October 6, 1978; most times hitting home run as leadoff batter, start of game (1), October 6, 1978.
Established American League Championship Series records for highest slugging average, seven-game Series (.826), 1985; most runs, total Series (16); most runs, seven-game Series (6), 1985; most hits, total Series (35); most home runs, four-game Series (3), 1978; highest slugging average, four-game Series (1.056), 1978; most hits, four-game Series (7), 1978; most home runs, seven-game Series (3), 1985; most total bases, four-game Series (19), 1978; most long hits, four-game Series (5), 1978 and seven-game Series (5), 1985; most long hits, two consecutive games, one series (4), October 6 and 7, 1978; most runs batted in, total Series (19); most total bases (19) and most bases on balls (7),

Tied American League Championship Series records for most at-bats, four-game Series (18), 1978; most Series, one or more home runs (4); most long hits, game (3), October 6, 1978 and October 11, 1985; most consecutive games, one or more hits (9); most home runs, three-game Series (2), 1980; most times on losing club (4).

Year Club	League	Pos.	G.	AB.	R.	H.	2B.	3B.	HR.	RBI.	B.A.	PO.	A.	E.	F.A.
1976—Kansas City	Amer.	3B	5	18	4	8	1	1	1	5	.444	3	7	3	.769
1977—Kansas City	Amer.	3B	5	20	2	6	0	2	0	2	.300	5	12	2	.895
1978—Kansas City	Amer.	3B	4	18	7	7	1	1	3	3	.389	3	8	1	.917
1980—Kansas City	Amer.	3B	3	11	3	3	1	0	2	4	.273	2	7	0	1.000
1984—Kansas City	Amer.	3B	3	13	0	3	0	0	0	0	.231	2	7	0	1.000
1985—Kansas City	Amer.	3B	7	23	6	8	2	0	3	5	.348	7	8	2	.882
Championship Series Totals—6 Years			27	103	22	35	5	4	9	19	.340	22	49	8	.899

WORLD SERIES RECORD

Tied World Series record for most times reached first base safely, game (batting 1.000) (5), October 22, 1985.

Year Club	League	Pos.	G.	AB.	R.	H.	2B.	3B.	HR.	RBI.	B.A.	PO.	A.	E.	F.A.
1980—Kansas City	Amer.	3B	6	24	3	9	2	1	1	3	.375	4	17	1	.955
1985—Kansas City	Amer.	3B	7	27	5	10	1	0	0	1	.370	10	19	1	.967
World Series Totals—2 Years			13	51	8	19	3	1	1	4	.373	14	36	2	.962

ALL-STAR GAME RECORD

Year League	Pos.	AB.	R.	H.	2B.	3B.	HR.	RBI.	B.A.	PO.	A.	E.	F.A.
1976—American	3B	2	0	0	0	0	0	0	.000	0	1	0	1.000
1977—American	3B	2	0	0	0	0	0	0	.000	2	1	0	1.000
1978—American	3B	3	1	2	1	0	0	2	.667	0	2	0	1.000
1979—American	3B	3	1	0	0	0	0	0	.000	1	2	0	1.000
1981—American	3B	3	0	0	0	0	0	0	.000	0	1	0	1.000
1982—American	3B	2	0	2	0	0	0	0	1.000	0	0	0	.000
1983—American	3B	4	2	2	1	1	0	1	.500	1	5	0	1.000
1984—American	3B	3	1	1	0	0	1	1	.333	3	0	0	1.000
1985—American	3B	1	0	0	0	0	0	1	.000	2	1	0	1.000
All-Star Game Totals—9 Years		23	5	7	2	1	1	5	.304	9	13	0	1.000

Named to American League All-Star Team in 1980; replaced due to injury.

MICHAEL QUINN BREWER
(Mike)

Born October 24, 1959, at Shreveport, La.
Height, 6.05. Weight, 190.
Throws and bats righthanded.
Attended Foothill College, Los Altos Hills, Calif.
Brother of Tony Brewer, outfielder in Los Angeles Dodgers' organization.

Led Gulf Coast League in total bases with 105 and tied for lead in caught stealing with 7 in 1979.
Named Gulf Coast League Most Valuable Player, 1979.

Year Club	League	Pos.	G.	AB.	R.	H.	2B.	3B.	HR.	RBI.	B.A.	PO.	A.	E.	F.A.
1979—Sarasota Gold	Gulf C.	OF	51	★205	38	★76	7	5	4	★47	★.371	72	5	●5	.939
1980—Fort Myers	Fla. St.	OF	123	426	54	102	13	4	6	63	.239	199	8	★11	.950
1981—Fort Myers	Fla. St.	OF	128	459	69	132	16	9	16	84	.288	209	12	9	.961
1982—Jacksonville	South	OF	121	438	74	109	15	4	20	68	.249	269	13	11	.962
1982—Omaha	A. A.	OF	18	56	10	16	5	0	1	7	.286	37	3	1	.976
1983—Omaha	A. A.	OF	120	412	63	104	23	3	9	42	.252	233	10	11	.957
1984—Omaha	A. A.	OF	104	330	46	67	10	4	11	41	.203	181	6	●10	.949
1984—Memphis†	South.	OF	35	129	17	29	4	0	2	23	.225	73	3	4	.950
1985—Maine	Int.	OF	119	413	58	97	17	2	17	53	.235	264	11	7	.975

Selected by Kansas City Royals' organization in 1st round (22nd player selected) of free-agent draft, January 9, 1979.

†Traded to Cleveland Indians' organization for a player to be named later or cash, April 5, 1985; returned, September 17, 1985.

BERNARDO BRITO

Born December 4, 1963, at Sabana Pelenque, Dominican Republic.
Height, 6.01. Weight, 190.
Throws and bats righthanded.

Led Midwest League in total bases with 244 in 1985.
Led New York-Pennsylvania League in total bases with 171 in 1984.

Year Club	League	Pos.	G.	AB.	R.	H.	2B.	3B.	HR.	RBI.	B.A.	PO.	A.	E.	F.A.
1981—Batavia	NYP	OF	12	29	1	6	0	0	0	2	.207	2	0	0	1.000
1982—Batavia	NYP	OF	41	123	10	29	2	0	4	15	.236	40	0	6	.870
1983—Waterloo	Midw.	OF	35	119	13	24	4	0	4	17	.202	41	2	3	.935
1983—Batavia	NYP	OF	60	206	18	50	10	3	7	34	.243	54	7	8	.884
1984—Batavia	NYP	OF	●76	★297	41	89	●19	3	★19	57	.300	100	8	8	.931
1985—Waterloo	Midw.	OF	135	498	66	128	27	1	★29	78	.257	160	15	9	.951

Signed as a free agent by Cleveland Indians' organization, October 8, 1980.

ANTHONY JOHN BRIZZOLARA

Name pronounced Briz-zoh-LAIR-uh.

(Tony)

Born January 14, 1957, at Santa Monica, Calif.
Height, 6.05. Weight, 217.
Throws and bats righthanded.
Received bachelor of business administration degree in acturial science
from University of Texas, Austin, Tex.

Major League saves: 1983 (1).
Led International League pitchers in games started with 30 in 1980 and 32 in 1982.

Year	Club	League	G.	IP.	W.	L.	Pct.	H.	R.	ER.	SO.	BB.	ERA.
1977—Kingsport	Ap'lachian	6	27	3	2	.600	21	8	7	27	10	2.33
1978—Greenwood	W. Carol.	3	20	3	0	1.000	9	3	2	21	8	0.90
1978—Savannah†	Southern	10	70	4	4	.500	57	19	15	55	21	1.93
1978—Richmond	Int'national	9	50	3	4	.429	57	34	33	40	18	5.94
1979—Richmond	Int'national	9	66	4	2	.667	47	15	14	42	28	1.91
1979—Atlanta	National	20	107	6	9	.400	133	70	63	64	33	5.30
1980—Richmond	Int'national	30	★206	10	●15	.400	198	102	85	128	56	3.71
1981—Richmond	Int'national	25	141	10	3	.769	138	62	56	59	44	3.57
1982—Richmond	Int'national	32	193	15	11	.577	★231	★119	★108	102	75	5.04
1983—Richmond	Int'national	21	127⅔	9	7	.563	136	58	53	90	44	3.74
1983—Atlanta	National	14	20⅓	1	0	1.000	22	8	8	17	6	3.54
1984—Richmond‡	Int'national	18	111⅓	7	7	.500	110	53	40	76	38	3.23
1984—Atlanta	National	10	29	1	2	.333	33	22	17	17	13	5.28
1985—Richmond§x	Int'national	33	165	10	12	.455	146	72	60	76	63	3.27
Major League Totals—3 Years		44	156⅓	8	11	.421	188	100	88	98	52	5.07

Selected by Atlanta Braves' organization in 2nd round of free-agent draft, June 7, 1977.
†On disabled list, June 20 to June 29, 1978.
‡On disabled list, April 30 to May 19, 1984.
§On suspended list, April 11 to April 19, 1985.
xGranted free agency, October 15, 1985.

GREGORY ALLEN BROCK

(Greg)

Born June 14, 1957, at McMinnville, Ore.
Height, 6.03. Weight, 205.
Throws right and bats lefthanded.
Attended University of Wyoming, Laramie, Wyo.
Brother of Eric Brock, shortstop in Los Angeles Dodgers' organization, 1983 and 1984.

Major League stolen bases: 1983 (5), 1984 (8), 1985 (4). Total—17.
Led Pacific Coast League in bases on balls received with 105 and intentional bases on balls received with 15 in 1982.
Led Pioneer League in bases on balls received with 54 in 1979.
Led Pacific Coast League first basemen in double plays with 106 in 1982.

Year	Club	League	Pos.	G.	AB.	R.	H.	2B.	3B.	HR.	RBI.	B.A.	PO.	A.	E.	F.A.
1979—Lethbridge	Pion.	1B	66	247	61	88	18	2	16	77	.356	543	★36	8	★.986
1980—Lodi	Calif.	1B	121	418	72	125	19	3	★29	95	.299	906	★79	5	★.995
1981—San Antonio	Texas	1B	128	499	86	147	25	3	★32	106	.295	1071	★90	9	.992
1982—Albuquerque	P. C.	1B	135	480	118	149	21	8	44	138	.310	★1076	★106	★20	.983
1982—Los Angeles	Nat.	1B	18	17	1	2	1	0	0	1	.118	9	0	0	1.000
1983—Los Angeles	Nat.	1B	146	455	64	102	14	2	20	66	.224	1162	106	12	.991
1984—Los Angeles†	Nat.	1B	88	271	33	61	6	0	14	34	.225	703	65	4	.995
1984—Albuquerque	P. C.	1B-3B	24	93	19	29	7	0	6	15	.312	134	38	11	.940
1985—Los Angeles	Nat.	1B	129	438	64	110	19	0	21	66	.251	1113	84	7	.994
Major League Totals—4 Years			381	1181	162	275	40	2	55	167	.233	2987	255	23	.993

Selected by Los Angeles Dodgers' organization in 13th round of free-agent draft, June 5, 1979.
†On disabled list, May 12 to June 7, 1984.

CHAMPIONSHIP SERIES RECORD

Year	Club	League	Pos.	G.	AB.	R.	H.	2B.	3B.	HR.	RBI.	B.A.	PO.	A.	E.	F.A.
1983—Los Angeles	Nat.	1B	3	9	1	0	0	0	0	0	.000	13	0	0	1.000
1985—Los Angeles	Nat.	1B-PH	5	12	2	1	0	0	1	2	.083	35	4	0	1.000
Championship Series Totals—2 Years			8	21	3	1	0	0	1	2	.048	48	4	0	1.000

ERIC ADRIAN BROERSMA

Born January 24, 1960, at Los Alamitos, Calif.
Height, 6.04. Weight, 225.
Throws and bats righthanded.
Attended El Camino College, Torrance, Calif., and received bachelor of arts degee
in economics from University of California, Los Angeles, Calif.

Year	Club	League	G.	IP.	W.	L.	Pct.	H.	R.	ER.	SO.	BB.	ERA.
1981—Wisconsin Rapids	Midwest	6	35	3	1	.750	21	13	12	48	19	3.09
1981—Orlando	Southern	8	43	2	4	.333	44	29	23	41	22	4.81
1982—Orlando	Southern	43	151⅓	7	5	.583	151	76	68	137	73	4.02
1983—Orlando	Southern	31	60	5	1	.833	45	21	21	38	22	3.15
1983—Toledo	Int'national	21	58	1	1	.500	62	31	30	46	30	4.66

Year Club	League	G.	IP.	W.	L.	Pct.	H.	R.	ER.	SO.	BB.	ERA.
1984—Toledo	Int'national	42	66	3	4	.429	56	30	29	78	32	3.95
1985—Toledo	Int'national	46	79⅓	4	5	.444	73	38	33	63	31	3.74

Selected by Oakland A's organization in 15th round of free-agent draft, June 3, 1980.
Selected by Minnesota Twins' organization in 3rd round of free-agent draft, June 8, 1981.

THOMAS DALE BROOKENS
(Tom)

Born August 10, 1953, at Chambersburg, Pa.
Height, 5.10. Weight, 170.
Throws and bats righthanded.
Attended Mansfield State College, Mansfield, Pa.

Twin brother of Tim Brookens, infielder-outfielder in Detroit Tigers' organization, 1975 through 1978; cousin of Ike Brookens, pitcher with Detroit Tigers, 1975.

Tied American League record for most errors by third baseman, game (4), September 6, 1980.
Major League stolen bases: 1979 (10), 1980 (13), 1981 (5), 1982 (5), 1983 (10), 1984 (6), 1985 (14). Total—63.
Tied for American League lead in errors by third basemen with 23 in 1985.

Year Club	League	Pos.	G.	AB.	R.	H.	2B.	3B.	HR.	RBI.	B.A.	PO.	A.	E.	F.A.
1975—Montgomery	South.	SS	100	329	37	73	11	2	7	36	.222	139	298	31	.934
1976—Montgomery	South.	2B	137	492	76	127	22	5	11	56	.258	310	★389	★25	.965
1977—Evansville	A. A.	3B-2B	118	440	70	127	22	5	8	52	.289	132	250	25	.939
1978—Evansville†	A. A.	3B-2B-1B	65	206	27	58	11	1	6	25	.282	76	100	20	.898
1979—Evansville	A. A.	3B-2B	77	265	51	81	23	2	14	46	.306	71	166	16	.937
1979—Detroit	Amer.	3B-2B	60	190	23	50	5	2	4	21	.263	76	141	11	.952
1980—Detroit	Amer.	★3-2-S	151	509	64	140	25	9	10	66	.275	127	307	★29	.937
1981—Detroit‡	Amer.	3B	71	239	19	58	10	1	4	25	.243	58	139	10	.952
1982—Detroit	Amer.	3-2-S-O	140	398	40	92	15	3	9	58	.231	119	276	20	.952
1983—Detroit	Amer.	3B-SS-2B	138	332	50	71	13	3	6	32	.214	97	254	22	.941
1984—Detroit§	Amer.	3B-SS-2B	113	224	32	55	11	4	5	26	.246	98	187	12	.960
1985—Detroit x	Amer.	3-S-2-C	156	485	54	115	34	6	7	47	.237	135	277	24	.944
Major League Totals—7 Years			829	2377	282	581	113	28	45	275	.244	710	1581	128	.947

Selected by Detroit Tigers' organization in 1st round (fourth player selected) of free-agent draft, January 9, 1975.
†On disabled list, April 14 to May 9 and June 4 to June 21, 1978.
‡On disabled list, March 30 to May 4, 1981.
§On disabled list, August 19 to September 4, 1984.
xGranted free agency, November 12, 1985; re-signed by Tigers, January 8, 1986.

CHAMPIONSHIP SERIES RECORD

Year Club	League	Pos.	G.	AB.	R.	H.	2B.	3B.	HR.	RBI.	B.A.	PO.	A.	E.	F.A.
1984—Detroit	Amer.	2B-3B	2	2	0	0	0	0	0	0	.000	0	2	1	.667

WORLD SERIES RECORD

Year Club	League	Pos.	G.	AB.	R.	H.	2B.	3B.	HR.	RBI.	B.A.	PO.	A.	E.	F.A.
1984—Detroit	Amer.	PH-3B	3	3	0	0	0	0	0	0	.000	0	3	0	1.000

HUBERT BROOKS JR.
(Hubie)

Born September 24, 1956, at Los Angeles, Calif.
Height, 6.00. Weight, 188.
Throws and bats righthanded.
Attended Mesa Community College, Mesa, Ariz., and received bachelor of science degree in health science from Arizona State University, Tempe, Ariz.
Grandson of Leandrus Brooks, player with Philadelphia of Negro National League; cousin of Donnie Moore, pitcher with California Angels.

Tied modern National League record for most errors in inning by third baseman (3), May 10, 1981 (fourth inning).
Major League stolen bases: 1980 (1), 1981 (9), 1982 (6), 1983 (6), 1984 (6), 1985 (6). Total—34.
Led International League in game-winning RBIs with 12 in 1980.
Named shortstop on THE SPORTING NEWS National League Silver Slugger team, 1985.
Named shortstop on THE SPORTING NEWS College Baseball All-America Team, 1978.
Named outfielder on THE SPORTING NEWS College Baseball All-America Team, 1977.

Year Club	League	Pos.	G.	AB.	R.	H.	2B.	3B.	HR.	RBI.	B.A.	PO.	A.	E.	F.A.
1978—Jackson	Texas	SS-OF-3B	45	153	19	33	8	1	3	16	.216	49	84	14	.905
1979—Jackson	Texas	3B-SS	112	406	68	124	21	2	3	28	.305	92	218	29	.942
1979—Tidewater	Int.	SS-3B-OF	5	15	1	6	1	0	1	3	.400	4	8	1	.923
1980—Tidewater	Int.	OF-3B-SS	113	417	50	124	18	5	3	50	.297	152	90	18	.931
1980—New York	Nat.	3B	24	81	8	25	2	1	1	10	.309	16	40	2	.966
1981—New York	Nat.	★3-O-S	98	358	34	110	21	2	4	38	.307	67	193	★21	.925
1982—New York†	Nat.	3B	126	457	40	114	21	2	2	40	.249	89	237	24	.931
1983—New York	Nat.	3B-2B	150	586	53	147	18	4	5	58	.251	116	303	21	.952
1984—New York‡	Nat.	3B-SS	153	561	61	159	23	2	16	73	.283	112	284	29	.932
1985—Montreal	Nat.	SS	156	605	67	163	34	7	13	100	.269	203	441	28	.958
Major League Totals—6 Years			707	2648	263	718	119	18	41	319	.271	603	1498	125	.944

Selected by Montreal Expos' organization in 19th round of free-agent draft, June 5, 1974.
Selected by Kansas City Royals' organization in secondary phase of free-agent draft, January 7, 1976.
Selected by Chicago White Sox' organization in secondary phase of free-agent draft, June 8, 1976.
Selected by Oakland A's organization in secondary phase of free-agent draft, January 11, 1977.

Selected by Chicago White Sox' organization in secondary phase of free-agent draft, June 7, 1977.
Selected by New York Mets' organization in 1st round (third player selected) of free-agent draft, June 6, 1978.
†On disabled list, June 28 to July 22, 1982.
‡Traded with Catcher Mike Fitzgerald, Outfielder Herm Winningham and Pitcher Floyd Youmans to Montreal Expos for Catcher Gary Carter, December 10, 1984.

MARK STEVEN BROUHARD

Name pronounced BRO-hard.
Born May 22, 1956, at Burbank, Calif.
Height, 6.01. Weight, 200.
Throws and bats righthanded.
Attended Pierce Junior College, Woodland Hills, Calif.

Major League stolen bases: 1980 (1), 1981 (1). Total—2.
Led Texas League in total bases with 308 and slugging percentage with .596 in 1979.
Tied for California League lead in being hit by pitch with 11 in 1978.
Named Texas League Most Valuable Player, 1979.

Year Club	League	Pos.	G.	AB.	R.	H.	2B.	3B.	HR.	RBI.	B.A.	PO.	A.	E.	F.A.
1976—Idaho Falls	Pion.	OF-1B	69	255	43	80	5	8	7	57	.314	46	2	5	.906
1977—Salinas	Calif.	OF	136	507	85	141	27	3	16	87	.278	216	8	9	.961
1978—Salinas	Calif.	OF-3B	133	532	86	165	29	5	21	91	.310	230	10	7	.972
1979—El Paso†	Texas	OF	132	517	97	●181	29	7	★28	★107	.350	171	10	5	.973
1980—Milwaukee	Amer.	OF-1B	45	125	12	29	6	0	5	16	.232	77	4	1	.988
1981—Vancouver	P. C.	OF	16	59	10	17	2	2	1	5	.288	33	3	0	1.000
1981—Milwaukee	Amer.	OF	60	186	19	51	6	3	2	20	.274	92	7	1	.990
1982—Milwaukee	Amer.	OF	40	108	16	29	4	1	4	10	.269	69	2	1	.986
1982—Vancouver	P. C.	OF	17	71	12	20	1	2	2	8	.282	30	3	1	.971
1983—Vancouver	P.C.	OF	45	165	23	53	15	0	5	30	.321	57	2	2	.967
1983—Milwaukee‡	Amer.	OF	56	185	25	51	10	1	7	23	.276	112	1	1	.991
1984—Milwaukee	Amer.	OF	66	197	20	47	7	0	6	22	.239	107	6	2	.983
1985—Milwaukee	Amer.	OF	37	108	11	28	7	2	1	13	.259	53	0	2	.964
1985—Vancouver§	P. C.	OF	15	64	7	14	3	0	0	7	.219	28	0	0	1.000
Major League Totals—6 Years			304	909	108	235	40	7	25	104	.259	510	20	8	.985

Selected by California Angels' organization in 4th round of free-agent draft, January 7, 1976.
†Drafted by Milwaukee Brewers, December 3, 1979.
‡On disabled list, June 21 to July 11, 1983.
§Sold to Yakult Swallows of Japanese baseball, November 22, 1985.

CHAMPIONSHIP SERIES RECORD

Tied Championship Series record for most runs, game (4), October 9, 1982.

Year Club	League	Pos.	G.	AB.	R.	H.	2B.	3B.	HR.	RBI.	B.A.	PO.	A.	E.	F.A.
1982—Milwaukee	Amer.	OF	1	4	4	3	1	0	1	3	.750	1	0	0	1.000

ROBERT RICHARD BROWER
(Bob)

Born January 10, 1960, at Queens, N.Y.
Height, 5.11. Weight, 185.
Throws and bats righthanded.
Attended Duke University, Durham, N.C.

Year Club	League	Pos.	G.	AB.	R.	H.	2B.	3B.	HR.	RBI.	B.A.	PO.	A.	E.	F.A.
1982—Sarasota Rangers	Gulf C.	OF	36	122	25	35	7	2	0	7	.287	53	3	0	1.000
1983—Burlington	Midw.	OF	43	138	35	43	4	6	5	28	.312	60	4	4	.941
1983—Tulsa	Texas	OF	69	252	41	59	4	1	3	17	.234	138	4	4	.973
1984—Tulsa	Texas	OF	96	344	69	98	14	9	7	30	.285	209	10	3	.986
1984—Oklahoma City	A. A.	OF	35	107	18	24	2	2	1	8	.224	69	7	2	.974
1985—Oklahoma City	A. A.	OF	133	445	56	111	13	★18	5	50	.249	282	8	3	.990

Signed as free agent by Texas Rangers' organization, July 1, 1982.

JOHN CHRISTOPHER BROWN
(Chris)

Born August 15, 1961, at Jackson, Miss.
Height, 6.00. Weight, 185.
Throws and bats righthanded.

Major League stolen bases: 1984 (2), 1985 (2). Total—4.
Led National League in being hit by pitch with 11 in 1985.

Year Club	League	Pos.	G.	AB.	R.	H.	2B.	3B.	HR.	RBI.	B.A.	PO.	A.	E.	F.A.
1979—Great Falls	Pion.	3B	47	171	24	46	5	3	5	30	.269	31	77	11	.908
1980—Clinton	Midw.	3B-1B	103	337	38	80	5	3	7	35	.237	352	132	19	.962
1981—Fresno	Calif.	3B-OF-1B	85	291	37	84	11	2	8	44	.289	89	156	23	.914
1982—Shreveport	Texas	3B-2B	58	185	26	49	14	0	1	21	.265	51	82	9	.937
1982—Fresno	Calif.	3B-1B-SS	41	133	22	39	9	1	4	31	.293	41	71	6	.949
1983—Shreveport	Texas	3B	102	322	44	88	21	0	10	58	.273	63	182	17	.935
1984—Phoenix†	P. C.	3B	84	283	41	80	13	5	9	64	.283	43	119	17	.905
1984—San Francisco	Nat.	3B	23	84	6	24	7	0	1	11	.286	23	40	7	.900
1985—San Francisco	Nat.	3B	131	432	50	117	20	3	16	61	.271	94	243	10	★.971
Major League Totals—2 Years			154	516	50	141	27	3	17	72	.273	117	283	17	.959

Selected by San Francisco Giants' organization in 2nd round of free-agent draft, June 5, 1979.
†On disabled list, April 11 to April 21 and July 30 to August 11, 1984.

MARK ANTHONY BROWN

Born July 13, 1959, at Bellows Falls, Vt.
Height, 6.03. Weight, 200.
Throws right and bats left and righthanded.
Attended University of Massachusetts, Amherst, Mass.

Year Club	League	G.	IP.	W.	L.	Pct.	H.	R.	ER.	SO.	BB.	ERA.
1980—Bluefield	Ap'lachian	6	19	1	0	1.000	11	5	2	16	8	0.95
1980—Miami	Florida St.	10	59	3	5	.375	58	40	31	40	35	4.73
1981—Miami†	Florida St.	17	53	3	3	.500	47	25	20	35	21	3.40
1981—Hagerstown	Carolina	10	21	1	0	1.000	19	7	5	16	8	2.14
1982—Hagerstown	Carolina	14	20⅓	0	0	.000	23	9	7	16	6	3.10
1982—Charlotte	Southern	19	73⅓	8	2	*.800	46	20	17	57	44	2.09
1982—Rochester	Int'national	3	6⅓	1	0	1.000	5	1	1	5	2	1.42
1983—Rochester‡	Int'national	19	53⅓	6	1	.857	41	23	21	44	20	3.54
1984—Rochester	Int'national	44	77	4	4	.500	85	39	32	50	41	3.74
1984—Baltimore§	American	9	23	1	2	.333	22	11	10	10	7	3.91
1985—Toledo	Int'national	26	67⅓	2	2	.500	71	30	22	26	22	2.94
1985—Minnesota	American	6	15⅔	0	0	.000	21	13	12	5	7	6.80
Major League Totals—2 Years		15	38⅔	1	2	.333	43	24	22	15	14	5.12

Selected by Baltimore Orioles' organization in 6th round of free-agent draft, June 3, 1980.
†On disabled list, April 10 to April 22, 1981.
‡On disabled list, May 31 to August 4, 1983.
§Traded to Minnesota Twins' organization for Pitcher Brad Havens, March 27, 1985.

MICHAEL CHARLES BROWN
(Mike)

Born December 29, 1959, at San Francisco, Calif.
Height, 6.02. Weight, 195.
Throws and bats righthanded.
Attended San Jose State University, San Jose, Calif.

Major League stolen bases: 1983 (1), 1985 (2). Total—3.

Year Club	League	Pos.	G.	AB.	R.	H.	2B.	3B.	HR.	RBI.	B.A.	PO.	A.	E.	F.A.
1980—Salinas	Calif.	OF-C	47	152	24	40	7	0	5	35	.263	72	4	5	.938
1981—Holyoke	East.	OF	135	499	64	160	25	8	6	83	.321	182	9	9	.955
1982—Spokane	P. C.	OF	134	476	74	135	30	7	11	73	.284	261	20	14	.957
1983—Edmonton	P. C.	OF	115	442	91	157	39	6	22	106	.355	190	11	2	.990
1983—California	Amer.	OF	31	104	12	24	5	1	3	9	.231	52	4	3	.949
1984—Edmonton	P. C.	OF	26	102	22	35	9	4	4	24	.343	50	5	0	1.000
1984—California	Amer.	OF	62	148	19	42	8	3	7	22	.284	57	4	2	.968
1985—California†	Amer.	OF	60	153	23	41	9	1	4	20	.268	78	3	0	1.000
1985—Pittsburgh	Nat.	OF	57	205	29	68	18	2	5	33	.332	87	3	6	.938
American League Totals—3 Years			153	405	54	107	22	5	14	51	.264	187	11	5	.975
National League Totals—1 Year			57	205	29	68	18	2	5	33	.332	87	3	6	.938
Major League Totals—3 Years			210	610	83	175	40	7	19	84	.287	274	14	11	.963

Selected by California Angels' organization in 7th round of free-agent draft, June 3, 1980.
†Traded with Pitcher Pat Clements and a player to be named later to Pittsburgh Pirates for Pitchers John Candelaria and Al Holland and Outfielder George Hendrick, August 2, 1985; Pittsburgh organization acquired Pitcher Bob Kipper to complete deal, August 16, 1985.

MICHAEL GARY BROWN
(Mike)

Born March 4, 1959, at Haddon Township, N.J.
Height, 6.02. Weight, 195.
Throws and bats righthanded.
Attended Clemson University, Clemson, S.C.

Led Carolina League in complete games with 12 and shutouts with 6 in 1981.
Tied for International League lead in hit basemen with 8 in 1985.
Named Carolina League Pitcher of the Year, 1981.

Year Club	League	G.	IP.	W.	L.	Pct.	H.	R.	ER.	SO.	BB.	ERA.
1980—Winter Haven	Florida St.	17	71	3	4	.429	79	37	34	50	32	4.31
1981—Winston-Salem	Carolina	21	145	*14	4	.778	94	32	24	144	39	*1.49
1982—Bristol†	Eastern	16	110	9	6	.600	92	39	30	113	35	2.45
1982—Boston†	American	3	6	1	0	1.000	7	0	0	4	1	0.00
1983—Boston‡	American	19	104	6	6	.500	110	62	54	35	43	4.67
1984—Boston	American	15	67	1	8	.111	104	63	51	32	19	6.85
1984—Pawtucket	Int'national	12	87⅓	6	3	.667	90	44	33	54	27	3.40
1985—Pawtucket§	Int'national	20	70⅔	2	5	.286	78	52	44	51	25	5.60
1985—Boston	American	2	3⅓	0	0	.000	9	8	8	3	3	21.60
Major League Totals—4 Years		39	180⅓	8	14	.364	230	133	113	74	66	5.64

Selected by Atlanta Braves' organization in 20th round of free-agent draft, June 7, 1977.

Selected by Boston Red Sox' organization in 2nd round of free-agent draft, June 3, 1980.
†On disabled list, April 27 to June 16, 1982.
‡On disabled list, July 28 to August 19, 1983.
§On suspended list, July 9 to July 26, 1985.

ROGERS LEE BROWN
(Bobby)

Born May 24, 1954, at Norfolk, Va.
Height, 6.01. Weight, 231.
Throws right and bats right and lefthanded.

Major League stolen bases: 1979 (2), 1980 (27), 1981 (4), 1982 (28), 1983 (27), 1984 (16), 1985 (6). Total—110.
Led Carolina League in caught stealing with 12 in 1976.
Named International League co-Most Valuable Player, 1979.

Year	Club	League	Pos.	G.	AB.	R.	H.	2B.	3B.	HR.	RBI.	B.A.	PO.	A.	E.	F.A.
1972—Bluefield	Appal.	OF	49	172	29	44	11	2	3	27	.256	53	4	8	.877
1973—Miami	Fla. St.	OF	100	279	35	79	8	3	3	17	.283	88	5	7	.930
1974—Miami	Fla. St.	OF	29	94	9	18	3	1	0	2	.191	50	1	4	.927
1974—Lodi	Calif.	OF-1B	95	359	44	108	7	6	8	58	.301	148	11	8	.952
1975—Lodi	Calif.	OF-1B-3B	133	491	77	146	15	8	6	64	.297	178	10	12	.940
1975—Asheville†	South.	OF	6	27	5	7	0	0	0	2	.259	13	2	0	1.000
1976—Peninsula	Carol.	OF-3B-1B	102	393	68	137	18	★10	8	41	★.349	299	89	21	.949
1977—Reading	East.	OF	56	238	38	69	12	5	5	28	.290	151	2	5	.968
1977—Oklahoma City	A. A.	OF	79	312	53	98	12	5	4	22	.314	78	184	6	.969
1978—Oklahoma City‡	A. A.	OF-3B	50	216	31	62	10	6	4	18	.287	105	20	7	.947
1978—Tacoma§x	P. C.	OF	66	261	51	81	11	4	10	39	.310	151	2	7	.956
1979—Tor.y-N.Y.z	Amer.	OF	34	78	8	17	3	1	0	3	.218	64	0	3	.955
1979—San Juan	Int.-Am.	PR	10	0	1	0	0	0	0	1	.000	0	0	0	.000
1979—Columbus	Int.	OF	70	258	53	90	14	3	8	41	.349	166	7	3	.983
1980—New York	Amer.	OF	137	412	65	107	12	5	14	47	.260	303	7	9	.972
1981—Columbus	Int.	OF	40	152	28	50	6	3	6	27	.329	78	3	3	.964
1981—New York a	Amer.	OF	31	62	5	14	1	0	0	6	.226	54	2	3	.949
1982—Salt Lake City	P. C.	OF	22	84	12	21	2	2	1	9	.250	44	2	1	.979
1982—Seattle bc	Amer.	OF	79	245	29	59	7	1	4	17	.241	148	5	5	.968
1983—Las Vegas	P.C.	OF	97	405	85	134	27	7	15	70	.331	166	4	5	.971
1983—San Diego	Nat.	OF	57	225	40	60	5	3	5	22	.267	103	1	4	.963
1984—San Diego	Nat.	OF	85	171	28	43	7	2	3	29	.251	100	2	3	.971
1985—San Diego	Nat.	OF	79	84	8	13	3	0	0	6	.155	20	2	0	1.000
American League Totals—4 Years			281	797	107	197	23	7	18	73	.247	569	14	20	.967
National League Totals—3 Years			221	480	76	116	15	5	8	57	.242	223	5	7	.970
Major League Totals—7 Years			502	1277	183	313	38	12	26	130	.245	792	19	27	.968

Selected by Baltimore Orioles' organization in 11th round of free-agent draft, June 6, 1972.
†Released, April 8, 1976; signed by Peninsula (Philadelphia Phillies' organization), May 14, 1976.
‡Traded with Outfielder Jay Johnstone to New York Yankees for Pitcher Rawly Eastwick, June 14, 1978.
§Drafted by New York Mets, December 4, 1978.
xSold on waivers to Toronto Blue Jays, March 25, 1979.
ySold to New York Yankees, April 19, 1979.
zLoaned to San Juan, April 20, 1979; returned, May 1, 1979.
aTraded to Seattle Mariners' organization, April 6, 1982, completing deal in which New York Yankees traded Pitchers Gene Nelson and Bill Caudill, a player to be named later and cash to Seattle for Pitcher Shane Rawley, April 1, 1982.
bOn disabled list, August 19 to September 9, 1982.
cReleased, March 28, 1983; signed by San Diego Padres' organization, April 19, 1983.

DIVISION SERIES RECORD

Year	Club	League	Pos.	G.	AB.	R.	H.	2B.	3B.	HR.	RBI.	B.A.	PO.	A.	E.	F.A.
1981—New York	Amer.	PR	1	0	0	0	0	0	0	0	.000	0	0	0	.000

CHAMPIONSHIP SERIES RECORD

Year	Club	League	Pos.	G.	AB.	R.	H.	2B.	3B.	HR.	RBI.	B.A.	PO.	A.	E.	F.A.
1980—New York	Amer.	OF	3	10	1	0	0	0	0	0	.000	7	0	0	1.000
1981—New York	Amer.	PR-OF	3	1	2	1	0	0	0	0	1.000	0	0	0	.000
1984—San Diego	Nat.	PH-OF	3	4	1	0	0	0	0	0	.000	3	0	0	1.000
Championship Series Totals—3 Years			9	15	4	1	0	0	0	0	.067	10	0	0	1.000

WORLD SERIES RECORD

Year	Club	League	Pos.	G.	AB.	R.	H.	2B.	3B.	HR.	RBI.	B.A.	PO.	A.	E.	F.A.
1981—New York	Amer.	PR-O-PH	4	1	1	0	0	0	0	0	.000	1	0	0	1.000
1984—San Diego	Nat.	OF	5	15	1	1	0	0	0	2	.067	13	0	0	1.000
World Series Totals—2 Years			9	16	2	1	0	0	0	2	.063	14	0	0	1.000

JEROME A. BROWNE
(Jerry)

Born February 13, 1966, at St. Croix, Virgin Islands.
Height, 5.10. Weight, 140.
Throws right and bats left and righthanded.

Led Carolina League second basemen in total chances with 675 in 1985.

Year Club League	Pos.	G.	AB.	R.	H.	2B.	3B.	HR.	RBI.	B.A.	PO.	A.	E.	F.A.
1983—Sarasota Rangers Gulf C.	2B	48	181	34	51	2	2	0	20	.282	92	123	14	.939
1984—Burlington .... Midw.	SS-2B	127	420	70	99	10	1	0	18	.236	231	311	43	.926
1985—Salem..................... Carol.	2B	122	460	69	123	18	4	3	58	.267	★265	★390	20	.970

Signed as free agent by Texas Rangers' organization, March 3, 1983.

THOMAS LEO BROWNING
(Tom)

Born April 28, 1960, at Casper, Wyo.
Height, 6.01. Weight, 190.
Throws and bats lefthanded.
Attended Tennessee Wesleyan College, Athens, Tenn., and
Le Moyne College, Syracuse, N.Y.

Pitched seven-inning, 2-0 no-hit victory against Iowa, July 31, 1984.
Tied for American Association lead in home runs allowed with 24 in 1984.
Named National League Rookie Pitcher of the Year by THE SPORTING NEWS, 1985.

Year Club League	G.	IP.	W.	L.	Pct.	H.	R.	ER.	SO.	BB.	ERA.
1982—Billings .... Pioneer	14	88	4	●8	.333	96	53	38	87	41	3.89
1983—Tampa .... Florida St.	11	78⅔	8	1	.889	53	19	13	101	36	1.49
1983—Waterbury .... Eastern	18	117⅓	4	10	.286	100	62	46	101	63	3.53
1984—Wichita .... Am. Assoc.	30	189½	12	10	.545	169	88	82	★160	73	3.05
1984—Cincinnati .... National	3	23⅓	1	0	1.000	27	4	4	14	5	1.54
1985—Cincinnati .... National	38	261⅓	20	9	.690	242	111	103	155	73	3.55
Major League Totals—2 Years	41	284⅔	21	9	.700	269	115	107	169	78	3.38

Selected by Cincinnati Reds' organization in 9th round of free-agent draft, June 7, 1982.

ANTHONY MICHAEL BRUMLEY
(Mike)

Born April 9, 1963, at Oklahoma City, Okla.
Height, 5.10. Weight, 165.
Throws right and bats left and righthanded.
Attended University of Texas, Austin, Tex.
Son of Mike Brumley, catcher with Washington Senators, 1964 through 1966.

Year Club League	Pos.	G.	AB.	R.	H.	2B.	3B.	HR.	RBI.	B.A.	PO.	A.	E.	F.A.
1983—Winter Haven .... Fla. St.	SS-OF	44	153	25	48	6	4	1	18	.314	51	92	20	.877
1984—New Britain† .... East.	OF-SS	34	121	14	28	6	2	0	9	.231	71	6	6	.928
1984—Midland .... Texas	OF	73	255	37	55	11	3	6	21	.216	128	4	5	.964
1985—Pittsfield .... East.	SS-OF	131	460	66	127	23	★14	3	58	.276	182	333	33	.940

Selected by Philadelphia Phillies' organization in 16th round of free-agent draft, June 3, 1980.
Selected by Boston Red Sox' organization in 2nd round of free-agent draft, June 6, 1983.
†Traded with Pitcher Dennis Eckersley to Chicago Cubs for First Baseman-Outfielder Bill Buckner, May 25, 1984.

GLENN EDWARD BRUMMER

Born November 23, 1954, at Olney, Ill.
Height, 6.00. Weight, 200.
Throws and bats righthanded.
Attended Lake Land College, Mattoon, Ill.
Brother of Tom Brummer, infielder in Boston Red Sox' organization, 1979 through 1981.

Major League stolen bases: 1982 (2), 1983 (1), 1985 (1). Total—4.
Led American Association in passed balls with 13 in 1980.

Year Club League	Pos.	G.	AB.	R.	H.	2B.	3B.	HR.	RBI.	B.A.	PO.	A.	E.	F.A.
1974—Sarasota Cards ..... Gulf C.	C	24	69	7	20	4	1	0	7	.290	118	15	2	.985
1975—Johnson City .... Appal.	C	50	183	27	47	7	1	5	23	.257	278	23	9	.971
1976—St. Petersburg....... Fla. St.	C	113	367	41	96	14	1	0	41	.262	★644	★77	10	.986
1977—Arkansas............... Texas	C	15	52	2	9	1	0	0	2	.173	97	6	6	.945
1977—St. Petersburg....... Fla. St.	C	21	51	7	11	1	0	0	1	.216	113	5	1	.992
1977—Lynchburg............ Carol.	C	40	137	16	45	3	2	0	16	.328	190	12	2	.990
1978—Arkansas............... Texas	C-OF	44	92	11	25	2	0	0	11	.272	135	14	3	.980
1979—Springfield† .... A. A.	C	44	104	19	22	2	0	1	11	.212	196	12	4	.981
1980—Springfield............ A. A.	C	110	323	36	83	12	0	1	40	.257	★562	55	12	.981
1981—Springfield............ A. A.	C	26	77	12	18	2	1	1	8	.234	153	13	4	.976
1981—St. Louis................. Nat.	C	21	30	2	6	1	0	0	2	.200	43	3	0	1.000
1982—St. Louis................. Nat.	C	35	64	4	15	4	0	0	8	.234	88	8	3	.970
1982—Louisville .... A. A.	C	8	28	2	3	0	0	1	2	.107	34	6	0	1.000
1983—St. Louis................. Nat.	C	45	87	7	24	7	0	0	9	.276	122	11	3	.978
1984—St. Louis‡.............. Nat.	C	28	58	3	12	0	0	1	3	.207	101	9	3	.973
1984—Louisville§ .... A. A.	C	16	53	3	11	2	0	1	4	.208	133	4	5	.965
1985—Oklahoma City ..... A. A.	C	1	4	0	0	0	0	0	0	.000	7	0	1	1.000
1985—Texas x .... Amer.	C-OF	49	108	7	30	4	0	0	5	.278	183	5	2	.989
National League Totals—4 Years		129	239	16	57	12	0	1	22	.238	354	31	9	.977
American League Totals—1 Year		49	108	7	30	4	0	0	5	.278	183	5	2	.989
Major League Totals—5 Years		178	347	23	87	16	0	1	27	.251	537	36	11	.981

Signed as free agent by St. Louis Cardinals' organization, May 20, 1974.
†On disabled list, July 17 to September 1, 1979.
‡On disabled list, July 22 to September 6, 1984; included rehabilitation disability assignment to Louisville, August 19 to September 6, 1984.

§Released, March 24, 1985; signed by Texas Rangers' organization, April 4, 1985.
xReleased, November 13, 1985.

WORLD SERIES RECORD

Year Club	League	Pos.	G.	AB.	R.	H.	2B.	3B.	HR.	RBI.	B.A.	PO.	A.	E.	F.A.
1982—St. Louis	Nat.	C	1	0	0	0	0	0	0	0	.000	0	0	0	.000

THOMAS ANDREW BRUNANSKY
(Tom)

Born August 20, 1960, at West Covina, Calif.
Height, 6.04. Weight, 210.
Throws and bats righthanded.

Major League stolen bases: 1981 (1), 1982 (1), 1983 (2), 1984 (4). 1985 (5). Total—13.
Led American League outfielders in double plays with 8 in 1983 and 6 in 1984.
Tied for Texas League lead in double plays by outfielders with 4 in 1980.
Received reported $100,000 bonus to sign with California Angels, 1978.

Year Club	League	Pos.	G.	AB.	R.	H.	2B.	3B.	HR.	RBI.	B.A.	PO.	A.	E.	F.A.
1978—Idaho Falls	Pioneer	OF	48	190	55	63	14	4	6	45	.332	85	1	8	.915
1979—Salinas	Calif.	OF	★140	485	85	131	23	1	23	76	.270	279	11	6	.980
1980—El Paso	Texas	OF	128	495	103	160	24	8	24	97	.323	306	17	★14	.958
1980—Salt Lake City	P. C.	OF	9	32	7	11	2	2	1	8	.344	28	1	0	1.000
1981—Salt Lake City†	P. C.	OF	96	343	61	114	17	10	22	81	.332	250	14	5	.981
1981—California	Amer.	OF	11	33	7	5	0	0	3	6	.152	27	3	2	.938
1982—Spokane‡	P. C.	OF	25	88	12	18	6	1	1	6	.205	44	7	1	.981
1982—Minnesota	Amer.	OF	127	463	77	126	30	1	20	46	.272	343	8	5	.986
1983—Minnesota	Amer.	OF	151	542	70	123	24	5	28	82	.227	375	16	6	.985
1984—Minnesota	Amer.	OF	155	567	75	144	21	0	32	85	.254	304	13	5	.984
1985—Minnesota	Amer.	OF	157	567	71	137	28	4	27	90	.242	300	14	5	.984
Major League Totals—5 Years			601	2172	300	535	103	10	110	309	.246	1349	54	23	.984

Selected by California Angels' organization in 1st round (14th player selected) of free-agent draft, June 6, 1978.
†On disabled list, August 8 to August 31, 1981.
‡Traded with Pitcher Mike Walters and cash to Minnesota Twins for Pitcher Doug Corbett and Second Baseman Rob Wilfong, May 12, 1982.

ALL-STAR GAME RECORD

Year League	Pos.	AB.	R.	H.	2B.	3B.	HR.	RBI.	B.A.	PO.	A.	E.	F.A.
1985—American	OF	1	0	0	0	0	0	0	.000	0	0	0	.000

WARREN SCOTT BRUSSTAR

Name pronounced BROO-stur.

Born February 2, 1952, at Oakland, Calif.
Height, 6.03. Weight, 200.
Throws and bats righthanded.
Attended Napa Junior College, Napa, Calif., and
Fresno State University, Fresno, Calif.

Major League saves: 1977 (3), 1979 (1), 1982 (2), 1983 (1), 1984 (3), 1985 (4). Total—14.
Led Eastern League in complete games with 19 in 1976.
Led Carolina League in wild pitches with 23 in 1975.
Tied for Eastern League lead in games started by pitchers with 27, intentional bases on balls issued with 12 and wild pitches with 13 in 1976.

Year Club	League	G.	IP.	W.	L.	Pct.	H.	R.	ER.	SO.	BB.	ERA.
1974—Spartanburg	W. Carol.	22	42	2	4	.333	39	23	9	34	24	1.93
1975—Rocky Mount†	Carolina	25	162	●14	8	.636	117	61	40	123	94	2.22
1976—Reading	Eastern	27	★199	10	★17	.370	167	83	60	119	★90	2.71
1977—Oklahoma City	Am. Assoc.	2	6	0	1	.000	3	3	1	5	5	1.50
1977—Philadelphia	National	46	71	7	2	.778	64	26	21	46	24	2.66
1978—Philadelphia	National	58	89	6	3	.667	74	25	23	60	30	2.33
1979—Philadelphia‡	National	13	14	1	0	1.000	23	12	11	3	2	7.07
1979—Reading	Eastern	1	2	0	0	.000	1	0	0	1	0	0.00
1980—Peninsula	Carolina	7	14	1	1	.500	16	7	7	8	2	4.61
1980—Philadelphia§	National	26	39	2	2	.500	42	16	16	21	13	3.69
1981—Oklahoma City	Am. Assoc.	46	93	3	2	.600	93	36	29	47	31	2.81
1981—Philadelphia	National	14	12	0	1	.000	12	6	6	8	10	4.50
1982—Philadelphia	National	22	22⅔	2	3	.400	31	12	12	11	5	4.76
1982—Oklahoma City x	Am. Assoc.	22	28	4	2	.667	25	11	8	13	14	2.57
1982—Chicago y	American	10	18⅓	2	0	1.000	19	7	7	7	3	3.44
1983—Chicago	National	59	80⅓	3	1	.750	67	21	21	46	37	2.35
1984—Chicago z	National	41	63⅔	1	1	.500	57	23	22	36	21	3.11
1985—Chicago	National	51	74⅓	4	3	.571	87	55	50	34	36	6.05
National League Totals—9 Years		330	466	26	16	.619	457	196	182	265	178	3.52
American League Totals—1 Year		10	18⅓	2	0	1.000	19	7	7	8	3	3.44
Major League Totals—10 Years		340	484⅓	28	16	.636	476	203	189	273	181	3.51

Selected by San Francisco Giants' organization in 27th round of free-agent draft, June 4, 1970.
Selected by San Francisco Giants' organization in secondary phase of free-agent draft, January 13, 1971.
Selected by New York Mets' organization in 33rd round of free-agent draft, June 5, 1973.
Selected by Philadelphia Phillies' organization in secondary phase of free-agent draft, January 9, 1974.

†On disabled list, May 29 to June 9, 1975.
‡On disabled list, March 29 to June 27, 1979.
§On disabled list, April 9 to July 12, 1980; included rehabilitation disability assignment to Peninsula, June 16 to July 5, 1980.
xSold to Chicago White Sox, August 30, 1982.
yTraded with Pitcher Steve Trout to Chicago Cubs for Pitchers Dick Tidrow and Randy Martz and Infielders Scott Fletcher and Pat Tabler, January 25, 1983.
zOn disabled list, April 1 to April 16, 1984.

DIVISION SERIES RECORD

Year Club	League	G.	IP.	W.	L.	Pct.	H.	R.	ER.	SO.	BB.	ERA.
1981—Philadelphia	National	2	3⅔	0	0	.000	5	2	2	3	1	4.91

CHAMPIONSHIP SERIES RECORD

Year Club	League	G.	IP.	W.	L.	Pct.	H.	R.	ER.	SO.	BB.	ERA.
1977—Philadelphia	National	2	2⅔	0	0	.000	2	1	1	2	1	3.38
1978—Philadelphia	National	3	2⅔	0	0	.000	2	0	0	1	1	0.00
1980—Philadelphia	National	2	2⅔	1	0	1.000	1	1	1	0	1	3.38
1984—Chicago	National	3	4⅓	0	0	.000	6	0	0	1	0	0.00
Championship Series Totals—4 Years		10	12⅓	1	0	1.000	11	2	2	3	3	1.46

WORLD SERIES RECORD

Year Club	League	G.	IP.	W.	L.	Pct.	H.	R.	ER.	SO.	BB.	ERA.
1980—Philadelphia	National	1	2⅓	0	0	.000	0	0	0	0	1	0.00

RALPH WENDALL BRYANT

Born May 20, 1961, at Fort Gaines, Ga.
Height, 6.02. Weight, 200.
Throws right and bats lefthanded.
Attended Abraham Baldwin Agriculture College, Tifton, Ga.

Led Texas League in slugging percentage with .581 in 1984.
Led Florida State League batters in strikeouts with 104 in 1982.

Year—Club	League	Pos.	G.	AB.	R.	H.	2B.	3B.	HR.	RBI.	B.A.	PO.	A.	E.	F.A.
1981—Lethbridge	Pion.	OF	50	181	31	48	12	4	5	29	.265	34	4	3	.927
1982—Vero Beach	Fla. St.	OF	122	409	71	125	22	7	9	71	.306	91	6	5	.951
1983—Vero Beach	Fla. St.	OF	130	489	74	129	27	11	10	65	.264	231	12	10	.960
1984—San Antonio	Texas	OF	115	434	71	130	21	4	★31	86	.300	191	11	★12	.944
1985—Albuquerque	P. C.	OF	120	400	62	107	27	3	15	64	.268	171	11	★13	.933
1985—Los Angeles	Nat.	OF	6	6	0	2	0	0	0	1	.333	0	0	0	.000
Major League Totals—1 Year			6	6	0	2	0	0	0	1	.333	0	0	0	.000

Selected by Los Angeles Dodgers' organization in 6th round of free-agent draft, January 8, 1980.
Selected by Minnesota Twins' organization in 13th round of free-agent draft, January 13, 1981.
Selected by Los Angeles Dodgers' organization in secondary phase of free-agent draft, June 8, 1981.

ROBERT GORDON BUCHANAN
(Bob)

Born May 3, 1961, at Ridley Park, Pa.
Height, 6.01. Weight, 185.
Throws and bats lefthanded.

Year—Club	League	G.	IP.	W.	L.	Pct.	H.	R.	ER.	SO.	BB.	ERA.
1979—Billings	Pioneer	14	91	7	5	.583	82	42	34	80	25	3.36
1980—Tampa	Florida St.	27	101	7	7	.500	102	53	48	62	40	4.28
1981—Cedar Rapids	Midwest	25	171	10	11	.476	174	81	61	125	64	3.21
1982—Waterbury	Eastern	27	165⅓	10	8	.556	174	90	71	78	68	3.86
1983—Indianapolis	Am. Assoc.	30	49	1	6	.143	69	42	36	22	31	6.61
1983—Waterbury	Eastern	14	18	0	1	.000	19	13	13	12	9	6.50
1984—Vermont	Eastern	14	20⅔	1	2	.333	14	8	5	18	14	2.18
1984—Wichita	Am. Assoc.	39	58⅔	1	2	.333	51	21	20	35	28	3.07
1985—Denver	Am. Assoc.	29	41⅓	4	3	.571	45	20	10	36	13	2.18
1985—Cincinnati†‡	National	14	16	1	0	1.000	25	15	15	3	9	8.44
Major League Totals—1 Year		14	16	1	0	1.000	25	15	15	3	9	8.44

Selected by Cincinnati Reds' organization in 2nd round of free-agent draft, June 5, 1979.
†On disabled list, August 8 to August 29, 1985.
‡Traded to San Francisco Giants for Pitcher Colin Ward, November 11, 1985.

KEVIN JOHN BUCKLEY

Born January 16, 1959, at Quincy, Mass.
Height, 6.01. Weight, 200.
Throws and bats righthanded.
Received bachelor of science degree in physical education from University of Maine, Orono, Me.

Led American Association batters in strikeouts with 171 in 1984.
Led American Association in passed balls with 12 in 1984.
Tied for Gulf Coast League lead in double plays by outfielders with 2 in 1981.

Year—Club	League	Pos.	G.	AB.	R.	H.	2B.	3B.	HR.	RBI.	B.A.	PO.	A.	E.	F.A.
1981—Sarasota Rangers	Gulf C.	OF	50	176	21	52	8	3	2	29	.295	52	●9	0	1.000
1982—Burlington	Midw.	OF-1B-3B	123	418	76	120	16	1	29	93	.287	232	22	16	.941

Year Club	League	Pos.	G.	AB.	R.	H.	2B.	3B.	HR.	RBI.	B.A.	PO.	A.	E.	F.A.
1983—Tulsa......	Texas	1B-OF-P	134	512	73	150	30	2	32	104	.293	616	61	12	.983
1984—Oklahoma City.....	A. A.	C-O-1-P	139	499	72	130	32	3	23	92	.261	458	54	14	.973
1984—Texas†	Amer.	PH	5	7	1	2	1	0	0	0	.286	0	0	0	.000
1985—Maine	Int.	C-1-O-P	86	294	39	65	10	0	15	45	.221	310	31	9	.974
Major League Totals			5	7	1	2	1	0	0	0	.286	0	0	0	.000

Selected by Texas Rangers' organization in 17th round of free-agent draft, June 8, 1981.

†Traded to Cleveland Indians' organization for a player to be named later, April 4, 1985; Texas Rangers' organization acquired Infielder Jeff Moronko to complete deal, April 29, 1985.

PITCHING RECORD

Year Club	League	G.	IP.	W.	L.	Pct.	H.	R.	ER.	SO.	BB.	ERA.
1983—Tulsa...............	Texas	4	5	0	0	.000	7	4	3	5	1	5.40
1984—Oklahoma City..............	Am. Assoc.	1	6	0	0	.000	10	8	8	3	3	12.00
1985—Maine	Int'national	1	1	0	0	.000	0	0	0	1	0	0.00

WILLIAM JOSEPH BUCKNER
(Bill)

Born December 14, 1949, at Vallejo, Calif.
Height, 6.01. Weight, 185.
Throws and bats lefthanded.
Attended University of Southern California, Los Angeles, Calif., and
Arizona State University, Tempe, Ariz.
Brother of Jim Buckner, minor league outfielder, 1972 through 1981;
and Bob Buckner, minor league infielder, 1966 through 1970;
and part-time scout with Chicago Cubs, 1977 through 1979.

Established major league record for most assists, first baseman, season (184), 1985.
Tied major league record for most games, first baseman, season (162), 1985.
Established National League record for most assists, first baseman, season (161), 1983.
Established National League record for fewest double plays, first baseman, season, 150 or more games (89), 1982.
Tied National League record for fewest errors by first baseman for leader in errors, season (13), 1983.
Major League stolen bases: 1971 (4), 1972 (10), 1973 (12), 1974 (31), 1975 (8), 1976 (28), 1977 (7), 1978 (7), 1979 (9), 1980 (1), 1981 (5), 1982 (15), 1983 (12), 1984 (2), 1985 (18). Total—169.
Led Pioneer League first basemen in double plays with 37 in 1968.

Year Club	League	Pos.	G.	AB.	R.	H.	2B.	3B.	HR.	RBI.	B.A.	PO.	A.	E.	F.A.
1968—Ogden	Pion.	1B	*64	*256	54	*88	10	*8	4	41	*.344	468	28	4	*.992
1969—Albuquerque.........	Texas	OF-1B	70	257	44	79	7	3	7	50	.307	220	15	3	.987
1969—Spokane	P. C.	OF-1B	36	143	21	45	1	1	2	27	.315	128	12	5	.966
1969—Los Angeles	Nat.	PH	1	1	0	0	0	0	0	0	.000	0	0	0	.000
1970—Spokane	P. C.	1B-OF	111	465	78	156	33	2	3	74	.335	582	22	7	.989
1970—Los Angeles	Nat.	OF-1B	28	68	6	13	3	1	0	4	.191	37	1	0	1.000
1971—Los Angeles	Nat.	OF-1B	108	358	37	99	15	1	5	41	.277	235	11	1	.996
1972—Los Angeles	Nat.	OF-1B	105	383	47	122	14	3	5	37	.319	434	22	4	.991
1973—Los Angeles	Nat.	1B-OF	140	575	68	158	20	0	8	46	.275	981	50	3	.997
1974—Los Angeles	Nat.	OF-1B	145	580	83	182	30	3	7	58	.314	284	5	7	.976
1975—Los Angeles†	Nat.	OF	92	288	30	70	11	2	6	31	.243	138	4	2	.986
1976—Los Angeles‡	Nat.	OF-1B	154	642	76	193	28	4	7	60	.301	315	7	5	.985
1977—Chicago§	Nat.	1B	122	426	40	121	27	0	11	60	.284	966	58	10	.990
1978—Chicago x..............	Nat.	1B	117	446	47	144	26	1	5	74	.323	1075	83	6	.995
1979—Chicago	Nat.	1B	149	591	72	168	34	7	14	66	.284	1258	124	7	.995
1980—Chicago	Nat.	1B-OF	145	578	69	187	41	3	10	68	*.324	916	78	8	.992
1981—Chicago	Nat.	1B	106	421	45	131	*35	3	10	75	.311	996	81	*17	.984
1982—Chicago	Nat.	1B	161	*657	93	201	34	5	15	105	.306	1547	*159	12	.993
1983—Chicago	Nat.	*●1B-OF	153	626	79	175	●38	6	16	66	.280	1391	*161	●13	.992
1984—Chicago y..............	Nat.	1B-OF	21	43	3	9	0	0	2	2	.209	71	6	0	1.000
1984—Boston..................	Amer.	1B	114	439	51	122	21	2	11	67	.278	974	96	●15	.986
1985—Boston..................	Amer.	1B	162	673	89	201	46	3	16	110	.299	1384	*184	12	.992
National League Totals—16 Years.........			1747	6683	795	1973	356	39	119	793	.295	10644	850	95	.992
American League Totals—2 Years.........			276	1112	140	323	67	5	27	177	.290	2358	280	27	.990
Major League Totals—17 Years..............			2023	7795	935	2296	423	44	146	970	.295	13002	1130	122	.991

Selected by Los Angeles Dodgers' organization in 2nd round of free-agent draft, June 7, 1968.

†On disabled list, April 21 to May 12, 1975.

‡Traded with Infielder Ivan DeJesus and Pitcher Jeff Albert to Chicago Cubs for Outfielder Rick Monday and Pitcher Mike Garman, January 11, 1977.

§On disabled list, March 28 to April 19, 1977.

xOn disabled list, June 22 to July 7, 1978.

yTraded to Boston Red Sox for Pitcher Dennis Eckersley and Outfielder Mike Brumley, May 25, 1984.

CHAMPIONSHIP SERIES RECORD

Year Club	League	Pos.	G.	AB.	R.	H.	2B.	3B.	HR.	RBI.	B.A.	PO.	A.	E.	F.A.
1974—Los Angeles	Nat.	OF	4	18	0	3	1	0	0	0	.167	6	0	0	1.000

WORLD SERIES RECORD

Year Club	League	Pos.	G.	AB.	R.	H.	2B.	3B.	HR.	RBI.	B.A.	PO.	A.	E.	F.A.
1974—Los Angeles	Nat.	OF	5	20	1	5	1	0	1	1	.250	11	0	0	1.000

ALL-STAR GAME RECORD

Year League	Pos.	AB.	R.	H.	2B.	3B.	HR.	RBI.	B.A.	PO.	A.	E.	F.A.
1981—National.............................	PH	1	0	0	0	0	0	0	.000	0	0	0	.000

STEVEN BERNARD BUECHELE

Name pronounced BOO-shell.

(Steve)

Born September 26, 1961, at Lancaster, Calif.
Height, 6.02. Weight, 190.
Throws and bats righthanded.
Attended Stanford University, Stanford, Calif.

Major League stolen bases: 1985 (3).
Named American Association Most Valuable Player, 1985.

Year Club	League	Pos.	G.	AB.	R.	H.	2B.	3B.	HR.	RBI.	B.A.	PO.	A.	E.	F.A.
1982—Tulsa	Texas	2B-3B	62	213	21	63	12	2	5	33	.296	111	174	8	.973
1983—Tulsa	Texas	2B-3B	117	437	62	121	12	4	14	62	.277	182	259	18	.961
1983—Oklahoma City	A. A.	2B-3B	9	34	6	9	5	0	1	4	.265	17	22	1	.975
1984—Oklahoma City	A. A.	2B-3B	131	447	48	118	25	3	7	59	.264	236	329	17	.971
1985—Oklahoma City	A. A.	3B-2B	89	350	56	104	20	7	9	64	.297	84	170	7	.973
1985—Texas	Amer.	3B-2B	69	219	22	48	6	3	6	21	.219	52	138	6	.969
Major League Totals—1 Year			69	219	22	48	6	3	6	21	.219	52	138	6	.969

Selected by Chicago White Sox' organization in 1st round (ninth player selected) of free-agent draft, June 5, 1979.
Selected by Texas Rangers' organization in 5th round of free-agent draft, June 7, 1982.

JAY CAMPBELL BUHNER

Born August 13, 1964, at Louisville, Ky.
Height, 6.03. Weight, 205.
Throws and bats righthanded.
Attended McLennan Community College, Waco, Tex.

Led Florida State League in game-winning RBIs with 15 in 1985.

Year Club	League	Pos.	G.	AB.	R.	H.	2B.	3B.	HR.	RBI.	B.A.	PO.	A.	E.	F.A.
1984—Watertown†	NYP	OF	65	229	43	74	16	3	9	●58	.323	106	8	1	.991
1985—Fort Lauderdale	Fla. St.	OF	117	409	65	121	18	10	11	76	.296	235	12	7	.972

Selected by Atlanta Braves' organization in 9th round of free-agent draft, June 6, 1983.
Selected by Pittsburgh Pirates' organization in secondary phase of free-agent draft, January 17, 1984.
†Traded with Infielder Dale Berra and Pitcher Alfonso Pulido to New York Yankees for Outfielder Steve Kemp, Infielder Tim Foli and $800,000, December 20, 1984.

ERIC GERALD BULLOCK

Born February 16, 1960, at Los Angeles, Calif.
Height, 5.11. Weight, 185.
Throws and bats righthanded.
Attended Los Angeles Harbor Junior College, Woodland Hills, Calif. and
California State University, Fullerton, Calif.
Son of Eddie Bullock, minor league outfielder, 1955.

Tied for Pacific Coast League lead in being hit by pitch with 7 in 1985.

Year Club	League	Pos.	G.	AB.	R.	H.	2B.	3B.	HR.	RBI.	B.A.	PO.	A.	E.	F.A.
1981—Sarasota Orange	Gulf C.	OF	56	184	38	54	8	3	1	15	.293	67	6	3	.961
1981—Daytona Beach	Fla. St.	DH	1	2	1	1	0	0	0	1	.500	0	0	0	.000
1982—Daytona Beach	Fla. St.	OF	117	442	90	150	24	11	5	●85	.339	180	11	5	.974
1982—Columbus	South.	OF	18	66	6	20	1	0	2	13	.303	21	1	0	1.000
1983—Columbus	South.	OF	130	475	65	131	15	6	9	59	.276	196	9	3	.986
1984—Columbus	South.	OF	71	265	47	77	15	2	3	41	.291	133	3	4	.971
1984—Tucson	P. C.	OF	60	185	22	51	6	2	1	16	.276	96	2	5	.951
1985—Tucson	P. C.	OF	124	467	81	149	26	8	4	57	.319	199	5	7	.967
1985—Houston	Nat.	OF	18	25	3	7	2	0	0	2	.280	6	0	2	.750
Major League Totals—1 Year			18	25	3	7	2	0	0	2	.280	6	0	2	.750

Selected by Los Angeles Dodgers' organization in 18th round of free-agent draft, June 6, 1978.
Selected by San Diego Padres' organization in 1st round (fifth player selected) of free-agent draft, January 13, 1981.
Selected by Houston Astros' organization in secondary phase of free-agent draft, June 8, 1981.

ALONZA BENJAMIN BUMBRY

(Al)

Born April 21, 1947, at Fredericksburg, Va.
Height, 5.08. Weight, 175.
Throws right and bats lefthanded.
Received bachelor of science degree in physical education from
Virginia State College, Petersburg, Va.

Tied modern major league record for most triples, game, (3), September 22, 1973.
Major League stolen bases: 1972 (1), 1973 (23), 1974 (12), 1975 (16), 1976 (42), 1977 (19), 1978 (5), 1979 (37), 1980 (44), 1981 (22), 1982 (10), 1983 (12), 1984 (9), 1985 (2). Total—254.
Named outfielder on THE SPORTING NEWS American League All-Star Team, 1980.
Named American League Rookie Player of the Year by THE SPORTING NEWS, 1973.

Named American League Rookie of the Year by Baseball Writers' Association of America, 1973.
Named Northern League Player of the Year, 1971.

Year	Club	League	Pos.	G.	AB.	R.	H.	2B.	3B.	HR.	RBI.	B.A.	PO.	A.	E.	F.A.
1969—Stockton†	Calif.	OF-1B	35	73	19	13	4	0	0	3	.178	31	3	2	.944
1970—							(In Military Service.)									
1971—Aberdeen	North.	OF	66	247	68	83	14	6	6	53	.336	85	5	5	.947
1972—Asheville	South.	OF	26	121	26	42	4	4	4	10	.347	60	4	3	.955
1972—Rochester	Int.	OF	108	435	83	150	29	★15	6	47	★.345	198	14	0	★1.000
1972—Baltimore	Amer.	OF	9	11	5	4	0	1	0	0	.364	4	0	0	1.000
1973—Baltimore	Amer.	OF	110	356	73	120	15	●11	7	34	.337	134	2	3	.978
1974—Baltimore	Amer.	OF	94	270	35	63	10	3	1	19	.233	115	7	6	.953
1975—Baltimore	Amer.	OF-3B	114	349	47	94	19	4	2	32	.269	70	2	0	1.000
1976—Baltimore	Amer.	OF	133	450	71	113	15	7	9	36	.251	251	9	3	.989
1977—Baltimore‡	Amer.	OF	133	518	74	164	31	3	4	41	.317	329	7	3	.991
1978—Baltimore§x	Amer.	OF	33	114	21	27	5	2	2	6	.237	62	2	1	.985
1979—Baltimore	Amer.	OF	148	569	80	162	29	1	7	49	.285	367	7	7	.982
1980—Baltimore	Amer.	OF	160	645	118	205	29	9	9	53	.318	488	7	5	.990
1981—Baltimore	Amer.	OF	101	392	61	107	18	2	1	27	.273	255	6	2	.992
1982—Baltimore	Amer.	OF	150	562	77	147	20	4	5	40	.262	404	9	6	.986
1983—Baltimore	Amer.	OF	124	378	63	104	14	4	3	31	.275	235	3	3	.988
1984—Baltimore y	Amer.	OF	119	344	47	93	12	1	3	24	.270	230	7	3	.988
1985—San Diego z	Nat.	OF	68	95	6	19	3	0	1	10	.200	31	0	2	.939
American League Totals—13 Years			1428	4958	772	1403	217	52	53	392	.283	2944	68	42	.986
National League Totals—1 Year			68	95	6	19	3	0	1	10	.200	31	0	2	.939
Major League Totals—14 Years			1496	5053	778	1422	220	52	54	402	.281	2975	68	44	.986

Selected by Baltimore Orioles' organization in 11th round of free-agent draft, June 7, 1968.
†On temporary inactive list, June 16, 1969; transferred to military list, July 22, 1969 through June 3, 1971.
‡On disabled list, July 28 to August 12, 1977.
§On disabled list, May 12 to September 1, 1978.
xGranted free agency, November 2, 1978; re-signed by Orioles, January 30, 1979.
yGranted free agency, November 8, 1984; signed by San Diego Padres, March 28, 1985.
zGranted free agency, November 12, 1985.

CHAMPIONSHIP SERIES RECORD

Year	Club	League	Pos.	G.	AB.	R.	H.	2B.	3B.	HR.	RBI.	B.A.	PO.	A.	E.	F.A.
1973—Baltimore	Amer.	OF	2	7	1	0	0	0	0	0	.000	4	1	1	.833
1974—Baltimore	Amer.	PR-PH	2	1	0	0	0	0	0	0	.000	0	0	0	.000
1979—Baltimore	Amer.	OF	4	16	5	4	0	1	0	0	.250	10	0	1	.909
1983—Baltimore	Amer.	OF-PR	3	8	0	1	1	0	0	1	.125	3	0	0	1.000
Championship Series Totals—4 Years			11	32	6	5	1	1	0	1	.156	17	1	2	.900

WORLD SERIES RECORD

Year	Club	League	Pos.	G.	AB.	R.	H.	2B.	3B.	HR.	RBI.	B.A.	PO.	A.	E.	F.A.
1979—Baltimore	Amer.	OF-PH	7	21	3	3	0	0	0	1	.143	14	1	1	.938
1983—Baltimore	Amer.	OF	4	11	0	1	1	0	0	1	.091	12	0	0	1.000
World Series Totals—2 Years			11	32	3	4	1	0	0	2	.125	26	1	1	.964

ALL-STAR GAME RECORD

Year	League	Pos.	AB.	R.	H.	2B.	3B.	HR.	RBI.	B.A.	PO.	A.	E.	F.A.
1980—American		OF	1	0	0	0	0	0	0	.000	2	0	0	1.000

RICHARD SCOTT BUONANTONY
(Rich)

Born November 28, 1962, at Hoboken, N.J.
Height, 6.04. Weight, 205.
Throws and bats righthanded.
Attended University of Nevada, Las Vegas, Nev.

Tied for Texas League lead in hit batsmen with 8 in 1985.

Year	Club	League	G.	IP.	W.	L.	Pct.	H.	R.	ER.	SO.	BB.	ERA.
1980—Sarasota Cubs	Gulf Coast	12	63	3	★8	.273	66	40	28	37	26	4.00
1981—Sarasota Cubs	Gulf Coast	13	64	2	6	.250	70	50	36	50	38	5.06
1982—Quad Cities	Midwest	26	161	12	4	.750	151	79	70	103	79	3.91
1983—Salinas	California	22	138	6	7	.462	136	73	53	97	62	3.46
1983—Midland†	Texas	4	24⅔	1	1	.500	24	15	15	13	20	5.47
1984—El Paso	Texas	8	34⅓	2	2	.500	46	39	36	17	31	9.44
1984—Stockton‡	California	20	129⅔	6	7	.462	127	61	55	121	72	3.82
1985—Arkansas	Texas	27	147⅓	10	11	.476	141	90	76	121	92	4.64

Selected by Chicago Cubs' organization in 14th round of free-agent draft, June 3, 1980.
†Traded to Milwaukee Brewers, October 24, 1983, completing deal in which Milwaukee traded Catcher Steve Lake to Chicago Cubs for player to be named later, April 1, 1983.
‡Traded with Pitcher Jim Koontz and Infielder Ron Koenigsfield to St. Louis Cardinals for Outfielders Paul Householder and Jim Adduci, October 2, 1984.

—DID YOU KNOW—

That Joe Niekro of the Astros established a Houston record with three sacrifice hits on June 19?

GUS EDWARD BURGESS

Born December 18, 1961, at Boynton Beach, Fla.
Height, 5.11. Weight, 189.
Throws and bats lefthanded.
Attended Palm Beach Junior College, Lake Worth, Fla.

Led International League in sacrifice flies with 12 in 1983.
Led Carolina League in stolen bases with 68 and tied for lead in sacrifice flies with 8 and caught stealing with 15 in 1981.

Year Club	League	Pos.	G.	AB.	R.	H.	2B.	3B.	HR.	RBI.	B.A.	PO.	A.	E.	F.A.
1980—Elmira..................	NYP	OF	58	130	23	27	6	1	2	18	.208	66	3	2	.972
1981—Winston-Salem	Carol.	OF	135	510	102	144	27	7	7	74	.282	250	8	★22	.921
1982—Bristol..................	East.	OF	133	477	71	138	25	5	11	62	.289	198	12	14	.938
1983—Pawtucket	Int.	OF	130	449	62	121	11	6	8	66	.269	195	★16	8	.963
1984—Pawtucket...........	Int.	OF	132	445	80	121	16	3	11	65	.272	234	10	8	.968
1985—Pawtucket†	Int.	●OF-P	106	359	36	81	11	0	2	19	.226	227	●13	9	.964

Selected by Montreal Expos' organization in 15th round of free-agent draft, June 5, 1979.
Selected by Boston Red Sox' organization in secondary phase of free-agent draft, January 9, 1980.
†On disabled list, July 16 to July 26, 1985.

PITCHING RECORD

Year Club	League	G.	IP.	W.	L.	Pct.	H.	R.	ER.	SO.	BB.	ERA.
1985—Pawtucket	Int'national	1	1	0	0	.000	1	2	2	1	4	18.00

TIMOTHY PHILIP BURKE
(Tim)

Born February 19, 1959, at Omaha, Neb.
Height, 6.03. Weight, 190.
Throws and bats righthanded.
Attended University of Nebraska, Lincoln, Neb.

Major League saves: 1985 (8).

Year Club	League	G.	IP.	W.	L.	Pct.	H.	R.	ER.	SO.	BB.	ERA.
1980—Salem†..............................	Carolina					(Did not play)						
1981—Alexandria	Carolina	23	149	8	10	.444	139	67	57	111	48	3.44
1982—Buffalo‡...	Eastern	25	144	7	10	.412	162	93	83	93	57	5.19
1983—Columbus	Eastern	4	12	1	0	1.000	15	9	9	6	8	6.75
1983—Nashville§x	Southern	20	129	12	4	.750	124	63	46	64	37	3.21
1984—Indianapolis	Am. Assoc.	35	180⅔	11	8	.579	192	81	70	108	61	3.49
1985—Montreal	National	★78	120⅓	9	4	.692	86	32	32	87	44	2.39
Major League Totals—1 Year.............................		78	120⅓	9	4	.692	86	32	32	87	44	2.39

Selected by Pittsburgh Pirates' organization in 2nd round of free-agent draft, June 3, 1980.
†On disabled list, July 12, 1980 through remainder of season.
‡Traded with Catcher John Holland, Infielder Jose Rivera and Outfielder Don Aubin to New York Yankees' organization for Outfielder Lee Mazzilli, December 22, 1982.
§On disabled list, May 4 to May 23, 1983.
xTraded to Montreal Expos' organization for Outfielder Pat Rooney, December 19, 1983.

ELLIS RENA BURKS

Born September 11, 1964, at Vicksburg, Miss.
Height, 6.02. Weight, 175.
Throws and bats righthanded.
Attended Ranger Junior College, Ranger, Tex.

Tied for Florida State League lead in double plays by outfielders with 6 in 1984.

Year Club	League	Pos.	G.	AB.	R.	H.	2B.	3B.	HR.	RBI.	B.A.	PO.	A.	E.	F.A.
1983—Elmira..................	NYP	OF	53	174	30	42	9	0	2	23	.241	89	5	2	.979
1984—Winter Haven.......	Fla. St.	OF	112	375	52	96	15	4	6	43	.256	196	12	5	.977
1985—New Britain	East.	OF	133	476	66	121	25	7	10	61	.254	306	9	8	.975

Selected by Boston Red Sox' organization in 1st round (20th player selected) of free agent draft, January 11, 1983.

RICHARD PAUL BURLESON
(Rick)

Born April 29, 1951, at Lynwood, Calif.
Height, 5.10. Weight, 160.
Throws and bats righthanded.
Attended Cerritos Junior College, Norwalk, Calif.

Established major league records for most double plays by shortstop, season (147), 1980; most assists by shortstop, game (15), April 13, 1982 (20 innings).
Major League stolen bases: 1974 (3), 1975 (8), 1976 (14), 1977 (13), 1978 (8), 1979 (9), 1980 (12), 1981 (4). Total—71.
Led American League shortstops in total chances with 851 in 1980 and 615 in 1981.
Led American League shortstops in double plays with 147 in 1980 and 88 in 1981.
Led International League shortstops in fielding percentage with .961 in 1973.
Led Eastern League shortstops in double plays with 80 in 1972.
Named shortstop on THE SPORTING NEWS American League All-Star Team, 1977 and 1981.
Named shortstop on THE SPORTING NEWS American League All-Star fielding team, 1979.
Named shortstop on THE SPORTING NEWS American League Silver Slugger team, 1981.

Year	Club	League	Pos.	G.	AB.	R.	H.	2B.	3B.	HR.	RBI.	B.A.	PO.	A.	E.	F.A.
1970—Winter Haven	Fla. St.		SS	118	419	42	92	13	4	1	29	.220	188	★400	38	.939
1971—Greenville	W. Car.		SS	29	118	24	31	4	2	2	12	.263	32	68	11	.901
1971—Winston-Salem†	Carol.		SS	77	299	35	82	14	2	4	30	.274	118	262	23	.943
1972—Pawtucket	East.		SS	136	488	59	115	26	0	9	51	.236	★191	380	23	★.961
1973—Pawtucket	Int.		SS-2B	★146	477	58	120	20	1	6	45	.252	241	431	25	.964
1974—Pawtucket	Int.		SS	10	41	7	14	4	0	1	4	.341	10	36	3	.939
1974—Boston	Amer.		SS-2B-3B	114	384	36	109	22	0	4	44	.284	209	329	21	.962
1975—Boston	Amer.		SS	158	580	66	146	25	1	6	62	.252	267	498	29	.963
1976—Boston	Amer.		SS	152	540	75	157	27	1	7	42	.291	274	478	34	.957
1977—Boston	Amer.		SS	154	★663	80	194	36	7	3	52	.293	★285	482	24	.970
1978—Boston‡	Amer.		SS	145	626	75	155	32	5	5	49	.248	285	482	15	.981
1979—Boston	Amer.		SS	153	627	93	174	32	5	5	60	.278	272	523	16	★.980
1980—Boston§	Amer.		SS	155	644	89	179	29	2	8	51	.278	★301	★528	22	.974
1981—California	Amer.		SS	●109	430	53	126	17	1	5	33	.293	★208	★394	13	.979
1982—California x	Amer.		SS	11	45	4	7	1	0	0	2	.156	19	51	1	.986
1983—California yz	Amer.		SS	33	119	22	34	7	0	0	11	.286	54	102	5	.969
1983—Edmonton	P. C.		SS	14	51	3	10	3	0	0	4	.196	17	16	3	.917
1984—California a	Amer.		PH-PR	7	4	2	0	0	0	0	0	.000	0	0	0	.000
1985—California b	Amer.								(Did not play)							
Major League Totals—11 Years				1191	4662	595	1281	228	22	43	406	.275	2174	3867	180	.971

Selected by Minnesota Twins' organization in 8th round of free-agent draft, June 5, 1969.
Selected by Boston Red Sox' organization in secondary phase of free-agent draft, January 17, 1970.
†On disabled list, June 1 to June 19, 1971.
‡On disabled list, July 14 to July 28, 1978.
§Traded with Third Baseman Butch Hobson to California Angels for Third Baseman Carney Lansford, Pitcher Mark Clear and Outfielder Rick Miller, December 10, 1980.
xOn disabled list, April 18, 1982 through remainder of season.
yOn disabled list, March 30 to June 30, 1983; included rehabilitation disability assignment to Edmonton, June 10 to June 27, 1983.
zOn disabled list, August 19 to September 3, 1983.
aOn disabled list, March 29 to September 1, 1984.
bOn disabled list, April 8, 1985 through remainder of season.

CHAMPIONSHIP SERIES RECORD

Year	Club	League	Pos.	G.	AB.	R.	H.	2B.	3B.	HR.	RBI.	B.A.	PO.	A.	E.	F.A.
1975—Boston	Amer.		SS	3	9	2	4	2	0	0	1	.444	4	12	1	.941

WORLD SERIES RECORD

Year	Club	League	Pos.	G.	AB.	R.	H.	2B.	3B.	HR.	RBI.	B.A.	PO.	A.	E.	F.A.
1975—Boston	Amer.		SS	7	24	1	7	1	0	0	2	.292	9	19	1	.966

ALL-STAR GAME RECORD

Year	League	Pos.	AB.	R.	H.	2B.	3B.	HR.	RBI.	B.A.	PO.	A.	E.	F.A.
1977—American		SS	2	0	0	0	0	0	0	.000	0	0	0	.000
1979—American		PR-SS	2	1	0	0	0	0	0	.000	0	1	0	1.000
1981—American		SS	1	0	0	0	0	0	0	.000	1	3	0	1.000
All-Star Game Totals—3 Years			5	1	0	0	0	0	0	.000	1	4	0	1.000

Named to American League All-Star Team for 1978 game; replaced due to injury by Jerry Remy.

ROBERT BRITT BURNS

(Known by middle name.)
Born June 8, 1959, at Houston, Tex.
Height, 6.05. Weight, 218.
Throws left and bats righthanded.

Major League saves: 1984 (3).
Tied for American League lead in balks with 4 in 1980.
Named American League Rookie Pitcher of the Year by THE SPORTING NEWS, 1980.

Year	Club	League	G.	IP.	W.	L.	Pct.	H.	R.	ER.	SO.	BB.	ERA.
1978—Appleton	Midwest		6	30	3	2	.600	25	8	8	28	2	2.40
1978—Chicago	American		2	8	0	2	.000	14	12	11	3	3	12.38
1978—Knoxville	Southern		4	21	1	1	.500	24	16	10	17	4	4.29
1979—Knoxville	Southern		20	110	6	10	.375	126	68	59	92	37	4.83
1979—Iowa	Am. Assoc.		7	41	2	3	.400	41	17	15	34	15	3.29
1979—Chicago	American		6	5	0	0	.000	10	5	3	2	1	5.40
1980—Chicago	American		34	238	15	13	.536	213	83	75	133	63	2.84
1981—Chicago	American		24	157	10	6	.625	139	52	46	108	49	2.64
1982—Chicago	American		28	169⅓	13	5	.722	168	89	76	116	67	4.04
1983—Chicago†	American		29	173⅔	10	11	.476	165	79	69	115	55	3.58
1984—Chicago‡	American		34	117	4	12	.250	130	74	65	85	45	5.00
1984—Appleton	Midwest		1	5	1	0	1.000	4	1	1	5	1	1.80
1984—Denver	Am. Assoc.		1	6	1	0	1.000	6	3	3	5	3	4.50
1985—Chicago§	American		36	227	18	11	.621	206	105	100	172	79	3.96
Major League Totals—8 Years			193	1095	70	60	.538	1045	499	445	734	362	3.66

Selected by Chicago White Sox' organization in 3rd round of free-agent draft, June 6, 1978.
†On disabled list, March 29 to May 9, 1983.
‡On disabled list, July 19 to August 20, 1984; included rehabilitation disability assignment to Appleton, August 10 to August 15, 1984, and Denver, August 16 to August 20, 1984.
§Traded with Shortstop Mike Soper and Outfielder Glen Braxton to New York Yankees for Catcher Ron Hassey and Pitcher Joe Cowley, December 12, 1985.

CHAMPIONSHIP SERIES RECORD

Year Club	League	G.	IP.	W.	L.	Pct.	H.	R.	ER.	SO.	BB.	ERA.
1983—Chicago	American	1	9⅓	0	1	.000	6	1	1	8	5	0.96

ALL-STAR GAME RECORD

Member of American League All-Star Team in 1981; did not play.

THOMAS EDWARD BURNS
(Tom)

Born September 30, 1961, at Jacksonville, Fla.
Height, 6.03. Weight, 200.
Throws and bats righthanded.

Led Midwest League in hit batsmen with 19 in 1983.
Led New York-Pennsylvania League in wild pitches with 15 in 1981.

Year Club	League	G.	IP.	W.	L.	Pct.	H.	R.	ER.	SO.	BB.	ERA.
1980—Batavia	NYP	17	56	2	4	.333	54	48	32	37	37	5.14
1981—Waterloo	Midwest	2	2	0	0	.000	2	4	4	2	4	18.00
1981—Batavia†	NYP	19	74	0	*11	.000	80	*71	*56	62	59	6.81
1982—	(Out of Organized Baseball)											
1983—Wausau	Midwest	46	134	6	9	.400	124	88	66	91	72	4.43
1984—Wausau‡	Midwest	28	167⅓	7	10	.412	162	88	65	90	63	3.50
1985—Lynchburg	Carolina	24	52	2	0	1.000	41	11	6	48	10	1.04
1985—Jackson§	Texas	31	51	7	1	.875	47	8	8	35	15	1.41

Signed as free agent by Cleveland Indians' organization, August 28, 1979.
†Released, April 1, 1982; signed by Wausau (Seattle Mariners' organization), April 8, 1983.
‡Traded to New York Mets' organization for First Baseman-Designated Hitter Paul Hollins, April 4, 1985.
§Drafted by Minnesota Twins, December 10, 1985.

BERTRAM RAY BURRIS
(Known by middle name.)

Born August 22, 1950, at Idabel, Okla.
Height, 6.05. Weight, 210.
Throws and bats righthanded.
Received bachelor of arts degree in recreational leadership from Southwestern State, Weatherford, Okla.

Major League saves: 1974 (1), 1978 (1), 1982 (2). Total—4.
Tied for National League lead in home runs allowed with 29 in 1977.

Year Club	League	G.	IP.	W.	L.	Pct.	H.	R.	ER.	SO.	BB.	ERA.
1972—Midland	Texas	14	95	7	5	.583	98	43	37	91	20	3.51
1973—Wichita	Am. Assoc.	8	59	4	3	.571	72	45	37	34	19	5.64
1973—Chicago	National	31	65	1	1	.500	65	22	21	57	27	2.91
1974—Wichita	Am. Assoc.	7	46	2	3	.400	52	33	26	34	23	5.09
1974—Chicago	National	40	75	3	5	.375	91	61	55	40	26	6.60
1975—Chicago	National	36	238	15	10	.600	259	121	109	108	73	4.12
1976—Chicago	National	37	249	15	13	.536	251	102	86	112	70	3.11
1977—Chicago	National	39	221	14	16	.467	270	132	116	105	67	4.72
1978—Chicago	National	40	199	7	13	.350	210	112	105	94	79	4.75
1979—Chicago†-New York§	National	18	43	0	2	.000	44	27	23	24	21	4.81
1979—New York‡	American	15	28	1	3	.250	40	22	19	19	10	6.11
1980—New York xy	National	29	170	7	13	.350	181	86	76	83	54	4.02
1981—Montreal	National	22	136	9	7	.563	117	56	46	52	41	3.04
1982—Montreal	National	37	123⅔	4	14	.222	143	77	65	55	53	4.73
1983—Montreal z	National	40	154	4	7	.364	139	68	63	100	56	3.68
1984—Oakland ab	American	34	211⅔	13	10	.565	193	84	74	93	90	3.15
1985—Milwaukee	American	29	170⅓	9	13	.409	182	95	91	81	53	4.81
American League Totals—3 Years		78	410	23	26	.469	415	201	184	193	153	4.04
National League Totals—11 Years		369	1673⅔	79	101	.439	1770	864	765	830	567	4.11
Major League Totals—13 Years		447	2083⅔	102	127	.445	2185	1065	949	1023	720	4.10

Selected by Chicago Cubs' organization in 17th round of free-agent draft, June 6, 1972.
†Traded to New York Yankees for Pitcher Dick Tidrow, May 23, 1979.
‡Sold on waivers to New York Mets, August 20, 1979.
§On disabled list, September 15 to October 3, 1979.
xOn disabled list, July 3 to August 4, 1980.
yGranted free agency, October 27, 1980; signed by Montreal Expos, February 18, 1981.
zTraded to Oakland A's for Outfielder Rusty McNealy and cash, December 8, 1983.
aAppeared in three games as a pinch-runner.
bTraded with Pitcher Eric Barry and a player to be named later to Milwaukee Brewers for Pitcher Don Sutton December 7, 1984; Milwaukee organization acquired Pitcher Ed Myers to complete deal, March 25, 1985.

DIVISION SERIES RECORD

Year Club	League	G.	IP.	W.	L.	Pct.	H.	R.	ER.	SO.	BB.	ERA.
1981—Montreal	National	1	5⅓	0	1	.000	7	4	3	4	4	5.06

CHAMPIONSHIP SERIES RECORD

Established National League Championship Series record for most innings pitched, five-game Series (17), 1981.

Year Club	League	G.	IP.	W.	L.	Pct.	H.	R.	ER.	SO.	BB.	ERA.
1981—Montreal	National	2	17	1	0	1.000	10	1	1	4	3	0.53

JEFFREY ALAN BURROUGHS
(Jeff)

Born March 7, 1951, at Long Beach, Calif.
Height, 6.01. Weight, 200.
Throws and bats righthanded.
Attended Long Beach City College, Long Beach, Calif.

Tied major league record for fewest caught stealing, season, 150 or more games (0), 1976.
Major League stolen bases: 1971 (1), 1974 (2), 1975 (4), 1977 (4), 1978 (1), 1979 (2), 1980 (1), 1982 (1). Total—16.
Hit three home runs in a game, August 14, 1981 (second game).
Led National League in bases on balls received with 117 in 1978.
Led American League batters in strikeouts with 155 in 1975.
Led American League in sacrifice flies with 11 in 1973.
Led American League outfielders in double plays with 5 in 1974.
Named American League Most Valuable Player by Baseball Writers' Association of America, 1974.
Named American League Player of the Year by THE SPORTING NEWS, 1974.
Named outfielder on THE SPORTING NEWS American League All-Star Team, 1974.
Received reported $88,000 bonus to sign with Washington Senators, 1969.

Year Club	League	Pos.	G.	AB.	R.	H.	2B.	3B.	HR.	RBI.	B.A.	PO.	A.	E.	F.A.
1969—Wytheville	Appal.	1B-OF	52	183	41	65	16	4	6	48	.355	192	12	10	.953
1970—Denver	A. A.	OF-3B-1B	115	390	64	105	17	6	17	71	.269	250	52	16	.950
1970—Washington	Amer.	OF	6	12	1	2	0	0	0	1	.167	5	0	0	1.000
1971—Denver	A. A.	OF	81	298	51	87	13	3	12	58	.292	108	7	10	.920
1971—Washington	Amer.	OF	59	181	20	42	9	0	5	25	.232	82	3	3	.966
1972—Texas†	Amer.	OF-1B	22	65	4	12	1	0	1	3	.185	33	2	2	.946
1972—Denver	A. A.	OF	84	307	60	93	13	2	24	59	.303	118	5	5	.961
1973—Texas	Amer.	OF-1B	151	526	71	147	17	1	30	85	.279	320	14	8	.977
1974—Texas	Amer.	OF-1B	152	554	84	167	33	2	25	★118	.301	242	11	8	.969
1975—Texas	Amer.	OF	152	585	81	132	20	0	29	94	.226	249	10	9	.966
1976—Texas‡	Amer.	OF	158	604	71	143	22	2	18	86	.237	289	12	4	.987
1977—Atlanta	Nat.	OF	154	579	91	157	19	1	41	114	.271	249	9	7	.974
1978—Atlanta	Nat.	OF	153	488	72	147	30	6	23	77	.301	224	13	6	.975
1979—Atlanta	Nat.	OF	116	397	49	89	14	1	11	47	.224	175	8	7	.963
1980—Atlanta§	Nat.	OF	99	278	35	73	14	0	13	51	.263	129	0	3	.977
1981—Seattle x	Amer.	OF	89	319	32	81	13	1	10	41	.254	127	4	2	.985
1982—Oakland	Amer.	OF	113	285	42	79	13	2	16	48	.277	52	0	1	.981
1983—Oakland	Amer.	DH	121	401	43	108	15	1	10	56	.269	0	0	0	.000
1984—Oakland y	Amer.	OF	58	71	5	15	1	0	2	8	.211	1	0	0	1.000
1985—Toronto z	Amer.	DH	86	191	19	49	9	3	6	28	.257	0	0	0	.000
American League Totals—12 Years			1167	3794	473	977	153	12	152	593	.258	1400	56	37	.975
National League Totals—4 Years			522	1742	247	466	77	8	88	289	.268	777	30	23	.972
Major League Totals—16 Years			1689	5536	720	1443	230	20	240	882	.261	2177	86	60	.974

Selected by Washington Senators' organization in 1st round (first player selected) of free-agent draft, June 5, 1969.
†On disabled list, April 27 to May 16, 1972.
‡Traded to Atlanta Braves for Outfielders Ken Henderson and Dave May, Pitchers Carl Morton, Roger Moret and Adrian Devine, and cash estimated at $250,000, December 9, 1976.
§Traded to Seattle Mariners for Pitcher Carlos Diaz, March 6, 1981.
xGranted free agency, November 13, 1981; signed by Oakland A's, April 7, 1982.
ySold to Toronto Blue Jays, December 22, 1984.
zGranted free agency, November 12, 1985.

CHAMPIONSHIP SERIES RECORD

Year Club	League	Pos.	G.	AB.	R.	H.	2B.	3B.	HR.	RBI.	B.A.	PO.	A.	E.	F.A.
1985—Toronto	Amer.	PH	1	1	0	0	0	0	0	0	.000	0	0	0	.000

ALL-STAR GAME RECORD

Year League	Pos.	AB.	R.	H.	2B.	3B.	HR.	RBI.	B.A.	PO.	A.	E.	F.A.
1974—American	OF	0	0	0	0	0	0	0	.000	1	0	0	1.000

Member of National League All-Star Team for 1978 game; did not play.

DENNIS ALLEN BURTT

Born November 29, 1957, at San Diego, Calif.
Height, 6.00. Weight, 187.
Throws right and bats left and righthanded.
Attended Santa Ana Junior College, Santa Ana, Calif.

Tied for International League lead in intentional bases on balls issued with 9 in 1982 and shutouts with 3 in 1985.

Year Club	League	G.	IP.	W.	L.	Pct.	H.	R.	ER.	SO.	BB.	ERA.
1976—Elmira	NYP	8	44	5	0	1.000	22	7	6	34	20	1.23
1977—Winter Haven†	Florida St.	7	32	2	1	.667	20	13	3	12	18	0.84
1978—Winter Haven	Florida St.	29	100	8	4	.667	76	35	29	76	39	2.61
1979—Winter Haven	Florida St.	35	152	11	10	.524	113	53	40	109	74	2.37
1980—Bristol	Eastern	31	165	11	8	.579	141	74	65	102	93	3.55
1981—Bristol	Eastern	27	170	10	8	.556	134	77	53	108	80	2.81
1982—Pawtucket	Int'national	25	150⅓	13	7	.650	163	96	80	79	98	4.79
1983—Pawtucket‡	Int'national	23	110⅓	4	5	.444	109	72	65	66	75	5.30
1984—Pawtucket§	Int'national	26	131⅓	6	8	.429	151	89	72	70	67	4.93
1985—Toledo	Int'national	27	172½	●14	8	.636	182	96	79	95	67	4.13
1985—Minnesota	American	5	28⅓	2	2	.500	20	13	12	9	7	3.81
Major League Totals—1 Year		5	28⅓	2	2	.500	20	13	12	9	7	3.81

†On disabled list, June 13 to August 8, 1977.
‡On disabled list, May 1 to May 31 and July 26 to August 5, 1983.
§Granted free agency, October 15, 1984; signed by Minnesota Twins' organization, December 31, 1984.

ROBERT RANDALL BUSH
(Randy)

Born October 5, 1958, at Dover, Del.
Height, 6.01. Weight, 184.
Throws and bats lefthanded.
Attended Miami-Dade North Community College, Miami, Fla.,
and University of New Orleans, New Orleans, La.

Major League stolen bases: 1984 (1), 1985 (3). Total—4.
Led Southern League in being hit by pitch with 8 in 1979 and 12 in 1981.

Year Club	League	Pos.	G.	AB.	R.	H.	2B.	3B.	HR.	RBI.	B.A.	PO.	A.	E.	F.A.
1979—Orlando	South.	1B	76	243	33	62	12	2	6	34	.255	653	38	13	.982
1980—Toledo†	Int.	OF-1B	40	108	11	21	1	0	1	7	.194	112	6	1	.992
1980—Orlando	South.	1B	51	175	32	41	2	1	7	26	.234	458	28	4	.992
1981—Orlando	South.	OF-1B	136	482	98	140	26	3	22	94	.290	174	7	5	.973
1982—Toledo	Int.	OF	49	160	21	52	14	0	8	27	.325	68	0	1	.986
1982—Minnesota	Amer.	OF	55	119	13	29	6	1	4	13	.011	7	0	0	1.000
1983—Minnesota	Amer.	1B	124	373	43	93	24	3	11	56	.249	21	3	0	1.000
1984—Minnesota	Amer.	1B	113	311	46	69	17	1	11	43	.222	5	0	0	1.000
1985—Minnesota	Amer.	OF-1B	97	234	26	56	13	3	10	35	.239	79	0	2	.975
Major League Totals—4 Years			389	1037	128	247	60	8	36	147	.238	112	3	2	.983

Selected by Minnesota Twins' organization in 2nd round of free-agent draft, June 5, 1979.
†On disabled list, May 25 to June 27, 1980.

JOHN DANIEL BUTCHER

Born March 8, 1957, at Glendale, Calif.
Height, 6.04. Weight, 190.
Throws and bats righthanded.
Attended Yavapai College, Prescott, Ariz.

Major League saves: 1982 (1), 1983 (5). Total—6.
Led International League in complete games with 14 in 1980.

Year Club	League	G.	IP.	W.	L.	Pct.	H.	R.	ER.	SO.	BB.	ERA.
1977—Sarasota Rangers	Gulf Coast	6	42	3	2	.600	28	10	6	23	11	1.29
1977—Asheville	W. Carol.	2	16	1	0	1.000	13	4	2	13	6	1.13
1978—Asheville	W. Carol.	24	154	10	9	.526	150	81	57	103	77	3.33
1979—Tulsa†	Texas	26	155	9	12	.429	197	106	88	82	53	5.11
1980—Charleston	Int'national	22	152	10	7	.588	141	57	56	71	50	3.32
1980—Texas	American	6	35	3	3	.500	34	19	16	27	13	4.11
1981—Wichita	Am. Assoc.	24	136	8	10	.444	171	100	85	87	60	5.63
1981—Texas	American	5	28	1	2	.333	18	6	5	19	8	1.61
1982—Denver	Am. Assoc.	8	59	5	1	.833	54	20	18	31	14	2.75
1982—Texas	American	18	94⅓	1	5	.167	102	53	51	39	34	4.87
1983—Texas‡	American	38	123	6	6	.500	128	50	48	58	41	3.51
1984—Minnesota	American	34	225	13	11	.542	242	98	86	83	53	3.44
1985—Minnesota	American	34	207⅔	11	14	.440	239	125	115	92	43	4.98
Major League Totals—6 Years		135	713	35	41	.461	763	351	321	318	192	4.05

Selected by St. Louis Cardinals' organization in 2nd round of free-agent draft, January 7, 1976.
Selected by Atlanta Braves' organization in secondary phase of free-agent draft, June 8, 1976.
Selected by Houston Astros' organization in secondary phase of free-agent draft, January 11, 1977.
Selected by Texas Rangers' organization in secondary phase of free-agent draft, June 7, 1977.
†On disabled list, July 30 to August 10, 1979.
‡Traded with Pitcher Mike Smithson and Catcher Sam Sorce to Minnesota Twins for Outfielder Gary Ward, December 7, 1983.

SALVATORE PHILIP BUTERA
(Sal)

Born September 25, 1952, at Richmond Hill, N.Y.
Height, 6.00. Weight, 189.
Throws and bats righthanded.
Attended Suffolk Community College, Selden, N.Y.

Led Carolina League in passed balls with 20 in 1974.
Tied for Carolina League lead in double plays by catchers with 9 in 1974.

Year Club	League	Pos.	G.	AB.	R.	H.	2B.	3B.	HR.	RBI.	B.A.	PO.	A.	E.	F.A.
1972—Sarasota W. Sox†	Gulf C.	C	36	114	18	28	7	0	0	16	.246	253	20	10	.965
1973—Fort Lauderdale	Fla. St.	C	99	319	21	76	12	1	1	32	.238	503	*86	10	.983
1974—Lynchburg	Carol.	C	124	417	35	90	16	2	3	55	.216	589	*102	7	*.990
1975—Orlando	South.	C	20	51	8	9	2	0	0	4	.176	61	14	0	1.000
1975—Tacoma	P. C.	C	73	215	21	52	9	0	2	26	.242	376	36	6	.986
1976—Orlando†	South.	C	90	267	45	73	8	0	3	28	.273	326	41	6	.984
1977—Tacoma	P. C.	C	87	252	27	70	13	0	4	45	.278	257	49	9	.971
1978—Toledo	Int.	C	74	206	20	52	7	0	4	28	.252	334	32	5	.987
1979—Toledo	Int.	C	78	236	20	70	13	0	2	29	.297	392	33	11	.975

Year Club	League	Pos.	G.	AB.	R.	H.	2B.	3B.	HR.	RBI.	B.A.	PO.	A.	E.	F.A.
1980—Minnesota	Amer.	C	34	85	4	23	1	0	0	2	.271	106	9	6	.950
1981—Minnesota	Amer.	C-1B	62	167	13	40	7	1	0	18	.240	256	41	9	.971
1982—Minnesota‡	Amer.	C	54	126	9	32	2	0	0	8	.254	230	26	3	.988
1983—Detroit	Amer.	C	4	5	1	1	0	0	0	0	.200	12	1	1	.929
1983—Evansville§	A. A.	C	67	219	23	65	11	0	2	21	.297	300	26	11	.967
1984—Indianapolis	A. A.	C	111	283	36	76	11	0	7	41	.269	588	54	6	★.991
1984—Montreal	Nat.	C	3	3	0	0	0	0	0	0	.000	9	0	0	1.000
1985—Indianapolis	A. A.	C	5	18	2	4	0	0	1	4	.222	27	4	0	1.000
1985—Montreal x	Nat.	C-P	67	120	11	24	1	0	3	12	.200	227	20	4	.984
American League Totals—4 Years			154	383	27	96	10	1	0	28	.251	604	77	19	.973
National League Totals—2 Years			70	123	11	24	1	0	3	12	.195	236	20	4	.985
Major League Totals—6 Years			224	506	38	120	11	1	3	40	.237	840	97	23	.976

Signed as free agent by Minnesota Twins' organization, May 15, 1972.

†Loaned to Sarasota White Sox (Chicago White Sox' organization), June 26, 1972; returned, September 14, 1972.

‡Traded to Detroit Tigers for Catcher Stine Poole, March 25, 1983.

§Released, October 21, 1983; signed by Indianapolis (Montreal Expos' organization), December 23, 1983.

xTraded with Pitcher Bill Gullickson to Cincinnati Reds for Pitchers Jay Tibbs, Andy McGaffigan and John Stuper and Catcher Dann Bilardello, December 19, 1985.

PITCHING RECORD

Year Club	League	G.	IP.	W.	L.	Pct.	H.	R.	ER.	SO.	BB.	ERA.
1985—Montreal	National	1	1	0	0	.000	0	0	0	0	0	0.00

BRETT MORGAN BUTLER

Born June 15, 1957, at Los Angeles, Calif.
Height, 5.10. Weight, 160.
Throws and bats lefthanded.
Attended Arizona State University, Tempe, Ariz., and received bachelor of science degree in education from Southeastern Oklahoma State University, Durant, Okla., in 1979.

Tied major league record for fewest double plays by outfielder, season, for leader in most double plays (4), 1983.
Major League stolen bases: 1981 (9), 1982 (21), 1983 (39), 1985 (47). Total—168.
Led American League in caught stealing with 22 in 1984 and 20 in 1985.
Tied for National League lead in double plays by outfielders with 4 in 1983.
Led International League in bases on balls received with 103 in 1981.
Named International League Most Valuable Player, 1981.

Year Club	League	Pos.	G.	AB.	R.	H.	2B.	3B.	HR.	RBI.	B.A.	PO.	A.	E.	F.A.
1979—Greenwood	W. Car.	OF	35	117	26	37	2	4	1	11	.316	45	2	0	1.000
1979—Dradenton	Gulf C.	OF	30	111	36	41	7	5	3	20	.369	66	5	0	1.000
1980—Anderson	S. Atl.	OF	70	255	73	76	12	6	1	26	.298	190	5	1	.995
1980—Durham	Carol.	OF	66	224	47	82	15	6	2	39	.366	156	4	3	.982
1981—Richmond	Int.	OF	125	466	★93	156	19	4	3	36	.335	286	15	3	.990
1981—Atlanta	Nat.	OF	40	126	17	32	2	3	0	4	.254	76	2	1	.987
1982—Atlanta	Nat.	OF	89	240	35	52	2	0	0	7	.217	129	2	0	1.000
1982—Richmond	Int.	OF	41	157	22	57	8	3	1	22	.363	101	2	1	.990
1983—Atlanta†	Nat.	OF	151	549	84	154	21	★13	5	37	.281	284	13	4	.987
1984—Cleveland	Amer.	OF	159	602	108	162	25	9	3	49	.269	448	13	4	.991
1985—Cleveland	Amer.	OF	152	591	106	184	28	14	5	50	.311	437	19	1	★.998
National League Totals—3 Years			280	915	136	238	25	16	5	48	.260	489	17	5	.990
American League Totals—2 Years			311	1193	214	346	53	23	8	99	.290	885	32	5	.995
Major League Totals—5 Years			591	2108	350	584	78	39	13	147	.277	1374	49	10	.993

Selected by Atlanta Braves' organization in 23rd round of free-agent draft, June 5, 1979.

†Traded with Infielder Brook Jacoby to Cleveland Indians, October 21, 1983, completing deal in which Atlanta Braves acquired Pitcher Len Barker for three players to be named later, August 28, 1983. Cleveland acquired Pitcher Rick Behenna as partial completion of deal, September 2, 1983.

CHAMPIONSHIP SERIES RECORD

Year Club	League	Pos.	G.	AB.	R.	H.	2B.	3B.	HR.	RBI.	B.A.	PO.	A.	E.	F.A.
1982—Atlanta	Nat.	OF-PH	2	1	0	0	0	0	0	0	.000	0	0	0	.000

MARTIN EUGENE BYSTROM
(Marty)

Born July 26, 1958, at Miami, Fla.
Height, 6.05. Weight, 210.
Throws and bats righthanded.
Attended Miami-Dade South Junior College, Miami, Fla.

Pitched 3-0 perfect game victory against Winston-Salem, August 12, 1978.
Led National League in hit batsmen with 7 in 1983.
Led American Association in balks with 5 and tied for lead in games started by pitchers with 26 in 1979.
Tied for Carolina League lead in complete games with 13 and shutouts with 5 in 1978.
Tied for Western Carolinas League lead in games started by pitchers with 27 in 1977.

Year Club	League	G.	IP.	W.	L.	Pct.	H.	R.	ER.	SO.	BB.	ERA.
1977—Spartanburg	W. Carol.	27	184	13	11	.542	★199	83	69	99	49	3.38
1978—Peninsula	Carolina	26	★197	●15	7	.682	170	71	62	★159	46	2.83
1979—Oklahoma City	Am. Assoc.	26	172	9	5	.643	174	102	78	108	69	4.08
1980—Oklahoma City†	Am. Assoc.	14	91	6	5	.545	89	49	37	68	27	3.66
1980—Philadelphia	National	6	36	5	0	1.000	26	6	6	21	9	1.50

Year Club	League	G.	IP.	W.	L.	Pct.	H.	R.	ER.	SO.	BB.	ERA.
1981—Philadelphia	National	9	54	4	3	.571	55	21	20	24	16	3.33
1981—Reading	Eastern	2	4	0	0	.000	5	2	2	2	1	4.50
1982—Philadelphia‡	National	19	89	5	6	.455	93	53	48	50	35	4.85
1983—Peninsula§	Carolina	1	6	1	0	1.000	5	1	0	9	1	0.00
1983—Philadelphia x	National	24	119⅓	6	9	.400	136	75	61	87	44	4.60
1984—Portland	P. Coast	5	22⅔	0	2	.000	26	17	14	10	9	5.56
1984—Philadelphia y	National	11	56⅔	4	4	.500	66	36	32	36	22	5.08
1984—New York z	American	7	39⅓	2	2	.500	34	16	13	24	13	2.97
1985—New York a	American	8	41	3	2	.600	44	29	26	16	19	5.71
1985—Columbus b	Int'national	4	24	2	0	1.000	13	7	5	16	9	1.88
National League Totals—5 Years		69	355	24	22	.522	376	191	167	218	126	4.23
American League Totals—2 Years		15	77⅓	5	4	.556	78	45	39	40	32	4.54
Major League Totals—6 Years		84	435⅓	29	26	.527	454	236	206	258	158	4.26

Signed as free agent by Philadelphia Phillies' organization, December 15, 1976.
†On disabled list, April 14 to May 16 and May 27 to June 12, 1980.
‡On disabled list, March 22 to June 8, 1982.
§On Philadelphia disabled list, March 27 to May 3, 1983; included rehabilitation disability assignment to Peninsula, April 28 to May 3, 1983.
xOn disabled list, August 21 to September 11, 1983.
yTraded with Outfielder Keith Hughes to New York Yankees for Pitcher Shane Rawley, June 30, 1984.
zOn disabled list, August 1 to September 3, 1984.
aOn disabled list, April 8 to July 23, 1985, included rehabilitation disability assignment to Columbus, June 16 to July 5, 1985.
bGranted free agency, November 12, 1985; re-signed by Yankees, November 13, 1985.

CHAMPIONSHIP SERIES RECORD

Year Club	League	G.	IP.	W.	L.	Pct.	H.	R.	ER.	SO.	BB.	ERA.
1980—Philadelphia	National	1	5⅓	0	0	.000	7	2	1	1	2	1.69

WORLD SERIES RECORD

Year Club	League	G.	IP.	W.	L.	Pct.	H.	R.	ER.	SO.	BB.	ERA.
1980—Philadelphia	National	1	5	0	0	.000	10	3	3	4	1	5.40
1983—Philadelphia	National	1	1	0	0	.000	0	0	0	1	0	0.00
World Series Totals—2 Years		2	6	0	0	.000	10	3	3	5	1	4.50

ENOS MILTON CABELL JR.

Name pronounced Kuh-BELL.

Born October 8, 1949, at Fort Riley, Kan.
Height, 6.05. Weight, 185.
Throws and bats righthanded.
Attended Los Angeles Harbor Junior College, Wilmington, Calif.
Cousin of Dick Davis, outfielder with Milwaukee Brewers, Philadelphia Phillies,
Pittsburgh Pirates and Toronto Blue Jays, 1977 through 1982, and currently with Kintetsu Buffaloes
of Japanese Baseball; and Ken Landreaux, outfielder with Los Angeles Dodgers.

Major League stolen bases: 1973 (1), 1974 (5), 1975 (12), 1976 (35), 1977 (42), 1978 (33), 1979 (37), 1980 (21), 1981 (6), 1982 (15), 1983 (3), 1984 (8), 1985 (9). Total—227.
Led National League third basemen in putouts with 140 and errors with 23 in 1977.
Led Appalachian League in total bases with 149 in 1969.
Led International League first basemen in assists with 90 and fielding percentage with .990 in 1972.
Led Texas League first basemen in assists with 121 in 1971.
Led California League first basemen in assists with 80 and errors with 26 in 1970.
Named Texas League Player of the Year, 1971.
Named Appalachian League Player of the Year, 1969.

Year Club	League	Pos.	G.	AB.	R.	H.	2B.	3B.	HR.	RBI.	B.A.	PO.	A.	E.	F.A.
1969—Bluefield	Appal.	1B	●69	★270	★62	★101	14	2	10	43	.374	★471	30	9	.982
1970—Stockton	Calif.	1B-OF	138	517	78	147	25	6	10	67	.284	844	81	33	.966
1971—Dall-Ft. Worth	Texas	●1-3-O	140	521	65	★162	24	6	6	79	★.311	1135	122	●20	.984
1972—Rochester	Int.	1-O-3-S	141	★540	82	145	26	9	8	66	.269	893	110	11	.989
1972—Baltimore	Amer.	1B	3	5	0	0	0	0	0	1	.000	7	0	0	1.000
1973—Rochester	Int.	1B-3B-2B	60	229	43	81	9	1	2	24	.354	510	47	10	.982
1973—Baltimore	Amer.	1B-3B	32	47	12	10	2	0	1	3	.213	111	4	1	.991
1974—Baltimore†	Amer.	1-O-3-2	80	174	24	42	4	2	3	17	.241	223	45	4	.985
1975—Houston	Nat.	OF-1B-3B	117	348	43	92	17	6	2	43	.264	197	58	6	.977
1976—Houston	Nat.	3B-1B	144	586	85	160	13	7	2	43	.273	263	17	959	.959
1977—Houston	Nat.	3B-1B-SS	150	625	101	176	36	7	16	68	.282	176	288	24	.951
1978—Houston	Nat.	3B-1B-SS	●162	★660	92	195	31	8	7	71	.295	211	277	18	.964
1979—Houston	Nat.	3B-1B	155	603	60	164	30	5	6	67	.272	396	199	14	.977
1980—Houston‡	Nat.	★3B-1B	152	604	69	167	23	8	2	55	.276	118	250	★29	.927
1981—San Francisco§	Nat.	1B-3B	96	396	41	101	20	1	2	36	.255	634	90	16	.978
1982—Detroit	Amer.	1B-3B-OF	125	464	45	121	17	3	2	37	.261	592	143	16	.979
1983—Detroit x	Amer.	1B-3B-SS	121	392	62	122	23	5	5	46	.311	830	79	3	.997
1984—Houston	Nat.	1B	127	436	52	135	17	3	8	44	.310	971	66	7	.993
1985—Hous.y-L.A.	Nat.	1B-3B-OF	117	335	40	91	19	1	2	36	.272	456	97	11	.980
American League Totals—5 Years			361	1082	143	295	46	10	11	104	.273	1763	271	24	.988
National League Totals—9 Years			1220	4593	583	1281	206	46	47	463	.279	3290	1588	142	.972
Major League Totals—14 Years			1581	5675	726	1576	252	56	58	567	.278	5053	1859	166	.977

Signed as free agent by Baltimore Orioles' organization, September 22, 1968.

†Traded with Second Baseman Rob Andrews to Houston Astros for First Baseman Lee May and Outfielder Jay Schlueter, December 3, 1974.
‡Traded to San Francisco Giants for Outfielder Chris Bourjos and Pitcher Bob Knepper, December 8, 1980.
§Traded with cash to Detroit Tigers for Outfielder Champ Summers, March 4, 1982.
xGranted free agency, November 7, 1983; signed by Houston Astros, February 14, 1984.
yTraded to Los Angeles Dodgers for Pitcher Rafael Montalvo and a player to be named later, July 10, 1985; Houston Astros' organization acquired Third Baseman German Rivera to complete deal, July 15, 1985.

CHAMPIONSHIP SERIES RECORD

Tied Championship Series record for most clubs, total Series (3).

Year Club	League	Pos.	G.	AB.	R.	H.	2B.	3B.	HR.	RBI.	B.A.	PO.	A.	E.	F.A.
1974—Baltimore .... Amer.		O-PH-PR	3	4	0	1	0	0	0	0	.250	2	0	0	1.000
1980—Houston .... Nat.		3B	5	21	1	5	1	0	0	0	.238	1	9	0	1.000
1985—Los Angeles .... Nat.		1B-PH	5	13	1	1	0	0	0	0	.077	20	3	0	1.000
Championship Series Totals—3 Years.....			13	38	2	7	1	0	0	0	.184	23	12	0	1.000

IVAN CALDERON (PEREZ)

Name pronounced Call-durh-OWN.

Born March 19, 1962, at Fajardo, Puerto Rico.
Height, 5.11. Weight, 160.
Throws and bats righthanded.

Major League stolen bases: 1984 (1), 1985 (4). Total—5.
Tied for Southern League lead in total bases with 267 in 1983.

Year Club	League	Pos.	G.	AB.	R.	H.	2B.	3B.	HR.	RBI.	B.A.	PO.	A.	E.	F.A.
1980—Bellingham .... N'west		OF	57	195	44	62	7	★9	4	32	.318	56	4	7	.896
1981—Wausau.................. Midw.		OF-SS	117	402	79	123	19	1	20	62	.306	130	17	6	.961
1982—Wausau.................. Midw.		S-O-3-1	126	461	91	132	22	5	24	89	.286	215	202	45	.903
1983—Chattanooga .... South.		OF	139	546	92	●170	34	★15	11	80	★.311	251	10	13	.953
1984—Salt Lake City†..... P. C.		OF	66	255	61	93	7	9	4	45	.365	132	9	8	.946
1984—Seattle‡................ Amer.		OF	11	24	2	5	1	0	1	1	.208	22	0	0	1.000
1985—Seattle.................. Amer.		OF-1B	67	210	37	60	16	4	8	28	.286	108	5	2	.983
Major League Totals—2 Years................			78	234	39	65	17	4	9	29	.278	130	5	2	.985

Signed as free agent by Seattle Mariners' organization, July 30, 1979.
†On disabled list, May 25 to July 2, 1984.
‡On disabled list, August 26 to September 12, 1984.

JEFFREY WILTON CALHOUN
(Jeff)

Born April 11, 1958, at LaGrange, Ga.
Height, 6.02. Weight, 190.
Throws and bats lefthanded.
Received degree from University of Mississippi, University, Miss. in 1980.

Major League saves: 1985 (4).
Led Florida State League in wild pitches with 17 in 1982.

Year Club	League	G.	IP.	W.	L.	Pct.	H.	R.	ER.	SO.	BB.	ERA.
1980—Sarasota Astros............................ Gulf Coast		8	50	2	2	.500	38	18	10	41	21	1.80
1981—Daytona Beach† .... Florida St.		21	111	6	6	.500	106	55	46	94	71	3.73
1982—Columbus..................................... Southern		7	34⅔	1	3	.250	44	35	22	32	28	5.71
1982—Daytona Beach .... Florida St.		21	116⅓	9	6	.600	126	71	60	62	55	4.64
1983—Columbus..................................... Southern		27	151⅓	6	11	.353	157	103	78	93	83	4.64
1984—Columbus..................................... Southern		37	63⅔	4	2	.667	52	21	20	51	26	2.83
1984—Tucson... P. Coast		14	21⅔	1	1	.500	16	4	4	20	12	1.66
1984—Houston....................................... National		9	15⅓	0	1	.000	5	3	2	11	2	1.17
1985—Houston‡..................................... National		44	63⅔	2	5	.286	56	21	18	47	24	2.54
Major League Totals—2 Years..........................		53	79	2	6	.250	61	24	20	58	26	2.28

Selected by California Angels' organization in 28th round of free-agent draft, June 8, 1976.
Selected by Houston Astros' organization in 3rd round of free-agent draft, June 3, 1980.
†On disabled list, May 4 to May 16, 1981.
‡On disabled list, June 7 to June 22, 1985.

ERNIE CARLOS CAMACHO

Born February 1, 1956, at Salinas, Calif.
Height, 6.01. Weight, 180.
Throws and bats righthanded.
Attended Hartnell Junior College, Salinas, Calif.

Major League saves: 1984 (23).

Year Club	League	G.	IP.	W.	L.	Pct.	H.	R.	ER.	SO.	BB.	ERA.
1976—Modesto....................................... California		10	56	3	4	.429	69	47	35	29	39	5.63
1977—Modesto†..................................... California		5	32	2	1	.667	30	19	14	21	23	3.94
1977—Chattanooga .... Southern		11	60	3	8	.273	74	50	43	20	28	6.45
1978—Modesto‡..................................... California		1	2	0	0	.000	0	0	0	2	2	0.00
1979—Ogden .... P. Coast		21	97	7	9	.438	102	86	71	60	70	6.59
1980—Ogden .... P. Coast		33	64	5	3	.625	60	29	28	58	26	3.94

Year Club	League	G.	IP.	W.	L.	Pct.	H.	R.	ER.	SO.	BB.	ERA.
1980—Oakland§	American	5	12	0	0	.000	20	9	9	9	5	6.75
1981—Portland x	P. Coast	18	38	2	3	.400	45	24	20	31	22	4.74
1981—Pittsburgh y	National	7	22	0	1	.000	23	13	12	11	15	4.91
1982—Edmonton zab	P. Coast	7	19⅔	0	0	.000	10	8	7	18	16	3.20
1982—Mexico City Reds	Mexican	15	20⅓	3	1	.750	21	12	12	15	6	5.31
1982—Rochester c	Int'national	8	17⅔	0	1	.000	16	7	4	11	10	2.04
1983—Vancouver d	P. Coast	11	23⅔	0	2	.000	31	21	18	16	12	6.85
1983—Charleston	Int'national	24	33⅓	4	0	1.000	19	5	5	27	17	1.35
1983—Cleveland	American	4	5⅓	0	1	.000	5	3	3	2	2	5.06
1984—Cleveland	American	69	100	5	9	.357	83	31	27	48	37	2.43
1985—Cleveland e	American	2	3⅓	0	1	.000	4	3	3	2	1	8.10
American League Totals—4 Years		80	120⅔	5	11	.313	112	46	42	61	45	3.13
National League Totals—1 Year		7	22	0	1	.000	23	13	12	11	15	4.91
Major League Totals—5 Years		87	142⅔	5	12	.294	135	59	54	72	60	3.41

Selected by Pittsburgh Pirates' organization in 12th round of free-agent draft, June 4, 1975.
Selected by California Angels' organization in secondary phase of free-agent draft, January 7, 1976.
Selected by Oakland A's organization in secondary phase of free-agent draft, June 8, 1976.
†On disabled list, April 23 to June 14, 1977.
‡On Jersey City temporary inactive list, April 14 to July 18, 1978; on Modesto temporary inactive list, July 18 to August 30, 1978.
§Traded to Pittsburgh Pirates, April 10, 1981, completing deal in which Pittsburgh traded Pitcher Bob Owchinko to Oakland A's for cash and player to be named later, April 6, 1981.
xOn disabled list, June 23 to July 15, 1981.
yTraded with Infielder Vance Law to Chicago White Sox for Pitchers Ross Baumgarten and Butch Edge, March 21, 1982.
zOn suspended list, April 5 to April 25, 1982.
aLoaned to Mexico City Reds, May 16, 1982; returned, August 2, 1982.
bLoaned to Rochester (Baltimore Orioles' organization), August 5, 1982; returned, September 17, 1982.
cGranted free agency, October 22, 1982; signed by Vancouver (Milwaukee Brewers' organization), December 19, 1982.
dTraded with Outfielder Gorman Thomas and Pitcher Jamie Easterly to Cleveland Indians for Outfielder Rick Manning and Pitcher Rick Waits, June 6, 1983.
eOn disabled list, April 13, 1985 through remainder of season.

RICK LAMAR CAMP

Born June 10, 1953, at Trion, Ga.
Height, 6.01. Weight, 198.
Throws and bats righthanded.
Attended West Georgia College, Carrollton, Ga.
Major League saves: 1977 (10), 1980 (22), 1981 (17), 1982 (5), 1985 (3). Total—57.
Led International League in balks with 5 in 1976.

Year Club	League	G.	IP.	W.	L.	Pct.	H.	R.	ER.	SO.	BB.	ERA.
1974—Kingsport	Ap'lachian	7	43	3	2	.600	44	23	15	52	16	3.14
1975—Savannah	Southern	25	176	12	10	.545	161	68	56	100	62	2.86
1976—Richmond	Int'national	49	164	10	11	.476	177	90	78	85	68	4.28
1976—Atlanta	National	5	11	0	1	.000	13	9	8	6	2	6.55
1977—Atlanta†	National	54	79	6	3	.667	89	47	35	51	47	3.99
1978—Atlanta	National	42	74	2	4	.333	99	42	31	23	32	3.77
1979—Richmond‡	Int'national	22	55	3	2	.600	59	31	26	33	12	4.25
1980—Atlanta	National	77	108	6	4	.600	92	26	23	33	29	1.92
1981—Atlanta	National	48	76	9	3	.750	68	17	15	47	12	1.78
1982—Atlanta	National	51	177⅓	11	13	.458	199	84	72	68	52	3.65
1983—Atlanta	National	40	140	10	9	.526	146	64	59	61	38	3.79
1984—Atlanta§	National	31	148⅔	8	6	.571	134	59	54	69	63	3.27
1985—Atlanta	National	66	127⅔	4	6	.400	130	72	56	49	61	3.95
Major League Totals—9 Years		414	941⅔	56	49	.533	970	420	353	407	336	3.37

Selected by Atlanta Braves' organization in 7th round of free-agent draft, June 5, 1974.
†On disabled list, July 28 to September 1, 1977.
‡On disabled list, April 13 to May 7 and August 7 to August 27, 1979.
§On disabled list, May 25 to June 9, 1984.

CHAMPIONSHIP SERIES RECORD

Year Club	League	G.	IP.	W.	L.	Pct.	H.	R.	ER.	SO.	BB.	ERA.
1982—Atlanta	National	1	1	0	1	.000	4	4	4	0	1	36.00

WILLIAM RICHARD CAMPBELL
(Bill)

Born August 9, 1948, at Highland Park, Mich.
Height, 6.04. Weight, 200.
Throws and bats righthanded.
Attended Mount San Antonio Junior College, Walnut, Calif.
Tied American League record for most games won, season, all as relief pitcher (17), 1976.
Major League saves: 1973 (7), 1974 (19), 1975 (5), 1976 (20), 1977 (31), 1978 (4), 1979 (9), 1981 (7), 1982 (8), 1983 (8), 1984 (1), 1985 (4). Total—123.
Led National League in intentional bases on balls issued with 18 in 1983.
Led American League in saves with 31 in 1977.

Led American League in games finished in relief with 68 in 1976 and tied for lead with 60 in 1977.
Led Southern League in complete games with 14 and tied for lead in games started by pitchers with 29 in 1972.
Named American League Fireman of the Year by THE SPORTING NEWS, 1976 and 1977.
Named Southern League Pitcher of the Year, 1972.

Year	Club	League	G.	IP.	W.	L.	Pct.	H.	R.	ER.	SO.	BB.	ERA.
1971—Wisconsin Rapids†	Midwest		9	63	5	3	.625	42	43	8	91	19	1.14
1972—Charlotte	Southern		29	219	13	10	.565	181	74	59	*204	69	2.42
1973—Tacoma	P. Coast		18	133	10	5	.667	123	63	54	110	46	3.65
1973—Minnesota	American		28	52	3	3	.500	44	20	18	42	20	3.12
1974—Minnesota	American		63	120	8	7	.533	109	37	35	89	55	2.63
1975—Minnesota	American		47	121	4	6	.400	119	58	51	76	46	3.79
1976—Minnesota‡	American		*78	168	17	5	*.773	145	63	56	115	62	3.00
1977—Boston	American		69	140	13	9	.591	112	48	46	114	60	2.96
1978—Boston	American		29	51	7	5	.583	62	25	22	47	17	3.88
1979—Boston	American		41	55	3	4	.429	55	28	26	25	23	4.25
1980—Boston§	American		23	41	4	0	1.000	44	26	22	17	22	4.83
1981—Boston x	American		30	48	1	1	.500	45	23	17	37	20	3.19
1982—Chicago	National		62	100	3	6	.333	89	44	41	71	40	3.69
1983—Chicago y	National		*82	121⅓	6	8	.429	128	65	61	97	49	4.49
1984—Philadelphia z	National		57	81⅓	6	5	.545	68	43	31	52	35	3.43
1985—St. Louis a	National		50	64⅓	5	3	.625	55	32	25	41	21	3.50
American League Totals—9 Years			408	796	60	40	.600	735	328	293	562	325	3.31
National League Totals—4 Years			251	368	20	22	.476	340	184	158	261	145	3.86
Major League Totals—13 Years			659	1164	80	62	.563	1075	512	451	823	470	3.49

Signed as free agent by Minnesota Twins' organization, September 25, 1970.
†On disabled list, June 14, 1971 through remainder of season.
‡Granted free agency, November 1, 1976; signed by Boston Red Sox, November 6, 1976.
§On disabled list, March 25 to June 20, 1980.
xGranted free agency, November 13, 1981; signed by Chicago Cubs, December 8, 1981.
yTraded with Catcher Mike Diaz to Philadelphia Phillies for Outfielders Bob Dernier and Gary Matthews and Pitcher Porfi Altamirano, March 27, 1984.
zTraded with Shortstop Ivan DeJesus to St. Louis Cardinals for Pitcher Dave Rucker, April 6, 1985.
aReleased, November 14, 1985.

CHAMPIONSHIP SERIES RECORD

Year	Club	League	G.	IP.	W.	L.	Pct.	H.	R.	ER.	SO.	BB.	ERA.
1985—St. Louis	National		3	2⅓	0	0	.000	3	0	0	2	0	0.00

WORLD SERIES RECORD

Year	Club	League	G.	IP.	W.	L.	Pct.	H.	R.	ER.	SO.	BB.	ERA.
1985—St. Louis	National		3	4	0	0	.000	4	1	1	5	2	2.25

ALL-STAR GAME RECORD

Year	League	IP.	W.	L.	Pct.	H.	R.	ER.	SO.	BB.	ERA.
1977—American		1	0	0	.000	0	0	0	2	1	0.00

SILVESTRE CAMPUSANO
(Sil)

Born December 31, 1966, at Mano Guayabo, D.R.
Height, 6.00. Weight, 160.
Throws and bats righthanded.

Tied for Gulf Coast League lead in stolen bases with 21 in 1984.
Led South Atlantic League outfielders in double plays with 5 in 1985.
Named South Atlantic League Most Valuable Player, 1985.

Year	Club	League	Pos.	G.	AB.	R.	H.	2B.	3B.	HR.	RBI.	B.A.	PO.	A.	E.	F.A.
1984—Bradenton Jays	Appal.	OF	●63	236	42	63	17	2	0	22	.267	128	7	*8	.944
1985—Florence	S. Atl.	OF	88	348	80	109	31	1	15	56	.313	188	12	4	.980
1985—Knoxville	South.	OF	45	178	30	54	9	0	6	29	.303	135	3	4	.972

Signed as free agent by Toronto Blue Jays' organization, November 14, 1983.

JOHN ROBERT CANDELARIA

Born November 6, 1953, at Brooklyn, N.Y.
Height, 6.07. Weight, 250.
Throws left and bats right and lefthanded.

Pitched 2-0 no-hit victory against Los Angeles Dodgers, August 9, 1976.
Major League saves: 1976 (1), 1978 (1), 1980 (1), 1982 (1), 1984 (2), 1985 (9). Total—15.
Tied for National League lead in home runs allowed with 29 in 1977.
Led Carolina League in home runs allowed with 17 in 1974.
Received reported $40,000 bonus to sign with Pittsburgh Pirates, 1973.

Year	Club	League	G.	IP.	W.	L.	Pct.	H.	R.	ER.	SO.	BB.	ERA.
1973—Charleston	W. Carol.		18	95	10	2	*.833	84	45	40	60	38	3.79
1974—Salem	Carolina		25	154	11	8	.579	146	80	63	147	63	3.68
1974—Charleston	Int'national		1	11	0	0	.000	7	2	2	10	1	1.64
1975—Charleston	Int'national		10	61	7	1	.875	53	15	12	48	17	1.77
1975—Pittsburgh	National		18	121	8	6	.571	95	47	37	95	36	2.75
1976—Pittsburgh	National		32	220	16	7	.696	173	87	77	138	60	3.15
1977—Pittsburgh	National		33	231	20	5	*.800	197	64	60	133	52	*2.34

Year	Club	League	G.	IP.	W.	L.	Pct.	H.	R.	ER.	SO.	BB.	ERA.
1978—Pittsburgh	National	30	189	12	11	.522	191	73	68	94	49	3.24
1979—Pittsburgh	National	33	207	14	9	.609	201	83	74	101	41	3.22
1980—Pittsburgh	National	35	233	11	14	.440	246	114	104	97	50	4.02
1981—Pittsburgh†	National	6	41	2	2	.500	42	17	16	14	11	3.51
1982—Pittsburgh	National	31	174⅔	12	7	.632	166	62	57	133	37	2.94
1983—Pittsburgh	National	33	197⅔	15	8	.652	191	73	71	157	45	3.23
1984—Pittsburgh	National	33	185⅓	12	11	.522	179	69	56	133	34	2.72
1985—Pittsburgh‡	National	37	54⅓	2	4	.333	57	23	22	47	14	3.64
1985—California	American	13	71	7	3	.700	70	33	30	53	24	3.80
National League Totals—11 Years		321	1854	124	84	.596	1738	712	642	1142	427	3.12
American League Totals—1 Year		13	71	7	3	.700	70	33	30	53	24	3.80
Major League Totals—11 Years		334	1925	131	87	.601	1808	745	672	1195	451	3.14

Selected by Pittsburgh Pirates' organization in 2nd round of free-agent draft, June 6, 1972.

†On disabled list, May 11, 1981 through remainder of season.

‡Traded with Pitcher Al Holland and Outfielder George Hendrick to California Angels for Pitcher Pat Clements, Outfielder Mike Brown and a player to be named later, August 2, 1985; Pittsburgh Pirates' organization acquired Pitcher Bob Kipper to complete deal, August 16, 1985.

CHAMPIONSHIP SERIES RECORD

Established Championship Series record for most strikeouts, three-game Series (14), 1975.

Tied Championship Series records for most strikeouts, game (14), October 7, 1975, most consecutive strikeouts, start of game (4), October 7, 1975.

Year	Club	League	G.	IP.	W.	L.	Pct.	H.	R.	ER.	SO.	BB.	ERA.
1975—Pittsburgh	National	1	7⅔	0	0	.000	3	3	3	14	2	3.52
1979—Pittsburgh	National	1	7	0	0	.000	5	2	2	4	1	2.57
Championship Series Totals—2 Years		2	14⅔	0	0	.000	8	5	5	18	3	3.07

WORLD SERIES RECORD

Year	Club	League	G.	IP.	W.	L.	Pct.	H.	R.	ER.	SO.	BB.	ERA.
1979—Pittsburgh	National	2	9	1	1	.500	14	6	5	4	2	5.00

ALL-STAR GAME RECORD

Member of National League All-Star Team in 1977; did not play.

THOMAS CAESAR CANDIOTTI
(Tom)

Born August 31, 1957, at Walnut Creek, Calif.
Height, 6.03. Weight, 205.
Throws and bats righthanded.
Received bachelor of science degree in business administration
from St. Mary's College, Moraga, Calif., in 1979.

Year	Club	League	G.	IP.	W.	L.	Pct.	H.	R.	ER.	SO.	BB.	ERA.
1979—Victoria†	Northwest	12	70	5	1	.833	63	23	19	66	16	2.44
1980—Fort Myers	Florida St.	7	44	3	2	.600	32	16	11	31	9	2.25
1980—Jacksonville‡§	Southern	17	117	7	8	.467	98	45	36	93	40	2.77
1981—El Paso x	Texas	21	119	7	6	.538	137	51	37	68	27	2.80
1982—Vancouver y	P. Coast					(Did not play)						
1983—El Paso	Texas	7	24⅔	1	0	1.000	23	10	8	18	7	2.92
1983—Vancouver	P. Coast	15	99⅓	6	4	.600	87	35	31	61	16	2.81
1983—Milwaukee	American	10	55⅔	4	4	.500	62	21	20	21	16	3.23
1984—Vancouver z	P. Coast	15	96⅔	8	4	.667	96	36	31	53	22	2.89
1984—Milwaukee a	American	8	32⅓	2	2	.500	38	21	19	23	10	5.29
1984—Beloit	Midwest	2	10	0	1	.000	12	5	3	12	5	2.70
1985—El Paso	Texas	4	29⅓	1	0	1.000	29	11	9	16	7	2.76
1985—Vancouver b	P. Coast	24	150⅔	9	13	.409	178	83	66	97	36	3.94
Major League Totals—2 Years		18	88	6	6	.500	100	42	39	44	26	3.99

Signed as free-agent by Victoria (Independent), July 17, 1979.

†Released, January 4, 1980; signed by Ft. Myers (Kansas City Royals' organization), January 5, 1980.

‡On disabled list, June 7 to June 26, 1980.

§Drafted by Vancouver (Milwaukee Brewers' organization), December 9, 1980.

xOn disabled list, April 10 to May 12, 1981.

yOn disabled list, April 13, 1982 through remainder of season.

zOn disabled list, May 30 to June 15, 1984.

aOn disabled list, August 2 to September 1, 1984; included rehabilitation disability assignment to Beloit, August 24 to August 31, 1984.

bGranted free agency, October 15, 1985; signed by Cleveland Indians, December 12, 1985.

JOHN ANTHONY CANGELOSI

Born March 10, 1963, at Brooklyn, N.Y.
Height, 5.08. Weight, 150.
Throws left and bats right and lefthanded.
Attended Miami-Dade Community College (North), Miami, Fla.

Led Eastern League in bases on balls received with 101 in 1984.
Led Midwest League in stolen bases with 87 and caught stealing with 35 in 1983.
Tied for New York-Pennsylvania League lead in bases on balls received with 56 in 1982.

Year Club	League	Pos.	G.	AB.	R.	H.	2B.	3B.	HR.	RBI.	B.A.	PO.	A.	E.	F.A.
1982—Niagara Falls	NYP	OF	●76	277	60	80	15	4	5	38	.289	118	5	4	.969
1983—Appleton	Midw.	OF	128	439	87	124	12	4	1	48	.282	262	10	6	.978
1984—Glens Falls†	East.	OF	138	464	91	133	17	1	1	38	.287	310	11	11	.967
1985—Mex. City Reds.....	Mex.	OF	61	201	46	71	9	4	1	30	.353	127	7	6	.957
1985—Chicago	Amer.	OF	5	2	2	0	0	0	0	0	.000	1	0	0	1.000
1985—Buffalo..................	A. A.	OF	78	244	34	58	8	5	1	21	.238	148	9	2	.987
Major League Totals—1 Year..................			5	2	2	0	0	0	0	0	.000	1	0	0	1.000

Selected by Chicago White Sox' organization in 4th round of free-agent draft, January 12, 1982.

†Loaned with Infielder Manny Salinas to Mexico City Reds, March 4, 1985, as part of deal in which Infielder Nelson Barrera was purchased by Chicago White Sox; returned, June 1, 1985.

JOSE CANSECO

Born July 2, 1964, at Havana, Cuba.
Height, 6.03. Weight, 215.
Throws and bats righthanded.
Twin brother of Ozzie Canseco, pitcher in New York Yankees' organization.

Major League stolen bases: 1985 (1).
Led Northwest League batters in strikeouts with 78 in 1983.
Led California League outfielders in double plays with 8 in 1984.
Named Minor League Player of the Year by THE SPORTING NEWS, 1985.
Named Southern League Most Valuable Player, 1985.

Year Club	League	Pos.	G.	AB.	R.	H.	2B.	3B.	HR.	RBI.	B.A.	PO.	A.	E.	F.A.
1982—Miami....................	Fla. St.	3B	6	9	0	1	0	0	0	0	.111	3	1	1	.800
1982—Idaho Falls...........	Pion.	3B-OF	28	57	13	15	3	0	2	7	.263	6	17	3	.885
1983—Madison	Midw.	OF	34	88	8	14	4	0	3	10	.159	23	2	1	.962
1983—Medford	N'west	OF	59	197	34	53	15	2	11	40	.269	46	5	5	.911
1984—Modesto.................	Calif.	OF	116	410	61	113	21	2	15	73	.276	216	17	9	.963
1985—Huntsville†...........	South.	OF	58	211	47	67	10	2	25	80	.318	117	9	7	.947
1985—Tacoma.................	P.C.	OF	60	233	41	81	16	1	11	47	.348	81	7	2	.978
1985—Oakland.................	Amer.	OF	29	96	16	29	3	0	5	13	.302	56	2	3	.951
Major League Total—1 Year			29	96	16	29	3	0	5	13	.302	56	2	3	.951

Selected by Oakland A's organization in 15th round of free-agent draft, June 7, 1982.
†On disabled list, May 14 to June 3, 1985.

NICK LEE CAPRA

Born March 8, 1958, at Denver, Colo.
Height, 5.08. Weight, 165.
Throws and bats righthanded.
Attended Blinn College, Brenham, Tex., Lamar Community College, Lamar, Colo. and University of Oklahoma, Norman, Okla.

Major League stolen bases: 1982 (2).
Led Texas League in stolen bases with 55 and tied for lead in game-winning RBIs with 13 in 1980.
Led American Association outfielders in total chances with 330 in 1983.
Named second baseman on THE SPORTING NEWS College Baseball All-America Team 1979.

Year Club	League	Pos.	G.	AB.	R.	H.	2B.	3B.	HR.	RBI.	B.A.	PO.	A.	E.	F.A.
1979—Tulsa†	Texas	3B-2B-SS	66	212	29	59	7	0	3	26	.278	60	173	22	.914
1980—Tulsa	Texas	2B-OF-SS	117	440	90	127	25	9	6	53	.289	288	303	19	.969
1981—Wichita..................	A. A.	OF	123	398	74	104	16	4	4	38	.261	226	6	7	.971
1982—Denver	A. A.	OF	121	416	82	117	15	10	9	40	.281	275	11	3	.990
1982—Texas.....................	Amer.	OF	13	15	2	4	0	0	1	1	.267	14	2	0	1.000
1983—Oklahoma City	A. A.	OF	124	441	84	113	17	4	13	41	.256	★307	12	11	.967
1983—Texas.....................	Amer.	OF	8	2	2	0	0	0	0	0	.000	0	0	0	.000
1984—Oklahoma City‡...	A. A.	OF-2B	123	442	68	113	18	1	2	21	.256	329	13	4	.988
1985—Oklahoma City	A. A.	OF-2B	97	353	53	96	17	1	0	27	.272	201	70	2	.993
1985—Texas§	Amer.	OF	8	8	1	1	0	0	0	0	.125	11	0	0	1.000
Major League Totals—3 Years.................			29	25	5	5	0	0	1	1	.200	25	2	0	1.000

Selected by Montreal Expos' organization in 12th round of free-agent draft, June 8, 1976.
Selected by Texas Rangers' organization in 3rd round of free-agent draft, June 5, 1979.
†On disabled list, July 4 to July 19, 1979.
‡On disabled list, May 14 to June 1, 1984.
§Granted free agency, October 15, 1985.

RAMON ANTONIO CARABALLO (LECLER)

Born August 20, 1962, at Loma de Cabrera, Dominican Republic.
Height, 6.04. Weight, 200.
Throws and bats righthanded.

Led South Atlantic League in games finished in relief with 46 in 1984.
Named South Atlantic League Pitcher of the Year, 1984.

Year Club	League	G.	IP.	W.	L.	Pct.	H.	R.	ER.	SO.	BB.	ERA.
1982—Helena..	Pioneer	17	31⅓	0	1	.000	29	22	12	21	14	3.45
1983—Bend..	Northwest	21	35⅔	2	3	.400	29	19	14	24	19	3.53
1984—Spartanburg....................................	S. Atlantic	52	70	6	2	.750	55	24	17	44	18	2.19
1984—Peninsula...	Carolina	1	1	0	0	.000	0	0	0	0	0	0.00
1985—Reading†..	Eastern	4	4⅓	0	0	.000	7	4	3	3	4	6.23

Signed as free agent by Philadelphia Phillies' organization, June 10, 1982.
†On disabled list, April 16 to April 26, April 30 to June 5 and June 13, 1985 through remainder of season.

RODNEY CLINE CAREW
(Rod)

Born October 1, 1945, at Gatun, Panama.
Height, 6.00. Weight, 182.
Throws right and bats lefthanded.

Tied major league records for most times stealing home, season (7), 1969; most stolen bases, inning (3), May 18, 1969 (3rd inning); most home runs with bases filled by pinch-hitter, game (1), September 9, 1976.

Established American League record for most games, one or more hits, season (131), 1977.

Tied American League records for most double plays, first baseman, extra-inning game (6), August 29, 1977 (1st game, 10 innings); most putouts by first baseman, game (32), April 13, 1982 (20 innings); most chances accepted by first baseman, game (34), April 13, 1982 (20 innings); most seasons leading league, intentional bases on balls (3).

Major League stolen bases: 1967 (5), 1968 (12), 1969 (19), 1970 (4), 1971 (6), 1972 (12), 1973 (41), 1974 (38), 1975 (35), 1976 (49), 1977 (23), 1978 (27), 1979 (18), 1980 (23), 1981 (16), 1982 (10), 1983 (6), 1984 (5), 1985 (5). Total—353.

Hit for the cycle, May 20, 1970.

Led American League in intentional bases on balls received with 18 in 1975, 15 in 1977 and 19 in 1978.

Led American League first basemen in double plays with 149 in 1976 and 161 in 1977.

Led American League first basemen in assists with 121 in 1977.

Led American League first basemen in total chances with 1,590 in 1977.

Named Major League Player of the Year by THE SPORTING NEWS, 1977.

Named American League Player of the Year by THE SPORTING NEWS, 1977.

Named American League Most Valuable Player by Baseball Writers' Association of America, 1977.

Named American League Rookie Player of the Year by THE SPORTING NEWS, 1967.

Named American League Rookie of the Year by Baseball Writers' Association of America, 1967.

Named first baseman on THE SPORTING NEWS American League All-Star Team, 1977 and 1978.

Named second baseman on THE SPORTING NEWS American League All-Star Team, 1967 through 1969 and 1972 through 1975.

Year—Club	League	Pos.	G.	AB.	R.	H.	2B.	3B.	HR.	RBI.	B.A.	PO.	A.	E.	F.A.
1964—Melbourne Twins	Coc. Rk.	2B	37	123	17	40	5	●3	0	21	.325	86	48	7	.950
1965—Orlando	Fla. St.	2B	125	439	57	133	20	8	1	52	.303	290	328	●28	.957
1966—Wilson	Carol.	2B	112	383	64	112	19	3	1	30	.292	248	275	21	.961
1967—Minnesota†	Amer.	2B	137	514	66	150	22	7	8	51	.292	289	314	15	.976
1968—Minnesota‡	Amer.	●2B-SS	127	461	46	126	27	2	1	42	.273	266	285	●18	.968
1969—Minnesota§	Amer.	2B	123	458	79	152	30	4	8	56	★.332	244	302	17	.970
1970—Minnesota x	Amer.	2B-1B	51	191	27	70	12	3	4	28	.366	79	122	8	.962
1971—Minnesota	Amer.	2B-3B	147	577	88	177	16	10	2	48	.307	324	331	16	.976
1972—Minnesota	Amer.	2B	142	535	61	170	21	6	0	51	★.318	331	378	16	.978
1973—Minnesota	Amer.	2B	149	580	98	★203	30	●11	6	62	★.350	383	413	13	.984
1974—Minnesota	Amer.	2B	153	599	86	★218	30	5	3	55	★.364	375	416	★33	.960
1975—Minnesota	Amer.	2B-1B	143	535	89	192	24	4	14	80	★.359	408	377	21	.974
1976—Minnesota	Amer.	1B-2B	156	605	97	200	29	12	9	90	.331	1398	110	16	.990
1977—Minnesota	Amer.	1B-2B	155	616	★128	★239	38	★16	14	100	★.388	1463	124	10	.994
1978—Minnesota y	Amer.	1B-2B-OF	152	564	85	188	26	10	5	70	★.333	1363	105	16	.989
1979—California z	Amer.	1B	110	409	78	130	15	3	3	44	.318	804	55	10	.988
1980—California	Amer.	1B	144	540	74	179	34	7	3	59	.331	897	57	6	.994
1981—California	Amer.	1B	93	364	57	111	17	1	2	21	.305	877	60	5	.995
1982—California	Amer.	1B	138	523	88	167	25	5	3	44	.319	1339	94	12	.992
1983—California a	Amer.	1B-2B	129	472	66	160	24	2	2	44	.339	891	42	6	.994
1984—California b	Amer.	1B	93	329	42	97	8	1	3	31	.295	724	59	●15	.981
1985—California cd	Amer.	1B	127	443	69	124	17	3	2	39	.280	1055	65	7	.994
Major League Totals—19 Years			2469	9315	1424	3053	445	112	92	1015	.328	13510	3709	260	.985

Signed as free agent by Minnesota Twins' organization, June 25, 1964.

†On military list, August 5 to August 21, 1967.

‡On military list, June 8 to June 24, 1968.

§On military list, August 17 to September 1, 1969.

xOn disabled list, June 24 to September 1, 1970.

yTraded to California Angels for Outfielder Ken Landreaux, Pitchers Paul Hartzell and Brad Havens and Third Baseman Dave Engle, February 3, 1979.

zOn disabled list, June 5 to July 19, 1979.

aGranted free agency, November 7, 1983; re-signed by Angels, November 22, 1983.

bOn disabled list, August 9 to September 1, 1984.

cOn disabled list, May 20 to June 10, 1985.

dGranted free agency, November 12, 1985.

CHAMPIONSHIP SERIES RECORD

Tied Championship Series record for most two-base hits, four-game Series (3), 1979.

Tied American League Championship Series records for most times on losing club (4); most hits, four-game Series (7), 1979.

Year—Club	League	Pos.	G.	AB.	R.	H.	2B.	3B.	HR.	RBI.	B.A.	PO.	A.	E.	F.A.
1969—Minnesota	Amer.	2B	3	14	0	1	0	0	0	0	.071	6	3	1	.900
1970—Minnesota	Amer.	PH	2	2	0	0	0	0	0	0	.000	0	0	0	.000
1979—California	Amer.	1B	4	17	4	7	3	0	0	1	.412	34	1	0	1.000
1982—California	Amer.	1B	5	17	2	3	1	0	0	0	.176	43	4	0	1.000
Championship Series Totals—4 Years			14	50	6	11	4	0	0	1	.220	83	8	1	.989

ALL-STAR GAME RECORD

Established All-Star Game record for most three-base hits, game (2), July 11, 1978.

Tied All-Star Game record for most at bats, nine-inning game (5), July 15, 1975.

Year League	Pos.	AB.	R.	H.	2B.	3B.	HR.	RBI.	B.A.	PO.	A.	E.	F.A.
1967—American	2B	3	0	0	0	0	0	0	.000	2	3	0	1.000
1968—American	2B	3	0	0	0	0	0	0	.000	2	2	0	1.000
1969—American	2B	3	0	0	0	0	0	0	.000	0	2	0	1.000
1971—American	2B	1	1	0	0	0	0	0	.000	1	2	0	1.000
1972—American	2B	2	0	1	0	0	0	1	.500	2	3	0	1.000
1973—American	2B	3	0	0	0	0	0	0	.000	5	1	0	1.000
1974—American	2B	1	1	0	0	0	0	0	.000	0	1	0	1.000
1975—American	2B	5	0	1	0	0	0	0	.200	3	1	0	1.000
1976—American	1B	3	0	0	0	0	0	0	.000	9	2	0	1.000
1977—American	1B	3	1	1	0	0	0	0	.333	7	0	0	1.000
1978—American	1B	4	2	2	0	2	0	0	.500	6	1	0	1.000
1980—American	1B	2	1	2	1	0	0	0	1.000	4	0	0	1.000
1981—American	1B	3	0	1	0	0	0	0	.333	12	0	0	1.000
1983—American	1B	3	2	2	0	0	0	1	.667	3	0	1	.750
1984—American	1B	2	0	0	0	0	0	0	.000	5	0	0	1.000
All-Star Game Totals—15 Years		41	8	10	1	2	0	2	.244	61	18	1	.988

Named to American League All-Star Team for 1970, 1979 and 1982 games; replaced due to injury.

STEVEN NORMAN CARLTON
(Steve)

Born December 22, 1944, at Miami, Fla.
Height, 6.05. Weight, 210.
Throws and bats lefthanded.
Attended Miami-Dade Community College, Miami, Fla.

Established major league records for most consecutive starting assignments, lifetime (512); most strikeouts, game by lefthanded pitcher and losing pitcher (19), September 15, 1969; most balks, season (11), 1979.

Tied major league record for most strikeouts, game (19), September 15, 1969.

Established National League records for most years, 100 or more strikeouts (18); most consecutive years, 100 or more strikeouts (18); most strikeouts, lifetime (3,920); most bases on balls issued, lifetime (1,656).

Tied modern National League record for most games won, season, by lefthander (27), 1972.

Led National League pitchers in games started with 41 in 1972, 38 in 1982 and tied for lead with 40 in 1973 and 38 in 1980.

Led National League in shutouts with 6 in 1982.

Led National League in complete games with 30 in 1972, 19 in 1982 and tied for lead with 18 in 1973.

Led National League in balks with 7 in 1977, 11 in 1979, 7 in 1980 and 9 in 1982 and 1983 and tied for lead with 7 in 1975, 1978 and 1984.

Led National League in wild pitches with 17 in 1980.

Led National League in home runs allowed with 30 in 1978.

Won National League Cy Young Memorial Award, 1972, 1977, 1980 and 1982.

Named National League Pitcher of the Year by THE SPORTING NEWS, 1972, 1977, 1980 and 1982.

Named lefthanded pitcher on THE SPORTING NEWS National League All-Star Team, 1969, 1971, 1972, 1977, 1979, 1980 and 1982.

Named pitcher on THE SPORTING NEWS National League All-Star fielding team, 1981.

Year Club	League	G.	IP.	W.	L.	Pct.	H.	R.	ER.	SO.	BB.	ERA.
1964—Rock Hill	W. Carol.	11	79	10	1	.909	39	17	9	91	36	1.03
1964—Winnipeg	Northern	12	75	4	4	.500	63	40	28	79	48	3.36
1964—Tulsa	Texas	4	24	1	1	.500	16	13	7	21	18	2.63
1965—St. Louis	National	15	25	0	0	.000	27	7	7	21	8	2.52
1966—Tulsa	P. Coast	19	128	9	5	.643	110	65	51	108	54	3.59
1966—St. Louis	National	9	52	3	3	.500	56	22	18	25	18	3.12
1967—St. Louis	National	30	193	14	9	.609	173	71	64	168	62	2.98
1968—St. Louis	National	34	232	13	11	.542	214	87	77	162	61	2.99
1969—St. Louis	National	31	236	17	11	.607	185	66	57	210	93	2.17
1970—St. Louis†	National	34	254	10	★19	.345	239	123	105	193	109	3.72
1971—St. Louis†	National	37	273	20	9	.690	275	120	108	172	98	3.56
1972—Philadelphia	National	41	★346	★27	10	.730	★257	84	76	★310	87	★1.98
1973—Philadelphia	National	40	●293	13	★20	.394	★293	★146	★127	223	113	3.90
1974—Philadelphia	National	39	291	16	13	.552	249	118	104	★240	★136	3.22
1975—Philadelphia	National	37	255	15	14	.517	217	116	101	192	104	3.56
1976—Philadelphia	National	35	253	20	7	★.741	224	94	88	195	72	3.13
1977—Philadelphia	National	36	283	★23	10	.697	229	99	83	198	89	2.64
1978—Philadelphia	National	34	247	16	13	.552	228	91	78	161	63	2.84
1979—Philadelphia	National	35	251	18	11	.621	202	112	101	213	89	3.62
1980—Philadelphia	National	38	★304	★24	9	.727	243	87	79	★286	90	2.34
1981—Philadelphia	National	24	190	13	4	.765	152	59	51	179	62	2.42
1982—Philadelphia	National	38	★295⅔	★23	11	.676	★253	114	102	★286	86	3.10
1983—Philadelphia	National	37	283⅔	15	16	.484	★277	117	98	★275	84	3.11
1984—Philadelphia	National	33	229	13	7	.650	214	104	91	163	79	3.58
1985—Philadelphia‡	National	16	92	1	8	.111	84	43	34	48	53	3.33
Major League Totals—21 Years		673	4878⅓	314	215	.594	4291	1880	1649	3920	1656	3.04

Signed as free agent by St. Louis Cardinals' organization, October 8, 1963.
†Traded to Philadelphia Phillies for Pitcher Rick Wise, February 25, 1972.
‡On disabled list, June 21 to September 2, 1985.

DIVISION SERIES RECORD

Year Club	League	G.	IP.	W.	L.	Pct.	H.	R.	ER.	SO.	BB.	ERA.
1981—Philadelphia	National	2	14	0	2	.000	14	6	6	13	8	3.86

CHAMPIONSHIP SERIES RECORD

Established Championship Series record for most bases on balls, total Series (28).

Tied Championship Series records for most games won, total Series (4); most games won, Series (2); most home runs hit by pitcher, total Series (1); most bases on balls, four-game Series (8), 1977; most bases on balls, five-game series (8), 1980.

Established National League Championship Series records for most strikeouts, total Series (39); most games started, total Series (8); most innings pitched, total Series (53⅔); most hits allowed, total Series (53); most earned runs allowed, total Series (21).

Tied National League Championship Series records for most strikeouts, four-game Series (13), 1983; most bases on balls, three-game Series (5), 1976.

Year Club	League	G.	IP.	W.	L.	Pct.	H.	R.	ER.	SO.	BB.	ERA.
1976—Philadelphia	National	1	7	0	1	.000	8	5	4	6	5	5.14
1977—Philadelphia	National	2	11⅔	0	1	.000	13	9	9	6	8	6.94
1978—Philadelphia	National	1	9	1	0	1.000	8	4	4	8	2	4.00
1980—Philadelphia	National	2	12⅓	1	0	1.000	11	3	3	6	8	2.19
1983—Philadelphia	National	2	13⅔	2	0	1.000	13	1	1	13	5	0.66
Championship Series Totals—5 Years		8	53⅔	4	2	.667	53	22	21	39	28	3.52

WORLD SERIES RECORD

Tied World Series record for most games won, losing none, six-game Series (2), 1980.

Year Club	League	G.	IP.	W.	L.	Pct.	H.	R.	ER.	SO.	BB.	ERA.
1967—St. Louis	National	1	6	0	1	.000	3	1	0	5	2	0.00
1968—St. Louis	National	2	4	0	0	.000	7	3	3	3	1	6.75
1980—Philadelphia	National	2	15	2	0	1.000	14	5	4	17	9	2.40
1983—Philadelphia	National	1	6⅔	0	1	.000	5	3	2	7	3	2.70
World Series Total—4 Years		6	31⅔	2	2	.500	29	12	9	32	15	2.56

ALL-STAR GAME RECORD

Year League	IP.	W.	L.	Pct.	H.	R.	ER.	SO.	BB.	ERA.
1968—National	1	0	0	.000	0	0	0	1	0	0.00
1969—National	3	1	0	1.000	2	2	2	2	1	6.00
1972—National	1	0	0	.000	0	0	0	1	0	0.00
1979—National	1	0	0	.000	2	3	3	0	1	27.00
1982—National	2	0	0	.000	1	0	0	4	2	0.00
All-Star Game Totals—5 Years	8	1	0	1.000	5	5	5	7	5	5.63

Member of National League All-Star Team in 1971, 1974, 1977, 1980 and 1981; did not play.

DONALD WAYNE CARMAN
(Don)

Born August 14, 1959, at Oklahoma City, Okla.
Height, 6.03. Weight, 190.
Throws and bats lefthanded.
Attended Seminole Junior College, Seminole, Okla.,
and University of Oklahoma, Norman, Okla.

Major League saves: 1983 (1), 1985 (7). Total—8.

Year Club	League	G.	IP.	W.	L.	Pct.	H.	R.	ER.	SO.	BB.	ERA.
1979—Spartanburg	W. Carol.	37	78	6	3	.667	72	36	34	70	28	3.92
1980—Peninsula	Carolina	27	150	14	5	.737	149	73	57	*141	53	3.42
1981—Reading	Eastern	28	176	12	13	.480	167	93	79	105	75	4.04
1982—Oklahoma City	Am. Assoc.	10	33	0	1	.000	37	29	25	29	23	6.82
1982—Reading	Eastern	20	97⅓	6	7	.462	99	58	45	81	62	4.16
1983—Reading	Eastern	*56	124⅓	8	5	.615	85	51	41	93	71	2.97
1983—Philadelphia	National	1	1	0	0	.000	0	0	0	0	0	0.00
1984—Portland	P. Coast	39	55⅔	3	3	.500	66	36	33	53	22	5.34
1984—Philadelphia	National	11	13⅓	0	1	.000	14	9	8	16	6	5.40
1985—Philadelphia	National	71	86⅓	9	4	.692	52	25	20	87	38	2.08
Major League Totals—3 Years		83	100⅔	9	5	.643	66	34	28	103	44	2.50

Signed as free agent by Philadelphia Phillies' organization, August 25, 1978.

NORMAN RAFAEL CARRASCO
(Norm)

Born August 6, 1962, at Caracas, Venezuela.
Height, 5.09. Weight, 170.
Throws and bats righthanded.

Led Eastern League in grounding into double plays with 19 in 1984.
Led Eastern League second basemen in total chances with 648 and tied for lead in double plays with 79 in 1984.
Led Midwest League second basemen in total chances with 720 and double plays with 85 in 1982.
Led Pioneer League second basemen in double plays with 52 in 1981.

Year Club	League	Pos.	G.	AB.	R.	H.	2B.	3B.	HR.	RBI.	B.A.	PO.	A.	E.	F.A.
1981—Idaho Falls	Pion.	2B	68	262	44	98	22	4	3	57	.374	*145	197	16	*.955
1982—Danville	Midw.	2B	136	*553	*115	154	*34	2	10	51	.278	*313	*379	28	.961
1983—Redwood	Calif.	2B	132	473	56	112	29	4	6	59	.237	*287	●363	28	.959
1984—Waterbury	East.	2B	136	516	78	147	23	3	9	64	.285	*286	346	16	.975
1985—Edmonton	P. C.	2B	114	402	41	95	13	3	3	47	.236	245	326	13	.978

Signed as free agent by California Angels' organization, March 18, 1981.

MATIAS CARRILLO (GARCIA)

Born February 24, 1964, at Los Mochis Sinaloa, Mex.
Height, 5.11. Weight, 185.
Throws and bats righthanded.

Led Mexican League in stolen bases with 30 and tied for lead in intentional bases on balls received with 16 in 1984.
Tied for Mexican League lead in double plays by outfielders with 4 in 1985.

Year—Club	League	Pos.	G.	AB.	R.	H.	2B.	3B.	HR.	RBI.	B.A.	PO.	A.	E.	F.A.
1982—Poza Rica	Mex.	OF-1B	99	301	59	93	9	5	0	29	.309	150	13	6	.964
1983—Poza Rica	Mex.	OF	91	360	54	112	13	11	6	39	.311	128	12	1	.993
1984—Mex. City Tigers	Mex.	OF	113	442	100	154	32	6	14	76	.348	281	13	12	.961
1985—Mex. City Tigers	Mex.	OF	126	465	114	164	21	8	20	102	.353	320	13	10	.971

Signed as free agent by Pittsburgh Pirates' organization, December 12, 1985.

GARY EDMUND CARTER

Born April 8, 1954, at Culver City, Calif.
Height, 6.02. Weight, 210.
Throws and bats righthanded.
Brother of Gordon Carter, outfielder in San Francisco Giants'
organization, 1972 and 1973.

Established major league record for fewest passed balls, season, 150 or more games (1), 1978.
Tied major league record for most home runs, two consecutive games (5), September 3 and 4, 1985.
Established National League records for most seasons leading league in games by catcher (6); most years leading league in putouts by catcher (7); most years leading league in chances accepted by catcher (7).
Major League stolen bases: 1974 (2), 1975 (5), 1977 (5), 1978 (10), 1979 (3), 1980 (3), 1981 (1), 1982 (2), 1983 (1), 1984 (2), 1985 (1). Total—35.
Hit three home runs in a game, April 20, 1977 and September 3, 1985.
Led National League catchers in assists with 107 in 1983.
Led National League catchers in total chances with 921 in 1977, 874 in 1978, 848 in 1979, 937 in 1980, 571 in 1981 and 1,068 in 1982.
Led National League in passed balls with 12 in 1979.
Led National League catchers in putouts with 811 in 1977, 781 in 1978, 509 in 1981, and 956 in 1985.
Led National League catchers in double plays with 14 in 1977, 9 in 1978, 12 in 1979 and 14 in 1983.
Led International League catchers in putouts with 794, assists with 65, double plays with 15 and fielding percentage with .990 in 1974.
Named National League Rookie Player of the Year by THE SPORTING NEWS, 1975.
Named catcher on THE SPORTING NEWS National League All-Star Team, 1980 through 1982, 1984 and 1985.
Named catcher on THE SPORTING NEWS National League All-Star fielding team, 1980 through 1982.
Named catcher on THE SPORTING NEWS National League Silver Slugger team, 1981, 1982, 1984 and 1985.

Year—Club	League	Pos.	G.	AB.	R.	H.	2B.	3B.	HR.	RBI.	B.A.	PO.	A.	E.	F.A.
1972—Cocoa Expos	Fla.E.C.	C-1B-3B	18	71	6	17	3	0	2	9	.239	111	12	10	.925
1972—W. Palm Beach	Fla. St.	C	20	50	9	16	2	2	0	5	.320	84	12	2	.980
1973—Quebec City	East.	C-1B-OF	130	439	65	111	16	1	15	68	.253	823	75	20	.978
1973—Peninsula	Int.	C	8	25	2	7	2	0	0	1	.280	5	1	0	1.000
1974—Memphis	Int.	C-1B-3B	135	441	62	118	14	7	23	83	.268	908	76	12	.988
1974—Montreal	Nat.	C-OF	9	27	5	11	0	1	1	6	.407	28	4	0	1.000
1975—Montreal	Nat.	OF-C-3B	144	503	58	136	20	1	17	68	.270	430	38	9	.981
1976—Montreal†	Nat.	C-OF	91	311	31	68	8	1	6	38	.219	364	42	2	.995
1977—Montreal	Nat.	★C-OF	154	522	86	148	29	2	31	84	.284	813	★101	9	.990
1978—Montreal	Nat.	C-1B	157	533	76	136	27	1	20	72	.255	787	83	10	.989
1979—Montreal	Nat.	C	141	505	74	143	26	5	22	75	.283	★751	★88	9	.989
1980—Montreal	Nat.	C-1B	154	549	76	145	25	5	29	101	.264	★822	★108	7	★.993
1981—Montreal	Nat.	C-1B	100	374	48	94	20	2	16	68	.251	515	58	4	.993
1982—Montreal	Nat.	C	154	557	91	163	32	1	29	97	.293	★954	★104	10	.991
1983—Montreal	Nat.	★C-1B	145	541	63	146	37	3	17	79	.270	855	108	5	★.995
1984—Montreal‡	Nat.	C-1B	159	596	75	175	32	1	27	●106	.294	990	78	7	.993
1985—New York	Nat.	C-1B-OF	149	555	83	156	17	1	32	100	.281	987	70	8	.992
Major League Totals—12 Years			1557	5573	766	1521	273	24	247	894	.273	8296	882	80	.991

Selected by Montreal Expos' organization in 3rd round of free-agent draft, June 6, 1972.
†On disabled list, June 6 to July 22, 1976.
‡Traded to New York Mets for Infielder Hubie Brooks, Catcher Mike Fitzgerald, Outfielder Herm Winningham and Pitcher Floyd Youmans, December 10, 1984.

DIVISION SERIES RECORD

Year—Club	League	Pos.	G.	AB.	R.	H.	2B.	3B.	HR.	RBI.	B.A.	PO.	A.	E.	F.A.
1981—Montreal	Nat.	C	5	19	3	8	3	0	2	6	.421	21	5	0	1.000

CHAMPIONSHIP SERIES RECORD

Year—Club	League	Pos.	G.	AB.	R.	H.	2B.	3B.	HR.	RBI.	B.A.	PO.	A.	E.	F.A.
1981—Montreal	Nat.	C	5	16	3	7	1	0	0	0	.438	27	3	0	1.000

ALL-STAR GAME RECORD

Tied All-Star Game record for most home runs, game (2), August 9, 1981.

Year—League	Pos.	AB.	R.	H.	2B.	3B.	HR.	RBI.	B.A.	PO.	A.	E.	F.A.
1975—National	OF	0	0	0	0	0	0	0	.000	1	0	0	1.000
1979—National	C	2	0	1	0	0	0	1	.500	6	1	0	1.000
1980—National	C	1	0	0	0	0	0	0	.000	1	0	0	1.000
1981—National	C	3	2	2	0	0	2	2	.667	5	1	0	1.000
1982—National	C	3	0	1	0	0	0	1	.333	7	0	0	1.000

Year League	Pos.	AB.	R.	H.	2B.	3B.	HR.	RBI.	B.A.	PO.	A.	E.	F.A.
1983—National	C	2	0	0	0	0	0	0	.000	3	0	0	1.000
1984—National	C	2	1	1	0	0	1	1	.500	9	0	0	1.000
All-Star Game Totals—7 Years		13	3	5	0	0	3	5	.385	32	2	0	1.000

Named to National League All-Star Team for 1985 game; replaced due to injury by Terry Kennedy.

JOSEPH CHRIS CARTER
(Joe)

Born March 7, 1960, at Oklahoma City, Okla.
Height, 6.03. Weight, 215.
Throws and bats righthanded.
Attended Wichita State University, Wichita, Kan.

Major League stolen bases: 1983 (1), 1984 (2), 1985 (24). Total—27.
Led American Association in total bases with 265 and tied for lead in strikeouts by batters with 103 in 1983.
Named College Player of the Year by THE SPORTING NEWS, 1981.
Named outfielder on THE SPORTING NEWS College Baseball All-America Team, 1980 and 1981.
Received reported $150,000 bonus to sign with Chicago Cubs, 1981.

Year Club	League	Pos.	G.	AB.	R.	H.	2B.	3B.	HR.	RBI.	B.A.	PO.	A.	E.	F.A.
1981—Midland	Texas	OF	67	249	42	67	15	3	5	35	.269	100	10	4	.965
1982—Midland†	Texas	OF	110	427	84	136	22	8	25	98	.319	182	6	5	.974
1983—Iowa	A. A.	OF	124	★522	82	160	27	6	22	83	.307	204	9	12	.947
1983—Chicago	Nat.	OF	23	51	6	9	1	1	0	1	.176	26	0	0	1.000
1984—Iowa‡	A. A.	OF	61	248	45	77	12	7	14	67	.310	142	6	2	.987
1984—Cleveland§	Amer.	OF-1B	66	244	32	67	6	1	13	41	.275	169	11	6	.968
1985—Cleveland	Amer.	O-1-2-3	143	489	64	128	27	0	15	59	.262	311	17	6	.982
National League Totals—1 Year			23	51	6	9	1	1	0	1	.176	26	0	0	1.000
American League Totals—2 Years			209	733	96	195	33	1	28	100	.266	480	28	12	.977
Major League Totals—3 Years			232	784	102	204	34	2	28	101	.260	506	28	12	.978

Selected by Chicago Cubs' organization in 1st round (second player selected) of free-agent draft, June 8, 1981.
†On disabled list, April 9 to April 19, 1982.
‡Traded with Outfielder Mel Hall and Pitchers Don Schulze and Darryl Banks to Cleveland Indians for Catcher Ron Hassey and Pitchers Rick Sutcliffe and George Frazier, June 13, 1984.
§On disabled list, July 2 to July 17, 1984.

CHARLES DOUGLAS CARY
(Chuck)

Born March 3, 1960, at Whittier, Calif.
Height, 6.04. Weight, 210.
Bats and throws lefthanded.
Attended University of California, Berkeley, Calif.

Major League saves: 1985 (2).
Tied for Southern League lead in balks with 3 in 1982.

Year Club	League	G.	IP.	W.	L.	Pct.	H.	R.	ER.	SO.	BB.	ERA.
1981—Macon	S. Atlantic	13	87	5	5	.500	77	32	25	55	19	2.59
1982—Birmingham	Southern	28	166	8	14	.364	162	93	77	125	64	4.17
1983—Birmingham†	Southern	17	104⅔	6	8	.429	103	50	42	69	42	3.61
1983—Evansville	Am. Assoc.	15	16⅓	1	1	.500	21	10	8	8	8	4.41
1984—Birmingham‡	Southern	22	108⅓	6	4	.600	118	61	58	62	46	4.82
1985—Nashville	Am. Assoc.	48	66	2	1	.667	55	27	22	54	27	3.00
1985—Detroit	American	16	23⅔	0	1	.000	16	9	9	22	8	3.42
Major League Totals—1 Year		16	23⅔	0	1	.000	16	9	9	22	8	3.42

Selected by Detroit Tigers' organization in 7th round of free-agent draft, June 8, 1981.
†On disabled list, April 18 to May 12, 1983.
‡On disabled list, June 24 to July 11 and August 4 to August 17, 1984.

JUAN CASTILLO

Name pronounced Cas-TEE-yo.

Born January 25, 1962, at San Pedro de Macoris, Dominican Republic.
Height, 5.11. Weight, 162.
Throws right and bats left and righthanded.

Led Texas League in caught stealing with 17 in 1983.
Led Texas League second basemen in assists with 359 in 1984.
Led Texas League second basemen in putouts with 247, assists with 360, errors with 27, double plays with 79 and total chances with 634 in 1983.
Led California League second basemen in double plays with 88 in 1982.

Year Club	League	Pos.	G.	AB.	R.	H.	2B.	3B.	HR.	RBI.	B.A.	PO.	A.	E.	F.A.
1980—Burlington	Midw.	2B	30	103	12	22	0	0	0	6	.214	60	72	3	.978
1980—Butte	Pion.	2B	59	183	28	53	9	3	0	20	.290	87	99	18	.912
1981—Burlington	Midw.	2B	110	365	36	90	8	4	4	34	.247	244	284	18	★.967
1982—Stockton	Calif.	2B	134	483	60	130	9	8	0	42	.269	273	273	23	.968
1983—El Paso	Texas	2B-SS-OF	123	461	79	125	24	2	8	62	.271	250	363	28	.956
1984—El Paso	Texas	2B-OF-SS	119	448	78	129	21	7	4	59	.288	273	360	17	.974
1984—Vancouver	P. C.	2B	8	30	6	10	0	0	0	2	.333	16	18	1	.971
1985—Vancouver	P. C.	SS-2B	118	440	71	119	17	3	1	32	.270	222	367	26	.958

Signed as free agent by Milwaukee Brewers' organization, October 11, 1979.

MARTIN HORACE CASTILLO

Name pronounced Cas-TEE-yo.

(Marty)

Born January 16, 1957, at Long Beach, Calif.
Height, 6.01. Weight, 190.
Throws and bats righthanded.
Attended Chapman College, Orange, Calif.
Brother of Art Castillo, outfielder in Minnesota Twins' organization, 1973 through 1975.

Major League stolen bases: 1983 (2), 1984 (1). Total—3.
Led American Association catchers in assists with 78, passed balls with 14 and stealers caught with 50 in 1982.
Led American Association in passed balls with 21 in 1981.

Year Club	League	Pos.	G.	AB.	R.	H.	2B.	3B.	HR.	RBI.	B.A.	PO.	A.	E.	F.A.
1978—Lakeland	Fla. St.	3B	67	205	24	53	4	2	5	25	.259	73	95	9	.949
1979—Montgomery†	South.	3B	74	274	47	84	17	1	9	47	.307	70	174	22	.917
1979—Evansville‡	A. A.	3B	31	103	11	24	4	1	1	6	.233	27	66	3	.969
1980—Evansville	A. A.	*3-C-1	132	455	59	114	28	4	12	62	.251	137	268	*26	.940
1981—Evansville	A. A.	C-3B-1B	120	396	63	105	23	2	17	68	.265	393	149	21	.945
1981—Detroit	Amer.	3B-OF	6	8	1	1	0	0	0	0	.125	4	8	0	1.000
1982—Evansville	A. A.	C-3-O-1	116	388	52	94	20	3	12	56	.242	525	117	13	.980
1982—Detroit	Amer.	C	1	0	0	0	0	0	0	0	.000	1	0	0	.000
1983—Evansville	A. A.	3B-SS	54	186	29	50	2	0	12	29	.269	33	71	7	.937
1983—Detroit	Amer.	3B-C	67	119	10	23	4	0	2	10	.193	73	69	1	.993
1984—Detroit	Amer.	C-3B	70	141	16	33	5	2	4	17	.234	161	37	7	.966
1985—Detroit§	Amer.	C-3B	57	84	4	10	2	0	2	5	.119	123	31	4	.975
Major League Totals—5 Years			201	352	31	67	11	2	8	32	.190	362	145	12	.977

Selected by Minnesota Twins' organization in 21st round of free-agent draft, June 4, 1975.
Selected by California Angels' organization in 8th round of free-agent draft, January 11, 1977.
Selected by Detroit Tigers' organization in 5th round of free-agent draft, June 6, 1978.
†On disabled list, April 21 to May 1, 1979.
‡On disabled list, July 30 to August 11, 1979.
§Released, January 16, 1986.

CHAMPIONSHIP SERIES RECORD

Year Club	League	Pos.	G.	AB.	R.	H.	2B.	3B.	HR.	RBI.	B.A.	PO.	A.	E.	F.A.
1984—Detroit	Amer.	3B	3	8	0	2	0	0	0	2	.250	3	4	0	1.000

WORLD SERIES RECORD

Year Club	League	Pos.	G.	AB.	R.	H.	2B.	3B.	HR.	RBI.	B.A.	PO.	A.	E.	F.A.
1984—Detroit	Amer.	3B	3	9	2	3	0	0	1	2	.333	3	3	0	1.000

MONTE CARMELO CASTILLO

Name pronounced Cas-TEE-yo.

(Carmen)

Born June 8, 1958, at San Francisco de Macoris, Dominican Republic.
Height, 6.01. Weight, 185.
Throws and bats righthanded.

Major League stolen bases: 1983 (1), 1984 (1), 1985 (3). Total—5.

Year Club	League	Pos.	G.	AB.	R.	H.	2B.	3B.	HR.	RBI.	B.A.	PO.	A.	E.	F.A.
1978—Auburn†	NYP	OF	53	174	37	41	10	2	4	21	.236	109	6	11	.913
1978—Helena	Pion.	OF	5	15	1	6	2	0	2	2	.400	2	0	1	.667
1979—Waterloo	Midw.	OF	49	138	25	28	5	1	3	12	.203	54	1	7	.887
1979—Batavia	NYP	OF	36	128	29	43	8	1	8	28	.336	56	4	5	.923
1980—Waterloo	Midw.	OF	117	390	69	103	14	1	11	64	.264	173	10	14	.929
1981—Chattanooga	South.	OF	119	441	63	124	17	6	11	58	.281	236	13	15	.943
1982—Charleston	Int.	OF	71	281	46	78	12	1	9	39	.278	159	10	11	.939
1982—Cleveland	Amer.	OF	47	120	11	25	4	0	2	11	.208	91	0	2	.978
1983—Charleston‡	Int.	OF	36	148	29	40	5	2	4	22	.270	85	6	6	.938
1983—Cleveland§	Amer.	OF	23	36	9	10	2	1	1	3	.278	23	3	2	.929
1984—Cleveland	Amer.	OF	87	211	36	55	9	2	10	36	.261	123	2	9	.933
1985—Cleveland	Amer.	OF	67	184	27	45	5	1	11	25	.245	101	0	5	.953
1985—Maine	Int.	OF	26	96	12	23	2	2	2	18	.240	9	0	0	1.000
Major League Totals—4 Years			224	551	83	135	20	4	24	75	.245	338	5	18	.950

Signed as free agent by Philadelphia Phillies' organization, June 30, 1978.
†Drafted by Chattanooga (Cleveland Indians' organization), December 5, 1978.
‡On disabled list, May 5 to July 4, 1983.

ROBERT ERNIE CASTILLO JR.

Name pronounced Cas-TEE-yo.

(Bobby)

Born April 18, 1955, at Los Angeles, Calif.
Height, 5.10. Weight, 180.
Throws and bats righthanded.
Attended Los Angeles Valley Junior College, Van Nuys, Calif.

Major League saves: 1978 (1), 1979 (7), 1980 (5), 1981 (5). Total—18.

Year Club	League	G.	IP.	W.	L.	Pct.	H.	R.	ER.	SO.	BB.	ERA.
1976—Reynosa	Mexican	13	72	5	5	.500	52	16	14	56	36	1.75
1977—Monterrey†	Mexican	34	255	19	11	.633	216	72	63	199	110	2.22
1977—Los Angeles	National	6	11	1	0	1.000	12	5	5	7	2	4.09
1978—Albuquerque	P. Coast	15	82	5	3	.625	81	54	49	65	51	5.38
1978—Los Angeles	National	18	34	0	4	.000	28	19	15	30	33	3.97
1979—Albuquerque‡	P. Coast	16	45	4	3	.571	49	34	28	42	31	5.60
1979—Los Angeles	National	19	24	2	0	1.000	26	5	3	25	13	1.13
1980—Los Angeles§	National	61	98	8	6	.571	70	31	30	60	45	2.76
1981—Los Angeles x	National	34	51	2	4	.333	50	31	30	35	24	5.29
1982—Minnesota	American	40	218⅔	13	11	.542	194	96	89	123	85	3.66
1983—Minnesota	American	27	158⅓	8	12	.400	170	91	84	90	65	4.77
1984—Minnesota yz	American	10	25⅓	2	1	.667	14	7	5	7	19	1.78
1985—Los Angeles a	National	35	68	2	2	.500	59	42	41	57	41	5.43
National League Totals—6 Years		173	286	15	16	.484	245	133	124	214	158	3.90
American League Totals—3 Years		77	402⅓	23	24	.489	378	194	178	220	169	3.98
Major League Totals—9 Years		250	688⅓	38	40	.487	623	327	302	434	327	3.95

Selected by Kansas City Royals' organization in 6th round of free-agent draft, January 9, 1974.
†Sold to Los Angeles Dodgers, June 16, 1977.
‡On disabled list, May 22 to July 21, 1979.
§Appeared in one game as an outfielder with no chances.
xTraded with Outfielder Bobby Mitchell to Minnesota Twins for Pitcher Paul Voigt and Catcher Scotti Madison, January 7, 1982.
yOn disabled list, March 29 to July 5, 1984.
zGranted free agency, November 8, 1984; signed by Los Angeles Dodgers, February 11, 1985.
aOn disabled list, April 2 to April 19, 1985.

CHAMPIONSHIP SERIES RECORD

Year Club	League	G.	IP.	W.	L.	Pct.	H.	R.	ER.	SO.	BB.	ERA.
1981—Los Angeles	National	1	1	0	0	.000	0	0	0	1	0	0.00
1985—Los Angeles	National	1	5⅓	0	0	.000	4	2	2	4	2	3.38
Championship Series Totals—2 Years		2	6⅓	0	0	.000	4	2	2	5	2	2.84

WORLD SERIES RECORD

Year Club	League	G.	IP.	W.	L.	Pct.	H.	R.	ER.	SO.	BB.	ERA.
1981—Los Angeles	National	1	1	0	0	.000	0	1	1	0	5	9.00

RECORD AS INFIELDER-OUTFIELDER

Year Club League	Pos.	G.	AB.	R.	H.	2B.	3B.	HR.	RBI.	B.A.	PO.	A.	E.	F.A.
1974—Sarasota Royals†..Gulf C.	●3B-OF	47	150	15	38	7	4	3	21	.253	31	70	●13	.886
1975—					(Out of Organized Baseball)									
1976—Reynosa .... Mex.	P-3B	1	2	0	0	0	0	0	0	.000	6	20	2	.929

†Released, April 7, 1975; signed by Reynosa of Mexican League, May 1, 1976.

WILLIAM HOLLAND CAUDILL
Name pronounced KAH-dull.

(Bill)

Born July 13, 1956, at Santa Monica, Calif.
Height, 6.01. Weight, 210.
Throws and bats righthanded.
Pitched six-inning, 4-0 no-hit victory against Winter Haven, May 14, 1975.
Major League saves: 1980 (1), 1982 (26), 1983 (26), 1984 (36), 1985 (14). Total—103.
Led Florida State League in complete games with 12 in 1975.

Year Club	League	G.	IP.	W.	L.	Pct.	H.	R.	ER.	SO.	BB.	ERA.
1974—Sarasota Cardinals	Gulf Coast	8	30	1	0	1.000	18	9	6	35	13	1.80
1975—St. Petersburg	Florida St.	25	163	●14	8	.636	123	63	57	★153	87	3.15
1976—Arkansas†	Texas	27	140	6	15	.286	128	79	69	★140	84	4.44
1977—Three Rivers‡	Eastern	19	114	13	4	★.765	97	56	53	93	72	4.18
1977—Indianapolis	Am. Assoc.	8	44	2	2	.500	31	20	18	25	31	3.68
1978—Wichita	Am. Assoc.	29	158	8	9	.471	151	103	97	124	105	5.53
1979—Wichita	Am. Assoc.	6	36	3	1	.750	27	11	11	36	17	2.75
1979—Chicago	National	29	90	1	7	.125	89	57	48	104	41	4.80
1980—Chicago	National	72	128	4	6	.400	100	37	31	112	59	2.18
1981—Chicago§x	National	30	71	1	5	.167	87	50	46	45	31	5.83
1982—Seattle	American	70	95⅔	12	9	.571	65	25	25	111	35	2.35
1983—Seattle yz	American	63	72⅔	2	8	.200	70	39	38	73	38	4.71
1984—Oakland ab	American	68	96⅓	9	7	.563	77	30	29	89	31	2.71
1985—Toronto	American	67	69⅓	4	6	.400	53	26	23	46	35	2.99
National League Totals—3 Years		131	289	6	18	.250	276	144	125	261	131	3.89
American League Totals—4 Years		268	334	27	30	.474	265	120	115	319	139	3.10
Major League Totals—7 Years		399	623	33	48	.407	541	264	240	580	270	3.47

Selected by St. Louis Cardinals' organization in 8th round of free-agent draft, June 5, 1974.
†Traded to Cincinnati Reds' organization for Infielder-Outfielder Joel Youngblood, March 28, 1977.
‡Traded with Pitcher Woodie Fryman to Chicago Cubs for Pitcher Bill Bonham, October 31, 1977.
§Traded to New York Yankees, April 1, 1982, as partial completion of deal in which Chicago Cubs acquired Second Baseman Pat Tabler from New York on waivers for two players to be named later, August 19, 1981; New York organization acquired Pitcher Jay Howell to complete deal, August 2, 1982.

xTraded with Pitcher Gene Nelson, a player to be named later and cash by New York Yankees to Seattle Mariners for Pitcher Shane Rawley, April 1, 1982; Seattle organization acquired Outfielder Bobby Brown to complete deal, April 6, 1982.

yOn disabled list, August 17 to September 4, 1983.

zTraded with a player to be named later to Oakland A's for Pitcher Dave Beard and Catcher Bob Kearney, November 21, 1983; Oakland acquired Pitcher Darrel Akerfelds to complete deal, December 7, 1983.

aHad one at-bat with a strikeout.

bTraded to Toronto Blue Jays for Outfielder Dave Collins, Shortstop Alfredo Griffin and cash, December 8, 1984.

ALL-STAR GAME RECORD

Year League	IP.	W.	L.	Pct.	H.	R.	ER.	SO.	BB.	ERA.
1984—American	1	0	0	.000	0	0	0	3	0	0.00

JOSE ISABEL CECENA

Born August 20, 1963, at Ciudad-Obregin, Sonora, Mex.
Height, 5.11. Weight, 180.
Throws and bats righthanded.

Year Club	League	G.	IP.	W.	L.	Pct.	H.	R.	ER.	SO.	BB.	ERA.
1983—Saltillo	Mexican	16	34⅓	1	2	.333	33	23	22	19	31	5.77
1984—Saltillo	Mexican	24	78½	1	4	.200	92	61	52	61	58	5.97
1985—Saltillo	Mexican	39	108⅔	7	13	.350	125	73	62	100	53	5.13

Signed as a free agent by Philadelphia Phillies' organization, December 10, 1985.

CESAR CEDENO

Name pronounced Suh-DAYN-yoh.

Born February 25, 1951, at Santo Domingo, Dominican Republic.
Height, 6.02. Weight, 200.
Throw and bats righthanded.

Tied major league record for most doubles, inning (2), April 9, 1973 (1st game, 6th inning).
Hit for the cycle, August 2, 1972 and August 9, 1976.
Major League stolen bases: 1970 (17), 1971 (20), 1972 (55), 1973 (56), 1974 (57), 1975 (50), 1976 (58), 1977 (61), 1978 (23), 1979 (30), 1980 (48), 1981 (12), 1982 (16), 1983 (13), 1984 (19), 1985 (14). Total—549.
Led National League in caught stealing with 21 in 1972 and 17 in 1975.
Led National League outfielders in double plays with 5 in 1976.
Led National League outfielders in total chances with 460 in 1974.
Tied for National League lead in sacrifice flies with 9 in 1979.
Tied for Carolina League lead in being hit by pitch with 14 in 1969.
Named outfielder on THE SPORTING NEWS National League All-Star Team, 1972, 1973, 1976 and 1980.
Named outfielder on THE SPORTING NEWS National League All-Star fielding team, 1972 through 1976.

Year Club	League	Pos.	G.	AB.	R.	H.	2B.	3B.	HR.	RBI.	B.A.	PO.	A.	E.	F.A.
1968—Covington	Appal.	OF	36	131	23	49	5	6	0	21	.374	49	●8	7	.891
1968—Cocoa	Fla. St.	OF	69	180	19	46	8	2	0	16	.256	70	4	7	.914
1969—Peninsula	Carol.	1B-OF	142	497	62	136	*32	3	5	39	.274	761	52	17	.980
1970—Okla. City	A. A.	OF	54	233	47	87	14	9	14	61	.373	113	6	4	.967
1970—Houston	Nat.	OF	90	355	46	110	21	4	7	42	.310	211	1	7	.968
1971—Houston	Nat.	OF-1B	161	611	85	161	*40	6	10	81	.264	348	6	4	.989
1972—Houston	Nat.	OF	139	559	103	179	●39	8	22	82	.320	345	9	7	.981
1973—Houston	Nat.	OF	139	525	86	168	35	2	25	70	.320	357	10	7	.981
1974—Houston	Nat.	OF	160	610	95	164	29	5	26	102	.269	★446	11	3	.993
1975—Houston†	Nat.	OF	131	500	93	144	31	3	13	63	.288	322	8	6	.982
1976—Houston	Nat.	OF	150	575	89	171	26	5	18	83	.297	377	11	8	.980
1977—Houston‡	Nat.	OF	141	530	92	148	36	8	14	71	.279	335	14	1	*.997
1978—Houston§	Nat.	OF	50	192	31	54	8	2	7	23	.281	149	2	2	.987
1979—Houston	Nat.	*1B-OF	132	470	57	123	27	4	6	54	.262	948	35	*17	.983
1980—Houston	Nat.	OF	137	499	71	154	32	8	10	73	.309	338	9	8	.977
1981—Houston x	Nat.	1B-OF	82	306	42	83	19	0	5	34	.271	510	28	5	.991
1982—Cincinnati	Carol.	OF-1B	138	492	52	142	35	1	8	57	.289	301	5	3	.990
1983—Cincinnati	Nat.	OF-1B	98	332	40	77	16	0	9	39	.232	258	10	1	.996
1984—Cincinnati y	Nat.	OF-1B	110	380	59	105	24	2	10	47	.276	355	21	7	.982
1985—Cinc.z-St.L.a	Nat.	1B-OF	111	296	38	86	16	1	9	49	.291	351	14	3	.992
Major League Totals—16 Years			1969	7232	1079	2069	434	59	199	970	.286	5951	194	89	.986

Signed as free agent by Houston Astros' organization, October 25, 1967.
†On disabled list, July 20 to August 8, 1975.
‡On disabled list, March 23 to April 13, 1977.
§On disabled list, June 17 to September 29, 1978.
xTraded to Cincinnati Reds for Third Baseman Ray Knight, December 18, 1981.
yOn disabled list, May 29 to June 13, 1984.
zTraded to St. Louis Cardinals for Outfielder Mark Jackson, August 29, 1985.
aGranted free agency, November 12, 1985.

DIVISION SERIES RECORD

Year Club	League	Pos.	G.	AB.	R.	H.	2B.	3B.	HR.	RBI.	B.A.	PO.	A.	E.	F.A.
1981—Houston	Nat.	1B	4	13	0	3	1	0	0	0	.231	36	2	1	.974

CHAMPIONSHIP SERIES RECORD

Year Club	League	Pos.	G.	AB.	R.	H.	2B.	3B.	HR.	RBI.	B.A.	PO.	A.	E.	F.A.
1980—Houston	Nat.	OF	3	11	1	2	0	0	0	1	.182	5	0	0	1.000
1985—St. Louis	Nat.	OF-PH	5	12	2	2	1	0	0	0	.167	5	0	0	1.000
Championship Series Totals—2 Years			8	23	3	4	1	0	0	1	.174	10	0	0	1.000

WORLD SERIES RECORD

Year	Club	League	Pos.	G.	AB.	R.	H.	2B.	3B.	HR.	RBI.	B.A.	PO.	A.	E.	F.A.
1985—St. Louis		Nat.	OF	5	15	1	2	1	0	0	1	.133	9	0	0	1.000

ALL-STAR GAME RECORD

Year	League	Pos.	AB.	R.	H.	2B.	3B.	HR.	RBI.	B.A.	PO.	A.	E.	F.A.
1972—National		OF	2	1	1	0	0	0	0	.500	0	0	0	.000
1973—National		OF	3	0	1	0	0	0	1	.333	3	0	0	1.000
1974—National		OF	2	0	0	0	0	0	0	.000	2	0	0	1.000
1976—National		OF	2	1	1	0	0	1	2	.500	1	0	0	1.000
All-Star Game Totals—4 Years			9	2	3	0	0	1	3	.333	6	0	0	1.000

VINICIO CEDENO

Born April 6, 1964, at LaRomana, Dominican Republic.
Height, 5.10. Weight, 185.
Throws and bats righthanded.

Year	Club	League	G.	IP.	W.	L.	Pct.	H.	R.	ER.	SO.	BB.	ERA.
1982—Salem		Northwest	2	4	0	0	.000	3	3	2	3	7	4.50
1983—Salem		Northwest	14	40	1	2	.333	39	31	18	32	29	4.05
1984—Salem		Northwest	23	33½	0	1	.000	26	23	15	37	20	4.05
1985—Quad Cities		Midwest	8	15	2	1	.667	10	6	3	20	16	1.80
1985—Redwood		California	38	47	4	7	.364	43	26	17	48	42	3.26

Signed as free agent by California Angels' organization, January 31, 1982.

RICHARD ALDO CERONE

(Rick)

Born May 19, 1954, at Newark, N. J.
Height, 5.11. Weight, 185.
Throws and bats righthanded.
Received bachelor of science degree in physical education from
Seton Hall University, South Orange, N. J. in 1975.

Major League stolen bases: 1979 (1), 1980 (1), 1984 (1). Total—3.
Named catcher on THE SPORTING NEWS American League All-Star Team, 1980.
Received reported $60,000 bonus to sign with Cleveland Indians, 1975.

Year	Club	League	Pos.	G.	AB.	R.	H.	2B.	3B.	HR.	RBI.	B.A.	PO.	A.	E.	F.A.
1975—Okla. City		A. A.	C-OF	46	140	22	35	6	1	2	13	.250	178	30	3	.986
1975—Cleveland		Amer.	C	7	12	1	3	1	0	0	0	.250	18	1	0	1.000
1976—Toledo†		Int.	C	96	339	38	86	19	0	11	49	.254	351	50	*18	.957
1976—Cleveland‡		Amer.	C	7	16	1	2	0	0	0	1	.125	25	1	1	.963
1977—Charleston		Int.	C-OF	70	231	30	54	10	1	6	40	.234	254	32	5	.983
1977—Toronto		Amer.	C	31	100	7	20	4	0	1	10	.200	146	15	1	.944
1978—Toronto		Amer.	C	88	282	25	63	8	2	3	20	.223	426	44	4	.992
1979—Toronto§		Amer.	C	136	469	47	112	27	4	7	61	.239	560	68	13	.980
1980—New York		Amer.	C	147	519	70	144	30	4	14	85	.277	800	73	9	.990
1981—New York x		Amer.	C	71	234	23	57	13	2	2	21	.244	353	26	3	.992
1982—New York y		Amer.	C	89	300	29	68	10	0	5	28	.227	509	25	6	.989
1983—New York z		Amer.	C-3B	80	246	18	54	7	0	2	22	.220	412	18	4	.991
1984—New York z		Amer.	C	38	120	8	25	3	0	2	13	.208	230	9	1	.996
1984—Columbus a		Int.	C	8	25	2	5	2	0	0	1	.200	42	5	1	.979
1985—Atlanta b		Nat.	C	96	282	15	61	9	0	3	25	.216	384	48	6	.986
American League Totals—10 Years				694	2298	229	548	103	12	36	261	.238	3479	280	42	.989
National League Total—1 Year				96	282	15	61	9	0	3	25	.216	384	48	6	.986
Major League Totals—11 Years				790	2580	244	609	112	12	39	286	.236	3863	328	48	.989

Selected by Cleveland Indians' organization in 1st round (seventh player selected) of free-agent draft, June 4, 1975.
†On disabled list, May 13 to May 24, 1976.
‡Traded with Infielder-Outfielder John Lowenstein to Toronto Blue Jays for Outfielder Rico Carty, December 6, 1976.
§Traded with Pitcher Tom Underwood and Outfielder Ted Wilborn to New York Yankees for First Baseman Chris Chambliss, Infielder Damaso Garcia and Pitcher Paul Mirabella, November 1, 1979.
xOn disabled list, April 19 to May 24, 1981.
yOn disabled list, May 12 to July 15, 1982.
zOn disabled list, May 7 to July 5, 1984; included rehabilitation disability assignment to Columbus, June 25 to July 5, 1984.
aTraded to Atlanta Braves for Pitcher Brian Fisher, December 5, 1984.
bOn disabled list, June 17 to July 2, 1985.

DIVISION SERIES RECORD

Year	Club	League	Pos.	G.	AB.	R.	H.	2B.	3B.	HR.	RBI.	B.A.	PO.	A.	E.	F.A.
1981—New York		Amer.	C	5	18	1	6	2	0	1	5	.333	42	1	1	.977

CHAMPIONSHIP SERIES RECORD

Tied Championsip Series record for hitting home run in first Series at-bat, October 8, 1980.

Year	Club	League	Pos.	G.	AB.	R.	H.	2B.	3B.	HR.	RBI.	B.A.	PO.	A.	E.	F.A.
1980—New York		Amer.	C	3	12	1	4	0	0	1	2	.333	14	4	0	1.000
1981—New York		Amer.	C	3	10	1	1	0	0	0	0	.100	23	2	0	1.000
Championship Series Totals—2 Years				6	22	2	5	0	0	1	2	.227	37	6	0	1.000

Year	Club	League	Pos.	G.	AB.	R.	H.	2B.	3B.	HR.	RBI.	B.A.	PO.	A.	E.	F.A.
1981—New York		Amer.	C	6	21	2	4	1	0	1	3	.190	42	4	0	1.000

JOHN JOSEPH CERUTTI

Born April 28, 1960, at Albany, N. Y.
Height, 6.02. Weight, 195.
Throws and bats lefthanded.
Received bachelor of arts degree in economics from Amherst College, Amherst, Mass.

Tied for Southern League lead in shutouts with 3 in 1983.
Tied for Pioneer League lead in home runs allowed with 8 and games started by pitchers with 14 in 1981.

Year	Club	League	G.	IP.	W.	L.	Pct.	H.	R.	ER.	SO.	BB.	ERA.
1981—Medicine Hat		Pioneer	14	*107	8	4	.667	87	45	36	120	43	3.03
1982—Kinston		Carolina	16	113	10	5	.667	88	47	40	136	49	3.19
1982—Knoxville		Southern	4	32⅓	4	0	1.000	18	4	4	17	10	1.11
1982—Syracuse		Int'national	6	30	0	3	.000	42	25	22	20	16	6.60
1983—Knoxville		Southern	29	188⅔	9	13	.409	182	89	72	131	65	3.43
1984—Syracuse		Int'national	29	148	7	●13	.350	152	89	73	114	52	4.44
1985—Syracuse		Int'national	28	182	11	9	.550	165	84	60	110	60	2.97
1985—Toronto		American	4	6⅔	0	2	.000	10	7	4	5	4	5.40
Major League Total—1 Year			4	6⅔	0	2	.000	10	7	4	5	4	5.40

Selected by Toronto Blue Jays' organization in 1st round (21st player selected) of free-agent draft, June 8, 1981.

RONALD CHARLES CEY

Name pronounced Say.

(Ron)

Born February 15, 1948, at Tacoma, Wash.
Height, 5.09. Weight, 185.
Throws and bats righthanded.
Attended Washington State University, Pullman, Wash., and Western
Washington State College, Bellingham, Wash.

Established major league record for fewest chances accepted by third baseman, season, 150 or more games (360), 1983.

Major League stolen bases: 1973 (1), 1974 (1), 1975 (5), 1977 (3), 1978 (2), 1979 (3), 1980 (2), 1982 (3), 1984 (3), 1985 (1). Total—24.

Led National League third basemen in double plays with 39 in 1973.
Led Pacific Coast League in bases on balls received with 117 in 1972.
Led Northwest League in sacrifice flies with 7 in 1968.
Led Pacific Coast League third baseman in putouts with 106, assists with 274 and tied for lead in double plays with 24 in 1972.
Led California League third basemen in double plays with 22 in 1969.
Tied for Pacific Coast League lead in being hit by pitch with 9 in 1971.

Year	Club	League	Pos.	G.	AB.	R.	H.	2B.	3B.	HR.	RBI.	B.A.	PO.	A.	E.	F.A.
1968—Tri-City		N'west	3B	74	254	50	76	11	4	9	*62	.299	46	*175	10	*.957
1969—Albuquerque		Texas	3B	13	32	8	5	1	0	0	2	.156	13	19	1	.970
1969—Bakersfield		Calif.	3B	98	353	68	117	16	1	22	56	.331	82	197	22	.927
1970—Albuquerque		Texas	3B	71	239	31	79	22	1	4	56	.331	44	132	10	.946
1971—Spokane		P. C.	3B	137	500	85	164	26	4	32	*123	.328	95	283	24	*.940
1971—Los Angeles		Nat.	PH	2	2	0	0	0	0	0	0	.000	0	0	0	.000
1972—Albuquerque		P. C.	3B-2B	142	496	99	163	25	7	23	103	.329	108	279	21	.949
1972—Los Angeles		Nat.	3B	11	37	3	10	1	0	1	3	.270	7	20	3	.900
1973—Los Angeles		Nat.	3B	152	507	60	124	18	4	15	80	.245	111	*328	18	.961
1974—Los Angeles		Nat.	3B	159	577	88	151	20	2	18	97	.262	155	365	22	.959
1975—Los Angeles		Nat.	3B	158	566	72	160	29	2	25	101	.283	144	309	19	.960
1976—Los Angeles		Nat.	3B	145	502	69	139	18	3	23	80	.277	111	334	16	.965
1977—Los Angeles		Nat.	3B	153	564	77	136	22	3	30	110	.241	138	346	18	.964
1978—Los Angeles		Nat.	3B	159	555	84	150	32	0	23	84	.270	116	336	16	.966
1979—Los Angeles		Nat.	3B	150	487	77	137	20	1	28	81	.281	128	325	9	*.977
1980—Los Angeles		Nat.	3B	157	551	81	140	25	0	28	77	.254	*127	317	13	.972
1981—Los Angeles		Nat.	3B	85	312	42	90	15	2	13	50	.288	71	184	16	.941
1982—Los Angeles†		Nat.	3B	150	556	62	141	23	1	24	79	.254	93	320	16	.963
1983—Chicago		Nat.	3B	159	581	73	160	33	1	24	90	.275	90	270	17	.955
1984—Chicago		Nat.	3B	146	505	71	121	27	0	25	97	.240	97	230	11	*.967
1985—Chicago		Nat.	3B	145	500	64	116	18	2	22	63	.232	75	273	*21	.943
Major League Totals—15 Years				1931	6802	923	1775	301	21	299	1092	.261	1458	3897	215	.961

Selected by New York Mets' organization in 24th round of free-agent draft, June 6, 1966.
Selected by Los Angeles Dodgers' organization in 3rd round of free-agent draft, June 7, 1968.
†Traded to Chicago Cubs for Outfielder Dan Cataline and Pitcher Vance Lovelace, January 19, 1983.

CHAMPIONSHIP SERIES RECORD

Tied Championship Series records for most two-base hits, total Series (7); most home runs with bases filled, game (1), October 4, 1977; most runs batted in, inning (4), October 4, 1977 (seventh inning); most two-base hits, four-game Series (3), 1974.
Tied National League Championship record for most hits, game (4), October 6, 1974.

Year	Club	League	Pos.	G.	AB.	R.	H.	2B.	3B.	HR.	RBI.	B.A.	PO.	A.	E.	F.A.
1974—Los Angeles		Nat.	3B	4	16	2	5	3	0	1	1	.313	2	4	2	.750

Year Club League	Pos.	G.	AB.	R.	H.	2B.	3B.	HR.	RBI.	B.A.	PO.	A.	E.	F.A.
1977—Los Angeles .... Nat.	3B	4	13	4	4	1	0	1	4	.308	7	14	1	.955
1978—Los Angeles .... Nat.	3B	4	16	4	5	1	0	1	3	.313	2	13	0	1.000
1981—Los Angeles .... Nat.	3B	5	18	1	5	1	0	0	3	.278	5	16	1	.955
1984—Chicago .... Nat.	3B	5	19	3	3	1	0	1	3	.158	1	6	0	1.000
Championship Series Totals—5 Years....		22	82	14	22	7	0	4	14	.268	17	53	4	.946

WORLD SERIES RECORD

Tied World Series record for batting in all club's runs, game, most (4), October 11, 1978.

Year Club League	Pos.	G.	AB.	R.	H.	2B.	3B.	HR.	RBI.	B.A.	PO.	A.	E.	F.A.
1974—Los Angeles .... Nat.	3B	5	17	1	3	0	0	0	0	.176	5	9	1	.933
1977—Los Angeles .... Nat.	3B	6	21	2	4	1	0	1	3	.190	5	7	0	1.000
1978—Los Angeles .... Nat.	3B	6	21	2	6	0	0	1	4	.286	2	12	0	1.000
1981—Los Angeles .... Nat.	3B	6	20	3	7	0	0	1	6	.350	4	11	0	1.000
World Series Totals—4 Years		23	79	8	20	1	0	3	13	.253	16	39	1	.982

ALL-STAR GAME RECORD

Year League	Pos.	AB.	R.	H.	2B.	3B.	HR.	RBI.	B.A.	PO.	A.	E.	F.A.
1974—National	3B	2	0	1	1	0	0	2	.500	0	0	0	.000
1975—National	3B	3	0	1	0	0	0	0	.333	0	1	0	1.000
1976—National	3B	0	0	0	0	0	0	0	.000	0	0	0	.000
1977—National	3B	2	0	0	0	0	0	0	.000	0	0	0	.000
1978—National	3B	1	0	0	0	0	0	0	.000	1	0	0	1.000
1979—National	3B	1	0	0	0	0	0	0	.000	2	1	0	1.000
All-Star Game Totals—6 Years....................		9	0	2	1	0	0	2	.222	3	2	0	1.000

RAY CHARLES CHADWICK

Born November 17, 1962, at Durham, N.C.
Height, 6.02. Weight, 180.
Throws right and bats left and righthanded.
Attended Winston-Salem State University, Winston-Salem, N.C.

Led Midwest League in balks with 5 in 1984.

Year Club	League	G.	IP.	W.	L.	Pct.	H.	R.	ER.	SO.	BB.	ERA.
1983—Salem...	Northwest	16	83⅓	3	5	.375	72	★63	●46	82	51	4.97
1984—Peoria†..	Midwest	26	153⅓	11	9	.550	138	87	68	133	85	3.99
1985—Redwood‡..	California	4	14	0	1	.000	13	14	10	10	11	6.43
1985—Midland...	Texas	10	60	5	2	.714	53	36	35	44	47	5.25
1985—Edmonton.......................................	P. Coast	2	11⅔	1	1	.500	9	7	4	9	6	3.09

Selected by California Angels' organization in 16th round of free-agent draft, June 6, 1983.
†On disabled list, May 17 to June 2, 1984.
‡On disabled list, April 9 to June 6, 1985.

ALBERT EUGENE CHAMBERS JR.
(Al)

Born March 24, 1961, at Harrisburg, Pa.
Height, 6.04. Weight, 217.
Throws and bats lefthanded.

Major League stolen bases: 1984 (2).
Led Eastern Deague in bases on balls received with 91 in 1981.

Year Club League	Pos.	G.	AB.	R.	H.	2B.	3B.	HR.	RBI.	B.A.	PO.	A.	E.	F.A.
1979—Bellingham .... N'west	OF	55	166	26	41	4	1	2	22	.247	63	1	3	.955
1980—San Jose .... Calif.	OF	115	426	76	128	18	★12	9	85	.300	122	3	5	.962
1981—Lynn....................... East.	OF	134	446	71	120	20	4	20	77	.269	178	5	9	.953
1982—Salt Lake City†..... P. C.	OF	97	343	57	96	28	5	8	50	.280	165	3	5	.971
1983—Salt Lake City....... P. C.	OF	99	347	77	115	26	6	12	75	.331	71	0	6	.922
1983—Seattle.................... Amer.	OF	31	67	11	14	3	0	1	7	.209	3	0	0	1.000
1984—Salt Lake City....... P. C.	OF	100	340	69	99	21	6	13	73	.291	25	1	1	.963
1984—Seattle.................... Amer.	OF	22	49	4	11	1	0	1	4	.224	18	0	1	.947
1985—Calgary .... P. C.	OF	100	354	64	109	31	3	9	64	.308	124	2	6	.955
1985—Seattle.................... Amer.	PH	4	4	0	0	0	0	0	0	.000	0	0	0	.000
Major League Totals—3 Years................		57	120	15	25	4	0	2	11	.208	21	0	1	.955

Selected by Seattle Mariners' organization in 1st round (first player selected) of free-agent draft, June 5, 1979.
†On disabled list, August 4 to August 14, 1983.

CARROLL CHRISTOPHER CHAMBLISS
(Chris)

Born December 26, 1948, at Dayton, O.
Height, 6.01. Weight, 220.
Throws right and bats lefthanded.
Attended Mira Costa Junior College, Oceanside, Calif., and University of California,
Los Angeles, Calif.; and received degree in physical education and recreation from
Montclair State College, Upper Montclair, N.J.
Cousin of Jo Jo White, guard with Boston Celtics, Golden State Warriors
and Kansas City Kings, 1969-70 through 1980-81.

Tied major league record for fewest caught stealing, season, 150 or more games (0), 1976 and 1977.

Major League stolen bases: 1971 (2), 1972 (3), 1973 (4), 1976 (1), 1977 (4), 1978 (2), 1979 (3), 1980 (7), 1981 (4), 1982 (7), 1983 (2), 1984 (1). Total—40.

Led National League first basemen in double plays with 144 in 1982.
Led National League first basemen in total chances with 1,739 in 1980 and 1,144 in 1981.
Led American League first basemen in total chances with 1,565 in 1973.
Named American League Rookie Player of the Year by THE SPORTING NEWS, 1971.
Named American League Rookie of the Year by Baseball Writers' Association of America, 1971.
Named first baseman on THE SPORTING NEWS American League All-Star Team, 1976.
Named first baseman on THE SPORTING NEWS American League All-Star fielding team, 1978.

Year—Club	League	Pos.	G.	AB.	R.	H.	2B.	3B.	HR.	RBI.	B.A.	PO.	A.	E.	F.A.
1970—Wichita†	A. A.	OF-1B	105	383	60	131	17	8	7	52	★.342	413	21	13	.971
1971—Wichita	A. A.	OF-1B	13	42	8	12	3	0	2	6	.286	42	3	0	1.000
1971—Cleveland	Amer.	1B	111	415	49	114	20	4	9	48	.275	943	55	8	.992
1972—Cleveland‡	Amer.	1B	121	466	51	136	27	2	6	44	.292	1109	56	8	.993
1973—Cleveland	Amer.	1B	155	572	70	156	30	2	11	53	.273	1437	114	★14	.991
1974—Cleve.§-N.Y.	Amer.	1B	127	467	46	119	20	3	6	50	.255	1035	84	11	.990
1975—New York	Amer.	1B	150	562	66	171	38	4	9	72	.304	1222	106	12	.991
1976—New York	Amer.	1B	156	641	79	188	32	6	17	96	.293	1440	109	9	.994
1977—New York	Amer.	1B	157	600	90	172	32	6	17	90	.287	1368	98	16	.989
1978—New York	Amer.	1B	162	625	81	171	26	3	12	90	.274	1366	111	4	★.997
1979—New York xy	Amer.	1B	149	554	61	155	27	3	18	63	.280	1299	95	7	.995
1980—Atlanta	Nat.	1B	158	602	83	170	37	2	18	72	.282	★1626	101	12	.993
1981—Atlanta	Nat.	1B	107	404	44	110	25	2	8	51	.272	1046	★94	4	.997
1982—Atlanta	Nat.	1B	157	534	57	144	25	2	20	86	.270	1352	138	10	.993
1983—Atlanta z	Nat.	1B	131	447	59	125	24	3	20	78	.280	1092	89	5	.996
1984—Atlanta	Nat.	1B	135	389	47	100	14	0	9	44	.257	996	70	8	.993
1985—Atlanta	Nat.	1B	101	170	16	40	7	0	3	21	.235	299	25	1	.997
American League Totals—9 Years			1288	4902	593	1382	252	33	105	606	.282	11219	828	89	.993
National League Totals—6 Years			789	2546	306	689	132	9	78	352	.271	6411	517	40	.994
Major League Totals—15 Years			2077	7448	899	2071	384	42	183	958	.278	17630	1345	129	.993

Selected by Cincinnati Reds' organization in 31st round of free-agent draft, June 6, 1967.
Selected by Cincinnati Reds' organization in secondary phase of free-agent draft, January 27, 1968.
Selected by Cleveland Indians' organization in 1st round (first player selected) of free-agent draft, January 17, 1970.

†On disabled list, May 25 to June 16, 1970.
‡On military list, June 23 to June 30, 1972.
§Traded with Pitchers Dick Tidrow and Cecil Upshaw to New York Yankees for Fritz Peterson, Steve Kline, Fred Beene and Tom Buskey, April 26, 1974.
xTraded with Infielder Damaso Garcia and Pitcher Paul Mirabella to Toronto Blue Jays for Catcher Rick Cerone, Pitcher Tom Underwood and Outfielder Ted Wilborn, November 1, 1979.
yTraded with Shortstop Luis Gomez to Atlanta Braves for Outfielder Barry Bonnell and Pitcher Joey McLaughlin, December 5, 1979.
zOn disabled list, August 8 to August 23, 1983.

CHAMPIONSHIP SERIES RECORD

Established Championship Series records for highest slugging average, five-game Series (.952), 1976; most total bases, five-game Series (20), 1976.
Tied Championship Series records for most hits, five-game Series (11), 1976; most hits, two consecutive games, one Series (6), October 3 and 4, 1978; most consecutive hits, one Series (5), 1978.
Tied American League Championship Series records for most consecutive hits, total Series (5); most one-base hits, four-game Series (6), 1978; most home runs, five-game Series (2), 1976.

Year—Club	League	Pos.	G.	AB.	R.	H.	2B.	3B.	HR.	RBI.	B.A.	PO.	A.	E.	F.A.
1976—New York	Amer.	1B	5	21	5	11	1	1	2	8	.524	50	3	1	.981
1977—New York	Amer.	1B	5	17	0	1	0	0	0	0	.059	35	7	0	1.000
1978—New York	Amer.	1B	4	15	1	6	0	0	0	2	.400	28	1	0	1.000
1982—Atlanta	Nat.	1B	3	10	0	0	0	0	0	0	.000	30	5	0	1.000
Championship Series Totals—4 Years			17	63	6	18	1	1	2	10	.286	143	16	1	.994

WORLD SERIES RECORD

Tied World Series records for most errors by first baseman, four-game Series (1), 1976; one or more hits, each game, four-game Series, 1976.

Year—Club	League	Pos.	G.	AB.	R.	H.	2B.	3B.	HR.	RBI.	B.A.	PO.	A.	E.	F.A.
1976—New York	Amer.	1B	4	16	1	5	1	0	0	1	.313	26	3	1	.967
1977—New York	Amer.	1B	6	24	4	7	2	0	1	4	.292	55	5	0	1.000
1978—New York	Amer.	1B	3	11	1	2	0	0	0	0	.182	17	1	0	1.000
World Series Totals—3 Years			13	51	6	14	3	0	1	5	.275	98	9	1	.991

ALL-STAR GAME RECORD

Year—League	Pos.	AB.	R.	H.	2B.	3B.	HR.	RBI.	B.A.	PO.	A.	E.	F.A.
1976—American	PH	1	0	0	0	0	0	0	.000	0	0	0	.000

—DID YOU KNOW—

That when the Mets' Keith Hernandez hit for the cycle against Atlanta on July 4, 1985, he connected off four different pitchers? His hits included a double against Rick Mahler, a two-run triple off Jeff Dedmon, a home run against Steve Shields and a 12th-inning single off Terry Forster.

KELVIN KEITH CHAPMAN

Born June 2, 1956, at Willits, Calif.
Height, 5.11. Weight, 173.
Throws and bats righthanded.
Attended Santa Rosa Junior College, Santa Rosa, Calif.

Major League stolen bases: 1984 (8), 1985 (5). Total—13.
Tied for International League lead in double plays by second basemen with 74 in 1979.

Year	Club	League	Pos.	G.	AB.	R.	H.	2B.	3B.	HR.	RBI.	B.A.	PO.	A.	E.	F.A.
1976—Marion		Appal.	2B	62	219	33	59	7	2	2	15	.269	138	164	8	★.974
1977—Wausau†		Midw.	2B-SS	127	493	96	151	28	5	12	47	.306	321	378	21	.971
1978—Jackson		Texas	2B	131	488	84	130	23	5	8	42	.266	★312	383	15	★.979
1979—Tidewater		Int.	●2B-SS	106	352	45	85	14	2	3	37	.241	248	303	●14	.975
1979—New York		Nat.	2B-3B	35	80	7	12	1	2	0	4	.150	51	46	2	.980
1980—Tidewater‡§		Int.	2B-3B	81	232	30	49	6	1	2	19	.211	62	118	10	.947
1981—Syracuse		Int.	2B	128	513	77	116	25	3	3	45	.226	292	404	14	.980
1982—Tidewater		Int.	2-O-3-S	101	329	53	92	13	2	5	40	.280	146	166	11	.966
1983—Tidewater x		Int.	2B-3B	72	223	41	61	8	3	4	28	.274	37	59	1	.990
1984—Tidewater		Int.	2B	12	40	4	11	2	1	0	6	.275	17	37	2	.964
1984—New York		Nat.	2B-3B	75	197	27	57	13	0	3	23	.289	105	134	6	.976
1985—New York		Nat.	2B-3B	62	144	16	25	3	0	0	7	.174	70	89	5	.970
1985—Tidewater y		Int.	2B-1B	17	54	9	10	3	0	0	2	.185	46	25	3	.959
Major League Totals—3 Years				172	421	50	94	17	2	3	34	.223	226	269	13	.974

Signed as free agent by New York Mets' organization, December 3, 1975.
†Suspended by league president, May 13 to May 16, 1977.
‡On temporary inactive list, May 15 to June 4, 1980.
§Loaned to Syracuse (Toronto Blue Jays' organization), April 3, 1981; returned, September 25, 1981.
xOn disabled list, April 12 to May 3, 1983.
yReleased, November 13, 1985.

FLOYD JOHN CHIFFER

Born April 20, 1956, at Glen Cove, N.Y.
Height, 6.02. Weight, 180.
Throws and bats righthanded.
Received bachelor of arts degree in history from University of California,
Los Angeles, Calif., in 1978.

Major League saves: 1982 (4), 1983 (1). Total—5.

Year	Club	League	G.	IP.	W.	L.	Pct.	H.	R.	ER.	SO.	BB.	ERA.
1978—Reno		California	15	103	6	5	.545	127	76	61	80	38	5.33
1979—Amarillo		Texas	43	82	3	2	.600	121	72	64	62	38	7.02
1980—Amarillo†		Texas	39	62	4	5	.444	41	17	15	61	28	2.18
1981—Hawaii		P. Coast	42	68	4	5	.444	63	33	26	51	22	3.44
1982—San Diego		National	51	79⅓	4	3	.571	73	33	26	48	34	2.95
1983—San Diego		National	15	22⅔	0	2	.000	17	10	8	15	10	3.18
1983—Las Vegas		P. Coast	42	78⅓	10	4	.714	74	38	28	62	33	3.22
1984—Las Vegas		P. Coast	36	55	5	4	.556	59	31	30	50	27	4.91
1984—San Diego‡		National	15	28	1	0	1.000	42	24	24	20	16	7.71
1985—Toledo§		Int'national	51	79⅔	9	7	.563	83	26	22	49	19	2.49
Major League Totals—3 Years			81	130	5	5	.500	132	67	58	83	60	4.02

Selected by California Angels' organization in 8th round of free-agent draft, June 5, 1974.
Selected by St. Louis Cardinals' organization in 23rd round of free-agent draft, June 7, 1977.
Selected by San Diego Padres' organization in 5th round of free-agent draft, June 6, 1978.
†On disabled list, June 26 to July 6, 1980.
‡Traded to Minnesota Twins for Catcher Ray Smith, December 7, 1984.
§Granted free agency, October 15, 1985.

RODNEY OSBORNE CHILDRESS
(Rocky)

Born February 18, 1962, at Santa Rosa, Calif.
Height, 6.02. Weight, 195.
Throws and bats righthanded.
Attended Santa Rosa Junior College, Santa Rosa, Calif.

Led Eastern League in intentional bases on balls issued with 13 in 1984.
Led Carolina League in saves with 16 and tied for lead in games finished in relief with 50 in 1983.

Year	Club	League	G.	IP.	W.	L.	Pct.	H.	R.	ER.	SO.	BB.	ERA.
1980—Helena		Pioneer	15	68	3	4	.429	79	32	19	43	20	2.51
1981—Bend		Northwest	25	46	4	5	.444	56	36	23	38	21	4.50
1982—Spartanburg		S. Atlantic	46	92	4	4	.500	101	53	41	54	44	4.01
1983—Peninsula		Carolina	★58	74⅓	4	7	.364	87	47	36	43	31	4.36
1984—Reading		Eastern	●62	103⅓	7	6	.538	107	38	34	50	40	2.96
1985—Portland		P. Coast	34	56⅔	4	5	.714	48	12	8	30	23	1.27
1985—Philadelphia		National	16	33⅓	0	1	.000	45	23	23	14	9	6.21
Major League Totals—1 Year			16	33⅓	0	1	.000	45	23	23	14	9	6.21

Selected by Philadelphia Phillies' organization in 21st round of free-agent draft, June 3, 1980.

JOHN LAWRENCE CHRISTENSEN

Born September 5, 1960, at Downey, Calif.
Height, 6.00. Weight, 180.
Throws and bats righthanded.
Attended California State University, Fullerton, Calif.
Brother of Jim Christensen, second baseman with Minnesota Twins' and
Oakland A's organizations, 1977 through 1983.

Major League stolen bases: 1985 (1).
Led International League outfielders in fielding percentage with .994 in 1984.

Year	Club	League	Pos.	G.	AB.	R.	H.	2B.	3B.	HR.	RBI.	B.A.	PO.	A.	E.	F.A.
1982—Shelby	S. Atl.		OF	125	440	100	147	24	2	22	★97	.334	156	9	2	.988
1982—Lynchburg	Carol.		OF	8	31	7	10	1	1	0	4	.323	11	1	1	.923
1983—Jackson	Texas		OF-1B-3B	109	405	76	135	26	2	12	72	.333	417	49	11	.977
1983—Tidewater	Int.		OF	20	80	12	21	0	0	2	15	.263	28	1	2	.935
1984—Tidewater	Int.		OF-1B	129	421	57	133	12	0	15	71	.316	177	7	1	.995
1984—New York	Nat.		OF	5	11	2	3	2	0	0	3	.273	1	0	1	.500
1985—New York	Nat.		OF	51	113	10	21	4	1	3	13	.186	41	2	2	.956
1985—Tidewater†	Int.		OF	43	156	14	33	4	1	1	13	.212	65	7	4	.947
Major League Totals—2 Years				56	124	12	24	6	1	3	16	.194	42	2	3	.936

Selected by California Angels' organization in 16th round of free-agent draft, June 6, 1978.
Selected by New York Mets' organization in 2nd round of free-agent draft, June 8, 1981.
†Traded with Pitchers Calvin Schiraldi and Wes Gardner and Outfielder LaSchelle Tarver to Boston Red Sox for Pitchers Bob Ojeda, Tom McCarthy, John Mitchell and Chris Bayer, November 13, 1985.

CLAY C. CHRISTIANSEN

Born June 28, 1958, at Wichita, Kan.
Height, 6.04. Weight, 220.
Throws and bats righthanded.
Attended University of Kansas, Lawrence, Kan.

Major League saves: 1984 (2).
Led International League in wild pitches with 16 in 1983.
Tied for International League lead in hit batsmen with 8 in 1985.

Year	Club	League	G.	IP.	W.	L.	Pct.	H.	R.	ER.	SO.	BB.	ERA.
1980—Oneonta	NYP	15	92	4	3	.571	89	43	26	62	24	2.54
1981—Fort Lauderdale	Florida St.	26	178	16	7	.696	158	59	45	98	46	2.28
1982—Nashville	Southern	29	214⅓	●16	8	.667	214	102	73	157	80	3.07
1983—Columbus	Int'national	32	160⅓	8	9	.471	★196	118	97	92	81	5.44
1984—Columbus	Int'national	22	107⅓	6	3	.667	109	44	37	56	39	3.10
1984—New York	American	24	38⅔	2	4	.333	50	28	26	27	12	6.05
1985—Columbus†	Int'national	28	137⅔	10	6	.625	128	66	56	67	59	3.66
Major League Totals—1 Year		24	38⅔	2	4	.333	50	28	26	27	12	6.05

Selected by New York Mets' organization in 29th round of free-agent draft, June 5, 1979.
Selected by New York Yankees' organization in 15th round of free-agent draft, June 8, 1980.
†On disabled list, July 23 to August 13, 1985.

STEPHEN RANDALL CHRISTMAS
(Steve)

Born December 9, 1957, at Orlando, Fla.
Height, 6.00. Weight, 190.
Throws right and bats lefthanded.
Attended Oklahoma City Southwestern Junior College, Oklahoma City, Okla.

Tied for American Association lead in sacrifice flies with 7 and grounded into double plays with 16 in 1985.
Led Eastern League catchers in total chances with 702 in 1981.
Led Eastern League catchers in fielding percentage with .984 in 1980.
Led Florida State League catchers in putouts with 646 and assists with 113 in 1979.
Led Western Carolinas League catchers in total chances with 627 in 1978.
Tied for Eastern League lead in passed balls with 15 in 1981.
Tied for Florida State League lead in passed balls with 17 in 1979.

Year	Club	League	Pos.	G.	AB.	R.	H.	2B.	3B.	HR.	RBI.	B.A.	PO.	A.	E.	F.A.
1977—Eugene	N'west		C-3B-1B	46	173	30	53	13	1	6	30	.306	214	24	7	.971
1978—Shelby	W. Car.		C	106	352	53	88	10	0	9	40	.250	★532	★77	18	.971
1979—Tampa	Fla. St.		●C-1B	122	377	50	99	18	2	6	39	.263	684	119	●17	.979
1980—Waterbury	East.		C-1B	115	347	44	84	15	2	7	44	.242	621	81	11	.985
1981—Waterbury	East.		C	126	395	40	104	21	0	7	63	.263	594	★95	13	.982
1982—Indianapolis†	A. A.		C-1B	85	252	31	77	14	1	7	37	.306	409	39	12	.974
1983—Tucson	P. C.		C-1B	48	164	18	47	6	0	2	18	.287	159	21	6	.968
1983—Indianapolis‡	A. A.		C-1B	31	98	14	24	6	1	4	20	.245	187	16	3	.985
1983—Cincinnati§	Nat.		C	9	17	0	1	0	0	0	1	.059	28	3	0	1.000
1984—Denver	A. A.		C-1B-OF	74	198	24	55	9	3	4	29	.278	248	22	3	.989
1984—Chicago x	Amer.		C	12	11	1	4	1	0	1	4	.364	2	0	0	1.000
1985—Buffalo y	A. A.		3B-1B-C	127	409	50	122	12	0	16	56	.298	360	119	11	.978
National League Totals—1 Year				9	17	0	1	0	0	0	1	.059	28	3	0	1.000
American League Totals—1 Year				12	11	1	4	1	0	1	4	.364	2	0	0	1.000
Major League Totals—2 Years				21	28	1	5	1	0	1	5	.179	30	3	0	1.000

Selected by Minnesota Twins' organization in 33rd round of free-agent draft, June 4, 1975.
Signed as free agent by Cincinnati Reds' organization, February 13, 1977.

†Loaned to Tucson (Houston Astros' organization), April 2, 1983; returned, June 27, 1983.
‡On disabled list, June 26 to July 22, 1983.
§Traded to Chicago White Sox for Infielder Fran Mullins, November 21, 1983.
xReleased, December 10, 1984; re-signed by Chicago White Sox' organization, January 14, 1985.
yGranted free agency, October 15, 1985.

MARK THOMAS CIARDI

Born August 19, 1961, at New Brunswick, N.J.
Height, 6.00. Weight, 180.
Throws and bats righthanded.
Attended University of Maryland, College Park, Md.

Year Club	League	G.	IP.	W.	L.	Pct.	H.	R.	ER.	SO.	BB.	ERA.
1983—Paintsville	Ap'lachian	13	69⅔	7	2	.778	62	33	25	80	17	3.23
1984—Beloit	Midwest	25	176	10	7	.588	160	76	59	*166	41	3.02
1985—Stockton	California	18	129⅓	10	6	.625	116	59	53	119	39	3.69
1985—El Paso	Texas	10	67⅔	8	1	.889	55	27	20	50	13	2.66

Selected by Milwaukee Brewers' organization in 27th round of free-agent draft, June 7, 1982.
Selected by Milwaukee Brewers' organization in 15th round of free-agent draft, June 6, 1983.

JOSEPH JOHN CIPOLLONI

Name pronounced Sip uh LOIIN-ee.

(Joe)

Born August 12, 1960, at Philadelphia, Pa.
Height, 5.08. Weight, 180.
Throws and bats righthanded.
Attended Phoenix College, Phoenix, Ariz., and
University of Arizona, Tucson, Ariz.

Led Carolina League catchers in double plays with 10 in 1983.

Year Club	League	Pos.	G.	AB.	R.	H.	2B.	3B.	HR.	RBI.	B.A.	PO.	A.	E.	F.A.
1981—Helena	Pion.	C	15	46	5	10	2	0	1	4	.217	85	14	2	.980
1982—Spartanburg	S. Atl.	C-3B	73	230	33	59	16	0	2	29	.257	422	64	12	.976
1983—Peninsula	Carol.	C	98	347	41	80	14	1	5	39	.231	625	76	14	.980
1984—Reading	East.	C	95	283	30	57	10	0	5	31	.201	440	61	10	.980
1985—Reading	East.	C	87	287	21	70	11	1	4	34	.244	437	67	7	.986

Selected by Pittsburgh Pirates' organization in 25th round of free-agent draft, June 3, 1980.
Signed as free agent by Philadelphia Phillies' oganization, August 8, 1981.

RALPH ALEXANDER CITARELLA

Born February 7, 1958, at East Orange, N.J.
Height, 6.00. Weight, 180.
Throws and bats righthanded.
Attended Florida Southern College, Lakeland, Fla., and Brevard Community College, Cocoa, Fla.

Year Club	League	G.	IP.	W.	L.	Pct.	H.	R.	ER.	SO.	BB.	ERA.
1979—Johnson City	Ap'lachian	4	21	0	2	.000	23	15	13	16	12	5.57
1979—St. Petersburg	Florida St.	7	26	0	0	.000	31	8	5	10	11	1.73
1980—Gastonia	S. Atlantic	*51	126	11	4	.733	87	35	23	113	49	*1.64
1981—Arkansas	Texas	31	125	8	9	.491	120	57	53	81	37	3.82
1981—Springfield	Am. Assoc.	1	7	0	0	.000	7	3	3	2	2	3.86
1982—Louisville	Am. Assoc.	28	153	*15	6	.714	171	95	83	82	62	4.88
1983—Louisville	Am. Assoc.	37	109⅔	7	6	.538	122	67	58	64	41	4.76
1983—St. Louis	National	6	11	0	0	.000	8	2	2	4	3	1.64
1984—Louisville	Am. Assoc.	16	89⅔	9	2	*.818	91	43	39	38	30	3.91
1984—St. Louis†‡	National	10	22⅓	0	1	.000	20	9	9	15	7	3.63
1985—Portland§	P. Coast	30	136	7	9	.438	128	67	52	86	58	3.44
Major League Totals—2 Years		16	33⅓	0	1	.000	28	11	11	19	10	2.97

Selected by Minnesota Twins' organization in 1st round (15th player selected) of free-agent draft, January 10, 1978.
Selected by Cincinnati Reds' organization in secondary phase of free-agent draft, June 6, 1978.
Selected by St. Louis Cardinals' organization in secondary phase of free-agent draft, June 5, 1979.
†On disabled list, July 2 to July 17, 1984.
‡Sold to Philadelphia Phillies' organization, January 23, 1985.
§Granted free agency, October 15, 1985; signed by Oakland A's, December 5, 1985.

JOSEPH ANDREW CITARI

(Joe)

Born August 31, 1963, at Oak Park, Ill.
Height, 6.02. Weight, 195.
Throws and bats righthanded.

Led Pioneer League in bases on balls received with 66 in 1982.
Led Southern League first basemen in total chances with 1,267 in 1985.

Year Club	League	Pos.	G.	AB.	R.	H.	2B.	3B.	HR.	RBI.	B.A.	PO.	A.	E.	F.A.
1981—Sar. Royals Gold	Gulf C.	1B	40	103	19	24	6	0	3	10	.233	155	5	3	.982
1982—Butte	Pion.	1B	●70	254	*75	83	16	4	18	64	.327	420	38	12	.974
1983—Fort Myers	Fla. St.	1B	111	361	45	84	6	1	4	43	.233	756	76	5	*.994
1984—Fort Myers	Fla. St.	1B	59	198	41	47	12	0	15	47	.237	400	35	4	.991

Year Club	League	Pos.	G.	AB.	R.	H.	2B.	3B.	HR.	RBI.	B.A.	PO.	A.	E.	F.A.
1984—Memphis...............	South.	1B	84	289	26	54	12	3	4	23	.187	84	273	59	.986
1985—Memphis...............	South.	*1B-OF	141	490	79	124	21	6	23	84	.253	*1147	*111	9	*.993

Selected by Kansas City Royals' organization in 16th round of free-agent draft, June 8, 1981.

JAMES CLANCY
(Jim)

Born December 18, 1955, at Chicago, Ill.
Height, 6.04. Weight, 220.
Throws and bats righthanded.
Led American League pitchers in games started with 40 in 1982 and tied for lead with 36 in 1984.
Tied for Gulf Coast League lead in shutouts with 2 in 1974.

Year Club	League	G.	IP.	W.	L.	Pct.	H.	R.	ER.	SO.	BB.	ERA.
1974—Sarasota Rangers.........................	Gulf Coast	9	53	3	3	.500	40	21	16	58	28	2.72
1975—Anderson.................................	W. Carol.	23	148	6	13	.316	139	85	63	109	91	3.83
1976—San Antonio†‡	Texas	23	125	6	8	.429	133	94	*89	77	98	6.41
1977—Jersey City	Eastern	20	118	5	13	.278	116	87	64	99	75	4.88
1977—Toronto	American	13	77	4	9	.308	80	47	43	44	47	5.03
1978—Toronto	American	31	194	10	12	.455	199	96	88	106	91	4.08
1979—Toronto§	American	12	64	2	7	.222	65	44	39	33	31	5.48
1980—Toronto	American	34	251	13	16	.448	217	108	92	152	*128	3.30
1981—Toronto	American	22	125	6	12	.333	126	77	68	56	64	4.90
1982—Toronto	American	40	266⅔	16	14	.533	251	122	110	139	77	3.71
1983—Toronto	American	34	223	15	11	.577	238	115	97	99	61	3.91
1984—Toronto	American	36	219⅔	13	15	.464	249	*132	*125	118	88	5.12
1985—Toronto x	American	23	128⅔	9	6	.600	117	54	54	66	37	3.78
1985—Knoxville	Southern	2	8	1	0	1.000	7	3	3	2	2	3.38
Major League Totals—9 Years.............................		245	1549	88	102	.463	1542	795	716	813	624	4.16

Selected by Texas Rangers' organization in 4th round of free-agent draft, June 5, 1974.
†On disabled list, June 15 to June 26, 1976.
‡Selected by Toronto Blue Jays from Texas Rangers in American League expansion draft, November 5, 1976.
§On disabled list, May 12 to July 4 and August 5, 1979 through remainder of season.
xOn disabled list, March 25 to April 30 and July 27 to September 2, 1985; included rehabilitation disability assignment to Knoxville, April 21 to April 30, 1985.

CHAMPIONSHIP SERIES RECORD

Year Club	League	G.	IP.	W.	L.	Pct.	H.	R.	ER.	SO.	BB.	ERA.
1985—Toronto	American	1	1	0	1	.000	2	1	1	0	1	9.00

ALL-STAR GAME RECORD

Year League	IP.	W.	L.	Pct.	H.	R.	ER.	SO.	BB.	ERA.
1982—American	1	0	0	.000	0	0	0	0	0	0.00

BRYAN DONALD CLARK

Born July 12, 1956, at Madera, Calif.
Height, 6.02. Weight, 200.
Throws and bats lefthanded.
Attended Fresno City College, Fresno, Calif.
Major League saves: 1981 (2), 1985 (2). Total—4.
Led Carolina League in wild pitches with 24 in 1977 and 27 in 1979.
Led Western Carolinas League in wild pitches with 31 in 1976.
Led New York-Pennsylvania League in wild pitches with 24 in 1975.
Tied for Carolina League lead in shutouts with 3 in 1979.
Tied for Gulf Coast League lead in shutouts with 2 in 1974.

Year Club	League	G.	IP.	W.	L.	Pct.	H.	R.	ER.	SO.	BB.	ERA.
1974—Bradenton Pirates	Gulf Coast	11	62	4	6	.400	49	35	23	47	*40	3.34
1975—Charleston.....................................	W. Carol.	12	57	4	7	.364	56	48	34	38	67	5.37
1975—Niagara Falls.....................................	NYP	13	74	3	*10	.231	47	49	37	59	*71	4.50
1976—Charleston.....................................	W. Carol.	22	103	1	13	.071	97	87	70	79	104	6.12
1977—Salem	Carolina	26	125	5	*13	.278	135	105	66	108	105	4.75
1978—Charleston†	W. Carol.	12	56	1	6	.143	55	53	38	44	55	6.11
1978—Bellingham	Northwest	2	4	0	0	.000	4	1	1	6	3	2.25
1978—Stockton	California	11	27	0	4	.000	30	32	22	18	39	7.33
1979—Alexandria	Carolina	23	167	●14	5	.737	124	57	49	116	*112	2.64
1980—Spokane	P. Coast	8	41	2	5	.286	43	35	24	19	37	5.27
1980—Lynn	Eastern	16	116	9	5	.643	102	49	40	93	50	3.10
1981—Seattle.....................................	American	29	93	2	5	.286	92	54	45	52	55	4.35
1982—Salt Lake City	P. Coast	4	5⅓	1	1	.500	5	6	6	2	5	10.13
1982—Seattle.....................................	American	37	114⅔	5	2	.714	104	44	35	70	58	2.75
1983—Seattle‡	American	41	161⅓	7	10	.412	160	82	71	76	72	3.94
1984—Syracuse	Int'national	6	34	3	1	.750	32	16	13	26	26	3.44
1984—Toronto§	American	20	45⅔	1	2	.333	66	33	30	21	22	5.91
1985—Maine	Int'national	4	18⅔	1	0	1.000	15	2	2	9	8	0.96
1985—Cleveland x	American	31	62⅔	3	4	.429	78	47	44	24	34	6.32
Major League Totals—5 Years.............................		158	478⅓	18	23	.439	500	260	225	243	241	4.23

Selected by Pittsburgh Pirates' organization in 10th round of free-agent draft, June 5, 1974.
†Sold to Seattle Mariners' organization, June 12, 1978.

‡Traded to Toronto Blue Jays for Outfielder Barry Bonnell, December 9, 1983.
§Released, April 1, 1985; signed by Cleveland Indians' organization, April 15, 1985.
xReleased, November 12, 1985.

DAVID EARL CLARK
(Dave)

Born September 3, 1962, at Tupelo, Miss.
Height, 6.02. Weight, 200.
Throws right and bats lefthanded.
Attended Jackson State University, Jackson, Miss.
Named outfielder on THE SPORTING NEWS College Baseball All-America Team, 1983.

Year	Club	League	Pos.	G.	AB.	R.	H.	2B.	3B.	HR.	RBI.	B.A.	PO.	A.	E.	F.A.
1983—Waterloo		Midw.	OF	58	159	20	44	8	1	4	20	.277	37	4	1	.976
1984—Waterloo		Midw.	OF	110	363	74	112	16	3	15	63	.309	128	10	4	.972
1984—Buffalo		East.	OF	17	56	12	10	1	0	3	10	.179	23	2	1	.962
1985—Waterbury		East.	OF	132	463	75	140	24	7	12	64	.302	204	11	11	.951

Selected by Cleveland Indians' organization in 1st round (11th player selected) of free-agent draft, June 6, 1983.

JACK ANTHONY CLARK

Born November 10, 1955, at New Brighton, Pa.
Height, 6.03. Weight, 205.
Throws and bats righthanded.

Major League stolen bases: 1975 (1), 1976 (6), 1977 (12), 1978 (15), 1979 (11), 1980 (2), 1981 (1), 1982 (6), 1983 (5), 1984 (1), 1985 (1). Total—61.
Led National League in game-winning RBIs with 18 in 1980 and tied for lead with 21 in 1982.
Tied for National League lead in double plays by outfielders with 5 in 1978, 7 in 1979 and 4 in 1981.
Led California League in total bases with 254 in 1974 and Texas League with 239 in 1975.
Led Texas League third basemen in putouts with 102, assists with 278, double plays with 29 and fielding percentage with .872 in 1975.
Named outfielder on THE SPORTING NEWS National League All-Star Team, 1978.
Named first baseman on THE SPORTING NEWS National League Silver Slugger team, 1985.

Year	Club	League	Pos.	G.	AB.	R.	H.	2B.	3B.	HR.	RBI.	B.A.	PO.	A.	E.	F.A.
1973—Great Falls		Pion.	OF-P-3B	65	234	46	75	20	1	9	54	.321	73	9	1	.988
1974—Fresno		Calif.	3B	131	495	88	156	23	9	19	★117	.315	100	204	★53	.852
1975—Lafayette		Texas	★3B-OF	126	466	94	141	25	2	●23	77	.303	107	279	★56	.873
1975—San Francisco		Nat.	OF-3B	8	17	3	4	0	0	0	2	.235	8	1	0	1.000
1976—Phoenix		P. C.	OF-3B	131	470	111	152	29	★16	17	86	.323	188	23	9	.959
1976—San Francisco		Nat.	OF	26	102	14	23	6	2	2	10	.225	71	3	1	.987
1977—San Francisco		Nat.	OF	136	413	64	104	17	4	13	51	.252	226	11	6	.975
1978—San Francisco		Nat.	OF	156	592	90	181	46	8	25	98	.306	320	16	6	.982
1979—San Francisco		Nat.	OF-3B	143	527	84	144	25	2	26	86	.273	262	13	5	.971
1980—San Francisco†		Nat.	OF	127	437	77	124	20	8	22	82	.284	229	7	8	.967
1981—San Francisco		Nat.	OF	99	385	60	103	19	2	17	53	.268	193	●14	4	.981
1982—San Francisco		Nat.	OF	157	563	90	154	30	3	27	103	.274	281	10	6	.980
1983—San Francisco		Nat.	OF-1B	135	492	82	132	25	0	20	66	.268	262	20	9	.969
1984—San Francisco‡§		Nat.	OF-1B	57	203	33	65	9	1	11	44	.320	120	9	2	.985
1985—St. Louis x		Nat.	★1B-OF	126	442	71	124	26	3	22	87	.281	1128	66	★14	.988
Major League Totals—11 Years				1170	4173	668	1158	223	33	185	682	.277	3100	170	61	.982

Selected by San Francisco Giants' organization in 13th round of free-agent draft, June 5, 1973.
†On disabled list, August 23 to September 8, 1980.
‡On disabled list, June 25 to September 5, 1984.
§Traded to St. Louis Cardinals for First Basemen David Green and Gary Rajsich, Pitcher Dave LaPoint and Shortstop Jose Gonzalez (Jose Uribe), February 1, 1985.
xOn disabled list, August 24 to September 8, 1985.

CHAMPIONSHIP SERIES RECORD

Tied Championship Series record for most hits, inning (2), October 13, 1985 (second inning).
Tied National League Championship Series records for most singles (7) and most bases on balls (5), six-game Series, 1985.

Year	Club	League	Pos.	G.	AB.	R.	H.	2B.	3B.	HR.	RBI.	B.A.	PO.	A.	E.	F.A.
1985—St. Louis		Nat.	1B	6	21	4	8	0	0	1	4	.381	55	0	0	1.000

WORLD SERIES RECORD

Year	Club	League	Pos.	G.	AB.	R.	H.	2B.	3B.	HR.	RBI.	B.A.	PO.	A.	E.	F.A.
1985—St. Louis		Nat.	1B	7	25	1	6	2	0	0	4	.240	49	4	0	1.000

ALL-STAR GAME RECORD

Year	League	Pos.	AB.	R.	H.	2B.	3B.	HR.	RBI.	B.A.	PO.	A.	E.	F.A.
1978—National		OF	1	0	0	0	0	0	0	.000	0	0	0	.000
1979—National		PH	1	0	0	0	0	0	0	.000	0	0	0	.000
1985—National		1B	1	0	0	0	0	0	0	.000	4	0	0	1.000
All-Star Game Totals—3 Years			3	0	0	0	0	0	0	.000	4	0	0	1.000

PITCHING RECORD

Year	Club	League	G.	IP.	W.	L.	Pct.	H.	R.	ER.	SO.	BB.	ERA.
1973—Great Falls		Pioneer	5	15	0	2	.000	24	24	10	17	19	6.00

ROBERT CALE CLARK
(Bobby)

Born June 13, 1955, at Sacramento, Calif.
Height, 6.00. Weight, 190.
Throws and bats righthanded.
Attended Riverside City Junior College, Riverside, Calif. and University of California, Riverside, Calif.
Major League stolen bases: 1979 (1), 1982 (1), 1984 (1), 1985 (1). Total—4.
Led Texas League in total bases with 297 in 1978.
Led Midwest League outfielders in double plays with 9 in 1977.
Led Pioneer League outfielders in fielding percentage with .978 in 1975.
Named Texas League Most Valuable Player, 1978.

Year	Club	League	Pos.	G.	AB.	R.	H.	2B.	3B.	HR.	RBI.	B.A.	PO.	A.	E.	F.A.
1975—Idaho Falls	Pion.	OF-1B-3B	•72	253	43	64	7	★9	4	38	.253	154	10	6	.965
1976—Quad Cities	Midw.	★OF-1B	•129	477	82	139	19	8	10	77	.291	365	★28	10	.975
1977—Salinas	Calif.	★O-C-1B	137	524	107	149	19	10	23	88	.284	311	11	7	★.979
1978—El Paso	Texas	OF	129	491	108	155	35	7	★31	★111	.316	261	★23	9	.969
1979—Salt Lake City	P. C.	OF	129	474	85	144	30	9	15	91	.304	★328	12	7	.980
1979—California	Amer.	OF	19	54	8	16	2	2	1	5	.296	41	4	1	.978
1980—Salt Lake City	P. C.	OF	33	113	18	39	6	4	4	21	.345	57	2	1	.983
1980—California	Amer.	OF	78	261	26	60	10	1	5	23	.230	213	6	4	.982
1981—California	Amer.	OF	34	88	12	22	2	1	4	19	.250	66	5	0	1.000
1982—California	Amer.	OF	102	90	11	19	1	0	2	8	.211	88	2	0	1.000
1983—California†	Amer.	OF-3B	76	212	17	49	9	1	5	21	.231	122	0	0	1.000
1983—Edmonton‡	P.C.	OF	7	31	3	8	2	0	2	7	.258	7	0	0	1.000
1984—Milwaukee§	Amer.	OF	58	169	17	44	7	2	2	16	.260	106	0	2	.981
1985—Vancouver	P. C.	OF	29	110	17	31	7	2	2	20	.282	194	14	6	.972
1985—Milwaukee	Amer.	OF	29	93	6	21	3	0	0	8	.226	72	1	0	1.000
Major League Totals—7 Years			396	967	97	231	34	7	19	100	.239	708	18	7	.990

Selected by Houston Astros' organization in 14th round of free-agent draft, June 5, 1973.
Selected by California Angels' organization in secondary phase of free-agent draft, January 9, 1975.
†On disabled list, July 20 to September 3, 1983; included rehabilitation disability assignment to Edmonton, August 16 to August 26, 1983.
‡Traded to Milwaukee Brewers for Pitcher Jim Slaton, December 20, 1983.
§On disabled list, March 29 to May 2, 1984.

CHAMPIONSHIP SERIES RECORD

Year	Club	League	Pos.	G.	AB.	R.	H.	2B.	3B.	HR.	RBI.	B.A.	PO.	A.	E.	F.A.
1979—California	Amer.	OF	1	3	0	0	0	0	0	0	.000	3	0	0	1.000
1982—California	Amer.	OF	2	0	0	0	0	0	0	0	.000	1	0	0	1.000
Championship Series Totals—2 Years			3	3	0	0	0	0	0	0	.000	4	0	0	1.000

WILLIAM N. CLARK JR.
(Will)

Born March 17, 1964, at New Orleans, La.
Height, 6.02. Weight, 190.
Throws and bats lefthanded.
Attended Mississippi State University, Mississippi State, Miss.

Named first baseman on THE SPORTING NEWS College Baseball All-America Team, 1985.
Member of 1984 U.S. Olympic baseball team.
Named designated hitter on THE SPORTING NEWS College Baseball All-America Team, 1984.

Year	Club	League	Pos.	G.	AB.	R.	H.	2B.	3B.	HR.	RBI.	B.A.	PO.	A.	E.	F.A.
1985—Fresno	Calif.	1B-OF	65	217	41	67	14	0	10	48	.309	523	51	6	.990

Selected by Kansas City Royals' organization in 4th round of free-agent draft, June 7, 1982.
Selected by San Francisco Giants' organization in 1st round (second player selected) of free-agent draft, June 3, 1985.

STANLEY MARTEN CLARKE
(Stan)

Born August 9, 1960, at Toledo, O.
Height, 6.01. Weight, 180.
Throws and bats lefthanded.
Attended University of Toledo, Toledo, O.

Led Pioneer League in balks with 6 and tied for lead in complete games with 6 in 1981.

Year	Club	League	G.	IP.	W.	L.	Pct.	H.	R.	ER.	SO.	BB.	ERA.
1981—Medicine Hat	Pioneer	17	94	8	4	.667	96	54	42	112	35	4.02
1982—Florence	S. Atlantic	50	95	6	4	.600	60	26	20	136	52	1.89
1982—Knoxville	Southern	11	16	0	1	.000	11	3	3	12	3	1.69
1983—Knoxville	Southern	26	43⅓	2	4	.333	30	18	12	51	20	2.49
1983—Toronto	American	10	11	1	1	.500	10	4	4	7	5	3.27
1983—Syracuse	Int'national	33	53	0	3	.000	39	26	17	58	34	2.89
1984—Syracuse†	Int'national	29	56⅔	2	3	.400	40	32	26	55	46	4.13
1985—Syracuse	Int'national	43	117⅔	•14	4	★.778	106	52	44	98	66	3.37
1985—Toronto	American	4	4	0	0	.000	3	2	2	2	2	4.50
Major League Totals—2 Years		14	15	1	1	.500	13	6	6	9	7	3.60

Selected by Toronto Blue Jays' organization in 6th round of free-agent draft, June 8, 1981.
†On disabled list, June 6 to July 3 and August 23, 1984 through remainder of season.

MARTIN KEITH CLARY
(Marty)

Born April 3, 1962, at Detroit, Mich.
Height, 6.04. Weight, 190.
Throws and bats righthanded.
Attended Northwestern University, Evanston, Ill.
Led Southern League pitchers in games started with 30 in 1984.

Year Club	League	G.	IP.	W.	L.	Pct.	H.	R.	ER.	SO.	BB.	ERA.
1983—Durham	Carolina	15	89⅔	3	8	.273	101	65	50	58	39	5.02
1984—Greenville	Southern	30	186½	14	9	.609	172	77	66	125	82	3.19
1985—Richmond	Int'national	26	156⅔	8	12	.400	155	81	73	76	77	4.19

Selected by Atlanta Braves' organization in 3rd round of free-agent draft, June 6, 1983.

MARK ALAN CLEAR

Born May 27, 1956, at Los Angeles, Calif.
Height, 6.04. Weight, 215.
Throws and bats righthanded.
Attended Mount San Antonio College, Walnut, Calif.
Nephew of Bob Clear, minor league pitcher, 1945 through 1955; minor league player-manager,
1956 through 1961; minor league manager, 1962 through 1973; scout with California Angels,
1974 and 1975; and coach with California Angels since 1976.
Major League saves: 1979 (14), 1980 (9), 1981 (9), 1982 (14), 1983 (4), 1984 (8), 1985 (3). Total—61.
Led Appalachian League in hit batsmen with 11 in 1974.
Named American League Rookie Pitcher of the Year by THE SPORTING NEWS, 1979.

Year Club	League	G.	IP.	W.	L.	Pct.	H.	R.	ER.	SO.	BB.	ERA.
1974—Pulaski†	Ap'lachian	14	51	0	7	.000	73	★69	49	38	43	8.65
1975—Idaho Falls	Pioneer	13	28	1	2	.333	24	14	6	29	30	1.93
1976—Quad Cities	Midwest	30	144	8	10	.444	135	84	63	109	111	3.94
1977—Quad Cities	Midwest	13	74	6	3	.667	64	47	40	48	50	4.86
1977—Salinas	California	13	44	1	4	.200	49	36	32	26	45	6.55
1978—Salinas	California	10	53	3	5	.375	51	38	32	55	40	5.43
1978—El Paso	Texas	31	52	4	2	.667	28	14	14	80	32	2.42
1979—California	American	52	109	11	5	.688	87	48	44	98	68	3.63
1980—California‡	American	58	106	11	11	.500	82	51	39	105	65	3.31
1981—Boston	American	34	77	8	3	.727	69	36	35	82	51	4.09
1982—Boston	American	55	105	14	9	.609	92	39	35	109	61	3.00
1983—Boston	American	48	96	4	5	.444	101	71	67	81	68	6.28
1984—Boston§	American	47	67	8	3	.727	47	38	30	76	70	4.03
1985—Boston§	American	41	55⅔	1	3	.250	45	26	23	55	50	3.72
Major League Totals—7 Years		335	615⅔	57	39	.594	523	309	273	606	433	3.99

Selected by Philadelphia Phillies' organization in 8th round of free-agent draft, June 5, 1974.
†Released, April 2, 1975; signed by California Angels' organization, June 16, 1975.
‡Traded with Third Baseman Carney Lansford and Outfielder Rick Miller to Boston Red Sox for Shortstop Rick Burleson and Third Baseman Butch Hobson, December 10, 1980.
§Traded to Milwaukee Brewers for Infielder Ed Romero, December 11, 1985.

CHAMPIONSHIP SERIES RECORD

Year Club	League	G.	IP.	W.	L.	Pct.	H.	R.	ER.	SO.	BB.	ERA.
1979—California	American	1	5⅔	0	0	.000	4	3	3	3	2	4.76

ALL-STAR GAME RECORD

Year League	IP.	W.	L.	Pct.	H.	R.	ER.	SO.	BB.	ERA.
1979—American	2	0	0	.000	2	1	1	0	1	4.50

Member of American League All-Star Team in 1982; did not play.

WILLIAM ROGER CLEMENS
(Known by middle name.)

Born August 4, 1962, at Dayton, O.
Height, 6.04. Weight, 205.
Throws and bats righthanded.
Attended San Jacinto College (North), Houston, Tex.,
and University of Texas, Austin, Tex.

Year Club	League	G.	IP.	W.	L.	Pct.	H.	R.	ER.	SO.	BB.	ERA.
1983—Winter Haven	Florida St.	4	29	3	1	.750	22	4	4	36	0	1.24
1983—New Britain	Eastern	7	52	4	1	.800	31	8	8	59	12	1.38
1984—Pawtucket	Int'national	7	46⅔	2	3	.400	39	12	10	50	14	1.93
1984—Boston	American	21	133⅓	9	4	.692	146	67	64	126	29	4.32
1985—Boston†	American	15	98⅓	7	5	.583	83	38	36	74	37	3.29
Major League Totals—2 Years		36	231⅔	16	9	.640	229	105	100	200	66	3.88

Selected by New York Mets' organization in 12th round of free-agent draft, June 8, 1981.
Selected by Boston Red Sox' organization in 1st round (19th player selected) of free-agent draft, June 6, 1983.
†On disabled list, July 8 to August 3 and August 21, 1985 through remainder of season.

PATRICK BRIAN CLEMENTS
(Pat)

Born February 2, 1962, at McCloud, Calif.
Height, 6.00. Weight, 175.
Throws left and bats righthanded.
Attended University of California, Los Angeles, Calif.

Major League saves: 1985 (3).

Year Club	League	G.	IP.	W.	L.	Pct.	H.	R.	ER.	SO.	BB.	ERA.
1983—Peoria	Midwest	15	92⅓	4	7	.364	113	56	46	67	24	4.48
1984—Waterbury	Eastern	43	67	4	2	.667	59	28	20	44	29	2.69
1985—California†	American	41	62	5	0	1.000	47	23	23	19	25	3.34
1985—Pittsburgh	National	27	34⅓	0	2	.000	39	14	14	17	15	3.67
American League Totals—1 Year		41	62	5	0	1.000	47	23	23	19	25	3.34
National League Totals—1 Year		27	34⅓	0	2	.000	39	14	14	17	15	3.67
Major League Totals—1 Year		68	96⅓	5	2	.714	86	37	37	36	40	3.46

Selected by New York Yankees' organization in 32nd round of free-agent draft, June 3, 1980.
Selected by California Angels' organization in 4th round of free-agent draft, June 6, 1983.
†Traded with Outfielder Mike Brown and a player to be named later to Pittsburgh Pirates for Pitchers John Candelaria and Al Holland and Outfielder George Hendrick, August 2, 1985; Pittsburgh organization acquired Pitcher Bob Kipper to complete deal, August 16, 1985.

STEWART WALKER CLIBURN
(Stu)

Born December 19, 1956, at Jackson, Miss.
Height, 6.00. Weight, 187.
Throws and bats righthanded.
Attended Delta State University, Cleveland, Miss.
Identical twin of Stan Cliburn, catcher in Pittsburgh Pirates' organization.

Major League saves: 1985 (6).

Year Club	League	G.	IP.	W.	L.	Pct.	H.	R.	ER.	SO.	BB.	ERA.
1977—Carolina	Carolina	15	97	8	5	.615	108	50	35	48	33	3.25
1978—Shreveport†	Texas	9	42	1	0	1.000	37	13	9	30	17	1.93
1979—Buffalo	Eastern	15	103	6	6	.500	110	50	37	62	43	3.23
1979—Portland‡	P. Coast	7	33	3	2	.600	43	19	18	17	17	4.91
1980—Buffalo§	Eastern	1	6	1	0	1.000	5	0	0	2	3	0.00
1980—Portland	P. Coast	17	82	2	9	.182	97	56	50	44	39	5.49
1981—Buffalo x	Eastern	28	85	5	8	.385	77	45	41	53	35	4.34
1981—Portland y	P. Coast	6	17	0	1	.000	32	18	18	7	6	9.53
1982—Holyoke	Eastern	22	103⅔	5	3	.625	91	48	41	78	42	3.56
1982—Spokane	P. Coast	8	38⅔	1	6	.143	51	37	33	28	17	7.68
1983—Nashua	Eastern	39	98⅔	6	7	.462	94	45	41	40	31	3.74
1984—Edmonton	P. Coast	45	75	7	7	.500	71	30	24	48	28	2.88
1984—California	American	1	2	0	0	.000	3	3	3	1	1	13.50
1985—Edmonton	P. Coast	2	3⅔	0	0	.000	3	0	0	2	0	0.00
1985—California	American	44	99	9	3	.750	87	25	23	48	26	2.09
Major League Totals—2 Years		45	101	9	3	.750	90	28	26	49	27	2.32

Selected by San Francisco Giants' organization in 16th round of free-agent draft, June 5, 1974.
Selected by Pittsburgh Pirates' organization in 4th round of free-agent draft, June 7, 1977.
†On disabled list, May 9 to May 24, May 26 to June 15 and July 2 to August 22, 1978.
‡On disabled list, July 22 to August 8, 1979.
§On disabled list, April 14 to April 26, 1980.
xOn disabled list, May 11 to May 27, 1981.
yReleased, April 8, 1982; signed by Holyoke (California Angels' organization), April 29, 1982.

BRYAN RICHARD CLUTTERBUCK

Born December 17, 1959, at Detroit, Mich.
Height, 6.04. Weight, 223.
Throws and bats righthanded.
Attended Eastern Michigan University, Ypsilanti, Mich.

Tied for Texas League lead in games started by pitchers with 27 in 1983 and 1984.
Tied for Midwest League lead in shutouts with 4 in 1982.

Year Club	League	G.	IP.	W.	L.	Pct.	H.	R.	ER.	SO.	BB.	ERA.
1981—Butte	Pioneer	6	16	1	1	.500	22	13	13	4	7	7.31
1982—Beloit	Midwest	26	173⅔	13	6	.684	165	84	70	138	56	3.63
1983—El Paso	Texas	27	166⅓	11	7	.611	204	118	96	86	78	5.19
1984—El Paso	Texas	27	179	10	9	.526	*198	*103	*79	112	52	3.97
1985—Vancouver	P. Coast	29	147⅔	11	7	.611	156	68	58	101	41	3.53

Selected by Milwaukee Brewers' organization in 7th round of free-agent draft, June 8, 1981.

—DID YOU KNOW—

That the Cardinals' John Tudor won each of his six starts in June, 1985? Tudor pitched 47 innings, recording two shutouts and an earned-run average of 1.34. His record improved to 7-7 after a 1-7 start.

JAMES STANLEY COCANOWER
(Jaime)
Nickname pronounced HI-me.

Born February 14, 1957, at Balboa Heights, Canal Zone
Height, 6.04. Weight, 200.
Throws and bats righthanded.
Received bachelor of business administration degree in accounting
from Baylor University, Waco, Tex., in 1980.

Led California League in balks with 6 in 1980.
Named California League co-Most Valuable Player, 1980.

Year Club	League	G.	IP.	W.	L.	Pct.	H.	R.	ER.	SO.	BB.	ERA.
1978—Burlington†	Midwest						(Did not play)					
1979—Stockton‡	California	20	78	2	4	.333	73	42	36	36	45	4.15
1980—Stockton	California	27	●198	17	5	.773	143	74	48	132	105	2.18
1981—Vancouver	P. Coast	26	137	6	12	.333	144	95	86	78	102	5.65
1982—Vancouver	P. Coast	14	74	4	3	.571	81	49	40	32	59	4.86
1982—El Paso§	Texas	9	62⅓	3	1	.750	73	36	23	29	30	3.32
1983—Vancouver x	P. Coast	23	153⅓	10	10	.500	177	100	82	79	59	4.81
1983—Milwaukee	American	5	30	2	0	1.000	21	8	6	8	12	1.80
1984—Milwaukee	American	33	174⅔	8	16	.333	188	99	78	65	78	4.02
1985—Vancouver	P. Coast	9	62⅔	5	2	.714	50	27	22	10	20	3.10
1985—Milwaukee	American	24	116⅓	6	8	.429	122	72	56	44	73	4.33
Major League Totals—3 Years		62	321	16	24	.400	331	179	140	117	163	3.93

Signed as free agent by Milwaukee Brewers' organization, June 7, 1978.
†On disabled list, June 17 to September 27, 1978.
‡On temporary inactive list, August 16 to September 8, 1979.
§On temporary inactive list, June 30 to July 15, 1982.
xOn disabled list, July 15 to July 24, 1983.

DAVID CARTER COCHRANE
(Dave)

Born January 31, 1963, at Riverside, Calif.
Height, 6.02. Weight, 180.
Throws right and bats left and righthanded.
Attended California State University, Fullerton, Calif.

Led Texas League batters in strikeouts with 133 in 1984.
Led Carolina League in game-winning RBIs with 18 in 1983.
Led New York-Pennsylvania League batters in strikeouts with 117 and intentional bases on balls received with 7 in 1982.

Year Club	League	Pos.	G.	AB.	R.	H.	2B.	3B.	HR.	RBI.	B.A.	PO.	A.	E.	F.A.
1982—Little Falls	NYP	3B	70	269	51	81	16	2	22	62	.301	49	110	★29	.846
1983—Lynchburg	Carol.	3B	120	445	73	117	16	1	25	★102	.263	66	167	26	.900
1984—Jackson	Texas	3B-SS	129	454	66	121	29	3	22	77	.267	79	167	32	.885
1985—Jackson†‡§	Texas	SS	33	103	14	23	1	0	4	20	.223	39	87	14	.900

Selected by New York Mets' organization in 4th round of free-agent draft, June 8, 1981.
†On disabled list, May 25 to July 16, 1985.
‡Traded to Chicago White Sox' organization for Outfielder Tom Paciorek, July 16, 1985.
§On Glens Falls disabled list, July 16, 1985 through remainder of season.

ATLEE ALAN COCKRELL
(Known by middle name.)

Born December 5, 1962, at Joplin, Mo.
Height, 6.02. Weight, 210.
Throws and bats righthanded.
Attended University of Tennessee, Knoxville, Tenn.

Led Texas League batters in strikeouts with 137 in 1985.
Received reported $100,000 bonus to sign with San Francisco Giants, 1984.
Named outfielder on THE SPORTING NEWS College Baseball All-America Team, 1984.

Year Club	League	Pos.	G.	AB.	R.	H.	2B.	3B.	HR.	RBI.	B.A.	PO.	A.	E.	F.A.
1984—Everett	N'west	OF	2	8	1	3	0	0	0	3	.375	6	0	0	1.000
1984—Fresno	Calif.	OF	61	214	20	46	6	0	1	32	.215	96	9	5	.955
1985—Shreveport	Texas	OF	126	455	53	115	25	3	11	68	.253	177	10	10	.949

Selected by Toronto Blue Jays' organization in 8th round of free-agent draft, June 8, 1981.
Selected by San Francisco Giants' organization in 1st round (ninth player selected) of free-agent draft, June 4, 1984.

CHRISTOPHER ALLEN CODIROLI
Name pronounced Coda-RO-lee.
(Chris)

Born March 26, 1958, at Oxnard, Calif.
Height, 6.01. Weight, 160.
Throws and bats righthanded.
Attended San Jose City College, San Jose, Calif.,
and San Jose State University, San Jose, Calif.

Major League saves: 1983 (1), 1984 (1). Total—2.
Tied for American League lead in games started by pitchers with 37 in 1985.

Year Club	League	G.	IP.	W.	L.	Pct.	H.	R.	ER.	SO.	BB.	ERA.
1978—Lakeland	Florida St.	16	102	4	6	.400	93	44	37	72	40	3.26
1978—Montgomery	Southern	10	78	5	2	.714	60	20	17	57	24	1.96
1979—Montgomery†	Southern	8	49	2	3	.400	41	24	18	34	27	3.31
1980—Lakeland‡	Florida St.	9	50	1	1	.500	33	13	10	26	19	1.80
1980—Montgomery§	Southern	2	4	0	1	.000	6	7	6	1	4	13.50
1981—San Jose	California	14	35	3	2	.600	23	8	6	26	24	1.54
1981—West Haven	Eastern	21	50	3	2	.600	35	25	15	47	25	2.70
1982—West Haven x	Eastern	12	45	6	1	.857	37	14	12	45	19	2.40
1982—Tacoma	P. Coast	16	123⅓	10	3	*.769	100	36	26	85	21	*1.90
1982—Oakland	American	3	16⅔	1	2	.333	16	8	8	5	4	4.32
1983—Oakland	American	37	205⅔	12	12	.500	208	115	102	85	72	4.46
1984—Oakland	American	28	89⅓	6	4	.600	111	67	58	44	34	5.84
1984—Tacoma	P. Coast	9	57	2	1	.667	49	35	24	52	30	3.79
1985—Oakland	American	37	226	14	14	.500	228	125	112	111	78	4.46
Major League Totals—4 Years		105	537⅔	33	32	.508	563	315	280	245	188	4.69

Selected by Detroit Tigers' organization in 1st round (11th player selected) of free-agent draft, January 10, 1978.
†On disabled list, May 25, 1979 through remainder of season.
‡On disabled list, April 11 to June 10, 1980.
§Released, April 3, 1981; signed by Oakland A's organization, April 14, 1981.
xOn disabled list, April 19 to April 29, 1982.

WILLIAM RODGERS COLE
(Rodger)

Born March 21, 1961, at Ann Arbor, Mich.
Height, 5.07. Weight, 160.
Throws and bats righthanded.
Attended Cochise County Community College, Douglas, Ariz.,
and Wiley College, Marshall, Tex.

Year Club	League	G.	IP.	W.	L.	Pct.	H.	R.	ER.	SO.	BB.	ERA.
1982—Helena	Pioneer	13	86⅔	7	3	.700	76	43	31	69	27	3.22
1983—Peninsula	Carolina	25	167⅓	9	13	.409	173	91	72	105	73	3.87
1983—Reading	Eastern	1	7	1	0	1.000	4	0	0	3	0	0.00
1984—Reading	Eastern	10	63⅔	3	4	.429	64	26	14	38	21	1.98
1984—Portland	P. Coast	17	96⅓	3	5	.375	110	66	57	46	41	5.33
1985—Portland†‡	P. Coast	40	86⅓	3	6	.333	101	57	45	47	50	4.69

Selected by Philadelphia Phillies' organization in 27th round of free-agent draft, June 7, 1982.
†On disabled list, May 7 to June 1, 1985.
‡Traded with First Baseman Ronnie Gideon to New York Mets for Catcher Ronn Reynolds and Pitcher Jeff Bittiger, January 16, 1986.

VINCENT MAURICE COLEMAN
(Vince)

Born September 22, 1961, at Jacksonville, Fla.
Height, 6.00. Weight, 170.
Throws right and bats left and righthanded.
Received degree in physical education from Florida A&M University, Tallahassee, Fla.
Cousin of Greg Coleman, punter with Minnesota Vikings.

Established major league records for most stolen bases (110) and most caught stealing (25), rookie season, 1985.
Established National League record for most strikeouts by switch-hitter, season (115), 1985.
Major League stolen bases: 1985 (110).
Led National League in stolen bases with 110 and caught stealing with 25 in 1985.
Led American Association in stolen bases with 101 and caught stealing with 36 in 1984.
Led South Atlantic League in stolen bases with 145 and caught stealing with 31 in 1983.
Tied for Appalachian League lead in stolen bases with 43 in 1982.
Led American Association outfielders in total chances with 381 in 1984.
Named National League Rookie Player of the Year by THE SPORTING NEWS, 1985.
Named National League Rookie of the Year by Baseball Writers' Association of America, 1985.
Named South Atlantic League Most Valuable Player, 1983.

Year Club	League	Pos.	G.	AB.	R.	H.	2B.	3B.	HR.	RBI.	B.A.	PO.	A.	E.	F.A.
1982—Johnson City	Appal.	OF	58	212	40	53	2	1	0	16	.250	123	7	8	.942
1983—Macon	S. Atl.	OF	113	446	99	156	8	7	0	53	*.350	225	18	8	.968
1984—Louisville	A. A.	OF	152	*608	*97	156	21	7	4	48	.257	357	14	●10	.974
1985—Louisville	A. A.	OF	5	21	1	3	0	0	0	0	.143	8	0	0	1.000
1985—St. Louis	Nat.	OF	151	636	107	170	20	10	1	40	.267	305	16	7	.979
Major League Totals—1 Year			151	636	107	170	20	10	1	40	.267	305	16	7	.979

Selected by Philadelphia Phillies' organization in 20th round of free-agent draft, June 8, 1981.
Selected by St. Louis Cardinals' organization in 10th round of free-agent draft, June 7, 1982.

CHAMPIONSHIP SERIES RECORD

Year Club	League	Pos.	G.	AB.	R.	H.	2B.	3B.	HR.	RBI.	B.A.	PO.	A.	E.	F.A.
1985—St. Louis	Nat.	OF	3	14	2	4	0	0	0	1	.286	8	0	0	1.000

DARNELL COLES

First name pronounced Darr-NELL.

Born June 2, 1962, at San Bernardino, Calif.
Height, 6.01. Weight, 185.
Throws and bats righthanded.
Attended Orange Coast College, Costa Mesa, Calif.

Major League stolen bases: 1984 (2).
Led Midwest League shortstops in double plays with 66 in 1981.

Year Club	League	Pos.	G.	AB.	R.	H.	2B.	3B.	HR.	RBI.	B.A.	PO.	A.	E.	F.A.
1980—Bellingham	N'west	SS	35	117	23	25	3	1	2	12	.214	37	80	★28	.807
1981—Wausau	Midw.	SS	111	354	53	97	20	3	9	48	.274	154	335	52	.904
1982—Bakersfield	Calif.	SS	136	482	91	146	24	4	11	55	.303	200	419	★73	.895
1983—Chattanooga	South.	SS	72	261	49	75	10	4	5	24	.287	131	232	30	.924
1983—Salt Lake City	P. C.	SS	61	234	43	74	12	5	10	41	.316	100	178	25	.917
1983—Seattle..................	Amer.	3B	27	92	9	26	7	0	1	6	.283	17	47	4	.941
1984—Salt Lake City†.....	P. C.	3B	69	242	57	77	22	3	14	68	.318	45	164	16	.929
1984—Seattle..................	Amer.	3B-OF	48	143	15	23	3	1	0	6	.161	31	63	8	.922
1985—Calgary	P. C.	3B-SS-OF	31	97	16	31	8	0	4	24	.320	16	49	5	.929
1985—Seattle‡..............	Amer.	SS-3B-OF	27	59	8	14	4	0	1	5	.237	25	44	6	.920
Major League Totals—3 Years................			102	294	32	63	14	1	2	17	.214	73	154	18	.927

Selected by Seattle Mariners' organization in 1st round (sixth player selected) of free-agent draft, June 3, 1980.
†On Seattle disabled list, March 29 to April 24, 1984; included rehabilitation disability assignment to Salt Lake City, April 12 to April 24, 1984.
‡Traded to Detroit Tigers for Pitcher Rich Monteleone, December 12, 1985.

DAVID S. COLLINS
(Dave)

Born October 20, 1952, at Rapid City, S. D.
Height, 5.10. Weight, 175.
Throws left and bats left and righthanded.
Attended Mesa Community College, Mesa, Ariz.

Major League stolen bases: 1975 (24), 1976 (32), 1977 (25), 1978 (7), 1979 (16), 1980 (79), 1981 (26), 1982 (13), 1983 (31), 1984 (60), 1985 (29). Total—342.
Led Pioneer League outfielders in double plays with 3 in 1972.
Named Pioneer League Most Valuable Player, 1972.

Year Club	League	Pos.	G.	AB.	R.	H.	2B.	3B.	HR.	RBI.	B.A.	PO.	A.	E.	F.A.
1972—Idaho Falls...........	Pion.	★OF-1B	68	252	40	69	8	★8	1	27	.274	101	★11	3	.974
1973—Quad Cities†.........	Midw.	OF	110	387	61	100	15	7	4	49	.258	229	10	11	.956
1974—Salinas..................	Calif.	OF-1B	39	143	30	49	3	5	1	21	.343	109	0	5	.956
1974—El Paso.................	Texas	1B-OF	82	324	64	114	15	4	4	49	★.352	381	14	12	.971
1975—Salt Lake City.......	P. C.	OF	51	193	41	60	7	6	0	24	.311	58	2	1	.984
1975—California..............	Amer.	OF	93	319	41	85	13	4	3	29	.266	159	3	2	.988
1976—Salt Lake City.......	P. C.	OF	35	136	28	49	13	4	0	12	.360	50	3	2	.964
1976—California‡............	Amer.	OF	99	365	45	96	12	1	4	28	.263	160	3	1	.994
1977—Seattle§................	Amer.	OF	120	402	46	96	9	3	5	28	.239	124	6	2	.985
1978—Cincinnati.............	Nat.	OF	102	102	13	22	1	0	0	7	.216	30	1	1	.969
1979—Cincinnati.............	Nat.	OF-1B	122	396	59	126	16	4	3	35	.318	223	3	4	.983
1980—Cincinnati.............	Nat.	OF	144	551	94	167	20	4	3	35	.303	337	5	5	.986
1981—Cincinnati x..........	Nat.	OF	95	360	63	98	18	6	3	23	.272	167	4	4	.977
1982—New York y.........	Amer.	OF-1B	111	348	41	88	12	3	3	25	.253	498	28	7	.987
1983—Toronto z.............	Amer.	OF-1B	118	402	55	109	12	4	1	34	.271	270	9	3	.989
1984—Toronto a.............	Amer.	OF-1B	128	441	59	136	24	●15	2	44	.308	237	11	2	.992
1985—Oakland b.............	Amer.	OF	112	379	52	95	16	4	4	29	.251	221	1	5	.978
National League Totals—4 Years...........			463	1409	229	413	55	14	9	100	.293	757	13	14	.982
American League Totals—7 Years........			781	2656	339	705	98	34	22	217	.265	1669	61	22	.987
Major League Totals—11 Years..............			1244	4065	568	1118	153	48	31	317	.275	2426	74	36	.986

Selected by Cincinnati Reds' organization in 23rd round of free-agent draft, June 8, 1971.
Selected by Kansas City Royals' organization in secondary phase of free-agent draft, January 12, 1972.
Selected by California Angels' organization in secondary phase of free-agent draft, June 6, 1972.
†On disabled list, May 21 to May 31, 1973.
‡Selected by Seattle Mariners in special American League expansion draft, November 5, 1976.
§Traded to Cincinnati Reds for Pitcher Shane Rawley, December 9, 1977.
xGranted free agency, November 13, 1981; signed by New York Yankees, December 23, 1981.
yTraded with Pitcher Mike Morgan, First Baseman Fred McGriff and a reported $400,000 to Toronto Blue Jays for Pitcher Dale Murray and Outfielder-Catcher Tom Dodd, December 9, 1982.
zOn disabled list, June 4 to June 22, 1983.
aTraded with Shortstop Alfredo Griffin and cash to Oakland A's for Pitcher Bill Caudill, December 8, 1984.
bTraded to Detroit Tigers for Infielder Barbaro Garbey, November 13, 1985.

CHAMPIONSHIP SERIES RECORD

Year Club	League	Pos.	G.	AB.	R.	H.	2B.	3B.	HR.	RBI.	B.A.	PO.	A.	E.	F.A.
1979—Cincinnati..............	Nat.	OF	3	14	0	5	1	0	0	1	.357	5	0	0	1.000

—DID YOU KNOW—

That the Phillies led the Mets, 16-0, after two innings in a 26-7 win on June 11?

DAVID ISMAEL CONCEPCION (BONITEZ)

Name pronounced Con-sep-see-OHN.

(Dave)

Born June 17, 1948, at Ocumare de la Costa, Aragua, Venezuela.
Height, 6.01. Weight, 190.
Throws and bats righthanded.
Attended College Augustin Codazzi, Aragua, Venezuela.

Tied major league records for most stolen bases by pinch-runner, inning, (2), July 7, 1974 (1st game, 7th inning); most double plays by shortstop, game, (5), June 25, 1975.
Established National League record for fewest chances accepted by shortstop, season, 150 or more games (616), 1985.
Tied National League record for fewest double plays by shortstop, season, 150 or more games (64), 1985.
Major League stolen bases: 1970 (10), 1971 (9), 1972 (13), 1973 (22), 1974 (41), 1975 (33), 1976 (21), 1977 (29), 1978 (23), 1979 (19), 1980 (12), 1981 (4), 1982 (13), 1983 (14), 1984 (22), 1985 (16). Total—301.
Led National League in game-winning RBIs with 14 in 1981.
Tied for National League lead in grounding into double plays with 21 in 1983.
Led National League shortstops in total chances with 805 in 1974 and 837 in 1976.
Tied for National League lead in double plays by shortstops with 102 in 1979.
Led Southern League shortstops in double plays with 64 in 1969.
Led Florida State League shortstops in fielding percentage with .953 in 1968.
Named shortstop on THE SPORTING NEWS National League All-Star Team, 1974, 1976, 1977 and 1981.
Named shortstop on THE SPORTING NEWS National League All-Star fielding team, 1974 through 1977 and 1979.
Named shortstop on THE SPORTING NEWS National League Silver Slugger team, 1981 and 1982.

Year—Club	League	Pos.	G.	AB.	R.	H.	2B.	3B.	HR.	RBI.	B.A.	PO.	A.	E.	F.A.
1968—Tampa	Fla. St.	SS-2B	120	329	47	77	11	1	0	22	.234	151	239	20	.951
1969—Asheville	South.	SS	96	340	47	100	11	5	1	37	.294	★157	★292	★29	★.939
1969—Indianapolis	A. A.	S-2-3-O	42	167	29	57	7	1	0	17	.341	76	128	9	.958
1970—Cincinnati	Nat.	SS-2B	101	265	38	69	6	3	1	19	.260	144	247	22	.947
1971—Cincinnati†	Nat.	S-2-3-O	130	327	24	67	4	4	1	20	.205	182	310	13	.974
1972—Cincinnati	Nat.	SS-3B-2B	119	378	40	79	13	2	2	29	.209	197	372	19	.968
1973—Cincinnati‡	Nat.	SS-OF	89	328	39	94	18	3	8	46	.287	167	292	12	.975
1974—Cincinnati	Nat.	★SS-OF	160	594	70	167	25	1	14	82	.281	239	★536	30	.963
1975—Cincinnati	Nat.	SS-3B	140	507	62	139	23	1	5	49	.274	241	446	16	.977
1976—Cincinnati	Nat.	SS	152	576	74	162	28	7	9	69	.281	★304	★506	27	.968
1977—Cincinnati	Nat.	SS	156	572	59	155	26	3	8	64	.271	280	490	11	★.986
1978—Cincinnati	Nat.	SS	153	565	75	170	33	4	6	67	.301	255	459	23	.969
1979—Cincinnati	Nat.	SS	149	590	91	166	25	3	16	84	.281	284	495	27	.967
1980—Cincinnati	Nat.	SS-2B	156	622	72	162	31	8	5	77	.260	265	451	16	.978
1981—Cincinnati	Nat.	SS	106	421	57	129	28	0	5	67	.306	208	322	22	.960
1982—Cincinnati	Nat.	SS-1B-3B	147	572	48	164	25	4	5	53	.287	271	459	17	.977
1983—Cincinnati	Nat.	SS-3B-1B	143	528	54	123	22	0	1	47	.233	227	387	13	.979
1984—Cincinnati	Nat.	SS-3B-1B	154	531	46	130	26	1	4	58	.245	213	324	17	.969
1985—Cincinnati	Nat.	SS-3B	155	560	59	141	19	2	7	48	.252	214	405	24	.963
Major League Totals—16 Years			2210	7936	908	2117	352	46	97	879	.267	3691	6501	309	.971

Signed as free agent by Cincinnati Reds' organization, September 12, 1967.
†On disabled list March 21 to April 20, 1971.
‡On disabled list July 22, 1973 through remainder of season.

CHAMPIONSHIP SERIES RECORD

Year—Club	League	Pos.	G.	AB.	R.	H.	2B.	3B.	HR.	RBI.	B.A.	PO.	A.	E.	F.A.
1970—Cincinnati	Nat.	PR-SS	3	0	0	0	0	0	0	0	.000	1	1	0	1.000
1972—Cincinnati	Nat.	PH-S-PR	3	2	0	0	0	0	0	0	.000	0	0	0	.000
1975—Cincinnati	Nat.	SS	3	11	2	5	0	0	1	1	.455	6	8	1	.933
1976—Cincinnati	Nat.	SS	3	10	4	2	1	0	0	0	.200	2	12	0	1.000
1979—Cincinnati	Nat.	SS	3	14	1	6	1	0	0	0	.429	3	14	0	1.000
Championship Series Totals—5 Years			15	37	7	13	2	0	1	1	.351	12	35	1	.979

WORLD SERIES RECORD

Tied World Series records for most sacrifice flies, total Series (3); fewest chances accepted by shortstop, game (0), October 16, 1975; one or more hits, each game, four-game Series, 1976.

Year—Club	League	Pos.	G.	AB.	R.	H.	2B.	3B.	HR.	RBI.	B.A.	PO.	A.	E.	F.A.
1970—Cincinnati	Nat.	SS	3	9	0	3	0	1	0	3	.333	2	2	0	1.000
1972—Cincinnati	Nat.	S-PR-PH	6	13	2	4	0	1	0	2	.308	4	11	1	.938
1975—Cincinnati	Nat.	SS	7	28	3	5	1	0	1	4	.179	12	22	1	.971
1976—Cincinnati	Nat.	SS	4	14	1	5	1	1	0	3	.357	6	11	1	.944
World Series Totals—4 Years			20	64	6	17	2	3	1	12	.266	24	46	3	.959

ALL STAR GAME RECORD

Year—League	Pos.	AB.	R.	H.	2B.	3B.	HR.	RBI.	B.A.	PO.	A.	E.	F.A.
1975—National	SS	2	0	1	0	0	0	0	.500	1	1	1	.667
1976—National	SS	2	0	1	0	0	0	0	.500	2	3	0	1.000
1977—National	SS	1	0	0	0	0	0	0	.000	1	1	0	1.000
1978—National	SS	0	1	0	0	0	0	0	.000	2	0	0	1.000
1980—National	SS	1	1	0	0	0	0	0	.000	0	2	0	1.000
1981—National	SS	3	0	0	0	0	0	0	.000	0	0	0	.000
1982—National	SS	3	1	1	0	0	1	2	.333	1	1	0	1.000
All-Star Game Totals—7 Years		12	3	3	0	0	1	2	.250	7	8	1	.938

Named to National League All-Star Team for 1973 game; replaced due to injury.
Named to National League All-Star Team for 1979 game; replaced due to injury by Larry Parrish.

ONIX CARDONA CONCEPCION (CARDONA)

Name pronounced Con-CEP-see-own.
Born October 5, 1958, at Dorado, Puerto Rico.
Height, 5.06. Weight, 180.
Throws and bats righthanded.
Major League stolen bases: 1982 (2), 1983 (10), 1984 (9), 1985 (4). Total—25.
Led California League shortstops in double plays with 85 in 1979.

Year Club	League	Pos.	G.	AB.	R.	H.	2B.	3B.	HR.	RBI.	B.A.	PO.	A.	E.	F.A.
1976—Jacksonville	South.	2B-SS	5	13	1	4	0	0	0	4	.308	10	18	2	.933
1976—Sarasota Royals	Gulf C.	SS	18	47	13	11	3	0	0	4	.234	16	40	8	.875
1977—Sarasota Royals	Gulf C.	2B-SS-1B	28	59	7	11	1	0	0	0	.186	45	37	5	.943
1978—Fort Myers	Fla. St.	SS-2B	79	213	29	50	7	0	0	13	.235	120	223	24	.935
1979—Bakersfield	Calif.	SS	127	504	88	151	25	3	14	75	.300	*227	*454	*55	.925
1980—Jacksonville	South.	SS	74	273	48	88	13	3	12	44	.322	117	249	16	.958
1980—Omaha	A. A.	SS	58	210	22	59	9	3	4	34	.281	74	135	11	.950
1980—Kansas City	Amer.	SS	12	15	1	2	0	0	0	2	.133	5	10	3	.833
1981—Omaha	A. A.	SS	118	438	62	112	15	2	6	57	.256	126	211	23	.936
1981—Kansas City	Amer.	SS	2	0	0	0	0	0	0	0	.000	0	0	0	.000
1982—Kansas City†	Amer.	SS-2B	74	205	17	48	9	1	0	15	.234	92	168	11	.959
1983—Kansas City	Amer.	3B-2B-SS	80	219	22	53	11	3	0	20	.242	92	175	15	.947
1984—Kansas City‡	Amer.	SS-2B-3B	90	287	36	81	9	2	1	23	.282	116	295	11	.974
1985—Kansas City	Amer.	SS-2B	131	314	32	64	5	1	2	20	.204	127	370	21	.960
Major League Totals—6 Years			389	1040	108	248	34	7	3	80	.238	432	1018	61	.960

Signed as free agent by Kansas City Royals' organization, March 10, 1976.
†On disabled list, April 2 to April 23, 1982.
‡On disabled list, June 21 to July 8 and August 11 to September 4, 1984.

CHAMPIONSHIP SERIES RECORD

Year Club	League	Pos.	G.	AB.	R.	H.	2B.	3B.	HR.	RBI.	B.A.	PO.	A.	E.	F.A.
1984—Kansas City	Amer.	SS	3	7	0	0	0	0	0	0	.000	0	6	1	.857
1985—Kansas City	Amer.	SS-PR	4	1	0	0	0	0	0	0	.000	2	4	0	1.000
Championship Series Totals—2 Years			7	8	0	0	0	0	0	0	.000	2	10	1	.923

WORLD SERIES RECORD

Year Club	League	Pos.	G.	AB.	R.	H.	2B.	3B.	HR.	RBI.	B.A.	PO.	A.	E.	F.A.
1980—Kansas City	Amer.	PR	3	0	0	0	0	0	0	0	.000	0	0	0	.000
1985—Kansas City	Amer.	PR-SS	3	0	1	0	0	0	0	0	.000	0	2	0	1.000
World Series Totals—2 Years			6	0	1	0	0	0	0	0	.000	0	2	0	1.000

DAVID BRIAN CONE

Born January 2, 1963, at Kansas City, Mo.
Height, 6.01. Weight, 180.
Throws right and bats lefthanded.
Led Southern League in wild pitches with 27 in 1984.

Year Club	League	G.	IP.	W.	L.	Pct.	H.	R.	ER.	SO.	BB.	ERA.
1981—Sarasota Royals-Blue	Gulf Coast	14	67	6	4	.600	52	24	19	45	33	2.55
1982—Charleston	S. Atlantic	16	104⅔	9	2	.818	84	38	24	87	47	2.06
1982—Fort Myers	Florida St.	10	72⅓	7	1	.875	56	21	17	57	25	2.12
1983—Jacksonville†	Southern					(Did not play)						
1984—Memphis	Southern	29	178⅔	8	12	.400	162	103	85	110	114	4.28
1985—Omaha	Am. Assoc.	28	158⅔	9	15	.375	157	90	82	115	*93	4.65

Selected by Kansas City Royals' organization in 3rd round of free-agent draft, June 8, 1981.
†On disabled list, April 8, 1983 through entire season.

FRITZIE LEE CONNALLY
(Fritz)

Born May 19, 1958, at Bryan, Tex.
Height, 6.04. Weight, 210.
Throws and bats righthanded.
Received bachelor of business administration degree in marketing
from Baylor University, Waco, Tex.
Led Pacific Coast League third basemen in fielding percentage with .959 in 1984.
Led American Association third basemen in putouts with 104, double plays with 16, total chances with 357 and fielding percentage with .947 in 1983.
Led Texas League third basemen in fielding percentage with .948 in 1982.

Year Club	League	Pos.	G.	AB.	R.	H.	2B.	3B.	HR.	RBI.	B.A.	PO.	A.	E.	F.A.
1980—Geneva	NYP	1B	67	229	46	70	*18	0	14	43	.306	*674	*46	1	*.999
1981—Quad Cities	Midw.	1B-3B	32	105	23	33	10	0	4	23	.314	240	39	3	.989
1981—Midland	Texas	3B-1B	94	344	61	106	21	0	12	57	.308	129	182	11	.966
1982—Midland	Texas	3B-1B-SS	123	428	75	124	23	3	24	91	.290	162	244	19	.955
1983—Iowa	A. A.	*3B-1B	128	451	74	130	25	2	22	85	.288	110	*234	19	.948
1983—Chicago†	Nat.	3B	8	10	0	1	0	0	0	0	.100	1	3	0	1.000
1984—Las Vegas ‡	P. C.	3B-1B	124	429	71	133	25	0	16	76	.310	340	197	13	.976

Year	Club	League	Pos.	G.	AB.	R.	H.	2B.	3B.	HR.	RBI.	B.A.	PO.	A.	E.	F.A.
1985—Baltimore	Amer.	3B-1B	50	112	16	26	4	0	3	15	.232	39	57	2	.980	
1985—Rochester	Int.	1B-3B	52	168	17	36	1	0	6	22	.214	413	48	1	.998	
National League Totals—1 Year			8	10	0	1	0	0	0	0	.100	1	3	0	1.000	
American League Totals—1 Year			50	112	16	26	4	0	3	15	.232	39	57	2	.980	
Major League Totals—2 Years			58	122	16	27	4	0	3	15	.221	40	60	2	.980	

Selected by Chicago Cubs' organization in 7th round of free-agent draft, June 3, 1980.

†Traded with First Baseman Carmelo Martinez and Pitcher Craig Lefferts to San Diego Padres for Pitcher Scott Sanderson, December 7, 1983.

‡Traded to Baltimore Orioles' organization for Second Baseman Vic Rodriguez, February 7, 1985.

JEFFREY DEAN CONNER
(Jeff)

Born June 26, 1959, at Biloxi, Miss.
Height, 6.01. Weight, 185.
Throws and bats lefthanded.
Attended Glendale Community College, Glendale, Ariz.

Led Eastern League in home runs allowed with 20 in 1981.
Tied for Eastern League lead in games started by pitchers with 27 in 1983.

Year	Club	League	G.	IP.	W.	L.	Pct.	H.	R.	ER.	SO.	BB.	ERA.
1977—Idaho Falls	Pioneer	12	40	1	5	.167	44	35	26	29	30	5.85
1978—Quad Cities	Midwest	22	146	4	9	.308	147	86	76	85	42	4.68
1979—Salinas	California	30	109	6	5	.545	110	64	53	67	60	4.38
1980—El Paso	Texas	8	30	0	3	.000	46	45	32	18	26	9.60
1980—Salinas	California	14	95	9	3	.750	93	42	31	55	43	2.94
1981—Holyoke	Eastern	26	183	11	13	.458	169	90	75	91	62	3.69
1982—Holyoke	Eastern	30	125	6	7	.462	135	62	51	76	55	3.67
1983—Nashua†	Eastern	27	★188	10	11	.476	182	84	75	87	78	3.59
1984—Evansville	Am. Assoc.	32	128⅓	6	11	.353	150	76	61	84	43	4.28
1985—Nashville	Am. Assoc.	33	105	8	7	.533	96	51	32	57	33	2.74

Selected by California Angels' organization in 3rd round of free-agent draft, June 7, 1977.
Selected by California Angels' organization in 3rd round of free-agent draft, June 7, 1977.

†Granted free agency, October 20, 1983; signed by Detroit Tigers' organization, December 1, 1983.

TIMOTHY JAMES CONROY
(Tim)

Born April 3, 1960, at Monroeville, Pa.
Height, 5.11. Weight, 185.
Throws and bats lefthanded.

Pitched seven-inning, 1-0 no-hit victory against Tucson, May 14, 1985 (first game).
Led Eastern League in wild pitches with 22 in 1979 and tied for lead with 16 in 1980.

Year	Club	League	G.	IP.	W.	L.	Pct.	H.	R.	ER.	SO.	BB.	ERA.
1978—Oakland	American	2	5	0	0	.000	3	6	4	0	9	7.20
1978—Vancouver†	P. Coast	3	9	0	1	.000	13	16	16	3	10	16.00
1979—Waterbury	Eastern	25	138	7	●14	.333	115	95	80	106	★119	5.22
1980—West Haven	Eastern	25	147	8	14	.364	160	119	101	72	93	6.18
1981—West Haven	Eastern	14	57	2	6	.250	59	50	38	51	43	6.00
1981—Modesto	California	8	39	1	3	.250	50	37	34	46	23	7.85
1982—Modesto	California	27	171⅔	15	4	.789	139	59	43	★184	62	2.25
1982—Oakland	American	5	25⅓	2	2	.500	20	13	10	17	18	3.55
1983—Oakland	American	39	162⅓	7	10	.412	141	89	71	112	98	3.94
1984—Oakland	American	38	93	1	6	.143	82	58	54	69	63	5.23
1985—Oakland	American	16	25⅓	0	1	.000	22	15	12	8	15	4.26
1985—Tacoma‡	P. Coast	22	129⅓	11	3	.786	106	52	47	166	71	3.27
Major League Totals—5 Years		100	311	10	19	.345	268	181	151	206	203	4.37

Selected by Oakland A's organization in 1st round (20th player selected) of free-agent draft, June 6, 1978.

†On disabled list, July 16 to September 1, 1978.

‡Traded with Catcher Mike Heath to St. Louis Cardinals for Pitcher Joaquin Andujar, December 10, 1985.

GLEN PATRICK COOK

Born September 8, 1959, at Buffalo, N.Y.
Height, 5.11. Weight, 180.
Throws and bats righthanded.
Received bachelor of science degree from Ithaca College, Ithaca, N.Y.

Led American Association in hit batsmen with 8 and tied for lead in home runs allowed with 24 in 1984.

Year	Club	League	G.	IP.	W.	L.	Pct.	H.	R.	ER.	SO.	BB.	ERA.
1981—Sarasota Rangers	Gulf Coast	14	43	2	2	.500	40	26	23	43	20	4.81
1982—Burlington†	Midwest	18	42⅔	2	3	.400	47	30	20	37	15	4.22
1983—Burlington	Midwest	9	52⅔	4	2	.667	50	28	24	59	24	4.10
1983—Tulsa	Texas	11	72	4	6	.400	60	33	25	70	26	3.13
1983—Oklahoma City	Am. Assoc.	3	20	0	1	.000	16	10	10	16	7	4.50
1984—Oklahoma City	Am. Assoc.	27	167	9	8	.529	159	92	90	124	57	4.85
1985—Oklahoma City	Am. Assoc.	18	120⅔	9	5	.643	92	50	43	80	32	3.21
1985—Texas	American	9	40	2	3	.400	53	42	42	19	18	9.45
Major League Totals—1 Year		9	40	2	3	.400	53	42	42	19	18	9.45

Selected by San Diego Padres' organization in 17th round of free-agent draft, June 3, 1980.
Selected by Texas Rangers' organization in 24th round of free-agent draft, June 8, 1981.
†On disabled list, June 22, 1982 through remainder of season.

CECIL CELESTER COOPER

Born December 20, 1949, at Brenham, Tex.
Height, 6.02. Weight, 190.
Throws and bats lefthanded.
Attended Blinn College, Brenham, Tex., and Prairie View A&M College, Prairie View, Tex.

Tied major league records for most strikeouts, extra-inning game (6), June 14, 1974 (15 innings); most at-bats, game (11), May 8, finished May 9, 1984 (25 innings).
Major League stolen bases: 1971 (1), 1973 (1), 1974 (2), 1975 (1), 1976 (7), 1977 (13), 1978 (3), 1979 (15), 1980 (17), 1981 (5), 1982 (2), 1983 (2), 1984 (8), 1985 (10). Total—87.
Hit three home runs in a game, July 27, 1979.
Led American League in total bases with 335 in 1980.
Led American League first basemen in total chances with 1,068 in 1981 and 1,550 in 1983.
Led American League first basemen in double plays with 160 in 1980, 111 in 1981, 156 in 1982 and 144 in 1983.
Tied for American League lead in game-winning RBIs with 16 in 1979.
Named first baseman on THE SPORTING NEWS American League All-Star Team, 1979 through 1982.
Named first baseman on THE SPORTING NEWS American League All-Star fielding team, 1979 and 1980.
Named first baseman on THE SPORTING NEWS American League Silver Slugger team, 1980 through 1982.
Named Midwest League Player of the Year, 1970.

Year—Club	League	Pos.	G.	AB.	R.	H.	2B.	3B.	HR.	RBI.	B.A.	PO.	A.	E.	F.A.
1968—Jamestown	NYP	1B	26	84	16	38	6	0	0	6	.452	130	0	1	.992
1969—Greenville†	W. Car.	1B-OF	62	212	27	63	12	2	1	18	.297	434	32	8	.983
1970—Danville‡	Midw.	1B-OF	114	420	86	141	16	8	3	39	★.336	535	33	12	.979
1971—Winston-Salem	Carol.	1B	42	153	31	58	6	3	6	26	.379	359	21	5	.987
1971—Pawtucket	East.	1B-OF	98	367	55	126	21	2	10	60	.343	740	35	12	.985
1971—Boston	Amer.	1B	14	42	9	13	4	1	0	3	.310	82	3	1	.988
1972—Louisville	Int.	1B	134	515	86	★162	★31	9	10	78	.315	1102	78	★17	.986
1972—Boston	Amer.	1B	12	17	0	4	1	0	0	2	.235	19	0	0	1.000
1973—Pawtucket	Int.	1B	128	450	68	132	27	1	15	77	.293	1082	84	12	.990
1973—Boston	Amer.	1B	30	101	12	24	2	0	3	11	.238	227	17	4	.984
1974—Boston	Amer.	1B	121	414	55	114	24	1	8	43	.275	637	40	12	.983
1975—Boston	Amer.	1B	106	305	49	95	17	6	14	44	.311	197	20	1	.995
1976—Boston§	Amer.	1B	123	451	66	127	22	6	15	78	.282	600	42	4	.994
1977—Milwaukee	Amer.	1B	160	643	86	193	31	7	20	78	.300	1386	118	12	.992
1978—Milwaukee x	Amer.	1B	107	407	60	127	23	2	13	54	.312	842	66	11	.988
1979—Milwaukee	Amer.	1B	150	590	83	182	●44	1	24	106	.308	1323	78	10	.993
1980—Milwaukee	Amer.	1B	153	622	96	219	33	4	25	★122	.352	1336	★106	5	★.997
1981—Milwaukee	Amer.	1B	106	416	70	133	★35	1	12	60	.320	★987	72	●9	.992
1982—Milwaukee	Amer.	1B	155	654	104	205	38	3	32	121	.313	1428	98	5	.997
1983—Milwaukee	Amer.	1B	160	661	106	203	37	3	30	●126	.307	★1452	87	11	.993
1984—Milwaukee	Amer.	1B	148	603	63	166	28	3	11	67	.275	1061	98	10	.991
1985—Milwaukee	Amer.	1B	154	631	82	185	39	8	16	99	.293	1087	94	17	.986
Major League Totals—15 Years			1699	6557	941	1990	378	46	223	1014	.303	12664	939	112	.992

Selected by Boston Red Sox' organization in 27th round of free-agent draft, June 7, 1968.
†On temporary inactive list, April 13 to June 4, 1969.
‡Drafted by St. Louis Cardinals, November 30, 1970; returned, April 5, 1971.
§Traded to Milwaukee Brewers for First Baseman George Scott and Outfielder Bernie Carbo, December 6, 1976.
xOn disabled list, June 9 to July 21, 1978.

DIVISION SERIES RECORD

Year—Club	League	Pos.	G.	AB.	R.	H.	2B.	3B.	HR.	RBI.	B.A.	PO.	A.	E.	F.A.
1981—Milwaukee	Amer.	1B	5	18	1	4	0	0	0	3	.222	47	4	1	.981

CHAMPIONSHIP SERIES RECORD

Year—Club	League	Pos.	G.	AB.	R.	H.	2B.	3B.	HR.	RBI.	B.A.	PO.	A.	E.	F.A.
1975—Boston	Amer.	1B	3	10	0	4	2	0	0	1	.400	24	1	1	.962
1982—Milwaukee	Amer.	1B	5	20	1	3	2	0	0	4	.150	37	3	2	.952
Championship Series Totals—2 Years			8	30	1	7	4	0	0	5	.233	61	4	3	.956

WORLD SERIES RECORD

Established World Series records for most assists by first baseman, seven-game Series (10), 1982; most chances accepted by first baseman, seven-game Series (81), 1982.

Year—Club	League	Pos.	G.	AB.	R.	H.	2B.	3B.	HR.	RBI.	B.A.	PO.	A.	E.	F.A.
1975—Boston	Amer.	1B-PH	5	19	0	1	1	0	0	1	.053	40	1	0	1.000
1982—Milwaukee	Amer.	1B	7	28	3	8	1	0	1	6	.286	71	10	1	.988
World Series Totals—2 Years			12	47	3	9	2	0	1	7	.191	111	11	1	.992

ALL-STAR GAME RECORD

Year—League	Pos.	AB.	R.	H.	2B.	3B.	HR.	RBI.	B.A.	PO.	A.	E.	F.A.
1979—American	PH	0	0	0	0	0	0	0	.000	0	0	0	.000
1980—American	1B	1	0	0	0	0	0	0	.000	6	0	0	1.000
1982—American	1B	2	0	1	0	0	0	0	.500	5	0	0	1.000
1983—American	PH	1	1	1	0	0	0	0	1.000	0	0	0	.000
1985—American	PH	0	0	0	0	0	0	0	.000	0	0	0	.000
All-Star Game Totals—5 Years		4	1	2	0	0	0	0	.500	11	0	0	1.000

DONALD JAMES COOPER
(Don)

Born January 15, 1957, at New York, N.Y.
Height, 6.00. Weight, 175.
Throws and bats righthanded.
Attended New York Institute of Technology, Old Westbury, N.Y.
Nephew of Robert Beier, minor league shortstop, 1952 through 1956.

Pitched 5-0, no-hit victory against Fort Myers, August 7, 1978.
Tied for International League lead in games finished in relief with 41 in 1983.
Tied for Eastern League lead in intentional bases on balls issued with 9 in 1979.

Year Club	League	G.	IP.	W.	L.	Pct.	H.	R.	ER.	SO.	BB.	ERA.
1978—Oneonta	NYP	5	20	1	2	.333	18	12	8	22	10	3.60
1978—Fort Lauderdale	Florida St.	10	52	2	3	.400	41	22	13	34	20	2.25
1979—West Haven	Eastern	28	54	6	4	.600	49	31	26	44	30	4.33
1979—Columbus	Int'national	8	18	0	0	.000	19	11	11	14	11	5.50
1980—Nashville	Southern	32	60	9	5	.643	43	18	12	62	29	1.80
1980—Columbus†	Int'national	12	38	3	2	.600	30	11	9	29	16	2.13
1981—Minnesota	American	27	59	1	5	.167	61	33	28	33	32	4.27
1982—Toledo	Int'national	28	176⅔	12	10	.545	196	105	91	★125	69	4.64
1982—Minnesota‡	American	6	11⅓	0	1	.000	14	12	12	5	11	9.53
1983—Syracuse	Int'national	46	87	10	5	.667	69	33	31	73	33	3.21
1983—Toronto§	American	4	5⅓	0	0	.000	8	4	4	5	0	6.75
1984—Columbus x	Int'national	41	88	8	6	.571	81	42	31	62	31	3.17
1985—Columbus	Int'national	33	68⅓	7	3	.700	61	23	18	59	21	2.37
1985—New York y	American	7	10	0	0	.000	12	6	6	4	3	5.40
Major League Totals—4 Years		44	85⅔	1	6	.143	95	55	50	47	46	5.25

Selected by New York Yankees' organization in 17th round of free-agent draft, June 6, 1978.
†Drafted by Minnesota Twins, December 8, 1980.
‡Traded to Syracuse (Toronto Blue Jays' organization) for Third Baseman Dave Baker, December 10, 1982.
§Traded to New York Yankees' organization for Outfielder Derwin McNealy, March 13, 1984.
xOn temporary inactive list, May 6 to May 18, 1984.
yReleased, November 12, 1985; signed by Oakland A's, December 5, 1985.

DOUGLAS MITCHELL CORBETT
(Doug)

Born November 4, 1952, at Sarasota, Fla.
Height, 6.01. Weight, 185.
Throws and bats righthanded.
Received bachelor of science degree in physical education from University of Florida, Gainesville, Fla.

Major League saves: 1980 (23), 1981 (17), 1982 (11), 1984 (4). Total—55.
Led American League in games finished in relief with 45 and intentional bases on balls issued with 13 in 1981.
Led American Association in saves with 12 in 1978.
Led Gulf Coast League in intentional bases on balls issued with 3 in 1974.

Year Club	League	G.	IP.	W.	L.	Pct.	H.	R.	ER.	SO.	BB.	ERA.
1974—Sarasota Royals†	Gulf Coast	11	42	4	2	.667	30	22	14	32	18	3.00
1975—Tampa	Florida St.	27	61	2	3	.400	42	11	10	48	21	1.48
1976—Tampa	Florida St.	45	85	10	5	.667	86	25	21	37	22	2.22
1977—Three Rivers	Eastern	39	88	4	5	.444	72	35	27	65	40	2.76
1978—Nashville	Southern	15	25	2	1	.667	18	11	7	33	7	2.52
1978—Indianapolis	Am. Assoc.	38	68	4	4	.500	54	22	15	46	17	1.99
1979—Indianapolis‡	Am. Assoc.	★69	110	3	6	.333	94	38	36	77	39	2.95
1980—Minnesota	American	73	136	8	6	.571	102	31	30	89	42	1.99
1981—Minnesota	American	★54	88	2	6	.250	80	29	25	60	34	2.56
1982—Minnesota§-California	American	43	79	1	9	.100	73	45	45	52	35	5.13
1982—Spokane	P. Coast	8	19	1	0	1.000	16	11	8	19	4	3.79
1983—California	American	11	17⅓	1	1	.500	26	10	7	18	4	3.63
1983—Edmonton	P. Coast	32	83	6	6	.500	95	55	43	61	29	4.66
1984—Edmonton	P. Coast	2	4⅔	1	0	1.000	2	0	0	5	0	0.00
1984—California	American	45	85	5	1	.833	76	22	20	48	30	2.12
1985—California x	American	30	46	3	3	.500	49	33	25	24	20	4.89
1985—Edmonton	P. Coast	1	3	0	1	.000	3	1	1	1	0	3.00
Major League Totals—6 Years		256	451⅓	20	26	.435	406	170	152	291	165	3.03

Signed as free agent by Kansas City Royals' organization, June 11, 1974.
†Released, April 10, 1975; signed by Cincinnati Reds' organization, May 6, 1975.
‡Drafted by Minnesota Twins, December 3, 1979.
§Traded with Second Baseman Rob Wilfong to California Angels for Outfielder Tom Brunansky, Pitcher Mike Walters and cash, May 12, 1982.
xOn disabled list, July 25 to August 29, 1985; included rehabilitation disability assignment to Edmonton, August 27 to August 29, 1985.

ALL-STAR GAME RECORD
Member of American League All-Star team in 1981; did not play.

—DID YOU KNOW—

That when Toronto reliever Bill Caudill recorded his 12th 1985 save on July 22, he established a team record?

TIMOTHY MICHAEL CORCORAN
(Tim)

Born March 19, 1953, at Glendale, Calif.
Height, 5.11. Weight, 180.
Throws and bats lefthanded.
Attended Mount San Antonio Junior College, Walnut, Calif. and California
State University, Los Angeles, Calif.
Brother of Pat Corcoran, infielder in Oakland A's organization, 1976 through 1978.

Major League stolen bases: 1978 (3), 1979 (1). Total—4.

Year—Club	League	Pos.	G.	AB.	R.	H.	2B.	3B.	HR.	RBI.	B.A.	PO.	A.	E.	F.A.
1974—Bristol	Appal.	OF	27	92	20	34	6	0	3	25	.370	32	0	0	1.000
1974—Lakeland	Fla. St.	OF	36	126	15	34	1	3	1	16	.270	71	3	1	.987
1975—Montgomery	South.	OF-1B	122	388	42	95	20	3	3	36	.245	283	21	4	.987
1976—Montgomery	South.	OF-1B	129	437	66	135	25	5	5	60	.309	607	49	5	.992
1977—Evansville	A. A.	1B-OF-P	39	136	27	47	11	3	7	33	.346	303	21	8	.976
1977—Detroit	Amer.	OF	55	103	13	29	3	0	3	15	.282	38	0	0	1.000
1978—Detroit	Amer.	OF	116	324	37	86	13	1	1	27	.265	186	6	3	.985
1979—Evansville	A. A.	OF-1B	87	287	40	97	15	0	4	50	.338	292	23	2	.994
1979—Detroit	Amer.	OF-1B	18	22	4	5	1	0	0	6	.227	45	2	0	1.000
1980—Detroit	Amer.	1B-OF	84	153	20	44	7	1	3	18	.288	274	19	5	.983
1981—Evansville†‡	A. A.	1B-OF	106	336	48	100	17	1	8	63	.298	644	41	12	.983
1001—Minnesota§	Amer.	1B	22	51	4	9	3	0	0	4	.176	108	9	0	1.000
1982—Oklahoma City	A. A.	OF-1B	120	433	60	125	28	5	7	69	.289	330	11	9	.974
1983—Portland	P. C.	OF-1B	128	454	75	141	30	7	9	93	.311	437	32	6	.987
1983—Philadelphia	Nat.	1B	3	0	0	0	0	0	0	0	.000	4	0	0	1.000
1984—Philadelphia x	Nat.	1B-OF	102	208	30	71	13	1	5	36	.341	338	21	1	.997
1985—Philadelphia y	Nat.	1B-OF	103	182	11	39	6	1	0	22	.214	389	25	3	.993
American League Totals—5 Years			295	653	78	173	27	2	7	70	.265	651	36	8	.988
National League Totals—3 Years			208	390	41	110	19	2	5	58	.282	731	46	4	.995
Major League Totals—8 Years			503	1043	119	283	46	4	12	128	.271	1382	82	12	.992

Signed as free agent by Detroit Tigers' organization, June 10, 1974.
†On disabled list, July 14 to July 24 and July 27 to August 10, 1981.
‡Traded to Minnesota Twins, September 4, 1981, completing deal in which Minnesota traded First Baseman-Outfielder Ron Jackson to Detroit Tigers for a player to be named later, August 23, 1981.
§Released, March 26, 1982; signed by Oklahoma City (Philadelphia Phillies' organization), April 13, 1982.
xOn disabled list, August 19 to September 3, 1984.
yReleased, December 22, 1985.

PITCHING RECORD

Year—Club	League	G.	IP.	W.	L.	Pct.	H.	R.	ER.	SO.	BB.	ERA.
1977—Evansville	Am. Assoc.	1	3	0	0	.000	2	2	2	2	1	6.00
1983—Portland	P. Coast	1	1	0	0	.000	3	2	2	0	0	18.00

EDWIN JOSUE CORREA
(Ed)

Born April 29, 1966, at Hato Rey, Puerto Rico.
Height, 6.02. Weight, 190.
Throws and bats righthanded.

Year—Club	League	G.	IP.	W.	L.	Pct.	H.	R.	ER.	SO.	BB.	ERA.
1982—Sarasota White Sox	Gulf Coast	10	59	5	2	.714	40	23	18	53	27	2.75
1983—Appleton†	Midwest	19	95	3	9	.250	81	59	47	87	61	4.45
1984—Appleton	Midwest	26	149⅓	10	6	.625	127	71	57	135	87	3.44
1985—Glens Falls	Eastern	8	40	1	5	.167	37	41	30	34	35	6.75
1985—Appleton	Midwest	18	139	13	3	●.813	93	45	39	128	56	2.53
1985—Chicago‡	American	5	10⅓	1	0	1.000	11	9	8	10	11	6.97
Major League Totals—1 Year		5	10⅓	1	0	1.000	11	9	8	10	11	6.97

Signed as free agent by Chicago White Sox' organization, July 11, 1982.
†On disabled list, May 22 to June 12, 1983.
‡Traded with Infielder Scott Fletcher and a player to be named later to Texas Rangers for Infielder Wayne Tolleson and Pitcher Dave Schmidt, November 25, 1985; Texas acquired Infielder Jose Mota to complete deal, December 12, 1985.

HENRY COTTO (SUAREZ)

Name pronounced KOTT-oh.

Born January 5, 1961, at New York, N. Y.
Height, 6.02. Weight, 180.
Throws and bats righthanded.

Major League stolen bases: 1984 (9), 1985 (1). Total—10.
Led Texas League in stolen bases with 52 in 1982.
Tied for American Association lead in caught stealing with 17 in 1983.
Led Texas League outfielders in total chances with 333 in 1982.

Year—Club	League	Pos.	G.	AB.	R.	H.	2B.	3B.	HR.	RBI.	B.A.	PO.	A.	E.	F.A.
1980—Sarasota Cubs	Gulf C.	OF	43	166	24	47	7	5	0	30	.283	93	6	3	.971
1980—Quad Cities	Midw.	OF	19	78	9	22	1	1	0	5	.282	27	2	4	.879
1981—Quad Cities	Midw.	OF	128	493	80	144	15	6	1	46	.292	249	*23	13	.954
1982—Midland	Texas	OF	130	524	103	161	12	5	1	36	.307	*310	16	7	.979

Year Club	League	Pos.	G.	AB.	R.	H.	2B.	3B.	HR.	RBI.	B.A.	PO.	A.	E.	F.A.
1983—Iowa†	A. A.	OF	104	426	52	111	7	10	0	35	.261	253	8	7	.974
1984—Chicago	Nat.	OF	105	146	24	40	5	0	0	8	.274	117	3	2	.984
1984—Iowa‡	A. A.	OF	8	30	3	6	2	0	0	0	.200	12	3	0	1.000
1985—New York§	Amer.	OF	34	56	4	17	1	0	1	6	.304	41	2	1	.977
1985—Columbus	Int.	OF	75	272	38	70	16	2	7	36	.257	158	5	2	.988
National League Totals—1 Year			105	146	24	40	5	0	0	8	.274	117	3	2	.984
American League Totals—1 Year			34	56	4	17	1	0	1	6	.304	41	2	1	.977
Major League Totals—2 Years			139	202	28	57	6	0	1	14	.282	158	5	3	.982

Signed as free agent by Chicago Cubs' organization, June 7, 1980.

†On disabled list, May 10 to May 30, 1983.

‡Traded with Catcher Ron Hassey and Pitchers Rich Bordi and Porfi Altamirano to New York Yankees for Pitcher Ray Fontenot and Outfielder Brian Dayett, December 4, 1984.

§On disabled list, May 25 to July 5, 1985; included rehabilitation disability assignment to Columbus, June 19 to July 5, 1985.

CHAMPIONSHIP SERIES RECORD

Year Club	League	Pos.	G.	AB.	R.	H.	2B.	3B.	HR.	RBI.	B.A.	PO.	A.	E.	F.A.
1984—Chicago	Nat.	OF-PR	3	1	1	1	0	0	0	0	1.000	2	0	0	1.000

ALFRED EDWARD COWENS JR.
(Al)

Born October 25, 1951, at Los Angeles, Calif.
Height, 6.02. Weight, 205.
Throws and bats righthanded.

Major League stolen bases: 1974 (5), 1975 (12), 1976 (23), 1977 (16), 1978 (14), 1979 (10), 1980 (6), 1981 (3), 1982 (11), 1983 (10), 1984 (9). Total—119.

Named outfielder on THE SPORTING NEWS American League All-Star fielding team, 1977.

Named Southern League Player of the Year, 1973.

Year Club	League	Pos.	G.	AB.	R.	H.	2B.	3B.	HR.	RBI.	B.A.	PO.	A.	E.	F.A.
1969—Kingsport	Appal.	3B-SS-OF	51	180	30	53	6	1	2	30	.294	48	85	16	.893
1970—Billings	Pion.	OF-SS	62	237	45	67	9	5	7	47	.283	82	20	5	.953
1971—Waterloo	Midw.	3B-1B-OF	16	48	5	14	5	0	0	5	.292	37	12	3	.942
1971—San Jose	Calif.	OF	99	380	60	108	14	5	8	66	.284	138	14	3	*.981
1972—Waterloo	Midw.	3B	8	31	5	7	1	0	0	3	.226	5	17	2	.917
1972—San Jose	Calif.	OF-3B-1B	83	307	36	86	17	2	5	53	.280	134	53	10	.949
1972—Jacksonville	South.	OF	35	120	17	24	2	1	4	9	.200	48	5	2	.964
1973—Jacksonville	South.	OF-1B-3B	135	491	91	142	25	7	16	81	.289	444	52	18	.965
1974—Kansas City	Amer.	OF-3B	110	269	28	65	7	1	1	25	.242	151	14	3	.982
1975—Kansas City	Amer.	OF	120	328	44	91	13	8	4	42	.277	214	4	5	.978
1976—Kansas City	Amer.	OF	152	581	71	154	23	6	3	59	.265	329	13	5	.986
1977—Kansas City	Amer.	OF	●162	606	98	189	32	14	23	112	.312	307	14	6	.982
1978—Kansas City†	Amer.	OF-3B	132	485	63	133	24	8	5	63	.274	280	20	4	.987
1979—Kansas City‡§	Amer.	OF	136	516	69	152	18	7	9	73	.295	288	3	4	.986
1980—Calif.x-Det.	Amer.	OF	142	522	69	140	20	3	6	59	.268	263	11	3	.989
1981—Detroit y	Amer.	OF	85	253	27	66	11	4	1	18	.261	166	3	1	.994
1982—Seattle z	Amer.	OF	146	560	72	151	39	8	20	78	.270	280	14	4	.987
1983—Seattle a	Amer.	OF	110	356	39	73	19	2	7	35	.205	124	7	2	.985
1984—Seattle	Amer.	OF	139	524	60	145	34	2	15	78	.277	228	8	3	.987
1985—Seattle b	Amer.	OF	122	452	59	120	32	5	14	69	.265	198	10	7	.967
Major League Totals—12 Years			1556	5452	699	1479	272	68	108	711	.271	2828	121	47	.984

Selected by Kansas City Royals' organization in 84th round of free agent draft, June 5, 1969.

†On disabled list, June 29 to July 24, 1978.

‡On disabled list, May 9 to May 30, 1979.

§Traded with Shortstop Todd Cruz and a player to be named later to California Angels for First Baseman Willie Aikens and Shortstop Rance Mulliniks, December 6, 1979; California organization acquired Pitcher Craig Eaton to complete deal, April 1, 1980.

xTraded to Detroit Tigers for First Baseman Jason Thompson, May 27, 1980.

ySold to Seattle Mariners, March 28, 1982.

zGranted free agency, November 10, 1982; re-signed by Mariners, January 14, 1983.

aOn disabled list, July 23 to August 21, 1983.

bReleased, December 20, 1985.

CHAMPIONSHIP SERIES RECORD

Year Club	League	Pos.	G.	AB.	R.	H.	2B.	3B.	HR.	RBI.	B.A.	PO.	A.	E.	F.A.
1976—Kansas City	Amer.	OF	5	21	3	4	0	1	0	0	.190	15	0	0	1.000
1977—Kansas City	Amer.	OF	5	19	2	5	0	0	1	5	.263	14	0	0	1.000
1978—Kansas City	Amer.	OF	4	15	2	2	0	0	0	1	.133	5	0	0	1.000
Championship Series Totals—3 Years			14	55	7	11	0	1	1	6	.200	34	0	0	1.000

JOSEPH ALAN COWLEY
(Joe)

Born August 15, 1958, at Lexington, Ky.
Height, 6.05. Weight, 210.
Throws and bats righthanded.

Led International League in shutouts with 4 in 1983.

Led Western Carolinas League in hit batsmen with 19 and tied for lead in balks with 3 in 1978.
Tied for Southern League lead in hit batsmen with 13 in 1979.

Year Club	League	G.	IP.	W.	L.	Pct.	H.	R.	ER.	SO.	BB.	ERA.
1976—Bradenton Braves	Gulf Coast	5	13	0	4	.000	17	16	13	12	19	9.00
1977—Greenwood	W. Carol.	10	32	1	0	1.000	31	29	29	25	43	8.16
1977—Kingsport	Ap'lachian	14	70	6	5	.545	73	59	48	59	50	6.17
1978—Greenwood	W. Carol.	25	161	11	7	.611	133	85	★71	141	★113	3.97
1979—Savannah	Southern	25	144	7	9	.438	115	74	60	103	81	3.75
1980—Savannah†	Southern	4	12	1	3	.250	24	18	17	13	9	12.75
1980—Durham	Carolina	10	64	6	0	1.000	57	26	20	44	25	2.81
1981—Savannah	Southern	11	69	6	0	1.000	47	22	21	56	16	2.74
1981—Richmond	Int'national	18	45	3	2	.600	33	15	14	39	16	2.80
1982—Atlanta‡	National	17	52½	1	2	.333	53	27	26	27	16	4.47
1982—Richmond	Int'national	9	51⅓	4	2	.667	46	24	23	33	30	4.03
1983—Richmond§	Int'national	28	124⅔	9	7	.563	106	69	61	108	72	4.40
1984—Columbus	Int'national	17	113	10	3	.769	100	59	46	96	50	3.66
1984—New York	American	16	83⅓	9	2	.818	75	34	33	71	31	3.56
1985—New York x	American	30	159⅔	12	6	.667	132	75	70	97	85	3.95
National League Totals—1 Year		17	52⅓	1	2	.333	53	27	26	27	16	4.47
American League Totals—2 Years		46	243	21	8	.724	207	109	103	168	116	3.81
Major League Totals—3 Years		63	295⅓	22	10	.688	260	136	129	195	132	3.93

Signed as free agent by Atlanta Braves' organization, July 22, 1970.
†On disabled list, April 26 to July 3, 1980.
‡On disabled list, May 10 to June 12, 1982.
§Granted free agency, October 20, 1983; signed by New York Yankees, November 22, 1983.
xTraded with Catcher Ron Hassey to Chicago White Sox for Pitcher Britt Burns, Shortstop Mike Soper and Outfielder Glen Braxton, December 12, 1985.

DANNY BRADFORD COX

Born September 21, 1959, at Northhampton, England.
Height, 6.04. Weight, 230.
Throws and bats righthanded.
Attended Chattahoochee Valley Community College, Phenix City, Ala.,
and Troy State University, Troy, Ala.
Pitched 11-0 no-hit victory against Bristol, August 9, 1981.
Tied for National League lead in hit batsmen with 7 in 1984.
Led Appalachian League in complete games with 10 and shutouts with 4 in 1981.
Named Appalachian League Player of the Year, 1981.

Year Club	League	G.	IP.	W.	L.	Pct.	H.	R.	ER.	SO.	BB.	ERA.
1981—Johnson City	Ap'lachian	13	★109	9	4	.692	80	27	25	★87	36	★2.06
1982—Springfield	Midwest	15	84⅓	5	3	.625	82	46	24	68	29	2.56
1983—St. Petersburg†	Florida St.	5	32	2	2	.500	26	10	9	22	14	2.53
1983—Arkansas	Texas	11	86⅓	8	3	.727	60	31	22	73	24	2.29
1983—Louisville	Am. Assoc.	2	11	0	0	.000	10	3	3	8	0	2.45
1983—St. Louis	National	12	83	3	6	.333	92	38	30	36	23	3.25
1984—St. Louis	National	29	156⅓	9	11	.450	171	81	70	70	54	4.03
1984—Louisville	Am. Assoc.	6	42⅓	4	1	.800	34	16	10	34	7	2.13
1985—St. Louis	National	35	241	18	9	.667	226	91	77	131	64	2.88
Major League Totals—3 Years		76	480⅓	30	26	.536	489	210	177	237	141	3.32

Selected by St. Louis Cardinals' organization in 13th round of free-agent draft, June 8, 1981.
†On Arkansas disabled list, April 8 to April 21, 1983.

CHAMPIONSHIP SERIES RECORD

Year Club	League	G.	IP.	W.	L.	Pct.	H.	R.	ER.	SO.	BB.	ERA.
1985—St. Louis	National	1	6	1	0	1.000	4	1	1	4	5	1.50

WORLD SERIES RECORD

Year Club	League	G.	IP.	W.	L.	Pct.	H.	R.	ER.	SO.	BB.	ERA.
1985—St. Louis	National	2	14	0	0	.000	14	2	2	13	4	1.29

STEVEN RAY CRAWFORD

(Steve)

Born April 29, 1958, at Pryor, Okla.
Height, 6.05. Weight, 225.
Throws and bats righthanded.
Attended Claremore Junior College, Claremore, Okla. and
Northeastern Oklahoma State University, Tahlequah, Okla.
Major League saves: 1984 (1), 1985 (12). Total—13.
Led Carolina League pitchers in games started with 28 and complete games with 15 in 1979.
Tied for Carolina League lead in shutouts with 3 in 1979.

Year Club	League	G.	IP.	W.	L.	Pct.	H.	R.	ER.	SO.	BB.	ERA.
1978—Winston-Salem	Carolina	19	110	9	5	.643	109	53	42	60	48	3.44
1979—Winston-Salem	Carolina	29	★211	11	11	.500	★208	88	●69	127	67	2.94
1980—Bristol†	Eastern	24	177	9	7	.563	170	68	52	97	64	2.64
1980—Boston	American	6	32	2	0	1.000	41	14	13	10	8	3.66
1981—Boston	American	14	58	0	5	.000	69	38	32	29	18	4.97

Year Club	League	G.	IP.	W.	L.	Pct.	H.	R.	ER.	SO.	BB.	ERA.
1982—Boston‡	American	5	9	1	0	1.000	14	3	2	2	0	2.00
1982—Pawtucket	Int'national	10	46	1	4	.200	55	25	21	20	15	4.11
1983—Pawtucket§	Int'national	27	154⅔	8	11	.421	181	98	89	104	80	5.18
1984—Pawtucket	Int'national	7	18⅓	2	1	.667	11	10	4	8	9	1.96
1984—Boston	American	35	62	5	0	1.000	69	31	23	21	21	3.34
1985—Boston x	American	44	91	6	5	.545	103	47	38	58	28	3.76
Major League Totals—5 Years		104	252	14	10	.583	296	133	108	120	75	3.86

Signed as free agent by Boston Red Sox' organization, May 6, 1978.
†On disabled list, April 14 to May 2, 1980.
‡On disabled list, April 1 to August 12, 1982; included rehabilitation disability assignment to Pawtucket, July 21 to August 9, 1982.
§On disabled list, July 26 to August 5, 1983.
xOn disabled list, May 7 to May 22 and June 23 to July 8, 1985.

STEVEN KEITH CREEL
(Known by middle name.)

Born February 4, 1959, at Dallas, Tex.
Height, 6.03. Weight, 190.
Throws and bats righthanded.
Attended University of Texas, Austin, Tex.
Cousin of Jack Creel, minor league third baseman-pitcher, 1938 through 1954.

Tied for American Association lead in shutouts with 3 and complete games with 10 in 1984.

Year Club	League	G.	IP.	W.	L.	Pct.	H.	R.	ER.	SO.	BB.	ERA.
1980—Fort Myers	Florida St.	6	26	2	2	.500	48	29	24	5	16	8.31
1980—Sarasota Royals-Blue	Gulf Coast	9	54	6	2	.750	46	21	13	39	9	2.17
1981—Jacksonville	Southern	20	149	12	7	.632	106	52	45	105	44	2.72
1981—Omaha	Am. Assoc.	6	38	4	1	.800	35	19	18	29	13	4.26
1982—Omaha	Am. Assoc.	18	114⅔	6	8	.429	120	69	56	56	67	4.40
1982—Kansas City	American	9	41⅔	1	4	.200	43	28	25	13	25	5.40
1983—Omaha	Am. Assoc.	7	53⅓	4	2	.667	44	18	18	41	24	3.04
1983—Kansas City	American	25	89⅓	2	5	.286	116	66	63	31	35	6.35
1984—Omaha†	Am. Assoc.	27	168	9	*15	.375	169	99	81	98	58	4.34
1985—Maine	Int'national	19	124	7	7	.500	121	59	51	58	38	3.70
1985—Cleveland	American	15	62	2	5	.286	73	35	33	31	23	4.79
Major League Totals—3 Years		49	193	5	14	.263	232	129	121	75	83	5.64

Selected by Oakland A's organization in 2nd round of free-agent draft, June 7, 1977.
Selected by Pittsburgh Pirates' organization in secondary phase of free-agent draft, January 8, 1980.
Selected by Kansas City Royals' organization in secondary phase of free-agent draft, June 3, 1980.
†Traded to Cleveland Indians for a player to be named later, March 19, 1985; Kansas City Royals' organization acquired Outfielder Dwight Taylor to complete deal, October 3, 1985.

CHARLES ROBERT CRIM
(Chuck)

Born July 23, 1961, at Van Nuys, Calif.
Height, 6.00. Weight, 170.
Throws and bats righthanded.
Attended University of Hawaii, Honolulu, Haw.

Led Appalachian League in complete games with 8 in 1982.
Tied for Midwest League lead in complete games with 11 in 1983.

Year Club	League	G.	IP.	W.	L.	Pct.	H.	R.	ER.	SO.	BB.	ERA.
1982—Pikeville	Ap'lachian	11	77⅓	4	6	.400	62	32	22	76	18	2.56
1983—Beloit	Midwest	25	163⅓	11	10	.524	150	83	63	154	50	3.47
1984—El Paso	Texas	55	90	7	4	.636	77	20	15	69	25	1.50
1985—Vancouver	P. Coast	48	106⅔	3	6	.333	110	58	54	68	38	4.56

Selected by Chicago Cubs' organization in 3rd round of free-agent draft, June 5, 1979.
Selected by Milwaukee Brewers' organization in 17th round of free-agent draft, June 7, 1982.

JOSE CRUZ (DILAN)

Born August 8, 1947, at Arroyo, Puerto Rico.
Height, 6.00. Weight, 185.
Throws and bats lefthanded.
Brother of Hector Cruz, third baseman-outfielder with St. Louis, Chicago N.L., San Francisco and Cincinnati, 1973 and 1975 through 1982, and Yomiuri Giants of Japanese baseball, 1983; and Cirilo (Tommy) Cruz, outfielder with St. Louis Cardinals and Chicago White Sox, 1973 and 1977, and currently with Nippon Ham Fighters in Japanese baseball.

Tied major league record for fewest double plays by outfielder, season, 150 or more games (0), 1978.
Major League stolen bases: 1971 (6), 1972 (9), 1973 (10), 1974 (4), 1975 (6), 1976 (28), 1977 (44), 1978 (37), 1979 (36), 1980 (36), 1981 (5), 1982 (21), 1983 (30), 1984 (22), 1985 (16). Total—310.
Led National League outfielders in double plays with 5 in 1972.
Tied for National League lead in sacrifice flies with 10 in 1977 and 1984.
Named outfielder on THE SPORTING NEWS National League All-Star Team, 1984.
Named outfielder on THE SPORTING NEWS National League Silver Slugger team, 1983 and 1984.
Led Texas League in total bases with 254 in 1970.

Year Club	League	Pos.	G.	AB.	R.	H.	2B.	3B.	HR.	RBI.	B.A.	PO.	A.	E.	F.A.
1967—St. Petersburg	Fla. St.	OF-1B	78	205	33	57	8	9	1	20	.278	113	5	7	.944
1968—Modesto	Calif.	OF-SS	133	504	101	144	24	10	13	53	.286	219	10	11	.954
1969—Arkansas†	Texas	OF	102	400	56	109	18	9	6	49	.273	235	16	9	.965
1970—Arkansas	Texas	OF	133	493	89	148	*29	7	21	90	.300	*276	10	12	.960
1970—St. Louis	Nat.	OF	6	17	2	6	1	0	0	1	.353	16	0	0	1.000
1971—Tulsa	A. A.	OF	67	254	56	83	15	7	15	49	.327	146	1	7	.955
1971—St. Louis	Nat.	OF	83	292	46	80	13	2	9	27	.274	197	2	5	.975
1972—St. Louis	Nat.	OF	117	332	33	78	14	4	2	23	.235	220	9	5	.979
1973—St. Louis	Nat.	OF	132	406	51	92	22	5	10	57	.227	276	2	6	.979
1974—St. Louis‡	Nat.	OF-1B	107	161	24	42	4	3	5	20	.261	81	2	2	.976
1975—Houston	Nat.	OF	120	315	44	81	15	2	9	49	.257	187	6	4	.980
1976—Houston	Nat.	OF	133	439	49	133	21	5	4	61	.303	265	10	8	.972
1977—Houston	Nat.	OF	157	579	87	173	31	10	17	87	.299	311	11	9	.973
1978—Houston	Nat.	OF-1B	153	565	79	178	34	9	10	83	.315	328	5	8	.977
1979—Houston	Nat.	OF	157	558	73	161	33	7	9	72	.289	320	7	14	.959
1980—Houston	Nat.	OF	160	612	79	185	29	7	11	91	.302	323	16	•11	.969
1981—Houston	Nat.	OF	107	409	53	109	16	5	13	55	.267	237	5	4	.984
1982—Houston	Nat.	OF	155	570	62	157	27	2	9	68	.275	340	9	*13	.964
1983—Houston	Nat.	OF	160	594	85	•189	28	8	14	92	.318	322	9	7	.979
1984—Houston	Nat.	OF	160	600	96	187	28	13	12	95	.312	310	11	8	.976
1985—Houston	Nat.	OF	141	544	69	163	34	4	9	79	.300	257	12	8	.971
Major League Totals—16 Years			2048	6993	922	2014	350	00	140	900	.288	3990	116	112	.973

Signed as free agent by St. Louis Cardinals' organization, October 27, 1966.
†On disabled list, April 8 to May 12, 1969.
‡Sold to Houston Astros, October 24, 1974.

DIVISION SERIES RECORD

Year Club	League	Pos.	G.	AB.	R.	H.	2B.	3B.	HR.	RBI.	B.A.	PO.	A.	E.	F.A.
1981—Houston	Nat.	OF	5	20	0	6	1	0	0	0	.300	15	0	1	.938

CHAMPIONSHIP SERIES RECORD

Established Championship Series record for most walks, five-game series (8), 1980.

Year Club	League	Pos.	G.	AB.	R.	H.	2B.	3B.	HR.	RBI.	B.A.	PO.	A.	E.	F.A.
1980—Houston	Nat.	OF	5	15	3	6	1	1	0	4	.400	19	0	0	1.000

ALL-STAR GAME RECORD

Year League	Pos.	AB.	R.	H.	2B.	3B.	HR.	RBI.	B.A.	PO.	A.	E.	F.A.
1985—National	OF	1	0	0	0	0	0	0	.000	2	0	0	1.000

Member of National League All-Star Team in 1980; did not play.

JULIO LUIS CRUZ

Born December 2, 1954, at Brooklyn, N. Y.
Height, 5.09. Weight, 167.
Throws right and bats right and lefthanded.
Attended San Bernardino Valley College, San Bernardino, Calif.

Tied major league records for most chances accepted by second baseman, nine-inning game (18), June 7, 1981; most at-bats, game (11), May 8, finished May 9, 1984 (25 innings); longest errorless game by second baseman (25 innings), May 8, finished May 9, 1984.

Established American League record for most games played with two clubs, season (160), Seattle (61), Chicago (99), 1983.

Tied American League records for most consecutive stolen bases without caught stealing (32); most innings played by second baseman, game (25), May 8, finished May 9, 1984.

Major League stolen bases: 1977 (15), 1978 (59), 1979 (49), 1980 (45), 1981 (43), 1982 (46), 1983 (57), 1984 (14), 1985 (8). Total—336.

Led American League second basemen in fielding percentage with .987 in 1978.

Led Pioneer League in stolen bases with 34, in being hit by pitch with 7 and tied for lead in caught stealing with 11 in 1974.

Tied for Pacific Coast League lead in sacrifice hits with 9 in 1977.

Tied for Midwest League lead in sacrifice hits with 11 in 1975.

Year Club	League	Pos.	G.	AB.	R.	H.	2B.	3B.	HR.	RBI.	B.A.	PO.	A.	E.	F.A.
1974—Idaho Falls	Pioneer	2B-SS-3B	72	237	44	57	4	1	0	27	.241	137	185	22	.936
1975—Quad Cities	Midw.	2B	108	368	79	96	6	6	0	35	.261	228	259	14	.972
1976—Salinas	Calif.	2B	96	348	92	107	12	3	1	45	.307	234	314	10	*.982
1976—El Paso	Texas	2B	13	49	9	16	4	1	0	9	.327	23	21	0	1.000
1976—Salt Lake City†	P. C.	2B-3B-OF	20	69	11	17	2	2	0	6	.246	30	47	1	.987
1977—Hawaii	P. C.	2B	75	303	71	111	9	9	0	33	.366	189	237	7	.984
1977—Seattle	Amer.	2B	60	199	25	51	3	1	1	7	.256	114	171	5	.983
1978—Seattle	Amer.	2B-SS	147	550	77	129	14	1	1	25	.235	295	482	11	.986
1979—Seattle‡	Amer.	2B	107	414	70	112	16	2	1	29	.271	258	361	13	.979
1980—Seattle§	Amer.	2B	119	422	66	88	9	3	2	16	.209	269	355	11	.983
1981—Seattle	Amer.	2B-SS	94	352	57	90	12	3	2	24	.256	240	297	11	.980
1982—Seattle	Amer.	2B-SS-3B	154	549	83	133	22	5	8	49	.242	322	438	10	.987
1983—Sea. x-Chi. y	Amer.	2B	160	515	71	130	19	5	3	52	.252	344	471	14	.983
1984—Chicago	Amer.	2B	143	415	42	92	14	4	5	43	.222	273	452	18	.976
1985—Chicago z	Amer.	2B	91	234	28	46	2	3	0	15	.197	158	220	7	.982
Major League Totals—9 Years			1075	3650	519	871	111	27	23	260	.239	2273	3247	100	.982

Signed as free agent by California Angels' organization, May 7, 1974.
†Selected by Seattle Mariners from California Angels in American League expansion draft, November 5, 1976.

‡On disabled list, June 5 to August 3, 1979.
§On disabled list, April 24 to May 9, 1980.
xTraded to Chicago White Sox for Second Baseman Tony Bernazard, June 15, 1983.
yGranted free agency, November 7, 1983; re-signed by White Sox, January 8, 1984.
zOn disabled list, May 17 to June 3, 1985.

CHAMPIONSHIP SERIES RECORD

Year Club	League	Pos.	G.	AB.	R.	H.	2B.	3B.	HR.	RBI.	B.A.	PO.	A.	E.	F.A.
1983—Chicago	Amer.	2B	4	12	0	4	0	0	0	0	.333	10	14	0	1.000

KALVOSKI DANIELS
(Kal)

Born August 20, 1963, at Vienna, Ga.
Height, 5.11. Weight, 185.
Throws right and bats lefthanded.
Attended Middle Georgia College, Cochran, Ga.

Led Eastern League in slugging percentage with .525 in 1984.
Tied for Pioneer League lead in game-winning RBIs with 9 and stolen bases with 27 in 1982.

Year Club	League	Pos.	G.	AB.	R.	H.	2B.	3B.	HR.	RBI.	B.A.	PO.	A.	E.	F.A.
1982—Billings	Pion.	OF	67	240	43	88	19	4	3	38	.367	104	4	5	.956
1983—Cedar Rapids	Midw.	OF	101	342	51	86	14	5	5	28	.251	130	5	2	.985
1984—Vermont	East.	OF	122	415	81	130	29	4	17	62	.313	143	2	5	.967
1985—Denver†	A. A.	OF	76	285	59	86	12	9	15	43	.302	83	5	4	.957

Selected by New York Mets' organization in 3rd round of free-agent draft, January 12, 1982.
Selected by Cincinnati Reds' organization in secondary phase of free-agent draft, June 7, 1982.
†On disabled list, July 7, 1985 through remainder of season.

RONALD MAURICE DARLING JR.
(Ron)

Born August 19, 1960, at Honolulu, Hawaii.
Height, 6.03. Weight, 195.
Throws and bats righthanded.
Attended Yale University, New Haven, Conn.
Brother of Eddie Darling, first baseman in New York Yankees' organization, 1981 and 1982.
Established major league record for fewest assists by pitcher, season, for leader in assists (47), 1985.

Year Club	League	G.	IP.	W.	L.	Pct.	H.	R.	ER.	SO.	BB.	ERA.
1981—Tulsa†	Texas	13	71	4	2	.667	72	43	35	53	33	4.44
1982—Tidewater	Int'national	26	152	7	9	.438	143	76	63	114	95	3.73
1983—Tidewater	Int'national	27	159	10	9	.526	137	83	71	107	102	4.02
1983—New York	National	5	35⅓	1	3	.250	31	11	11	23	17	2.80
1984—New York	National	33	205⅔	12	9	.571	179	97	87	136	104	3.81
1985—New York	National	36	248	16	6	.727	214	93	80	167	*114	2.90
Major League Totals—3 Years		74	489	29	18	.617	424	201	178	326	235	3.28

Selected by Texas Rangers' organization in 1st round (ninth player selected) of free-agent draft, June 8, 1981.
†Traded with Pitcher Walt Terrell to New York Mets' organization for Outfielder Lee Mazzilli, April 1, 1982.

ALL-STAR GAME RECORD
Member of National League All-Star Team in 1985; did not play.

DANNY WAYNE DARWIN

Born October 25, 1955, at Bonham, Tex.
Height, 6.03. Weight, 190.
Throws and bats righthanded.
Attended Grayson County College, Denison, Tex.

Major League saves: 1980 (8), 1982 (7), 1985 (2). Total—17.
Tied for American League lead in home runs allowed with 34 in 1985.
Tied for Texas League lead in shutouts with 4 and hit batsmen with 8 in 1977.
Tied for Western Carolinas League lead in balks with 5 in 1976.

Year Club	League	G.	IP.	W.	L.	Pct.	H.	R.	ER.	SO.	BB.	ERA.
1976—Asheville	W. Carol.	16	102	6	3	.667	96	54	41	76	48	3.62
1977—Tulsa†	Texas	23	154	13	4	.765	130	53	43	129	72	2.51
1978—Tucson	P. Coast	23	125	8	9	.471	147	100	87	126	83	6.26
1978—Texas	American	3	9	1	0	1.000	11	4	4	8	1	4.00
1979—Tucson	P. Coast	13	95	6	6	.500	89	43	38	65	42	3.60
1979—Texas	American	20	78	4	4	.500	50	36	35	58	30	4.04
1980—Texas‡	American	53	110	13	4	.765	98	37	32	104	50	2.62
1981—Texas	American	22	146	9	9	.500	115	67	59	98	57	3.64
1982—Texas	American	56	89	10	8	.556	95	38	34	61	37	3.44
1983—Texas§	American	28	183	8	13	.381	175	86	71	92	62	3.49
1984—Texas x	American x	35	223⅔	8	12	.400	249	110	98	123	54	3.94
1985—Milwaukee y	American	39	217⅔	8	18	.308	212	112	92	125	65	3.80
Major League Totals—8 Years		256	1056¼	61	68	.473	1005	490	425	669	356	3.62

Signed as free agent by Texas Rangers' organization, May 10, 1976.
†On disabled list, April 25 to May 4 and May 22 to June 11, 1977.

§On disabled list, March 25 to April 10 and August 9 to September 1, 1983.
xTraded with a player to be named later to Milwaukee Brewers as part of a six-player, four-team deal in which Kansas City Royals acquired Catcher Jim Sundberg from Milwaukee, Texas Rangers acquired Catcher Don Slaught from Kansas City, New York Mets' organization acquired Pitcher Frank Wills from Kansas City and Milwaukee organization acquired Pitcher Tim Leary from New York, January 18, 1985; Milwaukee organization acquired Catcher Bill Hance from Texas to complete deal, January 30, 1985.
yGranted free agency, November 12, 1985; re-signed by Brewers, December 22, 1985

RICHARD FREMONT DAUER

Name pronounced DOW-er.

(Rich)

Born July 27, 1952, at San Bernardino, Calif.
Height, 6.00. Weight, 180.
Throws and bats righthanded.
Attended San Bernardino Valley College, San Bernardino, Calif., and
University of Southern California, Los Angeles, Calif.

Established American League records for most consecutive errorless games by second baseman, season (86), 1978; most consecutive errorless chances accepted by second baseman, season (425), 1978.
Major League stolen bases: 1977 (1), 1980 (3), 1983 (1), 1984 (1). Total—6.
Led International League in fielding percentage with .976 in 1976.
Led Southern League third basemen in double plays with 28 in 1975.
Named International League co-Most Valuable Player, 1976.
Named third baseman on THE SPORTING NEWS College Baseball All-America Team, 1974.

Year Club	League	Pos.	G.	AB.	R.	H.	2B.	3B.	HR.	RBI.	B.A.	PO.	A.	E.	F.A.
1974—Asheville	South.	2B-3B	53	180	30	59	7	0	11	35	.328	72	104	3	.983
1975—Rochester	Int.	2B-3B	18	47	2	8	1	0	0	0	.170	17	30	2	.959
1975—Asheville	South.	★3B-2B	106	374	51	94	13	0	6	44	.251	98	195	6	★.980
1976—Rochester	Int.	2B-SS-1B	132	524	84	★176	26	3	11	78	★.336	276	402	18	.974
1976—Baltimore	Amer.	2B	11	39	0	4	0	0	0	3	.103	22	22	0	1.000
1977—Baltimore	Amer.	2B-3B	96	304	38	74	15	1	5	25	.243	182	233	7	.983
1978—Baltimore	Amer.	2B-3B	133	459	57	121	23	0	6	46	.264	222	321	7	.987
1979—Baltimore	Amer.	2B-3B	142	479	63	123	20	0	9	61	.257	234	355	17	.972
1980—Baltimore	Amer.	2B-3B	152	557	71	158	32	0	2	63	.284	334	418	8	.989
1981—Baltimore	Amer.	★2B-3B	96	369	41	97	27	0	4	38	.263	201	256	5	★.989
1982—Baltimore	Amer.	2B-3B	158	558	75	156	24	2	8	57	.280	289	354	8	.988
1983—Baltimore	Amer.	2B-3B	140	459	49	108	19	0	5	41	.235	280	333	8	.987
1984—Baltimore	Amer.	2B-3B	127	397	29	101	26	0	2	24	.254	225	329	11	.981
1985—Baltimore†	Amer.	2B-3B-1B	85	208	25	42	7	0	2	14	.202	126	202	4	.988
Major League Totals—10 Years			1140	3829	448	984	193	3	43	372	.257	2115	2823	75	.985

Selected by Oakland A's organization in 5th round of free agent draft, January 13, 1971.
Selected by Oakland A's organization in 9th round of free agent draft, January 12, 1972.
Selected by Cleveland Indians' organization in secondary phase of free agent draft, June 6, 1972.
Selected by Baltimore Orioles' organization in 1st round (24th player selected) of free agent draft, June 5, 1974.
†Granted free agency, November 12, 1985.

CHAMPIONSHIP SERIES RECORD

Year Club	League	Pos.	G.	AB.	R.	H.	2B.	3B.	HR.	RBI.	B.A.	PO.	A.	E.	F.A.
1979—Baltimore	Amer.	2B	4	11	0	2	0	0	0	0	.182	10	12	0	1.000
1983—Baltimore	Amer.	2B	4	14	0	0	0	0	0	1	.000	8	12	0	1.000
Championship Series Totals—2 Years			8	25	0	2	0	0	0	1	.080	18	24	0	1.000

WORLD SERIES RECORD

Year Club	League	Pos.	G.	AB.	R.	H.	2B.	3B.	HR.	RBI.	B.A.	PO.	A.	E.	F.A.
1979—Baltimore	Amer.	PH-2B	6	17	2	5	1	0	1	1	.294	10	10	0	1.000
1983—Baltimore	Amer.	2B-3B	5	19	2	4	1	0	0	3	.211	14	8	0	1.000
World Series Totals—2 Years			11	36	4	9	2	0	1	4	.250	24	18	0	1.000

DARREN ARTHUR DAULTON

Born January 3, 1962, at Arkansas City, Kan.
Height, 6.02. Weight, 190.
Throws right and bats lefthanded.
Attended Cowley County Community College, Arkansas City, Kan.

Major League stolen bases: 1985 (3).
Tied for Eastern League lead in sacrifice flies with 10 in 1983.

Year Club	League	Pos.	G.	AB.	R.	H.	2B.	3B.	HR.	RBI.	B.A.	PO.	A.	E.	F.A.
1980—Helena	Pion.	C	37	100	13	20	2	1	1	10	.200	224	17	4	.984
1981—Spartanburg	S. Atl.	C-OF-3B	98	270	44	62	11	1	3	29	.230	378	34	4	.990
1982—Peninsula	Carol.	C-1B	110	324	65	78	21	2	11	44	.241	654	63	9	.990
1983—Reading	East.	C-1B-OF	113	362	77	95	16	4	19	83	.262	557	57	14	.978
1983—Philadelphia	Nat.	C	2	3	1	1	0	0	0	0	.333	8	0	0	1.000
1984—Portland†	P. C.	C	80	252	45	75	19	4	7	38	.298	322	26	6	.983
1985—Portland	P. C.	C	23	64	13	19	5	3	2	10	.297	110	9	0	1.000
1985—Philadelphia‡	Nat.	C	36	103	14	21	3	1	4	11	.204	160	15	1	.994
Major League Totals—2 Years			38	106	15	22	3	1	4	11	.208	168	15	1	.995

Selected by Philadelphia Phillies' organization in 25th round of free-agent draft, June 3, 1980.

†On disabled list, July 20 to August 28, 1984.
‡On disabled list, May 17 to August 9, 1985; included rehabilitation disability assignment to Portland, July 20 to August 7, 1985.

ANDRE ANTER DAVID

Born May 18, 1958, at Hollywood, Calif.
Height, 6.00. Weight, 170.
Throws and bats lefthanded.
Attended Los Angeles Valley College, Van Nuys, Calif. and
California State University, Fullerton, Calif.

Tied major league record by hitting home run in first major league at-bat, June 29, 1984, first game.

Year Club	League	Pos.	G.	AB.	R.	H.	2B.	3B.	HR.	RBI.	B.A.	PO.	A.	E.	F.A.
1980—Visalia	Calif.	OF	63	210	33	68	9	2	0	32	.324	99	10	3	.973
1981—Orlando	South.	OF	133	475	57	111	13	5	10	54	.234	253	17	9	.968
1982—Toledo	Int.	OF	15	43	4	6	1	1	0	0	.140	26	1	2	.931
1982—Orlando	South.	OF-1B-3B	107	366	61	102	17	7	5	49	.279	195	9	7	.967
1983—Toledo	Int.	OF-1B	116	403	59	117	15	1	6	54	.290	107	7	4	.966
1984—Toledo	Int.	OF-1B	61	194	30	57	14	1	7	24	.294	87	4	3	.968
1984—Minnesota	Amer.	OF	33	48	5	12	2	0	1	5	.250	14	0	0	1.000
1985—Toledo†	Int.	1B-OF	102	331	40	88	15	1	8	48	.266	332	17	5	.986
Major League Totals—1 Year			33	48	5	12	2	0	1	5	.250	14	0	0	1.000

Selected by Minnesota Twins' organization in 14th round of free-agent draft, June 5, 1979.
Selected by Minnesota Twins' organization in 8th round of free-agent draft, June 3, 1980.
†On disabled list, July 31 to August 9, 1985.

JOHN MARK DAVIDSON

(Known by middle name.)

Born February 15, 1961, at Knoxville, Tenn.
Height, 6.02. Weight, 180.
Throws and bats righthanded.
Attended University of North Carolina, Charlotte, N.C.,
and Clemson University, Clemson, S.C.
Son of Max Davidson, minor league outfielder, 1947 through 1954.

Led Southern League in game-winning RBIs with 16 in 1985.

Year Club	League	Pos.	G.	AB.	R.	H.	2B.	3B.	HR.	RBI.	B.A.	PO.	A.	E.	F.A.
1982—Wis. Rapids	Midw.	OF	79	247	54	74	11	0	10	41	.300	166	13	5	.973
1983—Wis. Rapids†	Midw.	OF	111	363	63	80	15	1	13	48	.220	181	6	6	.969
1984—Orlando‡	South.	OF-1B-3B	114	348	55	99	11	6	4	37	.284	243	13	3	.988
1985—Orlando	South.	OF-3B	134	453	93	137	17	2	25	106	.302	305	14	6	.982

Selected by Minnesota Twins' organization in 11th round of free-agent draft, June 7, 1982.
†On disabled list, April 15 to May 4, 1983.
‡On disabled list, July 16 to July 26, 1984.

ALVIN GLENN DAVIS

(Al)

Born September 9, 1960, at Riverside, Calif.
Height, 6.01. Weight, 190.
Throws right and bats lefthanded.
Received bachelor of science degree in finance from Arizona State University, Tempe, Ariz.

Major League stolen bases: 1984 (5), 1985 (1). Total—6.
Led Southern League in bases on balls received with 120 and sacrifice flies with 12 in 1983.
Led Southern League first basemen in total chances with 1,348 and double plays with 118 in 1983.
Named American League Rookie Player of the Year by THE SPORTING NEWS, 1984.
Named American League Rookie of the Year by Baseball Writers' Association of America, 1984.

Year Club	League	Pos.	G.	AB.	R.	H.	2B.	3B.	HR.	RBI.	B.A.	PO.	A.	E.	F.A.
1982—Lynn	East	1B	74	225	37	64	10	1	12	56	.284	579	51	6	.991
1983—Chattanooga†	South.	★●1B-OF	131	422	87	125	24	3	18	83	.296	★1233	★99	●16	.988
1984—Salt Lake City	P. C.	1B	1	3	2	2	0	0	0	1	.667	2	0	0	1.000
1984—Seattle	Amer.	1B	152	567	80	161	34	3	27	116	.284	1271	94	11	.992
1985—Seattle	Amer.	1B	155	578	78	166	33	1	18	78	.287	1438	103	13	.992
Major League Totals—2 Years			307	1145	158	327	67	4	45	194	.286	2709	197	24	.992

Selected by San Francisco Giants' organization in 8th round of free-agent draft, June 6, 1978.
Selected by Oakland A's organization in 6th round of free-agent draft, June 8, 1981.
Selected by Seattle Mariners' organization in 6th round of free-agent draft, June 7, 1982.
†On disabled list, July 21 to July 31, 1983.

ALL-STAR GAME RECORD

Year League	Pos.	AB.	R.	H.	2B.	3B.	HR.	RBI.	B.A.	PO.	A.	E.	F.A.
1984—American	PH	1	0	0	0	0	0	0	.000	0	0	0	.000

—DID YOU KNOW—

That in the Phillies' 26-7 win over the Mets on June 11, Philadelphia tied a modern National League record for most extra base hits by one club with 14?

CHARLES THEODORE DAVIS
(Chili)

(Original nickname was Chili Bowl, which was prompted by a friend who saw Davis after he received a haircut back in the sixth grade. The nickname was later shortened to Chili.)

Born January 17, 1960, at Kingston, Jamaica.
Height, 6.03. Weight, 195.
Throws right and bats left and righthanded.
Tied National League record for most games, switch-hit home runs, season (1), June 5, 1983.
Major League stolen bases: 1981 (2), 1982 (24), 1983 (10), 1984 (12), 1985 (15). Total—63.

Year Club	League	Pos.	G.	AB.	R.	H.	2B.	3B.	HR.	RBI.	B.A.	PO.	A.	E.	F.A.
1978—Cedar Rapids........	Midw.	C-OF	124	424	63	119	18	5	16	73	.281	365	45	25	.943
1979—Fresno	Calif.	OF-C	134	490	91	132	24	5	21	95	.269	339	43	20	.950
1980—Shreveport	Texas	OF-C	129	442	50	130	30	4	12	67	.294	184	20	12	.944
1981—San Francisco	Nat.	OF	8	15	1	2	0	0	0	0	.133	7	0	0	1.000
1981—Phoenix†	P. C.	OF	88	334	76	117	16	6	19	75	.350	175	7	6	.968
1982—San Francisco	Nat.	OF	154	641	86	167	27	6	19	76	.261	404	●16	12	.972
1983—San Francisco	Nat.	OF	137	486	54	113	21	2	11	59	.233	357	7	9	.976
1983—Phoenix	P. C.	OF	10	44	12	13	2	0	2	9	.295	15	0	2	.882
1984—San Francisco	Nat.	OF	137	499	87	157	21	6	21	81	.315	292	9	9	.971
1985—San Francisco	Nat.	OF	136	481	53	130	25	2	13	56	.270	279	10	6	.980
Major League Totals—5 Years................			572	2122	281	569	94	16	64	272	.268	1339	42	36	.975

Selected by San Francisco Giants' organization in 11th round of free-agent draft, June 7, 1977.
†On disabled list, August 19 to August 28, 1982.

ALL-STAR GAME RECORD

Year League	Pos.	AB.	R.	H.	2B.	3B.	HR.	RBI.	B.A.	PO.	A.	E.	F.A.
1984—National	PH	1	0	0	0	0	0	0	.000	0	0	0	.000

ERIC KEITH DAVIS

Born May 29, 1962, at Los Angeles, Calif.
Height, 6.02. Weight, 170.
Throws and bats righthanded.
Major League stolen bases: 1984 (10), 1985 (16). Total—26.
Led Northwest League in stolen bases with 40 in 1981.

Year Club	League	Pos.	G.	AB.	R.	H.	2B.	3B.	HR.	RBI.	B.A.	PO.	A.	E.	F.A.
1980—Eugene	N'west	SS-2B	33	73	12	16	1	0	1	11	.219	24	35	11	.843
1981—Eugene	N'west	OF	62	214	★67	69	10	4	11	39	.322	94	11	4	.963
1982—Cedar Rapids........	Midw.	OF	111	434	80	120	20	5	15	56	.276	239	9	9	.965
1983—Waterbury	East.	OF	89	293	56	85	13	1	15	43	.290	214	8	2	.991
1983—Indianapolis	A. A.	OF	19	77	18	23	4	0	7	19	.299	61	1	1	.984
1984—Wichita	A. A.	OF	52	194	42	61	9	5	14	34	.314	110	5	5	.958
1984—Cincinnati†	Nat.	OF	57	174	33	39	10	1	10	30	.224	125	4	1	.992
1985—Cincinnati	Nat.	OF	56	122	26	30	3	3	8	18	.246	75	3	1	.987
1985—Denver	A. A.	OF	64	206	48	57	10	2	15	38	.277	94	5	3	.971
Major League Totals—2 Years..............			113	296	59	69	13	4	18	48	.233	200	7	2	.990

Selected by Cincinnati Reds' organization in 8th round of free-agent draft, June 3, 1980.
†On disabled list, August 16 to September 1, 1984.

GEORGE EARL DAVIS JR.
(Storm)

(Nicknamed by mother after character in book she was reading while pregnant with Storm.)

Born December 26, 1961, at Dallas, Tex.
Height, 6.04. Weight, 210.
Throws and bats righthanded.
Step-brother of Glenn Davis, first baseman with Houston Astros.
Major League saves: 1984 (1).

Year Club	League	G.	IP.	W.	L.	Pct.	H.	R.	ER.	SO.	BB.	ERA.
1979—Bluefield................	Ap'lachian.	10	58	4	4	.500	44	34	25	54	30	3.88
1980—Miami	Florida St.	25	151	9	12	.429	157	85	59	90	55	3.52
1981—Charlotte...............	Southern	28	187	14	10	.583	★215	86	72	119	65	3.47
1982—Rochester	Int'national	4	26⅔	2	1	.667	25	13	11	27	7	3.71
1982—Baltimore	American	29	100⅓	8	4	.667	96	40	39	67	28	3.49
1983—Baltimore	American	34	200⅓	13	7	.650	180	90	80	125	64	3.59
1984—Baltimore	American	35	225	14	9	.609	205	86	78	105	71	3.12
1985—Baltimore	American	31	175	10	8	.556	172	92	88	93	70	4.53
Major League Totals—4 Years..........................		129	701	45	28	.616	653	308	285	390	233	3.66

Selected by Baltimore Orioles' organization in 7th round of free-agent draft, June 5, 1979.

CHAMPIONSHIP SERIES RECORD

Year Club	League	G.	IP.	W.	L.	Pct.	H.	R.	ER.	SO.	BB.	ERA.
1983—Baltimore	American	1	6	0	0	.000	5	0	0	2	2	0.00

WORLD SERIES RECORD

Year Club	League	G.	IP.	W.	L.	Pct.	H.	R.	ER.	SO.	BB.	ERA.
1983—Baltimore	American	1	5	1	0	1.000	6	3	3	3	1	5.40

GERALD EDWARD DAVIS
(Jerry)

Born December 25, 1958, at Trenton, N.J.
Height, 6.00. Weight, 180.
Throws and bats righthanded.
Attended Howard University, Washington, D.C.

Major League stolen bases: 1983 (1).
Led Pacific Coast League in bases on balls received with 103 in 1984.
Led Carolina League in bases on balls received with 161 and being hit by pitch with 14 in 1981.
Tied for Pacific Coast League lead in being hit by pitch with 12 in 1983.

Year Club	League	Pos.	G.	AB.	R.	H.	2B.	3B.	HR.	RBI.	B.A.	PO.	A.	E.	F.A.
1980—Walla Walla	N'west	3B	54	197	39	60	4	1	8	50	.305	42	104	24	.859
1981—Salem	Carol.	OF-3B	★138	431	★114	132	24	3	★34	103	.306	140	49	30	.863
1982—Amarillo	Texas	OF	95	365	78	129	18	1	14	67	.353	158	4	10	.942
1982—Hawaii	P. C.	OF	41	145	26	39	8	0	3	19	.269	68	11	7	.919
1983—Las Vegas	P. C.	OF	139	503	113	150	29	8	23	100	.298	296	17	9	.972
1983—San Diego	Nat.	OF	5	15	3	5	2	0	0	1	.333	8	1	0	1.000
1984—Las Vegas	P. C.	OF	129	450	98	136	23	7	9	64	.302	240	17	12	.955
1985—San Diego	Nat.	OF	44	58	10	17	3	1	0	2	.293	18	2	1	.952
1985—Las Vegas	P. C.	OF	17	63	7	18	1	0	0	9	.286	50	3	0	1.000
Major League Totals—2 Years			49	73	13	22	5	1	0	3	.301	26	3	1	.961

Selected by Boston Red Sox' organization in 22nd round of free-agent draft, June 7, 1977.
Selected by San Diego Padres' organization in 6th round of free-agent draft, June 3, 1980.

GLENN EARL DAVIS

Born March 28, 1961, at Jacksonville, Fla.
Height, 6.03. Weight, 210.
Throws and bats righthanded.
Attended Manatee Junior College, Bradenton, Fla.,
and University of Georgia, Athens, Ga.
Step-brother of Storm Davis, pitcher with Baltimore Orioles.

Led Gulf Coast League first basemen in total chances with 520 and tied for lead in double plays with 35 in 1981.

Year Club	League	Pos.	G.	AB.	R.	H.	2B.	3B.	HR.	RBI.	B.A.	PO.	A.	E.	F.A.
1981—Sara. Astros-Or.	Gulf C.	★1B-OF	54	188	27	49	7	1	6	35	.261	★469	★37	★14	.973
1982—Daytona Beach	Fla. St.	1B-3B	103	378	70	119	28	3	●19	79	.315	759	70	16	.981
1982—Columbus	South.	1B	26	97	14	24	6	1	4	8	.247	257	11	2	.993
1983—Columbus	South.	OF	118	445	68	133	19	3	●25	85	.299	186	17	9	.958
1983—Tucson	P. C.	OF-1B-3B	15	57	5	12	3	0	1	8	.211	52	4	2	.966
1984—Tucson	P. C.	1B-OF	131	471	66	140	28	7	16	94	.297	922	94	22	.979
1984—Houston	Nat.	1B	18	61	6	13	5	0	2	8	.213	151	15	2	.988
1985—Tucson	P. C.	1B-OF	60	220	22	67	24	2	5	35	.305	420	29	5	.989
1985—Houston	Nat.	1B-OF	100	350	51	95	11	0	20	64	.271	766	57	12	.986
Major League Totals—2 Years			118	411	57	108	16	0	22	72	.263	917	72	14	.986

Selected by Baltimore Orioles' organization in 32nd round of free-agent draft, June 5, 1979.
Selected by Houston Astros' organization in secondary phase of free-agent draft, January 13, 1981.

JODY RICHARD DAVIS

Born November 12, 1956, at Gainesville, Ga.
Height, 6.03. Weight, 210.
Throws and bats righthanded.
Attended Middle Georgia College, Cochran, Ga.

Major League stolen bases: 1984 (5), 1985 (1). Total—6.
Led National League in passed balls with 21 in 1983.
Tied for National League lead in double plays by catchers with 11 in 1982.
Led Carolina League in sacrifice flies with 13 in 1978.
Led Carolina League catchers in double plays with 8 in 1978.

Year Club	League	Pos.	G.	AB.	R.	H.	2B.	3B.	HR.	RBI.	B.A.	PO.	A.	E.	F.A.
1976—Marion	Appal.	C	50	164	20	38	5	1	5	19	.232	290	30	★13	.961
1977—Little Falls	NYP	C-1B	64	214	37	62	11	2	11	46	.290	369	50	12	.972
1978—Lynchburg	Carol.	C-1B-3B	120	408	57	107	24	2	16	94	.262	595	79	15	.978
1979—Jackson†	Texas	C-1B	132	433	57	128	23	4	21	91	.296	661	81	15	.980
1980—St. Petersburg	Fla. St.	C-1B	45	155	27	43	4	0	6	27	.277	171	20	5	.974
1980—Springfield‡§	A. A.	C-1B	13	36	3	6	1	0	0	2	.167	59	7	1	.985
1981—Chicago	Nat.	C	56	180	14	46	5	1	4	21	.256	274	44	9	.972
1982—Chicago	Nat.	C	130	418	41	109	20	2	12	52	.261	598	89	11	.984
1983—Chicago	Nat.	C	151	510	56	138	31	2	24	84	.271	730	75	13	.984
1984—Chicago	Nat.	C	150	523	55	134	25	2	19	94	.256	811	89	★15	.984
1985—Chicago	Nat.	C	142	482	47	112	30	0	17	58	.232	694	84	8	.990
Major League Totals—5 Years			629	2113	213	539	111	7	76	309	.255	3107	381	56	.984

Selected by New York Mets' organization in 3rd round of free-agent draft, January 7, 1976.
†Traded to St. Louis Cardinals' organization for Pitcher Ray Searage, December 10, 1979.
‡On disabled list, April 14 to June 20, 1980.
§Drafted by Chicago Cubs, December 8, 1980.

CHAMPIONSHIP SERIES RECORD

Established National League Championship Series record for highest slugging average, five-game Series (.833), 1984.

Tied National League Championship Series record for most total bases, five-game Series (15), 1984.

Year	Club	League	Pos.	G.	AB.	R.	H.	2B.	3B.	HR.	RBI.	B.A.	PO.	A.	E.	F.A.
1984—Chicago		Nat.	C	5	18	3	7	2	0	2	6	.389	23	2	0	1.000

ALL-STAR GAME RECORD

Year	League	Pos.	AB.	R.	H.	2B.	3B.	HR.	RBI.	B.A.	PO.	A.	E.	F.A.
1984—National		C	1	0	0	0	0	0	0	.000	1	0	0	1.000

JOEL CLARK DAVIS

Born January 30, 1965, at Jacksonville, Fla.
Height, 6.05. Weight, 205.
Throws right and bats lefthanded.

Year	Club	League	G.	IP.	W.	L.	Pct.	H.	R.	ER.	SO.	BB.	ERA.
1983—Sarasota White Sox		Gulf Coast	12	75⅓	6	2	.750	51	23	16	95	26	1.91
1984—Appleton		Midwest	11	40⅓	1	2	.333	40	27	27	38	38	6.02
1984—Niagara Falls		NYP	11	69	3	4	.429	57	35	18	72	37	2.35
1985—Glens Falls		Eastern	4	11⅔	1	2	.333	12	13	10	9	14	7.71
1985—Glens Falls†		Eastern	4	25⅓	1	1	.500	21	8	8	20	16	2.84
1985—Buffalo		Am. Assoc.	10	56⅓	2	5	.286	61	39	29	31	35	4.63
1985—Chicago		American	12	71⅓	3	3	.500	71	34	33	37	26	4.16
Major League Totals—1 Year			12	71⅓	3	3	.500	71	34	33	37	26	4.16

Selected by Chicago White Sox' organization in 1st round (13th player selected) of free-agent draft, June 6, 1983.
†On disabled list, April 12 to May 28, 1985.

MARK WILLIAM DAVIS

Born October 19, 1960, at Livermore, Calif.
Height, 6.04. Weight, 195.
Throws and bats lefthanded.
Attended Chabot College, Hayward, Calif.

Major League saves: 1985 (7).
Led Western Carolinas League in shutouts with 5, home runs allowed with 18 and tied for lead in balks with 5 in 1979.
Tied for Eastern League lead in shutouts with 4 and in games started by pitchers with 28 in 1980.
Named Eastern League Player of the Year, 1980.

Year	Club	League	G.	IP.	W.	L.	Pct.	H.	R.	ER.	SO.	BB.	ERA.
1979—Spartanburg		W. Carol.	26	166	11	9	.550	147	76	59	135	49	3.20
1980—Reading		Eastern	28	*193	*19	6	*.760	140	63	53	*185	75	*2.47
1980—Philadelphia		National	2	7	0	0	.000	4	2	2	5	5	2.57
1981—Oklahoma City†		Am. Assoc.	13	65	5	2	.714	66	34	28	56	47	3.88
1981—Philadelphia		National	9	43	1	4	.200	49	37	37	29	24	7.74
1982—Oklahoma City‡§		Am. Assoc.	21	96⅔	5	12	.294	111	75	67	95	50	6.24
1983—Phoenix		P. Coast	13	72⅔	6	3	.667	89	57	51	64	33	6.32
1983—San Francisco		National	20	111	6	4	.600	93	51	43	83	50	3.49
1984—San Francisco		National	46	174⅔	5	17	.227	201	113	*104	124	54	5.36
1985—San Francisco		National	77	114⅓	5	12	.294	89	49	45	131	41	3.54
Major League Totals—5 Years			154	450	17	37	.315	436	252	231	372	174	4.62

Selected by New York Mets' organization in 21st round of free-agent draft, June 6, 1978.
Selected by Philadelphia Phillies' organization in secondary phase of free-agent draft, January 9, 1979.
†On disabled list, April 14 to June 11, 1981.
‡On disabled list, August 3 to August 30, 1982.
§Traded with Pitcher Mike Krukow and Outfielder Charles Penigar to San Francisco Giants for Second Baseman Joe Morgan and Pitcher Al Holland, December 14, 1982.

MICHAEL DWAYNE DAVIS
(Mike)

Born June 11, 1959, at San Diego, Calif.
Height, 6.03. Weight, 185.
Throws and bats lefthanded.
Attended San Diego Mesa College, San Diego, Calif.
Cousin of Dave Grayson, defensive back with Dallas Texans,
Kansas City Chiefs and Oakland Raiders, 1961 through 1970.

Major League stolen bases: 1980 (2), 1982 (3), 1983 (32), 1984 (14), 1985 (24). Total—75.

Year	Club	League	Pos.	G.	AB.	R.	H.	2B.	3B.	HR.	RBI.	B.A.	PO.	A.	E.	F.A.
1977—Medicine Hat		Pion.	*OF-1-2	59	213	53	67	5	3	2	18	.315	82	6	*15	.854
1978—Modesto		Calif.	OF-1B	106	406	74	136	12	4	2	35	.335	201	10	13	.942
1979—Modesto		Calif.	OF	41	161	48	63	10	4	0	19	.391	76	3	7	.919
1979—Waterbury		East.	OF	97	351	51	77	9	5	6	39	.219	208	7	15	.935
1980—Ogden		P. C.	OF	19	69	14	21	7	2	1	14	.304	34	2	1	.973
1980—Oakland		Amer.	OF-1B	51	95	11	20	2	1	1	8	.211	76	7	1	.988
1981—Tacoma		P. C.	OF-1B	133	515	84	148	28	6	6	71	.287	286	7	7	.977
1981—Oakland		Amer.	OF-1B	17	20	0	1	1	0	0	0	.050	3	0	0	1.000
1982—Tacoma†		P. C.	OF-1B	100	374	71	118	23	3	12	68	.316	197	13	9	.959
1982—Oakland		Amer.	OF-1B	23	75	12	30	4	0	1	10	.400	65	4	5	.932
1983—Oakland‡		Amer.	OF	128	443	61	122	24	4	8	62	.275	278	16	8	.974
1984—Oakland		Amer.	OF	134	382	47	88	18	3	9	46	.230	287	6	●12	.961
1985—Oakland		Amer.	OF	154	547	92	157	34	1	24	82	.287	370	6	8	.979
Major League Totals—6 Years				507	1562	223	418	83	9	43	208	.268	1079	39	34	.970

Selected by Minnesota Twins' organization in 31st round of free agent draft, June 8, 1976.
Selected by Oakland A's organization in 3rd round of free agent draft, June 7, 1977.
†On disabled list, April 13 to May 24, 1982.
‡On disabled list, July 13 to July 31, 1983.

CHAMPIONSHIP SERIES RECORD

Year Club	League	Pos.	G.	AB.	R.	H.	2B.	3B.	HR.	RBI.	B.A.	PO.	A.	E.	F.A.
1981—Oakland	Amer.	PH	1	1	0	1	0	0	0	0	1.000	0	0	0	.000

RONALD GENE DAVIS
(Ron)

Born August 6, 1955, at Houston Tex.
Height, 6.04. Weight, 198.
Throws and bats righthanded.
Attended Blinn Junior College, Brenham, Tex.

Established major league record for most consecutive strikeouts by relief pitcher, game (8), May 4, 1981.
Established American League record for most wins by rookie relief pitcher, season (14), 1979.
Tied American League record for most consecutive strikeouts, game (8), May 4, 1981.
Major League saves: 1979 (9), 1980 (7), 1981 (6), 1982 (22), 1983 (30), 1984 (29), 1985 (25). Total—128.
Led American League in intentional bases on balls issued with 12 in 1982.

Year Club	League	G.	IP.	W.	L.	Pct.	H.	R.	ER.	SO.	BB.	ERA.
1976—Pompano Beach	Florida St.	18	115	8	8	.500	110	62	48	78	51	3.76
1977—Midland†	Texas					(Did not play)						
1977—Pompano Beach	Florida St.	21	111	8	7	.533	119	63	51	58	59	4.14
1978—Midland‡	Texas	12	68	3	3	.500	80	51	48	45	38	6.35
1978—West Haven	Eastern	21	60	9	2	.818	41	14	10	39	27	1.50
1978—New York	American	4	2	0	0	.000	3	4	3	0	3	13.50
1979—Columbus	Int'national	11	19	0	1	.000	13	9	9	10	15	4.26
1979—New York	American	44	85	14	2	*.875	84	29	27	43	28	2.86
1980—New York	American	53	131	9	3	.750	121	50	43	65	32	2.95
1981—New York§	American	43	73	4	5	.444	47	22	22	83	25	2.71
1982—Minnesota	American	63	106	3	9	.250	106	53	52	89	47	4.42
1983—Minnesota	American	66	89	5	8	.385	89	34	33	84	33	3.34
1984—Minnesota	American	64	83	7	11	.389	79	44	42	74	41	4.55
1985—Minnesota	American	57	64⅔	2	6	.250	55	28	25	72	35	3.48
Major League Totals—8 Years		394	633⅔	44	44	.500	584	264	247	510	244	3.51

Selected by Chicago Cubs' organization in 3rd round of free-agent draft, January 7, 1976.
†On disabled list, April 9 to May 6, 1977.
‡Traded to New York Yankees' organization, June 12, 1978; completing deal in which New York traded Pitcher Ken Holtzman to Chicago Cubs for a player to be named later, June 10, 1978.
§Traded with Pitcher Paul Boris and Shortstop Greg Gagne and a reported $400,000 to Minnesota Twins for Shortstop Roy Smalley, April 10, 1982.

DIVISION SERIES RECORD

Year Club	League	G.	IP.	W.	L.	Pct.	H.	R.	ER.	SO.	BB.	ERA.
1981—New York	American	3	6	1	0	1.000	1	0	0	6	2	0.00

CHAMPIONSHIP SERIES RECORD

Year Club	League	G.	IP.	W.	L.	Pct.	H.	R.	ER.	SO.	BB.	ERA.
1980—New York	American	1	4	0	0	.000	3	1	1	3	1	2.25
1981—New York	American	2	3⅓	0	0	.000	0	0	0	4	2	0.00
Championship Series Totals—2 Years		3	7⅓	0	0	.000	3	1	1	7	3	1.23

WORLD SERIES RECORD

Year Club	League	G.	IP.	W.	L.	Pct.	H.	R.	ER.	SO.	BB.	ERA.
1981—New York	American	4	2⅓	0	0	.000	4	8	6	4	5	23.14

ALL-STAR GAME RECORD

Year League	IP.	W.	L.	Pct.	H.	R.	ER.	SO.	BB.	ERA.
1981—American	1	0	0	.000	1	1	1	1	0	9.00

STEVEN KENNON DAVIS
(Steve)

Born August 4, 1960, at San Antonio, Tex.
Height, 6.01. Weight, 170.
Throws and bats lefthanded.
Attended Texas A&M University, College Station, Tex.

Tied for Southern League lead in shutouts with 3 in 1985.
Named Southern League Pitcher of the Year, 1985.

Year Club	League	G.	IP.	W.	L.	Pct.	H.	R.	ER.	SO.	BB.	ERA.
1982—Medicine Hat	Pioneer	13	36⅔	5	1	.833	38	15	14	46	17	3.44
1983—Florence	S. Atlantic	23	153⅔	10	7	.588	129	66	55	167	52	3.22
1983—Knoxville	Southern	4	22	1	3	.250	26	17	17	18	14	6.95
1984—Knoxville	Southern	27	154⅔	9	6	.600	123	71	60	77	96	3.49
1985—Knoxville	Southern	27	154	*17	6	.739	114	49	42	107	72	*2.45

Year Club	League	G.	IP.	W.	L.	Pct.	H.	R.	ER.	SO.	BB.	ERA.
1985—Syracuse	Int'national	6	36	3	2	.600	19	11	10	34	17	2.50
1985—Toronto	American	10	28	2	1	.667	23	14	11	22	13	3.54
Major League Totals—1 Year		10	28	2	1	.667	23	14	11	22	13	3.54

Selected by Toronto Blue Jays' organization in 21st round of free-agent draft, June 7, 1982.

TRENCH NEAL DAVIS

Born September 12, 1960, at Baltimore, Md.
Height, 6.03. Weight, 171.
Throws and bats lefthanded.

Major League stolen bases: 1985 (1.)
Led Pacific Coast League in stolen bases with 53 in 1984.
Led Pacific Coast League in caught stealing with 22 in 1982.

Year Club	League	Pos.	G.	AB.	R.	H.	2B.	3B.	HR.	RBI.	B.A.	PO.	A.	E.	F.A.
1980—Bradenton Pir.	Gulf C.	1B	43	142	16	39	3	3	1	12	.275	184	15	10	.952
1981—Greenwood	S. Atl.	1B-OF	●141	●530	70	★158	24	9	4	73	.298	917	31	31	.968
1982—Portland	P. C.	OF	141	★571	80	153	16	5	2	46	.268	333	16	★14	.961
1983—Hawaii	P. C.	OF-1B	79	277	41	71	6	9	0	23	.256	147	9	3	.981
1983—Lynn	East.	OF-1B	59	219	37	61	7	4	2	16	.279	110	7	5	.959
1984—Hawaii	P. C.	OF	141	553	79	143	23	8	1	39	.259	311	18	★13	.962
1985—Hawaii	P. C.	OF	132	534	50	144	16	★12	2	56	.270	202	10	8	.074
1985—Pittsburgh	Nat.	OF	2	7	1	1	0	0	0	0	.143	2	0	1	.667
Major League Totals—1 Year		2	7	1	1	0	0	0	0	.143	2	0	1	.667

Signed as free agent by Pittsburgh Pirates' organization, June 23, 1980.

WALLACE McARTHUR DAVIS
(Butch)

Born June 19, 1958, at Williamston, N.C.
Height, 6.00. Weight, 185.
Throws and bats righthanded.
Attended St. Augustine's College, Raleigh, N.C., and received
bachelor of science degree from East Carolina University, Greenville, N.C. in 1980.

Major League stolen bases: 1983 (4), 1984 (4). Total—8.
Led Gulf Coast League in total bases with 105 and stolen bases with 31 in 1980.

Year Club	League	Pos.	G.	AB.	R.	H.	2B.	3B.	HR.	RBI.	B.A.	PO.	A.	E.	F.A.
1980—Sarasota Royals	Gulf C.	OF	61	235	46	★74	★17	4	2	35	.315	117	5	3	.976
1981—Fort Myers	Fla. St.	OF	126	464	★89	139	17	10	13	70	.300	239	5	12	.953
1982—Jacksonville	South.	OF	122	450	64	115	18	4	10	57	.256	231	7	2	.992
1983—Jacksonville	South.	OF-1B	90	331	51	105	15	7	14	63	.317	117	4	4	.968
1983—Omaha	A. A.	OF	46	171	27	54	10	3	5	21	.316	10	0	1	.909
1983—Kansas City	Amer.	OF	33	122	13	42	2	6	2	18	.344	83	1	2	.977
1984—Kansas City	Amer.	OF	41	116	11	17	3	0	2	12	.147	69	2	3	.959
1984—Omaha	A. A.	OF-1B	83	314	45	102	15	5	7	43	.325	153	13	6	.965
1985—Omaha	A. A.	OF-1B	109	403	58	106	26	10	6	34	.263	209	3	9	.959
Major League Totals—2 Years		74	238	24	59	5	6	4	30	.248	152	3	5	.969

Selected by Kansas City Royals' organization in 12th round of free-agent draft, June 3, 1980.

WILLIAM CHESTER DAWLEY
(Bill)

Born February 6, 1958, at Norwich, Conn.
Height, 6.04. Weight, 240.
Throws and bats righthanded.

Major League saves: 1983 (14), 1984 (5), 1985 (2). Total—21.
Led American Association pitchers in games started with 28 in 1982.

Year Club	League	G.	IP.	W.	L.	Pct.	H.	R.	ER.	SO.	BB.	ERA.
1976—Billings	Pioneer	13	78	6	4	.600	62	42	24	80	37	2.77
1977—Tampa	Florida St.	24	181	10	8	.556	151	69	57	110	69	2.83
1978—Nashville	Southern	27	141	7	13	.350	135	78	63	86	55	4.02
1979—Nashville†	Southern	25	140	9	9	.500	144	72	62	84	41	3.99
1980—Indianapolis	Am. Assoc.	25	77	4	6	.400	90	46	39	28	31	4.56
1980—Waterbury	Eastern	7	49	2	2	.500	43	18	16	33	25	2.94
1981—Indianapolis	Am. Assoc.	26	133	6	8	.429	141	77	73	109	69	4.94
1982—Indianapolis‡§	Am. Assoc.	29	★179	11	7	.611	196	86	76	106	48	3.82
1983—Houston	National	48	79⅔	6	6	.500	51	26	25	60	22	2.82
1984—Houston	National	60	98	11	4	.733	82	24	21	47	35	1.93
1985—Houston x	National	49	81	5	3	.625	76	35	32	48	37	3.56
Major League Totals—3 Years		157	258⅔	22	13	.629	209	85	78	155	94	2.71

Selected by Cincinnati Reds' organization in 7th round of free-agent draft, June 8, 1976.
†On temporary inactive list, May 21 to May 31, 1979.
‡Appeared in one game as an outfielder with no chances.
§Traded with Outfielder Anthony Walker to Houston Astros' organization for Catcher Alan Knicely, March 31, 1983.
xOn disabled list, July 6 to July 24, 1985.

Year League	IP.	W.	L.	Pct.	H.	R.	ER.	SO.	BB.	ERA.
1983—National	1⅓	0	0	.000	1	0	0	1	0	0.00

ANDRE FERNANDO DAWSON

Born July 10, 1954, at Miami, Fla.
Height, 6.03. Weight, 195.
Throws and bats righthanded.
Attended Florida A&M University, Tallahassee, Fla.
Nephew of Theodore Taylor, third baseman-outfielder in Pittsburgh Pirates'
organization, 1967 through 1969.

Tied major league records for most total bases, inning (8) and most home runs, inning (2), July 30, 1978 (third inning) and September 24, 1985 (fifth inning); most runs batted in, inning (6), September 24, 1985 (fifth inning).

Major League stolen bases: 1976 (1), 1977 (21), 1978 (28), 1979 (35), 1980 (34), 1981 (26), 1982 (39), 1983 (25), 1984 (13), 1985 (13). Total—235.

Hit three home runs in a game, September 24, 1985.

Led National League in being hit by pitch with 12 in 1978 and 7 in 1981.

Led National League in total bases with 341 and sacrifice flies with 18 in 1983.

Led National League outfielders in total chances with 344 in 1981, 435 in 1982 and 450 in 1983.

Tied for National League lead in being hit by pitch with 6 in 1980 and 9 in 1983.

Led Pioneer League in total bases with 166, in being hit by pitch with 6 and tied for lead in sacrifice flies with 5 in 1975.

Named National League Player of the Year by THE SPORTING NEWS, 1981.

Named National League Rookie Player of the Year by THE SPORTING NEWS, 1977.

Named National League Rookie of the Year by Baseball Writers' Association of America, 1977.

Named outfielder on THE SPORTING NEWS National League All-Star Team, 1981 and 1983.

Named outfielder on THE SPORTING NEWS National League All-Star fielding team, 1980 through 1985.

Named outfielder on THE SPORTING NEWS National League Silver Slugger team, 1980, 1981 and 1983.

Year—Club	League	Pos.	G.	AB.	R.	H.	2B.	3B.	HR.	RBI.	B.A.	PO.	A.	E.	F.A.
1975—Lethbridge	Pion.	OF	●72	★300	52	★99	14	7	★13	50	.330	★142	7	★10	.937
1976—Quebec City	East.	OF	40	143	27	51	6	0	8	27	.357	89	3	6	.939
1976—Denver	A. A.	OF	74	240	51	84	19	4	20	46	.350	97	2	2	.980
1976—Montreal	Nat.	OF	24	85	9	20	4	1	0	7	.235	61	1	2	.969
1977—Montreal	Nat.	OF	139	525	64	148	26	9	19	65	.282	352	9	4	.989
1978—Montreal	Nat.	OF	157	609	84	154	24	8	25	72	.253	411	17	5	.988
1979—Montreal	Nat.	OF	155	639	90	176	24	12	25	92	.275	394	7	5	.988
1980—Montreal	Nat.	OF	151	577	96	178	41	7	17	87	.308	410	14	6	.986
1981—Montreal	Nat.	OF	103	394	71	119	21	3	24	64	.302	★327	10	7	.980
1982—Montreal	Nat.	OF	148	608	107	183	37	7	23	83	.301	★419	8	8	.982
1983—Montreal	Nat.	OF	159	633	104	●189	36	10	32	113	.299	★435	6	9	.980
1984—Montreal	Nat.	OF	138	533	73	132	23	6	17	86	.248	297	11	8	.975
1985—Montreal	Nat.	OF	139	529	65	135	27	2	23	91	.255	248	9	7	.973
Major League Totals—10 Years			1313	5132	763	1434	263	65	205	760	.279	3354	92	61	.983

Selected by Montreal Expos' organization in 11th round of free-agent draft, June 4, 1975.

DIVISION SERIES RECORD

Year Club	League	Pos.	G.	AB.	R.	H.	2B.	3B.	HR.	RBI.	B.A.	PO.	A.	E.	F.A.
1981—Montreal	Nat.	OF	5	20	1	6	0	1	0	0	.300	12	1	1	.929

CHAMPIONSHIP SERIES RECORD

Year Club	League	Pos.	G.	AB.	R.	H.	2B.	3B.	HR.	RBI.	B.A.	PO.	A.	E.	F.A.
1981—Montreal	Nat.	OF	5	20	2	3	0	0	0	0	.150	12	0	0	1.000

ALL-STAR GAME RECORD

Year League	Pos.	AB.	R.	H.	2B.	3B.	HR.	RBI.	B.A.	PO.	A.	E.	F.A.
1981—National	OF	4	0	1	0	0	0	0	.250	4	0	0	1.000
1982—National	OF	4	0	1	0	0	0	0	.250	4	0	0	1.000
1983—National	OF	3	0	0	0	0	0	0	.000	3	0	0	1.000
All-Star Game Totals—3 Years		11	0	2	0	0	0	0	.182	11	0	0	1.000

RANDALL STEVEN DAY
(Randy)

Born December 30, 1960, at Fullerton, Calif.
Height, 6.02. Weight, 185.
Throws and bats righthanded.
Attended University of Texas, Austin, Tex.
Brother of Charlie Day, outfielder in Boston Red Sox' and
Kansas City Royals' organizations, 1968 through 1972.

Led Carolina League in total bases with 236 and game-winning RBIs with 13 in 1984.

Year Club	League	Pos.	G.	AB.	R.	H.	2B.	3B.	HR.	RBI.	B.A.	PO.	A.	E.	F.A.
1982—Bend	N'west	OF-1B	58	205	41	49	14	0	4	30	.239	107	6	5	.958
1983—Bend	N'west	3B-OF-1B	49	163	24	45	16	0	6	40	.276	62	38	10	.909
1984—Peninsula	Carol.	1B-3B-OF	132	468	84	124	25	0	★29	★103	.265	442	79	19	.965
1985—Reading†	East.	1B-3B	73	232	25	53	8	0	9	34	.228	537	55	5	.992

Signed as free agent by Philadelphia Phillies' organization, June 15, 1982.

†On disabled list, June 18 to July 22, 1985.

BRIAN KELLY DAYETT

Born January 22, 1957, at New London, Conn.
Height, 5.10. Weight, 180.
Throws and bats righthanded.
Attended St. Leo College, St. Leo, Fla.

Led International League in total bases with 281 in 1983.
Led Southern League in total bases with 285 and game-winning RBIs with 15 in 1982.
Tied for New York-Pennsylvania League lead in double plays by third basemen with 20 in 1978.
Named Southern League Most Valuable Player, 1982.

Year Club	League	Pos.	G.	AB.	R.	H.	2B.	3B.	HR.	RBI.	B.A.	PO.	A.	E.	F.A.
1978—Oneonta................	NYP	3B-C-1B	68	256	53	79	●20	4	11	63	.309	207	106	14	.957
1979—West Haven	East.	3B	135	465	58	119	21	4	11	74	.256	86	226	24	.929
1980—Nashville...............	South.	3B	35	100	15	21	8	0	0	9	.210	16	60	6	.927
1980—Alexandria	Carol.	3B-2B	13	48	12	21	5	1	3	17	.438	7	17	3	.889
1980—Fort Lauderdale ..	Fla. St.	3B	52	174	31	43	8	2	4	21	.247	51	103	11	.933
1981—Nashville...............	South.	3B-OF	112	338	53	91	15	3	18	62	.269	55	125	15	.923
1982—Nashville...............	South.	OF-3B	●144	536	89	150	29	2	34	96	.280	201	9	12	.946
1983—Columbus...............	Int.	OF-1B-3B	128	479	105	138	28	5	★35	★108	.288	224	10	6	.975
1983—New York.............	Amer.	OF	11	29	3	6	0	1	0	5	.207	22	1	0	1.000
1984—Columbus...............	Int.	OF	45	166	26	50	8	2	5	24	.301	91	1	2	.979
1984—New York†...........	Amer.	OF	64	127	14	31	8	0	4	23	.244	80	3	1	.988
1985—Chicago‡	Nat.	OF	22	26	1	6	0	0	1	4	.231	8	0	0	1.000
1985—Iowa	A. A.	OF-3B	14	37	5	14	4	0	1	11	.378	21	2	2	.920
American League Totals—2 Years			75	156	17	37	8	1	4	28	.237	102	4	1	.991
National League Totals—1 Year.............			22	26	1	6	0	0	1	4	.231	8	0	0	1.000
Major League Totals—3 Years...............			97	182	18	43	8	1	5	32	.236	110	4	1	.991

Selected by New York Yankees' organization in 16th round of free-agent draft, June 6, 1978.

†Traded with Pitcher Ray Fontenot to Chicago Cubs for Catcher Ron Hassey, Outfielder Henry Cotto and Pitcher Rich Bordi and Porfi Altamirano, December 4, 1984.

‡On disabled list, June 20, 1985 through remainder of season.

KENNETH GRANT DAYLEY II
(Ken)

Born February 25, 1959, at Jerome, Ida.
Height, 6.00. Weight, 171.
Throws and bats lefthanded.
Attended University of Portland, Portland, Ore.

Major League saves: 1985 (11).
Led International League pitchers in games started with 31 in 1981.
Received reported $100,000 bonus to sign with Atlanta Braves, 1980.
Named lefthanded pitcher on THE SPORTING NEWS College Baseball All-America Team, 1980.

Year Club	League	G.	IP.	W.	L.	Pct.	H.	R.	ER.	SO.	BB.	ERA.
1980—Savannah	Southern	16	105	8	3	.727	86	38	30	104	54	2.57
1981—Richmond.....................	Int'national	31	★200	●13	8	.619	180	82	74	★162	★117	3.33
1982—Richmond.....................	Int'national	13	98⅓	8	3	.727	89	43	34	79	47	3.11
1982—Atlanta	National	20	71⅓	5	6	.455	79	39	36	34	25	4.54
1983—Richmond.....................	Int'national	14	90⅔	9	3	.750	79	39	33	74	49	3.28
1983—Atlanta	National	24	104⅔	5	8	.385	100	59	50	70	39	4.30
1984—Atlanta†-St. Louis	National	7	23⅔	0	5	.000	44	28	21	10	11	7.99
1984—Richmond.....................	Int'national	9	62⅓	5	1	.833	66	31	28	45	24	4.04
1984—Louisville.....................	Am. Assoc.	13	96⅓	4	6	.400	86	42	35	79	22	3.27
1985—St. Louis.......................	National	57	65⅓	4	4	.500	65	24	20	62	18	2.76
Major League Totals—4 Years........................		108	265	14	23	.378	288	150	127	176	93	4.31

Selected by Atlanta Braves' organization in 1st round (third player selected) of free-agent draft, June 3, 1980.

†Traded with First Baseman Mike Jorgensen to St. Louis Cardinals for Third Baseman Ken Oberkfell, June 15, 1984.

CHAMPIONSHIP SERIES RECORD

Established National League Championship Series records for most games pitched (5) and most saves (2), six-game Series, 1985.

Year Club	League	G.	IP.	W.	L.	Pct.	H.	R.	ER.	SO.	BB.	ERA.
1985—St. Louis.....................	National	5	6	0	0	.000	2	0	0	3	1	0.00

WORLD SERIES RECORD

Year Club	League	G.	IP.	W.	L.	Pct.	H.	R.	ER.	SO.	BB.	ERA.
1985—St. Louis.........................	National	4	6	1	0	1.000	1	0	0	5	3	0.00

DOUGLAS VERNON DeCINCES

Name pronounced Duh-SIN-say.
(Doug)

Born August 29, 1950, at Burbank, Calif.
Height, 6.02. Weight, 195.
Throws and bats righthanded.
Attended Pierce Junior College, Woodland Hills, Calif., and University of California, Los Angeles, Calif.

Tied major league record for most times, three or more home runs, game, season (2), August 3 and August 8, 1982.
Tied American League record for most assists, third baseman, game (11), May 7, 1983, 12 innings.
Major League stolen bases: 1976 (8), 1977 (8), 1978 (7), 1979 (5), 1980 (11), 1982 (7), 1983 (2), 1984 (4), 1985 (1). Total—53.
Hit three home runs in a game, August 3 and August 8, 1982.
Led American League third basemen in assists with 330 in 1977 and 399 in 1982.
Led American League third basemen in total chances with 474 in 1977 and 479 in 1980.
Led American League third basemen in double plays with 34 in 1977, 41 in 1980 and 31 in 1981.
Tied for American League lead in putouts by third basemen with 86 in 1981.
Led Southern League second basemen in errors with 26 in 1972.
Named third baseman on THE SPORTING NEWS American League All-Star Team, 1982.
Named third baseman on THE SPORTING NEWS American League Silver Slugger team, 1982.

Year	Club	League	Pos.	G.	AB.	R.	H.	2B.	3B.	HR.	RBI.	B.A.	PO.	A.	E.	F.A.
1970—Bluefield	Appal.	S-1-2-3-P	54	164	28	48	10	0	4	27	.293	105	98	18	.919
1970—Dallas-Ft. W.	Texas	SS	11	35	3	6	1	0	0	2	.171	25	19	3	.936
1971—Dallas-Ft. W.†	Texas	2B-SS	78	235	29	61	10	1	5	29	.260	154	164	12	.964
1972—Asheville	South.	2B-SS	123	396	71	104	23	7	10	60	.263	254	314	28	.953
1973—Rochester	Int.	★3B-S-2	131	438	79	117	25	3	19	79	.267	150	264	17	★.961
1973—Baltimore	Amer.	3B-2B-SS	10	18	2	2	0	0	0	3	.111	4	19	2	.920
1974—Rochester	Int.	3B	132	444	70	125	17	4	11	66	.282	98	255	★32	.917
1974—Baltimore	Amer.	3B	1	1	0	0	0	0	0	0	.000	0	2	0	1.000
1975—Baltimore	Amer.	3-S-2-1	61	167	20	42	6	3	4	23	.251	92	115	7	.967
1976—Baltimore	Amer.	3-2-1-S	129	440	36	103	17	2	11	42	.234	191	257	20	.957
1977—Baltimore	Amer.	3B-1B-2B	150	522	63	135	28	3	19	69	.259	125	331	20	.958
1978—Baltimore	Amer.	3B-2B	142	511	72	146	37	1	28	80	.286	138	308	14	.970
1979—Baltimore‡	Amer.	3B	120	422	67	97	27	1	16	61	.230	99	247	13	.964
1980—Baltimore	Amer.	●3B-1B	145	489	64	122	23	2	16	64	.249	122	●340	19	.960
1981—Baltimore§	Amer.	●3-1-O	100	346	49	91	23	2	13	55	.263	91	191	●17	.943
1982—California	Amer.	3B-SS	153	575	94	173	42	5	30	97	.301	113	400	22	.959
1983—California x	Amer.	3B	95	370	49	104	19	3	18	65	.281	79	216	14	.955
1984—California	Amer.	3B	146	547	77	147	23	3	20	82	.269	107	266	14	.964
1985—California y	Amer.	3B	120	427	50	104	22	1	20	78	.244	95	202	13	.958
Major League Totals—13 Years			1372	4835	643	1266	267	26	195	719	.262	1256	2894	175	.960

Selected by San Diego Padres' organization in 3rd round of free-agent draft, June 5, 1969.
Selected by Baltimore Orioles' organization in secondary phase of free-agent draft, January 17, 1970.
†On disabled list, June 25 to July 27, 1971.
‡On disabled list, April 27 to June 5, 1979.
§Traded with Pitcher Jeff Schneider to California Angels for Outfielder Dan Ford, January 28, 1982.
xOn disabled list, July 14 to August 19, 1983.
yOn disabled list, May 15 to June 3, 1985.

CHAMPIONSHIP SERIES RECORD

Year	Club	League	Pos.	G.	AB.	R.	H.	2B.	3B.	HR.	RBI.	B.A.	PO.	A.	E.	F.A.
1979—Baltimore	Amer.	3B	4	13	4	4	1	0	0	3	.308	5	8	0	1.000
1982—California	Amer.	3B	5	19	5	6	2	0	0	0	.316	9	12	3	.875
Championship Series Totals—2 Years			9	32	9	10	3	0	0	3	.313	14	20	3	.919

WORLD SERIES RECORD

Tied World Series records for hitting home run in first series at bat, October 10, 1979; most errors by third baseman, inning (2), October 10, 1979 (sixth inning); most bases on balls, game (4), October 13, 1979.

Year	Club	League	Pos.	G.	AB.	R.	H.	2B.	3B.	HR.	RBI.	B.A.	PO.	A.	E.	F.A.
1979—Baltimore	Amer.	3B	7	25	2	5	0	0	1	3	.200	7	21	3	.903

ALL-STAR GAME RECORD

Year	League	Pos.	AB.	R.	H.	2B.	3B.	HR.	RBI.	B.A.	PO.	A.	E.	F.A.
1983—American		PH	1	0	0	0	0	0	0	.000	0	0	0	.000

PITCHING RECORD

Year	Club	League	G.	IP.	W.	L.	Pct.	H.	R.	ER.	SO.	BB.	ERA.
1970—Bluefield	Ap'lachian	1	2	0	1	.000	3	2	1	1	1	4.50

JEFFREY LINDEN DEDMON
(Jeff)

Born March 4, 1960, at Torrance, Calif.
Height, 6.02. Weight, 200.
Throws right and bats lefthanded.
Attended West Los Angeles College, Culver City, Calif.

Major League saves: 1984 (4).

Year	Club	League	G.	IP.	W.	L.	Pct.	H.	R.	ER.	SO.	BB.	ERA.
1980—Bradenton Braves	Gulf Coast	10	64	3	4	.429	55	26	21	28	11	2.95
1980—Anderson	S. Atlantic	2	11	1	0	1.000	10	3	1	8	3	0.82
1981—Durham	Carolina	28	165	7	8	.467	178	97	79	115	50	4.31
1982—Durham	Carolina	31	121⅓	5	6	.455	113	57	37	102	54	2.74
1983—Savannah	Southern	21	50	4	1	.800	46	18	16	26	16	2.88
1983—Richmond	Int'national	21	36	2	2	.500	28	9	7	33	14	1.75
1983—Atlanta	National	5	4	0	0	.000	10	6	6	3	0	13.50
1984—Atlanta	National	54	81	4	3	.571	86	39	34	51	35	3.78
1984—Richmond	Int'national	6	10	1	2	.333	11	10	9	10	13	8.10

Year Club	League	G.	IP.	W.	L.	Pct.	H.	R.	ER.	SO.	BB.	ERA.
1985—Richmond	Int'national	10	12	1	1	.500	12	2	2	7	3	1.50
1985—Atlanta	National	60	86	6	3	.667	84	52	39	41	49	4.08
Major League Totals—3 Years		119	171	10	6	.625	180	97	79	95	84	4.16

Selected by Houston Astros' organization in 1st round (seventh player selected), of free-agent draft, January 9, 1979.

Selected by Oakland A's organization in secondary phase of free-agent draft, June 5, 1979.

Selected by San Francisco Giants' organization in secondary phase of free-agent draft, January 8, 1980.

Selected by Atlanta Braves' organization in secondary phase of free-agent draft, June 3, 1980.

ROBERT GEORGE DEER
(Rob)

Born September 29, 1960, at Orange, Calif.
Height, 6.03. Weight, 210.
Throws and bats righthanded.
Attended Fresno City College, Fresno, Calif.

Major League stolen bases: 1984 (1).
Led Pacific Coast League batters in strikeouts with 175 in 1984.
Led Texas League batters in strikeouts with 177 in 1982 and 185 in 1983.
Tied for Texas League lead in game-winning RBIs with 13 in 1983.
Led California League batters in strikeouts with 146 in 1981.

Year Club	League	Pos.	G.	AB.	R.	H.	2B.	3B.	HR.	RBI.	B.A.	PO.	A.	E.	F.A.
1978—Great Falls	Pion.	OF	48	137	20	34	6	5	0	18	.248	83	3	4	.956
1979—Cedar Rapids	Midw.	OF	29	86	7	18	0	1	1	16	.209	35	1	4	.900
1979—Great Falls	Pion.	OF	63	218	49	69	18	7	7	44	.317	95	10	5	.955
1980—Clinton	Midw.	OF	127	434	60	114	31	5	13	58	.263	184	●17	11	.948
1981—Fresno	Calif.	OF	135	479	86	137	24	4	★33	107	.286	211	14	6	.974
1982—Shreveport	Texas	OF-1B	128	410	58	85	26	0	27	73	.207	184	10	11	.946
1983—Shreveport	Texas	OF	132	448	89	97	15	1	★35	99	.217	252	13	7	.974
1984—Phoenix	P. C.	OF	133	449	88	102	21	1	★31	69	.227	251	★19	9	.968
1984—San Francisco	Nat.	OF	13	24	5	4	0	0	3	3	.167	19	0	2	.905
1985—San Francisco†	Nat.	OF-1B	78	162	22	30	5	1	8	20	.185	127	2	2	.985
Major League Totals—2 Years			91	186	27	34	5	1	11	23	.183	146	2	4	.974

Selected by San Francisco Giants' organization in 4th round of free-agent draft, June 6, 1978.
†Traded to Milwaukee Brewers for Pitchers Dean Freeland and Eric Pilkington, December 18, 1985.

IVAN DeJESUS (ALVAREZ)
Name pronounced Day-HAY-soos.

Born January 9, 1953, at Santurce, Puerto Rico.
Height, 5.11. Weight, 185.
Throws and bats righthanded.
Attended University of Puerto Rico, Rio Piedras, Puerto Rico.

Tied Major League record for fewest double plays by shortstop, season, 150 or more games (64), 1983.
Major League stolen bases: 1975 (1), 1977 (24), 1978 (41), 1979 (24), 1980 (44), 1981 (21), 1982 (14), 1983 (11), 1984 (12), 1985 (2). Total—194.
Hit for the cycle, April 22, 1980.
Led National League shortstops in double plays with 81 in 1981.
Led Pacific Coast League shortstops in double plays with 114 in 1974.
Led California League shortstops in double plays with 87 in 1973.
Led California League shortstops in assists with 311, errors with 48 and double plays with 53 in 1971.
Led Florida State League shortstops in double plays with 56 in 1970.

Year Club	League	Pos.	G.	AB.	R.	H.	2B.	3B.	HR.	RBI.	B.A.	PO.	A.	E.	F.A.
1970—Daytona Beach	Fla. St.	SS	123	396	51	92	12	7	2	38	.232	164	361	38	.933
1971—Bakersfield	Calif.	SS-2B	126	462	77	108	16	2	6	30	.234	159	323	49	.908
1972—Daytona Beach	Fla. St.	SS	131	442	56	108	15	4	7	39	.244	187	★452	37	.945
1973—Bakersfield	Calif.	SS	132	519	77	125	17	1	7	57	.241	221	★403	★47	.930
1974—Albuquerque	P. C.	SS	140	510	81	152	17	5	7	55	.298	★268	★479	38	.952
1974—Los Angeles	Nat.	SS	3	3	1	1	0	0	0	0	.333	1	0	0	1.000
1975—Albuquerque	P. C.	SS	62	221	24	60	10	2	1	21	.271	97	265	24	.938
1975—Los Angeles	Nat.	SS	63	87	10	16	2	1	0	2	.184	45	107	4	.974
1976—Albuquerque	P. C.	SS-3B	108	405	69	123	27	7	7	64	.304	161	341	35	.935
1976—Los Angeles†	Nat.	SS-3B	22	41	4	7	2	1	0	2	.171	20	47	3	.957
1977—Chicago	Nat.	SS	155	624	91	166	31	7	3	40	.266	234	★595	33	.962
1978—Chicago	Nat.	SS	160	619	★104	172	24	7	3	35	.278	232	★558	27	.967
1979—Chicago	Nat.	SS	160	636	92	180	26	10	5	52	.283	235	507	32	.959
1980—Chicago	Nat.	SS	157	618	78	160	26	3	3	33	.259	229	529	24	.969
1981—Chicago‡	Nat.	SS	106	403	49	78	8	4	0	13	.194	★221	343	24	.959
1982—Philadelphia	Nat.	SS-3B	161	536	53	128	21	5	3	59	.239	222	488	21	.971
1983—Philadelphia	Nat.	SS	158	497	60	126	15	7	4	45	.254	214	438	23	.966
1984—Philadelphia§	Nat.	SS	144	435	40	112	15	3	0	35	.257	166	400	29	.951
1985—St. Louis x	Nat.	3B-SS	59	72	11	16	5	0	0	7	.222	15	40	2	.965
Major League Totals—12 Years			1348	4571	593	1162	175	48	21	323	.254	1834	4052	222	.964

Signed as free agent by Los Angeles Dodgers' organization, May 23, 1969.
†Traded with First Baseman Bill Buckner and Pitcher Jeff Albert to Chicago Cubs for Outfielder Rick Monday and Pitcher Mike Garman, January 11, 1977.
‡Traded to Philadelphia Phillies for Shortstop Larry Bowa and Infielder Ryne Sandberg, January 27, 1982.
§Traded with Pitcher Bill Campbell to St. Louis Cardinals for Pitcher Dave Rucker, April 6, 1985.
xGranted free agency, November 12, 1985.

Year Club League	Pos.	G.	AB.	R.	H.	2B.	3B.	HR.	RBI.	B.A.	PO.	A.	E.	F.A.
1983—Philadelphia .... Nat.	SS	4	12	0	3	0	0	0	1	.250	4	11	2	.882

WORLD SERIES RECORD

Year Club League	Pos.	G.	AB.	R.	H.	2B.	3B.	HR.	RBI.	B.A.	PO.	A.	E.	F.A.
1983—Philadelphia .... Nat.	SS	5	16	0	2	0	0	0	0	.125	5	14	1	.950
1985—St. Louis.................. Nat.	PH	1	1	0	0	0	0	0	0	.000	0	0	0	.000
World Series Totals—2 Years		6	17	0	2	0	0	0	0	.118	5	14	1	.950

JOSE LUIS DeJESUS (VELAZQUEZ)

(Formerly known as Jose Luis Velazquez.)

Born January 6, 1965, at Brooklyn, N.Y.
Height, 6.05. Weight, 170.
Throws and bats righthanded.

Led South Atlantic League pitchers in games started with 27 and hit batsmen with 13 in 1984.

Year Club	League	G.	IP.	W.	L.	Pct.	H.	R.	ER.	SO.	BB.	ERA.
1983—Sarasota Royals...........................	Gulf Coast	10	24	1	2	.333	17	18	11	10	17	4.13
1984—Charleston.....................................	S. Atlantic	27	163	11	12	.478	152	*98	*80	85	69	4.42
1985—Fort Myers†	Florida St.	27	129⅔	8	10	.444	119	70	62	94	59	4.30

Signed as free agent by Kansas City Royals' organization, May 9, 1983.
†Drafted by Toronto Blue Jays, December 10, 1985.

JOSE DeLEON (CHESTARO)

Born December 20, 1960, at LaVega, D.R.
Height, 6.03. Weight, 219.
Throws and bats righthanded.

Major League saves: 1985 (3).
Led Gulf Coast League in home runs allowed with 7 in 1979.
Tied for South Atlantic League lead in home runs allowed with 19 in 1980.
Tied for Gulf Coast League lead in wild pitches with 9 in 1979.

Year Club	League	G.	IP.	W.	L.	Pct.	H.	R.	ER.	SO.	BB.	ERA.
1979—Bradenton Pirates	Gulf Coast	11	59	2	4	.333	76	47	42	33	38	6.41
1980—Shelby..	S. Atlantic	26	168	10	15	.400	160	108	*90	118	69	4.82
1981—Buffalo...	Eastern	25	159	12	6	.667	136	72	55	158	94	3.11
1982—Portland†.......................................	P. Coast	24	119	10	7	.588	138	81	79	94	65	5.97
1983—Hawaii...	P. Coast	20	127⅓	11	6	.647	90	50	43	128	68	*3.04
1983—Pittsburgh.......................................	National	15	108	7	3	.700	75	36	34	118	47	2.83
1984—Pittsburgh.......................................	National	30	192⅓	7	13	.350	147	86	80	153	92	3.74
1985—Pittsburgh.......................................	National	31	162⅔	2	*19	.095	138	93	85	149	89	4.70
1985—Hawaii...	P. Coast	5	41	4	0	1.000	15	4	4	45	10	0.88
Major League Totals—3 Years...........................		76	463	16	35	.314	360	215	199	420	228	3.87

Selected by Pittsburgh Pirates' organization in 3rd round of free-agent draft June 5, 1979.
†On disabled list, July 5 to July 29, 1982.

LUIS ANTONIO DeLEON (TRICOCHE)

Born August 19, 1958, at Ponce, Puerto Rico.
Height, 6.01. Weight, 159.
Throws and bats righthanded.

Son of Luis A. DeLeon, minor league pitcher, 1957, 1958 and 1960; brother of Luis A. DeLeon, shortstop in
Boston Red Sox' and Cleveland Indians' organizations, 1974 through 1984;
and Desiderio DeLeon, minor league pitcher, 1977.

Major League saves: 1982 (15), 1983 (13), 1985 (3). Total—31.
Tied for Florida State League lead in saves with 14 and intentional bases on balls issued with 10 in 1979.
Tied for Appalachian League lead in shutouts with 2 in 1978.

Year Club	League	G.	IP.	W.	L.	Pct.	H.	R.	ER.	SO.	BB.	ERA.
1978—Johnson City..................................	Ap'lachian	13	84	7	6	.538	84	37	31	74	26	3.32
1979—St. Petersburg...............................	Florida St.	*59	92	8	3	.727	63	20	15	100	28	1.47
1979—Arkansas...	Texas	2	3	0	0	.000	1	2	2	4	2	6.00
1980—Arkansas...	Texas	*76	107	7	6	.538	85	46	39	92	49	3.28
1981—Springfield.....................................	Am. Assoc.	52	99	8	7	.533	73	34	28	96	35	2.55
1981—St. Louis†.......................................	National	10	15	0	1	.000	11	4	4	8	3	2.40
1982—San Diego	National	61	102	9	5	.643	77	25	23	60	16	2.03
1983—San Diego	National	63	111	6	6	.500	89	34	33	90	27	2.68
1984—San Diego‡	National	32	42⅔	2	2	.500	44	34	26	44	12	5.48
1984—Las Vegas.......................................	P. Coast	6	20⅔	1	1	.500	24	11	11	11	5	4.79
1985—San Diego	National	29	38⅔	0	3	.000	39	18	18	31	10	4.19
1985—Las Vegas.......................................	P. Coast	9	23⅓	2	1	.667	27	14	14	19	8	5.40
Major League Totals—5 Years...........................		195	309⅓	17	17	.500	260	115	104	233	68	3.03

Signed as free agent by St. Louis Cardinals' organization, November 21, 1977.
†Traded to San Diego Padres for Pitcher Al Olmsted, February 19, 1982, completing deal in which San Diego
traded Pitcher Steve Mura and a player to be named later to St. Louis Cardinals for Outfielder Sixto Lezcano and a
player to be named later, December 10, 1981.
‡On disabled list, May 6 to June 28 and July 21 to September 1, 1984; included rehabilitation disability assignment to
Las Vegas, June 8 to June 27, 1984.

JOHN RIKARD DEMPSEY
(Rick)

Born September 13, 1949, at Fayetteville, Tenn.
Height, 6.00. Weight, 184.
Throws and bats righthanded.
Attended Pierce Junior College, Woodland Hills, Calif.
Brother of Pat Dempsey, catcher in Minnesota Twins' organization.

Tied major league record for most double plays by catcher, game (3), June 1, 1977.
Major League stolen bases: 1974 (1), 1976 (1), 1977 (2), 1978 (7), 1980 (3), 1983 (1), 1984 (1). Total—16.
Tied for American League lead in double plays by catchers with 14 in 1978.
Led International League in passed balls with 14 in 1973.
Led New York-Pennsylvania League catchers in putouts with 468, assists with 35, fielding percentage with .990 and tied for lead in double plays with 4 in 1968.

Year	Club	League	Pos.	G.	AB.	R.	H.	2B.	3B.	HR.	RBI.	B.A.	PO.	A.	E.	F.A.
1967—Sarasota Twins	....	Gulf C.	C-OF-1B	40	102	9	21	4	3	0	9	.206	133	16	2	.987
1968—Wis. Rapids	....	Midw.	C	11	35	12	8	2	0	1	6	.229	68	2	1	.986
1968—Auburn	....	NYP	C-1B-OF	73	270	48	79	10	7	7	61	.293	505	38	7	.987
1969—Wis. Rapids	....	Midw.	C	50	151	35	55	11	2	6	31	.364	341	30	●13	.966
1969—Minnesota	....	Amer.	C	5	6	1	3	1	0	0	0	.500	5	0	1	.833
1970—Charlotte	....	South	C-OF-2B	105	351	28	86	20	6	4	42	.245	506	76	18	.970
1970—Minnesota	....	Amer.	C	5	7	1	0	0	0	0	0	.000	12	0	1	.923
1971—Charlotte	....	South	C-OF	105	338	39	82	16	2	8	47	.243	599	65	8	.988
1971—Minnesota	....	Amer.	C	6	13	2	4	1	0	0	0	.308	30	4	2	.944
1972—Minnesota†	....	Amer.	C	25	40	0	8	1	0	0	0	.200	67	5	1	.986
1972—Tacoma	....	P. C.	C-OF	48	161	13	38	6	2	3	18	.236	284	33	5	.984
1973—Syracuse	....	Int.	C-OF-3B	122	387	53	96	14	4	6	47	.248	585	69	9	.986
1973—New York	....	Amer.	C	6	11	0	2	0	0	0	0	.182	9	0	2	.818
1974—New York	....	Amer.	C-OF	43	109	12	26	3	0	2	12	.239	152	22	4	.978
1975—New York	....	Amer.	C-OF-3B	71	145	18	38	8	0	1	11	.262	92	9	3	.971
1976—N.Y.‡-Balt.	....	Amer.	C-OF	80	216	12	42	2	0	0	12	.194	302	39	4	.988
1977—Baltimore§	....	Amer.	C	91	270	27	61	7	4	3	34	.226	416	52	11	.977
1978—Baltimore	....	Amer.	C	136	441	41	114	25	0	6	32	.259	636	79	11	.985
1979—Baltimore	....	Amer.	C	124	368	48	88	23	0	6	41	.239	615	★81	7	.990
1980—Baltimore	....	Amer.	C-OF-1B	119	362	51	95	26	3	9	40	.262	544	55	8	.987
1981—Baltimore	....	Amer.	C	92	251	24	54	10	1	6	15	.215	384	35	1	★.998
1982—Baltimore	....	Amer.	C	125	344	35	88	15	1	5	36	.256	491	46	5	.991
1983—Baltimore	....	Amer.	C	128	347	33	80	16	2	4	32	.231	591	65	2	★.997
1984—Baltimore	....	Amer.	C	109	330	37	76	11	0	11	34	.230	453	43	4	.992
1985—Baltimore	....	Amer.	C	132	362	54	92	19	0	12	52	.254	575	49	8	.987
Major League Totals—17 Years				1297	3622	396	871	168	11	65	351	.240	5374	584	75	.988

Selected by Minnesota Twins' organization in 12th round of free-agent draft, June 6, 1967.

†Traded to New York Yankees' organization for Outfielder Danny Walton, October 27, 1972.

‡Traded with Pitchers Rudy May, Tippy Martinez, Dave Pagan and Scott McGregor to Baltimore Orioles for Pitchers Ken Holtzman, Doyle Alexander and Grant Jackson, Catcher Ellie Hendricks and Pitcher Jimmy Freeman, June 15, 1976.

§On disabled list, July 9 to August 21, 1977.

CHAMPIONSHIP SERIES RECORD

Year	Club	League	Pos.	G.	AB.	R.	H.	2B.	3B.	HR.	RBI.	B.A.	PO.	A.	E.	F.A.
1979—Baltimore	....	Amer.	C	3	10	3	4	2	0	0	2	.400	10	1	0	1.000
1983—Baltimore	....	Amer.	C	4	12	1	2	0	0	0	0	.167	29	5	1	.971
Championship Series Totals—2 Years				7	22	4	6	2	0	0	2	.273	39	6	1	.978

WORLD SERIES RECORD

Established World Series record for most long hits, five-game Series (5), 1983.
Tied World Series record for most two-base hits, five-game Series (4), 1983.

Year	Club	League	Pos.	G.	AB.	R.	H.	2B.	3B.	HR.	RBI.	B.A.	PO.	A.	E.	F.A.
1979—Baltimore	....	Amer.	C-PR	7	21	3	6	2	0	0	0	.286	38	2	0	1.000
1983—Baltimore	....	Amer.	C	5	13	3	5	4	0	1	2	.385	27	4	0	1.000
World Series Totals—2 Years				12	34	6	11	6	0	1	2	.324	65	6	0	1.000

BRIAN JOHN DENMAN

Born February 12, 1956, at Minneapolis, Minn.
Height, 6.04. Weight, 210.
Throws and bats righthanded.
Attended University of Minnesota, Minneapolis, Minn.

Pitched 4-1 no-hit victory against West Haven, July 6, 1981.
Led Eastern League in shutouts with 3 in 1979 and complete games with 13 in 1981.
Led International League in shutouts with 4 and tied for lead in complete games with 8 in 1985.

Year	Club	League	G.	IP.	W.	L.	Pct.	H.	R.	ER.	SO.	BB.	ERA.
1978—Winter Haven	....	Florida St.	27	189	★16	5	.762	147	51	43	122	34	2.05
1979—Bristol	....	Eastern	28	188	●14	10	.583	★194	88	77	97	54	3.69
1980—Bristol†	....	Eastern	10	58	6	0	1.000	71	26	20	35	12	3.10
1981—Pawtucket	....	Int'national	1	2	0	0	.000	1	1	1	3	0	4.50
1981—Bristol	....	Eastern	25	★188	●15	3	.833	172	65	51	109	51	★2.44
1982—Pawtucket	....	Int'national	20	92⅔	7	4	.636	120	56	52	41	30	5.05

Year	Club	League	G.	IP.	W.	L.	Pct.	H.	R.	ER.	SO.	BB.	ERA.
1982—Bristol	Eastern	5	38⅓	3	0	1.000	26	11	9	21	15	2.11
1982—Boston	American	9	49	3	4	.429	55	32	26	9	9	4.78
1983—Pawtucket‡	Int'national	26	154⅓	8	11	.421	182	99	86	76	66	5.02
1984—Pawtucket	Int'national	16	70⅓	3	5	.375	98	73	65	22	32	8.32
1984—New Britain§	Eastern	13	61	4	1	.800	63	21	17	39	10	2.51
1985—Nashville	Am. Assoc.	27	●181⅔	10	8	.556	198	93	82	65	51	4.06
Major League Totals—1 Year		9	49	3	4	.429	55	32	26	9	9	4.78

Selected by California Angels' organization in 14th round of free-agent draft, June 7, 1977.
Selected by Boston Red Sox' organization in secondary phase of free-agent draft, January 10, 1978.
†On disabled list, April 14 to July 14, 1980.
‡On disabled list, June 9 to June 29, 1983.
§Granted free agency, October 15, 1984; signed by Evansville (Detroit Tigers' organization), November 12, 1984.

JOHN ALLEN DENNY

Born November 8, 1952, at Prescott, Ariz.
Height, 6.03. Weight, 190.
Throws and bats righthanded.
Attended Yavapai College, Prescott, Ariz., and Southern Illinois University, Edwardsville, Ill.

Tied National League record for fewest games won, season, for leader in games won (19), 1983.
Pitched 8-1 no-hit victory against Midland, May 17, 1973.
Named National League Pitcher of the Year by THE SPORTING NEWS, 1983.
Won National League Cy Young Memorial Award, 1983.
Named National League Comeback Player of the Year by THE SPORTING NEWS, 1983.
Named righthanded pitcher on THE SPORTING NEWS National League All-Star Team, 1983.

Year	Club	League	G.	IP.	W.	L.	Pct.	H.	R.	ER.	SO.	BB.	ERA.
1970—Sarasota Cardinals	Gulf Coast	11	42	2	2	.500	32	14	6	43	9	1.29
1971—St. Petersburg	Florida St.	26	139	8	13	.381	123	58	47	77	62	3.04
1972—Modesto†	California	14	92	7	5	.583	95	54	45	65	39	4.40
1973—Arkansas‡	Texas	20	147	10	6	.625	128	57	51	81	52	3.12
1974—Tulsa	Am. Assoc.	21	132	9	8	.529	127	66	55	79	57	3.75
1974—St. Louis	National	2	2	0	0	.000	3	2	0	1	0	0.00
1975—Tulsa	Am. Assoc.	7	60	3	1	.750	47	12	12	44	32	1.80
1975—St. Louis	National	25	136	10	7	.588	149	73	60	72	51	3.97
1976—St. Louis	National	30	207	11	9	.550	189	71	58	74	74	★2.52
1977—St. Louis§	National	26	150	8	8	.500	165	85	75	60	62	4.50
1978—St. Louis	National	33	234	14	11	.560	200	81	77	103	74	2.96
1979—St. Louis x	National	31	206	8	11	.421	206	116	111	99	100	4.85
1980—Cleveland y	American	16	109	8	6	.571	116	54	53	59	47	4.38
1981—Cleveland z	American	19	146	10	6	.625	139	62	51	94	66	3.14
1982—Cleveland a	American	21	138⅓	6	11	.353	126	80	77	94	73	5.01
1982—Philadelphia	National	4	22⅓	0	2	.000	18	12	10	19	10	4.03
1983—Philadelphia	National	36	242⅔	★19	6	★.760	229	77	64	139	53	2.37
1984—Philadelphia b	National	22	154⅓	7	7	.500	122	53	·42	94	29	2.45
1985—Philadelphia c	National	33	230⅔	11	14	.440	252	112	98	123	83	3.82
National League Totals—10 Years		242	1585	88	75	.540	1533	682	595	784	536	3.38
American League Totals—3 Years		56	393⅓	24	23	.511	381	196	181	247	186	4.14
Major League Totals—12 Years		298	1978⅓	112	98	.533	1914	878	776	1031	722	3.53

Selected by St. Louis Cardinals' organization in 29th round of free-agent draft, June 4, 1970.
†On disabled list, July 17, 1972 through remainder of season.
‡On disabled list, August 11, 1973 through remainder of season.
§On disabled list, June 22 to July 29, 1977.
xTraded with Outfielder Jerry Mumphrey to Cleveland Indians for Outfielder Bobby Bonds, December 7, 1979.
yOn disabled list, July 15 to September 8, 1980.
zGranted free agency, November 13, 1981; re-signed by Indians, February 13, 1982.
aTraded to Philadelphia Phillies for Pitchers Jerry Reed and Roy Smith and Outfielder Wil Culmer, September 11, 1982.
bOn disabled list, May 31 to July 30, 1984.
cTraded with Pitcher Jeff Gray to Cincinnati Reds for Outfielder Gary Redus and Pitcher Tom Hume, December 11, 1985.

CHAMPIONSHIP SERIES RECORD

Year	Club	League	G.	IP.	W.	L.	Pct.	H.	R.	ER.	SO.	BB.	ERA.
1983—Philadelphia	National	1	6	0	1	.000	5	3	0	3	3	0.00

WORLD SERIES RECORD

Tied World Series record for most putouts, pitcher, inning (2), October 15, 1983 (fifth inning).

Year	Club	League	G.	IP.	W.	L.	Pct.	H.	R.	ER.	SO.	BB.	ERA.
1983—Philadelphia	National	2	13	1	1	.500	12	5	5	9	3	3.46

—DID YOU KNOW—

That when Chicago's Carlton Fisk homered on August 11, 1985, he became only the third catcher in baseball history to record 250 career home runs? Yankee catcher Yogi Berra and Cincinnati's Johnny Bench were the first two catchers to reach that career mark.

ROBERT EUGENE DERNIER

Name pronounced Dur-NEER.

(Bob)

Born January 5, 1957, at Kansas City, Mo.
Height, 6.00. Weight, 165.
Throws and bats righthanded.
Attended Longview Community College, Lee's Summit, Mo.

Major League stolen bases: 1980 (3), 1981 (2), 1982 (42), 1983 (35), 1984 (45), 1985 (31). Total—158.
Led Carolina League in stolen bases with 77 in 1979, Eastern League with 71 in 1980 and American Association with 72 in 1981.
Led Carolina League outfielders in putouts with 315 in 1979.
Tied for Carolina League lead in sacrifice hits with 12 in 1979.
Tied for Pioneer League lead in double plays by third basemen with 9 in 1978.
Named outfielder on THE SPORTING NEWS National League All-Star fielding team, 1984.
Named Carolina League Most Valuable Player, 1979.

Year Club	League	Pos.	G.	AB.	R.	H.	2B.	3B.	HR.	RBI.	B.A.	PO.	A.	E.	F.A.
1978—Spartanburg	W. Car.	SS	22	57	9	8	1	0	0	5	.140	23	61	16	.840
1978—Helena	Pion.	3B	53	186	49	56	6	2	4	27	.301	38	104	22	.866
1979—Peninsula	Carol.	OF-3B	135	491	102	143	19	2	4	42	.291	331	23	10	.973
1980—Reading	East.	OF	136	★536	★111	160	29	4	10	57	.299	★325	9	9	.974
1980—Philadelphia	Nat.	OF	10	7	5	4	0	0	0	1	.571	9	0	0	1.000
1981—Oklahoma City	A. A.	OF	127	497	★105	150	26	7	5	35	.302	★317	7	5	.985
1981—Philadelphia	Nat.	OF	10	4	0	3	0	0	0	0	.750	2	0	0	1.000
1982—Philadelphia	Nat.	OF	122	370	56	92	10	2	4	21	.249	255	5	5	.981
1983—Philadelphia	Nat.	OF	122	221	41	51	10	0	1	15	.231	164	3	2	.988
1983—Reading †	East.	OF	14	56	8	13	1	1	1	4	.232	36	0	0	1.000
1984—Chicago	Nat.	OF	143	536	94	149	26	5	3	32	.278	355	5	5	.986
1985—Chicago‡	Nat.	OF	121	469	63	119	20	3	1	21	.254	310	4	9	.972
Major League Totals—6 Years			528	1607	259	418	66	10	9	90	.260	1095	17	21	.981

Selected by Cincinnati Reds' organization in 12th round of free-agent draft, January 11, 1977.
Signed as free agent by Philadelphia Phillies' organization, August 5, 1977.
†Traded with Outfielder Gary Matthews and Pitcher Porfi Altamirano to Chicago Cubs for Pitcher Bill Campbell and Catcher Mike Diaz, March 27, 1984.
‡On disabled list, June 15 to July 7, 1985.

CHAMPIONSHIP SERIES RECORD

Tied Championship Series record for most times hitting home run as leadoff batter, start of game (1), October 2, 1984.

Year Club	League	Pos.	G.	AB.	R.	H.	2B.	3B.	HR.	RBI.	B.A.	PO.	A.	E.	F.A.
1983—Philadelphia	Nat.	OF	1	0	0	0	0	0	0	0	.000	0	0	0	.000
1984—Chicago	Nat.	OF	5	17	5	4	2	0	1	1	.235	12	1	0	1.000
Championship Series Totals—2 Years			6	17	5	4	2	0	1	1	.235	12	1	0	1.000

WORLD SERIES RECORD

Year Club	League	Pos.	G.	AB.	R.	H.	2B.	3B.	HR.	RBI.	B.A.	PO.	A.	E.	F.A.
1983—Philadelphia	Nat.	PR	1	0	1	0	0	0	0	0	.000	0	0	0	.000

JOSEPH DE SA

Name pronounced DAY-sah.

(Joe)

Born July 27, 1959, at Honolulu, Haw.
Height, 5.11. Weight, 170.
Throws and bats lefthanded.

Led American Association first basemen in putouts with 1,157, total chances with 1,285 and double plays with 131 in 1984.
Led American Association first basemen in putouts with 1,182, total chances with 1,297 and double plays with 124 in 1981.
Led Pioneer League first basemen in double plays with 65 in 1977.

Year Club	League	Pos.	G.	AB.	R.	H.	2B.	3B.	HR.	RBI.	B.A.	PO.	A.	E.	F.A.
1977—Calgary	Pion.	1B	★70	279	65	76	13	1	3	55	.272	★607	37	10	.985
1978—Gastonia	W. Car.	1B	42	149	23	39	11	0	4	25	.262	326	17	4	.988
1978—St. Petersburg	Fla. St.	1B	86	277	41	86	13	0	5	30	.310	722	53	1	.999
1979—Arkansas	Texas	1B	130	463	71	147	32	5	13	86	.317	★1129	★71	11	.991
1980—Springfield	A. A.	1B	123	423	54	124	25	2	9	74	.293	1005	★86	6	★.995
1980—St. Louis	Nat.	1B-OF	7	11	0	3	0	0	0	0	.273	3	0	0	1.000
1981—Springfield	A. A.	★1B-OF	132	497	60	145	30	2	12	73	.292	1185	★104	11	.992
1982—Louisville	A. A.	OF-1B	130	487	72	134	26	3	14	75	.275	488	38	10	.981
1983—Louisville†‡	A. A.	1B-OF	27	105	12	31	6	1	1	14	.295	176	21	1	.995
1984—Denver	A. A.	★1B-OF	141	511	73	144	32	7	10	81	.282	1165	★119	9	★.993
1985—Chicago	Amer.	1B-OF	28	44	5	8	2	0	2	7	.182	70	7	0	1.000
1985—Buffalo	A. A.	1B-OF	97	366	56	105	21	3	17	66	.287	729	49	8	.990
National League Totals—1 Year			7	11	0	3	0	0	0	0	.273	3	0	0	1.000
American League Totals—1 Year			28	44	5	8	2	0	2	7	.182	70	7	0	1.000
Major League Totals—2 Years			35	55	5	11	2	0	2	7	.200	73	7	0	1.000

Selected by St. Louis Cardinals' organization in 3rd round of free-agent draft, June 7, 1977.
†On disabled list, April 26 through May 6 and May 29 through September 12, 1983.
‡Granted free agency, October 20, 1983; signed by Chicago White Sox' organization, November 16, 1983.

JAMES JOSEPH DESHAIES

Name pronounced De-SHAYS.

(Jim)

Born June 23, 1960, at Massena, N.Y.
Height, 6.04. Weight, 222.
Throws and bats lefthanded.
Received bachelor of arts degree from Le Moyne College, Syracuse, N.Y., in 1982.

Pitched seven-inning, 5-1 no-hit victory against Columbus, May 4, 1984.
Led International League in balks with 4 in 1985.
Tied for International League lead in shutouts with 4 in 1984.

Year Club	League	G.	IP.	W.	L.	Pct.	H.	R.	ER.	SO.	BB.	ERA.
1982—Oneonta	NYP	15	108⅓	6	5	.545	93	50	40	★137	40	3.32
1983—Fort Lauderdale	Florida St.	20	117⅔	11	3	.786	105	44	33	128	58	2.52
1984—Nashville	Southern	7	45	3	2	.600	33	20	14	42	29	2.80
1984—Columbus	Int'national	18	135⅔	10	5	.667	99	45	36	117	62	★2.39
1984—New York	American	2	7	0	1	.000	14	9	9	5	7	11.57
1985—Columbus†‡	Int'national	21	131⅔	8	6	.571	124	67	63	106	59	4.31
1985—Houston	National	2	3	0	0	.000	1	0	0	2	0	0.00
American League Totals—1 Year		2	7	0	1	.000	14	9	9	5	7	11.57
National League Totals—1 Year		2	3	0	0	.000	1	0	0	2	0	0.00
Major League Totals—2 Years		4	10	0	1	.000	15	9	9	7	7	8.10

Selected by Montreal Expos' organization in 13th round of free-agent draft, June 6, 1978.
Selected by New York Yankees' organization in 21st round of free-agent draft, June 7, 1982.
†On disabled list, April 10 to April 26 and August 4 to August 14, 1985.
‡Traded with a player to be named later to Houston Astros for Pitcher Joe Niekro, September 15, 1985; Houston organization acquired Infielder Neder Horta, September 24, 1985, and Pitcher Dody Rather, January 11, 1986, to complete deal.

ORESTES DESTRADE

Name pronounced Des-TRAD-a.

Born May 8, 1962, at Santiago, Cuba.
Height, 6.04. Weight, 210.
Throws right and bats right and lefthanded.
Attended Florida College, Temple Terrace, Fla.

Led Eastern League batters in strikeouts with 129 in 1985.
Tied for Florida State League lead in bases on balls received with 82 and game-winning RBIs with 15 in 1983.
Led Eastern League first basemen in total chances with 1,194 and double plays with 99 in 1985.
Tied for Appalachian League lead in double plays by first basemen with 42 in 1981.

Year Club	League	Pos.	G.	AB.	R.	H.	2B.	3B.	HR.	RBI.	B.A.	PO.	A.	E.	F.A.
1981—Paintsville	Appal.	1B	63	208	51	57	12	1	★14	46	.274	461	22	11	.978
1982—Greensboro	S. Atl.	1B	43	122	9	22	4	1	1	14	.180	359	15	4	.989
1982—Oneonta	NYP	1B	64	194	44	45	12	1	4	30	.232	298	33	10	.971
1983—Fort Lauderdale	Fla. St.	OF-1B	127	425	61	124	24	5	18	74	.292	425	24	9	.980
1984—Nashville	South.	OF-1B	35	121	15	29	6	0	6	12	.240	56	2	3	.951
1984—Fort Lauderdale	Fla. St.	1B	95	308	40	68	14	2	12	57	.221	764	41	●16	.981
1985—Albany	East.	1B	136	471	82	119	24	5	23	72	.253	★1103	73	18	.985

Selected by California Angels' organization in 23rd round of free-agent draft, June 3, 1980.
Signed as free agent by New York Yankees' organization, May 17, 1981.

JEFFREY ALLEN DeWILLIS

(Jeff)

Born April 13, 1965, at Houston, Tex.
Height, 6.02. Weight, 170.
Throws and bats righthanded.

Led Carolina League catchers in total chances with 932 and double plays with 8 in 1984.

Year Club	League	Pos.	G.	AB.	R.	H.	2B.	3B.	HR.	RBI.	B.A.	PO.	A.	E.	F.A.
1983—Medicine Hat	Pion.	C-OF-1B	56	190	34	46	8	0	5	21	.242	317	26	8	.977
1984—Kinston	Carol.	C	122	356	47	84	11	1	1	31	.236	★848	69	15	.984
1984—Knoxville	South.	C	1	2	1	0	0	0	0	0	.000	2	2	0	1.000
1985—Kinston	Carol.	C	27	87	12	16	3	1	1	8	.184	206	26	3	.987
1985—Knoxville	South.	C	68	196	22	43	7	1	2	22	.219	377	45	3	.993
1985—Syracuse	Int.	C	19	48	3	11	1	0	1	3	.229	106	9	3	.975

Selected by Toronto Blue Jays' organization in 3rd round of free-agent draft, June 6, 1983.

BAUDILIO JOSE DIAZ (SEIJAS)

Name pronounced DEE-az.

(Bo)

Born March 23, 1953, at Cua, Miranda, Venezuela.
Height, 5.11. Weight, 200.
Throws and bats righthanded.

Major League stolen bases: 1980 (1), 1981 (2), 1982 (3), 1983 (1). Total—7.
Tied for International League lead in double plays by catchers with 7 in 1977.

Year Club	League	Pos.	G.	AB.	R.	H.	2B.	3B.	HR.	RBI.	B.A.	PO.	A.	E.	F.A.
1971—Winter Haven	Fla. St.	C	4	10	1	0	0	0	0	0	.000	25	1	0	1.000
1971—Williamsport	NYP	PH	1	1	0	0	0	0	0	0	.000	0	0	0	.000
1971—Pawtucket	East.	C	1	2	0	0	0	0	0	0	.000	4	0	0	1.000
1971—Greenville	W. Car.	C	10	25	2	5	1	0	0	0	.200	35	2	2	.949
1972—Winter Haven	Fla. St.	C	14	44	3	7	1	0	0	0	.159	72	7	0	1.000
1973—Elmira	NYP	C	25	69	3	17	3	0	0	9	.246	107	16	1	.992
1974—Winter Haven	Fla. St.	C-3B	97	327	31	79	20	1	1	38	.242	476	75	14	.975
1975—Winston-Salem	Carol.	C	59	179	22	47	8	1	6	29	.263	271	45	9	.972
1976—Rhode Island	Int.	C-OF	62	117	10	29	1	0	4	18	.248	222	28	3	.988
1977—Pawtucket	Int.	*C-3B	105	308	37	81	14	1	7	54	.263	459	67	6	*.989
1977—Boston†	Amer.	C	2	1	0	0	0	0	0	0	.000	5	0	0	1.000
1978—Cleveland‡	Amer.	C	44	127	12	30	4	0	2	11	.236	183	18	6	.971
1979—Tacoma	P. C.	C	34	115	5	28	7	0	2	11	.243	223	24	5	.980
1979—Cleveland§	Amer.	C	15	32	0	5	2	0	0	1	.156	63	6	3	.958
1980—Cleveland	Amer.	C	76	207	15	47	11	2	3	32	.227	317	35	4	.989
1981—Cleveland x	Amer.	C	63	182	25	57	19	0	7	38	.313	247	27	7	.975
1982—Philadelphia	Nat.	C	144	525	69	151	29	1	18	85	.288	850	80	10	.989
1983—Philadelphia	Nat.	C	136	471	49	111	17	0	15	64	.236	903	97	*14	.986
1984—Philadelphia y	Nat.	C	27	75	5	16	4	0	1	9	.213	114	9	1	.992
1984—Reading	East.	C	3	7	2	3	0	0	1	3	.429	11	4	1	.938
1985—Phi.za-Cinc.	Nat.	C	77	237	21	58	13	1	5	31	.245	428	42	8	.983
American League Totals—5 Years			200	549	52	139	36	2	12	82	.253	815	86	20	.978
National League Totals—4 Years			384	1308	144	336	63	2	39	189	.257	2295	228	33	.987
Major League Totals—9 Years			584	1857	196	475	99	4	51	271	.256	3110	314	53	.985

Signed as free agent by Boston Red Sox' organization, November 25, 1970.
†Traded with Pitchers Rick Wise and Mike Paxton and Third Baseman Ted Cox to Cleveland Indians for Pitcher Dennis Eckersley and Catcher Fred Kendall, March 30, 1978.
‡On disabled list, April 16 to June 16, 1978.
§On disabled list, March 31 to April 17 and June 8 to July 20, 1979.
xTraded to Philadelphia Phillies for Outfielder Lonnie Smith and a player to be named later, November 20, 1981; Cleveland organization acquired Pitcher Scott Munninghoff to complete deal, December 9, 1981.
yOn disabled list, May 1 to May 31, June 21 to July 16 and August 20, 1984 through remainder of season; included rehabilitation disability assignment to Reading, July 11 to July 16, 1984.
zOn disabled list, April 19 to June 1, 1985.
aTraded with Pitcher Greg Simpson to Cincinnati Reds for Shortstop Tom Foley, Catcher Alan Knicely, a player to be named later and cash, August 8, 1985; Philadelphia Phillies acquired Pitcher Freddie Toliver to complete deal, August 27, 1985.

CHAMPIONSHIP SERIES RECORD

Year Club	League	Pos.	G.	AB.	R.	H.	2B.	3B.	HR.	RBI.	B.A.	PO.	A.	E.	F.A.
1983—Philadelphia	Nat.	C	4	13	0	2	1	0	0	0	.154	32	2	0	1.000

WORLD SERIES RECORD

Year Club	League	Pos.	G.	AB.	R.	H.	2B.	3B.	HR.	RBI.	B.A.	PO.	A.	E.	F.A.
1983—Philadelphia	Nat.	C	5	15	1	5	1	0	0	0	.333	37	1	1	.974

ALL-STAR GAME RECORD

Year League	Pos.	AB.	R.	H.	2B.	3B.	HR.	RBI.	B.A.	PO.	A.	E.	F.A.
1981—American	C	1	0	0	0	0	0	0	.000	2	0	0	1.000

CARLOS ANTONIO DIAZ JR.

Name pronounced DEE-az.

Born January 7, 1958, at Kaneohe, Haw.
Height, 6.00. Weight, 170.
Throws left and bats righthanded.
Attended Allan Hancock Junior College, Santa Maria, Calif.

Major League saves: 1982 (1), 1983 (2), 1984 (1). Total—4.

Year Club	League	G.	IP.	W.	L.	Pct.	H.	R.	ER.	SO.	BB.	ERA.
1979—Bellingham	Northwest	2	8	0	0	.000	5	0	0	8	2	0.00
1979—San Jose	California	26	24	4	1	.800	26	18	17	36	13	6.38
1980—Spokane†	P. Coast	*58	64	3	5	.375	72	31	28	51	27	3.94
1981—Richmond	Int'national	35	49	3	3	.500	32	17	15	29	20	2.81
1982—Richmond	Int'national	31	53⅓	3	4	.429	52	21	16	52	17	2.70
1982—Atlanta‡-New York	National	23	29	3	2	.600	37	17	13	16	13	4.03
1983—New York§	National	54	83⅓	3	1	.750	62	22	19	64	35	2.05
1984—Los Angeles	National	37	41	1	0	1.000	47	26	25	36	24	5.49
1984—Albuquerque	P. Coast	20	46⅓	1	2	.333	48	30	23	35	20	4.47
1985—Los Angeles	National	46	79⅓	6	3	.667	70	28	23	73	18	2.61
Major League Totals—4 Years		160	232⅔	13	6	.684	216	93	80	189	90	3.09

Selected by Seattle Mariners' organization in 3rd round of free-agent draft, January 9, 1979.
Selected by Seattle Mariners' organization in secondary phase of free-agent draft, June 5, 1979.
†Traded to Atlanta Braves' organization for Outfielder Jeff Burroughs, March 6, 1981.
‡Traded to New York Mets for Pitcher Tom Hausman, September 10, 1982.
§Traded with a player to be named later to Los Angeles Dodgers for Pitcher Sid Fernandez and Infielder Ross Jones, December 8, 1983; Los Angeles acquired Infielder Bob Bailor to complete deal, December 12, 1983.

Year	Club	League	G.	IP.	W.	L.	Pct.	H.	R.	ER.	SO.	BB.	ERA.
1985—Los Angeles		National	2	3	0	0	.000	5	1	1	2	1	3.00

EDGAR SERRANO DIAZ

Born February 8, 1964, at Santurce, Puerto Rico.
Height, 6.00. Weight, 165.
Throws and bats righthanded.

Led Texas League shortstops in total chances with 743 and double plays with 101 in 1985.

Year	Club	League	Pos.	G.	AB.	R.	H.	2B.	3B.	HR.	RBI.	B.A.	PO.	A.	E.	F.A.
1982—Pikeville		Appal.	SS	15	24	4	2	0	0	0	0	.083	12	30	3	.933
1983—Beloit		Midw.	SS	107	307	29	64	2	0	0	15	.208	173	258	42	.911
1984—Stockton		Calif.	SS	123	419	58	108	1	7	0	35	.258	189	381	40	.934
1985—El Paso		Texas	SS	132	501	90	134	14	4	0	55	.267	*217	*489	37	.950

Signed as free agent by Milwaukee Brewers' organization, March 3, 1982.

MICHAEL ANTHONY DIAZ

Name pronounced DEE-az.

(Mike)

Born April 15, 1960, at San Francisco, Calif.
Height, 6.02. Weight, 195.
Throws and bats righthanded.

Tied for Pacific Coast League lead in being hit by pitch with 7 in 1985.
Led Texas League catchers in total chances with 684 in 1981.

Year	Club	League	Pos.	G.	AB.	R.	H.	2B.	3B.	HR.	RBI.	B.A.	PO.	A.	E.	F.A.
1978—Bradenton Cubs		Gulf C.	C-OF	26	68	10	19	3	0	1	7	.279	54	8	3	.954
1979—Geneva		NYP	C	63	237	45	74	*19	1	7	36	.312	*423	35	7	.985
1980—Davenport		Midw.	C	105	386	51	113	17	1	8	47	.293	*627	63	*16	.977
1981—Midland		Texas	C	110	390	56	103	19	2	10	60	.264	*593	*75	16	.977
1982—Midland		Texas	C	121	443	54	128	23	4	22	75	.289	417	42	15	.968
1983—Iowa		A. A.	C-1B-OF	74	238	43	77	13	3	15	47	.324	223	14	12	.952
1983—Chicago†		Nat.	C	6	7	2	2	1	0	0	1	.286	5	0	0	1.000
1984—Portland		P. C.	C-OF-1B	105	341	52	92	15	1	14	46	.270	373	16	14	.965
1985—Port.‡-Haw.		P. C.	C-O-1-3	128	445	65	139	29	4	22	85	.312	698	37	7	.991
Major League Totals—1 Year				6	7	2	2	1	0	0	1	.286	5	0	0	1.000

Selected by Chicago Cubs' organization in 30th round of free-agent draft, June 6, 1978.
†Traded with Pitcher Bill Campbell to Philadelphia Phillies for Outfielders Bob Dernier and Gary Matthews and Pitcher Porfi Altamirano, March 27, 1984.
‡Traded to Pittsburgh Pirates' organization for Catcher Steve Herz, April 27, 1985.

MIGUEL ANGEL DILONE (REYES)

Name pronounced Me-GUELL Dee-loh-NAY.

Born November 1, 1954, at Santiago, Dominican Republic.
Height, 5.11. Weight, 175.
Throws right and bats left and righthanded.

Established National League record for most stolen bases with no caught stealing, season (12), 1977.
Major League stolen bases: 1974 (2), 1975 (2), 1976 (5), 1977 (12), 1978 (50), 1979 (21), 1980 (61), 1981 (29), 1982 (33), 1983 (8), 1984 (27), 1985 (17). Total—267.
Led American League in caught stealing with 23 in 1978.
Led Western Carolinas League in stolen bases with 95 in 1973, Carolina League with 84 in 1974 and International League with 48 in 1975 and 61 in 1976.
Led Western Carolinas League in caught stealing with 18 in 1973, Carolina League with 23 in 1974 and International League with 21 in 1976.
Led New York-Pennsylvania League in caught stealing with 10 in 1972.
Named Carolina League Most Valuable Player, 1974.

Year	Club	League	Pos.	G.	AB.	R.	H.	2B.	3B.	HR.	RBI.	B.A.	PO.	A.	E.	F.A.
1972—Niagara Falls		NYP	OF	61	223	50	50	6	0	0	16	.224	83	4	5	.946
1973—Charleston		W. Car.	OF	115	438	*94	119	8	5	1	24	.272	228	11	7	.972
1974—Salem		Carol.	OF	132	532	106	*176	28	9	1	47	.331	271	8	13	.955
1974—Pittsburgh		Nat.	PR-OF	12	2	3	0	0	0	0	0	.000	1	0	0	1.000
1975—Charleston		Int.	OF	125	471	61	102	12	5	1	26	.217	275	11	6	.978
1975—Pittsburgh		Nat.	OF	18	6	8	0	0	0	0	0	.000	3	0	0	1.000
1976—Charleston		Int.	OF-3B	100	408	63	137	7	6	1	17	.336	202	26	9	.962
1976—Pittsburgh		Nat.	OF	16	17	7	4	0	0	0	0	.235	11	0	0	1.000
1977—Pittsburgh†		Nat.	OF	29	44	5	6	0	0	0	0	.136	21	1	0	1.000
1977—Columbus‡		Int.	OF	38	144	28	31	5	1	0	7	.215	101	2	1	.990
1978—Oakland		Amer.	OF-3B	135	258	34	59	8	0	1	14	.229	196	4	5	.976
1979—Oakland§		Amer.	OF	30	91	15	17	1	2	1	6	.187	47	0	2	.959
1979—Ogden		P. C.	OF	6	29	5	8	1	1	0	6	.276	14	0	0	1.000
1979—Chicago		Nat.	OF	43	36	14	11	0	0	0	1	.306	27	0	0	1.000
1980—Wichita x		A. A.	OF-2B	20	84	12	20	5	0	0	2	.238	48	0	1	.980
1980—Cleveland		Amer.	OF	132	528	82	180	30	9	0	40	.341	249	7	7	.973
1981—Cleveland		Amer.	OF	72	269	33	78	5	5	0	19	.290	126	7	4	.971
1982—Cleveland y		Amer.	OF	104	379	50	89	12	3	3	25	.235	187	3	7	.964
1983—Clev.-z-Chi. ab		Amer.	OF	36	71	16	13	3	1	0	7	.183	47	0	0	1.000

Year Club League	Pos.	G.	AB.	R.	H.	2B.	3B.	HR.	RBI.	B.A.	PO.	A.	E.	F.A.
1983—Charleston............ Int.	OF	34	141	39	48	4	1	0	14	.340	69	1	1	.986
1983—Pittsburgh.............. Nat.	PR-PH	7	0	1	0	0	0	0	0	.000	0	0	0	.000
1984—Montreal c.............. Nat.	OF	88	169	28	47	8	2	1	10	.278	76	1	1	.987
1985—Mont.d-S.D.e.......... Nat.	OF	78	130	18	26	0	3	0	7	.200	57	2	3	.952
1985—Las Vegas............. P. C.	OF	11	43	6	14	5	0	1	4	.326	9	0	1	.900
American League Totals—6 Years........		509	1596	230	436	59	20	5	111	.273	852	21	25	.972
National League Totals—8 Years..............		291	404	84	94	8	5	1	18	.233	196	4	4	.980
Major League Totals—12 Years..............		800	2000	314	530	67	25	6	129	.265	1048	25	29	.974

Originally signed as a free agent by Pittsburgh Pirates but on a later date the St. Louis Cardinals also signed him not realizing that the Pittsburgh club had a valid contract. The National Association ruled in favor of the Pirates, April 20, 1972.

†On disabled list, May 16 to June 25, 1977.

‡Traded with Pitcher Elias Sosa and a player to be named later to Oakland A's for Catcher Manny Sanguillen, April 4, 1978; Oakland acquired Infielder Mike Edwards to complete deal, April 10, 1978.

§Sold to Chicago Cubs, July 4, 1979.

xSold to Cleveland Indians, May 7, 1980.

yGranted free agency, November 10, 1982; re-signed by Indians, February 9, 1983.

zTraded to Chicago White Sox, September 1, 1983, completing deal in which Chicago traded Pitcher Richard Barnes to Cleveland Indians' organization for a player to be named later, August 25, 1983.

aTraded with Pitcher Mike Maitland to Pittsburgh Pirates for Pitcher Randy Niemann, September 7, 1983.

bGranted free agency, November 7, 1983; signed by Montreal Expos, January 17, 1984.

cGranted free agency, November 8, 1984; re-signed by Expos, March 4, 1985.

dReleased, July 10, 1985; signed by Las Vegas (San Diego Padres' organization), July 27, 1985.

eGranted free agency, November 12, 1985.

FRANK MICHAEL DiPINO

Born October 22, 1956, at Syracuse, N.Y.
Height, 6.00. Weight, 180.
Throws and bats lefthanded.
Attended St. Leo College, St. Leo, Fla.

Pitched seven-inning, 6-0 no-hit victory against Reading, June 8, 1980 (second game).
Major League saves: 1983 (20), 1984 (14), 1985 (6). Total—40.

Year Club	League	G.	IP.	W.	L.	Pct.	H.	R.	ER.	SO.	BB.	ERA.
1977—Newark	NYP	14	29	1	3	.250	14	12	8	41	22	2.48
1978—Burlington	Midwest	15	88	5	4	.556	98	58	46	68	36	4.70
1979—Stockton†	California	16	99	5	3	.625	92	45	38	67	46	3.45
1980—Holyoke	Eastern	16	76	7	0	1.000	46	13	11	58	27	1.30
1980—Vancouver..................................	P. Coast	24	28	3	1	.750	24	10	7	32	14	2.25
1981—Vancouver‡................................	P. Coast	27	81	3	5	.375	83	45	39	81	39	4.33
1981—Milwaukee§................................	American	2	2	0	0	.000	0	0	0	3	3	0.00
1982—Vancouver§................................	P. Coast	26	189⅔	13	9	.591	187	102	85	115	86	4.03
1982—Houston......................................	National	6	28⅓	2	2	.500	32	20	19	25	11	6.04
1983—Houston......................................	National	53	71⅓	3	4	.429	52	21	21	67	20	2.65
1984—Houston......................................	National	57	75⅓	4	9	.308	74	32	28	65	36	3.35
1985—Houston......................................	National	54	76	3	7	.300	69	44	34	49	43	4.03
American League Totals—1 Year		2	2	0	0	.000	0	0	0	3	3	0.00
National League Totals—4 Years......................		170	251	12	22	.353	227	117	102	206	110	3.66
Major League Totals—5 Years............................		172	253	12	22	.353	227	117	102	209	113	3.63

Signed as free agent by Milwaukee Brewers' organization, July 11, 1977.

†On disabled list, May 19 to June 11, 1979.

‡On disabled list, May 9 to June 10, 1981.

§Traded with Outfielder Kevin Bass and Pitcher Mike Madden to Houston Astros, September 3, 1982, completing deal in which Houston traded Pitcher Don Sutton to Milwaukee Brewers for three players to be named later, August 30, 1982.

BENITO JAMES DISTEFANO JR.

Name pronounced Dis-tuh-FAHN-oh.

(Benny)

Born January 23, 1962, at Brooklyn, N.Y.
Height, 6.01. Weight, 205.
Throws and bats lefthanded.
Attended Alvin Community College, Alvin, Tex.

Year Club League	Pos.	G.	AB.	R.	H.	2B.	3B.	HR.	RBI.	B.A.	PO.	A.	E.	F.A.
1982—Greenwood............ S. Atl.	1B	136	477	74	138	23	●8	15	89	.289	★1184	★104	19	.985
1983—Lynn........................ East.	OF-1B	★137	480	71	130	19	7	25	92	.271	271	13	13	.956
1984—Hawaii .... P. C.	1B-OF	66	240	40	73	13	8	6	33	.304	334	30	0	1.000
1984—Pittsburgh.............. Nat.	OF-1B	45	78	10	13	1	2	3	9	.167	88	9	3	.970
1985—Hawaii .... P. C.	OF-1B	136	480	74	114	27	8	14	67	.238	375	18	8	.980
Major League Totals—1 Year		45	78	10	13	1	2	3	9	.167	88	9	3	.970

Selected by Los Angeles Dodgers' organization in 16th round of free-agent draft, January 13, 1981.

Selected by Toronto Blue Jays' organization in secondary phase of free-agent draft, June 8, 1981.

Selected by Pittsburgh Pirates' organization in secondary phase of free-agent draft, January 12, 1982.

KENNETH JOHN DIXON
(Ken)

Born October 17, 1960, at Monroe, Va.
Height, 5.11. Weight, 166.
Throws right and bats left and righthanded.

Major League saves: 1985 (1).
Led Southern League in complete games with 20 and tied for lead in home runs allowed with 20 in 1984.
Tied for Appalachian League lead in hit batsmen with 5 in 1980.
Named Southern League Pitcher of the Year, 1984.

Year	Club	League	G.	IP.	W.	L.	Pct.	H.	R.	ER.	SO.	BB.	ERA.
1980—Bluefield	Ap'lachian	13	78	4	5	.444	69	46	40	62	★48	4.62
1981—Miami	Florida St.	11	60	1	8	.111	57	41	29	40	42	4.35
1981—Bluefield	Ap'lachian	3	18	2	1	.667	23	12	12	22	11	6.00
1981—Hagerstown	Carolina	9	65	3	5	.375	44	25	21	73	30	2.91
1982—Hagerstown	Carolina	15	97⅔	7	8	.467	97	59	50	71	50	4.61
1982—Charlotte	Southern	13	76⅔	3	8	.273	72	44	39	61	42	4.58
1983—Charlotte	Southern	20	130	8	7	.533	123	64	57	73	70	3.95
1983—Rochester	Int'national	11	64⅓	3	6	.333	65	41	32	34	26	4.48
1984—Charlotte	Southern	31	★240	●16	8	.667	198	92	76	★211	78	2.85
1984—Baltimore	American	2	13	0	1	.000	14	6	6	8	4	4.15
1985—Baltimore†	American	34	162	8	4	.667	144	68	66	108	64	3.67
Major League Totals—2 Years		36	175	8	5	.615	158	74	72	116	68	3.70

Selected by Baltimore Orioles' organization in 3rd round of free-agent draft, June 3, 1980.
†Appeared in three games as pinch-runner.

REGINALD TERRENCE DOBIE
(Reggie)

Born August 17, 1964, at Rosedale, Miss.
Height, 6.01. Weight, 175.
Throws and bats righthanded.
Attended Triton College, River Grove, Ill., and
Chicago State University, Chicago, Ill.

Tied for Carolina League lead in games started by pitchers with 26 in 1985.
Tied for Gulf Coast League lead in balks with 3 in 1983.

Year	Club	League	G.	IP.	W.	L.	Pct.	H.	R.	ER.	SO.	BB.	ERA.
1983—Sarasota Mets	Gulf Coast	12	44	0	4	.000	47	21	16	44	31	3.27
1984—Columbia	S. Atlantic	25	172⅓	10	9	.526	123	75	58	★128	★119	3.03
1985—Lynchburg	Carolina	26	167⅔	12	5	.706	118	61	49	144	77	2.63

Selected by New York Mets' organization in 8th round of free-agent draft, January 11, 1983.

JOHN ROBERT DOPSON JR.

Born July 14, 1963, at Baltimore, Md.
Height, 6.04. Weight, 205.
Throws and bats righthanded.

Year	Club	League	G.	IP.	W.	L.	Pct.	H.	R.	ER.	SO.	BB.	ERA.
1982—Jamestown	NYP	15	106⅔	6	●8	.429	117	58	47	62	34	3.97
1983—West Palm Beach	Florida St.	23	146⅔	13	6	.684	141	82	56	69	38	3.44
1984—Jacksonville†	Southern	26	170⅔	10	8	.556	198	83	70	76	41	3.69
1985—Jacksonville	Southern	5	32⅓	3	0	1.000	27	5	4	20	10	1.11
1985—Indianapolis‡	Am. Assoc.	18	95⅓	4	7	.364	88	44	40	48	44	3.78
1985—Montreal	National	4	13	0	2	.000	25	17	16	4	4	11.08
Major League Totals—1 Year		4	13	0	2	.000	25	17	16	4	4	11.08

Selected by Montreal Expos' organization in 2nd round of free-agent draft, June 7, 1982.
†On suspended list, May 24 to May 31, 1984.
‡On disabled list, June 24 to July 15, 1985.

WILLIAM DONALD DORAN

Name pronounced DOOR-un.

(Bill)

Born May 28, 1958, at Cincinnati, Ohio.
Height, 6.00. Weight, 175.
Throws right and bats right and lefthanded.
Attended Miami University, Oxford, Ohio.

Major League stolen bases: 1982 (5), 1983 (12), 1984 (21), 1985 (23). Total—61.
Led Pacific Coast League second basemen in double plays with 123 in 1982.
Led Gulf Coast League second basemen in double plays with 33 in 1979.

Year	Club	League	Pos.	G.	AB.	R.	H.	2B.	3B.	HR.	RBI.	B.A.	PO.	A.	E.	F.A.
1979—Sarasota Astros	Gulf C.	2B	44	164	21	42	6	0	1	16	.256	107	★144	11	.958
1980—Daytona Beach	Fla. St.	2B-SS	102	369	62	90	11	3	2	45	.244	232	259	21	.959
1981—Columbus	South.	2B-SS	124	427	83	120	17	7	5	56	.281	263	355	17	.973
1982—Tucson	P. C.	2B	★142	559	100	169	32	7	1	65	.302	★361	★424	★23	.972
1982—Houston	Nat.	2B	26	97	11	27	3	0	0	6	.278	41	78	3	.975
1983—Houston	Nat.	2B	154	535	70	145	12	7	8	39	.271	★347	461	17	.979

Year Club	League	Pos.	G.	AB.	R.	H.	2B.	3B.	HR.	RBI.	B.A.	PO.	A.	E.	F.A.
1984—Houston	Nat.	2B-SS	147	548	92	143	18	11	4	41	.261	274	440	12	.983
1985—Houston	Nat.	2B	148	578	84	166	31	6	14	59	.287	345	440	16	.980
Major League Totals—4 Years			475	1758	257	481	64	24	26	145	.274	1007	1419	48	.981

Selected by Houston Astros' organization in 6th round of free-agent draft, June 5, 1979.

BRIAN RICHARD DORSETT

Born April 9, 1961, at Terre Haute, Ind.
Height, 6.03. Weight, 215.
Throws and bats righthanded.
Attended Indiana State University, Terre Haute, Ind.

Year Club	League	Pos.	G.	AB.	R.	H.	2B.	3B.	HR.	RBI.	B.A.	PO.	A.	E.	F.A.
1983—Medford	N'west	C	14	48	11	13	2	1	1	10	.271	85	8	2	.979
1983—Madison	Midw.	C	58	204	16	52	7	0	3	27	.255	337	51	6	.985
1984—Modesto†	Calif.	C-1B	99	375	39	99	19	0	8	52	.264	511	76	13	.978
1985—Madison	Midw.	C	40	161	15	43	11	0	2	30	.267	194	40	5	.979
1985—Huntsville	South.	C	88	313	38	84	18	3	11	43	.268	437	51	10	.980

Selected by Oakland A's organization in 10th round of free-agent draft, June 6, 1983.
†On disabled list, June 18 to July 24, 1984.

JAMES EDWARD DORSEY III
(Jim)

Born August 2, 1955, at Chicago, Ill.
Height, 6.02. Weight, 200.
Throws and bats righthanded.
Attended Los Angeles Valley Junior College, Van Nuys, Calif.

Pitched 4-0, seven-inning no-hit victory against Clinton, May 20, 1975.

Year Club	League	G.	IP.	W.	L.	Pct.	H.	R.	ER.	SO.	BB.	ERA.
1975—Quad Cities	Midwest	25	161	15	3	.833	114	49	38	161	56	2.12
1976—El Paso	Texas	26	164	9	9	.500	188	104	82	101	77	4.50
1977—El Paso	Texas	25	144	10	9	.526	167	*105	80	73	70	5.00
1978—El Paso	Texas	9	59	5	2	.714	62	42	38	56	33	5.80
1978—Salt Lake City	P. Coast	19	132	11	7	.611	118	57	49	83	77	3.34
1979—Salt Lake City	P. Coast	28	168	10	12	.455	176	113	*103	92	100	5.52
1980—Salt Lake City	P. Coast	27	173	14	7	.667	177	89	77	109	93	4.01
1980—California†	American	4	16	1	2	.333	25	16	16	8	8	9.00
1981—Pawtucket	Int'national	27	137	4	10	.286	116	59	51	97	70	3.35
1982—Pawtucket‡	Int'national	22	97	5	7	.417	115	52	47	81	50	4.36
1983—Pawtucket§	Int'national	29	67⅓	5	7	.417	59	33	30	63	40	4.01
1984—Pawtucket	Int'national	41	105⅓	6	4	.600	87	41	34	83	49	2.91
1984—Boston	American	2	2⅔	0	0	.000	6	3	3	4	2	10.13
1985—Pawtucket	Int'national	32	146⅓	8	8	.500	136	73	.70	110	53	4.31
1985—Boston x	American	2	5⅓	0	1	.000	12	12	12	2	10	20.25
Major League Totals—3 Years		8	24	1	3	.250	43	31	31	14	20	11.63

Selected by California Angels' organization in 21st round of free-agent draft, June 5, 1973.
Selected by Los Angeles Dodgers' organization in secondary phase of free-agent draft, January 9, 1974.
Selected by California Angels' organization in 2nd round of free-agent draft, January 9, 1975.
†Traded with Pitcher Frank Tanana and Outfielder Joe Rudi to Boston Red Sox for Outfielder Fred Lynn and Pitcher Steve Renko, January 23, 1981.
‡On disabled list, May 5 to May 30, 1982.
§On disabled list, April 12 to May 1 and June 11 to July 14, 1983.
xReleased, November 14, 1985.

ARNOLD WAYNE DOTSON
(Known by middle name.)

Born March 18, 1965, at Lubbock, Tex.
Height, 6.01. Weight, 175.
Throws and bats righthanded.

Year Club	League	G.	IP.	W.	L.	Pct.	H.	R.	ER.	SO.	BB.	ERA.
1983—Bristol	Ap'lachian	12	54⅓	4	2	.667	63	54	46	49	39	7.62
1984—Lakeland†‡	Florida St.	18	60	3	7	.300	60	45	35	34	55	5.25
1985—Lakeland	Florida St.	17	101	6	8	.429	107	78	61	71	61	5.44

Selected by Detroit Tigers' organization in 1st round (15th player selected) of free-agent draft, June 6, 1983.
†On disabled list, April 6 to April 16, 1984.
‡On suspended list, July 25 to August 4, 1984.

RICHARD ELLIOTT DOTSON

Born January 10, 1959, at Cincinnati, O.
Height, 6.00. Weight, 203.
Throws and bats righthanded.

Tied for American League lead in shutouts with 4 in 1981.

Year Club	League	G.	IP.	W.	L.	Pct.	H.	R.	ER.	SO.	BB.	ERA.
1977—Idaho Falls†	Pioneer	13	66	4	5	.444	65	61	42	83	63	5.73
1978—Knoxville	Southern	26	145	11	10	.524	128	85	69	152	*105	4.28

Year Club	League	G.	IP.	W.	L.	Pct.	H.	R.	ER.	SO.	BB.	ERA.
1979—Knoxville	Southern	25	163	9	9	.500	133	81	67	133	88	3.70
1979—Chicago	American	5	24	2	0	1.000	28	13	10	13	6	3.75
1980—Chicago	American	33	198	12	10	.545	185	105	94	109	87	4.27
1981—Chicago	American	24	141	9	8	.529	145	67	59	73	49	3.77
1982—Chicago	American	34	196⅔	11	15	.423	219	97	84	109	73	3.84
1983—Chicago	American	35	240	22	7	★.759	209	92	86	137	★106	3.23
1984—Chicago‡	American	32	245⅔	14	15	.483	216	110	98	120	103	3.59
1985—Chicago§	American	9	52⅓	3	4	.429	53	30	26	33	17	4.47
Major League Totals—7 Years		172	1097⅔	73	59	.553	1055	514	457	594	441	3.75

Selected by California Angels' organization in 1st round (seventh player selected) of free-agent draft, June 7, 1977.

†Traded with Outfielders Bobby Bonds and Thad Bosley to Chicago White Sox for Catcher Brian Downing and Pitchers Chris Knapp and Dave Frost, December 5, 1977.

‡Appeared in one game as a pinch-runner.

§On disabled list, April 7 to April 22 and June 11, 1985 through remainder of season.

CHAMPIONSHIP SERIES RECORD

Year Club	League	G.	IP.	W.	L.	Pct.	H.	R.	ER.	SO.	BB.	ERA.
1983—Chicago	American	1	5	0	1	.000	6	6	6	3	3	10.80

ALL-STAR GAME RECORD

Year League		IP.	W.	L.	Pct.	H.	R.	ER.	SO.	BB.	ERA.
1984—American		2	0	0	.000	2	0	0	2	1	0.00

BRIAN JAY DOWNING

Born October 9, 1950, at Los Angeles, Calif.
Height, 5.10. Weight, 200.
Throws and bats righthanded.
Attended Cypress Junior College, Cypress, Calif.

Tied major league records for highest fielding percentage by outfielder, season, 150 or more games (1.000), 1982; fewest errors by outfielder, season, 150 or more games (0), 1982; fewest double plays by outfielder, season, 150 or more games (0), 1982.

Established American League record for most consecutive errorless games by an outfielder (244), May 25, 1981 through July 21, second game, 1983.

Major League stolen bases: 1975 (13), 1976 (7), 1977 (1), 1978 (3), 1979 (3), 1981 (1), 1982 (2), 1983 (1), 1985 (5). Total—36.

Year Club	League	Pos.	G.	AB.	R.	H.	2B.	3B.	HR.	RBI.	B.A.	PO.	A.	E.	F.A.
1970—Sarasota W. S.	Gulf C.	C-OF	34	96	16	21	1	1	0	14	.219	167	11	1	.994
1971—Appleton	Midw.	3B-C-OF	99	333	51	82	6	3	3	22	.246	353	98	13	.972
1972—Knoxville	South.	OF-3B-C	135	442	75	123	24	7	15	67	.278	250	123	21	.947
1973—Iowa	A. A.	3B-OF-C	68	228	34	56	6	1	7	27	.246	84	90	8	.956
1973—Chicago†	Amer.	OF-C-3B	34	73	5	13	1	0	2	4	.178	72	17	5	.947
1974—Chicago	Amer.	C-OF	108	293	41	66	12	1	10	39	.225	337	30	2	.995
1975—Chicago	Amer.	C	138	420	58	101	12	1	7	41	.240	730	84	8	.990
1976—Chicago‡	Amer.	C	104	317	38	81	14	0	3	30	.256	450	38	6	.988
1977—Chicago§	Amer.	C-OF	69	169	28	48	4	2	4	25	.284	325	28	6	.983
1978—California	Amer.	C	133	412	42	105	15	0	7	46	.255	681	82	5	.993
1979—California	Amer.	C	148	509	87	166	27	3	12	75	.326	669	35	11	.985
1980—California x	Amer.	C	30	93	5	27	6	0	2	25	.290	69	6	0	1.000
1981—California	Amer.	OF-C	93	317	47	79	14	0	9	41	.249	237	18	2	.992
1982—California	Amer.	OF	158	623	109	175	37	2	28	84	.281	321	9	0	●1.000
1983—California y	Amer.	OF	113	403	68	99	15	1	19	53	.246	160	9	1	.994
1984—California	Amer.	OF	156	539	65	148	28	2	23	91	.275	272	5	0	★1.000
1985—California	Amer.	OF	150	520	80	137	23	1	20	85	.263	244	5	2	.992
Major League Totals—13 Years			1434	4688	673	1245	208	13	146	639	.266	4567	384	48	.990

Signed as free-agent by Chicago White Sox' organization, August 19, 1969.

†On disabled list, June 1 to July 9, 1973.

‡On disabled list, July 30 to August 15, 1976.

§Traded with Pitchers Chris Knapp and Dave Frost to California Angels for Outfielders Bobby Bonds and Thad Bosley and Pitcher Dick Dotson, December 5, 1977.

xOn disabled list, April 20 to September 1, 1980.

yOn disabled list, May 10 to June 20, 1983.

CHAMPIONSHIP SERIES RECORD

Year Club	League	Pos.	G.	AB.	R.	H.	2B.	3B.	HR.	RBI.	B.A.	PO.	A.	E.	F.A.
1979—California	Amer.	C	4	15	1	3	0	0	1	1	.200	27	0	0	1.000
1982—California	Amer.	C	5	19	3	3	1	0	0	0	.158	5	0	0	1.000
Championship Series Totals—2 Years			9	34	4	6	1	0	0	1	.176	32	0	0	1.000

ALL-STAR GAME RECORD

Year League		Pos.	AB.	R.	H.	2B.	3B.	HR.	RBI.	B.A.	PO.	A.	E.	F.A.
1979—American		C	1	0	1	0	0	0	0	1.000	3	0	0	1.000

KELLY ROBERT DOWNS

Born October 25, 1960, at Ogden, Utah.
Height, 6.04. Weight, 195.
Throws and bats righthanded.
Brother of Dave Downs, pitcher with Philadelphia Phillies, 1972.

Tied for Pacific Coast League lead in games started by pitchers with 29 in 1983.

Year Club	League	G.	IP.	W.	L.	Pct.	H.	R.	ER.	SO.	BB.	ERA.
1980—Spartanburg	W. Carol.	14	90	5	7	.417	85	41	26	40	17	2.60
1981—Peninsula	Carolina	25	175	13	7	.650	176	79	58	124	35	2.98
1982—Oklahoma City	Am. Assoc.	32	156⅔	2	*15	.118	182	*116	93	70	72	5.34
1983—Portland	P. Coast	29	159⅓	9	●13	.409	186	98	79	71	61	4.46
1984—Portland†	P. Coast	30	163	7	12	.368	166	106	96	104	65	5.30
1985—Phoenix	P. Coast	37	137	9	10	.474	138	69	61	109	56	4.01

Selected by Philadelphia Phillies' organization in 26th round of free-agent draft, June 5, 1979.

†Traded with Pitcher George Riley to San Francisco Giants for First Baseman Al Oliver and a player to be named later, August 20, 1984; Philadelphia Phillies acquired Pitcher Renie Martin to complete deal, August 30, 1984.

RICHARD MICHAEL DOYLE
(Rich)

Born February 4, 1964, at LaMirada, Calif.
Height, 6.05. Weight, 205.
Throws and bats righthanded.
Attended University of Southern California, Los Angeles, Calif.

Pitched 6-1 no-hit victory against Albany, June 7, 1983 (first game).
Led Eastern League in home runs allowed with 19 in 1984.

Year Club	League	G.	IP.	W.	L.	Pct.	H.	R.	ER.	SO.	BB.	ERA.
1981—Batavia	NYP	15	58	2	6	.250	68	49	32	36	38	4.97
1982—Waterloo†	Midwest	21	121	7	6	.538	113	61	53	124	55	3.94
1983—Buffalo‡	Eastern	18	98⅔	5	7	.417	95	55	51	80	50	4.65
1984—Buffalo	Eastern	25	119⅓	7	11	.389	125	86	75	67	56	5.66
1985—Waterbury§	Eastern	15	86⅓	8	4	.667	95	47	42	50	26	4.38
1985—Maine	Int'national	8	38	1	3	.250	47	27	21	16	18	4.97

Selected by Cleveland Indians' organization in 5th round of free-agent draft, June 8, 1981.

†On disabled list, April 9 to April 22, 1982.

‡On disabled list, June 14 to July 7, 1983.

§On disabled list, April 24 to May 5 and June 25 to July 5, 1985.

THOMAS DEAN DOZIER
(Tom)

Born September 5, 1961, at Richmond, Calif.
Height, 6.02. Weight, 190.
Throws and bats righthanded.

Year Club	League	G.	IP.	W.	L.	Pct.	H.	R.	ER.	SO.	BB.	ERA.
1979—Johnson City	Ap'lachian	11	35	1	3	.250	48	28	20	12	15	5.14
1980—Johnson City	Ap'lachian	11	40	3	2	.600	38	25	22	19	14	4.95
1981—St. Petersburg	Florida St.	15	37	2	2	.500	38	23	23	13	21	5.59
1981—Gastonia	S. Atlantic	11	43	1	0	1.000	26	8	7	26	10	1.47
1982—Springfield	Midwest	26	133	11	6	.647	131	74	62	87	52	4.20
1983—St. Petersburg	Florida St.	26	153	11	7	.611	133	63	50	109	60	2.94
1983—Springfield†	Midwest	1	6⅔	0	0	.000	3	2	1	9	5	1.35
1984—Albany	Eastern	44	89⅓	6	5	.545	74	37	29	57	34	2.92
1985—Tacoma‡	P. Coast	6	34	0	0	.000	27	18	16	22	14	4.24
1985—Huntsville	Southern	12	59⅔	5	2	.714	42	28	21	54	26	3.17

Selected by St. Louis Cardinals' organization in 11th round of free-agent draft, June 5, 1979.

†Traded with pitcher Jim Strichek to Oakland A's organization, September 14, 1983, completing deal in which Oakland traded Pitcher Steve Baker to St. Louis Cardinals for two players to be named later, September 2, 1983.

‡On disabled list, April 22 to June 18, 1985.

DOUGLAS DEAN DRABEK
(Doug)

Born July 25, 1962, at Victoria, Tex.
Height, 6.01. Weight, 185.
Throws and bats righthanded.
Attended University of Houston, Houston, Tex.

Year Club	League	G.	IP.	W.	L.	Pct.	H.	R.	ER.	SO.	BB.	ERA.
1983—Niagara Falls	NYP	16	103⅔	6	7	.462	99	52	42	103	48	3.65
1984—Appleton	Midwest	1	5	1	0	1.000	3	1	1	6	3	1.80
1984—Glens Falls†	Eastern	19	124⅔	12	5	.706	90	34	31	75	44	2.24
1984—Nashville	Southern	4	31	1	2	.333	30	11	8	22	10	2.32
1985—Albany	Eastern	26	*192⅔	13	7	.650	153	71	64	*153	55	2.99

Selected by Cleveland Indians' organization in 4th round of free-agent draft, June 3, 1980.
Selected by Chicago White Sox' organization in 11th round of free-agent draft, June 6, 1983.

†Traded with Pitcher Kevin Hickey to New York Yankees' organization, August 13, 1984, completing deal in which New York traded Infielder Roy Smalley to Chicago White Sox for two players to be named later, July 18, 1984.

DAVID FRANCIS DRAVECKY
(Dave)

Born February 14, 1956, at Youngstown, O.
Height, 6.01. Weight, 193.
Throws left and bats righthanded.
Attended Youngstown State University, Youngstown, Ohio.

Major League saves: 1982 (2), 1983 (8). Total—10.
Led Texas League in shutouts with 4 in 1981.

Year	Club	League	G.	IP.	W.	L.	Pct.	H.	R.	ER.	SO.	BB.	ERA.
1978—Charleston	W. Carol.	20	52	4	2	.667	54	30	24	31	32	4.15
1979—Buffalo	Eastern	35	114	6	7	.462	125	71	54	81	59	4.26
1980—Buffalo†	Eastern	27	161	13	7	.650	165	76	60	64	60	3.35
1981—Amarillo	Texas	30	172	●15	5	.750	157	69	51	141	45	2.67
1982—Hawaii	P. Coast	16	36⅓	4	1	.800	28	15	10	26	14	2.48
1982—San Diego	National	31	105	5	3	.625	86	37	30	59	33	2.57
1983—San Diego	National	28	183⅔	14	10	.583	181	78	73	74	44	3.58
1984—San Diego	National	50	156⅔	9	8	.529	125	53	51	71	51	2.93
1985—San Diego	National	34	214⅔	13	11	.542	200	79	70	105	57	2.93
Major League Totals—4 Years		143	660	41	32	.562	592	247	244	309	185	3.05

Selected by Pittsburgh Pirates' organization in 21st round of free-agent draft, June 6, 1978.
†Traded to San Diego Padres' organization for Outfielder Robert D. (Bobby) Mitchell, April 5, 1981.

CHAMPIONSHIP SERIES RECORD

Year	Club	League	G.	IP.	W.	L.	Pct.	H.	R.	ER.	SO.	BB.	ERA.
1984—San Diego	National	3	6	0	0	.000	2	0	0	5	0	0.00

WORLD SERIES RECORD

Year	Club	League	G.	IP.	W.	L.	Pct.	H.	R.	ER.	SO.	BB.	ERA.
1984—San Diego	National	2	4⅔	0	0	.000	3	0	0	5	1	0.00

ALL-STAR GAME RECORD

Year	League	IP.	W.	L.	Pct.	H.	R.	ER.	SO.	BB.	ERA.
1983—National		2	0	0	.000	1	0	0	2	0	0.00

DANIEL DRIESSEN
(Dan)

Born July 29, 1951, at Hilton Head, S. C.
Height, 5.11. Weight, 200.
Throws right and bats lefthanded.
Uncle of Gerald Perry, first baseman-outfielder with Atlanta Braves;
cousin of Reggie Kinlaw, nose guard with Seattle Seahawks.

Major League stolen bases: 1973 (8), 1974 (10), 1975 (10), 1976 (14), 1977 (31), 1978 (28), 1979 (11), 1980 (19), 1981 (2), 1982 (11), 1983 (6), 1984 (2), 1985 (2). Total—154.
Tied for National League lead in bases on balls received with 93 and in being hit by pitch with 6 in 1980.
Led Eastern League first basemen in fielding percentage with .994 in 1972.

Year	Club	League	Pos.	G.	AB.	R.	H.	2B.	3B.	HR.	RBI.	B.A.	PO.	A.	E.	F.A.
1970—Tampa	Fla. St.	1B	93	242	28	54	2	1	0	20	.223	473	37	5	.990
1971—Tampa	Fla. St.	1B	136	468	72	153	27	9	4	62	.327	1064	86	15	.987
1972—Three Rivers	East.	1B-3B	136	481	62	155	37	4	4	65	.322	805	138	9	.991
1973—Indianapolis	A. A.	3B-1B	47	181	42	74	14	4	6	46	.409	50	97	6	.961
1973—Cincinnati	Nat.	3B-1B-OF	102	366	40	110	15	2	4	47	.301	160	157	12	.964
1974—Cincinnati	Nat.	3B-1B-OF	150	470	63	132	23	6	7	56	.281	186	206	26	.938
1975—Cincinnati†	Nat.	1B-OF	88	210	38	59	8	1	7	38	.281	309	20	5	.985
1976—Cincinnati	Nat.	1B-OF	98	219	32	54	11	1	7	44	.247	314	23	2	.994
1977—Cincinnati	Nat.	1B	151	536	75	161	31	4	17	91	.300	1182	75	7	.994
1978—Cincinnati	Nat.	1B	153	524	68	131	23	3	16	70	.250	1264	93	6	★.996
1979—Cincinnati	Nat.	1B	150	515	72	129	24	3	18	75	.250	1289	79	9	.993
1980—Cincinnati	Nat.	1B	154	524	81	139	36	1	14	74	.265	1349	85	7	.995
1981—Cincinnati	Nat.	1B	82	233	35	55	14	0	7	33	.236	558	30	3	.995
1982—Cincinnati	Nat.	1B	149	516	64	139	25	1	17	57	.269	1239	78	3	★.998
1983—Cincinnati‡	Nat.	1B	122	386	57	107	17	1	12	57	.277	917	71	4	★.996
1984—Cinc.§-Mont.	Nat.	1B	132	387	47	104	24	0	16	60	.269	870	52	7	.992
1985—Mont.x-S.F.	Nat.	1B	145	493	53	120	26	0	9	47	.243	1203	91	4	.997
Major League Totals—13 Years			1676	5379	734	1440	277	23	151	749	.268	10843	1060	95	.992

Signed as free agent by Cincinnati Reds' organization, August 28, 1969.
†On disabled list, March 23 to April 15, 1975.
‡On disabled list, June 11 to July 1, 1983.
§Traded to Montreal Expos for Pitchers Andy McGaffigan and Jim Jefferson, July 26, 1984.
xTraded to San Francisco Giants for Pitcher Bill Laskey, First Baseman Scot Thompson and a player to be named later, August 1, 1985; deal settled when Laskey was traded back to San Francisco for Pitcher George Riley and Outfielder Alonzo Powell, October 24, 1985.

CHAMPIONSHIP SERIES RECORD

Year	Club	League	Pos.	G.	AB.	R.	H.	2B.	3B.	HR.	RBI.	B.A.	PO.	A.	E.	F.A.
1973—Cincinnati	Nat.	3B-PR	4	12	0	2	1	0	0	1	.167	3	2	1	.833
1976—Cincinnati	Nat.	PH	1	1	0	0	0	0	0	0	.000	0	0	0	.000
1979—Cincinnati	Nat.	1B	3	12	1	1	0	0	0	0	.083	32	0	0	1.000
Championship Series Totals—3 Years			8	25	1	3	1	0	0	1	.120	35	2	1	.974

WORLD SERIES RECORD

Year	Club	League	Pos.	G.	AB.	R.	H.	2B.	3B.	HR.	RBI.	B.A.	PO.	A.	E.	F.A.
1975—Cincinnati	Nat.	PH	2	2	0	0	0	0	0	0	.000	0	0	0	.000
1976—Cincinnati	Nat.	DH	4	14	4	5	2	0	1	1	.357	0	0	0	.000
World Series Totals—2 Years			6	16	4	5	2	0	1	1	.313	0	0	0	.000

THOMAS JEROME DUNBAR
(Tommy)

Born November 24, 1959, at Graniteville, S. C.
Height, 6.02. Weight, 190.
Throws and bats lefthanded.
Attended Middle Georgia College, Cochran, Ga.
Major League stolen bases: 1983 (3), 1984 (1). Total—4

Year Club	League	Pos.	G.	AB.	R.	H.	2B.	3B.	HR.	RBI.	B.A.	PO.	A.	E.	F.A.
1980—Asheville	S. Atl.	OF	75	262	39	79	9	6	1	39	.302	101	9	11	.909
1981—Asheville	S. Atl.	OF	138	•530	101	157	*33	7	15	76	.296	184	15	13	.939
1982—Tulsa	Texas	OF	131	461	93	149	*44	4	16	85	.323	201	5	7	.967
1983—Oklahoma City	A. A.	OF	*135	498	73	140	34	5	4	65	.281	244	13	5	.981
1983—Texas	Amer.	OF	12	24	3	6	0	0	0	3	.250	7	0	1	.875
1984—Oklahoma City	A. A.	OF	105	368	69	124	21	5	12	61	*.337	184	10	4	.980
1984—Texas	Amer.	OF	34	97	9	25	2	0	2	10	.258	31	0	2	.939
1985—Texas†	Amer.	OF	45	104	7	21	4	0	1	5	.202	14	0	1	.933
1985—Oklahoma City	A. A.	OF	49	164	12	37	7	1	0	16	.226	70	2	1	.986
Major League Totals—3 Years			91	225	19	52	6	0	3	18	.231	52	0	4	.929

Selected by Boston Red Sox' organization in 11th round of free-agent draft, June 5, 1979.
Selected by Texas Rangers' organization in secondary phase of free-agent draft, January 8, 1980.
†On disabled list, May 18 to June 3, 1985.

MARIANO DUNCAN

Born March 13, 1963, at San Pedro de Macoris, Dominican Republic.
Height, 6.00. Weight, 160.
Throws right and bats left and righthanded.
Major League stolen bases: 1985 (38).
Led Florida State League in stolen bases with 56 in 1983.
Led Texas League second basemen in double plays with 84 in 1984.

Year Club	League	Pos.	G.	AB.	R.	H.	2B.	3B.	HR.	RBI.	B.A.	PO.	A.	E.	F.A.
1982—Lethbridge	Pion.	SS-2B	30	55	9	13	3	1	1	8	.236	23	35	15	.795
1983—Vero Beach	Fla. St.	OF-SS-2B	109	384	73	102	10	*15	0	42	.266	169	157	37	.898
1984—San Antonio	Texas	2B-OF-SS	125	502	80	127	14	•11	2	44	.253	283	335	22	.966
1985—Los Angeles	Nat.	SS-2B	142	562	74	137	24	6	6	39	.244	224	430	30	.956
Major League Totals—1 Year			142	562	74	137	24	6	6	39	.244	224	430	30	.956

Signed as free agent by Los Angeles Dodgers' organization, January 17, 1982.

CHAMPIONSHIP SERIES RECORD

Year Club	League	Pos.	G.	AB.	R.	H.	2B.	3B.	HR.	RBI.	B.A.	PO.	A.	E.	F.A.
1985—Los Angeles	Nat.	SS	5	18	2	4	2	1	0	1	.222	7	16	1	.958

GREGORY JON DUNN
(Greg)

Born January 7, 1962, at Atwater, Calif.
Height, 6.00. Weight, 180.
Throws and bats righthanded.
Pitched 11-1 no-hit victory against Batavia, August 3, 1981.

Year Club	League	G.	IP.	W.	L.	Pct.	H.	R.	ER.	SO.	BB.	ERA.
1981—Erie	NYP	13	75	7	1	•.875	50	42	34	84	54	4.08
1982—Springfield	Midwest	27	162⅔	12	7	.632	149	92	78	116	90	4.32
1983—Springfield†	Midwest	27	95	2	7	.222	86	66	47	84	52	4.45
1984—St. Petersburg	Florida St.	30	126⅔	5	12	.294	120	75	60	99	90	4.26
1985—Springfield	Midwest	55	80	4	9	.308	56	29	22	115	62	2.48

Selected by St. Louis Cardinals' organization in 21st round of free-agent draft, June 3, 1980.
†On disabled list, September 1 to September 12, 1983.

MICHAEL DENNIS DUNNE
(Mike)

Born October 27, 1962, at Peoria, Ill.
Height, 6.04. Weight, 190.
Throws and bats righthanded.
Attended Bradley University, Peoria, Ill.
Member of 1984 U.S. Olympic baseball team.
Named righthanded pitcher on THE SPORTING NEWS College Baseball All-America Team, 1984.

Year Club	League	G.	IP.	W.	L.	Pct.	H.	R.	ER.	SO.	BB.	ERA.
1985—Arkansas†	Texas	23	146	4	9	.308	133	72	50	91	57	3.08

Selected by St. Louis Cardinals' organization in 1st round (seventh player selected) of free-agent draft, June 4, 1984.
†On disabled list, May 31 to June 10, 1985.

SHAWON DONNELL DUNSTON

Born March 21, 1963, at Brooklyn, N.Y.
Height, 6.01. Weight, 175.
Throws and bats righthanded.

Major League stolen bases: 1985 (11).
Received reported $150,000 bonus to sign with Chicago Cubs, 1982.

Year Club	League	Pos.	G.	AB.	R.	H.	2B.	3B.	HR.	RBI.	B.A.	PO.	A.	E.	F.A.
1982—Sarasota Cubs.......	Gulf C.	SS-3B	53	190	27	61	11	0	2	28	.321	61	129	24	.888
1983—Quad Cities†.........	Midw.	SS	117	455	65	141	17	8	4	62	.310	172	326	47	.914
1984—Midland..................	Texas	SS	73	298	44	98	13	3	3	34	.329	164	203	32	.920
1984—Iowa	A. A.	SS	61	210	25	49	11	1	7	27	.233	90	165	26	.907
1985—Chicago	Nat.	SS	74	250	40	65	12	4	4	18	.260	144	248	17	.958
1985—Iowa	A. A.	SS	73	272	24	73	9	6	2	28	.268	138	176	12	.963
Major League Totals—1 Year..................			74	250	40	65	12	4	4	18	.260	144	248	17	.958

Selected by Chicago Cubs' organization in 1st round (first player selected) of free-agent draft, June 7, 1982.
†On disabled list, May 31 to June 10, 1983.

BRYAN RODNEY DUQUETTE

Born November 24, 1960, at Los Angeles, Calif.
Height, 6.00. Weight, 190.
Throws and bats lefthanded.
Attended University of Hawaii, Honolulu, Haw.

Year Club	League	G.	IP.	W.	L.	Pct.	H.	R.	ER.	SO.	BB.	ERA.
1982—Beloit	Midwest	22	56⅓	3	4	.429	52	32	25	59	28	3.99
1983—Stockton	California	14	23	4	0	1.000	11	4	2	31	11	0.78
1983—El Paso...	Texas	37	46⅓	2	2	.500	52	35	30	36	30	5.83
1984—El Paso...	Texas	48	66	4	4	.500	53	29	24	45	34	3.27
1984—Vancouver......................................	P. Coast	7	11⅓	0	0	.000	12	4	4	9	7	3.18
1985—Vancouver......................................	P. Coast	41	63⅔	5	3	.625	61	25	23	48	29	3.25

Selected by Milwaukee Brewers' organization in 2nd round of free-agent draft, June 7, 1982.

LEON DURHAM

Born July 31, 1957, at Cincinnati, O.
Height, 6.02. Weight, 210.
Throws and bats lefthanded.

Major League stolen bases: 1980 (8), 1981 (25), 1982 (28), 1983 (12), 1984 (16), 1985 (7). Total—96.
Tied for National League lead in intentional bases on balls received with 24 in 1985.
Led Texas League first basemen in double plays with 96 in 1978.
Led Gulf Coast League first basemen in errors with 10 in 1976.
Named outfielder on THE SPORTING NEWS National League Silver Slugger team, 1982.

Year Club	League	Pos.	G.	AB.	R.	H.	2B.	3B.	HR.	RBI.	B.A.	PO.	A.	E.	F.A.
1976—Sarasota Cards.....	Gulf C.	1B-OF	44	156	25	35	3	5	2	18	.224	296	5	12	.962
1977—Gastonia.................	W. Car.	1B	63	239	45	88	18	3	4	44	.368	492	28	8	.985
1977—St. Petersburg.......	Fla. St.	1B	63	209	26	60	3	6	0	25	.287	533	27	9	.984
1978—Arkansas†..............	Texas	1B	102	367	72	116	21	5	12	70	.316	931	42	8	*.992
1979—Springfield.............	A. A.	OF-1B	127	449	84	139	33	4	23	88	.310	304	19	6	.982
1980—Springfield.............	A. A.	OF-1B	32	128	20	33	5	5	5	23	.258	96	8	4	.963
1980—St. Louis‡...............	Nat.	OF-1B	96	303	42	82	15	4	8	42	.271	180	22	3	.985
1981—Chicago§	Nat.	OF-1B	87	328	42	95	14	6	10	35	.290	175	4	5	.973
1982—Chicago	Nat.	OF-1B	148	539	84	168	33	7	22	90	.312	311	12	12	.964
1983—Chicago x...............	Nat.	OF-1B	100	337	58	87	18	8	12	55	.258	203	4	6	.972
1984—Chicago y..............	Nat.	1B	137	473	86	132	30	4	23	96	.279	1162	96	7	.994
1985—Chicago	Nat.	1B	153	542	58	153	32	2	21	75	.282	1421	107	7	.995
Major League Totals—6 Years.................			721	2522	370	717	142	31	96	393	.284	3452	245	40	.989

Selected by St. Louis Cardinals' organization in 1st round (15th player selected) of free-agent draft, June 8, 1976.
†On disabled list, April 23 to May 25, 1978.
‡Traded with Third Baseman Ken Reitz and a player to be named later to Chicago Cubs for Pitcher Bruce Sutter, December 9, 1980; Chicago acquired Third Baseman Tye Waller to complete deal, December 22, 1980.
§On disabled list, June 2 to August 9, 1981.
xOn disabled list, June 9 to June 24, 1983.
yOn disabled list, June 24 to July 12, 1984.

CHAMPIONSHIP SERIES RECORD

Year Club	League	Pos.	G.	AB.	R.	H.	2B.	3B.	HR.	RBI.	B.A.	PO.	A.	E.	F.A.
1984—Chicago	Nat.	1B	5	20	2	3	0	0	2	4	.150	47	3	1	.980

ALL-STAR GAME RECORD

Year League	Pos.	AB.	R.	H.	2B.	3B.	HR.	RBI.	B.A.	PO.	A.	E.	F.A.
1983—National	OF	2	0	0	0	0	0	0	.000	0	0	0	.000

Member of National League All-Star Team in 1982; did not play.

—DID YOU KNOW—

That in 1975, the Royals' George Brett went 15 for 17 against Angels pitcher Ed Figueroa? In 15 consecutive plate appearances, Brett collected 13 hits and walked twice.

JAMES EDWARD DWYER
(Jimmy)

Born January 3, 1950, at Evergreen Park, Ill.
Height, 5.10. Weight, 175.
Throws and bats lefthanded.
Received bachelor of arts degree in accounting from Southern Illinois University, Carbondale, Ill., in 1973.
Nephew of Don Dwyer, second baseman in New York Giants' organization, 1947.

Major League stolen bases: 1975 (4), 1978 (7), 1979 (3), 1980 (3), 1982 (2), 1983 (1). Total—20.
Tied for American Association lead in caught stealing with 13 in 1977.

Year Club	League	Pos.	G.	AB.	R.	H.	2B.	3B.	HR.	RBI.	B.A.	PO.	A.	E.	F.A.
1971—Cedar Rapids........	Midw.	OF	58	201	30	63	6	6	2	15	.313	73	3	3	.962
1972—Modesto	Calif.	OF	92	354	87	115	15	*13	9	45	.325	149	8	4	.975
1972—Arkansas...............	Texas	OF	44	162	16	41	1	0	2	14	.253	101	6	2	.982
1973—Tulsa......................	A. A.	OF	87	349	63	135	22	8	1	40	*.387	127	8	5	.964
1973—St. Louis.................	Nat.	OF	28	57	7	11	1	1	0	0	.193	32	0	0	1.000
1974—Tulsa......................	A. A.	OF-1B	36	119	20	40	7	2	1	15	.336	120	13	3	.978
1974—St. Louis.................	Nat.	OF-1B	74	86	13	24	1	0	2	11	.279	31	3	0	1.000
1975—Tulsa......................	A. A.	OF	33	109	17	44	8	2	1	17	.404	49	2	2	.962
1975—St.L.†-Mont.	Nat.	OF	81	206	26	56	8	1	3	21	.272	104	8	4	.966
1976—Mont.‡-N.Y.§.........	Nat.	OF-PH	61	105	9	19	3	1	0	5	.181	35	0	1	.972
1976—Tidewater..............	Int.	OF	8	26	0	5	1	0	0	1	.192	14	0	1	.933
1077 Wichita x	A. A.	OF	130	464	*113	*154	*38	12	18	70	*.332	245	6	8	.969
1977—St. Louis.................	Nat.	OF	13	31	3	7	1	0	0	2	.226	16	0	0	1.000
1978—St.L. y-S.F. z	Nat.	OF-1B	107	238	30	53	12	2	6	26	.223	216	15	3	.987
1979—Boston.....................	Amer.	1B-OF	76	113	19	30	7	0	2	14	.265	167	16	4	.979
1980—Boston a	Amer.	OF-1B	93	260	41	74	11	1	9	38	.285	143	15	4	.975
1981—Baltimore	Amer.	OF-1B	68	134	16	30	0	1	3	10	.224	97	2	2	.980
1982—Baltimore	Amer.	OF-1B	71	148	28	45	4	3	6	15	.304	87	0	2	.978
1983—Baltimore	Amer.	OF-1B	100	196	37	56	17	1	8	38	.286	123	2	4	.969
1984—Baltimore b	Amer.	OF	76	161	22	41	9	1	2	21	.255	83	3	3	.966
1985—Baltimore c	Amer.	OF	101	233	35	58	8	3	7	36	.249	131	4	1	.993
National League Totals—6 Years........			364	723	88	170	26	5	11	65	.235	434	26	8	.983
American League Totals—7 Years........			585	1245	198	334	56	10	37	172	.268	831	42	20	.978
Major League Totals—13 Years.............			949	1968	286	504	82	15	48	237	.256	1265	68	28	.979

Selected by St. Louis Cardinals' organization in 11th round of free-agent draft, June 8, 1971.
†Traded to Montreal Expos for Infielder Larry Lintz, July 25, 1975.
‡Traded with Outfielder Jose (Pepe) Mangual to New York Mets for Outfielder Del Unser and Infielder Wayne Garrett, July 21, 1976.
§In three-club deal, Chicago Cubs traded Outfielder-First Baseman Pete LaCock to Kansas City Royals, the New York Mets traded Outfielder Jim Dwyer to Chicago Cubs' organization, and New York received a player to be named later, December 8, 1976; New York acquired Outfielder Sheldon Mallory from Kansas City to complete deal, December 13, 1976.
xReleased, September 7, 1977, signed by St. Louis Cardinals, September 13, 1977.
yTraded to San Francisco Giants, June 15, 1978, completing deal in which San Francisco traded Pitcher Frank Riccelli to St. Louis Cardinals for a player to be named later, October 25, 1977.
zSold to Boston Red Sox, March 15, 1979.
aGranted free agency, October 22, 1980; signed by Baltimore Orioles, December 23, 1980.
bOn disabled list, July 19 to August 29, 1984.
cGranted free agency, November 12, 1985.

CHAMPIONSHIP SERIES RECORD

Year Club	League	Pos.	G.	AB.	R.	H.	2B.	3B.	HR.	RBI.	B.A.	PO.	A.	E.	F.A.
1983—Baltimore	Amer.	PH-OF	2	4	1	1	1	0	0	0	.250	4	0	0	1.000

WORLD SERIES RECORD

Tied World Series record for hitting home run in first Series at-bat, October 11, 1983 (first inning).

Year Club	League	Pos.	G.	AB.	R.	H.	2B.	3B.	HR.	RBI.	B.A.	PO.	A.	E.	F.A.
1983—Baltimore	Amer.	OF	2	8	3	3	1	0	1	1	.375	2	0	0	1.000

JEROME MATTHEW DYBZINSKI

Name pronounced Dib-ZIN-ski.

(Jerry)

Born July 7, 1955, at Cleveland, O.
Height, 6.02. Weight, 188.
Throws and bats righthanded.
Received bachelor of arts degree in physical education and health
from Cleveland State University, Cleveland, O., in 1977.

Major League stolen bases: 1980 (4), 1981 (7), 1982 (3), 1983 (11), 1984 (7). Total—32.
Led New York-Pennsylvania League shortstops in double plays with 51 in 1977.
Tied for Pacific Coast League lead in being hit by pitch with 7 in 1979.

Year Club	League	Pos.	G.	AB.	R.	H.	2B.	3B.	HR.	RBI.	B.A.	PO.	A.	E.	F.A.
1977—Batavia..................	NYP	SS	58	169	39	37	7	0	0	16	.219	*117	*198	19	*.943
1978—Waterloo...............	Midw.	SS	134	508	96	144	15	2	12	63	.283	*191	412	*47	.928
1979—Tacoma..................	P. C.	SS	132	469	58	119	16	3	1	25	.254	*269	409	30	.958
1980—Cleveland...............	Amer.	SS-2B-3B	114	248	32	57	11	1	1	23	.230	140	263	13	.969
1981—Cleveland...............	Amer.	SS-2B-3B	48	57	10	17	0	0	0	6	.298	35	70	5	.955
1982—Cleveland...............	Amer.	SS-3B	80	212	19	49	6	2	0	22	.231	120	244	17	.955

Year Club League	Pos.	G.	AB.	R.	H.	2B.	3B.	HR.	RBI.	B.A.	PO.	A.	E.	F.A.
1982—Charleston†‡........ Int.	SS	30	107	14	32	6	1	2	12	.299	71	107	8	.957
1983—Chicago............... Amer.	SS-3B	127	256	30	59	10	1	1	32	.230	141	258	14	.966
1984—Chicago§ .... Amer.	SS-3B-2B	94	132	17	31	5	1	1	10	.235	69	160	7	.970
1985—Hawaii.................... P. C.	3-S-2-O	55	176	19	35	6	2	1	13	.199	48	90	6	.958
1985—Pittsburgh x .... Nat.	SS	5	4	0	0	0	0	0	0	.000	4	5	1	.900
American League Totals—5 Years		463	905	108	213	32	5	3	93	.235	505	995	56	.964
National League Totals—1 Year.............		5	4	0	0	0	0	0	0	.000	4	5	1	.900
Major League Totals—6 Years...................		468	909	108	213	32	5	3	93	.234	509	1000	57	.964

Selected by Cleveland Indians' organization in 15th round of free-agent draft, June 7, 1977.
†On suspended list, July 7 to July 31, 1982.
‡Traded to Chicago White Sox for Infielder Pat Tabler, April 1, 1983.
§Released, April 1, 1985; signed by Pittsburgh Pirates' organization, April 11, 1985.
xReleased, October 4, 1985; signed by Seattle Mariners' organization, January 18, 1986.

CHAMPIONSHIP SERIES RECORD

Year Club League	Pos.	G.	AB.	R.	H.	2B.	3B.	HR.	RBI.	B.A.	PO.	A.	E.	F.A.
1983—Chicago.................. Amer.	SS	2	4	0	1	0	0	0	0	.250	3	8	0	1.000

LEONARD KYLE DYKSTRA

Name pronounced DYK-struh.

(Lenny)

Born February 10, 1963, at Santa Ana, Calif.
Height, 5.10. Weight, 160.
Throws and bats lefthanded.
Grandson of Pete Leswick, forward with New York Americans and Boston Bruins
of NHL, 1936-37 and 1944-45; nephew of Tony Leswick, forward with
New York Rangers, Detroit Red Wings and Chicago Black
Hawks of NHL, 1945-46 through 1955-56 and 1957-58.

Major League stolen bases: 1985 (15).
Led Carolina League in bases on balls received with 107, stolen bases with 105 and caught stealing with 23 in 1983.
Named Carolina League Player of the Year, 1983.

Year Club League	Pos.	G.	AB.	R.	H.	2B.	3B.	HR.	RBI.	B.A.	PO.	A.	E.	F.A.
1981—Shelby.................... S. Atl.	OF-SS	48	157	34	41	7	2	0	18	.261	86	3	4	.957
1982—Shelby.................... S. Atl.	OF	120	413	95	120	13	7	3	38	.291	239	11	14	.947
1983—Lynchburg............. Carol.	OF	●136	*525	*132	*188	24	*14	8	81	*.358	268	9	7	.975
1984—Jackson .... Texas	OF	131	501	*100	138	25	7	6	52	.275	256	5	2	*.992
1985—Tidewater.............. Int.	OF	58	229	44	71	8	6	1	25	.310	184	4	5	.974
1985—New York.............. Nat.	OF	83	236	40	60	9	3	1	19	.254	165	6	1	.994
Major League Totals—1 Year..................		83	236	40	60	9	3	1	19	.254	165	6	1	.994

Selected by New York Mets' organization in 12th round of free-agent draft, June 8, 1981.

WILLIAM SCOTT EARL

(Scotty)

Born September 18, 1960, at Seymour, Ind.
Height, 5.11. Weight, 165.
Throws and bats righthanded.
Attended Glen Oaks Community College, Centerville, Mich., and received
degree in liberal arts from Eastern Kentucky University, Richmond, Ky., in 1981.

Major League stolen bases: 1984 (1).
Tied for American Association lead in bases on balls received with 77 in 1984.
Led American Association second basemen in putouts with 277 in 1984 and 263 in 1985.
Led American Association second basemen in assists with 423, total chances with 721 and double plays with 105 in 1984.
Led Southern League second basemen in putouts with 318, errors with 31, total chances with 765 and tied for lead in assists with 416 in 1983.
Led Florida State League second basemen in double plays with 96 and total chances with 742 in 1982.

Year Club League	Pos.	G.	AB.	R.	H.	2B.	3B.	HR.	RBI.	B.A.	PO.	A.	E.	F.A.
1981—Bristol..................... Appal.	2B	52	181	38	47	6	0	3	18	.260	89	169	13	.952
1982—Lakeland................ Fla. St.	2B	*136	464	86	133	17	5	12	47	.287	*298	419	25	.966
1983—Birmingham .... South.	2B-SS	144	529	96	138	22	10	10	60	.261	325	424	32	.959
1984—Evansville .... A. A.	2B-3B-SS	●153	534	82	134	21	8	11	51	.251	296	472	26	.967
1984—Detroit.................... Amer.	2B	14	35	3	4	0	1	0	1	.114	23	24	2	.959
1985—Nashville................ A. A.	*2B-3B	125	381	55	90	19	3	7	44	.236	265	338	*11	.982
Major League Totals—1 Year..................		14	35	3	4	0	1	0	1	.114	23	24	2	.959

Selected by Detroit Tigers' organization in 14th round of free-agent draft, June 8, 1981.

MICHAEL ANTHONY EASLER

(Mike)

Born November 29, 1950, at Cleveland, O.
Height, 6.01. Weight, 196.
Throws right and bats lefthanded.
Attended Cleveland State University, Cleveland, O.
Brother-in-law of Cliff Johnson, first baseman-designated hitter with Toronto Blue Jays.

Major League stolen bases: 1976 (1), 1980 (5), 1981 (4), 1982 (1), 1983 (4), 1984 (1). Total—16.
Hit for the cycle, June 12, 1980.
Tied for Southern League lead in being hit by pitch with 8 in 1972.
Tied for American Association lead in double plays by outfielders with 4 in 1976.

Year Club	League	Pos.	G.	AB.	R.	H.	2B.	3B.	HR.	RBI.	B.A.	PO.	A.	E.	F.A.
1969—Covington	Appal.	OF-3B	33	113	21	36	7	2	0	11	.319	25	10	4	.897
1970—Cocoa†	Fla. St.	OF	96	314	30	79	11	4	1	24	.252	142	5	7	.955
1971—Cocoa‡	Fla. St.	OF	109	392	61	115	15	5	11	68	.293	153	14	8	.954
1972—Columbus	South.	OF	106	372	52	100	11	4	13	46	.269	149	7	8	.951
1973—Columbus	South.	OF	48	168	27	52	11	1	6	32	.310	81	2	1	.988
1973—Denver	A. A.	OF	48	176	24	50	11	2	7	26	.284	74	2	6	.927
1973—Houston	Nat.	OF	6	7	1	0	0	0	0	0	.000	1	0	1	.500
1974—Denver	A. A.	OF	100	367	75	104	18	8	19	63	.283	172	7	5	.973
1974—Houston	Nat.	PH	15	15	0	1	0	0	0	0	.067	0	0	0	.000
1975—Iowa§-Tulsa	A. A.	OF	113	415	69	130	31	6	15	69	.313	161	6	8	.954
1975—Houston x	Nat.	PH	5	5	0	0	0	0	0	0	.000	0	0	0	.000
1976—Tulsa y	A. A.	OF	118	378	75	133	31	2	26	77	*.352	172	*16	8	.959
1976—California z	Amer.	DH	21	54	6	13	1	1	0	4	.241	0	0	0	.000
1977—Columbus	Int.	OF	127	451	83	136	29	5	18	75	.302	171	7	3	.983
1977—Pittsburgh	Nat.	OF	10	18	3	8	2	0	1	5	.444	7	0	0	1.000
1978—Columbus ab	Int.	OF-1B	126	448	84	148	26	3	18	84	*.330	378	31	5	.988
1979—Pittsburgh	Nat.	OF	55	54	8	15	1	1	2	11	.278	0	0	0	.000
1980—Pittsburgh	Nat.	OF	132	393	66	133	27	3	21	74	.338	201	6	3	.996
1981—Pittsburgh	Nat.	OF	95	339	43	97	18	5	7	42	.286	188	13	4	.980
1982—Pittsburgh	Nat.	OF	142	475	52	131	27	2	15	58	.276	243	8	7	.973
1983—Pittsburgh cd	Nat.	OF	115	381	44	117	17	2	10	54	.307	158	6	6	.965
1984—Boston	Amer.	1B	156	601	87	188	31	5	27	91	.313	256	29	7	.976
1985—Boston	Amer.	OF	155	568	71	149	29	4	16	74	.262	32	0	3	.914
National League Totals—9 Years			575	1687	217	502	92	13	56	244	.298	798	33	21	.975
American League Totals—3 Years			332	1223	164	350	61	10	43	169	.286	288	29	10	.969
Major League Totals—12 Years			907	2910	381	852	153	23	99	413	.293	1086	62	31	.974

Selected by Houston Astros' organization in 6th round of free-agent draft, June 5, 1969.
†On temporary inactive list, May 13 to May 25, 1970.
‡On temporary inactive list, May 25 to June 14, 1971.
§Loaned to St. Louis Cardinals' organization, June 25, 1975.
xTraded to St. Louis Cardinals for Pitcher Mike Barlow, September 30, 1975.
yTraded to California Angels for a player to be named later, September 3, 1976; St. Louis Cardinals acquired Infielder Ron Farkas to complete deal, September 7, 1976.
zTraded to Pittsburgh Pirates for Pitcher Randy Sealy, April 4, 1977.
aSold to Boston Red Sox, October 27, 1978.
bTraded to Pittsburgh Pirates for Outfielder George Hill and Pitcher Martin Rivas, March 15, 1979.
cOn disabled list, August 11 to September 2, 1983.
dTraded to Boston Red Sox for Pitcher John Tudor, December 6, 1983.

CHAMPIONSHIP SERIES RECORD

Year Club	League	Pos.	G.	AB.	R.	H.	2B.	3B.	HR.	RBI.	B.A.	PO.	A.	E.	F.A.
1979—Pittsburgh	Nat.	PH	1	1	0	0	0	0	0	0	.000	0	0	0	.000

WORLD SERIES RECORD

Year Club	League	Pos.	G.	AB.	R.	H.	2B.	3B.	HR.	RBI.	B.A.	PO.	A.	E.	F.A.
1979—Pittsburgh	Nat.	PH	2	1	0	0	0	0	0	0	.000	0	0	0	.000

ALL-STAR GAME RECORD

Year League	Pos.	AB.	R.	H.	2B.	3B.	HR.	RBI.	B.A.	PO.	A.	E.	F.A.
1981—National	OF	1	1	0	0	0	0	0	.000	0	0	0	.000

JAMES MORRIS EASTERLY
(Jamie)

Born February 17, 1953, at Houston, Tex.
Height, 5.10. Weight, 180.
Throws and bats lefthanded.
Attended Sam Houston State University, Huntsville, Tex.

Pitched seven-inning, 10-0 perfect game against Iowa, July 14, 1979.
Major League saves: 1977 (1), 1978 (1), 1981 (4), 1982 (2), 1983 (4), 1984 (2). Total—14.

Year Club	League	G.	IP.	W.	L.	Pct.	H.	R.	ER.	SO.	BB.	ERA.
1971—Greenwood	W. Carol.	8	29	3	0	1.000	14	3	2	33	9	0.62
1972—Greenwood	W. Carol.	7	24	1	0	1.000	11	0	0	29	13	0.00
1972—Savannah†	Southern	2	4	0	1	.000	7	2	2	4	4	4.50
1973—Savannah‡	Southern	15	67	5	3	.625	62	40	28	53	41	3.76
1974—Richmond	Int'national	26	138	9	6	.600	115	48	39	84	75	2.54
1974—Atlanta	National	3	3	0	0	.000	6	7	5	0	4	15.00
1975—Atlanta	Int'national	2	10	1	1	.500	11	3	2	4	6	1.80
1975—Atlanta	National	21	69	2	9	.182	73	47	38	34	42	4.96
1976—Richmond	Int'national	33	137	7	6	.583	133	56	45	91	88	2.96
1976—Atlanta	National	4	22	1	1	.500	23	12	12	11	13	4.91
1977—Atlanta§	National	22	59	2	4	.333	72	46	40	37	30	6.10
1978—Atlanta	National	37	78	3	6	.333	91	52	49	42	45	5.65
1979—Richmond	Int'national	10	13	0	0	.000	5	0	0	12	7	0.00
1979—Atlanta xy	National	4	3	0	0	.000	7	6	4	3	3	12.00

Year Club	League	G.	IP.	W.	L.	Pct.	H.	R.	ER.	SO.	BB.	ERA.
1979—Denver	Am. Assoc.	20	88	5	6	.455	100	40	32	55	39	3.27
1980—Denver z	Am. Assoc.	56	134	9	8	.529	118	64	54	105	56	3.63
1981—Milwaukee	American	44	62	3	3	.500	46	23	22	31	34	3.19
1982—Milwaukee a	American	28	30⅔	0	2	.000	39	19	16	16	15	4.70
1983—Milwaukee bc-Cleveland d	American	53	68⅔	4	3	.571	83	32	28	45	32	3.67
1984—Cleveland e	American	26	69⅓	3	1	.750	74	31	26	42	23	3.38
1985—Cleveland f	American	50	98⅔	4	1	.800	96	52	43	58	53	3.92
National League Totals—6 Years		91	234	8	20	.286	272	170	148	127	137	5.69
American League Totals—5 Years		201	329⅓	14	10	.583	338	157	135	192	157	3.69
Major League Totals—11 Years		292	563⅓	22	30	.423	610	327	283	319	294	4.52

Selected by Atlanta Braves' organization in 2nd round of free-agent draft, June 8, 1971.

†On disabled list, April 11 to April 27, July 7 to July 28 and August 5, 1972 through remainder of season.

‡On disabled list, April 24 to May 12 and May 24 to July 9, 1973.

§On disabled list, June 6 to July 4 and July 21 to September 19, 1977.

xLoaned to Denver (Montreal Expos' organization), June 6, 1979; returned, August 31, 1979.

ySold to Montreal Expos, October 17, 1979.

zSold to Milwaukee Brewers, September 22, 1980.

aOn disabled list, July 12 to September 1, 1982.

bHad a sacrifice bunt and a ground out in only plate appearances during season when designated hitter took the field.

cTraded with Outfielder Gorman Thomas and Pitcher Ernie Camacho to Cleveland Indians for Outfielder Rick Manning and Pitcher Rick Waits, June 6, 1983.

dGranted free agency, November 7, 1983; re-signed by Indians, January 17, 1984.

eOn disabled list, March 25 to June 15, 1984.

fGranted free agency, November 12, 1985; re-signed by Indians, January 8, 1986.

DIVISION SERIES RECORD

Year Club	League	G.	IP.	W.	L.	Pct.	H.	R.	ER.	SO.	BB.	ERA.
1981—Milwaukee	American	2	1⅓	0	0	.000	2	1	1	1	0	6.75

DENNIS LEE ECKERSLEY

Born October 3, 1954, at Oakland, Calif.
Height, 6.02. Weight, 195.
Throws and bats righthanded.
Son-in-law of Al Jacinto, second baseman in Chicago White Sox' organization, 1947 through 1954.

Tied American League record for most low-hit (no-hit and one-hit) games, season (3), 1977.
Pitched 1-0 no-hit victory against California Angels, May 30, 1977.
Major League saves: 1975 (2), 1976 (1). Total—3.
Led American League in home runs allowed with 30 in 1978.
Tied for American League lead in intentional bases on balls issued with 11 in 1977.
Led Texas League in hit batsmen with 10 in 1974.
Led California League pitchers in games started with 31 and tied for lead in shutouts with 5 in 1973.
Named American League Rookie Pitcher of the Year by THE SPORTING NEWS, 1975.
Received reported $32,000 bonus to sign with Cleveland Indians, 1972.

Year Club	League	G.	IP.	W.	L.	Pct.	H.	R.	ER.	SO.	BB.	ERA.
1972—Reno	California	12	75	5	5	.500	87	46	40	56	33	4.80
1973—Reno	California	31	202	12	8	.600	182	97	82	218	91	3.65
1974—San Antonio	Texas	23	167	●14	3	*.824	141	66	63	*163	60	3.40
1975—Cleveland	American	34	187	13	7	.650	147	61	54	152	90	2.60
1976—Cleveland	American	36	199	13	12	.520	155	82	76	200	78	3.44
1977—Cleveland†	American	33	247	14	13	.519	214	100	97	191	54	3.53
1978—Boston	American	35	268	20	8	.714	258	99	89	162	71	2.99
1979—Boston	American	33	247	17	10	.630	234	89	82	150	59	2.99
1980—Boston	American	30	198	12	14	.462	188	101	94	121	44	4.27
1981—Boston	American	23	154	9	8	.529	160	82	73	79	35	4.27
1982—Boston	American	33	224⅓	13	13	.500	228	101	93	127	43	3.73
1983—Boston	American	28	176½	9	13	.409	223	119	110	77	39	5.61
1984—Boston‡	American	9	64⅔	4	4	.500	71	38	36	33	13	5.01
1984—Chicago§	National	24	160⅓	10	8	.556	152	59	54	81	36	3.03
1985—Chicago x	National	25	169⅓	11	7	.611	145	61	58	117	19	3.08
American League Totals—10 Years		294	1965⅓	124	102	.549	1878	872	804	1292	526	3.68
National League Totals—2 Years		49	329⅔	21	15	.583	297	120	112	198	55	3.06
Major League Totals—11 Years		343	2295	145	117	.553	2175	992	916	1490	581	3.59

Selected by Cleveland Indians' organization in 3rd round of free-agent draft, June 6, 1972.

†Traded with Catcher Fred Kendall to Boston Red Sox for Pitchers Rick Wise and Mike Paxton, Third Baseman Ted Cox and Catcher Bo Diaz, March 30, 1978.

‡Traded with Outfielder Mike Brumley to Chicago Cubs for First Baseman-Outfielder Bill Buckner, May 25, 1984.

§Granted free agency, November 8, 1984; re-signed by Cubs, November 28, 1984.

xOn disabled list, August 11 to September 7, 1985.

CHAMPIONSHIP SERIES RECORD

Year Club	League	G.	IP.	W.	L.	Pct.	H.	R.	ER.	SO.	BB.	ERA.
1984—Chicago	National	1	5⅓	0	1	.000	9	5	5	0	0	8.44

Year League	IP.	W.	L.	Pct.	H.	R.	ER.	SO.	BB.	ERA.
1977—American	2	0	0	.000	0	0	0	1	0	0.00
1982—American	3	0	1	.000	2	3	3	1	2	9.00
All-Star Game Totals—2 Years	5	0	1	.000	2	3	3	2	2	5.40

KEVIN DANIEL ELSTER

Born August 3, 1964, at San Pedro, Calif.
Height, 6.02. Weight, 180.
Throws and bats righthanded.
Attended Golden West College, Huntington Beach, Calif.

Led New York-Pennsylvania League shortstops in double plays with 45 and total chances with 358 in 1984.

Year Club	League	Pos.	G.	AB.	R.	H.	2B.	3B.	HR.	RBI.	B.A.	PO.	A.	E.	F.A.
1984—Little Falls	NYP	SS	71	257	35	66	7	3	3	35	.257	★128	214	16	★.955
1985—Lynchburg	Carol.	SS	59	224	41	66	9	0	7	26	.295	82	195	16	.945
1985—Jackson†	Texas	SS	59	214	30	55	13	0	2	22	.257	107	220	10	.970

Selected by New York Mets' organization in 2nd round of free-agent draft, January 17, 1984.
†On disabled list, August 11, 1985 through remainder of season.

STEVEN MICHAEL ENGEL
(Steve)

Born December 31, 1961, at Cincinnati, O.
Height, 6.00. Weight, 180.
Throws left and bats righthanded.
Attended Eastern Kentucky University, Richmond, Ky.

Major League saves: 1985 (1).

Year Club	League	G.	IP.	W.	L.	Pct.	H.	R.	ER.	SO.	BB.	ERA.
1983—Geneva	NYP	11	72	7	2	.778	61	31	29	77	21	3.63
1984—Lodi	California	27	171	11	7	.611	141	63	51	153	78	2.68
1985—Pittsfield	Eastern	12	76⅓	3	6	.333	67	36	33	52	44	3.89
1985—Iowa	Am. Assoc.	10	61⅓	4	2	.667	55	26	22	53	34	3.23
1985—Chicago	National	11	51⅔	1	5	.167	61	36	32	29	26	5.57
Major League Totals—1 Year		11	51⅔	1	5	.167	61	36	32	29	26	5.57

Selected by Milwaukee Brewers' organization in 9th round of free-agent draft, June 3, 1980.
Selected by Chicago Cubs' organization in 5th round of free-agent draft, June 6, 1983.

RALPH DAVID ENGLE
(Dave)

Born November 30, 1956, at San Diego, Calif.
Height, 6.03. Weight, 216.
Throws and bats righthanded.
Attended University of Southern California, Los Angeles, Calif.

Major League stolen bases: 1983 (2), 1985 (2). Total—4.

Year Club	League	Pos.	G.	AB.	R.	H.	2B.	3B.	HR.	RBI.	B.A.	PO.	A.	E.	F.A.
1978—Salinas†	Calif.	3B	53	203	34	62	11	0	6	40	.305	20	65	10	.895
1979—Toledo	Int.	3B	106	363	46	104	17	1	7	51	.287	72	197	23	.921
1980—Toledo	Int.	OF	133	489	74	150	27	3	7	73	★.307	225	16	5	.980
1981—Minnesota	Amer.	OF-3B	82	248	29	64	14	4	5	32	.258	144	4	3	.980
1982—Minnesota	Amer.	OF	58	186	20	42	7	2	4	16	.226	63	3	1	.985
1982—Toledo	Int.	OF	9	34	14	15	1	1	5	12	.441	15	4	0	1.000
1983—Minnesota	Amer.	C-OF	120	374	46	114	22	4	8	43	.305	306	26	9	.974
1984—Minnesota	Amer.	C	109	391	56	104	20	1	4	38	.266	376	34	8	.981
1985—Minnesota‡	Amer.	C-OF	70	172	28	44	8	2	7	25	.256	66	4	1	.986
Major League Totals—5 Years			439	1371	179	368	71	13	28	154	.268	955	71	22	.979

Selected by California Angels' organization in 2nd round of free-agent draft, June 6, 1978.
†Traded with Outfielder Ken Landreaux and Pitchers Paul Hartzell and Brad Havens to Minnesota Twins for First Baseman Rod Carew, February 3, 1979.
‡Traded to Detroit Tigers for Infielder Chris Pittaro and Outfielder Alex Sanchez, January 16, 1986.

Member of American League All-Star Team in 1984; did not play.

JAMES GERHARD EPPARD
(Jim)

Born April 27, 1960, at South Bend, Ind.
Height, 6.02. Weight, 180.
Throws and bats lefthanded.
Attended Citrus College, Azusa, Calif., and University of California, Berkeley, Calif.

Tied for California League lead in grounding into double plays with 19 in 1985.
Led California League first basemen in total chances with 1,341 in 1985.

Year	Club	League	Pos.	G.	AB.	R.	H.	2B.	3B.	HR.	RBI.	B.A.	PO.	A.	E.	F.A.
1982—Medford	N'west	★1B-OF	64	242	58	★91	13	2	1	41	★.376	459	★38	10	.980
1983—Modesto	Calif.	1B	134	488	68	138	18	4	4	45	.283	1086	74	10	★.991
1984—Albany	East.	OF-1B	118	417	58	130	14	6	0	51	.312	551	41	4	.993
1985—Modesto	Calif.	1B	141	531	97	★183	23	4	3	88	★.345	1204	★125	12	.991

Selected by Chicago Cubs' organization in 11th round of free-agent draft, January 8, 1980.
Selected by Oakland A's organization in 13th round of free-agent draft, June 7, 1982.

NICHOLAS ANDREW ESASKY

Name pronounced Ee-SASS-kee.

(Nick)

Born February 24, 1960, at Hialeah, Fla.
Height, 6.03. Weight, 200.
Throws and bats righthanded.

Major League stolen bases: 1983 (6), 1984 (1), 1985 (3). Total—10.
Led Eastern League batters in strikeouts with 131 and game-winning RBIs with 14 in 1980.

Year	Club	League	Pos.	G.	AB.	R.	H.	2B.	3B.	HR.	RBI.	B.A.	PO.	A.	E.	F.A.
1978—Billings	Pion.	3B	64	213	38	65	10	5	4	48	.305	★62	88	22	.872
1979—Tampa	Fla. St.	3B	124	439	52	118	16	3	10	66	.269	91	234	27	.923
1980—Waterbury	East.	3B	135	425	79	115	18	4	★30	79	.271	98	241	23	.936
1981—Indianapolis	A. A.	3B	121	423	55	112	22	4	17	62	.265	99	220	★37	.896
1982—Indianapolis	A. A.	3B	105	341	59	90	15	3	27	62	.264	77	150	21	★.915
1983—Indianapolis	A. A.	3B	49	158	33	44	5	0	14	37	.278	27	71	14	.875
1983—Cincinnati	Nat.	3B	85	302	41	80	10	5	12	46	.265	53	133	13	.935
1984—Cincinnati	Nat.	3B-1B	113	322	30	62	10	5	10	45	.193	220	137	18	.952
1985—Cincinnati	Nat.	3B-OF-1B	125	413	61	108	21	0	21	66	.262	169	106	8	.972
Major League Totals—3 Years			323	1037	132	250	41	10	43	157	.241	442	376	39	.954

Selected by Cincinnati Reds' organization in 1st round (17th player selected) of free-agent draft, June 6, 1978.

ANGEL RUBEN ESCOBAR (RIVAS)

Born May 12, 1965, at La Sabana, Venezuela.
Height, 6.01. Weight, 160.
Throws right and bats left and righthanded.

Led Midwest League shortstops in double plays with 71 in 1984.

Year	Club	League	Pos.	G.	AB.	R.	H.	2B.	3B.	HR.	RBI.	B.A.	PO.	A.	E.	F.A.
1983—Great Falls	Pion.	SS-2B	44	109	15	23	3	1	0	6	.211	50	64	17	.870
1984—Clinton	Midw.	SS	99	311	47	70	16	2	2	25	.225	175	295	★48	.907
1985—Fresno	Calif.	SS-2B	109	386	62	97	13	2	1	34	.251	174	290	36	.928

Signed as free agent by San Francisco Giants' organization, June 10, 1982.

JOSE ELIAS ESCOBAR (SANCHEZ)

Born October 30, 1960, at Las Flores, Venezuela.
Height, 5.10. Weight, 140.
Throws and bats righthanded.

Led Carolina League in sacrifice hits with 13 in 1983.

Year	Club	League	Pos.	G.	AB.	R.	H.	2B.	3B.	HR.	RBI.	B.A.	PO.	A.	E.	F.A.
1979—Utica	NYP	SS-2B	62	204	44	54	5	3	2	21	.265	123	131	22	.920
1980—Utica	NYP	SS-2B	67	231	23	54	5	3	2	27	.234	90	182	24	.919
1981—Kinston	Carol.	SS-2B	56	192	22	48	5	0	1	16	.250	75	154	16	.935
1981—Florence	S. Atl.	SS-3B	35	105	12	25	3	0	0	4	.238	31	72	12	.896
1982—Kinston	Carol.	SS-2B	84	225	30	54	9	0	0	16	.240	89	175	17	.940
1983—Kinston	Carol.	SS-2B-3B	125	458	47	122	18	4	2	49	.266	211	382	27	.956
1984—Knoxville†	South.	S-3-2-O	96	340	40	80	13	4	1	45	.235	119	275	15	.963
1985—Reading	East.	SS-3B-2B	40	122	17	31	4	0	1	8	.254	39	85	10	.925
1985—Portland‡	P. C.	SS-2B-3B	46	109	21	35	4	2	1	8	.321	50	114	7	.959

Signed as free agent by Toronto Blue Jays' organization, November 27, 1978.

†Traded with Outfielder Ken Kinnard and Pitcher Dave Shipanoff to Philadelphia Phillies' organization for First Baseman Len Matuszek, April 1, 1985.

‡Released, December 12, 1985.

JUAN ESPINO (REYES)

Born March 16, 1956, at Bonao, Dominican Republic.
Height, 6.00. Weight, 185.
Throws and bats righthanded.

Led New York-Pennsylvania League batters in strikeouts with 61 in 1975.
Led International League in passed balls with 13 in 1985 and tied for lead with 10 in 1983.

Year	Club	League	Pos.	G.	AB.	R.	H.	2B.	3B.	HR.	RBI.	B.A.	PO.	A.	E.	F.A.
1975—Oneonta	NYP	C-OF	48	157	24	36	5	5	2	23	.229	26	3	2	.935
1976—Fort Lauderdale†	Fla. St.	C	39	118	18	30	5	3	4	20	.254	170	20	3	.984
1977—Fort Lauderdale	Fla. St.	C	52	141	8	28	8	0	0	16	.199	266	40	9	.971
1978—West Haven	East.	C	82	261	32	73	14	0	6	37	.280	426	44	6	★.987
1979—West Haven	East.	C	95	296	40	70	11	1	8	44	.236	509	57	13	.978
1980—Nashville	South.	C	17	56	3	9	1	0	0	9	.161	115	6	2	.984
1980—Columbus	Int.	C	48	129	11	27	7	1	1	16	.209	238	29	5	.982
1981—Columbus	Int.	C	80	253	22	59	8	2	7	32	.233	434	53	8	.984

Year Club	League	Pos.	G.	AB.	R.	H.	2B.	3B.	HR.	RBI.	B.A.	PO.	A.	E.	F.A.
1982—Columbus‡...........	Int.	C	54	163	30	46	10	1	3	27	.282	264	34	5	.983
1982—New York.............	Amer.	C	3	2	0	0	0	0	0	0	.000	4	0	0	1.000
1983—Columbus...........	Int.	C	77	211	35	59	10	1	10		.280	326	42	7	.981
1983—New York§.........	Amer.	C	10	23	1	6	0	0	1	3	.261	38	1	0	1.000
1984—Maine x	Int.	C	97	327	38	82	6	1	7	41	.251	432	47	11	.978
1985—Columbus.........	Int.	C	74	224	30	56	11	0	3	20	.250	349	46	7	.983
1985—New York..........	Amer.	C	9	11	0	4	0	0	0	0	.364	16	4	0	1.000
Major League Totals—3 Years.................			22	36	1	10	0	0	1	3	.278	58	5	0	1.000

Signed as free agent by New York Yankees' organization, December 26, 1974.
†On disabled list, May 26 to June 9, 1976.
‡On disabled list, August 3 to August 23, 1982.
§Sold to Cleveland Indians' organization, March 31, 1984.
xSold to Columbus (New York Yankees' organization), January 8, 1985.

ALVARO ALBERTO ESPINOZA (RAMIREZ)
Name pronounced Ess-pin-OH-zuh.

Born February 19, 1962, at Valencia, Carabobo, Venezuela.
Height, 6.00. Weight, 170.
Throws and bats righthanded.
Tied for International League lead in sacrifice hits with 16 in 1984.
Led California League shortstops in total chances with 000 in 1983.
Led Gulf Coast League shortstops in assists with 217, double plays with 33 and total chances with 356 in 1980.

Year Club	League	Pos.	G.	AB.	R.	H.	2B.	3B.	HR.	RBI.	B.A.	PO.	A.	E.	F.A.
1979—Sarasota Astros....	Gulf C.	SS-2B-3B	11	32	3	7	0	0	0	5	.219	18	27	1	.978
1980—Sara. Astros-O.†....	Gulf C.	*SS-3B	59	200	24	43	5	0	0	14	.215	*114	219	*25	.930
1981—..................................						(Out of Organized Baseball)									
1982—Wis. Rapids...........	Midw.	SS-3B-1B	112	379	41	101	9	0	5	29	.266	237	241	33	.935
1983—Visalia	Calif.	SS	130	486	57	155	20	1	4	57	.319	*256	364	40	.939
1984—Toledo‡	Int.	SS	104	344	22	80	12	5	0	30	.233	157	293	19	.959
1985—Toledo§	Int.	SS	82	266	24	61	11	0	1	33	.229	132	245	16	.959
1985—Minnesota...........	Amer.	SS	32	57	5	15	2	0	0	9	.263	25	69	5	.949
Major League Totals—1 Year.................			32	57	5	15	2	0	0	9	.263	25	69	5	.949

Signed as free agent by Houston Astros' organization, October 30, 1978.
†Released, September 30, 1980; signed by Wisconsin Rapids (Minnesota Twins' organization), March 18, 1982.
‡On disabled list, June 7 to June 25, 1984.
§On disabled list, June 6 to July 2, 1985.

CECIL EDWARD ESPY

Born January 20, 1963, at San Diego, Calif.
Height, 6.03. Weight, 190.
Throws right and bats left and righthanded.
Son of Cecil Espy, scout with St. Louis Cardinals since 1979.
Led Florida State League in stolen bases with 74 in 1982.
Tied for Texas League lead in caught stealing with 17 in 1985.
Led Texas League shortstops in errors with 50 in 1985.
Led Texas League outfielders in total chances with 365 in 1984.

Year Club	League	Pos.	G.	AB.	R.	H.	2B.	3B.	HR.	RBI.	B.A.	PO.	A.	E.	F.A.
1980—Sarasota W. Sox...	Gulf C.	OF	58	212	33	58	7	3	0	26	.274	138	4	7	.953
1981—Appleton	Midw.	OF	72	273	37	55	2	2	1	19	.201	143	5	5	.967
1981—Sarasota W. Sox†.	Gulf C.	OF	43	142	24	40	3	1	0	16	.282	54	1	4	.932
1982—Vero Beach..........	Fla. St.	OF	131	*523	*100	*166	14	7	1	34	.317	275	9	10	.966
1983—San Antonio..........	Texas	OF	133	*564	88	151	16	11	4	38	.268	258	12	10	.964
1983—Los Angeles	Nat.	OF	20	11	4	3	1	0	0	1	.273	11	0	0	1.000
1984—San Antonio.........	Texas	*O-2-S	*133	*535	99	146	19	8	8	60	.273	*348	16	5	.986
1985—San Antonio‡.........	Texas	SS-OF	124	461	64	129	24	3	5	49	.280	183	346	51	.912
Major League Totals—1 Year.................			20	11	4	3	1	0	0	1	.273	11	0	0	1.000

Selected by Chicago White Sox' organization in 1st round (eighth player selected) of free-agent draft, June 3, 1980.
†Traded with Pitcher Burt Geiger to Los Angeles Dodgers' organization for Outfielder Rudy Law, March 30, 1982.
‡Traded with First Baseman Sid Bream to Pittsburgh Pirates, September 9, 1985, completing deal in which Los Angeles Dodgers acquired Third Baseman Bill Madlock for three players to be named later, R. J. Reynolds as partial completion of deal, September 3, 1985.

FRANK ANTHONY EUFEMIA III

Born December 23, 1959, at Bronx, N.Y.
Height, 5.11. Weight, 180.
Throws and bats righthanded.
Attended Ramapo College of New Jersey, Mahwah, N. J.
Major League saves: 1985 (2).
Led California League in games finished in relief with 53 in 1983.

Year Club	League	G.	IP.	W.	L.	Pct.	H.	R.	ER.	SO.	BB.	ERA.
1982—Wisconsin Rapids.........	Midwest	27	58	2	1	.667	47	18	11	36	17	1.71
1983—Visalia	California	*64	95⅔	10	4	.714	79	27	26	78	29	2.45
1984—Orlando	Southern	45	75	6	4	.600	74	30	24	42	23	2.88
1985—Toledo	Int'national	14	36⅓	3	1	.750	23	6	6	23	12	1.49
1985—Minnesota	American	39	61⅔	4	2	.667	56	27	26	30	21	3.79
Major League Totals—1 Year..............		39	61⅔	4	2	.667	56	27	26	30	21	3.79

Selected by Minnesota Twins' organization in 18th round of free-agent draft, June 7, 1982.

DARRELL WAYNE EVANS

Born May 26, 1947, at Pasadena, Calif.
Height, 6.02. Weight, 205.
Throws right and bats lefthanded.
Attended Pasadena City College, Pasadena, Calif. and
California State University, Los Angeles, Calif.
Grandson of David Salazar, former minor league player.

Established National League records for most double plays, third baseman, (45), 1974; most games, consecutive, one or more bases on balls (15), April 9 through 27, 1976.

Tied modern National League record for most errors in inning by third baseman (3), April 11, 1980 (7th inning).

Major League stolen bases: 1971 (2), 1972 (4), 1973 (6), 1974 (4), 1975 (12), 1976 (9), 1977 (9), 1978 (4), 1979 (6), 1980 (17), 1981 (2), 1982 (5), 1983 (6), 1984 (2). Total—88.

Hit three home runs in a game, June 15, 1983.

Led National League in bases on balls received with 124 in 1973 and 126 in 1974.

Led National League third basemen in putouts with 161 and assists with 381 in 1975.

Led National League third basemen in double plays with 45 in 1974 and 41 in 1975.

Led National League third basemen in total chances with 471 in 1973, 578 in 1974, 578 in 1975, 520 in 1978 and 528 in 1979.

Led International League third basemen in fielding percentage with .951 in 1970.

Named third baseman on THE SPORTING NEWS National League All-Star Team, 1973.

Named Player of the Year in Gulf Coast League, 1967.

Year Club	League	Pos.	G.	AB.	R.	H.	2B.	3B.	HR.	RBI.	B.A.	PO.	A.	E.	F.A.
1967—Peninsula	Carol.	3B	8	28	4	11	1	1	0	6	.393	6	13	2	.905
1967—Bradenton A's	Gulf C.	3B-SS	14	45	13	22	3	3	2	11	.489	25	30	2	.965
1967—Leesburg	Fla. St.	3B-SS	39	142	18	37	4	2	0	12	.261	49	81	11	.922
1968—Birmingham†	South.	3B-1B-2B	56	187	18	45	6	3	3	25	.241	103	101	10	.953
1969—Richmond	Int.	3B	59	211	43	76	12	4	7	45	.360	51	103	19	.890
1969—Shreveport	Texas	3B-SS-OF	24	79	14	22	5	4	2	14	.278	25	40	3	.956
1969—Atlanta	Nat.	3B	12	26	3	6	0	0	0	1	.231	4	7	1	.917
1970—Richmond	Int.	3B-1B-OF	120	447	92	134	20	7	20	83	.300	99	220	16	.952
1970—Atlanta	Nat.	3B	12	44	4	14	1	1	0	9	.318	6	26	2	.941
1971—Richmond	Int.	OF-3B	31	101	20	31	2	2	6	30	.307	59	11	1	.986
1971—Atlanta	Nat.	3B-OF	89	260	42	63	11	1	12	38	.242	77	138	14	.939
1972—Atlanta‡	Nat.	3B	125	418	67	106	12	0	19	71	.254	126	273	25	.941
1973—Atlanta	Nat.	3B-1B	161	595	114	167	25	8	41	104	.281	266	335	24	.962
1974—Atlanta	Nat.	3B	160	571	99	137	21	3	25	79	.240	★185	367	26	.955
1975—Atlanta	Nat.	★3B-1B	156	567	82	138	22	2	22	73	.243	164	382	★36	.938
1976—Atl.§-S.F.	Nat.	1B-3B	136	396	53	81	9	1	11	46	.205	978	110	10	.991
1977—San Francisco	Nat.	OF-1B-3B	144	461	64	117	18	3	17	72	.254	324	83	13	.969
1978—San Francisco	Nat.	3B	159	547	82	133	24	2	20	78	.243	★147	★348	★25	.952
1979—San Francisco	Nat.	3B	160	562	68	142	23	2	17	70	.253	★129	★369	★30	.943
1980—San Francisco	Nat.	3B-1B	154	556	69	147	23	0	20	78	.264	232	340	27	.955
1981—San Francisco	Nat.	3B-1B	102	357	51	92	13	4	12	48	.258	188	202	14	.965
1982—San Francisco	Nat.	3B-1B-SS	141	465	64	119	20	4	16	61	.256	471	233	21	.971
1983—San Francisco y	Nat.	1B-3B-SS	142	523	94	145	29	3	30	82	.277	1001	164	19	.984
1984—Detroit	Amer.	1B-3B	131	401	60	93	11	1	16	63	.232	331	62	2	.995
1985—Detroit	Amer.	1B-3B	151	505	81	125	17	0	★40	94	.248	831	125	20	.980
National League Totals—15 Years			1853	6348	956	1607	251	34	262	910	.253	4298	3377	287	.964
American League Totals—2 Years			282	906	141	218	28	1	56	157	.241	1162	187	22	.984
Major League Totals—17 Years			2135	7254	1097	1825	279	35	318	1067	.252	5460	3564	309	.967

Selected by Chicago Cubs' organization in 8th round of free-agent draft, June 22, 1965.

Selected by New York Yankees' organization in secondary phase of free-agent draft, January 29, 1966.

Selected by Detroit Tigers' organization in 5th round of free-agent draft, June 6, 1966.

Selected by Philadelphia Phillies' organization in 3rd round of free-agent draft, January 28, 1967.

Selected by Kansas City A's organization in secondary phase of free-agent draft, June 7, 1967.

†Drafted by Atlanta Braves, December 2, 1968.

‡On military list, June 17 to July 3, 1972.

§Traded with Shortstop Marty Perez to San Francisco Giants for First Baseman-Outfielder Willie Montanez, Shortstop Craig Robinson, Infielder Mike Eden and Outfielder Jake Brown, June 13, 1976.

xGranted free agency, November 2, 1978; re-signed by Giants, December 5, 1978.

yGranted free agency, November 7, 1983; signed by Detroit Tigers, December 17, 1983.

CHAMPIONSHIP SERIES RECORD

Year Club	League	Pos.	G.	AB.	R.	H.	2B.	3B.	HR.	RBI.	B.A.	PO.	A.	E.	F.A.
1984—Detroit	Amer.	1B-3B	3	10	1	3	1	0	0	1	.300	22	4	0	1.000

WORLD SERIES RECORD

Year Club	League	Pos.	G.	AB.	R.	H.	2B.	3B.	HR.	RBI.	B.A.	PO.	A.	E.	F.A.
1984—Detroit	Amer.	1B-3B	5	15	1	1	0	0	0	1	.067	18	5	0	1.000

ALL-STAR GAME RECORD

Year League	Pos.	AB.	R.	H.	2B.	3B.	HR.	RBI.	B.A.	PO.	A.	E.	F.A.
1973—National	PH	0	0	0	0	0	0	0	.000	0	0	0	.000
1983—National	1B	1	0	0	0	0	0	0	.000	2	1	0	1.000
All-Star Game Totals—2 Years		1	0	0	0	0	0	0	.000	2	1	0	1.000

—DID YOU KNOW—
That the 1985 California Angels were 30-13 in one-run games?

DWIGHT MICHAEL EVANS

Born November 3, 1951, at Santa Monica, Calif.
Height, 6.03. Weight, 205.
Throws and bats righthanded.

Major League stolen bases: 1973 (5), 1974 (4), 1975 (3), 1976 (6), 1977 (4), 1978 (8), 1979 (6), 1980 (3), 1981 (3), 1982 (3), 1983 (3), 1984 (3), 1985 (7). Total—58.
Hit for the cycle, June 28, 1984.
Led American League in bases on balls received with 85 in 1981 and 114 in 1985.
Led American League in total bases with 215 in 1981.
Led American League outfielders in double plays with 8 in 1975 and 7 in 1980.
Led Western Carolinas League in sacrifice flies with 8 in 1970.
Tied for Carolina League lead in double plays by outfielders with 3 in 1971.
Named outfielder on THE SPORTING NEWS American League All-Star Team, 1982 and 1984.
Named outfielder on THE SPORTING NEWS American League All-Star fielding team, 1976, 1978, 1979 and 1981 through 1985.
Named outfielder on THE SPORTING NEWS American League Silver Slugger team, 1981.
Named International League Most Valuable Player, 1972.

Year	Club	League	Pos.	G.	AB.	R.	H.	2B.	3B.	HR.	RBI.	B.A.	PO.	A.	E.	F.A.
1969—Jamestown		NYP	OF-3B	34	100	13	28	3	2	1	12	.280	44	10	3	.947
1970—Greenville		W. Car.	OF-3B	108	355	69	98	14	*11	7	68	.276	130	11	7	.953
1971—Winston-Salem		Carol.	OF-1B	118	402	63	115	20	4	12	63	.286	219	17	10	.959
1972—Louisville		Int.	OF	●144	496	90	149	22	8	17	●95	.300	270	13	6	.070
1972—Boston		Amer.	OF	18	57	2	15	3	1	1	6	.263	25	3	0	1.000
1973—Boston		Amer.	OF	119	282	46	63	13	1	10	32	.223	178	4	1	.995
1974—Boston		Amer.	OF	133	463	60	130	19	8	10	70	.281	294	8	3	.990
1975—Boston		Amer.	OF	128	412	61	113	24	6	13	56	.274	281	15	4	.987
1976—Boston		Amer.	OF	146	501	61	121	34	5	17	62	.242	324	15	2	*.994
1977—Boston†		Amer.	OF	73	230	39	66	9	2	14	36	.287	126	2	1	.992
1978—Boston		Amer.	OF	147	497	75	123	24	2	24	63	.247	305	14	6	.982
1979—Boston		Amer.	OF	152	489	69	134	24	1	21	58	.274	307	15	4	.988
1980—Boston		Amer.	OF	148	463	72	123	37	5	18	60	.266	281	11	5	.982
1981—Boston		Amer.	OF	108	412	84	122	19	4	●22	71	.296	259	9	2	.993
1982—Boston		Amer.	OF	●162	609	122	178	37	7	32	98	.292	346	9	10	.973
1983—Boston‡		Amer.	OF	126	470	74	112	19	4	22	58	.238	222	6	3	.987
1984—Boston		Amer.	OF	●162	630	*121	186	37	8	32	104	.295	311	7	2	.994
1985—Boston		Amer.	OF	159	617	110	162	29	1	29	78	.263	291	9	3	.990
Major League Totals—14 Years				1781	6132	996	1648	328	55	265	852	.269	3537	127	46	.988

Selected by Boston Red Sox' organization in 5th round of free-agent draft, June 5, 1969.
†On disabled list, June 21 to July 8 and August 25 to September 21, 1977.
‡On disabled list, August 13 to September 1, 1983.

CHAMPIONSHIP SERIES RECORD

Year	Club	League	Pos.	G.	AB.	R.	H.	2B.	3B.	HR.	RBI.	B.A.	PO.	A.	E.	F.A.
1975—Boston		Amer.	OF	3	10	1	1	1	0	0	0	.100	7	0	0	1.000

WORLD SERIES RECORD

Tied World Series record for highest fielding average by outfielder, seven-game Series (1.000 with 24 chances), 1975.

Year	Club	League	Pos.	G.	AB.	R.	H.	2B.	3B.	HR.	RBI.	B.A.	PO.	A.	E.	F.A.
1975—Boston		Amer.	OF	7	24	3	7	1	1	1	5	.292	23	1	0	1.000

ALL-STAR GAME RECORD

Year	League	Pos.	AB.	R.	H.	2B.	3B.	HR.	RBI.	B.A.	PO.	A.	E.	F.A.
1978—American		OF	1	0	0	0	0	0	0	.000	3	0	0	1.000
1981—American		PH-OF	2	1	1	0	0	0	0	.500	2	0	0	1.000
All-Star Game Totals—2 Years			3	1	1	0	0	0	0	.333	5	0	0	1.000

ROBERT JOSEPH FALLON
(Bob)

Born February 18, 1960, at New York, N.Y.
Height, 6.03. Weight, 205.
Throws and bats lefthanded.
Attended Miami-Dade Community College-North, Miami, Fla.

Tied for Eastern League lead in games started by pitchers with 27 in 1982.

Year	Club	League	G.	IP.	W.	L.	Pct.	H.	R.	ER.	SO.	BB.	ERA.
1979—Niagara Falls		NYP	15	83	3	7	.300	70	48	32	52	66	3.47
1980—Appleton		Midwest	22	122	11	5	.688	103	62	48	103	82	3.54
1981—Glens Falls		Eastern	26	135	11	9	.550	155	*112	81	81	78	5.40
1982—Glens Falls		Eastern	28	147⅔	9	9	.500	142	90	78	119	87	4.75
1983—Denver†		Am. Assoc.	24	138⅓	10	5	.667	119	74	66	105	73	4.29
1984—Denver‡		Am. Assoc.	19	115½	5	8	.385	101	63	48	101	58	3.75
1984—Chicago		American	3	14⅔	0	0	.000	12	7	6	10	11	3.68
1985—Buffalo		Am. Assoc.	15	80	3	8	.273	94	53	38	60	40	4.28
1985—Chicago		American	10	16	0	0	.000	25	11	11	17	9	6.19
Major League Totals—2 Years			13	30⅔	0	0	.000	37	18	17	27	20	4.99

Selected by Oakland A's organization in 2nd round of free-agent draft, January 9, 1979.

Selected by Chicago White Sox' organization in secondary phase of free-agent draft, June 5, 1979.
†On disabled list, July 13 to July 24, 1983.
‡On disabled list, August 20 to September 3, 1984.

STANLEY ROBERT FANSLER
(Stan)

Born February 12, 1965, at Elkins, W. Va.
Height, 5.11. Weight, 180.
Throws and bats righthanded.

Year Club	League	G.	IP.	W.	L.	Pct.	H.	R.	ER.	SO.	BB.	ERA.
1983—Watertown	NYP	14	57	0	*10	.000	79	69	51	49	28	8.05
1984—Watertown	NYP	14	98⅔	5	1	.833	68	32	22	78	38	2.01
1985—Nashua	Eastern	24	158⅔	9	7	.563	137	67	53	74	75	3.01

Selected by Pittsburgh Pirates' organization in 2nd round of free-agent draft, June 6, 1983.

STEVEN MICHAEL FARR
(Steve)

Born December 12, 1956, at Cheverly, Md.
Height, 5.11. Weight, 190.
Throws and bats righthanded.
Attended American University, Washington, D.C.

Major League saves: 1984 (1), 1985 (1). Total—2.

Year Club	League	G.	IP.	W.	L.	Pct.	H.	R.	ER.	SO.	BB.	ERA.
1977—Niagara Falls	NYP	10	52	1	5	.167	53	30	23	43	30	3.98
1978—Charleston	W. Carol.	21	77	5	3	.625	72	45	36	54	63	4.21
1978—Salem	Ap'lacian	2	16	2	0	1.000	13	2	1	12	1	0.56
1979—Salem†	Carolina	26	119	3	10	.231	138	81	66	105	47	4.99
1980—Buffalo	Eastern	23	161	11	6	.647	158	84	71	71	64	3.97
1980—Portland	P. Coast	2	7	0	1	.000	11	9	8	0	2	10.29
1981—Buffalo	Eastern	29	106	8	3	.727	102	50	44	82	48	3.74
1981—Portland	P. Coast	4	23	0	3	.000	39	28	20	19	12	7.83
1982—Buffalo‡§	Eastern	25	76⅓	5	8	.385	72	40	34	84	38	4.01
1983—Buffalo	Eastern	18	112	13	1	*.929	88	28	20	108	50	*1.61
1984—Maine	Int'national	6	45	4	0	1.000	37	14	13	40	8	2.60
1984—Cleveland xy	American	31	116	3	11	.214	106	61	59	83	46	4.58
1985—Omaha	Am. Assoc.	17	133⅔	10	4	.714	105	36	30	98	41	*2.02
1985—Kansas City	American	16	37⅔	2	1	.667	34	15	13	36	20	3.11
Major League Totals—2 Years		47	153⅔	5	12	.294	140	76	72	119	66	4.22

Signed as a free agent by Pittsburgh Pirates' organization, December 13, 1976.
†On disabled list, June 6 to June 22, 1979.
‡On Lynn suspended list, April 16, 1983; then transferred to restricted list, April 27 to June 8, 1983.
§Traded to Buffalo (Cleveland Indians' organization) for Catcher John Malkin, June 8, 1983.
xOn disabled list, June 20 to July 5, 1984.
yReleased, March 31, 1985; signed by Kansas City Royals' organization, May 9, 1985.

CHAMPIONSHIP SERIES RECORD

Year Club	League	G.	IP.	W.	L.	Pct.	H.	R.	ER.	SO.	BB.	ERA.
1985—Kansas City	American	2	6⅓	1	0	1.000	4	1	1	3	1	1.42

MICHAEL OTIS FELDER
(Mike)

Born November 18, 1962, at Vallejo, Calif.
Height, 5.08. Weight, 160.
Throws right and bats left and righthanded.
Attended Contra Costa College, San Pablo, Calif.

Major League stolen bases: 1985 (4).
Led Pacific Coast League in stolen bases with 61 in 1985.
Led Texas League in sacrifice flies with 9 in 1984.
Led Texas League in stolen bases with 71 in 1983 and 58 in 1984.
Led California League in stolen bases with 92 in 1982.
Led Texas League outfielders in putouts with 332, total chances with 363 and tied for lead in assists with 18 in 1983.

Year Club	League	Pos.	G.	AB.	R.	H.	2B.	3B.	HR.	RBI.	B.A.	PO.	A.	E.	F.A.
1981—Stockton	Calif.	2B-OF	91	338	66	91	8	1	3	30	.269	172	162	13	.963
1982—Stockton	Calif.	OF	137	524	102	138	18	11	7	47	.263	314	9	10	.970
1983—El Paso	Texas	●OF-2B	133	554	108	156	23	10	9	78	.282	334	24	●13	.965
1984—El Paso†	Texas	OF	122	496	98	144	19	2	9	72	.290	321	13	6	.982
1985—Vancouver	P. C.	OF-2B	137	563	91	177	16	11	2	43	.314	294	15	4	.987
1985—Milwaukee	Amer.	OF	15	56	8	11	1	0	0	0	.196	32	1	0	1.000
Major League Totals—1 Year			15	56	8	11	1	0	0	0	.196	32	1	0	1.000

Selected by Milwaukee Brewers' organization in 3rd round of free-agent draft, January 13, 1981.
†On disabled list, April 15 to April 26, 1984.

GREGORY JAMES FERLENDA
(Greg)

Born August 7, 1964, at Syracuse, N.Y.
Height, 6.01. Weight, 185.
Throws and bats righthanded.
Attended Onondaga Community College, Syracuse, N.Y.

Year Club	League	G.	IP.	W.	L.	Pct.	H.	R.	ER.	SO.	BB.	ERA.
1983—Medicine Hat	Pioneer	16	70⅓	4	6	.400	76	58	47	83	41	6.01
1984—Florence	S. Atlantic	28	89⅔	2	11	.154	92	74	57	70	67	5.72
1985—Florence†	S. Atlantic	35	165⅓	12	5	.706	152	83	60	160	75	3.27

Selected by Toronto Blue Jays' organization in 14th round of free-agent draft, January 11, 1983.
†Traded to Texas Rangers, November 14, 1985, completing deal in which Texas traded Designated Hitter Cliff Johnson to Toronto Blue Jays for three players to be named later, August 28, 1985. Toronto organization acquired Pitchers Matt Williams and Jeff Mays as partial completion of deal, August 29, 1985.

CHARLES SIDNEY FERNANDEZ
(Sid)

Born October 12, 1962, at Honolulu, Hawaii.
Height, 6.01. Weight, 220.
Throws and bats lefthanded.

Pitched 1-0 no-hit victory against Fort Lauderdale, June 8, 1982.
Pitched 5-0 no-hit victory against Winter Haven, April 24, 1982.
Named Texas League Pitcher of the Year, 1983.

Year Club	League	G.	IP.	W.	L.	Pct.	H.	R.	ER.	SO.	BB.	ERA.
1981—Lethbridge	Pioneer	11	76	5	1	.833	43	21	13	★128	31	★1.54
1982—Vero Beach	Florida St.	12	84⅔	8	1	.889	38	19	18	★137	38	1.91
1982—Albuquerque	P. Coast	13	88	6	5	.545	76	54	53	86	52	5.42
1983—San Antonio	Texas	24	153	●13	4	.765	111	61	48	★209	96	★2.82
1983—Los Angeles†	National	2	6	0	1	.000	7	4	4	9	7	6.00
1984—Tidewater	Int'national	17	105⅔	6	5	.545	69	39	30	123	63	2.56
1984—New York	National	15	90	6	6	.500	74	40	35	62	34	3.50
1985—Tidewater	Int'national	5	35⅓	4	1	.800	17	8	8	42	21	2.04
1985—New York	National	26	170⅓	9	9	.500	108	56	53	180	80	2.80
Major League Totals—3 Years		43	266⅓	15	16	.484	189	100	92	251	121	3.11

Selected by Los Angeles Dodgers' organization in 3rd round of free-agent draft, June 8, 1981.
†Traded with Infielder Ross Jones to New York Mets for Pitcher Carlos Diaz and a player to be named later, December 8, 1983; Los Angeles Dodgers acquired Infielder Bob Bailor to complete deal, December 12, 1983.

OCTAVIO ANTONIO FERNANDEZ (CASTRO)
(Tony)

Born August 6, 1962, at San Pedro de Macoris, Dominican Republic.
Height, 6.02. Weight, 165.
Throws right and bats right and lefthanded.

Major League stolen bases: 1984 (5), 1985 (13). Total—18.
Led American League shortstops in total chances with 791 in 1985.
Led International League shortstops in double plays with 87 in 1983.

Year Club	League	Pos.	G.	AB.	R.	H.	2B.	3B.	HR.	RBI.	B.A.	PO.	A.	E.	F.A.
1980—Kinston	Carol.	SS	62	187	28	52	6	2	0	12	.278	93	205	28	.914
1981—Kinston	Carol.	SS	75	280	57	89	10	6	1	13	.318	121	227	19	.948
1981—Syracuse†	Int.	SS	31	115	13	32	6	2	1	9	.278	69	80	3	.980
1982—Syracuse	Int.	SS	134	523	78	158	21	6	4	56	.302	★246	364	23	★.964
1983—Syracuse	Int.	SS	117	437	65	131	18	6	5	38	.300	★211	361	26	.957
1983—Toronto	Amer.	SS	15	34	5	9	1	1	0	2	.265	16	17	0	1.000
1984—Syracuse	Int.	SS	26	94	12	24	1	0	0	6	.255	46	72	5	.959
1984—Toronto	Amer.	SS-3B	88	233	29	63	5	3	3	19	.269	119	195	9	.972
1985—Toronto	Amer.	SS	161	564	71	163	31	10	2	51	.289	283	★478	30	.962
Major League Totals—3 Years			264	831	105	235	37	14	5	72	.283	418	690	39	.966

Signed as free agent by Toronto Blue Jays' organization, April 24, 1979.
†On disabled list, August 10 to August 27, 1981.

CHAMPIONSHIP SERIES RECORD

Year Club	League	Pos.	G.	AB.	R.	H.	2B.	3B.	HR.	RBI.	B.A.	PO.	A.	E.	F.A.
1985—Toronto	Amer.	SS	7	24	2	8	2	0	0	2	.333	11	15	2	.929

ANTHONY ROSS FERREIRA
Name pronounced Fer-AIR-a.
(Tony)

Born October 4, 1962, at Riverside, Calif.
Height, 6.02. Weight, 160.
Throws and bats lefthanded.
Cousin of Derek Diaz, pitcher in Milwaukee Brewers' organization.

Pitched 6-0 no-hit victory against Knoxville, July 9, 1983.

Year Club	League	G.	IP.	W.	L.	Pct.	H.	R.	ER.	SO.	BB.	ERA.
1981—Sarasota Royals-Gold	Gulf Coast	12	48	4	0	1.000	40	19	12	45	22	2.25
1982—Fort Myers	Florida St.	22	150⅓	12	7	.632	144	64	48	120	66	2.87
1982—Jacksonville	Southern	6	37⅓	2	4	.333	38	20	17	30	14	4.10
1983—Jacksonville	Southern	35	136⅓	7	11	.389	122	77	64	85	68	4.22
1984—Omaha	Am. Assoc.	40	114⅓	7	10	.412	128	65	58	69	52	4.57
1985—Omaha	Am. Assoc.	27	173⅔	11	10	.524	142	73	62	105	89	3.21
1985—Kansas City	American	2	5⅔	0	0	.000	6	5	5	5	2	7.94
Major League Totals—1 Year		2	5⅔	0	0	.000	6	5	5	5	2	7.94

Selected by Kansas City Royals' organization in 2nd round of free-agent draft, June 8, 1981.

CECIL GRANT FIELDER

Born September 21, 1963, at Los Angeles, Calif.
Height, 6.03. Weight, 230.
Throws and bats righthanded.
Attended University of Nevada, Las Vegas, Nev.

Led Pioneer League in total bases with 176 and being hit by pitch with 8 in 1982.

Year Club	League	Pos.	G.	AB.	R.	H.	2B.	3B.	HR.	RBI.	B.A.	PO.	A.	E.	F.A.
1982—Butte†	Pion.	1B	69	273	73	88	*28	0	*20	68	.322	247	18	4	.985
1983—Florence	S. Atl.	1B	140	500	81	156	28	2	16	94	.312	957	64	16	.985
1984—Kinston	Carol.	1B	61	222	42	63	12	1	19	49	.284	533	24	9	.984
1984—Knoxville	South.	1B	64	236	33	60	12	2	9	44	.254	173	10	4	.979
1985—Knoxville	South.	1B	96	361	52	106	26	2	18	81	.294	444	26	6	.987
1985—Toronto	Amer.	1B	30	74	6	23	4	0	4	16	.311	171	17	4	.979
Major League Totals—1 Year			30	74	6	23	4	0	4	16	.311	171	17	4	.979

Selected by Baltimore Orioles' organization in 31st round of free-agent draft, June 8, 1981.
Selected by Kansas City Royals' organization in secondary phase of free-agent draft, June 7, 1982.
†Traded to Toronto Blue Jays' organization for Outfielder Leon Roberts, February 4, 1983.

CHAMPIONSHIP SERIES RECORD

Year Club	League	Pos.	G.	AB.	R.	H.	2B.	3B.	HR.	RBI.	B.A.	PO.	A.	E.	F.A.
1985—Toronto	Amer.	PH	3	3	0	1	1	0	0	0	.333	0	0	0	.000

THOMAS CARSON FILER
(Tom)

Born December 1, 1956, at Philadelphia, Pa.
Height, 6.01. Weight, 198.
Throws and bats righthanded.
Received bachelor of science degree in marketing from
La Salle College, Philadelphia, Pa., in 1978.

Tied for American Association lead in wild pitches with 11 in 1981.

Year Club	League	G.	IP.	W.	L.	Pct.	H.	R.	ER.	SO.	BB.	ERA.
1978—Oneonta	NYP	9	43	2	3	.400	30	14	8	34	14	1.67
1979—West Haven	Eastern	24	154	12	8	.600	132	73	62	80	53	3.62
1980—Nashville†	Southern	27	187	13	9	.591	168	94	61	112	86	2.94
1981—Columbus‡	Int'national	1	3	0	1	.000	6	5	5	3	4	15.00
1981—Iowa	Am. Assoc.	21	109	4	9	.308	123	64	58	61	57	4.79
1982—Iowa	Am. Assoc.	17	92⅓	6	7	.462	109	74	69	51	31	6.73
1982—Chicago	National	8	40⅔	1	2	.333	50	25	25	15	18	5.53
1983—Iowa	Am. Assoc.	27	108	5	6	.455	128	56	50	56	44	4.17
1984—Iowa §x	Am. Assoc.	26	123⅓	9	7	.563	149	86	67	80	48	4.89
1985—Syracuse y	Int'national	12	78⅓	7	2	.778	67	24	22	31	22	2.53
1985—Toronto z	American	11	48⅔	7	0	1.000	38	21	21	24	18	3.88
National League Totals—1 Year		8	40⅔	1	2	.333	50	25	25	15	18	5.53
American League Totals—1 Year		11	48⅔	7	0	1.000	38	21	21	24	18	3.88
Major League Totals—2 Years		19	89⅓	8	2	.800	88	46	46	39	36	4.63

Signed as free agent by New York Yankees' organization, June 28, 1978.
†Drafted by Oakland A's, December 8, 1980; returned, April 9, 1981.
‡Traded with cash to Chicago Cubs' organization for Catcher Barry Foote, April 27, 1981.
§On disabled list, April 20 to May 12 and August 11 to August 22, 1984.
xGranted free agency, October 15, 1984; signed by Syracuse (Toronto Blue Jays' organization), November 21, 1984.
yOn disabled list, April 24 to May 4, 1985.
zOn disabled list, August 28 to September 12, 1985.

WILLIAM PETER FILSON
(Pete)

Born September 28, 1958, at Darby, Pa.
Height, 6.02. Weight, 195.
Throws left and bats left and righthanded.
Attended Temple University, Philadelphia, Pa.

Pitched seven-inning, 4-0 no-hit victory against Gastonia, April 25, 1980 (first game).
Pitched seven-inning, 10-0 no-hit victory against Kingsport, August 7, 1979 (second game).
Major League saves: 1983 (1), 1984 (1), 1985 (2). Total—4.
Led International League in complete games with 11 and balks with 8 in 1982.
Led Appalachian League in complete games with 9, shutouts with 3 and balks with 4 in 1979.

Year—Club	League	G.	IP.	W.	L.	Pct.	H.	R.	ER.	SO.	BB.	ERA.
1979—Paintsville	Ap'lachian	13	*91	*9	0	*1.000	51	19	17	*118	39	*1.68
1979—Oneonta	NYP	1	1	0	0	.000	0	0	0	1	0	0.00
1980—Greensboro	S. Atlantic	4	27	3	0	1.000	13	5	5	34	14	1.67
1980—Fort Lauderdale	Florida St.	23	144	10	9	.526	105	56	48	86	69	3.00
1981—Fort Lauderdale	Florida St.	11	68	7	1	.875	56	20	15	68	20	1.99
1981—Nashville	Southern	14	99	10	2	●.833	73	30	20	77	28	1.82
1982—Columbus†-Toledo	Int'national	23	150⅔	8	10	.444	168	87	77	84	53	4.60
1982—Minnesota	American	5	12⅓	0	2	.000	17	12	12	10	8	8.76
1983—Minnesota‡	American	26	90	4	1	.800	87	34	34	49	29	3.40
1983—Toledo	Int'national	2	7	0	1	.000	8	6	6	6	3	7.71
1984—Minnesota	American	55	118⅔	6	5	.545	106	56	54	59	54	4.10
1985—Minnesota	American	40	95⅔	4	5	.444	93	42	39	42	30	3.67
Major League Totals—4 Years		126	316⅔	14	13	.519	303	144	139	160	121	3.95

Selected by New York Yankees' organization in 8th round of free-agent draft, June 5, 1979.

†Traded with Infielder Larry Milbourne and Pitcher John Pacella to Minnesota Twins for Catcher Butch Wynegar and Pitcher Roger Erickson, May 12, 1982.

‡On disabled list, July 13 to August 3, 1983.

JOHN JOSEPH FIMPLE
(Jack)

Born February 10, 1959, at Darby, Pa.
Height, 6.02. Weight, 185.
Throws and bats righthanded.
Attended Humboldt State University, Arcata, Calif.

Major League stolen bases: 1983 (1).
Led Midwest League in sacrifice flies with 8 in 1981.
Led Pacific Coast League in passed balls with 16 in 1984.
Led Florida State League catchers in putouts with 542 and assists with 54 in 1982.
Led Midwest League in passed balls with 36 in 1981.

Year—Club	League	Pos.	G.	AB.	R.	H.	2B.	3B.	HR.	RBI.	B.A.	PO.	A.	E.	F.A.
1980—Bat.†-Auburn	NYP	2B-3B	61	215	27	52	7	0	5	24	.242	113	121	14	.944
1981—Waterloo‡	Midw.	C-1B	108	371	53	107	21	2	10	76	.288	676	92	10	.987
1982—Vero Beach	Fla. St.	C-1B	111	359	53	101	14	5	9	54	.281	610	58	11	.984
1983—Albuquerque	P. C.	C	80	235	44	58	12	3	10	51	.247	397	*73	14	.971
1983—Los Angeles	Nat.	C	54	148	16	37	8	1	2	22	.250	336	32	4	.989
1984—Albuquerque	P. C.	C	107	334	39	83	15	3	11	60	.249	481	45	8	.985
1984—Los Angeles	Nat.	C	12	26	2	5	1	0	0	3	.192	54	4	1	.983
1985—Albuquerque	P. C.	C-3B	95	231	25	53	11	0	5	29	.229	304	63	4	.989
Major League Totals—2 Years			66	174	18	42	9	1	2	25	.241	390	36	5	.988

Selected by Cleveland Indians' organization in 29th round of free-agent draft, June 3, 1980.

†Loaned to Auburn (Co-op), July 27, 1980; returned, September 5, 1980.

‡Traded with Pitcher Larry White and Outfielder Jorge Orta to Los Angeles Dodgers for Pitcher Rick Sutcliffe and Second Baseman Jack Perconte, December 9, 1981.

CHAMPIONSHIP SERIES RECORD

Year—Club	League	Pos.	G.	AB.	R.	H.	2B.	3B.	HR.	RBI.	B.A.	PO.	A.	E.	F.A.
1983—Los Angeles	Nat.	C	3	7	0	1	0	0	0	1	.143	14	2	0	1.000

ROLAND GLEN FINGERS
(Rollie)

Born August 25, 1946, at Steubenville, O.
Height, 6.04. Weight, 200.
Throws and bats righthanded.
Attended Chaffey Junior College, Alta Loma, Calif.
Son of George M. Fingers, former minor league player in St. Louis Cardinals' organization; brother of Gordon Fingers, pitcher in Oakland Athletics' organization, 1970; uncle of Bob Fingers, pitcher in Milwaukee Brewers' organization.

Established major league record for most saves, lifetime (324).
Major League saves: 1969 (12), 1970 (2), 1971 (17), 1972 (21), 1973 (22), 1974 (18), 1975 (24), 1976 (20), 1977 (35), 1978 (37), 1979 (13), 1980 (23), 1981 (28), 1982 (29), 1984 (23), 1985 (17). Total—341.
Led American League in saves with 28 in 1981.
Led National League in saves with 35 in 1977 and 37 in 1978.
Led National League in games finished in relief with 69 in 1977.
Led American League in games finished in relief with 59 in 1975.
Tied for Southern League lead in shutouts with 3 in 1968.
Named American League Most Valuable Player by Baseball Writers' Association of America, 1981.
Won American League Cy Young Memorial Award, 1981.
Named American League Fireman of the Year by THE SPORTING NEWS, 1981.
Named National League Fireman of the Year by THE SPORTING NEWS, 1977 and 1978.
Named National League co-Fireman of the Year by THE SPORTING NEWS, 1980.

Year—Club	League	G.	IP.	W.	L.	Pct.	H.	R.	ER.	SO.	BB.	ERA.
1965—Leesburg	Florida St.	25	175	8	15	.348	148	83	58	108	69	2.98
1966—Modesto	California	22	159	11	6	.647	120	61	49	152	43	2.77
1967—Birmingham†‡	Southern	18	102	6	5	.545	75	34	25	61	36	2.21
1968—Birmingham	Southern	18	108	10	4	.714	94	38	36	93	28	3.00
1968—Oakland	American	1	1	0	0	.000	4	4	4	0	1	36.00

Year Club	League	G.	IP.	W.	L.	Pct.	H.	R.	ER.	SO.	BB.	ERA.
1969—Oakland	American	60	119	6	7	.462	116	60	49	61	41	3.71
1970—Oakland	American	45	148	7	9	.438	137	65	60	79	48	3.65
1971—Oakland	American	48	129	4	6	.400	94	46	43	98	30	3.00
1972—Oakland	American	65	111	11	9	.550	85	35	31	113	32	2.51
1973—Oakland	American	62	127	7	8	.467	107	41	27	110	39	1.91
1974—Oakland	American	★76	119	9	5	.643	104	41	35	95	29	2.65
1975—Oakland	American	★75	127	10	6	.625	95	43	42	115	33	2.98
1976—Oakland§	American	70	135	13	11	.542	118	40	37	113	40	2.47
1977—San Diego	National	★78	132	8	9	.471	123	47	44	113	36	3.00
1978—San Diego	National	67	107	6	13	.316	84	33	30	72	29	2.52
1979—San Diego	National	54	84	9	9	.500	91	47	42	65	37	4.50
1980—San Diego xy	National	66	103	11	9	.550	101	35	32	69	32	2.80
1981—Milwaukee	American	47	78	6	3	.667	55	9	9	61	13	1.04
1982—Milwaukee	American	50	79⅔	5	6	.455	63	23	23	71	20	2.60
1983—Milwaukee z	American					(Did not play)						
1984—Milwaukee ab	American	33	46	1	2	.333	38	13	10	40	13	1.96
1985—Milwaukee c	American	47	55⅓	1	6	.143	59	33	31	24	19	5.04
National League Totals—4 Years		265	426	34	40	.459	399	162	148	319	134	3.13
American League Totals—13 Years		679	1275	80	78	.506	1075	453	401	980	358	2.83
Major League Totals—17 Years		944	1701	114	118	.491	1474	615	549	1299	492	2.90

Signed as free agent by Kansas City A's organization, December 24, 1964.
†On disabled list, April 18 to June 1, 1967.
‡On military list, December 29, 1967 through May 12, 1968.
§Played out option year and granted free agency, November 1, 1976; signed as free agent with San Diego Padres, December 14, 1976.
xTraded with Pitcher Bob Shirley, Catcher-First Baseman Gene Tenace and a player to be named later to St. Louis Cardinals for Catchers Terry Kennedy and Steve Swisher, Pitchers John Littlefield, Al Olmsted, Kim Seaman and John Urrea and Infielder Mike Phillips, December 8, 1980; St. Louis organization acquired Catcher Bob Geren to complete deal, December 10, 1980.
yTraded with Catcher Ted Simmons and Pitcher Pete Vuckovich to Milwaukee Brewers for Outfielders Sixto Lezcano and David Green and Pitchers Lary Sorensen and Dave LaPoint, December 12, 1980.
zOn disabled list, March 26, 1983 through remainder of season.
aOn disabled list, July 24, 1984 through remainder of season.
bGranted free agency, November 8, 1984; re-signed by Brewers, January 16, 1985.
cReleased, November 14, 1985.

DIVISION SERIES RECORD

Year Club	League	G.	IP.	W.	L.	Pct.	H.	R.	ER.	SO.	BB.	ERA.
1981—Milwaukee	American	3	4⅔	1	0	1.000	7	3	2	5	1	3.86

CHAMPIONSHIP SERIES RECORD

Established American League Championship Series record for most games pitched, total Series (11).
Tied American League Championship Series record for most saves, total Series (2).

Year Club	League	G.	IP.	W.	L.	Pct.	H.	R.	ER.	SO.	BB.	ERA.
1971—Oakland	American	2	2⅓	0	0	.000	2	2	2	2	1	7.71
1972—Oakland	American	3	5⅓	1	0	1.000	4	1	1	3	1	1.69
1973—Oakland	American	3	4⅔	0	1	.000	4	1	1	4	2	1.93
1974—Oakland	American	2	3	0	0	.000	3	1	1	3	1	3.00
1975—Oakland	American	1	4	0	1	.000	5	3	3	3	1	6.75
Championship Series Totals—5 Years		11	19⅓	1	2	.333	18	8	8	15	6	3.72

WORLD SERIES RECORD

Established World Series record for most saves, total Series (6); most games as relief pitcher, total Series (16).
Tied World Series record for most saves, five-game Series (2), 1974.

Year Club	League	G.	IP.	W.	L.	Pct.	H.	R.	ER.	SO.	BB.	ERA.
1972—Oakland	American	6	10⅓	1	1	.500	4	2	2	11	4	1.74
1973—Oakland	American	6	13⅔	0	1	.000	13	5	1	8	4	0.66
1974—Oakland	American	4	9⅓	1	0	1.000	8	2	2	6	2	1.93
World Series Totals—3 Years		16	33⅓	2	2	.500	25	9	5	25	10	1.35

ALL-STAR GAME RECORD

Year League	IP.	W.	L.	Pct.	H.	R.	ER.	SO.	BB.	ERA.
1973—American	1	0	0	.000	0	0	0	0	0	0.00
1974—American	1	0	0	.000	1	2	2	0	1	18.00
1978—National	2	0	0	.000	1	0	0	1	0	0.00
1981—American	⅓	0	1	.000	2	2	2	0	2	54.00
1982—American	1	0	0	.000	2	0	0	0	0	0.00
All-Star Game Totals—5 Years	5⅓	0	1	.000	6	4	4	1	3	6.75

Member of American League All-Star Team in 1975 and 1976; did not play.

—DID YOU KNOW—

That Giants pitcher Jim Gott connected for two home runs in a May 12 game against St. Louis? The 1985 season marked Gott's major league batting debut after spending his first three seasons with Toronto in the American League.

STEPHEN JOHN FIREOVID

Name pronounced FYR-oh-vid.

(Steve)

Born June 6, 1957, at Bryan, O.
Height, 6.02. Weight, 195.
Throws right and bats left and righthanded.
Attended Miami University, Oxford, O.

Year Club	League	G.	IP.	W.	L.	Pct.	H.	R.	ER.	SO.	BB.	ERA.
1978—Walla Walla	Northwest	14	106	9	2	.818	82	45	29	99	52	2.46
1979—Reno	California	26	168	13	9	.591	182	92	76	135	65	4.07
1980—Amarillo	Texas	27	164	12	6	.667	196	100	86	106	52	4.72
1981—Hawaii	P. Coast	25	162	11	7	.611	173	77	57	57	55	3.17
1981—San Diego	National	5	26	0	1	.000	30	8	8	11	7	2.77
1982—Hawaii	P. Coast	25	135⅔	10	8	.556	171	87	81	56	39	5.37
1983—Las Vegas	P. Coast	28	184⅔	14	10	.583	*212	124	98	80	63	4.78
1983—San Diego†	National	3	5	0	0	.000	4	2	1	1	2	1.80
1984—Portland	P. Coast	46	111⅔	5	9	.357	133	71	54	45	44	4.35
1984—Philadelphia‡	National	6	5⅔	0	0	.000	4	1	1	3	0	1.59
1985—Buffalo	Am. Assoc.	24	137⅓	8	7	.533	154	50	46	57	34	3.01
1985—Chicago§	American	4	7	0	0	.000	17	4	4	2	2	5.14
National League Totals 3 Years		14	00⅔	0	1	.000	38	11	10	15	9	2.45
American League Totals—1 Year		4	7	0	0	.000	17	4	4	2	2	5.14
Major League Totals—4 Years		18	43⅔	0	1	.000	55	15	14	17	11	2.89

Selected by San Diego Padres' organization in 7th round of free-agent draft, June 6, 1978.

†Traded to Philadelphia Phillies' organization, October 11, 1983, completing deal in which San Diego Padres traded Outfielder Sixto Lezcano and a player to be named later to Philadelphia for four players to be named later, August 31, 1983; San Diego acquired Pitchers Marty Decker, Ed Wojna, Darren Burroughs and Lance McCullers as partial completion of deal, September 20, 1983.

‡Released, November 9, 1984; signed by Buffalo (Chicago White Sox' organization), January 12, 1985.

§Granted free agency, October 15, 1985; signed by Seattle Mariners' organization, January 18, 1986.

MICHAEL THOMAS FISCHLIN

(Mike)

Born September 13, 1955, at Sacramento, Calif.
Height, 6.01. Weight, 165.
Throws and bats righthanded.
Attended Cosumnes River Junior College, Sacramento, Calif.,
and Sacramento State University, Sacramento, Calif.

Major League stolen bases: 1978 (1), 1981 (3), 1982 (9), 1983 (9), 1984 (2). Total—24.

Tied National League record for fewest chances offered by shortstop, two consecutive games (1), June 18 and 20, 1978.

Led International League in sacrifice hits with 15 in 1981.

Led Pacific Coast League shortstops in putouts with 200 and double plays with 88 in 1980.

Year Club	League	Pos.	G.	AB.	R.	H.	2B.	3B.	HR.	RBI.	B.A.	PO.	A.	E.	F.A.
1975—Oneonta	NYP	SS	35	135	22	31	4	3	0	6	.230	34	128	15	.915
1975—Fort Lauderdale	Fla. St.	SS	29	104	7	19	4	0	0	7	.183	54	90	10	.935
1976—West Haven	East.	SS-3B-2B	91	248	16	38	7	1	2	20	.153	149	243	27	.936
1976—Oneonta	NYP	SS	14	55	13	14	3	0	0	5	.255	36	48	7	.923
1977—Fort Lauderdale†	Fla. St.	SS-2B	53	201	28	59	6	4	0	20	.294	84	188	16	.944
1977—Columbus	South.	SS	66	223	23	54	5	0	1	16	.242	104	204	16	.951
1977—Houston	Nat.	SS	13	15	0	3	0	0	0	0	.200	3	17	0	1.000
1978—Charleston	Int.	SS	82	280	38	59	10	2	0	19	.211	141	279	13	.970
1978—Houston	Nat.	SS	44	86	3	10	1	0	0	0	.116	49	67	9	.928
1979—Charleston‡	Int.	SS	44	138	13	31	4	1	0	8	.225	73	134	8	.963
1980—Tucson	P. C.	*SS-OF	131	417	65	117	24	7	3	49	.281	201	*437	*40	*.941
1980—Houston§	Nat.	SS	1	1	0	0	0	0	0	0	.000	0	0	0	.000
1981—Charleston	Int.	SS-2B	136	463	83	110	14	7	5	43	.238	224	433	31	.955
1981—Cleveland	Amer.	SS-2B	22	43	3	10	1	0	0	5	.233	33	39	4	.947
1982—Cleveland	Amer.	S-3-2-C	112	276	34	74	12	1	0	21	.268	142	257	13	.968
1983—Cleveland	Amer.	2B-SS-3B	95	225	31	47	5	2	2	23	.209	169	226	14	.966
1984—Cleveland	Amer.	2B-3B-SS	85	133	17	30	4	2	1	14	.226	104	146	8	.969
1985—Cleveland x	Amer.	2-S-1-3	73	60	12	12	4	1	0	2	.200	73	89	4	.976
National League Totals—3 Years			58	102	3	13	1	0	0	0	.127	52	84	9	.938
American League Totals—5 Years			387	737	97	173	26	6	3	65	.235	521	757	43	.967
Major League Totals—8 Years			445	839	100	186	27	6	3	65	.222	573	841	52	.965

Selected by New York Yankees' organization in 7th round of free-agent draft, June 4, 1975.

†Traded with Pitcher Randy Niemann and a player to be named later to Houston Astros' organization for Catcher-First Baseman Cliff Johnson, June 15, 1977; Houston acquired First Baseman-Outfielder Dave Bergman to complete deal, November 23, 1977.

‡On disabled list, June 18 to August 28, 1979.

§Traded to Cleveland Indians' organization for cash and a player to be named later, April 3, 1981; Houston Astros' organization acquired Outfielder Jim Lentine to complete deal, September 28, 1981.

xTraded to New York Yankees for a player to be named later, December 11, 1985.

BRIAN KEVIN FISHER

Born March 18, 1962, at Honolulu, Hawaii.
Height, 6.04. Weight, 210.
Throws and bats righthanded.
Attended Columbia College, Aurora, Col.

Major League saves: 1985 (14).
Led International League pitchers in games started with 29 in 1984.
Tied for South Atlantic League lead in balks with 4 in 1981.

Year Club	League	G.	IP.	W.	L.	Pct.	H.	R.	ER.	SO.	BB.	ERA.
1980—Bradenton Braves	Gulf Coast	12	61	5	3	.625	55	34	26	48	★53	3.84
1981—Anderson	S. Atlantic	25	152	6	8	.429	139	96	72	152	94	4.26
1982—Durham†	Carolina	18	104	6	6	.500	72	43	32	129	43	2.77
1983—Savannah	Southern	27	150	8	11	.421	172	101	87	103	56	5.22
1984—Richmond‡	Int'national	29	183	9	11	.450	188	●101	★87	122	●100	4.28
1985—Columbus	Int'national	7	11⅓	0	0	.000	8	4	3	12	7	2.38
1985—New York	American	55	98⅓	4	4	.500	77	32	26	85	29	2.38
Major League Totals—1 Year		55	98⅓	4	4	.500	77	32	26	85	29	2.38

Selected by Atlanta Braves' organization in 2nd round of free-agent draft, June 3, 1980.
†On disabled list, May 18 to July 1, 1982.
‡Traded to New York Yankees for Catcher Rick Cerone, December 5, 1984.

CARLTON ERNEST FISK

Born December 26, 1947, at Bellows Falls, Vt.
Height, 6.02. Weight, 217.
Throws and bats righthanded.
Attended University of New Hampshire, Durham, N. H.
Brother of Calvin Fisk, former catcher in Baltimore Orioles' organization;
brother-in-law of Rick Miller, outfielder with Boston Red Sox; cousin of
Dave Jennings, punter with New York Jets.

Established major league records for longest game with no passed balls (25 innings), and most innings played by catcher, game (25), May 8, finished May 9, 1984.
Tied major league records for most at-bats (11) and plate appearances (12), game, May 8, finished May 9, 1984 (25 innings), most home runs, opening game of season (2), April 6, 1973.
Tied modern major league record for most long hits, inning (2), May 15, 1975 (eighth inning) and June 30, 1977 (eighth inning).
Established American League record for most home runs by catcher, season (33), 1985.
Tied American League record for fewest passed balls, season, 150 or more games (4), 1977.
Major League stolen bases: 1972 (5), 1973 (7), 1974 (5), 1975 (4), 1976 (12), 1977 (7), 1978 (7), 1979 (3), 1980 (11), 1981 (3), 1982 (17), 1983 (9), 1984 (6), 1985 (17). Total—113.
Hit for the cycle, May 16, 1984.
Led American League in being hit by pitch with 13 in 1980.
Led American League catchers in passed balls with 11 in 1983.
Led American League catches in putouts with 470 and double plays with 10 in 1981.
Led American League catchers in errors with 10 in 1980.
Led American League catchers in total chances with 933 in 1972, 803 in 1973, 519 in 1981 and 871 in 1985.
Led International League catchers in double plays with 12 in 1971.
Named THE SPORTING NEWS American League Rookie Player of the Year, 1972.
Named American League Rookie of the Year by Baseball Writers' Association of America, 1972.
Named catcher on THE SPORTING NEWS American League All-Star Team, 1972, 1977, 1983 and 1985.
Named catcher on THE SPORTING NEWS American League All-Star fielding team, 1972.
Named catcher on THE SPORTING NEWS American League Silver Slugger team, 1981 and 1985.

Year Club	League	Pos.	G.	AB.	R.	H.	2B.	3B.	HR.	RBI.	B.A.	PO.	A.	E.	F.A.
1967—Greenville†	W. Car.														
1968—Waterloo‡	Midw.					(In Military Service)									
1969—Pittsfield	East.	C	62	195	31	66	11	2	12	34	.338	385	42	8	.982
1969—Boston	Amer.	C	97	309	38	75	18	3	10	41	.243	551	65	★22	.966
1970—Pawtucket	East.	C	2	5	0	0	0	0	0	0	.000	2	0	0	1.000
1971—Louisville	Int.	C-OF-1B	93	284	43	65	18	1	12	44	.229	482	50	7	.987
1971—Boston	Amer.	C-OF-3B	94	308	45	81	10	4	10	43	.263	588	51	13	.980
1972—Boston	Amer.	C	14	48	7	15	2	1	2	6	.313	72	6	2	.975
1973—Boston	Amer.	C	131	457	74	134	28	●9	22	61	.293	★846	★72	●15	.984
1974—Boston§	Amer.	C	135	508	65	125	21	0	26	71	.246	★739	50	★14	.983
1975—Boston x	Amer.	C	52	187	36	56	12	1	11	26	.299	267	26	6	.980
1976—Boston	Amer.	C	79	263	47	87	14	4	10	52	.331	347	30	8	.979
1977—Boston	Amer.	C	134	487	76	124	17	5	17	58	.255	649	73	12	.984
1978—Boston	Amer.	C	152	536	106	169	26	3	20	102	.315	779	69	11	.987
1979—Boston y	Amer.	★C-OF	157	571	94	162	39	5	20	88	.284	734	90	★17	.980
1980—Boston z	Amer.	C-OF	91	320	49	87	23	2	10	42	.272	155	8	3	.982
1981—Chicago	Amer.	C-1-O-3	96	338	44	89	12	0	7	45	.263	479	46	6	.989
1982—Chicago	Amer.	C-1B	135	476	66	127	17	3	14	65	.267	648	63	5	.993
1983—Chicago	Amer.	C	138	488	85	141	26	4	26	86	.289	★709	46	7	.991
1984—Chicago a	Amer.	C	102	359	54	83	20	1	21	43	.231	421	38	6	.987
1985—Chicago b	Amer.	C	153	543	85	129	23	1	37	107	.238	★801	60	10	.989
Major League Totals—16 Years			1702	6064	961	1666	305	42	267	914	.275	8191	733	133	.985

Selected by Baltimore Orioles' organization in 36th round of free-agent draft, June, 1965.
Selected by Boston Red Sox' organization in 1st round (fourth player selected) of free-agent draft, January, 1967.
†On temporary inactive list, April 17, 1967; transferred to military list, May 18, 1967 through April 9, 1968.
‡On temporary inactive list, August 5 to August 20, 1968.
§On disabled list, March 21 to April 26 and June 28, 1974 through remainder of season.

xOn disabled list, March 24 to June 23, 1975.
yOn disabled list, April 14 to May 21, 1979.
zGranted free agency by arbitrator's ruling, February 12, 1981; signed by Chicago White Sox, March 18, 1981.
aOn disabled list, June 13 to July 5, 1984.
bGranted free agency, November 12, 1985; re-signed by White Sox, January 8, 1986.

CHAMPIONSHIP SERIES RECORD

Year Club	League	Pos.	G.	AB.	R.	H.	2B.	3B.	HR.	RBI.	B.A.	PO.	A.	E.	F.A.
1975—Boston	Amer.	C	3	12	4	5	1	0	0	2	.417	15	0	0	1.000
1983—Chicago	Amer.	C	4	17	0	3	1	0	0	0	.176	27	3	0	1.000
Championship Series Totals—2 Years.....			7	29	4	8	2	0	0	2	.276	42	3	0	1.000

WORLD SERIES RECORD

Tied World Series records for most at bats inning and most times faced pitcher inning (2), October 15, 1975 (fourth inning); most errors by catcher, game (2), October 14, 1975.

Year Club	League	Pos.	G.	AB.	R.	H.	2B.	3B.	HR.	RBI.	B.A.	PO.	A.	E.	F.A.
1975—Boston	Amer.	C	7	25	5	6	0	0	2	4	.240	37	3	2	.952

ALL-STAR GAME RECORD

Year League	Pos.	AB.	R.	H.	2B.	3B.	HR.	RBI.	B.A.	PO.	A.	E.	F.A.
1972—American..................................	C	2	1	1	0	0	0	0	.500	2	0	0	1.000
1973—American..................................	C	2	0	0	0	0	0	0	.000	3	0	0	1.000
1976—American..................................	C	1	0	0	0	0	0	0	.000	1	0	0	1.000
1977—American..................................	C	2	0	0	0	0	0	0	.000	6	1	0	1.000
1978—American	C	2	0	0	0	0	0	1	.000	4	0	0	1.000
1980—American..................................	C	2	0	0	0	0	0	0	.000	5	0	0	1.000
1981—American	C	3	1	1	0	0	0	0	.333	4	0	0	1.000
1982—American	C	2	0	0	0	0	0	0	.000	2	0	0	1.000
1985—American	C	2	0	0	0	0	0	0	.000	2	0	0	1.000
All-Star Game Totals—9 Years....................		18	2	2	0	0	0	1	.111	29	1	0	1.000

Named to American League All-Star Team for 1974 game; replaced due to injury.

MICHAEL ROY FITZGERALD
(Mike)

Born July 13, 1960, at Long Beach, Calif.
Height, 6.00. Weight, 185.
Throws and bats righthanded.
Nephew of Dan Gausepohl, outfielder in San Diego
Padres' organization, 1979 through 1982.

Tied major league record by hitting home run in first major league at-bat, September 13, 1983.
Major League stolen bases: 1984 (1), 1985 (5). Total—6.
Led Carolina League in sacrifice flies with 11 in 1979.

Year Club	League	Pos.	G.	AB.	R.	H.	2B.	3B.	HR.	RBI.	B.A.	PO.	A.	E.	F.A.
1978—Little Falls.............	NYP	C	48	140	25	36	10	0	5	21	.257	230	37	1	.996
1979—Lynchburg.............	Carol.	C	117	368	55	93	16	4	13	★75	.253	424	60	10	.980
1980—Alex.†-Lynch.........	Carol.	C-1B-OF	105	338	36	71	10	2	10	44	.210	438	45	7	.986
1981—Jackson	Texas	C-1-O-3	66	218	28	68	14	2	4	29	.312	344	52	3	.992
1981—Tidewater.............	Int.	C-OF	24	58	9	9	2	0	1	3	.155	124	9	2	.985
1982—Tidewater.............	Int.	C-1-O-3	94	302	33	74	9	2	4	36	.245	451	34	7	986
1983—Tidewater.............	Int.	C-1-3-O	111	370	64	105	17	1	14	65	.284	588	62	8	.988
1983—New York.............	Nat.	C	8	20	1	2	0	0	1	2	.100	37	8	2	.957
1984—New York‡...........	Nat.	C	112	360	20	87	15	1	2	33	.242	715	47	4	★.995
1985—Montreal	Nat.	C	108	295	25	61	7	1	5	34	.207	542	46	8	.987
Major League Totals—3 Years.................			228	675	46	150	22	2	8	69	.222	1294	101	14	.990

Selected by New York Mets' organization in 6th round of free-agent draft, June 6, 1978.
†Loaned to Alexandria (Co-op), April 8, 1980; returned, May 31, 1980.
‡Traded with Infielder Hubie Brooks, Outfielder Herm Winningham and Pitcher Floyd Youmans to Montreal Expos for Catcher Gary Carter, December 10, 1984.

MICHAEL KENDALL FLANAGAN
(Mike)

Born December 16, 1951, at Manchester, N. H.
Height, 6.00. Weight, 195.
Throws and bats lefthanded.
Attended University of Massachusetts, Amherst, Mass.
Son of Ed Flanagan, Jr., minor league pitcher, 1947 through 1952.

Major League saves: 1977 (1).
Tied for American League lead in shutouts with 5 in 1979.
Tied for American League lead in games started by pitchers with 40 in 1978.
Tied for International League lead in shutouts with 4 in 1975.
Tied for Southern League lead in shutouts with 3 in 1974.
Named American League Pitcher of the Year by THE SPORTING NEWS, 1979.
Won American League Cy Young Memorial Award, 1979.
Named lefthanded pitcher on THE SPORTING NEWS American League All-Star Team, 1979.

Year Club	League	G.	IP.	W.	L.	Pct.	H.	R.	ER.	SO.	BB.	ERA.
1973—Miami	Florida St.	11	61	4	1	.800	39	21	15	61	25	2.21
1974—Miami	Florida St.	14	103	6	6	.500	67	32	24	119	48	2.10
1974—Asheville	Southern	11	84	6	4	.600	61	19	17	62	18	1.82
1975—Rochester	Int'national	27	173	13	4	★.765	155	58	48	135	56	2.50
1975—Baltimore	American	2	10	0	1	.000	9	4	3	7	6	2.70
1976—Baltimore	American	20	85	3	5	.375	83	41	39	56	33	4.13
1976—Rochester	Int'national	7	51	6	1	.857	40	16	12	24	14	2.12
1977—Baltimore	American	36	235	15	10	.600	235	100	95	149	70	3.64
1978—Baltimore	American	40	281	19	15	.559	271	128	★126	167	87	4.04
1979—Baltimore	American	39	266	★23	9	.719	245	107	91	190	70	3.08
1980—Baltimore	American	37	251	16	13	.552	★278	121	115	128	71	4.12
1981—Baltimore	American	20	116	9	6	.600	108	55	54	72	37	4.19
1982—Baltimore	American	36	236	15	11	.577	233	110	104	103	76	3.97
1983—Baltimore†	American	20	125⅓	12	4	.750	135	53	46	50	31	3.30
1984—Baltimore	American	34	226⅔	13	13	.500	213	103	89	115	81	3.53
1985—Hagerstown‡	Carolina	1	6	0	0	.000	1	0	0	5	4	0.00
1985—Baltimore	American	15	86	4	5	.444	101	49	49	42	28	5.13
Major League Totals—11 Years		299	1918	129	92	.584	1911	871	811	1079	590	3.81

Selected by Houston Astros' organization in 15th round of free-agent draft, June 8, 1971.
Selected by Baltimore Orioles' organization in 7th round of free-agent draft, June 5, 1973.
†On disabled list, May 18 to August 7, 1983.
‡On Baltimore disabled list, March 26 to July 20, 1985; included rehabilitation disability assignment to Hagerstown, July 10 to July 20, 1985.

CHAMPIONSHIP SERIES RECORD

Year Club	League	G.	IP.	W.	L.	Pct.	H.	R.	ER.	SO.	BB.	ERA.
1979—Baltimore	American	1	7	1	0	1.000	6	6	4	2	1	5.14
1983—Baltimore	American	1	5	1	0	1.000	5	1	1	1	0	1.80
Championship Series Total—2 Years		2	12	2	0	1.000	11	7	5	3	1	3.75

WORLD SERIES RECORD

Year Club	League	G.	IP.	W.	L.	Pct.	H.	R.	ER.	SO.	BB.	ERA.
1979—Baltimore	American	3	15	1	1	.500	18	7	5	13	2	3.00
1983—Baltimore	American	1	4	0	0	.000	6	2	2	1	1	4.50
World Series Totals—2 Years		4	19	1	1	.500	24	9	7	14	3	3.32

ALL-STAR GAME RECORD

Named to American League All-Star Team for 1978 game; did not play.

TIMOTHY EARL FLANNERY
(Tim)

Born September 29, 1957, at Tulsa, Okla.
Height, 5.11. Weight, 176.
Throws right and bats lefthanded.
Attended Chapman College, Orange, Calif.
Nephew of Hal Smith, catcher with St. Louis Cardinals and Pittsburgh Pirates, 1956 through 1961 and 1965; minor league manager, 1966; coach, Pittsburgh Pirates, 1967; coach, Cincinnati Reds, 1968 and 1969; and scout with St. Louis Cardinals, 1970 through 1975 and since 1978.

Major League stolen bases: 1980 (2), 1981 (1), 1982 (1), 1983 (2), 1984 (4), 1985 (2). Total—12.

Year Club	League	Pos.	G.	AB.	R.	H.	2B.	3B.	HR.	RBI.	B.A.	PO.	A.	E.	F.A.
1978—Reno	Calif.	2B-P	84	340	65	119	11	5	2	49	.350	213	269	19	.962
1979—Amarillo	Texas	2B-SS	125	524	88	●181	23	6	6	71	.345	287	374	28	.959
1979—San Diego	Nat.	2B	22	65	2	10	0	1	0	4	.154	45	60	1	.991
1980—Hawaii	P. C.	2B	47	182	27	63	10	3	1	16	.346	102	146	5	.980
1980—San Diego	Nat.	2B-3B	95	292	15	70	12	0	0	25	.240	140	204	8	.977
1981—Hawaii	P. C.	2B	21	78	16	22	3	1	0	10	.282	47	62	2	.982
1981—San Diego	Nat.	3B-2B	37	67	4	17	4	1	0	6	.254	16	32	2	.960
1982—San Diego	Nat.	2B-3B-SS	122	379	40	100	11	7	0	30	.264	226	278	14	.973
1983—San Diego	Nat.	3B-2B-SS	92	214	24	50	7	3	3	19	.234	63	156	4	.982
1984—San Diego	Nat.	2B-SS-3B	86	128	24	35	3	3	2	10	.273	36	69	5	.955
1985—San Diego	Nat.	2B-3B	126	384	50	108	14	3	1	40	.281	261	287	13	.977
Major League Totals—7 Years			580	1529	159	390	51	18	6	134	.255	787	1086	47	.976

Selected by San Diego Padres' organization in 6th round of free-agent draft, June 6, 1978.

CHAMPIONSHIP SERIES RECORD

Year Club	League	Pos.	G.	AB.	R.	H.	2B.	3B.	HR.	RBI.	B.A.	PO.	A.	E.	F.A.
1984—San Diego	Nat.	PH	3	2	2	1	0	0	0	0	.500	0	0	0	.000

WORLD SERIES RECORD

Year Club	League	Pos.	G.	AB.	R.	H.	2B.	3B.	HR.	RBI.	B.A.	PO.	A.	E.	F.A.
1984—San Diego	Nat.	PH-2B	1	1	0	1	0	0	0	0	1.000	1	0	0	1.000

PITCHING RECORD

Year Club	League	G.	IP.	W.	L.	Pct.	H.	R.	ER.	SO.	BB.	ERA.
1978—Reno	California	1	⅓	0	1	.000	3	6	5	0	1	135.00

SCOTT BRIAN FLETCHER

Born July 30, 1958, at Fort Walton Beach, Fla.
Height, 5.11. Weight, 173.
Throws and bats righthanded.
Attended University of Toledo, Toledo, Ohio; Valencia Community College,
Orlando, Fla., and Georgia Southern College, Statesboro, Ga.
Son of Richard W. Fletcher, minor league pitcher, 1952 through 1959.

Major League stolen bases: 1982 (1), 1983 (5), 1985 (5). Total—21.
Led American Association in being hit by pitch with 9 and grounding into double plays with 20 in 1981.
Led American Association shortstops in total chances with 607 in 1982.
Led Texas League second basemen in double plays with 112 in 1980.

Year Club	League	Pos.	G.	AB.	R.	H.	2B.	3B.	HR.	RBI.	B.A.	PO.	A.	E.	F.A.
1979—Geneva	NYP	SS	67	261	59	81	12	3	4	43	.310	99	195	18	*.942
1980—Midland	Texas	*2B-SS	130	501	*111	164	16	*11	6	65	.327	*354	*390	*29	.962
1981—Iowa	A. A.	SS	119	458	66	117	26	4	4	33	.255	*222	337	28	.952
1981—Chicago	Nat.	2B-SS-3B	19	46	6	10	4	0	0	1	.217	34	44	3	.963
1982—Iowa	A. A.	SS	129	502	90	157	26	3	4	60	.313	224	●357	26	.957
1982—Chicago†	Nat.	SS	11	24	4	4	0	0	0	1	.167	11	23	0	1.000
1983—Chicago	Amer.	SS-2B-3B	114	262	42	62	16	5	3	31	.237	126	308	16	.964
1984—Chicago	Amer.	SS-2B-3B	149	456	46	114	13	3	3	35	.250	234	439	19	.973
1985—Chicago‡	Amer.	3B-SS-2B	119	301	38	77	8	1	2	31	.256	123	208	8	.976
National League Totals—2 Years			30	70	10	14	4	0	0	2	.200	45	67	3	.974
American League Totals—3 Years			382	1019	126	253	37	9	8	97	.248	483	955	43	.971
Major League Totals—5 Years			412	1089	136	267	41	9	8	99	.245	528	1022	46	.971

Selected by Los Angeles Dodgers' organization in 33rd round of free-agent draft, June 8, 1976.
Selected by Oakland A's organization in secondary phase of free-agent draft, January 10, 1978.
Selected by Houston Astros' organization in secondary phase of free-agent draft, June 6, 1978.
Selected by Chicago Cubs' organization in secondary phase of free-agent draft, June 5, 1979.

†Traded with Pitchers Dick Tidrow and Randy Martz and Infielder Pat Tabler to Chicago White Sox for Pitchers Steve Trout and Warren Brusstar, January 25, 1983.

‡Traded with Pitcher Ed Correa and a player to be named later to Texas Rangers for Infielder Wayne Tolleson and Pitcher Dave Schmidt, November 25, 1985; Texas acquired Infielder Jose Mota to complete deal, December 12, 1985.

CHAMPIONSHIP SERIES RECORD

Year Club	League	Pos.	G.	AB.	R.	H.	2B.	3B.	HR.	RBI.	B.A.	PO.	A.	E.	F.A.
1983—Chicago	Amer.	SS	3	7	0	0	0	0	0	0	.000	3	8	0	1.000

ROBERT DOUGLAS FLYNN JR.
(Doug)

Born April 18, 1951, at Lexington, Ky.
Height, 5.11. Weight, 172.
Throws and bats righthanded.
Attended University of Kentucky, Lexington, Ky., and Somerset
Community College, Somerset, Ky.
Son of Robert Douglas Flynn, Sr., player in Brooklyn Dodgers' organization, 1949.

Tied modern major league record for most three-base hits, game (3), August 5, 1980.
Major League stolen bases: 1975 (3), 1976 (2), 1977 (1), 1978 (3), 1980 (2), 1981 (1), 1982 (6), 1983 (2). Total—20.
Led National League second basemen in putouts with 369, total chances with 762 and double plays with 98 in 1979.
Led American Association shortstops in double plays with 91 in 1974.
Led Eastern League shortstops in double plays with 97 in 1973.
Tied for Eastern League lead in sacrifice flies with 9 in 1973.
Named second baseman on THE SPORTING NEWS National League All-Star fielding team, 1980.

Year Club	League	Pos.	G.	AB.	R.	H.	2B.	3B.	HR.	RBI.	B.A.	PO.	A.	E.	F.A.
1972—Tampa	Fla. St.	3-S-2-P	98	313	32	66	12	2	1	37	.211	109	240	18	.951
1973—Three Rivers	East.	SS	*139	*500	52	129	11	0	3	42	.258	*231	*453	34	.953
1974—Indianapolis	A. A.	SS	134	458	57	116	13	6	2	34	.253	213	*392	33	.948
1975—Cincinnati	Nat.	3B-2B-SS	89	127	17	34	7	0	1	20	.268	57	118	2	.989
1976—Cincinnati	Nat.	2B-3B-SS	93	219	20	62	5	2	1	20	.283	107	152	4	.985
1977—Cinc.†-N.Y.	Nat.	SS-2B-3B	126	314	14	62	7	2	0	19	.197	171	235	14	.967
1978—New York	Nat.	2B-SS	156	532	37	126	12	8	0	36	.237	332	426	15	.981
1979—New York	Nat.	2B-SS	157	555	35	135	19	5	4	61	.243	402	421	16	.981
1980—New York‡	Nat.	*2B-SS	128	443	46	113	9	8	0	24	.255	284	374	6	*.991
1981—New York§	Nat.	2B-SS	105	325	24	72	12	4	1	20	.222	229	319	7	.987
1982—Texas x	Amer.	2B-SS	88	270	13	57	6	2	0	19	.211	161	254	9	.979
1982—Montreal	Nat.	2B	58	193	13	47	6	2	0	20	.244	135	157	5	.983
1983—Montreal	Nat.	2B-SS	143	452	44	107	18	4	0	26	.237	249	375	11	.983
1984—Montreal	Nat.	2B-SS	124	366	23	89	12	1	0	17	.243	189	291	13	.974
1985—Montreal y	Nat.	2B-SS	9	6	0	1	0	0	0	0	.167	3	2	0	1.000
1985—Detroit z	Amer.	2B-SS-3B	32	51	2	13	2	1	0	2	.255	39	44	1	.988
National League Totals—11 Years			1188	3532	273	848	107	36	7	263	.240	2158	2870	93	.982
American League Totals—2 Years			120	321	15	70	8	3	0	21	.218	200	298	10	.980
Major League Totals—11 Years			1308	3853	288	918	115	39	7	284	.238	2358	3168	103	.982

Signed as free agent by Cincinnati Reds' organization, August 25, 1971.

†Traded with Outfielders Dan Norman and Steve Henderson and Pitcher Pat Zachry to New York Mets for Pitcher Tom Seaver, June 15, 1977.

‡On disabled list, August 20 to September 6, 1980.

§Traded with Pitcher Dan Boitano to Texas Rangers for Pitcher Jim Kern, December 11, 1981.

yReleased, June 11, 1985; signed by Detroit Tigers, June 20, 1985.
zGranted free agency, November 12, 1985; re-signed by Tigers, November 21, 1985.

CHAMPIONSHIP SERIES RECORD

Year Club	League	Pos.	G.	AB.	R.	H.	2B.	3B.	HR.	RBI.	B.A.	PO.	A.	E.	F.A.
1976—Cincinnati	Nat.	2B	1	0	0	0	0	0	0	0	.000	0	0	0	.000

PITCHING RECORD

Year Club	League	G.	IP.	W.	L.	Pct.	H.	R.	ER.	SO.	BB.	ERA.
1972—Tampa..	Florida St.	1	3	0	0	.000	3	1	1	3	1	3.00

THOMAS MICHAEL FOLEY
(Tom)

Born September 9, 1959, at Columbus, Ga.
Height, 6.01. Weight, 171.
Throws right and bats lefthanded.
Attended Miami-Dade Community College South, Miami, Fla.

Major League stolen bases: 1983 (1), 1984 (3), 1985 (2). Total—6.
Led Pioneer League in caught stealing with 10 in 1977.
Led Florida State League shortstops in double plays with 71 in 1979.
Led Western Carolinas League shortstops in double plays with 98 in 1978.

Year Club	League	Pos.	G.	AB.	R.	H.	2B.	3B.	HR.	RBI.	B.A.	PO.	A.	E.	F.A.
1977—Billings	Pion.	3B-SS	59	209	37	53	7	1	2	21	.254	53	109	24	.871
1978—Shelby....................	W. Car.	SS	124	424	55	98	19	1	2	41	.231	★217	●352	30	★.950
1979—Tampa....................	Fla. St.	SS	125	414	38	95	12	6	0	37	.229	223	★394	35	.946
1980—Waterbury............	East.	2B	131	477	49	119	16	4	4	41	.249	★222	329	31	.947
1981—Indianapolis.........	A. A.	SS	103	347	47	81	12	2	6	27	.233	175	267	27	.942
1982—Indianapolis.........	A. A.	SS	129	427	65	115	20	9	8	63	.269	★227	343	27	.955
1983—Cincinnati.............	Nat.	SS-2B	68	98	7	20	4	1	0	9	.204	54	76	2	.985
1984—Cincinnati.............	Nat.	SS-2B-3B	106	277	26	70	8	3	5	27	.253	119	228	11	.969
1985—Cinc.†-Phil.	Nat.	SS-2B-3B	89	250	24	60	13	1	3	23	.240	127	202	7	.979
Major League Totals—3 Years................			263	625	57	150	25	5	8	59	.240	300	506	20	.976

Selected by Cincinnati Reds' organization in 7th round of free-agent draft, June 7, 1977.

†Traded with Catcher Alan Knicely, a player to be named later and cash to Philadelphia Phillies for Catcher Bo Diaz and Pitcher Greg Simpson, August 8, 1985; Philadelphia acquired Pitcher Freddie Toliver to complete deal, August 27, 1985.

TIMOTHY JOHN FOLI
(Tim)

Born December 8, 1950, at Culver City, Calif.
Height, 6.00. Weight, 175.
Throws and bats righthanded.
Brother of Ernie Foli, minor league infielder-outfielder, 1962 through 1968.

Major League stolen bases: 1971 (5), 1972 (11), 1973 (6), 1974 (8), 1975 (13), 1976 (6), 1977 (2), 1978 (2), 1979 (6), 1980 (11), 1981 (7), 1982 (2), 1983 (2). Total—81.
Hit for the cycle, April 21, 1976.
Led American League in sacrifice hits with 26 in 1982.
Led American League shortstops in fielding percentage with .985 in 1982.
Led National League shortstops in putouts with 260 in 1975.
Led National League shortstops in total chances with 795 in 1972 and 778 in 1975.
Led National League shortstops in double plays with 104 in 1975 and 102 in 1976.
Tied for National League lead in being hit by pitch with 6 in 1980.
Led California League shortstops in double plays with 72 in 1969.
Led Appalachian League shortstops in putouts with 97, fielding percentage with .920 and double plays with 29 in 1968.
Received reported $75,000 bonus to sign with New York Mets, 1968.

Year Club	League	Pos.	G.	AB.	R.	H.	2B.	3B.	HR.	RBI.	B.A.	PO.	A.	E.	F.A.
1968—Marion...................	Appal.	★SS-1B	63	235	38	66	10	3	4	36	.281	105	★167	23	.922
1968—Memphis†.............	Texas	SS	5	20	4	5	0	0	0	1	.250	8	10	2	.900
1969—Visalia	Calif.	SS	95	383	60	116	10	0	15	62	.303	154	280	36	.923
1970—Tidewater..............	Int.	SS-2B	103	375	63	98	10	4	6	30	.261	181	289	20	.959
1970—New York..............	Nat.	SS-3B	5	11	0	4	0	0	0	1	.364	4	10	0	1.000
1971—New York‡§..........	Nat.	2-3-S-O	97	288	32	65	12	2	0	24	.226	150	199	12	.967
1972—Montreal	Nat.	★SS-2B	149	540	45	130	12	2	2	35	.241	★281	487	27	.966
1973—Montreal x	Nat.	SS-2B-O	126	458	37	110	11	0	2	36	.240	248	399	27	.960
1974—Montreal y	Nat.	SS-3B	121	441	41	112	10	3	0	39	.254	220	412	19	.971
1975—Montreal	Nat.	★SS-2B	152	572	64	136	25	2	1	29	.238	261	★497	21	.973
1976—Montreal	Nat.	SS-3B	149	546	41	144	36	1	6	54	.264	249	470	18	.976
1977—Mont. z-S.F. ab....	Nat.	S-2-3-O	117	425	32	94	22	4	4	30	.221	217	345	13	.977
1978—New York c...........	Nat.	SS	113	413	37	106	21	1	1	27	.257	190	314	18	.966
1979—N.Y. d-Pitts...........	Nat.	SS	136	532	70	153	23	1	1	65	.288	259	410	15	.978
1980—Pittsburgh e	Nat.	SS	127	495	61	131	22	0	3	38	.265	212	402	12	★.981
1981—Pittsburgh f	Nat.	SS	86	316	32	78	12	2	0	20	.247	140	247	14	.965
1982—California..............	Amer.	SS-2B-3B	150	480	46	121	14	2	3	56	.252	247	462	12	.983
1983—California gh........	Amer.	SS-3B	88	330	29	83	10	0	2	29	.252	131	298	13	.971
1984—New York i...........	Amer.	S-2-3-1	61	163	8	41	11	0	0	16	.252	88	122	6	.972

Year	Club	League	Pos.	G.	AB.	R.	H.	2B.	3B.	HR.	RBI.	B.A.	PO.	A.	E.	F.A.
1985—Pittsburgh jk		Nat.	SS	19	37	1	7	0	0	0	2	.189	16	34	1	.980
1985—Miami l		Fla. St.	SS	1	4	0	1	0	0	0	0	.250	1	5	0	1.000
National League Totals— 13 Years				1397	5074	493	1270	206	18	20	400	.250	2447	4226	197	.971
American League Totals—3 Years				299	973	83	245	35	2	5	101	.252	466	882	31	.978
Major League Totals—16 Years				1696	6047	576	1515	241	20	25	501	.251	2913	5108	228	.972

Selected by New York Mets' organization in 1st round (first player selected) of free-agent draft, June 7, 1968.

†On military list, January 13 to May 24, 1969.

‡On military list, August 16 to September 1, 1971.

§Traded with Outfielder Ken Singleton and First Baseman Mike Jorgensen to Montreal Expos for Outfielder Rusty Staub, April 5, 1972.

xOn disabled list, July 9 to August 7, 1973.

yOn disabled list, May 13 to May 29, 1974.

zTraded to San Francisco Giants for Shortstop Chris Speier, April 27, 1977.

aOn disabled list, June 21 to July 21, 1977.

bSold to New York Mets, December 7, 1977.

cOn disabled list, April 26 to May 22, 1978.

dTraded with Pitcher Greg Field to Pittsburgh Pirates for Shortstop Frank Taveras, April 19, 1979.

eOn disabled list, May 29 to June 13, 1980.

fTraded to California Angels for Catcher Brian Harper, December 11, 1981.

gOn suspended list, September 1 to September 13, 1983.

hTraded to New York Yankees for Pitcher Curt Kaufman and cash, December 8, 1983.

iTraded with Outfielder Steve Kemp and $800,000 to Pittsburgh Pirates for Infielder Dale Berra, Pitcher Alfonso Pulido and Outfielder Jay Buhner, December 20, 1984.

jOn disabled list, April 23 to May 17, 1985.

kReleased, June 17, 1985; signed by Miami Marlins (Independent) July 2, 1985.

lReleased, July 4, 1985; named coach of Texas Rangers for 1986 season, October 28, 1985.

CHAMPIONSHIP SERIES RECORD

Year	Club	League	Pos.	G.	AB.	R.	H.	2B.	3B.	HR.	RBI.	B.A.	PO.	A.	E.	F.A.
1979—Pittsburgh		Nat.	SS	3	12	1	4	1	0	0	3	.333	3	9	0	1.000
1982—California		Amer.	SS	5	16	0	2	0	0	0	1	.125	6	7	0	1.000
Championship Series Totals—2 Years				8	28	1	6	1	0	0	4	.214	9	16	0	1.000

WORLD SERIES RECORD

Established World Series records for fewest strikeouts, most at bats, Series (0 and 30), 1979; most assists by shortstop, seven-game Series (32), 1979.

Tied World Series records for most double plays by shortstop, seven-game Series (7), 1979; most double plays started by shortstop, seven-game Series (4), 1979; most assists by shortstop, inning (3), October 12, 1979 (second inning).

Year	Club	League	Pos.	G.	AB.	R.	H.	2B.	3B.	HR.	RBI.	B.A.	PO.	A.	E.	F.A.
1979—Pittsburgh		Nat.	SS	7	30	6	10	1	1	0	3	.333	8	32	3	.930

SILTON RAY FONTENOT

Name pronounced FON-ten-oh.

(Known by middle name.)

Born August 8, 1957, at Lake Charles, La.

Height, 6.00. Weight, 175.

Throws and bats lefthanded.

Attended McNeese State University, Lake Charles, La.

Year	Club	League	G.	IP.	W.	L.	Pct.	H.	R.	ER.	SO.	BB.	ERA.
1979—Sarasota Rangers†		Gulf Coast	8	31	3	1	.750	28	20	14	42	12	4.06
1980—Greensboro‡		S. Atlantic	11	49	2	2	.500	41	27	20	50	19	3.67
1981—Greensboro§		S. Atlantic	9	59	4	2	.667	53	22	18	62	23	2.75
1981—Fort Lauderdale x		Florida St.	8	45	1	4	.200	50	34	28	37	31	5.60
1982—Fort Lauderdale		Florida St.	12	74	6	5	.545	57	29	24	71	31	2.92
1982—Nashville		Southern	14	91⅓	5	6	.455	85	34	22	69	17	2.17
1983—Columbus		Int'national	26	35	3	2	.600	25	16	11	36	17	2.83
1983—New York		American	15	97⅓	8	2	.800	101	41	36	27	25	3.33
1984—New York y		American	35	169⅓	8	9	.471	189	77	68	85	58	3.61
1985—Chicago		National	38	154⅔	6	10	.375	177	86	75	70	45	4.36
American League Totals—2 Years			50	266⅔	16	11	.593	290	118	104	112	83	3.51
National League Totals—1 Year			38	154⅔	6	10	.375	177	86	75	70	45	4.36
Major League Totals—3 Years			88	421⅓	22	21	.512	467	204	179	182	128	3.82

Selected by Texas Rangers' organization in 34th round of free-agent draft, June 5, 1979.

†Traded with Pitcher Gene Nelson to New York Yankees' organization for Pitchers Bob Polinsky, Neal Mersch and Mark Softy, October 8, 1979; completing deal in which New York traded Outfielder Mickey Rivers and three players to be named later to Texas Rangers for Third Baseman Amos Lewis and two players to be named later, August 1, 1979.

‡On disabled list, April 22 to May 12 and July 14, 1980 through remainder of season.

§On disabled list, April 9 to May 5, 1981.

xOn disabled list, August 27, 1981 through remainder of season.

yTraded with Outfielder Brian Dayett to Chicago Cubs for Catcher Ron Hassey, Outfielder Henry Cotto and Pitchers Rich Bordi and Porfi Altamirano, December 4, 1984.

CURTIS GLENN FORD
(Curt)

Born October 11, 1960, at Jackson, Miss.
Height, 5.10. Weight, 150.
Throws right and bats lefthanded.
Attended Jackson State University, Jackson, Miss.

Major League stolen bases: 1985 (1).
Led American Association in stolen bases with 45 and tied for lead in caught stealing with 17 in 1985.
Led Midwest League in total bases with 236 in 1983.
Named Midwest League Most Valuable Player, 1983.

Year	Club	League	Pos.	G.	AB.	R.	H.	2B.	3B.	HR.	RBI.	B.A.	PO.	A.	E.	F.A.
1981—Johnson City	Appal.	★2B-1B	63	218	36	65	11	2	5	38	.298	115	149	★18	.936
1982—St. Petersburg	Fla. St.	2B-OF	133	447	59	123	18	8	1	49	.275	292	294	22	.964
1983—Springfield	Midw.	OF-2B	126	465	80	135	27	7	20	★91	.290	181	7	8	.960
1984—Arkansas	Texas	OF-2B-3B	118	442	62	143	23	1	10	78	.324	224	102	8	.976
1984—Louisville	A. A.	OF-2B	13	38	5	10	2	0	0	1	.263	13	2	0	1.000
1985—Louisville	A. A.	OF-3B	127	475	73	121	20	6	7	45	.255	243	25	8	.971
1985—St. Louis	Nat.	OF	11	12	2	6	2	0	0	3	.500	3	0	1	.750
Major League Totals—1 Year			11	12	2	6	2	0	0	3	.500	3	0	1	.750

Selected by St. Louis Cardinals' organization in 4th round of free-agent draft, June 8, 1981.

DARNELL GLENN FORD SR.
(Dan)

Born May 19, 1952, at Los Angeles, Calif.
Height, 6.01. Weight, 185.
Throws and bats righthanded.
Attended Southwestern College, Chula Vista, Calif., and Mesa Community College, Mesa, Ariz.

Major League stolen bases: 1975 (6), 1976 (17), 1977 (6), 1978 (7), 1979 (8), 1981 (2), 1982 (5), 1983 (9), 1984 (1). Total—61.
Hit three home runs in a game, July 20, 1983.
Hit for the cycle, August 10, 1979.
Tied for American League lead in sacrifice flies with 13 in 1979.
Led Midwest League in being hit by pitch with 12 in 1971.
Led Pacific Coast League outfielders in double plays with 7 in 1973.

Year	Club	League	Pos.	G.	AB.	R.	H.	2B.	3B.	HR.	RBI.	B.A.	PO.	A.	E.	F.A.
1971—Burlington	Midw.	OF	107	397	75	106	21	4	14	80	.267	186	11	10	.952
1972—Burlington†	Midw.	OF	72	246	55	87	15	4	18	61	.354	137	4	8	.946
1973—Tucson‡	P. C.	OF	128	465	80	136	21	12	14	70	.292	310	●16	11	.967
1974—Tucson§x	P. C.	OF	115	428	62	117	11	9	12	65	.273	263	11	14	.951
1975—Minnesota	Amer.	OF	130	440	72	123	21	1	15	59	.280	246	3	3	.988
1976—Minnesota	Amer.	OF	145	514	87	137	24	7	20	86	.267	267	6	9	.968
1977—Minnesota	Amer.	OF	144	453	66	121	25	7	11	60	.267	205	9	8	.964
1978—Minnesota y	Amer.	OF	151	592	78	162	36	10	11	82	.274	376	6	9	.977
1979—California z	Amer.	OF	142	569	100	165	26	5	21	101	.290	332	10	8	.977
1980—California	Amer.	OF	65	226	22	63	11	0	7	26	.279	75	3	5	.940
1981—California a	Amer.	OF	97	375	53	104	14	1	15	48	.277	188	3	●8	.960
1982—Baltimore	Amer.	OF	123	421	46	99	21	3	10	43	.235	263	6	7	.975
1983—Baltimore bc	Amer.	OF	103	407	63	114	30	4	9	55	.280	218	2	3	.987
1984—Baltimore d	Amer.	OF	25	91	7	21	4	0	1	5	.231	36	1	0	1.000
1985—Baltimore e	Amer.	DH	28	75	4	14	2	0	1	1	.187	0	0	0	.000
Major League Totals—11 Years			1153	4163	598	1123	214	38	121	566	.270	2206	49	60	.974

Selected by Oakland A's organization in 1st round (16th player selected) of free-agent draft, June 4, 1970.
†On temporary inactive list, April 15 to May 20, 1972.
‡On temporary inactive list, April 13 to April 16, 1973.
§On temporary inactive list, July 12 to August 2, 1974.
xTraded with Pitcher Dennis Myers to Minnesota Twins for First Baseman Pat Bourque, October 23, 1974.
yTraded to California Angels for Third Baseman Ron Jackson and Catcher Danny Goodwin, December 4, 1978.
zOn disabled list, June 3 to August 5, 1979.
aTraded to Baltimore Orioles for Third Baseman Doug DeCinces and Pitcher Jeff Schneider, January 28, 1982.
bOn disabled list, June 22 to July 20, 1983.
cGranted free agency, November 7, 1983; re-signed by Orioles, January 23, 1984.
dOn disabled list, April 16 to July 19 and August 17 to September 17, 1984.
eOn disabled list, June 8, 1985 through remainder of season.

CHAMPIONSHIP SERIES RECORD

Tied Championship Series record by hitting home run in first Series at-bat, October 3, 1979.

Year	Club	League	Pos.	G.	AB.	R.	H.	2B.	3B.	HR.	RBI.	B.A.	PO.	A.	E.	F.A.
1979—California	Amer.	OF	4	17	2	5	1	0	2	4	.294	6	0	1	.857
1983—Baltimore	Amer.	OF-PH	2	5	0	1	1	0	0	0	.200	1	0	0	1.000
Championship Series Totals—2 Years			6	22	2	6	2	0	2	4	.273	7	0	1	.875

WORLD SERIES RECORD

Year	Club	League	Pos.	G.	AB.	R.	H.	2B.	3B.	HR.	RBI.	B.A.	PO.	A.	E.	F.A.
1983—Baltimore	Amer.	PH-OF	5	12	1	2	0	0	1	1	.167	5	1	0	1.000

KENNETH ROTH FORSCH
(Ken)

Born September 8, 1946, at Sacramento, Calif.
Height, 6.04. Weight, 215.
Throws and bats righthanded.
Attended Sacramento City College, Sacramento, Calif., and Oregon
State University, Corvallis, Ore.
Brother of Bob Forsch, pitcher with St. Louis Cardinals.

Pitched 6-0 no-hit victory against Atlanta Braves, April 7, 1979.
Major League saves: 1973 (4), 1974 (10), 1975 (2), 1976 (19), 1977 (8), 1978 (7). Total—50.
Led American League in hit batsmen with 11 in 1982.
Tied for American League lead in shutouts with 4 in 1981.
Led Southern League in shutouts with 5 in 1970.

Year Club	League	G.	IP.	W.	L.	Pct.	H.	R.	ER.	SO.	BB.	ERA.
1968—Greensboro	Carolina	3	6	0	0	.000	6	2	2	6	3	3.00
1968—Williamsport	NYP	4	26	1	2	.333	14	6	4	40	9	1.38
1969—Peninsula†	Carolina	17	94	6	5	.545	67	40	33	100	53	3.16
1970—Columbus	Southern	22	167	•13	8	.619	135	48	38	152	39	2.05
1970—Oklahoma City	Am. Assoc.	5	40	4	0	1.000	25	7	7	37	10	1.58
1970—Houston	National	4	24	1	2	.333	28	15	15	13	5	5.63
1971—Houston	National	33	188	8	8	.500	162	60	53	131	53	2.54
1972 Houston	National	30	156	0	0	.429	100	75	68	113	62	3.92
1973—Houston	National	46	201	9	12	.429	197	101	94	149	74	4.21
1974—Houston	National	70	103	8	7	.533	98	38	32	48	37	2.80
1975—Houston‡	National	34	109	4	8	.333	114	42	39	54	30	3.22
1976—Houston	National	52	92	4	3	.571	76	23	22	49	26	2.15
1977—Houston	National	42	86	5	8	.385	80	32	26	45	28	2.72
1978—Houston	National	52	133	10	6	.625	136	44	40	71	37	2.71
1979—Houston§	National	26	178	11	6	.647	155	67	60	58	35	3.03
1980—Houston x	National	32	222	12	13	.480	230	90	79	84	41	3.20
1981—California	American	20	153	11	7	.611	143	54	49	55	27	2.88
1982—California	American	37	228	13	11	.542	225	108	98	73	57	3.87
1983—California y	American	31	219⅓	11	12	.478	226	107	99	81	61	4.06
1984—California y	American	2	16⅓	1	1	.500	14	4	4	10	3	2.20
1985—California za	American					(Did not play)						
American League Totals—4 Years		90	616⅔	36	31	.537	608	273	250	219	148	3.66
National League Totals—11 Years		421	1492	78	81	.491	1439	587	528	815	428	3.18
Major League Totals—15 Years		511	2108⅔	114	112	.504	2047	860	778	1034	576	3.32

Selected by California Angels' organization in 13th round of free-agent draft, June, 1966.
Selected by Chicago Cubs' organization in secondary phase of free-agent draft, June 7, 1967.
Selected by Houston Astros' organization in 18th round of free-agent draft, June, 1968.
†On disabled list, June 11 to July 11, 1969.
‡On disabled list, July 31 to September 22, 1975.
§On disabled list, May 23 to June 26, 1979.
xTraded to California Angels for Second Baseman Dickie Thon, April 1, 1981.
yOn disabled list, April 11, 1984 through remainder of season.
zOn disabled list, April 1, 1985 through entire season.
aReleased, December 20, 1985.

CHAMPIONSHIP SERIES RECORD

Year Club	League	G.	IP.	W.	L.	Pct.	H.	R.	ER.	SO.	BB.	ERA.
1980—Houston	National	2	8⅔	0	1	.000	10	4	4	6	1	4.15

ALL-STAR GAME RECORD

Year League	IP.	W.	L.	Pct.	H.	R.	ER.	SO.	BB.	ERA.
1976—National	1	0	0	.000	0	0	0	1	0	0.00
1981—American	1	0	0	.000	1	1	1	0	0	9.00
All-Star Game Totals—2 Years	2	0	0	.000	1	1	1	1	0	4.50

ROBERT HERBERT FORSCH
(Bob)

Born January 13, 1950, at Sacramento, Calif.
Height, 6.03. Weight, 215.
Throws and bats righthanded.
Attended Sacramento City College, Sacramento, Calif.
Brother of Ken Forsch, pitcher with Houston Astros and California Angels, 1970 through 1984.

Pitched 3-0 no-hit victory against Montreal Expos, September 26, 1983.
Pitched 5-0 no-hit victory against Philadelphia Phillies, April 16, 1978.
Pitched 5-0 no-hit victory against Denver, May 25, 1973.
Pitched seven-inning, 4-0 no-hit victory against Memphis, May 13, 1972.
Major League saves: 1982 (1), 1985 (2). Total—3.
Led Midwest League in hit batsmen with 11 in 1971.
Tied for Texas League lead in hit batsmen with 10 in 1972.
Named pitcher on THE SPORTING NEWS National League Silver Slugger team, 1980.
Received reported $25,000 bonus to sign with St. Louis Cardinals, 1968.

Year	Club	League	G.	IP.	W.	L.	Pct.	H.	R.	ER.	SO.	BB.	ERA.
1970—Cedar Rapids	Midwest	1	3	0	0	.000	6	4	4	1	2	12.00
1970—Lewiston	Northwest	7	28	2	3	.400	32	22	13	15	17	4.18
1971—Cedar Rapids	Midwest	23	158	11	7	.611	140	74	55	134	41	3.13
1972—Arkansas	Texas	24	153	8	10	.444	158	85	*74	109	47	4.35
1973—Tulsa	Am. Assoc.	27	166	12	12	.500	169	91	81	124	66	4.36
1974—Tulsa	Am. Assoc.	15	103	8	5	.615	95	49	42	71	33	3.67
1974—St. Louis	National	19	100	7	4	.636	84	38	33	39	34	2.97
1975—St. Louis	National	34	230	15	10	.600	213	89	73	108	70	2.86
1976—St. Louis	National	33	194	8	10	.444	209	112	85	76	71	3.94
1977—St. Louis	National	35	217	20	7	.741	210	97	84	95	69	3.48
1978—St. Louis	National	34	234	11	17	.393	205	110	96	114	97	3.69
1979—St. Louis	National	33	219	11	11	.500	215	102	93	92	52	3.82
1980—St. Louis	National	31	215	11	10	.524	225	102	90	87	33	3.77
1981—St. Louis	National	20	124	10	5	.667	106	47	44	41	29	3.19
1982—St. Louis	National	36	233	15	9	.625	238	95	90	69	54	3.48
1983—St. Louis	National	34	187	10	12	.455	190	104	89	56	54	4.28
1984—St. Louis†	National	16	52⅓	2	5	.286	64	38	35	21	19	6.02
1985—St. Louis	National	34	136	9	6	.600	132	63	59	48	47	3.90
Major League Totals—12 Years		359	2141⅓	129	106	.549	2091	997	871	846	629	3.66

Selected by St. Louis Cardinals' organization in 38th round of free-agent draft, June 7, 1968.
†On disabled list, June 1 to September 3, 1984.

CHAMPIONSHIP SERIES RECORD

Year	Club	League	G.	IP.	W.	L.	Pct.	H.	R.	ER.	SO.	BB.	ERA.
1982—St. Louis	National	1	9	1	0	1.000	3	0	0	6	0	0.00
1985—St. Louis	National	1	3⅓	0	0	.000	3	2	2	0	2	5.40
Championship Series Totals—2 Years		2	12⅓	1	0	1.000	6	2	2	6	2	1.46

WORLD SERIES RECORD

Tied World Series record for most games lost, seven-game Series (2), 1982.

Year	Club	League	G.	IP.	W.	L.	Pct.	H.	R.	ER.	SO.	BB.	ERA.
1982—St. Louis	National	2	12⅔	0	2	.000	18	10	7	4	3	4.97
1985—St. Louis	National	2	3	0	1	.000	6	4	4	3	1	12.00
World Series Totals—2 Years		4	15⅔	0	3	.000	24	14	11	7	4	6.32

RECORD AS INFIELDER

Year	Club	League	Pos.	G.	AB.	R.	H.	2B.	3B.	HR.	RBI.	B.A.	PO.	A.	E.	F.A.
1968—Sarasota Cards	Gulf C.	3B	44	143	17	32	5	0	0	16	.224	29	80	12	*.901
1969—Lewiston	N'west	3B-OF-2B	26	74	11	15	3	0	3	10	.203	12	45	13	.814
1969—Modesto	Calif.	3B-OF	33	119	8	28	2	0	1	7	.235	33	58	6	.938
1970—Modesto	Calif.	3B-OF	20	47	4	7	3	0	1	1	.149	19	20	3	.929
1970—Cedar Rapids	Midw.	3B-1B-P	19	34	2	3	2	0	0	1	.088	9	19	3	.903
1970—Lewiston	N'west	P-S-2-3	18	30	5	4	0	1	0	3	.133	9	13	6	.786

TERRY JAY FORSTER

Born January 14, 1952, at Sioux Falls, S. D.
Height, 6.04. Weight, 220.
Throws and bats lefthanded.
Attended Grossmont College, El Cajon, Calif.; and San Diego State University, San Diego, Calif.

Major League saves: 1971 (1), 1972 (29), 1973 (16), 1974 (24), 1975 (4), 1976 (1), 1977 (1), 1978 (22), 1979 (2), 1982 (3), 1983 (13), 1984 (5), 1985 (1) Total—122.
Led American League in saves with 24 in 1974.
Named American League Fireman of the Year by THE SPORTING NEWS, 1974.

Year	Club	League	G.	IP.	W.	L.	Pct.	H.	R.	ER.	SO.	BB.	ERA.
1970—Appleton	Midwest	10	54	6	1	.857	30	11	8	42	29	1.33
1971—Chicago	American	45	50	2	3	.400	46	23	22	48	23	3.96
1972—Chicago	American	62	100	6	5	.545	75	31	25	104	44	2.25
1973—Chicago	American	51	173	6	11	.353	174	69	62	120	78	3.23
1974—Chicago	American	59	134	7	8	.467	120	57	54	105	48	3.63
1975—Chicago†	American	17	37	3	3	.500	30	12	9	32	24	2.19
1976—Chicago‡	American	29	111	2	12	.143	126	61	54	70	41	4.38
1977—Pittsburgh§	National	33	87	6	4	.600	90	47	43	58	32	4.45
1978—Los Angeles	National	47	65	5	4	.556	56	19	14	46	23	1.94
1979—Los Angeles x	National	17	16	1	2	.333	18	11	10	8	11	5.63
1980—Los Angeles y	National	9	12	0	0	.000	10	4	4	2	4	3.00
1981—Los Angeles	National	21	31	0	1	.000	37	14	14	17	15	4.06
1982—Los Angeles z	National	56	83	5	6	.455	66	38	28	52	31	3.04
1983—Atlanta	National	56	79⅓	3	2	.600	60	19	19	54	31	2.16
1984—Atlanta a	National	25	26⅔	2	0	1.000	30	9	8	10	7	2.70
1985—Atlanta	National	46	59⅓	2	3	.400	49	22	15	37	28	2.28
American League Totals—6 Years		263	605	26	42	.382	571	253	226	479	258	3.36
National League Totals—9 Years		310	459⅓	24	22	.522	416	183	155	284	182	3.04
Major League Totals—15 Years		573	1064⅓	50	64	.439	987	436	381	763	440	3.22

Selected by Chicago White Sox' organization in 2nd round of free-agent draft, June 4, 1970.
†On disabled list, May 25 to July 1, July 26 to August 17 and August 18 to September 29, 1975.
‡Traded with Pitcher Rich Gossage to Pittsburgh Pirates for Outfielder Richie Zisk and Pitcher Silvio Martinez, December 10, 1976.

xOn disabled list, March 21 to May 25 and August 13, 1979 through remainder of season.
yOn disabled list, April 2 to July 14 and August 5 to September 15, 1980.
zGranted free agency, November 10, 1982; signed by Atlanta Braves, December 1, 1982.
aOn disabled list, March 28 to April 19, June 24 to August 4 and August 11 to September 1, 1984.

DIVISION SERIES RECORD

Year Club	League	G.	IP.	W.	L.	Pct.	H.	R.	ER.	SO.	BB.	ERA.
1981—Los Angeles	National	1	⅓	0	0	.000	0	0	0	0	0	0.00

CHAMPIONSHIP SERIES RECORD

Year Club	League	G.	IP.	W.	L.	Pct.	H.	R.	ER.	SO.	BB.	ERA.
1978—Los Angeles	National	1	1	1	0	1.000	1	0	0	2	0	0.00
1981—Los Angeles	National	1	⅓	0	0	.000	0	0	0	1	0	0.00
Championship Series Totals—2 Years		2	1⅓	1	0	1.000	1	0	0	3	0	0.00

WORLD SERIES RECORD

Year Club	League	G.	IP.	W.	L.	Pct.	H.	R.	ER.	SO.	BB.	ERA.
1978—Los Angeles	National	3	4	0	0	.000	5	0	0	6	1	0.00
1981—Los Angeles	National	2	2	0	0	.000	1	0	0	0	3	0.00
World Series Totals—2 Years		5	6	0	0	.000	6	0	0	6	4	0.00

GEORGE ARTHUR FOSTER

Born December 1, 1948, at Tuscaloosa, Ala.
Height, 6.01. Weight, 198.
Throws and bats righthanded.
Attended El Camino College, Torrance, Calif.

Established major league record for most home runs, righthanded batter on road (31), 1977.
Tied major league record for most consecutive seasons leading league in runs batted in (3), 1976, 1977 and 1978.
Tied National League record for most home runs, bases filled, month (2), August, 1983.
Major League stolen bases: 1971 (7), 1972 (2), 1974 (3), 1975 (2), 1976 (17), 1977 (6), 1978 (4), 1980 (1), 1981 (4), 1982 (1), 1983 (1), 1984 (2). Total—50.
Hit three home runs in a game, July 14, 1977.
Led National League in total bases with 388 and slugging percentage with .631 in 1977.
Led California League outfielders in total chances with 285 in 1969.
Led Northwest League outfielders in double plays with 4 in 1968.
Named National League Player of the Year by THE SPORTING NEWS, 1976 and 1977.
Named National League Most Valuable Player by Baseball Writers' Association of America, 1977.
Named outfielder on THE SPORTING NEWS National League All-Star Team, 1976 through 1978 and 1981.
Named outfielder on THE SPORTING NEWS National League Silver Slugger team, 1981.

Year Club	League	Pos.	G.	AB.	R.	H.	2B.	3B.	HR.	RBI.	B.A.	PO.	A.	E.	F.A.
1968—Medford	N'west	OF	72	253	47	70	9	5	3	30	.277	★142	6	5	.967
1969—Fresno	Calif.	OF	121	449	68	144	5	8	14	85	.321	★267	14	4	★.986
1969—San Francisco	Nat.	OF	9	5	1	2	0	0	0	1	.400	3	0	0	1.000
1970—Phoenix†	P. C.	OF	114	403	54	124	18	6	8	66	.308	202	5	9	.958
1970—San Francisco	Nat.	OF	9	19	2	6	1	1	1	4	.316	10	0	0	1.000
1971—S.F.‡-Cin.	Nat.	OF	140	473	50	114	23	4	13	58	.241	315	9	5	.985
1972—Cincinnati	Nat.	OF	59	145	15	29	4	1	2	12	.200	71	1	2	.973
1973—Indianapolis	A. A.	OF	134	496	77	130	26	1	15	60	.262	★332	7	10	.971
1973—Cincinnati	Nat.	OF	17	39	6	11	3	0	4	9	.282	19	1	0	1.000
1974—Cincinnati	Nat.	OF	106	276	31	73	18	0	7	41	.264	172	2	2	.989
1975—Cincinnati	Nat.	OF-1B	134	463	71	139	24	4	23	78	.300	299	11	3	.990
1976—Cincinnati	Nat.	★OF-1B	144	562	86	172	21	9	29	★121	.306	322	9	2	★.994
1977—Cincinnati	Nat.	OF	158	615	★124	197	31	2	★52	★149	.320	352	12	3	.992
1978—Cincinnati	Nat.	OF	158	604	97	170	26	7	★40	★120	.281	319	10	10	.971
1979—Cincinnati§	Nat.	OF	121	440	68	133	18	3	30	98	.302	214	7	4	.982
1980—Cincinnati	Nat.	OF	144	528	79	144	21	5	25	93	.273	295	6	1	.997
1981—Cincinnati x	Nat.	OF	108	414	64	122	23	2	22	90	.295	224	8	2	.991
1982—New York	Nat.	OF	151	550	64	136	23	2	13	70	.247	289	12	8	.974
1983—New York	Nat.	OF	157	601	74	145	19	2	28	90	.241	314	12	4	.988
1984—New York	Nat.	OF	146	553	67	149	22	1	24	86	.269	278	6	7	.976
1985—New York	Nat.	OF	129	452	57	119	24	1	21	77	.263	198	7	5	.976
Major League Totals—17 Years			1890	6739	956	1861	301	44	334	1197	.276	3694	113	58	.985

Selected by San Francisco Giants' organization in 3rd round of free-agent draft, January 27, 1968.
†On disabled list, June 10 to June 30, 1970.
‡Traded to Cincinnati Reds for Shortstop Frank Duffy and Pitcher Vern Geishert, May 29, 1971.
§On disabled list, July 22 to August 12, 1979.
xTraded to New York Mets for Catcher Alex Trevino and Pitchers Jim Kern and Greg Harris, February 10, 1982.

CHAMPIONSHIP SERIES RECORD

Tied Championship Series record for most consecutive games, one or more runs batted in (4).

Year Club	League	Pos.	G.	AB.	R.	H.	2B.	3B.	HR.	RBI.	B.A.	PO.	A.	E.	F.A.
1972—Cincinnati	Nat.	PR	1	0	1	0	0	0	0	0	.000	0	0	0	.000
1975—Cincinnati	Nat.	OF	3	11	3	4	0	0	0	0	.364	7	0	0	1.000
1976—Cincinnati	Nat.	OF	3	12	2	2	0	0	2	4	.167	7	0	0	1.000
1979—Cincinnati	Nat.	OF	3	10	1	2	0	0	1	2	.200	6	2	0	1.000
Championships Series Totals—4 Years			10	33	7	8	0	0	3	6	.242	20	2	0	1.000

— 168 —

Established World Series records for most putouts by left fielder, game (8), October 21, 1976; most chances accepted by left fielder, game (8), October 21, 1976.

Tied World Series record for most times caught stealing, four-game Series (2), 1976; one or more hits, each game, four-game Series, 1976; most putouts by outfielder, game (8), October 21, 1976.

Year Club	League	Pos.	G.	AB.	R.	H.	2B.	3B.	HR.	RBI.	B.A.	PO.	A.	E.	F.A.
1972—Cincinnati	Nat.	PR-OF	2	0	0	0	0	0	0	0	.000	0	0	0	.000
1975—Cincinnati	Nat.	OF	7	29	1	8	1	0	0	2	.276	13	1	0	1.000
1976—Cincinnati	Nat.	OF	4	14	3	6	1	0	0	4	.429	14	0	0	1.000
World Series Totals—3 Years			13	43	4	14	2	0	0	6	.326	27	1	0	1.000

ALL-STAR GAME RECORD

Year League	Pos.	AB.	R.	H.	2B.	3B.	HR.	RBI.	B.A.	PO.	A.	E.	F.A.
1976—National	OF	3	1	1	0	0	1	3	.333	0	0	0	.000
1977—National	OF	3	1	1	1	0	0	1	.333	2	0	0	1.000
1978—National	OF	2	1	0	0	0	0	0	.000	2	0	0	1.000
1979—National	OF	1	0	1	1	0	0	1	1.000	0	0	0	.000
1981—National	OF	2	0	0	0	0	0	0	.000	0	0	0	.000
All-Star Game Totals—5 Years		11	3	3	2	0	1	5	.273	4	0	0	1.000

ALAN KIM FOWLKES

Name pronounced Folks.

Born August 8, 1958, at Brawley, Calif.
Height, 6.02. Weight, 190.
Throws and bats righthanded.
Attended California State Poly University, Pomona, Calif.
Brother of George Fowlkes, pitcher in Philadelphia Phillies' organization, 1965 through 1967.

Named Texas League Pitcher of the Year, 1981.

Year Club	League	G.	IP.	W.	L.	Pct.	H.	R.	ER.	SO.	BB.	ERA.
1980—Great Falls	Pioneer	4	19	2	0	1.000	18	5	5	22	5	2.37
1980—Fresno	California	18	88	5	5	.500	69	26	20	90	16	2.05
1981—Shreveport	Texas	32	*203	14	10	.583	186	81	63	*152	51	2.79
1982—San Francisco	National	21	85	4	2	.667	111	55	49	50	24	5.19
1982—Phoenix	P. Coast	13	73⅓	6	3	.667	78	26	22	31	14	2.70
1983—Phoenix†	P. Coast	27	134	9	11	.450	181	118	97	78	58	6.51
1984—Phoenix‡§	P. Coast	16	79	4	4	.500	83	41	33	52	17	3.76
1985—Edmonton	P. Coast	23	142⅓	9	8	.529	171	75	60	69	39	3.79
1985—California x	American	2	7	0	0	.000	8	7	7	5	4	9.00
National League Totals—1 Year		21	85	4	2	.667	111	55	49	50	24	5.19
American League Totals—1 Year		2	7	0	0	.000	8	7	7	5	4	9.00
Major League Totals—2 Years		23	92	4	2	.667	119	62	56	55	28	5.48

Selected by San Francisco Giants' organization in 8th round of free-agent draft, June 3, 1980.
†On San Francisco disabled list, March 27 to April 21, 1983.
‡On disabled list, June 6 to August 5, 1984.
§Released, April 9, 1985; signed by California Angels' organization, May 2, 1985.
xOn disabled list, August 29, 1985 through remainder of season.

JOHN ANTHONY FRANCO

Born September 17, 1960, at Brooklyn, N.Y.
Height, 5.10. Weight, 175.
Throws and bats lefthanded.
Attended St. John's University, Jamaica, N.Y.

Major League saves: 1984 (4), 1985 (12). Total—16.

Year Club	League	G.	IP.	W.	L.	Pct.	H.	R.	ER.	SO.	BB.	ERA.
1981—Vero Beach	Florida St.	13	79	7	4	.636	78	41	31	60	41	3.53
1982—Albuquerque	P. Coast	5	27⅓	1	2	.333	41	22	22	24	15	7.24
1982—San Antonio	Texas	17	105⅓	10	5	.667	137	70	58	76	46	4.96
1983—Albuquerque†	P. Coast	11	15	0	0	.000	10	11	9	8	11	5.40
1983—Indianapolis	Am. Assoc.	23	115	6	10	.375	148	69	62	54	42	4.85
1984—Wichita	Am. Assoc.	6	9⅓	1	0	1.000	8	6	6	11	4	5.79
1984—Cincinnati	National	54	79⅓	6	2	.750	74	28	23	55	36	2.61
1985—Cincinnati	National	67	99	12	3	.800	83	27	24	61	40	2.18
Major League Totals—2 Years		121	178⅓	18	5	.783	157	55	47	116	76	2.37

Selected by Los Angeles Dodgers' organization in 5th round of free-agent draft, June 8, 1981.
†Traded with Pitcher Brett Wise to Cincinnati Reds' organization for Infielder Rafael Landestoy, May 9, 1983.

JULIO CESAR FRANCO

Name pronounced FRANHK-oh.

Born August 23, 1961, at San Pedro de Macoris, Dominican Republic.
Height, 6.00. Weight, 160.
Throws and bats righthanded.

Major League stolen bases: 1983 (32), 1984 (19), 1985 (13). Total—64.
Led American League shortstops in errors with 35 in 1985.
Led Northwest League in total bases with 153 in 1979.
Led Carolina League shortstops in double plays with 73 in 1980.

Led Northwest League shortstops in double plays with 45 in 1979.
Named Carolina League Most Valuable Player, 1980.

Year Club	League	Pos.	G.	AB.	R.	H.	2B.	3B.	HR.	RBI.	B.A.	PO.	A.	E.	F.A.
1978—Butte	Pion.	SS	47	141	34	43	5	2	3	28	.305	37	52	25	.781
1979—Central Ore.	N'west	SS	•71	299	57	*98	15	5	•10	45	.328	103	*256	31	.921
1980—Peninsula	Carol.	SS	•140	*555	105	178	25	6	11	*99	.321	179	*412	42	.934
1981—Reading.................	East.	SS	*139	*532	70	160	17	3	8	74	.301	246	437	30	.958
1982—Oklahoma City	A. A.	*SS-3B	120	463	80	139	19	5	21	66	.300	211	350	*42	.930
1982—Philadelphia†	Nat.	SS-3B	16	29	3	8	1	0	0	3	.276	8	25	0	1.000
1983—Cleveland..............	Amer.	SS	149	560	68	153	24	8	8	80	.273	247	438	28	.961
1984—Cleveland..............	Amer.	SS	160	*658	82	188	22	5	3	79	.286	280	481	*36	.955
1985—Cleveland..............	Amer.	SS-2B	160	636	97	183	33	4	6	90	.288	252	437	36	.950
National League Totals—1 Year.............			16	29	3	8	1	0	0	3	.276	8	25	0	1.000
American League Totals—3 Years			469	1854	247	524	79	17	17	249	.283	779	1356	100	.955
Major League Totals—4 Years.................			485	1883	250	532	80	17	17	252	.283	787	1381	100	.956

Signed as free agent by Philadelphia Phillies' organization, June 23, 1978.
†Traded with Second Baseman Manny Trillo, Outfielder George Vukovich, Pitcher Jay Baller and Catcher Gerry Willard to Cleveland Indians for Outfielder Von Hayes, December 9, 1982.

TERRY JON FRANCONA

Born April 22, 1959, at New Brighton, Pa.
Height, 6.01. Weight, 175.
Throws and bats lefthanded.
Attended University of Arizona, Tucson, Ariz.
Son of John (Tito) Francona, outfielder-first baseman with Baltimore, Chicago A.L., Detroit,
Cleveland, St. Louis, Philadelphia, Atlanta, Oakland and Milwaukee, 1956 through 1970.
Major League stolen bases: 1981 (1), 1982 (2), 1985 (5). Total—8.
Named College Player of the Year by THE SPORTING NEWS, 1980.
Named outfielder on THE SPORTING NEWS College Baseball All-America Team, 1980.

Year Club	League	Pos.	G.	AB.	R.	H.	2B.	3B.	HR.	RBI.	B.A.	PO.	A.	E.	F.A.
1980—Memphis................	South.	OF	60	210	20	63	13	2	1	23	.300	59	4	4	.940
1981—Memphis................	South.	OF-1B	41	161	20	56	8	1	0	18	.348	102	7	5	.956
1981—Denver	A. A.	OF	93	355	53	125	17	*9	1	58	.352	158	7	3	.982
1981—Montreal	Nat.	OF-1B	34	95	11	26	0	1	1	8	.274	41	5	0	1.000
1982—Montreal†	Nat.	OF-1B	46	131	14	42	3	0	0	9	.321	65	0	3	.956
1983—Montreal	Nat.	OF-1B	120	230	21	59	11	1	3	22	.257	172	10	3	.984
1984—Montreal‡	Nat.	1B-OF	58	214	18	74	19	2	1	18	.346	431	50	3	.994
1985—Montreal	Nat.	1B-OF-3B	107	281	19	75	15	1	2	31	.267	431	40	6	.987
Major League Totals—5 Years.................			365	951	83	276	48	5	7	88	.290	1140	105	15	.988

Selected by Chicago Cubs' organization in 2nd round of free-agent draft, June 7, 1977.
Selected by Montreal Expos' organization in 1st round (22nd player selected) of free-agent draft, June 3, 1980.
†On disabled list, June 17 to September 27, 1982.
‡On disabled list, June 15 to September 5, 1984.

DIVISION SERIES RECORD

Year Club	League	Pos.	G.	AB.	R.	H.	2B.	3B.	HR.	RBI.	B.A.	PO.	A.	E.	F.A.
1981—Montreal	Nat.	OF	5	12	0	4	0	0	0	0	.333	8	0	0	1.000

CHAMPIONSHIP SERIES RECORD

Year Club	League	Pos.	G.	AB.	R.	H.	2B.	3B.	HR.	RBI.	B.A.	PO.	A.	E.	F.A.
1981—Montreal	Nat.	PH-OF	2	1	0	0	0	0	0	0	.000	0	0	0	.000

GEORGE ALLEN FRAZIER

Born October 13, 1954, at Oklahoma City, Okla.
Height, 6.05. Weight, 200.
Throws and bats righthanded.
Attended University of Oklahoma, Norman, Okla.
Major League saves: 1980 (3), 1981 (3), 1982 (1), 1983 (8), 1984 (4), 1985 (2). Total—21.

Year Club	League	G.	IP.	W.	L.	Pct.	H.	R.	ER.	SO.	BB.	ERA.
1976—Newark	NYP	6	15	2	1	.667	11	3	3	17	4	1.80
1976—Burlington	Midwest	20	36	7	2	.778	30	9	7	28	14	1.75
1977—Spokane	P. Coast	7	11	2	2	.500	9	5	5	9	5	4.09
1977—Holyoke†	Eastern	45	98	12	7	.632	94	44	36	71	29	3.31
1978—Springfield.................	Am. Assoc.	32	69	6	5	.545	59	33	26	52	25	3.39
1978—St. Louis.................	National	14	22	0	3	.000	22	14	10	8	6	4.09
1979—Springfield.................	Am. Assoc.	24	56	1	2	.333	40	17	15	56	23	2.41
1979—St. Louis.................	National	25	32	2	4	.333	35	19	16	14	12	4.50
1980—Springfield.................	Am. Assoc.	35	60	1	3	.250	44	22	20	55	23	3.00
1980—St. Louis.................	National	22	23	1	4	.200	24	10	7	11	7	2.74
1981—Springfield‡.................	Am. Assoc.	21	31	1	2	.333	35	14	11	28	11	3.19
1981—Columbus.....................	Int'national	27	59	4	1	.800	58	23	21	50	12	3.20
1981—New York	American	16	28	0	1	.000	26	7	5	17	11	1.61
1982—New York.....................	American	63	111⅔	4	4	.500	103	51	43	69	39	3.47
1983—New York§.....................	American	61	115⅓	4	4	.500	94	44	44	78	45	3.43
1984—Cleveland x.................	American	22	44⅓	3	2	.600	45	19	18	24	14	3.65

Year Club	League	G.	IP.	W.	L.	Pct.	H.	R.	ER.	SO.	BB.	ERA.
1984—Chicago	National	37	63⅔	6	3	.667	53	30	29	58	26	4.10
1985—Chicago	National	51	76	7	8	.467	88	57	54	46	52	6.39
National League Totals—5 Years		149	216⅔	16	22	.421	222	130	116	137	103	4.82
American League Totals—4 Years		162	299⅓	11	11	.500	268	121	110	188	109	3.31
Major League Totals—8 Years		311	516	27	33	.450	490	251	226	325	212	3.94

Selected by Texas Rangers' organization in 13th round of free-agent draft, June 6, 1976.

Selected by Milwaukee Brewers' organization in 9th round of free-agent draft, June 8, 1976.

†Traded to St. Louis Cardinals' organization for Catcher Buck Martinez, December 9, 1977.

‡Traded to New York Yankees' organization, June 7, 1981, completing deal in which New York organization traded Shortstop Rafael Santana to St. Louis Cardinals for a player to be named later, February 16, 1981.

§Traded with Outfielder Otis Nixon and a player to be named later to Cleveland Indians for Third Baseman Toby Harrah and a player to be named later, February 5, 1984; New York organization acquired Pitcher Rick Browne and Cleveland organization acquired Pitcher Guy Elston to complete deal, February 8, 1984.

xTraded with Catcher Ron Hassey and Pitcher Rick Sutcliffe to Chicago Cubs for Outfielders Mel Hall and Joe Carter and Pitchers Don Schulze and Darryl Banks, June 13, 1984.

CHAMPIONSHIP SERIES RECORD

Tied American League Championship Series record for most strikeouts by a relief pitcher, game (5), October 14, 1981.

Year Club	League	G.	IP.	W.	L.	Pct.	H.	R.	ER.	SO.	BB.	ERA.
1981—New York	American	1	5⅔	1	0	1.000	5	0	0	5	1	0.00
1984—Chicago	National	1	1⅔	0	0	.000	2	2	2	1	0	10.80
Championship Series Totals—2 Years		2	7⅓	1	0	1.000	7	2	2	6	1	2.45

WORLD SERIES RECORD

Established World Series record for most games lost, six-game Series (3), 1981.

Year Club	League	G.	IP.	W.	L.	Pct.	H.	R.	ER.	SO.	BB.	ERA.
1981—New York	American	3	3⅔	0	3	.000	9	7	7	2	3	17.18

MARVIN FREEMAN

Born April 10, 1963, at Chicago, Ill.
Height, 6.06. Weight, 182.
Throws and bats righthanded.
Attended Jackson State University, Jackson, Miss.

Tied for Northwest League lead in games started by pitchers with 15 in 1984.

Year Club	League	G.	IP.	W.	L.	Pct.	H.	R.	ER.	SO.	BB.	ERA.
1984—Bend	Northwest	15	89⅔	8	5	.615	64	41	26	79	52	2.61
1985—Clearwater	Florida St.	14	88⅓	6	5	.545	72	32	30	55	36	3.06
1985—Reading	Eastern	11	65⅓	1	7	.125	51	41	39	35	52	5.37

Selected by Montreal Expos' organization in 9th round of free-agent draft, June 8, 1981.

Selected by Philadelphia Phillies' organization in 2nd round of free-agent draft, June 4, 1984.

MICHAEL EUGENE FRIEDERICH
(Mike)

Born February 26, 1965, in Winfield, Ill.
Height, 6.05. Weight, 225.
Throws right and bats left and righthanded.

Pitched 2-0 no-hit victory against Lakeland, August 4, 1985 (first game).

Year Club	League	G.	IP.	W.	L.	Pct.	H.	R.	ER.	SO.	BB.	ERA.
1983—Sarasota Astros	Gulf Coast	3	21	3	0	1.000	11	4	4	20	3	1.71
1983—Auburn	NYP	9	70⅓	6	2	.750	58	20	14	75	12	*1.79
1984—Daytona Beach	Florida St.	25	147⅓	12	9	.571	121	69	57	80	94	3.48
1985—Osceola	Florida St.	24	142⅓	8	9	.471	130	74	52	125	62	3.29

Selected by Houston Astros' organization in 3rd round of free-agent draft, June 6, 1983.

DOUGLAS STEVEN FROBEL

Name pronounced Froh-bul.

(Doug)

Born June 6, 1959, at Ottawa, Ont., Can.
Height, 6.04. Weight, 193.
Throws right and bats lefthanded.

Major League stolen bases: 1982 (1), 1983 (1), 1984 (7), 1985 (4). Total—13.

Year Club	League	Pos.	G.	AB.	R.	H.	2B.	3B.	HR.	RBI.	B.A.	PO.	A.	E.	F.A.
1978—Charleston	W. Car.	OF-1B	93	287	30	68	15	1	2	33	.237	80	12	9	.911
1979—Shelby	W. Car.	OF-1B-3B	48	130	11	24	3	0	3	13	.185	153	33	3	.984
1979—Auburn	NYP	3B-1B	35	118	16	34	4	2	4	31	.288	18	30	11	.814
1980—Shelby†	S. Atl.	1B-3B-2B	67	246	42	80	14	1	13	41	.325	220	56	13	.955
1980—Salem	Carol.	1B-3B-OF	40	144	21	34	8	1	7	18	.236	294	29	8	.976
1981—Buffalo	East.	OF-1B	135	479	72	120	17	3	28	78	.251	624	57	19	.973
1982—Portland	P. C.	OF	135	472	76	123	38	3	23	75	.261	229	11	11	.956
1982—Pittsburgh	Nat.	OF	16	34	5	7	2	0	2	3	.206	18	0	0	1.000
1983—Hawaii	P. C.	OF	101	378	66	115	18	6	24	80	.304	169	11	9	.952
1983—Pittsburgh	Nat.	OF	32	60	10	17	4	1	3	11	.283	27	0	1	.964

Year Club	League	Pos.	G.	AB.	R.	H.	2B.	3B.	HR.	RBI.	B.A.	PO.	A.	E.	F.A.
1984—Pittsburgh.............	Nat.	OF	126	276	33	56	9	3	12	28	.203	188	9	9	.956
1985—Pitts.‡-Mont..........	Nat.	OF	65	132	17	25	6	0	1	11	.189	58	2	4	.938
1985—Indianapolis........	A. A.	OF	23	74	9	21	6	1	2	11	.284	29	1	0	1.000
Major League Totals—4 Years................			239	502	65	105	21	4	18	53	.209	291	11	14	.956

Signed as free agent by Pittsburgh Pirates' organization, August 18, 1977.
†On disabled list, May 19 to June 4, 1980.
‡Sold to Indianapolis (Montreal Expos' organization), August 12, 1985.

MICHAEL JAY FUENTES
(Mike)

Born July 11, 1958, at Miami, Fla.
Height, 6.03. Weight, 190.
Throws and bats righthanded.
Received degree in finance from Florida State University, Tallahassee, Fla.

Led American Association in game-winning RBIs with 13 in 1984.
Tied for American Association lead in strikeouts by batters with 103 in 1983.

Year Club	League	Pos.	G.	AB.	R.	H.	2B.	3B.	HR.	RBI.	B.A.	PO.	A.	E.	F.A.
1981—W. Palm Beach....	Fla. St.	OF	67	223	43	65	6	1	15	45	.291	127	5	2	.985
1981—Memphis...............	South.	OF	3	13	0	3	1	0	0	0	.231	0	0	0	.000
1982—Memphis...............	South.	OF	142	*539	*104	144	24	2	*37	*115	.267	284	*22	5	.984
1982—Wichita.................	A. A.	OF	1	2	0	0	0	0	0	0	.000	6	0	0	1.000
1983—Wichita.................	A. A.	OF	132	448	*96	134	23	3	30	91	.299	244	13	6	.977
1983—Montreal...............	Nat.	PH-PR	6	4	1	1	0	0	0	0	.250	0	0	0	.000
1984—Indianapolis........	A. A.	OF	148	522	88	131	22	4	22	80	.251	227	10	3	.988
1984—Montreal...............	Nat.	OF	3	4	0	1	0	0	0	0	.250	4	0	0	1.000
1985—Indianapolis†........	A. A.	OF	121	391	58	100	11	0	12	58	.256	173	6	4	.978
Major League Totals—2 Years................			9	8	1	2	0	0	0	0	.250	4	0	0	1.000

Selected by Minnesota Twins' organization in 5th round of free-agent draft, June 3, 1980.
Selected by Montreal Expos' organization in 2nd round of free-agent draft, June 8, 1981.
†Traded to Oakland A's for Outfielder Tom Romano, January 13, 1986.

WILLIAM DAVID FULTON
(Bill)

Born October 22, 1963, at Pittsburgh, Pa.
Height, 6.03. Weight, 195.
Throws and bats righthanded.
Attended Pensacola Junior College, Pensacola, Fla.

Pitched 5-0 no-hit victory against Lakeland, July 2, 1985 (first game).
Pitched 1-0 no-hit victory against Geneva, July 25, 1983.

Year Club	League	G.	IP.	W.	L.	Pct.	H.	R.	ER.	SO.	BB.	ERA.
1983—Oneonta..	NYP	14	84⅓	4	7	.364	73	49	35	77	35	3.74
1984—Greensboro†.................................	S. Atlantic	10	52	2	3	.400	45	26	24	29	26	4.15
1985—Fort Lauderdale	Florida St.	15	112	11	2	.846	91	31	20	71	30	1.61

Selected by Baltimore Orioles' organization in 1st round (25th player selected) of free-agent draft, January 11, 1983.
Selected by New York Yankees' organization in secondary phase of free-agent draft, June 6, 1983.
†On disabled list, June 12 to July 13, 1984.

MARK CLIFFORD FUNDERBURK

Born May 16, 1957, at Charlotte, N. C.
Height, 6.05. Weight, 230.
Throws and bats righthanded.
Attended Louisburg College, Louisburg, N. C.

Led Southern League in total bases with 272 in 1985.
Led International League in grounding into double plays with 17 in 1981.
Led Midwest League batters in strikeouts with 129 in 1978.

Year Club	League	Pos.	G.	AB.	R.	H.	2B.	3B.	HR.	RBI.	B.A.	PO.	A.	E.	F.A.
1976—Elizabethton	Appal.	OF	61	225	25	53	7	4	7	33	.236	82	8	4	.957
1977—Wisc. Rapids........	Midw.	OF	38	124	14	33	4	2	3	17	.266	32	1	2	.943
1977—Elizabethton	Appal.	OF	47	177	23	49	5	2	7	31	.277	61	2	6	.913
1978—Wisc. Rapids........	Midw.	*1B-OF	132	497	76	128	19	1	25	78	.258	1022	46	*20	.982
1979—Visalia	Calif.	1B-OF	128	484	106	150	20	1	*31	109	.310	1038	77	21	.982
1980—Orlando	South.	OF-1B	139	525	70	131	21	2	26	87	.250	223	15	6	.975
1981—Toledo	Int.	OF	119	394	47	88	14	1	18	52	.223	166	5	11	.940
1981—Minnesota.............	Amer.	OF	8	15	2	3	1	0	0	2	.200	4	1	0	1.000
1982—Orlando†	South.	OF-1B	121	402	80	106	23	1	23	85	.264	224	19	5	.980
1983—Omaha‡.................	A. A.	1B	17	59	4	10	0	0	2	4	.169	172	3	6	.967
1983—Mex. C. Tigers....	Mex.	OF-1B	36	129	24	47	7	1	8	33	.364	73	2	2	.974
1984—Rimini	Italy						Figures unavailable								
1985—Orlando	South.	OF-1B	140	523	70	148	20	1	*34	*116	.283	496	28	4	.992
1985—Minnesota.............	Amer.	OF-1B	23	70	7	22	7	1	2	13	.314	15	0	0	1.000
Major League Totals—2 Years................			31	85	9	25	8	1	2	15	.294	19	1	0	1.000

†Released, October 21, 1982; signed by Omaha (Kansas City Royals' organization), February 1, 1983.
‡Released, May 22, 1983; signed by Orlando (Minnesota Twins' organization), November 30, 1984.

GARY JOSEPH GAETTI

Name pronounced Guy-ETT-ee.

Born August 19, 1958, at Centralia, Ill.
Height, 6.00. Weight, 192.
Throws and bats righthanded.
Attended Lake Land College, Mattoon, Ill., and Northwest
Missouri State University, Maryville, Mo.

Tied major league records by hitting home run in first major league at-bat, September 20, 1981; most home runs, opening day of season (2), April 6, 1982; most sacrifice flies, rookie season (13), 1982.

Major League stolen bases: 1983 (7), 1984 (11), 1985 (13). Total—31.
Led American League in sacrifice flies with 13 in 1982.
Led American League third basemen in putouts with 142 in 1984 and 146 in 1985.
Led American League third basemen in assists with 334, total chances with 496 and tied for lead in errors with 20 in 1984.
Led American League third basemen in double plays with 46 in 1983.
Led Southern League third basemen in putouts with 122 and assists with 281 in 1981.
Led Midwest League third basemen in double plays with 35 in 1980.
Tied for Appalachian League lead in errors by third basemen with 18 in 1979.

Year Club	League	Pos.	G.	AB.	R.	H.	2B.	3B.	HR.	RBI.	B.A.	PO.	A.	E.	F.A.
1979—Elizabethton	Appal.	3B-SS	66	230	50	59	15	2	14	42	.257	70	134	21	.907
1980—Wis. Rapids	Midw.	3B	138	503	77	134	27	3	★22	82	.266	★94	★363	●35	.929
1981—Orlando	South.	★3B-1B	137	561	92	137	19	2	30	93	.277	143	283	★32	.930
1981—Minnesota	Amer.	3B	9	26	4	5	0	0	2	3	.192	5	17	0	1.000
1982—Minnesota	Amer.	3B-SS	145	508	59	117	25	4	25	84	.230	106	291	17	.959
1983—Minnesota	Amer.	3B-SS	157	584	81	143	30	3	21	78	.245	★131	361	17	.967
1984—Minnesota	Amer.	3B-OF-SS	●162	588	55	154	29	4	5	65	.262	163	335	21	.960
1985—Minnesota	Amer.	3B-OF-1B	160	560	71	138	31	0	20	63	.246	162	316	18	.964
Major League Totals—5 Years			633	2266	270	557	115	11	73	293	.246	567	1320	73	.963

Selected by St. Louis Cardinals' organization in 4th round of free-agent draft, January 10, 1978.
Selected by Chicago White Sox' organization in secondary phase of free-agent draft, June 6, 1978.
Selected by Minnesota Twins' organization in secondary phase of free-agent draft, June 5, 1979.

GREGORY CARPENTER GAGNE

(Greg)

Born November 12, 1961, at Fall River, Mass.
Height, 5.11. Weight, 185.
Throws and bats righthanded.

Major League stolen bases: 1985 (10).
Led International League shortstops in total chances with 599 in 1983.

Year Club	League	Pos.	G.	AB.	R.	H.	2B.	3B.	HR.	RBI.	B.A.	PO.	A.	E.	F.A.
1979—Paintsville	Appal.	SS	41	106	10	19	2	3	0	7	.179	28	62	14	.865
1980—Greensboro†	S. Atl.	SS-3B-2B	98	337	39	91	20	5	3	32	.270	133	233	35	.913
1981—Greensboro	S. Atl.	2B-SS-3B	104	364	71	108	21	3	9	48	.297	172	280	25	.948
1982—Fort Lauderdale‡	Fla. St.	SS	1	3	0	1	0	0	0	0	.333	3	5	0	1.000
1982—Orlando	South.	SS-2B	136	504	73	117	23	4	11	57	.232	185	403	39	.938
1983—Toledo	Int.	SS	119	392	61	100	22	4	17	66	.255	201	★364	★34	.943
1983—Minnesota	Amer.	SS	10	27	2	3	1	0	0	3	.111	10	14	2	.923
1984—Toledo§	Int.	3B-SS-2B	70	236	31	66	7	2	9	27	.280	58	168	20	.926
1984—Minnesota	Amer.	PR-PH	2	1	0	0	0	0	0	0	.000	0	0	0	.000
1985—Minnesota x	Amer.	SS	114	293	37	66	15	3	2	23	.225	149	269	14	.968
Major League Totals—3 Years			126	321	39	69	16	3	2	26	.215	159	283	16	.965

Selected by New York Yankees' organization in 5th round of free-agent draft, June 5, 1979.
†On disabled list, September 4 to September 22, 1980.
‡Traded with Pitchers Ron Davis and Paul Boris and a reported $400,000 to Minnesota Twins for Shortstop Roy Smalley, April 10, 1982.
§On disabled list, June 13 to July 18, 1984.
xOn disabled list, August 10 to September 1, 1985.

TELMANCH GAINEY

(Ty)

Born December 25, 1960, at Cheraw, S. C.
Height, 6.01. Weight, 190.
Throws and bats lefthanded.

Year Club	League	Pos.	G.	AB.	R.	H.	2B.	3B.	HR.	RBI.	B.A.	PO.	A.	E.	F.A.
1979—Sarasota Astros	Gulf C.	OF	21	61	5	14	1	1	0	7	.230	13	1	1	.933
1980—Sarasota Astros	Gulf C.	OF	47	167	41	47	4	2	2	26	.281	48	2	3	.943
1980—Daytona Beach	Fla. St.	OF	5	12	3	1	0	0	0	0	.083	4	0	0	1.000
1981—Daytona Beach	Fla. St.	OF	114	347	40	86	11	8	6	38	.248	127	7	3	.978
1982—Daytona Beach	Fla. St.	OF	106	425	92	145	20	11	10	58	★.341	161	6	9	.949
1982—Columbus	South.	OF	16	58	9	17	5	0	1	5	.293	19	1	0	1.000
1983—Columbus	South.	OF	110	397	65	107	15	1	9	43	.270	56	1	0	1.000
1984—Columbus	South.	OF	133	467	85	129	28	2	13	78	.276	240	8	4	.984
1985—Tucson†	P. C.	OF	68	232	42	78	14	2	5	46	.336	119	4	4	.969
1985—Houston	Nat.	OF	13	37	5	6	0	0	0	0	.162	21	0	2	.913
Major League Totals—1 Year			13	37	5	6	0	0	0	0	.162	21	0	2	.913

Selected by Houston Astros' organization in 2nd round of free-agent draft, June 5, 1979.
†On disabled list, May 24 to June 14, 1985.

ANDRES JOSE GALARRAGA
Name pronounced Gahl-ah-RAH-guh.

Born June 18, 1961, at Caracas, Venezuela.
Height, 6.03. Weight, 209.
Throws and bats righthanded.

Major League stolen bases: 1985 (1).
Led Southern League in total bases with 271, slugging percentage with .508, intentional bases on balls received with 10 and tied for lead in being hit by pitch with 9 in 1984.
Tied for American Association lead in game-winning RBIs with 13 in 1985.
Led Southern League first basemen in total chances with 1,428 and double plays with 130 in 1984.
Named Southern League Most Valuable Player, 1984.

Year Club	League	Pos.	G.	AB.	R.	H.	2B.	3B.	HR.	RBI.	B.A.	PO.	A.	E.	F.A.
1979—W. Palm Beach....	Fla. St.	1B	7	23	3	3	0	0	0	1	.130	2	1	0	1.000
1979—Calgary	Pion.	1B-3B-C	42	112	14	24	3	1	4	16	.214	187	21	5	.976
1980—Calgary	Pion.	1-3-C-O	59	190	27	50	11	4	4	22	.263	287	52	21	.942
1981—Jamestown	NYP	C-1-O-3	47	154	24	40	5	4	6	26	.260	154	15	0	1.000
1982—W. Palm Beach....	Fla. St.	1B-OF	105	338	39	95	20	2	14	51	.281	462	36	9	.982
1983—W. Palm Beach....	Fla. St.	1B-OF-3B	104	401	55	116	18	3	10	66	.289	861	77	13	.986
1984—Jacksonville	South.	1B	143	533	81	154	28	4	27	87	.289	*1302	*110	16	.989
1985—Indianapolis	A. A.	1B-OF	121	439	*75	118	15	8	25	87	.269	930	63	14	.986
1985—Montreal	Nat.	1B	24	75	9	14	1	0	2	4	.187	173	22	1	.995
Major League Totals—1 Year			24	75	9	14	1	0	2	4	.187	173	22	1	.995

Signed as free agent by Montreal Expos' organization, January 19, 1979.

DAVID THOMAS GALLAGHER
(Dave)

Born September 20, 1960, at Trenton, N.J.
Height, 6.00. Weight, 180.
Throws and bats righthanded.
Attended Mercer County Community College, Trenton, N.J.

Led Midwest League in sacrifice hits with 21 in 1982.
Led International League outfielders in total chances with 369 in 1985.
Tied for Eastern League lead in double plays by outfielders with 4 in 1983.

Year Club	League	Pos.	G.	AB.	R.	H.	2B.	3B.	HR.	RBI.	B.A.	PO.	A.	E.	F.A.
1980—Batavia	NYP	OF	69	241	33	66	6	3	5	36	.274	114	4	2	.983
1981—Waterloo	Midw.	OF-3B	127	435	55	102	22	1	3	34	.234	224	22	7	.972
1982—Chattanooga	South.	OF	15	54	10	12	2	1	0	4	.222	32	1	0	1.000
1982—Waterloo	Midw.	OF	110	409	61	118	25	7	6	47	.289	232	15	4	*.984
1983—Buffalo†	East.	OF-3B	107	376	64	127	21	3	2	47	*.338	223	13	5	.979
1984—Maine	Int.	OF	116	380	49	94	19	5	6	49	.247	208	7	3	.986
1985—Maine	Int.	OF	132	488	71	118	22	3	9	55	.242	*357	9	3	*.992

Selected by Oakland A's organization in 1st round (third player selected) of free-agent draft, January 8, 1980.
Selected by Cleveland Indians' organization in secondary phase of free-agent draft, June 3, 1980.
†On disabled list, May 2 to June 6, 1983.

MICHAEL ANTHONY GALLEGO
(Mike)

Born October 31, 1960, at Whittier, Calif.
Height, 5.08. Weight, 160.
Throws and bats righthanded.
Attended University of California, Los Angeles, Calif.

Major League stolen bases: 1985 (1).

Year Club	League	Pos.	G.	AB.	R.	H.	2B.	3B.	HR.	RBI.	B.A.	PO.	A.	E.	F.A.
1981—Modesto	Calif.	2B	60	202	38	55	9	3	0	23	.272	127	161	13	.957
1982—West Haven	East.	2B-SS	54	139	17	25	1	0	0	5	.180	85	111	4	.980
1982—Tacoma	P. C.	2B-3B-SS	44	136	12	30	3	1	0	11	.221	73	111	8	.958
1983—Tacoma†	P. C.	2B	2	2	0	0	0	0	0	0	.000	0	1	0	1.000
1983—Albany	East.	2B-SS-3B	90	274	31	61	6	0	0	18	.223	184	260	4	.991
1984—Tacoma	P. C.	2B-SS-3B	101	288	29	70	8	1	0	18	.243	167	231	13	.968
1985—Oakland	Amer.	2B-SS-3B	76	77	13	16	5	1	1	9	.208	57	94	1	.993
1985—Modesto	Calif.	2B-SS-3B	6	25	1	5	1	0	0	2	.200	12	11	1	.958
Major League Totals—1 Year			76	77	13	16	5	1	1	9	.208	57	94	1	.993

Selected by Oakland A's organization in 2nd round of free-agent draft., June 8, 1981.
†On temporary inactive list, April 10 to May 20, 1983.

BALVINO GALVEZ

Born March 31, 1964, at San Pedro de Macoris, Dominican Republic.
Height, 6.00. Weight, 170.
Throws and bats righthanded.

Year Club	League	G.	IP.	W.	L.	Pct.	H.	R.	ER.	SO.	BB.	ERA.
1982—Lethbridge	Pioneer	10	20⅓	0	0	.000	33	21	13	11	17	5.75
1983—Bradenton Dodgers	Gulf Coast	13	66⅓	4	3	.571	62	33	22	51	19	2.98
1984—Vero Beach	Florida St.	26	156⅔	12	11	.522	152	68	63	76	62	3.62
1985—San Antonio	Texas	26	170⅔	10	9	.526	181	99	86	111	79	4.54

Signed as free agent by Los Angeles Dodgers' organization, September 10, 1981.

OSCAR CHARLES GAMBLE

Born December 20, 1949, at Ramer, Ala.
Height, 5.11. Weight, 177.
Throws right and bats lefthanded.

Major League stolen bases: 1970 (5), 1971 (5), 1973 (3), 1974 (5), 1975 (11), 1976 (5), 1977 (1), 1978 (1), 1979 (2), 1980 (2), 1982 (6), 1984 (1). Total—47.

Year Club	League	Pos.	G.	AB.	R.	H.	2B.	3B.	HR.	RBI.	B.A.	PO.	A.	E.	F.A.
1968—Caldwell	Pion.	OF	34	94	18	25	2	0	2	12	.266	42	4	4	.920
1969—San Antonio	Texas	OF	119	477	62	142	*32	3	7	32	.298	247	10	8	.970
1969—Chicago†	Nat.	OF	24	71	6	16	1	1	1	5	.225	41	1	4	.913
1970—Eugene	P. C.	OF	28	108	26	32	7	2	1	8	.296	54	3	0	1.000
1970—Philadelphia	Nat.	OF	88	275	31	72	12	4	1	19	.262	148	4	7	.956
1971—Eugene	P. C.	OF	39	138	30	40	5	2	4	20	.290	65	4	3	.958
1971—Philadelphia	Nat.	OF	92	280	24	62	11	1	6	23	.221	125	4	4	.970
1972—Eugene	P. C.	OF	42	144	30	42	8	1	8	20	.292	67	8	1	.987
1972—Philadelphia‡	Nat.	OF-1B	74	135	17	32	5	2	1	13	.237	54	2	0	1.000
1973—Cleveland	Amer.	OF	113	390	56	104	11	3	20	44	.267	67	1	2	.971
1974—Cleveland	Amer.	OF	135	454	74	132	16	4	19	59	.291	19	1	0	1.000
1975—Cleveland§	Amer.	OF	121	348	60	91	16	3	15	45	.261	146	8	2	.987
1976—New York x	Amer.	OF	110	340	43	79	13	1	17	57	.232	199	10	4	.981
1977—Chicago y	Amer.	OF	137	408	75	121	22	2	31	83	.297	73	1	1	.987
1978—San Diego z	Nat.	OF	126	375	46	103	15	3	7	47	.275	172	12	4	.979
1979—Tex. a-N.Y.	Amer.	OF	100	274	48	98	10	1	19	64	.358	88	5	3	.969
1980—New York b	Amer.	OF	78	194	40	54	10	2	14	50	.278	65	2	0	1.000
1981—New York	Amer.	OF	80	189	24	45	8	0	10	27	.238	77	0	0	1.000
1982—New York	Amer.	OF	108	316	49	86	21	2	18	57	.272	59	6	0	1.000
1983—New York c	Amer.	OF	74	180	26	47	10	2	7	26	.261	64	1	4	.942
1984—New York de	Amer.	OF	54	125	17	23	2	0	10	27	.184	15	1	0	1.000
1985—Chicago f	Amer.	DH	70	148	20	30	5	0	4	20	.203	0	0	0	.000
National League Totals—5 Years			404	1136	124	285	44	11	16	107	.251	540	23	19	.967
American League Totals—12 Years			1180	3366	532	910	144	20	184	559	.270	872	36	16	.983
Major League Totals—17 Years			1584	4502	656	1195	188	31	200	666	.265	1412	59	35	.977

Selected by Chicago Cubs' organization in 16th round of free-agent draft, June 7, 1968.

†Traded with Pitcher Dick Selma to Philadelphia Phillies for Outfielder Johnny Callison, November 17, 1969.

‡Traded with Outfielder Roger Freed to Cleveland Indians for Outfielder Del Unser and Infielder Terry Wedgewood, November 30, 1972.

§Traded to New York Yankees for Pitcher Pat Dobson, November 22, 1975.

xTraded with Pitchers Bob Polinsky and LaMarr Hoyt, and cash estimated at $250,000 to Chicago White Sox for Shortstop Bucky Dent, April 5, 1977.

yGranted free agency, October 28, 1977; signed by San Diego Padres, November 29, 1977.

zTraded with Catcher Dave Roberts to Texas Rangers for Third Baseman Kurt Bevacqua, Catcher Bill Fahey, First Baseman Mike Hargrove and cash estimated at $300,000, October 25, 1978.

aTraded with Third Baseman Amos Lewis and two players to be named later to New York Yankees for Outfielder Mickey Rivers and three players to be named later, August 1, 1979; New York sent Pitchers Bob Polinsky, Neal Mersch and Mark Softy and Texas sent Pitchers Gene Nelson and Ray Fontenot to complete deal, October 8, 1979.

bOn disabled list, May 14 to June 23, 1980.

cGranted free agency, November 7, 1983; re-signed by Yankees, April 17, 1984.

dOn disabled list, July 17 to September 3, 1984.

eGranted free agency, November 8, 1984; signed by Chicago White Sox, March 23, 1985.

fReleased, August 12, 1985.

DIVISION SERIES RECORD

Year Club	League	Pos.	G.	AB.	R.	H.	2B.	3B.	HR.	RBI.	B.A.	PO.	A.	E.	F.A.
1981—New York	Amer.	DH	4	9	2	5	1	0	2	3	.555	0	0	0	.000

CHAMPIONSHIP SERIES RECORD

Year Club	League	Pos.	G.	AB.	R.	H.	2B.	3B.	HR.	RBI.	B.A.	PO.	A.	E.	F.A.
1976—New York	Amer.	OF-PH	3	8	1	2	1	0	0	1	.250	4	0	2	.667
1980—New York	Amer.	O-DH-PH	2	5	1	1	0	0	0	0	.200	1	0	0	1.000
1981—New York	Amer.	DH-OF	3	6	2	1	0	0	0	1	.167	4	0	0	1.000
Championship Series Totals—3 Years			8	19	4	4	1	0	0	2	.211	9	0	2	.818

WORLD SERIES RECORD

Year Club	League	Pos.	G.	AB.	R.	H.	2B.	3B.	HR.	RBI.	B.A.	PO.	A.	E.	F.A.
1976—New York	Amer.	PH-OF	3	8	0	1	0	0	1	.125	3	0	0	1.000
1981—New York	Amer.	OF-PH	3	6	1	2	0	0	0	1	.333	4	0	0	1.000
World Series Totals—2 Years			6	14	1	3	0	0	0	2	.214	7	0	0	1.000

JAMES ELMER GANTNER
(Jim)

Born January 5, 1954, at Fond du Lac, Wis.
Height, 5.11. Weight, 175.
Throws right and bats lefthanded.
Attended University of Wisconsin, Oshkosh, Wis.

Tied major league record for longest errorless game by second baseman (25 innings), May 8, finished May 9, 1984; fielded 24⅓ innings.

Tied American League record for most innings played by second baseman, game (25), May 8, finished May 9, 1984; fielded 24⅓ innings.

Major League stolen bases: 1976 (1), 1977 (2), 1978 (2), 1979 (3), 1980 (11), 1981 (3), 1982 (6), 1983 (5), 1984 (6), 1985 (11). Total—50.

Led American League second basemen in total chances with 613 in 1981, 900 in 1983 and 844 in 1984.
Led American League second basemen in double plays with 95 in 1981 and 128 in 1983.
Led Pacific Coast League third basemen in putouts with 136 and in fielding percentage with .936 in 1977.
Led Eastern League third basemen in fielding percentage with .953 in 1976.
Led Eastern League third basemen in putouts with 118 and assists with 310 in 1975.

Year	Club	League	Pos.	G.	AB.	R.	H.	2B.	3B.	HR.	RBI.	B.A.	PO.	A.	E.	F.A.
1974—Newark	NYP	SS-3B	62	177	35	54	6	2	5	21	.305	64	134	14	.934
1975—Thetford Mines	East.	3B-SS	●138	456	61	117	17	0	12	48	.257	129	317	33	.931
1976—Berkshire	East.	3B-SS	126	403	56	118	21	1	6	53	.293	120	294	20	.954
1976—Milwaukee	Amer.	3B	26	69	6	17	1	0	0	7	.246	17	37	1	.982
1977—Spokane	P. C.	★3B-OF	●143	541	98	152	35	5	15	80	.281	137	★321	31	.937
1977—Milwaukee	Amer.	3B	14	47	4	14	1	0	1	2	.298	8	29	4	.902
1978—Milwaukee	Amer.	2-3-S-1	43	97	14	21	1	0	1	8	.216	46	82	5	.962
1979—Milwaukee	Amer.	3-2-S-P	70	208	29	59	10	3	2	22	.284	80	161	7	.972
1980—Milwaukee	Amer.	3B-2B-SS	132	415	47	117	21	3	4	40	.282	159	335	15	.971
1981—Milwaukee	Amer.	2B	107	352	35	94	14	1	2	33	.267	251	352	10	.984
1982—Milwaukee	Amer.	2B	132	447	48	132	17	2	4	43	.295	307	398	13	.982
1983—Milwaukee	Amer.	2B	161	603	85	170	23	8	11	74	.282	374	★512	14	.984
1984—Milwaukee	Amer.	2B	153	613	61	173	27	1	3	56	.282	★362	469	13	.985
1985—Milwaukee	Amer.	2B-3B-SS	143	523	63	133	15	4	5	44	.254	278	436	11	.985
Major League Totals 10 Years			001	0074	092	930	130	22	33	329	.276	1882	2811	93	.981

Selected by Milwaukee Brewers' organization in 12th round of free-agent draft, June 5, 1974.

DIVISION SERIES RECORD

Year	Club	League	Pos.	G.	AB.	R.	H.	2B.	3B.	HR.	RBI.	B.A.	PO.	A.	E.	F.A.
1981—Milwaukee	Amer.	2B	4	14	1	2	1	0	0	0	.143	3	15	2	.900

CHAMPIONSHIP SERIES RECORD

Year	Club	League	Pos.	G.	AB.	R.	H.	2B.	3B.	HR.	RBI.	B.A.	PO.	A.	E.	F.A.
1982—Milwaukee	Amer.	2B	5	16	1	3	0	0	0	2	.188	12	8	0	1.000

WORLD SERIES RECORD

Established World Series records for most assists by second baseman, seven-game Series (33), 1982; most errors by second baseman, seven-game Series (5), 1982.

Year	Club	League	Pos.	G.	AB.	R.	H.	2B.	3B.	HR.	RBI.	B.A.	PO.	A.	E.	F.A.
1982—Milwaukee	Amer.	2B	7	24	5	8	4	1	0	4	.333	9	33	5	.894

PITCHING RECORD

Year	Club	League	G.	IP.	W.	L.	Pct.	H.	R.	ER.	SO.	BB.	ERA.
1979—Milwaukee	American	1	1	0	0	.000	2	0	0	0	0	0.00

HENRY EUGENE GARBER
(Gene)

Born November 13, 1947, at Lancaster, Pa.
Height, 5.10. Weight, 172.
Throws and bats righthanded.
Received bachelor of arts degree in history and political science from
Elizabethtown College, Elizabethtown, Pa. in 1969.

Established major league record for most games lost by relief pitcher, season (16), 1979.
Tied major league record for most consecutive games won by relief pitcher, three consecutive games (3), May 15 through 17, 1975.
Major League saves: 1973 (11), 1974 (5), 1975 (14), 1976 (11), 1977 (19), 1978 (25), 1979 (25), 1980 (7), 1981 (2), 1982 (30), 1983 (9), 1984 (11), 1985 (1). Total—170.
Led National League in games finished in relief with 47 in 1975.
Tied for International League lead in complete games with 13 in 1972.
Named International League Pitcher of the Year, 1972.

Year	Club	League	G.	IP.	W.	L.	Pct.	H.	R.	ER.	SO.	BB.	ERA.
1965—Salem	Ap'lachian	1	⅔	0	0	.000	0	0	0	2	2	0.00
1965—Batavia	NYP	11	72	4	3	.571	71	42	28	40	31	3.50
1966—Raleigh	Carolina	16	94	4	4	.500	106	53	48	76	28	4.60
1967—Raleigh	Carolina	18	138	8	6	.571	103	41	29	68	47	1.89
1968—York	Eastern	16	118	7	2	.778	79	33	21	86	30	1.60
1968—Columbus	Int'national	23	59	5	1	.833	62	21	16	32	17	2.44
1969—York	Eastern	11	73	5	3	.625	61	40	25	57	40	3.08
1969—Pittsburgh	National	2	5	0	0	.000	6	3	3	3	1	5.40
1969—Columbus†	Int'national	17	123	7	6	.538	116	51	42	74	37	3.07
1970—Columbus	Int'national	30	95	5	2	.714	96	57	50	75	38	4.74
1970—Pittsburgh	National	14	22	0	3	.000	22	13	13	7	10	5.32
1971—Charleston‡	Int'national	24	170	14	6	.700	★184	85	79	105	54	4.18
1972—Charleston	Int'national	20	163	14	3	★.824	131	49	41	103	45	★2.26
1972—Pittsburgh§	National	4	6	0	0	.000	7	5	5	3	3	7.50
1973—Kansas City	American	48	153	9	9	.500	164	78	72	60	49	4.24
1974—Kansas City x	American	17	28	1	2	.333	35	21	15	14	13	4.82
1974—Toledo	Int'national	3	22	2	1	.667	19	7	1	17	3	0.41
1974—Philadelphia	National	34	48	4	0	1.000	39	15	11	27	31	2.06
1975—Philadelphia	National	★71	110	10	12	.455	104	48	44	69	27	3.60

Year Club	League	G.	IP.	W.	L.	Pct.	H.	R.	ER.	SO.	BB.	ERA.
1976—Philadelphia	National	59	93	9	3	.750	78	33	29	92	30	2.81
1977—Philadelphia	National	64	103	8	6	.571	82	30	27	78	23	2.36
1978—Philadelphia y-Atlanta	National	65	117	6	5	.545	84	32	28	85	24	2.15
1979—Atlanta	National	68	106	6	16	.273	121	66	51	56	24	4.33
1980—Atlanta	National	68	82	5	5	.500	95	42	35	51	24	3.84
1981—Atlanta z	National	35	59	4	6	.400	49	23	17	34	20	2.59
1982—Atlanta	National	69	119⅓	8	10	.444	100	40	31	68	32	2.34
1983—Atlanta a	National	43	60⅔	4	5	.444	72	37	31	45	23	4.60
1984—Atlanta	National	62	106	3	6	.333	103	45	36	55	24	3.06
1985—Atlanta	National	59	97⅓	6	6	.500	98	41	39	66	25	3.61
American League Totals—2 Years		65	181	10	11	.476	199	99	87	74	62	4.33
National League Totals—15 Years		717	1134⅓	73	83	.468	1060	473	400	739	321	3.17
Major League Totals—16 Years		782	1315⅓	83	94	.469	1259	572	487	813	383	3.33

Selected by Pittsburgh Pirates' organization in 13th round of free-agent draft, June 14, 1965.
†On military list, September 2, 1969, through February 18, 1970.
‡On temporary inactive list, June 24 to July 12, 1971.
§Traded to Kansas City Royals for Pitcher Jim Rooker, October 25, 1972.
xSold to Philadelphia Phillies, July 12, 1974.
yTraded to Atlanta Braves for Pitcher Dick Ruthven, June 15, 1978.
zOn disabled list, May 4 to August 9, 1981.
aOn disabled list, June 25 to July 27, 1983.

CHAMPIONSHIP SERIES RECORD

Year Club	League	G.	IP.	W.	L.	Pct.	H.	R.	ER.	SO.	BB.	ERA.
1976—Philadelphia	National	2	⅔	0	1	.000	2	2	1	0	1	13.50
1977—Philadelphia	National	3	5⅓	1	1	.500	4	3	2	3	0	3.38
1982—Atlanta	National	2	3⅓	0	1	.000	4	3	3	3	1	8.10
Championship Series Totals—3 Years		7	9⅓	1	3	.250	10	8	6	6	2	5.79

BARBARO GARBEY GARBEY

Name pronounced BAR-bar-o Gar-BAY.

Born December 4, 1956, at Santiago, Cuba.
Height, 5.10. Weight, 170.
Throws and bats righthanded.

Major League stolen bases: 1984 (6), 1985 (3). Total—9.
Tied for Southern League lead in double plays by outfielders with 5 in 1982.

Year Club	League	Pos.	G.	AB.	R.	H.	2B.	3B.	HR.	RBI.	B.A.	PO.	A.	E.	F.A.
1980—Lakeland	Fla. St.	OF	26	88	15	32	4	0	1	16	.364	60	4	3	.955
1981—Birmingham†	South.	OF	107	391	56	112	17	4	6	55	.286	106	3	5	.956
1981—Evansville	A. A.	OF	4	12	4	1	0	0	0	0	.083	7	0	0	1.000
1982—Birmingham‡	South.	OF-1B	120	480	69	143	32	4	17	99	.298	206	22	11	.956
1983—Evansville§	A. A.	OF-3B-1B	101	377	60	121	21	6	14	59	.321	147	55	12	.944
1984—Detroit	Amer.	1-3-0-2	110	327	45	94	17	1	5	52	.287	411	58	12	.975
1985—Detroit x	Amer.	1B-OF-3B	86	237	27	61	9	1	6	29	.257	228	20	3	.988
Major League Totals—2 Years			196	564	72	155	26	2	11	81	.275	639	78	15	.980

Signed as free agent by Detroit Tigers' organization, June 6, 1980.
†On disabled list, April 16 to May 4, 1981.
‡On disabled list, August 22, 1982 through remainder of season.
§On suspended list, July 1 to July 31, 1983.
xTraded to Oakland A's for Outfielder Dave Collins, November 13, 1985.

CHAMPIONSHIP SERIES RECORD

Year Club	League	Pos.	G.	AB.	R.	H.	2B.	3B.	HR.	RBI.	B.A.	PO.	A.	E.	F.A.
1984—Detroit	Amer.	DH-PH	3	9	1	3	0	0	0	0	.333	0	0	0	.000

WORLD SERIES RECORD

Tied World Series record for most at-bats, inning (2), October 12, 1984 (second inning).

Year Club	League	Pos.	G.	AB.	R.	H.	2B.	3B.	HR.	RBI.	B.A.	PO.	A.	E.	F.A.
1984—Detroit	Amer.	DH-PH	4	12	0	0	0	0	0	0	.000	0	0	0	.000

ALFONSO RAFAEL GARCIA
(Kiko)

(Nicknamed by grandparents.)

Born October 14, 1953, at Martinez, Calif.
Height, 5.11. Weight, 178.
Throws and bats righthanded.

Major League stolen bases: 1976 (2), 1977 (2), 1978 (7), 1979 (11), 1980 (8), 1981 (2), 1982 (1), 1983 (1). Total—34.
Led International League shortstops in double plays with 112 in 1976.
Led International League second basemen in double plays with 71 in 1975.
Led Southern League shortstops in double plays with 105 in 1974.

Year Club	League	Pos.	G.	AB.	R.	H.	2B.	3B.	HR.	RBI.	B.A.	PO.	A.	E.	F.A.
1971—Bluefield	Appal.	SS	56	203	35	51	3	*5	2	23	.251	95	128	24	.503
1971—Stockton	Calif.	SS	4	14	1	4	0	1	0	2	.286	8	13	2	.913
1972—Miami	Fla. St.	SS-3B	126	445	51	112	15	6	2	39	.252	176	416	40	.937

Year Club	League	Pos.	G.	AB.	R.	H.	2B.	3B.	HR.	RBI.	B.A.	PO.	A.	E.	F.A.
1973—Lodi	Calif.	SS	129	494	89	128	15	10	3	36	.259	*237	361	43	.933
1974—Asheville	South.	SS	135	511	68	140	18	5	7	53	.274	*250	*510	48	.941
1975—Rochester	Int.	2B-SS	122	405	34	99	11	1	3	32	.244	260	255	25	.953
1976—Rochester	Int.	SS	130	450	75	124	11	*10	3	44	.276	*241	*473	*38	.949
1976—Baltimore	Amer.	SS	11	32	2	7	1	1	1	4	.219	15	27	0	1.000
1977—Baltimore	Amer.	SS-2B	65	131	20	29	6	0	2	10	.221	78	152	8	.966
1978—Baltimore	Amer.	SS-2B	79	186	17	49	6	4	0	13	.263	87	175	16	.942
1979—Baltimore	Amer.	S-2-O-3	126	417	54	103	15	9	5	24	.247	209	321	27	.952
1980—Baltimore†‡	Amer.	3B-2B-OF	111	311	27	62	8	0	1	27	.199	177	292	11	.977
1981—Houston§	Nat.	SS-2B-3B	48	136	9	37	6	1	0	15	.272	58	119	11	.941
1982—Houston xy	Nat.	SS-3B-2B	34	76	5	16	5	0	1	5	.211	29	62	5	.948
1983—Portland	P. C.	SS-3B-1B	35	113	19	39	7	1	1	16	.345	47	76	3	.976
1983—Philadelphia	Amer.	2B-SS-3B	84	118	22	34	7	1	2	9	.288	94	115	6	.972
1984—Philadelphia z	Nat.	SS-3B-2B	57	60	6	14	2	0	0	5	.233	25	54	2	.975
1985—Philadelphia a	Nat.	SS-3B	4	3	0	0	0	0	0	0	.000	0	2	0	1.000
American League Totals—5 Years			392	1077	120	250	36	14	9	78	.232	566	967	62	.961
National League Totals—5 Years			227	393	42	101	20	2	3	34	.257	206	352	24	.959
Major League Totals—10 Years			619	1470	162	351	56	16	12	112	.239	772	1319	86	.960

Selected by Baltimore Orioles' organization in 3rd round of free-agent draft, June 8, 1971.

†On disabled list, May 23 to June 7, 1980.

‡Traded to Houston Astros for Outfielder Chris Bourjos and cash, April 1, 1981.

§On disabled list, April 4 to April 19, 1981.

xOn disabled list, August 21 to September 5, 1982.

yGranted free agency, November 10, 1982; signed by Philadelphia Phillies' organization, March 1, 1983.

zReleased, April 3, 1985; re-signed by Phillies, April 5, 1985.

aReleased, May 17, 1985.

DIVISION SERIES RECORD

Year Club	League	Pos.	G.	AB.	R.	H.	2B.	3B.	HR.	RBI.	B.A.	PO.	A.	E.	F.A.
1981—Houston	Nat.	SS	2	4	0	0	0	0	0	0	.000	2	4	0	1.000

CHAMPIONSHIP SERIES RECORD

Year Club	League	Pos.	G.	AB.	R.	H.	2B.	3B.	HR.	RBI.	B.A.	PO.	A.	E.	F.A.
1979—Baltimore	Amer.	SS	3	11	1	3	0	0	0	2	.273	6	16	2	.917

WORLD SERIES RECORD

Tied World Series records for most times reached first base safely, game (5), October 12, 1979; most at bats and most times faced pitcher, inning (2), October 13, 1979 (eighth inning); most three-base hits, game, batting in three runs (1), October 12, 1979.

Year Club	League	Pos.	G.	AB.	R.	H.	2B.	3B.	HR.	RBI.	B.A.	PO.	A.	E.	F.A.
1979—Baltimore	Amer.	SS	6	20	4	8	2	1	0	6	.400	10	17	1	.964

DAMASO DOMINGO GARCIA

First name pronounced Da-MAH-so.

Born February 7, 1957, at Moca, Dominican Republic.
Height, 6.00. Weight, 175.
Throws and bats righthanded.
Attended Madre y Maestra University, Santiago, Dominican Republic.

Major League stolen bases: 1978 (1), 1979 (2), 1980 (13), 1981 (13), 1982 (54), 1983 (31), 1984 (46), 1985 (28). Total—188.

Led Florida State League second baseman in double plays with 83 in 1976.

Tied for New York-Pennsylvania League lead in double plays by second basemen with 33 in 1975.

Named second baseman on THE SPORTING NEWS American League All-Star Team, 1982 and 1985.

Named second baseman on THE SPORTING NEWS American League Silver Slugger team, 1982.

Year Club	League	Pos.	G.	AB.	R.	H.	2B.	3B.	HR.	RBI.	B.A.	PO.	A.	E.	F.A.
1975—Oneonta	NYP	2B	50	157	28	42	4	2	0	17	.268	143	118	*17	.929
1976—Fort Lauderdale†	Fla.St.	2B	124	412	55	109	•22	4	1	41	.265	*273	353	21	*.968
1977—West Haven	East.	2B	129	445	62	118	13	9	0	53	.265	263	382	19	.971
1978—Tacoma	P. C.	2B-SS	102	385	51	103	18	6	1	53	.268	217	345	25	.957
1978—New York	Amer.	2B-SS	18	41	5	8	0	0	0	1	.195	36	35	4	.947
1979—Columbus ‡	Int.	SS-1B	39	118	18	32	1	0	1	3	.271	53	85	6	.958
1979—New York §	Amer.	SS-3B	11	38	3	10	1	0	0	4	.263	9	28	4	.902
1980—Toronto	Amer.	2B	140	543	50	151	30	7	4	46	.278	316	471	16	.980
1981—Toronto x	Amer.	2B	64	250	24	63	8	1	1	13	.252	132	181	9	.972
1982—Toronto	Amer.	2B	147	597	89	185	32	3	5	42	.310	273	461	15	.980
1983—Toronto	Amer.	2B	131	525	84	161	23	6	3	38	.307	266	360	12	.981
1984—Toronto	Amer.	2B	152	633	79	180	32	5	5	46	.284	267	427	14	.980
1985—Toronto	Amer.	2B	146	600	70	169	25	4	8	65	.282	302	371	13	.981
Major League Totals—8 Years			809	3227	404	927	151	26	26	255	.287	1601	2334	87	.978

Signed as free agent by New York Yankees' organization, March 10, 1975.

†On suspended list, June 4 to June 7, 1976.

‡On disabled list, May 14 to July 24 and July 31 to August 13, 1979.

§Traded with First Baseman Chris Chambliss and Pitcher Paul Mirabella to Toronto Blue Jays for Catcher Rick Cerone, Pitcher Tom Underwood and Outfielder Ted Wilborn, November 1, 1979.

xOn disabled list, August 22, 1981 through remainder of season.

Established American League Championship Series record for most doubles, seven-game Series (4), 1985.

Year	Club	League	Pos.	G.	AB.	R.	H.	2B.	3B.	HR.	RBI.	B.A.	PO.	A.	E.	F.A.
1985—Toronto		Amer.	2B	7	30	4	7	4	0	0	1	.233	10	12	0	1.000

ALL-STAR GAME RECORD

Year	League	Pos.	AB.	R.	H.	2B.	3B.	HR.	RBI.	B.A.	PO.	A.	E.	F.A.
1984—American		2B	1	0	0	0	0	0	0	.000	1	0	0	1.000
1985—American		2B	2	0	1	0	0	0	0	.500	0	3	0	1.000
All-Star Game Totals—2 Years			3	0	1	0	0	0	0	.333	1	3	0	1.000

RONALD CLYDE GARDENHIRE
(Ron)

Born October 24, 1957, at Butzbach, Germany.
Height, 6.00. Weight, 174.
Throws and bats righthanded.
Attended Paris Junior College, Paris, Tex., and University of Texas, Austin, Tex.

Major League stolen bases: 1981 (2), 1982 (5), 1984 (6). Total—13.
Led Texas League shortstops in assists with 406 and errors with 40 in 1980.

Year	Club	League	Pos.	G.	AB.	R.	H.	2B.	3B.	HR.	RBI.	B.A.	PO.	A.	E.	F.A.
1979—Lynchburg		Carol.	SS	70	277	36	82	13	3	4	27	.296	120	252	21	.947
1980—Jackson		Texas	SS-2B	127	458	58	118	16	6	6	64	.258	168	411	41	.934
1981—Tidewater		Int.	SS-2B-3B	125	414	52	105	17	8	2	40	.254	206	373	33	.946
1981—New York		Nat.	SS-2B-3B	27	48	2	13	1	0	0	3	.271	28	50	2	.975
1982—New York		Nat.	SS-2B-3B	141	384	29	92	17	1	3	33	.240	235	399	29	.956
1983—New York		Nat.	SS	17	32	1	2	0	0	0	1	.063	13	30	0	1.000
1983—Tidewater†		Int.	SS	102	387	63	111	20	6	4	39	.287	202	321	27	.951
1984—New York‡		Nat.	SS-2B-3B	74	207	20	51	7	1	1	10	.246	98	154	12	.955
1985—New York§		Nat.	SS-2B-3B	26	39	5	7	2	1	0	2	.179	21	32	4	.930
1985—Tidewater		Int.	3B-SS-2B	22	71	3	15	2	0	1	10	.211	20	36	5	.918
Major League Totals—5 Years				285	710	57	165	27	3	4	49	.232	395	665	47	.958

Selected by New York Mets' organization in 6th round of free-agent draft, June 5, 1979.
†On disabled list, July 21 to July 31, 1983.
‡On disabled list, July 20 to August 9 and August 20 to September 10, 1984.
§On disabled list, May 2 to May 17, May 25 to July 19 and August 16 to September 1, 1985; included rehabilitation disability assignment to Tidewater, June 24 to July 13, 1985.

WESLEY BRIAN GARDNER
(Wes)

Born April 29, 1961, at Benton, Ark.
Height, 6.04. Weight, 197.
Throws and bats righthanded.
Attended University of Central Arkansas, Conway, Ark.

Major League saves: 1984 (1).
Led International League in saves with 20 in 1984 and tied for lead with 18 in 1985.
Led International League in games finished in relief with 37 in 1984.

Year	Club	League	G.	IP.	W.	L.	Pct.	H.	R.	ER.	SO.	BB.	ERA.
1982—Little Falls		NYP	23	77⅔	3	6	.333	73	48	32	77	29	3.71
1983—Lynchburg		Carolina	49	62⅔	6	3	.667	55	16	13	67	32	1.87
1984—Tidewater		Int'national	40	56	1	2	.333	40	11	10	36	19	1.61
1984—New York		National	21	25⅓	1	1	.500	34	19	18	19	8	6.39
1985—Tidewater		Int'national	53	76⅔	7	6	.538	57	31	24	75	34	2.82
1985—New York†		National	9	12	0	2	.000	18	14	7	11	8	5.25
Major League Totals—2 Years			30	37⅓	1	3	.250	52	33	25	30	16	6.03

Selected by New York Mets' organization in 22nd round of free-agent draft, June 7, 1982.
†Traded with Pitcher Calvin Schiraldi and Outfielders John Christensen and LaSchelle Tarver to Boston Red Sox for Pitchers Bob Ojeda, Tom McCarthy, John Mitchell and Chris Bayer, November 13, 1985.

PHILIP MASON GARNER
(Phil)

Born April 30, 1949, at Jefferson City, Tenn.
Height, 5.10. Weight, 177.
Throws and bats righthanded.
Received bachelor of science degree in general business from
University of Tennessee, Knoxville, Tenn., in 1973.

Tied major league record for most home runs, bases filled, two consecutive games (2), September 14 and 15, 1978.
Tied National League record for most home runs, bases filled, month (2), September, 1978.
Major League stolen bases: 1974 (1), 1975 (4), 1976 (35), 1977 (32), 1978 (27), 1979 (17), 1980 (32), 1981 (10), 1982 (24), 1983 (18), 1984 (3), 1985 (4). Total—207.
Led American League second basemen in total chances with 865 in 1976.
Led National League second basemen in assists with 499, total chances with 869 and double plays with 116 in 1980.
Led Pacific Coast League third basemen in putouts with 104, assists with 261 and double plays with 23 in 1973.

Year	Club	League	Pos.	G.	AB.	R.	H.	2B.	3B.	HR.	RBI.	B.A.	PO.	A.	E.	F.A.
1971—Burlington		Midw.	3B	116	439	73	122	22	4	11	70	.278	∗122	203	29	.918
1972—Birmingham		South.	3B	71	264	45	74	10	6	12	40	.280	74	116	13	.936

Year Club	League	Pos.	G.	AB.	R.	H.	2B.	3B.	HR.	RBI.	B.A.	PO.	A.	E.	F.A.
1972—Iowa	A. A.	3B	70	247	33	60	18	4	9	22	.243	50	140	10	.950
1973—Tucson	P. C.	*3B-2B	138	516	87	149	23	12	14	73	.289	107	270	*35	.915
1973—Oakland	Amer.	3B	9	5	0	0	0	0	0	0	.000	2	3	0	1.000
1974—Tucson	P. C.	3B-SS	96	388	78	128	29	10	11	51	.330	92	182	15	.948
1974—Oakland	Amer.	3B-SS-2B	30	28	4	5	1	0	0	1	.179	11	24	1	.972
1975—Oakland	Amer.	*2B-SS	●160	488	46	120	21	5	6	54	.246	355	427	*26	.968
1976—Oakland†	Amer.	2B	159	555	54	145	29	12	8	74	.261	378	*465	22	.975
1977—Pittsburgh	Nat.	3B-2B-SS	153	585	99	152	35	10	17	77	.260	223	351	17	.971
1978—Pittsburgh	Nat.	3B-2B-SS	154	528	66	138	25	9	10	66	.261	258	389	28	.959
1979—Pittsburgh	Nat.	3B-2B-SS	150	549	76	161	32	8	11	59	.293	234	396	22	.966
1980—Pittsburgh	Nat.	*2B-SS	151	548	62	142	27	6	5	58	.259	349	500	*21	.976
1981—Pitt‡§-Hou.	Nat.	2B	87	294	35	73	9	3	1	26	.248	183	250	12	.973
1982—Houston	Nat.	2B-3B	155	588	65	161	33	8	13	83	.274	285	464	17	.978
1983—Houston	Nat.	3B	154	567	76	135	24	2	14	79	.238	100	311	24	.945
1984—Houston	Nat.	3B-2B	128	374	60	104	17	6	4	45	.278	136	251	12	.970
1985—Houston	Nat.	3B-2B	135	463	65	124	23	10	6	51	.268	101	229	21	.940
American League Totals—4 Years			358	1076	104	270	51	17	14	129	.251	746	919	49	.971
National League Totals—9 Years			1267	4496	604	1190	225	62	81	544	.265	1869	3141	174	.966
Major League Totals—13 Years			1625	5572	708	1460	276	79	95	673	.262	2615	4060	223	.968

Selected by Montreal Expos' organization in 8th round of free-agent draft, June 4, 1970.

Selected by Oakland A's organization in secondary phase of free-agent draft, January 13, 1971.

†Traded with Infielder Tommy Helms and Pitcher Chris Batton to Pittsburgh Pirates for Pitchers Doc Medich, Dave Giusti, Rick Langford and Doug Bair and Outfielders Mitchell Page and Tony Armas, March 15, 1977.

‡On disabled list, April 2 to April 23, 1981.

§Traded to Houston Astros for Second Baseman Johnny Ray and two players to be named later, August 31, 1981; Pittsburgh Pirates' organization acquired Outfielder Kevin Houston and Pitcher Randy Niemann to complete deal, September 9, 1981.

DIVISION SERIES RECORD

Year Club	League	Pos.	G.	AB.	R.	H.	2B.	3B.	HR.	RBI.	B.A.	PO.	A.	E.	F.A.
1981—Houston	Nat.	2B	5	18	1	2	0	0	0	0	.111	6	8	1	.933

CHAMPIONSHIP SERIES RECORD

Year Club	League	Pos.	G.	AB.	R.	H.	2B.	3B.	HR.	RBI.	B.A.	PO.	A.	E.	F.A.
1975—Oakland	Amer.	2B	3	5	0	0	0	0	0	0	.000	7	4	1	.917
1979—Pittsburgh	Nat.	2B-SS	3	12	4	5	0	1	1	1	.417	8	9	0	1.000
Championship Series Totals—2 Years			6	17	4	5	0	1	1	1	.294	15	13	1	.966

WORLD SERIES RECORD

Established World Series record for most double plays by second baseman, seven-game Series (9), 1979.

Tied World Series records for highest batting average, seven-game Series (.500), 1979; one or more hits, each game, seven-game Series, 1979; most assists by second baseman, inning (3), October 13, 1979 (ninth inning).

Year Club	League	Pos.	G.	AB.	R.	H.	2B.	3B.	HR.	RBI.	B.A.	PO.	A.	E.	F.A.
1979—Pittsburgh	Nat.	2B	7	24	4	12	4	0	0	5	.500	21	23	2	.957

ALL-STAR GAME RECORD

Year League		Pos.	AB.	R.	H.	2B.	3B.	HR.	RBI.	B.A.	PO.	A.	E.	F.A.
1976—American		2B	1	0	0	0	0	0	0	.000	1	1	0	1.000
1980—National		2B	2	1	1	0	0	0	0	.500	1	3	0	1.000
1981—National		2B	0	0	0	0	0	0	0	.000	0	0	0	.000
All-Star Game Totals—3 Years			3	1	1	0	0	0	0	.333	2	4	0	1.000

SCOTT WILLIAM GARRELTS

Name pronounced Guh-RELTZ.

Born October 30, 1961, at Urbana, Ill.

Height, 6.04. Weight, 195.

Throws and bats righthanded.

Pitched seven-inning, 1-0 no-hit victory against Tacoma, August 20, 1983.

Major League saves: 1985 (13).

Tied for Midwest League lead in games started by pitchers with 27 in 1980.

Year Club	League	G.	IP.	W.	L.	Pct.	H.	R.	ER.	SO.	BB.	ERA.
1979—Great Falls	Pioneer	8	43	1	4	.200	45	37	28	26	40	5.86
1980—Clinton	Midwest	27	176	11	11	.500	155	98	76	*159	*149	3.89
1981—Shreveport†	Texas	14	71	3	8	.273	56	43	35	73	43	4.44
1982—Shreveport	Texas	27	151⅓	9	10	.474	131	76	64	159	90	3.81
1982—San Francisco	National	1	2	0	0	.000	3	3	3	4	2	13.50
1983—Phoenix‡	P. Coast	21	97⅔	5	5	.500	86	64	50	89	81	4.61
1983—San Francisco	National	5	35⅔	2	2	.500	33	11	10	16	19	2.52
1984—Phoenix	P. Coast	21	97⅔	5	7	.417	97	75	64	69	82	5.90
1984—San Francisco	National	21	43	2	3	.400	45	33	27	32	34	5.65
1985—San Francisco	National	74	105⅔	9	6	.600	76	37	27	106	58	2.30
Major League Totals—4 Years		101	186⅓	13	11	.542	157	84	67	158	113	3.24

Selected by San Francisco Giants' organization in 1st round (15th player selected) of free-agent draft, June 5, 1979.

†On disabled list, July 15 to August 16, 1981.

‡On disabled list, May 12 to June 6 and July 8 to July 24, 1983.

ALL-STAR GAME RECORD

Member of National League All-Star Team in 1985; did not play.

STEVEN PATRICK GARVEY
(Steve)

Born December 22, 1948, at Tampa, Fla.
Height, 5.10. Weight, 190.
Throws and bats righthanded.
Received bachelor of science degree in education from
Michigan State University, East Lansing, Mich. in 1971.

Established major league records for most seasons leading league in games by first baseman (9); highest fielding percentage by first baseman, season, 100 and 150 or more games (1.000), 1984; fewest errors by first baseman, season, 150 or more games (0), 1984; highest lifetime fielding percentage by first baseman (.996); most consecutive errorless games by first baseman, season (159), April 3 through September 29, 1984; most consecutive errorless games by first baseman, lifetime (193), June 26, second game, 1983 through April 14, 1985; most consecutive chances accepted, season, no errors, by first baseman (1,319), April 3 through September 29, 1984.

Tied major league records for most games, first baseman, season (162), 1976, 1979, 1980 and 1985; most unassisted double plays, first baseman, game (2), August 31, 1976; most long hits, consecutive, game (5), August 28, 1977; most long hits, game (5), August 28, 1977.

Established National League records for most consecutive years playing in all clubs' games (7); most consecutive games played (1,207); most consecutive chances accepted, lifetime, no errors, by first baseman (1,633), June 26, first game, 1983, through April 15, 1985.

Tied National League records for most long hits, consecutive, season (5), August 28, 1977; most years leading league in games played (6).

Major League stolen bases: 1970 (1), 1971 (1), 1972 (4), 1974 (5), 1975 (11), 1976 (19), 1977 (9), 1978 (10), 1979 (3), 1980 (6), 1981 (3), 1982 (5), 1983 (4), 1984 (1). Total—82.

Led National League in grounding into double plays with 25 in 1979 and 1984.

Tied for National League lead in sacrifice flies with 10 in 1984.

Led National League first basemen in double plays with 138 in 1985.

Led National League first basemen in total chances with 1,606 in 1974, 1,585 in 1975, 1,669 in 1977, 1,629 in 1978 and 1,539 in 1985.

Led Pacific Coast League third basemen in errors with 24 in 1970.

Led Pioneer League in total bases with 151 and tied for league lead in sacrifice flies with 4 in 1968.

Led Pioneer League third basemen in double plays with 10 in 1968.

Named National League Most Valuable Player by Baseball Writers' Association of America, 1974.

Named first baseman on THE SPORTING NEWS National League All-Star Team, 1974, 1975, 1977 and 1978.

Named first baseman on THE SPORTING NEWS National League All-Star fielding team, 1974 through 1977.

Named third baseman on THE SPORTING NEWS College Baseball All-America Team, 1968.

Year Club	League	Pos.	G.	AB.	R.	H.	2B.	3B.	HR.	RBI.	B.A.	PO.	A.	E.	F.A.
1968—Ogden	Pion.	3B	62	216	49	73	12	3	⋆20	⋆59	.338	⋆51	⋆109	⋆23	.874
1969—Albuquerque	Texas	3B-1B	83	316	51	118	18	2	14	85	.373	348	86	20	.956
1969—Los Angeles	Nat.	PH	3	3	0	1	0	0	0	0	.333	0	0	0	.000
1970—Spokane	P. C.	3B-2B-OF	95	376	71	120	26	5	15	87	.319	103	178	26	.915
1970—Los Angeles	Nat.	3B-2B	34	93	8	25	5	0	1	6	.269	23	59	5	.943
1971—Los Angeles†	Nat.	3B	81	225	27	51	12	1	7	26	.227	53	161	14	.939
1972—Los Angeles	Nat.	⋆3B-1B	96	294	36	79	14	2	9	30	.269	104	189	⋆28	.913
1973—Los Angeles	Nat.	1B-OF	114	349	37	106	17	3	8	50	.304	731	27	7	.991
1974—Los Angeles	Nat.	1B	156	642	95	200	32	3	21	111	.312	⋆1536	62	8	.995
1975—Los Angeles	Nat.	1B	160	659	85	210	38	6	18	95	.319	⋆1500	77	8	⋆.995
1976—Los Angeles	Nat.	1B	162	631	85	200	37	4	13	80	.317	⋆1583	67	3	⋆.998
1977—Los Angeles	Nat.	1B ●162	646	91	192	25	3	33	115	.297	⋆1606	55	8	⋆.995
1978—Los Angeles	Nat.	1B ●162	639	89	⋆202	36	9	21	113	.316	⋆1546	74	9	.994
1979—Los Angeles	Nat.	1B	162	648	92	204	32	1	28	110	.315	1402	93	7	.995
1980—Los Angeles	Nat.	1B ⋆163	658	78	⋆200	27	1	26	106	.304	1502	112	6	.996
1981—Los Angeles	Nat.	1B ●110	431	63	122	23	1	10	64	.283	1019	55	1	⋆.999
1982—Los Angeles‡	Nat.	1B ●162	625	66	176	35	1	16	86	.282	1539	111	8	.995
1983—San Diego§	Nat.	1B	100	388	76	114	22	0	14	59	.294	888	49	6	.994
1984—San Diego	Nat.	1B	161	617	72	175	27	2	8	86	.284	1232	87	0	⋆1.000
1985—San Diego	Nat.	1B ●162	654	80	184	34	6	17	81	.281	⋆1442	92	5	.997
Major League Totals—17 Years			2150	8202	1080	2441	416	43	250	1218	.298	17706	1370	123	.994

Selected by Minnesota Twins' organization in 3rd round of free-agent draft, June, 1966.

Selected by Los Angeles Dodgers' organization in secondary phase of free-agent draft, June 7, 1968.

†On disabled list, June 23 to July 26, 1971.

‡Granted free agency, November 10, 1982; signed by San Diego Padres, December 21, 1982.

§On disabled list, July 30, 1983 through remainder of season.

DIVISION SERIES RECORD

Year	Club	League	Pos.	G.	AB.	R.	H.	2B.	3B.	HR.	RBI.	B.A.	PO.	A.	E.	F.A.
1981—Los Angeles		Nat.	1B	5	19	4	7	0	1	2	4	.368	49	5	0	1.000

CHAMPIONSHIP SERIES RECORD

Established Championship Series records for most consecutive hits, total Series (6); most long hits, Series (6), 1978; most total bases, four-game Series (22), 1978; most runs batted in, total Series (21).

Tied Championship Series records for most home runs, four-game Series (4), 1978; most runs, game (4), October 9, 1974; most Series, two or more home runs (2); most runs batted in, game (5), October 6, 1984.

Established National League Championship Series records for most runs, four-game Series (6), 1978; highest slugging average, total Series, 10 or more games and 30 or more at bats (.678); most home runs, total Series (8); most runs batted in, five-game Series (7), 1984; most long hits, total Series (12).

Tied National League Championship Series record for most hits, game (4), October 9, 1974 and October 6, 1984.

Year	Club	League	Pos.	G.	AB.	R.	H.	2B.	3B.	HR.	RBI.	B.A.	PO.	A.	E.	F.A.
1974—Los Angeles		Nat.	1B	4	18	4	7	1	0	2	5	.389	40	2	1	.977
1977—Los Angeles		Nat.	1B	4	13	2	4	0	0	0	0	.308	40	1	0	1.000
1978—Los Angeles		Nat.	1B	4	18	6	7	1	1	4	7	.389	44	5	0	1.000

Year Club League	Pos.	G.	AB.	R.	H.	2B.	3B.	HR.	RBI.	B.A.	PO.	A.	E.	F.A.
1981—Los Angeles .... Nat.	1B	5	21	2	6	0	0	1	2	.286	49	2	0	1.000
1984—San Diego .... Nat.	1B	5	20	1	8	1	0	1	7	.400	35	3	0	1.000
Championship Series Totals—5 Years....		22	90	15	32	3	1	8	21	.356	208	13	1	.995

WORLD SERIES RECORD

Tied World Series record for most unassisted double plays by first baseman, game (1), October 9, 1984.
Tied World Series record for most singles, five-game Series, (8), 1974; one or more hits, each game, five-game Series, 1974.

Year Club League	Pos.	G.	AB.	R.	H.	2B.	3B.	HR.	RBI.	B.A.	PO.	A.	E.	F.A.
1974—Los Angeles .... Nat.	1B	5	21	2	8	0	0	0	1	.381	34	3	0	1.000
1977—Los Angeles .... Nat.	1B	6	24	5	9	1	1	1	3	.375	59	6	0	1.000
1978—Los Angeles .... Nat.	1B	6	24	1	5	1	0	0	0	.208	58	3	1	.984
1981—Los Angeles .... Nat.	1B	6	24	3	10	1	0	0	0	.417	44	3	0	1.000
1984—San Diego .... Nat.	1B	5	20	2	4	2	0	0	2	.200	34	3	0	1.000
World Series Totals—5 Years		28	113	13	36	5	1	1	6	.319	229	18	1	.996

ALL-STAR GAME RECORD

Tied All-Star game record for most games played at first base (8).

Year League	Pos.	AB.	R.	H.	2B.	3B.	HR.	RBI.	B.A.	PO.	A.	E.	F.A.
1974—National	1B	4	1	2	1	0	0	1	.500	6	2	0	1.000
1975—National	1B	3	1	2	0	0	1	1	.667	4	1	0	1.000
1976—National	1B	3	1	1	0	1	0	1	.333	6	0	0	1.000
1977—National	1B	3	1	1	0	0	1	1	.333	1	0	0	1.000
1978—National	1B	3	1	2	0	1	0	2	.667	7	1	0	1.000
1979—National	1B	2	1	0	0	0	0	0	.000	5	0	0	1.000
1980—National	1B	2	0	0	0	0	0	0	.000	7	0	0	1.000
1981—National	1B	2	0	1	0	0	0	0	.500	3	1	0	1.000
1984—National	1B	3	1	1	0	0	0	0	.333	5	1	0	1.000
1985—National	1B	3	0	1	0	0	0	1	.333	5	0	0	1.000
All-Star Game Totals—10 Years		28	7	11	2	2	2	7	.393	49	6	0	1.000

RICHARD LEO GEDMAN JR.

(Rich)

Born September 26, 1959, at Worcester, Mass.
Height, 6.00. Weight, 215.
Throws right and bats lefthanded.

Major League stolen bases: 1985 (2).
Hit for the cycle, September 18, 1985.
Led International League catchers in double plays with 13 in 1980.
Named American League Rookie Player of the Year by THE SPORTING NEWS, 1981.

Year Club League	Pos.	G.	AB.	R.	H.	2B.	3B.	HR.	RBI.	B.A.	PO.	A.	E.	F.A.
1978—Winter Haven....... Fla. St.	C	98	297	35	89	17	3	3	32	.300	377	39	2	*.995
1979—Bristol..................... East.	C	130	470	48	129	25	1	12	63	.274	497	58	11	*.981
1980—Pawtucket .... Int.	C	111	347	43	82	18	2	11	29	.236	367	*65	7	.984
1980—Boston.................... Amer.	C	9	24	2	5	0	0	0	1	.208	13	0	2	.867
1981—Pawtucket .... Int.	C	25	81	8	24	3	0	2	11	.296	176	20	6	.969
1981—Boston.................... Amer.	C	62	205	22	59	15	0	5	26	.288	275	30	3	.990
1982—Boston.................... Amer.	C	92	289	30	72	17	2	4	26	.249	397	29	10	.977
1983—Boston.................... Amer.	C	81	204	21	60	16	1	2	18	.294	274	26	6	.980
1984—Boston.................... Amer.	C	133	449	54	121	26	4	24	72	.269	693	58	*18	.977
1985—Boston.................... Amer.	C	144	498	66	147	30	5	18	80	.295	768	*78	*15	.983
Major League Totals—6 Years		521	1669	195	464	104	12	53	223	.278	2420	221	54	.980

Signed as free agent by Boston Red Sox' organization, August 5, 1977.

ALL-STAR GAME RECORD

Year League	Pos.	AB.	R.	H.	2B.	3B.	HR.	RBI.	B.A.	PO.	A.	E.	F.A.
1985—American	C	1	0	0	0	0	0	0	.000	4	0	0	1.000

JOHN DAVID GEISEL

Name pronounced GUY-sul.

(Dave)

Born January 18, 1955, at Windber, Pa.
Height, 6.03. Weight, 205.
Throws and bats lefthanded.

Major League saves: 1983 (5), 1984 (3). Total—8.

Year Club League	G.	IP.	W.	L.	Pct.	H.	R.	ER.	SO.	BB.	ERA.
1974—Midland............................. Texas	24	150	12	7	.632	170	72	63	92	37	3.78
1975—Midland............................. Texas	35	132	8	5	.615	149	67	59	75	44	4.02
1976—Midland............................. Texas	20	107	5	8	.385	114	59	44	59	45	3.70
1976—Wichita............................. Am. Assoc.	9	50	2	4	.333	50	33	28	27	25	5.04
1977—Wichita†........................... Am. Assoc.	28	94	4	6	.400	95	49	46	57	62	4.40
1978—Wichita............................. Am. Assoc.	19	107	6	9	.400	102	68	59	62	65	4.96
1978—Chicago............................. National	18	23	1	0	1.000	27	12	11	15	11	4.30
1979—Wichita‡........................... Am. Assoc.	45	79	5	5	.500	76	29	22	49	47	2.51
1979—Chicago............................. National	7	15	0	0	.000	10	1	1	5	4	0.60

Year Club	League	G.	IP.	W.	L.	Pct.	H.	R.	ER.	SO.	BB.	ERA.
1980—Wichita§	Am. Assoc.	9	15	1	0	1.000	14	12	11	17	13	6.60
1981—Iowa x	Am. Assoc.	28	38	1	2	.333	38	24	19	43	31	4.50
1981—Chicago y	National	11	16	2	0	1.000	11	3	1	7	10	0.56
1982—Syracuse	Int'national	21	80⅔	4	2	.667	74	38	35	43	38	3.90
1982—Toronto	American	16	31⅔	1	1	.500	32	15	14	22	17	3.98
1983—Toronto z	American	47	52⅓	0	3	.000	47	28	27	50	31	4.64
1984—Salt Lake City	P. Coast	26	72	4	2	.667	81	41	39	52	40	4.88
1984—Seattle	American	20	43⅓	1	1	.500	47	22	20	28	9	4.15
1985—Seattle	American	12	27	0	0	.000	40	35	21	19	17	15	6.33
1985—Calgary a	P. Coast	20	114⅓	5	7	.417	153	92	73	69	45	5.75
National League Totals—3 Years		36	54	3	0	1.000	48	16	13	27	25	2.17
American League Totals—4 Years		95	154⅓	2	5	.286	161	86	80	117	72	4.67
Major League Totals—7 Years		131	208⅓	5	5	.500	209	102	93	144	97	4.02

Selected by Chicago Cubs' organization in 5th round of free-agent draft, June 5, 1973.
†On disabled list, April 15 to May 6, 1977.
‡On disabled list, June 17 to June 28, 1979.
§On disabled list, April 14 to July 29, 1980.
xOn temporarily inactive list, April 14 to May 28, 1981.
yTraded to Toronto Blue Jays' organization, March 25, 1982, completing deal in which Toronto traded Pitcher Paul Mirabella to Chicago Cubs' organization for a player to be named later, December 28, 1981.
zDrafted by Seattle Mariners, December 5, 1983.
aGranted free agency, October 15, 1985.

STEPHEN EDWARD GEORGE
(Steve)

Born October 18, 1961, at St. Louis, Mo.
Height, 6.00. Weight, 160.
Throws left and bats left and righthanded.
Attended Broward Community College, Fort Lauderdale,
Fla., and Florida Southern College, Lakeland, Fla.

Pitched five-inning, 6-0 no-hit victory against Miami, August 14, 1985.
Led Florida State League in shutouts with 5 and complete games with 12 in 1985.

Year Club	League	G.	IP.	W.	L.	Pct.	H.	R.	ER.	SO.	BB.	ERA.
1982—Paintsville	Ap'lachian	13	63⅓	3	4	.429	62	45	35	64	38	4.97
1983—Greensboro	S. Atlantic	35	84	5	4	.556	93	65	47	78	64	5.04
1984—Greensboro†	S. Atlantic	24	48⅔	2	4	.333	30	31	28	46	55	5.18
1985—Fort Lauderdale	Florida St.	24	164⅔	13	7	.650	120	48	32	141	76	1.75

Selected by New York Yankees' organization in 15th round of free-agen draft, June 7, 1982.
†On temporarily inactive list, April 9 to April 19, 1984.

CRAIG STUART GERBER

Born January 8, 1959, at Chicago, Ill.
Height, 6.00. Weight, 175.
Throws right and bats lefthanded.
Attended California State Poly University, San Luis Obispo, Calif.

Tied for California League lead in caught stealing with 20 in 1982.
Tied for Pioneer League lead in caught stealing with 9 in 1981.
Led Pacific Coast League shortstops in fielding percentage with .976 in 1984.
Led Eastern League second basemen in putouts with 311, assists with 441, double plays with 107 and total chances with 762 in 1983.
Led Pioneer League third basemen in putouts with 61 and double plays with 23 in 1981.

Year Club	League	Pos.	G.	AB.	R.	H.	2B.	3B.	HR.	RBI.	B.A.	PO.	A.	E.	F.A.
1981—Idaho Falls	Pion.	3B-2B-SS	●70	★288	52	77	13	1	0	15	.267	73	145	11	.952
1982—Redwood	Calif.	S-2-3-O	131	493	71	145	21	6	0	39	.294	178	385	23	.961
1982—Spokane	P. C.	2B-3B	2	8	2	5	2	0	0	0	.625	4	6	0	1.000
1983—Nashua	East.	★2B-C-SS	132	502	65	119	18	9	1	40	.237	316	442	10	★.987
1983—Edmonton	P. C.	3B	2	6	2	1	0	0	0	0	.167	1	6	0	1.000
1984—Edmonton	P. C.	SS-2B-OF	114	365	55	84	18	7	1	40	.230	186	339	14	.974
1985—California	Amer.	SS-3B-2B	65	91	8	24	1	2	0	6	.264	56	112	5	.971
Major League Totals—1 Year			65	91	8	24	1	2	0	6	.264	56	112	5	.971

Selected by California Angels' organization in 20th round of free-agent draft, June 8, 1981.

HAROLD KENNETH GERHART
(Ken)

Born May 19, 1961, at Charleston, S.C.
Height, 6.00. Weight, 190.
Throws and bats righthanded.
Attended Middle Tennessee State University, Murfreesboro, Tenn.

Led Carolina League in total bases with 275 in 1983.
Led Appalachian League in sacrifice flies with 8 in 1982.

Year Club	League	Pos.	G.	AB.	R.	H.	2B.	3B.	HR.	RBI.	B.A.	PO.	A.	E.	F.A.
1982—Bluefield	Appal.	OF	66	228	57	59	13	0	12	43	.259	105	3	2	.982
1983—Hagerstown	Carol.	OF	130	501	131	137	29	8	★31	86	.273	274	11	13	.956
1984—Charlotte	South.	OF	85	264	40	53	8	3	13	40	.201	183	5	4	.979

Year Club	League	Pos.	G.	AB.	R.	H.	2B.	3B.	HR.	RBI.	B.A.	PO.	A.	E.	F.A.
1984—Hagerstown	Carol.	OF	47	168	39	54	18	3	6	21	.321	108	1	5	.956
1985—Charlotte...............	South.	OF	68	222	55	61	16	1	17	52	.275	177	4	1	.995

Selected by Baltimore Orioles' organization in 5th round of free-agent draft, June 7, 1982.

JOHN MICHAEL GIBBONS

Born June 8, 1962, at Great Falls, Mont.
Height, 5.11. Weight, 185.
Throws and bats righthanded.

Tied for Appalachian League lead in being hit by pitch with 7 in 1980.
Led South Atlantic League catchers in double plays with 8 in 1982.
Tied for Appalachian League lead in passed balls with 11 in 1980.

Year Club	League	Pos.	G.	AB.	R.	H.	2B.	3B.	HR.	RBI.	B.A.	PO.	A.	E.	F.A.
1980—Kingsport...............	Appal.	C	53	181	28	50	7	1	7	34	.276	177	11	7	.964
1981—Shelby....................	S. Atl.	C	109	360	33	68	11	4	8	57	.189	629	65	18	.975
1982—Shelby....................	S. Atl.	C-1B	99	321	60	85	13	2	12	67	.265	559	72	17	.974
1982—Jackson	Texas	C	6	18	1	5	0	1	0	3	.278	21	1	0	1.000
1983—Jackson	Texas	C	110	373	63	111	25	1	18	67	.298	575	62	12	.982
1984—New York†...........	Nat.	C	10	31	1	2	0	0	0	1	.065	54	5	1	.983
1984—Tidewater.............	Int.	C	65	211	31	54	9	1	6	27	.256	199	20	4	.982
1985—Tidewater.............	Int.	C	108	370	35	96	10	2	9	30	.259	531	36	6	★.990
Major League Totals—1 Year..................			10	31	1	2	0	0	0	1	.065	54	5	1	.983

Selected by New York Mets' organization in 1st round (24th player selected) of free-agent draft, June 3, 1980.
†On disabled list, March 26 to April 10 and May 2 to June 4, 1984.

KIRK HAROLD GIBSON

Born May 28, 1957, at Pontiac, Mich.
Height, 6.03. Weight, 215.
Throws and bats lefthanded.
Attended Michigan State University, East Lansing, Mich.

Major League stolen bases: 1979 (3), 1980 (4), 1981 (17), 1982 (9), 1983 (14), 1984 (29), 1985 (30). Total—106.
Named as wide receiver on THE SPORTING NEWS College Football All-America Team, 1978.
Selected by St. Louis Cardinals in 7th round (173rd player selected) of 1979 NFL draft.
Received reported $200,000 bonus to sign with Detroit Tigers, 1978.
Named outfielder on THE SPORTING NEWS College Baseball All-America Team, 1978.

Year Club	League	Pos.	G.	AB.	R.	H.	2B.	3B.	HR.	RBI.	B.A.	PO.	A.	E.	F.A.
1978—Lakeland†	Fla. St.	OF	54	175	27	42	5	4	8	40	.240	115	2	6	.951
1979—Evansville‡	A. A.	OF	89	327	50	80	13	5	9	42	.245	100	5	9	.921
1979—Detroit..................	Amer.	OF	12	38	3	9	3	0	1	4	.237	15	0	0	1.000
1980—Detroit§.................	Amer.	OF	51	175	23	46	2	1	9	16	.263	122	1	1	.992
1981—Detroit..................	Amer.	OF	83	290	41	95	11	3	9	40	.328	142	1	4	.973
1982—Detroit x	Amer.	OF	69	266	34	74	16	2	8	35	.278	167	4	1	.994
1983—Detroit..................	Amer.	OF	128	401	60	91	12	9	15	51	.227	116	2	3	.975
1984—Detroit..................	Amer.	OF	149	531	92	150	23	10	27	91	.282	245	4	●12	.954
1985—Detroit y................	Amer.	OF	154	581	96	167	37	5	29	97	.287	286	1	●11	.963
Major League Totals—7 Years................			646	2282	349	632	104	30	98	334	.277	1093	13	32	.972

Selected by Detroit Tigers' organization in 1st round (12th player selected) of free-agent draft, June 6, 1978.
†On restricted list, August 15, 1978, to March 1, 1979.
‡On disabled list, April 13 to May 21, 1979.
§On disabled list, June 18 to October 6, 1980.
xOn disabled list, July 11, 1982 through remainder of season.
yGranted free agency, November 12, 1985; re-signed by Tigers, January 8, 1986.

CHAMPIONSHIP SERIES RECORD

Year Club	League	Pos.	G.	AB.	R.	H.	2B.	3B.	HR.	RBI.	B.A.	PO.	A.	E.	F.A.
1984—Detroit...................	Amer.	OF	3	12	2	5	1	0	1	2	.417	7	0	0	1.000

WORLD SERIES RECORD

Year Club	League	Pos.	G.	AB.	R.	H.	2B.	3B.	HR.	RBI.	B.A.	PO.	A.	E.	F.A.
1984—Detroit...................	Amer.	OF	5	18	4	6	0	0	2	7	.333	5	1	2	.750

ROBERT LOUIS GIBSON
(Bob)

Born June 19, 1957, at Philadelphia, Pa.
Height, 6.00. Weight, 195.
Throws and bats righthanded.
Attended Bloomsburg University, Bloomsburg, Pa.

Major League saves: 1983 (2), 1985 (11). Total—13.

Year Club	League	G.	IP.	W.	L.	Pct.	H.	R.	ER.	SO.	BB.	ERA.
1979—Burlington	Midwest	25	137	5	12	.294	152	99	84	111	64	5.52
1980—Stockton	California	33	67	6	3	.667	45	32	29	59	58	3.90
1981—Stockton	California	49	66	6	8	.429	61	31	22	67	38	3.00
1982—El Paso	Texas	47	66⅓	6	2	.750	55	23	16	66	39	2.17
1982—Vancouver..	P. Coast	6	8	1	1	.500	3	2	1	6	10	1.13
1983—Milwaukee..	American	27	80⅔	3	4	.429	71	40	35	46	46	3.90

Year Club	League	G.	IP.	W.	L.	Pct.	H.	R.	ER.	SO.	BB.	ERA.
1984—Vancouver†	P. Coast	14	73⅓	3	4	.429	50	40	37	75	39	4.54
1984—Milwaukee	American	18	69	2	5	.286	61	43	38	54	47	4.96
1985—Milwaukee	American	41	92⅓	6	7	.462	86	44	40	53	49	3.90
Major League Totals—3 Years		86	242	11	16	.407	218	127	113	153	142	4.20

Signed as free agent by Milwaukee Brewers' organization, March 7, 1979.
†On temporary inactive list, July 17 to August 10, 1984.

MARK DAVID GILBERT

Born August 22, 1956, At Atlanta, Ga.
Height, 6.00. Weight, 175.
Throws right and bats left and righthanded.
Attended Miami-Dade Community College (North), Miami, Fla., and received
bachelor of science degree in finance from Florida State University, Tallahassee, Fla.
Son of Herb Gilbert, minor league infielder, 1952, 1953, 1956 and 1957.

Led Midwest League in caught stealing with 22 in 1979.
Tied for American Association lead in bases on balls received with 77 in 1984.
Tied for American Association lead in double plays by outfielders with 4 in 1984.

Year Club	League	Pos.	G.	AB.	R.	H.	2B.	3B.	HR.	RBI.	B.A.	PO.	A.	E.	F.A.
1978—Geneva	NYP	OF	65	263	*83	89	14	2	0	37	.338	122	●10	6	.957
1979—Quad Cities†	Midw.	OF	117	407	80	128	12	7	0	55	.314	198	3	5	*.976
1980—Waterbury‡	East.	OF	49	154	12	31	2	0	0	6	.201	108	5	2	.983
1981—Waterbury§	East.	OF-P	105	360	60	89	15	5	5	31	.247	203	12	6	.973
1982—Waterbury x	East.	OF-2B	109	380	65	114	17	1	5	41	.300	149	27	3	.983
1983—Indianapolis	A. A.	OF	117	445	73	124	16	1	1	62	.279	212	11	3	.987
1984—Wichita y	A. A.	OF	137	486	84	136	18	7	6	46	.280	234	*19	6	.977
1985—Buffalo	A. A.	OF	119	428	67	114	20	5	3	33	.266	227	11	6	.975
1985—Chicago z	Amer.	OF	7	22	3	6	1	0	0	3	.273	14	0	0	1.000
Major League Totals—1 Year			7	22	3	6	1	0	0	3	.273	14	0	0	1.000

Selected by Chicago Cubs' organization in 14th round of free-agent draft, June 6, 1978.
†Traded to Cincinnati Reds' organization, October 12, 1979, completing deal in which Cincinnati traded Pitcher Doug Capilla to Chicago Cubs for a player to be named later, May 3, 1979.
‡On disabled list, April 16 to July 14, 1980.
§On disabled list, August 10, 1981 through remainder of season.
xOn disabled list, June 22 to July 18, 1982.
yGranted free agency, October 15, 1984; signed by Buffalo (Chicago White Sox' organization), December 25, 1984.
zGranted free agency, October 15, 1985.

PITCHING RECORD

Year Club	League	G.	IP.	W.	L.	Pct.	H.	R.	ER.	SO.	BB.	ERA.
1981—Waterbury	Eastern	2	5	0	0	.000	5	5	3	1	5	5.40

BRIAN JEFFREY GILES

Born April 27, 1960, at Manhattan, Kan.
Height, 6.01. Weight, 162.
Throws and bats righthanded.
Grandson of George F. Giles, first baseman in Negro National and American Leagues,
1927 through 1938; son of George F. Giles, Jr., minor league infielder, 1953 through 1955.

Major League stolen bases: 1982 (6), 1983 (17), 1985 (2). Total—25.

Year Club	League	Pos.	G.	AB.	R.	H.	2B.	3B.	HR.	RBI.	B.A.	PO.	A.	E.	F.A.
1978—Little Falls	NYP	2B	61	195	36	44	5	5	4	21	.226	*135	144	16	.946
1979—Lynchburg†	Carol.	2B	86	278	40	83	16	2	2	33	.299	180	271	13	.972
1980—Jackson	Texas	2B	132	448	76	128	30	8	10	57	.286	291	325	26	.960
1981—Tidewater	Int.	2B-SS	121	400	60	107	17	3	7	40	.268	267	384	24	.964
1981—New York	Nat.	SS-2B	9	7	0	0	0	0	0	0	.000	5	8	0	1.000
1982—Tidewater	Int.	2B-SS	108	352	48	98	32	4	11	54	.278	240	354	17	.972
1982—New York	Nat.	2B-SS	45	138	14	29	5	0	3	10	.210	122	133	2	.992
1983—New York	Nat.	2B-SS	145	400	39	98	15	0	2	27	.245	309	390	14	.980
1984—Tidewater‡	Int.	2B-SS-3B	118	384	59	93	24	1	6	37	.242	248	344	16	.974
1985—Milwaukee	Amer.	SS-2B	34	58	6	10	1	0	1	1	.172	48	58	2	.981
1985—Vancouver§	P. C.	SS	40	128	21	30	7	1	2	15	.234	47	125	9	.950
National League Totals—3 Years			199	545	53	127	20	0	5	37	.233	436	531	16	.984
American League Totals—1 Year			34	58	6	10	1	0	1	1	.172	48	58	2	.981
Major League Totals—4 Years			233	603	59	137	21	0	6	38	.227	484	589	18	.984

Selected by New York Mets' organization in 2nd round of free-agent draft, June 6, 1978.
†On disabled list, July 10 to August 11, 1979.
‡Drafted by Milwaukee Brewers, December 3, 1984.
§Granted free agency, October 15, 1985.

—DID YOU KNOW—

That when the Yankees' Rickey Henderson and the Rangers' Oddibe McDowell led off their respective first innings with home runs on July 27, 1985, it marked only the third time in 30 years that such a feat had occurred? Henderson also was one of two players to lead off a 1983 game with a home run.

CLINTON DANIEL GLADDEN III
(Dan)

Born July 7, 1957, at San Jose, Calif.
Height, 5.11. Weight, 180.
Throws and bats righthanded.
Attended DeAnza College, Cupertino, Calif., and
Fresno State University, Fresno, Calif.
Brother of Jeff Gladden, pitcher in Kansas City Royals'
and San Francisco Giants' organization, 1980 through 1984.

Major League stolen bases: 1983 (4), 1984 (31), 1985 (32). Total—67.
Led Texas League in stolen bases with 52 and caught stealing with 26 in 1981.

Year Club	League	Pos.	G.	AB.	R.	H.	2B.	3B.	HR.	RBI.	B.A.	PO.	A.	E.	F.A.
1979—Fresno	Calif.	OF-2B-SS	60	228	41	70	9	1	3	31	.307	56	16	3	.960
1980—Fresno	Calif.	OF	62	237	46	72	10	2	9	41	.304	68	3	1	.986
1980—Shreveport	Texas	OF-SS	74	292	51	86	11	2	9	35	.295	169	14	5	.973
1981—Shreveport	Texas	OF-SS-2B	124	472	81	148	23	9	8	44	.314	211	12	3	.987
1982—Phoenix	P. C.	OF	130	503	93	155	40	5	10	74	.308	264	16	7	.976
1983—Phoenix	P. C.	OF	127	505	113	153	30	9	12	80	.303	319	6	7	.979
1983—San Francisco	Nat.	OF	18	63	6	14	2	0	1	9	.222	53	0	0	1.000
1984—Phoenix†	P. C.	OF	59	234	70	93	11	7	3	27	.397	130	4	2	.985
1984—San Francisco	Nat.	OF	86	342	71	120	17	2	4	31	.351	232	8	3	.988
1985—San Francisco	Nat.	OF	142	502	64	122	15	8	7	41	.243	273	3	7	.975
Major League Totals—3 Years			246	907	141	256	34	10	12	81	.282	558	11	10	.983

Signed as free agent by San Francisco Giants' organization, June 17, 1979.
†On disabled list, April 19 to May 1, 1984.

JERRY DON GLEATON
(Jerry Don)

Born September 14, 1957, at Brownwood, Tex.
Height, 6.03. Weight, 210.
Throws and bats lefthanded.
Attended University of Texas, Austin, Tex.

Major League saves: 1984 (2), 1985 (1). Total—3.
Tied for Eastern League lead in complete games with 13 in 1982.
Tied for Texas League lead in home runs allowed with 17 in 1980.

Year Club	League	G.	IP.	W.	L.	Pct.	H.	R.	ER.	SO.	BB.	ERA.
1979—Tulsa	Texas	5	35	3	2	.600	37	19	19	21	15	4.89
1979—Texas	American	5	10	0	1	.000	15	7	7	2	2	6.30
1980—Tulsa	Texas	25	178	13	7	.650	179	83	72	138	68	3.64
1980—Texas†	American	5	7	0	0	.000	5	2	2	2	4	2.57
1981—Seattle	American	20	85	4	7	.364	88	50	45	31	38	4.76
1981—Spokane	P. Coast	13	91	5	7	.417	104	53	42	57	39	4.15
1982—Lynn	Eastern	24	182	15	7	.682	175	71	55	132	54	2.72
1982—Seattle	American	3	4⅔	0	0	.000	7	7	7	1	2	13.50
1983—Salt Lake City	P. Coast	24	137⅓	9	9	.500	189	112	102	73	81	6.68
1984—Salt Lake City‡	P. Coast	29	49⅔	4	1	.800	62	39	32	39	17	5.80
1984—Denver	Am. Assoc.	12	20	1	1	.500	20	5	4	10	4	1.80
1984—Chicago	American	11	18⅓	1	2	.333	20	12	7	4	6	3.44
1985—Buffalo	Am. Assoc.	38	55⅓	8	2	★.800	62	17	15	37	21	2.44
1985—Chicago	American	31	29⅔	1	0	1.000	37	19	19	22	13	5.76
Major League Totals—6 Years		75	154⅔	6	10	.375	172	97	87	62	65	5.06

Selected by Baltimore Orioles' organization in 2nd round of free-agent draft, June 8, 1976.
Selected by Texas Rangers' organization in 1st round (17th player selected) of free-agent draft, June 5, 1979.
†Traded with Pitchers Brian Allard, Ken Clay and Steve Finch, Shortstop Rick Auerbach and Outfielder Richie Zisk to Seattle Mariners for Catcher Larry Cox, Pitcher Rick Honeycutt, Outfielders Willie Horton and Leon Roberts and Shortstop Mario Mendoza, December 12, 1980.
‡Traded with Pitcher Gene Nelson to Chicago White Sox for Pitcher Salome Barojas, June 27, 1984.

EDWARD PAUL GLYNN
(Ed)

Born June 3, 1953, at Flushing, N. Y.
Height, 6.02. Weight, 180.
Throws left and bats righthanded.
Attended York College, Jamaica, N. Y.

Pitched seven-inning, 3-0 no-hit victory against Iowa, July 15, 1976.
Major League saves: 1979 (7), 1980 (1), 1982 (4). Total—12.
Led American Association in intentional bases on balls issued with 11 in 1978.
Tied for American Association lead in balks with 4 in 1977.

Year Club	League	G.	IP.	W.	L.	Pct.	H.	R.	ER.	SO.	BB.	ERA.
1972—Lakeland	Florida St.	15	57	1	4	.200	52	30	28	54	50	4.42
1972—Bristol	Ap'alachian	11	57	4	2	.667	38	35	30	67	46	4.74
1973—Clinton	Midwest	24	135	9	6	.600	117	68	68	130	84	4.53
1974—Clinton	Midwest	15	114	8	4	.667	104	46	38	104	46	3.00
1974—Montgomery	Southern	9	49	1	4	.200	60	44	30	31	29	5.51
1975—Montgomery	Southern	19	127	10	5	.667	116	50	44	66	72	3.12
1975—Evansville	Am. Assoc.	7	40	1	2	.333	40	18	11	23	19	2.48

Year Club	League	G.	IP.	W.	L.	Pct.	H.	R.	ER.	SO.	BB.	ERA.
1975—Detroit	American	3	15	0	2	.000	11	8	7	8	8	4.20
1976—Evansville	Am. Assoc.	24	148	9	7	.563	146	76	59	92	82	3.59
1976—Detroit	American	5	24	1	3	.250	22	18	16	17	20	6.00
1977—Evansville	Am. Assoc.	28	156	6	8	.429	163	97	86	125	71	4.96
1977—Detroit	American	8	27	2	1	.667	36	17	16	13	12	5.33
1978—Evansville	Am. Assoc.	27	38	3	2	.600	32	14	14	28	32	3.32
1978—Detroit†	American	10	15	0	0	.000	11	5	5	9	4	3.00
1979—Tidewater	Int'national	17	29	0	1	.000	22	10	7	16	9	2.17
1979—New York	National	46	60	1	4	.200	57	22	20	32	40	3.00
1980—New York‡§	National	38	52	3	3	.500	49	26	24	32	23	4.15
1981—Charleston	Int'national	42	71	4	6	.400	50	34	28	70	42	3.55
1981—Cleveland	American	4	8	0	0	.000	5	1	1	4	4	1.13
1982—Charleston	Int'national	7	9⅔	3	1	.750	7	5	5	17	2	4.66
1982—Cleveland	American	47	49⅔	5	2	.714	43	27	23	54	30	4.17
1983—Cleveland	American	11	12⅓	0	2	.000	22	11	8	13	6	5.84
1983—Charleston	Int'national	37	47	3	5	.375	43	30	26	51	28	4.98
1984—Maine x-Tidewater y	Int'national	45	55	2	4	.333	38	17	16	76	30	2.62
1985—Pawtucket z	Int'national	5	5	0	0	.000	7	3	3	8	2	5.40
1985—Montreal	National	3	2⅓	0	0	.000	5	5	5	2	4	19.29
1985—Indianapolis a	Am. Assoc	28	42	4	2	.667	25	11	8	48	17	1.71
American League Totals—7 Years		88	151	8	10	.444	150	87	76	118	84	4.53
National League Totals—3 Years		87	114⅓	4	7	.364	111	53	49	66	67	3.86
Major League Totals—10 Years		175	265⅓	12	17	.414	261	140	125	184	151	4.24

Signed as free agent by Detroit Tigers' organization, September 25, 1971.
†Traded to New York Mets for Pitcher Mardie Cornejo, March 13, 1979.
‡On disabled list, August 16 to September 6, 1980.
§Traded to Cleveland Indians' organization for a player to be named later, April 6, 1981; New York Mets' organization acquired Pitcher Dominick Bullinger to complete deal, December 14, 1981.
xSold to Tidewater (New York Mets' organization), June 22, 1984.
ySold to Boston Red Sox, November 9, 1984.
zTraded to Montreal Expos for a player to be named later, May 1, 1985.
aGranted free agency, October 15, 1985.

RANDALL SCOTT GOMEZ
(Randy)

Born February 4, 1958, at San Mateo, Calif.
Height, 5.09. Weight, 185.
Throws and bats righthanded.
Attended College of San Mateo, San Mateo, Calif., and
University of Utah, Salt Lake City, Utah.

Led Texas League in grounding into double plays with 23 in 1983.
Led Pacific Coast League catchers in double plays with 11 in 1985.
Led Texas League catchers in total chances with 812 in 1983.
Led Pioneer League catchers in total chances with 497 in 1980.

Year Club	League	Pos.	G.	AB.	R.	H.	2B.	3B.	HR.	RBI.	B.A.	PO.	A.	E.	F.A.
1980—Great Falls	Pion.	C	66	241	63	87	14	4	8	53	.361	★447	★42	8	.984
1981—Fresno†	Calif.	C-3B	105	399	59	122	14	4	3	43	.306	518	82	23	.963
1982—Shreveport	Texas	C-3B	84	274	33	72	15	1	2	25	.263	380	58	10	.978
1983—Shreveport	Texas	C	119	418	57	116	18	1	5	48	.278	★699	★98	15	.982
1984—Phoenix	P. C.	C	99	307	41	84	11	3	2	40	.274	558	56	★15	.976
1984—San Francisco	Nat.	C	14	30	0	5	1	0	0	0	.167	69	8	4	.951
1985—Phoenix‡	P. C.	C	79	279	25	74	14	2	1	34	.265	502	47	11	.980
Major League Totals—1 Year			14	30	0	5	1	0	0	0	.167	69	8	4	.951

Selected by Cincinnati Reds' organization in 13th round of free-agent draft, June 5, 1979.
Selected by San Francisco Giants' organization in 23th round of free-agent draft, June 3, 1980.
†On disabled list, July 17 to August 7, 1981.
‡On disabled list, May 6 to May 27, 1985.

RENE ADRIAN GONZALES

Born September 3, 1961, at Austin, Tex.
Height, 6.03. Weight, 180.
Throws and bats righthanded.
Attended Glendale College, Glendale, Calif.; and California State University, Los Angeles, Calif.

Led American Association shortstops in double plays with 79 in 1985.
Led Southern League shortstops in double plays with 102 in 1983.

Year Club	League	Pos.	G.	AB.	R.	H.	2B.	3B.	HR.	RBI.	B.A.	PO.	A.	E.	F.A.
1982—Memphis	South.	SS	56	183	10	39	3	1	1	11	.213	77	183	14	.949
1983—Memphis	South.	SS	144	476	67	128	12	2	2	44	.269	★258	449	20	★.972
1984—Indianapolis	A. A.	SS-3B-2B	114	359	41	84	12	2	2	32	.234	161	349	13	.975
1984—Montreal	Nat.	SS	29	30	5	7	1	0	0	2	.233	17	28	2	.957
1985—Indianapolis	A. A.	SS	130	340	21	77	11	1	0	25	.226	203	★345	23	.960
Major League Totals—1 Year			29	30	5	7	1	0	0	2	.233	17	28	2	.957

Selected by Montreal Expos' organization in 5th round of free-agent draft, June 7, 1982.

ARTURO GONZALEZ (MATA)

Born October 29, 1955, at Nuevo Leon, Mexico.
Height, 6.03. Weight, 205.
Throws and bats righthanded.
Pitched 2-0 no-hit victory against Union Laguna, June 28, 1978.
Pitched 10⅓ inning 0-0 no-hit tie against Ciudad Juarez, March 28, 1979.
Tied for Pacific Coast League lead in shutouts with 3 in 1985.
Led Mexican League pitchers in games started with 29 in 1982.

Year Club	League	G.	IP.	W.	L.	Pct.	H.	R.	ER.	SO.	BB.	ERA.
1976—Monterrey	Mexican	2	4	0	0	.000	4	0	0	1	0	0.00
1977—Monterrey	Mexican	26	47	2	2	.500	56	38	27	34	36	5.17
1978—Monterrey	Mexican	35	229	18	12	.600	206	95	68	134	101	2.67
1979—Monterrey§	Mexican	36	243	12	●18	.400	253	113	99	144	105	3.67
1980—Chattanooga xy	Southern	13	82	5	5	.500	66	33	24	44	31	2.63
1981—Monterrey	Mexican	30	215	14	13	.519	202	79	55	144	68	2.30
1982—Monterrey z	Mexican	31	214⅓	13	12	.520	203	89	67	118	80	2.81
1982—El Paso a	Texas	6	35	3	2	.600	51	19	18	16	7	4.63
1983—Monterrey	Mexican	23	173⅓	12	8	.600	135	52	37	104	33	★1.92
1984—Monterrey b	Mexican	28	197	13	12	.520	203	87	72	121	58	3.29
1984—Reading	Eastern	7	47	3	3	.500	46	24	18	24	18	3.45
1985—Portland	P. Coast	28	164⅔	10	10	.500	168	63	59	85	40	3.22

RECORD AS OUTFIELDER

Year Club	League	Pos.	G.	AB.	R.	H.	2B.	3B.	HR.	RBI.	B.A.	PO.	A.	E.	F.A.
1972—Monterrey	M. Cen.	OF-1B	31	86	13	22	0	1	3	11	.256	55	2	1	.983
1973—Ciudad Victoria†	M. Cen.	OF	9	30	6	11	3	3	0	5	.367	14	1	1	.938
1973—Cedar Rapids	Midw.	OF	59	124	10	20	1	0	0	6	.161	47	5	0	1.000
1974—Cedar Rapids‡	Midw.	OF	41	113	12	22	2	1	0	8	.195	46	3	0	1.000
1974—Monterrey	Mex.	OF	14	38	4	11	0	0	0	2	.289	29	2	1	.969
1975—Monterrey	Mex.	OF	111	313	21	74	11	5	3	39	.236	178	12	8	.960
1976—Monterrey	Mex.	OF-P	84	202	12	37	7	2	0	10	.183	129	6	3	.978

Signed as free agent by Monterrey (Mexican League), March 14, 1972.
†Sold to Cincinnati Reds, March 16, 1973.
‡Sold to Monterrey (Mexican League), June 14, 1974.
§Sold to Cleveland Indians, December 4, 1979.
xOn disabled list, June 2 to July 24, 1980.
ySold to Monterrey (Mexican League), December 10, 1980.
zSold to Milwaukee Brewers, August 2, 1982.
aSold to Monterrey (Mexican League), September 30, 1982.
bSold to Philadelphia Phillies, July 27, 1984.

DENIO MARIANO GONZALEZ (MANZUETA)
(Denny)

Born July 22, 1963, at Sabana Grande Boya, D.R.
Height 5.11. Weight, 165.
Throws and bats righthanded.
Major League stolen bases: 1984 (1), 1985 (2). Total—3.

Year Club	League	Pos.	G.	AB.	R.	H.	2B.	3B.	HR.	RBI.	B.A.	PO.	A.	E.	F.A.
1981—Bradenton Pir.	Gulf C.	2B-3B	50	179	32	62	5	3	2	24	.346	102	113	14	.939
1982—Portland	P. C.	2B-3B	51	164	23	37	4	6	0	9	.226	106	133	20	.923
1982—Buffalo	East.	2B	68	252	28	70	5	4	3	21	.278	137	176	11	.966
1983—Hawaii	P. C.	SS-2B	125	449	76	121	18	8	9	48	.269	193	319	34	.938
1984—Hawaii	P. C.	OF-3B-2B	113	380	61	114	22	7	15	67	.300	121	84	5	.976
1984—Pittsburgh	Nat.	3B-SS-OF	26	82	9	15	3	1	0	4	.183	26	53	3	.963
1985—Hawaii	P. C.	3-O-2-S	106	365	68	105	21	6	12	57	.288	97	183	15	.949
1985—Pittsburgh	Nat.	3B-OF-2B	35	124	11	28	4	0	4	12	.226	44	42	8	.915
Major League Totals—2 Years			61	206	20	43	7	1	4	16	.209	70	95	11	.938

Signed as free agent by Pittsburgh Pirates' organization, June 25, 1981.

JOSE RAFAEL GONZALEZ

Born November 23, 1964, at Puerto Plata, Dominican Republic.
Height, 6.03. Weight, 190.
Throws and bats righthanded.
Major League stolen bases: 1985 (1).
Tied for Texas League lead in caught stealing with 17 in 1985.
Led Texas League outfielders in total chances with 320 in 1985.

Year Club	League	Pos.	G.	AB.	R.	H.	2B.	3B.	HR.	RBI.	B.A.	PO.	A.	E.	F.A.
1981—Lethbridge	Pion.	OF	34	103	11	14	1	1	0	7	.136	65	6	5	.934
1982—Lethbridge	Pion.	OF	55	209	35	63	14	1	4	47	.301	112	7	1	.992
1983—Lodi†	Calif.	OF	76	310	48	91	17	4	6	36	.294	182	7	4	.979
1984—Bakersfield	Calif.	OF	129	484	86	107	26	1	11	59	.221	264	13	9	.969
1985—San Antonio	Texas	OF	128	448	82	137	22	6	13	62	.306	★294	15	11	.966
1985—Los Angeles	Nat.	OF	23	11	6	3	2	0	0	0	.273	10	0	0	1.000
Major League Totals—1 Year			23	11	6	3	2	0	0	0	.273	10	0	0	1.000

Signed as free agent by Los Angeles Dodgers' organization, August 12, 1980.
†On disabled list, July 7, 1983 through remainder of season.

JULIAN GONZALEZ

Born August 20, 1964, at Puerto Plata, Dominican Republic.
Height, 6.04. Weight, 200.
Throws and bats righthanded.

Year—Club	League	G.	IP.	W.	L.	Pct.	H.	R.	ER.	SO.	BB.	ERA.
1981—Idaho Falls	Pioneer	6	11	0	2	.000	17	18	14	14	15	11.45
1982—Salem	Northwest	10	16⅓	0	1	.000	17	18	15	6	19	8.27
1983—Peoria	Midwest	44	86⅓	2	4	.333	85	72	48	67	42	5.00
1984—Redwood	California	52	72⅔	8	6	.571	57	25	22	54	45	2.72
1985—Midland	Texas	53	77⅔	8	5	.615	84	38	33	45	50	3.82

Signed as free agent by California Angels' organization, February 10, 1981.

DWIGHT EUGENE GOODEN

Born November 16, 1964, at Tampa, Fla.
Height, 6.03. Weight, 198.
Throws and bats righthanded

Established major league record for most strikeouts by rookie, season (276), 1984.
Tied modern major league record for most strikeouts, two consecutive games (32), September 12, 17, 1984.
Established National League record for most strikeouts, three consecutive games (43), September 7, 12, 17, 1984.
Led National League in complete games with 16 in 1985.
Tied for National League lead in balks with 7 in 1984.
Led Carolina League in shutouts with 6 in 1983.
Named National League Pitcher of the Year by THE SPORTING NEWS, 1985.
Won National League Cy Young Memorial Award, 1985.
Named righthanded pitcher on THE SPORTING NEWS National League All-Star Team, 1985.
Named National League Rookie Pitcher of the Year by THE SPORTING NEWS, 1984.
Named National League Rookie of the Year by Baseball Writers' Association of America, 1984.
Named Carolina League Pitcher of the Year, 1983.
Received reported $125,000 bonus to sign with New York Mets, 1982.

Year—Club	League	G.	IP.	W.	L.	Pct.	H.	R.	ER.	SO.	BB.	ERA.
1982—Kingsport	Ap'lachian	9	65⅓	5	4	.556	34	18	66	25	2.47	
1982—Little Falls	NYP	2	13	0	1	.000	11	6	6	18	3	4.15
1983—Lynchburg	Carolina	27	191	*19	4	.826	121	58	53	*300	*112	*2.50
1984—New York	National	31	218	17	9	.654	161	72	63	*276	73	2.60
1985—New York	National	35	*276⅔	*24	4	.857	198	51	47	*268	69	*1.53
Major League Totals—2 Years		66	494⅔	41	13	.759	359	123	110	544	142	2.00

Selected by New York Mets' organization in 1st round (fifth player selected) of free-agent draft, June 7, 1982.

ALL-STAR GAME RECORD

Year—League	IP.	W.	L.	Pct.	H.	R.	ER.	SO.	BB.	ERA.
1984—National	2	0	0	.000	1	0	0	3	0	0.00

Member of National League All-Star Team in 1985; did not play.

DONALD THOMAS GORDON
(Don)

Born October 10, 1959, at New York, N.Y.
Height, 6.01. Weight, 175.
Throws and bats righthanded.
Attended The Citadel, Charleston, S.C., and University
of South Carolina, Columbia, S.C.

Year—Club	League	G.	IP.	W.	L.	Pct.	H.	R.	ER.	SO.	BB.	ERA.
1982—Bristol	Ap'lachian	22	65⅔	4	4	.500	48	17	16	42	14	2.19
1983—Birmingham	Southern	43	102⅔	9	5	.643	104	50	39	50	23	3.42
1984—Birmingham†-Knoxville	Southern	54	109⅔	6	4	.600	103	47	41	51	21	3.36
1985—Syracuse	Int'national	51	113	8	5	.615	93	39	26	43	21	*2.07

Selected by Detroit Tigers' organization in 31st round of free-agent draft, June 7, 1982.
†Released, June 23, 1984; signed by Knoxville (Toronto Blue Jays' organization), June 25, 1984.

THOMAS PATRICK GORMAN
(Tom)

Born December 16, 1957, at Woodburn, Ore.
Height, 6.04. Weight, 200.
Throws and bats lefthanded.
Received degree from Gonzaga University, Spokane, Wash.

Tied for Southern League lead in saves with 22 in 1981.

Year—Club	League	G.	IP.	W.	L.	Pct.	H.	R.	ER.	SO.	BB.	ERA.
1980—Memphis	Southern	25	69	6	4	.600	64	34	21	45	22	2.74
1981—Memphis	Southern	52	91	12	9	.571	82	39	31	91	30	3.07
1981—Montreal	National	9	15	0	0	.000	12	7	7	13	6	4.20
1982—Wichita	Am. Assoc.	23	119⅓	8	7	.533	131	77	69	69	35	5.20
1982—Montreal†-New York	National	8	16⅓	1	1	.500	16	5	5	13	4	2.76
1982—Tidewater	Int'national	4	11⅓	1	1	.500	12	8	8	6	4	6.35
1983—Tidewater	Int'national	10	61⅔	6	1	.857	54	25	20	58	18	2.92
1983—New York	National	25	49⅓	1	4	.200	45	29	27	30	15	4.93
1984—Tidewater	Int'national	3	18	1	2	.333	17	8	6	13	4	3.00

Year—Club	League	G.	IP.	W.	L.	Pct.	H.	R.	ER.	SO.	BB.	ERA.
1984—New York	National	36	57⅔	6	0	1.000	51	20	19	40	13	2.97
1985—New York	National	34	52⅔	4	4	.500	56	32	30	32	18	5.13
Major League Totals—5 Years		112	191	12	9	.571	180	93	88	128	56	4.15

Selected by Montreal Expos' organization in 4th round of free-agent draft, June 3, 1980.

†Traded to New York Mets' organization, August 14, 1982, completing deal in which New York traded Outfielder Joel Youngblood to Montreal Expos for a player to be named later, August 4, 1982.

RICHARD MICHAEL GOSSAGE
(Rich or Goose)

Born July 5, 1951, at Colorado Springs, Colo.
Height, 6.03. Weight, 220.
Throws and bats righthanded.
Attended Southern Colorado State College, Pueblo, Colo.

Established National League record for most strikeouts by relief pitcher, season (151), 1977.
Major League saves: 1972 (2), 1974 (1), 1975 (26), 1976 (1), 1977 (26), 1978 (27), 1979 (18), 1980 (33), 1981 (20), 1982 (30), 1983 (22), 1984 (25), 1985 (26). Total—257.
Led American League in saves with 26 in 1975 and 27 in 1978.
Led American League in games finished in relief with 55 in 1978.
Tied for American League lead in saves with 33 in 1980.
Tied for American League lead in intentional bases on balls issued with 15 in 1975.
Led Midwest League in complete games with 15 and shutouts with 7 in 1971.
Named American League Fireman of the Year by THE SPORTING NEWS, 1975 and 1978.
Named Midwest League Player of the Year, 1971.

Year—Club	League	G.	IP.	W.	L.	Pct.	H.	R.	ER.	SO.	BB.	ERA.
1970—Sarasota White Sox	Gulf Coast	3	16	0	0	.000	11	6	5	21	4	2.81
1970—Appleton	Midwest	10	35	0	3	.000	41	27	23	21	19	5.91
1971—Appleton	Midwest	25	187	★18	2	★.900	141	48	38	149	50	★1.83
1972—Chicago	American	36	80	7	1	.875	72	44	38	57	44	4.28
1973—Iowa	Am. Assoc.	12	71	5	4	.556	59	32	29	66	28	3.68
1973—Chicago	American	20	50	0	4	.000	57	44	41	33	37	7.38
1974—Appleton	Midwest	2	8	0	2	.000	8	6	3	5	4	3.38
1974—Chicago	American	39	89	4	6	.400	92	45	41	64	47	4.15
1975—Chicago	American	61	142	9	8	.529	99	32	29	130	70	1.84
1976—Chicago†	American	31	224	9	17	.346	214	104	98	135	90	3.94
1977—Pittsburgh‡	National	72	133	11	9	.550	78	27	24	151	49	1.62
1978—New York	American	63	134	10	11	.476	87	41	30	122	59	2.01
1979—New York§	American	36	58	5	3	.625	48	18	17	41	19	2.64
1980—New York	American	64	99	6	2	.750	74	29	25	103	37	2.27
1981—New York	American	32	47	3	2	.600	22	6	4	48	14	0.77
1982—New York	American	56	93	4	5	.444	63	23	23	102	28	2.23
1983—New York x	American	57	87⅓	13	5	.722	82	27	22	90	25	2.27
1984—San Diego	National	62	102⅓	10	6	.625	75	34	33	84	36	2.90
1985—San Diego y	National	50	79	5	3	.625	64	21	16	52	17	1.82
National League Totals—3 Years		184	314⅓	26	18	.591	217	82	73	287	102	2.09
American League Totals—11 Years		496	1103⅓	70	64	.522	910	413	368	925	470	3.00
Major League Totals—14 Years		680	1417⅔	96	82	.539	1127	495	441	1212	572	2.80

Selected by Chicago White Sox' organization in 9th round of free-agent draft, June 4, 1970.

†Traded with Pitcher Terry Forster to Pittsburgh Pirates for Outfielder Richie Zisk and Pitcher Silvio Martinez, December 10, 1976.

‡Granted free agency, October 28, 1977; signed by New York Yankees, November 23, 1977.

§On disabled list, April 21 to July 9, 1979.

xGranted free agency, November 7, 1983; signed by San Diego Padres, January 6, 1984.

yOn disabled list, August 8 to September 1, 1985.

DIVISION SERIES RECORD

Year—Club	League	G.	IP.	W.	L.	Pct.	H.	R.	ER.	SO.	BB.	ERA.
1981—New York	American	3	6⅔	0	0	.000	3	0	0	8	2	0.00

CHAMPIONSHIP SERIES RECORD

Tied American League Championship Series record for most saves, total Series (2).

Year—Club	League	G.	IP.	W.	L.	Pct.	H.	R.	ER.	SO.	BB.	ERA.
1978—New York	American	2	4	1	0	1.000	3	2	2	3	0	4.50
1980—New York	American	1	⅓	0	1	.000	3	2	2	0	0	54.00
1981—New York	American	2	2⅔	0	0	.000	1	0	0	2	0	0.00
1984—San Diego	National	3	4	0	0	.000	5	2	2	5	1	4.50
Championship Series Totals—4 Years		8	11	1	1	.500	12	6	6	10	1	4.91

WORLD SERIES RECORD

Tied World Series record for most saves, six-game Series (2), 1981.

Year—Club	League	G.	IP.	W.	L.	Pct.	H.	R.	ER.	SO.	BB.	ERA.
1978—New York	American	3	6	1	0	1.000	1	0	0	4	1	0.00
1981—New York	American	3	5	0	0	.000	2	0	0	5	2	0.00
1984—San Diego	National	2	2⅔	0	0	.000	3	4	4	2	1	13.50
World Series Totals—3 Years		8	13⅔	1	0	1.000	6	4	4	11	4	2.63

Established All-Star game record for most games finished (5).

Year League	IP.	W.	L.	Pct.	H.	R.	ER.	SO.	BB.	ERA.
1975—American	1	0	0	.000	1	1	1	0	0	9.00
1977—National	1	0	0	.000	1	2	2	2	1	18.00
1978—American	1	0	1	.000	4	4	4	1	1	36.00
1980—American	1	0	0	.000	1	0	0	0	0	0.00
1984—National	1	0	0	.000	1	0	0	2	0	0.00
1985—National	1	0	0	.000	0	0	0	2	1	0.00
All-Star Game Totals—6 Years	6	0	1	.000	8	7	7	7	3	10.50

Named to American League All-Star Team for 1981 game; replaced due to injury.
Member of American League All-Star Team in 1976 and 1982; did not play.

JAMES WILLIAM GOTT
(Jim)

Born August 3, 1959, at Hollywood, Calif.
Height, 6.04. Weight, 210.
Throws and bats righthanded.

Major League saves: 1984 (2).
Led Western Carolinas League in wild pitches with 21 in 1979.
Tied for Pioneer League lead in games started by pitchers with 14 in 1978.

Year Club	League	G.	IP.	W.	L.	Pct.	H.	R.	ER.	SO.	BB.	ERA.
1977—Calgary	Pioneer	14	65	3	4	.429	71	★82	★69	60	★83	9.55
1978—Gastonia	W. Carol.	22	145	9	6	.600	100	67	64	130	●113	3.97
1978—St. Petersburg	Florida St.	5	28	1	3	.250	23	9	4	15	12	1.29
1979—St. Petersburg	Florida St.	4	18	0	3	.000	18	13	13	9	13	6.50
1979—Gastonia	W. Carol.	19	77	5	5	.500	63	57	48	102	88	5.61
1979—Arkansas†	Texas	2	5	0	1	.000	3	6	3	7	13	5.40
1980—St. Petersburg	Florida St.	25	137	5	11	.313	138	96	70	103	113	4.60
1981—Arkansas‡	Texas	28	131	5	9	.357	133	68	50	93	65	3.44
1982—Toronto	American	30	136	5	10	.333	134	76	67	82	66	4.43
1983—Toronto	American	34	176⅔	9	14	.391	195	103	93	121	68	4.74
1984—Toronto§	American	35	109⅔	7	6	.538	93	54	49	73	49	4.02
1985—San Francisco	National	26	148⅓	7	10	.412	144	73	64	78	51	3.88
American League Totals—3 Years		99	421⅓	21	30	.412	422	233	209	276	183	4.45
National League Totals—1 Year		26	148⅓	7	10	.412	144	73	64	78	51	3.88
Major League Totals—4 Years		125	570⅔	28	40	.412	566	306	273	354	234	4.31

Selected by St. Louis Cardinals' organization in 4th round of free-agent draft, June 7, 1977.
†On disabled list, August 16 to September 1, 1979.
‡Drafted by Toronto Blue Jays, December 7, 1981.
§Traded with Pitcher Jack McKnight and Infielder Augie Schmidt to San Francisco Giants for Pitcher Gary Lavelle, January 26, 1985.

MARK ANDREW GRANT

Born October 24, 1963, at Aurora, Ill.
Height, 6.02. Weight, 195.
Throws and bats righthanded.

Cousin of Rick Ramos, pitcher in Montreal Expos' organization, 1978 through 1983; and nephew of Richard Ramos, pitcher in Chicago White Sox' organization, 1953 through 1958.

Pitched 9-0 no-hit victory against Danville, August 12, 1982.
Major League saves: 1984 (1).
Led Pacific Coast League pitchers in wild pitches with 18 and tied for league lead in games started with 29 and shutouts with 3 in 1985.
Tied for Midwest League lead in shutouts with 4 in 1982.

Year Club	League	G.	IP.	W.	L.	Pct.	H.	R.	ER.	SO.	BB.	ERA.
1981—Great Falls	Pioneer	10	64	2	6	.250	63	36	31	50	35	4.36
1982—Clinton	Midwest	27	★198⅔	★16	5	★.762	139	63	52	★243	60	2.36
1983—Shreveport	Texas	26	★186⅔	10	8	.556	182	83	76	159	71	3.66
1984—Phoenix	P. Coast	17	111⅓	5	7	.417	102	64	49	78	61	3.96
1984—San Francisco†	National	11	53⅔	1	4	.200	56	40	38	32	19	6.37
1985—Phoenix	P. Coast	29	183	8	●15	.348	182	101	92	133	90	4.52
Major League Totals—1 Year		11	53⅓	1	4	.200	56	40	38	32	19	6.37

Selected by San Francisco Giants' organization in 1st round (10th player selected) of free-agent draft, June 8, 1981.
†On disabled list, May 4 to May 23, 1984.

RICHARD RAY GRAPENTHIN

Name pronounced GRAPP-un-thin.

(Dick)

Born April 16, 1958, at Linn Grove, Iowa.
Height, 6.02. Weight, 210.
Throws and bats righthanded.
Attended Mesa Community College, Mesa, Ariz., and received bachelor of science degree in physical education from Indiana State University, Terre Haute, Ind., in 1980.

Major League saves: 1984 (2).
Led American Association in saves with 18 and games finished in relief with 39 in 1984.
Tied for American Association lead in intentional bases on balls issued with 7 in 1985.

Year Club	League	G.	IP.	W.	L.	Pct.	H.	R.	ER.	SO.	BB.	ERA.
1980—Jamestown	NYP	7	27	2	2	.500	30	17	17	24	14	5.67
1981—West Palm Beach	Florida St.	31	80	5	4	.556	96	47	40	44	22	4.50
1982—San Jose	California	27	45	2	1	.667	41	7	4	39	19	0.80
1982—Wichita	Am. Assoc.	20	32⅓	2	2	.500	36	21	17	23	16	4.73
1983—Montreal	National	1	4	0	1	.000	4	4	4	3	1	9.00
1983—Wichita	Am. Assoc.	40	70⅓	5	5	.500	72	35	30	33	26	3.84
1984—Indianapolis	Am. Assoc.	53	91	6	7	.462	81	38	31	44	33	3.07
1984—Montreal	National	13	23	1	2	.333	19	9	9	9	7	3.52
1985—Indianapolis	Am. Assoc.	48	84⅓	5	7	.417	77	38	35	24	31	3.74
1985—Montreal	National	5	7	0	0	.000	13	11	11	4	8	14.14
Major League Totals—3 Years		19	34	1	3	.250	36	24	24	16	16	6.35

Signed as free agent by Montreal Expos' organization, July 9, 1980.

JEFFREY EDWARD GRAY
(Jeff)

Born April 10, 1963, at Richmond, Va.
Height, 6.01. Weight, 175.
Throws and bats righthanded.
Attended Florida State University, Tallahassee, Fla.

Led Florida State League in games finished in relief with 47 in 1985.
Tied for Gulf Coast League lead in intentional bases on balls issued with 5 in 1984.

Year Club	League	G.	IP.	W.	L.	Pct.	H.	R.	ER.	SO.	BB.	ERA.
1984—Sarasota Phillies	Gulf Coast	26	41⅓	6	4	.600	35	9	6	26	10	1.31
1985—Clearwater†	Florida St.	55	87⅔	5	9	.357	80	38	31	80	33	3.18

Signed as free agent by Philadelphia Phillies' organization, June 14, 1984.
†Traded with Pitcher John Denny to Cincinnati Reds for Outfielder Gary Redus and Pitcher Tom Hume, December 11, 1985.

CHRISTOPHER DeWAYNE GREEN
(Chris)

Born September 5, 1960, at Los Angeles, Calif.
Height, 6.04. Weight, 207.
Throws and bats lefthanded.

Led Carolina League in balks with 4 in 1982.

Year Club	League	G.	IP.	W.	L.	Pct.	H.	R.	ER.	SO.	BB.	ERA.
1979—Bradenton Pirates	Gulf Coast	9	32	1	2	.333	28	28	22	31	40	6.19
1980—Shelby†‡	W. Carol.	19	95	6	7	.462	103	57	45	57	28	4.26
1981—Greenwood	S. Atlantic	27	184	15	7	.682	148	87	63	128	86	3.08
1982—Alexandria	Carolina	14	86⅓	9	1	★.900	76	29	24	84	33	2.50
1982—Buffalo	Eastern	13	99⅓	7	5	.583	71	41	36	82	52	3.26
1983—Hawaii	P. Coast	13	77⅓	0	9	.000	94	53	45	49	36	5.24
1983—Lynn	Eastern	23	74⅔	5	6	.455	76	38	33	73	31	3.98
1984—Pittsburgh	National	4	3	0	0	.000	5	2	2	3	1	6.00
1984—Hawaii§	P. Coast	13	16⅔	2	2	.500	15	15	11	18	8	5.94
1985—Hawaii x	P. Coast	35	97⅔	3	6	.333	108	50	46	91	28	4.24
Major League Totals—1 Year		4	3	0	0	.000	5	2	2	3	1	6.00

Selected by Pittsburgh Pirates' organization in 4th round of free-agent draft, June 5, 1979.
†On disabled list, April 21 to May 9, 1980.
‡On suspended list, May 9 to May 13, 1980.
§On temporary inactive list, June 12 to July 26, 1984.
xOn disabled list, April 11 to April 23, 1985.

DAVID ALEJANDRO GREEN (CASAYA)

Born December 4, 1960, at Managua, Nicaragua.
Height, 6.03. Weight, 185.
Throws and bats righthanded.

Major League stolen bases: 1982 (11), 1983 (34), 1984 (17), 1985 (6). Total—68.

Year Club	League	Pos.	G.	AB.	R.	H.	2B.	3B.	HR.	RBI.	B.A.	PO.	A.	E.	F.A.
1979—Stockton	Calif.	OF	136	500	68	131	16	9	8	70	.262	282	8	6	.980
1980—Holyoke†	East.	OF	129	446	71	130	13	★19	8	67	.291	261	18	13	.955
1981—Springfield‡	A. A.	OF	106	430	66	116	26	3	10	67	.270	251	12	4	.985
1981—St. Louis	Nat.	OF	21	34	6	5	1	0	0	2	.147	31	1	1	.970
1982—St. Louis§	Nat.	OF	76	166	21	47	7	1	2	23	.283	111	4	1	.991
1982—Louisville	A. A.	OF	46	174	45	60	5	4	9	40	.345	111	17	1	.992
1983—St. Louis	Nat.	OF	146	422	52	120	14	10	8	69	.284	214	10	7	.970
1984—St. Louis xy	Nat.	1B-OF	126	452	49	121	14	4	15	65	.268	1103	70	10	.992
1985—San Francisco z	Nat.	1B-OF	106	294	36	73	10	2	5	20	.248	645	42	10	.986
Major League Totals—5 Years			475	1368	164	366	46	17	30	179	.268	2104	127	29	.987

Signed as free agent by Milwaukee Brewers' organization, September 24, 1978.
†Traded with Outfielder Sixto Lezcano and Pitchers Lary Sorensen and Dave LaPoint to St. Louis Cardinals for Catcher Ted Simmons and Pitchers Pete Vuckovich and Rollie Fingers, December 12, 1980.
‡On disabled list, June 20 to July 2, 1981.
§On disabled list, May 8 to May 23, 1982.
xOn disabled list, May 24 to June 15, 1984.

yTraded with First Baseman Gary Rajsich, Pitcher Dave LaPoint and Shortstop Jose Gonzalez (Jose Uribe) to San Francisco Giants for Outfielder-First Baseman Jack Clark, February 1, 1985.

zTraded to Milwaukee Brewers for a player to be named later, December 4, 1985; San Francisco Giants acquired Shortstop Hector Quinones to complete deal, December 11, 1985.

CHAMPIONSHIP SERIES RECORD

Year	Club	League	Pos.	G.	AB.	R.	H.	2B.	3B.	HR.	RBI.	B.A.	PO.	A.	E.	F.A.
1982—St. Louis		Nat.	OF	2	1	1	1	0	0	0	0	1.000	0	0	0	.000

WORLD SERIES RECORD

Year	Club	League	Pos.	G.	AB.	R.	H.	2B.	3B.	HR.	RBI.	B.A.	PO.	A.	E.	F.A.
1982—St. Louis		Nat.	O-PH-DH	7	10	3	2	1	1	0	0	.200	4	0	0	1.000

OTIS ANDRE GREEN

Born March 11, 1964, at Miami, Fla.
Height, 6.02. Weight, 180.
Throws and bats lefthanded.
Attended Miami-Dade Community College North, Miami, Fla.

Year	Club	League	Pos.	G.	AB.	R.	H.	2B.	3B.	HR.	RBI.	B.A.	PO.	A.	E.	F.A.
1983—Medicine Hat	Pion.	OF	59	241	44	76	8	2	10	37	.315	102	1	7	.936
1984—Florence	S. Atl.	OF	43	158	31	42	6	4	5	26	.266	70	4	2	.974
1984—Kinston	Carol.	OF	84	305	40	79	18	3	6	34	.259	120	7	5	.962
1985—Knoxville†	South.	OF	115	442	68	128	19	5	11	68	.290	221	4	3	.987

Selected by Chicago White Sox' organization in 5th round of free-agent draft, June 7, 1982.
Selected by Chicago White Sox' organization in secondary phase of free-agent draft, January 11, 1983.
Selected by Toronto Blue Jays' organization in secondary phase of free-agent draft, June 6, 1983.
†On disabled list, July 18 to August 14, 1985.

MICHAEL LEWIS GREENWELL
(Mike)

Born July 18, 1963, at Louisville, Ky.
Height, 6.00. Weight, 170.
Throws right and bats lefthanded.

Major League stolen bases: 1985 (1).
Led Carolina League in being hit by pitch with 15 in 1984.

Year	Club	League	Pos.	G.	AB.	R.	H.	2B.	3B.	HR.	RBI.	B.A.	PO.	A.	E.	F.A.
1982—Elmira	NYP	3B-2B	72	268	57	72	10	1	6	36	.269	96	151	31	.888
1983—Winston-Salem†	Carol.	OF	48	158	23	44	8	0	3	21	.278	28	1	1	.967
1984—Winston-Salem	Carol.	3B-OF	130	454	70	139	23	6	16	84	.306	126	132	30	.896
1985—Pawtucket	Int.	OF	117	418	47	107	21	1	13	52	.256	178	8	7	.964
1985—Boston	Amer.	OF	17	31	7	10	1	0	4	8	.323	14	0	0	1.000
Major League Totals—1 Year			17	31	7	10	1	0	4	8	.323	14	0	0	1.000

Selected by Boston Red Sox' organization in 3rd round of free-agent draft, June 7, 1982.
†On disabled list, April 21 to May 2 and May 13 to July 25, 1983.

ROBERT ANTHONY GRICH
(Bobby)

Born January 15, 1949, at Muskegon, Mich.
Height, 6.02. Weight, 190.
Throws and bats righthanded.
Attended University of California, Los Angeles, Calif., and
Fresno State University, Fresno, Calif.

Established major league records for highest fielding average by second baseman, season, 100 or more games (.9967), 1985; most putouts, second baseman, season (484), 1974.

Tied major league records for fewest errors by second baseman (800 or more chances), season (5), 1973; highest fielding average, second baseman, lifetime (.984).

Tied American League record for most games, second baseman, season (162), 1973.

Major League stolen bases: 1970 (1), 1971 (1), 1972 (13), 1973 (17), 1974 (17), 1975 (14), 1976 (14), 1977 (6), 1978 (4), 1979 (1), 1980 (3), 1981 (2), 1982 (3), 1983 (2), 1984 (2), 1985 (3). Total—103.

Hit three home runs in a game, June 18, 1974.
Led American League in slugging percentage with .543 in 1981.
Led American League in being hit by pitch with 20 in 1974.
Led American League second basemen in fielding percentage with .997 in 1985.
Led American League second basemen in double plays with 130 in 1973, 132 in 1974 and 122 in 1975.
Led American League second basemen in total chances with 945 in 1973, 957 in 1974 and 928 in 1975.
Led International League in total bases with 299 in 1971.
Led International League shortstops in double plays with 81 in 1971.
Named Minor League Player of the Year by THE SPORTING NEWS, 1971.
Named International League Most Valuable Player, 1971.
Named Texas League co-Most Valuable Player, 1969.
Named second baseman on THE SPORTING NEWS American League All-Star Team, 1976, 1979 and 1981.
Named second baseman on THE SPORTING NEWS American League All-Star fielding team, 1973 through 1976.
Named second baseman on THE SPORTING NEWS American League Silver Slugger team, 1981.
Received reported $40,000 bonus to sign with Baltimore Orioles, 1967.

Year Club League	Pos.	G.	AB.	R.	H.	2B.	3B.	HR.	RBI.	B.A.	PO.	A.	E.	F.A.
1967—Bluefield .... Appal.	SS	58	213	43	54	10	4	3	26	.254	74	126	24	.893
1968—Stockton .... Calif.	SS	113	426	63	97	18	2	8	44	.228	205	*379	35	.943
1969—Dal.-Ft. Worth† .... Texas	SS	121	413	60	128	16	8	2	50	.310	*199	368	29	.951
1970—Rochester .... Int.	2B-SS	63	235	67	90	11	3	9	42	.383	144	199	9	.974
1970—Baltimore .... Amer.	SS-2-3	30	95	11	20	1	3	0	8	.211	56	79	7	.951
1971—Rochester .... Int.	SS	130	473	*124	159	26	9	*32	83	*.336	*238	*394	17	*.974
1971—Baltimore .... Amer.	SS-2	7	30	7	9	0	0	1	6	.300	11	31	0	1.000
1972—Baltimore .... Amer.	S-2-1-3	133	460	66	128	21	3	12	50	.278	299	338	20	.970
1973—Baltimore .... Amer.	2B	●162	581	82	146	29	7	12	50	.251	*431	*509	5	*.995
1974—Baltimore .... Amer.	2B	160	582	92	153	29	6	19	82	.263	*484	*453	20	.979
1975—Baltimore .... Amer.	2B	150	524	81	136	26	4	13	57	.260	*423	*484	21	.977
1976—Baltimore‡ .... Amer.	*2B-3B	144	518	93	138	31	4	13	54	.266	*389	400	12	.985
1977—California§ .... Amer.	SS	52	181	24	44	6	0	7	23	.243	88	141	4	.983
1978—California .... Amer.	2B	144	487	68	122	16	2	6	42	.251	325	419	13	.983
1979—California .... Amer.	2B	153	534	78	157	30	5	30	101	.294	340	438	13	.984
1980—California .... Amer.	2B-1B	150	498	60	135	22	2	14	62	.271	353	464	9	.989
1981—California x .... Amer.	2B	100	352	56	107	14	2	●22	61	.304	230	349	10	.983
1982—California .... Amer.	2B	145	506	74	132	28	5	19	65	.261	338	450	11	.986
1983—California y .... Amer.	*2B-SS	120	387	65	113	17	0	16	62	.292	271	415	*22	.969
1984—California .... Amer.	2B-1B-3B	116	363	60	93	15	1	18	58	.256	311	282	12	.980
1985—California z .... Amer.	2B-1B-3B	144	479	74	116	17	3	13	53	.242	331	408	3	.996
Major League Totals—16 Years		1910	6577	997	1749	302	47	215	834	.266	4680	5660	182	.983

Selected by Baltimore Orioles' organization in 1st round (18th player selected) of free-agent draft, June 6, 1967.
†On military list, September 2, 1969 through April 1, 1970.
‡Granted free agency, November 1, 1976; signed by California Angels, November 24, 1976.
§On disabled list, June 9, 1977 through remainder of season.
xOn disabled list, June 10 to August 8, 1981.
yOn disabled list, August 30, 1983 through remainder of season.
zGranted free agency, November 12, 1985; re-signed by Angels, November 26, 1985.

CHAMPIONSHIP SERIES RECORD

Tied American League Championship Series records for most times on losing club (4); most strikeouts, five-game Series (7), 1982; most consecutive strikeouts, one Series, consecutive at-bats and plate appearances (4), 1982.

Year Club League	Pos.	G.	AB.	R.	H.	2B.	3B.	HR.	RBI.	B.A.	PO.	A.	E.	F.A.
1973—Baltimore .... Amer.	2B	5	20	1	2	0	0	1	1	.100	16	9	0	1.000
1974—Baltimore .... Amer.	2B	4	16	2	4	1	0	1	2	.250	13	12	1	.962
1979—California .... Amer.	2B	4	13	0	2	1	0	0	2	.154	4	12	1	.941
1982—California .... Amer.	2B	5	15	1	3	1	0	0	1	.200	10	17	0	1.000
Championship Series Totals—4 Years		18	64	4	11	3	0	2	6	.172	43	50	2	.979

ALL-STAR GAME RECORD

Year League	Pos.	AB.	R.	H.	2B.	3B.	HR.	RBI.	B.A.	PO.	A.	E.	F.A.
1972—American	SS	4	0	0	0	0	0	0	.000	0	3	0	1.000
1974—American	2B	3	0	1	0	0	0	0	.333	0	2	0	1.000
1976—American	2B	2	0	0	0	0	0	0	.000	1	1	0	1.000
1979—American	2B	1	0	0	0	0	0	0	.000	2	0	0	1.000
1980—American	2B	0	0	0	0	0	0	0	.000	0	1	0	1.000
1982—American‡	2B	1	0	0	0	0	0	0	.000	2	2	0	1.000
All-Star Game Totals—6 Years		11	0	1	0	0	0	0	.091	5	9	0	1.000

GEORGE KENNETH GRIFFEY
(Ken)

Born April 10, 1950, at Donora, Pa.
Height, 6.00. Weight, 200.
Throws and bats lefthanded.

Tied major league record for most at bats, game, since 1900 (7), June 13, 1975.
Major League stolen bases: 1973 (4), 1974 (9), 1975 (16), 1976 (34), 1977 (17), 1978 (23), 1979 (12), 1980 (23), 1981 (12), 1982 (10), 1983 (5), 1984 (2), 1985 (7). Total—174.
Led American Association in stolen bases with 43 in 1973.
Tied for Eastern League lead in double plays by outfielders with 6 in 1972.
Named as outfielder on THE SPORTING NEWS National League All-Star Team, 1976.

Year Club League	Pos.	G.	AB.	R.	H.	2B.	3B.	HR.	RBI.	B.A.	PO.	A.	E.	F.A.
1969—Bradenton Reds....Gulf C.	*OF-1B	49	153	22	43	*11	1	1	12	.281	57	4	*10	.859
1970—Sioux Falls .... North.	OF	51	164	20	40	2	1	2	24	.244	76	2	7	.918
1971—Tampa .... Fla. St.	OF	88	281	60	96	7	11	3	33	.342	137	13	8	.949
1971—Three Rivers .... East.	OF	9	32	1	13	1	2	0	4	.406	17	0	1	.944
1972—Three Rivers .... East.	●OF-SS	128	472	*96	150	21	3	14	52	.318	212	10	●15	.937
1973—Indianapolis .... A. A.	OF	107	397	88	130	18	5	10	58	.327	171	11	6	.968
1973—Cincinnati .... Nat.	OF	25	86	19	33	5	1	3	14	.384	25	1	0	1.000
1974—Indianapolis .... A. A.	OF	43	162	34	54	6	4	5	18	.333	70	4	1	.987
1974—Cincinnati .... Nat.	OF	88	227	24	57	9	5	2	19	.251	115	5	0	1.000
1975—Cincinnati .... Nat.	OF	132	463	95	141	15	9	4	46	.305	202	6	7	.967
1976—Cincinnati .... Nat.	OF	148	562	111	189	28	9	6	74	.336	270	10	6	.976
1977—Cincinnati .... Nat.	OF	154	585	117	186	35	8	12	57	.318	298	10	3	.990
1978—Cincinnati .... Nat.	OF	158	614	90	177	33	8	10	63	.288	296	13	10	.969
1979—Cincinnati† .... Nat.	OF	95	380	62	120	27	4	8	32	.316	175	8	3	.984
1980—Cincinnati .... Nat.	OF	146	544	89	160	28	10	13	85	.294	266	5	6	.978

Year Club League	Pos.	G.	AB.	R.	H.	2B.	3B.	HR.	RBI.	B.A.	PO.	A.	E.	F.A.
1981—Cincinnati‡........... Nat.	OF	101	396	65	123	21	6	2	34	.311	268	8	3	.989
1982—New York............ Amer.	OF	127	484	70	134	23	2	12	54	.277	282	8	5	.983
1983—New York§........... Amer.	1B-OF	118	458	60	140	21	3	11	46	.306	870	57	8	.991
1984—New York.............. Amer.	OF-1B	120	399	44	109	20	1	7	56	.273	422	22	16	.965
1985—New York x .... Amer.	OF-1B	127	438	68	120	28	4	10	69	.274	227	8	7	.971
National League Totals—9 Years...........		1047	3857	672	1186	201	60	60	424	.307	1915	66	38	.981
American League Totals—4 Years		492	1779	242	503	92	10	40	225	.283	1801	95	36	.981
Major League Totals—13 Years..............		1539	5636	914	1689	293	70	100	649	.300	3716	161	74	.981

Selected by Cincinnati Reds' organization in 29th round of free-agent draft, June 5, 1969.

†On disabled list, August 14 to September 7, 1979.

‡Traded to New York Yankees for Pitcher Brian Ryder and a player to be named later, November 4, 1981; Cincinnati Reds' organization acquired Pitcher Freddie Toliver to complete deal, December 10, 1981.

§On disabled list, July 2 to August 2, 1983.

xOn disabled list, May 28 to June 12, 1985.

CHAMPIONSHIP SERIES RECORD

Tied Championship Series record for most stolen bases, game (3), October 5, 1975.

Year Club League	Pos.	G.	AB.	R.	H.	2B.	3B.	HR.	RBI.	B.A.	PO.	A.	E.	F.A.
1973—Cincinnati............. Nat.	OF-PH	3	7	0	1	1	0	0	0	.143	2	0	0	1.000
1975—Cincinnati............. Nat.	OF	3	12	3	4	1	0	0	4	.333	4	1	0	1.000
1976—Cincinnati............. Nat.	OF	3	13	2	5	0	1	0	2	.385	11	0	0	1.000
Championship Series Totals—3 Years....		9	32	5	10	2	1	0	6	.313	17	1	0	1.000

WORLD SERIES RECORD

Tied World Series record for fewest chances accepted by outfielder, extra-inning game (0), October 21, 1975 (12 innings); most at-bats, game, no hits (5), October 21, 1976.

Year Club League	Pos.	G.	AB.	R.	H.	2B.	3B.	HR.	RBI.	B.A.	PO.	A.	E.	F.A.
1975—Cincinnati............. Nat.	OF	7	26	4	7	3	1	0	4	.269	10	1	0	1.000
1976—Cincinnati............. Nat.	OF	4	17	2	1	0	0	0	1	.059	5	0	0	1.000
World Series Totals—2 Years		11	43	6	8	3	1	0	5	.186	15	1	0	1.000

ALL-STAR GAME RECORD

Year League	Pos.	AB.	R.	H.	2B.	3B.	HR.	RBI.	B.A.	PO.	A.	E.	F.A.
1976—National	OF	1	1	1	0	0	0	1	1.000	1	0	0	1.000
1980—National	OF	3	1	2	0	0	1	1	.667	0	0	0	.000
All-Star Game Totals—2 Years....................		4	2	3	0	0	1	2	.750	1	0	0	1.000

Member of National League All-Star Team in 1977; did not play.

ALFREDO CLAUDINO GRIFFIN

Born March 6, 1957, at Dominican Republic City, Dominican Republic.
Height, 5.11. Weight, 165.
Throws right and bats left and righthanded.

Tied American League record for most games by shortstop, season (162), 1982 and 1985.

Major League stolen bases: 1977 (2), 1979 (21), 1980 (18), 1981 (8), 1982 (10), 1983 (8), 1984 (11), 1985 (24). Total—102.

Led American League shortstops in putouts with 280 in 1983.

Led American League shortstops in total chances with 824 in 1982.

Named shortstop on THE SPORTING NEWS American League All-Star fielding team, 1985.

Named American League Co-Rookie of the Year by the Baseball Writers' Association of America, 1979.

Year Club League	Pos.	G.	AB.	R.	H.	2B.	3B.	HR.	RBI.	B.A.	PO.	A.	E.	F.A.
1974—Reno .... Calif.	SS	11	35	4	9	0	0	0	1	.257	10	22	9	.780
1974—Sarasota Ind.......... Gulf C.	SS	49	158	17	41	1	0	0	11	.259	67	133	*25	.889
1975—San Jose .... Calif.	SS	124	358	42	82	4	3	0	25	.229	189	281	47	.909
1976—San Jose .... Calif.	SS	64	224	40	58	3	1	0	17	.259	91	145	24	.908
1976—Williamsport......... East.	SS	58	200	22	55	3	0	0	17	.275	86	172	17	.938
1976—Toledo .... Int.	SS	22	88	5	19	7	1	0	6	.216	44	71	7	.943
1976—Cleveland.............. Amer.	SS	12	4	0	1	0	0	0	0	.250	1	2	1	.750
1977—Toledo .... Int.	SS	125	457	60	114	14	5	1	32	.249	*223	398	*49	.927
1977—Cleveland.............. Amer.	SS	14	41	5	6	1	0	0	3	.146	17	30	3	.940
1978—Portland .... P. C.	*SS-OF	133	474	82	138	22	10	5	48	.291	201	395	*40	.937
1978—Cleveland†............. Amer.	SS	5	4	1	2	1	0	0	0	.500	4	7	1	.917
1979—Toronto .... Amer.	SS	153	624	81	179	22	10	2	31	.287	272	501	*36	.956
1980—Toronto .... Amer.	SS	155	653	63	166	26	●15	2	41	.254	295	489	*37	.955
1981—Toronto .... Amer.	*SS-3B-2B	101	388	30	81	19	6	0	21	.209	191	279	*31	.938
1982—Toronto .... Amer.	SS	●162	539	57	130	20	8	1	48	.241	*319	479	●26	.968
1983—Toronto .... Amer.	SS-2B	●162	528	62	132	22	9	4	47	.250	287	422	25	.966
1984—Toronto‡ .... Amer.	SS-2B	140	419	53	101	8	2	4	30	.241	230	320	21	.963
1985—Oakland................. Amer.	SS	162	614	75	166	18	7	2	64	.270	278	440	30	.960
Major League Totals—10 Years..............		1066	3814	427	964	137	57	15	285	.253	1894	2969	211	.958

Signed as free agent by Cleveland Indians' organization, August 22, 1973.

†Traded with Third Baseman Phil Lansford to Toronto Blue Jays for Pitcher Victor Cruz, December 6, 1978.

‡Traded with Outfielder Dave Collins and cash to Oakland A's for Pitcher Bill Caudill, December 8, 1984.

ALL-STAR GAME RECORD

Year League	Pos.	AB.	R.	H.	2B.	3B.	HR.	RBI.	B.A.	PO.	A.	E.	F.A.
1984—American	SS	0	0	0	0	0	0	0	.000	0	1	0	1.000

MICHAEL LEROY GRIFFIN
(Mike)

Born June 26, 1957, at Colusa, Calif.
Height, 6.05. Weight, 195.
Throws and bats righthanded.
Attended American River College, Sacramento, Calif.

Led Texas League in wild pitches with 26 in 1978.
Led Western Carolinas League in complete games with 19 and tied for lead in games started by pitchers with 27 in 1977.

Year Club	League	G.	IP.	W.	L.	Pct.	H.	R.	ER.	SO.	BB.	ERA.
1976—Asheville	W. Carol.	11	65	6	3	.667	71	36	35	26	25	4.85
1977—Asheville	W. Carol.	27	*209	*17	9	.654	189	100	81	*201	75	3.49
1978—Tulsa†	Texas	27	169	6	*19	.240	*217	140	114	112	85	6.07
1979—West Haven	Eastern	17	125	8	7	.533	120	53	41	66	26	2.95
1979—Columbus	Int'national	6	41	3	1	.750	35	9	8	34	13	1.76
1979—New York	American	3	4	0	0	.000	5	2	2	5	2	4.50
1980—Columbus	Int'national	13	83	7	2	.778	88	37	32	47	22	3.47
1980—New York	American	13	54	2	4	.333	64	36	29	25	23	4.83
1981—Columbus	Int'national	17	48	3	1	.750	39	14	13	34	16	2.44
1981—New York‡	American	2	4	0	0	.000	5	1	1	4	0	2.25
1981—Chicago§	National	16	52	2	5	.286	64	27	26	20	9	4.50
1982—Wichita	Am. Assoc.	28	136⅓	8	7	.533	166	99	90	88	24	5.93
1982—Montreal x-San Diego y	National	7	10⅓	0	1	.000	9	4	4	4	3	3.48
1983—Oklahoma City	Am. Assoc.	35	144⅔	7	8	.467	155	79	68	87	43	4.23
1984—Oklahoma City z	Am. Assoc.	31	113	8	5	.615	138	67	56	69	41	4.46
1985—Omaha	Am. Assoc.	24	135	7	8	.467	115	58	49	69	43	3.27
American League Totals—3 Years		18	62	2	4	.333	74	39	32	34	25	4.65
National League Totals—2 Years		23	62⅓	2	6	.250	73	31	30	24	12	4.33
Major League Totals—4 Years		41	124⅓	4	10	.286	147	70	62	58	37	4.49

Selected by Texas Rangers' organization in 3rd round of free-agent draft, June 8, 1976.

†Traded with Outfielders Juan Beniquez and Greg Jemison and Pitchers Paul Mirabella and Dave Righetti to New York Yankees for Pitchers Sparky Lyle, Larry McCall and Dave Rajsich, Shortstop Domingo Ramos, Catcher Mike Heath and cash, November 10, 1978.

‡Traded to Chicago Cubs, August 5, 1981; completing deal in which New York Yankees traded Pitcher Doug Bird, $400,000 and a player to be named later to Chicago for Pitcher Rick Reuschel, June 12, 1981.

§Traded to Montreal Expos' organization, March 26, 1982, completing deal in which Montreal traded Outfielder Dan Briggs to Chicago Cubs for a player to be named later, March 15, 1982.

xTraded to San Diego Padres' organization, August 30, 1982, completing deal in which San Diego organization traded infielder Jerry Manuel to Montreal Expos' organization for a player to be named later, June 8, 1982.

yReleased, March 27, 1983; signed by Oklahoma City (Texas Rangers' organization), April 5, 1983.

zGranted free agency, October 15, 1984; signed by Omaha (Kansas City Royals' organization), December 25, 1984.

GREGORY EUGENE GROSS
(Greg)

Born August 1, 1952, at York, Pa.
Height, 5.11. Weight, 175.
Throws and bats lefthanded.

Major League stolen bases: 1973 (2), 1974 (12), 1975 (2), 1976 (2), 1978 (3), 1979 (5), 1980 (1), 1981 (2), 1982 (4), 1983 (3), 1984 (1), 1985 (1). Total—38.
Tied for Appalachian League lead in double plays by outfielders with 3 in 1970.
Named National League Rookie Player of the Year by THE SPORTING NEWS, 1974.
Named Appalachian League Player of the Year, 1970.

Year Club	League	Pos.	G.	AB.	R.	H.	2B.	3B.	HR.	RBI.	B.A.	PO.	A.	E.	F.A.
1970—Covington	Appal.	OF	54	211	40	*74	8	3	2	27	.351	93	*10	3	.972
1971—Columbus	South.	OF-1B	132	494	57	144	14	4	2	33	.291	244	13	9	.966
1972—Columbus	South.	OF	101	367	55	111	14	2	0	25	.302	172	9	3	.984
1972—Okla. City	A. A.	OF	28	109	15	27	4	0	0	8	.248	64	4	1	.986
1973—Denver	A. A.	OF	131	528	98	*174	25	6	0	55	.330	226	11	10	.960
1973—Houston	Nat.	OF	14	39	5	9	2	1	0	1	.231	13	2	0	1.000
1974—Houston	Nat.	OF	156	589	78	185	21	8	0	36	.314	296	15	2	.994
1975—Houston†	Nat.	OF	132	483	67	142	14	10	0	41	.294	216	14	10	.958
1976—Houston‡	Nat.	OF	128	426	52	122	12	3	0	27	.286	208	13	5	.978
1977—Chicago	Nat.	OF	115	239	43	77	10	4	5	32	.322	109	3	1	.991
1978—Chicago§	Nat.	OF	124	347	34	92	12	7	1	39	.265	182	6	4	.979
1979—Philadelphia x	Nat.	OF	111	174	21	58	6	3	0	15	.333	82	5	2	.978
1980—Philadelphia	Nat.	OF-1B	127	154	19	37	7	2	0	12	.240	69	5	2	.974
1981—Philadelphia	Nat.	OF	83	102	14	23	6	1	0	7	.225	48	7	1	.982
1982—Philadelphia	Nat.	OF	119	134	14	40	4	0	0	10	.299	55	3	1	.983
1983—Philadelphia	Nat.	OF-1B	136	245	25	74	12	3	0	29	.302	105	1	1	.991
1984—Philadelphia	Nat.	OF-1B	112	202	19	65	9	1	0	16	.322	195	13	2	.990
1985—Philadelphia y	Nat.	OF-1B	93	169	21	44	5	2	0	14	.260	66	8	0	1.000
Major League Totals—13 Years			1450	3303	412	968	120	45	6	279	.293	1644	95	31	.982

Selected by Houston Astros' organization in 4th round of free-agent draft, June 4, 1970.

†On disabled list, April 2 to April 24, 1975.

‡Traded to Chicago Cubs for infielder Julio Gonzalez, December 8, 1976.

§Traded with Second Baseman Manny Trillo and Catcher Dave Rader to Philadelphia Phillies for Outfielder Jerry Martin, Catcher Barry Foote, Second Baseman Ted Sizemore and Pitchers Derek Botelho and Henry Mack, February 23, 1979.

xGranted free agency, November 1, 1979; re-signed by Phillies, December 13, 1979.
yOn disabled list, September 6, 1985 through remainder of season.

DIVISION SERIES RECORD

Year	Club	League	Pos.	G.	AB.	R.	H.	2B.	3B.	HR.	RBI.	B.A.	PO.	A.	E.	F.A.
1981—Philadelphia		Nat.	PH-OF	4	4	0	0	0	0	0	0	.000	0	0	0	.000

CHAMPIONSHIP SERIES RECORD

Year	Club	League	Pos.	G.	AB.	R.	H.	2B.	3B.	HR.	RBI.	B.A.	PO.	A.	E.	F.A.
1980—Philadelphia		Nat.	PH-OF	4	4	2	3	0	0	0	1	.750	1	0	0	1.000
1983—Philadelphia		Nat.	OF-PH	4	5	1	0	0	0	0	0	.000	4	0	0	1.000
Championship Series Totals—2 Years				8	9	3	3	0	0	0	1	.333	5	0	0	1.000

WORLD SERIES RECORD

Year	Club	League	Pos.	G.	AB.	R.	H.	2B.	3B.	HR.	RBI.	B.A.	PO.	A.	E.	F.A.
1980—Philadelphia		Nat.	PH-OF	4	2	0	0	0	0	0	0	.000	1	0	0	1.000
1983—Philadelphia		Nat.	OF	2	6	0	0	0	0	0	0	.000	8	0	0	1.000
World Series Totals—2 Years				6	8	0	0	0	0	0	0	.000	9	0	0	1.000

KEVIN FRANK GROSS

Born June 8, 1961, at Downey, Calif.
Height, 6.05. Weight, 203.
Throws and bats righthanded.
Attended Oxnard College, Oxnard, Calif.,
and California Lutheran College, Thousand Oaks, Calif.

Major League saves: 1984 (1).
Tied for South Atlantic League lead in games started by pitchers with 28 in 1981.

Year	Club	League	G.	IP.	W.	L.	Pct.	H.	R.	ER.	SO.	BB.	ERA.
1981—Spartanburg		S. Atlantic	28	192	13	12	.520	173	94	76	123	62	3.56
1982—Reading		Eastern	26	151	10	15	.400	138	81	71	136	89	4.23
1983—Portland		P. Coast	15	80	3	5	.375	82	60	60	61	45	6.75
1983—Philadelphia		National	17	96	4	6	.400	100	46	38	66	35	3.56
1984—Philadelphia		National	44	129	8	5	.615	140	66	59	84	44	4.12
1985—Philadelphia		National	38	205⅔	15	13	.536	194	86	78	151	81	3.41
Major League Totals—3 Years			99	430⅔	27	24	.529	434	198	175	301	160	3.66

Selected by Baltimore Orioles' organization in 32nd round of free-agent draft, June 5, 1979.
Selected by Philadelphia Phillies' organization in secondary phase of free-agent draft, January 13, 1981.

WAYNE DALE GROSS

Born January 14, 1952, at Riverside, Calif.
Height, 6.02. Weight, 205.
Throws right and bats lefthanded.
Attended California Poly State University, Pomona, Calif.

Major League stolen bases: 1977 (5), 1979 (4), 1980 (5), 1981 (2), 1982 (3), 1983 (3), 1984 (1), 1985 (1). Total—24.

Year	Club	League	Pos.	G.	AB.	R.	H.	2B.	3B.	HR.	RBI.	B.A.	PO.	A.	E.	F.A.
1973—Lewiston		N'west.	1B	8	29	4	7	2	0	1	1	.241	58	4	0	1.000
1973—Burlington		Midw.	1B-OF	56	187	27	44	8	3	4	36	.235	426	19	4	.991
1974—Birmingham		South.	1B-OF-3B	105	316	36	77	12	2	14	54	.244	503	42	15	.973
1975—Birmingham		South.	OF-1B	130	435	69	121	23	2	19	71	.278	193	16	13	.941
1976—Tucson		P. C.	3B-1B-OF	115	395	77	128	30	7	19	75	.324	273	164	16	.965
1976—Oakland		Amer.	1B-OF	10	18	0	4	0	0	0	1	.222	30	1	1	.969
1977—Oakland		Amer.	*3B-1B	146	485	66	113	21	1	22	63	.233	127	242	*27	.932
1978—Vancouver		P. C.	3B-1B-OF	17	56	20	23	5	0	3	10	.411	32	33	5	.929
1978—Oakland		Amer.	3B-1B	118	285	18	57	10	2	7	23	.200	120	150	22	.925
1979—Oakland		Amer.	3B-1B-OF	138	442	54	99	19	1	14	50	.224	252	225	21	.958
1980—Oakland		Amer.	3B-1B	113	366	45	103	20	3	14	61	.281	125	136	11	.960
1981—Oakland		Amer.	3B-1B	82	243	29	50	7	1	10	31	.206	68	127	12	.942
1982—Oakland		Amer.	3B-1B	129	386	43	97	14	0	9	41	.251	203	189	11	.973
1983—Oakland†		Amer.	1B-3B-P	137	339	34	79	18	0	12	44	.233	473	113	9	.985
1984—Baltimore		Amer.	3B-1B	127	342	53	74	9	1	22	64	.216	69	205	18	.938
1985—Baltimore		Amer.	3B-1B	103	217	31	51	8	0	11	18	.235	81	102	10	.948
Major League Totals—10 Years				1103	3123	373	727	126	9	121	396	.233	1548	1490	142	.955

Selected by Oakland A's organization in 9th round of free-agent draft, June 5, 1973.
†Traded to Baltimore Orioles for Pitcher Tim Stoddard, December 9, 1983.

DIVISION SERIES RECORD

Year	Club	League	Pos.	G.	AB.	R.	H.	2B.	3B.	HR.	RBI.	B.A.	PO.	A.	E.	F.A.
1981—Oakland		Amer.	3B-PH	2	5	1	2	0	0	1	3	.400	1	4	0	1.000

CHAMPIONSHIP SERIES RECORD

Year	Club	League	Pos.	G.	AB.	R.	H.	2B.	3B.	HR.	RBI.	B.A.	PO.	A.	E.	F.A.
1981—Oakland		Amer.	PH-3B	3	5	0	0	0	0	0	0	.000	2	0	0	1.000

ALL-STAR GAME RECORD

Member of American League All-Star Team in 1977; did not play.

PITCHING RECORD

Year	Club	League	G.	IP.	W.	L.	Pct.	H.	R.	ER.	SO.	BB.	ERA.
1983—Oakland		American	1	2⅓	0	0	.000	2	0	0	0	1	0.00

LARRY WAYNE GROVES

Born December 16, 1958, at Kansas City, Kan.
Height, 6.01. Weight, 185.
Throws and bats righthanded.
Attended Emporia State University, Emporia, Kan.,
and Wichita State University, Wichita, Kan.

Year	Club	League	G.	IP.	W.	L.	Pct.	H.	R.	ER.	SO.	BB.	ERA.
1980—Jamestown		NYP	13	99	7	5	.583	92	51	42	49	37	3.82
1981—West Palm Beach		Florida St.	33	105	2	8	.200	111	56	44	42	43	3.77
1982—San José†		California	15	85	5	5	.500	88	44	37	42	37	3.92
1983—West Palm Beach‡		Florida St.	23	67	5	3	.625	63	26	21	43	18	2.82
1984—Jacksonville§		Southern	5	14	0	1	.000	19	10	7	9	9	4.50
1985—Jacksonville		Southern	36	67⅓	6	4	.600	42	13	10	33	20	1.34
1985—Indianapolis		Am. Assoc.	12	18⅔	2	1	.667	23	14	13	8	9	6.27

Selected by Milwaukee Brewers' organization in 16th round of free-agent draft, June 7, 1977.
Selected by Montreal Expos' organization in 13th round of free-agent draft, June 3, 1980.
†On disabled list, July 25, 1982 through remainder of season.
‡On disabled list, April 8 to May 4, 1983.
§On disabled list, April 10 to April 29 and May 27, 1984 through remainder of season.

JOHN MAYWOOD GRUBB JR.

Born August 4, 1948, at Richmond, Va.
Height, 6.03. Weight, 180.
Throws right and bats lefthanded.
Attended Manatee Junior College, West Bradenton, Fla., and received degree from
Florida State University, Tallahassee, Fla.

Major League stolen bases: 1973 (9), 1974 (4), 1975 (2), 1976 (1), 1978 (6), 1979 (2), 1980 (2), 1984 (1). Total—27.
Tied for Texas League lead in double plays by outfielders with 4 in 1972.

Year	Club	League	Pos.	G.	AB.	R.	H.	2B.	3B.	HR.	RBI.	B.A.	PO.	A.	E.	F.A.
1971—Lodi		Calif.	OF-3B-2B	116	409	69	126	23	5	12	56	.308	158	84	14	.945
1972—Alexandria		Texas	★OF-1B	126	446	66	132	25	2	10	61	.296	205	12	2	★.991
1972—San Diego		Nat.	OF	7	21	4	7	1	1	0	1	.333	16	0	0	1.000
1973—San Diego		Nat.	OF-3B	113	389	52	121	22	3	8	37	.311	229	11	3	.988
1974—San Diego		Nat.	OF-3B	140	444	53	127	20	4	8	42	.286	321	8	8	.976
1975—San Diego		Nat.	OF	144	553	72	149	36	2	4	38	.269	334	3	3	.991
1976—San Diego†‡		Nat.	OF-1B-2B	109	384	54	109	22	1	5	27	.284	248	7	6	.977
1977—Cleveland§		Amer.	OF	34	93	8	28	3	3	2	14	.301	47	2	0	1.000
1978—Cleve. x-Tex.		Amer.	OF	134	411	62	113	19	6	15	67	.275	213	16	6	.974
1979—Texas y		Amer.	OF	102	289	42	79	14	0	10	37	.273	135	8	2	.986
1980—Texas		Amer.	OF	110	274	40	76	12	1	9	32	.277	112	6	6	.952
1981—Texas		Amer.	OF	67	199	26	46	9	1	3	26	.231	95	2	1	.990
1982—Texas za		Amer.	OF	103	308	35	86	13	3	3	26	.279	135	4	5	.965
1983—Detroit b		Amer.	OF	57	134	20	34	5	2	4	22	.254	34	1	0	1.000
1984—Detroit c		Amer.	OF	86	176	25	47	5	0	8	17	.267	47	0	0	1.000
1985—Detroit d		Amer.	OF	78	155	19	38	7	1	5	25	.245	23	0	0	1.000
National League Totals—5 Years				513	1791	235	513	101	11	25	145	.286	1148	29	20	.983
American League Totals—9 Years				771	2039	277	547	87	17	59	266	.268	841	39	20	.978
Major League Totals—14 Years				1284	3830	512	1060	188	28	84	411	.277	1989	68	40	.981

Selected by Boston Red Sox' organization in 3rd round of free-agent draft, February 1, 1969.
Selected by Cincinnati Reds' organization in secondary phase of free-agent draft, June 5, 1969.
Selected by Atlanta Braves' organization in secondary phase of free-agent draft, June 4, 1970.
Selected by San Diego Padres' organization in secondary phase of free-agent draft, January 13, 1971.
†On disabled list, April 26 to May 28, 1976.
‡Traded with Catcher Fred Kendall and Shortstop Hector Torres to Cleveland Indians for Outfielder George Hendrick, December 8, 1976.
§On disabled list, April 1 to April 23 and July 8, 1977 through remainder of season.
xTraded to Texas Rangers for a player to be named later, August 31, 1978; Cleveland Indians acquired Pitcher Bobby Cuellar and Outfielder David Rivera to complete deal, October 3, 1978.
yOn disabled list, August 6 to September 1, 1979.
zOn disabled list, March 27 to April 26, 1982.
aTraded to Detroit Tigers for Pitcher Dave Tobik, March 24, 1983.
bOn disabled list, July 27 to September 13, 1983.
cGranted free agency, November 8, 1984; re-signed by Tigers, December 23, 1984.
dOn disabled list, July 5 to July 20, 1985.

CHAMPIONSHIP SERIES RECORD

Year	Club	League	Pos.	G.	AB.	R.	H.	2B.	3B.	HR.	RBI.	B.A.	PO.	A.	E.	F.A.
1984—Detroit		Amer.	DH	1	4	0	1	1	0	0	2	.250	0	0	0	.000

WORLD SERIES RECORD

Year	Club	League	Pos.	G.	AB.	R.	H.	2B.	3B.	HR.	RBI.	B.A.	PO.	A.	E.	F.A.
1984—Detroit		Amer.	PH-DH	4	3	0	1	0	0	0	0	.333	0	0	0	.000

Year	League	Pos.	AB.	R.	H.	2B.	3B.	HR.	RBI.	B.A.	PO.	A.	E.	F.A.
1974—National		OF	1	0	0	0	0	0	0	.000	0	20	0	.000

KELLY WAYNE GRUBER

Born February 26, 1962, at Bellaire, Tex.
Height, 6.00. Weight, 180.
Throws and bats righthanded.
Attended University of Texas, Austin, Tex.

Led International League in slugging percentage with .500 in 1984.
Led International League third basemen in total chances with 309 in 1985.
Led Southern League shortstops in errors with 43 in 1982.

Year	Club	League	Pos.	G.	AB.	R.	H.	2B.	3B.	HR.	RBI.	B.A.	PO.	A.	E.	F.A.
1980—Batavia	NYP	SS	61	212	27	46	3	2	2	19	.217	87	155	21	.920
1981—Waterloo	Midw.	SS	127	458	64	133	25	4	14	59	.290	★180	★389	★56	.910
1982—Chattanooga	South.	SS-3B	128	441	53	107	18	4	13	54	.243	161	333	44	.918
1983—Buffalo†	East.	3B-SS-OF	111	403	60	106	20	4	15	54	.263	98	170	27	.908
1984—Toronto	Amer.	3B-OF-SS	15	16	1	1	0	0	1	2	.063	6	12	2	.900
1984—Syracuse	Int.	3B-OF	97	342	53	92	12	2	21	55	.269	76	156	18	.928
1985—Syracuse	Int.	3B	121	473	71	118	16	5	21	69	.249	78	★217	14	.955
1985—Toronto	Amer.	3B-2B	5	13	0	3	0	0	0	1	.231	2	6	0	1.000
Major League Totals—2 Years			20	29	1	4	0	0	1	3	.138	8	18	2	.929

Selected by Cleveland Indians' organization in 1st round (10th player selected) of free-agent draft, June 3, 1980.
†Drafted by Toronto Blue Jays, December 5, 1983.

CECILIO GUANTE (MAGALLANES)

Name pronounced Goo-AHN-tay.

Born February 2, 1960, at Villa Mella, D.R.
Height, 6.03. Weight, 200.
Throws and bats righthanded.

Major League saves: 1983 (9), 1984 (2), 1985 (5). Total—16.
Led South Atlantic League in saves with 19 in 1980.

Year	Club	League	G.	IP.	W.	L.	Pct.	H.	R.	ER.	SO.	BB.	ERA.
1980—Shelby	S. Atlantic	39	90	6	6	.500	58	32	29	114	25	2.90
1980—Salem	Carolina	6	14	0	0	.000	7	2	2	18	8	1.29
1981—Buffalo	Eastern	10	14	1	1	.500	8	3	1	17	9	0.64
1981—Portland†	P. Coast	19	104	6	6	.500	110	64	62	70	58	5.37
1982—Portland	P. Coast	21	35	3	2	.600	34	17	15	29	26	3.86
1982—Pittsburgh	National	10	27	0	0	.000	28	16	10	26	5	3.33
1983—Hawaii	P. Coast	15	25⅔	2	1	.667	22	12	10	24	12	3.51
1983—Pittsburgh	National	49	100⅓	2	6	.250	90	45	37	82	46	3.32
1984—Pittsburgh‡	National	27	41⅓	2	3	.400	32	12	12	30	16	2.61
1984—Nashua	Eastern	1	3	0	0	.000	5	1	1	2	0	3.00
1985—Pittsburgh	National	63	109	4	6	.400	84	34	33	92	40	2.72
Major League Totals—4 Years		149	277⅔	8	15	.348	234	107	92	230	107	2.98

Signed as free agent by Pittsburgh Pirates' organization, November 24, 1979.
†On disabled list, July 25 to August 5, 1981.
‡On disabled list, July 13 to July 30, 1984.

MARK STEVEN GUBICZA

Name pronounced GOO-ba-zah.

Born August 14, 1962, at Philadelphia, Pa.
Height, 6.05. Weight, 210.
Throws and bats righthanded.
Son of Anthony F. Gubicza, minor league pitcher, 1950 and 1951.

Year	Club	League	G.	IP.	W.	L.	Pct.	H.	R.	ER.	SO.	BB.	ERA.
1981—Sarasota Royals-Gold	Gulf Coast	11	56	●8	1	★.889	39	18	14	40	23	2.25
1982—Fort Myers†	Florida St.	11	48	2	5	.286	49	33	22	36	25	4.13
1983—Jacksonville	Southern	28	196	14	12	.538	146	81	67	★146	93	3.08
1984—Kansas City	American	29	189	10	14	.417	172	90	85	111	75	4.05
1985—Kansas City	American	29	177⅓	14	10	.583	160	88	80	99	77	4.06
Major League Totals—2 Years		58	366⅓	24	24	.500	332	178	165	210	152	4.05

Selected by Kansas City Royals' organization in 2nd round of free-agent draft, June 8, 1981.
†On disabled list, June 29, 1982 through remainder of season.

CHAMPIONSHIP SERIES RECORD

Year	Club	League	G.	IP.	W.	L.	Pct.	H.	R.	ER.	SO.	BB.	ERA.
1985—Kansas City	American	2	8⅓	1	0	1.000	4	3	3	4	4	3.24

INOCENCIO GUERRERO

Born December 28, 1960, at Higueral, Dominican Republic.
Height 6.00. Weight, 185.
Throws and bats righthanded.

Year Club	League	Pos.	G.	AB.	R.	H.	2B.	3B.	HR.	RBI.	B.A.	PO.	A.	E.	F.A.
1979—Bradenton Brav...	Gulf C.	C	23	80	16	18	3	0	1	15	.225	41	5	2	.958
1980—Bradenton Brav...	Gulf C.	1B-C	41	118	7	23	3	1	0	14	.195	173	18	10	.950
1981—Anderson†	S. Atl.	C-1B	60	146	21	29	4	1	3	11	.199	214	10	8	.966
1982—Anderson	S. Atl.	DH	131	441	70	127	25	4	14	81	.288	0	0	0	.000
1982—Durham	Carol.	DH	1	3	0	0	0	0	0	0	.000	0	0	0	.000
1983—Durham	Carol.	1B	62	217	45	72	11	2	11	44	.332	370	30	12	.971
1983—Savannah	South.	1B	71	247	23	58	14	1	7	31	.235	325	20	10	.972
1984—Greenville	South.	1B	132	444	78	119	23	4	10	80	.268	389	19	3	.993
1985—Greenville	South.	1B	118	419	72	117	27	5	16	68	.279	825	41	13	.985
1985—Richmond	Int.	1B	6	15	0	6	1	0	0	3	.400	11	0	0	1.000

Signed as free agent by Atlanta Braves' organization, November 2, 1978.
†On disabled list, July 29 to August 13, 1981.

PEDRO GUERRERO

Name pronounced Guh-RAIR-oh.

Born June 29, 1956, at San Pedro de Macoris, Dominican Republic.
Height, 6.00. Weight, 195.
Throws and bats righthanded.
Cousin of Domingo Michel, second baseman in Los Angeles Dodgers' organization.

Established National League record for most home runs, month of June (15), 1985.
Major League stolen bases: 1979 (2), 1980 (2), 1981 (5), 1982 (22), 1983 (23), 1984 (9), 1985 (12). Total—75.
Led National League in slugging percentage with .577 in 1985.
Led National League third basemen in errors with 30 and tied for lead in total chances with 458 in 1983.
Led Pacific Coast League in sacrifice flies with 15 in 1978.
Tied for Northwest League lead in double plays by third basemen with 13 in 1974.
Named outfielder on THE SPORTING NEWS National League All-Star Team, 1981 and 1982.
Named outfielder on THE SPORTING NEWS National League Silver Slugger team, 1982.

Year Club	League	Pos.	G.	AB.	R.	H.	2B.	3B.	HR.	RBI.	B.A.	PO.	A.	E.	F.A.
1973—Sarasota Ind.†	Gulf C.	3B-SS	44	153	13	39	2	3	2	22	.255	32	82	11	.912
1974—Orangeburg	W. Car.	3B	19	55	3	8	1	0	0	1	.145	11	22	5	.868
1974—Bellingham	N'west	3B	82	297	49	94	●23	2	3	55	.316	★69	124	23	.894
1975—Danville	Midw.	3B-OF	104	351	81	121	25	5	10	76	★.345	111	168	31	.900
1976—Waterbury	East.	1B	132	495	73	151	★30	10	5	66	.305	1129	★96	★19	.985
1977—Albuquerque‡	P. C.	1B	32	129	30	52	11	4	4	39	.403	329	17	10	.972
1978—Albuquerque	P. C.	1B-3B	134	492	92	166	28	4	14	★116	.337	982	80	10	.991
1978—Los Angeles	Nat.	1B	5	8	3	5	0	1	0	1	.625	25	1	0	1.000
1979—Albuquerque	P. C.	OF-3B-1B	113	453	94	151	33	9	22	★103	.333	188	9	5	.975
1979—Los Angeles	Nat.	OF-1B-3B	25	62	7	15	2	0	2	9	.242	53	4	1	.983
1980—Los Angeles§	Nat.	O-2-3-1	75	183	27	59	9	1	7	31	.322	103	110	3	.986
1981—Los Angeles	Nat.	OF-3B-1B	98	347	46	104	17	2	12	48	.300	165	55	11	.952
1982—Los Angeles	Nat.	OF-3B	150	575	87	175	27	5	32	100	.304	282	53	12	.965
1983—Los Angeles	Nat.	3B-1B	160	584	87	174	28	6	32	103	.298	130	308	31	.934
1984—Los Angeles x	Nat.	3B-OF-1B	144	535	85	162	29	4	16	72	.303	271	151	22	.950
1985—Los Angeles	Nat.	OF-3B-1B	137	487	99	156	22	2	33	87	.320	251	123	13	.966
Major League Totals—8 Years			794	2781	441	850	134	21	134	451	.306	1280	805	93	.957

Signed as free agent by Cleveland Indians' organization, January 15, 1973.
†Traded to Los Angeles Dodgers for Pitcher Bruce Ellingsen, April 4, 1974.
‡On disabled list, May 19 to August 30, 1977.
§On disabled list, August 23 to September 15, 1980.
xOn disabled list, July 22 to August 6, 1984.

DIVISION SERIES RECORD

Year Club	League	Pos.	G.	AB.	R.	H.	2B.	3B.	HR.	RBI.	B.A.	PO.	A.	E.	F.A.
1981—Los Angeles	Nat.	3B	5	17	1	3	1	0	1	1	.176	3	15	0	1.000

CHAMPIONSHIP SERIES RECORD

Tied National League Championship Series records for most bases on balls (5) and most stolen bases (2), six-game Series, 1985.

Year Club	League	Pos.	G.	AB.	R.	H.	2B.	3B.	HR.	RBI.	B.A.	PO.	A.	E.	F.A.
1981—Los Angeles	Nat.	OF	5	19	1	2	0	0	1	2	.105	9	2	0	1.000
1983—Los Angeles	Nat.	3B	4	12	1	3	1	1	0	2	.250	0	9	0	1.000
1985—Los Angeles	Nat.	OF	6	20	2	5	1	0	0	4	.250	11	0	0	1.000
Championship Series Totals—3 Years			15	51	4	10	2	1	1	8	.196	20	11	0	1.000

WORLD SERIES RECORD

Year Club	League	Pos.	G.	AB.	R.	H.	2B.	3B.	HR.	RBI.	B.A.	PO.	A.	E.	F.A.
1981—Los Angeles	Nat.	OF	6	21	2	7	1	1	2	7	.333	17	1	0	1.000

ALL-STAR GAME RECORD

Year League	Pos.	AB.	R.	H.	2B.	3B.	HR.	RBI.	B.A.	PO.	A.	E.	F.A.
1981—National	PH	1	0	0	0	0	0	0	.000	0	0	0	.000
1983—National	3B-OF	1	0	0	0	0	0	0	.000	0	0	1	.000
All-Star Game Totals—2 Years		2	0	0	0	0	0	0	.000	0	0	1	.000

Named to National League All-Star Team for 1985 game; replaced due to injury by Glenn Wilson.

ARTHUR LEE GUETTERMAN

(Known by middle name.)

Born November 22, 1958, at Chattanooga, Tenn.
Height, 6.08. Weight, 225.
Throws and bats lefthanded.
Received bachelor of science degree in physical education from
Liberty Baptist College, Lynchburg, Va. in 1981.

Year Club	League	G.	IP.	W.	L.	Pct.	H.	R.	ER.	SO.	BB.	ERA.
1981—Bellingham	Northwest	13	84	6	4	.600	85	36	25	55	42	2.68
1982—Bakersfield	California	26	154	7	11	.389	172	100	76	82	69	4.44
1983—Bakersfield	California	25	156⅓	12	6	.667	164	72	56	93	45	3.22
1984—Chattanooga†	Southern	24	157	11	7	.611	174	68	59	47	38	3.38
1984—Seattle	American	3	4⅓	0	0	.000	9	2	2	2	2	4.15
1985—Calgary‡	P. Coast	20	110⅓	5	8	.385	138	86	71	48	44	5.79
Major League Totals—1 Year		3	4⅓	0	0	.000	9	2	2	2	2	4.15

Selected by Seattle Mariners' organization in 4th round of free-agent draft, June 8, 1981.
†On disabled list, August 1 to August 15, 1984.
‡On disabled list, April 11 to May 31, 1985.

RONALD AMES GUIDRY

(Ron)

Born August 28, 1950, at Lafayette, La.
Height, 5.11. Weight, 160.
Throws and bats lefthanded.
Attended University of Southwestern Louisiana, Lafayette, La.

Established major league records for highest winning percentage, season, 20 or more wins (.893), 1978; highest winning percentage, lifetime, 200 or more decisions (.694).
Tied major league record for striking out side on nine pitches, August 7, 1984, second game (ninth inning).
Established American League record for most strikeouts by lefthanded pitcher, game (18), June 17, 1978.
Tied American League record for most shutouts by lefthanded pitcher, season (9), 1978.
Major League saves: 1977 (1), 1979 (2), 1980 (1). Total—4.
Led American League in complete games with 21 in 1983.
Led American League in shutouts with 9 in 1978.
Named Man of the Year by THE SPORTING NEWS, 1978.
Named Major League Player of the Year by THE SPORTING NEWS, 1978.
Named American League Pitcher of the Year by THE SPORTING NEWS, 1978.
Won American League Cy Young Memorial Award, 1978.
Named lefthanded pitcher on THE SPORTING NEWS American League All-Star Team, 1978, 1981, 1983 and 1985.
Named pitcher on THE SPORTING NEWS American League All-Star fielding team, 1982 through 1985.

Year Club	League	G.	IP.	W.	L.	Pct.	H.	R.	ER.	SO.	BB.	ERA.
1971—Johnson City	Ap'lachian	7	47	2	2	.500	34	13	11	61	27	2.11
1972—Fort Lauderdale†	Florida St.	15	66	2	4	.333	53	35	28	61	50	3.82
1973—Kinston‡	Carolina	20	101	7	6	.538	85	53	36	97	70	3.21
1974—West Haven§	Eastern	37	77	2	4	.333	80	48	45	79	53	5.26
1975—Syracuse	Int'national	42	62	6	5	.545	46	24	20	76	37	2.90
1975—New York	American	10	16	0	1	.000	15	6	6	15	9	3.38
1976—New York	American	7	16	0	0	.000	20	12	10	12	4	5.63
1976—Syracuse	Int'national	22	40	5	1	.833	16	5	3	50	13	0.68
1977—New York	American	31	211	16	7	.696	174	72	66	176	65	2.82
1978—New York	American	35	274	*25	3	*.893	187	61	53	248	72	*1.74
1979—New York x	American	33	236	18	8	.692	203	83	73	201	71	*2.78
1980—New York	American	37	220	17	10	.630	215	97	87	166	80	3.56
1981—New York y	American	23	127	11	5	.688	100	41	39	104	26	2.76
1982—New York	American	34	222	14	8	.636	216	104	94	162	69	3.81
1983—New York x	American	31	250⅓	21	9	.700	232	99	95	156	60	3.42
1984—New York za	American	29	195⅔	10	11	.476	223	102	98	127	44	4.51
1985—New York	American	34	259	*22	6	*.786	243	104	94	143	42	3.27
Major League Totals—11 Years		304	2027	154	68	.694	1828	781	715	1510	542	3.17

Selected by New York Yankees' organization in 3rd round of free-agent draft, June 8, 1971.
†Appeared as outfielder in one game with one putout.
‡On temporary inactive list, July 13 to August 3, 1973.
§Appeared as outfielder with no chances.
xAppeared as outfielder in one game with no chances.
yGranted free agency, November 13, 1981; re-signed by Yankees, December 15, 1981.
zOn disabled list, August 16 to September 3, 1984.
aAppeared in one game as a pinch-runner.

DIVISION SERIES RECORD

Year Club	League	G.	IP.	W.	L.	Pct.	H.	R.	ER.	SO.	BB.	ERA.
1981—New York	American	2	8⅓	0	0	.000	11	5	5	8	3	5.40

CHAMPIONSHIP SERIES RECORD

Year Club	League	G.	IP.	W.	L.	Pct.	H.	R.	ER.	SO.	BB.	ERA.
1977—New York	American	2	11⅓	1	0	1.000	9	5	5	8	3	3.97
1978—New York	American	1	8	1	0	1.000	7	1	1	7	1	1.13
1980—New York	American	1	3	0	1	.000	5	4	4	2	4	12.00
Championship Series Totals—3 Years		4	22⅓	2	1	.667	21	10	10	17	8	4.03

Appeared as pinch-runner for New York Yankees in one game of 1976 Championship Series.

Tied World Series record for most consecutive home runs allowed, inning (2), October 25, 1981 (seventh inning).

Year	Club	League	G.	IP.	W.	L.	Pct.	H.	R.	ER.	SO.	BB.	ERA.
1977—New York	American		1	9	1	0	1.000	4	2	2	7	3	2.00
1978—New York	American		1	9	1	0	1.000	8	1	1	4	7	1.00
1981—New York	American		2	14	1	1	.500	8	3	3	15	4	1.93
World Series Totals—3 Years			4	32	3	1	.750	20	6	6	26	14	1.69

ALL-STAR GAME RECORD

Year	League	IP.	W.	L.	Pct.	H.	R.	ER.	SO.	BB.	ERA.
1978—American		⅓	0	0	.000	0	0	0	0	0	0.00
1979—American		⅓	0	0	.000	0	0	0	0	1	0.00
All-Star Game Totals—2 Years		⅔	0	0	.000	0	0	0	0	1	0.00

Member of American League All-Star Team in 1982; did not play.
Named to American League All-Star Team for 1983 game; replaced due to injury by Tippy Martinez.

OSWALDO JOSE GUILLEN (BARRIOS)
Name pronounced Geeh-JEN.
(Ozzie)

Born January 20, 1964, at Ocumare del Tuv, Miranda, Venezuela
Height, 5.10. Weight, 160.
Throws right and bats lefthanded.

Tied major league record for fewest bases on balls received, 150 or more games, season (12), 1985.
Established American League record for fewest putouts, shortstop, season, 150 or more games (220), 1985.
Major League stolen bases: 1985 (7).
Led Pacific Coast League shortstops in assists with 362 and total chances with 549 in 1984.
Tied for California League lead in sacrifice hits with 14 in 1982.
Named American League Rookie Player of the Year by THE SPORTING NEWS, 1985.
Named American League Rookie of the Year by Baseball Writers' Association of America, 1985.

Year	Club	League	Pos.	G.	AB.	R.	H.	2B.	3B.	HR.	RBI.	B.A.	PO.	A.	E.	F.A.
1981—Bradenton Padr.†	Gulf C.	SS-2B	55	189	26	49	4	1	0	16	.259	105	135	15	.941
1982—Reno†	Calif.	SS	130	528	★103	★183	33	1	2	54	.347	★240	399	41	.940
1983—Beaumont†	Texas	SS	114	427	62	126	20	4	2	48	.295	185	327	★38	.931
1984—Las Vegas†‡	P. C.	SS-2B	122	463	81	137	26	6	5	53	.296	172	364	17	.969
1985—Chicago	Amer.	SS	150	491	71	134	21	9	1	33	.273	220	382	12	★.980
Major League Totals—1 Year			150	491	71	134	21	9	1	33	.273	220	382	12	.980

Signed as free agent by San Diego Padres' organization, December 17, 1980.
†Switch-hitter.
‡Traded with Pitchers Tim Lollar and Bill Long and Third Baseman Luis Salazar to Chicago White Sox for Pitchers LaMarr Hoyt, Kevin Kristan and Todd Simmons, December 6, 1984.

BRADLEY LEE GULDEN
(Brad)

Born June 10, 1956, at New Ulm, Minn.
Height, 5.11. Weight, 182.
Throws right and bats lefthanded.

Major League stolen bases: 1984 (2).
Led Pacific Coast League in passed balls with 22 and tied for lead in double plays by catchers with 11 in 1978.
Led California League in passed balls with 18 in 1977.
Led Northwest League catchers in double plays with 9 and passed balls with 23 in 1975.

Year	Club	League	Pos.	G.	AB.	R.	H.	2B.	3B.	HR.	RBI.	B.A.	PO.	A.	E.	F.A.
1975—Bellingham	N'west	C	66	203	25	33	4	0	2	15	.163	★319	★70	★33	.922
1976—Danville	Midw.	★C-OF	103	334	42	95	20	2	3	51	.284	521	90	★39	.939
1977—Lodi	Calif.	C	118	423	76	127	23	2	15	86	.300	★704	★66	★24	.970
1978—Albuquerque	P. C.	C	125	436	69	128	21	4	8	72	.294	★610	★88	★23	.968
1978—Los Angeles†	Nat.	C	3	4	0	0	0	0	0	0	.000	8	1	0	1.000
1979—Columbus	Int.	C	80	230	28	57	10	0	6	34	.248	326	22	3	.991
1979—New York	Amer.	C	40	92	10	15	4	0	0	6	.163	178	24	1	.995
1980—Columbus	Int.	C	14	51	6	8	2	0	2	10	.157	54	13	4	.944
1980—Nashville‡	South.	C-OF	85	295	34	70	13	6	6	46	.237	543	80	12	.981
1980—New York§	Amer.	C	2	3	1	1	0	0	1	2	.333	3	0	0	1.000
1981—Seattle	Amer.	C	8	16	0	3	2	0	0	1	.188	24	3	0	1.000
1981—Spokane	P. C.	C	15	51	9	14	5	0	2	9	.275	37	3	5	.889
1981—Columbus x	Int.	C-OF	73	237	37	70	13	4	17	42	.295	362	39	7	.983
1982—Wichita	A. A.	C-OF	64	212	37	61	16	2	7	35	.288	219	20	6	.976
1982—Montreal y	Nat.	C	5	6	1	0	0	0	0	0	.000	6	2	0	1.000
1983—Columbus z	Int.	C	94	275	45	87	16	1	9	47	.316	512	45	●13	.977
1984—Cincinnati	Nat.	C	107	292	31	66	8	2	4	33	.226	485	53	14	.975
1985—Denver a	A. A.	C-1B	45	143	20	35	7	0	4	16	.245	263	24	5	.983
1985—Tucson bc	P. C.	C-1B	47	153	20	41	10	2	3	21	.268	203	25	5	.979
National League Totals—3 Years			115	302	32	66	8	2	4	33	.219	499	56	14	.975
American League Totals—3 Years			50	111	11	19	6	0	1	9	.171	205	27	1	.996
Major League Totals—6 Years			165	413	43	85	14	2	5	42	.206	704	83	15	.981

Selected by Los Angeles Dodgers' organization in 17th round of free-agent draft, June 4, 1975.
†Traded to New York Yankees for Outfielder Gary Thomasson, February 15, 1979.

‡On disabled list, August 7 to August 17, 1980.
§Traded with cash to Seattle Mariners for Infielder Larry Milbourne and a player to be named later, November 18, 1980; Seattle traded Gulden back to New York Yankees to complete deal, May 18, 1981.
xTraded to Montreal Expos' organization for Catcher Bobby Ramos, April 5, 1982.
ySold to New York Yankees, October 26, 1982.
zGranted free agency, October 20, 1983; signed by Cincinnati Reds, November 4, 1983.
aSold to Tucson (Houston Astros' organization), June 12, 1985.
bOn disabled list, August 16, 1985 through remainder of season.
cGranted free agency, October 15, 1985; signed by San Francisco Giants, December 12, 1985.

WILLIAM LEE GULLICKSON
(Bill)

Born February 20, 1959, at Marshall, Minn.
Height, 6.03. Weight, 220.
Throws and bats righthanded.
Tied modern major league record for most wild pitches, game (6), April 10, 1982.
Led National League in home runs allowed with 27 in 1984.
Named National League Rookie Pitcher of the Year by THE SPORTING NEWS, 1980.

Year Club	League	G.	IP.	W.	L.	Pct.	H.	R.	ER.	SO.	BB.	ERA.
1977—West Palm Beach	Florida St.	10	56	3	3	.500	67	30	25	35	17	4.02
1978—West Palm Beach	Florida St.	20	148	9	9	.500	121	45	30	127	52	1.82
1978—Memphis	Southern	8	50	1	4	.200	44	19	17	43	19	3.06
1979—Denver	Am. Assoc.	11	54	3	3	.500	65	44	40	31	26	6.67
1979—Memphis	Southern	16	116	10	3	.769	110	52	47	115	42	3.65
1979—Montreal	National	1	1	0	0	.000	2	0	0	0	0	0.00
1980—Denver	Am. Assoc.	9	66	6	2	.750	47	14	14	64	29	1.91
1980—Montreal	National	24	141	10	5	.667	127	53	47	120	50	3.00
1981—Montreal	National	22	157	7	9	.438	142	54	49	115	34	2.81
1982—Montreal	National	34	236⅔	12	14	.462	231	101	94	155	61	3.57
1983—Montreal	National	34	242⅓	17	12	.586	230	108	101	120	59	3.75
1984—Montreal†	National	32	226⅔	12	9	.571	230	100	91	100	37	3.61
1985—Montreal‡§	National	29	181⅓	14	12	.538	187	78	71	68	47	3.52
Major League Totals—7 Years		176	1186	72	61	.541	1149	494	453	678	288	3.44

Selected by Montreal Expos' organization in 1st round (second player selected) of free-agent draft, June 7, 1977.
†On disabled list, April 20 to May 8, 1984.
‡On disabled list, June 17 to July 8, 1985.
§Traded with Catcher Sal Butera to Cincinnati Reds for Pitchers Jay Tibbs, Andy McGaffigan and John Stuper and Catcher Dann Bilardello, December 19, 1985.

DIVISION SERIES RECORD

Year Club	League	G.	IP.	W.	L.	Pct.	H.	R.	ER.	SO.	BB.	ERA.
1981—Montreal	National	1	7⅔	1	0	1.000	6	1	1	3	1	1.17

CHAMPIONSHIP SERIES RECORD

Tied Championship Series record for most games lost, Series (2), 1981.

Year Club	League	G.	IP.	W.	L.	Pct.	H.	R.	ER.	SO.	BB.	ERA.
1981—Montreal	National	2	14⅓	0	2	.000	12	5	4	12	6	2.51

DAVID LAWRENCE GUMPERT
(Dave)

Born May 5, 1958, at South Haven, Mich.
Height, 6.03. Weight, 190.
Throws and bats righthanded.
Received degree from Aquinas College, Grand Rapids, Mich.
Major League saves: 1982 (1), 1983 (2). Total—3.
Tied for American Association lead in intentional bases on balls issued with 7 in 1985.

Year Club	League	G.	IP.	W.	L.	Pct.	H.	R.	ER.	SO.	BB.	ERA.
1981—Lakeland	Florida St.	14	108	8	5	.615	97	33	30	75	26	2.50
1981—Birmingham	Southern	11	74	6	3	.667	78	39	34	25	16	4.14
1981—Evansville	Am. Assoc.	1	4	0	0	.000	5	2	2	3	2	4.50
1982—Birmingham	Southern	42	70⅔	9	6	.600	56	20	17	52	23	2.17
1982—Evansville	Am. Assoc.	2	5⅔	1	0	1.000	0	0	0	2	3	0.00
1982—Detroit	American	5	2	0	0	.000	7	6	6	0	2	27.00
1983—Evansville	Am. Assoc.	14	27⅔	5	1	.833	23	8	7	17	9	2.28
1983—Detroit	American	26	44⅓	0	2	.000	43	16	13	14	7	2.64
1984—Evansville†	Am. Assoc.	56	87⅓	7	4	.636	105	51	48	48	40	4.95
1985—Iowa	Am. Assoc.	42	66⅔	3	4	.429	74	36	31	33	23	4.19
1985—Chicago‡	National	9	10⅓	1	0	1.000	12	7	4	4	7	3.48
American League Totals—2 Years		31	46⅓	0	2	.000	50	22	19	14	9	3.69
National League Totals—1 Year		9	10⅓	1	0	1.000	12	7	4	4	7	3.48
Major League Totals—3 Years		40	56⅔	1	2	.333	62	29	23	18	16	3.65

Signed as free agent by Detroit Tigers' organization, November 4, 1980.
†Released, March 30, 1985; signed by Iowa (Chicago Cubs' organization), April 7, 1985.
‡On disabled list, August 23 to September 18, 1985.

LAWRENCE CYRIL GURA
(Larry)

Born November 26, 1947, at Joliet, Ill.
Height, 6.01. Weight, 185.
Throws and bats lefthanded.
Received bachelor of arts degree in physical education from
Arizona State University, Tempe, Ariz., in 1969.

Established major league record for most sacrifice flies allowed, season (17), 1983.
Tied for International League lead in shutouts with 4 in 1974.
Major League saves: 1970 (1), 1971 (1), 1976 (1), 1977 (10), 1985 (1). Total—14.
Received reported $50,000 bonus to sign with Chicago Cubs, 1969.
Named lefthanded pitcher on THE SPORTING NEWS College Baseball All-America Team, 1969.

Year	Club	League	G.	IP.	W.	L.	Pct.	H.	R.	ER.	SO.	BB.	ERA.
1969—Tacoma		P. Coast	16	88	4	8	.333	79	39	31	47	24	3.17
1970—Tacoma		P. Coast	10	61	3	4	.429	55	32	27	32	17	3.98
1970—Chicago		National	20	38	1	3	.250	35	18	16	21	23	3.79
1971—Tacoma		P. Coast	30	190	11	8	.579	199	93	75	140	50	3.55
1971—Chicago		National	6	3	0	0	.000	6	3	2	2	1	6.00
1972—Wichita		Am. Assoc.	26	130	11	4	*.733	127	60	53	109	38	3.65
1972—Chicago		National	7	12	0	0	.000	11	5	5	13	3	3.75
1973—Wichita		Am. Assoc.	5	31	1	2	.333	38	18	16	29	11	4.65
1973—Chicago†		National	21	65	2	4	.333	79	39	35	43	11	4.85
1974—Spokane‡		P. Coast	7	29	1	1	.500	34	14	10	25	9	3.10
1974—Syracuse		Int'national	17	118	7	7	.500	89	32	28	97	19	*2.14
1974—New York		American	8	56	5	1	.833	54	17	15	17	12	2.41
1975—New York§		American	26	151	7	8	.467	173	65	59	65	41	3.52
1976—Kansas City x		American	20	63	4	0	1.000	47	20	16	22	20	2.29
1977—Kansas City		American	52	106	8	5	.615	108	43	37	46	28	3.14
1978—Kansas City y		American	35	222	16	4	.800	183	73	67	81	60	2.72
1979—Kansas City		American	39	234	13	12	.520	226	137	116	85	73	4.46
1980—Kansas City		American	36	283	18	10	.643	272	107	93	113	76	2.96
1981—Kansas City		American	23	172	11	8	.579	139	61	52	61	35	2.72
1982—Kansas City		American	37	248	18	12	.600	251	124	111	98	64	4.03
1983—Kansas City z		American	34	200⅓	11	*18	.379	220	119	109	57	76	4.90
1984—Kansas City		American	31	168⅔	12	9	.571	175	102	97	68	67	5.18
1985—Kansas City a		American	3	4⅓	0	0	.000	7	6	6	2	4	12.46
1985—Chicago		National	5	20⅓	0	3	.000	34	19	19	7	6	8.41
1985—Iowa b		Am. Assoc.	10	71	7	3	.700	69	24	20	45	8	2.54
National League Totals—5 Years			59	138⅓	3	10	.231	165	84	77	86	44	5.01
American League Totals—12 Years			344	1908⅓	123	87	.586	1855	874	778	715	556	3.67
Major League Totals—16 Years			403	2046⅔	126	97	.565	2020	958	855	801	600	3.76

Selected by Chicago Cubs' organization in 2nd round of free-agent draft, June 5, 1969.
†Traded to Texas Rangers, November 14, 1973, completing deal in which Texas traded Pitcher Mike Paul to Chicago Cubs for a player to be named later, August 31, 1973.
‡Traded to New York Yankees for Catcher Duke Sims, May 8, 1974.
§Traded to Kansas City Royals for Catcher Fran Healy, May 15, 1976.
xOn disabled list, June 1 to June 23, 1976.
yGranted free agency, November 2, 1978; re-signed by Royals, November 13, 1978.
zAppeared in one game as a pinch-runner.
aReleased, May 18, 1985; signed by Chicago Cubs, May 28, 1985.
bReleased by Chicago Cubs, August 14, 1985.

DIVISION SERIES RECORD

Year	Club	League	G.	IP.	W.	L.	Pct.	H.	R.	ER.	SO.	BB.	ERA.
1981—Kansas City		American	1	3⅔	0	1	.000	7	4	3	3	3	7.36

CHAMPIONSHIP SERIES RECORD

Established Championship Series record for most hits allowed, game (12), October 9, 1976.
Established American League Championship Series record for most hits allowed, five-game Series (18), 1976.

Year	Club	League	G.	IP.	W.	L.	Pct.	H.	R.	ER.	SO.	BB.	ERA.
1976—Kansas City		American	2	10⅔	0	1	.000	18	6	5	4	1	4.22
1977—Kansas City		American	2	2	0	1	.000	7	5	4	2	1	18.00
1978—Kansas City		American	1	6⅓	1	0	1.000	8	2	2	2	2	2.84
1980—Kansas City		American	1	9	1	0	1.000	10	2	2	4	1	2.00
Championship Series Totals—4 Years			6	28	2	2	.500	43	15	13	12	5	4.18

WORLD SERIES RECORD

Tied World Series record for most double plays by pitcher, six-game Series (2), 1980.

Year	Club	League	G.	IP.	W.	L.	Pct.	H.	R.	ER.	SO.	BB.	ERA.
1980—Kansas City		American	2	12⅓	0	0	.000	8	4	3	4	3	2.19

ALL-STAR GAME RECORD

Named to American League All-Star Team in 1980; did not play.

—DID YOU KNOW—

That 14 one-hitters were pitched in 1985, including two by the Dodgers' Orel Hershiser?

DIMAS J. GUTIERREZ (MARTE)

Born March 25, 1966, at Punto Fijo Edo Falcon, Venezuela.
Height, 5.11. Weight, 172.
Throws and bats righthanded.
Tied for Carolina League lead in sacrifice flies with 10 in 1985.
Tied for Gulf Coast League lead in game-winning RBIs with 8 in 1983.
Led Gulf Coast League third basemen in fielding percentage with .897 in 1983.

Year Club	League	Pos.	G.	AB.	R.	H.	2B.	3B.	HR.	RBI.	B.A.	PO.	A.	E.	F.A.
1983—Bradenton Pir.	Gulf C.	3B-SS	49	191	27	48	9	3	●8	33	.251	42	96	14	.908
1984—Macon	S. Atl.	3B	66	242	26	60	13	2	1	19	.248	40	122	19	.895
1984—Watertown	NYP	3B-SS	70	264	33	67	14	3	7	33	.254	56	161	13	.943
1985—Prince William	Carol.	3-S-2-O	121	419	62	111	24	4	3	49	.265	80	210	17	.945

Signed as free agent by Pittsburgh Pirates' organization, November 29, 1982.

JOAQUIN FERNANDO GUTIERREZ

Name pronounced Wah-KEEN Goo-TEE-erz.

(Jackie)

Born June 27, 1960, at Cartagena, Colombia.
Height, 6.01. Weight, 175.
Throws and bats righthanded.
Brother-in-law of Orlando Ramirez, shortstop with California Angels, 1974 through 1977 and 1979;
son of Campo Gutierrez, who competed in javelin event for Columbia in 1936 Olympics;
and brother of Freddie Gutierrez, who competed in 100 meter race in 1964 Olympics.

Established major league records for fewest assists (347), and chances accepted (575) by shortstop, season, 150 or more games, 1984.
Major League stolen bases: 1984 (12), 1985 (10). Total—22.
Led Carolina League shortstops in assists with 423 and tied for lead in putouts with 205 and errors with 53 in 1981.

Year Club	League	Pos.	G.	AB.	R.	H.	2B.	3B.	HR.	RBI.	B.A.	PO.	A.	E.	F.A.
1978—Elmira	NYP	SS	63	216	23	42	8	0	0	18	.194	★131	197	20	★.943
1979—Elmira	NYP	SS-2B	63	183	29	46	4	2	0	14	.251	97	157	12	.955
1980—Winter Haven	Fla. St.	3B-SS-2B	111	368	46	94	4	1	1	40	.255	103	179	19	.937
1981—Winston-Salem	Carol.	SS-3B	137	507	56	126	14	5	1	45	.249	207	428	55	.920
1982—Bristol	East.	SS	138	468	64	130	20	2	1	44	.278	★199	368	37	★.939
1983—New Britain	East.	SS	67	248	36	69	7	2	4	25	.278	116	194	13	.960
1983—Pawtucket	Int.	SS	66	233	30	62	11	1	1	17	.266	109	211	20	.941
1983—Boston	Amer.	SS	5	10	2	3	0	0	0	0	.300	9	6	1	.938
1984—Boston	Amer.	SS	151	449	55	118	12	3	2	29	.263	228	347	31	.949
1985—Boston†	Amer.	SS	103	275	33	60	5	2	2	21	.218	143	238	23	.943
Major League Totals—3 Years			259	734	90	181	17	5	4	50	.247	380	591	55	.946

Signed as free agent by Boston Red Sox' organization, January 14, 1978.
†Traded to Baltimore Orioles for Pitcher Sammy Stewart, December 17, 1985.

JOSE ALBERTO GUZMAN (MIRABEL)

Born April 9, 1963, at Santa Isabel, Puerto Rico.
Height, 6.03. Weight, 185.
Throws and bats righthanded.

Year Club	League	G.	IP.	W.	L.	Pct.	H.	R.	ER.	SO.	BB.	ERA.
1981—Sarasota Rangers	Gulf Coast	14	39	3	3	.500	44	30	23	13	14	5.31
1982—Sarasota Rangers	Gulf Coast	12	66	5	4	.556	51	21	16	42	13	2.18
1983—Burlington	Midwest	25	154⅔	12	8	.600	135	68	51	146	52	2.97
1984—Tulsa	Texas	25	140⅓	7	9	.438	137	75	65	82	55	4.17
1985—Oklahoma City	Am. Assoc.	25	149⅔	10	5	.667	131	60	52	76	40	3.13
1985—Texas	American	5	32⅔	3	2	.600	27	13	10	24	14	2.76
Major League Totals—1 Year		5	32⅔	3	2	.600	27	13	10	24	14	2.76

Signed as free agent by Texas Rangers' organization, February 10, 1981.

DOUGLAS WAYNE GWOSDZ

Name pronounced Goosh.

(Doug)

Born June 20, 1960, at Houston, Tex.
Height, 5.11. Weight, 180.
Throws and bats righthanded.

Year Club	League	Pos.	G.	AB.	R.	H.	2B.	3B.	HR.	RBI.	B.A.	PO.	A.	E.	F.A.
1978—Walla Walla	N'west	C	48	170	25	42	6	0	5	26	.247	256	51	5	★.984
1979—Reno	Calif.	C-OF	85	258	37	67	7	3	6	40	.260	583	51	8	.988
1980—Amarillo	Texas	C	97	286	40	70	18	2	7	43	.245	597	66	14	.979
1981—Hawaii	P. C.	C-1B	66	201	36	53	12	1	8	28	.264	322	42	8	.978
1981—San Diego	Nat.	C	16	24	1	4	2	0	0	3	.167	40	5	0	1.000
1982—San Diego	Nat.	C	7	17	1	3	0	0	0	0	.176	34	2	0	1.000
1982—Hawaii†	P. C.	C-OF	29	86	11	16	5	0	2	12	.186	133	16	4	.974
1983—San Diego	Nat.	C	39	55	7	6	1	0	1	4	.109	95	5	3	.971
1984—San Diego	Nat.	C	7	8	0	2	0	0	0	1	.250	25	1	1	.963
1984—Las Vegas‡	P. C.	C	61	197	20	45	10	0	6	27	.228	300	32	5	.985

Year Club League	Pos.	G.	AB.	R.	H.	2B.	3B.	HR.	RBI.	B.A.	PO.	A.	E.	F.A.
1985—San Francisco....... Nat.					(Did not play)									
1985—Phoenix§................ P. C.	C	52	143	25	36	12	1	6	25	.252	243	22	1	.996
Major League Totals—4 Years...............		69	104	9	15	3	0	1	8	.144	194	13	4	.981

Selected by San Diego Padres' organization in 2nd round of free-agent draft, June 6, 1978.
†On disabled list, July 15 to September 3, 1982.
‡Drafted by San Francisco Giants, December 3, 1984.
§Granted free agency, October 15, 1985.

ANTHONY KEITH GWYNN

Name pronounced Gwin.

(Tony)

Born May 9, 1960, at Los Angeles, Calif.
Height, 5.11. Weight, 206.
Throws and bats lefthanded.
Attended San Diego State University, San Diego, Calif.
Brother of Chris Gwynn, outfielder in Los Angeles Dodgers' organization.

Major League stolen bases: 1982 (8), 1983 (7), 1984 (33), 1985 (14). Total—62.
Named outfielder on THE SPORTING NEWS National League All-Star Team, 1984.
Named outfielder on THE SPORTING NEWS National League Silver Slugger team, 1984.
Named Northwest League Most Valuable Player, 1981.
Drafted by San Diego Clippers in 10th round (210th player selected) of NBA draft, June 9, 1981.

Year Club League	Pos.	G.	AB.	R.	H.	2B.	3B.	HR.	RBI.	B.A.	PO.	A.	E.	F.A.
1981—Walla Walla .... N'west	OF	42	178	46	59	12	1	12	37	★.331	76	2	3	.963
1981—Amarillo................. Texas	OF	23	91	22	42	8	2	4	19	.462	41	1	0	1.000
1982—Hawaii................... P. C.	OF	93	366	65	120	23	2	5	46	.328	208	11	4	.982
1982—San Diego† .... Nat.	OF	54	190	33	55	12	2	1	17	.289	110	1	1	.991
1983—Las Vegas‡........... P. C.	OF	17	73	15	25	6	0	0	7	.342	23	2	3	.893
1983—San Diego .... Nat.	OF	86	304	34	94	12	2	1	37	.309	163	9	1	.994
1984—San Diego .... Nat.	OF	158	606	88	★213	21	10	5	71	★.351	345	11	4	.989
1985—San Diego .... Nat.	OF	154	622	90	197	29	5	6	46	.317	337	14	4	.989
Major League Totals—4 Years................		452	1722	245	559	74	19	13	171	.325	955	35	10	.990

Selected by San Diego Padres' organization in 3rd round of free-agent draft, June 8, 1981.
†On disabled list, August 26 to September 10, 1982.
‡On San Diego disabled list, March 26 to June 21, 1983; included rehabilitation assignment to Las Vegas, May 31 to June 20, 1983.

CHAMPIONSHIP SERIES RECORD

Tied Championship Series record for most runs, five-game Series (6), 1984.

Year Club League	Pos.	G.	AB.	R.	H.	2B.	3B.	HR.	RBI.	B.A.	PO.	A.	E.	F.A.
1984—San Diego .... Nat.	OF	5	19	6	7	3	0	0	3	.368	9	0	0	1.000

WORLD SERIES RECORD

Year Club League	Pos.	G.	AB.	R.	H.	2B.	3B.	HR.	RBI.	B.A.	PO.	A.	E.	F.A.
1984—San Diego .... Nat.	OF	5	19	1	5	0	0	0	0	.263	12	1	1	.929

ALL-STAR GAME RECORD

Year League	Pos.	AB.	R.	H.	2B.	3B.	HR.	RBI.	B.A.	PO.	A.	E.	F.A.
1984—National...	OF	3	0	1	0	0	0	0	.333	0	0	0	.000
1985—National...	OF	1	0	0	0	0	0	0	.000	1	0	0	1.000
All-Star Game Totals—2 Years....................		4	0	1	0	0	0	0	.250	1	0	0	1.000

CHRISTOPHER KARLTON GWYNN

Name pronounced Gwin.

(Chris)

Born October 13, 1964, at Long Beach, Calif.
Height, 6.00. Weight, 201.
Throws and bats lefthanded.
Attended San Diego State University, San Diego, Calif.
Brother of Tony Gwynn, outfielder with San Diego Padres.

Named outfielder on THE SPORTING NEWS College Baseball All-America Team, 1985.
Member of 1984 U.S. Olympic baseball team.

Year Club League	Pos.	G.	AB.	R.	H.	2B.	3B.	HR.	RBI.	B.A.	PO.	A.	E.	F.A.
1985—Vero Beach........... Fla. St.	OF	52	179	19	46	8	6	0	17	.257	43	2	0	1.000

Selected by California Angels' organization in 5th round of free-agent draft, June 7, 1982.
Selected by Los Angeles Dodgers' organization in 1st round (10th player selected) of free-agent draft, June 3, 1985.

—DID YOU KNOW—

That four players with the Reds early in the 1985 season had more than 2,000 career hits? The players were Pete Rose (4,204), Tony Perez (2,681), Cesar Cedeno (2,069) and Dave Concepcion (2,117).

BRYAN EDMUND HAAS
(Moose)

Born April 22, 1956, at Baltimore, Md.
Height, 6.00. Weight, 170.
Throws and bats righthanded.
Attended Catonsville Junior College, Catonsville, Md.

Major League saves: 1978 (1), 1982 (1). Total—2.

Year Club	League	G.	IP.	W.	L.	Pct.	H.	R.	ER.	SO.	BB.	ERA.
1974—Newark	NYP	13	96	5	5	.500	91	43	34	89	41	3.19
1975—Burlington	Midwest	25	171	11	8	.579	149	66	39	146	49	2.05
1976—Spokane	P. Coast	30	172	13	9	.591	208	116	★106	130	86	5.55
1976—Milwaukee	American	5	16	0	1	.000	12	8	7	9	12	3.94
1977—Milwaukee	American	32	198	10	12	.455	195	104	95	113	84	4.32
1978—Milwaukee†	American	7	31	2	3	.400	33	22	21	32	8	6.10
1979—Milwaukee	American	29	185	11	11	.500	198	112	98	95	59	4.77
1980—Milwaukee	American	33	252	16	15	.516	246	96	87	146	56	3.11
1981—Milwaukee	American	24	137	11	7	.611	146	69	68	64	40	4.47
1982—Milwaukee	American	32	193⅓	11	8	.517	232	101	96	104	39	4.47
1983—Milwaukee‡	American	25	179	13	3	.813	170	66	65	75	42	3.27
1984—Milwaukee	American	31	189¼	9	11	.450	205	91	84	84	43	3.99
1985—Milwaukee	American	27	161⅔	8	8	.500	165	85	69	78	25	3.84
Major League Totals—10 Years		245	1542⅓	91	79	.535	1602	754	690	800	408	4.03

Selected by Milwaukee Brewers' organization in 2nd round of free-agent draft, June 5, 1974.
†On disabled list, April 20 to June 21 and June 27 to September 15, 1978.
‡Appeared in one game as a pinch-runner.

DIVISION SERIES RECORD

Year Club	League	G.	IP.	W.	L.	Pct.	H.	R.	ER.	SO.	BB.	ERA.
1981—Milwaukee	American	2	6⅔	0	2	.000	13	7	7	1	1	9.45

CHAMPIONSHIP SERIES RECORD

Year Club	League	G.	IP.	W.	L.	Pct.	H.	R.	ER.	SO.	BB.	ERA.
1982—Milwaukee	American	1	7⅓	1	0	1.000	5	5	4	7	5	4.91

WORLD SERIES RECORD

Year Club	League	G.	IP.	W.	L.	Pct.	H.	R.	ER.	SO.	BB.	ERA.
1982—Milwaukee	American	2	7⅓	0	0	.000	8	7	6	4	3	7.36

JOHN GABRIEL HABYAN

Name pronounced HAY-bee-un.

Born January 29, 1964, at Bayshore, N.Y.
Height, 6.01. Weight, 195.
Throws and bats righthanded.

Pitched 6-0 no-hit victory against Columbus, May 13, 1985.

Year Club	League	G.	IP.	W.	L.	Pct.	H.	R.	ER.	SO.	BB.	ERA.
1982—Bluefield	Ap'lachian	12	81⅓	●9	2	.818	68	35	32	55	24	3.54
1982—Hagerstown	Carolina	1	⅔	0	0	.000	5	5	5	1	2	67.50
1983—Hagerstown	Carolina	11	48	2	3	.400	54	41	31	42	29	5.81
1983—Newark	NYP	11	71⅔	5	3	.625	68	34	27	64	29	3.39
1984—Hagerstown	Carolina	13	81⅓	9	4	.692	64	41	32	81	33	3.54
1984—Charlotte	Southern	13	77	4	7	.364	84	46	38	55	34	4.44
1985—Charlotte	Southern	28	189⅔	13	5	.722	157	73	69	123	90	3.27
1985—Baltimore	American	2	2⅔	1	0	1.000	3	1	0	2	0	0.00
Major League Totals—1 Year		2	2⅔	1	0	1.000	3	1	0	2	0	0.00

Selected by Baltimore Orioles' organization in 3rd round of free-agent draft, June 7, 1982.

KEVIN EUGENE HAGEN

Born March 8, 1960, at Renton, Wash.
Height, 6.02. Weight, 185.
Throws and bats righthanded.
Attended Bellevue Community College, Bellevue, Wash.

Led Texas League in hit batsmen with 9 and tied for lead in balks with 4 in 1981.
Tied for American Association lead in games started by pitchers with 28 and hit batsmen with 10 in 1985.
Tied for American Association lead in shutouts with 2 in 1983.
Tied for Texas League lead in balks with 4 in 1982.

Year Club	League	G.	IP.	W.	L.	Pct.	H.	R.	ER.	SO.	BB.	ERA.
1980—Gastonia	S. Atlantic	29	177	14	8	.636	171	91	78	104	71	3.97
1981—Arkansas	Texas	27	165	8	11	.421	179	95	73	66	69	3.98
1982—Arkansas	Texas	27	189⅔	11	10	.524	176	88	76	102	75	3.61
1983—Louisville	Am. Assoc.	21	131⅓	6	9	.400	122	72	63	60	46	4.32
1983—St. Louis	National	9	22⅓	2	2	.500	34	15	12	7	7	4.84
1984—Louisville	Am. Assoc.	29	176⅔	10	9	.526	174	88	68	77	57	3.46
1984—St. Louis	National	4	7⅓	1	0	1.000	9	2	2	1	2.45
1985—Louisville†	Am. Assoc.	28	170	10	9	.526	162	72	64	63	87	3.39
Major League Totals—2 Years		13	29⅔	3	2	.600	43	17	14	9	8	4.25

Selected by St. Louis Cardinals' organization in 4th round of free-agent draft, January 3, 1980.
†Sold to Cleveland Indians' organization, January 3, 1986.

JERRY WAYNE HAIRSTON

Born February 16, 1952, at Birmingham, Ala.
Height, 5.10. Weight, 190.
Throws right and bats left and righthanded.
Attended Lawson State Junior College, Birmingham, Ala.
Son of Sam Hairston, Sr., catcher with Chicago White Sox, 1951; and scout and minor league instructor with
Chicago White Sox, 1961 through 1982 and 1985; brother of John Hairston, catcher-outfielder
with Chicago Cubs, 1969; and Sam Hairston, Jr., second baseman
in Chicago White Sox' organization, 1966.

Major League stolen bases: 1975 (1), 1976 (1), 1984 (2). Total—4.
Led Mexican League in bases on balls received with 122 in 1978, 77 in 1980 and 122 in 1981.
Led Midwest League second baseman in double plays with 77 in 1971.
Tied for Mexican League lead in double plays by outfielders with 4 in 1981.

Year	Club	League	Pos.	G.	AB.	R.	H.	2B.	3B.	HR.	RBI.	B.A.	PO.	A.	E.	F.A.
1970—Sarasota W. Sox	Gulf C.		2B	56	183	37	61	8	2	1	36	.333	129	130	*19	.932
1971—Appleton	Midw.		2B	121	448	86	120	15	4	0	39	.268	*260	*333	*31	.950
1972—Knoxville	South.		2-1-O-3	132	459	82	134	19	●9	10	64	.292	591	225	27	.968
1973—Iowa	A. A.		O-2-3-1	84	274	51	95	18	6	9	65	.347	70	36	7	.938
1973—Chicago	Amer.		OF-1B	60	210	25	57	11	1	0	23	.271	194	13	5	.976
1974—Iowa	A. A.		OF	42	140	31	53	10	2	5	42	.379	48	1	2	.961
1974—Chicago†	Amer.		OF	45	109	8	25	7	0	0	8	.229	24	1	2	.926
1975—Denver	A. A.		DH	40	139	28	51	9	0	3	31	.367	0	0	0	.000
1975—Chicago	Amer.		OF	69	219	26	62	8	0	0	23	.283	111	6	6	.951
1976—Iowa	A. A.		OF-INF	94	325	53	94	24	3	5	64	.289	199	13	5	.977
1976—Chicago	Amer.		OF	44	119	20	27	2	2	0	10	.227	71	1	2	.973
1977—Chicago‡	Amer.		OF	13	26	3	8	2	0	0	4	.308	15	1	0	1.000
1977—Pittsburgh§	Nat.		OF-2B	51	52	5	10	2	0	2	6	.192	13	0	1	.929
1978—Durango	Mex.		OF	144	488	97	177	21	7	9	77	.363	297	19	11	.966
1979—Durango	Mex.		OF	128	427	87	151	22	5	12	56	.354	295	8	6	.981
1980—Campeche	Mex.		OF-1B	77	235	50	74	15	2	7	28	.315	189	11	3	.985
1981—Mex. C. Reds x	Mex.		OF	123	536	74	118	14	8	7	73	.296	*334	11	6	.983
1981—Chicago	Amer.		OF	9	25	5	7	1	0	1	6	.280	14	0	1	.933
1982—Chicago	Amer.		OF	85	90	11	21	5	0	5	18	.233	34	2	0	1.000
1983—Chicago	Amer.		OF	101	126	17	37	9	1	5	22	.294	29	1	1	.968
1984—Chicago	Amer.		OF	115	227	41	59	13	2	5	19	.260	57	2	2	.967
1985—Chicago	Amer.		OF	95	140	9	34	8	0	2	20	.243	5	0	0	1.000
American League Totals—10 Years				636	1291	165	337	66	6	18	153	.261	554	27	19	.968
National League Totals—1 Year				51	52	5	10	2	0	2	6	.192	13	0	1	.929
Major League Totals—10 Years				687	1343	170	347	68	6	20	159	.258	567	27	20	.967

Selected by Chicago White Sox' organization in 3rd round of free-agent draft, June 4, 1970.
†On disabled list, June 27 to July 12, 1974.
‡Sold to Pittsburgh Pirates, June 13, 1977.
§Sold to Durango of Mexican League, March 2, 1978.
xSold to Chicago White Sox, September 10, 1981.

CHAMPIONSHIP SERIES RECORD

Year	Club	League	Pos.	G.	AB.	R.	H.	2B.	3B.	HR.	RBI.	B.A.	PO.	A.	E.	F.A.
1983—Chicago	Amer.		PH-OF	2	3	0	0	0	0	0	0	.000	0	0	1	.000

ALBERT HALL

Born March 7, 1959, at Birmingham, Ala.
Height, 5.11. Weight, 155.
Throws right and bats left and righthanded.

Major League stolen bases: 1983 (1), 1984 (6), 1985 (1). Total—8.
Led International League in stolen bases with 62 in 1982.
Led Carolina League in being hit by pitch with 9, stolen bases with 100 and caught stealing with 27 in 1980.
Led Western Carolinas League in stolen bases with 66 in 1979.
Led Gulf Coast League shortstops in double plays with 23 in 1978.
Tied for Southern League lead in caught stealing with 17 in 1981.

Year	Club	League	Pos.	G.	AB.	R.	H.	2B.	3B.	HR.	RBI.	B.A.	PO.	A.	E.	F.A.
1977—Kingsport	Appal.		SS	35	68	11	11	0	0	0	3	.162	10	28	10	.792
1978—Bradenton Brav	Gulf C.		SS	34	123	15	36	4	2	0	14	.293	55	100	●15	.912
1979—Greenwood	W. Car.		SS	105	368	84	106	10	3	0	38	.288	120	288	*72	.850
1980—Durham	Carol.		OF-SS	125	491	95	139	16	7	4	41	.283	166	32	16	.925
1981—Savannah	South.		OF	133	487	83	150	28	10	5	27	.308	263	16	10	.965
1981—Atlanta	Nat.		OF	6	2	1	0	0	0	0	0	.000	0	0	0	.000
1982—Richmond	Int.		OF	129	528	97	139	18	*15	3	42	.263	297	6	7	.977
1982—Atlanta	Nat.		PR	5	0	1	0	0	0	0	0	.000	0	0	0	.000
1983—Richmond	Int.		*OF-SS	130	521	120	153	28	*11	1	42	.294	280	10	*12	.960
1983—Atlanta	Nat.		OF	10	8	2	0	0	0	0	0	.000	3	0	1	.750
1984—Atlanta	Nat.		OF	87	142	25	37	6	1	1	9	.261	64	4	5	.932
1985—Atlanta	Nat.		OF	54	47	5	7	0	1	0	3	.149	7	2	1	.900
1985—Richmond†	Int.		OF	38	98	12	22	0	3	0	5	.224	77	2	3	.963
Major League Totals—5 Years				162	199	34	44	6	2	1	12	.221	74	6	7	.920

Selected by Atlanta Braves' organization in 6th round of free-agent draft, June 7, 1977.
†On disabled list, July 12 to July 26, 1985.

MELVIN HALL JR.
(Mel)

Born September 16, 1960, at Lyons, N.Y.
Height, 6.01. Weight, 185.
Throws and bats lefthanded.
Son of Melvin Hall Sr., minor league player in Cincinnati Reds' organization, 1949.

Major League stolen bases: 1983 (6), 1984 (3). Total—9.
Led American Association in game-winning RBIs with 17 in 1982.
Led Texas League in total bases with 286 in 1981.
Led American Association outfielders in total chances with 339 in 1982.
Led Texas League outfielders in total chances with 324 and double plays with 5 in 1981.

Year	Club	League	Pos.	G.	AB.	R.	H.	2B.	3B.	HR.	RBI.	B.A.	PO.	A.	E.	F.A.
1978—Bradenton Cubs	...	Gulf C.	OF	43	145	30	42	7	3	2	17	.290	★97	5	4	.962
1979—Geneva		NYP	OF	66	251	49	79	18	5	3	53	.315	113	5	7	.944
1980—Midland		Texas	OF	37	128	17	34	7	3	1	14	.266	58	3	3	.953
1980—Quad Cities		Midw.	OF	97	347	54	102	14	4	6	42	.294	171	9	5	.973
1981—Midland		Texas	OF	131	533	●98	★170	34	5	24	95	.319	★302	14	8	.975
1981—Chicago		Nat.	OF	10	11	1	1	0	0	1	2	.091	0	0	0	.000
1982—Iowa		A. A.	OF	133	502	★116	165	★34	6	32	125	.329	★317	13	●9	.973
1982—Chicago		Nat.	OF	24	80	6	21	3	2	0	4	.263	42	4	3	.939
1983—Chicago†		Nat.	OF	112	410	60	116	23	5	17	56	.283	239	8	3	.988
1983—Midland		Texas	OF	6	19	9	9	2	1	3	7	.474	8	0	0	1.000
1984—Chicago‡		Nat.	OF	48	150	25	42	11	3	4	22	.280	69	5	3	.961
1984—Cleveland		Amer.	OF	83	257	43	66	13	1	7	30	.257	143	3	1	.993
1985—Cleveland§		Amer.	OF	23	66	7	21	6	0	0	12	.318	18	0	0	1.000
National League Totals—4 Years				194	651	92	180	37	10	22	84	.276	350	17	9	.976
American League Totals—2 Years				106	323	50	87	19	1	7	42	.269	161	3	1	.994
Major League Totals—5 Years				300	974	142	267	56	11	29	126	.274	511	20	10	.982

Selected by Chicago Cubs' organization in 2nd round of free-agent draft, June 6, 1978.
†On disabled list, April 15 to May 31, 1983; included rehabilitation disability assignment to Midland, May 25 to May 31, 1983.
‡Traded with Outfielder Joe Carter and Pitchers Don Schulze and Darryl Banks to Cleveland Indians for Catcher Ron Hassey and Pitchers Rick Sutcliffe and George Frazier, June 13, 1984.
§On disabled list, May 10, 1985 through remainder of season.

CARLTON BYRON HAMILTON
(Carl)

Born November 4, 1964, at Gary, Ind.
Height, 6.02. Weight, 175.
Throws and bats lefthanded.
Attended Triton College, River Grove, Ill.

Led Carolina League in complete games with 11 in 1985.

Year	Club	League	G.	IP.	W.	L.	Pct.	H.	R.	ER.	SO.	BB.	ERA.
1983—Pikesville		Ap'lachian	5	13	0	2	.000	12	11	9	16	18	6.23
1984—Quad Cities		Midwest	18	109	5	7	.417	69	48	34	104	76	2.81
1985—Winston-Salem		Carolina	25	155⅔	11	10	.524	110	61	47	152	108	2.72

Selected by Chicago Cubs' organization in 8th round of free-agent draft, January 11, 1983.
Selected by Chicago Cubs' organization in secondary phase of free-agent draft, June 6, 1983.

JEFFREY ROBERT HAMILTON
(Jeff)

Born March 19, 1964, at Flint, Mich.
Height, 6.03. Weight, 190.
Throws and bats righthanded.

Led Florida State League third basemen in total chances with 395 and double plays with 25 in 1984.
Led Pioneer League third basemen in double plays with 16 in 1983.

Year	Club	League	Pos.	G.	AB.	R.	H.	2B.	3B.	HR.	RBI.	B.A.	PO.	A.	E.	F.A.
1983—Lodi		Calif.	3B-OF	44	141	15	28	4	0	0	10	.199	26	62	17	.838
1983—Lethbridge		Pion.	3B	68	★281	48	●94	★23	2	3	61	.335	38	118	17	.902
1984—Vero Beach		Fla. St.	3B	127	466	51	121	31	4	4	59	.260	★109	★259	★27	★.932
1985—San Antonio		Texas	3B-OF	101	377	48	125	14	3	13	59	.332	69	186	16	.941

Selected by Los Angeles Dodgers' organization in 29th round of free-agent draft, June 7, 1982.

CHARLTON ATLEE HAMMAKER
(Known by middle name.)

Born January 24, 1958, at Carmel, Calif.
Height, 6.02. Weight, 195.
Throws and bats lefthanded.
Attended East Tennessee State University, Johnson City, Tenn.

Year	Club	League	G.	IP.	W.	L.	Pct.	H.	R.	ER.	SO.	BB.	ERA.
1979—Sarasota Royals-Gold		Gulf Coast	1	5	1	0	1.000	3	1	1	6	1	1.80
1979—Fort Myers†		Florida St.	1	5	0	1	.000	9	5	1	5	0	1.80
1980—Jacksonville‡		Southern	20	137	8	9	.471	131	64	51	88	37	3.35
1981—Omaha		Am. Assoc.	21	146	11	5	.688	147	70	59	63	40	3.64

Year Club	League	G.	IP.	W.	L.	Pct.	H.	R.	ER.	SO.	BB.	ERA.
1981—Kansas City§	American	10	39	1	3	.250	44	24	24	11	12	5.54
1982—Phoenix	P. Coast	1	5⅔	0	1	.000	13	5	4	6	2	6.35
1982—San Francisco	National	29	175	12	8	.600	189	86	80	102	28	4.11
1983—San Francisco x	National	23	171⅓	10	9	.526	147	57	43	127	32	★2.25
1984—Phoenix y	P. Coast	2	8	0	1	.000	14	7	4	5	2	4.50
1984—San Francisco	National	6	33	2	0	1.000	32	10	8	24	9	2.18
1985—San Francisco	National	29	170⅔	5	12	.294	161	81	71	100	47	3.74
American League Totals—1 Year		10	39	1	3	.250	44	24	24	11	12	5.54
National League Totals—4 Years		87	551	29	29	.500	529	234	202	353	116	3.30
Major League Totals—5 Years		97	590	30	32	.484	573	258	226	364	128	3.45

Selected by Kansas City Royals' organization in 1st round (21st player selected) of free-agent draft, June 5, 1979.
†On disabled list, July 6 to October 26, 1979.
‡On disabled list, August 3 to August 22, 1980.
§Traded with Pitchers Craig Chamberlain and Renie Martin and a player to be named later to San Francisco Giants for Pitchers Vida Blue and Bob Tufts, March 30, 1982; San Francisco organization acquired Second Baseman Brad Wellman to complete deal, April 19, 1982.
xOn disabled list, July 26 to August 21, 1983.
yOn San Francisco disabled list, April 2 to June 26 and August 4 to September 1, 1984; included rehabilitation disability assignment to Phoenix, June 16 to June 25, 1984.

ALL-STAR GAME RECORD

Established All-Star Game and inning records for most runs and earned runs allowed (7), July 6, 1983 (third inning).
Tied All-Star Game record for most home runs allowed, inning (2), July 6, 1983 (third inning).

Year League	IP.	W.	L.	Pct.	H.	R.	ER.	SO.	BB.	ERA.
1983—National	⅔	0	0	.000	6	7	7	0	1	94.50

ERIC JOHN HARDGRAVE

Born October 5, 1960, at Fresno, Calif.
Height, 6.03. Weight, 210.
Throws and bats righthanded.
Attended Stanford University, Stanford, Calif.

Named California League Most Valuable Player, 1985.

Year Club	League	Pos.	G.	AB.	R.	H.	2B.	3B.	HR.	RBI.	B.A.	PO.	A.	E.	F.A.
1983—Spokane	N'west	1B-OF	37	125	25	37	7	2	4	17	.296	198	18	6	.973
1983—Reno	Calif.	1B	20	69	3	18	0	1	1	5	.261	100	4	4	.963
1984—Reno	Calif.	1B	125	443	58	125	20	0	9	90	.282	982	62	24	.978
1985—Reno	Calif.	1B	77	291	58	109	24	1	●24	85	.375	553	36	5	.992
1985—Beaumont	Texas	1B-3B-SS	46	155	23	40	9	1	5	26	.258	356	21	8	.979

Selected by Cleveland Indians' organization in 3rd round of free-agent draft, June 5, 1979.
Selected by San Diego Padres' organization in 6th round of free-agent draft, June 6, 1983.

ALAN ROBERT HARGESHEIMER

Name pronounced HAHR-guh-shy-mer.

(Al)

Born November 21, 1956, at Chicago, Ill.
Height, 6.03. Weight, 200.
Throws and bats righthanded.
Attended Mayfair Junior College, Chicago, Ill. and received bachelor of arts degree
in physical education from Northeastern Illinois University, Chicago, Ill.

Tied for California League lead in games started by pitchers with 28 in 1978.

Year Club	League	G.	IP.	W.	L.	Pct.	H.	R.	ER.	SO.	BB.	ERA.
1978—Fresno	California	29	176	7	11	.389	★216	117	96	109	82	4.91
1979—Shreveport	Texas	24	141	6	10	.375	165	96	71	80	60	4.53
1980—Shreveport	Texas	12	81	2	6	.250	67	28	16	40	30	1.78
1980—Phoenix	P. Coast	2	17	1	1	.500	18	8	8	13	13	4.24
1980—San Francisco	National	15	75	4	6	.400	82	38	36	40	32	4.32
1981—Phoenix†	P. Coast	20	118	6	8	.429	127	58	48	64	41	3.66
1981—San Francisco	National	6	19	1	2	.333	20	9	9	6	9	4.26
1982—Phoenix‡	P. Coast	29	152⅔	6	12	.333	★214	111	89	95	65	6.54
1983—Iowa	Am. Assoc.	49	78⅓	7	4	.636	78	35	30	50	48	3.45
1983—Chicago§	National	5	4	0	0	.000	6	4	4	5	2	9.00
1984—Omaha x	Am. Assoc.	11	14⅔	1	2	.333	13	7	5	9	10	3.07
1985—Omaha	Am. Assoc.	32	151⅔	11	10	.524	136	60	49	91	72	2.91
Major League Totals—3 Years		26	98	5	8	.385	108	51	49	51	43	4.50

Signed as free agent by San Francisco Giants' organization, March 21, 1978.
†On disabled list, June 13 to July 12, 1981.
‡Traded to Chicago Cubs' organization for Pitcher Herman Segelke, October 15, 1982.
§Traded to Kansas City Royals for Pitcher Derek Botelho, March 30, 1984.
xOn disabled list, May 16, 1984 through remainder of season.

DUDLEY MICHAEL HARGROVE
(Mike)

Born October 26, 1949, at Perryton, Tex.
Height, 6.00. Weight, 195.
Throws and bats lefthanded.
Received bachelor of science degree in physical education and social sciences
from Northwestern State University, Alva, Okla.

Major League stolen bases: 1975 (4), 1976 (2), 1977 (2), 1978 (2), 1979 (2), 1980 (4), 1981 (5), 1982 (2), 1985 (1). Total—24.
Led American League in bases on balls received with 97 in 1976 and 107 in 1978.
Led American League first basemen in total chances with 1,489 in 1980.
Led Western Carolinas League in total bases with 247 in 1973.
Led Western Carolinas League first basemen in double plays with 118 in 1973 and led New York-Pennsylvania League first basemen with 58 in 1972.
Named American League Rookie Player of the Year by THE SPORTING NEWS, 1974.
Named American League Rookie of the Year by Baseball Writers' Association of America, 1974.
Named Western Carolinas League Player of the Year, 1973.

Year Club	League	Pos.	G.	AB.	R.	H.	2B.	3B.	HR.	RBI.	B.A.	PO.	A.	E.	F.A.
1972—Geneva	NYP	1B	●70	243	38	65	8	0	4	37	.267	★537	●40	10	★.983
1973—Gastonia	W. Car.	1B	●130	456	88	★160	★35	8	12	82	★.351	★1121	★77	14	★.988
1974—Texas	Amer.	1B-OF	131	415	57	134	18	6	4	66	.323	638	72	9	.987
1975—Texas	Amer.	OF-1B	145	519	82	157	22	2	11	62	.303	513	45	13	.977
1976—Texas	Amer.	1B	151	541	80	155	30	1	7	58	.287	1222	110	★21	.984
1977—Texas	Amer.	1B	153	525	98	160	28	4	18	69	.305	1393	100	11	.993
1978—Texas†	Amer.	1B	146	494	63	124	24	1	7	40	.251	1221	★116	★17	.987
1979—San Diego‡	Nat.	1B	52	125	15	24	5	0	0	8	.192	323	17	5	.986
1979—Cleveland	Amer.	OF-1B	100	338	60	110	21	4	10	56	.325	356	16	2	.995
1980—Cleveland	Amer.	1B	160	589	86	179	22	2	11	85	.304	★1391	88	10	.993
1981—Cleveland	Amer.	1B	94	322	43	102	21	0	2	49	.317	766	76	●9	.989
1982—Cleveland	Amer.	1B	160	591	67	160	26	1	4	65	.271	1293	★123	5	.996
1983—Cleveland	Amer.	1B	134	469	57	134	21	4	3	57	.286	1098	115	7	.994
1984—Cleveland	Amer.	1B	133	352	44	94	14	2	2	44	.267	790	83	8	.991
1985—Cleveland§	Amer.	1B-OF	107	284	31	81	14	1	1	27	.285	599	66	6	.991
American League Totals—12 Years			1614	5439	768	1590	261	28	80	678	.292	11280	1010	118	.990
National League Totals—1 Year			52	125	15	24	5	0	0	8	.192	323	17	5	.986
Major League Totals—12 Years			1666	5564	783	1614	266	28	80	686	.290	11603	1027	123	.990

Selected by Texas Rangers' organization in 25th round of free-agent draft, June 6, 1972.
†Traded with Third Baseman Kurt Bevacqua and Catcher Bill Fahey to San Diego Padres for Outfielder Oscar Gamble, Catcher Dave Roberts and cash estimated at $300,000, October 25, 1978.
‡Traded to Cleveland Indians for Outfielder Paul Dade, June 14, 1979.
§Granted free agency, November 12, 1985.

ALL-STAR GAME RECORD

Year League	Pos.	AB.	R.	H.	2B.	3B.	HR.	RBI.	B.A.	PO.	A.	E.	F.A.
1975—American	PH	1	0	0	0	0	0	0	.000	0	0	0	.000

BRIAN DAVID HARPER

Born October 16, 1959, at Los Angeles, Calif.
Height, 6.02. Weight, 195.
Throws and bats righthanded.

Major League stolen bases: 1981 (1).
Led Pacific Coast League in total bases with 339 in 1981.
Led Pacific Coast League catchers in errors with 19 in 1981.
Led Texas League in passed balls with 19 in 1979.

Year Club	League	Pos.	G.	AB.	R.	H.	2B.	3B.	HR.	RBI.	B.A.	PO.	A.	E.	F.A.
1977—Idaho Falls	Pion.	C	52	186	28	60	9	3	1	33	.323	352	36	13	.968
1978—Quad Cities	Midw.	C	129	508	80	149	31	2	24	★101	.293	430	46	16	.967
1979—El Paso	Texas	C	132	531	85	167	★37	3	14	90	.315	443	66	★29	.946
1979—California	Amer.	DH	1	2	0	0	0	0	0	0	.000	0	0	0	.000
1980—El Paso†	Texas	C	105	400	61	114	23	3	12	66	.285	214	30	7	.972
1981—Salt Lake City	P. C.	C-OF-1B	134	549	99	★192	45	9	28	122	.350	421	30	24	.949
1981—California‡	Amer.	OF	4	11	1	3	0	0	1	1	.273	5	0	1	.833
1982—Pittsburgh	Nat.	OF	20	29	4	8	1	0	2	4	.276	10	0	0	1.000
1982—Portland	P. C.	OF-3B-C	101	395	71	112	29	8	17	73	.284	164	36	8	.962
1983—Pittsburgh	Nat.	OF-1B	61	131	16	29	4	1	7	20	.221	40	0	0	1.000
1984—Pittsburgh§ x	Nat.	OF-C	46	112	4	29	4	0	2	11	.259	57	3	1	.984
1985—St. Louis	Nat.	O-3-C-1	43	52	5	13	4	0	0	8	.250	15	5	0	1.000
American League Totals—2 Years			5	13	1	3	0	0	0	1	.231	5	0	1	.833
National League Totals—4 Years			170	324	29	79	13	1	11	43	.244	122	8	1	.992
Major League Totals—6 Years			175	337	30	82	13	1	11	44	.243	127	8	2	.985

Selected by California Angels' organization in 4th round of free-agent draft, June 7, 1977.
†On disabled list, July 1 to July 17, 1980.
‡Traded to Pittsburgh Pirates for Shortstop Tim Foli, December 11, 1981.
§On disabled list, April 12 to May 10 and May 16 to June 4, 1984.
xTraded with Pitcher John Tudor to St. Louis Cardinals for Outfielder-First Baseman George Hendrick and Catcher Steve Barnard, December 12, 1984.

Year Club	League	Pos.	G.	AB.	R.	H.	2B.	3B.	HR.	RBI.	B.A.	PO.	A.	E.	F.A.
1985—St. Louis	Nat.	PH	1	1	0	0	0	0	0	0	.000	0	0	0	.000

WORLD SERIES RECORD

Year Club	League	Pos.	G.	AB.	R.	H.	2B.	3B.	HR.	RBI.	B.A.	PO.	A.	E.	F.A.
1985—St. Louis	Nat.	PH	4	4	0	1	0	0	0	1	.250	0	0	0	.000

TERRY JOE HARPER

Born August 19, 1955, at Douglasville, Ga.
Height, 6.01. Weight, 202.
Throws and bats righthanded.

Major League stolen bases: 1980 (2), 1981 (5), 1982 (7), 1983 (6), 1984 (4), 1985 (9). Total—33.
Led International League in caught stealing with 18 in 1980.
Led International League outfielders in double plays with 5 in 1980.

Year Club	League	Pos.	G.	AB.	R.	H.	2B.	3B.	HR.	RBI.	B.A.	PO.	A.	E.	F.A.
1973—Wytheville	Appal.	P	13	17	3	4	0	0	0	2	.235	3	7	4	.714
1974—Greenwood†	W. Car.	P	15	15	0	4	0	1	0	1	.267	1	11	2	.857
1975—Greenwood‡	W. Car.	P	14	0	0	0	0	0	0	0	.000	6	17	0	1.000
1976—Greenwood§	W. Car.	P	2	0	0	0	0	0	0	0	.000	1	0	0	1.000
1976—Brad. Braves	Gulf C.	OF-3B-1B	51	185	21	48	6	6	1	37	.259	87	8	6	.941
1977—Greenwood	W. Car.	OF-3B-1B	70	261	45	74	12	3	4	43	.295	200	10	4	.981
1977—Savannah	South.	OF	54	149	14	36	3	5	1	18	.242	94	8	2	.981
1978—Savannah	South.	OF	47	174	17	46	9	1	4	21	.264	85	10	2	.979
1978—Richmond	Int.	OF	73	205	21	52	5	3	0	24	.254	137	5	2	.986
1979—Richmond x	Int.	OF	108	327	49	99	18	3	10	58	.303	164	9	9	.951
1980—Richmond	Int.	OF	*140	512	66	143	19	8	13	72	.279	315	19	6	.982
1980—Atlanta	Nat.	OF	21	54	3	10	2	1	0	3	.185	30	0	1	.968
1981—Atlanta	Nat.	OF	40	73	9	19	1	0	2	8	.260	38	2	1	.976
1981—Richmond	Int.	OF	10	44	3	10	3	0	2	4	.227	22	0	0	1.000
1982—Richmond	Int.	OF	37	146	25	56	12	2	9	42	.384	77	8	1	.988
1982—Atlanta yz	Nat.	OF	48	150	16	43	3	0	2	16	.287	74	4	1	.987
1983—Atlanta	Nat.	OF	80	201	19	53	13	1	3	26	.264	95	5	5	.952
1984—Atlanta a	Nat.	OF	40	102	4	16	3	1	0	8	.157	60	3	0	1.000
1984—Richmond	Int.	OF	59	216	41	70	3	3	10	38	.324	118	7	4	.969
1985—Atlanta	Nat.	OF	138	492	58	130	15	2	17	72	.264	215	10	5	.978
Major League Totals—6 Years			367	1072	109	271	37	5	24	133	.253	512	24	13	.976

Selected by Atlanta Braves' organization in 16th round of free-agent draft, June 5, 1973.
†On disabled list, May 5 to May 31 and June 24 to July 9, 1974.
‡On disabled list, June 18 to July 7 and August 2 to August 16, 1975.
§On disabled list, April 27 to June 25, 1976.
xOn disabled list, August 20 to September 26, 1979.
yOn disabled list, June 1 to July 1 and July 23 to July 31, 1982.
zOn disabled list, July 8 to July 23, 1982.
aOn disabled list, March 25 to April 24, 1984.

CHAMPIONSHIP SERIES RECORD

Year Club	League	Pos.	G.	AB.	R.	H.	2B.	3B.	HR.	RBI.	B.A.	PO.	A.	E.	F.A.
1982—Atlanta	Nat.	PR-OF	1	1	1	0	0	0	0	0	.000	0	0	0	.000

PITCHING RECORD

Year Club	League	G.	IP.	W.	L.	Pct.	H.	R.	ER.	SO.	BB.	ERA.
1973—Wytheville	Ap'lachian	12	58	3	3	.500	60	36	25	42	36	3.88
1974—Greenwood	W. Carol.	15	43	4	2	.667	44	23	19	37	25	3.98
1975—Greenwood	W. Carol.	14	69	1	5	.167	95	48	40	27	39	5.22
1976—Greenwood	W. Carol.	2	8	1	1	.500	9	10	10	4	7	11.25

COLBERT DALE HARRAH

Name pronounced HAIR-uh.

(Toby)

Born October 26, 1948, at Sissonville, W. Va.
Height, 6.00. Weight, 180.
Throws and bats righthanded.
Attended Ohio Northern University, Ada, O.

Established major league records for most innings by third baseman, no assists, game (17), September 17, 1977; fewest chances offered by shortstop, doubleheader (0), June 25, 1976.
Tied major league record for fewest chances offered by shortstop, two consecutive games (0), June 25, 1976 (doubleheader).
Major League stolen bases: 1971 (10), 1972 (16), 1973 (10), 1974 (15), 1975 (23), 1976 (8), 1977 (27), 1978 (31), 1979 (20), 1980 (17), 1981 (12), 1982 (17), 1983 (4), 1984 (3), 1985 (11). Total—236.
Led American League in bases on balls received with 109 in 1977.
Led American League shortstops in putouts with 281 in 1974 and tied for lead with 290 in 1976.
Led American League shortstops in errors with 36 in 1976.
Named shortstop on THE SPORTING NEWS American League All-Star Team, 1975.

Year Club	League	Pos.	G.	AB.	R.	H.	2B.	3B.	HR.	RBI.	B.A.	PO.	A.	E.	F.A.
1967—Huron†	North.	2B-SS	63	207	34	53	6	0	3	22	.256	136	163	23	.929
1968—Burlington	Carol.	SS	135	468	73	112	16	3	6	39	.239	217	356	*50	.920

Year Club League	Pos.	G.	AB.	R.	H.	2B.	3B.	HR.	RBI.	B.A.	PO.	A.	E.	F.A.
1969—Burlington‡ .... Carol.	SS-2B	46	147	27	45	4	2	4	12	.306	76	152	10	.958
1969—Savannah .... South.	SS	28	80	8	19	2	0	2	7	.238	36	78	11	.912
1969—Washington .... Amer.	SS	8	1	4	0	0	0	0	0	.000	0	0	0	.000
1970—Pittsfield§ .... East.	SS-3B	95	359	57	99	18	1	3	37	.276	159	293	27	.944
1971—Washington .... Amer.	SS-3B	127	383	45	88	11	3	2	22	.230	187	321	24	.955
1972—Texas x .... Amer.	SS	116	374	47	97	14	3	1	31	.259	166	308	20	.960
1973—Texas y .... Amer.	SS-3B	118	461	64	120	16	1	10	50	.260	155	332	27	.947
1974—Texas .... Amer.	●SS-3B	161	573	79	149	23	2	21	74	.260	283	474	●29	.963
1975—Texas .... Amer.	SS-3B-2B	151	522	81	153	24	1	20	93	.293	253	481	29	.962
1976—Texas .... Amer.	SS-3B	155	584	64	152	21	1	15	67	.260	294	481	37	.954
1977—Texas .... Amer.	3B-SS	159	539	90	142	25	5	27	87	.263	108	278	15	.963
1978—Texas z .... Amer.	3B-SS	139	450	56	103	17	3	12	59	.229	129	330	11	.977
1979—Cleveland .... Amer.	3B-SS	149	527	99	147	25	1	20	77	.279	113	215	19	.947
1980—Cleveland .... Amer.	3B-SS	160	561	100	150	22	4	11	72	.267	121	319	13	.971
1981—Cleveland .... Amer.	3B-SS	103	361	64	105	12	4	5	44	.291	64	180	13	.949
1982—Cleveland .... Amer.	3B-2B-SS	●162	602	100	183	29	4	25	78	.304	126	279	12	.971
1983—Cleveland ab........ Amer.	★3B-2B	138	526	81	140	23	1	9	53	.266	101	273	11	★.971
1984—New York cd........ Amer.	3B-2B-OF	88	253	40	55	9	4	1	26	.217	52	132	6	.968
1985—Texas .... Amer.	2B-SS	126	396	65	107	18	1	9	44	.270	212	351	6	.989
Major League Totals—16 Years		2060	7113	1079	1891	289	38	188	877	.266	2364	4754	272	.963

Signed as free agent by Philadelphia Phillies' organization, December 27, 1966.
†Drafted by Washington Senators' organization, November 28, 1967.
‡On military list, January 28 to June 2, 1969.
§On temporary inactive list, July 24 to August 11, 1970.
xOn disabled list, August 14 to September 6, 1972.
yOn disabled list, July 2 to August 7, 1973.
zTraded to Cleveland Indians for Third Baseman Buddy Bell, December 8, 1978.
aOn disabled list, April 17 to May 14, 1983.
bTraded with a player to be named later to New York Yankees for Pitcher George Frazier, Outfielder Otis Nixon and a player to be named later, February 5, 1984; New York organization acquired Pitcher Rick Browne and Cleveland organization acquired Pitcher Guy Elston to complete deal, February 8, 1984.
cOn disabled list, July 3 to July 20, 1984.
dTraded to Texas Rangers for Outfielder Billy Sample and a player to be named later, February 27, 1985; New York Yankees' organization acquired Pitcher Eric Dersin to complete deal, July 14, 1985.

ALL-STAR GAME RECORD

Year League	Pos.	AB.	R.	II.	2B.	3B.	HR.	RBI.	B.A.	PO.	A.	F.	F.A.
1976—American...	SS	2	0	0	0	0	0	0	.000	0	0	0	.000

Named to American League All-Star Team for the 1972 game; replaced due to an injury.
Member of American League All-Star Team in 1975 and 1982; did not play.

GREG ALLEN HARRIS

Brn November 2, 1955, at Lynwood, Calif.
Height, 6.00. Weight, 165.
Throws right and bats left and righthanded.
Attended Long Beach City College, Long Beach, Calif.

Major League saves: 1981 (1), 1982 (1), 1984 (3), 1985 (11). Total—16.

Year Club League	G.	IP.	W.	L.	Pct.	H.	R.	ER.	SO.	BB.	ERA.
1977—Jackson .... Texas	30	83	3	6	.333	96	63	50	56	36	5.42
1978—Lynchburg.................................. Carolina	21	154	8	9	.471	114	52	37	102	74	2.16
1978—Jackson .... Texas	6	33	2	3	.400	24	13	11	18	10	3.00
1979—Jackson .... Texas	25	163	9	11	.450	125	58	41	89	81	★2.26
1980—Tidewater................................. Int'national	39	110	2	9	.182	99	45	33	92	40	2.70
1981—Tidewater................................. Int'national	7	48	4	0	1.000	37	14	11	26	16	2.06
1981—New York†................................ National	16	69	3	5	.375	65	36	34	54	28	4.43
1982—Indianapolis .... Am. Assoc.	8	48	4	1	.800	27	18	16	44	24	3.00
1982—Cincinnati .... National	34	91⅓	2	6	.250	96	56	49	67	37	4.83
1983—Indianapolis .... Am. Assoc.	28	152⅓	9	12	.429	155	83	70	★146	66	4.14
1983—Cincinnati‡ .... National	1	1	0	0	.000	2	3	3	1	3	27.00
1984—Montreal§-San Diego...................National	34	54⅓	2	2	.500	38	18	15	45	25	2.48
1984—Indianapolis x .... Am. Assoc.	14	44⅔	4	4	.500	44	27	22	45	29	4.43
1985—Texas.. American	58	113	5	4	.556	74	35	31	111	43	2.47
National League Totals—4 Years........................	85	215⅔	7	13	.350	201	113	101	167	93	4.21
American League Totals—1 Year........................	58	113	5	4	.556	74	35	31	111	43	2.47
Major League Totals—5 Years............................	143	328⅔	12	17	.414	275	148	132	278	136	3.61

Selected by California Angels' organization in 10th round of free-agent draft, June 5, 1974.
Selected by New York Mets' organization in secondary phase of free-agent draft, January 9, 1975.
Selected by New York Mets' organization in 7th round of free-agent draft, January 7, 1976.
Signed as free agent by New York Mets' organization, September 17, 1976.
†Traded with Catcher Alex Trevino and Pitcher Jim Kern to Cincinnati Reds for Outfielder George Foster, February 10, 1982.
‡Claimed on waivers by Montreal Expos, September 27, 1983.
§Traded to San Diego Padres for Infielder Al Newman, July 20, 1984.
xSold to Texas Rangers, February 13, 1985.

CHAMPIONSHIP SERIES RECORD

Tied Championship Series records for most runs, most earned runs and most hits allowed, inning (6), October 2, 1984 (fifth inning); most earned runs allowed, game (7), October 2, 1984.

Tied National League Championship Series record for most runs allowed, five-game Series (8), 1984.

Year	Club	League	G.	IP.	W.	L.	Pct.	H.	R.	ER.	SO.	BB.	ERA.
1984—San Diego		National	1	2	0	0	.000	9	8	7	2	3	31.50

WORLD SERIES RECORD

Year	Club	League	G.	IP.	W.	L.	Pct.	H.	R.	ER.	SO.	BB.	ERA.
1984—San Diego		National	1	5⅓	0	0	.000	3	0	0	5	3	0.00

LEONARD ANTHONY HARRIS
(Lenny)

Born October 28, 1964, at Miami, Fla.
Height, 5.11. Weight, 180.
Throws right and bats lefthanded.
Attended Miami-Dade Community College (North), Miami, Fla.

Led Florida State League third basemen in double plays with 34 in 1985.

Year	Club	League	Pos.	G.	AB.	R.	H.	2B.	3B.	HR.	RBI.	B.A.	PO.	A.	E.	F.A.
1983—Billings		Pion.	3B	56	224	37	63	8	1	1	26	.281	34	95	22	.854
1984—Cedar Rapids		Midw.	3B	132	468	52	115	15	3	6	53	.246	111	204	★34	.903
1985—Tampa		Fla. St.	3B	132	499	66	129	11	8	3	51	.259	89	★277	★35	.913

Selected by Cincinnati Reds' organization in 5th round of free-agent draft, June 6, 1983.

RONALD DWAYNE HARRISON
(Ron)

Born October 15, 1960, at Sacramento, Calif.
Height, 6.02. Weight, 170.
Throws right and bats lefthanded.
Attended Contra Costa College, San Pablo, Calif.

Tied for Eastern League lead in sacrifice hits with 12 in 1983.
Led Midwest League outfielders in double plays with 6 in 1982.

Year	Club	League	Pos.	G.	AB.	R.	H.	2B.	3B.	HR.	RBI.	B.A.	PO.	A.	E.	F.A.
1981—Medford		N'west	OF	32	90	10	16	5	1	1	7	.178	32	3	5	.875
1982—Madison		Midw.	OF	127	447	59	125	20	4	8	64	.280	238	15	12	.955
1983—Albany		Eastern	OF	106	398	65	116	17	3	11	50	.291	215	12	11	.954
1984—Madison†		Midw.	OF	19	66	10	13	4	0	0	9	.197	36	2	1	.974
1984—Tacoma		P. C.	OF	55	222	36	60	10	2	2	24	.270	135	5	4	.972
1985—Tacoma		P. C.	OF	119	387	55	97	13	2	7	42	.251	184	12	4	.980

Signed as free agent by Oakland A's organization, May 19, 1981.
†On Albany disabled list, March 21 to May 21, 1984.

MICHAEL LAWRENCE HART
(Mike)

Born February 17, 1958, at Milwaukee, Wis.
Height, 5.11. Weight, 185.
Throws and bats lefthanded.
Received degree in physical education from University of Wisconsin, Madison, Wis. in 1979.
Nephew of Bill Mosser Sr., minor league pitcher, 1946 through 1952.

Year	Club	League	Pos.	G.	AB.	R.	H.	2B.	3B.	HR.	RBI.	B.A.	PO.	A.	E.	F.A.
1979—Bellingham		N'west	OF	4	8	0	1	0	0	0	0	.125	8	1	1	.900
1979—Wausau		Midw.	OF	52	177	34	46	9	1	1	21	.260	79	3	0	1.000
1980—Lynn		East.	OF	117	399	69	119	15	6	10	61	.298	204	5	6	.972
1981—Spokane†		P. C.	OF	105	357	51	99	19	4	6	48	.277	237	7	3	.988
1982—Salt Lake City‡		P. C.	OF	134	472	86	127	15	6	10	74	.269	268	10	5	.982
1983—Toledo		Int.	OF	137	487	95	141	18	7	17	66	.290	311	12	10	.970
1984—Toledo		Int.	OF	92	329	37	89	11	4	9	48	.271	193	6	3	.985
1984—Minnesota		Amer.	OF	13	29	0	5	0	0	0	5	.172	24	1	0	1.000
1985—Toledo		Int.	OF	135	496	71	133	22	4	24	83	.268	345	11	5	.986
Major League Totals—1 Year				13	29	0	5	0	0	0	5	.172	24	1	0	1.000

Selected by Seattle Mariners' organization in 13th round of free-agent draft, June 5, 1979.
†On disabled list, April 8 to May 14, 1981.
‡Released, January 28, 1983; signed by Toledo (Minnesota Twins' organization), January 31, 1983.

RONALD KYLE HARTSHORN
(Known by middle name.)

Born October 3, 1964, at Trenton, N.J.
Height, 6.02. Weight, 185.
Throws right and bats lefthanded.
Attended Mercer County Community College, Trenton, N.J.

Tied for Carolina League lead in hit batsmen with 9 in 1985.
Tied for South Atlantic League lead in complete games with 10 and shutouts with 4 in 1984.
Named Carolina League Pitcher of the Year, 1985.

Year	Club	League	G.	IP.	W.	L.	Pct.	H.	R.	ER.	SO.	BB.	ERA.
1982—Little Falls		NYP	13	54	5	2	.714	65	53	41	52	30	6.83

Year Club	League	G.	IP.	W.	L.	Pct.	H.	R.	ER.	SO.	BB.	ERA.
1983—Columbia	S. Atlantic	9	32⅔	1	3	.250	46	32	25	20	22	6.89
1983—Little Falls	NYP	15	80⅓	4	7	.364	83	53	40	63	36	4.48
1984—Columbia	S. Atlantic	24	160	14	4	*.778	126	64	44	100	83	*2.48
1985—Lynchburg	Carolina	25	170⅔	*17	4	*.810	125	45	32	98	53	*1.69
1985—Jackson	Texas	3	15⅔	0	2	.000	22	12	12	6	5	6.89

Selected by New York Mets' organization in 6th round of free-agent draft, June 7, 1982.

RONALD WILLIAM HASSEY
(Ron)

Born February 27, 1953, at Tucson, Ariz.
Height, 6.02. Weight, 195.
Throws right and bats lefthanded.
Received degree in public administration from University of Arizona, Tucson, Ariz.
Son of Bill Hassey, minor league outfielder, 1949 through 1952.

Major League stolen bases: 1978 (2), 1979 (1), 1982 (3), 1983 (2), 1984 (1). Total—9.
Led American League in passed balls with 15 in 1985.

Year Club	League	Pos.	G.	AB.	R.	H.	2B.	3B.	HR.	RBI.	B.A.	PO.	A.	E.	F.A.
1976—San Jose	Calif.	C-3B	22	62	7	19	4	0	1	7	.306	55	2	2	.966
1976—Williamsport	East.	C	21	68	6	19	3	0	0	8	.279	63	10	4	.948
1977—Toledo	Int.	C-3-1-O	129	446	50	132	21	1	10	57	.296	484	82	21	.964
1978—Portland	P. C.	C-3B	72	235	42	76	12	1	12	52	.323	312	32	7	.980
1978—Cleveland	Amer.	C	25	74	5	15	0	0	2	9	.203	130	15	1	.993
1979—Tacoma	P. C.	C-3B	44	157	25	53	10	0	3	27	.338	282	44	2	.994
1979—Cleveland	Amer.	C-1B	75	223	20	64	14	0	4	32	.287	368	29	3	.993
1980—Cleveland	Amer.	C-1B	130	390	43	124	18	4	8	65	.318	564	52	4	.994
1981—Cleveland	Amer.	C-1B	61	190	8	44	4	0	1	25	.232	327	44	3	.992
1982—Cleveland	Amer.	C-1B	113	323	33	81	18	0	5	34	.251	566	38	4	.993
1983—Cleveland	Amer.	C	117	341	48	92	21	0	6	42	.270	514	43	3	.995
1984—Cleveland†	Amer.	C-1B	48	149	11	38	5	1	0	19	.255	210	16	1	.996
1984—Chicago‡§	Nat.	C-1B	19	33	5	11	0	0	2	5	.333	53	2	1	.982
1985—New York x	Amer.	C-1B	92	267	31	79	16	1	13	42	.296	420	20	7	.984
American League Totals—8 Years			661	1957	199	537	96	6	39	268	.274	3099	257	26	.992
National League Totals—1 Year			19	33	5	11	0	0	2	5	.333	53	2	1	.982
Major League Totals—9 Years			680	1990	204	548	96	6	41	273	.275	3152	259	27	.992

Selected by Cincinnati Reds' organization in 23rd round of free-agent draft, June 6, 1972.
Selected by Kansas City Royals' organization in 22nd round of free-agent draft, June 4, 1975.
Selected by Cleveland Indians' organization in 18th round of free-agent draft, June 8, 1976.
†Traded with Pitchers Rick Sutcliffe and George Frazier to Chicago Cubs for Outfielders Mel Hall and Joe Carter and Pitchers Don Schulze and Darryl Banks, June 13, 1984.
‡On disabled list, July 5 to September 1, 1984.
§Traded with Outfielder Henry Cotto and Pitchers Rich Bordi and Porfi Altamirano to New York Yankees for Pitcher Ray Fontenot and Outfielder Brian Dayett, December 4, 1984.
xTraded with Pitcher Joe Cowley to Chicago White Sox for Pitcher Britt Burns, Shortstop Mike Soper and Outfielder Glen Braxton, December 12, 1985.

ANDREW EARL HASSLER
(Andy)

Born October 18, 1951, at Texas City, Tex.
Height, 6.05 Weight, 220.
Throws and bats lefthanded.

Major League saves: 1974 (1), 1978 (1), 1979 (4), 1980 (10), 1981 (5), 1982 (4), 1983 (4). Total—29.
Led American Association in intentional bases on balls issued with 8 in 1984.
Tied for Pacific Coast League lead in games started by pitchers with 31 and wild pitches with 14 in 1972.

Year Club	League	G.	IP.	W.	L.	Pct.	H.	R.	ER.	SO.	BB.	ERA.
1970—El Paso†	Texas	22	144	10	7	.588	138	80	62	122	87	3.88
1971—Salt Lake City‡	P. Coast	9	51	5	1	.833	50	34	26	42	39	4.59
1971—California	American	6	19	0	3	.000	25	10	8	13	15	3.79
1972—Salt Lake City	P. Coast	32	174	9	10	.474	163	106	85	150	*114	4.40
1973—Salt Lake City	P. Coast	24	163	13	8	.619	166	93	76	127	81	4.20
1973—California	American	7	32	0	4	.000	33	23	13	19	19	3.66
1974—Salt Lake City	P. Coast	12	79	5	7	.417	98	61	52	52	48	5.92
1974—California	American	23	162	7	11	.389	132	64	47	76	79	2.61
1975—California	American	30	133	3	12	.200	158	94	88	82	53	5.95
1976—Calif.§-K. C.	American	33	147	5	12	.294	139	68	59	61	56	3.61
1977—Kansas City x	American	29	156	9	6	.600	166	88	73	83	75	4.21
1978—Kan. City y-Boston	American	24	88	3	5	.375	114	49	38	49	37	3.89
1979—Boston z	American	8	15	1	2	.333	23	17	15	7	7	9.00
1979—New York a	National	29	80	4	5	.444	74	35	33	53	42	3.71
1980—Pittsburgh b	National	6	12	0	0	.000	9	6	5	4	4	3.75
1980—California	American	41	83	5	1	.833	67	25	23	75	37	2.49
1981—California	American	42	76	4	3	.571	72	29	27	44	33	3.20
1982—California	American	54	71⅓	2	1	.667	58	24	22	38	40	2.78
1983—California c	American	42	36⅓	0	5	.000	42	22	22	20	17	5.45
1984—Arkansas	Texas	9	10⅓	1	1	.500	9	6	6	9	5	5.23
1984—Louisville	Am. Assoc.	38	64	7	4	.636	47	19	15	51	24	2.11
1984—St. Louis	National	3	2⅓	1	0	1.000	4	3	3	1	2	11.57

Year	Club	League	G.	IP.	W.	L.	Pct.	H.	R.	ER.	SO.	BB.	ERA.
1985—St. Louis	National	10	10	0	1	.000	9	5	2	5	4	1.80
1985—Louisville de	Am. Assoc.	26	41	4	5	.444	39	17	15	32	19	3.29
National League Totals—4 Years		48	104⅓	5	6	.455	96	49	43	63	52	3.71
American League Totals—12 Years		339	1018⅔	39	65	.375	1029	513	435	567	468	3.84
Major League Totals—14 Years		387	1123	44	71	.383	1125	562	478	630	520	3.83

Selected by California Angels' organization in 25th round of free-agent draft, June 5, 1969.
†On disabled list, August 10 to September 6, 1970.
‡On disabled list April 27 to May 12 and June 28 to August 31, 1971.
§Sold to Kansas City Royals, July 5, 1976.
xOn disabled list, April 27 to May 25, 1977.
ySold to Boston Red Sox, July 24, 1978.
zSold to New York Mets, June 15, 1979.
aGranted free agency, November 1, 1979; signed by Pittsburgh Pirates, November 21, 1979.
bSold to California Angels, June 10, 1980.
cReleased, April 1, 1984; signed by Arkansas (St. Louis Cardinals' organization), May 2, 1984.
dOn temporary inactive list, August 4, 1985 through remainder of season.
eReleased, October 15, 1985.

CHAMPIONSHIP SERIES RECORD

Year	Club	League	G.	IP.	W.	L.	Pct.	H.	R.	ER.	SO.	BB.	ERA.
1976—Kansas City	American	2	7⅓	0	1	.000	8	6	5	4	6	6.14
1977—Kansas City	American	1	5⅔	0	1	.000	5	3	3	3	0	4.76
1982—California	American	2	2⅔	0	0	.000	0	0	0	2	0	0.00
Championship Series Totals—3 Years		5	15⅔	0	2	.000	13	9	8	9	6	4.60

MICHAEL VAUGHN HATCHER JR.
(Mickey)

Born March 15, 1955, at Cleveland, O.
Height, 6.02. Weight, 199.
Throws and bats righthanded.
Attended Mesa Community College, Mesa, Ariz., and
University of Oklahoma, Norman, Okla.
Brother of Hal Hatcher, catcher in Kansas City Royals' organization.

Tied American League record for most hits, two consecutive games (9), April 27 and 28, 1985.
Major League stolen bases: 1979 (1), 1981 (3), 1983 (2). Total—6.

Year	Club	League	Pos.	G.	AB.	R.	H.	2B.	3B.	HR.	RBI.	B.A.	PO.	A.	E.	F.A.
1977—Clinton	Midw.	OF	78	288	47	89	12	4	11	53	.309	126	9	4	.971
1978—San Antonio†	Texas	3B	83	334	60	111	12	6	8	62	.332	55	124	22	.891
1978—Albuquerque	P. C.	3B-OF	41	155	25	51	11	5	7	39	.329	24	63	8	.916
1979—Albuquerque	P. C.	3B-OF	103	420	88	156	29	12	10	93	★.371	127	156	12	.959
1979—Los Angeles	Nat.	OF-3B	33	93	9	25	4	1	1	5	.269	47	24	5	.934
1980—Albuquerque	P. C.	OF-3B	43	181	28	65	7	2	7	40	.359	52	32	9	.903
1980—Los Angeles‡	Nat.	3B-OF	57	84	4	19	2	0	1	5	.226	31	23	3	.947
1981—Minnesota	Amer.	OF-1B-3B	99	377	36	96	23	2	3	37	.255	296	11	3	.990
1982—Minnesota	Amer.	OF-3B	84	277	23	69	13	2	3	26	.249	81	17	1	.990
1983—Minnesota§	Amer.	OF-1B-3B	106	375	50	119	15	3	9	47	.317	199	11	3	.986
1984—Minnesota	Amer.	OF-1B-3B	152	576	61	174	35	5	5	69	.302	364	20	9	.977
1985—Minnesota x	Amer.	OF-1B	116	444	46	125	28	0	3	49	.282	246	7	3	.988
National League Totals—2 Years			90	177	13	44	6	1	2	10	.249	78	47	8	.940
American League Totals—5 Years			557	2049	216	583	114	12	23	228	.285	1186	66	19	.985
Major League Totals—7 Years			647	2226	229	627	120	13	25	238	.282	1264	113	27	.981

Selected by Houston Astros' organization in 14th round of free-agent draft, June 5, 1974.
Selected by New York Mets' organization in 2nd round of free-agent draft, January 7, 1976.
Selected by Los Angeles Dodgers' organization in 5th round of free-agent draft, June 7, 1977.
†On disabled list, July 13 to July 23, 1978.
‡Traded with First Baseman Kelly Snider and Pitcher Matt Reeves to Minnesota Twins for Outfielder Ken Landreaux, March 30, 1981.
§On disabled list, June 21 to July 8 and August 1 to August 23, 1983.
xOn disabled list, July 10 to July 25, 1985.

WILLIAM AUGUSTUS HATCHER
(Billy)

Born October 4, 1960, at Williams, Ariz.
Height, 5.09. Weight, 175.
Throws and bats righthanded.
Attended Yavapai Community College, Prescott, Ariz.

Major League stolen bases: 1984 (2), 1985 (2). Total—4.
Led American Association in being hit by pitch with 9 in 1984.
Led New York-Pennsylvania League in being hit by pitch with 8 in 1981.

Year	Club	League	Pos.	G.	AB.	R.	H.	2B.	3B.	HR.	RBI.	B.A.	PO.	A.	E.	F.A.
1981—Geneva	NYP	OF	●75	289	57	81	15	3	4	40	.280	138	7	11	.930
1982—Salinas	Calif.	OF	138	549	92	171	18	8	8	59	.311	235	10	12	.953
1983—Midland	Texas	OF	135	545	★132	163	33	11	10	80	.299	286	17	●13	.959
1984—Iowa	A. A.	OF	150	595	96	164	27	18	9	59	.276	303	15	7	.978
1984—Chicago	Nat.	OF	8	9	1	1	0	0	0	0	.111	2	1	0	1.000

Year	Club	League	Pos.	G.	AB.	R.	H.	2B.	3B.	HR.	RBI.	B.A.	PO.	A.	E.	F.A.
1985—Iowa	A. A.		OF	67	279	39	78	14	5	5	19	.280	157	4	4	.976
1985—Chicago†‡	Nat.		OF	53	163	24	40	12	1	2	10	.245	77	2	1	.988
Major League Totals—2 Years				61	172	25	41	12	1	2	10	.238	79	3	1	.988

Selected by Chicago Cubs' organization in 6th round of free-agent draft, January 13, 1981.

†On disabled list, August 19 to September 3, 1985.

‡Traded with a player to be named later to Houston Astros for Outfielder Jerry Mumphrey, December 16, 1985.

BRADLEY DAVID HAVENS
(Brad)

Born November 17, 1959, at Highland Park, Mich.
Height, 6.01. Weight, 190.
Throws and bats lefthanded.

Led International League in complete games with 12 in 1984.
Led California League in complete games with 12 in 1980.
Led Midwest League in complete games with 17 in 1978.
Tied for California League lead in games started by pitchers with 28 in 1980.
Named International League Pitcher of the Year, 1984.

Year	Club	League	G.	IP.	W.	L.	Pct.	H.	R.	ER.	SO.	BB.	ERA.
1978—Quad Cities†	Midwest		26	★200	13	10	.565	171	80	59	★197	74	2.66
1979—Orlando	Southern		19	94	4	10	.286	128	85	76	63	50	7.28
1979—Wisconsin Rapids	Midwest		10	73	6	1	.857	62	35	34	80	18	4.19
1980—Visalia	California		28	195	14	9	.609	186	90	72	★179	82	3.32
1981—Orlando	Southern		11	74	6	2	.750	81	38	29	58	20	3.53
1981—Minnesota	American		14	78	3	6	.333	76	33	31	43	24	3.58
1982—Minnesota	American		33	208⅔	10	14	.417	201	112	100	129	80	4.31
1983—Minnesota	American		16	80⅓	5	8	.385	110	75	73	40	38	8.18
1983—Toledo	Int'national		11	69⅔	6	3	.667	60	34	30	64	37	3.88
1984—Toledo‡	Int'national		25	169	11	10	.524	142	56	49	★169	70	2.61
1985—Rochester	Int'national		34	133⅔	8	10	.444	135	79	72	★129	52	4.85
1985—Baltimore	American		8	14⅓	0	1	.000	20	14	14	19	10	8.79
Major League Totals—4 Years			71	381⅓	18	29	.383	407	234	218	231	152	5.15

Selected by California Angels' organization in 8th round of free-agent draft, June 7, 1977.

†Traded with Outfielder Ken Landreaux, Pitcher Paul Hartzell and Third Baseman Dave Engle to Minnesota Twins for First Baseman Rod Carew, February 3, 1979.

‡Traded to Baltimore Orioles' organization for Pitcher Mark Brown, March 27, 1985.

MELTON ANDREW HAWKINS
(Andy)

Born January 21, 1960, at Waco, Tex.
Height, 6.03. Weight, 205.
Throws and bats righthanded.

Led Pacific Coast League in shutouts with 6 in 1982.
Led Texas League in complete games with 14 and tied for lead in games started by pitchers with 27 in 1981.
Led Northwest League in balks with 4 in 1978.

Year	Club	League	G.	IP.	W.	L.	Pct.	H.	R.	ER.	SO.	BB.	ERA.
1978—Walla Walla	Northwest		14	102	8	3	.727	95	52	24	73	45	2.12
1979—Reno	California		27	188	8	13	.381	★232	143	★117	130	97	5.60
1980—Reno	California		26	171	13	10	.565	183	108	81	124	79	4.26
1981—Amarillo	Texas		27	200	11	10	.524	★209	100	★93	144	48	4.19
1982—Hawaii	P. Coast		18	132⅔	9	7	.563	108	49	32	91	47	2.17
1982—San Diego	National		15	63⅔	2	5	.286	66	33	29	25	27	4.10
1983—Las Vegas	P. Coast		14	85⅓	6	4	.600	110	67	61	50	27	6.43
1983—San Diego	National		21	119⅔	5	7	.417	106	50	39	59	48	2.93
1984—San Diego	National		36	146	8	9	.471	143	90	76	77	72	4.68
1985—San Diego	National		33	228⅔	18	8	.692	229	88	80	69	65	3.15
Major League Totals—4 Years			105	558	33	29	.532	544	261	224	230	212	3.61

Selected by San Diego Padres' organization in 1st round (fifth player selected) of free-agent draft, June 6, 1978.

CHAMPIONSHIP SERIES RECORD

Year	Club	League	G.	IP.	W.	L.	Pct.	H.	R.	ER.	SO.	BB.	ERA.
1984—San Diego	National		3	3⅔	0	0	.000	0	0	0	1	2	0.00

WORLD SERIES RECORD

Year	Club	League	G.	IP.	W.	L.	Pct.	H.	R.	ER.	SO.	BB.	ERA.
1984—San Diego	National		3	12	1	1	.500	4	1	1	4	6	0.75

GARY WILLIAM HAWLEY JR.
(Billy)

Born March 12, 1964, at Columbia, S.C.
Height, 6.03. Weight, 195.
Throws right and bats lefthanded.

Led Florida State League in complete games with 12 and tied for lead in shutouts with 5 in 1984.
Named Florida State League Most Valuable Player, 1984.

Year Club	League	G.	IP.	W.	L.	Pct.	H.	R.	ER.	SO.	BB.	ERA.
1982—Billings	Pioneer	13	53⅓	2	6	.250	75	49	41	41	18	6.92
1983—Cedar Rapids	Midwest	26	152⅔	11	9	.550	173	83	66	99	31	3.89
1984—Tampa	Florida St.	26	178	*18	5	.783	151	52	37	95	44	*1.87
1985—Vermont†	Eastern	17	101	7	8	.467	102	60	52	52	30	4.63

Selected by Cincinnati Reds' organization in 1st round (23rd player selected) of free-agent draft, June 7, 1982.
†On disabled list, June 29 to July 9, 1985.

CHARLES DEWAYNE HAYES
(Charlie)

Born May 29, 1965, at Hattiesburg, Miss.
Height, 6.00. Weight, 195.
Throws and bats righthanded.

Year Club	League	Pos.	G.	AB.	R.	H.	2B.	3B.	HR.	RBI.	B.A.	PO.	A.	E.	F.A.
1983—Great Falls†	Pion.	3B-OF	34	111	9	29	4	2	0	9	.261	13	32	9	.833
1984—Clinton	Midw.	3B	116	392	41	96	17	2	2	51	.245	68	216	28	.910
1985—Fresno	Calif.	3B	131	467	73	132	17	2	4	68	.283	*100	233	18	*.949

Selected by San Francisco Giants' organization in 4th round of free-agent draft, June 6, 1983.
†On disabled list, July 20, 1983 through remainder of season.

VON FRANCIS HAYES

Born August 31, 1958, at Stockton, Calif.
Height, 6.05. Weight, 180.
Throws right and bats lefthanded.
Attended St. Mary's College, Moraga, Calif.

Tied major league record for most home runs (2) and most total bases (8), inning, June 11, 1985 (first inning).
Major League stolen bases: 1981 (8), 1982 (32), 1983 (20), 1984 (48), 1985 (21). Total—129.
Led Midwest League third basemen in fielding percentage with .930 in 1980.
Named Midwest League Most Valuable Player, 1980.

Year Club	League	Pos.	G.	AB.	R.	H.	2B.	3B.	HR.	RBI.	B.A.	PO.	A.	E.	F.A.
1980—Waterloo	Midw.	3B-SS	134	492	105	*162	*33	3	15	90	*.329	94	291	30	.928
1981—Cleveland	Amer.	OF-3B	43	109	21	28	8	2	1	17	.257	30	4	3	.919
1981—Charleston	Int.	3B-1B	105	382	58	120	19	6	10	73	.314	96	222	19	.944
1982—Cleveland†	Amer.	OF-3B-1B	150	527	65	132	25	3	14	82	.250	323	17	6	.983
1983—Philadelphia‡	Nat.	OF	124	351	45	93	9	5	6	32	.265	165	7	5	.972
1984—Philadelphia	Nat.	OF	152	561	85	164	27	6	16	67	.292	341	2	4	.988
1985—Philadelphia	Nat.	OF	152	570	76	150	30	4	13	70	.263	368	9	6	.984
American League Totals—2 Years			193	636	86	160	33	5	15	99	.252	353	21	9	.977
National League Totals—3 Years			428	1482	206	407	66	15	35	169	.275	874	18	15	.983
Major League Totals—5 Years			621	2118	292	567	99	20	50	268	.268	1227	39	24	.981

Selected by Cleveland Indians' organization in 7th round of free-agent draft, June 5, 1979.
†Traded to Philadelphia Phillies for Second Baseman Manny Trillo, Outfielder George Vukovich, Infielder Julio Franco, Pitcher Jay Baller and Catcher Gerry Willard, December 9, 1982.
‡On disabled list, March 27 to April 12, 1983.

CHAMPIONSHIP SERIES RECORD

Year Club	League	Pos.	G.	AB.	R.	H.	2B.	3B.	HR.	RBI.	B.A.	PO.	A.	E.	F.A.
1983—Philadelphia	Nat.	PH-OF	2	2	0	0	0	0	0	0	.000	0	0	0	.000

WORLD SERIES RECORD

Year Club	League	Pos.	G.	AB.	R.	H.	2B.	3B.	HR.	RBI.	B.A.	PO.	A.	E.	F.A.
1983—Philadelphia	Nat.	PH-OF	4	3	0	0	0	0	0	0	.000	1	0	0	1.000

RAYMOND ALTON HAYWARD JR.
(Ray)

Born April 27, 1961, at Enid, Okla.
Height, 6.01. Weight, 190.
Throws and bats lefthanded.
Received degree in finance from University of Oklahoma, Norman, Okla., in 1983.

Tied for Pacific Coast League lead in hit batsmen with 6 in 1985.
Tied for Pacific Coast League lead in wild pitches with 16 in 1984.
Named lefthanded pitcher on THE SPORTING NEWS College Baseball All-America Team, 1983.

Year Club	League	G.	IP.	W.	L.	Pct.	H.	R.	ER.	SO.	BB.	ERA.
1983—Beaumont	Texas	10	66⅓	5	1	.833	45	16	13	71	30	1.76
1984—Las Vegas	P. Coast	26	129⅓	9	6	.600	129	78	70	91	79	4.87
1985—Las Vegas	P. Coast	28	*191⅓	11	10	.524	198	104	85	150	79	4.00

Selected by Pittsburgh Pirates' organization in 12th round of free-agent draft, June 7, 1982.
Selected by San Diego Padres' organization in 1st round (10th player selected) of free-agent draft, June 6, 1983.

EDWARD JOHN HEARN
(Ed)

Born August 23, 1960, at Stuart, Fla.
Height, 6.03. Weight, 215.
Throws and bats righthanded.

Year	Club	League	Pos.	G.	AB.	R.	H.	2B.	3B.	HR.	RBI.	B.A.	PO.	A.	E.	F.A.
1978—Helena	Pion.		C	47	173	34	49	3	1	13	45	.283	274	35	9	.972
1979—Helena†	Pion.						(Did not play)									
1980—Spartanburg	S. Atl.		1B	66	217	25	65	12	2	3	32	.300	68	7	1	.987
1981—Peninsula	Carol.		1B	101	317	61	96	29	2	10	44	.303	538	25	12	.979
1982—Peninsula	Carol.		C-1B	21	76	15	25	2	0	6	14	.329	69	2	2	.973
1982—Reading‡§	East.		1B-C	43	135	16	37	6	2	3	27	.274	204	16	7	.969
1983—Jackson	Texas		1B-C	5	20	4	6	1	0	0	2	.300	40	1	1	.976
1983—Lynchburg	Carol.		C-1-3-O	91	290	37	79	16	1	5	47	.272	333	37	9	.976
1984—Jackson x	Texas		C-1B	86	311	46	97	19	2	11	51	.312	613	54	6	.991
1985—Tidewater	Int.		C-1B	112	418	35	110	29	1	5	57	.263	543	45	5	.992

Selected by Philadelphia Phillies' organization in 4th round of free-agent draft, June 6, 1978.
†On temporary inactive list, June 22, 1979 through remainder of season.
‡On disabled list, June 15 to July 6, 1982.
§Released, January 7, 1983; signed by Lynchburg (New York Mets' organization), February 3, 1983.
xGranted free agency, October 15, 1984; re-signed by Mets' organization, December 13, 1984.

JEFFREY VERNON HEARRON
(Jeff)

Born November 19, 1961, at Long Beach, Calif.
Height, 6.02. Weight, 190.
Throws and bats righthanded.
Attended University of Texas, Austin, Tex.

Year	Club	League	Pos.	G.	AB.	R.	H.	2B.	3B.	HR.	RBI.	B.A.	PO.	A.	E.	F.A.
1983—Florence	S. Atl.		C	47	144	19	41	11	0	5	20	.285	235	40	7	.975
1984—Knoxville†	South.		C	81	240	30	60	9	0	7	28	.250	387	45	14	.969
1985—Knoxville‡	South.		C	45	130	17	29	6	1	5	15	.223	190	20	3	.986
1985—Toronto	Amer.		C	4	7	0	1	0	0	0	0	.143	16	1	0	1.000
Major League Totals—1 Year				4	7	0	1	0	0	0	0	.143	16	1	0	1.000

Selected by Toronto Blue Jays' organization in 4th round of free-agent draft, June 6, 1983.
†On disabled list, May 2 to May 12, July 2 to July 17 and September 2 to September 14, 1984.
‡On disabled list, April 11 to April 28, 1985.

CHAMPIONSHIP SERIES RECORD

Year	Club	League	Pos.	G.	AB.	R.	H.	2B.	3B.	HR.	RBI.	B.A.	PO.	A.	E.	F.A.
1985—Toronto	Amer.		C	2	0	0	0	0	0	0	0	.000	2	0	0	1.000

DAVID LANIER HEATH

Born June 19, 1960, at Ozark, Ala.
Height, 6.02. Weight, 215.
Throws and bats righthanded.
Attended Auburn University, Auburn, Ala.

Led Eastern League catchers in putouts with 508 and total chances with 573 in 1984.
Led Midwest League catchers in double plays with 10 in 1983.

Year	Club	League	Pos.	G.	AB.	R.	H.	2B.	3B.	HR.	RBI.	B.A.	PO.	A.	E.	F.A.
1983—Peoria	Midw.		★C-1B	121	417	70	113	28	3	★27	71	.271	643	97	★22	.971
1984—Waterbury	East.		★C-3B	121	426	35	79	12	0	9	41	.185	509	53	★13	.977
1985—Midland	Texas		C	98	362	49	112	21	1	12	54	.309	360	70	10	.977

Selected by California Angels' organization in 26th round of free-agent draft, June 7, 1982.

KELLY MARK HEATH

Born September 4, 1957, at Plattsburg, N.Y.
Height, 5.08. Weight, 155.
Throws and bats righthanded.
Attended Louisburg College, Louisburg, N.C.

Year	Club	League	Pos.	G.	AB.	R.	H.	2B.	3B.	HR.	RBI.	B.A.	PO.	A.	E.	F.A.
1977—Daytona Beach	Fla. St.		SS	59	181	13	42	4	4	2	30	.232	108	147	19	.931
1978—Jacksonville†	South.		SS	70	231	29	62	6	0	3	24	.268	115	217	31	.915
1979—Jacksonville	South.		SS-2B	129	422	67	115	26	3	7	61	.273	167	348	31	.943
1980—Omaha	A. A.		SS	56	182	22	46	10	1	3	22	.253	75	128	11	.949
1980—Jacksonville	South.		SS	55	205	26	63	10	2	5	27	.307	75	186	12	.956
1981—Omaha	A. A.		2B-SS	111	387	52	93	21	5	3	37	.240	222	282	10	.978
1982—Omaha	A. A.		2B-SS	106	361	48	86	14	2	11	41	.238	232	285	17	.968
1982—Kansas City	Amer.		2B	1	1	0	0	0	0	0	0	.000	1	2	0	1.000
1983—Omaha‡	A. A.		2B-SS	129	460	71	110	16	6	13	61	.239	263	371	13	.980
1984—Columbus	Int.		2-3-S-O	108	350	72	87	17	5	8	38	.249	138	151	23	.926
1985—Columbus§	Int.		OF-2B	121	377	83	97	21	4	18	53	.257	151	55	7	.967
Major League Totals—1 Year				1	1	0	0	0	0	0	0	.000	1	2	0	1.000

Selected by Kansas City Royals' organization in 7th round of free-agent draft, June 7, 1977.
†On disabled list, May 8 to June 30, 1978.
‡Granted free agency, October 20, 1983; signed by New York Yankees' organization, December 2, 1983.
§Granted free agency, October 15, 1985; signed by Atlanta Braves, December 26, 1985.

MICHAEL THOMAS HEATH
(Mike)

Born February 5, 1955, at Tampa, Fla.
Height, 5.11. Weight, 190.
Throws and bats righthanded.

Major League stolen bases: 1979 (1), 1980 (3), 1981 (3), 1982 (8), 1983 (3), 1984 (7), 1985 (7). Total—32.
Led New York-Pennsylvania League shortstops in double plays with 42 in 1974.
Tied for Appalachian League lead in sacrifice hits with 7 in 1973.

Year Club	League	Pos.	G.	AB.	R.	H.	2B.	3B.	HR.	RBI.	B.A.	PO.	A.	E.	F.A.
1973—Johnson City	Appal.	SS-2B-3B	48	166	17	29	5	2	0	10	.175	83	137	24	.902
1974—Oneonta	NYP	SS	65	234	51	66	6	3	3	34	.282	114	170	*27	.913
1975—Fort Lauderdale†	Fla. St.	SS	98	376	43	87	7	3	1	23	.231	184	256	31	.934
1976—Fort Lauderdale‡	Fla. St.	SS-3B-C-P	80	267	28	71	16	3	2	30	.266	143	121	16	.943
1977—West Haven	East.	C-3B	98	352	58	94	13	5	8	42	.267	492	72	16	.972
1978—West Haven	East.	C-SS	66	217	43	64	16	1	8	27	.295	335	53	10	.975
1978—New York§	Amer.	C	33	92	6	21	3	1	0	8	.228	151	11	5	.970
1979—Tucson x	P. C.	C	54	196	21	53	8	2	1	28	.270	183	24	7	.967
1979—Oakland	Amer.	OF-C-3B	74	258	19	66	8	0	3	27	.256	167	32	5	.975
1980—Oakland	Amer.	C-OF	92	305	27	74	10	2	1	33	.243	292	20	4	.987
1981—Oakland	Amer.	*C-OF	84	301	26	71	7	1	8	30	.236	399	45	*10	.978
1982—Oakland y	Amer.	C-OF-3B	101	318	43	77	18	4	3	39	.242	368	54	12	.972
1983—Oakland z	Amer.	C-OF-3B	96	345	45	97	17	0	6	33	.281	362	47	11	.974
1984—Oakland	Amer.	C-O-3-S	140	475	49	118	21	5	13	64	.248	495	56	8	.986
1985—Oakland a	Amer.	C-OF-3B	138	436	71	109	18	6	13	55	.250	539	67	12	.981
Major League Totals—8 Years			758	2530	286	633	102	19	47	289	.250	2773	332	67	.979

Selected by New York Yankees' organization in 2nd round of free-agent draft, June 5, 1973.
†On Syracuse disabled list, August 2 to September 16, 1975.
‡On disabled list, June 29 to July 13, 1976.
§Traded with Pitchers Sparky Lyle, Larry McCall and Dave Rajsich, Shortstop Domingo Ramos and cash to Texas Rangers for Outfielders Juan Beniquez and Greg Jemison and Pitchers Mike Griffin, Paul Mirabella and Dave Righetti, November 10, 1978.
xTraded with Third Baseman Dave Chalk and cash to Oakland A's for Pitcher John Henry Johnson, June 15, 1979.
yOn disabled list, March 28 to April 20, 1982.
zOn disabled list, April 25 to May 25, 1983.
aTraded with Pitcher Tim Conroy to St. Louis Cardinals for Pitcher Joaquin Andujar, December 10, 1985.

DIVISION SERIES RECORD

Year Club	League	Pos.	G.	AB.	R.	H.	2B.	3B.	HR.	RBI.	B.A.	PO.	A.	E.	F.A.
1981—Oakland	Amer.	C	2	8	0	0	0	0	0	0	.000	9	1	0	1.000

CHAMPIONSHIP SERIES RECORD

Year Club	League	Pos.	G.	AB.	R.	H.	2B.	3B.	HR.	RBI.	B.A.	PO.	A.	E.	F.A.
1981—Oakland	Amer.	C-OF	3	6	1	2	0	0	0	0	.333	3	1	0	1.000

WORLD SERIES RECORD

Year Club	League	Pos.	G.	AB.	R.	H.	2B.	3B.	HR.	RBI.	B.A.	PO.	A.	E.	F.A.
1978—New York	Amer.	C	1	0	0	0	0	0	0	0	.000	0	0	0	.000

PITCHING RECORD

Year Club	League	G.	IP.	W.	L.	Pct.	H.	R.	ER.	SO.	BB.	ERA.
1976—Fort Lauderdale	Florida St.	1	1	0	0	.000	1	0	0	1	0	0.00

RONALD JEFFREY HEATHCOCK
(Jeff)

Born November 18, 1959, at West Covina, Calif.
Height, 6.04. Weight, 195.
Throws and bats righthanded.
Attended Golden West College, Huntington Beach, Calif.,
and Oral Roberts University, Tulsa, Okla.

Major League saves: 1983 (1), 1985 (1). Total—2.
Led Southern League in home runs allowed with 26 in 1982.
Tied for Southern League lead in shutouts with 3 in 1983.

Year Club	League	G.	IP.	W.	L.	Pct.	H.	R.	ER.	SO.	BB.	ERA.
1981—Daytona Beach	Florida St.	11	85	9	0	1.000	67	20	12	77	21	1.27
1981—Columbus	Southern	16	101	4	7	.364	104	57	52	59	35	4.63
1982—Columbus	Southern	29	191	13	13	.500	216	*119	*101	108	56	4.76
1983—Columbus	Southern	14	91⅓	4	4	.500	82	32	23	69	22	2.27
1983—Tucson	P. Coast	15	110⅓	10	3	.769	104	45	34	65	26	2.77
1983—Houston	National	6	28	2	1	.667	19	14	10	12	4	3.21
1984—Tucson†	P. Coast	4	16⅔	1	1	.500	12	8	8	8	6	4.32
1985—Tucson	P. Coast	23	141⅔	7	10	.412	180	91	80	59	27	5.08
1985—Houston	National	14	56⅓	3	1	.750	50	25	21	25	13	3.36
Major League Totals—2 Years		20	84⅓	5	2	.714	69	39	31	37	17	3.31

Selected by Milwaukee Brewers' organization in 2nd round of free-agent draft, January 9, 1979.
Selected by San Diego Padres' organization in secondary phase of free-agent draft, June 5, 1979.
Selected by Houston Astros' organization in secondary phase of free-agent draft, June 3, 1980.
†On disabled list, April 25, 1984 through remainder of season.

NEAL HEATON

Born March 3, 1960, at Jamaica, N.Y.
Height, 6.01. Weight, 205.
Throws and bats lefthanded.
Attended University of Miami, Coral Gables, Fla.

Major League saves: 1983 (7).
Named lefthanded pitcher on THE SPORTING NEWS College Baseball All-America Team, 1981.

Year Club	League	G.	IP.	W.	L.	Pct.	H.	R.	ER.	SO.	BB.	ERA.
1981—Chattanooga	Southern	11	77	4	4	.500	61	42	34	50	27	3.97
1982—Charleston	Int'national	29	172⅔	10	5	.667	194	97	77	105	66	4.01
1982—Cleveland	American	8	31	0	2	.000	32	21	18	14	16	5.23
1983—Cleveland	American	39	149½	11	7	.611	157	79	69	75	44	4.16
1984—Cleveland	American	38	198⅔	12	15	.444	231	128	115	75	75	5.21
1985—Cleveland	American	36	207⅔	9	17	.346	244	119	113	82	80	4.90
Major League Totals—4 Years		121	586⅔	32	41	.438	664	347	315	246	215	4.83

Selected by New York Mets' organization in 1st round (first player selected) of free-agent draft, January 9, 1979.
Selected by Cleveland Indians' organization in 2nd round of free-agent draft, June 8, 1981.

RICHARD JOSEPH HEBNER
(Richie)

Born November 26, 1947, at Norwood, Mass.
Height, 6.01. Weight, 200.
Throws right and bats lefthanded.
Brother of William Hebner, umpire in Florida State League, Eastern League
and International League, 1967 through 1972.

Tied major league record for most bases on balls, inning (2), August 27, 1974 (third inning).
Tied modern major league record for most at bats, game (7), September 16, 1975.
Major League stolen bases: 1969 (4), 1970 (2), 1971 (2), 1976 (1), 1977 (7), 1978 (4), 1979 (3), 1981 (1), 1982 (5), 1983 (8), 1984 (1). Total—38.
Led International League third basemen in errors with 19 in 1968.
Received reported $40,000 bonus to sign with Pittsburgh Pirates, 1966.

Year Club	League	Pos.	G.	AB.	R.	H.	2B.	3B.	HR.	RBI.	B.A.	PO.	A.	E.	F.A.
1966—Salem†‡	Appal.	1B	26	92	17	33	9	3	4	20	.359	167	10	2	.989
1967—Raleigh§	Carol.	3B	78	274	45	92	15	6	2	33	.336	69	135	17	.923
1968—Columbus x	Int.	3B-SS	104	381	50	105	20	5	6	51	.276	77	224	23	.929
1968—Pittsburgh	Nat.	PH	2	1	0	0	0	0	0	0	.000	0	0	0	.000
1969—Pittsburgh	Nat.	3B-1B	129	459	72	138	23	4	8	47	.301	81	240	19	.944
1970—Pittsburgh y	Nat.	3B	120	420	60	122	24	8	11	46	.290	64	235	19	.940
1971—Pittsburgh z	Nat.	3B	112	388	50	105	17	8	17	67	.271	89	172	14	.949
1972—Pittsburgh	Nat.	3B	124	427	63	128	24	4	19	72	.300	76	210	9	.969
1973—Pittsburgh	Nat.	3B	144	509	73	138	28	1	25	74	.271	92	260	23	.939
1974—Pittsburgh	Nat.	3B	146	550	97	160	21	6	18	68	.291	115	304	★28	.937
1975—Pittsburgh	Nat.	3B	128	472	65	116	16	4	15	57	.246	86	244	19	.946
1976—Pittsburgh a	Nat.	3B	132	434	60	108	21	3	8	51	.249	87	236	16	.953
1977—Philadelphia b	Nat.	1B-3B-2B	118	397	67	113	17	4	18	62	.285	933	85	11	.989
1978—Philadelphia c	Nat.	1B-3B-2B	137	435	61	123	22	3	17	71	.283	994	94	8	.993
1979—New York d	Nat.	3B-1B	136	473	54	127	25	2	10	79	.268	125	248	23	.942
1980—Detroit	Amer.	1B-3B	104	341	48	99	10	7	12	82	.290	485	84	4	.993
1981—Detroit	Amer.	1B	78	226	19	51	8	2	5	28	.226	531	29	3	.995
1982—Detroit e	Amer.	1B	68	179	25	49	6	0	8	18	.274	286	25	3	.990
1982—Pittsburgh	Nat.	OF-1B-3B	25	70	6	21	2	0	2	12	.300	52	3	1	.982
1983—Pittsburgh f	Nat.	3B-1B-OF	78	162	23	43	4	1	5	26	.265	63	45	2	.982
1984—Chicago g	Nat.	3B-1B-OF	44	81	12	27	3	0	2	8	.333	39	26	1	.985
1985—Chicago h	Nat.	1B-OF	83	120	10	26	2	0	3	22	.217	110	24	4	.971
National League Totals—16 Years			1658	5398	773	1495	249	48	178	762	.277	3006	2426	197	.965
American League Totals—3 Years			250	746	92	199	24	9	25	128	.267	1302	138	10	.993
Major League Totals—18 Years			1908	6144	865	1694	273	57	203	890	.276	4308	2564	207	.971

Selected by Pittsburgh Pirates' organization in 1st round (15th player selected) of free-agent draft, June 28, 1966.
†On temporary inactive list, August 9 to August 18, 1966.
‡On military list, August 18, 1966 through April 6, 1967.
§On temporary inactive list, May 13 to May 15, June 10 to June 24 and July 20 to August 16, 1967.
xOn temporary inactive list, July 13 to July 29, 1968.
yOn military list, August 8 to August 24, 1970.
zOn military list, July 25 to August 9, 1971.
aPlayed out option year and granted free agency, November 1, 1976; signed as free agent by Philadelphia Phillies, December 15, 1976.
bOn disabled list, March 27 to April 29, 1977.
cTraded with Second Baseman Jose Moreno to New York Mets for Pitcher Nino Espinosa, March 27, 1979.
dTraded to Detroit Tigers for Third Baseman Phil Mankowski and Outfielder Jerry Morales, October 31, 1979.
eSold to Pittsburgh Pirates, August 16, 1982.
fGranted free agency, November 7, 1983; signed by Chicago Cubs, January 5, 1984.
gOn disabled list, July 13 to September 9, 1984.
hGranted free agency, November 12, 1985.

CHAMPIONSHIP SERIES RECORD

Established Championship Series record for most times on losing club (7).
Tied Championship Series record for most two-base hits, total Series (7); most clubs, total Series (3).
Established National League Championship Series record for most Series played (8).

Tied National League Championship Series record for most Series, one or more hits (7).

Year Club	League	Pos.	G.	AB.	R.	H.	2B.	3B.	HR.	RBI.	B.A.	PO.	A.	E.	F.A.
1970—Pittsburgh	Nat.	3B	2	6	0	4	2	0	0	0	.667	0	4	0	1.000
1971—Pittsburgh	Nat.	PH-3B	4	17	3	5	1	0	2	4	.294	4	3	1	.875
1972—Pittsburgh	Nat.	3B	5	16	2	3	1	0	0	1	.188	5	11	0	1.000
1974—Pittsburgh	Nat.	3B	4	13	1	3	0	0	1	4	.231	5	7	0	1.000
1975—Pittsburgh	Nat.	3B	3	12	2	4	1	0	0	2	.333	0	2	0	1.000
1977—Philadelphia	Nat.	1B-PH	4	14	2	5	2	0	0	0	.357	32	0	0	1.000
1978—Philadelphia	Nat.	1B-PH	3	9	0	1	0	0	0	1	.111	21	0	0	1.000
1984—Chicago	Nat.	PH	2	1	0	0	0	0	0	0	.000	0	0	0	.000
Championship Series Totals—8 Years			27	88	10	25	7	0	3	12	.284	67	27	1	.989

WORLD SERIES RECORD

Year Club	League	Pos.	G.	AB.	R.	H.	2B.	3B.	HR.	RBI.	B.A.	PO.	A.	E.	F.A.
1971—Pittsburgh	Nat.	3B	3	12	2	2	0	0	1	3	.167	1	3	1	.800

DANIEL WILLIAM HEEP
(Danny)

Born July 3, 1957, at San Antonio, Tex.
Height, 5.11. Weight, 105.
Throws and bats lefthanded.
Received degree in teaching and political science from St. Mary's University, San Antonio, Tex.

Major League stolen bases: 1983 (3), 1984 (3), 1985 (2). Total—8.
Led Southern League in total bases with 274 in 1979.
Named Southern League co-Most Valuable Player, 1979.

Year Club	League	Pos.	G.	AB.	R.	H.	2B.	3B.	HR.	RBI.	B.A.	PO.	A.	E.	F.A.
1978—Daytona Beach	Fla. St.	OF	66	212	29	72	18	2	2	24	.340	89	9	2	.980
1979—Columbus	South.	OF	138	523	103	*171	30	5	16	84	.327	211	12	6	.974
1979—Houston	Nat.	OF	14	14	0	2	0	0	0	2	.143	7	0	0	1.000
1980—Tucson	P. C.	1B-OF	96	376	63	129	28	5	17	69	*.343	810	53	8	.991
1980—Houston	Nat.	1B	33	87	6	24	8	0	0	6	.276	188	8	2	.990
1981—Houston†	Nat.	1B-OF	33	96	6	24	3	0	0	11	.250	198	9	2	.990
1981—Tuscon	P. C.	1B-OF	78	285	55	96	23	5	11	60	.337	635	44	12	.983
1982—Houston‡	Nat.	OF-1B	85	198	16	47	14	1	4	22	.237	192	6	1	.995
1983—New York	Nat.	OF-1B	115	253	30	64	12	0	8	21	.253	159	11	0	1.000
1984—New York	Nat.	OF-1B	99	199	36	46	9	2	1	12	.231	137	7	4	.973
1985—New York	Nat.	OF-1B	95	271	26	76	17	0	7	42	.280	154	5	4	.975
Major League Totals—7 Years			474	1118	120	283	63	3	20	116	.253	1035	46	13	.988

Selected by Houston Astros' organization in 2nd round of free-agent draft, June 6, 1978.
†On disabled list, April 19 to May 4, 1981.
‡Traded to New York Mets for Pitcher Mike Scott, December 10, 1982.

CHAMPIONSHIP SERIES RECORD

Year Club	League	Pos.	G.	AB.	R.	H.	2B.	3B.	HR.	RBI.	B.A.	PO.	A.	E.	F.A.
1980—Houston	Nat.	PH	1	1	0	0	0	0	0	0	.000	0	0	0	.000

ROBERT HILMER HEGMAN
(Bob)

Born February 26, 1958, at Springfield, Minn.
Height, 6.01. Weight, 180.
Throws and bats righthanded.
Received bachelor of science degree in management
from St. Cloud State University, St. Cloud, Minn.

Year Club	League	Pos.	G.	AB.	R.	H.	2B.	3B.	HR.	RBI.	B.A.	PO.	A.	E.	F.A.
1980—Sarasota Royals	Gulf C.	SS-2B	54	212	30	49	6	2	0	13	.231	91	179	18	.938
1981—Charleston	S. Atl.	S-3-2-O	100	311	43	81	8	1	0	22	.260	151	262	30	.932
1982—Jacksonville	South.	3-2-S-O	87	262	36	55	1	0	0	15	.210	90	167	15	.945
1983—Jacksonville	South.	3-O-S-2	74	235	33	56	8	1	1	26	.238	71	94	8	.954
1983—Omaha	A. A.	3B	4	4	2	0	0	0	0	0	.000	1	2	1	.750
1984—Memphis	South.	SS	135	475	62	120	9	5	0	45	.253	*239	361	24	*.962
1985—Omaha	A. A.	2-S-O-3-1	89	207	16	48	5	1	0	19	.232	121	142	10	.963
1985—Kansas City	Amer.	2B	1	0	0	0	0	0	0	0	.000	0	0	0	.000
Major League Totals—1 Year			1	0	0	0	0	0	0	0	.000	0	0	0	.000

Selected by Kansas City Royals' organization in 15th round of free-agent draft, June 3, 1980.

DAVID LEE HENDERSON
(Dave)

Born July 21, 1958, at Dos Palos, Calif.
Height, 6.02. Weight, 210.
Throws and bats righthanded.
Nephew of Joe Henderson, pitcher with Chicago
White Sox and Cincinnati Reds, 1974, 1976 and 1977.
Major League stolen bases: 1981 (2), 1982 (2), 1983 (9), 1984 (5), 1985 (6). Total—24.

Year Club	League	Pos.	G.	AB.	R.	H.	2B.	3B.	HR.	RBI.	B.A.	PO.	A.	E.	F.A.
1977—Bellingham	N'west.	OF	65	251	47	79	14	2	•16	63	.315	136	5	⋆11	.928
1978—Stockton	Calif.	OF	117	409	48	95	16	4	7	63	.232	204	12	14	.939
1979—San Jose	Calif.	OF	136	507	103	152	23	3	27	99	.300	264	18	4	.986
1980—Spokane†	P. C.	OF	109	341	48	95	26	1	7	50	.279	258	9	7	.974
1981—Seattle	Amer.	OF	59	126	17	21	3	0	6	13	.167	105	4	0	1.000
1981—Spokane	P. C.	OF	80	272	47	76	23	1	12	50	.279	146	7	3	.981
1982—Seattle‡	Amer.	OF	104	324	47	82	17	1	14	48	.253	249	11	4	.985
1983—Seattle	Amer.	OF	137	484	50	130	24	5	17	55	.269	304	17	6	.982
1984—Seattle§	Amer.	OF	112	350	42	98	23	0	14	43	.280	242	11	3	.988
1985—Seattle	Amer.	OF	139	502	70	121	28	2	14	68	.241	335	8	5	.986
Major League Totals—5 Years			551	1786	226	452	95	8	65	227	.253	1235	51	18	.986

Selected by Seattle Mariners' organization in 1st round (26th player selected) of free-agent draft, June 7, 1977.

†On disabled list, June 26 to July 22, 1980.

‡On disabled list, May 3 to May 18, 1982.

§On disabled list, August 10 to August 29, 1984.

RICKEY HENLEY HENDERSON

Born December 25, 1958, at Chicago, Ill.
Height, 5.10. Weight, 195.
Throws left and bats righthanded.

Established modern major league record for most stolen bases, season (130), 1982.

Established major league record for most times caught stealing, season (42), 1982.

Established American League records for most home runs as leadoff batter, season (7), 1985; most consecutive years, 50 or more stolen bases (6).

Tied American League record for most stolen bases, two consecutive games (7), July 3, 4, 1983.

Major League stolen bases: 1979 (33), 1980 (100), 1981 (56), 1982 (130), 1983 (108), 1984 (66), 1985 (80). Total—573.

Led American League in bases on balls received with 116 in 1982 and 103 in 1983.

Led American League in stolen bases with 100 in 1980, 56 in 1981, 130 in 1982, 108 in 1983, 66 in 1984 and 80 in 1985.

Led American League in caught stealing with 26 in 1980, 22 in 1981, 42 in 1982 and 19 in 1983.

Led American League outfielders in total chances with 341 in 1981.

Led Eastern League in stolen bases with 81 and caught stealing with 28 in 1978.

Led California League in stolen bases with 95 and caught stealing with 22 in 1977.

Led Eastern League outfielders in double plays with 4 in 1978.

Won THE SPORTING NEWS Golden Shoe Award, 1983.

Won THE SPORTING NEWS Silver Shoe Award, 1982.

Named outfielder on THE SPORTING NEWS American League All-Star Team, 1981 and 1985.

Named outfielder on THE SPORTING NEWS American League All-Star fielding team, 1981.

Named outfielder on THE SPORTING NEWS American League Silver Slugger team, 1981 and 1985.

Year Club	League	Pos.	G.	AB.	R.	H.	2B.	3B.	HR.	RBI.	B.A.	PO.	A.	E.	F.A.
1976—Boise	N'west.	OF	46	140	34	47	13	2	3	23	.336	99	3	⋆12	.895
1977—Modesto	Calif.	OF	134	481	120	166	18	4	11	69	.345	278	15	⋆20	.936
1978—Jersey City	East.	OF	133	455	81	141	14	4	0	34	.310	305	•15	7	.979
1979—Ogden	P. C.	OF	71	259	66	80	11	8	3	26	.309	149	6	6	.963
1979—Oakland	Amer.	OF	89	351	49	96	13	3	1	26	.274	215	5	6	.973
1980—Oakland	Amer.	OF	158	591	111	179	22	4	9	53	.303	407	15	7	.984
1981—Oakland	Amer.	OF	108	423	⋆89	⋆135	18	7	6	35	.319	⋆327	7	7	.979
1982—Oakland	Amer.	OF	149	536	119	143	24	4	10	51	.267	379	2	9	.977
1983—Oakland	Amer.	OF	145	513	105	150	25	7	9	48	.292	349	9	3	.992
1984—Oakland†	Amer.	OF	142	502	113	147	27	4	16	58	.293	341	7	11	.969
1985—Fort Lauderdale‡	Fla. St.	OF	3	6	5	1	0	1	0	3	.167	6	0	0	1.000
1985—New York	Amer.	OF	143	547	⋆146	172	28	5	24	72	.314	439	7	9	.980
Major League Totals—7 Years			934	3463	732	1022	157	34	75	343	.295	2457	52	52	.980

Selected by Oakland A's organization in 4th round of free-agent draft, June 8, 1976.

†Traded with Pitcher Bert Bradley and cash to New York Yankees for Outfielder Stan Javier and Pitchers Jay Howell, Jose Rijo, Eric Plunk and Tim Birtsas, December 5, 1984.

‡On New York disabled list, March 30 to April 22, 1985; included rehabilitation disability assignment to Fort Lauderdale, April 19 to April 22, 1985.

DIVISION SERIES RECORD

Year Club	League	Pos.	G.	AB.	R.	H.	2B.	3B.	HR.	RBI.	B.A.	PO.	A.	E.	F.A.
1981—Oakland	Amer.	OF	3	11	3	2	0	0	0	0	.182	8	0	0	1.000

CHAMPIONSHIP SERIES RECORD

Tied American League Championship Series record for most stolen bases, three-game Series (2), 1981.

Year Club	League	Pos.	G.	AB.	R.	H.	2B.	3B.	HR.	RBI.	B.A.	PO.	A.	E.	F.A.
1981—Oakland	Amer.	OF	3	11	0	4	2	1	0	1	.364	6	0	1	.857

ALL-STAR GAME RECORD

Tied All-Star Game record for most one-base hits, game (3), July 13, 1982.

Year League	Pos.	AB.	R.	H.	2B.	3B.	HR.	RBI.	B.A.	PO.	A.	E.	F.A.
1980—American	OF	1	0	0	0	0	0	0	.000	0	0	0	.000
1982—American	OF	4	1	3	0	0	0	0	.750	3	0	1	.750
1983—American	OF	1	0	0	0	0	0	1	.000	0	0	0	.000
1984—American	OF	2	0	0	0	0	0	0	.000	0	0	0	.000
1985—American	OF	3	1	1	0	0	0	0	.333	1	0	0	1.000
All-Star Game Totals—5 Years		11	2	4	0	0	0	1	.364	4	0	1	.800

STEPHEN CURTIS HENDERSON
(Steve)

Born November 18, 1952, at Houston, Tex.
Height, 6.01. Weight, 185.
Throws and bats righthanded.
Attended Prairie View A & M University, Prairie View, Tex.

Major League stolen bases: 1977 (6), 1978 (13), 1979 (13), 1980 (23), 1981 (5), 1982 (6), 1983 (10), 1984 (2). Total—78.
Led National League in grounding into double plays with 24 in 1978.
Led Eastern League in total bases with 255 and caught stealing with 17 in 1976.

Year	Club	League	Pos.	G.	AB.	R.	H.	2B.	3B.	HR.	RBI.	B.A.	PO.	A.	E.	F.A.
1974—Billings		Pion.	OF	72	249	★60	72	19	5	●8	●44	.289	114	6	6	★.952
1975—Tampa		Fla. St.	OF-SS	123	413	59	115	9	★16	0	54	.278	263	7	8	.971
1976—Three Rivers		East.	OF	134	506	90	●158	24	★11	17	61	.312	260	12	8	.971
1977—Indianapolis†		A. A.	OF	60	233	35	76	12	6	7	25	.326	107	3	3	.973
1977—New York		Nat.	OF	99	350	67	104	16	6	12	65	.297	189	4	4	.980
1978—New York		Nat.	OF	157	587	83	156	30	9	10	65	.266	315	18	11	.968
1979—New York‡		Nat.	OF	98	350	42	107	16	8	5	39	.306	201	6	2	.990
1980—New York§		Nat.	OF	143	513	75	149	17	8	8	58	.290	299	7	6	.981
1981—Chicago x		Nat.	OF	82	287	32	84	9	5	5	35	.293	152	4	★8	.951
1982—Chicago y		Nat.	OF	92	257	23	60	12	4	2	29	.233	126	5	6	.956
1983—Seattle z		Amer.	OF	121	436	50	128	32	3	10	54	.294	182	15	6	.970
1984—Seattle ab		Amer.	OF	109	325	42	85	12	3	10	35	.262	84	4	6	.936
1985—Oakland		Amer.	OF	85	193	25	58	8	3	3	31	.301	79	3	4	.953
National League Totals—6 Years				671	2344	322	660	100	40	42	291	.282	1282	44	37	.973
American League Totals—3 Years				315	954	117	271	52	9	23	120	.284	345	22	16	.958
Major League Totals—9 Years				986	3298	439	931	152	49	65	411	.282	1627	66	53	.970

Selected by Cincinnati Reds' organization in 5th round of free-agent draft, June 5, 1974.
†Traded with Infielder Doug Flynn, Outfielder Dan Norman and Pitcher Pat Zachry to New York Mets for Pitcher Tom Seaver, June 15, 1977.
‡On disabled list, July 31 to September 17, 1979.
§Traded with cash to Chicago Cubs for Outfielder Dave Kingman, February 28, 1981.
xOn disabled list, May 29 to August 11, 1981.
yTraded to Seattle Mariners for Pitcher Rich Bordi, December 9, 1982.
zGranted free agency, November 7, 1983; re-signed by Mariners, January 26, 1984.
aOn disabled list, June 10 to June 25, 1984.
bGranted free agency, November 8, 1984; signed by Oakland A's, March 31, 1985.

GEORGE ANDREW HENDRICK JR.

Born October 18, 1949, at Los Angeles, Calif.
Height, 6.03. Weight, 195.
Throws and bats righthanded.
Attended East Los Angeles Junior College, Los Angeles, Calif.

Major League stolen bases: 1972 (3), 1973 (7), 1974 (6), 1975 (6), 1976 (4), 1977 (11), 1978 (2), 1979 (2), 1980 (6), 1981 (4), 1982 (3), 1983 (3), 1985 (1). Total—58.
Hit three home runs in a game, June 19, 1973.
Led National League in sacrifice flies with 14 in 1982.
Led American League outfielders in double plays with 6 in 1976.
Tied for National League lead in double plays by outfielders with 7 in 1979.
Named first baseman on THE SPORTING NEWS National League All-Star Team, 1983.
Named outfielder on THE SPORTING NEWS National League All-Star Team, 1980.
Named first baseman on THE SPORTING NEWS National League Silver Slugger team, 1983.
Named outfielder on THE SPORTING NEWS National League Silver Slugger team, 1980.

Year	Club	League	Pos.	G.	AB.	R.	H.	2B.	3B.	HR.	RBI.	B.A.	PO.	A.	E.	F.A.
1968—Burlington		Midw.	OF	103	364	58	119	●25	4	5	60	★.327	134	8	8	.947
1969—Lodi		Calif.	OF	86	316	47	97	13	2	4	28	.307	121	5	4	.969
1970—Burlington		Midw.	OF	54	198	37	61	9	3	12	43	.308	80	1	5	.942
1970—Birmingham		South.	OF	54	199	30	57	12	0	6	20	.286	115	4	5	.960
1971—Iowa		A. A.	OF	63	249	57	83	9	2	21	63	.333	113	5	3	.975
1971—Oakland		Amer.	OF	42	114	8	27	4	1	0	8	.237	52	1	1	.981
1972—Iowa		A. A.	OF	8	33	0	9	0	0	0	4	.273	14	2	0	1.000
1972—Oakland†		Amer.	OF	58	121	10	22	1	1	4	15	.182	68	0	0	1.000
1973—Cleveland‡		Amer.	OF	113	440	64	118	18	0	21	61	.268	242	7	3	.988
1974—Cleveland		Amer.	OF	139	495	65	138	23	1	19	67	.279	355	9	4	.989
1975—Cleveland		Amer.	OF	145	561	82	145	21	2	24	86	.258	338	4	6	.983
1976—Cleveland§		Amer.	OF	149	551	72	146	20	3	25	81	.265	288	13	4	.987
1977—San Diego		Nat.	OF	152	541	75	168	25	2	23	81	.311	386	11	7	.983
1978—S.D. x-St.L.		Nat.	OF	138	493	64	137	31	1	20	75	.278	313	6	2	.994
1979—St. Louis		Nat.	OF	140	493	67	148	27	1	16	75	.300	254	★20	2	.993
1980—St. Louis		Nat.	OF	150	572	73	173	33	2	25	109	.302	322	10	2	.994
1981—St. Louis		Nat.	OF	101	394	67	112	19	3	18	61	.284	227	6	4	.983
1982—St. Louis		Nat.	OF	136	515	65	145	20	5	19	104	.282	238	6	5	.980
1983—St. Louis		Nat.	1B-OF	144	529	73	168	33	3	18	97	.318	904	79	8	.992
1984—St. Louis y		Nat.	OF-1B	120	441	57	122	28	1	9	69	.277	189	9	2	.990
1985—Pittsburgh z		Nat.	OF	69	256	23	59	15	0	2	25	.230	133	2	4	.971
1985—California		Amer.	OF	16	41	5	5	1	0	2	6	.122	18	1	0	1.000
American League Totals—7 Years				662	2323	306	601	88	8	95	324	.259	1361	35	18	.987
National League Totals—9 Years				1150	4234	564	1232	231	18	150	696	.291	2966	149	36	.989
Major League Totals—15 Years				1812	6557	870	1833	319	26	245	1020	.280	4327	184	54	.988

Selected by Oakland A's organization in 1st round (first player selected) of free-agent draft, January 27, 1968.
†Traded with Catcher Dave Duncan to Cleveland Indians for Catcher Ray Fosse and Infielder Jack Heidemann, March 24, 1973.
‡On disabled list, August 14 to September 29, 1973.
§Traded to San Diego Padres for Outfielder John Grubb, Catcher Fred Kendall and Shortstop Hector Torres, December 8, 1976.
xTraded to St. Louis Cardinals for Pitcher Eric Rasmussen, May 26, 1978.
yTraded with Catcher Steve Barnard to Pittsburgh Pirates for Pitcher John Tudor and Outfielder Brian Harper, December 12, 1984.
zTraded with Pitchers John Candelaria and Al Holland to California Angels for Pitcher Pat Clements, Outfielder Mike Brown and a player to be named later, August 2, 1985; Pittsburgh Pirates' organization acquired Pitcher Bob Kipper to complete deal, August 16, 1985.

CHAMPIONSHIP SERIES RECORD

Year Club	League	Pos.	G.	AB.	R.	H.	2B.	3B.	HR.	RBI.	B.A.	PO.	A.	E.	F.A.
1972—Oakland	Amer.	PH-OF	5	7	2	1	0	0	0	0	.143	1	0	0	1.000
1982—St. Louis	Nat.	OF	3	13	2	4	0	0	0	2	.308	5	0	0	1.000
Championship Series Totals—2 Years			8	20	4	5	0	0	0	2	.250	6	0	0	1.000

WORLD SERIES RECORD

Tied World Series record for most times awarded first base on catcher's interference, game (1), October 15, 1982.

Year Club	League	Pos.	G.	AB.	R.	H.	2B.	3B.	HR.	RBI.	B.A.	PO.	A.	E.	F.A.
1972—Oakland	Amer.	OF	5	15	3	2	0	0	0	0	.133	12	0	0	1.000
1982—St. Louis	Nat.	OF	7	28	5	9	0	0	0	5	.321	10	1	0	1.000
World Series Totals—2 Years			12	43	8	11	0	0	0	5	.256	22	1	0	1.000

ALL-STAR GAME RECORD

Year League	Pos.	AB.	R.	H.	2B.	3B.	HR.	RBI.	B.A.	PO.	A.	E.	F.A.
1974—American	OF	2	1	1	0	0	0	0	.500	3	0	0	1.000
1975—American	PR-OF	1	1	1	0	0	0	0	1.000	0	0	0	.000
1980—National	OF	2	0	1	0	0	0	1	.500	0	0	0	.000
All-Star Game Totals—3 Years		5	1	3	0	0	0	1	.600	3	0	0	1.000

Member of National League All-Star Team in 1983; did not play.

DAVID LEE HENGEL
(Dave)

Born December 18, 1961, at Oakland, Calif.
Height, 6.00. Weight, 185.
Throws and bats righthanded.
Attended University of California, Berkeley, Calif.

Led Midwest League in slugging percentage with .565 in 1984.

Year Club	League	Pos.	G.	AB.	R.	H.	2B.	3B.	HR.	RBI.	B.A.	PO.	A.	E.	F.A.
1983—Bellingham	N'west	OF	9	27	4	9	4	0	0	6	.333	10	0	0	1.000
1984—Wausau	Midw.	OF	120	441	68	136	31	2	26	98	.308	109	9	9	.929
1985—Chattanooga	South.	OF	122	460	71	132	30	5	17	89	.287	277	14	6	.980
1985—Calgary	P. C.	OF	6	23	1	2	1	0	0	3	.087	13	0	0	1.000

Selected by San Francisco Giants' organization in 6th round of free-agent draft, June 3, 1980.
Selected by Seattle Mariners' organization in 3rd round of free-agent draft, June 6, 1983.

THOMAS ANTHONY HENKE
Name pronounced HEN-key.
(Tom)

Born December 21, 1957, at Kansas City, Mo.
Height, 6.05. Weight, 215.
Throws and bats righthanded.
Attended East Central College, Union, Mo.

Major League saves: 1983 (1), 1984 (2), 1985 (13). Total—16.
Tied for International League lead in saves with 18 in 1985.
Named International League Pitcher of the Year, 1985.

Year Club	League	G.	IP.	W.	L.	Pct.	H.	R.	ER.	SO.	BB.	ERA.
1980—Sarasota Rangers	Gulf Coast	8	38	3	3	.500	33	11	4	34	12	0.95
1980—Asheville	S. Atlantic	5	23	0	2	.000	25	21	20	19	20	7.83
1981—Asheville	S. Atlantic	28	92	8	6	.571	77	36	30	67	35	2.93
1981—Tulsa	Texas	15	32	4	3	.571	31	16	14	37	14	3.94
1982—Tulsa	Texas	★52	87⅔	3	6	.333	69	35	26	100	40	2.67
1982—Texas	American	8	15⅔	1	0	1.000	14	2	2	9	8	1.15
1983—Oklahoma City	Am. Assoc.	47	77⅔	9	6	.600	71	33	26	90	33	3.01
1983—Texas	American	8	16	1	0	1.000	16	6	6	17	4	3.38
1984—Texas	American	25	28⅓	1	1	.500	36	21	20	25	20	6.35
1984—Oklahoma City†	Am. Assoc.	39	64⅔	6	2	.750	59	21	19	65	25	2.64
1985—Syracuse	Int'national	39	51⅓	2	1	.667	13	5	5	60	18	0.88
1985—Toronto	American	28	40	3	3	.500	29	12	9	42	8	2.03
Major League Totals—4 Years		69	100	6	4	.600	95	41	37	93	40	3.33

Selected by Seattle Mariners' organization in 20th round of free-agent draft, June 5, 1979.
Selected by Chicago Cubs' organization in secondary phase of free-agent draft, January 8, 1980.

Selected by Texas Rangers' organization in secondary phase of free-agent draft, June 3, 1980.

†Selected by Toronto Blue Jays' organization in player compensation pool draft, January 24, 1985. (Toronto received compensation for Texas Rangers' signing of free agent Designated Hitter Cliff Johnson, a Type A player, December 5, 1984.

CHAMPIONSHIP SERIES RECORD

Tied Championship Series record for most games won, six-game Series (2), 1985.

Year Club	League	G.	IP.	W.	L.	Pct.	H.	R.	ER.	SO.	BB.	ERA.
1985—Toronto	American	3	6⅓	2	0	1.000	5	3	3	4	4	4.26

DWAYNE ALLEN HENRY

Born February 16, 1962, at Elkton, Md.
Height, 6.03. Weight, 205.
Throws and bats righthanded.

Major League saves: 1985 (3).

Year Club	League	G.	IP.	W.	L.	Pct.	H.	R.	ER.	SO.	BB.	ERA.
1980—Sarasota Rangers	Gulf Coast	11	54	5	1	.833	36	23	16	47	28	2.67
1981—Asheville	S. Atlantic	25	134	8	7	.533	120	81	66	86	58	4.43
1982—Burlington†	Midwest	4	18⅔	2	0	1.000	6	0	0	25	6	0.00
1983—Tulsa‡	Texas	9	14	0	0	.000	16	14	9	14	19	5.79
1983—Sarasota Rangers	Gulf Coast	3	9	0	0	.000	10	6	4	11	1	4.00
1984—Tulsa	Texas	33	85	5	8	.385	65	42	32	79	60	3.39
1984—Texas	American	3	4⅓	0	1	.000	5	4	4	2	7	8.31
1985—Tulsa	Texas	34	81⅓	7	6	.538	51	32	24	97	44	2.66
1985—Texas	American	16	21	2	2	.500	16	7	6	20	7	2.57
Major League Totals—2 Years		19	25⅓	2	3	.400	21	11	10	22	14	3.55

Selected by Texas Rangers' organization in 2nd round of free-agent draft, June 3, 1980.
†On disabled list, May 4, 1982 through remainder of season.
‡On disabled list, April 8 to July 9, 1983.

HECTOR HEREDIA (HINOSTROZA)

Born May 20, 1960, at Huata Sonora, Mex.
Height, 6.02. Weight, 185.
Throws and bats righthanded.

Year Club	League	G.	IP.	W.	L.	Pct.	H.	R.	ER.	SO.	BB.	ERA.
1981—Monterrey	Mexican	21	64	2	3	.400	55	31	20	20	32	2.81
1982—Monterrey	Mexican	28	79⅓	0	4	.000	92	45	39	24	35	4.42
1983—Monterrey†	Mexican					Figures unavailable						
1984—Monterrey‡	Mexican	39	66⅔	3	7	.300	56	37	31	41	31	4.18
1985—San Antonio§	Texas	3	4⅔	1	0	1.000	4	1	1	2	0	1.93

Signed as free agent by Monterrey (Mexican League), March 23, 1981.
†Under contract but played for different minor league club in Mexico.
‡Sold to Los Angeles Dodgers, December 5, 1984.
§On disabled list, April 18, 1985 through remainder of season.

GUILLERMO HERNANDEZ (VILLANUEVA)
(Willie)

Born November 14, 1955, at Aguada, Puerto Rico.
Height, 6.02. Weight, 185.
Throws and bats lefthanded.

Tied National League record for most consecutive strikeouts by relief pitcher, game (6), July 3, 1983.
Major League saves: 1977 (4), 1978 (3), 1981 (2), 1982 (10), 1983 (8), 1984 (32), 1985 (31). Total—90.
Led American League in games finished in relief with 68 in 1984.
Led Western Carolinas League pitchers in games started with 26 and complete games with 13 in 1977.
Named American League Most Valuable Player by Baseball Writers' Association of America, 1984.
Named American League Pitcher of the Year by THE SPORTING NEWS, 1984.
Won American League Cy Young Memorial Award, 1984.
Named lefthanded pitcher on THE SPORTING NEWS American League All-Star Team, 1984.
Received reported $25,000 bonus to sign with Philadelphia Phillies, 1974.

Year Club	League	G.	IP.	W.	L.	Pct.	H.	R.	ER.	SO.	BB.	ERA.
1974—Spartanburg	W. Carol.	26	★190	11	11	.500	169	82	58	★179	49	2.75
1975—Reading	Eastern	13	91	8	2	.800	79	32	30	46	25	2.97
1975—Toledo	Int'national	13	80	6	4	.600	86	43	29	46	26	3.26
1976—Oklahoma City†	Am. Assoc.	25	135	8	9	.471	154	82	68	88	30	4.53
1977—Chicago	National	67	110	8	7	.533	94	42	37	78	28	3.03
1978—Chicago	National	54	60	8	2	.800	57	26	25	38	35	3.75
1979—Chicago	National	51	79	4	4	.500	85	50	44	53	39	5.01
1980—Chicago	National	53	108	1	9	.100	115	58	53	75	45	4.42
1981—Iowa	Am. Assoc.	18	74	4	5	.444	84	39	32	41	27	3.89
1981—Chicago	National	12	14	0	0	.000	14	7	6	13	8	3.86
1982—Chicago	National	75	75	4	6	.400	74	26	25	54	24	3.00
1983—Chicago‡-Philadelphia§	National	74	115⅓	9	4	.692	109	47	42	93	32	3.28
1984—Detroit	American	★80	140½	9	3	.750	96	30	30	112	36	1.92
1985—Detroit x	American	74	106⅔	8	10	.444	82	38	32	76	14	2.70
National League Totals—7 Years		386	561⅓	34	32	.515	548	256	232	404	211	3.72
American League Totals—2 Years		154	247	17	13	.567	178	68	62	188	50	2.26
Major League Totals—9 Years		540	808⅓	51	45	.531	726	324	294	592	261	3.27

Signed as free agent by Philadelphia Phillies' organization, September 11, 1973.
†Drafted by Chicago Cubs, December 6, 1976.
‡Traded to Philadelphia Phillies for Pitchers Dick Ruthven and Bill Johnson, May 22, 1983.
§Traded with First Baseman Dave Bergman to Detroit Tigers for Outfielder Glenn Wilson and Catcher-First Baseman John Wockenfuss, March 24, 1984.
xGrounded out on only at-bat.

CHAMPIONSHIP SERIES RECORD

Tied Championship Series record for most games pitched, three-game Series (3), 1984.

Year Club	League	G.	IP.	W.	L.	Pct.	H.	R.	ER.	SO.	BB.	ERA.
1984—Detroit	American	3	4	0	0	.000	3	1	1	3	1	2.25

WORLD SERIES RECORD

Tied World Series record for most saves, five-game Series (2), 1984.

Year Club	League	G.	IP.	W.	L.	Pct.	H.	R.	ER.	SO.	BB.	ERA.
1983—Philadelphia	National	3	4	0	0	.000	0	0	0	4	1	0.00
1984—Detroit	American	3	5⅓	0	0	.000	4	1	1	0	0	1.69
World Series Totals—2 Years		6	9⅓	0	0	.000	4	1	1	4	1	0.96

ALL-STAR GAME RECORD

Year League	IP.	W.	L.	Pct.	H.	R.	ER.	SO.	BB.	ERA.
1984—American	1	0	0	.000	1	1	1	1	0	9.00
1985—American	⅔	0	0	.000	1	0	0	2	1	0.00
All-Star Game Totals—2 Years	1⅔	0	0	.000	2	1	1	3	1	5.40

KEITH HERNANDEZ

Born October 20, 1953, at San Francisco, Calif.
Height, 6.00. Weight, 195.
Throws and bats lefthanded.
Attended College of San Mateo, San Mateo, Calif.
Son of John Hernandez, minor league infielder, 1941 through 1950; and brother of Gary Hernandez,
first baseman-outfielder in St. Louis Cardinals' organization, 1972 through 1975.

Established major league records for most game-winning RBIs, season (24), 1985; most years leading league in double plays by first baseman (6).
Established National League record for most game-winning RBIs, lifetime (94).
Tied National League records for most home runs with bases filled, month (2), September, 1977; fewest errors by first baseman for leader in errors, season (13), 1983.
Major League stolen bases: 1976 (4), 1977 (7), 1978 (13), 1979 (11), 1980 (14), 1981 (12), 1982 (19), 1983 (9), 1984 (2), 1985 (3). Total—94.
Hit for the cycle, July 4, 1985.
Led National League in intentional bases on balls received with 19 in 1982.
Led National League first basemen in putouts with 1,054 in 1981 and 1,586 in 1982.
Led National League first basemen in double plays with 146 in 1977, 145 in 1979, 146 in 1980, 99 in 1981, 147 in 1983 and 127 in 1984.
Led National League first basemen in total chances with 1,643 in 1979, 1,732 in 1982 and 1,578 in 1983.
Led National League in game-winning RBIs with 24 in 1985 and tied for lead with 21 in 1982.
Led Texas League first basemen in double plays with 101 in 1973.
Named National League Player of the Year by THE SPORTING NEWS, 1979.
Named National League co-Most Valuable Player by Baseball Writers' Association of America, 1979.
Named first baseman on THE SPORTING NEWS National League All-Star Team, 1979, 1980, 1984 and 1985.
Named first baseman on THE SPORTING NEWS National League All-Star fielding team, 1978 through 1985.
Named first baseman on THE SPORTING NEWS National League Silver Slugger team, 1980 and 1984.

Year Club	League	Pos.	G.	AB.	R.	H.	2B.	3B.	HR.	RBI.	B.A.	PO.	A.	E.	F.A.
1972—St. Petersburg†	Fla. St.	1B	84	309	38	79	16	5	5	41	.256	682	52	7	.991
1972—Tulsa	A. A.	1B	11	29	5	7	1	0	0	1	.241	54	2	0	1.000
1973—Arkansas	Texas	1B	105	388	62	101	20	2	3	52	.260	960	61	9	*.991
1973—Tulsa	A. A.	1B	31	120	20	40	6	1	5	25	.333	289	15	1	.997
1974—Tulsa‡	A. A.	1B-OF	102	353	67	124	18	6	14	63	*.351	690	50	12	.984
1974—St. Louis	Nat.	1B	14	34	3	10	1	2	0	2	.294	70	1	2	.973
1975—Tulsa	A. A.	●1B-OF	85	324	70	107	29	3	10	48	.330	597	53	●13	.980
1975—St. Louis	Nat.	1B	64	188	20	47	8	2	3	20	.250	469	36	2	.996
1976—St. Louis	Nat.	1B	129	374	54	108	21	5	7	46	.289	862	●107	10	.990
1977—St. Louis	Nat.	1B	161	560	90	163	41	4	15	91	.291	1453	106	12	.992
1978—St. Louis	Nat.	1B	159	542	90	138	32	4	11	64	.255	1436	96	10	.994
1979—St. Louis	Nat.	1B	161	610	*116	210	*48	11	11	105	*.344	*1489	*146	8	.995
1980—St. Louis	Nat.	1B	159	595	*111	191	39	8	16	99	.321	1572	115	9	.995
1981—St. Louis	Nat.	1B-OF	103	376	65	115	27	4	8	48	.306	1054	86	3	.997
1982—St. Louis	Nat.	1B-OF	160	579	79	173	33	6	7	94	.299	1591	135	11	.994
1983—St.L.§-N.Y.	Nat.	1B	150	538	77	160	23	7	12	63	.297	*1418	147	●13	.992
1984—New York	Nat.	1B	154	550	83	171	31	0	15	94	.311	1214	*142	8	.997
1985—New York	Nat.	1B	158	593	87	183	34	4	10	91	.309	1310	*139	4	*.997
Major League Totals—12 Years			1572	5539	875	1669	338	57	115	817	.301	13940	1256	92	.994

Selected by St. Louis Cardinals' organization in 42nd round of free-agent draft, June 8, 1971.
†On disabled list, April 10 to May 30, 1972.
‡On disabled list, April 16 to May 20, 1974.
§Traded to New York Mets for Pitchers Neil Allen and Rick Ownbey, June 15, 1983.

CHAMPIONSHIP SERIES RECORD

Year Club	League	Pos.	G.	AB.	R.	H.	2B.	3B.	HR.	RBI.	B.A.	PO.	A.	E.	F.A.
1982—St. Louis	Nat.	1B	3	12	3	4	0	0	0	1	.333	35	1	0	1.000

Year	Club	League	Pos.	G.	AB.	R.	H.	2B.	3B.	HR.	RBI.	B.A.	PO.	A.	E.	F.A.
1982—St. Louis		Nat.	1B	7	27	4	7	2	0	1	8	.259	62	7	2	.972

ALL-STAR GAME RECORD

Year	League	Pos.	AB.	R.	H.	2B.	3B.	HR.	RBI.	B.A.	PO.	A.	E.	F.A.
1979—National		PH	1	0	0	0	0	0	0	.000	0	0	0	.000
1980—National		PH-1B	2	0	2	0	0	0	0	1.000	5	0	0	1.000
1984—National		1B	1	0	0	0	0	0	0	.000	1	0	0	1.000
All-Star Game Totals—3 Years			4	0	2	0	0	0	0	.500	6	0	0	1.000

LEONARDO JESUS HERNANDEZ
(Leo)

Born November 6, 1959, at Santa Lucia, Estado Miranda, Venezuela.
Height, 5.11. Weight, 170.
Throws and bats righthanded.

Major League stolen bases: 1983 (1).
Led International League in total bases with 237 in 1984.
Tied for Texas League lead in game-winning RBIs with 12 in 1981.
Led International League outfielders in errors with 12 in 1984.

Year	Club	League	Pos.	G.	AB.	R.	H.	2B.	3B.	HR.	RBI.	B.A.	PO.	A.	E.	F.A.
1978—Clinton		Midw.	3B	112	444	65	123	21	4	17	73	.277	86	222	20	*.939
1979—Clinton		Midw.	3B	29	113	24	38	8	1	2	23	.336	22	66	6	.936
1979—Lodi		Calif.	3B	61	257	48	82	12	2	8	52	.319	52	143	29	.871
1979—San Antonio		Texas	3B	36	128	19	32	7	0	2	11	.250	19	51	8	.897
1980—San Antonio		Texas	3B	41	136	27	33	9	2	2	26	.243	23	77	14	.877
1980—Vero Beach		Fla. St.	3B-OF-1B	82	307	53	95	13	3	10	46	.309	99	102	9	.957
1981—San Antonio		Texas	3B	131	497	90	148	34	3	25	91	.298	*107	271	*25	.938
1982—San Antonio†		Texas	3B-1B	19	75	8	24	4	1	3	14	.320	39	35	6	.925
1982—Charlotte		South.	3-1-O-2	68	270	46	78	18	2	20	62	.289	159	104	11	.960
1982—Rochester		Int.	3B-OF-2B	53	202	29	64	10	3	11	43	.317	41	98	6	.959
1982—Baltimore		Amer.	PH	2	2	0	0	0	0	0	0	.000	0	0	0	.000
1983—Baltimore		Amer.	3B	64	203	21	50	6	1	6	26	.246	44	109	13	.922
1983—Rochester		Int.	3B-OF-2B	57	201	24	69	13	2	8	25	.343	57	66	10	.925
1984—Rochester		Int.	OF-3B-1B	136	512	66	141	25	4	21	83	.275	248	42	15	.951
1985—Rochester		Int.	OF-3B-1B	124	475	59	128	31	2	17	69	.269	182	75	10	.963
1985—Baltimore‡		Amer.	1B-OF	12	21	0	1	0	0	0	0	.048	2	0	0	1.000
Major League Totals—3 Years				78	226	21	51	6	1	6	26	.226	46	109	13	.923

Signed as free agent by Los Angeles Dodgers' organization, January 18, 1978.
†Traded to Baltimore Orioles' organization for Catcher-First Baseman Jose Morales, April 28, 1982.
‡Traded to New York Yankees, December 16, 1985, completing deal in which New York traded Pitcher Rich Bordi and Infielder Rex Hudler to Baltimore Orioles for Outfielder Gary Roenicke and a player to be named later, December 12, 1985.

MANUEL ANTONIO HERNANDEZ
(Manny)

Born May 7, 1961, at La Romana, Dominican Republic.
Height, 6.00. Weight, 150.
Throws and bats righthanded.

Tied for Pacific Coast League lead in balks with 5 in 1984.

Year	Club	League	G.	IP.	W.	L.	Pct.	H.	R.	ER.	SO.	BB.	ERA.
1979—Sarasota Astros		Gulf Coast	9	14	2	0	1.000	17	6	4	10	10	2.57
1980—Sarasota Astros Blue		Gulf Coast	11	62	5	2	.714	65	26	21	37	15	3.05
1981—Daytona Beach		Florida St.	13	79	6	5	.545	67	36	30	61	24	3.42
1982—Daytona Beach		Florida St.	21	99⅓	6	6	.500	114	70	55	50	52	4.98
1983—Daytona Beach		Florida St.	18	102⅓	10	3	.769	86	46	34	73	27	2.99
1984—Tucson		P. Coast	28	146⅔	6	9	.400	153	96	80	107	65	4.91
1985—Tucson†		P. Coast	11	37⅔	1	1	.500	35	19	15	25	10	3.58

Signed as free agent by Houston Astros' organization, November 23, 1978.
†On disabled list, May 9 to July 18, 1985.

LARRY LEE HERNDON

Born November 3, 1953, at Sunflower, Miss.
Height, 6.03. Weight, 200.
Throws and bats righthanded.
Attended Tennessee State University, Nashville, Tenn. and Skyline College, San Bruno, Calif.

Tied major league record for most consecutive home runs, two consecutive games (4), May 16 and 18, 1982.
Major League stolen bases: 1976 (12), 1977 (4), 1978 (13), 1979 (8), 1980 (8), 1981 (15), 1982 (12), 1983 (9), 1984 (6), 1985 (2). Total—89.
Hit three home runs in a game, May 18, 1982.
Led Texas League in stolen bases with 50 and caught stealing with 16 in 1974.
Tied for Texas League lead in double plays by outfielders with 4 in 1974.
Named National League Rookie Player of the Year by THE SPORTING NEWS, 1976.

Year Club	League	Pos.	G.	AB.	R.	H.	2B.	3B.	HR.	RBI.	B.A.	PO.	A.	E.	F.A.
1971—Sarasota Cards.....	Gulf C.	OF	40	138	13	33	2	0	0	8	.239	68	4	3	.960
1972—St. Petersburg	Fla. St.	OF	7	28	2	4	0	0	0	0	.143	12	1	2	.867
1972—Sarasota R. B........	Gulf C.	OF	31	113	16	29	5	3	0	9	.257	50	5	3	.948
1972—Cedar Rapids†......	Midw.	OF	7	21	1	6	0	0	0	1	.286	10	0	0	1.000
1973—St. Petersburg	Fla. St.	OF	141	485	83	139	9	5	3	41	.287	233	10	8	.968
1974—Arkansas...............	Texas	OF	132	498	74	142	16	●10	2	41	.285	325	★24	16	.956
1974—St. Louis................	Nat.	OF	12	1	3	1	0	0	0	0	1.000	1	0	0	1.000
1975—Tulsa‡....................	A. A.	OF	22	96	13	23	5	0	1	5	.240	35	2	3	.925
1975—Phoenix.................	P. C.	OF	115	427	49	115	6	4	2	44	.269	287	10	10	.967
1976—Phoenix.................	P. C.	OF	14	57	8	14	2	1	1	5	.246	38	3	0	1.000
1976—San Francisco	Nat.	OF	115	337	42	97	11	3	2	23	.288	226	8	8	.967
1977—San Francisco§x...	Nat.	OF	49	109	13	26	4	3	1	5	.239	87	2	4	.957
1978—San Francisco	Nat.	OF	151	471	52	122	15	9	1	32	.259	369	3	10	.974
1979—San Francisco	Nat.	OF	132	354	35	91	14	5	7	36	.257	196	10	8	.963
1980—San Francisco	Nat.	OF	139	493	54	127	17	11	8	49	.258	247	8	●11	.959
1981—San Francisco y...	Nat.	OF	96	364	48	105	15	8	5	41	.288	207	8	5	.977
1982—Detroit..................	Amer.	OF	157	614	92	179	21	13	23	88	.292	328	11	6	.983
1983—Detroit..................	Amer.	OF	153	603	88	182	28	9	20	92	.302	283	6	★15	.951
1984—Detroit..................	Amer.	OF	125	407	52	114	18	5	7	43	.280	199	7	3	.986
1985—Detroit..................	Amer.	OF	137	442	45	108	12	7	12	37	.244	273	7	7	.976
National League Totals—7 Years			694	2129	247	569	76	39	24	186	.267	1333	39	46	.968
American League Totals—4 Years			572	2066	277	583	79	34	62	260	.282	1083	31	31	.973
Major League Totals—11 Years			1266	4195	524	1152	155	73	86	446	.275	2416	70	77	.970

Selected by St. Louis Cardinals' organization in 3rd round of free-agent draft, June 8, 1971.

†On disabled list, August 11, 1972 through remainder of season.

‡Traded with Pitcher Tony Gonzalez to San Francisco Giants for Pitcher Ron Bryant, May 9, 1975.

§On disabled list, June 19 to August 26, 1977.

xOn disqualified list, August 26, 1977 through remainder of season.

yTraded to Detroit Tigers for Pitchers Dan Schatzeder and Mike Chris, December 9, 1981.

CHAMPIONSHIP SERIES RECORD

Year Club	League	Pos.	G.	AB.	R.	H.	2B.	3B.	HR.	RBI.	B.A.	PO.	A.	E.	F.A.
1984—Detroit...............	Amer.	OF	2	5	1	1	0	0	1	1	.200	6	0	0	1.000

WORLD SERIES RECORD

Year Club	League	Pos.	G.	AB.	R.	H.	2B.	3B.	HR.	RBI.	B.A.	PO.	A.	E.	F.A.
1984—Detroit..................	Amer.	OF-PH	5	15	1	5	0	0	1	3	.333	6	0	0	1.000

THOMAS MITCHELL HERR
(Tom)

Born April 4, 1956, at Lancaster, Pa.
Height, 6.00. Weight, 185.
Throws right and bats left and righthanded.
Attended University of Delaware, Newark, Del.

Major League stolen bases: 1979 (1), 1980 (9), 1981 (23), 1982 (25), 1983 (6), 1984 (13), 1985 (31). Total—108.
Led National League in sacrifice flies with 13 in 1985.
Led National League second basemen in double plays with 74 in 1981 and 106 in 1984.
Led National League second basemen in total chances with 590 in 1981.
Led Florida State League in stolen bases with 50 in 1977.
Led Florida State League second basemen in double plays with 91 in 1977.
Named second baseman on THE SPORTING NEWS National League All-Star Team, 1985.

Year Club	League	Pos.	G.	AB.	R.	H.	2B.	3B.	HR.	RBI.	B.A.	PO.	A.	E.	F.A.
1975—Johnson City	Appal.	2B-SS	42	133	29	41	8	1	0	15	.308	74	125	5	.975
1976—St. Petersburg	Fla. St.	SS-2B	82	275	47	74	6	1	0	21	.269	133	211	18	.950
1977—St. Petersburg	Fla. St.	2B	136	★515	★80	★156	13	7	1	53	.303	★348	★430	21	★.974
1978—Arkansas...............	Texas	2B	89	335	70	98	23	4	3	45	.293	207	280	13	.974
1978—Springfield.............	A. A.	2B	33	86	16	24	6	1	0	8	.279	45	63	7	.939
1979—Springfield.............	A. A.	2B	109	423	74	124	20	6	6	48	.293	225	324	10	★.982
1979—St. Louis................	Nat.	2B	14	10	4	2	0	0	0	1	.200	12	11	0	1.000
1980—Springfield.............	A. A.	2B-3B	37	141	29	44	6	2	1	16	.312	29	52	1	.988
1980—St. Louis................	Nat.	2B-SS	76	222	29	55	12	5	0	15	.248	124	184	7	.978
1981—St. Louis................	Nat.	2B	103	411	50	110	14	9	0	46	.268	211	★374	5	★.992
1982—St. Louis................	Nat.	2B	135	493	83	131	19	4	0	36	.266	263	427	9	.987
1983—St. Louis†...............	Nat.	2B	89	313	43	101	14	4	2	31	.323	178	245	6	.986
1983—Arkansas...............	Texas	2B	3	9	0	4	3	0	0	1	.444	4	9	0	1.000
1984—St. Louis................	Nat.	2B	145	558	67	154	23	2	4	49	.276	328	452	6	.992
1985—St. Louis................	Nat.	2B	159	596	97	180	38	3	8	110	.302	337	448	12	.985
Major League Totals—7 Years			721	2603	373	733	120	27	14	288	.282	1453	2141	45	.988

Signed as free agent by St. Louis Cardinals' organization, August 22, 1974.

†On disabled list, March 25 to April 29 and August 9, 1983 through remainder of season; included rehabilitation disability assignment to Arkansas, April 18 to April 29, 1983.

CHAMPIONSHIP SERIES RECORD

Tied Championship Series record for most consecutive games, one or more runs batted in (4), 1985.

Established National League Championship Series records for most doubles (4) and most long hits (5), six-game Series, 1985.

Tied National League Championship Series record for most bases on balls, six-game Series (5), 1985.

Year	Club	League	Pos.	G.	AB.	R.	H.	2B.	3B.	HR.	RBI.	B.A.	PO.	A.	E.	F.A.
1982—St. Louis		Nat.	2B	3	13	1	3	1	0	0	0	.231	6	10	0	1.000
1985—St. Louis		Nat.	2B	6	21	2	7	4	0	1	6	.333	13	12	0	1.000
Championship Series Totals—2 Years				9	34	3	10	5	0	1	6	.294	19	22	0	1.000

WORLD SERIES RECORD

Established World Series record for most double plays started, second baseman, seven-game Series (5), 1985.
Established World Series record for most runs batted in on sacrifice fly (2), October 16, 1982 (second inning).

Year	Club	League	Pos.	G.	AB.	R.	H.	2B.	3B.	HR.	RBI.	B.A.	PO.	A.	E.	F.A.
1982—St. Louis		Nat.	2B	7	25	2	4	2	0	0	5	.160	11	19	1	.968
1985—St. Louis		Nat.	2B	7	26	2	4	2	0	0	0	.154	11	13	0	1.000
World Series Totals—2 Years				14	51	4	8	4	0	0	5	.157	22	32	1	.982

ALL-STAR GAME RECORD

Year	League	Pos.	AB.	R.	H.	2B.	3B.	HR.	RBI.	B.A.	PO.	A.	E.	F.A.
1985—National		2B	3	1	1	1	0	0	0	.333	0	1	0	1.000

OREL LEONARD HERSHISER IV

Name pronounced Hersh-HYZ-ur.
Born September 16, 1958, at Buffalo, N.Y.
Height, 6.03. Weight, 190.
Throws and bats righthanded.
Attended Bowling Green State University, Bowling Green, O.

Major League saves: 1983 (1), 1984 (2). Total—3.
Tied for National League lead in shutouts with 4 in 1984.
Led Pacific Coast League in intentional bases on balls issued with 8 in 1983.

Year	Club	League	G.	IP.	W.	L.	Pct.	H.	R.	ER.	SO.	BB.	ERA.
1979—Clinton		Midwest	15	43	4	0	1.000	33	15	10	33	17	2.09
1980—San Antonio		Texas	49	109	5	9	.357	120	59	43	75	59	3.55
1981—San Antonio		Texas	42	102	7	6	.538	94	54	53	95	50	4.68
1982—Albuquerque		P. Coast	47	123⅔	9	6	.600	121	73	51	93	63	3.71
1983—Albuquerque		P. Coast	49	134⅓	10	8	.556	132	73	61	95	57	4.09
1983—Los Angeles		National	8	8	0	0	.000	7	6	3	5	6	3.38
1984—Los Angeles		National	45	189⅔	11	8	.579	160	65	56	150	50	2.66
1985—Los Angeles		National	36	239⅔	19	3	★.864	179	72	54	157	68	2.03
Major League Totals—3 Years			89	437⅓	30	11	.732	346	143	113	312	124	2.33

Selected by Los Angeles Dodgers' organization in 17th round of free-agent draft, June 5, 1979.

CHAMPIONSHIP SERIES RECORD

Established National League Championship Series records for most innings pitched (15⅓) and most hits allowed (17), six-game Series, 1985.

Year	Club	League	G.	IP.	W.	L.	Pct.	H.	R.	ER.	SO.	BB.	ERA.
1985—Los Angeles		National	2	15⅓	1	0	1.000	17	6	6	5	6	3.52

JOSEPH THOMAS HESKETH

(Joe)

Born February 15, 1959, at Lackawanna, N.Y.
Height, 6.02. Weight, 170.
Throws and bats lefthanded.
Attended State University of New York, Buffalo, N.Y.

Major League saves: 1984 (1).
Tied for American Association lead in shutouts with 2 in 1983.
Named American Association Pitcher of the Year, 1984.

Year	Club	League	G.	IP.	W.	L.	Pct.	H.	R.	ER.	SO.	BB.	ERA.
1980—West Palm Beach		Florida St.	11	75	8	2	.800	71	30	16	43	32	1.92
1980—Memphis		Southern	3	20	1	0	1.000	20	13	9	20	7	4.05
1981—Memphis†		Southern					(Did Not Play)						
1982—Memphis‡		Southern					(Did Not Play)						
1982—West Palm Beach		Florida St.	8	45⅔	3	2	.600	41	16	14	24	16	2.76
1983—Memphis		Southern	11	74	6	4	.600	82	38	25	22	25	3.04
1983—Wichita		Am. Assoc.	15	88⅓	5	5	.500	98	53	50	41	46	5.09
1984—Indianapolis		Am. Assoc.	22	147⅔	12	3	.800	120	60	50	135	54	3.05
1984—Montreal		National	11	45	2	2	.500	38	12	9	32	15	1.80
1985—Montreal§		National	25	155⅓	10	5	.667	125	52	43	113	45	2.49
Major League Totals—2 Years			36	200⅓	12	7	.632	163	64	52	145	60	2.34

Selected by Montreal Expos' organization in 2nd round of free-agent draft, June 3, 1980.
†On disabled list, April 9, 1981, through remainder of season.
‡On disabled list, April 8 to July 8, 1982.
§On disabled list, August 24, 1985 through remainder of season.

—DID YOU KNOW—

That the National League's opening-day crowd of 52,971 in Cincinnati on April 8, 1985, was the largest in Riverfront Stadium history for a season opener?

TEODORO VALENZUELA HIGUERA (VALENZUELA)

Name pronounced Tea-O-door-RO Val-en-ZWAY-luh Hugh-gare-a.

(Teddy)

Born November 9, 1958, at Las Mochis, Mexico.
Height, 5.10. Weight, 180.
Throws left and bats left and righthanded.

Tied for Mexican League lead in games started by pitchers with 27 and complete games with 18 in 1983.
Named American League Rookie Pitcher of the Year by THE SPORTING NEWS, 1985.

Year Club	League	G.	IP.	W.	L.	Pct.	H.	R.	ER.	SO.	BB.	ERA.
1979—Ciudad Juarez	Mexican	2	1	0	1	.000	4	5	5	1	4	45.00
1980—Ciudad Juarez†	Mexican	19	117	8	3	.727	111	30	24	76	59	1.85
1980—Ciudad Juarez‡	Mexican	8	49	2	5	.286	44	22	20	29	17	3.67
1981—Ciudad Juarez	Mexican	16	36	1	2	.333	45	29	28	19	24	7.00
1982—Ciudad Juarez	Mexican	24	142⅓	9	12	.429	163	77	64	74	53	4.05
1983—Ciudad Juarez§	Mexican	27	*222	●17	8	.680	177	61	50	*165	68	2.03
1984—El Paso	Texas	19	121	8	7	.533	116	57	35	99	43	*2.60
1984—Vancouver	P. Coast	8	40	1	4	.200	49	26	21	29	14	4.73
1985—Milwaukee	American	32	212⅓	15	8	.652	186	105	92	127	63	3.90
Major League Totals—1 Year		32	212⅓	15	8	.652	186	105	92	127	63	3.90

†20-team season.
‡6-team season.
§Sold to Vancouver (Milwaukee Brewers' organization), September 13, 1983.

DONALD EARL HILL

(Donnie)

Born November 20, 1960, at Pomona, Calif.
Height, 5.10. Weight, 160.
Throws right and bats left and righthanded.
Attended Orange Coast College, Costa Mesa, Calif.; and Arizona State University, Tempe, Ariz.

Major League stolen bases: 1983 (1), 1984 (1), 1985 (9). Total—11.
Tied for Eastern League lead in sacrifice flies with 8 in 1982.

Year Club	League	Pos.	G.	AB.	R.	H.	2B.	3B.	HR.	RBI.	B.A.	PO.	A.	E.	F.A.
1981—Modesto	Calif.	SS-2B	46	149	21	29	3	0	6	22	.195	44	84	22	.853
1982—West Haven†	East.	SS-3B	132	405	66	103	21	3	10	59	.254	141	301	29	.938
1983—Tacoma‡	P. C.	SS	93	322	45	101	19	2	14	63	.314	148	256	18	.957
1983—Oakland	Amer.	SS	53	158	20	42	7	0	2	15	.266	87	136	9	.961
1984—Oakland§	Amer.	SS-2B-3B	73	174	21	40	6	0	2	16	.230	102	128	12	.950
1984—Tacoma	P. C.	SS-2B	42	141	28	46	12	3	2	24	.326	71	92	4	.976
1985—Oakland	Amer.	2B	123	393	45	112	13	2	3	48	.285	228	320	15	.973
Major League Totals—3 Years			249	725	86	194	26	2	7	79	.268	417	584	36	.965

Selected by Houston Astros' organization in 5th round of free-agent draft, January 8, 1980.
Selected by San Francisco Giants' organization in secondary phase of free-agent draft, June 3, 1980.
Selected by Oakland A's organization in secondary phase of free-agent draft, June 8, 1981.
†On temporary inactive list, April 13 to April 23, 1982.
‡On disabled list, April 30 to May 10, 1983.
§On disabled list, May 3 to May 18, 1984.

GLENALLEN HILL

(Glen)

Born March 22, 1965, at Santa Cruz, Calif.
Height, 6.02. Weight, 190.
Throws and bats righthanded.

Led Carolina League batters in strikeouts with 211 in 1985.
Led South Atlantic League batters in strikeouts with 150 in 1984.

Year Club	League	Pos.	G.	AB.	R.	H.	2B.	3B.	HR.	RBI.	B.A.	PO.	A.	E.	F.A.
1983—Medicine Hat	Pion.	OF	46	133	34	63	3	4	6	27	.256	63	3	6	.917
1984—Florence	S. Atl.	OF	129	440	75	105	19	5	16	64	.239	281	9	16	.948
1985—Kinston	Carol.	OF	131	466	57	98	13	0	20	56	.210	234	12	13	.950

Selected by Toronto Blue Jays' organization in 9th round of free-agent draft, June 6, 1983.

MARC KEVIN HILL

Born February 18, 1952, at Louisiana, Mo.
Height, 6.03. Weight, 240.
Throws and bats righthanded.

Major League stolen bases: 1978 (1).
Led American Association catchers in double plays with 18 in 1974.
Led Florida State League catchers in total chances with 983 and double plays with 14 in 1972.
Led Gulf Coast League catchers in double plays with 5 in 1970.

Year Club	League	Pos.	G.	AB.	R.	H.	2B.	3B.	HR.	RBI.	B.A.	PO.	A.	E.	F.A.
1970—Sarasota Cards	Gulf C.	C	28	78	6	15	3	0	0	6	.192	176	24	2	.990
1971—Cedar Rapids	Midw.	C	87	272	21	63	9	1	1	27	.232	572	57	8	.987
1972—St. Petersburg	Fla. St.	C	124	421	34	104	12	1	8	65	.247	*876	*92	15	.985
1972—Modesto	Calif.	C-1B	7	24	2	8	2	0	0	4	.333	39	3	0	1.000
1973—Arkansas	Texas	C	122	403	41	97	19	2	9	49	.241	*670	64	8	.989

Year—Club	League	Pos.	G.	AB.	R.	H.	2B.	3B.	HR.	RBI.	B.A.	PO.	A.	E.	F.A.
1973—Tulsa	A. A.	C	9	29	4	12	1	0	3	8	.414	61	5	0	1.000
1973—St. Louis	Nat.	C	1	3	0	0	0	0	0	0	.000	5	0	0	1.000
1974—Tulsa	A. A.	C-1B	96	327	46	91	16	1	14	58	.278	553	61	9	.986
1974—St. Louis†	Nat.	C	10	21	2	5	1	0	0	2	.238	41	5	0	1.000
1975—San Francisco	Nat.	C-3B	72	182	14	39	4	0	5	23	.214	282	27	2	.994
1976—San Francisco‡	Nat.	C-1B	54	131	11	24	5	0	3	15	.183	186	24	1	.995
1977—San Francisco	Nat.	C	108	320	28	80	10	0	9	50	.250	505	57	6	.989
1978—San Francisco	Nat.	C-1B	117	358	20	87	15	1	3	36	.243	592	56	9	.986
1979—San Francisco§	Nat.	C-1B	63	169	20	35	3	0	3	15	.207	285	31	3	.991
1980—San Francisco x	Nat.	C	17	41	1	7	2	0	0	0	.171	61	8	2	.972
1980—Seattle y	Amer.	C	29	70	8	16	2	1	2	9	.229	101	10	1	.991
1981—Chicago	Amer.	C-1B-3B	16	6	0	0	0	0	0	0	.000	11	1	0	1.000
1981—Glens Falls	East.	C	2	7	1	3	0	0	0	3	.429	6	1	0	1.000
1982—Chicago	Amer.	C-1B-3B	53	88	9	23	2	0	3	13	.261	136	16	1	.993
1983—Chicago	Amer.	C-1B	58	133	11	30	6	0	1	11	.226	215	12	2	.991
1984—Chicago	Amer.	C-1B	77	193	15	45	10	1	5	20	.233	315	17	3	.991
1985—Chicago	Amer.	C-3B	40	75	5	10	2	0	0	4	.133	185	13	3	.985
National League Totals—8 Years			442	1225	96	277	40	1	23	141	.226	1957	208	23	.989
American League Totals—6 Years			273	565	48	124	22	2	11	57	.219	963	69	10	.990
Major League Totals—13 Years			715	1790	144	401	62	3	34	198	.224	2920	277	33	.990

Selected by St. Louis Cardinals' organization in 10th round of free-agent draft, June 4, 1970.
†Traded to San Francisco Giants for Pitcher Elias Sosa and Catcher Ken Rudolph, October 14, 1974.
‡On disabled list, August 4, 1976 through remainder of season.
§On disabled list, July 25, 1979 through remainder of season.
xSold on waivers to Seattle Mariners, June 20, 1980.
yGranted free agency, October 28, 1980; signed by Chicago White Sox, February 12, 1981.

GEORGE ADDISON HINSHAW

Born October 23, 1959, at Los Angeles, Calif.
Height, 6.00. Weight, 185.
Throws and bats righthanded.
Attended LaVerne College, LaVerne, Calif.

Major League stolen bases: 1983 (1).
Led California League in total bases with 298 in 1981.

Year—Club	League	Pos.	G.	AB.	R.	H.	2B.	3B.	HR.	RBI.	B.A.	PO.	A.	E.	F.A.
1980—Walla Walla	N'west	OF-SS	63	230	46	66	10	4	3	29	.287	115	66	22	.892
1981—Reno	Calif.	OF-SS	128	510	113	★189	20	7	25	★131	.371	202	18	15	.936
1982—Amarillo	Texas	●OF-3B	129	519	90	154	24	3	18	89	.297	246	17	●17	.939
1982—San Diego	Nat.	OF	6	15	1	4	0	0	0	1	.267	9	1	0	1.000
1983—Las Vegas	P. C.	★3B-OF	133	480	92	136	19	5	16	67	.283	86	249	★41	.891
1983—San Diego	Nat.	3B-2B	7	16	1	7	1	0	0	4	.438	6	5	0	1.000
1984—Las Vegas	P. C.	OF-3B-2B	121	420	57	113	16	4	12	53	.269	164	193	24	.937
1985—Las Vegas†	P. C.	OF	101	337	41	94	13	6	3	49	.279	207	9	11	.952
Major League Totals—2 Years			13	31	2	11	1	0	0	5	.355	15	6	0	1.000

Selected by San Diego Padres' organization in 11th round of free-agent draft, June 3, 1980.
†On disabled list, July 19 to August 8, 1985.

MICHAEL JAY HOCUTT
(Mike)

Born September 11, 1961, at Laporte, Ind.
Height, 6.02. Weight, 200.
Throws right and bats lefthanded.
Attended Iowa State University, Ames, Iowa.

Led Southern League first basemen in double plays with 125 in 1985.

Year—Club	League	Pos.	G.	AB.	R.	H.	2B.	3B.	HR.	RBI.	B.A.	PO.	A.	E.	F.A.
1982—Jamestown	NYP	3B	35	127	28	41	5	3	12	39	.323	25	77	12	.895
1982—W. Palm Beach	Fla. St.	1B-3B	24	77	10	22	2	2	3	15	.286	133	9	6	.959
1983—W. Palm Beach	Fla. St	1B-3B	105	364	41	75	15	2	6	49	.206	404	41	12	.974
1984—W. Palm Beach	Fla. St.	1B-3B	●143	523	70	146	19	4	12	★100	.279	852	122	22	.978
1984—Jacksonville	South.	1B	4	12	1	1	1	0	0	2	.083	8	1	0	1.000
1985—Jacksonville	South.	1B	139	495	85	128	22	8	28	92	.259	1144	104	10	.992

Selected by Cleveland Indians' organization in 16th round of free-agent draft, June 5, 1979.
Selected by Montreal Expos' organization in 28th round of free-agent draft, June 7, 1982.

ED OLIVER HODGE

Born April 19, 1958, at Bellflower, Calif.
Height, 6.02. Weight, 192.
Throws and bats lefthanded.
Attended Cerritos College, Norwalk, Calif.

Year—Club	League	G.	IP.	W.	L.	Pct.	H.	R.	ER.	SO.	BB.	ERA.
1979—Elizabethton	Ap'lachian	14	81	8	4	.667	82	46	39	56	21	4.33
1980—Orlando	Southern	27	186	14	9	.609	188	95	77	90	62	3.73
1981—Toledo	Int'national	29	163	8	★17	.320	173	92	82	84	60	4.53
1982—Toledo	Int'national	5	18	1	3	.250	23	17	17	20	13	8.50
1982—Orlando	Southern	39	79	6	9	.400	91	49	43	77	39	4.90

Year Club	League	G.	IP.	W.	L.	Pct.	H.	R.	ER.	SO.	BB.	ERA.
1983—Toledo	Int'national	28	143	11	6	.647	137	72	63	72	64	3.97
1984—Toledo	Int'national	3	22⅓	2	0	1.000	15	5	5	16	5	2.01
1984—Minnesota	American	25	100	4	3	.571	116	59	53	59	29	4.77
1985—Toledo†	Int'national	29	152	9	7	.563	183	87	76	80	45	4.50
Major League Totals—1 Year		25	100	4	3	.571	116	59	53	59	29	4.77

Selected by Minnesota Twins' organization in 5th round of free-agent draft, January 9, 1979.
†Released, December 20, 1985.

GLENN EDWARD HOFFMAN

Born July 7, 1958, at Orange, Calif.
Height, 6.02. Weight, 190.
Throws and bats righthanded.

Major League stolen bases: 1980 (2), 1983 (1), 1985 (2). Total—5.
Led International League shortstops in double plays with 87 in 1978.
Tied for Florida State League lead in putouts by shortstops with 220 in 1977.

Year Club	League	Pos.	G.	AB.	R.	H.	2B.	3B.	HR.	RBI.	B.A.	PO.	A.	E.	F.A.
1976—Elmira	NYP	SS	60	191	29	52	7	2	3	34	.272	★83	139	17	.925
1977—Winter Haven	Fla. St.	SS-3B-1B	126	425	51	123	17	2	3	61	.289	225	377	36	.944
1977—Pawtucket	Int.	SS	4	9	2	4	1	0	0	2	.444	4	10	1	.933
1978—Pawtucket	Int.	★SS-P	131	411	27	116	17	1	2	48	.282	★211	★391	45	.930
1979—Pawtucket	Int.	3B-SS-P	139	520	70	148	13	3	11	54	.285	172	286	19	.960
1980—Boston	Amer.	3B-SS-2B	114	312	37	89	15	4	4	42	.285	78	202	17	.943
1981—Boston	Amer.	SS-3B	78	242	28	56	10	0	1	20	.231	132	234	15	.961
1982—Boston	Amer.	SS	150	469	53	98	23	2	7	49	.209	246	439	20	.972
1983—Boston	Amer.	SS	143	473	56	123	24	1	4	41	.260	240	417	26	.962
1984—Boston	Amer.	SS-3B-2B	64	74	8	14	4	0	0	4	.189	43	74	5	.959
1985—Boston†	Amer.	SS-3B-2B	96	279	40	77	17	2	6	34	.276	157	232	11	.973
Major League Totals—6 Years			645	1849	222	457	93	9	22	190	.247	896	1598	94	.964

Selected by Boston Red Sox' organization in 2nd round of free-agent draft, June 8, 1976.
†On disabled list, July 25 to August 21, 1985.

PITCHING RECORD

Year Club	League	G.	IP.	W.	L.	Pct.	II.	R.	ER.	SO.	BB.	ERA.
1978—Pawtucket	Int'national	1	⅓	0	0	.000	0	0	0	0	0	0.00
1979—Pawtucket	Int'national	1	1	0	0	.000	1	1	1	0	1	9.00

ALFRED WILLIS HOLLAND
(Al)

Born August 16, 1952, at Roanoke, Va.
Height, 5.11. Weight, 210.
Throws left and bats righthanded.
Received bachelor of science degree in recreation from
North Carolina A&T University, Greensboro, N. C. in 1975.

Major League saves: 1980 (7), 1981 (7), 1982 (5), 1983 (25), 1984 (29), 1985 (5). Total—78.
Led New York-Pennsylvania League in balks with 5 and tied for lead in shutouts with 2 in 1975.
Named National League co-Fireman of the Year by THE SPORTING NEWS, 1983.

Year Club	League	G.	IP.	W.	L.	Pct.	H.	R.	ER.	SO.	BB.	ERA.
1975—Bradenton Pirates	Gulf Coast	5	40	2	2	.500	24	6	5	39	20	1.13
1975—Niagara Falls	NYP	6	49	4	2	.667	44	20	14	50	14	2.57
1976—Salem	Carolina	39	76	4	2	.667	59	32	25	72	45	2.96
1977—Shreveport	Texas	21	36	4	1	.800	23	7	5	25	17	1.25
1977—Columbus	Int'national	27	86	6	4	.600	83	44	34	73	36	3.56
1977—Pittsburgh	National	2	2	0	0	.000	4	2	2	1	0	9.00
1978—Columbus†	Int'national	20	91	8	5	.615	102	59	54	65	34	5.34
1979—Portland‡-Phoenix	P. Coast	29	174	10	10	.500	173	99	87	140	87	4.50
1979—San Francisco	National	3	7	0	0	.000	3	0	0	7	5	0.00
1980—San Francisco	National	54	82	5	3	.625	71	21	16	65	34	1.76
1981—San Francisco	National	47	101	7	5	.583	87	31	27	78	44	2.41
1982—San Francisco§x	National	58	129⅔	7	3	.700	115	56	48	97	40	3.33
1983—Philadelphia y	National	68	91⅔	8	4	.667	63	26	23	100	30	2.26
1984—Philadelphia	National	68	98⅓	5	10	.333	82	38	37	61	30	3.39
1985—Philadelphia z-Pittsburgh a	National	41	62⅔	1	4	.200	53	24	24	48	21	3.45
1985—California b	American	15	24⅓	0	1	.000	17	4	4	14	10	1.48
National League Totals—8 Years		341	574⅓	33	29	.532	478	198	177	457	204	2.77
American League Totals—1 Year		15	24⅓	0	1	.000	17	4	4	14	10	1.48
Major League Totals—8 Years		356	598⅔	33	30	.524	495	202	181	471	214	2.72

Selected by Texas Rangers' organization in 30th round of free-agent draft, June 5, 1974.
Selected by San Diego Padres' organization in secondary phase of free-agent draft, January 9, 1975.
Signed as free agent by Pittsburgh Pirates' organization, June 28, 1975.
†On disabled list, April 14 to May 28 and July 20 to July 31, 1978.
‡Traded with Pitchers Ed Whitson and Fred Breining to San Francisco Giants for Third Basemen Bill Madlock and Lenny Randle and Pitcher Dave Roberts, June 28, 1979.
§On disabled list, May 11 to June 4, 1982.
xTraded with Second Baseman Joe Morgan to Philadelphia Phillies for Pitchers Mike Krukow and Mark Davis and Outfielder Charles Penigar, December 14, 1982.
yOn disabled list, March 31 to April 29, 1983.

zTraded with Pitcher Frankie Griffin to Pittsburgh Pirates for Pitcher Kent Tekulve, April 20, 1985.

aTraded with Pitcher John Candelaria and Outfielder George Hendrick to California Angels for Pitcher Pat Clements, Outfielder Mike Brown and a player to be named later, August 2, 1985; Pittsburgh Pirates' organization acquired Pitcher Bob Kipper to complete deal, August 16, 1985.

bGranted free agency, November 12, 1985.

CHAMPIONSHIP SERIES RECORD

Year Club	League	G.	IP.	W.	L.	Pct.	H.	R.	ER.	SO.	BB.	ERA.
1983—Philadelphia	National	2	3	0	0	.000	1	0	0	3	0	0.00

WORLD SERIES RECORD

Year Club	League	G.	IP.	W.	L.	Pct.	H.	R.	ER.	SO.	BB.	ERA.
1983—Philadelphia	National	2	3⅔	0	0	.000	1	0	0	5	0	0.00

ALL-STAR GAME RECORD

Member of National League All-Star Team in 1984; did not play.

BRIAN JOHN HOLTON

Born November 29, 1959, at McKeesport, Pa.
Height, 6.02. Weight, 190.
Throws and bats righthanded.
Attended Louisburg College, Louisburg, N.C.

Tied for Texas League lead in complete games with 16 in 1980.
Tied for California League lead in shutouts with 3 in 1979.

Year Club	League	G.	IP.	W.	L.	Pct.	H.	R.	ER.	SO.	BB.	ERA.
1978—Clinton†	Midwest	14	79	6	4	.600	94	51	38	54	23	4.33
1979—Lodi	California	10	72	7	0	1.000	47	26	21	72	32	2.63
1979—San Antonio	Texas	13	51	3	5	.375	50	24	21	40	25	3.71
1980—San Antonio	Texas	27	207	●15	10	.600	204	93	79	139	65	3.43
1981—Albuquerque	P. Coast	26	191	16	6	.727	215	94	73	73	51	3.44
1982—Albuquerque	P. Coast	32	161⅓	12	8	.600	191	102	92	76	60	5.13
1983—Albuquerque‡	P. Coast	20	97⅔	7	5	.583	113	76	69	70	50	6.36
1984—Albuquerque §x	P. Coast	12	32	0	0	.000	39	23	20	15	9	5.63
1985—Albuquerque	P. Coast	27	179⅔	9	10	.474	183	83	72	86	40	3.61
1985—Los Angeles	National	3	4	1	1	.500	9	7	4	1	1	9.00
Major League Totals—1 Year		3	4	1	1	.500	9	7	4	1	1	9.00

Selected by Los Angeles Dodgers' organization in 1st round (22nd player selected) of free-agent draft, January 10, 1978.

†On temporary inactive list, June 12 to July 7, 1978.
‡On disabled list, June 28 to July 15, 1983.
§On disabled list, April 7 to July 11, 1984.
xGranted free agency, October 15, 1984; re-signed by Dodgers' organization, October 22, 1984.

FREDERICK WAYNE HONEYCUTT
(Rick)

Born June 29, 1954, at Chattanooga, Tenn.
Height, 5.11. Weight, 190.
Throws and bats lefthanded.
Received bachelor of science degree in health education from
University of Tennessee, Knoxville, Tenn.

Major League saves: 1985 (1).
Tied for New York-Pennsylvania League lead in complete games with 7 in 1976.

Year Club	League	G.	IP.	W.	L.	Pct.	H.	R.	ER.	SO.	BB.	ERA.
1976—Niagara Falls†	NYP	13	★97	5	3	.625	91	36	28	★98	20	2.60
1977—Shreveport‡§	Texas	21	135	10	6	.625	144	53	37	82	42	★2.47
1977—Seattle	American	10	29	0	1	.000	26	16	14	17	11	4.34
1978—Seattle x	American	26	134	5	11	.313	150	81	73	50	49	4.90
1979—Seattle	American	33	194	11	12	.478	201	103	87	83	67	4.04
1980—Seattle y	American	30	203	10	17	.370	221	99	89	79	60	3.95
1981—Texas	American	20	128	11	6	.647	120	49	47	40	17	3.30
1982—Texas	American	30	164	5	17	.227	201	103	96	64	54	5.27
1983—Texas z	American	25	174⅔	14	8	.636	168	59	47	56	37	★2.42
1983—Los Angeles	National	9	39	2	3	.400	46	26	25	18	13	5.77
1984—Los Angeles	National	29	183⅔	10	9	.526	180	72	58	75	51	2.84
1985—Los Angeles	National	31	142	8	12	.400	141	71	54	67	49	3.42
American League Totals—7 Years		174	1026⅔	56	72	.438	1087	510	453	389	295	3.97
National League Totals—3 Years		69	364⅔	20	24	.455	367	169	137	160	113	3.38
Major League Totals—9 Years		243	1391⅓	76	96	.442	1454	679	590	549	408	3.82

Selected by Baltimore Orioles' organization in 14th round of free-agent draft, June 6, 1972.
Selected by Pittsburgh Pirates' organization in 17th round of free-agent draft, June 8, 1976.

†Played two games as first baseman and one game as shortstop.
‡Traded to Seattle Mariners, August 22, 1977, completing deal in which Seattle traded Pitcher Dave Pagan to Pittsburgh Pirates for a player to be named later, July 27, 1977.
§Appeared as shortstop with no chances.
xOn disabled list, May 20 to June 26, 1978.
yTraded with Catcher Larry Cox, Outfielders Willie Horton and Leon Roberts and Shortstop Mario Mendoza to

Texas Rangers for Pitchers Brian Allard, Ken Clay, Steve Finch and Jerry Don Gleaton, Shortstop Rick Auerbach and Outfielder Richie Zisk, December 12, 1980.

zTraded to Los Angeles Dodgers for Pitcher Dave Stewart and a player to be named later, August 19, 1983; Texas Rangers acquired Pitcher Ricky Wright to complete deal, September 16, 1983.

CHAMPIONSHIP SERIES RECORD

Year Club	League	G.	IP.	W.	L.	Pct.	H.	R.	ER.	SO.	BB.	ERA.
1983—Los Angeles	National	2	1⅔	0	0	.000	4	4	4	2	0	21.60
1985—Los Angeles	National	2	1⅓	0	0	.000	4	2	2	1	2	13.50
Championship Series Totals—2 Years		4	3	0	0	.000	8	6	6	3	2	18.00

ALL-STAR GAME RECORD

Year League	IP.	W.	L.	Pct.	H.	R.	ER.	SO.	BB.	ERA.
1983—American	2	0	0	.000	5	2	2	0	0	9.00

Member of American League All-Star Team in 1980; did not play.

BURT CARLTON HOOTON

Born February 7, 1950, at Greenville, Tex.
Height, 6.01. Weight, 210.
Throws and bats righthanded.
Attended University of Texas, Austin, Tex.

Pitched 4-0 no-hit victory against Philadelphia Phillies, April 16, 1972.
Major League saves: 1974 (1), 1977 (1), 1980 (1), 1984 (4). Total—7.
Received reported $50,000 bonus to sign with Chicago Cubs, 1971.
Named righthanded pitcher on THE SPORTING NEWS College Baseball All-America Team, 1969 and 1971.

Year Club	League	G.	IP.	W.	L.	Pct.	H.	R.	ER.	SO.	BB.	ERA.
1971—Tacoma	P. Coast	12	102	7	4	.636	73	26	19	135	19	1.68
1971—Chicago	National	3	21	2	0	1.000	8	5	5	22	10	2.14
1972—Chicago	National	33	218	11	14	.440	201	78	68	132	81	2.81
1973—Chicago	National	42	240	14	17	.452	248	107	98	134	73	3.68
1974—Chicago	National	48	176	7	11	.389	214	112	94	94	51	4.81
1975—Chicago†-Los Angeles	National	34	235	18	9	.667	190	88	80	153	68	3.06
1976—Los Angeles	National	33	227	11	15	.423	203	93	82	116	60	3.25
1977—Los Angeles	National	32	223	12	7	.632	184	74	65	153	60	2.62
1978—Los Angeles	National	32	236	19	10	.655	196	74	71	104	61	2.71
1979—Los Angeles	National	29	212	11	10	.524	191	85	70	129	63	2.97
1980—Los Angeles	National	34	207	14	8	.636	194	90	84	118	64	3.65
1981—Los Angeles	National	23	142	11	6	.647	124	42	36	74	33	2.28
1982—Los Angeles‡	National	21	120⅔	4	7	.364	130	57	54	51	33	4.03
1983—Los Angeles	National	33	160	9	8	.529	156	86	75	87	59	4.22
1984—Los Angeles §	National	54	110	3	6	.333	109	43	42	62	43	3.44
1985—Texas	American	29	124	5	8	.385	149	78	72	62	40	5.23
National League Totals—14 Years		451	2527⅔	146	128	.533	2348	1034	924	1429	759	3.29
American League Totals—1 Year		29	124	5	8	.385	149	78	72	62	40	5.23
Major League Totals—15 Years		480	2651⅔	151	136	.526	2497	1112	996	1491	799	3.38

Selected by New York Mets' organization in 5th round of free-agent draft, June 7, 1968.
Selected by Chicago Cubs' organization in secondary phase of free-agent draft, June 8, 1971.
†Traded to Los Angeles Dodgers for Pitchers Geoff Zahn and Eddie Solomon, May 2, 1975.
‡On disabled list, May 18 to June 8 and June 21 to August 8, 1982.
§Granted free agency, November 8, 1984; signed by Texas Rangers, December 20, 1984.

DIVISION SERIES RECORD

Year Club	League	G.	IP.	W.	L.	Pct.	H.	R.	ER.	SO.	BB.	ERA.
1981—Los Angeles	National	1	7	1	0	1.000	3	1	1	2	3	1.29

CHAMPIONSHIP SERIES RECORD

Tied Championship Series record for most games won, Series (2), 1981; most bases on balls, inning (4), October 7, 1977 (second inning).
Tied National League Championship Series record for most hits allowed, game (10), October 4, 1978.

Year Club	League	G.	IP.	W.	L.	Pct.	H.	R.	ER.	SO.	BB.	ERA.
1977—Los Angeles	National	1	1⅔	0	0	.000	2	3	3	1	4	16.20
1978—Los Angeles	National	1	4½	0	0	.000	10	4	4	5	0	7.71
1981—Los Angeles	National	2	14⅔	2	0	1.000	11	1	0	7	6	0.00
Championship Series Totals—3 Years		4	21	2	0	1.000	23	8	7	13	10	3.00

WORLD SERIES RECORD

Year Club	League	G.	IP.	W.	L.	Pct.	H.	R.	ER.	SO.	BB.	ERA.
1977—Los Angeles	National	2	12	1	1	.500	8	5	5	9	2	3.75
1978—Los Angeles	National	2	8⅓	1	1	.500	13	7	6	6	3	6.48
1981—Los Angeles	National	2	11⅓	1	1	.500	8	3	2	3	9	1.59
World Series Totals—3 Years		6	31⅔	3	3	.500	29	15	13	18	14	3.69

ALL-STAR GAME RECORD

Year League	IP.	W.	L.	Pct.	H.	R.	ER.	SO.	BB.	ERA.
1981—National	1⅔	0	0	.000	5	3	3	1	0	16.20

SAMUEL LEE HORN
(Sam)

Born November 2, 1963, at Fort Thomas, Ky.
Height, 6.05. Weight, 215.
Throws and bats lefthanded.

Led Carolina League in slugging percentage with .538 in 1984.

Year Club	League	Pos.	G.	AB.	R.	H.	2B.	3B.	HR.	RBI.	B.A.	PO.	A.	E.	F.A.
1982—Elmira	NYP	1B	61	213	47	64	13	1	11	48	.300	368	29	11	.973
1983—Winston-Salem†	Carol.	1B	68	217	33	52	9	0	9	29	.240	363	24	10	.975
1984—Winston-Salem	Carol.	1B	127	403	67	126	22	3	21	89	.313	978	★70	★29	.973
1985—New Britain	East.	1B	134	457	64	129	★32	0	11	82	.282	751	63	★23	.973

Selected by Boston Red Sox' organization in 1st round (16th player selected) of free-agent draft, June 7, 1982.
†On disabled list, April 28 to June 23, 1983.

JAMES ROBERT HORNER
(Bob)

Born August 6, 1957, at Junction City, Kan.
Height, 6.01. Weight, 215.
Throws and bats righthanded
Attended Arizona State University, Tempe, Ariz.

Major League stolen bases: 1980 (3), 1981 (2), 1982 (3), 1983 (4), 1985 (1). Total—13.
Named National League Rookie Player of the Year by THE SPORTING NEWS, 1978.
Named National League Rookie of the Year by Baseball Writers' Association of America, 1978.
Named College Player of the Year by THE SPORTING NEWS, 1978.
Received reported $175,000 bonus to sign with Atlanta Braves, 1978.
Named second baseman on THE SPORTING NEWS College Baseball All-America Team, 1977 and 1978.

Year Club	League	Pos.	G.	AB.	R.	H.	2B.	3B.	HR.	RBI.	B.A.	PO.	A.	E.	F.A.
1978—Atlanta	Nat.	3B	89	323	50	86	17	1	23	63	.266	81	199	13	.956
1979—Atlanta†	Nat.	3B-1B	121	487	66	153	15	1	33	98	.314	470	167	22	.967
1980—Atlanta‡	Nat.	3B-1B	124	463	81	124	14	1	35	89	.268	80	253	23	.935
1981—Atlanta	Nat.	3B	79	300	42	83	10	0	15	42	.277	51	129	12	.938
1982—Atlanta	Nat.	3B	140	499	85	130	24	0	32	97	.261	102	217	10	.970
1983—Atlanta§	Nat.	3B-1B	104	386	75	117	25	1	20	68	.303	78	153	10	.959
1984—Atlanta x	Nat.	3B	32	113	15	31	8	0	3	19	.274	21	61	3	.965
1985—Atlanta	Nat.	1B-3B	130	483	61	129	25	3	27	89	.267	917	119	11	.989
Major League Totals—8 Years			819	3054	475	853	138	7	188	565	.279	1800	1298	104	.968

Selected by Oakland A's organization in 15th round of free-agent draft, June 4, 1975.
Selected by Atlanta Braves' organization in 1st round (first player selected) of free-agent draft, June 6, 1978.
†On disabled list, April 11 to April 26, 1979.
‡On disqualified list when refused option to Richmond (International), April 28, 1980; reinstated May 10, 1980.
§On disabled list, August 16, 1983 through remainder of season.
xOn disabled list, April 28 to May 17 and June 4, 1984 through remainder of season.

CHAMPIONSHIP SERIES RECORD

Year Club	League	Pos.	G.	AB.	R.	H.	2B.	3B.	HR.	RBI.	B.A.	PO.	A.	E.	F.A.
1982—Atlanta	Nat.	3B	3	11	0	1	0	0	0	0	.091	2	5	0	1.000

ALL-STAR GAME RECORD

Year League	Pos.	AB.	R.	H.	2B.	3B.	HR.	RBI.	B.A.	PO.	A.	E.	F.A.
1982—National	PH	1	0	0	0	0	0	0	.000	0	0	0	.000

RICKY NEAL HORTON
(Rick)

Born July 30, 1959, at Poughkeepsie, N.Y.
Height, 6.02. Weight, 197.
Throws and bats lefthanded.
Received bachelor of science degree in engineering from
University of Virginia, Charlottesville, Va. in 1982.

Major League saves: 1984 (1), 1985 (1). Total—2.
Led American Association in balks with 7 in 1983.

Year Club	League	G.	IP.	W.	L.	Pct.	H.	R.	ER.	SO.	BB.	ERA.
1980—St. Petersburg	Florida St.	6	25	0	2	.000	29	18	17	13	17	6.12
1980—Gastonia	S. Atlantic	14	42	2	4	.333	30	21	17	30	25	3.64
1981—St. Petersburg	Florida St.	28	100	7	3	.700	101	52	49	66	49	4.41
1982—Arkansas	Texas	16	108⅔	9	6	.600	83	45	38	90	52	3.15
1982—Louisville	Am. Assoc.	8	36⅓	2	3	.400	47	31	27	37	11	6.69
1983—Louisville	Am. Assoc.	30	157	10	6	.625	177	99	84	92	58	4.82
1984—St. Louis	National	37	125⅔	9	4	.692	140	53	48	76	39	3.44
1985—St. Louis	National	49	89⅔	3	2	.600	84	30	29	59	34	2.91
Major League Totals—2 Years		86	215⅓	12	6	.667	224	83	77	135	73	3.22

Selected by San Francisco Giants' organization in 20th round of free-agent draft, June 7, 1977.
Selected by St. Louis Cardinals' organization in 4th round of free-agent draft, June 3, 1980.

CHAMPIONSHIP SERIES RECORD

Year	Club	League	G.	IP.	W.	L.	Pct.	H.	R.	ER.	SO.	BB.	ERA.
1985—St. Louis	National	3	3	0	0	.000	4	4	4	1	2	12.00

WORLD SERIES RECORD

Year	Club	League	G.	IP.	W.	L.	Pct.	H.	R.	ER.	SO.	BB.	ERA.
1985—St. Louis	National	3	4	0	0	.000	4	3	3	5	5	6.75

CHARLES OLIVER HOUGH

Name pronounced Huff.

(Charlie)

Born January 5, 1948, at Honolulu, Hawaii.
Height, 6.02. Weight, 190.
Throws and bats righthanded.

Major League saves: 1970 (2), 1973 (5), 1974 (1), 1975 (4), 1976 (18), 1977 (22), 1978 (7), 1980 (1), 1981 (1). Total—61.
Led American League pitchers in complete games with 17 and tied for lead in games started with 36 in 1984.
Led Pacific Coast League in intentional bases on balls issued with 13 in 1972.
Led Pacific Coast League in saves with 18 in 1970.
Led Texas League in home runs allowed with 17 in 1969.
Named Pacific Coast League Pitcher of the Year, 1972.

Year	Club	League	G.	IP.	W.	L.	Pct.	H.	R.	ER.	SO.	BB.	ERA.
1966—Ogden	Pioneer	21	68	5	●7	.417	82	56	36	68	29	4.76
1967—Santa Barbara	California	20	165	14	4	★.778	129	50	41	138	43	2.24
1967—Albuquerque	Texas	7	36	2	1	.667	57	31	28	25	10	7.00
1968—Albuquerque†	Texas	27	121	6	10	.375	145	72	53	74	26	3.94
1969—Albuquerque	Texas	27	163	10	9	.526	190	87	74	113	42	4.09
1970—Spokane	P. Coast	49	134	12	8	.600	98	43	29	90	44	1.95
1970—Los Angeles	National	8	17	0	0	.000	18	11	10	8	11	5.29
1971—Spokane‡	P. Coast	47	117	10	8	.556	95	56	51	104	52	3.92
1971—Los Angeles	National	4	4	0	0	.000	3	3	2	4	3	4.50
1972—Albuquerque§	P. Coast	58	125	14	5	.737	109	47	33	95	60	2.38
1972—Los Angeles	National	2	3	0	0	.000	2	1	1	4	2	3.00
1973—Los Angeles	National	37	72	4	2	.667	52	24	22	70	45	2.75
1974—Los Angeles	National	49	96	9	4	.692	65	45	40	63	40	3.75
1975—Los Angeles	National	38	61	3	7	.300	43	25	20	34	34	2.95
1976—Los Angeles	National	77	143	12	8	.600	102	43	35	81	77	2.20
1977—Los Angeles	National	70	127	6	12	.333	98	53	47	105	70	3.33
1978—Los Angeles	National	55	93	5	5	.500	69	38	34	66	48	3.29
1979—Los Angeles	National	42	151	7	5	.583	152	88	80	76	66	4.77
1980—Los Angeles x	National	19	32	1	3	.250	37	21	20	25	21	5.63
1980—Texas	American	16	61	2	2	.500	54	30	27	47	37	3.98
1981—Texas	American	21	82	4	1	.800	61	30	27	69	31	2.96
1982—Texas	American	34	228	16	13	.552	217	111	100	128	72	3.95
1983—Texas	American	34	252	15	13	.536	219	96	89	152	95	3.18
1984—Texas	American	36	266	16	14	.533	★260	127	111	164	94	3.76
1985—Texas	American	34	250⅓	14	16	.467	198	102	92	141	83	3.31
National League Totals—11 Years		401	799	47	46	.505	641	352	311	536	417	3.50
American League Totals—6 Years		175	1139⅓	67	59	.532	1009	496	446	701	412	3.52
Major League Totals—16 Years		576	1938⅓	114	105	.521	1650	848	757	1237	829	3.51

Selected by Los Angeles Dodgers' organization in 8th round of free-agent draft, June 9, 1966.
†On temporary inactive list, June 19 to July 1, 1968.
‡On temporary inactive list, July 10 to July 24, 1971.
§On temporary inactive list June 12 to June 15, July 22 to July 24 and August 7 to August 12, 1972.
xSold to Texas Rangers, July 11, 1980.

CHAMPIONSHIP SERIES RECORD

Year	Club	League	G.	IP.	W.	L.	Pct.	H.	R.	ER.	SO.	BB.	ERA.
1974—Los Angeles	National	1	2⅓	0	0	.000	4	2	2	2	0	7.71
1977—Los Angeles	National	1	2	0	0	.000	2	1	1	3	0	4.50
1978—Los Angeles	National	1	2	0	0	.000	1	1	1	1	0	4.50
Championship Series Totals—3 Years		3	6⅓	0	0	.000	7	4	4	6	0	5.68

WORLD SERIES RECORD

Tied World Series record for most wild pitches, inning and game (2), October 15, 1978 (seventh inning).

Year	Club	League	G.	IP.	W.	L.	Pct.	H.	R.	ER.	SO.	BB.	ERA.
1974—Los Angeles	National	1	2	0	0	.000	0	0	0	4	1	0.00
1977—Los Angeles	National	2	5	0	0	.000	3	1	1	5	0	1.80
1978—Los Angeles	National	2	5⅓	0	0	.000	10	5	5	5	2	8.44
World Series Totals—3 Years		5	12⅓	0	0	.000	13	6	6	14	3	4.38

BATTING RECORD

Year	Club	League	Pos.	G.	AB.	R.	H.	2B.	3B.	HR.	RBI.	B.A.	PO.	A.	E.	F.A.
1967—Santa Barbara	Calif.	P-1B	28	72	8	14	2	0	0	4	.194	15	25	2	.953
1968—Albuquerque	Texas	P-1B-3B	56	83	10	21	4	0	0	6	.253	43	25	4	.944
1969—Albuquerque	Texas	P-3B	31	57	10	12	0	0	1	9	.211	10	19	2	.935
1970—Spokane	P. C.	P-OF-1B	49	33	1	6	0	0	1	3	.182	7	28	3	.921
1971—Spokane	P. C.	P-OF	48	36	2	10	0	0	0	3	.278	6	20	1	.963
1972—Albuquerque	P. C.	P-OF	58	34	4	9	1	0	0	5	.265	3	27	0	1.000

PAUL WESLEY HOUSEHOLDER

Born September 4, 1958, at Columbus, O.
Height, 6.00. Weight, 185.
Throws right and bats right and lefthanded.

Major League stolen bases: 1980 (1), 1981 (3), 1982 (17), 1983 (12), 1984 (1), 1985 (1). Total—35.
Led Western Carolinas League batters in strikeouts with 130 in 1977.
Led American Association outfielders in total chances with 332 in 1981.
Led Southern League outfielders in fielding percentage with .989 and double plays with 5 in 1979.
Tied for American Association lead in game-winning RBIs with 11 in 1981.

Year Club	League	Pos.	G.	AB.	R.	H.	2B.	3B.	HR.	RBI.	B.A.	PO.	A.	E.	F.A.
1976—Billings	Pion.	OF-3B	50	149	23	38	3	2	2	19	.255	74	8	6	.932
1977—Shelby	W. Car.	OF	137	500	72	116	15	•9	10	63	.232	278	10	8	.973
1978—Tampa	Fla. St.	OF	123	415	59	103	8	10	10	42	.248	213	8	11	.953
1979—Nashville	South.	OF-3B	142	488	93	138	24	7	20	95	.283	247	18	4	.985
1980—Indianapolis	A. A.	OF-3B	125	464	74	137	26	5	9	50	.295	249	10	8	.970
1980—Cincinnati	Nat.	OF	20	45	3	11	1	1	0	7	.244	16	2	0	1.000
1981—Indianapolis	A. A.	OF	124	453	72	136	19	6	19	77	.300	315	10	7	.979
1981—Cincinnati	Nat.	OF	23	69	12	19	4	0	2	9	.275	32	1	0	1.000
1982—Cincinnati	Nat.	OF	138	417	40	88	11	5	9	34	.211	220	14	2	.992
1983—Cincinnati†	Nat.	OF	123	380	40	97	24	4	6	43	.255	221	5	2	★.991
1984—Cinc.‡-St.L.	Nat.	OF	27	26	4	3	1	0	0	0	.115	9	1	0	1.000
1984—Wichita§	A. A.	OF	118	408	64	101	14	7	18	64	.248	209	9	4	.982
1985 Milwaukee	Amer.	OF	95	299	41	77	15	0	11	34	.258	202	5	3	.986
National League Totals—5 Years			331	937	99	218	41	10	17	93	.233	498	23	4	.992
American League Totals—1 Year			95	299	41	77	15	0	11	34	.258	202	5	3	.986
Major League Totals—6 Years			426	1236	140	295	56	10	28	127	.239	700	28	7	.990

Selected by Cincinnati Reds' organization in 2nd round of free-agent draft, June 8, 1976.

†On disabled list, March 23 to April 26, 1983.

‡Traded to St. Louis Cardinals for a player to be named later, September 9, 1984; Cincinnati Reds acquired Pitcher John Stuper to complete deal, September 10, 1984.

§Traded with Outfielder Jim Adduci to Milwaukee Brewers for Pitchers Rich Buonantony and Jim Koontz and Infielder Ron Koenigsfeld, October 3, 1984.

ARTHUR HENRY HOWE JR.
(Art)

Born December 15, 1946, at Pittsburgh, Pa.
Height, 6.01. Weight, 185.
Throws and bats righthanded.
Received bachelor of science degree in business administration
from University of Wyoming, Laramie, Wyo.

Major League stolen bases: 1975 (1), 1978 (2), 1979 (3), 1980 (1), 1981 (1), 1982 (2). Total—10.
Led International League third basemen in errors with 22 and double plays with 24 in 1972.
Tied for Carolina League lead in putouts by third basemen with 95 in 1971.

Year Club	League	Pos.	G.	AB.	R.	H.	2B.	3B.	HR.	RBI.	B.A.	PO.	A.	E.	F.A.
1971—Salem	Carol.	3B-SS	114	382	77	133	27	7	12	79	★.348	110	221	21	.940
1972—Charleston†	Int.	3B-2B-SS	109	365	68	99	21	3	14	53	.271	105	248	24	.936
1973—Charleston‡	Int.	3B-2B-SS	119	372	50	85	20	1	8	44	.228	141	229	21	.946
1974—Charleston	Int.	3B	60	207	26	70	17	4	8	36	.338	35	90	9	.933
1974—Pittsburgh	Nat.	3B-SS	29	74	10	18	4	1	1	5	.243	11	49	4	.938
1975—Charleston	Int.	3B-2B	11	42	4	15	1	3	0	3	.357	15	23	1	.974
1975—Pittsburgh§	Nat.	3B-SS	63	146	13	25	9	0	1	10	.171	19	89	7	.939
1976—Memphis	Int.	3B-1B	74	259	50	92	21	3	12	59	.355	93	120	14	.934
1976—Houston	Nat.	3B-2B	21	29	0	4	1	0	0	0	.138	17	16	1	.970
1977—Houston	Nat.	2B-3B-SS	125	413	44	109	23	7	8	58	.264	213	333	8	.986
1978—Houston	Nat.	2B-3B-1B	119	420	46	123	33	3	7	55	.293	240	302	13	.977
1979—Houston	Nat.	2B-3B-1B	118	355	32	88	15	2	6	33	.248	188	261	7	.985
1980—Houston	Nat.	1-3-2-S	110	321	34	91	12	5	10	46	.283	598	86	10	.986
1981—Houston	Nat.	3B-1B	103	361	43	107	22	4	3	36	.296	67	206	9	.968
1982—Houston x	Nat.	3B-1B	110	365	29	87	15	1	5	38	.238	344	174	7	.987
1983—Houston yz	Nat.				(Did not play)										
1984—St. Louis	Nat.	3-1-2-S	89	139	17	30	5	0	2	12	.216	71	80	3	.981
1985—St. Louis a	Nat.	1B-3B	4	3	0	0	0	0	0	0	.000	5	1	0	1.000
Major League Totals—12 Years			891	2626	268	682	139	23	43	293	.260	1773	1597	69	.980

Signed as free agent by Pittsburgh Pirates' organization, June, 1971.

†On disabled list, August 17 to September 2, 1972.

‡On disabled list, April 13 to May 6, 1973.

§Traded to Houston Astros, January 6, 1976, completing deal in which Houston traded Second Baseman Tommy Helms to Pittsburgh Pirates for a player to be named later, December 12, 1975.

xOn disabled list, May 12 to June 19, 1982.

yOn disabled list, March 27, 1983 through remainder of season.

zGranted free agency, November 7, 1983; signed by St. Louis Cardinals, March 21, 1984.

aReleased, April 22, 1985; named coach of Texas Rangers, May 22, 1985.

DIVISION SERIES RECORD

Year Club	League	Pos.	G.	AB.	R.	H.	2B.	3B.	HR.	RBI.	B.A.	PO.	A.	E.	F.A.
1981—Houston	Nat.	3B	5	17	1	4	0	0	1	1	.235	6	9	0	1.000

Year	Club	League	Pos.	G.	AB.	R.	H.	2B.	3B.	HR.	RBI.	B.A.	PO.	A.	E.	F.A.
1974—Pittsburgh	....	Nat.	PH	1	1	0	0	0	0	0	0	.000	0	0	0	.000
1980—Houston	....	Nat.	1B-PH	5	15	0	3	1	1	0	2	.200	29	3	0	1.000
Champion Series Totals—2 Years	....			6	16	0	3	1	1	0	2	.188	29	3	0	1.000

STEVEN ROY HOWE
(Steve)

Born March 10, 1958, at Pontiac, Mich.
Height, 5.11. Weight, 190.
Throws and bats lefthanded.
Attended University of Michigan, Ann Arbor, Mich.

Major League saves: 1980 (17), 1981 (8), 1982 (13), 1983 (18), 1985 (3). Total—59.
Named National League Rookie of the Year by Baseball Writers' Association of America, 1980.
Named lefthanded pitcher on THE SPORTING NEWS College Baseball All-America Team, 1979.

Year	Club	League	G.	IP.	W.	L.	Pct.	H.	R.	ER.	SO.	BB.	ERA.
1979—San Antonio	....	Texas	13	95	6	2	.750	78	36	33	57	22	3.13
1980—Los Angeles	....	National	59	85	7	9	.438	83	33	25	39	22	2.65
1981—Los Angeles	....	National	41	54	5	3	.625	51	17	15	32	18	2.50
1982—Los Angeles	....	National	66	99⅓	7	5	.583	87	27	23	49	17	2.08
1983—Los Angeles†‡§	....	National	46	68⅔	4	7	.364	55	15	11	52	12	1.44
1984—Los Angeles	....	National				(Did	not	play)				
1985—Los Angeles xy	....	National	19	22	1	1	.500	30	17	12	11	5	4.91
1985—Minnesota z	....	American	13	19	2	3	.400	28	16	13	10	7	6.16
National League Totals—6 Years	....		231	329	24	25	.490	306	109	86	183	74	2.35
American League Totals—1 Year	....		13	19	2	3	.400	28	16	13	10	7	6.16
Major League Totals—6 Years	....		244	348	26	28	.481	334	125	99	193	81	2.56

Selected by Los Angeles Dodgers' organization in 1st round (16th player selected) of free-agent draft, June 5, 1979.
†On disabled list, May 28 to June 29, 1983.
‡On suspended list, July 16 to July 17 and September 23, 1983 through remainder of season.
§On suspended list, December 15, 1983 through entire 1984 season.
xOn restricted list, July 1 to July 3, 1985.
yReleased, July 3, 1985; signed by Minnesota Twins, August 12, 1985.
zReleased, September 17, 1985.

Year	Club	League	G.	IP.	W.	L.	Pct.	H.	R.	ER.	SO.	BB.	ERA.
1981—Los Angeles	....	National	2	2	0	0	.000	1	0	0	2	0	0.00

Year	Club	League	G.	IP.	W.	L.	Pct.	H.	R.	ER.	SO.	BB.	ERA.
1981—Los Angeles	....	National	2	2	0	0	.000	1	0	0	2	0	0.00

Year	Club	League	G.	IP.	W.	L.	Pct.	H.	R.	ER.	SO.	BB.	ERA.
1981—Los Angeles	....	National	3	7	1	0	1.000	7	3	3	4	1	3.86

Year	League	IP.	W.	L.	Pct.	H.	R.	ER.	SO.	BB.	ERA.
1982—National	....	⅓	0	0	.000	0	0	0	0	0	0.00

JACK ROBERT HOWELL

Born August 18, 1961, at Tucson, Ariz.
Height, 6.00. Weight, 185.
Throws right and bats lefthanded.

Major League stolen bases: 1985 (1).
Led California League third basemen in fielding percentage with .943, assists with 259, double plays with 23 and total chances with 368 in 1984.

Year	Club	League	Pos.	G.	AB.	R.	H.	2B.	3B.	HR.	RBI.	B.A.	PO.	A.	E.	F.A.
1983—Salem	....	N'west	3B-2B	21	76	23	30	2	5	3	12	.395	19	32	11	.823
1984—Redwood	....	Calif.	3B-1B	135	451	62	111	21	5	5	64	.246	96	260	21	.944
1985—Edmonton†	....	P. C.	3B-SS	79	284	55	106	22	3	13	48	.373	67	130	12	.943
1985—California	....	Amer.	3B	43	137	19	27	4	0	5	18	.197	33	75	8	.931
Major League Totals—1 Year	....			43	137	19	27	4	0	5	18	.197	33	75	8	.931

Signed as free agent by California Angels' organization, August 6, 1983.
†On disabled list, June 21 to July 7, 1985.

JAY CANFIELD HOWELL

Born November 26, 1955, at Miami, Fla.
Height, 6.03. Weight, 205.
Throws and bats righthanded.
Attended University of Colorado, Boulder, Colo.

Major League saves: 1984 (7), 1985 (29). Total—36.
Tied for American Association lead in shutouts with 2 in 1982.
Tied for American Association lead in balks with 6 in 1981.

Named American Association Pitcher of the Year, 1982.

Year Club	League	G.	IP.	W.	L.	Pct.	H.	R.	ER.	SO.	BB.	ERA.
1976—Eugene	Northwest	13	73	5	4	.556	65	30	24	79	34	2.96
1977—Tampa	Florida St.	23	158	7	13	.350	141	60	52	99	52	2.96
1978—Nashville	Southern	28	166	9	14	.391	134	70	57	*173	55	3.09
1979—Indianapolis	Am. Assoc.	24	128	10	10	.500	121	82	73	79	84	5.13
1980—Indianapolis	Am. Assoc.	25	98	5	11	.313	95	70	55	73	71	5.05
1980—Cincinnati†	National	5	3	0	0	.000	8	5	5	1	0	15.00
1981—Iowa	Am. Assoc.	23	144	5	10	.333	141	74	60	90	62	3.75
1981—Chicago	National	10	22	2	0	1.000	23	13	12	10	10	4.91
1982—Iowa‡	Am. Assoc.	20	141⅓	13	4	*.765	102	45	37	139	48	*2.36
1982—Columbus	Int'national	5	37⅓	2	1	.667	18	13	10	33	19	2.41
1982—New York	American	6	28	2	3	.400	42	25	24	21	13	7.71
1983—New York§	American	19	82	1	5	.167	89	53	49	61	35	5.38
1984—New York x	American	61	103⅔	9	4	.692	86	33	31	109	34	2.69
1985—Oakland	American	63	98	9	8	.529	98	32	31	68	81	2.85
National League Totals—2 Years		15	25	2	0	1.000	31	18	17	11	10	6.12
American League Totals—4 Years		149	311⅔	21	20	.512	315	143	135	259	113	3.90
Major League Totals—6 Years		164	336⅔	23	20	.535	346	161	152	270	123	4.06

Selected by Cincinnati Reds' organization in 12th round of free-agent draft, June 5, 1973.
Selected by Cincinnati Reds' organization in 31st round of free-agent draft, June 8, 1976.
†Traded to Chicago Cubs for Catcher Mike O'Berry, October 17, 1980.
†Traded to New York Yankees' organization, August 2, 1982, completing deal in which Chicago Cubs acquired Second Baseman Pat Tabler from New York on waivers for two players to be named later, August 19, 1981; New York acquired Pitcher Bill Caudill as partial completion of deal, April 1, 1982.
§On disabled list, August 3, 1983 through remainder of season.
xTraded with Outfielder Stan Javier and Pitchers Jose Rijo, Eric Plunk and Tim Birtsas to Oakland A's for Outfielder Rickey Henderson, Pitcher Bert Bradley and cash, December 5, 1984.

ALL-STAR GAME RECORD
Member of American League All-Star Team in 1985; did not play.

KENNETH HOWELL JR.
(Ken)

Born November 28, 1960, at Detroit, Mich.
Height, 6.03. Weight, 200.
Throws and bats righthanded.
Attended Tuskegee Institute, Tuskegee Institute, Ala.

Major League saves: 1984 (6), 1985 (12). Total—18.
Tied for Texas League lead in games started by pitchers with 27 in 1983.

Year Club	League	G.	IP.	W.	L.	Pct.	H.	R.	ER.	SO.	BB.	ERA.
1982—Vero Beach	Florida St.	11	59⅔	5	4	.556	58	40	28	37	36	4.22
1983—San Antonio	Texas	27	169⅓	8	11	.421	171	98	83	116	101	4.41
1983—Albuquerque	P. Coast	1	3	0	0	.000	4	3	3	1	1	9.00
1984—Albuquerque†	P. Coast	18	72⅓	8	2	.800	79	48	37	58	37	4.60
1984—Los Angeles	National	32	51⅓	5	5	.500	51	21	19	54	9	3.33
1985—Los Angeles	National	56	86	4	7	.364	66	41	36	85	35	3.77
Major League Totals—2 Years		88	137⅓	9	12	.429	117	62	55	139	44	3.60

Selected by Los Angeles Dodgers' organization in 3rd round of free-agent draft, June 7, 1982.
†On disabled list, April 7 to April 17, 1984.

CHAMPIONSHIP SERIES RECORD

Year Club	League	G.	IP.	W.	L.	Pct.	H.	R.	ER.	SO.	BB.	ERA.
1985—Los Angeles	National	1	2	0	0	.000	0	0	0	2	0	0.00

DEWEY LaMARR HOYT
(Known by middle name.)

Born January 1, 1955, at Columbia, S. C.
Height, 6.02. Weight, 244.
Throws and bats righthanded.
Son of Dewey Hoyt, minor league pitcher, 1947 and 1948.

Major League saves: 1981 (10).
Led Midwest League pitchers in games started with 27 and tied for lead in shutouts with 3 in 1978.
Tied for Florida State League lead in balks with 3 in 1974.
Named American League Pitcher of the Year by THE SPORTING NEWS, 1983.
Won American League Cy Young Memorial Award, 1983.
Named righthanded pitcher on THE SPORTING NEWS American League All-Star Team, 1983.

Year Club	League	G.	IP.	W.	L.	Pct.	H.	R.	ER.	SO.	BB.	ERA.
1973—Johnson City	Ap'lachian	12	76	6	6	.500	73	44	33	58	40	3.91
1974—Fort Lauderdale	Florida St.	23	161	13	4	.765	143	66	43	77	60	2.40
1975—Fort Lauderdale†	Florida St.	7	26	2	1	.667	24	14	13	12	8	4.50
1975—West Haven	Eastern	8	44	2	4	.333	45	25	15	22	13	3.07
1976—West Haven‡	Eastern	25	180	15	8	.652	169	66	50	103	46	2.50
1977—Knoxville	Southern	25	132	4	●13	.235	160	70	62	67	35	4.23
1977—Iowa	Am. Assoc.	6	25	1	2	.333	30	20	20	14	9	7.20
1978—Appleton	Midwest	28	189	*18	4	*.818	*187	74	61	115	60	2.90

Year—Club	League	G.	IP.	W.	L.	Pct.	H.	R.	ER.	SO.	BB.	ERA.
1979—Iowa	Am. Assoc.	9	43	1	4	.200	50	29	22	27	24	4.60
1979—Knoxville	Southern	37	82	9	5	.643	80	29	27	60	35	2.96
1979—Chicago	American	2	3	0	0	.000	2	0	0	0	0	0.00
1980—Iowa	Am. Assoc.	18	62	5	2	.714	61	22	20	36	24	2.90
1980—Chicago	American	24	112	9	3	.750	123	66	57	55	41	4.58
1981—Chicago	American	43	91	9	3	.750	80	40	36	60	28	3.56
1982—Chicago	American	39	239⅔	★19	15	.559	248	104	94	124	48	3.53
1983—Chicago	American	36	260⅔	★24	10	.706	236	115	106	148	31	3.66
1984—Chicago§x	American	34	235⅔	13	★18	.419	244	127	117	126	43	4.47
1985—San Diego	National	31	210⅓	16	8	.667	210	85	81	83	20	3.47
American League Totals—6 Years		178	942	74	49	.602	933	452	410	513	191	3.92
National League Totals—1 Year		31	210⅓	16	8	.667	210	85	81	83	20	3.47
Major League Totals—7 Years		209	1152⅓	90	57	.612	1143	537	491	596	211	3.83

Selected by New York Yankees' organization in 5th round of free-agent draft, June 5, 1973.

†On disabled list, April 16 to June 6, 1975.

‡Traded with Outfielder Oscar Gamble, Pitcher Bob Polinsky and cash estimated at $250,000 to Chicago White Sox for Shortstop Bucky Dent, April 5, 1977.

§Appeared in one game as an outfielder with no chances.

xTraded with Pitchers Kevin Kristan and Todd Simmons to San Diego Padres for Pitchers Tim Lollar and Bill Long, Third Baseman Luis Salazar and Shortstop Ozzie Guillen, December 6, 1984.

CHAMPIONSHIP SERIES RECORD

Year—Club	League	G.	IP.	W.	L.	Pct.	H.	R.	ER.	SO.	BB.	ERA.
1983—Chicago	American	1	9	1	0	1.000	5	1	1	4	0	1.00

ALL-STAR GAME RECORD

Year—League	IP.	W.	L.	Pct.	H.	R.	ER.	SO.	BB.	ERA.
1985—National	3	1	0	1.000	2	1	0	0	0	0.00

KENT ALAN HRBEK

Name pronounced HER-beck.

Born May 21, 1960, at Bloomington, Minn.
Height, 6.04. Weight, 229.
Throws right and bats lefthanded.

Major League stolen bases: 1982 (3), 1983 (4), 1984 (1), 1985 (1). Total—9.
Led California League in slugging percentage with .630 and tied for lead in sacrifice flies with 9 in 1981.
Named California League Most Valuable Player, 1981.

Year—Club	League	Pos.	G.	AB.	R.	H.	2B.	3B.	HR.	RBI.	B.A.	PO.	A.	E.	F.A.
1979—Elizabethton†‡	Appal.	1B	17	59	5	12	2	0	1	11	.203	126	11	2	.986
1980—Wisc. Rapids§	Midw.	1B	115	419	74	112	16	0	19	76	.267	1005	81	★20	.982
1981—Visalia	Calif.	1B	121	462	119	175	25	5	27	111	★.379	1034	53	11	★.989
1981—Minnesota	Amer.	1B	24	67	5	16	5	0	1	7	.239	124	4	0	1.000
1982—Minnesota	Amer.	1B	140	532	82	160	21	4	23	92	.301	1174	88	9	.993
1983—Minnesota	Amer.	1B	141	515	75	153	41	5	16	84	.297	1151	89	13	.990
1984—Minnesota	Amer.	1B	149	559	80	174	31	3	27	107	.311	1320	99	14	.990
1985—Minnesota	Amer.	1B	158	593	78	165	31	2	21	93	.278	1339	114	8	.995
Major League Totals—5 Years			612	2266	320	668	129	14	88	383	.295	5108	394	44	.992

Selected by Minnesota Twins' organization in 17th round of free-agent draft, June 6, 1978.

†On Wisconsin Rapids disabled list, April 13 to June 21, 1979.

‡On Elizabethton disabled list, July 22 to September 6, 1979.

§On disabled list, May 27 to June 6, 1980.

ALL-STAR GAME RECORD

Year—League	Pos.	AB.	R.	H.	2B.	3B.	HR.	RBI.	B.A.	PO.	A.	E.	F.A.
1982—American	PH	1	0	0	0	0	0	0	.000	0	0	0	.000

GLENN DEE HUBBARD

Born September 25, 1957, at Hann Air Force Base, Germany.
Height, 5.08, Weight, 169.
Throws and bats righthanded.

Tied major league record for most assists by second baseman, nine-inning game (12), April 14, 1985.
Major League stolen bases: 1978 (2), 1980 (7), 1981 (4), 1982 (4), 1983 (3), 1984 (4), 1985 (4). Total—28.
Led National League in sacrifice hits with 20 in 1982.
Led National League second basemen in total chances with 888 in 1985.
Led National League second basemen in double plays with 111 in 1982 and 127 in 1985.
Led Appalachian League third basemen in fielding percentage with .932 in 1975.
Named second baseman on THE SPORTING NEWS National League All-Star Team, 1983.

Year—Club	League	Pos.	G.	AB.	R.	H.	2B.	3B.	HR.	RBI.	B.A.	PO.	A.	E.	F.A.
1975—Kingsport	Appal.	3B-SS-2B	53	136	31	39	6	4	2	21	.287	44	88	9	.936
1976—Kingsport	Appal.	2B	37	136	29	40	8	0	2	15	.294	96	122	1	.995
1976—Greenwood†	W. Car.	2B	33	126	26	40	8	1	4	21	.317	62	83	6	.960
1977—Greenwood	W. Car.	2B	45	182	39	70	10	1	5	44	.385	114	133	4	.984
1977—Savannah	South.	2B	87	298	49	67	15	2	6	32	.225	209	239	10	.978
1978—Richmond	Int.	2B	80	301	58	101	12	3	14	36	.336	208	243	11	.976
1978—Atlanta‡	Nat.	2B	44	163	15	42	4	0	2	13	.258	102	130	5	.979
1979—Richmond	Int.	3B-2B	34	125	21	42	5	1	2	17	.336	83	109	7	.965

Year Club	League	Pos.	G.	AB.	R.	H.	2B.	3B.	HR.	RBI.	B.A.	PO.	A.	E.	F.A.
1979—Atlanta	Nat.	2B	97	325	34	75	12	0	3	29	.231	193	268	●15	.968
1980—Richmond	Int.	2B	38	143	23	45	11	2	2	25	.315	89	127	4	.982
1980—Atlanta	Nat.	2B	117	431	55	107	21	3	9	43	.248	268	405	15	.978
1981—Atlanta	Nat.	2B	99	361	39	85	13	5	6	33	.235	188	344	5	.991
1982—Atlanta	Nat.	2B	145	532	75	132	25	1	9	59	.248	312	505	14	.983
1983—Atlanta	Nat.	2B	148	517	65	136	24	6	12	70	.263	313	484	12	.985
1984—Atlanta	Nat.	2B	120	397	53	93	27	2	9	43	.234	237	405	8	.988
1985—Atlanta	Nat.	2B	142	439	51	102	21	0	5	39	.232	339	★539	10	.989
Major League Totals—8 Years			912	3165	387	772	147	17	55	329	.244	1952	3080	84	.984

Selected by Atlanta Braves' organization in 20th round of free-agent draft, June 4, 1975.
†On temporary inactive list, May 17 to June 22, 1976.
‡On disabled list, July 22 to August 23, 1978.

CHAMPIONSHIP SERIES RECORD

Year Club	League	Pos.	G.	AB.	R.	H.	2B.	3B.	HR.	RBI.	B.A.	PO.	A.	E.	F.A.
1982—Atlanta	Nat.	2B	3	9	1	2	0	0	0	1	.222	4	11	0	1.000

ALL-STAR GAME RECORD

Year League	Pos.	AB.	R.	H.	2B.	3B.	HR.	RBI.	B.A.	PO.	A.	E.	F.A.
1983—National	2B	1	0	1	0	0	0	0	1.000	0	0	0	.000

REX ALLEN HUDLER

Born September 2, 1960, at Tempe, Ariz.
Height, 6.02. Weight, 180.
Throws and bats righthanded.
Led International League second basemen in double plays with 95 in 1984.

Year Club	League	Pos.	G.	AB.	R.	H.	2B.	3B.	HR.	RBI.	B.A.	PO.	A.	E.	F.A.
1978—Oneonta	NYP	SS	58	221	33	62	5	5	0	24	.281	123	21	22	.906
1979—Fort Lauderdale†	Fla. St.	S-3-2-O	116	414	37	104	14	1	1	25	.251	164	314	45	.914
1980—Fort Lauderdale‡	Fla. St.	3-2-O-1	37	125	14	26	4	0	0	6	.208	55	71	5	.962
1980—Greensboro	S. Atl.	2B	20	75	7	17	3	1	2	9	.227	51	52	5	.954
1981—Fort Lauderdale§	Fla. St.	2-S-3-O	79	259	35	77	11	1	2	26	.297	104	238	19	.947
1982—Nashville	South.	2B-SS-OF	89	299	27	71	14	1	0	24	.237	136	219	20	.947
1982—Fort Lauderdale	Fla. St.	2B	9	32	2	8	1	0	1	6	.250	23	25	2	.960
1983—Fort Lauderdale	Fla. St.	2B-SS	91	345	55	93	15	2	2	50	.270	195	245	15	.967
1983—Columbus	Int.	2B-3B-SS	40	118	17	36	5	0	1	11	.305	55	95	4	.974
1984—Columbus	Int.	2B	114	394	49	115	26	1	1	35	.292	266	348	16	.975
1984—New York	Amer.	2B	9	7	2	1	1	0	0	0	.143	4	7	0	1.000
1985—Columbus	Int.	2-S-O-3-1	106	380	62	95	13	4	3	18	.250	192	234	17	.962
1985—New York x	Amer.	2B-1B-SS	20	51	4	8	0	1	0	1	.157	42	51	2	.979
Major League Totals—2 Years			29	58	6	9	1	1	0	1	.155	46	58	2	.981

Selected by New York Yankees' organization in 1st round (18th player selected) of free-agent draft, June 6, 1978.
†On disabled list, May 18 to May 31, 1979.
‡On disabled list, May 10 to June 15, 1980.
§On disabled list, May 11 to June 11, 1981.
xTraded with Pitcher Rich Bordi to Baltimore Orioles for Outfielder Gary Roenicke and a player to be named later, December 12, 1985; New York Yankees acquired Outfielder Leo Hernandez to complete deal, December 16, 1985.

CHARLES LYNN HUDSON

Born March 16, 1959, at Ennis, Tex.
Height, 6.03. Weight, 185.
Throws right and bats left and righthanded.
Received bachelor of business administration degree in management from
Prairie View A&M University, Prairie View, Tex., in 1981.
Tied for Carolina League lead in shutouts with 3 in 1982.
Tied for Carolina League lead in games started by pitchers with 14 in 1981.
Named Carolina League Pitcher of the Year, 1982.

Year Club	League	G.	IP.	W.	L.	Pct.	H.	R.	ER.	SO.	BB.	ERA.
1981—Helena	Pioneer	14	87	5	5	.500	92	53	37	67	27	3.83
1982—Peninsula	Carolina	27	185	●15	5	.750	143	56	38	147	64	★1.85
1983—Portland	P. Coast	10	64	6	3	.667	48	19	19	51	16	2.67
1983—Philadelphia	National	26	169⅓	8	8	.500	158	73	63	101	53	3.35
1984—Philadelphia†	National	30	173⅔	9	11	.450	181	101	78	94	52	4.04
1985—Philadelphia	National	38	193	8	13	.381	188	92	81	122	74	3.78
Major League Totals—3 Years		94	536	25	32	.439	527	266	222	317	179	3.73

Selected by Philadelphia Phillies' organization in 12th round of free-agent draft, June 8, 1981.
†On disabled list, August 10 to September 1, 1984.

CHAMPIONSHIP SERIES RECORD

Year Club	League	G.	IP.	W.	L.	Pct.	H.	R.	ER.	SO.	BB.	ERA.
1983—Philadelphia	National	1	9	1	0	1.000	4	2	2	9	2	2.00

WORLD SERIES RECORD

Tied World Series records for most games lost, five-game Series (2), 1983; most home runs allowed, five-game Series (4), 1983.

Year Club	League	G.	IP.	W.	L.	Pct.	H.	R.	ER.	SO.	BB.	ERA.
1983—Philadelphia	National	2	8⅓	0	2	.000	9	8	8	6	1	8.64

PHILLIP LEE HUFFMAN
(Phil)

Born January 20, 1958, at Freeport, Tex.
Height, 6.02. Weight, 185.
Throws and bats righthanded.

Year Club	League	G.	IP.	W.	L.	Pct.	H.	R.	ER.	SO.	BB.	ERA.
1977—Great Falls†	Pioneer	10	67	7	3	.700	79	47	39	59	29	5.24
1978—Jersey City	Eastern	5	33	3	0	1.000	27	8	8	10	3	2.18
1978—Vancouver‡	P. Coast	17	123	7	6	.538	145	66	53	46	45	3.88
1978—Syracuse	Int'national	2	11	1	1	.500	14	6	6	7	6	4.91
1979—Toronto	American	31	173	6	★18	.250	220	130	111	56	68	5.77
1980—Syracuse§	Int'national	16	93	3	9	.250	98	45	41	47	35	3.97
1981—Syracuse x	Int'national	27	131	5	9	.357	150	91	80	57	43	5.50
1982—Omaha y	Am. Assoc.	9	38⅓	3	4	.429	42	31	24	13	16	5.63
1982—Jacksonville z	Southern	8	49⅔	3	3	.500	47	24	22	41	22	3.99
1983—Jackson	Texas	17	113⅔	7	8	.467	105	56	49	88	44	3.88
1984—Tidewater a	Int'national	17	45	0	2	.000	51	32	30	42	16	6.00
1984—Charlotte	Southern	11	64⅔	6	1	.857	64	30	26	37	17	3.62
1985—Rochester b	Int'national	23	152	10	10	.500	140	73	59	78	48	3.49
1985—Baltimore	American	2	4⅔	0	0	.000	7	8	8	2	5	15.43
Major League Totals—2 Years		33	177⅔	6	18	.250	227	138	119	58	73	6.03

Selected by San Francisco Giants' organization in 2nd round of free-agent draft, June 7, 1977.

†Traded with Outfielder Gary Thomasson, Catcher Gary Alexander, Pitchers Dave Heaverlo, Alan Wirth and John Johnson, a player to be named later and cash estimated at $390,000 to Oakland A's for Pitcher Vida Blue, March 15, 1978; Oakland acquired Shortstop Mario Guerrero to complete deal, April 7, 1978.

‡Traded with Outfielder-Designated Hitter Willie Horton to Toronto Blue Jays for Designated Hitter Rico Carty, August 15, 1978.

§On disabled list, July 9 to August 8, 1980.

xTraded to Kansas City Royals' organization for Shortstop Rance Mulliniks, March 25, 1982.

yOn disabled list, April 13 to May 9, 1982.

zReleased, April 2, 1983; signed by Jackson (New York Mets' organization), May 24, 1983.

aSold to Charlotte (Baltimore Orioles' organization), July 13, 1984.

bOn Baltimore disabled list, July 10 to July 20, 1985; included rehabilitation disability assignment to Hagerstown, July 10 to July 20, 1985.

MARK LAWRENCE HUISMANN

Born May 11, 1958, at Lincoln, Neb.
Height, 6.03. Weight, 195.
Throws and bats righthanded.
Received bachelor of science degree in business and finance from
Colorado State University, Fort Collins, Colo., in 1980.

Major League saves: 1984 (3).
Led American Association in saves with 33 and games finished in relief with 56 in 1985.
Named American Association Pitcher of the Year, 1985.

Year Club	League	G.	IP.	W.	L.	Pct.	H.	R.	ER.	SO.	BB.	ERA.
1980—Sarasota Royals Blue	Gulf Coast	28	59	1	2	.333	50	20	16	46	14	2.44
1981—Charleston	S. Atlantic	28	44	3	2	.600	36	16	8	42	17	1.64
1981—Fort Myers	Florida St.	14	21	3	1	.750	15	9	8	19	16	3.43
1982—Fort Myers	Florida St.	14	23	3	1	.750	16	1	1	21	4	0.39
1982—Jacksonville	Southern	36	54⅔	4	4	.500	52	18	13	60	15	2.14
1983—Jacksonville	Southern	37	61⅓	6	3	.667	60	25	22	46	25	3.23
1983—Omaha	Am. Assoc.	17	24⅓	0	2	.000	16	7	5	25	9	1.85
1983—Kansas City	American	13	30⅔	2	1	.667	29	20	19	20	17	5.58
1984—Kansas City	American	38	75	3	3	.500	84	38	35	54	21	4.20
1984—Omaha	Am. Assoc.	15	19	2	0	1.000	11	0	0	18	5	0.00
1985—Omaha	Am. Assoc.	★59	89⅓	5	5	.500	70	20	20	70	14	2.01
1985—Kansas City	American	9	18⅔	1	0	1.000	14	4	4	9	3	1.93
Major League Totals—3 Years		60	124⅓	6	4	.600	127	62	58	83	41	4.20

Selected by Chicago Cubs' organization in 23rd round of free-agent draft, June 5, 1979.
Signed as free agent by Kansas City Royals' organization, June 16, 1980.

CHAMPIONSHIP SERIES RECORD

Year Club	League	G.	IP.	W.	L.	Pct.	H.	R.	ER.	SO.	BB.	ERA.
1984—Kansas City	American	1	2⅔	0	0	.000	6	3	2	2	1	6.75

TIMOTHY CRAIG HULETT
Name pronounced HUGH-lit.

(Tim)

Born January 12, 1960, at Springfield, Ill.
Height, 6.00. Weight, 185.
Throws and bats righthanded.
Attended Miami-Dade Community College (North), Miami, Fla.,
and University of South Florida, Tampa, Fla.

Major League stolen bases: 1983 (1), 1984 (1), 1985 (6). Total—8.
Tied for American League lead in errors by third basemen with 23 in 1985.
Led American Association in sacrifice flies with 9 in 1983.

Led American Association second basemen in total chances with 730 in 1983.
Led Eastern League second basemen in putouts with 343, assists with 386, double plays with 95, fielding percentage with .975 and total chances with 748 in 1982.
Led Eastern League second basemen in putouts with 332, assists with 415, double plays with 112 and total chances with 763 in 1981.

Year	Club	League	Pos.	G.	AB.	R.	H.	2B.	3B.	HR.	RBI.	B.A.	PO.	A.	E.	F.A.
1980—Glens Falls	East.		SS	6	23	2	4	0	0	0	0	.174	14	13	2	.931
1980—Iowa	A. A.		3B	3	8	1	2	0	0	0	0	.250	0	6	3	.667
1980—Appleton	Midw.		2B-3B-SS	79	278	49	72	11	1	13	47	.259	162	258	17	.961
1981—Glens Falls	East.		2B-3B	134	437	59	99	27	1	10	55	.227	333	422	16	.979
1982—Glens Falls	East.		2B-SS	•140	★536	★113	145	28	5	22	87	.271	352	398	21	.973
1983—Denver	A. A.		2B	133	477	77	130	19	4	21	88	.273	★286	★424	★20	.973
1983—Chicago	Amer.		2B	6	5	0	1	0	0	0	0	.200	8	6	2	.875
1984—Chicago	Amer.		3B-2B	8	7	1	0	0	0	0	0	.000	4	15	0	1.000
1984—Denver	A. A.		2B-3B-SS	139	475	72	125	32	6	16	80	.263	269	371	28	.958
1985—Chicago	Amer.		3B-2B-OF	141	395	52	106	19	4	5	37	.268	117	256	24	.940
Major League Totals—3 Years				155	407	53	107	19	4	5	37	.263	129	277	26	.940

Selected by Texas Rangers' organization in 39th round of free-agent draft, June 6, 1978.
Selected by Chicago White Sox' organization in secondary phase of free-agent draft, January 8, 1980.

THOMAS HUBERT HUME JR.

Name pronounced Hyoom.

(Tom)

Born March 29, 1953, at Cincinnati, O.
Height, 6.01. Weight, 185.
Throws and bats righthanded.
Attended Manatee Junior College, West Bradenton, Fla.

Major League saves: 1978 (1), 1979 (17), 1980 (25), 1981 (13), 1982 (17), 1983 (9), 1984 (3), 1985 (3). Total—88.
Led National League in games finished in relief with 62 in 1980.
Tied for Eastern League lead in games started by pitchers with 27 in 1973.
Named National League co-Fireman of the Year by THE SPORTING NEWS, 1980.

Year	Club	League	G.	IP.	W.	L.	Pct.	H.	R.	ER.	SO.	BB.	ERA.
1972—Tampa†	Florida St.	23	141	7	11	.389	135	69	54	112	68	3.45
1973—Three Rivers	Eastern	27	170	7	8	.467	186	97	81	103	99	4.29
1974—Three Rivers	Eastern	26	157	7	12	.368	★167	91	77	109	90	4.41
1975—Three Rivers	Eastern	7	45	3	2	.600	43	20	15	19	15	3.00
1975—Indianapolis	Am. Assoc.	17	100	6	6	.500	106	49	45	56	36	4.05
1976—Indianapolis	Am. Assoc.	27	182	9	12	.429	178	91	83	111	62	4.10
1977—Indianapolis	Am. Assoc.	28	106	5	6	.455	99	40	30	76	37	2.55
1977—Cincinnati	National	14	43	3	3	.500	54	36	34	22	17	7.12
1978—Cincinnati	National	42	174	8	11	.421	198	89	80	90	50	4.41
1979—Cincinnati	National	57	163	10	9	.526	162	54	50	80	33	2.76
1980—Cincinnati	National	78	137	9	10	.474	121	44	39	68	38	2.56
1981—Cincinnati	National	51	68	9	4	.692	63	27	26	27	31	3.44
1982—Cincinnati‡	National	46	63⅔	2	6	.250	57	24	22	22	21	3.11
1983—Cincinnati§	National	48	66	3	5	.375	66	40	35	34	41	4.77
1984—Cincinnati	National	54	113⅓	4	13	.235	142	83	71	59	41	5.64
1985—Cincinnati x	National	56	80	3	5	.375	65	33	29	50	35	3.26
Major League Totals—9 Years		446	908	51	66	.436	928	430	386	452	307	3.83

Selected by Los Angeles Dodgers' organization in 35th round of free-agent draft, June 8, 1971.
Selected by Cincinnati Reds' organization in secondary phase of free-agent draft, January 12, 1972.

†Appeared in one game as a second basemen with three putouts and two assists and in one game as a third basemen with one assist.
‡On disabled list, July 27, 1982 through remainder of season.
§On disabled list, May 25 to June 19, 1983.
xTraded with Outfielder Gary Redus to Philadelphia Phillies for Pitchers John Denny and Jeff Gray, December 11, 1985.

CHAMPIONSHIP SERIES RECORD

Year	Club	League	G.	IP.	W.	L.	Pct.	H.	R.	ER.	SO.	BB.	ERA.
1979—Cincinnati	National	3	4	0	1	.000	6	3	3	2	0	6.75

ALL-STAR GAME RECORD

Year	League	IP.	W.	L.	Pct.	H.	R.	ER.	SO.	BB.	ERA.
1982—National		⅓	0	0	.000	0	0	0	0	0	0.00

JAMES RANDALL HUNT

(Randy)

Born January 3, 1960, at Montgomery, Ala.
Height, 6.00. Weight, 185.
Throws and bats righthanded.
Attended Chattahoochee Valley Community College, Phenix City, Ala., and University of Alabama, University, Ala.

Led Florida State League in sacrifice flies with 10 in 1984.
Tied for Midwest League lead in game-winning RBIs with 14 in 1982.
Led New York-Pennsylvania League catchers in double plays with 6 and tied for lead in passed balls with 13 in 1981.

Tied for Midwest League lead in passed balls with 23 in 1982.

Year Club League	Pos.	G.	AB.	R.	H.	2B.	3B.	HR.	RBI.	B.A.	PO.	A.	E.	F.A.
1981—Erie.......................... NYP	C	60	195	43	58	6	2	8	27	.297	345	●46	9	.978
1982—Springfield............ Midw.	C-OF	134	494	72	143	17	3	15	79	.289	557	90	18	.973
1983—Arkansas................ Texas	★C-OF	105	338	36	76	21	2	4	51	.225	543	67	★20	.968
1984—St. Petersburg....... Fla. St.	C-OF-1B	100	336	43	92	15	3	5	59	.274	577	78	17	.975
1984—Arkansas................ Texas	C	27	90	7	20	6	0	0	4	.222	143	8	4	.974
1985—Louis.†-Okla. C...... A. A.	C	63	182	18	49	14	2	1	23	.269	333	38	5	.987
1985—St. Louis.................. Nat.	C	14	19	1	3	0	0	0	1	.158	33	1	0	1.000
Major League Totals—1 Year..................		14	19	1	3	0	0	0	1	.158	33	1	0	1.000

Selected by Detroit Tigers' organization in 5th round of free-agent draft, January 8, 1980.
Selected by New York Yankees' organization in secondary phase of free-agent draft, June 3, 1980.
Selected by St. Louis Cardinals' organization in secondary phase of free-agent draft, June 8, 1981.
†Loaned to Oklahoma City (Texas Rangers' organization), July 28, 1985; returned, September 2, 1985.

DAVID BLAIN HUPPERT
(Dave)

Born April 1, 1957, at Southgate, Calif.
Height, 6.01. Weight, 190.
Throws and bats righthanded.

Led Texas League catchers in total chances with 691 in 1985.
Tied for Florida State League lead in double plays by catchers with 7 in 1978.

Year Club League	Pos.	G.	AB.	R.	H.	2B.	3B.	HR.	RBI.	B.A.	PO.	A.	E.	F.A.
1977—Bluefield................. Appal.	C	51	125	21	29	4	0	6	12	.232	★292	★46	6	.983
1978—Miami.................... Fla. St.	C	47	184	28	42	5	2	2	15	.228	375	56	7	.984
1978—Charlotte†............... South.	C	24	63	9	15	1	0	0	4	.238	104	21	4	.969
1979—Charlotte............... South.	C	102	300	37	67	12	2	5	37	.223	543	73	10	.984
1980—Charlotte............... South.	C	107	319	43	70	15	2	3	23	.219	521	61	★20	.967
1981—Roch.-Toledo .... Int.	C	68	176	22	32	6	1	2	12	.182	374	46	★13	.970
1981—Hagerstown‡ .... Carol.	C	1	2	0	1	0	0	0	0	.500	5	2	0	1.000
1982—Charlotte............... South.	C-1B	83	220	28	49	9	0	4	24	.223	400	70	7	.986
1983—Rochester............. Int.	C	68	155	21	30	7	2	0	11	.194	367	58	9	.979
1983—Baltimore§ .... Amer.	C	2	0	0	0	0	0	0	0	.000	3	0	0	1.000
1984—Vancouver........... P. C.	C	60	150	17	25	3	0	0	7	.167	288	29	8	.975
1985—El Paso.................. Texas	C	96	309	46	70	14	1	5	34	.227	★612	70	9	.987
1985—Milwaukee........... Amer.	C	15	21	1	1	0	0	0	0	.048	45	3	2	.960
1985—Vancouver x........ P. C.	C	9	26	3	8	0	0	0	1	.308	63	8	1	.986
Major League Totals—2 Years...............		17	21	1	1	0	0	0	0	.048	48	3	2	.962

Signed as free agent by Baltimore Orioles' organization, May 22, 1977.
†On disabled list, August 2 to October 11, 1978.
‡Loaned to Toledo (Minnesota Twins' organization), July 26, 1981; returned, August 28, 1981.
§Released, October 28, 1983; signed by Vancouver (Milwaukee Brewers' organization), January 10, 1984.
xReleased, November 22, 1985.

CLINTON MERRICK HURDLE
(Clint)

Born July 30, 1957, at Big Rapids, Mich.
Height, 6.03. Weight, 195.
Throws right and bats lefthanded.

Major League stolen bases: 1978 (1).
Led International League in intentional bases on balls received with 12 and tied for lead in game-winning hits with 14 in 1983.
Led American Association outfielders in double plays with 4 in 1977.
Tied for Gulf Coast League lead in being hit by pitch with 6 in 1975.
Tied for American Association lead in double plays by outfielders with 4 in 1979.
Received reported $50,000 bonus to sign with Kansas City Royals, 1975.

Year Club League	Pos.	G.	AB.	R.	H.	2B.	3B.	HR.	RBI.	B.A.	PO.	A.	E.	F.A.
1975—Sarasota Royals... Gulf C.	OF	49	175	34	48	4	4	1	★31	.274	94	5	2	.980
1976—Waterloo .... Midw.	OF	127	429	89	101	22	5	19	89	.235	179	12	7	.965
1977—Omaha.................. A. A.	OF	129	442	85	145	35	3	16	66	.328	198	★17	6	.973
1977—Kansas City........... Amer.	OF	9	26	5	8	0	0	2	7	.308	17	0	0	1.000
1978—Kansas City......... Amer.	OF-1B-3B	133	417	48	110	25	5	7	56	.264	544	30	12	.980
1979—Omaha.................. A. A.	OF	68	220	30	52	13	0	6	29	.236	124	14	4	.972
1979—Kansas City.......... Amer.	OF-3B	59	171	16	41	10	3	3	30	.240	89	2	3	.968
1980—Kansas City.......... Amer.	OF	130	395	50	116	31	2	10	60	.294	233	8	10	.960
1981—Kansas City†‡....... Amer.	OF	28	76	12	25	3	1	4	15	.329	59	1	0	1.000
1982—Cincinnati .... Nat.	OF	19	34	2	7	1	0	0	1	.206	17	2	1	.950
1982—Indianapolis§x...... A. A.	OF-1B	88	261	38	64	18	0	12	58	.245	113	7	4	.968
1983—Tidewater............. Int.	3B-1B-OF	139	477	82	136	★33	4	22	106	.285	130	149	22	.927
1983—New York .... Nat.	3B-OF	13	33	3	6	2	0	0	2	.182	1	15	4	.800
1984—Tidewater............. Int.	1-C-3-O	128	412	60	100	15	1	21	64	.243	1036	60	9	.992
1985—Tidewater............. Int.	C-OF	43	82	7	16	4	0	3	7	.195	89	7	1	.990
American League Totals—5 Years		359	1085	131	300	69	11	26	168	.276	942	41	25	.975
National League Totals—3 Years		75	149	12	29	7	0	3	10	.195	107	24	6	.956
Major League Totals—8 Years.................		434	1234	143	329	76	11	29	178	.267	1049	65	31	.973

Selected by Kansas City Royals' organization in 1st round (ninth player selected) of free-agent draft, June 4, 1975.
†On disabled list, April 20 to May 30 and August 9 to September 13, 1981.

‡Traded to Cincinnati Reds for Pitcher Scott Brown, December 11, 1981.
§Released, November 15, 1982; invited to Seattle Mariners' spring training, February, 1983.
xReleased, April 4, 1983; signed by New York Mets' organization, April 7, 1983.
yDrafted by St. Louis Cardinals, December 10, 1985.

DIVISION SERIES RECORD

Year Club	League	Pos.	G.	AB.	R.	H.	2B.	3B.	HR.	RBI.	B.A.	PO.	A.	E.	F.A.
1981—Kansas City..........	Amer.	OF	3	11	0	3	0	0	0	0	.273	6	0	0	1.000

CHAMPIONSHIP SERIES RECORD

Year Club	League	Pos.	G.	AB.	R.	H.	2B.	3B.	HR.	RBI.	B.A.	PO.	A.	E.	F.A.
1978—Kansas City..........	Amer.	PH-OF	4	8	1	3	0	1	0	1	.375	6	1	0	1.000
1980—Kansas City..........	Amer.	OF	3	2	0	0	0	0	0	0	.000	1	0	0	1.000
Championship Series Totals—2 Years.....			7	10	1	3	0	1	0	1	.300	7	1	0	1.000

WORLD SERIES RECORD

Year Club	League	Pos.	G.	AB.	R.	H.	2B.	3B.	HR.	RBI.	B.A.	PO.	A.	E.	F.A.
1980—Kansas City..........	Amer.	OF	4	12	1	5	1	0	0	0	.417	8	0	0	1.000

BRUCE VEE HURST

Born March 24, 1958, at St. George, Utah.
Height, 6.03. Weight, 215.
Throws and bats lefthanded.
Attended Dixie College, St. George, Utah.

Led American League in balks with 4 in 1985.

Year Club	League	G.	IP.	W.	L.	Pct.	H.	R.	ER.	SO.	BB.	ERA.
1976—Elmira...............	NYP	9	42	3	2	.600	25	18	14	40	38	3.00
1977—Winter Haven†............	Florida St.	13	91	5	4	.556	77	28	21	69	25	2.08
1978—Bristol‡	Eastern	6	33	1	3	.250	32	15	10	35	17	2.73
1979—Winter Haven............	Florida St.	12	84	8	2	.800	57	22	18	64	20	1.93
1979—Bristol............	Eastern	16	113	9	4	.692	108	56	45	91	49	3.58
1980—Pawtucket............	Int'national	17	105	8	6	.571	101	52	46	54	50	3.94
1980—Boston............	American	12	31	2	2	.500	39	33	31	16	9	9.00
1981—Pawtucket............	Int'national	32	157	12	7	.632	143	68	50	99	71	2.87
1981—Boston............	American	5	23	2	0	1.000	23	11	11	11	12	4.30
1982—Boston............	American	28	117	3	7	.300	161	87	75	53	40	5.77
1983—Boston............	American	33	211⅓	12	12	.500	241	102	96	115	62	4.09
1984—Boston............	American	33	218	12	12	.500	232	106	95	136	88	3.92
1985—Boston............	American	35	229⅓	11	13	.458	243	123	115	189	70	4.51
Major League Totals—6 Years............		146	829⅔	42	46	.477	939	462	423	520	288	4.59

Selected by Boston Red Sox' organization in 1st round (22nd player selected) of free-agent draft, June 8, 1976.
†On disabled list, August 8 to September 14, 1977.
‡On disabled list, May 23 to September 21, 1978.

PETER JOSEPH INCAVIGLIA
(Pete)

Born April 2, 1964, at Pebble Beach, Calif.
Height, 6.01. Weight, 225.
Throws and bats righthanded.
Attended Oklahoma State University, Stillwater, Okla.

Son of Tom Incaviglia, minor league infielder, 1948 through 1950 and 1955; and
brother of Tony Incaviglia, minor league third baseman, 1979 through 1983.

Received reported $175,000 bonus to sign with Texas Rangers.
Named designated hitter on THE SPORTING NEWS College Baseball All-America Team, 1985.

Year Club	League	Pos.	G.	AB.	R.	H.	2B.	3B.	HR.	RBI.	B.A.	PO.	A.	E.	F.A.
		(Has no professional record)													

Selected by San Francisco Giants' organization in 6th round of free-agent draft, June 7, 1982.
Selected by Montreal Expos' organization in 1st round (eighth player selected) of free-agent draft, June 3, 1985.
Traded to Texas Rangers' organization for Pitcher Bob Sebra and Infielder Jim Anderson, November 2, 1985.

DANE CHARLES IORG

Name pronounced Orj.

Born May 11, 1950, at Eureka, Calif.
Height, 6.00. Weight, 180.
Throws right and bats lefthanded.
Attended Brigham Young University, Provo, Utah.
Brother of Garth Iorg, third baseman with Toronto Blue Jays; and
Lee Iorg, outfielder in New York Mets' organization, 1974 through 1977.

Major League stolen bases: 1979 (1), 1980 (1), 1981 (2), 1983 (1). Total—5.
Tied for Northwest League lead in sacrifice flies with 6 in 1971.
Led Eastern League first basemen in double plays with 78 in 1975.
Tied for Northwest League lead in double plays by outfielders with 2 in 1971.
Named Northwest League Most Valuable Player, 1971.
Named outfielder on THE SPORTING NEWS College Baseball All-America Team, 1971.

Year	Club	League	Pos.	G.	AB.	R.	H.	2B.	3B.	HR.	RBI.	B.A.	PO.	A.	E.	F.A.
1971—Walla Walla	N'west	OF	77	275	64	101	●15	6	7	65	★.367	135	10	6	.960
1972—Reading	East.	OF	15	43	2	6	2	0	0	1	.140	18	0	1	.947
1972—Burlington	Carol.	OF-P	92	324	61	104	20	3	8	37	.321	119	5	5	.961
1973—Reading	East.	OF	116	386	64	119	21	6	7	49	.308	149	8	5	.969
1974—Toledo	Int.	★1B-OF	133	444	53	110	19	3	10	59	.248	947	★91	9	.991
1975—Toledo	Int.	1B-3B	13	36	7	7	2	0	0	2	.194	76	2	0	1.000
1975—Reading	East.	1B	97	319	47	88	19	5	6	59	.276	★827	44	9	★.990
1976—Oklahoma City	A. A.	1B-OF-C	120	396	65	129	25	11	11	68	.326	741	68	11	.987
1977—Okla. City-N.O.	A. A.	OF-1B-3B	75	273	47	90	14	4	9	48	.330	246	20	6	.978
1977—Phil.†-St.L.	Nat.	1B-OF	42	62	5	15	2	0	0	6	.242	71	4	2	.974
1978—Springfield	A. A.	1B-OF-3B	89	345	73	128	20	0	24	87	★.371	643	64	12	.983
1978—St. Louis	Nat.	OF	35	85	6	23	4	1	0	4	.271	33	5	0	1.000
1979—St. Louis	Nat.	OF-1B	79	179	12	52	11	1	1	21	.291	121	7	2	.985
1980—St. Louis	Nat.	OF-1B	105	251	33	76	23	1	3	36	.303	133	2	1	.993
1981—St. Louis	Nat.	OF-1B-3B	75	217	23	71	11	2	2	39	.327	125	7	3	.978
1982—St. Louis	Nat.	OF-1B-3B	102	238	17	70	14	1	0	34	.294	177	10	3	.984
1983—St. Louis‡	Nat.	OF-1B	58	116	6	31	9	1	0	11	.267	127	5	3	.978
1983—Louisville	A. A.	1B	3	10	2	2	0	0	0	0	.200	21	0	0	1.000
1984—St. Louis§	Nat.	1B-OF	15	28	3	4	2	0	0	3	.143	35	2	0	1.000
1984—Kansas City	Amer.	1B-OF-3B	78	235	27	60	16	2	5	30	.255	399	22	3	.993
1985—Kansas City xy	Amer.	OF-1B-3B	64	130	7	29	9	1	1	21	.223	55	4	0	1.000
National League Totals—8 Years			511	1176	105	342	76	7	6	154	.291	822	42	14	.984
American League Totals—2 Years			142	365	34	89	25	3	6	51	.244	454	26	3	.994
Major League Totals—9 Years			653	1541	139	431	101	10	12	205	.280	1276	68	17	.988

Selected by Kansas City Royals' organization in 13th round of free-agent draft, June 7, 1968.
Selected by Philadelphia Phillies' organization in secondary phase of free-agent draft, June 8, 1971.
†Traded with Outfielder Rick Bosetti and Pitcher Tom Underwood to St. Louis Cardinals for Outfielder Bake McBride and Pitcher Steve Waterbury, June 15, 1977.
‡On disabled list, July 17 to August 15, 1983; included rehabilitation disability assignment to Louisville, August 11 to August 15, 1983.
§Sold to Kansas City Royals, May 9, 1984.
xOn disabled list, August 25 to September 9, 1985.
yGranted free agency, November 12, 1985.

CHAMPIONSHIP SERIES RECORD

Year	Club	League	Pos.	G.	AB.	R.	H.	2B.	3B.	HR.	RBI.	B.A.	PO.	A.	E.	F.A.
1984—Kansas City	Amer.	PH	2	2	0	1	0	0	0	1	.500	0	0	0	.000
1985—Kansas City	Amer.	PH	4	2	0	1	1	0	0	0	.500	0	0	0	.000
Championship Series Totals—2 Years			6	4	0	2	1	0	0	1	.500	0	0	0	.000

WORLD SERIES RECORD

Tied World Series record for most at-bats, inning (2), October 19, 1982 (sixth inning).

Year	Club	League	Pos.	G.	AB.	R.	H.	2B.	3B.	HR.	RBI.	B.A.	PO.	A.	E.	F.A.
1982—St. Louis	Nat.	DH	5	17	4	9	4	1	0	1	.529	0	0	0	.000
1985—Kansas City	Amer.	PH	2	2	0	1	0	0	0	2	.500	0	0	0	.000
World Series Totals—2 Years			7	19	4	10	4	1	0	3	.526	0	0	0	.000

PITCHING RECORD

Year	Club	League	G.	IP.	W.	L.	Pct.	H.	R.	ER.	SO.	BB.	ERA.
1972—Burlington	Carolina	1	1	0	0	.000	3	3	3	0	1	27.00

GARTH RAY IORG
Name pronounced Orj.

Born October 12, 1954, at Arcata, Calif.
Height, 5.11. Weight, 175.
Throws and bats righthanded.
Attended College of the Redwoods, Eureka, Calif.
Brother of Dane Iorg, first baseman-outfielder with Kansas City Royals; and Lee Iorg, outfielder in New York Mets' organization, 1974 through 1977.

Major League stolen bases: 1980 (2), 1981 (2), 1982 (3), 1983 (7), 1984 (1), 1985 (3). Total—18.
Led Florida State League in sacrifice hits with 20 in 1974.

Year	Club	League	Pos.	G.	AB.	R.	H.	2B.	3B.	HR.	RBI.	B.A.	PO.	A.	E.	F.A.
1973—Johnson City	Appal.	SS-2B	51	169	20	40	3	0	3	13	.237	88	120	20	.912
1974—Fort Lauderdale	Fla. St.	SS-2B-3B	102	325	30	70	11	4	0	38	.215	134	245	28	.931
1975—Fort Lauderdale	Fla. St.	3-2-O-S	50	186	10	47	4	2	0	16	.253	67	78	11	.929
1975—West Haven	East.	3B-SS-2B	76	236	19	59	6	2	0	21	.250	79	202	26	.915
1976—West Haven†	East.	2B	78	273	31	75	17	1	1	24	.275	172	236	18	.958
1977—Charleston‡	Int.	2B-SS	70	262	35	77	8	3	1	34	.294	158	234	18	.956
1978—Syracuse§	Int.	3B-2B-SS	89	324	29	70	16	2	6	25	.216	141	204	11	.969
1978—Toronto	Amer.	2B	19	49	3	8	0	0	0	3	.163	34	51	3	.966
1979—Syracuse	Int.	2-3-S-O	121	430	65	121	23	4	5	39	.281	150	250	20	.952
1980—Syracuse	Int.	2B-3B	32	134	17	40	6	3	1	14	.299	60	99	4	.975
1980—Toronto	Amer.	2-3-O-1-S	80	222	24	55	10	1	2	14	.248	122	155	3	.989
1981—Toronto	Amer.	2-3-S-1	70	215	17	52	11	0	0	10	.242	99	182	12	.959
1982—Toronto	Amer.	3B-2B	129	417	45	119	20	5	1	36	.285	114	236	14	.962
1983—Toronto	Amer.	3B-2B-SS	122	375	40	103	22	5	2	39	.275	106	223	9	.973

— 247 —

Year Club	League	Pos.	G.	AB.	R.	H.	2B.	3B.	HR.	RBI.	B.A.	PO.	A.	E.	F.A.
1984—Toronto	Amer.	3B-2B-SS	121	247	24	56	10	3	1	25	.227	66	117	10	.948
1985—Toronto	Amer.	3B-2B	131	288	33	90	22	1	7	37	.313	71	192	9	.967
Major League Totals—7 Years			672	1813	186	483	95	15	13	164	.266	612	1156	60	.967

Selected by New York Yankees' organization in 8th round of free-agent draft, June 5, 1973.
†Selected by Toronto Blue Jays in American League expansion draft, November 5, 1976.
‡On disabled list, June 29 to September 1, 1977.
§On disabled list, June 18 to June 28, 1978.

CHAMPIONSHIP SERIES RECORD

Year Club	League	Pos.	G.	AB.	R.	H.	2B.	3B.	HR.	RBI.	B.A.	PO.	A.	E.	F.A.
1985—Toronto	Amer.	3B-PH	6	15	1	2	0	0	0	0	.133	5	10	0	1.000

DANNY LYNN JACKSON

Born January 5, 1962, at San Antonio, Tex.
Height, 6.00. Weight, 190.
Throws left and bats righthanded.
Attended University of Oklahoma, Norman, Okla., and
Trinidad State Junior College, Trinidad, Colo.
Brother of Mike Jackson, fourth-round selection of Kansas City Kings in 1983 NBA draft.
Tied for American Association lead in complete games with 10 in 1984.
Tied for American Association lead in shutouts with 2 in 1983 and 3 in 1984.

Year Club	League	G.	IP.	W.	L.	Pct.	H.	R.	ER.	SO.	BB.	ERA.
1982—Charleston	S. Atlantic	13	96⅓	10	1	.909	80	37	28	62	39	2.62
1982—Jacksonville†	Southern	14	98	7	2	.778	78	30	26	74	42	2.39
1983—Omaha	Am. Assoc.	23	136	7	8	.467	126	74	60	93	73	3.97
1983—Kansas City	American	4	19	1	1	.500	26	12	11	9	6	5.21
1984—Kansas City	American	15	76	2	6	.250	84	41	36	40	35	4.26
1984—Omaha	Am. Assoc.	16	110⅓	5	8	.385	91	50	45	82	45	3.67
1985—Kansas City	American	32	208	14	12	.538	209	94	79	114	76	3.42
Major League Totals—3 Years		51	303	17	19	.472	319	147	126	163	117	3.74

Selected by Oakland A's organization in 24th round of free-agent draft, June 3, 1980.
Selected by Kansas City Royals' organization in secondary phase of free-agent draft, January 17, 1982.
†On disabled list, September 8, 1982 through remainder of season.

CHAMPIONSHIP SERIES RECORD

Year Club	League	G.	IP.	W.	L.	Pct.	H.	R.	ER.	SO.	BB.	ERA.
1985—Kansas City	American	2	10	1	0	1.000	10	0	0	7	1	0.00

WORLD SERIES RECORD

Tied World Series record for most consecutive times striking out, Series (5), 1985.

Year Club	League	G.	IP.	W.	L.	Pct.	H.	R.	ER.	SO.	BB.	ERA.
1985—Kansas City	American	2	16	1	1	.500	9	3	3	12	5	1.69

DARRIN JAY JACKSON

Born August 22, 1962, at Los Angeles, Calif.
Height, 6.00. Weight, 175.
Throws and bats righthanded.
Led Gulf Coast League outfielders in total chances with 127 in 1981.
Tied for Texas League lead in double plays with 6 in 1984.

Year Club	League	Pos.	G.	AB.	R.	H.	2B.	3B.	HR.	RBI.	B.A.	PO.	A.	E.	F.A.
1981—Sarasota Cubs	Gulf C.	OF	62	210	29	39	5	0	1	15	.186	*121	5	1	.992
1982—Quad Cities	Midw.	OF	132	529	86	146	23	5	5	48	.276	266	9	8	.972
1983—Salinas	Calif.	OF	129	509	70	126	18	5	6	54	.248	237	15	13	.951
1984—Midland	Texas	OF	132	496	63	134	18	2	15	54	.270	286	*19	8	.974
1985—Iowa	A. A.	OF	10	40	0	7	2	1	0	1	.175	19	0	0	1.000
1985—Pittsfield	East.	OF	91	325	38	82	10	1	3	30	.252	221	5	0	1.000
1985—Chicago	Nat.	OF	5	11	0	1	0	0	0	0	.091	7	0	0	1.000
Major League Totals—1 Year			5	11	0	1	0	0	0	0	.091	7	0	0	1.000

Selected by Chicago Cubs' organization in 2nd round of free-agent draft, June 8, 1981.

REGINALD MARTINEZ JACKSON
(Reggie)

Born May 18, 1946, at Wyncote, Pa.
Height, 6.00. Weight, 206.
Throws and bats lefthanded.
Attended Arizona State University, Tempe, Ariz.

Established major league records for most strikeouts, lifetime (2,385); most strikeouts by lefthanded batter, season (171), 1968; most years, 100 or more strikeouts (17); most consecutive years, 100 or more strikeouts (13).
Tied major league records for most consecutive years leading league in strikeouts (4), 1968 through 1971; most strikeouts, nine-inning game (5), September 27, 1968.
Tied American League records for most times, four or more strikeouts, game, season (5), April 7 (second game)—

April 21—May 18—June 4—September 21 (first game), 1971; most consecutive games, one or more home runs (6), July 18 through 23, 1976; most seasons leading league, errors, outfielder (5), 1968, 1970, 1972, 1975 and 1976; fewest errors, season, for leader in most errors (9), 1972.

Hit three home runs in a game, July 2, 1969.

Hit home runs in all 12 parks, 1975.

Major League stolen bases: 1967 (1), 1968 (14), 1969 (13), 1970 (26), 1971 (16), 1972 (9), 1973 (22), 1974 (25), 1975 (17), 1976 (28), 1977 (17), 1978 (14), 1979 (9), 1980 (1), 1982 (4), 1984 (8), 1985 (1). Total—225.

Led American League batters in strikeouts with 171 in 1968, 142 in 1969, 135 in 1970, 161 in 1971 and 156 in 1982.

Led American League in slugging percentage with .608 in 1969, .531 in 1973 and .502 in 1976.

Led American League in intentional bases on balls received with 20 in 1974 and tied for lead with 20 in 1969.

Led American League in caught stealing with 17 in 1970.

Tied for American League lead in double plays by outfielders with 5 in 1972.

Led Southern League in total bases with 232 in 1967.

Named Major League Player of the Year by THE SPORTING NEWS, 1973.

Named American League Player of the Year by THE SPORTING NEWS, 1973.

Named American League Most Valuable Player by Baseball Writers' Association of America, 1973.

Named outfielder on THE SPORTING NEWS American League All-Star Team, 1969, 1973, 1975, 1976 and 1980.

Named outfielder on THE SPORTING NEWS American League Silver Slugger team, 1982.

Named designated hitter on THE SPORTING NEWS American League Silver Slugger team, 1980.

Named Southern League Player of the Year, 1967.

Named College Player of the Year by THE SPORTING NEWS, 1966.

Received reported $85,000 bonus to sign with Kansas City Athletics, 1966.

Named outfielder on THE SPORTING NEWS College Baseball All-America Team, 1966.

Year	Club	League	Pos.	G.	AB.	R.	H.	2B.	3B.	HR.	RBI.	B.A.	PO.	A.	E.	F.A.
1966—Lewiston	N'west	OF	12	48	14	14	3	2	2	11	.292	23	0	1	.958
1966—Modesto	Calif.	OF	56	221	50	66	6	0	21	60	.299	108	3	9	.925
1967—Birmingham	South.	OF	114	413	*84	121	26	*17	17	58	.293	228	3	*18	.928
1967—Kansas City	Amer.	OF	35	118	13	21	4	4	1	6	.178	55	1	4	.933
1968—Oakland	Amer.	OF	154	553	82	138	13	6	29	74	.250	269	14	*12	.959
1969—Oakland	Amer.	OF	152	549	*123	151	36	3	47	118	.275	278	14	11	.964
1970—Oakland	Amer.	OF	149	426	57	101	21	2	23	66	.237	251	8	●12	.956
1971—Oakland†	Amer.	OF	150	567	87	157	29	3	32	80	.277	285	15	7	.977
1972—Oakland†	Amer.	OF	135	499	72	132	25	2	25	75	.265	301	5	*9	.971
1973—Oakland	Amer.	OF	151	539	*99	158	28	2	*32	*117	.293	302	4	9	.971
1974—Oakland	Amer.	OF	148	506	90	146	25	1	29	93	.289	296	8	10	.968
1975—Oakland‡	Amer.	OF	157	593	91	150	39	3	●36	104	.253	315	13	*12	.965
1976—Baltimore§x	Amer.	OF	134	498	84	138	27	2	27	91	.277	284	8	*11	.964
1977—New York	Amer.	OF	146	525	93	150	39	2	32	110	.286	236	7	13	.949
1978—New York	Amer.	OF	139	511	82	140	13	5	27	97	.274	212	6	3	.986
1979—New York y	Amer.	OF	131	465	78	138	24	2	29	89	.297	274	7	4	.986
1980—New York	Amer.	OF	143	514	94	154	22	4	●41	111	.300	174	3	7	.962
1981—New York za	Amer.	OF	94	334	33	79	17	1	15	54	.237	111	3	3	.974
1982—California	Amer.	OF	153	530	92	146	17	1	●39	101	.275	200	6	6	.972
1983—California	Amer.	OF	116	397	43	77	14	1	14	49	.194	66	4	1	.986
1984—California	Amer.	OF	143	525	67	117	17	2	25	81	.223	7	0	0	1.000
1985—California	Amer.	OF	143	460	64	116	27	0	27	85	.252	112	6	7	.944
Major League Totals—19 Years				2573	9109	1444	2409	437	46	530	1601	.264	4028	132	141	.967

Selected by Kansas City A's organization in 1st round (second player selected) of free-agent draft, June 13, 1966.

†On disabled list, August 10 to August 25, 1972.

‡Traded with Pitchers Ken Holtzman and Bill Van Bommel to Baltimore Orioles for Outfielder Don Baylor and Pitchers Mike Torrez and Paul Mitchell, April 2, 1976.

§On disqualified list, April 9 to May 2, 1976.

xPlayed out option year and granted free agency, November 1, 1976; signed as free agent with New York Yankees, November 29, 1976.

yOn disabled list, June 3 to June 27, 1979.

zOn disabled list, April 2 to April 17, 1981.

aGranted free agency, November 13, 1981; signed by California Angels, January 22, 1982.

DIVISION SERIES RECORD

Year	Club	League	Pos.	G.	AB.	R.	H.	2B.	3B.	HR.	RBI.	B.A.	PO.	A.	E.	F.A.
1981—New York	Amer.	OF	5	20	4	6	0	0	2	4	.300	7	0	0	1.000

CHAMPIONSHIP SERIES RECORD

Established Championship Series records for most Series played (10); most Series, one or more hits (9); most Series played all games (9); most games, total Series (39); most at-bats, total Series (137); most times stealing home, game (1), October 12, 1972; most strikeouts, total Series (34).

Tied Championship Series records for most clubs, total Series (3); most times on winning club (6); most times reached first base safely, game (5), October 3, 1978.

Established American League Championship Series records for most one-base hits, total Series (21); highest batting average, four-game Series (.462), 1978; most runs batted in, four-game Series (6), 1978; most bases on balls, total Series (15).

Tied American League Championship Series records for most times on losing club (4); most home runs, three-game Series (2), 1971; most Series, one or more home runs (4); most total bases, three-game Series (11), 1971; highest slugging average, three-game Series (.917), 1971; most strikeouts, five-game Series (7), 1982; most bases on balls, four-game Series (5), 1974.

Year	Club	League	Pos.	G.	AB.	R.	H.	2B.	3B.	HR.	RBI.	B.A.	PO.	A.	E.	F.A.
1971—Oakland	Amer.	OF	3	12	2	4	1	0	2	2	.333	9	1	0	1.000
1972—Oakland	Amer.	OF	5	18	1	5	1	0	0	2	.278	14	0	1	.933
1973—Oakland	Amer.	OF	5	21	0	3	0	0	0	0	.143	19	0	0	1.000
1974—Oakland	Amer.	DH-OF	4	12	0	2	1	0	0	1	.167	0	0	0	.000
1975—Oakland	Amer.	OF	3	12	1	5	0	0	1	3	.417	5	1	0	1.000

Year	Club	League	Pos.	G.	AB.	R.	H.	2B.	3B.	HR.	RBI.	B.A.	PO.	A.	E.	F.A.
1977—New York	Amer.	O-D-PH	5	16	1	2	0	0	0	1	.125	10	1	0	1.000
1978—New York	Amer.	DH-OF	4	13	5	6	1	0	2	6	.462	4	0	0	1.000
1980—New York	Amer.	OF	3	11	1	3	1	0	0	0	.273	5	0	0	1.000
1981—New York	Amer.	OF	2	4	1	0	0	0	1	1	.000	1	0	0	1.000
1982—California	Amer.	OF	5	18	2	2	0	0	1	2	.111	2	0	0	1.000
Championship Series Totals—10 Years...			39	137	14	32	5	0	6	18	.234	69	3	1	.986

WORLD SERIES RECORD

Established World Series records for most home runs, two consecutive Series, two consecutive years (7), 1977 and 1978; highest slugging percentage, six-game Series (1.250), 1977; most home runs, Series (5), 1977; most total bases, Series (25), 1977; most runs, Series (10), 1977; most long hits, six-game Series (6), 1977 (tied record for any length Series); most extra bases on long hits, Series (16), 1977; most home runs, three consecutive games, one Series (5), 1977; most home runs, two consecutive games, Series (4), October 16 and 18, 1977; most consecutive home runs, two consecutive games (4), October 16 and 18, 1977; most home runs, four consecutive games, one in each game (6); highest slugging average, total Series, 20 or more games (.755).

Tied World Series records for most times reached first base safely, game (batting 1.000) (5), October 24, 1981; most home runs, game (3), October 18, 1977 (consecutive, each on first pitch); most home runs, two consecutive innings (2), October 18, 1977 (fourth and fifth inning); most total bases, game (12), October 18, 1977; most runs, game (4), October 18, 1977; most consecutive games, one or more runs batted in (6); one or more hits, each game, six-game Series, 1978; most times hit by pitch, total Series (3).

Year	Club	League	Pos.	G.	AB.	R.	H.	2B.	3B.	HR.	RBI.	B.A.	PO.	A	F	F A
1973 Oakland	Amer.	OF	7	29	3	9	3	1	1	6	.310	17	0	0	1.000
1974—Oakland	Amer.	OF	5	14	3	4	1	0	1	1	.286	6	1	1	.875
1977—New York	Amer.	OF	6	20	10	9	1	0	5	8	.450	9	0	0	1.000
1978—New York	Amer.	DH	6	23	2	9	1	0	2	8	.391	0	0	0	.000
1981—New York	Amer.	OF	3	12	3	4	1	0	1	1	.333	5	0	1	.832
World Series Totals—5 Years			27	98	21	35	7	1	10	24	.357	37	1	2	.950

ALL-STAR GAME RECORD

Tied All-Star Game record for most home runs by pinch-hitter, game (1), July 13, 1971.

Year	League	Pos.	AB.	R.	H.	2B.	3B.	HR.	RBI.	B.A.	PO.	A.	E.	F.A.
1969—American		OF	2	0	0	0	0	0	0	.000	2	0	0	1.000
1971—American		PH	1	1	1	0	0	1	2	1.000	0	0	0	.000
1972—American		OF	4	0	2	1	0	0	0	.500	5	0	0	1.000
1973—American		OF	4	1	1	1	0	0	0	.250	0	0	0	.000
1974—American		OF	3	0	0	0	0	0	0	.000	3	0	0	1.000
1975—American		OF	3	0	1	0	0	0	0	.333	2	0	0	1.000
1977—American		OF	2	0	1	0	0	0	0	.500	0	0	0	.000
1979—American		PH-OF	1	0	0	0	0	0	0	.000	0	0	0	.000
1980—American		OF	2	0	1	0	0	0	0	.500	0	0	0	.000
1981—American		OF	1	0	0	0	0	0	0	.000	0	0	0	.000
1982—American		OF	1	0	0	0	0	0	1	.000	3	0	0	1.000
1984—American		OF	2	0	0	0	0	0	0	.000	0	0	1	.000
All-Star Game Totals—12 Years			26	2	7	2	0	1	3	.269	15	0	1	.938

Named to American League All-Star Team for 1978 game; replaced due to injury by Graig Nettles.
Named to American League All-Star Team for 1983 game; replaced due to injury by Ben Oglivie.

ROY LEE JACKSON

Born May 1, 1954, at Opelika, Ala.
Height, 6.02. Weight, 205.
Throws and bats righthanded.
Attended Tuskegee Institute, Tuskegee, Ala.

Major league saves: 1980 (1), 1981 (7), 1982 (6), 1983 (7), 1984 (10), 1985 (2). Total—33.

Year	Club	League	G.	IP.	W.	L.	Pct.	H.	R.	ER.	SO.	BB.	ERA.
1975—Marion	Ap'lachian	8	50	4	2	.667	35	10	8	35	14	1.44
1975—Wausau	Midwest	5	38	1	3	.250	29	12	10	35	7	2.37
1976—Lynchburg	Carolina	7	55	2	3	.400	51	26	21	19	15	3.44
1976—Jackson	Texas	20	132	8	6	.571	136	51	44	82	39	3.00
1977—Tidewater	Int'national	28	168	13	7	.650	174	78	69	110	73	3.70
1977—New York	National	4	24	0	2	.000	25	16	16	13	15	6.00
1978—Tidewater	Int'national	27	176	11	10	.524	176	91	73	132	51	3.73
1978—New York	National	4	13	0	0	.000	21	13	13	6	6	9.00
1979—Tidewater	Int'national	33	137	12	7	.632	143	63	57	89	33	3.74
1979—New York	National	8	16	1	0	1.000	11	4	4	10	5	2.25
1980—Tidewater	Int'national	22	78	3	5	.375	63	33	20	56	51	2.31
1980—New York†	National	24	71	1	7	.125	78	37	33	58	20	4.18
1981—Toronto	American	39	62	1	2	.333	65	23	18	27	25	2.61
1982—Toronto	American	48	97	8	8	.500	77	37	33	71	31	3.06
1983—Toronto	American	49	92	8	3	.727	92	48	46	48	41	4.50
1984—Toronto‡	American	54	86	7	8	.467	73	40	34	58	31	3.56
1985—Rochester§	Int'national	15	27	1	1	.500	26	12	9	25	8	3.00
1985—Las Vegas	P. Coast	3	5⅔	1	0	1.000	3	1	1	3	0	1.59
1985—San Diego	National	22	40	2	3	.400	32	13	12	28	13	2.70
National League Totals—5 Years		62	164	4	12	.250	167	83	78	115	59	4.28
American League Totals—4 Years		190	337	24	21	.533	307	148	131	204	128	3.50
Major League Totals—9 Years		252	501	28	33	.459	474	231	209	319	187	3.75

Selected by Houston Astros' organization in 12th round of free-agent draft, June 6, 1972.

Signed as free agent by New York Mets' organization, June 27, 1975.
†Traded to Toronto Blue Jays for Outfielder Bob Bailor, December 12, 1980.
‡Released, April 1, 1985; signed by Rochester (Baltimore Orioles' organization), May 1, 1985.
§Traded with a player to be named later to San Diego Padres' organization for Second Baseman Alan Wiggins, June 27, 1985; San Diego acquired Pitcher Rich Caldwell to complete deal, September 16, 1985.

BROOK WALLACE JACOBY JR.

Born November 23, 1959, at Philadelphia, Pa.
Height, 5.11. Weight, 175.
Throws and bats righthanded.
Attended Ventura College, Ventura, Calif.
Son of Brook Jacoby Sr., minor league pitcher, 1956 through 1958.

Major League stolen bases: 1984 (3), 1985 (2). Total—5.
Led International League third basemen in total chances with 331 and double plays with 22 in 1982.

Year Club	League	Pos.	G.	AB.	R.	H.	2B.	3B.	HR.	RBI.	B.A.	PO.	A.	E.	F.A.
1979—Kingsport	Appal.	OF	8	28	3	7	2	0	0	1	.250	9	0	0	1.000
1979—Bradenton	Gulf C.	OF	42	160	24	43	11	1	3	35	.269	65	7	4	.947
1980—Anderson	S. Atl.	OF-3B	132	496	82	147	*40	4	19	*108	.296	219	30	10	.961
1980—Savannah	South.	3B	3	8	0	1	0	0	0	0	.125	0	2	0	1.000
1981—Savannah	South.	3B-OF	140	507	59	148	28	3	24	82	.292	103	232	31	.915
1981—Atlanta	Nat.	3B	11	10	0	2	0	0	0	1	.200	3	4	0	1.000
1982—Richmond	Int.	3B	134	501	74	150	21	3	18	58	.299	83	*229	*19	*.943
1983—Richmond	Int.	3B	133	489	88	154	32	2	25	100	.315	62	247	18	.945
1983—Atlanta†	Nat.	3B	4	8	0	0	0	0	0	0	.000	0	2	0	1.000
1984—Cleveland‡	Amer.	3B-SS	126	439	64	116	19	3	7	40	.264	86	188	14	.951
1985—Cleveland	Amer.	3B-2B	161	606	72	166	26	3	20	87	.274	114	319	19	.958
National League Totals—2 Years			15	18	0	2	0	0	0	1	.111	3	6	0	1.000
American League Totals—2 Years			287	1045	136	282	45	6	27	127	.270	200	507	33	.955
Major League Totals—4 Years			302	1063	136	284	45	6	27	128	.267	203	513	33	.956

Selected by Atlanta Braves' organization in 7th round of free-agent draft, January 9, 1979.
†Traded with Outfielder Brett Butler to Cleveland Indians, October 21, 1983, completing deal in which Atlanta Braves acquired Pitcher Len Barker for three players to be named later, August 28, 1983. Cleveland acquired Pitcher Rick Behenna as partial completion of deal, September 2, 1983.
‡On disabled list, August 20, 1984 through remainder of season.

DION JAMES

Born November 9, 1962, at Philadelphia, Pa.
Height, 6.01. Weight, 170.
Throws and bats lefthanded.

Major League stolen bases: 1983 (1), 1984 (10). Total—11.
Led California League outfielders in fielding percentage with .988 in 1981.

Year Club	League	Pos.	G.	AB.	R.	H.	2B.	3B.	HR.	RBI.	B.A.	PO.	A.	E.	F.A.
1980—Butte	Pion.	OF-1B	59	224	57	71	14	1	0	27	.317	80	4	7	.923
1980—Burlington	Midw.	OF	3	10	0	1	0	0	0	1	.100	8	1	0	1.000
1981—Stockton	Calif.	OF-1B	124	451	70	137	17	3	2	49	.304	250	10	3	.989
1982—El Paso†	Texas	OF	106	422	103	136	25	3	9	72	.322	237	9	7	.972
1983—Vancouver	P. C.	OF	129	467	84	157	29	5	8	68	.336	289	6	2	.993
1983—Milwaukee	Amer.	OF	11	20	1	2	0	0	0	1	.100	12	1	0	1.000
1984—Milwaukee	Amer.	OF	128	387	52	114	19	5	1	30	.295	252	7	3	.989
1985—Vancouver‡	P. C.	OF	10	37	2	4	2	0	0	5	.108	17	0	0	1.000
1985—Milwaukee	Amer.	OF	18	49	5	11	1	0	0	3	.224	20	0	0	1.000
Major League Totals—3 Years			157	456	58	127	20	5	1	34	.279	284	8	3	.990

Selected by Milwaukee Brewers' organization in 1st round (25th player selected) of free-agent draft, June 3, 1980.
†On disabled list, July 1 to August 1, 1982.
‡On Milwaukee disabled list, March 31 to April 28 and May 20 to September 1, 1985; included rehabilitation disability assignment to Vancouver, April 12 to April 28, 1985.

DONALD CHRISTOPHER JAMES
(Chris)

Born October 4, 1962, at Rusk, Tex.
Height, 6.01. Weight, 190.
Throws and bats righthanded.
Attended Blinn College, Brenham, Tex.
Brother of Craig James, running back with New England Patriots.

Tied for Pacific Coast League lead in being hit by pitch with 7 in 1985.
Led South Atlantic League in total bases with 257 and tied for lead in being hit by pitch with 12 in 1983.
Led Pacific Coast League outfielders in total chances with 351 in 1985.

Year Club	League	Pos.	G.	AB.	R.	H.	2B.	3B.	HR.	RBI.	B.A.	PO.	A.	E.	F.A.
1982—Bend	N'west	3B-OF	63	227	47	72	*19	3	12	50	.317	93	54	10	.936
1983—Spartanburg	S. Atl.	OF-3B	129	499	94	148	23	4	26	*121	.297	150	88	16	.937
1984—Reading	East.	*3B-OF	128	457	66	117	19	*12	8	57	.256	104	209	*39	.889
1985—Portland	P. C.	OF	135	507	78	160	35	8	11	73	.316	*328	16	7	.980

Signed as free agent by Philadelphia Phillies' organization, October 30, 1981.

ROBERT HARVEY JAMES
(Bob)

Born August 15, 1958, at Glendale, Calif.
Height, 6.04. Weight, 230.
Throws and bats righthanded.

Major League saves: 1983 (7), 1984 (10), 1985 (32). Total—49.
Led American Association in balks with 7 in 1980.
Led Florida State League in wild pitches with 19 in 1978.
Tied for American Association lead in games started by pitchers with 26 in 1979.

Year Club	League	G.	IP.	W.	L.	Pct.	H.	R.	ER.	SO.	BB.	ERA.
1976—Lethbridge	Pioneer	3	8	0	1	.000	7	8	4	11	9	4.50
1977—West Palm Beach†	Florida St.	21	100	5	5	.500	99	51	37	83	76	3.33
1978—West Palm Beach‡	Florida St.	21	127	10	7	.588	99	53	44	139	86	3.11
1978—Memphis	Southern	3	20	2	1	.667	14	5	1	25	11	0.45
1978—Montreal	National	4	4	0	1	.000	4	4	4	3	4	9.00
1979—Denver	Am. Assoc.	26	132	8	13	.381	139	*112	*98	122	*123	6.68
1979—Montreal	National	2	2	0	0	.000	2	3	3	1	3	13.50
1980—Denver§	Am. Assoc.	17	87	9	2	.818	66	42	37	79	74	3.83
1981—Denver	Am. Assoc.	20	57	1	2	.333	43	43	36	46	69	5.68
1982—Montreal x	National	7	9	0	0	.000	10	6	6	11	8	6.00
1982—Evansville	Am. Assoc.	9	21⅔	1	1	.500	9	6	5	30	14	2.08
1982—Detroit	American	12	19⅔	0	2	.000	22	12	11	20	8	5.03
1983—Detroit y	American	4	4	0	0	.000	5	5	5	4	3	11.25
1983—Wichita	Am. Assoc.	22	31	4	2	.667	27	17	16	40	25	4.65
1983—Montreal	National	27	50	1	0	1.000	37	17	16	56	23	2.88
1984—Montreal z	National	62	96	6	6	.500	92	47	39	91	45	3.66
1985—Chicago	American	69	110	8	7	.533	90	31	26	88	23	2.13
National League Totals—5 Years		102	161	7	7	.500	145	77	68	162	83	3.80
American League Totals—3 Years		85	133⅔	8	9	.471	117	49	42	112	34	2.83
Major League Totals—6 Years		187	294⅔	15	16	.484	262	126	110	274	117	3.36

Selected by Montreal Expos' organization in 1st round (ninth player selected) of free-agent draft, June 8, 1976.
†On temporary inactive list, April 13 to May 6, 1977.
‡On disabled list, April 10 to April 21, 1978.
§On disabled list, July 13 to September 1, 1980.
xSold to Evansville (Detroit Tigers' organization), June 10, 1982.
ySold to Wichita (Montreal Expos' organization), May 3, 1983.
zTraded to Chicago White Sox for Infielder Vance Law, December 7, 1984.

JAMES MICHAEL JEFFCOAT
(Mike)

Born August 3, 1959, at Pine Bluff, Ark.
Height, 6.02. Weight, 189.
Throws and bats lefthanded.
Attended Louisiana Tech University, Ruston, La.

Major League saves: 1984 (1).

Year Club	League	G.	IP.	W.	L.	Pct.	H.	R.	ER.	SO.	BB.	ERA.
1980—Waterloo	Midwest	4	6	0	0	.000	12	12	4	7	3	6.00
1980—Batavia	NYP	12	68	4	3	.571	65	40	30	71	45	3.97
1981—Waterloo	Midwest	25	147	10	8	.556	151	71	63	109	78	3.86
1982—Waterloo	Midwest	9	62	5	4	.556	58	29	28	68	15	4.06
1982—Chattanooga	Southern	18	128⅓	8	8	.500	122	49	41	107	51	2.88
1983—Charleston	Int'natonal	26	167	12	8	.600	187	95	84	96	46	4.53
1983—Cleveland	American	11	32⅔	1	3	.250	32	13	12	9	13	3.31
1984—Cleveland	American	63	75⅓	5	2	.714	82	28	25	41	24	2.99
1985—Cleveland†	American	9	9⅔	0	0	.000	8	5	3	4	6	2.79
1985—Phoenix	P. Coast	10	59⅔	4	5	.444	64	26	24	28	9	3.62
1985—San Francisco	National	19	22	0	2	.000	27	13	13	10	6	5.32
American League Totals—3 Years		83	117⅔	6	5	.545	122	46	40	54	43	3.06
National League Totals—1 Year		19	22	0	2	.000	27	13	13	10	6	5.32
Major League Totals—3 Years		102	139⅔	6	7	.462	149	59	53	64	49	3.42

Selected by St. Louis Cardinals' organization in 30th round of free-agent draft, June 7, 1977.
Selected by Cleveland Indians' organization in 13th round of free-agent draft, June 3, 1980.
†Traded with Infielder Luis Quinones to San Francisco Giants' organization for Shortstop Johnnie LeMaster, May 7, 1985.

STANLEY JEFFERSON
(Stan)

Born December 4, 1962, at New York, N.Y.
Height, 5.11. Weight, 175.
Throws and bats righthanded.
Attended Bethune-Cookman College, Daytona Beach, Fla.

Led Texas League in stolen bases with 39 in 1985.
Led New York-Pennsylvania League in stolen bases with 35 in 1983.
Named outfielder on THE SPORTING NEWS College Baseball All-America Team, 1983.

Year Club	League	Pos.	G.	AB.	R.	H.	2B.	3B.	HR.	RBI.	B.A.	PO.	A.	E.	F.A.
1983—Little Falls............	NYP	OF	71	281	57	90	5	1	9	36	.320	*153	7	4	.976
1984—Lynchburg............	Carol.	OF	128	493	*113	142	20	●9	5	47	.288	265	11	8	.972
1985—Jackson	Texas	OF	133	524	97	145	21	6	8	30	.277	276	9	7	.976

Selected by New York Mets' organization in 1st round (20th player selected) of free-agent draft, June 6, 1983.

LARRY STEVEN JELTZ
(Steve)

Born May 28, 1959, at Paris, France.
Height, 5.11. Weight, 170.
Throws right and bats left and righthanded.
Attended University of Kansas, Lawrence, Kan.

Major League stolen bases: 1984 (2), 1985 (1). Total—3.
Led Carolina League second basemen in double plays with 84 in 1981.
Tied for Carolina League lead in caught stealing with 15 in 1981.

Year Club	League	Pos.	G.	AB.	R.	H.	2B.	3B.	HR.	RBI.	B.A.	PO.	A.	E.	F.A.
1980—Spartanburg†........	S. Atl.	2B	31	107	19	31	2	1	0	8	.290	51	61	4	.966
1981—Peninsula	Carol.	2B	133	482	81	112	18	0	2	32	.232	*293	*369	25	.964
1982—Reading................	East.	2B-SS-3B	126	380	61	92	10	3	7	28	.242	251	297	22	.961
1983—Portland...............	P. C.	3-2-S-O	71	181	34	48	6	1	0	16	.265	106	113	11	.952
1983—Philadelphia	Nat.	2B-SS-3B	13	8	0	1	0	1	0	1	.125	4	5	0	1.000
1984—Portland...............	P. C.	S-2-O-3	134	436	68	96	10	9	2	46	.220	270	349	28	.957
1984—Philadelphia	Nat.	SS-3B	28	68	7	14	0	1	1	7	.206	37	93	1	.992
1985—Philadelphia	Nat.	SS	89	196	17	37	4	1	0	12	.189	106	215	14	.958
1985—Portland...............	P. C.	SS	21	71	6	21	4	1	1	9	.296	28	66	4	.959
Major League Totals—3 Years................			130	272	24	52	4	3	1	20	.191	147	313	15	.968

Selected by Philadelphia Phillies' organization in 9th round of free-agent draft, June 3, 1980.
†On disabled list, July 27, 1980 through remainder of season.

THOMAS EDWARD JOHN
(Tommy)

Born May 22, 1943, at Terre Haute, Ind.
Height, 6.03. Weight, 203.
Throws left and bats righthanded.
Attended Indiana State College, Terre Haute, Ind.

Tied American League record for most hit batsmen, game, nine-innings (4), June 15, 1968.
Major League saves: 1978 (1).
Led American League in shutouts with 6 in 1980.
Tied for American League lead in shutouts with 5 in 1966 and 6 in 1967.
Tied for American League lead in wild pitches with 17 and in intentional bases on balls issued with 16 in 1970.
Named National League Comeback Player of the Year by THE SPORTING NEWS, 1976.
Named lefthanded pitcher on THE SPORTING NEWS American League All-Star Team, 1980.
Received reported $40,000 bonus to sign with Cleveland Indians, 1961.

Year Club	League	G.	IP.	W.	L.	Pct.	H.	R.	ER.	SO.	BB.	ERA.
1961—Dubuque..........................	Midwest	14	88	10	4	.714	74	47	31	99	59	3.17
1962—Charleston	Eastern	21	128	6	8	.429	129	67	55	114	71	3.87
1962—Jacksonville	Int'national	8	34	2	2	.500	29	20	18	27	16	4.76
1963—Charleston	Eastern	12	95	9	2	.818	85	25	17	45	12	1.61
1963—Jacksonville	Int'national	18	102	6	8	.429	115	53	40	63	39	3.53
1963—Cleveland.......................	American	6	20	0	2	.000	23	10	5	9	6	2.25
1964—Cleveland.......................	American	25	94	2	9	.182	97	53	41	65	35	3.93
1964—Portland†	P. Coast	13	74	6	6	.500	75	38	35	72	24	4.26
1965—Chicago	American	39	184	14	7	.667	162	67	63	126	58	3.08
1966—Chicago	American	34	223	14	11	.560	195	76	65	138	57	2.62
1967—Chicago	American	31	178	10	13	.435	143	62	49	110	47	2.48
1968—Chicago‡	American	25	177	10	5	.667	135	45	39	117	49	1.98
1969—Chicago	American	33	232	9	11	.450	230	91	84	128	90	3.26
1970—Chicago	American	37	269	12	17	.414	253	117	98	138	101	3.28
1971—Chicago§	American	38	229	13	16	.448	244	115	92	131	58	3.62
1972—Los Angeles..................	National	29	187	11	5	.688	172	68	60	117	40	2.89
1973—Los Angeles..................	National	36	218	16	7	*.696	202	88	75	116	50	3.10
1974—Los Angeles x...............	National	22	153	13	3	.813	133	51	44	78	42	2.59
1975—Los Angeles y...............	National					(Did not play)						
1976—Los Angeles..................	National	31	207	10	10	.500	207	76	71	91	61	3.09
1977—Los Angeles..................	National	31	220	20	7	.741	225	82	68	123	50	2.78
1978—Los Angeles z...............	National	33	213	17	10	.630	230	95	78	124	53	3.30
1979—New York.......................	American	37	276	21	9	.700	268	109	91	111	65	2.97
1980—New York.......................	American	36	265	22	9	.710	270	115	101	78	56	3.43
1981—New York a....................	American	20	140	9	8	.529	135	50	41	50	39	2.64
1982—New York b-California.......	American	37	221⅔	14	12	.538	239	102	91	68	39	3.69
1983—California.......................	American	34	234⅓	11	13	.458	*287	126	113	65	49	4.33
1984—California.......................	American	32	181⅓	7	13	.350	223	97	91	47	56	4.52
1985—California c-Oakland.......	American	23	86⅓	4	10	.286	117	59	53	25	28	5.53
1985—Modesto	California	2	4	0	0	.000	12	8	7	11	6	5.73
1985—Madison d	Midwest	1	6	0	0	.000	4	2	2	3	4	3.00
American League Totals—16 Years		487	3011	172	165	.510	3021	1294	1117	1406	833	3.34
National League Totals—6 Years......................		182	1198	87	42	.674	1169	460	396	649	296	2.97
Major League Totals—22 Years...........................		669	4209	259	207	.556	4190	1754	1513	2055	1129	3.24

Signed as free agent by Cleveland Indians' organization, June 12, 1961.

†Traded to Chicago White Sox with Catcher John Romano and Outfielder Tommie Agee for Catcher Camilo Carreon and Outfielder Rocky Colavito, January 20, 1965, as part of three-way deal which saw Chicago obtain Colavito from Kansas City Athletics earlier same day for Outfielders Jim Landis and Mike Hershberger and a pitcher to be named later; Kansas City acquired Pitcher Fred Talbot to complete deal, February 10, 1965.

‡On disabled list, August 22, 1968 through remainder of season.

§Traded with Infielder Steve Huntz to Los Angeles Dodgers for Infielder-Outfielder Richie Allen, December 2, 1971.

xOn disabled list, July 17, 1974 through remainder of season.

yOn disabled list, April 6, 1975 through remainder of season.

zGranted free agency, November 2, 1978; signed by New York Yankees, November 21, 1978.

aOn disabled list, June 1 to August 5, 1981.

bTraded to California Angels for a player to be named later, August 31, 1982; New York Yankees acquired Pitcher Dennis Rasmussen to complete deal, November 24 1982.

cReleased, June 19, 1985; signed by Modesto (Oakland A's organization), July 12, 1985.

dGranted free agency, November 12, 1985.

DIVISION SERIES RECORD

Year—Club	League	G.	IP.	W.	L.	Pct.	H.	R.	ER.	SO.	BB.	ERA.
1981—New York	American	1	7	0	1	.000	8	5	5	0	2	6.43

CHAMPIONSHIP SERIES RECORD

Established Championship Series record for most runs allowed, five-game Series (9), 1982.
Tied Championship Series record for most games won, total Series (4).
Tied National League Championship Series record for most complete games, total Series (2).

Year—Club	League	G.	IP.	W.	L.	Pct.	H.	R.	ER.	SO.	BB.	ERA.
1977—Los Angeles	National	2	13⅔	1	0	1.000	11	5	1	11	5	0.66
1978—Los Angeles	National	1	9	1	0	1.000	4	0	0	4	2	0.00
1980—New York	American	1	6⅔	0	0	.000	8	2	2	3	1	2.70
1981—New York	American	1	6	1	0	1.000	6	1	1	3	1	1.50
1982—California	American	2	12⅓	1	1	.500	11	9	7	6	6	5.11
Championship Series Totals—5 Years		7	47⅔	4	1	.800	40	17	11	27	15	2.08

WORLD SERIES RECORD

Year—Club	League	G.	IP.	W.	L.	Pct.	H.	R.	ER.	SO.	BB.	ERA.
1977—Los Angeles	National	1	6	0	1	.000	9	5	4	7	3	6.00
1978—Los Angeles	National	2	14⅔	1	0	1.000	14	8	5	6	4	3.07
1981—New York	American	3	13	1	0	1.000	11	1	1	8	0	0.69
World Series Totals—3 Years		6	33⅔	2	1	.667	34	14	10	21	7	2.67

ALL-STAR GAME RECORD

Year—League	IP.	W.	L.	Pct.	H.	R.	ER.	SO.	BB.	ERA.
1968—American	⅔	0	0	.000	0	0	0	0	0	0.00
1980—American	2⅓	0	1	.000	4	3	3	1	0	11.57
All-Star Game Totals—2 Years	3	0	1	.000	5	3	3	1	0	9.00

Member of National League All-Star Team for 1978 game; did not play.
Member of American League All-Star Team for 1979 game; did not play.

CLIFFORD JOHNSON JR.
(Cliff)

Born July 22, 1947, at San Antonio, Tex.
Height, 6.04. Weight, 225.
Throws and bats righthanded.
Brother-in-law of Mike Easler, designated hitter-first baseman with Boston Red Sox;
Cousin of Elijah Johnson, infielder-outfielder in Houston Astros' and Baltimore Orioles'
organizations, 1961 through 1970 and 1972.

Established major league record for most home runs by pinch-hitter, lifetime (19).

Tied major league records for most home runs, inning (2) and most total bases, inning (8), June 30, 1977 (eighth inning).

Tied modern major league record for most long hits, inning (2), May 31, 1975 (eighth inning) and June 30, 1977 (eighth inning).

Major League stolen bases: 1975 (1), 1979 (2), 1981 (5), 1982 (1). Total—9.

Hit three home runs in a game, June 30, 1977.

Led National League in passed balls with 12 in 1976.

Led American Association in total bases with 285 and being hit by pitch with 16 in 1973.

Led American Association in passed balls with 17 and tied for lead in errors with 13 in 1972.

Tied for Southern League lead in being hit by pitch with 8 in 1972.

Tied for Southern League lead in passed balls with 15 in 1971.

Tied for Appalachian League lead in double plays by catchers with 3 in 1967.

Named American Association Most Valuable Player, 1973.

Named Carolina League Most Valuable Player, 1970.

Year—Club	League	Pos.	G.	AB.	R.	H.	2B.	3B.	HR.	RBI.	B.A.	PO.	A.	E.	F.A.
1967—Cocoa	Fla. St.	C-OF	53	156	13	41	5	1	4	20	.263	168	13	10	.948
1967—Covington	Appal.	OF-C-1B	36	110	21	34	7	2	5	24	.309	103	10	6	.950
1968—Cocoa	Fla. St.	★C-OF-1B	117	353	60	102	17	3	10	61	.289	641	55	★26	.964
1969—Peninsula	Carol.	C	103	327	37	75	16	1	11	54	.229	615	68	21	.970
1970—Raleigh-Durham	Carol.	C-OF	102	343	74	114	24	0	★27	★91	.332	474	40	9	.983
1970—Oklahoma City	A. A.	C-OF-1B	22	55	12	21	4	1	1	5	.382	63	9	2	.973
1971—Oklahoma City	A. A.	C-1B	31	105	16	26	5	2	5	15	.248	219	20	2	.992

Year Club	League	Pos.	G.	AB.	R.	H.	2B.	3B.	HR.	RBI.	B.A.	PO.	A.	E.	F.A.
1971—Columbus...............	South.	C-1B	58	164	16	30	10	0	4	21	.183	350	35	5	.987
1972—Columbus...............	South.	C-3B-1B	42	160	28	46	11	2	10	38	.288	235	36	8	.971
1972—Oklahoma City.....	A. A.	C-1B	89	313	55	88	12	5	17	59	.281	600	59	15	.978
1972—Houston..................	Nat.	C	5	4	0	1	0	0	0	0	.250	6	0	0	1.000
1973—Denver	A. A.	1B	133	490	*105	148	30	4	*33	*117	.302	132	15	4	.974
1973—Houston..................	Nat.	1B	7	20	6	6	2	0	2	6	.300	47	2	0	1.000
1974—Houston..................	Nat.	C-1B	83	171	26	39	4	1	10	29	.228	270	18	4	.986
1975—Houston..................	Nat.	1B-C-OF	122	340	52	94	16	1	20	65	.276	604	38	12	.982
1976—Houston..................	Nat.	C-OF-1B	108	318	36	72	21	2	10	49	.226	468	35	9	.982
1977—Houston†...............	Nat.	OF-1B	51	144	22	43	8	0	10	23	.299	113	11	3	.976
1977—New York.............	Amer.	C-1B	56	142	24	42	8	0	12	31	.296	145	14	1	.994
1978—New York.............	Amer.	C-1B	76	174	20	32	9	1	6	19	.184	71	10	2	.976
1979—N.Y.‡-Cleve.	Amer.	C	100	304	48	82	16	0	20	67	.270	10	1	0	1.000
1980—Cleveland§............	Amer.	DH	54	174	25	40	3	1	6	28	.230	0	0	0	.000
1980—Chicago x.............	Nat.	1B-C	68	196	28	46	8	0	10	34	.235	469	16	4	.992
1981—Oakland.................	Amer.	1B	84	273	40	71	8	0	17	59	.260	42	1	0	1.000
1982—Oakland yz............	Amer.	1B	73	214	19	51	10	0	7	31	.238	66	8	1	.987
1983—Toronto	Amer.	1B	142	407	59	108	23	1	22	76	.265	47	4	0	1.000
1984—Toronto a..............	Amer.	1B	127	359	51	109	23	1	16	61	.304	26	0	0	1.000
1985—Tex.bc-Tor.............	Amer.	1B	106	369	35	96	17	1	13	66	.260	17	1	1	.947
National League Totals—7 Years...........			444	1193	170	301	59	4	62	206	.252	1977	120	32	.985
American League Totals—9 Years.........			818	2416	321	631	117	5	119	438	.261	424	39	5	.989
Major League Totals—14 Years...............			1262	3609	491	932	176	9	181	644	.258	2401	159	37	.986

Selected by Houston Astros' organization in 5th round of free-agent draft, June 7, 1966.

†Traded to New York Yankees for Infielder Mike Fischlin, Pitcher Randy Niemann and a player to be named later, June 15, 1977; Houston Astros acquired First Baseman-Outfielder Dave Bergman to complete deal, November 23, 1977.

‡Traded to Cleveland Indians for Pitcher Don Hood, June 15, 1979.

§Traded to Chicago Cubs for two players to be named later, June 23, 1980; Cleveland Indians acquired Outfielder-First Baseman Karl Pagel and cash to complete deal, June 30, 1980.

xTraded with Infielder Keith Drumright to Oakland A's for Pitcher Mike King, December 11, 1980.

yOn disabled list, August 5 to September 1, 1982.

zTraded to Toronto Blue Jays for Outfielder Al Woods, November 5, 1982.

aGranted free agency, November 8, 1984; signed by Texas Rangers, December 20, 1984 (Pitcher Tom Henke selected from player compensation pool by Texas Rangers' organization, January 24, 1985.)

bOn disabled list, June 20 to July 22, 1985.

cTraded to Toronto Blue Jays for three players to be named later, August 28, 1985; Texas Rangers acquired Pitchers Matt Williams and Jeff Mays, August 29, 1985, and Pitcher Greg Ferlenda, November 14, 1985, to complete deal.

DIVISION SERIES RECORD

Year Club	League	Pos.	G.	AB.	R.	H.	2B.	3B.	HR.	RBI.	B.A.	PO.	A.	E.	F.A.
1981—Oakland.................	Amer.	DH	2	7	0	2	1	0	0	0	.286	0	0	0	.000

CHAMPIONSHIP SERIES RECORD

Tied Championship Series record for most clubs, total Series (3).

Established American League Championship Series record for highest batting average, seven-game Series (.368), 1985.

Year Club	League	Pos.	G.	AB.	R.	H.	2B.	3B.	HR.	RBI.	B.A.	PO.	A.	E.	F.A.
1977—New York.............	Amer.	DH-PH	5	15	2	6	2	0	1	2	.400	0	0	0	.000
1978—New York.............	Amer.	PH	1	1	0	0	0	0	0	0	.000	0	0	0	.000
1981—Oakland.................	Amer.	DH	2	6	0	0	0	0	0	0	.000	0	0	0	.000
1985—Toronto	Amer.	DH-PH	7	19	1	7	2	0	0	2	.368	0	0	0	.000
Championship Series Totals—4 Years.....			15	41	3	13	4	0	1	4	.317	0	0	0	.000

WORLD SERIES RECORD

Year Club	League	Pos.	G.	AB.	R.	H.	2B.	3B.	HR.	RBI.	B.A.	PO.	A.	E.	F.A.
1977—New York.............	Amer.	PH-C	2	1	0	0	0	0	0	0	.000	0	0	0	.000
1978—New York.............	Amer.	PH	2	2	0	0	0	0	0	0	.000	0	0	0	.000
World Series Totals—2 Years			4	3	0	0	0	0	0	0	.000	0	0	0	.000

HOWARD MICHAEL JOHNSON

Born November 29, 1960, at Clearwater, Fla.
Height, 5.10. Weight, 175.
Throws right and bats right and lefthanded.
Attended St. Petersburg Junior College, St. Petersburg, Fla.

Major League stolen bases: 1982 (7), 1984 (10), 1985 (6). Total—23.
Led Florida State League in sacrifice hits with 16 in 1980.
Led American Association third basemen in double plays with 19 in 1982.
Led Florida State League third basemen in double plays with 21 in 1980.

Year Club	League	Pos.	G.	AB.	R.	H.	2B.	3B.	HR.	RBI.	B.A.	PO.	A.	E.	F.A.
1979—Lakeland................	Fla. St.	3B-SS-OF	132	456	49	107	9	6	3	49	.235	130	240	36	.911
1980—Lakeland................	Fla. St.	3B	130	474	83	135	*28	1	10	69	.285	*110	*264	13	*.966
1981—Birmingham	South.	3B	138	488	84	130	28	7	22	83	.266	103	218	26	.925
1982—Evansville	A. A.	3B-OF	98	366	70	116	16	4	23	67	.317	69	139	23	.900
1982—Detroit...................	Amer.	3B-OF	54	155	23	49	5	0	4	14	.316	36	40	7	.916
1983—Detroit...................	Amer.	3B	27	66	11	14	0	0	3	5	.212	10	30	7	.851

Year Club League	Pos.	G.	AB.	R.	H.	2B.	3B.	HR.	RBI.	B.A.	PO.	A.	E.	F.A.
1983—Evansville† .... A. A.	3B	3	9	1	2	1	0	0	0	.222	1	11	2	.857
1984—Detroit‡................. Amer.	3-S-1-O	116	355	43	88	14	1	12	50	.248	63	150	14	.938
1985—New York.............. Nat.	3B-SS-OF	126	389	38	94	18	4	11	46	.242	78	190	18	.937
American League Totals—3 Years		197	576	77	151	19	1	19	69	.262	109	220	28	.922
National League Totals—1 Year............		126	389	38	94	18	4	11	46	.242	78	190	18	.937
Major League Totals—4 Years................		323	965	115	245	37	5	30	115	.254	187	410	46	.928

Selected by New York Yankees' organization in 23rd round of free-agent draft, June 6, 1978.
Selected by Detroit Tigers' organization in secondary phase of free-agent draft, January 9, 1979.
†On disabled list, June 2 to August 8, 1983.
‡Traded to New York Mets for Pitcher Walt Terrell, December 7, 1984.

WORLD SERIES RECORD

Year Club League	Pos.	G.	AB.	R.	H.	2B.	3B.	HR.	RBI.	B.A.	PO.	A.	E.	F.A.
1984—Detroit.................... Amer.	PH	1	1	0	0	0	0	0	0	.000	0	0	0	.000

JOSEPH RICHARD JOHNSON
(Joe)

Born October 30, 1961, at Brookline, Mass.
Height, 6.02. Weight, 195.
Throws and bats righthanded.
Attended University of Maine, Orono, Me.

Year Club League	G.	IP.	W.	L.	Pct.	H.	R.	ER.	SO.	BB.	ERA.
1982—Savannah.................... Southern	6	28⅔	2	1	.667	32	14	12	15	10	3.77
1983—Savannah.................... Southern	26	157⅓	10	9	.526	162	82	66	94	59	3.78
1983—Richmond.................... Int'national	1	5	0	0	.000	7	4	4	2	3	7.20
1984—Richmond.................... Int'national	4	20⅓	0	2	.000	27	18	13	11	4	5.75
1984—Greenville .... Southern	24	151	8	10	.444	155	70	63	72	41	3.75
1985—Greenville .... Southern	12	59⅔	6	3	.667	78	30	27	29	12	4.07
1985—Richmond.................... Int'national	9	72	7	1	.875	60	22	17	50	10	2.13
1985—Atlanta .... National	15	85⅔	4	4	.500	95	44	39	34	24	4.10
Major League Totals—1 Year	15	85⅔	4	4	.500	95	44	39	34	24	4.10

Selected by Atlanta Braves' organization in 2nd round of free-agent draft, June 7, 1982.

ROY EDWARD JOHNSON

Born June 27, 1959, at Parkin, Ark.
Height, 6.04. Weight, 220.
Throws and bats lefthanded.
Attended Tennessee State University, Nashville, Tenn.

Major League stolen bases: 1984 (1).
Tied for New York-Pennsylvania League lead in caught stealing with 6 in 1980.

Year Club League	Pos.	G.	AB.	R.	H.	2B.	3B.	HR.	RBI.	B.A.	PO.	A.	E.	F.A.
1980—Jamestown .... NYP	OF	36	126	29	41	6	3	6	19	.325	63	1	3	.955
1980—W. Palm Beach.... Fla. St.	OF	24	85	11	19	4	1	1	12	.224	44	1	1	.978
1981—Memphis............... South.	OF	130	477	83	126	19	10	18	90	.264	★340	8	11	.969
1982—Wichita................. A. A.	OF	102	376	73	138	19	6	14	76	★.367	238	4	8	.968
1982—Montreal .... Nat.	OF	17	32	2	7	2	0	0	2	.219	18	0	0	1.000
1983—Wichita† .... A. A.	OF	79	248	39	72	13	1	5	43	.290	89	1	3	.968
1984—Indianapolis‡ .... A. A.	OF	107	356	48	96	17	4	9	49	.270	160	3	4	.976
1984—Montreal .... Nat.	OF	16	33	2	5	2	0	1	2	.152	15	0	1	.938
1985—Montreal .... Nat.	OF	3	5	0	0	0	0	0	0	.000	0	0	0	.000
1985—Indianapolis§xy.... A. A.	OF	26	90	15	25	6	0	3	12	.278	51	3	4	.931
Major League Totals—3 Years................		36	70	4	12	4	0	1	4	.171	33	0	1	.971

Selected by Montreal Expos' organization in 5th round of free-agent draft, June 3, 1980.
†On temporary inactive list, April 19 to May 21, 1983.
‡On disabled list, May 24 to June 15, 1984.
§On suspended list, May 16 to May 23, 1985.
xOn disabled list, May 25 to June 5, 1985.
yDrafted by Buffalo (Chicago White Sox' organization), December 11, 1985.

JOHN WILLIAM JOHNSTONE JR.
(Jay)

Born November 20, 1946, at Manchester, Conn.
Height, 6.01. Weight, 190.
Throws right and bats lefthanded.
Attended Mount San Antonio Junior College, Walnut, Calif.

Major League stolen bases: 1966 (3), 1967 (3), 1968 (2), 1969 (3), 1970 (1), 1971 (10), 1972 (2), 1974 (5), 1975 (7), 1976 (5), 1977 (3), 1979 (2), 1980 (3), 1983 (1). Total—50.

Year Club League	Pos.	G.	AB.	R.	H.	2B.	3B.	HR.	RBI.	B.A.	PO.	A.	E.	F.A.
1963—San Jose .... Calif.	OF-SS-3B	48	155	21	39	5	3	1	18	.252	51	31	9	.901
1964—San Jose .... Calif.	OF	126	454	66	132	27	●11	4	48	.291	250	14	12	.957
1965—El Paso .... Texas	OF	35	137	21	39	9	2	1	21	.285	82	4	4	.956
1965—San Jose .... Calif.	OF	97	356	53	107	17	6	6	60	.301	198	11	10	.954
1966—El Paso .... Texas	OF	7	25	5	9	2	0	1	1	.360	19	0	0	1.000
1966—Seattle .... P. C.	OF	81	318	60	108	14	7	7	42	.340	170	7	4	.978

Year Club League	Pos.	G.	AB.	R.	H.	2B.	3B.	HR.	RBI.	B.A.	PO.	A.	E.	F.A.
1966—California.............. Amer.	OF	61	254	35	67	12	4	3	17	.264	114	2	3	.975
1967—California.............. Amer.	OF	79	230	18	48	7	1	2	10	.209	141	3	4	.973
1967—Seattle .... P. C.	OF	49	184	21	58	11	1	4	21	.315	117	3	4	.968
1968—California.............. Amer.	OF	41	115	11	30	4	1	0	3	.261	58	4	1	.984
1968—Seattle .... P. C.	OF	84	314	45	87	15	4	13	56	.277	203	11	9	.960
1969—California.............. Amer.	OF	148	540	64	146	20	5	10	59	.270	331	12	6	.983
1970—California†............. Amer.	OF	119	320	34	76	10	5	11	39	.238	200	7	4	.981
1971—Chicago .... Amer.	OF	124	388	53	101	14	1	16	40	.260	232	9	8	.968
1972—Chicago‡................. Amer.	OF	113	261	27	49	9	0	4	17	.188	154	5	2	.988
1973—Tucson .... P. C.	OF	69	242	58	84	15	5	9	44	.347	125	2	6	.955
1973—Oakland§.............. Amer.	OF-2B	23	28	1	3	1	0	0	3	.107	7	0	0	1.000
1974—Toledo .... Int.	OF-1B	57	155	31	49	15	1	8	25	.316	77	6	3	.965
1974—Philadelphia .... Nat.	OF	64	200	30	59	10	4	6	30	.295	88	4	3	.968
1975—Philadelphia .... Nat.	OF	122	350	50	115	19	2	7	54	.329	152	10	4	.976
1976—Philadelphia .... Nat.	OF-1B	129	440	62	140	38	4	5	53	.318	293	10	8	.974
1977—Philadelphia .... Nat.	OF-1B	112	363	64	103	18	4	15	59	.284	294	15	1	.997
1978—Philadelphia x...... Nat.	1B-OF	35	56	3	10	2	0	0	4	.179	77	7	1	.988
1978—New York............. Amer.	OF	36	65	6	17	0	0	1	6	.262	31	0	0	1.000
1979—New York y .... Amer.	OF	23	48	7	10	1	0	1	7	.208	32	0	0	1.000
1979—San Diego z .... Nat.	OF-1B	75	201	10	59	8	2	0	32	.294	185	18	4	.981
1980—Los Angeles .... Nat.	OF	109	251	31	77	15	2	2	20	.307	100	9	4	.965
1981—Los Angeles .... Nat.	OF-1B	61	83	8	17	3	0	3	6	.205	33	4	1	.974
1982—L.A. a-Chi. .... Nat.	OF	119	282	40	68	14	1	10	45	.241	154	8	3	.982
1983—Chicago .... Nat.	OF	86	140	16	36	7	0	6	22	.257	55	3	4	.935
1984—Chicago bc .... Nat.	OF	52	73	8	21	2	2	0	3	.288	12	0	0	1.000
1985—Los Angeles de..... Nat.	PH	17	15	0	2	1	0	0	2	.133	0	0	0	.000
National League Totals—12 Years.........		981	2454	322	707	137	21	54	330	.288	1443	88	33	.979
American League Totals—10 Years		767	2249	256	547	78	17	48	201	.243	1300	42	28	.980
Major League Totals—20 Years..............		1748	4703	578	1254	215	38	102	531	.267	2743	130	61	.979

Signed as free agent by California Angels' organization, June 30, 1963.

†Traded with Pitcher Tom Bradley and Catcher Tom Egan to Chicago White Sox for Outfielder Ken Berry, Second Baseman Syd O'Brien and Pitcher Billy Wynne, November 30, 1970.

‡Released, March 7, 1973; signed by Oakland Athletics, March 31, 1973.

§Conditionally released to St. Louis Cardinals, January 9, 1974; released by St. Louis, March 26, 1974; signed by Philadelphia Phillies, April 3, 1974.

xTraded with Outfielder Bobby Brown to New York Yankees for Pitcher Rawly Eastwick, June 14, 1978.

yTraded to San Diego Padres for Pitcher Dave Wehrmeister, June 15, 1979.

zGranted free agency, November 1, 1979; signed by Los Angeles Dodgers, December 4, 1979.

aReleased, May 25, 1982; signed by Chicago Cubs, June 1, 1982.

bOn disabled list, April 12 to May 15, 1984.

cReleased, September 9, 1984; signed by Los Angeles Dodgers, February 20, 1985.

dOn disabled list, April 23 to June 21 and July 10 to September 1, 1985.

eReleased, October 31, 1985.

DIVISION SERIES RECORD

Year Club League	Pos.	G.	AB.	R.	H.	2B.	3B.	HR.	RBI.	B.A.	PO.	A.	E.	F.A.
1981—Los Angeles .... Nat.	PH	1	1	0	0	0	0	0	0	.000	0	0	0	.000

CHAMPIONSHIP SERIES RECORD

Established Championship Series record for highest batting average, three-game Series (.778), 1976.

Tied Championship Series records for most hits, three-game Series (7), 1976; most hits, two consecutive games, one Series (6), October 10 and 12, 1976.

Year Club League	Pos.	G.	AB.	R.	H.	2B.	3B.	HR.	RBI.	B.A.	PO.	A.	E.	F.A.
1976—Philadelphia .... Nat.	PH-OF	3	9	1	7	1	1	0	2	.778	3	0	0	1.000
1977—Philadelphia .... Nat.	OF-PH	2	5	0	1	0	0	0	0	.200	4	0	0	1.000
1981—Los Angeles .... Nat.	PH	2	2	0	0	0	0	0	0	.000	0	0	0	.000
1985—Los Angeles .... Nat.	PH	1	1	0	0	0	0	0	0	.000	0	0	0	.000
Championship Series Totals—4 Years....		8	17	1	8	1	1	0	2	.471	7	0	0	1.000

WORLD SERIES RECORD

Tied World Series record for most home runs as pinch-hitter, game (1), October 24, 1981.

Year Club League	Pos.	G.	AB.	R.	H.	2B.	3B.	HR.	RBI.	B.A.	PO.	A.	E.	F.A.
1978—New York............. Amer.	OF	2	0	0	0	0	0	0	0	.000	1	0	0	1.000
1981—Los Angeles .... Nat.	PH	3	3	1	2	0	0	1	3	.667	0	0	0	1.000
World Series Totals—2 Years		5	3	1	2	0	0	1	3	.667	1	0	0	1.000

ALFORNIA JONES
(Al)

Born February 10, 1959, at Charleston, Miss.
Height, 5.11. Weight, 178.
Throws and bats righthanded.
Attended Alcorn State University, Lorman, Miss.

Major League saves: 1984 (5).
Led Midwest League in games finished in relief with 50 in 1983.

Year Club	League	G.	IP.	W.	L.	Pct.	H.	R.	ER.	SO.	BB.	ERA.
1981—Sarasota White Sox.......................	Gulf Coast	11	58	3	5	.375	50	19	9	41	20	1.40
1982—Appleton	Midwest	26	57	2	4	.333	53	27	21	64	34	3.32

Year Club	League	G.	IP.	W.	L.	Pct.	H.	R.	ER.	SO.	BB.	ERA.
1983—Appleton	Midwest	*55	102	11	1	*.917	54	13	11	124	39	0.97
1983—Chicago	American	2	2⅓	0	0	.000	3	1	1	2	2	3.86
1984—Denver	Am. Assoc.	24	28⅔	2	3	.400	26	16	15	20	20	4.71
1984—Chicago	American	20	20⅓	1	1	.500	23	10	10	15	11	4.43
1985—Chicago†	American	5	6	1	0	1.000	3	2	1	2	3	1.50
1985—Buffalo	Am. Assoc.	4	2⅔	0	1	.000	3	3	3	1	3	10.13
Major League Totals—3 Years		27	28⅔	2	1	.667	29	13	12	19	16	3.77

Selected by Chicago White Sox' organization in 13th round of free-agent draft, June 8, 1981.

†On disabled list, April 22 to September 3, 1985; included rehabilitation disability assignment to Buffalo, August 19 to September 3, 1985.

BARRY LOUIS JONES

Born February 15, 1963, at Centerville, Ind.
Height, 6.02. Weight, 215.
Throws and bats righthanded.
Attended Indiana University, Bloomington, Ind.

Year Club	League	G.	IP.	W.	L.	Pct.	H.	R.	ER.	SO.	BB.	ERA.
1984—Watertown	NYP	14	86⅔	6	3	.667	75	41	33	61	49	3.43
1985—Prince William	Carolina	28	37⅓	3	2	.600	26	7	5	42	19	1.21
1985—Nashua	Eastern	23	29	3	2	.600	19	6	5	24	10	1.55
1985—Hawaii	P. Coast	1	3	0	0	.000	3	3	3	2	1	9.00

Selected by Texas Rangers' organization in 6th round of free-agent draft, June 8, 1981.
Selected by Pittsburgh Pirates' organization in 3rd round of free-agent draft, June 4, 1984.

CHRISTOPHER DALE JONES
(Chris)

Born July 13, 1957, at Los Angeles, Calif.
Height, 6.00. Weight, 183.
Throws and bats lefthanded.
Attended San Diego State University, San Diego, Calif.

Year Club	League	Pos.	G.	AB.	R.	H.	2B.	3B.	HR.	RBI.	B.A.	PO.	A.	E.	F.A.
1979—Sarasota Astros	Gulf C.	OF-1B	31	93	15	24	3	1	0	6	.258	76	3	4	.952
1980—Daytona Beach	Fla. St.	OF-1B	124	413	77	103	9	9	5	54	.249	133	6	4	.972
1981—Columbus	South.	OF	●143	535	102	171	25	9	7	65	.320	178	9	2	*.989
1982—Tucson†	P. C.	OF	36	115	17	26	6	2	0	9	.226	58	1	2	.967
1983—Tucson	P. C.	OF	86	234	41	66	8	5	3	21	.282	119	2	0	1.000
1984—Tucson	P. C.	OF	120	452	78	138	29	10	6	49	.305	262	6	2	.993
1985—Tucson	P. C.	OF	76	281	44	95	21	8	2	33	.338	142	7	1	.993
1985—Houston‡	Nat.	OF	31	25	0	5	0	0	0	1	.200	15	0	0	1.000
Major League Totals—1 Year			31	25	0	5	0	0	0	1	.200	15	0	0	1.000

Selected by Baltimore Orioles' organization in 23rd round of free-agent draft, June 7, 1977.
Selected by Houston Astros' organization in 25th round of free-agent draft, June 5, 1979.
†On disabled list, May 5 to August 4, 1982.
‡Released, November 13, 1985.

LYNN MORRIS JONES

Born January 1, 1953, at Meadville, Pa.
Height, 5.09. Weight, 170.
Throws and bats righthanded.
Received bachelor of arts degree in sociology
from Thiel College, Greenville, Pa.
Brother of Darryl Jones, outfielder with New York Yankees, 1979.

Major League stolen bases: 1979 (9), 1980 (1), 1981 (1), 1984 (1). Total—13.
Tied for Eastern League lead in sacrifice flies with 8 in 1976.

Year Club	League	Pos.	G.	AB.	R.	H.	2B.	3B.	HR.	RBI.	B.A.	PO.	A.	E.	F.A.
1974—Seattle	N'west.	OF	76	282	53	74	15	2	2	37	.262	166	*13	4	.978
1975—Three Rivers	East.	OF-SS	53	141	12	29	3	1	1	14	.206	89	25	6	.950
1975—Eugene	N'west.	OF-3B	62	211	53	71	13	3	13	63	.336	90	9	6	.943
1976—Three Rivers	East.	OF	131	418	41	105	17	0	2	36	.251	196	5	8	.962
1977—Three Rivers†	East.	OF	94	324	49	87	14	2	5	32	.269	229	14	1	*.996
1978—Indianapolis‡	A. A.	OF-2B	126	482	81	158	28	4	9	62	.328	246	14	3	.989
1979—Detroit	Amer.	OF	95	213	33	63	8	0	4	26	.296	142	3	3	.980
1980—Evansville	A. A.	OF	34	121	10	33	4	0	0	11	.273	29	1	1	.968
1980—Detroit§	Amer.	OF	30	55	9	14	2	2	0	6	.255	31	0	0	1.000
1981—Detroit	Amer.	OF	71	174	19	45	5	0	2	19	.259	85	5	1	.989
1982—Detroit	Amer.	OF	58	139	15	31	3	1	0	14	.223	86	3	0	1.000
1983—Detroit x	Amer.	OF	49	64	9	17	1	2	0	6	.266	28	2	1	.968
1984—Kansas City y	Amer.	OF	47	103	11	31	6	0	1	10	.301	51	0	2	.962
1984—Omaha	A. A.	OF	17	63	8	16	6	0	1	3	.254	38	0	0	1.000
1985—Kansas City z	Amer.	OF	110	152	12	32	7	0	0	9	.211	115	2	2	.983
Major League Totals—7 Years			460	900	108	233	32	5	7	90	.259	538	15	9	.984

Selected by Cincinnati Reds' organization in 10th round of free-agent draft, June 5, 1974.
†On disabled list, July 8 to August 8, 1977.
‡Drafted by Detroit Tigers, December 4, 1978.
§On disabled list, April 30 to July 25, 1980.

xGranted free agency when he refused option to minors, December 1, 1983; signed by Kansas City Royals, December 6, 1983.

yOn disabled list, March 28 to May 2 and June 6 to August 1, 1984; included rehabilitation disability assignment to Omaha, July 12 to August 1, 1984.

zGranted free agency, November 12, 1985; re-signed by Royals, December 2, 1985.

CHAMPIONSHIP SERIES RECORD

Year Club League	Pos.	G.	AB.	R.	H.	2B.	3B.	HR.	RBI.	B.A.	PO.	A.	E.	F.A.
1984—Kansas City........... Amer.	PH-OF	3	5	1	1	0	0	0	0	.200	2	0	0	1.000
1985—Kansas City........... Amer.	OF	5	0	0	0	0	0	0	0	.000	2	0	0	1.000
Championship Series Totals—2 Years.....		8	5	1	1	0	0	0	0	.200	4	0	0	1.000

WORLD SERIES RECORD

Year Club League	Pos.	G.	AB.	R.	H.	2B.	3B.	HR.	RBI.	B.A.	PO.	A.	E.	F.A.
1985—Kansas City........... Amer.	PH-OF	6	3	0	2	1	1	0	0	.667	4	0	0	1.000

MICHAEL CARL JONES
(Mike)

Born July 30, 1959, at Pittsford, N.Y.
Height, 6.05. Weight, 230.
Throws and bats lefthanded.
Nephew of Bert Jones, catcher selected by Baltimore Orioles' organization
in free-agent draft, 1966.

Led Southern League in wild pitches with 16 in 1979.
Tied for Gulf Coast League lead in complete games with 4 in 1977.

Year Club	League	G.	IP.	W.	L.	Pct.	H.	R.	ER.	SO.	BB.	ERA.
1977—Sarasota Royals............................	Gulf Coast	8	55	5	1	.833	41	19	15	52	43	2.45
1977—Daytona Beach	Florida St.	1	7	1	0	1.000	6	2	2	5	3	2.57
1978—Fort Myers.....................................	Florida St.	25	169	13	9	.591	150	80	69	118	★117	3.67
1979—Jacksonville..................................	Southern	26	167	9	13	.409	142	92	76	116	★109	4.10
1980—Jacksonville..................................	Southern	24	158	13	6	.684	152	79	68	116	83	3.87
1980—Kansas City...................................	American	3	5	0	1	.000	6	7	6	2	5	10.80
1981—Omaha†..	Am. Assoc.	20	134	11	7	.611	102	55	44	101	79	2.96
1981—Kansas City...................................	American	12	76	6	3	.667	74	30	27	29	28	3.20
1982—Kansas City‡.................................	American					(Did not play)						
1983—Fort Myers§..................................	Florida St.	18	116	5	8	.385	135	47	42	68	31	3.26
1984—Omaha..	Am. Assoc.	11	73⅓	4	5	.444	65	39	38	38	27	3.44
1984—Kansas City...................................	American	23	81	2	3	.400	86	48	44	43	36	4.89
1985—Kansas City...................................	American	33	64	3	3	.500	62	40	34	32	39	4.78
Major League Totals—4 Years............................		71	226	11	10	.524	228	125	111	106	108	4.42

Selected by Kansas City Royals' organization in 1st round (21st player selected) of free-agent draft, June 7, 1977.

†On suspended list, July 23 to July 26, 1981.

‡On disabled list, April 5, 1982 through remainder of season.

§On Omaha disabled list, August 15 to September 7, 1983; included rehabilitation disability assignment to Ft. Myers, August 15 to September 7, 1983.

DIVISION SERIES RECORD

Year Club	League	G.	IP.	W.	L.	Pct.	H.	R.	ER.	SO.	BB.	ERA.
1981—Kansas City....................................	American	1	8	0	1	.000	9	2	2	2	0	2.25

CHAMPIONSHIP SERIES RECORD

Year Club	League	G.	IP.	W.	L.	Pct.	H.	R.	ER.	SO.	BB.	ERA.
1984—Kansas City....................................	American	1	1⅓	0	0	.000	1	1	1	0	0	6.75

ODELL JONES JR.

Born January 13, 1953, at Tulare, Calif.
Height, 6.03. Weight, 175.
Throws and bats righthanded.
Attended Compton College, Compton, Calif.
Cousin of Charles Jackson, linebacker with New York Jets.

Pitched 7-0 no-hit victory against Pittsfield, April 29, 1974.
Major League saves: 1983 (10), 1984 (2). Total—12.
Led Eastern League in balks with 3 in 1974.

Year Club	League	G.	IP.	W.	L.	Pct.	H.	R.	ER.	SO.	BB.	ERA.
1972—Niagara Falls	NYP	11	79	7	3	.700	78	34	27	53	20	3.08
1973—Charleston....................................	W. Carol.	10	62	2	3	.400	42	22	10	62	29	1.45
1973—Salem	Carolina	11	67	5	4	.556	64	40	36	55	38	4.84
1974—Thetford Mines	Eastern	24	161	11	8	.579	103	63	58	153	★120	3.24
1975—Charleston....................................	Int'national	26	★188	●14	9	.609	133	67	56	★157	88	2.68
1975—Pittsburgh.....................................	National	2	3	0	0	.000	1	0	0	2	0	0.00
1976—Charleston†..................................	Int'national	16	84	2	7	.222	81	49	46	47	43	4.93
1977—Pittsburgh.....................................	National	34	108	3	7	.300	118	63	61	66	31	5.08
1978—Columbus......................................	Int'national	28	181	12	9	.571	174	100	★92	★169	69	4.57
1978—Pittsburgh‡...................................	National	3	9	2	0	1.000	7	3	2	10	4	2.00
1979—Seattle§...	American	25	119	3	11	.214	151	90	80	72	58	6.05
1980—Portland x	P. Coast	19	98	6	7	.462	96	49	45	89	46	4.13
1981—Portland..	P. Coast	23	153	12	6	.667	138	73	60	★135	68	3.53

Year Club	League	G.	IP.	W.	L.	Pct.	H.	R.	ER.	SO.	BB.	ERA.
1981—Pittsburgh	National	13	54	4	5	.444	51	23	20	30	23	3.33
1982—Portland y	P. Coast	28	190⅓	*16	9	.640	162	103	90	*172	94	4.26
1983—Texas z	American	42	67	3	6	.333	56	28	23	50	22	3.09
1984—Texas	American	33	59⅓	2	4	.333	62	28	24	28	23	3.64
1985—Rochester	Int'national	41	105	4	6	.400	97	52	49	104	45	4.20
National League Totals—4 Years		52	174	9	12	.429	177	89	83	108	58	4.29
American League Totals—3 Years		100	245⅓	8	21	.276	269	146	127	150	103	4.66
Major League Totals—7 Years		152	419⅓	17	33	.340	446	235	210	258	161	4.51

Signed as free agent by Pittsburgh Pirates' organization, November 25, 1971.

†On disabled list, July 13 to August 24, 1976.

‡Traded with Shortstop Mario Mendoza and Pitcher Rafael Vasquez to Seattle Mariners for Pitchers Enrique Romo and Rick Jones and Shortstop Tom McMillan, December 5, 1978.

§Traded to Pittsburgh Pirates' organization for a player to be named later, April 1, 1980; Seattle Mariners acquired Pitcher Larry Andersen to complete deal, October 29, 1980.

xOn disabled list, June 16 to July 6 and July 13 to August 3, 1980.

yDrafted by Texas Rangers, December 6, 1982.

zOn disabled list, August 19 to September 9, 1983.

ROBERT OLIVER JONES JR.

(Bobby)

Born October 11, 1949, at Elkton, Md.

Height, 6.03. Weight, 215.

Throws and bats lefthanded.

Tied major league record for most two-base hits, inning (2), July 3, 1983 (fifteenth inning).

Major League stolen bases: 1976 (3), 1984 (1), 1985 (1). Total—5.

Tied for American Association lead in game-winning RBIs with 11 in 1981.

Year Club	League	Pos.	G.	AB.	R.	H.	2B.	3B.	HR.	RBI.	B.A.	PO.	A.	E.	F.A.
1967—Geneva	NYP	1B	19	60	5	13	2	1	0	2	.217	115	5	0	1.000
1968—Salisbury	W. Car.	OF-1B	102	354	33	87	11	5	5	39	.246	327	24	17	.954
1969—Burlington	Carol.	OF-1B	39	111	7	22	1	0	1	6	.198	73	3	3	.962
1969—Shelby†	W. Car.	OF-1B	20	74	9	20	3	0	1	7	.270	50	2	1	.981
1970—							(In Military Service)								
1971—Anderson	W. Car.	1B-OF	116	424	82	136	19	5	23	77	.321	721	27	10	.987
1972—Denver	A. A.	OF	118	345	46	99	15	6	5	46	.287	159	6	4	.976
1973—Spokane	P. C.	OF	121	437	57	121	25	7	9	71	.277	186	6	1	*.995
1974—Spokane	P. C.	OF	131	466	87	140	18	5	16	91	.300	221	9	5	.979
1974—Texas	Amer.	OF	2	5	0	0	0	0	0	0	.000	5	0	0	1.000
1975—Spokane	P. C.	OF-1B	109	404	69	112	12	6	17	67	.277	210	4	3	.986
1975—Texas	Amer.	OF	9	11	2	1	0	0	0	0	.091	6	0	0	1.000
1976—Sacramento‡	P. C.	OF	26	93	16	33	5	2	10	29	.355	51	4	1	.982
1976—California	Amer.	OF-DH	78	166	22	35	6	0	6	17	.211	98	6	1	.990
1977—California	DH	14	17	3	3	0	0	1	3	.176	0	0	0	.000
1977—Salt Lake City	P. C.	OF-1B	94	353	71	120	28	10	18	85	.340	224	4	5	.979
1978—Salt Lake City§x	P. C.	OF-1B	122	460	79	141	31	6	14	102	.307	344	13	5	.986
1979-80—							(Out of Organized Baseball)								
1981—Wichita	A. A.	OF-1B	117	352	53	111	15	3	20	72	.315	332	19	2	.994
1981—Texas	Amer.	OF	10	34	4	9	1	0	3	7	.265	20	4	0	1.000
1982—Denver	A. A.	OF	82	261	44	83	19	5	12	51	.318	120	5	2	.984
1983—Oklahoma City	A. A.	1B	46	171	25	61	14	3	4	29	.357	268	22	2	.993
1983—Texas	Amer.	OF-1B	41	72	5	16	4	0	1	11	.222	24	0	0	1.000
1984—Texas y	Amer.	OF-1B	64	143	14	37	4	0	4	22	.259	139	7	1	.993
1985—Texas	Amer.	OF-1B	83	134	14	30	2	0	5	23	.224	44	0	0	1.000
Major League Totals—8 Years			301	582	64	131	17	0	20	83	.225	336	17	2	.994

Selected by Washington Senators' organization in 36th round of free-agent draft, June 6, 1967.

†On military list, August 18, 1969 through February 15, 1971.

‡Sold on waivers to California Angels, May 17, 1976.

§On disabled list, July 11 to July 21, 1978.

xReleased, January 29, 1979; signed by Wichita (Texas Rangers' organization), December 18, 1980.

yOn disabled list, July 23 to August 10, 1984.

RUPPERT SANDERSON JONES

Born March 12, 1955, at Dallas, Tex.

Height, 5.10. Weight, 171.

Throws and bats lefthanded.

Tied major league records for most strikeouts, two consecutive games (8), July 16 and 17, 1982; most putouts by outfielder, game (12), May 16, 1978, 16 innings.

Tied American League record for most chances accepted by outfielder, game (12), May 16, 1978, 16 innings.

Major League stolen bases: 1977 (13), 1978 (22), 1979 (33), 1980 (18), 1981 (7), 1982 (18), 1983 (11), 1984 (2), 1985 (7). Total—131.

Tied for Pioneer League lead in double plays by outfielders with 1 in 1973.

Year Club	League	Pos.	G.	AB.	R.	H.	2B.	3B.	HR.	RBI.	B.A.	PO.	A.	E.	F.A.
1973—Billings	Pion.	OF	61	193	45	58	10	4	4	31	.301	55	5	5	.923
1974—Waterloo	Midw.	OF	68	249	44	88	15	0	13	43	.353	94	7	3	.971
1974—San Jose	Calif.	OF	53	191	29	53	7	3	8	45	.277	101	2	4	.963
1975—Omaha	A. A.	OF	119	403	62	98	25	5	13	54	.243	171	15	*13	.935
1976—Omaha	A. A.	OF	102	359	65	94	15	9	19	73	.262	243	2	8	.968
1976—Kansas City†	Amer.	OF	28	51	9	11	1	1	1	7	.216	21	0	0	1.000

Year Club	League	Pos.	G.	AB.	R.	H.	2B.	3B.	HR.	RBI.	B.A.	PO.	A.	E.	F.A.
1977—Seattle	Amer.	OF	160	597	85	157	26	8	24	76	.263	465	11	9	.981
1978—Seattle‡	Amer.	OF	129	472	48	111	24	3	6	46	.235	393	10	6	.985
1979—Seattle§	Amer.	OF ●162		622	109	166	29	9	21	78	.267	453	13	5	.989
1980—New York xy	Amer.	OF	83	328	38	73	11	3	9	42	.223	246	4	3	.988
1981—San Diego	Nat.	OF	105	397	53	99	34	1	4	39	.249	295	9	2	.993
1982—San Diego z	Nat.	OF	116	424	69	120	20	2	12	61	.283	314	3	5	.984
1983—San Diego a	Nat.	OF-1B	133	335	42	78	12	3	12	49	.233	268	6	6	.979
1984—Evansville	A. A.	OF	48	160	30	50	9	3	9	45	.313	97	1	4	.961
1984—Detroit b	Amer.	OF	79	215	26	61	12	1	12	37	.284	150	4	0	1.000
1985—California	Amer.	OF	125	389	66	90	17	2	21	67	.231	179	12	1	.995
American League Totals—7 Years			766	2674	381	669	120	27	94	353	.250	1907	54	24	.988
National League Totals—3 Years			354	1156	164	297	66	6	28	149	.257	877	18	13	.986
Major League Totals—10 Years			1120	3830	545	966	186	33	122	502	.252	2784	72	37	.987

Selected by Kansas City Royals' organization in 3rd round of free-agent draft, June 5, 1973.
†Selected by Seattle Mariners in American League expansion draft, November 5, 1976.
‡On disabled list, June 16 to July 20, 1978.
§Traded with Pitcher Jim Lewis to New York Yankees for Outfielder Juan Beniquez, Pitchers Jim Beattie and Rick Anderson and Catcher Jerry Narron, November 1, 1979.
xOn disabled list, May 27 to July 10 and August 26, 1980 through remainder of season.
yTraded with Outfielder Joe Lefebvre and Pitchers Tim Lollar and Chris Welsh to San Diego Padres for Outfielder Jerry Mumphrey and Pitcher John Pacella, April 1, 1981.
zOn disabled list, August 6 to August 21, 1982.
aGranted free agency, November 7, 1983; signed by Detroit Tigers, April 10, 1984.
bGranted free agency, November 8, 1984; signed by California Angels, January 30, 1985.

CHAMPIONSHIP SERIES RECORD

Year Club	League	Pos.	G.	AB.	R.	H.	2B.	3B.	HR.	RBI.	B.A.	PO.	A.	E.	F.A.
1984—Detroit	Amer.	PH-OF	2	5	1	0	0	0	0	0	.000	5	0	0	1.000

WORLD SERIES RECORD

Year Club	League	Pos.	G.	AB.	R.	H.	2B.	3B.	HR.	RBI.	B.A.	PO.	A.	E.	F.A.
1984—Detroit	Amer.	OF	2	3	0	0	0	0	0	0	.000	3	0	0	1.000

ALL-STAR GAME RECORD

Year League	Pos.	AB.	R.	H.	2B.	3B.	HR.	RBI.	B.A.	PO.	A.	E.	F.A.
1977—American	PH	1	0	0	0	0	0	0	.000	0	0	0	.000
1982—National	PH	1	1	1	0	1	0	0	1.000	0	0	0	.000
All-Star Game Totals—2 Years...................		2	1	1	0	1	0	0	.500	0	0	0	.000

TRACY DONALD JONES

Born March 31, 1961, at Inglewood, Calif.
Height, 6.03. Weight, 180.
Throws and bats righthanded.
Attended Loyola Marymount University, Los Angeles, Calif.

Year Club	League	Pos.	G.	AB.	R.	H.	2B.	3B.	HR.	RBI.	B.A.	PO.	A.	E.	F.A.
1983—Tampa	Fla. St.	O-3-1-S	53	118	27	32	5	3	1	15	.271	54	12	11	.857
1983—Eugene	N'west	2B-3B-OF	55	203	42	54	12	0	1	26	.266	81	68	12	.925
1984—Tampa†	Fla. St.	OF	86	307	50	95	14	3	4	41	.309	150	6	0	1.000
1985—Vermont	East.	OF	75	284	40	90	12	3	4	31	.317	117	4	1	.992
1985—Denver	A. A.	OF	51	205	43	69	12	0	10	31	.337	93	2	0	1.000

Selected by New York Mets' organization in 4th round of free-agent draft, June 7, 1982.
Selected by Cincinnati Reds' organization in secondary phase of free-agent draft, January 11, 1983.
†On disabled list, July 18 to September 18, 1984.

MICHAEL JORGENSEN

(Mike)

Born August 16, 1948, at Passaic, N. J.
Height, 6.00. Weight, 187.
Throws and bats lefthanded.
Attended St. John's University, Jamaica, N. Y.

Major League stolen bases: 1970 (2), 1971 (1), 1972 (12), 1973 (16), 1974 (3), 1975 (3), 1976 (7), 1977 (3), 1978 (3), 1981 (4), 1982 (2), 1985 (2). Total—58.
Tied for International League lead in sacrifice flies with 8 in 1969.
Named first baseman on THE SPORTING NEWS National League All-Star fielding team, 1973.

Year Club	League	Pos.	G.	AB.	R.	H.	2B.	3B.	HR.	RBI.	B.A.	PO.	A.	E.	F.A.
1966—Marion..................	Appal.	1B	46	150	30	47	0	0	8	37	.313	298	16	4	.987
1967—Winter Haven.......	Fla. St.	1B-OF	84	302	56	89	11	4	5	41	.295	639	29	7	.990
1968—New York.............	Nat.	1B	8	14	0	2	1	0	0	0	.143	32	1	0	1.000
1968—Memphis.............	Texas	1B	28	100	7	16	1	2	0	10	.160	211	11	0	1.000
1968—Raleigh-Dur.	Carol.	1B-OF	57	213	34	67	13	4	3	27	.315	311	25	3	.991
1969—Tidewater.............	Int.	1B	105	359	75	104	15	5	21	69	.290	882	50	5	★.995
1970—New York.............	Nat.	1B-OF	76	87	15	17	3	1	3	4	.195	145	12	3	.981
1971—Tidewater.............	Int.	1B-OF	65	228	50	78	12	1	15	41	.342	157	7	3	.982
1971—New York†...........	Nat.	OF-1B	45	118	16	26	1	1	5	11	.220	64	2	3	.957
1972—Montreal‡.............	Nat.	1B-OF	113	372	48	86	12	3	13	47	.231	801	57	6	.993
1973—Montreal.............	Nat.	★1B-OF	138	413	49	95	16	2	9	47	.230	1002	80	5	★.995

Year Club	League	Pos.	G.	AB.	R.	H.	2B.	3B.	HR.	RBI.	B.A.	PO.	A.	E.	F.A.
1974—Montreal	Nat.	1B-OF	131	287	45	89	16	1	11	59	.310	653	54	1	.999
1975—Montreal	Nat.	1B-OF	144	445	58	116	18	0	18	67	.261	1153	91	7	.994
1976—Montreal	Nat.	1B-OF	125	343	36	87	13	0	6	23	.254	651	58	8	.989
1977—Montreal§	Nat.	1B	19	20	3	4	1	0	0	0	.200	23	4	0	1.000
1977—Oakland xy	Amer.	1B-OF	66	203	18	50	4	1	8	32	.246	365	32	4	.990
1978—Texas	Amer.	1B-OF	96	97	20	19	3	0	1	9	.196	317	31	2	.994
1979—Texas za	Amer.	1B-OF	90	157	21	35	7	0	6	16	.223	320	31	4	.989
1980—New York	Nat.	1B-OF	119	321	43	82	11	0	7	43	.255	562	37	4	.993
1981—New York	Nat.	1B-OF	86	122	8	25	5	2	3	15	.205	143	9	1	.993
1982—New York	Nat.	1B-OF	120	114	16	29	6	0	2	14	.254	131	5	2	.986
1983—N.Y.b-Atl.	Nat.	1B-OF	95	72	10	18	4	0	2	11	.250	81	6	0	1.000
1984—Atl. c-St.L.	Nat.	1B-OF	90	124	9	31	5	2	1	17	.250	222	19	2	.992
1985—St. Louis d	Nat.	1B-OF	72	112	14	22	6	0	0	11	.196	318	17	2	.994
National League Totals—15 Years			1381	2964	370	729	118	12	80	369	.246	5981	432	44	.993
American League Totals—3 Years			252	457	59	104	14	1	15	57	.228	1002	94	10	.991
Major League Totals—17 Years			1633	3421	429	833	132	13	95	426	.243	6983	526	54	.993

Selected by New York Mets' organization in free-agent draft, June 30, 1966.

†Traded with Infielder Tim Foli and Outfielder Ken Singleton to Montreal Expos for Outfielder Rusty Staub, April 6, 1972.

‡On military list, July 7 to July 10 and July 20 to August 6, 1972.

§Traded to Oakland Athletics for Pitcher Stan Bahnsen, May 22, 1977.

xOn disabled list, July 11 to August 31, 1977.

yGranted free agency, October 20, 1977; signed by Texas Rangers, January 21, 1978.

zOn disabled list, June 1 to July 1, 1979.

aTraded to New York Mets, October 23, 1979; completing deal in which the Texas Rangers acquired First Baseman Willie Montanez for two players to be named later, August 12, 1979; New York organization acquired Pitcher Ed Lynch as partial completion of deal, September 18, 1979.

bSold to Atlanta Braves, June 15, 1983.

cTraded with Pitcher Ken Dayley to St. Louis Cardinals for Third Baseman Ken Oberkfell, June 15, 1984.

dGranted free agency, November 12, 1985.

CHAMPIONSHIP SERIES RECORD

Year Club	League	Pos.	G.	AB.	R.	H.	2B.	3B.	HR.	RBI.	B.A.	PO.	A.	E.	F.A.
1985—St. Louis	Nat.	PH	2	2	0	0	0	0	0	0	.000	0	0	0	.000

WORLD SERIES RECORD

Year Club	League	Pos.	G.	AB.	R.	H.	2B.	3B.	HR.	RBI.	B.A.	PO.	A.	E.	F.A.
1985—St. Louis	Nat.	PH-OF	2	3	0	0	0	0	0	0	.000	1	0	0	1.000

WALLACE KEITH JOYNER

(Wally)

Born June 16, 1962, at Atlanta, Ga.
Height, 6.02. Weight, 185.
Throws and bats lefthanded.
Attended Brigham Young University, Provo, Utah.

Tied for Eastern League lead in intentional bases on balls received with 8 in 1984.
Led Pacific Coast League first basemen in total chances with 1,229 and double plays with 121 in 1985.

Year Club	League	Pos.	G.	AB.	R.	H.	2B.	3B.	HR.	RBI.	B.A.	PO.	A.	E.	F.A.
1983—Peoria	Midw.	1B	54	192	25	63	16	2	3	33	.328	480	45	6	.989
1984—Waterbury	East.	1B-OF	134	467	81	148	24	7	12	72	.317	906	86	9	.991
1985—Edmonton	P. C.	1B	126	477	68	135	29	5	12	73	.283	★1107	★107	●15	.988

Selected by California Angels' organization in 3rd round of free-agent draft, June 6, 1983.

EDWARD JAMES JURAK

Name pronounced YOU-rack.

(Ed)

Born October 24, 1957, at Los Angeles, Calif.
Height, 6.02. Weight, 185.
Throws and bats righthanded.

Major League stolen bases: 1983 (1).
Led Eastern League shortstops in double plays with 76 in 1979.

Year Club	League	Pos.	G.	AB.	R.	H.	2B.	3B.	HR.	RBI.	B.A.	PO.	A.	E.	F.A.
1975—Elmira	NYP	SS	68	250	41	63	9	3	0	25	.252	104	192	★43	.873
1976—Winston-Salem	Carol.	SS	113	401	49	88	6	2	4	35	.219	168	346	★55	.903
1977—Bristol	East.	SS	123	441	74	116	12	8	1	36	.263	173	345	26	.952
1978—Pawtucket	Int.	SS-3B	23	46	9	12	1	1	0	6	.261	11	34	8	.849
1978—Winter Haven†	Fla. St.	SS-3B-1B	38	139	14	37	0	1	0	11	.266	49	99	16	.902
1979—Bristol	East.	SS	135	435	50	96	17	2	0	41	.221	★208	★374	★40	.936
1980—Pawtucket‡	Int.	SS-3B	83	221	16	58	8	1	3	31	.262	72	130	19	.914
1981—Bristol§	East.	SS-3B-2B	87	297	63	101	19	3	1	25	★.340	114	194	29	.914
1981—Pawtucket	Int.	SS	23	90	13	27	3	2	1	9	.300	39	81	10	.923
1982—Pawtucket	Int.	3B-SS	81	284	39	84	14	1	9	43	.296	53	177	17	.931
1982—Boston	Amer.	3B-OF	12	21	3	7	0	0	0	7	.333	7	17	2	.923
1983—Boston	Amer.	S-1-3-2	75	159	19	44	8	4	0	18	.277	197	117	11	.966
1984—Boston	Amer.	1-2-3-S	47	66	6	16	3	1	1	7	.242	92	40	3	.978

Year Club	League	Pos.	G.	AB.	R.	H.	2B.	3B.	HR.	RBI.	B.A.	PO.	A.	E.	F.A.
1985—Pawtucket............ Int.	3B-OF-1B	72	263	33	68	11	2	6	38	.259	183	75	8	.970	
1985—Boston.................... Amer.	3-S-1-O	26	13	4	3	0	0	0	0	.231	5	10	2	.882	
Major League Totals—4 Years................		160	259	32	70	11	5	1	32	.270	301	184	18	.964	

Selected by Boston Red Sox' organization in 3rd round of free-agent draft, June 4, 1975.
†On disabled list, May 4 to June 16, 1978.
‡On disabled list, April 16 to April 28 and May 28 to June 7, 1980.
§On disabled list, June 10 to July 4, 1981.

JEFFREY PATRICK KAISER
(Jeff)

Born July 24, 1960, at Wyandotte, Mich.
Height, 6.03. Weight, 195.
Throws left and bats righthanded.
Received bachelor of arts degree in business administration from
Western Michigan University, Kalamazoo, Mich.

Year Club	League	G.	IP.	W.	L.	Pct.	H.	R.	ER.	SO.	BB.	ERA.
1982—Medford	Northwest	15	78	8	1	★.889	91	56	46	69	57	5.31
1983—Modesto............................	California	25	164⅔	12	9	.571	160	84	70	102	80	3.83
1984—Albany..............................	Eastern	7	47⅔	5	1	.833	36	11	10	20	15	1.89
1984—Tacoma†............................	P. Coast	14	74⅔	4	7	.364	81	52	38	38	28	4.58
1985—Oakland............................	American	15	16⅔	0	0	.000	25	32	27	10	20	14.58
1985—Tacoma‡............................	P. Coast	27	46⅓	4	2	.667	33	10	9	36	18	1.75
Major League Totals—1 Year..............................		15	16⅔	0	0	.000	25	32	27	10	20	14.58

Selected by Toronto Blue Jays' organization in 7th round of free-agent draft, June 8, 1981.
Selected by Oakland A's organization in 10th round of free-agent draft, June 7, 1982.
†On disabled list, July 20 to August 3, 1984.
‡On disabled list, June 21 to July 7, 1985.

ROBERT HENRY KEARNEY
Name pronounced KERN-ee.
(Bob)

Born October 3, 1956, at San Antonio, Tex.
Height, 6.00. Weight, 185.
Throws and bats righthanded.
Attended University of Texas, Austin, Tex.

Major League stolen bases: 1983 (1), 1984 (7), 1985 (1). Total—9.
Led American League catchers in total chances with 897 in 1984.
Tied for Pioneer League lead in double plays by catchers with 4 in 1977.

Year Club	League	Pos.	G.	AB.	R.	H.	2B.	3B.	HR.	RBI.	B.A.	PO.	A.	E.	F.A.
1977—Great Falls........... Pion.	C	58	211	49	50	7	0	7	34	.237	★417	★56	10	.979	
1978—Cedar Rapids....... Midw.	C	28	89	8	24	3	0	1	15	.270	182	23	2	.990	
1978—Waterbury........... East.	C	38	125	10	21	3	0	1	8	.168	195	33	9	.962	
1979—Shreveport .... Texas	C	63	224	27	60	9	1	4	24	.268	312	49	7	.981	
1979—Phoenix .... P. C.	C	38	124	11	17	2	1	2	10	.137	183	27	7	.968	
1979—San Francisco ...... Nat.	C	2	0	0	0	0	0	0	0	.000	0	0	0	.000	
1980—Phoenix†.............. P. C.	C	92	298	42	68	8	3	2	24	.228	358	68	11	.975	
1981—Tacoma................. P. C.	C	86	278	38	70	13	2	3	29	.252	487	73	9	.984	
1981—Oakland................ Amer.	C	1	0	0	0	0	0	0	0	.000	0	0	0	.000	
1982—Oakland................ Amer.	C	22	71	7	12	3	0	0	5	.169	114	14	4	.970	
1982—Tacoma................. P. C.	C	115	388	41	98	13	3	7	55	.253	589	93	9	.987	
1983—Oakland‡.............. Amer.	C	108	298	33	76	11	0	8	32	.255	437	41	9	.982	
1984—Seattle.................. Amer.	C	133	431	39	97	24	1	7	43	.225	★823	63	11	.988	
1985—Seattle.................. Amer.	C	108	305	24	74	14	1	6	27	.243	529	50	3	★.995	
National League Totals—1 Year.............		2	0	0	0	0	0	0	0	.000	0	0	0	.000	
American League Totals—5 Years		372	1105	103	259	52	2	21	107	.234	1903	168	27	.987	
Major League Totals—6 Years................		374	1105	103	259	52	2	21	107	.234	1903	168	27	.987	

Selected by San Francisco Giants' organization in 14th round of free-agent draft, June 7, 1977.
†Drafted by Tacoma (Oakland A's organization), December 9, 1980.
‡Traded with Pitcher Dave Beard to Seattle Mariners for Pitcher Bill Caudill and a player to be named later, November 21, 1983; Oakland A's acquired Pitcher Darrel Akerfelds to complete deal, December 7, 1983.

CHARLES PATRICK KEEDY
(Pat)

Born January 10, 1959, at Birmingham, Ala.
Height, 6.04. Weight, 205.
Throws and bats righthanded.
Attended Auburn University, Auburn, Ala.

Led Eastern League third basemen in double plays with 25 in 1981.

Year Club	League	Pos.	G.	AB.	R.	H.	2B.	3B.	HR.	RBI.	B.A.	PO.	A.	E.	F.A.
1979—Salinas .... Calif.	3B-SS	52	125	22	26	3	0	4	15	.208	47	109	9	.945	
1980—El Paso................. Texas	SS-3B	26	98	11	14	3	0	1	10	.143	29	87	14	.892	
1980—Salinas† .... Calif.	SS-3B	42	118	16	26	4	0	4	17	.220	32	89	11	.917	
1981—Holyoke................. East.	3B-2B-1B	107	367	45	90	14	2	6	34	.245	63	239	23	.929	

Year Club	League	Pos.	G.	AB.	R.	H.	2B.	3B.	HR.	RBI.	B.A.	PO.	A.	E.	F.A.
1982—Holyoke................	East.	3B-SS	125	437	68	108	19	6	19	73	.247	91	279	30	.925
1983—Edmonton‡..........	P. C.	3-O-1-2-S	66	210	38	47	13	1	14	40	.224	46	123	17	.909
1984—Edmonton.............	P. C.	3-O-S-1	100	348	64	90	20	4	17	53	.259	119	124	18	.931
1985—Edmonton.............	P. C.	I-O-P-C	107	365	59	101	24	4	17	61	.277	201	116	12	.964
1985—California..............	Amer.	3B-OF	3	4	1	2	1	0	1	1	.500	1	0	0	1.000
Major League Totals—1 Year.................			3	4	1	2	1	0	1	1	.500	1	0	0	1.000

Selected by Chicago White Sox' organization in 13th round of free-agent draft, June 8, 1976.
Selected by California Angels' organization in 5th round of free-agent draft, June 5, 1979.
†On disabled list, August 13, 1980 through remainder of season.
‡On disabled list, May 17 to June 17 and July 5 to July 20, 1983.

PITCHING RECORD

Year Club	League	G.	IP.	W.	L.	Pct.	H.	R.	ER.	SO.	BB.	ERA.
1985—Edmonton......................	P. Coast	2	3	0	0	.000	1	1	1	0	2	3.00

STEVEN F. KEMP
(Steve)

Born August 7, 1954, at San Angelo, Tex.
Height, 6.00. Weight, 190.
Throws and bats lefthanded.
Attended University of Southern California, Los Angeles, Calif.

Major League stolen bases: 1977 (3), 1978 (2), 1979 (5), 1980 (5), 1981 (9), 1982 (7), 1983 (1), 1984 (4), 1985 (1). Total—37.
Received reported $50,000 bonus to sign with Detroit Tigers, 1976.
Named outfielder on THE SPORTING NEWS College Baseball All-America Team, 1975.

Year Club	League	Pos.	G.	AB.	R.	H.	2B.	3B.	HR.	RBI.	B.A.	PO.	A.	E.	F.A.
1976—Montgomery.........	South.	OF-1B	73	256	41	74	17	2	8	43	.289	91	4	2	.979
1976—Evansville	A. A.	OF	52	171	37	66	14	3	11	38	.386	91	2	5	.945
1977—Detroit...................	Amer.	OF	151	552	75	142	29	4	18	88	.257	252	10	5	.981
1978—Detroit...................	Amer.	OF	159	582	75	161	18	4	15	79	.277	325	11	8	.977
1979—Detroit...................	Amer.	OF	134	490	88	156	26	3	26	105	.318	229	12	6	.976
1980—Detroit...................	Amer.	OF	135	508	88	149	23	3	21	101	.293	197	4	1	.995
1981—Detroit†.................	Amer.	OF	105	372	52	103	18	4	9	49	.277	207	4	3	.986
1982—Chicago‡...............	Amer.	OF	160	580	91	166	23	1	19	98	.286	280	6	7	.976
1983—New York§...........	Amer.	OF	109	373	53	90	17	3	12	49	.241	215	5	3	.987
1984—New York xy	Amer.	OF	94	313	37	91	12	1	7	41	.291	138	2	4	.972
1985—Pittsburgh z	Nat.	OF	92	236	19	59	13	2	2	21	.250	105	1	0	1.000
American League Totals—8 Years			1047	3770	559	1058	166	23	127	610	.281	1843	54	37	.981
National League Totals—1 Year..............			92	236	19	59	13	2	2	21	.250	105	1	0	1.000
Major League Totals—9 Years...............			1139	4006	578	1117	179	25	129	631	.279	1948	55	37	.982

Selected by Detroit Tigers' organization in 1st round (first player selected) of free-agent draft, January 7, 1976.
†Traded to Chicago White Sox for Outfielder Chet Lemon, November 27, 1981.
‡Granted free agency, November 10, 1982; signed by New York Yankees as Type A player, December 8, 1982. (Pitcher Steve Mura was selected from player compensation pool by Chicago White Sox, January 26, 1983.)
§On disabled list, September 15, 1983 through remainder of season.
xOn disabled list, April 4 to April 20, 1984.
yTraded with Infielder Tim Foli and $800,000 to Pittsburgh Pirates for Infielder Dale Berra, Pitcher Alfonso Pulido and Outfielder Jay Buhner, December 20, 1984.
zOn disabled list, April 6 to April 21, 1985.

ALL-STAR GAME RECORD

Year League	Pos.	AB.	R.	H.	2B.	3B.	HR.	RBI.	B.A.	PO.	A.	E.	F.A.
1979—American	PH	1	0	0	0	0	0	0	.000	0	0	0	.000

TERRENCE EDWARD KENNEDY
(Terry)

Born June 4, 1956, at Euclid, O.
Height, 6.04. Weight, 224.
Throws right and bats lefthanded.
Attended Florida State University, Tallahassee, Fla.

Son of Bob Kennedy, third baseman-outfielder with Chicago AL, Cleveland, Baltimore, Detroit and Brooklyn, 1939 through 1957; scout, Cleveland, 1958 through 1961; minor league manager, Chicago Cubs' organization, 1962; coach, Chicago Cubs, 1963 and 1964; Chicago Cubs executive, 1965; minor league manager, Los Angeles Dodgers' organization, 1966; coach, Atlanta Braves, 1967; manager, Oakland A's, 1968; Director of Player Development, St. Louis Cardinals, 1969 through 1976; Executive Vice President, Chicago Cubs, 1977 through 1981, and Houston Astros Vice-President-Baseball Operations since 1982; brother of Bob Kennedy Jr., pitcher in St. Louis Cardinals' organization, 1971 through 1975; scout, Seattle Mariners, 1976; scout, Chicago Cubs, 1977 through 1981, and scout with Houston Astros since 1982.

Tied National League record for most two-base hits by catcher, season (40), 1982.
Major League stolen bases: 1982 (1), 1983 (1), 1984 (1). Total—3.
Led Major League catchers in double plays with 12 in 1981 and tied for lead with 11 in 1982 and 12 in 1985.
Named catcher on THE SPORTING NEWS National League Silver Slugger team, 1983.
Named College Player of the Year by THE SPORTING NEWS, 1977.
Received reported $100,000 bonus to sign with St. Louis Cardinals, 1977.
Named catcher on THE SPORTING NEWS College Baseball All-America Team, 1976 and 1977.

Year Club	League	Pos.	G.	AB.	R.	H.	2B.	3B.	HR.	RBI.	B.A.	PO.	A.	E.	F.A.
1977—Johnson City	Appal.	C-1B	12	39	14	23	7	2	3	15	.590	66	3	1	.986
1977—St. Petersburg	Fla. St.	C	45	166	22	41	8	0	4	22	.247	168	22	6	.969
1978—Arkansas	Texas	C-OF	69	239	55	69	14	0	10	54	.289	365	30	7	.983
1978—Springfield	A. A.	C-1B	64	230	35	76	13	0	10	46	.330	331	26	7	.981
1978—St. Louis	Nat.	C	10	29	0	5	0	0	0	2	.172	46	4	1	.980
1979—Springfield	A. A.	C	84	294	35	86	18	1	13	64	.293	434	38	13	.973
1979—St. Louis	Nat.	C	33	109	11	31	7	0	2	17	.284	135	7	1	.993
1980—St. Louis†	Nat.	C-OF	84	248	28	63	12	3	4	34	.254	231	22	7	.973
1981—San Diego	Nat.	C	101	382	32	115	24	1	2	41	.301	465	63	★20	.964
1982—San Diego	Nat.	C-1B	153	562	75	166	42	1	21	97	.295	777	66	9	.989
1983—San Diego	Nat.	C-1B	149	549	47	156	27	2	17	98	.284	807	82	12	.987
1984—San Diego	Nat.	C	148	530	54	127	16	1	14	57	.240	708	54	14	.982
1985—San Diego	Nat.	C-1B	143	532	54	139	27	1	10	74	.261	662	68	10	.986
Major League Totals—8 Years			821	2941	301	802	155	9	70	420	.273	3831	366	74	.983

Selected by St. Louis Cardinals' organization in 1st round (sixth player selected) of free-agent draft, June 7, 1977.

†Traded with Catcher Steve Swisher, Pitchers John Littlefield, Al Olmsted, Kim Seaman and John Urrea and Infielder Mike Phillips to San Diego Padres for Pitchers Rollie Fingers and Bob Shirley, Catcher-First Baseman Gene Tenace and a player to be named later, December 8, 1980; St. Louis Cardinals' organization acquired catcher Bob Geren to complete deal, December 10, 1980.

CHAMPIONSHIP SERIES RECORD

Year Club	League	Pos.	G.	AB.	R.	H.	2B.	3B.	HR.	RBI.	B.A.	PO.	A.	E.	F.A.
1984—San Diego	Nat.	C	5	18	2	4	0	0	0	1	.222	28	4	0	1.000

WORLD SERIES RECORD

Year Club	League	Pos.	G.	AB.	R.	H.	2B.	3B.	HR.	RBI.	B.A.	PO.	A.	E.	F.A.
1984—San Diego	Nat.	C	5	19	2	4	1	0	1	3	.211	30	2	0	1.000

ALL-STAR GAME RECORD

Year League	Pos.	AB.	R.	H.	2B.	3B.	HR.	RBI.	B.A.	PO.	A.	E.	F.A.
1981—National	PH	1	0	0	0	0	0	0	.000	0	0	0	.000
1985—National	C	2	0	1	0	0	0	1	.500	0	0	1	.000
All-Star Game Totals—2 Years		3	0	1	0	0	0	1	.333	0	0	1	.000

Member of National League All-Star Team in 1983; did not play.

MATTHEW LON KEOUGH

Name pronounced KEE-oh.

(Matt)

Born July 3, 1955, at Pomona, Calif.
Height, 6.02. Weight, 175.
Throws and bats righthanded.
Attended University of California, Los Angeles, Calif.
Son of Marty Keough, outfielder-first baseman with Boston, Cleveland, Washington, Cincinnati, Atlanta and Chicago N.L., 1956 through 1966; minor league manager, San Diego Padres' organization, 1970; scout, San Diego Padres, 1969 through 1976; scout, Los Angeles Dodgers, 1977 through 1979; and scout St. Louis Cardinals since 1980; nephew of Joe Keough, outfielder with Oakland A's, Kansas City Royals and Chicago White Sox, 1968 through 1973.

Tied major league record for most consecutive games lost, start of season (14), 1979.
Led American League in home runs allowed with 38 in 1982.
Tied for California League lead in sacrifice flies with 9 in 1975.
Named American League Comeback Player of the Year by THE SPORTING NEWS, 1980.

Year Club	League	G.	IP.	W.	L.	Pct.	H.	R.	ER.	SO.	BB.	ERA.
1976—Chattanooga	Southern	2	2	0	0	.000	1	0	0	2	0	0.00
1977—Chattanooga	Southern	26	175	9	12	.429	162	87	74	★153	67	3.81
1977—Oakland	American	7	43	1	3	.250	39	25	23	23	22	4.81
1978—Oakland	American	32	197	8	15	.348	178	90	71	108	85	3.24
1979—Oakland	American	30	177	2	17	.105	220	115	99	95	78	5.03
1980—Oakland	American	34	250	16	13	.552	218	94	81	121	94	2.92
1981—Oakland	American	19	140	10	6	.625	125	56	53	60	45	3.41
1982—Oakland	American	34	209⅓	11	●18	.379	233	★144	★133	75	101	5.72
1983—Oakland†-New York	American	26	99⅔	5	7	.417	109	71	59	54	51	5.33
1984—Nashville‡§	Southern	7	40	2	4	.333	41	32	30	32	32	6.75
1985—Louisville xy	Am. Assoc.	19	110	3	7	.300	88	44	41	92	42	3.35
1985—St. Louis z	National	4	10	0	1	.000	10	5	5	10	4	4.50
American League Totals—7 Years		182	1116	53	79	.402	1122	595	519	536	476	4.19
National League Totals—1 Year		4	10	0	1	.000	10	5	5	10	4	4.50
Major League Totals—8 Years		186	1126	53	80	.398	1132	600	524	546	480	4.19

Selected by Oakland A's organization in 7th round of free-agent draft, June 5, 1973.
†Traded to New York Yankees for First Baseman Marshall Brant and Pitcher Ben Callahan, June 15, 1983.
‡On disabled list, May 22 to September 10, 1984.
§Released, November 5, 1984; signed by St. Louis Cardinals' organization, April 21, 1985.
xOn temporary inactive list, April 21 to May 7, 1985.
yOn disabled list, June 3 to June 21, 1985.
zGranted free agency, November 12, 1985.

Year Club	League	G.	IP.	W.	L.	Pct.	H.	R.	ER.	SO.	BB.	ERA.
1981—Oakland	American	1	8⅓	0	1	.000	7	2	1	4	6	1.08

ALL-STAR GAME RECORD

Year League	IP.	W.	L.	Pct.	H.	R.	ER.	SO.	BB.	ERA.
1978—American	⅓	0	0	.000	1	0	0	0	0	0.00

RECORD AS INFIELDER

Led Southern League third basemen in putouts with 110 and assists with 252 in 1976.
Led California League shortstops in errors with 56 in 1975.

Year—Club	League	Pos.	G.	AB.	R.	H.	2B.	3B.	HR.	RBI.	B.A.	PO.	A.	E.	F.A.
1974—Burlington	Midw.	SS-1B	98	323	31	64	14	2	4	24	.198	143	207	34	.911
1975—Modesto	Calif.	SS-3B	123	445	73	135	∗34	2	13	81	.303	191	312	57	.898
1976—Chattanooga	South.	3-S-O-1-P	124	420	43	88	13	3	6	52	.210	125	274	25	.941

KURT DAVID KEPSHIRE

Born July 3, 1959, at Bridgeport, Conn.
Height, 6.01. Weight, 180.
Throws right and bats lefthanded.
Attended University of New Haven, New Haven, Conn.

Tied for Pioneer League lead in intentional bases on balls issued with 4 in 1979.

Year Club	League	G.	IP.	W.	L.	Pct.	H.	R.	ER.	SO.	BB.	ERA.
1979—Billings	Pioneer	24	50	4	0	1.000	30	16	14	57	27	2.52
1980—Tampa	Florida St.	29	54	5	4	.556	48	20	12	26	19	2.00
1980—Eugene	Northwest	8	42	3	3	.500	54	36	29	18	15	6.21
1981—Cedar Rapids	Midwest	39	98	7	5	.583	98	63	47	94	32	4.32
1982—Cedar Rapids	Midwest	21	33	3	1	.750	23	11	8	29	10	2.18
1982—Waterbury	Eastern	30	46⅓	1	4	.200	35	22	21	31	22	4.08
1982—Indianapolis†	Am. Assoc.	5	9	0	0	.000	7	5	5	5	2	5.00
1983—Arkansas	Texas	19	35⅔	3	2	.600	35	17	14	23	5	3.53
1983—Louisville	Am. Assoc.	21	83⅓	6	2	.750	88	44	34	52	24	3.67
1984—Louisville	Am. Assoc.	16	107⅔	7	5	.583	87	56	55	85	63	4.60
1984—St. Louis	National	17	109	6	5	.545	100	47	40	71	44	3.30
1985—St. Louis	National	32	153⅓	10	9	.526	155	89	81	67	71	4.75
Major League Totals—2 Years		49	262⅓	16	14	.533	255	136	121	138	115	4.15

Selected by Cincinnati Reds' organization in 24th round of free-agent draft, June 5, 1979.
†Drafted by St. Louis Cardinals, December 6, 1982.

CHARLES PATRICK KERFELD
(Charlie)

Born September 28, 1963, at Carson City, Nev.
Height, 6.06. Weight, 225.
Throws and bats righthanded.
Attended Yavapai College, Prescott, Ariz.

Led South Atlantic League pitchers in complete games with 12 and tied for lead in games started with 28 in 1983.
Named South Atlantic League Pitcher of the Year, 1983.

Year Club	League	G.	IP.	W.	L.	Pct.	H.	R.	ER.	SO.	BB.	ERA.
1983—Asheville	S. Atlantic	28	∗192	∗16	10	.615	171	84	62	189	85	2.91
1984—Columbus†	Southern	24	162⅔	14	9	.609	140	80	54	118	79	2.99
1984—Tucson	P. Coast	1	3⅔	0	1	.000	6	4	4	3	1	9.82
1985—Tucson	P. Coast	26	163⅓	10	11	.476	176	95	80	123	74	4.41
1985—Houston	National	11	44⅓	4	2	.667	44	22	20	30	25	4.06
Major League Totals—1 Year		11	44⅓	4	2	.667	44	22	20	30	25	4.06

Selected by Philadelphia Phillies' organization in 24th round of free-agent draft, June 8, 1981.
Selected by Seattle Mariners' organization in secondary phase of free-agent draft, January 12, 1982.
Selected by Houston Astros' organization in secondary phase of free-agent draft, June 7, 1982.
†On disabled list, June 4 to June 28, 1984.

JAMES LESTER KERN
(Jim)

Born March 15, 1949, at Gladwin, Mich.
Height, 6.05. Weight, 195.
Throws and bats righthanded.
Attended Delta Junior College, University Center, Mich., and
Michigan State University, East Lansing, Mich.

Pitched seven-inning, 2-0 no-hit victory against San Jose, May 29, 1971.
Major League saves: 1976 (15), 1977 (18), 1978 (13), 1979 (29), 1980 (2), 1981 (6), 1982 (5). Total—88.
Led Western Carolinas League in wild pitches with 25 in 1970.
Tied for American Association lead in wild pitches with 17 and balks with 2 in 1974.
Tied for California League lead in balks with 2 in 1971.
Named American League co-Fireman of the Year by THE SPORTING NEWS, 1979.
Named righthanded pitcher on THE SPORTING NEWS American League All-Star Team, 1979.
Named American Association Pitcher of the Year, 1974.

Year Club	League	G.	IP.	W.	L.	Pct.	H.	R.	ER.	SO.	BB.	ERA.
1968—Rock Hill	W. Carol.	12	28	0	3	.000	29	30	21	25	26	6.75
1968—Sarasota Indians	Gulf Coast	12	45	4	4	.500	44	32	19	48	32	3.80
1969—†						(In Military Service)						
1970—Reno	California	4	15	0	0	.000	9	12	10	20	20	6.00
1970—Sumter	W. Carol.	14	72	5	6	.455	57	47	39	71	70	4.88
1971—Reno	California	24	100	7	9	.438	99	91	73	109	100	6.57
1972—Elmira	Eastern	22	104	3	11	.214	87	55	50	90	73	4.33
1973—San Antonio	Texas	25	166	11	7	.611	130	76	55	182	★129	2.98
1974—Oklahoma City	Am. Assoc.	25	189	★17	7	.708	139	63	53	★220	104	2.52
1974—Cleveland	American	4	15	0	1	.000	16	9	8	11	14	4.80
1975—Oklahoma City	Am. Assoc.	3	14	1	1	.500	12	10	10	11	11	6.43
1975—Cleveland	American	13	72	1	2	.333	60	31	30	55	45	3.75
1976—Cleveland	American	50	118	10	7	.588	91	38	31	111	50	2.36
1977—Cleveland	American	60	92	8	10	.444	85	39	35	91	47	3.42
1978—Cleveland‡	American	58	99	10	10	.500	77	36	34	95	58	3.09
1979—Texas	American	71	143	13	5	.722	99	35	25	136	62	1.57
1980—Texas§	American	38	63	3	11	.214	65	38	34	40	45	4.86
1981—Texas xyz	American	23	30	1	2	.333	21	10	9	20	22	2.70
1981—Wichita	Am. Assoc.	2	6	0	0	.000	2	0	0	6	5	0.00
1982—Cincinnati a	National	50	76	3	5	.375	61	27	24	43	48	2.84
1982—Chicago	American	13	28	2	1	.667	20	16	16	23	12	5.14
1983—Chicago bc	American	1	⅔	0	0	.000	1	1	0	0	0	0.00
1984—Philadelphia d	National	8	13⅓	0	1	.000	20	16	15	8	10	10.13
1984—El Paso	Texas	8	15	2	0	1.000	19	10	10	13	8	6.00
1984—Milwaukee e	American	6	4⅔	1	0	1.000	6	0	0	4	3	0.00
1985—Vancouver	P. Coast	5	9⅓	0	0	.000	3	3	3	4	8	2.89
1985—Milwaukee	American	5	11	0	1	.000	14	8	8	3	5	6.55
American League Totals—12 Years		342	676½	49	50	.495	555	261	230	589	363	3.06
National League Totals—2 Years		58	89⅓	3	6	.333	81	43	39	51	58	3.93
Major League Totals—12 Years		400	765⅔	52	56	.481	636	304	269	640	421	3.16

Signed as free agent by Cleveland Indians' organization, September 4, 1967.

†On military list, May 11, 1969 through January 7, 1970.

‡Traded with Infielder Larvell Blanks to Texas Rangers for Outfielder Bobby Bonds and Pitcher Len Barker, October 3, 1978.

§On disabled list, August 19 to September 15, 1980.

xOn disabled list, April 30 to June 2, 1981; included rehabilitation disability assignment to Wichita, May 26 to June 2, 1981.

yTraded to New York Mets for Second Baseman Doug Flynn and Pitcher Dan Boitano, December 11, 1981.

zTraded with Catcher Alex Trevino and Pitcher Greg Harris by New York Mets to Cincinnati Reds for Outfielder George Foster, February 10, 1982.

aTraded to Chicago White Sox for two players to be named later, August 23, 1982; Cincinnati Reds' organization acquired Third Baseman Wade Rowdon and Outfielder Leo Garcia to complete deal, September 7, 1982.

bOn disabled list, April 6, 1983 through remainder of season.

cReleased, March 1, 1984; signed by Philadelphia Phillies, June 3, 1984.

dReleased, July 27, 1984; signed by El Paso (Milwaukee Brewers' organization), August 8, 1984.

eGranted free agency, November 8, 1984; re-signed by Brewers' organization, January 8, 1985.

ALL-STAR GAME RECORD

Year League	IP.	W.	L.	Pct.	H.	R.	ER.	SO.	BB.	ERA.
1977—American	1	0	0	.000	0	0	0	2	0	0.00
1978—American	⅔	0	0	.000	1	0	0	1	1	0.00
1979—American	2⅔	0	1	.000	2	2	2	3	3	6.75
All-Star Game Totals—3 Years	4⅓	0	1	.000	3	2	2	6	4	4.15

JAMES EDWARD KEY
(Jimmy)

Born April 22, 1961, at Huntsville, Ala.
Height, 6.01. Weight, 185.
Throws left and bats righthanded.
Attended Clemson University, Clemson, S.C.

Major League saves: 1984 (10).

Year Club	League	G.	IP.	W.	L.	Pct.	H.	R.	ER.	SO.	BB.	ERA.
1982—Medicine Hat	Pioneer	5	31⅓	2	1	.667	27	12	8	25	10	2.30
1982—Florence	S. Atlantic	9	58	5	2	.714	59	33	24	49	18	3.72
1983—Knoxville	Southern	14	101	6	5	.545	86	35	32	57	40	2.85
1983—Syracuse	Int'national	16	89⅓	4	8	.333	87	58	41	71	33	4.13
1984—Toronto	American	63	62	4	5	.444	70	37	32	44	32	4.65
1985—Toronto†	American	35	212⅔	14	6	.700	188	77	71	85	50	3.00
Major League Totals—2 Years		98	274⅔	18	11	.621	258	114	103	129	82	3.37

Selected by Chicago White Sox' organization in 10th round of free-agent draft, June 5, 1979.

Selected by Toronto Blue Jays' organization in 3rd round of free-agent draft, June 7, 1982.

†Appeared in one game as a pinch-runner.

CHAMPIONSHIP SERIES RECORD

Year Club	League	G.	IP.	W.	L.	Pct.	H.	R.	ER.	SO.	BB.	ERA.
1985—Toronto	American	2	8⅔	0	1	.000	15	5	5	5	2	5.19

Year League	IP.	W.	L.	Pct.	H.	R.	ER.	SO.	BB.	ERA.
1985—American	⅓	0	0	.000	0	0	0	0	0	0.00

SAM KHALIFA
Name pronounced Kuh-LEE-fuh.
(Sammy)

Born December 5, 1963, at Fontana, Calif.
Height, 5.11. Weight, 170.
Throws and bats righthanded.

Major League stolen bases: 1985 (5).

Year Club	League	Pos.	G.	AB.	R.	H.	2B.	3B.	HR.	RBI.	B.A.	PO.	A.	E.	F.A.
1982—Bradenton Pir.	Gulf. C.	SS	6	25	1	2	0	0	0	0	.080	12	26	4	.905
1982—Greenwood...........	S. Atl.	SS	48	177	29	54	6	1	0	19	.305	69	136	19	.915
1983—Alexandria†	Carol.	★SS-2B	103	356	42	96	19	6	1	49	.270	156	279	★33	.929
1983—Lynn....................	East.	SS	5	15	1	3	0	0	0	1	.200	8	9	0	1.000
1984—Nashua‡	East.	SS	91	344	39	82	12	4	1	36	.238	151	266	24	.946
1985—Hawaii..................	P. C.	SS-2B	67	217	36	61	14	5	1	22	.281	89	193	11	.962
1985—Pittsburgh.............	Nat.	SS	95	.320	30	76	14	3	2	31	.238	156	316	16	.967
Major League Totals—1 Year................			95	320	30	76	14	3	2	31	.238	156	316	16	.967

Selected by Pittsburgh Pirates' organization in 1st round (seventh player selected) of free-agent draft, June 7, 1982.
†On disabled list, May 6 to May 21, 1983.
‡On disabled list, April 13 to May 9 and August 11, 1984 through remainder of season.

STEVEN GEORGE KIEFER
(Steve)

Born October 18, 1960, at Chicago, Ill.
Height, 6.01. Weight, 180.
Throws and bats righthanded.
Attended Cerritos College, Norwalk, Calif. and Fullerton College, Fullerton, Calif.

Led Pacific Coast League shortstops in errors with 35 in 1984.
Tied for Eastern League lead in sacrifice hits with 12 in 1983.

Year League		Pos.	G.	AB.	R.	H.	2B.	3B.	HR.	RBI.	B.A.	PO.	A.	E.	F.A.
1981—Medford	N'west	SS-3B	55	192	38	47	7	5	4	22	.245	68	175	17	.935
1982—Madison	Midw.	SS	124	415	72	97	24	1	15	58	.234	173	395	44	.928
1983—Albany..................	East.	SS-3B-OF	123	415	68	102	18	1	19	81	.246	186	306	38	.928
1984—Tacoma.................	P. C.	SS-3B	125	455	63	122	18	3	16	54	.268	189	328	38	.932
1984—Oakland................	Amer.	SS-3B	23	40	7	7	1	2	0	2	.175	15	35	5	.909
1985—Tacoma†..............	P. C.	3B-SS	85	331	41	87	25	2	12	53	.263	80	171	13	.951
1985—Oakland................	Amer.	3B	40	66	8	13	1	1	1	10	.197	15	37	7	.881
Major League Totals—2 Years................			63	106	15	20	2	3	1	12	.189	30	72	12	.895

Selected by Oakland A's organization in 1st round (16th player selected) of free-agent draft, January 13, 1981.
†On disabled list, May 6 to May 20, 1985.

DAVID ARTHUR KINGMAN
(Dave)

Born December 21, 1948, at Pendleton, Ore.
Height, 6.06. Weight, 215.
Throws and bats righthanded.
Attended Harper College, Palatine, Ill., and University of Southern
California, Los Angeles, Calif.

Tied major league records for most home runs, two consecutive games (5), July 27 and 28, 1979; most times, three or more home runs, game, season (2), May 17 and July 28, 1979; most strikeouts, nine-inning game (5), May 28, 1982; most unassisted double plays by first baseman, game (2), July 25, 1982.
Tied modern major league record for most clubs played on, season, major leagues (4), 1977.
Tied National League record for fewest errors by first baseman for leader in errors, season (13), 1974.
Major League stolen bases: 1971 (5), 1972 (16), 1973 (8), 1974 (8), 1975 (7), 1976 (7), 1977 (5), 1978 (3), 1979 (4), 1980 (2), 1981 (6), 1982 (4), 1983 (2), 1984 (2), 1985 (3). Total—82.
Hit three home runs in a game June 4, 1976, May 14, 1978 and May 17, July 28, 1979 and April 16, 1984.
Hit for the cycle, April 16, 1972.
Led American League in sacrifice flies with 14 in 1984.
Led National League batters in strikeouts with 131 in 1979, 105 in 1981 and 156 in 1982.
Led National League in slugging percentage with .613 in 1979.
Led National League first basemen in errors with 13 in 1974.
Named American League Comeback Player of the Year by THE SPORTING NEWS, 1984.
Named designated hitter on THE SPORTING NEWS American League All-Star Team, 1984.
Named outfielder on THE SPORTING NEWS National League All-Star Team, 1979.
Named outfielder on THE SPORTING NEWS College Baseball All-America Team, 1970.

Year Club	League	Pos.	G.	AB.	R.	H.	2B.	3B.	HR.	RBI.	B.A.	PO.	A.	E.	F.A.
1970—Amarillo.................	Texas	1B-OF	60	210	41	62	9	1	15	41	.295	226	9	9	.963
1971—Phoenix	P. C.	OF-1B	105	392	89	109	29	5	26	99	.278	785	40	8	.990
1971—San Francisco	Nat.	1B-OF	41	115	17	32	10	2	6	24	.278	168	9	4	.978
1972—San Francisco	Nat.	3B-1B-OF	135	472	65	106	17	4	29	83	.225	496	159	22	.968
1973—San Francisco	Nat.	3B-1B-P	112	305	54	62	10	1	24	55	.203	313	146	22	.954
1974—San Francisco†	Nat.	1B-3B-OF	121	350	41	78	18	2	18	55	.223	696	98	25	.969

Year—Club	League	Pos.	G.	AB.	R.	H.	2B.	3B.	HR.	RBI.	B.A.	PO.	A.	E.	F.A.
1975—New York............	Nat.	OF-1B-3B	134	502	65	116	22	1	36	88	.231	526	69	14	.977
1976—New York‡...........	Nat.	OF-1B	123	474	70	113	14	1	37	86	.238	293	18	9	.972
1977—N.Y.§-S.D. x..........	Nat.	OF-1B-3B	114	379	38	84	16	0	20	67	.222	333	24	7	.981
1977—Cal. y-N.Y. z.........	Amer.	1B-OF	18	60	9	13	4	0	6	11	.217	73	5	2	.975
1978—Chicago a...............	Nat.	OF-1B	119	395	65	105	17	4	28	79	.266	226	10	6	.975
1979—Chicago	Nat.	OF	145	532	97	153	19	5	*48	115	.288	240	11	12	.954
1980—Chicago bcd	Nat.	OF-1B	81	255	31	71	8	0	18	57	.278	119	10	8	.942
1981—New York..............	Nat.	1B-OF	100	353	40	78	11	3	22	59	.221	548	34	20	.967
1982—New York..............	Nat.	1B	149	535	80	109	9	1	*37	99	.204	1232	69	18	.986
1983—New York e	Nat.	1B-OF	100	248	25	49	7	0	13	29	.198	450	28	3	.994
1984—Oakland f.............	Amer.	1B	147	549	68	147	23	1	35	118	.268	55	2	0	1.000
1985—Oakland g	Amer.	1B	158	592	66	141	16	0	30	91	.238	50	1	0	1.000
National League Totals—13 Years.........			1474	4915	688	1156	178	24	336	896	.235	5640	685	170	.974
American League Totals—3 Years			323	1201	143	301	43	1	71	220	.251	178	8	2	.989
Major League Totals—15 Years..............			1797	6116	831	1457	221	25	407	1116	.238	5818	693	172	.974

Selected by California Angels' organization in 2nd round of free-agent draft, June 6, 1967.
Selected by Baltimore Orioles' organization in secondary phase of free-agent draft, January 27, 1968.
Selected by San Francisco Giants' organization in secondary phase of free-agent draft, June 4, 1970.
†Sold to New York Mets for an estimated $125,000, February 28, 1975.
‡On disabled list, July 20 to August 27, 1976.
§Traded to San Diego Padres for Third Baseman-Outfielder Bobby Valentine and Pitcher Paul Siebert, June 15, 1977.

xSold on waivers to California Angels, September 6, 1977.
ySold to New York Yankees, September 15, 1977.
zGranted free agency, November 2, 1977; signed by Chicago Cubs, November 30, 1977.
aOn disabled list, July 1 to July 26, 1978.
bOn supplemental disabled list, June 13 to June 28 and July 10 to August 6, 1980.
cOn disabled list, August 6 to August 12, 1980.
dTraded to New York Mets for Outfielder Steve Henderson and cash, February 28, 1981.
eReleased, January 30, 1984; signed by Oakland A's, March 29, 1984.
fGranted free agency, November 8, 1984; re-signed by A's, December 19, 1984.
gReleased, December 20, 1985; re-signed by A's, January 20, 1986.

CHAMPIONSHIP SERIES RECORD

Year—Club	League	Pos.	G.	AB.	R.	H.	2B.	3B.	HR.	RBI.	B.A.	PO.	A.	E.	F.A.
1971—San Francisco	Nat.	PH-OF	4	9	0	1	0	0	0	0	.111	5	0	0	1.000

ALL-STAR GAME RECORD

Year	League	Pos.	AB.	R.	H.	2B.	3B.	HR.	RBI.	B.A.	PO.	A.	E.	F.A.
1976—National		OF	2	0	0	0	0	0	0	.000	1	0	0	1.000
1980—National		OF	1	0	0	0	0	0	0	.000	0	0	0	.000
All-Star Game Totals—2 Years....................			3	0	0	0	0	0	0	.000	1	0	0	1.000

Named to National League All-Star Team for 1979 game; replaced due to injury by Keith Hernandez.

PITCHING RECORD

Year—Club	League	G.	IP.	W.	L.	Pct.	H.	R.	ER.	SO.	BB.	ERA.
1973—San Francisco................................	National	2	4	0	0	.000	3	4	4	4	6	9.00

ROBERT WAYNE KIPPER
(Bob)

Born July 8, 1964, at Aurora, Ill.
Height, 6.02. Weight, 200.
Throws left and bats righthanded.

Pitched seven-inning, 9-0 no-hit victory against San Jose, June 10, 1984 (second game).
Named California League Pitcher of the Year, 1984.

Year—Club	League	G.	IP.	W.	L.	Pct.	H.	R.	ER.	SO.	BB.	ERA.
1982—Salem...	Northwest	13	76⅔	6	5	.545	62	46	38	65	52	4.46
1983—Peoria†...	Midwest	22	127⅔	5	8	.385	112	77	66	105	52	4.65
1984—Redwood.......................................	California	26	185	*18	8	.692	147	61	42	98	65	*2.04
1985—California.......................................	American	2	3⅓	0	1	.000	7	8	8	0	3	21.60
1985—Midland‡...	Texas	9	49⅔	3	3	.500	52	22	17	31	10	3.08
1985—Edmonton§x-Hawaii.....................	P. Coast	7	49⅔	3	0	1.000	36	15	11	42	12	1.99
1985—Pittsburgh.......................................	National	5	24⅔	1	2	.333	21	16	14	13	7	5.11
American League Totals—1 Year......................		2	3⅓	0	1	.000	7	8	8	0	3	21.60
National League Totals—1 Year........................		5	24⅔	1	2	.333	21	16	14	13	7	5.11
Major League Totals—1 Year...........................		7	28.	1	3	.250	28	24	22	13	10	7.07

Selected by California Angels' organization in 1st round (eighth player selected) of free-agent draft, June 7, 1982.
†On disabled list, July 20 to August 8, 1983.
‡On disabled list, May 31 to June 10, 1985.
§Loaned to Hawaii (Pittsburgh Pirates' organization), August 2, 1985; returned, August 16, 1985.

xTraded to Pittsburgh Pirates' organization, August 16, 1985, completing deal in which Pittsburgh traded Pitchers John Candelaria and Al Holland and Outfielder George Hendrick to California Angels for Pitcher Pat Clements, Outfielder Mike Brown and a player to be named later, August 2, 1985.

BRUCE EUGENE KISON

Name pronounced KEE-son.

Born February 18, 1950, at Pasco, Wash.
Height, 6.04. Weight, 173.
Throws and bats righthanded.
Attended Columbia Basin Junior College, Pasco, Wash., Manatee Junior College,
West Bradenton, Fla., and Central Washington State
College, Ellensburgh, Wash.

Major League saves: 1972 (3), 1974 (2), 1976 (1), 1982 (1), 1983 (2), 1984 (2), 1985 (1). Total—12.
Led International League in hit batsmen with 14 in 1973.
Led Eastern League in hit batsmen with 21 in 1970.

Year Club	League	G.	IP.	W.	L.	Pct.	H.	R.	ER.	SO.	BB.	ERA.
1968—Bradenton Pirates	Gulf Coast	10	24	2	1	.667	24	9	6	9	6	2.25
1969—Geneva†	NYP	13	94	5	2	.714	84	48	33	77	39	3.16
1970—Salem	Carolina	5	33	3	1	.750	17	5	3	26	7	0.82
1970—Waterbury	Eastern	19	130	10	4	.714	93	42	33	82	54	2.28
1971—Charleston	Int'national	12	85	10	1	.909	53	29	27	57	38	2.86
1971—Pittsburgh	National	18	95	6	5	.545	93	40	36	60	36	3.41
1972—Pittsburgh‡	National	32	152	9	7	.563	123	61	55	102	69	3.26
1973—Pittsburgh§	National	7	44	3	0	1.000	36	17	15	26	24	3.07
1973—Charleston x	Int'national	20	114	8	6	.571	94	59	50	70	8?	3.95
1974—Pittsburgh	National	40	129	9	8	.529	123	64	50	71	57	3.49
1975—Pittsburgh	National	33	192	12	11	.522	160	89	69	89	92	3.23
1976—Pittsburgh	National	31	193	14	9	.609	180	83	66	98	52	3.08
1977—Pittsburgh	National	33	193	9	10	.474	209	113	105	122	55	4.90
1978—Pittsburgh y	National	28	96	6	6	.500	81	40	34	62	39	3.19
1979—Pittsburgh z	National	33	172	13	7	.650	157	70	61	105	45	3.19
1980—California a	American	13	73	3	6	.333	73	46	40	28	32	4.93
1981—California b	American	11	44	1	1	.500	40	18	17	19	14	3.48
1982—California	American	33	142	10	5	.667	120	54	50	86	44	3.17
1983—California c	American	26	126⅔	11	5	.688	128	59	57	83	43	4.05
1984—California de	American	20	65⅓	4	5	.444	72	42	39	66	28	5.37
1985—Boston fg	American	22	92	5	3	.625	98	43	42	56	32	4.11
National League Totals—9 Years		255	1266	81	63	.563	1162	577	491	735	469	3.49
American League Totals—6 Years		125	543	34	25	.576	531	262	245	338	193	4.06
Major League Totals—15 Years		380	1809	115	88	.567	1693	839	736	1073	662	3.66

Selected by Pittsburgh Pirates' organization in 6th round of free-agent draft, June 7, 1968.
†On restricted list, March 13 to June 18, 1969.
‡On disabled list, March 29 to April 20, 1972.
§On disabled list, March 23 to April 21, 1973.
xOn disabled list, June 14 to July 5, 1973.
yOn disabled list, May 28 to July 6, 1978.
zGranted free agency, November 1, 1979; signed by California Angels, November 16, 1979.
aOn disabled list, June 11 to July 14 and July 15, 1980 through remainder of season.
bOn disabled list, April 7 to August 8, 1981.
cOn disabled list, May 30 to June 27, 1983.
dOn disabled list, March 29 to June 6, 1984.
eGranted free agency, November 8, 1984; signed by Boston Red Sox, January 14, 1985.
fOn disabled list, April 15 to May 7, 1985.
gGranted free agency, November 12, 1985.

CHAMPIONSHIP SERIES RECORD

Tied Championship Series record for most games won, total series (4).
Established National League Championship Series record for most bases on balls, game (6), October 8, 1974.
Tied National League Championship Series record for most games won, total Series (3).

Year Club	League	G.	IP.	W.	L.	Pct.	H.	R.	ER.	SO.	BB.	ERA.
1971—Pittsburgh	National	1	4⅔	1	0	1.000	2	0	0	3	2	0.00
1972—Pittsburgh	National	2	2⅓	1	0	1.000	1	0	0	3	0	0.00
1974—Pittsburgh	National	1	6⅔	1	0	1.000	2	0	0	5	6	0.00
1975—Pittsburgh	National	1	2	0	0	.000	2	1	1	1	1	4.50
1982—California	American	2	14	1	0	1.000	8	4	3	12	3	1.93
Championship Series Totals—5 Years		7	29⅔	4	0	1.000	15	5	4	24	12	1.21

WORLD SERIES RECORD

Established World Series record for most hit batsmen, game (3), October 13, 1971.
Tied World Series record for most hit batsmen, Series (3), 1971.

Year Club	League	G.	IP.	W.	L.	Pct.	H.	R.	ER.	SO.	BB.	ERA.
1971—Pittsburgh	National	2	6⅓	1	0	1.000	1	0	0	3	2	0.00
1979—Pittsburgh	National	1	⅓	0	1	.000	3	5	4	0	2	108.00
World Series Totals—2 Years		3	6⅔	1	1	.500	4	5	4	3	4	5.40

RONALD DALE KITTLE

(Ron)

Born January 5, 1958, at Gary, Indiana.
Height, 6.04. Weight, 220.
Throws and bats righthanded.

Tied major league record for most home runs, month of October (4), 1985.

Major League stolen bases: 1983 (8), 1984 (3), 1985 (1). Total—12.
Led American League batters in strikeouts with 150 in 1983.
Led Pacific Coast League in total bases with 355, slugging percentage with .752 and tied for lead in being hit by pitch with 10 in 1982.
Led Eastern League in total bases with 270 and slugging percentage with .694 in 1981.
Named American League Rookie Player of the Year by THE SPORTING NEWS, 1983.
Named American League Rookie of the Year by Baseball Writers' Association of America, 1983.
Named Minor League Player of the Year by THE SPORTING NEWS, 1982.
Named Pacific Coast League Most Valuable Player, 1982.
Named Eastern League Player of the Year, 1981.

Year	Club	League	Pos.	G.	AB.	R.	H.	2B.	3B.	HR.	RBI.	B.A.	PO.	A.	E.	F.A.
1977—Clinton†	Midw.		OF	22	53	9	10	4	0	0	3	.189	16	0	0	1.000
1977—Lethbridge	Pion.		OF	34	100	22	25	3	0	7	21	.250	29	2	6	.838
1978—Clinton‡	Midw.		OF	13	35	2	5	2	1	0	4	.143	4	1	1	.833
1979—Knoxville	South.		OF-C	53	157	28	43	9	1	6	26	.274	44	1	6	.980
1979—Appleton	Midw.		OF-C	35	120	18	31	3	1	2	12	.258	33	1	2	.972
1980—Appleton	Midw.		C-OF	61	209	31	66	15	3	12	56	.316	56	9	1	.985
1980—Glens Falls§	East.		OF	17	65	11	20	3	1	4	9	.308	24	4	3	.903
1981—Glens Falls x	East.		OF	109	389	97	127	17	3	★40	★103	.326	28	0	3	.903
1982—Edmonton	P. C.		OF-C	127	472	★121	163	22	10	★50	★144	.345	149	15	8	.953
1982—Chicago	Amer.		OF	20	29	3	7	2	0	1	7	.241	3	0	0	1.000
1983—Chicago	Amer.		OF	145	520	75	132	19	3	35	100	.254	234	7	9	.964
1984—Chicago	Amer.		OF	139	466	67	100	15	0	32	74	.215	226	14	7	.972
1985—Chicago y	Amer.		OF	116	379	51	87	12	0	26	58	.230	88	2	1	.989
1985—Buffalo	A. A.		OF	6	21	3	7	2	0	2	5	.333	2	0	0	1.000
Major League Totals—4 Years				420	1394	196	326	48	3	94	239	.234	551	23	17	.971

Signed as free agent by Los Angeles Dodgers' organization, July 5, 1977.
†On disabled list, April 30 to May 14, 1977.
‡Released, July 7, 1978; signed by Knoxville (Chicago White Sox' organization), September 4, 1978.
§On disabled list, July 27 to August 31, 1980.
xOn disabled list, April 21 to May 10, 1981.
yOn disabled list, July 4 to July 25, 1985; included rehabilitation disability assignment to Buffalo, July 19 to July 25, 1985.

CHAMPIONSHIP SERIES RECORD

Year	Club	League	Pos.	G.	AB.	R.	H.	2B.	3B.	HR.	RBI.	B.A.	PO.	A.	E.	F.A.
1983—Chicago	Amer.		OF	3	7	1	2	1	0	0	0	.286	3	0	0	1.000

ALL-STAR GAME RECORD

Year	League	Pos.	AB.	R.	H.	2B.	3B.	HR.	RBI.	B.A.	PO.	A.	E.	F.A.
1983—American		OF	2	1	1	0	0	0	0	.500	1	0	0	1.000

THOMAS CARL KLAWITTER
(Tom)

Born June 24, 1958, at LaCrosse, Wis.
Height, 6.03. Weight, 195.
Throws left and bats righthanded.
Attended University of Wisconsin, LaCrosse, Wis.

Led Pioneer League in hit batsmen with 10 in 1980.

Year	Club	League	G.	IP.	W.	L.	Pct.	H.	R.	ER.	SO.	BB.	ERA.
1980—Lethbridge	Pioneer		13	66	5	4	.556	69	50	30	61	47	4.09
1981—Lodi	California		27	162	11	7	.611	150	102	81	100	110	4.50
1982—San Antonio	Texas		28	163	9	★14	.391	189	★122	96	83	93	5.30
1983—San Antonio†	Texas		7	17⅓	1	0	1.000	21	16	13	3	19	6.75
1983—Wisconsin Rapids	Midwest		23	156⅓	10	5	.667	146	64	52	90	71	2.99
1984—Toledo	Int'national		26	168	10	6	.625	167	80	67	91	60	3.59
1985—Minnesota‡	American		7	9⅓	0	0	.000	7	7	7	5	13	6.75
Major League Totals—1 Year			7	9⅓	0	0	.000	7	7	7	5	13	6.75

Selected by Los Angeles Dodgers' organization in 19th round of free-agent draft, June 3, 1980.
†Released, May 2, 1983; signed by Wisconsin Rapids (Minnesota Twins' organization), May 12, 1983.
‡On disabled list, June 1 to September 9, 1985.

ROBERT WESLEY KNEPPER
Name pronounced NEPP-ur.
(Bob)

Born May 25, 1954, at Akron, O.
Height, 6.02. Weight, 210.
Throws and bats lefthanded.

Major League saves: 1982 (1).
Led National League in shutouts with 6 in 1978.
Tied for National League lead in hit batsmen with 8 in 1980.
Led California League pitchers in games started with 30 and tied for lead in complete games with 16 in 1974.
Tied for Pacific Coast League lead in shutouts with 3 in 1976.
Named National League Comeback Player of the Year by THE SPORTING NEWS, 1981.

Year	Club	League	G.	IP.	W.	L.	Pct.	H.	R.	ER.	SO.	BB.	ERA.
1972—Great Falls	Pioneer		12	68	7	1	.875	53	20	11	75	19	1.46
1973—Decatur	Midwest		11	79	7	2	.778	65	28	17	68	23	1.94

Year	Club	League	G.	IP.	W.	L.	Pct.	H.	R.	ER.	SO.	BB.	ERA.
1973—Fresno	California	13	71	2	8	.200	78	54	32	66	35	4.06
1974—Fresno	California	30	*238	*20	5	●.800	*239	103	84	*247	80	3.18
1975—Phoenix	P. Coast	26	155	11	11	.500	169	101	79	94	78	4.59
1976—Phoenix	P. Coast	29	205	14	10	.583	209	105	98	130	64	4.30
1976—San Francisco	National	4	25	1	2	.333	26	9	9	11	7	3.24
1977—Phoenix	P. Coast	10	51	3	6	.333	68	51	42	24	25	7.41
1977—San Francisco	National	27	166	11	9	.550	151	73	62	100	72	3.36
1978—San Francisco	National	36	260	17	11	.607	218	85	76	147	85	2.63
1979—San Francisco	National	34	207	9	12	.429	241	117	107	123	77	4.65
1980—San Francisco†	National	35	215	9	16	.360	242	114	98	103	61	4.10
1981—Houston	National	22	157	9	5	.643	128	41	38	75	38	2.18
1982—Houston	National	33	180	5	15	.250	193	100	89	108	60	4.45
1983—Houston	National	35	203	6	13	.316	202	93	72	125	71	3.19
1984—Houston	National	35	233⅔	15	10	.600	223	93	83	140	55	3.20
1985—Houston	National	37	241	15	13	.536	253	●119	95	131	54	3.55
Major League Totals—10 Years		298	1887⅔	97	106	.478	1877	844	729	1063	580	3.48

Selected by San Francisco Giants' organization in 2nd round of free-agent draft, June 6, 1972.

†Traded with Outfielder Chris Bourjos to Houston Astros for Third Baseman Enos Cabell, December 8, 1980.

DIVISION SERIES RECORD

Year	Club	League	G.	IP.	W.	L.	Pct.	H.	R.	ER.	SO.	BB.	ERA.
1981—Houston	National	1	5	0	1	.000	6	3	3	4	2	5.40

ALL-STAR GAME RECORD

Year	League	IP.	W.	L.	Pct.	H.	R.	ER.	SO.	BB.	ERA.
1981—National		2	0	0	.000	1	0	0	3	2	0.00

ALAN LEE KNICELY

Name pronounced NYSS-lee.

Born May 19, 1955, at Harrisonburg, Va.
Height, 6.00. Weight, 194.
Throws and bats righthanded.
Brother of Harold Knicely, catcher in Houston Astros' organization, 1974.

Led American Association in total bases with 326 and tied for lead in sacrifice flies with 11 in 1984.
Led Pacific Coast League in passed balls with 16 in 1980.
Tied for Southern League lead in strikeouts by batters with 112 in 1978.
Tied for Pacific Coast League lead in double plays by catchers with 8 in 1980.
Named Minor League Player of the Year by THE SPORTING NEWS, 1984.
Named American Association Most Valuable Player, 1984.
Named Southern League co-Most Valuable Player, 1979.

Year	Club	League	Pos.	G.	AB.	R.	H.	2B.	3B.	HR.	RBI.	B.A.	PO.	A.	E.	F.A.
1974—Covington	Appal.	P	15	41	5	9	2	1	0	6	.220	3	*19	3	.880
1975—Dubuque	Midw.	P	27	35	5	11	1	0	1	9	.314	11	15	1	.963
1976—Dubuque	Midw.	P-1B	77	156	23	45	9	1	4	20	.288	84	23	3	.973
1977—Columbus	South.	3B-P	99	277	28	73	10	3	6	35	.264	84	140	24	.903
1978—Columbus	South.	OF	140	427	51	97	13	2	15	50	.227	262	22	10	.966
1979—Columbus	South.	C	120	422	77	122	12	3	*33	76	.289	446	51	15	.971
1979—Houston	Nat.	C-3B	7	6	0	0	0	0	0	0	.000	2	0	0	1.000
1980—Tucson	P. C.	C	133	468	69	149	18	4	22	*105	.318	511	*93	●23	.963
1980—Houston	Nat.	PH	1	1	0	0	0	0	0	0	.000	0	0	0	.000
1981—Tucson	P. C.	C-OF	138	490	81	150	32	5	18	96	.306	549	81	15	.977
1981—Houston	Nat.	C-OF	3	7	2	4	0	0	2	2	.571	11	2	0	1.000
1982—Houston†	Nat.	C-OF-3B	59	133	10	25	2	0	2	12	.188	128	15	4	.973
1983—Cincinnati	Nat.	C-OF-1B	59	98	11	22	3	0	2	10	.224	124	13	0	1.000
1984—Wichita	A. A.	*1-C-3	152	570	94	*190	29	4	33	*126	.333	967	92	*18	.983
1984—Cincinnati	Nat.	1B-C	10	29	0	4	0	0	0	5	.138	60	5	1	.985
1985—Denver	A. A.	C-1B	29	109	20	45	10	0	7	29	.413	106	15	4	.968
1985—Cinc.‡-Phil.	Nat.	C-1B	55	165	17	40	9	0	5	26	.242	235	13	8	.969
1985—Portland	P. C.	C-1B	21	77	11	22	2	0	3	11	.286	127	8	4	.971
Major League Totals—7 Years			194	439	40	95	14	0	11	55	.216	560	48	13	.979

Selected by Houston Astros' organization in 3rd round of free-agent draft, June 5, 1974.

†Traded to Cincinnati Reds for Pitcher Bill Dawley and Outfielder Anthony Walker, March 31, 1983.

‡Traded with Shortstop Tom Foley, a player to be named later and cash to Philadelphia Phillies for Catcher Bo Diaz and Pitcher Greg Simpson, August 8, 1985; Philadelphia acquired Pitcher Freddie Toliver to complete deal, August 27, 1985.

PITCHING RECORD

Year	Club	League	G.	IP.	W.	L.	Pct.	H.	R.	ER.	SO.	BB.	ERA.
1974—Covington	Ap'lachian	12	81	7	3	.700	78	35	31	53	42	3.44
1975—Dubuque	Midwest	26	122	4	10	.286	113	59	49	87	62	3.61
1976—Dubuque	Midwest	24	107	7	3	.700	100	58	47	87	62	3.95
1977—Columbus	Southern	14	42	1	5	.167	40	32	24	25	25	5.14

—DID YOU KNOW—

That the Cardinals' Tom Herr drove in his 50th 1985 run in the team's 54th game? His previous season high was 49 in 1984.

CHARLES RAY KNIGHT
(Known by middle name.)

Born December 28, 1952, at Albany, Ga.
Height, 6.02. Weight, 190.
Throws and bats righthanded.
Attended Albany Junior College, Albany, Ga.
Husband of Nancy Lopez Knight, professional golfer.

Tied major league records for most home runs, inning (2) and most total bases, inning (8), May 13, 1980 (fifth inning).
Major League stolen bases: 1977 (1), 1979 (4), 1980 (1), 1981 (2), 1982 (2), 1985 (1). Total—11.
Led National League in grounding into double plays with 18 in 1981 and tied for lead with 24 in 1980.
Led American Association third basemen in putouts with 102 in 1976.
Tied for American Association lead in double plays by third basemen with 24 in 1974.

Year	Club	League	Pos.	G.	AB.	R.	H.	2B.	3B.	HR.	RBI.	B.A.	PO.	A.	E.	F.A.
1971—Sioux Falls	North.		O-INF-P	64	239	34	68	5	2	6	31	.285	69	79	17	.897
1972—Three Rivers	East.		O-INF-P	97	302	25	64	8	1	2	35	.212	102	142	20	.924
1973—Three Rivers	East.		O-3-1-2	57	193	41	54	14	2	2	22	.280	76	57	7	.950
1973—Indianapolis	A. A.		3-O-1-P	78	253	20	55	10	4	1	16	.217	72	126	11	.947
1974—Indianapolis	A. A.		★3B-OF	107	352	36	80	13	4	5	37	.227	94	177	11	★.961
1974—Cincinnati	Nat.		3B	14	11	1	2	1	0	0	2	.182	2	8	0	1.000
1975—Cincinnati	A. A.		★3B-1B	123	434	58	118	16	5	4	48	.272	★116	227	17	.953
1976—Indianapolis†	A. A.		3B-1B	110	396	47	106	24	3	10	41	.268	136	181	13	.961
1977—Cincinnati	Nat.		3-2-O-S	80	92	8	24	5	1	1	13	.261	45	45	4	.957
1978—Cincinnati‡	Nat.		3-2-O-S-1	83	65	7	13	3	0	1	4	.200	13	41	7	.885
1979—Cincinnati	Nat.		3B	150	551	64	175	37	4	10	79	.318	120	262	15	.962
1980—Cincinnati	Nat.		3B	162	618	71	163	39	7	14	78	.264	120	291	13	.969
1981—Cincinnati§	Nat.		3B	106	386	43	100	23	1	6	34	.259	69	176	11	.957
1982—Houston	Nat.		1B-3B	158	609	72	179	36	6	6	70	.294	1002	186	17	.986
1983—Houston	Nat.		1B	145	507	43	154	36	4	9	70	.304	1285	73	9	.993
1984—Hou. x-N.Y.	Nat.		3B-1B	115	371	28	88	14	0	3	35	.237	256	132	9	.977
1985—New York y	Nat.		3B-2B-1B	90	271	22	59	12	0	6	36	.218	56	113	7	.960
Major League Totals—10 Years				1103	3481	359	957	206	23	56	421	.275	2968	1327	92	.979

Selected by Cincinnati Reds' organization in 10th round of free-agent draft, June 4, 1970.
†On disabled list, June 21 to July 2, 1976.
‡On disabled list, April 17 to May 8, 1978.
§Traded to Houston Astros for First Baseman-Outfielder Cesar Cedeno, December 18, 1981.
xTraded to New York Mets for three players to be named later, August 28, 1984; Houston Astros acquired Outfielder Gerald Young and Infielder Manny Lee, August 31, 1984, and Pitcher Mitch Cook, September 10, 1984, to complete deal.
yOn disabled list, March 30 to April 20, 1985.

CHAMPIONSHIP SERIES RECORD

Year	Club	League	Pos.	G.	AB.	R.	H.	2B.	3B.	HR.	RBI.	B.A.	PO.	A.	E.	F.A.
1979—Cincinnati	Nat.		3B	3	14	0	4	1	0	0	0	.286	0	5	0	1.000

ALL-STAR GAME RECORD

Year	League	Pos.	AB.	R.	H.	2B.	3B.	HR.	RBI.	B.A.	PO.	A.	E.	F.A.
1980—National		3B	1	1	1	0	0	0	0	1.000	0	1	0	1.000
1982—National		3B	3	0	0	0	0	0	0	.000	1	4	0	1.000
All-Star Game Totals—2 Years			4	1	1	0	0	0	0	.250	1	5	0	1.000

PITCHING RECORD

Year	Club	League	G.	IP.	W.	L.	Pct.	H.	R.	ER.	SO.	BB.	ERA.
1971—Sioux Falls	Northern		3	4	1	1	.500	5	6	5	4	5	11.25
1972—Three Rivers	Eastern		2	4	0	0	.000	3	1	1	2	4	2.25
1973—Indianapolis	Am. Assoc.		1	2	0	0	.000	2	1	1	0	4	4.50

MARK RICHARD KNUDSON

Name pronounced NOOD-sun.

Born October 28, 1960, at Denver, Colo.
Height, 6.05. Weight, 215.
Throws and bats righthanded.
Attended Colorado State University, Fort Collins, Colo.

Year	Club	League	G.	IP.	W.	L.	Pct.	H.	R.	ER.	SO.	BB.	ERA.
1982—Daytona Beach	Florida St.		12	60⅓	2	6	.250	75	35	32	15	23	4.77
1983—Daytona Beach	Florida St.		12	78⅔	5	3	.625	80	29	21	47	22	2.40
1983—Columbus	Southern		13	69⅔	4	5	.444	82	40	33	28	21	4.26
1984—Columbus	Southern		14	101	4	5	.444	100	32	25	54	27	2.23
1984—Tucson	P. Coast		13	84	4	6	.400	93	41	34	42	20	3.64
1985—Tucson	P. Coast		24	146	8	5	.615	171	69	65	68	37	4.01
1985—Houston†	National		2	11	0	2	.000	21	11	11	4	3	9.00
Major League Totals—1 Year			2	11	0	2	.000	21	11	11	4	3	9.00

Selected by Houston Astros' organization in 3rd round of free-agent draft, June 7, 1982.
†On disabled list, July 15 to August 5, 1985.

BRAD LYNN KOMMINSK

Name pronounced KOMM-insk.
Born April 4, 1961, at Lima, Ohio.
Height, 6.02. Weight, 205.
Throws and bats righthanded.

Major League stolen bases: 1984 (18), 1985 (10). Total—28.
Led International League in slugging percentage with .596 and tied for lead in game-winning RBIs with 14 in 1983.
Led Carolina League in total bases with 278 and grounding into double plays with 24 in 1981.
Led Appalachian League batters in strikeouts with 74 and stolen bases with 20 in 1979.
Named Carolina League Most Valuable Player, 1981.
Received reported $72,000 bonus to sign with Atlanta Braves, 1979.

Year Club	League	Pos.	G.	AB.	R.	H.	2B.	3B.	HR.	RBI.	B.A.	PO.	A.	E.	F.A.
1979—Kingsport	Appal.	OF	59	185	37	41	9	1	7	34	.222	112	1	2	.983
1980—Anderson	S. Atl.	OF	121	425	86	111	17	5	20	67	.261	217	5	12	.949
1981—Durham	Carol.	OF	132	459	108	•148	27	2	33	★104	★.322	154	7	10	.942
1982—Savannah	South.	OF	133	454	88	124	18	7	26	78	.273	158	6	10	.943
1982—Richmond	Int.	OF	5	17	4	6	1	0	2	5	.353	10	0	0	1.000
1983—Richmond	Int.	OF	117	413	94	138	24	6	24	103	.334	179	4	3	.984
1983—Atlanta	Nat.	OF	19	36	2	8	2	0	0	4	.222	16	1	1	.944
1984—Richmond	Int.	OF	42	144	23	37	11	3	5	28	.257	66	4	3	.959
1984—Atlanta	Nat.	OF	90	301	37	61	10	0	8	36	.203	135	2	1	.993
1985—Atlanta	Nat.	OF	106	300	52	00	12	3	4	21	.227	161	2	7	.959
Major League Totals—3 Years			215	637	91	137	24	3	12	61	.215	312	5	9	.972

Selected by Atlanta Braves' organization in 1st round (fourth player selected) of free-agent draft, June 5, 1979.

JEROME MARTIN KOOSMAN
(Jerry)

Born December 23, 1942, at Appleton, Minn.
Height, 6.02. Weight, 220.
Throws left and bats righthanded.
Attended University of Minnesota, Morris, Minn., and
State School of Science, Wahpeton, N.D.

Established National League record for most strikeouts, season, by pitcher as batter (62), 1968.
Tied modern National League record for most shutout games won or tied, rookie season (7), 1968.
Major League saves: 1972 (1), 1975 (2), 1978 (2), 1980 (2), 1981 (5), 1982 (3), 1983 (2). Total—17.
Tied for National League lead in balks with 3 in 1970 and 7 in 1975.
Named National League Rookie Pitcher of the Year by THE SPORTING NEWS, 1968.

Year Club	League	G.	IP.	W.	L.	Pct.	H.	R.	ER.	SO.	BB.	ERA.
1965—Greenville	W. Carol.	27	107	5	11	.313	101	70	56	128	56	4.71
1965—Williamsport	Eastern	2	12	0	2	.000	11	7	5	11	11	3.75
1966—Auburn	NYP	24	170	12	7	.632	109	43	26	174	43	★1.38
1967—New York	National	9	22	0	2	.000	22	17	15	11	19	6.14
1967—Jacksonville	Int'national	25	178	11	10	.524	137	60	48	★183	46	2.43
1968—New York	National	35	264	19	12	.613	221	72	61	178	69	2.08
1969—New York	National	32	241	17	9	.684	187	66	61	180	68	2.28
1970—New York	National	30	212	12	7	.632	189	87	74	118	71	3.14
1971—New York†	National	26	166	6	11	.353	160	66	56	96	51	3.04
1972—New York	National	34	163	11	12	.478	155	81	75	147	52	4.14
1973—New York	National	35	263	14	15	.483	234	93	83	156	76	2.84
1974—New York	National	35	265	15	11	.577	258	113	99	188	85	3.36
1975—New York	National	36	240	14	13	.519	234	106	91	173	98	3.41
1976—New York	National	34	247	21	10	.677	205	81	74	200	66	2.70
1977—New York	National	32	227	8	•20	.286	195	102	88	192	81	3.49
1978—New York‡	National	38	235	3	15	.167	221	110	98	160	84	3.75
1979—Minnesota	American	37	264	20	13	.606	268	108	99	157	83	3.38
1980—Minnesota	American	38	243	16	13	.552	252	119	109	149	60	4.04
1981—Minnesota§-Chicago	American	27	121	4	•13	.235	125	59	54	76	41	4.02
1982—Chicago	American	42	173⅓	11	7	.611	194	81	74	88	38	3.84
1983—Chicago xy	American	37	169⅔	11	7	.611	176	96	90	90	53	4.77
1984—Philadelphia	National	36	224	14	15	.483	232	95	81	137	60	3.25
1985—Philadelphia za	National	19	99⅓	6	4	.600	107	56	51	60	34	4.62
National League Totals—14 Years		431	2868⅓	160	156	.506	2620	1145	1007	1996	914	3.16
American League Totals—5 Years		181	971	62	53	.539	1015	463	426	560	284	3.95
Major League Totals—19 Years		612	3839⅓	222	209	.515	3635	1608	1433	2556	1198	3.36

Signed as free agent by New York Mets' organization, August 27, 1964.
†On disabled list, July 7 to August 9, 1971.
‡Traded to Minnesota Twins for Pitcher Greg Field and a player to be named later, December 8, 1978; New York Mets acquired Pitcher Jesse Orosco to complete deal, February 7, 1979.
§Traded to Chicago White Sox for Shortstop Ivan Mesa, Third Baseman Ron Perry, a player to be named later and cash, August 30, 1981; Minnesota Twins' organization acquired Outfielder Randy Johnson to complete deal, September 2, 1981. (Pitcher Kevin Flannery replaced Perry due to injuries, October 18, 1982.)
xGranted free agency, November 7, 1983; re-signed by White Sox, December 2, 1983.
yTraded to Philadelphia Phillies, February 15, 1984, completing deal in which Philadelphia traded Pitcher Ron Reed to Chicago White Sox for a player to be named later, December 5, 1983.
zOn disabled list, May 4 to June 8 and August 22, 1985 through remainder of season.
aReleased, December 6, 1985.

CHAMPIONSHIP SERIES RECORD

Year Club	League	G.	IP.	W.	L.	Pct.	H.	R.	ER.	SO.	BB.	ERA.
1969—New York	National	1	4⅔	0	0	.000	7	6	6	5	4	11.57
1973—New York	National	1	9	1	0	1.000	8	2	2	9	0	2.00
1983—Chicago	American	1	⅓	0	0	.000	1	3	2	0	2	54.00
Championship Series Totals—3 Years		3	14	1	0	1.000	16	11	10	14	6	6.43

WORLD SERIES RECORD

Year Club	League	G.	IP.	W.	L.	Pct.	H.	R.	ER.	SO.	BB.	ERA.
1969—New York	National	2	17⅔	2	0	1.000	7	4	4	9	4	2.04
1973—New York	National	2	8⅔	1	0	1.000	9	3	3	8	7	3.12
World Series Totals—2 Years		4	26⅓	3	0	1.000	16	7	7	17	11	2.39

ALL-STAR GAME RECORD

Year League	IP.	W.	L.	Pct.	H.	R.	ER.	SO.	BB.	ERA.
1968—National	⅓	0	0	.000	0	0	0	1	0	0.00
1969—National	1⅔	0	0	.000	1	0	0	1	0	0.00
All-Star Game Totals—2 Years	2	0	0	.000	1	0	0	2	0	0.00

RAYMOND ALLEN KRAWCZYK

Name pronounced KRAH-sick.

(Ray)

Born October 9, 1959, at Pittsburgh, Pa.
Height, 6.01. Weight, 184.
Throws and bats righthanded.
Attended Golden West College, Huntington Beach, Calif.,
and Oral Roberts University, Tulsa, Okla.

Led Pacific Coast League in saves with 20 in 1985.

Year Club	League	G.	IP.	W.	L.	Pct.	H.	R.	ER.	SO.	BB.	ERA.
1981—Bradenton Pirates	Gulf Coast	4	18	0	1	.000	11	5	3	14	7	1.50
1981—Alexandria	Carolina	8	46	2	4	.333	48	32	25	41	14	4.89
1982—Alexandria	Carolina	6	18⅔	1	0	1.000	10	1	1	25	13	0.48
1982—Buffalo	Eastern	38	101⅓	3	5	.375	93	59	53	102	59	4.71
1983—Hawaii	P. Coast	41	88⅔	5	7	.417	80	46	37	88	33	3.76
1984—Hawaii	P. Coast	43	72	4	5	.444	57	21	17	77	36	2.13
1984—Pittsburgh	National	4	5⅓	0	0	.000	7	2	2	3	4	3.38
1985—Hawaii†	P. Coast	38	55⅔	5	3	.625	35	15	14	54	22	2.26
1985—Pittsburgh	National	8	8⅓	0	2	.000	20	13	13	9	6	14.04
Major League Totals—2 Years		12	13⅔	0	2	.000	27	15	15	12	10	9.88

Selected by Boston Red Sox' organization in 1st round (23rd player selected) of free-agent draft, January 8, 1980.
Selected by St. Louis Cardinals' organization in secondary phase of free-agent draft, June 3, 1980.
Selected by Pittsburgh Pirates' organization in secondary phase of free-agent draft, June 8, 1981.
†Appeared in one game as a first baseman with no chances.

WAYNE RICHARD KRENCHICKI

Name pronounced Kren-CHIK-ee.

Born September 17, 1954, at Trenton, N.J.
Height, 6.01. Weight, 180.
Throws right and bats lefthanded.
Attended University of Miami, Miami, Fla.
Brother of Tom Krenchicki, shortstop in Los Angeles Dodgers' organization, 1968.

Major League stolen bases: 1982 (5).
Led Southern League second basemen in double plays with 114 in 1977.
Led Florida State League shortstops in assists with 378, double plays with 60 and fielding percentage with .968 in 1976.

Year Club	League	Pos.	G.	AB.	R.	H.	2B.	3B.	HR.	RBI.	B.A.	PO.	A.	E.	F.A.
1976—Miami	Fla. St.	SS-3B	133	459	38	109	14	1	0	35	.237	190	439	19	.971
1977—Charlotte	South.	2B	131	510	69	140	17	9	3	42	.275	★325	★455	25	.969
1978—Rochester	Int.	3B-2B-SS	★140	520	★93	154	26	1	12	71	.296	204	389	32	.949
1979—Rochester†	Int.	2B-SS-3B	66	249	21	65	7	2	0	22	.261	129	173	9	.971
1979—Baltimore	Amer.	3B-2B	16	21	1	4	1	0	0	0	.190	12	12	2	.923
1980—Rochester‡	Int.	2B-3B-SS	87	311	42	82	13	3	2	39	.264	137	230	10	.973
1980—Baltimore	Amer.	SS-2B	9	14	1	2	0	0	0	0	.143	9	9	0	1.000
1981—Baltimore	Amer.	2B-3B-SS	33	56	7	12	4	0	0	6	.214	23	56	3	.963
1981—Rochester§	Int.	2B-3B-SS	16	56	5	10	0	0	0	4	.179	28	58	1	.988
1982—Cincinnati	Nat.	3B-2B	94	187	19	53	6	1	2	21	.283	40	103	6	.960
1983—Cincinnati x	Nat.	3B-2B	51	77	6	21	2	0	0	11	.273	7	41	1	.980
1983—Detroit y	Amer.	3-2-S-1	59	133	18	37	7	0	1	16	.278	43	75	8	.937
1984—Wichita	A. A.	2B-3B	18	64	14	18	7	0	2	5	.281	38	44	3	.965
1984—Cincinnati	Nat.	3B-1B-2B	97	181	18	54	9	2	6	22	.298	35	92	5	.962
1985—Cincinnati	Nat.	3B-2B	90	173	16	47	9	0	4	25	.272	35	87	4	.968
American League Totals—4 Years			117	224	27	55	12	0	1	22	.246	87	152	13	.948
National League Totals—4 Years			332	618	59	175	26	3	12	79	.283	117	323	16	.965
Major League Totals—7 Years			449	842	86	230	38	3	13	101	.273	204	475	29	.959

Selected by Philadelphia Phillies' organization in 8th round of free-agent draft, June 6, 1972.
Selected by Baltimore Orioles' organization in secondary phase of free-agent draft, January 7, 1976.
†On disabled list, May 10 to June 1 and August 5 to August 15, 1979.
‡On disabled list, July 12 to August 1, 1980.
§Traded to Cincinnati Reds, February 16, 1982, completing deal in which Cincinnati traded Pitcher Paul Moskau to Baltimore Orioles for a player to be named later, February 9, 1982.
xTraded to Detroit Tigers for Pitcher Pat Underwood, June 30, 1983.
ySold to Cincinnati Reds, November 18, 1983.

WILLIAM CULP KRUEGER
Name pronounced KREW-ger.
(Bill)

Born April 24, 1958, at Waukegan, Ill.
Height, 6.05. Weight, 210.
Throws and bats lefthanded.
Received bachelor of arts degree in business administration from
University of Portland, Portland, Ore. in 1979.

Tied for Eastern League lead in games started by pitchers with 27 and shutouts with 3 in 1982.

Year—Club	League	G.	IP.	W.	L.	Pct.	H.	R.	ER.	SO.	BB.	ERA.
1980—Medford	Northwest	9	44	0	4	.000	54	38	25	48	29	5.11
1981—Modesto	California	10	98	3	5	.375	87	49	40	76	52	3.67
1981—West Haven	Eastern	11	68	3	6	.333	74	36	27	36	31	3.57
1982—West Haven	Eastern	28	181	15	9	.625	160	69	57	163	81	2.83
1983—Oakland†	American	17	109⅔	7	6	.538	104	54	44	58	53	3.61
1984—Tacoma	P. Coast	5	31⅔	2	2	.500	29	17	13	20	21	3.69
1984—Oakland	American	26	142	10	10	.500	156	95	75	61	85	4.75
1985—Oakland	American	32	151⅓	9	10	.474	165	95	76	56	69	4.52
1985—Tacoma	P. Coast	2	9⅔	0	1	.000	12	10	10	10	6	9.31
Major League Totals—3 Years		75	403	26	26	.500	425	244	195	175	207	4.35

Signed as free agent by Oakland A's organization, July 12, 1980.
†On disabled list, August 5, 1983 through remainder of season.

JOHN MARTIN KRUK

Born February 9, 1961, at Charleston, W. Va.
Height, 5.10. Weight, 170.
Throws and bats lefthanded.
Attended Allegany Community College, Cumberland, Md.

Led Texas League in sacrifice flies with 13 in 1983.
Led Pacific Coast League outfielders in double plays with 4 in 1984.

Year—Club	League	Pos.	G.	AB.	R.	H.	2B.	3B.	HR.	RBI.	B.A.	PO.	A.	E.	F.A.
1981—Walla Walla	N'west	OF-1B	63	157	31	38	10	0	1	13	.242	108	5	2	.983
1982—Reno	Calif.	OF-1B	125	441	82	137	30	8	11	92	.311	253	11	7	.974
1983—Beaumont	Texas	OF-1B-P	133	498	94	170	41	9	10	88	.341	304	22	8	.976
1984—Las Vegas	P. C.	OF	115	340	56	111	25	6	11	57	.326	183	7	2	.990
1985—Las Vegas	P. C.	OF-1B	123	422	61	148	29	4	7	59	*.351	356	18	7	.982

Selected by Pittsburgh Pirates' organization in 3rd round of free-agent draft, January 13, 1981.
Selected by San Diego Padres' organization in secondary phase of free-agent draft, June 8, 1981.

PITCHING RECORD

Year—Club	League	G.	IP.	W.	L.	Pct.	H.	R.	ER.	SO.	BB.	ERA.
1983—Beaumont	Texas	3	5	0	0	.000	5	0	0	3	2	0.00

MICHAEL EDWARD KRUKOW
Name pronounced KROO-koh.
(Mike)

Born January 21, 1952, at Long Beach, Calif.
Height, 6.04. Weight, 205.
Throws and bats righthanded.
Attended California Poly State University, San Luis Obispo, Calif.

Major League saves: 1984 (1).
Tied for National League lead in games started by pitchers with 25 in 1981.
Tied for National League lead in hit batsmen with 8 in 1980.
Led Gulf Coast League in intentional bases on balls issued with 4 and tied for lead in complete games with 4 in 1973.

Year—Club	League	G.	IP.	W.	L.	Pct.	H.	R.	ER.	SO.	BB.	ERA.
1973—Bradenton Cubs	Gulf Coast	13	77	4	3	.571	76	32	27	*80	28	3.16
1974—Midland	Texas	6	30	1	1	.500	42	24	17	21	19	5.10
1974—Key West	Florida St.	20	130	5	10	.333	121	66	46	94	47	3.18
1975—Midland†	Texas	24	153	13	6	.684	143	65	58	100	66	3.41
1976—Wichita	Am. Assoc.	26	144	7	9	.438	142	61	53	108	47	3.31
1976—Chicago	National	2	4	0	0	.000	6	4	4	1	2	9.00
1977—Chicago	National	34	172	8	14	.364	195	96	84	106	61	4.40
1978—Wichita	Am. Assoc.	7	53	2	3	.400	51	27	23	29	21	3.91
1978—Chicago	National	27	138	9	3	.750	125	62	60	81	53	3.91
1979—Chicago	National	28	165	9	9	.500	172	84	77	119	81	4.20

Year—Club	League	G.	IP.	W.	L.	Pct.	H.	R.	ER.	SO.	BB.	ERA.
1980—Chicago	National	34	205	10	15	.400	200	117	100	130	80	4.39
1981—Chicago‡	National	25	144	9	9	.500	146	68	59	101	55	3.69
1982—Philadelphia§	National	33	208	13	11	.542	211	87	72	138	82	3.12
1983—San Francisco x	National	31	184⅓	11	11	.500	189	95	81	136	76	3.95
1984—San Francisco	National	35	199⅓	11	12	.478	★234	★117	101	141	78	4.56
1985—San Francisco	National	28	194⅔	8	11	.421	176	80	73	150	49	3.38
Major League Totals—10 Years		277	1614⅓	88	95	.481	1654	810	711	1103	617	3.96

Selected by California Angels' organization in 32nd round of free-agent draft, June 4, 1970.

Selected by Chicago Cubs' organization in 8th round of free-agent draft, June 5, 1973.

†On disabled list, May 19 to June 7, 1975.

‡Traded with cash to Philadelphia Phillies for Catcher Keith Moreland and Pitchers Dan Larson and Dickie Noles, December 8, 1981.

§Traded with Pitcher Mark Davis and Outfielder Charles Penigar to San Francisco Giants for Second Baseman Joe Morgan and Pitcher Al Holland, December 14, 1982.

xOn disabled list, April 11 to May 8, 1983.

DUANE EUGENE KUIPER

Name pronounced KIPE-er.

Born June 19, 1950, at Racine, Wis.
Height, 6.00. Weight, 175.
Throws right and bats lefthanded.
Attended Indian Hills Community College, Centerville, Ia., and received
bachelor of arts degree from Southern Illinois University, Carbondale, Ill. in 1972;
Cousin of Dick Bosman, pitcher with Washington Senators, Texas Rangers,
Cleveland Indians and Oakland Athletics, 1966 through 1976.

Tied major league record for most triples, bases filled, game (2), July 27, 1978.
Major League stolen bases: 1974 (1), 1975 (19), 1976 (10), 1977 (11), 1978 (4), 1979 (4), 1981 (1), 1982 (2). Total—52.
Led American League second basemen in fielding percentage with .987 in 1976.
Led American Association in stolen bases with 28 in 1974.

Year—Club	League	Pos.	G.	AB.	R.	H.	2B.	3B.	HR.	RBI.	B.A.	PO.	A.	E.	F.A.
1972—Reno	Calif.	2B-SS-3B	124	496	89	149	20	3	2	53	.300	264	283	18	.968
1973—Okla. City	A. A.	2B	18	56	6	9	1	1	0	6	.161	42	34	3	.962
1973—San Antonio	Texas	2B	107	395	46	113	11	2	1	42	.286	220	317	19	.966
1974—Okla. City	A. A.	2B	●135	★554	83	172	27	5	3	53	.310	291	★365	11	★.984
1974—Cleveland	Amer.	2B	10	22	7	11	2	0	0	4	.500	16	19	0	1.000
1975—Okla. City	A. A.	2B	40	164	18	40	5	0	1	12	.244	110	94	3	.986
1975—Cleveland†	Amer.	2B	90	346	42	101	11	1	0	25	.292	192	230	12	.972
1976—Cleveland	Amer.	2B-1B	135	506	47	133	13	6	0	37	.263	321	367	11	.984
1977—Cleveland	Amer.	2B	148	610	62	169	15	8	1	50	.277	334	449	12	.985
1978—Cleveland	Amer.	2B	149	547	52	155	18	6	0	43	.283	341	408	16	.979
1979—Cleveland	Amer.	2B	140	479	46	122	9	5	0	39	.255	345	380	9	★.988
1980—Cleveland‡	Amer.	2B	42	149	10	42	5	0	0	9	.282	87	111	1	.995
1981—Cleveland§x	Amer.	2B	72	206	15	53	6	0	0	14	.257	118	174	5	.983
1982—San Francisco	Nat.	2B	107	218	26	61	9	1	0	17	.280	101	124	5	.978
1983—San Francisco y	Nat.	2B	72	176	14	44	2	2	0	14	.250	107	140	3	.988
1984—San Francisco	Nat.	2B-1B	83	115	8	23	1	0	0	11	.200	62	66	4	.970
1985—San Francisco za	Nat.	PH	9	5	0	3	0	0	0	0	.600	0	0	0	.000
American League Totals—8 Years			786	2865	281	786	79	26	1	221	.274	1754	2138	66	.983
National League Totals—4 Years			271	514	48	131	12	3	0	42	.255	270	330	12	.980
Major League Totals—12 Years			1057	3379	329	917	91	29	1	263	.271	2024	2468	78	.983

Selected by New York Yankees' organization in 12th round of free-agent draft, June 7, 1968.

Selected by Seattle Pilots' organization in secondary phase of free-agent draft, February 1, 1969.

Selected by Chicago White Sox' organization in 1st round (fifth player selected) of free-agent draft, January 17, 1970.

Selected by Cincinnati Reds' organization in secondary phase of free-agent draft, June 4, 1970.

Selected by Boston Red Sox' organization in secondary phase of free-agent draft, June 8, 1971.

Selected by Cleveland Indians' organization in secondary phase of free-agent draft, January 12, 1972.

†On disabled list, July 22 to August 11, 1975.

‡On disabled list, June 2, 1980 through remainder of season.

§On disabled list, March 31 to April 30, 1981.

xTraded to San Francisco Giants for Pitcher Ed Whitson, November 16, 1981.

yOn disabled list, May 28 to July 8, 1983.

zOn disabled list, April 5 to May 7, 1985.

aReleased, June 28, 1985.

JEFFREY WILLIAM KUNKEL
(Jeff)

Born March 25, 1962, at West Palm Beach, Fla.
Height, 6.02. Weight, 180.
Throws and bats righthanded.
Attended Rider College, Lawrenceville, N.J.
Son of Bill Kunkel, pitcher with Kansas City A's and New York Yankees, 1961 through 1963; umpire, Florida
State League, 1966; Southern League, 1967 and 1968; and American League umpire, 1968 through 1984.

Major League stolen bases: 1984 (4).

Named shortstop on THE SPORTING NEWS College Baseball All-America Team, 1983.

Year Club	League	Pos.	G.	AB.	R.	H.	2B.	3B.	HR.	RBI.	B.A.	PO.	A.	E.	F.A.
1983—Burlington	Midw.	SS	31	122	22	35	7	1	6	18	.287	38	88	13	.906
1983—Tulsa	Texas	SS-2B	37	130	21	37	14	0	5	25	.285	68	106	9	.951
1984—Tulsa†	Texas	SS	47	177	30	56	16	1	4	22	.316	64	103	16	.913
1984—Texas	Amer.	SS	50	142	13	29	2	3	3	7	.204	81	120	17	.922
1985—Oklahoma City	A. A.	SS-OF	99	370	40	72	8	6	5	43	.195	152	308	26	.947
1985—Texas	Amer.	SS	2	4	1	1	0	0	0	0	.250	2	5	0	1.000
Major League Totals—2 Years			52	146	14	30	2	3	3	7	.205	83	125	17	.924

Selected by Texas Rangers' organization in 1st round (third player selected) of free-agent draft, June 6, 1983.
†On disabled list, April 10 to May 12 and May 17 to June 4, 1984.

RUSSELL JAY KUNTZ

Name pronounced COON-ts.

(Rusty)

Born February 4, 1955, at Orange, Calif.
Height, 6.03. Weight, 190.
Throws and bats righthanded.
Attended Cuesta College, San Luis Obispo, Calif.,
and California State College (Stanislaus), Turlock, Calif.

Major League stolen bases: 1980 (1), 1981 (1), 1983 (1), 1984 (2). Total—5.
Led American Association batters in strikeouts with 111 in 1979.
Led Gulf Coast League in sacrifice flies with 6 and bases on balls received with 40 in 1977.

Year Club	League	Pos.	G.	AB.	R.	H.	2B.	3B.	HR.	RBI.	B.A.	PO.	A.	E.	F.A.
1977—Sara. W. Sox	Gulf C.	OF	51	174	●49	50	9	5	3	33	.287	87	●9	3	.970
1978—Knoxville	South.	OF	113	395	68	104	25	7	10	57	.263	244	9	3	.988
1979—Iowa	A. A.	OF	122	394	67	116	27	5	15	57	.294	287	12	5	.984
1979—Chicago	Amer.	OF	5	11	0	1	0	0	0	0	.091	12	1	0	1.000
1980—Iowa†	A. A.	OF	91	339	47	99	20	2	11	54	.292	198	9	7	.967
1980—Chicago	Amer.	OF	36	62	5	14	4	0	0	3	.226	45	2	1	.979
1981—Chicago	Amer.	OF	67	55	15	14	2	0	0	4	.255	54	0	0	1.000
1982—Edmonton‡	P. C.	OF	69	193	35	52	11	2	7	34	.269	134	3	5	.965
1982—Chicago	Amer.	OF	21	26	4	5	1	0	0	3	.192	21	0	0	1.000
1983—Chi.§-Minn.	Amer.	OF	59	142	19	30	4	0	3	6	.211	106	3	2	.982
1983—Denver x	A. A.	OF	13	43	6	15	2	1	1	8	.349	25	0	1	.962
1984—Detroit	Amer.	OF	84	140	32	40	12	0	2	22	.286	74	2	1	.987
1984—Evansville	A. A.	OF-3B	10	27	4	5	0	0	0	0	.185	18	0	0	1.000
1985—Detroit	Amer.	1B	5	5	0	0	0	0	0	0	.000	0	0	1	.000
1985—Nashville y	A. A.	OF-1B	74	167	24	37	5	0	7	29	.222	93	4	0	1.000
Major League Totals—7 Years			277	441	75	104	23	0	5	38	.236	312	8	5	.985

Selected by Chicago White Sox' organization in 11th round of free-agent draft, June 7, 1977.
†On disabled list, May 24 to June 17, 1980.
‡On disabled list, April 30 to May 31, 1982.
§Traded to Minnesota Twins for Third Baseman Mike Sodders, June 21, 1983.
xTraded to Detroit Tigers for Pitcher Larry Pashnick, December 5, 1983.
yReleased, October 9, 1985; signed by Oakland A's, December 8, 1985.

CHAMPIONSHIP SERIES RECORD

Year Club	League	Pos.	G.	AB.	R.	H.	2B.	3B.	HR.	RBI.	B.A.	PO.	A.	E.	F.A.
1984—Detroit	Amer.	PH-OF	1	1	0	0	0	0	0	0	.000	0	0	0	.000

WORLD SERIES RECORD

Year Club	League	Pos.	G.	AB.	R.	H.	2B.	3B.	HR.	RBI.	B.A.	PO.	A.	E.	F.A.
1984—Detroit	Amer.	PH	2	1	0	0	0	0	0	1	.000	0	0	0	.000

FRANK JOSEPH LaCORTE JR.

Name pronounced Luh-KORT-ee.

Born October 13, 1952, at San Jose, Calif.
Height, 6.01. Weight, 180.
Throws and bats righthanded.
Attended Gavilan College, Gilroy, Calif.

Major League saves: 1980 (11), 1981 (5), 1982 (7), 1983 (3). Total—26.

Year Club	League	G.	IP.	W.	L.	Pct.	H.	R.	ER.	SO.	BB.	ERA.
1973—Greenwood	W. Carol.	18	105	7	8	.467	70	44	30	109	51	2.57
1973—Savannah	Southern	7	30	2	1	.667	19	14	12	34	22	3.60
1974—Savannah	Southern	23	120	7	8	.467	106	76	63	106	89	4.73
1975—Richmond	Int'national	24	128	9	7	.563	121	65	61	108	71	4.29
1975—Atlanta	National	3	14	0	3	.000	13	10	8	10	6	5.14
1976—Richmond	Int'national	14	78	3	3	.500	91	55	46	77	47	5.31
1976—Atlanta	National	19	105	3	12	.200	97	58	55	79	53	4.71
1977—Richmond†	Int'national	8	37	2	3	.400	38	25	25	40	29	6.08
1977—Atlanta	National	14	37	1	8	.111	67	51	48	28	29	11.68
1978—Richmond‡	Int'national	23	130	6	7	.462	125	67	61	99	66	4.22
1978—Atlanta	National	2	15	0	1	.000	9	6	6	7	4	3.60
1979—Atlanta§-Houston	National	18	35	1	2	.333	30	23	22	30	15	5.66
1979—Charleston	Int'national	12	79	4	7	.364	68	32	24	57	31	2.73
1980—Houston	National	55	83	8	5	.615	61	29	26	66	43	2.82

Year Club	League	G.	IP.	W.	L.	Pct.	H.	R.	ER.	SO.	BB.	ERA.
1981—Houston	National	37	42	4	2	.667	41	18	17	40	21	3.64
1982—Houston	National	55	76⅓	1	5	.167	71	44	38	51	46	4.48
1983—Houston xy	National	37	53⅓	4	4	.500	35	32	30	48	28	5.06
1984—California z	American	13	29⅓	1	2	.333	33	26	23	13	13	7.06
1984—Edmonton	P. Coast	7	9⅔	0	1	.000	16	16	12	7	5	11.17
1985—California a	American					(Did not play)						
National League Totals—9 Years		240	460⅔	22	42	.344	424	271	250	359	245	4.88
American League Totals—1 Year		13	29⅓	1	2	.333	33	26	23	13	13	7.06
Major League Totals—10 Years		253	490	23	44	.343	457	297	273	372	258	5.01

Signed as free agent by Atlanta Braves' organization, September 5, 1972.
†On disabled list, July 31 to August 11, 1977.
‡On disabled list, August 2 to August 16, 1978.
§Traded to Houston Astros for Pitcher Bo McLaughlin, May 25, 1979.
xOn disabled list, July 25 to September 1, 1983.
yGranted free agency, November 7, 1983; signed by California Angels, December 8, 1983.
zOn disabled list, June 13 to September 1, 1984; included rehabilitation disability assignment to Edmonton, July 23 to August 10, 1984.
aOn disabled list, April 1, 1985 through entire season.

DIVISION SERIES RECORD

Year Club	League	G.	IP.	W.	L.	Pct.	H.	R.	ER.	SO.	BB.	ERA.
1981—Houston	National	2	3⅔	0	0	.000	2	0	0	5	1	0.00

CHAMPIONSHIP SERIES RECORD

Year Club	League	G.	IP.	W.	L.	Pct.	H.	R.	ER.	SO.	BB.	ERA.
1980—Houston	National	2	3	1	1	.500	7	2	1	2	2	3.00

MICHAEL JAMES LaCOSS
(Mike)

Born May 30, 1956, at Glendale, Calif.
Height, 6.04. Weight, 190.
Throws and bats righthanded.

Major League saves: 1981 (1), 1983 (1), 1984 (3), 1985 (1). Total—6.
Tied for American Association lead in shutouts with 3 in 1978.

Year Club	League	G.	IP.	W.	L.	Pct.	H.	R.	ER.	SO.	BB.	ERA.
1974—Billings	Pioneer	13	87	6	5	.545	81	40	27	58	38	2.79
1975—Tampa	Florida St.	23	151	4	7	.412	131	61	48	72	41	2.86
1976—Three Rivers	Eastern	25	162	12	10	.545	148	66	53	80	53	2.94
1977—Indianapolis	Am. Assoc.	27	186	11	★13	.458	181	93	80	104	65	3.87
1978—Indianapolis	Am. Assoc.	19	130	11	5	.688	129	62	50	67	49	3.46
1978—Cincinnati	National	16	96	4	8	.333	104	56	48	31	46	4.50
1979—Cincinnati	National	35	206	14	8	.636	202	92	80	73	79	3.50
1980—Cincinnati	National	34	169	10	12	.455	207	101	87	59	68	4.63
1981—Cincinnati†	National	20	78	4	7	.364	102	55	53	22	30	6.12
1982—Houston	National	41	115	6	6	.500	107	41	37	51	54	2.90
1983—Houston‡	National	38	138	5	7	.417	142	81	68	53	56	4.43
1984—Houston§	National	39	132	7	5	.583	132	64	59	86	55	4.02
1985—Kansas City	American	21	40⅔	1	1	.500	49	25	23	26	29	5.09
1985—Omaha	Am. Assoc.	4	22⅓	1	2	.333	23	12	8	11	15	3.22
National League Totals—7 Years		223	934	50	53	.485	996	490	432	375	388	4.16
American League Totals—1 Year		21	40⅔	1	1	.500	49	25	23	26	29	5.09
Major League Totals—8 Years		244	974⅔	51	54	.486	1045	515	455	401	417	4.20

Selected by Cincinnati Reds' organization in 3rd round of free-agent draft, June 5, 1974.
†Sold on waivers to Houston Astros, April 4, 1982.
‡On disabled list, June 17 to July 8, 1983.
§Granted free agency, November 8, 1984; signed by Kansas City Royals' organization, February 19, 1985.

CHAMPIONSHIP SERIES RECORD

Year Club	League	G.	IP.	W.	L.	Pct.	H.	R.	ER.	SO.	BB.	ERA.
1979—Cincinnati	National	1	1⅔	0	1	.000	1	2	2	0	4	10.80

ALL-STAR GAME RECORD

Year League		IP.	W.	L.	Pct.	H.	R.	ER.	SO.	BB.	ERA.
1979—National		1⅓	0	0	.000	1	0	0	0	0	0.00

LEONDAUS LACY
(Lee)

Born April 10, 1949, at Longview, Tex.
Height, 6.01. Weight, 185.
Throws and bats righthanded.
Attended Laney Junior College, Oakland, Calif.

Tied major league record for most home runs by pinch-hitter, consecutive at-bats (3), May 2, 6 and 17, 1978 (includes one base on balls during streak).
Major League stolen bases: 1972 (5), 1973 (2), 1974 (2), 1975 (5), 1976 (3), 1977 (4), 1978 (7), 1979 (6), 1980 (18), 1981 (24), 1982 (40), 1983 (31), 1984 (21), 1985 (10). Total—178.

Led National League outfielders in fielding percentage with .996 in 1984.
Led California League shortstops in errors with 63 in 1970.
Led Pioneer League third basemen in putouts with 50, assists with 116, errors with 26 and double plays with 9 in 1969.

Year	Club	League	Pos.	G.	AB.	R.	H.	2B.	3B.	HR.	RBI.	B.A.	PO.	A.	E.	F.A.
1969—Ogden	Pion	3B-SS-2B	71	239	43	70	6	7	1	38	.293	54	121	27	.866
1970—Bakersfield	Calif.	SS-3B	124	502	96	151	19	5	4	49	.301	189	291	66	.879
1971—Albuquerque	Texas	2-3-S-O	132	488	54	150	17	7	0	57	.307	263	358	31	.952
1972—El Paso	Texas	2B-SS	68	258	39	96	22	4	1	35	.372	123	191	7	.978
1972—Los Angeles	Nat.	2B	60	243	34	63	7	3	0	12	.259	125	161	8	.973
1973—Los Angeles	Nat.	2B	57	135	14	28	2	0	0	8	.207	80	85	6	.965
1974—Los Angeles	Nat.	2B-3B	48	78	13	22	6	0	0	8	.282	38	53	3	.968
1975—Los Angeles†	Nat.	2B-OF-SS	101	306	44	96	11	5	7	40	.314	152	75	13	.946
1976—Atl.‡-L.A.	Nat.	2B-OF-3B	103	338	42	91	11	3	3	34	.269	193	111	9	.971
1977—Los Angeles§	Nat.	OF-2B-3B	75	169	28	45	7	0	6	21	.266	56	69	4	.969
1978—Los Angeles x	Nat.	O-2-3-S	103	245	29	64	16	4	13	40	.261	114	64	9	.952
1979—Pittsburgh	Nat.	OF-2B	84	182	17	45	9	3	5	15	.247	77	8	3	.966
1980—Pittsburgh	Nat.	OF-3B	109	278	45	93	20	4	7	33	.335	175	11	3	.984
1981—Pittsburgh	Nat.	OF-3B	78	213	31	57	11	4	2	10	.268	121	8	3	.977
1982—Pittsburgh	Nat.	OF-3B	121	359	66	112	16	3	5	31	.312	186	9	7	.965
1983—Pittsburgh	Nat.	OF	108	288	40	87	12	3	4	13	.302	167	2	0	1.000
1984—Pittsburgh y	Nat.	OF-2B	138	474	66	152	26	3	12	70	.321	272	18	2	.993
1985—Baltimore z	Amer.	OF	121	492	69	144	22	4	0	48	.293	201	9	4	.984
National League Totals—13 Years			1185	3308	469	955	154	35	64	335	.289	1756	674	70	.972
American League Totals—1 Year			121	492	69	144	22	4	9	48	.293	231	9	4	.984
Major League Totals—14 Years			1306	3800	538	1099	176	39	73	383	.289	1987	683	74	.973

Selected by Los Angeles Dodgers' organization in 2nd round of free-agent draft, February 1, 1969.
†Traded with Outfielder Jimmy Wynn, First Baseman-Outfielder Tom Paciorek and Infielder Jerry Royster to Atlanta Braves for Outfielder Dusty Baker and First Baseman-Third Baseman Ed Goodson, November 17, 1975.
‡Traded with Pitcher Elias Sosa to Los Angeles Dodgers for Pitcher Mike Marshall, June 23, 1976.
§On disabled list, June 20 to July 15, 1977.
xGranted free agency, November 2, 1978; signed by Pittsburgh Pirates, January 19, 1979.
yGranted free agency, November 8, 1984; signed by Baltimore Orioles, December 7, 1984.
zOn disabled list, March 28 to May 13, 1985.

CHAMPIONSHIP SERIES RECORD

Year	Club	League	Pos.	G.	AB.	R.	H.	2B.	3B.	HR.	RBI.	B.A.	PO.	A.	E.	F.A.
1974—Los Angeles	Nat.	PR	1	0	0	0	0	0	0	0	.000	0	0	0	.000
1977—Los Angeles	Nat.	PH	1	1	1	1	0	0	0	0	1.000	0	0	0	.000
1978—Los Angeles	Nat.	PH	2	2	0	0	0	0	0	0	.000	0	0	0	.000
Championship Series Totals—3 Years			4	3	1	1	0	0	0	0	.333	0	0	0	.000

WORLD SERIES RECORD

Year	Club	League	Pos.	G.	AB.	R.	H.	2B.	3B.	HR.	RBI.	B.A.	PO.	A.	E.	F.A.
1974—Los Angeles	Nat.	PH	1	1	0	0	0	0	0	0	.000	0	0	0	.000
1977—Los Angeles	Nat.	PH-OF	4	7	1	3	0	0	0	2	.429	2	0	0	1.000
1978—Los Angeles	Nat.	DH	4	14	0	2	0	0	0	1	.143	0	0	0	.000
1979—Pittsburgh	Nat.	PH	4	4	0	1	0	0	0	0	.250	0	0	0	.000
World Series Totals—4 Years			13	26	1	6	0	0	0	3	.231	2	0	0	1.000

PETER LINWOOD LADD
(Pete)

Born July 17, 1956, at Portland, Me.
Height, 6.03. Weight, 235.
Throws and bats righthanded.
Attended University of Mississippi, University, Miss.

Major League saves: 1982 (3), 1983 (25), 1984 (3), 1985 (2). Total—33.
Led Florida State League in saves with 18 in 1978.

Year	Club	League	G.	IP.	W.	L.	Pct.	H.	R.	ER.	SO.	BB.	ERA.
1977—Winter Haven	Florida St.	19	27	4	1	.800	19	8	5	27	7	1.67
1978—Winter Haven	Florida St.	44	85	8	2	.800	69	36	30	66	30	3.18
1979—Bristol†	Eastern	18	29	3	1	.750	11	2	2	26	8	0.62
1979—Columbus‡	Southern	13	41	6	1	.857	24	13	12	31	23	2.63
1979—Houston	National	10	12	1	1	.500	8	5	4	6	8	3.00
1980—Columbus	Southern	33	55	6	5	.545	47	27	21	38	29	3.44
1980—Tucson	P. Coast	18	21	1	2	.333	18	7	6	24	4	2.57
1981—Tucson§	P. Coast	47	96	5	4	.556	90	43	36	68	44	3.38
1982—Vancouver	P. Coast	34	55⅔	10	2	.833	42	19	18	63	18	2.91
1982—Milwaukee	American	16	18	1	3	.250	16	8	8	12	6	4.00
1983—Milwaukee	American	44	49⅓	3	4	.429	30	17	14	41	16	2.55
1983—Vancouver	P. Coast	12	13⅓	0	0	.000	10	2	2	16	4	1.35
1984—Milwaukee	American	54	91	4	9	.308	94	58	53	75	38	5.24
1985—Milwaukee	American	29	45⅔	0	0	.000	58	26	23	22	10	4.53
1985—Vancouver x	P. Coast	5	9	0	0	.000	6	2	2	5	1	2.00
National League Totals—1 Year		10	12	1	1	.500	8	5	4	6	8	3.00
American League Totals—4 Years		143	204	8	16	.333	198	109	98	150	70	4.32
Major League Totals—5 Years		153	216	9	17	.346	206	114	102	156	78	4.25

Selected by Boston Red Sox' organization in 25th round of free-agent draft, June 7, 1977.

‡On disabled list, July 4 to July 18, 1979.
§Traded to Milwaukee Brewers' organization for Pitcher Rickey (Buster) Keeton, October 23, 1981.
xReleased, November 25, 1985; signed by Seattle Mariners' organization, January 18, 1986.

CHAMPIONSHIP SERIES RECORD

Tied Championship Series record for most saves, five-game Series (2), 1982.
Tied American League Championship Series record for most saves, total Series (2), 1982.

Year Club	League	G.	IP.	W.	L.	Pct.	H.	R.	ER.	SO.	BB.	ERA.
1982—Milwaukee	American	3	3⅓	0	0	.000	0	0	0	5	0	0.00

WORLD SERIES RECORD

Year Club	League	G.	IP.	W.	L.	Pct.	H.	R.	ER.	SO.	BB.	ERA.
1982—Milwaukee	American	1	⅔	0	0	.000	1	0	0	0	2	0.00

MICHAEL RUSSELL LAGA
(Mike)

Born June 14, 1960, at Ridgewood, N. J.
Height, 6.02. Weight, 210.
Throws and bats lefthanded.
Attended Bergen Community College, Paramus, N. J.,
and Fairleigh Dickinson University, Teaneck, N. J.

Major League stolen bases: 1982 (1).
Led American Association in sacrifice flies with 7 in 1985.
Led American Association first basemen in total chances with 1,146 and double plays with 101 in 1985.
Led American Association in being hit by pitch with 13 in 1982.
Led American Association first basemen in total chances with 1,221 in 1982.

Year Club	League	Pos.	G.	AB.	R.	H.	2B.	3B.	HR.	RBI.	B.A.	PO.	A.	E.	F.A.
1980—Lakeland	Fla. St.	1B	122	407	60	111	14	6	12	74	.273	1025	84	*18	.984
1981—Birmingham	South.	1B	142	547	89	158	28	7	31	86	.289	1193	*105	*23	.983
1982—Evansville	A. A.	1B	126	444	77	111	15	3	34	90	.250	*1135	68	18	.985
1982—Detroit	Amer.	1B	27	88	6	23	9	0	3	11	.261	163	4	1	.994
1983—Evansville	A. A.	1B	105	355	46	82	24	1	16	58	.231	835	62	*11	.988
1983—Detroit	Amer.	1B	12	21	2	4	0	0	0	2	.190	9	1	0	1.000
1984—Evansville	A. A.	1B	●153	569	86	151	30	9	30	94	.265	1008	92	14	.987
1984—Detroit	Amer.	1B	9	11	1	6	0	0	0	1	.545	12	1	0	1.000
1985—Nashville	A. A.	1B	117	430	58	113	30	2	20	79	.263	*1024	*111	11	.990
1985—Detroit	Amer.	1B	9	36	3	6	1	0	2	6	.167	33	5	1	.974
Major League Totals—4 Years			57	156	12	39	10	0	5	20	.250	217	11	2	.991

Selected by Detroit Tigers' organization in 1st round (17th player selected) of free-agent draft, January 8, 1980.

JEFFREY ALLEN LAHTI
Name pronounced LOT-ee.
(Jeff)

Born October 8, 1956, at Oregon City, Ore.
Height, 6.00. Weight, 180.
Throws and bats righthanded.
Attended Treasure Valley Community College, Ontario, Ore. and
Portland State University, Portland, Ore.

Major League saves: 1984 (1), 1985 (19). Total—20.
Tied for Western Carolinas League lead in saves with 13 in 1979.

Year Club	League	G.	IP.	W.	L.	Pct.	H.	R.	ER.	SO.	BB.	ERA.
1978—Eugene	Northwest	16	53	1	5	.167	58	34	26	32	21	4.42
1979—Greensboro	W. Carol.	53	92	7	2	.778	83	43	29	89	33	2.84
1979—Nashville	Southern	6	16	2	0	1.000	10	4	3	12	5	1.69
1980—Waterbury	Eastern	55	91	7	8	.467	75	34	28	78	40	2.77
1981—Indianapolis†	Am. Assoc.	50	100	6	6	.500	78	38	33	70	31	2.97
1982—Louisville	Am. Assoc.	21	30⅓	3	2	.600	27	15	15	17	7	4.45
1982—St. Louis	National	33	56⅔	5	4	.556	53	27	24	22	21	3.81
1983—St. Louis‡	National	53	74	3	3	.500	64	31	26	26	29	3.16
1983—Louisville	Am. Assoc.	1	2	0	0	.000	2	1	1	0	0	4.50
1984—St. Louis	National	63	84⅔	4	2	.667	69	36	35	45	34	3.72
1985—St. Louis§	National	52	68⅓	5	2	.714	63	15	14	41	26	1.84
Major League Totals—4 Years		201	283⅔	17	11	.607	249	109	99	134	110	3.14

Selected by Philadelphia Phillies' organization in 12th round of free-agent draft, January 7, 1976.
Selected by San Francisco Giants' organization in 7th round of free-agent draft, January 11, 1977.
Selected by Cincinnati Reds' organization in 5th round of free-agent draft, June 6, 1978.
†Traded with Pitcher Jose Brito to St. Louis Cardinals' organization for Pitcher Bob Shirley, April 1, 1982.
‡On disabled list, June 1 to June 22, 1983; included rehabilitation disability assignment to Louisville, June 19 to June 22, 1983.
§On disabled list, April 3 to April 21, 1985.

CHAMPIONSHIP SERIES RECORD

Year Club	League	G.	IP.	W.	L.	Pct.	H.	R.	ER.	SO.	BB.	ERA.
1985—St. Louis	National	2	2	1	0	1.000	2	0	0	1	0	0.00

Year Club	League	G.	IP.	W.	L.	Pct.	H.	R.	ER.	SO.	BB.	ERA.
1982—St. Louis	National	2	1⅓	0	0	.000	4	2	2	1	1	10.80
1985—St. Louis	National	3	3⅔	0	0	.000	10	6	5	2	0	12.27
World Series Totals—2 Years		5	5⅓	0	0	.000	14	8	7	3	1	11.81

STEVEN MICHAEL LAKE
(Steve)

Born March 14, 1957, at Inglewood, Calif.
Height, 6.01. Weight, 190.
Throws and bats righthanded.
Cousin of Mike Lake, minor league pitcher, 1941 through 1946.

Major League stolen bases: 1985 (1).
Led Appalachian League in passed balls with 15 in 1975.

Year Club	League	Pos.	G.	AB.	R.	H.	2B.	3B.	HR.	RBI.	B.A.	PO.	A.	E.	F.A.
1975—Bluefield	Appal.	C	49	162	17	45	12	0	3	24	.278	254	★39	9	.970
1976—Miami	Fla. St.	PH	1	1	0	1	0	0	0	1	1.000	0	0	0	.000
1977—Miami	Fla. St.	C	79	232	25	55	10	1	2	24	.237	357	47	6	.985
1978—Miami†‡	Fla. St.	C	69	223	19	57	10	0	2	26	.256	300	49	6	.983
1979—Stockton§	Calif.	C	94	329	36	93	12	3	6	40	.283	504	73	8	.986
1980—Holyoke	East	C-OF	102	325	36	81	0	0	2	44	.258	445	107	10	.982
1981—Vancouver x	P. C.	C	109	348	27	80	14	1	2	38	.230	502	102	7	.989
1982—Tucson y	P. C.	C	112	378	42	100	15	4	3	45	.265	504	91	12	.980
1983—Chicago	Nat.	C	38	85	9	22	4	1	1	7	.259	115	22	0	1.000
1984—Chicago z	Nat.	C	25	54	4	12	4	0	2	7	.222	72	13	4	.955
1984—Midland	Texas	C	9	25	2	4	0	0	1	1	.160	46	7	0	1.000
1985—Chicago	Nat.	C	58	119	5	18	2	0	1	11	.151	182	25	1	.995
Major League Totals—3 Years			121	258	18	52	10	1	4	25	.202	369	60	5	.988

Selected by Baltimore Orioles' organization in 3rd round of free-agent draft, June 4, 1975.
†On disabled list, April 17 to May 16, 1978.
‡Sold to Milwaukee Brewers' organization, December 21, 1978.
§On disabled list, June 20 to July 6, 1979.
xLoaned to Tucson (Houston Astros' organization), April 5, 1982; returned, September 7, 1982.
yTraded to Chicago Cubs for a player to be named later, April 1, 1983; Milwaukee Brewers' organization acquired Pitcher Rich Buonantony to complete deal, October 24, 1983.
zOn disabled list, May 14 to August 3, 1984; included rehabilitation disability assignment to Midland, July 23 to August 3, 1984.

CHAMPIONSHIP SERIES RECORD

Year Club	League	Pos.	G.	AB.	R.	H.	2B.	3B.	HR.	RBI.	B.A.	PO.	A.	E.	F.A.
1984—Chicago	Nat.	C	1	1	0	1	1	0	0	0	1.000	0	0	0	.000

DENNIS PATRICK LAMP

Born September 23, 1952, at Los Angeles, Calif.
Height, 6.03. Weight, 215.
Throws and bats righthanded.

Established National League record for most games taken out as starting pitcher, season (35), 1980.
Major League saves: 1982 (5), 1983 (15), 1984 (9), 1985 (2). Total—31.

Year Club	League	G.	IP.	W.	L.	Pct.	H.	R.	ER.	SO.	BB.	ERA.
1971—Caldwell	Pioneer	14	46	1	2	.333	51	39	33	43	32	6.46
1972—Bradenton Cubs	Gulf Coast	14	70	7	2	.778	56	20	15	56	21	1.93
1973—Quincy	Midwest	13	89	6	4	.600	67	32	26	71	29	2.63
1973—Midland	Texas	9	48	2	4	.333	54	29	25	23	11	4.69
1974—Key West	Florida St.	8	49	1	5	.167	39	15	8	20	14	1.47
1974—Midland	Texas	24	60	1	1	.500	70	38	31	42	22	4.65
1975—Midland	Texas	37	127	7	5	.583	112	52	47	71	54	3.33
1976—Wichita	Am. Assoc.	30	153	8	★14	.364	182	94	69	98	52	4.06
1977—Wichita	Am. Assoc.	20	129	11	★4	.733	116	54	42	52	23	2.93
1977—Chicago	National	11	30	0	2	.000	43	21	21	12	8	6.30
1978—Chicago	National	37	224	7	15	.318	221	96	82	73	56	3.29
1979—Chicago	National	38	200	11	10	.524	223	96	78	86	46	3.51
1980—Chicago†	National	41	203	10	14	.417	259	★123	★117	83	82	5.19
1981—Chicago	American	27	127	7	6	.538	103	41	34	71	43	2.41
1982—Chicago	American	44	189⅔	11	8	.579	206	96	84	78	59	3.99
1983—Chicago‡	American	49	116⅓	7	7	.500	123	52	48	44	29	3.71
1984—Toronto	American	56	85	8	8	.500	97	53	43	45	38	4.55
1985—Toronto	American	53	105⅔	11	0	1.000	96	42	39	68	27	3.32
National League Totals—4 Years		127	657	28	41	.406	746	336	298	254	192	4.08
American League Totals—5 Years		229	623⅔	44	29	.603	625	284	248	306	196	3.58
Major League Totals—9 Years		356	1280⅔	72	70	.507	1371	620	546	560	388	3.84

Selected by Chicago Cubs' organization in 3rd round of free-agent draft, June 8, 1971.
†Traded to Chicago White Sox for Pitcher Ken Kravec, March 28, 1981.
‡Granted free agency, November 7, 1983; signed by Toronto Blue Jays as Type A player, January 10, 1984. (Pitcher Tom Seaver selected from player compensation pool by Chicago White Sox, January 20, 1984.)

CHAMPIONSHIP SERIES RECORD

Tied American League Championship Series records for most games pitched, four-game Series (3), 1983; most strikeouts by a relief pitcher, game (5), October 15, 1985.

Year Club	League	G.	IP.	W.	L.	Pct.	H.	R.	ER.	SO.	BB.	ERA.
1983—Chicago	American	3	2	0	0	.000	0	1	0	1	2	0.00
1985—Toronto	American	3	9⅓	0	0	.000	2	0	0	10	1	0.00
Championship Series Totals—2 Years		6	11⅓	0	0	.000	2	1	0	11	3	0.00

KENNETH FRANCIS LANDREAUX

Name pronounced LAN-droh.

(Ken)

Born December 22, 1954, at Los Angeles, Calif.
Height, 5.11. Weight, 190.
Throws right and bats lefthanded.
Attended Arizona State University, Tempe, Ariz.
Cousin of Enos Cabell, infielder with Los Angeles Dodgers.

Tied major league record for most two-base hits, inning (2), July 3, 1979 (seventh inning).
Tied modern major league record for most three-base hits, game (3), July 3, 1980.
Major League stolen bases: 1977 (1), 1978 (7), 1979 (10), 1980 (8), 1981 (18), 1982 (31), 1983 (30), 1984 (10), 1985 (15). Total—130.
Named Minor League Player of the Year by THE SPORTING NEWS, 1977.
Named outfielder on THE SPORTING NEWS College Baseball All-America Team, 1976.

Year Club	League	Pos.	G.	AB.	R.	H.	2B.	3B.	HR.	RBI.	B.A.	PO.	A.	E.	F.A.
1976—El Paso†	Texas	OF	21	59	15	13	3	1	2	11	.220	32	4	0	1.000
1977—El Paso	Texas	OF	57	209	57	74	17	4	16	59	.354	117	6	6	.953
1977—Salt Lake City	P. C.	OF	62	256	67	92	16	4	11	57	.359	164	3	4	.977
1977—California	Amer.	OF	23	76	6	19	5	1	0	5	.250	59	5	2	.970
1978—California‡	Amer.	OF	93	260	37	58	7	5	5	23	.223	138	6	2	.986
1979—Minnesota	Amer.	OF	151	564	81	172	27	5	15	83	.305	292	10	6	.981
1980—Minnesota§	Amer.	OF	129	484	56	136	23	11	7	62	.281	231	8	6	.976
1981—Los Angeles	Nat.	OF	99	390	48	98	16	4	7	41	.251	210	4	0	•1.000
1982—Los Angeles	Nat.	OF	129	461	71	131	23	7	7	50	.284	281	3	4	.986
1983—Los Angeles	Nat.	OF	141	481	63	135	25	3	17	66	.281	299	4	3	.990
1984—Los Angeles x	Nat.	OF	134	438	39	110	11	5	11	47	.251	212	3	3	.986
1985—Los Angeles	Nat.	OF	147	482	70	129	26	2	12	50	.268	267	4	7	.975
American League Totals—4 Years			396	1384	180	385	62	22	27	173	.278	720	29	16	.979
National League Totals—5 Years			650	2252	291	603	101	21	54	254	.268	1269	18	17	.987
Major League Totals—9 Years			1046	3636	471	988	163	43	81	427	.272	1989	47	33	.984

Selected by Houston Astros' organization in 8th round of free-agent draft, June 5, 1973.
Selected by California Angels' organization in 1st round (sixth player selected) of free-agent draft, June 8, 1976.
†On disabled list, July 17 to August 4, 1976.
‡Traded with Pitchers Paul Hartzell and Brad Havens and Third Baseman Dave Engle to Minnesota Twins for First Baseman Rod Carew, February 3, 1979.
§Traded to Los Angeles Dodgers for Third Baseman-Outfielder Mickey Hatcher, First Baseman Kelly Snider and Pitcher Matt Reeves, March 30, 1981.
xOn disabled list, April 27 to May 12, 1984.

DIVISION SERIES RECORD

Year Club	League	Pos.	G.	AB.	R.	H.	2B.	3B.	HR.	RBI.	B.A.	PO.	A.	E.	F.A.
1981—Los Angeles	Nat.	OF	5	20	1	4	1	0	0	1	.200	16	0	0	1.000

CHAMPIONSHIP SERIES RECORD

Year Club	League	Pos.	G.	AB.	R.	H.	2B.	3B.	HR.	RBI.	B.A.	PO.	A.	E.	F.A.
1981—Los Angeles	Nat.	OF	5	10	0	1	1	0	0	0	.100	4	0	0	1.000
1983—Los Angeles	Nat.	OF	4	14	0	2	0	0	0	1	.143	12	0	0	1.000
1985—Los Angeles	Nat.	PH-OF	5	18	4	7	3	0	0	2	.389	7	0	0	1.000
Championship Series Totals—3 Years			14	42	4	10	4	0	0	3	.238	23	0	0	1.000

WORLD SERIES RECORD

Year Club	League	Pos.	G.	AB.	R.	H.	2B.	3B.	HR.	RBI.	B.A.	PO.	A.	E.	F.A.
1981—Los Angeles	Nat.	PH-O-PR	5	6	1	1	1	0	0	0	.167	6	0	0	1.000

ALL-STAR GAME RECORD

Year League	Pos.	AB.	R.	H.	2B.	3B.	HR.	RBI.	B.A.	PO.	A.	E.	F.A.
1980—American	PH-OF	1	0	0	0	0	0	0	.000	1	0	0	1.000

TERRY LEE LANDRUM

(Tito)

Born October 25, 1954, at Joplin, Mo.
Height, 5.11. Weight, 175.
Throws and bats righthanded.
Attended Eastern Oklahoma State, Wilburton, Okla.

Major League stolen bases: 1980 (3), 1981 (4), 1983 (1), 1984 (3), 1985 (1). Total—12.
Led Florida State League in stolen bases with 68 in 1978.

Year Club	League	Pos.	G.	AB.	R.	H.	2B.	3B.	HR.	RBI.	B.A.	PO.	A.	E.	F.A.
1973—Orangeburg	W. Car.	OF	70	262	30	73	7	3	1	27	.279	168	7	1	.994
1974—St. Petersburg†	Fla. St.	OF	87	309	38	73	5	9	3	39	.236	214	7	8	.965
1975—St. Petersburg	Fla. St.	OF	132	435	76	96	21	4	11	45	.221	*313	5	7	.978
1976—Arkansas‡	Texas	OF	99	359	49	99	13	3	7	45	.276	201	12	7	.968

Year—Club	League	Pos.	G.	AB.	R.	H.	2B.	3B.	HR.	RBI.	B.A.	PO.	A.	E.	F.A.
1976—Tulsa	A. A.	OF	9	24	1	6	1	0	0	1	.250	17	0	0	1.000
1977—Arkansas	Texas	OF	26	84	11	18	3	1	2	13	.214	50	5	1	.982
1977—St. Petersburg	Fla. St.	OF	67	249	40	61	15	3	4	40	.245	157	7	1	.994
1978—St. Petersburg	Fla. St.	OF	117	434	66	129	★25	1	4	45	.297	★305	8	3	.991
1979—Arkansas	Texas	OF	71	265	44	71	20	5	3	33	.268	134	7	4	.972
1979—Springfield	A. A.	OF	61	193	28	50	8	2	6	34	.259	126	5	2	.985
1980—Springfield	A. A.	OF	93	350	55	106	23	6	12	46	.303	193	6	4	.980
1980—St. Louis	Nat.	OF	35	77	6	19	2	2	0	7	.247	40	1	1	.976
1981—St. Louis	Nat.	OF	81	119	13	31	5	4	0	10	.261	72	6	0	1.000
1982—St. Louis	Nat.	OF	79	72	12	20	3	0	2	14	.278	50	2	0	1.000
1982—Louisville	A. A.	OF	25	94	10	19	2	1	0	6	.202	46	0	2	.958
1983—St. Louis	Nat.	OF	6	5	0	1	0	1	0	0	.200	1	0	0	1.000
1983—Louisville§	A. A.	OF	111	431	79	126	23	★12	18	77	.292	286	8	8	.974
1983—Baltimore x	Amer.	OF	26	42	8	13	2	0	1	4	.310	39	0	0	1.000
1984—St. Louis	Nat.	OF	105	173	21	47	9	1	3	26	.272	93	1	2	.979
1985—St. Louis y	Nat.	OF	85	161	21	45	8	2	4	21	.280	91	2	0	1.000
National League Totals—6 Years			391	607	73	163	27	10	9	78	.269	347	12	3	.992
American League Totals—1 Year			26	42	8	13	2	0	1	4	.310	39	0	0	1.000
Major League Totals—7 Years			417	649	81	176	29	10	10	82	.271	386	12	3	.993

Signed as free agent by St. Louis Cardinals' organization, October 10, 1972.
†On disabled list, July 19 to September 20, 1974.
‡On disabled list, April 24 to May 10, 1976.
§Sold to Baltimore Orioles, August 31, 1983, completing deal in which Baltimore traded Infielder-Catcher Floyd Rayford to St. Louis Cardinals for a player to be named later, June 13, 1983.
xTraded to St. Louis Cardinals for Pitcher Jose Brito and cash, March 25, 1984.
yOn disabled list, April 17 to May 8, 1985.

CHAMPIONSHIP SERIES RECORD

Tied Championship Series record for most hits, inning (2), October 13, 1985 (second inning).
Tied National League Championship Series record for most hits, game (4), October 13, 1985.

Year—Club	League	Pos.	G.	AB.	R.	H.	2B.	3B.	HR.	RBI.	B.A.	PO.	A.	E.	F.A.
1983—Baltimore	Amer.	PR-O-PH	4	10	2	2	0	0	1	1	.200	5	0	0	1.000
1985—St. Louis	Nat.	PH-OF	5	14	2	6	0	0	0	4	.429	6	0	0	1.000
Championship Series Totals—2 Years			9	24	4	8	0	0	1	5	.333	11	0	0	1.000

WORLD SERIES RECORD

Year—Club	League	Pos.	G.	AB.	R.	H.	2B.	3B.	HR.	RBI.	B.A.	PO.	A.	E.	F.A.
1983—Baltimore	Amer.	PR-OF	3	0	0	0	0	0	0	0	.000	1	0	0	1.000
1985—St. Louis	Nat.	OF	7	25	3	9	2	0	1	1	.360	12	1	0	1.000
World Series Totals—2 Years			10	25	3	9	2	0	1	1	.360	13	1	0	1.000

JAMES RICK LANGFORD
(Known by middle name.)

Born March 20, 1952, at Farmville, Va.
Height, 6.00. Weight, 185.
Throws and bats righthanded.
Attended Manatee Junior College, Bradenton, Fla., and
Florida State University, Tallahassee, Fla.

Pitched 11-0 no-hit victory against Memphis, May 30, 1976.
Led American League in wild pitches with 16 in 1979.
Led American League in complete games with 28 in 1980 and 18 in 1981.

Year—Club	League	G.	IP.	W.	L.	Pct.	H.	R.	ER.	SO.	BB.	ERA.
1973—Bradenton Pirates†	Gulf Coast	3	10	1	0	1.000	5	3	0	10	7	0.00
1974—Salem	Carolina	26	174	11	7	.611	143	63	52	125	74	2.69
1975—Shreveport	Texas	16	42	5	2	.714	40	25	17	39	22	3.64
1975—Charleston	Int'national	13	65	7	2	.778	55	26	24	41	20	3.32
1976—Charleston	Int'national	16	121	9	5	.643	106	51	43	95	48	3.20
1976—Pittsburgh‡	National	12	23	0	1	.000	27	17	16	17	14	6.26
1977—Oakland	American	37	208	8	●19	.296	223	107	93	141	73	4.02
1978—Oakland	American	37	176	7	13	.350	169	77	67	92	56	3.43
1979—Oakland	American	34	219	12	16	.429	233	114	104	101	57	4.27
1980—Oakland	American	35	★290	19	12	.613	276	119	105	102	64	3.26
1981—Oakland	American	24	195	12	10	.545	190	81	65	84	58	3.00
1982—Oakland§	American	32	237⅓	11	16	.407	265	121	111	79	49	4.21
1983—Oakland x	American	7	20	0	4	.000	43	28	27	2	10	12.15
1983—Modesto	California	1	6	0	0	.000	4	2	2	2	2	3.00
1984—Tacoma y	P. Coast	3	15	0	2	.000	22	11	10	3	2	6.00
1984—Oakland	American	3	8⅔	0	0	.000	15	8	8	2	2	8.31
1985—Modesto z	California	1	6	0	0	.000	10	5	4	3	2	6.00
1985—Oakland	American	23	59	3	5	.375	60	24	23	21	15	3.51
National League Totals—1 Year		12	23	0	1	.000	27	17	16	17	14	6.26
American League Totals—9 Years		232	1413	72	95	.431	1474	679	603	624	384	3.84
Major League Totals—10 Years		244	1436	72	96	.429	1501	696	619	641	398	3.88

Selected by St. Louis Cardinals' organization in 11th round of free-agent draft, January 13, 1971.
Selected by Cleveland Indians' organization in 36th round of free-agent draft, June 6, 1972.
Signed as free agent by Pittsburgh Pirates' organization, June 17, 1973.

†On suspended list, July 17, 1973 through remainder of season.
‡Traded with Pitchers Doc Medich, Dave Giusti and Doug Bair, and Outfielders Mitchell Page and Tony Armas to Oakland A's for Infielders Phil Garner and Tommy Helms, and Pitcher Chris Batton, March 15, 1977.
§Appeared in one game as outfielder with one putout and had one at-bat with no hits.
xOn disabled list, April 5 to May 2, May 20 to July 17 and July 31, 1983 through remainder of season.
yOn Oakland disabled list, March 31 to September 1, 1984; included rehabilitation disability assignment to Tacoma, June 5 to June 18, 1984.
zOn Oakland disabled list, April 9 to June 13, 1985; included rehabilitation disability assignment to Modesto, June 9 to June 13, 1985.

DIVISION SERIES RECORD

Year	Club	League	G.	IP.	W.	L.	Pct.	H.	R.	ER.	SO.	BB.	ERA.
1981—Oakland		American	1	7⅓	1	0	1.000	10	1	1	3	0	1.23

MARK EDWARD LANGSTON

Born August 20, 1960, at San Diego, Calif.
Height, 6.02. Weight, 183.
Throws left and bats righthanded.
Attended San Jose State University, San Jose, Calif.

Named American League Rookie Pitcher of the Year by THE SPORTING NEWS, 1984.

Year	Club	League	G.	IP.	W.	L.	Pct.	H.	R.	ER.	SO.	BB.	ERA.
1981—Bellingham		Northwest	13	85	7	3	.700	81	37	32	97	46	3.39
1982—Bakersfield		California	26	177⅓	12	7	.632	143	71	50	161	102	2.54
1983—Chattanooga		Southern	28	198	14	9	.609	187	104	79	142	102	3.59
1984—Seattle		American	35	225	17	10	.630	188	99	85	★204	★118	3.40
1985—Seattle†		American	24	126⅔	7	14	.333	122	85	77	72	91	5.47
Major League Totals—2 Years			59	351⅔	24	24	.500	310	184	162	276	209	4.15

Selected by Chicago Cubs' organization in 15th round of free-agent draft, June 6, 1978.
Selected by Seattle Mariners' organization in 3rd round of free-agent draft, June 8, 1981.
†On disabled list, June 7 to July 22, 1985.

CARNEY RAY LANSFORD

Born February 7, 1957, at San Jose, Calif.
Height, 6.02. Weight, 195.
Throws and bats righthanded.
Brother of Phil Lansford, infielder in Cleveland Indians' and Toronto Blue Jays' organizations, 1978 through 1981; and Joe Lansford, first baseman in Oakland A's organization.

Major League stolen bases: 1978 (20), 1979 (20), 1980 (14), 1981 (15), 1982 (9), 1983 (3), 1984 (9), 1985 (2). Total—92.
Hit three home runs in a game, September 1, 1979.
Led American League in sacrifice flies with 11 in 1980.
Led Texas League third basemen in double plays with 16 in 1977.
Named third baseman on THE SPORTING NEWS American League Silver Slugger team, 1981.

Year	Club	League	Pos.	G.	AB.	R.	H.	2B.	3B.	HR.	RBI.	B.A.	PO.	A.	E.	F.A.
1975—Idaho Falls†		Pion.	3B-SS	8	27	5	6	2	0	1	1	.222	8	14	9	.710
1976—Quad Cities		Midw.	3B-OF-SS	121	418	87	120	19	5	14	86	.287	130	215	36	.906
1977—El Paso		Texas	3B	120	443	98	147	17	3	18	94	.332	★110	★210	15	★.955
1978—California‡		Amer.	3B-SS	121	453	63	133	23	2	8	52	.294	94	186	18	.940
1979—California		Amer.	3B	157	654	114	188	30	5	19	79	.287	★135	263	7	★.983
1980—California§		Amer.	3B	151	602	87	157	27	3	15	80	.261	★151	250	19	.955
1981—Boston		Amer.	3B	102	399	61	134	23	3	4	52	★.336	70	180	13	.951
1982—Boston xy		Amer.	3B	128	482	65	145	28	4	11	63	.301	83	216	10	.968
1983—Oakland z		Amer.	3B-SS	80	299	43	92	16	2	10	45	.308	60	163	10	.957
1984—Oakland		Amer.	3B	151	597	70	179	31	5	14	74	.300	137	268	18	.957
1985—Oakland a		Amer.	3B	98	401	51	111	18	2	13	46	.277	85	119	5	.976
Major League Totals—8 Years				988	3887	554	1139	196	26	94	491	.293	815	1645	100	.961

Selected by California Angels' organization in 3rd round of free-agent draft, June 4, 1975.
†On disabled list, July 21 to September 30, 1975.
‡On disabled list, June 11 to July 7, 1978.
§Traded with Pitcher Mark Clear and Outfielder Rick Miller to Boston Red Sox for Shortstop Rick Burleson and Third Baseman Butch Hobson, December 10, 1980.
xOn disabled list, June 24 to July 21, 1982.
yTraded with Outfielder Garry Hancock and a player to be named later to Oakland A's for Outfielder Tony Armas and Catcher Jeff Newman, December 6, 1982; Oakland acquired Pitcher Jerry King to complete deal, December 20, 1982.
zOn disabled list, May 19 to June 7, 1983.
aOn disabled list, July 26 to August 28, 1985.

CHAMPIONSHIP SERIES RECORD

Year	Club	League	Pos.	G.	AB.	R.	H.	2B.	3B.	HR.	RBI.	B.A.	PO.	A.	E.	F.A.
1979—California		Amer.	3B	4	17	2	5	0	0	0	3	.294	4	8	0	1.000

DAVID JEFFREY LaPOINT
(Dave)

Born July 29, 1959, at Glens Falls, N. Y.
Height, 6.03. Weight, 215.
Throws and bats lefthanded.

Pitched 4-0 no-hit victory against Reno, July 25, 1979.
Major League saves: 1980 (1).
Led National League in wild pitches with 15 in 1984.
Tied for American Association lead in complete games with 9 in 1981.
Tied for California League lead in shutouts with 3 and complete games with 11 in 1979.
Tied for Midwest League lead in home runs allowed with 20 in 1978.

Year Club	League	G.	IP.	W.	L.	Pct.	H.	R.	ER.	SO.	BB.	ERA.
1977—Newark	NYP	13	69	5	2	.714	73	40	36	60	22	4.70
1978—Burlington	Midwest	25	161	12	12	.500	177	98	72	134	41	4.02
1979—Stockton	California	27	180	12	10	.545	144	74	63	★208	85	3.15
1980—Vancouver†	P. Coast	17	93	7	4	.636	71	48	29	64	45	2.81
1980—Milwaukee‡	American	5	15	1	0	1.000	17	14	10	5	13	6.00
1981—Springfield	Am. Assoc.	25	172	13	9	.591	160	83	61	★129	66	3.19
1981—St. Louis	National	3	11	1	0	1.000	12	5	5	4	2	4.09
1982—St. Louis	National	42	152⅔	9	3	.750	170	63	58	81	52	3.42
1983—St. Louis	National	37	191⅓	12	9	.571	191	92	84	113	84	3.95
1984—St. Louis§x	National	33	193	12	10	.545	205	94	85	130	77	3.96
1985—San Francisco y	National	31	206⅔	7	17	.292	215	99	82	122	74	3.57
American League Totals—1 Year		5	15	1	0	1.000	17	14	10	5	13	6.00
National League Totals—5 Years		146	754⅔	41	39	.513	793	353	314	450	289	3.74
Major League Totals—6 Years		151	769⅔	42	39	.519	810	367	324	455	302	3.79

Selected by Milwaukee Brewers' organization in 10th round of free-agent draft, June 7, 1977.
†On disabled list, May 6 to May 17 and June 6 to July 15, 1980.
‡Traded with Pitcher Lary Sorensen and Outfielders Sixto Lezcano and David Green to St. Louis Cardinals for Pitchers Pete Vuckovich and Rollie Fingers and Catcher Ted Simmons, December 12, 1980.
§On disabled list, June 15 to June 30, 1984.
xTraded with First Basemen David Green and Gary Rajsich and Shortstop Jose Gonzalez (Jose Uribe) to San Francisco Giants for Outfielder-First Baseman Jack Clark, February 1, 1985.
yTraded with Catcher Matt Nokes and Pitcher Eric King to Detroit Tigers for Pitcher Juan Berenguer, Catcher Bob Melvin and a player to be named later, October 7, 1985; San Francisco Giants acquired Pitcher Scott Medvin to complete deal, December 11, 1985.

WORLD SERIES RECORD

Year Club	League	G.	IP.	W.	L.	Pct.	H.	R.	ER.	SO.	BB.	ERA.
1982—St. Louis	National	2	8⅓	0	0	.000	10	6	3	3	2	3.24

BARRY LOUIS LARKIN

Born April 28, 1964, at Cincinnati, O.
Height, 6.00. Weight, 180.
Throws and bats righthanded.
Attended University of Michigan, Ann Arbor, Mich.
Brother of Byron Larkin, guard at Xavier University;
and Mike Larkin, defensive back at University of Notre Dame.

Named shortstop on THE SPORTING NEWS College Baseball All-America Team, 1985.
Member of 1984 U.S. Olympic baseball team.

Year Club	League	Pos.	G.	AB.	R.	H.	2B.	3B.	HR.	RBI.	B.A.	PO.	A.	E.	F.A.
1985—Vermont	East.	SS	72	255	42	68	13	2	1	31	.267	110	166	17	.942

Selected by Cincinnati Reds' organization in 2nd round of free-agent draft, June 7, 1982.
Selected by Cincinnati Reds' organization in 1st round (fourth player selected) of free-agent draft, June 3, 1985.

WILLIAM ALAN LASKEY
(Bill)

Born December 20, 1957, at Toledo, O.
Height, 6.05. Weight, 190.
Throws and bats righthanded.
Attended Monroe County Community College, Monroe, Mich., and
Kent State University, Kent, O.

Year Club	League	G.	IP.	W.	L.	Pct.	H.	R.	ER.	SO.	BB.	ERA.
1978—Sarasota Royals	Gulf Coast	4	23	1	2	.333	13	7	5	9	11	1.96
1978—Jacksonville	Southern	7	27	3	2	.600	23	14	13	13	15	4.33
1979—Fort Myers	Florida St.	13	93	7	4	.636	71	24	23	72	35	2.23
1979—Jacksonville	Southern	15	97	4	3	.571	78	44	38	53	46	3.53
1980—Omaha	Am. Assoc.	27	145	5	8	.385	155	81	67	77	72	4.16
1981—Omaha†	Am. Assoc.	23	138	10	8	.556	136	67	60	87	52	3.91
1982—Phoenix	P. Coast	2	14	1	0	1.000	12	5	2	10	2	1.29
1982—San Francisco	National	32	189⅓	13	12	.520	186	74	66	88	43	3.14
1983—San Francisco	National	25	148⅓	13	10	.565	151	75	69	81	45	4.19
1984—San Francisco	National	35	207⅔	9	14	.391	222	112	100	71	50	4.33
1985—San Francisco‡-Montreal§	National	30	148⅓	5	16	.238	165	91	81	60	53	4.91
Major League Totals—4 Years		122	693⅔	40	52	.435	724	352	316	300	191	4.10

Selected by Detroit Tigers' organization in 8th round of free-agent draft, January 11, 1977.
Selected by Detroit Tigers' organization in secondary phase of free-agent draft, June 7, 1977.
Selected by Kansas City Royals' organization in secondary phase of free-agent draft, June 6, 1978.
†Traded with Pitcher Rich Gale to San Francisco Giants for Outfielder Jerry Martin, December 10, 1981.
‡Traded with First Baseman Scot Thompson and a player to be named later to Montreal Expos for First Baseman Dan Driessen, August 1, 1985.
§Traded to San Francisco Giants for Pitcher George Riley and Outfielder Alonzo Powell, October 24, 1985 (this deal settled earlier deal of Laskey going from San Francisco to Montreal on August 1, 1985).

WILLIAM CAROL LATHAM JR.
(Bill)

Born August 29, 1960, at Birmingham, Ala.
Height, 6.02. Weight, 190.
Throws and bats lefthanded.
Received bachelor of science degree in transportation
from Auburn University, Auburn, Ala. in 1981.

Year Club	League	G.	IP.	W.	L.	Pct.	H.	R.	ER.	SO.	BB.	ERA.
1981—Little Falls	NYP	13	88	5	5	.500	91	52	38	70	38	3.89
1982—Shelby	S. Atlantic	24	143⅓	9	7	.563	145	81	70	114	53	4.40
1983—Lynchburg	Carolina	13	84⅓	8	4	.667	81	34	20	54	22	2.13
1983—Jackson	Texas	12	72⅔	4	4	.500	72	38	35	37	35	4.33
1984—Jackson	Texas	7	44⅓	2	2	.500	38	15	11	27	9	2.22
1984—Tidewater	Int'national	21	132⅓	11	3	.786	119	49	45	57	42	3.06
1985—New York	National	7	22⅔	1	3	.250	21	10	10	10	7	3.97
1985—Tidewater†	Int'national	24	157⅔	13	8	.619	144	61	47	66	57	2.68
Major League Totals—1 Year		7	22⅔	1	3	.250	21	10	10	10	7	3.97

Selected by Seattle Mariners' organization in 11th round of free-agent draft, June 7, 1977.
Signed as free agent by New York Mets' organization, June 15, 1981.
†Traded with Outfielder Billy Beane and Pitcher Joe Klink to Minnesota Twins for Second Baseman Tim Teufel and Outfielder Pat Crosby, January 16, 1986.

TIMOTHY JON LAUDNER
Name pronounced LAWD-ner.
(Tim)

Born June 7, 1958, at Mason City, Ia.
Height, 6.03. Weight, 208.
Throws and bats righthanded.
Attended University of Missouri, Columbia, Mo.

Tied American League record for most home runs, first two major league games (2), August 28 and 29, 1981.
Led Southern League in slugging percentage with .628 and game-winning RBIs with 14 in 1981.
Named Southern League Most Valuable Player, 1981.

Year Club	League	Pos.	G.	AB.	R.	H.	2B.	3B.	HR.	RBI.	B.A.	PO.	A.	E.	F.A.
1979—Orlando	South.	C	45	141	17	34	7	0	3	20	.241	224	29	6	.977
1980—Orlando†	South.	C	17	61	7	14	5	0	2	5	.230	81	10	1	.989
1980—Visalia	Calif.	C	56	186	23	42	13	0	10	29	.226	251	36	5	.983
1981—Orlando	South.	C-1B	130	433	87	123	21	1	*42	104	.284	631	66	15	.979
1981—Minnesota	Amer.	C	14	43	4	7	2	0	2	5	.163	49	5	0	1.000
1982—Toledo	Int.	C	20	71	4	12	2	0	2	12	.169	121	9	0	1.000
1982—Minnesota	Amer.	C	93	306	37	78	19	1	7	33	.255	454	41	*12	.976
1983—Minnesota	Amer.	C	62	168	20	31	9	0	6	18	.185	259	22	4	.986
1984—Minnesota	Amer.	C	87	262	31	54	16	1	10	35	.206	362	38	9	.978
1985—Minnesota	Amer.	C-1B	72	164	16	39	5	0	7	19	.238	236	19	8	.970
Major League Totals—5 Years			328	943	108	209	51	2	32	110	.222	1360	125	33	.978

Selected by Cincinnati Reds' organization in 33rd round of free-agent draft, June 8, 1976.
Selected by Minnesota Twins' organization in 3rd round of free-agent draft, June 5, 1979.
†On disabled list, April 11 to April 21, 1980.

MICHAEL EUGENE LAVALLIERE
(Mike)

Born August 18, 1960, at Charlotte, N.C.
Height, 5.10. Weight, 200.
Throws right and bats lefthanded.
Attended University of Lowell, Lowell, Mass.
Son of Guy Lavalliere, minor league catcher, 1952 and 1955 through 1961.

Year Club	League	Pos.	G.	AB.	R.	H.	2B.	3B.	HR.	RBI.	B.A.	PO.	A.	E.	F.A.
1981—Spartanburg	S. Atl.	3B-OF	39	123	15	33	9	0	2	23	.268	16	32	5	.906
1982—Peninsula	Carol.	C-3B	66	178	20	49	4	2	2	23	.275	306	35	6	.983
1983—Reading	East.	C-3B-P	81	218	24	64	16	2	4	43	.294	243	59	4	.987
1984—Reading	East.	C-3-2-P	55	147	19	37	6	0	6	22	.252	113	45	2	.988
1984—Portland	P. C.	C	37	122	20	38	6	3	5	21	.311	186	16	1	.995
1984—Philadelphia†‡	Nat.	C	6	7	0	0	0	0	0	0	.000	20	2	0	1.000
1985—St. Louis	Nat.	C	12	34	2	5	1	0	0	6	.147	48	5	0	1.000
1985—Louisville§	A. A.	C	83	231	19	47	12	1	4	26	.203	420	53	5	.990
Major League Totals—2 Years			18	41	2	5	1	0	0	6	.122	68	7	0	1.000

Signed as free agent by Philadelphia Phillies' organization, July 12, 1981.
†Traded to St. Louis Cardinals for a player to be named later, December 3, 1984; returned due to injured status, December 13, 1984.
‡Granted free agency, December 23, 1984; signed by Louisville (St. Louis Cardinals' organization), January 23, 1985.
§On disabled list, July 18 to July 29, 1985.

PITCHING RECORD

Year Club	League	G.	IP.	W.	L.	Pct.	H.	R.	ER.	SO.	BB.	ERA.
1983—Reading	Eastern	4	3⅓	0	0	.000	3	3	2	2	2	5.40
1984—Reading	Eastern	1	1	0	0	.000	3	2	2	1	1	18.00

GARY ROBERT LAVELLE

Born January 3, 1949, at Scranton, Pa.
Height, 6.01. Weight, 200.
Throws left and bats righthanded.

Pitched seven-inning, 4-0 no-hit game against Clinton, August 15, 1969.
Major League saves: 1975 (8), 1976 (12), 1977 (20), 1978 (14), 1979 (20), 1980 (9), 1981 (4), 1982 (8), 1983 (20), 1984 (12), 1985 (8). Total—135.
Led National League in intentional bases on balls issued with 18 in 1977.
Tied for Pacific Coast League lead in shutouts with 3 in 1974.

Year—Club	League	G.	IP.	W.	L.	Pct.	H.	R.	ER.	SO.	BB.	ERA.
1967—Salt Lake City	Pioneer	17	37	3	2	.600	37	18	12	32	23	2.92
1968—Medford	Northwest	13	60	3	3	.500	53	33	23	67	42	3.45
1969—Decatur†	Midwest	7	48	4	2	.667	41	17	9	30	24	1.69
1970—Amarillo	Texas	21	100	6	12	.333	99	75	60	64	72	5.40
1971—Amarillo	Texas	23	136	11	8	.579	132	65	53	77	56	3.50
1972—Phoenix	P. Coast	37	147	11	14	.440	161	91	69	107	55	4.22
1973—Phoenix‡	P. Coast	36	101	5	7	.417	112	56	51	61	43	4.54
1974—Phoenix	P. Coast	35	182	8	●16	.333	228	119	106	105	76	5.24
1974—San Francisco	National	10	17	0	3	.000	14	7	4	12	10	2.12
1975—San Francisco	National	65	82	6	3	.667	80	30	27	51	48	2.96
1976—San Francisco	National	65	110	10	6	.625	102	37	33	71	52	2.70
1977—San Francisco	National	73	118	7	7	.500	106	35	35	93	27	2.06
1978—San Francisco	National	67	98	13	10	.565	96	41	36	63	44	3.31
1979—San Francisco	National	70	97	7	9	.438	86	31	27	80	42	2.51
1980—San Francisco	National	62	100	6	8	.429	106	43	38	66	36	3.42
1981—San Francisco	National	34	66	2	6	.250	58	33	28	45	23	3.82
1982—San Francisco	National	68	104⅔	10	7	.588	97	35	31	76	29	2.67
1983—San Francisco§	National	56	87	7	4	.636	73	33	25	68	19	2.59
1984—San Francisco x	National	77	101	5	4	.556	92	34	31	71	42	2.76
1985—Toronto	American	69	72⅔	5	7	.417	54	30	25	50	36	3.10
National League Totals—11 Years		647	980⅔	73	67	.521	910	359	307	696	382	2.82
American League Totals—1 Year		69	72⅔	5	7	.417	54	30	25	50	36	3.10
Major League Totals—12 Years		716	1053⅓	78	74	.513	964	389	332	746	418	2.84

Selected by San Francisco Giants' organization in 34th round of free-agent draft, June 6, 1967.
†On suspended list, April 11, 1969; transferred to military list through July 5, 1969.
‡On temporary inactive list, June 2 to June 20, 1973.
§On disabled list, July 15 to August 5, 1983.
xTraded to Toronto Blue Jays for Pitchers Jim Gott and Jack McKnight and Infielder Augie Schmidt, January 26, 1985.

CHAMPIONSHIP SERIES RECORD

Year—Club	League	G.	IP.	W.	L.	Pct.	H.	R.	ER.	SO.	BB.	ERA.
1985—Toronto	American	1	0	0	0	.000	0	0	0	0	1	0.00

ALL-STAR GAME RECORD

Year—League		IP.	W.	L.	Pct.	H.	R.	ER.	SO.	BB.	ERA.
1977—National		2	0	0	.000	1	0	0	2	0	0.00

Member of National League All-Star Team in 1983; did not play.

RUDY KARL LAW

Born October 7, 1956, at Waco, Tex.
Height, 6.02. Weight, 180.
Throws and bats lefthanded.

Tied major league records for most at-bats (11) and plate appearances (12), game, May 8, finished May 9, 1984 (25 innings).
Tied American League records for longest errorless game and most innings by outfielder, game (25), May 8, finished May 9, 1984.
Major League stolen bases: 1978 (3), 1980 (40), 1982 (36), 1983 (77), 1984 (29), 1985 (29). Total—214.
Led Pacific Coast League in stolen bases with 79 and caught stealing with 20 in 1978.

Year—Club	League	Pos.	G.	AB.	R.	H.	2B.	3B.	HR.	RBI.	B.A.	PO.	A.	E.	F.A.
1976—Bellingham	N'west.	OF-1B	54	161	40	54	7	1	1	16	.335	58	2	4	.938
1977—Lodi	Calif.	OF	122	451	124	174	22	5	9	88	★.386	107	2	6	.948
1978—Albuquerque	P. C.	OF	138	★573	118	179	21	9	4	72	.312	236	10	10	.961
1978—Los Angeles	Nat.	OF	11	12	2	3	0	0	0	1	.250	3	0	0	1.000
1979—Albuquerque†	P. C.	OF	72	270	46	80	4	2	0	28	.296	142	2	3	.980
1980—Los Angeles	Nat.	OF	128	388	55	101	5	4	1	23	.260	233	6	3	.988
1981—Albuquerque‡	P. C.	OF	107	397	75	133	16	9	0	39	.335	158	5	5	.970
1982—Chicago	Amer.	OF	121	336	55	107	15	8	3	32	.318	215	2	6	.973
1983—Chicago	Amer.	OF	141	501	95	142	20	7	3	34	.283	302	5	2	★.994
1984—Chicago	Amer.	OF	136	487	68	122	14	7	6	37	.251	322	5	5	.985
1985—Chicago§	Amer.	OF	125	390	62	101	21	6	4	36	.259	226	7	3	.987
National League Totals—2 Years			139	400	57	104	5	4	1	24	.260	236	6	3	.988
American League Totals—4 Years			523	1714	280	472	70	28	16	139	.275	1065	19	16	.985
Major League Totals—6 Years			662	2114	337	576	75	32	17	163	.272	1301	25	19	.986

Signed as free agent by Los Angeles Dodgers' organization, September 1, 1975.
†On disabled list, June 22 to August 31, 1979.
‡Traded to Chicago White Sox for Outfielder Cecil Espy and Pitcher Bert Geiger, March 30, 1982.
§On disabled list, July 20 to August 4, 1985.

Tied American League Championship Series records for most at-bats, four-game Series (18), 1983; most hits, four-game Series (7), 1983; most one-base hits, four-game Series (6), 1983.

Year Club	League	Pos.	G.	AB.	R.	H.	2B.	3B.	HR.	RBI.	B.A.	PO.	A.	E.	F.A.
1983—Chicago	Amer.	OF	4	18	1	7	1	0	0	0	.389	10	0	0	1.000

VANCE AARON LAW

Born October 1, 1956, at Boise, Ida.
Height, 6.02. Weight, 190.
Throws and bats righthanded.
Attended Brigham Young University, Provo, Utah.
Son of Vern Law, pitcher with Pittsburgh Pirates, 1950, 1951 and 1954 through 1967.

Established American League record for longest errorless game by third baseman (25 innings), May 8, finished May 9, 1984.
Tied American League record for most innings played by third baseman, game (25), May 8, finished May 9, 1984.
Major League stolen bases: 1980 (2), 1981 (1), 1982 (4), 1983 (3), 1984 (4), 1985 (6). Total—20.
Led Pacific Coast League in sacrifice hits with 14 in 1979.

Year Club	League	Pos.	G.	AB.	R.	H.	2B.	3B.	HR.	RBI.	B.A.	PO.	A.	E.	F.A.
1978—Bradenton Pir.	Gulf C.	SS	1	3	0	1	0	0	0	0	.333	2	5	0	1.000
1978—Salem	Carol.	SS	60	213	48	68	13	7	2	30	.319	96	180	22	.926
1979—Portland	P. C.	SS-3B-2B	131	448	62	139	16	8	2	52	.310	201	308	22	.959
1980—Portland	P. C.	SS	96	339	59	100	23	5	5	54	.295	169	295	14	.971
1980—Pittsburgh	Nat.	2B-SS-3B	25	74	11	17	2	2	0	3	.230	31	54	3	.966
1981—Pittsburgh	Nat.	2B-SS-3B	30	67	1	9	0	1	0	3	.134	50	58	0	1.000
1981—Portland†‡	P. C.	2B-SS-3B	88	310	55	86	14	9	5	43	.277	168	218	9	.977
1982—Chicago	Amer.	S-3-2-O	114	359	40	101	20	1	5	54	.281	156	313	26	.947
1983—Chicago	Amer.	3-2-S-O	145	408	55	99	21	5	4	42	.243	94	311	14	.967
1984—Chicago§	Amer.	3-2-O-S	151	481	60	121	18	2	17	59	.252	119	246	16	.958
1985—Montreal	Nat.	2-1-3-O	147	519	75	138	30	6	10	52	.266	420	402	12	.986
National League Totals—3 Years			202	660	87	164	32	9	10	58	.248	501	514	15	.985
American League Totals—3 Years			410	1248	155	321	59	8	26	155	.257	369	870	56	.957
Major League Totals—6 Years			612	1908	242	485	91	17	36	213	.254	870	1384	71	.969

Selected by Pittsburgh Pirates' organization in 38th round of free-agent draft, June 6, 1978.
†On disabled list, July 5 to July 15, 1981.
‡Traded with Pitcher Ernie Camacho to Chicago White Sox for Pitchers Ross Baumgarten and Butch Edge, March 21, 1982.
§Traded to Montreal Expos for Pitcher Bob James, December 7, 1984.

CHAMPIONSHIP SERIES RECORD

Year Club	League	Pos.	G.	AB.	R.	H.	2B.	3B.	HR.	RBI.	B.A.	PO.	A.	E.	F.A.
1983—Chicago	Amer.	3B	4	11	0	2	0	0	0	1	.182	1	9	1	.909

THOMAS JAMES LAWLESS
(Tom)

Born December 19, 1956, at Erie, Pa.
Height, 5.11. Weight, 170.
Throws and bats righthanded.
Received bachelor of arts degree in political science from
Pennsylvania State University-Behrend, Erie, Pa.

Major League stolen bases: 1982 (16), 1984 (7), 1985 (2). Total—25.
Led American Association in stolen bases with 46 in 1983.
Led Florida State League in sacrifice hits with 13 and stolen bases with 60 in 1979.
Led Pioneer League shortstops in putouts with 116 in 1978.

Year Club	League	Pos.	G.	AB.	R.	H.	2B.	3B.	HR.	RBI.	B.A.	PO.	A.	E.	F.A.
1978—Billings	Pioneer	SS-2B	63	254	64	70	5	●7	5	35	.276	117	186	24	.927
1979—Tampa	Fla. St.	2B	131	469	66	126	9	5	1	39	.269	★296	376	17	★.975
1980—Waterbury	East.	2B	130	498	83	137	20	7	2	29	.275	★316	333	14	.979
1981—Waterbury	East.	2B	136	522	77	152	20	10	8	50	.291	323	379	15	.979
1982—Indianapolis	A. A.	2B-SS	86	351	76	108	18	6	2	28	.308	185	251	13	.971
1982—Cincinnati	Nat.	2B	49	165	19	35	6	0	0	4	.212	87	136	5	.978
1983—Indianapolis	A. A.	2B	115	423	93	118	23	3	13	35	.279	255	303	17	.970
1984—Cinc.†-Mont.		2B-3B	54	97	11	23	3	0	1	2	.237	50	52	1	.990
1984—Wich.-Ind.‡	A. A.	3B-2B-SS	50	173	36	47	5	5	4	23	.272	53	103	4	.975
1985—Louisville	A. A.	3B-OF	31	124	16	36	9	1	1	12	.290	20	58	3	.963
1985—St. Louis	Nat.	3B-2B	47	58	8	12	3	1	0	8	.207	19	44	1	.984
Major League Totals—3 Years			150	320	38	70	12	1	1	14	.219	156	232	7	.982

Selected by Cincinnati Reds' organization in 17th round of free-agent draft, June 6, 1978.
†Traded to Montreal Expos' organization for First Baseman-Outfielder Pete Rose, August 16, 1984.
‡Sold to Louisville (St. Louis Cardinals' organization), March 25, 1985, completing deal in which St. Louis traded Pitcher Mickey Mahler to Montreal Expos for a player to be named later, February 6, 1985.

WORLD SERIES RECORD

Year Club	League	Pos.	G.	AB.	R.	H.	2B.	3B.	HR.	RBI.	B.A.	PO.	A.	E.	F.A.
1985—St. Louis	Nat.	PR	1	0	0	0	0	0	0	0	.000	0	0	0	.000

JACK THOMAS LAZORKO

Name pronounced La-ZOR-ko.

Born March 30, 1956, at Hoboken, N.J.
Height, 5.11. Weight, 200.
Throws and bats righthanded.
Attended Miami-Dade South Community College, Miami, Fla.; and received bachelor
of science degree in business administration and management
from Mississippi State University, Starkville, Miss. in 1978.

Major League saves: 1984 (1), 1985 (1). Total—2.
Led Texas League in intentional bases on balls issued with 12 in 1980.
Led Texas League in games finished in relief with 37 in 1981.
Tied for Pacific Coast League lead in hit batsmen with 6 in 1985.

Year Club	League	G.	IP.	W.	L.	Pct.	H.	R.	ER.	SO.	BB.	ERA.
1978—Sarasota Astros	Gulf Coast	3	4	0	1	.000	7	2	1	5	2	2.25
1978—Daytona Beach	Florida St.	13	27	3	0	1.000	21	8	8	8	10	2.67
1979—Daytona Beach†	Florida St.	17	29	2	1	.667	38	15	15	17	12	4.66
1979—Asheville	W. Carolinas	23	37	4	3	.571	33	19	13	22	12	3.16
1980—Tulsa	Texas	55	82	6	5	.545	78	50	34	47	53	3.73
1981—Tulsa	Texas	47	67	4	8	.333	54	31	25	36	23	3.36
1981—Wichita	Am. Assoc.	8	13	1	0	1.000	14	4	4	9	8	2.77
1982—Denver	Am. Assoc.	23	43½	1	2	.333	63	38	33	32	23	6.85
1982—Tulsa‡	Texas	15	39⅔	2	2	.500	27	9	9	40	7	2.04
1983—El Paso§	Texas	46	80⅓	7	1	.875	102	62	53	55	34	5.94
1984—Vancouver	P. Coast	28	52⅔	2	3	.400	43	24	22	35	15	3.76
1984—Milwaukee x	American	15	39⅔	0	1	.000	37	19	19	24	22	4.31
1985—Phoenix y-Calgary z	P. Coast	44	74⅓	5	5	.500	56	20	17	52	21	2.06
1985—Seattle a	American	15	20⅓	0	0	.000	23	10	8	7	8	3.54
Major League Totals—2 Years		30	60	0	1	.000	60	29	27	31	30	4.05

Selected by Philadelphia Phillies' organization in 8th round of free-agnt draft, January 9, 1975.
Selected by Philadelphia Phillies' organization in 1st round (18th player selected) of free-agent draft, January 7, 1976.
Selected by Philadelphia Phillies' organization in secondary phase of free-agent draft, June 8, 1976.
Selected by New York Yankees' organization in secondary phase of free-agent draft, June 7, 1977.
Selected by Houston Astros' organization in 11th round of free-agent draft, June 6, 1978.
†Sold to Texas Rangers' organization, June 27, 1979.
‡Released, April 5, 1983; signed by El Paso (Milwaukee Brewers' organization), April 10, 1984.
§On disabled list, April 27 to May 7, 1984.
xGranted free agency, October 15, 1984; signed by Phoenix (San Francisco Giants' organization), April 10, 1985.
ySold to Calgary (Seattle Mariners' organization), June 13, 1985.
zAppeared in one game as a third baseman and outfielder with no chances.
aReleased, November 1, 1985.

CHARLES WILLIAM LEA

Name pronounced Lee.

(Charlie)

Born December 25, 1956, at Orleans, France.
Height, 6.04. Weight, 200.
Throws and bats righthanded.
Attended University of Mississippi, University, Miss., Shelby State Community College,
Memphis, Tenn., and Memphis State University, Memphis, Tenn.

Pitched 4-0 no-hit victory against San Francisco Giants, May 10, 1981 (second game).

Year Club	League	G.	IP.	W.	L.	Pct.	H.	R.	ER.	SO.	BB.	ERA.
1978—Memphis	Southern	12	68	3	3	.500	57	34	27	37	32	3.57
1979—Memphis	Southern	24	162	8	8	.500	161	88	79	81	71	4.39
1980—Memphis	Southern	9	75	9	0	1.000	34	10	7	54	21	0.84
1980—Denver	Am. Assoc.	2	12	0	0	.000	8	2	2	9	5	1.50
1980—Montreal	National	21	74	7	5	.583	103	51	43	56	55	3.72
1981—Montreal	National	16	64	5	4	.556	63	34	33	31	26	4.64
1982—Montreal	National	27	177⅔	12	10	.545	145	70	64	115	56	3.24
1983—Montreal	National	33	222	16	11	.593	195	87	77	137	84	3.12
1984—Montreal	National	30	224⅓	15	10	.600	198	82	72	123	68	2.89
1985—Montreal†	National					(Did not play)						
Major League Totals—5 Years		127	792	55	40	.579	704	324	289	462	289	3.28

Selected by New York Mets' organization in 15th round of free-agent draft, June 4, 1975.
Selected by St. Louis Cardinals' organization in secondary phase of free-agent draft, June 8, 1976.
Selected by Chicago White Sox' organization in secondary phase of free-agent draft, January 11, 1977.
Selected by Montreal Expos' organization in 9th round of free-agent draft, June 6, 1978.
†On disabled list, March 24, 1985 through entire season.

ALL-STAR GAME RECORD

Year League	IP.	W.	L.	Pct.	H.	R.	ER.	SO.	BB.	ERA.
1984—National	2	1	0	1.000	3	1	1	2	0	4.50

—DID YOU KNOW—

That the Yankees' Rickey Henderson led off seven games with home runs in 1985?

RICHARD MAX LEACH JR.
(Rick)

Born May 4, 1957, at Ann Arbor, Mich.
Height, 6.00. Weight, 195.
Throws and bats lefthanded.
Attended University of Michigan, Ann Arbor, Mich.

Major League stolen bases: 1982 (4), 1983 (2). Total—6.
Led International League in sacrifice flies with 12 in 1985.
Tied for International League lead in assists by outfielders with 13 in 1985.
Selected by Denver Broncos in 5th round of 1979 NFL draft.
Received reported $200,000 bonus to sign with Detroit Tigers, 1979.
Named outfielder on THE SPORTING NEWS College Baseball All-America Team, 1979.

Year	Club	League	Pos.	G.	AB.	R.	H.	2B.	3B.	HR.	RBI.	B.A.	PO.	A.	E.	F.A.
1979—Lakeland†	Fla. St.	OF	48	168	21	51	10	1	2	23	.304	104	8	3	.974
1980—Evansville	A. A.	1B-OF	126	430	69	117	14	1	5	58	.272	767	62	9	.989
1981—Evansville	A. A.	1B	13	44	8	18	5	0	2	16	.409	129	16	2	.986
1981—Detroit	Amer.	1B-OF	54	83	9	16	3	1	1	11	.193	149	14	0	1.000
1982—Detroit‡	Amer.	1B-OF	82	218	23	52	7	2	3	12	.239	430	29	2	.996
1982—Evansville	A. A.	DH	11	38	6	11	2	0	0	2	.289	0	0	0	.000
1983—Detroit§	Amer.	1B-OF	99	242	22	60	17	0	3	26	.248	465	45	4	.992
1984—Syracuse	Int.	OF-1B	23	79	16	24	6	2	3	8	.304	70	4	2	.974
1984—Toronto	Amer.	OF-1B-P	65	88	11	23	6	2	0	7	.261	92	14	0	1.000
1985—Syracuse	Int.	OF-1B	136	533	77	151	24	2	15	79	.283	675	66	10	.987
1985—Toronto	Amer.	1B-OF	16	35	2	7	0	1	0	1	.200	78	6	1	.988
Major League Totals—5 Years			316	666	67	158	33	6	7	57	.237	1214	108	7	.995

Selected by Philadelphia Phillies' organization in 11th round of free-agent draft, June 4, 1975.
Selected by Philadelphia Phillies' organization in 24th round of free-agent draft, June 6, 1978.
Selected by Detroit Tigers' organization in 1st round (13th player selected) of free-agent draft, June 5, 1979.
†On disabled list, June 18 to June 29, 1979.
‡On disabled list, April 12 to May 17, 1982; included rehabilitation disability assignment to Evansville, May 6 to May 17, 1982.
§Released, March 24, 1984; signed by Toronto Blue Jays' organization, April 3, 1984.

PITCHING RECORD

Year	Club	League	G.	IP.	W.	L.	Pct.	H.	R.	ER.	SO.	BB.	ERA.
1984—Toronto	American	1	1	0	0	.000	2	3	3	0	2	27.00

TERRY HESTER LEACH

Born March 13, 1954, at Selma, Ala.
Height, 6.00. Weight, 205.
Throws and bats righthanded.
Received business administration degree in personnel management-industrial relations
from Auburn University, Auburn University, Ala.

Major League saves: 1982 (3), 1985 (1). Total—4.
Led Gulf States League in home runs allowed with 12 in 1976.

Year	Club	League	G.	IP.	W.	L.	Pct.	H.	R.	ER.	SO.	BB.	ERA.
1976—Baton Rouge†‡	Gulf States	5	19	2	0	1.000	43	21	13	15	14	6.16
1977—Greenwood	W. Carol.	20	67	3	2	.600	47	25	19	67	24	2.55
1978—Savannah§	Southern	9	25	1	0	1.000	24	17	14	21	13	5.04
1978—Kinston	Carolina	34	66	5	4	.556	57	29	24	46	25	3.27
1979—Savannah	Southern	40	92	2	9	.182	77	33	20	68	26	1.96
1979—Richmond	Int'national	7	14	3	1	.750	14	3	3	12	4	1.93
1980—Savannah xy	Southern	22	87	5	1	.833	83	36	31	58	17	3.21
1980—Jackson	Texas	8	54	5	1	.833	50	16	9	30	15	1.50
1981—Tidewater	Int'national	15	76	5	2	.714	63	27	23	42	19	2.72
1981—Jackson	Texas	8	58	5	1	.833	47	14	11	43	12	1.71
1981—New York	National	21	35	1	1	.500	26	11	10	16	12	2.57
1982—Tidewater	Int'national	30	48⅔	4	1	.800	48	20	16	34	19	2.96
1982—New York	National	21	45⅓	2	1	.667	46	22	21	30	18	4.17
1983—Tidewater	Int'national	37	113	5	7	.417	120	66	56	66	42	4.46
1984—Richmond b-Tidewater	Int'national	43	95	11	4	.733	98	42	32	59	30	3.03
1985—Tidewater	Int'national	24	45⅓	1	0	1.000	33	12	8	25	8	1.59
1985—New York	National	22	55⅔	3	4	.429	48	19	18	30	14	2.91
Major League Totals—3 Years		64	136	6	6	.500	120	52	49	76	44	3.24

Selected by Boston Red Sox' organization in 7th round of free-agent draft, January 7, 1976.
†Signed as free agent by Baton Rouge (Independent), June 29, 1976; released when Baton Rouge withdrew from league, August 13, 1976.
‡Signed by Greenwood (Atlanta Braves' organization) as free agent, May 28, 1977.
§Loaned to Kinston (Independent), June 3, 1978; returned, October 25, 1978.
xOn disabled list, June 12 to July 23, 1980.
yReleased, July 23, 1980; signed by Jackson (New York Mets' organization), July 27, 1980.
zTraded to Chicago Cubs' organization for Pitchers Jim Adamczak and Mitch Cook, September 26, 1983.
aTraded by Chicago Cubs' organization to Atlanta Braves' organization for Pitcher Ron Meridith, April 4, 1984.
bReleased, May 25, 1984; signed by New York Mets' organization, May 26, 1984.

LUIS ENRIQUE LEAL

Named pronounced LEE-al.
Born March 21, 1957, at Barquisimento, Venezuela.
Height, 6.03. Weight, 220.
Throws and bats righthanded.
Brother of Carlos Leal, outfielder in Toronto Blue Jays' organization, 1979 through 1982.

Tied American League record for most consecutive hits allowed, start of game (5), June 2, 1980.
Pitched 2-0 no-hit victory against Tampa, May 11, 1979.
Major League saves: 1981 (1).

Year Club	League	G.	IP.	W.	L.	Pct.	H.	R.	ER.	SO.	BB.	ERA.
1979—Dunedin	Florida St.	21	150	12	2	.857	137	51	44	90	45	2.64
1979—Syracuse	Int'national	1	6	1	0	1.000	4	3	3	2	2	4.50
1980—Syracuse	Int'national	16	110	6	5	.545	102	44	40	76	31	3.27
1980—Toronto	American	13	60	3	4	.429	72	35	30	26	31	4.50
1981—Toronto	American	29	130	7	●13	.350	127	63	53	71	44	3.67
1982—Toronto	American	38	249⅔	12	15	.444	250	113	109	111	79	3.93
1983—Toronto	American	35	217⅓	13	12	.520	216	113	104	116	65	4.31
1984—Toronto	American	35	221⅓	13	8	.619	221	106	96	134	77	3.89
1985—Toronto	American	15	67⅓	3	6	.333	82	46	43	33	24	5.75
1985—Syracuse	Int'national	12	69	6	2	.750	69	32	30	43	20	3.91
Major League Totals—6 Years		165	946⅔	51	58	.468	968	476	435	491	320	4.14

Signed as free agent by Toronto Blue Jays organization, 1979.

TIMOTHY JAMES LEARY
(Tim)

Born December 23, 1958, at Santa Monica, Calif.
Height, 6.03. Weight, 190.
Throws and bats righthanded.
Attended University of California, Los Angeles, Calif.

Led Texas League in shutouts with 6 in 1980.
Named Texas League Most Valuable Player, 1980.
Named righthanded pitcher on THE SPORTING NEWS College Baseball All-America Team, 1979.

Year Club	League	G.	IP.	W.	L.	Pct.	H.	R.	ER.	SO.	BB.	ERA.
1979—Jackson†	Texas					(Did not play)						
1980—Jackson	Texas	26	173	●15	8	.652	150	67	53	138	62	2.76
1981—New York‡	National	1	2	0	0	.000	0	0	0	3	1	0.00
1981—Tidewater	Int'national	6	34	1	3	.250	27	16	14	15	27	3.71
1982—Tidewater§	Int'national					(Did not play)						
1983—Tidewater	Int'national	27	160⅓	8	*16	.333	170	100	78	106	73	4.38
1983—New York	National	2	10⅔	1	1	.500	15	10	4	9	4	3.38
1984—New York	National	20	53⅔	3	3	.500	61	28	24	29	18	4.02
1984—Tidewater x	Int'national	10	53⅓	4	4	.500	47	26	24	27	42	4.05
1985—Vancouver	P. Coast	27	177⅔	10	7	.588	174	85	79	136	57	4.00
1985—Milwaukee	American	5	33⅓	1	4	.200	40	18	15	29	8	4.05
National League Totals—3 Years		23	66⅓	4	4	.500	76	38	28	41	23	3.80
American League Totals—1 Year		5	33⅓	1	4	.200	40	18	15	29	8	4.05
Major League Totals—4 Years		28	99⅔	5	8	.385	116	56	43	70	31	3.88

Selected by New York Mets' organization in 1st round (second player selected) of free-agent draft, June 5, 1979.
†On disabled list, July 19 to October 1, 1979.
‡On disabled list, April 16 to August 1, 1981.
§On disabled list, April 13, 1982 through remainder of season.
xTraded to Milwaukee Brewers' organization as part of a six-player, four-team deal in which Kansas City Royals acquired Catcher Jim Sundberg from Milwaukee, Texas Rangers acquired Catcher Don Slaught from Kansas City, New York Mets' organization acquired Pitcher Frank Wills from Kansas City and Milwaukee acquired Pitcher Danny Darwin and a player to be named later from Texas, January 18, 1985; Milwaukee organization acquired Catcher Bill Hance from Texas to complete deal, January 30, 1985.

MANUEL LORA LEE
(Manny)

Born June 17, 1965, at San Pedro de Macoris, Dominican Republic.
Height, 5.09. Weight, 150.
Throws right and bats left and righthanded.

Major League stolen bases: 1985 (1).

Year Club	League	Pos.	G.	AB.	R.	H.	2B.	3B.	HR.	RBI.	B.A.	PO.	A.	E.	F.A.
1982—Kingsport	Appal.	2B-SS	16	54	2	12	1	0	0	3	.222	34	34	6	.919
1983—Sarasota Mets	Gulf C.	2B-SS	32	97	8	24	2	1	0	12	.247	44	79	8	.939
1983—Little Falls	NYP	2B	17	45	10	13	0	0	0	5	.289	34	40	3	.961
1984—Columbia†‡§	S. Atl.	SS-2B	102	346	84	114	12	5	2	33	*.329	126	277	34	.922
1985—Toronto	Amer.	2B-SS-3B	64	40	9	8	0	0	0	0	.200	34	56	3	.968
Major League Totals—1 Year			64	40	9	8	0	0	0	0	.200	34	56	3	.968

Signed as free agent by New York Mets' organization, May 10, 1982.
†On disabled list, April 9 to April 22, 1984.
‡Traded with Outfielder Gerald Young to Houston Astros, August 31, 1984, as partial completion of deal in which New York Mets acquired Infielder Ray Knight for three players to be named later, August 28, 1984; Houston acquired Pitcher Mitch Cook to complete deal, September 10, 1984.
§Drafted by Toronto Blue Jays, December 3, 1984.

Year	Club	League	Pos.	G.	AB.	R.	H.	2B.	3B.	HR.	RBI.	B.A.	PO.	A.	E.	F.A.
1985—Toronto		Amer.	PR-2B	1	0	0	0	0	0	0	0	.000	0	0	0	.000

DAVID DALE LEEPER
Name pronounced LEE-per.

(Dave)

Born October 30, 1959, at Santa Ana, Calif.
Height, 5.11. Weight, 170.
Throws and bats lefthanded.
Attended University of Southern California, Los Angeles, Calif.
Son of Dale Leeper, minor league pitcher, 1946 through 1950.

Named outfielder on THE SPORTING NEWS College Baseball All-America Team, 1981.

Year	Club	League	Pos.	G.	AB.	R.	H.	2B.	3B.	HR.	RBI.	B.A.	PO.	A.	E.	F.A.
1981—Jacksonville		South.	OF	67	227	19	61	7	0	2	21	.269	117	6	7	.946
1982—Jacksonville		South.	OF	132	502	59	147	23	5	3	50	.293	210	8	10	.956
1983—Jacksonville		South.	OF	36	147	22	43	9	1	3	25	.293	58	5	0	1.000
1983—Omaha		A. A.	OF	106	405	52	112	20	8	9	58	.277	199	0	8	.961
1984—Omaha		A. A.	OF-1B	149	534	67	137	26	11	16	79	.257	207	6	6	.973
1984—Kansas City		Amer.	OF	4	6	1	0	0	0	0	0	.000	4	0	0	1.000
1985—Omaha		A. A.	OF-1B	98	380	52	106	21	2	10	52	.279	180	7	2	.989
1985—Kansas City		Amer.	OF	15	34	1	3	0	0	0	4	.088	13	0	1	.929
Major League Totals—2 Years				19	40	2	3	0	0	0	4	.075	17	0	1	.944

Selected by Minnesota Twins' organization in 3rd round of free-agent draft, June 6, 1978.
Selected by Kansas City Royals' organization in 1st round (23rd player selected) of free-agent draft, June 8, 1981.

JOSEPH HENRY LEFEBVRE
Name pronounced Luh-FAY.

(Joe)

Born Feburary 22, 1956, at Penacook, N.H.
Height, 5.10. Weight, 180.
Throws right and bats lefthanded.
Attended Eckerd College, St. Petersburg, Fla.

Tied American League record for most home runs, first two major league games (2), May 22 and 23, 1980.
Major League stolen bases: 1981 (6), 1983 (5). Total—11.
Collected six hits in one game, September 13, 1982 (16 innings).
Tied for Eastern League lead in assists by outfielders with 16 in 1979.

Year	Club	League	Pos.	G.	AB.	R.	H.	2B.	3B.	HR.	RBI.	B.A.	PO.	A.	E.	F.A.
1977—Fort Lauderdale		Fla. St.	OF-P	48	172	20	53	6	9	2	29	.308	76	4	2	.976
1977—West Haven		East.	OF	6	22	8	8	2	0	0	3	.364	7	2	0	1.000
1978—West Haven		East.	OF-3B-C	134	459	*102	122	21	●11	19	70	.266	240	48	14	.954
1979—West Haven		East.	O-I-P-C	138	487	85	142	28	10	21	●107	.292	248	31	10	.965
1980—Columbus		Int.	OF-3B	56	198	37	55	11	3	10	26	.278	89	3	5	.948
1980—New York†		Amer.	OF	74	150	26	34	1	1	8	21	.227	75	3	2	.975
1981—San Diego		Nat.	OF	86	246	31	63	13	4	8	31	.256	167	6	1	.994
1982—San Diego		Nat.	3B-OF-C	102	239	25	57	9	0	4	21	.238	72	74	3	.980
1982—Hawaii		P. C.	OF-3B	8	32	7	11	3	1	0	5	.344	14	6	1	.952
1983—S. D.‡-Phila.		Nat.	OF-3B-C	119	278	35	85	20	8	8	39	.306	105	22	5	.962
1984—Philadelphia§		Nat.	OF-3B	52	160	22	40	9	0	3	18	.250	83	4	3	.967
1984—Reading		East.	OF	6	12	5	4	1	0	0	0	.333	11	1	0	1.000
1985—Philadelphia x		Nat.								(Did not play)						
American League Totals—1 Year				74	150	26	34	1	1	8	21	.227	75	3	2	.975
National League Totals—4 Years				359	923	113	245	51	12	23	109	.265	427	106	12	.978
Major League Totals—5 Years				433	1073	139	279	52	13	31	130	.260	502	109	14	.978

Selected by New York Yankees' organization in 3rd round of free-agent draft, June 7, 1977.

†Traded with Outfielder Ruppert Jones and Pitchers Tim Lollar and Chris Welsh to San Diego Padres for Outfielder Jerry Mumphrey and Pitcher John Pacella, April 1, 1981.

‡Traded to Philadelphia Phillies for Pitcher Sid Monge, May 22, 1983.

§On disabled list, June 18, 1984 through remainder of season; included rehabilitation disability assignment to Reading, July 31 to August 10, 1984.

xOn disabled list, March 26, 1985 through entire season.

CHAMPIONSHIP SERIES RECORD

Year	Club	League	Pos.	G.	AB.	R.	H.	2B.	3B.	HR.	RBI.	B.A.	PO.	A.	E.	F.A.
1980—New York		Amer.	OF	1	0	0	0	0	0	0	0	.000	0	0	0	.000
1983—Philadelphia		Nat.	PH-OF	2	2	0	0	0	0	0	1	.000	2	0	0	1.000
Championship Series Totals—2 Years				3	2	0	0	0	0	0	1	.000	2	0	0	1.000

WORLD SERIES RECORD

Year	Club	League	Pos.	G.	AB.	R.	H.	2B.	3B.	HR.	RBI.	B.A.	PO.	A.	E.	F.A.
1983—Philadelphia		Nat.	PH-OF	3	5	0	1	1	0	0	2	.200	3	0	0	1.000

PITCHING RECORD

Year	Club	League	G.	IP.	W.	L.	Pct.	H.	R.	ER.	SO.	BB.	ERA.
1977—Fort Lauderdale		Florida St.	1	1	0	0	.000	1	1	1	1	2	9.00
1979—West Haven		Eastern	2	5	0	0	.000	5	2	2	4	1	3.60

CRAIG LINDSAY LEFFERTS

Born September 29, 1957, in Munich, West Germany.
Height, 6.01. Weight, 196.
Throws and bats lefthanded.
Attended University of Arizona, Tucson, Ariz.

Major League saves: 1983 (1), 1984 (10), 1985 (2). Total—13.

Year Club	League	G.	IP.	W.	L.	Pct.	H.	R.	ER.	SO.	BB.	ERA.
1980—Geneva	NYP	12	94	9	1	*.900	74	35	29	*99	24	2.78
1981—Midland	Texas	26	185	12	●12	.500	203	95	85	135	36	4.14
1982—Iowa†	Am. Assoc.	18	97⅓	8	5	.615	97	50	33	71	25	3.05
1983—Chicago‡	National	56	89	3	4	.429	80	35	31	60	29	3.13
1984—San Diego	National	62	105⅔	3	4	.429	88	29	25	56	24	2.13
1985—San Diego	National	60	83⅓	7	6	.538	75	34	31	48	30	3.35
Major League Totals—3 Years		178	278	13	14	.481	243	98	87	164	83	2.82

Selected by Kansas City Royals' organization in 6th round of free-agent draft, June 5, 1979.
Selected by Chicago Cubs' organization in 9th round of free-agent draft, June 3, 1980.
†On disabled list, April 24 to June 4, 1982.
‡Traded with First Baseman Carmelo Martinez and Third Baseman Fritz Connally to San Diego Padres for Pitcher Scott Sanderson, December 7, 1983.

CHAMPIONSHIP SERIES RECORD

Tied Championship Series record for most games won, Series (2), 1984.

Year Club	League	G.	IP.	W.	L.	Pct.	H.	R.	ER.	SO.	BB.	ERA.
1984—San Diego	National	3	4	2	0	1.000	1	0	0	1	1	0.00

WORLD SERIES RECORD

Year Club	League	G.	IP.	W.	L.	Pct.	H.	R.	ER.	SO.	BB.	ERA.
1984—San Diego	National	3	6	0	0	.000	2	0	0	7	1	0.00

CHARLES LOUIS LEIBRANDT JR.
(Charlie)

Born October 4, 1956, at Chicago, Ill.
Height, 6.03. Weight, 200.
Throws left and bats righthanded.
Received bachelor of science degree in management from
Miami University, Oxford, O.

Major League saves: 1982 (2).
Tied for American Association lead in shutouts with 3 in 1984.
Tied for American Association lead in games started by pitchers with 26 in 1979.

Year Club	League	G.	IP.	W.	L.	Pct.	H.	R.	ER.	SO.	BB.	ERA.
1978—Eugene	Northwest	3	20	2	0	1.000	24	13	9	18	5	4.05
1978—Tampa	Florida St.	6	47	4	1	.800	26	4	4	40	17	0.77
1978—Indianapolis	Am. Assoc	4	29	2	1	.667	20	9	9	12	12	2.79
1979—Indianapolis	Am. Assoc.	27	162	8	*14	.364	146	67	53	100	65	2.94
1979—Cincinnati	National	3	4	0	0	.000	2	2	0	1	2	0.00
1980—Cincinnati	National	36	174	10	9	.526	200	84	82	62	54	4.24
1981—Indianapolis	Am. Assoc.	25	169	9	7	.563	149	76	55	101	75	2.93
1981—Cincinnati	National	7	30	1	1	.500	28	12	12	9	15	3.60
1982—Cincinnati	National	36	107⅔	5	7	.417	130	68	61	34	48	5.10
1983—Indianapolis†-Omaha	Am. Assoc.	27	185⅓	9	10	.474	181	113	88	128	77	4.27
1984—Omaha	Am. Assoc.	9	72⅔	7	1	.875	51	14	10	38	16	1.24
1984—Kansas City	American	23	143⅔	11	7	.611	158	65	58	53	38	3.63
1985—Kansas City	American	33	237⅔	17	9	.654	223	86	71	108	68	2.69
National League Totals—4 Years		82	315⅔	16	17	.485	360	166	155	106	119	4.42
American League Totals—2 Years		56	381⅓	28	16	.636	381	151	129	161	106	3.04
Major League Totals—6 Years		138	697	44	33	.571	741	317	284	267	225	3.67

Selected by Cincinnati Reds' organization in 9th round of free-agent draft, June 6, 1978.
†Traded to Kansas City Royals for Pitcher Bob Tufts, June 7, 1983.

CHAMPIONSHIP SERIES RECORD

Established American League Championship Series record for most hits allowed, seven-game Series (17), 1985.
Tied Championship Series record for most games lost, Series (2), 1985.
Tied American League Championship Series records for most games lost, total Series (3); most strikeouts by a relief pitcher, game (5), October 16, 1985.

Year Club	League	G.	IP.	W.	L.	Pct.	H.	R.	ER.	SO.	BB.	ERA.
1979—Cincinnati	National	1	⅓	0	0	.000	0	0	0	0	0	0.00
1984—Kansas City	American	1	8	0	1	.000	3	1	1	6	4	1.13
1985—Kansas City	American	3	15⅓	1	2	.333	17	9	9	6	4	5.28
Championship Series Totals—3 Years		5	23⅔	1	3	.250	20	10	10	12	8	3.80

WORLD SERIES RECORD

Year Club	League	G.	IP.	W.	L.	Pct.	H.	R.	ER.	SO.	BB.	ERA.
1985—Kansas City	American	2	16⅓	0	1	.000	10	5	5	10	4	2.76

JOHNNIE LEE LeMASTER

Born June 19, 1954, at Portsmouth, O.
Height, 6.02. Weight, 180.
Throws and bats righthanded.
Cousin of Ron Salyer, minor league pitcher, 1970 through 1977;
and Frank LeMaster, linebacker with Philadelphia Eagles, 1974 through 1982.

Major League stolen bases: 1975 (2), 1976 (2), 1977 (2), 1978 (6), 1979 (9), 1981 (3), 1982 (13), 1983 (39), 1984 (17), 1985 (1). Total—94.
Tied major league record by hitting home run in first major league at-bat, September 2, 1975 (inside the park).
Led Pioneer League batters in strikeouts with 71 in 1973.
Led Pacific Coast League shortstops in double plays with 107 in 1975.
Led Pioneer League shortstops in double plays with 32 in 1973.

Year—Club	League	Pos.	G.	AB.	R.	H.	2B.	3B.	HR.	RBI.	B.A.	PO.	A.	E.	F.A.
1973—Great Falls	Pion.	SS	70	250	34	61	8	2	2	33	.244	★106	★178	★38	.882
1974—Decatur	Midw.	SS	104	399	51	103	14	4	3	28	.258	145	280	★48	.899
1974—Fresno	Calif.	SS	21	84	15	24	3	0	1	4	.286	30	68	8	.925
1975—Phoenix	P. C.	SS	143	520	75	152	26	8	4	58	.292	207	★489	33	.955
1975—San Francisco	Nat.	SS	22	74	4	14	4	0	2	9	.189	26	62	3	.967
1976—Phoenix	P. C.	SS	105	380	60	94	14	5	4	35	.247	151	349	26	.951
1976—San Francisco	Nat.	SS	33	100	9	21	3	2	0	9	.210	54	109	11	.937
1977—Phoenix	P. C.	SS-2B	22	70	12	22	7	2	0	13	.314	37	71	6	.947
1977—San Francisco	Nat.	SS-3B	68	134	13	20	5	1	0	8	.149	66	134	14	.935
1978—San Francisco	Nat.	SS-2B	101	272	23	64	18	3	1	14	.235	135	261	14	.966
1979—San Francisco	Nat.	SS	108	343	42	87	11	2	3	29	.254	160	303	20	.959
1980—San Francisco	Nat.	SS	135	405	33	87	16	6	3	31	.215	200	372	26	.957
1981—San Francisco	Nat.	SS	104	324	27	82	9	1	0	28	.253	166	294	17	.964
1982—San Francisco†	Nat.	SS	130	436	34	94	14	1	2	30	.216	223	382	23	.963
1983—San Francisco	Nat.	SS	141	534	81	128	16	1	6	30	.240	215	402	23	.964
1984—San Francisco	Nat.	SS	132	451	46	98	13	2	4	32	.217	222	391	23	.964
1985—San Fran.‡-Pitt. x.	Nat.	SS	34	74	5	9	0	0	1	6	.122	55	80	3	.978
1985—Cleveland§	Amer.	SS	11	20	0	3	0	0	0	2	.150	19	18	2	.949
National League Totals—11 Years			1008	3147	317	704	109	19	22	226	.224	1522	2790	177	.961
American League Totals—1 Year			11	20	0	3	0	0	0	2	.150	19	18	2	.949
Major League Totals—11 Years			1019	3167	317	707	109	19	22	228	.223	1541	2808	179	.960

Selected by San Francisco Giants' organization in 1st round (sixth player selected) of free-agent draft, June 5, 1973.
†On disabled list, August 15 to September 1, 1982.
‡Traded to Cleveland Indians for Pitcher Mike Jeffcoat and Infielder Luis Quinones, May 7, 1985.
§Traded to Pittsburgh Pirates for a player to be named later, May 30, 1985; Cleveland Indians' organization acquired Pitcher Scott Bailes to complete deal, July 3, 1985.
xOn disabled list, June 21 to August 5 and August 8 to September 9, 1985.

CHESTER EARL LEMON
(Chet)

Born February 12, 1955, at Jackson, Miss.
Height, 6.00. Weight, 190.
Throws and bats righthanded.
Attended Pepperdine University, Malibu, Calif., and Cerritos College, Norwalk, Calif.

Established American League records for most chances accepted by outfielder, season (524), 1977; most putouts by outfielder, season (512), 1977; most years by outfielder, 400 or more putouts (5).
Tied American League record for most years by outfielder, 500 or more putouts (1), 1977.
Major League stolen bases: 1975 (1), 1976 (13), 1977 (8), 1978 (5), 1979 (7), 1980 (6), 1981 (5), 1982 (1), 1984 (5). Total—51.
Led American League in being hit by pitch with 13 in 1979, 13 in 1981, 15 in 1982 and 20 in 1983.
Led American League outfielders in total chances with 536 in 1977.

Year—Club	League	Pos.	G.	AB.	R.	H.	2B.	3B.	HR.	RBI.	B.A.	PO.	A.	E.	F.A.
1972—Coos Bay-N. B.	N'west	SS-3B	38	140	33	40	8	1	2	16	.286	56	94	16	.904
1972—Burlington	Midw.	3B-SS	33	129	18	33	5	0	1	8	.256	24	62	13	.869
1973—Burlington	Midw.	3B-SS	113	392	73	121	21	1	19	★88	.309	102	215	36	.898
1974—Birmingham†	South.	3B-SS	79	272	52	79	22	2	10	61	.290	84	135	23	.905
1975—Tucson‡	P. C.	3B-OF	65	243	43	68	7	2	5	33	.280	60	70	19	.872
1975—Denver	A. A.	3B-OF	70	254	40	78	15	6	8	49	.307	39	76	19	.858
1975—Chicago	Amer.	3B-OF	9	35	2	9	2	0	0	1	.257	5	7	1	.923
1976—Chicago	Amer.	OF	132	451	46	111	15	5	4	38	.246	353	12	3	.992
1977—Chicago	Amer.	OF	150	553	99	151	38	4	19	67	.273	★512	12	12	.978
1978—Chicago§	Amer.	OF	105	357	51	107	24	6	13	55	.300	284	8	5	.983
1979—Chicago	Amer.	OF	148	556	79	177	●44	2	17	86	.318	411	10	10	.977
1980—Chicago	Amer.	OF-2B	147	514	76	150	32	6	11	51	.292	347	11	7	.981
1981—Chicago x	Amer.	OF	94	328	50	99	23	6	9	50	.302	240	2	4	.984
1982—Detroit	Amer.	OF	125	436	75	116	20	1	19	52	.266	242	11	4	.984
1983—Detroit	Amer.	OF	145	491	78	125	21	5	24	69	.255	406	6	5	.988
1984—Detroit	Amer.	OF	141	509	77	146	34	6	20	76	.287	427	6	2	.995
1985—Detroit	Amer.	OF	145	517	69	137	28	4	18	68	.265	411	6	4	.990
Major League Totals—11 Years			1341	4747	702	1328	281	45	154	613	.280	3638	91	57	.985

Selected by Oakland A's organization in 1st round (20th player selected) of free-agent draft, June 6, 1972.
†On disabled list, July 16 to September 16, 1974.
‡Traded with Pitcher Dave Hamilton to Chicago White Sox for Pitchers Stan Bahnsen and Lee (Skip) Pitlock, June 15, 1975.
§On disabled list, August 12 to August 27, 1978.
xTraded to Detroit Tigers for Outfielder Steve Kemp, November 27, 1981.

Year Club	League	Pos.	G.	AB.	R.	H.	2B.	3B.	HR.	RBI.	B.A.	PO.	A.	E.	F.A.
1984—Detroit	Amer.	OF	3	13	1	0	0	0	0	0	.000	9	0	0	1.000

WORLD SERIES RECORD

Year Club	League	Pos.	G.	AB.	R.	H.	2B.	3B.	HR.	RBI.	B.A.	PO.	A.	E.	F.A.
1984—Detroit	Amer.	OF	5	17	1	5	0	0	0	1	.294	15	0	0	1.000

ALL-STAR GAME RECORD

Year League	Pos.	AB.	R.	H.	2B.	3B.	HR.	RBI.	B.A.	PO.	A.	E.	F.A.
1978—American	OF	0	0	0	0	0	0	0	.000	0	0	1	.000
1979—American	OF	2	1	0	0	0	0	0	.000	2	0	0	1.000
1984—American	OF	2	0	1	0	0	0	0	.500	0	0	0	.000
All-Star Game Totals—3 Years		4	1	1	0	0	0	0	.250	2	0	1	.667

DENNIS PATRICK LEONARD

Born May 8, 1951, at Brooklyn, N. Y.
Height, 6.01. Weight, 195.
Throws and bats righthanded.
Attended Iona College, New Rochelle, N. Y.

Pitched 2-0 no-hit victory against Visalia, April 26, 1973.
Pitched seven-inning 3-0 no-hit victory against Quincy, July 15, 1972.
Major League saves: 1977 (1).
Led American League in home runs allowed with 30 in 1980.
Led American League pitchers in games started with 38 in 1980, 26 in 1981 and tied for lead with 40 in 1978.
Tied for American League lead in shutouts with 5 in 1979.
Led American Association in complete games with 18, shutouts with 4 and tied for lead in games started by pitchers with 29 in 1974.
Tied for California League lead in complete games with 16 and shutouts with 5 in 1973.

Year Club	League	G.	IP.	W.	L.	Pct.	H.	R.	ER.	SO.	BB.	ERA.
1972—Kingsport	Ap'lachian	4	22	2	1	.667	19	9	8	31	6	3.27
1972—Waterloo	Midwest	10	67	4	3	.571	58	28	23	63	26	3.09
1973—San Jose	California	29	206	★15	9	.625	152	70	59	212	81	2.58
1974—Omaha	Am. Assoc.	29	★223	12	13	.480	178	96	86	193	91	3.47
1974—Kansas City	American	5	22	0	4	.000	28	15	13	8	12	5.32
1975—Omaha	Am. Assoc.	3	19	0	2	.000	19	11	9	14	10	4.26
1975—Kansas City	American	32	212	15	7	.682	212	98	89	146	90	3.78
1976—Kansas City	American	35	259	17	10	.630	247	113	101	150	70	3.51
1977—Kansas City	American	38	293	●20	12	.625	246	117	99	244	79	3.04
1978—Kansas City	American	40	295	21	17	.553	★283	125	109	183	78	3.33
1979—Kansas City	American	32	236	14	12	.538	226	117	107	126	56	4.08
1980—Kansas City	American	38	280	20	11	.645	271	127	★118	155	80	3.79
1981—Kansas City	American	26	★202	13	11	.542	★202	79	67	107	41	2.99
1982—Kansas City†	American	21	130⅔	10	6	.625	145	82	74	58	46	5.10
1982—Fort Myers	Florida St.	1	5	0	0	.000	4	0	0	3	2	0.00
1982—Sarasota Royals	Gulf Coast	1	5	0	1	.000	5	3	3	2	1	5.40
1982—Omaha	Am. Assoc.	3	20⅔	1	2	.333	19	17	17	13	9	7.40
1983—Kansas City‡	American	10	63	6	3	.667	69	29	26	31	19	3.71
1984—Kansas City§	American					(Did not play)						
1985—Fort Myers x	Florida St.	3	16⅓	2	0	1.000	5	3	2	10	2	1.10
1985—Memphis	Southern	1	5	0	0	.000	9	4	4	1	1	7.20
1985—Kansas City	American	2	2	0	0	.000	1	0	0	1	0	0.00
Major League Totals—11 Years		279	1994⅔	136	93	.594	1930	902	803	1209	571	3.62

Selected by Kansas City Royals' organization in 2nd round of free-agent draft, June 6, 1972.
†On disabled list, May 22 to August 8, 1982; included rehabilitation disability assignment to Ft. Myers, July 8 to July 12, 1982; Sarasota, July 13 to July 14, 1982, and Omaha, July 23 to August 4, 1982.
‡On disabled list, May 29, 1983 through remainder of season.
§On disabled list, March 29, 1984 through entire season.
xOn Kansas City disabled list, April 8 to September 3, 1985; included rehabilitation disability assignment to Fort Myers, August 12 to August 28, and Memphis, August 29, 1985.

DIVISION SERIES RECORD

Year Club	League	G.	IP.	W.	L.	Pct.	H.	R.	ER.	SO.	BB.	ERA.
1981—Kansas City	American	1	8	0	1	.000	7	4	1	3	1	1.13

CHAMPIONSHIP SERIES RECORD

Tied Championship Series record for most games lost, Series (2), 1978.
Established American League Championship Series record for most hits allowed, four-game Series (13), 1978.
Tied American League Championship Series record for most games lost, total Series (3).

Year Club	League	G.	IP.	W.	L.	Pct.	H.	R.	ER.	SO.	BB.	ERA.
1976—Kansas City	American	2	2⅓	0	0	.000	9	5	5	0	2	19.29
1977—Kansas City	American	2	9	1	1	.500	5	4	3	4	2	3.00
1978—Kansas City	American	2	12	0	2	.000	13	5	5	11	2	3.75
1980—Kansas City	American	1	8	1	0	1.000	7	2	2	8	1	2.25
Championship Series Totals—4 Years		7	31⅓	2	3	.400	34	16	15	23	7	4.31

WORLD SERIES RECORD

Year Club	League	G.	IP.	W.	L.	Pct.	H.	R.	ER.	SO.	BB.	ERA.
1980—Kansas City	American	2	10⅔	1	1	.500	15	9	8	5	2	6.75

JEFFREY N. LEONARD
(Jeff)

Born September 22, 1955, at Philadelphia, Pa.
Height, 6.04. Weight, 200.
Throws and bats righthanded.
Major League stolen bases: 1979 (23), 1980 (4), 1981 (5), 1982 (18), 1983 (26), 1984 (17), 1985 (11). Total—104.
Hit for the cycle, June 27, 1985.
Named National League Rookie Player of the Year by THE SPORTING NEWS, 1979.

Year Club	League	Pos.	G.	AB.	R.	H.	2B.	3B.	HR.	RBI.	B.A.	PO.	A.	E.	F.A.
1973—Bellingham	N'west	OF	55	187	30	52	4	3	2	20	.278	46	2	5	.906
1974—Orangeburg	W. Car.	OF	8	15	0	1	0	0	0	1	.067	5	1	1	.857
1974—Bellingham	N'west	OF	78	278	47	90	12	4	3	43	.324	115	7	6	.953
1975—Bakersfield	Calif.	OF	106	320	44	89	11	3	4	37	.278	137	5	7	.953
1976—Lodi	Calif.	OF	133	509	93	168	29	9	8	85	.330	214	13	*15	.938
1976—Albuquerque	P. C.	OF	7	27	2	8	2	1	1	6	.296	14	0	0	1.000
1977—San Antonio	Texas	OF	122	468	75	147	17	10	12	70	.314	241	12	8	.969
1977—Los Angeles	Nat.	OF	11	10	1	3	0	1	0	2	.300	7	0	0	1.000
1978—Albuquerque†	P. C.	OF	133	502	111	*183	23	14	11	93	*.365	216	8	6	.974
1978—Houston	Nat.	OF	8	26	2	10	2	0	0	4	.385	16	1	0	1.000
1979—Houston	Nat.	OF	134	411	47	119	15	5	0	47	.290	227	6	10	.959
1980—Houston	Nat.	OF	88	216	29	46	7	5	3	20	.213	161	9	3	.983
1981—Hou.‡-S.F.	Nat.	OF-1B	44	145	21	42	12	4	4	29	.290	152	5	1	.994
1981—Phoenix	P. C.	OF	47	187	38	75	17	3	7	45	.401	90	2	2	.979
1982—San Francisco§	Nat.	OF-1B	80	278	32	72	16	1	9	49	.259	137	2	9	.939
1982—Phoenix	P. C.	OF	17	59	14	21	5	0	4	12	.356	5	0	0	1.000
1983—San Francisco	Nat.	OF	139	516	74	144	17	7	21	87	.279	253	17	7	.975
1984—San Francisco	Nat.	OF	136	514	76	155	27	2	21	86	.302	247	14	8	.970
1985—San Francisco	Nat.	OF	133	507	49	122	20	3	17	62	.241	203	10	5	.977
Major League Totals—9 Years			773	2623	331	713	116	28	75	386	.272	1403	64	43	.972

Signed as free agent by Los Angeles Dodgers' organization, June 7, 1973.
†Traded to Houston Astros, September 11, 1978, completing deal in which Los Angeles Dodgers acquired Catcher Joe Ferguson for two players to be named later, July 1, 1978; Houston acquired Shortstop Rafael Landestoy as partial completion of deal, July 7, 1978.
‡Traded with First Baseman-Outfielder Dave Bergman to San Francisco Giants for First Baseman Mike Ivie, April 20, 1981.
§On disabled list, May 23 to July 19, 1982; included rehabilitation disability assignment to Phoenix, July 1 to July 19, 1982.

CHAMPIONSHIP SERIES RECORD

Year Club	League	Pos.	G.	AB.	R.	H.	2B.	3B.	HR.	RBI.	B.A.	PO.	A.	E.	F.A.
1980—Houston	Nat.	PH-OF	3	3	0	0	0	0	0	0	.000	2	1	0	1.000

BRADLEY JAY LESLEY
(Brad)

Born September 11, 1958, at Turlock, Calif.
Height, 6.06. Weight, 230.
Throws and bats righthanded.
Attended Merced Junior College, Merced, Calif.
Major League saves: 1982 (4), 1984 (2). Total—6.
Tied for American Association lead in saves with 14 and intentional bases on balls issued with 8 in 1982.

Year Club	League	G.	IP.	W.	L.	Pct.	H.	R.	ER.	SO.	BB.	ERA.
1978—Eugene	Northwest	13	79	5	4	.556	97	47	44	60	26	5.01
1979—Greensboro†	W. Carol.	19	101	3	7	.300	112	67	52	62	34	4.63
1980—Tampa	Florida St.	37	76	4	2	.667	67	23	17	44	40	2.01
1981—Cedar Rapids	Midwest	22	34	4	1	.800	14	4	3	51	21	0.79
1981—Waterbury	Eastern	26	45	4	1	.800	45	17	13	37	15	2.60
1982—Indianapolis	Am. Assoc.	40	59⅔	6	4	.600	55	27	24	47	25	3.62
1982—Cincinnati	National	28	38⅓	0	2	.000	27	13	11	29	13	2.58
1983—Indianapolis‡	Am. Assoc.	13	17⅔	3	1	.750	11	5	5	19	5	2.55
1983—Cincinnati	National	5	8⅓	0	0	.000	9	2	2	5	0	2.16
1984—Wichita	Am. Assoc.	27	36	3	3	.500	26	21	13	33	29	3.25
1984—Cincinnati§	National	16	19⅓	0	1	.000	17	11	11	7	14	5.12
1984—Vancouver x	P. Coast	5	7⅔	0	0	.000	3	1	0	6	4	0.00
1985—Vancouver y	P. Coast	48	56⅓	3	5	.375	41	15	14	50	26	2.24
1985—Milwaukee	American	5	6⅓	1	0	1.000	8	7	7	5	2	9.95
National League Totals—3 Years		49	66	0	3	.000	53	26	24	41	27	3.27
American League Totals—1 Year		5	6⅓	1	0	1.000	8	7	7	5	2	9.95
Major League Totals—4 Years		54	72⅓	1	3	.250	61	33	31	46	29	3.86

Selected by Minnesota Twins' organization in 7th round of free-agent draft, January 11, 1977.
Selected by Cincinnati Reds' organization in 1st round (18th player selected) of free-agent draft, January 10, 1978.
Selected by Cincinnati Reds' organization in secondary phase of free-agent draft, June 6, 1978.
†On disabled list, May 5 to May 19, 1979.
‡On disabled list, July 4 to July 29, 1983.
§Loaned to Vancouver (Milwaukee Brewers' organization), August 10, 1984; returned, August 31, 1984.
xSold to Milwaukee Brewers, November 12, 1984.
yReleased, November 22, 1985.

JAMES MARTIN LEWIS
(Jim)

Born October 12, 1955, at Miami, Fla.
Height, 6.03. Weight, 205.
Throws and bats righthanded.
Attended Miami-Dade Community College, Miami, Fla.,
and University of South Carolina, Columbia, S. C.

Led Pacific Coast League pitchers in games started with 30 in 1984.
Tied for California League lead in shutouts with 5 in 1978.
Tied for International League lead in intentional bases on balls issued with 13 in 1980.

Year	Club	League	G.	IP.	W.	L.	Pct.	H.	R.	ER.	SO.	BB.	ERA.
1977—Bellingham	Northwest	12	27	3	2	.600	33	23	17	31	14	5.67
1978—Stockton	California	26	212	12	11	.522	166	70	50	★189	61	★2.12
1979—Spokane	P. Coast	28	183	13	11	.542	206	95	75	98	56	3.69
1979—Seattle†	American	2	2	0	0	.000	10	7	4	0	1	18.00
1980—Columbus	Int'national	47	93	10	7	.588	73	34	24	76	45	2.32
1981—Columbus	Int'national	54	150	8	7	.533	147	89	83	100	65	4.98
1982—Columbus	Int'national	32	166	12	6	.667	139	61	48	107	64	★2.60
1982—New York‡	American	1	⅔	0	0	.000	3	7	4	0	3	54.00
1983—Toledo	Int'national	38	123	11	9	.550	128	81	69	76	86	5.05
1983—Minnesota§	American	6	18	0	0	.000	24	13	13	8	7	6.50
1984—Salt Lake City	P. Coast	30	207	15	9	.625	★249	117	102	122	79	4.43
1985—Calgary x	P. Coast	20	103	7	7	.500	130	83	74	52	37	6.47
1985—Seattle y	American	2	4⅔	0	1	.000	8	4	4	1	1	7.71
Major League Totals—4 Years		11	25⅓	0	1	.000	45	31	25	9	12	8.88

Signed as free agent by Seattle Mariners' organization, June 22, 1977.
†Traded with Outfielder Ruppert Jones to New York Yankees for Pitchers Rick Anderson and Jim Beattie, Outfielder Juan Beniquez and Catcher Jerry Narron, November 1, 1979.
‡Drafted by Toledo (Minnesota Twins' organization), December 7, 1982.
§Granted free agency, October 20, 1983; signed by Seattle Mariners' organization, February 21, 1984.
xOn disabled list, May 20 to June 22, 1985.
yReleased, November 1, 1985.

SIXTO LEZCANO

Name pronounced Lezz-KAHN-oh.

Born November 28, 1953, at Arecibo, Puerto Rico.
Height, 5.10. Weight, 190.
Throws and bats righthanded.
Cousin of Carlos Lezcano, outfielder with Chicago Cubs, 1980 and 1981.

Tied major league record for most home runs, opening day of season (2), April 10, 1980.
Major League stolen bases: 1974 (1), 1975 (5), 1976 (14), 1977 (6), 1978 (3), 1979 (4), 1980 (1), 1982 (2), 1983 (1). Total—37.
Led National League outfielders in double plays with 8 in 1982.
Named outfielder on THE SPORTING NEWS American League All-Star fielding team, 1979.

Year	Club	League	Pos.	G.	AB.	R.	H.	2B.	3B.	HR.	RBI.	B.A.	PO.	A.	E.	F.A.
1971—Newark	NYP	OF-3B	53	152	24	44	5	1	7	23	.289	55	11	5	.930
1972—Danville	Midw.	OF	114	423	67	114	20	5	10	56	.270	147	13	10	.941
1973—Shreveport	Texas	OF	134	458	69	134	★35	★7	18	90	.293	264	★17	13	.956
1974—Sacramento	P. C.	OF	131	508	100	165	23	8	34	99	.325	245	24	3	.989
1974—Milwaukee	Amer.	OF	15	54	5	13	2	0	2	9	.241	32	3	1	.972
1975—Milwaukee	Amer.	OF	134	429	55	106	19	3	11	43	.247	240	10	6	.977
1976—Milwaukee	Amer.	OF	145	513	53	146	19	5	7	56	.285	345	10	10	.973
1977—Milwaukee†	Amer.	OF	109	400	50	109	21	4	21	49	.273	238	11	3	.988
1978—Milwaukee	Amer.	OF	132	442	62	129	21	4	15	61	.292	262	★18	6	.979
1979—Milwaukee	Amer.	OF	138	473	84	152	29	3	28	101	.321	281	10	4	.986
1980—Milwaukee‡	Amer.	OF	112	411	51	94	19	3	18	55	.229	228	8	4	.983
1981—St. Louis§	Nat.	OF	72	214	26	57	8	2	5	28	.266	103	5	3	.973
1982—San Diego	Nat.	OF	138	470	73	136	26	6	16	84	.289	275	●16	3	.990
1983—S.D. x-Phila	Nat.	OF	115	356	49	85	12	2	8	56	.239	189	10	6	.971
1984—Philadelphia y	Nat.	OF	109	256	36	71	6	2	14	40	.277	151	3	3	.981
1985—Pittsburgh	Nat.	OF	72	116	16	24	2	0	3	9	.207	57	2	2	.967
American League Totals—7 Years			785	2722	360	749	130	22	102	374	.275	1626	70	34	.980
National League Totals—5 Years			506	1412	200	373	54	12	46	217	.264	775	36	17	.979
Major League Totals—12 Years			1291	4134	560	1122	184	34	148	591	.271	2401	106	51	.980

Signed as free agent by Milwaukee Brewers' organization, October 1, 1970.
†On disabled list, July 23 to August 16, 1977.
‡Traded with Pitchers Lary Sorensen and Dave LaPoint and Outfielder David Green to St. Louis Cardinals for Catcher Ted Simmons and Pitchers Pete Vuckovich and Rollie Fingers, December 12, 1980.
§Traded with a player to be named later to San Diego Padres for Pitcher Steve Mura and a player to be named later, December 10, 1981; San Diego acquired Pitcher Luis DeLeon and St. Louis Cardinals' organization acquired Pitcher Al Olmsted to complete deal, February 19, 1982.
xTraded with a player to be named later to Philadelphia Phillies for four players to be named later, August 31, 1983; San Diego Padres acquired Pitchers Marty Decker, Ed Wojna, Darren Burroughs and Lance McCullers, September 20, 1983, and Philadelphia organization acquired Pitcher Steve Fireovid to complete deal, October 11, 1983.
yGranted free agency, November 8, 1984; signed by Pittsburgh Pirates, January 22, 1985.

Year Club	League	Pos.	G.	AB.	R.	H.	2B.	3B.	HR.	RBI.	B.A.	PO.	A.	E.	F.A.
1983—Philadelphia	Nat.	OF-PH	4	13	2	4	0	0	1	2	.308	5	1	1	.857

WORLD SERIES RECORD

Year Club	League	Pos.	G.	AB.	R.	H.	2B.	3B.	HR.	RBI.	B.A.	PO.	A.	E.	F.A.
1983—Philadelphia	Nat.	PH-OF	4	8	0	1	0	0	0	0	.125	2	0	0	1.000

RUFINO AUGUSTO LINARES

Name pronounced Luh-NAHR-ess.
Born February 28, 1951, at San Pedro de Macoris, Dominican Republic.
Height 6.01. Weight, 190.
Throws and bats righthanded.
Brother of Felix Linares, first baseman-pitcher in Atlanta Braves' organization, 1977, 1978 and 1982.
Major League stolen bases: 1981 (8), 1982 (5), 1985 (2). Total—15.

Year Club	League	Pos.	G.	AB.	R.	H.	2B.	3B.	HR.	RBI.	B.A.	PO.	A.	E.	F.A.
1974—Kingsport..............	Appal.	OF	56	220	32	64	7	1	6	41	.291	106	5	6	.949
1975—Greenwood...........	W. Car.	OF	106	302	36	77	12	2	2	35	.255	178	6	10	.948
1976—Greenwood...........	W. Car.	OF-1B	109	389	57	127	20	4	3	54	.326	52	4	1	.982
1977—Savannah	South.	OF	85	262	32	76	12	5	2	29	.290	93	9	5	.953
1978—Savannah	South.	OF	116	400	49	121	15	5	8	51	.303	158	12	3	.983
1978—Richmond..............	Int.	DH	4	9	1	1	0	1	0	3	.111	0	0	0	.000
1979—Savannah	South.	OF	53	198	35	65	11	1	8	37	.328	40	1	2	.953
1979—Richmond†...........	Int.	OF	36	104	9	31	4	1	1	13	.298	22	1	5	.821
1980—Richmond..............	Int.	OF	63	234	31	77	12	4	3	41	.329	56	5	0	1.000
1980—Savannah	South.	OF	51	200	37	85	18	6	2	38	.425	100	4	5	.954
1981—Atlanta	Nat.	OF	78	253	27	67	9	2	5	25	.265	124	6	5	.963
1982—Atlanta	Nat.	OF	77	191	28	57	7	1	2	17	.298	92	4	0	1.000
1983—Richmond‡...........	Int.	OF	29	107	10	24	6	2	1	24	.224	20	1	1	.955
1984—Richmond..............	Int.	OF	57	216	26	64	13	5	3	39	.296	24	0	1	.960
1984—Atlanta§ x..............	Nat.	OF	34	58	4	12	3	0	1	10	.207	21	2	1	.958
1985—Edmonton...............	P. C.	OF	98	383	64	119	13	8	16	65	.311	52	1	2	.964
1985—California...............	Amer.	OF	18	43	7	11	2	0	3	11	.256	1	0	0	1.000
National League Totals—3 Years			189	502	59	136	19	3	8	52	.271	237	12	6	.976
American League Totals—1 Year			18	43	7	11	2	0	3	11	.256	1	0	0	1.000
Major League Totals—4 Years.................			207	545	66	147	21	3	11	63	.270	238	12	6	.977

Signed as free agent by Atlanta Braves' organization, December 30, 1973.
†On disabled list, August 3 to August 13, 1979.
‡On Atlanta disabled list, March 24 to August 15, 1983; included rehabilitation disability assignment to Richmond, July 26 to August 15, 1983.
§Released, November 13, 1984; signed by Edmonton (California Angels' organization) as a non-player coach, April 12, 1985.
xReleased, May 4, 1985; re-signed by Edmonton as a player, May 20, 1985.

JAMES WILLIAM LINDEMAN
(Jim)

Born January 10, 1962, at Evanston, Ill.
Height, 6.01. Weight, 200.
Throws and bats righthanded.
Attended Bradley University, Peoria, Ill.

Year Club	League	Pos.	G.	AB.	R.	H.	2B.	3B.	HR.	RBI.	B.A.	PO.	A.	E.	F.A.
1983—St. Petersburg.......	Fla. St.	3B	70	232	45	64	13	1	8	37	.276	36	98	26	.838
1984—Springfield.............	Midw.	3B-SS	94	354	69	169	15	2	18	66	.271	78	175	30	.894
1984—Arkansas................	Texas	3B	40	137	14	26	4	3	0	13	.190	24	67	6	.939
1985—Arkansas................	Texas	3B	128	450	54	127	30	6	10	63	.282	74	238	24	.929

Selected by St. Louis Cardinals' organization in 1st round (24th player selected) of free-agent draft, June 6, 1983.

RICHARD BRYAN LITTLE

(Known by middle name.)
Born October 8, 1959, at Houston, Tex.
Height, 5.10. Weight, 160.
Throws right and bats right and lefthanded.
Attended Louisburg College, Louisburg, N.C., and
Texas A & M University, College Station, Tex.
Brother of Grady Little, catcher in Atlanta Braves' and Los Angeles Dodgers' organizations,
1968 through 1973; minor league manager, Baltimore Orioles' organization,
1980 through 1984; Toronto Blue Jays' organization, 1985; and currently manager in Atlanta Braves' organization.
brother of Tom Little, pitcher in
Oakland A's organization, 1976.
Major League stolen bases' 1982 (2), 1983 (4), 1984 (2). Total—8.

Year Club	League	Pos.	G.	AB.	R.	H.	2B.	3B.	HR.	RBI.	B.A.	PO.	A.	E.	F.A.
1980—Jamestown............	NYP	2B-SS	7	27	6	8	0	0	0	3	.296	11	21	2	.941
1980—W. Palm Beach....	Fla. St.	SS	64	195	23	43	2	0	0	11	.221	95	212	12	.962
1981—Memphis................	South.	SS	●143	553	98	162	15	3	1	46	.293	★237	399	24	★.964
1982—Wichita..................	A. A.	SS-2B	99	388	67	111	13	3	1	35	.286	165	305	17	.965

Year Club	League	Pos.	G.	AB.	R.	H.	2B.	3B.	HR.	RBI.	B.A.	PO.	A.	E.	F.A.
1982—Montreal	Nat.	2B-3B	29	42	6	9	0	0	0	3	.214	21	32	1	.981
1983—Montreal	Nat.	SS-2B	106	350	48	91	15	3	1	36	.260	181	248	9	.979
1984—Montreal	Nat.	2B-SS	85	266	31	65	11	1	0	9	.244	137	199	6	.982
1984—Indianapolis†	A. A.	2B-SS-3B	35	106	15	31	2	1	0	5	.292	57	84	3	.979
1985—Buffalo	A. A.	2B	49	183	30	56	13	2	1	20	.306	98	145	3	.988
1985—Chicago	Amer.	2B-3B-SS	73	188	35	47	9	1	2	27	.250	101	165	5	.982
National League Totals—3 Years			220	658	85	165	26	4	1	48	.251	339	479	16	.981
American League Totals—1 Year			73	188	35	47	9	1	2	27	.250	101	165	5	.982
Major League Totals—4 Years			293	846	120	212	35	5	3	75	.251	440	644	21	.981

Selected by Los Angeles Dodgers' organization in 5th round of free-agent draft, January 10, 1978.
Selected by Montreal Expos' organization in 9th round of free-agent draft, June 3, 1980.
†Traded to Chicago White Sox for Pitcher Bert Roberge, December 7, 1984.

WILLIAM TIMOTHY LOLLAR
(Tim)

Born March 17, 1956, at Poplar Bluff, Mo.
Height, 6.03. Weight, 195.
Throws and bats lefthanded.
Attended Mineral Area Community College, Flat River, Mo.,
and University of Arkansas, Fayetteville, Ark.

Major League saves: 1980 (2), 1981 (1), 1985 (1). Total—4.

Year Club	League	G.	IP.	W.	L.	Pct.	H.	R.	ER.	SO.	BB.	ERA.
1978—West Haven†	Eastern	8	31	1	1	.500	40	24	20	20	14	5.81
1979—West Haven	Eastern	22	119	8	5	.615	122	55	42	60	36	3.18
1980—Columbus	Int'national	21	49	2	1	.667	29	15	14	50	27	2.57
1980—New York‡	American	14	32	1	0	1.000	33	14	12	13	20	3.38
1981—San Diego	National	24	77	2	8	.200	87	56	52	38	51	6.08
1982—San Diego	National	34	232⅔	16	9	.640	192	82	81	150	87	3.13
1983—San Diego	National	30	175⅔	7	12	.368	170	98	90	135	85	4.61
1984—San Diego§	National	31	195⅔	11	13	.458	168	89	85	131	105	3.91
1985—Chicago x-Boston y	American	34	150	8	10	.444	140	85	77	105	98	4.62
American League Totals—2 Years		48	182	9	10	.474	173	99	89	118	118	4.40
National League Totals—4 Years		119	681	36	42	.462	617	325	308	454	328	4.07
Major League Totals—6 Years		167	863	45	52	.464	790	424	397	572	446	4.14

Selected by Cleveland Indians' organization in 5th round of free-agent draft, June 6, 1977.
Selected by New York Yankees' organization in 4th round of free-agent draft, June 6, 1978.
†On disabled list, August 2 to August 14, 1978.
‡Traded with Outfielder Ruppert Jones and Joe Lefebvre and Pitcher Chris Welsh to San Diego Padres for Outfielder Jerry Mumphrey and Pitcher John Pacella, April 1, 1981.
§Traded with Pitcher Bill Long, Third Baseman Luis Salazar and Shortstop Ozzie Guillen to Chicago White Sox for Pitchers LaMarr Hoyt, Kevin Kristan and Todd Simmons, December 6, 1984.
xTraded to Boston Red Sox for Outfielder Reid Nichols and a player to be named later, July 11, 1985.
yHad one at-bat with no hits.

CHAMPIONSHIP SERIES RECORD

Year Club	League	G.	IP.	W.	L.	Pct.	H.	R.	ER.	SO.	BB.	ERA.
1984—San Diego	National	1	4⅓	0	0	.000	3	3	3	3	4	6.23

WORLD SERIES RECORD

Year Club	League	G.	IP.	W.	L.	Pct.	H.	R.	ER.	SO.	BB.	ERA.
1984—San Diego	National	1	1⅔	0	1	.000	4	4	4	0	4	21.60

RECORD AS INFIELDER

Year Club	League	Pos.	G.	AB.	R.	H.	2B.	3B.	HR.	RBI.	B.A.	PO.	A.	E.	F.A.
1978—West Haven	East.	P-1B	28	55	11	14	2	1	2	7	.255	16	3	0	1.000
1979—West Haven	East.	P-1B	65	122	16	28	3	0	5	15	.230	137	9	1	.993

DOUGLAS EDWARD LOMAN
(Doug)

Born May 9, 1958, at Bakersfield, Calif.
Height, 5.11. Weight, 185.
Throws and bats lefthanded.
Attended Bakersfield College, Bakersfield, Calif.

Led Pacific Coast League in intentional bases on balls received with 13 in 1984.
Tied for Pacific Coast League lead in sacrifice flies with 8 in 1985.

Year Club	League	Pos.	G.	AB.	R.	H.	2B.	3B.	HR.	RBI.	B.A.	PO.	A.	E.	F.A.
1978—Burlington	Midw.	OF	125	409	67	100	23	4	9	63	.244	221	14	8	.967
1979—Stockton	Calif.	OF	138	521	76	144	22	9	9	65	.276	258	12	9	.968
1980—Holyoke	East.	OF	●138	471	78	123	20	9	8	62	.261	271	16	13	.957
1981—El Paso	Texas	OF	71	271	50	83	17	2	7	42	.306	118	15	9	.937
1981—Vancouver	P. C.	OF	62	214	23	53	11	5	3	19	.248	166	5	3	.983
1982—Vancouver	P. C.	OF	118	411	57	106	19	6	14	64	.258	176	12	8	.959
1983—Vancouver	P. C.	OF	130	465	69	122	20	4	19	78	.262	199	6	5	.976
1984—Vancouver	P. C.	OF	★142	524	79	★170	34	9	18	102	.324	267	15	3	.989

— 300 —

Year	Club	League	Pos.	G.	AB.	R.	H.	2B.	3B.	HR.	RBI.	B.A.	PO.	A.	E.	F.A.
1984—Milwaukee		Amer.	OF	23	76	13	21	4	0	2	12	.276	54	4	2	.967
1985—Milwaukee		Amer.	OF	24	66	10	14	3	2	0	7	.212	41	4	0	1.000
1985—Vancouver†		P. C.	OF	104	385	61	113	23	6	10	66	.294	204	9	5	.977
Major League Totals—2 Years				47	142	23	35	7	2	2	19	.246	95	8	2	.981

Selected by Milwaukee Brewers' organization in 2nd round of free-agent draft, January 10, 1978.
†Released, September 27, 1985.

PHILLIP ARDEN LOMBARDI
(Phil)

Born February 20, 1963, at Granada Hills, Calif.
Height, 6.02. Weight, 200.
Throws and bats righthanded.

Led Florida State League catchers in fielding percentage with .985 in 1984.

Year	Club	League	Pos.	G.	AB.	R.	H.	2B.	3B.	HR.	RBI.	B.A.	PO.	A.	E.	F.A.
1981—Bradenton Yanks	Gulf C.		C	20	53	9	13	3	0	0	6	.245	94	17	4	.965
1982—Paintsville		Appal.	C	50	180	26	45	8	0	0	14	.250	323	★50	8	.979
1983—Greensboro		S. Atl.	C-OF	94	330	63	99	15	0	7	43	.300	564	52	14	.978
1983—Fort Lauderdale		Fla. St.	C	17	49	1	11	2	0	0	3	.224	77	6	5	.943
1984—Fort Lauderdale		Fla. St.	C-O-1-3	127	393	58	115	20	2	8	70	.293	669	61	14	.990
1985—Albany†		East.	C-O-3-S	76	250	44	64	13	2	5	32	.256	390	48	11	.976

Selected by New York Yankees' organization in 3rd round of free-agent draft, June 8, 1981.
†On disabled list, July 20 to September 16, 1985.

STEPHEN PAUL LOMBARDOZZI
(Steve)

Born April 26, 1960, at Malden, Mass.
Height, 6.00. Weight, 175.
Throws and bats righthanded.
Attended Gulf Coast Community College, Panama City, Fla.,
and University of Florida, Gainesville, Fla.

Major League stolen bases: 1985 (3).
Led California League shortstops in fielding percentage with .947 in 1982.

Year	Club	League	Pos.	G.	AB.	R.	H.	2B.	3B.	HR.	RBI.	B.A.	PO.	A.	E.	F.A.
1981—Elizabethton		Appal.	SS	65	246	48	79	13	2	6	38	.321	89	192	14	★.953
1982—Visalia		Calif.	SS-OF-P	122	441	81	131	24	1	6	67	.297	185	393	33	.946
1983—Orlando		South.	SS-2B	137	492	76	143	23	6	3	52	.291	203	364	33	.945
1984—Toledo		Int.	2B-SS	119	385	57	96	15	1	9	31	.249	237	310	14	.975
1985—Toledo		Int.	2B-3B-SS	118	451	55	119	21	3	14	48	.264	272	324	17	.972
1985—Minnesota		Amer.	2B	28	54	10	20	4	1	0	6	.370	31	80	2	.982
Major League Totals—1 Year				28	54	10	20	4	1	0	6	.370	31	80	2	.982

Selected by Minnesota Twins' organization in 9th round of free-agent draft, June 8, 1981.

PITCHING RECORD

Year	Club	League	G.	IP.	W.	L.	Pct.	H.	R.	ER.	SO.	BB.	ERA.
1982—Visalia		California	1	1	0	1	.000	5	4	4	2	0	36.00

ROBERT EARL LONG

Born November 11, 1954, at Jasper, Tenn.
Height, 6.03. Weight, 185.
Throws and bats righthanded.
Attended Carson-Newman College, Jefferson City, Tenn., and Shorter College, Rome, Ga.

Year	Club	League	G.	IP.	W.	L.	Pct.	H.	R.	ER.	SO.	BB.	ERA.
1976—Niagara Falls		NYP	11	68	3	5	.375	74	44	31	32	35	4.10
1977—Charleston		W. Carol.	17	85	6	4	.600	78	42	32	57	43	3.39
1978—Salem		Carolina	33	93	8	4	.667	74	42	29	81	40	2.81
1979—Buffalo		Eastern	44	92	4	10	.286	98	52	35	73	54	3.42
1980—Portland†		P. Coast	33	93	4	4	.500	86	48	44	54	41	4.26
1981—Portland		P. Coast	26	157	15	3	.833	122	56	52	97	59	2.98
1981—Pittsburgh		National	5	20	1	2	.333	23	14	13	8	10	5.85
1982—Portland‡§		P. Coast	31	157⅓	5	13	.278	146	110	101	91	73	5.78
1983—Chattanooga		Southern	33	48⅔	4	5	.444	31	21	18	44	26	3.33
1984—Salt Lake City		P. Coast	50	90⅔	6	3	.667	93	53	52	73	37	5.16
1985—Calgary		P. Coast	19	34⅓	3	1	.750	24	9	8	32	15	2.10
1985—Seattle x		American	28	38⅓	0	0	.000	30	17	16	29	17	3.76
National League Totals—1 Year			5	20	1	2	.333	23	14	13	8	10	5.85
American League Totals—1 Year			28	38⅓	0	0	.000	30	17	16	29	17	3.76
Major League Totals—2 Years			33	58⅓	1	2	.333	53	31	29	37	27	4.47

Selected by Pittsburgh Pirates' organization in 24th round of free-agent draft, June 8, 1976.
†On disabled list, July 31 to August 10, 1980.
‡Granted free agency, October 20, 1982; signed by Denver (Chicago White Sox' organization), March 15, 1983.
§Released, April 3, 1983; signed by Chattanooga (Seattle Mariners' organization), May 31, 1983.
xReleased, November 1, 1985; signed by Atlanta Braves, January, 1986.

WILLIAM DOUGLAS LONG
(Bill)

Born February 29, 1960, at Cincinnati, O.
Height, 6.00. Weight, 185.
Throws and bats righthanded.
Attended Miami University, Oxford, O.

Year Club	League	G.	IP.	W.	L.	Pct.	H.	R.	ER.	SO.	BB.	ERA.
1981—Salem	Carolina	14	87	9	2	.818	81	31	27	80	28	2.79
1982—Amarillo	Texas	27	*198⅓	12	10	.545	*222	116	97	117	53	4.40
1983—Las Vegas	P. Coast	18	62⅓	5	5	.500	99	66	53	41	28	7.65
1983—Beaumont	Texas	10	65⅓	2	5	.286	80	47	41	33	28	5.65
1984—Beaumont†	Texas	25	159⅔	●14	5	.737	149	56	52	114	67	2.93
1985—Buffalo	Am. Assoc.	25	151⅓	*13	6	.684	146	69	59	71	43	3.51
1985—Chicago	American	4	14	0	1	.000	25	17	16	13	5	10.29
Major League Totals—1 Year		4	14	0	1	.000	25	17	16	13	5	10.29

Selected by San Diego Padres' organization in 2nd round of free-agent draft, June 8, 1981.

†Traded with Pitcher Tim Lollar, Third Baseman Luis Salazar and Shortstop Ozzie Guillen to Chicago White Sox for Pitchers LaMarr Hoyt, Kevin Kristan and Todd Simmons, December 6, 1984.

DAVID EARL LOPES
Name rhymes with Ropes.
(Davey)

Born May 3, 1946, at East Providence, R. I.
Height, 5.09. Weight, 170.
Throws and bats righthanded.
Attended Iowa Wesleyan College, Mt. Pleasant, Iowa, and received bachelor of science degree
in education from Washburn University, Topeka, Kan. in 1969.

Established major league record for most consecutive stolen bases, season (38), June 10 through August 24, 1975.
Tied major league record for most errors, inning, second baseman, (3), June 2, 1973 (1st inning).
Tied National League records for most stolen bases, game, since 1900 (5), August 24, 1974; most double plays, second baseman, game (5), May 18, 1975.
Hit three home runs in a game, August 20, 1974.
Major League stolen bases: 1972 (4), 1973 (36), 1974 (59), 1975 (77), 1976 (63), 1977 (47), 1978 (45), 1979 (44), 1980 (23), 1981 (20), 1982 (28), 1983 (22), 1984 (15), 1985 (47). Total—530.
Led National League in stolen bases with 77 in 1975 and 63 in 1976.
Led Pacific Coast League in stolen bases with 48 in 1972.
Led Pacific Coast League second basemen in errors with 18 in 1972.
Tied for Pacific Coast League lead in errors by outfielders with 10 in 1970.
Named second baseman on THE SPORTING NEWS National League All-Star Team, 1978 and 1979.
Named second baseman on THE SPORTING NEWS National League All-Star fielding team, 1978.

Year Club	League	Pos.	G.	AB.	R.	H.	2B.	3B.	HR.	RBI.	B.A.	PO.	A.	E.	F.A.
1968—Daytona Beach†	Fla. St.	OF	82	271	39	67	6	6	5	33	.247	109	7	4	.967
1969—Daytona Bea.‡§	Fla. St.	OF	72	264	53	74	7	4	9	33	.280	138	16	7	.957
1970—Spokane x	P. C.	OF-2B	100	343	48	90	15	4	6	35	.262	202	19	12	.948
1971—Spokane y	P. C.	OF-2B	94	353	78	108	9	9	6	36	.306	157	103	11	.959
1972—Albuquerque z	P. C.	2B-OF-SS	104	397	94	126	18	6	11	53	.317	213	270	21	.958
1972—Los Angeles	Nat.	2B	11	42	6	9	4	0	0	1	.214	27	27	2	.964
1973—Los Angeles	Nat.	2-O-S-3	142	535	77	147	13	5	6	37	.275	323	380	11	.985
1974—Los Angeles	Nat.	2B	145	530	95	141	26	3	10	35	.266	309	360	*24	.965
1975—Los Angeles	Nat.	2B-OF-SS	155	618	108	162	24	6	8	41	.262	360	386	16	.979
1976—Los Angeles a	Nat.	2B-OF	117	427	72	103	17	7	4	20	.241	254	268	15	.965
1977—Los Angeles	Nat.	2B	134	502	85	142	19	5	11	53	.283	287	380	14	.979
1978—Los Angeles	Nat.	*2B-OF	151	587	93	163	25	4	17	58	.278	340	424	*20	.974
1979—Los Angeles	Nat.	2B	153	582	109	154	20	6	28	73	.265	341	*384	14	.981
1980—Los Angeles	Nat.	2B	141	553	79	139	15	3	10	49	.251	304	416	15	.980
1981—Los Angeles bc	Nat.	2B	58	214	35	44	2	0	5	17	.206	129	161	2	.993
1982—Oakland	Amer.	2B-OF	128	450	58	109	19	3	11	42	.242	295	338	15	.977
1983—Oakland	Amer.	2B-OF-3B	147	494	64	137	13	4	17	67	.277	267	287	9	.984
1984—Oakland de	Amer.	OF-2B-3B	72	230	32	59	11	1	9	36	.257	99	47	6	.961
1984—Chicago	Nat.	OF-2B	16	17	5	4	1	0	0	0	.235	6	2	0	1.000
1985—Chicago	Nat.	OF-3B-2B	99	275	52	78	11	0	11	44	.284	115	6	1	.992
National League Totals—12 Years			1322	4882	816	1286	177	39	110	428	.263	2795	3194	138	.977
American League Totals—3 Years			347	1174	154	305	43	8	37	145	.260	661	672	30	.978
Major League Totals—14 Years			1669	6056	970	1591	220	47	147	573	.263	3456	3866	168	.978

Selected by San Francisco Giants' organization in 28th round of free-agent draft, June 6, 1967.
Selected by Los Angeles Dodgers' organization in secondary phase of free-agent draft, January 27, 1968.
†On restricted list, April 11 to June 13, 1968.
‡On temporary inactive list, April 11 to April 27, 1969.
§On military list, July 22, 1969 to April 8, 1970.
xOn temporary inactive list, June 9 to June 30, 1970.
yOn temporary inactive list, April 26 to April 29 and June 8 to July 2, 1971.
zOn temporary inactive list, June 16 to June 30 and August 28 to September 1, 1972.
aOn disabled list, March 31 to May 3, 1976.
bOn disabled list, August 18 to September 2, 1981.
cTraded to Oakland A's for Second Baseman Lance Hudson, February 8, 1982.
dOn disabled list, July 7 to August 8, 1984.
eTraded to Chicago Cubs, August 31, 1984, as partial completion of deal in which Chicago traded Pitcher Chuck Rainey and a player to be named later to Oakland A's for a player to be named later, July 15, 1984; Oakland organization acquired Outfielder Damon Farmar to complete deal, March 18, 1985.

Year	Club	League	Pos.	G.	AB.	R.	H.	2B.	3B.	HR.	RBI.	B.A.	PO.	A.	E.	F.A.
1981—Los Angeles		Nat.	2B	5	20	1	4	1	0	0	0	.200	7	12	0	1.000

CHAMPIONSHIP SERIES RECORD

Established Championship Series records for most stolen bases, total Series (9); most stolen bases, four-game Series (3), 1974 and five-game Series (5), 1981.

Tied Championship Series records for most consecutive games, one or more runs batted in, total Series (4); most hits, two consecutive games, one Series (6), October 4 and 5, 1978.

Tied National League Championship Series record for most three-base hits, total Series (2).

Year	Club	League	Pos.	G.	AB.	R.	H.	2B.	3B.	HR.	RBI.	B.A.	PO.	A.	E.	F.A.
1974—Los Angeles		Nat.	2B	4	15	4	4	0	1	0	3	.267	9	18	1	.964
1977—Los Angeles		Nat.	2B	4	17	2	4	0	0	0	3	.235	9	10	1	.950
1978—Los Angeles		Nat.	2B	4	18	3	7	1	1	2	5	.389	10	10	2	.909
1981—Los Angeles		Nat.	2B	5	18	0	5	0	0	0	0	.278	13	13	0	1.000
1984—Chicago		Nat.	OF-PH	2	1	0	0	0	0	0	0	.000	0	0	0	.000
Championship Series Totals—5 Years....				19	69	9	20	1	2	2	11	.290	41	51	4	.958

WORLD SERIES RECORD

Established World Series records for most stolen bases, six-game Series (4), 1981; most putouts by second baseman, six-game Series (26), 1981; most chances accepted by second baseman, six-game Series (40), 1981; most errors by second baseman, six-game Series (6), 1981.

Tied World Series records for most stolen bases, inning (2), October 15, 1974 (first inning); most putouts by second baseman, game (8), October 16, 1974; most chances accepted by second baseman, game (13), October 16, 1974; most putouts by second baseman, inning (3), October 16, 1974 (sixth inning) and October 21 1981 (fourth inning); most times home run as leadoff batter, start of game (1), October 17, 1978; most errors by second baseman, game (3), October 25, 1981; most errors by second baseman, inning (2), October 25, 1981 (fourth inning).

Year	Club	League	Pos.	G.	AB.	R.	H.	2B.	3B.	HR.	RBI.	B.A.	PO.	A.	E.	F.A.
1974—Los Angeles		Nat.	2B	5	18	2	2	0	0	0	0	.111	19	9	0	1.000
1977—Los Angeles		Nat.	2B	6	24	3	4	0	1	1	2	.167	12	22	0	1.000
1978—Los Angeles		Nat.	2B	6	26	7	8	0	0	3	7	.308	10	19	1	.967
1981—Los Angeles		Nat.	2B	6	22	6	5	1	0	0	2	.227	26	14	6	.870
World Series Totals—4 Years				23	90	18	19	1	1	4	11	.211	67	64	7	.949

ALL-STAR GAME RECORD

Year	League	Pos.	AB.	R.	H.	2B.	3B.	HR.	RBI.	B.A.	PO.	A.	E.	F.A.
1978—National		PH-2B	1	0	1	0	0	0	1	1.000	0	1	0	1.000
1979—National		2B	3	0	1	0	0	0	0	.333	4	1	0	1.000
1980—National		2B	1	0	0	0	0	0	0	.000	0	2	0	1.000
1981—National		2B	0	0	0	0	0	0	0	.000	1	0	0	.000
All-Star Game Totals—4 Years			5	0	2	0	0	0	1	.400	5	4	0	1.000

AURELIO ALEJANDRO LOPEZ (RIOS)

Born October 5, 1948, at Tecamachalco, Puebla, Mexico.
Height, 6.00. Weight, 225.
Throws and bats righthanded.

Pitched 1-0 no-hit victory against Carmen, May 24, 1969.
Major League saves: 1979 (21), 1980 (21), 1981 (3), 1982 (3), 1983 (18), 1984 (14), 1985 (5). Total—85.
Led Mexican League in wild pitches with 18 in 1975.
Led Mexican League in saves with 20 in 1974, 23 in 1975 and 16 in 1976.
Named Mexican League Most Valuable Player, 1977.

Year	Club	League	G.	IP.	W.	L.	Pct.	H.	R.	ER.	SO.	BB.	ERA.
1967—Las Choapas		Mex. SE.	27	96	5	3	.625	93	62	46	80	66	4.31
1968—Mexico City Reds		Mexican	31	162	10	10	.500	154	73	47	99	64	2.61
1969—Minatitlan		Mex. SE.	16	83	7	4	.636	56	29	18	64	40	1.95
1969—Mexico City Reds		Mexican	21	105	10	4	.714	131	53	45	76	49	3.86
1970—Mexico City Reds		Mexican	37	172	16	11	.593	153	64	57	127	100	2.98
1971—Mexico City Reds†		Mexican	21	83	4	7	.364	86	49	45	36	59	4.88
1972—Mexico City Reds		Mexican	46	121	5	7	.417	109	57	49	89	58	3.64
1973—Mexico City Reds		Mexican	53	127	12	10	.545	115	58	47	117	82	3.33
1974—Mexico City Reds‡		Mexican	*60	113	7	7	.500	94	50	32	134	70	2.55
1974—Kansas City§		American	8	16	0	0	.000	21	12	10	5	10	5.63
1975—Mexico City Reds		Mexican	*71	114	10	8	.556	97	46	36	114	68	2.84
1976—Mexico City Reds		Mexican	*59	98	4	11	.267	111	61	49	65	49	4.50
1977—Mexico City Reds x		Mexican	*73	157	19	8	.704	132	39	35	165	49	2.01
1978—Springfield		Am. Assoc.	34	76	6	6	.500	72	37	30	81	39	3.55
1978—St. Louis y		National	25	65	4	2	.667	52	35	31	46	32	4.29
1979—Detroit		American	61	127	10	5	.667	95	37	34	106	51	2.41
1980—Detroit		American	67	124	13	6	.684	125	56	52	97	45	3.77
1981—Detroit		American	29	82	5	2	.714	70	34	33	53	31	3.62
1982—Detroit z		American	19	41	3	1	.750	41	27	24	26	19	5.27
1982—Evansville		Am. Assoc.	12	30⅔	4	0	1.000	23	6	6	30	10	1.76
1983—Detroit		American	57	115⅓	9	8	.529	87	36	36	90	49	2.81
1984—Detroit		American	71	137⅔	10	1	.909	109	51	45	94	52	2.94
1985—Detroit a		American	51	86⅓	3	7	.300	82	50	46	53	41	4.80
American League Totals—8 Years			363	729⅓	53	30	.639	630	303	280	524	298	3.46
National League Totals—1 Year			25	65	4	2	.667	52	35	31	46	32	4.29
Major League Totals—9 Years			388	794⅓	57	32	.640	682	338	311	570	330	3.52

Signed as free agent by Las Choapas, March 28, 1967.

†On disabled list, April 30 to May 27 and June 28 to July 12, 1971.

‡Sold to Kansas City Royals, August 29, 1974.

§Sold to Mexico City Reds, March 27, 1975.

xSold to St. Louis Cardinals, October 26, 1977.

yTraded with Outfielder Jerry Morales to Detroit Tigers for Pitchers Bob Sykes and Jack Murphy, December 4, 1978.

zOn disabled list, March 23 to May 13, 1982; included rehabilitation disability assignment to Evansville, April 19 to May 11, 1982.

aGranted free agency, November 12, 1985.

CHAMPIONSHIP SERIES RECORD

Year Club	League	G.	IP.	W.	L.	Pct.	H.	R.	ER.	SO.	BB.	ERA.
1984—Detroit	American	1	3	1	0	1.000	4	0	0	2	1	0.00

WORLD SERIES RECORD

Year Club	League	G.	IP.	W.	L.	Pct.	H.	R.	ER.	SO.	BB.	ERA.
1984—Detroit	American	2	3	1	0	1.000	1	0	0	4	1	0.00

ALL-STAR GAME RECORD

Member of American League All-Star Team in 1983; did not play.

SCOTT GREGORY LOUCKS

Name pronounced Laucks.

Born November 11, 1956, at Anchorage, Alaska.
Height, 6.00. Weight, 178.
Throws and bats righthanded.
Attended Southeastern Oklahoma State University, Durant, Okla.

Major League stolen bases: 1981 (1), 1982 (4), 1983 (2). Total—7.
Led Pacific Coast League in stolen bases with 71 in 1983.
Led Florida State League in bases on balls received with 77 in 1979.

Year Club	League	Pos.	G.	AB.	R.	H.	2B.	3B.	HR.	RBI.	B.A.	PO.	A.	E.	F.A.
1977—Sara. Astros	Gulf C.	OF	46	142	41	38	2	7	1	20	.268	46	5	●4	.927
1978—Daytona Beach	Fla. St.	OF	43	128	21	26	3	2	0	9	.203	71	4	7	.915
1978—Columbus	South.	OF	76	232	38	45	4	4	3	17	.194	131	1	5	.964
1979—Daytona Beach	Fla. St.	OF	108	338	80	83	6	3	2	18	.246	164	13	3	.983
1979—Columbus	South.	OF	9	8	3	1	0	0	0	1	.125	6	0	1	.857
1980—Columbus	South.	OF	137	515	90	125	13	6	10	45	.243	264	12	6	.979
1980—Houston	Nat.	OF	8	3	4	1	0	0	0	0	.333	1	0	0	1.000
1981—Tucson†	P. C.	OF-3B	88	339	60	92	11	5	3	22	.271	158	7	5	.971
1981—Houston	Nat.	OF	10	7	2	4	0	0	0	0	.571	5	0	0	1.000
1982—Tucson	P. C.	OF	74	310	48	82	12	5	1	21	.265	173	6	6	.968
1982—Houston	Nat.	OF	44	49	6	11	2	0	0	3	.224	41	3	1	.978
1983—Tucson	P. C.	OF	138	541	107	155	33	●13	8	58	.287	338	12	9	.975
1983—Houston	Nat.	OF	7	14	2	3	0	0	0	0	.214	12	1	0	1.000
1984—Tucson‡§	P. C.	OF	28	109	17	27	1	2	0	3	.248	62	6	2	.971
1984—Indianapolis x	A. A.	OF	54	138	19	28	5	2	2	20	.203	83	3	1	.989
1985—Hawaii y	P. C.	OF	91	330	61	93	21	2	5	27	.282	127	3	2	.985
1985—Pittsburgh	Nat.	OF	4	7	1	2	2	0	0	1	.286	2	0	0	1.000
Major League Totals—5 Years			73	80	15	21	4	0	0	4	.263	61	4	1	.985

Selected by Houston Astros' organization in 5th round of free-agent draft, June 7, 1977.

†On disabled list, April 24 to May 20, 1981.

‡On Houston disabled list, April 1 to June 22, 1984; included rehabilitation disability assignment to Tucson, June 2 to June 21, 1984.

§Traded to Indianapolis (Montreal Expos' organization) for Third Baseman Brad Mills, July 6, 1984.

xGranted free agency, October 15, 1984; signed by Hawaii (Pittsburgh Pirates' organization), March 1, 1985.

yOn disabled list, June 20 to July 18, 1985.

JOHN LEE LOWENSTEIN

Name pronounced LOW-in-stine.

Born January 27, 1947, at Wolf Point, Mont.
Height, 6.01. Weight, 180.
Throws right and bats lefthanded.
Received bachelor of arts degree in anthropology from
University of California, Riverside, Calif.

Major League stolen bases: 1970 (1), 1971 (1), 1972 (2), 1973 (5), 1974 (36), 1975 (15), 1976 (11), 1977 (1), 1978 (16), 1979 (16) 1980 (7), 1981 (7), 1982 (7), 1983 (2), 1984 (1). Total—128.

Year Club	League	Pos.	G.	AB.	R.	H.	2B.	3B.	HR.	RBI.	B.A.	PO.	A.	E.	F.A.
1968—Waterbury	East.	PH	3	2	0	0	0	0	0	0	.000	0	0	0	.000
1968—Reno	Calif.	2B-3B	48	164	22	53	8	2	7	38	.323	71	106	8	.957
1969—Reno†	Calif.	1B-OF	26	67	7	19	4	2	1	11	.284	93	5	2	.980
1970—Wichita	A. A.	3-S-O-2	108	369	69	109	15	6	18	52	.295	130	218	13	.964
1970—Cleveland	Amer.	2-3-O-S	17	43	5	11	3	1	1	6	.256	15	37	2	.963
1971—Wichita	A. A.	OF-3B	37	125	27	40	8	0	8	24	.320	55	4	2	.967
1971—Cleveland	Amer.	2B-OF-SS	58	140	15	26	5	0	4	9	.186	103	66	4	.977
1972—Cleveland	Amer.	OF-1B	68	151	16	32	8	1	6	21	.212	82	7	0	1.000
1973—Cleveland	Amer.	O-2-3-1	98	305	42	89	16	1	6	40	.292	124	85	7	.968

Year Club	League	Pos.	G.	AB.	R.	H.	2B.	3B.	HR.	RBI.	B.A.	PO.	A.	E.	F.A.
1974—Cleveland..............	Amer.	O-3-1-2	140	508	65	123	14	2	8	48	.242	314	84	6	.985
1975—Cleveland..............	Amer.	OF-3B-2B	91	265	37	64	5	1	12	33	.242	61	16	2	.975
1976—Cleveland‡§.........	Amer.	OF-1B	93	229	33	47	8	2	2	14	.205	178	10	7	.964
1977—Cleveland x..........	Amer.	OF-1B	81	149	24	36	6	1	4	12	.242	63	1	0	1.000
1978—Texas y..................	Amer.	3B-OF	77	176	28	39	8	3	5	21	.222	34	42	6	.927
1979—Baltimore z..........	Amer.	OF-1B-3B	97	197	33	50	8	2	11	34	.254	124	7	1	.992
1980—Baltimore a..........	Amer.	OF	104	196	38	61	8	0	4	27	.311	128	3	1	.992
1981—Baltimore	Amer.	OF	83	189	19	47	7	0	6	20	.249	100	3	1	.990
1982—Baltimore b..........	Amer.	OF	122	322	69	103	15	2	24	66	.320	202	2	0	●1.000
1983—Baltimore	Amer.	OF-2B	122	310	52	87	13	2	15	60	.281	155	8	3	.982
1984—Baltimore c..........	Amer.	OF-1B	105	270	34	64	13	0	8	28	.237	113	5	3	.975
1985—Baltimore d..........	Amer.	OF	12	26	0	2	0	0	0	2	.077	7	0	0	1.000
Major League Totals—16 Years..............			1368	3476	510	881	137	18	116	441	.253	1803	376	43	.981

Selected by Cleveland Indians' organization in 18th round of free-agent draft, June 7, 1968.
†On military list, January 31 to August 2, 1969.
‡Traded with Catcher Rick Cerone to Toronto Blue Jays for Outfielder Rico Carty, December 6, 1976.
§Traded to Cleveland Indians for Infielder Hector Torres, March 29, 1977.
xTraded with Pitcher Tom Buskey to Texas Rangers for Outfielder-Designated Hitter Willie Horton and Pitcher David Clyde, February 28, 1978.
ySold on waivers to Baltimore Orioles, November 27, 1978.
zOn disabled list, August 9 to August 24, 1979.
aOn disabled list, May 19 to June 11, 1980.
bGranted free agency, November 10, 1982; re-signed by Orioles, February 24, 1983.
cOn disabled list, August 2 to August 20, 1984.
dReleased, May 21, 1985.

CHAMPIONSHIP SERIES RECORD

Tied Championship Series records for hitting home run in first Series at-bat, October 3, 1979; most home runs by pinch-hitter, game (1), October 3, 1979.

Year Club	League	Pos.	G.	AB.	R.	H.	2B.	3B.	HR.	RBI.	B.A.	PO.	A.	E.	F.A.
1979—Baltimore	Amer.	PH-OF	4	6	2	1	0	0	1	3	.167	6	0	0	1.000
1983—Baltimore	Amer.	OF-PH	3	6	0	1	1	0	0	2	.167	4	0	0	1.000
Championship Series Totals—2 Years.....			7	12	2	2	1	0	1	5	.167	10	0	0	1.000

WORLD SERIES RECORD

Year Club	League	Pos.	G.	AB.	R.	H.	2B.	3B.	HR.	RBI.	B.A.	PO.	A.	E.	F.A.
1979—Baltimore	Amer.	OF-PH	6	13	2	3	1	0	0	3	.231	6	0	1	.857
1983—Baltimore	Amer.	OF	4	13	2	5	1	0	1	1	.385	4	0	1	.800
World Series Totals—2 Years..................			10	26	4	8	2	0	1	4	.308	10	0	2	.833

GARY PAUL LUCAS

Born November 8, 1954, at Riverside, Calif.
Height, 6.05. Weight, 200.
Throws and bats lefthanded.
Attended Chapman College, Orange, Calif.

Major League saves: 1980 (3), 1981 (13), 1982 (16), 1983 (17), 1984 (8), 1985 (1). Total—58.
Tied for National League lead in intentional bases on balls issued with 15 in 1981.

Year Club	League	G.	IP.	W.	L.	Pct.	H.	R.	ER.	SO.	BB.	ERA.
1976—Walla Walla	Northwest	14	93	7	3	.700	91	40	32	49	30	3.10
1977—Reno	California	28	176	13	7	.650	205	114	90	98	48	4.60
1978—Amarillo..........................	Texas	25	159	8	17	.320	182	104	86	115	26	4.87
1979—Hawaii†	P. Coast	24	178	10	7	.588	151	64	55	98	58	2.78
1980—San Diego	National	46	150	5	8	.385	138	59	54	85	43	3.24
1981—San Diego	National	★57	90	7	7	.500	78	26	20	53	36	2.00
1982—San Diego	National	65	97⅓	1	10	.091	89	42	35	64	29	3.24
1983—San Diego‡	National	62	91	5	8	.385	85	38	29	60	34	2.87
1984—Montreal	National	55	53	0	3	.000	54	20	16	42	20	2.72
1985—West Palm Beach§	Florida St.	3	5	0	0	.000	4	5	4	3	1	7.20
1985—Indianapolis	Am. Assoc.	1	2	0	0	.000	1	0	0	2	2	0.00
1985—Montreal x..................................	National	49	67⅔	6	2	.750	63	29	24	31	24	3.19
Major League Totals—6 Years..........................		334	549	24	38	.387	507	214	178	335	186	2.92

Selected by Cincinnati Reds' organization in 1st round (21st player selected) of free-agent draft, January 10, 1973.
Selected by Cincinnati Reds' organization in secondary phase of free-agent draft, June 5, 1973.
Selected by San Diego Padres' organization in 19th round of free-agent draft, June 8, 1976.
†On disabled list, August 5 to August 30, 1979.
‡Traded to Montreal Expos for Pitcher Scott Sanderson and Infielder Al Newman, December 7, 1983.
§On Montreal disabled list, March 27 to May 19, 1985; included rehabilitation disability assignment to West Palm Beach, May 1 to May 14, and Indianapolis, May 15 to May 19, 1985.
xTraded to California Angels for Pitcher Luis Sanchez and Catcher Tim Arnold, December 27, 1985.

URBANO RAFAEL LUGO

Born August 12, 1962, at Caracas, Venezuela.
Height, 6.00. Weight, 185.
Throws and bats righthanded.
Son of Urbano Lugo, pitcher in Mexican League, 1967 through 1970 and 1973.

Year Club	League	G.	IP.	W.	L.	Pct.	H.	R.	ER.	SO.	BB.	ERA.
1982—Danville	Midwest	10	24	0	2	.000	35	30	27	13	16	10.13
1982—Salem	Northwest	14	90⅔	7	3	.700	74	45	29	62	61	2.88
1983—Peoria	Midwest	15	107	8	5	.615	82	39	30	96	28	2.52
1983—Redwood	California	11	64⅔	5	5	.500	59	36	28	58	31	3.90
1984—Waterbury	Eastern	24	164⅓	13	8	.619	135	63	51	117	68	2.79
1985—Edmonton	P. Coast	4	25⅔	2	0	1.000	20	14	13	19	14	4.56
1985—California†	American	20	83	3	4	.429	86	36	34	42	29	3.69
Major League Totals—1 Year		20	83	3	4	.429	86	36	34	42	29	3.69

Signed as free agent by California Angels' organization, January 31, 1982.
†On disabled list, August 22 to September 6, 1985.

EDWARD FRANCIS LYNCH
(Ed)

Born February 25, 1956, at Brooklyn, N.Y.
Height, 6.05. Weight, 210.
Throws and bats righthanded.
Received bachelor of science degree in finance from University of South Carolina, Columbia, S.C.,
and master's degree in business administration from University of Miami, Coral Gables, Fla.
Major League saves: 1982 (2), 1984 (2). Total—4.

Year Club	League	G.	IP.	W.	L.	Pct	H.	R.	ER.	SO.	BB.	ERA.
1977—Sarasota Rangers	Gulf Coast	13	56	1	4	.200	61	31	23	36	15	3.70
1978—Asheville	W. Carol.	18	123	7	9	.438	122	55	45	79	33	3.29
1978—Tulsa	Texas	7	54	4	3	.571	64	25	16	44	14	2.67
1979—Tucson†	P. Coast	27	156	10	11	.476	184	96	84	65	37	4.85
1980—Tidewater	Int'national	24	163	13	6	.684	151	69	57	91	42	3.15
1980—New York	National	5	19	1	1	.500	24	12	11	9	5	5.21
1981—Tidewater	Int'national	15	99	7	6	.538	93	46	43	54	29	3.91
1981—New York	National	17	80	4	5	.444	79	32	26	27	21	2.93
1982—New York	National	43	139⅓	4	8	.333	145	57	55	51	40	3.55
1983—New York	National	30	174⅔	10	10	.500	208	94	83	44	41	4.28
1984—New York	National	40	124	9	8	.529	169	77	62	62	24	4.50
1985—New York	National	31	191	10	8	.556	188	76	73	65	27	3.44
Major League Totals—6 Years		166	728	38	40	.487	813	348	310	258	158	3.83

Selected by Texas Rangers' organization in 22nd round of free-agent draft, June 7, 1977.
†Traded to New York Mets' organization, September 18, 1979, as partial completion of deal in which Texas Rangers acquired First Baseman Willie Montanez for two players to be named later, August 12, 1979; New York acquired First Baseman Mike Jorgensen to complete deal, October 23, 1979.

FREDRIC MICHAEL LYNN
(Fred)

Born February 3, 1952, at Chicago, Ill.
Height, 6.01. Weight, 190.
Throws and bats lefthanded.
Attended University of Southern California, Los Angeles, Calif.
Established American League record for most doubles, rookie season (47), 1975.
Tied American League record for most total bases, game (16), June 18, 1975.
Major League stolen bases: 1975 (10), 1976 (14), 1977 (2), 1978 (3), 1979 (2), 1980 (12), 1981 (1), 1982 (7), 1983 (2), 1984 (2), 1985 (7). Total—62.
Hit three home runs in a game, June 18, 1975.
Hit for the cycle, May 13, 1980.
Led American League in slugging percentage with .566 in 1975 and .637 in 1979.
Named American League Player of the Year by THE SPORTING NEWS, 1975.
Named American League Most Valuable Player by Baseball Writers' Association of America, 1975.
Named American League Rookie of the Year by Baseball Writers' Association of America, 1975.
Named American League Rookie Player of the Year by THE SPORTING NEWS, 1975.
Named outfielder on THE SPORTING NEWS American League All-Star Team, 1975, 1978 and 1979.
Named outfielder on THE SPORTING NEWS American League All-Star fielding team, 1975 and 1978 through 1980.
Received reported $40,000 bonus to sign with Boston Red Sox, 1973.
Named outfielder on THE SPORTING NEWS College Baseball All-America Team, 1972 and 1973.

Year Club	League	Pos.	G.	AB.	R.	H.	2B.	3B.	HR.	RBI.	B.A.	PO.	A.	E.	F.A.
1973—Bristol	East.	OF	53	162	26	42	9	4	6	36	.259	79	3	5	.943
1974—Pawtucket	Int.	OF	124	415	65	117	19	2	21	68	.282	247	12	7	.974
1974—Boston	Amer.	OF	15	43	5	18	2	2	2	10	.419	18	2	0	1.000
1975—Boston	Amer.	OF	145	528	*103	175	*47	7	21	105	.331	404	11	7	.983
1976—Boston	Amer.	OF	132	507	76	159	32	8	10	65	.314	367	13	6	.984
1977—Boston†	Amer.	OF	129	497	81	129	29	5	18	76	.260	333	7	2	.994
1978—Boston	Amer.	OF	150	541	75	161	33	3	22	82	.298	408	11	7	.984
1979—Boston	Amer.	OF	147	531	116	177	42	1	39	122	*.333	381	10	5	.987
1980—Boston‡	Amer.	OF	110	415	67	125	32	3	12	61	.301	302	11	2	.994
1981—California	Amer.	OF	76	256	28	56	8	1	5	31	.219	176	4	4	.978
1982—California	Amer.	OF	138	472	89	141	38	1	21	86	.299	317	6	3	.991
1983—California	Amer.	OF	117	437	56	119	20	3	22	74	.272	274	8	2	.993
1984—California§	Amer.	OF	142	517	84	140	28	3	23	79	.271	321	12	6	.982
1985—Baltimore	Amer.	OF	124	448	59	118	12	1	23	68	.263	314	6	2	.994
Major League Totals—12 Years			1425	5192	839	1518	323	39	218	859	.292	3615	101	46	.988

Selected by New York Yankees' organization in 3rd round of free-agent draft, June 4, 1970.

Selected by Boston Red Sox' organization in 2nd round of free-agent draft, June 5, 1973.
†On disabled list, March 24 to May 6, 1977.
‡Traded with Pitcher Steve Renko to California Angels for Pitchers Frank Tanana and Jim Dorsey and Outfielder Joe Rudi, January 23, 1981.
§Granted free agency, November 8, 1984; signed by Baltimore Orioles, December 11, 1984. (Pitcher Donnie Moore selected from player compensation pool by California Angels, January 24, 1985.)

CHAMPIONSHIP SERIES RECORD

Established Championship Series record for highest batting average, five-game Series (.611), 1982.
Tied Championship Series records for most hits, five-game Series (11), 1982; most one-base hits, five-game Series (8), 1982.
Established American League Championship Series record for most hits, two consecutive Series (15), 1975 and 1982.

Year Club	League	Pos.	G.	AB.	R.	H.	2B.	3B.	HR.	RBI.	B.A.	PO.	A.	E.	F.A.
1975—Boston	Amer.	OF	3	11	1	4	1	0	0	3	.364	12	1	1	.929
1982—California	Amer.	OF	5	18	5	11	2	0	1	5	.611	16	0	1	.941
Championship Series Totals—2 Years			8	29	6	15	3	0	1	8	.517	28	1	2	.935

WORLD SERIES RECORD

Tied World Series record for highest fielding average by outfielder, seven-game Series (1.000 with 24 chances), 1975.

Year Club	League	Pos.	G.	AB.	R.	H.	2B.	3B.	HR.	RBI.	B.A.	PO.	A.	E.	F.A.
1975—Boston	Amer.	OF	7	25	3	7	1	0	1	5	.280	23	1	0	1.000

ALL-STAR GAME RECORD

Hit only All-Star Game home run with bases loaded, July 6, 1983.
Established All-Star Game record for most runs batted in, inning (4), July 6, 1983.

Year League	Pos.	AB.	R.	H.	2B.	3B.	HR.	RBI.	B.A.	PO.	A.	E.	F.A.
1975—American	PH-OF	2	0	0	0	0	0	0	.000	1	0	0	1.000
1976—American	OF	3	1	1	0	0	1	1	.333	0	0	0	1.000
1977—American	OF	1	1	0	0	0	0	0	.000	2	0	0	1.000
1978—American	OF	4	0	1	0	0	0	0	.250	3	0	0	1.000
1979—American	OF	1	1	1	0	0	1	2	1.000	0	0	0	.000
1980—American	OF	3	1	1	0	0	1	2	.333	2	0	0	1.000
1981—American	PH	1	0	1	0	0	0	1	1.000	0	0	0	.000
1982—American	OF	2	0	0	0	0	0	0	.000	0	0	0	.000
1983—American	OF	3	1	1	0	0	1	4	.333	1	0	0	1.000
All-Star Game Totals—9 Years		20	5	6	0	0	4	10	.300	9	0	0	1.000

BARRY STEPHEN LYONS

Born June 3, 1960, at Biloxi, Miss.
Height, 6.01. Weight, 205.
Throws and bats righthanded.
Attended Delta State University, Cleveland, Miss.

Led Texas League in grounding into double plays with 19 and tied for lead in game-winning RBIs with 16 in 1985.
Led Texas League catchers in errors with 19 in 1985.
Led Carolina League catchers in assists with 72 and fielding percentage with .989 in 1984.
Named Carolina League Player of the Year, 1984.

Year Club	League	Pos.	G.	AB.	R.	H.	2B.	3B.	HR.	RBI.	B.A.	PO.	A.	E.	F.A.
1982—Shelby	S. Atl.	C-1B	45	164	23	46	12	0	4	46	.280	226	21	8	.969
1983—Lynchburg	Carol.	C	2	7	0	1	0	0	0	2	.143	21	4	0	1.000
1983—Columbia	S. Atl.	C-1B-OF	92	316	55	94	9	2	5	45	.297	387	33	17	.961
1984—Lynchburg	Carol.	C-1B-OF	115	412	59	130	17	3	12	87	.316	894	86	13	.987
1985—Jackson	Texas	C-1B	126	486	69	149	34	6	11	108	.307	834	65	23	.975

Selected by Detroit Tigers' organization in 25th round of free-agent draft, June 8, 1981.
Selected by New York Mets' organization in 15th round of free-agent draft, June 7, 1982.

STEPHEN JOHN LYONS
(Steve)

Born June 3, 1960, at Tacoma, Wash.
Height, 6.03. Weight, 190.
Throws right and bats lefthanded.
Attended Oregon State University, Corvallis, Ore.

Major League stolen bases: 1985 (12).
Led International League third basemen in putouts with 98, errors with 25 and total chances with 332 in 1984.

Year Club	League	Pos.	G.	AB.	R.	H.	2B.	3B.	HR.	RBI.	B.A.	PO.	A.	E.	F.A.
1981—Winston-Salem	Carol.	OF-SS	64	252	43	61	9	3	6	40	.242	137	23	8	.952
1982—Bristol	East.	OF-SS	135	460	86	112	23	3	13	58	.243	275	11	9	.969
1983—New Britain	East.	3-O-S-P	132	456	83	112	24	7	7	62	.246	145	207	17	.954
1984—Pawtucket	Int.	3B-OF-SS	131	444	80	119	21	2	17	62	.268	141	211	26	.931
1985—Boston	Amer.	OF-3B-SS	133	371	52	98	14	3	5	30	.264	253	6	7	.974
Major League Totals—1 Year			133	371	52	98	14	3	5	30	.264	253	6	7	.974

Selected by Boston Red Sox' organization in 1st round (19th player selected) of free-agent draft, June 8, 1981.

PITCHING RECORD

Year Club	League	G.	IP.	W.	L.	Pct.	H.	R.	ER.	SO.	BB.	ERA.
1983—New Britain	Eastern	3	3⅔	1	0	1.000	3	1	1	2	1	2.45

RICHARD EUGENE LYSANDER
(Rick)

Born February 21, 1953, at Huntington Park, Calif.
Height, 6.02. Weight, 190.
Throws and bats righthanded.
Attended Citrus Junior College, Azusa, Calif., San Jose State University, San Jose, Calif.,
and attending California State University, Los Angeles, Calif.

Major League saves: 1983 (3), 1984 (5), 1985 (3). Total—11.
Led Pacific Coast League in intentional bases on balls issued with 13 in 1980.

Year Club	League	G.	IP.	W.	L.	Pct.	H.	R.	ER.	SO.	BB.	ERA.
1974—Lewiston	Northwest	11	58	5	3	.625	54	28	17	25	18	2.64
1975—Modesto	California	21	131	8	8	.500	152	92	70	82	38	4.81
1975—Birmingham	Southern	8	57	5	2	.714	58	24	21	25	20	3.32
1976—Tucson	P. Coast	17	28	2	2	.500	41	21	20	21	15	6.43
1976—Chattanooga	Southern	18	118	7	6	.538	108	47	46	31	34	3.20
1977—Chattanooga	Southern	14	84	4	5	.444	104	55	46	41	31	4.93
1977—San Jose	P. Coast	29	61	3	3	.500	68	38	29	38	26	4.28
1978—Vancouver	P. Coast	14	29	0	0	.000	42	26	26	12	12	8.07
1978—Jersey City	Eastern	17	127	9	6	.600	128	58	36	58	40	2.55
1979—Ogden	P. Coast	50	84	10	3	.769	94	54	41	60	46	4.39
1980—Ogden	P. Coast	35	81	4	5	.444	103	55	46	46	43	5.11
1980—Oakland	American	5	14	0	0	.000	24	12	12	6	4	7.71
1981—Tacoma†	P. Coast	25	161	9	3	.750	159	80	71	91	53	3.97
1982—Tucson‡	P. Coast	42	162⅓	10	7	.588	203	95	73	99	49	4.05
1983—Minnesota	American	61	125	5	12	.294	132	63	47	58	43	3.38
1984—Toledo	Int'national	28	37	3	2	.600	22	14	14	23	11	3.41
1984—Minnesota	American	36	56⅔	4	3	.571	62	23	22	22	27	3.49
1985—Minnesota	American	35	61	0	2	.000	72	43	41	26	22	6.05
1985—Toledo§	Int'national	7	10⅓	1	0	1.000	7	1	1	8	5	0.87
Major League Totals—4 Years		137	256⅔	9	17	.346	290	142	122	111	96	4.28

Selected by Oakland A's organization in 19th round of free-agent draft, June 5, 1974.
†Traded to Houston Astros, September 17, 1981, completing deal in which Houston traded Infielder Jimmy Sexton to Oakland A's for a player to be named later, February 12, 1981.
‡Traded to Minnesota Twins' organization for Pitcher Bob Veselic, January 12, 1983.
§Released, December 20, 1985.

SHANE LEE MACK

Born December 7, 1963, at Los Angeles, Calif.
Height, 6.00. Weight, 185.
Throws and bats righthanded.
Attended University of California, Los Angeles, Calif.

Member of 1984 U.S. Olympic baseball team.
Named outfielder on THE SPORTING NEWS College Baseball All-America Team, 1984.

Year Club	League	Pos.	G.	AB.	R.	H.	2B.	3B.	HR.	RBI.	B.A.	PO.	A.	E.	F.A.
1985—Beaumont	Texas	OF-3B	125	430	59	112	23	3	6	55	.260	252	12	7	.974

Selected by Kansas City Royals' organization in 4th round of free-agent draft, June 8, 1981.
Selected by San Diego Padres' organization in 1st round (11th player selected) of free-agent draft, June 4, 1984.

TONY LYNN MACK

Born April 30, 1961, at Lexington, Ky.
Height, 5.10. Weight, 175.
Throws and bats righthanded.
Attended Lamar University, Beaumont, Tex.

Tied for Pacific Coast League lead in shutouts with 3 in 1985.
Tied for California League lead in complete games with 15 in 1983.

Year Club	League	G.	IP.	W.	L.	Pct.	H.	R.	ER.	SO.	BB.	ERA.
1982—Salem	Northwest	13	92	3	*8	.273	92	56	41	70	50	4.23
1983—Redwood	California	27	*196⅓	13	9	.591	191	92	76	133	77	3.48
1984—Waterbury	Eastern	25	171⅓	11	8	.579	155	67	62	83	74	3.26
1985—Edmonton	P. Coast	25	153⅔	8	14	.364	179	103	81	100	81	4.74
1985—California	American	1	2⅓	0	1	.000	8	4	4	0	0	15.43
Major League Totals—1 Year		1	2⅓	0	1	.000	8	4	4	0	0	15.43

Selected by California Angels' organization in 3rd round of free-agent draft, June 7, 1982.

MICHAEL ANTHONY MADDEN
(Mike)

Born January 13, 1958, at Denver, Colo.
Height, 6.01. Weight, 190.
Throws and bats lefthanded.
Attended University of Northern Colorado, Greeley, Colo.

Year Club	League	G.	IP.	W.	L.	Pct.	H.	R.	ER.	SO.	BB.	ERA.
1979—Burlington	Midwest	5	32	2	1	.667	21	11	7	23	15	1.97
1980—Stockton	California	29	134	12	4	.750	88	46	29	92	63	*1.95
1981—El Paso†	Texas	22	125	6	8	.429	154	94	79	140	40	5.69
1982—Vancouver‡	P. Coast	18	80⅔	3	8	.273	92	69	63	41	60	7.03

Year	Club	League	G.	IP.	W.	L.	Pct.	H.	R.	ER.	SO.	BB.	ERA.
1983—Houston§	National	28	94⅔	9	5	.643	76	37	33	44	45	3.14
1983—Tucson	P. Coast	4	22	1	1	.500	25	9	9	15	8	3.68
1984—Houston	National	17	40⅔	2	3	.400	46	27	25	29	35	5.53
1984—Tucson	P. Coast	11	60⅔	4	3	.571	60	29	29	38	30	4.30
1985—Tucson x	P. Coast	6	23	2	0	1.000	24	11	9	14	11	3.52
1985—Houston	National	13	19	0	0	.000	29	15	9	16	11	4.26
Major League Totals—3 Years			58	154⅓	11	8	.579	151	79	67	89	91	3.91

Selected by Pittsburgh Pirates' organization in 3rd round of free-agent draft, June 8, 1976.
Signed as free agent by Milwaukee Brewers' organization, July 18, 1979.
†On disabled list, July 9 to August 5, 1981.
‡Traded with Outfielder Kevin Bass and Pitcher Frank DiPino to Houston Astros, September 3, 1982, completing deal in which Houston traded Pitcher Don Sutton to Milwaukee Brewers for three players to be named later, August 30, 1982.
§On disabled list, June 1 to June 22, 1983.
xOn Houston disabled list, April 4 to June 28, 1985; included rehabilitation disability assignment to Tucson, June 9 to June 28, 1985.

GARRY LEE MADDOX

Born September 1, 1949, at Cincinnati, O.
Height, 6.03. Weight, 190.
Throws and bats righthanded.
Attended Harbor College, Wilmington, Calif.

Tied major league record for most putouts by outfielder, game (12), (12 innings), June 10, 1984.
Major League stolen bases: 1972 (13), 1973 (24), 1974 (21), 1975 (25), 1976 (29), 1977 (22), 1978 (33), 1979 (26), 1980 (25), 1981 (9), 1982 (7), 1983 (7), 1984 (3), 1985 (4). Total—248.
Led National League in sacrifice flies with 8 in 1981.
Led National League outfielders in total chances with 456 in 1976 and 459 in 1978.
Tied for National League lead in double plays by outfielders with 4 in 1981.
Led Pioneer League batters in strikeouts with 68 in 1968.
Led Pioneer League outfielders in double plays with 2 in 1968.
Named outfielder on THE SPORTING NEWS National League All-Star fielding team, 1975 through 1982.

Year	Club	League	Pos.	G.	AB.	R.	H.	2B.	3B.	HR.	RBI.	B.A.	PO.	A.	E.	F.A.
1968—Salt Lake City	Pion.	OF	58	206	34	52	11	2	5	29	.252	98	6	★10	.912
1968—Fresno†	Calif.	OF	5	19	2	6	0	0	0	5	.316	7	0	0	1.000
1969-70—						(In Military Service)									
1971—Fresno	Calif.	OF	120	475	105	142	25	5	30	106	.299	215	13	0	.962
1972—Phoenix	P. C.	OF	11	48	16	21	3	2	9	22	.438	22	1	2	.920
1972—San Francisco	Nat.	OF	125	458	62	122	26	7	12	58	.266	279	7	6	.979
1973—San Francisco	Nat.	OF	144	587	81	187	30	10	11	76	.319	370	4	●12	.969
1974—San Francisco	Nat.	OF	135	538	74	153	31	3	8	50	.284	345	3	5	.986
1975—S.F.‡-Phil.§	Nat.	OF	116	426	54	116	26	8	5	50	.272	325	13	5	.985
1976—Philadelphia	Nat.	OF	146	531	75	175	37	6	6	68	.330	★441	10	5	.989
1977—Philadelphia x	Nat.	OF	139	571	85	167	27	10	14	74	.292	383	7	9	.977
1978—Philadelphia	Nat.	OF	155	598	62	172	34	3	11	68	.288	★444	7	8	.983
1979—Philadelphia	Nat.	OF	148	548	70	154	28	6	13	61	.281	433	13	2	.996
1980—Philadelphia	Nat.	OF	143	549	59	142	31	3	11	73	.259	405	7	10	.976
1981—Philadelphia	Nat.	OF	94	323	37	85	7	1	5	40	.263	249	8	6	.977
1982—Philadelphia y	Nat.	OF	119	412	39	117	27	2	8	61	.284	253	8	2	★.992
1983—Philadelphia z	Nat.	OF	97	324	27	89	14	2	4	32	.275	216	1	5	.977
1984—Philadelphia a	Nat.	OF	77	241	29	68	11	0	5	19	.282	160	3	0	1.000
1985—Philadelphia b	Nat.	OF	105	218	22	52	8	1	4	23	.239	143	3	3	.980
Major League Totals—14 Years			1743	6324	776	1799	337	62	117	753	.284	4446	94	78	.983

Selected by San Francisco Giants' organization in 2nd round of free-agent draft, January 27, 1968.
†On military list, October 31, 1968 through February 21, 1971.
‡Traded to Philadelphia Phillies for First Baseman Willie Montanez, May 4, 1975.
§On disabled list, May 25 to June 30, 1975.
xOn disabled list, August 13 to August 28, 1977.
yOn disabled list, June 20 to July 5 and July 18 to August 5, 1982.
zOn disabled list, June 23 to July 8, 1983.
aOn disabled list, August 3 to August 18 and August 20, 1984 through remainder of season.
bGranted free agency, November 12, 1985; re-signed by Phillies, December 6, 1985.

DIVISION SERIES RECORD

Year	Club	League	Pos.	G.	AB.	R.	H.	2B.	3B.	HR.	RBI.	B.A.	PO.	A.	E.	F.A.
1981—Philadelphia	Nat.	OF	2	3	0	1	1	0	0	0	.333	3	0	0	1.000

CHAMPIONSHIP SERIES RECORD

Tied Championship Series records for most consecutive games, one or more runs batted in, total Series (4); most at bats, four-game Series (19), 1978.

Year	Club	League	Pos.	G.	AB.	R.	H.	2B.	3B.	HR.	RBI.	B.A.	PO.	A.	E.	F.A.
1976—Philadelphia	Nat.	OF	3	13	2	3	1	0	0	1	.231	9	0	0	1.000
1977—Philadelphia	Nat.	OF	2	7	1	3	0	0	0	2	.429	6	0	0	1.000
1978—Philadelphia	Nat.	OF	4	19	1	5	0	0	0	2	.263	16	0	1	.941
1980—Philadelphia	Nat.	OF	5	20	2	6	2	0	0	3	.300	23	0	0	1.000
1983—Philadelphia	Nat.	OF	3	11	0	3	1	0	0	1	.273	8	0	1	.889
Championship Series Totals—5 Years			17	70	6	20	4	0	0	9	.286	62	0	2	.969

Year	Club	League	Pos.	G.	AB.	R.	H.	2B.	3B.	HR.	RBI.	B.A.	PO.	A.	E.	F.A.
1980—Philadelphia	....	Nat.	OF	6	22	1	5	2	0	0	1	.227	11	1	0	1.000
1983—Philadelphia	....	Nat.	PH-OF	4	12	1	3	1	0	1	1	.250	7	0	0	1.000
World Series Totals—2 Years	....			10	34	2	8	3	0	1	2	.235	18	1	0	1.000

CHARLES SCOTT MADISON
(Scotti)

Born September 12, 1958, at Pensacola, Fla.
Height, 5.11. Weight, 185.
Throws right and bats left and righthanded.
Attended Vanderbilt University, Nashville, Tenn.

Led American Association in slugging percentage with .590 in 1985.
Named catcher on THE SPORTING NEWS College Baseball All-America Team, 1980.

Year	Club	League	Pos.	G.	AB.	R.	H.	2B.	3B.	HR.	RBI.	B.A.	PO.	A.	E.	F.A.
1980—Orlando	....	South.	C-1B-OF	81	282	31	65	9	4	6	32	.230	185	24	4	.981
1981—Visalia†	....	Calif.	*C-1B	133	459	109	157	*32	3	26	110	.342	542	66	11	*.982
1982—San Antonio‡	....	Texas	3-C-2-O	88	294	39	69	11	2	7	35	.235	167	75	16	.938
1982—Albuquerque	....	P. C.	C	11	36	5	8	1	0	0	2	.222	6	0	0	1.000
1983—San Antonio	....	Texas	C-3B	80	259	54	79	11	4	11	57	.305	423	55	11	.078
1983—Albuquerque§	P C		C 3D	20	03	10	19	2	0	2	12	.292	103	18	7	.945
1984—Birmingham	....	South.	C-1-3-2	133	473	82	129	23	4	15	83	.273	773	109	18	.980
1985—Birmingham	....	South	C-1B-3B	37	121	28	39	8	1	5	25	.322	205	27	2	.991
1985—Nashville	....	A. A.	C-3-1-O	86	317	59	108	23	4	16	54	*.341	352	74	11	.975
1985—Detroit	....	Amer.	C	6	11	0	0	0	0	0	1	.000	1	0	0	1.000
Major League Totals—1 Year	....			6	11	0	0	0	0	0	1	.000	1	0	0	1.000

Selected by Cincinnati Reds' organization in 35th round of free-agent draft, June 8, 1976.
Selected by San Francisco Giants' organization in 10th round of free-agent draft, June 5, 1979.
Selected by Minnesota Twins' organization in 3rd round of free-agent draft, June 3, 1980.
†Traded with Pitcher Paul Voigt to Los Angeles Dodgers' organization for Pitcher Bobby Castillo and Outfielder Bobby Mitchell, January 7, 1982.
‡On disabled list, June 25 to July 16, 1982.
§Sold to Birmingham (Detroit Tigers' organization), March 19, 1984.

BILL MADLOCK JR.

Born January 12, 1951, at Memphis, Tenn.
Height, 5.11. Weight, 206.
Throws and bats righthanded.
Attended Southeastern Community College, Keokuk, Ia.

Collected six hits in one game, July 26, 1975 (10 innings).
Major League stolen bases: 1973 (3), 1974 (11), 1975 (9), 1976 (15), 1977 (13), 1978 (16), 1979 (32), 1980 (16), 1981 (18), 1982 (18), 1983 (3), 1984 (3), 1985 (10). Total—167.
Tied for National League lead in grounding into double plays with 25 in 1977.
Tied for National League lead in being hit by pitch with 11 in 1976.
Led Pacific Coast League in total bases with 268 in 1973.
Led Eastern League third basemen in errors with 33 in 1971.
Led New York-Pennsylvania League shortstops in putouts with 107 in 1970.
Named third baseman on THE SPORTING NEWS National League All-Star Team, 1975.

Year	Club	League	Pos.	G.	AB.	R.	H.	2B.	3B.	HR.	RBI.	B.A.	PO.	A.	E.	F.A.
1970—Geneva	....	NYP	SS-3B	66	234	44	63	5	1	6	29	.269	123	132	25	.911
1971—Pittsfield	....	East.	3-2-S-O	112	376	62	88	14	2	10	37	.234	100	214	34	.902
1972—Pittsfield	....	East.	2B-3B	42	131	29	43	13	3	4	26	.328	81	88	7	.960
1972—Denver	....	A. A.	3B-2B	26	61	7	13	3	0	1	9	.213	10	30	2	.952
1973—Spokane	....	P. C.	2-3-O	123	491	*119	166	22	7	22	90	.338	172	245	25	.943
1973—Texas†	....	Amer.	3B	21	77	16	27	5	3	1	5	.351	13	32	4	.918
1974—Chicago‡	....	Nat.	3B	128	453	65	142	21	5	9	54	.313	84	229	18	.946
1975—Chicago	....	Nat.	3B	130	514	77	182	29	7	7	64	*.354	79	250	20	.943
1976—Chicago§	....	Nat.	3B	142	514	68	174	36	1	15	84	*.339	107	234	14	.961
1977—San Francisco	......	Nat.	3B-2B	140	533	70	161	28	1	12	46	.302	101	234	18	.949
1978—San Francisco	......	Nat.	2B-1B	122	447	76	138	26	3	15	44	.309	234	300	14	.974
1979—S. F.x-Pitts.	......	Nat.	3B-2B-1B	154	560	85	167	26	5	14	85	.298	209	297	14	.973
1980—Pittsburgh y	......	Nat.	3B-1B	137	494	62	137	22	4	10	53	.277	159	217	7	.982
1981—Pittsburgh	....	Nat.	3B	82	279	35	95	23	1	6	45	*.341	50	147	9	.956
1982—Pittsburgh	....	Nat.	3B-1B	154	568	92	181	33	3	19	95	.319	114	267	18	.955
1983—Pittsburgh	....	Nat.	3B	130	473	68	153	21	0	12	68	*.323	59	193	11	.958
1984—Pittsburgh z	....	Nat.	3B-1B	103	403	38	102	16	0	4	44	.253	76	176	15	.944
1985—Pitts. a-L.A.	....	Nat.	3B-1B	144	513	69	141	27	1	12	56	.275	155	243	19	.954
American League Totals—1 Year	....			21	77	16	27	5	3	1	5	.351	13	32	4	.918
National League Totals—12 Years	....			1566	5751	805	1773	308	31	135	738	.308	1427	2787	177	.960
Major League Totals—13 Years	....			1587	5828	821	1800	313	34	136	743	.309	1440	2819	181	.959

Selected by St. Louis Cardinals' organization in 14th round of free-agent draft, June 5, 1969.
Selected by Washington Senators' organization in secondary phase of free-agent draft, January 17, 1970.
†Traded with Infielder-Outfielder Vic Harris to Chicago Cubs for Pitcher Ferguson Jenkins, October 25, 1973.
‡On disabled list, May 4 to June 4, 1974.
§Traded with Infielder Rob Sperring to San Francisco Giants for Outfielder Bobby Murcer, Infielder Steve Onti-veros and Pitcher Andrew Muhlstock, February 11, 1977.

xTraded with Third Baseman Lenny Randle and Pitcher Dave Roberts to Pittsburgh Pirates for Pitchers Ed Whitson, Fred Breining and Al Holland, June 28, 1979.
yOn suspended list, June 5 to June 20, 1980.
zOn disabled list, August 13, 1984 through remainder of season.
aTraded to Los Angeles Dodgers for three players to be named later, August 31, 1985; Pittsburgh Pirates acquired Outfielder R. J. Reynolds, September 3, 1985, and Outfielder Cecil Espy and First Baseman Sid Bream, September 9, 1985, to complete deal.

CHAMPIONSHIP SERIES RECORD

Established National League Championship Series records for highest slugging average (.750), most home runs (3), most total bases (18) and most runs batted in (7), six-game Series, 1985.

Year	Club	League	Pos.	G.	AB.	R.	H.	2B.	3B.	HR.	RBI.	B.A.	PO.	A.	E.	F.A.
1979—Pittsburgh		Nat.	3B	3	12	1	3	0	0	1	2	.250	1	7	0	1.000
1985—Los Angeles		Nat.	3B	6	24	5	8	1	0	3	7	.333	6	9	0	1.000
Championship Series Totals—2 Years				9	36	6	11	1	0	4	9	.306	7	16	0	1.000

WORLD SERIES RECORD

Tied World Series records for most double plays by third baseman, seven-game Series (4), 1979; fewest chances offered by third baseman, game (0), October 12, 1979.

Year	Club	League	Pos.	G.	AB.	R.	H.	2B.	3B.	HR.	RBI.	B.A.	PO.	A.	E.	F.A.
1979—Pittsburgh		Nat.	3B	7	24	2	9	1	0	0	3	.375	3	10	1	.929

ALL-STAR GAME RECORD

Year	League	Pos.	AB.	R.	H.	2B.	3B.	HR.	RBI.	B.A.	PO.	A.	E.	F.A.
1975—National		3B	2	0	1	0	0	0	2	.500	0	0	0	.000
1981—National		3B	1	0	0	0	0	0	0	.000	0	1	0	.000
1983—National		PH-3B	1	0	0	0	0	0	0	.000	0	0	0	.000
All-Star Game Totals—3 Years			4	0	1	0	0	0	2	.250	0	1	0	1.000

DAVID JOSEPH MAGADAN
(Dave)

Born September 30, 1962, at Tampa, Fla.
Height, 6.03. Weight, 190.
Throws right and bats lefthanded.
Attended University of Alabama, University, Ala.
Cousin of Lou Piniella, manager of New York Yankees.

Led Texas League in bases on balls received with 106 in 1985.
Led Carolina League in intentional bases on balls received with 10 in 1984.
Led Texas League third basemen in putouts with 87, assists with 275 and total chances with 393 in 1985.
Named designated hitter on THE SPORTING NEWS College Baseball All-America Team, 1983.

Year	Club	League	Pos.	G.	AB.	R.	H.	2B.	3B.	HR.	RBI.	B.A.	PO.	A.	E.	F.A.
1983—Columbia		S. Atl.	1B	64	220	41	74	13	1	3	32	.336	520	37	7	.988
1984—Lynchburg†		Carol.	1B	112	371	78	130	22	4	0	62	*.350	896	64	16	.984
1985—Jackson		Texas	*3B-1B	134	466	84	144	22	0	0	76	.309	106	276	*31	.925

Selected by Boston Red Sox' organization in 12th round of free-agent draft, June 3, 1980.
Selected by New York Mets' organization in 2nd round of free-agent draft, June 6, 1983.
†On disabled list, August 7 to September 10, 1984.

MICHAEL JAMES MAHLER

Name pronounced MAY-ler.

(Mickey)

Born July 30, 1952, at Montgomery, Ala.
Height, 6.03. Weight, 190.
Throws left and bats right and lefthanded.
Attended Trinity University, San Antonio, Tex.
Brother of Rick Mahler, pitcher with Atlanta Braves.

Pitched seven-inning, 6-0 no-hit victory against Birmingham, July 25, 1974.
Pitched 7-0 no-hit victory against Toledo, June 1, 1977.
Major League saves: 1985 (1).
Led Pacific Coast League in complete games with 14 in 1980.
Led International League pitchers in games started with 31 in 1977.
Tied for American Association lead in wild pitches with 15 in 1984.
Tied for International League lead in home runs allowed with 15 in 1975.

Year	Club	League	G.	IP.	W.	L.	Pct.	H.	R.	ER.	SO.	BB.	ERA.
1974—Savannah		Southern	14	77	8	1	.889	38	13	11	62	35	1.29
1975—Richmond		Int'national	27	166	6	14	.300	167	82	71	129	70	3.85
1976—Richmond		Int'national	17	84	5	9	.357	95	63	54	52	40	5.79
1976—Savannah		Southern	8	53	3	5	.375	44	21	19	38	20	3.23
1977—Richmond		Int'national	31	*217	13	10	.565	202	101	85	145	80	3.53
1977—Atlanta		National	5	23	1	2	.333	31	19	16	14	9	6.26
1978—Atlanta		National	34	135	4	11	.267	130	82	70	92	66	4.67
1979—Atlanta†		National	26	100	5	11	.313	123	72	65	71	47	5.85
1980—Portland		P. Coast	25	173	14	8	.636	143	67	51	*140	85	2.65
1980—Pittsburgh‡		National	2	1	0	0	.000	4	7	7	1	3	63.00
1981—Salt Lake City§		P. Coast	23	127	10	4	.714	164	75	70	63	47	4.96
1981—California		American	6	6	0	0	.000	1	0	0	5	2	0.00

Year Club	League	G.	IP.	W.	L.	Pct.	H.	R.	ER.	SO.	BB.	ERA.
1982—Spokane x	P. Coast	20	134⅔	9	7	.563	156	90	85	116	75	5.68
1982—California	American	6	8	2	0	1.000	9	1	1	5	6	1.13
1983—Edmonton yza	P. Coast	1	5	1	0	1.000	3	2	2	3	2	3.60
1984—Louisville b	Am. Assoc.	26	153⅓	8	12	.400	149	83	73	142	88	4.28
1985—Indianapolis-Nashville	Am. Assoc.	14	98	7	2	.778	93	38	35	92	39	3.21
1985—Montreal c	National	9	48½	1	4	.200	40	22	19	32	24	3.54
1985—Detroit d	American	3	20⅔	1	2	.333	19	8	4	14	4	1.74
National League Totals—5 Years		76	307½	11	28	.282	328	202	177	210	149	5.18
American League Totals—3 Years		15	34⅔	3	2	.600	29	9	5	24	12	1.30
Major League Totals—7 Years		91	342	14	30	.318	357	211	182	234	161	4.79

Selected by Atlanta Braves' organization in 10th round of free-agent draft, June 5, 1974.
†Released, March 29, 1980; signed by Pittsburgh Pirates' organization, April 10, 1980.
‡Traded with Catcher Ed Ott to California Angels for First Baseman Jason Thompson, April 1, 1981.
§On suspended list, April 14, 1981.
xOn suspended list, August 5 and August 6, 1982.
yOn California disabled list, April 6, 1983 through remainder of season; included rehabilitation disability assignment to Edmonton, April 9 to April 28, 1983.
zReleased, November 8, 1983; signed by Tidewater (New York Mets' organization), January 25, 1984.
aReleased, March 16, 1984; signed by Louisville (St. Louis Cardinals' organization), March 17, 1984.
bTraded to Montreal Expos for a player to be named later, February 6, 1985; Louisville (St. Louis Cardinals' organization) purchased Infielder Tom Lawless to complete deal, March 25, 1985.
cReleased, July 23, 1985; signed by Nashville (Detroit Tigers' organization), August 3, 1985.
dReleased, October 9, 1985; signed by Texas Rangers, January 16, 1986.

RICHARD KEITH MAHLER

Name pronounced MAY-ler.

(Rick)

Born August 5, 1953, at Austin, Tex.
Height, 6.01. Weight, 202.
Throws and bats righthanded.
Attended Trinity University, San Antonio, Tex.
Brother of Mickey Mahler, pitcher with Texas Rangers.

Established major league record for most game-winning runs batted in by pitcher, season (3), 1985.
Major League saves: 1981 (2).
Led National League pitchers in games started with 39 in 1985.

Year Club	League	G.	IP.	W.	L.	Pct.	H.	R.	ER.	SO.	BB.	ERA.
1975—Kingsport	Ap'lachian	26	64	2	2	.500	52	23	21	58	26	2.95
1976—Greenwood	W. Carol.	31	105	6	6	.500	96	49	34	68	49	2.91
1977—Savannah	Southern	17	86	6	2	.750	71	31	22	53	38	2.30
1977—Richmond	Int'national	14	40	0	2	.000	45	29	27	25	23	6.08
1978—Richmond	Int'national	32	126	9	5	.643	130	65	55	66	53	3.93
1979—Richmond	Int'national	24	54	4	6	.400	46	26	20	40	18	3.33
1979—Atlanta	National	15	22	0	0	.000	28	16	15	12	11	6.14
1980—Richmond	Int'national	29	188	12	6	.667	172	68	54	101	80	2.59
1980—Atlanta	National	2	4	0	0	.000	2	1	1	1	0	2.25
1981—Atlanta	National	34	112	8	6	.571	109	41	35	54	43	2.81
1982—Atlanta	National	39	205⅓	9	10	.474	213	105	96	105	62	4.21
1983—Atlanta	National	10	14⅓	0	0	.000	16	8	8	7	9	5.02
1983—Richmond	In'national	24	162⅔	12	7	.632	165	102	89	103	85	4.92
1984—Atlanta	National	38	222	13	10	.565	209	86	77	106	62	3.12
1985—Atlanta	National	39	266⅔	17	15	.531	★272	116	103	107	79	3.48
Major League Totals—7 Years		177	846⅓	47	41	.534	849	373	335	392	266	3.56

Signed as free agent by Atlanta Braves' organization, June 16, 1975.

CHAMPIONSHIP SERIES RECORD

Year Club	League	G.	IP.	W.	L.	Pct.	H.	R.	ER.	SO.	BB.	ERA.
1982—Atlanta	National	1	1⅔	0	0	.000	3	0	0	0	2	0.00

CANDIDO MALDONADO (GUADARRAMA)

(Candy)

Born September 5, 1960, at Humacao, Puerto Rico.
Height, 5.11. Weight, 195.
Throws and bats righthanded.

Major League stolen bases: 1985 (1).
Led California League in total bases with 247 in 1980.
Tied for Pioneer League lead in sacrifice flies with 6 in 1978.
Named California League co-Most Valuable Player, 1980.

Year Club	League	Pos.	G.	AB.	R.	H.	2B.	3B.	HR.	RBI.	B.A.	PO.	A.	E.	F.A.
1978—Lethbridge	Pion.	OF	57	210	45	61	15	5	12	48	.290	112	6	8	.937
1979—Clinton	Midw.	OF	50	158	25	37	13	1	2	26	.234	81	5	2	.977
1979—Lethbridge	Pion.	OF	59	234	42	70	★20	3	5	33	.299	81	5	4	.956
1980—Lodi†	Calif.	OF	121	456	75	139	27	3	25	★102	.305	211	13	11	.953
1981—Albuquerque	P. C.	OF	126	460	96	154	40	9	21	104	.335	221	21	8	.968
1981—Los Angeles	Nat.	OF	11	12	0	1	0	0	0	0	.083	8	0	0	1.000
1982—Albuquerque	P. C.	OF	138	541	91	163	28	6	24	96	.301	303	15	10	.970

Year	Club	League	Pos.	G.	AB.	R.	H.	2B.	3B.	HR.	RBI.	B.A.	PO.	A.	E.	F.A.
1982—Los Angeles	Nat.		OF	6	4	0	0	0	0	0	0	.000	5	0	0	1.000
1983—Los Angeles	Nat.		OF	42	62	5	12	1	1	1	6	.194	26	0	0	1.000
1983—Albuquerque	P. C.		OF-3B	38	144	23	46	6	1	4	20	.319	66	11	4	.951
1984—Los Angeles	Nat.		OF-3B	116	254	25	68	14	0	5	28	.268	124	5	8	.942
1985—Los Angeles‡	Nat.		OF	121	213	20	48	7	1	5	19	.225	121	6	2	.984
Major League Totals—5 Years				296	545	50	129	22	2	11	53	.237	284	11	10	.967

Signed as free agent by Los Angeles Dodgers' organization, June 6, 1978.
†On disabled list, August 16 to September 16, 1980.
‡Traded to San Francisco Giants for Catcher Alex Trevino, December 11, 1985.

CHAMPIONSHIP SERIES RECORD

Year	Club	League	Pos.	G.	AB.	R.	H.	2B.	3B.	HR.	RBI.	B.A.	PO.	A.	E.	F.A.
1983—Los Angeles	Nat.		PH	2	2	0	0	0	0	0	0	.000	0	0	0	.000
1985—Los Angeles	Nat.		OF-PH	4	7	0	1	0	0	0	1	.143	4	0	1	.800
Championship Series Totals—2 Years				6	9	0	1	0	0	0	1	.111	4	0	1	.800

ROBIN DALE MALLICOAT
(Rob)

Born November 16, 1964, at St. Helens, Ore.
Height, 6.03. Weight, 178.
Throws and bats lefthanded.
Attended Taft College, Taft, Calif.

Year	Club	League	G.	IP.	W.	L.	Pct.	H.	R.	ER.	SO.	BB.	ERA.
1984—Auburn	NYP	1	5	0	0	.000	8	3	3	6	3	5.40
1984—Asheville	S. Atlantic	11	64⅓	3	4	.429	49	30	28	57	36	3.92
1985—Osceola	Florida St.	26	178⅔	★16	6	.727	119	41	27	★158	74	1.36

Selected by Detroit Tigers' organization in 8th round of free-agent draft, June 6, 1983.
Selected by Houston Astros' organization in secondary phase of free-agent draft, January 17, 1984.

RICHARD EUGENE MANNING
(Rick)

Born September 2, 1954, at Niagara Falls, N. Y.
Height, 6.01. Weight, 180.
Throws right and bats lefthanded.

Tied major league records for most strikeouts, nine-inning game (5), May 15, 1977; most putouts by outfielder, game (12), July 11, 1983, 15 innings; fewest double plays by outfielder, season, 150 or more games (0), 1983.
Tied American League record for most chances accepted by outfielder, game (12), July 11, 1983, 15 innings.
Major league stolen bases: 1975 (19), 1976 (16), 1977 (9), 1978 (12), 1979 (30), 1980 (12), 1981 (25), 1982 (12), 1983 (18), 1984 (5), 1985 (1). Total—159.
Led American League outfielders in total chances with 478 in 1983.
Named outfielder on THE SPORTING NEWS American League All-Star fielding team, 1976.
Received reported $65,000 bonus to sign with Cleveland Indians, 1972.

Year	Club	League	Pos.	G.	AB.	R.	H.	2B.	3B.	HR.	RBI.	B.A.	PO.	A.	E.	F.A.
1972—Reno	Calif.		OF-SS	57	216	45	52	4	4	3	23	.241	71	45	19	.859
1973—Reno	Calif.		OF-SS	137	486	★101	136	40	★14	6	67	.280	184	8	7	.965
1974—Oklahoma City	A. A.		OF	122	402	58	108	16	5	5	39	.269	207	12	8	.965
1975—Oklahoma City	A. A.		OF	30	117	18	37	5	2	0	15	.316	62	4	0	1.000
1975—Cleveland	Amer.		OF	120	480	69	137	16	5	3	35	.285	331	12	9	.974
1976—Cleveland	Amer.		OF	138	552	73	161	24	7	6	43	.292	359	8	5	.987
1977—Cleveland†	Amer.		OF	68	252	33	57	7	3	5	18	.226	191	2	2	.990
1978—Cleveland	Amer.		OF	148	566	65	149	27	3	3	50	.263	377	7	2	.995
1979—Cleveland	Amer.		OF	144	560	67	145	12	2	3	51	.259	417	9	6	.986
1980—Cleveland	Amer.		OF	140	471	55	110	17	4	3	52	.234	379	7	4	.990
1981—Cleveland	Amer.		OF	103	360	47	88	15	3	4	33	.244	305	6	4	.987
1982—Cleveland‡	Amer.		OF	152	562	71	152	18	2	8	44	.270	387	10	9	.978
1983—Clev.§-Milw.	Amer.		OF	158	569	60	140	20	4	4	43	.246	★471	2	5	.990
1984—Milwaukee	Amer.		OF	119	341	53	85	10	5	7	31	.249	231	2	3	.987
1985—Milwaukee x	Amer.		OF	79	216	19	47	9	1	2	18	.218	160	2	4	.976
Major League Totals—11 Years				1369	4929	612	1271	175	39	48	418	.258	3608	67	53	.986

Selected by Cleveland Indians' organization in 1st round (second player selected) of free-agent draft, June 6, 1972.
†On disabled list, June 21 to September 1, 1977.
‡Granted free agency, November 10, 1982; re-signed with Indians, December 15, 1982.
§Traded with Pitcher Rick Waits to Milwaukee Brewers for Outfielder Gorman Thomas and Pitchers Jamie Easterly and Ernie Camacho, June 6, 1983.
xOn disabled list, April 28 to May 17, 1985.

REYES FRED ELOY MANRIQUE

Name pronounced Man-ree-KEE.
Born November 5, 1961, at Bolivar, Venezuela.
Height, 6.01. Weight, 175.
Throws and bats righthanded.
Led International League second basemen in errors with 22 in 1983 and 24 in 1984.

Year Club	League	Pos.	G.	AB.	R.	H.	2B.	3B.	HR.	RBI.	B.A.	PO.	A.	E.	F.A.
1979—Dunedin	Fla. St.	SS	5	15	0	2	0	0	0	0	.133	4	7	3	.786
1979—Medicine Hat.......	Pion.	SS	66	270	47	81	8	●10	2	30	.300	103	208	*37	.894
1980—Kinston..................	Carol.	SS-OF	111	390	49	108	9	5	7	50	.277	120	192	37	.894
1981—Knoxville†	South.	SS	115	469	62	131	15	6	5	42	.279	161	330	45	.916
1981—Toronto	Amer.	SS-3B	14	28	1	4	0	0	0	1	.143	10	27	3	.925
1982—Syracuse‡	Int.	2B-3B-SS	103	362	41	91	9	2	4	37	.251	186	255	24	.948
1983—Syracuse	Int.	2-S-3-O	128	485	55	130	22	8	10	50	.268	211	351	36	.940
1984—Syracuse§	Int.	2B-SS-3B	129	517	63	146	15	5	6	45	.282	233	389	28	.957
1984—Toronto§	Amer.	2B	10	9	0	3	0	0	0	1	.333	5	10	1	.938
1985—Indianapolis	A. A.	3B-SS-2B	123	409	46	98	21	5	8	37	.240	126	249	19	.952
1985—Montreal	Nat.	2B-SS-3B	9	13	5	4	1	1	1	1	.308	5	10	0	1.000
American League Totals—2 Years			24	37	1	7	0	0	0	2	.189	15	37	4	.929
National League Totals—1 Year..............			9	13	5	4	1	1	1	1	.308	5	10	0	1.000
Major League Totals—3 Years			33	50	6	11	1	1	1	3	.220	20	47	4	.944

Signed as free agent by Toronto Blue Jays' organization, November 24, 1978.
†On disabled list, April 9 to April 19, 1981.
‡On disabled list, June 27 to July 12, 1982.
§Sold to Montreal Expos, April 7, 1985.

MICHAEL ALLEN MARSHALL
(Mike)

Born January 12, 1960, at Libertyville, Ill.
Height, 6.05. Weight, 220.
Throws and bats righthanded.

Major League stolen bases: 1982 (2), 1983 (7), 1984 (4), 1985 (3). Total—16.
Led California League in total bases with 301 in 1979.
Led Pacific Coast League first basemen in double plays with 136 in 1981.
Led Texas League first basemen in double plays with 120 in 1980.
Named Minor League Player of the Year by THE SPORTING NEWS, 1981.
Named Pacific Coast League Most Valuable Player, 1981.
Named California League co-Most Valuable Player, 1979.

Year Club	League	Pos.	G.	AB.	R.	H.	2B.	3B.	HR.	RBI.	B.A.	PO.	A.	E.	F.A.
1978—Lethbridge	Pion.	1B-OF	65	256	48	83	15	2	12	70	.324	308	16	7	.979
1979—Lodi	Calif.	1B	137	525	101	*186	*37	3	24	116	*.354	1173	71	20	.984
1980—San Antonio..........	Texas	1B	134	470	95	151	21	6	16	82	.321	*1157	64	●16	.987
1981—Albuquerque........	P. C.	1B	128	467	*114	174	25	7	*34	*137	*.373	1127	54	9	.992
1981—Los Angeles	Nat.	1B-3B-OF	14	25	2	5	3	0	0	1	.200	14	2	0	1.000
1982—Albuquerque........	P. C.	OF-1B-3B	66	255	74	99	20	1	14	58	.388	113	3	4	.966
1982—Los Angeles	Nat.	OF-1B	49	95	10	23	3	0	5	9	.242	122	5	2	.984
1983—Los Angeles	Nat.	OF-1B	140	465	47	132	17	1	17	65	.284	395	21	6	.986
1984—Los Angeles†	Nat.	OF-1B	134	495	68	127	27	0	21	65	.257	331	17	5	.986
1985—Los Angeles‡	Nat.	OF-1B	135	518	72	152	27	2	28	95	.293	265	12	4	.986
Major League Totals—5 Years			472	1598	199	439	77	3	71	235	.275	1127	57	17	.986

Selected by Los Angeles Dodgers' organization in 6th round of free-agent draft, June 6, 1978.
†On disabled list, May 13 to June 3, 1984.
‡On disabled list, June 20 to July 18, 1985.

DIVISION SERIES RECORD

Year Club	League	Pos.	G.	AB.	R.	H.	2B.	3B.	HR.	RBI.	B.A.	PO.	A.	E.	F.A.
1981—Los Angeles	Nat.	PH	1	1	0	0	0	0	0	0	.000	0	0	0	.000

CHAMPIONSHIP SERIES RECORD

Year Club	League	Pos.	G.	AB.	R.	H.	2B.	3B.	HR.	RBI.	B.A.	PO.	A.	E.	F.A.
1983—Los Angeles	Nat.	1B-OF	4	15	1	2	1	0	1	2	.133	22	2	0	1.000
1985—Los Angeles	Nat.	OF	6	23	1	5	2	0	1	3	.217	8	0	0	1.000
Championship Series Totals—2 Years.....			10	38	2	7	3	0	2	5	.184	30	2	0	1.000

ALL-STAR GAME RECORD

Member of National League All-Star Team in 1984; did not play.

ALEXIS DeJESUS MARTE (PEGUERO)
(Alex)

Born December 12, 1962, at Santo Domingo, D.R.
Height, 6.00. Weight, 160.
Throws and bats lefthanded.

Led Southern League in stolen bases with 64 and caught stealing with 21 in 1985.
Led Gulf Coast League in stolen bases with 50 in 1981.

Year Club	League	Pos.	G.	AB.	R.	H.	2B.	3B.	HR.	RBI.	B.A.	PO.	A.	E.	F.A.
1981—Bradenton Jays....	Gulf C.	OF	49	157	35	46	4	2	0	15	.293	92	5	4	.960
1981—Florence	S. Atl.	OF	14	51	9	16	0	0	0	0	.314	18	0	2	.900
1982—Florence†	S. Atl.	OF-1B	83	264	47	67	8	3	1	22	.254	102	4	4	.964
1983—Kinston‡................	Carol.	OF	116	409	53	105	7	3	2	36	.257	180	13	8	.960
1984—Visalia	Calif.	OF	127	510	80	140	11	5	0	30	.275	286	7	6	.980
1985—Orlando	South.	OF	141	534	*117	*171	15	9	0	33	.320	320	*18	12	.966

Signed as free agent by Toronto Blue Jays' organization, May 13, 1980.
†On disabled list, April 20 to May 10 and May 18 to June 2, 1982.
‡Drafted by Orlando (Minnesota Twins' organization), December 6, 1983.

CARMELO MARTINEZ (SALGADO)
(Bitu)

Born July 28, 1960, at Dorado, Puerto Rico.
Height, 6.02. Weight, 210.
Throws and bats righthanded.
Attended Central College of Bayamon, Bayamon, Puerto Rico.
Cousin of Edgar Martinez, third baseman in Seattle Mariners' organization.

Tied major league record by hitting home run in first major league at-bat, August 22, 1983.
Major League stolen bases: 1984 (1).
Tied for National League lead in sacrifice flies with 10 in 1984.
Led American Association first basemen in total chances with 1,283 and tied for lead in double plays with 99 in 1983.
Led Texas League first basemen in putouts with 1,087, total chances with 1,180 and double plays with 102 in 1982.

Year Club	League	Pos.	G.	AB.	R.	H.	2B.	3B.	HR.	RBI.	B.A.	PO.	A.	E.	F.A.
1979—Sarasota Cubs	Gulf C.	OF-1B	40	143	18	29	4	0	1	23	.203	139	9	6	.961
1980—Quad Cities	Midw.	O-1-3-2-S	128	460	65	118	23	0	12	64	.257	433	99	13	.976
1981—Midland	Texas	3-O-2-1	116	392	65	116	22	1	21	84	.296	61	80	24	.855
1982—Midland	Texas	1B-OF	131	467	100	156	35	4	27	93	.334	1098	78	17	.986
1983—Iowa	A. A.	*1B-2B	123	458	76	115	25	1	*31	94	.251	*1191	*83	9	.993
1983—Chicago†	Nat.	1B-3B-OF	29	89	8	23	3	0	6	16	.258	233	17	2	.992
1984—San Diego	Nat.	OF-1B	149	488	64	122	28	2	13	66	.250	317	15	8	.976
1985—San Diego‡	Nat.	OF-1B	150	514	64	130	28	1	21	72	.253	302	14	7	.978
Major League Totals—3 Years			328	1091	136	275	59	3	40	154	.252	852	46	17	.981

Signed as free agent by Chicago Cubs' organization, December 9, 1978.
†Traded with Pitcher Craig Lefferts and Third Baseman Fritz Connally to San Diego Padres for Pitcher Scott Sanderson, December 7, 1983.
‡On disabled list, March 31 to April 15, 1985.

CHAMPIONSHIP SERIES RECORD

Year Club	League	Pos.	G.	AB.	R.	H.	2B.	3B.	HR.	RBI.	B.A.	PO.	A.	E.	F.A.
1984—San Diego	Nat.	OF	5	17	1	3	0	0	0	0	.176	6	0	0	1.000

WORLD SERIES RECORD

Established World Series record for most strikeouts, five-game Series (9), 1984.

Year Club	League	Pos.	G.	AB.	R.	H.	2B.	3B.	HR.	RBI.	B.A.	PO.	A.	E.	F.A.
1984—San Diego	Nat.	OF	5	17	0	3	0	0	0	0	.176	7	0	1	.875

FELIX ANTHONY MARTINEZ
(Tippy)

Born May 31, 1950, at La Junta, Colo.
Height, 5.10. Weight, 175.
Throws and bats lefthanded.
Attended Colorado State University, Fort Collins, Colo.

Major League saves: 1975 (8), 1976 (10), 1977 (9), 1978 (5), 1979 (3), 1980 (10), 1981 (11), 1982 (16), 1983 (21), 1984 (17), 1985 (4). Total—114.
Led American League in intentional bases on balls issued with 13 in 1984.
Tied for Carolina League lead in saves with 15 and wild pitches with 17 in 1973.

Year Club	League	G.	IP.	W.	L.	Pct.	H.	R.	ER.	SO.	BB.	ERA.
1972—Oneonta	NYP	2	9	1	0	1.000	3	2	2	9	10	2.00
1972—Kinston	Carolina	5	20	0	0	.000	22	10	10	18	13	4.50
1973—Kinston	Carolina	54	105	13	8	.619	74	38	31	160	61	2.66
1974—Syracuse	Int'national	36	64	7	5	.583	49	29	27	70	32	3.80
1974—New York	American	10	13	0	0	.000	14	7	6	10	9	4.15
1975—Syracuse	Int'national	14	110	8	2	.800	91	39	25	105	35	2.05
1975—New York	American	23	37	1	2	.333	27	15	11	20	32	2.68
1976—New York†-Baltimore	American	39	70	5	1	.833	50	19	18	45	42	2.31
1977—Baltimore	American	41	50	5	1	.833	47	17	15	29	27	2.70
1978—Baltimore	American	42	69	3	3	.500	77	41	37	57	40	4.83
1979—Baltimore	American	39	78	10	3	.769	59	29	25	61	31	2.88
1980—Baltimore	American	53	81	4	4	.500	69	30	27	68	34	3.00
1981—Baltimore	American	37	59	3	3	.500	48	21	19	50	32	2.90
1982—Baltimore	American	76	95	8	8	.500	81	39	36	78	37	3.41
1983—Baltimore‡	American	65	103⅓	9	3	.750	76	30	27	81	37	2.35
1984—Baltimore	American	55	89⅔	4	9	.308	88	42	39	72	51	3.91
1985—Baltimore	American	49	70	3	3	.500	70	48	42	47	37	5.40
Major League Totals—12 Years		529	815	55	40	.579	706	338	302	618	409	3.33

Selected by Washington Senators' organization in 35th round of free-agent draft, June 5, 1969.
Signed as free agent by New York Yankees' organization, July 22, 1972.
†Traded with Pitchers Rudy May, Dave Pagan and Scott McGregor and Catcher Rick Dempsey to Baltimore Orioles for Pitchers Ken Holtzman, Doyle Alexander and Grant Jackson, Catcher Ellie Hendricks and Pitcher Jimmy Freeman, June 15, 1976.
‡On disabled list, July 9 to July 31, 1983.

Year Club	League	G.	IP.	W.	L.	Pct.	H.	R.	ER.	SO.	BB.	ERA.
1983—Baltimore	American	2	6	1	0	1.000	5	0	0	5	3	0.00

WORLD SERIES RECORD

Tied World Series record for most saves, five-game Series (2), 1983.

Year Club	League	G.	IP.	W.	L.	Pct.	H.	R.	ER.	SO.	BB.	ERA.
1979—Baltimore	American	3	1⅓	0	0	.000	3	1	1	1	0	6.75
1983—Baltimore	American	3	3	0	0	.000	3	1	1	0	0	3.00
World Series Totals—2 Years		6	4⅓	0	0	.000	6	2	2	1	0	4.15

ALL-STAR GAME RECORD

Member of American League All-Star Team in 1983; did not play.

JOHN ALBERT MARTINEZ
(Buck)

Born November 7, 1948, at Redding, Calif.
Height, 5.11. Weight, 200.
Throws and bats righthanded.
Attended Sacramento City College, Sacramento, Calif. and
Sacramento State College, Sacramento, Calif.

Major League stolen bases: 1975 (1), 1978 (1), 1980 (1), 1981 (1), 1982 (1). Total—5.
Led American Association catchers in fielding percentage with .994 in 1973.

Year Club	League	Pos.	G.	AB.	R.	H.	2B.	3B.	HR.	RBI.	B.A.	PO.	A.	E.	F.A.
1967—Eugene	N'west	●C-OF-3B	77	269	53	96	16	4	2	46	.357	294	●48	8	.977
1968—Spartanburg	W. Car.	C	8	28	6	11	4	0	0	11	.393	51	2	0	1.000
1968—Tidewater†‡	Carol.	C	36	110	10	31	12	1	1	14	.282	272	16	1	.997
1969—Kansas City§	Amer.	C-OF	72	205	14	47	6	1	4	23	.229	292	26	9	.972
1970—Kansas City x	Amer.	C	6	9	1	1	0	0	0	0	.111	20	3	1	.958
1971—Omaha	A. A.	C	75	269	34	77	23	1	5	39	.286	502	37	8	.985
1971—Kansas City	Amer.	C	22	46	3	7	2	0	0	1	.152	84	6	3	.968
1972—Omaha y	A. A.	C	67	195	23	34	9	0	4	12	.174	493	47	6	.989
1973—Omaha	A. A.	C-1B	82	254	24	69	13	0	5	38	.272	522	47	3	.995
1973—Kansas City	Amer.	C	14	32	2	8	1	0	1	6	.250	52	4	2	.966
1974—Kansas City	Amer.	C	43	107	10	23	3	1	1	8	.215	151	16	4	.977
1975—Kansas City	Amer.	C	80	226	15	51	9	2	3	23	.226	361	39	8	.980
1976—Kansas City z	Amer.	C	95	267	24	61	13	3	5	34	.228	420	40	4	.991
1977—Kansas City a	Amer.	C	29	80	3	18	4	0	1	9	.225	133	8	1	.993
1978—Milwaukee	Amer.	C	89	256	26	56	10	1	1	20	.219	327	32	8	.978
1979—Milwaukee	Amer.	C-P	69	196	17	53	8	0	4	26	.270	198	39	8	.967
1980—Milwaukee b	Amer.	C	76	219	16	49	9	0	3	17	.224	293	33	5	.985
1981—Toronto c	Amer.	C	45	128	13	29	8	1	4	21	.227	192	22	2	.991
1982—Toronto	Amer.	C	96	260	26	63	17	0	10	37	.242	382	35	5	.988
1983—Toronto	Amer.	C	88	221	27	56	14	0	10	33	.253	331	25	4	.989
1984—Toronto	Amer.	C	102	232	24	51	13	1	5	37	.220	360	34	2	.995
1985—Toronto d	Amer.	C	42	99	11	16	3	0	4	14	.162	155	16	2	.988
Major League Totals—16 Years			968	2583	232	589	120	10	56	309	.228	3751	378	68	.984

Selected by Philadelphia Phillies' organization in 7th round of free-agent draft, January 28, 1967.
†Drafted by Houston Astros, December 2, 1968.
‡Traded with Infielder Mickey Sinnerud and Catcher Tommie Smith by Houston Astros to Kansas City Royals for Catcher John Jones, December 16, 1968.
§On restricted list, April 7 to June 17, 1969.
xOn military list, April 2 to August 10, 1970.
yOn disabled list, July 9 to August 25, 1972.
zOn disabled list, May 20 to June 5, 1976.
aTraded with Pitcher Mark Littell to St. Louis Cardinals for Pitcher Al Hrabosky, December 8, 1977; traded by St. Louis to Milwaukee Brewers for Pitcher George Frazier, December 8, 1977.
bTraded to Toronto Blue Jays for Outfielder Gil Kubski, May 10, 1981 (appeared in no games with Milwaukee).
cGranted free agency, November 13, 1981; re-signed by Blue Jays, December 6, 1981.
dOn disabled list, July 10, 1985 through remainder of season.

CHAMPIONSHIP SERIES RECORD

Year Club	League	Pos.	G.	AB.	R.	H.	2B.	3B.	HR.	RBI.	B.A.	PO.	A.	E.	F.A.
1976—Kansas City	Amer.	C	5	15	0	5	0	0	0	4	.333	15	4	0	1.000

PITCHING RECORD

Year Club	League	G.	IP.	W.	L.	Pct.	H.	R.	ER.	SO.	BB.	ERA.
1979—Milwaukee	American	1	1	0	0	.000	1	1	1	0	1	9.00

JOSE DENNIS MARTINEZ
(Known by middle name.)

Born May 14, 1955, at Granada, Nicaragua.
Height, 6.01. Weight, 183.
Throws and bats righthanded.

Major League saves: 1977 (4), 1980 (1). Total—5.
Led American League pitchers in games started with 39 and complete games with 18 in 1979.

Led International League in complete games with 16 in 1976.
Named International League Pitcher of the Year, 1976.

Year Club	League	G.	IP.	W.	L.	Pct.	H.	R.	ER.	SO.	BB.	ERA.
1974—Miami	Florida St.	25	179	15	6	.714	124	48	41	162	53	2.06
1975—Miami	Florida St.	20	145	12	4	.750	125	54	42	114	35	2.61
1975—Asheville	Southern	6	45	4	1	.800	45	16	13	18	12	2.60
1975—Rochester	Int'national	2	5	0	0	.000	7	4	3	4	2	5.40
1976—Rochester	Int'national	25	180	*14	8	.636	148	64	50	*140	50	*2.50
1976—Baltimore	American	4	28	1	2	.333	23	8	8	18	8	2.57
1977—Baltimore	American	42	167	14	7	.667	157	86	76	107	64	4.10
1978—Baltimore	American	40	276	16	11	.593	257	121	108	142	93	3.25
1979—Baltimore	American	40	*292	15	16	.484	279	129	119	132	78	3.67
1980—Baltimore†	American	25	100	6	4	.600	103	44	44	42	44	3.96
1980—Miami	Florida St.	2	12	0	0	.000	3	1	0	7	5	0.00
1981—Baltimore	American	25	179	●14	5	.737	173	84	66	88	62	3.32
1982—Baltimore	American	40	252	16	12	.571	262	123	118	111	87	4.21
1983—Baltimore	American	32	153	7	16	.304	209	108	94	71	45	5.53
1984—Baltimore	American	34	141⅔	6	9	.400	145	81	79	77	37	5.02
1985—Baltimore	American	33	180	13	11	.542	203	110	103	68	63	5.15
Major League Totals—10 Years		315	1768⅔	108	93	.537	1811	894	815	856	581	4.15

Signed as free agent by Baltimore Orioles' organization, December 10, 1973.
†On disabled list, March 28 to April 20 and June 3 to July 10, 1980; included rehabilitation disability assignment to Miami, July 1 to July 10, 1980.

CHAMPIONSHIP SERIES RECORD

Year Club	League	G.	IP.	W.	L.	Pct.	H.	R.	ER.	SO.	BB.	ERA.
1979—Baltimore	American	1	8⅓	0	0	.000	8	3	3	4	0	3.24

WORLD SERIES RECORD

Year Club	League	G.	IP.	W.	L.	Pct.	H.	R.	ER.	SO.	BB.	ERA.
1979—Baltimore	American	2	2	0	0	.000	6	4	4	0	0	18.00

MICHAEL PAUL MASON
(Mike)

Born November 21, 1958, at Fairbault, Minn.
Height, 6.02. Weight, 205.
Throws and bats lefthanded.
Attended Normandale Community College, Bloomington, Minn., and
Oral Roberts University, Tulsa, Okla.

Tied for Texas League lead in balks with 4 in 1982.

Year Club	League	G.	IP.	W.	L.	Pct.	H.	R.	ER.	SO.	BB.	ERA.
1980—Sarasota Rangers	Gulf Coast	12	61	6	1	.857	40	17	14	*55	46	2.07
1981—Asheville†	S. Atlantic	12	85	8	3	.727	58	28	20	39	35	2.12
1982—Tulsa	Texas	26	155	10	9	.526	153	84	67	111	46	3.89
1982—Texas	American	4	23	1	2	.333	21	13	13	8	9	5.09
1983—Texas	American	5	10⅔	0	2	.000	10	7	7	9	6	5.91
1983—Oklahoma City‡	Am. Assoc.	16	88⅔	5	5	.500	100	50	41	50	26	4.16
1984—Texas	American	36	184⅓	9	13	.409	159	78	74	113	51	3.61
1985—Texas	American	38	179	8	15	.348	212	113	96	92	73	4.83
Major League Totals—4 Years		83	397	18	32	.360	402	211	190	222	139	4.31

Selected by Detroit Tigers' organization in 14th round of free-agent draft, June 6, 1978.
Selected by Minnesota Twins' organization in secondary phase of free-agent draft, January 9, 1979.
Selected by St. Louis Cardinals' organization in secondary phase of free-agent draft, June 5, 1979.
Selected by Texas Rangers' organization in secondary phase of free-agent draft, June 3, 1980.
†On disabled list, July 26, 1981 through remainder of season.
‡On disabled list, June 17 to July 15, 1983.

ROGER LeROY MASON

Born September 18, 1958, at Bellaire, Mich.
Height, 6.06. Weight, 215.
Throws and bats righthanded.
Attended Saginaw Valley State College, University Center, Mich.

Major League saves: 1984 (1).

Year Club	League	G.	IP.	W.	L.	Pct.	H.	R.	ER.	SO.	BB.	ERA.
1981—Macon	S. Atlantic	26	148	10	10	.500	153	77	64	105	50	3.89
1982—Lakeland	Florida St.	22	132⅔	7	7	.500	124	60	51	72	52	3.46
1983—Birmingham	Southern	17	126⅔	7	4	.636	116	45	29	83	43	*2.06
1983—Evansville	Am. Assoc.	11	78⅔	5	5	.500	84	39	37	43	21	4.23
1984—Evansville†	Am. Assoc.	25	151⅔	9	7	.563	175	78	64	88	64	3.80
1984—Detroit‡	American	5	22	1	1	.500	23	11	11	15	10	4.50
1985—Phoenix	P. Coast	24	167⅓	12	1	*.923	145	62	62	120	72	3.33
1985—San Francisco	National	5	29⅔	1	3	.250	28	13	7	26	11	2.12
American League Totals—1 Year		5	22	1	1	.500	23	11	11	15	10	4.50
National League Totals—1 Year		5	29⅔	1	3	.250	28	13	7	26	11	2.12
Major League Totals—2 Years		10	51⅔	2	4	.333	51	24	18	41	21	3.14

Signed as free agent by Detroit Tigers' organization, September 21, 1980.
†On disabled list, May 3 to May 19, 1984.
‡Traded to San Francisco Giants' organization for Outfielder Alejandro Sanchez, April 5, 1985.

VICTOR JOSE MATA (ABREU)
(Vic)

Born June 17, 1961, at Santiago, Dominican Republic.
Height, 6.01. Weight, 165.
Throws and bats righthanded.

Major League stolen bases: 1984 (1).
Tied for South Atlantic League lead in double plays by outfielders with 4 in 1981.

Year	Club	League	Pos.	G.	AB.	R.	H.	2B.	3B.	HR.	RBI.	B.A.	PO.	A.	E.	F.A.
1978—Oneonta	NYP	OF	34	57	9	13	0	0	0	3	.228	34	1	0	1.000
1979—Oneonta	NYP	OF	60	224	36	60	6	1	2	23	.268	100	9	4	.965
1980—Greensboro	S. Atl.	OF	101	346	43	96	11	2	5	47	.277	164	9	6	.966
1981—Greensboro	S. Atl.	O-3-2-1	102	353	59	92	11	4	2	39	.261	165	32	10	.952
1982—Greensboro	S. Atl.	OF-2B-3B	123	481	89	151	25	5	5	64	.314	278	24	14	.956
1983—Nashville	South.	OF-2B-1B	130	465	79	141	19	5	10	63	.303	257	28	28	.936
1984—Columbus	Int.	OF	87	314	42	87	13	5	10	49	.277	200	6	3	.986
1984—New York	Amer.	OF	30	70	8	23	5	0	1	6	.329	49	0	3	.942
1985—New York	Amer.	OF	6	7	1	1	0	0	0	0	.143	1	0	0	1.000
1985—Columbus	Int.	OF-3B	104	375	39	98	14	2	3	27	.261	243	5	★13	.950
Major League Totals—2 Years			36	77	9	24	5	0	1	6	.312	50	0	3	.943

Signed as free agent by New York Yankees' organization, March 16, 1978.

GREGORY INMAN MATHEWS
(Greg)

Born May 17, 1963, at Harbor City, Calif.
Height, 6.02. Weight, 180.
Throws left and bats left and righthanded.
Attended Santa Ana College, Santa Ana, Calif.; and
California State University, Fullerton, Calif.

Year	Club	League	G.	IP.	W.	L.	Pct.	H.	R.	ER.	SO.	BB.	ERA.
1984—Erie	NYP	3	15	0	1	.000	16	15	15	9	8	9.00
1984—Johnson City	Ap'lachian	5	31⅓	2	3	.400	27	12	9	21	13	2.59
1984—Savannah	S. Atlantic	6	27⅓	1	0	1.000	24	10	9	21	15	2.96
1985—St. Petersburg	Florida St.	16	122	13	1	★.929	76	17	15	96	47	★1.11
1985—Louisville	Am. Assoc.	12	74	6	4	.600	61	33	24	47	26	2.92

Selected by Minnesota Twins' organization in 9th round of free-agent draft, January 12, 1982.
Selected by St. Louis Cardinals' organization in 10th round of free-agent draft, June 4, 1984.

RONALD VANCE MATHIS
(Ron)

Born September 25, 1958, at Kansas City, Mo.
Height, 6.00. Weight, 180.
Throws and bats righthanded.
Received bachelor of arts degree in computer science from
University of Missouri, Columbia, Mo., in 1980.

Major League saves: 1985 (1).
Led Pacific Coast League in shutouts with 3 in 1983.

Year	Club	League	G.	IP.	W.	L.	Pct.	H.	R.	ER.	SO.	BB.	ERA.
1980—Bristol	Ap'lachian	3	16	1	2	.333	19	11	11	18	5	6.19
1980—Macon	S. Atlantic	12	86	9	2	.818	60	25	20	78	38	2.09
1980—Montgomery	Southern	1	3	0	1	.000	4	4	4	3	4	12.00
1981—Birmingham†	Southern	23	134	8	8	.500	129	79	68	125	53	4.57
1982—Birmingham‡-Columbus	Southern	12	71⅓	6	2	.750	59	26	26	69	29	3.28
1982—Tucson	P. Coast	14	84½	4	8	.333	90	50	42	79	42	4.48
1983—Tucson	P. Coast	28	182⅔	11	●13	.458	179	101	88	137	73	4.34
1984—Tucson§	P. Coast	12	67⅓	5	2	.714	62	26	25	47	12	3.34
1985—Houston	National	23	70	3	5	.375	83	54	47	34	27	6.04
1985—Tucson	P. Coast	7	44	4	2	.667	45	24	22	29	19	4.50
Major League Totals—1 Year			23	70	3	5	.375	83	54	47	34	27	6.04

Selected by Detroit Tigers' organization in 30th round of free-agent draft, June 7, 1980.
†On disabled list, August 3 to August 18, 1981.
‡Released April 19, 1982; signed by Columbus (Houston Astros' organization), May 5, 1982.
§On disabled list, April 28 to June 5 and July 17 to August 27, 1984.

GARY NATHANIEL MATTHEWS

Born July 5, 1950, at San Fernando, Calif.
Height, 6.03. Weight, 205.
Throws and bats righthanded.

Hit three home runs in a game, September 25, 1976.
Major League stolen bases: 1973 (17), 1974 (11), 1975 (13), 1976 (12), 1977 (22), 1978 (8), 1979 (18), 1980 (11), 1981 (15), 1982 (21), 1983 (13), 1984 (17), 1985 (2). Total—180.
Led National League in grounding into double plays with 23 in 1982.
Led National League in bases on balls received with 103, game-winning RBIs with 19 and tied for lead in sacrifice flies with 10 in 1984.
Led Texas League in total bases with 232 and tied for lead in sacrifice flies with 10 in 1971.
Tied for California League lead in double plays by outfielders with 3 in 1970.

Named National League Rookie Player of the Year by THE SPORTING NEWS , 1973.
Named National League Rookie of the Year by Baseball Writers' Association of America, 1973.

Year Club League	Pos.	G.	AB.	R.	H.	2B.	3B.	HR.	RBI.	B.A.	PO.	A.	E.	F.A.
1969—Decatur................. Midw.	OF	53	174	31	56	11	2	8	30	.322	63	7	8	.897
1970—Fresno.................. Calif.	OF	117	380	77	106	11	5	23	74	.279	133	15	★15	.908
1971—Amarillo................. Texas	OF	●142	493	82	138	★37	6	15	★86	.280	290	10	5	★.984
1972—Phoenix................. P. C.	OF	136	480	101	150	27	8	21	108	.313	218	●16	★13	.947
1972—San Francisco...... Nat.	OF	20	62	11	18	1	1	4	14	.290	34	0	1	.971
1973—San Francisco...... Nat.	OF	148	540	74	162	22	10	12	58	.300	277	11	5	.983
1974—San Francisco...... Nat.	OF	154	561	87	161	27	6	16	82	.287	281	9	9	.970
1975—San Francisco†.... Nat.	OF	116	425	67	119	22	3	12	58	.280	225	11	8	.967
1976—San Francisco‡.... Nat.	OF	156	587	79	164	28	4	20	84	.279	265	8	7	.975
1977—Atlanta.................. Nat.	OF	148	555	89	157	25	5	17	64	.283	262	11	10	.965
1978—Atlanta§............... Nat.	OF	129	474	75	135	20	5	18	62	.285	238	10	8	.969
1979—Atlanta................. Nat.	OF	156	631	97	192	34	5	27	90	.304	292	12	8	.974
1980—Atlanta x.............. Nat.	OF	155	571	79	159	17	3	19	75	.278	258	8	●11	.960
1981—Philadelphia........ Nat.	OF	101	359	62	108	21	3	9	67	.301	170	11	7	.963
1982—Philadelphia........ Nat.	OF	●162	616	89	173	31	1	19	83	.281	268	14	10	.966
1983—Philadelphia y...... Nat.	OF	132	446	66	115	18	2	10	50	.258	174	11	5	.974
1984—Chicago .... Nat.	OF	147	491	101	143	21	2	14	82	.291	224	7	●11	.955
1985—Chicago z............. Nat.	OF	97	298	45	70	12	0	13	40	.235	119	7	3	.977
Major League Totals—14 Years...............		1821	6616	1021	1876	299	50	210	909	.284	3087	130	103	.969

Selected by San Francisco Giants' organization in 1st round (17th player selected) of free-agent draft, June 7, 1968.
†On disabled list, June 5 to July 18, 1975.
‡Granted free agency, November 1, 1976; signed by Atlanta Braves, November 17, 1976.
§On disabled list, April 15 to May 2, 1978.
xTraded to Philadelphia Phillies for Pitcher Bob Walk, March 25, 1981.
yTraded with Outfielder Bob Dernier and Pitcher Porfi Altamirano to Chicago Cubs for Pitcher Bill Campbell and Catcher Mike Diaz, March 27, 1984.
zOn disabled list, May 27 to June 20 and July 8 to July 23, 1985.

DIVISION SERIES RECORD

Year Club League	Pos.	G.	AB.	R.	H.	2B.	3B.	HR.	RBI.	B.A.	PO.	A.	E.	F.A.
1981—Philadelphia......... Nat.	OF	5	20	3	8	0	1	1	1	.400	6	0	0	1.000

CHAMPIONSHIP SERIES RECORD

Tied Championship Series records for most runs batted in, four-game Series (8), 1983; most Series, two or more home runs (2); most consecutive hits, one Series (5), 1983.

Year Club League	Pos.	G.	AB.	R.	H.	2B.	3B.	HR.	RBI.	B.A.	PO.	A.	E.	F.A.
1983—Philadelphia......... Nat.	OF	4	14	4	6	0	0	3	8	.429	6	0	0	1.000
1984—Chicago .... Nat.	OF	5	15	4	3	0	0	2	5	.200	10	0	0	1.000
Championship Series Totals—2 Years.....		9	29	8	9	0	0	5	13	.310	16	0	0	1.000

WORLD SERIES RECORD

Year Club League	Pos.	G.	AB.	R.	H.	2B.	3B.	HR.	RBI.	B.A.	PO.	A.	E.	F.A.
1983—Philadelphia .... Nat.	OF	5	16	1	4	0	0	1	1	.250	15	0	0	1.000

ALL-STAR GAME RECORD

Year League	Pos.	AB.	R.	H.	2B.	3B.	HR.	RBI.	B.A.	PO.	A.	E.	F.A.
1979—National...	OF	2	0	0	0	0	0	0	.000	2	0	0	1.000

DONALD ARTHUR MATTINGLY
(Don)

Born April 20, 1961, at Evansville, Ind.
Height, 5.11. Weight, 185.
Throws and bats lefthanded.

Major League stolen bases: 1984 (1), 1985 (2). Total—3.
Led American League in total bases with 370, game-winning RBIs with 21 and sacrifice flies with 15 in 1985.
Led American League first basemen in fielding percentage with .996 in 1984.
Tied for American League lead in double plays by first basemen with 154 in 1985.
Led South Atlantic League in sacrifice flies with 12 in 1980.
Named Major League Player of the Year by THE SPORTING NEWS, 1985.
Named American League Player of the Year by THE SPORTING NEWS, 1984 and 1985.
Named American League Most Valuable Player by Baseball Writers' Association of America, 1985.
Named first baseman on THE SPORTING NEWS American League All-Star Team, 1984 and 1985.
Named first baseman on THE SPORTING NEWS American League All-Star fielding team, 1985.
Named first baseman on THE SPORTING NEWS American League Silver Slugger team, 1985.
Named South Atlantic League Most Valuable Player, 1980.
Received reported $22,000 bonus to sign with New York Yankees, 1979.

Year Club League	Pos.	G.	AB.	R.	H.	2B.	3B.	HR.	RBI.	B.A.	PO.	A.	E.	F.A.
1979—Oneonta.................. NYP	OF-1B	53	166	20	58	10	2	3	31	.349	29	2	2	.939
1980—Greensboro........... S. Atl.	OF-1B	133	494	92	★177	35	5	9	105	★.358	205	16	8	.976
1981—Nashville.............. South.	OF-1B	141	547	74	173	★35	4	7	98	.316	846	69	12	.987
1982—Columbus.............. Int.	OF-1B	130	476	67	150	24	2	10	75	.315	271	17	5	.983
1982—New York.............. Amer.	OF-1B	7	12	0	2	0	0	0	1	.167	15	1	0	1.000
1983—New York.............. Amer.	OF-1B-2B	91	279	34	79	15	4	4	32	.283	350	15	3	.992
1983—Columbus.............. Int.	1B-OF	43	159	35	54	11	3	8	37	.340	325	29	1	.997
1984—New York.............. Amer.	1B-OF	153	603	91	★207	★44	2	23	110	★.343	1143	126	6	.995
1985—New York.............. Amer.	1B	159	652	107	211	★48	3	35	★145	.324	1318	87	7	★.995
Major League Totals—4 Years.................		410	1546	232	499	107	9	62	288	.323	2826	229	16	.995

Selected by New York Yankees' organization in 19th round of free-agent draft, June 5, 1979.

ALL-STAR GAME RECORD

Year	League	Pos.	AB.	R.	H.	2B.	3B.	HR.	RBI.	B.A.	PO.	A.	E.	F.A.
1984—American		PH	1	0	0	0	0	0	0	.000	0	0	0	.000
1985—American		1B	1	0	0	0	0	0	0	.000	4	0	0	1.000
All-Star Game Totals—2 Years			2	0	0	0	0	0	0	.000	4	0	0	1.000

LEONARD JAMES MATUSZEK

Named pronounced Mu-TU-zek.

(Len)

Born September 27, 1954, at Toledo, O.
Height, 6.02. Weight, 195.
Throws right and bats lefthanded.
Attended University of Toledo, Toledo, O.

Tied major league record for fewest putouts by first baseman, game (0), June 1, 1984.
Major League stolen bases: 1984 (4), 1985 (2). Total—6.
Led American Association in intentional bases on balls received with 22 in 1981.

Year	Club	League	Pos.	G.	AB.	R.	H.	2B.	3B.	HR	RBI	B.A.	PO.	A.	E.	F.A.
1976—Peninsula	Carol.	1B	47	166	23	46	9	1	3	21	.277	426	34	1	.998
1977—Peninsula	Carol.	1B	122	410	56	94	18	4	10	56	.229	1051	74	12	*.989
1978—Reading†	East.	1B-3B	92	294	41	80	16	4	5	36	.272	556	85	13	.980
1979—Reading	East.	1B-3B	32	108	19	31	9	4	3	16	.287	145	42	5	.974
1979—Oklahoma City	A. A.	1B-3B	72	228	31	60	9	3	4	31	.263	421	55	10	.979
1980—Oklahoma City‡	A. A.	1B-3B	67	256	38	78	16	5	7	35	.305	580	55	6	.991
1981—Oklahoma City	A. A.	*1B-3B	129	463	87	146	27	2	21	91	.315	1146	101	6	*.995
1981—Philadelphia	Nat.	1B-3B	13	11	1	3	1	0	0	1	.273	5	4	0	1.000
1982—Philadelphia§	Nat.	3B-1B	25	39	1	3	1	0	0	3	.077	12	8	3	.870
1982—Oklahoma City	A. A.	1B	67	231	41	67	16	4	7	46	.290	560	59	8	.987
1983—Philadelphia	Nat.	1B	28	80	12	22	6	1	4	16	.275	144	9	0	1.000
1983—Portland	P. C.	1B-OF	113	412	82	136	28	6	24	92	.330	811	67	10	.989
1984—Philadelphia xy	Nat.	1B-OF	101	262	40	65	17	1	12	43	.248	644	55	8	.989
1985—Toronto z	Amer.	1B	62	151	23	32	6	2	2	15	.212	19	2	0	1.000
1985—Los Angeles	Nat.	OF-1B-3B	43	63	10	14	2	1	3	13	.222	47	2	0	1.000
National League Totals—5 Years			210	455	64	107	27	3	19	76	.235	852	78	11	.988
American League Totals—1 Year			62	151	23	32	6	2	2	15	.212	19	2	0	1.000
Major League Totals—5 Years			272	606	87	139	33	5	21	91	.229	871	80	11	.989

Selected by Philadelphia Phillies' organization in 5th round of free-agent draft, June 8, 1976.
†On disabled list, June 23 to July 26, 1978.
‡On disabled list, April 14 to May 16 and May 17 to June 21, 1980.
§On disabled list, April 29 to May 15, 1982.
xOn disabled list, June 9 to July 22, 1984.
yTraded to Toronto Blue Jays for Infielder Jose Escobar, Outfielder Ken Kinnard and Pitcher Dave Shipanoff, April 1, 1985.
zTraded to Los Angeles Dodgers for First Baseman-Outfielder Al Oliver, July 9, 1985.

CHAMPIONSHIP SERIES RECORD

Year	Club	League	Pos.	G.	AB.	R.	H.	2B.	3B.	HR.	RBI.	B.A.	PO.	A.	E.	F.A.
1985—Los Angeles	Nat.	PH-OF-1B	3	1	1	1	0	0	0	0	1.000	0	0	0	.000

LEE LOUIS MAZZILLI

Born March 25, 1955, at Brooklyn, N.Y.
Height, 6.01. Weight, 190.
Throws right and bats left and righthanded.
Son of Libero Mazzilli, former professional welterweight boxer.

Major League stolen bases: 1976 (5), 1977 (22), 1978 (20), 1979 (34), 1980 (41), 1981 (17), 1982 (13), 1983 (15), 1984 (8), 1985 (4). Total—179.
Led Texas League in bases on balls received with 111, caught stealing with 15 and tied for lead in being hit by pitch with 7 in 1976.
Led California League in caught stealing with 16 in 1975.
Received reported $50,000 bonus to sign with New York Mets, 1973.

Year	Club	League	Pos.	G.	AB.	R.	H.	2B.	3B.	HR.	RBI.	B.A.	PO.	A.	E.	F.A.
1974—Anderson	W. Car.	OF	132	472	82	127	24	3	11	48	.269	227	9	9	.963
1975—Visalia	Calif.	OF-1B	125	430	103	121	10	4	13	52	.281	185	9	9	.956
1976—Jackson	Texas	OF	131	439	91	128	21	6	13	43	.292	262	8	8	.971
1976—New York	Nat.	OF	24	77	9	15	2	0	2	7	.195	55	2	1	.983
1977—New York	Nat.	OF	159	537	66	134	24	3	6	46	.250	386	9	3	.992
1978—New York	Nat.	OF	148	542	78	148	28	5	16	61	.273	386	8	5	.987
1979—New York	Nat.	OF-1B	158	597	78	181	34	4	15	79	.303	480	24	5	.990
1980—New York†	Nat.	1B-OF	152	578	82	162	31	4	16	76	.280	874	53	14	.985
1981—New York†	Nat.	OF	95	324	36	74	14	5	6	34	.228	192	5	6	.970
1982—Tex.‡§-N.Y. x	Amer.	OF-1B	95	323	43	81	10	0	10	34	.251	234	8	4	.984
1983—Pittsburgh	Nat.	OF-1B	109	246	37	59	9	0	5	24	.240	173	3	4	.978

Year Club League	Pos.	G.	AB.	R.	H.	2B.	3B.	HR.	RBI.	B.A.	PO.	A.	E.	F.A.
1984—Pittsburgh y .... Nat.	OF-1B	111	266	37	63	11	1	4	21	.237	103	2	1	.991
1985—Pittsburgh.............. Nat.	1B-OF	92	117	20	33	8	0	1	9	.282	152	6	3	.981
National League Totals—9 Years...........		1048	3284	443	869	161	22	71	357	.265	2801	112	42	.986
American League Totals—1 Year..........		95	323	43	81	10	0	10	34	.251	234	8	4	.984
Major League Totals—10 Years...............		1143	3607	486	950	171	22	81	391	.263	3035	120	46	.986

Selected by New York Mets' organization in 1st round (14th player selected) of free-agent draft, June 5, 1973.

†Traded to Texas Rangers for Pitchers Ron Darling and Walt Terrell, April 1, 1982.

‡On disabled list, May 20 to June 29, 1982.

§Traded to New York Yankees for Shortstop Bucky Dent, August 8, 1982.

xTraded to Pittsburgh Pirates for Outfielder Don Aubin, Pitcher Tim Burke, Catcher John Holland and Infielder Jose Rivera, December 22, 1982.

yOn disabled list, August 28 to September 11, 1984.

ALL-STAR GAME RECORD

Tied All-Star Game record for most home runs by pinch-hitter, game (1), July 17, 1979.

Year League	Pos.	AB.	R.	H.	2B.	3B.	HR.	RBI.	B.A.	PO.	A.	E.	F.A.
1979—National........................	PH-OF	1	1	1	0	0	1	2	1.000	0	0	0	.000

THOMAS MICHAEL McCARTHY
(Tom)

Born June 18, 1961, at Lundstahl, W. Germany.
Height, 6.00. Weight, 180.
Throws and bats righthanded.

Year Club League	G.	IP.	W.	L.	Pct.	H.	R.	ER.	SO.	BB.	ERA.
1979—Elmira............................... NYP	18	46	2	6	.250	67	50	36	26	37	7.04
1980—Elmira............................... NYP	3	20	2	1	.667	10	7	7	14	13	3.15
1980—Winston-Salem .... Carolina	11	61	4	4	.500	55	32	27	28	46	3.98
1981—Winston-Salem .... Carolina	28	105	3	7	.300	123	99	85	75	99	7.29
1982—Winston-Salem .... Carolina	30	103⅓	3	11	.214	128	95	75	75	65	6.53
1983—Winston-Salem .... Carolina	35	98	8	6	.571	91	56	45	100	54	4.13
1984—New Britain .... Eastern	38	79⅓	8	5	.615	71	35	27	65	56	3.06
1985—Pawtucket...................... Int'national	26	85⅓	5	6	.455	72	48	34	65	62	3.59
1985—Boston†........................... American	3	5	0	0	.000	7	6	6	2	4	10.80
Major League Totals—1 Year......................	3	5	0	0	.000	7	6	6	2	4	10.80

Selected by Boston Red Sox' organization in 7th round of free-agent draft, June 5, 1979.

†Traded with Pitchers Bob Ojeda, John Mitchell and Chris Bayer to New York Mets for Pitchers Calvin Schiraldi and Wes Gardner and Outfielders John Christensen and LaSchelle Tarver, November 13, 1985.

KIRK EDWARD McCASKILL

Born April 9, 1961, at Kapuskasing, Ontario, Canada.
Height, 6.01. Weight, 195.
Throws and bats righthanded.
Attended University of Vermont, Burlington, Vt.
Son of Ted McCaskill, center with Minnesota North Stars (NHL)
and Los Angeles Sharks (WHA), 1967-68, 1972-73 and 1973-74.

Year Club League	G.	IP.	W.	L.	Pct.	H.	R.	ER.	SO.	BB.	ERA.
1982—Salem............................... Northwest	11	71⅓	5	5	.500	63	43	34	87	51	4.29
1983—Redwood........................ California	16	108⅓	6	5	.545	78	39	28	100	60	2.33
1983—Nashua†.......................... Eastern	13	87	4	8	.333	90	47	43	63	43	4.45
1984—Edmonton...................... P. Coast	24	143	7	11	.389	162	104	91	75	74	5.73
1985—Edmonton...................... P. Coast	3	17⅔	1	1	.500	17	7	4	18	6	2.04
1985—California....................... American	30	189⅔	12	12	.500	189	105	99	102	64	4.70
Major League Totals—1 Year....................	30	189⅔	12	12	.500	189	105	99	102	64	4.70

Selected by California Angels' organization in 4th round of free-agent draft, June 7, 1982.

†On suspended list, August 30, 1983; then transferred to disqualified list, September 26, 1983 through April 25, 1984.

RECORD AS HOCKEY PLAYER

Year Team	League	Games	G.	A.	Pts.	Pen.
1983-84—Sherbrooke Jets (a)	AHL	78	10	12	22	21

(a)—June, 1981—Drafted by Winnipeg Jets in 1981 NHL entry draft. Fourth Jets pick, 64th overall, fourth round.

STEVEN EARL McCATTY
(Steve)

Born March 20, 1954, at Detroit, Mich.
Height, 6.03. Weight, 205.
Throws and bats righthanded.
Attended Macomb Community College, Warren, Mich.

Major League saves: 1983 (5).

Tied for American League lead in shutouts with 4 in 1981.

Year Club League	G.	IP.	W.	L.	Pct.	H.	R.	ER.	SO.	BB.	ERA.
1973—Lewiston .... Northwest	19	70	2	2	.500	83	48	37	49	31	4.76
1974—Lewiston .... Northwest	15	96	8	3	.727	99	58	35	62	42	3.28

Year Club	League	G.	IP.	W.	L.	Pct.	H.	R.	ER.	SO.	BB.	ERA.
1975—Modesto	California	37	126	4	8	.333	138	80	64	75	54	4.57
1976—Chattanooga	Southern	36	77	5	4	.556	73	44	27	40	31	3.16
1976—Tucson	P. Coast	5	10	1	1	.500	13	8	7	5	7	6.30
1977—Chattanooga	Southern	14	56	4	2	.667	46	14	12	39	10	1.93
1977—San Jose	P. Coast	23	146	7	8	.467	175	105	93	78	69	5.73
1977—Oakland	American	4	14	0	0	.000	16	9	8	9	7	5.14
1978—Vancouver†	P. Coast	39	55	7	4	.636	53	23	19	51	23	3.11
1978—Oakland	American	9	20	0	0	.000	26	14	10	10	9	4.50
1979—Ogden	P. Coast	8	20	1	1	.500	12	7	7	16	18	3.15
1979—Oakland	American	31	186	11	12	.478	207	106	87	87	80	4.21
1980—Oakland	American	33	222	14	14	.500	202	104	95	114	99	3.85
1981—Oakland	American	22	186	●14	7	.667	140	50	48	91	61	⋆2.32
1982—Oakland‡	American	21	128⅔	6	3	.667	124	62	57	66	70	3.99
1983—Oakland§	American	38	167	6	9	.400	156	79	74	65	82	3.99
1984—Oakland	American	33	179⅔	8	14	.364	206	101	95	63	71	4.76
1985—Oakland x	American	30	85⅔	4	4	.500	95	56	53	36	41	5.57
Major League Totals—9 Years		221	1189	63	63	.500	1172	581	527	541	520	3.99

Signed as free agent by Oakland A's organization, June 24, 1973.
†Appeared as outfielder with no chances.
‡On disabled list, June 4 to June 25, 1982.
§Appeared in one game as a pinch-runner.
xGranted free agency, November 12, 1985.

DIVISION SERIES RECORD

Year Club	League	G.	IP.	W.	L.	Pct.	H.	R.	ER.	SO.	BB.	ERA.
1981—Oakland	American	1	9	1	0	1.000	6	1	1	3	4	1.00

CHAMPIONSHIP SERIES RECORD

Year Club	League	G.	IP.	W.	L.	Pct.	H.	R.	ER.	SO.	BB.	ERA.
1981—Oakland	American	1	3⅓	0	1	.000	6	5	5	2	2	13.50

ROBERT CRAIG McCLURE
(Bob)

Born April 29, 1952, at Oakland, Calif.
Height, 5.11. Weight, 170.
Throws left and bats left and righthanded.
Attended College of San Mateo, San Mateo, Calif.

Major League saves: 1975 (1), 1977 (6), 1978 (9), 1979 (5), 1980 (10), 1984 (1), 1985 (3). Total—35.
Led American League in balks with 6 in 1983.
Tied for Pioneer League lead in shutouts with 3 in 1973.

Year Club	League	G.	IP.	W.	L.	Pct.	H.	R.	ER.	SO.	BB.	ERA.
1973—Billings	Pioneer	14	94	⋆10	2	.833	64	41	22	110	67	2.11
1974—Omaha	Am. Assoc.	21	136	5	8	.385	140	71	58	88	65	3.84
1975—Jacksonville†	Southern	9	42	3	2	.600	31	18	11	39	23	2.36
1975—Kansas City	American	12	15	1	0	1.000	4	0	0	15	14	0.00
1976—Omaha	Am. Assoc.	21	133	9	8	.529	133	61	44	91	41	2.98
1976—Kansas City‡	American	8	4	0	0	.000	3	4	4	3	8	9.00
1977—Milwaukee	American	68	71	2	1	.667	64	25	20	57	34	2.54
1978—Milwaukee	American	44	65	2	6	.250	53	30	27	47	30	3.74
1979—Milwaukee	American	36	51	5	2	.714	53	29	22	37	24	3.88
1980—Milwaukee	American	52	91	5	8	.385	83	34	31	47	37	3.07
1981—Burlington	Midwest	4	14	0	2	.000	19	15	15	11	11	9.64
1981—Milwaukee§	American	4	8	0	0	.000	7	3	3	6	4	3.38
1982—Milwaukee x	American	34	172⅔	12	7	.632	160	90	81	99	74	4.22
1983—Milwaukee y	American	24	142	9	9	.500	152	75	71	68	68	4.50
1984—Milwaukee	American	39	139⅔	4	8	.333	154	76	68	68	52	4.38
1985—Milwaukee	American	38	85⅔	4	1	.800	91	43	41	57	30	4.31
Major League Totals—11 Years		359	845	44	42	.512	824	409	368	504	375	3.92

Selected by Los Angeles Dodgers' organization in 3rd round of free-agent draft, January 10, 1973.
Selected by Kansas City Royals' organization in secondary phase of free-agent draft, June 5, 1973.
†On disabled list, April 15 to May 13 and June 5 to July 25, 1975.
‡Traded to Milwaukee Brewers, March 15, 1977; completing deal in which Kansas City Royals traded Infielder Jamie Quirk, Outfielder Jim Wohlford and a player to be named later to Milwaukee for Pitcher Jim Colborn and Catcher Darrell Porter, December 6, 1976.
§On disabled list, March 28 to September 1, 1981; included rehabilitation disability assignment to Burlington, August 7 to August 24, 1981.
xGranted free agency, November 10, 1982; re-signed by Brewers, December 6, 1982.
yOn disabled list, August 22 to September 12, 1983.

DIVISION SERIES RECORD

Year Club	League	G.	IP.	W.	L.	Pct.	H.	R.	ER.	SO.	BB.	ERA.
1981—Milwaukee	American	3	3⅓	0	0	.000	4	0	0	2	0	0.00

CHAMPIONSHIP SERIES RECORD

Year Club	League	G.	IP.	W.	L.	Pct.	H.	R.	ER.	SO.	BB.	ERA.
1982—Milwaukee	American	1	1⅔	1	0	1.000	2	0	0	0	0	0.00

Tied World Series record for most games lost, seven-game Series (2), 1982.

Year Club	League	G.	IP.	W.	L.	Pct.	H.	R.	ER.	SO.	BB.	ERA.
1982—Milwaukee	American	5	4⅓	0	2	.000	5	2	2	5	3	4.15

LANCE GRAYE McCULLERS

Born March 8, 1964, at Tampa, Fla.
Height, 6.01. Weight, 185.
Throws right and bats right and lefthanded.

Major League saves: 1985 (5).
Tied for Pacific Coast League lead in hit batsmen with 6 in 1985.

Year Club	League	G.	IP.	W.	L.	Pct.	H.	R.	ER.	SO.	BB.	ERA.
1982—Helena	Pioneer	13	87	6	4	.600	89	44	36	62	33	3.72
1983—Spartanburg†	S. Atlantic	22	136⅓	9	6	.600	139	79	61	87	57	4.03
1984—Miami	Florida St.	22	106⅓	6	4	.600	92	37	30	94	45	2.54
1984—Beaumont‡	Texas	8	55⅓	4	1	.800	38	13	13	48	35	2.11
1985—Las Vegas	P. Coast	24	149⅓	11	8	.579	135	75	66	148	83	3.98
1985—San Diego	National	21	35	0	2	.000	23	15	9	27	16	2.31
Major League Totals—1 Year		21	35	0	2	.000	23	15	9	27	16	2.31

Selected by Philadelphia Phillies' organization in 2nd round of free-agent draft, June 7, 1982.

†Traded with Pitchers Marty Decker, Darren Burroughs and Ed Wojna to San Diego Padres, September 20, 1983, as partial completion of deal in which San Diego traded Outfielder Sixto Lezcano and a player to be named later to Philadelphia Phillies for four players to be named later, August 31, 1983; Philadelphia organization acquired Pitcher Steve Fireovid to complete deal, October 11, 1983.

‡On disabled list, September 7, 1984 through remainder of season.

ODDIBE McDOWELL JR.

First name pronounced OH-da-bee.

Born August 25, 1962, at Hollywood, Fla.
Height, 5.09. Weight, 160.
Throws and bats lefthanded.
Attended Miami-Dade Community College (North), Miami, Fla., and
Arizona State University, Tempe, Ariz.

Tied major league record for most putouts by outfielder, game (12), July 20, 1985, 15 innings.
Tied American League record for most chances accepted by outfielder, game (12), July 20, 1985, 15 innings.
Major League stolen bases: 1985 (25).
Hit for the cycle, July 23, 1985.
Member of 1984 U.S. Olympic baseball team.
Named outfielder on THE SPORTING NEWS College Baseball All-America Team, 1983 and 1984.

Year Club	League	Pos.	G.	AB.	R.	H.	2B.	3B.	HR.	RBI.	B.A.	PO.	A.	E.	F.A.
1985—Oklahoma City	A. A.	OF	31	125	32	50	7	8	2	18	.400	72	4	1	.987
1985—Texas	Amer.	OF	111	406	63	97	14	5	18	42	.239	282	9	2	.993
Major League Totals—1 Year			111	406	63	97	14	5	18	42	.239	282	9	2	.993

Selected by St. Louis Cardinals' organization in 4th round of free-agent draft, January 13, 1981.
Selected by Texas Rangers' organization in secondary phase of free-agent draft, June 8, 1981.
Selected by New York Yankees' organization in secondary phase of free-agent draft, January 12, 1982.
Selected by Toronto Blue Jays' organization in secondary phase of free-agent draft, June 7, 1982.
Selected by Minnesota Twins' organization in secondary phase of free-agent draft, June 6, 1983.
Selected by Texas Rangers' organization in 1st round (12th player selected) of free-agent draft, June 4, 1984.

ROGER ALAN McDOWELL

Born December 21, 1960, at Cincinnati, O.
Height, 6.01. Weight, 175.
Throws and bats righthanded.
Attended Bowling Green State University, Bowling Green, O.

Major League saves: 1985 (17).

Year Club	League	G.	IP.	W.	L.	Pct.	H.	R.	ER.	SO.	BB.	ERA.
1982—Shelby	S. Atlantic	12	71⅓	6	4	.600	61	34	26	40	30	3.28
1982—Lynchburg	Carolina	4	29⅓	2	0	1.000	26	12	7	23	11	2.15
1983—Jackson	Texas	27	172⅓	11	12	.478	203	111	93	115	71	4.86
1984—Jackson†	Texas	3	7⅓	0	0	.000	9	3	3	8	1	3.68
1985—New York	National	62	127⅓	6	5	.545	108	43	40	70	37	2.83
Major League Totals—1 Year		62	127⅓	6	5	.545	108	43	40	70	37	2.83

Selected by New York Mets' organization in 3rd round of free-agent draft, June 7, 1982.
†On disabled list, April 10 to August 14, 1984.

ANDREW JOSEPH McGAFFIGAN
(Andy)

Born October 25, 1956, at West Palm Beach, Fla.
Height, 6.03. Weight, 195.
Throws and bats righthanded.
Attended Palm Beach Junior College, Lake Worth, Fla., and
received degree from Florida Southern College, Lakeland, Fla., in 1978.

Major League saves: 1983 (2), 1984 (1). Total—3.

Named Southern League Pitcher of the Year, 1980.

Year Club	League	G.	IP.	W.	L.	Pct.	H.	R.	ER.	SO.	BB.	ERA.
1978—Oneonta	NYP	2	12	0	1	.000	14	8	6	13	9	4.50
1978—Fort Lauderdale	Florida St.	11	66	4	5	.444	45	28	21	36	20	2.86
1979—West Haven	Eastern	23	144	10	6	.625	136	75	61	113	54	3.81
1980—Nashville†	Southern	31	170	15	5	.750	139	62	45	125	62	*2.38
1981—Columbus‡	Int'national	17	103	8	6	.571	85	45	37	57	37	3.23
1981—New York§	American	2	7	0	0	.000	5	3	2	2	3	2.57
1982—Phoenix x	P. Coast	18	96	1	6	.143	115	72	64	64	51	6.00
1982—San Francisco	National	4	8	1	0	1.000	5	1	0	4	1	0.00
1983—San Francisco y	National	43	134⅓	3	9	.250	131	67	64	93	39	4.29
1984—Montreal z-Cincinnati	National	30	69	3	6	.333	60	28	27	57	23	3.52
1985—Denver	Am. Assoc.	26	106⅔	11	5	.688	105	43	35	91	37	2.95
1985—Cincinnati a	National	15	94⅓	3	3	.500	88	40	39	83	30	3.72
American League Totals—1 Year		2	7	0	0	.000	5	3	2	2	3	2.57
National League Totals—4 Years		92	305⅔	10	18	.357	284	136	130	237	93	3.83
Major League Totals—5 Years		94	312⅔	10	18	.357	289	139	132	239	96	3.80

Selected by Cincinnati Reds' organization in 36th round of free-agent draft, June 5, 1974.
Selected by Chicago White Sox' organization in 5th round of free-agent draft, January 7, 1976.
Selected by New York Yankees' organization in 6th round of free-agent draft, June 6, 1978.
†On disabled list, September 1 to September 22, 1980.
‡On disabled list, April 10 to June 14, 1981.
§Traded with Outfielder Ted Wilborn to San Francisco Giants' organization for Pitcher Doyle Alexander, March 30, 1982.
xOn disabled list, June 20 to August 13, 1982.
yTraded to Montreal Expos, March 31, 1984, as compensation for the injury that Pitcher Fred Breining arrived with in trade of February 27, 1984, which sent Breining and Outfielder Max Venable to Montreal for First Baseman Al Oliver. (Breining remained with Montreal.)
zTraded with Pitcher Jim Jefferson to Cincinnati Reds for First Baseman Dan Driessen, July 26, 1984.
aTraded with Pitchers Jay Tibbs and John Stuper and Catcher Dann Bilardello to Montreal Expos for Pitcher Bill Gullickson and Catcher Sal Butera, December 19, 1985.

WILLIE DEAN McGEE

Born November 2, 1958, at San Francisco, Calif.
Height, 6.01. Weight, 176.
Throws right and bats right and lefthanded.
Attended Diablo Valley College, Pleasant Hill, Calif.

Established modern National League record for highest batting average, switch-hitter, season, 100 or more games (.353), 1985.
Major League stolen bases: 1982 (24), 1983 (39), 1984 (43), 1985 (56). Total—162.
Hit for the cycle, June 23, 1984.
Named National League Player of the Year by THE SPORTING NEWS, 1985.
Named National League Most Valuable Player by Baseball Writers' Association of America, 1985.
Named outfielder on THE SPORTING NEWS National League All-Star Team, 1985.
Named outfielder on THE SPORTING NEWS National League All-Star fielding team, 1983 and 1985.
Named outfielder on THE SPORTING NEWS National League Silver Slugger team, 1985.

Year Club	League	Pos.	G.	AB.	R.	H.	2B.	3B.	HR.	RBI.	B.A.	PO.	A.	E.	F.A.
1977—Oneonta	NYP	OF	65	225	31	53	4	3	2	22	.236	103	5	10	.915
1978—Fort Lauderdale	Fla. St.	OF	124	423	62	106	6	6	0	37	.251	243	12	9	.966
1979—West Haven	East.	OF	49	115	21	28	3	1	1	8	.243	88	3	3	.968
1979—Fort Lauderdale	Fla. St.	OF	46	176	25	56	8	3	1	18	.318	103	3	2	.981
1980—Nashville†	South.	OF	78	223	35	63	4	5	1	22	.283	127	6	6	.957
1981—Nashville‡§	South.	OF	100	388	77	125	20	5	7	63	.322	203	10	6	.973
1982—Louisville x	A. A.	OF	13	55	11	16	2	2	1	3	.291	40	0	1	.976
1982—St. Louis	Nat.	OF	123	422	43	125	12	8	4	56	.296	245	3	11	.958
1983—St. Louis y	Nat.	OF	147	601	75	172	22	8	5	75	.286	385	7	5	.987
1983—Arkansas	Texas	OF	7	29	5	8	1	1	0	2	.276	7	0	0	1.000
1984—St. Louis z	Nat.	OF	145	571	82	166	19	11	6	50	.291	374	10	6	.985
1985—St. Louis	Nat.	OF	152	612	114	*216	26	*18	10	82	*.353	382	11	9	.978
Major League Totals—4 Years			567	2206	314	679	79	45	25	263	.308	1386	31	31	.979

Selected by Chicago White Sox' organization in 7th round of free-agent draft, June 8, 1976.
Selected by New York Yankees' organization in secondary phase of free-agent draft, January 11, 1977.
†On disabled list, May 22 to June 7 and July 14 to August 7, 1980.
‡On disabled list, April 24 to June 4, 1981.
§Traded to St. Louis Cardinals' organization for Pitcher Bob Sykes, October 21, 1981.
xOn disabled list, April 13 to April 23, 1982.
yOn disabled list, March 30 to April 29, 1983; included rehabilitation disability assignment to Arkansas, April 18 to April 29, 1983.
zOn disabled list, July 12 to July 27, 1984.

CHAMPIONSHIP SERIES RECORD

Tied Championship Series record for most three-base hits, Series (2), 1982.
Established National League Championship Series records for most at-bats (26), most runs (6) and most strikeouts (6), six-game Series, 1985.
Tied National League Championship Series records for most three-base hits, total Series (2); most stolen bases, six-game Series (2), 1985.

Year Club	League	Pos.	G.	AB.	R.	H.	2B.	3B.	HR.	RBI.	B.A.	PO.	A.	E.	F.A.
1982—St. Louis	Nat.	OF	3	13	4	4	0	2	1	5	.308	12	0	1	.923
1985—St. Louis	Nat.	OF	6	26	6	7	1	0	0	3	.269	18	0	0	1.000
Championship Series Totals—2 Years			9	39	10	11	1	2	1	8	.282	30	0	1	.968

Tied World Series records for most home runs, game, by rookie (2), October 15, 1982; highest fielding average by outfielder, seven-game Series (1.000 with 24 chances), 1982; most putouts by outfielder, seven-game Series (24), 1982.

Year	Club	League	Pos.	G.	AB.	R.	H.	2B.	3B.	HR.	RBI.	B.A.	PO.	A.	E.	F.A.
1982—St. Louis	Nat.		OF	6	25	6	6	0	0	2	5	.240	24	0	0	1.000
1985—St. Louis	Nat.		OF	7	27	2	7	2	0	1	2	.259	15	0	0	1.000
World Series Totals—2 Years				13	52	8	13	2	0	3	7	.250	39	0	0	1.000

ALL-STAR GAME RECORD

Year	League	Pos.	AB.	R.	H.	2B.	3B.	HR.	RBI.	B.A.	PO.	A.	E.	F.A.
1983—National		OF	2	0	1	0	0	0	0	.500	2	0	0	1.000
1985—National		OF	2	0	1	1	0	0	2	.500	1	0	0	1.000
All-Star Game Totals—2 Years			4	0	2	1	0	0	2	.500	3	0	0	1.000

SCOTT HOUSTON McGREGOR

Born January 18, 1954, at Inglewood, Calif.
Height, 6.01. Weight, 190.
Throws left and bats right and lefthanded.
Attended El Camino Junior College, Torrance, Calif. and Loyola Marymount University, Los Angeles, Calif.

Major League saves: 1977 (4), 1978 (1). Total—5.
Tied for American League lead in home runs allowed with 34 in 1985.
Led International League in complete games with 12 and tied for lead in balks with 3 in 1974.
Led Eastern League pitchers in complete games with 14 and tied for lead in games started with 27 in 1973.
Led International League in shutouts with 6 in 1976.
Named International League Pitcher of the Year, 1974.
Received reported $80,000 bonus to sign with New York Yankees, 1972.

Year	Club	League	G.	IP.	W.	L.	Pct.	H.	R.	ER.	SO.	BB.	ERA.
1972—Fort Lauderdale	Florida St.		11	79	7	3	.700	66	30	24	54	25	2.73
1973—West Haven	Eastern		27	★197	●12	●13	.480	★197	95	72	126	63	3.29
1974—Syracuse	Int'national		27	★199	13	10	.565	204	88	76	124	75	3.44
1975—Syracuse†	Int'national		21	124	6	9	.400	134	73	55	72	60	3.99
1976—Syracuse‡-Rochester	Int'national		24	162	12	6	.667	159	59	55	83	40	3.06
1976—Baltimore	American		3	15	0	1	.000	17	7	6	6	5	3.60
1977—Baltimore	American		29	114	3	5	.375	119	57	56	55	30	4.42
1978—Baltimore	American		35	233	15	13	.536	217	98	86	94	47	3.32
1979—Baltimore	American		27	175	13	6	.684	165	70	65	81	23	3.34
1980—Baltimore	American		36	252	20	8	.714	254	101	93	119	58	3.32
1981—Baltimore	American		24	160	13	5	.722	167	63	58	82	40	3.26
1982—Baltimore	American		37	226⅓	14	12	.538	238	126	116	84	52	4.61
1983—Baltimore	American		36	260	18	7	.720	271	101	92	86	45	3.18
1984—Baltimore§	American		30	196⅓	15	12	.556	216	93	86	67	54	3.94
1985—Baltimore	American		35	204	14	14	.500	226	118	109	86	65	4.81
Major League Totals—10 Years			292	1835⅔	125	83	.601	1890	834	767	760	419	3.76

Selected by New York Yankees' organization in 1st round (14th player selected) of free-agent draft, June 6, 1972.
†On disabled list, August 1 to August 29, 1975.
‡Traded with Pitchers Rudy May, Felix Martinez and Dave Pagan, and Catcher Rich Dempsey to Baltimore Orioles for Pitchers Ken Holtzman, Doyle Alexander and Grant Jackson, Catcher Ellie Hendricks and Pitcher Jimmy Freeman, June 15, 1976.
§On disabled list, August 29, 1984 through remainder of season.

CHAMPIONSHIP SERIES RECORD

Year	Club	League	G.	IP.	W.	L.	Pct.	H.	R.	ER.	SO.	BB.	ERA.
1979—Baltimore	American		1	9	1	0	1.000	6	0	0	4	1	0.00
1983—Baltimore	American		1	6⅔	0	1	.000	6	2	1	2	3	1.35
Championship Series Totals—2 Years			2	15⅔	1	1	.500	12	2	1	6	4	0.57

WORLD SERIES RECORD

Year	Club	League	G.	IP.	W.	L.	Pct.	H.	R.	ER.	SO.	BB.	ERA.
1979—Baltimore	American		2	17	1	1	.500	16	6	6	8	2	3.18
1983—Baltimore	American		2	17	1	1	.500	9	2	2	12	2	1.06
World Series Totals—2 Years			4	34	2	2	.500	25	8	8	20	4	2.12

ALL-STAR GAME RECORD

Member of American League All-Star Team in 1981; did not play.

MARK DAVID McGWIRE

Born October 1, 1963, at Claremont, Calif.
Height, 6.05. Weight, 215.
Throws and bats righthanded.
Attended University of Southern California, Los Angeles, Calif.

Led California League third basemen in assists with 239 and total chances with 354 in 1985.
Member of 1984 U.S. Olympic baseball team.
Named College Player of the Year by THE SPORTING NEWS, 1984.
Named first baseman on THE SPORTING NEWS College Baseball All-America Team, 1984.

Year	Club	League	Pos.	G.	AB.	R.	H.	2B.	3B.	HR.	RBI.	B.A.	PO.	A.	E.	F.A.
1984—Modesto	Calif.		1B	16	55	7	11	3	0	1	1	.200	107	6	1	.991
1985—Modesto	Calif.		3B-1B	138	489	95	134	23	3	●24	●106	.274	105	240	33	.913

Selected by Montreal Expos' organization in 8th round of free-agent draft, June 8, 1981.
Selected by Oakland A's organization in 1st round (10th player selected) of free-agent draft, June 4, 1984.

JONATHAN ANDREW McKNIGHT
(Jack)

Born June 7, 1961, at Alvin, Tex.
Height, 6.02. Weight, 180.
Throws and bats righthanded.
Attended Westark Community College, Fort Smith, Ark.
Son of Jim McKnight Sr., infielder-outfielder with Chicago Cubs, 1960 and 1961; scout, San Francisco Giants, 1971; and minor league player-manager, San Francisco Giants' organization, 1972; brother of Jim McKnight Jr., minor league infielder, 1978 through 1982.

Year Club	League	G.	IP.	W.	L.	Pct.	H.	R.	ER.	SO.	BB.	ERA.
1981—Florence	S. Atlantic	27	172	9	8	.529	139	73	62	119	77	3.24
1982—Kinston	Carolina	26	167⅔	●15	6	.714	149	78	64	124	●87	3.44
1983—Knoxville	Southern	30	172	8	12	.400	162	97	79	96	107	4.13
1984—Knoxville†	Southern	24	151	11	8	.579	128	75	64	93	83	3.81
1985—Shreveport‡	Texas	5	38	2	1	.667	28	10	7	40	10	1.66
1985—Phoenix	P. Coast	17	99⅓	8	4	.667	89	47	38	55	65	3.44

Signed as free agent by Toronto Blue Jays' organization, October 12, 1980.
†Traded with Pitcher Jim Gott and Infielder Augie Schmidt to San Francisco Giants for Pitcher Gary Lavelle, January 26, 1985.
‡On Phoenix disabled list, April 11 to May 1, 1985.

JOE CRAIG McMURTRY

(Known by middle name.)
Born November 5, 1959, at Troy, Tex.
Height, 6.05. Weight, 195.
Throws and bats righthanded.
Attended McLennan Community College, Waco, Tex.

Major League saves: 1985 (1).
Tied for International League lead in games started by pitchers with 32 in 1982.
Named National League Rookie Pitcher of the Year by THE SPORTING NEWS, 1983.
Named International League Pitcher of the Year, 1982.

Year Club	League	G.	IP.	W.	L.	Pct.	H.	R.	ER.	SO.	BB.	ERA.
1980—Savannah	Southern	14	86	7	4	.636	82	40	34	37	35	3.56
1981—Savannah	Southern	28	202	★15	11	.577	168	87	62	111	95	2.76
1982—Richmond	Int'national	32	★210	★17	9	.654	198	98	89	96	107	3.81
1983—Atlanta	National	36	224⅔	15	9	.625	204	86	77	105	88	3.08
1984—Atlanta	National	37	183⅓	9	17	.346	184	100	88	99	102	4.32
1985—Atlanta	National	17	45	0	3	.000	56	36	33	28	27	6.60
1985—Richmond	Int'national	16	107⅓	7	5	.583	88	43	39	74	51	3.27
Major League Totals—3 Years		90	453	24	29	.453	444	222	198	232	217	3.93

Selected by Atlanta Braves' organization in 1st round (fourth player selected) of free-agent draft, January 8, 1980.

HAROLD ABRAHAM McRAE
(Hal)

Born July 10, 1946, at Avon Park, Fla.
Height, 5.11. Weight, 185.
Throws and bats righthanded.
Attended Florida A&M University, Tallahassee, Fla.
Father of Brian McRae, shortstop in Kansas City Royals' organization.

Tied major league record for most long hits, doubleheader, (6), August 27, 1974 (5 doubles, 1 home run).
Major League stolen bases: 1968 (1), 1971 (3), 1973 (2), 1974 (11), 1975 (11), 1976 (22), 1977 (18), 1978 (17), 1979 (5), 1980 (10), 1981 (3), 1982 (4), 1983 (2). Total—109.
Led American League in being hit by pitch with 13 in 1977.
Named designated hitter on THE SPORTING NEWS American League All-Star Team, 1976, 1977 and 1982.
Named designated hitter on THE SPORTING NEWS American League Silver Slugger team, 1982.

Year Club	League	Pos.	G.	AB.	R.	H.	2B.	3B.	HR.	RBI.	B.A.	PO.	A.	E.	F.A.
1965—Tampa	Fla. St.	OF	22	65	3	10	3	0	0	4	.154	19	0	0	1.000
1966—Peninsula†	Carol.	2B	109	394	65	113	19	4	11	56	.287	252	226	★28	.945
1967—Buffalo‡	Int.	2B	73	259	30	65	14	3	10	34	.251	133	208	23	.937
1967—Knoxville	South.	2B	51	186	26	54	10	3	6	25	.290	140	136	12	.958
1968—Indianapolis	P. C.	2B-OF	119	444	64	131	31	11	16	65	.295	222	307	14	.974
1968—Cincinnati	Nat.	2B	17	51	1	10	1	0	0	2	.196	33	30	5	.926
1969—Indianapolis§	A. A.	OF	17	41	2	9	1	0	0	4	.220	0	0	0	.000
1970—Cincinnati	Nat.	OF-3B-2B	70	165	18	41	6	1	8	23	.248	53	7	1	.984
1971—Cincinnati	Nat.	OF	99	337	39	89	24	2	9	34	.264	167	6	6	.966
1972—Cincinnati x	Nat.	OF-3B	61	97	9	27	4	0	5	26	.278	16	14	6	.833
1973—Kansas City	Amer.	OF-3B	106	338	36	79	18	3	9	50	.234	101	6	5	.955
1974—Kansas City	Amer.	OF-3B	148	539	71	167	36	4	15	88	.310	132	3	7	.951
1975—Kansas City	Amer.	OF-3B	126	480	57	147	38	6	5	71	.306	207	7	3	.986
1976—Kansas City	Amer.	OF	149	527	75	175	34	5	8	73	.332	63	2	2	.970
1977—Kansas City	Amer.	OF	●162	641	104	191	★54	11	21	92	.298	81	8	4	.957
1978—Kansas City	Amer.	OF	156	623	90	170	39	5	16	72	.273	3	1	0	1.000
1979—Kansas City y	Amer.	DH	101	393	55	113	32	4	10	74	.288	0	0	0	.000
1980—Kansas City z	Amer.	OF	124	489	73	145	39	5	14	83	.297	17	0	0	1.000
1981—Kansas City	Amer.	OF	101	389	38	106	23	2	7	36	.272	10	0	1	.909
1982—Kansas City a	Amer.	OF	159	613	91	189	●46	8	27	★133	.308	1	0	1	.500

Year Club League	Pos.	G.	AB.	R.	H.	2B.	3B.	HR.	RBI.	B.A.	PO.	A.	E.	F.A.
1983—Kansas City.......... Amer.	DH	157	589	84	183	41	6	12	82	.311	0	0	0	.000
1984—Kansas City.......... Amer.	DH	106	317	30	96	13	4	3	42	.303	0	0	0	.000
1985—Kansas City b ...... Amer.	DH	112	320	41	83	19	0	14	70	.259	0	0	0	.000
National League Totals—4 Years...........		247	650	67	167	35	3	22	85	.257	269	57	18	.948
American League Totals—13 Years		1707	6258	846	1844	432	63	161	966	.295	615	27	23	.965
Major League Totals—17 Years...............		1954	6908	913	2011	467	66	183	1051	.291	884	84	41	.959

Selected by Cincinnati Reds' organization in 6th round of free-agent draft, June, 1965.
†On disabled list, June 23 to July 6, 1966.
‡On disabled list, April 26 to May 7, 1967.
§On disabled list, April 18 to May 28 and July 4 to August 5, 1969.
xTraded with Pitcher Wayne Simpson to Kansas City Royals for Pitcher Roger Nelson and Outfielder Richie Scheinblum, November 30, 1972.
yOn disabled list, June 11 to August 2, 1979.
zOn disabled list, May 13 to June 2, 1980.
aGranted free agency, November 10, 1982; re-signed by Royals, November 15, 1982.
bGranted free agency, November 12, 1985; re-signed by Royals, December 8, 1985.

DIVISION SERIES RECORD

Year Club League	Pos.	G.	AB.	R.	H.	2B.	3B.	HR.	RBI.	B.A.	PO.	A.	E.	F.A.
1981—Kansas City.......... Amer.	DH	3	11	0	1	1	0	0	0	.091	0	0	0	.000

CHAMPIONSHIP SERIES RECORD

Established Championship Series record for most runs, five-game Series (6), 1977.
Tied Championship Series record for most doubles, total Series (7).
Tied American League Championship Series record for most times on losing club (4).

Year Club League	Pos.	G.	AB.	R.	H.	2B.	3B.	HR.	RBI.	B.A.	PO.	A.	E.	F.A.
1970—Cincinnati.............. Nat.	PH-OF	2	4	0	0	0	0	0	0	.000	2	0	0	1.000
1972—Cincinnati.............. Nat.	PH	1	0	0	0	0	0	0	0	.000	0	0	0	.000
1976—Kansas City.......... Amer.	DH	5	17	2	2	1	1	0	1	.118	5	1	0	1.000
1977—Kansas City.......... Amer.	OF-DH	5	18	6	8	3	0	1	2	.444	2	1	0	1.000
1978—Kansas City.......... Amer.	DH	4	14	0	3	0	0	0	2	.214	0	0	0	.000
1980—Kansas City.......... Amer.	DH	3	10	0	2	0	0	0	0	.200	0	0	0	.000
1984—Kansas City.......... Amer.	PH	2	2	0	2	1	0	0	1	1.000	0	0	0	.000
1985—Kansas City.......... Amer.	DH	6	23	1	6	2	0	0	3	.261	0	0	0	.000
Championship Series Totals—8 Years....		28	88	9	23	7	1	1	9	.261	9	2	0	1.000

WORLD SERIES RECORD

Year Club League	Pos.	G.	AB.	R.	H.	2B.	3B.	HR.	RBI.	B.A.	PO.	A.	E.	F.A.
1970—Cincinnati.............. Nat.	OF	3	11	1	5	2	0	0	3	.455	2	1	0	1.000
1972—Cincinnati.............. Nat.	PH-OF	5	9	1	4	1	0	0	2	.444	4	0	0	1.000
1980—Kansas City.......... Amer.	DH	6	24	3	9	3	0	0	1	.375	0	0	0	.000
1985—Kansas City.......... Amer.	PH	3	1	0	0	0	0	0	0	.000	0	0	0	.000
World Series Totals—4 Years		17	45	5	18	6	0	0	6	.400	6	1	0	1.000

ALL-STAR GAME RECORD

Year League	Pos.	AB.	R.	H.	2B.	3B.	HR.	RBI.	B.A.	PO.	A.	E.	F.A.
1975—American.......................................	PH	1	0	0	0	0	0	0	.000	0	0	0	.000
1976—American.......................................	PH	1	0	0	0	0	0	0	.000	0	0	0	.000
1982—American.......................................	PH	0	0	0	0	0	0	0	.000	0	0	0	.000
All-Star Game Totals—3 Years...................		2	0	0	0	0	0	0	.000	0	0	0	.000

WALTER KEVIN McREYNOLDS

(Known by middle name.)
Born October 16, 1959, at Little Rock, Ark.
Height, 6.01. Weight, 205.
Throws and bats righthanded.
Attended University of Arkansas, Fayetteville, Ark.

Major League stolen bases: 1983 (2), 1984 (3), 1985 (4). Total—9.
Led National League outfielders in total chances with 436 in 1984 and 445 in 1985.
Led Pacific Coast League in total bases with 328 in 1983.
Named Minor League Player of the Year by THE SPORTING NEWS, 1983.
Named Pacific Coast League Player of the Year, 1983.
Named California League Most Valuable Player, 1982.
Received reported $125,000 bonus to sign with San Diego Padres, 1982.
Named outfielder on THE SPORTING NEWS College Baseball All-America Team, 1981.

Year Club League	Pos.	G.	AB.	R.	H.	2B.	3B.	HR.	RBI.	B.A.	PO.	A.	E.	F.A.
1982—Reno .... Calif.	OF	90	338	83	127	17	5	★28	98	★.376	52	7	3	.952
1982—Amarillo................. Texas	OF	40	162	30	57	8	3	5	39	.352	76	3	2	.975
1983—Las Vegas.............. P. C.	OF	113	446	98	168	★46	9	●32	116	.377	257	3	9	.967
1983—San Diego .... Nat.	OF	39	140	15	31	3	1	4	14	.221	87	4	1	.989
1984—San Diego .... Nat.	OF	147	525	68	146	26	6	20	75	.278	★422	10	4	.991
1985—San Diego .... Nat.	OF	152	564	61	132	24	4	15	75	.234	★430	12	3	.993
Major League Totals—3 Years.................		338	1229	144	309	53	11	39	164	.251	939	26	8	.992

Selected by Milwaukee Brewers' organization in 18th round of free-agent draft, June 6, 1978.
Selected by San Diego Padres' organization in 1st round (sixth player selected) of free-agent draft, June 8, 1981.

Year	Club	League	Pos.	G.	AB.	R.	H.	2B.	3B.	HR.	RBI.	B.A.	PO.	A.	E.	F.A.
1984—San Diego		Nat.	OF	4	10	2	3	0	0	1	4	.300	10	0	0	1.000

LARRY DEAN McWILLIAMS

Born February 10, 1954, at Wichita, Kan.
Height, 6.05. Weight, 181.
Throws and bats lefthanded.
Attended Paris Junior College, Paris, Tex.

Tied major league record for most strikeouts by batter, inning (2), April 22, 1979 (fourth inning).
Major League saves: 1982 (1), 1984 (1). Total—2.
Named lefthanded pitcher on THE SPORTING NEWS National League All-Star Team, 1983.

Year	Club	League	G.	IP.	W.	L.	Pct.	H.	R.	ER.	SO.	BB.	ERA.
1974—Greenwood†		W. Carol.	11	64	4	3	.571	64	26	20	61	23	2.81
1975—Greenwood‡		W. Carol.	17	93	8	4	.667	83	36	29	71	18	2.81
1976—Greenwood		W. Carol.	8	48	2	2	.500	40	19	14	44	13	2.63
1976—Savannah		Southern	16	74	3	8	.273	82	41	38	37	33	4.62
1977—Savannah		Southern	26	158	8	9	.471	153	70	59	139	64	3.36
1978—Richmond		Int'national	15	108	6	5	.545	87	36	34	78	41	2.83
1978—Atlanta		National	15	99	9	3	.750	84	38	31	42	35	2.82
1979—Atlanta§		National	13	66	3	7	.600	60	41	41	32	22	5.59
1980—Atlanta		National	30	164	9	14	.391	188	97	90	77	39	4.94
1981—Richmond		Int'national	29	178	●13	10	.565	174	98	●86	157	79	4.35
1981—Atlanta		National	6	38	2	1	.667	31	13	13	23	8	3.08
1982—Atlanta x-Pittsburgh		National	46	159⅓	8	8	.500	158	79	68	118	44	3.84
1983—Pittsburgh		National	35	238	15	8	.652	205	99	86	199	87	3.25
1984—Pittsburgh		National	34	227⅓	12	11	.522	226	86	74	149	78	2.93
1985—Pittsburgh y		National	30	126⅓	7	9	.438	139	70	66	52	62	4.70
Major League Totals—8 Years			209	1118	65	56	.537	1100	523	469	692	375	3.78

Selected by Atlanta Braves' organization in 1st round (sixth player selected) of free-agent draft, January 9, 1974.
†On disabled list, July 22 to September 25, 1974.
‡On disabled list, April 11 to June 3, 1975.
§On disabled list, May 18 to June 15 and July 7 to September 1, 1979.
xTraded to Pittsburgh Pirates for Pitcher Pascual Perez and a player to be named later, June 30, 1982; Atlanta Braves' organization acquired Shortstop Carlos Rios to complete deal, September 8, 1982.
yOn disabled list, May 17 to June 8 and August 18 to September 3, 1985.

ROBERT ANDREW MEACHAM
(Bobby)

Born August 25, 1960, at Los Angeles, Calif.
Height, 6.01. Weight, 180.
Throws right and bats left and righthanded.
Attended San Diego State University, San Diego, Calif.

Major League stolen bases: 1983 (8), 1984 (9), 1985 (25). Total—42.
Led American League in sacrifice hits with 14 in 1984 and 23 in 1985.
Named shortstop on THE SPORTING NEWS College Baseball All-America Team, 1981.

Year	Club	League	Pos.	G.	AB.	R.	H.	2B.	3B.	HR.	RBI.	B.A.	PO.	A.	E.	F.A.
1981—Gastonia		S. Atl.	SS	74	274	24	50	8	2	1	18	.182	107	235	25	.932
1982—St. Petersburg†		Fla. St.	SS	120	421	57	109	15	4	0	37	.259	201	306	★47	.915
1983—Columbus		Int.	SS	120	423	58	111	18	3	9	60	.262	206	348	30	.949
1983—New York		Amer.	SS-3B	22	51	5	12	2	0	0	4	.235	16	64	6	.930
1984—Nashville		South.	SS	8	31	3	9	0	0	0	3	.290	16	25	1	.976
1984—Columbus		Int.	SS	46	187	35	53	13	●6	2	13	.283	67	133	14	.935
1984—New York		Amer.	SS-2B	99	360	62	91	13	4	2	25	.253	140	272	19	.956
1985—New York		Amer.	SS	156	481	70	105	16	2	1	47	.218	236	390	24	.963
Major League Totals—3 Years				277	892	137	208	31	6	3	76	.233	392	726	49	.958

Selected by Chicago White Sox' organization in 14th round of free agent draft, June 6, 1978.
Selected by St. Louis Cardinals' organization in 1st round (eighth player selected) of free-agent draft, June 8, 1981.
†Traded with Outfielder Stan Javier to New York Yankees' organization for Pitchers Marty Mason and Steve Fincher and Outfielder Bob Helsom, December 14, 1982.

DAVID KEITH MEIER

Name pronounced MY-er.

(Dave)

Born August 8, 1959, at Helena, Mont.
Height, 6.00. Weight, 185.
Throws and bats righthanded.
Attended Fresno City College, Fresno, Calif., and received bachelor of arts degree
in economics from Stanford University, Stanford, Calif. in 1981.

Tied for Southern League lead in double plays by outfielders with 5 in 1982.

Year	Club	League	Pos.	G.	AB.	R.	H.	2B.	3B.	HR.	RBI.	B.A.	PO.	A.	E.	F.A.
1981—Visalia		Calif.	SS-OF-3B	71	273	53	92	12	0	9	50	.337	65	85	13	.920
1982—Orlando		South.	O-3-2-S	134	474	71	136	19	7	8	63	.287	254	27	6	.979
1983—Toledo		Int.	OF-P	126	426	63	143	21	6	8	68	.336	224	6	7	.970

Year Club	League	Pos.	G.	AB.	R.	H.	2B.	3B.	HR.	RBI.	B.A.	PO.	A.	E.	F.A.
1984—Minnesota............	Amer.	OF-3B	59	147	18	35	8	1	0	13	.238	87	2	2	.978
1985—Minnesota†..........	Amer.	OF	71	104	15	27	6	0	1	8	.260	77	1	1	.987
Major League Totals—2 Years.................			130	251	33	62	14	1	1	21	.247	164	3	3	.982

Selected by California Angels' organization in 31st round of free-agent draft, June 7, 1977.
Selected by St. Louis Cardinals' organization in secondary phase of free-agent draft, January 10, 1978.
Selected by Minnesota Twins' organization in 5th round of free-agent draft, June 8, 1981.
†Released, December 20, 1985.

PITCHING RECORD

Year Club	League	G.	IP.	W.	L.	Pct.	H.	R.	ER.	SO.	BB.	ERA.
1983—Toledo	Int'national	1	1	0	0	.000	2	1	1	0	0	9.00

FRANCISCO JAVIER MELENDEZ (VILLEGAS)

Born January 25, 1964, at Rio Piedras, Puerto Rico.
Height, 6.00. Weight, 185.
Throws and bats lefthanded.

Led Pacific Coast League first basemen in putouts with 1,085 in 1984.
Led Eastern League first basemen in putouts with 1,081, total chances with 1,166 and double plays with 99 in 1983.

Year Club	League	Pos.	G.	AB.	R.	H.	2B.	3B.	HR.	RBI.	B.A.	PO.	A.	E.	F.A.
1981—Peninsula..............	Carol.	1B-OF	32	74	6	10	3	0	0	6	.135	154	13	6	.965
1981—Spartanburg..........	S. Atl.	1B-OF	85	306	44	82	13	1	3	36	.268	760	57	17	.980
1982—Peninsula..............	Carol.	1B	118	424	54	124	*33	3	4	69	.292	739	75	11	.987
1983—Reading.................	East.	1B-OF	126	450	81	134	17	4	5	75	.298	1082	73	12	.990
1984—Portland................	P. C.	*1B-OF	128	506	63	158	36	8	3	65	.312	1090	85	11	*.991
1984—Philadelphia	Nat.	1B	21	23	0	3	0	0	0	2	.130	37	4	0	1.000
1985—Portland................	P. C.	●1B-OF	130	397	41	111	25	2	2	54	.280	974	69	●15	.986
Major League Totals—1 Year.................			21	23	0	3	0	0	0	2	.130	37	4	0	1.000

Signed as free agent by Philadelphia Phillies' organization, October 4, 1980.

ROBERT PAUL MELVIN
(Bob)

Born October 28, 1961, at Palo Alto, Calif.
Height, 6.04. Weight, 205.
Throws and bats righthanded.
Attended University of California, Berkeley, Calif.,
and Canada College, Redwood City, Calif.

Year Club	League	Pos.	G.	AB.	R.	H.	2B.	3B.	HR.	RBI.	B.A.	PO.	A.	E.	F.A.
1981—Macon.....................	S. Atl.	C	114	412	56	112	19	1	14	64	.272	456	67	2	*.996
1982—Birmingham†........	South.	*C-1B-3B	98	364	33	86	12	1	13	52	.236	638	54	9	*.987
1983—Birmingham	South.	C-1B-2B	78	285	43	82	14	2	10	56	.288	404	30	2	.995
1983—Evansville	A. A.	C-1B	45	142	10	27	6	0	2	11	.190	213	16	1	.996
1984—Evansville	A. A.	C-1B	44	141	12	35	13	0	0	11	.248	214	21	1	.996
1984—Birmingham	South.	C-1B-3B	69	271	34	73	14	1	2	33	.269	341	38	4	.990
1985—Nashville	A. A.	C-1B-OF	53	177	27	48	7	1	9	24	.271	276	28	2	.993
1985—Detroit‡.................	Amer.	C	41	82	10	18	4	1	0	4	.220	175	13	2	.989
Major League Totals—1 Year.................			41	82	10	18	4	1	0	4	.220	175	13	2	.989

Selected by Baltimore Orioles' organization in 3rd round of free-agent draft, June 5, 1979.
Selected by Detroit Tigers' organization in secondary phase of free-agent draft, January 13, 1981.
†On disabled list, May 1 to May 25, 1982.
‡Traded with Pitcher Juan Berenguer and a player to be named later to San Francisco Giants for Pitchers Dave LaPoint and Eric King and Catcher Matt Nokes, October 7, 1985; San Francisco acquired Pitcher Scott Medvin to complete deal, December 11, 1985.

RONALD KNOX MERIDITH
(Ron)

Born November 26, 1956, at San Pedro, Calif.
Height, 6.00. Weight, 175.
Throws and bats lefthanded.
Attended Oral Roberts University, Tulsa, Okla.

Major League saves: 1985 (1).

Year Club	League	G.	IP.	W.	L.	Pct.	H.	R.	ER.	SO.	BB.	ERA.
1978—Sarasota Astros............................	Gulf Coast	2	12	2	0	1.000	12	6	4	6	3	3.00
1978—Daytona Beach	Florida St.	9	56	3	6	.333	59	28	27	31	17	4.34
1979—Columbus	Southern	26	149	9	11	.450	150	75	71	63	78	4.29
1980—Columbus	Southern	25	145	9	5	.643	143	48	41	82	40	2.54
1981—Tucson†..	P. Coast	34	132	7	6	.538	166	93	80	70	63	5.45
1982—Hawaii	P. Coast	37	111⅓	6	2	.750	105	53	47	68	41	3.80
1983—Tucson‡§......................................	P. Coast	37	91	2	3	.400	128	74	65	59	33	6.43
1984—Iowa	Am. Assoc.	49	93⅔	7	3	.700	88	33	33	78	33	3.17
1984—Chicago	National	3	5⅓	0	0	.000	6	5	2	4	2	3.38
1985—Iowa	Am. Assoc.	25	41	4	1	.800	29	9	6	29	7	1.32
1985—Chicago	National	32	46⅓	3	2	.600	53	24	23	23	24	4.47
Major League Totals—2 Years...........................		35	51⅔	3	2	.600	59	29	25	27	26	4.35

Selected by Houston Astros' organization in 4th round of free-agent draft, June 6, 1978.
†Loaned to Hawaii (San Diego Padres' organization), April 6, 1982; returned, September 17, 1982.
‡Traded to Atlanta Braves' organization for Pitcher Jose Alvarez, February 16, 1984.
§Traded to Chicago Cubs' organization for Pitcher Terry Leach, April 4, 1984.

DANIEL THOMAS MEYER
(Dan)

Born August 3, 1952, at Hamilton, O.
Height, 5.11. Weight, 180.
Throws right and bats lefthanded.
Attended Santa Ana College, Santa Ana, Calif., and University
of Arizona, Tucson, Ariz.

Tied major league record for most times awarded first base on catcher's interference, game (2), May 3, 1977.
Major League stolen bases: 1974 (1), 1975 (8), 1976 (10), 1977 (11), 1978 (7), 1979 (11), 1980 (8), 1981 (4), 1982 (1). Total—61.
Led Appalachian League in total bases with 158 in 1972.
Tied for American Association lead in sacrifice flies with 9 in 1974.
Led Appalachian League third basemen in assists with 97 in 1972.
Named Appalachian League Player of the Year, 1972.

Year Club	League	Pos.	G.	AB.	R.	H.	2B.	3B.	HR.	RBI.	B.A.	PO.	A.	E.	F.A.
1972—Bristol	Appal.	3B-2B-OF	65	235	54	*93	11	6	14	46	*.396	69	124	13	.937
1973—Lakeland	Fla. St.	2B	133	473	63	114	17	6	10	59	.241	205	207	21	.900
1974 Evansville	A. A.	3B-OF-1B	129	484	75	146	26	7	9	57	.302	238	153	22	.947
1974—Detroit	Amer.	OF	13	50	5	10	1	1	3	7	.200	29	0	1	.967
1975—Detroit†	Amer.	OF-1B	122	470	56	111	17	3	8	47	.236	571	41	12	.981
1976—Detroit‡	Amer.	OF-1B	105	294	37	74	8	4	2	16	.252	244	14	2	.992
1977—Seattle	Amer.	1B	159	582	75	159	24	4	22	90	.273	1407	109	12	.992
1978—Seattle§	Amer.	1B-OF	123	444	38	101	18	1	8	56	.227	1107	79	13	.989
1979—Seattle	Amer.	3B-OF-1B	144	525	72	146	21	7	20	74	.278	198	205	22	.948
1980—Seattle	Amer.	OF-3B-1B	146	531	56	146	25	6	11	71	.275	219	22	10	.960
1981—Seattle xy	Amer.	3B-OF-1B	83	252	26	66	10	1	3	22	.262	79	88	7	.960
1982—Oakland	Amer.	1B-OF	120	383	28	92	17	3	8	59	.240	387	32	5	.988
1983—Oakland z	Amer.	1B-OF-3B	69	169	15	32	9	0	1	13	.189	305	16	4	.988
1984—Tacoma	P. C.	1B-3B-OF	124	457	63	134	19	2	7	57	.293	425	85	11	.979
1984—Oakland a	Amer.	1B	20	22	1	7	3	1	0	4	.318	15	2	1	.944
1985—Oakland b	Amer.	OF-3B	14	12	2	0	0	0	0	0	.000	1	0	0	1.000
Major League Totals—12 Years			1118	3734	411	944	153	31	86	459	.253	4562	608	89	.983

Selected by Detroit Tigers' organization in 4th round of free-agent draft, June 6, 1972.
†On disabled list, July 20 to August 6, 1975.
‡Selected by Seattle Mariners in American League expansion draft, November 5, 1976.
§On disabled list, May 24 to June 8, 1978.
xOn disabled list, April 8 to April 21, 1981.
yTraded to Oakland A's for Pitcher Rich Bordi, December 9, 1981.
zOn disabled list, July 24 to September 1, 1983.
aGranted free agency, November 8, 1984; re-signed by A's, January 15, 1985.
bReleased, May 26, 1985.

TANNER JOE MEYER JR.
(Known by middle name.)

Born May 10, 1962, at Kailua, Haw.
Height, 6.03. Weight, 250.
Throws and bats righthanded.
Attended University of Hawaii, Honolulu, Haw.

Led Midwest League in total bases with 264 in 1984.
Named Midwest League Most Valuable Player, 1984.

Year Club	League	Pos.	G.	AB.	R.	H.	2B.	3B.	HR.	RBI.	B.A.	PO.	A.	E.	F.A.
1984—Beloit	Midw.	1B	128	475	73	152	22	0	*30	*102	*.320	560	34	11	.982
1985—El Paso	Texas	1B	131	506	79	154	17	2	*37	123	.304	252	15	6	.978

Selected by California Angels' organization in 8th round of free-agent draft, June 8, 1981.
Selected by Milwaukee Brewers' organization in 5th round of free-agent draft, June 6, 1983.

LAWRENCE WILLIAM MILBOURNE
Name pronounced MILL-born.
(Larry)

Born February 14, 1951, at Port Norris, N.J.
Height, 6.00. Weight, 165.
Throws right and bats left and righthanded.
Attended Glassboro State College, Glassboro, N.J., and Cumberland
County Junior College, Vineland, N.J.
Cousin of George Jamison, linebacker with Baltimore Stars.

Major League stolen bases: 1974 (6), 1975 (1), 1976 (6), 1977 (3), 1978 (5), 1979 (5), 1980 (7), 1981 (2), 1982 (3), 1983 (3). Total—41.

Year Club	League	Pos.	G.	AB.	R.	H.	2B.	3B.	HR.	RBI.	B.A.	PO.	A.	E.	F.A.
1969—Bluefield†	Appal.	SS	●69	246	49	75	10	●6	4	35	.305	94	171	*28	.904
1970—							(Out of Organized Baseball)								

Year Club	League	Pos.	G.	AB.	R.	H.	2B.	3B.	HR.	RBI.	B.A.	PO.	A.	E.	F.A.
1971—Decatur‡	Midw.	*2-S-3	*123	*518	69	*156	23	5	5	38	.301	267	256	27	*.951
1972—Shreveport§	Texas	2B	122	416	50	110	14	5	2	36	.264	273	314	25	.959
1973—Tulsa x	A. A.	2-3-O-S	111	367	55	104	13	6	5	43	.283	158	197	16	.957
1974—Houston	Nat.	2B-SS-OF	112	136	31	38	2	1	0	9	.279	102	148	7	.973
1975—Iowa	A. A.	2B	24	77	9	17	3	1	1	6	.221	33	47	8	.909
1975—Houston	Nat.	2B-SS	73	151	17	32	1	2	1	9	.212	95	136	10	.959
1976—Houston	Nat.	2B	59	145	22	36	4	0	0	7	.248	67	100	6	.965
1976—Memphis y	Int.	2B-SS	71	292	45	95	12	2	5	31	.325	132	245	13	.967
1977—Seattle	Amer.	2B-SS-3B	86	242	24	53	10	0	2	21	.219	120	209	12	.965
1978—Seattle	Amer.	3B-SS-2B	93	234	31	53	6	2	2	20	.226	92	169	9	.967
1979—Seattle	Amer.	SS-2B-3B	123	356	40	99	13	4	2	26	.278	144	265	12	.971
1980—Seattle z	Amer.	SS-3B-2B	106	258	31	68	6	6	0	26	.264	103	195	8	.987
1981—New York	Amer.	SS-2B-3B	61	163	24	51	7	2	1	12	.313	74	121	8	.961
1982—N.Y.a-Min.b-Cle.c.	Amer.	2B-SS-3B	125	416	40	107	13	5	2	26	.257	210	297	18	.966
1983—Philadelphia d	Nat.	2B-SS-3B	41	66	3	16	0	1	0	4	.242	40	48	3	.967
1983—New York e	Amer.	2B-SS-3B	31	70	5	14	4	0	0	2	.200	46	57	1	.990
1984—Seattle f	Amer.	3B-2B-SS	79	211	22	56	5	1	1	22	.265	53	86	12	.921
1985—Calgary gh	P. C.	2B	9	36	5	10	0	0	0	0	.278	2	1	2	.600
National League Totals—4 Years			285	498	73	122	7	4	1	29	.245	304	432	26	.966
American League Totals—8 Years			704	1950	217	501	64	20	10	155	.257	842	1399	80	.966
Major League Totals—11 Years			989	2448	290	623	71	24	11	184	.254	1146	1831	106	.966

Signed as free agent by Baltimore Orioles' organization, June 18, 1969.

†Released, April 7, 1970; signed by Decatur (San Francisco Giants' organization), April 2, 1971.

‡Drafted by Salt Lake City (California Angels' organization), November 29, 1971.

§Drafted by Tulsa (St. Louis Cardinals' organization), November 27, 1972.

xDrafted by Houston Astros, December 3, 1973.

yTraded to Seattle Mariners for Pitcher Roy Thomas, March 30, 1977.

zTraded with a player to be named later to New York Yankees for Catcher Brad Gulden and cash, November 18, 1980; Seattle Mariners traded Gulden back to New York Yankees to complete deal, May 18, 1981.

aTraded with Pitchers John Pacella and Pete Filson to Minnesota Twins for Catcher Butch Wynegar and Pitcher Roger Erickson, May 12, 1982.

bTraded to Cleveland Indians for Outfielder Larry Littleton, July 3, 1982.

cTraded to Philadelphia Phillies for a player to be named later, December 9, 1982; deal settled with cash.

dSold to New York Yankees, July 16, 1983.

eTraded to Seattle Mariners for Pitchers Scott Nielsen and Eric Parent, February 14, 1984.

fOn disabled list, June 25 to July 10, 1984.

gOn Seattle disabled list, April 8 to July 23, 1985; included rehabilitation disability assignment to Calgary, May 7 to May 20 and June 29 to July 5, 1985.

hReleased, August 2, 1985.

DIVISION SERIES RECORD

Year Club	League	Pos.	G.	AB.	R.	H.	2B.	3B.	HR.	RBI.	B.A.	PO.	A.	E.	F.A.
1981—New York	Amer.	SS	5	19	4	6	1	0	0	0	.316	5	14	0	1.000

CHAMPIONSHIP SERIES RECORD

Year Club	League	Pos.	G.	AB.	R.	H.	2B.	3B.	HR.	RBI.	B.A.	PO.	A.	E.	F.A.
1981—New York	Amer.	SS	3	13	4	6	0	0	0	1	.462	2	7	0	1.000

WORLD SERIES RECORD

Year Club	League	Pos.	G.	AB.	R.	H.	2B.	3B.	HR.	RBI.	B.A.	PO.	A.	E.	F.A.
1981—New York	Amer.	SS	6	20	2	5	2	0	0	3	.250	5	16	2	.913

DARRELL KEITH MILLER

Born February 26, 1959, at Washington, D.C.
Height, 6.02. Weight, 200.
Throws and bats righthanded.
Attended California State Poly University, Pomona, Calif.
Brother of Cheryl Miller, member of 1984 U.S. Olympic
Gold Medal women's basketball team and forward at University of Southern California;
and Reggie Miller, forward at University of California at Los Angeles.

Year Club	League	Pos.	G.	AB.	R.	H.	2B.	3B.	HR.	RBI.	B.A.	PO.	A.	E.	F.A.
1979—Idaho Falls	Pion.	C-1B	60	205	35	55	10	2	6	34	.268	254	40	12	.961
1980—Salinas	Calif.	C-1B-OF	64	195	26	56	6	3	4	28	.287	289	57	8	.977
1980—Salt Lake City	P. C.	C	30	101	10	30	2	2	0	11	.297	113	18	6	.956
1981—Holyoke	East.	C-OF-1B	126	443	61	117	26	9	10	62	.264	507	50	24	.959
1982—Holyoke†	East.	OF	119	450	76	118	25	*10	11	60	.262	187	8	8	.961
1983—Edmonton‡	P. C.	O-C-1-3	51	142	29	43	5	1	2	23	.303	146	24	8	.955
1984—Edmonton§	P. C.	C-OF-1B	92	328	65	107	19	9	12	67	.326	270	27	4	.987
1984—California	Amer.	1B-OF	17	41	5	7	0	0	0	1	.171	92	7	1	.990
1985—California x	Amer.	OF-C-3B	51	48	8	18	2	1	2	7	.375	39	3	2	.955
1985—Edmonton	P. C.	OF-C	17	71	10	20	3	1	1	6	.282	43	5	1	.980
Major League Totals—2 Years			68	89	13	25	2	1	2	8	.281	131	10	3	.979

Selected by California Angels' organization in 9th round of free-agent draft, June 5, 1979.

†On disabled list, May 6 to May 20, 1982.

‡On disabled list, May 4 to May 31, 1983.

§On disabled list, July 17 to August 7, 1984.

xOn disabled list, June 13 to July 5, 1985.

RICHARD ALAN MILLER
(Rick)

Born April 19, 1948, at Grand Rapids, Mich.
Height, 6.00. Weight, 180.
Throws and bats lefthanded.
Attended Michigan State University, East Lansing, Mich.
Brother-in-law of Carlton Fisk, catcher with Chicago White Sox.

Major League stolen bases: 1973 (12), 1974 (13), 1975 (3), 1976 (11), 1977 (11), 1978 (3), 1979 (5), 1980 (7), 1981 (3), 1982 (5), 1983 (3), 1984 (1), 1985 (1). Total—78.
Led International League in bases on balls received with 106 in 1971.
Named outfielder on THE SPORTING NEWS American League All-Star fielding team, 1978.
Named outfielder on THE SPORTING NEWS College Baseball All-America Team, 1969.

Year Club	League	Pos.	G.	AB.	R.	H.	2B.	3B.	HR.	RBI.	B.A.	PO.	A.	E.	F.A.
1969—Pittsfield	East.	OF	77	221	25	58	7	1	6	32	.262	150	8	3	.981
1970—Pawtucket	East.	OF	113	381	69	94	16	4	12	56	.247	227	5	5	.979
1971—Louisville	Int.	OF	133	461	79	114	24	2	15	58	.247	267	21	6	.980
1971—Boston	Amer.	OF	15	33	9	11	5	0	1	7	.333	30	1	1	.969
1972—Boston	Amer.	OF	89	98	13	21	4	1	3	15	.214	80	7	3	.967
1973—Boston	Amer.	OF	143	441	65	115	17	7	6	43	.261	301	4	7	.978
1974—Boston	Amer.	OF	114	280	41	73	8	1	5	22	.261	253	7	3	.989
1975—Boston	Amer.	OF	77	108	21	21	2	1	0	15	.194	101	2	2	.981
1976—Boston	Amer.	OF	105	269	40	76	15	3	0	27	.283	220	4	2	.991
1977 Boston†‡	Amer.	OF	86	189	34	48	9	3	0	24	.254	118	5	1	.992
1978—California	Amer.	OF	132	475	66	125	25	4	1	37	.263	353	9	4	.989
1979—California§	Amer.	OF	120	427	60	125	15	5	2	28	.293	349	3	4	.989
1980—California x	Amer.	OF	129	412	52	113	14	3	2	38	.274	299	11	5	.984
1981—Boston	Amer.	OF	97	316	38	92	17	2	2	33	.291	219	5	3	.987
1982—Boston	Amer.	OF	135	409	50	104	13	2	4	38	.254	277	6	5	.983
1983—Boston	Amer.	OF-1B	104	262	41	75	10	2	2	21	.286	151	5	1	.994
1984—Boston	Amer.	OF-1B	95	123	17	32	5	1	0	12	.260	80	5	1	.988
1985—Boston yz	Amer.	OF	41	45	5	15	2	0	0	9	.333	9	0	0	1.000
Major League Totals—15 Years			1482	3887	552	1046	161	35	28	369	.269	2840	74	42	.986

Selected by Boston Red Sox' organization in 2nd round of free-agent draft, June 5, 1969.
†On disabled list, May 3 to May 30, 1977.
‡Granted free agency, November 2, 1977; signed by California Angels, December 21, 1977.
§On disabled list, June 2 to July 9, 1979.
xTraded with Pitcher Mark Clear and Third Baseman Carney Lansford to Boston Red Sox for Shortstop Rick Burleson and Third Baseman Butch Hobson, December 10, 1980.
yOn disabled list, August 3 to September 1, 1985.
zGranted free agency, November 12, 1985.

CHAMPIONSHIP SERIES RECORD

Year Club	League	Pos.	G.	AB.	R.	H.	2B.	3B.	HR.	RBI.	B.A.	PO.	A.	E.	F.A.
1979—California	Amer.	OF	4	16	2	4	0	0	0	0	.250	14	2	0	1.000

WORLD SERIES RECORD

Year Club	League	Pos.	G.	AB.	R.	H.	2B.	3B.	HR.	RBI.	B.A.	PO.	A.	E.	F.A.
1975—Boston	Amer.	OF-PH	3	2	0	0	0	0	0	0	.000	1	0	0	1.000

EDDIE JAMES MILNER JR.

Born May 21, 1955, at Columbus, O.
Height, 5.11. Weight, 170.
Throws and bats lefthanded.
Attended Muskingum College, New Concord, O., and received bachelor of science degree
in business from Central State University, Wilberforce, O. in 1978.
Brother of Hobson Milner, 12th round selection of Minnesota Vikings in 1982 NFL draft;
cousin of John Milner, first baseman-outfielder with New York Mets,
Pittsburgh Pirates and Montreal Expos, 1971 through 1982.

Major League stolen bases: 1982 (18), 1983 (41), 1984 (21), 1985 (35). Total—115.
Tied for Pioneer League lead in double plays by outfielders with 1 in 1976.
Named Florida State League Most Valuable Player, 1978.

Year Club	League	Pos.	G.	AB.	R.	H.	2B.	3B.	HR.	RBI.	B.A.	PO.	A.	E.	F.A.
1976—Billings	Pion.	OF	67	231	51	59	14	3	2	27	.255	*149	*12	7	.958
1977—Shelby	W. Car.	OF	110	414	62	111	15	8	3	30	.268	254	10	10	.964
1978—Tampa	Fla. St.	OF	133	497	79	141	16	*16	8	44	.284	283	7	6	.980
1979—Indianapolis	A. A.	OF	30	98	9	18	0	2	0	5	.184	49	2	2	.962
1979—Nashville	South.	OF	104	369	70	97	12	12	11	51	.263	259	9	5	.982
1980—Indianapolis	A. A.	OF	130	468	63	118	11	7	5	37	.252	*363	6	7	.981
1980—Cincinnati	Nat.	PH-PR	6	3	1	0	0	0	0	0	.000	0	0	0	.000
1981—Indianapolis	A. A.	OF	127	453	69	130	14	6	3	42	.287	228	12	4	.984
1981—Cincinnati	Nat.	OF	8	5	0	1	1	0	0	1	.200	2	0	0	1.000
1982—Cincinnati†	Nat.	OF	113	407	61	109	23	5	4	31	.268	215	8	3	.987
1983—Cincinnati	Nat.	OF	146	502	77	131	23	6	9	33	.261	392	9	4	.990
1984—Cincinnati‡	Nat.	OF	117	336	44	78	8	4	7	29	.232	285	8	5	.983
1985—Cincinnati	Nat.	OF	145	453	82	115	19	7	3	33	.254	340	12	6	.983
Major League Totals—6 Years			535	1706	265	434	74	22	23	127	.254	1234	37	18	.986

Selected by Cincinnati Reds' organization in 21st round of free-agent draft, June 8, 1976.
†On disabled list, August 11 to September 7, 1982.
‡On disabled list, June 30 to August 6, 1984.

GREGORY BRIAN MINTON
(Greg)

Born July 29, 1951, at Lubbock, Tex.
Height, 6.02.   Weight, 191.
Throws right and bats left and righthanded.
Attended San Diego Mesa College, San Diego, Calif.

Major League saves: 1979 (4), 1980 (19), 1981 (21), 1982 (30), 1983 (22), 1984 (19), 1985 (4). Total—119.
Led National League in intentional bases on balls issued with 20 in 1984 and 18 in 1985.
Led National League in games finished in relief with 44 in 1981 and 66 in 1982.
Led Pacific Coast League in wild pitches with 18 in 1977.
Led Pacific Coast League in balks with 6 in 1975.

Year Club	League	G.	IP.	W.	L.	Pct.	H.	R.	ER.	SO.	BB.	ERA.
1970—Billings†	Pioneer	16	40	1	4	.200	37	23	14	36	16	3.15
1971—Waterloo	Midwest	27	124	11	6	.647	118	52	42	117	55	3.05
1972—San Jose‡	California	28	178	12	12	.500	182	117	78	153	77	3.94
1973—Phoenix	P. Coast	5	13	0	0	.000	11	6	6	4	8	4.15
1973—Amarillo	Texas	38	122	5	11	.313	138	87	61	77	48	4.50
1974—Fresno	California	13	96	10	1	.909	85	32	24	81	18	2.25
1974—Amarillo	Texas	6	29	1	4	.200	42	26	19	21	10	5.90
1975—Phoenix	P. Coast	42	177	10	6	.625	178	73	51	76	76	2.59
1975—San Francisco	National	4	17	1	1	.500	19	14	13	6	11	6.88
1976—San Francisco	National	10	26	0	3	.000	32	18	14	7	12	4.85
1976—Phoenix§	P. Coast	13	74	4	5	.444	91	57	46	31	32	5.59
1977—Phoenix	P. Coast	29	161	14	6	*.700	188	93	87	77	70	4.86
1977—San Francisco	National	2	14	1	1	.500	14	8	7	5	4	4.50
1978—Phoenix	P. Coast	14	92	7	4	.636	97	54	46	32	38	4.50
1978—San Francisco	National	11	16	0	1	.000	22	14	14	6	8	7.88
1979—San Francisco x	National	46	80	4	3	.571	59	25	16	33	27	1.80
1980—San Francisco	National	68	91	4	6	.400	81	28	25	42	34	2.47
1981—San Francisco	National	55	84	4	5	.444	84	28	27	29	36	2.89
1982—San Francisco	National	78	123	10	4	.714	108	29	25	58	42	1.83
1983—San Francisco	National	73	106⅔	7	11	.389	117	51	42	38	47	3.54
1984—San Francisco	National	74	124⅓	4	9	.308	130	60	52	48	57	3.76
1985—San Francisco	National	68	96⅔	5	4	.556	98	42	38	37	54	3.54
Major League Totals—11 Years		489	778⅔	40	48	.455	764	317	273	309	332	3.16

Selected by Kansas City Royals' organization in 3rd round of free-agent draft, January 17, 1970.
†Appeared in two games as an outfielder with one putout.
‡Traded to San Francisco Giants for Catcher Fran Healy, April 2, 1973.
§On disabled list, July 24 to August 5, 1976.
xOn disabled list, March 26 to May 31, 1979.

ALL-STAR GAME RECORD

Year League	IP.	W.	L.	Pct.	H.	R.	ER.	SO.	BB.	ERA.
1982—National	⅔	0	0	.000	0	0	0	0	1	0.00

PAUL THOMAS MIRABELLA

Born March 20, 1954, at Belleville, N. J.
Height, 6.02. Weight, 196.
Throws and bats lefthanded.
Attended Montclair State University, Upper Montclair, N. J.

Major League saves: 1982 (3), 1984 (3). Total—6
Tied for Pacific Coast League lead in balks with 4 in 1978.
Tied for Texas League lead in shutouts with 4 and games started by pitchers with 26 in 1977.
Tied for Western Carolinas League lead in balks with 5 in 1976.

Year Club	League	G.	IP.	W.	L.	Pct.	H.	R.	ER.	SO.	BB.	ERA.
1976—Asheville	W. Carol.	22	149	10	7	.588	149	77	66	*136	69	3.99
1977—Tulsa	Texas	26	176	12	7	.632	167	90	75	112	70	3.83
1978—Tucson	P. Coast	22	143	9	6	.600	158	77	63	85	68	3.97
1978—Texas†	American	10	28	3	2	.600	30	18	18	23	17	5.79
1979—Columbus‡	Int'national	22	144	11	7	.611	129	75	62	98	50	3.88
1979—New York‡	American	10	14	0	4	.000	16	15	14	4	10	9.00
1980—Syracuse	Int'national	4	31	1	2	.333	28	13	9	23	8	2.61
1980—Toronto	American	33	131	5	12	.294	151	73	63	53	66	4.33
1981—Syracuse	Int'national	22	153	11	7	.611	150	63	52	79	53	3.06
1981—Toronto§x	American	8	15	0	0	.000	20	16	12	9	7	7.20
1982—Texas y	American	40	50⅔	1	1	.500	46	28	27	29	22	4.80
1983—Rochester	Int'national	19	76⅓	3	5	.375	87	44	31	32	29	3.66
1983—Baltimore z	American	3	9⅔	0	0	.000	9	6	6	4	7	5.59
1983—Portland a	P. Coast	5	14⅓	0	1	.000	19	13	12	11	10	7.53
1984—Seattle	American	52	68	2	5	.286	74	39	33	41	32	4.37
1985—Calgary	P. Coast	53	68⅓	4	4	.556	84	34	31	42	29	4.08
1985—Seattle	American	10	13⅔	0	0	.000	9	4	2	8	4	1.32
Major League Totals—8 Years		166	330	11	24	.314	355	199	175	171	165	4.77

Selected by Minnesota Twins' organization in 16th round of free-agent draft, June 4, 1975.
Selected by Texas Rangers' organization in secondary phase of free-agent draft, January 7, 1976.
†Traded with Pitchers Mike Griffin and Dave Righetti and Outfielders Juan Beniquez and Greg Jemison to New York Yankees for Pitchers Sparky Lyle, Larry McCall and Dave Rajsich, Catcher Mike Heath, Shortstop Domingo Ramos and cash, November 10, 1978.

‡Traded with First Baseman Chris Chambliss and Infielder Damaso Garcia to Toronto Blue Jays for Catcher Rick Cerone, Pitcher Tom Underwood and Outfielder Ted Wilborn, November 1, 1979.
§Traded to Chicago Cubs' organization for a player to be named later, December 28, 1981; Toronto Blue Jays' organization acquired Pitcher Dave Geisel to complete deal, March 25, 1982.
xTraded with a player to be named later and cash to Texas Rangers for Second Baseman Bump Wills, March 26, 1982; Texas organization acquired Pitcher Paul Semall to complete deal, April 21, 1982.
yReleased, March 26, 1983; signed by Rochester (Baltimore Orioles' organization), April 16, 1983.
zSold to Portland (Philadelphia Phillies' organization), August 12, 1983.
aGranted free agency, October 20, 1983; signed by Seattle Mariners, January 23, 1984.

CHARLES ROSS MITCHELL
(Charlie)

Born June 24, 1962, at Dickson, Tenn.
Height, 6.03. Weight, 170.
Throws and bats righthanded.
Attended Columbia State Community College, Columbia, Tenn.
Brother of John Mitchell, pitcher in New York Mets' organization.

Led International League in games finished in relief with 56 and tied for lead in intentional bases on balls issued with 8 in 1985.

Year Club	League	G.	IP.	W.	L.	Pct.	H.	R.	ER.	SO.	BB.	ERA.
1982—Elmira	NYP	33	00⅓	4	3	.571	70	34	26	45	14	3.53
1983—New Britain	Eastern	49	100	2	4	.333	82	39	32	54	36	2.88
1984—Pawtucket	Int'national	37	59⅔	10	4	.714	48	20	14	43	14	2.11
1984—Boston	American	10	16⅓	0	0	.000	14	7	5	7	6	2.76
1985—Pawtucket	Int'national	*63	111⅔	5	9	.357	117	39	36	65	43	2.90
1985—Boston†	American	2	1⅔	0	0	.000	5	3	3	2	0	16.20
Major League Totals—2 Years		12	18	0	0	.000	19	10	8	9	6	4.00

Selected by Boston Red Sox' organization in 4th round of free-agent draft, January 12, 1982.
†Traded to Minnesota Twins for Outfielder Mike Stenhouse, December 12, 1985.

KEVIN DARRELL MITCHELL

Born January 13, 1962, at San Diego, Calif.
Height, 5.11. Weight, 210.
Throws and bats righthanded.

Led International League third basemen in assists with 215 in 1984.

Year Club	League	Pos.	G.	AB.	R.	H.	2B.	3B.	HR.	RBI.	B.A.	PO.	A.	E.	F.A.
1981—Kingsport	Appal.	3B-OF	62	221	39	74	9	2	7	45	.335	44	102	18	.890
1982—Lynchburg†	Carol.	3B	29	85	19	27	5	1	1	16	.318	11	33	10	.815
1983—Jackson	Texas	*3B-OF	120	441	75	132	25	2	15	85	.299	81	*224	21	.936
1984—Tidewater	Int.	3B-1B-OF	120	432	51	105	21	3	10	54	.243	114	220	22	.938
1984—New York	Nat.	3B	7	14	0	3	0	0	0	1	.214	1	4	1	.833
1985—Tidewater‡	Int.	*3B-1B	95	348	44	101	24	2	9	43	.290	56	209	*22	.923
Major League Totals—1 Year			7	14	0	3	0	0	0	1	.214	1	4	1	.833

Signed as free agent by New York Mets' organization, November 16, 1980.
†On disabled list, July 21, 1982 through remainder of season.
‡On disabled list, July 12 to July 30, 1985.

JOHN JOSEPH MIZEROCK

Name pronounced MIZZ-rock.

Born December 8, 1960, at Punxsutawney, Pa.
Height, 5.11. Weight, 190.
Throws right and bats lefthanded.

Led Southern League in intentional bases on balls received with 12 in 1982.
Led Southern League catchers in putouts with 762 and total chances with 865 in 1982.
Led Florida State League catchers in fielding percentage with .993 and passed balls with 13 in 1981.
Tied for Florida State League lead in double plays by catchers with 8 in 1980.

Year Club	League	Pos.	G.	AB.	R.	H.	2B.	3B.	HR.	RBI.	B.A.	PO.	A.	E.	F.A.
1979—Daytona Beach	Fla. St.	C	53	152	13	39	6	1	3	12	.257	255	25	5	.982
1980—Daytona Beach	Fla. St.	C	99	299	37	66	11	1	2	39	.221	532	52	9	.985
1981—Daytona Beach	Fla. St.	C-1B-OF	92	304	36	67	11	0	1	42	.220	515	50	4	.993
1981—Columbus	South.	C	11	35	6	8	2	0	0	2	.229	80	11	2	.979
1982—Columbus	South.	*C-1B	128	420	46	96	14	1	12	48	.229	785	*87	17	.981
1983—Houston†	Nat.	C	33	85	8	13	4	1	1	10	.153	154	24	6	.967
1983—Tucson	P. C.	C-1B	53	176	18	46	12	2	5	31	.261	298	29	5	.985
1984—Columbus‡	South.	C-O-1-3	61	181	19	43	7	0	4	23	.238	165	19	5	.974
1985—Tucson	P. C.	C	75	223	24	47	11	1	1	19	.211	333	43	5	.987
1985—Houston	Nat.	C	15	38	6	9	4	0	0	6	.237	77	8	3	.966
Major League Totals—2 Years			48	123	14	22	8	1	1	16	.179	231	32	9	.967

Selected by Houston Astros' organization in 1st round (eighth player selected) of free-agent draft, June 5, 1979.
†On disabled list, July 3 to July 26, 1983.
‡On Houston disabled list, April 1 to June 20, 1984; included rehabilitation disability assignment to Columbus, May 31 to June 19, 1984.

PAUL LEO MOLITOR

Born August 22, 1956, at St. Paul, Minn.
Height, 6.00. Weight, 175.
Throws and bats righthanded.
Attended University of Minnesota, Minneapolis, Minn.

Hit three home runs in a game, May 12, 1982.
Major League stolen bases: 1978 (30), 1979 (33), 1980 (34), 1981 (10), 1982 (41), 1983 (41), 1984 (1), 1985 (21). Total—211.
Led American League third basemen in errors with 29 and double plays with 48 in 1982.
Named American League Rookie Player of the Year by THE SPORTING NEWS, 1978.
Named Midwest League Most Valuable Player, 1977.
Received reported $100,000 bonus to sign with Milwaukee Brewers, 1977.
Named shortstop on THE SPORTING NEWS College Baseball All-America Team, 1977.

Year Club League	Pos.	G.	AB.	R.	H.	2B.	3B.	HR.	RBI.	B.A.	PO.	A.	E.	F.A.
1977—Burlington .... Midw.	SS	64	228	52	79	12	0	8	50	.346	83	207	28	.912
1978—Milwaukee............ Amer.	2B-SS-3B	125	521	73	142	26	4	6	45	.273	253	401	22	.967
1979—Milwaukee............ Amer.	2B-SS	140	584	88	188	27	16	9	62	.322	309	440	16	.979
1980—Milwaukee†........... Amer.	2B-SS-3B	111	450	81	137	29	2	9	37	.304	260	336	20	.968
1981—Milwaukee‡.......... Amer.	OF	64	251	45	67	11	0	2	19	.267	119	4	3	.976
1982—Milwaukee............ Amer.	3B-SS	160	∗666	∗136	201	26	8	19	71	.302	134	350	32	.938
1983—Milwaukee............ Amer.	3B	152	608	95	164	28	6	15	47	.270	105	343	16	.966
1984—Milwaukee§.......... Amer.	3B	13	46	3	10	1	0	0	6	.217	7	21	2	.933
1985—Milwaukee x .... Amer.	3B	140	576	93	171	28	3	10	48	.297	126	263	19	.953
Major League Totals—8 Years.................		905	3702	614	1080	176	39	70	335	.292	1313	2158	130	.964

Selected by St. Louis Cardinals' organization in 28th round of free-agent draft, June 5, 1974.
Selected by Milwaukee Brewers' organization in 1st round (third player selected) of free-agent draft, June 7, 1977.
†On disabled list, June 24 to July 18, 1980.
‡On disabled list, May 3 to August 12, 1981.
§On disabled list, May 2, 1984 through remainder of season.
xOn disabled list, August 13 to August 28, 1985.

DIVISION SERIES RECORD

Year Club League	Pos.	G.	AB.	R.	H.	2B.	3B.	HR.	RBI.	B.A.	PO.	A.	E.	F.A.
1981—Milwaukee............ Amer.	OF	5	20	2	5	0	0	1	1	.250	12	7	0	1.000

CHAMPIONSHIP SERIES RECORD

Tied American League Championship Series record for most home runs, five-game Series (2), 1982.

Year Club League	Pos.	G.	AB.	R.	H.	2B.	3B.	HR.	RBI.	B.A.	PO.	A.	E.	F.A.
1982—Milwaukee............ Amer.	3B	5	19	4	6	1	0	2	5	.316	4	11	2	.882

WORLD SERIES RECORD

Established World Series records for most hits, game (5), October 12, 1982; most one-base hits, game (5), October 12, 1982.
Tied World Series records for most at-bats, nine-inning game (6), October 12, 1982; most hits, two consecutive games, one Series (7), October 12, 13, 1982.

Year Club League	Pos.	G.	AB.	R.	H.	2B.	3B.	HR.	RBI.	B.A.	PO.	A.	E.	F.A.
1982—Milwaukee............ Amer.	3B	7	31	5	11	0	0	0	3	.355	4	9	0	1.000

ALL-STAR GAME RECORD

Year League	Pos.	AB.	R.	H.	2B.	3B.	HR.	RBI.	B.A.	PO.	A.	E.	F.A.
1985—American	3B-OF	1	0	0	0	0	0	0	.000	0	0	0	.000

Named to American League All-Star Team in 1980; replaced due to injury.

JOHN JOSEPH MONTEFUSCO JR.

Name pronounced Mon-tuh-FYOOS-koh.
Born May 25, 1950, at Long Branch, N. J.
Height, 6.01. Weight, 185.
Throws and bats righthanded.
Attended Brookdale Community College, Lincroft, N. J.

Pitched 9-0 no-hit victory against Atlanta Braves, September 29, 1976.
Hit home run on first official major league time at bat, September 3, 1974.
Struck out eight consecutive batters against Salt Lake City, August 11, 1974.
Major League saves: 1981 (1), 1983 (4). Total—5.
Tied for National League lead in shutouts by pitchers with 6 in 1976.
Led Texas League in shutouts with 4 in 1974.
Tied for Pacific Coast League lead in shutouts with 3 in 1974.
Named National League Rookie of the Year by Baseball Writers' Association of America, 1975.
Named National League Rookie Pitcher of the Year by THE SPORTING NEWS, 1975.

Year Club	League	G.	IP.	W.	L.	Pct.	H.	R.	ER.	SO.	BB.	ERA.
1973—Decatur	Midwest	24	120	9	2	.818	94	40	29	126	44	2.18
1974—Amarillo..	Texas	19	144	8	9	.471	143	61	50	107	37	3.13
1974—Phoenix	P. Coast	11	77	7	3	.700	60	35	28	90	26	3.27
1974—San Francisco................................	National	7	39	3	2	.600	41	22	21	34	19	4.85
1975—San Francisco................................	National	35	244	15	9	.625	210	85	78	215	86	2.88
1976—San Francisco................................	National	37	253	16	14	.533	224	90	80	172	74	2.85
1977—San Francisco†..............................	National	26	157	7	12	.368	170	82	61	110	46	3.50
1978—San Francisco	National	36	239	11	9	.550	233	110	101	177	68	3.80

Year Club	League	G.	IP.	W.	L.	Pct.	H.	R.	ER.	SO.	BB.	ERA.
1979—San Francisco‡	National	22	137	3	8	.273	145	64	60	76	51	3.94
1980—San Francisco§x	National	22	113	4	8	.333	120	61	55	85	39	4.38
1981—Atlanta y	National	26	77	2	3	.400	76	32	30	34	27	3.51
1982—San Diego	National	32	184⅓	10	11	.476	177	93	82	83	41	4.00
1983—San Diego z	National	31	95⅓	9	4	.692	94	38	35	52	32	3.30
1983—New York	American	6	38	5	0	1.000	39	14	14	15	10	3.32
1984—New York a	American	11	55⅓	5	3	.625	55	26	22	23	13	3.58
1984—Columbus	Int'national	3	13	1	0	1.000	6	1	1	7	1	0.69
1985—New York bc	American	3	7	0	0	.000	12	8	8	2	2	10.29
National League Totals—10 Years		274	1538⅔	80	80	.500	1489	677	603	1038	483	3.53
American League Totals—3 Years		20	100⅓	10	3	.769	106	48	44	40	25	3.95
Major League Totals—12 Years		294	1639	90	83	.520	1595	725	647	1078	508	3.55

Signed as free agent by San Francisco Giants' organization, October 6, 1972.

†On disabled list, May 27 to July 6, 1977.

‡On disabled list, April 26 to June 13, 1979.

§On disabled list, July 17 to August 24, 1980.

xTraded with Outfielder Craig Landis to Atlanta Braves for Pitcher Doyle Alexander, December 12, 1980.

yGranted free agency, November 13, 1981; signed by San Diego Padres, March 6, 1982.

zTraded to New York Yankees for two players to be named later, August 26, 1983; San Diego Padres acquired Pitcher Dennis Rasmussen and Second Baseman Edwin Rodriguez to complete deal, September 12, 1983.

aOn disabled list, April 29 to August 16, 1984; included rehabilitation disability assignment to Columbus, August 4 to August 16, 1984.

bOn disabled list, April 1 to April 29 and May 15, 1985 through remainder of season.

cReleased, November 12, 1985.

ALL-STAR GAME RECORD

Year League	IP.	W.	L.	Pct.	H.	R.	ER.	SO.	BB.	ERA.
1976—National	2	0	0	.000	0	0	0	2	2	0.00

RICHARD MONTELEONE
(Rich)

Born March 22, 1963, at Tampa, Fla.
Height, 6.02. Weight, 205.
Throws and bats righthanded.
Led Appalachian League pitchers in home runs allowed with 8 in 1982.

Year Club	League	G.	IP.	W.	L.	Pct.	H.	R.	ER.	SO.	BB.	ERA.
1982—Bristol	Ap'lachian	12	71⅔	4	6	.400	66	41	31	52	23	3.89
1983—Lakeland	Florida St.	24	142⅓	9	8	.529	146	80	65	124	80	4.11
1983—Birmingham	Southern	3	15	1	1	.500	25	12	12	9	6	7.20
1984—Birmingham	Southern	19	123⅔	7	8	.467	116	69	64	74	67	4.66
1984—Evansville	Am. Assoc.	11	64	5	3	.625	64	33	32	42	36	4.50
1985—Nashville	Am. Assoc.	27	145⅓	6	12	.333	149	89	82	97	87	5.08

Selected by Detroit Tigers' organization in 1st round (20th player selected) of free-agent draft, June 7, 1982.

†Traded to Seattle Mariners for Third Baseman Darnell Coles, December 12, 1985.

REGINALD LAVANCE MONTGOMERY
(Reggie)

Born August 4, 1962, at Los Angeles, Calif.
Height, 6.04. Weight, 220.
Throws and bats righthanded.
Attended University of Southern California, Los Angeles, Calif.

Year Club	League	Pos.	G.	AB.	R.	H.	2B.	3B.	HR.	RBI.	B.A.	PO.	A.	E.	F.A.
1983—Salem	N'west	OF-1B	68	265	39	81	10	4	5	∗47	.306	140	18	7	.958
1984—Redwood	Calif.	OF	120	447	81	130	28	1	14	79	.291	152	5	3	∗.981
1985—Midland†	Texas	OF	112	450	57	130	23	1	22	101	.289	119	15	5	.964

Selected by Chicago White Sox' organization in 1st round (eighth player selected) of free-agent draft, January 13, 1981.

Selected by California Angels' organization in 1st round (26th player selected) of free-agent draft, June 8, 1981.

Selected by California Angels' organization in 25th round of free-agent draft, June 6, 1983.

†On disabled list, August 8, 1985 through remainder of season.

WILLIAM CRAIG MOONEYHAM
(Bill)

Born August 16, 1960, at Livermore, Calif.
Height, 6.00. Weight, 175.
Throws and bats righthanded.
Attended Merced Community College, Merced, Calif.

Year Club	League	G.	IP.	W.	L.	Pct.	H.	R.	ER.	SO.	BB.	ERA.
1980—Salinas	California	12	74	4	7	.364	66	44	31	88	64	3.77
1981—Holyoke	Eastern	25	135	9	11	.450	124	90	68	155	∗131	4.53
1982—Holyoke†	Eastern	8	49	2	3	.400	44	26	23	46	24	4.22
1983—Nashua	Eastern	19	110	8	6	.571	99	67	56	76	83	4.58
1983—Edmonton	P. Coast	7	35⅔	2	0	1.000	51	39	39	26	22	9.84
1984—Edmonton‡§	P. Coast	16	72⅔	5	3	.625	99	55	48	40	46	5.94

Year Club	League	G.	IP.	W.	L.	Pct.	H.	R.	ER.	SO.	BB.	ERA.
1985—Modesto.........................	California	8	14⅓	2	0	1.000	9	3	2	13	8	1.26
1985—Huntsville	Southern	10	36⅓	2	1	.667	27	13	8	28	15	1.98
1985—Tacoma..........................	P. Coast	21	60⅓	2	6	.250	56	28	28	49	38	4.18

Selected by Montreal Expos' organization in 6th round of free-agent draft, June 6, 1978.
Selected by St. Louis Cardinals' organization in secondary phase of free-agent draft, January 9, 1979.
Selected by New York Mets' organization in secondary phase of free-agent draft, June 5, 1979.
Selected by Seattle Mariners' organization in secondary phase of free-agent draft, January 8, 1980.
Selected by California Angels' organization in secondary phase of free-agent draft, June 3, 1980.
†On disabled list, March 26 to July 22, 1982.
‡On disabled list, May 1 to May 21, 1984.
§Released, March 31, 1985; signed by Modesto (Oakland A's organization), April 26, 1985.

CHARLES WILLIAM MOORE JR.
(Charlie)

Born June 21, 1953, at Birmingham, Ala.
Height, 5.11. Weight, 180.
Throws and bats righthanded.
Attended Mesa Junior College, Mesa, Ariz., and University of Alabama, Birmingham, Ala.
Son of Charles William Moore, Sr., minor league pitcher, 1948 through 1952.

Major League stolen bases: 1974 (3), 1975 (1), 1976 (1), 1977 (1), 1978 (4), 1979 (8), 1980 (10), 1981 (1), 1982 (2), 1983 (11), 1985 (4). Total—46.
Hit for the cycle, October 1, 1980.
Led American League outfielders in double plays with 6 in 1982.
Led American League in passed balls with 14 in 1977.
Led Midwest League catchers in putouts with 721, assists with 91, double plays with 12 and tied for lead in passed balls with 30 in 1972.
Led New York-Pennsylvania League in passed balls with 16 in 1971.

Year Club	League	Pos.	G.	AB.	R.	H.	2B.	3B.	HR.	RBI.	B.A.	PO.	A.	E.	F.A.
1971—Newark	NYP	C	60	209	36	62	12	3	6	27	.297	★439	★34	5	.990
1972—Danville	Midw.	★C-1B	106	348	56	90	14	4	12	44	.259	723	92	★25	.970
1973—Shreveport	Texas	C	76	271	47	69	14	2	8	45	.255	402	46	14	.970
1973—Evansville	A. A.	C	50	178	27	52	9	1	7	25	.292	274	30	2	.993
1973—Milwaukee............	Amer.	C	8	27	0	5	0	1	0	3	.185	48	5	1	.981
1974—Milwaukee............	Amer.	C	72	204	17	50	10	4	0	19	.245	229	28	4	.985
1975—Milwaukee............	Amer.	C-OF	73	241	26	70	20	1	1	29	.290	234	23	10	.963
1976—Milwaukee............	Amer.	C-O-3	87	241	33	46	7	4	3	16	.191	249	45	9	.970
1977—Milwaukee............	Amer.	C	138	375	42	93	15	6	5	45	.248	566	78	●13	.980
1978—Milwaukee............	Amer.	C	96	268	30	72	7	1	5	31	.269	314	41	6	.983
1979—Milwaukee............	Amer.	C	111	337	45	101	16	2	5	38	.300	414	58	10	.979
1980—Milwaukee............	Amer.	C	111	320	42	93	13	2	2	30	.291	319	28	4	.989
1981—Milwaukee............	Amer.	C-OF	48	156	16	47	8	3	1	9	.301	160	7	5	.973
1982—Milwaukee............	Amer.	OF-C-2B	133	456	53	116	22	4	6	45	.254	317	23	7	.980
1983—Milwaukee............	Amer.	OF-C	151	529	65	150	27	6	2	49	.284	309	10	7	.979
1984—Milwaukee†..........	Amer.	OF-C	70	188	13	44	7	1	2	17	.234	145	3	3	.980
1985—Milwaukee............	Amer.	C-OF	105	349	35	81	13	4	0	31	.232	511	54	13	.978
Major League Totals—13 Years...............			1203	3691	417	968	165	39	32	362	.262	3815	413	92	.979

Selected by Milwaukee Brewers' organization in 4th round of free-agent draft, June 8, 1971.
†On disabled list, July 6 to July 23, 1984.

DIVISION SERIES RECORD

Year Club	League	Pos.	G.	AB.	R.	H.	2B.	3B.	HR.	RBI.	B.A.	PO.	A.	E.	F.A.
1981—Milwaukee............	Amer.	DH-OF	4	9	0	2	0	0	0	1	.222	7	0	0	1.000

CHAMPIONSHIP SERIES RECORD

Year Club	League	Pos.	G.	AB.	R.	H.	2B.	3B.	HR.	RBI.	B.A.	PO.	A.	E.	F.A.
1982—Milwaukee............	Amer.	OF	5	13	3	6	0	0	0	0	.462	7	1	0	1.000

WORLD SERIES RECORD

Tied World Series record for most putouts by right fielder, inning (3), October 12, 1982 (eighth inning).

Year Club	League	Pos.	G.	AB.	R.	H.	2B.	3B.	HR.	RBI.	B.A.	PO.	A.	E.	F.A.
1982—Milwaukee............	Amer.	OF	7	26	3	9	3	0	0	2	.346	13	0	0	1.000

DONNIE RAY MOORE

Born February 13, 1954, at Lubbock, Tex.
Height, 6.00. Weight, 185.
Throws right and bats lefthanded.
Attended Ranger Junior College, Ranger, Tex.
Cousin of Hubie Brooks, shortstop with Montreal Expos.

Major League saves: 1978 (4), 1979 (1), 1982 (1), 1983 (6), 1984 (16), 1985 (31). Total—59.
Led American Association in home runs allowed with 25 in 1976.
Led Texas League pitchers in games started with 27 and tied for lead in shutouts with 3 and home runs allowed with 16 in 1975.
Received reported $50,000 bonus to sign with Chicago Cubs, 1973.

Year Club	League	G.	IP.	W.	L.	Pct.	H.	R.	ER.	SO.	BB.	ERA.
1973—Bradenton Cubs	Gulf Coast	4	10	0	1	.000	9	5	4	6	6	3.60
1974—Key West†	Florida St.	26	174	11	12	.478	167	73	54	97	69	2.79

Year Club	League	G.	IP.	W.	L.	Pct.	H.	R.	ER.	SO.	BB.	ERA.
1974—Midland	Texas	5	22	0	4	.000	32	18	17	9	5	6.95
1975—Midland	Texas	28	●185	14	8	.636	191	79	61	123	67	2.97
1975—Chicago	National	4	9	0	0	.000	12	4	4	4	4	4.00
1976—Wichita	Am. Assoc.	24	152	7	11	.389	170	96	80	92	61	4.74
1977—Wichita	Am. Assoc.	11	66	4	4	.500	68	38	36	34	22	4.91
1977—Chicago	National	27	49	4	2	.667	51	27	22	34	18	4.04
1978—Chicago	National	71	103	9	7	.563	117	55	47	50	31	4.11
1979—Wichita	Am. Assoc.	5	29	1	3	.250	29	26	26	16	20	8.07
1979—Chicago‡	National	39	73	1	4	.200	95	46	42	43	25	5.18
1980—St. Louis	National	11	22	1	1	.500	25	15	15	10	5	6.14
1980—Springfield	Am. Assoc.	14	85	6	5	.545	74	32	29	49	32	3.07
1981—Springfield§xy	Am. Assoc.	21	108	8	6	.571	115	49	41	47	31	3.42
1981—Milwaukee	American	3	4	0	0	.000	4	3	3	2	4	6.75
1982—Richmond	Int'national	36	58	5	3	.625	51	17	14	45	18	2.29
1982—Atlanta	National	16	27⅔	3	1	.750	32	13	13	17	7	4.23
1983—Richmond	Int'national	12	16⅔	0	2	.000	12	6	6	9	7	3.24
1983—Atlanta z	National	43	68⅔	2	3	.400	72	30	28	41	10	3.67
1984—Atlanta ab	National	47	64⅓	4	5	.444	63	27	21	47	18	2.94
1985—California c	American	65	103	8	8	.500	91	28	22	72	21	1.92
National League Totals—8 Years		258	416⅔	24	23	.511	467	217	192	250	118	4.15
American League Totals—2 Years		68	107	8	8	.500	95	31	25	74	25	2.10
Major League Totals—10 Years		326	523⅔	32	31	.508	562	248	217	324	143	3.73

Selected by Boston Red Sox' organization in 10th round of free-agent draft, June 6, 1972.
Signed as free agent by Chicago Cubs' organization, June 3, 1973.
†Appeared in two games as an outfielder with two putouts.
‡Traded to St. Louis Cardinals for Second Baseman Mike Tyson, October 17, 1979.
§On temporary inactive list, April 14 to May 11, 1981.
xSold conditionally to Milwaukee Brewers, September 3, 1981; returned, October 23, 1981.
yTraded to Atlanta Braves' organization for Pitcher Dan Morogiello, February 1, 1982.
zOn disabled list, August 3 to August 24, 1983.
aOn disabled list, April 19 to May 24, 1984.
bSelected by California Angels in player compensation pool draft, January 24, 1985. (California received compensation for Baltimore Orioles' signing free agent Outfielder Fred Lynn, a Type A player, December 11, 1984.)
cGranted free agency, November 12, 1985; re-signed by Angels, January 8, 1986.

CHAMPIONSHIP SERIES RECORD

Year Club	League	G.	IP.	W.	L.	Pct.	H.	R.	ER.	SO.	BB.	ERA.
1982—Atlanta	National	2	2⅔	0	0	.000	2	0	0	1	0	0.00

ALL-STAR GAME RECORD

Year League		IP.	W.	L.	Pct.	H.	R.	ER.	SO.	BB.	ERA.
1985—American		2	0	0	.000	0	0	0	1	0	0.00

MICHAEL WAYNE MOORE
(Mike)

Born November 26, 1959, at Eakly, Okla.
Height, 6.04. Weight, 205.
Throws and bats righthanded.
Attended Oral Roberts University, Tulsa, Okla.
Received reported $100,000 bonus to sign with Seattle Mariners, 1981.
Named righthanded pitcher on THE SPORTING NEWS College Baseball All-America Team, 1981.

Year Club	League	G.	IP.	W.	L.	Pct.	H.	R.	ER.	SO.	BB.	ERA.
1981—Lynn	Eastern	13	94	6	5	.545	83	42	38	81	34	3.64
1982—Seattle	American	28	144⅓	7	14	.333	159	91	86	73	79	5.36
1982—Salt Lake City	P. Coast	1	8	0	0	.000	9	4	4	6	5	4.50
1983—Seattle	American	22	128	6	8	.429	130	75	67	108	60	4.71
1983—Salt Lake City	P. Coast	11	82⅓	4	4	.500	78	48	33	80	54	3.61
1984—Seattle	American	34	212	7	17	.292	236	127	117	158	85	4.97
1985—Seattle	American	35	247	17	10	.630	230	100	95	155	70	3.46
Major League Totals—4 Years		119	731⅓	37	49	.430	755	393	365	494	294	4.49

Selected by St. Louis Cardinals' organization in 3rd round of free-agent draft, June 6, 1978.
Selected by Seattle Mariners' organization in 1st round (first player selected) of free-agent draft, June 8, 1981.

ROBERT DEVELL MOORE
(Bob)

Born November 8, 1958, at Jena, La.
Height, 6.04. Weight, 190.
Throws and bats righthanded.

Year Club	League	G.	IP.	W.	L.	Pct.	H.	R.	ER.	SO.	BB.	ERA.
1976—Boise	Northwest	14	22	0	0	.000	23	23	13	20	18	5.32
1977—Medicine Hat	Pioneer	9	45	0	6	.000	55	59	37	45	50	7.40
1977—Modesto†	California	10	23	0	1	.000	24	27	19	28	32	7.43
1978—Modesto	California	23	117	2	10	.167	102	104	87	123	136	6.69
1979—Waterbury	Eastern	17	85	5	7	.417	86	64	56	42	69	5.93
1980—West Haven	Eastern	5	23	0	4	.000	32	25	23	7	15	9.00

Year Club	League	G.	IP.	W.	L.	Pct.	H.	R.	ER.	SO.	BB.	ERA.
1980—Modesto	California	18	109	4	6	.400	107	72	56	72	84	4.62
1981—Modesto‡-San Jose	California	30	190	9	★15	.375	176	122	108	169	115	5.12
1982—Madison	Midwest	9	52⅓	3	5	.375	47	34	25	41	29	4.30
1982—Modesto	California	7	14	3	1	.750	11	2	1	8	4	0.64
1982—West Haven§x	Eastern	16	47⅓	1	3	.250	55	41	31	34	24	5.89
1983—Glens Falls y	Eastern	24	63	2	6	.250	82	54	46	59	40	6.57
1983—Stockton z	California	5	25⅔	1	2	.333	25	13	10	15	5	3.51
1984—Shreveport	Texas	52	85⅓	7	5	.583	85	36	29	69	24	3.06
1984—Phoenix	P. Coast	6	14⅓	1	2	.333	16	10	10	8	10	6.28
1985—Phoenix	P. Coast	50	79⅔	6	2	.750	69	31	31	60	41	3.50
1985—San Francisco	National	11	16⅔	0	0	.000	18	6	6	10	10	3.24
Major League Totals—1 Year		11	16⅔	0	0	.000	18	6	6	10	10	3.24

Selected by Oakland A's organization in 11th round of free-agent draft, June 8, 1976.
†On disabled list, May 18 to May 28, 1977.
‡Loaned to San Jose (Co-op), May 7, 1981; returned, August 31, 1981.
§On disabled list, August 6 to August 16, 1982.
xTraded to Chicago White Sox' organization for Pitcher Jesse Anderson, December 8, 1982.
yReleased, July 14, 1983; signed by Stockton (Milwaukee Brewers' organization), August 5, 1983.
zReleased, March 28, 1984; signed by Shreveport (San Francisco Giants' organization), April 2, 1984.

WILLIAM ROSS MOORE
(Bill)

Born October 10, 1960, at Los Angeles, Calif.
Height, 6.01. Weight, 185.
Throws left and bats righthanded.
Attended California State University, Fullerton, Calif.

Led Florida State League in total bases with 245, bases on balls received with 112, slugging percentage with .506, game-winning RBIs with 17 and tied for lead in intentional bases on balls received with 11 in 1984.

Year Club	League	Pos.	G.	AB.	R.	H.	2B.	3B.	HR.	RBI.	B.A.	PO.	A.	E.	F.A.
1983—Calgary	Pion.	OF-1B	59	199	63	72	19	1	13	51	.362	125	12	6	.958
1984—W. Palm Beach	Fla. St.	OF-1B	●143	484	★102	145	26	4	★22	94	.300	300	14	7	.978
1985—Jacksonville	South.	OF-1B	140	509	83	132	30	2	33	104	.259	311	21	9	.974

Selected by Kansas City Royals' organization in 10th round for free-agent draft, June 5, 1979.
Selected by Montreal Expos' organization in 6th round of free-agent draft, June 6, 1983.

BOBBY KEITH MORELAND
(Known by middle name.)

Born May 2, 1954, at Dallas, Tex.
Height, 6.00. Weight, 200.
Throws and bats righthanded.
Attended University of Texas, Austin, Texas.

Major League stolen bases: 1980 (3), 1981 (1), 1984 (1), 1985 (12). Total—17.
Led American Association in sacrifice flies with 10 in 1978 and with 13 in 1979.
Led American Association catchers in double plays with 10 in 1978.
Led American Association in passed balls with 11 in 1979 and tied for lead with 10 in 1978.
Led Eastern League in passed balls with 18 in 1977.
Tied for Carolina League lead in double plays by third basemen with 19 in 1976.

Year Club	League	Pos.	G.	AB.	R.	H.	2B.	3B.	HR.	RBI.	B.A.	PO.	A.	E.	F.A.
1975—Spartanburg	W. Car.	3B	69	246	28	68	13	1	1	41	.276	52	128	17	.914
1976—Peninsula	Carol.	●3B-SS	78	294	38	83	12	2	4	47	.282	50	221	●26	.912
1976—Reading	East.	3B-2B	61	199	7	52	5	0	0	7	.261	62	99	13	.925
1977—Reading	East.	C-3B	104	401	61	131	19	1	8	55	.327	339	60	8	.980
1977—Oklahoma City	A. A.	C	7	13	3	1	0	0	0	1	.077	17	1	0	1.000
1978—Oklahoma City	A. A.	C-1-3-O	130	501	73	145	25	4	16	98	.289	641	75	13	.982
1978—Philadelphia	Nat.	C	1	2	0	0	0	0	0	0	.000	4	0	0	1.000
1979—Oklahoma City	A. A.	C-3B-OF	130	494	86	149	●34	3	20	109	.302	397	44	13	.971
1979—Philadelphia	Nat.	C	14	48	3	18	3	2	0	8	.375	71	3	0	1.000
1980—Philadelphia	Nat.	C-OF	62	159	13	50	8	0	4	29	.314	186	22	7	.967
1981—Philadelphia†	Nat.	C-3-1-O	61	196	16	50	7	0	6	37	.255	267	31	9	.971
1982—Chicago	Nat.	OF-C-3B	138	476	50	124	17	2	15	68	.261	384	38	8	.981
1983—Chicago	Nat.	OF-C	154	533	76	161	30	3	16	70	.302	244	7	6	.977
1984—Chicago	Nat.	O-1-3-C	140	495	59	138	17	3	16	80	.279	393	30	10	.977
1985—Chicago	Nat.	O-1-3-C	161	587	74	180	30	3	14	106	.307	313	29	13	.963
Major League Totals—8 Years		731	2496	291	721	112	13	71	398	.289	1862	160	53	.974

Selected by Philadelphia Phillies' organization in 7th round of free-agent draft, June 4, 1975.
†Traded with Pitchers Dan Larson and Dickie Noles to Chicago Cubs for Pitcher Mike Krukow and cash, December 8, 1981.

DIVISION SERIES RECORD

Year Club	League	Pos.	G.	AB.	R.	H.	2B.	3B.	HR.	RBI.	B.A.	PO.	A.	E.	F.A.
1981—Philadelphia	Nat.	C	4	13	2	6	0	0	1	3	.462	30	2	1	.970

Year	Club	League	Pos.	G.	AB.	R.	H.	2B.	3B.	HR.	RBI.	B.A.	PO.	A.	E.	F.A.
1980—Philadelphia		Nat.	C-PH	2	1	0	0	0	0	0	1	.000	0	0	0	.000
1984—Chicago		Nat.	OF	5	18	3	6	2	0	0	2	.333	9	0	0	1.000
Championship Series Totals—2 Years				7	19	3	6	2	0	0	3	.316	9	0	0	1.000

WORLD SERIES RECORD

Year	Club	League	Pos.	G.	AB.	R.	H.	2B.	3B.	HR.	RBI.	B.A.	PO.	A.	E.	F.A.
1980—Philadelphia		Nat.	DH	3	12	1	4	0	0	1	1	.333	0	0	0	.000

ARMANDO MORENO (CLEMENTE)

Born December 25, 1963, at Santurce, Puerto Rico.
Height, 5.10. Weight, 160.
Throws and bats righthanded.

Year	Club	League	Pos.	G.	AB.	R.	H.	2B.	3B.	HR.	RBI.	B.A.	PO.	A.	E.	F.A.
1982—Calgary		Pion.	2B	66	213	52	72	18	1	5	42	.338	138	163	★23	.929
1983—Gastonia		S. Atl.	2B	115	367	89	120	19	1	8	63	.327	218	262	30	.941
1984—Jacksonville		South.	2B	126	400	51	92	12	1	10	55	.230	255	375	26	.960
1985—Jacksonville†		South.	2B	105	371	67	106	25	0	8	32	.286	262	258	14	.974

Signed as free agent by Montreal Expos' organization, August 28, 1981.
†On disabled list, July 8 to August 1, 1985.

OMAR RENAN MORENO (QUINTERO)

Born October 24, 1953, at Puerto Armuelles, Panama.
Height, 6.03. Weight, 185.
Throws and bats lefthanded.

Major League stolen bases: 1975 (1), 1976 (15), 1977 (53), 1978 (71), 1979 (77), 1980 (96), 1981 (39), 1982 (60), 1983 (37), 1984 (20), 1985 (1). Total—470.
Led National League in caught stealing with 33 in 1980 and 14 in 1981.
Led National League in stolen bases with 71 in 1978 and 77 in 1979.
Led National League outfielders in total chances with 514 in 1979 and 499 in 1980.
Tied for National League lead in caught stealing with 26 in 1982.
Led Carolina League in stolen bases with 77 in 1973.
Led Eastern League in stolen bases with 67 in 1974.
Named outfielder on THE SPORTING NEWS National League All-Star Team, 1979.

Year	Club	League	Pos.	G.	AB.	R.	H.	2B.	3B.	HR.	RBI.	B.A.	PO.	A.	E.	F.A.
1969—Bradenton Pir.		Gulf C.	OF	25	62	7	18	1	0	0	4	.290	22	0	3	.880
1970—Bradenton Pir.		Gulf C.	OF-1B	51	219	32	51	7	4	1	19	.233	129	9	8	.945
1970—Niagara Falls		NYP	OF	10	23	1	4	0	0	0	3	.174	10	0	0	1.000
1971—Bradenton Pir.		Gulf C.	OF	38	101	11	33	5	2	0	9	.327	35	4	2	.951
1972—Gastonia		W. Car.	OF	51	144	18	31	5	2	1	17	.215	95	3	3	.970
1972—Niagara Falls		NYP	OF	68	259	52	75	11	6	2	34	.290	87	4	5	.948
1973—Salem		Carol.	OF	136	529	★112	150	22	8	9	56	.284	242	14	13	.952
1973—Charleston		Int.	OF	3	12	1	4	0	1	1	3	.333	4	0	0	1.000
1974—Thetford Mines		East.	OF	112	407	88	122	15	6	7	39	.300	193	13	9	.958
1974—Charleston		Int.	OF	23	82	16	18	3	0	0	4	.220	40	2	1	.977
1975—Charleston		Int.	OF	130	447	73	127	20	2	9	51	.284	★328	10	6	.983
1975—Pittsburgh		Nat.	OF	6	6	1	1	0	0	0	0	.167	0	0	1	1.000
1976—Charleston		Int.	OF	94	330	70	104	11	7	3	36	.315	200	★17	1	★.955
1976—Pittsburgh		Nat.	OF	48	122	24	33	4	1	2	12	.270	93	3	4	.960
1977—Pittsburgh		Nat.	OF	150	492	69	118	19	9	7	34	.240	366	10	9	.977
1978—Pittsburgh		Nat.	OF	155	515	95	121	15	7	2	33	.235	409	9	7	.984
1979—Pittsburgh		Nat.	OF	162	★695	110	196	21	12	8	69	.282	★490	11	13	.975
1980—Pittsburgh		Nat.	OF	162	★676	87	168	20	●13	2	36	.249	★479	15	5	.990
1981—Pittsburgh		Nat.	OF	103	434	62	120	18	8	1	35	.276	302	6	1	.997
1982—Pittsburgh†		Nat.	OF	158	645	82	158	18	9	3	44	.245	396	10	7	.983
1983—Houston		Nat.	OF	97	405	48	98	12	11	0	25	.242	251	8	6	.977
1983—New York		Amer.	OF	48	152	17	38	9	1	1	17	.250	120	1	1	.992
1984—New York		Amer.	OF	117	355	37	92	12	6	4	38	.259	262	9	4	.985
1985—N.Y.§-K.C. x		Amer.	OF	58	136	21	30	5	4	3	16	.221	86	3	0	1.000
National League Totals—9 Years				1041	3990	578	1013	127	70	25	288	.254	2786	72	53	.982
American League Totals—3 Years				223	643	75	160	26	11	8	71	.249	468	13	5	.990
Major League Totals—11 Years				1264	4633	653	1173	153	81	33	359	.253	3254	85	58	.983

Signed as free agent by Pittsburgh Pirates' organization, March 30, 1969.
†Granted free agency, November 10, 1982; signed by Houston Astros, December 10, 1982.
‡Traded to New York Yankees for Outfielder Jerry Mumphrey, August 10, 1983.
§Released, August 16, 1985; signed by Kansas City Royals, September 3, 1985.
xReleased, November 15, 1985.

CHAMPIONSHIP SERIES RECORD

Year	Club	League	Pos.	G.	AB.	R.	H.	2B.	3B.	HR.	RBI.	B.A.	PO.	A.	E.	F.A.
1979—Pittsburgh		Nat.	OF	3	12	3	3	0	1	0	0	.250	7	0	0	1.000

WORLD SERIES RECORD

Tied World Series record for most at bats, seven-game Series (33), 1979.

Year	Club	League	Pos.	G.	AB.	R.	H.	2B.	3B.	HR.	RBI.	B.A.	PO.	A.	E.	F.A.
1979—Pittsburgh		Nat.	OF	7	33	4	11	2	0	0	3	.333	20	1	0	1.000

MICHAEL THOMAS MORGAN
(Mike)

Born October 8, 1959, at Tulare, Calif.
Height, 6.02. Weight, 185.
Throws and bats righthanded.

Tied for International League lead in shutouts with 4 in 1984.
Received reported $50,000 bonus to sign with Oakland A's, 1978.

Year Club	League	G.	IP.	W.	L.	Pct.	H.	R.	ER.	SO.	BB.	ERA.
1978—Oakland	American	3	12	0	3	.000	19	12	10	0	8	7.50
1978—Vancouver	P. Coast	14	92	5	6	.455	109	67	57	31	54	5.58
1979—Ogden	P. Coast	13	101	5	5	.500	93	48	39	42	49	3.48
1979—Oakland	American	13	77	2	10	.167	102	57	51	17	50	5.96
1980—Ogden†‡	P. Coast	20	115	6	9	.400	135	79	69	46	77	5.40
1981—Nashville§	Southern	26	169	8	7	.533	164	97	83	100	83	4.42
1982—New York x	American	30	150⅓	7	11	.389	167	77	73	71	67	4.37
1983—Toronto y	American	16	45⅓	0	3	.000	48	26	26	22	21	5.16
1983—Syracuse	Int'national	5	19⅓	0	3	.000	20	12	12	17	13	5.59
1984—Syracuse z	Int'national	34	★185⅔	13	11	.542	167	●101	84	105	●100	4.07
1985—Seattle a	American	2	6	1	1	.500	11	8	8	2	5	12.00
1985—Calgary	P. Coast	1	2	0	0	.000	3	1	1	0	0	4.50
Major League Totals—5 Years		64	290⅔	10	28	.263	347	180	168	112	151	5.20

Selected by Oakland A's organizaton in 1st round (fourth player selected) of free-agent draft, June 6, 1978.
†On disabled list, May 14 to June 27, 1980.
‡Traded to New York Yankees for Shortstop Fred Stanley and a player to be named later, November 3, 1980; Oakland A's acquired Second Baseman Brian Doyle to complete deal, November 17, 1980.
§On disabled list, April 9 to April 22, 1981.
xTraded with Outfielder-First Baseman Dave Collins, First Baseman Fred McGriff and a reported $400,000 to Toronto Blue Jays for Pitcher Dale Murray and Outfielder-Catcher Tom Dodd, December 9, 1982.
yOn disabled list, July 2 to August 23, 1983; included rehabilitation disability assignment to Syracuse, August 1 to August 18, 1983.
zDrafted by Seattle Mariners, December 3, 1984.
aOn disabled list, April 17, 1985 through remainder of season; included rehabilitation disability assignment to Calgary, July 19 to July 22, 1985.

RUSSELL LEE MORMAN
(Russ)

Born April 28, 1962, at Independence, Mo.
Height, 6.04. Weight, 215.
Throws and bats righthanded.
Attended Iowa Western Community College, Clarinda, Ia.,
and Wichita State University, Wichita, Kan.

Led Eastern League in slugging percentage with .512 in 1985.
Led Midwest League in game-winning RBIs with 15 in 1984.
Led Eastern League first basemen in assists with 79 in 1985.
Named first baseman on THE SPORTING NEWS College Baseball All-America Team, 1983.

Year Club	League	Pos.	G.	AB.	R.	H.	2B.	3B.	HR.	RBI.	B.A.	PO.	A.	E.	F.A.
1983—Glens Falls	East.	1B	71	233	29	57	9	1	3	32	.245	591	43	7	.989
1984—Appleton	Midw.	1B-OF	122	424	68	111	17	7	7	80	.262	823	43	10	.989
1985—Glens Falls	East.	★1-3-OF	119	422	64	131	24	5	17	81	.310	905	81	12	★.988
1985—Buffalo	A. A.	1B	21	64	16	19	3	1	7	14	.297	144	7	2	.987

Selected by Kansas City Royals' organization in 7th round of free-agent draft, January 13, 1981.
Selected by Chicago White Sox' organization in 1st round (28th player selected) of free-agent draft, June 6, 1983.

JOHN DANIEL MORRIS

Born February 23, 1961, at Freeport, N.Y.
Height, 6.01. Weight, 185.
Throws and bats lefthanded.
Attended Seton Hall University, South Orange, N.J.

Led Southern League outfielders in total chances with 343 in 1985.
Named Southern League Most Valuable Player, 1983.
Named outfielder on THE SPORTING NEWS College Baseball All-America Team, 1982.

Year Club	League	Pos.	G.	AB.	R.	H.	2B.	3B.	HR.	RBI.	B.A.	PO.	A.	E.	F.A.
1982—Fort Myers	Fla. St.	OF	45	137	21	39	7	2	2	17	.285	64	2	2	.971
1983—Jacksonville	South.	OF	140	490	96	141	27	8	23	92	.288	260	8	3	★.989
1984—Omaha	A. A.	OF	148	492	77	133	24	4	15	60	.270	★359	7	4	★.989
1985—Omaha†-Louis.	A. A.	OF	130	466	64	117	25	6	5	50	.251	★330	11	2	★.994

Selected by Kansas City Royals' organization in 1st round (10th player selected) of free-agent draft, June 7, 1982.
†Traded to St. Louis Cardinals' organization for Outfielder Lonnie Smith, May 17, 1985.

JOHN SCOTT MORRIS
(Jack)

Born May 16, 1955, at St. Paul, Minn.
Height, 6.03. Weight, 200.
Throws and bats righthanded.
Attended Brigham Young University, Provo, Utah.

Tied American League record for most seasons leading league, wild pitches (3).
Pitched 4-0 no-hit victory against Chicago White Sox, April 7, 1984.
Led American League in wild pitches with 18 in 1983, 14 in 1984 and 15 in 1985.
Named American League Pitcher of the Year by THE SPORTING NEWS, 1981.
Named righthanded pitcher on THE SPORTING NEWS American League All-Star Team, 1981.

Year	Club	League	G.	IP.	W.	L.	Pct.	H.	R.	ER.	SO.	BB.	ERA.
1976—Montgomery		Southern	12	36	2	3	.400	37	31	25	18	36	6.25
1977—Evansville		Am. Assoc.	20	135	6	7	.462	141	68	54	95	42	3.60
1977—Detroit		American	7	46	1	1	.500	38	20	19	28	23	3.72
1978—Detroit		American	28	106	3	5	.375	107	57	51	48	49	4.33
1979—Evansville		Am. Assoc.	5	34	2	2	.500	22	13	9	28	18	2.38
1979—Detroit		American	27	198	17	7	.708	179	76	72	113	59	3.27
1980—Detroit		American	36	250	16	15	.516	252	125	116	112	87	4.18
1981—Detroit		American	25	198	●14	7	.667	153	69	67	97	★78	3.05
1982—Detroit		American	37	266⅓	17	16	.515	247	131	120	135	96	4.06
1983—Detroit†		American	37	★293⅔	20	13	.606	257	117	109	★232	83	3.34
1984—Detroit		American	35	240⅓	19	11	.633	221	108	96	148	87	3.60
1985—Detroit‡		American	35	257	16	11	.593	212	102	95	191	110	3.33
Major League Totals—9 Years			267	1855⅓	123	86	.589	1666	805	745	1104	672	3.61

Selected by Detroit Tigers' organization in 5th round of free-agent draft, June 8, 1976.
†Appeared in seven games as a pinch-runner.
‡Appeared in one game as a pinch-runner.

CHAMPIONSHIP SERIES RECORD

Year	Club	League	G.	IP.	W.	L.	Pct.	H.	R.	ER.	SO.	BB.	ERA.
1984—Detroit		American	1	7	1	0	1.000	5	1	1	4	1	1.29

WORLD SERIES RECORD

Established World Series record for most putouts, pitcher, five-game Series (5), 1984.
Tied World Series record for most wild pitches, game (2), October 13, 1984.

Year	Club	League	G.	IP.	W.	L.	Pct.	H.	R.	ER.	SO.	BB.	ERA.
1984—Detroit		American	2	18	2	0	1.000	13	4	4	13	3	2.00

ALL-STAR GAME RECORD

Year	League	IP.	W.	L.	Pct.	H.	R.	ER.	SO.	BB.	ERA.
1981—American		2	0	0	.000	2	0	0	2	1	0.00
1984—American		2	0	0	.000	2	0	0	2	1	0.00
1985—American		2⅔	0	1	.000	5	2	2	1	1	6.75
All-Star Game Totals—3 Years		6⅔	0	1	.000	9	2	2	5	3	2.70

JAMES FORREST MORRISON
(Jim)

Born September 23, 1952, at Pensacola, Fla.
Height, 5.11. Weight, 185.
Throws and bats righthanded.
Attended Georgia Southern College, Statesboro, Ga.

Tied major league record for fewest three-base hits, most at-bats, season (0 and 604), 1980.
Major League stolen bases: 1978 (1), 1979 (11), 1980 (9), 1981 (3), 1982 (2), 1983 (2), 1985 (3). Total—31.
Led American League second basemen in assists with 481, total chances with 932 and double plays with 117 in 1980.
Led Carolina League in total bases with 239 in 1975.
Led American Association third basemen in assists with 236 in 1977.
Led American Association third basemen in double plays with 22 in 1976.
Led Carolina League third basemen in assists with 311, errors with 32 and double plays with 35 in 1975.

Year	Club	League	Pos.	G.	AB.	R.	H.	2B.	3B.	HR.	RBI.	B.A.	PO.	A.	E.	F.A.
1974—Spartanburg	W. Car.		3B	3	8	1	3	1	0	1	3	.375	4	5	1	.900
1974—Rocky Mount	Carol.		3B	72	265	30	67	9	1	4	24	.253	54	157	19	.917
1975—Rocky Mount	Carol.		3B-SS	140	497	★98	143	24	6	★20	88	.288	135	331	35	.930
1976—Oklahoma City	A. A.		★3B-SS	126	422	79	122	17	6	18	71	.289	100	★239	24	.934
1977—Oklahoma City	A. A.		3B-2B-OF	127	452	72	133	23	4	12	71	.294	99	272	25	.937
1977—Philadelphia	Nat.		3B	5	7	3	3	0	0	0	1	.429	0	7	1	.875
1978—Oklahoma City	A. A.		2B-3B-1B	54	189	37	52	6	1	10	28	.275	111	134	10	.961
1978—Philadelphia	Nat.		2B-3B-OF	53	108	12	17	1	1	3	10	.157	88	97	6	.969
1979—Oklahoma City†	A. A.		2B-3B-OF	79	281	59	90	15	0	22	61	.320	129	226	17	.954
1979—Chicago	Amer.		2B-3B	67	240	38	66	14	0	14	35	.275	121	185	9	.971
1980—Chicago	Amer.		★2B-SS	162	604	66	171	40	0	15	57	.283	★422	482	★29	.969
1981—Chicago	Amer.		3B-2B	90	290	27	68	8	1	10	34	.234	64	200	12	.957
1982—Chicago‡	Amer.		3B	51	166	17	37	7	3	7	19	.223	19	87	10	.914
1982—Pittsburgh	Nat.		3-2-O-S	44	86	10	24	4	1	4	15	.279	17	43	2	.968
1983—Pittsburgh	Nat.		2B-3B-SS	66	158	16	48	7	2	6	25	.304	56	99	7	.957
1984—Pittsburgh	Nat.		3-2-S-1	100	304	38	87	14	2	11	45	.286	86	166	10	.962
1985—Pittsburgh	Nat.		3B-2B-OF	92	244	17	62	10	0	4	22	.254	73	121	5	.975
National League Totals—6 Years				360	907	96	241	36	6	28	118	.266	320	533	31	.965
American League Totals—4 Years				370	1300	148	342	69	4	46	145	.263	626	954	60	.963
Major League Totals—9 Years				730	2207	244	583	105	10	74	263	.264	946	1487	91	.964

Selected by Pittsburgh Pirates' organization in 5th round of free-agent draft, January 12, 1972.
Selected by Pittsburgh Pirates' organization in secondary phase of free-agent draft, June 6, 1972.
Selected by Philadelphia Phillies' organization in 5th round of free-agent draft, June 5, 1974.

†Traded to Chicago White Sox, July 10, 1979, completing deal in which Chicago traded Pitcher Jack Kucek to Philadelphia Phillies for a player to be named later, April 13, 1979.
‡Traded to Pittsburgh Pirates for Pitcher Eddie Solomon, June 14, 1982.

CHAMPIONSHIP SERIES RECORD

Year	Club	League	Pos.	G.	AB.	R.	H.	2B.	3B.	HR.	RBI.	B.A.	PO.	A.	E.	F.A.
1978—Philadelphia		Nat.	PH	1	1	0	0	0	0	0	0	.000	0	0	0	.000

LLOYD ANTHONY MOSEBY

Born November 5, 1959, at Portland, Ark.
Height, 6.03. Weight, 200.
Throws right and bats lefthanded.
Major League stolen bases: 1980 (4), 1981 (11), 1982 (11), 1983 (27), 1984 (39), 1985 (37). Total—129.
Led Florida State League in total bases with 237 and tied for lead in being hit by pitch with 10 in 1979.
Led Pioneer League in being hit by pitch with 11 and tied for lead in caught stealing with 7 in 1978.
Named outfielder on THE SPORTING NEWS American League All-Star Team, 1983.
Named outfielder on THE SPORTING NEWS American League Silver Slugger team, 1983.

Year	Club	League	Pos.	G.	AB.	R.	H.	2B.	3B.	HR.	RBI.	B.A.	PO.	A.	E.	F.A.
1978—Medicine Hat		Pion.	OF	67	253	65	77	12	4	10	38	.304	76	3	6	.929
1979—Dunedin		Fla. St.	OF	129	446	*89	*148	23	6	18	84	.332	190	11	9	.957
1980—Syracuse		Int.	OF	37	146	28	47	8	6	3	19	.322	83	1	3	.966
1980—Toronto		Amer.	OF	114	389	44	89	24	1	9	46	.229	208	12	4	.982
1981—Toronto		Amer.	OF	100	378	36	88	16	2	9	43	.233	259	4	3	.989
1982—Toronto		Amer.	OF	147	487	51	115	20	9	9	52	.236	361	4	3	.992
1983—Toronto		Amer.	OF	151	539	104	170	31	7	18	81	.315	399	10	7	.983
1984—Toronto		Amer.	OF	158	592	97	166	28	•15	18	92	.280	473	8	5	.990
1985—Toronto		Amer.	OF	152	584	92	151	30	7	18	70	.259	394	7	8	.980
Major League Totals—6 Years				822	2969	424	779	149	41	81	384	.262	2094	45	30	.986

Selected by Toronto Blue Jays' organization in 1st round (second player selected) of free-agent draft, June 6, 1978.

CHAMPIONSHIP SERIES RECORD

Established American League Championship Series record for most at-bats, seven-game Series (31), 1985.

Year	Club	League	Pos.	G.	AB.	R.	H.	2B.	3B.	HR.	RBI.	B.A.	PO.	A.	E.	F.A.
1985—Toronto		Amer.	OF	7	31	5	7	1	0	0	4	.226	16	0	0	1.000

JOHN WILLIAM MOSES

Born August 9, 1957, at Los Angeles, Calif.
Height, 5.09. Weight, 165.
Throws left and bats left and righthanded.
Attended Golden West College, Huntington Beach, Calif., and
University of Arizona, Tucson, Ariz.
Major League stolen bases: 1982 (5), 1983 (11), 1984 (1), 1985 (5). Total—22.
Led Midwest League in caught stealing with 21 and bases on balls received with 103 in 1981.
Tied for Midwest League lead in sacrifice hits with 13 in 1981.
Led Eastern League outfielders in double plays with 6 in 1982.

Year	Club	League	Pos.	G.	AB.	R.	H.	2B.	3B.	HR.	RBI.	B.A.	PO.	A.	E.	F.A.
1980—Bellingham		N'west	OF	60	227	55	60	5	2	2	32	.264	92	6	3	.970
1981—Wausau		Midw.	OF	123	429	*102	120	24	3	3	48	.280	204	10	5	.977
1982—Lynn		East.	OF	128	466	87	133	25	6	6	52	.285	259	*20	0	*1.000
1982—Seattle		Amer.	OF	22	44	7	14	5	1	1	3	.318	16	2	1	.947
1983—Seattle		Amer.	OF	93	130	19	27	4	1	0	6	.208	87	8	2	.979
1983—Salt Lake City		P. C.	OF	16	65	14	17	4	0	0	10	.262	26	0	0	1.000
1984—Chattanooga		South.	OF	53	182	27	46	6	3	0	12	.253	107	4	2	.982
1984—Salt Lake City		P. C.	OF	70	276	45	76	11	5	0	27	.275	161	8	1	.994
1984—Seattle		Amer.	OF	19	35	3	12	1	1	0	2	.343	26	1	0	1.000
1985—Calgary		P. C.	OF-1B	113	473	75	152	*37	1	5	47	.321	316	12	4	.988
1985—Seattle		Amer.	OF	33	62	4	12	0	0	0	3	.194	35	1	0	1.000
Major League Totals—4 Years				167	271	33	65	10	3	1	14	.240	164	12	3	.983

Selected by Seattle Mariners' organization in 16th round of free-agent draft, June 3, 1980.

JOSE MANUEL MOTA

Born March 16, 1965, at Santo Domingo, Dominican Republic.
Height, 5.09. Weight, 160.
Throws right and bats left and righthanded.
Attended California State University, Fullerton, Calif.
Son of Manny Mota, outfielder with San Francisco Giants, Pittsburgh Pirates,
Montreal Expos and Los Angeles Dodgers, 1962 through 1979, 1980 and 1982;
and coach with Los Angeles Dodgers since 1980.
Named second baseman on THE SPORTING NEWS College Baseball All-America Team, 1985.

Year	Club	League	Pos.	G.	AB.	R.	H.	2B.	3B.	HR.	RBI.	B.A.	PO.	A.	E.	F.A.
1985—Niagara Falls		NYP	2B	65	254	35	77	9	2	0	27	.303	154	156	16	.951
1985—Buffalo†		A. A.	2B	6	18	3	5	0	0	1	.278	10	12	0	1.000

Selected by Chicago White Sox' organization in 2nd round of free-agent draft, June 3, 1985.
†Traded to Texas Rangers, December 12, 1985, completing deal in which Texas traded Infielder Wayne Tolleson and Pitcher Dave Schmidt to Chicago White Sox for Pitcher Ed Correa, Infielder Scott Fletcher and a player to be named later, November 25, 1985.

DARRYL DeWAYNE MOTLEY

Born January 21, 1960, at Muskogee, Okla.
Height, 5.09. Weight, 196.
Throws and bats righthanded.

Major League stolen bases: 1981 (1), 1983 (2), 1984 (10), 1985 (6). Total—19.

Year Club	League	Pos.	G.	AB.	R.	H.	2B.	3B.	HR.	RBI.	B.A.	PO.	A.	E.	F.A.
1978—Sarasota Royals...	Gulf C.	OF	10	41	10	20	1	0	2	9	.488	23	1	1	.960
1978—Fort Myers	Fla. St.	OF	49	151	13	36	3	2	0	12	.238	100	1	4	.962
1979—Fort Myers	Fla. St.	3B	123	447	47	106	20	2	8	45	.237	★109	183	●29	.910
1980—Fort Myers†	Fla. St.	3B-OF-SS	32	119	20	36	7	0	4	24	.303	33	56	9	.908
1980—Jacksonville‡	South.	3B	51	182	30	58	15	1	5	31	.319	43	100	10	.935
1981—Omaha	A. A.	OF	109	410	63	118	18	5	18	64	.288	201	7	3	.986
1981—Kansas City	Amer.	OF	42	125	15	29	4	0	2	8	.232	88	3	3	.968
1982—Omaha§	A. A.	OF	114	409	51	104	12	6	8	52	.254	216	4	3	.987
1983—Evansville	A. A.	OF	130	506	89	142	32	5	16	60	.281	282	14	5	.983
1983—Kansas City	Amer.	OF	19	68	9	16	1	2	3	11	.235	42	2	1	.978
1984—Kansas City	Amer.	OF	146	522	64	148	25	6	15	70	.284	301	7	5	.984
1985—Kansas City	Amer.	OF	123	383	45	85	20	1	17	49	.222	198	4	7	.967
Major League Totals—4 Years			330	1098	133	278	50	9	37	138	.253	629	16	16	.976

Selected by Kansas City Royals' organization in 2nd round of free-agent draft, June 6, 1978.
†On disabled list, April 11 to May 18, 1980.
‡On disabled list, August 9, 1980 through remainder of season.
§Loaned to Evansville (Detroit Tigers organization), April 2, 1983; returned, September 1, 1983.

CHAMPIONSHIP SERIES RECORD

Year Club	League	Pos.	G.	AB.	R.	H.	2B.	3B.	HR.	RBI.	B.A.	PO.	A.	E.	F.A.
1984—Kansas City	Amer.	OF	3	12	0	2	0	0	0	1	.167	11	0	0	1.000
1985—Kansas City	Amer.	OF	2	3	1	1	0	0	0	1	.333	4	0	0	1.000
Championship Series Totals—2 Years			5	15	1	3	0	0	0	2	.200	15	0	0	1.000

WORLD SERIES RECORD

Year Club	League	Pos.	G.	AB.	R.	H.	2B.	3B.	HR.	RBI.	B.A.	PO.	A.	E.	F.A.
1985—Kansas City	Amer.	OF-PH	5	11	1	4	0	0	1	3	.364	4	0	0	1.000

TERENCE JOHN MULHOLLAND
(Terry)

Born March 9, 1963, at Uniontown, Pa.
Height, 6.03. Weight, 200.
Throws left and bats righthanded.
Attended Marietta College, Marietta, O.

Led Texas League in shutouts with 3 in 1985.

Year Club	League	G.	IP.	W.	L.	Pct.	H.	R.	ER.	SO.	BB.	ERA.
1984—Fresno	California	9	42⅔	5	2	.714	32	17	14	39	36	2.95
1985—Shreveport	Texas	26	176⅔	9	8	.529	166	79	57	122	87	2.90

Selected by San Francisco Giants' organization in 1st round (24th player selected) of free-agent draft, June 4, 1984.

STEVEN RANCE MULLINIKS

Name pronounced MUL-in-iks.

(Known by middle name.)

Born January 15, 1956, at Tulare, Calif.
Height, 6.00. Weight, 170.
Throws right and bats lefthanded.
Son of Harvey Mulliniks, pitcher in New York Yankees' organization, 1956 and 1957.

Major League stolen bases: 1977 (1), 1978 (2), 1982 (3), 1984 (2), 1985 (2). Total—10.
Led American League third basemen in fielding percentage with .968 in 1984.
Led Pacific Coast League shortstops in fielding percentage with .968 in 1979.

Year Club	League	Pos.	G.	AB.	R.	H.	2B.	3B.	HR.	RBI.	B.A.	PO.	A.	E.	F.A.
1974—Idaho Falls	Pion.	SS	66	202	28	44	8	3	0	24	.218	★110	★170	★33	.895
1975—Quad Cities	Midw.	SS	52	186	34	50	6	2	1	21	.269	82	136	17	.928
1975—Salinas	Calif.	SS-2B	59	209	38	54	8	0	0	10	.258	88	146	14	.944
1976—El Paso†	Texas	SS-2B	90	333	81	105	22	4	7	51	.315	140	247	20	.951
1977—Salt Lake City	P. C.	SS	58	220	48	68	17	3	11	51	.309	116	207	15	.956
1977—California	Amer.	SS	78	271	36	73	13	2	5	21	.269	112	229	13	.963
1978—Salt Lake City	P. C.	SS	34	127	34	39	6	2	3	21	.307	65	109	12	.935
1978—California	Amer.	SS	50	119	6	22	3	1	1	6	.185	68	93	8	.953
1979—Salt Lake City	P. C.	SS-2B	116	402	94	138	21	7	3	59	.343	204	331	17	.969
1979—California‡	Amer.	SS	22	68	7	10	0	0	1	8	.147	46	43	4	.957
1980—Kansas City	Amer.	SS-2B	36	54	8	14	3	0	0	6	.259	30	53	1	.988
1981—Kansas City§	Amer.	2B-SS-3B	24	44	6	10	3	0	0	5	.227	25	39	5	.928
1982—Toronto	Amer.	3B-SS	112	311	32	76	25	0	4	35	.244	69	154	14	.941
1983—Toronto	Amer.	3B-SS-2B	129	364	54	100	34	3	10	49	.275	77	185	7	.974
1984—Toronto	Amer.	3B-SS-2B	125	343	41	111	21	5	3	42	.324	67	152	8	.965
1985—Toronto	Amer.	3B	129	366	55	108	26	1	10	57	.295	75	162	7	★.971
Major League Totals—9 Years			705	1940	245	524	128	12	32	229	.270	569	1110	67	.962

Selected by California Angels' organization in 3rd round of free-agent draft, June 5, 1974.
†On disabled list, May 4 to June 9 and September 2 to September 24, 1976.

‡Traded with First Baseman Willie Aikens to Kansas City Royals for Outfielder Al Cowens, Shortstop Todd Cruz and a player to be named later, December 6, 1979; California Angels acquired Pitcher Craig Eaton to complete deal, April 1, 1980.

§Traded to Toronto Blue Jays for Pitcher Phil Huffman, March 25, 1982.

CHAMPIONSHIP SERIES RECORD

Year Club	League	Pos.	G.	AB.	R.	H.	2B.	3B.	HR.	RBI.	B.A.	PO.	A.	E.	F.A.
1985—Toronto	Amer.	PH-3B	5	11	1	4	1	0	1	3	.364	1	4	0	1.000

JERRY WAYNE MUMPHREY

Born September 9, 1952, at Tyler, Tex.
Height, 6.02. Weight, 200.
Throws right and bats left and righthanded.

Major League stolen bases: 1976 (22), 1977 (22), 1978 (14), 1979 (8), 1980 (52), 1981 (14), 1982 (11), 1983 (7), 1984 (15), 1985 (6). Total—171.

Led American Association in stolen bases with 44 and caught stealing with 21 in 1975.

Led Gulf Coast League batters in strikeouts with 45 in 1971.

Year Club	League	Pos.	G.	AB.	R.	H.	2B.	3B.	HR.	RBI.	B.A.	PO.	A.	E.	F.A.
1971—Sarasota Cards	Gulf C.	OF	38	141	20	36	3	2	0	6	.255	52	1	3	.946
1972—Sarasota Cards	Gulf C.	OF	26	111	21	38	5	2	0	12	.342	63	2	0	1.000
1972—Cedar Rapids	Midw.	OF	11	33	6	6	2	0	0	1	.182	15	0	0	1.000
1972—St. Petersburg	Fla. St.	OF	17	44	7	15	2	1	0	1	.341	11	1	1	.923
1973—St. Petersburg	Fla. St.	OF	142	★556	★93	★159	20	●9	5	52	.286	210	6	4	982
1974—Arkansas	Tex.	OF	130	507	87	147	21	6	10	54	.290	209	11	9	.961
1974—St. Louis	Nat.	OF	5	2	2	0	0	0	0	0	.000	0	0	0	.000
1975—Tulsa	A. A.	OF	127	495	87	141	19	6	8	59	.285	248	7	6	.977
1975—St. Louis	Nat.	OF	11	16	2	6	2	0	0	1	.375	9	0	0	1.000
1976—Tulsa	A. A.	OF	19	68	14	23	9	1	1	8	.338	42	4	0	1.000
1976—St. Louis	Nat.	OF	112	384	51	99	15	5	1	26	.258	261	6	2	.993
1977—St. Louis	Nat.	OF	145	463	73	133	20	10	2	38	.287	291	8	9	.971
1978—St. Louis	Nat.	OF	125	367	41	96	13	4	2	37	.262	178	10	1	.995
1979—St. Louis ††§	Nat.	OF	124	339	53	100	10	3	3	32	.295	180	3	3	.984
1980—San Diego x	Nat.	OF	160	564	61	168	24	3	4	59	.298	398	10	●11	.974
1981—New York	Amer.	OF	80	319	44	98	11	5	6	32	.307	219	5	●8	.966
1982—New York y	Amer.	OF	123	477	76	143	24	10	9	68	.300	336	5	5	.986
1983—New York z	Amer.	OF	83	267	41	70	11	4	7	36	.262	227	7	4	.983
1983—Houston	Nat.	OF	44	143	17	48	10	2	1	17	.336	103	1	1	.990
1984—Houston	Nat.	OF	151	524	66	152	20	3	9	83	.290	317	5	4	.988
1985—Houston a	Nat.	OF	130	444	52	123	25	2	8	61	.277	248	6	8	.969
National League Totals—10 Years			1007	3246	418	925	139	32	30	354	.285	1985	49	39	.981
American League Totals—3 Years			286	1063	161	311	46	19	22	136	.293	782	17	17	.979
Major League Totals—12 Years			1293	4309	579	1236	185	51	52	490	.287	2767	66	56	.981

Selected by St. Louis Cardinals' organization in 4th round of free-agent draft, June 8, 1971.

†On disabled list, March 29 to April 20, 1979.

‡Traded with Pitcher John Denny to Cleveland Indians for Outfielder Bobby Bonds, December 7, 1979.

§Traded by Cleveland Indians to San Diego Padres for Pitcher Bob Owchinko and Outfielder Jim Wilhelm, February 15, 1980.

xTraded with Pitcher John Pacella to New York Yankees for Outfielders Ruppert Jones and Joe Lefebvre and Pitchers Tim Lollar and Chris Welsh, April 1, 1981.

yOn disabled list, May 10 to June 21, 1982.

zTraded to Houston Astros for Outfielder Omar Moreno, August 10, 1983.

aTraded to Chicago Cubs for Outfielder Billy Hatcher and a player to be named later, December 16, 1985.

DIVISION SERIES RECORD

Year Club	League	Pos.	G.	AB.	R.	H.	2B.	3B.	HR.	RBI.	B.A.	PO.	A.	E.	F.A.
1981—New York	Amer.	OF	5	21	2	2	0	0	0	0	.095	15	1	0	1.000

CHAMPIONSHIP SERIES RECORD

Year Club	League	Pos.	G.	AB.	R.	H.	2B.	3B.	HR.	RBI.	B.A.	PO.	A.	E.	F.A.
1981—New York	Amer.	OF	3	12	2	6	1	0	0	0	.500	4	0	0	1.000

WORLD SERIES RECORD

Year Club	League	Pos.	G.	AB.	R.	H.	2B.	3B.	HR.	RBI.	B.A.	PO.	A.	E.	F.A.
1981—New York	Amer.	OF	5	15	2	3	0	0	0	0	.200	6	0	0	1.000

ALL-STAR GAME RECORD

Year League	Pos.	AB.	R.	H.	2B.	3B.	HR.	RBI.	B.A.	PO.	A.	E.	F.A.
1984—National	PH	1	0	0	0	0	0	0	.000	0	0	0	.000

STEPHEN ANDREW MURA

Name pronounced MYUR-uh.

(Steve)

Born February 12, 1955, at New Orleans, La.
Height, 6.02. Weight, 188.
Throws and bats righthanded.
Attended Tulane University, New Orleans, La.

Major League saves: 1979 (2), 1980 (2), 1985 (1). Total—5.

Led Pacific Coast League in complete games with 16 in 1978.
Tied for Pacific Coast League lead in shutouts with 3 in 1977.
Named righthanded pitcher on THE SPORTING NEWS College Baseball All-America Team, 1976.

Year Club	League	G.	IP.	W.	L.	Pct.	H.	R.	ER.	SO.	BB.	ERA.
1976—Walla Walla	Northwest	8	59	7	0	*1.000	41	14	9	68	18	*1.37
1976—Amarillo	Texas	7	59	4	2	.667	48	22	17	50	27	2.59
1977—Hawaii	P. Coast	28	165	12	10	.545	164	106	87	123	122	4.75
1978—Hawaii	P. Coast	26	177	10	*16	.385	177	94	82	*158	90	4.17
1978—San Diego	National	5	8	0	2	.000	15	10	10	5	5	11.25
1979—San Diego†	National	38	73	4	4	.500	57	30	25	59	37	3.08
1980—San Diego	National	37	169	8	7	.533	149	74	69	109	86	3.67
1981—San Diego‡	National	23	139	5	●14	.263	156	72	66	70	50	4.27
1982—St. Louis§	National	35	184⅓	12	11	.522	196	89	83	84	80	4.05
1983—Chicago	American	6	12⅓	0	0	.000	13	11	6	4	6	4.38
1983—Denver xy	Am. Assoc.	19	121⅓	3	11	.214	121	73	65	85	49	4.82
1984—Portland z	P. Coast	48	99	9	4	.692	94	57	55	82	53	5.00
1985—Tacoma	P. Coast	16	111	7	5	.583	103	55	45	89	35	3.65
1985—Oakland a	American	23	48	1	1	.500	41	25	22	29	25	4.13
American League Totals—2 Years		29	60⅓	1	1	.500	54	36	28	33	31	4.18
National League Totals—5 Years		138	573⅓	29	38	.433	573	275	253	327	258	3.97
Major League Totals—7 Years		167	633⅔	30	39	.435	627	311	281	360	289	3.99

Selected by San Diego Padres' organization in 2nd round of free-agent draft, June 8, 1976.
†On disabled list, May 23 to June 28, 1979.

‡Traded with a player to be named later to St. Louis Cardinals for Outfielder Sixto Lezcano and a player to be named later, December 10, 1981; St. Louis organization acquired Pitcher Al Olmsted and San Diego Padres acquired Pitcher Luis DeLeon to complete deal, February 19, 1982.

§Selected by Chicago White Sox' organization in player compensation pool draft, January 26, 1983. (Chicago received compensation for New York Yankees' signing of free-agent Outfielder Steve Kemp, a Type A player, December 9, 1982.)

xOn disabled list, June 29 to July 10, 1983.

yReleased, March 26, 1984; signed by Portland (Philadelphia Phillies' organization), April 5, 1984.

zReleased, October 31, 1984; signed by Tacoma (Oakland A's organization), March 11, 1985.

aReleased, December 20, 1985.

DALE BRYAN MURPHY

Born March 12, 1956, at Portland, Ore.
Height, 6.05. Weight, 215.
Throws and bats righthanded.
Attended Portland Community College, Portland, Ore. and Brigham Young University, Provo, Utah.

Tied major league records for fewest double plays by outfielder, season, 150 or more games (0), 1983; fewest double plays by outfielder, season, for leader in double plays (4), 1981 and 1985.

Major league stolen bases: 1978 (11), 1979 (6), 1980 (9), 1981 (14), 1982 (23), 1983 (30), 1984 (19), 1985 (10). Total—122.

Hit three home runs in a game, May 18, 1979.

Led National League in bases on balls received with 90 in 1985.

Led National League in total bases with 332 in 1984.

Led National League in slugging percentage with .540 in 1983 and .547 in 1984.

Led National League batters in strikeouts with 145 in 1978, 133 in 1980 and tied for lead with 141 in 1985.

Led National League first basemen in errors with 20 in 1978.

Tied for National League lead in double plays by outfielders with 4 in 1981 and 1985.

Tied for International League lead in total bases with 249 in 1977.

Led International League catchers in putouts with 510, passed balls with 14 and tied for lead in double plays with 7 in 1977.

Named National League Player of the Year by THE SPORTING NEWS, 1982 and 1983.

Named National League Most Valuable Player by Baseball Writers' Association of America, 1982 and 1983.

Named outfielder on THE SPORTING NEWS National League All-Star Team, 1982 through 1985.

Named outfielder on THE SPORTING NEWS National League All-Star fielding team, 1982 through 1985.

Named outfielder on THE SPORTING NEWS National League Silver Slugger team, 1982 through 1985.

Year Club	League	Pos.	G.	AB.	R.	H.	2B.	3B.	HR.	RBI.	B.A.	PO.	A.	E.	F.A.
1974—Kingsport	Appal.	C	54	181	28	46	7	0	5	31	.254	389	28	7	.983
1975—Greenwood	W. Car.	C-1B	131	443	48	101	20	1	5	48	.228	723	81	18	.978
1976—Savannah	South.	C	104	352	37	94	13	5	12	55	.267	444	40	10	.980
1976—Richmond	Int.	C-OF	18	50	10	13	1	1	4	8	.260	60	9	4	.945
1976—Atlanta	Nat.	C	19	65	3	17	6	0	0	9	.262	100	13	3	.974
1977—Richmond	Int.	C-1B	127	466	71	142	●33	4	22	*90	.305	600	50	15	.977
1977—Atlanta	Nat.	C	18	76	5	24	8	1	2	14	.316	114	11	6	.954
1978—Atlanta	Nat.	1B-C	151	530	66	120	14	3	23	79	.226	1220	105	23	.983
1979—Atlanta†	Nat.	1B-C	104	384	53	106	7	2	21	57	.276	812	57	20	.978
1980—Atlanta	Nat.	OF-1B	156	569	98	160	27	2	33	89	.281	384	15	6	.985
1981—Atlanta	Nat.	OF-1B	104	369	43	91	12	1	13	50	.247	264	11	5	.982
1982—Atlanta	Nat.	OF	●162	598	113	168	23	2	36	●109	.281	407	6	9	.979
1983—Atlanta	Nat.	OF	*162	589	131	178	24	4	36	*121	.302	373	10	6	.985
1984—Atlanta	Nat.	OF	*162	607	94	176	32	8	●36	100	.290	369	10	5	.987
1985—Atlanta	Nat.	OF	●162	616	*118	185	32	2	*37	111	.300	334	8	7	.980
Major League Totals—10 Years			1200	4403	724	1225	185	25	237	739	.278	4377	246	90	.981

Selected by Atlanta Braves' organization in 1st round (fifth player selected) of free-agent draft, June 5, 1974.
†On disabled list, May 25 to July 19, 1979.

Year Club League	Pos.	G.	AB.	R.	H.	2B.	3B.	HR.	RBI.	B.A.	PO.	A.	E.	F.A.
1982—Atlanta .... Nat.	OF	3	11	1	3	0	0	0	0	.273	8	0	0	1.000

ALL-STAR GAME RECORD

Year League	Pos.	AB.	R.	H.	2B.	3B.	HR.	RBI.	B.A.	PO.	A.	E.	F.A.
1980—National	OF	1	0	0	0	0	0	0	.000	0	0	0	.000
1982—National	OF	2	1	0	0	0	0	0	.000	2	0	0	1.000
1983—National	OF	3	0	1	0	0	0	1	.333	0	0	0	.000
1984—National	OF	3	1	2	0	0	1	1	.667	0	0	0	.000
1985—National	OF	3	0	1	1	0	0	0	.333	1	0	0	1.000
All-Star Game Totals—5 Years..................		12	2	4	1	0	1	2	.333	3	0	0	1.000

DANIEL LEE MURPHY
(Dan)

Born September 18, 1964, at Artesia, Calif.
Height, 6.02. Weight, 195.
Throws and bats righthanded.

Year Club	League	G.	IP.	W.	L.	Pct.	H.	R.	ER.	SO.	BB.	ERA.
1983—Paintsville	Ap'lachian	11	38⅔	3	1	.750	43	22	16	29	26	3.72
1983—Beloit	Midwest	8	24⅔	0	0	.000	21	14	11	22	14	4.01
1984—Beloit	Midwest	26	112⅔	9	4	.692	116	59	45	79	44	3.59
1985—Stockton	California	24	132	9	7	.563	114	65	58	157	84	3.95

Signed as free agent by Milwaukee Brewers' organization, December 2, 1982.

DWAYNE KEITH MURPHY

Born March 18, 1955, at Merced, Calif.
Height, 6.01. Weight, 185.
Throws right and bats lefthanded.

Tied major league record for fewest double plays by outfielder, season, 150 or more games (0), 1980 and 1985.
Major League stolen bases: 1979 (15), 1980 (26), 1981 (10), 1982 (26), 1983 (7), 1984 (4), 1985 (4). Total—92.
Led American League in sacrifice hits with 22 in 1980 and game-winning RBIs with 15 in 1981.
Led American League outfielders in total chances with 525 in 1980, 474 in 1982 and 494 in 1984.
Led Southern League in bases on balls received with 97 in 1977.
Tied for Southern League lead in double plays by outfielders with 4 in 1977.
Named outfielder on THE SPORTING NEWS American League All-Star Team, 1981.
Named outfielder on THE SPORTING NEWS American League All-Star fielding team, 1980 through 1985.

Year Club	League	Pos.	G.	AB.	R.	H.	2B.	3B.	HR.	RBI.	B.A.	PO.	A.	E.	F.A.
1973—Lewiston	N'west	OF	68	215	25	50	7	2	3	19	.233	102	*13	6	.950
1974—Burlington†	Midw.	OF	53	150	16	33	6	2	2	10	.220	55	2	3	.959
1975—Modesto	Calif.	OF	126	429	81	125	20	7	8	71	.291	250	7	9	.966
1976—Chattanooga	South.	OF	68	200	32	52	6	0	1	23	.260	138	6	1	.993
1976—Tucson	P. C.	OF	52	179	32	42	7	2	3	11	.235	125	6	4	.970
1977—Chattanooga	South.	OF	132	406	53	104	11	9	5	53	.256	320	14	5	*.985
1978—Vancouver...........	P. C.	OF-SS	42	148	35	39	4	1	7	17	.264	125	9	3	.978
1978—Oakland‡.............	Amer.	OF	60	52	15	10	2	0	0	5	.192	49	1	0	1.000
1979—Oakland‡.............	Amer.	OF	121	388	57	99	10	4	11	40	.255	322	10	4	.988
1980—Oakland.............	Amer.	OF	159	573	86	157	18	2	13	68	.274	*507	13	5	.990
1981—Oakland.............	Amer.	OF	107	390	58	98	10	3	15	60	.251	326	6	5	.985
1982—Oakland.............	Amer.	*OF-SS	151	543	84	129	15	1	27	94	.238	*452	18	8	.983
1983—Oakland§.............	Amer.	OF	130	471	55	107	17	2	17	75	.227	365	7	8	.979
1984—Oakland.............	Amer.	OF	153	559	93	143	18	2	33	88	.256	*474	14	6	.988
1985—Oakland.............	Amer.	OF	152	523	77	122	21	3	20	59	.233	432	6	5	.989
Major League Totals—8 Years...............		1033	3499	525	865	111	17	136	489	.247	2927	75	41	.987

Selected by Oakland A's organization in 15th round of free-agent draft, June 5, 1973.
†On disabled list, July 16 to September 16, 1974.
‡On disabled list, June 21 to July 14, 1979.
§On disabled list, June 24 to July 11, 1983.

DIVISION SERIES RECORD

Year Club	League	Pos.	G.	AB.	R.	H.	2B.	3B.	HR.	RBI.	B.A.	PO.	A.	E.	F.A.
1981—Oakland.................	Amer.	OF	3	11	4	6	1	0	1	2	.545	13	0	0	1.000

CHAMPIONSHIP SERIES RECORD

Year Club	League	Pos.	G.	AB.	R.	H.	2B.	3B.	HR.	RBI.	B.A.	PO.	A.	E.	F.A.
1981—Oakland.................	Amer.	OF	3	8	0	2	1	0	0	1	.250	9	0	0	1.000

ROBERT ALBERT MURPHY JR.
(Rob)

Born May 26, 1960, at Miami, Fla.
Height, 6.02. Weight, 200.
Throws and bats lefthanded.
Attended University of Florida, Gainesville, Fla.

Tied for Eastern League lead in saves with 15 in 1984.

Year—Club	League	G.	IP.	W.	L.	Pct.	H.	R.	ER.	SO.	BB.	ERA.
1981—Tampa	Florida St.	25	105	6	8	.429	109	73	53	58	67	4.54
1982—Cedar Rapids	Midwest	31	89	3	7	.300	92	62	40	96	61	4.04
1983—Cedar Rapids	Midwest	36	140⅔	6	10	.375	120	66	52	137	69	3.33
1984—Vermont	Eastern	45	69⅔	2	3	.400	57	23	21	69	35	2.71
1985—Denver	Am. Assoc.	41	84	5	5	.500	94	55	43	66	57	4.61
1985—Cincinnati	National	2	3	0	0	.000	2	2	2	1	2	6.00
Major League Totals—1 Year		2	3	0	0	.000	2	2	2	1	2	6.00

Selected by Milwaukee Brewers' organization in 29th round of free-agent draft, June 6, 1978.
Selected by Cincinnati Reds' organization in secondary phase of free-agent draft, January 13, 1981.

DALE ALBERT MURRAY

Born February 2, 1950, at Cuero, Tex.
Height, 6.04. Weight, 225.
Throws and bats righthanded.
Attended Blinn Junior College, Brenham, Tex., and Victoria College, Victoria, Tex.

Tied major league record for most intentional bases on balls allowed, season (23), 1978.
Major League saves: 1974 (10), 1975 (9), 1976 (13), 1977 (4), 1978 (7), 1979 (5), 1982 (11), 1983 (1). Total—60.
Led National League in intentional bases on balls issued with 23 in 1978.
Led International League in saves with 16 in 1981.
Led Northern League in intentional bases on balls issued with 6 in 1970.

Year—Club	League	G.	IP.	W.	L.	Pct.	H.	R.	ER.	SO.	BB.	ERA.
1970—Watertown	Northern	22	51	4	6	.400	50	41	32	48	39	5.65
1971—West Palm Beach†	Florida St.	1	1	0	1	.000	4	4	4	2	2	36.00
1972—West Palm Beach	Florida St.	7	10	3	1	.750	10	6	6	8	7	5.40
1972—Quebec City	Eastern	39	108	11	5	.688	85	41	29	64	53	2.42
1973—Peninsula	Int'national	28	150	8	●13	.381	145	77	71	89	75	4.26
1974—Memphis	Int'national	30	43	4	2	.667	34	11	7	36	19	1.47
1974—Montreal	National	32	70	1	1	.500	46	12	8	31	23	1.03
1975—Montreal‡	National	63	111	15	8	.652	134	59	49	43	39	3.97
1976—Montreal§	National	★81	113	4	9	.308	117	47	41	35	37	3.27
1977—Cincinnati	National	61	102	7	2	.778	125	60	56	42	46	4.94
1978—Cincinnati x-New York	National	68	119	9	6	.600	119	59	50	62	53	3.78
1979—New York y-Montreal	National	67	110	5	10	.333	119	62	56	41	55	4.58
1980—Denver	Am. Assoc.	16	44	4	1	.800	31	13	8	25	17	1.64
1980—Montreal z	National	16	29	0	1	.000	39	23	20	16	12	6.21
1981—Syracuse	Int'national	52	78	5	4	.556	57	23	16	57	28	1.85
1981—Toronto	American	11	15	1	0	1.000	12	2	2	12	5	1.20
1982—Toronto x	American	56	111	8	7	.533	115	48	39	60	32	3.16
1983—New York b	American	40	94⅓	2	4	.333	113	56	47	45	22	4.48
1984—New York c	American	19	23⅔	1	2	.333	30	15	13	13	5	4.94
1984—Columbus	Int'national	8	16⅔	3	0	.000	18	12	11	13	7	5.94
1985—New York d-Texas	American	4	3	0	0	.000	7	5	5	0	0	15.00
1985—Oklahoma City	Am. Assoc.	26	35	1	4	.200	29	17	11	20	7	2.83
National League Totals—7 Years		388	654	41	37	.526	699	322	280	270	265	3.85
American League Totals—5 Years		130	247	12	13	.480	277	126	106	130	64	3.86
Major League Totals—12 Years		518	901	53	50	.515	976	448	386	400	329	3.86

Selected by Montreal Expos' organization in 18th round of free-agent draft, June 4, 1970.
†On disabled list, April 16 to September 30, 1971.
‡On disabled list, May 12 to June 17, 1975.
§Traded with Pitcher Woodie Fryman to Cincinnati Reds for First Baseman Tony Perez and Pitcher Will McEnaney, December 16, 1976.
xTraded to New York Mets for Outfielder Ken Henderson, May 19, 1978.
ySold to Montreal Expos, August 30, 1979.
zReleased, August 28, 1980; signed by Toronto Blue Jays' organization, January 20, 1981.
aTraded with Outfielder-Catcher Tom Dodd to New York Yankees for Outfielder-First Baseman Dave Collins, Pitcher Mike Morgan, First Baseman Fred McGriff and a reported $400,000, December 9, 1982.
bGranted free agency, November 7, 1983; re-signed by Yankees, November 21, 1983.
cOn disabled list, May 10 to August 14, 1984; included rehabilitation disability assignment to Columbus, July 23 to August 11, 1984.
dReleased, April 29, 1985; signed by Texas Rangers' organization, May 7, 1985.

RECORD AS OUTFIELDER

Year—Club	League	Pos.	G.	AB.	R.	H.	2B.	3B.	HR.	RBI.	B.A.	PO.	A.	E.	F.A.
1970—W. Palm Beach	Fla. St.	OF	4	3	0	1	0	0	0	0	.333	0	0	0	.000

EDDIE CLARENCE MURRAY

Born February 24, 1956, at Los Angeles, Calif.
Height, 6.02. Weight, 200.
Throws right and bats left and righthanded.
Attended California State University, Los Angeles, Calif.
Brother of Rich Murray, first baseman in Kansas City Royals' organization;
Leon Murray, first baseman in San Franciso Giants' organization, 1970;
Charles Murray, minor league outfielder, 1962 through 1966
and 1969; and Venice Murray, first baseman in
San Francisco Giants' organization, 1978.

Established major league record for most game-winning runs batted in, lifetime (97).
Tied major league records for most games, switch-hit home runs, season (2), 1982; most intentional bases on balls by switch-hitter, season (25), 1984.

Established American League record for most consecutive games, one or more hits by switch-hitter, season (22), 1984.
Major League stolen bases: 1978 (6), 1979 (10), 1980 (7), 1981 (2), 1982 (7), 1983 (5), 1984 (10), 1985 (5). Total—52.
Hit three home runs in a game, August 29, 1979 (second game), September 14, 1980 (13 innings) and August 26, 1985.
Switch-hit home runs in one game six times: August 3, 1977, August 29, 1979 (two righthanded and one lefthanded); August 16, 1981, April 24, 1982 , August 26, 1982 and August 26, 1985 (two lefthanded and one righthanded).
Led American League in bases on balls received with 107 and game-winning RBIs with 19 in 1984.
Led American League in intentional bases on balls received with 25 in 1984 and tied for lead with 18 in 1982.
Led American League first basemen in double plays with 152 in 1984 and tied for lead with 154 in 1985.
Led American League first basemen in total chances with 1,615 in 1978 and 1,694 in 1984.
Led American League first basemen in putouts with 1,504 in 1978.
Led Florida State League in total bases with 212 in 1974.
Led Florida State League first basemen in double plays with 113 in 1974.
Named American League Rookie of the Year by Baseball Writers' Association of America, 1977.
Named first baseman on THE SPORTING NEWS American League All-Star Team, 1983.
Named first baseman on THE SPORTING NEWS American League All-Star fielding team, 1982 through 1984.
Named first baseman on THE SPORTING NEWS American League Silver Slugger team, 1983 and 1984.
Named Appalachian League Player of the Year, 1973.

Year Club	League	Pos.	G.	AB.	R.	H.	2B.	3B.	HR.	RBI.	B.A.	PO.	A.	E.	F.A.
1973—Bluefield	Appal.	1B	50	188	34	54	6	0	11	32	.287	421	14	13	.971
1974—Miami	Fla. St.	1B	131	460	64	133	*29	7	12	63	.289	*1114	*51	*25	.979
1974—Asheville	South.	1B	2	7	1	2	2	0	0	2	.286	17	0	0	1.000
1975—Asheville	South.	1B-3B	124	436	66	115	13	5	17	68	.264	637	58	15	.979
1976—Charlotte	South.	1B	88	299	46	89	15	2	12	46	.298	746	45	9	.989
1976—Rochester	Int.	1B-OF-3B	54	168	35	46	6	2	11	40	.274	291	13	5	.984
1977—Baltimore	Amer.	OF-1B	160	611	81	173	29	2	27	88	.283	482	20	4	.992
1978—Baltimore	Amer.	1B-3B	161	610	85	174	32	3	27	95	.285	1507	112	6	.996
1979—Baltimore	Amer.	1B	159	606	90	179	30	2	25	99	.295	*1456	107	10	.994
1980—Baltimore	Amer.	1B	158	621	100	186	36	2	32	116	.300	1369	77	9	.994
1981—Baltimore	Amer.	1B	99	378	57	111	21	2	●22	*78	.294	899	*91	1	*.999
1982—Baltimore	Amer.	1B	151	550	87	174	30	1	32	110	.316	1269	97	4	*.997
1983—Baltimore	Amer.	1B	156	582	115	178	30	3	33	111	.306	1393	114	10	.993
1984—Baltimore	Amer.	1B	●162	588	97	180	26	3	29	110	.306	*1538	*143	13	.992
1985—Baltimore	Amer.	1B	156	583	111	173	37	1	31	124	.297	1338	152	*19	.987
Major League Totals—9 Years			1362	5129	823	1528	271	19	258	931	.298	11251	913	76	.994

Selected by Baltimore Orioles' organization in 3rd round of free-agent draft, June 5, 1973.

CHAMPIONSHIP SERIES RECORD

Tied Championship Series record for most runs, game (4), October 7, 1983.
Tied American League Championship Series record for most bases on balls, four-game Series (5), 1979.

Year Club	League	Pos.	G.	AB.	R.	H.	2B.	3B.	HR.	RBI.	B.A.	PO.	A.	E.	F.A.
1979—Baltimore	Amer.	1B	4	12	3	5	0	0	1	5	.417	44	3	2	.959
1983—Baltimore	Amer.	1B	4	15	5	4	0	0	1	3	.267	34	3	1	.974
Championship Series Totals—2 Years			8	27	8	9	0	0	2	8	.333	78	6	3	.966

WORLD SERIES RECORD

Established World Series record for most double plays started by first baseman, game (2), October 11, 1979.

Year Club	League	Pos.	G.	AB.	R.	H.	2B.	3B.	HR.	RBI.	B.A.	PO.	A.	E.	F.A.
1979—Baltimore	Amer.	1B	7	26	3	4	1	0	1	2	.154	60	7	0	1.000
1983—Baltimore	Amer.	1B	5	20	2	5	0	0	2	3	.250	46	1	1	.979
World Series Totals—2 Years			12	46	5	9	1	0	3	5	.196	106	8	1	.991

ALL-STAR GAME RECORD

Year League	Pos.	AB.	R.	H.	2B.	3B.	HR.	RBI.	B.A.	PO.	A.	E.	F.A.
1981—American	PH-1B	2	0	0	0	0	0	0	.000	2	1	0	1.000
1982—American	PH-1B	1	0	0	0	0	0	0	.000	4	0	0	1.000
1983—American	1B	2	0	0	0	0	0	0	.000	4	0	0	1.000
1984—American	1B	2	0	1	1	0	0	0	.500	3	0	0	1.000
1985—American	1B	3	0	0	0	0	0	0	.000	5	2	0	1.000
All-Star Game Totals—5 Years		10	0	1	1	0	0	0	.100	18	3	0	1.000

Named to American League All-Star Team for 1978 game; did not play.

RALPH RONALD MUSSELMAN
(Ron)

Born November 11, 1954, at Wilmington, N.C.
Height, 6.02. Weight, 185.
Throws and bats righthanded.
Attended Louisburg Junior College, Louisburg, N.C., and
Clemson University, Clemson, S.C.

Major League saves: 1984 (1).
Led Pacific Coast League in games finished in relief with 44 in 1982.

Year Club	League	G.	IP.	W.	L.	Pct.	H.	R.	ER.	SO.	BB.	ERA.
1977—Bellingham	Northwest	12	70	4	4	.500	75	44	36	67	26	4.63
1978—Alexandria	Carolina	25	161	6	12	.333	182	96	76	111	69	4.25
1979—Alexandria	Carolina	27	90	3	4	.429	87	44	31	60	30	3.10
1980—Lynn	Eastern	53	86	6	6	.500	75	49	37	47	34	3.87
1981—Spokane†	P. Coast	43	67	1	8	.111	69	31	28	25	27	3.76

Year Club	League	G.	IP.	W.	L.	Pct.	H.	R.	ER.	SO.	BB.	ERA.
1982—Salt Lake City	P. Coast	●51	68⅔	5	4	.556	68	25	25	40	19	3.28
1982—Seattle‡	American	12	15⅔	1	0	1.000	18	7	6	9	6	3.45
1983—Oklahoma City	Am. Assoc.	28	137⅔	9	12	.429	166	99	84	85	50	5.49
1984—Oklahoma City§x	Am. Assoc.	13	26⅔	1	2	.333	29	13	12	18	8	4.05
1984—Syracuse	Int'national	26	31	1	2	.333	27	10	10	19	12	2.90
1984—Toronto	American	11	21⅓	0	2	.000	18	7	5	9	10	2.11
1985—Toronto	American	25	52⅓	3	0	1.000	59	28	26	29	24	4.47
1985—Syracuse y	Int'national	2	11	1	0	1.000	13	7	6	5	1	4.91
Major League Totals—3 Years		48	89⅓	4	2	.667	95	42	37	47	40	3.73

Selected by California Angels' organization in 22nd round of free-agent draft, June 4, 1975.
Selected by Houston Astros' organization in secondary phase of free-agent draft, June 8, 1976.
Selected by Seattle Mariners' organization in 5th round of free-agent draft, June 7, 1977.
†On disabled list, April 23 to May 7, 1981.
‡Traded to Texas Rangers for First Baseman Pat Putnam, December 21, 1982.
§On disabled list, April 19 to May 11, 1984.
xSold to Syracuse (Toronto Blue Jays' organization), June 8, 1984.
yGranted free agency, October 15, 1985; signed by Cleveland Indians, December 12, 1985.

RANDALL KIRK MYERS
(Randy)

Born September 19, 1962, at Vancouver, Wash.
Height, 6.01. Weight, 190.
Throws and bats lefthanded.
Attended Clark College, Vancouver, Wash.

Tied for Carolina League lead in complete games with 7 in 1984.
Tied for South Atlantic League lead in games started by pitchers with 28 in 1983.
Tied for Appalachian League lead in games started by pitchers with 13 and balks with 3 in 1982.
Named Carolina League Pitcher of the Year, 1984.

Year Club	League	G.	IP.	W.	L.	Pct.	H.	R.	ER.	SO.	BB.	ERA.
1982—Kingsport	Ap'lachian	13	74⅓	6	3	.667	68	49	34	●86	69	4.12
1983—Columbia	S. Atlantic	28	173⅓	14	10	.583	146	94	70	164	108	3.63
1984—Lynchburg	Carolina	23	157	13	5	.722	123	46	36	171	61	*2.06
1984—Jackson	Texas	5	35	2	1	.667	29	14	8	35	16	2.06
1985—Jackson	Texas	19	120⅓	4	8	.333	99	61	53	116	69	3.96
1985—Tidewater	Int'national	8	44	1	1	.500	40	13	9	25	20	1.84
1985—New York	National	1	2	0	0	.000	0	0	0	2	1	0.00
Major League Totals—1 Year		1	2	0	0	.000	0	0	0	2	1	0.00

Selected by Cincinnati Reds' organization in 3rd round of free-agent draft, January 12, 1982.
Selected by New York Mets' organization in secondary phase of free-agent draft, June 7, 1982.

JERRY AUSTIN NARRON

Born January 15, 1956, at Goldsboro, N. C.
Height, 6.03. Weight, 205.
Throws right and bats lefthanded.
Attends East Carolina University, Greenville, N. C.
Brother of John Narron, Jr., first baseman in New York Yankees' and Chicago White
Sox' organizations, 1974 and 1975; nephew of Sam Narron, catcher with St. Louis Cardinals,
1935, 1942 and 1943; coach, Pittsburgh Pirates, 1951 through 1964; and part-time scout with Pittsburgh Pirates
since 1982; nephew of Milton Narron, former minor league catcher-outfielder.

Led Pacific Coast League in intentional bases on balls received with 15 in 1983.
Tied for Florida State League lead in being hit by pitch with 10 in 1975.
Led Florida State League catchers in fielding percentage with .986 and double plays with 7 in 1976.
Tied for Pacific Coast League lead in double plays by catchers with 11 in 1978.

Year Club	League	Pos.	G.	AB.	R.	H.	2B.	3B.	HR.	RBI.	B.A.	PO.	A.	E.	F.A.
1974—Johnson City	Appal.	C-OF	66	226	43	68	15	3	7	49	.301	249	19	8	.971
1975—Fort Lauderdale	Fla. St.	1B-C-OF	113	360	39	76	12	0	2	34	.211	425	33	2	.996
1976—Fort Lauderdale	Fla. St.	C-1B	119	412	35	101	17	0	6	56	.245	563	56	8	.987
1977—West Haven	East.	C-1B	121	438	80	131	16	0	28	93	.299	625	40	7	.990
1978—Tacoma	P. C.	C-1B	120	435	67	121	25	1	15	84	.278	552	78	18	.972
1979—New York†	Amer.	C	61	123	17	21	3	1	4	18	.171	167	15	5	.973
1980—Spokane	P. C.	C-1B	67	233	40	66	14	2	9	39	.283	223	19	6	.976
1980—Seattle	Amer.	C	48	107	7	21	3	0	4	18	.196	115	11	1	.992
1981—Seattle‡	Amer.	C	76	203	13	45	5	0	3	17	.222	248	11	1	.996
1982—Spokane	P. C.	C	110	408	60	127	24	2	12	61	.311	446	46	12	.976
1983—Edmonton	P. C.	1B-C	139	532	93	160	30	5	27	102	.301	1298	70	13	.991
1983—California	Amer.	C	10	22	1	3	0	0	1	4	.136	14	3	2	.895
1984—California	Amer.	C-1B	69	150	9	37	5	0	3	17	.247	184	12	1	.995
1985—California	Amer.	C-1B	67	132	12	29	4	0	5	14	.220	146	14	0	1.000
Major League Totals—6 Years			331	737	59	156	20	1	20	88	.212	874	66	10	.989

Selected by New York Yankees' organization in 6th round of free-agent draft, June 5, 1974.
†Traded with Outfielder Juan Beniquez and Pitchers Jim Beattie and Rick Anderson to Seattle Mariners for
Outfielder Ruppert Jones and Pitcher Jim Lewis, November 1, 1979.
‡Released, March 30, 1982; signed by California Angels' organization, April 1, 1982.

RICKY LEE NELSON

Born May 8, 1959, at Eloy, Ariz.
Height, 6.00. Weight, 195.
Throws right and bats lefthanded.
Attended Arizona State University, Tempe, Ariz.

Major League stolen bases: 1983 (7).
Tied for California League lead in total bases with 245 and game-winning RBIs with 15 in 1982.

Year Club	League	Pos.	G.	AB.	R.	H.	2B.	3B.	HR.	RBI.	B.A.	PO.	A.	E.	F.A.
1981—Bellingham	N'west	OF	56	197	35	56	5	0	6	37	.284	49	7	3	.949
1982—Bakersfield	Calif.	OF	★140	★566	65	174	★36	1	11	★101	.307	197	13	9	.959
1983—Salt Lake City	P. C.	OF-3B	29	102	20	34	6	3	5	27	.333	55	4	1	.983
1983—Seattle	Amer.	OF	98	291	32	74	13	3	5	36	.254	122	10	4	.971
1984—Salt Lake City†	P. C.	OF	75	310	54	91	11	4	11	42	.294	141	3	2	.986
1984—Seattle	Amer.	OF	9	15	2	3	0	0	1	2	.200	2	0	0	1.000
1985—Calgary	P. C.	OF	120	489	75	131	30	4	16	70	.268	210	5	6	.973
1985—Seattle	Amer.	OF	6	2	2	0	0	0	0	0	.000	1	0	0	1.000
Major League Totals—3 Years			113	308	36	77	13	3	6	38	.250	125	10	4	.971

Selected by California Angels' organization in 24th round of free-agent draft, June 3, 1980.
Selected by Seattle Mariners' organization in 4th round of free-agent draft, June 8, 1981.
†On disabled list, June 8 to July 19, 1984.

ROBERT AUGUSTUS NELSON II
(Rob)

Born May 17, 1964, at Pasadena, Calif.
Height, 6.04. Weight, 215.
Throws and bats lefthanded.
Attended Mount San Antonio College, Walnut, Calif.

Led Midwest League batters in strikeouts with 140 in 1984.
Led Midwest League first basemen in double plays with 111 and total chances with 1,279 in 1984.

Year Club	League	Pos.	G.	AB.	R.	H.	2B.	3B.	HR.	RBI.	B.A.	PO.	A.	E.	F.A.
1983—Idaho Falls	Pion.	1B	54	196	42	57	12	2	12	38	.291	418	32	6	.986
1984—Madison	Midw.	1B	136	487	71	120	25	2	19	85	.246	★1173	★89	17	.987
1985—Huntsville	South.	1B	140	499	68	116	25	0	32	98	.232	1101	86	★23	.981

Selected by Houston Astros' organization in 27th round of free-agent draft, June 7, 1982.
Selected by Atlanta Braves' organization in secondary phase of free-agent draft, January 11, 1983.
Selected by Oakland A's organization in secondary phase of free-agent draft, June 6, 1983.

WAYLAND EUGENE NELSON II
(Gene)

Born December 3, 1960, at Tampa, Fla.
Height, 6.00. Weight, 172.
Throws and bats righthanded.

Major League saves: 1984 (1), 1985 (2). Total—3.
Led Florida State League in shutouts with 5 and complete games with 16 in 1980.

Year Club	League	G.	IP.	W.	L.	Pct.	H.	R.	ER.	SO.	BB.	ERA.
1978—Sarasota Rangers	Gulf Coast	14	52	5	0	●1.000	41	18	13	28	20	2.25
1979—Asheville†	W. Carol.	33	155	13	5	★.722	149	77	62	96	44	3.60
1980—Fort Lauderdale	Florida St.	27	196	★20	3	★.870	146	51	43	130	70	1.97
1981—New York‡	American	8	39	3	1	.750	40	24	21	16	23	4.85
1981—Fort Lauderdale	Florida St.	2	10	0	0	.000	9	6	6	8	5	5.40
1981—Columbus§	Int'national	5	32	4	0	1.000	25	9	9	37	14	2.53
1982—Seattle	American	22	122⅔	6	9	.400	133	70	70	60	71	4.62
1982—Salt Lake City	P. Coast	5	37⅔	1	3	.250	36	18	14	22	28	3.35
1983—Salt Lake City x	P. Coast	16	99	9	4	.692	115	65	57	74	28	5.18
1983—Seattle	American	10	32	0	3	.000	38	29	28	11	21	7.88
1984—Salt Lake City y	P. Coast	17	112	6	8	.429	138	75	70	89	54	5.63
1984—Chicago	American	20	74⅔	3	5	.375	72	38	37	36	17	4.46
1985—Chicago z	American	46	145⅖	10	10	.500	144	74	69	101	67	4.26
Major League Totals—5 Years		106	414	22	28	.440	427	235	218	235	188	4.74

Selected by Texas Rangers' organization in 29th round of free-agent draft, June 6, 1978.
†Traded with Pitcher Ray Fontenot to New York Yankees' organization for Pitchers Bob Polinsky, Neal Mersch and Mark Softy, October 8, 1979; completing deal in which New York traded Outfielder Mickey Rivers and three players to be named later to Texas Rangers for Third Baseman Amos Lewis and two players to be named later, August 1, 1979.
‡On disabled list, April 10 to May 4, 1981; included rehabilitation disability assignment to Ft. Lauderdale, April 17 to May 4, 1981.
§Traded with Pitcher Bill Caudill, a player to be named later and cash to Seattle Mariners for Pitcher Shane Rawley, April 1, 1982; Seattle organization acquired Outfielder Bobby Brown to complete deal, April 6, 1982.
xOn disabled list, June 25 to July 31, 1983.
yTraded with Pitcher Jerry Don Gleaton to Chicago White Sox for Pitcher Salome Barojas, June 27, 1984.
zHad one at-bat with no hits.

GRAIG NETTLES

Born August 20, 1944, at San Diego, Calif.
Height, 6.00. Weight, 187.
Throws right and bats lefthanded.
Attended San Diego State College, San Diego, Calif.
Brother of Jim Nettles, outfielder with Minnesota, Detroit, Kansas City and Oakland,
1970 through 1972, 1974, 1979 and 1981; minor league coach, Oakland A's organization,
1982 and 1983; and minor league manager in Oakland A's organization since 1984.

Established major league records for most assists by third baseman, season (412), and most double plays by third baseman, season (54), 1971.

Tied major league records for most home runs month of April (11), 1974; fewest three-base hits, season, 150 or more games (0), 1972 and 1973.

Established American League record for most home runs by third baseman, lifetime (319).

Tied American League record for most home runs, doubleheader (4), April 14, 1974.

Major League stolen bases: 1969 (1), 1970 (3), 1971 (7), 1972 (2), 1974 (1), 1975 (1), 1976 (11), 1977 (2), 1978 (1), 1979 (1), 1982 (1). Total—31.

Led American League in sacrifice flies with 11 in 1975.

Led American League third basemen in total chances with 587 in 1971, 553 in 1973, 545 in 1974 and 539 in 1976.

Led American League third basemen in double plays with 54 in 1971, 30 in 1976 and tied for lead with 30 in 1978.

Led American League third basemen in assists with 383 in 1976.

Led Southern League third basemen in double plays with 34 in 1967 and led Pacific Coast League third basemen with 20 in 1968.

Named third baseman on THE SPORTING NEWS American League All Star Team, 1975, 1977 and 1978.

Named third baseman on THE SPORTING NEWS American League All-Star fielding team, 1977 and 1978.

Year Club	League	Pos.	G.	AB.	R.	H.	2B.	3B.	HR.	RBI.	B.A.	PO.	A.	E.	F.A.
1966—Wis. Rapids	Midw.	2B-3B	117	413	84	111	19	6	★28	75	.269	240	245	28	.945
1967—Charlotte	South.	3B	140	499	69	116	18	4	●19	86	.232	107	★318	24	.947
1967—Minnesota	Amer.	PH	3	3	0	1	1	0	0	0	.333	0	0	0	.000
1968—Denver	P. C.	3B-OF-1B	130	451	84	134	17	●12	22	83	.297	125	266	17	.958
1968—Minnesota	Amer.	OF-3B-1B	22	76	13	17	2	1	5	8	.224	50	9	2	.967
1969—Minnesota†	Amer.	OF-3B	96	225	27	50	9	2	7	26	.222	88	44	2	.985
1970—Cleveland	Amer.	★3B-OF	157	549	81	129	13	1	26	62	.235	135	358	17	★.967
1971—Cleveland	Amer.	3B	158	598	78	156	18	1	28	86	.261	★159	★412	16	.973
1972—Cleveland‡	Amer.	3B	150	557	65	141	28	0	17	70	.253	114	★358	★21	.957
1973—New York	Amer.	3B	160	552	65	129	18	0	22	81	.234	117	★410	26	.953
1974—New York	Amer.	★3B-SS	155	566	74	139	21	1	22	75	.246	★147	377	21	.961
1975—New York	Amer.	3B	157	581	71	155	24	4	21	91	.267	135	★379	19	.964
1976—New York	Amer.	3B-SS	158	583	88	148	29	2	★32	93	.254	137	384	19	.965
1977—New York	Amer.	3B	158	589	99	150	23	4	37	107	.255	132	321	12	.974
1978—New York	Amer.	3B-SS	159	587	81	162	23	2	27	93	.276	110	326	11	.975
1979—New York	Amer.	3B	145	521	71	132	15	1	20	73	.253	110	339	16	.966
1980—New York§	Amer.	3B-SS	89	324	52	79	14	0	16	45	.244	59	183	10	.960
1981—New York	Amer.	3B	103	349	46	85	7	1	15	46	.244	63	214	8	.972
1982—New York x	Amer.	3B	122	405	47	94	11	2	18	55	.232	73	255	23	.934
1983—New York y	Amer.	3B	129	462	56	123	17	3	20	75	.266	78	273	16	.956
1984—San Diego	Nat.	3B	124	395	56	90	11	1	20	65	.228	93	201	20	.936
1985—San Diego	Nat.	3B	137	440	66	115	23	1	15	61	.261	122	229	15	.959
American League Totals—17 Years			2121	7527	1014	1890	273	25	333	1086	.251	1707	4642	239	.964
National League Totals—2 Years			261	835	122	205	34	2	35	126	.246	215	430	35	.949
Major League Totals—19 Years			2382	8362	1136	2095	307	27	368	1212	.251	1922	5072	274	.962

Selected by Minnesota Twins' organization in 4th round of free-agent draft, June 9, 1965.

†Traded with Pitchers Dean Chance and Robert L. Miller and Outfielder Ted Uhlaender to Cleveland Indians for Pitchers Luis Tiant and Stan Williams, December 12, 1969.

‡Traded with Catcher Jerry Moses to New York Yankees for Catcher-First Baseman John Ellis, Infielder Jerry Kenney and Outfielders Charlie Spikes and Rosendo Torres, November 27, 1972.

§On disabled list, July 27 to October 2, 1980.

xOn disabled list, April 26 to May 17, 1982.

yTraded to San Diego Padres for Pitcher Dennis Rasmussen and a player to be named later, March 30, 1984; New York Yankees' organization acquired Pitcher Darin Cloninger to complete deal, April 26, 1984.

DIVISION SERIES RECORD

Year Club	League	Pos.	G.	AB.	R.	H.	2B.	3B.	HR.	RBI.	B.A.	PO.	A.	E.	F.A.
1981—New York	Amer.	3B	5	17	1	1	0	0	0	1	.059	7	7	0	1.000

CHAMPIONSHIP SERIES RECORD

Established Championship Series records for most hits, inning (2), October 14, 1981; most runs batted in, three-game Series (9), 1981.

Tied Championship Series records for most times reached first base safely, game (5), October 14, 1981; most clubs, total Series (3).

Tied American League Championship Series records for most home runs, five-game Series (2), 1976; highest slugging average, three-game Series (.917), 1981; most Series, one or more home runs (4).

Year Club	League	Pos.	G.	AB.	R.	H.	2B.	3B.	HR.	RBI.	B.A.	PO.	A.	E.	F.A.
1969—Minnesota	Amer.	PH	1	1	0	1	0	0	0	0	1.000	0	0	0	.000
1976—New York	Amer.	3B	5	17	2	4	1	0	2	4	.235	5	14	0	1.000
1977—New York	Amer.	3B	5	20	1	3	0	0	0	1	.150	2	12	0	1.000
1978—New York	Amer.	3B	4	15	3	5	0	1	1	2	.333	6	7	0	1.000
1980—New York	Amer.	3B-PH	2	6	1	1	0	0	1	1	.167	0	2	0	1.000
1981—New York	Amer.	3B	3	12	2	6	2	0	1	9	.500	4	4	1	.889
1984—San Diego	Nat.	3B	4	14	1	2	0	0	0	2	.143	5	8	0	1.000
Championship Series Totals—7 Years			24	85	10	22	3	1	5	19	.259	22	47	1	.986

WORLD SERIES RECORD

Established World Series records for most double plays by third baseman, four-game Series (3), 1976; most assists by third baseman, six-game Series (20), 1977; highest fielding average by third baseman, six-game Series, most chances accepted (1.000 and 26), 1978; most double plays by third baseman, total Series (7); most double plays and double plays started by third baseman, six-game Series (3), 1978; most assists by third baseman, total Series (68); most chances accepted by third baseman, total Series (96).

Tied World Series records for most double plays started by third baseman, four-game Series (2), 1976; most double plays started, game (2), October 19, 1976; fewest chances accepted by third baseman, game (0), October 18, 1977.

Year Club	League	Pos.	G.	AB.	R.	H.	2B.	3B.	HR.	RBI.	B.A.	PO.	A.	E.	F.A.
1976—New York	Amer.	3B	4	12	0	3	0	0	0	2	.250	8	8	0	1.000
1977—New York	Amer.	3B	6	21	1	4	1	0	0	2	.190	2	20	1	.957
1978—New York	Amer.	3B	6	25	2	4	0	0	0	1	.160	8	18	0	1.000
1981—New York	Amer.	3B	3	10	1	4	1	0	0	0	.400	3	10	1	.929
1984—San Diego	Nat.	3B	5	12	2	3	0	0	0	2	.250	7	12	0	1.000
World Series Totals—5 Years			24	80	6	18	2	0	0	7	.225	28	68	2	.980

ALL-STAR GAME RECORD

Year League	Pos.	AB.	R.	H.	2B.	3B.	HR.	RBI.	B.A.	PO.	A.	E.	F.A.
1975—American	3B	4	0	1	0	0	0	0	.250	2	2	0	1.000
1977—American	3B	2	0	0	0	0	0	0	.000	0	1	0	1.000
1978—American†	3B	0	0	0	0	0	0	0	.000	0	1	0	1.000
1979—American	3B	1	0	1	0	0	0	0	1.000	1	2	0	1.000
1980—American	3B	2	0	0	0	0	0	0	.000	0	1	0	1.000
1985—National	3B	2	0	0	0	0	0	0	.000	0	1	0	1.000
All-Star Game Totals—6 Years	11	0	2	0	0	0	0	.182	3	8	0	1.000

†Originally replaced due to injury by Larry Hisle, then re-named to replace Reggie Jackson.

ALBERT DWAYNE NEWMAN
(Al)

Born June 30, 1960, at Kansas City, Mo.
Height, 5.09. Weight, 175.
Throws right and bats left and righthanded.
Attended Chaffey College, Alta Loma, Calif., and
San Diego State University, San Diego, Calif.

Major League stolen bases: 1985 (2).
Led Southern League in sacrifice hits with 18 in 1982.
Led Texas League shortstops in double plays with 58 in 1984.
Led Southern League second basemen in total chances with 776 in 1982.

Year Club	League	Pos.	G.	AB.	R.	H.	2B.	3B.	HR.	RBI.	B.A.	PO.	A.	E.	F.A.
1982—Memphis	South.	2B	142	494	85	136	16	8	1	41	.275	★356	●388	★32	.959
1983—Wichita	A. A.	2B	38	124	20	30	6	1	0	16	.242	73	96	5	.971
1983—Memphis†‡	South.	2B	52	194	18	49	5	2	0	13	.253	111	123	14	.944
1984—Beaumont§	Texas	SS	88	318	69	80	8	0	0	23	.252	138	250	27	.935
1984—Indianapolis	A. A.	2-3-O-S	37	123	13	37	3	0	0	11	.301	49	79	2	.985
1985—Indianapolis	A. A.	2B-SS	87	301	42	85	16	2	0	23	.282	144	250	10	.975
1985—Montreal	Nat.	2B-SS	25	29	7	5	1	0	0	1	.172	19	36	0	1.000
Major League Totals—1 Year			25	29	7	5	1	0	0	1	.172	19	36	0	1.000

Selected by California Angels' organization in 3rd round of free-agent draft, January 9, 1979.
Selected by Texas Rangers' organization in 3rd round of free-agent draft, January 8, 1980.
Selected by New York Mets' organization in secondary phase of free-agent draft, June 3, 1980.
Selected by Montreal Expos' organization in secondary phase of free-agent draft, June 8, 1981.
†On disabled list, July 23 to August 16, 1983.
‡Traded with Pitcher Scott Sanderson to San Diego Padres for Pitcher Gary Lucas, December 7, 1983.
§Traded to Montreal Expos' organization for Pitcher Greg Harris, July 20, 1984.

CARL EDWARD NICHOLS

Born October 14, 1962, at Los Angeles, Calif.
Height, 6.00. Weight, 184.
Throws and bats righthanded.

Led California League catchers in total chances with 897 in 1984.
Led New York-Pennsylvania League catchers in assists with 47 and tied for lead in double plays with 6 in 1983.

Year Club	League	Pos.	G.	AB.	R.	H.	2B.	3B.	HR.	RBI.	B.A.	PO.	A.	E.	F.A.
1980—Bluefield	Appal.	C-1B-OF	37	85	24	18	2	2	0	10	.212	129	13	2	.986
1981—Miami	Fla. St.	C-1-S-3-O	16	31	1	6	0	0	0	3	.194	34	9	6	.878
1981—Hagerstown†	Carol.	C-O-S-2	38	81	8	22	4	0	1	6	.272	131	21	3	.981
1982—Macon	S. Atl.	C-OF-1B	84	257	33	55	10	2	0	30	.214	391	49	21	.954
1983—San Jose	Calif.	C-OF-3B	54	152	16	31	4	0	1	12	.204	204	39	17	.935
1983—Newark	NYP	C-O-3-S	66	217	40	63	14	0	5	26	.290	348	56	10	.976
1984—S.J.‡-Red.§	Calif.	★C-OF	121	389	53	88	14	2	4	54	.226	★769	★112	17	.981
1985—Charlotte	South.	C-OF-1B	115	331	45	78	11	2	2	37	.236	496	71	15	.984

Selected by Baltimore Orioles' organization in 4th round of free-agent draft, June 3, 1980.
†Loaned to Macon (Detroit Tigers' organization), April 8, 1982; returned, September 15, 1982.
‡Loaned to San Jose (Independent), April 10, 1984; returned, June 9, 1984.
§Loaned to Redwood (California Angels' organization), June 9, 1984; returned, September 10, 1984.

THOMAS REID NICHOLS

(Known by middle name.)

Born August 5, 1958, at Ocala, Fla.
Height, 5.11. Weight, 165.
Throws and bats righthanded.
Attended Snead State Junior College, Boaz, Ala.

Major League stolen bases: 1982 (5), 1983 (7), 1984 (2), 1985 (6). Total—20.
Led Carolina League in total bases with 227 and being hit by pitch with 12 in 1979.
Led Carolina League outfielders in assists with 23 in 1979.

Year	Club	League	Pos.	G.	AB.	R.	H.	2B.	3B.	HR.	RBI.	B.A.	PO.	A.	E.	F.A.
1976—Elmira	NYP	2B-3B-OF	23	53	8	18	1	0	0	9	.340	11	12	2	.920
1977—Winter Haven	Fla. St.	OF-2B	116	387	41	102	15	7	4	34	.264	166	41	7	.967
1978—Winter Haven	Fla. St.	OF-3B	125	413	52	102	20	1	5	34	.247	200	24	9	.961
1979—Winston-Salem	Carol.	OF-3B	134	*532	*107	*156	25	5	12	59	.293	240	23	10	.963
1980—Pawtucket	Int.	OF	134	511	68	141	27	5	4	42	.276	250	12	6	.978
1980—Boston	Amer.	OF	12	36	5	8	0	1	0	3	.222	24	1	1	.961
1981—Boston	Amer.	OF-3B	39	48	13	9	0	1	0	3	.188	35	4	0	1.000
1982—Boston†	Amer.	OF	92	245	35	74	16	1	7	33	.302	169	9	2	.989
1983—Boston	Amer.	OF-SS	100	274	35	78	22	1	6	22	.285	168	5	1	.994
1984—Boston	Amer.	OF	74	124	14	28	5	1	1	14	.226	79	3	1	.988
1985—Bos.‡-Chic.	Amer.	OF-2B	72	150	23	41	8	1	2	18	.273	85	2	1	.989
Major League Totals—6 Years			389	877	125	238	51	6	16	00	.271	500	24	6	.990

Selected by Boston Red Sox' organization in 12th round of free-agent draft, June 8, 1976.
†On disabled list, July 21 to August 6, 1982.
‡Traded with a player to be named later to Chicago White Sox for Pitcher Tim Lollar, July 11, 1985.

STEVEN RICHARD NICOSIA

Name pronounced Nuh-KOH-see-uh.

(Steve)

Born August 6, 1955, at Paterson, N. J.
Height, 5.10. Weight, 185.
Throws and bats righthanded.

Major League stolen bases: 1981 (3), 1984 (1), 1985 (1). Total—5.
Led Texas League catchers in putouts with 525 in 1975.
Led Carolina League catchers in putouts with 833 and errors with 12 in 1974.

Year	Club	League	Pos.	G.	AB.	R.	H.	2B.	3B.	HR.	RBI.	B.A.	PO.	A.	E.	F.A.
1973—Charleston	W. Car.	C-OF	54	165	22	38	8	2	2	21	.230	389	25	7	.983
1973—Sherbrooke	East.	C	3	9	1	1	0	0	0	0	.111	29	1	0	1.000
1974—Salem	Carol.	C-1B-OF	118	413	63	126	16	9	15	92	.305	860	89	13	.986
1975—Shreveport	Tex.	*C-OF	110	370	52	99	15	6	6	39	.268	527	45	8	*.986
1976—Charleston	Int.	*C-1B	117	378	29	99	20	0	8	49	.262	*616	57	8	.988
1977—Columbus†	Int.	C	25	85	12	18	5	0	4	12	.212	132	16	2	.987
1978—Columbus	Int.	C-O-1-3	111	366	66	118	20	5	12	74	.322	486	38	9	.983
1978—Pittsburgh	Nat.	C	3	5	0	0	0	0	0	0	.000	8	1	0	1.000
1979—Pittsburgh	Nat.	C	70	191	22	55	16	0	4	13	.288	320	25	3	.991
1980—Pittsburgh	Nat.	C	60	176	16	38	8	0	1	22	.216	284	25	5	.984
1981—Pittsburgh	Nat.	C	54	169	21	39	10	1	2	18	.231	257	23	5	.982
1982—Pittsburgh	Nat.	C-OF	39	100	6	28	3	0	1	7	.280	183	22	2	.990
1983—Pitt.‡§-S.F.	Nat.	C	36	79	8	17	2	0	1	7	.215	131	9	2	.986
1984—San Francisco xy.	Nat.	C	48	132	9	40	11	2	2	19	.303	190	11	3	.985
1985—Montreal za	Nat.	C-1B	42	71	4	12	2	0	0	1	.169	86	5	1	.989
1985—Toronto b	Amer.	C	6	15	0	4	0	0	0	1	.267	23	2	0	1.000
National League Totals—8 Years			352	923	86	229	52	3	11	87	.248	1459	121	21	.987
American League Totals—1 Year			6	15	0	4	0	0	0	1	.267	23	2	0	1.000
Major League Totals—8 Years			358	938	86	233	52	3	11	88	.248	1482	123	21	.987

Selected by Pittsburgh Pirates' organization in 1st round (24th player selected) of free-agent draft, June 5, 1973.
†On disabled list, May 17 to August 23, 1977.
‡On disabled list, July 13 to August 8, 1983.
§Traded to San Francisco Giants for Catcher Milt May and cash, August 19, 1983.
xOn disabled list, August 21 to September 5, 1984.
yGranted free agency, November 8, 1984; signed by Montreal Expos, February 15, 1985.
zOn disabled list, April 22 to May 18, 1985.
aReleased, August 22, 1985; signed by Toronto Blue Jays, September 1, 1985.
bGranted free agency, November 12, 1985.

WORLD SERIES RECORD

Year	Club	League	Pos.	G.	AB.	R.	H.	2B.	3B.	HR.	RBI.	B.A.	PO.	A.	E.	F.A.
1979—Pittsburgh	Nat.	C	4	16	1	1	0	0	0	0	.063	23	2	0	1.000

—DID YOU KNOW—

That on May 31, Cardinals rookie Vince Coleman swiped two bases against the Reds, giving him 31 for the 1985 season and eclipsing the St. Louis rookie mark established by Bake McBride in 1974?

THOMAS EDWARD NIEDENFUER

Name pronounced NEED-un-fyoor.

(Tom)

Born August 13, 1959, at St. Louis Park, Minn.
Height, 6.04. Weight, 220.
Throws and bats righthanded.
Attended Washington State University, Pullman, Wash.

Major League saves: 1981 (2), 1982 (9), 1983 (11), 1984 (11), 1985 (19). Total—52.

Year	Club	League	G.	IP.	W.	L.	Pct.	H.	R.	ER.	SO.	BB.	ERA.
1981—San Antonio	Texas	36	90	13	3	*.813	61	19	18	95	34	1.80
1981—Los Angeles	National	17	26	3	1	.750	25	11	11	12	6	3.81
1982—Albuquerque	P. Coast	4	10⅔	2	0	1.000	6	0	0	15	2	0.00
1982—Los Angeles	National	55	69⅔	3	4	.429	71	22	21	60	25	2.71
1983—Los Angeles	National	66	94⅔	8	3	.727	55	22	20	66	29	1.90
1984—Los Angeles†	National	33	47⅓	2	5	.286	39	14	13	45	23	2.47
1985—Los Angeles	National	64	106⅓	7	9	.438	86	32	32	102	24	2.71
Major League Totals—5 Years		235	344	23	22	.511	276	101	97	285	107	2.54

Selected by Los Angeles Dodgers' organization in 36th round of free-agent draft, June 7, 1977.
Signed as free agent by Los Angeles Dodgers' organization, August 14, 1980.
†On disabled list, July 16 to July 31 and August 5 to September 11, 1984.

DIVISION SERIES RECORD

Year	Club	League	G.	IP.	W.	L.	Pct.	H.	R.	ER.	SO.	BB.	ERA.
1981—Los Angeles	National	1	⅓	0	0	.000	1	0	0	1	1	0.00

CHAMPIONSHIP SERIES RECORD

Tied Championship Series record for most games lost, Series (2), 1985.

Year	Club	League	G.	IP.	W.	L.	Pct.	H.	R.	ER.	SO.	BB.	ERA.
1981—Los Angeles	National	1	⅓	0	0	.000	2	0	0	0	0	0.00
1983—Los Angeles	National	2	2	0	0	.000	0	0	0	3	1	0.00
1985—Los Angeles	National	3	5⅔	0	2	.000	5	4	4	5	2	6.35
Championship Series Totals—3 Years		6	8	0	2	.000	7	4	4	8	3	4.50

WORLD SERIES RECORD

Year	Club	League	G.	IP.	W.	L.	Pct.	H.	R.	ER.	SO.	BB.	ERA.
1981—Los Angeles	National	2	5	0	0	.000	3	2	0	0	1	0.00

JOSEPH FRANKLIN NIEKRO

Name pronounced NEE-krow.

(Joe)

Born November 7, 1944, at Martins Ferry, O.
Height, 6.01. Weight, 190.
Throws and bats righthanded.
Attended West Liberty State College, West Liberty, W. Va.
Brother of Phil Niekro, pitcher with New York Yankees.

Pitched seven-inning, 2-0 perfect game against Tidewater, July 16, 1972 (second game).
Major League saves: 1971 (1), 1972 (1), 1973 (3), 1975 (4), 1977 (5). Total—14.
Led National League pitchers in games started with 38 in 1983 and 1984.
Led National League in wild pitches with 19 in 1982, 14 in 1983, 21 in 1985 and tied for lead with 19 in 1979.
Tied for National League lead in shutouts with 5 in 1979.
Named National League Pitcher of the Year by THE SPORTING NEWS, 1979.
Named righthanded pitcher on THE SPORTING NEWS National League All-Star Team, 1979.

Year	Club	League	G.	IP.	W.	L.	Pct.	H.	R.	ER.	SO.	BB.	ERA.
1966—Treasure Valley	Pioneer	1	4	0	0	.000	4	0	0	7	1	0.00
1966—Quincy	Midwest	4	25	1	2	.333	17	7	3	14	6	1.08
1966—Dallas-Fort Worth	Texas	12	79	5	4	.556	71	28	22	50	15	2.51
1967—Chicago	National	36	170	10	7	.588	171	68	63	77	32	3.34
1968—Chicago	National	34	177	14	10	.583	204	93	85	65	59	4.32
1969—Chicago†-San Diego‡	National	41	221	8	18	.308	237	100	91	62	51	3.71
1970—Detroit	American	38	213	12	13	.480	221	107	96	101	72	4.06
1971—Detroit	American	31	122	6	7	.462	136	62	61	43	49	4.28
1972—Toledo§	Int'national	2	14	2	0	1.000	6	1	1	11	3	0.64
1972—Detroit	American	18	47	3	2	.600	62	20	20	24	8	3.83
1973—Toledo x	Int'national	26	143	7	10	.412	148	74	59	77	47	3.71
1973—Atlanta	National	20	24	2	4	.333	23	11	11	12	11	4.13
1974—Richmond	Int'national	30	52	8	1	.889	44	14	12	50	18	2.08
1974—Atlanta y	National	27	43	3	2	.600	36	19	17	31	18	3.56
1975—Iowa	Am. Assoc.	7	9	1	0	1.000	7	6	5	9	7	5.00
1975—Houston	National	40	88	6	4	.600	79	32	30	54	39	3.07
1976—Houston	National	36	118	4	8	.333	107	60	44	77	56	3.36
1977—Houston	National	44	181	13	8	.619	155	66	61	101	64	3.03
1978—Houston	National	35	203	14	14	.500	190	97	87	97	73	3.86
1979—Houston	National	38	264	●21	11	.656	221	102	88	119	107	3.00
1980—Houston	National	37	256	20	12	.625	268	119	101	127	79	3.55
1981—Houston	National	24	166	9	9	.500	150	60	52	77	47	2.82
1982—Houston	National	35	270	17	12	.586	224	79	74	130	64	2.47

Year Club	League	G.	IP.	W.	L.	Pct.	H.	R.	ER.	SO.	BB.	ERA.
1983—Houston	National	38	263⅔	15	14	.517	238	115	102	152	101	3.48
1984—Houston	National	38	248⅓	16	12	.571	223	104	84	127	89	3.04
1985—Houston z	National	32	213	9	12	.429	197	100	88	117	99	3.72
1985—New York a	American	3	12⅓	2	1	.667	14	8	8	4	8	5.84
National League Totals—16 Years		555	2906	181	157	.536	2723	1225	1078	1425	989	3.34
American League Totals—4 Years		90	394⅓	23	23	.500	433	197	185	172	137	4.22
Major League Totals—19 Years		645	3300⅓	204	180	.531	3156	1422	1263	1597	1126	3.44

Selected by Cleveland Indians' organization in 7th round of free-agent draft, January, 1966.
Selected by Chicago Cubs' organization in 3rd round of free-agent draft, June, 1966.
†Traded with Pitcher Gary Ross and Infielder Francisco Libran to San Diego Padres for Pitcher Dick Selma, April 24, 1969. Libran remained on Cubs' San Antonio farm team but became San Diego property.
‡Traded to Detroit Tigers for Pitcher Pat Dobson and Shortstop-Outfielder Dave Campbell, December 4, 1969.
§On disabled list, August 7 to September 1, 1972.
xSold on waivers to Atlanta Braves, August 7, 1973.
ySold to Houston Astros, April 5, 1975.
zTraded to New York Yankees for Pitcher Jim Deshaies and two players to be named later, September 15, 1985; Houston Astros' organization acquired Infielder Neder Horta, September 24, 1985, and Pitcher Dody Rather, January 11, 1986, to complete deal.
aGranted free agency, November 12, 1985; re-signed by Yankees, January 8, 1986.

<h3 align="center">DIVISION SERIES RECORD</h3>

Year Club	League	G.	IP.	W.	L.	Pct.	H.	R.	ER.	SO.	BB.	ERA.
1981—Houston	National	1	8	0	0	.000	7	0	0	4	3	0.00

<h3 align="center">CHAMPIONSHIP SERIES RECORD</h3>

Established National League Championship Series record for most innings pitched, game (10), October 10, 1980.

Year Club	League	G.	IP.	W.	L.	Pct.	H.	R.	ER.	SO.	BB.	ERA.
1980—Houston	National	1	10	0	0	.000	6	0	0	2	1	0.00

<h3 align="center">ALL-STAR GAME RECORD</h3>

Member of National League All-Star Team for 1979 game; did not play.

<h2 align="center">PHILIP HENRY NIEKRO</h2>

Name pronounced NEE-krow.

<h3 align="center">(Phil)</h3>

Born April 1, 1939, at Blaine, O.
Height, 6.02. Weight, 195.
Throws and bats righthanded.
Brother of Joe Niekro, pitcher with New York Yankees.

Established major league records for fewest sacrifice flies allowed, season, most innings (0 and 284), 1969; most seasons and most consecutive seasons leading major leagues, runs allowed (3); most wild pitches, lifetime (207); most putouts by pitcher, lifetime (364).

Tied major league records for most strikeouts, inning (4), July 29, 1977 (sixth inning); most seasons and most consecutive seasons leading league, runs allowed (3), 1977 through 1979; most wild pitches, inning (4), August 4, 1979, second game (fifth inning); most seasons and most consecutive seasons leading league, games lost (4), 1977 through 1980.

Tied modern major league record for most wild pitches, game (6), August 4, 1979, second game.

Established National League records for most putouts by pitcher, lifetime (340); most games started, no relief appearances, season (44), 1979.

Established modern National League record for most games lost, lifetime (230).

Pitched 9-0 no-hit victory against San Diego Padres, August 5, 1973.

Major League saves: 1969 (1), 1971 (2), 1973 (4), 1974 (1), 1978 (1), 1980 (1). Total—10.

Led National League in home runs allowed with 40 in 1970, 29 in 1975, 41 in 1979 and 30 in 1980.

Led National League in hit batsmen with 11 in 1975, 13 in 1978 and 11 in 1979.

Led National League in complete games with 18 in 1974, 20 in 1977, 22 in 1978 and 23 in 1979.

Led National League in wild pitches with 19 in 1967, 14 in 1976 and 17 in 1977.

Led National League pitchers in games started with 43 in 1977, 42 in 1978, 44 in 1979, and tied for lead with 38 in 1980.

Led National League batters in sacrifice hits with 18 in 1968.

Tied for National League lead in balks with 3 in 1968 and 3 in 1972.

Named pitcher on THE SPORTING NEWS National League All-Star fielding team, 1978 through 1980, 1982 and 1983.

Year Club	League	G.	IP.	W.	L.	Pct.	H.	R.	ER.	SO.	BB.	ERA.
1959—Wellsville	NYP	10	35	2	1	.667	47	38	29	16	24	7.46
1959—McCook	Neb. State	★23	52	7	1	.875	35	20	18	48	29	3.12
1960—Jacksonville	Sally	38	84	6	4	.600	66	36	26	52	52	2.79
1960—Louisville	Am. Assoc.	6	10	1	0	1.000	11	5	4	2	9	3.60
1961—Austin	Texas	★51	110	4	4	.500	100	45	36	84	53	2.95
1962—Louisville	Am. Assoc.	49	98	9	6	.600	111	50	42	48	41	3.86
1963—Denver	P. Coast					(In Military Service)						
1964—Milwaukee	National	10	15	0	0	.000	15	10	8	8	7	4.80
1964—Denver	P. Coast	29	172	11	5	.688	172	79	66	119	45	3.45
1965—Milwaukee	National	41	75	2	3	.400	73	32	24	49	26	2.88
1966—Atlanta	National	28	50	4	3	.571	48	32	23	17	23	4.14
1966—Richmond	Int'national	17	54	3	4	.429	43	27	22	36	16	3.67
1967—Atlanta	National	46	207	11	9	.550	164	64	43	129	55	★1.87
1968—Atlanta	National	37	257	14	12	.538	228	83	74	140	45	2.59
1969—Atlanta	National	40	284	23	13	.639	235	93	81	193	57	2.57

Year Club	League	G	IP	W	L	Pct.	H	R	ER	SO	BB	ERA.
1970—Atlanta	National	34	230	12	18	.400	222	124	109	168	68	4.27
1971—Atlanta	National	42	269	15	14	.517	248	112	89	173	70	2.98
1972—Atlanta	National	38	282	16	12	.571	254	112	96	164	53	3.06
1973—Atlanta	National	42	245	13	10	.565	214	103	90	131	89	3.31
1974—Atlanta	National	41	*302	●20	13	.606	249	91	80	195	88	2.38
1975—Atlanta	National	39	276	15	15	.500	285	115	98	144	72	3.20
1976—Atlanta	National	38	271	17	11	.607	249	116	99	173	101	3.29
1977—Atlanta	National	44	*330	16	●20	.444	*315	*166	*148	*262	*164	4.04
1978—Atlanta	National	44	*334	19	*18	.514	*295	*129	●107	248	102	2.83
1979—Atlanta	National	44	*342	●21	*20	.512	*311	*160	129	208	*113	3.39
1980—Atlanta	National	40	275	15	*18	.455	256	119	111	176	85	3.63
1981—Atlanta	National	22	139	7	7	.500	120	56	48	62	56	3.11
1982—Atlanta†	National	35	234⅓	17	4	*.810	225	106	94	144	73	3.61
1983—Atlanta‡	National	34	201⅔	11	10	.524	212	94	89	128	105	3.97
1984—New York	American	32	215⅔	16	8	.667	219	85	74	136	76	3.09
1985—New York§	American	33	220	16	12	.571	203	110	100	149	*120	4.09
American League Totals—2 Years		65	435⅔	32	20	.615	422	195	174	285	196	3.59
National League Totals—20 Years		739	4619	268	230	.538	4218	1917	1640	2912	1452	3.20
Major League Totals—22 Years		804	5054⅔	300	250	.545	4640	2112	1814	3197	1648	3.23

Signed as free agent by Milwaukee Braves' organization, July 19, 1958.
†On disabled list, March 31 to April 21, 1982.
‡Released, October 7, 1983; signed by New York Yankees, January 5, 1984.
§Granted free agency, November 12, 1985; re-signed by Yankees, January 8, 1986.

CHAMPIONSHIP SERIES RECORD

Established Championship Series record for most runs allowed, game (9), October 4, 1969.
Tied Championship Series record for most runs allowed, three-game Series (9), 1969.

Year Club	League	G	IP	W	L	Pct.	H	R	ER	SO	BB	ERA.
1969—Atlanta	National	1	8	0	1	.000	9	9	4	4	4	4.50
1982—Atlanta	National	1	6	0	0	.000	6	2	2	5	4	3.00
Championship Series Totals—2 Years		2	14	0	1	.000	15	11	6	9	8	3.86

ALL-STAR GAME RECORD

Year League	IP	W	L	Pct.	H	R	ER	SO	BB	ERA.
1969—National	1	0	0	.000	0	0	0	2	0	0.00
1978—National	⅓	0	0	.000	0	0	0	0	0	0.00
All-Star Game Totals—2 Years	1⅓	0	0	.000	0	0	0	2	0	0.00

Member of American League All-Star Team in 1984; did not play.
Member of National League All-Star Team in 1975 and 1982; did not play.

JEFFREY SCOTT NIELSEN

(Known by middle name.)

Born December 18, 1958, at Salt Lake City, Utah.
Height, 6.01. Weight, 190.
Throws and bats righthanded.
Attended Brigham Young University, Provo, Utah.

Year Club	League	G	IP	W	L	Pct.	H	R	ER	SO	BB	ERA.
1983—Bellingham	Northwest	2	13	2	0	1.000	11	4	3	13	2	2.08
1983—Chattanooga†	Southern	13	63½	2	4	.333	81	49	45	24	27	6.39
1984—Fort Lauderdale‡	Florida St.	4	16⅔	2	1	.667	16	8	2	7	5	1.08
1984—Nashville	Southern	10	73⅔	6	3	.667	55	34	20	27	15	2.44
1984—Columbus	Int'national	11	56⅔	5	4	.556	59	27	25	21	23	3.97
1985—Albany§	Eastern	11	73⅓	6	1	.857	60	26	24	31	14	2.95

Selected by Seattle Mariners' organization in 6th round of free-agent draft, June 6, 1983.
†Traded with Pitcher Eric Parent to New York Yankees' organization for Infielder Larry Milbourne, February 14, 1984.
‡On disabled list, April 6 to April 23, 1984.
§On disabled list, May 30 to June 21 and June 27 to September 16, 1985.

RANDY HAROLD NIEMANN

Born November 15, 1955, at Fortuna, Calif.
Height, 6.05. Weight, 215.
Throws left and bats righthanded.
Attended College of the Redwoods, Eureka, Calif.

Major League saves: 1979 (1), 1980 (1), 1982 (1). Total—3.
Tied for American Association lead in games started by pitchers with 29 in 1984.
Tied for Florida State League lead in hit batsmen with 14 in 1976.

Year Club	League	G	IP	W	L	Pct.	H	R	ER	SO	BB	ERA.
1975—Oneonta	NYP	8	55	3	3	.500	53	26	15	23	20	2.45
1976—Fort Lauderdale	Florida St.	25	190	9	10	.474	173	74	60	79	73	2.84
1977—West Haven†	Eastern	13	62	4	4	.500	73	44	38	18	26	5.52
1977—Columbus	Southern	15	34	0	3	.000	36	22	18	15	19	4.76
1978—Columbus	Southern	29	123	9	5	.643	125	44	28	53	39	2.05
1979—Charleston	Int'national	8	47	3	2	.600	49	25	21	17	10	4.02
1979—Houston	National	26	67	3	2	.600	68	32	28	24	22	3.76

Year Club	League	G.	IP.	W.	L.	Pct.	H.	R.	ER.	SO.	BB.	ERA.
1980—Tucson	P. Coast	9	52	4	1	.800	64	36	28	26	26	4.85
1980—Houston	National	22	33	0	1	.000	40	21	20	18	12	5.45
1981—Tucson‡§x-Portland	P. Coast	10	57	4	2	.667	68	40	31	39	38	4.89
1982—Portland	P. Coast	8	44⅔	3	2	.600	41	22	19	28	26	3.83
1982—Pittsburgh	National	20	35⅓	1	1	.500	34	22	20	26	17	5.09
1983—Pittsburgh	National	8	13⅔	0	1	.000	20	14	14	8	7	9.22
1983—Hawaii y	P. Coast	16	82	2	3	.400	95	49	41	52	45	4.50
1984—Denver	Am. Assoc.	32	*190⅓	10	12	.455	*235	*136	*124	110	86	5.86
1984—Chicago z	American	5	5⅓	0	0	.000	5	1	1	5	5	1.69
1985—Tidewater	Int'national	30	159⅔	11	6	.647	152	65	49	76	51	2.76
1985—New York	National	4	4⅔	0	0	.000	5	0	0	2	0	0.00
National League Totals—5 Years		80	153⅔	4	5	.444	167	89	82	78	58	4.80
American League Totals—1 Year		5	5⅓	0	0	.000	5	1	1	5	5	1.69
Major League Totals—6 Years		85	159	4	5	.444	172	90	83	83	63	4.70

Selected by Montreal Expos' organization in 5th round of free-agent draft, January 9, 1974.
Selected by Minnesota Twins' organization in 3rd round of free-agent draft, January 9, 1975.
Selected by New York Yankees' organization in secondary phase of free-agent draft, June 4, 1975.
†Traded with Infielder Mike Fischlin and a player to be named later to Houston Astros for Catcher Cliff Johnson, June 15, 1977; Houston Astros acquired First Baseman-Outfielder Dave Bergman to complete deal, November 23, 1977.
‡On Houston disabled list, March 28 to May 11, 1981.
§On disabled list, July 1 to September 1, 1981.
xTraded with Outfielder Kevin Houston to Pittsburgh Pirates' organization, September 9, 1981, completing deal in which Houston Astros traded Second Baseman Johnny Ray and two players to be named later to Pittsburgh for Second Baseman Phil Garner, August 31, 1981.
yTraded to Chicago White Sox for Outfielder Miguel Dilone and Pitcher Mike Maitland, September 7, 1983.
zTraded to New York Mets' organization for Pitcher Ken Reed and Third Baseman Gene Autry, March 30, 1985.

THOMAS ANDREW NIETO

Name pronounced Nee-AY-toh.

(Tom)

Born October 27, 1960, at Downey, Calif.
Height, 6.01. Weight, 205.
Throws and bats righthanded.
Attended Cerritos College, Norwalk, Calif., and
Oral Roberts University, Tulsa, Okla.

Tied for American Association lead in being hit by pitch with 8 in 1983.

Year Club	League	Pos.	G.	AB.	R.	H.	2B.	3B.	HR.	RBI.	B.A.	PO.	A.	E.	F.A.
1981—Arkansas	Texas	C	62	184	12	33	2	0	2	19	.179	270	37	8	.975
1982—Arkansas†	Texas	C	96	298	33	72	11	3	5	31	.242	466	58	3	*.994
1983—Louisville	A. A.	C	115	383	44	104	17	1	5	52	.272	605	71	*15	.978
1984—Louisville	A. A.	C	77	253	23	70	12	1	7	34	.277	446	43	8	.984
1984—St. Louis	Nat.	C	33	86	7	24	4	0	3	12	.279	135	18	1	.994
1985—St. Louis	Nat.	C	95	253	15	57	10	2	0	34	.225	384	28	4	.990
Major League Totals—2 Years			128	339	22	81	14	2	3	46	.239	519	46	5	.991

Selected by Minnesota Twins' organization in 31st round of free-agent draft, June 5, 1979.
Selected by Pittsburgh Pirates' organization in secondary phase of free-agent draft, January 8, 1980.
Selected by St. Louis Cardinals' organization in 3rd round of free-agent draft, June 8, 1981.
†On disabled list, June 19 to June 30, 1982.

CHAMPIONSHIP SERIES RECORD

Year Club	League	Pos.	G.	AB.	R.	H.	2B.	3B.	HR.	RBI.	B.A.	PO.	A.	E.	F.A.
1985—St. Louis	Nat.	C	1	3	1	0	0	0	0	0	.000	7	0	0	1.000

WORLD SERIES RECORD

Year Club	League	Pos.	G.	AB.	R.	H.	2B.	3B.	HR.	RBI.	B.A.	PO.	A.	E.	F.A.
1985—St. Louis	Nat.	C	2	5	0	0	0	0	0	1	.000	23	1	0	1.000

JUAN MANUEL NIEVES

Born January 5, 1965, at Santurce, Puerto Rico.
Height, 6.03. Weight, 175.
Throws and bats lefthanded.
Named Texas League Pitcher of the Year, 1985.
Received reported $150,000 bonus to sign with Milwaukee Brewers, 1983.

Year Club	League	G.	IP.	W.	L.	Pct.	H.	R.	ER.	SO.	BB.	ERA.
1983—Beloit	Midwest	12	69⅓	7	1	.875	43	11	10	89	15	1.30
1984—Stockton	California	24	139⅔	10	3	.769	137	75	55	133	63	3.54
1985—El Paso	Texas	17	120	8	2	*.800	106	53	47	91	44	3.53
1985—Vancouver	P. Coast	12	68⅔	8	3	.727	56	30	29	54	44	3.80

Signed as free agent by Milwaukee Brewers' organization, July 1, 1983.

—DID YOU KNOW—

That over the past two seasons, Dwight Gooden of the Mets has posted 10 or more strikeouts in 26 of his 66 games started, a 39.4 per cent rate?

ALBERT SAMUEL NIPPER
(Al)

Born April 2, 1959, at San Diego, Calif.
Height, 6.00. Weight, 194.
Throws and bats righthanded.
Attended Northeast Missouri State University, Kirksville, Mo.

Led Florida State League in complete games with 15 in 1981.

Year Club	League	G.	IP.	W.	L.	Pct.	H.	R.	ER.	SO.	BB.	ERA.
1980—Winter Haven	Florida St.	16	85	6	4	.600	82	29	24	48	49	2.54
1981—Winter Haven	Florida St.	29	*212	14	8	.636	191	59	40	139	60	*1.70
1982—Bristol†	Eastern	19	115	6	7	.462	108	50	47	66	45	3.68
1983—New Britain	Eastern	10	67	4	3	.571	46	26	21	42	25	2.82
1983—Pawtucket	Int'national	18	109⅓	9	4	.692	108	62	54	58	54	4.45
1983—Boston	American	3	16	1	1	.500	17	4	4	5	7	2.25
1984—Boston	American	29	182⅔	11	6	.647	183	86	79	84	52	3.89
1985—Boston‡	American	25	162	9	12	.429	157	83	73	85	82	4.06
Major League Totals—3 Years		57	360⅔	21	19	.525	357	173	156	174	141	3.89

Selected by Boston Red Sox' organization in 8th round of free-agent draft, June 3, 1980.
†On disabled list, June 26 to July 25, 1982.
‡On disabled list, March 25 to April 15, 1985; included rehabilitation disability assignment to Pawtucket, March 31 to April 15, 1985.

OTIS JUNIOR NIXON

Born January 9, 1959, at Columbus County, N.C.
Height, 6.02. Weight, 180.
Throws right and bats right and lefthanded.
Attended Louisburg College, Louisburg, N.C.
Brother of Donell Nixon, infielder with Seattle Mariners.

Major League stolen bases: 1984 (12), 1985 (20). Total—32.
Led International League in stolen bases with 94 and caught stealing with 29 in 1983.
Led Southern League in bases on balls received with 110 in 1981.
Led South Atlantic League in bases on balls received with 113 and stolen bases with 67 in 1980.
Led Appalachian League in bases on balls received with 57 in 1979.
Led International League outfielders in fielding percentage with .992, putouts with 363 and total chances with 371 in 1983.
Led Appalachian League third basemen in fielding percentage with .945, putouts with 52, assists with 120, and double plays with 12 in 1979.

Year Club	League	Pos.	G.	AB.	R.	H.	2B.	3B.	HR.	RBI.	B.A.	PO.	A.	E.	F.A.
1979—Paintsville	Appal.	3B-SS	63	203	58	58	10	3	1	25	.286	54	122	11	.941
1980—Greensboro	S. Atl.	3B-SS	136	493	*124	137	12	5	3	48	.278	164	308	36	.929
1981—Nashville	South.	SS	127	407	89	102	9	2	0	20	.251	198	348	*56	.907
1982—Nashville	South.	SS-2B	72	283	47	80	3	2	0	20	.283	126	211	23	.936
1982—Columbus	Int.	2B-SS	59	207	43	58	4	0	0	14	.280	104	169	14	.951
1983—Columbus	Int.	OF-2B	138	*557	*129	*162	11	6	0	41	.291	385	24	4	.990
1983—New York†	Amer.	OF	13	14	2	2	0	0	0	0	.143	14	1	1	.938
1984—Cleveland	Amer.	OF	49	91	16	14	0	0	0	1	.154	81	3	0	1.000
1984—Maine	Int.	OF	72	253	42	70	5	1	0	22	.277	206	7	1	.995
1985—Cleveland	Amer.	OF	104	162	34	38	4	0	3	9	.235	129	5	4	.971
Major League Totals—3 Years			166	267	52	54	4	0	3	10	.202	224	9	5	.979

Selected by Cincinnati Reds' organization in 21st round of free-agent draft, June 6, 1978.
Selected by California Angels' organization in secondary phase of free-agent draft, January 9, 1979.
Selected by New York Yankees' organization in secondary phase of free-agent draft, June 5, 1979.
†Traded with Pitcher George Frazier and a player to be named later to Cleveland Indians for Third Baseman Toby Harrah and a player to be named later, February 5, 1984; New York organization acquired Pitcher Rick Browne and Cleveland organization acquired Pitcher Guy Elston to complete deal, February 8, 1984.

ROBERT DONELL NIXON

(Known by middle name.)
Born December 31, 1961, at Evergreen, N. C.
Height, 6.01. Weight, 185.
Throws and bats righthanded.
Attended Louisburg College, Louisburg, N. C.
Brother of Otis Nixon, outfielder with Cleveland Indians.

Led Southern League in stolen bases with 102 in 1984.
Led California League in stolen bases with 144 and caught stealing with 24 in 1983.
Led Midwest League in stolen bases with 85 in 1982.

Year Club	League	Pos.	G.	AB.	R.	H.	2B.	3B.	HR.	RBI.	B.A.	PO.	A.	E.	F.A.
1981—Wausau†	Midw.	1B-2B-OF	59	204	35	58	7	2	5	26	.284	252	9	3	.989
1982—Wausau	Midw.	*3B-1B	116	461	102	156	18	7	11	56	.338	*87	187	*49	.848
1982—Lynn	Midw.	3B	6	24	5	7	2	1	0	1	.292	0	2	0	1.000
1983—Bakersfield	Calif.	*3B-OF	135	542	*116	174	27	4	4	51	.321	98	249	*51	.872
1984—Chattanooga	South.	OF-3B	140	536	99	144	25	5	4	57	.269	262	6	8	.971
1985—Seattle‡	Amer.						(Did not play)								

Selected by Seattle Mariners' organization in 10th round of free-agent draft, June 3, 1980.
†On disabled list, July 7, 1981 through remainder of season.
‡On disabled list, April 8, 1985 through entire season.

MILCIADES ARTURO NOBOA JR.
Name pronounced Nah-BO-ah.
(Junior)

Born November 10, 1964, at Santo Domingo, Dominican Republic.
Height, 5.09. Weight, 160.
Throws and bats righthanded.

Major League stolen bases: 1984 (1).
Led Eastern League in sacrifice hits with 17 in 1984.
Led Midwest League in sacrifice hits with 18 in 1983.
Led Midwest League second basemen in putouts with 257 and double plays with 81 in 1983.

Year Club	League	Pos.	G.	AB.	R.	H.	2B.	3B.	HR.	RBI.	B.A.	PO.	A.	E.	F.A.
1981—Batavia	NYP	2B	50	162	15	49	8	0	0	6	.302	82	100	*18	.910
1982—Waterloo	Midw.	SS	121	385	69	96	12	5	0	23	.249	*207	306	46	.918
1983—Waterloo	Midw.	2B-SS	132	449	64	115	22	3	1	29	.256	260	355	24	.962
1984—Buffalo	East.	2B	117	383	55	97	18	4	1	45	.253	228	305	*18	.967
1984—Cleveland	Amer.	2B	23	11	3	4	0	0	0	0	.364	7	13	0	1.000
1985—Maine	Int.	2B	122	403	62	116	11	2	5	32	.288	270	379	14	.979
Major League Totals—1 Year			23	11	3	4	0	0	0	0	.364	7	13	0	1.000

Signed as free agent by Cleveland Indians' organization, May 26, 1981.

MATTHEW DODGE NOKES
(Matt)

Born October 31, 1963, at San Diego, Calif.
Height, 6.01. Weight, 185.
Throws right and bats lefthanded.

Led Texas League catchers in double plays with 6 in 1985.
Led California League catchers in double plays with 9 in 1983.
Led Pioneer League in passed balls with 19 in 1981.

Year Club	League	Pos.	G.	AB.	R.	H.	2B.	3B.	HR.	RBI.	B.A.	PO.	A.	E.	F.A.
1981—Great Falls	Pion.	C	44	146	14	33	6	2	0	13	.226	288	35	*13	.961
1982—Clinton	Midw.	C	82	247	19	53	12	0	3	23	.215	363	41	13	.969
1983—Fresno	Calif.	C	125	429	62	138	26	6	14	82	.322	595	62	16	.976
1984—Shreveport	Texas	C	97	308	32	89	19	2	11	61	.289	400	31	8	.982
1985—Shreveport	Texas	C	105	344	52	101	24	1	14	56	.294	520	40	12	.980
1985—San Francisco†	Nat.	C	19	53	3	11	2	0	2	5	.208	84	2	2	.977
Major League Totals—1 Year			19	53	3	11	2	0	2	5	.208	84	2	2	.977

Selected by San Francisco Giants' organization in 20th round of free-agent draft, June 8, 1981.
†Traded with Pitchers Dave LaPoint and Eric King to Detroit Tigers for Pitcher Juan Berenguer, Catcher Bob Melvin and a player to be named later, October 7, 1985; San Francisco Giants acquired Pitcher Scott Medvin to complete deal, December 11, 1985.

JOSEPH WILLIAM NOLAN JR.
(Joe)

Born May 12, 1951, at St. Louis, Mo.
Height, 6.00. Weight, 190.
Throws right and bats lefthanded.

Major League stolen bases: 1977 (1), 1978 (3), 1979 (1), 1981 (1), 1982 (1). Total—7.
Led National League in passed balls with 14 in 1978.
Led Texas League catchers in double plays with 10 in 1972.
Led California League catchers in putouts with 728 in 1971.
Tied for Appalachian League lead in double plays by catchers with 3 in 1969.

Year Club	League	Pos.	G.	AB.	R.	H.	2B.	3B.	HR.	RBI.	B.A.	PO.	A.	E.	F.A.
1969—Marion	Appal.	C	52	160	33	40	5	0	2	19	.250	312	30	6	.983
1970—Pompano Beach	Fla. St.	*C-OF-3B	95	281	38	65	6	4	0	30	.231	438	59	*18	.965
1971—Visalia	Calif.	C-3B-OF	120	393	76	109	17	3	13	75	.277	746	95	17	.980
1972—Memphis	Texas	C	130	418	51	90	13	3	4	41	.215	*868	67	12	.987
1972—New York	Nat.	C	4	10	0	0	0	0	0	0	.000	12	3	1	.938
1973—Tidewater	Int.	C	97	287	34	69	9	1	4	29	.240	526	43	10	.983
1974—Tidewater†	Int.	C	57	145	18	39	8	0	5	20	.269	274	24	8	.974
1975—Richmond	Int.	C-3-O-2	111	342	41	92	13	0	6	53	.269	572	51	7	.989
1975—Atlanta	Nat.	C	4	4	0	1	0	0	0	0	.250	2	0	0	1.000
1976—Richmond‡	Int.	C	32	87	9	25	6	1	0	9	.287	134	14	0	1.000
1977—Atlanta§	Nat.	C	62	82	13	23	3	0	3	9	.280	80	7	0	1.000
1978—Atlanta	Nat.	C	95	213	22	49	7	3	4	22	.230	295	24	7	.979
1979—Atlanta	Nat.	C	89	230	28	57	9	3	4	21	.248	328	27	6	.983
1980—Atl.x-Cin.	Nat.	C	70	176	16	54	8	0	3	26	.307	271	26	5	.983
1981—Cincinnati y	Nat.	C	81	236	25	73	18	1	1	26	.309	393	18	2	*.995
1982—Baltimore z	Amer.	C	77	219	24	51	7	1	6	35	.233	292	22	7	.978
1983—Baltimore a	Amer.	C	73	184	25	51	11	1	5	24	.277	223	16	5	.980
1984—Baltimore b	Amer.	C	35	62	2	18	1	1	1	9	.290	22	3	1	.962
1985—Baltimore cd	Amer.	C	31	38	1	5	2	0	0	6	.132	22	2	0	1.000
National League Totals—7 Years			405	951	104	257	45	7	15	104	.270	1381	105	21	.986
American League Totals—4 Years			216	503	52	125	21	3	12	74	.249	559	43	13	.979
Major League Totals—11 Years			621	1454	156	382	66	10	27	178	.263	1940	148	34	.984

Selected by New York Mets' organization in 2nd round of free-agent draft, June 5, 1969.

†Traded to Atlanta Braves for Infielder Leo Foster, April 4, 1975.
‡On disabled list, April 21 to July 14, 1976.
§On disabled list, May 4 to May 19, 1977.
xGranted free agency when refused waiver option to minors, June 12, 1980; signed by Cincinnati Reds, June 13, 1980.
yTraded to Baltimore Orioles for Pitcher Brooks Carey and Outfielder Dallas Williams, March 26, 1982.
zGranted free agency, November 10, 1982; re-signed by Orioles, January 15, 1983.
aOn disabled list, June 22 to July 14, 1983.
bOn disabled list, May 7 to August 5, 1984.
cOn disabled list, July 2, 1985 through remainder of season.
dReleased, October 9, 1985.

CHAMPIONSHIP SERIES RECORD

Year Club	League	Pos.	G.	AB.	R.	H.	2B.	3B.	HR.	RBI.	B.A.	PO.	A.	E.	F.A.
1983—Baltimore	Amer.	PH	1	0	0	0	0	0	0	1	.000	0	0	0	.000

WORLD SERIES RECORD

Year Club	League	Pos.	G.	AB.	R.	H.	2B.	3B.	HR.	RBI.	B.A.	PO.	A.	E.	F.A.
1983—Baltimore	Amer.	PH-C	2	2	0	0	0	0	0	0	.000	3	0	0	1.000

DICKIE RAY NOLES

Born November 19, 1956, at Charlotte, N. C.
Height, 6.02. Weight, 190.
Throws and bats righthanded.

Major League saves: 1980 (6), 1985 (1). Total—7.
Led Eastern League in hit batsmen with 15 in 1978.
Led Carolina League in games started by pitchers with 27 in 1977.
Led Western Carolinas League in hit batsmen with 13 in 1976.
Tied for Carolina League lead in hit batsmen with 11 in 1977.
Tied for Western Carolinas League lead in home runs allowed with 13 in 1976.

Year Club	League	G.	IP.	W.	L.	Pct.	H.	R.	ER.	SO.	BB.	ERA.
1975—Auburn	NYP	9	50	2	2	.500	49	30	20	31	27	3.60
1976—Spartanburg	W. Carol.	24	137	4	★16	.200	166	★110	★90	95	65	5.91
1977—Peninsula	Carolina	27	★199	10	11	.476	188	103	81	114	78	3.66
1978—Reading	Eastern	27	159	12	8	.600	177	100	75	78	72	4.25
1979—Oklahoma City†	Am. Assoc.	12	76	6	4	.600	69	38	33	48	28	3.91
1979—Philadelphia	National	14	90	3	4	.429	80	40	38	42	38	3.80
1979—Reading	Eastern	1	9	0	1	.000	7	5	4	2	4	4.00
1980—Philadelphia	National	48	81	1	4	.200	80	42	35	57	42	3.89
1981—Oklahoma City‡	Am. Assoc.	22	104	6	6	.500	85	45	38	82	46	3.29
1981—Philadelphia§	National	13	58	2	2	.500	57	30	27	34	23	4.19
1982—Chicago x	National	31	171	10	13	.435	180	99	84	85	61	4.42
1983—Chicago	National	24	116⅓	5	10	.333	133	69	61	59	37	4.72
1983—Quad Cities	Midwest	3	12	0	1	.000	19	11	7	12	5	5.25
1984—Chicago z	National	21	50⅔	2	2	.500	60	29	29	14	16	5.15
1984—Texas	American	18	57⅔	2	3	.400	60	38	33	39	30	5.15
1985—Texas ab	American	28	110⅓	4	8	.333	129	67	62	59	33	5.06
National League Totals—6 Years		151	567	23	35	.397	590	309	274	291	217	4.35
American League Totals—2 Years		46	168	6	11	.353	189	105	95	98	63	5.09
Major League Totals—7 Years		197	735	29	46	.387	779	414	369	389	280	4.52

Selected by Philadelphia Phillies' organization in 4th round of free-agent draft, June 4, 1975.
†On disabled list, April 13 to April 24, 1979.
‡Appeared as outfielder with no chances.
§Traded with Catcher Keith Moreland and Pitcher Dan Larson to Chicago Cubs for Pitcher Mike Krukow and cash, December 8, 1981.
xOn disabled list, June 13 to July 4, 1982.
yOn disabled list, April 12 to June 4, 1983; included rehabilitation disability assignment to Quad Cities, May 21 to June 4, 1983.
zTraded to Texas Rangers for two players to be named later, July 2, 1984; Chicago Cubs' organization acquired Pitcher Tim Henry and Infielder Jorge Gomez to complete deal, December 11, 1984.
aOn disabled list, June 24 to July 14, 1985.
bReleased, December 20, 1985.

DIVISION SERIES RECORD

Year Club	League	G.	IP.	W.	L.	Pct.	H.	R.	ER.	SO.	BB.	ERA.
1981—Philadelphia	National	1	4	0	0	.000	4	2	2	5	2	4.50

CHAMPIONSHIP SERIES RECORD

Year Club	League	G.	IP.	W.	L.	Pct.	H.	R.	ER.	SO.	BB.	ERA.
1980—Philadelphia	National	2	2⅔	0	0	.000	1	0	0	0	3	0.00

WORLD SERIES RECORD

Year Club	League	G.	IP.	W.	L.	Pct.	H.	R.	ER.	SO.	BB.	ERA.
1980—Philadelphia	National	1	4⅔	0	0	.000	5	1	1	6	2	1.93

—DID YOU KNOW—

That when the Montreal Expos defeated Rick Sutcliffe on April 19, they snapped the Cub righthander's 16-game winning streak that dated back to July 4, 1984?

MICHAEL KELVIN NORRIS
(Mike)

Born March 19, 1955, at San Francisco, Calif.
Height, 6.02. Weight, 172.
Throws and bats righthanded.
Attended City College of San Francisco, San Francisco, Calif.

Pitched shutout in first major league game, April 10, 1975.
Led American League in wild pitches with 14 in 1981.
Tied for American League lead in balks with 4 in 1980 and 5 in 1981.
Named pitcher on THE SPORTING NEWS American League All-Star fielding team, 1980 and 1981.
Received reported $25,000 bonus to sign with Oakland Athletics, 1973.

Year Club	League	G.	IP.	W.	L.	Pct.	H.	R.	ER.	SO.	BB.	ERA.
1973—Burlington	Midwest	20	110	8	4	.667	81	38	27	130	40	2.21
1974—Birmingham†	Southern	21	109	7	8	.467	107	64	49	103	65	4.05
1975—Oakland‡	American	4	17	1	0	1.000	6	2	0	5	8	0.00
1976—Tucson	P. Coast	5	33	2	1	.667	28	15	14	19	23	3.82
1976—Oakland	American	24	96	4	5	.444	91	53	51	44	56	4.78
1977—San Jose§	P. Coast	6	46	3	2	.600	42	18	18	35	18	3.52
1977—Oakland	American	16	77	2	7	.222	77	45	41	35	31	4.79
1978—Vancouver	P. Coast	7	42	3	3	.500	42	28	27	32	27	5.79
1978—Jersey City x	Eastern	9	66	2	6	.250	58	35	25	51	36	3.41
1978—Oakland	American	14	49	0	5	.000	46	31	00	30	35	5.51
1979—Oakland y	American	29	146	5	8	.385	146	87	78	96	94	4.81
1980—Oakland	American	33	284	22	9	.710	215	88	80	180	83	2.54
1981—Oakland	American	23	173	12	9	.571	145	77	72	78	63	3.75
1982—Oakland z	American	28	166⅓	7	11	.389	154	103	88	83	84	4.76
1983—Oakland a	American	16	88⅔	4	5	.444	68	42	37	63	36	3.76
1983—Tacoma	P. Coast	1	4	0	0	.000	6	6	4	3	1	9.00
1984—Oakland b	American						(Did not play)					
1985—Modesto cd	California	2	13	1	0	1.000	4	1	0	6	1	0.00
Major League Totals—9 Years		187	1097	57	59	.491	948	531	477	620	490	3.91

Selected by Oakland A's organization in 1st round (24th player selected) of free-agent draft, January 10, 1973.
†On disabled list, June 14 to June 24, 1974.
‡On disabled list, April 28 to September 19, 1975.
§On disabled list, August 27 to September 6, 1977.
xOn suspended list, May 19 to May 28, 1978.
yOn disabled list, July 12 to August 7, 1979.
zOn disabled list, June 17 to July 8, 1982.
aOn disabled list, June 18 to July 26 and August 11, 1983 through remainder of season; included rehabilitation disability assignment to Tacoma, July 6 to July 26, 1983.
bOn disabled list, March 31, 1984 through entire season.
cOn Oakland disabled list, March 29, 1985 through entire season; included rehabilitation disability assignment to Modesto, June 13 to June 25, 1985.
dGranted free agency, November 12, 1985.

DIVISION SERIES RECORD

Year Club	League	G.	IP.	W.	L.	Pct.	H.	R.	ER.	SO.	BB.	ERA.
1981—Oakland	American	1	9	1	0	1.000	4	0	0	2	3	0.00

CHAMPIONSHIP SERIES RECORD

Year Club	League	G.	IP.	W.	L.	Pct.	H.	R.	ER.	SO.	BB.	ERA.
1981—Oakland	American	1	7⅓	0	1	.000	6	3	3	4	2	3.68

ALL-STAR GAME RECORD

Year League	IP.	W.	L.	Pct.	H.	R.	ER.	SO.	BB.	ERA.
1981—American	1	0	0	.000	2	1	1	1	0	9.00

EDWIN NUNEZ (MARTINEZ)

Name pronounced NOON-yez.

Born May 27, 1963, at Humacao, Puerto Rico.
Height, 6.05. Weight, 235.
Throws and bats righthanded.

Major League saves: 1984 (7), 1985 (16). Total—23.
Led Midwest League in complete games with 13 in 1981.

Year Club	League	G.	IP.	W.	L.	Pct.	H.	R.	ER.	SO.	BB.	ERA.
1979—Bellingham	Northwest	6	39	4	1	.800	39	14	9	30	5	2.08
1980—Wausau	Midwest	22	138	9	7	.563	145	71	57	91	58	3.72
1981—Wausau	Midwest	25	*186	*16	3	.842	143	61	51	*205	58	2.47
1982—Seattle†	American	8	35⅓	1	2	.333	36	18	18	27	16	4.58
1982—Salt Lake City‡	P. Coast	11	55⅓	4	3	.571	40	26	21	42	23	3.42
1983—Seattle	American	14	37	0	4	.000	40	21	18	35	22	4.38
1983—Salt Lake City§	P. Coast	14	77⅓	4	4	.500	99	70	61	52	36	7.10
1984—Salt Lake City x	P. Coast	18	27⅔	3	2	.600	24	12	11	26	12	3.58
1984—Seattle	American	37	67⅔	2	2	.500	55	26	24	57	21	3.19
1985—Seattle	American	70	90⅓	7	3	.700	79	36	31	58	34	3.09
Major League Totals—4 Years		129	230⅓	10	11	.476	210	101	91	177	93	3.56

Signed as free agent by Seattle Mariners' organization, March 17, 1979.

†On disabled list, April 23 to May 15, 1982.
‡On disabled list, June 4 to June 29, 1982.
§On disabled list, June 30 to July 14, 1983.
xOn disabled list, May 12 to June 3, 1984.

KENNETH RAY OBERKFELL

Name pronounced OH-burk-fell.

(Ken)

Born May 4, 1956, at Maryville, Illinois.
Height, 6.01. Weight, 210.
Throws right and bats lefthanded.
Attended Belleville Area Junior College, Belleville, Ill.

Major League stolen bases: 1979 (4), 1980 (4), 1981 (13), 1982 (11), 1983 (12), 1984 (2), 1985 (1). Total—47.
Led National League third basemen in double plays with 23 and tied for lead in total chances with 338 in 1981.
Led National League second basemen in fielding percentage with .985 in 1979.

Year	Club	League	Pos.	G.	AB.	R.	H.	2B.	3B.	HR.	RBI.	B.A.	PO.	A.	E.	F.A.
1975—Johnson City	Appal.	SS	17	54	15	19	3	0	1	8	.352	21	58	4	.952
1975—St. Petersburg	Fla. St.	SS	41	134	14	47	6	1	0	22	.351	71	107	6	.967
1976—Arkansas	Texas	2B-SS	128	456	64	131	19	2	3	47	.287	259	321	18	.970
1977—New Orleans	A. A.	2B-SS	120	418	67	105	18	5	4	32	.251	205	325	17	.969
1977—St. Louis	Nat.	2B	9	9	0	1	0	0	0	1	.111	3	4	0	1.000
1978—Springfield	A. A.	3B-2B-SS	64	242	41	69	13	4	6	38	.285	77	113	6	.969
1978—St. Louis	Nat.	2B-3B	24	50	7	6	1	0	0	0	.120	30	48	1	.987
1979—St. Louis	Nat.	2B-3B-SS	135	369	53	111	19	5	1	35	.301	223	343	9	.984
1980—St. Louis†	Nat.	2B-3B	116	422	58	128	27	6	3	46	.303	227	340	7	.988
1981—St. Louis	Nat.	3B-SS	102	376	43	110	12	6	2	45	.293	77	247	15	.956
1982—St. Louis‡	Nat.	★3B-2B	137	470	55	136	22	5	2	34	.289	80	305	11	★.972
1983—St. Louis	Nat.	★3B-2B-SS	151	488	62	143	26	5	3	38	.293	132	303	18	★.960
1984—St. Louis§-Atl.x	Nat.	3B-2B-SS	100	324	38	87	19	2	1	21	.269	64	173	8	.967
1985—Atlanta	Nat.	3B-2B	134	412	30	112	19	4	3	35	.272	88	257	12	.966
Major League Totals—9 Years			908	2920	346	834	145	33	15	255	.286	924	2020	81	.973

Signed as free agent by St. Louis Cardinals' organization, May 4, 1975.
†On disabled list, May 11 to June 20, 1980.
‡On disabled list, March 31 to April 23, 1982.
§Traded to Atlanta Braves for Pitcher Ken Dayley and First Baseman Mike Jorgensen, June 15, 1984.
xOn disabled list, August 27, 1984 through remainder of season.

CHAMPIONSHIP SERIES RECORD

Tied Championship Series record for most at-bats, three-game Series (15).

Year	Club	League	Pos.	G.	AB.	R.	H.	2B.	3B.	HR.	RBI.	B.A.	PO.	A.	E.	F.A.
1982—St. Louis	Nat.	3B	3	15	1	3	0	0	0	2	.200	2	4	1	.857

WORLD SERIES RECORD

Year	Club	League	Pos.	G.	AB.	R.	H.	2B.	3B.	HR.	RBI.	B.A.	PO.	A.	E.	F.A.
1982—St. Louis	Nat.	3B	7	24	4	7	1	0	0	1	.292	3	21	1	.960

PRESTON MICHAEL O'BERRY

(Mike)

Born April 20, 1954, at Birmingham, Ala.
Height, 6.02. Weight, 195.
Throws and bats righthanded.
Received bachelor of science degree in education from
University of South Alabama, Mobile, Ala., and attended
University of Alabama, Birmingham, Ala.

Major League stolen bases: 1985 (1).
Led Eastern League catchers in double plays with 10 in 1977.
Led Carolina League catchers in double plays with 10 in 1976.
Tied for Pacific Coast League lead in passed balls with 13 in 1983.

Year	Club	League	Pos.	G.	AB.	R.	H.	2B.	3B.	HR.	RBI.	B.A.	PO.	A.	E.	F.A.
1975—Winter Haven	Fla. St.	C	39	96	5	8	2	1	0	5	.083	120	24	11	.929
1976—Winston-Salem	Carol.	C	111	330	51	66	12	4	4	32	.200	★608	★69	★13	.981
1977—Bristol	East.	C	125	352	46	72	10	2	2	25	.205	682	★89	★16	.980
1978—Bristol	East.	C	114	339	41	80	12	1	6	41	.236	★648	★76	13	.982
1979—Pawtucket	Int.	C-1B	34	78	6	13	1	0	1	5	.167	168	16	8	.958
1979—Boston†	Amer.	C	43	59	8	10	1	0	1	4	.169	103	7	5	.957
1980—Midland	Texas	C	57	173	31	42	9	3	1	23	.243	337	39	11	.972
1980—Wichita	A. A.	C-OF	9	23	4	6	2	0	0	6	.261	26	5	2	.939
1980—Chicago‡	Nat.	C	19	48	7	10	1	0	0	5	.208	94	16	2	.982
1981—Cincinnati	Nat.	C	55	111	6	20	3	1	1	5	.180	208	22	4	.983
1982—Cincinnati	Nat.	C	21	45	5	10	2	0	0	3	.222	84	12	1	.990
1982—Indianapolis§x	A. A.	C-1B-OF	45	105	11	20	3	1	0	5	.190	172	18	4	.979
1983—Edmonton	P. C.	C-3B	57	179	43	55	8	1	4	24	.307	289	19	8	.975
1983—California y	Amer.	C	26	60	7	10	1	0	1	5	.167	77	8	0	1.000
1984—Columbus	Int.	C-3B	70	187	17	42	4	1	4	26	.225	356	44	9	.978
1984—New York	Amer.	C-3B	13	32	3	8	2	0	0	5	.250	53	5	0	1.000
1985—Columbus z	Int.	C	18	57	7	13	2	0	1	7	.228	88	9	2	.980

Year Club League	Pos.	G.	AB.	R.	H.	2B.	3B.	HR.	RBI.	B.A.	PO.	A.	E.	F.A.
1985—Indianapolis .... A. A.	C	44	121	8	21	4	0	1	10	.174	213	23	6	.975
1985—Montreal .... Nat.	C	20	21	2	4	0	0	0	0	.190	53	6	0	1.000
American League Totals—3 Years		82	151	18	28	4	0	2	14	.185	233	20	5	.981
National League Totals—4 Years		115	225	20	44	6	1	1	13	.196	439	56	7	.986
Major League Totals—7 Years		197	376	38	72	10	1	3	27	.191	672	76	12	.984

Selected by Boston Red Sox' organization in 22nd round of free-agent draft, June 4, 1975.

†Traded to Chicago Cubs, October 23, 1979, completing deal in which Chicago traded Second Baseman Ted Sizemore to Boston Red Sox for a player to be named later, August 17, 1979.

‡Traded to Cincinnati Reds for Pitcher Jay Howell, October 17, 1980.

§On suspended list, June 14 to June 19, 1982.

xTraded to California Angels' organization for First Baseman John Harris, January 7, 1983.

yGranted free agency when refused option to minors, November 15, 1983; signed by New York Yankees, December 7, 1983.

zReleased, May 25, 1985; signed by Indianapolis (Montreal Expos' organization), June 21, 1985.

CHARLES HUGH O'BRIEN
(Charlie)

Born May 1, 1960, at Tulsa, Okla.
Height, 6.02. Weight, 195.
Throws and bats righthanded.
Attended Wichita State University, Wichita, Kan.

Year Club League	Pos.	G.	AB.	R.	H.	2B.	3B.	HR.	RBI.	B.A.	PO.	A.	E.	F.A.
1982—Medford .... N'west	C	17	60	11	17	3	0	3	14	.283	116	18	4	.971
1982—Modesto................ Calif.	C	41	140	23	42	6	0	3	32	.300	239	44	5	.983
1983—Albany†................ East.	C-1B	92	285	50	83	12	1	14	56	.291	478	82	11	.981
1984—Modesto‡.............. Calif.	C	9	32	8	9	2	0	1	5	.281	41	8	0	1.000
1984—Tacoma................ P. C.	C-OF	69	195	33	44	11	0	9	22	.226	260	39	0	1.000
1985—Huntsville .... South.	C	33	115	20	24	5	0	7	16	.209	182	29	5	.977
1985—Oakland................ Amer.	C	16	11	3	3	1	0	0	1	.273	23	0	1	.958
1985—Modesto................ Calif.	C	9	27	5	8	4	1	1	2	.296	33	8	1	.976
1985—Tacoma................ P. C.	C	18	57	5	9	4	0	0	7	.158	110	9	3	.975
Major League Totals—1 Year		16	11	3	3	1	0	0	1	.273	23	0	1	.958

Selected by Texas Rangers' organization in 14th round of free-agent draft, June 6, 1978.

Selected by Seattle Mariners' organization in 21st round of free-agent draft, June 8, 1981.

Selected by Oakland A's organization in 5th round of free-agent draft, June 7, 1982.

†On disabled list, July 31, 1983 through remainder of season.

‡On Albany disabled list, April 13 to May 15, 1984.

PETER MICHAEL O'BRIEN
(Pete)

Born February 9, 1958, at Santa Monica, Calif.
Height, 6.01. Weight, 198.
Throws and bats lefthanded.
Attended Monterrey Peninsula College, Monterrey, Calif.; and
University of Nebraska, Lincoln, Neb.

Tied major league record for most double plays started by first baseman, nine-inning game (3), May 22, 1984.
Major League stolen bases: 1982 (1), 1983 (5), 1984 (3), 1985 (5). Total—14.
Led American League first basemen in assists with 120 in 1983.

Year Club League	Pos.	G.	AB.	R.	H.	2B.	3B.	HR.	RBI.	B.A.	PO.	A.	E.	F.A.
1979—Sarasota Rangers Gulf C.	1B	50	189	39	46	10	2	0	31	.243	*465	*44	7	.986
1980—Asheville............... S. Atl.	1B	134	505	98	149	34	2	17	94	.295	*1227	*96	14	.990
1981—Tulsa .... Texas	1B	110	382	57	109	19	3	17	78	.285	973	95	11	.990
1982—Denver .... A. A.	OF-1B	128	477	92	148	21	1	25	102	.310	418	37	8	.983
1982—Texas.................... Amer.	OF-1B	20	67	13	16	4	1	4	13	.239	39	3	0	1.000
1983—Texas.................... Amer.	1B-OF	154	524	53	124	24	5	8	53	.237	1191	121	11	.992
1984—Texas.................... Amer.	1B-OF	142	520	57	149	26	2	18	80	.287	1271	105	11	.992
1985—Texas.................... Amer.	1B	159	573	69	153	34	3	22	92	.267	1457	98	8	.995
Major League Totals—4 Years		475	1684	192	442	88	11	52	238	.262	3958	327	30	.993

Selected by Texas Rangers' organization in 15th round of free-agent draft, June 5, 1979.

JACK WILLIAM O'CONNOR

Born June 2, 1958, at Yucca Valley, Calif.
Height, 6.03. Weight, 210.
Throws and bats lefthanded.

Pitched 1-0 no-hit victory against Fort Myers, June 28, 1979.

Year Club League	G.	IP.	W.	L.	Pct.	H.	R.	ER.	SO.	BB.	ERA.
1976—Lethbridge .... Pioneer	5	21	2	3	.400	22	16	15	17	20	6.43
1977—Jamestown .... NYP	13	77	6	6	.500	72	36	30	56	30	3.51
1978—West Palm Beach .... Florida St.	29	76	4	6	.400	78	42	34	53	46	4.03
1979—West Palm Beach .... Florida St.	24	146	9	7	.563	125	60	46	87	63	2.84
1980—Memphis......................... Southern	7	29	1	2	.333	30	27	25	17	20	7.76
1980—West Palm Beach .... Florida St.	17	139	9	6	.600	105	46	37	93	70	2.40
1980—Denver† .... Am. Assoc.	2	5	0	0	.000	3	1	1	7	6	1.80
1981—Minnesota....................... American	28	35	3	2	.600	46	27	23	16	30	5.91

Year Club	League	G.	IP.	W.	L.	Pct.	H.	R.	ER.	SO.	BB.	ERA.
1982—Toledo	Int'national	12	42⅓	3	3	.500	42	22	16	42	17	3.40
1982—Minnesota	American	23	126	8	9	.471	122	63	60	56	57	4.29
1983—Minnesota	American	27	83	2	3	.400	107	59	54	56	36	5.86
1983—Toledo	Int'national	14	43½	2	1	.667	52	30	24	39	23	4.98
1984—Toledo	Int'national	48	92⅔	9	5	.643	62	28	21	96	41	2.04
1984—Minnesota‡	American	2	4⅔	0	0	.000	1	1	1	0	4	1.93
1985—Indianapolis	Am. Assoc.	42	68⅔	3	4	.429	62	39	36	63	28	4.72
1985—Montreal	National	20	23⅔	0	2	.000	21	14	13	16	13	4.94
American League Totals—4 Years		80	248⅔	13	14	.481	276	150	138	128	127	4.99
National League Totals—1 Year		20	23⅔	0	2	.000	21	14	13	16	13	4.94
Major League Totals—5 Years		100	272⅓	13	16	.448	297	164	151	144	140	4.99

Selected by Montreal Expos' organization in 9th round of free-agent draft, June 8, 1976.
†Drafted by Minnesota Twins, December 8, 1980.
‡Traded to Montreal Expos' organization for Outfielder-First Baseman Mike Stenhouse, January 9, 1985.

BRYAN ALOIS OELKERS

Name pronounced ELK-ers.
Born March 11, 1961, at Zaragoza, Spain.
Height, 6.03. Weight, 205.
Throws and bats lefthanded.
Attended Wichita State University, Wichita, Kan.

Led Southern League in shutouts with 4 in 1984.
Received reported $69,500 bonus to sign with Minnesota Twins, 1982.

Year Club	League	G.	IP.	W.	L.	Pct.	H.	R.	ER.	SO.	BB.	ERA.
1982—Visalia	California	5	33	2	2	.500	27	15	13	17	17	3.55
1982—Orlando	Southern	3	25	1	0	1.000	16	6	4	14	9	1.44
1983—Minnesota	American	10	34⅓	0	5	.000	56	34	33	13	17	8.65
1983—Toledo	Int'national	17	104½	5	7	.417	121	68	60	60	49	5.18
1984—Orlando	Southern	29	219⅔	●16	11	.593	199	★104	83	139	74	3.40
1985—Toledo†	Int'national	12	48	0	4	.000	58	39	36	30	26	6.75
1985—Orlando‡	Southern	6	33	2	3	.400	46	27	22	15	18	6.00
Major League Totals—1 Year		10	34⅓	0	5	.000	56	34	33	13	17	8.65

Selected by Chicago Cubs' organization in 20th round of free-agent draft, June 5, 1979.
Selected by Minnesota Twins' organization in 1st round (fourth player selected) of free-agent draft, June 7, 1982.
†On disabled list, April 10 to May 22, 1985.
‡Traded with Pitcher Ken Schrom to Cleveland Indians for Pitchers Roy Smith and Ramon Romero, January 7, 1986.

RONALD JOHN OESTER

Name pronounced O-ster.

(Ron)

Born May 5, 1956, at Cincinnati, O.
Height, 6.02. Weight, 190.
Throws right and bats left and righthanded.

Major League stolen bases: 1980 (6), 1981 (2), 1982 (5), 1983 (2), 1984 (7), 1985 (5). Total—27.
Led American Association shortstops in double plays with 102 in 1978.
Led Eastern League shortstops in double plays with 84 in 1976.
Led Pioneer League shortstops in double plays with 27 in 1974.

Year Club	League	Pos.	G.	AB.	R.	H.	2B.	3B.	HR.	RBI.	B.A.	PO.	A.	E.	F.A.
1974—Billings	Pion.	SS	53	167	23	52	11	1	0	21	.311	87	141	27	.894
1975—Tampa	Fla. St.	SS	117	375	40	82	3	4	0	25	.219	174	358	34	.940
1976—Three Rivers	East.	SS	138	447	57	110	14	4	0	44	.246	★233	★408	38	.944
1977—Indianapolis	A. A.	SS	134	455	60	116	16	5	3	33	.255	203	★386	39	.938
1978—Indianapolis	A. A.	SS	●135	514	78	133	21	4	7	49	.259	★300	★428	32	.958
1978—Cincinnati	Nat.	SS	6	8	1	3	0	0	0	1	.375	3	9	0	1.000
1979—Cincinnati	A. A.	SS	●136	509	62	143	19	6	2	33	.281	★244	397	31	.954
1979—Cincinnati	Nat.	SS	6	3	0	0	0	0	0	0	.000	1	2	0	1.000
1980—Cincinnati	Nat.	2B-SS-3B	100	303	40	84	16	2	2	20	.277	161	224	10	.975
1981—Cincinnati	Nat.	2B-SS	105	354	45	96	16	7	5	42	.271	213	341	11	.981
1982—Cincinnati	Nat.	2B-SS-3B	151	549	63	143	19	4	9	47	.260	304	403	22	.970
1983—Cincinnati	Nat.	2B	157	549	63	145	23	5	11	58	.264	315	413	17	.977
1984—Cincinnati	Nat.	2B-SS	150	553	54	134	26	3	3	38	.242	357	388	15	.980
1985—Cincinnati	Nat.	2B	152	526	59	155	26	3	1	34	.295	366	457	9	.989
Major League Totals—8 Years			827	2845	325	760	126	24	31	240	.267	1720	2237	84	.979

Selected by Cincinnati Reds' organization in 9th round of free-agent draft, June 5, 1974.

BENJAMIN A. OGLIVIE

(Ben)

Born February 11, 1949, at Colon, Panama.
Height, 6.02. Weight, 170.
Throws and bats lefthanded.
Attended Bronx Community College, Bronx, N. Y., Northeastern University, Boston, Mass.,
and Wayne State University, Detroit, Mich.

Tied American League records for longest errorless game and most innings by outfielder, game (25), May 8, finished May 9, 1984 (fielded 24⅓ innings).

Major League stolen bases: 1972 (1), 1973 (1), 1974 (12), 1975 (11), 1976 (9), 1977 (9), 1978 (11), 1979 (12), 1980 (11), 1981 (2), 1982 (3), 1983 (4). Total—86.

Hit three home runs in a game, July 8, 1979 (first game), June 20, 1982 and May 14, 1983.

Led American League in intentional bases on balls received with 19 in 1980.

Led Eastern League outfielders in double plays with 5 in 1970.

Named outfielder on THE SPORTING NEWS American League All-Star Team, 1980.

Named outfielder on THE SPORTING NEWS American League Silver Slugger team, 1980.

Year Club	League	Pos.	G.	AB.	R.	H.	2B.	3B.	HR.	RBI.	B.A.	PO.	A.	E.	F.A.
1968—Jamestown	NYP	1B-OF	16	45	7	13	1	0	1	5	.289	66	2	2	.971
1969—Greenville	W. Car.	OF	106	363	48	115	15	●7	8	62	.317	128	6	12	.918
1969—Winter Haven	Fla. St.	OF	11	32	4	8	1	0	0	5	.250	13	1	1	.933
1970—Pawtucket	East.	OF	115	391	62	91	15	0	10	51	.233	172	14	5	.974
1971—Louisville	Int.	OF	134	474	82	144	27	7	17	86	.304	215	∗26	12	.953
1971—Boston	Amer.	OF	14	38	2	10	3	0	0	4	.263	22	1	1	.958
1972—Boston	Amer.	OF	94	253	27	61	10	2	8	30	.241	98	5	2	.981
1973—Boston†	Amer.	OF	58	147	16	32	9	1	2	9	.218	56	2	1	.983
1974—Detroit	Amer.	OF-1B	92	252	28	68	11	3	4	29	.270	162	11	5	.972
1975—Detroit	Amer.	OF-1B	100	332	45	95	14	1	9	36	.286	232	8	5	.980
1976—Detroit	Amer.	OF-1B	115	305	36	87	12	3	15	47	.285	234	8	3	.988
1977—Detroit‡	Amer.	OF	132	450	63	118	24	2	21	61	.262	236	10	6	.976
1978—Milwaukee	Amer.	OF-1B	128	469	71	142	29	4	18	72	.303	275	0	0	.979
1979—Milwaukee	Amer.	OF-1B	130	514	88	145	30	4	29	81	.282	320	10	5	.985
1980—Milwaukee	Amer.	OF	156	592	94	180	26	2	●41	118	.304	384	18	9	.978
1981—Milwaukee	Amer.	OF	107	400	53	97	15	2	14	72	.243	211	3	4	.982
1982—Milwaukee	Amer.	OF	159	602	92	147	22	1	34	102	.244	359	15	7	.982
1983—Milwaukee	Amer.	OF	125	411	49	115	19	3	13	66	.280	259	8	4	.985
1984—Milwaukee	Amer.	OF	131	461	49	121	16	2	12	60	.262	256	6	8	.970
1985—Milwaukee	Amer.	OF	101	341	40	99	17	2	10	61	.290	190	4	7	.965
Major League Totals—15 Years			1651	5567	753	1517	257	32	230	848	.272	3294	117	73	.979

Selected by Boston Red Sox' organization in 7th round of free-agent draft, June 7, 1968.

†Traded to Detroit Tigers for Second Baseman Dick McAuliffe, October 23, 1973.

‡Traded to Milwaukee Brewers for Pitchers Jim Slaton and Rich Folkers, December 9, 1977.

DIVISION SERIES RECORD

Year Club	League	Pos.	G.	AB.	R.	H.	2B.	3B.	HR.	RBI.	B.A.	PO.	A.	E.	F.A.
1981—Milwaukee	Amer.	OF	5	18	0	3	1	0	0	1	.167	13	1	0	1.000

CHAMPIONSHIP SERIES RECORD

Year Club	League	Pos.	G.	AB.	R.	H.	2B.	3B.	HR.	RBI.	B.A.	PO.	A.	E.	F.A.
1982—Milwaukee	Amer.	OF	4	15	1	2	0	0	1	1	.133	5	0	2	.714

WORLD SERIES RECORD

Tied World Series records for most putouts by left fielder, inning (3), October 19, 1982 (seventh inning); most consecutive putouts by outfielder (4), October 19, 1982.

Year Club	League	Pos.	G.	AB.	R.	H.	2B.	3B.	HR.	RBI.	B.A.	PO.	A.	E.	F.A.
1982—Milwaukee	Amer.	OF	7	27	4	6	0	1	1	1	.222	13	0	1	.929

ALL-STAR GAME RECORD

Year League	Pos.	AB.	R.	H.	2B.	3B.	HR.	RBI.	B.A.	PO.	A.	E.	F.A.
1980—American	OF	2	0	0	0	0	0	0	.000	1	0	0	1.000
1982—American	PH	1	0	0	0	0	0	0	.000	0	0	0	.000
1983—American	OF	1	0	0	0	0	0	0	.000	0	0	0	.000
All-Star Game Totals—3 Years		4	0	0	0	0	0	0	.000	1	0	0	1.000

ROBERT MICHAEL OJEDA

Name pronounced Oh-HEED-a.

(Bob)

Born December 17, 1957, at Los Angeles, Calif.
Height, 6.01. Weight, 190.
Throws and bats lefthanded.
Attended College of the Sequoias, Visalia, Calif.

Major League saves: 1985 (1).

Tied for American League lead in shutouts with 5 in 1984.

Tied for International League lead in balks with 3 in 1980.

Tied for Florida State League lead in games started by pitchers with 29 in 1979.

Named International League Pitcher of the Year, 1981.

Year Club	League	G.	IP.	W.	L.	Pct.	H.	R.	ER.	SO.	BB.	ERA.
1978—Elmira	NYP	18	43	1	6	.143	45	32	23	35	43	4.81
1979—Winter Haven	Florida St.	29	200	15	7	.682	163	66	54	150	84	2.43
1980—Pawtucket	Int'national	19	123	6	7	.462	107	54	44	78	56	3.22
1980—Boston	American	7	26	1	1	.500	39	20	20	12	14	6.92
1981—Pawtucket	Int'national	25	173	12	9	.571	136	52	41	113	73	∗2.13
1981—Boston	American	10	66	6	2	.750	50	25	23	28	25	3.14
1982—Boston†	American	22	78⅓	4	6	.400	95	53	49	52	29	5.63
1983—Boston	American	29	173⅔	12	7	.632	173	85	78	94	73	4.04

Year Club	League	G.	IP.	W.	L.	Pct.	H.	R.	ER.	SO.	BB.	ERA.
1984—Boston‡	American	33	216⅔	12	12	.500	211	106	96	137	96	3.99
1985—Boston§	American	39	157⅔	9	11	.450	166	74	70	102	48	4.00
Major League Totals—6 Years		140	718⅓	44	39	.530	734	363	336	425	285	4.21

Signed as free agent by Boston Red Sox' organization, May 20, 1978.
†On disabled list, August 20 to September 10, 1982.
‡On disabled list, August 16 to September 1, 1984.
§Traded with Pitchers Tom McCarthy, John Mitchell and Chris Bayer to New York Mets for Pitchers Calvin Schiraldi and Wes Gardner and Outfielders John Christensen and LaSchelle Tarver, November 13, 1985.

ALBERT OLIVER JR.
(Al)

Born October 14, 1946, at Portsmouth, O.
Height, 6.01. Weight, 185.
Throws and bats lefthanded.
Attended Kent State University, Kent, O.

Tied major league records for most home runs, opening day of season (2), April 6, 1983; most errors by first baseman, inning (3), May 23, 1969 (fourth inning); most long hits, doubleheader (6), August 17, 1980; most extra bases on long hits, doubleheader (15), August 17, 1980.
Tied modern major league record for most at bats, game (7), September 16, 1975.
Established American League record for most total bases, doubleheader (21), August 17, 1980.
Tied American League record for most home runs, doubleheader, home run in each game (4), August 17, 1980.
Tied National League record for fewest errors by first baseman for leader in errors, season (13), 1983.
Major League stolen bases: 1969 (8), 1970 (1), 1971 (4), 1972 (2), 1973 (6), 1974 (10), 1975 (4), 1976 (6), 1977 (13), 1978 (8), 1979 (4), 1980 (5), 1981 (3), 1982 (5), 1983 (1), 1984 (3), 1985 (1). Total—84.
Hit three home runs in a game, May 23, 1979 and August 17, 1980 (second game).
Led National League in total bases with 317 in 1982.
Tied for National League lead in grounding into double plays with 21 in 1983.
Led Western Carolinas League first basemen in double plays with 93 in 1965.
Named first baseman on THE SPORTING NEWS National League All-Star Team, 1982.
Named outfielder on THE SPORTING NEWS National League All-Star Team, 1975.
Named first baseman on THE SPORTING NEWS National League Silver Slugger team, 1982.
Named outfielder on THE SPORTING NEWS American League Silver Slugger team, 1980.
Named designated hitter on THE SPORTING NEWS American League Silver Slugger team, 1981.

Year Club	League	Pos.	G.	AB.	R.	H.	2B.	3B.	HR.	RBI.	B.A.	PO.	A.	E.	F.A.
1964—Salem†	Appal.				(Did not play)										
1965—Gastonia	W. Car.	1B	123	*515	77	*159	19	5	10	71	.309	*1031	*64	21	.981
1966—Raleigh‡	Carol.	1B	117	458	66	137	25	4	10	57	.299	1035	*75	16	.986
1967—Macon§	South.	1B-OF	38	126	18	28	1	2	1	4	.222	267	21	6	.980
1967—Raleigh x	Carol.	1B	40	145	20	43	4	4	2	15	.297	365	17	0	1.000
1968—Columbus	Int.	1B-OF	132	473	61	149	22	13	14	74	.315	968	28	16	.984
1968—Pittsburgh	Nat.	OF	4	8	1	1	0	0	0	0	.125	3	0	0	1.000
1969—Pittsburgh	Nat.	1B-OF	129	463	55	132	19	2	17	70	.285	911	50	9	.991
1970—Pittsburgh	Nat.	OF-1B	151	551	63	149	33	5	12	83	.270	718	52	9	.988
1971—Pittsburgh	Nat.	OF-1B	143	529	69	149	31	7	14	64	.282	497	15	6	.988
1972—Pittsburgh	Nat.	OF-1B	140	565	88	176	27	4	12	89	.312	353	4	5	.986
1973—Pittsburgh	Nat.	OF-1B	158	654	90	191	38	7	20	99	.292	692	36	13	.982
1974—Pittsburgh	Nat.	OF-1B	147	617	96	198	38	12	11	85	.321	702	26	7	.990
1975—Pittsburgh	Nat.	OF-1B	155	628	90	176	39	8	18	84	.280	409	6	5	.988
1976—Pittsburgh	Nat.	OF-1B	121	443	62	143	22	5	12	61	.323	327	4	5	.985
1977—Pittsburgh y	Nat.	OF	154	568	75	175	29	6	19	82	.308	305	6	6	.981
1978—Texas z	Amer.	OF	133	525	65	170	35	5	14	89	.324	219	8	3	.987
1979—Texas	Amer.	OF	136	492	69	159	28	4	12	76	.323	260	9	7	.975
1980—Texas	Amer.	OF-1B	*163	656	96	209	43	3	19	117	.319	315	9	9	.973
1981—Texas a	Amer.	1B	102	421	53	130	29	1	4	55	.309	2	0	0	1.000
1982—Montreal	Nat.	1B	160	617	90	*204	*43	2	22	●109	*.331	1286	92	*19	.986
1983—Montreal b	Nat.	●1B-OF	157	614	70	184	●38	3	8	84	.300	1207	118	●13	.990
1984—S.F. cd-Phila. e	Nat.	1B-OF	119	432	36	130	26	2	0	48	.301	818	61	13	.985
1985—Los Angeles fg	Nat.	OF	35	79	1	20	5	0	0	8	.253	13	2	2	.882
1985—Toronto h	Amer.	1B	61	187	20	47	6	1	5	23	.251	3	0	0	1.000
National League Totals—14 Years			1773	6768	886	2028	388	63	165	966	.300	8241	472	112	.987
American League Totals—5 Years			595	2281	303	715	141	14	54	360	.313	799	26	19	.977
Major League Totals—18 Years			2368	9049	1189	2743	529	77	219	1326	.303	9040	498	131	.986

Signed as free agent by Pittsburgh Pirates' organization, June 13, 1964.
†On disabled list, June 23 to July 1 and July 16 to September 22, 1964.
‡On temporary inactive list, May 26 to June 15, 1966.
§On military list, January 7 to May 7, 1967.
xOn temporary inactive list, June 21 to July 15, 1967.
yTraded with infielder Nelson Norman to Texas Rangers for Pitcher Bert Blyleven and First Baseman-Outfielder John Milner, December 8, 1977.
zOn disabled list, June 15 to July 13, 1978.
aTraded to Montreal Expos for Third Baseman Larry Parrish and First Baseman Dave Hostetler, March 31, 1982.
bTraded to San Francisco Giants for Pitcher Fred Breining and a player to be named later, February 27, 1984; Montreal Expos' organization acquired Outfielder Max Venable to complete deal, March 31, 1984. (San Francisco traded Pitcher Andy McGaffigan to Montreal, March 31, 1984, as compensation for the injury that Breining arrived with. Breining remained with Montreal.)
cOn disabled list, July 23 to August 7, 1984.
dTraded with a player to be named later to Philadelphia Phillies for Pitchers Kelly Downs and George Riley, August 20, 1984; Philadelphia acquired Pitcher Renie Martin to complete deal, August 30, 1984.

eTraded to Los Angeles Dodgers for Pitcher Pat Zachry, February 4, 1985.
fOn disabled list, May 18 to June 7, 1985.
gTraded to Toronto Blue Jays for First Baseman Len Matuszek, July 9, 1985.
hGranted free agency, November 12, 1985.

CHAMPIONSHIP SERIES RECORD

Year—Club	League	Pos.	G.	AB.	R.	H.	2B.	3B.	HR.	RBI.	B.A.	PO.	A.	E.	F.A.
1970—Pittsburgh	Nat.	1B	2	8	0	2	0	0	0	1	.250	22	1	0	1.000
1971—Pittsburgh	Nat.	PH-OF	4	12	2	3	0	0	1	5	.250	5	0	0	1.000
1972—Pittsburgh	Nat.	OF	5	20	3	5	2	1	1	3	.250	17	1	0	1.000
1974—Pittsburgh	Nat.	OF	4	14	1	2	0	0	0	1	.143	9	0	0	1.000
1975—Pittsburgh	Nat.	OF	3	11	1	2	0	0	1	2	.182	5	0	0	1.000
1985—Toronto	Amer.	PH-DH	5	8	0	3	1	0	0	3	.375	0	0	0	.000
Championship Series Totals—6 Years			23	73	7	17	3	1	3	15	.233	58	2	0	1.000

WORLD SERIES RECORD

Year—Club	League	Pos.	G.	AB.	R.	H.	2B.	3B.	HR.	RBI.	B.A.	PO.	A.	E.	F.A.
1971—Pittsburgh	Nat.	PH-OF	5	19	1	4	2	0	0	2	.211	11	0	1	.917

ALL-STAR GAME RECORD

Year—League	Pos.	AB.	R.	H.	2B.	3B.	HR.	RBI.	B.A.	PO.	A.	E.	F.A.
1972—National	OF	1	0	0	0	0	0	0	.000	0	0	0	.000
1975—National	PH-OF	1	1	1	1	0	0	0	1.000	0	0	0	.000
1970—National	OF	1	0	0	0	0	0	0	.000	1	0	0	1.000
1980—American	OF	1	0	0	0	0	0	0	.000	0	0	0	.000
1981—American	PH	1	0	0	0	0	0	0	.000	0	0	0	.000
1982—National	1B	2	1	2	1	0	0	0	1.000	2	0	0	1.000
1983—National	1B	2	1	1	1	0	0	0	.500	2	1	0	1.000
All-Star Game Totals—7 Years		9	3	4	3	0	0	0	.444	5	1	0	1.000

JOSEPH MELTON OLIVER
(Joe)

Born July 24, 1965, at Memphis, Tenn.
Height, 6.03. Weight, 205.
Throws and bats righthanded.

Led Florida State League catchers in assists with 84 and passed balls with 33 in 1985.
Led Midwest League catchers in passed balls with 30 and total chances with 855 in 1984.
Led Pioneer League catchers in putouts with 425, assists with 38 and total chances with 468 in 1983.

Year—Club	League	Pos.	G.	AB.	R.	H.	2B.	3B.	HR.	RBI.	B.A.	PO.	A.	E.	F.A.
1983—Billings	Pion.	★C-1B	56	186	21	40	4	0	4	28	.215	426	39	5	★.989
1984—Cedar Rapids	Midw.	C	102	335	34	73	11	0	3	29	.218	★757	85	13	.985
1985—Tampa	Fla. St.	C-1B	112	386	38	104	23	2	7	62	.269	615	94	16	.978

Selected by Cincinnati Reds' organization in 2nd round of free-agent draft, June 6, 1983.

GREGORY WILLIAM OLSON
(Greg)

Born September 6, 1960, at Marshall, Minn.
Height 6.00. Weight, 190.
Throws and bats righthanded.
Attended University of Minnesota, Minneapolis, Minn.

Led Carolina League catchers in total chances with 973 in 1983.

Year—Club	League	Pos.	G.	AB.	R.	H.	2B.	3B.	HR.	RBI.	B.A.	PO.	A.	E.	F.A.
1982—Lynchburg	Carol.	C-3B	32	91	10	24	1	0	0	5	.264	149	26	6	.967
1983—Lynchburg	Carol.	C	107	318	56	73	7	0	0	22	.230	★881	★82	10	★.990
1984—Jackson	Texas	C	74	234	27	55	9	0	0	22	.235	511	51	9	.984
1985—Jackson	Texas	C	69	211	21	57	7	0	1	32	.270	353	56	6	.986

Selected by New York Mets' organization in 7th round of free-agent draft, June 7, 1982.

EDWARD R. OLWINE
(Ed)

Born May 28, 1958, at Greenville, O.
Height, 6.02. Weight, 165.
Throws left and bats righthanded.
Attended Morehead State University, Morehead, Ky.

Led South Atlantic League in saves with 19 in 1981.

Year—Club	League	G.	IP.	W.	L.	Pct.	H.	R.	ER.	SO.	BB.	ERA.
1980—Oneonta	NYP	6	9	2	1	.667	8	4	1	8	6	1.00
1980—Paintsville	Ap'lachian	13	35	5	2	.714	32	11	10	47	11	2.57
1980—Fort Lauderdale	Florida St.	2	1	0	0	.000	5	4	1	0	0	9.00
1981—Greensboro	S. Atlantic	51	75	8	5	.615	67	35	25	73	25	3.00
1982—Fort Lauderdale	Florida St.	39	67⅔	4	5	.556	70	32	25	48	21	3.33
1983—Nashville	Southern	29	82⅔	2	4	.333	90	53	40	66	38	4.35
1983—Columbus†	Int'national	8	10⅓	2	0	1.000	21	11	11	11	6	9.58
1984—Tidewater‡	Int'national	50	68	4	2	.667	47	26	18	50	25	2.38
1985—Tidewater	Int'national	55	66	4	7	.364	60	23	21	50	26	2.86

Signed as free agent by New York Yankees' organization, June 15, 1980.
†Drafted by Tidewater (New York Mets' organization), December 6, 1983.
‡Drafted by Philadelphia Phillies, December 3, 1984; returned, March 28, 1985.

THOMAS PATRICK O'MALLEY
(Tom)

Born December 25, 1960, at Orange, N. J.
Height, 6.00. Weight, 185.
Throws right and bats lefthanded.

Major League stolen bases: 1983 (2).
Led International League third basemen in putouts with 90 and fielding percentage with .964 in 1985.

Year	Club	League	Pos.	G.	AB.	R.	H.	2B.	3B.	HR.	RBI.	B.A.	PO.	A.	E.	F.A.
1979—Great Falls	Pion.	2-S-O-3		42	119	13	29	6	1	1	20	.244	41	34	9	.893
1980—Fresno	Calif.	3B		122	435	67	125	20	9	3	74	.287	69	253	22	★.936
1981—Shreveport	Texas	3B		123	467	50	135	23	6	6	53	.289	94	237	15	.957
1982—Phoenix	P. C.	3B		26	96	23	43	11	1	3	15	.448	12	44	6	.903
1982—San Francisco†	Nat.	3B-SS-2B		92	291	26	80	12	4	2	27	.275	60	161	8	.965
1983—San Francisco	Nat.	3B		135	410	40	106	16	1	5	45	.259	70	213	18	.940
1984—Phoenix	P. C.	3B-1B		105	387	44	134	20	2	5	72	.346	227	134	15	.960
1984—San Francisco‡	Nat.	3B		13	25	2	3	0	0	0	0	.120	5	8	0	1.000
1984—Chicago§	Amer.	3B		12	16	0	2	0	0	0	3	.125	2	1	0	1.000
1985—Nashville x	A. A	3B		33	128	13	39	8	0	1	12	.305	16	62	9	.897
1985—Rochester	Int.	3B-1B		102	358	62	108	13	1	10	44	.302	92	207	11	.965
1985—Baltimore	Amer.	3B		8	14	1	1	0	0	1	2	.071	2	3	1	.833
National League Totals—3 Years				240	726	68	189	28	5	7	72	.260	135	382	26	.952
American League Totals—2 Years				20	30	1	3	0	0	1	5	.100	4	4	1	.889
Major League Totals—4 Years				260	756	69	192	28	5	8	77	.254	139	386	27	.951

Selected by San Francisco Giants' organization in 16th round of free-agent draft, June 5, 1979.
†On disabled list, August 16 to September 6, 1982.
‡Traded to Chicago White Sox for two players to be named later, September 1, 1984; San Francisco Giants acquired Pitcher Mike Trujillo and First Baseman Pat Adams to complete deal, September 7, 1984.
§Released, April 1, 1985; signed by Nashville (Detroit Tigers' organization), April 8, 1985.
xTraded to Rochester (Baltimore Orioles' organization) for Catcher Papo Rosado, May 21, 1985.

RANDALL JEFFREY O'NEAL
(Randy)

Born August 30, 1960, at Ashland, Ky.
Height, 6.02. Weight, 195.
Throws and bats righthanded.
Attended Palm Beach Junior College, Lake Worth, Fla.,
and University of Florida, Gainesville, Fla.

Pitched seven-inning, 4-0 no-hit victory against Winter Haven, August 23, 1981 (first game).
Major League saves: 1985 (1).
Tied for American Association lead in balks with 6 in 1984.

Year	Club	League	G.	IP.	W.	L.	Pct.	H.	R.	ER.	SO.	BB.	ERA.
1981—Lakeland	Florida St.	13	69	4	5	.444	59	27	22	31	18	2.87
1982—Birmingham	Southern	27	185	11	7	.611	169	83	70	105	71	3.41
1983—Evansville	Am. Assoc.	23	140⅓	8	10	.444	159	80	66	70	45	4.23
1984—Evansville	Am. Assoc.	25	166⅓	9	10	.474	152	82	66	110	59	3.57
1984—Detroit	American	4	18⅔	2	1	.667	16	7	7	12	6	3.38
1985—Nashville	Am. Assoc.	10	67⅔	5	4	.556	57	29	27	44	19	3.59
1985—Detroit	American	28	94⅓	5	5	.500	82	42	34	52	36	3.24
Major League Totals—2 Years		32	113	7	6	.538	98	49	41	64	42	3.27

Selected by Montreal Expos' organization in 4th round of free-agent draft, January 9, 1979.
Selected by Minnesota Twins' organization in secondary phase of free-agent draft, June 5, 1979.
Selected by Milwaukee Brewers' organization in secondary phase of free-agent draft, January 8, 1980.
Selected by Cincinnati Reds' organization in secondary phase of free-agent draft, June 3, 1980.
Selected by Detroit Tigers' organization in secondary phase of free-agent draft, June 8, 1981.

PAUL ANDREW O'NEILL

Born February 25, 1963, at Columbus, O.
Height, 6.04. Weight, 205.
Throws and bats lefthanded.
Attended Otterbein College, Westerville, O.
Son of Charles W. O'Neill, minor league pitcher, 1945 through 1948.

Tied for American Association lead in game-winning RBIs with 13 in 1985.
Led American Association outfielders in assists with 19 and double plays with 8 in 1985.

Year	Club	League	Pos.	G.	AB.	R.	H.	2B.	3B.	HR.	RBI.	B.A.	PO.	A.	E.	F.A.
1981—Billings	Pion.	OF		66	241	37	76	7	2	3	29	.315	87	4	5	.948
1982—Cedar Rapids	Midw.	OF		116	386	50	105	19	2	8	71	.272	137	7	8	.947
1983—Tampa	Fla. St.	OF-1B		121	413	62	115	23	7	8	51	.278	218	14	10	★.959
1983—Waterbury	East.	OF		14	43	6	12	0	0	0	6	.279	26	0	0	1.000
1984—Vermont	East.	OF		134	475	70	126	31	5	16	76	.265	246	5	7	.973
1985—Denver	A. A.	OB-1B		★137	★509	63	★155	★32	3	7	74	.305	248	20	7	.975
1985—Cincinnati	Nat.	OF		5	12	1	4	1	0	0	1	.333	3	1	0	1.000
Major League Totals—1 Year				5	12	1	4	1	0	0	1	.333	3	1	0	1.000

Selected by Cincinnati Reds' organization in 4th round of free-agent draft, June 8, 1981.

STEVEN ONTIVEROS
(Steve)

Born March 5, 1961, at Tularosa, N.M.
Height, 6.00. Weight, 180.
Throws and bats righthanded.
Received bachelor of science degree in physical education
from University of Michigan, Ann Arbor, Mich.

Major League saves: 1985 (8).

Year Club	League	G.	IP.	W.	L.	Pct.	H.	R.	ER.	SO.	BB.	ERA.
1982—Medford	Northwest	4	8	1	0	1.000	3	0	0	9	4	0.00
1982—West Haven†	Eastern	16	27	2	2	.500	34	26	19	28	12	6.33
1983—Albany	Eastern	32	129⅔	8	4	.667	131	62	54	91	36	3.75
1984—Tacoma‡	P. Coast	2	11⅓	1	1	.500	18	11	10	6	5	7.94
1985—Madison	Midwest	5	30⅔	3	1	.750	23	10	7	26	6	2.05
1985—Tacoma§	P. Coast	15	33⅔	3	0	1.000	26	13	11	30	21	2.94
1985—Oakland	American	39	74⅔	1	3	.250	45	17	16	36	19	1.93
Major League Totals—1 Year		39	74⅔	1	3	.250	45	17	16	36	19	1.93

Selected by Oakland A's organization in 2nd round of free-agent draft, June 7, 1982.
†On temporarily inactive list, July 27 to August 6, 1982.
‡On disabled list, April 16 to August 8, 1984.
§On disabled list, April 16 to April 28, 1985.

JOSE MANUEL OQUENDO

Name pronounced Oh-KEN-doh.

Born July 4, 1963, at Rio Piedras, Puerto Rico.
Height, 5.10. Weight, 156.
Throws right and bats left and righthanded.

Major League stolen bases: 1983 (8), 1984 (10). Total—18.
Led American Association in sacrifice hits with 15 in 1985.
Led International League in sacrifice hits with 14 in 1982.
Led Carolina League in sacrifice hits with 13 in 1980.
Led American Association shortstops in total chances with 591 in 1985.
Led Northwest League shortstops in errors with 40 in 1979.

Year Club	League	Pos.	G.	AB.	R.	H.	2B.	3B.	HR.	RBI.	B.A.	PO.	A.	E.	F.A.
1979—Grays Harbor	N'west	*SS-2B	64	220	24	50	8	0	1	14	.227	90	177	*40	.870
1980—Lynchburg	Carol.	SS	109	301	38	51	10	3	0	26	.169	126	358	31	*.940
1981—Lynchburg	Carol.	SS	124	393	59	98	8	6	0	38	.249	169	390	23	*.961
1982—Tidewater	Int.	SS	114	337	40	72	8	3	0	22	.214	186	337	25	.954
1983—Tidewater	Int.	SS	13	34	3	4	0	0	0	3	.118	20	23	4	.915
1983—New York	Nat.	SS	120	328	29	70	7	0	1	17	.213	182	326	21	.960
1984—New York	Nat.	SS	81	189	23	42	5	0	0	10	.222	95	152	7	.972
1984—Tidewater†	Int.	SS	38	113	8	18	1	0	1	8	.159	54	111	2	.988
1985—Louisville	A. A.	SS	133	384	38	81	8	1	1	30	.211	*227	341	23	.961
Major League Totals—2 Years			201	517	52	112	12	0	1	27	.217	277	478	28	.964

Signed as free agent by New York Mets' organization, April 15, 1979.
†Traded with Pitcher Mark Jason Davis to St. Louis Cardinals' organization for Shortstop Argenis Salazar and Pitcher John Young, April 2, 1985.

JESSE OROSCO

Name pronounced Oh-ROSS-koh.

Born April 21, 1957, at Santa Barbara, Calif.
Height, 6.02. Weight, 185.
Throws left and bats righthanded.
Attended Santa Barbara City College, Santa Barbara, Calif.

Major League saves: 1981 (1), 1982 (4), 1983 (17), 1984 (31), 1985 (17). Total—70.
Led Appalachian League in intentional bases on balls issued with 5 in 1978.

Year Club	League	G.	IP.	W.	L.	Pct.	H.	R.	ER.	SO.	BB.	ERA.
1978—Elizabethton†	Ap'lachian	20	40	4	4	.500	29	7	5	48	20	1.13
1979—Tidewater	Int'national	16	81	4	4	.500	82	45	35	55	43	3.89
1979—New York	National	18	35	1	2	.333	33	20	19	22	22	4.89
1980—Jackson	Texas	37	71	4	4	.500	52	36	29	85	62	3.68
1981—Tidewater	Int'national	46	87	9	5	.643	80	39	32	81	32	3.31
1981—New York	National	8	17	0	1	.000	13	4	3	18	6	1.59
1982—New York	National	54	109⅓	4	10	.286	92	37	33	89	40	2.72
1983—New York	National	62	110	13	7	.650	76	27	18	84	38	1.47
1984—New York	National	60	87	10	6	.625	58	29	25	85	34	2.59
1985—New York	National	54	79	8	6	.571	66	26	24	68	34	2.73
Major League Totals—6 Years		256	437⅓	36	32	.529	338	143	122	366	174	2.51

Selected by St. Louis Cardinals' organization in 7th round of free-agent draft, January 11, 1977.
Selected by Minnesota Twins' organization in 2nd round of free-agent draft, January 10, 1978.
†Traded to New York Mets, February 7, 1979, completing deal in which Minnesota Twins traded Pitcher Greg Field and a player to be named later to New York for Pitcher Jerry Koosman, December 8, 1978.

ALL-STAR GAME RECORD

Year League	IP.	W.	L.	Pct.	H.	R.	ER.	SO.	BB.	ERA.
1983—National	⅓	0	0	.000	0	0	0	1	0	0.00

Member of National League All-Star Team in 1984; did not play.

JOSEPH MICHAEL ORSULAK
(Joe)

Born May 31, 1962, at Parsippany, N.J.
Height, 6.01. Weight, 186.
Throws and bats lefthanded.

Major League stolen bases: 1984 (3), 1985 (24). Total—27.
Led Pacific Coast League outfielders in total chances with 367 and double plays with 8 in 1983.
Tied for South Atlantic League lead in double plays by outfielders with 4 in 1981.

Year—Club	League	Pos.	G.	AB.	R.	H.	2B.	3B.	HR.	RBI.	B.A.	PO.	A.	E.	F.A.
1981—Greenwood†	S. Atl.	OF	118	460	80	145	18	8	6	70	.315	249	16	4	★.985
1982—Alexandria	Carol.	OF-1B	129	463	92	134	18	4	14	65	.289	286	7	10	.967
1983—Hawaii	P. C.	OF	139	538	87	154	12	●13	10	58	.286	★341	●18	8	.978
1983—Pittsburgh	Nat.	OF	7	11	0	2	0	0	0	1	.182	2	2	0	1.000
1984—Hawaii	P. C.	OF	98	388	51	110	19	12	3	53	.284	258	6	2	.992
1984—Pittsburgh	Nat.	OF	32	67	12	17	1	2	0	3	.254	41	1	0	1.000
1985—Pittsburgh‡	Nat.	OF	121	397	54	119	14	6	0	21	.300	229	10	6	.976
Major League Totals—3 Years			160	475	66	138	15	8	0	25	.291	272	13	6	.979

Selected by Pittsburgh Pirates' organization in 6th round of free-agent draft, June 3, 1980.
†On temporarily inactive list, July 10 to July 27, 1981.
‡On disabled list, May 25 to June 9, 1985.

JORGE ORTA (NUNEZ)
Named pronounced OR-ta.

Born November 26, 1950, at Mazatlan, Mexico.
Height, 5.10. Weight, 175.
Throws right and bats lefthanded.

Major League stolen bases: 1972 (3), 1973 (8), 1974 (9), 1975 (16), 1976 (24), 1977 (4), 1978 (1), 1979 (1), 1980 (6), 1981 (4), 1983 (1), 1985 (2). Total—79.
Collected six hits in one game, June 15, 1980.

Year—Club	League	Pos.	G.	AB.	R.	H.	2B.	3B.	HR.	RBI.	B.A.	PO.	A.	E.	F.A.
1968—Fresnillo	Mex. Cen.	2B-SS	20	68	8	18	6	0	0	1	.265	29	39	4	.944
1969—S. Luis Potosi	Mex. C.					(Did not play)									
1970—Puerto Mex.	Mex. S.E.	2B-SS	18	43	6	13	1	0	0	3	.302	29	28	1	.983
1971—S. Luis Potosi	Mex. Cen.	2B	59	182	55	77	17	★7	7	53	★.423	115	108	15	.937
1971—Mexicali†	Mex. No.		58	207	45	75	14	2	16	48	.362	figures unavailable			
1972—Knoxville	South.	2B	53	196	41	62	6	7	7	34	.316	113	142	9	.966
1972—Chicago	Amer.	SS-2B-3B	51	124	20	25	3	1	3	11	.202	50	85	8	.944
1973—Chicago	Amer.	2B-SS	128	425	46	113	9	10	6	40	.266	255	301	18	.969
1974—Chicago	Amer.	2B-SS	139	525	73	166	31	2	10	67	.316	297	313	18	.971
1975—Chicago	Amer.	2B	140	542	64	165	26	10	11	83	.304	354	354	16	.978
1976—Chicago	Amer.	OF-3B	158	636	74	174	29	8	14	72	.274	187	111	15	.952
1977—Chicago	Amer.	2B	144	564	71	159	27	8	11	84	.282	287	335	19	.970
1978—Chicago	Amer.	2B	117	420	45	115	19	2	13	53	.274	275	290	9	.984
1979—Chicago‡	Amer.	2B	113	325	49	85	18	3	11	46	.262	57	75	3	.978
1980—Cleveland	Amer.	OF	129	481	78	140	18	3	10	64	.291	269	10	5	.982
1981—Cleveland§	Amer.	OF	88	338	50	92	14	3	5	34	.272	150	11	1	.994
1982—Los Angeles xy	Nat.	OF	86	115	13	25	5	0	2	8	.217	35	1	2	.947
1983—Toronto z	Amer.	OF	103	245	30	58	6	3	10	38	.237	16	1	0	1.000
1984—Kansas City	Amer.	OF-2B	122	403	50	120	23	7	9	50	.298	48	0	1	.980
1985—Kansas City	Amer.	DH	110	300	32	80	21	1	4	45	.267	0	0	0	.000
American League Totals—13 Years			1542	5328	682	1492	244	61	117	687	.280	2347	1886	113	.974
National League Totals—1 Year			86	115	13	25	5	0	2	8	.217	35	1	2	.947
Major League Totals—14 Years			1628	5443	695	1517	249	61	119	695	.279	2382	1887	115	.974

Signed as free agent by Fresnillo, June 13, 1968.
†Sold to Appleton (Chicago White Sox' organization), November 30, 1971.
‡Granted free agency, November 1, 1979; signed by Cleveland Indians, December 19, 1979.
§Traded with Catcher Jack Fimple and Pitcher Larry White to Los Angeles Dodgers for Pitcher Rick Sutcliffe and Second Baseman Jack Perconte, December 9, 1981.
xTraded to New York Mets for Pitcher Pat Zachry, December 28, 1982.
yTraded to Toronto Blue Jays for Pitcher Steve Senteney, February 4, 1983.
zTraded to Kansas City Royals for First Baseman Willie Aikens, December 19, 1983.

CHAMPIONSHIP SERIES RECORD

Year—Club	League	Pos.	G.	AB.	R.	H.	2B.	3B.	HR.	RBI.	B.A.	PO.	A.	E.	F.A.
1984—Kansas City	Amer.	DH	3	10	1	1	0	1	0	1	.100	0	0	0	.000
1985—Kansas City	Amer.	DH-PH	2	5	0	0	0	0	0	0	.000	0	0	0	.000
Championship Series Totals—2 Years			5	15	1	1	0	1	0	1	.067	0	0	0	.000

WORLD SERIES RECORD

Year—Club	League	Pos.	G.	AB.	R.	H.	2B.	3B.	HR.	RBI.	B.A.	PO.	A.	E.	F.A.
1985—Kansas City	Amer.	PH	3	3	0	1	0	0	0	0	.333	0	0	0	.000

Named to American League All-Star Team for 1975 game; replaced due to injury.
Member of American League All-Star Team in 1980; did not play.

ADALBERTO ORTIZ JR. (COLON)

Name pronounced Orr-TEEZ.

(Junior)

Born October 24, 1959, at Humacao, Puerto Rico.
Height, 5.11. Weight, 176.
Throws and bats righthanded.
Brother of Alexander Ortiz, minor league outfielder, 1978 and 1979.

Major League stolen bases: 1983 (1), 1984 (1), 1985 (1). Total—3.
Led Pacific Coast League catchers in putouts with 744 and double plays with 17 in 1982.
Led Carolina League catchers in double plays with 12 in 1979.
Tied for Western Carolinas League lead in passed balls with 22 in 1978.

Year Club	League	Pos.	G.	AB.	R.	H.	2B.	3B.	HR.	RBI.	B.A.	PO.	A.	E.	F.A.
1977—Charleston†	W. Car.	C	21	53	2	14	3	0	0	10	.264	93	13	4	.964
1977—Bradenton Pir.	Gulf C.	C	34	118	11	24	5	1	1	12	.203	76	14	4	.957
1978—Charleston‡	W. Car.	C	41	122	12	26	4	0	1	16	.213	198	44	7	.972
1979—Salem	Carol.	★C-1B	108	396	35	112	21	2	5	66	.283	602	★84	★17	.977
1980—Buffalo	East.	C	130	513	79	★178	25	1	12	78	★.346	497	91	16	.974
1980—Portland	P. C.	C	8	27	1	3	0	1	0	3	.111	42	10	0	1.000
1981—Portland	P. C.	C	105	346	49	93	14	7	2	46	.269	606	76	15	.978
1982—Portland	P. C.	C-OF-1B	124	449	46	131	22	0	6	57	.292	751	★110	★19	.978
1982—Pittsburgh	Nat.	C	7	15	1	3	1	0	0	0	.200	27	3	0	1.000
1983—Pitt.§-N.Y.	Nat.	C	73	193	11	48	5	0	0	12	.249	293	31	11	.967
1984—New York x	Nat.	C	40	91	6	18	3	0	0	11	.198	136	13	3	.980
1985—Pittsburgh	Nat.	C	23	72	4	21	2	0	1	5	.292	115	14	2	.985
Major League Totals—4 Years			143	371	22	90	11	0	1	28	.243	571	61	16	.975

Signed as free agent by Pittsburgh Pirates' organization, January 18, 1977.
†On temporary inactive list, June 18 to June 22, 1977.
‡On disabled list, June 16 to September 5, 1978.
§Traded with Pitcher Art Ray to New York Mets for Outfielder Marvell Wynne and Pitcher Steve Senteney, June 14, 1983.
xDrafted by Pittsburgh Pirates, December 3, 1984.

PHILIP ROLAND OUELLETTE

Name pronounced Well-LETT.

(Phil)

Born November 10, 1961, at Salem, Ore.
Height, 6.00. Weight, 190.
Throws right and bats left and righthanded.
Attended Citrus College, Azusa, Calif.
Cousin of Dan Simmons, member of U.S. Olympic ski team, 1980 and 1984.

Year Club	League	Pos.	G.	AB.	R.	H.	2B.	3B.	HR.	RBI.	B.A.	PO.	A.	E.	F.A.
1981—Great Falls	Pion.	C-1B	42	129	17	34	6	1	1	28	.264	234	21	4	.985
1982—Clinton	Midw.	C	109	351	59	96	18	1	13	74	.274	681	65	6	★.992
1983—Fresno†	Calif.	C-1B	71	210	37	57	7	2	5	35	.271	334	18	1	.997
1984—Phoenix	P. C.	C-P	70	171	32	45	8	4	7	29	.263	265	25	3	.990
1985—Phoenix‡	P. C.	C	27	79	7	14	0	0	0	8	.177	114	10	1	.992

Signed as free agent by San Francisco Giants' organization, May 17, 1981.
†On disabled list, August 2, 1983 through remainder of season.
‡On disabled list, May 27, 1985 through remainder of season.

PITCHING RECORD

Year Club	League	G.	IP.	W.	L.	Pct.	H.	R.	ER.	SO.	BB.	ERA.
1984—Phoenix	P. Coast	3	7⅔	0	1	.000	6	2	2	2	3	2.35

DAVE OWEN

Born April 25, 1958, at Cleburne, Tex.
Height, 6.01. Weight, 175.
Throws right and bats left and righthanded.
Attended University of Texas, Arlington, Tex.
Brother of Spike Owen, shortstop with Seattle Mariners.

Major League stolen bases: 1983 (1), 1984 (1), 1985 (1). Total—3.

Year Club	League	Pos.	G.	AB.	R.	H.	2B.	3B.	HR.	RBI.	B.A.	PO.	A.	E.	F.A.
1979—Sarasota Cubs	Gulf C.	SS	10	23	8	7	0	0	0	4	.304	17	26	7	.860
1979—Quad Cities	Midw.	SS	45	129	23	18	3	0	0	4	.140	56	139	11	.947
1980—Midland	Texas	SS	78	257	45	74	8	0	3	31	.288	96	213	32	.906
1980—Quad Cities	Midw.	SS	56	188	43	49	5	1	0	17	.261	88	155	17	.935
1981—Midland	Texas	SS-2B-3B	80	247	40	53	8	1	0	23	.215	109	205	26	.924
1982—Midland	Texas	SS-3B	125	427	59	135	12	9	4	40	.316	183	309	29	.944
1983—Iowa	A. A.	SS	126	425	67	110	21	3	6	39	.259	203	★431	25	★.962
1983—Chicago	Nat.	SS-3B	16	22	1	2	0	1	0	2	.091	10	29	0	1.000
1984—Iowa	A. A.	SS-2B-OF	43	136	18	31	5	1	1	9	.228	65	111	7	.962

Year Club	League	Pos.	G.	AB.	R.	H.	2B.	3B.	HR.	RBI.	B.A.	PO.	A.	E.	F.A.
1984—Chicago	Nat.	SS-3B-2B	47	93	8	18	2	2	1	10	.194	40	91	7	.949
1985—Iowa	A. A.	2-S-3-O	100	321	60	73	13	5	11	40	.227	157	280	7	.984
1985—Chicago†	Nat.	SS-3B-2B	22	19	6	7	0	0	0	4	.368	6	14	2	.909
Major League Totals—3 Years			85	134	15	27	2	3	1	16	.201	56	134	9	.955

Selected by Chicago Cubs' organization in 10th round of free-agent draft, June 5, 1979.
†Traded to San Francisco Giants for Second Baseman Manny Trillo, December 11, 1985.

LAWRENCE THOMAS OWEN
(Larry)

Born May 31, 1955, at Cleveland, O.
Height, 5.10. Weight, 190.
Throws and bats righthanded.
Attended Bowling Green State University, Bowling Green, O.

Led International League catchers in total chances with 648 in 1984.
Tied for International League lead in passed balls with 15 in 1979.

Year Club	League	Pos.	G.	AB.	R.	H.	2B.	3B.	HR.	RBI.	B.A.	PO.	A.	E.	F.A.
1977—Greenwood	W. Car.	C	61	170	26	48	9	2	3	24	.282	295	47	11	.969
1978—Savannah	South.	C	112	364	35	78	9	1	11	45	.214	★545	★89	★25	.962
1978—Richmond	Int.	C	14	40	2	10	1	0	0	3	.250	59	9	6	.919
1979—Richmond	Int.	C	110	358	32	70	7	3	7	29	.196	★615	●73	★13	.981
1980—Savannah	South.	C-3B	76	228	27	48	8	1	6	20	.211	304	44	7	.980
1981—Savannah	South.	C	90	279	30	64	8	3	5	23	.229	450	77	★23	.958
1981—Atlanta	Nat.	C	13	16	0	0	0	0	0	0	.000	23	4	1	.964
1982—Richmond	Int.	C	58	178	21	37	5	0	5	26	.208	265	37	6	.981
1982—Atlanta	Nat.	C	2	3	1	1	1	0	0	0	.333	2	1	0	1.000
1983—Atlanta	Nat.	C	17	17	0	2	0	0	0	1	.118	30	2	1	.970
1983—Richmond	Int.	C	5	12	4	5	0	1	1	2	.417	20	0	0	1.000
1984—Richmond	Int.	C	94	314	33	76	13	0	7	45	.242	572	★62	★14	.978
1985—Richmond	Int.	C	83	247	21	57	15	0	5	32	.231	436	65	12	.977
1985—Atlanta	Nat.	C	26	71	7	17	3	0	2	12	.239	129	11	5	.966
Major League Totals—4 Years			58	107	8	20	4	0	2	13	.187	184	18	7	.967

Selected by California Angels' organization in 18th round of free-agent draft, June 8, 1976.
Selected by Atlanta Braves' organization in 17th round of free-agent draft, June 7, 1977.

SPIKE DEE OWEN

Born April 19, 1961, at Cleburne, Tex.
Height, 5.10. Weight, 165.
Throws right and bats left and righthanded.
Attended University of Texas, Austin, Tex.
Brother of Dave Owen, shortstop with San Francisco Giants.

Major League stolen bases: 1983 (10), 1984 (16), 1985 (11). Total—37.
Named shortstop on THE SPORTING NEWS College Baseball All-America Team, 1982.

Year Club	League	Pos.	G.	AB.	R.	H.	2B.	3B.	HR.	RBI.	B.A.	PO.	A.	E.	F.A.
1982—Lynn	East.	SS	78	241	32	64	9	2	1	27	.266	106	207	9	.972
1983—Salt Lake City	P. C.	SS	72	256	58	68	8	9	1	32	.266	111	212	14	.958
1983—Seattle	Amer.	SS	80	306	36	60	11	3	2	21	.196	122	233	11	.970
1984—Seattle	Amer.	SS	152	530	67	130	18	8	3	43	.245	245	463	17	.977
1985—Seattle†	Amer.	SS	118	352	41	91	10	6	6	37	.259	196	361	14	.975
Major League Totals—3 Years			350	1188	144	281	39	17	11	101	.237	563	1057	42	.975

Selected by Seattle Mariners' organization in 1st round (sixth player selected) of free-agent draft, June 7, 1982.
†On disabled list, July 15 to August 1, 1985.

RICHARD WAYNE OWNBEY
(Rick)

Born October 20, 1957, at Corona, Calif.
Height, 6.03. Weight, 185.
Throws and bats righthanded.
Attended Santa Ana College, Santa Ana, Calif.

Year Club	League	G.	IP.	W.	L.	Pct.	H.	R.	ER.	SO.	BB.	ERA.
1980—Lynchburg	Carolina	12	92	8	1	.889	66	24	19	93	35	1.86
1980—Jackson	Texas	2	13	1	0	1.000	7	3	2	12	7	1.38
1981—Jackson†	Texas	20	133	10	7	.588	110	49	41	125	62	2.77
1982—Tidewater	Int'national	23	150⅓	8	7	.533	107	64	56	122	112	3.35
1982—New York	National	8	50⅓	1	2	.333	44	23	21	28	43	3.75
1983—New York‡	National	10	34⅔	1	3	.250	31	19	18	19	21	4.67
1983—Louisville	Am. Assoc.	16	104	7	5	.583	100	47	42	77	51	3.63
1984—Louisville§	Am. Assoc.	17	96⅓	6	6	.500	75	52	43	111	61	4.02
1984—St. Louis	National	4	19	0	3	.000	23	13	10	11	8	4.74
1985—Louisville x	Am. Assoc.	25	166	10	9	.526	154	68	63	122	74	3.42
Major League Totals—3 Years		22	104	2	8	.200	98	55	49	58	72	4.24

Selected by Pittsburgh Pirates' organization in 4th round of free-agent draft, January 9, 1979.
Selected by New York Mets' organization in 13th round of free-agent draft, June 3, 1980.
†On disabled list, May 24 to June 9, 1981.
‡Traded with Pitcher Neil Allen to St. Louis Cardinals for First Baseman Keith Hernandez, June 15, 1983.

§On disabled list, April 6 to April 20 and May 3 to June 4, 1984.
xOn St. Louis disabled list, March 28 to May 20, 1985; included rehabilitation disability assignment to Louisville, April 30 to May 20, 1985.

JOHN LEWIS PACELLA

Name pronounced Puh-SELL-uh.

Born September 15, 1956, at Brooklyn, N.Y.
Height, 6.02. Weight, 184.
Throws and bats righthanded.

Pitched 3-0 no-hit victory against Tulsa, April 15, 1977.
Major League saves: 1982 (2).

Year Club	League	G.	IP.	W.	L.	Pct.	H.	R.	ER.	SO.	BB.	ERA.
1974—Marion	Ap'lachian	12	43	1	7	.125	48	31	24	19	32	5.02
1975—Wausau	Midwest	19	132	9	8	.529	124	71	56	73	58	3.82
1976—Lynchburg	Carolina	26	185	12	11	.522	151	*97	67	119	83	3.26
1977—Tidewater	Int'national	17	93	7	5	.583	100	50	41	46	54	3.97
1977—Jackson	Texas	11	73	3	4	.429	75	47	33	49	39	4.07
1977—New York	National	3	4	0	0	.000	2	2	0	1	2	0.00
1978—Jackson	Texas	7	48	4	3	.571	31	16	14	44	16	2.63
1978—Tidewater	Int'national	19	102	4	11	.267	110	71	57	77	40	5.03
1979—Tidewater	Int'national	26	142	7	10	.412	129	65	58	95	61	3.61
1979—New York	National	4	16	0	2	.000	16	8	8	12	4	4.50
1980—New York‡	National	02	84	3	4	.429	89	51	48	68	59	5.14
1981—Columbus	Int'national	27	155	11	9	.550	149	84	77	135	91	4.47
1982—New York§-Minnesota xy	American	24	61⅔	1	3	.250	74	56	50	22	46	7.30
1982—Columbus z	Int'national	6	5⅓	0	2	.000	6	9	4	2	12	6.75
1983—Charlotte	Southern	10	28⅓	0	5	.000	34	30	20	17	28	6.35
1984—Charlotte	Southern	12	27⅓	0	0	.000	27	21	13	21	28	4.28
1984—Rochester	Int'national	22	113	6	3	.667	92	45	39	120	48	3.11
1984—Baltimore a	American	6	14⅔	0	1	.000	15	13	11	8	9	6.75
1985—Nashville	Southern	37	122⅔	7	7	.500	90	47	44	79	54	3.23
National League Totals—3 Years		39	104	3	6	.333	107	61	56	81	65	4.85
American League Totals—2 Years		30	76⅓	1	4	.200	89	69	61	30	55	7.19
Major League Totals—5 Years		69	180⅓	4	10	.286	196	130	117	111	120	5.84

Selected by New York Mets' organization in 4th round of free-agent draft, June 5, 1974.
†Traded with Infielder Jose Moreno to San Diego Padres for Pitcher Randy Jones, December 15, 1980.
‡Traded by San Diego Padres with Outfielder Jerry Mumphrey and a player to be named later to New York Yankees for Outfielders Ruppert Jones and Joe Lefebvre and Pitchers Tim Lollar and Chris Welsh, April 1, 1981; New York organization acquired Outfielder Dave Stegman to complete deal, April 30, 1981.
§Traded with Infielder Larry Milbourne and Pitcher Pete Filson to Minnesota Twins for Catcher Butch Wynegar and Pitcher Roger Erickson, May 12, 1982.
xOn disabled list, August 8 to September 1, 1982.
yTraded to Texas Rangers for Pitcher Len Whitehouse, November 1, 1982.
zReleased, April 6, 1983; signed by Charlotte (Baltimore Orioles' organization), July 11, 1983.
aReleased, December 10, 1984; signed by Nashville (Detroit Tigers' organization), December 28, 1984.

THOMAS MARIAN PACIOREK

Name pronounced Pah-CHOR-eck.

(Tom)

Born November 2, 1946, at Detroit, Mich.
Height, 6.04. Weight, 205.
Throws and bats righthanded.
Received bachelor of science degree in education from University of Houston, Houston, Tex.
Brother of Jim Paciorek, outfielder in Milwaukee Brewers' organization;
Mike Paciorek, first baseman in Los Angeles Dodgers'
and Atlanta Braves' organizations, 1973 through 1977;
and John Paciorek, outfielder with Houston Astros, 1963.

Major League stolen bases: 1972 (1), 1973 (3), 1974 (1), 1975 (4), 1976 (2), 1977 (1), 1978 (2), 1979 (6), 1980 (3), 1981 (13), 1982 (3), 1983 (6), 1984 (6), 1985 (3). Total—54.
Led Pacific Coast League in total bases with 310 and tied for lead in sacrifice flies with 12 in 1972.
Named Minor League Player of the Year by THE SPORTING NEWS, 1972.
Named Pacific Coast League Most Valuable Player, 1972.
Named outfielder on THE SPORTING NEWS College Baseball All-America Team, 1967 and 1968.
Selected by Miami Dolphins in 9th round of 1968 NFL draft.

Year Club	League	Pos.	G.	AB.	R.	H.	2B.	3B.	HR.	RBI.	B.A.	PO.	A.	E.	F.A.
1968—Ogden	Pion.	OF-1B	29	101	25	39	6	3	5	23	.386	45	3	2	.960
1968—Bakersfield	Calif.	OF-1B	38	116	16	32	1	1	0	10	.276	44	1	0	1.000
1969—Bakersfield†	Calif.	OF-3B	91	359	59	114	20	3	15	53	.318	111	44	16	.906
1970—Spokane	P. C.	OF	●146	549	88	179	36	12	17	101	.326	262	5	6	.978
1970—Los Angeles	Nat.	OF	8	9	2	2	1	0	0	0	.222	1	0	0	1.000
1971—Spokane	P. C.	OF-3B	144	564	89	172	31	*14	15	105	.305	240	9	8	.969
1971—Los Angeles	Nat.	OF	2	2	0	1	0	0	0	1	.500	1	0	0	1.000
1972—Albuquerque	P. C.	1B	147	*605	*125	*186	*33	5	*27	107	.307	*1239	80	●13	.990
1972—Los Angeles	Nat.	1B-OF	11	47	4	12	4	0	1	6	.255	53	3	1	.982
1973—Los Angeles	Nat.	OF-1B	96	195	26	51	8	0	5	18	.262	117	3	2	.984
1974—Los Angeles	Nat.	OF-1B	85	175	23	42	8	6	1	24	.240	85	1	5	.945
1975—Los Angeles‡	Nat.	OF	62	145	14	28	8	0	1	5	.193	69	0	2	.972
1976—Atlanta	Nat.	OF-1B-3B	111	324	39	94	10	4	4	36	.290	216	10	3	.987

— 374 —

Year—Club	League	Pos.	G.	AB.	R.	H.	2B.	3B.	HR.	RBI.	B.A.	PO.	A.	E.	F.A.
1977—Atlanta§	Nat.	1B-OF-3B	72	155	20	37	8	0	3	15	.239	248	16	5	.981
1978—Atlanta x	Nat.	1B	5	9	2	3	0	0	0	0	.333	21	0	0	1.000
1978—San Jose	P. C.	OF	16	57	7	16	1	2	3	17	.281	32	1	1	.971
1978—Seattle y	Amer.	OF-1B	70	251	32	75	20	3	4	30	.299	115	5	2	.984
1979—Seattle	Amer.	OF-1B	103	310	38	89	23	4	6	42	.287	237	12	1	.996
1980—Seattle	Amer.	OF-1B	126	418	44	114	19	1	15	59	.273	360	22	5	.987
1981—Seattle z	Amer.	OF	104	405	50	132	28	2	14	66	.326	253	10	7	.974
1982—Chicago a	Amer.	1B-OF	104	382	49	119	27	4	11	55	.312	835	66	6	.993
1983—Chicago	Amer.	1B-OF	115	420	65	129	32	3	9	63	.307	629	38	1	.999
1984—Chicago b	Amer.	1B-OF	111	363	35	93	21	2	4	29	.256	596	25	6	.990
1985—Chicago c	Amer.	OF-1B	46	122	14	30	2	0	0	9	.246	76	6	1	.988
1985—New York d	Nat.	OF-1B	46	116	14	33	3	1	1	11	.284	76	3	0	1.000
American League Totals—8 Years			779	2671	327	781	172	19	63	353	.292	3101	184	29	.991
National League Totals—10 Years			498	1177	144	303	50	11	16	116	.257	887	36	18	.981
Major League Totals—16 Years			1277	3848	471	1084	222	30	79	469	.282	3988	220	47	.989

Selected by Los Angeles Dodgers' organization in 42nd round of free-agent draft, June 7, 1968.

†On restricted list, April 3 to June 3, 1969.

‡Traded with Outfielder Jimmy Wynn, Second Baseman Lee Lacy and Infielder Jerry Royster to Atlanta Braves for Outfielder Dusty Baker and First Baseman-Third Baseman Ed Goodson, November 17, 1975.

§Released March 30, 1978; re-signed by Atlanta Braves, April 7, 1978.

xReleased, May 23, 1978; signed by Seattle Mariners' organization, May 31, 1978.

yGranted free agency, November 2, 1978; re-signed by Mariners, January 6, 1979.

zTraded to Chicago White Sox for Catcher Jim Essian, Shortstop Todd Cruz and Outfielder Rod Allen, December 11, 1981.

aOn disabled list, July 27 to August 11 and August 28 to September 17, 1982.

bOn disabled list, June 30 to July 28, 1984.

cTraded to New York Mets for Infielder Dave Cochrane, July 16, 1985.

dReleased, November 13, 1985; signed by Texas Rangers, December 10, 1985.

CHAMPIONSHIP SERIES RECORD

Year—Club	League	Pos.	G.	AB.	R.	H.	2B.	3B.	HR.	RBI.	B.A.	PO.	A.	E.	F.A.
1974—Los Angeles	Nat.	PH-OF	1	1	0	1	0	0	0	0	1.000	0	0	0	.000
1983—Chicago	Amer.	1B-OF	4	16	1	4	0	0	0	1	.250	30	3	0	1.000
Championship Series Totals—2 Years			5	17	1	5	0	0	0	1	.294	30	3	0	1.000

WORLD SERIES RECORD

Year—Club	League	Pos.	G.	AB.	R.	H.	2B.	3B.	HR.	RBI.	B.A.	PO.	A.	E.	F.A.
1974—Los Angeles	Nat.	PH-PR	3	2	1	1	1	0	0	0	.500	0	0	0	.000

ALL-STAR GAME RECORD

Year—League	Pos.	AB.	R.	H.	2B.	3B.	HR.	RBI.	B.A.	PO.	A.	E.	F.A.
1981—American	PH	1	0	1	0	0	0	0	1.000	0	0	0	.000

MICHAEL TIMOTHY PAGLIARULO
Name pronounced PAG-lee-a-rule-oh.

(Mike)

Born March 15, 1960, at Medford, Mass.
Height, 6.02. Weight, 195.
Throws right and bats lefthanded.
Attended University of Miami, Coral Gables, Fla.
Son of Charles Pagliarulo, infielder in Chicago Cubs' organization, 1958.

Led New York-Pennsylvania League in intentional bases on balls received with 8 in 1981.
Led Southern League third basemen in total chances with 433 in 1983.
Led New York-Pennsylvania League third basemen in total chances with 214 in 1981.

Year—Club	League	Pos.	G.	AB.	R.	H.	2B.	3B.	HR.	RBI.	B.A.	PO.	A.	E.	F.A.
1981—Oneonta	NYP	3B	72	245	32	53	9	4	2	28	.216	40	★159	15	.930
1982—Greensboro	S. Atl.	3B	123	403	79	113	22	0	22	79	.280	73	★278	27	.929
1983—Nashville	South.	3B	135	450	82	117	19	4	19	80	.260	★98	★315	20	★.954
1984—Columbus	Int.	3B-SS	58	146	24	31	5	1	7	25	.212	27	95	13	.904
1984—New York	Amer.	3B	67	201	24	48	15	3	7	34	.239	44	106	7	.955
1985—New York	Amer.	3B	138	380	55	91	16	2	19	62	.239	67	187	13	.951
Major League Totals—2 Years			205	581	79	139	31	5	26	96	.239	111	293	20	.953

Selected by New York Yankees' organization in 6th round of free-agent draft, June 8, 1981.

THOMAS ALAN PAGNOZZI

(Tom)

Born July 30, 1962, at Tucson, Ariz.
Height, 6.01. Weight, 190.
Throws and bats righthanded.
Attended Central Arizona College, Coolidge, Ariz.,
and University of Arkansas, Fayetteville, Ark.
Brother of Tim Pagnozzi, shortstop in Philadelphia Phillies' organization, 1976;
and Mike Pagnozzi, pitcher in Baltimore Orioles' organization, 1975 through 1978.

Year Club	League	Pos.	G.	AB.	R.	H.	2B.	3B.	HR.	RBI.	B.A.	PO.	A.	E.	F.A.
1983—Erie	NYP	C	45	168	28	52	9	1	6	22	.310	183	20	3	.985
1983—Macon	S. Atl.	C	18	57	7	14	2	1	0	6	.246	125	18	8	.947
1984—Springfield	Midw.	C	114	396	57	112	20	4	10	68	.283	667	*90	12	.984
1985—Arkansas	Texas	C-1B	41	139	15	43	7	1	5	29	.309	243	27	1	.996
1985—Louisville	A. A.	C	76	268	29	72	13	2	5	40	.269	266	25	4	.986

Selected by Milwaukee Brewers' organization in 24th round of free-agent draft, January 12, 1982.
Selected by St. Louis Cardinals' organization in 8th round of free agent draft, June 6, 1983.

DAVID WILLIAM PALMER JR.

Born October 19, 1957, at Glens Falls, N.Y.
Height, 6.01. Weight, 205.
Throws and bats righthanded.

Pitched five-inning, 4-0 perfect game against St. Louis Cardinals, April 21, 1984 (second game).
Major League saves: 1979 (2).
Tied for Pioneer League lead in home runs allowed with 6 in 1976.

Year Club	League	G.	IP.	W.	L.	Pct.	H.	R.	ER.	SO.	BB.	ERA.
1976—Lethbridge	Pioneer	13	45	0	5	.000	58	49	36	44	28	7.20
1977—West Palm Beach	Florida St.	25	119	6	8	.429	120	49	38	88	44	2.87
1978—West Palm Beach	Florida St.	7	51	4	2	.667	44	23	11	58	4	1.94
1978—Memphis	Southern	19	130	8	10	.444	107	57	44	78	44	3.05
1978—Montreal	National	5	10	0	1	.000	9	4	3	7	2	2.70
1979—Montreal	National	36	123	10	2	.833	110	41	36	72	30	2.63
1980—Montreal†	National	24	130	8	6	.571	124	53	43	73	30	2.98
1981—West Palm Beach‡	Florida St.	3	11	0	0	.000	9	1	1	7	5	0.82
1981—Memphis	Southern	1	0	0	0	.000	0	1	1	0	1	0.00
1982—Memphis	Southern	9	51⅓	3	2	.600	38	21	20	44	33	3.51
1982—Montreal §	National	13	73⅔	6	4	.600	60	34	26	46	36	3.18
1983—West Palm Beach x	Florida St.					(Did not play)						
1984—Montreal y	National	20	105⅓	7	3	.700	101	45	45	66	44	3.84
1985—Montreal za	National	24	135⅔	7	10	.412	128	60	56	106	67	3.71
Major League Totals—6 Years		122	577⅔	38	26	.594	532	237	209	370	209	3.26

Selected by Montreal Expos' organization in 21st round of free-agent draft, June 8, 1976.
†On disabled list, July 21 to August 27, 1980.
‡On Montreal disabled list, March 25 to August 9, 1981; included rehabilitation disability assignment to West Palm Beach, May 6 to May 25, 1981.
§On disabled list, August 14 to September 27, 1982.
xOn Montreal disabled list, March 28 to September 20, 1983; included rehabilitation disability assignment to West Palm Beach, August 6 to August 26, 1983.
yOn disabled list, August 5 to September 1, 1984.
zOn disabled list, August 9 to September 1, 1985.
aGranted free agency, November 12, 1985.

JAMES FRANKLIN PANKOVITS
(Jim)

Born August 6, 1955, at Pennington Gap, Va.
Height, 5.10. Weight, 175.
Throws and bats righthanded.
Attended University of South Carolina, Columbia, S.C.

Major League stolen bases: 1984 (2), 1985 (1). Total—3.
Led Appalachian League second basemen in assists with 212 and double plays with 47 in 1976.
Named third baseman on THE SPORTING NEWS College Baseball All-America Team, 1976.

Year Club	League	Pos.	G.	AB.	R.	H.	2B.	3B.	HR.	RBI.	B.A.	PO.	A.	E.	F.A.
1976—Covington	Appal.	2B	●70	275	50	68	9	2	5	31	.247	165	212	18	.954
1977—Cocoa†	Fla. St.	SS-3B	91	326	27	74	9	3	2	20	.227	2	3	0	1.000
1978—Columbus	South.	SS	137	509	67	122	19	7	10	43	.240	4	8	2	.857
1978—Charleston	Int.	2B	3	7	0	1	0	0	0	0	.143	5	3	0	1.000
1979—Columbus	South.	SS	92	346	53	91	10	3	10	45	.263	0	13	0	1.000
1979—Charleston	Int.	2B	22	59	7	10	3	1	0	3	.169	43	53	4	.960
1980—Tucson	P. C.	2B-3B-SS	64	213	36	53	8	4	2	26	.249	110	128	9	.964
1981—Tucson	P. C.	O-3-2-S	122	450	83	127	34	9	7	64	.282	93	75	22	.884
1982—Hawaii‡§	P. C.	3B-2B-OF	139	494	84	132	25	7	15	77	.267	192	162	22	.941
1983—Tucson	P. C.	2B	126	450	77	129	25	6	11	62	.287	215	322	25	.956
1984—Tucson	P. C.	2B	49	187	41	62	12	3	7	39	.332	103	176	8	.972
1984—Houston	Nat.	2B-SS-OF	53	81	6	23	7	0	1	14	.284	22	22	3	.936
1985—Houston x	Nat.	O-2-S-3	75	172	24	42	3	0	4	14	.244	81	38	2	.983
Major League Totals—2 Years		128	253	30	65	10	0	5	28	.257	103	60	5	.970

Selected by Houston Astros' organization in 4th round of free-agent draft, June 8, 1976.
†On disabled list, May 22 to June 24, 1977.
‡Loaned to Hawaii (San Diego Padres' organization), March 28, 1982; returned, September 17, 1982.
§Granted free agency, October 22, 1982; re-signed by Astros' organization, January 23, 1983.
xOn disabled list, July 3 to July 18 and July 27 to August 22, 1985.

—DID YOU KNOW—
That the St. Louis Cardinals used five pitchers in one inning three times in 1985?

ALBERTO JUDAS PARDO
(Al)

Born September 8, 1962, at Oviedo, Spain.
Height, 6.02. Weight, 195.
Throws right and bats left and righthanded.
Brother of Braulio Pardo, minor league catcher, 1980.

Led Southern League in game-winning RBIs with 17 in 1984.

Year	Club	League	Pos.	G.	AB.	R.	H.	2B.	3B.	HR.	RBI.	B.A.	PO.	A.	E.	F.A.
1980—Bluefield	Appal.	C-1B	48	151	26	52	6	2	3	23	.344	66	8	0	1.000
1981—Miami	Fla. St.	C	91	291	25	63	9	3	3	32	.216	396	41	6	.987
1981—Hagerstown	Carol.	C	21	76	11	24	3	1	1	7	.316	37	7	2	.957
1982—Hagerstown	Carol.	C-1B-OF	130	492	76	142	24	4	17	86	.289	685	74	11	.986
1983—Rochester	Int.	C	69	220	25	56	11	2	1	31	.255	223	18	9	.964
1983—Charlotte	South.	C	37	141	20	44	11	3	4	19	.312	129	18	4	.974
1984—Charlotte	South.	C-OF-1B	138	483	72	128	23	2	13	81	.265	397	32	14	.968
1985—Rochester	Int.	C	60	194	23	49	14	1	8	35	.253	258	19	6	.979
1985—Baltimore	Amer.	C	34	75	3	10	1	0	0	1	.133	131	7	3	.979
Major League Totals—1 Year			34	75	3	10	1	0	0	1	.133	131	7	3	.979

Selected by Baltimore Orioles' organization in 2nd round of free-agent draft, June 3, 1980.

MARK ALLEN PARENT

Born September 16, 1961, at Ashland, Ore.
Height, 6.05. Weight, 215.
Throws and bats righthanded.

Led Carolina League catchers in double plays with 16 in 1981.
Led Northwest League catchers in fielding percentage with .979 in 1980.

Year	Club	League	Pos.	G.	AB.	R.	H.	2B.	3B.	HR.	RBI.	B.A.	PO.	A.	E.	F.A.
1979—Walla Walla	N'west	C-OF	40	126	8	24	4	0	1	11	.190	229	34	6	.978
1980—Reno	Calif.	C	30	99	8	20	3	0	0	12	.202	128	23	2	.987
1980—Grays Harbor	N'west	C-1B	66	230	29	55	11	2	7	32	.230	381	38	9	.979
1981—Salem	Carol.	C	123	438	44	103	16	3	6	47	.235	★694	87	★28	.965
1982—Amarillo	Texas	C	26	89	12	17	3	1	1	13	.191	100	6	2	.981
1982—Salem	Carol.	C-1B	99	360	39	81	15	2	6	41	.225	475	64	12	.978
1983—Beaumont†	Texas	C	81	282	38	71	22	1	7	33	.252	464	71	10	★.982
1984—Beaumont‡	Texas	C-1B	111	380	52	109	24	3	7	60	.287	674	68	7	.991
1985—Las Vegas	P. C.	C-1B	105	361	36	87	23	3	7	45	.241	586	54	6	.991

Selected by San Diego Padres' organization in 4th round of free-agent draft, June 5, 1979.
†On suspended list, August 27, 1983 through remainder of season.
‡On disabled list, September 4, 1984 through remainder of season.

KELLY JAY PARIS

Born October 17, 1957, at Encino, Calif.
Height, 6.00. Weight, 175.
Throws and bats righthanded.
Brother of Brett Paris, infielder in San Francisco Giants' and
St. Louis Cardinals' organizations, 1975 and 1976.

Led Appalachian League in sacrifice flies with 7 in 1977.
Led Florida State League third basemen in double plays with 24 and tied for lead in errors with 29 in 1979.

Year	Club	League	Pos.	G.	AB.	R.	H.	2B.	3B.	HR.	RBI.	B.A.	PO.	A.	E.	F.A.
1975—Sarasota Cards	Gulf C.	SS	34	123	14	29	2	0	2	13	.236	59	92	14	.915
1976—Johnson City†	Appal.	1B	●70	247	40	68	7	3	5	30	.275	621	43	7	.990
1977—St. Petersburg‡	Fla. St.	1B-3B	44	124	14	22	3	0	0	9	.177	269	22	3	.990
1977—Johnson City‡	Appal.	1B-3B	51	169	32	53	8	1	2	28	.314	355	37	5	.987
1978—St. Petersburg	Fla. St.	1B	42	155	14	32	6	0	1	12	.206	319	23	5	.986
1978—Gastonia	W. Car.	1B-3B	79	297	48	75	9	3	2	20	.253	593	49	12	.982
1979—St. Petersburg	Fla. St.	3B-1B	118	388	52	110	15	3	2	53	.284	291	229	30	.945
1980—Arkansas	Texas	SS	116	399	63	120	28	3	4	49	.301	181	349	38	.933
1981—Springfield§	A. A.	SS-3B	90	292	38	78	10	1	6	31	.267	119	237	36	.908
1982—Louisville	A. A.	SS-3B-1B	129	482	71	158	32	5	11	83	.328	208	364	29	.952
1982—St. Louis x	Nat.	3B-2B	12	29	1	3	0	0	0	1	.103	9	25	4	.895
1983—Cincinnati	Nat.	3-2-S-1	56	120	13	30	6	0	0	7	.250	60	62	6	.953
1983—Indianapolis yz	A. A.	SS-2B-3B	8	35	9	11	1	0	2	9	.314	10	26	0	1.000
1984—Hawaii a	P. C.	SS-2B	127	460	65	115	26	3	10	58	.250	203	313	32	.942
1985—Rochester	Int.	S-2-3-O	126	440	69	121	25	2	18	67	.275	169	376	34	.941
1985—Baltimore	Amer.	2B	5	9	0	0	0	0	0	0	.000	3	3	1	.857
National League Totals—2 Years			68	149	14	33	6	0	0	8	.221	69	87	10	.940
American League Totals—1 Year			5	9	0	0	0	0	0	0	.000	3	3	1	.857
Major League Totals—3 Years			73	158	14	33	6	0	0	8	.209	72	90	11	.936

Selected by St. Louis Cardinals' organization in 2nd round of free-agent draft, June 4, 1975.
†On temporarily inactive list, April 16 to May 7, 1976.
‡Batted as switchhitter.
§On disabled list, July 25, 1981 through remainder of season.
xTraded to Cincinnati Reds' organization for Pitcher James Strichek, March 31, 1983.
ySold to Chicago White Sox, November 28, 1983.
zReleased, March 21, 1984; signed by Pittsburgh Pirates' organization, March 28, 1984.
aGranted free agency, October 15, 1984; signed by Rochester (Baltimore Orioles' organization), November 12, 1984.

DAVID GENE PARKER
(Dave)

Born June 9, 1951, at Jackson, Miss.
Height, 6.05. Weight, 230.
Throws right and bats lefthanded.

Tied major league record for most home runs, month of October (4), 1985.
Major League stolen bases: 1973 (1), 1974 (3), 1975 (8), 1976 (19), 1977 (17), 1978 (20), 1979 (20), 1980 (10), 1981 (6), 1982 (7), 1983 (12), 1984 (11), 1985 (5). Total—139.
Led National League in grounding into double plays with 26 in 1985.
Led National League in total bases with 340 in 1978 and 350 in 1985.
Led National League in slugging percentage with .541 in 1975 and .585 in 1978.
Led National League in intentional bases on balls received with 23 in 1978 and tied for lead with 24 in 1985.
Tied for National League lead in sacrifice flies with 9 in 1979.
Led National League outfielders in total chances with 430 and double plays with 9 in 1977.
Led Carolina League in total bases with 270 and stolen bases with 38 in 1972.
Tied for Gulf Coast League lead in total bases with 107 in 1970.
Named National League Player of the Year by THE SPORTING NEWS, 1978.
Named National League Most Valuable Player by Baseball Writers' Association of America, 1978.
Named outfielder on THE SPORTING NEWS National League All-Star Team, 1975, 1977, 1978 and 1985.
Named outfielder on THE SPORTING NEWS National League All-Star fielding team, 1977 through 1979.
Named outfielder on THE SPORTING NEWS National League Silver Slugger team, 1985.
Named Carolina League Most Valuable Player, 1972.

Year	Club	League	Pos.	G.	AB.	R.	H.	2B.	3B.	HR.	RBI.	B.A.	PO.	A.	E.	F.A.
1970—Bradenton Pir.	Gulf C.	●OF-P	61	239	34	75	8	3	●6	41	.314	92	11	●8	.928
1971—Waterbury	East.	OF	30	114	10	26	4	1	0	7	.228	43	5	6	.889
1971—Monroe	W. Car.	OF	71	268	49	96	16	4	11	48	.358	104	8	10	.918
1972—Salem	Carol.	OF	135	*523	*91	*162	*30	6	22	*101	*.310	*250	*20	*20	.931
1973—Charleston	Int.	OF	84	309	44	98	20	7	9	57	.317	144	11	7	.957
1973—Pittsburgh	Nat.	OF	54	139	17	40	9	1	4	14	.288	77	3	3	.964
1974—Pittsburgh†	Nat.	OF-1B	73	220	27	62	10	3	4	29	.282	154	8	4	.976
1975—Pittsburgh	Nat.	OF	148	558	75	172	35	10	25	101	.308	311	7	9	.972
1976—Pittsburgh	Nat.	OF	138	537	82	168	28	10	13	90	.313	294	13	*14	.956
1977—Pittsburgh	Nat.	*OF-2B	159	637	107	*215	*44	8	21	88	*.338	*389	*26	*15	.965
1978—Pittsburgh‡	Nat.	OF	148	581	102	194	32	12	30	117	*.334	302	12	*13	.960
1979—Pittsburgh	Nat.	OF	158	622	109	193	45	7	25	94	.310	341	15	*15	.960
1980—Pittsburgh	Nat.	OF	139	518	71	153	31	1	17	79	.295	235	14	9	.965
1981—Pittsburgh§	Nat.	OF	67	240	29	62	14	3	9	48	.258	110	1	7	.941
1982—Pittsburgh x	Nat.	OF	73	244	41	66	19	3	6	29	.270	108	2	5	.957
1983—Pittsburgh y	Nat.	OF	144	552	68	154	29	4	12	69	.279	282	3	8	.973
1984—Cincinnati	Nat.	OF	156	607	73	173	28	0	16	94	.285	296	6	8	.974
1985—Cincinnati	Nat.	OF	160	635	88	198	*42	4	34	*125	.312	329	12	10	.972
Major League Totals—13 Years				1617	6090	889	1850	366	66	216	977	.304	3228	121	120	.965

Selected by Pittsburgh Pirates' organization in 14th round of free-agent draft, June 4, 1970.
†On disabled list, June 7 to June 28 and July 5 to July 31, 1974.
‡On disabled list, July 1 to July 16, 1978.
§On disabled list, May 14 to May 29, 1981.
xOn disabled list, May 12 to June 7 and July 29 to September 7, 1982.
yGranted free agency, November 7, 1983; signed by Cincinnati Reds, December 7, 1983.

CHAMPIONSHIP SERIES RECORD

Year	Club	League	Pos.	G.	AB.	R.	H.	2B.	3B.	HR.	RBI.	B.A.	PO.	A.	E.	F.A.
1974—Pittsburgh	Nat.	OF-PH	3	8	0	1	0	0	0	0	.125	4	1	0	1.000
1975—Pittsburgh	Nat.	OF	3	10	2	0	0	0	0	0	.000	13	1	0	1.000
1979—Pittsburgh	Nat.	OF	3	12	2	4	0	0	0	2	.333	9	0	0	1.000
Championship Series Totals—3 Years				9	30	4	5	0	0	0	2	.167	26	2	0	1.000

WORLD SERIES RECORD

Year	Club	League	Pos.	G.	AB.	R.	H.	2B.	3B.	HR.	RBI.	B.A.	PO.	A.	E.	F.A.
1979—Pittsburgh	Nat.	OF	7	29	2	10	3	0	0	4	.345	13	1	1	.933

ALL-STAR GAME RECORD

Established All-Star Game record for most assists by outfielder, game (2), July 17, 1979.

Year	League	Pos.	AB.	R.	H.	2B.	3B.	HR.	RBI.	B.A.	PO.	A.	E.	F.A.
1977—National		OF	3	1	1	0	0	0	0	.333	2	0	0	1.000
1979—National		OF	3	0	1	0	0	0	1	.333	0	2	0	1.000
1980—National		OF	2	0	0	0	0	0	0	.000	0	0	0	.000
1981—National		OF	3	1	1	0	0	1	1	.333	1	0	0	1.000
1985—National		OF	2	0	0	0	0	0	0	.000	1	0	0	1.000
All-Star Game Totals—5 Years			13	2	3	0	0	1	2	.231	4	2	0	1.000

PITCHING RECORD

Year	Club	League	G.	IP.	W.	L.	Pct.	H.	R.	ER.	SO.	BB.	ERA.
1970—Bradenton Pirates	Gulf Coast	1	4	0	0	.000	7	2	2	2	1	4.50

—DID YOU KNOW—

That Red Sox third baseman Mike Greenwell's first three hits in the major leagues were home runs?

GARY LEE PARMENTER

Born June 24, 1962, in Bennington, Vt.
Height, 6.02. Weight, 190.
Throws and bats righthanded.
Attended Middle Georgia College, Cochran, Ga., and
University of South Carolina, Columbia, S.C.

Pitched 6-0 no-hit victory against Nashua, June 8, 1985.

Year—Club	League	G.	IP.	W.	L.	Pct.	H.	R.	ER.	SO.	BB.	ERA.
1983—Quad Cities	Midwest	11	39⅔	1	2	.333	43	29	20	32	9	4.54
1984—Lodi	California	27	143½	8	9	.471	152	81	61	132	59	3.83
1985—Pittsfield	Eastern	17	121⅔	6	5	.545	81	40	33	62	49	2.44

Selected by Seattle Mariners' organization in 4th round of free-agent draft, January 13, 1981.
Selected by Seattle Mariners' organization in 8th round of free-agent draft, June 7, 1982.
Selected by Chicago Cubs' organization in secondary phase of free-agent draft, June 6, 1983.

JEFFREY DALE PARRETT
(Jeff)

Born August 26, 1961, at Indianapolis, Ind.
Height, 6.04. Weight, 185.
Throws and bats righthanded.
Attended University of Kentucky, Lexington, Ky.

Year—Club	League	G.	IP.	W.	L.	Pct.	H.	R.	ER.	SO.	BB.	ERA.
1983—Paintsville	Ap'lachian	3	17	2	0	1.000	12	6	4	21	8	2.12
1983—Beloit	Midwest	10	47	2	2	.500	40	26	21	34	29	4.02
1984—Beloit	Midwest	29	91⅔	4	3	.571	76	50	46	95	71	4.52
1985—Stockton†	California	45	127⅔	7	4	.636	97	50	39	120	75	★2.75

Selected by Milwaukee Brewers' organization in 9th round of free-agent draft, June 6, 1983.
†Drafted by Montreal Expos, December 10, 1985.

LANCE MICHAEL PARRISH

Born June 15, 1956, at McKeesport, Pa.
Height, 6.03. Weight, 220.
Throws and bats righthanded.

Major League stolen bases: 1979 (6), 1980 (6), 1981 (2), 1982 (3), 1983 (1), 1984 (2), 1985 (2). Total—22.
Led American League in sacrifice flies with 13 in 1983.
Led American League catchers in double plays with 11 in 1984.
Led American League catchers in total chances with 772 in 1983.
Led American League in passed balls with 21 in 1979.
Tied for American League lead in passed balls with 17 in 1980.
Led Appalachian League batters in strikeouts with 92 in 1974.
Led American Association in double plays with 10 and passed balls with 21 in 1977.
Led Southern League in passed balls with 22 in 1976.
Led Florida State League catchers in double plays with 8 and passed balls with 31 in 1975.
Named catcher on THE SPORTING NEWS American League All-Star Team, 1982 and 1984.
Named catcher on THE SPORTING NEWS American League All-Star fielding team, 1983 through 1985.
Named catcher on THE SPORTING NEWS American League Silver Slugger team, 1980 and 1982 through 1984.

Year—Club	League	Pos.	G.	AB.	R.	H.	2B.	3B.	HR.	RBI.	B.A.	PO.	A.	E.	F.A.
1974—Bristol	Appal.	3B-OF	68	253	45	54	11	1	11	46	.213	36	83	22	.844
1975—Lakeland	Fla. St.	C	100	341	30	75	15	2	5	37	.220	460	50	7	.986
1976—Montgomery	South.	C	107	340	46	75	9	2	14	55	.221	★600	★79	11	★.984
1977—Evansville	A. A.	C	115	416	74	116	21	2	25	90	.279	★722	★82	11	★.987
1977—Detroit	Amer.	C	12	46	10	9	2	0	3	7	.196	76	6	0	1.000
1978—Detroit	Amer.	C	85	288	37	63	11	3	14	41	.219	353	39	5	.987
1979—Detroit	Amer.	C	143	493	65	136	26	3	19	65	.276	707	★79	9	.989
1980—Detroit	Amer.	C-1B-OF	144	553	79	158	34	6	24	82	.286	607	67	7	.990
1981—Detroit	Amer.	C	96	348	39	85	18	2	10	46	.244	407	40	3	.993
1982—Detroit	Amer.	C-OF	133	486	75	138	19	2	32	87	.284	627	76	8	.989
1983—Detroit	Amer.	C	155	605	80	163	42	3	27	114	.269	695	73	4	.995
1984—Detroit	Amer.	C	147	578	75	137	16	2	33	98	.237	720	67	7	.991
1985—Detroit	Amer.	C	140	549	64	150	27	1	28	98	.273	695	53	5	.993
Major League Totals—9 Years			1055	3946	524	1039	195	22	190	638	.263	4887	500	48	.991

Selected by Detroit Tigers' organization in 1st round (16th player selected) of free-agent draft, June 5, 1974.

CHAMPIONSHIP SERIES RECORD

Year—Club	League	Pos.	G.	AB.	R.	H.	2B.	3B.	HR.	RBI.	B.A.	PO.	A.	E.	F.A.
1984—Detroit	Amer.	C	3	12	1	3	1	0	1	3	.250	21	2	0	1.000

WORLD SERIES RECORD

Year—Club	League	Pos.	G.	AB.	R.	H.	2B.	3B.	HR.	RBI.	B.A.	PO.	A.	E.	F.A.
1984—Detroit	Amer.	C	5	18	3	5	1	0	1	2	.278	30	3	1	.971

ALL-STAR GAME RECORD

Established All-Star Game record for most assists by catcher, game (3), July 13, 1982.

Year—League	Pos.	AB.	R.	H.	2B.	3B.	HR.	RBI.	B.A.	PO.	A.	E.	F.A.
1980—American	C	1	0	0	0	0	0	0	.000	0	0	0	.000
1982—American	C	2	0	1	1	0	0	0	.500	2	3	0	1.000

Year League	Pos.	AB.	R.	H.	2B.	3B.	HR.	RBI.	B.A.	PO.	A.	E.	F.A.
1983—American	C	2	0	0	0	0	0	0	.000	1	0	0	1.000
1984—American	C	2	0	0	0	0	0	0	.000	3	1	1	.800
All Star Game Totals 4 Years		7	0	1	1	0	0	0	.143	6	4	1	.909

Named to American League All-Star Team for 1985 game; replaced due to injury by Rich Gedman.

LARRY ALTON PARRISH

Born November 10, 1953, at Winter Haven, Fla.
Height, 6.03. Weight, 215.
Throws and bats righthanded.
Attended Seminole Community College, Sanford, Fla.

Tied major league records for most home runs, bases filled, month (3), July, 1982; most home runs, bases filled, week (3), July 4 through 10 (first game), 1982.
Major League stolen bases' 1975 (4), 1976 (2), 1977 (2), 1978 (2), 1979 (5), 1980 (2), 1982 (5), 1984 (2). Total—24.
Hit three home runs in a game, May 29, 1977, July 30, 1978, April 25, 1980 and April 29, 1985.
Tied for National League lead in double plays by third basemen with 35 in 1976.
Led Florida State League in sacrifice flies with 9 in 1973.
Led Eastern League third basemen in double plays with 32 in 1974.
Led Florida State League third basemen in putouts with 95 and assists with 285 in 1973.
Named Florida State League Most Valuable Player, 1973.

Year Club	League	Pos.	G.	AB.	R.	H.	2B.	3B.	HR.	RBI.	B.A.	PO.	A.	E.	F.A.
1972—W. Palm D'ch	Fla. St.	OF	2	4	0	1	0	0	0	0	.250	2	0	0	1.000
1972—Jamestown	NYP	OF	62	223	32	58	4	3	4	28	.260	69	3	3	.960
1973—W. Palm B'ch	Fla. St.	★3B-SS	138	481	82	141	14	6	16	33	.293	100	292	32	★.925
1974—Quebec City	East.	3B	119	437	61	124	14	2	13	77	.284	★108	★277	●31	.925
1974—Montreal	Nat.	3B	25	69	9	14	5	0	0	4	.203	20	51	1	.986
1975—Montreal	Nat.	3B-SS-2B	145	532	50	146	32	5	10	65	.274	105	291	35	.919
1976—Montreal	Nat.	3B	154	543	65	126	28	5	11	61	.232	122	310	25	.945
1977—Montreal	Nat.	3B	123	402	50	99	19	2	11	46	.246	81	225	21	.936
1978—Montreal	Nat.	3B	144	520	68	144	39	4	15	70	.277	122	288	23	.947
1979—Montreal	Nat.	3B	153	544	83	167	39	2	30	82	.307	119	290	23	.947
1980—Montreal†	Nat.	3B	126	452	55	115	27	3	15	72	.254	106	231	18	.949
1981—Montreal‡	Nat.	3B	97	349	41	85	19	3	8	44	.244	★91	141	16	.935
1982—Texas	Amer.	OF-3B	128	440	59	116	15	0	17	62	.264	190	12	8	.962
1983—Texas	Amer.	OF	145	555	76	151	26	4	26	88	.272	215	11	9	.962
1984—Texas	Amer.	OF-3B	156	613	72	175	42	1	22	101	.285	155	35	4	.979
1985—Texas§	Amer.	OF-3B	94	346	44	86	11	1	17	51	.249	111	7	1	.992
National League Totals—8 Years			967	3411	421	896	207	24	100	444	.263	866	1827	162	.943
American League Totals—4 Years			523	1954	251	528	95	6	82	302	.270	671	65	22	.971
Major League Totals—12 Years			1490	5365	672	1424	302	30	182	746	.265	1537	1892	184	.949

Signed as free agent by Montreal Expos' organization, May 21, 1972.
†On disabled list, June 2 to June 30, 1980.
‡Traded with First Baseman Dave Hostetler to Texas Rangers for First Baseman-Outfielder Al Oliver, March 31, 1982.
§On disabled list, July 6 to September 1, 1985.

DIVISION SERIES RECORD

Year Club	League	Pos.	G.	AB.	R.	H.	2B.	3B.	HR.	RBI.	B.A.	PO.	A.	E.	F.A.
1981—Montreal	Nat.	3B	5	20	3	3	1	0	0	1	.150	7	6	0	1.000

CHAMPIONSHIP SERIES RECORD

Year Club	League	Pos.	G.	AB.	R.	H.	2B.	3B.	HR.	RBI.	B.A.	PO.	A.	E.	F.A.
1981—Montreal	Nat.	3B	5	19	2	5	2	0	0	2	.263	3	13	1	.941

ALL-STAR GAME RECORD

Year League	Pos.	AB.	R.	H.	2B.	3B.	HR.	RBI.	B.A.	PO.	A.	E.	F.A.
1979—National	3B	0	0	0	0	0	0	0	.000	0	0	0	.000

DANIEL ANTHONY PASQUA

Name Pronounced PASS-quah.

(Dan)

Born October 17, 1961, at Harrington Park, N.J.
Height, 6.00. Weight, 205.
Throws and bats lefthanded.
Attended William Paterson College, Wayne, N.J.

Led International League in slugging percentage with .599 in 1985.
Led Southern League batters in strikeouts with 148 in 1984.
Named International League Player of the Year, 1985.
Named Appalachian League Player of the Year, 1982.

Year Club	League	Pos.	G.	AB.	R.	H.	2B.	3B.	HR.	RBI.	B.A.	PO.	A.	E.	F.A.
1982—Paintsville	Appal.	OF	60	239	43	72	10	2	★16	●63	.301	114	4	4	.967
1982—Oneonta	NYP	OF	4	17	3	5	1	0	2	4	.294	2	1	1	.750
1983—Fort Lauderdale	Fla. St.	OF	131	451	83	123	25	10	19	84	.273	213	8	5	.978
1983—Columbus	Int.	OF	1	3	0	0	0	0	0	0	.000	5	0	0	1.000
1984—Nashville	South.	OF	136	460	78	112	14	3	★33	91	.243	244	11	★12	.955

Year Club	League	Pos.	G.	AB.	R.	H.	2B.	3B.	HR.	RBI.	B.A.	PO.	A.	E.	F.A.
1985—Columbus	Int.	OF	78	287	52	92	16	5	18	69	.321	141	9	4	.974
1985—New York	Amer.	OF	60	148	17	31	3	1	9	25	.209	72	2	0	1.000
Major League Totals—1 Year			60	148	17	31	3	1	9	25	.209	72	2	0	1.000

Selected by New York Yankees' organization in 3rd round of free-agent draft, June 7, 1982.

FRANK ENRICO PASTORE

Name pronounced Pass-TORR-ee.

Born August 21, 1957, at Alhambra, Calif.
Height, 6.03. Weight, 215.
Throws and bats righthanded.
Attended Cal Poly Pomona State University, Pomona, Calif.; and Stanford University, Palo Alto, Calif.

Major League saves: 1979 (4).

Year Club	League	G.	IP.	W.	L.	Pct.	H.	R.	ER.	SO.	BB.	ERA.
1975—Billings	Pioneer	15	88	5	●7	.417	89	47	25	69	27	2.56
1976—Tampa	Florida St.	21	107	5	7	.417	101	50	37	54	34	3.11
1977—Tampa	Florida St.	14	95	4	5	.444	78	31	24	36	22	2.27
1977—Three Rivers	Eastern	15	94	6	6	.500	98	43	38	51	32	3.64
1978—Indianapolis	Am. Assoc.	4	12	0	2	.000	24	15	9	8	5	6.75
1978—Nashville†	Southern	22	129	6	8	.429	106	58	50	120	46	3.49
1979—Cincinnati	National	30	95	6	7	.462	102	47	45	63	23	4.26
1979—Indianapolis	Am. Assoc.	10	68	7	2	.778	51	21	21	69	17	2.78
1980—Cincinnati‡	National	27	185	13	7	.650	161	72	67	110	42	3.26
1981—Cincinnati	National	22	132	4	9	.308	125	73	59	81	35	4.02
1982—Cincinnati§	National	31	188⅓	8	13	.381	210	86	83	94	57	3.97
1983—Cincinnati	National	36	184⅓	9	12	.429	207	104	100	93	64	4.88
1984—Cincinnati x	National	24	98⅓	3	8	.273	110	74	71	53	40	6.50
1984—Wichita	Am. Assoc.	2	13	0	1	.000	6	4	4	12	8	2.77
1985—Cincinnati y	National	17	54	2	1	.667	60	23	23	29	16	3.83
Major League Totals—7 Years		187	937	45	57	.441	975	479	448	523	277	4.30

Selected by Cincinnati Reds' organization in 2nd round of free-agent draft, June 4, 1975.
†On disabled list, August 24 to August 31, 1978.
‡On disabled list, July 27 to August 22, 1980.
§On disabled list, June 24 to July 19, 1982.
xOn disabled list, July 9 to July 31, 1984; included rehabilitation disability assignment to Wichita, July 19 to July 31, 1984.
yOn disabled list, July 20, 1985 through remainder of season.

CHAMPIONSHIP SERIES RECORD

Year Club	League	G.	IP.	W.	L.	Pct.	H.	R.	ER.	SO.	BB.	ERA.
1979—Cincinnati	National	1	7	0	0	.000	7	2	2	1	3	2.57

REGINALD ALLEN PATTERSON
(Reggie)

Born November 7, 1958, at Birmingham, Ala.
Height, 6.04. Weight, 180.
Throws right and bats lefthanded.

Pitched 2-0 no-hit victory against Omaha, August 21, 1984.
Led American Association in games started by pitchers with 28 and tied for lead in shutouts with 2 in 1983.
Led Pacific Coast League pitchers in games started with 29 in 1982.
Tied for American Association lead in games started by pitchers with 29 in 1984.

Year Club	League	G.	IP.	W.	L.	Pct.	H.	R.	ER.	SO.	BB.	ERA.
1979—Niagara Falls	NYP	10	55	5	1	.833	43	17	14	44	21	2.29
1979—Knoxville	Southern	4	25	2	1	.667	22	12	9	7	15	3.24
1980—Glens Falls	Eastern	13	89	6	3	.667	80	46	37	52	45	3.74
1980—Iowa	Am. Assoc.	13	71	4	8	.333	84	54	50	56	28	6.34
1981—Edmonton	P. Coast	20	136	10	8	.556	111	63	50	80	71	3.31
1981—Chicago	American	6	7	0	1	.000	14	11	11	2	6	14.14
1981—Appleton	Midwest	1	5	0	0	.000	2	1	1	2	0	1.80
1982—Edmonton†	P. Coast	29	186⅔	14	10	.583	212	125	101	109	89	4.87
1983—Iowa	Am. Assoc.	28	172	10	10	.500	201	★116	100	114	84	5.23
1983—Chicago	National	5	18⅔	1	2	.333	17	12	10	10	6	4.82
1984—Iowa	Am. Assoc.	32	178⅔	★14	7	.667	185	105	86	116	65	4.33
1984—Chicago	National	3	6	0	1	.000	10	7	7	5	2	10.50
1985—Iowa‡	Am. Assoc.	22	132	8	10	.444	142	86	70	78	51	4.77
1985—Chicago	National	8	39	3	0	1.000	36	13	13	17	10	3.00
American League Totals—1 Year		6	7	0	1	.000	14	11	11	2	6	14.14
National League Totals—3 Years		16	63⅔	4	3	.571	63	32	30	32	18	4.24
Major League Totals—4 Years		22	70⅔	4	4	.500	77	43	41	34	24	5.22

Signed as free agent by Chicago White Sox' organization, June 20, 1979.
†Traded to Chicago Cubs' organization for Infielder-Outfielder Tye Waller, December 10, 1982.
‡On disabled list, April 23 to May 12, 1985.

ROBERT CHANDLER PATTERSON
(Bob)

Born May 16, 1959, at Jacksonville, Fla.
Height, 6.02. Weight, 185.
Throws left and bats righthanded.
Received degree from East Carolina University, Greenville, N.C.

Year Club	League	G.	IP.	W.	L.	Pct.	H.	R.	ER.	SO.	BB.	ERA.
1982—Sarasota Padres	Gulf Coast	8	52	4	3	.571	60	18	17	65	7	2.94
1982—Reno	California	4	25⅓	1	0	1.000	28	11	10	10	5	3.55
1983—Beaumont	Texas	43	116⅔	8	4	.667	107	61	52	97	36	4.01
1984—Las Vegas	P. Coast	∗60	143⅓	8	9	.471	129	63	52	97	37	3.27
1985—Las Vegas	P. Coast	42	186⅓	10	11	.476	187	80	65	146	52	3.14
1985—San Diego	National	3	4	0	0	.000	13	11	11	1	3	24.75
Major League Totals—1 Year		3	4	0	0	.000	13	11	11	1	3	24.75

Selected by San Diego Padres' organization in 21st round of free-agent draft, June 7, 1982.

SCOTT GORDON PATTERSON

Born September 11, 1958, at Philadelphia, Pa.
Height, 6.02. Weight, 180.
Throws and bats righthanded.
Attended Long Beach City College, Long Beach, Calif., Rutgers University, New Brunswick, N.J.,
Mesa Community College, Mesa, Ariz., and University of Southern California, Los Angeles, Calif.

Year Club	League	G.	IP.	W.	L.	Pct.	H.	R.	ER.	SO.	BB.	ERA.
1980—Anderson	S. Atlantic	28	165	7	10	.412	185	99	82	120	64	4.47
1981—Durham	Carolina	13	98	9	0	1.000	74	27	23	89	42	2.11
1981—Savannah	Southern	13	94	5	8	.385	94	56	46	55	36	4.40
1982—Richmond†-Columbus	Int'national	29	155⅓	7	12	.368	163	106	95	104	85	5.50
1983—Nashville	Southern	13	98⅓	8	4	.667	88	37	30	40	30	2.75
1983—Columbus	Int'national	15	89⅔	6	2	.750	113	65	59	43	47	5.92
1984—Nashville	Southern	32	64	5	4	.556	72	42	34	47	38	4.78
1984—Columbus	Int'national	11	36	1	3	.250	47	26	26	18	15	6.50
1985—Albany‡	Eastern	27	46⅓	7	2	.778	32	12	8	35	17	1.55
1985—Columbus§	Int'national	21	37⅔	5	2	.714	30	16	14	26	12	3.35

Selected by Toronto Blue Jays' organization in 1st round (fourth player selected) of free-agent draft, January 9, 1979.
Selected by Oakland A's organization in secondary phase of free-agent draft, June 5, 1979.
Selected by Atlanta Braves' organization in secondary phase of free-agent draft, January 8, 1980.
†Traded to New York Yankees' organization for First Baseman Bob Watson, April 23, 1982.
‡On disabled list, May 28 to June 6, 1985.
§Drafted by Texas Rangers, December 10, 1985.

MICHAEL EARL PAYNE
(Mike)

Born November 15, 1961, at Woonsocket, R.I.
Height, 5.11. Weight, 181.
Throws and bats righthanded.

Year Club	League	G.	IP.	W.	L.	Pct.	H.	R.	ER.	SO.	BB.	ERA.
1979—Kingsport	Ap'lachian	7	30	2	3	.400	30	23	13	14	17	3.90
1980—Anderson†	S. Atlantic	21	126	12	6	.667	129	76	61	70	73	4.36
1981—Durham	Carolina	29	105	6	6	.500	107	76	61	84	65	5.23
1982—Durham	Carolina	21	126	8	7	.533	127	66	57	88	55	4.07
1983—Savannah	Southern	25	145	10	7	.588	144	71	63	97	80	3.91
1984—Richmond	Int'national	26	145⅓	10	10	.500	155	68	53	80	89	3.28
1984—Atlanta	National	3	5⅔	0	1	.000	7	4	4	3	3	6.35
1985—Richmond	Int'national	13	60	5	4	.556	65	41	34	18	64	5.10
1985—Greenville‡	Southern	2	7⅔	0	1	.000	8	5	5	4	4	5.87
Major League Totals—1 Year		3	5⅔	0	1	.000	7	4	4	3	3	6.35

Selected by Atlanta Braves' organization in 6th round of free-agent draft, June 5, 1979.
†On disabled list, August 21, 1980 through remainder of season.
‡On disabled list, July 29, 1985 through remainder of season.

STUART RUSSELL PEDERSON
(Stu)

Born January 28, 1960, at Palo Alto, Calif.
Height, 6.00. Weight, 185.
Throws and bats lefthanded.
Attended University of Southern California, Los Angeles, Calif.

Led Florida State League in total bases with 229 in 1982.
Named Florida State League Most Valuable Player, 1982.

Year Club	League	Pos.	G.	AB.	R.	H.	2B.	3B.	HR.	RBI.	B.A.	PO.	A.	E.	F.A.
1981—Lodi	Calif.	OF	56	182	47	67	14	1	8	35	.368	84	8	1	.989
1982—Vero Beach	Fla. St.	OF	134	464	95	156	16	∗18	7	79	.336	211	14	6	.974
1983—San Antonio	Texas	OF	120	406	92	125	21	12	10	66	.308	169	14	3	.984
1983—Albuquerque	P. C.	OF	1	2	0	0	0	0	0	0	.000	0	0	0	.000
1984—San Antonio	Texas	OF-P	131	476	78	137	25	●11	11	86	.288	182	13	7	.965

Year Club	League	Pos.	G.	AB.	R.	H.	2B.	3B.	HR.	RBI.	B.A.	PO.	A.	E.	F.A.
1985—Albuquerque	P. C.	OF-P	111	287	54	94	20	3	8	55	.328	110	5	8	.935
1985—Los Angeles	Nat.	OF	8	4	1	0	0	0	0	1	.000	2	0	0	1.000
Major League Totals—1 Year..................			8	4	1	0	0	0	0	1	.000	2	0	0	1.000

Selected by Los Angeles Dodgers' organization in 9th round of free-agent draft, June 8, 1981.

PITCHING RECORD

Year Club	League	G.	IP.	W.	L.	Pct.	H.	R.	ER.	SO.	BB.	ERA.
1984—San Antonio....................................	Texas	1	1	0	0	.000	0	1	0	1	3	0.00
1985—Albuquerque	P. Coast	1	1	0	0	.000	1	0	0	0	1	0.00

ADALBERTO PENA (RIVERA)
(Bert)

Born July 11, 1959, at Santurce, Puerto Rico.
Height, 5.11. Weight, 165.
Throws and bats righthanded.

Led Southern League shortstops in double plays with 78 in 1980.
Led Florida State League shortstops in double plays with 66 in 1977.

Year Club	League	Pos.	G.	AB.	R.	H.	2B.	3B.	HR.	RBI.	B.A.	PO.	A.	E.	F.A.
1977—Cocoa......................	Fla. St.	SS	93	285	28	65	9	2	1	21	.228	161	279	29	.938
1978—Columbus..............	South.	SS	141	410	24	66	10	0	2	24	.161	★229	352	39	.937
1979—Daytona Beach ...	Fla. St.	SS	113	341	26	66	11	1	1	23	.194	152	290	★45	.908
1980—Columbus..............	South.	SS	124	386	47	97	20	0	9	49	.251	193	363	26	.955
1981—Tucson...................	P. C.	SS	135	468	69	122	24	12	7	66	.261	224	464	39	.946
1981—Houston.................	Nat.	SS	4	2	0	1	0	0	0	0	.500	1	1	0	1.000
1982—Tucson†.................	P. C.	SS-OF	97	362	53	78	17	5	5	33	.215	182	299	32	.938
1983—Tucson..................	P. C.	SS	112	382	45	94	21	3	5	63	.246	166	290	19	★.960
1983—Houston.................	Nat.	SS	4	8	0	1	0	0	0	0	.125	1	7	0	1.000
1984—Tucson..................	P. C.	SS	89	281	34	73	10	3	5	35	.260	152	254	14	.967
1984—Houston‡..............	Nat.	SS	24	39	3	8	1	0	1	4	.205	26	39	3	.956
1985—Tucson§................	P. C.	SS-2B	59	204	24	53	10	0	1	19	.260	87	169	17	.938
1985—Houston.................	Nat.	3B-SS-2B	20	29	7	8	2	0	0	4	.276	9	15	1	.960
Major League Totals—4 Years................			52	78	10	18	3	0	1	8	.231	37	62	4	.961

Signed as free agent by Houston Astros' organization, May 2, 1977.
†On disabled list, August 13 to September 1, 1982.
‡On disabled list, August 4 to August 19, 1984.
§On Houston disabled list, April 8 to May 20 and June 8 to July 19, 1985; included rehabilitation disability assignment to Tucson, April 29 to May 18, 1985.

ALEJANDRO PENA (VASQUEZ)

Born June 25, 1959, at Cambiaso, Dominican Republic.
Height, 6.01. Weight, 205.
Throws and bats righthanded.

Major League saves: 1981 (2), 1983 (1). Total—3.
Tied for National League lead in shutouts with 4 in 1984.
Led Pacific Coast League in saves with 22 in 1981.

Year Club	League	G.	IP.	W.	L.	Pct.	H.	R.	ER.	SO.	BB.	ERA.
1979—Clinton	Midwest	21	71	3	3	.500	53	39	33	57	44	4.18
1980—Vero Beach..................................	Florida St.	35	73	10	3	.769	57	32	26	46	41	3.21
1981—Albuquerque	P. Coast	38	56	2	5	.286	36	12	10	40	21	1.61
1981—Los Angeles	National	14	25	1	1	.500	18	8	8	14	11	2.88
1982—Los Angeles	National	29	35⅔	0	2	.000	37	24	19	20	21	4.79
1982—Albuquerque	P. Coast	16	28⅔	1	1	.500	37	18	17	27	10	5.34
1983—Los Angeles	National	34	177	12	9	.571	152	67	54	120	51	2.75
1984—Los Angeles	National	28	199⅓	12	6	.667	186	67	55	135	46	★2.48
1985—Los Angeles†	National	2	4⅓	0	1	.000	7	5	4	2	3	8.31
Major League Totals—5 Years..........................		107	441⅓	25	19	.568	400	171	140	291	132	2.85

Signed as free agent by Los Angeles Dodgers' organization, September 10, 1978.
†On disabled list, April 8 to September 5, 1985.

CHAMPIONSHIP SERIES RECORD

Year Club	League	G.	IP.	W.	L.	Pct.	H.	R.	ER.	SO.	BB.	ERA.
1981—Los Angeles	National	2	2⅓	0	0	.000	1	0	0	0	0	0.00
1983—Los Angeles	National	1	2⅔	0	0	.000	4	2	2	3	1	6.75
Championship Series Totals—2 Years................		3	5	0	0	.000	5	2	2	3	1	3.60

ANTONIO FRANCISCO PENA (PADILLA)
(Tony)

Born June 4, 1957, at Monte Cristi, Dominican Republic.
Height, 6.00. Weight, 184.
Throws and bats righthanded.
Brother of Ramon Pena, pitcher in Detroit Tigers' organization.

Major League stolen bases: 1981 (1), 1982 (2), 1983 (6), 1984 (12), 1985 (12). Total—33.
Led National League catchers in assists with 100 in 1985.
Led National League catchers in double plays with 15 in 1984.

Led National League catchers in total chances with 1,075 in 1983, 999 in 1984 and 1,034 in 1985.
Led Eastern League catchers in double plays with 14 in 1979.
Led Carolina League catchers in double plays with 9 in 1977.
Tied for Carolina League lead in passed balls with 16 in 1977.
Named catcher on THE SPORTING NEWS National League All-Star Team, 1983.
Named catcher on THE SPORTING NEWS National League All-Star fielding team, 1983 through 1985.

Year—Club	League	Pos.	G.	AB.	R.	H.	2B.	3B.	HR.	RBI.	B.A.	PO.	A.	E.	F.A.
1976—Bradenton Pir.	Gulf C.	O-1-C-3	33	110	10	23	2	2	1	11	.209	108	14	4	.968
1976—Charleston	W. Car.	C	14	49	4	11	2	0	1	8	.224	64	7	2	.973
1977—Charleston	W. Car.	C	29	101	10	24	4	0	3	16	.238	172	19	6	.970
1977—Salem	Carol.	C	84	319	36	88	15	3	7	46	.276	★470	★66	★17	.969
1978—Shreveport	Texas	C	104	348	34	80	14	0	8	42	.230	637	54	★25	.965
1979—Buffalo	East.	C	134	515	89	161	16	4	34	97	.313	★768	★120	★26	.972
1980—Portland	P. C.	C	124	452	57	148	24	13	9	77	.327	★639	85	●23	.969
1980—Pittsburgh	Nat.	C	8	21	1	9	1	1	0	1	.429	38	2	2	.952
1981—Pittsburgh	Nat.	C	66	210	16	63	9	1	2	17	.300	286	41	5	.985
1982—Pittsburgh	Nat.	C	138	497	53	147	28	4	11	63	.296	763	89	16	.982
1983—Pittsburgh	Nat.	C	151	542	51	163	22	3	15	70	.301	★976	90	9	.992
1984—Pittsburgh	Nat.	C	147	546	77	156	27	2	15	78	.286	★895	★95	9	.991
1985—Pittsburgh	Nat.	C-1B	147	546	53	136	27	2	10	59	.249	925	102	12	.988
Major League Totals—6 Years			657	2362	251	674	114	13	53	288	.285	3883	419	53	.988

Signed as free agent by Pittsburgh Pirates' organization, July 22, 1975.

ALL-STAR GAME RECORD

Year—League	Pos.	AB.	R.	H.	2B.	3B.	HR.	RBI.	B.A.	PO.	A.	E.	F.A.
1982—National	PR-C	1	0	0	0	0	0	0	.000	3	0	0	1.000
1984—National	C	0	0	0	0	0	0	0	.000	2	0	0	1.000
1985—National	C	1	0	0	0	0	0	0	.000	4	1	0	1.000
All-Star Game Totals—3 Years		2	0	0	0	0	0	0	.000	9	1	0	1.000

TERRY LEE PENDLETON

Born July 16, 1960, at Los Angeles, Calif.
Height, 5.09. Weight, 178.
Throws right and bats left and righthanded.
Attended Oxnard College, Oxnard, Calif. and
Fresno State University, Fresno, Calif.

Major League stolen bases: 1984 (20), 1985 (17). Total—37.
Led American Association third basemen in putouts with 88 and fielding percentage with .964 in 1984.

Year—Club	League	Pos.	G.	AB.	R.	H.	2B.	3B.	HR.	RBI.	B.A.	PO.	A.	E.	F.A.
1982—Johnson City	Appal.	2B	43	181	38	58	14	●4	4	27	.320	79	105	17	.915
1982—St. Petersburg	Fla. St.	2B	20	69	4	18	2	1	1	7	.261	41	51	2	.979
1983—Arkansas†	Texas	2B	48	185	29	51	10	3	4	20	.276	94	135	7	.970
1984—Louisville	A. A.	3B-2B	91	330	52	98	23	5	4	44	.297	91	157	10	.961
1984—St. Louis	Nat.	3B	67	262	37	85	16	3	1	33	.324	59	155	13	.943
1985—St. Louis‡	Nat.	3B	149	559	56	134	16	3	5	69	.240	129	361	18	.965
Major League Totals—2 Years			216	821	93	219	32	6	6	102	.267	188	516	31	.958

Selected by St. Louis Cardinals' organization in 7th round of free-agent draft, June 7, 1982.
†On disabled list, April 8 to May 23 and July 16 to September 5, 1983.
‡On disabled list June 15 to June 30, 1985.

CHAMPIONSHIP SERIES RECORD

Year—Club	League	Pos.	G.	AB.	R.	H.	2B.	3B.	HR.	RBI.	B.A.	PO.	A.	E.	F.A.
1985—St. Louis	Nat.	3B	6	24	2	5	1	0	0	4	.208	6	18	1	.960

WORLD SERIES RECORD

Tied World Series record for most doubles, driving in three runs, game (1), October 20, 1985.

Year—Club	League	Pos.	G.	AB.	R.	H.	2B.	3B.	HR.	RBI.	B.A.	PO.	A.	E.	F.A.
1985—St. Louis	Nat.	3B	7	23	3	6	1	1	0	3	.261	6	14	1	.952

JOHN PATRICK PERCONTE

Name pronounced PURR-con-tee.

(Jack)

Born August 31, 1954, at Joliet, Ill.
Height, 5.10. Weight, 165.
Throws right and bats lefthanded.
Received bachelor of science degree in sociology from
Murray State University, Murray, Ky. in 1976.

Major League stolen bases: 1980 (3), 1981 (1), 1982 (9), 1983 (3), 1984 (29), 1985 (31). Total—76.

Year—Club	League	Pos.	G.	AB.	R.	H.	2B.	3B.	HR.	RBI.	B.A.	PO.	A.	E.	F.A.
1976—Lodi	Calif.	2B	68	252	58	72	7	1	1	19	.286	141	223	12	.968
1977—Lodi	Calif.	2B	131	515	★132	172	21	12	6	58	.334	292	390	22	.969
1978—San Antonio	Texas	2B	134	538	90	148	20	8	2	52	.275	286	357	21	.968
1979—Albuquerque	P. C.	2B	143	521	104	168	25	7	2	68	.322	278	403	★35	.951
1980—Albuquerque†	P. C.	2B	120	439	84	143	16	7	2	46	.326	291	320	15	.976
1980—Los Angeles	Nat.	2B	14	17	2	4	0	0	0	2	.235	13	18	0	1.000
1981—Albuquerque	P. C.	2B	127	448	107	155	26	6	1	58	.346	286	321	23	.963

Year	Club	League	Pos.	G.	AB.	R.	H.	2B.	3B.	HR.	RBI.	B.A.	PO.	A.	E.	F.A.
1981—Los Angeles‡		Nat.	OF	8	9	2	2	0	1	0	1	.222	4	13	0	1.000
1982—Cleveland		Amer.	2B	93	219	27	52	4	4	0	15	.237	131	199	8	.976
1983—Charleston		Int.	*2B-3B	94	341	76	118	17	2	4	45	*.346	177	323	6	*.988
1983—Cleveland§		Amer.	2B	14	26	1	7	1	0	0	0	.269	20	37	3	.950
1984—Seattle		Amer.	2B	155	612	93	180	24	4	0	31	.294	303	438	14	.981
1985—Seattle		Amer.	2B	125	485	60	128	17	7	2	23	.264	244	381	9	.986
1985—Calgary		P. C.	2B	14	52	17	15	2	2	0	9	.288	31	47	2	.975
National League Totals—2 Years				22	26	4	6	0	1	0	3	.231	17	31	0	1.000
American League Totals—4 Years				387	1342	181	367	46	15	2	69	.273	698	1055	34	.981
Major League Totals—6 Years				409	1368	185	373	46	16	2	72	.273	715	1086	34	.981

Selected by Los Angeles Dodgers' organization in 16th round of free-agent draft, June 8, 1976.

†On disabled list, May 18 to June 9, 1980.

‡Traded with Pitcher Rick Sutcliffe to Cleveland Indians for Outfielder Jorge Orta, Catcher Jack Fimple and Pitcher Larry White, December 9, 1981.

§Traded with Outfielder Gorman Thomas to Seattle Mariners for Second Baseman Tony Bernazard, December 7, 1983.

ATANASIO RIGAL PEREZ

Name pronounced PER-ez.

(Tony)

Born May 14, 1942, at Ciego de Avila, Camaguey, Cuba.
Height, 6.02. Weight, 205.
Throws and bats righthanded.

Tied modern major league record for most at bats, game (7), June 13, 1975.

Tied National League records for most home runs through May 31 (18), 1970; fewest errors by first baseman for leader in errors, season (13), 1973.

Major League stolen bases: 1966 (1), 1968 (3), 1969 (4), 1970 (8), 1971 (4), 1972 (4), 1973 (3), 1974 (1), 1975 (1), 1976 (10), 1977 (4), 1978 (2), 1979 (2), 1980 (1), 1983 (1). Total—49.

Led American League in grounding into double plays with 25 in 1980.

Led National League first basemen in double plays with 131 and total chances with 1,416 in 1973.

Led National League third basemen in assists with 304 and total chances with 435 in 1971.

Led National League third basemen in double plays with 35 in 1969 and tied for lead with 33 in 1968.

Led Carolina League third basemen in double plays with 23 in 1962.

Named first baseman on THE SPORTING NEWS National League All-Star Team, 1973.

Named third baseman on THE SPORTING NEWS National League All-Star Team, 1970.

Named Pacific Coast League Most Valuable Player, 1964.

Year	Club	League	Pos.	G.	AB.	R.	H.	2B.	3B.	HR.	RBI.	B.A.	PO.	A.	E.	F.A.
1960—Geneva†		NYP	INF-OF	104	384	82	107	21	4	6	43	.279	199	197	31	.927
1961—Geneva		NYP	3B	121	460	110	*160	32	7	27	*132	*.348	107	*232	*42	.890
1962—Rocky Mount‡§		Carol.	3B	100	384	72	112	20	8	18	74	.292	88	178	30	.899
1963—San Diego		P. C.	3B	8	29	4	11	3	1	1	5	.379	6	8	1	.933
1963—Macon x		Sally	3B	69	256	44	79	19	3	11	48	.309	57	100	18	.897
1964—San Diego		P. C.	1B-3B-OF	124	479	96	148	20	8	34	107	.309	816	104	19	.980
1964—Cincinnati		Nat.	1B	12	25	1	2	1	0	0	1	.080	51	0	1	.981
1965—Cincinnati		Nat.	1B	104	281	40	73	14	4	12	47	.260	525	40	6	.989
1966—Cincinnati		Nat.	1B	99	257	25	68	10	4	4	39	.265	530	23	6	.989
1967—Cincinnati		Nat.	3B-1B-2B	156	600	78	174	28	7	26	102	.290	249	234	13	.974
1968—Cincinnati		Nat.	3B	160	625	93	176	25	7	18	92	.282	*151	343	*25	.952
1969—Cincinnati		Nat.	3B	160	629	103	185	31	2	37	122	.294	136	*342	*32	.937
1970—Cincinnati		Nat.	*3B-1B	158	587	107	186	28	6	40	129	.317	167	292	*35	.929
1971—Cincinnati		Nat.	3B-1B	158	609	72	164	22	3	25	91	.269	281	308	20	.967
1972—Cincinnati		Nat.	1B	136	515	64	146	33	7	21	90	.283	1207	68	9	.993
1973—Cincinnati		Nat.	1B	151	564	73	177	33	3	27	101	.314	*1318	85	*13	.991
1974—Cincinnati		Nat.	1B	158	596	81	158	28	2	28	101	.265	1292	75	6	*.996
1975—Cincinnati		Nat.	1B	137	511	74	144	28	3	20	109	.282	1192	72	9	.993
1976—Cincinnati y		Nat.	1B	139	527	77	137	32	6	19	91	.260	1158	73	5	.996
1977—Montreal		Nat.	1B	154	559	71	158	32	6	19	91	.283	1312	110	11	.992
1978—Montreal		Nat.	1B	148	544	63	158	38	3	14	78	.290	1181	82	11	.991
1979—Montreal z		Nat.	1B	132	489	58	132	29	4	13	73	.270	1114	65	11	.991
1980—Boston		Amer.	1B	151	585	73	161	31	3	25	105	.275	1301	87	10	.993
1981—Boston		Amer.	1B	84	306	35	77	11	3	9	39	.252	519	37	4	.993
1982—Boston a		Amer.	1B	69	196	18	51	14	2	6	31	.260	5	1	1	.857
1983—Philadelphia b		Nat.	1B	91	253	18	61	11	2	6	43	.241	514	40	1	.998
1984—Cincinnati c		Nat.	1B	71	137	9	33	6	1	2	15	.241	186	12	2	.990
1985—Cincinnati d		Nat.	1B	72	183	25	60	8	0	6	33	.328	340	22	2	.995
National League Totals—19 Years				2396	8491	1132	2392	437	70	337	1448	.282	12904	2286	218	.986
American League Totals—3 Years				304	1087	126	289	56	8	40	175	.266	1825	125	15	.992
Major League Totals—22 Years				2700	9578	1258	2681	493	78	377	1623	.280	14729	2411	233	.987

Signed as free agent by Cincinnati Reds' organization, March 12, 1960.

†On disabled list, June 25 to July 5, 1960.

‡On suspended list, April 13 to April 16, 1962.

§On disabled list, July 30 to September 4, 1962.

xOn suspended list, April 11, 1963; transferred to restricted list, April 23 to June 25, 1963.

yTraded with Pitcher Will McEnaney to Montreal Expos for Pitchers Woodie Fryman and Dale Murray, December 16, 1976.

zGranted free agency, November 1, 1979; signed by Boston Red Sox, November 16, 1979.

aReleased, November 1, 1982; signed by Philadelphia Phillies, January 31, 1983.

bTraded to Cincinnati Reds for a player to be named later, December 5, 1983; deal settled in cash.

CHAMPIONSHIP SERIES RECORD

Tied Championship Series records for most consecutive games, one or more runs batted in, total Series (4); most at bats, extra-inning game (6), October 9, 1973 (12 innings); most strikeouts, five-game Series (7), 1972.

Year Club	League	Pos.	G.	AB.	R.	H.	2B.	3B.	HR.	RBI.	B.A.	PO.	A.	E.	F.A.
1970—Cincinnati	Nat.	3B-1B	3	12	1	4	2	0	1	2	.333	6	6	1	.923
1972—Cincinnati	Nat.	1B	5	20	0	4	1	0	0	2	.200	45	3	0	1.000
1973—Cincinnati	Nat.	1B	5	22	1	2	0	0	1	2	.091	47	4	0	1.000
1975—Cincinnati	Nat.	1B	3	12	3	5	0	0	1	4	.417	27	5	0	1.000
1976—Cincinnati	Nat.	1B	3	10	1	2	0	0	0	3	.200	27	2	1	.967
1983—Philadelphia	Nat.	PH	1	1	0	1	0	0	0	0	1.000	0	0	0	.000
Championship Series Totals—6 Years			20	77	6	18	3	0	3	13	.234	152	20	2	.989

WORLD SERIES RECORD

Tied World Series record for one or more hits, each game, seven-game Series, 1972; most unassisted double plays by first baseman, game (1), October 11, 1975.

Year Club	League	Pos.	G.	AB.	R.	H.	2B.	3B.	HR.	RBI.	B.A.	PO.	A.	E.	F.A.
1970—Cincinnati	Nat.	3B	5	18	2	1	0	0	0	0	.056	3	13	1	.941
1972—Cincinnati	Nat.	1B	7	23	3	10	2	0	0	2	.435	73	3	1	.987
1975—Cincinnati	Nat.	1B	7	28	4	5	0	0	3	7	.170	66	5	1	.980
1976—Cincinnati	Nat.	1B	4	16	1	5	1	0	0	2	.313	32	4	0	1.000
1983—Philadelphia	Nat.	PH-1B	4	10	0	2	0	0	0	0	.200	13	1	0	1.000
World Series Totals—5 Years			27	95	10	23	3	0	3	11	.242	187	26	3	.986

ALL-STAR GAME RECORD

Year League	Pos.	AB.	R.	H.	2B.	3B.	HR.	RBI.	B.A.	PO.	A.	E.	F.A.
1967—National	3B	2	1	1	0	0	1	1	.500	0	3	0	1.000
1968—National	3B	0	0	0	0	0	0	0	.000	0	1	0	1.000
1969—National	3B	1	0	0	0	0	0	0	.000	1	1	0	1.000
1970—National	3B	3	0	0	0	0	0	0	.000	1	1	0	1.000
1974—National	PH	1	0	0	0	0	0	0	.000	0	0	0	.000
1975—National	1B	1	0	0	0	0	0	0	.000	1	1	0	1.000
1976—National	1B	0	0	0	0	0	0	0	.000	2	0	0	1.000
All-Star Game Totals—7 Years		8	1	1	0	0	1	1	.125	5	7	0	1.000

PASCUAL GROSS PEREZ

Born May 17, 1957, at San Cristobal, Dominican Republic.
Height, 6.03. Weight, 162.
Throws and bats righthanded.
Brother of Melido Perez, pitcher in Kansas City Royals' organization; and Valerio Perez, pitcher in Kansas City Royals' organization, 1983 and 1984.

Led Western Carolinas League in balks with 6 in 1977.
Tied for Carolina League lead in shutouts with 5 in 1978.

Year Club	League	G.	IP.	W.	L.	Pct.	H.	R.	ER.	SO.	BB.	ERA.
1976—Bradenton Pirates†	Gulf Coast	10	56	2	5	.286	51	41	29	34	35	4.66
1977—Charleston	W. Carol.	25	156	10	5	.667	153	80	69	96	60	3.98
1978—Salem	Carolina	24	152	11	7	.611	133	70	44	126	51	2.61
1978—Columbus	Int'national	1	5	0	0	.000	4	0	0	4	1	0.00
1979—Portland‡	P. Coast	20	103	9	7	.563	121	70	63	51	47	5.50
1980—Portland	P. Coast	24	160	12	10	.545	172	76	72	105	48	4.05
1980—Pittsburgh	National	2	12	0	1	.000	15	6	5	7	2	3.75
1981—Portland	P. Coast	5	31	1	2	.333	40	19	17	11	14	4.94
1981—Pittsburgh	National	17	86	2	7	.222	92	50	38	46	34	3.98
1982—Portland§	P. Coast	19	106⅓	4	9	.308	111	59	57	59	37	4.82
1982—Richmond	Int'national	5	43	5	0	1.000	32	7	6	27	8	1.26
1982—Atlanta	National	16	79½	4	4	.500	85	35	27	29	17	3.06
1983—Atlanta	National	33	215⅓	15	8	.652	213	88	82	144	51	3.43
1984—Atlanta x	National	30	211⅔	14	8	.636	208	96	88	145	51	3.74
1985—Atlanta yz	National	22	95⅓	1	13	.071	115	72	65	57	57	6.14
Major League Totals—6 Years		120	699⅔	36	41	.468	728	347	305	428	212	3.92

Signed as free agent by Pittsburgh Pirates' organization, January 27, 1976.
†On suspended list, August 26 to August 28, 1976.
‡On disabled list, July 16 to August 14, 1979.
§Traded with a player to be named later to Atlanta Braves' organization for Pitcher Larry McWilliams, June 30, 1982; Atlanta organization acquired Shortstop Carlos Rios to complete deal, September 8, 1982.
xOn suspended list, April 3 to May 1, 1984.
yOn disabled list, May 5 to May 25, June 1 to June 22 and August 13 to September 3, 1985.
zOn suspended list, July 22, 1985; then transferred to restricted list, July 25 to August 4, 1985.

CHAMPIONSHIP SERIES RECORD

Year Club	League	G.	IP.	W.	L.	Pct.	H.	R.	ER.	SO.	BB.	ERA.
1982—Atlanta	National	2	8⅔	0	1	.000	10	5	5	4	2	5.19

ALL-STAR GAME RECORD

Year League			IP.	W.	L.	Pct.	H.	R.	ER.	SO.	BB.	ERA.
1983—National			⅔	0	0	.000	3	2	2	1	1	27.00

JONATHAN SAMUEL PERLMAN
(Jon)

Born December 13, 1956, at Dallas, Tex.
Height, 6.03. Weight, 185.
Throws right and bats lefthanded.
Received bachelor of business administration degree in finance and
management from Baylor University, Waco, Tex.

Led Texas League pitchers in games started with 30 in 1980.
Tied for Texas League lead in hit batsmen with 13 in 1982.

Year	Club	League	G.	IP.	W.	L.	Pct.	H.	R.	ER.	SO.	BB.	ERA.
1979—Midland		Texas	18	96	4	8	.333	133	76	49	34	32	4.59
1980—Midland		Texas	30	200	13	7	.650	★230	115	95	78	76	4.28
1981—Iowa		Am. Assoc.	16	62	2	7	.222	74	53	44	16	37	6.39
1981—Midland		Texas	12	58	1	4	.200	90	62	49	29	22	7.60
1982—Midland		Texas	26	184⅓	●13	7	.650	196	89	75	81	50	3.66
1983—Iowa		Am. Assoc.	31	115⅔	4	11	.267	138	78	58	34	29	4.51
1984—Iowa		Am. Assoc.	24	147⅓	11	6	.647	131	69	62	61	51	3.79
1985—Iowa		Am. Assoc.	32	151⅓	7	12	.368	181	91	79	64	45	4.70
1985—Chicago†		National	6	8⅔	1	0	1.000	10	11	11	4	8	11.42
Major League Totals—1 Year			6	8⅔	1	0	1.000	10	11	11	4	8	11.42

Selected by Chicago Cubs' organization in 5th round of free-agent draft, June 6, 1978.
Selected by Chicago Cubs' organization in 1st round (12th player selected) of free-agent draft, June 5, 1979.
†Released, October 8, 1985.

GERALD JUNE PERRY

Born October 30, 1960, at Savannah, Ga.
Height, 6.00. Weight, 190.
Throws right and bats lefthanded.
Nephew of Dan Driessen, first baseman with San Francisco Giants.

Major League stolen bases: 1984 (15), 1985 (9). Total—24.
Led Carolina League first basemen in double plays with 109 in 1980.
Led Gulf Coast League first basemen in double plays with 46 in 1978.

Year	Club	League	Pos.	G.	AB.	R.	H.	2B.	3B.	HR.	RBI.	B.A.	PO.	A.	E.	F.A.
1978—Bradenton Brav...		Gulf C.	1B	★55	191	32	51	★12	3	1	26	.267	★479	★37	6	★.989
1979—Greenwood		W. Car.	1B	109	400	69	133	17	4	9	71	★.333	881	59	19	.980
1980—Durham		Carol.	1B	138	497	102	124	19	5	15	92	.249	★1296	93	16	.989
1981—Savannah		South.	1B	137	476	71	132	18	3	19	84	.277	1221	86	18	.986
1982—Richmond		Int.	1B	133	492	94	146	22	4	15	92	.297	1110	94	●17	.986
1983—Richmond		Int.	1B	113	423	81	133	21	8	13	71	.314	943	88	11	.989
1983—Atlanta		Nat.	1B-OF	27	39	5	14	2	0	1	6	.359	55	0	1	.982
1984—Atlanta		Nat.	1B-OF	122	347	52	92	12	2	7	47	.265	550	28	12	.980
1985—Atlanta		Nat.	1B-OF	110	238	22	51	5	0	3	13	.214	541	37	9	.985
Major League Totals—3 Years				259	624	79	157	19	2	11	66	.252	1146	65	22	.982

Selected by Atlanta Braves' organization in 11th round of free-agent draft, June 6, 1978.

WILLIAM PATRICK PERRY
(Pat)

Born February 4, 1959, at Taylorville, Ill.
Height, 6.01. Weight, 170.
Throws and bats lefthanded.
Attended Lincoln Land Community College, Springfield, Ill.

Tied for Gulf Coast League lead in shutouts with 2 in 1978.

Year	Club	League	G.	IP.	W.	L.	Pct.	H.	R.	ER.	SO.	BB.	ERA.
1978—Sarasota Astros		Gulf Coast	12	35	2	4	.333	29	15	9	35	14	2.31
1979—Daytona Beach		Florida St.	12	51	2	3	.400	64	31	30	30	16	5.29
1979—Sarasota Astros		Gulf Coast	9	49	3	1	.750	55	21	20	24	16	3.67
1980—Daytona Beach		Florida St.	22	115	9	5	.643	121	51	38	54	46	2.97
1981—Columbus		Southern	27	51	3	1	.750	54	40	36	35	38	6.35
1981—Daytona Beach		Florida St.	9	20	2	0	1.000	11	6	6	22	7	2.70
1982—Columbus†		Southern	22	37⅔	4	0	1.000	32	19	17	28	18	4.06
1983—Columbus‡§		Southern	11	49	5	2	.714	60	30	22	27	21	4.04
1983—Buffalo x		Eastern	4	5⅓	0	0	.000	8	5	4	4	4	6.75
1983—Springfield		Midwest	6	24⅓	1	1	.500	17	6	6	31	5	2.22
1984—Arkansas		Texas	25	48⅔	4	2	.667	34	8	6	51	17	1.11
1984—Louisville		Am. Assoc.	21	44⅔	4	3	.571	35	12	11	43	21	2.22
1985—Louisville		Am. Assoc.	45	91	4	3	.571	56	33	24	63	39	2.37
1985—St. Louis		National	6	12⅓	1	0	1.000	3	0	0	6	3	0.00
Major League Totals—1 Year			6	12⅓	1	0	1.000	3	0	0	6	3	0.00

Selected by Houston Astros' organization in 2nd round of free-agent draft, January 10, 1978.
†On disabled list, May 6 to May 24 and August 1, 1982 through remainder of season.
‡On disabled list, May 24 to June 15, 1983.
§Released, June 24, 1983; signed by Buffalo (Cleveland Indians' organization), July 1, 1983.
xReleased, July 12, 1983; signed by Springfield (St. Louis Cardinals' organization), August 3, 1983.

EUGENE JAMES PETRALLI JR.
(Geno)

Born September 25, 1959, at Sacramento, Calif.
Height, 6.01. Weight, 180.
Throws right and bats left and righthanded.
Attended Sacramento City College, Sacramento, Calif.
Son of Gene Petralli, minor league first baseman, 1948 through 1951 and 1953.

Major League stolen bases: 1983 (1), 1985 (1). Total—2.
Led International League catchers in putouts with 633, assists with 86, errors with 19, double plays with 10 and total chances with 738 in 1982.
Tied for Pioneer League lead in passed balls with 27 in 1978.

Year—Club	League	Pos.	G.	AB.	R.	H.	2B.	3B.	HR.	RBI.	B.A.	PO.	A.	E.	F.A.
1978—Medicine Hat	Pion.	C-3B	65	242	42	68	14	5	2	40	.281	238	68	19	.942
1979—Dunedin†	Fla. St.	C-3B-OF	52	184	18	53	13	0	1	24	.288	206	42	5	.980
1979—Syracuse	Int.	C	18	56	6	13	0	1	0	7	.232	67	12	1	.988
1980—Knoxville	South.	C-1B-OF	116	382	42	109	20	2	3	38	.285	569	82	18	.973
1981—Syracuse‡	Int.	C	45	151	17	40	11	0	0	16	.265	188	30	6	.973
1982—Syracuse	Int.	C-1B-3B	126	395	57	114	19	3	9	58	.289	674	89	20	.974
1982—Toronto	Amer.	C-3B	16	44	3	16	2	0	0	1	.364	51	4	1	.982
1983—Syracuse	Int.	C-1B	104	327	39	80	9	2	3	40	.245	541	68	7	.989
1983—Toronto	Amer.	C	6	4	0	0	0	0	0	0	.000	7	0	0	1.000
1984—Toronto§	Amer.	C	3	3	0	0	0	0	0	0	.000	1	1	0	1.000
1984—Maine x	Int.	C-O-1	23	83	9	18	3	0	0	5	.217	122	11	6	.957
1985—Maine y	Int.	C	2	7	0	1	0	0	0	1	.143	12	1	1	.929
1985—Oklahoma City	A. A.	C	27	80	11	21	8	0	1	5	.263	108	14	3	.976
1985—Texas	Amer.	C	42	100	7	27	2	0	0	11	.270	179	16	2	.990
Major League Totals—4 Years			67	151	10	43	4	0	0	12	.285	238	21	3	.989

Selected by Toronto Blue Jays' organization in 3rd round of free-agent draft, January 10, 1978.
†On suspended list, April 13 to April 27, 1979.
‡On disabled list, May 6 to June 1 and June 28 to August 18, 1981.
§Sold to Maine (Cleveland Indians' organization), May 8, 1984.
xOn disabled list, July 11, 1984 through remainder of season.
yReleased, April 23, 1985; signed by Oklahoma City (Texas Rangers' organization), May 17, 1985.

DANIEL JOSEPH PETRY

Name pronounced PEE-tree.

(Dan)

Born November 13, 1958, at Palo Alto, Calif.
Height, 6.04. Weight, 200.
Throws and bats righthanded.

Led American League pitchers in games started with 38 and home runs allowed with 37 in 1983.

Year—Club	League	G.	IP.	W.	L.	Pct.	H.	R.	ER.	SO.	BB.	ERA.
1976—Bristol	Ap'lachian	14	79	2	3	.400	54	42	33	51	★56	3.76
1977—Lakeland	Florida St.	25	145	10	11	.476	139	68	55	68	68	3.41
1978—Montgomery	Southern	14	92	6	7	.462	70	38	25	69	41	2.45
1978—Evansville	Am. Assoc.	13	71	4	3	.571	59	38	36	50	33	4.56
1979—Evansville	Am. Assoc.	15	91	4	3	.571	92	60	49	55	37	4.85
1979—Detroit	American	15	98	6	5	.545	90	46	43	43	33	3.95
1980—Evansville	Am. Assoc.	4	30	2	0	1.000	21	11	9	16	12	2.70
1980—Detroit	American	27	165	10	9	.526	82	72	88	83	3.93	
1981—Detroit	American	23	141	10	9	.526	115	53	47	79	57	3.00
1982—Detroit	American	35	246	15	9	.625	220	98	88	132	100	3.22
1983—Detroit	American	38	266⅓	19	11	.633	256	126	116	122	99	3.92
1984—Detroit	American	35	233⅓	18	8	.692	231	94	84	144	66	3.24
1985—Detroit	American	34	238⅔	15	13	.536	190	98	89	109	81	3.36
Major League Totals—7 Years		207	1388⅓	93	64	.592	1258	597	539	717	519	3.49

Selected by Detroit Tigers' organization in 4th round of free-agent draft, June 8, 1976.

CHAMPIONSHIP SERIES RECORD

Year—Club	League	G.	IP.	W.	L.	Pct.	H.	R.	ER.	SO.	BB.	ERA.
1984—Detroit	American	1	7	0	0	.000	4	2	2	4	1	2.57

WORLD SERIES RECORD

Year—Club	League	G.	IP.	W.	L.	Pct.	H.	R.	ER.	SO.	BB.	ERA.
1984—Detroit	American	2	8	0	1	.000	14	8	8	4	5	9.00

ALL-STAR GAME RECORD

Year—League		IP.	W.	L.	Pct.	H.	R.	ER.	SO.	BB.	ERA.
1985—American		⅓	0	0	.000	0	2	2	1	3	54.00

GARY GEORGE PETTIS

Born April 3, 1958, at Oakland, Calif.
Height, 6.01. Weight, 160.
Throws right and bats left and righthanded.
Attended Laney College, Oakland, Calif.
Brother of Stacey Pettis, outfielder in California Angels' organization.

Major League stolen bases: 1983 (8), 1984 (48), 1985 (56). Total—112.
Led Pacific Coast League in stolen bases with 53 in 1982.
Named outfielder on THE SPORTING NEWS American League All-Star fielding team, 1985.

Year	Club	League	Pos.	G.	AB.	R.	H.	2B.	3B.	HR.	RBI.	B.A.	PO.	A.	E.	F.A.
1979—Idaho Falls	Pion.	3B-SS-2B	50	198	39	63	10	●10	3	26	.318	59	94	24	.864
1980—Salinas	Calif.	OF-SS-3B	118	393	71	94	15	3	2	31	.239	206	36	13	.949
1981—Holyoke	East.	OF	120	421	77	112	8	9	3	36	.266	237	5	4	.984
1982—Spokane	P. C.	OF	133	528	108	152	22	★14	1	59	.288	★345	9	6	★.983
1982—California	Amer.	OF	10	5	5	1	0	0	1	1	.200	5	1	0	1.000
1983—Edmonton	P. C.	OF	132	529	★138	151	27	8	11	52	.285	325	10	5	.985
1983—California	Amer.	OF	22	85	19	25	2	3	3	6	.294	49	5	1	.982
1984—California	Amer.	OF	140	397	63	90	11	6	2	29	.227	337	11	6	.983
1985—California†	Amer.	OF	125	443	67	114	10	8	1	32	.257	368	13	4	.990
Major League Totals—4 Years			297	930	154	230	23	17	7	68	.247	759	30	11	.986

Selected by California Angels' organization in 6th round of free-agent draft, January 9, 1979.
†On disabled list, July 5 to July 31, 1985.

KENNETH ALLEN PHELPS
(Ken)

Born August 6, 1954, at Seattle, Wash.
Height, 6.01. Weight, 204.
Throws and bats lefthanded.
Attended Washington State University, Pullman, Wash.; Mesa Community College,
Mesa, Ariz., and received bachelor of science degree in physical education from
Arizona State University, Tempe, Ariz.

Major League stolen bases: 1984 (3), 1985 (2). Total—5.
Led American Association in total bases with 320 in 1982.
Led American Association in bases on balls received with 128 in 1980 and 108 in 1982.
Led Southern League in bases on balls received with 99 in 1978.
Tied for American Association lead in intentional bases on balls received with 12 in 1982.
Led American Association first basemen in double plays with 111 in 1979, 103 in 1980 and 108 in 1982.
Named American Association Most Valuable Player, 1982.

Year	Club	League	Pos.	G.	AB.	R.	H.	2B.	3B.	HR.	RBI.	B.A.	PO.	A.	E.	F.A.
1976—Sarasota Royals	Gulf C.	1B	28	98	20	29	6	3	3	28	.296	166	16	2	.989
1976—Waterloo	Midw.	1B	25	72	12	19	8	0	1	10	.264	205	12	3	.986
1977—Daytona Beach	Fla. St.	1B	40	145	22	50	7	0	5	32	.345	341	31	8	.979
1977—Jacksonville	South.	1B	81	262	30	51	6	3	5	40	.195	691	38	10	.986
1978—Jacksonville	South.	1B	124	381	65	94	20	0	16	61	.247	1028	66	16	.986
1979—Omaha	A. A.	1B	130	430	71	114	26	3	20	77	.265	★1129	80	★13	.989
1980—Omaha	A. A.	1B	133	442	80	130	30	3	23	72	.294	★1154	51	12	.990
1980—Kansas City	Amer.	1B	3	4	0	0	0	0	0	0	.000	14	0	0	1.000
1981—Kansas City	Amer.	1B	21	22	1	3	0	1	0	1	.136	4	1	0	1.000
1981—Omaha†	A. A.	1B	19	66	9	22	8	1	5	21	.333	169	15	2	.989
1982—Wichita	A. A.	1B	132	453	112	151	23	4	★46	★141	.333	1047	74	14	.988
1982—Montreal‡	Nat.	PH	10	8	0	2	0	0	0	0	.250	0	0	0	.000
1983—Seattle	Amer.	1B	50	127	10	30	4	1	7	16	.236	164	16	0	1.000
1983—Salt Lake City	P. C.	1B	74	270	81	92	29	6	24	82	.341	535	37	7	.988
1984—Seattle§	Amer.	1B	101	290	52	70	9	0	24	51	.241	72	4	1	.987
1984—Salt Lake City	P. C.	1B	12	45	7	14	3	0	3	13	.311	25	5	0	1.000
1985—Seattle	Amer.	1B	61	116	18	24	3	0	9	24	.207	31	2	0	1.000
American League Totals—5 Years			236	559	81	127	16	2	40	92	.227	285	23	1	.997
National League Totals—1 Year			10	8	0	2	0	0	0	0	.250	0	0	0	.000
Major League Totals—6 Years			246	567	81	129	16	2	40	92	.228	285	23	1	.997

Selected by Atlanta Braves' organization in 8th round of free-agent draft, June 6, 1972.
Selected by New York Yankees' organization in 1st round (11th player selected) of free-agent draft, January 9, 1974.
Selected by Philadelphia Phillies' organization in secondary phase of free-agent draft, June 5, 1974.
Selected by Kansas City Royals' organization in 15th round of free-agent draft, June 8, 1976.
†Traded to Montreal Expos' organization for Pitcher Grant Jackson, January 19, 1982.
‡Sold to Seattle Mariners, March 31, 1983.
§On disabled list, April 7 to May 18, 1984; included rehabilitation disability assignment to Salt Lake City, May 4 to May 18, 1984.

KEITH ANTHONY PHILLIPS
(Tony)

Born April 25, 1959, at Atlanta, Ga.
Height, 5.10. Weight, 160.
Throws right and bats right and lefthanded.
Attended New Mexico Military Institute, Roswell, N.M.

Major League stolen bases: 1982 (2), 1983 (16), 1984 (10), 1985 (3). Total—31.
Led Eastern League in being hit by pitch with 10 in 1981.
Led Southern League in bases on balls received with 98 in 1980.

Year	Club	League	Pos.	G.	AB.	R.	H.	2B.	3B.	HR.	RBI.	B.A.	PO.	A.	E.	F.A.
1978—W. Palm Beach†	Fla. St.	3B-SS-2B	32	54	8	9	0	0	0	3	.167	13	33	5	.902
1978—Jamestown	NYP	SS-2B-3B	52	152	24	29	5	2	1	17	.191	73	146	16	.932
1979—W. Palm Beach	Fla. St.	2B-SS	60	203	30	47	5	1	0	18	.232	120	156	21	.929
1979—Memphis	South.	SS-2B	52	156	31	44	4	2	3	11	.282	68	134	18	.914

Year—Club	League	Pos.	G.	AB.	R.	H.	2B.	3B.	HR.	RBI.	B.A.	PO.	A.	E.	F.A.
1980—Memphis‡§	South.	*SS-2B	136	502	100	125	18	4	5	41	.249	226	408	*42	.938
1981—West Haven	East.	SS	131	461	79	114	25	3	9	64	.247	200	391	*33	.947
1981—Tacoma	P. C.	2B-SS	4	11	1	4	1	0	0	2	.364	8	10	0	1.000
1982—Tacoma	P. C.	SS	86	300	76	89	18	5	4	47	.297	138	236	30	.926
1982—Oakland	Amer.	SS	40	81	11	17	2	2	0	8	.210	46	95	7	.953
1983—Oakland	Amer.	SS-2B-3B	148	412	54	102	12	3	4	35	.248	218	383	30	.952
1984—Oakland	Amer.	SS-2B-OF	154	451	62	120	24	3	4	37	.266	255	391	28	.958
1985—Tacoma x	P. C.	3B-2B	20	69	9	9	1	0	0	5	.130	15	36	4	.927
1985—Oakland	Amer.	3B-2B	42	161	23	45	12	2	4	17	.280	54	103	3	.981
Major League Totals—4 Years			384	1105	150	284	50	10	12	97	.257	573	972	68	.958

Selected by Seattle Mariners' organization in 16th round of free-agent draft, June 7, 1977.
Selected by Montreal Expos' organization in secondary phase of free-agent draft, January 10, 1978.
†On temporary inactive list, April 11 to May 4, 1978.
‡Traded with cash to San Diego Padres for First Baseman Willie Montanez, August 31, 1980.
§Traded with Pitcher Eric Mustad and Infielder Kevin Bell to Oakland A's organization for Pitcher Bob Lacey and Pitcher Roy Moretti, March 27, 1981.
xOn Oakland disabled list, March 26 to August 22, 1985; included rehabilitation disability assignment to Tacoma, July 30 to August 5 and August 7 to August 20, 1985.

ROBERT MICHAEL PICCIOLO

Name pronounced PEACH alo.

(Rob)

Born February 4, 1953, at Santa Monica, Calif.
Height, 6.02. Weight, 180.
Throws and bats righthanded.
Attended Santa Monica City College, Santa Monica, Calif. and received
bachelor of arts degree in journalism from Pepperdine University, Malibu, Calif.

Major League stolen bases: 1977 (1), 1978 (1), 1979 (2), 1980 (1), 1982 (1), 1985 (3). Total—9.
Led Southern League shortstops in double plays with 91 in 1975.

Year—Club	League	Pos.	G.	AB.	R.	H.	2B.	3B.	HR.	RBI.	B.A.	PO.	A.	E.	F.A.
1975—Birmingham	South.	SS	133	488	55	135	23	6	3	62	.277	*278	*404	18	*.974
1976—Tucson	P. C.	SS	139	*570	78	170	19	4	5	54	.298	220	*429	22	*.967
1977—San Jose	P. C.	SS	10	38	5	8	1	0	1	4	.211	23	25	0	1.000
1977—Oakland	Amer.	SS	148	419	35	84	12	3	2	22	.200	213	381	21	.966
1978—Vancouver	P. C.	SS	26	90	14	23	3	3	2	17	.256	53	87	3	.979
1978—Oakland	Amer.	SS-2B-3B	78	93	16	21	1	0	2	7	.226	74	90	7	.959
1979—Oakland	Amer.	S-2-3-O	115	348	37	88	16	2	2	27	.253	203	288	17	.967
1980—Oakland	Amer.	SS-2B-OF	95	271	32	65	9	2	5	18	.240	164	208	6	.984
1981—Oakland	Amer.	SS	82	179	23	48	5	3	4	13	.268	99	157	5	.981
1982—Oak.†-Milw.	Amer.	SS-2B	40	70	10	17	2	0	0	4	.243	47	72	3	.975
1983—Milwaukee‡	Amer.	S-2-3-1	14	27	2	6	3	0	0	1	.222	27	20	1	.979
1984—California§	Amer.	S-3-2-O	87	119	18	24	6	0	1	9	.202	69	135	6	.971
1985—Oakland xy	Amer.	3-2-1-S-O	71	102	19	28	2	0	1	8	.275	56	66	5	.961
Major League Totals—9 Years			730	1628	192	381	56	10	17	109	.234	952	1417	71	.971

Selected by San Francisco Giants' organization in 2nd round of free-agent draft, January 10, 1973.
Selected by Kansas City Royals' organization in secondary phase of free-agent draft, June 5, 1973.
Selected by Detroit Tigers' organization in secondary phase of free-agent draft, June 5, 1974.
Selected by Oakland A's organization in secondary phase of free-agent draft, January 9, 1975.
†Traded to Milwaukee Brewers for Pitcher Mike Warren and First Baseman John Evans, May 14, 1982.
‡Granted free agency, November 7, 1983; signed by California Angels, February 6, 1984.
§Released, January 11, 1985; signed by Oakland A's, February 5, 1985.
xOn disabled list, August 10 to September 1, 1985.
yGranted free agency, November 12, 1985.

DIVISION SERIES RECORD

Year—Club	League	Pos.	G.	AB.	R.	H.	2B.	3B.	HR.	RBI.	B.A.	PO.	A.	E.	F.A.
1981—Oakland	Amer.	SS	1	3	0	1	0	0	0	0	.333	1	2	0	1.000

CHAMPIONSHIP SERIES RECORD

Year—Club	League	Pos.	G.	AB.	R.	H.	2B.	3B.	HR.	RBI.	B.A.	PO.	A.	E.	F.A.
1981—Oakland	Amer.	SS	2	5	1	1	0	0	0	0	.200	5	5	1	.909

CRAIG STEVEN PIPPIN

Born August 4, 1956, at Bristol, Tenn.
Height, 6.02. Weight, 180.
Throws and bats righthanded.
Attended University of Florida, Gainesville, Fla.

Led Gulf Coast League in saves with 6 in 1978.
Led Eastern League in wild pitches with 15 in 1983.

Year—Club	League	G.	IP.	W.	L.	Pct.	H.	R.	ER.	SO.	BB.	ERA.
1978—Sarasota Royals	Gulf Coast	18	27	3	1	.750	20	10	8	31	10	2.67
1979—Fort Myers	Florida St.	34	68	4	4	.500	56	23	20	47	43	2.65
1980—Fort Myers	Florida St.	45	82	4	5	.444	66	25	22	48	37	2.41
1981—Jacksonville	Southern	26	34	1	2	.333	34	47	40	16	18	8.74
1981—Fort Myers†	Florida St.	21	31	0	3	.000	28	12	12	30	17	3.48
1982—Buffalo	Eastern	23	51	0	4	.000	52	24	16	53	34	2.82

Year Club	League	G.	IP.	W.	L.	Pct.	H.	R.	ER.	SO.	BB.	ERA.
1983—Lynn	Eastern	37	102⅓	13	3	.813	78	49	41	88	76	3.61
1984—Nashua	Eastern	16	68⅔	3	4	.429	52	30	16	52	31	2.10
1984—Hawaii‡	P. Coast	6	15⅓	1	2	.333	10	7	7	12	7	4.11
1985—Waterbury	Eastern	18	39⅓	3	3	.500	32	13	13	47	17	2.97
1985—Maine	Int'national	36	60	7	3	.700	41	20	18	52	35	2.70

Selected by Kansas City Royals' organization in 30th round of free-agent draft, June 6, 1978.
†Released, April 4, 1982; signed by Buffalo (Pittsburgh Pirates' organization), May 29, 1982.
‡Granted free agency, October 15, 1984; signed by Maine (Cleveland Indians' organization), December 25, 1984.

CHRISTOPHER FRANCIS PITTARO
(Chris)

Born September 16, 1961, at Trenton, N.J.
Height, 5.11. Weight, 170.
Throws right and bats left and righthanded.
Attended University of North Carolina, Chapel Hill, N.C.
Son of Francis (Sonny) Pittaro, infielder in Washington Senators'
and Minnesota Twins' organizations, 1960 through 1962.

Major League stolen bases: 1985 (1).

Year Club	League	Pos.	G.	AB.	R.	H.	2B.	3B.	HR.	RBI.	B.A.	PO.	A.	E.	F.A.
1982—Macon	S. Atl.	SS	68	218	25	50	6	0	2	25	.229	99	212	24	.928
1983—Lakeland	Fla. St.	∗2B-SS	107	392	43	106	19	4	1	39	.270	224	310	12	∗.978
1984—Birmingham	South.	2B-SS	137	517	85	147	27	7	11	61	.284	260	417	22	.969
1985—Detroit†	Amer.	3B-2B	28	62	10	15	3	1	0	7	.242	15	36	6	.895
1985—Nashville‡	A. A.	3B-SS-2B	60	175	22	34	4	1	3	19	.194	63	126	6	.969
Major League Totals—1 Year			28	62	10	15	3	1	0	7	.242	15	36	6	.895

Selected by Detroit Tigers' organization in 6th round of free-agent draft, June 7, 1982.
†On disabled list, May 27 to June 14, 1985.
‡Traded with Outfielder Alex Sanchez to Minnesota Twins for Catcher Dave Engle, January 16, 1986.

DANIEL THOMAS PLESAC
(Dan)

Born February 4, 1962, at Gary, Ind.
Height, 6.05. Weight, 205.
Throws and bats lefthanded.
Attended North Carolina State University, Raleigh, N.C.

Led Appalachian League pitchers in balks with 3 and tied for lead in games started with 14 in 1983.

Year Club	League	G.	IP.	W.	L.	Pct.	H.	R.	ER.	SO.	BB.	ERA.
1983—Paintsville	Ap'lachian	14	82⅓	∗9	1	∗.900	76	44	32	∗85	57	3.50
1984—Stockton	California	16	108⅓	6	6	.500	106	51	40	101	50	3.32
1984—El Paso	Texas	7	39	2	2	.500	43	19	15	24	16	3.46
1985—El Paso	Texas	25	150⅓	12	5	.706	171	91	83	128	68	4.97

Selected by St. Louis Cardinals' organization in 2nd round of free-agent draft, June 3, 1980.
Selected by Milwaukee Brewers' organization in 1st round (26th player selected) of free-agent draft, June 6, 1983.

ERIC VAUGHN PLUNK

Born September 3, 1963, at Wilmington, Calif.
Height, 6.05. Weight, 210.
Throws and bats righthanded.
Attended California State University at Dominguez Hills, Carson, Calif.

Tied for Florida State League lead in shutouts with 4 in 1983 and balks with 7 in 1984.

Year Club	League	G.	IP.	W.	L.	Pct.	H.	R.	ER.	SO.	BB.	ERA.
1981—Bradenton Yankees	Gulf Coast	11	54	3	4	.429	56	29	23	47	20	3.83
1982—Paintsville	Ap'lachian	12	64	6	3	.667	63	35	33	59	30	4.64
1983—Fort Lauderdale†	Florida St.	20	125	8	10	.444	115	55	38	109	63	2.74
1984—Fort Lauderdale‡	Florida St.	28	176⅓	12	12	.500	153	85	56	∗152	∗123	2.86
1985—Huntsville	Southern	13	79⅓	8	2	.800	61	36	30	68	56	3.40
1985—Tacoma	P. Coast	11	53	0	5	.000	51	41	34	43	50	5.77

Selected by New York Yankees' organization in 4th round of free-agent draft, June 8, 1981.
†On disabled list, August 11 to August 26, 1983.
‡Traded with Outfielder Stan Javier and Pitchers Jay Howell, Jose Rijo and Tim Birtsas to Oakland A's for Outfielder Rickey Henderson, Pitcher Bert Bradley and cash, December 5, 1984.

MICHAEL WAYNE POEHL

Name pronounced Pale.

(Mike)

Born August 28, 1964, at Houston, Tex.
Height, 6.04. Weight, 195.
Throws and bats righthanded.
Attended University of Texas, Austin, Tex.

Year Club	League	G.	IP.	W.	L.	Pct.	H.	R.	ER.	SO.	BB.	ERA.
1985—Batavia	NYP	10	55⅔	3	2	.600	48	22	13	48	21	2.10

Selected by Cleveland Indians' organization in 1st round (ninth player selected) of free-agent draft, June 3, 1985.

GUSTAVO POLIDOR
(Gus)

Born October 26, 1961, at Caracas, Venezuela.
Height, 6.01. Weight, 175.
Throws and bats righthanded.

Led Pacific Coast League shortstops in total chances with 669 and double plays with 93 in 1985.
Tied for Eastern League lead in double plays by shortstops with 69 in 1983.

Year	Club	League	Pos.	G.	AB.	R.	H.	2B.	3B.	HR.	RBI.	B.A.	PO.	A.	E.	F.A.
1981—Holyoke	East.	SS	130	479	46	119	17	3	2	47	.248	192	375	32	.947	
1982—Holyoke†	East.	SS	56	208	17	47	7	0	2	23	.226	74	149	21	.914	
1983—Nashua	East.	★SS-3B	105	329	32	69	7	2	0	21	.210	208	283	★37	.930	
1984—Waterbury	East.	★SS-P	119	394	42	88	11	1	1	32	.223	★200	322	27	★.951	
1985—Edmonton	P. C.	SS	132	460	56	131	18	7	2	51	.285	★250	★396	23	.966	
1985—California	Amer.	SS-OF	2	1	1	1	0	0	0	0	1.000	0	2	0	1.000	
Major League Totals—1 Year			2	1	1	1	0	0	0	0	1.000	0	2	0	1.000	

Signed as free agent by California Angels' organization, January 5, 1981.
†On disabled list, June 22 to July 14 and July 26, 1982 through remainder of season.

PITCHING RECORD

Year	Club	League	G.	IP.	W.	L.	Pct.	H.	R.	ER.	SO.	BB.	ERA.
1984—Waterbury	Eastern	1	1	0	0	.000	0	0	0	0	1	0.00	

CARLOS ANTONIO PONCE
Name pronounced PON-say.

Born February 7, 1959, at Rio Piedras, P.R.
Height, 5.10. Weight, 185.
Throws and bats righthanded.
Attended Universidad Interamericana, Hato Rey, P.R.,
and Abraham Baldwin Agricultural College, Tifton, Ga.

Led Pacific Coast League in sacrifice flies with 12 in 1985.
Led Texas League in total bases with 299 in 1983.
Led Pioneer League in total bases with 143 in 1980.
Tied for California League lead in game-winning RBIs with 15 and sacrifice flies with 12 in 1982.
Led Texas League first basemen in double plays with 99 in 1983.
Led California League first basemen in double plays with 112 in 1982.

Year	Club	League	Pos.	G.	AB.	R.	H.	2B.	3B.	HR.	RBI.	B.A.	PO.	A.	E.	F.A.
1980—Butte	Pion.	1B-OF	69	259	48	90	18	7	7	55	.347	360	24	12	.970	
1981—Burlington	Midw.	1B	130	487	70	131	25	7	15	62	.269	1111	58	★25	.979	
1982—Stockton	Calif.	1B	132	489	59	140	31	★13	6	79	.286	★1225	78	19	.986	
1983—El Paso	Texas	1B	129	506	114	★176	★50	5	21	111	.348	1133	69	●22	.982	
1984—Vancouver	P. C.	1B	112	414	50	102	20	5	7	55	.246	567	31	11	.982	
1985—Vancouver	P. C.	3B-1B	109	394	53	126	25	5	12	78	.320	375	81	14	.970	
1985—Milwaukee	Amer.	1B-OF	21	62	4	10	2	0	1	5	.161	67	3	0	1.000	
Major League Totals—1 Year			21	62	4	10	2	0	1	5	.161	67	3	0	1.000	

Signed as free-agent by Milwaukee Brewers' organization, January 15, 1982.

MARK ALLAN POOLE

Born April 15, 1959, at Denison, Tex.
Height, 6.00. Weight, 185.
Throws and bats righthanded.
Attended Glendale Community College, Glendale, Ariz.;
and Oklahoma State University, Stillwater, Okla.

Year	Club	League	Pos.	G.	AB.	R.	H.	2B.	3B.	HR.	RBI.	B.A.	PO.	A.	E.	F.A.
1981—Medicine Hat	Pion.	C-2B	56	212	36	58	12	1	6	45	.274	242	61	9	.971	
1982—Florence	S. Atl.	C	106	355	54	93	19	0	7	43	.262	★757	47	15	.982	
1983—Kinston	Carol.	C-1-2-3	94	339	56	82	14	1	13	53	.242	506	71	11	.981	
1983—Syracuse	Int.	C-2B	19	54	7	10	1	1	2	7	.185	128	13	1	.993	
1984—Knoxville	South.	C	78	247	31	71	11	0	4	25	.287	394	52	3	★.993	
1984—Syracuse	Int.	C	10	39	5	12	3	0	0	3	.308	44	8	0	1.000	
1985—Syracuse	Int.	C	75	237	29	70	9	0	8	37	.295	370	24	6	.985	

Selected by Toronto Blue Jays' organization in 9th round of free-agent draft, June 8, 1981.

CHARLES WILLIAM PORTER III
(Chuck)

Born January 12, 1956, at Baltimore, Md.
Height, 6.03. Weight, 187.
Throws and bats righthanded.
Attending Clemson University, Clemson, S.C.

Tied for Pacific Coast League lead in complete games with 12 in 1982.
Tied for Pacific Coast League lead in hit batsmen with 7 in 1979.

Year	Club	League	G.	IP.	W.	L.	Pct.	H.	R.	ER.	SO.	BB.	ERA.
1976—Quad Cities	Midwest	13	101	5	4	.556	90	42	36	65	27	3.21	
1977—Salinas	California	13	96	11	1	.917	84	37	35	66	24	3.28	
1977—El Paso	Texas	14	93	9	1	.900	106	45	40	45	16	3.87	

Year—Club	League	G.	IP.	W.	L.	Pct.	H.	R.	ER.	SO.	BB.	ERA.
1978—Salt Lake City	P. Coast	8	24	0	5	.000	34	29	26	7	12	9.75
1978—El Paso	Texas	18	124	10	5	.667	131	56	50	51	36	3.63
1979—Salt Lake City†	P. Coast	31	137	5	9	.357	164	100	87	41	44	5.72
1980—Burlington	Midwest	7	38	0	4	.000	40	25	14	22	5	3.32
1980—Holyoke	Eastern	14	90	8	2	.800	84	32	29	30	16	2.90
1981—Vancouver	P. Coast	27	140	7	10	.412	142	67	59	54	40	3.79
1981—Milwaukee	American	3	4	0	0	.000	6	2	2	1	1	4.50
1982—Vancouver‡	P. Coast	25	183⅓	8	12	.400	196	98	81	102	59	3.98
1982—Milwaukee	American	3	3⅔	0	0	.000	3	2	2	3	1	4.91
1983—Vancouver	P. Coast	7	19	0	1	.000	30	15	10	10	12	4.74
1983—Milwaukee	American	25	134	7	9	.438	162	72	67	76	38	4.50
1984—Milwaukee§	American	17	81⅓	6	4	.600	92	37	35	48	12	3.87
1985—Milwaukee x	American	6	13⅔	0	0	.000	15	8	3	8	2	1.98
1985—Beloit	Midwest	3	13⅔	1	0	1.000	15	5	5	12	5	3.29
Major League Totals—5 Years		54	236⅔	13	13	.500	278	121	109	136	54	4.15

Selected by California Angels' organization in 7th round of free-agent draft, June 8, 1976.

†Released, March 31, 1980; signed by Burlington (Milwaukee Brewers' organization), May 16, 1980.

‡On temporary inactive list, April 25 to May 9, 1982.

§On disabled list, June 3 to June 23 and July 23, 1984 through remainder of season.

xOn disabled list, March 22 to September 1, 1985; included rehabilitation disability assignment to Beloit, August 13 to September 1, 1985.

DARRELL RAY PORTER

Born January 17, 1952, at Joplin, Mo.
Height, 6.01. Weight, 202.
Throws right and bats lefthanded.

Major League stolen bases: 1971 (2), 1973 (5), 1974 (8), 1975 (2), 1976 (2), 1977 (1), 1979 (3), 1980 (1), 1981 (1), 1982 (1), 1983 (1), 1984 (5), 1985 (6). Total—38.

Led American League in bases on balls received with 121 in 1979.

Led American League catchers in double plays with 15 in 1979.

Led American League in passed balls with 15 in 1975, 9 in 1978 and tied for lead with 12 in 1976.

Tied for American League lead in sacrifice flies with 13 in 1979.

Led Midwest League in passed balls with 19 in 1971.

Named catcher on THE SPORTING NEWS American League All-Star Team, 1979.

Received bonus reported in excess of $70,000 to sign with Milwaukee Brewers, 1970.

Year—Club	League	Pos.	G.	AB.	R.	H.	2B.	3B.	HR.	RBI.	B.A.	PO.	A.	E.	F.A.
1970—Clinton	Midw.	C	62	185	24	37	11	0	4	21	.200	380	42	10	.977
1971—Danville	Midw.	C	101	332	75	90	9	7	24	70	.271	674	★69	★19	.975
1971—Milwaukee	Amer.	C	22	70	4	15	2	0	2	9	.214	108	18	3	.977
1972—Evansville	A. A.	C	88	255	37	55	7	2	13	45	.216	541	★56	7	.988
1972—Milwaukee	Amer.	C	18	56	2	7	1	0	1	2	.125	113	8	3	.976
1973—Milwaukee	Amer.	C	117	350	50	89	19	2	16	67	.254	372	47	10	.977
1974—Milwaukee	Amer.	C	131	432	59	104	15	4	12	56	.241	484	60	12	.978
1975—Milwaukee†	Amer.	C	130	409	66	95	12	5	18	60	.232	532	82	13	.979
1976—Milwaukee†	Amer.	C	119	389	43	81	14	1	5	32	.208	491	52	4	.975
1977—Kansas City	Amer.	C	130	425	61	117	21	3	16	60	.275	663	61	●13	.982
1978—Kansas City	Amer.	C	150	520	77	138	27	6	18	78	.265	608	62	8	.988
1979—Kansas City	Amer.	C	157	533	101	155	23	10	20	112	.291	628	68	13	.982
1980—Kansas City‡§	Amer.	C	118	418	51	104	14	2	7	51	.249	322	37	8	.978
1981—St. Louis x	Nat.	C	61	174	22	39	10	2	6	31	.224	206	31	5	.979
1982—St. Louis y	Nat.	C	120	373	46	86	18	5	12	48	.231	469	64	9	.983
1983—St. Louis	Nat.	C	145	443	57	116	24	3	15	66	.262	578	70	7	.989
1984—St. Louis	Nat.	C	127	422	56	98	16	3	11	68	.232	620	58	11	.984
1985—St. Louis z	Nat.	C	84	240	30	53	12	2	10	36	.221	386	26	4	.990
1985—Louisville a	A. A.	C	7	20	3	3	0	0	1	2	.150	2	0	0	1.000
American League Totals—10 Years			1092	3602	514	905	148	33	115	527	.251	4321	495	97	.980
National League Totals—5 Years			537	1652	211	392	80	15	54	249	.237	2259	249	36	.986
Major League Totals—15 Years			1629	5254	725	1297	228	48	169	776	.247	6580	744	133	.982

Selected by Milwaukee Brewers' organization in 1st round (fourth player selected) of free-agent draft, June 4, 1970.

†Traded with Pitcher Jim Colborn to Kansas City Royals for Outfielder Jim Wohlford, Infielder Jamie Quirk and a player to be named later, December 6, 1976; Milwaukee Brewers acquired Pitcher Bob McClure to complete deal, March 15, 1977.

‡On disabled list, April 4 to May 2, 1980.

§Granted free agency, October 24, 1980; signed by St. Louis Cardinals, December 13, 1980.

xOn disabled list, May 18 to August 19, 1981.

yOn disabled list, May 15 to June 5, 1982.

zOn disabled list, April 12 to April 27 and June 3 to July 16, 1985; included rehabilitation disability assignment to Louisville, July 9 to July 16, 1985.

aReleased, November 14, 1985.

CHAMPIONSHIP SERIES RECORD

Tied Championship Series record for most two-base hits, three-game Series (3), 1982.

Tied National League Championship Series record for most bases on balls, six-game Series (5), 1985.

Year—Club	League	Pos.	G.	AB.	R.	H.	2B.	3B.	HR.	RBI.	B.A.	PO.	A.	E.	F.A.
1977—Kansas City	Amer.	C	5	15	3	5	0	0	0	0	.333	18	0	0	1.000
1978—Kansas City	Amer.	C	4	14	1	5	1	0	0	3	.357	21	1	0	1.000
1980—Kansas City	Amer.	C	3	10	2	1	0	0	0	0	.100	17	1	0	1.000

Year	Club	League	Pos.	G.	AB.	R.	H.	2B.	3B.	HR.	RBI.	B.A.	PO.	A.	E.	F.A.
1982—St. Louis		Nat.	C	3	9	3	5	3	0	0	1	.556	15	3	0	1.000
1985—St. Louis		Nat.	C	5	15	1	4	1	0	0	0	.267	25	2	1	.964
Championship Series Totals—5 Years				20	63	10	20	5	0	0	4	.317	96	7	1	.990

WORLD SERIES RECORD

Year	Club	League	Pos.	G.	AB.	R.	H.	2B.	3B.	HR.	RBI.	B.A.	PO.	A.	E.	F.A.
1980—Kansas City		Amer.	PH-C	5	14	1	2	0	0	0	0	.143	13	2	0	1.000
1982—St. Louis		Nat.	C	7	28	1	8	2	0	1	5	.286	33	2	0	1.000
1985—St. Louis		Nat.	C	5	15	0	2	0	0	0	0	.133	36	4	0	1.000
World Series Totals—3 Years				17	57	2	12	2	0	1	5	.211	82	8	0	1.000

ALL-STAR GAME RECORD

Year	League	Pos.	AB.	R.	H.	2B.	3B.	HR.	RBI.	B.A.	PO.	A.	E.	F.A.
1978—American		PH	1	0	0	0	0	0	0	.000	0	0	0	.000
1979—American		C	3	0	1	1	0	0	0	.333	2	0	0	1.000
1980—American		C	1	0	0	0	0	0	0	.000	0	1	0	.000
All-Star Game Totals—3 Years			5	0	1	1	0	0	0	.200	2	1	0	1.000

Member of American League All-Star Team in 1974; did not play.

MARK STEVEN PORTUGAL

Born October 30, 1962, at Los Angeles, Calif.
Height, 6.00. Weight, 190.
Throws and bats righthanded.

Led Appalachian League in wild pitches with 12, home runs allowed with 11 and tied for lead in hit batsmen with 5 in 1981.

Year	Club	League	G.	IP.	W.	L.	Pct.	H.	R.	ER.	SO.	BB.	ERA.
1981—Elizabethton		Ap'lachian	14	85	7	1	.875	65	41	35	65	39	3.71
1982—Wisconsin Rapids		Midwest	36	119	9	8	.529	110	62	53	95	62	4.01
1983—Visalia		California	24	131⅓	10	5	.667	142	77	61	132	84	4.18
1984—Orlando		Southern	27	196	14	7	.667	171	80	65	110	113	2.98
1985—Toledo†		Int'national	19	128⅔	8	5	.615	129	60	54	89	60	3.78
1985—Minnesota		American	6	24⅓	1	3	.250	24	16	15	12	14	5.55
Major League Totals—1 Year			6	24⅓	1	3	.250	24	16	15	12	14	5.55

Signed as free agent by Minnesota Twins' organization, October 23, 1980.
†On disabled list, July 22 to August 2, 1985.

DENNIS CLAY POWELL

Born August 13, 1963, at Moultrie, Ga.
Height, 6.03. Weight, 200.
Throws left and bats righthanded.

Major League saves: 1985 (1).
Led Gulf Coast League in shutouts with 2 in 1983.

Year	Club	League	G.	IP.	W.	L.	Pct.	H.	R.	ER.	SO.	BB.	ERA.
1983—Bradenton Dodgers		Gulf Coast	11	74	8	2	.800	52	22	12	*103	23	1.46
1984—Vero Beach		Florida St.	4	26	1	1	.500	19	7	4	14	12	1.38
1984—San Antonio		Texas	24	168	9	8	.529	153	81	63	82	87	3.38
1985—Albuquerque		P. Coast	18	111⅔	9	0	1.000	106	40	34	55	48	2.74
1985—Los Angeles		National	16	29⅓	1	1	.500	30	19	17	19	13	5.22
Major League Totals—1 Year			16	29⅓	1	1	.500	30	19	17	19	13	5.22

Signed as free agent by Los Angeles Dodgers' organization, May 17, 1983.

TED HENRY POWER

Born January 31, 1955, at Guthrie, Okla.
Height, 6.04. Weight, 220.
Throws and bats righthanded.
Attended Kansas State University, Manhattan, Kan.

Major League saves: 1983 (2), 1984 (11), 1985 (27). Total—40.

Year	Club	League	G.	IP.	W.	L.	Pct.	H.	R.	ER.	SO.	BB.	ERA.
1976—Lodi		California	13	51	1	3	.250	46	34	26	58	44	4.59
1977—San Antonio†		Texas	12	72	5	3	.625	51	35	31	60	55	3.88
1978—San Antonio‡		Texas	25	101	6	5	.545	92	57	45	97	75	4.01
1979—San Antonio		Texas	10	64	5	1	.833	69	44	37	52	43	5.20
1979—Albuquerque		P. Coast	18	101	5	5	.500	95	59	52	69	82	4.63
1980—Albuquerque		P. Coast	26	155	13	7	.650	160	93	78	113	95	4.53
1981—Albuquerque		P. Coast	27	187	*18	3	*.857	165	84	74	*111	*103	3.56
1981—Los Angeles		National	5	14	1	3	.250	16	6	5	7	7	3.21
1982—Los Angeles		National	12	33⅔	1	1	.500	38	27	25	15	23	6.68
1982—Albuquerque§		P. Coast	14	73	5	4	.556	77	51	42	54	49	5.18
1983—Cincinnati		National	49	111	5	6	.455	120	62	56	57	49	4.54
1984—Cincinnati		National	*78	108⅔	9	7	.563	93	37	34	81	46	2.82
1985—Cincinnati		National	64	80	8	6	.571	65	27	24	42	45	2.70
Major League Totals—5 Years			208	347⅓	24	23	.511	332	159	144	202	170	3.73

Selected by Los Angeles Dodgers' organization in 5th round of free-agent draft, June 8, 1976.

†On disabled list, July 18 to July 29 and August 20 to September 4, 1977.
‡On disabled list, July 5 to July 21, 1978.
§Traded to Cincinnati Reds for cash and Infielder Michael James Ramsey, October 15, 1982.

JAMES ARTHUR PRESLEY
(Jim)

Born October 23, 1961, at Pensacola, Fla.
Height, 6.01. Weight, 200.
Throws and bats righthanded.
Attended Pensacola Junior College, Pensacola, Fla.

Established major league record for fewest putouts by third baseman, season, 150 or more games (82), 1985.
Major League stolen bases: 1984 (1), 1985 (2). Total—3.
Led Eastern League in game-winning RBIs with 16 in 1982.
Led Midwest League in being hit by pitch with 12 in 1980.
Led Eastern League third basemen in assists with 247 and total chances with 365 in 1982.
Led Southern League third basemen in double plays with 29 in 1983.

Year Club	League	Pos.	G.	AB.	R.	H.	2B.	3B.	HR.	RBI.	B.A.	PO.	A.	E.	F.A.
1979—Bellingham	N'west	SS	48	138	20	27	4	1	1	12	.196	42	127	27	.862
1980—Wausau	Midw.	3-S-2-1	126	429	45	105	21	1	12	52	.245	161	235	22	.947
1981—Wausau	Midw.	3B	57	208	48	58	10	0	12	53	.279	32	105	9	.938
1981—Lynn	East.	3B-2B	64	210	32	54	7	1	8	36	.257	49	110	11	.935
1982—Lynn	East.	★3B-OF	133	462	65	123	24	0	22	79	.266	84	250	★35	.905
1983—Chattanooga	South.	3B-SS	131	461	70	122	31	5	14	90	.265	122	329	27	.944
1984—Salt Lake City	P. C.	3B	69	265	43	84	13	4	13	56	.317	53	140	12	.941
1984—Seattle	Amer.	3B	70	251	27	57	12	1	10	36	.227	48	113	7	.958
1985—Seattle	Amer.	3B	155	570	71	157	33	1	28	84	.275	82	335	17	.961
Major League Totals—2 Years			225	821	98	214	45	2	38	120	.261	130	448	24	.960

Selected by Seattle Mariners' organization in 4th round of free-agent draft, June 5, 1979.

JOSEPH WALTER PRICE
(Joe)

Born November 29, 1956, at Inglewood, Calif.
Height, 6.04. Weight, 220.
Throws left and bats righthanded.
Attended Oklahoma State University, Stillwater, Okla., and
University of Oklahoma, Norman, Okla.

Major League saves: 1981 (4), 1982 (3), 1985 (1). Total—8.

Year Club	League	G.	IP.	W.	L.	Pct.	H.	R.	ER.	SO.	BB.	ERA.
1977—Billings	Pioneer	15	94	6	5	.545	83	50	39	97	42	3.73
1978—Tampa	Florida St.	23	165	10	4	.714	123	40	27	128	51	1.47
1978—Nashville	Southern	2	10	0	0	.000	7	3	3	10	3	2.70
1979—Nashville	Southern	22	109	6	6	.500	101	58	48	69	41	3.96
1980—Indianapolis	Am. Assoc.	11	79	4	4	.500	64	36	34	83	30	3.87
1980—Cincinnati	National	24	111	7	3	.700	95	45	44	44	37	3.57
1981—Cincinnati	National	41	54	6	1	.857	42	19	15	41	18	2.50
1982—Cincinnati	National	59	72⅔	3	4	.429	73	26	23	71	32	2.85
1983—Cincinnati†	National	21	144	10	6	.625	118	46	46	83	46	2.88
1984—Cincinnati	National	30	171⅔	7	13	.350	176	91	80	129	61	4.19
1985—Cincinnati†	National	26	64⅔	2	2	.500	59	35	28	52	23	3.90
Major League Totals—6 Years		201	618	35	29	.547	563	262	236	420	217	3.44

Selected by Cincinnati Reds' organization in 4th round of free-agent draft, June 7, 1977.
†On disabled list, August 7 to September 1, 1983.
‡On disabled list, July 23 to August 8 and August 29 to September 13, 1985.

GREGORY RUSSELL PRYOR
(Greg)

Born October 2, 1949, at Marietta, O.
Height, 6.00. Weight, 175.
Throws and bats righthanded.
Received bachelor of science degree in industrial management from
Florida Southern College, Lakeland, Fla.
Brother of Jeff Pryor, pitcher in California Angels' organization, 1968 through 1972.

Major League stolen bases: 1978 (3), 1979 (3), 1980 (2), 1982 (2). Total—10.
Led International League shortstops in assists with 417 and double plays with 87 in 1977.
Tied for Pacific Coast League lead in double plays by shortstop with 90 in 1976.

Year Club	League	Pos.	G.	AB.	R.	H.	2B.	3B.	HR.	RBI.	B.A.	PO.	A.	E.	F.A.
1971—Geneva	NYP	3-2-S-O	60	226	40	64	10	4	4	28	.283	76	138	21	.911
1972—Pittsfield	East.	SS	65	208	23	43	10	2	1	16	.207	89	155	29	.894
1972—Burlington	Carol.	SS-OF	39	119	16	28	2	1	1	15	.235	49	110	11	.935
1973—Rocky Mount	Carol.	SS-2B	126	443	53	130	20	9	2	44	.293	203	349	50	.917
1974—Pittsfield	East.	3B-SS-2B	122	441	61	104	20	1	5	37	.236	113	255	26	.934
1975—Spokane	P. C.	SS-3B-2B	135	481	59	117	21	2	5	53	.243	184	411	33	.947
1976—Sacramento	P. C.	SS	122	495	71	136	21	3	9	51	.275	158	409	32	.947
1976—Texas†	Amer.	2B-3B-SS	5	8	2	3	0	0	0	1	.375	4	8	0	1.000
1977—Syracuse‡	Int.	★S-3-2	124	461	60	125	18	6	7	52	.271	213	420	21	★.968

Year Club	League	Pos.	G.	AB.	R.	H.	2B.	3B.	HR.	RBI.	B.A.	PO.	A.	E.	F.A.
1978—Chicago	Amer.	2B-3B-SS	82	222	27	58	11	0	2	15	.261	100	202	11	.965
1979—Chicago	Amer.	SS-2B-3B	143	476	60	131	23	3	3	34	.275	218	447	26	.962
1980—Chicago	Amer.	SS-3B-2B	122	338	32	81	18	4	1	29	.240	130	344	16	.967
1981—Chicago§	Amer.	3B-SS-2B	47	76	4	17	1	0	0	6	.224	27	65	6	.939
1982—Kansas City	Amer.	3-2-1-S	73	152	23	41	10	1	2	12	.270	78	112	5	.974
1983—Kansas City	Amer.	3B-1B-2B	68	115	9	25	4	0	1	14	.217	38	100	5	.965
1984—Kansas City x	Amer.	3-2-S-1	123	270	32	71	11	1	4	25	.263	87	190	8	.972
1985—Kansas City	Amer.	3-2-S-1	63	114	8	25	3	0	1	3	.219	47	87	5	.964
Major League Totals—9 Years			726	1771	197	452	81	9	14	139	.255	729	1555	82	.965

Selected by Washington Senators' organization in 6th round of free-agent draft, June 8, 1971.

†Traded with Infielder Brian Doyle and cash estimated at $25,000 to New York Yankees for Infielder Sandy Alomar, February 17, 1977.

‡Granted free agency, November 5, 1977; signed by Chicago White Sox, November 28, 1977.

§Traded to Kansas City Royals for Pitcher Jeff Schattinger, March 24, 1982.

xGranted free agency, November 8, 1984; re-signed by Royals, December 20, 1984.

CHAMPIONSHIP SERIES RECORD

Year Club	League	Pos.	G.	AB.	R.	H.	2B.	3B.	HR.	RBI.	B.A.	PO.	A.	E.	F.A.
1984—Kansas City	Amer.	PR-3B	1	0	0	0	0	0	0	0	.000	1	0	0	1.000

WORLD SERIES RECORD

Year Club	League	Pos.	G.	AB.	R.	H.	2B.	3B.	HR.	RBI.	B.A.	PO.	A.	E.	F.A.
1985—Kansas City	Amer.	3B	1	0	0	0	0	0	0	0	.000	0	1	0	1.000

KIRBY PUCKETT

Born March 14, 1961, at Chicago, Ill.
Height, 5.08. Weight, 178.
Throws and bats righthanded.
Attended Bradley University, Peoria, Ill., and Triton College, River Grove, Ill.

Tied modern major league record for most hits, first game in majors, nine innings (4), May 8, 1984.
Major League stolen bases: 1984 (14), 1985 (21). Total—35.
Led American League outfielders in total chances with 492 in 1985.
Led Appalachian League in total bases with 135 and tied for lead in stolen bases with 43 in 1982.
Led California League outfielders in double plays with 5 in 1983.
Named California League Player of the Year, 1983.

Year Club	League	Pos.	G.	AB.	R.	H.	2B.	3B.	HR.	RBI.	B.A.	PO.	A.	E.	F.A.
1982—Elizabethton	Appal.	OF	65	★275	★65	★105	15	3	3	35	★.382	133	★11	5	.966
1983—Visalia	Calif.	OF	138	★548	105	172	29	7	9	97	.314	253	★22	5	.982
1984—Toledo	Int.	OF	21	80	9	21	2	0	1	5	.263	35	1	3	.923
1984—Minnesota	Amer.	OF	128	557	63	165	12	5	0	31	.296	438	★16	3	.993
1985—Minnesota	Amer.	OF	161	★691	80	199	29	13	4	74	.288	★465	19	8	.984
Major League Totals—2 Years			289	1248	143	364	41	18	4	105	.292	903	35	11	.988

Selected by Minnesota Twins' organization in 1st round (third player selected) of free-agent draft, January 12, 1982.

TERRANCE STEPHEN PUHL

Name pronounced Pool.

(Terry)

Born July 8, 1956, at Melville, Saskatchewan, Canada.
Height, 6.02. Weight, 197.
Throws right and bats lefthanded.

Established major league record for highest fielding percentage by outfielder, lifetime, 1,000 or more games (.993).
Tied major league records for highest fielding percentage by outfielder, season, 150 or more games (1.000), 1979; fewest errors by outfielder, season, 150 or more games (0), 1979.
Major League stolen bases: 1977 (10), 1978 (32), 1979 (30), 1980 (27), 1981 (22), 1982 (17), 1983 (24), 1984 (13), 1985 (6). Total—181.

Year Club	League	Pos.	G.	AB.	R.	H.	2B.	3B.	HR.	RBI.	B.A.	PO.	A.	E.	F.A.
1974—Covington	Appal.	OF	59	211	42	60	11	0	0	21	.284	89	2	2	.978
1975—Dubuque	Midw.	OF-1B	104	346	57	115	10	2	0	28	.332	230	11	7	.971
1976—Columbus..............	South.	OF	28	98	13	28	5	0	1	14	.286	76	1	2	.975
1976—Memphis...............	Int.	OF	105	372	50	99	17	3	1	39	.266	191	5	3	.985
1977—Charleston	Int.	OF	78	285	53	87	12	6	4	33	.305	189	4	3	.985
1977—Houston	Nat.	OF	60	229	40	69	13	5	0	10	.301	119	3	1	.992
1978—Houston	Nat.	OF	149	585	87	169	25	6	3	35	.289	386	6	3	.992
1979—Houston	Nat.	OF	157	600	87	172	22	4	8	49	.287	352	7	0	★1.000
1980—Houston	Nat.	OF	141	535	75	151	24	5	13	55	.282	311	14	3	.991
1981—Houston	Nat.	OF	96	350	43	88	19	4	3	28	.251	185	5	0	●1.000
1982—Houston	Nat.	OF	145	507	64	133	17	9	8	50	.262	257	4	3	.989
1983—Houston	Nat.	OF	137	465	66	136	25	7	8	44	.292	220	4	2	.991
1984—Houston†	Nat.	OF	132	449	66	135	19	7	9	55	.301	213	6	3	.986
1985—Houston‡	Nat.	OF	57	194	34	55	14	3	2	23	.284	92	3	0	1.000
Major League Totals—9 Years			1074	3914	562	1108	178	50	54	349	.283	2135	52	15	.993

Signed as free agent by Houston Astros' organization, September 19, 1973.

†On disabled list, April 13 to April 30, 1984.

‡On disabled list, April 22 to May 7, June 13 to June 28, July 19 to August 15 and August 26, 1985 through remainder of season.

Year	Club	League	Pos.	G.	AB.	R.	H.	2B.	3B.	HR.	RBI.	B.A.	PO.	A.	E.	F.A.
1981—Houston		Nat.	OF	5	21	2	4	1	0	0	0	.190	7	1	0	1.000

CHAMPIONSHIP SERIES RECORD

Tied Championship Series records for most at-bats, extra-inning game (6), October 8, 1980; most one-base hits, five-game Series (8), 1980.

Established National League Championship Series records for highest batting average, five-game Series (.526), 1980; most hits, five-game Series (10), 1980.

Tied National League Championship Series record for most hits, game (4), October 12, 1980.

Year	Club	League	Pos.	G.	AB.	R.	H.	2B.	3B.	HR.	RBI.	B.A.	PO.	A.	E.	F.A.
1980—Houston		Nat.	PH-OF	5	19	4	10	2	0	0	3	.526	13	0	0	1.000

ALL-STAR GAME RECORD

Member of National League All-Star Team for 1978 game; did not play.

LUIS BIENVENIDO PUJOLS (TORIBIA)

Name pronounced POO-hols.

Born November 18, 1955, at Santiago Rodriguez, Dominican Republic
Height, 6.01. Weight, 195.
Throws and bats righthanded.

Major League stolen bases: 1981 (1).
Led National League in passed balls with 20 in 1982.
Led Appalachian League in sacrifice flies with 9 in 1974.
Tied for Appalachian League lead in double plays by catchers with 3 and passed balls with 24 in 1973.

Year	Club	League	Pos.	G.	AB.	R.	H.	2B.	3B.	HR.	RBI.	B.A.	PO.	A.	E.	F.A.
1973—Covington		Appal.	C	26	86	8	23	2	0	1	4	.267	187	21	6	.972
1974—Cedar Rapids		Midw.	C	26	86	4	17	0	1	0	10	.198	186	19	2	.990
1974—Covington		Appal.	C	60	218	26	58	7	1	1	27	.266	★408	★49	★11	.976
1975—Dubuque		Midw.	C-OF-1B	102	341	23	75	13	1	0	31	.220	598	62	9	.987
1976—Columbus†		South.	C-3B-OF	53	142	12	28	2	0	2	16	.197	186	21	1	.995
1977—Charleston‡		Int.	C	58	180	15	41	4	0	1	19	.228	239	26	4	.985
1977—Houston		Nat.	C	6	15	0	1	0	0	0	0	.067	18	4	0	1.000
1978—Charleston		Int.	C	61	196	22	43	6	1	2	24	.219	277	19	3	.990
1978—Houston		Nat.	C-1B	56	153	11	20	8	1	1	11	.131	272	33	6	.981
1979—Charleston		Int.	C	105	345	29	86	18	2	6	41	.249	487	41	6	.989
1979—Houston		Nat.	C	26	75	7	17	2	1	0	8	.227	136	6	1	.993
1980—Houston		Nat.	C-3B	78	221	15	44	6	1	0	20	.199	349	35	4	.990
1981—Houston		Nat.	C	40	117	5	28	3	1	1	14	.239	192	14	1	.995
1982—Houston		Nat.	C	65	176	8	35	6	2	4	15	.199	295	39	3	.991
1983—Houston		Nat.	C	40	87	4	17	2	0	0	12	.195	180	20	6	.971
1983—Tucson		P. C.	C	33	112	18	28	7	0	1	9	.250	189	14	2	.990
1984—Tucson§		P. C.	★C-1B	110	375	39	104	22	2	10	58	.277	578	★69	6	★.991
1984—Kansas City x		Amer.	C	4	5	0	1	0	0	0	1	.200	9	0	0	1.000
1985—Texas y		Amer.	C	1	1	0	1	0	0	0	0	1.000	1	0	0	1.000
National League Totals—7 Years				311	844	50	162	27	6	6	80	.192	1442	151	21	.987
American League Totals—2 Years				5	6	0	2	0	0	0	1	.333	10	0	0	1.000
Major League Totals—9 Years				316	850	50	164	27	6	6	81	.193	1452	151	21	.987

Signed as free agent by Houston Astros' organization, January 9, 1973.

†On disabled list, June 11 to June 25, July 28 to August 14 and August 22 to September 15, 1976.

‡On disabled list, April 15 to April 25, 1977.

§Traded to Kansas City Royals for Pitcher Jim Miner, September 1, 1984.

xGranted free agency when refused option to minors, October 19, 1984; signed by Texas Rangers' organization, December 19, 1984.

yOn disabled list, April 18 to May 20 and June 3, 1985 through remainder of season.

DIVISION SERIES RECORD

Year	Club	League	Pos.	G.	AB.	R.	H.	2B.	3B.	HR.	RBI.	B.A.	PO.	A.	E.	F.A.
1981—Houston		Nat.	C	2	6	0	0	0	0	0	0	.000	12	1	0	1.000

CHAMPIONSHIP SERIES RECORD

Year	Club	League	Pos.	G.	AB.	R.	H.	2B.	3B.	HR.	RBI.	B.A.	PO.	A.	E.	F.A.
1980—Houston		Nat.	C	4	10	1	1	0	1	0	0	.100	21	2	0	1.000

CHARLES MICHAEL PULEO

Name pronounced Puh-LAY-oh.

(Charlie)

Born February 7, 1955, at Glen Ridge, N. J.
Height, 6.03. Weight, 190.
Throws and bats righthanded.
Received bachelor of science degree in physical education and science from
Seton Hall University, South Orange, N. J. in 1977.

Pitched seven-inning, 3-0 no-hit victory against St. Petersburg, August 13, 1979 (second game).
Major League saves: 1982 (1).

Year Club	League	G.	IP.	W.	L.	Pct.	H.	R.	ER.	SO.	BB.	ERA.
1978—Utica	NYP	16	104	10	3	.769	81	46	31	★125	48	2.68
1979—Dunedin	Florida St.	22	123	10	10	.500	126	72	61	77	61	4.46
1980—Knoxville†‡	Southern	19	108	8	7	.533	87	51	34	97	66	2.83
1981—Tidewater	Int'national	26	169	12	9	.571	132	74	65	133	73	3.46
1981—New York	National	4	13	0	0	.000	8	1	0	8	8	0.00
1982—New York§	National	36	171	9	9	.500	179	99	85	98	90	4.47
1983—Cincinnati x	National	27	143⅔	6	12	.333	145	86	78	71	91	4.89
1984—Wichita	Am. Assoc.	19	104⅓	8	9	.471	117	71	62	59	59	5.35
1984—Cincinnati	National	5	22	1	2	.333	27	15	14	6	15	5.73
1985—Denver y	Am. Assoc.	11	61	1	5	.167	70	42	31	40	37	4.57
1985—Richmond	Int'national	16	71	5	4	.556	50	23	22	63	37	2.79
Major League Totals—4 Years		72	349⅔	16	23	.410	359	201	177	183	204	4.56

Selected by Detroit Tigers' organization in 13th round of free-agent draft, June 5, 1973.
Signed as free agent by Toronto Blue Jays' organization, March 14, 1978.
†On disabled list, April 24 to June 14, 1980.
‡Traded to New York Mets' organization, April 14, 1981; completing deal in which New York traded Pitcher Mark Bomback to Toronto Blue Jays for a player to be named later, April 6, 1981.
§Traded with Catcher Lloyd McClendon and Outfielder Jason Felice to Cincinnati Reds for Pitcher Tom Seaver, December 16, 1982.
xOn disabled list, March 20 to May 2, 1983.
ySold to Richmond (Atlanta Braves' organization), June 6, 1985.

ALFONSO PULIDO (MANZO)
Name pronounced Puh-LEE-doh.

Born January 23, 1959, at Vera Cruz, Mex.
Height, 5.11. Weight, 175.
Throws and bats lefthanded.

Led Pacific Coast League in complete games with 16 and shutouts with 4 in 1984.
Led Mexican Center League in games started by pitchers with 16 in 1978 and tied for lead with 14 in 1977.
Tied for Mexican Center League lead in shutouts with 3 in 1978.

Year Club	League	G.	IP.	W.	L.	Pct.	H.	R.	ER.	SO.	BB.	ERA.
1977—Arandas	Mex. Cent.	14	99	6	6	.500	124	61	48	46	18	4.36
1978—Matamoras	Mex. Cent.	18	111	10	3	.769	103	39	26	81	16	2.11
1978—Cordoba	Mexican	5	12	2	0	1.000	5	1	1	10	2	0.75
1979—Cordoba	Mexican	20	47	3	2	.600	50	22	22	23	19	4.21
1980—Reynosa†	Mexican	26	132	9	6	.600	142	58	52	69	39	3.55
1980—Reynosa‡	Mexican	7	47	3	4	.429	59	18	12	19	13	2.30
1981—Mexico City Reds	Mexican	31	126	5	6	.455	121	46	43	46	25	3.07
1982—Mexico City Reds	Mexican	43	93⅓	8	8	.500	94	34	25	50	31	2.41
1983—Mexico City Reds§	Mexican	29	187⅓	●17	3	.850	170	46	42	83	31	2.02
1983—Pittsburgh	National	1	2	0	0	.000	4	3	2	1	1	9.00
1984—Hawaii	P. Coast	28	★216	18	6	.750	190	73	61	123	46	2.54
1984—Pittsburgh x	National	1	2	0	0	.000	3	2	2	2	1	9.00
1985—Columbus	Int'national	31	146	11	8	.579	154	66	55	67	34	3.39
Major League Totals—2 Years		2	4	0	0	.000	7	5	4	3	2	9.00

†20-team season.
‡6-team season.
§Sold to Pittsburgh Pirates, July 22, 1983; remained with Mexico City Reds on loan until September 1, 1983.
xTraded with Infielder Dale Berra and Outfielder Jay Buhner to New York Yankees for Outfielder Steve Kemp, Infielder Tim Foli and $800,000, December 20, 1984.

HECTOR APONTE QUINONES
Name pronounced Key-NO-nez.

Born October 14, 1964, at Florida, Puerto Rico.
Height, 6.02. Weight, 165.
Throws and bats righthanded.

Led California League shortstops in total chances with 606 in 1985.
Led Appalachian League shortstops in double plays with 26 in 1983.

Year Club	League	Pos.	G.	AB.	R.	H.	2B.	3B.	HR.	RBI.	B.A.	PO.	A.	E.	F.A.
1982—Pikeville†	Appal.	SS-3B	8	18	2	4	0	0	0	0	.222	7	6	2	.867
1983—Beloit	Midw.	SS-2B-3B	27	72	9	15	1	0	1	6	.208	32	60	18	.836
1983—Paintsville	Appal.	SS	63	197	32	53	8	0	1	29	.269	80	146	28	★.890
1984—Beloit	Midw.	SS	99	309	27	69	6	0	0	15	.223	119	234	38	.903
1985—Stockton‡	Calif.	SS	132	449	70	108	23	7	0	62	.241	195	★355	★56	.908

Signed as free agent by Milwaukee Brewers' organization, March 9, 1982.
†On temporarily inactive list, June 25 to July 12, 1982.
‡Traded to San Francisco Giants, December 11, 1985, completing deal in which San Francisco traded First Baseman-Outfielder David Green to Milwaukee Brewers for a player to be named later, December 4, 1985.

LUIS RAUL QUINONES
Name pronounced Key-NO-nez.

Born April 28, 1962, at Ponce, Puerto Rico.
Height, 5.11. Weight, 165.
Throws right and bats left and righthanded.

Major League stolen bases: 1983 (1).

Led Carolina League shortstops in double plays with 77 in 1981.
Tied for Northwest League lead in double plays by shortstops with 33 in 1980.

Year	Club	League	Pos.	G.	AB.	R.	H.	2B.	3B.	HR.	RBI.	B.A.	PO.	A.	E.	F.A.
1980—Grays Harbor	N'west		SS	56	156	33	35	2	2	0	11	.224	70	157	24	.904
1981—Salem	Carol.		●SS-2B	123	455	64	102	10	4	7	37	.224	208	341	●53	.912
1982—Salem	Carol.		SS	41	173	32	48	1	4	5	28	.277	41	99	15	.903
1982—Amarillo†	Texas		SS	95	411	69	120	19	7	11	60	.292	164	288	31	.936
1983—Albany	East.		2B-OF-SS	56	213	35	51	5	0	6	23	.239	101	138	13	.948
1983—Oakland	Amer.		2-O-3-S	19	42	5	8	2	1	0	4	.190	22	24	1	.979
1983—Tacoma‡	P. C.		SS-OF-2B	45	133	14	35	3	1	2	14	.263	62	97	9	.946
1984—Maine	Int.		★SS-OF-2B	131	473	71	127	27	3	8	60	.268	217	330	★43	.927
1985—Maine§	Int.		SS-OF	14	45	4	8	2	1	1	2	.178	19	12	0	1.000
1985—Phoenix	P. C.		SS-2B-3B	85	304	46	78	13	7	8	47	.257	106	236	13	.963
Major League Totals—1 Year				19	42	5	8	2	1	0	4	.190	22	24	1	.979

Signed as free agent by San Diego Padres' organization, April 28, 1980.

†Drafted by Oakland A's, December 6, 1982.

‡Traded to Cleveland Indians, December 8, 1983, completing deal in which Cleveland traded Catcher Jim Essian to Oakland A's for a player to be named later, December 5, 1983.

§Traded with Pitcher Mike Jeffcoat to San Francisco Giants' organization for Shortstop Johnnie LeMaster, May 7, 1985.

REY FRANCISCO QUINONEZ

Name pronounced Key-NO-nez.

Born November 11, 1963, at Rio Piedras, Puerto Rico.
Height, 5.11. Weight, 160.
Throws and bats righthanded.

Led Eastern League in being hit by pitch with 9 in 1985.
Led Carolina League in grounding into double plays with 20 in 1984.
Led Eastern League shortstops in double plays with 75 in 1985.
Led Carolina League shortstops in total chances with 718 and double plays with 84 in 1984.

Year	Club	League	Pos.	G.	AB.	R.	H.	2B.	3B.	HR.	RBI.	B.A.	PO.	A.	E.	F.A.
1983—Elmira	NYP		SS	67	234	38	69	11	0	12	55	.295	107	226	27	.925
1984—Winston-Salem	Carol.		SS	132	458	53	128	★30	6	11	69	.279	★240	★428	★50	.930
1985—New Britain	East.		SS	134	439	67	113	19	5	9	50	.257	207	★402	★34	.947

Signed as free agent by Boston Red Sox' organization, September 8, 1982.

JAMES PATRICK QUIRK
(Jamie)

Born October 22, 1954, at Whittier, Calif.
Height, 6.04. Weight, 200.
Throws right and bats lefthanded.
Attended Whittier College, Whittier, Calif.

Major League stolen bases: 1980 (3).
Led American Association in passed balls with 23 in 1985.
Led American Association third basemen in double plays with 31 in 1975.
Led Pioneer League shortstops in double plays with 16 in 1972.

Year	Club	League	Pos.	G.	AB.	R.	H.	2B.	3B.	HR.	RBI.	B.A.	PO.	A.	E.	F.A.
1972—Billings	Pion.		SS	55	208	29	53	9	4	5	37	.255	★63	★162	★28	★.889
1973—San Jose	Calif.		SS	132	429	58	99	12	7	8	45	.231	160	330	39	.926
1974—Jacksonville	South.		SS	46	163	16	37	7	2	3	21	.227	75	133	20	.912
1974—Omaha	A. A.		SS-3B-2B	53	203	27	57	10	2	10	31	.281	64	141	14	.936
1975—Omaha	A. A.		3B	127	445	62	122	23	4	13	64	.274	109	★254	16	★.958
1975—Kansas City	Amer.		OF-3B	14	39	2	10	0	0	1	5	.256	19	3	2	.917
1976—Kansas City†	Amer.		SS-3B-1B	64	114	11	28	6	0	1	15	.246	9	14	2	.920
1977—Milwaukee	Amer.		OF-3B	93	221	16	48	14	1	3	13	.217	19	4	2	.920
1978—Spokane‡	P. C.		3B-1B	97	343	58	100	20	2	12	63	.292	235	142	20	.950
1978—Kansas City§	Amer.		3B-SS	17	29	3	6	2	0	0	2	.207	11	16	2	.931
1979—Kansas City	Amer.		C-SS-3B	51	79	8	24	6	1	1	11	.304	16	9	1	.960
1980—Kansas City	Amer.		C-3-O-1	62	163	13	45	5	0	5	21	.276	78	66	8	.947
1981—Kansas City	Amer.		C-3-2-O	46	100	8	25	7	0	0	10	.250	63	23	4	.956
1982—Kansas City xy	Amer.		C-1-3-O	36	78	8	18	3	0	1	5	.231	110	12	0	1.000
1983—St. Louis za	Nat.		C-3B-SS	48	86	3	18	2	1	2	11	.209	68	13	6	.931
1984—Denver	A. A.		C-3-O-1-P	70	201	23	42	6	3	2	24	.209	212	67	11	.962
1984—Chi. b-Cle. c	Amer.		3B-C	4	3	1	1	0	0	1	2	.333	1	0	0	1.000
1985—Omaha	A. A.		C-1B-3B	104	324	33	79	5	1	8	48	.244	525	67	14	.977
1985—Kansas City d	Amer.		C-1B	19	57	3	16	3	1	0	4	.281	66	8	1	.987
American League Totals—10 Years				406	883	73	221	46	3	13	88	.250	392	155	22	.961
National League Totals—1 Year				48	86	3	18	2	1	2	11	.209	68	13	6	.931
Major League Totals—11 Years				454	969	76	239	48	4	15	99	.247	460	168	28	.957

Selected by Kansas City Royals' organization in 1st round (18th player selected) of free-agent draft, June 6, 1972.

†Traded with Outfielder Jim Wohlford and a player to be named later to Milwaukee Brewers for Pitcher Jim Colborn and Catcher Darrell Porter, December 6, 1976; Milwaukee acquired Pitcher Bob McClure to complete deal, March 15, 1977.

‡Traded to Kansas City Royals for Pitcher Gerry Ako and cash, August 3, 1978.

§On disabled list, August 14 to September 5, 1978.

xOn disabled list, August 10 to September 1, 1982.

yGranted free agency, November 10, 1982; signed by St. Louis Cardinals, February 16, 1983.

zReleased, March 26, 1984; named St. Louis Cardinals coach, April 13, 1984.
aSigned by Chicago White Sox' organization, May 23, 1984.
bSold to Cleveland Indians, September 24, 1984.
cReleased, October 15, 1984; signed by Kansas City Royals' organization, February 25, 1985.
dGranted free agency, November 12, 1985; re-signed by Royals, November 27, 1985.

CHAMPIONSHIP SERIES RECORD

Year Club	League	Pos.	G.	AB.	R.	H.	2B.	3B.	HR.	RBI.	B.A.	PO.	A.	E.	F.A.
1976—Kansas City	Amer.	PH-DH	4	7	1	1	0	1	0	2	.143	0	0	0	.000
1985—Kansas City	Amer.	PH	1	1	0	0	0	0	0	0	.000	0	0	0	.000
Championship Series Totals—2 Years			5	8	1	1	0	1	0	2	.125	0	0	0	.000

PITCHING RECORD

Year Club	League	G.	IP.	W.	L.	Pct.	H.	R.	ER.	SO.	BB.	ERA.
1984—Denver	Am. Assoc.	2	2	0	0	.000	6	3	3	0	0	13.50

DANIEL RAYMOND QUISENBERRY
Name pronounced QUIZ-en-berry.
(Dan)

Born February 7, 1953, at Santa Monica, Calif.
Height, 6.02. Weight, 190.
Throws and bats righthanded.
Attended Orange Coast College, Costa Mesa, Calif., LaVerne College, LaVerne, Calif.,
and Fresno Pacific College, Fresno, Calif.

Tied major league record for most saves, season (45), 1983.
Major League saves: 1979 (5), 1980 (33), 1981 (18), 1982 (35), 1983 (45), 1984 (44), 1985 (37). Total—217.
Led American League in games finished in relief with 68 in both 1980 and 1982, 62 in 1983 and 76 in 1985.
Led American League in saves with 35 in 1982, 45 in 1983, 44 in 1984, 37 in 1985 and tied for lead with 33 in 1980.
Tied for Southern League lead in saves with 15 in 1978.
Named American League Fireman of the Year by THE SPORTING NEWS, 1980 and 1982 through 1985.

Year Club	League	G.	IP.	W.	L.	Pct.	H.	R.	ER.	SO.	BB.	ERA.
1975—Waterloo	Midwest	20	44	3	2	.600	40	16	12	31	6	2.45
1975—Jacksonville	Southern	6	8	0	1	.000	5	3	2	2	4	2.25
1976—Jacksonville	Southern	9	12	0	1	.000	8	6	3	6	2	2.25
1976—Waterloo	Midwest	34	42	2	1	.667	28	4	3	19	9	0.64
1977—Jacksonville	Southern	33	74	3	1	.750	61	18	11	33	11	1.34
1978—Jacksonville	Southern	48	64	4	2	.667	62	22	17	29	12	2.39
1979—Omaha	Am. Assoc.	26	35	2	1	.667	29	15	14	16	10	3.60
1979—Kansas City	American	32	40	3	2	.600	42	16	14	13	7	3.15
1980—Kansas City	American	★75	128	12	7	.632	129	47	44	37	27	3.09
1981—Kansas City	American	40	62	1	4	.200	59	16	12	20	15	1.74
1982—Kansas City	American	72	136⅔	9	7	.563	126	43	39	46	12	2.57
1983—Kansas City	American	★69	139	5	3	.625	118	35	30	48	11	1.94
1984—Kansas City	American	72	129⅓	6	3	.667	121	39	38	41	12	2.64
1985—Kansas City	American	★84	129	8	9	.471	142	41	34	54	16	2.37
Major League Totals—7 Years		444	764	44	35	.557	737	237	211	259	100	2.49

Signed as free agent by Kansas City Royals' organization, June 7, 1975.

DIVISION SERIES RECORD

Year Club	League	G.	IP.	W.	L.	Pct.	H.	R.	ER.	SO.	BB.	ERA.
1981—Kansas City	American	1	1	0	0	.000	1	0	0	0	0	0.00

CHAMPIONSHIP SERIES RECORD

Established American League Championship Series record for most games pitched, seven-game Series (4), 1985.
Tied American League Championship Series record for most saves, total Series (2), 1985.

Year Club	League	G.	IP.	W.	L.	Pct.	H.	R.	ER.	SO.	BB.	ERA.
1980—Kansas City	American	2	4⅔	1	0	1.000	4	1	0	1	2	0.00
1984—Kansas City	American	1	3	0	1	.000	2	2	1	1	1	3.00
1985—Kansas City	American	4	4⅔	0	1	.000	7	4	2	3	0	3.86
Championship Series Totals—3 Years		7	12⅓	1	2	.333	13	7	3	5	3	2.19

WORLD SERIES RECORD

Established World Series records for most games pitched in relief, six-game Series (6), 1980; most games finished, six-game Series (6), 1980.

Year Club	League	G.	IP.	W.	L.	Pct.	H.	R.	ER.	SO.	BB.	ERA.
1980—Kansas City	American	6	10⅓	1	2	.333	10	6	6	0	3	5.23
1985—Kansas City	American	4	4⅓	1	0	1.000	5	1	1	3	3	2.08
World Series Totals—2 Years		10	14⅔	2	2	.500	15	7	7	3	6	4.30

ALL-STAR GAME RECORD

Year League		IP.	W.	L.	Pct.	H.	R.	ER.	SO.	BB.	ERA.
1982—American		2	0	0	.000	3	1	1	1	0	4.50
1983—American		1	0	0	.000	1	0	0	1	0	0.00
All-Star Game Totals—2 Years		3	0	0	.000	4	1	1	2	0	3.00

Member of American League All-Star Team in 1984; did not play.

JOHN ANDREW RABB

Born June 23, 1960, at Los Angeles, Calif.
Height, 6.01. Weight, 179.
Throws and bats righthanded.
Attended El Camino Junior College, Torrance, Calif.

Major League stolen bases: 1983 (1), 1984 (1). Total—2.
Led International League in being hit by pitch with 10 in 1985.
Led California League catchers in putouts with 661 and tied for lead in passed balls with 17 in 1980.
Tied for Texas League lead in double plays by catchers with 6 in 1981.

Year Club	League	Pos.	G.	AB.	R.	H.	2B.	3B.	HR.	RBI.	B.A.	PO.	A.	E.	F.A.
1978—Great Falls	Pion.	C-O-3-1	54	184	32	52	5	3	8	32	.283	185	22	6	.972
1979—Cedar Rapids	Midw.	C-OF	125	447	63	118	19	1	19	90	.264	384	50	15	.967
1980—Fresno	Calif.	*C-OF-3B	128	395	69	96	21	2	19	80	.243	*661	70	11	.985
1981—Shreveport	Texas	*C-OF	102	355	51	98	16	2	16	58	.276	533	42	*18	.970
1982—Phoenix	P. C.	C-OF	119	413	66	115	27	2	22	73	.278	552	55	16	.974
1982—San Francisco	Nat.	OF	2	2	0	1	0	1	0	0	.500	1	0	0	1.000
1983—Phoenix	P. C.	C-OF	62	216	50	74	11	1	10	51	.343	291	17	5	.984
1983—San Francisco	Nat.	C-OF	40	104	10	24	9	0	1	14	.231	176	13	5	.974
1984—San Francisco	Nat.	1B-OF-C	54	82	10	16	1	0	3	9	.195	107	7	3	.974
1985—Phoenix†	P. C.	OF	6	22	3	7	1	0	0	0	.318	13	0	1	.929
1985—Richmond	Int.	O-C-3-1	111	369	55	93	12	5	21	62	.252	151	5	5	.969
1985—Atlanta	Nat.	OF	3	2	0	0	0	0	0	0	.000	0	0	0	.000
Major League Totals—4 Years			99	190	20	41	10	1	4	23	.216	284	20	8	.974

Selected by San Francisco Giants' organization in 11th round of free-agent draft, June 6, 1978.
†Traded to Atlanta Braves' organization for Catcher Alex Trevino, April 17, 1985.

TIMOTHY RAINES

(Tim)

Born September 16, 1959, at Sanford, Fla.
Height, 5.08. Weight, 170.
Throws right and bats left and righthanded.
Brother of Ned Raines, minor league outfielder, 1978 through 1980.

Established major league record for highest stolen base percentage, lifetime, 300 or more attempts (.867).
Tied major league record for fewest double plays by outfielder, season, for leader in double plays (4), 1985.
Major League stolen bases: 1979 (2), 1980 (5), 1981 (71), 1982 (78), 1983 (90), 1984 (75), 1985 (70). Total—391.
Led National League in stolen bases with 71 in 1981, 78 in 1982, 90 in 1983 and 75 in 1984.
Led National League outfielders in assists with 21 in 1983.
Led American Association in stolen bases with 77 in 1980.
Won THE SPORTING NEWS Gold Shoe Award, 1984.
Named outfielder on THE SPORTING NEWS National League All-Star Team, 1983.
Named National League Rookie Player of the Year by THE SPORTING NEWS, 1981.
Named Minor League Player of the Year by THE SPORTING NEWS, 1980.

Year Club	League	Pos.	G.	AB.	R.	H.	2B.	3B.	HR.	RBI.	B.A.	PO.	A.	E.	F.A.
1977—Sarasota Expos	Gulf C.	2B-3B-OF	49	161	28	45	6	2	0	21	.280	79	72	13	.921
1978—W. Palm Beach†	Fla. St.	2B-SS	100	359	67	103	10	0	0	23	.287	219	273	24	.953
1979—Memphis	South.	2B	●145	552	●104	160	25	10	5	50	.290	*341	*413	*23	.970
1979—Montreal	Nat.	PR	6	0	3	0	0	0	0	0	.000	0	0	0	.000
1980—Denver	A. A.	2B	108	429	105	152	23	●11	6	64	*.354	226	338	16	.972
1980—Montreal	Nat.	2B-OF	15	20	5	1	0	0	0	0	.050	15	16	0	1.000
1981—Montreal	Nat.	OF-2B	88	313	61	95	13	7	5	37	.304	162	8	4	.977
1982—Montreal	Nat.	OF-2B	156	647	90	179	32	8	4	43	.277	293	126	8	.981
1983—Montreal	Nat.	OF-2B	156	615	●133	183	32	8	11	71	.298	314	23	4	.988
1984—Montreal	Nat.	OF-2B	160	622	106	192	●38	9	8	60	.309	420	8	6	.986
1985—Montreal	Nat.	OF	150	575	115	184	30	13	11	41	.320	284	8	2	.993
Major League Totals—7 Years			731	2792	513	834	145	45	39	252	.299	1488	189	24	.986

Selected by Montreal Expos' organization in 5th round of free-agent draft, June 7, 1977.
†On disabled list, May 23 to June 5, 1978.

CHAMPIONSHIP SERIES RECORD

Year Club	League	Pos.	G.	AB.	R.	H.	2B.	3B.	HR.	RBI.	B.A.	PO.	A.	E.	F.A.
1981—Montreal	Nat.	OF	5	21	1	5	2	0	0	1	.238	9	0	0	1.000

ALL-STAR GAME RECORD

Year League	Pos.	AB.	R.	H.	2B.	3B.	HR.	RBI.	B.A.	PO.	A.	E.	F.A.
1981—National	PR-OF	0	0	0	0	0	0	0	.000	1	0	0	1.000
1982—National	OF	1	0	0	0	0	0	0	.000	0	0	0	.000
1983—National	OF	3	0	0	0	0	0	0	.000	2	0	0	1.000
1984—National	OF	1	0	0	0	0	0	0	.000	4	0	0	1.000
1985—National	PH-OF	0	1	0	0	0	0	0	.000	0	0	0	.000
All-Star Game Totals—5 Years		5	1	0	0	0	0	0	.000	7	0	0	1.000

—DID YOU KNOW—

That on April 29, 1985, Texas outfielder Larry Parrish became the third player in baseball history to hit three consecutive homers in one game in both leagues? His other consecutive three-homer game came May 29, 1977, with the Expos.

GARY LOUIS RAJSICH
Name pronounced RAY-sich.

Born October 28, 1954, at Youngstown, O.
Height, 6.02. Weight, 190.
Throws and bats lefthanded.
Attended Arizona State University, Tempe, Ariz.
Brother of Dave Rajsich, pitcher with New York Yankees and Texas Rangers, 1978 through 1980; and Tim Rajsich, minor league shortstop, 1971 and 1972.
Major League stolen bases: 1982 (1).
Led American Association in slugging percentage with .575 and intentional bases on balls received with 9 in 1984.
Tied for International League lead in being hit by pitch with 9 in 1983.
Led Florida State League first basemen in double plays with 115 in 1977.
Led Appalachian League first basemen in double plays with 58 in 1976.

Year Club	League	Pos.	G.	AB.	R.	H.	2B.	3B.	HR.	RBI.	B.A.	PO.	A.	E.	F.A.
1976—Covington	Appal.	1B	66	244	33	54	8	3	6	27	.221	*649	*75	*14	.981
1977—Cocoa	Fla. St.	*1B-OF	136	486	50	119	19	5	8	53	.245	1153	*119	25	.981
1978—Columbus	South.	OF-1B	80	286	37	69	12	5	7	34	.241	359	28	2	.995
1978—Charleston	Int.	OF	46	126	19	29	4	1	2	13	.230	74	3	1	.987
1979—Columbus	South.	OF-2B	66	232	43	68	25	4	14	53	.293	105	7	4	.966
1979—Charleston	Int.	OF	65	218	27	45	8	2	6	28	.206	114	1	4	.966
1980—Tucson†	P. C.	OF	134	445	94	143	22	14	21	99	.321	205	10	1	.995
1981—Tidewater‡	Int.	OF-1B	74	253	47	70	11	1	24	56	.277	188	13	4	.980
1982—New York	Nat.	OF-1B	80	162	17	42	8	3	2	12	.259	70	1	0	1.000
1983—Tidewater	Int	*1B-OF	120	430	00	110	15	2	28	83	.270	927	*120	10	*.991
1983—New York§	Nat.	1B	11	36	5	12	3	0	1	3	.333	94	6	0	1.000
1984—Louisville	A. A.	1B	117	416	71	119	29	2	29	95	.286	965	93	8	.992
1984—St. Louis a	Nat.	1B	7	7	1	1	0	0	0	2	.143	13	0	0	1.000
1985—San Francisco	Nat.	1B	51	91	5	15	6	0	0	10	.165	185	11	2	.990
1985—Phoenix bc	P. C.	1B-OF	10	40	8	15	3	1	3	12	.375	35	4	0	1.000
1985—Louisville d	A. A.	1B	49	173	27	42	3	1	10	37	.243	401	43	5	.989
Major League Totals—4 Years			149	296	28	70	17	3	3	27	.236	362	18	2	.995

Selected by Houston Astros' organization in 11th round of free-agent draft, June 8, 1976.
†Traded to New York Mets' organization for Outfielder John Csefalvay, April 3, 1981.
‡On disabled list, July 16, 1981 through remainder of season.
§Sold to Louisville (St. Louis Cardinals' organization), April 5, 1984.
aTraded with First Baseman David Green, Pitcher Dave LaPoint and Shortstop Jose Gonzalez (Jose Uribe) to San Francisco Giants for Outfielder-First Baseman Jack Clark, February 1, 1985.
bLoaned to Louisville (St. Louis Cardinals' organization), July 16, 1985; returned, July 22, 1985.
cSold to Louisville (St. Louis Cardinals), July 22, 1985.
dSold to Chunichi Dragons of Japanese baseball, December 6, 1985.

ROBERT CHAUNCEY RALSTON
(Bob)

Born July 9, 1962, at Santa Cruz, Calif.
Height, 5.10. Weight, 165.
Throws and bats righthanded.
Attended Chabot College, Hayward, Calif., and University of Arizona, Tucson, Ariz.
Led Southern League shortstops in errors with 35 in 1985.

Year Club	League	Pos.	G.	AB.	R.	H.	2B.	3B.	HR.	RBI.	B.A.	PO.	A.	E.	F.A.
1984—Orlando	South.	3B-2B-SS	82	298	38	82	4	3	0	24	.275	73	192	15	.946
1985—Orlando	South.	SS-2B-3B	126	419	66	126	11	1	0	28	.301	206	357	40	.934

Selected by Kansas City Royals' organization in 1st round (ninth player selected) of free-agent draft, January 12, 1982.
Selected by San Francisco Giants' organization in 17th round of free-agent draft, June 6, 1983.
Selected by Minnesota Twins' organization in 6th round of free-agent draft, June 4, 1984.

MARIO RAMIREZ (TORRES)

Born September 12, 1957, at Yauco, Puerto Rico.
Height, 5.09. Weight, 155.
Throws and bats righthanded.
Led International League shortstops in fielding percentage with .983 in 1979.

Year Club	League	Pos.	G.	AB.	R.	H.	2B.	3B.	HR.	RBI.	B.A.	PO.	A.	E.	F.A.
1976—Wausau	Midw.	SS	89	287	48	66	16	1	2	28	.230	145	253	46	.896
1977—Lynchburg	Carol.	SS	72	272	41	62	11	3	8	36	.228	123	186	19	.942
1977—Jackson	Texas	SS	60	206	23	52	5	1	6	21	.252	110	170	14	.952
1978—Tidewater	Int.	SS	126	389	43	81	14	4	5	41	.208	176	382	*46	.924
1979—Tidewater	Int.	SS-2B	132	376	42	82	10	2	6	31	.218	190	432	9	.986
1980—New York	Nat.	SS-2B-3B	18	24	2	5	0	0	0	0	.208	13	21	0	1.000
1980—Tidewater†	Int.	SS-2B-OF	71	208	17	42	7	2	0	15	.202	129	173	17	.947
1981—Hawaii	P. C.	SS	118	411	51	103	13	7	5	49	.251	192	390	18	.970
1981—San Diego	Nat.	SS-2B	13	13	1	1	0	0	0	1	.077	5	11	0	1.000
1982—San Diego	Nat.	SS-3B-2B	13	23	1	4	1	0	0	1	.174	10	21	1	.969
1982—Hawaii	P. C.	SS	22	70	14	18	6	0	1	9	.257	29	64	5	.949
1983—Las Vegas	P. C.	SS	16	54	7	12	2	2	1	8	.222	25	46	1	.986
1983—San Diego	Nat.	SS-3B	55	107	11	21	6	3	0	12	.196	50	86	2	.986
1984—San Diego	Nat.	SS-3B-2B	48	59	12	7	1	0	2	9	.119	34	45	3	.963

Year	Club	League	Pos.	G.	AB.	R.	H.	2B.	3B.	HR.	RBI.	B.A.	PO.	A.	E.	F.A.
1985—San Diego	Nat.		SS-2B	37	60	6	17	0	0	2	5	.283	25	38	5	.926
1985—Las Vegas	P. C.		SS	13	47	6	13	4	2	0	6	.277	16	20	2	.947
Major League Totals—6 Years				184	286	33	55	8	3	4	28	.192	137	222	11	.970

Signed as free agent by New York Mets' organization, March 5, 1976.
†Drafted by San Diego Padres, December 8, 1980.

CHAMPIONSHIP SERIES RECORD

Year	Club	League	Pos.	G.	AB.	R.	H.	2B.	3B.	HR.	RBI.	B.A.	PO.	A.	E.	F.A.
1984—San Diego	Nat.		PH	2	2	0	0	0	0	0	0	.000	0	0	0	.000

RAFAEL EMILIO RAMIREZ (PEGUERO)

Born February 18, 1959, at San Pedro de Macoris, Dominican Republic.
Height, 6.00. Weight, 170.
Throws and bats righthanded.

Tied major league record for most double plays by shortstop, extra-inning game (6), June 27, 1982 (14 innings).
Established National League record for fewest putouts by shortstop, season, for leader in most putouts (251), 1984.
Major League stolen bases: 1980 (2), 1981 (7), 1982 (27), 1983 (16), 1984 (14), 1985 (2). Total—68.
Led National League shortstops in double plays with 130 in 1982, 116 in 1983, 115 in 1985 and tied for lead with 94 in 1984.
Led National League shortstops in total chances with 866 in 1982 and 724 in 1984.

Year	Club	League	Pos.	G.	AB.	R.	H.	2B.	3B.	HR.	RBI.	B.A.	PO.	A.	E.	F.A.
1977—Brad. Braves	Gulf C.		SS-OF	49	175	20	31	2	1	4	19	.177	52	94	32	.820
1978—Greenwood	W. Car.		SS	81	282	54	77	15	3	6	46	.273	119	229	★43	.890
1978—Savannah	South.		SS	38	131	14	27	4	0	2	13	.206	61	123	15	.925
1979—Savannah†	South.		SS	113	386	47	80	17	3	10	39	.207	134	282	★38	.916
1980—Richmond‡	Int.		SS	80	281	33	79	15	3	5	38	.281	117	294	23	.947
1980—Atlanta	Nat.		SS	50	165	17	44	6	1	2	11	.267	63	140	11	.949
1981—Atlanta	Nat.		SS	95	307	30	67	16	2	2	20	.218	181	306	★30	.942
1982—Atlanta	Nat.		SS	157	609	74	169	24	4	10	52	.278	★300	528	★38	.956
1983—Atlanta	Nat.		SS	152	622	82	185	13	5	7	58	.297	232	490	★39	.949
1984—Atlanta	Nat.		SS	145	591	51	157	22	4	2	48	.266	★251	443	●30	.959
1985—Atlanta	Nat.		SS	138	568	54	141	25	4	5	58	.248	214	451	★32	.954
Major League Totals—6 Years				737	2862	308	763	106	20	28	247	.267	1241	2358	180	.952

Signed as free agent by Atlanta Braves' organization, September 28, 1976.
†On disabled list, April 16 to April 27, 1979.
‡On disabled list, June 23 to July 17, 1980.

CHAMPIONSHIP SERIES RECORD

Year	Club	League	Pos.	G.	AB.	R.	H.	2B.	3B.	HR.	RBI.	B.A.	PO.	A.	E.	F.A.
1982—Atlanta	Nat.		SS	3	11	1	2	0	0	0	1	.182	5	11	1	.941

ALL-STAR GAME RECORD

Member of National League All-Star Team in 1984; did not play.

DOMINGO ANTONIO RAMOS

Born March 29, 1958, at Santiago, Dominican Republic.
Height, 5.10. Weight, 154.
Throws and bats righthanded.

Major League stolen bases: 1983 (3), 1984 (2). Total—5.
Tied for International League lead in sacrifice flies with 6 in 1981.

Year	Club	League	Pos.	G.	AB.	R.	H.	2B.	3B.	HR.	RBI.	B.A.	PO.	A.	E.	F.A.
1975—Oneonta	NYP		SS-3B	49	166	29	39	4	1	0	21	.235	60	143	14	.935
1976—Fort Lauderdale	Fla. St.		SS	103	328	34	79	11	3	0	29	.241	150	343	35	.934
1976—Syracuse	Int.		SS	11	39	7	10	2	1	0	8	.256	13	20	2	.943
1977—West Haven	East.		SS	129	431	55	106	18	6	2	50	.246	222	433	23	★.966
1978—Tacoma	P. C.		SS	91	314	43	74	13	3	0	30	.236	155	290	28	.941
1978—West Haven	East.		SS	40	134	16	34	2	2	1	13	.254	40	128	6	.966
1978—New York†‡	Amer.		SS	1	0	0	0	0	0	0	0	.000	0	0	0	.000
1979—Syr.§-Colum. x	Int.		SS	115	376	38	92	11	4	1	28	.245	211	323	26	.954
1980—Syracuse	Int.		SS	84	319	45	80	8	4	4	27	.251	160	240	28	.935
1980—Toronto	Amer.		SS-2B	5	16	0	2	0	0	0	0	.125	5	10	0	1.000
1981—Syracuse y	Int.		SS-3B-2B	96	320	42	82	4	5	0	31	.256	158	248	19	.955
1982—Salt Lake City	P. C.		SS	112	427	75	134	19	8	6	56	.314	174	288	19	.960
1982—Seattle	Amer.		SS	8	26	3	4	2	0	0	1	.154	9	14	2	.920
1983—Seattle	Amer.		2B-SS-3B	53	127	14	36	4	0	2	10	.283	51	109	8	.952
1984—Seattle	Amer.		3-S-1-2	59	81	6	15	2	0	0	2	.185	51	49	5	.952
1985—Seattle	Amer.		S-2-1-3	75	168	19	33	6	0	1	15	.196	87	119	10	.954
Major League Totals—6 Years				201	418	42	90	14	0	3	28	.215	203	301	25	.953

Signed as free agent by New York Yankees' organization, May 27, 1975.
†Traded with Pitchers Sparky Lyle, Larry McCall and Dave Rajsich, Catcher Mike Heath and cash to Texas Rangers for Outfielders Juan Beniquez and Greg Jemison and Pitchers Mike Griffin, Paul Mirabella and Dave Righetti, November 10, 1978.
‡Loaned to Toronto Blue Jays' organization, April 5, 1979.
§Loaned to New York Yankees' organization, July 30, 1979; returned to Texas Rangers, September 28, 1979.
xSold to Toronto Blue Jays, November 5, 1979.
yDrafted by Seattle Mariners, December 7, 1981.

MICHAEL JEFFREY RAMSEY
(Mike)

Born March 29, 1954, at Roanoke, Va.
Height, 6.01. Weight, 170.
Throws right and bats left and righthanded.
Attended Appalachian State University, Boone, N.C.

Major League stolen bases: 1981 (4), 1982 (6), 1983 (4). Total—14.
Led Appalachian League in sacrifice hits with 12 in 1975.
Led Appalachian League shortstops in fielding percentage with .937 in 1975.

Year	Club	League	Pos.	G.	AB.	R.	H.	2B.	3B.	HR.	RBI.	B.A.	PO.	A.	E.	F.A.
1975—Johnson City	Appal.		SS-2B	65	*277	43	79	14	1	0	25	.285	98	183	17	.943
1976—Arkansas†	Texas		SS	84	288	26	79	6	1	0	24	.274	109	231	32	.914
1977—Arkansas	Texas		SS	121	484	51	121	21	4	1	28	.250	166	317	*44	.917
1978—Springfield‡	A. A.		SS	99	382	53	92	8	4	2	30	.241	172	223	*41	.906
1978—St. Louis	Nat.		SS	12	5	4	1	0	0	0	0	.200	4	6	1	.909
1979—Springfield	A. A.		SS	97	281	28	62	9	3	1	27	.221	134	198	24	.933
1980—Springfield	A. A.		SS-OF	21	69	7	18	1	0	0	6	.261	34	47	6	.931
1980—St. Louis	Nat.		2B-3B-SS	59	126	11	33	8	1	0	8	.262	62	94	9	.945
1981—St. Louis§	Nat.		S-3-2-O	47	124	19	32	3	0	0	9	.258	56	126	6	.968
1982—St. Louis	Nat.		2-3-S-O	112	256	18	59	8	2	1	21	.230	135	219	10	.973
1983—St. Louis x	Nat.		2-S-3-O	97	175	25	46	4	3	1	16	.263	94	149	8	.968
1984—St. L.y-Mon. z	Nat.		SS-2B-3B	58	85	3	16	2	0	0	3	.188	44	79	3	.976
1985—Los Angeles a	Nat.		SS-2B	9	15	1	2	1	0	0	0	.133	5	11	3	.880
1985—Charlotte b	South.		2B-3B-SS	6	14	2	2	1	0	0	1	.143	4	7	0	1.000
Major League Totals—7 Years				394	786	81	189	26	6	2	57	.240	400	684	39	.965

Selected by Chicago Cubs' organization in 26th round of free-agent draft, June 6, 1972.
Selected by St. Louis Cardinals' organization in 3rd round of free-agent draft, June 4, 1975.
†On disabled list, July 17 to September 7, 1976.
‡On disabled list, May 13 to May 25, 1978.
§On disabled list, June 5 to August 5, 1981.
xOn disabled list, June 14 to June 29, 1983.
yTraded to Montreal Expos for Shortstop Chris Speier and cash, July 1, 1984.
zReleased, April 6, 1985; signed by Los Angeles Dodgers, April 30, 1985.
aReleased, June 2, 1985; signed by Charlotte (Baltimore Orioles' organization), July 8, 1985.
bOn disabled list, July 9 to August 9, 1985.

WORLD SERIES RECORD

Year	Club	League	Pos.	G.	AB.	R.	H.	2B.	3B.	HR.	RBI.	B.A.	PO.	A.	E.	F.A.
1982—St. Louis	Nat.		3B-PR	3	1	1	0	0	0	0	0	.000	0	0	0	.000

WILLIAM LARRY RANDOLPH JR.
(Willie)

Born July 6, 1954, at Holly Hill, S. C.
Height, 5.11. Weight, 163.
Throws and bats righthanded.
Brother of Terry Randolph, defensive back with Green Bay Packers, 1977.

Tied major league record for most assists by second baseman in extra-inning game since 1900 (13), August 25, 1976 (19 innings).
Established American League record for most chances accepted by second baseman in extra-inning game (20), August 25, 1976 (19 innings).
Major League stolen bases: 1975 (1), 1976 (37), 1977 (13), 1978 (36), 1979 (33), 1980 (30), 1981 (14), 1982 (16), 1983 (12), 1984 (10), 1985 (16). Total—218.
Led American League in bases on balls received with 119 in 1980.
Led American League second basemen in double plays with 128 in 1979 and 112 in 1984.
Led American League second basemen in total chances with 846 in 1979.
Led Eastern League in bases on balls received with 110 in 1974.
Led Western Carolinas League in bases on balls received with 90 and tied for lead in sacrifice flies with 8 in 1973.
Named second baseman on THE SPORTING NEWS American League All-Star Team, 1977 and 1980.
Named second baseman on THE SPORTING NEWS American League Silver Slugger team, 1980.

Year	Club	League	Pos.	G.	AB.	R.	H.	2B.	3B.	HR.	RBI.	B.A.	PO.	A.	E.	F.A.
1972—Bradenton Pir.	Gulf C.		SS-OF	44	167	21	53	6	5	0	10	.317	85	116	24	.893
1973—Charleston	W. Car.		2B	121	428	93	120	25	6	8	51	.280	*285	308	*24	.961
1974—Thetford Mines	East.		2B	135	461	*103	117	28	6	12	53	.254	269	319	21	.966
1975—Charleston	Int.		2B	91	313	41	106	13	5	7	42	.339	189	250	16	.965
1975—Pittsburgh†	Nat.		2B-3B	30	61	9	10	1	0	0	3	.164	34	45	6	.929
1976—New York	Amer.		2B	125	430	59	115	15	4	1	40	.267	307	415	19	.974
1977—New York	Amer.		2B	147	551	91	151	28	11	4	40	.274	350	454	16	.980
1978—New York‡	Amer.		2B	134	499	87	139	18	6	3	42	.279	296	400	16	.978
1979—New York	Amer.		2B	153	574	98	155	15	13	5	61	.270	*355	*478	13	.985
1980—New York	Amer.		2B	138	513	99	151	23	7	7	46	.294	361	401	19	.976
1981—New York	Amer.		2B	93	357	59	83	14	3	2	24	.232	205	268	*11	.977
1982—New York	Amer.		2B	144	553	85	155	21	4	3	36	.280	352	380	14	.981
1983—New York§	Amer.		2B	104	420	73	117	21	1	2	38	.279	265	298	12	.979
1984—New York	Amer.		2B	142	564	86	162	24	2	2	31	.287	334	419	13	.983
1985—New York	Amer.		2B	143	497	75	137	21	2	5	40	.276	303	425	11	.985
National League Totals—1 Year				30	61	9	10	1	0	0	3	.164	34	45	6	.929
American League Totals—10 Years				1323	4958	812	1365	200	53	34	398	.275	3128	3938	144	.980
Major League Totals—11 Years				1353	5019	821	1375	201	53	34	401	.274	3162	3983	150	.979

Selected by Pittsburgh Pirates' organization in 7th round of free-agent draft, June 6, 1972.
†Traded with Pitchers Ken Brett and Dock Ellis to New York Yankees for Pitcher Doc Medich, December 11, 1975.
‡On disabled list, June 23 to July 14, 1978.
§On disabled list, June 27 to July 12 and July 13 to August 5, 1983.

DIVISION SERIES RECORD

Year Club	League	Pos.	G.	AB.	R.	H.	2B.	3B.	HR.	RBI.	B.A.	PO.	A.	E.	F.A.
1981—New York..............	Amer.	2B	5	20	0	4	0	0	0	1	.200	7	10	0	1.000

CHAMPIONSHIP SERIES RECORD

Year Club	League	Pos.	G.	AB.	R.	H.	2B.	3B.	HR.	RBI.	B.A.	PO.	A.	E.	F.A.
1975—Pittsburgh	Nat.	PH-PR-2	2	2	1	0	0	0	0	0	.000	0	1	0	1.000
1976—New York..............	Amer.	2B	5	17	0	2	0	0	0	1	.118	8	14	0	1.000
1977—New York..............	Amer.	2B	5	18	4	5	1	0	0	2	.278	13	9	0	1.000
1980—New York..............	Amer.	2B	3	13	0	5	2	0	0	1	.385	2	9	0	1.000
1981—New York..............	Amer.	2B	3	12	2	4	0	0	1	2	.333	12	12	0	1.000
Championship Series Totals—5 Years....			18	62	7	16	3	0	1	6	.258	35	45	0	1.000

WORLD SERIES RECORD

Established World Series record for most bases on balls, six-game Series (9), 1981.
Tied World Series record for fewest chances accepted by second baseman, game (0), October 25, 1981.

Year Club	League	Pos.	G.	AB.	R.	H.	2B.	3B.	HR.	RBI.	B.A.	PO.	A.	E.	F.A.
1976—New York..............	Amer.	2B	4	14	1	1	0	0	0	0	.071	13	8	0	1.000
1977—New York..............	Amer.	2B	6	25	5	4	2	0	1	1	.160	13	14	0	1.000
1981—New York..............	Amer.	2B	6	18	5	4	1	1	2	3	.222	13	11	0	1.000
World Series Totals—3 Years			16	57	11	9	3	1	3	4	.158	39	33	0	1.000

ALL-STAR GAME RECORD

Established All-Star Game record for most assists by second baseman, nine-inning game (6), July 19, 1977.
Tied All-Star Game records for most at bats, nine-inning game (5), July 19, 1977; most errors, game (2), July 8, 1980.

Year League	Pos.	AB.	R.	H.	2B.	3B.	HR.	RBI.	B.A.	PO.	A.	E.	F.A.
1977—American..	2B	5	0	1	0	0	0	1	.200	2	6	0	1.000
1980—American	2B	4	0	2	0	0	0	0	.500	0	3	2	.600
1981—American	2B	3	0	1	0	0	0	0	.333	0	5	0	1.000
All-Star Game Totals—3 Years....................		12	0	4	0	0	0	1	.333	2	14	2	.888

Named to American League All-Star Team for 1976 game; replaced due to injury.

DENNIS LEE RASMUSSEN

Born April 18, 1959, at Los Angeles, Calif.
Height, 6.07. Weight, 225.
Throws and bats lefthanded.
Attended Creighton University, Omaha, Neb.
Grandson of Wilbur Lee (Bill) Brubaker, infielder with Pittsburgh
Pirates and Boston Braves, 1932 through 1940 and 1943.

Led Eastern League in wild pitches with 18 in 1981.
Tied for International League lead in games started by pitchers with 28 in 1983.

Year Club	League	G.	IP.	W.	L.	Pct.	H.	R.	ER.	SO.	BB.	ERA.
1980—Salinas...	California	11	76	4	6	.400	69	51	46	63	52	5.45
1981—Holyoke..	Eastern	24	156	8	12	.400	134	95	69	125	99	3.98
1982—Spokane†	P. Coast	27	171⅔	11	8	.579	166	110	96	162	★113	5.03
1983—Columbus‡..	Int'national	28	181	●13	10	.565	161	106	92	★187	108	4.57
1983—San Diego§	National	4	13⅔	0	0	.000	10	5	3	13	8	1.98
1984—Columbus	Int'national	6	43⅔	4	1	.800	24	15	15	30	27	3.09
1984—New York..	American	24	147⅔	9	6	.600	127	79	75	110	60	4.57
1985—New York..	American	22	101⅔	3	5	.375	97	56	45	63	42	3.98
1985—Columbus	Int'national	7	45	0	3	.000	41	24	19	43	25	3.80
National League Totals—1 Year		4	13⅔	0	0	.000	10	5	3	13	8	1.98
American League Totals—2 Years		46	249⅓	12	11	.522	224	135	120	173	102	4.33
Major League Totals—3 Years.............................		50	263	12	11	.522	234	140	123	186	110	4.21

Selected by Pittsburgh Pirates' organization in 18th round of free-agent draft, June 7, 1977.
Selected by California Angels' organization in 1st round (17th player selected) of free-agent draft, June 3, 1980.
†Traded to New York Yankees, November 24, 1982, completing deal in which New York traded Pitcher Tommy John to California Angels for a player to be named later, August 31, 1982.
‡Traded with Second Baseman Edwin Rodriguez to San Diego Padres, September 12, 1983, completing deal in which San Diego traded Pitcher John Montefusco to New York Yankees for two players to be named later, August 26, 1983.
§Traded with a player to be named later to New York Yankees' organization for Third Baseman Graig Nettles, March 30, 1984; New York organization acquired Pitcher Darin Cloninger to complete deal, April 26, 1984.

DODY EUGENE RATHER

Born August 13, 1964, at Houston, Tex.
Height, 6.00. Weight, 180.
Throws and bats righthanded.
Attended San Jacinto College (North), Houston, Tex.

Pitched 6-0 no-hit victory against Watertown, July 24, 1985.

Year Club	League	G.	IP.	W.	L.	Pct.	H.	R.	ER.	SO.	BB.	ERA.
1984—Oneonta	NYP	13	38	0	4	.000	34	29	25	59	35	5.92
1985—Oneonta	NYP	8	58	8	0	1.000	22	5	2	88	16	0.31
1985—Fort Lauderdale†	Florida St.	6	36⅓	2	3	.400	31	17	14	35	20	3.47

Selected by New York Yankees' organization in 4th round of free-agent draft, January 17, 1984.

Selected by New York Yankees' organization in secondary phase of free-agent draft, June 4, 1984.

†Traded to Houston Astros, January 11, 1986, completing deal in which Houston traded Pitcher Joe Niekro to New York Yankees for Pitcher Jim Deshaies and two players to be named later, September 15, 1985; New York organization acquired Infielder Neder Horta as partial completion of deal, September 24, 1985.

SHANE WILLIAM RAWLEY

Born July 27, 1955, at Racine, Wis.
Height, 6.00. Weight, 155.
Throws and bats lefthanded.
Attended Indian Hills Community College, Centerville, Ia.

Major League saves: 1978 (4), 1979 (11), 1980 (13), 1981 (8), 1982 (3), 1983 (1). Total—40.

Led American League in intentional bases on balls issued with 16 in 1980.

Year Club	League	G.	IP.	W.	L.	Pct.	H.	R.	ER.	SO.	BB.	ERA.
1974—Sarasota Expos	Gulf Coast	2	12	0	1	.000	12	9	3	16	4	2.25
1974—Kinston	Carolina	5	19	0	2	.000	22	15	13	11	12	6.16
1975—West Palm Beach	Florida St.	24	165	8	12	.400	148	80	56	113	73	3.05
1976—Quebec City	Eastern	25	164	11	7	.611	143	55	49	113	70	2.60
1977—Denver†-Indianapolis‡§	Am. Assoc.	26	152	6	10	.375	150	89	80	92	68	4.74
1978—Seattle	American	52	111	4	9	.308	114	57	51	66	51	4.14
1979—Seattle x	American	48	84	5	9	.357	88	40	36	48	40	3.86
1980—Seattle	American	59	114	7	7	.500	103	44	42	68	63	3.32
1981—Spokane	P. Coast	3	6	0	0	.000	3	0	0	3	3	0.00
1981—Seattle yz	American	46	68	4	6	.400	64	31	30	35	38	3.97
1982—New York	American	47	164	11	10	.524	165	79	74	111	54	4.06
1983—New York	American	34	238⅓	14	14	.500	246	111	100	124	79	3.78
1984—New York ab	American	11	42	2	3	.400	46	33	29	24	27	6.21
1984—Philadelphia	National	18	120⅓	10	6	.625	117	55	51	58	27	3.81
1985—Philadelphia	National	36	198⅔	13	8	.619	188	82	73	106	81	3.31
American League Totals—7 Years		297	821⅓	47	58	.448	826	395	362	476	352	3.97
National League Totals—2 Years		54	319	23	14	.622	305	137	124	164	108	3.50
Major League Totals—8 Years		351	1140⅓	70	72	.493	1131	532	486	640	460	3.84

Selected by Los Angeles Dodgers' organization in 4th round of free-agent draft, January 9, 1974.

Selected by Montreal Expos' organization in secondary phase of free-agent draft, June 5, 1974.

†Traded with Pitcher Angel Torres to Cincinnati Reds' organization, May 27, 1977, completing deal in which Cincinnati traded Pitcher Santo Alcala to Montreal Expos for two players to be named later, May 21, 1977.

‡Appeared with Indianapolis in one game as an outfielder with no chances.

§Traded to Seattle Mariners for Outfielder Dave Collins, December 9, 1977.

xOn disabled list, June 30 to August 21, 1979.

yOn disabled list, April 1 to April 24, 1981; included rehabilitation disability assignment to Spokane, April 16 to April 24, 1981.

zTraded to New York Yankees for Pitchers Gene Nelson and Bill Caudill, a player to be named later and cash, April 1, 1982; Seattle Mariners' organization acquired Outfielder Bobby Brown to complete deal, April 6, 1982.

aOn disabled list, May 20 to June 4, 1984.

bTraded to Philadelphia Phillies for Pitcher Marty Bystrom and Outfielder Keith Hughes, June 30, 1984.

JOHNNY CORNELIUS RAY

Born March 1, 1957, at Chouteau, Okla.
Height, 5.11. Weight, 175.
Throws right and bats right and lefthanded.
Attended Northeastern Oklahoma A & M, Miami, Okla.; and
University of Arkansas, Fayetteville, Ark.

Major League stolen bases: 1982 (16), 1983 (18), 1984 (11), 1985 (13). Total—58.

Led National League second basemen in total chances with 914 in 1982.

Named National League Rookie Player of the Year by THE SPORTING NEWS, 1982.

Named second baseman on THE SPORTING NEWS National League Silver Slugger team, 1983.

Year Club	League	Pos.	G.	AB.	R.	H.	2B.	3B.	HR.	RBI.	B.A.	PO.	A.	E.	F.A.
1979—Sarasota Astros	Gulf C.	3B-2B	37	132	25	41	8	1	3	25	.311	25	51	11	.874
1979—Daytona Beach	Fla. St.	3B-SS-2B	24	68	6	15	1	2	1	10	.221	21	38	8	.881
1980—Columbus	South.	2B-3B-OF	138	497	86	161	32	6	10	72	.324	203	331	24	.957
1981—Tucson†	P. C.	2B	131	525	111	183	★50	10	5	83	.349	309	369	19	.973
1981—Pittsburgh	Nat.	2B	31	102	10	25	11	0	0	6	.245	52	96	2	.987
1982—Pittsburgh	Nat.	2B	●162	647	79	182	30	7	7	63	.281	★381	★512	★21	.977
1983—Pittsburgh	Nat.	2B	151	576	68	163	●38	7	5	53	.283	319	452	13	.983
1984—Pittsburgh	Nat.	2B	155	555	75	173	●38	6	6	67	.312	331	400	12	.984
1985—Pittsburgh	Nat.	2B	154	594	67	163	33	3	7	70	.274	305	423	18	.976
Major League Totals—5 Years			653	2474	299	706	150	23	25	259	.285	1388	1883	66	.980

Selected by Houston Astros' organization in 12th round of free-agent draft, June 5, 1979.

†Traded with two players to be named later to Pittsburgh Pirates for Second Baseman Phil Garner, August 31, 1981; Pittsburgh organization acquired Pitcher Randy Niemann and Outfielder Kevin Houston to complete deal, September 9, 1981.

FLOYD KINNARD RAYFORD

Born July 27, 1957, at Memphis, Tenn.
Height, 5.10. Weight, 195.
Throws and bats righthanded.

Major League stolen bases: 1983 (1), 1985 (3). Total—4.
Led International League third basemen in fielding percentage with .942 in 1980.
Led Texas League third basemen in putouts with 95 and in assists with 216 in 1978.
Led California League third basemen in assists with 202, double plays with 21 and fielding percentage with .944 in 1976.
Tied for California League lead in double plays by third basemen with 21 in 1977.

Year	Club	League	Pos.	G.	AB.	R.	H.	2B.	3B.	HR.	RBI.	B.A.	PO.	A.	E.	F.A.
1975—Idaho Falls		Pion.	3-C-1-O-S	●72	272	43	77	12	5	2	43	.283	244	100	21	.942
1976—Salinas		Calif.	3B-C-2B	125	462	73	126	19	6	5	67	.273	162	216	16	.959
1977—Salinas		Calif.	3B	51	205	37	53	7	3	6	39	.259	40	117	7	.957
1977—El Paso		Texas	1-2-3-S-O	79	320	65	95	17	3	11	60	.297	427	133	12	.979
1978—El Paso		Texas	3-2-1-S	126	483	78	151	36	2	17	87	.313	113	230	14	.961
1979—Salt Lake City†		P. C.	★3-S-1-2	135	551	98	162	28	6	13	80	.294	134	316	20	★.957
1980—Rochester		Int.	3B-2B-SS	107	387	51	89	22	0	9	46	.230	86	213	19	.940
1980—Baltimore		Amer.	3B-2B	8	18	1	4	0	0	0	1	.222	3	11	2	.875
1981—Rochester		Int.	3B-C-SS	96	311	50	77	18	2	11	45	.248	208	106	11	.966
1982—Baltimore		Amer.	3B-C	34	53	7	7	0	0	3	5	.132	11	43	6	.900
1982—Rochester		Int.	2B	3	12	1	3	0	0	1	2	.250	2	6	0	1.000
1983—Rochester‡		Int.	2B-C-3B	42	140	24	52	16	1	2	38	.371	54	44	5	.951
1983—St. Louis§		Nat.	3B	56	104	5	22	4	0	3	14	.212	13	40	7	.883
1984—Rochester		Int.	C	7	18	1	1	0	0	1	1	.056	25	5	1	.968
1984—Baltimore		Amer.	C-3B-1B	86	250	24	64	14	0	4	27	.256	310	67	6	.984
1985—Baltimore		Amer.	3B-C	105	359	55	110	21	1	18	48	.306	176	152	7	.979
American League Totals—4 Years				233	680	87	185	35	1	25	81	.272	500	273	21	.974
National League Totals—1 Year				56	104	5	22	4	0	3	14	.212	13	40	7	.883
Major League Totals—5 Years				289	784	92	207	39	1	28	95	.264	513	313	28	.967

Selected by California Angels' organization in 4th round of free-agent draft, June 4, 1975.
†Traded with cash to Baltimore Orioles' organization for Outfielder Larry Harlow, June 5, 1979. (Remained on option to Salt Lake City.)
‡Traded to St. Louis Cardinals for a player to be named later, June 13, 1983; Baltimore Orioles purchased Outfielder Tito Landrum to complete deal, August 31, 1983.
§Sold to Baltimore Orioles' organization, March 30, 1984.

RANDY MAX READY

Born January 8, 1960, at San Mateo, Calif.
Height, 5.11. Weight, 175.
Throws and bats righthanded.
Attended California State University, Hayward,
Calif., and Mesa College, Grand Junction, Colo.

Tied American League record for most innings played by third baseman, game (25), May 8, finished May 9, 1984 (fielded 24⅓ innings).
Led Pacific Coast League in bases on balls received with 99 in 1983.
Led Texas League in total bases with 281 in 1982.
Led Texas League third basemen in double plays with 27 and total chances with 456 in 1982.
Led Midwest League third basemen in double plays with 22 in 1981.

Year	Club	League	Pos.	G.	AB.	R.	H.	2B.	3B.	HR.	RBI.	B.A.	PO.	A.	E.	F.A.
1980—Butte		Pion.	SS-2B-3B	61	226	★65	85	★23	4	8	50	★.376	86	174	22	.922
1981—Burlington		Midw.	3B	110	367	74	113	17	0	17	56	.308	72	216	21	★.932
1982—El Paso		Texas	3B	132	475	★122	★178	33	5	20	99	★.375	★115	★312	●29	.936
1983—Vancouver		P. C.	3B	116	407	82	134	28	1	13	59	.329	136	231	24	.939
1983—Milwaukee		Amer.	3B	12	37	8	15	3	2	1	6	.405	5	8	0	1.000
1984—Milwaukee		Amer.	3B	37	123	13	23	6	1	3	13	.187	29	76	6	.946
1984—Vancouver†		P. C.	2B-3B	43	151	48	49	7	4	3	18	.325	74	125	6	.971
1985—Milwaukee‡		Amer.	OF-3B-2B	48	181	29	48	9	5	1	21	.265	93	14	1	.991
1985—Vancouver		P. C.	OF-3B-2B	52	190	33	62	12	3	4	29	.326	60	35	7	.931
Major League Totals—3 Years				97	341	50	86	18	8	5	40	.252	127	98	7	.970

Selected by Milwaukee Brewers' organization in 5th round of free-agent draft, June 3, 1980.
†On disabled list, August 21, 1984 through remainder of season.
‡On disabled list, April 30 to June 19, 1985; included rehabilitation disability assignment to Vancouver, June 1 to June 19, 1985.

JEFFREY JAMES REARDON
(Jeff)

Born October 1, 1955, at Pittsfield, Mass.
Height, 6.01. Weight, 190.
Throws and bats righthanded.
Attended University of Massachusetts, Amherst, Mass.

Major League saves: 1979 (2), 1980 (6), 1981 (8), 1982 (26), 1983 (21), 1984 (23), 1985 (41). Total—127.
Led National League in saves with 41 in 1985.
Led Carolina League in shutouts with 3 in 1977.
Named National League Fireman of the Year by THE SPORTING NEWS, 1985.

Year Club	League	G.	IP.	W.	L.	Pct.	H.	R.	ER.	SO.	BB.	ERA.
1977—Lynchburg	Carolina	16	101	8	3	.727	89	42	37	60	30	3.30
1978—Jackson	Texas	28	163	*17	4	*.810	128	56	46	115	65	2.53
1979—Tidewater†	Int'national	30	69	5	2	.714	46	18	16	64	21	2.09
1979—New York	National	18	21	1	2	.333	12	7	4	10	9	1.71
1980—New York	National	61	110	8	7	.533	96	36	32	101	47	2.62
1981—New York‡-Montreal	National	43	70	3	0	1.000	48	17	17	49	21	2.19
1982—Montreal	National	75	109	7	4	.636	87	28	25	86	36	2.06
1983—Montreal	National	66	92	7	9	.438	87	34	31	78	44	3.03
1984—Montreal	National	68	87	7	7	.500	70	31	28	79	37	2.90
1985—Montreal	National	63	87⅔	2	8	.200	68	31	31	67	26	3.18
Major League Totals—7 Years		394	576⅔	35	37	.486	468	184	168	470	220	2.62

Selected by Montreal Expos' organization in 23rd round of free-agent draft, June 5, 1973.
Signed as free agent by New York Mets' organization, June 14, 1977.
†On disabled list, June 13 to June 24 and June 29 to July 26, 1979.
‡Traded with Outfielder Dan Norman to Montreal Expos for Outfielder Ellis Valentine, May 29, 1981.

DIVISION SERIES RECORD

Year Club	League	G.	IP.	W.	L.	Pct.	H.	R.	ER.	SO.	BB.	ERA.
1981—Montreal	National	3	4⅓	0	1	.000	1	1	1	2	1	2.08

CHAMPIONSHIP SERIES RECORD

Year Club	League	G.	IP.	W.	L.	Pct.	H.	R.	ER.	SO.	BB.	ERA.
1981—Montreal	National	1	1	0	0	.000	3	3	3	0	0	27.00

ALL-STAR GAME RECORD

Year League		IP.	W.	L.	Pct.	H.	R.	ER.	SO.	BB.	ERA.
1985—National		1	0	0	.000	1	0	0	1	0	0.00

GARY EUGENE REDUS

Name pronounced REE-dus.

Born November 1, 1956, at Athens, Ala.
Height, 6.01. Weight, 180.
Throws and bats righthanded.
Attended Calhoun Junior College, Decatur, Ala., and Athens State College, Athens, Ala.
Brother of Jeff Redus, outfielder in Kansas City Royals' organization, 1984 and 1985.

Major League stolen bases: 1982 (11), 1983 (39), 1984 (48), 1985 (48). Total—146.
Led American Association in stolen bases with 54 and tied for lead in sacrifice flies with 9 in 1982.
Led Florida State League in total bases with 220 in 1980.
Led Pioneer League in total bases with 199, stolen bases with 42 and tied for lead in sacrifice flies with 6 in 1978.
Tied for Western Carolinas League lead in errors by second basemen with 20 in 1979.
Named Pioneer League Player of the Year, 1978.

Year Club	League	Pos.	G.	AB.	R.	H.	2B.	3B.	HR.	RBI.	B.A.	PO.	A.	E.	F.A.
1978—Billings	Pion.	2B	68	253	*100	*117	19	6	17	62	*.462	124	*185	*28	.917
1979—Nashville	South.	OF	36	109	7	19	2	1	0	7	.174	74	3	3	.963
1979—Greensboro	W. Car.	2B-OF	83	309	79	86	17	1	16	52	.278	172	193	21	.946
1980—Tampa	Fla. St.	OF-3B-1B	128	452	78	136	18	9	16	68	.301	213	84	27	.917
1981—Waterbury	East.	OF-1B	138	477	71	119	26	4	20	75	.249	667	34	14	.980
1982—Indianapolis	A. A.	OF	122	439	112	146	29	9	24	93	.333	223	10	7	.971
1982—Cincinnati	Nat.	OF	20	83	12	18	3	2	1	7	.217	29	3	1	.970
1983—Cincinnati	Nat.	OF	125	453	90	112	20	9	17	51	.247	235	11	7	.972
1984—Cincinnati	Nat.	OF	123	394	69	100	21	3	7	22	.254	200	6	7	.967
1985—Cincinnati†	Nat.	OF	101	246	51	62	14	4	6	28	.252	140	3	2	.986
Major League Totals—4 Years			369	1176	222	292	58	18	31	108	.248	604	23	17	.974

Selected by Boston Red Sox' organization in 17th round of free-agent draft, June 7, 1977.
Selected by Cincinnati Reds' organization in 15th round of free-agent draft, June 6, 1978.
†Traded with Pitcher Tom Hume to Philadelphia Phillies for Pitchers John Denny and Jeff Gray, December 11, 1985.

THAD WILLIAM REECE

Born November 15, 1958, at San Francisco, Calif.
Height, 5.10. Weight, 170.
Throws right and bats lefthanded.
Received bachelor of arts degree in communications from University of Hawaii, Honolulu, Haw.

Year Club	League	Pos.	G.	AB.	R.	H.	2B.	3B.	HR.	RBI.	B.A.	PO.	A.	E.	F.A.
1981—San Jose	Calif.	2B	47	139	18	36	8	1	0	6	.259	78	119	7	.966
1982—Modesto	Calif.	2B-3B-OF	80	182	28	50	10	2	0	16	.275	110	110	7	.969
1983—Madison	Midw.	2-3-O-S	118	393	69	116	27	2	2	44	.295	106	142	16	.939
1984—Albany	East.	3-2-S-O	120	420	70	139	22	4	2	46	*.331	150	188	12	.966
1985—Tacoma	P. C	*2-S-P-O	130	474	51	124	20	2	2	50	.262	247	362	13	*.979

Selected by Texas Rangers' organization in 24th round of free-agent draft, June 7, 1977.
Selected by Oakland A's organization in 17th round of free-agent draft, June 8, 1981.

PITCHING RECORD

Year Club	League	G.	IP.	W.	L.	Pct.	H.	R.	ER.	SO.	BB.	ERA.
1985—Tacoma	P. Coast	2	1⅔	0	0	.000	0	0	0	0	1	0.00

JEFFREY SCOTT REED
(Jeff)

Born November 12, 1962, at Joliet, Ill.
Height, 6.02. Weight, 185.
Throws right and bats lefthanded.
Brother of Curtis Reed, outfielder in San Diego Padres' and
Chicago White Sox' organizations, 1977 through 1984.
Led International League catchers in total chances with 720 in 1985.
Led Southern League catchers in total chances with 714 and double plays with 12 in 1983.
Led California League catchers in total chances with 758 and tied for lead in double plays with 9 in 1982.

Year Club	League	Pos.	G.	AB.	R.	H.	2B.	3B.	HR.	RBI.	B.A.	PO.	A.	E.	F.A.
1980—Elizabethton	Appal.	C	65	225	39	64	15	1	1	20	.284	269	★41	9	.972
1981—Wisconsin Rapids	Midw.	C	106	312	63	73	12	1	4	34	.234	547	★93	7	.989
1981—Orlando	South.	C	3	4	0	1	0	0	0	0	.250	4	1	0	1.000
1982—Visalia	Calif.	C	125	395	69	130	19	2	5	54	.329	★642	●106	10	.987
1983—Orlando	South.	C	118	379	52	100	16	5	6	45	.264	★618	★88	8	★.989
1983—Toledo	Int.	C	14	41	5	7	1	1	0	3	.171	77	6	1	.988
1984—Minnesota	Amer.	C	18	21	3	3	3	0	0	1	.143	41	2	1	.977
1984—Toledo	Int.	C	94	301	30	80	16	3	3	35	.266	546	43	5	★.992
1985—Toledo	Int.	C	122	404	53	100	15	3	5	36	.248	★627	★81	12	.983
1985—Minnesota	Amer.	C	7	10	2	2	0	0	0	0	.200	9	3	0	1.000
Major League Totals—2 Years			25	31	5	5	3	0	0	1	.161	50	5	1	.982

Selected by Minnesota Twins' organization in 1st round (12th player selected) of free-agent draft, June 3, 1980.

JERRY MAXWELL REED

Born October 8, 1955, at Bryson City, N.C.
Height, 6.01. Weight, 190.
Throws and bats righthanded.
Received bachelor of science degree in education from
Western Carolina University, Cullowhee, N.C. in 1977.
Major League saves: 1985 (8).
Tied for Eastern League lead in intentional bases on balls issued with 9 in 1979.

Year Club	League	G.	IP.	W.	L.	Pct.	H.	R.	ER.	SO.	BB.	ERA.
1977—Auburn	NYP	★32	56	3	5	.375	63	35	30	36	24	4.82
1978—Spartanburg	W. Carol.	39	66	7	2	.778	36	22	10	31	34	1.36
1978—Peninsula	Carolina	15	24	1	0	1.000	9	3	2	11	5	0.75
1979—Reading	Eastern	45	80	11	4	.733	67	25	17	37	28	1.91
1980—Oklahoma City	Am. Assoc.	33	97	6	5	.545	128	62	53	36	42	4.92
1980—Reading	Eastern	8	17	1	1	.500	17	6	6	10	10	3.18
1981—Reading	Eastern	56	80	5	4	.556	80	34	29	62	29	3.26
1981—Philadelphia	National	4	5	0	1	.000	7	4	4	5	6	7.20
1982—Oklahoma City	Am. Assoc.	25	131⅔	6	7	.462	135	78	64	73	59	4.37
1982—Philadelphia†	National	7	8⅔	1	0	1.000	11	6	5	1	3	5.19
1982—Cleveland	American	6	15⅔	1	1	.500	15	6	6	10	3	3.45
1983—Charleston	Int'national	21	145⅓	10	6	.625	141	70	58	57	67	3.59
1983—Cleveland	American	7	21⅓	0	0	.000	26	19	17	11	9	7.17
1984—Maine	Int'national	27	179⅓	12	6	.667	★193	86	72	77	57	3.61
1985—Maine	Int'national	14	95⅓	8	5	.615	88	41	36	47	37	3.40
1985—Cleveland	American	33	72⅓	3	5	.375	67	41	33	37	19	4.11
National League Totals—2 Years		11	13⅔	1	1	.500	18	10	9	6	9	5.93
American League Totals—3 Years		46	109⅓	4	6	.400	108	66	56	58	31	4.61
Major League Totals—4 Years		57	123	5	7	.417	126	76	65	64	40	4.76

Selected by Minnesota Twins' organization in 11th round of free-agent draft, June 5, 1973.
Selected by Philadelphia Phillies' organization in 22nd round of free-agent draft, June 7, 1977.
†Traded with Pitcher Roy Smith and Outfielder Wil Culmer to Cleveland Indians for Pitcher John Denny, September 12, 1982.

JESSIE THOMAS REID

Born June 1, 1962, at Honolulu, Haw.
Height, 6.01. Weight, 200.
Throws and bats lefthanded.

Year Club	League	Pos.	G.	AB.	R.	H.	2B.	3B.	HR.	RBI.	B.A.	PO.	A.	E.	F.A.
1980—Great Falls	Pion.	OF-1B	59	227	57	83	15	6	5	48	.366	137	7	4	.973
1981—Fresno	Calif.	OF-1B	124	426	68	105	15	3	1	40	.246	222	13	8	.967
1982—Fresno	Calif.	OF-1B	127	476	78	139	20	5	6	73	.292	385	27	14	.967
1983—Shreveport	Texas	OF	125	389	59	101	22	0	13	50	.260	157	7	4	.976
1984—Shreveport	Texas	OF	88	296	33	62	10	1	6	32	.209	129	9	2	.986
1984—Phoenix	P. C.	OF	36	121	13	28	5	0	1	9	.231	70	0	1	.986
1985—Fresno	Calif.	OF-1B	72	254	45	82	14	2	8	55	.323	139	6	4	.973
1985—Phoenix	P. C.	OF	54	179	26	47	6	3	7	32	.263	101	3	3	.972

Selected by San Francisco Giants' organization in 1st round (seventh player selected) of free-agent draft, June 3, 1980.

GERALD PETER REMY
(Jerry)

Born November 8, 1952, at Fall Rivers, Mass.
Height, 5.09. Weight, 165.
Throws right and bats lefthanded.
Attended Roger Williams College, Bristol, R. I.

Collected six hits in one game, September 3, 1981 (20 innings).
Major League stolen bases: 1975 (34), 1976 (35), 1977 (41), 1978 (30), 1979 (14), 1980 (14), 1981 (9), 1982 (16), 1983 (11), 1984 (4). Total—208.
Led American League second basemen in double plays with 114 in 1978.
Led California League in caught stealing with 18 in 1972.
Led Midwest League second basemen in double plays with 73 in 1973.
Led California League second basemen in assists with 402 and double plays with 86 in 1972.
Named Most Valuable Player in Midwest League, 1973.

Year—Club	League	Pos.	G.	AB.	R.	H.	2B.	3B.	HR.	RBI.	B.A.	PO.	A.	E.	F.A.
1971—Magic Valley†	Pion.	2B-OF	32	104	25	32	5	3	0	6	.308	61	54	5	.958
1972—Stockton	Calif.	2B-SS	133	532	59	141	18	3	4	43	.265	275	404	28	.960
1973—Quad Cities	Midw.	2B	117	478	66	★160	23	10	4	36	★.335	★277	★330	24	.962
1974—El Paso	Texas	2B	91	394	74	133	34	5	4	46	.338	233	267	18	.965
1974—Salt Lake City	P. C.	2B	48	195	33	57	6	5	0	21	.292	108	135	7	.972
1975—California	Amer.	2B	147	569	82	147	17	5	1	46	.258	336	427	14	.982
1976—California	Amer.	2B	140	502	64	132	14	3	0	28	.263	279	406	16	.977
1977—California‡	Amer.	2B-3B	154	575	74	145	19	10	4	44	.252	307	420	19	.975
1978—Boston	Amer.	2B-SS	148	583	87	162	24	6	2	44	.278	328	446	13	.983
1979—Boston§	Amer.	2B	80	306	49	91	11	2	0	29	.297	147	205	11	.970
1980—Boston x	Amer.	2B-OF	63	230	24	72	7	2	0	9	.313	109	189	7	.977
1981—Boston y	Amer.	2B	88	358	55	110	9	1	0	31	.307	162	272	7	.984
1982—Boston	Amer.	2B	155	636	89	178	22	3	0	47	.280	290	432	13	.982
1983—Boston z	Amer.	2B	146	592	73	163	16	5	0	43	.275	295	376	7	.990
1984—Boston a	Amer.	2B	30	104	8	26	1	1	0	8	.250	40	70	3	.973
1985—Boston bc	Amer.						(Did not play)								
Major League Totals—10 Years			1154	4455	605	1226	140	38	7	329	.275	2293	3243	110	.981

Selected by Washington Senators' organization in 19th round of free-agent draft, June 4, 1970.
Selected by California Angels' organization in secondary phase of free-agent draft, January 13, 1971.
†On disabled list, August 12, 1971 through remainder of season.
‡Traded to Boston Red Sox for Pitcher Don Aase and cash, December 8, 1977.
§On disabled list, July 2 to August 8 and August 17 to September 1, 1979.
xOn disabled list, July 15, 1980 through remainder of season.
yGranted free agency, November 13, 1981; re-signed by Red Sox, December 8, 1981.
zOn disabled list, March 27 to April 15, 1983.
aOn disabled list, May 19, 1984 through remainder of season.
bOn disabled list, April 7, 1985 through entire season.
cReleased, December 10, 1985.

ALL-STAR GAME RECORD

Named to American League All-Star Team for 1978 game to replace injured Rick Burleson; did not play.

RICHARD AVINA RENTERIA
Name pronounced Ren-ter-REE-ah.
(Rich)

Born December 25, 1961, at Harbor City, Calif.
Height, 5.09. Weight, 172.
Throws and bats righthanded.

Led South Atlantic League third basemen in errors with 39 in 1981.
Tied for Carolina League in grounding into double plays with 19 in 1982.

Year—Club	League	Pos.	G.	AB.	R.	H.	2B.	3B.	HR.	RBI.	B.A.	PO.	A.	E.	F.A.
1980—Bradenton Pir.	Gulf C.	3B-SS	46	176	19	40	6	1	2	23	.227	32	87	16	.882
1981—Greenwood	S. Atl.	3B-SS	127	510	90	146	19	5	4	48	.286	87	232	39	.891
1982—Alexandria	Carol.	2B	127	508	80	★168	24	5	14	★100	★.331	196	346	28	.951
1983—Lynn†	East.	3B	115	424	47	121	25	0	4	40	.285	83	170	19	.930
1984—Nashua	East.	2B	113	443	63	121	22	7	1	34	.273	208	283	12	.976
1984—Hawaii‡	P. C.	2B	19	77	8	19	3	1	0	11	.247	22	45	2	.971
1985—Mex. C. Tigers	Mex.	3B-2B	125	484	89	169	29	11	19	★125	.349	121	241	19	.950
1985—Hawaii	P. C.	2B	7	31	2	6	2	0	0	2	.194	5	15	0	1.000

Selected by Pittsburgh Pirates' organization in 1st round (20th player selected) of free-agent draft, June 3, 1980.
†On disabled list, May 10 to June 1, 1983.
‡Loaned to Mexico City Tigers, March 11, 1985; returned, August 21, 1985.

RICKY EUGENE REUSCHEL
Name pronounced RUSH-ul.
(Rick)

Born May 16, 1949, at Quincy, Ill.
Height, 6.03. Weight, 230.
Throws and bats righthanded.
Attended Western Illinois University, Macomb, Ill.
Brother of Paul Reuschel, pitcher with Chicago Cubs and Cleveland Indians, 1975 through 1978.

Tied major league record for most putouts, pitcher, inning (3), April 25, 1975 (third inning).
Major League saves: 1975 (1), 1976 (1), 1977 (1), 1985 (1). Total—4.
Tied for National League lead in games started by pitchers with 38 in 1980.
Led Northern League pitchers in complete games with 7 and tied for lead in games started with 14 in 1970.
Named righthanded pitcher on THE SPORTING NEWS National League All-Star Team, 1977.
Named National League Comeback Player of the Year by THE SPORTING NEWS, 1985.
Named pitcher on THE SPORTING NEWS National League All-Star fielding team, 1985.

Year Club	League	G.	IP.	W.	L.	Pct.	H.	R.	ER.	SO.	BB.	ERA.
1970—Huron	Northern	14	102	9	2	.818	96	52	40	88	22	3.52
1971—San Antonio†	Texas	16	121	8	4	.667	105	40	31	81	15	2.31
1972—Wichita	Am. Assoc.	12	102	9	2	.818	78	30	15	72	30	1.32
1972—Chicago	National	21	129	10	8	.556	127	46	42	87	29	2.93
1973—Chicago	National	36	237	14	15	.483	244	95	79	168	62	3.00
1974—Chicago	National	41	241	13	12	.520	262	130	115	160	83	4.29
1975—Chicago	National	38	234	11	*17	.393	244	116	97	155	67	3.73
1976—Chicago	National	38	260	14	12	.538	260	*117	100	146	64	3.46
1977—Chicago	National	39	252	20	10	.667	233	84	78	166	74	2.79
1978—Chicago	National	35	243	14	15	.483	235	98	92	115	54	3.41
1979—Chicago	National	36	239	18	12	.600	251	104	96	125	75	3.62
1980—Chicago	National	38	257	11	13	.458	*281	111	97	140	76	3.40
1981—Chicago‡	National	13	86	4	7	.364	87	40	33	53	23	3.45
1981—New York	American	12	71	4	4	.500	75	24	21	22	10	2.66
1982—New York§	American					(Did not play)						
1983—Columbus xy	Int'national	4	16	0	1	.000	21	9	9	7	6	5.06
1983—Quad Cities	Midwest	13	70⅔	3	4	.429	73	29	19	56	9	2.42
1983—Chicago	National	4	20⅔	1	1	.500	18	9	9	9	10	3.92
1984—Chicago za	National	19	92⅓	5	5	.500	123	57	53	43	23	5.17
1985—Hawaii	P. Coast	8	54	6	2	.750	52	18	15	46	12	2.50
1985—Pittsburgh	National	31	194	14	8	.636	153	58	49	138	52	2.27
National League Totals—13 Years		389	2485	149	135	.525	2518	1065	940	1505	692	3.40
American League Totals—1 Year		12	71	4	4	.500	75	24	21	22	10	2.66
Major League Totals—13 Years		401	2556	153	139	.524	2593	1089	961	1527	702	3.38

Selected by Chicago Cubs' organization in 3rd round of free-agent draft, June 4, 1970.
†On temporary inactive list, July 2, 1971; transferred to military list, July 8, 1971 through April 10, 1972.
‡Traded to New York Yankees for Pitcher Doug Bird, $400,000 and a player to be named later, June 12, 1981; Chicago Cubs acquired Pitcher Mike Griffin to complete deal, August 5, 1981.
§On disabled list, March 23, 1982 through remainder of season.
xOn New York disabled list, April 4 to June 9, 1983; included rehabilitation disability assignment to Columbus, May 23 to June 9, 1983.
yReleased, June 9, 1983; signed by Quad Cities (Chicago Cubs' organization), June 28, 1983.
zOn disabled list, March 27 to April 21 and August 23 to September 1, 1984.
aGranted free agency, November 8, 1984; signed by Pittsburgh Pirates' organization, February 28, 1985.

DIVISION SERIES RECORD

Year Club	League	G.	IP.	W.	L.	Pct.	H.	R.	ER.	SO.	BB.	ERA.
1981—New York	American	1	6	0	1	.000	4	2	2	3	1	3.00

WORLD SERIES RECORD

Year Club	League	G.	IP.	W.	L.	Pct.	H.	R.	ER.	SO.	BB.	ERA.
1981—New York	American	2	3⅔	0	0	.000	7	3	2	2	3	4.91

ALL-STAR GAME RECORD

Year League		IP.	W.	L.	Pct.	H.	R.	ER.	SO.	BB.	ERA.
1977—National		1	0	0	.000	1	0	0	0	0	0.00

JERRY REUSS

Name pronounced Royce.

Born June 19, 1949, at St. Louis, Mo.
Height, 6.05.   Weight, 217.
Throws and bats lefthanded.
Attended Southern Illinois University, Carbondale, Ill., Central Missouri State College,
Warrensburg, Mo., and University of California, Santa Barbara, Calif.

Tied major league record for most home runs allowed, bases filled, lifetime (9).
Pitched 8-0 no-hit victory against San Francisco Giants, June 27, 1980.
Major League saves: 1972 (1), 1976 (2), 1979 (3), 1980 (3), 1984 (1). Total—10.
Led National League in shutouts with 6 in 1980.
Led National League in hit batsmen with 10 in 1972.
Tied for National League lead in games started by pitchers with 40 in 1973.
Led American Association pitchers in games started with 29 in 1969.
Led Texas League in wild pitches with 16 in 1968.
Named National League Comeback Player of the Year by THE SPORTING NEWS, 1980.
Received reported $30,000 bonus to sign with St. Louis Cardinals, 1967.

Year Club	League	G.	IP.	W.	L.	Pct.	H.	R.	ER.	SO.	BB.	ERA.
1967—Sarasota Cards	Gulf Coast	2	7	0	0	.000	7	6	4	6	3	5.14
1967—Cedar Rapids	Midwest	9	58	2	5	.286	44	20	12	63	19	1.86
1967—Tulsa	P. Coast	1	1	0	0	.000	2	6	6	1	4	54.00
1968—Arkansas	Texas	17	112	7	8	.467	75	43	27	86	45	2.17
1969—Tulsa	Am. Assoc.	30	*186	●13	11	.542	188	●112	84	*151	116	4.06

Year Club	League	G.	IP.	W.	L.	Pct.	H.	R.	ER.	SO.	BB.	ERA.
1969—St. Louis	National	1	7	1	0	1.000	2	0	0	3	3	0.00
1970—Tulsa	Am. Assoc.	11	85	7	2	.778	69	26	20	69	28	2.12
1970—St. Louis	National	20	127	7	8	.467	132	62	58	74	49	4.11
1971—St. Louis†	National	36	211	14	14	.500	228	125	112	131	109	4.78
1972—Houston	National	33	192	9	13	.409	177	101	89	174	83	4.17
1973—Houston‡	National	41	279	16	13	.552	271	123	116	177	★117	3.74
1974—Pittsburgh	National	35	260	16	11	.593	259	115	101	105	101	3.50
1975—Pittsburgh	National	32	237	18	11	.621	224	73	67	131	78	2.54
1976—Pittsburgh	National	31	209	14	9	.609	209	98	82	108	51	3.53
1977—Pittsburgh	National	33	208	10	13	.435	225	109	95	116	71	4.11
1978—Pittsburgh§	National	23	83	3	2	.600	97	48	45	42	23	4.88
1979—Los Angeles	National	39	160	7	14	.333	178	88	63	83	60	3.54
1980—Los Angeles	National	37	229	18	6	.750	193	74	64	111	40	2.52
1981—Los Angeles	National	22	153	10	4	.714	138	44	39	51	27	2.29
1982—Los Angeles	National	39	254⅔	18	11	.621	232	98	88	138	50	3.11
1983—Los Angeles x	National	32	223⅓	12	11	.522	233	94	73	143	50	2.94
1984—Los Angeles x	National	30	99	5	7	.417	102	51	42	44	31	3.82
1985—Los Angeles	National	34	212⅔	14	10	.583	210	78	69	84	58	2.92
Major League Totals—17 Years		518	3144⅔	192	157	.550	3110	1381	1203	1715	1001	3.44

Selected by St. Louis Cardinals' organization in 2nd round of free-agent draft, June 6, 1967.
†Traded to Houston Astros for Pitchers Scipio Spinks and Lance Clemons, April 15, 1972.
‡Traded to Pittsburgh Pirates for Catcher Milt May, October 31, 1973.
§Traded to Los Angeles Dodgers for Pitcher Rick Rhoden, April 9, 1979.
xOn disabled list, June 8 to July 12, 1984.

DIVISION SERIES RECORD

Year Club	League	G.	IP.	W.	L.	Pct.	H.	R.	ER.	SO.	BB.	ERA.
1981—Los Angeles	National	2	18	1	0	1.000	10	0	0	7	5	0.00

CHAMPIONSHIP SERIES RECORD

Established Championship Series records for most games lost, total Series (7); most runs allowed, inning (7), October 13, 1985 (second inning).

Tied Championship Series records for most runs allowed, total Series (25); most games lost, Series (2), 1974, 1983; most bases on balls, four-game Series (8), 1974.

Year Club	League	G.	IP.	W.	L.	Pct.	H.	R.	ER.	SO.	BB.	ERA.
1974—Pittsburgh	National	2	9⅔	0	2	.000	7	4	4	3	8	3.72
1975—Pittsburgh	National	1	2⅔	0	1	.000	4	4	4	1	4	13.50
1981—Los Angeles	National	1	7	0	1	.000	7	4	4	2	1	5.14
1983—Los Angeles	National	2	12	0	2	.000	14	6	6	4	3	4.50
1985—Los Angeles	National	1	1⅔	0	1	.000	5	7	2	0	1	10.80
Championship Series Totals—5 Years		7	33	0	7	.000	37	25	20	10	17	5.45

WORLD SERIES RECORD

Year Club	League	G.	IP.	W.	L.	Pct.	H.	R.	ER.	SO.	BB.	ERA.
1981—Los Angeles	National	2	11⅔	1	1	.500	10	5	5	8	3	3.86

ALL-STAR GAME RECORD

Year League	IP.	W.	L.	Pct.	H.	R.	ER.	SO.	BB.	ERA.
1975—National	3	0	0	.000	3	0	0	2	0	0.00
1980—National	1	1	0	1.000	0	0	0	3	0	0.00
All-Star Game Totals—2 Years	4	1	0	1.000	3	0	0	5	0	0.00

GILBERTO R. REYES (POLANCO)

Name pronounced RAY-us.

(Gil)

Born December 10, 1963, at Santo Domingo, Dominican Republic.
Height, 6.03. Weight, 195.
Throws and bats righthanded.

Tied for Pacific Coast League lead in sacrifice flies with 8 in 1985.
Led Pacific Coast League in passed balls with 24 in 1985.
Led Texas League catchers in total chances with 718, double plays with 13 and passed balls with 31 in 1984.
Tied for California League lead in assists by catchers with 106 and double plays with 9 in 1982.

Year Club	League	Pos.	G.	AB.	R.	H.	2B.	3B.	HR.	RBI.	B.A.	PO.	A.	E.	F.A.
1980—Lethbridge	Pion.	1B	6	11	0	2	0	0	0	1	.182	16	0	2	.889
1981—Vero Beach	Fla. St.	1B-C	21	58	3	12	3	0	1	6	.207	71	6	2	.975
1981—Lethbridge	Pion.	C-1B	44	155	28	40	9	0	6	24	.258	240	24	4	.985
1982—Lodi	Calif.	C-3B	127	424	65	119	18	1	15	55	.281	493	106	20	.968
1983—San Antonio†	Texas	C	33	124	10	35	7	0	1	16	.282	167	30	5	.975
1983—Los Angeles	Nat.	C	19	31	1	5	2	0	0	0	.161	59	9	4	.944
1983—Albuquerque	P. C.	C	20	62	8	19	1	2	2	15	.306	103	17	8	.938
1984—San Antonio	Texas	C	120	433	55	131	16	2	10	78	.303	★598	★101	★19	.974
1984—Los Angeles	Nat.	C	4	5	0	0	0	0	0	0	.000	5	0	0	1.000
1985—Albuquerque	P. C.	★C-1B	111	366	35	97	20	0	6	54	.265	439	66	★21	.960
1985—Los Angeles	Nat.	C	6	1	0	0	0	0	0	0	.000	6	4	0	1.000
Major League Totals—3 Years			29	37	1	5	2	0	0	0	.135	70	13	4	.954

Signed as free agent by Los Angeles Dodgers' organization, January 15, 1980.
†On disabled list, May 11 to June 1, 1983.

GORDON CRAIG REYNOLDS
(Known by middle name.)

Born December 27, 1952, at Houston, Tex.
Height, 6.01. Weight, 175.
Throws right and bats lefthanded.
Attended Houston Baptist College, Houston, Tex.

Tied modern major league record for most three-base hits, game (3), May 16, 1981.
Major League stolen bases: 1977 (6), 1978 (9), 1979 (12), 1980 (2), 1981 (3), 1982 (3), 1984 (7), 1985 (4). Total—46.
Led National League in sacrifice hits with 34 in 1979, 18 in 1981 and 16 in 1984.
Led National League shortstops in assists with 472 in 1984.
Tied for Gulf Coast League lead in sacrifice flies with 4 in 1971.
Led Carolina League shortstops in double plays with 81 in 1973 and tied for International League lead with 64 in 1975.

Year—Club	League	Pos.	G.	AB.	R.	H.	2B.	3B.	HR.	RBI.	B.A.	PO.	A.	E.	F.A.
1971—Bradenton Pir.	Gulf C.	SS	48	192	26	61	8	0	0	16	.318	*87	112	*25	.888
1972—Gastonia†	W. Car.	SS	41	146	18	35	4	1	0	9	.240	55	94	12	.925
1973—Salem	Carol.	SS-2B	138	*558	75	*160	18	5	13	86	.287	200	395	50	.922
1973—Charleston	Int.	SS-3B	4	14	2	3	0	0	0	0	.214	4	11	1	.938
1974—Thetford Mines	East.	SS	64	234	31	66	7	0	6	29	.282	76	170	13	.950
1974—Charleston‡	Int.	SS-2B	36	107	12	36	5	0	0	5	.336	40	71	3	.974
1975—Charleston	Int.	SS	108	425	51	131	22	3	6	42	.308	151	287	26	.944
1975—Pittsburgh	Nat.	SS	31	76	8	17	3	0	0	4	.224	43	82	4	.969
1976—Charleston	Int.	SS-2B	126	497	57	144	18	1	2	47	.290	198	262	31	.937
1976—Pittsburgh§	Nat.	SS-2B	7	4	1	1	0	0	1	1	.250	2	6	1	.889
1977—Seattle	Amer.	SS	135	420	41	104	12	3	4	28	.248	197	397	28	.955
1978—Seattle x	Amer.	SS	148	548	57	160	16	7	5	44	.292	243	461	29	.960
1979—Houston	Nat.	SS	146	555	63	147	20	9	0	39	.265	208	428	23	.965
1980—Houston	Nat.	SS	137	381	34	86	9	6	3	28	.226	162	362	17	.969
1981—Houston	Nat.	SS	87	323	43	84	10	●12	4	31	.260	139	261	11	.973
1982—Houston y	Nat.	SS-3B	54	118	16	30	2	3	1	7	.254	45	98	6	.960
1983—Houston	Nat.	2-3-S-O	65	98	10	21	3	0	1	6	.214	37	57	3	.969
1984—Houston	Nat.	SS-3B	146	527	61	137	15	11	6	60	.260	212	473	25	.965
1985—Houston	Nat.	SS-2B	107	379	43	103	18	8	4	32	.272	159	319	11	.978
American League Totals—2 Years			283	968	98	264	28	10	9	72	.273	440	858	57	.958
National League Totals—9 Years			780	2461	279	626	80	49	20	208	.254	1007	2086	101	.968
Major League Totals—11 Years			1063	3429	377	890	108	59	29	280	.260	1447	2944	158	.965

Selected by Pittsburgh Pirates' organization in 1st round (22nd player selected) of free-agent draft, June 8, 1971.
†On disabled list, June 6 to August 30, 1972.
‡On disabled list, July 31 to August 21, 1974.
§Traded with Infielder Jim Sexton to Seattle Mariners for Pitcher Grant Jackson, December 7, 1976.
xTraded to Houston Astros for Pitcher Floyd Bannister, December 8, 1978.
yOn disabled list, April 11 to May 5, 1982.

DIVISION SERIES RECORD

Year—Club	League	Pos.	G.	AB.	R.	H.	2B.	3B.	HR.	RBI.	B.A.	PO.	A.	E.	F.A.
1981—Houston	Nat.	PH	2	3	1	1	0	0	0	0	.333	1	0	0	1.000

CHAMPIONSHIP SERIES RECORD

Year—Club	League	Pos.	G.	AB.	R.	H.	2B.	3B.	HR.	RBI.	B.A.	PO.	A.	E.	F.A.
1975—Pittsburgh	Nat.	SS	2	1	0	0	0	0	0	0	.000	0	0	1	.000
1980—Houston	Nat.	SS	4	13	2	2	1	0	0	0	.154	8	12	1	.952
Championship Series Totals—2 Years			6	14	2	2	1	0	0	0	.143	8	12	2	.909

ALL-STAR GAME RECORD

Year—League	Pos.	AB.	R.	H.	2B.	3B.	HR.	RBI.	B.A.	PO.	A.	E.	F.A.
1979—National	SS	2	0	0	0	0	0	0	.000	0	1	0	1.000

Named to American League All-Star Team for 1978 game; did not play.

HAROLD CRAIG REYNOLDS

Born November 26, 1960, at Eugene, Ore.
Height, 5.11. Weight, 165.
Throws right and bats left and righthanded.
Attended San Diego State University, San Diego, Calif.;
Canada College, Redwood City, Calif., and
California State University, Long Beach, Calif.

Brother of Larry Reynolds, shortstop-outfielder in Texas Rangers' and St. Louis Cardinals' organizations, 1979 through 1984; and Don Reynolds, outfielder with San Diego Padres, 1978 and 1979.

Major League stolen bases: 1984 (1), 1985 (3). Total—4.
Led Pacific Coast League in sacrifice hits with 14 in 1983.
Led Eastern League in caught stealing with 20 in 1982.
Led Midwest League in stolen bases with 69 in 1981.
Tied for Pacific Coast League lead in caught stealing with 17 in 1984.
Led Pacific Coast League second basemen in double plays with 104 and total chances with 747 in 1984.
Led Pacific Coast League second basemen in putouts with 286 and total chances with 723 in 1983.
Led Midwest League second basemen in double plays with 82 in 1981.

Year—Club	League	Pos.	G.	AB.	R.	H.	2B.	3B.	HR.	RBI.	B.A.	PO.	A.	E.	F.A.
1981—Wausau	Midw.	2B-OF-3B	127	493	98	146	23	3	11	59	.296	259	386	27	.960

Year	Club	League	Pos.	G.	AB.	R.	H.	2B.	3B.	HR.	RBI.	B.A.	PO.	A.	E.	F.A.
1982—Lynn	East.		2B	102	375	58	102	14	4	2	48	.272	202	232	19	.958
1983—Salt Lake City	P. C.		*2B-SS	136	534	84	165	20	9	1	72	.309	287	*410	*27	.963
1983—Seattle	Amer.		2B	20	59	8	12	4	1	0	1	.203	30	48	2	.975
1984—Salt Lake City	P. C.		2B	135	*558	94	165	22	6	3	54	.296	*326	*396	*25	*.967
1984—Seattle	Amer.		2B	10	10	3	3	0	0	0	0	.300	8	12	0	1.000
1985—Seattle	Amer.		2B	67	104	15	15	3	1	0	6	.144	69	123	8	.960
1985—Calgary	P. C.		2B	52	212	36	77	11	3	5	30	.363	119	171	13	.957
Major League Totals—3 Years				97	173	26	30	7	2	0	7	.173	107	183	10	.967

Selected by San Diego Padres' organization in 5th round of free-agent draft, June 5, 1979.
Selected by Seattle Mariners' organization in secondary phase of free-agent draft, June 3, 1980.

ROBERT JAMES REYNOLDS
(R. J.)

Born April 19, 1959, at Sacramento, Calif.
Height, 6.00. Weight, 180.
Throws right and bats left and righthanded.
Attended Cosumnes River College, Sacramento, Calif.;
and Sacramento City College, Sacramento, Calif.

Major League stolen bases: 1983 (5), 1984 (7), 1985 (18). Total—30.
Led Texas League outfielders in double plays with 8 in 1983
Led Florida State League outfielders in double plays with 6 and total chances with 395 in 1981.
Led California League outfielders in double plays with 6 in 1980.

Year	Club	League	Pos.	G.	AB.	R.	H.	2B.	3B.	HR.	RBI.	B.A.	PO.	A.	E.	F.A.
1980—Lodi	Calif.		OF	86	299	33	84	6	3	4	31	.281	188	10	12	.943
1981—Vero Beach	Fla. St.		OF	132	502	62	139	9	11	2	49	.277	*368	20	7	.982
1982—Lodi	Calif.		OF	108	403	67	126	19	3	6	35	.313	212	12	6	.974
1982—San Antonio	Texas		OF	3	12	3	2	0	0	1	2	.167	10	1	0	1.000
1983—San Antonio	Texas		OF	133	504	103	170	25	3	18	89	.337	255	●18	12	.958
1983—Los Angeles	Nat.		OF	24	55	5	13	0	0	2	11	.236	25	2	2	.931
1984—Albuquerque	P. C.		OF	47	199	38	69	10	4	3	30	.347	104	4	6	.947
1984—Los Angeles†			OF	73	240	24	62	12	2	2	24	.258	104	4	3	.973
1985—L.A.‡§-Pitt.	Nat.		OF	104	337	44	95	15	7	3	42	.282	159	6	6	.965
Major League Totals—3 Years				201	632	73	170	27	9	7	77	.269	288	12	11	.965

Selected by Los Angeles Dodgers' organization in 2nd round of free-agent draft, January 8, 1980.
†On disabled list, July 2 to July 17, 1984.
‡On disabled list, April 8 to April 23 and July 18 to August 2, 1985.
§Traded to Pittsburgh Pirates, September 3, 1985, as partial completion of deal in which Los Angeles Dodgers acquired Third Baseman Bill Madlock for three players to be named later, August 31, 1985; Pittsburgh acquired Outfielder Cecil Espy and First Baseman Sid Bream to complete deal, September 9, 1985.

RONN DWAYNE REYNOLDS

Born September 28, 1958, at Wichita, Kan.
Height, 6.00. Weight, 200.
Throws and bats righthanded.
Attended Garden City Community College, Garden City, Kan.,
and University of Arkansas, Fayetteville, Ark.

Tied for Texas League lead in being hit by pitch with 10 in 1982.
Led Texas League catchers in putouts with 583 and total chances with 651 in 1982.

Year	Club	League	Pos.	G.	AB.	R.	H.	2B.	3B.	HR.	RBI.	B.A.	PO.	A.	E.	F.A.
1980—Little Falls	NYP		C	15	44	6	8	1	1	1	8	.182	85	3	2	.978
1980—Lynchburg	Carol.		C	36	105	14	21	3	0	2	17	.200	206	23	3	.987
1981—Jackson	Texas		C	88	272	16	64	12	1	2	30	.235	493	67	12	.979
1982—Jackson	Texas		C-3B-OF	123	431	50	110	13	1	10	43	.255	585	57	14	.979
1982—New York	Nat.		C	2	4	0	0	0	0	0	0	.000	3	0	0	1.000
1983—Tidewater	Int.		C	40	128	8	27	8	0	0	9	.211	209	27	1	.996
1983—New York	Nat.		C	24	66	4	13	1	0	0	2	.197	99	14	7	.942
1984—Tidewater	Int.		C-1B	90	280	35	73	11	0	11	46	.261	457	25	7	.986
1985—New York	Nat.		C	28	43	4	9	2	0	0	1	.209	86	9	1	.990
1985—Tidewater†	Int.		C	3	10	0	3	1	0	0	2	.300	5	2	0	1.000
Major League Totals—3 Years				54	113	8	22	3	0	0	3	.195	188	23	8	.963

Selected by Oakland A's organization in 5th round of free-agent draft, June 5, 1979.
Selected by New York Mets' organization in 5th round of free-agent draft, June 3, 1980.
†Traded with Pitcher Jeff Bittiger to Philadelphia Phillies for Pitcher Rodger Cole and First Baseman Ronnie Gideon, January 16, 1986.

RICHARD ALAN RHODEN

Name pronounced ROH-dun.

(Rick)

Born May 16, 1953, at Boynton Beach, Fla.
Height, 6.03. Weight, 195.
Throws and bats righthanded.

Pitched seven-inning, 1-0 no-hit victory against Phoenix, April 23, 1980 (first game).
Major League saves: 1983 (1).
Named pitcher on THE SPORTING NEWS National League Silver Slugger team, 1984 and 1985.

Year Club	League	G.	IP.	W.	L.	Pct.	H.	R.	ER.	SO.	BB.	ERA.
1971—Daytona Beach	Florida St.	11	61	4	6	.400	59	32	27	67	29	3.98
1972—El Paso	Texas	13	87	6	4	.600	70	36	32	89	30	3.31
1972—Albuquerque	P. Coast	13	80	7	1	.875	83	41	34	55	34	3.83
1973—Albuquerque†	P. Coast	20	116	4	9	.308	117	66	58	68	70	4.50
1974—Albuquerque	P. Coast	26	178	9	10	.474	197	103	87	106	65	4.40
1974—Los Angeles	National	4	9	1	0	1.000	5	2	2	7	4	2.00
1975—Los Angeles	National	26	99	3	3	.500	94	40	34	40	32	3.09
1976—Los Angeles	National	27	181	12	3	.800	165	66	60	77	53	2.98
1977—Los Angeles	National	31	216	16	10	.615	223	98	90	122	63	3.75
1978—Los Angeles‡	National	30	165	10	8	.556	160	77	67	79	51	3.65
1979—Pittsburgh§	National	1	5	0	1	.000	5	4	4	2	2	7.20
1980—Portland	P. Coast	10	52	6	3	.667	47	22	17	24	21	2.94
1980—Pittsburgh	National	20	127	7	5	.583	133	58	54	70	40	3.83
1981—Pittsburgh	National	21	136	9	4	.692	147	66	59	76	53	3.90
1982—Pittsburgh	National	35	230⅓	11	14	.440	239	115	106	128	70	4.14
1983—Pittsburgh	National	36	241⅓	13	13	.500	256	95	84	153	68	3.09
1984—Pittsburgh	National	33	238⅓	14	9	.609	216	81	72	136	62	2.72
1985—Pittsburgh	National	35	213⅓	10	15	.400	254	●119	★106	128	69	4.47
Major League Totals—12 Years		299	1864⅓	106	85	.555	1897	821	738	1018	567	3.56

Selected by Los Angeles Dodgers' organization in 1st round (20th player selected) of free-agent draft, June 8, 1971.
†On disabled list, July 20 to August 15, 1973.
‡Traded to Pittsburgh Pirates for Pitcher Jerry Reuss, April 9, 1979.
§On disabled list, May 12 to October 4, 1979.

CHAMPIONSHIP SERIES RECORD

Year Club	League	G.	IP.	W.	L.	Pct.	H.	R.	ER.	SO.	BB.	ERA.
1977—Los Angeles	National	1	4⅓	0	0	.000	2	0	0	0	2	0.00
1978—Los Angeles	National	1	4	0	0	.000	2	1	1	3	1	2.25
Championship Series Totals—2 Years		2	8⅓	0	0	.000	4	1	1	3	3	1.08

WORLD SERIES RECORD

Year Club	League	G.	IP.	W.	L.	Pct.	H.	R.	ER.	SO.	BB.	ERA.
1977—Los Angeles	National	2	7	0	1	.000	4	2	2	5	1	2.57

ALL-STAR GAME RECORD

Year League		IP.	W.	L.	Pct.	H.	R.	ER.	SO.	BB.	ERA.
1976—National		1	0	0	.000	1	0	0	0	0	0.00

JAMES EDWARD RICE
(Jim)

Born March 8, 1953, at Anderson, S. C.
Height, 6.02. Weight, 205.
Throws and bats righthanded.

Established major league record for most times grounding into double plays, season (36), 1984.
Tied major league record for most consecutive seasons leading major leagues, total bases (2).
Tied American League records for most consecutive seasons leading league, total bases (3); most years leading league in grounding into double plays (3).
Major League stolen bases: 1975 (10), 1976 (8), 1977 (5), 1978 (7), 1979 (9), 1980 (8), 1981 (2), 1984 (4), 1985 (2). Total—55.
Hit three home runs in a game, August 29, 1977 and August 29, 1983 (second game).
Led American League in grounding into double plays with 29 in 1982, 36 in 1984, 35 in 1985 and tied for lead with 31 in 1983.
Led American League in total bases with 382 in 1977, 406 in 1978, 369 in 1979 and 344 in 1983.
Led American League in slugging percentage with .593 in 1977 and .600 in 1978.
Led American League batters in strikeouts with 123 in 1976.
Led International League in total bases with 249 in 1974.
Led Florida State League in total bases with 240 in 1972.
Named American League Player of the Year by THE SPORTING NEWS, 1978.
Named American League Most Valuable Player by Baseball Writers' Association of America, 1978.
Named outfielder on THE SPORTING NEWS American League All-Star Team, 1975, 1977 through 1979 and 1983.
Named outfielder on THE SPORTING NEWS American League Silver Slugger team, 1983 and 1984.
Named Minor League Player of the Year by THE SPORTING NEWS, 1974.
Named International League Most Valuable Player, 1974.
Received reported $45,000 bonus to sign with Boston Red Sox, 1971.

Year Club	League	Pos.	G.	AB.	R.	H.	2B.	3B.	HR.	RBI.	B.A.	PO.	A.	E.	F.A.
1971—Williamsport	NYP	OF	60	223	34	57	9	5	5	27	.256	86	2	6	.936
1972—Winter Haven	Fla. St.	OF	130	★491	★80	★143	20	13	17	87	.291	190	10	9	.957
1973—Bristol	East.	OF	119	423	66	134	25	4	27	93	★.317	169	13	12	.938
1973—Pawtucket	Int.	OF	10	37	7	14	2	0	4	10	.378	21	0	0	1.000
1974—Pawtucket	Int.	OF	117	430	69	145	21	4	★25	★93	★.337	181	10	11	.946
1974—Boston	Amer.	OF	24	67	6	18	2	1	1	13	.269	4	0	1	.800
1975—Boston	Amer.	OF	144	564	92	174	29	4	22	102	.309	162	6	0	1.000
1976—Boston	Amer.	OF	153	581	75	164	25	8	25	85	.282	199	8	7	.967
1977—Boston	Amer.	OF	160	644	104	206	29	15	★39	114	.320	83	4	4	.956
1978—Boston	Amer.	OF	★163	★677	121	★213	25	★15	★46	★139	.315	245	13	3	.989
1979—Boston	Amer.	OF	158	619	117	201	39	6	39	130	.325	241	8	4	.984
1980—Boston†	Amer.	OF	124	504	81	148	22	6	24	86	.294	233	10	3	.988

Year Club League	Pos.	G.	AB.	R.	H.	2B.	3B.	HR.	RBI.	B.A.	PO.	A.	E.	F.A.
1981—Boston................. Amer.	OF	108	*451	51	128	18	1	17	62	.284	237	9	3	.988
1982—Boston................. Amer.	OF	145	573	86	177	24	5	24	97	.309	273	10	9	.969
1983—Boston................. Amer.	OF	155	626	90	191	34	1	*39	●126	.305	339	21	6	.984
1984—Boston................. Amer.	OF	159	657	98	184	25	7	28	122	.280	336	12	4	.989
1985—Boston................. Amer.	OF	140	546	85	159	20	3	27	103	.291	236	8	9	.964
Major League Totals—12 Years.............		1633	6509	1006	1963	292	72	331	1179	.302	2588	109	53	.981

Selected by Boston Red Sox' organization in 1st round (15th player selected) of free-agent draft, June 8, 1971.
†On disabled list, June 22 to July 27, 1980.

ALL-STAR GAME RECORD

Tied All-Star Game record for most at bats, game (5), July 17, 1979.

Year League	Pos.	AB.	R.	H.	2B.	3B.	HR.	RBI.	B.A.	PO.	A.	E.	F.A.
1977—American	OF	2	0	1	0	0	0	0	.500	1	0	0	1.000
1978—American	OF	4	0	0	0	0	0	0	.000	2	0	0	1.000
1979—American	OF	5	0	1	1	0	0	0	.200	3	0	0	1.000
1983—American	OF	4	1	2	0	0	1	1	.500	1	0	0	1.000
1984—American	PH-OF	1	0	0	0	0	0	0	.000	1	0	0	1.000
1985—American	OF	3	0	0	0	0	0	0	.000	1	0	0	1.000
All-Star Game Totals—6 Years....................		19	1	4	1	0	1	1	.211	9	0	0	1.000

Named to American League All-Star Team in 1980; replaced due to injury.

MICHAEL ANTHONY RICHARDT

Name pronounced Richard.

(Mike)

Born May 24, 1958, at Los Angeles, Calif.
Height, 6.00. Weight, 170.
Throws and bats righthanded.
Attended Fresno City College, Fresno, Calif.

Major League stolen bases: 1982 (9), 1983 (2). Total—11.
Tied for Gulf Coast League lead in sacrifice hits with 6 in 1978.
Led Gulf Coast League second basemen in fielding percentage with .982 and tied for lead in double plays with 24 in 1978.
Tied for International League lead in double plays by second basemen with 74 in 1980.

Year Club League	Pos.	G.	AB.	R.	H.	2B.	3B.	HR.	RBI.	B.A.	PO.	A.	E.	F.A.
1978—Sara. Rangers....... Gulf C.	2B-3B	45	160	30	45	9	2	0	14	.281	90	94	7	.963
1979—Asheville............... W. Car.	2B	75	283	61	88	15	3	4	41	.311	173	212	16	.960
1979—Tulsa .... Texas	2B	68	272	50	89	17	5	5	24	.327	162	218	6	.984
1980—Charleston............ Int.	2B	124	487	74	136	21	13	12	46	.279	*262	385	10	*.985
1980—Texas..................... Amer.	2B	22	71	2	16	2	0	0	8	.225	32	55	2	.978
1981—Wichita.................. A. A.	2B-3B-OF	90	350	53	124	17	2	8	60	*.354	86	151	8	.967
1982—Texas†.................. Amer.	2B-OF	119	402	34	97	10	0	3	43	.241	253	279	6	.989
1983—Texas‡................... Amer.	2B	22	83	9	13	2	1	1	7	.157	56	61	1	.992
1983—Oklahoma City ..... A. A.	2B-OF	30	116	7	31	5	0	2	13	.267	42	60	2	.981
1984—Oklahoma City ..... A. A.	2B	17	65	14	20	7	0	1	5	.308	29	42	1	.986
1984—Texas§ .... Amer.	2B	6	9	0	1	0	0	0	0	.111	5	6	0	1.000
1984—Tucson x .... P. C.	2B	38	122	24	36	9	2	3	20	.295	69	84	2	.987
1984—Houston y .... Nat.	PH-PR	16	15	1	4	1	0	0	2	.267	0	0	0	.000
1985—Tucson za............. P. C.	DH	13	16	4	4	2	0	0	3	.250	0	0	0	.000
American League Totals—4 Years........		169	565	45	127	14	1	4	58	.225	346	401	9	.988
National League Totals—1 Year.............		16	15	1	4	1	0	0	2	.267	0	0	0	.000
Major League Totals—4 Years.................		185	580	46	131	15	1	4	60	.226	346	401	9	.988

Selected by Toronto Blue Jays' organization in 2nd round of free-agent draft, January 10, 1978.
Selected by Texas Rangers' organization in secondary phase of free-agent draft, June 6, 1978.
†On disabled list, May 6 to May 21, 1982.
‡On disabled list, April 22 to July 14, 1983; included rehabilitation disability assignment to Oklahoma City, July 8 to July 14, 1983.
§Traded to Houston Astros' organization for Infielder-Outfielder Alan Bannister, May 25, 1984.
xOn disabled list, June 20 to July 17, 1984.
yOn disabled list, August 19 to September 3, 1984.
zOn Houston disabled list, March 25, 1985 through entire season; included rehabilitation disability assignment to Tucson, August 14 to September 2, 1985.
aReleased, November 13, 1985.

DAVID ALLAN RIGHETTI

Name pronounced Ri-GET-tee.

(Dave)

Born November 28, 1958, at San Jose, Calif.
Height, 6.03. Weight, 195.
Throws and bats lefthanded.
Attended San Jose City College, San Jose, Calif.
Son of Leo Righetti, minor league infielder, 1944 through 1949 and 1951 through 1957;
Brother of Steven Righetti, third baseman in Texas Rangers' organization, 1977 through 1979.

Pitched 4-0 no-hit victory against Boston Red Sox, July 4, 1983.
Major League saves: 1982 (1), 1984 (31), 1985 (29). Total—61.

Named American League Rookie Pitcher of the Year by THE SPORTING NEWS, 1981.
Named American League Rookie of the Year by Baseball Writers' Association of America, 1981.

Year Club	League	G.	IP.	W.	L.	Pct.	H.	R.	ER.	SO.	BB.	ERA.
1977—Asheville	W. Carol.	17	109	11	3	*.786	98	47	38	101	53	3.14
1978—Tulsa†‡	Texas	13	91	5	5	.500	66	40	32	127	49	3.16
1979—West Haven§	Eastern	11	69	4	3	.571	45	23	15	78	45	1.96
1979—Columbus x	Int'national	8	40	3	2	.600	22	13	13	44	19	2.93
1979—New York	American	3	17	0	1	.000	10	7	7	13	10	3.71
1980—Columbus	Int'national	24	142	6	10	.375	124	79	73	139	*101	4.63
1981—Columbus	Int'national	7	45	5	0	1.000	30	8	5	50	26	1.00
1981—New York	American	15	105	8	4	.667	75	25	24	89	38	2.06
1982—New York	American	33	183	11	10	.524	155	88	77	163	*108	3.79
1982—Columbus	Int'national	4	25⅔	1	0	1.000	22	11	8	33	12	2.81
1983—New York	American	31	217	14	8	.636	194	96	83	169	67	3.44
1984—New York y	American	64	96⅓	5	6	.455	79	29	25	90	37	2.34
1985—New York	American	74	107	12	7	.632	96	36	33	92	45	2.78
Major League Totals—6 Years		220	725⅓	50	36	.581	609	281	249	616	305	3.09

Selected by Texas Rangers' organization in 1st round (ninth player selected) of free-agent draft, January 11, 1977.
†On disabled list, July 31 to September 2, 1978.
‡Traded with Pitchers Mike Griffin and Paul Mirabella and Outfielders Juan Beniquez and Greg Jemison to New York Yankees for Pitchers Sparky Lyle, Larry McCall and Dave Rajsich, Catcher Mike Heath, Shortstop Domingo Ramos and cash, November 10, 1978.
§On disabled list, May 21 to June 28, 1979.
xOn disabled list, June 28 to July 20 and August 2 to August 23, 1979.
yOn disabled list, June 17 to July 2, 1984.

DIVISION SERIES RECORD

Year Club	League	G.	IP.	W.	L.	Pct.	H.	R.	ER.	SO.	BB.	ERA.
1981—New York	American	2	9	2	0	1.000	8	1	1	10	3	1.00

CHAMPIONSHIP SERIES RECORD

Year Club	League	G.	IP.	W.	L.	Pct.	H.	R.	ER.	SO.	BB.	ERA.
1981—New York	American	1	6	1	0	1.000	4	0	0	4	2	0.00

WORLD SERIES RECORD

Year Club	League	G.	IP.	W.	L.	Pct.	H.	R.	ER.	SO.	BB.	ERA.
1981—New York	American	1	2	0	0	.000	5	3	3	1	2	13.50

JOSE ANTONIO RIJO (ABREU)

Born May 13, 1965, at San Cristobal, Dominican Republic.
Height, 6.01. Weight, 160.
Throws and bats righthanded.

Major League saves: 1984 (2).
Led Pacific Coast League in balks with 11 in 1985.
Led Florida State League in complete games with 15 and tied for lead in shutouts with 4 in 1983.
Named Florida State League Most Valuable Player, 1983.

Year Club	League	G.	IP.	W.	L.	Pct.	H.	R.	ER.	SO.	BB.	ERA.
1981—Bradenton Yankees	Gulf Coast	11	22	3	3	.500	37	16	11	22	7	4.50
1982—Paintsville	Ap'lachian	13	79⅓	8	4	.667	76	33	22	66	22	2.50
1983—Fort Lauderdale	Florida St.	21	160⅓	*15	5	.750	129	38	30	152	43	*1.68
1983—Nashville	Southern	5	40⅓	3	2	.600	31	12	12	32	22	2.68
1984—New York	American	24	62⅓	2	8	.200	74	40	33	47	33	4.76
1984—Columbus†	Int'national	11	65⅓	3	3	.500	67	35	32	47	40	4.41
1985—Tacoma	P. Coast	24	149	7	10	.412	116	64	48	*179	*108	2.90
1985—Oakland	American	12	63⅔	6	4	.600	57	26	25	65	28	3.53
Major League Totals—2 Years		36	126	8	12	.400	131	66	58	112	61	4.14

Signed as free agent by New York Yankees' organization, August 1, 1980.
†Traded with Outfielder Stan Javier and Pitchers Jay Howell, Eric Plunk and Tim Birtsas to Oakland A's for Outfielder Rickey Henderson, Pitcher Bert Bradley and cash, December 5, 1984.

ERNEST RILES

Born October 2, 1960, at Cairo, Ga.
Height, 6.00. Weight, 180.
Throws right and bats lefthanded.
Attended Middle Georgia College, Cochran, Ga.

Major League stolen bases: 1985 (2).
Led California League in bases on balls received with 84 in 1982.
Led Texas League shortstops in total chances with 670 and double plays with 77 in 1983.
Led California League shortstops in double plays with 95 and tied for lead in total chances with 692 in 1982.

Year Club	League	Pos.	G.	AB.	R.	H.	2B.	3B.	HR.	RBI.	B.A.	PO.	A.	E.	F.A.
1981—Butte	Pion.	SS-3B-2B	67	256	63	89	11	2	4	43	.348	97	217	27	.921
1982—Stockton	Calif.	SS	138	447	60	128	23	6	2	56	.286	204	*451	37	.947
1983—El Paso	Texas	SS	130	476	109	166	31	3	13	91	*.349	*193	*445	32	*.952
1984—Vancouver	P. C.	SS	123	424	59	113	19	7	3	54	.267	*190	316	17	.967
1985—Vancouver	P. C.	SS	30	118	19	41	7	1	2	20	.347	47	120	6	.965
1985—Milwaukee	Amer.	SS	116	448	54	128	12	7	5	45	.286	183	310	22	.957
Major League Totals—1 Year			116	448	54	128	12	7	5	45	.286	183	310	22	.957

Selected by Seattle Mariners' organization in 21st round of free-agent draft, June 3, 1980.
Selected by Milwaukee Brewers' organization in secondary phase of free-agent draft, January 13, 1981.

GEORGE MICHAEL RILEY

Born October 6, 1956, at Philadelphia, Pa.
Height, 6.04. Weight, 200.
Throws and bats lefthanded.

Pitched 10-0, seven-inning no-hit victory against Fort Lauderdale, July 11, 1976 (first game).
Led Florida State League in games started with 26 in 1975.

Year Club	League	G.	IP.	W.	L.	Pct.	H.	R.	ER.	SO.	BB.	ERA.
1974—Bradenton Cubs	Gulf Coast	5	21	0	3	.000	18	14	8	16	8	3.43
1975—Key West	Florida St.	28	155	10	10	.500	141	75	62	84	81	3.60
1976—Pompano Beach	Florida St.	20	114	7	10	.412	122	73	49	76	47	3.87
1976—Midland	Texas	8	47	1	5	.167	61	37	34	29	36	6.51
1977—Midland	Texas	30	75	3	1	.750	79	41	36	57	36	4.32
1977—Wichita	Am. Assoc.	9	13	0	0	.000	15	7	7	11	8	4.85
1978—Wichita	Am. Assoc.	24	36	3	5	.375	47	31	29	17	23	7.25
1978—Midland	Texas	10	69	5	3	.625	77	37	34	50	39	4.43
1979—Wichita†	Am. Assoc.	38	74	3	8	.273	75	53	50	53	53	6.08
1979—Chicago	National	4	13	0	1	.000	16	9	8	5	6	5.54
1980—Wichita	Am. Assoc.	28	47	3	3	.500	60	23	23	32	19	4.40
1980—Chicago‡	National	22	36	0	4	.000	41	29	23	18	20	5.75
1981—Appleton§	Midwest	7	30	0	3	.000	30	13	12	27	13	3.60
1982—Reading	Eastern	37	58⅔	2	3	.400	56	27	23	46	25	3.53
1983—Reading	Eastern	27	81⅔	8	3	.727	69	27	22	58	44	2.42
1983—Portland	P. Coast	9	47	5	2	.714	48	36	33	27	32	6.32
1984—Portland x	P. Coast	36	163⅔	11	7	.611	127	65	54	138	52	2.97
1984—San Francisco	National	5	29⅓	1	0	1.000	39	14	13	12	7	3.99
1985—Phoenix y	P. Coast	46	89⅓	6	7	.462	97	52	48	64	43	4.84
Major League Totals—3 Years		31	78⅓	1	5	.167	96	52	44	35	33	5.06

Selected by Chicago Cubs' organization in 4th round of free-agent draft, June 5, 1974.
†On disabled list, April 17 to April 27, 1979.
‡Released, February 26, 1981; signed by Appleton (Chicago White Sox' organization), July 18, 1981.
§Released, March 29, 1982; signed by Reading (Philadelphia Phillies' organization), June 5, 1982.
xTraded with Pitcher Kelly Downs to San Francisco Giants for First Baseman Al Oliver and a player to be named later, August 20, 1984; Philadelphia Phillies acquired Pitcher Renie Martin to complete deal, August 30, 1984.
yTraded with Outfielder Alonzo Powell to Montreal Expos' organization for Pitcher Bill Laskey, October 24, 1985.

CALVIN EDWIN RIPKEN JR.

(Cal)

Born August 24, 1960, at Havre de Grace, Md.
Height, 6.04. Weight, 200.
Throws and bats righthanded.

Son of Cal Ripken, minor league catcher-outfielder, 1957 through 1964; minor league player-manager, Baltimore Orioles' organization, 1961, 1962 and 1964; minor league manager, Baltimore Orioles' organization, 1963 and 1965 through 1974; scout, Baltimore Orioles, 1975; and coach with Baltimore Orioles since 1976; brother of Billy Ripken, shortstop in Baltimore Orioles' organization; nephew of Bill Ripken, minor league outfielder, 1947 through 1949.

Established major league record for fewest stolen bases, season, most at-bats (0 and 663), 1983.
Established American League record for most assists by shortstop, season (583), 1984.
Tied American League record for most games by shortstop, season (162), 1983 and 1984.
Major League stolen bases: 1982 (3), 1984 (2), 1985 (2). Total—7.
Hit for the cycle, May 6, 1984.
Led American League shortstops in total chances with 831 in 1983 and 906 in 1984.
Led American League shortstops in double plays with 113 in 1983, 122 in 1984 and 123 in 1985.
Tied for Southern League lead in sacrifice flies with 9 in 1980.
Led Southern League third basemen in fielding percentage with .933, putouts with 119, assists with 268, and double plays with 34 in 1980.
Tied for Appalachian League lead in double plays by shortstops with 31 in 1978.
Named Major League Player of the Year by THE SPORTING NEWS, 1983.
Named American League Player of the Year by THE SPORTING NEWS, 1983.
Named American League Most Valuable Player by Baseball Writers' Association of America, 1983.
Named American League Rookie Player of the Year by THE SPORTING NEWS, 1982.
Named American League Rookie of the Year by Baseball Writers' Association of America, 1982.
Named shortstop on THE SPORTING NEWS American League All-Star Team, 1983 through 1985.
Named shortstop on THE SPORTING NEWS Silver Slugger team, 1983 through 1985.

Year Club	League	Pos.	G.	AB.	R.	H.	2B.	3B.	HR.	RBI.	B.A.	PO.	A.	E.	F.A.
1978—Bluefield	Appal.	SS	63	239	27	63	7	1	0	24	.264	★92	204	★33	.900
1979—Miami	Fla. St.	3B-SS-2B	105	393	51	119	★28	1	5	54	.303	149	260	30	.932
1979—Charlotte	South.	3B	17	61	6	11	0	1	3	8	.180	13	26	3	.929
1980—Charlotte	South.	3B-SS	●144	522	91	144	28	5	25	78	.276	151	341	35	.934
1981—Rochester	Int.	3B-SS	114	437	74	126	31	4	23	75	.288	128	320	21	.955
1981—Baltimore	Amer.	SS-3B	23	39	1	5	0	0	0	0	.128	13	30	3	.935
1982—Baltimore	Amer.	SS-3B	160	598	90	158	32	5	28	93	.264	221	440	19	.972
1983—Baltimore	Amer.	SS	●162	★663	★121	★211	★47	2	27	102	.318	272	★534	25	.970
1984—Baltimore	Amer.	SS	●162	641	103	195	37	7	27	86	.304	★297	★583	26	.971
1985—Baltimore†	Amer.	SS	161	642	116	181	32	5	26	110	.282	★286	474	26	.967
Major League Totals—5 Years			668	2583	431	750	148	19	108	391	.290	1089	2061	99	.970

Selected by Baltimore Orioles' organization in 2nd round of free-agent draft, June 6, 1978.

Year Club League	Pos.	G.	AB.	R.	H.	2B.	3B.	HR.	RBI.	B.A.	PO.	A.	E.	F.A.
1983—Baltimore .... Amer.	SS	4	15	5	6	2	0	0	1	.400	7	11	0	1.000

WORLD SERIES RECORD

Year Club League	Pos.	G.	AB.	R.	H.	2B.	3B.	HR.	RBI.	B.A.	PO.	A.	E.	F.A.
1983—Baltimore .... Amer.	SS	5	18	2	3	0	0	0	1	.167	6	14	0	1.000

ALL-STAR GAME RECORD

Year League	Pos.	AB.	R.	H.	2B.	3B.	HR.	RBI.	B.A.	PO.	A.	E.	F.A.
1983—American	SS	0	0	0	0	0	0	0	.000	1	0	0	1.000
1984—American	SS	3	0	0	0	0	0	0	.000	0	0		.000
1985—American	SS	3	0	1	0	0	0	0	.333	2	1	0	1.000
All-Star Game Totals—3 Years...................		6	0	1	0	0	0	0	.167	3	1	0	1.000

REGGIE BLAKE RITTER

Born January 23, 1960, at Malvern, Ark.
Height, 6.02. Weight, 195.
Throws right and bats lefthanded.
Attended Henderson State University, Arkadelphia, Ark.

Year Club	League	G.	IP.	W.	L.	Pct.	H.	R.	ER.	SO.	BB.	ERA.
1983—Waterloo.....................................	Midwest	31	110	4	7	.364	111	61	45	85	55	3.68
1984—Waterloo.....................................	Midwest	37	128⅔	6	6	.500	145	82	68	89	50	4.76
1985—Waterbury..................................	Eastern	15	101	7	6	.538	91	40	36	31	33	3.21
1985—Maine†......................................	Int'national	10	53	4	3	.571	51	26	25	24	17	4.25

Signed as free agent by Cleveland Indians' organization, August 12, 1982.
†On disabled list, August 3 to August 14, 1985.

GERMAN RIVERA (DIAZ)

Born July 6, 1960, at Santurce, Puerto Rico.
Height, 6.02. Weight, 170.
Throws and bats righthanded.

Major League stolen bases: 1984 (1).
Led Pacific Coast League third basemen in double plays with 21 in 1985.
Led Florida State League in sacrifice flies with 10 in 1980.
Led Pacific Coast League third basemen in assists with 333, double plays with 31 and total chances with 478 in 1983.
Led Texas League third basemen in errors with 29 in 1982.
Tied for Pioneer League lead in double plays by third basemen with 9 in 1978.

Year Club	League	Pos.	G.	AB.	R.	H.	2B.	3B.	HR.	RBI.	B.A.	PO.	A.	E.	F.A.
1978—Clinton....................	Midw.	3B-OF	36	108	11	22	3	1	3	13	.204	27	31	5	.921
1978—Lethbridge	Pion.	3B	66	252	61	79	15	2	7	45	.313	50	★120	12	★.934
1979—Lodi	Calif.	3B	36	139	26	26	6	1	1	17	.187	24	84	19	.850
1979—Clinton...................	Midw.	3B	100	338	43	82	18	5	4	42	.243	74	199	17	.941
1980—Vero Beach..........	Fla. St.	3B	137	530	77	137	19	10	4	★80	.258	81	203	●29	.907
1981—Lodi	Calif.	3B-SS	128	478	78	127	31	2	13	71	.266	157	419	40	.935
1982—San Antonio†........	Texas	SS-3B	136	474	63	137	17	4	15	60	.289	171	342	61	.894
1983—Albuquerque........	P. Coast	3B-SS	138	515	109	169	27	5	24	103	.328	116	343	34	.931
1983—Los Angeles	Nat.	3B	13	17	1	6	1	0	0	0	.353	2	11	1	.929
1984—Los Angeles	Nat.	3B	94	227	20	59	12	2	2	17	.260	55	167	15	.937
1984—Albuquerque........	P. C.	3B-SS	51	181	30	57	12	3	4	39	.315	53	117	14	.924
1985—Alb.‡-Tucson	P. C.	3B	108	384	45	108	22	2	8	44	.281	76	191	18	★.937
1985—Houston..................	Nat.	3B	13	36	3	7	2	1	0	2	.194	7	25	2	.941
Major League Totals—3 Years................			120	280	24	72	15	3	2	19	.257	64	203	18	.937

Signed as free agent by Los Angeles Dodgers' organization, December 20, 1977.
†Drafted by Oakland A's, December 6, 1982; returned, March 25, 1983.
‡Traded to Houston Astros' organization, July 15, 1985, completing deal in which Houston traded Infielder Enos Cabell to Los Angeles Dodgers for Pitcher Rafael Montalvo and a player to be named later, July 10, 1985.

LUIS ANTONIO RIVERA

Born January 3, 1964, at Cidra, Puerto Rico.
Height, 5.11. Weight, 165.
Throws and bats righthanded.

Led Southern League shortstops in total chances with 643 and double plays with 107 in 1985.
Led Florida State League shortstops in assists with 436, errors with 51, total chances with 704 and double plays with 95 in 1983.
Tied for Florida State League lead in total chances by shortstops with 626 in 1984.

Year Club	League	Pos.	G.	AB.	R.	H.	2B.	3B.	HR.	RBI.	B.A.	PO.	A.	E.	F.A.
1982—San Jose	Calif.	SS	130	476	53	123	20	3	3	49	.258	226	389	55	.918
1983—W. Palm Beach....	Fla. St.	SS	129	419	63	95	18	5	5	53	.227	217	436	51	.928
1984—W. Palm Beach....	Fla. St.	SS	124	439	54	100	23	0	6	43	.228	★198	★389	39	.938
1985—Jacksonville..........	South.	SS	138	★538	74	129	20	2	16	72	.240	★198	★412	33	.949

Signed as free agent by Montreal Expos' organization, September 22, 1981.

BERTRAND ROLAND ROBERGE

Name pronounced ROW-berj.

(Bert)

Born October 3, 1954, at Lewiston, Me.
Height, 6.04. Weight, 190.
Throws and bats righthanded.
Received bachelor of science degree in zoology from
University of Maine, Orono, Me.

Major League saves: 1979 (4), 1982 (3), 1985 (2). Total—9.
Led National League in balks with 5 in 1985.

Year Club	League	G.	IP.	W.	L.	Pct.	H.	R.	ER.	SO.	BB.	ERA.
1976—Covington†	Ap'lachian	14	36	2	2	.500	33	21	13	40	12	3.25
1976—Memphis	Int'national	2	10	0	0	.000	11	5	3	8	3	2.70
1977—Columbus	Southern	6	7	0	0	.000	13	5	5	9	3	6.43
1977—Cocoa	Florida St.	33	60	4	5	.444	54	24	17	35	26	2.55
1978—Columbus	Southern	21	32	0	3	.000	37	15	12	24	10	3.38
1979—Columbus	Southern	13	88	7	1	.875	80	34	29	86	37	2.97
1979—Houston‡	National	26	32	3	0	1.000	20	6	6	13	17	1.69
1980—Tucson	P. Coast	34	49	5	3	.625	44	28	26	47	28	4.78
1980—Houston	National	14	24	2	0	1.000	24	16	16	9	10	6.00
1981—Tucson	P. Coast	50	87	5	4	.556	85	43	35	62	32	3.62
1982—Tucson	P. Coast	34	46⅔	4	4	.500	49	21	17	21	23	3.28
1982—Houston	National	22	25⅔	1	2	.333	29	12	12	18	6	4.21
1983—Tucson§	P. Coast	47	68⅔	3	8	.273	66	37	35	63	30	4.59
1984—Denver	Am. Assoc.	26	37	5	1	.833	27	8	8	36	10	1.95
1984—Chicago xy	American	21	40⅔	3	3	.500	36	18	17	25	15	3.76
1985—Montreal z	National	42	68	3	3	.500	58	28	26	34	22	3.44
1985—Indianapolis	Am. Assoc.	1	2	0	0	.000	2	1	1	2	1	4.50
National League Totals—4 Years		104	149⅔	9	5	.643	131	62	60	74	55	3.61
American League Totals—1 Year		21	40⅔	3	3	.500	36	18	17	25	15	3.76
Major League Totals—5 Years		125	190⅓	12	8	.600	167	80	77	99	70	3.64

Selected by Houston Astros' organization in 17th round of free-agent draft, June 8, 1976.
†Appeared in one game as outfielder with three putouts.
‡On disabled list, August 16 to September 6, 1979.
§Granted free agency, October 20, 1983; signed by Chicago White Sox, December 5, 1983.
xOn disabled list, June 23 to July 25, 1984; included rehabilitation disability assignment to Denver, July 5 to July 24, 1984.
yTraded to Montreal Expos for Infielder Bryan Little, December 7, 1984.
zOn disabled list, May 30 to July 8, 1985; included rehabilitation disability assignment to Indianapolis, July 4 to July 8, 1985.

LEON JOSEPH ROBERTS III

Born October 27, 1963, at Berkley, Calif.
Height, 5.07. Weight, 150.
Throws right and bats left and righthanded.
Attended Chabot College, Hayward, Calif.; and University of Nevada, Las Vegas, Nev.

Tied for Eastern League lead in stolen bases with 40 in 1985.
Led Carolina League second basemen in total chances with 654 and double plays with 91 in 1984.
Led South Atlantic League second basemen in fielding percentage with .962 and tied for lead in double plays with 76 in 1983.

Year Club	League	Pos.	G.	AB.	R.	H.	2B.	3B.	HR.	RBI.	B.A.	PO.	A.	E.	F.A.
1982—Bradenton Pir.	Gulf C.	2B	6	23	4	7	1	0	0	1	.304	14	15	0	1.000
1982—Greenwood	S. Atl.	2B	33	107	15	23	3	1	0	6	.215	52	82	7	.950
1983—Greenwood	S. Atl.	2B-SS	122	438	78	140	20	5	6	63	.320	273	311	24	.961
1984—Prince William	Carol.	2B	134	498	81	∗150	25	5	8	77	.301	∗282	352	20	∗.969
1985—Nashua†‡	East.	2B	105	401	64	109	19	5	1	23	.272	217	249	●29	.941

Selected by Pittsburgh Pirates' organization in 5th round of free-agent draft, June 8, 1981.
Selected by Pittsburgh Pirates' organization in secondary phase of free-agent draft, June 7, 1982.
†On suspended list, June 30 to July 3, 1985.
‡Drafted by San Diego Padres, December 10, 1985.

SCOTT ANTHONY ROBERTS

Born October 7, 1959, at Seattle, Wash.
Height, 6.05. Weight, 220.
Throws and bats righthanded.
Attended University of Hawaii, Honolulu, Haw.

Led Pioneer League in hit batsmen with 12 in 1981.

Year Club	League	G.	IP.	W.	L.	Pct.	H.	R.	ER.	SO.	BB.	ERA.
1981—Butte	Pioneer	12	78	6	1	∗.857	51	23	16	74	28	1.85
1982—Stockton	California	24	174⅓	14	6	.700	151	65	49	137	41	2.53
1983—Vancouver†	P. Coast	21	109	6	10	.375	135	90	77	69	63	6.36
1984—Vancouver	P. Coast	26	151	8	6	.571	156	72	60	89	74	3.58
1985—Vancouver	P. Coast	12	27⅓	1	2	.333	33	21	19	17	13	6.26
1985—El Paso‡	Texas	12	76	7	2	.778	93	53	48	47	26	5.68

Selected by Pittsburgh Pirates' organization in 7th round of free-agent draft, June 6, 1978.
Selected by Milwaukee Brewers' organization in 2nd round of free-agent draft, June 8, 1981.
†On disabled list, May 20 to May 30, 1983.
‡Traded to Cleveland Indians for Pitcher Rich Thompson, December 16, 1985.

ANDRE LEVETT ROBERTSON

Born October 2, 1957, at Orange, Tex.
Height, 5.10. Weight, 160.
Throws and bats righthanded.
Attending University of Texas, Austin, Tex.

Major League stolen bases: 1981 (1), 1983 (2), 1985 (1). Total—4.

Year Club	League	Pos.	G.	AB.	R.	H.	2B.	3B.	HR.	RBI.	B.A.	PO.	A.	E.	F.A.
1979—Dunedin	Fla. St.	SS-2B	70	264	35	57	14	2	2	18	.216	132	245	22	.945
1979—Syracuse†	Int.	SS	1	4	0	0	0	0	0	0	.000	1	4	0	1.000
1980—Fort Lauderdale ..	Fla. St.	SS	63	233	30	58	7	4	0	22	.249	109	184	10	.967
1980—Columbus..............	Int.	SS	68	215	22	54	7	3	3	19	.251	88	222	13	.960
1980—Nashville...............	South.	SS	13	46	7	12	2	1	1	11	.261	23	43	5	.930
1981—Columbus‡	Int.	SS	123	402	55	104	13	6	9	49	.259	★210	★362	17	★.971
1981—New York.............	Amer.	SS-2B	10	19	1	5	1	0	0	0	.263	9	24	0	1.000
1982—Columbus..............	Int.	SS-2B	57	202	28	41	7	3	3	26	.203	115	144	12	.956
1982—New York.............	Amer.	SS-2B-3B	44	118	16	26	5	0	2	9	.220	84	98	6	.968
1983—New York§...........	Amer.	SS-2B	98	322	37	80	16	3	1	22	.248	163	302	15	.969
1984—Columbus..............	Int.	SS-3B-2B	69	226	30	54	8	1	6	19	.239	109	220	12	.965
1984—New York.............	Amer.	SS-2B	52	140	10	30	5	1	0	6	.214	68	142	16	.929
1985—Columbus x...........	Int.	SS	9	28	3	11	1	0	0	1	.393	18	32	2	.962
1985—New York.............	Amer.	3B-SS-2B	50	125	16	41	5	0	2	17	.328	32	67	10	.908
Major League Totals—5 Years.................			254	724	80	182	32	4	5	54	.251	356	633	47	.955

Selected by Texas Rangers' organization in 12th round of free-agent draft, June 8, 1976.
Selected by Toronto Blue Jays' organization in 4th round of free-agent draft, June 5, 1979.
†Sold to New York Yankees' organization, December 10, 1979.
‡On disabled list, April 18 to May 3, 1981.
§On disabled list, August 18, 1983 through remainder of season.
xOn New York disabled list, March 24 to May 29, 1985; included rehabilitation disability assignment to Columbus, May 20 to May 29, 1985.

CHAMPIONSHIP SERIES RECORD

Year Club	League	Pos.	G.	AB.	R.	H.	2B.	3B.	HR.	RBI.	B.A.	PO.	A.	E.	F.A.
1981—New York.............	Amer.	PH-SS	1	1	0	0	0	0	0	0	.000	2	1	0	1.000

WORLD SERIES RECORD

Year Club	League	Pos.	G.	AB.	R.	H.	2B.	3B.	HR.	RBI.	B.A.	PO.	A.	E.	F.A.
1981—New York.............	Amer.	PR	1	0	0	0	0	0	0	0	.000	0	0	0	.000

WILLIAM JOSEPH ROBIDOUX

Name pronounced ROW-ba-doe.

(Billy Joe)

Born January 13, 1964, at Ware, Mass.
Height, 6.01. Weight, 200.
Throws right and bats lefthanded.

Led Texas League in total bases with 297 and slugging percentage with .577 in 1985.
Led Texas League first basemen in putouts with 1,025, assists with 68, fielding percentage with .988, total chances with 1,106 and double plays with 102 in 1985.
Named Texas League Most Valuable Player, 1985.

Year Club	League	Pos.	G.	AB.	R.	H.	2B.	3B.	HR.	RBI.	B.A.	PO.	A.	E.	F.A.
1982—Pikeville†	Appal.	3B-1B	54	167	28	48	10	1	0	13	.287	57	54	15	.881
1983—Beloit	Midw.	3B-1B-2B	126	435	70	138	30	1	10	61	.317	104	163	25	.914
1984—Stockton	Calif.	3B-1B	97	333	50	93	18	1	5	67	.279	323	98	15	.966
1985—El Paso	Texas	1B-OF-3B	133	515	★111	★176	★46	3	23	★132	★.342	1030	69	15	.987
1985—Milwaukee.............	Amer.	OF-1B	18	51	5	9	2	0	3	8	.176	64	6	0	1.000
Major League Totals—1 Year..................			18	51	5	9	2	0	3	8	.176	64	6	0	1.000

Selected by Milwaukee Brewers' organization in 6th round of free-agent draft, June 7, 1982.
†On disabled list, June 21 to July 1, 1982.

DON ALLEN ROBINSON

Born June 8, 1957, at Ashland, Ky.
Height, 6.04. Weight, 231.
Throws and bats righthanded.

Major League saves: 1978 (1), 1980 (1), 1981 (2), 1984 (10), 1985 (3). Total—17.
Tied for National League lead in home runs allowed with 26 in 1982.
Led Western Carolinas League in complete games with 11 in 1976.
Tied for Gulf Coast League lead in hit batsmen with 6 in 1975.
Named National League Rookie Pitcher of the Year by THE SPORTING NEWS, 1978.
Named pitcher on THE SPORTING NEWS National League Silver Slugger team, 1982.

Year Club	League	G.	IP.	W.	L.	Pct.	H.	R.	ER.	SO.	BB.	ERA.
1975—Bradenton Pirates........................	Gulf Coast	10	66	2	3	.400	51	23	18	★70	31	2.45
1976—Charleston	W. Carol.	25	★172	12	9	.571	146	79	62	132	64	3.24
1977—Shreveport......................................	Texas	18	112	7	6	.538	113	58	51	103	41	4.06
1977—Columbus†	Int'national	1	5	1	0	1.000	7	0	0	3	1	0.00
1978—Pittsburgh.......................................	National	35	228	14	6	.700	203	98	88	135	57	3.47
1979—Pittsburgh.......................................	National	29	161	8	8	.500	171	74	69	96	52	3.86
1980—Pittsburgh‡.....................................	National	29	160	7	10	.412	157	74	71	103	45	3.99

Year Club	League	G.	IP.	W.	L.	Pct.	H.	R.	ER.	SO.	BB.	ERA.
1981—Pittsburgh§	National	16	38	0	3	.000	47	27	25	17	23	5.92
1982—Pittsburgh	National	38	227	15	13	.536	213	*123	108	165	103	4.28
1983—Pittsburgh x	National	9	36½	2	2	.500	43	21	18	28	21	4.46
1983—Lynn	Eastern	2	6⅔	0	1	.000	9	6	6	5	2	8.10
1984—Pittsburgh y	National	51	122	5	6	.455	99	45	41	110	49	3.02
1985—Pittsburgh	National	44	95⅓	5	11	.313	95	49	41	65	42	3.87
Major League Totals— 8 Years		251	1067⅔	56	59	.487	1028	511	461	719	392	3.89

Selected by Pittsburgh Pirates' organization in 3rd round of free-agent draft, June 4, 1975.
†On disabled list, July 28 to September 6, 1977.
‡On disabled list, March 31 to May 1, 1980.
§On disabled list, May 2 to June 6 and August 2 to August 26, 1981.
xOn disabled list, March 29 to June 10 and July 29 to September 2, 1983; included rehabilitation disability assignment to Lynn, April 29 to May 18, 1983.
yAppeared in one game as an outfielder with two putouts.

CHAMPIONSHIP SERIES RECORD

Year Club	League	G.	IP.	W.	L.	Pct.	H.	R.	ER.	SO.	BB.	ERA.
1979—Pittsburgh	National	2	2	1	0	1.000	0	0	0	3	1	0.00

WORLD SERIES RECORD

Year Club	League	G.	IP.	W.	L.	Pct.	H.	R.	ER.	SO.	BB.	ERA.
1979—Pittsburgh	National	4	5	1	0	1.000	4	3	3	3	6	5.40

JEFFREY DANIEL ROBINSON
(Jeff)

Born December 13, 1960, at Santa Ana, Calif.
Height, 6.04. Weight, 195.
Throws and bats righthanded.
Attended California State University, Fullerton, Calif.

Tied for National League lead in hit batsmen with 7 in 1984.
Tied for Pacific Coast League lead in games started by pitchers with 29 in 1985.

Year Club	League	G.	IP.	W.	L.	Pct.	H.	R.	ER.	SO.	BB.	ERA.
1983—Fresno	California	14	94⅔	7	6	.538	88	35	24	78	21	2.28
1984—San Francisco	National	34	171⅔	7	15	.318	195	99	87	102	52	4.56
1985—Phoenix	P. Coast	29	161	9	9	.500	192	107	92	80	60	5.14
1985—San Francisco	National	8	12⅓	0	0	.000	16	11	7	8	10	5.11
Major League Totals—2 Years		42	184	7	15	.318	211	110	94	110	62	4.60

Selected by Toronto Blue Jays' organization in 17th round of free-agent draft, June 5, 1979.
Selected by Detroit Tigers' organization in 14th round of free-agent draft, June 7, 1982.
Selected by San Francisco Giants' organization in 2nd round of free-agent draft, June 6, 1983.

RONALD DEAN ROBINSON
(Ron)

Born March 24, 1962, at Exeter, Calif.
Height, 6.04. Weight, 200.
Throws and bats righthanded.

Major League saves: 1985 (1).

Year Club	League	G.	IP.	W.	L.	Pct.	H.	R.	ER.	SO.	BB.	ERA.
1980—Tampa	Florida St.	13	76	4	6	.400	76	32	28	44	16	3.32
1981—Cedar Rapids	Midwest	24	169	10	8	.556	136	58	42	165	55	2.24
1982—Waterbury	Eastern	32	178⅓	13	7	.650	166	78	65	149	65	3.28
1983—Waterbury	Eastern	20	142⅔	7	9	.438	132	66	57	82	60	3.60
1983—Indianapolis	Am. Assoc.	4	30⅔	4	0	1.000	22	13	11	20	7	3.23
1984—Wichita	Am. Assoc.	25	150⅓	9	6	.600	168	86	77	98	60	4.61
1984—Cincinnati	National	12	39⅔	1	2	.333	35	18	12	24	13	2.72
1985—Denver	Am. Assoc.	6	39⅔	2	1	.667	39	17	12	24	12	2.72
1985—Cincinnati	National	33	108⅓	7	7	.500	107	53	48	76	32	3.99
Major League Totals—2 Years		45	148	8	9	.471	142	71	60	100	45	3.65

Selected by Cincinnati Reds' organization in 1st round (19th player selected) of free-agent draft, June 3, 1980.

MICHAEL JOSEPH ROCHFORD
(Mike)

Born March 14, 1963, at Methuen, Mass.
Height, 6.04. Weight, 205.
Throws and bats lefthanded.
Attended Santa Fe Community College, Gainsville, Fla.

Led International League in balks with 5 in 1984.
Tied for Carolina League lead in games started by pitchers with 29 in 1983.

Year Club	League	G.	IP.	W.	L.	Pct.	H.	R.	ER.	SO.	BB.	ERA.
1982—Elmira	NYP	16	85⅔	6	4	.600	99	53	40	66	26	4.20
1983—Winston-Salem	Carolina	29	210⅓	16	11	.593	182	85	70	165	57	3.00
1984—Pawtucket	Int'national	31	141⅓	8	10	.444	156	88	77	73	59	4.90
1985—New Britain	Eastern	14	93⅓	8	5	.615	84	39	31	42	41	2.99
1985—Pawtucket	Int'national	12	72	5	2	.714	74	34	33	47	32	4.13

Selected by Boston Red Sox' organization in 1st round (17th player selected) of free-agent draft, January 12, 1982.

EDWIN RODRIGUEZ (MORALES)
(Ed)

Born August 14, 1960, at Ponce, Puerto Rico.
Height, 5.10. Weight, 175.
Throws and bats righthanded.

Year Club	League	Pos.	G.	AB.	R.	H.	2B.	3B.	HR.	RBI.	B.A.	PO.	A.	E.	F.A.
1980—Bradenton Yanks	Gulf C.	1B-2B	47	157	22	39	4	2	1	16	.248	179	9	6	.969
1981—Oneonta	NYP	2B-3B-SS	50	146	27	45	5	3	0	19	.308	81	120	4	.980
1982—Greensboro	S. Atl.	2B	115	425	88	126	23	3	4	62	.296	227	320	25	.956
1982—Nashville	South.	SS	10	34	4	7	0	1	0	3	.206	19	38	4	.934
1982—New York	Amer.	2B	3	9	2	3	0	0	0	1	.333	2	12	2	.875
1983—Columbus†	Int.	2B-SS-3B	112	393	73	98	7	8	2	54	.249	207	329	25	.955
1983—San Diego	Nat.	2B-SS-3B	7	12	1	2	1	0	0	0	.167	8	8	0	1.000
1984—Las Vegas‡	P. C.	2B-SS-3B	105	341	45	80	10	8	6	38	.235	205	246	14	.970
1985—Las Vegas	P. C.	2B-SS	115	436	78	126	21	6	6	35	.289	207	286	26	.950
1985—San Diego	Nat.	PH	1	1	0	0	0	0	0	0	.000	0	0	0	.000
American League Totals—1 Year			3	9	2	3	0	0	0	1	.333	2	12	2	.875
National League Totals—2 Years			8	13	1	2	1	0	0	0	.154	8	8	0	1.000
Major League Totals—3 Years			11	22	3	5	1	0	0	1	.227	10	20	2	.938

Signed as free agent by New York Yankees' organization, June 3, 1980.

†Traded with Pitcher Dennis Rasmussen to San Diego Padres, September 12, 1983, completing deal in which San Diego traded Pitcher John Montefusco to New York Yankees for two players to be named later, August 26, 1983.

‡On disabled list, May 6 to May 18, 1985.

RUBEN DARIO RODRIGUEZ (MARTINEZ)

Born August 4, 1964, at Cabrera, Dominican Republic.
Throws and bats righthanded.

Led Eastern League in passed balls with 17 in 1985.
Led Eastern League catchers in double plays with 10 in 1984.

Year Club	League	Pos.	G.	AB.	R.	H.	2B.	3B.	HR.	RBI.	B.A.	PO.	A.	E.	F.A.
1982—Greenwood	S. Atl.	C	69	218	26	54	13	0	1	15	.248	351	60	19	.956
1983—Alexandria	Carol.	C-1B	79	254	19	58	14	1	4	31	.228	496	70	11	.981
1984—Nashua	East.	C	87	242	26	53	13	1	4	32	.219	409	58	11	.977
1985—Nashua	East.	C	104	341	28	73	9	4	3	40	.214	498	96	11	.982
1985—Hawaii	P. C.	C	1	4	0	1	0	0	0	0	.250	9	0	0	1.000

Signed as free agent by Pittsburgh Pirates' organization, November 6, 1981.

VICTOR MANUEL RODRIGUEZ (RIVERA)
(Vic)

Born July 14, 1961, at New York, N.Y.
Height, 5.11. Weight, 160.
Throws and bats righthanded.

Led International League in grounding into double plays with 23 in 1984.
Led International League second basemen in total chances with 689 in 1984.

Year Club	League	Pos.	G.	AB.	R.	H.	2B.	3B.	HR.	RBI.	B.A.	PO.	A.	E.	F.A.
1977—Bluefield	Appal.	3B-SS	53	188	28	55	10	4	3	23	.293	1	6	1	.875
1978—Bluefield	Appal.	OF-3B-SS	59	209	26	67	4	2	2	28	.321	39	14	5	.914
1979—Miami	Fla. St.	2B-3B-OF	67	228	23	70	10	2	1	31	.307	71	105	11	.941
1980—Alexandria†	Carol.	2B	33	130	20	39	4	2	2	15	.300	62	94	6	.963
1980—Charlotte	South.	3B	19	65	4	15	0	0	0	4	.231	14	37	2	.962
1980—Miami	Fla. St.	2B	50	184	21	60	10	2	2	21	.326	103	144	14	.946
1981—Charlotte	South.	2B	138	553	68	169	22	1	9	65	.306	337	357	18	.975
1982—Rochester	Int.	2B	87	300	26	74	10	2	0	18	.247	189	273	17	.965
1982—Charlotte	South.	2B	47	165	17	48	13	0	3	18	.291	95	116	10	.955
1983—Charlotte	South.	2B-3B	140	★571	80	●170	26	1	14	77	.298	291	386	19	.973
1984—Rochester	Int.	2B	132	478	54	131	22	●6	6	46	.274	★272	★403	14	.980
1984—Baltimore‡	Amer.	2B	11	17	4	7	3	0	0	2	.412	8	15	1	.958
1985—Las Vegas§	P. C.	2B-3B-SS	127	462	56	144	31	3	11	58	.312	183	311	16	.969
Major League Totals—1 Year			11	17	4	7	3	0	0	2	.412	8	15	1	.958

Signed as free agent by Baltimore Orioles' organization, February 11, 1977.

†Loaned to Alexandria (Co-op), April 6, 1980; returned, May 23, 1980.

‡Traded to San Diego Padres' organization for Third Baseman Fritz Connally, February 7, 1985.

§Granted free agency, October 15, 1985; invited to St. Louis Cardinals' spring training.

GARY STEVEN ROENICKE

Name pronounced RENN-uh-kee.

Born December 5, 1954, at Covina, Calif.
Height, 6.03. Weight, 200.
Throws and bats righthanded.
Attended California Poly State University, Pomona, Calif., Whittier College,
Whittier, Calif., and University of California at Los Angeles, Los Angeles, Calif.
Brother of Ron Roenicke, outfielder with San Francisco Giants.

Major League stolen bases: 1979 (1), 1980 (2), 1981 (1), 1982 (6), 1983 (2), 1984 (1), 1985 (2). Total—15.
Led American Association in being hit by pitch with 13 in 1977.
Led Florida State League in being hit by pitch with 11 in 1974.

Tied for Eastern League lead in being hit by pitch with 12 in 1975.
Tied for Florida State League lead in double plays by third basemen with 32 in 1974.
Named Eastern League Most Valuable Player, 1975.

Year	Club	League	Pos.	G.	AB.	R.	H.	2B.	3B.	HR.	RBI.	B.A.	PO.	A.	E.	F.A.
1973—Jamestown	NYP	3B	68	255	48	76	17	6	3	40	.298	*71	92	11	*.937
1974—W. Palm Beach	Fla. St.	3B-OF-1B	131	470	68	130	24	0	14	*82	.277	152	216	31	.922
1974—Quebec City	East.	3B	1	3	0	1	0	0	0	0	.333	1	2	0	1.000
1975—Quebec City	East.	OF	131	466	67	133	23	0	14	*74	.285	223	*22	10	.961
1976—Denver	A. A.	OF	77	252	56	73	11	5	12	44	.290	110	9	5	.960
1976—Montreal	Nat.	OF	29	90	9	20	3	1	2	5	.222	39	3	2	.955
1977—Denver†	A. A.	OF-3B-1B	124	448	87	144	31	4	11	72	.321	174	113	17	.944
1978—Rochester	Int.	OF-1B-3B	98	329	49	101	15	1	13	64	.307	219	25	2	.992
1978—Baltimore	Amer.	OF	27	58	5	15	3	0	3	15	.259	22	1	0	1.000
1979—Baltimore	Amer.	OF	133	376	60	98	16	1	25	64	.261	246	10	5	.981
1980—Baltimore‡	Amer.	OF	118	297	40	71	13	0	10	28	.239	197	8	0	*1.000
1981—Baltimore	Amer.	OF	85	219	31	59	16	0	3	20	.269	175	2	3	.983
1982—Baltimore	Amer.	OF-1B	137	393	58	106	25	1	21	74	.270	363	13	3	.992
1983—Baltimore	Amer.	OF-1B-3B	115	323	45	84	13	0	19	64	.260	219	9	3	.987
1984—Baltimore	Amer.	OF	121	326	36	73	19	1	10	44	.224	197	6	1	.995
1985—Baltimore§	Amer.	OF	114	225	36	49	9	0	15	43	.218	134	6	1	.993
American League Totals—8 Years			850	2217	311	555	114	3	106	352	.250	1553	55	16	.990
National League Totals—1 Year			29	90	9	20	3	1	2	5	.222	39	3	2	.955
Major League Totals—9 Years			879	2307	320	575	117	4	108	357	.249	1592	58	18	.989

Selected by Montreal Expos' organization in 1st round (eighth player selected) of free-agent draft, June 5, 1973.
†Traded with Pitchers Joe Kerrigan and Don Stanhouse to Baltimore Orioles for Pitchers Rudy May, Randy Miller and Bryn Smith, December 7, 1977.
‡On disabled list, June 10 to July 15, 1980.
§Traded with a player to be named later to New York Yankees for Pitcher Rich Bordi and Infielder Rex Hudler, December 12, 1985; New York acquired Outfielder Leo Hernandez to complete deal, December 16, 1985.

CHAMPIONSHIP SERIES RECORD

Tied Championship Series record for most consecutive games, one or more runs batted in, total Series (4).
Tied American League Championship Series record for most bases on balls, four-game Series (5), 1983.

Year	Club	League	Pos.	G.	AB.	R.	H.	2B.	3B.	HR.	RBI.	B.A.	PO.	A.	E.	F.A.
1979—Baltimore	Amer.	OF-PH	2	5	1	1	0	0	0	1	.200	3	1	0	1.000
1983—Baltimore	Amer.	OF-PH	3	4	4	3	1	0	1	4	.750	4	1	0	1.000
Championship Series Totals—2 Years			5	9	5	4	1	0	1	5	.444	7	2	0	1.000

WORLD SERIES RECORD

Year	Club	League	Pos.	G.	AB.	R.	H.	2B.	3B.	HR.	RBI.	B.A.	PO.	A.	E.	F.A.
1979—Baltimore	Amer.	OF-PH	6	16	1	2	1	0	0	0	.125	14	1	0	1.000
1983—Baltimore	Amer.	PH-OF	3	7	0	0	0	0	0	0	.000	2	1	0	1.000
World Series Totals—2 Years			9	23	1	2	1	0	0	0	.087	16	2	0	1.000

RONALD JON ROENICKE

Name pronounced RENN-uh-kee.

(Ron)

Born August 19, 1956, at Covina, Calif.
Height, 6.00. Weight, 180.
Throws left and bats left and righthanded.
Attended Mount San Antonio College, Walnut, Calif., and
University of California, Los Angeles, Calif.
Brother of Gary Roenicke, outfielder with New York Yankees.

Major League stolen bases: 1981 (1), 1982 (5), 1983 (9), 1985 (6). Total—21.
Led Pacific Coast League in on-base percentage with .464, bases on balls received with 110, and sacrifice flies with 16 in 1981.
Led Texas League outfielders in fielding percentage with .993 in 1979.

Year	Club	League	Pos.	G.	AB.	R.	H.	2B.	3B.	HR.	RBI.	B.A.	PO.	A.	E.	F.A.
1977—Clinton	Midw.	OF-1B	76	250	35	64	12	0	5	25	.256	253	7	4	.985
1978—Lodi†	Calif.	OF	61	215	61	78	13	5	9	51	.363	100	8	6	.947
1978—San Antonio	Texas	OF	30	109	16	26	2	2	1	11	.239	51	4	2	.965
1979—San Antonio	Texas	OF-1B	130	464	82	140	24	6	13	69	.302	426	18	4	.991
1980—Albuquerque‡	P. C.	OF-1B	77	270	60	80	18	3	7	47	.296	167	9	8	.957
1981—Albuquerque	P. C.	OF-1B	126	411	100	130	23	9	15	94	.316	217	14	4	.983
1981—Los Angeles	Nat.	OF	22	47	6	11	0	0	0	0	.234	38	1	0	1.000
1982—Albuquerque	P. C.	OF	23	78	18	24	5	1	4	15	.308	14	1	0	1.000
1982—Los Angeles	Nat.	OF	109	143	18	37	8	0	1	12	.259	59	1	1	.984
1983—Los Angeles§	Nat.	OF	81	145	12	32	4	0	2	12	.221	75	1	1	.987
1983—Seattle x	Amer.	OF-1B	59	198	23	50	12	0	4	23	.253	168	13	2	.989
1984—Las Vegas y	P. C.	OF-1B	90	290	65	90	14	3	8	45	.310	161	7	1	.994
1984—San Diego z	Nat.	OF	12	20	4	6	1	0	1	2	.300	10	0	0	1.000
1985—Phoenix	P. C.	OF-1B	60	214	36	66	16	0	5	48	.308	130	6	1	.993
1985—San Francisco	Nat.	OF	65	133	23	34	9	1	3	13	.256	63	0	1	.984
National League Totals—5 Years			289	488	63	120	22	1	7	39	.246	245	3	3	.988
American League Totals—1 Year			59	198	23	50	12	0	4	23	.253	168	13	2	.989
Major League Totals—5 Years			348	686	86	170	34	1	11	62	.248	413	16	5	.988

Selected by Oakland A's organization in 7th round of free-agent draft, June 5, 1974.

Selected by Detroit Tigers' organization in secondary phase of free-agent draft, January 7, 1976.
Selected by Atlanta Braves' organization in secondary phase of free-agent draft, June 8, 1976.
Selected by Los Angeles Dodgers' organization in secondary phase of free agent draft, June 7, 1977.
†On disabled list, June 11 to July 17, 1978.
‡On disabled list, July 1 to August 27, 1980.
§Released, July 18, 1983; signed by Seattle Mariners, July 26, 1983.
xReleased, March 23, 1984; signed by Las Vegas (San Diego Padres' organization), April 5, 1984.
yOn disabled list, June 19 to July 29, 1984.
zReleased, March 30, 1985; signed by Phoenix (San Francisco Giants' organization), May 3, 1985.

WORLD SERIES RECORD

Year	Club	League	Pos.	G.	AB.	R.	H.	2B.	3B.	HR.	RBI.	B.A.	PO.	A.	E.	F.A.
1984—San Diego	Nat.	OF-PR	2	0	0	0	0	0	0	0	0	.000	0	0	0	.000

KENNETH SCOTT ROGERS
(Kenny)

Born November 10, 1964, at Savannah, Ga.
Height, 6.00. Weight, 165.
Throws and bats lefthanded.

Year	Club	League	G.	IP.	W.	L.	Pct.	H.	R.	ER.	SO.	BB.	ERA.
1982—Sarasota Rangers	Gulf Coast	2	3	0	0	.000	0	0	0	4	0	0.00
1983—Sarasota Rangers	Gulf Coast	15	53⅓	4	1	.800	40	21	14	36	20	2.36
1984—Burlington	Midwest	39	92⅔	4	7	.364	87	52	41	93	33	3.98
1985—Daytona Beach	Florida St.	6	10	0	1	.000	12	9	8	9	11	7.20
1985—Burlington	Midwest	33	95	2	5	.286	67	34	30	96	62	2.84

Selected by Texas Rangers' organization in 39th round of free-agent draft, June 7, 1982.

STEPHEN DOUGLAS ROGERS
(Steve)

Born October 26, 1949, at Jefferson City, Mo.
Height, 6.01. Weight, 175.
Throws and bats righthanded.
Received bachelor of science degree in petroleum engineering from Tulsa University, Tulsa, Okla.

Established major league record for fewest complete games for leader in complete games (14), 1980.
Major League saves: 1976 (1), 1978 (1). Total—2.
Led National League in sacrifice hits with 20 in 1983.
Led National League in shutouts with 5 in 1983 and tied for lead with 5 in 1979.
Led National League in complete games with 14 in 1980.
Named National League Rookie Pitcher of the Year by THE SPORTING NEWS, 1973.
Named righthanded pitcher on THE SPORTING NEWS National League All-Star Team, 1982.

Year	Club	League	G.	IP.	W.	L.	Pct.	H.	R.	ER.	SO.	BB.	ERA.
1971—Winnipeg	Int'national	15	102	3	10	.231	109	51	45	67	40	3.97
1972—Peninsula†	Int'national	13	64	2	6	.250	75	32	29	39	25	4.08
1973—Quebec City	Eastern	11	77	4	5	.444	61	29	23	64	33	2.69
1973—Peninsula	Int'national	4	29	3	1	.750	18	6	6	22	8	1.86
1973—Montreal	National	17	134	10	5	.667	93	28	23	64	49	1.54
1974—Montreal	National	38	254	15	•22	.405	255	★139	★126	154	80	4.46
1975—Montreal	National	35	252	11	12	.478	248	104	92	137	88	3.29
1976—Montreal‡	National	33	230	7	•17	.292	212	93	82	150	69	3.21
1977—Montreal	National	40	302	17	16	.515	272	122	104	206	81	3.10
1978—Montreal	National	30	219	13	10	.565	186	64	60	126	64	2.47
1979—Montreal	National	37	249	13	12	.520	232	97	83	143	78	3.00
1980—Montreal	National	37	281	16	11	.593	247	101	93	147	85	2.98
1981—Montreal	National	22	161	12	8	.600	149	64	61	87	41	3.41
1982—Montreal	National	35	277	19	8	.704	245	84	74	179	65	★2.40
1983—Montreal	National	36	273	17	12	.586	258	108	98	146	78	3.23
1984—Montreal§	National	31	169⅓	6	15	.286	171	93	81	64	78	4.31
1985—Montreal x	National	8	38	2	4	.333	51	25	24	18	20	5.68
1985—Edmonton y	P. Coast	5	35⅓	1	2	.333	42	19	16	20	13	4.08
1985—Buffalo	Am. Assoc.	4	20⅔	1	2	.333	21	12	10	13	9	4.35
Major League Totals—13 Years		399	2839⅓	158	152	.510	2619	1122	1001	1621	876	3.17

Selected by New York Yankees' organization in 60th round of free-agent draft, June 6, 1967.
Selected by Montreal Expos' organization in secondary phase of free-agent draft, June 8, 1971.
†On temporary inactive list, April 14 to June 9, 1972.
‡On disabled list, May 26 to June 28, 1976.
§On disabled list, March 25 to April 19, 1984.
xReleased, May 21, 1985; signed by California Angels' organization, June 3, 1985.
yReleased, July 2, 1985; signed by Chicago White Sox' organization, August 8, 1985.

DIVISION SERIES RECORD

Year	Club	League	G.	IP.	W.	L.	Pct.	H.	R.	ER.	SO.	BB.	ERA.
1981—Montreal	National	2	17⅔	2	0	1.000	16	1	1	5	3	0.51

CHAMPIONSHIP SERIES RECORD

Year	Club	League	G.	IP.	W.	L.	Pct.	H.	R.	ER.	SO.	BB.	ERA.
1981—Montreal	National	2	10	1	1	.500	8	2	2	6	1	1.80

Year League	IP.	W.	L.	Pct.	H.	R.	ER.	SO.	BB.	ERA.
1978—National	2	0	0	.000	2	0	0	2	0	0.00
1979—National	2	0	0	.000	0	0	0	2	0	0.00
1982—National	3	1	0	1.000	4	1	1	2	0	3.00
All-Star Game Totals—3 Years	7	1	0	1.000	6	1	1	6	0	1.29

Member of National League All-Star Team in 1974 and 1983; did not play.

DANIEL JAY ROHN
(Dan)

Born January 10, 1956, at Alpena, Mich.
Height, 5.09. Weight, 165.
Throws right and bats lefthanded.
Attended Central Michigan University, Mt. Pleasant, Mich.

Major League stolen bases: 1983 (1).
Led International League in bases on balls received with 116 in 1985.
Led Texas League in bases on balls received with 105 in 1979.
Led Florida State League in bases on balls received with 117 in 1978.
Tied for American Association lead in caught stealing with 17 in 1983.
Led American Association second basemen in fielding percentage with .990 in 1983.
Led American Association second basemen in double plays with 104 in 1980.
Led Texas League second basemen in double plays with 120 in 1979.
Led Florida State League second basemen in double plays with 83 in 1978.

Year Club	League	Pos.	G.	AB.	R.	H.	2B.	3B.	HR.	RBI.	B.A.	PO.	A.	E.	F.A.
1977—Geneva	NYP	2B	21	72	8	15	0	0	1	5	.208	66	63	5	.963
1977—Pompano Beach	Fla. St.	2B-SS	54	173	23	48	6	3	0	22	.277	103	160	9	.967
1978—Pompano Beach	Fla. St.	2B	132	421	★95	116	17	2	2	48	.276	★302	400	26	.964
1979—Midland	Texas	2B	128	489	★122	150	26	6	5	52	.307	★315	★429	19	975
1980—Wichita	A. A.	2B	130	480	81	117	18	1	4	22	.244	★295	★434	●19	.975
1981—Iowa	A. A.	2B-3B	131	488	73	130	23	4	7	43	.266	194	278	10	.979
1982—Iowa	A. A.	2B-3B-SS	107	364	85	100	20	4	8	32	.275	178	241	9	.979
1983—Iowa	A. A.	2-3-S-O-P	117	413	84	130	29	5	8	56	.315	189	315	6	.988
1983—Chicago	Nat.	2B-SS	23	31	3	12	3	2	0	6	.387	12	12	2	.923
1984—Iowa	A. A.	S-2-3-O	109	370	74	99	22	1	8	46	.268	169	298	17	.965
1984—Chicago†	Nat.	3B-2B-SS	25	31	1	4	0	0	1	3	.129	5	15	0	1.000
1985—Maine	Int.	S-3-2-O	137	444	68	116	22	1	9	56	.261	212	373	20	.967
Major League Totals—2 Years			48	62	4	16	3	2	1	9	.258	17	27	2	.957

Selected by Chicago Cubs' organization in 4th round of free-agent draft, June 7, 1977.
†Traded to Cleveland Indians' organization for Pitcher Jay Baller, April 1, 1985.

PITCHING RECORD

Year Club	League	G.	IP.	W.	L.	Pct.	H.	R.	ER.	SO.	BB.	ERA.
1983—Iowa	Am. Assoc.	1	3⅓	0	0	.000	11	8	5	1	3	13.50

JOSE RAFAEL ROMAN
Name pronounced Ro-MON.

Born May 21, 1963, at Santo Domingo, Dominican Republic.
Height, 6.00. Weight, 160.
Throws and bats righthanded.
Brother of Miguel Roman, outfielder in Cleveland Indians' organization.

Led New York-Pennsylvania League in home runs allowed with 15 in 1981.

Year Club	League	G.	IP.	W.	L.	Pct.	H.	R.	ER.	SO.	BB.	ERA.
1981—Batavia	NYP	20	55	0	3	.000	63	45	39	46	27	6.38
1982—Waterloo	Midwest	24	57⅔	2	5	.286	64	42	33	56	37	5.15
1983—Waterloo	Midwest	34	126⅓	6	7	.462	103	49	36	132	56	2.56
1984—Buffalo	Eastern	27	143⅔	14	6	.700	130	69	62	105	63	3.88
1984—Cleveland	American	3	6	0	2	.000	9	12	12	3	11	18.00
1985—Cleveland	American	5	16⅓	0	4	.000	13	17	12	12	14	6.61
1985—Maine†	Int'national	11	49⅓	4	1	.800	46	23	20	27	30	3.65
Major League Totals—2 Years		8	22⅓	0	6	.000	22	29	24	15	25	9.67

Signed as free agent by Cleveland Indians' organization, May 23, 1981.
†On disabled list, July 8 to August 6, 1985.

PEDRO MIGUEL ROMAN
Name promounced Ro-MON.
(Known by middle name.)

Born June 18, 1964, at Puerto Plata, Dominican Republic.
Height, 6.03. Weight, 170.
Throws right and bats left and righthanded.
Brother of Jose Roman, pitcher in Cleveland Indians' organization.

Led Midwest League outfielders in total chances with 316 in 1985.

Year Club	League	Pos.	G.	AB.	R.	H.	2B.	3B.	HR.	RBI.	B.A.	PO.	A.	E.	F.A.
1981—Batavia	NYP	OF	17	35	1	4	0	0	0	1	.114	19	0	1	.950
1982—Batavia	NYP	OF-3B	59	200	21	59	9	2	6	27	.295	64	39	7	.936

Year	Club	League	Pos.	G.	AB.	R.	H.	2B.	3B.	HR.	RBI.	B.A.	PO.	A.	E.	F.A.
1983—Waterloo	Midw.	OF-3B	9	30	2	5	0	0	0	1	.167	8	1	0	1.000
1983—Batavia	NYP	OF	●75	283	34	71	14	0	9	27	.251	135	9	8	.947
1984—Waterloo	Midw.	OF	32	82	9	19	5	0	2	10	.232	25	2	0	1.000
1984—Batavia	NYP	OF	70	283	48	72	13	1	16	53	.254	143	11	9	.945
1985—Waterloo	Midw.	★OF-3B	136	★548	81	144	19	2	19	76	.263	★299	8	10	.968

Signed as free agent by Cleveland Indians' organization, May 23, 1981.

RONALD JAMES ROMANICK
(Ron)

Born November 6, 1960, at Burley, Ida.
Height, 6.04. Weight, 200.
Throws and bats righthanded.
Attended Arizona State University, Tempe, Ariz., and University of Washington, Seattle, Wash.

Pitched 1-0 no-hit victory against Buffalo, April 27, 1982.
Tied for Eastern League lead in games started by pitchers with 27 in 1983.
Received reported $70,000 bonus to sign with California Angels, 1981.

Year	Club	League	G.	IP.	W.	L.	Pct.	H.	R.	ER.	SO.	BB.	ERA.
1981—Redwood	California	28	★207	15	10	.600	173	88	67	178	76	★2.91
1982—Holyoke†	Eastern	16	86⅔	6	3	.667	104	52	41	62	26	4.26
1983—Nashua	Eastern	27	174	9	12	.429	★200	105	94	112	80	4.86
1984—California	American	33	229⅔	12	12	.500	240	107	96	87	61	3.76
1985—California	American	31	195	14	9	.609	210	101	89	64	62	4.11
Major League Totals—2 Years		64	424⅔	26	21	.553	450	208	185	151	123	3.92

Selected by Toronto Blue Jays' organization in 3rd round of free-agent draft, June 5, 1979.
Selected by San Diego Padres' organization in secondary phase of free-agent draft, June 3, 1980.
Selected by California Angels' organization in secondary phase of free-agent draft, January 13, 1981.
†On disabled list, May 31 to July 29, 1982.

THOMAS MICHAEL ROMANO
(Tom)

Born October 25, 1958, at Syracuse, N.Y.
Height, 5.10. Weight, 170.
Throws and bats righthanded.
Received bachelor of arts degree in physical education from
Coastal Carolina College, Conway, S.C.

Led Eastern League in total bases with 278 in 1983.
Led Midwest League in caught stealing with 23 in 1982.
Led New York-Pennsylvania League in total bases with 155 in 1981.
Tied for Pacific Coast League lead in grounding into double plays with 16 in 1984.
Named Midwest League Most Valuable Player, 1982.

Year	Club	League	Pos.	G.	AB.	R.	H.	2B.	3B.	HR.	RBI.	B.A.	PO.	A.	E.	F.A.
1980—Sarasota Blue†	Gulf C.	OF	58	186	32	48	10	4	4	37	.258	104	8	5	.957
1981—Utica‡	NYP	OF	66	243	49	82	14	4	17	53	.377	113	5	11	.915
1982—Madison	Midw.	OF	128	485	102	165	32	4	26	98	.340	179	13	●15	.928
1983—Albany	East.	OF	134	★512	90	★164	28	7	24	89	.320	287	8	12	.961
1984—Tacoma	P. C.	OF	133	503	81	141	28	7	15	75	.280	298	10	10	.969
1985—Tacoma§	P. C.	OF	118	415	66	109	28	5	10	54	.263	161	8	5	.971

Selected by Kansas City Royals' organization in 17th round of free-agent draft, June 3, 1980.
†Released, April 2, 1981; signed by Utica (Independent), June 19, 1981.
‡Sold to West Haven (Oakland A's organization), December 9, 1981.
§Traded to Indianapolis (Montreal Expos' organization) for Outfielder Mike Fuentes, January 13, 1986.

EDGARDO ROMERO
(Ed)

Born December 9, 1957, at Santurce, Puerto Rico.
Height, 5.11. Weight, 150.
Throws and bats righthanded.

Major League stolen bases: 1980 (2), 1983 (1), 1984 (3), 1985 (1). Total—7.
Led Pacific Coast League shortstops in double plays with 97 in 1979.
Led Midwest League shortstops in total chances with 647 and double plays with 64 in 1976.

Year	Club	League	Pos.	G.	AB.	R.	H.	2B.	3B.	HR.	RBI.	B.A.	PO.	A.	E.	F.A.
1976—Burlington	Midwest	SS	●129	462	58	101	23	1	1	32	.219	187	★419	41	.937
1977—Holyoke	East.	SS	121	457	63	118	19	6	1	38	.258	203	372	41	.933
1977—Milwaukee	Amer.	SS	10	25	4	7	1	0	0	2	.280	9	24	1	.971
1978—Spokane	P. C.	SS-3B	129	440	73	123	27	2	4	52	.280	221	349	32	.947
1979—Vancouver	P. C.	SS	139	515	65	134	26	6	0	39	.260	215	★414	26	.960
1980—Vancouver	P. C.	SS-2B	50	172	19	47	7	1	0	16	.273	72	153	6	.974
1980—Milwaukee	Amer.	SS-2B-3B	42	104	20	27	7	0	1	10	.260	60	102	12	.931
1981—Milwaukee	Amer.	SS-3B-2B	44	91	6	18	3	0	1	10	.198	61	102	6	.964
1982—Milwaukee	Amer.	2-S-3-O	52	144	18	36	8	0	1	7	.250	103	113	7	.969
1983—Milwaukee	Amer.	S-O-3-2	59	145	17	46	7	0	1	18	.317	59	58	5	.959
1984—Milwaukee	Amer.	3-S-2-O	116	357	36	90	12	0	1	31	.252	141	256	18	.957
1985—Milwaukee†	Amer.	S-2-O-3	88	251	24	63	11	1	0	21	.251	157	219	8	.979
Major League Totals—7 Years		411	1117	125	287	49	1	5	99	.257	590	874	57	.963

Signed as free agent by Milwaukee Brewers' organization, November 14, 1975.
†Traded to Boston Red Sox for Pitcher Mark Clear, December 11, 1985.

DIVISION SERIES RECORD

Year Club	League	Pos.	G.	AB.	R.	H.	2B.	3B.	HR.	RBI.	B.A.	PO.	A.	E.	F.A.
1981—Milwaukee	Amer.	2B	1	2	1	1	0	0	0	0	.500	2	2	0	1.000

RAMON ROMERO (De Los SANTOS)

Born January 22, 1959, at San Pedro de Macoris, D.R.
Height, 6.04. Weight, 170.
Throws and bats lefthanded.

Year Club	League	G.	IP.	W.	L.	Pct.	H.	R.	ER.	SO.	BB.	ERA.
1977—Batavia	NYP	1	1	0	0	.000	0	0	0	0	1	0.00
1977—Pulaski	Ap'lachian	16	48	0	0	.000	52	41	37	28	25	6.94
1978—Batavia	NYP	12	31	1	2	.333	33	24	18	30	32	5.23
1978—Waterloo	Midwest	1	3	0	0	.000	3	0	0	2	4	0.00
1979—Wausau	Midwest	17	66	4	1	.800	77	53	48	53	53	6.55
1980—Waterloo	Midwest	31	98	5	5	.500	78	53	40	87	62	3.67
1981—Waterloo	Midwest	8	19	0	2	.000	19	12	11	14	13	5.21
1981—Hagerstown	Carolina	17	29	1	3	.250	18	9	8	22	15	2.48
1981—Chattanooga	Southern	19	19	2	2	.500	23	11	11	16	11	5.21
1982—Waterloo	Midwest	7	31	3	1	.750	22	11	7	30	21	2.03
1982—Chattanooga	Southern	20	89	5	5	.500	87	49	39	55	39	3.94
1983—Buffalo	Eastern	44	98	10	4	.714	85	50	43	92	77	3.95
1984—Maine	Int'national	27	59⅔	1	1	.500	47	18	17	50	38	2.56
1984—Buffalo	Eastern	11	51⅓	3	4	.429	56	35	32	41	33	5.61
1984—Cleveland	American	1	3	0	0	.000	0	0	0	3	0	0.00
1985—Cleveland	American	19	64⅓	2	3	.400	69	48	47	38	38	6.58
1985—Maine†	Int'national	15	42	0	2	.000	35	17	14	23	23	3.00
Major League Totals—2 Years		20	67⅓	2	3	.400	69	48	47	41	38	6.28

Signed as free agent by Cleveland Indians' organization, October 1, 1976.
†Traded with Pitcher Roy Smith to Minnesota Twins for Pitchers Ken Schrom and Bryan Oelkers, January 7, 1986.

KEVIN ANDREW ROMINE

Name pronounced Ro-MINE.

Born May 23, 1961, at Exeter, N.H.
Height, 5.11. Weight, 185.
Throws and bats righthanded.
Attended Orange Coast College, Costa Mesa, Calif., and
Arizona State University, Tempe, Ariz.

Major League stolen bases: 1985 (1).
Tied for Eastern League lead in double plays by outfielders with 4 in 1983.
Named outfielder on THE SPORTING NEWS College Baseball All-America Team, 1982.

Year Club	League	Pos.	G.	AB.	R.	H.	2B.	3B.	HR.	RBI.	B.A.	PO.	A.	E.	F.A.
1982—Winter Haven	Fla. St.	OF	55	201	24	51	4	4	3	22	.254	97	6	3	.972
1983—New Britain	East.	OF	132	467	74	122	26	5	11	80	.261	211	12	4	.982
1984—Pawtucket†	Int.	OF	113	336	62	85	10	1	12	72	.253	202	12	5	.977
1985—Pawtucket‡	Int.	OF	106	403	43	98	20	1	5	33	.243	246	9	8	.970
1985—Boston	Amer.	OF	24	28	3	6	2	0	0	1	.214	20	1	0	1.000
Major League Totals—1 Year		24	28	3	6	2	0	0	1	.214	20	1	0	1.000

Selected by California Angels' organization in 3rd round of free-agent draft, January 8, 1980.
Selected by Philadelphia Phillies' organization in secondary phase of free-agent draft, June 3, 1980.
Selected by Boston Red Sox' organization in second round of free-agent draft, June 7, 1982.
†On disabled list, July 18 to July 31, 1984.
‡On disabled list, July 6 to July 17, 1985.

NELSON WILEY ROOD

Born June 15, 1960, at West Palm Beach, Fla.
Height, 5.10. Weight, 170.
Throws and bats righthanded.
Attended Florida Southern College, Lakeland, Fla.

Led New York-Pennsylvania League shortstops in total chances with 478 and double plays with 46 in 1983.

Year Club	League	Pos.	G.	AB.	R.	H.	2B.	3B.	HR.	RBI.	B.A.	PO.	A.	E.	F.A.
1983—Auburn	NYP	SS	73	292	46	68	11	2	1	26	.233	★121	★228	29	.923
1984—Daytona Beach	Fla. St.	SS	89	329	84	95	12	5	1	28	.289	154	289	21	.955
1984—Columbus	South.	SS	50	169	37	58	1	3	0	12	.343	86	177	16	.943
1985—Columbus	South.	SS	64	225	31	59	8	3	1	17	.262	119	204	12	.964
1985—Tucson	P. C.	SS-2B-OF	69	269	46	66	6	2	0	16	.245	120	176	12	.961

Selected by Houston Astros' organization in 13th round of free-agent draft, June 6, 1983.

—DID YOU KNOW—

That when Pete Rose broke Ty Cobb's record of 4,191 hits on September 11, it was exactly 57 years to the day that Cobb last appeared in a major league game?

PETER EDWARD ROSE
(Pete)

Born April 14, 1941, at Cincinnati, O.
Height, 5.11. Weight, 203.
Throws right and bats right and lefthanded.
Brother of David Rose, pitcher in Cincinnati Reds' organization, 1967 and 1968.

Established major league records for most games, lifetime (3,490); most singles, lifetime (3,173); most seasons and most consecutive seasons, 100 or more games (23); most seasons, 200 or more hits (10); most seasons, 150 or more games (17); most at-bats, lifetime (13,816); most plate appearances, lifetime (15,618); most consecutive seasons, 600 or more at-bats (13); most seasons, 600 or more at-bats (17); most plate appearances, season (771), 1974; most hits, lifetime (4,204); most doubles by switch-hitter, season (51), 1978.

Tied major league records for most 20-game hitting streaks, lifetime (7); most consecutive seasons leading major leagues in runs scored (3); fewest sacrifice flies, season, most at-bats (0 and 680), 1973; most hits by switch-hitter, season (230), 1973; most games, first baseman, season (162), 1980 and 1982; most stolen bases, inning (3), May 11, 1980, seventh inning.

Established National League records for most consecutive years played (23); most years playing in all clubs' games (10); most runs, lifetime (2,150); most seasons leading league, hits (7); most doubles, lifetime (738); most singles by switch-hitter, season (181), 1973; fewest stolen bases, season, most at-bats (0 and 662), 1975.

Tied National League records for most times five or more hits in one game, lifetime (9); most consecutive games, one or more hits, season (44), 1978; most games, switch hit home runs, lifetime (2); most seasons leading league in at-bats (4); most seasons played (23).

Tied modern National League records for most seasons leading league in fielding percentage by outfielder, 100 or more games (3); most consecutive years leading league in fielding percentage by outfielder, 100 or more games (2).

Major League stolen bases: 1963 (13), 1964 (4), 1965 (8), 1966 (4), 1967 (11), 1968 (3), 1969 (7), 1970 (12), 1971 (13), 1972 (10), 1973 (10), 1974 (2), 1976 (9), 1977 (16), 1978 (13), 1979 (20), 1980 (12), 1981 (4), 1982 (8), 1983 (7), 1984 (1), 1985 (8). Total—195.

Hit three home runs in a game, April 29, 1978.
Tied for National League lead in being hit by pitch with 6 in 1980.
Led Florida State League in total bases with 246 in 1961.
Named Player of the Decade for 1970-79 by THE SPORTING NEWS.
Named Man of the Year by THE SPORTING NEWS, 1985.
Named National League Player of the Year by THE SPORTING NEWS, 1968.
Named National League Most Valuable Player by Baseball Writers' Association of America, 1973.
Named National League Rookie Player of the Year by THE SPORTING NEWS, 1963.
Named National League Rookie of the Year by Baseball Writers' Association of America, 1963.
Named first baseman on THE SPORTING NEWS National League All-Star Team, 1981.
Named third baseman on THE SPORTING NEWS National League All-Star Team, 1978.
Named outfielder on THE SPORTING NEWS National League All-Star Team, 1968 and 1973.
Named second baseman on THE SPORTING NEWS National League All-Star Team, 1965 and 1966.
Named outfielder on THE SPORTING NEWS National League All-Star fielding team, 1969 and 1970.
Named first baseman on THE SPORTING NEWS National League Silver Slugger team, 1981.

Year Club	League	Pos.	G.	AB.	R.	H.	2B.	3B.	HR.	RBI.	B.A.	PO.	A.	E.	F.A.
1960—Geneva	NYP	2B	85	321	60	89	8	5	1	43	.277	198	193	★36	.916
1961—Tampa	Fla. St.	2B	130	484	105	★160	20	★30	2	77	.331	256	294	21	.963
1962—Macon	Sally	2B	139	540	★136	178	31	★17	9	71	.330	317	368	24	.966
1963—Cincinnati†	Nat.	2B-OF	157	623	101	170	25	9	6	41	.273	360	360	22	.971
1964—Cincinnati	Nat.	2B	136	516	64	139	13	2	4	34	.269	263	301	12	.979
1965—Cincinnati	Nat.	2B	162	★670	117	★209	35	11	11	81	.312	★382	403	20	.975
1966—Cincinnati	Nat.	2B-3B	156	654	97	205	38	5	16	70	.313	409	374	18	.978
1967—Cincinnati	Nat.	OF-2B	148	585	86	176	32	8	12	76	.301	287	93	11	.972
1968—Cincinnati‡	Nat.	●O-2-1	149	626	94	●210	42	6	10	49	★.335	270	●20	3	.990
1969—Cincinnati	Nat.	OF-2B	156	627	●120	218	33	11	16	82	★.348	317	10	4	.988
1970—Cincinnati	Nat.	OF	159	649	120	●205	37	9	15	52	.316	309	8	1	★.997
1971—Cincinnati	Nat.	OF	160	632	86	192	27	4	13	44	.304	306	13	2	●.994
1972—Cincinnati	Nat.	OF	★154	★645	107	★198	31	11	6	57	.307	330	●15	2	.994
1973—Cincinnati	Nat.	OF	160	★680	115	★230	36	8	5	64	★.338	343	15	3	.992
1974—Cincinnati	Nat.	OF	★163	652	★110	185	★45	7	3	51	.284	346	11	1	★.997
1975—Cincinnati	Nat.	3B-OF	●162	662	★112	210	★47	4	7	74	.317	161	230	14	.965
1976—Cincinnati	Nat.	★3B-OF	162	665	★130	★215	★42	6	10	63	.323	115	293	13	★.969
1977—Cincinnati	Nat.	3B	●162	★655	95	204	38	7	9	64	.311	98	268	16	.958
1978—Cincinnati§	Nat.	3B-OF-1B	159	655	103	198	★51	3	7	52	.302	135	256	15	.963
1979—Philadelphia	Nat.	1B-3B-2B	163	628	90	208	40	5	4	59	.331	1429	93	10	.993
1980—Philadelphia	Nat.	1B	162	655	95	185	★42	1	1	64	.282	1427	★123	5	★.997
1981—Philadelphia	Nat.	1B	107	431	73	★140	18	5	0	33	.325	929	91	4	.996
1982—Philadelphia	Nat.	1B	●162	634	80	172	25	4	3	54	.271	1428	123	8	.995
1983—Philadelphia x	Nat.	1B-OF	151	493	52	121	14	3	0	45	.245	827	74	10	.989
1984—Mont. y-Cin.	Nat.	1B-OF	121	374	43	107	15	2	0	34	.286	530	53	8	.986
1985—Cincinnati	Nat.	1B	119	405	60	107	12	2	2	46	.264	870	73	5	.995
Major League Totals—23 Years			3490	13816	2150	4204	738	133	160	1289	.304	11871	3306	207	.987

Signed as free agent by Cincinnati Reds' organization, July 8, 1960.
†On military list, October 1, 1963 through March 14, 1964.
‡On disabled list, July 6 to July 27, 1968.
§Granted free agency, November 2, 1978; signed by Philadelphia Phillies, December 5, 1978.
xReleased, October 19, 1983; signed by Montreal Expos, January 20, 1984.
yTraded to Cincinnati Reds for Infielder Tom Lawless, August 16, 1984.

DIVISION SERIES RECORD

Year Club	League	Pos.	G.	AB.	R.	H.	2B.	3B.	HR.	RBI.	B.A.	PO.	A.	E.	F.A.
1981—Philadelphia	Nat.	1B	5	20	1	6	1	0	0	2	.300	29	8	0	1.000

CHAMPIONSHIP SERIES RECORD

Established Championship Series records for most positions played, total Series (4); most consecutive games, one or more hits (15); most hits, total Series (45); most one-base hits, total Series (34); most hits, two consecutive Series (17), 1972 and 1973.

Tied Championship Series records for most times on winning club (6); most one-base hits, five-game Series (8), 1980; most two-base hits, total Series (7); most two-base hits, five-game Series (4), 1972.

Established National League Championship Series records for most games, total Series (28); most Series, played all games (7); highest batting average, total Series, 10 or more games and 30 or more at-bats (.381); most at-bats, total Series (118); most runs, total Series (17); most total bases, total Series (63).

Tied National League Championship Series records for most Series, one or more hits (7); most total bases, five-game Series (15), 1973.

Year	Club	League	Pos.	G.	AB.	R.	H.	2B.	3B.	HR.	RBI.	B.A.	PO.	A.	E.	F.A.
1970—Cincinnati		Nat.	OF	3	13	1	3	0	0	0	1	.231	3	0	0	1.000
1972—Cincinnati		Nat.	OF	5	20	1	9	4	0	0	2	.450	10	0	0	1.000
1973—Cincinnati		Nat.	OF	5	21	3	8	1	0	2	2	.381	10	1	0	1.000
1975—Cincinnati		Nat.	3B	3	14	3	5	0	0	1	2	.357	2	1	0	1.000
1976—Cincinnati		Nat.	3B	3	14	3	6	2	1	0	2	.429	2	5	1	.875
1980—Philadelphia		Nat.	1B	5	20	3	8	0	0	0	2	.400	53	7	0	1.000
1983—Philadelphia		Nat.	1B	4	16	3	6	0	0	0	0	.375	29	2	0	1.000
Championship Series Totals—7 Years....				28	118	17	45	7	1	3	11	.381	109	16	1	.992

WORLD SERIES RECORD

Tied World Series records for most positions played, total Series (4); most double plays by first baseman, six-game Series (8), 1000, most double plays by first baseman, nine-inning game (4), October 15, 1980; most times awarded first base on catcher's interference, game (1), October 10, 1970; most times home run as leadoff batter in game (1), October 20, 1972.

Year	Club	League	Pos.	G.	AB.	R.	H.	2B.	3B.	HR.	RBI.	B.A.	PO.	A.	E.	F.A.
1970—Cincinnati		Nat.	OF	5	20	2	5	1	0	1	2	.250	14	1	1	.938
1972—Cincinnati		Nat.	OF	7	28	3	6	0	0	1	2	.214	14	1	0	1.000
1975—Cincinnati		Nat.	3B	7	27	3	10	1	1	0	2	.370	7	9	0	1.000
1976—Cincinnati		Nat.	3B	4	16	1	3	1	0	0	1	.188	6	3	0	1.000
1980—Philadelphia		Nat.	1B	6	23	2	6	1	0	0	1	.261	49	6	0	1.000
1983—Philadelphia		Nat.	PH-1B-OF	5	16	1	5	1	0	0	1	.313	26	4	0	1.000
World Series Totals—6 Years				34	130	12	35	5	1	2	9	.269	116	24	1	.993

ALL-STAR GAME RECORD

Established All-Star Game record for most positions played, total games (5).

Year	League	Pos.	AB.	R.	H.	2B.	3B.	HR.	RBI.	B.A.	PO.	A.	E.	F.A.
1965—National		2B	2	0	0	0	0	0	0	.000	2	4	0	1.000
1967—National		2B	1	0	0	0	0	0	0	.000	1	0	0	1.000
1969—National		OF	1	0	0	0	0	0	0	.000	2	0	0	1.000
1970—National		OF	3	1	1	0	0	0	0	.333	3	0	0	1.000
1971—National		OF	0	0	0	0	0	0	0	.000	0	0	0	.000
1973—National		OF	3	1	0	0	0	0	0	.000	1	0	0	1.000
1974—National		OF	2	0	0	0	0	0	0	.000	1	0	0	1.000
1975—National		OF	4	0	2	0	0	0	1	.500	4	0	0	1.000
1976—National		3B	3	1	2	1	0	0	0	.667	0	1	0	1.000
1977—National		PH-3B	2	0	0	0	0	0	0	.000	0	1	0	1.000
1978—National		3B	4	0	1	1	0	0	0	.250	1	0	0	1.000
1979—National		PH-1B	2	0	0	0	0	0	0	.000	2	0	0	1.000
1980—National		PH	1	0	0	0	0	0	0	.000	0	0	0	.000
1981—National		1B	3	0	1	0	0	0	0	.333	5	0	0	1.000
1982—National		1B	1	0	0	0	0	0	1	.000	4	0	0	1.000
1985—National		PH	1	0	0	0	0	0	0	.000	0	0	0	.000
All-Star Game Totals—16 Years			33	3	7	1	1	0	2	.212	26	6	0	1.000

Named to National League All-Star Team for 1968 game; replaced due to injury.

RECORD AS MANAGER

Year	Club	League	Position	W.	L.
1984—Cincinnati†		Nat.	Fifth (W)	19	22
1985—Cincinnati		Nat.	Second (W)	89	72
Major League Totals—2 Years				108	94

†Replaced Vern Rapp with club in fifth place (record of 51-70), August 16, 1984.

MARK JOSEPH ROSS

Born August 8, 1957, at Galveston, Tex.
Height, 6.00. Weight, 195.
Throws and bats righthanded.
Received bachelor of business degree from Texas A&M University, College Station, Tex. in 1979.

Major League saves: 1985 (1).
Led Pacific Coast League in games finished in relief with 45 and saves with 20 in 1984.
Led Southern League in games finished in relief with 59, intentional bases on balls issued with 12 and tied for lead in saves with 22 in 1981.

Year	Club	League	G.	IP.	W.	L.	Pct.	H.	R.	ER.	SO.	BB.	ERA.
1979—Sarasota Astros		Gulf Coast	2	7	1	0	1.000	5	3	3	2	1	3.86
1980—Daytona Beach		Florida St.	30	58	5	3	.625	50	14	11	39	11	1.71
1980—Columbus		Southern	14	27	2	2	.500	30	11	11	13	4	3.67

Year Club	League	G.	IP.	W.	L.	Pct.	H.	R.	ER.	SO.	BB.	ERA.
1981—Columbus	Southern	*64	116	8	10	.444	103	35	29	70	32	*2.25
1982—Tucson	P. Coast	43	83	4	3	.571	106	55	45	35	32	4.88
1982—Houston	National	4	6	0	0	.000	3	1	1	4	0	1.50
1983—Columbus†	Southern	13	27⅓	1	1	.500	27	8	8	12	16	2.63
1983—Tucson	P. Coast	6	6⅓	0	2	.000	14	10	7	2	4	9.95
1984—Tucson	P. Coast	57	92	5	6	.455	88	35	30	32	24	2.93
1984—Houston	National	2	2⅓	1	0	1.000	1	0	0	1	0	0.00
1985—Tucson	P. Coast	46	77	8	5	.615	109	38	31	31	21	3.62
1985—Houston‡	National	8	13	0	2	.000	12	7	7	3	2	4.85
Major League Totals—3 Years		14	21⅓	1	2	.333	16	8	8	8	2	3.38

Selected by Houston Astros' organization in 7th round of free-agent draft, June 5, 1979.
†On Tucson disabled list, April 11 to June 27, 1983.
‡Traded to St. Louis Cardinals for a player to be named later, December 9, 1985.

WADE LEE ROWDON

Born September 7, 1960, at Riverhead, N.Y.
Height, 6.02. Weight, 170.
Throws and bats righthanded.
Attended Stetson University, Deland, Fla.

Led American Association in total bases with 230 in 1985.
Led Eastern League third basemen in fielding percentage with .940 in 1983.
Led Midwest League third basemen in total chances with 362 and double plays with 24 in 1982.

Year Club League	Pos.	G.	AB.	R.	H.	2B.	3B.	HR.	RBI.	B.A.	PO.	A.	E.	F.A.
1981—Sarasota W. Sox ... Gulf C.	SS	3	6	2	3	0	0	0	1	.500	1	3	0	1.000
1982—Appleton† .... Midw.	3B	126	433	75	123	19	8	12	79	.284	81	*264	17	*.953
1983—Waterbury .... East.	3B-2B-1B	135	480	62	112	29	1	21	76	.233	173	231	22	.948
1984—Wichita .... A. A.	SS-3B	144	479	78	120	30	4	16	72	.251	175	295	28	.944
1984—Cincinnati .... Nat.	SS-3B	4	7	0	2	0	0	0	0	.286	3	5	0	1.000
1985—Denver .... A. A.	3B-SS-2B	128	457	61	132	31	5	19	78	.289	148	277	25	.944
1985—Cincinnati .... Nat.	3B	5	9	2	2	0	0	0	2	.222	1	3	2	.667
Major League Totals—2 Years		9	16	2	4	0	0	0	2	.250	4	8	2	.857

Selected by Chicago White Sox' organization in 8th round of free-agent draft, June 8, 1981.
†Traded with Outfielder Leo Garcia to Cincinnati Reds' organization, September 7, 1982, completing deal in which Cincinnati traded Pitcher Jim Kern to Chicago White Sox for two players to be named later, August 23, 1982.

JERON KENNIS ROYSTER
(Jerry)

Born October 18, 1952, at Sacramento, Calif.
Height, 6.00. Weight, 165.
Throws and bats righthanded.
Attended Healds Business College, Sacramento, Calif.

Major League stolen bases: 1973 (1), 1975 (1), 1976 (24), 1977 (28), 1978 (27), 1979 (35), 1980 (22), 1981 (7), 1982 (14), 1983 (11), 1984 (6), 1985 (6). Total—182.
Led National League third basemen in putouts with 156 in 1976.
Tied for National League lead in double plays by third basemen with 35 in 1976.
Tied for Pacific Coast League lead in stolen bases with 33 in 1975.
Led Pacific Coast League third basemen in fielding percentage with .962 in 1974.
Led Texas League third basemen in double plays with 26 in 1972.
Named Pacific Coast League Player of the Year in 1975.

Year Club League	Pos.	G.	AB.	R.	H.	2B.	3B.	HR.	RBI.	B.A.	PO.	A.	E.	F.A.
1971—Bakersfield .... Calif.	3B	7	20	2	2	1	0	0	2	.100	1	5	1	.857
1971—Daytona Beach .... Fla. St.	3B-SS-2B	111	371	68	100	13	7	8	42	.270	90	265	29	.925
1972—El Paso .... Texas	*3-S-O	127	479	*89	123	28	3	18	59	.257	103	209	24	.899
1973—Albuquerque .... P. C.	3B-SS-OF	122	463	78	140	24	11	6	68	.302	167	222	24	.942
1973—Los Angeles .... Nat.	3B-2B	10	19	1	4	0	0	0	2	.211	3	14	3	.850
1974—Albuquerque .... P. C.	3B-2B-SS	125	458	69	126	19	1	10	65	.275	121	257	14	.964
1974—Los Angeles .... Nat.	2B-OF-3B	6	0	2	0	0	0	0	0	.000	0	3	0	1.000
1975—Albuquerque .... P. C.	SS-3B	133	487	*91	162	31	7	10	65	*.333	183	349	38	.933
1975—Los Angeles† .... Nat.	O-2-3-S	13	36	2	9	2	1	0	1	.250	12	15	2	.931
1976—Atlanta .... Nat.	3B-SS	149	533	65	132	13	1	5	45	.248	158	310	19	.961
1977—Atlanta .... Nat.	3-S-2-O	140	445	64	96	10	2	6	28	.216	182	267	28	.941
1978—Atlanta .... Nat.	SS-2B-3B	140	529	67	137	17	8	2	35	.259	284	376	23	.966
1979—Atlanta .... Nat.	3B-2B	154	601	103	164	25	6	3	51	.273	261	405	22	.968
1980—Atlanta .... Nat.	2B-3B-OF	123	392	42	95	17	5	1	20	.242	195	166	18	.953
1981—Atlanta .... Nat.	3B-2B	64	93	13	19	4	1	0	9	.204	35	48	4	.954
1982—Atlanta .... Nat.	3-O-2-S	108	261	43	77	13	2	2	25	.295	105	112	11	.952
1983—Atlanta‡ .... Nat.	3-2-O-S	91	268	32	63	10	3	3	30	.235	112	156	10	.964
1984—Atlanta§ .... Nat.	2-3-S-O	81	227	22	47	13	2	1	21	.207	99	162	9	.967
1985—San Diego .... Nat.	2-3-S-O	90	249	31	70	13	2	5	31	.281	130	214	8	.977
Major League Totals—13 Years		1169	3653	487	913	137	33	28	298	.250	1576	2248	157	.961

Signed as free agent by Los Angeles Dodgers' organization, August 21, 1970.
†Traded with Outfielder Jimmy Wynn, Second Baseman Lee Lacy and First Baseman-Outfielder Tom Paciorek to Atlanta Braves for Outfielder Dusty Baker and First Baseman-Third Baseman Ed Goodson, November 17, 1975.
‡On disabled list, August 19 to September 9, 1983.
§Granted free agency, November 8, 1984; signed by San Diego Padres, January 3, 1985.

Year	Club	League	Pos.	G.	AB.	R.	H.	2B.	3B.	HR.	RBI.	B.A.	PO.	A.	E.	F.A.
1982—Atlanta		Nat.	OF-3B	3	11	0	2	0	0	0	0	.182	4	0	0	1.000

DAVID SCOTT ROZEMA

Name pronounced ROZE-mah.

(Dave)

Born August 5, 1956, at Grand Rapids, Mich.
Height, 6.04 Weight, 200.
Throws and bats righthanded.
Attended Grand Rapids Junior College, Grand Rapids, Mich.

Major League saves: 1980 (4), 1981 (3), 1982 (1), 1983 (2), 1985 (7). Total—17.
Tied for Southern League lead in shutouts with 4 in 1976.
Tied for Midwest League lead in shutouts with 5 in 1975.
Named American League Rookie Pitcher of the Year by THE SPORTING NEWS, 1977.

Year	Club	League	G.	IP.	W.	L.	Pct.	H.	R.	ER.	SO.	BB.	ERA.
1975—Clinton		Midwest	27	164	14	5	.737	128	50	38	123	32	2.09
1976—Montgomery†		Southern	19	126	12	4	.750	98	29	22	96	15	*1.57
1977—Detroit		American	28	218	15	7	.682	222	87	75	92	34	3.10
1978—Detroit		American	28	209	9	12	.429	205	83	73	57	41	3.14
1979—Detroit‡		American	16	97	4	4	.500	101	52	38	33	30	3.53
1980—Detroit		American	42	145	6	9	.400	152	68	63	49	49	3.91
1981—Detroit		American	28	104	5	5	.500	99	42	42	46	25	3.63
1982—Detroit§		American	8	27⅔	3	0	1.000	17	5	5	15	7	1.63
1983—Detroit		American	29	105	8	3	.727	100	50	40	63	29	3.43
1984—Detroit x		American	29	101	7	6	.538	110	49	42	48	18	3.74
1985—Texas y		American	34	88	3	7	.300	100	45	41	42	22	4.19
Major League Totals—9 Years			242	1094⅔	60	53	.531	1106	481	419	445	255	3.44

Selected by San Francisco Giants' organization in 22nd round of free-agent draft, June 5, 1974.
Selected by Detroit Tigers' organization in secondary phase of free-agent draft, January 9, 1975.
†On disabled list, May 9 to June 21, 1976.
‡On disabled list, June 16 to August 27, 1979.
§On disabled list, May 15, 1982 through remainder of season.
xGranted free agency, November 8, 1984; signed by Texas Rangers, December 28, 1984.
yOn disabled list, August 12 to September 14, 1985.

DAVID MICHAEL RUCKER

(Dave)

Born September 1, 1957, at San Bernardino, Calif.
Height, 6.01. Weight, 185.
Throws and bats lefthanded.
Attended University of California, Los Angeles, Calif., and
LaVerne College, LaVerne, Calif.

Major League saves: 1985 (1).

Year	Club	League	G.	IP.	W.	L.	Pct.	H.	R.	ER.	SO.	BB.	ERA.
1978—Bristol		Ap'lachian	3	7	1	0	1.000	10	5	4	7	2	5.14
1978—Lakeland		Florida St.	18	31	6	3	.667	26	13	11	18	13	3.19
1979—Montgomery		Southern	28	96	4	7	.364	97	56	49	64	66	4.59
1979—Evansville		Am. Assoc.	2	13	1	1	.500	11	4	4	8	1	2.77
1980—Evansville		Am. Assoc.	52	92	7	8	.467	94	53	35	53	52	3.42
1981—Detroit		American	2	4	0	0	.000	3	4	3	2	1	6.75
1981—Evansville		Am. Assoc.	35	67	7	4	.636	60	30	28	36	42	3.76
1982—Evansville		Am. Assoc.	30	58⅓	4	1	.800	53	27	22	42	29	3.39
1982—Detroit		American	27	64	5	6	.455	62	26	24	31	23	3.38
1983—Detroit		American	4	9	1	2	.333	18	17	17	6	8	17.00
1983—Evansville†		Am. Assoc.	18	29⅔	2	4	.333	25	12	11	30	21	3.34
1983—St. Louis		National	34	37	5	3	.625	36	14	10	22	18	2.43
1984—St. Louis‡		National	50	73	2	3	.400	62	23	17	38	34	2.10
1985—Portland		P. Coast	10	16	1	0	1.000	15	9	8	17	4	4.50
1985—Philadelphia		National	39	79⅓	3	2	.600	83	42	38	41	40	4.31
American League Totals—3 Years			33	77	6	8	.429	83	47	44	39	32	5.14
National League Totals—3 Years			123	189⅓	10	8	.556	181	79	65	101	92	3.09
Major League Totals—5 Years			156	266⅓	16	16	.500	264	126	109	140	124	3.68

Selected by Philadelphia Phillies' organization in 19th round of free-agent draft, June 4, 1975.
Selected by Detroit Tigers' organization in 16th round of free-agent draft, June 6, 1978.
†Traded to St. Louis Cardinals, July 5, 1983, completing deal in which St. Louis traded Pitcher Doug Bair to Detroit Tigers for a player to be named later, June 21, 1983.
‡Traded to Philadelphia Phillies' organization for Pitcher Bill Campbell and Shortstop Ivan DeJesus, April 6, 1985.

—DID YOU KNOW—

That 38-year-old Darrell Evans hit 40 home runs in 1985 and became the oldest A.L. home-run champion ever? Evans, who captured his first home run title, also became the first player to produce 40-homer seasons in both leagues.

VERNON GERALD RUHLE

Name pronounced Rule.

(Vern)

Born January 25, 1951, at Coleman, Mich.
Height, 6.01. Weight, 187.
Throws and bats righthanded.
Attended Olivet College, Olivet, Mich.

Major League saves: 1981 (1), 1982 (1), 1983 (3), 1984 (2), 1985 (3). Total—10.

Year Club	League	G.	IP.	W.	L.	Pct.	H.	R.	ER.	SO.	BB.	ERA.
1972—Bristol	Ap'lachian	4	28	0	2	.000	24	6	4	30	5	1.29
1972—Rocky Mount	Carolina	13	72	5	8	.385	87	53	38	53	28	4.75
1973—Lakeland	Florida St.	15	96	6	5	.545	81	27	22	67	24	2.06
1973—Montgomery	Southern	10	81	6	2	.750	72	33	26	34	17	2.89
1974—Montgomery	Southern	5	45	5	0	1.000	29	6	3	32	12	0.60
1974—Evansville	Am. Assoc.	22	156	13	5	.722	178	80	70	94	42	4.04
1974—Detroit	American	5	33	2	0	1.000	35	13	10	10	6	2.73
1975—Detroit	American	32	190	11	12	.478	199	104	85	67	65	4.03
1976—Detroit	American	32	200	9	12	.429	227	99	87	88	59	3.92
1977—Evansville†	Am. Assoc.	10	21	1	4	.200	31	19	16	15	9	6.86
1977—Detroit‡§	American	14	66	3	5	.375	83	44	42	27	15	5.73
1978—Columbus	Southern	5	39	4	1	.800	32	9	8	25	8	1.85
1978—Charleston	Int'national	13	94	4	4	.500	89	36	29	48	16	2.78
1978—Houston	National	13	68	3	3	.500	57	17	16	27	20	2.12
1979—Houston x	National	13	66	2	6	.250	64	33	30	33	8	4.09
1980—Houston	National	28	159	12	4	.750	148	51	42	55	29	2.38
1981—Houston y	National	20	102	4	6	.400	97	36	33	39	20	2.91
1982—Houston	National	31	149	9	13	.409	169	81	65	56	24	3.93
1983—Houston	National	41	114⅔	8	5	.615	107	49	47	43	36	3.69
1984—Houston z	National	40	90⅓	1	9	.100	112	58	46	60	29	4.58
1985—Cleveland ab	American	42	125	2	10	.167	139	65	60	54	30	4.32
American League Totals—5 Years		125	614	27	39	.409	683	325	284	246	175	4.16
National League Totals—7 Years		186	749	39	46	.459	754	325	279	313	166	3.35
Major League Totals—12 Years		311	1363	66	85	.437	1437	650	563	559	341	3.72

Selected by Detroit Tigers' organization in 17th round of free-agent draft, June 6, 1972.
†On disabled list, July 24 to August 5, 1977.
‡On disabled list, May 21 to June 16, 1977.
§Released, March 27, 1978; signed by Houston Astros' organization, March 29, 1978.
xOn disabled list, May 14 to September 1, 1979.
yOn disabled list, April 30 to May 21, 1981.
zGranted free agency, November 8, 1984; signed by Cleveland Indians, December 22, 1984.
aOn disabled list, April 27 to May 12 and May 29 to June 16, 1985.
bGranted free agency, November 12, 1985.

DIVISION SERIES RECORD

Year Club	League	G.	IP.	W.	L.	Pct.	H.	R.	ER.	SO.	BB.	ERA.
1981—Houston	National	1	8	0	1	.000	4	2	2	1	2	2.25

CHAMPIONSHIP SERIES RECORD

Year Club	League	G.	IP.	W.	L.	Pct.	H.	R.	ER.	SO.	BB.	ERA.
1980—Houston	National	1	7	0	0	.000	8	3	3	3	1	3.86

PAUL WILLIAM RUNGE

Name pronounced RUNG-ee.

Born May 21, 1958, at Kingston, N.Y.
Height, 6.00. Weight, 165.
Throws and bats righthanded.
Attended Jacksonville University, Jacksonville, Fla.

Major League stolen bases: 1984 (5).
Led International League in bases on balls received with 95 in 1982.
Led International League second basemen in total chances with 747 in 1982.
Led International League shortstops in double plays with 67 in 1981.
Led Appalachian League shortstops in double plays with 38 in 1979.

Year Club	League	Pos.	G.	AB.	R.	H.	2B.	3B.	HR.	RBI.	B.A.	PO.	A.	E.	F.A.
1979—Kingsport	Appal.	SS	66	229	57	67	11	0	6	45	.293	*104	*194	*24	.925
1980—Durham	Carol.	SS	74	245	37	64	8	4	8	37	.261	105	280	25	.939
1980—Savannah	South.	SS	75	248	32	68	11	3	9	34	.274	115	196	17	.948
1981—Richmond	Int.	SS	134	426	49	98	20	5	9	41	.230	191	450	*35	.948
1981—Atlanta	Nat.	SS	10	27	2	7	1	0	0	2	.259	14	27	4	.911
1982—Richmond	Int.	2B	134	507	*106	142	25	6	15	71	.280	*318	412	●17	.977
1982—Atlanta	Nat.	PH-PR	4	2	0	0	0	0	0	0	.000	0	0	0	.000
1983—Richmond	Int.	2B	137	472	76	129	17	4	15	72	.273	269	392	14	.979
1983—Atlanta	Nat.	2B	5	8	0	2	0	0	0	1	.250	4	3	0	1.000
1984—Atlanta	Nat.	2B-SS-3B	28	90	5	24	3	1	0	3	.267	53	101	5	.969
1984—Richmond	Int.	2-3-S-1	91	301	44	72	9	3	8	41	.239	163	264	16	.964
1985—Atlanta	Nat.	3B-SS-2B	50	87	15	19	3	0	1	5	.218	15	66	7	.920
Major League Totals—5 Years			97	214	22	52	7	1	1	11	.243	86	197	16	.946

Selected by Atlanta Braves' organization in 8th round of free-agent draft, June 5, 1979.

THOMAS WILLIAM RUNNELLS
(Tom)

Born April 17, 1955, at Greeley, Colo.
Height, 6.00. Weight, 175.
Throws right and bats right and lefthanded.
Received bachelor of arts degree in physical education from
University of Northern Colorado, Greeley, Colo.

Led American Association second basemen in total chances with 654 and double plays with 83 in 1985.
Led American Association second basemen in fielding percentage with .993 in 1984.

Year Club	League	Pos.	G.	AB.	R.	H.	2B.	3B.	HR.	RBI.	B.A.	PO.	A.	E.	F.A.
1977—Great Falls†	Pion.	2-3-O-S	63	241	61	70	8	1	1	53	.290	117	144	16	.942
1978—Fresno	Calif.	2B-SS-3B	139	564	83	163	15	7	0	55	.289	289	437	37	.952
1979—Shreveport	Texas	SS	128	435	45	102	10	2	4	32	.234	190	413	19	*.969
1980—Shreveport	Texas	SS	73	258	27	50	4	1	0	10	.194	117	240	18	.952
1980—Phoenix	P. C.	SS-2B	37	149	21	45	4	0	0	10	.302	51	121	4	.977
1981—Phoenix	P. C.	SS-OF-2B	131	467	40	128	11	2	0	51	.274	240	392	28	.958
1982—Phoenix	P. C.	S-3-2-O	108	347	52	93	8	11	0	48	.268	164	259	23	.948
1983—Phoenix‡§	P. C.	SS-2B-1B	74	244	43	74	11	4	1	28	.303	119	188	13	.959
1984—Wichita	A. A.	2-3-O-S	125	438	67	108	21	3	6	61	.247	229	350	5	.991
1985—Denver	A. A.	2B	114	466	55	135	22	8	5	51	.290	256	*391	7	*.989
1985—Cincinnati	Nat.	SS-2B	28	35	3	7	1	0	0	0	.200	10	22	0	1.000
Major League Totals—1 Year			28	35	3	7	1	0	0	0	.200	10	22	0	1.000

Signed as free agent by San Francisco Giants' organization, June 16, 1977.
†Batted righthanded only.
‡On disabled list, July 24, 1983 through remainder of season.
§Granted free agency, October 20, 1983; signed by Indianapolis (Cincinnati Reds' organization), October 30, 1983.

JEFFREY LEE RUSSELL
(Jeff)

Born September 2, 1961, at Cincinnati, O.
Height, 6.04. Weight, 200.
Throws and bats righthanded.
Attended Gulf Coast Community College, Panama City, Fla.

Year Club	League	G.	IP.	W.	L.	Pct.	H.	R.	ER.	SO.	BB.	ERA.
1980—Eugene	Northwest	13	90	6	5	.545	80	47	30	75	50	3.00
1981—Tampa	Florida St.	22	143	10	4	.714	109	51	32	92	48	2.01
1982—Waterbury†	Eastern	14	79⅔	6	4	.600	67	27	21	88	23	2.37
1983—Indianapolis	Am. Assoc.	18	119	5	5	.500	106	51	47	98	44	3.55
1983—Cincinnati	National	10	68⅓	4	5	.444	58	30	23	40	22	3.03
1984—Cincinnati	National	33	181⅔	6	*18	.250	186	97	86	101	65	4.26
1985—Denver‡§-Oklahoma City	Am. Assoc.	18	115⅓	7	4	.636	105	55	52	94	51	4.06
1985—Texas	American	13	62	3	6	.333	85	55	52	44	27	7.55
National League Totals—2 Years		43	250	10	23	.303	244	127	109	141	87	3.92
American League Totals—1 Year		13	62	3	6	.333	85	55	52	44	27	7.55
Major League Totals—3 Years		56	312	13	29	.310	329	182	161	185	114	4.64

Selected by Cincinnati Reds' organization in 5th round of free-agent draft, June 5, 1979.
†On disabled list, May 5 to June 10 and July 28, 1982 through remainder of season.
‡On disabled list, May 22 to June 10, 1985.
§Traded to Texas Rangers' organization, July 23, 1985, completing deal in which Texas traded Third Baseman Buddy Bell to Cincinnati Reds for Outfielder Duane Walker and a player to be named later, July 19, 1985.

JOHN WILLIAM RUSSELL

Born January 5, 1961, at Oklahoma City, Okla.
Height, 6.00. Weight, 200.
Throws and bats righthanded.
Attended University of Oklahoma, Norman, Okla.

Major League stolen bases: 1985 (2).
Tied for Pacific Coast League lead in passed balls with 13 in 1983.

Year Club	League	Pos.	G.	AB.	R.	H.	2B.	3B.	HR.	RBI.	B.A.	PO.	A.	E.	F.A.
1982—Reading	East.	C-OF-1B	77	263	26	53	10	5	6	30	.202	354	44	12	.971
1983—Portland	P. C.	C-O-3	128	445	71	113	23	3	27	76	.254	551	58	12	.981
1984—Portland	P. C.	OF-1B-C	93	350	75	101	22	5	19	77	.289	182	18	5	.976
1984—Philadelphia	Nat.	OF-C	39	99	11	28	8	1	2	11	.283	51	1	0	1.000
1985—Philadelphia	Nat.	OF-1B	81	216	22	47	12	0	9	23	.218	170	9	4	.978
1985—Portland	P. C.	OF-C-1B	16	49	8	15	2	2	4	11	.306	24	1	1	.962
Major League Totals—2 Years			120	315	33	75	20	1	11	34	.238	221	10	4	.983

Selected by Montreal Expos' organization in 4th round of free-agent draft, June 5, 1979.
Selected by Philadelphia Phillies' organization in 1st round (13th player selected) of free-agent draft, June 7, 1982.

—DID YOU KNOW—

That Yankee outfielder Rickey Henderson has stolen 573 bases in his first seven major league seasons? That compares to 334 by all-time career leader Lou Brock in his first seven seasons. Brock finished his career with 938.

WILLIAM ELLIS RUSSELL
(Bill)

Born October 21, 1948, at Pittsburg, Kan.
Height, 6.00. Weight, 175.
Throws and bats righthanded.
Attended Kansas State College, Pittsburg, Kan.

Established major league records for fewest putouts by shortstop, season, 150 or more games (194), 1974.
Tied major league record for most strikeouts, nine-inning game (5), June 9, 1971; fewest double plays by shortstop, season, 150 or more games (64), 1982.
Major League stolen bases: 1969 (4), 1970 (9), 1971 (6), 1972 (14), 1973 (15), 1974 (14), 1975 (5), 1976 (15), 1977 (16), 1978 (10), 1979 (6), 1980 (13), 1981 (2), 1982 (10), 1983 (13), 1984 (4), 1985 (4). Total—160.
Led National League in intentional bases on balls received with 25 in 1974.
Led National League shortstops in double plays with 102 in 1977.
Led National League shortstops in total chances with 834 in 1973.
Tied for California League lead in double plays by outfielders with 4 in 1968.
Named shortstop on THE SPORTING NEWS National League All-Star Team, 1973.

Year	Club	League	Pos.	G.	AB.	R.	H.	2B.	3B.	HR.	RBI.	B.A.	PO.	A.	E.	F.A.
1966—Ogden		Pion.	OF	39	87	19	31	5	1	3	21	.356	25	3	2	.933
1967—Dubuque		Midw.	OF	67	263	29	58	11	1	5	21	.221	98	11	10	.916
1968—Bakersfield	Calif.		OF	115	439	76	123	16	3	17	55	.280	255	★22	7	.975
1969—Los Angeles†	Nat.		OF	98	212	35	48	6	2	5	15	.226	132	4	3	.978
1970—Spokane	P. C.		OF-3B-SS	55	237	48	86	13	5	3	30	.363	112	39	6	.962
1970—Los Angeles‡	Nat.		OF-SS	81	278	30	72	11	9	0	28	.259	167	10	3	.983
1971—Los Angeles§	Nat.		2B-OF-SS	91	211	29	48	7	4	2	15	.227	131	124	8	.970
1972—Los Angeles x	Nat.		★SS-OF	129	434	47	118	19	5	4	34	.272	202	439	★34	.950
1973—Los Angeles	Nat.		SS	●162	615	55	163	26	3	4	56	.265	243	★560	31	.963
1974—Los Angeles	Nat.		★SS-OF	160	553	61	149	17	6	5	65	.269	194	491	★39	.946
1975—Los Angeles y	Nat.		SS	84	252	24	52	9	2	0	14	.206	94	230	11	.967
1976—Los Angeles	Nat.		SS	149	554	53	152	17	3	5	65	.274	251	476	28	.963
1977—Los Angeles	Nat.		SS	153	634	84	176	28	6	4	51	.278	234	523	29	.963
1978—Los Angeles	Nat.		SS	155	625	72	179	32	4	3	46	.286	245	533	31	.962
1979—Los Angeles	Nat.		SS	153	627	72	170	26	4	7	56	.271	218	452	30	.957
1980—Los Angeles	Nat.		SS	130	466	38	123	23	2	3	34	.264	179	387	19	.968
1981—Los Angeles	Nat.		SS	82	262	20	61	9	2	0	22	.233	128	261	14	.965
1982—Los Angeles	Nat.		SS	153	497	64	136	20	2	3	46	.274	216	502	29	.961
1983—Los Angeles	Nat.		SS	131	451	47	111	13	1	1	30	.246	192	392	22	.964
1984—Los Angeles z	Nat.		SS-OF-2B	89	262	25	70	12	1	0	19	.267	115	173	9	.970
1985—Los Angeles	Nat.		S-O-2-3	76	169	19	44	6	1	0	13	.260	60	82	10	.934
Major League Totals—17 Years				2076	7102	775	1872	282	57	46	609	.264	3001	5639	350	.961

Selected by Los Angeles Dodgers' organization in 37th round of free-agent draft, June 12, 1966.
†On military list, August 1 to August 19, 1969.
‡On military list, July 3 to July 19, 1970.
§On military list, June 19 to July 3, 1971.
xOn military list, July 7 to July 22, 1972.
yOn disabled list, April 13 to May 6 and May 11 to June 30, 1975.
zOn disabled list, May 14 to June 4 and August 12 to August 27, 1984.

DIVISION SERIES RECORD

Year	Club	League	Pos.	G.	AB.	R.	H.	2B.	3B.	HR.	RBI.	B.A.	PO.	A.	E.	F.A.
1981—Los Angeles	Nat.		SS	5	16	1	4	1	0	0	2	.250	10	15	2	.926

CHAMPIONSHIP SERIES RECORD

Established Championship Series record for most one-base hits, four-game Series (7), 1974.

Year	Club	League	Pos.	G.	AB.	R.	H.	2B.	3B.	HR.	RBI.	B.A.	PO.	A.	E.	F.A.
1974—Los Angeles	Nat.		SS	4	18	1	7	0	0	0	3	.389	13	16	0	1.000
1977—Los Angeles	Nat.		SS	4	18	3	5	1	0	0	2	.278	11	12	2	.920
1978—Los Angeles	Nat.		SS	4	17	1	7	1	0	0	2	.412	4	14	0	1.000
1981—Los Angeles	Nat.		SS	5	16	2	5	0	1	0	1	.313	10	13	0	1.000
1983—Los Angeles	Nat.		SS	4	14	1	4	0	0	0	0	.286	4	10	1	.933
Championship Series Totals—5 Years				21	83	8	28	2	1	0	8	.337	42	65	3	.973

WORLD SERIES RECORD

Established World Series record for most assists by shortstop, six-game Series (26), 1981.
Tied World Series record for one or more hits, each game, six-game Series, 1978.

Year	Club	League	Pos.	G.	AB.	R.	H.	2B.	3B.	HR.	RBI.	B.A.	PO.	A.	E.	F.A.
1974—Los Angeles	Nat.		SS	5	18	0	4	0	1	0	2	.222	4	11	1	.938
1977—Los Angeles	Nat.		SS	6	26	3	4	0	1	0	2	.154	9	21	0	1.000
1978—Los Angeles	Nat.		SS	6	26	1	11	2	0	0	2	.423	11	20	3	.912
1981—Los Angeles	Nat.		SS	6	25	1	6	0	0	0	2	.240	4	26	1	.968
World Series Totals—4 Years				23	95	5	25	2	2	0	8	.263	28	78	5	.955

ALL-STAR GAME RECORD

Year	League	Pos.	AB.	R.	H.	2B.	3B.	HR.	RBI.	B.A.	PO.	A.	E.	F.A.
1973—National		SS	2	0	0	0	0	0	0	.000	0	2	0	1.000
1976—National		SS	1	0	0	0	0	0	0	.000	1	2	0	1.000
1980—National		SS	2	0	0	0	0	0	0	.000	0	2	0	1.000
All-Star Game Totals—3 Years			5	0	0	0	0	0	0	.000	1	6	0	1.000

RICHARD DAVID RUTHVEN
(Dick)

Born March 27, 1951, at Sacramento, Calif.
Height, 6.03. Weight, 190.
Throws and bats righthanded.
Attended Fresno State University, Fresno, Calif.
Brother-in-law of Tommy Hutton, first baseman-outfielder with Los Angeles, Philadelphia,
Toronto and Montreal, 1966, 1969 and 1972 through 1981, and broadcaster with Montreal Expos since 1982.

Tied National League record for most putouts by pitcher, nine-inning game (5), April 19, 1978.
Major League saves: 1973 (1).
Tied for National League lead in balks with 5 in 1976.
Named righthanded pitcher on THE SPORTING NEWS College Baseball All-America Team, 1972.

Year—Club	League	G.	IP.	W.	L.	Pct.	H.	R.	ER.	SO.	BB.	ERA.
1973—Philadelphia†	National	25	128	6	9	.400	125	69	60	98	75	4.22
1974—Philadelphia	National	35	213	9	13	.409	182	106	95	153	116	4.01
1975—Toledo	Int'national	23	153	10	12	.455	148	72	54	114	69	3.18
1975—Philadelphia‡	National	11	41	2	2	.500	37	22	19	26	22	4.17
1976—Atlanta	National	36	240	14	●17	.452	255	★112	112	142	90	4.20
1977—Atlanta§	National	25	151	7	13	.350	158	86	71	84	62	4.23
1978—Atlanta x-Philadelphia	National	33	232	15	11	.577	214	95	87	120	56	3.38
1979—Philadelphia y	National	20	122	7	5	.583	121	59	58	58	37	4.28
1980—Philadelphia	National	33	223	17	10	.630	241	99	88	86	74	3.55
1981—Philadelphia	National	23	147	12	7	.632	162	★94	★84	80	54	5.14
1982—Philadelphia	National	33	204⅓	11	11	.500	189	99	86	115	59	3.79
1983—Philadelphia z-Chicago	National	32	183	13	12	.520	202	101	89	99	38	4.38
1984—Chicago a	National	23	126⅔	6	10	.375	154	75	71	55	41	5.04
1984—Lodi	California	2	9	1	0	1.000	9	4	4	8	2	4.00
1985—Chicago b	National	20	87⅓	4	7	.364	103	49	44	26	37	4.53
Major League Totals—13 Years		349	2098⅓	123	127	.492	2143	1066	964	1152	761	4.13

Selected by Baltimore Orioles' organization in 20th round of free-agent draft, June 5, 1969.
Selected by Minnesota Twins' organization in 1st round (eighth player selected) of free-agent draft, June 6, 1972.
Selected by Philadelphia Phillies' organization in secondary phase of free-agent draft, January 10, 1973.
†On disabled list, August 3 to September 1, 1973.
‡Traded with Pitcher Roy Thomas and Infielder-Outfielder Alan Bannister to Chicago White Sox for Pitcher Jim Kaat and Shortstop Mike Buskey, December 10, 1975. Traded with Outfielder Ken Henderson and Pitcher Danny Osborn by Chicago White Sox to Atlanta Braves for Outfielder Ralph Garr and Infielder Larvell Blanks, December 12, 1975.
§On disabled list, May 2 to July 4, 1977.
xTraded to Philadelphia Phillies for Pitcher Gene Garber, June 15, 1978.
yOn disabled list, July 2 to July 25 and August 16 to October 4, 1979.
zTraded with Pitcher Bill Johnson to Chicago Cubs for Pitcher Willie Hernandez, May 22, 1983.
aOn disabled list, May 20 to July 15, 1984; included rehabilitation disability assignment to Lodi, June 29 to July 15, 1984.
bOn disabled list, August 11 to October 1, 1985.

DIVISION SERIES RECORD

Year—Club	League	G.	IP.	W.	L.	Pct.	H.	R.	ER.	SO.	BB.	ERA.
1981—Philadelphia	National	1	4	0	1	.000	3	3	2	0	1	4.50

CHAMPIONSHIP SERIES RECORD

Year—Club	League	G.	IP.	W.	L.	Pct.	H.	R.	ER.	SO.	BB.	ERA.
1978—Philadelphia	National	1	4⅔	0	1	.000	6	3	3	3	0	5.79
1980—Philadelphia	National	2	9	1	0	1.000	3	2	2	4	5	2.00
Championship Series Totals—2 Years		3	13⅔	1	1	.500	9	5	5	7	5	3.29

WORLD SERIES RECORD

Year—Club	League	G.	IP.	W.	L.	Pct.	H.	R.	ER.	SO.	BB.	ERA.
1980—Philadelphia	National	1	9	0	0	.000	9	3	3	7	0	3.00

ALL-STAR GAME RECORD

Year—League		IP.	W.	L.	Pct.	H.	R.	ER.	SO.	BB.	ERA.
1981—National		⅓	0	0	.000	0	0	0	0	0	0.00

Member of National League All-Star Team in 1976; did not play.

MARK DWAYNE RYAL

Name pronounced Rile.

Born April 28, 1960, at Henryetta, Okla.
Height, 6:01. Weight, 185.
Throws and bats lefthanded.

Led American Association in grounding into double plays with 21 in 1983.
Tied for American Association lead in intentional bases on balls received with 12 in 1982.

Year—Club	League	Pos.	G.	AB.	R.	H.	2B.	3B.	HR.	RBI.	B.A.	PO.	A.	E.	F.A.
1978—Sarasota Royals	Gulf C.	OF	27	83	11	20	0	1	0	10	.241	37	4	0	1.000
1979—Fort Myers	Fla. St.	OF	107	360	27	79	12	1	4	34	.219	199	15	3	.986
1980—Fort Myers	Fla. St.	OF	123	440	60	117	21	3	5	51	.266	174	8	2	.989
1981—Jacksonville	South.	OF	123	457	50	122	15	2	14	69	.267	237	8	11	.957

Year	Club	League	Pos.	G.	AB.	R.	H.	2B.	3B.	HR.	RBI.	B.A.	PO.	A.	E.	F.A.
1981—Omaha		A. A.	OF	6	19	2	4	0	0	0	1	.211	9	1	0	1.000
1982—Omaha		A. A.	*OF-1B	129	473	69	135	27	2	20	77	.285	242	*18	6	.977
1982—Kansas City		Amer.	OF	6	13	0	1	0	0	0	0	.077	9	0	1	.900
1983—Omaha		A. A.	OF-1B	132	454	61	118	28	5	9	57	.260	203	11	8	.964
1984—Omaha†		A. A.	1B-OF	131	435	56	103	18	1	13	64	.237	680	58	16	.979
1985—Buffalo		A. A.	OF	106	392	50	104	21	1	13	66	.265	175	10	2	.989
1985—Chicago‡		Amer.	OF	12	33	4	5	3	0	0	3	.152	21	0	0	1.000
Major League Totals—2 Years				18	46	4	6	3	0	0	3	.130	30	0	1	.968

Selected by Kansas City Royals' organization in 3rd round of free-agent draft, June 6, 1978.
†Released, September 4, 1984, signed by Chicago White Sox' organization, December 28, 1984.
‡Granted free agency, October 15, 1985.

LYNN NOLAN RYAN JR.

(Known by middle name.)

Born January 31, 1947, at Refugio, Tex.
Height, 6.02. Weight, 195.
Throws and bats righthanded.
Attended Alvin Junior College, Alvin, Tex.

Established major league records for most strikeouts, lifetime (4,083); most games, 15 or more strikeouts, lifetime (19); most games, 10 or more strikeouts, lifetime (158); most seasons, 300 or more strikeouts (5); most games, 10 or more strikeouts, season (23), 1973; most strikeouts, three consecutive games (including extra innings—27⅓) (47), August 12, 16 and 20, 1974; most strikeouts by losing pitcher, extra-inning game (19), August 20, 1974 (11 innings); most seasons leading league, bases on balls allowed (8); most bases on balls, lifetime (2,186); most no-hit games, lifetime (5).

Established modern major league records for most consecutive seasons, 300 or more strikeouts (3); most strikeouts, season (383), 1973.

Tied major league records for striking out side on nine pitches, April 19, 1968 (third inning) and July 9, 1972 (second inning); most no-hit games, season (2), 1973; most strikeouts game (19), August 12, 1974; most clubs shut out, season (8), 1972; most consecutive seasons leading major leagues, bases on balls allowed (3); most strikeouts, three consecutive nine-inning games (41), August 7, 12 and 16, 1974.

Established American League record for most games, 10 or more strikeouts, lifetime (114); most games, 15 or more strikeouts, lifetime (19).

Tied American League records for most seasons, 200 or more strikeouts (7); most consecutive strikeouts, game (8), July 9, 1972 and July 15, 1973; most strikeouts, two consecutive games (32), August 7 (13), 12 (19), 1974; most low-hit (no-hit and one-hit) games, season (3), 1973; most wild pitches, season (21), 1977; most seasons leading league, errors by pitcher (4); most seasons leading league, wild pitches (3).

Pitched 5-0 no-hit victory against Los Angeles Dodgers, September 26, 1981.
Pitched 1-0 no-hit victory against Baltimore Orioles, June 1, 1975.
Pitched 4-0 no-hit victory against Minnesota Twins, September 28, 1974.
Pitched 6-0 no-hit victory against Detroit Tigers, July 15, 1973.
Pitched 3-0 no-hit victory against Kansas City Royals, May 15, 1973.
Major League saves: 1969 (1), 1970 (1), 1973 (1). Total—3.
Led National League in hit batsmen with 8 in 1982.
Led National League in wild pitches with 16 in 1981.
Led American League in shutouts with 9 in 1972, 7 in 1976, and tied for lead with 5 in 1979.
Led American League in wild pitches with 18 in 1972, 21 in 1977 and 13 in 1978.
Tied for American League lead in complete games with 22 in 1977.
Tied for National League lead in sacrifice hits by hitters with 14 in 1985.
Led Western Carolinas League pitchers in games started with 28 in 1966.
Tied for Appalachian League lead in hit batsmen with 8 in 1965.
Named American League Pitcher of the Year by THE SPORTING NEWS, 1977.
Named righthanded pitcher on THE SPORTING NEWS American League All-Star Team, 1977.
Named Western Carolinas Pitcher of the Year, 1966.

Year	Club	League	G.	IP.	W.	L.	Pct.	H.	R.	ER.	SO.	BB.	ERA.
1965—Marion		Ap'lachian	13	78	3	6	.333	61	47	38	115	56	4.38
1966—Greenville		W. Carol.	29	183	*17	2	.895	109	59	51	*272	*127	2.51
1966—Williamsport		Eastern	3	19	0	2	.000	9	6	2	35	12	0.95
1966—New York		National	2	3	0	1	.000	5	5	5	6	3	15.00
1967—Winter Haven†		Florida St.	1	4	0	0	.000	1	1	1	5	2	2.25
1967—Jacksonville‡		Int'national	3	7	1	0	1.000	3	1	0	18	3	0.00
1968—New York§		National	21	134	6	9	.400	93	50	46	133	75	3.09
1969—New York		National	25	89	6	3	.667	60	38	35	92	53	3.54
1970—New York		National	27	132	7	11	.389	86	59	50	125	97	3.41
1971—New York x		National	30	152	10	14	.417	125	78	67	137	116	3.97
1972—California		American	39	284	19	16	.543	166	80	72	*329	*157	2.28
1973—California		American	41	326	21	16	.568	238	113	104	*383	*162	2.87
1974—California		American	42	*333	22	16	.579	221	127	107	*367	*202	2.89
1975—California		American	28	198	14	12	.538	152	90	76	186	132	3.45
1976—California		American	39	284	17	*18	.486	193	117	106	*327	*183	3.36
1977—California		American	37	299	19	16	.543	198	110	92	*341	*204	2.77
1978—California y		American	31	235	10	13	.435	183	106	97	*260	*148	3.71
1979—California z		American	34	223	16	14	.533	169	104	89	*223	114	3.59
1980—Houston		National	35	234	11	10	.524	205	100	87	200	*98	3.35
1981—Houston		National	21	149	11	5	.688	99	34	28	140	68	*1.69
1982—Houston		National	35	250⅓	16	12	.571	196	100	88	245	*109	3.16
1983—Houston a		National	29	196⅓	14	9	.609	134	74	65	183	101	2.98

Year Club	League	G.	IP.	W.	L.	Pct.	H.	R.	ER.	SO.	BB.	ERA.
1984—Houston b	National	30	183⅔	12	11	.522	143	78	62	197	69	3.04
1985—Houston	National	35	232	10	12	.455	205	108	98	209	95	3.80
National League Totals—11 Years		290	1755⅓	103	97	.515	1351	724	631	1667	884	3.24
American League Totals—8 Years		291	2182	138	121	.533	1520	847	743	2416	1302	3.06
Major League Totals—19 Years		581	3937⅓	241	218	.525	2871	1571	1374	4083	2186	3.14

Selected by New York Mets' organization in 8th round of free-agent draft, June, 1965.
†On military list, January 3 to May 13, 1967.
‡On disabled list, July 16 to August 30, 1967.
§On disabled list, July 30 to August 30, 1968.
xTraded with Pitcher Don Rose, Outfielder Leroy Stanton and Catcher Francisco Estrada to California Angels for Infielder Jim Fregosi, December 10, 1971.
yOn disabled list, June 14 to July 5, 1978.
zGranted free agency, November 1, 1979; signed by Houston Astros, November 19, 1979.
aOn disabled list, March 25 to April 17 and May 3 to June 6, 1983.
bOn disabled list, June 2 to June 17 and June 18 to July 3, 1984.

DIVISION SERIES RECORD

Year Club	League	G.	IP.	W.	L.	Pct.	H.	R.	ER.	SO.	BB.	ERA.
1981—Houston	National	2	15	1	1	.500	6	4	3	14	3	1.80

CHAMPIONSHIP SERIES RECORD

Established Championship Series record for most strikeouts by relief pitcher, game (7), October 6, 1969.
Tied Championship Series records for most clubs, total Series (3); most earned runs allowed, five-game Series (8), 1980; most consecutive strikeouts, start of game (4), October 3, 1979.
Established National League Championship Series records for most runs allowed, five-game Series (8), 1980; most hits allowed, five-game Series (16), 1980.

Year Club	League	G.	IP.	W.	L.	Pct.	H.	R.	ER.	SO.	BB.	ERA.
1969—New York	National	1	7	1	0	1.000	3	2	2	7	2	2.57
1979—California	American	1	7	0	0	.000	4	3	1	8	3	1.29
1980—Houston	National	2	13⅓	0	0	.000	16	8	8	14	3	5.40
Championship Series Totals—3 Years		4	27⅓	1	0	1.000	23	13	11	29	8	3.62

WORLD SERIES RECORD

Year Club	League	G.	IP.	W.	L.	Pct.	H.	R.	ER.	SO.	BB.	ERA.
1969—New York	National	1	2⅓	0	0	.000	1	0	0	3	2	0.00

ALL-STAR GAME RECORD

Year League	IP.	W.	L.	Pct.	H.	R.	ER.	SO.	BB.	ERA.
1973—American	2	0	0	.000	2	2	2	2	2	9.00
1979—American	2	0	0	.000	5	3	3	2	1	13.50
1981—National	1	0	0	.000	0	0	0	1	0	0.00
1985—National	3	0	0	.000	2	0	0	2	2	0.00
All-Star Game Totals—4 Years	8	0	0	.000	9	5	5	7	5	5.63

Member of American League All-Star Team for the 1972 and 1975 games; did not play.
Named to American League All-Star Team to replace Frank Tanana for 1977 game; declined.

BRET WILLIAM SABERHAGEN

Born April 13, 1964, at Chicago Heights, Ill.
Height, 6.01. Weight, 160.
Throws and bats righthanded.

Major League saves: 1984 (1).
Named American League Pitcher of the Year by THE SPORTING NEWS, 1985.
Won American League Cy Young Memorial Award, 1985.
Named righthanded pitcher on THE SPORTING NEWS American League All-Star Team, 1985.

Year Club	League	G.	IP.	W.	L.	Pct.	H.	R.	ER.	SO.	BB.	ERA.
1983—Fort Myers	Florida St.	16	109⅔	10	5	.667	98	34	28	82	19	2.30
1983—Jacksonville	Southern	11	77⅓	6	2	.750	66	31	25	48	29	2.91
1984—Kansas City†	American	38	157⅔	10	11	.476	138	71	61	73	36	3.48
1985—Kansas City	American	32	235⅓	20	6	.769	211	79	75	158	38	2.87
Major League Totals—2 Years		70	393	30	17	.638	349	150	136	231	74	3.11

Selected by Kansas City Royals' organization in 19th round of free-agent draft, June 7, 1982.
†Appeared in one game as a pinch-runner.

CHAMPIONSHIP SERIES RECORD

Year Club	League	G.	IP.	W.	L.	Pct.	H.	R.	ER.	SO.	BB.	ERA.
1984—Kansas City	American	1	8	0	0	.000	6	3	2	5	1	2.25
1985—Kansas City	American	2	7⅓	0	0	.000	12	5	5	6	2	6.14
Championship Series Totals—2 Years		3	15⅓	0	0	.000	18	8	7	11	3	4.11

WORLD SERIES RECORD

Year Club	League	G.	IP.	W.	L.	Pct.	H.	R.	ER.	SO.	BB.	ERA.
1985—Kansas City	American	2	18	2	0	1.000	11	1	1	10	1	0.50

RANDY ANTHONY ST. CLAIRE

Born August 23, 1960, at Glens Falls, N.Y.
Height, 6.03. Weight, 180.
Throws and bats righthanded.
Son of Ebba St. Claire, catcher with Boston Braves,
Milwaukee Braves and New York Giants, 1951 through 1954;
and brother of Steve St. Claire, pitcher in Montreal Expos' organization.

Led Southern League in intentional bases on balls issued with 14 in 1984.

Year Club	League	G.	IP.	W.	L.	Pct.	H.	R.	ER.	SO.	BB.	ERA.
1979—Calgary	Pioneer	6	33	1	2	.333	30	22	16	17	15	4.36
1980—Calgary	Pioneer	21	57	5	7	.417	65	36	27	51	23	4.26
1981—Jamestown	NYP	13	51	4	1	.800	53	22	11	36	17	1.94
1982—San Jose	California	9	61	2	5	.286	58	32	28	44	20	4.13
1982—W. Palm Beach	Florida St.	19	65	3	8	.273	74	41	38	38	17	5.26
1983—W. Palm Beach	Florida St.	42	98	5	7	.417	72	33	23	77	31	2.11
1984—Jacksonville	Southern	48	75	10	7	.588	64	35	24	56	29	2.88
1984—Indianapolis	Am. Assoc.	13	17⅔	1	1	.500	15	2	2	17	6	1.02
1984—Montreal	National	4	8	0	0	.000	11	4	4	4	2	4.50
1985—Indianapolis†	Am. Assoc.	11	19⅔	0	1	.000	21	5	4	11	3	1.83
1985—Montreal	National	42	68⅔	5	3	.625	69	32	30	25	26	3.93
Major League Totals—2 Years		46	76⅔	5	3	.625	80	36	34	29	28	3.99

Signed as free agent by Montreal Expos' organization, September 9, 1978.
†On disabled list, May 7 to May 17, 1985.

LENN HARUKI SAKATA

Name pronounced Lenn Ha-ROO-key Sah-KAH-tah.

Born June 8, 1953, at Honolulu, Hawaii
Height, 5.09. Weight, 160.
Throws and bats righthanded.
Attended Treasure Valley Community College, Ontario, Ore. and
Gonzaga University, Spokane, Wash.

Major League stolen bases: 1977 (1), 1978 (1), 1980 (2), 1981 (4), 1982 (7), 1983 (8), 1984 (4), 1985 (3). Total—30.

Year Club	League	Pos.	G.	AB.	R.	H.	2B.	3B.	HR.	RBI.	B.A.	PO.	A.	E.	F.A.
1975—Thetford Mines†	East.	2B	121	421	63	108	9	3	9	43	.257	243	304	16	.972
1976—Spokane	P. C.	2B	141	510	64	143	23	5	10	70	.280	•327	428	•22	.972
1977—Spokane	P. C.	2B	94	345	52	105	19	4	4	73	.304	221	352	13	★.978
1977—Milwaukee	Amer.	2B	53	154	13	25	2	0	2	12	.162	102	159	4	.985
1978—Spokane	P. C.	2B	45	156	24	42	14	3	0	20	.269	73	160	5	.979
1978—Milwaukee	Amer.	2B	30	78	8	15	4	0	0	3	.192	50	66	3	.975
1979—Vancouver‡	P. C.	2B-3B	118	454	59	136	21	3	6	64	.300	266	409	14	.980
1979—Milwaukee§	Amer.	2B	4	14	1	7	2	0	0	1	.500	10	13	0	1.000
1980—Rochester x	Int.	2B	26	93	19	32	6	1	3	8	.344	45	87	4	.971
1980—Baltimore	Amer.	2B-SS	43	83	12	16	3	2	1	9	.193	55	73	2	.985
1981—Baltimore y	Amer.	SS-2B	61	150	19	34	4	0	5	15	.227	82	148	7	.970
1982—Baltimore	Amer.	2B-SS	136	343	40	89	18	1	6	31	.259	182	299	16	.968
1983—Baltimore	Amer.	2B-C	66	134	23	34	7	0	3	12	.254	84	117	2	.990
1984—Baltimore	Amer.	2B-OF	81	157	23	30	1	0	3	11	.191	80	161	3	.988
1985—Baltimore	Amer.	2B	55	97	15	22	3	0	3	6	.227	58	87	6	.960
1985—Rochester z	Int.	2B	16	56	7	12	1	0	0	2	.214	28	48	3	.962
Major League Totals—9 Years			529	1210	154	272	44	3	23	100	.225	703	1123	43	.977

Selected by San Francisco Giants' organization in 14th round of free-agent draft, June 6, 1972.
Selected by San Diego Padres' organization in 5th round of free-agent draft, June 5, 1974.
Selected by Milwaukee Brewers' organization in secondary phase of free-agent draft, January 9, 1975.
†On disabled list, August 26 to September 5, 1975.
‡On disabled list, April 30 to May 18, 1979.
§Traded to Baltimore Orioles for Pitcher John Flinn, December 6, 1979.
xOn suspended list, April 16 to April 21, 1980.
yOn disabled list, November 9, 1980 through May 28, 1981.
zGranted free agency, November 12, 1985.

WORLD SERIES RECORD

Year Club	League	Pos.	G.	AB.	R.	H.	2B.	3B.	HR.	RBI.	B.A.	PO.	A.	E.	F.A.
1983—Baltimore	Amer.	PR-2B	1	1	0	0	0	0	0	0	.000	2	2	0	1.000

MARK BRUCE SALAS

Name pronounced SAL-us.

Born March 8, 1961, at Montebello, Calif.
Height, 6.00. Weight, 180.
Throws right and bats lefthanded.

Tied for Florida State League lead in sacrifice flies with 10 in 1981.
Tied for Appalachian League lead in passed balls with 10 in 1979.

Year Club	League	Pos.	G.	AB.	R.	H.	2B.	3B.	HR.	RBI.	B.A.	PO.	A.	E.	F.A.
1979—Johnson City	Appal.	C	53	144	23	35	4	2	5	23	.243	194	19	6	.973
1980—Gastonia	S. Atl.	C	98	267	42	67	8	3	9	46	.251	452	41	5	★.990
1981—St. Petersburg	Fla St.	•C-1B	100	321	26	78	9	2	2	52	.243	387	66	•13	.972
1982—Arkansas	Texas	C	27	76	4	17	4	0	0	5	.224	88	15	1	.990

Year Club	League	Pos.	G.	AB.	R.	H.	2B.	3B.	HR.	RBI.	B.A.	PO.	A.	E.	F.A.
1982—Louisville†	A. A.	C	7	22	1	4	0	0	0	1	.182	16	3	1	.950
1982—Nashville	South.	C	43	137	19	35	7	0	6	20	.255	267	24	7	.977
1983—Arkansas	Texas	C-OF	131	473	76	144	25	4	20	82	.304	334	41	4	.989
1984—Louisville	A. A.	C-OF	95	316	28	77	20	2	12	48	.244	260	28	7	.976
1984—St. Louis‡	Nat.	C-OF	14	20	1	2	1	0	0	1	.100	13	2	0	1.000
1985—Minnesota	Amer.	C	120	360	51	108	20	5	9	41	.300	529	39	5	.991
National League Totals—1 Year			14	20	1	2	1	0	0	1	.100	13	2	0	1.000
American League Totals—1 Year			120	360	51	108	20	5	9	41	.300	529	39	5	.991
Major League Totals—2 Years			134	380	52	110	21	5	9	42	.289	542	41	5	.991

Selected by St. Louis Cardinals' organization in 18th round of free-agent draft, June 5, 1979.

†Loaned to Nashville (New York Yankees' organization), June 30, 1982; returned, September 13, 1982.

‡Drafted by Minnesota Twins, December 3, 1984.

ARGENIS ANTONIO SALAZAR
(Angel)

Born November 4, 1961, at El Tigre, Venezuela.
Height, 6.00. Weight, 173.
Throws and bats righthanded.

Major League stolen bases: 1984 (1).
Tied for Pioneer League lead in double plays by shortstops with 45 in 1981.

Year Club	League	Pos.	G.	AB.	R.	H.	2B.	3B.	HR.	RBI.	B.A.	PO.	A.	E.	F.A.
1980—W. Palm Beach†	Fla. St.					(Did not play)									
1980—Calgary	Pion.	S-2-1-C	51	169	29	41	2	0	0	11	.243	60	126	17	.916
1981—Calgary	Pion.	SS	63	259	37	64	5	3	2	25	.247	89	*228	13	*.961
1982—W. Palm Beach	Fla. St.	SS	112	408	63	109	15	2	2	36	.267	176	*364	35	.939
1983—Wichita	A. A.	SS	98	341	47	103	23	7	1	54	.302	152	256	24	.944
1983—Montreal	Nat.	SS	36	37	5	8	1	1	0	1	.216	28	28	2	.966
1984—Montreal	Nat.	SS	80	174	12	27	4	2	0	12	.155	88	155	10	.960
1984—Indianapolis†§	A. A.	SS-3B	50	156	11	43	8	1	1	14	.276	54	117	3	.983
1985—Tidewater x	Int.	SS-2B	84	230	25	58	10	1	0	18	.252	119	244	16	.958
Major League Totals—2 Years			116	211	17	35	5	3	0	13	.166	116	183	12	.961

Signed as free agent by Montreal Expos' organization, January 20, 1980.

†On temporarily inactive list, April 10 to June 1, 1980.

‡Selected by St. Louis Cardinals' organization in player compensation pool draft, January 24, 1985. (St. Louis received compensation for Atlanta Braves' signing of free agent Pitcher Bruce Sutter, a Type A player, December 7, 1984.)

§Traded with Pitcher John Young to New York Mets' organization for Shortstop Jose Oquendo and Pitcher Mark Jason Davis, April 2, 1985.

xOn disabled list, April 13 to April 27 and June 16 to July 2, 1985.

LUIS ERNESTO SALAZAR

Born May 19, 1956, at Barcelona, Venezuela.
Height, 6.00. Weight, 185.
Throws and bats righthanded.

Major League stolen bases: 1980 (11), 1981 (11), 1982 (32), 1983 (24), 1984 (11), 1985 (14). Total—103.
Led National League third basemen in errors with 26 and tied for lead in double plays with 28 in 1982.
Led Eastern League outfielders in putouts with 312 and tied for lead in double plays with 3 in 1979.

Year Club	League	Pos.	G.	AB.	R.	H.	2B.	3B.	HR.	RBI.	B.A.	PO.	A.	E.	F.A.
1974—Sarasota Royals†	Gulf C.	SS	2	4	0	1	0	0	0	1	.250	0	2	0	1.000
1976—Niagara Falls	NYP	SS-OF	42	151	18	36	3	4	1	17	.238	71	49	17	.876
1977—Salem	Carol.	SS-3B-2B	116	433	72	117	17	5	11	48	.270	157	294	45	.909
1978—Salem	Carol.	OF-3B-SS	126	472	55	138	20	4	3	49	.292	160	77	19	.926
1979—Buffalo	East.	OF-3B	*139	*561	*108	*181	17	5	27	86	.323	321	42	13	.965
1980—Port.‡-Hawaii	P. C.	OF	127	497	91	157	23	15	9	64	.316	304	11	8	.975
1980—San Diego	Nat.	3B-OF	44	169	28	57	4	7	1	25	.337	39	88	7	.948
1981—San Diego	Nat.	3B-OF	109	400	37	121	19	6	3	38	.303	108	191	14	.955
1982—San Diego	Nat.	3B-SS-OF	145	524	55	127	15	5	8	62	.242	133	326	29	.941
1983—San Diego	Nat.	3B-SS	134	481	52	124	16	2	14	45	.258	122	274	21	.950
1984—San Diego§x		3B-OF-SS	93	228	20	55	7	2	3	17	.241	87	97	6	.968
1985—Chicago	Amer.	OF-3B-1B	122	327	39	80	18	2	10	45	.245	180	57	10	.960
National League Totals—5 Years			525	1802	192	484	61	22	29	187	.269	489	976	77	.950
American League Totals—1 Year			122	327	39	80	18	2	10	45	.245	180	57	10	.960
Major League Totals—6 Years			647	2129	231	564	79	24	39	232	.265	669	1033	87	.951

Signed as free agent by Kansas City Royals' organization, November 29, 1973.

†Released, July 8, 1974; signed by Pittsburgh Pirates' organization, November 23, 1975.

‡Traded with Outfielder Rick Lancellotti to San Diego Padres' organization for Infielder Kurt Bevacqua and a player to be named later, August 4, 1980; Pittsburgh Pirates' organization acquired Pitcher Mark Lee to complete deal, August 12, 1980.

§On disabled list, May 15 to June 11, 1984.

xTraded with Pitchers Tim Lollar and Bill Long and Shortstop Ozzie Guillen to Chicago White Sox for Pitchers LaMarr Hoyt, Kevin Kristan and Todd Simmons, December 6, 1984.

CHAMPIONSHIP SERIES RECORD

Year Club	League	Pos.	G.	AB.	R.	H.	2B.	3B.	HR.	RBI.	B.A.	PO.	A.	E.	F.A.
1984—San Diego	Nat.	3B-PH-OF	3	5	0	1	0	1	0	0	.200	1	3	0	1.000

Year	Club	League	Pos.	G.	AB.	R.	H.	2B.	3B.	HR.	RBI.	B.A.	PO.	A.	E.	F.A.
1984—San Diego†		Nat.	3B-OF	4	3	0	1	0	0	0	0	.333	1	0	0	1.000

†Also appeared as a pinch-runner and pinch-hitter.

JOSEPH CHARLES SAMBITO

Name pronounced Sam-BEET-oh.

(Joe)

Born June 28, 1952, at Brooklyn, N.Y.
Height, 6.01. Weight, 190.
Throws and bats lefthanded.
Attended Adelphi University, Garden City, N.Y.

Major League saves: 1976 (1), 1977 (7), 1978 (11), 1979 (22), 1980 (17), 1981 (10), 1982 (4). Total—72.
Led Southern League in wild pitches with 14 and tied for lead in games started by pitchers with 28 in 1975.
Tied for Appalachian League lead in shutouts with 2 in 1973.

Year	Club	League	G.	IP.	W.	L.	Pct.	H.	R.	ER.	SO.	BB.	ERA.
1973—Columbus	Southern	1	2	0	0	.000	4	4	4	2	1	18.00
1973—Covington	Ap'lachian	11	55	4	2	.667	32	18	9	57	13	1.47
1974—Cedar Rapids	Midwest	23	156	11	8	.579	133	59	52	182	49	3.00
1975—Columbus	Southern	30	*209	12	9	.571	*200	85	70	*140	85	3.01
1976—Memphis	Int'national	5	27	3	0	1.000	37	19	19	17	13	6.33
1976—Columbus	Southern	12	100	8	2	.800	77	27	20	61	23	1.80
1976—Houston	National	20	53	3	2	.600	45	21	21	26	14	3.57
1977—Houston	National	54	89	5	5	.500	77	34	23	67	24	2.33
1978—Houston	National	62	88	4	9	.308	85	32	30	96	32	3.07
1979—Houston	National	63	91	8	7	.533	80	20	18	83	23	1.78
1980—Houston	National	64	90	8	4	.667	65	26	22	75	22	2.20
1981—Houston	National	49	64	5	5	.500	43	17	13	41	22	1.83
1982—Houston†	National	9	12⅔	0	0	.000	7	2	1	7	2	0.71
1983—Houston‡	National					(Did not play)						
1984—Tucson§	P. Coast	8	8	0	0	.000	5	2	2	5	4	2.25
1984—Houston x	National	32	47⅔	0	0	.000	39	16	16	26	16	3.02
1985—New York	National	8	10⅔	0	0	.000	21	18	15	3	8	12.66
1985—Tidewater y	Int'national	19	20⅔	0	3	.000	31	15	10	12	11	4.35
Major League Totals—10 Years		361	546	33	32	.508	462	186	159	424	163	2.62

Selected by Houston Astros' organization in 17th round of free-agent draft, June 5, 1973.
†On disabled list, May 20, 1982 through remainder of season.
‡On disabled list, March 30, 1983 through remainder of season.
§On Houston disabled list, April 2 to May 25, 1984; included rehabilitation disability assignment to Tucson, May 9 to May 25, 1984.
xReleased, April 8, 1985; signed by New York Mets, April 26, 1985.
yReleased, August 23, 1985.

DIVISION SERIES RECORD

Year	Club	League	G.	IP.	W.	L.	Pct.	H.	R.	ER.	SO.	BB.	ERA.
1981—Houston	National	2	1⅔	1	0	1.000	5	3	3	2	2	16.20

CHAMPIONSHIP SERIES RECORD

Year	Club	League	G.	IP.	W.	L.	Pct.	H.	R.	ER.	SO.	BB.	ERA.
1980—Houston	National	3	3⅔	0	1	.000	4	2	2	6	2	4.91

ALL-STAR GAME RECORD

Year	League	IP.	W.	L.	Pct.	H.	R.	ER.	SO.	BB.	ERA.
1979—National		⅔	0	0	.000	0	0	0	0	1	0.00

WILLIAM AMOS SAMPLE

(Billy)

Born April 2, 1955, at Roanoke, Va.
Height, 5.09. Weight, 175.
Throws and bats righthanded.
Received bachelor of science degree in psychology from
James Madison University, Harrisonburg, Va.

Tied major league records for highest fielding percentage by outfielder, season, 100 or more games (1.000), 1979; most assists by outfielder, inning (2), April 28, 1979 (fourth inning).
Major League stolen bases: 1979 (8), 1980 (8), 1981 (4), 1982 (10), 1983 (44), 1984 (18), 1985 (2). Total—94.
Led Pacific Coast League in bases on balls received with 109 in 1978.
Led Gulf Coast League in total bases with 86 in 1976.
Led Texas League second basemen in errors with 23 in 1977.

Year	Club	League	Pos.	G.	AB.	R.	H.	2B.	3B.	HR.	RBI.	B.A.	PO.	A.	E.	F.A.
1976—Sarasota Rang	Gulf C.	2B	45	152	35	58	7	*9	1	33	*.382	81	113	8	.960
1977—Tulsa	Texas	2B-OF-3B	113	408	86	142	26	*13	7	72	.348	169	122	26	.918
1978—Tucson	P. C.	OF-2B	131	483	*141	170	27	13	18	99	.352	234	11	6	.976
1978—Texas	Amer.	OF	8	15	2	7	2	0	0	3	.467	0	0	0	.000
1979—Texas	Amer.	OF	128	325	60	95	21	2	5	35	.292	173	7	0	1.000
1980—Texas	Amer.	OF	99	204	29	53	10	0	4	19	.260	105	2	3	.973
1981—Texas†	Amer.	OF	66	230	36	65	16	0	3	25	.283	132	4	1	.993

Year Club	League	Pos.	G.	AB.	R.	H.	2B.	3B.	HR.	RBI.	B.A.	PO.	A.	E.	F.A.
1981—Wichita	A. A.	OF	3	14	2	5	1	0	0	2	.357	9	0	0	1.000
1982—Texas	Amer.	OF	97	360	56	94	14	2	10	29	.261	196	6	4	.981
1983—Texas	Amer.	OF	147	554	80	152	28	3	12	57	.274	329	8	4	.988
1984—Texas‡	Amer.	OF	130	489	67	121	20	2	5	33	.247	285	3	4	.986
1985—New York§	Amer.	OF	59	139	18	40	5	0	1	15	.288	89	1	1	.989
Major League Totals—8 Years			734	2316	348	627	116	9	40	216	.271	1309	31	17	.987

Selected by Texas Rangers' organization in 28th round of free-agent draft, June 5, 1973.
Selected by Texas Rangers' organization in 10th round of free-agent draft, June 8, 1976.
†On disabled list, May 6 to June 2, 1981; included rehabilitation disability assignment to Wichita, May 28 to June 2, 1981.
‡Traded with a player to be named later to New York Yankees for Third Baseman Toby Harrah, February 27, 1985; New York organization acquired Pitcher Eric Dersin to complete deal, July 14, 1985.
§Traded to Atlanta Braves for Infielder Miguel Sosa, December 6, 1985.

JUAN MILTON SAMUEL

Name pronounced SAHM-well.

Born December 9, 1960, at San Pedro de Macoris, D.R.
Height, 5.11. Weight, 170.
Throws and bats righthanded.

Established major league records for most at-bats by righthander, season (701), 1984; fewest sacrifice hits, most at-bats, season (0 and 701), 1984.
Tied major league record for most assists by second baseman, nine-inning game (12), April 20, 1985.
Established National League record for most at-bats, season (701), 1984.
Major League stolen bases: 1983 (3), 1984 (72), 1985 (53). Total—128.
Led National League batters in strikeouts with 168 in 1984 and tied for lead with 141 in 1985.
Led Carolina League in total bases with 283 and tied for lead in being hit by pitch with 15 in 1982.
Led Northwest League batters in strikeouts with 87 and caught stealing with 10 in 1980.
Led Carolina League second basemen in double plays with 82 and total chances with 721 in 1982.
Led South Atlantic League second basemen in double plays with 82 and total chances with 737 in 1981.
Named National League Rookie Player of the Year by THE SPORTING NEWS, 1984.
Named Carolina League Most Valuable Player, 1982.

Year Club	League	Pos.	G.	AB.	R.	H.	2B.	3B.	HR.	RBI.	B.A.	PO.	A.	E.	F.A.
1980—Cen. Oregon	N'west	2B	69	★298	66	84	11	2	17	44	.282	162	188	★30	.921
1981—Spartanburg	S. Atl.	2B	135	512	88	127	22	8	11	74	.248	★280	★409	★50	.932
1982—Peninsula	Carol.	2B	135	494	★111	158	29	6	28	94	.320	★244	★442	★35	.951
1983—Reading	East.	2B	47	184	36	43	10	0	11	39	.234	121	127	14	.947
1983—Portland	P. C.	2B	65	261	59	86	14	8	15	52	.330	110	168	15	.949
1983—Philadelphia	Nat.	2B	18	65	14	18	1	2	2	5	.277	44	54	9	.916
1984—Philadelphia	Nat.	2B	160	★701	105	191	36	●19	15	69	.272	388	438	★33	.962
1985—Philadelphia	Nat.	2B	161	★663	101	175	31	13	19	74	.264	★389	463	15	.983
Major League Totals—3 Years			339	1429	220	384	68	34	36	148	.269	821	955	57	.969

Signed as free agent by Philadelphia Phillies' organization, April 29, 1980.

CHAMPIONSHIP SERIES RECORD

Year Club	League	Pos.	G.	AB.	R.	H.	2B.	3B.	HR.	RBI.	B.A.	PO.	A.	E.	F.A.
1983—Philadelphia	Nat.	PR	1	0	0	0	0	0	0	0	.000	0	0	0	.000

WORLD SERIES RECORD

Year Club	League	Pos.	G.	AB.	R.	H.	2B.	3B.	HR.	RBI.	B.A.	PO.	A.	E.	F.A.
1983—Philadelphia	Nat.	PR-PH	3	1	0	0	0	0	0	0	.000	0	0	0	.000

ALL-STAR GAME RECORD

Member of National League All-Star Team in 1984; did not play.

ALEJANDRO SANCHEZ (PIMENTEL)
(Alex)

Born February 26, 1959, at San Pedro, Dominican Republic.
Height, 6.00. Weight, 175.
Throws and bats righthanded.

Tied American League record for most home runs by pinch-hitter, consecutive at-bats (2), July 20 and 23, 1985.
Major League stolen bases: 1984 (2), 1985 (2). Total—4.
Led Pacific Coast League in total bases with 294 in 1984.
Named Pacific Coast League Player of the Year, 1984.

Year Club	League	Pos.	G.	AB.	R.	H.	2B.	3B.	HR.	RBI.	B.A.	PO.	A.	E.	F.A.
1978—Helena	Pion.	OF	6	24	4	5	0	1	0	5	.208	2	1	0	1.000
1978—Auburn	NYP	OF	58	242	30	58	9	5	4	28	.240	120	6	★14	.900
1979—Cen. Oregon	N'west	OF	54	204	31	55	10	2	3	38	.270	97	6	5	.954
1980—Spartanburg	S. Atl.	OF	127	490	84	140	26	8	15	76	.286	223	15	●16	.937
1981—Reading	East.	OF	138	495	77	136	19	★17	13	76	.275	216	13	15	.939
1982—Oklahoma City†	A. A.	OF	88	320	57	98	24	7	13	46	.306	155	10	●9	.948
1982—Philadelphia	Nat.	OF	7	14	3	4	1	0	2	4	.286	7	0	0	1.000
1983—Portland	P. C.	OF	125	458	75	113	21	5	17	74	.247	219	●18	★12	.952
1983—Philadelphia‡	Nat.	OF	8	7	2	2	0	0	0	2	.286	1	0	1	.500
1984—Phoenix	P. C.	OF	135	532	98	169	29	9	26	108	.318	249	10	12	.956
1984—San Francisco§	Nat.	OF	13	41	3	8	0	1	0	2	.195	18	2	1	.952

Year Club League	Pos.	G.	AB.	R.	H.	2B.	3B.	HR.	RBI.	B.A.	PO.	A.	E.	F.A.
1985—Nashville................. A. A.	OF	10	38	6	9	1	0	2	5	.237	17	0	0	1.000
1985—Detroit x .... Amer.	OF	71	133	19	33	6	2	6	12	.248	35	1	3	.923
National League Totals—3 Years...........		28	62	8	14	1	1	2	8	.226	26	2	2	.933
American League Totals—1 Year..........		71	133	19	33	6	2	6	12	.248	35	1	3	.923
Major League Totals—4 Years.................		99	195	27	47	7	3	8	20	.241	61	3	5	.928

Signed as free agent by Philadelphia Phillies' organization, April 10, 1978.
†On disabled list, July 1 to August 5, 1982.
‡Traded to San Francisco Giants' organization for First Baseman Dave Bergman, March 24, 1984.
§Traded to Detroit Tigers' organization for Pitcher Roger Mason, April 5, 1985.
xTraded with Infielder Chris Pittaro to Minnesota Twins for Catcher Dave Engle, January 16, 1986.

LUIS MERCEDES SANCHEZ

Born August 24, 1953, at Cariaco, Sucre, Venezuela.
Height, 6.02. Weight, 170.
Throws and bats righthanded.

Major League saves: 1981 (2), 1982 (5), 1983 (7), 1984 (11), 1985 (2). Total—27.
Led American League in intentional bases on balls issued with 14 in 1983.
Led Florida East Coast League in complete games with 6 in 1972.
Tied for Mexican League lead in complete games with 16 in 1980.

Year Club League	G.	IP.	W.	L.	Pct.	H.	R.	ER.	SO.	BB.	ERA.
1972—Cocoa Astros.................... Fla. E. C.	11	71	6	3	.667	55	29	20	49	31	2.54
1973—Cedar Rapids.................... Midwest	26	130	5	9	.357	140	75	61	93	43	4.22
1974—Cedar Rapids.................... Midwest	25	147	9	4	.692	122	39	26	130	44	★1.59
1975—Columbus........................ Southern	21	132	6	12	.333	137	76	59	60	64	4.02
1975—Dubuque†......................... Midwest	6	31	2	3	.400	25	19	12	19	10	3.48
1976—Tampa‡§x........................ Florida St.	2	8	0	2	.000	11	4	4	5	4	4.50
1977-78........................					(Did not play)						
1979—Caracas y........................ Int.-Amer.	13	35	2	4	.333	39	25	19	25	19	4.89
1980—Aguila z........................ Mexican	24	177	14	9	.609	149	47	40	●155	35	2.03
1980—Albuquerque a................ P. Coast	5	22	2	1	.667	27	14	13	15	10	5.32
1981—California........................ American	17	34	0	2	.000	39	16	11	13	11	2.91
1981—Salt Lake City.................. P. Coast	6	8	0	0	.000	12	7	7	7	7	7.88
1982—California........................ American	46	92⅔	7	4	.636	89	36	33	58	34	3.21
1982—Spokane......................... P. Coast	2	9⅔	0	1	.000	13	13	10	5	8	9.31
1983—California........................ American	56	98⅓	10	8	.556	92	42	40	49	40	3.66
1984—California........................ American	49	83⅔	9	7	.563	84	34	31	62	33	3.33
1985—California b...................... American	26	61⅓	2	0	1.000	67	41	39	34	27	5.72
1985—Edmonton c..................... P. Coast	4	5⅓	0	0	.000	7	6	6	4	2	10.13
Major League Totals—5 Years.............................	194	370	28	21	.571	371	169	154	216	145	3.75

Signed as free agent by Houston Astros' organization, September 1, 1971.
†Traded with Pitcher Carlos Alfonso to Cincinnati Reds' organization, December 12, 1975, completing deal in which Cincinnati Reds traded Pitcher Joaquin Andujar to Houston Astros for two players to be named later, October 24, 1975.
‡On disabled list, April 17 to May 18, 1976.
§On temporary inactive list, May 28 to July 28, 1976.
xOn disqualified list, July 28, 1976 through March 30, 1979; signed by Caracas of Inter-American League, March 30, 1979.
ySigned by Aguila, December 29, 1979.
zLoaned to Los Angeles Dodgers' organization, July 31, 1980; returned, October 15, 1980.
aSold to California Angels, February 10, 1981.
bOn disabled list, April 24 to June 13, 1985; included rehabilitation disability assignment to Edmonton, May 29 to June 10, 1985.
cTraded with Catcher Tim Arnold to Montreal Expos for Pitcher Gary Lucas, December 27, 1985.

CHAMPIONSHIP SERIES RECORD

Year Club League	G.	IP.	W.	L.	Pct.	H.	R.	ER.	SO.	BB.	ERA.
1982—California........................ American	2	2⅔	0	1	.000	4	2	2	1	1	6.75

RYNE DEE SANDBERG

Born September 18, 1959, at Spokane, Wash.
Height, 6.01. Weight, 175.
Throws and bats righthanded.

Tied major league record for most assists by second baseman, nine-inning game (12), June 12, 1983.
Major League stolen bases: 1982 (32), 1983 (37), 1984 (32), 1985 (54). Total—155.
Led National League second basemen in total chances with 914 in 1983 and 870 in 1984.
Led National League second basemen in assists with 571 and double plays with 126 in 1983.
Led Eastern League shortstops in fielding percentage with .964, assists with 386 and double plays with 81 in 1980.
Led Western Carolinas League shortstops in double plays with 80 in 1979.
Led Pioneer League shortstops in double plays with 39 in 1978.
Named Major League Player of the Year by THE SPORTING NEWS, 1984.
Named National League Player of the Year by THE SPORTING NEWS, 1984.
Named National League Most Valuable Player by Baseball Writers' Association of America, 1984.
Named second baseman on THE SPORTING NEWS National League All-Star Team, 1984.
Named second baseman on THE SPORTING NEWS National League All-Star fielding team, 1983 through 1985.
Named second baseman on THE SPORTING NEWS National League Silver Slugger team, 1984 and 1985.
Received reported $30,000 bonus to sign with Philadelphia Phillies, 1978.

Year Club	League	Pos.	G.	AB.	R.	H.	2B.	3B.	HR.	RBI.	B.A.	PO.	A.	E.	F.A.
1978—Helena	Pion.	SS	56	190	34	59	6	6	1	23	.311	92	*200	24	.924
1979—Spartanburg	W. Car.	SS	*138	*539	83	133	21	7	4	47	.247	134	*467	35	*.945
1980—Reading	East.	SS-3B	129	490	95	152	21	12	11	79	.310	156	388	20	.965
1981—Oklahoma City	A. A.	SS-2B	133	519	78	152	17	5	9	62	.293	229	396	21	.967
1981—Philadelphia†	Nat.	SS-2B	13	6	2	1	0	0	0	0	.167	7	7	0	1.000
1982—Chicago	Nat.	3B-2B	156	635	103	172	33	5	7	54	.271	136	373	12	.977
1983—Chicago	Nat.	*2B-SS	158	633	94	165	25	4	8	48	.261	330	572	13	*.986
1984—Chicago	Nat.	2B	156	636	*114	200	36	●19	19	84	.314	314	*550	6	*.993
1985—Chicago	Nat.	2B-SS	153	609	113	186	31	6	26	83	.305	353	501	12	.986
Major League Totals—5 Years			636	2519	426	724	125	34	60	269	.287	1140	2003	43	.987

Selected by Philadelphia Phillies' organization in 20th round of free-agent draft, June 6, 1978.
†Traded with Shortstop Larry Bowa to Chicago Cubs for Shortstop Ivan DeJesus, January 27, 1982.

CHAMPIONSHIP SERIES RECORD

Year Club	League	Pos.	G.	AB.	R.	H.	2B.	3B.	HR.	RBI.	B.A.	PO.	A.	E.	F.A.
1984—Chicago	Nat.	2B	5	19	3	7	2	0	0	2	.368	13	18	1	.969

ALL-STAR GAME RECORD

Year League	Pos.	AB.	R.	H.	2B.	3B.	HR.	RBI.	B.A.	PO.	A.	E.	F.A.
1984—National	2B	4	0	1	0	0	0	0	.250	0	0	0	.000
1985—National	2B	1	1	0	0	0	0	0	.000	0	3	0	1.000
All-Star Game Totals—2 Years		5	1	1	0	0	0	0	.200	0	3	0	1.000

SCOTT DOUGLAS SANDERSON

Born July 22, 1956, at Dearborn, Mich.
Height, 6.05. Weight, 198.
Throws and bats righthanded.
Attended Vanderbilt University, Nashville, Tenn.

Tied National League record for most consecutive home runs allowed, inning (3), July 11, 1982 (second inning).
Major League saves: 1979 (1), 1983 (1). Total—2.

Year Club	League	G.	IP.	W.	L.	Pct.	H.	R.	ER.	SO.	BB.	ERA.
1977—West Palm Beach	Florida St.	10	57	5	2	.714	58	22	17	37	23	2.68
1978—Memphis	Southern	9	58	5	3	.625	55	32	26	44	19	4.03
1978—Denver	Am. Assoc.	9	49	4	2	.667	47	35	33	36	30	6.06
1978—Montreal	National	10	61	4	2	.667	52	20	17	50	21	2.51
1979—Montreal	National	34	168	9	8	.529	148	69	64	138	54	3.43
1980—Montreal	National	33	211	16	11	.593	206	76	73	125	56	3.11
1981—Montreal	National	22	137	9	7	.563	122	50	45	77	31	2.96
1982—Montreal	National	32	224	12	12	.500	212	98	86	158	58	3.46
1983—Montreal†‡	National	18	81⅓	6	7	.462	98	50	42	55	20	4.65
1984—Chicago§	National	24	140⅔	8	5	.615	140	54	49	76	24	3.14
1984—Lodi	California	1	5	0	1	.000	7	2	2	2	0	3.60
1985—Chicago x	National	19	121	5	6	.455	100	49	42	80	27	3.12
Major League Totals—8 Years		192	1144	69	58	.543	1078	466	418	759	291	3.29

Selected by Kansas City Royals' organization in 11th round of free-agent draft, June 5, 1974.
Selected by Montreal Expos' organization in 3rd round of free-agent draft, June 7, 1977.
†On disabled list, July 5 to September 1, 1983.
‡Traded with Infielder Al Newman to San Diego Padres for Pitcher Gary Lucas, December 7, 1983; Traded by San Diego to Chicago Cubs for First Baseman Carmelo Martinez, Pitcher Craig Lefferts and Third Baseman Fritz Connally, December 7, 1983.
§On disabled list, June 1 to July 5, 1984; included rehabilitation disability assignment to Lodi, June 29 to July 5, 1984.
xOn disabled list, August 14, 1985 through remainder of season.

DIVISION SERIES RECORD

Year Club	League	G.	IP.	W.	L.	Pct.	H.	R.	ER.	SO.	BB.	ERA.
1981—Montreal	National	1	2⅔	0	0	.000	4	4	2	2	2	6.75

CHAMPIONSHIP SERIES RECORD

Year Club	League	G.	IP.	W.	L.	Pct.	H.	R.	ER.	SO.	BB.	ERA.
1984—Chicago	National	1	4⅔	0	0	.000	6	3	3	2	1	5.79

RAFAEL FRANCISCO SANTANA (DeLaCRUZ)

Born January 31, 1958, at La Romana, Dominican Republic.
Height, 6.01. Weight, 156.
Throws and bats righthanded.

Established National League record for fewest assists by shortstop, season, 150 or more games (396), 1985.
Major League stolen bases: 1985 (1).
Led New York-Pennsylvania League in sacrifice hits with 8 in 1977.
Led Texas League shortstops in fielding percentage with .955 and tied for lead in double plays with 79 in 1981.

Year Club	League	Pos.	G.	AB.	R.	H.	2B.	3B.	HR.	RBI.	B.A.	PO.	A.	E.	F.A.
1977—Oneonta	NYP	SS	60	157	26	41	5	0	0	23	.261	62	162	*27	.892
1978—Fort Lauderdale	Fla. St.	SS	131	431	37	111	8	5	0	35	.258	166	372	*48	.918
1979—Fort Lauderdale	Fla. St.	SS-3B-2B	133	472	62	124	9	6	0	41	.263	160	351	16	.970
1980—Nashville	South.	SS	86	275	33	64	4	3	0	20	.233	125	247	25	.937
1980—Fort Lauderdale†	Fla. St.	SS	51	168	20	38	2	0	1	17	.226	81	158	9	.964
1981—Arkansas	Texas	SS-3B-2B	110	326	34	76	14	3	0	19	.233	154	350	23	.956

— 444 —

Year Club	League	Pos.	G.	AB.	R.	H.	2B.	3B.	HR.	RBI.	B.A.	PO.	A.	E.	F.A.
1981—Springfield............	A. A.	SS-3B	2	8	3	4	1	0	1	2	.500	1	8	3	.750
1982—Louisville	A. A.	3B-2B-SS	121	430	65	123	15	3	3	53	.286	163	275	11	.976
1983—St. Louis.................	Nat.	2B-SS-3B	30	14	1	3	0	0	0	2	.214	3	8	4	.733
1983—Louisville‡	A. A.	3-2-S-1	45	167	19	47	9	1	0	20	.281	60	117	10	.947
1984—Tidewater.............	Int.	S-3-2-1	77	255	34	71	6	0	1	23	.278	107	232	14	.960
1984—New York§...........	Nat.	SS	51	152	14	42	11	1	1	12	.276	92	104	6	.970
1985—New York...........	Nat.	SS	154	529	41	136	19	1	1	29	.257	*301	396	25	.965
Major League Totals—3 Years...............			235	695	56	181	30	2	2	43	.260	396	508	35	.963

Signed as free agent by New York Yankees' organization, August 31, 1976.
†Traded to St. Louis Cardinals for a player to be named later, February 16, 1981; New York Yankees' organization acquired Pitcher George Frazier to complete deal, June 7, 1981.
‡Released, January 17, 1984; signed by Tidewater (New York Mets' organization), January 17, 1984.
§On disabled list, August 25 to September 9, 1984.

BENITO SANTIAGO (RIVERA)

Born September 3, 1965, at Ponce, P.R.
Height, 6.01. Weight, 180.
Throws and bats righthanded.

Led Texas League in passed balls with 16 in 1985.
Led Florida State League catchers in double plays with 12 and passed balls with 26 in 1983.

Year Club	League	Pos.	G.	AB.	R.	H.	2B.	3B.	HR.	RBI.	B.A.	PO.	A.	E.	F.A.
1983—Miami	Fla. St.	C	122	429	34	106	25	3	5	56	.247	471	*69	*21	.963
1984—Reno	Calif.	C	114	416	64	116	20	6	16	83	.279	692	96	25	.969
1985—Beaumont†	Texas	*C-1B-3B	101	372	55	111	16	6	5	52	.298	525	*78	15	.976

Signed as free agent by San Diego Padres' organization, September 1, 1982.
†On disabled list, June 21 to July 2, 1985.

MANUEL EDUARDO SARMIENTO (APONTE)

Name pronounced Sar-mee-EN-toh.

(Manny)

Born February 2, 1956, at Cagua, Aragua, Venezuela.
Height, 5.11. Weight, 170.
Throws and bats righthanded.

Major League saves: 1977 (1), 1978 (5), 1980 (1), 1982 (1), 1983 (4). Total—12.
Led Northwest League in saves with 14 in 1973 and Eastern League with 15 in 1975.

Year Club	League	G.	IP.	W.	L.	Pct.	H.	R.	ER.	SO.	BB.	ERA.
1972—Bradenton Reds...........................	Gulf Coast	18	40	2	6	.250	40	22	13	34	15	2.93
1973—Seattle..	Northwest	*36	67	2	6	.250	53	22	16	60	24	2.15
1974—Tampa..	Florida St.	39	126	10	9	.526	112	42	40	80	47	2.86
1975—Three Rivers	Eastern	*64	129	6	8	.429	104	41	37	114	51	2.58
1976—Indianapolis	Am. Assoc.	43	65	11	5	.688	49	21	20	51	24	2.77
1976—Cincinnati	National	22	44	5	1	.833	36	14	10	20	12	2.05
1977—Indianapolis†	Am. Assoc.	25	35	3	4	.429	45	26	26	35	12	6.69
1977—Cincinnati	National	24	40	0	0	.000	28	13	11	23	11	2.48
1978—Cincinnati	National	63	127	9	7	.563	109	65	62	72	54	4.39
1979—Indianapolis	Am. Assoc.	19	38	1	0	1.000	41	14	10	34	11	2.37
1979—Cincinnati‡	National	23	39	0	4	.000	47	21	20	23	7	4.62
1980—Spokane..	P. Coast	51	63	8	7	.533	57	27	21	66	20	3.00
1980—Seattle§...	American	9	15	0	1	.000	14	7	6	15	6	3.60
1981—Pawtucket x...................................	Int'national	47	96	7	5	.583	71	27	25	99	27	2.34
1982—Portland	P. Coast	6	9	1	0	1.000	10	2	1	8	4	1.00
1982—Pittsburgh......................................	National	35	164⅔	9	4	.692	153	69	62	81	46	3.39
1983—Pittsburgh......................................	National	52	84⅓	3	5	.375	74	35	28	49	36	2.99
1984—Pittsburgh y...................................	National					(Did not play)						
1985—Hawaii z..	P. Coast	18	107⅔	5	8	.385	102	48	38	81	31	3.18
National League Totals—6 Years.............		219	499	26	21	.553	447	217	193	268	166	3.48
American League Totals—1 Year		9	15	0	1	.000	14	7	6	15	6	3.60
Major League Totals—7 Years............................		228	514	26	22	.542	461	224	199	283	172	3.48

Signed as free agent by Cincinnati Reds' organization, March 25, 1972.
†On disabled list, April 13 to May 4 and May 28 to June 17, 1977.
‡Released, April 2, 1980; signed by Seattle Mariners' organization, April 14, 1980.
§Traded to Boston Red Sox' organization for Pitcher Dick Drago, April 8, 1981.
xSold to Pittsburgh Pirates, October 23, 1981.
yOn disabled list, March 29, 1984 through entire season.
zOn disabled list, April 21 to June 18, 1985.

CHAMPIONSHIP SERIES RECORD

Year Club	League	G.	IP.	W.	L.	Pct.	H.	R.	ER.	SO.	BB.	ERA.
1976—Cincinnati	National	1	1	0	0	.000	2	2	2	0	1	18.00

—DID YOU KNOW—

That the Cardinals' nine-run inning in the fourth game of the National League Championship Series against the Dodgers was the biggest in playoff history?

DAVID JOHN SAX
(Dave)

Born September 22, 1958, at Sacramento, Calif.
Height, 6.00. Weight, 185.
Throws and bats righthanded.
Brother of Steve Sax, second baseman with Los Angeles Dodgers.

Year Club	League	Pos.	G.	AB.	R.	H.	2B.	3B.	HR.	RBI.	B.A.	PO.	A.	E.	F.A.
1978—Lethbridge	Pion.	2-3-S-O	44	145	31	39	10	2	4	31	.269	79	80	13	.924
1979—Clinton..................	Midw.	C-3-O-1	97	282	37	76	18	1	6	49	.270	226	32	7	.974
1980—Lodi....................	Calif.	C-1-O-3	43	123	9	21	3	0	1	11	.171	159	25	8	.958
1980—Vero Beach.........	Fla. St.	OF-C-1B	58	193	33	68	8	5	2	33	.352	156	18	2	.989
1981—San Antonio†.......	Texas	C-OF	62	221	43	68	13	2	4	31	.308	231	17	5	.980
1982—Albuquerque	P. C.	C-3-1-O	117	417	71	132	29	1	12	75	.317	403	57	12	.975
1982—Los Angeles	Nat.	OF	2	2	0	0	0	0	0	0	.000	1	0	0	1.000
1983—Albuquerque	P. C.	C-1B	75	280	59	96	22	3	8	59	.343	159	18	3	.983
1983—Los Angeles	Nat.	C	7	8	0	0	0	0	0	1	.000	11	0	1	.917
1984—Albuquerque‡.......	P. C.	C-O-1-3	106	294	54	76	14	1	10	41	.259	297	27	11	.967
1985—Boston..................	Amer.	C-OF	22	36	2	11	3	0	0	6	.306	66	0	1	.985
1985—Pawtucket	Int.	C-OF-3B	20	61	6	13	2	0	1	4	.213	42	9	2	.962
National League Totals—2 Years...........			9	10	0	0	0	0	0	1	.000	12	0	1	.923
American League Totals—1 Year			22	36	2	11	3	0	0	6	.306	66	0	1	.985
Major League Totals—3 Years.................			31	46	2	11	3	0	0	7	.239	78	0	2	.975

Signed as free agent by Los Angeles Dodgers' organization, June 16, 1978.
†On disabled list, July 3 to September 15, 1981.
‡Granted free agency, October 15, 1984; signed by Pawtucket (Boston Red Sox' organization), January 23, 1985.

STEPHEN LOUIS SAX
(Steve)

Born January 29, 1960, at Sacramento, Calif.
Height, 5.11. Weight, 185.
Throws and bats righthanded.
Brother of David Sax, catcher with Boston Red Sox.

Major League stolen bases: 1981 (5), 1982 (49), 1983 (56), 1984 (34), 1985 (27). Total—171.
Led National League in caught stealing with 30 in 1983.
Led Florida State League second basemen in double plays with 91 in 1980.
Named National League Rookie of the Year by Baseball Writers' Association of America, 1982.
Named Texas League Most Valuable Player, 1981.

Year Club	League	Pos.	G.	AB.	R.	H.	2B.	3B.	HR.	RBI.	B.A.	PO.	A.	E.	F.A.
1978—Lethbridge	Pion.	SS	39	131	24	43	6	3	0	21	.328	21	40	9	.871
1979—Clinton..................	Midw.	OF-2B-3B	115	386	64	112	15	2	2	52	.290	111	75	18	.912
1980—Vero Beach..........	Fla. St.	*2B-OF	●139	●530	78	150	18	8	3	61	.283	*360	*438	20	*.976
1981—San Antonio..........	Texas	2B	115	485	94	168	23	3	8	52	*.346	255	298	17	.970
1981—Los Angeles	Nat.	2B	31	119	15	33	2	0	2	9	.277	64	93	4	.975
1982—Los Angeles	Nat.	2B	150	638	88	180	23	7	4	47	.282	347	452	19	.977
1983—Los Angeles	Nat.	2B	155	623	94	175	18	5	5	41	.281	331	399	*30	.961
1984—Los Angeles	Nat.	2B	145	569	70	138	24	4	1	35	.243	318	450	21	.973
1985—Los Angeles†	Nat.	*2B-3B	136	488	62	136	8	4	1	42	.279	330	358	*22	.969
Major League Totals—5 Years.................			617	2437	329	662	75	20	13	174	.272	1390	1752	96	.970

Selected by Los Angeles Dodgers' organization in 9th round of free-agent draft, June 6, 1978.
†On disabled list, April 19 to May 4, 1985.

DIVISION SERIES RECORD

Year Club	League	Pos.	G.	AB.	R.	H.	2B.	3B.	HR.	RBI.	B.A.	PO.	A.	E.	F.A.
1981—Los Angeles	Nat.	2B	1	0	0	0	0	0	0	0	.000	0	0	0	.000

CHAMPIONSHIP SERIES RECORD

Year Club	League	Pos.	G.	AB.	R.	H.	2B.	3B.	HR.	RBI.	B.A.	PO.	A.	E.	F.A.
1981—Los Angeles	Nat.	2B	1	0	0	0	0	0	0	0	.000	0	1	0	1.000
1983—Los Angeles	Nat.	2B	4	16	0	4	0	0	0	0	.250	11	12	0	1.000
1985—Los Angeles	Nat.	2B	6	20	1	6	3	0	0	1	.300	11	21	0	1.000
Championship Series Totals—3 Years.....			11	36	1	10	3	0	0	1	.278	22	34	0	1.000

WORLD SERIES RECORD

Year Club	League	Pos.	G.	AB.	R.	H.	2B.	3B.	HR.	RBI.	B.A.	PO.	A.	E.	F.A.
1981—Los Angeles	Nat.	PH-PR-2	2	1	0	0	0	0	0	0	.000	0	0	0	.000

ALL-STAR GAME RECORD

Year League		Pos.	AB.	R.	H.	2B.	3B.	HR.	RBI.	B.A.	PO.	A.	E.	F.A.
1982—National............................		PR-2B	1	0	1	0	0	0	0	1.000	2	0	1	.667
1983—National............................		2B	3	1	1	0	0	0	1	.333	2	0	1	.667
All-Star Game Totals—2 Years...................			4	1	2	0	0	0	1	.500	4	0	2	.667

—DID YOU KNOW—

That American League batting champ Wade Boggs tied the major league record by hitting safely in 135 contests in 1985? Chuck Klein first accomplished that feat in 1930.

DANIEL ERNEST SCHATZEDER

Name pronounced Shotz-AY-dur.

(Dan)

Born December 1, 1954, at Elmhurst, Ill.
Height, 6.00. Weight, 195.
Throws and bats lefthanded.
Received degree in business administration from University of Denver, Denver, Colo., in 1976.

Major League saves: 1979 (1), 1983 (2), 1984 (1). Total—4.

Year Club	League	G.	IP.	W.	L.	Pct.	H.	R.	ER.	SO.	BB.	ERA.
1976—West Palm Beach	Florida St.	10	64	5	3	.625	49	22	19	49	20	2.67
1976—Quebec City	Eastern	5	28	2	3	.400	38	16	14	19	10	4.50
1977—Quebec City	Eastern	8	62	5	3	.625	39	20	19	59	15	2.76
1977—Denver†	Am. Assoc.	9	36	2	2	.500	45	25	24	28	14	6.00
1977—Montreal	National	6	22	2	1	.667	16	6	6	14	13	2.45
1978—Denver	Am. Assoc.	4	28	3	0	1.000	24	11	9	19	11	2.89
1978—Montreal	National	29	144	7	7	.500	108	54	49	69	68	3.06
1979—Montreal‡	National	32	162	10	5	.667	136	57	51	106	59	2.83
1980—Detroit§	American	32	193	11	13	.458	178	88	86	94	58	4.01
1981—Detroit x	American	17	71	6	8	.429	74	49	48	20	29	6.08
1982—San Francisco y-Montreal	National	39	69⅓	1	6	.143	84	46	41	33	24	5.23
1982—Phoenix	P. Coast	1	3⅔	0	0	.000	10	6	5	1	3	12.27
1983—Montreal z	National	58	87	5	2	.714	88	34	31	48	25	3.21
1984—Montreal	National	36	136	7	7	.500	112	44	41	89	36	2.71
1985—Montreal a	National	24	104⅓	3	5	.375	101	52	44	64	31	3.80
1985—Indianapolis	Am. Assoc.	1	3	0	0	.000	2	0	0	3	1	0.00
National League Totals—7 Years		224	724⅔	35	33	.515	645	293	263	423	256	3.27
American League Totals—2 Years		49	264	17	21	.447	252	137	134	114	87	4.57
Major League Totals—9 Years		273	988⅔	52	54	.491	897	430	397	537	343	3.61

Selected by Montreal Expos' organization in 3rd round of free-agent draft, June 8, 1976.
†On disabled list, July 5 to August 30, 1977.
‡Traded to Detroit Tigers for Outfielder Ron LeFlore, December 7, 1979.
§On disabled list, May 27 to June 17, 1980.
xTraded with Pitcher Mike Chris to San Francisco Giants for Outfielder Larry Herndon, December 9, 1981.
ySold to Montreal Expos, June 15, 1982.
zGranted free agency, November 7, 1983; re-signed by Expos, December 19, 1983.
aOn disabled list, June 21 to July 23 and August 7 to September 1, 1985; included rehabilitation disability assignment to Indianapolis, July 19 to July 23, 1985.

WILLIAM JOSEPH SCHERRER

Named pronounced SHURR-ur.

(Bill)

Born January 20, 1958, at Tonawanda, N. Y.
Height, 6.04. Weight, 180.
Throws and bats lefthanded.
Attended University of Nevada, Las Vegas, Nev.

Major League saves: 1983 (10), 1984 (1). Total—11.
Led American League in intentional bases on balls issued with 13 in 1985.
Tied for American Association lead in shutouts with 2 in 1982.
Tied for Northwest League lead in shutouts with 2 in 1978.

Year Club	League	G.	IP.	W.	L.	Pct.	H.	R.	ER.	SO.	BB.	ERA.
1977—Shelby	W. Carol.	27	158	9	9	.500	132	87	62	122	105	3.53
1978—Shelby	W. Carol.	10	31	0	2	.000	27	19	14	18	26	4.06
1978—Eugene	Northwest	13	84	6	4	.600	61	43	33	87	42	3.54
1979—Tampa	Florida St.	25	159	12	3	.800	126	43	32	140	65	1.81
1980—Waterbury	Eastern	25	151	7	8	.467	139	58	56	84	58	3.34
1981—Waterbury	Eastern	50	119	5	9	.357	121	70	57	89	62	4.31
1982—Tampa	Florida St.	7	47⅓	3	2	.600	37	13	12	45	18	2.28
1982—Waterbury	Eastern	5	31	1	3	.250	30	15	13	18	15	3.77
1982—Indianapolis	Am. Assoc.	19	88⅔	6	4	.600	68	43	40	81	32	4.06
1982—Cincinnati	National	5	17⅓	0	1	.000	17	7	5	7	0	2.60
1983—Cincinnati	National	73	92	2	3	.400	73	31	28	57	33	2.74
1984—Cincinnati†	National	36	52⅓	1	1	.500	64	31	29	35	15	4.99
1984—Wichita‡§	Am. Assoc.	10	16⅔	2	3	.400	16	6	6	14	11	3.24
1984—Detroit	American	18	19	1	0	1.000	14	4	4	16	8	1.89
1985—Detroit	American	48	66	3	2	.600	62	35	32	46	41	4.36
National League Totals—3 Years		114	161⅔	3	5	.375	154	69	62	99	48	3.45
American League Totals—2 Years		66	85	4	2	.667	76	39	36	62	49	3.81
Major League Totals—4 Years		180	246⅔	7	7	.500	230	108	98	161	97	3.58

Selected by Cleveland Indians' organization in 6th round of free-agent draft, June 8, 1976.
Selected by Cincinnati Reds' organization in secondary phase of free-agent draft, January 11, 1977.
†On disabled list, April 18 to May 3, 1984.
‡On disabled list, July 31 to August 10, 1984.
§Traded to Detroit Tigers for cash and a player to be named later, August 27, 1984; Cincinnati Reds acquired Pitcher Carl Willis to complete deal, September 1, 1984.

Year Club	League	G.	IP.	W.	L.	Pct.	H.	R.	ER.	SO.	BB.	ERA.
1984—Detroit	American	3	3	0	0	.000	5	1	1	0	0	3.00

CALVIN DREW SCHIRALDI

Born June 16, 1962, at Houston, Tex.
Height, 6.04. Weight, 200.
Throws and bats righthanded.
Attended University of Texas, Austin, Tex.
Named Texas League Pitcher of the Year, 1984.

Year Club	League	G.	IP.	W.	L.	Pct.	H.	R.	ER.	SO.	BB.	ERA.
1983—Jackson	Texas	7	38⅔	3	3	.500	41	28	25	26	29	5.82
1983—Lynchburg	Carolina	6	30⅓	4	1	.800	28	16	15	41	17	4.45
1984—Jackson	Texas	23	156⅓	●14	3	*.824	118	58	50	131	69	2.88
1984—Tidewater	Int'national	4	31⅓	3	1	.750	18	6	4	24	10	1.15
1984—New York	National	5	17⅓	0	2	.000	20	13	11	16	10	5.71
1985—Tidewater	Int'national	17	100⅓	4	5	.444	91	50	39	76	56	3.50
1985—New York†‡	National	10	26⅓	2	1	.667	43	27	26	21	11	8.89
Major League Totals—2 Years		15	43⅔	2	3	.400	63	40	37	37	21	7.63

Selected by Chicago White Sox' organization in 17th round of free-agent draft, June 3, 1980.
Selected by New York Mets' organization in 1st round (27th player selected) of free-agent draft, June 6, 1983.
†On disabled list, May 15 to May 30, 1985.
‡Traded with Pitcher Wes Gardner and Outfielders John Christensen and LaSchelle Tarver to Boston Red Sox for Pitchers Bob Ojeda, Tom McCarthy, John Mitchell and Chris Bayer, November 13, 1985.

DAVID JOSEPH SCHMIDT
(Dave)

Born April 22, 1957, at Niles, Mich.
Height, 6.01. Weight, 185.
Throws and bats righthanded.
Attended Los Angeles Valley College, Van Nuys, Calif., and University of California, Los Angeles, Calif.
Major League saves: 1981 (1), 1982 (6), 1983 (2), 1984 (12), 1985 (5). Total—26.

Year Club	League	G.	IP.	W.	L.	Pct.	H.	R.	ER.	SO.	BB.	ERA.
1979—Sarasota Rangers	Gulf Coast	7	30	2	2	.500	30	19	14	27	8	4.20
1980—Asheville	S. Atlantic	12	91	8	1	.889	76	32	20	67	13	1.98
1980—Tulsa	Texas	12	73	4	6	.400	90	42	36	46	28	4.44
1981—Tulsa	Texas	3	24	1	1	.500	17	5	5	17	6	1.88
1981—Texas	American	14	32	0	1	.000	31	11	11	13	11	3.09
1981—Wichita	Am. Assoc.	12	87	2	5	.286	90	47	47	49	26	4.86
1982—Texas	American	33	109⅔	4	6	.400	118	45	39	69	25	3.20
1983—Texas†	American	31	46⅓	3	3	.500	42	20	20	29	14	3.88
1984—Texas	American	43	70⅓	6	6	.500	69	30	20	46	20	2.56
1985—Texas‡	American	51	85⅔	7	6	.538	81	36	30	46	22	3.15
Major League Totals—5 Years		172	344	20	22	.476	341	142	120	203	92	3.14

Selected by Texas Rangers' organization in 26th round of free-agent draft, June 5, 1979.
†On disabled list, March 25 to May 1, 1983.
‡Traded with Infielder Wayne Tolleson to Chicago White Sox for Pitcher Ed Correa, Infielder Scott Fletcher and a player to be named later, November 25, 1985; Texas Rangers acquired Infielder Jose Mota to complete deal, December 12, 1985.

ERIC LEWIS SCHMIDT

Born August 19, 1962, at Southgate, Calif.
Height, 6.04. Weight, 210.
Throws right and bats left and righthanded.
Attended Antelope Valley College, Lancaster, Calif., and
Oklahoma State University, Stillwater, Okla.

Year Club	League	G.	IP.	W.	L.	Pct.	H.	R.	ER.	SO.	BB.	ERA.
1984—Appleton	Midwest	21	123⅓	9	4	.692	124	56	44	66	48	3.21
1985—Glens Falls	Eastern	27	173⅓	11	12	.478	187	80	65	97	74	3.38

Selected by Kansas City Royals' organization in 2nd round of free-agent draft, January 12, 1982.
Selected by Chicago White Sox' organization in 7th round of free-agent draft, June 6, 1983.

MICHAEL JACK SCHMIDT
(Mike)

Born September 27, 1949, at Dayton, O.
Height, 6.02. Weight, 203.
Throws and bats righthanded.
Received bachelor of arts degree in business administration from Ohio University, Athens, O. in 1971.

Established major league records for most total bases, extra-inning game (17), April 17, 1976 (10 innings); most home runs by third baseman, season (48), 1980.

Tied major league records for most home runs, extra-inning game (4), April 17, 1976 (10 innings); most consecutive home runs, extra-inning game (4), April 17, 1976 (10 innings); most home runs, consecutive plate appearances (4), April 17, 1976 and July 6 and 7, 1979; most extra bases on long hits, game (12), April 17, 1976 (10 innings); most home runs, two consecutive games (5), April 17 and 18, 1976; most home runs, three consecutive games (6), April 17-20, 1976; most home runs, month of April (11), 1976; most consecutive seasons leading major leagues in strikeouts (3), 1974 through 1976; most home runs, month of October (4), 1980.

Established National League record for most assists, third baseman, season (404), 1974; fewest singles, season, 150 or more games (63), 1979.

Tied National League records for most years leading league in home runs (7); most home runs, bases full, one month, 2, June, 1973; most home runs through July 31 (36), 1979; most home runs, five consecutive games, one or more homer each game (7), July 6 through 10, 1979; most years leading league in extra bases on long hits (6); most consecutive years leading league in extra bases on long hits (3, performed twice); most consecutive years leading league in bases on balls (3); most years leading league in assists by third baseman (7).

Hit three home runs in a game, July 7, 1979.

Hit home runs in all 12 National League parks, 1979.

Major League stolen bases: 1973 (8), 1974 (23), 1975 (29), 1976 (14), 1977 (15), 1978 (19), 1979 (9), 1980 (12), 1981 (12), 1982 (14), 1983 (7), 1984 (5), 1985 (1). Total—168.

Led National League in intentional bases on balls received with 18 in 1981.

Led National League in total bases with 306 in 1976, 342 in 1980 and 228 in 1981.

Led National League in slugging percentage with .546 in 1974, .624 in 1980, .644 in 1981 and .547 in 1982.

Led National League batters in strikeouts with 138 in 1974, 180 in 1975, 149 in 1976 and 148 in 1983.

Led National League in bases on balls received with 120 in 1979, 73 in 1981, 107 in 1982 and 128 in 1983.

Led National League in sacrifice flies with 13 in 1980 and tied for lead with 9 in 1979.

Tied for National League lead in being hit by pitch with 11 in 1976.

Led National League third basemen in total chances with 537 in 1976, 521 in 1977, 497 in 1980, 457 in 1982 and tied for lead with 338 in 1981 and 458 in 1983.

Led National League third basemen in double plays with 34 in 1978, 36 in 1979, 31 in 1980, 29 in 1983 and tied for lead with 28 in 1982.

Led National League third basemen in assists with 396 in 1977 and 332 in 1983.

Led Pacific Coast League batters in strikeouts with 145 in 1972.

Named National League Player of the Year by THE SPORTING NEWS, 1980.

Named National League Most Valuable Player by Baseball Writers' Association of America, 1980 and 1981.

Named third baseman on THE SPORTING NEWS National League All-Star Team, 1974, 1976, 1977 and 1979 through 1984.

Named third baseman on THE SPORTING NEWS National League All-Star fielding team, 1976 through 1984.

Named third baseman on THE SPORTING NEWS National League Silver Slugger team, 1980 through 1984.

Named shortstop on THE SPORTING NEWS College Baseball All-America Team, 1971.

Year Club	League	Pos.	G.	AB.	R.	H.	2B.	3B.	HR.	RBI.	B.A.	PO.	A.	E.	F.A.
1971—Reading	East.	SS-3B	74	237	27	50	7	1	8	31	.211	100	224	23	.934
1972—Eugene	P. C.	2B-3B-SS	131	436	80	127	23	6	26	91	.291	271	324	25	.960
1972—Philadelphia†	Nat.	3B-2B	13	34	2	7	0	0	1	3	.206	10	25	2	.946
1973—Philadelphia‡	Nat.	3-2-1-S	132	367	43	72	11	0	18	52	.196	119	256	18	.954
1974—Philadelphia	Nat.	3B	162	568	108	160	28	7	★36	116	.282	134	★404	26	.954
1975—Philadelphia	Nat.	3B-SS	158	562	93	140	34	3	★38	95	.249	139	390	26	.953
1976—Philadelphia	Nat.	3B	160	584	112	153	31	4	★38	107	.262	139	★377	21	.961
1977—Philadelphia	Nat.	3B-SS-2B	154	544	114	149	27	11	38	101	.274	109	401	20	.962
1978—Philadelphia	Nat.	3B-SS	145	513	93	129	27	2	21	78	.251	98	325	16	.964
1979—Philadelphia	Nat.	3B-SS	160	541	109	137	25	4	45	114	.253	115	363	23	.954
1980—Philadelphia	Nat.	3B	150	548	104	157	25	8	★48	★121	.286	98	★372	27	.946
1981—Philadelphia	Nat.	3B	102	354	★78	112	19	2	★31	★91	.316	74	★249	15	.956
1982—Philadelphia§	Nat.	3B	148	514	108	144	26	3	35	87	.280	110	★324	23	.950
1983—Philadelphia	Nat.	3B-SS	154	534	104	136	16	4	★40	109	.255	108	333	19	.959
1984—Philadelphia	Nat.	3B-1B-SS	151	528	93	146	23	3	●36	●106	.277	93	330	26	.942
1985—Philadelphia	Nat.	1B-3B-SS	158	549	89	152	31	5	33	93	.277	911	193	18	.984
Major League Totals—14 Years			1947	6740	1250	1794	323	56	458	1273	.266	2257	4342	280	.959

Selected by Philadelphia Phillies' organization in 2nd round of free-agent draft, June 8, 1971.

†On disabled list, August 21 to September 2, 1972.

‡On disabled list, March 28 to April 21, 1973.

§On disabled list, April 14 to April 29, 1982.

DIVISION SERIES RECORD

Year Club	League	Pos.	G.	AB.	R.	H.	2B.	3B.	HR.	RBI.	B.A.	PO.	A.	E.	F.A.
1981—Philadelphia	Nat.	3B	5	16	3	4	1	0	1	2	.250	6	10	1	.941

CHAMPIONSHIP SERIES RECORD

Established Championship Series record for most at-bats, five-game Series (24), 1980.

Tied Championship Series records for highest batting average, four-game Series (.467), 1983; most at-bats, extra-inning game (6), October 8, 1980; most two-base hits, total Series (7).

Year Club	League	Pos.	G.	AB.	R.	H.	2B.	3B.	HR.	RBI.	B.A.	PO.	A.	E.	F.A.
1976—Philadelphia	Nat.	3B	3	13	1	4	2	0	0	2	.308	4	9	1	.929
1977—Philadelphia	Nat.	3B	4	16	2	1	0	0	0	1	.063	4	15	0	1.000
1978—Philadelphia	Nat.	3B	4	15	1	3	2	0	0	1	.200	3	18	2	.913
1980—Philadelphia	Nat.	3B	5	24	1	5	1	0	1	1	.208	3	17	1	.952
1983—Philadelphia	Nat.	3B	4	15	5	7	2	0	1	2	.467	6	7	1	.929
Championship Series Totals—5 Years			20	83	10	20	7	0	1	7	.241	20	66	5	.945

WORLD SERIES RECORD

Tied World Series record for fewest chances accepted by third baseman, game (0), October 21, 1980.

Year Club	League	Pos.	G.	AB.	R.	H.	2B.	3B.	HR.	RBI.	B.A.	PO.	A.	E.	F.A.
1980—Philadelphia	Nat.	3B	6	21	6	8	1	0	2	7	.381	9	8	0	1.000
1983—Philadelphia	Nat.	3B	5	20	0	1	0	0	0	0	.050	1	10	1	.917
World Series Totals—2 Years			11	41	6	9	1	0	2	7	.220	10	18	1	.966

Year League	Pos.	AB.	R.	H.	2B.	3B.	HR.	RBI.	B.A.	PO.	A.	E.	F.A.
1974—National	PH-3B	0	1	0	0	0	0	0	.000	0	1	0	1.000
1976—National	3B	1	0	0	0	0	0	0	.000	0	0	0	.000
1977—National	PR	0	0	0	0	0	0	0	.000	0	0	0	.000
1979—National	3B	3	2	2	1	1	0	1	.667	1	1	1	.667
1981—National	3B	4	1	2	1	0	1	2	.500	0	2	1	.667
1982—National	3B	1	0	0	0	0	0	0	.000	0	0	0	.000
1983—National	3B	3	0	0	0	0	0	0	.000	0	0	1	.000
1984—National	3B	3	0	0	0	0	0	0	.000	0	4	0	1.000
All-Star Game Totals—8 Years		15	4	4	2	1	1	3	.267	1	8	3	.750

Named to National League All-Star Team in 1980; replaced due to injury by Ray Knight.

RICHARD CRAIG SCHOFIELD
(Dick)

Born November 21, 1962, at Springfield, Ill.
Height, 5.10. Weight, 175.
Throws and bats righthanded.
Son of John Richard (Dick) Schofield, infielder with St. Louis Cardinals, Pittsburgh, San Francisco, New York Yankees, Los Angeles Dodgers, Boston and Milwaukee Brewers, 1953 through 1971.

Major League stolen bases: 1984 (5), 1985 (11). Total—16.
Led Pioneer League in bases on balls received with 68 in 1981.
Received reported $100,000 bonus to sign with California Angels, 1981.

Year Club	League	Pos.	G.	AB.	R.	H.	2B.	3B.	HR.	RBI.	B.A.	PO.	A.	E.	F.A.
1981—Idaho Falls	Pion.	*SS-2B	66	226	59	63	10	1	6	31	.279	*102	201	22	.932
1982—Danville	Midw.	SS	92	308	80	111	21	*10	12	53	*.360	129	249	23	.943
1982—Redwood	Calif.	SS	33	102	15	25	3	3	1	8	.245	35	103	3	.979
1982—Spokane	P. C.	SS-3B	7	30	4	9	4	1	1	12	.300	7	20	0	1.000
1983—Edmonton	P. C.	SS-3B	139	521	91	148	30	7	16	94	.284	220	402	30	.954
1983—California	Amer.	SS	21	54	4	11	2	0	3	4	.204	24	67	7	.929
1984—California†	Amer.	SS	140	400	39	77	10	3	4	21	.193	218	420	12	*.982
1985—California	Amer.	SS	147	438	50	96	19	3	8	41	.219	261	397	25	.963
Major League Totals—3 Years			308	892	93	184	31	6	15	66	.206	503	884	44	.969

Selected by California Angels' organization in 1st round (third player selected) of free-agent draft, June 8, 1981.
†On disabled list, July 1 to July 24, 1984.

ALFRED WILLIAM SCHROEDER III
Name pronounced SHRO-der.

(Bill)

Born September 7, 1958, at Baltimore, Md.
Height, 6.02. Weight, 210.
Throws and bats righthanded.
Attended Clemson University, Clemson, S. C.

Led Pacific Coast League batters in strikeouts with 136 and game-winning RBIs with 15 in 1982.
Led California League batters in strikeouts with 141 in 1980.
Led Pioneer League in total bases with 170 in 1979.
Led California League catchers in total chances with 759 in 1980.
Tied for Pacific Coast League lead in passed balls with 13 in 1983.

Year Club	League	Pos.	G.	AB.	R.	H.	2B.	3B.	HR.	RBI.	B.A.	PO.	A.	E.	F.A.
1979—Butte	Pion.	C-1B	65	242	73	86	16	7	18	77	.355	474	50	9	.983
1980—Stockton	Calif.	*C-1B	123	437	68	117	20	3	18	97	.268	669	96	7	*.991
1981—El Paso	Texas	C-OF	95	335	41	87	20	2	15	61	.260	511	49	10	.982
1982—Vancouver	P. C.	C	116	425	66	113	16	3	22	77	.266	569	77	7	*.989
1983—Vancouver	P. C.	C	82	304	51	87	13	3	20	70	.286	399	68	6	*.987
1983—Milwaukee	Amer.	C	23	73	7	13	2	1	3	7	.178	92	5	2	.980
1984—Milwaukee	Amer.	C-1B	61	210	29	54	6	0	14	25	.257	277	24	4	.987
1985—Milwaukee†	Amer.	C-1B	53	194	18	47	8	0	8	25	.242	216	23	3	.988
Major League Totals—3 Years			137	477	54	114	16	1	25	57	.239	585	52	9	.986

Selected by Milwaukee Brewers' organization in 8th round of free-agent draft, June 5, 1979.
†On disabled list, May 15 to June 14 and June 22 to July 19, 1985.

KENNETH MARVIN SCHROM
(Ken)

Born November 23, 1954, at Grangeville, Ida.
Height, 6.02. Weight, 195.
Throws and bats righthanded.
Attended University of Idaho, Moscow, Ida.

Major League saves: 1980 (1).
Tied for Texas League lead in home runs allowed with 24 in 1978.

Year Club	League	G.	IP.	W.	L.	Pct.	H.	R.	ER.	SO.	BB.	ERA.
1976—Idaho Falls	Pioneer	16	48	1	5	.167	42	31	20	46	32	3.75
1977—Quad Cities	Midwest	16	44	3	1	.750	22	10	7	40	20	1.43
1977—Salinas	California	15	21	1	1	.500	22	8	8	22	11	3.43

Year Club	League	G.	IP.	W.	L.	Pct.	H.	R.	ER.	SO.	BB.	ERA.
1977—El Paso	Texas	10	18	1	0	1.000	14	4	4	7	8	2.00
1978—El Paso	Texas	33	165	9	6	.600	180	93	86	126	52	4.69
1979—El Paso	Texas	25	168	7	8	.467	204	111	97	107	75	5.20
1979—Salt Lake City	P. Coast	3	4	0	0	.000	3	0	0	3	3	0.00
1980—Salt Lake City†	P. Coast	14	23	0	1	.000	32	25	20	11	17	7.83
1980—Syracuse	Int'national	26	46	0	2	.000	41	19	17	32	20	3.33
1980—Toronto	American	17	31	1	0	1.000	32	18	18	13	19	5.23
1981—Syracuse	Int'national	42	104	4	6	.400	86	44	43	72	41	3.72
1982—Syracuse	Int'national	27	98	4	5	.444	102	61	56	49	41	5.14
1982—Toronto‡	American	6	15⅓	1	0	1.000	13	11	10	8	15	5.87
1983—Toledo	Int'national	5	31⅔	3	1	.750	30	19	16	20	14	4.55
1983—Minnesota§	American	33	196⅓	15	8	.652	196	92	81	80	80	3.71
1984—Orlando x	Southern	2	10	0	0	.000	10	8	3	10	6	2.70
1984—Minnesota	American	25	137	5	11	.313	156	75	68	49	41	4.47
1985—Minnesota y	American	29	160⅔	9	12	.429	164	95	89	74	59	4.99
Major League Totals—5 Years		110	540⅓	31	31	.500	561	291	266	224	214	4.43

Selected by Minnesota Twins' organization in 10th round of free-agent draft, June 5, 1973.
Selected by California Angels' organization in 17th round of free-agent draft, June 8, 1976.
†Traded to Toronto Blue Jays' organization, June 10, 1980, completing deal in which Toronto traded Pitcher Dave Lemanczyk to California Angels for a player to be named later, June 3, 1980.
‡Released, August 30, 1982; signed by Minnesota Twins' organization, December 1, 1982.
§Appeared in one game as a pinch-runner.
xOn Minnesota disabled list, March 29 to May 22, 1984; included rehabilitation disability assignment to Orlando, April 18 to April 26, 1984.
yTraded with Pitcher Bryan Oelkers to Cleveland Indians for Pitchers Roy Smith and Ramon Romero, January 7, 1986.

RICHARD SPENCER SCHU

Name pronounced Shoo.

(Rick)

Born January 26, 1962, at Philadelphia, Pa.
Height, 6.00. Weight, 170.
Throws and bats righthanded.
Attended Sacramento City College, Sacramento, Calif.
Son of Ken Schu, minor league pitcher, 1955 and 1956.

Major League stolen bases: 1985 (8).
Led Pacific Coast League third basemen in total chances with 390 in 1984.

Year Club	League	Pos.	G.	AB.	R.	H.	2B.	3B.	HR.	RBI.	B.A.	PO.	A.	E.	F.A.
1981—Bend	N'west	3B-2B-SS	68	258	41	69	10	0	2	42	.267	55	137	24	.889
1982—Spartanburg	S. Atl.	3B-2B-SS	125	429	78	117	28	1	12	60	.273	157	257	45	.902
1983—Peninsula	Carol.	3B-SS-2B	122	444	69	119	22	3	14	63	.268	82	252	30	.918
1983—Portland	P. C.	3B-SS	9	29	7	11	2	1	1	3	.379	6	12	2	.900
1984—Portland	P. C.	3B	140	552	70	166	35	●14	12	82	.301	★109	★254	★27	.931
1984—Philadelphia	Nat.	3B	17	29	12	8	2	1	2	5	.276	7	13	1	.952
1985—Portland	P. C.	SS-3B	42	150	19	42	8	3	4	22	.280	36	91	11	.920
1985—Philadelphia	Nat.	3B	112	416	54	105	21	4	7	24	.252	86	191	20	.933
Major League Totals—2 Years			129	445	66	113	23	5	9	29	.254	93	204	21	.934

Signed as free agent by Philadelphia Phillies' organization, November 25, 1980.

DAVID PAUL SCHULER

(Dave)

Born October 4, 1953, at Framingham, Mass.
Height, 6.05. Weight, 215.
Throws left and bats righthanded.
Received bachelor of science degree in general business management
from University of New Haven, West Haven, Conn.

Year Club	League	G.	IP.	W.	L.	Pct.	H.	R.	ER.	SO.	BB.	ERA.
1976—San Jose	California	54	89	4	7	.364	126	82	47	62	38	4.75
1977—Waterloo†	Midwest	8	15	1	2	.333	23	11	10	8	2	6.00
1977—Salinas	California	8	55	5	1	.833	53	12	11	25	5	1.80
1977—El Paso	Texas	17	90	8	2	.800	88	42	37	46	21	3.70
1978—Salt Lake City‡	P. Coast	6	23	0	1	.000	41	28	24	4	8	9.39
1979—Salt Lake City§	P. Coast	26	118	10	4	.714	120	64	57	36	34	4.35
1979—California	American	1	2	0	0	.000	2	2	2	0	0	9.00
1980—Salt Lake City	P. Coast	45	71	11	4	.733	54	23	18	42	23	2.28
1980—California	American	8	13	0	1	.000	13	5	5	7	2	3.46
1981—Salt Lake City x	P. Coast	34	68	4	5	.444	100	45	36	35	22	4.76
1982—Omaha	Am. Assoc.	32	107⅓	6	2	.750	123	39	37	87	23	3.10
1983—Omaha y	Am. Assoc.	38	107⅔	6	7	.462	99	45	39	59	32	3.26
1984—Indianapolis z	Am. Assoc.	42	47	8	0	1.000	48	16	16	42	7	3.06
1985—Richmond	Int'national	41	73⅓	4	3	.571	52	23	21	61	23	2.58
1985—Atlanta a	National	9	10⅔	0	0	.000	19	8	8	10	3	6.75
American League Totals—2 Years		9	15	0	1	.000	15	7	7	7	2	4.20
National League Totals—1 Year		9	10⅔	0	0	.000	19	8	8	10	3	6.75
Major League Totals—3 Years		18	25⅔	0	1	.000	34	15	15	17	5	5.26

Selected by Cleveland Indians' organization in 10th round of free-agent draft, June 4, 1975.

†Traded with Pitcher Dave LaRoche to California Angels' organization for First Baseman-Outfielder Bruce Bochte, Pitcher Sid Monge and cash estimated at $250,000, May 11, 1977.

‡On disabled list, May 26 to October 5, 1978.

§On disabled list, April 11 to May 17, 1979.

xReleased, April 16, 1982; signed by Omaha (Kansas City Royals' organization), April 29, 1982.

yGranted free agency, October 20, 1983; signed by Indianapolis (Montreal Expos' organization), May 13, 1984.

zGranted free agency, October 15, 1984; signed by Atlanta Braves' organization, January, 27, 1985.

aReleased, November 12, 1985.

DONALD ARTHUR SCHULZE
Name pronounced SHULL-zee.

(Don)

Born September 27, 1962, at Roselle, Ill.
Height, 6.04. Weight, 230.
Throws and bats righthanded.

Led Gulf Coast League in complete games with 3 in 1980.
Tied for American Association lead in shutouts with 2 in 1983.

Year Club	League	G.	IP.	W.	L.	Pct.	H.	R.	ER.	SO.	BB.	ERA.
1980—Sarasota Cubs	Gulf Coast	12	66	2	7	.222	58	38	30	30	36	4.09
1981—Quad Cities†	Midwest	17	105	8	5	.615	89	33	27	61	51	2.31
1982—Salinas	California	24	165	13	7	.650	150	61	52	122	59	2.84
1983—Iowa	Am. Assoc.	25	168⅔	11	9	.550	170	88	80	103	63	4.27
1983—Chicago	National	4	14	0	1	.000	19	11	11	8	7	7.07
1984—Iowa	Am. Assoc.	13	79	5	5	.500	79	40	38	44	29	4.33
1984—Chicago‡	National	1	3	0	0	.000	8	4	4	2	1	12.00
1984—Maine	Int'national	2	9⅓	1	1	.500	14	12	9	7	3	8.68
1984—Cleveland	American	19	85⅔	3	6	.333	105	53	46	39	27	4.83
1985—Cleveland	American	19	94⅓	4	10	.286	128	75	63	37	19	6.01
1985—Maine	Int'national	15	115⅓	6	4	.600	105	41	34	45	29	2.65
National League Totals—2 Years		5	17	0	1	.000	27	15	15	10	8	7.94
American League Totals—2 Years		38	180	7	16	.304	233	128	109	76	46	5.45
Major League Totals—3 Years		43	197	7	17	.292	260	143	124	86	54	5.66

Selected by Chicago Cubs' organization in 1st round (11th player selected) of free-agent draft, June 3, 1980.

†On disabled list, June 22 to July 16, 1981.

‡Traded with Outfielders Mel Hall and Joe Carter and Pitcher Darryl Banks to Cleveland Indians for Catcher Ron Hassey and Pitchers Rick Sutcliffe and George Frazier, June 13, 1984.

MICHAEL LORRI SCIOSCIA
Name pronounced SO-sha.

(Mike)

Born November 27, 1958, at Upper Darby, Pa.
Height, 6.02. Weight, 200.
Throws right and bats lefthanded.
Attended Pennsylvania State University, University Park, Pa.

Major League stolen bases: 1980 (1), 1982 (2), 1984 (2), 1985 (3). Total—8.
Led National League in passed balls with 11 in 1981.
Tied for Pacific Coast League lead in being hit by pitch with 7 in 1979.
Led Pacific Coast League catchers in double plays with 19 and passed balls with 22 in 1979.
Led Midwest League catchers in errors with 20 and double plays with 12 in 1978.

Year Club	League	Pos.	G.	AB.	R.	H.	2B.	3B.	HR.	RBI.	B.A.	PO.	A.	E.	F.A.
1976—Bellingham	N'west.	C	46	151	25	42	6	0	7	26	.278	202	35	14	.944
1977—Clinton	Midw.	C-1B	121	364	58	92	20	1	7	44	.253	764	95	22	.975
1978—San Antonio†	Texas	C	58	204	29	61	16	0	2	34	.299	214	17	4	.983
1979—Albuquerque	P. C.	C	143	461	80	155	34	0	3	68	.336	★690	★86	★15	.981
1980—Albuquerque	P. C.	C	52	160	33	53	11	1	3	33	.331	207	19	5	.978
1980—Los Angeles‡	Nat.	C-3B	54	134	8	34	5	1	1	8	.254	226	26	2	.992
1981—Los Angeles	Nat.	C	93	290	27	80	10	0	2	29	.276	493	48	7	.987
1982—Los Angeles	Nat.	C	129	365	31	80	11	1	5	38	.219	631	57	10	.986
1983—Los Angeles§	Nat.	C	12	35	3	11	3	0	1	7	.314	55	4	0	1.000
1984—Los Angeles x	Nat.	C	114	341	29	93	18	0	5	38	.273	701	64	12	.985
1985—Los Angeles	Nat.	C	141	429	47	127	26	3	7	53	.296	818	66	●13	.986
Major League Totals—6 Years			543	1594	145	425	73	5	21	173	.267	2924	265	44	.986

Selected by Los Angeles Dodgers' organization in 1st round (19th player selected) of free-agent draft, June 8, 1976.

†On disabled list, May 19 to August 4, 1978.

‡On disabled list, April 10 to April 20, 1980.

§On disabled list, May 15, 1983 through remainder of season.

xOn disabled list, May 6 to May 21, 1984.

DIVISION SERIES RECORD

Year Club	League	Pos.	G.	AB.	R.	H.	2B.	3B.	HR.	RBI.	B.A.	PO.	A.	E.	F.A.
1981—Los Angeles	Nat.	C	4	13	0	2	0	0	0	1	.154	21	3	0	1.000

CHAMPIONSHIP SERIES RECORD

Year Club	League	Pos.	G.	AB.	R.	H.	2B.	3B.	HR.	RBI.	B.A.	PO.	A.	E.	F.A.
1981—Los Angeles	Nat.	C	5	15	1	2	0	0	1	1	.133	27	1	0	1.000
1985—Los Angeles	Nat.	C	6	16	2	4	0	0	0	1	.250	31	4	1	.972
Championship Series Totals—2 Years			11	31	3	6	0	0	1	2	.194	58	5	1	.984

Year	Club	League	Pos.	G.	AB.	R.	H.	2B.	3B.	HR.	RBI.	B.A.	PO.	A.	E.	F.A.
1981—Los Angeles		Nat.	C-PH	3	4	1	1	0	0	0	0	.250	7	1	0	1.000

DARYL ANTHONY SCONIERS

Name pronounced SCON-yers.

Born October 3, 1958, at San Bernardino, Calif.
Height, 6.02. Weight, 185.
Throws and bats lefthanded.
Attended Orange Coast College, Costa Mesa, Calif.

Tied American League record for most home runs by pinch-hitter, consecutive at-bats (2), April 30, May 7, 1983.
Major League stolen bases: 1983 (4), 1984 (1), 1985 (2). Total—7.
Led Texas League in total bases with 296 in 1980.
Led Midwest League first basemen in double plays with 106 in 1978.

Year	Club	League	Pos.	G.	AB.	R.	H.	2B.	3B.	HR.	RBI.	B.A.	PO.	A.	E.	F.A.
1977—Idaho Falls	Pion.		1B	49	158	34	49	10	1	0	24	.310	343	19	7	.961
1978—Quad Cities	Midw.		1B	126	466	88	133	*35	7	19	86	.285	*1194	52	16	.987
1979—Salinas†	Calif.		1B	108	365	60	105	17	6	11	50	.288	804	42	7	*.992
1980—El Paso	Texas		1B	●136	506	95	*187	*48	8	15	87	*.370	887	46	●16	.983
1981—Salt Lake City	P. C.		1B	108	410	91	145	24	8	13	74	.354	866	36	6	.993
1981—California	Amer.		1B	15	52	6	14	1	1	1	7	.269	95	8	0	1.000
1982—California	Amer.		1B	12	13	0	2	0	0	0	2	.154	23	1	0	1.000
1982—Spokane‡	P. C.		1B	98	383	64	126	33	10	5	73	.329	842	32	11	.988
1983—California	Amer.		1B-OF	106	314	49	86	19	3	8	46	.274	473	23	8	.984
1984—California§	Amer.		1B	57	160	14	39	4	0	4	17	.244	355	26	4	.990
1985—Midland x	Texas		1B	15	58	7	13	6	0	1	10	.224	84	3	1	.989
1985—California yz	Amer.		1B	44	98	14	28	6	1	2	12	.286	35	1	1	.973
1985—Edmonton	P. C.		DH	6	20	3	7	2	0	0	4	.350	0	0	0	.000
Major League Totals—5 Years				234	637	83	169	30	5	15	84	.265	981	59	13	.988

Selected by California Angels' organization in 3rd round of free-agent draft, January 11, 1977.
†On temporary inactive list, April 6 to May 9, 1979.
‡On suspended list, April 27 to May 12, 1982.
§On disabled list, April 12 to July 13, 1984.
xOn California special rehabilitation list, April 7 to May 21, 1985; including rehabilitation disability assignment to Midland, May 1 to May 21, 1985.
yOn disabled list, July 15 to September 6, 1985; including rehabilitation disability assignment to Edmonton, August 20 to August 26, 1985.
zReleased, December 20, 1985.

DONALD MALCOLM SCOTT

(Donnie)

Born August 16, 1961, at Dunedin, Fla.
Height, 5.11. Weight, 185.
Throws right and bats left and righthanded.

Major League stolen bases: 1985 (1).
Switch-hit home runs in one game, April 29, 1985.
Led American League in passed balls with 18 in 1984.
Led American Association in passed balls with 22 in 1983.
Led Texas League in passed balls with 21 in 1982.
Led South Atlantic League in passed balls with 41 and tied for lead in double plays by catchers with 7 in 1980.

Year	Club	League	Pos.	G.	AB.	R.	H.	2B.	3B.	HR.	RBI.	B.A.	PO.	A.	E.	F.A.
1979—Sarasota Rang	Gulf C.		*C-OF	45	146	18	45	7	1	1	29	.308	190	19	4	*.981
1980—Asheville	S. Atl.		C	115	421	57	124	22	1	13	78	.295	593	*81	17	.975
1981—Tulsa	Texas		C-3B-OF	114	385	44	91	16	2	5	41	.236	509	103	19	.970
1982—Tulsa	Texas		*C-3B	108	367	55	104	19	3	12	61	.283	537	75	*21	.967
1983—Oklahoma City	A. A.		C	112	371	44	94	14	3	4	54	.253	596	*74	12	.982
1983—Texas	Amer.		C	2	4	0	0	0	0	0	0	.000	8	2	0	1.000
1984—Oklahoma City	A. A.		C	46	168	25	55	14	2	3	25	.327	222	46	4	.985
1984—Texas†	Amer.		C	81	235	16	52	9	0	3	20	.221	400	41	12	.974
1985—Calgary	P. C.		C	7	26	6	12	3	1	0	9	.462	39	5	3	.936
1985—Seattle	Amer.		C	80	185	18	41	13	0	4	23	.222	277	31	6	.981
Major League Totals—3 Years				163	424	34	93	22	0	7	43	.219	685	74	18	.977

Selected by Texas Rangers' organization in 2nd round of free-agent draft, June 5, 1979.
†Traded to Seattle Mariners' organization for Catcher Orlando Mercado, April 4, 1985.

MICHAEL WARREN SCOTT

(Mike)

Born April 26, 1955, at Santa Monica, Calif.
Height, 6.03. Weight, 215.
Throws and bats righthanded.
Attended Pepperdine University, Malibu, Calif.

Major League saves: 1982 (3).
Led Texas League in complete games with 14 and tied for lead in balks with 3 in 1977.
Tied for International League lead in games started by pitchers with 29 in 1978 and balks with 3 in 1980.

Year Club	League	G.	IP.	W.	L.	Pct.	H.	R.	ER.	SO.	BB.	ERA.
1976—Jackson	Texas	7	44	3	3	.500	34	20	14	19	14	2.86
1977—Jackson	Texas	25	*187	*14	10	.583	132	77	61	97	55	2.94
1977—Tidewater	Int'national	2	2	0	1	.000	4	5	4	0	3	18.00
1978—Tidewater	Int'national	29	192	10	10	.500	196	105	84	93	83	3.94
1979—Tidewater	Int'national	18	99	8	4	.667	103	37	35	40	27	3.18
1979—New York	National	18	52	1	3	.250	59	35	31	21	20	5.37
1980—Tidewater	Int'national	27	170	13	7	.650	165	69	56	88	64	2.96
1980—New York	National	6	29	1	1	.500	40	14	14	13	8	4.34
1981—New York	National	23	136	5	10	.333	130	65	59	54	34	3.90
1982—New York†	National	37	147	7	13	.350	185	100	84	63	60	5.14
1983—Houston‡	National	24	145	10	6	.625	143	67	60	73	46	3.72
1984—Houston	National	31	154	5	11	.313	179	96	80	83	43	4.68
1985—Houston	National	36	221⅔	18	8	.692	194	91	81	137	80	3.29
Major League Totals—7 Years		175	884⅔	47	52	.475	930	468	409	444	291	4.16

Selected by New York Mets' organization in 2nd round of free-agent draft, June 8, 1976.
†Traded to Houston Astros for Outfielder-First Baseman Danny Heep, December 10, 1982.
‡On disabled list, April 5 to May 4, 1983.

JAMES DEAN SCRANTON
(Jim)

Born April 5, 1960, at Torrance, Calif.
Height, 6.00. Weight, 185.
Throws right and bats left and righthanded.
Attended Palomar College, San Marcos, Calif., and
University of Arizona, Tucson, Ariz.

Led American Association in sacrifice hits with 17 in 1984.
Led Southern League shortstops in double plays with 76 in 1982.
Led Florida State League second basemen in double plays with 65 in 1981.
Led South Atlantic League shortstops in fielding percentage with .952 in 1980.

Year Club	League	Pos.	G.	AB.	R.	H.	2B.	3B.	HR.	RBI.	B.A.	PO.	A.	E.	F.A.
1980—Charleston	S. Atl.	SS-2B-OF	121	450	69	114	16	3	2	33	.253	227	341	28	.953
1981—Fort Myers	Fla. St.	SS	107	355	37	76	6	1	2	32	.214	*206	*346	30	.949
1982—Jacksonville	South.	SS	128	413	44	97	7	4	0	41	.235	*210	364	26	*.957
1983—Jacksonville	South.	SS	141	450	43	98	10	1	2	31	.218	211	469	*40	.944
1984—Omaha	A. A.	SS	136	430	47	108	16	5	3	37	.251	197	373	31	.948
1984—Kansas City	Amer.	SS-3B	2	2	0	0	0	0	0	0	.000	0	1	0	1.000
1985—Omaha	A. A.	*SS-P	121	378	36	74	10	1	1	29	.196	216	297	*27	.950
1985—Kansas City	Amer.	SS	6	4	1	0	0	0	0	0	.000	1	8	0	1.000
Major League Totals—2 Years			8	6	1	0	0	0	0	0	.000	1	9	0	1.000

Selected by Oakland A's organization in 14th round of free-agent draft, June 6, 1978.
Signed as free agent by Kansas City Royals' organization, February 27, 1980.

PITCHING RECORD

Year Club	League	G.	IP.	W.	L.	Pct.	H.	R.	ER.	SO.	BB.	ERA.
1985—Omaha	Am. Assoc.	1	2	0	0	.000	3	1	1	1	1	4.50

RODNEY GRANT SCURRY
Name pronounced SKUR-ee.
(Rod)

Born March 17, 1956, at Sacramento, Calif.
Height, 6.02. Weight, 180.
Throws and bats lefthanded.

Pitched seven-inning, 2-0 no-hit victory against Richmond, July 25, 1977.
Major League saves: 1981 (7), 1982 (14), 1983 (7), 1984 (4), 1985 (3). Total—35.
Led Carolina League pitchers in games started with 26 in 1975.
Led New York-Pennsylvania League in hit batsmen with 7 in 1974.

Year Club	League	G.	IP.	W.	L.	Pct.	H.	R.	ER.	SO.	BB.	ERA.
1974—Niagara Falls	NYP	14	89	5	6	.455	55	36	34	102	*74	3.44
1975—Salem	Carolina	26	150	9	12	.429	128	79	61	143	118	3.66
1976—Shreveport	Texas	24	123	8	8	.500	120	71	53	83	83	3.88
1977—Shreveport	Texas	18	113	3	11	.214	97	54	36	111	48	2.87
1977—Columbus	Int'national	8	37	3	2	.600	30	31	19	39	32	4.62
1978—Columbus†	Int'national	16	63	3	3	.500	69	44	40	57	43	5.71
1978—Shreveport	Texas	5	29	1	4	.200	27	19	15	38	24	4.66
1979—Portland‡	P. Coast	35	122	5	5	.500	121	64	56	94	72	4.13
1980—Pittsburgh	National	20	38	0	2	.000	23	12	9	28	17	2.13
1981—Pittsburgh	National	27	74	4	5	.444	74	33	31	65	40	3.77
1982—Pittsburgh	National	76	103⅔	4	5	.444	79	26	20	94	64	1.74
1983—Pittsburgh	National	61	68	4	9	.308	63	45	42	67	53	5.56
1984—Pittsburgh§	National	43	46⅓	5	6	.455	28	14	13	48	22	2.53
1985—Pittsburgh x	National	30	47⅔	0	1	.000	42	22	17	43	28	3.21
1985—New York	American	5	12⅔	1	0	1.000	5	4	4	17	10	2.84
National League Totals—6 Years		257	377⅔	17	28	.378	309	152	132	345	224	3.15
American League Totals—1 Year		5	12⅔	1	0	1.000	5	4	4	17	10	2.84
Major League Totals—6 Years		262	390⅓	18	28	.391	314	156	136	362	234	3.14

Selected by Pittsburgh Pirates' organization in 1st round (11th player selected) of free-agent draft, June 5, 1974.
†On disabled list, June 12 to July 11, 1978.
‡On disabled list, August 4 to August 14, 1979.
§On disabled list, April 7 to May 13 and August 5 to August 27, 1984.
xSold to New York Yankees, September 14, 1985.

RAYMOND MARK SEARAGE
(Ray)

Born May 1, 1955, at Freeport, N.Y.
Height, 6.01. Weight, 180.
Throws and bats lefthanded.
Attended West Liberty State College, West Liberty, W. Va.

Major League saves: 1981 (1), 1984 (6), 1985 (1). Total—8.
Led International League in wild pitches with 14 in 1982.

Year Club	League	G.	IP.	W.	L.	Pct.	H.	R.	ER.	SO.	BB.	ERA.
1976—Sara. W. Sox-Sara. Cards	Gulf Coast	11	32	1	3	.250	24	17	15	31	22	4.22
1977—St. Petersburg	Florida St.	13	19	0	0	.000	11	7	6	12	12	2.84
1977—Johnson City	Ap'lachian	8	41	3	2	.600	38	23	22	27	21	4.83
1978—Gastonia	W. Carol.	39	110	8	3	.727	86	40	34	86	68	2.78
1979—Arkansas†	Texas	42	89	10	4	.714	73	27	22	63	46	2.22
1980—Tidewater	Int'national	19	30	1	0	1.000	35	24	23	20	20	6.90
1980—Jackson	Texas	14	70	4	5	.444	54	32	26	71	26	3.34
1981—Tidewater	Int'national	18	27	2	0	1.000	29	10	7	23	13	2.33
1981—New York‡	National	26	37	1	0	1.000	34	16	15	16	17	3.65
1982—Charleston§	Int'national	38	114	2	7	.222	112	73	62	87	87	4.89
1983—Charleston x	Int'national	31	134	7	7	.500	146	94	84	77	76	5.64
1984—Vancouver	P. Coast	33	76⅓	6	3	.667	62	29	26	59	44	3.07
1984—Milwaukee	American	21	38⅓	2	1	.667	20	3	3	29	16	0.70
1985—Milwaukee	American	33	38	1	4	.200	54	27	25	36	24	5.92
1985—Vancouver	P. Coast	23	26	2	0	1.000	22	10	7	31	12	2.42
National League Totals—1 Year		26	37	1	0	1.000	34	16	15	16	17	3.65
American League Totals—2 Years		54	76⅓	3	5	.375	74	30	28	65	40	3.30
Major League Totals—3 Years		80	113⅓	4	5	.444	108	46	43	81	57	3.41

Selected by St. Louis Cardinals' organization in 22nd round of free-agent draft, June 8, 1976.
†Traded to New York Mets' organization for Catcher Jody Davis, December 10, 1979.
‡Traded to Cleveland Indians for Shortstop Tom Veryzer, January 8, 1982.
§Traded on a conditional basis to San Diego Padres for a player to be named later, December 15, 1982; returned, March 28, 1983.
xGranted free agency, October 20, 1983; signed by Vancouver (Milwaukee Brewers' organization), November 4, 1983.

GEORGE THOMAS SEAVER
(Tom)

Born November 17, 1944, at Fresno, Calif.
Height, 6.01. Weight, 210.
Throws and bats righthanded.
Attended Fresno City College, Fresno, Calif., and received bachelor of science degree in public relations from University of Southern California, Los Angeles, Calif. in 1974.
Son of Charles Seaver, former U.S. Walker Cup golfer.

Established major league records for most seasons, 200 or more strikeouts (10); most consecutive seasons, 200 or more strikeouts (9), 1968 through 1976; most consecutive strikeouts, game (10), April 22, 1970; most times pitched opening game of season (15).
Tied major league record for most strikeouts game (19), April 22, 1970.
Established National League records for lowest earned run average, 200 or more games won, lifetime (2.73); most strikeouts, by righthanded pitcher, lifetime (3,272).
Tied National League record for most season opening games won, lifetime (6).
Pitched 4-0 no-hit victory against St. Louis Cardinals, June 16, 1978.
Led National League in shutouts with 7 in 1977.
Tied for National League lead in shutouts with 5 in 1979.
Tied for National League lead in complete games with 18 in 1973.
Led International League pitchers in games started with 32 in 1966.
Named National League Pitcher of the Year by THE SPORTING NEWS, 1969 and 1975.
Won National League Cy Young Memorial Award, 1969, 1973 and 1975.
Named National League Rookie of the Year by Baseball Writers' Association of America, 1967.
Named righthanded pitcher on THE SPORTING NEWS National League All-Star Team, 1969, 1973, 1975 and 1981.

Year Club	League	G.	IP.	W.	L.	Pct.	H.	R.	ER.	SO.	BB.	ERA.
1966—Jacksonville	Int'national	34	210	12	12	.500	184	87	73	188	66	3.13
1967—New York	National	35	251	16	13	.552	224	85	77	170	78	2.76
1968—New York	National	36	278	16	12	.571	224	73	68	205	48	2.20
1969—New York	National	36	273	*25	7	*.781	202	75	67	208	82	2.21
1970—New York	National	37	291	18	12	.600	230	103	91	*283	83	*2.81
1971—New York	National	36	286	20	10	.667	210	61	56	*289	61	*1.76
1972—New York	National	35	262	21	12	.636	215	92	85	249	77	2.92
1973—New York	National	36	290	19	10	.655	219	74	67	*251	64	*2.08
1974—New York	National	32	236	11	11	.500	199	89	84	201	75	3.20
1975—New York	National	36	280	*22	9	.710	217	81	74	*243	88	2.38
1976—New York	National	35	271	14	11	.560	211	83	78	*235	77	2.59

Year Club	League	G.	IP.	W.	L.	Pct.	H.	R.	ER.	SO.	BB.	ERA.
1977—New York†-Cincinnati	National	33	261	21	6	.778	199	78	75	196	66	2.59
1978—Cincinnati	National	36	260	16	14	.533	218	97	83	226	89	2.87
1979—Cincinnati	National	32	215	16	6	*.727	187	85	75	131	61	3.14
1980—Cincinnati‡	National	26	168	10	8	.556	140	74	68	101	59	3.64
1981—Cincinnati	National	23	166	*14	2	*.875	120	51	47	87	66	2.55
1982—Cincinnati§	National	21	111⅓	5	13	.278	136	75	68	62	44	5.50
1983—New York x	National	34	231	9	14	.391	201	104	91	135	86	3.55
1984—Chicago	American	34	236⅔	15	11	.577	216	108	104	131	61	3.95
1985—Chicago	American	35	238⅔	16	11	.593	223	103	84	134	69	3.17
National League Totals—17 Years		559	4130⅓	273	170	.616	3352	1380	1254	3272	1204	2.73
American League Totals—2 Years		69	475⅓	31	22	.585	439	211	188	265	130	3.56
Major League Totals—19 Years		628	4605⅔	304	192	.613	3791	1591	1442	3537	1334	2.82

Selected by Los Angeles Dodgers' organization in 22nd round of free-agent draft, June, 1965.

Signed by Atlanta Braves to Richmond contract for reported $40,000 bonus, February, 1966; subsequently, Commissioner William Eckert nullified the contract because the signing violated the college rule. However, since the University of Southern California then declared Seaver ineligible, Eckert decreed that any club other than the Braves which was willing to match terms of his Richmond contract would be eligible to draw for negotiation rights. Cleveland Indians, Philadelphia Phillies and New York Mets expressed that willingness, and Eckert drew the name of the Mets in a special drawing, April 3, 1966; Mets then signed Seaver to Jacksonville contract for reported $50,000 bonus.

†Traded to Cincinnati Reds for Infielder Doug Flynn, Pitcher Pat Zachry and Outfielders Dan Norman and Steve Henderson, June 15, 1977.

‡On disabled list, July 1 to August 4, 1980.

§Traded to New York Mets for Pitcher Charlie Puleo, Catcher Lloyd McClendon and Outfielder Jason Felice, December 16, 1982.

xSelected by Chicago White Sox in player compensation pool draft, January 20, 1984. (Chicago received compensation for Toronto Blue Jays' signing of Pitcher Dennis Lamp, a Type A player, January 10, 1984.

CHAMPIONSHIP SERIES RECORD

Established Championship Series record for most strikeouts, five-game Series (17), 1973.

Year Club	League	G.	IP.	W.	L.	Pct.	H.	R.	ER.	SO.	BB.	ERA.
1969—New York	National	1	7	1	0	1.000	8	5	5	2	3	6.43
1973—New York	National	2	16⅔	1	1	.500	13	4	3	17	5	1.62
1979—Cincinnati	National	1	8	0	0	.000	5	2	2	5	2	2.25
Championship Series Totals—3 Years		4	31⅔	2	1	.667	26	11	10	24	10	2.84

WORLD SERIES RECORD

Year Club	League	G.	IP.	W.	L.	Pct.	H.	R.	ER.	SO.	BB.	ERA.
1969—New York	National	2	15	1	1	.500	12	5	5	9	3	3.00
1973—New York	National	2	15	0	1	.000	13	4	4	18	3	2.40
World Series Totals—2 Years		4	30	1	2	.333	25	9	9	27	6	2.70

ALL-STAR GAME RECORD

Year League		IP.	W.	L.	Pct.	H.	R.	ER.	SO.	BB.	ERA.
1967—National		1	0	0	.000	0	0	0	1	1	0.00
1968—National		2	0	0	.000	2	0	0	5	0	0.00
1970—National		3	0	0	.000	1	0	0	4	0	0.00
1973—National		1	0	0	.000	0	0	0	1	1	0.00
1975—National		1	0	0	.000	2	3	3	2	1	27.00
1976—National		2	0	0	.000	2	1	1	1	0	4.50
1977—National		2	0	0	.000	4	3	2	2	1	9.00
1981—National		1	0	0	.000	3	1	1	1	0	9.00
All-Star Game Totals—8 Years		13	0	0	.000	14	8	7	16	4	4.85

Member of National League All-Star Team for 1969, 1971, 1972 and 1978 games; did not play.

ROBERT BUSH SEBRA

(Bob)

Born December 11, 1961, at Ridgewood, N.J.
Height, 6.02. Weight, 200.
Throws and bats righthanded.
Attended University of Nebraska, Lincoln, Neb.

Tied for American Association lead in home runs allowed with 17 in 1985.

Year Club	League	G.	IP.	W.	L.	Pct.	H.	R.	ER.	SO.	BB.	ERA.
1983—Tri-Cities	Northwest	12	58⅓	4	3	.571	48	36	26	70	29	4.01
1984—Tulsa	Texas	17	100⅓	10	5	.667	86	45	38	90	41	3.41
1984—Oklahoma City	Am. Assoc.	9	53⅓	4	4	.500	37	23	20	38	25	3.38
1985—Oklahoma City	Am. Assoc.	22	138⅔	10	6	.625	121	62	59	84	57	3.83
1985—Texas†	American	7	20⅓	0	2	.000	26	17	17	13	14	7.52
Major League Totals—1 Year		7	20⅓	0	2	.000	26	17	17	13	14	7.52

Selected by Detroit Tigers' organization in 4th round of free-agent draft, June 3, 1980.

Selected by Texas Rangers' organization in 5th round of free-agent draft, June 6, 1983.

†Traded with Infielder Jim Anderson to Montreal Expos for Third Baseman Pete Incaviglia, November 2, 1985.

JEFFREY DOYLE SELLERS
(Jeff)

Born May 11, 1964, at Compton, Calif.
Height, 6.01. Weight, 175.
Throws and bats righthanded.

Led Eastern League in shutouts with 5 and complete games with 15 in 1985.
Led Florida State League pitchers in games started with 29 in 1984.

Year Club	League	G.	IP.	W.	L.	Pct.	H.	R.	ER.	SO.	BB.	ERA.
1982—Elmira	NYP	17	61⅔	1	4	.200	55	31	21	45	39	3.06
1983—Winter Haven	Florida St.	21	117⅔	8	9	.471	149	77	59	68	47	4.51
1984—Winter Haven	Florida St.	29	182	12	10	.545	182	87	69	94	80	3.41
1985—New Britain	Eastern	25	184⅔	●14	7	.667	165	67	57	115	67	2.78
1985—Boston	American	4	22⅓	2	0	1.000	24	10	9	6	7	3.63
Major League Totals—1 Year		4	22⅓	2	0	1.000	24	10	9	6	7	3.63

Selected by Boston Red Sox' organization in 8th round of free-agent draft, June 7, 1982.

MICHAEL HAROLD SHADE
(Mike)

Born March 7, 1961, at Pottstown, Pa.
Height, 6.02. Weight, 205.
Throws and bats righthanded.
Attended West Chester University, West Chester, Pa.

Year Club	League	G.	IP.	W.	L.	Pct.	H.	R.	ER.	SO.	BB.	ERA.
1982—Erie	NYP	13	45⅓	3	4	.429	38	24	20	63	16	3.97
1983—Springfield	Midwest	47	78⅔	9	5	.643	69	39	25	85	32	2.86
1984—St. Petersburg	Florida St.	28	45⅔	0	2	.000	35	12	7	43	26	1.38
1984—Arkansas	Texas	27	46⅔	2	4	.333	35	18	16	48	30	3.09
1984—Louisville	Am. Assoc.	2	2⅔	0	1	.000	5	4	3	3	3	10.13
1985—Louisville	Am. Assoc.	14	31⅓	0	2	.000	23	20	20	31	29	5.74
1985—Arkansas	Texas	32	41	0	7	.000	44	27	20	36	20	4.39

Selected by St. Louis Cardinals' organization in 4th round of free-agent draft, June 7, 1982.

MICHAEL TYRONE SHARPERSON
(Mike)

Born October 4, 1960, at Orangeburg, S.C.
Height, 6.01. Weight, 175.
Throws and bats righthanded.
Attended DeKalb Community College South, Decatur, Ga.

Led International League second basemen in putouts with 286 and total chances with 666 in 1985.
Led Southern League second basemen in total chances with 775 and double plays with 103 in 1984.

Year Club	League	Pos.	G.	AB.	R.	H.	2B.	3B.	HR.	RBI.	B.A.	PO.	A.	E.	F.A.
1982—Florence	S. Atl.	SS-3B	111	326	51	83	16	1	3	33	.255	136	261	33	.923
1983—Kinston†	Carol.	S-3-2-C	90	361	55	96	8	1	5	41	.266	148	286	19	.958
1984—Knoxville	South.	2B	140	542	86	165	25	7	4	48	.304	★331	★423	21	.973
1985—Syracuse	Int.	2B-SS	134	★536	★86	★155	19	★7	1	59	.289	291	372	17	.975

Selected by Pittsburgh Pirates' organization in 41st round of free-agent draft, June 5, 1979.
Selected by Montreal Expos' organization in secondary phase of free-agent draft, January 8, 1980.
Selected by Detroit Tigers' organization in 4th round of free-agent draft, January 13, 1981.
Selected by Toronto Blue Jays' organization in secondary phase of free-agent draft, June 8, 1981.
†On disabled list, August 14, 1983 through remainder of season.

LARRY KENT SHEETS

Born December 6, 1959, at Staunton, Va.
Height, 6.04. Weight, 210.
Throws right and bats lefthanded.
Attended Eastern Mennonite College, Harrisonburg, Va.

Led International League outfielders in double plays with 5 in 1984.

Year Club	League	Pos.	G.	AB.	R.	H.	2B.	3B.	HR.	RBI.	B.A.	PO.	A.	E.	F.A.
1978—Bluefield	Appal.	OF-1B	67	225	32	60	9	2	11	★48	.267	121	8	4	.970
1979—Miami†	Fla. St.						(Did not play)								
1979—Bluefield	Appal.	OF	3	12	2	4	2	0	0	2	.333	1	0	0	1.000
1980—Bluefield‡	Appal.	OF	37	124	29	47	9	1	★14	47	.379	40	3	2	.956
1980—Charlotte	South.	OF	13	48	1	9	4	0	0	5	.188	4	1	0	1.000
1981—Rochester§	Int.						(Did not play)								
1982—Rochester x	Int.						(Did not play)								
1982—Hagerstown y	Carol.	OF	88	324	46	96	21	0	18	59	.296	123	5	6	.955
1983—Charlotte	South.	OF-1B	138	503	72	145	★37	3	●25	87	.288	256	15	7	.975
1983—Rochester	Int.	OF	3	13	1	2	1	0	0	2	.154	5	0	1	.833
1984—Rochester	Int.	OF	134	431	76	130	26	4	13	67	.302	201	★19	2	.991
1984—Baltimore	Amer.	OF	8	16	3	7	1	0	1	2	.438	12	1	0	1.000
1985—Baltimore	Amer.	OF-1B	113	328	43	86	8	0	17	50	.262	12	1	1	.929
Major League Totals—2 Years			121	344	46	93	9	0	18	52	.270	24	2	1	.963

Selected by Baltimore Orioles' organization in 2nd round of free-agent draft, June 6, 1978.

†On suspended list, May 1 to August 29, 1979.
‡On restricted list, June 18 to June 23, 1980.
§On restricted list, April 14 to May 28 and June 18, 1981 through remainder of season.
xOn suspended list, April 13, 1982; then transferred to restricted list, April 23 to May 13, 1982.
yOn disabled list, August 23, 1982 through remainder of season.

JOHN T. SHELBY

Born February 23, 1958, at Lexington, Ky.
Height, 6.01. Weight, 175.
Throws right and bats right and lefthanded.
Attended Columbia State Community College, Columbia, Tenn.

Major League stolen bases: 1981 (2), 1983 (15), 1984 (12), 1985 (5). Total—34.
Led Florida State League outfielders in double plays with 7 in 1979.
Led Appalachian League outfielders in double plays with 3 in 1978.

Year Club	League	Pos.	G.	AB.	R.	H.	2B.	3B.	HR.	RBI.	B.A.	PO.	A.	E.	F.A.
1977—Bluefield	Appal.	OF	60	211	28	54	9	1	0	1	.256	90	●12	7	.936
1978—Miami	Fla. St.	OF	13	26	4	6	1	0	0	3	.231	14	2	2	.889
1978—Bluefield	Appal.	OF	64	248	49	70	9	1	6	25	.282	128	*11	6	.959
1979—Miami	Fla. St.	OF	132	478	50	96	11	6	3	38	.201	*252	●22	8	.972
1980—Charlotte	South.	OF	134	*560	66	135	27	11	6	51	.241	*361	21	*16	.960
1981—Charlotte	South.	OF	62	251	40	59	11	4	2	21	.235	120	3	10	.925
1981—Rochester	Int.	OF	76	326	42	86	21	8	3	32	.264	189	8	6	.970
1981—Baltimore	Amer.	OF	7	3	2	0	0	0	0	0	.000	1	0	0	1.000
1982—Rochester	Int.	OF	133	*548	92	153	26	6	16	52	.279	331	13	8	.977
1982—Baltimore	Amer.	OF	26	35	8	11	3	0	1	2	.314	20	1	0	1.000
1983—Baltimore	Amer.	OF	126	325	52	84	15	2	5	27	.258	200	9	4	.981
1984—Baltimore	Amer.	OF	128	383	44	80	12	5	6	30	.209	261	9	2	.993
1985—Rochester	Int.	OF	52	206	31	59	16	4	8	21	.286	124	4	1	.992
1985—Baltimore	Amer.	OF-2B	69	205	28	58	6	2	7	27	.283	148	4	3	.981
Major League Totals—5 Years			356	950	134	233	36	9	19	86	.245	630	23	9	.986

Selected by Baltimore Orioles' organization in 1st round (19th player selected) of free-agent draft, January 11, 1977.

CHAMPIONSHIP SERIES RECORD

Year Club	League	Pos.	G.	AB.	R.	H.	2B.	3B.	HR.	RBI.	B.A.	PO.	A.	E.	F.A.
1983—Baltimore	Amer.	OF-PH	3	9	1	2	0	0	0	0	.222	3	0	0	1.000

WORLD SERIES RECORD

Year Club	League	Pos.	G.	AB.	R.	H.	2B.	3B.	HR.	RBI.	B.A.	PO.	A.	E.	F.A.
1983—Baltimore	Amer.	PH-OF	5	9	1	4	0	0	0	1	.444	10	0	0	1.000

RONALD WAYNE SHEPHERD
(Ron)

Born October 27, 1960, at Longview, Tex.
Height, 6.04. Weight, 180.
Throws and bats righthanded.
Attended Kilgore College, Kilgore, Tex.
Brother of Larry Shepherd, wide receiver at University of Houston.

Major League stolen bases: 1985 (3).

Year Club	League	Pos.	G.	AB.	R.	H.	2B.	3B.	HR.	RBI.	B.A.	PO.	A.	E.	F.A.
1979—Medicine Hat	Pion.	OF	49	178	21	37	6	2	3	20	.208	92	5	8	.924
1980—Kinston	Carol.	OF	110	384	53	80	16	4	11	61	.208	239	7	●13	.950
1981—Kinston	Carol.	OF	135	486	71	114	15	3	16	66	.235	*280	9	12	.960
1982—Knoxville	South.	OF	136	482	62	119	19	8	15	65	.247	260	4	9	.967
1983—Syracuse	Int.	OF	119	404	60	110	20	3	13	62	.272	254	6	4	.985
1984—Syracuse	Int.	OF	113	363	37	80	16	3	12	50	.220	241	7	10	.961
1984—Toronto	Amer.	OF	12	4	0	0	0	0	0	0	.000	2	1	0	1.000
1985—Toronto†	Amer.	OF	38	35	7	4	2	0	0	1	.114	24	0	0	1.000
1985—Syracuse	Int.	OF	37	133	23	41	12	2	2	16	.308	60	0	3	.952
Major League Totals—2 Years			50	39	7	4	2	0	0	1	.103	26	1	0	1.000

Selected by Toronto Blue Jays' organization in 2nd round of free-agent draft, June 5, 1979.
†On disabled list, April 7 to April 22, 1985.

PATRICK ARTHUR SHERIDAN
(Pat)

Born December 4, 1957, at Ann Arbor, Mich.
Height, 6.03. Weight, 180.
Throws right and bats lefthanded.
Attended Eastern Michigan University, Ypsilanti, Mich.
Son of Arthur Sheridan, minor league pitcher, 1952 through 1956.

Major League stolen bases: 1983 (12), 1984 (19), 1985 (11). Total—42.

Year Club	League	Pos.	G.	AB.	R.	H.	2B.	3B.	HR.	RBI.	B.A.	PO.	A.	E.	F.A.
1979—Fort Myers	Fla. St.	OF	67	235	25	66	4	3	0	16	.281	142	8	1	.993
1980—Fort Myers	Fla. St.	OF-C	20	79	17	32	1	0	1	13	.405	37	4	1	.976
1980—Jacksonville†	South.	OF	97	367	63	112	17	7	5	42	.305	201	7	9	.959
1981—Omaha‡	A. A.	OF	86	315	49	94	15	8	5	31	.298	193	2	3	.985
1981—Kansas City	Amer.	OF	3	1	0	0	0	0	0	0	.000	2	0	0	1.000

Year Club League	Pos.	G.	AB.	R.	H.	2B.	3B.	HR.	RBI.	B.A.	PO.	A.	E.	F.A.
1982—Omaha§.................. A. A.	OF	41	135	8	34	8	1	0	13	.252	92	3	0	1.000
1983—Omaha.................. A. A.	OF	20	75	16	23	4	5	4	14	.307	53	2	0	1.000
1983—Kansas City.......... Amer.	OF	109	333	43	90	12	2	7	36	.270	237	6	3	.988
1984—Kansas City.......... Amer.	OF	138	481	64	136	24	4	8	53	.283	273	8	4	.986
1985—Kansas City x ...... Amer.	OF	78	206	18	47	9	2	3	17	.228	116	3	2	.983
1985—Omaha.................. A. A.	OF	8	28	1	10	1	0	0	1	.357	8	1	0	1.000
Major League Totals—4 Years.................		328	1021	125	273	45	8	18	106	.267	628	17	9	.986

Selected by Cincinnati Reds' organization in 36th round of free-agent draft, June 8, 1976.
Selected by Kansas City Royals' organization in 3rd round of free-agent draft, June 5, 1979.
†On disabled list, May 16 to June 2, 1980.
‡On disabled list, May 25 to June 25, 1981.
§On disabled list, April 27 to June 25 and June 27 to July 19, 1982.
xOn disabled list, June 19 to July 4 and August 5 to September 3, 1985; included rehabilitation disability assignment to Omaha, August 26 to September 3, 1985.

CHAMPIONSHIP SERIES RECORD

Tied Championship Series record for most home runs by pinch-hitter, game (1), October 9, 1985.

Year Club League	Pos.	G.	AB.	R.	H.	2B.	3B.	HR.	RBI.	B.A.	PO.	A.	E.	F.A.
1984—Kansas City.......... Amer.	OF	3	6	1	0	0	0	0	0	.000	9	0	1	.900
1985—Kansas City.......... Amer.	OF-PH	7	20	4	3	0	0	2	3	.150	13	0	0	1.000
Championship Series Totals—2 Years.....		10	26	5	3	0	0	2	3	.115	22	0	1	.957

WORLD SERIES RECORD

Year Club League	Pos.	G.	AB.	R.	H.	2B.	3B.	HR.	RBI.	B.A.	PO.	A.	E.	F.A.
1985—Kansas City.......... Amer.	PH-OF	5	18	0	4	2	0	0	1	.222	6	0	0	1.000

STEPHEN MACK SHIELDS
(Steve)

Born November 30, 1958, in Etowah County, Ala.
Height, 6.05. Weight, 220.
Throws and bats righthanded.

Tied for International League lead in shutouts with 3 and hit batsmen with 8 in 1985.
Tied for Eastern League lead in complete games with 13 and shutouts with 3 in 1982.
Tied for Eastern League lead in intentional bases on balls issued with 10 in 1981.

Year Club	League	G.	IP.	W.	L.	Pct.	H.	R.	ER.	SO.	BB.	ERA.
1977—Elmira...............................	NYP	15	81	1	6	.143	72	45	37	108	37	4.11
1978—Winter Haven†...............	Florida St.	14	51	3	3	.500	52	14	11	34	9	1.94
1979—Winston-Salem	Carolina	24	152	11	8	.579	149	78	51	152	80	3.02
1980—Bristol...........................	Eastern	39	113	5	6	.455	128	79	61	63	77	4.86
1981—Bristol...........................	Eastern	29	126	5	*14	.263	136	75	65	87	65	4.64
1982—Bristol...........................	Eastern	29	170⅓	10	13	.435	172	100	67	125	71	3.54
1983—Pawtucket‡...................	Int'national	36	143	4	12	.250	171	94	74	115	63	4.66
1984—Richmond....................	Int'national	39	110	9	4	.692	122	69	58	101	39	4.75
1985—Richmond....................	Int'national	18	133	6	7	.462	110	53	39	88	54	2.64
1985—Atlanta........................	National	23	68	1	2	.333	86	46	39	29	32	5.16
Major League Totals—1 Year..............................		23	68	1	2	.333	86	46	39	29	32	5.16

Selected by Boston Red Sox' organization in 10th round of free-agent draft, June 7, 1977.
†On disabled list, April 10 to June 14, 1978.
‡Granted free agency, October 20, 1983; signed by Richmond (Atlanta Braves' organization), October 26, 1983.

ANTHONY RAYMOND SHINES
(Razor)

Born July 18, 1956, at Durham, N.C.
Height, 6.01. Weight, 210.
Throws right and bats left and righthanded.
Attended St. Augustine's College, Raleigh, N.C.

Year Club League	Pos.	G.	AB.	R.	H.	2B.	3B.	HR.	RBI.	B.A.	PO.	A.	E.	F.A.
1978—Jamestown............ NYP	1B	63	224	39	66	12	0	9	39	.295	514	26	14	.975
1979—W. Palm Beach†.. Fla. St.	1B	122	406	44	104	13	0	4	53	.256	860	53	16	.983
1980—W. Palm Beach‡.. Fla. St.	C-1B	73	267	27	64	15	1	6	40	.240	506	64	13	.978
1981—Memphis............... South.	1-3-C-O	119	359	50	79	7	4	10	42	.220	673	108	20	.975
1981—W. Palm Beach.... Fla. St.	3B-1B-C	8	26	4	6	0	0	3	6	.231	24	7	6	.838
1982—Memphis............... South.	1B-C-3B	122	432	67	121	18	2	16	66	.280	573	63	14	.979
1983—Memphis............... South.	1B-C-3B	109	388	72	111	27	2	20	63	.286	611	83	20	.972
1983—Wichita................. A. A.	1B-C	29	112	14	31	6	1	1	11	.277	196	18	1	.995
1983—Montreal.............. Nat.	OF	3	2	0	1	0	0	0	0	.500	0	0	0	.000
1984—Indianapolis§....... A. A.	1-3-C-P	131	443	73	125	26	1	18	80	.282	735	141	16	.982
1984—Montreal.............. Nat.	1B-3B	12	20	0	6	1	0	0	2	.300	26	0	0	1.000
1985—Montreal.............. Nat.	1B-P	47	50	0	6	0	0	0	3	.120	34	4	2	.950
1985—Indianapolis....... A. A.	1B-3B-OF	65	240	39	74	15	2	7	45	.308	158	40	2	.990
Major League Totals—3 Years............		62	72	0	13	1	0	0	5	.181	60	4	2	.970

Selected by Montreal Expos' organization in 18th round of free-agent draft, June 6, 1978.
†On disabled list, June 12 to June 23, 1979.
‡On disabled list, May 4 to May 14, June 12 to June 23 and July 10, 1980 through remainder of season.
§On disabled list, July 1 to July 12, 1984.

Year Club	League	G.	IP.	W.	L.	Pct.	H.	R.	ER.	SO.	BB.	ERA.
1984—Indianapolis	Am. Assoc.	1	1	0	0	.000	1	1	0	1	0	0.00
1985—Montreal	National	1	1	0	0	.000	1	0	0	0	0	0.00
Major League Totals—1 Year		1	1	0	0	.000	1	0	0	0	0	0.00

DAVID NOEL SHIPANOFF
(Dave)

Born November 13, 1959, at Edmonton, Alberta.
Height, 6.02. Weight, 185.
Throws and bats righthanded.
Attended Wabash Valley College, Mt. Carmel, Ill.

Major League saves: 1985 (3).
Led Southern League in saves with 18 and games finished in relief with 46 in 1983.
Led Carolina League in saves with 30 and games finished in relief with 56 in 1982.

Year Club	League	G.	IP.	W.	L.	Pct.	H.	R.	ER.	SO.	BB.	ERA.
1980—Medicine Hat	Pioneer	8	36	1	4	.200	49	37	31	19	23	7.75
1981—Florence	S. Atlantic	52	101	7	7	.500	78	40	30	101	44	2.67
1982—Kinston	Carolina	*63	92⅔	7	3	.700	57	22	20	105	46	1.94
1983—Knoxville	Southern	●61	69⅔	6	3	.667	53	32	26	73	51	3.36
1983—Syracuse	Int'national	8	11	0	1	.000	0	4	4	18	9	3.27
1984—Syracuse	Int'national	5	8⅓	0	0	.000	9	15	12	8	18	12.96
1984—Knoxville†	Southern	36	130⅔	5	9	.357	108	60	52	108	68	3.58
1985—Portland	P. Coast	51	91⅔	8	5	.615	73	30	27	115	40	2.65
1985—Philadelphia	National	26	36⅓	1	2	.333	33	15	13	26	16	3.22
Major League Totals—1 Year		26	36⅓	1	2	.333	33	15	13	26	16	3.22

Signed as free agent by Toronto Blue Jays' organization, July 19, 1980.
†Traded with Infielder Jose Escobar and Outfielder Ken Kinnard to Philadelphia Phillies' organization for First Baseman Len Matuszek, April 1, 1985.

CRAIG BARRY SHIPLEY

Born January 7, 1963, at Parramatta, Australia.
Height, 6.01. Weight, 175.
Throws right and bats left and righthanded.
Attended University of Alabama, University, Ala.

Year Club	League	Pos.	G.	AB.	R.	H.	2B.	3B.	HR.	RBI.	B.A.	PO.	A.	E.	F.A.
1984—Vero Beach†	Fla. St.	SS	85	293	56	82	11	2	0	28	.280	137	216	17	.954
1985—Albuquerque	P. C.	SS	124	414	50	100	9	2	0	30	.242	202	367	21	.964

Signed as a free agent by Los Angeles Dodgers' organization, May 28, 1984.
†Batted righthanded.

ROBERT CHARLES SHIRLEY
(Bob)

Born June 25, 1954, at Oklahoma City, Okla.
Height, 5.11. Weight, 180.
Throws left and bats righthanded.
Attended University of Oklahoma, Norman, Okla.

Major League saves: 1978 (5), 1980 (7), 1981 (1), 1985 (2). Total—15.

Year Club	League	G.	IP.	W.	L.	Pct.	H.	R.	ER.	SO.	BB.	ERA.
1976—Amarillo	Texas	16	111	9	5	.643	113	55	41	90	39	3.32
1976—Hawaii	P. Coast	13	81	5	5	.500	91	62	47	47	24	5.22
1977—San Diego	National	39	214	12	18	.400	215	107	88	146	100	3.70
1978—San Diego	National	50	166	8	11	.421	164	75	68	102	61	3.69
1979—San Diego	National	49	205	8	16	.333	196	89	77	117	59	3.38
1980—San Diego†	National	59	137	11	12	.478	143	58	54	67	54	3.55
1981—St. Louis‡	National	28	79	6	4	.600	78	42	36	36	34	4.10
1982—Cincinnati§	National	41	152⅔	8	13	.381	138	74	61	89	73	3.60
1983—New York	American	25	108	5	8	.385	122	71	61	53	36	5.08
1984—New York	American	41	114⅓	3	3	.500	119	47	43	48	38	3.38
1985—New York	American	48	109	5	5	.500	103	34	32	55	26	2.64
National League Totals—6 Years		266	953⅔	53	74	.417	934	445	384	557	381	3.62
American League Totals—3 Years		114	331⅓	13	16	.448	344	152	136	156	100	3.69
Major League Totals—9 Years		380	1285	66	90	.423	1278	597	520	713	481	3.64

Selected by Los Angeles Dodgers' organization in 38th round of free-agent draft, June 6, 1972.
Selected by San Francisco Giants' organization in 5th round of free-agent draft, June 4, 1975.
Selected by San Diego Padres' organization in secondary phase of free-agent draft, January 7, 1976.
†Traded with Pitcher Rollie Fingers, Catcher-First Baseman Gene Tenace and a player to be named later to St. Louis Cardinals for Catchers Terry Kennedy and Steve Swisher, Pitchers John Littlefield, Al Olmsted, John Urrea and Kim Seaman and Infielder Mike Phillips, December 8, 1980; St. Louis organization acquired Catcher Bob Geren to complete deal, December 10, 1980.
‡Traded to Cincinnati Reds for Pitchers Jeff Lahti and Jose Brito, April 1, 1982.
§Granted free agency, November 10, 1982; signed by New York Yankees, December 10, 1982.

ERIC VAUGHN SHOW

Name rhymes with Chow.

Born May 19, 1956, at Riverside, Calif.
Height, 6.01. Weight, 185.
Throws and bats righthanded.
Attended University of California, Riverside, Calif.

Major League saves: 1981 (3), 1982 (3). Total—6.
Led Texas League in hit batsmen with 10 in 1980.

Year Club	League	G.	IP.	W.	L.	Pct.	H.	R.	ER.	SO.	BB.	ERA.
1978—Walla Walla	Northwest	11	60	5	2	.714	47	28	19	43	20	2.85
1979—Reno	California	28	169	13	9	.591	144	79	67	186	92	3.57
1980—Amarillo	Texas	26	166	12	6	.667	141	81	69	144	81	3.74
1981—Hawaii	P. Coast	34	85	7	3	.700	67	30	24	70	35	2.54
1981—San Diego	National	15	23	1	3	.250	17	9	8	22	9	3.13
1982—San Diego	National	47	150	10	6	.625	117	49	44	88	48	2.64
1983—San Diego	National	35	200⅔	15	12	.556	201	97	93	120	74	4.17
1984—San Diego	National	32	206⅔	15	9	.625	175	88	78	104	88	3.40
1985—San Diego	National	35	233	12	11	.522	212	95	80	141	87	3.09
Major League Totals—5 Years		164	813⅓	53	41	.564	722	338	303	475	306	3.35

Selected by Minnesota Twins' organization in 36th round of free-agent draft, June 5, 1974.
Selected by San Diego Padres' organization in 18th round of free-agent draft, June 6, 1978.

CHAMPIONSHIP SERIES RECORD

Tied Championship Series record for most earned runs allowed, five-game Series (8), 1984.
Tied National League Championship Series record for most runs allowed, five-game Series (8), 1984.

Year Club	League	G.	IP.	W.	L.	Pct.	H.	R.	ER.	SO.	BB.	ERA.
1984—San Diego	National	2	5⅓	0	1	.000	8	8	8	2	4	13.50

WORLD SERIES RECORD

Year Club	League	G.	IP.	W.	L.	Pct.	H.	R.	ER.	SO.	BB.	ERA.
1984—San Diego	National	1	2⅔	0	1	.000	4	4	3	2	1	10.13

RUBEN ANGEL SIERRA (GARCIA)

Born October 6, 1965, at Rio Piedras, Puerto Rico.
Height, 6.01. Weight, 175.
Throws right and bats left and righthanded.

Year Club	League	Pos.	G.	AB.	R.	H.	2B.	3B.	HR.	RBI.	B.A.	PO.	A.	E.	F.A.
1983—Sarasota Ran.†	Gulf C.	OF	48	182	26	44	7	3	1	26	.242	67	6	4	.948
1984—Burlington	Midw.	OF	●138	482	55	127	33	5	6	75	.263	239	18	★20	.928
1985—Tulsa	Texas	OF	★137	★545	63	138	34	★8	13	74	.253	234	12	★15	.943

Signed as free agent by Texas Rangers' organization, November 21, 1982.
†Batted righthanded.

ULISES SIERRA (PIZARRO)

(Candy)

Born March 27, 1967, at Rio Piedras, Puerto Rico.
Height, 6.02. Weight, 190.
Throws and bats righthanded.

Pitched seven-inning, 2-0 no-hit victory against Modesto, June 15, 1984 (first game).

Year Club	League	G.	IP.	W.	L.	Pct.	H.	R.	ER.	SO.	BB.	ERA.
1983—Spokane	Northwest	23	37	1	5	.167	44	33	22	31	21	5.35
1984—Reno	California	28	135⅓	11	4	.733	133	67	56	106	57	3.72
1985—Beaumont	Texas	23	104⅓	3	6	.333	109	65	55	93	60	4.74

Signed as free agent by San Diego Padres' organization, May 29, 1983.

NELSON BERNARD SIMMONS III

Born June 27, 1963, at Washington, D. C.
Height, 6.01. Weight, 195.
Throws right and bats left and righthanded.

Switch-hit home runs in one game, September 16, 1985.
Major League stolen bases: 1984 (1), 1985 (1). Total—2.
Led Florida State League in bases on balls received with 96 and intentional bases on balls received with 13 in 1982.

Year Club	League	Pos.	G.	AB.	R.	H.	2B.	3B.	HR.	RBI.	B.A.	PO.	A.	E.	F.A.
1981—Bristol	Appal.	OF	69	★267	36	79	14	1	10	45	.296	62	7	8	.896
1982—Lakeland	Fla. St.	OF	133	491	68	144	24	8	9	61	.293	178	7	●12	.939
1982—Birmingham	South.	OF	8	30	2	6	0	0	0	4	.200	11	0	0	1.000
1983—Birmingham†	South.	OF	118	404	57	110	17	1	11	64	.272	174	11	★14	.930
1984—Evansville	A. A.	OF	142	501	79	154	★41	5	22	83	.307	232	10	6	.976
1984—Detroit	Amer.	OF	9	30	4	13	2	0	0	3	.433	8	0	0	1.000
1985—Detroit‡	Amer.	OF	75	251	31	60	11	0	10	33	.239	67	2	4	.945
1985—Nashville	A. A.	OF	49	188	17	46	14	0	9	26	.245	93	7	1	.990
Major League Totals—2 Years		84	281	35	73	13	0	10	36	.260	75	2	4	.951

Selected by Detroit Tigers' organization in 2nd round of free-agent draft, June 8, 1981.
†On disabled list, September 7 to September 19, 1983.
‡On disabled list, April 9 to April 30, 1985.

TED LYLE SIMMONS

Born August 9, 1949, at Highland Park, Mich.
Height, 6.00. Weight, 200.
Throws right and bats left and righthanded.
Attended Wayne State University, Detroit, Mich. and
University of Michigan, Ann Arbor, Mich.

Tied major league record for most intentional bases on balls by switch-hitter, season (25), 1977.
Established National League records for most home runs by switch hitter, career (172); fewest errors by catcher, season, for leader in errors (15), 1975.
Tied National League record for most games, switch-hit home runs, season (1), April 17, 1975 and June 11, 1979; most games switch-hit home runs, league (2).
Established American League records for longest errorless game and most innings played by first baseman, game (25), May 8, finished May 9, 1984 (fielded 24⅓ innings).
Major League stolen bases: 1970 (2), 1971 (1), 1972 (1), 1973 (2), 1975 (1), 1977 (2), 1978 (1), 1980 (1), 1983 (4), 1984 (3), 1985 (1). Total—19.
Switch-hit home runs in one game three times: April 17, 1975, June 11, 1979 and May 2, 1982.
Led National League in intentional bases on balls received with 19 in 1976 and 25 in 1977.
Led National League in grounding into double plays with 29 in 1973.
Led National League catchers in putouts with 842 in 1972 and 888 in 1973.
Led National League catchers in assists with 78 in 1972 and 74 in 1973.
Led National League catchers in total chances with 928 in 1972, 975 in 1973 and 880 in 1975.
Led National League in passed balls with 25 in 1973, 28 in 1975 and 14 in 1979.
Led California League catchers in putouts with 984 in 1968.
Tied for California League lead in being hit by pitch with 9 in 1968.
Named catcher on THE SPORTING NEWS National League All-Star Team, 1977 through 1979.
Named catcher on THE SPORTING NEWS National League Silver Slugger team, 1980.
Named California League Most Valuable Player, 1968.
Received reported $50,000 bonus to sign with St. Louis Cardinals, 1967.

Year Club	League	Pos.	G.	AB.	R.	H.	2B.	3B.	HR.	RBI.	B.A.	PO.	A.	E.	F.A.
1967—Sarasota Cards.....	Gulf C.	C	6	20	5	7	1	1	2	8	.350	33	0	0	1.000
1967—Cedar Rapids.....	Midw.	OF-C	47	171	15	46	11	2	4	34	.269	119	8	3	.977
1968—Modesto	Calif.	*C-OF	136	493	86	163	30	2	28	*117	*.331	989	79	*16	.985
1968—St. Louis.....	Nat.	C	2	3	0	1	0	0	0	0	.333	3	1	0	1.000
1969—Tulsa.....	A. A.	C-3-O-1	129	499	80	158	33	4	16	88	.317	463	92	19	.967
1969—St. Louis†	Nat.	C	5	14	0	3	0	1	0	3	.214	22	0	1	.957
1970—Tulsa.....	A. A.	C	15	51	10	19	4	1	1	8	.373	99	7	0	1.000
1970—St. Louis.....	Nat.	C	82	284	29	69	8	2	3	24	.243	466	37	5	.990
1971—St. Louis‡	Nat.	C	133	510	64	155	32	4	7	77	.304	747	52	9	.989
1972—St. Louis.....	Nat.	C-1B	152	594	70	180	36	6	16	96	.303	967	93	13	.988
1973—St. Louis.....	Nat.	C-1B-OF	161	619	62	192	36	2	13	91	.310	932	78	14	.986
1974—St. Louis.....	Nat.	C-1B	152	599	66	163	33	6	20	103	.272	813	87	15	.984
1975—St. Louis.....	Nat.	*C-1B-OF	157	581	80	193	32	3	18	100	.332	818	64	*15	.983
1976—St. Louis.....	Nat.	C-1-O-3	150	546	60	159	35	3	5	75	.291	726	88	10	.988
1977—St. Louis.....	Nat.	C-OF	150	516	82	164	25	3	21	95	.318	683	75	10	.987
1978—St. Louis.....	Nat.	*C-OF	152	516	71	148	40	5	22	80	.287	703	*88	10	.988
1979—St. Louis§.....	Nat.	C	123	448	68	127	22	0	26	87	.283	606	69	10	.985
1980—St. Louis x	Nat.	C-OF	145	495	84	150	33	2	21	98	.303	528	71	10	.984
1981—Milwaukee.....	Amer.	C-1B	100	380	45	82	13	3	14	61	.216	333	41	8	.979
1982—Milwaukee.....	Amer.	C	137	539	73	145	29	0	23	97	.269	570	62	3	*.995
1983—Milwaukee y	Amer.	C	153	600	76	185	39	3	13	108	.308	395	41	11	.975
1984—Milwaukee.....	Amer.	1B-3B	132	497	44	110	23	2	4	52	.221	352	52	8	.981
1985—Milwaukee.....	Amer.	1B-C-3B	143	528	60	144	28	2	12	76	.273	291	26	3	.991
National League Totals—13 Years			1564	5725	736	1704	332	37	172	929	.298	8014	803	122	.986
American League Totals—5 Years			665	2544	298	666	132	10	66	394	.262	1941	222	33	.985
Major League Totals—18 Years			2229	8269	1034	2370	464	47	238	1323	.287	9955	1025	155	.986

Selected by St. Louis Cardinals' organization in 1st round (10th player selected) of free-agent draft, June 6, 1967.
†On military list, December 12, 1969 through May 9, 1970.
‡On military list, June 19 to July 4, 1971.
§On disabled list, June 25 to July 24, 1979.
xTraded with Pitchers Rollie Fingers and Pete Vuckovich to Milwaukee Brewers for Pitchers Lary Sorensen and Dave LaPoint and Outfielders Sixto Lezcano and David Green, December 12, 1980.
yGranted free agency, November 7, 1983; re-signed by Brewers, January 16, 1984.

DIVISION SERIES RECORD

Year Club	League	Pos.	G.	AB.	R.	H.	2B.	3B.	HR.	RBI.	B.A.	PO.	A.	E.	F.A.
1981—Milwaukee.....	Amer.	C	5	18	1	4	1	0	1	4	.222	23	2	1	.962

CHAMPIONSHIP SERIES RECORD

Year Club	League	Pos.	G.	AB.	R.	H.	2B.	3B.	HR.	RBI.	B.A.	PO.	A.	E.	F.A.
1982—Milwaukee.....	Amer.	C	5	18	3	3	0	0	0	1	.167	36	3	0	1.000

WORLD SERIES RECORD

Tied World Series record for fewest putouts by catcher, game (1), October 15, 1982.

Year Club	League	Pos.	G.	AB.	R.	H.	2B.	3B.	HR.	RBI.	B.A.	PO.	A.	E.	F.A.
1982—Milwaukee.....	Amer.	C	7	23	2	4	0	0	2	3	.174	28	2	1	.968

—DID YOU KNOW—

That the White Sox' Harold Baines hit .335 on the road in 1985?

Year League	Pos.	AB.	R.	H.	2B.	3B.	HR.	RBI.	B.A.	PO.	A.	E.	F.A.
1973—National	PH-C	1	0	0	0	0	0	0	.000	1	1	0	1.000
1977—National	C	3	0	0	0	0	0	0	.000	5	0	0	1.000
1978—National	C	3	0	1	0	0	0	0	.333	4	1	0	1.000
1981—American	PH	1	0	1	0	0	0	1	1.000	0	0	0	.000
1983—American	C	2	0	0	0	0	0	0	.000	4	0	0	1.000
All-Star Game Totals—5 Years		10	0	2	0	0	0	1	.200	14	2	0	1.000

Member of National League All-Star Team for 1972 and 1974 games; did not play.
Named to National League All-Star Team for 1979 game; replaced due to injury.

TODD ELDON SIMMONS

Born September 11, 1963, at Lakewood, Calif.
Height, 6.04. Weight, 210.
Throws and bats righthanded.
Attended California State University, Fullerton, Calif.

Year Club	League	G.	IP.	W.	L.	Pct.	H.	R.	ER.	SO.	BB.	ERA.
1984—Appleton†	Midwest	7	37	1	3	.250	46	30	28	22	14	6.81
1985—Reno	California	24	142	8	10	.444	133	70	54	117	73	3.42
1985—Las Vegas	P. Coast	6	5⅔	0	1	.000	8	11	7	5	9	11.12

Selected by Philadelphia Phillies' organization in 15th round of free-agent draft, June 8, 1981.
Selected by Chicago White Sox' organization in 4th round of free-agent draft, June 4, 1984.
†Traded with Pitchers LaMarr Hoyt and Kevin Kristan to San Diego Padres for Pitchers Tim Lollar and Bill Long, Third Baseman Luis Salazar and Shortstop Ozzie Guillen, December 6, 1984.

DOUGLAS RANDALL SISK
(Doug)

Born September 26, 1957, at Renton, Wash.
Height, 6.02. Weight, 210.
Throws and bats righthanded.
Attended Green River Community College, Auburn, Wash. and received bachelor of science degree
in criminal justice from Washington State University, Pullman, Wash.

Major League saves: 1982 (1), 1983 (11), 1984 (15), 1985 (2). Total—29.
Led Appalachian League pitchers in games started with 15 in 1980.

Year Club	League	G.	IP.	W.	L.	Pct.	H.	R.	ER.	SO.	BB.	ERA.
1980—Kingsport	Ap'lachian	15	*98	●8	5	.615	*91	46	29	41	45	2.66
1981—Lynchburg	Carolina	36	83	3	2	.600	78	35	30	61	32	3.25
1981—Jackson	Texas	14	25	3	0	1.000	23	11	10	15	12	3.60
1982—Jackson	Texas	44	138	11	8	.611	136	59	41	53	58	*2.67
1982—New York	National	8	8⅔	0	1	.000	5	1	1	4	4	1.04
1983—New York	National	67	104⅓	5	4	.556	88	38	26	33	59	2.24
1984—New York†	National	50	77⅔	1	3	.250	57	24	18	32	54	2.09
1985—New York	National	42	73	4	5	.444	86	48	43	26	40	5.30
1985—Tidewater	Int'national	4	15	0	2	.000	15	12	12	4	13	7.20
Major League Totals—4 Years		167	263⅔	10	13	.435	236	111	88	95	157	3.00

Signed as free agent by New York Mets' organization, June 10, 1980.
†On disabled list, August 9 to August 29, 1984.

JOEL PATRICK SKINNER

Born February 21, 1961, at San Diego, Calif.
Height, 6.04. Weight, 205.
Throws and bats righthanded.
Attended San Diego Mesa College, San Diego, Calif.
Son of Bob Skinner, outfielder-first baseman with Pittsburgh Pirates, Cincinnati Reds and St. Louis
Cardinals, 1954 through 1966; manager, Philadelphia Phillies, 1968 and 1969, manager,
San Diego Padres, 1977; coach, San Diego Padres, 1977; coach, California Angels, 1978;
and coach with Pittsburgh Pirates since 1979.

Major League stolen bases: 1984 (1).
Led American Association batters in strikeouts with 115 and tied for lead in grounding into double plays with 16 in 1985.
Led American Association catchers in total chances with 698 and double plays with 13 in 1985.
Tied for South Atlantic League lead in double plays by catchers with 7 in 1980.

Year Club	League	Pos.	G.	AB.	R.	H.	2B.	3B.	HR.	RBI.	B.A.	PO.	A.	E.	F.A.
1980—Shelby	S. Atl.	C	100	324	36	73	15	2	7	27	.225	536	63	18	.971
1981—Greenwood†‡	S. Atl.	C	117	428	48	114	25	2	11	63	.266	766	42	*22	.974
1982—Glens Falls	East.	C	120	422	49	107	11	6	7	65	.254	726	80	12	.985
1983—Denver	A. A.	C	108	361	55	94	15	5	12	50	.260	550	54	5	.992
1983—Chicago	Amer.	C	6	11	2	3	0	0	0	1	.273	20	4	1	.960
1984—Denver§	A. A.	C	42	141	27	40	6	0	10	27	.284	255	24	5	.982
1984—Chicago	Amer.	C	43	80	4	17	2	0	0	3	.213	171	11	2	.989
1985—Buffalo	A. A.	C	115	390	47	94	13	0	12	59	.241	*623	*65	10	.986
1985—Chicago	Amer.	C	22	44	9	15	4	1	1	5	.341	94	8	3	.971
Major League Totals—3 Years			71	135	15	35	6	1	1	9	.259	285	23	6	.981

Selected by Pittsburgh Pirates' organization in 36th round of free-agent draft, June 5, 1979.
†On disabled list, June 1 to June 13, 1981.
‡Selected by Chicago White Sox' organization in player compensation pool draft, February 2, 1982. (Chicago

received compensation for Philadelphia Phillies' signing of free agent Pitcher Ed Farmer, a Type A player, January 28, 1982.)
§On disabled list, July 23, 1984 through remainder of season.

MICHAEL ROSS SKINNER
(Mike)

Born August 5, 1964, at Teaneck, N.J.
Height, 6.01. Weight, 195.
Throws and bats righthanded.
Attended County College of Morris, Randolph Township,
N.J., and Jacksonville University, Jacksonville, Fla.
Tied for New York-Pennsylvania League lead in complete games with 7 in 1983.

Year Club	League	G.	IP.	W.	L.	Pct.	H.	R.	ER.	SO.	BB.	ERA.
1983—Bluefield	Ap'lachian	7	22⅔	2	1	.667	13	9	9	30	14	3.57
1984—Bluefield	Ap'lachian	3	14	1	1	.500	25	13	7	13	7	4.50
1984—Newark	NYP	11	79⅓	7	2	.778	65	25	18	55	25	2.04
1985—Hagerstown	Carolina	11	74	5	4	.556	69	40	37	70	16	4.50
1985—Charlotte	Southern	16	111⅓	11	1	*.917	97	37	32	70	43	2.59

Selected by Baltimore Orioles' organization in 12th round of free-agent draft, June 6, 1983.

JAMES MICHAEL SLATON
(Jim)

Born June 19, 1950, at Long Beach, Calif.
Height, 6.00. Weight, 185.
Throws and bats righthanded.
Attended Antelope Valley College, Lancaster, Calif.
Pitched 5-0 no-hit victory against Wichita, August 3, 1972.
Major League saves: 1982 (6), 1983 (5), 1985 (1). Total—12.

Year Club	League	G.	IP.	W.	L.	Pct.	H.	R.	ER.	SO.	BB.	ERA.
1969—Billings	Pioneer	2	8	1	0	1.000	1	0	0	16	0	0.00
1969—Clinton	Midwest	13	82	6	3	.667	65	27	26	83	34	2.85
1970—Clinton†	Midwest	2	18	1	1	.500	9	4	3	15	5	1.50
1971—Evansville	Am. Assoc.	4	32	1	0	1.000	22	9	5	26	9	1.39
1971—Milwaukee	American	26	148	10	8	.556	140	67	62	63	71	3.77
1972—Evansville	Am. Assoc.	16	114	11	2	.846	97	39	37	68	37	2.92
1972—Milwaukee	American	9	44	1	6	.143	50	31	27	17	21	5.52
1973—Milwaukee	American	38	276	13	15	.464	266	127	114	134	99	3.72
1974—Milwaukee	American	40	250	13	16	.448	255	117	109	126	102	3.92
1975—Milwaukee	American	37	217	11	18	.379	238	129	109	119	90	4.52
1976—Milwaukee	American	38	293	14	15	.483	*287	●126	112	138	94	3.44
1977—Milwaukee‡	American	32	221	10	14	.417	223	104	88	104	77	3.58
1978—Detroit§	American	35	234	17	11	.607	235	117	107	92	85	4.12
1979—Milwaukee	American	32	213	15	9	.625	229	95	86	80	54	3.63
1980—Milwaukee x	American	3	16	1	1	.500	17	10	8	4	5	4.50
1981—Milwaukee	American	24	117	5	7	.417	120	60	57	47	50	4.38
1982—Milwaukee y	American	39	117⅔	10	6	.625	117	48	43	59	41	3.29
1983—Milwaukee z	American	46	112⅓	14	6	.700	112	57	54	38	56	4.33
1984—California	American	32	163	7	10	.412	192	95	90	67	56	4.97
1985—California	American	29	148⅓	6	10	.375	162	82	72	60	63	4.37
Major League Totals—15 Years		460	2570⅓	147	152	.492	2643	1265	1138	1148	964	3.98

Selected by Seattle Pilots' organization in 14th round of free-agent draft, June 5, 1969.
†On military list, May 8, 1970 through remainder of season.
‡Traded with Pitcher Rich Folkers to Detroit Tigers for Outfielder Ben Oglivie, December 9, 1977.
§Granted free agency, November 2, 1978; signed by Milwaukee Brewers, November 28, 1978.
xOn disabled list, May 25 to October 1, 1980.
yOn disabled list, April 1 to April 23, 1982.
zTraded to California Angels for Outfielder Bobby Clark, December 20, 1983.

DIVISION SERIES RECORD

Year Club	League	G.	IP.	W.	L.	Pct.	H.	R.	ER.	SO.	BB.	ERA.
1981—Milwaukee	American	4	6	0	0	.000	6	2	2	2	0	3.00

CHAMPIONSHIP SERIES RECORD

Year Club	League	G.	IP.	W.	L.	Pct.	H.	R.	ER.	SO.	BB.	ERA.
1982—Milwaukee	American	2	4⅔	0	0	.000	3	2	1	3	1	1.93

WORLD SERIES RECORD

Year Club	League	G.	IP.	W.	L.	Pct.	H.	R.	ER.	SO.	BB.	ERA.
1982—Milwaukee	American	2	2⅔	1	0	1.000	1	0	0	1	2	0.00

ALL-STAR GAME RECORD
Member of American League All-Star Team in 1977; did not play.

DONALD MARTIN SLAUGHT
(Don)

Born September 11, 1959, at Long Beach, Calif.
Height, 6.00. Weight, 185.
Throws and bats righthanded.
Attended El Camino College, Torrance, Calif., and
University of California, Los Angeles, Calif.
Major League stolen bases: 1983 (3), 1985 (5). Total—8.

Year Club League	Pos.	G.	AB.	R.	H.	2B.	3B.	HR.	RBI.	B.A.	PO.	A.	E.	F.A.
1980—Fort Myers........... Fla. St.	C	50	176	13	46	9	0	2	16	.261	175	34	4	.981
1981—Jacksonville......... South.	C-1B	96	379	45	127	21	2	6	44	.335	482	61	9	.984
1981—Omaha†................. A. A.	C	22	71	10	21	4	0	2	8	.296	91	7	3	.970
1982—Omaha‡................. A. A.	C	53	206	29	55	10	1	4	16	.267	216	25	5	.980
1982—Kansas City.......... Amer.	C	43	115	14	32	6	0	3	8	.278	156	7	1	.994
1983—Kansas City§........ Amer.	C	83	276	21	86	13	4	0	28	.312	299	18	12	.964
1984—Kansas City x ...... Amer.	C	124	409	48	108	27	4	4	42	.264	547	44	11	.982
1985—Texas y............... Amer.	C	102	343	34	96	17	4	8	35	.280	550	33	6	.990
Major League Totals—4 Years...............		352	1143	117	322	63	12	15	113	.282	1552	102	30	.982

Selected by Milwaukee Brewers' organization in 19th round of free-agent draft, June 5, 1979.
Selected by Kansas City Royals' organization in 7th round of free-agent draft, June 3, 1980.
†On disabled list, August 16 to September 29, 1981.
‡On disabled list, April 21 to May 15, 1982.
§On disabled list, May 16 to June 1, 1983.
xTraded to Texas Rangers as part of a six-player, four-team deal in which Kansas City Royals acquired Catcher Jim Sundberg from Milwaukee Brewers, New York Mets' organization acquired Pitcher Frank Wills from Kansas City, Milwaukee acquired Pitcher Danny Darwin and a player to be named later from Texas and Pitcher Tim Leary from New York, January 18, 1985; Milwaukee organization acquired Catcher Bill Hance from Texas to complete deal, January 30, 1985.
yOn disabled list, August 9 to August 26, 1985.

CHAMPIONSHIP SERIES RECORD

Year Club League	Pos.	G.	AB.	R.	H.	2B.	3B.	HR.	RBI.	B.A.	PO.	A.	E.	F.A.
1984—Kansas City........... Amer.	C	3	11	0	4	0	0	0	0	.364	17	0	3	.850

ROY FREDERICK SMALLEY III

Born October 25, 1952, at Los Angeles, Calif.
Height, 6.01. Weight, 182.
Throws right and bats left and righthanded.
Attended Los Angeles City Community College, Los Angeles, Calif., and
University of Southern California, Los Angeles, Calif.
Son of Roy Smalley, Jr., infielder with Chicago Cubs, Milwaukee Braves and
Philadelphia Phillies, 1948 through 1958; nephew of Gene Mauch, manager of California Angels.

Tied major league record for most strikeouts, two consecutive games (8), August 28 and 29, 1976 (26 innings).
Major League stolen bases: 1975 (4), 1976 (2), 1977 (5), 1978 (2), 1979 (2), 1980 (3), 1983 (3), 1984 (3). Total—24.
Switch-hit home runs in one game, September 5, 1982.
Led American League in sacrifice hits with 25 in 1976.
Led American League shortstops in double plays with 116 in 1977, with 121 in 1978 and with 144 in 1979.
Led American League shortstops in putouts with 296 in 1979.
Led American League shortstops in total chances with 792 in 1977, 839 in 1978 and 897 in 1979.
Named shortstop on THE SPORTING NEWS American League All-Star Team, 1979.
Received reported $100,000 bonus to sign with Texas Rangers, 1974.

Year Club League	Pos.	G.	AB.	R.	H.	2B.	3B.	HR.	RBI.	B.A.	PO.	A.	E.	F.A.
1974—Pittsfield .... East.	SS	125	406	74	102	22	5	14	42	.251	146	376	*42	.926
1975—Spokane .... P. C.	SS-2B	43	162	26	55	8	1	2	19	.340	88	151	10	.960
1975—Texas..................... Amer.	SS-2B-C	78	250	22	57	8	0	3	33	.228	108	232	20	.944
1976—Tex.†-Minn. .... Amer.	SS-2B	144	513	61	133	18	3	3	44	.259	274	447	26	.965
1977—Minnesota............. Amer.	SS	150	584	93	135	21	5	6	56	.231	255	*504	33	.958
1978—Minnesota............. Amer.	SS	158	586	80	160	31	3	19	77	.273	*287	*527	25	.970
1979—Minnesota............. Amer.	*SS-1B	●162	621	94	168	28	3	24	95	.271	305	*572	29	.968
1980—Minnesota............. Amer.	SS-1B	133	486	64	135	24	1	12	63	.278	226	448	17	.990
1981—Minnesota............. Amer.	SS-1B	56	167	24	44	7	1	7	22	.263	62	89	8	.950
1982—Minn.‡-N.Y. .... Amer.	SS-3B-2B	146	499	57	127	15	2	20	67	.255	142	367	15	.971
1983—New York.............. Amer.	SS-3B-1B	130	451	70	124	24	1	18	62	.275	289	295	21	.965
1984—N.Y.§-Chic. x .... Amer.	3B-SS-1B	114	344	32	73	12	1	11	39	.212	90	158	16	.939
1985—Minnesota............. Amer.	SS-3B-1B	129	388	57	100	20	0	12	45	.258	70	133	3	.985
Major League Totals—11 Years...............		1400	4889	654	1256	208	20	135	603	.257	2108	3772	213	.965

Selected by Montreal Expos' organization in 35th round of free-agent draft, June 4, 1970.
Selected by Boston Red Sox' organization in secondary phase of free-agent draft, January 13, 1971.
Selected by St. Louis Cardinals' organization in secondary phase of free-agent draft, June 8, 1971.
Selected by Boston Red Sox' organization in secondary phase of free-agent draft, January 12, 1972.
Selected by Texas Rangers' organization in 1st round (first player selected) of free-agent draft, January 9, 1974.
†Traded with Pitchers Bill Singer and Jim Gideon, Infielder Mike Cubbage, and $250,000 cash to Minnesota Twins for Pitcher Bert Blyleven and Shortstop Danny Thompson, June 1, 1976.
‡Traded to New York Yankees for Pitchers Ron Davis and Paul Boris, Shortstop Greg Gagne and a reported $400,000, April 10, 1982.
§Traded to Chicago White Sox for two players to be named later, July 18, 1984; New York Yankees' organization acquired Pitchers Kevin Hickey and Doug Drabek to complete deal, August 13, 1984.
xTraded to Minnesota Twins for First Baseman Randall Stuart (Randy) Johnson and outfielder Ron Scheer, February 19, 1985.

Year League	Pos.	AB.	R.	H.	2B.	3B.	HR.	RBI.	B.A.	PO.	A.	E.	F.A.
1979—American	SS	3	0	0	0	0	0	0	.000	2	2	0	1.000

BRYN NELSON SMITH

First name pronounced Brin.

Born August 11, 1955, at Marietta, Ga.
Height, 6.02. Weight, 200.
Throws and bats righthanded.
Attended Allan Hancock College, Santa Maria, Calif.

Major League saves: 1982 (3), 1983 (3). Total—6.
Tied for American Association lead in complete games with 9 in 1981.
Tied for Southern League lead in complete games with 16 in 1977 and 12 in 1980.
Named American Association Pitcher of the Year, 1981.

Year Club	League	G.	IP.	W.	L.	Pct.	H.	R.	ER.	SO.	BB.	ERA.
1975—Miami	Florida St.	26	139	11	7	.611	117	48	33	93	59	2.14
1976—Miami	Florida St.	23	164	10	10	.500	140	72	51	119	62	2.80
1977—Charlotte†	Southern	27	*206	*15	11	.577	*195	78	63	103	57	2.75
1978—Denver	Am. Assoc.	11	54	0	6	.000	79	48	41	25	14	6.83
1978—Memphis‡	Southern	11	69	4	6	.400	53	28	19	48	31	2.48
1979—Memphis	Southern	27	184	11	10	.524	175	80	69	115	74	3.38
1980—Memphis	Southern	27	181	10	9	.526	179	75	56	110	54	2.78
1981—Denver	Am. Assoc.	29	*183	*15	5	*.750	166	80	62	127	42	3.03
1981—Montreal	National	7	13	1	0	1.000	14	4	4	9	3	2.77
1982—Wichita	Am. Assoc.	3	23⅔	2	0	1.000	21	5	5	15	2	1.90
1982—Montreal	National	47	79⅓	2	4	.333	81	43	37	50	23	4.20
1983—Montreal	National	49	155⅓	6	11	.353	142	51	43	101	43	2.49
1984—Montreal	National	28	179	12	13	.480	178	72	66	101	51	3.32
1985—Montreal	National	32	222⅓	18	5	.783	193	85	72	127	41	2.91
Major League Totals—5 Years		163	649	39	33	.542	608	255	222	388	161	3.08

Selected by St. Louis Cardinals' organization in the 49th round of free-agent draft, June 5, 1973.
Signed as free agent by Baltimore Orioles' organization, December 18, 1974.
†Traded with Pitchers Rudy May and Randy Miller by Baltimore Orioles' organization to Montreal Expos' organization for Pitchers Don Stanhouse and Joe Kerrigan and Outfielder Gary Roenicke, December 7, 1977.
‡On disabled list, August 5 to August 17, 1978.

DAVID LEE SMITH

Born October 20, 1962, at Lynwood, Calif.
Height, 6.02. Weight, 175.
Throws and bats righthanded.
Attended University of California, Riverside, Calif.

Year Club	League	Pos.	G.	AB.	R.	H.	2B.	3B.	HR.	RBI.	B.A.	PO.	A.	E.	F.A.
1984—Newark	NYP	SS-2B-3B	71	229	38	55	9	1	1	31	.240	101	223	22	.936
1985—Hagerstown	Carol.	SS	122	393	48	92	16	1	0	29	.234	186	*394	22	*.963

Selected by Baltimore Orioles' organization in 6th round of free-agent draft, June 4, 1984.

DAVID STANLEY SMITH JR.
(Dave)

Born January 21, 1955, at San Francisco, Calif.
Height, 6.01. Weight, 195.
Throws and bats righthanded.
Attended San Diego State University, San Diego, Calif.

Major League saves: 1980 (10), 1981 (8), 1982 (11), 1983 (6), 1984 (5), 1985 (27). Total—67.

Year Club	League	G.	IP.	W.	L.	Pct.	H.	R.	ER.	SO.	BB.	ERA.
1976—Covington	Ap'lachian	15	97	5	5	.500	80	40	29	71	28	2.69
1977—Cocoa	Florida St.	14	93	7	5	.583	97	40	32	81	31	3.10
1977—Columbus	Southern	9	54	3	5	.375	52	2	21	29	24	3.50
1978—Columbus	Southern	26	181	10	13	.435	170	89	70	114	88	3.48
1979—Charleston	Int'national	34	160	7	8	.467	159	80	65	90	44	3.66
1980—Houston	National	57	103	7	5	.583	90	24	22	85	32	1.92
1981—Houston	National	42	75	5	3	.625	54	26	23	52	23	2.76
1982—Houston†	National	49	63⅓	5	4	.556	69	30	27	28	31	3.84
1983—Houston	National	42	72⅔	3	1	.750	72	32	25	41	36	3.10
1984—Houston	National	53	77⅓	5	4	.556	60	22	19	45	20	2.21
1985—Houston	National	64	79⅓	9	5	.643	69	26	20	40	17	2.27
Major League Totals—6 Years		307	470⅔	34	22	.607	414	160	136	291	159	2.60

Selected by Houston Astros' organization in 8th round of free-agent draft, June 8, 1976.
†On disabled list, June 27 to July 18, 1982.

DIVISION SERIES RECORD

Year Club	League	G.	IP.	W.	L.	Pct.	H.	R.	ER.	SO.	BB.	ERA.
1981—Houston	National	2	2⅓	0	0	.000	2	1	1	4	0	3.86

CHAMPIONSHIP SERIES RECORD

Year Club	League	G.	IP.	W.	L.	Pct.	H.	R.	ER.	SO.	BB.	ERA.
1980—Houston	National	3	2⅓	1	0	1.000	4	1	1	4	2	3.86

DAVID WAYNE SMITH

Born August 30, 1957, at Tomball, Tex.
Height, 6.01. Weight, 190.
Throws and bats righthanded.
Attended Lamar University, Beaumont, Tex.

Year Club	League	G.	IP.	W.	L.	Pct.	H.	R.	ER.	SO.	BB.	ERA.
1979—Grays Harbor	Northwest	14	70	3	5	.375	81	40	34	60	31	4.37
1980—Lynchburg	Carolina	29	113	8	7	.533	121	60	42	63	63	3.35
1981—Lynchburg†	Carolina	28	61	5	2	.714	59	25	16	41	26	2.36
1981—Jackson†	Texas	24	56	4	4	.500	55	32	28	42	25	4.50
1982—Holyoke	Eastern	39	142⅔	4	9	.308	154	80	54	104	70	3.41
1983—Nashua	Eastern	24	36⅓	2	2	.500	32	9	8	30	15	1.98
1983—Edmonton	P. Coast	23	38⅓	6	3	.667	40	24	22	26	23	5.17
1984—Edmonton	P. Coast	50	69	6	3	.667	71	30	24	37	30	3.13
1984—California	American	1	1	0	0	.000	4	2	2	0	0	18.00
1985—Edmonton	P. Coast	42	72	6	7	.462	78	32	30	29	20	3.75
1985—California	American	4	5	0	0	.000	5	4	4	3	1	7.20
Major League Totals—2 Years		5	6	0	0	.000	9	6	6	3	1	9.00

Selected by New York Mets' organization in 27th round of free-agent draft, June 5, 1979.
†Drafted by Salt Lake City (California Angels' organization), December 8, 1981.

KENNETH EARL SMITH
(Ken)

Born Feburary 12, 1958, at Youngstown, O.
Height, 6.01. Weight, 195.
Throws right and bats lefthanded.
Attended Youngstown State University, Youngstown, O.

Major League stolen bases: 1983 (1).
Led International League batters in strikeouts with 106 in 1980.
Led Southern League in bases on balls received with 102 in 1979.
Led International League first basemen in total chances with 1,228 and double plays with 121 in 1984.
Led International League first basemen in putouts with 1,158, assists with 84 and double plays with 95 in 1980.

Year Club	League	Pos.	G.	AB.	R.	H.	2B.	3B.	HR.	RBI.	B.A.	PO.	A.	E.	F.A.
1976—Bradenton Brav...	Gulf C.	OF-1B	32	94	24	24	3	1	1	12	.255	78	6	4	.955
1977—Greenwood†	W. Car.	OF-1B	67	212	38	64	7	0	1	25	.302	89	5	4	.959
1978—Savannah	South.	OF	138	462	55	110	19	5	2	40	.238	225	10	10	.959
1979—Savannah	South.	1B-OF	141	449	71	112	12	4	10	51	.249	1188	85	7	.995
1980—Richmond	Int.	1-O-2-3	132	418	61	103	17	4	12	53	.246	1167	86	15	.988
1981—Richmond	Int.	1B-OF	129	478	64	128	9	6	11	60	.268	1062	84	12	.990
1981—Atlanta	Nat.	1B	5	3	0	1	1	0	0	0	.333	6	1	0	1.000
1982—Atlanta	Nat.	1B-OF	48	41	6	12	1	0	0	3	.293	15	1	0	1.000
1982—Richmond	Int.	OF	43	129	24	34	3	0	8	25	.264	27	2	1	.967
1983—Atlanta	Nat.	1B	30	12	2	2	0	0	1	2	.167	27	6	0	1.000
1983—Richmond‡	Int.	1B-OF	52	174	36	49	8	2	4	31	.282	281	16	2	.993
1984—Richmond	Int.	1B	136	453	72	123	17	4	9	59	.272	*1159	56	*13	.989
1985—Richmond	Int.	1B-OF	22	36	8	6	0	0	1	7	.167	98	5	3	.972
1985—Greenville§	South.	OF-1B-C	66	183	38	55	11	1	10	43	.301	177	9	1	.995
Major League Totals—3 Years			83	56	8	15	2	0	1	5	.268	48	8	0	1.000

Selected by Atlanta Braves' organization in 1st round (third player selected) of free-agent draft, June 8, 1976.
†On disabled list, April 27 to June 24, 1977.
‡Granted free agency, October 20, 1983; re-signed by Braves, January 23, 1984.
§Granted free agency, October 15, 1985.

LEE ARTHUR SMITH

Born December 4, 1957, at Jamestown, La.
Height, 6.05. Weight, 220.
Throws and bats righthanded.
Attended Northwestern State University, Natchitoches, La.

Major League saves: 1981 (1), 1982 (17), 1983 (29), 1984 (33), 1985 (33). Total—113.
Led National League in games finished in relief with 57 in 1985 and tied for lead with 56 in 1983.
Led National League in saves with 29 in 1983.
Tied for American Association lead in wild pitches with 16 in 1980.
Named National League co-Fireman of the Year by THE SPORTING NEWS, 1983.

Year Club	League	G.	IP.	W.	L.	Pct.	H.	R.	ER.	SO.	BB.	ERA.
1975—Bradenton Cubs	Gulf Coast	10	62	3	5	.375	35	23	16	35	*49	2.32
1976—Pompano Beach	Florida St.	26	101	4	8	.333	120	76	60	52	74	5.35
1977—Pompano Beach	Florida St.	26	130	10	4	.714	131	67	62	82	85	4.29
1978—Midland	Texas	30	155	8	10	.444	161	122	103	71	*128	5.98
1979—Midland	Texas	35	104	9	5	.643	122	65	57	46	85	4.93
1980—Wichita	Am. Assoc.	50	90	4	7	.364	70	49	37	63	56	3.70
1980—Chicago	National	18	22	2	0	1.000	21	9	7	17	14	2.86
1981—Chicago	National	40	67	3	6	.333	57	31	26	50	31	3.49
1982—Chicago	National	72	117	2	5	.286	105	38	35	99	37	2.69
1983—Chicago	National	66	103⅓	4	10	.286	70	23	19	91	41	1.65
1984—Chicago	National	69	101	9	7	.563	98	42	41	86	35	3.65
1985—Chicago	National	65	97⅔	7	4	.636	87	35	33	112	32	3.04
Major League Totals—6 Years		330	508	27	32	.458	438	178	161	455	190	2.85

Selected by Chicago Cubs' organization in 2nd round of free-agent draft, June 4, 1975.

CHAMPIONSHIP SERIES RECORD

Year Club	League	G.	IP.	W.	L.	Pct.	H.	R.	ER.	SO.	BB.	ERA.
1984—Chicago	National	2	2	0	1	.000	3	2	2	3	0	9.00

ALL-STAR GAME RECORD

Year League	IP.	W.	L.	Pct.	H.	R.	ER.	SO.	BB.	ERA.
1983—National	1	0	0	.000	2	2	1	1	0	9.00

LEROY PURDY SMITH III
(Roy)

Born September 6, 1961, at Mt. Vernon, N.Y.
Height, 6.03. Weight, 205.
Throws and bats righthanded.
Attended Fordham University, Bronx, N.Y.

Tied for Carolina League lead in shutouts with 3 in 1980.
Named Carolina League Pitcher of the Year, 1980.

Year Club	League	G.	IP.	W.	L.	Pct.	H.	R.	ER.	SO.	BB.	ERA.
1979—Helena	Pioneer	5	36	5	0	1.000	21	16	10	42	16	2.50
1980—Peninsula	Carolina	27	163	*17	6	.739	101	54	47	134	63	2.60
1981—Reading	Eastern	27	161	11	8	.579	123	92	79	117	97	4.42
1982—Reading†	Eastern	26	166	10	8	.556	141	81	71	122	82	3.85
1983—Charleston	Int'national	27	155½	6	8	.429	166	101	89	95	75	5.16
1984—Maine	Int'national	12	80⅔	5	4	.556	77	47	39	48	29	4.35
1984—Cleveland	American	22	86⅓	5	5	.500	91	49	44	55	40	4.59
1985—Maine	Int'national	15	109⅓	10	4	.714	84	33	29	65	29	2.39
1985—Cleveland‡§	American	12	62⅓	1	4	.200	84	40	37	28	17	5.34
Major League Totals—2 Years		34	148⅔	6	9	.400	175	89	81	83	57	4.90

Selected by Philadelphia Phillies' organization in 3rd round of free-agent draft, June 5, 1979.

†Traded with Pitcher Jerry Reed and Outfielder Wil Culmer to Cleveland Indians for Pitcher John Denny, September 12, 1982.

‡On disabled list, July 3 to August 1, 1985; included rehabilitation disability assignment to Maine, July 27 to July 30, 1985.

§Traded with Pitcher Ramon Romero to Minnesota Twins for Pitchers Ken Schrom and Bryan Oelkers, January 7, 1986.

LONNIE SMITH

Born December 22, 1955, at Chicago, Ill.
Height, 5.09. Weight, 170.
Throws and bats righthanded.

Tied major league record for fewest double plays by outfielder, season, for leader in double plays (4), 1983.
Tied modern National League record for most stolen bases, game, (5), September 4, 1982.
Major League stolen bases: 1978 (4), 1979 (2), 1980 (33), 1981 (21), 1982 (68), 1983 (43), 1984 (50), 1985 (52). Total—273.
Led National League in being hit by pitch with 9 in 1982 and 1984 and tied for lead with 9 in 1983.
Tied for National League lead in caught stealing with 26 in 1982.
Tied for National League lead in double plays by outfielders with 4 in 1983.
Led American Association in stolen bases with 66 and caught stealing with 19 in 1978.
Led Western Carolinas League in stolen bases with 56 and tied for lead in caught stealing with 14 in 1975.
Led American Association outfielders in double plays with 5 in 1978.
Named National League Rookie Player of the Year by THE SPORTING NEWS, 1980.
Named outfielder on THE SPORTING NEWS National League All-Star Team, 1982.

Year Club	League	Pos.	G.	AB.	R.	H.	2B.	3B.	HR.	RBI.	B.A.	PO.	A.	E.	F.A.
1974—Auburn	NYP	OF	61	210	48	60	10	4	5	27	.286	143	6	●9	.943
1975—Spartanburg	W. Car.	OF	131	465	*114	*150	23	4	7	40	.323	*317	9	11	.967
1976—Oklahoma City	A. A.	OF	134	483	*93	149	24	9	8	54	.308	200	4	*14	.936
1977—Oklahoma City	A. A.	OF	125	477	91	132	14	10	4	41	.277	231	8	*13	.948
1978—Oklahoma City†	A. A.	OF	125	480	103	151	20	5	7	43	.315	274	*21	*12	.961
1978—Philadelphia	Nat.	OF	17	4	6	0	0	0	0	0	.000	5	1	0	1.000
1979—Oklahoma City	A. A.	OF	110	451	*106	149	26	9	7	44	.330	268	13	*12	.959
1979—Philadelphia	Nat.	OF	17	30	4	5	2	0	0	3	.167	19	1	0	1.000
1980—Philadelphia	Nat.	OF	100	298	69	101	14	4	3	20	.339	121	2	4	.969
1981—Philadelphia‡	Nat.	OF	62	176	40	57	14	3	2	11	.324	91	10	3	.971
1982—St. Louis	Nat.	OF	156	592	*120	182	35	8	8	69	.307	303	●16	10	.970
1983—St. Louis§	Nat.	OF	130	492	83	158	31	5	8	45	.321	225	14	*15	.941
1984—St. Louis	Nat.	OF	145	504	77	126	20	4	6	49	.250	184	*18	●11	.948
1985—St. Louis x	Nat.	OF	28	96	15	25	2	2	0	7	.260	43	1	0	1.000
1985—Kansas City	Amer.	OF	120	448	77	115	23	4	6	41	.257	195	10	9	.958
National League Totals—8 Years			655	2192	414	654	118	26	27	204	.298	991	63	43	.961
American League Totals—1 Year			120	448	77	115	23	4	6	41	.257	195	10	9	.958
Major League Totals—8 Years			775	2640	491	769	141	30	33	245	.291	1186	73	52	.960

Selected by Philadelphia Phillies' organization in 1st round (third player selected) of free-agent draft, June 5, 1974.

†On disabled list, April 14 to April 25, 1978.

‡Traded with a player to be named later to Cleveland Indians for Catcher Bo Diaz, November 20, 1981; Traded by Cleveland to St. Louis Cardinals for Pitchers Lary Sorensen and Silvio Martinez, November 20, 1981. Cleveland organization acquired Pitcher Scott Munninghoff to complete first deal, December 9, 1981.

§On disabled list, June 11 to July 8, 1983.
xTraded to Kansas City Royals for Outfielder John Morris, May 17, 1985.

DIVISION SERIES RECORD

Year	Club	League	Pos.	G.	AB.	R.	H.	2B.	3B.	HR.	RBI.	B.A.	PO.	A.	E.	F.A.
1981—Philadelphia		Nat.	OF	5	19	1	5	1	0	0	0	.263	6	1	0	1.000

CHAMPIONSHIP SERIES RECORD

Tied Championship Series record for most clubs, total Series (3).

Year	Club	League	Pos.	G.	AB.	R.	H.	2B.	3B.	HR.	RBI.	B.A.	PO.	A.	E.	F.A.
1980—Philadelphia		Nat.	PR-OF	3	5	2	3	0	0	0	0	.600	2	1	0	1.000
1982—St. Louis		Nat.	OF	3	11	1	3	0	0	0	1	.273	2	0	0	1.000
1985—Kansas City		Amer.	OF	7	28	2	7	2	0	0	1	.250	8	3	1	.917
Championship Series Totals—3 Years				13	44	5	13	2	0	0	2	.295	12	4	1	.941

WORLD SERIES RECORD

Tied World Series record for most clubs, total Series (3).

Year	Club	League	Pos.	G.	AB.	R.	H.	2B.	3B.	HR.	RBI.	B.A.	PO.	A.	E.	F.A.
1980—Philadelphia		Nat.	PR-O-DH	6	19	2	5	1	0	0	1	.263	4	1	0	1.000
1982—St. Louis		Nat.	OF-DH	7	28	6	9	4	1	0	1	.321	11	0	0	1.000
1985—Kansas City		Amer.	OF	7	27	4	9	3	0	0	4	.333	7	2	0	1.000
World Series Totals—3 Years				20	74	12	23	8	1	0	6	.311	22	3	0	1.000

ALL-STAR GAME RECORD

Year	League	Pos.	AB.	R.	H.	2B.	3B.	HR.	RBI.	B.A.	PO.	A.	E.	F.A.
1982—National		OF	0	0	0	0	0	0	0	.000	1	0	0	1.000

MICHAEL ANTHONY SMITH
(Mike)

Born February 23, 1961, at Jackson, Miss.
Height, 6.01. Weight, 195.
Throws right and bats right and lefthanded.
Attended Utica Junior College, Utica, Miss.

Led Florida State League in saves with 21 in 1982.

Year	Club	League	G.	IP.	W.	L.	Pct.	H.	R.	ER.	SO.	BB.	ERA.
1981—Billings		Pioneer	22	46	5	5	.500	39	21	7	52	19	1.37
1982—Tampa		Florida St.	48	80⅓	7	1	.875	55	17	11	80	42	1.23
1983—Waterbury†		Eastern	22	28⅔	2	5	.286	18	13	9	16	25	2.83
1984—Cincinnati		National	8	10⅓	1	0	1.000	12	6	6	7	5	5.23
1984—Wichita		Am. Assoc.	12	18	3	2	.600	17	8	8	20	13	4.00
1984—Vermont		Eastern	35	51	3	3	.500	51	28	19	49	20	3.35
1985—Denver		Am. Assoc.	47	68⅔	5	4	.556	65	40	37	67	38	4.85
1985—Cincinnati		National	2	3⅓	0	0	.000	2	2	2	2	1	5.40
Major League Totals—2 Years			10	13⅔	1	0	1.000	14	8	8	9	6	5.27

Signed as free agent by Cincinnati Reds' organization, May 11, 1981.
†On disabled list, June 28, 1983 through remainder of season.

OSBORNE EARL SMITH
(Ozzie)

Born December 26, 1954, at Mobile, Ala.
Height, 5.10. Weight, 150.
Throws right and bats left and righthanded.
Received degree from California Polytechnic State University, San Luis Obispo, Calif.

Established major league record for most assists by shortstop, season (621), 1980.
Tied major league records for most years with 500 or more assists, shortstop (6); most double plays by shortstop, extra-inning game (6), August 25, 1979 (19 innings).
Tied National League records for most years (5) and most consecutive years (4) leading league in assists, shortstop; most years leading league in chances accepted, shortstop (5).
Major League stolen bases: 1978 (40), 1979 (28), 1980 (57), 1981 (22), 1982 (25), 1983 (34), 1984 (35), 1985 (31) Total—272.
Led National League in sacrifice hits with 28 in 1978 and 23 in 1980.
Led National League shortstops in total chances with 933 in 1980, 658 in 1981, 844 in 1983 and 827 in 1985.
Led National League shortstops in double plays with 113 in 1980 and tied for lead with 94 in 1984.
Led Northwest League in stolen bases with 30 in 1977.
Led Northwest League shortstops in double plays with 40 in 1977.
Named shortstop on THE SPORTING NEWS National League All-Star Team, 1982, 1984 and 1985.
Named shortstop on THE SPORTING NEWS National League All-Star fielding team, 1980 through 1985.

Year	Club	League	Pos.	G.	AB.	R.	H.	2B.	3B.	HR.	RBI.	B.A.	PO.	A.	E.	F.A.
1977—Walla Walla		N'west	SS	●68	★287	★69	87	10	2	1	35	.303	130	★254	23	★.943
1978—San Diego		Nat.	SS	159	590	69	152	17	6	1	46	.258	264	548	25	.970
1979—San Diego		Nat.	SS	156	587	77	124	18	6	0	27	.211	256	★555	20	.976
1980—San Diego		Nat.	SS	158	609	67	140	18	5	0	35	.230	★288	★621	24	.974
1981—San Diego†		Nat.	SS	●110	★450	53	100	11	2	0	21	.222	220	★422	16	★.976
1982—St. Louis		Nat.	SS	140	488	58	121	24	1	2	43	.248	279	★535	13	★.984
1983—St. Louis		Nat.	SS	159	552	69	134	30	6	3	50	.243	★304	519	21	.975
1984—St. Louis‡		Nat.	SS	124	412	53	106	20	5	1	44	.257	233	437	12	★.982
1985—St. Louis		Nat.	SS	158	537	70	148	22	3	6	54	.276	264	★549	14	★.983
Major League Totals—8 Years				1164	4225	516	1025	160	34	13	320	.243	2108	4186	145	.977

Selected by Detroit Tigers' organization in 7th round of free-agent draft, June 8, 1976.
Selected by San Diego Padres' organization in 4th round of free-agent draft, June 7, 1977.
†Traded to St. Louis Cardinals for Shortstop Garry Templeton, February 11, 1982.
‡On disabled list, July 14 to August 19, 1984.

CHAMPIONSHIP SERIES RECORD

Established National League Championship Series records for highest batting average (.435) and most hits (10), six-game Series, 1985.
Tied National League Championship Series record for most singles, six-game Series (7), 1985.

Year Club	League	Pos.	G.	AB.	R.	H.	2B.	3B.	HR.	RBI.	B.A.	PO.	A.	E.	F.A.
1982—St. Louis	Nat.	SS	3	9	0	5	0	0	0	3	.556	4	11	0	1.000
1985—St. Louis	Nat.	SS	6	23	4	10	1	1	1	3	.435	6	16	0	1.000
Championship Series Totals—2 Years			9	32	4	15	1	1	1	6	.469	10	27	0	1.000

WORLD SERIES RECORD

Established World Series record for most putouts by shortstop, seven-game Series (22), 1982.
Tied World Series record for fewest chances accepted, shortstop, game (0), October 23, 1985.

Year Club	League	Pos.	G.	AB.	R.	H.	2B.	3B.	HR.	RBI.	B.A.	PO.	A.	E.	F.A.
1982—St. Louis	Nat.	SS	7	24	3	5	0	0	0	1	.208	22	11	0	1.000
1985—St. Louis	Nat.	SS	7	23	1	2	0	0	0	0	.087	10	16	1	.963
World Series Totals—2 Years			14	47	4	7	0	0	0	1	.149	32	33	1	.985

ALL-STAR GAME RECORD

Year League	Pos.	AB.	R.	H.	2B.	3B.	HR.	RBI.	B.A.	PO.	A.	E.	F.A.
1981—National	SS	0	0	0	0	0	0	0	.000	1	0	0	1.000
1982—National	PR-SS	0	0	0	0	0	0	0	.000	0	1	0	1.000
1983—National	SS	2	1	1	0	0	0	0	.500	0	0	0	.000
1984—National	SS	3	0	0	0	0	0	0	.000	3	0	0	1.000
1985—National	SS	4	0	0	0	0	0	0	.000	1	3	0	1.000
All-Star Game Totals—5 Years		9	1	1	0	0	0	0	.111	5	4	0	1.000

PATRICK KEITH SMITH
(Known by middle name.)

Born October 20, 1961, at Los Angeles, Calif.
Height, 6.01. Weight, 175.
Throws and bats righthanded.
Attended College of the Canyons, Valencia, Calif.
Brother of Dave Smith, first baseman in Seattle Mariners' organization.

Led Southern League in sacrifice hits with 17 in 1984.
Led New York-Pennsylvania League in sacrifice hits with 9 in 1980.
Led Southern League shortstops in total chances with 724 and double plays with 97 in 1984.

Year Club	League	Pos.	G.	AB.	R.	H.	2B.	3B.	HR.	RBI.	B.A.	PO.	A.	E.	F.A.
1979—Oneonta	NYP	SS	56	119	19	29	0	0	0	9	.244	65	115	21	.896
1980—Greensboro†	S. Atl.	SS	21	63	10	12	3	0	0	1	.190	23	47	5	.933
1980—Oneonta	NYP	SS	65	193	32	47	2	0	0	11	.244	★104	186	21	★.932
1981—Oneonta	NYP	SS	19	50	8	10	1	0	0	3	.200	30	52	7	.921
1981—Greensboro	S. Atl.	SS-3B	33	60	14	12	0	0	0	4	.200	25	67	4	.958
1982—Fort Lauderdale	Fla. St.	S-2-3-1	94	178	26	39	8	0	0	11	.219	130	184	13	.960
1982—Nashville	South.	SS	4	12	0	0	0	0	0	0	.000	4	13	1	.944
1983—Nashville	South.	SS-2B	141	426	78	110	8	4	8	38	.258	240	445	37	.949
1984—New York	Amer.	SS	2	4	0	0	0	0	0	0	.000	2	10	1	.923
1984—Nashville	South.	SS	138	460	80	128	15	1	3	42	.278	238	★440	★46	.936
1985—Columbus	Int.	SS-2B-3B	123	307	40	74	9	1	4	21	.241	176	302	27	.947
1985—New York	Amer.	SS	4	0	1	0	0	0	0	0	.000	0	1	0	1.000
Major League Totals—2 Years			6	4	1	0	0	0	0	0	.000	2	11	1	.929

Selected by New York Yankees' organization in 15th round of free-agent draft, June 5, 1979.
†On disabled list, June 5 to June 15, 1980.

PETER JOHN SMITH
(Pete)

Born February 27, 1966, at Abington, Mass.
Height, 6.02. Weight, 185.
Throws and bats righthanded.

Year Club	League	G.	IP.	W.	L.	Pct.	H.	R.	ER.	SO.	BB.	ERA.
1984—Sarasota Phillies	Gulf Coast	8	37	1	2	.333	28	11	6	35	16	1.46
1985—Clearwater†	Florida St.	26	153	12	10	.545	135	68	56	86	80	3.29

Selected by Philadelphia Phillies' organization in 1st round (21st player selected) of free-agent draft, June 4, 1984.
†Traded with Catcher Ozzie Virgil to Atlanta Braves for Pitcher Steve Bedrosian and Outfielder Milt Thompson, December 10, 1985.

—DID YOU KNOW—

That Ozzie Smith's homer in the ninth inning of the fifth game of the National League Championship Series was his first professional lefthanded round-tripper? His other 13 homers were hit righthanded.

RAYMOND EDWARD SMITH
(Ray)

Born September 18, 1955, at Glendale, Calif.
Height, 6.01. Weight, 188.
Throws and bats righthanded.
Attended Mira Costa College, Oceanside, Calif., and received bachelor of science degree
in recreation administration from University of Oregon, Eugene, Ore in 1976.

Major League stolen bases: 1983 (1).

Year Club	League	Pos.	G.	AB.	R.	H.	2B.	3B.	HR.	RBI.	B.A.	PO.	A.	E.	F.A.
1977—Visalia	Calif.	SS	33	120	23	43	6	0	1	20	.358	54	101	19	.891
1977—Elizabethton	Appal.	C-1-3-S	63	234	50	71	13	1	7	42	.303	371	39	4	.990
1978—Orlando†	South.	C	72	216	26	58	10	0	2	31	.269	310	23	13	.962
1979—Toledo	Int.	C-3B	78	233	24	58	7	3	3	24	.249	358	28	11	.972
1980—Toledo	Int.	C	115	398	36	109	14	4	0	46	.274	461	64	7	.987
1981—Minnesota‡	Amer.	C	15	40	4	8	1	0	1	1	.200	65	3	0	1.000
1982—Toledo	Int.	C	94	305	25	83	13	2	6	43	.272	449	59	11	.979
1982—Minnesota	Amer.	C	9	23	1	5	0	1	0	1	.217	44	2	0	1.000
1983—Minnesota	Amer.	C	59	152	11	34	5	0	0	8	.224	272	27	5	.984
1984—Toledo§	Int.	C-1B	80	247	24	57	10	0	3	26	.231	395	41	3	.993
1985—Las Vegas x	P. C.	C-O-1-3-P	104	397	48	129	32	3	7	42	.325	560	52	11	.982
Major League Totals—3 Years			83	215	16	47	6	1	1	10	.219	381	32	5	.988

Signed as free agent by Minnesota Twins' organization, January 24, 1977.
†On disabled list, May 23 to June 3, 1978.
‡On disabled list, May 8, 1981 through remainder of season.
§Traded to San Diego Padres for Pitcher Floyd Chiffer, December 7, 1984.
xGranted free agency, October 15, 1985; signed by Oakland A's, December 9, 1985.

PITCHING RECORD

Year Club	League	G.	IP.	W.	L.	Pct.	H.	R.	ER.	SO.	BB.	ERA.
1985—Las Vegas	P. Coast	1	1	0	0	.000	1	0	0	0	0	0.00

ZANE WILLIAM SMITH

Born December 28, 1960, at Madison, Wis.
Height, 6.02. Weight, 195.
Throws and bats lefthanded.
Attended Indiana State University, Terre Haute, Ind.

Year Club	League	G.	IP.	W.	L.	Pct.	H.	R.	ER.	SO.	BB.	ERA.
1982—Anderson	S. Atlantic	12	63	5	3	.625	65	53	48	32	34	6.86
1983—Durham	Carolina	27	170⅔	9	●15	.375	183	109	93	126	83	4.90
1984—Greenville	Southern	9	60	7	0	1.000	47	13	11	35	23	1.65
1984—Richmond	Int'national	19	123⅔	7	4	.636	113	62	57	68	65	4.15
1984—Atlanta	National	3	20	1	0	1.000	16	7	5	16	13	2.25
1985—Atlanta†	National	42	147	9	10	.474	135	70	62	85	80	3.80
Major League Totals—2 Years		45	167	10	10	.500	151	77	67	101	93	3.61

Selected by Atlanta Braves' organization in 3rd round of free-agent draft, June 7, 1982.
†On disabled list, August 5 to September 1, 1985.

BILLY MIKE SMITHSON
(Known by middle name.)

Born January 21, 1955, at Centerville, Tenn.
Height, 6.08. Weight, 215.
Throws right and bats lefthanded.
Attended University of Tennessee, Knoxville, Tenn.

Led American League in hit batsmen with 15 in 1985.
Led American League in home runs allowed with 35 in 1984.
Tied for American League lead in games started by pitchers with 36 in 1984 and 37 in 1985.
Tied for International League lead in intentional bases on balls issued with 13 in 1980.

Year Club	League	G.	IP.	W.	L.	Pct.	H.	R.	ER.	SO.	BB.	ERA.
1976—Winter Haven	Florida St.	11	64	4	3	.571	63	27	22	29	20	3.09
1977—Winter Haven	Florida St.	25	172	13	8	.619	170	56	53	92	41	2.77
1977—Bristol	Eastern	1	3	0	1	.000	8	7	7	1	0	21.00
1978—Bristol	Eastern	27	160	11	10	.524	178	92	81	86	76	4.56
1979—Bristol	Eastern	*48	132	8	12	.400	128	82	69	89	53	4.70
1980—Pawtucket	Int'national	*50	99	5	9	.357	95	50	32	73	45	2.91
1981—Pawtucket†	Int'national	34	91	2	4	.333	74	44	39	82	45	3.86
1982—Denver	Am. Assoc.	29	152⅔	11	7	.611	149	82	77	*144	47	4.54
1982—Texas	American	8	46⅔	3	4	.429	51	26	26	24	13	5.01
1983—Texas‡	American	33	223⅓	10	14	.417	233	102	97	135	71	3.91
1984—Minnesota	American	36	252	15	13	.536	246	113	103	144	54	3.68
1985—Minnesota	American	37	257	15	14	.517	264	134	*124	127	78	4.34
Major League Totals—4 Years		114	779	43	45	.489	794	375	350	430	216	4.04

Selected by Boston Red Sox' organization in 5th round of free-agent draft, June 8, 1976.
†Traded to Texas Rangers' organization for Pitcher John Henry Johnson, April 9, 1982.
‡Traded with Pitcher John Butcher and Catcher Sam Sorce to Minnesota Twins for Outfielder Gary Ward, December 7, 1983.

NATHANIEL SNELL
(Nate)

Born September 2, 1952, at Orangeburg, S.C.
Height, 6.04. Weight, 190.
Throws and bats righthanded.
Attended Tennessee State University, Nashville, Tenn.

Major League saves: 1985 (5).
Led Southern League in games finished in relief with 48 and tied for lead in saves with 17 in 1984.
Led Southern League in home runs allowed with 20 in 1978.

Year—Club	League	G.	IP.	W.	L.	Pct.	H.	R.	ER.	SO.	BB.	ERA.
1977—Miami	Florida St.	16	106	7	7	.500	106	41	20	68	15	1.70
1978—Charlotte	Southern	28	193	7	13	.350	*193	91	78	97	44	3.64
1979—Charlotte	Southern	10	65	5	2	.714	65	30	27	42	29	3.74
1979—Rochester†‡	Int'national	12	76	4	7	.364	72	44	37	35	22	4.38
1980—Shreveport§	Texas	33	64	4	4	.500	77	38	32	44	18	4.50
1981—Charlotte	Southern	8	38	1	2	.333	32	14	11	19	10	2.61
1981—Rochester	Int'national	15	41	1	3	.250	33	14	12	20	7	2.63
1982—Rochester x	Int'national	37	83⅓	4	6	.400	83	40	34	31	26	3.67
1983—Charlotte	Southern	15	22⅔	1	0	1.000	15	0	0	7	6	0.00
1983—Rochester y	Int'national	39	70	6	2	.750	71	29	28	46	17	3.60
1984—Rochester	Int'national	6	9⅓	0	2	.000	13	6	5	6	7	4.82
1984—Charlotte	Southern	52	81⅔	9	4	.692	68	30	22	45	28	2.42
1984—Baltimore	American	5	7⅔	1	1	.500	8	2	2	7	1	2.35
1985—Baltimore z	American	43	100⅓	3	2	.600	100	44	30	41	30	2.69
1985—Rochester	Int'national	2	4⅔	0	0	.000	4	0	0	3	0	0.00
Major League Totals—2 Years		48	108	4	3	.571	108	46	32	48	31	2.67

Selected by Baltimore Orioles' organization in 18th round of free-agent draft, June 6, 1972.
Selected by Atlanta Braves' organization in 22nd round of free-agent draft, June 4, 1975.
Signed as free agent by Baltimore Orioles' organization, September 5, 1976.
†On disabled list, July 17 to August 5, 1979.
‡Drafted by Phoenix (San Francisco Giants' organization), December 4, 1979.
§Released, March 27, 1981; signed by Charlotte (Baltimore Orioles' organization), May 26, 1981.
xOn disabled list, May 3 to June 9, 1982.
yGranted free agency, October 20, 1983; re-signed by Orioles, January 17, 1984.
zOn disabled list, July 10 to August 9, 1985; included rehabilitation disability assignment to Rochester, August 2 to August 7, 1985.

VAN VOORHEES SNIDER

Born August 11, 1963, at Birmingham, Ala.
Height, 6.03. Weight, 185.
Throws right and bats lefthanded.
Attended Gadsden State Junior College, Gadsden, Ala.

Led South Atlantic League outfielders in double plays with 7 in 1983.
Tied for Pioneer League lead in double plays by outfielder with 2 in 1982.

Year—Club	League	Pos.	G.	AB.	R.	H.	2B.	3B.	HR.	RBI.	B.A.	PO.	A.	E.	F.A.
1982—Butte	Pion.	OF	67	237	46	71	13	5	9	53	.300	99	*14	9	.926
1983—Charleston	S. Atl.	OF	123	467	86	136	26	2	20	94	.291	207	17	*22	.911
1983—Jacksonville	South.	OF	13	33	2	6	3	0	0	2	.182	28	0	2	.933
1984—Memphis	South.	OF	132	488	52	120	23	9	7	62	.246	319	*24	4	*.988
1985—Memphis†	South.	OF	85	292	43	69	15	4	8	39	.236	166	9	*13	.931

Signed as free agent by Kansas City Royals' organization, November 2, 1981.
†On disabled list, May 3 to July 1, 1985.

BRIAN ROBERT SNYDER

Born February 20, 1958, at Flemington, N.J.
Height, 6.03. Weight, 185.
Throws and bats lefthanded.
Attended Clemson University, Clemson, S.C.

Pitched 4-0 no-hit victory against Modesto, June 24, 1980.
Major League saves: 1985 (1).
Led Pacific Coast League in intentional bases on balls issued with 11 in 1982.

Year—Club	League	G.	IP.	W.	L.	Pct.	H.	R.	ER.	SO.	BB.	ERA.
1979—Alexandria	Carolina	6	31	3	3	.500	23	11	7	20	22	2.03
1980—San Jose	California	25	127	7	5	.583	139	96	80	97	92	5.67
1981—Wausau†	Midwest	27	67	3	1	.750	34	21	11	77	37	1.48
1982—Salt Lake City	P. Coast	●51	57⅓	4	3	.571	64	32	30	56	45	4.71
1983—Salt Lake City‡	P. Coast	28	49⅓	5	2	.714	53	25	24	37	31	4.38
1984—Salt Lake City	P. Coast	27	129⅔	8	9	.471	155	105	90	83	80	6.25

—DID YOU KNOW—

That the St. Louis Cardinals, who stole 314 bases in 1985, would have led the major leagues even if Vince Coleman's 110 thefts were omitted?

Year Club	League	G.	IP.	W.	L.	Pct.	H.	R.	ER.	SO.	BB.	ERA.
1985—Calgary	P. Coast	20	69⅔	4	2	.667	76	36	31	46	26	4.00
1985—Seattle§..................................	American	15	35⅓	1	2	.333	44	28	25	23	19	6.37
Major League Totals—1 Year................................		15	35⅓	1	2	.333	44	28	25	23	19	6.37

Selected by Texas Rangers' organization in 16th round of free-agent draft, June 8, 1976.
Selected by Seattle Mariners' organization in 7th round of free-agent draft, June 5, 1979.
†On disabled list, April 15 to May 5, 1981.
‡On disabled list, July 30, 1983 through remainder of season.
§Released, November 1, 1985.

JAMES CORY SNYDER
(Known by middle name.)
Born November 11, 1962, at Canyon Country, Calif.
Height, 6.04. Weight, 175.
Throws and bats righthanded.
Attended Brigham Young University, Provo, Utah.

Led Eastern League in total bases with 255, game-winning RBIs with 14 and sacrifice flies with 12 in 1985.
Led Eastern League third basemen in putouts with 132, total chances with 391 and double plays with 26 in 1985.
Named Eastern League Most Valuable Player, 1985.
Member of 1984 U.S. Olympic baseball team.
Named shortstop on THE SPORTING NEWS College Baseball All-America Team, 1984.

Year Club	League	Pos.	G.	AB.	R.	H.	2B.	3B.	HR.	RBI.	B.A.	PO.	A.	E.	F.A.
1985—Waterbury............	East.	3B-SS	★139	512	77	144	25	1	★28	★94	.281	134	231	33	.917

Selected by Cleveland Indians' organization in 1st round (fourth player selected) of free-agent draft, June 4, 1984.

JULIO CESAR SOLANO
Born January 8, 1960, at Agua Blanca, Dominican Republic.
Height, 6.01. Weight, 155.
Throws and bats righthanded.

Led South Atlantic League in hit batsmen with 11 and tied for lead in games started by pitchers with 27 and shutouts with 3 in 1982.

Year Club	League	G.	IP.	W.	L.	Pct.	H.	R.	ER.	SO.	BB.	ERA.
1980—Sarasota Astros-Orange................	Gulf Coast	18	38	5	2	.714	31	16	11	29	23	2.61
1981—Sarasota Astros-Blue	Gulf Coast	17	74	4	4	.500	71	47	32	45	36	3.89
1982—Asheville..	S. Atlantic	28	178	10	7	.588	165	89	70	163	116	3.54
1983—Houston..	National	4	6	0	2	.000	5	5	4	3	4	6.00
1983—Tucson..	P. Coast	29	161⅔	10	7	.588	183	104	89	123	71	4.95
1984—Tucson..	P. Coast	17	80⅔	3	5	.375	74	41	23	55	37	2.57
1984—Houston..	National	31	50⅔	1	3	.250	31	13	11	33	18	1.95
1985—Houston..	National	20	33⅔	2	2	.500	34	13	13	17	13	3.48
1985—Tucson..	P. Coast	23	31⅔	2	3	.400	25	16	14	23	21	3.98
Major League Totals—3 Years............................		55	90⅓	3	7	.300	70	31	28	53	35	2.79

Signed as free agent by Houston Astros' organization, November 21, 1979.

ALAN MARTIN SONTAG
Born October 21, 1963, at Valley Stream, N.Y.
Height, 6.05. Weight, 195.
Throws and bats righthanded.
Attended Indian River Community College, Fort Pierce, Fla.

Led Midwest League in shutouts with 6 and complete games with 15 in 1985.

Year Club	League	G.	IP.	W.	L.	Pct.	H.	R.	ER.	SO.	BB.	ERA.
1984—Kenosha......................................	Midwest	20	143⅓	7	7	.500	118	51	44	110	57	2.76
1985—Kenosha......................................	Midwest	28	★220⅓	15	11	.577	171	65	57	★213	59	2.33

Selected by Baltimore Orioles' organization in 9th round of free-agent draft, January 11, 1983.
Selected by Baltimore Orioles' organization in secondary phase of free-agent draft, June 6, 1983.
Selected by Minnesota Twins' organization in secondary phase of free-agent draft, January 17, 1984.

MICHAEL DAVIS SOPER
(Mike)

Born May 23, 1965, at Miami, Fla.
Height, 6.01. Weight, 165.
Throws and bats righthanded.

Led Gulf Coast League in being hit by pitch with 7 in 1983.
Led Midwest League shortstops in total chances with 568 in 1984.

Year Club	League	Pos.	G.	AB.	R.	H.	2B.	3B.	HR.	RBI.	B.A.	PO.	A.	E.	F.A.
1983—Sarasota W. Sox ...	Gulf C.	SS	53	199	22	55	11	0	0	26	.276	65	150	17	.927
1984—Appleton	Midw.	SS	128	444	47	105	18	2	1	48	.236	★189	★350	29	.949
1985—Glens Falls†	East.	SS	132	480	50	142	16	0	4	49	.296	208	325	31	.945

Selected by Chicago White Sox' organization in 3rd round of free-agent draft, June 6, 1983.
†Traded with Pitcher Britt Burns and Outfielder Glen Braxton to New York Yankees for Catcher Ron Hassey and Pitcher Joe Cowley, December 12, 1985.

LARY ALAN SORENSEN

Born October 4, 1955, at Detroit, Mich.
Height, 6.02. Weight, 200.
Throws and bats righthanded.
Attended University of Michigan, Ann Arbor, Mich.

Major League saves: 1978 (1), 1980 (1), 1984 (1). Total—3.
Tied for American League lead in balks with 4 in 1984.
Tied for National League lead in balks with 5 in 1981.
Tied for Pacific Coast League lead in shutouts with 3 in 1977.
Tied for New York-Pennsylvania league lead in complete games with 7 and shutouts with 2 in 1976.

Year Club	League	G.	IP.	W.	L.	Pct.	H.	R.	ER.	SO.	BB.	ERA.
1976—Newark	NYP	13	75	6	2	.750	58	22	19	65	27	2.28
1976—Berkshire	Eastern	7	41	0	3	.000	44	19	15	25	16	3.29
1977—Spokane	P. Coast	12	72	5	5	.500	79	41	37	43	31	4.63
1977—Milwaukee	American	23	142	7	10	.412	147	72	69	57	36	4.37
1978—Milwaukee	American	37	281	18	12	.600	277	111	100	78	50	3.20
1979—Milwaukee	American	34	235	15	14	.517	250	113	104	63	42	3.98
1980—Milwaukee†	American	35	196	12	10	.545	242	91	80	54	45	3.67
1981—St. Louis‡	National	23	140	7	7	.500	149	59	51	52	26	3.28
1982—Cleveland	American	32	189⅓	10	15	.400	251	130	118	62	55	5.61
1983—Cleveland§	American	36	222⅔	12	11	.522	238	112	105	76	65	4.24
1984—Oakland x	American	46	183⅓	6	13	.316	240	117	100	63	44	4.91
1985—Chicago y	National	45	82½	3	7	.300	96	44	30	31	24	4.20
American League Totals—7 Years		243	1449⅓	80	85	.485	1645	746	676	453	337	4.20
National League Totals—2 Years		68	222⅓	10	14	.417	235	103	90	86	50	3.64
Major League Totals—9 Years		311	1671½	90	99	.476	1880	849	766	539	387	4.12

Selected by Milwaukee Brewers' organization in 8th round of free-agent draft, June 8, 1976.
†Traded with Outfielders Sixto Lezcano and David Green and Pitcher Dave LaPoint to St. Louis Cardinals for Pitchers Rollie Fingers and Pete Vuckovich and Catcher Ted Simmons, December 12, 1980.
‡Traded with Pitcher Silvio Martinez to Cleveland Indians for Outfielder Lonnie Smith, November 20, 1981.
§Granted free agency, November 7, 1983; signed by Oakland A's, January 23, 1984.
xReleased, October 16, 1984; signed by Chicago Cubs, December 13, 1984.
yReleased, December 20, 1985.

ALL-STAR GAME RECORD

Year League	IP.	W.	L.	Pct.	H.	R.	ER.	SO.	BB.	ERA.
1978—American	3	0	0	.000	1	0	0	0	0	0.00

MIGUEL OLEA SOSA

Born May 15, 1960, at La Ramona, Dominican Republic.
Height, 5.10. Weight, 165.
Throws and bats righthanded.

Led International League second basemen in errors with 24 in 1985.
Led Carolina League shortstops in double plays with 83 in 1983.
Led South Atlantic League shortstops in double plays with 78 in 1980.

Year Club	League	Pos.	G.	AB.	R.	H.	2B.	3B.	HR.	RBI.	B.A.	PO.	A.	E.	F.A.
1979—Bradenton Brav.	Gulf C.	SS	44	171	25	48	8	2	5	26	.281	52	128	★22	.891
1980—Anderson	S. Atl.	SS	125	511	81	137	23	3	18	92	.268	186	★397	49	.922
1980—Durham	Carol.	SS	5	23	5	8	3	0	1	5	.348	15	15	3	.909
1981—Durham	Carol.	SS	118	479	63	132	22	4	17	70	.276	128	315	51	.897
1982—Durham	Carol.	SS	132	507	77	146	18	4	25	69	.288	185	★354	33	.942
1983—Savannah	South.	2B-SS	125	490	54	120	16	0	17	★93	.245	196	291	22	.957
1983—Richmond	Int.	2B	2	9	2	3	1	0	0	2	.333	5	8	0	1.000
1984—Greenville	South.	2B	53	187	30	55	6	1	11	31	.294	71	115	12	.939
1984—Richmond	Int.	2B	64	258	34	76	11	0	15	41	.295	131	169	6	.980
1985—Richmond†	Int.	2B-SS-OF	119	433	49	83	13	2	14	49	.192	183	312	26	.950

Signed as free agent by Atlanta Braves' organization, December 8, 1978.
†Traded to New York Yankees for Outfielder Billy Sample, December 6, 1985.

MARIO MELVIN SOTO

Born July 12, 1956, Bani, Dominican Republic.
Height, 6.00. Weight, 185.
Throws and bats righthanded.

Tied major league record for most strikeouts, inning (4), May 17, 1984 (third inning).
Major League saves: 1980 (4).
Led National League in complete games with 18 in 1983 and 13 in 1984.
Led National League in home runs allowed with 28 in 1983, 30 in 1985 and tied for lead with 13 in 1981.
Tied for National League lead in games started by pitchers with 25 in 1981.
Led Florida State League in balks with 6 in 1976.
Tied for American Association lead in balks with 6 in 1978.

Year Club	League	G.	IP.	W.	L.	Pct.	H.	R.	ER.	SO.	BB.	ERA.
1974—Billings†	Pioneer					(Did not play)						
1975—Eugene	Northwest	5	30	2	3	.400	33	21	14	11	18	4.20
1976—Tampa	Florida St.	26	★197	13	7	.650	142	54	41	★124	80	1.87
1977—Indianapolis	Am. Assoc.	18	123	11	5	.688	100	51	42	109	61	3.07
1977—Cincinnati	National	12	61	2	6	.250	60	38	36	44	26	5.31
1978—Indianapolis	Am. Assoc.	26	160	9	12	.429	129	102	89	121	95	5.01

— 474 —

Year Club	League	G.	IP.	W.	L.	Pct.	H.	R.	ER.	SO.	BB.	ERA.
1978—Cincinnati	National	5	18	1	0	1.000	13	5	5	13	13	2.50
1979—Indianapolis‡	Am. Assoc.	15	25	1	1	.500	20	11	11	38	18	3.96
1979—Cincinnati	National	25	37	3	2	.600	33	25	22	32	30	5.35
1980—Cincinnati	National	53	190	10	8	.556	126	72	65	182	84	3.08
1981—Cincinnati	National	25	175	12	9	.571	142	69	64	151	61	3.29
1982—Cincinnati	National	35	257⅔	14	13	.519	202	88	80	274	71	2.79
1983—Cincinnati	National	34	273¾	17	13	.567	207	96	82	242	95	2.70
1984—Cincinnati	National	33	237⅓	18	7	.720	181	102	93	185	87	3.53
1985—Cincinnati	National	36	256⅔	12	15	.444	196	109	102	214	104	3.58
Major League Totals—9 Years		258	1506⅓	89	73	.549	1160	604	549	1337	571	3.28

Signed as free agent by Cincinnati Reds' organization, December 3, 1973.
†On disabled list, July 1 to September 17, 1974.
‡On disabled list, April 13 to May 21, 1979.

CHAMPIONSHIP SERIES RECORD

Year Club	League	G.	IP.	W.	L.	Pct.	H.	R.	ER.	SO.	BB.	ERA.
1979—Cincinnati	National	1	2	0	0	.000	0	0	0	1	0	0.00

ALL-STAR GAME RECORD

Year League	IP.	W.	L.	Pct.	H.	R.	ER.	SO.	BB.	ERA.
1982—National	2	0	0	.000	3	0	0	4	0	0.00
1983—National	2	0	1	.000	2	2	0	2	2	0.00
1984—National	2	0	0	.000	0	0	0	1	0	0.00
All-Star Game Totals—3 Years	6	0	1	.000	5	2	0	7	2	0.00

ROBERT CLIFFORD SPECK
(Cliff)

Born August 8, 1956, at Portland, Ore.
Height, 6.04. Weight, 195.
Throws and bats righthanded.

Tied for Appalachian League lead in games started by pitchers with 13 in 1974.

Year Club	League	G.	IP.	W.	L.	Pct.	H.	R.	ER.	SO.	BB.	ERA.
1974—Marion	Ap'lachian	13	79	4	4	.500	58	34	26	70	48	2.96
1975—Wausau†	Midwest	8	38	2	6	.250	36	33	28	28	37	6.63
1976—Lynchburg‡	Carolina	10	55	4	2	.667	37	32	26	31	47	4.25
1977—Lynchburg§	Carolina	20	91	5	7	.417	90	62	54	49	64	5.34
1978—Peninsula	Carolina	29	97	7	4	.636	88	43	34	67	47	3.15
1979—Peninsula	Carolina	26	77	6	3	.667	65	30	24	58	39	2.81
1979—Reading	Eastern	9	56	3	5	.375	60	33	27	39	21	4.34
1980—Reading	Eastern	9	51	4	3	.571	39	25	22	43	25	3.88
1980—Oklahoma City x	Am. Assoc.	20	74	1	5	.167	81	58	50	27	52	6.08
1981—Charlotte	Southern	12	33	1	0	1.000	29	11	10	24	11	2.73
1981—Rochester y	Int'national	27	76	6	3	.667	81	35	32	51	37	3.79
1982—Rochester	Int'national	31	156⅔	8	10	.444	148	77	60	88	72	3.45
1983—Rochester z	Int'national	29	148⅓	8	12	.400	136	95	83	130	105	5.04
1984—Denver	Am. Assoc.	29	176⅔	12	11	.522	186	117	102	148	73	5.20
1985—Buffalo ab	Am. Assoc.	21	122⅓	6	7	.462	113	66	66	88	67	4.86

Selected by New York Mets' organization in 1st round (17th player selected) of free-agent draft, June 5, 1974.
†On disabled list, June 12 to July 12, 1975.
‡On disabled list, June 17, 1976 through remainder of season.
§Released, April 1, 1978; signed by Peninsula (Philadelphia Phillies' organization), April 13, 1978.
xReleased, January 15, 1981; signed by Charlotte (Baltimore Orioles' organization), March 13, 1981.
yOn disabled list, July 3 to July 13, 1981.
zGranted free agency, October 20, 1983; signed by Chicago White Sox, December 16, 1983.
aOn Chicago disabled list, March 25 to May 20, 1985.
bGranted free agency, October 15, 1985; signed by Richmond (Atlanta Braves' organization), November 15, 1985.

CHRIS EDWARD SPEIER

Name pronounced Spire.

Born June 28, 1950, at Alameda, Calif.
Height, 6.01. Weight, 175.
Throws and bats righthanded.
Attended University of Santa Barbara, Santa Barbara, Calif.

Major League stolen bases: 1971 (4), 1972 (9), 1973 (4), 1974 (3), 1975 (4), 1976 (2), 1977 (1), 1978 (1), 1981 (1), 1982 (1), 1983 (2), 1985 (1). Total—33.
Hit for the cycle, July 20, 1978.
Led Texas League shortstops in putouts with 223 and assists with 325 in 1970.
Named shortstop on THE SPORTING NEWS National League All-Star Team, 1972.

Year Club	League	Pos.	G.	AB.	R.	H.	2B.	3B.	HR.	RBI.	B.A.	PO.	A.	E.	F.A.
1970—Amarillo	Texas	SS-3B-OF	129	460	44	130	20	5	6	66	.283	224	327	38	.935
1971—San Francisco	Nat.	SS	157	601	74	141	17	6	8	46	.235	239	517	●33	.953
1972—San Francisco	Nat.	SS	150	562	74	151	25	2	15	71	.269	243	*517	20	.974
1973—San Francisco	Nat.	●SS-2B	153	542	58	135	17	4	11	71	.249	255	471	●33	.957
1974—San Francisco	Nat.	SS-2B	141	501	55	125	19	5	9	53	.250	215	453	21	.970
1975—San Francisco	Nat.	*SS-3B	141	487	60	132	30	5	10	69	.271	247	421	12	*.982
1976—San Francisco	Nat.	S-2-3-1	145	495	51	112	18	4	3	40	.226	241	464	19	.974

Year—Club	League	Pos.	G.	AB.	R.	H.	2B.	3B.	HR.	RBI.	B.A.	PO.	A.	E.	F.A.
1977—S.F.†-Mont.............	Nat.	SS	145	548	59	128	31	6	5	38	.234	239	455	23	.968
1978—Montreal...............	Nat.	SS	150	501	47	126	18	3	5	51	.251	245	467	18	.975
1979—Montreal‡.............	Nat.	SS	113	344	31	78	13	1	7	26	.227	194	355	17	.970
1980—Montreal...............	Nat.	SS-3B	128	388	35	103	14	4	1	32	.265	187	397	21	.965
1981—Montreal§.............	Nat.	SS	96	307	33	69	10	2	2	25	.225	175	280	17	.964
1982—Montreal...............	Nat.	SS	156	530	41	136	26	4	7	60	.257	291	405	13	.982
1983—Montreal x........	Nat.	SS-3B-2B	88	261	31	67	12	2	2	22	.257	117	203	14	.958
1984—Mont. y-St.L. z.....	Nat.	SS-3B	63	158	10	27	7	1	3	9	.171	56	152	4	.981
1984—Minnesota ab.......	Amer.	SS	12	33	2	7	0	0	0	1	.212	14	28	1	.977
1985—Chicago...............	Nat.	SS-3B-2B	106	218	16	53	11	0	4	24	.243	87	177	11	.960
National League Totals—15 Years.........			1932	6443	675	1583	268	49	92	637	.246	3031	5734	276	.969
American League Totals—1 Year			12	33	2	7	0	0	0	1	.212	14	28	1	.977
Major League Totals—15 Years...............			1944	6476	677	1590	268	49	92	638	.246	3045	5762	277	.970

Selected by Washington Senators' organization in 11th round of free-agent draft, June 7, 1968.
Selected by San Francisco Giants' organization in secondary phase of free-agent draft, January 17, 1970.
†Traded to Montreal Expos for Shortstop Tim Foli, April 27, 1977.
‡On disabled list, July 8 to July 27, 1979.
§Granted free agency, November 13, 1981; re-signed by Expos, January 12, 1982.
xOn disabled list, May 29 to June 13, 1983.
yTraded with cash to St. Louis Cardinals for Infielder Mike Ramsey, July 1, 1984.
zTraded to Minnesota Twins for a player to be named later and cash, August 19, 1984; St. Louis Cardinals' organization acquired Pitcher Jay Pettibone to complete deal, October 2, 1984.
aOn disabled list, August 22 to September 7, 1984.
bGranted free agency, November 8, 1984; signed by Chicago Cubs, April 8, 1985.

DIVISION SERIES RECORD

Year—Club	League	Pos.	G.	AB.	R.	H.	2B.	3B.	HR.	RBI.	B.A.	PO.	A.	E.	F.A.
1981—Montreal...............	Nat.	SS	5	15	4	6	2	0	0	3	.400	16	15	0	1.000

CHAMPIONSHIP SERIES RECORD

Year—Club	League	Pos.	G.	AB.	R.	H.	2B.	3B.	HR.	RBI.	B.A.	PO.	A.	E.	F.A.
1971—San Francisco	Nat.	SS	4	14	4	5	1	0	1	1	.357	3	14	1	.944
1981—Montreal...............	Nat.	SS	5	16	0	3	0	0	0	0	.188	15	16	2	.939
Championship Series Totals—2 Years.....			9	30	4	8	1	0	1	1	.267	18	30	3	.941

ALL-STAR GAME RECORD

Year—League	Pos.	AB.	R.	H.	2B.	3B.	HR.	RBI.	B.A.	PO.	A.	E.	F.A.
1972—National	SS	2	0	0	0	0	0	0	.000	1	5	0	1.000
1973—National	SS	2	0	0	0	0	0	0	.000	1	1	0	1.000
All-Star Game Totals—2 Years....................		4	0	0	0	0	0	0	.000	2	6	0	1.000

Member of National League All-Star Team in 1974 game; did not play.

DANIEL RAY SPILLNER
(Dan)

Born November 27, 1951, at Casper, Wyo.
Height, 6.01. Weight, 190.
Throws and bats righthanded.
Attended Green River Community College, Auburn, Wash.

Major League saves: 1975 (1), 1977 (6), 1978 (3), 1979 (1), 1981 (7), 1982 (21), 1983 (8), 1984 (2), 1985 (1). Total—50.
Led Pacific Coast League in home runs allowed with 27 in 1973.
Led Texas League in home runs allowed with 21 in 1972.

Year—Club	League	G.	IP.	W.	L.	Pct.	H.	R.	ER.	SO.	BB.	ERA.
1970—Tri-City...............	Northwest	7	29	1	1	.500	37	21	18	21	15	5.59
1971—Lodi....................	California	25	148	10	5	.667	177	102	87	96	55	5.29
1972—Alexandria............	Texas	27	180	16	7	.696	156	75	68	126	∗85	3.41
1973—Hawaii................	P. Coast	32	188	10	11	.476	188	105	86	124	85	4.12
1974—Hawaii................	P. Coast	7	54	4	2	.667	49	24	22	47	18	3.67
1974—San Diego	National	30	148	9	11	.450	153	78	66	95	70	4.01
1975—San Diego	National	37	167	5	13	.278	194	93	79	104	63	4.26
1976—San Diego†..........	National	32	107	2	11	.154	120	70	60	57	55	5.05
1977—Hawaii................	P. Coast	3	16	1	1	.500	21	6	6	8	4	3.38
1977—San Diego	National	76	123	7	6	.538	130	61	51	74	60	3.73
1978—San Diego‡..........	National	17	26	1	0	1.000	32	15	13	16	7	4.50
1978—Cleveland..............	American	36	56	3	1	.750	54	26	23	48	21	3.70
1979—Cleveland..............	American	49	158	9	5	.643	153	82	81	97	64	4.61
1980—Cleveland§.............	American	34	194	16	11	.593	225	122	114	100	74	5.29
1981—Cleveland..............	American	32	97	4	4	.500	86	41	34	59	39	3.15
1982—Cleveland..............	American	65	133⅔	12	10	.545	117	44	37	90	45	2.49
1983—Cleveland..............	American	60	92⅓	2	9	.182	117	54	52	48	38	5.07
1984—Cleveland x-Chicago y....	American	36	99⅓	1	5	.167	121	61	54	49	36	4.89
1985—Chicago za............	American	52	91⅔	4	3	.571	83	39	35	41	33	3.44
American League Totals—8 Years		364	922	51	48	.515	956	469	430	532	350	4.20
National League Totals—5 Years.....................		192	571	24	41	.369	629	317	269	346	255	4.24
Major League Totals—12 Years.....................		556	1493	75	89	.457	1585	786	699	878	605	4.21

Selected by San Diego Padres' organization in 2nd round of free-agent draft, June 4, 1970.
†On disabled list, August 3, 1976 through remainder of season.

‡Traded to Cleveland Indians for Pitcher Dennis Kinney, June 14, 1978.
§Granted free agency, October 24, 1980; re-signed by Indians, December 8, 1980.
xTraded to Chicago White Sox for a player to be named later, June 21, 1984; Cleveland Indians' organization acquired Pitcher Jim Siwy to complete deal, June 26, 1984.
yAppeared in one game as a pinch-runner.
zWalked as pinch-hitter in only plate appearance.
aGranted free agency, November 12, 1985.

WILLIAM HARRY SPILMAN

(Known by middle name.)

Born July 18, 1954, at Albany, Ga.
Height, 6.01. Weight, 190.
Throws right and bats lefthanded.
Son of Harry Spilman, catcher in Los Angeles Dodgers' organization, 1952.

Led Eastern League in total bases with 277 and intentional bases on balls received with 19 in 1977.
Named Eastern League Player of the Year, 1977.

Year Club	League	Pos.	G.	AB.	R.	H.	2B.	3B.	HR.	RBI.	B.A.	PO.	A.	E.	F.A.
1974—Billings	Pion.	1B-3B	54	178	29	55	12	2	2	30	.309	92	8	3	.971
1975—Tampa	Fla. St.	1B	115	348	33	90	13	1	1	38	.259	946	56	●17	.983
1976—Tampa	Fla. St.	1B	118	361	50	90	12	5	6	35	.249	986	70	16	.985
1977—Three Rivers	East.	1B	133	493	*94	*184	*39	3	16	78	*.373	1095	78	7	.994
1978—Indianapolis	A. A.	3B-1B	133	488	95	144	26	4	13	79	.295	262	184	23	.951
1978—Cincinnati	Nat.	PH	4	4	1	1	0	0	0	0	.250	0	0	0	.000
1979—Indianapolis	A. A.	3B-1B	71	267	42	77	13	3	3	27	.288	154	92	8	.969
1979—Cincinnati	Nat.	1B-3B-OF	43	56	7	12	3	0	0	5	.214	64	11	0	1.000
1980—Cincinnati	Nat.	1-3-O-C	65	101	14	27	4	0	4	19	.267	132	15	2	.987
1981—Cinc.†-Hou.	Nat.	1B	51	58	9	14	1	0	0	4	.241	62	5	1	.985
1982—Tucson	P. C.	1B-3B	53	190	34	63	16	3	6	33	.332	307	13	3	.991
1982—Houston	Nat.	1B	38	61	7	17	2	0	3	11	.279	86	5	1	.989
1983—Houston	Nat.	1B-C	42	78	7	13	3	0	1	9	.167	138	8	0	1.000
1984—Houston‡	Nat.	1B-C	32	72	14	19	2	0	2	15	.264	143	9	3	.981
1985—Houston§	Nat.	1B-C	44	66	3	9	1	0	1	4	.136	134	4	0	1.000
Major League Totals—8 Years			319	496	62	112	16	0	11	67	.226	759	57	7	.991

Signed as free agent by Cincinnati Reds' organization, June 25, 1974.
†Traded to Houston Astros for Second Baseman Rafael Landestoy, June 8, 1981.
‡On disabled list, July 16, 1984 through remainder of season.
§Granted free agency, November 12, 1985.

DIVISION SERIES RECORD

Year Club	League	Pos.	G.	AB.	R.	H.	2B.	3B.	HR.	RBI.	B.A.	PO.	A.	E.	F.A.
1981—Houston	Nat.	PH	1	1	0	0	0	0	0	0	.000	0	0	0	.000

CHAMPIONSHIP SERIES RECORD

Year Club	League	Pos.	G.	AB.	R.	H.	2B.	3B.	HR.	RBI.	B.A.	PO.	A.	E.	F.A.
1979—Cincinnati	Nat.	PH	2	2	0	0	0	0	0	0	.000	0	0	0	.000

MICHAEL LYNN SQUIRES

(Mike)

Born March 5, 1952, at Kalamazoo, Mich.
Height, 5.11. Weight, 185.
Throws and bats lefthanded.
Attended Kalamazoo Valley Community College, Kalamazoo, Mich.
and Western Michigan University, Kalamazoo, Mich.
Son of Lynn Squires, scout with Chicago White Sox, 1981 through 1985.

Major League stolen bases: 1975 (3), 1978 (4), 1979 (15), 1980 (8), 1981 (7), 1982 (3), 1983 (3), 1984 (2). Total—45.
Tied for American Association lead in caught stealing with 13 in 1977.
Led American Association first basemen in fielding percentage with .995 in 1978.
Named first baseman on THE SPORTING NEWS American League All-Star fielding team, 1981.
Named Southern League Most Valuable Player, 1975.

Year Club	League	Pos.	G.	AB.	R.	H.	2B.	3B.	HR.	RBI.	B.A.	PO.	A.	E.	F.A.
1973—Appleton	Midw.	1B-OF-P	68	228	42	68	7	3	3	37	.298	479	44	4	.992
1974—Knoxville	South.	1B	136	481	74	138	23	5	6	69	.287	*1173	*80	5	*.996
1975—Knoxville	South.	1B	129	448	68	136	23	5	3	50	.304	1085	78	6	*.995
1975—Chicago	Amer.	1B	20	65	5	15	0	0	0	4	.231	155	12	2	.988
1976—Iowa	A. A.	*1B-P	124	336	37	85	18	1	2	40	.253	823	47	4	*.995
1977—Iowa	A. A.	1B-OF-P	126	415	67	134	29	4	1	45	.323	897	65	7	.993
1977—Chicago	Amer.	1B	3	3	0	0	0	0	0	0	.000	8	1	0	1.000
1978—Iowa	A. A.	1B-OF	115	449	70	140	24	3	5	48	.312	922	71	6	.994
1978—Chicago	Amer.	1B	46	150	25	42	9	2	0	19	.280	361	20	1	.997
1979—Chicago	Amer.	1B-OF	122	295	44	78	10	1	2	22	.264	744	60	4	.995
1980—Chicago	Amer.	1B-C	131	343	38	97	11	3	2	33	.283	905	68	5	.995
1981—Chicago	Amer.	1B-OF	92	294	35	78	9	0	0	25	.265	729	58	6	.992
1982—Chicago	Amer.	1B	116	195	33	52	9	3	1	21	.267	512	48	3	.995
1983—Chicago	Amer.	*1B-3B	143	153	21	34	4	1	1	11	.222	515	40	2	*.996
1984—Chicago†	Amer.	1-3-O-P	104	82	9	15	1	0	0	6	.183	234	25	0	1.000
1985—Glens Falls	East.	1B	4	15	0	1	0	0	0	0	.067	31	3	0	1.000
1985—Chicago	Amer.	PR	2	0	1	0	0	0	0	0	.000	0	0	0	.000
Major League Totals—10 Years			779	1580	211	411	53	10	6	141	.260	4163	332	23	.995

Selected by Chicago White Sox' organization in 18th round of free-agent draft, June 5, 1973.
†Released, March 26, 1985 to become scout for Chicago White Sox; re-signed by White Sox, September 1, 1985.

CHAMPIONSHIP SERIES RECORD

Year Club	League	Pos.	G.	AB.	R.	H.	2B.	3B.	HR.	RBI.	B.A.	PO.	A.	E.	F.A.
1983—Chicago	Amer.	1B-PH-PR	4	4	0	0	0	0	0	0	.000	6	0	0	1.000

PITCHING RECORD

Year Club	League	G.	IP.	W.	L.	Pct.	H.	R.	ER.	SO.	BB.	ERA.
1973—Appleton	Midwest	1	⅓	0	0	.000	0	0	0	1	1	0.00
1976—Iowa	Am. Assoc.	1	2	0	0	.000	5	4	4	1	1	18.00
1977—Iowa	Am. Assoc.	1	1	0	0	.000	1	0	0	1	0	0.00
1984—Chicago	American	1	⅓	0	0	.000	0	0	0	0	0	0.00
Major League Totals—1 Year		1	⅓	0	0	.000	0	0	0	0	0	0.00

STEPHEN BLAIR STANICEK

Name pronounced Stan-i-sek.

(Steve)

Born June 19, 1961, at Lake Forest, Ill.
Height, 6.00. Weight, 195.
Throws and bats righthanded.
Attended University of Nebraska, Lincoln, Neb.

Named designated hitter on THE SPORTING NEWS College Baseball All-America Team, 1982.

Year Club	League	Pos.	G.	AB.	R.	H.	2B.	3B.	HR.	RBI.	B.A.	PO.	A.	E.	F.A.
1982—Fresno	Calif.	1B-3B	22	69	9	17	3	0	3	6	.246	122	11	2	.985
1983—Fresno	Calif.	1B	126	438	68	106	15	3	16	77	.242	596	63	15	.978
1984—Shreveport	Texas	1B	94	271	36	63	12	2	5	34	.232	609	43	11	.983
1985—Shreveport	Texas	1B-3B	119	401	57	113	17	2	13	54	.282	516	140	35	.949

Selected by St. Louis Cardinals' organization in 16th round of free-agent draft, June 5, 1979.
Selected by San Francisco Giants' organization in 1st round (11th player selected) of free-agent draft, June 7, 1982.

ROBERT WILLIAM STANLEY

(Bob)

Born November 10, 1954, at Portland, Me.
Height, 6.04. Weight, 205.
Throws and bats righthanded.

Established American League record for most innings pitched by relief pitcher, season (168⅓), 1982.
Major League saves: 1977 (3), 1978 (10), 1979 (1), 1980 (14), 1982 (14), 1983 (33), 1984 (22), 1985 (10). Total—107.
Led American League in hit batsmen with 11 and tied for lead in games started by pitchers with 27 in 1976.
Led New York-Pennsylvania League pitchers in games started with 15 in 1974.
Tied for Florida State League lead in games started by pitchers with 26 in 1975.

Year Club	League	G.	IP.	W.	L.	Pct.	H.	R.	ER.	SO.	BB.	ERA.
1974—Elmira	NYP	15	86	6	6	.500	94	57	44	45	40	4.60
1975—Winter Haven	Florida St.	27	169	5	*17	.227	136	76	55	73	74	2.93
1976—Bristol†	Eastern	27	186	15	9	.625	176	76	55	78	83	2.66
1977—Boston	American	41	151	8	7	.533	176	74	67	44	43	3.99
1978—Boston	American	52	142	15	2	.882	142	50	41	38	34	2.60
1979—Boston	American	40	217	16	12	.571	250	110	96	56	44	3.98
1980—Boston	American	52	175	10	8	.556	186	75	66	71	52	3.39
1981—Boston	American	35	99	10	8	.556	110	46	42	28	38	3.82
1982—Boston	American	48	168⅓	12	7	.632	161	60	58	83	50	3.10
1983—Boston	American	64	145⅓	8	10	.444	145	56	46	65	38	2.85
1984—Boston	American	57	106⅔	9	10	.474	113	57	42	52	23	3.54
1985—Boston	American	48	87⅔	6	6	.500	76	30	28	46	30	2.87
Major League Totals—9 Years		437	1292	94	70	.573	1359	558	486	483	352	3.39

Selected by Los Angeles Dodgers' organization in 9th round of free-agent draft, June 5, 1973.
Selected by Boston Red Sox' organization in secondary phase of free-agent draft, January 9, 1974.
†On disabled list, June 19 to June 24, 1976.

ALL-STAR GAME RECORD

Year League	IP.	W.	L.	Pct.	H.	R.	ER.	SO.	BB.	ERA.
1979—American	2	0	0	.000	1	1	1	0	0	4.50
1983—American	2	0	0	.000	2	0	0	0	0	0.00
All-Star Game Totals—2 Years	4	0	0	.000	3	1	1	0	0	2.25

MICHAEL THOMAS STANTON

(Mike)

Born September 25, 1952, at St. Louis, Mo.
Height, 6.02. Weight, 200.
Throws and bats righthanded.
Attended Miami-Dade Community College (South), Miami, Fla.

Major League saves: 1975 (1), 1980 (5), 1981 (2), 1982 (7), 1983 (7), 1984 (8), 1985 (1). Total—31.
Tied for Southern League lead in games started by pitchers with 27 in 1974.

Year Club	League	G.	IP.	W.	L.	Pct.	H.	R.	ER.	SO.	BB.	ERA.
1973—Covington	Ap'lachian	7	51	2	3	.400	34	26	11	70	21	1.94
1973—Cedar Rapids	Midwest	7	53	3	2	.600	40	16	8	59	18	1.36
1974—Columbus	Southern	27	179	11	*15	.423	158	85	61	*146	*121	3.07
1975—Iowa	Am. Assoc.	18	107	5	11	.313	95	56	49	105	66	4.12
1975—Houston	National	7	17	0	2	.000	20	14	14	16	20	7.41
1975—Columbus	Southern	10	39	2	3	.400	31	13	10	41	19	2.31
1976—Memphis	Int'national	21	128	6	11	.353	135	88	69	101	67	4.85
1977—Charleston†‡	Int'national	20	116	8	7	.533	115	53	44	81	47	3.41
1978—Syracuse§	Int'national	31	143	6	12	.333	155	*110	87	116	105	5.48
1979—Maracaibo x	Inter-Amer.	5	30	3	2	.600	24	15	9	7	7	2.70
1979—Tacoma	P. Coast	8	45	3	3	.500	43	17	12	34	23	2.40
1980—Cleveland	American	51	86	1	3	.250	98	57	51	74	44	5.34
1981—Cleveland yza	American	24	43	3	3	.500	43	21	21	34	18	4.40
1982—Seattle	American	56	71⅓	2	4	.333	70	37	33	49	21	4.16
1983—Seattle	American	50	65	2	3	.400	65	26	24	47	28	3.32
1984—Seattle	American	54	61	4	4	.500	55	28	24	55	22	3.54
1985—Seattle bc-Chicago d	American	35	40⅔	1	3	.250	47	34	29	29	29	6.42
National League Totals—1 Year		7	17	0	2	.000	20	14	14	16	20	7.41
American League Totals—6 Years		270	367	13	20	.394	378	203	182	288	162	4.46
Major League Totals—7 Years		277	384	13	22	.371	398	217	196	304	182	4.59

Selected by Atlanta Braves' organization in 9th round of free-agent draft, June 8, 1971.
Selected by Kansas City Royals' organization in secondary phase of free-agent draft, January 12, 1972.
Selected by Texas Rangers' organization in secondary phase of free-agent draft, June 6, 1972.
Selected by Houston Astros' organization in secondary phase of free-agent draft, January 10, 1973.
†On disabled list, June 19 to July 4, 1977.
‡Sold to Toronto Blue Jays' organization, March 29, 1978.
§Sold to Maracaibo of Inter-American League, April 7, 1979.
xSigned as free agent by Cleveland Indians' organization after Inter-American League folded, July 18, 1979.
ySold to St. Louis Cardinals, December 7, 1981.
zSold to Cleveland Indians' organization, February 8, 1982.
aReleased, February 13, 1982; signed by Seattle Mariners, April 5, 1982.
bOn disabled list, June 5 to June 20, 1985.
cReleased, June 20, 1985; signed by Chicago White Sox, June 26, 1985.
dReleased, August 12, 1985.

DAVID LESLIE STAPLETON
(Dave)

Born January 16, 1954, at Fairhope, Ala.
Height, 6.01. Weight, 170.
Throws and bats righthanded.
Attended Faulkner State Junior College, Bay Minette, Ala., and
received bachelor of science degree in education from
University of South Alabama, Mobile, Ala.

Major League stolen bases: 1980 (3), 1982 (2), 1983 (1). Total—6.
Led International League in total bases with 249 in 1979.
Named International League co-Most Valuable Player, 1979.

Year Club	League	Pos.	G.	AB.	R.	H.	2B.	3B.	HR.	RBI.	B.A.	PO.	A.	E.	F.A.
1975—Winter Haven	Fla. St.	2B-SS-OF	56	199	23	48	8	1	1	14	.241	106	143	14	.947
1976—Winter Haven	Fla. St.	3-2-1-S-O	118	400	67	115	13	2	4	38	.288	164	248	17	.960
1977—Bristol	East.	2B-3B	86	304	52	93	21	4	8	28	.306	147	174	14	.958
1977—Pawtucket	Int.	3-1-2-S-O	25	74	9	18	5	0	1	9	.243	34	29	2	.969
1978—Pawtucket†	Int.	3-2-1-S	113	432	69	112	26	3	11	49	.259	155	224	21	.948
1979—Pawtucket	Int.	1-3-2-O-S	140	*553	*88	*169	*33	1	15	64	.306	651	231	9	.990
1980—Pawtucket	Int.	1-2-3-O	37	150	25	51	3	1	3	19	.340	239	53	8	.973
1980—Boston	Amer.	2-1-O-3	106	449	61	144	33	5	7	45	.321	269	338	12	.981
1981—Boston	Amer.	S-3-2-1	93	355	45	101	17	1	10	42	.285	260	204	17	.965
1982—Boston	Amer.	1-S-2-3-O	150	538	66	142	28	1	14	65	.264	1032	179	13	.989
1983—Boston	Amer.	1B-2B	151	542	54	134	31	1	10	66	.247	1249	105	10	.993
1984—Boston‡	Amer.	1B	13	39	4	9	2	0	0	1	.231	86	8	0	1.000
1985—Boston§	Amer.	2B-1B	30	66	4	15	6	0	0	2	.227	41	36	1	.987
1985—Pawtucket	Int.	3B	5	14	1	3	1	0	0	0	.214	2	11	0	1.000
Major League Totals—6 Years			543	1989	234	545	117	8	41	221	.274	2937	870	53	.986

Selected by Boston Red Sox' organization in 10th round of free-agent draft, June 4, 1975.
†On disabled list, April 10 to May 5, 1978.
‡On disabled list, April 29, 1984 through remainder of season.
§On disabled list, May 16 to June 7, 1985; included rehabilitation disability assignment to Pawtucket, May 31 to June 7, 1985.

DANIEL JOSEPH STAUB
(Rusty)
(Named by nurses in hospital of birth for his hair.)

Born April 1, 1944, at New Orleans, La.
Height, 6.02. Weight, 215.
Throws right and bats lefthanded.

Established major league records for most games, pinch-hitter, season (94), 1983; most at-bats pinch-hitter, season (81), 1983.

Tied major league records for most seasons, consecutive, leading league, grounded into double plays (2), 1976 and 1977; most consecutive hits during season by pinch-hitter (8), June 11 through June 26, first game, 1983.

Major League stolen bases: 1964 (1), 1965 (3), 1966 (2), 1968 (2), 1969 (3), 1970 (12), 1971 (9), 1973 (1), 1974 (2), 1975 (2), 1976 (3), 1977 (1), 1978 (3), 1979 (1), 1980 (1), 1981 (1). Total—47.

Led American League in grounding into double plays with 23 in 1976 and 27 in 1977.

Tied for National League lead in double plays by outfielders with 5 in 1971, 5 in 1973 and 5 in 1974.

Led Carolina League first basemen in double plays with 123 in 1962.

Named designated hitter on The Sporting News American League All-Star Team, 1978.

Named Carolina League Most Valuable Player, 1962.

Received reported $100,000 bonus to sign with Houston Colt .45s, 1961.

Year—Club	League	Pos.	G.	AB.	R.	H.	2B.	3B.	HR.	RBI.	B.A.	PO.	A.	E.	F.A.
1962—Durham	Carol.	1B	●140	509	●115	149	20	4	23	93	.293	★1247	★76	★20	.985
1963—Houston	Nat.	1B-OF	150	513	43	115	17	4	6	45	.224	963	63	11	.989
1964—Houston	Nat.	1B-OF	89	292	26	63	10	2	8	35	.216	512	30	9	.984
1964—Oklahoma City	P. C.	OF-1B	71	226	55	71	13	1	20	45	.314	306	22	5	.985
1965—Houston	Nat.	OF-1B	131	410	43	105	20	1	14	63	.256	203	12	11	.951
1966—Houston	Nat.	OF-1B	153	554	60	155	28	3	13	81	.280	291	15	12	.962
1967—Houston	Nat.	OF	149	546	71	182	★44	1	10	74	.333	269	10	11	.962
1968—Houston†	Nat.	1B-OF	161	591	54	172	37	1	6	72	.291	1336	94	13	.991
1969—Montreal	Nat.	OF	158	549	89	166	26	5	29	79	.302	265	★16	11	.966
1970—Montreal	Nat.	OF	160	569	98	156	23	7	30	94	.274	308	14	5	.985
1971—Montreal‡	Nat.	OF	★162	599	94	186	34	6	19	97	.311	290	★20	★18	.945
1972—New York§	Nat.	OF	66	239	32	70	11	0	9	38	.293	108	4	2	.982
1973—New York	Nat.	OF	152	585	77	163	36	1	15	76	.279	297	17	7	.978
1974—New York	Nat.	OF	151	561	65	145	22	2	19	78	.258	262	★19	5	.983
1975—New York x	Nat.	OF	155	574	93	162	30	4	19	105	.282	267	★15	4	.986
1976—Detroit	Amer.	OF	●161	589	73	176	28	3	15	96	.299	218	8	7	.970
1977—Detroit	Amer.	DH	158	623	84	173	34	3	22	101	.278	0	0	0	.000
1978—Detroit	Amer.	DH	162	642	75	175	30	1	24	121	.273	0	0	0	.000
1979—Detroit yz	Amer.	DH	68	246	32	58	12	1	9	40	.236	0	0	0	.000
1979—Montreal a	Nat.	1B-OF	38	86	9	23	3	0	3	14	.267	156	7	1	.994
1980—Texas bc	Amer.	1B-OF	109	340	42	102	23	2	9	55	.300	262	14	6	.979
1981—New York	Nat.	1B	70	161	9	51	9	0	5	21	.317	339	20	4	.989
1982—New York d	Nat.	OF-1B	112	219	11	53	9	0	3	27	.242	172	19	2	.990
1983—New York	Nat.	1B-OF	104	115	5	34	6	0	3	28	.296	40	5	2	.957
1984—New York e	Nat.	1B	78	72	2	19	4	0	1	18	.264	13	0	0	1.000
1985—New York f	Nat.	OF	54	45	2	12	3	0	1	8	.267	1	0	0	1.000
American League Totals—5 Years			658	2440	306	684	127	10	79	413	.280	480	22	13	.975
National League Totals—19 Years			2293	7280	883	2032	372	37	213	1053	.279	6092	380	127	.981
Major League Totals—23 Years			2951	9720	1189	2716	499	47	292	1466	.279	6572	402	140	.980

Signed as free agent by Houston Colt .45s' organization, September 11, 1961.

†Traded to Montreal Expos for First Baseman Donn Clendenon and Outfielder Jesus Alou, January 22, 1969. Clendenon refused to report to Houston; Pitchers John Billingham and Drannon (Skip) Guinn and cash sent to Houston to complete deal, April 8, 1969.

‡Traded to New York Mets for Outfielder Ken Singleton, First Baseman Mike Jorgensen and Infielder Tim Foli, April 6, 1972.

§On disabled list, July 21 to September 1, 1972.

xTraded with Pitcher Bill Laxton to Detroit Tigers for Pitcher Mickey Lolich and Outfielder Billy Baldwin, December 12, 1975.

yOn disqualified list, April 5 to May 1, 1979.

zSold to Montreal Expos, July 20, 1979.

aTraded to Texas Rangers for Second Baseman LaRue Washington and Third Baseman Chris Smith, March 31, 1980.

bOn disabled list, May 1 to June 5, 1980.

cGranted free agency, October 23, 1980; signed by New York Mets, December 16, 1980.

dPlayer-coach.

eGranted free agency when refused option to minors, November 12, 1984; re-signed by Mets, January 3, 1985.

fGranted free agency, November 12, 1985.

CHAMPIONSHIP SERIES RECORD

Established Championship Series records for most home runs, five-game Series (3), 1973; most home runs, two consecutive innings (2), October 8, 1973 (first and second innings).

Year—Club	League	Pos.	G.	AB.	R.	H.	2B.	3B.	HR.	RBI.	B.A.	PO.	A.	E.	F.A.
1973—New York	Nat.	OF	4	15	4	3	0	0	3	5	.200	10	0	0	1.000

WORLD SERIES RECORD

Tied World Series record for most times reached first base safely, game (batting 1.000) (5), October 4, 1973.

Year—Club	League	Pos.	G.	AB.	R.	H.	2B.	3B.	HR.	RBI.	B.A.	PO.	A.	E.	F.A.
1973—New York	Nat.	OF-PH	7	26	1	11	2	0	1	6	.423	5	0	0	1.000

ALL-STAR GAME RECORD

Year—League	Pos.	AB.	R.	H.	2B.	3B.	HR.	RBI.	B.A.	PO.	A.	E.	F.A.
1967—National	PH	1	0	1	0	0	0	0	1.000	0	0	0	.000
1968—National	PH	1	0	0	0	0	0	0	.000	0	0	0	.000
1970—National	PH	1	0	0	0	0	0	0	.000	0	0	0	.000
1976—American	OF	2	0	2	0	0	0	0	1.000	1	0	0	1.000
All-Star Game Totals—4 Years		5	0	3	0	0	0	0	.600	1	0	0	1.000

Member of National League All-Star Team for 1969 and 1971 games; did not play.

JAMES EARL STEELS
(Jim)

Born May 30, 1961, at Jackson, Miss.
Height, 5.10. Weight, 185.
Throws and bats lefthanded.

Named Texas League Most Valuable Player, 1984.

Year Club	League	Pos.	G.	AB.	R.	H.	2B.	3B.	HR.	RBI.	B.A.	PO.	A.	E.	F.A.
1980—Reno†	Calif.	OF	73	285	42	86	8	4	3	27	.302	78	9	5	.946
1981—Amarillo	Texas	OF-1B	127	485	58	138	28	5	3	59	.285	206	14	8	.965
1982—Amarillo	Texas	1B	86	371	61	118	16	8	6	57	.318	789	61	★20	.977
1982—Hawaii	P. C.	OF-1B	52	196	33	49	10	6	4	26	.250	103	2	4	.963
1983—Las Vegas	P. C.	OF-1B	28	95	17	23	5	1	1	14	.242	47	4	0	1.000
1983—Beaumont	Texas	OF-1B	83	313	57	84	17	4	10	61	.268	188	10	7	.966
1984—Beaumont	Texas	OF-P-1B	127	474	90	161	26	10	12	81	★.340	195	15	5	.977
1985—Las Vegas‡	P. C.	OF	111	394	39	103	19	4	5	46	.261	163	12	3	.983

Selected by San Diego Padres' organization in 8th round of free-agent draft, June 5, 1979.
†On disabled list, April 29 to June 16, 1980.
‡On disabled list, July 6 to July 24, 1985.

PITCHING RECORD

Year Club	League	G.	IP.	W.	L.	Pct.	H.	R.	ER.	SO.	BB.	ERA.
1984—Beaumont	Texas	3	4⅔	0	0	.000	3	4	4	2	10	7.71

JOHN ROBERT STEFERO

Born September 22, 1959, at Sumter, S.C.
Height, 5.08. Weight, 185.
Throws right and bats lefthanded.

Tied for Appalachian League lead in errors by third baseman with 18 in 1979.

Year Club	League	Pos.	G.	AB.	R.	H.	2B.	3B.	HR.	RBI.	B.A.	PO.	A.	E.	F.A.
1979—Bluefield	Appal.	3B-C	59	200	37	55	11	2	8	42	.275	58	95	19	.890
1980—Miami	Fla. St.	C	101	307	32	66	9	4	5	30	.215	352	63	★14	.967
1981—Hagerstown†	Carol.	C-3B-OF	111	338	69	97	16	2	25	82	.287	630	74	16	.978
1982—Charlotte	South.	C-OF-3B	115	357	45	82	9	2	17	60	.230	435	51	17	.966
1983—Charlotte	South.	C-OF	61	205	33	63	9	0	16	34	.307	261	40	12	.962
1983—Baltimore	Amer.	C	9	11	2	5	1	0	0	4	.455	20	3	2	.920
1983—Rochester	Int.	C	35	97	13	19	5	0	2	5	.196	153	26	4	.978
1984—Rochester	Int.	C	5	15	0	1	0	0	0	1	.067	18	1	2	.905
1984—Hagerstown	Carol.	C-OF	41	134	9	28	3	0	1	17	.209	171	21	2	.990
1984—Charlotte‡	South.	C	51	164	25	34	6	1	7	14	.207	195	30	3	.987
1985—Charlotte	South.	C-OF	57	169	31	37	8	0	7	19	.219	203	30	0	1.000
1985—Rochester	Int.	C	49	128	16	24	5	0	10	23	.188	192	24	4	.982
Major League Totals—1 Year			9	11	2	5	1	0	0	4	.455	20	3	2	.920

Signed as free agent by Baltimore Orioles' organization, June 26, 1979.
†On disabled list, August 31 to September 11, 1981.
‡On disabled list, August 28 to September 4, 1984.

DAVID WILLIAM STEGMAN
(Dave)

Born January 30, 1954, at Inglewood, Calif.
Height, 5.11. Weight, 190.
Throws and bats righthanded.
Received bachelor of science degree in engineering and math from University of Arizona, Tucson, Ariz.

Major League stolen bases: 1979 (1), 1980 (1), 1984 (3). Total—5.
Led American Association in bases on balls received with 100 in 1983.
Named outfielder on THE SPORTING NEWS College Baseball All-America Team, 1975 and 1976.

Year Club	League	Pos.	G.	AB.	R.	H.	2B.	3B.	HR.	RBI.	B.A.	PO.	A.	E.	F.A.
1976—Montgomery	South.	OF	61	188	31	50	8	0	0	20	.266	105	2	3	.973
1977—Montgomery	South.	OF	67	226	55	78	19	5	11	59	.345	132	6	1	.993
1977—Evansville	A. A.	OF	50	153	25	34	12	0	6	18	.222	99	4	6	.945
1978—Evansville	A. A.	★OF-C	●135	462	95	122	30	1	14	67	.264	299	8	3	★.990
1978—Detroit	Amer.	OF	8	14	3	4	2	0	1	3	.286	11	0	0	1.000
1979—Evansville	A. A.	OF	133	506	95	153	33	2	11	60	.302	★322	12	5	.985
1979—Detroit	Amer.	OF	12	31	6	6	0	0	3	5	.194	35	0	0	1.000
1980—Evansville	A. A.	OF	18	59	11	12	2	1	1	6	.203	37	1	1	.974
1980—Detroit††‡	Amer.	OF	65	130	12	23	5	0	2	9	.177	82	1	1	.988
1981—Columbus	Int.	OF	90	227	42	66	15	1	6	24	.291	128	2	3	.977
1982—Columbus	Int.	OF-3B	115	383	71	104	18	2	10	53	.272	206	29	4	.983
1982—New York§	Amer.	PR	2	0	0	0	0	0	0	0	.000	0	0	0	.000
1983—Denver	A A	OF	111	395	94	132	30	6	7	54	.334	231	11	3	.988
1983—Chicago	Amer.	OF	30	53	5	9	2	0	4	4	.170	31	1	0	1.000
1984—Chicago	Amer.	OF	55	92	13	24	1	2	2	11	.261	65	1	1	.985
1984—Denver x	A. A.	OF-2B-3B	34	105	17	30	10	1	2	9	.286	60	8	4	.944
1985—Syracuse	Int.	OF	89	257	36	82	15	4	10	45	.319	123	8	1	.992
Major League Totals—6 Years			172	320	39	66	10	2	8	32	.206	224	3	2	.991

Selected by Minnesota Twins' organization in 10th round of free-agent draft, June 6, 1972.
Selected by Boston Red Sox' organization in 9th round of free-agent draft, June 4, 1975.

Selected by Atlanta Braves' organization in secondary phase of free-agent draft, January 7, 1976.
Selected by Detroit Tigers' organization in secondary phase of free-agent draft, June 8, 1976.
†Traded to San Diego Padres for Pitcher Dennis Kinney, December 12, 1980.
‡Traded by San Diego to New York Yankees' organization, April 30, 1981, completing deal in which New York organization traded Pitcher Byron Ballard to San Diego organization for a player to be named later, April 6, 1981.
§Granted free agency, October 22, 1982; signed by Chicago White Sox' organization, January 26, 1983.
xGranted free agency, October 15, 1984; signed by Syracuse (Toronto Blue Jays' organization), February 6, 1985.
yGranted free agency, October 15, 1985.

WILLIAM ALLEN STEIN
(Bill)

Born January 21, 1947, at Battle Creek, Mich.
Height, 5.10. Weight, 175.
Throws and bats righthanded.
Attended Brevard Junior College, Cocoa, Fla.,
and Southern Illinois University, Carbondale, Ill.

Established American League record for most consecutive hits during season by pinch-hitter (7), April 14 through May 25, 1981.

Major League stolen bases: 1972 (1), 1975 (2), 1976 (4), 1977 (3), 1978 (1), 1979 (1), 1980 (1), 1981 (1), 1983 (2). Total—16.

Led American Association in total bases with 274 in 1974.

Year—Club	League	Pos.	G.	AB.	R.	H.	2B.	3B.	HR.	RBI.	B.A.	PO.	A.	E.	F.A.
1969—Tulsa	A. A.	2B-3B-SS	62	183	24	54	11	5	1	20	.295	81	97	9	.952
1970—Arkansas	Texas	2B-OF-SS	114	429	56	124	21	2	8	52	.289	179	198	17	.957
1971—Tulsa†	A. A.	O-3-2-P	103	389	50	106	22	4	8	67	.272	154	86	13	.949
1972—Tulsa	A. A.	O-2-3-1	103	360	49	100	26	4	5	36	.278	146	52	5	.975
1972—St. Louis	Nat.	3B-OF	14	35	2	11	0	1	2	3	.314	5	4	0	1.000
1973—St. Louis	Nat.	OF-1B-3B	32	55	4	12	2	0	0	2	.218	37	1	0	1.000
1973—Tulsa‡§	A. A.	3B	21	81	12	23	2	1	0	8	.284	8	37	1	.978
1974—Iowa	A. A.	3B-OF	●135	543	★107	★178	32	8	16	74	.328	89	204	13	.958
1974—Chicago	Amer.	3B	13	43	5	12	1	0	0	5	.279	7	20	4	.871
1975—Chicago	Amer.	2B-3B-OF	76	226	23	61	7	1	3	21	.270	87	118	9	.958
1976—Chicago x	Amer.	2-3-1-S-O	117	392	32	105	15	2	4	36	.268	161	243	19	.955
1977—Seattle	Amer.	★3B-SS	151	556	53	144	26	5	13	46	.259	★146	255	15	.964
1978—Seattle	Amer.	3B	114	403	41	105	24	4	4	37	.261	72	244	24	.929
1979—Seattle y	Amer.	3B-2B-SS	88	250	28	62	9	2	7	27	.248	64	162	7	.970
1980—Seattle za	Amer.	3B-2B-1B	67	198	16	53	5	1	5	27	.268	119	115	4	.983
1981—Texas	Amer.	1-O-3-2-S	53	115	21	38	6	0	2	22	.330	166	26	2	.990
1982—Texas	Amer.	2-3-S-1-O	85	184	14	44	8	0	1	16	.239	72	122	6	.970
1983—Texas	Amer.	2B-1B-3B	78	232	21	72	15	1	2	33	.310	222	103	5	.985
1984—Texas b	Amer.	2B-1B-3B	27	43	3	12	1	0	0	3	.279	16	17	1	.971
1985—Texas cd	Amer.	3-1-O-2	44	79	5	20	3	1	1	12	.253	52	20	2	.973
American League Totals—12 Years			913	2721	262	728	120	17	42	306	.268	1184	1445	98	.964
National League Totals—2 Years			46	90	6	23	2	1	2	5	.256	42	5	0	1.000
Major League Totals—14 Years			959	2811	268	751	122	18	44	311	.267	1226	1450	98	.965

Selected by Baltimore Orioles' organization in 33rd round of free-agent draft, June 7, 1968.
Selected by St. Louis Cardinals' organization in 27th round of free-agent draft, June 5, 1969.
†On temporary inactive list, July 1 to July 12, 1971.
‡Traded to California Angels' organization for Infielder Jerry DaVanon, September 25, 1973.
§Sold by California Angels to Chicago White Sox, April 3, 1974; California acquired Pitcher Steve Blateric to complete deal, August 1, 1974.
xSelected by Seattle Mariners in American League expansion draft, November 5, 1976.
yOn disabled list, May 25 to June 15, 1979.
zOn disabled list, June 2 to July 22, 1980.
aGranted free agency, October 22, 1980; signed by Texas Rangers, December 18, 1980.
bOn disabled list, May 5 to June 13 and August 9 to September 3, 1984.
cOn disabled list, August 26 to September 10, 1985.
dGranted free agency, November 12, 1985.

PITCHING RECORD

Year—Club	League	G.	IP.	W.	L.	Pct.	H.	R.	ER.	SO.	BB.	ERA.
1971—Tulsa	Am. Assoc.	1	6	0	0	.000	8	3	3	6	0	4.50

MICHAEL STEVEN STENHOUSE
(Mike)

Born May 29, 1958, at Pueblo, Colo.
Height, 6.01. Weight, 185.
Throws right and bats lefthanded.
Received bachelor of arts degree in economics from Harvard University, Cambridge, Mass.
Son of David Stenhouse, pitcher with Washington Senators, 1962 through 1964;
brother of David Stenhouse, Jr., catcher in Toronto Blue Jays' organization.

Major League stolen bases: 1985 (1).
Led American Association in slugging percentage with .681 in 1983.
Led Florida State League in game-winning RBIs with 12 and bases on balls received with 123 in 1980.
Named American Association Most Valuable Player, 1983.
Named designated hitter on THE SPORTING NEWS College Baseball All-America Team, 1979.

Year—Club	League	Pos.	G.	AB.	R.	H.	2B.	3B.	HR.	RBI.	B.A.	PO.	A.	E.	F.A.
1980—W. Palm Beach	Fla. St.	1B-OF	133	439	77	120	17	7	13	71	.273	912	56	12	.988

Year Club	League	Pos.	G.	AB.	R.	H.	2B.	3B.	HR.	RBI.	B.A.	PO.	A.	E.	F.A.
1980—Memphis................	South.	OF-1B	1	3	0	0	0	0	0	0	.000	2	0	0	1.000
1981—Memphis†.............	South.	OF-1B	118	397	64	108	25	7	14	72	.272	407	26	6	.986
1982—Wichita..................	A. A.	OF	134	436	94	126	25	3	25	80	.289	243	6	6	.976
1982—Montreal...............	Nat.	PH	1	1	0	0	0	0	0	0	.000	0	0	0	.000
1983—Wichita..................	A. A.	1B-OF	109	361	93	128	33	5	25	93	*.355	681	48	8	.989
1983—Montreal...............	Nat.	OF-1B	24	40	2	5	1	0	0	2	.125	37	2	0	1.000
1984—Montreal...............	Nat.	OF-1B	80	175	14	32	8	0	4	16	.183	118	5	2	.984
1984—Indianapolis‡........	A. A.	1B-OF	27	93	22	31	4	2	8	27	.333	128	16	4	.973
1985—Minnesota§...........	Amer.	OF-1B	81	179	23	40	5	0	5	21	.223	83	10	3	.969
National League Totals—3 Years...........			105	216	16	37	9	0	4	18	.171	155	7	2	.988
American League Totals—1 Year..........			81	179	23	40	5	0	5	21	.223	83	10	3	.969
Major League Totals—4 Years.................			186	395	39	77	14	0	9	39	.195	238	17	5	.981

Selected by Oakland A's organization in 1st round (26th player selected) of free-agent draft, June 5, 1979.
Selected by Montreal Expos' organization in secondary phase of free-agent draft, January 8, 1980.
†On disabled list, April 9 to April 29, 1981.
‡Traded to Minnesota Twins for Pitcher Jack O'Connor, January 9, 1985.
§Traded to Boston Red Sox for Pitcher Charlie Mitchell, December 12, 1985.

RUSSELL JOHN STEPHANS
(Russ)

Born May 20, 1959, at Pontiac, Mich.
Height, 6.00. Weight, 190.
Throws and bats righthanded.
Attended Los Angeles Valley College, Van Nuys, Calif.
and Arizona State University, Tempe, Ariz.

Year Club	League	Pos.	G.	AB.	R.	H.	2B.	3B.	HR.	RBI.	B.A.	PO.	A.	E.	F.A.
1980—Charleston.............	S. Atl.	C-3B	8	21	2	3	0	0	0	1	.143	23	10	1	.971
1981—Charleston.............	S. Atl.	C	47	163	23	49	2	0	2	19	.301	173	21	5	.975
1981—Omaha...................	A. A.	C	2	3	0	1	0	0	0	0	.333	7	0	0	1.000
1981—Jacksonville†........	South.	C	4	12	1	2	0	0	0	1	.167	27	3	0	1.000
1982—Jacksonville.........	South.	*C-1B	120	384	47	101	14	0	10	42	.263	730	64	*19	.977
1983—Omaha‡.................	A. A.	C	61	175	25	42	4	2	3	22	.240	327	42	7	.981
1984—Omaha..................	A. A.	C-1B	109	334	54	97	21	3	9	48	.290	500	49	6	.989
1985—Omaha§................	A. A.	DH	10	28	6	8	2	1	0	5	.286	0	0	0	.000

Selected by California Angels' organization in 7th round of free-agent draft, January 9, 1979.
Selected by Philadelphia Phillies' organization in secondary phase of free-agent draft, June 5, 1979.
Selected by Kansas City Royals' organization in secondary phase of free-agent draft, June 3, 1980.
†On disabled list, July 20, 1981 through remainder of season.
‡On disabled list, July 16 to July 27 and July 28, 1983 through remainder of season.
§On disabled list, April 12 to July 1 and July 26, 1985 through remainder of season.

DAVID KEITH STEWART
(Dave)

Born February 19, 1957, at Oakland, Calif.
Height, 6.02. Weight, 200.
Throws and bats righthanded.

Major League saves: 1981 (6), 1982 (1), 1983 (8), 1985 (4). Total—19.
Led Pacific Coast League pitchers in games started with 29 in 1980.
Tied for Texas League lead in games started by pitchers with 28 in 1978.
Tied for Midwest League lead in complete games with 15, shutouts with 3 and balks with 3 in 1977.

Year Club	League	G.	IP.	W.	L.	Pct.	H.	R.	ER.	SO.	BB.	ERA.
1975—Bellingham...............................	Northwest	22	49	0	5	.000	59	46	30	37	49	5.51
1976—Danville...................................	Midwest	4	10	0	2	.000	17	20	18	10	16	16.20
1976—Bellingham...............................	Northwest	24	50	1	1	.500	47	35	28	53	58	5.04
1977—Clinton....................................	Midwest	24	176	*17	4	.810	152	52	42	144	72	2.15
1977—Albuquerque..........................	P. Coast	1	6	1	0	1.000	4	3	3	3	6	4.50
1978—San Antonio...........................	Texas	28	*193	14	12	.538	181	99	79	130	97	3.68
1978—Los Angeles	National	1	2	0	0	.000	1	0	0	1	0	0.00
1979—Albuquerque..........................	P. Coast	28	170	11	12	.478	198	112	99	105	81	5.24
1980—Albuquerque..........................	P. Coast	31	*202	●15	10	.600	189	94	83	125	89	3.70
1981—Los Angeles	National	32	43	4	3	.571	40	13	12	29	14	2.51
1982—Los Angeles	National	45	146⅓	9	8	.529	137	72	62	80	49	3.81
1983—Los Angeles†	National	46	76	5	2	.714	67	28	25	54	33	2.96
1983—Texas.....................................	American	8	63	5	2	.714	50	15	14	24	17	2.14
1984—Texas.....................................	American	32	192⅓	7	14	.333	193	106	101	119	87	4.73
1985—Texas‡....................................	American	42	81⅓	0	6	.000	86	53	49	64	37	5.42
1985—Philadelphia	National	4	4⅓	0	0	.000	5	4	3	2	4	6.23
National League Totals—5 Years......................		128	271⅔	18	13	.581	250	117	102	166	100	3.38
American League Totals—3 Years.....................		82	332⅔	12	22	.353	329	174	164	207	141	4.44
Major League Totals—6 Years............................		210	604⅓	30	35	.462	579	291	266	373	241	3.96

Selected by Los Angeles Dodgers' organization in 16th round of free-agent draft, June 4, 1975.
†Traded with a player to be named later to Texas Rangers for Pitcher Rick Honeycutt, August 19, 1983; Texas acquired Pitcher Ricky Wright to complete deal, September 16, 1983.
‡Traded to Philadelphia Phillies for Pitcher Rick Surhoff, September 13, 1985.

Year	Club	League	G.	IP.	W.	L.	Pct.	H.	R.	ER.	SO.	BB.	ERA.
1981—Los Angeles		National	2	⅔	0	2	.000	4	3	3	1	0	40.50

WORLD SERIES RECORD

Year	Club	League	G.	IP.	W.	L.	Pct.	H.	R.	ER.	SO.	BB.	ERA.
1981—Los Angeles		National	2	1⅔	0	0	.000	1	0	0	1	2	0.00

SAMUEL LEE STEWART JR.
(Sammy)

Born October 28, 1954, at Asheville, N.C.
Height, 6.03. Weight, 208.
Throws and bats righthanded.
Attended Montreat-Anderson Junior College, Montreat, N.C.

Established major league record for most consecutive strikeouts, first major league game (7), September 1, 1978 (second game).

Pitched seven-inning, 1-0 no-hit victory against Winter Haven, July 20, 1976.

Major League saves: 1979 (1), 1980 (3), 1981 (4), 1982 (5), 1983 (7), 1984 (13), 1985 (9). Total—42.

Year	Club	League	G.	IP.	W.	L.	Pct.	H.	R.	ER.	SO.	BB.	ERA.
1975—Bluefield	Ap'lachian	18	43	3	3	.500	62	44	29	29	26	6.07
1976—Miami	Florida St.	23	182	12	8	.600	147	65	49	79	⋆86	2.42
1977—Rochester	Int'national	10	54	0	5	.000	68	41	38	28	35	6.33
1977—Charlotte	Southern	16	117	9	6	.600	93	32	27	56	43	⋆2.08
1978—Rochester	Int'national	27	173	13	10	.565	168	90	73	111	93	3.80
1978—Baltimore	American	2	11	1	1	.500	10	5	4	11	3	3.27
1979—Baltimore	American	31	118	8	5	.615	96	47	46	71	71	3.51
1980—Baltimore	American	33	119	7	7	.500	103	51	47	78	60	3.55
1981—Baltimore	American	29	112	4	8	.333	89	33	29	57	57	2.33
1982—Baltimore†	American	38	139	10	9	.526	140	68	64	69	62	4.14
1982—Hagerstown	Carolina	2	8	0	0	.000	8	2	2	6	1	2.25
1983—Baltimore‡	American	58	141⅓	9	4	.692	138	60	58	95	67	3.62
1984—Baltimore§	American	60	93	7	4	.636	81	42	34	56	47	3.29
1985—Baltimore§	American	56	129⅔	5	7	.417	117	60	52	77	66	3.61
Major League Totals—8 Years		307	866	51	45	.531	774	366	334	514	433	3.47

Selected by Kansas City Royals' organization in 28th round of free-agent draft, June 5, 1974.

Signed as free agent by Baltimore Orioles' organization, June 15, 1975.

†On disabled list, June 22 to July 15, 1982; included rehabilitation disability assignment to Hagerstown, July 7 to July 15, 1982.

‡Appeared in one game as a pinch-runner.

§Traded to Boston Red Sox for Shortstop Jackie Gutierrez, December 17, 1985.

CHAMPIONSHIP SERIES RECORD

Year	Club	League	G.	IP.	W.	L.	Pct.	H.	R.	ER.	SO.	BB.	ERA.
1983—Baltimore		American	2	4⅓	0	0	.000	2	0	0	2	1	0.00

WORLD SERIES RECORD

Year	Club	League	G.	IP.	W.	L.	Pct.	H.	R.	ER.	SO.	BB.	ERA.
1979—Baltimore		American	1	2⅔	0	0	.000	4	0	0	0	1	0.00
1983—Baltimore		American	3	5	0	0	.000	2	0	0	6	2	0.00
World Series Totals—2 Years			4	7⅔	0	0	.000	6	0	0	6	3	0.00

DAVID ANDREW STIEB

Name pronounced Steeb.

(Dave)

Born July 22, 1957, at Santa Ana, Calif.
Height, 6.01. Weight, 185.
Throws and bats righthanded.
Attended Santa Ana College, Santa Ana, Calif., and
Southern Illinois University, Carbondale, Ill.
Brother of Steve Stieb, catcher in Atlanta Braves' organization, 1979 through 1981.

Led American League in hit batsmen with 14 in 1983, 11 in 1984 and tied for lead with 11 in 1981.

Led American League in complete games with 19 and shutouts with 5 in 1982.

Named American League Pitcher of the Year by THE SPORTING NEWS, 1982.

Named righthanded pitcher on THE SPORTING NEWS American League All-Star Team, 1982.

Named outfielder on THE SPORTING NEWS College Baseball All-America Team, 1978.

Year	Club	League	G.	IP.	W.	L.	Pct.	H.	R.	ER.	SO.	BB.	ERA.
1978—Dunedin	Florida St.	4	26	2	0	1.000	23	10	6	8	1	2.08
1979—Dunedin	Florida St.	8	51	5	0	1.000	54	30	24	38	28	4.24
1979—Syracuse	Int'national	7	51	5	2	.714	39	15	12	20	14	2.12
1979—Toronto	American	18	129	8	8	.500	139	70	62	52	48	4.33
1980—Toronto†	American	34	243	12	15	.444	232	108	100	108	83	3.70
1981—Toronto	American	25	184	11	10	.524	148	70	65	89	61	3.18
1982—Toronto	American	38	⋆288⅓	17	14	.548	⋆271	116	104	141	75	3.25
1983—Toronto	American	36	278	17	12	.586	223	105	94	187	93	3.04
1984—Toronto	American	35	⋆267	16	8	.667	215	87	84	198	88	2.83
1985—Toronto	American	36	265	14	13	.519	206	89	73	167	96	⋆2.48
Major League Totals—7 Years		222	1654⅓	95	80	.543	1434	645	582	942	544	3.17

Selected by Toronto Blue Jays' organization in 5th round of free-agent draft, June 6, 1978.
†Appeared in one game as outfielder with no chances.

CHAMPIONSHIP SERIES RECORD

Established Championship Series record for most games started, Series (3), 1985.
Established American League Championship Series records for most innings pitched (20⅓), most bases on balls (10) and most strikeouts (18), seven-game Series, 1985.

Year	Club	League	G.	IP.	W.	L.	Pct.	H.	R.	ER.	SO.	BB.	ERA.
1985—Toronto		American	3	20⅓	1	1	.500	11	7	7	18	10	3.10

ALL-STAR GAME RECORD

Tied All-Star Game record for most wild pitches, inning and game (2), July 8, 1980 (seventh inning).

Year	League	IP.	W.	L.	Pct.	H.	R.	ER.	SO.	BB.	ERA.
1980—American		1	0	0	.000	1	1	0	0	2	0.00
1981—American		1⅔	0	0	.000	1	0	0	1	1	0.00
1983—American		3	1	0	1.000	0	1	0	4	1	0.00
1984—American		2	0	1	.000	3	2	1	2	0	4.50
1985—American		1	0	0	.000	0	0	0	2	1	0.00
All-Star Game Totals—5 Years		8⅔	1	1	.500	5	4	1	9	5	1.04

RECORD AS OUTFIELDER

Year	Club	League	Pos.	G.	AB.	R.	H.	2B.	3B.	HR.	RBI.	B.A.	PO.	A.	E.	F.A.
1978—Dunedin		Fla. St.	OF-P	35	99	10	19	3	0	1	9	.192	85	7	3	.968

KURT ANDREW STILLWELL

Born June 4, 1965, at Glendale, Calif.
Height, 5.11. Weight, 165.
Throws right and bats left and righthanded.
Son of Ron Stillwell, infielder with Washington Senators, 1961 and 1962.

Year	Club	League	Pos.	G.	AB.	R.	H.	2B.	3B.	HR.	RBI.	B.A.	PO.	A.	E.	F.A.
1983—Billings		Pion.	SS	65	250	47	81	10	1	2	44	.324	73	137	*30	.875
1984—Cedar Rapids		Midw.	SS	112	382	63	96	15	1	4	33	.251	156	245	25	.941
1985—Denver†		A. A.	SS-3B	59	182	28	48	7	4	1	22	.264	103	135	25	.905

Selected by Cincinnati Reds' organization in 1st round (second player selected) of free-agent draft, June 6, 1983.
†On disabled list, August 9, 1985 through remainder of season.

ROBERT LYLE STODDARD
(Bob)

Born March 8, 1957, at Morgan Hill, Calif.
Height, 6.01. Weight, 190.
Throws and bats righthanded.
Attended Gavilan College, Gilroy, Calif., and
Fresno State University, Fresno, Calif.

Major League saves: 1985 (1).

Year	Club	League	G.	IP.	W.	L.	Pct.	H.	R.	ER.	SO.	BB.	ERA.
1978—Stockton		California	10	51	1	6	.143	46	36	31	47	39	5.47
1979—Stockton		California	20	120	7	5	.583	78	45	40	104	58	3.00
1980—Spokane†		P. Coast	21	124	4	9	.308	147	84	68	84	53	4.94
1981—Spokane‡		P. Coast	19	121	10	4	.714	117	47	39	70	41	2.90
1981—Seattle		American	5	35	2	1	.667	35	10	10	22	9	2.57
1982—Salt Lake City		P. Coast	24	147	7	11	.389	158	91	85	86	65	5.20
1982—Seattle		American	9	67⅓	3	3	.500	48	22	18	24	18	2.41
1983—Seattle		American	35	175⅔	9	17	.346	182	95	86	87	58	4.41
1984—Seattle		American	27	79	2	3	.400	86	51	45	39	37	5.13
1984—Salt Lake City		P. Coast	9	58⅔	4	4	.500	47	34	32	29	20	4.91
1985—Calgary§x		P. Coast	7	39⅔	1	3	.250	55	31	26	33	13	5.90
1985—Nashville		Am. Assoc.	22	30⅔	2	1	.667	15	3	2	31	14	0.59
1985—Detroit y		American	8	13⅓	0	0	.000	15	11	10	11	5	6.75
Major League Totals—5 Years			84	370⅓	16	24	.400	366	189	169	183	127	4.11

Selected by Milwaukee Brewers' organization in 19th round of free-agent draft, June 4, 1975.
Selected by Atlanta Braves' organization in secondary phase of free-agent draft, January 7, 1976.
Selected by Oakland A's organization in secondary phase of free-agent draft, June 8, 1976.
Selected by Seattle Mariners' organization in 10th round of free-agent draft, June 6, 1978.
†On disabled list, April 10 to April 24 and May 14 to May 26, 1980.
‡On disabled list, April 15 to April 27, June 7 to June 19 and July 24 to August 9, 1981.
§On disabled list, May 27 to June 28, 1985.
xReleased, June 28, 1985; signed by Nashville (Detroit Tigers' organization), July 1, 1985.
yReleased, October 9, 1985.

TIMOTHY PAUL STODDARD
(Tim)

Born January 24, 1953, at East Chicago, Ind.
Height, 6.07. Weight, 250.
Throws and bats righthanded.
Attended North Carolina State University, Raleigh, N. C.

Major League saves: 1979 (3), 1980 (26), 1981 (7), 1982 (12), 1983 (9), 1984 (7), 1985 (1). Total—65.
Tied for Southern League lead in wild pitches with 17 in 1977.

Year—Club	League	G.	IP.	W.	L.	Pct.	H.	R.	ER.	SO.	BB.	ERA.
1975—Knoxville	Southern	31	66	3	4	.429	66	40	31	37	43	4.23
1975—Chicago	American	1	1	0	0	.000	2	1	1	0	0	9.00
1976—Knoxville	Southern	20	140	9	8	.529	147	55	45	62	60	2.89
1976—Iowa†	Am. Assoc.	12	29	0	2	.000	37	20	18	20	15	5.59
1977—Charlotte	Southern	36	174	10	7	.588	175	75	62	94	66	3.21
1978—Rochester‡	Int'national	45	76	7	3	.700	80	28	22	70	32	2.61
1978—Baltimore	American	8	18	0	1	.000	22	17	12	14	8	6.00
1979—Baltimore§	American	29	58	3	1	.750	44	12	11	47	19	1.71
1980—Baltimore	American	64	86	5	3	.625	72	27	24	64	38	2.51
1981—Baltimore	American	31	37	4	2	.667	38	16	16	32	18	3.89
1982—Baltimore xy	American	50	56	3	4	.429	53	26	25	42	29	4.02
1982—Rochester	Int'national	5	6	0	0	.000	2	1	1	6	2	1.50
1983—Baltimore za	American	47	57⅔	4	3	.571	65	39	39	50	29	6.09
1984—Chicago b	National	58	92	10	6	.625	77	41	39	87	57	3.82
1985—San Diego	National	44	60	1	6	.143	63	35	31	42	37	4.65
American League Totals—7 Years		230	313⅓	19	14	.576	296	138	128	249	141	3.67
National League Totals—2 Years		102	152	11	12	.478	140	76	70	129	94	4.14
Major League Totals—9 Years		332	465⅔	30	26	.536	436	214	198	378	235	3.83

Selected by Texas Rangers' organization in 24th round of free-agent draft, June 5, 1974.
Selected by Chicago White Sox' organization in secondary phase of free-agent draft, January 9, 1975.
†Released, March 28, 1977; signed by Charlotte (Baltimore Orioles' organization), April 8, 1977.
‡On disabled list, June 15 to July 9, 1978.
§On disabled list, July 21 to September 1, 1979.
xOn disabled list, March 31 to May 5, 1982; included rehabilitation disability assignment to Rochester, April 27 to May 5, 1982.
yOn disabled list, September 7, 1982 through remainder of season.
zTraded to Oakland A's for Third Baseman Wayne Gross, December 9, 1983.
aTraded to Chicago Cubs for Pitcher Stan Kyles and a player to be named later, March 26, 1984; Oakland A's acquired Outfielder Stan Boderick to complete deal, March 31, 1984.
bGranted free agency, November 8, 1984; signed by San Diego Padres, January 8, 1985.

CHAMPIONSHIP SERIES RECORD

Year—Club	League	G.	IP.	W.	L.	Pct.	H.	R.	ER.	SO.	BB.	ERA.
1984—Chicago	National	2	2	0	0	.000	1	2	1	2	2	4.50

WORLD SERIES RECORD

Year—Club	League	G.	IP.	W.	L.	Pct.	H.	R.	ER.	SO.	BB.	ERA.
1979—Baltimore	American	4	5	1	0	1.000	6	3	3	3	1	5.40

RICHARD JAY STOLL
(Rich)

Born September 23, 1962, at Williamsport, Ind.
Height, 5.11. Weight, 180.
Throws and bats righthanded.
Attended University of Michigan, Ann Arbor, Mich.

Pitched seven-inning, 3-0 no-hit victory against Buffalo, August 27, 1985.
Led American Association in balks with 10 and tied for lead in complete games with 8 in 1985.

Year—Club	League	G.	IP.	W.	L.	Pct.	H.	R.	ER.	SO.	BB.	ERA.
1983—West Palm Beach	Florida St.	13	83⅔	8	3	.727	71	30	28	60	34	3.01
1983—Wichita	Am. Assoc.	2	3	0	1	.000	5	6	5	3	4	15.00
1984—Jacksonville	Southern	17	114⅓	10	5	.667	105	47	35	59	37	2.76
1984—Indianapolis	Am. Assoc.	9	64	4	2	.667	41	17	14	29	18	1.97
1985—Indianapolis†	Am. Assoc.	23	145⅔	9	9	.500	148	83	66	57	46	4.08

Selected by Montreal Expos' organization in 1st round (14th player selected) of free-agent draft, June 6, 1983.
†On disabled list, May 4 to May 25, 1985.

JEFFERY GLEN STONE
(Jeff)

Born December 26, 1960, at Kennett, Mo.
Height, 6.00. Weight, 175.
Throws right and bats lefthanded.

Major League stolen bases: 1983 (4), 1984 (27), 1985 (15). Total—46.
Led Carolina League in stolen bases with 94 in 1982.
Led South Atlantic League in being hit by pitch with 15 and stolen bases with 123 in 1981.
Led South Atlantic League outfielders in total chances with 290 in 1981.
Named Eastern League Most Valuable Player, 1983.

Year—Club	League	Pos.	G.	AB.	R.	H.	2B.	3B.	HR.	RBI.	B.A.	PO.	A.	E.	F.A.
1980—Central Oregon	N'west	OF	55	241	52	63	12	4	0	19	.261	116	4	4	.968
1981—Spartanburg	S. Atl.	OF	134	516	★108	143	13	9	3	53	.277	★264	11	15	.948
1982—Peninsula	Carol.	OF	★137	★559	110	166	18	★13	2	50	.297	●276	9	8	.973
1983—Reading†	East.	OF	125	492	★109	156	25	10	9	67	.317	226	6	9	.963
1983—Philadelphia	Nat.	OF	9	4	2	3	0	2	0	3	.750	0	0	0	.000
1984—Portland	P. C.	OF	82	355	59	109	15	●14	7	34	.307	194	7	12	.944
1984—Philadelphia‡	Nat.	OF	51	185	27	67	4	6	1	15	.362	75	1	7	.916

Year Club League	Pos.	G.	AB.	R.	H.	2B.	3B.	HR.	RBI.	B.A.	PO.	A.	E.	F.A.
1985—Philadelphia .... Nat.	OF	88	264	36	70	4	3	3	11	.265	82	4	3	.966
1985—Portland................ P. C.	OF	67	252	58	83	16	8	2	28	.329	103	6	6	.948
Major League Totals—3 Years...............		148	453	65	140	8	11	4	29	.309	157	5	10	.942

Signed as free agent by Philadelphia Phillies' organization, August 26, 1979.

†On disabled list, May 11 to May 21, 1983.

‡On disabled list, July 7 to August 6, 1984; included rehabilitation disability assignment to Portland, August 2 to August 6, 1984.

LESTER P. STRAKER
(Les)

Born October 10, 1959, at Ciudad Bolivar, Venezuela.
Height, 6.01. Weight, 178.
Throws and bats righthanded.

Pitched 4-0 no-hit victory against Winter Haven, July 17, 1982.
Led Southern League in complete games with 12 and tied for lead in shutouts with 3 in 1985.
Tied for Pioneer League lead in shutouts with 1 in 1978.

Year Club League	G.	IP.	W.	L.	Pct.	H.	R.	ER.	SO.	BB.	ERA.
1977—Eugene... Northwest	7	26	1	2	.333	25	10	8	18	20	2.77
1978—Billings...................................... Pioneer	12	69	7	2	.778	46	29	18	54	37	2.35
1979—Greensboro................................... W. Carol.	29	141	7	10	.412	123	83	62	121	75	3.96
1980—Cedar Rapids............................ Midwest	34	135	6	5	.545	135	74	56	89	66	3.73
1981—Waterbury†................................ Eastern	19	45	1	5	.167	50	35	32	33	34	6.40
1982—Tampa....................................... Florida St.	25	154⅓	9	9	.500	137	58	44	99	60	2.57
1983—Waterbury‡§.............................. Eastern	3	10	0	2	.000	16	10	10	5	6	9.00
1984—Albany x.................................... Eastern	28	95⅔	6	5	.545	97	55	45	60	43	4.23
1985—Orlando..................................... Southern	27	★193	16	6	.727	164	75	66	106	79	3.08

Signed as free agent by Cincinnati Reds' organization, February 10, 1977.

†On Tampa disabled list, August 3, 1981 through remainder of season.

‡On disabled list, May 5, 1983 through remainder of season.

§Granted free agency, October 20, 1983; signed by Tacoma (Oakland A's organization), November 26, 1983.

xReleased, December 12, 1984; signed by Orlando (Minnesota Twins' organization), January 10, 1985.

DARRYL EUGENE STRAWBERRY

Born March 12, 1962, at Los Angeles, Calif.
Height, 6.05. Weight, 190.
Throws and bats lefthanded.

Brother of Michael Strawberry, outfielder in Los Angeles Dodgers' organization, 1980 and 1981.

Hit three home runs in a game, August 5, 1985.
Major League stolen bases: 1983 (19), 1984 (27), 1985 (26). Total—72.
Led Texas League in slugging percentage with .602, bases on balls received with 100 and caught stealing with 22 in 1982.
Named National League Rookie Player of the Year by THE SPORTING NEWS, 1983.
Named National League Rookie of the Year by Baseball Writers' Association of America, 1983.
Named Texas League Most Valuable Player, 1982.
Received reported $200,000 bonus to sign with New York Mets, 1980.

Year Club League	Pos.	G.	AB.	R.	H.	2B.	3B.	HR.	RBI.	B.A.	PO.	A.	E.	F.A.
1980—Kingsport............... Appal.	OF	44	157	27	42	5	2	5	20	.268	55	4	3	.952
1981—Lynchburg............ Carol.	OF	123	420	84	107	22	6	13	78	.255	173	8	13	.933
1982—Jackson .... Texas	OF	129	435	93	123	19	9	★34	97	.283	211	8	9	.961
1983—Tidewater............. Int.	OF	16	57	12	19	4	1	3	13	.333	22	0	4	.846
1983—New York............. Nat.	OF	122	420	63	108	15	7	26	74	.257	232	8	4	.984
1984—New York............. Nat.	OF	147	522	75	131	27	4	26	97	.251	276	11	6	.980
1985—New York†........... Nat.	OF	111	393	78	109	15	4	29	79	.277	211	5	2	.991
Major League Totals—3 Years.............		380	1335	216	348	57	15	81	250	.261	719	24	12	.984

Selected by New York Mets' organization in 1st round (first player selected) of free-agent draft, June 3, 1980.

†On disabled list, May 12 to June 28, 1985.

ALL-STAR GAME RECORD

Year League	Pos.	AB.	R.	H.	2B.	3B.	HR.	RBI.	B.A.	PO.	A.	E.	F.A.
1984—National	OF	2	0	1	0	0	0	0	.500	0	0	0	.000
1985—National	OF	1	2	1	0	0	0	0	1.000	3	0	0	1.000
All-Star Game Totals—2 Years....................		3	2	2	0	0	0	0	.667	3	0	0	1.000

FRANKLIN LEE STUBBS

Born October 21, 1960, at Laurinburg, N.C.
Height, 6.02. Weight, 205.
Throws and bats lefthanded.
Attended Virginia Tech., Blacksburg, Va.

Major League stolen bases: 1984 (2).
Named first baseman on THE SPORTING NEWS College Baseball All-America Team, 1982.

Year Club League	Pos.	G.	AB.	R.	H.	2B.	3B.	HR.	RBI.	B.A.	PO.	A.	E.	F.A.
1982—Vero Beach†........ Fla. St.	1B	16	54	6	11	1	1	3	5	.204	134	3	3	.979
1983—San Antonio.......... Texas	1B-OF	47	173	35	54	8	3	12	52	.312	425	23	5	.989
1983—Albuquerque .... P. C.	OF-1B	76	267	49	74	16	3	16	58	.277	106	3	6	.948
1984—Albuquerque .... P. C.	OF-1B	29	108	26	35	5	5	6	24	.324	36	4	2	.952

Year Club	League	Pos.	G.	AB.	R.	H.	2B.	3B.	HR.	RBI.	B.A.	PO.	A.	E.	F.A.
1984—Los Angeles	Nat.	1B-OF	87	217	22	42	2	3	8	17	.194	417	37	4	.991
1985—Albuquerque	P. C.	1B-OF	132	421	86	118	23	5	32	93	.280	945	87	14	.987
1985—Los Angeles	Nat.	1B	10	9	0	2	0	0	0	2	.222	11	0	0	1.000
Major League Totals—2 Years..............			97	226	22	44	2	3	8	19	.195	428	37	4	.991

Selected by Los Angeles Dodgers' organization in 1st round (19th player selected) of free-agent draft, June 7, 1982.
†On disabled list, July 5, 1982 through remainder of season.

JOHN ANTON STUPER

Born May 9, 1957, at Butler, Pa.
Height, 6.02. Weight, 200.
Throws and bats righthanded.
Attended Butler County Community College, Butler, Pa., Point Park College, Pittsburgh, Pa.,
and received bachelor of arts degree in English from LaRoche College, Pittsburgh, Pa., in 1980.
Major League saves: 1983 (1).
Tied for American Association lead in shutouts with 2 in 1982.

Year Club	League	G.	IP.	W.	L.	Pct.	H.	R.	ER.	SO.	BB.	ERA.
1978—Charleston†	W. Carol.	13	76	4	8	.333	85	59	45	36	62	5.33
1979—St. Petersburg..................	Florida St.	42	93	2	5	.286	84	38	28	62	54	2.71
1980—St. Petersburg..................	Florida St.	24	39	1	4	.200	38	12	10	28	19	2.31
1980—Arkansas...............................	Texas	25	88	7	2	.778	77	28	24	57	40	2.45
1981—Springfield.........................	Am. Assoc.	28	161	6	14	.300	175	101	88	59	85	4.92
1982—Louisville	Am. Assoc.	8	61⅓	7	1	.875	49	11	10	42	16	1.46
1982—St. Louis............................	National	23	136⅔	9	7	.563	137	55	51	53	55	3.36
1983—St. Louis............................	National	40	198	12	11	.522	202	95	81	81	71	3.68
1984—Louisville	Am. Assoc.	2	11⅔	0	0	.000	10	6	6	8	7	4.63
1984—St. Louis‡..........................	National	15	61⅓	3	5	.375	73	39	36	19	20	5.28
1984—Vancouver§........................	P. Coast	10	63	2	3	.400	58	28	27	30	26	3.86
1985—Cincinnati x	National	33	99	8	5	.615	116	60	50	38	37	4.55
Major League Totals—4 Years..............		111	495	32	28	.533	528	249	218	191	183	3.96

Selected by Pittsburgh Pirates' organization in 18th round of free-agent draft, June 6, 1978.
†Traded to St. Louis Cardinals' organization for Infielder Tommy Sandt, January 25, 1979.
‡Loaned to Vancouver (Milwaukee Brewers' organization), July 3, 1984; returned, September 3, 1984.
§Traded to Cincinnati Reds, September 10, 1984, completing deal in which Cincinnati traded Outfielder Paul Householder to St. Louis Cardinals for a player to be named later, September 9, 1984.
xTraded with Pitchers Jay Tibbs and Andy McGaffigan and Catcher Dann Bilardello to Montreal Expos for Pitcher Bill Gullickson and Catcher Sal Butera, December 19, 1985.

CHAMPIONSHIP SERIES RECORD

Year Club	League	G.	IP.	W.	L.	Pct.	H.	R.	ER.	SO.	BB.	ERA.
1982—St. Louis.............................	National	1	6	0	0	.000	4	3	2	4	1	3.00

WORLD SERIES RECORD

Tied World Series records for most wild pitches, game (2), October 13, 1982; most wild pitches, Series (3), 1982.

Year Club	League	G.	IP.	W.	L.	Pct.	H.	R.	ER.	SO.	BB.	ERA.
1982—St. Louis.............................	National	2	13	1	0	1.000	10	5	5	5	5	3.46

MARC COOPER SULLIVAN

Born July 25, 1958, at Quincy, Mass.
Height, 6.04. Weight, 198.
Throws and bats righthanded.
Attended University of Florida, Gainesville, Fla.
Son of Haywood Sullivan, catcher with Boston Red Sox and Kansas City A's, 1955, 1957 and 1959 through 1963;
manager, Kansas City A's, 1965; Vice-President of Player Personnel, Boston Red Sox, 1966 through 1977;
Executive Vice-President, General Manager and General Partner, Boston Red Sox,
1978 through 1984; and Chief Executive Officer, Boston Red Sox, since 1985.
Led International League catchers in putouts with 574 in 1984.
Led Eastern League catchers in double plays with 13 in 1982.
Led Carolina League catchers in putouts with 788 in 1981.
Named catcher on THE SPORTING NEWS College Baseball All-America Team, 1979.

Year Club	League	Pos.	G.	AB.	R.	H.	2B.	3B.	HR.	RBI.	B.A.	PO.	A.	E.	F.A.
1979—Winter Haven.......	Fla. St.	C	31	92	8	19	2	1	0	10	.207	146	20	2	.988
1980—Winter Haven.......	Fla. St.	C-1B	94	293	32	66	8	3	4	30	.225	482	75	11	.981
1981—Winston-Salem	Carol.	★C-OF-1B	120	406	67	109	21	1	14	64	.268	792	★114	15	★.984
1982—Bristol..................	East.	★C-1B	117	369	31	75	8	2	1	33	.203	728	★89	13	.984
1982—Pawtucket.............	Int.	C	4	10	0	2	0	0	0	1	.200	19	4	1	.958
1982—Boston....................	Amer.	C	2	6	0	2	0	0	0	0	.333	9	2	0	1.000
1983—New Britain...........	East.	C-1B	73	231	30	53	15	1	7	43	.229	503	32	7	.987
1983—Pawtucket†...........	Int.	C-1B	27	70	9	13	3	0	1	7	.186	107	14	2	.984
1984—Pawtucket.............	Int.	C-1B	116	383	54	78	14	1	15	63	.204	600	59	9	.987
1984—Boston....................	Amer.	C	2	6	1	3	0	0	0	1	.500	19	0	1	.950
1985—Boston‡.................	Amer.	C	32	69	10	12	2	0	2	3	.174	129	8	1	.993
1985—Pawtucket.............	Int.	C	2	4	0	1	0	0	0	0	.250	10	0	0	1.000
Major League Totals—3 Years...............			36	81	11	17	2	0	2	4	.210	157	10	2	.988

Selected by Boston Red Sox' organization in 2nd round of free-agent draft, June 5, 1979.
†On disabled list, August 15, 1983 through remainder of season.
‡On disabled list, June 1 to June 20 and July 3 to July 30, 1985; included rehabilitation disability assignment to Pawtucket, June 16 to June 20, 1985.

JAMES HOWARD SUNDBERG
(Jim)

Born May 18, 1951, at Galesburg, Ill.
Height, 6.00. Weight, 196.
Throws and bats righthanded.
Attended University of Iowa, Iowa City, Iowa.

Tied major league records for most seasons leading league in assists by catcher (6); most assists by catcher, inning (3), September 3, 1976 (fifth inning); fewest errors by catcher, season (4), 1979.
Established American League record for highest fielding percentage by catcher, season (.995), 1979.
Tied American League record for most games, catcher, season (155), 1975.
Major League stolen bases: 1974 (2), 1975 (3), 1977 (2), 1978 (2), 1979 (3), 1980 (2), 1981 (2), 1982 (2), 1984 (1). Total—19.
Led American League in passed balls with 8 in 1981 and 16 in 1982.
Led American League catchers in total chances with 909 in 1975, 822 in 1976, 909 in 1977, 863 in 1978, 833 in 1979 and 936 in 1980.
Led American League catchers in double plays with 15 in 1974, 11 in 1976 and 15 in 1982.
Tied for American League lead in passed balls with 17 in 1980.
Tied for American League lead in double plays by catchers with 12 in 1977 and 14 in 1978.
Named catcher on THE SPORTING NEWS American League All-Star Team, 1978 and 1981.
Named catcher on THE SPORTING NEWS American League All-Star fielding team, 1976 through 1981.

Year Club	League	Pos.	G.	AB.	R.	H.	2B.	3B.	HR.	RBI.	B.A.	PO.	A.	E.	F.A.
1973—Pittsfield	East.	C	91	242	39	72	14	0	5	40	.298	449	52	3	★.994
1974—Texas	Amer.	C	132	368	45	91	13	3	3	36	.247	722	69	8	.990
1975—Texas	Amer.	C	155	472	45	94	9	0	6	36	.199	★791	★101	17	.981
1976—Texas	Amer.	C	140	448	33	102	24	2	3	34	.228	★719	★96	7	★.991
1977—Texas	Amer.	C	149	453	61	132	20	3	6	65	.291	★801	★103	5	★.994
1978—Texas	Amer.	C	149	518	54	144	23	6	6	58	.278	★769	★91	3	★.997
1979—Texas	Amer.	C	150	495	50	136	23	4	5	64	.275	★754	75	4	★.995
1980—Texas	Amer.	C	151	505	59	138	24	1	10	63	.273	★853	★76	7	.993
1981—Texas	Amer.	★C-OF	102	339	42	94	17	2	3	28	.277	465	★52	2	★.996
1982—Texas	Amer.	C-OF	139	470	37	118	22	5	10	47	.251	612	69	6	.991
1983—Texas†	Amer.	C	131	378	30	76	14	0	2	28	.201	618	56	5	.993
1984—Milwaukee‡§	Amer.	C	110	348	43	91	19	4	7	43	.261	556	55	3	★.995
1985—Kansas City	Amer.	C	115	367	38	90	12	4	10	35	.245	572	41	5	.992
Major League Totals—12 Years			1623	5161	537	1306	220	34	71	537	.253	8232	884	72	.992

Selected by Oakland A's organization in 14th round of free-agent draft, June 5, 1969.
Selected by Texas Rangers' organization in 8th round of free-agent draft, June 6, 1972.
Selected by Texas Rangers' organization in secondary phase of free-agent draft, January 10, 1973.
†Traded to Milwaukee Brewers for Catcher Ned Yost and Pitcher Dan Scarpetta, December 8, 1983.
‡On disabled list, August 6 to September 1, 1984.
§Traded to Kansas City Royals as part of a six-player, four-team deal in which Texas Rangers acquired Catcher Don Slaught from Kansas City, New York Mets' organization acquired Pitcher Frank Wills from Kansas City, Milwaukee Brewers acquired Pitcher Danny Darwin and a player to be named later from Texas and Pitcher Tim Leary from New York, January 18, 1985; Milwaukee organization acquired Catcher Bill Hance from Texas to complete deal, January 30, 1985.

CHAMPIONSHIP SERIES RECORD

Established American League Championship Series record for most runs batted in, seven-game series (6), 1985.

Year Club	League	Pos.	G.	AB.	R.	H.	2B.	3B.	HR.	RBI.	B.A.	PO.	A.	E.	F.A.
1985—Kansas City	Amer.	C	7	24	3	4	1	1	1	6	.167	41	2	1	.977

WORLD SERIES RECORD

Year Club	League	Pos.	G.	AB.	R.	H.	2B.	3B.	HR.	RBI.	B.A.	PO.	A.	E.	F.A.
1985—Kansas City	Amer.	C	7	24	6	6	2	0	0	1	.250	47	3	0	1.000

ALL-STAR GAME RECORD

Year League	Pos.	AB.	R.	H.	2B.	3B.	HR.	RBI.	B.A.	PO.	A.	E.	F.A.
1978—American	C	0	0	0	0	0	0	0	.000	2	1	0	1.000
1984—American	C	1	0	0	0	0	0	0	.000	6	0	0	1.000
All-Star Game Totals—2 Years		1	0	0	0	0	0	0	.000	8	1	0	1.000

Member of American League All-Star Team in 1974 game; did not play.

RICHARD CLIFFORD SURHOFF
(Rich)

Born October 3, 1962, at Bronx, N.Y.
Height, 6.03. Weight, 210.
Throws and bats righthanded.
Attended St. John's River Community College, Palatka, Fla.
Son of Dick Surhoff, forward with New York Knicks and Milwaukee Hawks of the National Basketball Association, 1952-53 and 1953-54; and brother of B. J. Surhoff, catcher in Milwaukee Brewers' organization.

Major League saves: 1985 (2).
Led Pacific Coast League in games finished in relief with 41 in 1985.
Led Eastern League in games finished in relief with 50 and tied for lead in saves with 15 in 1984.

Year Club	League	G.	IP.	W.	L.	Pct.	H.	R.	ER.	SO.	BB.	ERA.
1982—Spartanburg	S. Atlantic	21	35⅓	4	2	.667	31	13	10	21	14	2.55
1983—Peninsula	Carolina	29	51⅓	3	2	.600	50	16	14	35	15	2.45

Year Club	League	G.	IP.	W.	L.	Pct.	H.	R.	ER.	SO.	BB.	ERA.
1983—Reading	Eastern	40	63	5	1	.833	58	24	22	36	26	3.14
1984—Reading	Eastern	•62	87⅓	7	6	.538	79	42	30	75	39	3.09
1985—Portland	P. Coast	⋆70	110⅔	7	8	.467	107	44	39	91	44	3.17
1985—Philadelphia†	National	2	1	1	0	1.000	2	0	0	1	0	0.00
1985—Texas	American	7	8⅓	0	1	.000	12	7	7	8	3	7.56
National League Totals—1 Year		2	1	1	0	1.000	2	0	0	1	0	0.00
American League Totals—1 Year		7	8⅓	0	1	.000	12	7	7	8	3	7.56
Major League Totals—1 Year		9	9⅓	1	1	.500	14	7	7	9	3	6.75

Selected by Philadelphia Phillies' organization in 20th round of free-agent draft, January 12, 1982.
†Traded to Texas Rangers for Pitcher Dave Stewart, September 13, 1985.

WILLIAM JAMES SURHOFF
(B. J.)

Born August 4, 1964, at Rye, N.Y.
Height, 6.01. Weight, 185.
Throws right and bats lefthanded.
Attended University of North Carolina, Chapel Hill, N.C.
Son of Dick Surhoff, forward with New York Knicks and Milwaukee Hawks of the
National Basketball Association, 1952-53 and 1953-54; and brother of
Rich Surhoff, pitcher in Texas Rangers' organization.
Named College Player of the Year by THE SPORTING NEWS, 1985.
Member of 1984 U. S. Olympic baseball team.
Named catcher on THE SPORTING NEWS College Baseball All-America Team, 1985.

Year Club	League	Pos.	G.	AB.	R.	H.	2B.	3B.	HR.	RBI.	B.A.	PO.	A.	E.	F.A.
1985—Beloit	Midw.	C	76	289	39	96	13	4	7	58	.332	475	44	3	.994

Selected by New York Yankees' organization in 5th round of free-agent draft, June 7, 1982.
Selected by Milwaukee Brewers' organization in 1st round (first player selected) of free-agent draft, June 3, 1985.

RICHARD LEE SUTCLIFFE
(Rick)

Born June 21, 1956, at Independence, Mo.
Height, 6.06. Weight, 200.
Throws right and bats lefthanded.
Brother of Terry Sutcliffe, pitcher in Los Angeles Dodgers' organization, 1979 through 1981.
Major League saves: 1980 (5), 1982 (1). Total—6.
Led California League pitchers in games started with 28 in 1975.
Tied for Northwest League lead in shutouts with 2 in 1974.
Named National League Pitcher of the Year by THE SPORTING NEWS, 1984.
Won National League Cy Young Memorial Award, 1984.
Named righthanded pitcher on THE SPORTING NEWS National League All-Star Team, 1984.
Named National League Rookie Pitcher of the Year by THE SPORTING NEWS, 1979.
Named National League Rookie of the Year by Baseball Writers' Association of America, 1979.
Received reported $80,000 bonus to sign with Los Angeles Dodgers, 1974.

Year Club	League	G.	IP.	W.	L.	Pct.	H.	R.	ER.	SO.	BB.	ERA.
1974—Bellingham	Northwest	17	95	10	3	.769	79	42	35	69	48	3.32
1975—Bakersfield	California	28	193	8	⋆16	.333	⋆214	⋆115	⋆89	91	68	4.15
1976—Waterbury	Eastern	30	187	10	11	.476	⋆187	90	66	121	45	3.18
1976—Los Angeles	National	1	5	0	0	.000	2	0	0	3	1	0.00
1977—Albuquerque†	P. Coast	17	77	3	10	.231	96	67	55	48	63	6.43
1978—Albuquerque	P. Coast	30	184	13	6	.684	179	101	91	99	92	4.45
1978—Los Angeles	National	2	2	0	0	.000	2	0	0	0	1	0.00
1979—Los Angeles	National	39	242	17	10	.630	217	104	93	117	97	3.46
1980—Los Angeles	National	42	110	3	9	.250	122	73	68	59	55	5.56
1981—Los Angeles‡§	National	14	47	2	2	.500	41	24	21	16	20	4.02
1982—Cleveland	American	34	216	14	8	.636	174	81	71	142	98	⋆2.96
1983—Cleveland	American	36	243⅓	17	11	.607	251	131	116	160	102	4.29
1984—Cleveland x	American	15	94⅓	4	5	.444	111	60	54	58	46	5.15
1984—Chicago y	National	20	150⅓	16	1	⋆.941	123	53	45	155	39	2.69
1985—Chicago z	National	20	130	8	8	.500	119	51	46	102	44	3.18
National League Totals—7 Years		138	686⅓	46	30	.605	626	305	273	452	257	3.58
American League Totals—3 Years		85	553⅔	35	24	.593	536	272	241	360	246	3.92
Major League Totals—9 Years		223	1240	81	54	.600	1162	577	514	812	503	3.73

Selected by Los Angeles Dodgers' organization in 1st round (21st player selected) of free-agent draft, June 5, 1974.
†On disabled list, May 3 to May 24, 1977.
‡On disabled list, August 14 to September 5, 1981.
§Traded with Second Baseman Jack Perconte to Cleveland Indians for Outfielder Jorge Orta, Catcher Jack Fimple and Pitcher Larry White, December 9, 1981.
xTraded with Catcher Ron Hassey and Pitcher George Frazier to Chicago Cubs for Outfielders Mel Hall and Joe Carter and Pitchers Don Schulze and Darryl Banks, June 13, 1984.
yGranted free agency, November 8, 1984; re-signed by Cubs, December 14, 1984.
zOn disabled list, May 20 to June 7, July 8 to July 23 and July 29 to September 27, 1985.

CHAMPIONSHIP SERIES RECORD

Tied Championship Series records for hitting home run in first Series at-bat, October 2, 1984; most home runs hit by pitcher, total Series (1); most bases on balls, five-game Series (8), 1984.

Year Club	League	G.	IP.	W.	L.	Pct.	H.	R.	ER.	SO.	BB.	ERA.
1984—Chicago	National	2	13⅓	1	1	.500	9	6	5	10	8	3.38

ALL-STAR GAME RECORD

Member of American League All-Star Team in 1983; did not play.

HOWARD BRUCE SUTTER

Name pronounced SUIT-er.

(Known by middle name.)

Born January 8, 1953, at Lancaster, Pa.
Height, 6.02. Weight, 190.
Throws and bats righthanded.

Tied major league records for most saves, season (45), 1984; striking out side on 9 pitches, September 8, 1977 (ninth inning).

Established National League record for most saves, lifetime (283).

Tied National League records for most consecutive strikeouts by relief pitcher, game (6), September 8, 1977.

Major League saves: 1976 (10), 1977 (31), 1978 (27), 1979 (37), 1980 (28), 1981 (25), 1982 (36), 1983 (21), 1984 (45), 1985 (23). Total—283.

Led National League in saves with 37 in 1979, 28 in 1980, 25 in 1981, 36 in 1982 and 45 in 1984.

Led National League in games finished in relief with 63 in 1984.

Tied for Texas League lead in saves with 13 in 1975.

Won National League Cy Young Memorial Award, 1979.

Named National League Fireman of the Year by THE SPORTING NEWS, 1979, 1981, 1982 and 1984.

Year Club	League	G.	IP.	W.	L.	Pct.	H.	R.	ER.	SO.	BB.	ERA.
1972—Bradenton Cubs	Gulf Coast	2	5	0	0	.000	3	0	0	4	0	0.00
1973—Quincy	Midwest	40	85	3	3	.500	94	52	39	76	27	4.13
1974—Key West†	Florida St.	18	40	1	5	.167	26	9	6	50	13	1.35
1974—Midland	Texas	8	25	1	2	.333	22	6	4	14	6	1.44
1975—Midland	Texas	41	67	5	7	.417	64	26	16	50	21	2.15
1976—Wichita	Am. Assoc.	7	12	2	1	.667	9	3	2	16	4	1.50
1976—Chicago	National	52	83	6	3	.667	63	27	25	73	26	2.71
1977—Chicago‡	National	62	107	7	3	.700	69	21	16	129	23	1.35
1978—Chicago	National	64	99	8	10	.444	82	44	35	106	34	3.18
1979—Chicago	National	62	101	6	6	.500	67	29	25	110	32	2.23
1980—Chicago§	National	60	102	5	8	.385	90	35	30	76	34	2.65
1981—St. Louis	National	48	82	3	5	.375	64	24	24	57	24	2.63
1982—St. Louis	National	70	102⅓	9	8	.529	88	38	33	61	34	2.90
1983—St. Louis	National	60	89⅓	9	10	.474	90	45	42	64	30	4.23
1984—St. Louis x	National	71	122⅔	5	7	.417	109	26	21	77	23	1.54
1985—Atlanta	National	58	88⅓	7	7	.500	91	46	44	52	29	4.48
Major League Totals—10 Years		607	976⅔	65	67	.492	813	335	295	805	289	2.72

Selected by Washington Senators' organization in 21st round of free-agent draft, June 4, 1970.

Signed as free agent by Chicago Cubs' organization, September 9, 1971.

†On disabled list, May 22 to July 28, 1974.

‡On disabled list, August 2 to August 23, 1977.

§Traded to St. Louis Cardinals for Third Baseman Ken Reitz, Outfielder-First Baseman Leon Durham and a player to be named later, December 9, 1980; Chicago Cubs acquired Third Baseman Tye Waller to complete deal, December 22, 1980.

xGranted free agency, November 8, 1984; signed by Atlanta Braves, December 7, 1984 (Shortstop Argenis Salazar selected from player compensation pool by St. Louis Cardinals' organization, January 24, 1985).

CHAMPIONSHIP SERIES RECORD

Year Club	League	G.	IP.	W.	L.	Pct.	H.	R.	ER.	SO.	BB.	ERA.
1982—St. Louis	National	2	4⅓	1	0	1.000	0	0	0	1	0	0.00

WORLD SERIES RECORD

Year Club	League	G.	IP.	W.	L.	Pct.	H.	R.	ER.	SO.	BB.	ERA.
1982—St. Louis	National	4	7⅔	1	0	1.000	6	4	4	6	3	4.70

ALL-STAR GAME RECORD

Year League	IP.	W.	L.	Pct.	H.	R.	ER.	SO.	BB.	ERA.
1978—National	1⅔	1	0	1.000	0	0	0	2	0	0.00
1979—National	2	1	0	1.000	2	0	0	3	2	0.00
1980—National	2	0	0	.000	0	0	0	1	1	0.00
1981—National	1	0	0	.000	0	0	0	1	0	0.00
All-Star Game Totals—4 Years	6⅔	2	0	1.000	2	0	0	7	3	0.00

Member of National League All-Star Team in 1984; did not play.

Named to National League All-Star Team in 1977; replaced due to injury.

DONALD HOWARD SUTTON

(Don)

Born April 2, 1945, at Clio, Ala.
Height, 6.01. Weight, 190.
Throws and bats righthanded.
Attended Gulf Coast Community College, Panama City, Fla.;
Mississippi College, Clinton, Miss.; University of Southern California, Los Angeles, Calif.
and Whittier College, Whittier, Calif.

Established major league records for most consecutive games lost to one club, lifetime (13), 1966 through 1969, (vs. Chicago); most years and most consecutive years with 100 or more strikeouts (20).
Tied National League record for most consecutive home runs allowed, inning (3), May 27, 1980 (third inning).
Tied modern National League record for most one-hit games, lifetime (5).
Major League saves: 1971 (1), 1979 (1), 1980 (1). Total—3.
Led National League pitchers in games started with 40 in 1974.
Led National League in shutouts with 9 in 1972.
Tied for National League lead in balks with 3 in 1968.
Named National League Rookie Pitcher of the Year by THE SPORTING NEWS, 1966.
Named righthanded pitcher on THE SPORTING NEWS National League All-Star Team, 1976.
Named Texas League Player of the Year, 1965.

Year—Club	League	G.	IP.	W.	L.	Pct.	H.	R.	ER.	SO.	BB.	ERA.
1965—Santa Barbara	California	10	84	8	1	.889	59	18	14	101	15	1.50
1965—Albuquerque	Texas	21	165	15	6	*.714	151	60	51	138	30	2.78
1966—Los Angeles	National	37	226	12	12	.500	192	82	75	209	52	2.99
1967—Los Angeles	National	37	233	11	15	.423	223	106	102	169	57	3.94
1968—Spokane	P. Coast	2	16	1	1	.500	11	2	2	19	5	1.13
1968—Los Angeles	National	35	208	11	15	.423	179	64	60	162	59	2.60
1969—Los Angeles	National	41	293	17	18	.486	269	123	113	217	91	3.47
1970—Los Angeles	National	38	260	15	13	.536	251	127	●118	201	78	4.08
1971—Los Angeles	National	38	265	17	12	.586	231	85	75	194	55	2.55
1972—Los Angeles	National	33	273	19	9	.679	186	78	63	207	63	2.08
1973—Los Angeles	National	33	256	18	10	.643	196	78	69	200	56	2.43
1974—Los Angeles	National	40	276	19	9	.679	241	111	99	170	80	3.00
1975—Los Angeles	National	35	254	16	13	.552	202	87	81	175	62	2.87
1976—Los Angeles §	National	35	268	21	10	.677	231	98	91	161	82	3.06
1977—Los Angeles	National	33	240	14	8	.636	207	93	85	150	69	3.19
1978—Los Angeles	National	34	238	15	11	.577	228	109	94	154	54	3.55
1979—Los Angeles	National	33	226	12	15	.444	201	109	96	146	61	3.82
1980—Los Angeles†	National	32	212	13	5	.722	163	56	52	128	47	*2.21
1981—Houston	National	23	159	11	9	.550	132	51	46	104	29	2.60
1982—Houston‡	National	27	195	13	8	.619	169	75	65	139	46	3.00
1982—Milwaukee	American	7	54⅔	4	1	.800	55	21	20	36	18	3.29
1983—Milwaukee	American	31	220⅓	8	13	.381	209	109	100	134	54	4.08
1984—Milwaukee§	American	33	212⅔	14	12	.538	224	103	89	143	51	3.77
1985—Oakland x-California y	American	34	226	15	10	.600	221	101	97	107	59	3.86
National League Totals—17 Years		584	4082	254	192	.570	3501	1532	1384	2895	1041	3.05
American League Totals—4 Years		105	713⅔	41	36	.532	709	334	306	420	182	3.86
Major League Totals—20 Years		689	4795⅔	295	228	.564	4210	1866	1690	3315	1223	3.17

Signed as free agent by Los Angeles Dodgers' organization, September 11, 1964.
†Granted free agency, October 23, 1980; signed by Houston Astros, December 4, 1980.
‡Traded to Milwaukee Brewers for three players to be named later, August 30, 1982; Houston Astros acquired Pitchers Frank DiPino and Mike Madden and Outfielder Kevin Bass to complete deal, September 3, 1982.
§Traded to Oakland A's for Pitchers Ray Burris, Eric Barry and a player to be named later, December 7, 1984; Milwaukee Brewers' organization acquired Pitcher Ed Myers to complete deal, March 25, 1985.
xTraded to California Angels for two players to be named later, September 10, 1985; Oakland A's organization acquired Pitcher Robert Sharpnack and Outfielder Jerome Nelson to complete deal, September 25, 1985.
yGranted free agency, November 12, 1985; re-signed by Angels, December 5, 1985.

CHAMPIONSHIP SERIES RECORD

Established Championship Series records for most consecutive scoreless innings, Series (15⅔), 1974; most innings pitched, four-game Series (17), 1974.
Tied Championship Series records for most games won, Series (2), 1974; most games won, total Series (4).
Established National League Championship Series record for most consecutive scoreless innings, total Series (15⅔).
Tied National League Championship Series records for most games won, total Series (3); most complete games, total Series (2); most strikeouts four-game Series (13), 1974.

Year—Club	League	G.	IP.	W.	L.	Pct.	H.	R.	ER.	SO.	BB.	ERA.
1974—Los Angeles	National	2	17	2	0	1.000	7	1	1	13	2	0.53
1977—Los Angeles	National	1	9	1	0	1.000	9	1	1	4	0	1.00
1978—Los Angeles	National	1	5⅔	0	1	.000	7	7	4	0	2	6.35
1982—Milwaukee	American	1	7⅔	1	0	1.000	8	3	3	9	2	3.52
Championship Series Totals—4 Years		5	39⅓	4	1	.800	31	12	9	26	6	2.06

WORLD SERIES RECORD

Tied World Series records for most consecutive home runs allowed, inning (2), October 16, 1977 (eighth inning); most runs allowed, six-game Series (10), 1978.

Year—Club	League	G.	IP.	W.	L.	Pct.	H.	R.	ER.	SO.	BB.	ERA.
1974—Los Angeles	National	2	13	1	0	1.000	9	4	4	12	3	2.77
1977—Los Angeles	National	2	16	1	0	1.000	17	7	7	6	1	3.94
1978—Los Angeles	National	2	12	0	2	.000	17	10	10	8	4	7.50
1982—Milwaukee	American	2	10⅓	0	1	.000	12	11	9	5	1	7.84
World Series Totals—4 Years		8	51⅓	2	3	.400	55	32	30	31	9	5.26

ALL-STAR GAME RECORD

Year—League	IP.	W.	L.	Pct.	H.	R.	ER.	SO.	BB.	ERA.
1972—National	2	0	0	.000	1	0	0	2	0	0.00
1973—National	1	0	0	.000	0	0	0	0	0	0.00
1975—National	2	0	0	.000	3	0	0	1	0	0.00
1977—National	3	1	0	1.000	1	0	0	4	1	0.00
All-Star Game Totals—4 Years	8	1	0	1.000	5	0	0	7	1	0.00

DALE CURTIS SVEUM

Born November 23, 1963, at Richmond, Calif.
Height, 6.02. Weight, 185.
Throws right and bats left and righthanded.

Led Texas League in total bases with 256 in 1984.
Led Texas League third basemen in putouts with 111 in 1984.
Led California League third basemen in assists with 261 in 1983.

Year	Club	League	Pos.	G.	AB.	R.	H.	2B.	3B.	HR.	RBI.	B.A.	PO.	A.	E.	F.A.
1982—Pikeville	Appal.	SS-3B	58	223	29	52	13	1	2	21	.233	84	158	36	.871
1983—Stockton	Calif.	3B-SS	135	533	70	139	26	5	5	70	.261	105	281	40	.906
1984—El Paso	Texas	*3B-SS	131	523	92	*172	*41	8	9	84	.329	113	259	*30	.925
1985—Vancouver	P. C.	3B-SS	122	415	42	98	17	3	6	48	.236	81	200	26	.915

Selected by Milwaukee Brewers' organization in 1st round (25th player selected) of free-agent draft, June 7, 1982.

WILLIAM DAVID SWAGGERTY
(Bill)

Born December 5, 1956, at Sanford, Fla.
Height, 6.02. Weight, 190.
Throws and bats righthanded.
Attended St. John's River Community College, Palatka, Fla., and Stetson University, Deland, Fla.

Led International League in complete games with 10 in 1985.

Year	Club	League	G.	IP.	W.	L.	Pct.	H.	R.	ER.	SO.	BB.	ERA.
1979—Bluefield	Ap'lachian	17	68	5	3	.625	76	45	36	36	28	4.79
1980—Miami	Florida St.	19	43	3	1	.750	39	16	11	25	22	2.30
1980—Charlotte	Southern	26	51	3	6	.333	47	20	14	23	24	2.47
1981—Charlotte†	Southern	35	49	8	5	.615	35	15	11	26	19	2.02
1982—Rochester‡	Int'national	29	92	6	5	.545	111	63	55	27	59	5.38
1983—Rochester§	Int'national	25	118⅓	9	6	.600	136	67	61	25	37	4.64
1983—Baltimore	American	7	21⅔	1	1	.500	23	8	7	7	6	2.91
1984—Rochester	Int'national	11	64⅓	6	2	.750	53	25	19	22	30	2.66
1984—Baltimore x	American	23	57	3	2	.600	68	41	33	18	21	5.21
1985—Rochester	Int'national	30	*189	11	●13	.458	*187	73	68	58	52	3.24
1985—Baltimore	American	1	1⅔	0	0	.000	3	1	1	2	2	5.40
Major League Totals—3 Years		31	80⅓	4	3	.571	94	50	41	27	29	4.59

Selected by Baltimore Orioles' organization in 25th round of free-agent draft, June 5, 1979.
†On disabled list, June 1 to June 24, 1981.
‡On disabled list, August 27, 1982 through remainder of season.
§On disabled list, April 12 to May 6, 1983.
xAppeared in one game as a pinch-runner.

WILLIAM CHARLES SWIFT
(Bill)

Born December 27, 1961, at Portland, Maine.
Height, 6.00. Weight, 170.
Throws and bats righthanded.
Attended University of Maine, Orono, Maine.

Member of 1984 U.S. Olympic baseball team.

Year	Club	League	G.	IP.	W.	L.	Pct.	H.	R.	ER.	SO.	BB.	ERA.
1985—Chattanooga†	Southern	7	39	2	1	.667	34	16	16	21	21	3.69
1985—Seattle	American	23	120⅔	6	10	.375	131	71	64	55	48	4.77
Major League Totals—1 Year		23	120⅔	6	10	.375	131	71	64	55	48	4.77

Selected by Minnesota Twins' organization in 2nd round of free-agent draft, June 6, 1983.
Selected by Seattle Mariners' organization in 1st round (second player selected) of free-agent draft, June 4, 1984.
†On disabled list, May 6 to May 21, 1985.

PATRICK SEAN TABLER
(Pat)

Born February 2, 1958, at Hamilton, O.
Height, 6.03. Weight, 185.
Throws and bats righthanded.

Major League stolen bases: 1983 (2), 1984 (3). Total—5.
Led Southern League in game-winning RBIs with 13 in 1980.
Led American Association third basemen in total chances with 361 in 1982.
Tied for American Association lead in sacrifice flies with 9 in 1982.

Year	Club	League	Pos.	G.	AB.	R.	H.	2B.	3B.	HR.	RBI.	B.A.	PO.	A.	E.	F.A.
1976—Oneonta	NYP	3B-OF	65	238	27	55	3	0	1	20	.231	79	71	12	.926
1977—Fort Lauderdale	Fla. St.	3B	110	391	35	93	7	1	1	36	.238	87	209	*35	.894
1978—Fort Lauderdale	Fla. St.	1B-3B-OF	138	455	56	124	9	5	5	70	.273	855	88	15	.984
1979—Fort Lauderdale	Fla. St.	O-3-2-1	75	247	39	78	12	4	2	33	.316	102	41	11	.929
1979—West Haven	East.	2B-OF	56	190	33	57	15	3	6	36	.300	124	169	13	.958
1980—Nashville	South.	2B	136	479	82	142	38	8	16	83	.296	262	361	*27	.958
1981—Columbus†‡	Int.	2B-3B	52	179	41	53	14	3	11	33	.296	66	116	14	.929
1981—Iowa	A. A.	2B	63	222	41	68	13	3	6	37	.306	110	141	4	.984
1981—Chicago	Nat.	2B	35	101	11	19	3	1	1	5	.188	70	93	3	.982

Year Club	League	Pos.	G.	AB.	R.	H.	2B.	3B.	HR.	RBI.	B.A.	PO.	A.	E.	F.A.
1982—Iowa	A. A.	*3B-1B	129	441	89	151	32	*11	17	105	.342	*112	*215	*34	.906
1982—Chicago§x	Nat.	3B	25	85	9	20	4	2	1	7	.235	23	33	3	.949
1983—Charleston	Int.	3B	4	14	2	3	0	1	0	2	.214	2	4	3	.667
1983—Cleveland	Amer.	OF-3B-2B	124	430	56	125	23	5	6	65	.291	197	55	11	.958
1984—Cleveland	Amer.	1-O-3-2	144	473	66	137	21	3	10	68	.290	532	89	7	.989
1985—Cleveland	Amer.	1B-3B-2B	117	404	47	111	18	3	5	59	.275	744	77	14	.983
National League Totals—2 Years			60	186	20	39	7	3	2	12	.210	93	126	6	.973
American League Totals—3 Years			385	1307	169	373	62	11	21	192	.285	1473	221	32	.981
Major League Totals—5 Years			445	1493	189	412	69	14	23	204	.276	1566	347	38	.981

Selected by New York Yankees' organization in 1st round (16th player selected) of free-agent draft, June 8, 1976.

†Loaned to Iowa (Chicago Cubs' organization), June 12, 1981; returned, August 19, 1981.

‡Acquired on waivers by Chicago Cubs for two players to be named later, August 19, 1981; New York Yankees acquired Pitcher Bill Caudill, April 1, 1982, and New York organization acquired Pitcher Jay Howell, August 2, 1982, to complete deal.

§Traded with Pitchers Dick Tidrow and Randy Martz and Infielder Scott Fletcher to Chicago White Sox for Pitchers Steve Trout and Warren Brusstar, January 25, 1983.

xTraded to Cleveland Indians for Shortstop Jerry Dybzinski, April 1, 1983.

GREGORY STEVEN TABOR
(Greg)

Born May 21, 1961, at Castro Valley, Calif,
Height, 6.00. Weight, 165.
Throws and bats righthanded.
Attended Chabot College, Hayward, Calif.

Led Texas League in caught stealing with 18 in 1984.
Led Texas League in sacrifice hits with 15 in 1983.

Year Club	League	Pos.	G.	AB.	R.	H.	2B.	3B.	HR.	RBI.	B.A.	PO.	A.	E.	F.A.
1981—Sarasota Rangers	Gulf C.	SS	9	25	4	8	1	0	0	5	.320	15	29	3	.936
1981—Asheville	S. Atl.	SS-2B	39	136	13	23	3	1	0	4	.169	90	131	23	.906
1982—Burlington	Midw.	2B-SS	98	326	58	81	12	5	2	21	.248	238	258	19	.963
1982—Tulsa	Texas	2B	23	66	6	13	1	1	1	6	.197	38	50	4	.957
1983—Tulsa	Texas	2-S-O-3	112	370	57	99	14	8	1	40	.268	199	295	22	.957
1984—Tulsa	Texas	2B-SS-OF	123	462	69	138	27	2	6	53	.299	241	390	25	.962
1985—Oklahoma City†	A. A.	2B	25	81	16	18	1	0	0	10	.222	49	92	2	.986

Selected by Texas Rangers' organization in 1st round (10th player selected) of free-agent draft, January 13, 1981.

†On disabled list, May 12 to September 8, 1985.

FRANK DARYL TANANA
Name rhymes with Banana.

Born July 3, 1953, at Detroit, Mich.
Height, 6.03. Weight, 195.
Throws and bats lefthanded.
Attended California State University, Fullerton, Calif.
Son of Frank Richard Tanana, minor league outfielder, 1952 through 1956.

Established American League record for most balks, season (8), 1978.
Tied American League record for most consecutive hits allowed, start of game (5), May 18, 1980.
Led American League in balks with 8 in 1978 and tied for lead with 4 in 1984.
Led American League in shutouts with 7 in 1977.
Led Texas League in complete games with 15 in 1973.
Named American League Rookie Pitcher of the Year by THE SPORTING NEWS, 1974.
Named lefthanded pitcher on THE SPORTING NEWS American League All-Star Team, 1976 and 1977.
Named Texas League Pitcher of the Year, 1973.

Year Club	League	G.	IP.	W.	L.	Pct.	H.	R.	ER.	SO.	BB.	ERA.
1971—Idaho Falls†	Pioneer	....	....	....	....	....	....	....	....	....	....	....
1972—Quad Cities	Midwest	19	129	7	2	.778	111	48	40	134	57	2.79
1973—El Paso	Texas	26	*206	16	6	.727	170	72	62	*197	63	2.71
1973—Salt Lake City	P. Coast	2	14	1	0	1.000	11	5	4	15	2	2.57
1973—California	American	4	26	2	2	.500	20	11	9	22	8	3.12
1974—California	American	39	269	14	19	.424	262	104	93	180	77	3.11
1975—California	American	34	257	16	9	.640	211	80	75	*269	73	2.63
1976—California	American	34	288	19	10	.655	212	88	78	261	73	2.44
1977—California	American	31	241	15	9	.625	201	72	68	205	61	*2.54
1978—California	American	33	239	18	12	.600	239	108	97	137	60	3.65
1979—California‡	American	18	90	7	5	.583	93	44	39	46	25	3.90
1980—California§	American	32	204	11	12	.478	223	107	94	113	45	4.15
1981—Boston x	American	24	141	4	10	.286	142	70	63	78	43	4.02
1982—Texas	American	30	194⅓	7	●18	.280	199	102	91	87	55	4.21
1983—Texas	American	29	159⅓	7	9	.438	144	70	56	108	49	3.16
1984—Texas	American	35	246⅓	15	15	.500	234	117	89	141	81	3.25
1985—Texas y-Detroit	American	33	215	12	14	.462	220	112	102	159	57	4.27
Major League Totals—13 Years		376	2570	147	144	.505	2400	1085	954	1806	707	3.34

Selected by California Angels' organization in 1st round (13th player selected) of free-agent draft, June 8, 1971.

†Appeared in one game as pinch-runner (did not pitch due to a sore arm).

‡On disabled list, July 9 to September 4, 1979.

§Traded with Pitcher Jim Dorsey and Outfielder Joe Rudi to Boston Red Sox for Outfielder Fred Lynn and Pitcher Steve Renko, January 23, 1981.

xGranted free agency, November 13, 1981; signed by Texas Rangers, January 6, 1982.
yTraded to Detroit Tigers for Pitcher Duane James, June 20, 1985.

CHAMPIONSHIP SERIES RECORD

Year Club	League	G.	IP.	W.	L.	Pct.	H.	R.	ER.	SO.	BB.	ERA.
1979—California	American	1	5	0	0	.000	6	2	2	3	2	3.60

ALL-STAR GAME RECORD

Year League	IP.	W.	L.	Pct.	H.	R.	ER.	SO.	BB.	ERA.
1976—American	2	0	0	.000	3	3	3	0	1	6.00

Named to American League All-Star Team for the 1977 game; replaced due to injury.
Named to American League All-Star Team for 1978 game; did not play.

BRUCE MATTHEW TANNER

Born December 9, 1961, at New Castle, Pa.
Height, 6.03. Weight, 220.
Throws right and bats lefthanded.
Attended Florida State University, Tallahassee, Fla.
Son of Chuck Tanner, manager of Atlanta Braves; and brother of Mark Tanner, pitcher in
Chicago Cubs', Chicago White Sox' and Texas Rangers' organizations, 1972 through 1975.

Year Club	League	G.	IP.	W.	L.	Pct.	H.	R.	ER.	SO.	BB.	ERA.
1983—Niagara Falls	NYP	16	25	2	3	.400	30	16	10	31	17	3.60
1983—Glens Falls	Eastern	5	6	0	0	.000	2	1	1	1	5	1.50
1983—Appleton	Midwest	4	3	0	1	.000	3	1	1	1	3	3.00
1984—Appleton	Midwest	37	123⅔	12	4	.750	96	32	27	91	30	*1.96
1985—Buffalo	Am. Assoc.	20	109⅓	5	7	.417	99	49	42	49	44	3.46
1985—Chicago	American	10	27	1	2	.333	34	17	16	9	13	5.33
Major League Totals—1 Year		10	27	1	2	.333	34	17	16	9	13	5.33

Selected by Chicago Cubs' organization in 33rd round of free-agent draft, June 3, 1980.
Selected by Chicago White Sox' organization in 4th round of free-agent draft, June 6, 1983.

DANILO TARTABULL (MORA)
(Dan)

Born October 30, 1962, at San Juan, P.R.
Height, 6.01. Weight, 185.
Throws and bats righthanded.
Son of Jose Tartabull, outfielder with Kansas City A's, Boston Red Sox and Oakland A's, 1962 through 1970;
and Yucatan of Mexican League, 1972; and minor league manager,
Houston Astros' organization, 1982 through 1984.

Major League stolen bases: 1985 (1).
Led Pacific Coast League in slugging percentage with .615 and total bases with 291 in 1985.
Led Pacific Coast League shortstops in errors with 35 in 1985.
Led Pacific Coast League shortstops in double plays with 68 in 1984.
Led Florida State League third basemen in errors with 29 in 1981.
Named Pacific Coast League Player of the Year, 1985.
Named Florida State League Most Valuable Player, 1981.

Year Club	League	Pos.	G.	AB.	R.	H.	2B.	3B.	HR.	RBI.	B.A.	PO.	A.	E.	F.A.
1980—Billings	Pion.	3B-OF-2B	59	157	33	47	10	0	2	27	.299	34	54	14	.863
1981—Tampa	Fla. St.	3B-2B	127	422	86	131	*28	10	14	81	*.310	150	248	39	.911
1982—Waterbury†	East.	2B	126	409	64	93	17	3	17	63	.227	237	306	*32	.944
1983—Chattanooga	South.	2B	128	481	95	145	32	7	13	66	.301	252	405	23	.966
1984—Salt Lake City	P. C.	SS	116	418	69	127	22	9	13	73	.304	181	333	24	.955
1984—Seattle	Amer.	SS-2B	10	20	3	6	1	0	2	7	.300	8	21	2	.935
1985—Calgary	P. C.	SS-3B	125	473	102	142	14	3	*43	*109	.300	181	399	36	.942
1985—Seattle	Amer.	SS-3B	19	61	8	20	7	1	1	7	.328	28	43	4	.947
Major League Totals—2 Years			29	81	11	26	8	1	3	14	.321	36	64	6	.943

Selected by Cincinnati Reds' organization in 3rd round of free-agent draft, June 3, 1980.
†Selected by Seattle Mariners' organization in player compensation pool draft, January 20, 1983. (Seattle received compensation for Chicago White Sox' signing of free-agent Pitcher Floyd Bannister, December 13, 1982.)

LaSCHELLE TARVER

Born January 30, 1959, at Modesto, Calif.
Height, 5.11. Weight, 165.
Throws and bats lefthanded.
Attended Reedley College, Reedley, Calif., and California State University, Sacramento, Calif.

Year Club	League	Pos.	G.	AB.	R.	H.	2B.	3B.	HR.	RBI.	B.A.	PO.	A.	E.	F.A.
1981—Shelby	S. Atl.	OF	110	427	78	134	14	5	0	27	.314	247	9	4	.985
1981—Lynchburg	Carol.	OF	5	22	3	10	2	0	0	3	.455	10	0	0	1.000
1982—Lynchburg	Carol.	OF	99	399	75	123	14	2	1	34	.308	140	3	8	.947
1982—Jackson	Texas	OF	24	74	15	15	2	0	0	8	.203	18	0	0	1.000
1982—Tidewater	Int.	OF	3	8	1	2	0	0	0	0	.250	4	0	1	.800
1983—Jackson	Texas	OF	121	481	95	152	19	2	0	36	.316	127	3	7	.949
1983—Tidewater	Int.	DH	3	10	4	5	1	0	0	0	.500	0	0	0	.000
1984—Tidewater	Int.	OF	108	368	63	120	13	1	0	26	.326	97	0	0	1.000
1985—Tidewater†	Int.	OF	126	457	73	142	17	3	1	40	.311	151	5	5	.969

Selected by California Angels' organization in 32nd round of free-agent draft, June 7, 1977.

Signed as free agent by New York Mets' organization, August 18, 1980.

†Traded with Pitchers Calvin Schiraldi and Wes Gardner and Outfielder John Christensen to Boston Red Sox for Pitchers Bob Ojeda, Tom McCarthy, John Mitchell and Chris Bayer, November 13, 1985.

DWIGHT BERNARD TAYLOR

Born March 24, 1960, at Los Angeles, Calif.
Height, 5.09. Weight, 166.
Throws and bats lefthanded.
Attended University of Arizona, Tucson, Ariz.

Led International League in stolen bases with 52 in 1985.
Led Eastern League in stolen bases with 95 in 1983.

Year Club	League	Pos.	G.	AB.	R.	H.	2B.	3B.	HR.	RBI.	B.A.	PO.	A.	E.	F.A.
1981—Waterloo	Midw.	OF	49	153	25	33	4	0	0	13	.216	51	6	2	.966
1982—Waterloo	Midw.	OF	27	101	28	27	4	1	0	6	.267	49	3	1	.981
1982—Chattanooga	South.	OF	110	426	71	123	10	9	2	33	.289	256	9	14	.950
1983—Buffalo	East.	OF	131	451	95	136	13	4	8	38	.302	223	10	9	.963
1984—Maine†	Int.	OF	108	406	64	110	16	2	4	50	.271	234	9	3	.988
1985—Maine‡	Int.	OF	118	427	67	107	7	4	2	32	.251	266	4	11	.961

Selected by Philadelphia Phillies' organization in 11th round of free-agent draft, June 6, 1978.

Selected by Cleveland Indians' organization in 7th round of free-agent draft, June 8, 1981.

†On disabled list, June 1 to June 20, 1984.

‡Traded to Kansas City Royals' organization, October 3, 1985, completing deal in which Kansas City traded Pitcher Keith Creel to Cleveland Indians for a player to be named later, March 19, 1985.

TERRY DERRELL TAYLOR

Born July 28, 1964, at Crestview, Fla.
Height, 6.01. Weight, 180.
Throws and bats righthanded.

Tied for Southern League lead in hit batsmen with 16 in 1985.

Year Club	League	G.	IP.	W.	L.	Pct.	H.	R.	ER.	SO.	BB.	ERA.
1982—Bellingham	Northwest	14	86⅔	6	4	.600	75	53	42	61	54	4.36
1983—Wausau	Midwest	24	130⅔	9	9	.500	131	94	79	118	79	5.44
1984—Salinas	California	17	104⅓	7	6	.538	87	48	34	73	55	2.93
1985—Chattanooga	Southern	28	165⅓	4	15	.211	171	*114	*97	107	96	5.28

Selected by Seattle Mariners' organization in 4th round of free-agent draft, June 7, 1982.

WILLIAM HOWELL TAYLOR
(Billy)

Born October 16, 1961, at Monticello, Fla.
Height, 6.08. Weight, 200.
Throws right and bats left and righthanded.
Attended Abraham Baldwin Agricultural College, Tifton, Ga.

Year Club	League	G.	IP.	W.	L.	Pct.	H.	R.	ER.	SO.	BB.	ERA.
1980—Asheville	S. Atlantic	6	14	0	2	.000	24	24	17	12	9	10.93
1980—Sarasota Rangers	Gulf Coast	14	35	0	0	.000	36	14	9	22	16	2.31
1981—Asheville	S. Atlantic	14	64	1	7	.175	76	43	33	44	35	4.64
1981—Sarasota Rangers†	Gulf Coast	13	35	1	3	.250	28	13	5	13	16	1.29
1982—Wausau-Burlington	Midwest	37	112	7	9	.438	100	64	52	95	63	4.18
1983—Salem	Carolina	7	41⅔	1	1	.500	30	34	29	42	42	6.26
1983—Tulsa	Texas	21	76	5	8	.385	86	65	58	75	51	6.87
1984—Tulsa	Texas	42	80	5	3	.625	65	38	34	80	51	3.83
1985—Tulsa	Texas	20	103⅔	3	9	.250	84	55	40	87	48	3.47

Selected by Texas Rangers' organization in 2nd round of free-agent draft, January 8, 1980.

†Loaned to Wausau (Seattle Mariners' organization), April 5, 1982; returned, June 23, 1982.

FELIX TEJEDA (SANCHEZ)

Born February 28, 1963, at Joachin, Mexico.
Height, 6.00. Weight, 160.
Throws left and bats left and righthanded.

Year Club	League	G.	IP.	W.	L.	Pct.	H.	R.	ER.	SO.	BB.	ERA.
1981—Coatzacoalcos	Mexican	21	34	1	0	1.000	31	17	14	17	16	3.71
1982—Coatzacoalcos	Mexican	18	44	0	2	.000	46	20	18	32	11	3.68
1983—Coatzacoalcos†	Mexican	24	76⅔	5	4	.556	80	38	31	59	20	3.64
1983—Lodi	California	9	29⅔	0	3	.000	40	25	21	30	16	6.37
1983—San Antonio	Texas	3	8⅓	1	2	.333	9	4	4	3	6	4.32
1984—Vero Beach	Florida St.	15	50⅓	2	0	1.000	51	24	16	27	20	2.86
1984—Bakersfield‡	California	13	60⅔	5	2	.714	57	20	19	38	14	2.82
1985—Bakersfield§	California	7	23⅓	1	0	1.000	16	11	7	18	4	2.70
1985—Albuquerque x	P. Coast	9	16⅓	2	0	1.000	24	16	14	14	8	7.71

Signed as free agent by Coatzacoalcos (Mexican League), March 23, 1981.

†Sold to Los Angeles Dodgers' organization, June 23, 1983.

‡On disabled list, August 30, 1984 through remainder of season.

§On disabled list, April 18 to June 14, 1985.

xOn disabled list, August 8, 1985 through remainder of season.

KENTON CHARLES TEKULVE
Name pronounced Tuh-KULL-vee.

(Kent)

Born March 5, 1947, at Cincinnati, O.
Height, 6.04. Weight, 175.
Throws and bats righthanded.
Received bachelor of science degree in physical education
from Marietta College, Marietta, O.

Tied major league records for most intentional bases on balls allowed, season (23), 1982; most consecutive games won by relief pitcher, three consecutive games (3), May 6, 7, 9, 1980.

Major League saves: 1975 (5), 1976 (9), 1977 (7), 1978 (31), 1979 (31), 1980 (21), 1981 (3), 1982 (20), 1983 (18), 1984 (13), 1985 (14). Total—172.

Led National League in intentional bases on balls issued with 20 in 1979, 23 in 1982 and tied for lead with 16 in 1980.
Led National League in games finished in relief with 65 in 1978, 67 in 1979 and tied for lead with 56 in 1983.

Year Club	League	G.	IP.	W.	L.	Pct.	H.	R.	ER.	SO.	BB.	ERA.
1969—Geneva	NYP	9	53	6	2	.750	40	15	10	60	22	1.70
1970—Salem	Carolina	41	79	4	6	.400	68	29	17	75	51	1.94
1971—Salem	Carolina	47	75	11	5	.688	77	36	29	62	31	3.48
1971—Waterbury	Eastern	2	3	0	0	.000	3	0	0	0	2	0.00
1972—Sherbrooke	Eastern	31	72	7	6	.538	61	24	21	54	22	2.63
1972—Charleston	Int'national	9	22	2	1	.667	22	10	10	9	10	4.09
1973—Sherbrooke	Eastern	*57	94	●12	4	*.750	70	24	16	89	35	1.53
1974—Charleston	Int'national	35	60	6	3	.667	50	20	15	38	21	2.25
1974—Pittsburgh	National	8	9	1	1	.500	12	6	6	6	5	6.00
1975—Charleston	Int'national	24	71	5	4	.556	47	23	14	46	19	1.77
1975—Pittsburgh	National	34	56	1	2	.333	43	20	14	28	23	2.25
1976—Pittsburgh	National	64	103	5	3	.625	91	30	28	68	25	2.45
1977—Pittsburgh	National	72	103	10	1	.909	89	41	35	59	33	3.06
1978—Pittsburgh	National	*91	135	8	7	.533	115	44	35	77	55	2.33
1979—Pittsburgh†	National	*94	134	10	8	.556	109	46	41	75	49	2.75
1980—Pittsburgh	National	78	93	8	12	.400	96	39	35	47	40	3.39
1981—Pittsburgh	National	45	65	5	5	.500	61	19	18	34	17	2.49
1982—Pittsburgh	National	*85	128⅔	12	8	.600	113	47	41	66	46	2.87
1983—Pittsburgh‡	National	76	99	7	5	.583	78	27	18	52	36	1.64
1984—Pittsburgh	National	72	88	3	9	.250	86	30	26	36	33	2.66
1985—Pittsburgh §-Philadelphia	National	61	75⅔	4	10	.286	74	35	30	40	30	3.57
Major League Totals—12 Years		780	1089⅓	74	71	.510	967	384	327	588	392	2.70

Signed as free agent by Pittsburgh Pirates' organization, July 16, 1969.
†Appeared in one game as an outfielder with one putout.
‡Granted free agency, November 7, 1983; re-signed by Pirates, December 22, 1983.
§Traded to Philadelphia Phillies for Pitchers Al Holland and Frankie Griffin, April 20, 1985.

CHAMPIONSHIP SERIES RECORD

Year Club	League	G.	IP.	W.	L.	Pct.	H.	R.	ER.	SO.	BB.	ERA.
1975—Pittsburgh	National	2	1⅓	0	0	.000	3	1	1	2	1	6.75
1979—Pittsburgh	National	2	2⅔	0	0	.000	2	1	1	2	2	3.38
Championship Series Totals—2 Years		4	4	0	0	.000	5	2	2	4	3	4.50

WORLD SERIES RECORD

Established World Series record for most saves, seven-game Series (3), 1979.

Year Club	League	G.	IP.	W.	L.	Pct.	H.	R.	ER.	SO.	BB.	ERA.
1979—Pittsburgh	National	5	9⅓	0	1	.000	4	3	3	10	3	2.89

ALL-STAR GAME RECORD

Member of National League All-Star Team in 1980; did not play.

ALONSO TELLEZ

Born September 9, 1961, at Casas Grandes, Chihuahua, Mex.
Height, 5.11. Weight, 180.
Throws and bats righthanded.

Led Mexican League outfielders in total chances with 346 in 1985.

Year Club	League	Pos.	G.	AB.	R.	H.	2B.	3B.	HR.	RBI.	B.A.	PO.	A.	E.	F.A.
1985—Cordoba	Mex.	OF	130	476	78	146	19	4	16	85	.307	*333	6	7	.980

Signed as free agent by Los Angeles Dodgers' organization, December 11, 1985.

THOMAS JOHN TELLMANN
(Tom)

Born March 29, 1954, at Warren, Pa.
Height, 6.04. Weight, 185.
Throws and bats righthanded.
Received bachelor of arts degree in physical education from
Grand Canyon College, Phoenix, Ariz.

Major League saves: 1980 (1), 1983 (8), 1984 (4). Total—13.
Led Pacific Coast League in shutouts with 4 in 1980.

Led California League in saves with 12 and intentional bases on balls issued with 9 in 1977.

Year Club	League	G.	IP.	W.	L.	Pct.	H.	R.	ER.	SO.	BB.	ERA.
1976—Walla Walla	Northwest	17	69	3	4	.429	56	37	25	46	33	3.26
1977—Reno	California	48	88	8	7	.533	92	50	33	82	32	3.38
1978—Amarillo	Texas	48	76	5	6	.455	74	29	22	48	25	2.61
1979—Hawaii	P. Coast	44	83	4	8	.333	98	37	27	51	40	2.93
1979—San Diego	National	1	3	0	0	.000	7	5	5	1	0	15.00
1980—Hawaii	P. Coast	24	170	13	5	.722	155	74	61	83	58	3.23
1980—San Diego	National	6	22	3	0	1.000	23	5	4	9	8	1.64
1981—Hawaii	P. Coast	25	176	12	11	.522	189	78	71	67	53	3.63
1982—Hawaii†	P. Coast	41	104	7	7	.500	113	56	44	55	36	3.81
1983—Milwaukee	American	44	99⅔	9	4	.692	95	34	31	48	35	2.80
1984—Milwaukee‡§	American	50	81	6	3	.667	82	28	25	28	31	2.78
1985—Tacoma	P. Coast	8	12⅓	0	2	.000	12	8	8	6	3	5.84
1985—Oakland x	American	11	21⅓	0	0	.000	33	12	12	8	9	5.06
National League Totals—2 Years		7	25	3	0	1.000	30	10	9	10	8	3.24
American League Totals—3 Years		105	202	15	7	.682	210	74	68	84	75	3.03
Major League Totals—5 Years		112	227	18	7	.720	240	84	77	94	83	3.05

Selected by San Diego Padres' organization in 11th round of free-agent draft, June 8, 1976.
†Traded to Milwaukee Brewers' organization for Pitchers Weldon Swift and Tim Cook, October 15, 1982.
‡On disabled list, May 20 to June 10, 1984.
§Released, March 30, 1985; signed by Oakland A's organization, April 11, 1985.
xOn disabled list, June 10, 1985 through remainder of season; included rehabilitation disability assignment to Tacoma, July 20 to August 5, 1985.

GARRY LEWIS TEMPLETON

Born March 24, 1956, at Lockey, Tex.
Height, 5.11. Weight, 190.
Throws right and bats left and righthanded.
Brother of Ken Templeton, outfielder in Oakland A's organization, 1972 through 1974; son of Spiavia Templeton, former infielder in the Negro Leagues.

Tied major league records by collecting 100 or more hits righthanded and lefthanded, season, 1979; most consecutive seasons leading league, three-base hits (3), 1977 through 1979; most intentional bases on balls, game (4), July 5, 1985 (12 innings).
Tied modern major league record for most three-base hits by switch hitter, season, (19), 1979; most intentional bases on balls, game (4), July 5, 1985 (12 innings).
Major League stolen bases: 1976 (11), 1977 (28), 1978 (34), 1979 (26), 1980 (31), 1981 (8), 1982 (27), 1983 (16), 1984 (8), 1985 (16). Total—205.
Led National League in intentional bases on balls received with 23 in 1984 and tied for lead with 24 in 1985.
Led National League shortstops in total chances with 848 in 1978 and 851 in 1979.
Led National League shortstops in double plays with 108 in 1978.
Tied for National League lead in caught stealing with 24 in 1977.
Tied for National League lead in double plays by shortstops with 102 in 1979.
Named shortstop on THE SPORTING NEWS National League All-Star Team, 1977, 1979 and 1980.
Named shortstop on THE SPORTING NEWS National League Silver Slugger team, 1980 and 1984.
Received reported $40,000 bonus to sign with St. Louis Cardinals, 1974.

Year Club	League	Pos.	G.	AB.	R.	H.	2B.	3B.	HR.	RBI.	B.A.	PO.	A.	E.	F.A.
1974—Sarasota Cards	Gulf C.	SS	18	71	11	19	1	0	3	10	.268	15	41	3	.949
1974—St. Petersburg	Fla. St.	SS	23	95	3	20	1	0	0	2	.211	42	64	7	.938
1975—St. Petersburg	Fla. St.	SS	82	349	50	92	7	8	1	32	.264	130	253	29	.930
1975—Arkansas	Texas	SS	42	177	36	71	9	4	2	20	.401	60	131	18	.914
1976—Tulsa	A. A.	*S-3-O	106	443	65	142	24	*15	6	38	.321	*178	319	34	.936
1976—St. Louis	Nat.	SS	53	213	32	62	8	2	1	17	.291	111	172	24	.922
1977—St. Louis	Nat.	SS	153	621	94	200	19	*18	8	79	.322	285	453	32	.958
1978—St. Louis	Nat.	SS	155	647	82	181	31	*13	2	47	.280	*285	523	*40	.953
1979—St. Louis	Nat.	SS	154	672	105	*211	32	*19	9	62	.314	*292	525	*34	.960
1980—St. Louis†	Nat.	SS	118	504	83	161	19	9	4	43	.319	223	451	*29	.959
1981—St. Louis‡§	Nat.	SS	80	333	47	96	16	8	1	33	.288	160	272	18	.960
1982—San Diego	Nat.	SS	141	563	76	139	25	8	6	64	.247	220	422	26	.961
1983—San Diego x	Nat.	SS	126	460	39	121	20	2	3	40	.263	219	355	24	.960
1984—San Diego	Nat.	SS	148	493	40	127	19	3	2	35	.258	225	407	26	.960
1985—San Diego	Nat.	SS	148	546	63	154	30	2	6	55	.282	245	460	23	.968
Major League Totals—10 Years			1276	5052	661	1452	219	84	42	475	.287	2265	4040	276	.958

Selected by St. Louis Cardinals' organization in 1st round (13th player selected) of free-agent draft, June 5, 1974.
†On disabled list, July 24 to August 14 and August 24 to September 8, 1980.
‡On suspended list, August 26, 1981; then transferred to disabled list, August 28 to September 14, 1981.
§Traded to San Diego Padres for Shortstop Ozzie Smith, February 11, 1982.
xOn disabled list, April 28 to May 17, 1983.

CHAMPIONSHIP SERIES RECORD

Year Club	League	Pos.	G.	AB.	R.	H.	2B.	3B.	HR.	RBI.	B.A.	PO.	A.	E.	F.A.
1984—San Diego	Nat.	SS	5	15	2	5	1	0	0	2	.333	19	11	1	.968

WORLD SERIES RECORD

Year Club	League	Pos.	G.	AB.	R.	H.	2B.	3B.	HR.	RBI.	B.A.	PO.	A.	E.	F.A.
1984—San Diego	Nat.	SS	5	19	1	6	1	0	0	0	.316	8	11	0	1.000

ALL-STAR GAME RECORD

Year League	Pos.	AB.	R.	H.	2B.	3B.	HR.	RBI.	B.A.	PO.	A.	E.	F.A.
1977—National	SS	1	1	1	0	0	0	0	1.000	1	2	1	.750
1985—National	PH	1	0	1	0	0	0	0	1.000	0	0	0	.000
All-Star Game Totals—2 Years		2	1	2	1	0	0	0	1.000	1	2	1	.750

Named to National League All-Star Team for 1979 game; declined.

CHARLES WALTER TERRELL

Name pronounced TEAR-el.

(Walt)

Born May 11, 1958, at Jeffersonville, Ind.
Height, 6.02. Weight, 205.
Throws right and bats lefthanded.
Received degree from Morehead State University, Morehead, Ky. in 1980.

Tied for International League lead in intentional bases on balls issued with 9 in 1982.
Named International League Pitcher of the Year, 1983.

Year Club	League	G.	IP.	W.	L.	Pct.	H.	R.	ER.	SO.	BB.	ERA.
1980—Sarasota Rangers	Gulf Coast	7	38	3	2	.600	20	11	6	23	12	1.42
1980—Asheville	S. Atlantic	3	8	1	1	.500	11	9	6	5	8	6.75
1981—Tulsa†	Texas	27	174	●15	7	.682	158	74	60	123	63	3.10
1982—Tidewater‡	Int'national	21	138⅔	7	8	.467	130	69	61	74	72	3.96
1982—New York	National	3	21	0	3	.000	22	12	8	8	14	3.43
1983—Tidewater	Int'national	12	86⅔	10	1	★.909	76	34	30	58	44	3.12
1983—New York	National	21	133⅔	8	8	.500	123	57	53	59	55	3.57
1984—New York§	National	33	215	11	12	.478	232	99	84	114	80	3.52
1985—Detroit	American	34	229	15	10	.600	221	107	98	130	95	3.85
National League Totals—3 Years		57	369⅔	19	23	.452	377	168	145	181	149	3.53
American League Totals—1 Year		34	229	15	10	.600	221	107	98	130	95	3.85
Major League Totals—4 Years		91	598⅔	34	33	.507	598	275	243	311	244	3.65

Selected by New York Mets' organization in 15th round of free-agent draft, June 5, 1979.
Selected by Texas Rangers' organization in 33rd round of free-agent draft, June 3, 1980.
†Traded with Pitcher Ron Darling to New York Mets' organization for Outfielder Lee Mazzilli, April 1, 1982.
‡On disabled list, July 19 to August 2, 1982.
§Traded to Detroit Tigers for Third Baseman Howard Johnson, December 7, 1984.

SCOTT RAY TERRY

Born November 11, 1959, at Hobbs, N.M.
Height, 5.10. Weight, 185.
Throws and bats righthanded.
Attended Southwestern University, Georgetown, Tex.

Tied for American Association lead in games started by pitchers with 28 and wild pitches with 14 in 1985.
Led Eastern League in shutouts with 6 in 1984.

Year Club	League	G.	IP.	W.	L.	Pct.	H.	R.	ER.	SO.	BB.	ERA.
1983—Tampa	Florida St.	30	59⅓	3	3	.500	60	34	28	52	30	4.25
1984—Vermont	Eastern	20	144	14	3	★.824	110	31	24	100	43	★1.50
1984—Wichita†	Am. Assoc.	2	9⅓	0	0	.000	13	6	6	6	7	5.79
1985—Denver	Am. Assoc.	28	178⅔	11	12	.478	★203	★105	★88	101	76	4.43

Selected by Cincinnati Reds' organization in 12th round of free-agent draft, June 3, 1980.
†On disabled list, August 8 to September 18, 1984.

RECORD AS OUTFIELDER

Year Club	League	Pos.	G.	AB.	R.	H.	2B.	3B.	HR.	RBI.	B.A.	PO.	A.	E.	F.A.
1980—Billings	Pion.	OF	67	251	39	65	9	3	4	45	.259	104	●10	5	.958
1981—Cedar Rapids	Midw.	OF	113	351	32	68	9	0	5	31	.194	147	5	5	.968
1982—Cedar Rapids	Midw.	OF	108	335	50	85	16	3	12	54	.254	156	10	8	.954
1983—Tampa	Fla. St.	OF-P	66	105	14	25	6	2	0	12	.238	60	16	3	.962

MICKEY LEE TETTLETON

Born September 16, 1960, at Oklahoma City, Okla.
Height, 6.02. Weight, 200.
Throws right and bats left and righthanded.
Attended Oklahoma State University, Stillwater, Okla.

Major League stolen bases: 1985 (2).
Tied for Eastern League lead in intentional bases on balls received with 8 in 1984.

Year Club	League	Pos.	G.	AB.	R.	H.	2B.	3B.	HR.	RBI.	B.A.	PO.	A.	E.	F.A.
1981—Modesto	Calif.	C-OF-1B	48	138	28	34	3	0	5	19	.246	235	31	14	.950
1982—Modesto†	Calif.	C-OF	88	253	44	63	18	0	8	37	.249	424	36	8	.983
1983—Modesto	Calif.	C-OF	124	378	55	92	18	2	7	62	.243	582	46	11	.983
1984—Albany	East.	★C-O-1-3-S	86	281	32	65	18	0	5	47	.231	368	42	3	★.993
1984—Oakland	Amer.	C	33	76	10	20	2	1	1	5	.263	112	10	1	.992
1985—Oakland‡	Amer.	C	78	211	23	53	12	0	3	15	.251	344	24	4	.989
1985—Modesto	Calif.	C	4	14	1	3	3	0	0	2	.214	20	1	0	1.000
Major League Totals—2 Years			111	287	33	73	14	1	4	20	.254	456	34	5	.990

Selected by Oakland A's organization in 5th round of free-agent draft, June 8, 1981.
†On disabled list, July 16 to August 13, 1982.
‡On disabled list, August 4 to August 25, 1985; included rehabilitation disability assignment to Modesto, August 21 to August 25, 1985.

TIMOTHY SHAWN TEUFEL
Name pronounced TUFF-el.
(Tim)
Born July 7, 1958, at Greenwich, Conn.
Height, 6.00. Weight, 175.
Throws and bats righthanded.
Attended St. Petersburg Junior College, St. Petersburg, Fla.,
and Clemson University, Clemson, S. C.

Established American League record for fewest double plays by second baseman, season, 150 or more games (81), 1984.

Major League stolen bases: 1984 (1), 1985 (4). Total—5.

Led International League second basemen in putouts with 304, assists with 394, total chances with 711 and double plays with 109 in 1983.

Named International League Player of the Year, 1983.

Named second baseman on THE SPORTING NEWS College Baseball All-America Team, 1980.

Year Club	League	Pos.	G.	AB.	R.	H.	2B.	3B.	HR.	RBI.	B.A.	PO.	A.	E.	F.A.
1980—Orlando	South.	2B	86	287	38	76	15	3	11	47	.265	196	246	17	.963
1981—Orlando	South.	2B	128	416	69	103	21	5	17	60	.248	312	376	20	.972
1982—Orlando	South.	2B	100	340	52	96	12	4	9	56	.282	231	185	15	.965
1982—Toledo	Int.	2B	45	149	25	42	10	4	6	20	.282	99	139	3	.988
1983—Toledo	Int.	2B-SS	136	471	103	152	27	6	27	100	.323	306	401	14	.981
1983—Minnesota	Amer.	2B-SS	21	78	11	24	7	1	3	6	.308	47	58	1	.991
1984—Minnesota	Amer.	2B	157	568	76	149	30	3	14	61	.262	315	★485	13	.984
1985—Minnesota†	Amer.	2B	138	434	58	113	24	3	10	50	.260	237	352	12	.980
Major League Totals—3 Years			316	1080	145	286	61	7	27	117	.265	599	895	26	.983

Selected by Milwaukee Brewers' organization in 16th round of free-agent draft, June 6, 1978.
Selected by Chicago White Sox' organization in secondary phase of free-agent draft, June 5, 1979.
Selected by Minnesota Twins' organization in 2nd round of free-agent draft, June 3, 1980.
†Traded with Outfielder Pat Crosby to New York Mets for Outfielder Billy Beane and Pitchers Bill Latham and Joe Klink, January 16, 1986.

ROBERT ALAN TEWKSBURY
(Bob)
Born November 30, 1960, at Concord, N. H.
Height, 6.04. Weight, 200.
Throws and bats righthanded.
Attended Rutgers University, New Brunswick, N.J., and St. Leo College, St. Leo, Fla.

Led Florida State League in shutouts with 5 and tied for lead in complete games with 13 in 1982.

Year Club	League	G.	IP.	W.	L.	Pct.	H.	R.	ER.	SO.	BB.	ERA.
1981—Oneonta	NYP	14	85	7	3	.700	85	43	34	62	37	3.40
1982—Fort Lauderdale	Florida St.	24	181⅓	★15	4	.789	146	46	38	92	47	★1.88
1983—Fort Lauderdale†	Florida St.	2	16	2	0	1.000	6	1	0	5	1	0.00
1983—Nashville	Southern	7	51	5	1	.833	49	20	16	15	10	2.82
1984—Nashville‡	Southern	26	172	11	9	.550	185	69	54	78	42	2.83
1985—Albany§	Eastern	17	106⅔	6	5	.545	101	48	42	63	19	3.54
1985—Columbus	Int'national	6	44	3	0	1.000	27	5	5	21	5	1.02

Selected by New York Yankees' organization in 19th round of free-agent draft, June 8, 1981.
†On disabled list, April 8 to June 7, 1983.
‡On disabled list, April 9 to April 27, 1984.
§On disabled list, June 10 to June 25, 1985.

ANDRES PERES THOMAS
Born November 10, 1963, at Boca Chica, Dominican Republic.
Height, 6.01. Weight, 170.
Throws and bats righthanded.

Year Club	League	Pos.	G.	AB.	R.	H.	2B.	3B.	HR.	RBI.	B.A.	PO.	A.	E.	F.A.
1982—Bradenton Brav...	Gulf C.	SS	44	143	18	37	2	1	1	14	.259	61	136	20	.908
1983—Anderson	S. Atl.	SS	61	251	33	79	8	4	1	20	.315	61	197	24	.915
1983—Durham	Carol.	SS	70	290	17	72	14	0	2	41	.248	107	222	32	.911
1984—Durham†	Carol.	SS	114	460	64	121	18	4	7	44	.263	156	361	34	.938
1985—Greenville	South.	SS-OF	114	458	53	114	18	4	9	59	.249	155	339	31	.941
1985—Richmond	Int.	SS	11	28	3	5	0	0	1	6	.179	15	30	3	.938
1985—Atlanta	Nat.	SS	15	18	6	5	0	0	0	2	.278	6	17	2	.920
Major League Totals—1 Year			15	18	6	5	0	0	0	2	.278	6	17	2	.920

Signed as free agent by Atlanta Braves' organization, December 16, 1981.
†On suspended list, August 28, 1984 through remainder of season.

DERREL OSBON THOMAS

Born January 14, 1951, at Los Angeles, Calif.
Height, 6.00. Weight, 160.
Throws right and bats right and lefthanded.

Major League stolen bases: 1972 (9), 1973 (15), 1974 (7), 1975 (28), 1976 (10), 1977 (15), 1978 (11), 1979 (18), 1980 (7), 1981 (7), 1982 (2), 1983 (9), 1985 (2). Total—140.
Led American Association second basemen in putouts with 226 and fielding percentage with .979 in 1971.

Year	Club	League	Pos.	G.	AB.	R.	H.	2B.	3B.	HR.	RBI.	B.A.	PO.	A.	E.	F.A.
1969—Cocoa	Fla. St.	SS	33	114	17	33	5	3	0	8	.289	57	75	22	.857
1969—Okla. City	A. A.	SS-OF	36	154	21	48	4	6	0	17	.312	50	64	11	.912
1970—Columbus	South.	SS-2B	38	156	24	38	5	4	4	12	.244	60	95	14	.917
1970—Okla. City	A. A.	SS-2B-OF	75	272	39	73	5	6	4	21	.268	126	156	20	.934
1971—Okla. City	A. A.	2B-SS	122	486	74	139	22	8	3	42	.286	257	325	15	.975
1971—Houston†	Nat.	2B	5	5	0	0	0	0	0	0	.000	3	2	0	1.000
1972—Hawaii	P. C.	OF-2B	6	27	2	4	2	0	0	3	.148	13	6	2	.905
1972—San Diego	Nat.	2B-SS-OF	130	500	48	115	15	5	5	36	.230	290	357	26	.961
1973—San Diego	Nat.	SS-2B	113	404	41	96	7	1	0	22	.238	211	324	37	.935
1974—San Diego‡	Nat.	2-3-O-S	141	523	48	129	24	6	3	41	.247	310	336	18	.973
1975—San Francisco	Nat.	2B-OF	144	540	99	149	21	9	6	48	.276	349	372	19	.974
1976—San Francisco§	Nat.	2-O-3-S	81	272	38	63	5	4	2	19	.232	163	215	15	.962
1977—San Francisco x	Nat.	O-2-S-3-1	148	506	75	135	13	10	8	44	.267	307	158	14	.971
1978—San Diego yz	Nat.	O-2-3-1	128	352	36	80	10	2	3	26	.227	328	168	12	.976
1979—Los Angeles	Nat.	0-3-2-S-1	141	406	47	104	15	4	5	44	.256	298	38	5	.985
1980—Los Angeles	Nat.	O-S-2-C-3	117	297	32	79	18	3	1	22	.266	203	175	14	.964
1981—Los Angeles	Nat.	2-S-O-3	80	218	25	54	4	0	4	24	.248	133	144	14	.952
1982—Los Angeles a	Nat.	O-2-3-S	66	98	13	26	2	1	0	2	.265	58	58	4	.967
1983—Los Angeles bc	Nat.	O-S-2-3	118	192	38	48	6	6	2	8	.250	134	51	5	.974
1984—Montreal d	Nat.	S-O-2-3-1	108	243	26	62	12	2	0	20	.255	118	135	10	.962
1984—California e	Amer.	OF-SS-3B	14	29	3	4	0	1	0	2	.138	12	1	1	.929
1985—Miami fg	Fla. St.	OF-SS	27	89	6	26	2	0	0	9	.292	11	9	2	.909
1985—Philadelphia h	Nat.	S-O-C-2-3	63	92	16	19	2	0	4	12	.207	31	38	7	.908
National League Totals—15 Years			1583	4648	582	1159	154	53	43	468	.249	2936	2571	200	.965
American League Totals—1 Year			14	29	3	4	0	1	0	2	.138	12	1	1	.929
Major League Totals—15 Years			1597	4677	585	1163	154	54	43	470	.249	2948	2572	201	.965

Selected by Houston Astros' organization in 1st round (first player selected) of free-agent draft, February 1, 1969.
†Traded with Pitchers Bill Greif and Mark Schaeffer to San Diego Padres for Pitcher Dave Roberts, December 3, 1971.
‡Traded to San Francisco Giants for Second Baseman Tito Fuentes and Pitcher Butch Metzger, December 6, 1974.
§On disabled list, July 12 to September 15, 1976.
xTraded to San Diego Padres for Catcher-Infielder Mike Ivie, February 28, 1978.
yOn disabled list, July 3 to July 22, 1978.
zGranted free agency, November 2, 1978; signed by Los Angeles Dodgers November 14, 1978.
aOn disabled list, June 25 to September 1, 1982.
bOn disabled list, May 3 to June 4, 1983.
cGranted free agency, November 7, 1983; signed by Montreal Expos, February 2, 1984.
dTraded to California Angels for cash and a conditional player to be named later, September 6, 1984.
eGranted free agency, November 8, 1984; signed by Miami (Independent), April 3, 1985.
fPlayer-coach, May 12 to May 14, 1985.
gSold to Philadelphia Phillies, May 15, 1985.
hGranted free agency, November 12, 1985.

DIVISION SERIES RECORD

Year	Club	League	Pos.	G.	AB.	R.	H.	2B.	3B.	HR.	RBI.	B.A.	PO.	A.	E.	F.A.
1981—Los Angeles	Nat.	OF	4	2	1	0	0	0	0	0	.000	0	0	0	.000

CHAMPIONSHIP SERIES RECORD

Year	Club	League	Pos.	G.	AB.	R.	H.	2B.	3B.	HR.	RBI.	B.A.	PO.	A.	E.	F.A.
1981—Los Angeles	Nat.	PR-3-OF	2	1	2	1	0	0	0	0	1.000	1	0	0	1.000
1983—Los Angeles	Nat.	OF-PH	4	9	0	4	1	0	0	0	.444	7	0	0	1.000
Championship Series Totals—2 Years			6	10	2	5	1	0	0	0	.500	8	0	0	1.000

WORLD SERIES RECORD

Tied World Series record for most positions played, Series (3), 1981 (shortstop, centerfield, third base).

Year	Club	League	Pos.	G.	AB.	R.	H.	2B.	3B.	HR.	RBI.	B.A.	PO.	A.	E.	F.A.
1981—Los Angeles	Nat.	PH-S-O-3	5	7	2	0	0	0	0	1	.000	4	1	0	1.000

JAMES GORMAN THOMAS III

(Known by middle name.)

Born December 12, 1950, at Charleston, S. C.
Height, 6.03. Weight, 200.
Throws and bats righthanded.
Attended Baptist College, Charleston, S. C.

Tied major league records for most strikeouts, two consecutive games (8), July 27 and 28, 1975; most strikeouts, three consecutive games (10), July 27 through 29, 1975.
Tied American League records for most consecutive strikeouts (8), July 27 through 29, 1975; most strikeouts, season (175), 1979; most years with 400 or more putouts, outfielder (4).
Hit three home runs in a game, April 11, 1985.

Major League stolen bases: 1973 (5), 1974 (4), 1975 (4), 1976 (2), 1978 (3), 1979 (1), 1980 (8), 1981 (4), 1982 (3), 1983 (10), 1985 (3). Total—47.

Led American League batters in strikeouts with 175 in 1979, 170 in 1980 and tied for lead with 133 in 1978.
Led Pacific Coast League in total bases with 320 in 1977.
Led Pacific Coast League batters in strikeouts with 175 in 1974.
Led Texas League batters in strikeouts with 171 in 1972.
Led Midwest League batters in strikeouts with 170 in 1971.
Tied for Texas League lead in double plays by outfielders with 4 in 1972.
Named outfielder on THE SPORTING NEWS American League All-Star Team, 1982.
Named American League Comeback Player of the Year by THE SPORTING NEWS, 1985.

Year Club	League	Pos.	G.	AB.	R.	H.	2B.	3B.	HR.	RBI.	B.A.	PO.	A.	E.	F.A.
1969—Billings	Pion.	SS-1B	41	142	23	42	10	3	4	28	.296	94	82	27	.867
1970—Clinton†	Midw.	SS-3B-2B	85	297	36	63	5	4	8	39	.212	105	186	28	.912
1971—Danville	Midw.	OF-3B	121	457	82	112	20	4	⋆31	83	.245	195	14	10	.954
1972—San Antonio	Texas	⋆OF-1B	135	465	70	112	22	2	⋆26	68	.241	⋆305	⋆24	6	⋆.982
1973—Evansville	A. A.	OF	46	146	26	31	6	0	8	18	.212	66	3	4	.945
1973—Milwaukee	Amer.	OF-3B	59	155	16	29	7	1	2	11	.187	87	1	4	.957
1974—Sacramento	P. C.	OF	138	474	117	141	15	1	51	122	.297	302	16	10	.970
1974—Milwaukee	Amer.	OF	17	46	10	12	4	0	2	11	.261	26	0	0	1.000
1975—Milwaukee	Amer.	OF	121	240	34	43	12	2	10	28	.179	215	5	9	.961
1976—Milwaukee	Amer.	OF-3B	99	227	27	45	9	2	8	36	.198	211	4	4	.982
1977—Spokane‡§	P. C.	OF	143	500	114	161	41	5	36	114	.322	325	13	7	⋆.980
1978—Milwaukee	Amer.	OF	137	452	70	111	24	1	32	86	.246	345	5	6	.983
1979—Milwaukee	Amer.	OF	156	557	97	136	29	0	⋆45	123	.244	435	4	4	.991
1980—Milwaukee	Amer.	OF	162	628	78	150	26	3	38	105	.239	455	6	7	.985
1981—Milwaukee	Amer.	OF	103	363	54	94	22	0	21	65	.259	221	8	5	.979
1982—Milwaukee	Amer.	OF	158	567	96	139	29	1	●39	112	.245	427	11	4	.991
1983—Milw. x-Clev. y	Amer.	OF	152	535	72	112	23	1	22	69	.209	439	7	7	.985
1984—Seattle z	Amer.	OF	35	108	6	17	3	0	1	13	.157	45	2	0	1.000
1985—Seattle a	Amer.	DH	135	484	76	104	16	1	32	87	.215	0	0	0	.000
Major League Totals—12 Years			1334	4362	636	992	204	12	252	746	.227	2906	53	50	.983

Selected by Seattle Pilots' organization in 1st round (21st player selected) of free-agent draft, June 5, 1969.
†On restricted list, March 4 to May 30, 1970.
‡Traded to Texas Rangers, October 25, 1977, completing deal in which Texas traded Outfielder-First Baseman Ed Kirkpatrick to Milwaukee Brewers for a player to be named later, August 20, 1977.
§Sold to Milwaukee Brewers, February 8, 1978.
xTraded with Pitchers Jamie Easterly and Ernie Camacho to Cleveland Indians for Outfielder Rick Manning and Pitcher Rick Waits, June 6, 1983.
yTraded with Second Baseman Jack Perconte to Seattle Mariners for Second Baseman Tony Bernazard, December 7, 1983.
zOn disabled list, May 16, 1984 through remainder of season.
aOn disabled list, May 22 to June 11, 1985.

DIVISION SERIES RECORD

Year Club	League	Pos.	G.	AB.	R.	H.	2B.	3B.	HR.	RBI.	B.A.	PO.	A.	E.	F.A.
1981—Milwaukee	Amer.	OF	5	18	2	2	0	0	1	1	.111	12	0	0	1.000

CHAMPIONSHIP SERIES RECORD

Tied Championship Series record for hitting home run in first Series at-bat, October 5, 1982.

Year Club	League	Pos.	G.	AB.	R.	H.	2B.	3B.	HR.	RBI.	B.A.	PO.	A.	E.	F.A.
1982—Milwaukee	Amer.	OF	5	16	1	1	0	0	1	3	.063	13	0	0	1.000

WORLD SERIES RECORD

Tied World Series record for most at-bats, inning (2), October 16, 1982 (seventh inning).

Year Club	League	Pos.	G.	AB.	R.	H.	2B.	3B.	HR.	RBI.	B.A.	PO.	A.	E.	F.A.
1982—Milwaukee	Amer.	OF	7	26	0	3	0	0	0	3	.115	15	0	0	1.000

ALL-STAR GAME RECORD

Year League	Pos.	AB.	R.	H.	2B.	3B.	HR.	RBI.	B.A.	PO.	A.	E.	F.A.
1981—American	PH	1	0	0	0	0	0	0	.000	0	0	0	.000

ROY JUSTIN THOMAS

Born June 22, 1953, at Quantico, Va.
Height, 6.05. Weight, 215.
Throws and bats righthanded.
Attended University of Tampa, Tampa, Fla., and De Anza College, Cupertino, Calif.

Pitched seven-inning, 2-0 no-hit victory against West Haven, August 20, 1974 (second game).
Major League saves: 1978 (3), 1979 (1), 1983 (1), 1984 (1), 1985 (1). Total—7.
Led Pacific Coast League in wild pitches with 27 and tied for lead in hit batsmen with 10 in 1983.
Led American Association in wild pitches with 17 in 1976.
Led Eastern League in games started by pitchers with 27 in 1974.
Led Carolina League in shutouts with 6 in 1973.
Received reported $75,000 bonus to sign with Philadelphia Phillies, 1971.

Year Club	League	G.	IP.	W.	L.	Pct.	H.	R.	ER.	SO.	BB.	ERA.
1971—Walla Walla	Northwest	7	12	0	3	.000	19	22	14	8	16	10.50
1972—Spartanburg	W. Carol.	24	152	11	7	.611	128	67	58	128	62	3.43
1973—Rocky Mount	Carolina	26	169	●15	8	.652	119	53	42	⋆193	77	⋆2.24
1973—Reading	Eastern	2	16	2	0	1.000	11	2	2	14	7	1.13

Year Club	League	G.	IP.	W.	L.	Pct.	H.	R.	ER.	SO.	BB.	ERA.
1974—Reading	Eastern	27	●191	14	11	.560	154	77	55	★168	89	2.59
1974—Toledo	Int'national	2	7	0	0	.000	5	3	1	5	2	1.29
1975—Toledo	Int'national	19	119	4	9	.308	112	63	53	95	49	4.01
1975—Reading†	Eastern	10	67	6	3	.667	50	22	19	53	29	2.55
1976—Iowa‡§	Am. Assoc.	27	168	6	11	.353	167	89	70	103	72	3.75
1977—Charleston	Int'national	44	168	11	6	.647	151	63	59	71	65	3.16
1977—Houston	National	4	6	0	0	.000	5	2	2	4	3	3.00
1978—Charleston x	Int'national	28	66	9	4	.692	63	28	23	40	30	3.14
1978—St. Louis	National	16	28	1	1	.500	21	14	12	16	16	3.86
1979—Springfield	Am. Assoc.	17	74	5	6	.455	79	55	48	85	31	5.84
1979—St. Louis	National	26	77	3	4	.429	66	29	25	44	24	2.92
1980—St. Louis	National	24	55	2	3	.400	59	32	29	22	25	4.75
1980—Springfield y	Am. Assoc.	19	37	5	1	.833	34	18	14	36	18	3.41
1981—Tacoma z	P. Coast	36	165	12	8	.600	137	61	56	111	49	3.05
1982—Salt Lake City	P. Coast	33	156⅔	8	9	.471	195	112	98	96	84	5.63
1983—Seattle	American	43	88⅔	3	1	.750	95	44	34	77	32	3.45
1984—Seattle a	American	21	49⅔	3	2	.600	52	33	29	42	37	5.26
1984—Salt Lake City b	P. Coast	7	18⅓	0	0	.000	15	10	8	13	12	3.93
1985—Calgary	P. Coast	15	29⅔	2	2	.500	29	15	15	40	13	4.55
1985—Seattle	American	40	93⅔	7	0	1.000	66	37	35	70	48	3.36
National League Totals—4 Years		70	166	6	8	.429	151	77	68	86	68	3.69
American League Totals—3 Years		104	232	13	3	.813	213	114	98	189	117	3.80
Major League Totals—7 Years		174	398	19	11	.633	364	191	166	275	185	3.75

Selected by Philadelphia Phillies' organization in 1st round (sixth player selected) of free-agent draft, June 8, 1971.

†Traded with Pitcher Dick Ruthven and Infielder-Outfielder Alan Bannister by Philadelphia Phillies to Chicago White Sox for Pitcher Jim Kaat and Shortstop Mike Buskey, December 10, 1975.

‡Selected by Seattle Mariners in American League expansion draft, November 5, 1976.

§Traded to Houston Astros for Infielder Larry Milbourne, March 30, 1977.

xSold on waivers to St. Louis Cardinals, June 23, 1978.

yDrafted by Oakland A's, December 8, 1980.

zTraded to Seattle Mariners' organization for Outfielder Rusty McNealy and Pitcher Tim Hallgren, December 9, 1981.

aOn disabled list, June 12 to July 4, 1984.

bGranted free agency, October 15, 1984; signed by Calgary (Seattle Mariners' organization), February 28, 1985.

JASON DOLPH THOMPSON

Born July 6, 1954, at Hollywood, Calif.
Height, 6.03. Weight, 210.
Throws and bats lefthanded.
Attended California State University, Northridge, Calif.

Major League stolen bases: 1976 (2), 1979 (2), 1980 (2), 1982 (1), 1983 (1). Total—8.
Led National League first basemen in total chances with 1,425 in 1984.
Led American League first basemen in double plays with 153 in 1978.
Led American League first basemen in total chances with 1,712 in 1977.

Year Club	League	Pos.	G.	AB.	R.	H.	2B.	3B.	HR.	RBI.	B.A.	PO.	A.	E.	F.A.
1975 Montgomery	South	1B	75	222	42	72	12	1	10	38	.324	633	47	10	.986
1976—Evansville	A. A.	1B	4	16	3	5	0	0	3	6	.313	29	7	0	1.000
1976—Detroit	Amer.	1B	123	412	45	90	12	1	17	54	.218	1157	88	8	.994
1977—Detroit	Amer.	1B	158	585	87	158	24	5	31	105	.270	★1599	97	16	.991
1978—Detroit	Amer.	1B	153	589	79	169	25	3	26	96	.287	1503	92	11	.993
1979—Detroit	Amer.	1B	145	492	58	121	16	1	20	79	.246	1176	91	8	.994
1980—Det.†-Calif.‡	Amer.	1B	138	438	69	126	19	0	21	90	.288	679	51	0	1.000
1981—Pittsburgh	Nat.	1B	86	223	36	54	13	0	15	42	.242	590	46	7	.989
1982—Pittsburgh	Nat.	1B	156	550	87	156	32	0	31	101	.284	1395	105	10	.993
1983—Pittsburgh	Nat.	1B	152	517	70	134	20	1	18	76	.259	1266	89	9	.993
1984—Pittsburgh	Nat.	1B	154	543	61	138	22	0	17	74	.254	★1337	74	★14	.990
1985—Pittsburgh	Nat.	1B	123	402	42	97	17	1	12	61	.241	995	82	9	.992
American League Totals—5 Years			717	2516	338	664	96	10	115	424	.264	6114	419	43	.993
National League Totals—5 Years			671	2235	296	579	104	2	93	354	.259	5583	396	49	.992
Major League Totals—10 Years			1388	4751	634	1243	200	12	208	778	.262	11697	815	92	.993

Selected by Los Angeles Dodgers' organization in 15th round of free-agent draft, June 6, 1972.

Selected by Detroit Tigers' organization in 4th round of free-agent draft, June 4, 1975.

†Traded to California Angels for Outfielder Al Cowens, May 27, 1980.

‡Traded to Pittsburgh Pirates for Catcher Ed Ott and Pitcher Mickey Mahler, April 1, 1981.

ALL-STAR GAME RECORD

Year League	Pos.	AB.	R.	H.	2B.	3B.	HR.	RBI.	B.A.	PO.	A.	E.	F.A.
1978—American	PH	1	0	0	0	0	0	0	.000	0	0	0	.000
1982—National	PH	1	0	0	0	0	0	0	.000	0	0	0	.000
All-Star Game Totals—2 Years		2	0	0	0	0	0	0	.000	0	0	0	.000

Member of American League All-Star Team in 1977; did not play.

—DID YOU KNOW—

That Don Mattingly is the first Yankee to have consecutive 200-hit seasons since Joe DiMaggio and Lou Gehrig in the 1936 and 1937 seasons?

MILTON BERNARD THOMPSON
(Milt)

Born January 5, 1959, at Washington, D.C.
Height, 5.11. Weight, 160.
Throws right and bats lefthanded.
Attended Howard University, Washington, D.C.

Major League stolen bases: 1984 (14), 1985 (9). Total—23.
Led International League outfielders in total chances with 341 in 1984.
Led Southern League in stolen bases with 68 and caught stealing with 19 in 1982.
Led Southern League outfielders in total chances with 336 in 1982.

Year	Club	League	Pos.	G.	AB.	R.	H.	2B.	3B.	HR.	RBI.	B.A.	PO.	A.	E.	F.A.
1979—Greenwood	W. Car.	OF	53	145	31	27	4	1	2	16	.186	85	8	3	.969
1979—Kingsport	Appal.	OF	26	94	22	31	8	4	1	11	.330	58	4	1	.984
1980—Durham	Carol.	OF	68	255	49	74	12	3	2	36	.290	159	8	5	.971
1980—Savannah	South.	OF	71	278	35	83	7	3	1	15	.299	133	11	6	.960
1981—Savannah	South.	OF	140	493	92	135	18	2	4	31	.274	226	17	8	.968
1982—Savannah	South.	OF	●144	526	83	132	20	7	6	45	.251	★312	10	14	.958
1982—Richmond	Int.	OF	3	6	2	1	0	0	0	0	.167	4	0	0	1.000
1983—Richmond	Int.	OF	12	32	12	8	1	0	0	3	.250	30	0	1	.968
1983—Savannah	South.	OF-1B	115	386	84	117	21	4	5	36	.303	295	15	7	.978
1984—Richmond	Int.	OF	134	503	●91	145	11	3	4	40	.288	★317	13	11	.968
1984—Atlanta	Nat.	OF	25	99	16	30	1	0	2	4	.303	37	6	2	.956
1985—Richmond	Int.	OF	82	312	52	98	10	1	2	22	.314	209	3	4	.981
1985—Atlanta†	Nat.	OF	73	182	17	55	7	2	0	6	.302	78	2	3	.964
Major League Totals—2 Years			98	281	33	85	8	2	2	10	.302	115	8	5	.961

Selected by Atlanta Braves' organization in 2nd round of free-agent draft, January 9, 1979.
†Traded with Pitcher Steve Bedrosian to Philadelphia Phillies for Catcher Ozzie Virgil and Pitcher Pete Smith, December 10, 1985.

RICHARD NEIL THOMPSON
(Rich)

Born November 1, 1958, at New York, N.Y.
Height, 6.03. Weight, 225.
Throws right and bats left and righthanded.
Received bachelor of arts degree in economics from Amherst College, Amherst, Mass. in 1980,
and attending Baylor University School of Law, Waco, Tex.

Major League saves: 1985 (5).

Year	Club	League	G.	IP.	W.	L.	Pct.	H.	R.	ER.	SO.	BB.	ERA.
1980—Batavia	NYP	7	12	2	0	1.000	12	3	1	16	6	0.75
1981—Waterloo	Midwest	28	122	5	6	.455	112	67	56	109	55	4.13
1982—Chattanooga	Southern	50	78	7	6	.538	69	39	35	55	36	4.04
1983—Buffalo	Eastern	43	78⅔	3	7	.300	67	33	25	61	46	2.86
1984—Buffalo†	Eastern	51	104⅔	9	7	.563	96	48	39	81	47	3.35
1985—Maine	Int'national	4	9	0	0	.000	6	1	1	2	2	1.00
1985—Cleveland‡	American	57	80	3	8	.273	95	63	56	30	48	6.30
Major League Totals—1 Year		57	80	3	8	.273	95	63	56	30	48	6.30

Selected by Cleveland Indians' organization in 7th round of free-agent draft, June 3, 1980.
†On disabled list August 9 to August 19, 1984.
‡Traded to Milwaukee Brewers for Pitcher Scott Roberts, December 16, 1985.

ROBERT RANDALL THOMPSON
(Rob)

Born May 10, 1962, at West Palm Beach, Fla.
Height, 5.11. Weight, 165.
Throws and bats righthanded.
Attended Palm Beach Junior College, Lake Worth, Fla.,
and University of Florida, Gainesville, Fla.

Led Texas League second basemen in putouts with 291, total chances with 664 and double plays with 91 in 1985.

Year	Club	League	Pos.	G.	AB.	R.	H.	2B.	3B.	HR.	RBI.	B.A.	PO.	A.	E.	F.A.
1983—Fresno	Calif.	2B	64	220	33	57	8	1	4	23	.259	118	185	11	.965
1984—Fresno	Calif.	2B-SS-3B	102	325	53	81	11	0	8	43	.249	182	280	24	.951
1985—Shreveport	Texas	★2B-SS	121	449	85	117	20	7	9	40	.261	292	366	12	★.982

Selected by Oakland A's organization in 2nd round of free-agent draft, January 12, 1982.
Selected by Seattle Mariners' organization in secondary phase of free-agent draft, June 7, 1982.
Selected by San Francisco Giants' organization in secondary phase of free-agent draft, June 6, 1983.

VERNON SCOT THOMPSON
(Known by middle name.)

Born December 7, 1955, at Grove City, Pa.
Height, 6.03. Weight, 175.
Throws and bats lefthanded.
Son of William K. Thompson, minor league first baseman-outfielder, 1953 through 1962;
brother of Joe Thompson, minor league first baseman, 1976.

Major League stolen bases: 1979 (4), 1980 (6), 1981 (2), 1984 (5). Total—17.

Led American Association first basemen in fielding percentage with .994 in 1977.

Year Club League	Pos.	G.	AB.	R.	H.	2B.	3B.	HR.	RBI.	B.A.	PO.	A.	E.	F.A.
1974—Bradenton Cubs....Gulf C.	OF-1B	47	169	22	43	6	3	1	19	.254	86	7	5	.948
1975—Key West .... Fla. St.	OF-1B	123	424	40	95	6	3	3	41	.224	186	10	12	.942
1976—Midland.................. Texas	1B-OF	116	425	47	121	11	2	7	54	.285	766	50	12	.985
1977—Wichita.................. A. A.	1B-OF	124	446	77	136	24	5	11	54	.305	920	62	7	.993
1978—Wichita.................. A. A.	1B-OF ●135	★519	83	169	★33	7	10	64	.326	873	59	13	.986
1978—Chicago .... Nat.	OF-1B	19	36	7	15	3	0	0	2	.417	14	1	0	1.000
1979—Chicago .... Nat.	OF	128	346	36	100	13	5	2	29	.289	161	7	5	.971
1980—Chicago† .... Nat.	OF-1B	102	226	26	48	10	1	2	13	.212	149	6	4	.975
1981—Chicago .... Nat.	OF-1B	57	115	8	19	5	0	0	8	.209	56	1	2	.966
1981—Iowa .... A. A.	OF	69	277	35	74	10	0	2	29	.267	177	3	6	.968
1982—Iowa .... A. A.	1B-OF	29	93	17	32	6	0	2	11	.344	40	3	3	.935
1982—Chicago‡ .... Nat.	OF-1B	49	74	11	27	5	1	0	7	.365	39	3	0	1.000
1983—Chicago .... Nat.	OF-1B	53	88	4	17	3	1	0	10	.193	29	0	0	1.000
1983—Iowa§ .... A. A.	OF-1B	25	86	9	18	3	0	1	8	.209	56	2	0	1.000
1984—San Francisco ...... Nat.	1B-OF	120	245	30	75	7	1	1	31	.306	562	36	2	.997
1985—S.F. x-Montreal..... Nat.	1B-OF	98	143	10	32	6	0	0	10	.224	180	18	1	.995
Major League Totals—8 Years................		626	1273	132	333	52	9	5	110	.262	1190	72	14	.989

Selected by Chicago Cubs' organization in 1st round (seventh player selected) of free-agent draft, June 5, 1974.

†On disabled list, July 10 to August 6, 1980.

‡On disabled list, June 18 to July 22, 1982.

§Granted free agency, October 15, 1983; signed by Phoenix (San Francisco Giants' organization), January 12, 1984.

xTraded with Pitcher Bill Laskey and a player to be named later to Montreal Expos for First Baseman Dan Driessen, August 1, 1985; deal settled when Laskey was traded back to San Francisco Giants for Pitcher George Riley and Outfielder Alonzo Powell, October 24, 1985.

RICHARD WILLIAM THON
(Dickie)

Born June 20, 1958, at South Bend, Ind.
Height, 5.11. Weight, 150.
Throws and bats righthanded.
Grandson of Fred Thon, minor league pitcher, 1940.

Tied National League record for fewest triples, season, for league leader in triples (10), 1982.
Major League stolen bases: 1980 (7), 1981 (6), 1982 (37), 1983 (34), 1985 (8). Total—92.
Led National League in game-winning RBIs with 18 in 1983.
Named shortstop on THE SPORTING NEWS National League All-Star Team, 1983.
Named shortstop on THE SPORTING NEWS National League Silver Slugger team, 1983.

Year Club League	Pos.	G.	AB.	R.	H.	2B.	3B.	HR.	RBI.	B.A.	PO.	A.	E.	F.A.
1976—Quad Cities........... Midw.	SS	69	246	46	68	11	4	1	32	.276	96	193	32	.900
1977—Salinas................... Calif.	SS	56	225	48	71	13	2	4	44	.316	95	162	13	.952
1977—Salt Lake City....... P. C.	SS	77	274	47	79	9	3	8	43	.288	129	242	26	.935
1978—Salt Lake City....... P. C.	2B-SS	130	439	67	113	17	3	1	47	.257	273	380	26	.962
1979—Salt Lake City....... P. C.	SS-2B	38	162	25	47	3	1	2	21	.290	70	120	11	.945
1979—California.............. Amer.	2B-SS-3B	35	56	6	19	3	0	0	8	.339	38	46	8	.913
1980—Salt Lake City....... P. C.	2B-SS	40	155	28	61	14	2	2	28	.394	81	107	12	.940
1980—California†........... Amer.	S-2-3-1	80	267	32	68	12	2	0	15	.255	70	124	10	.951
1981—Houston .... Nat.	2B-SS-3B	49	95	13	26	6	0	0	3	.274	53	63	6	.951
1982—Houston .... Nat.	SS-3B-2B	136	496	73	137	31	★10	3	36	.276	183	412	17	.972
1983—Houston .... Nat.	SS	154	619	81	177	28	9	20	79	.286	258	★533	28	.966
1984—Houston‡ .... Nat.	SS	5	17	3	6	0	1	0	1	.353	8	13	0	1.000
1985—Houston§x............ Nat.	SS	84	251	26	63	6	1	6	29	.251	106	218	11	.967
American League Totals—2 Years		115	323	38	87	15	2	0	23	.269	108	170	18	.939
National League Totals—5 Years...........		428	1478	196	409	71	21	29	148	.277	608	1239	62	.968
Major League Totals—7 Years................		543	1801	234	496	86	23	29	171	.275	716	1409	80	.964

Signed as free agent by California Angels' organization, November 23, 1975.

†Traded to Houston Astros for Pitcher Ken Forsch, April 1, 1981.

‡On disabled list, April 9, 1984 through remainder of season.

§On disabled list, May 19 to June 8, 1985.

xGranted free agency, November 12, 1985; re-signed by Astros, January 7, 1986.

DIVISION SERIES RECORD

Year Club League	Pos.	G.	AB.	R.	H.	2B.	3B.	HR.	RBI.	B.A.	PO.	A.	E.	F.A.
1981—Houston .... Nat.	SS-PH	4	11	0	2	0	0	0	0	.182	5	10	1	.938

CHAMPIONSHIP SERIES RECORD

Year Club League	Pos.	G.	AB.	R.	H.	2B.	3B.	HR.	RBI.	B.A.	PO.	A.	E.	F.A.
1979—California.............. Amer.	PR-SS	1	0	1	0	0	0	0	0	.000	0	0	0	.000

ALL-STAR GAME RECORD

Year League	Pos.	AB.	R.	H.	2B.	3B.	HR.	RBI.	B.A.	PO.	A.	E.	F.A.
1983—National	PH-SS	3	0	1	0	0	0	0	.333	0	2	0	1.000

—DID YOU KNOW—

That in the 26-7 win by Philadelphia over New York on June 11, the Phillies set team marks for hits (27), runs (26) and total bases (47)?

ANDRE THORNTON

Born August 13, 1949, at Tuskegee, Ala.
Height, 6.02. Weight, 205.
Throws and bats righthanded.
Attended Cheyney State College, Cheyney, Pa.
Brother-in-law of Pat Kelly, outfielder with Minnesota, Kansas City, Chicago AL,
Baltimore and Cleveland, 1967 through 1981.

Tied major league record for most assists, first baseman, inning (3), August 22, 1975 (5th inning).
Major League stolen bases: 1974 (2), 1975 (3), 1976 (4), 1977 (3), 1978 (4), 1979 (5), 1981 (3), 1982 (6), 1983 (4), 1984 (6), 1985 (3). Total—43.
Hit for the cycle, April 22, 1978.
Tied for American League lead in intentional bases on balls received with 18 in 1982.
Led Western Carolinas League first basemen in errors with 19 in 1969.
Led Northwest League first basemen in double plays with 35 in 1968.
Tied for Eastern League lead in caught stealing with 8 in 1971.
Named American League Comeback Player of the Year by THE SPORTING NEWS, 1982.
Named designated hitter on THE SPORTING NEWS American League Silver Slugger team, 1984.

Year Club	League	Pos.	G.	AB.	R.	H.	2B.	3B.	HR.	RBI.	B.A.	PO.	A.	E.	F.A.
1967—Huron†	North.	3B-OF	19	55	3	10	1	2	1	3	.182	7	9	10	.615
1968—Eugene‡	N'west.	1B	56	185	27	46	9	2	5	31	.249	*427	*24	10	*.978
1969—Spartanburg§	W. Car.	1B-3B-OF	90	299	56	75	13	4	13	51	.251	701	45	20	.974
1970—Peninsula x	Carol.	1B	67	193	24	48	7	2	5	23	.249	499	30	5	.991
1971—Reading y	East.	1B	116	367	67	98	18	1	26	76	.267	1006	48	15	.986
1972—Eugene z	P. C.	1D-0D	40	141	22	45	8	2	6	29	.319	224	46	11	.961
1972—Richmond abc	Int.	1B-OF	49	159	30	42	5	0	14	36	.264	379	33	6	.986
1973—Richmond d	Int.	3B-1B-OF	16	49	8	10	2	0	4	8	.204	67	17	5	.944
1973—Wichita	A. A.	1B	40	135	34	39	2	0	17	45	.289	362	23	1	.997
1973—Chicago	Nat.	1B	17	35	3	7	3	0	0	2	.200	81	10	1	.989
1974—Chicago	Nat.	1B-3B	107	303	41	79	16	4	10	46	.261	760	70	7	.992
1975—Chicago e	Nat.	1B-3B	120	372	70	109	21	4	18	60	.293	984	77	13	.988
1976—Chi. f-Mont. gh	Nat.	1B-OF	96	268	28	52	11	2	11	38	.194	542	46	6	.990
1977—Cleveland	Amer.	1B	131	433	77	114	20	5	28	70	.263	1026	71	6	.995
1978—Cleveland	Amer.	1B	145	508	97	133	22	4	33	105	.262	1327	106	7	.995
1979—Cleveland	Amer.	1B	143	515	89	120	31	1	26	93	.233	1089	82	7	.994
1980—Cleveland i	Amer.					(Did not play)									
1981—Cleveland j	Amer.	1B	69	226	22	54	12	0	6	30	.239	67	5	1	.986
1982—Cleveland	Amer.	1B	161	589	90	161	26	1	32	116	.273	76	5	0	1.000
1983—Cleveland	Amer.	1B	141	508	78	143	27	1	17	77	.281	201	21	2	.991
1984—Cleveland k	Amer.	1B	155	587	91	159	26	0	33	99	.271	86	9	2	.979
1985—Cleveland l	Amer.	DH	124	461	49	109	13	0	22	88	.236	0	0	0	.000
American League Totals—8 Years			1069	3827	593	993	177	12	197	678	.259	3872	299	25	.994
National League Totals—4 Years			340	978	142	247	51	10	39	146	.252	2367	203	27	.990
Major League Totals—12 Years			1409	4805	735	1240	228	22	236	824	.258	6239	502	52	.992

Signed as free agent by Philadelphia Phillies' organization, August 6, 1967.
†On military list, December 29, 1967 through May 1, 1968.
‡On temporary inactive list, June 1 to July 2, 1968.
§On temporary inactive list, June 4 to June 24, 1969.
xOn temporary inactive list, June 11 to June 30, 1970.
yOn temporary inactive list, June 7 to June 26, 1971.
zTraded with Pitcher Joe Hoerner to Atlanta Braves for Pitchers Jim Nash and Gary Neibauer, June 15, 1972.
aOn temporary inactive list, June 28 to July 1, 1972.
bOn disabled list, July 5 to July 16, 1972.
cOn temporary inactive list, August 1 to August 4, 1972.
dTraded to Chicago Cubs for First Baseman Joe Pepitone, May 19, 1973.
eOn disabled list, April 1 to May 4, 1975.
fTraded to Montreal Expos for Pitcher Steve Renko and Outfielder-First Baseman Larry Biittner, May 17, 1976.
gOn disabled list, June 10 to July 1, 1976.
hTraded to Cleveland Indians for Pitcher Jackie Brown, December 10, 1976.
iOn disabled list, March 28 to June 9 and June 19 to October 13, 1980.
jOn disabled list, March 30 to April 17 and August 24 to September 8, 1981.
kGranted free agency, November 8, 1984; re-signed by Indians, December 4, 1984.
lOn disabled list, March 24 to April 25, 1985.

ALL-STAR GAME RECORD

Year League	Pos.	AB.	R.	H.	2B.	3B.	HR.	RBI.	B.A.	PO.	A.	E.	F.A.
1982—American	PH	1	0	0	0	0	0	0	.000	0	0	0	.000
1984—American	PH	1	0	1	0	0	0	0	1.000	0	0	0	.000
All-Star Game Totals—2 Years		2	0	1	0	0	0	0	.500	0	0	0	.000

LOUIS THORNTON JR.
(Lou)

Born April 26, 1963, at Montgomery, Ala.
Height, 6.00. Weight, 175.
Throws right and bats lefthanded.

Major League stolen bases: 1985 (1).
Led Appalachian League outfielders in errors with 9 in 1982.

Year Club	League	Pos.	G.	AB.	R.	H.	2B.	3B.	HR.	RBI.	B.A.	PO.	A.	E.	F.A.
1981—Kingsport	Appal.	1B	48	153	23	32	7	0	2	17	.209	338	43	16	.960

Year Club	League	Pos.	G.	AB.	R.	H.	2B.	3B.	HR.	RBI.	B.A.	PO.	A.	E.	F.A.
1982—Kingsport...........	Appal.	OF-1B-3B	57	210	29	44	9	2	5	29	.210	182	7	13	.940
1983—Columbia	S. Atl.	OF	119	448	80	120	24	6	11	73	.268	193	18	11	.950
1984—Lynchburg†.........	Carolina	OF-1B	131	505	78	139	25	7	6	67	.275	250	13	11	.960
1985—Toronto	Amer.	OF	56	72	18	17	1	1	1	8	.236	44	0	2	.957
Major League Totals—1 Year..................			56	72	18	17	1	1	1	8	.236	44	0	2	.957

Selected by New York Mets' organization in 19th round of free-agent draft, June 8, 1981.
†Drafted by Toronto Blue Jays, December 3, 1984.

CHAMPIONSHIP SERIES RECORD

Year Club	League	Pos.	G.	AB.	R.	H.	2B.	3B.	HR.	RBI.	B.A.	PO.	A.	E.	F.A.
1985—Toronto	Amer.	PR	2	0	1	0	0	0	0	0	.000	0	0	0	.000

GARY MONTEZ THURMAN JR.

Born November 12, 1964, at Indianapolis, Ind.
Height, 5.10. Weight, 165.
Throws and bats righthanded.

Led Florida State League in stolen bases with 70 in 1985.
Led Gulf Coast League batters in strikeouts with 58 in 1983.
Tied for South Atlantic League lead in caught stealing with 17 in 1984.
Led Gulf Coast League outfielders in total chances with 143 in 1983, South Atlantic League outfielders with 329 in 1984 and Florida State League outfielders with 396 in 1985.

Year Club	League	Pos.	G.	AB.	R.	H.	2B.	3B.	HR.	RBI.	B.A.	PO.	A.	E.	F.A.
1983—Sarasota Royals...	Gulf C.	OF	59	203	32	52	8	2	0	19	.256	★127	★13	3	.979
1984—Charleston	S. Atl.	OF	129	478	71	109	6	8	6	51	.228	★311	5	13	.960
1985—Fort Myers	Fla. St.	OF	134	453	68	137	9	9	0	45	.302	★368	18	10	.975

Selected by Kansas City Royals' organization in 1st round (21st player selected) of free-agent draft, June 6, 1983.

MARK ANTHONY THURMOND

Born September 12, 1956, at Houston, Tex.
Height, 6.00. Weight, 190.
Throws and bats lefthanded.
Received bachelor of science degree in finance from
Texas A&M University, College Station, Tex. in 1979.

Major League saves: 1985 (2).
Named lefthanded pitcher on THE SPORTING NEWS National League All-Star Team, 1984.
Tied for Texas League lead in games started by pitchers with 27 in 1981.

Year Club	League	G.	IP.	W.	L.	Pct.	H.	R.	ER.	SO.	BB.	ERA.
1979—Amarillo..................................	Texas	17	62	3	5	.375	89	52	39	64	31	5.66
1980—Amarillo†..............................	Texas	26	156	10	9	.526	164	80	67	125	61	3.87
1981—Amarillo..................................	Texas	27	193	12	5	.706	202	86	70	128	56	3.26
1982—Hawaii.....................................	P. Coast	28	194⅓	12	10	.545	202	88	77	106	58	3.57
1983—Las Vegas..............................	P. Coast	19	63	6	1	.857	63	28	23	38	24	3.29
1983—San Diego	National	21	115⅓	7	3	.700	104	40	34	49	33	2.65
1984—San Diego	National	32	178⅔	14	8	.636	174	70	59	57	55	2.97
1985—San Diego	National	36	138⅓	7	11	.389	154	70	61	57	44	3.97
Major League Totals—3 Years.............................		89	432⅓	28	22	.560	432	180	154	163	132	3.21

Selected by San Diego Padres' organization in 24th round of free-agent draft, June 6, 1978.
Selected by San Diego Padres' organization in 5th round of free-agent draft, June 5, 1979.
†On disabled list, July 5 to July 16, 1980.

CHAMPIONSHIP SERIES RECORD

Year Club	League	G.	IP.	W.	L.	Pct.	H.	R.	ER.	SO.	BB.	ERA.
1984—San Diego	National	1	3⅔	0	1	.000	7	4	4	1	2	9.82

WORLD SERIES RECORD

Year Club	League	G.	IP.	W.	L.	Pct.	H.	R.	ER.	SO.	BB.	ERA.
1984—San Diego	National	2	5⅓	0	1	.000	12	6	6	2	3	10.13

JAY LINDSEY TIBBS

Born January 4, 1962, at Birmingham, Ala.
Height, 6.03. Weight, 185.
Throws and bats righthanded.

Year Club	League	G.	IP.	W.	L.	Pct.	H.	R.	ER.	SO.	BB.	ERA.
1980—Kingsport..................................	Ap'lachian	12	76	3	7	.300	88	54	37	45	32	4.38
1981—Lynchburg...............................	Carolina	15	72	2	7	.222	89	65	55	41	34	6.88
1981—Shelby.....................................	W. Carol.	13	89	4	8	.333	87	56	38	57	33	3.84
1982—Lynchburg†.............................	Carolina	7	38⅓	2	4	.333	42	28	24	31	23	5.63
1982—Jackson	Texas	1	3⅓	0	0	.000	2	1	0	3	1	0.00
1983—Lynchburg‡.............................	Carolina	28	203⅔	14	8	.636	172	94	66	170	96	2.92
1984—Jackson	Texas	6	37⅓	1	2	.333	28	15	13	31	19	3.13
1984—Tidewater§..............................	Int'national	8	41⅓	3	5	.375	44	27	24	27	23	5.23
1984—Wichita....................................	Am. Assoc.	4	27⅔	3	0	1.000	22	13	11	14	8	3.58
1984—Cincinnati...............................	National	14	100⅔	6	2	.750	87	34	32	40	33	2.86

Year	Club	League	G.	IP.	W.	L.	Pct.	H.	R.	ER.	SO.	BB.	ERA.
1985—Cincinnati		National	35	218	10	16	.385	216	111	95	98	83	3.92
1985—Denver x		Am. Assoc.	4	31⅔	1	2	.333	20	10	8	15	12	2.27
Major League Totals—2 Years			49	318⅔	16	18	.471	303	145	127	138	116	3.59

Selected by New York Mets' organization in 2nd round of free-agent draft, June 3, 1980.

†On disabled list, July 21 to August 29, 1982.

‡Drafted by Philadelphia Phillies, December 5, 1983; returned, March 29, 1984.

§Traded with Third Baseman Eddie Williams and Pitcher Matt Bullinger to Cincinnati Reds' organization for Pitcher Bruce Berenyi, June 15, 1984.

xTraded with Pitchers Andy McGaffigan and John Stuper and Catcher Dann Bilardello to Montreal Expos for Pitcher Bill Gullickson and Catcher Sal Butera, December 19, 1985.

KERRY JEROME TILLMAN
(Rusty)

Born August 29, 1960, at Jacksonville, Fla.
Height, 6.00. Weight, 175.
Throws and bats righthanded.
Attended Florida Junior College, Temple Terrace, Fla.

Year	Club	League	Pos.	G.	AB.	R.	H.	2B.	3B.	HR.	RBI.	B.A.	PO.	A.	E.	F.A.
1979—Little Falls		NYP	OF	6	22	4	7	0	1	0	4	.318	4	1	0	1.000
1979—Grays Harbor		N'west	OF	60	217	33	64	10	1	3	30	.295	140	7	5	.967
1980—Lynchburg		Carol.	OF	135	526	94	166	27	11	8	79	.316	173	10	5	*.973
1981—Jackson		Texas	OF-1B	122	464	66	129	21	4	6	59	.278	126	8	4	.971
1982—Tidewater		Int.	OF	108	404	60	130	10	6	5	54	.322	156	10	3	.982
1982—New York		Nat.	OF	12	13	4	2	1	0	0	0	.154	2	0	0	1.000
1983—Tidewater		Int.	OF	126	483	67	123	20	7	8	63	.255	220	13	7	.971
1984—Tidewater†		Int.	OF-3B	44	151	17	33	5	1	3	13	.219	56	8	2	.970
1984—Denver‡		A. A.	OF	75	255	43	78	6	3	9	43	.306	114	8	5	.961
1985—Las Vegas		P. C.	O-1-3-P	115	412	66	139	27	7	12	75	.337	193	7	6	.971
Major League Totals—1 Year				12	13	4	2	1	0	0	0	.154	2	0	0	1.000

Selected by New York Mets' organization in 10th round of free-agent draft, January 9, 1979.

†Loaned to Denver (Chicago White Sox' organization), June 14, 1984; returned, September 16, 1984.

‡Traded to San Diego Padres' organization for Outfielder-First Baseman Rick Lancellotti, March 31, 1985.

PITCHING RECORD

Year	Club	League	G.	IP.	W.	L.	Pct.	H.	R.	ER.	SO.	BB.	ERA.
1985—Las Vegas		P. Coast	1	1	0	0	.000	5	6	3	1	1	27.00

DONALD FITZGERALD TIMBERLAKE
(Don)

Born January 14, 1964, at Credmoor, N.C.
Height 6.03. Weight, 210.
Throws and bats righthanded.

Year	Club	League	G.	IP.	W.	L.	Pct.	H.	R.	ER.	SO.	BB.	ERA.
1982—Salem		Northwest	11	69⅔	5	4	.556	63	37	30	52	35	3.88
1983—Peoria†		Midwest	23	127	7	10	.412	156	86	67	68	44	4.75
1984—Redwood		California	25	156⅔	15	5	.750	149	67	53	111	57	3.04
1985—Midland‡		Texas	23	120⅔	5	12	.294	168	*110	90	45	65	6.71

Selected by California Angels' organization in 7th round of free-agent draft, June 7, 1982.

†On disabled list, April 30 to May 23, 1983.

‡On disabled list, June 21 to July 12, 1985.

RONALD IRVIN TINGLEY
(Ron)

Born May 27, 1959, at Presque Isle, Maine.
Height, 6.02. Weight, 160.
Throws and bats righthanded.

Year	Club	League	Pos.	G.	AB.	R.	H.	2B.	3B.	HR.	RBI.	B.A.	PO.	A.	E.	F.A.
1977—Walla Walla		N'west	OF	21	33	8	5	0	0	1	3	.152	5	2	0	1.000
1978—Walla Walla		N'west	OF-C	43	140	22	29	2	0	2	21	.207	149	16	8	.954
1979—Santa Clara		Calif.	C-OF-P	52	143	11	29	4	1	0	17	.203	258	42	8	.974
1979—Amarillo		Texas	C-OF	30	90	16	23	4	1	1	6	.256	133	17	4	.974
1980—Reno†		Calif.	C-OF	65	204	37	61	3	3	3	35	.299	333	46	10	.974
1981—Amarillo		Texas	C-1B-OF	116	379	72	109	9	*10	13	60	.288	607	41	11	.983
1982—Hawaii		P. C.	C	115	362	45	95	13	8	6	42	.262	540	77	12	.981
1982—San Diego		Nat.	C	8	20	0	2	0	0	0	0	.100	40	4	2	.957
1983—Las Vegas		P. C.	C	92	294	44	83	15	6	10	48	.282	449	55	12	.977
1984—Salt Lake City‡§		P. C.	C	3	2	1	1	0	0	1	1	.500	3	0	0	1.000
1985—Calgary x		P. C.	C-OF	83	277	36	70	11	3	11	47	.253	399	51	10	.978
Major League Totals—1 Year				8	20	0	2	0	0	0	0	.100	40	4	2	.957

Selected by San Diego Padres' organization in 10th round of free-agent draft, June 7, 1977.

†On disabled list, April 10 to April 29, 1980.

‡On disabled list, April 7 to August 10, 1984.

§Granted free agency, October 15, 1984; signed by Calgary (Seattle Mariners' organization), January 15, 1985.

xGranted free agency, October 15, 1985; signed by Richmond (Atlanta Braves' organization), November 19, 1985.

Year Club	League	G.	IP.	W.	L.	Pct.	H.	R.	ER.	SO.	BB.	ERA.
1979—Santa Clara	California	1	1	0	0	.000	4	5	1	2	2	9.00

DAVID VANCE TOBIK

Name pronounced TOE-bick.

(Dave)

Born March 2, 1953, at Euclid, O.
Height, 6.01. Weight, 195.
Throws and bats righthanded.
Received bachelor of business administration degree from Ohio University, Athens, O.

Major League saves: 1979 (3), 1981 (1), 1982 (9), 1983 (9), 1984 (5), 1985 (1). Total—28.

Year Club	League	G.	IP.	W.	L.	Pct.	H.	R.	ER.	SO.	BB.	ERA.
1975—Lakeland........................	Florida St.	5	36	1	4	.200	29	14	10	22	19	2.50
1975—Montgomery..................	Southern	20	99	6	9	.400	7	57	48	62	44	4.36
1976—Lakeland........................	Florida St.	6	42	3	1	.750	28	11	5	29	15	1.07
1976—Montgomery†................	Southern	18	63	4	5	.444	56	33	26	44	32	3.71
1977—Montgomery..................	Southern	27	48	4	4	.500	31	17	14	42	17	2.63
1977—Evansville	Am. Assoc.	13	19	4	1	.800	19	8	7	17	9	3.32
1978—Evansville	Am. Assoc.	33	79	5	4	.556	71	43	30	70	26	3.42
1978—Detroit...........................	American	5	12	0	0	.000	2	5	5	11	3	3.75
1979—Evansville	Am. Assoc.	19	38	4	0	1.000	24	6	2	45	13	0.47
1979—Detroit...........................	American	37	69	3	5	.375	59	34	33	48	25	4.30
1980—Evansville	Am. Assoc.	30	48	3	3	.500	35	22	21	49	26	3.94
1980—Detroit...........................	American	17	61	1	0	1.000	61	27	27	34	21	3.98
1981—Detroit...........................	American	27	60	2	2	.500	47	19	18	32	33	2.70
1982—Detroit‡........................	American	51	98⅔	4	9	.308	86	45	39	63	38	3.56
1983—Texas.............................	American	27	44	2	1	.667	36	18	18	30	13	3.68
1983—Oklahoma City..............	Am. Assoc.	12	20⅓	3	0	1.000	13	8	8	14	10	3.54
1984—Texas.............................	American	24	42⅓	1	6	.143	44	20	17	30	17	3.61
1984—Oklahoma City§	Am. Assoc.	14	32⅓	1	1	.500	34	12	11	30	9	3.06
1985—Calgary	P. Coast	56	88⅔	12	6	.667	98	59	51	97	58	5.18
1985—Seattle x	American	8	9	1	0	1.000	10	8	6	8	3	6.00
Major League Totals—8 Years............................		196	396	14	23	.378	355	176	163	256	153	3.70

Selected by Montreal Expos' organization in 3rd round of free-agent draft, June 5, 1974.
Selected by Detroit Tigers' organization in secondary phase of free-agent draft, January 9, 1975.
†On disabled list, June 3 to June 24, 1976.
‡Traded to Texas Rangers for Outfielder Johnny Grubb, March 24, 1983.
§Granted free agency, October 15, 1985; signed by Calgary (Seattle Mariners' organization), April 4, 1985.
xReleased, November 1, 1985.

FREDDIE LEE TOLIVER

(Fred)

Born February 3, 1961, at Natchez, Miss.
Height, 6.01. Weight, 170.
Throws and bats righthanded.

Major League saves: 1985 (1).

Year Club	League	G.	IP.	W.	L.	Pct.	H.	R.	ER.	SO.	BB.	ERA.
1979—Oneonta..........................	NYP	13	77	*10	2	.833	46	28	18	71	66	2.10
1980—Fort Lauderdale	Florida St.	3	8	0	2	.000	14	15	13	4	10	14.63
1980—Greensboro†..................	S. Atlantic	20	126	6	8	.429	98	60	40	96	89	2.86
1981—Greensboro‡§................	S. Atlantic	17	80	5	3	.625	67	38	31	62	56	3.49
1982—Cedar Rapids.................	Midwest	23	115	6	7	.462	114	77	54	117	66	4.23
1982—Indianapolis...................	Am. Assoc.	4	20⅔	2	2	.500	20	10	9	19	13	3.92
1983—Indianapolis...................	Am. Assoc.	26	166⅔	8	10	.444	151	93	84	112	*110	4.54
1984—Wichita..........................	Am. Assoc.	32	164	11	6	.647	142	90	88	113	*116	4.83
1984—Cincinnati......................	National	3	10	0	0	.000	7	2	1	4	7	0.90
1985—Denver xy......................	Am. Assoc.	19	121⅓	11	3	.786	113	50	44	84	56	3.24
1985—Philadelphia	National	11	25	0	4	.000	27	15	13	23	17	4.68
Major League Totals—2 Years............................		14	35	0	4	.000	34	17	14	27	24	3.60

Selected by New York Yankees' organization in 3rd round of free-agent draft, June 5, 1979.
†On disabled list, May 23 to June 6, 1980.
‡On disabled list, April 9 to May 27, 1981.
§Traded to Cincinnati Reds' organization, December 10, 1981, completing deal in which Cincinnati traded Outfielder Ken Griffey to New York Yankees for Pitcher Brian Ryder and a player to be named later, November 4, 1981.
xOn disabled list, July 5 to August 10, 1985.
yTraded to Philadelphia Phillies, August 27, 1985, completing deal in which Philadelphia traded Catcher Bo Diaz and Pitcher Greg Simpson to Cincinnati Reds for Shortstop Tom Foley, Catcher Alan Knicely, a player to be named later and cash, August 8, 1985.

JIMMY WAYNE TOLLESON

(Known by middle name.)

Born November 22, 1955, at Spartanburg, S. C.
Height, 5.09. Weight, 160.
Throws right and bats left and righthanded.
Attended Western Carolina University, Cullowhee, N. C.

Major League stolen bases: 1981 (2), 1982 (1), 1983 (33), 1984 (22), 1985 (21). Total—79.

Year Club	League	Pos.	G.	AB.	R.	H.	2B.	3B.	HR.	RBI.	B.A.	PO.	A.	E.	F.A.
1978—Asheville	W. Car.	3B-SS	70	212	35	57	4	1	0	21	.269	85	175	20	.929
1979—Tulsa	Texas	SS	130	418	43	98	9	7	1	36	.234	179	413	*41	.935
1980—Tulsa	Texas	SS	131	452	69	124	19	7	1	30	.274	161	395	31	.947
1981—Wichita	A. A.	3-S-2-O	107	375	58	98	9	4	3	38	.261	96	259	15	.959
1981—Texas	Amer.	3B-SS	14	24	6	4	0	0	0	1	.167	5	8	0	1.000
1982—Texas	Amer.	SS-3B-2B	38	70	6	8	1	0	0	2	.114	47	70	5	.959
1982—Denver	A. A.	SS	71	266	48	64	9	3	4	27	.241	97	195	6	.980
1983—Texas	Amer.	2B-SS	134	470	64	122	13	2	3	20	.260	268	372	17	.974
1984—Texas	Amer.	2-S-3-O	118	338	35	72	9	2	0	9	.213	195	287	10	.980
1985—Texas†	Amer.	SS-2B-3B	123	323	45	101	9	5	1	18	.313	149	255	14	.967
Major League Totals—5 Years			427	1225	156	307	32	9	4	50	.251	664	992	46	.973

Selected by Pittsburgh Pirates' organization in 12th round of free-agent draft, June 7, 1977.
Selected by Texas Rangers' organization in 8th round of free-agent draft, June 6, 1978.

†Traded with Pitcher Dave Schmidt to Chicago White Sox for Pitcher Ed Correa, Infielder Scott Fletcher and a player to be named later, November 25, 1985; Texas Rangers acquired Infielder Jose Mota to complete deal, December 12, 1985.

TIMOTHY LEE TOLMAN
(Tim)

Born April 20, 1956, at Santa Monica, Calif.
Height, 6.00. Weight, 190.
Throws and bats righthanded.
Attended University of Southern California, Los Angeles, Calif.

Led Gulf Coast League in being hit by pitch with 5 in 1978.
Led Southern League first basemen in assists with 90 in 1980.
Led Florida State League first basemen in errors with 17 in 1979.

Year Club	League	Pos.	G.	AB.	R.	H.	2B.	3B.	HR.	RBI.	B.A.	PO.	A.	E.	F.A.
1978—Sarasota Astros	Gulf C.	1B	39	122	25	42	5	6	0	23	*.344	292	21	4	.987
1978—Daytona Beach	Fla. St.	OF-1B	7	25	2	7	2	0	0	5	.280	24	2	0	1.000
1979—Daytona Beach	Fla. St.	1B-3B-OF	131	422	62	122	13	3	1	53	.289	688	93	26	.968
1980—Columbus	South.	1B-OF	139	481	67	142	37	4	7	73	.295	980	93	15	.986
1981—Tucson	P. C.	OF-1B	137	479	85	154	28	8	14	99	.322	735	49	10	.987
1981—Houston	Nat.	OF	4	8	0	1	0	0	0	0	.125	2	0	0	1.000
1982—Tucson	P. C.	OF-1B-3B	125	473	93	143	31	6	15	82	.302	525	46	15	.974
1982—Houston	Nat.	OF-1B	15	26	4	5	2	0	1	3	.192	17	1	0	1.000
1983—Houston	Nat.	1B-OF	43	56	4	11	4	0	2	10	.196	55	2	0	1.000
1983—Tucson	P. C.	1B-OF	7	24	4	9	2	0	1	6	.375	31	3	0	1.000
1984—Tucson	P. C.	OF-1B-3B	102	363	63	106	27	7	9	54	.292	299	25	13	.961
1984—Houston	Nat.	OF-1B	14	17	2	3	1	0	0	0	.176	6	0	0	1.000
1985—Houston	Nat.	OF	31	43	4	6	1	0	2	8	.140	12	0	0	1.000
1985—Tucson†	P. C.	OF-1B	40	149	30	45	10	1	4	27	.302	133	5	4	.972
Major League Totals—5 Years			107	150	14	26	8	0	5	21	.173	92	3	0	1.000

Selected by Houston Astros' organization in 12th round of free-agent draft, June 6, 1978.
†Released, November 13, 1985.

DAVID ALLEN TOMLIN
(Dave)

Born June 22, 1949, at Maysville, Ky.
Height, 6.02. Weight, 185.
Throws and bats lefthanded.

Led Appalachian League pitchers in games started with 13 and tied for lead in complete games with 6 in 1967.
Major League saves: 1973 (1), 1974 (2), 1975 (1), 1977 (3), 1978 (4), 1979 (1). Total—12.

Year Club	League	G.	IP.	W.	L.	Pct.	H.	R.	ER.	SO.	BB.	ERA.
1967—Wytheville	Ap'lachian	14	85	●7	6	.538	*93	55	41	47	43	4.34
1968—Tampa	Florida St.	37	56	6	3	.667	47	19	15	38	16	2.41
1969—Tampa	Florida St.	23	44	5	1	.833	34	18	14	25	22	2.86
1970—Asheville	Southern	25	139	6	10	.375	135	62	48	73	58	3.11
1971—Indianapolis	Am. Assoc.	41	61	7	4	.636	46	19	15	50	24	2.23
1972—Indianapolis	Am. Assoc.	36	90	5	6	.455	83	30	28	86	36	2.79
1972—Cincinnati	National	3	4	0	0	.000	7	4	4	2	1	9.00
1973—Indianapolis	Am. Assoc.	25	31	1	3	.250	29	15	12	26	11	3.52
1973—Cincinnati†	National	16	28	1	2	.333	24	15	15	20	15	4.82
1974—Hawaii	P. Coast	25	48	5	1	.833	33	10	9	48	20	1.69
1974—San Diego	National	47	58	2	0	1.000	59	29	28	29	30	4.34
1975—San Diego	National	67	83	4	2	.667	87	38	30	48	31	3.25
1976—San Diego	National	49	73	0	1	.000	62	24	23	43	20	2.84
1977—San Diego‡§	National	76	102	4	4	.500	98	38	34	55	32	3.00
1978—Cincinnati	National	57	62	9	1	.900	88	54	40	32	30	5.81
1979—Cincinnati	National	53	58	2	2	.500	59	29	17	30	18	2.64
1980—Cincinnati x	National	27	26	3	0	1.000	38	17	16	6	11	5.54
1981—Syracuse y	Int'national	38	57	2	3	.400	67	25	23	36	19	3.63
1982—Indianapolis z	Am. Assoc.	*64	91⅔	9	2	.818	96	39	36	67	30	3.53
1982—Montreal	National	1	2	0	0	.000	1	1	1	2	1	4.50
1983—Wichita a	Am. Assoc.	41	52⅓	4	1	.800	44	21	21	44	18	3.61
1983—Pittsburgh b	National	5	4	0	0	.000	6	4	3	5	1	6.75

Year	Club	League	G.	IP.	W.	L.	Pct.	H.	R.	ER.	SO.	BB.	ERA.
1984—Hawaii	P. Coast	22	50⅔	3	2	.600	45	17	15	43	21	2.66
1985—Hawaii	P. Coast	33	82	8	2	.800	62	22	19	65	35	2.09
1985—Pittsburgh	National	1	1	0	0	.000	1	0	0	0	1	0.00
Major League Totals—12 Years		402	501	25	12	.676	530	253	211	272	191	3.79

Selected by Cincinnati Reds' organization in 29th round of free-agent draft, June 6, 1967.
†Traded with Outfielder Bobby Tolan to San Diego Padres for Pitcher Clay Kirby, November 9, 1973.
‡Traded with $125,000 to Texas Rangers for Pitcher Gaylord Perry, February 15, 1978.
§Sold to Cincinnati Reds, March 28, 1978.
xReleased, September 2, 1980; signed by Syracuse (Toronto Blue Jays' organization), February 26, 1981.
yReleased, April 8, 1982; signed by Indianapolis (Cincinnati Reds' organization), April 22, 1982.
zSold to Montreal Expos, September 8, 1982.
aSold to Pittsburgh Pirates, August 2, 1983.
bGranted free agency, November 7, 1983; re-signed by Pirates' organization, January 12, 1984.

CHAMPIONSHIP SERIES RECORD

Year	Club	League	G.	IP.	W.	L.	Pct.	H.	R.	ER.	SO.	BB.	ERA.
1973—Cincinnati	National	1	1⅔	0	0	.000	5	3	3	1	1	16.20
1979—Cincinnati	National	3	3	0	0	.000	3	1	0	3	2	0.00
Championship Series Totals—2 Years		4	4⅔	0	0	.000	8	4	3	4	3	5.79

JAMES JOSEPH TRABER
(Jim)

Born December 26, 1961, at Columbus, O.
Height, 6.00. Weight, 194.
Throws and bats lefthanded.
Attended Oklahoma State University, Stillwater, Okla.

Led Appalachian League in game-winning RBIs with 10 in 1982.
Led Carolina League first basemen in putouts with 1,006, double plays with 96 and total chances with 1,070 in 1983.
Led Appalachian League first basemen in double plays with 44 and total chances with 581 in 1982.

Year	Club	League	Pos.	G.	AB.	R.	H.	2B.	3B.	HR.	RBI.	B.A.	PO.	A.	E.	F.A.
1982—Bluefield	Appal.	1B	61	235	41	76	18	3	9	●63	.323	★540	★34	7	.988
1982—Hagerstown	Carol.	OF-1B	7	26	1	9	2	0	0	2	.346	12	0	0	1.000
1983—Hagerstown	Carol.	★1B-OF	128	449	73	123	22	1	14	79	.274	1012	54	10	★.991
1984—Hagerstown†	Carol.	1B-OF	48	165	33	59	15	0	2	29	.358	361	30	7	.982
1984—Charlotte	South.	1B	75	296	50	104	17	2	16	56	.351	663	44	7	.990
1984—Baltimore	Amer.	DH-PH	10	21	3	5	0	0	0	2	.238	0	0	0	.000
1985—Rochester‡	Int.	OF-1B	80	279	32	74	13	2	7	37	.265	220	22	4	.984
Major League Totals			10	21	3	5	0	0	0	2	.238	0	0	0	.000

Selected by Baltimore Orioles' organization in 21st round of free-agent draft, June 7, 1982.
†On suspended list, June 7 to June 17, 1984.
‡On disabled list, May 21 to July 8, 1985.

ALAN STUART TRAMMELL
Name pronounced TRAM-mull.

Born February 21, 1958, at Garden Grove, Calif.
Height, 6.00. Weight, 170.
Throws and bats righthanded.

Major League stolen bases: 1978 (3), 1979 (17), 1980 (12), 1981 (10), 1982 (19), 1983 (30), 1984 (19), 1985 (14). Total—124.
Led American League in sacrifice hits with 16 in 1981 and 15 in 1983.
Named American League Comeback Player of the Year by THE SPORTING NEWS, 1983.
Named shortstop on THE SPORTING NEWS American League All-Star fielding team, 1980, 1981, 1983 and 1984.
Named Southern League Most Valuable Player, 1977.

Year	Club	League	Pos.	G.	AB.	R.	H.	2B.	3B.	HR.	RBI.	B.A.	PO.	A.	E.	F.A.
1976—Bristol	Appal.	SS	41	140	27	38	2	2	0	7	.271	59	131	12	.941
1976—Montgomery	South.	SS	21	56	4	10	0	0	0	2	.179	40	64	2	.981
1977—Montgomery	South.	SS	134	454	78	132	9	★19	3	50	.291	188	397	27	.956
1977—Detroit	Amer.	SS	19	43	6	8	0	0	0	0	.186	15	34	2	.961
1978—Detroit	Amer.	SS	139	448	49	120	14	6	2	34	.268	239	421	14	.979
1979—Detroit	Amer.	SS	142	460	68	127	11	4	6	50	.276	245	388	26	.961
1980—Detroit	Amer.	SS	146	560	107	168	21	5	9	65	.300	225	412	13	.980
1981—Detroit	Amer.	SS	105	392	52	101	15	3	2	31	.258	181	347	9	.983
1982—Detroit	Amer.	SS	157	489	66	126	34	3	9	57	.258	259	459	16	.978
1983—Detroit	Amer.	SS	142	505	83	161	31	2	14	66	.319	236	367	13	.979
1984—Detroit†	Amer.	SS	139	555	85	174	34	5	14	69	.314	180	314	10	.980
1985—Detroit	Amer.	SS	149	605	79	156	21	7	13	57	.258	225	400	15	.977
Major League Totals—9 Years			1138	4057	595	1141	181	35	69	429	.281	1805	3142	118	.977

Selected by Detroit Tigers' organization in 2nd round of free-agent draft, June 8, 1976.
†On disabled list, July 9 to July 31, 1984.

CHAMPIONSHIP SERIES RECORD

Year	Club	League	Pos.	G.	AB.	R.	H.	2B.	3B.	HR.	RBI.	B.A.	PO.	A.	E.	F.A.
1984—Detroit	Amer.	SS	3	11	2	4	0	1	1	3	.364	1	8	0	1.000

Tied World Series records for batting in all club's runs, game, most (4), October 13, 1984; most hits, five-game Series (9), 1984.

Year Club	League	Pos.	G.	AB.	R.	H.	2B.	3B.	HR.	RBI.	B.A.	PO.	A.	E.	F.A.
1984—Detroit.................... Amer.		SS	5	20	5	9	1	0	2	6	.450	8	9	1	.944

ALL-STAR GAME RECORD

Year League	Pos.	AB.	R.	H.	2B.	3B.	HR.	RBI.	B.A.	PO.	A.	E.	F.A.
1980—American	SS	0	0	0	0	0	0	0	.000	0	0	0	.000
1985—American	SS	1	0	0	0	0	0	0	.000	0	0	0	.000
All-Star Game Totals—2 Years....................		1	0	0	0	0	0	0	.000	0	0	0	.000

Named to American League All-Star Team for 1984 game; replaced due to injury by Alfredo Griffin.

ALEJANDRO TREVINO (CASTRO)

(Alex)

Born August 26, 1957, at Monterrey, Mexico.
Height, 5.10. Weight, 165.
Throws and bats righthanded.
Attended University of Nuevo Leon, Monterrey, Mexico.
Brother of Bobby Trevino, outfielder with California Angels, 1968; outfielder in Mexican League, 1970 through 1979; manager, Tabasco, 1977, Tampico, 1979, and Toluca, 1980.

Major League stolen bases: 1979 (2), 1981 (3), 1982 (3), 1984 (5). Total—13
Led Midwest League catchers in putouts with 847 and assists with 102 in 1977.
Led Carolina League in passed balls with 18 in 1976.

Year Club	League	Pos.	G.	AB.	R.	H.	2B.	3B.	HR.	RBI.	B.A.	PO.	A.	E.	F.A.
1973—Victoria† .... Mx. Cen.		C-OF	12	26	3	6	1	0	0	2	.231	26	5	1	.969
1974—Marion .... Appal.		C-SS	12	16	0	1	0	0	0	1	.063	15	0	0	1.000
1975—Marion .... Appal.		C-2B-OF	22	60	10	12	1	0	0	3	.200	96	8	6	.963
1976—Lynchburg .... Carol.		C-3-2-S	94	284	17	57	11	2	0	31	.201	400	130	18	.967
1977—Wausau .... Midw.		C-2-1-3	128	422	57	100	10	0	2	36	.237	865	110	15	.985
1978—Tidewater .... Int.		C-3B	87	262	44	77	13	2	5	37	.294	303	68	11	.971
1978—New York .... Nat.		C-3B	6	12	3	3	0	0	0	0	.250	12	4	0	1.000
1979—New York .... Nat.		C-3B-2B	79	207	24	56	11	1	0	20	.271	229	71	9	.971
1980—New York .... Nat.		C-3B-2B	106	355	26	91	11	2	0	37	.256	450	76	16	.970
1981—New York‡ .... Nat.		C-2-O-3	56	149	17	39	2	0	0	10	.262	215	25	9	.964
1982—Cincinnati .... Nat.		★C-3B	120	355	24	89	10	3	1	33	.251	725	61	★17	.979
1983—Cincinnati .... Nat.		C-3B-2B	74	167	14	36	8	1	1	13	.216	359	32	5	.987
1984—Cinc.§-Atl. .... Nat.		C	85	272	36	66	16	0	3	28	.243	403	61	5	.989
1985—Atl. x-S.F. y .... Nat.		C-3B	57	157	17	34	10	1	6	19	.217	299	19	7	.978
Major League Totals—8 Years................			583	1674	161	414	68	8	11	160	.247	2692	349	68	.978

Signed as free agent by Victoria, May 16, 1974.
†Sold to New York Mets' organization, May 22, 1974.
‡Traded with Pitchers Jim Kern and Greg Harris to Cincinnati Reds for Outfielder George Foster, February 10, 1982.
§Traded to Atlanta Braves for player to be named later, April 24, 1984; deal settled with reported $50,000 in July, 1984.
xTraded to San Francisco Giants for Catcher-Outfielder John Rabb, April 17, 1985.
yTraded to Los Angeles Dodgers for Outfielder Candy Maldonado, December 11, 1985.

JESUS MANUEL TRILLO (MARCANO)

Name pronounced TREE-yo.

(Manny)

Born December 25, 1950, at Caritito, Monagas, Venezuela.
Height, 6.01. Weight, 164.
Throws and bats righthanded.
Attended Colegio Libertador Bolivar, Maturin, Monagas, Venz.

Established major league records for most consecutive errorless games by second baseman, season (89), 1982; most consecutive errorless chances accepted by second baseman, season (479), 1982.
Major League stolen bases: 1975 (1), 1976 (17), 1977 (3), 1979 (4), 1980 (8), 1981 (10), 1982 (8), 1983 (1), 1985 (2). Total—54.
Led National League second basemen in double plays with 99 in 1978.
Led National League second basemen in total chances with 822 in 1977 and 878 in 1978.
Led Pacific Coast League second basemen in double plays with 113 in 1973.
Named second baseman on THE SPORTING NEWS National League All-Star Team, 1980 through 1982.
Named second baseman on THE SPORTING NEWS National League All-Star fielding team, 1979, 1981 and 1982.
Named second baseman on THE SPORTING NEWS National League Silver Slugger team, 1980 and 1981.

Year Club	League	Pos.	G.	AB.	R.	H.	2B.	3B.	HR.	RBI.	B.A.	PO.	A.	E.	F.A.
1968—Huron† .... North.		SS-3B-C	35	92	8	24	2	1	0	4	.261	35	48	5	.943
1969—Spartanburg‡....... W. Car.		3-C-S-2	83	275	41	77	18	0	1	26	.280	188	98	12	.960
1970—Birmingham .... South.		3B-2B-SS	84	241	26	63	10	1	2	19	.261	101	130	14	.943
1971—Birmingham§ .... South.		3B-SS	107	371	37	104	18	1	5	44	.280	110	212	31	.912
1972—Iowa .... A. A.		3B-2B-SS	133	509	67	153	27	6	9	53	.301	176	304	28	.945
1973—Tucson.................... P. C.		★2B-OF	135	519	76	162	25	7	8	78	.312	★304	★373	19	★.973
1973—Oakland.................. Amer.		2B	17	12	0	3	2	0	0	3	.250	15	17	2	.941
1974—Tucson.................... P. C.		2B	85	320	31	81	19	1	2	39	.253	198	256	12	.974
1974—Oakland x............. Amer.		2B	21	33	3	5	0	0	0	2	.152	31	43	4	.949
1975—Chicago .... Nat.		★2B-SS	154	545	55	135	12	2	7	70	.248	350	★509	★29	.967

Year	Club	League	Pos.	G.	AB.	R.	H.	2B.	3B.	HR.	RBI.	B.A.	PO.	A.	E.	F.A.
1976—Chicago	Nat.	⋆2B-SS	158	582	42	139	24	3	4	59	.239	350	⋆527	17	.981
1977—Chicago	Nat.	2B	152	504	51	141	18	5	7	57	.280	330	⋆467	⋆25	.970
1978—Chicago y	Nat.	2B	152	552	53	144	17	5	4	55	.261	354	⋆505	19	.978
1979—Philadelphia z	Nat.	2B	118	431	40	112	22	1	6	42	.260	270	368	10	.985
1980—Philadelphia a	Nat.	2B	141	531	68	155	25	9	7	43	.292	⋆360	467	11	.987
1981—Philadelphia	Nat.	2B	94	349	37	100	14	3	6	36	.287	⋆245	286	7	.987
1982—Philadelphia b	Nat.	2B	149	549	52	149	24	1	0	39	.271	343	441	5	⋆.994
1983—Cleveland cd	Amer.	2B	88	320	33	87	13	1	1	29	.272	172	269	5	.989
1983—Montreal e	Nat.	2B	31	121	16	32	8	0	2	16	.264	57	86	3	.979
1984—San Francisco f	Nat.	2B-3B	98	401	45	102	21	1	4	36	.254	218	294	6	.988
1985—San Francisco g	Nat.	2B-3B	125	451	36	101	16	2	3	25	.224	263	361	13	.980
American League Totals—3 Years			126	365	36	95	15	1	1	34	.260	218	329	11	.980
National League Totals—11 Years			1372	5016	495	1310	201	32	50	478	.261	3140	4311	145	.981
Major League Totals—13 Years			1498	5381	531	1405	216	33	51	512	.261	3358	4640	156	.981

Signed as free agent by Philadelphia Phillies' organization, January 26, 1968.

†On disabled list, August 16 to September 3, 1968.

‡Drafted by Birmingham (Oakland Athletics' organization), December 1, 1969.

§On disabled list, May 1 to May 20, 1971.

xTraded with Pitchers Darold Knowles and Bob Locker to Chicago Cubs for First Baseman-Outfielder Billy Williams, October 23, 1974.

yTraded with Outfielder Greg Gross and Catcher Dave Rader to Philadelphia Phillies for Outfielder Jerry Martin, Catcher Barry Foote, Second Baseman Ted Sizemore and Pitchers Derek Botelho and Henry Mack, February 23, 1979.

zOn disabled list, May 4 to June 16, 1979.

aOn disabled list, April 20 to May 7, 1980.

bTraded with Outfielder George Vukovich, Infielder Julio Franco, Pitcher Jay Baller and Catcher Gerry Willard to Cleveland Indians for Outfielder Von Hayes, December 9, 1982.

cOn disabled list, July 24 to August 8, 1983.

dTraded to Montreal Expos for outfielder Don Carter and cash, August 17, 1983.

eGranted free agency, November 7, 1983; signed by San Francisco Giants, December 20, 1983.

fOn disabled list, May 13 to July 7, 1984.

gTraded to Chicago Cubs for Infielder Dave Owen, December 11, 1985.

DIVISION SERIES RECORD

Year	Club	League	Pos.	G.	AB.	R.	H.	2B.	3B.	HR.	RBI.	B.A.	PO.	A.	E.	F.A.
1981—Philadelphia	Nat.	2B	5	16	1	3	0	0	0	1	.188	15	10	0	1.000

CHAMPIONSHIP SERIES RECORD

Year	Club	League	Pos.	G.	AB.	R.	H.	2B.	3B.	HR.	RBI.	B.A.	PO.	A.	E.	F.A.
1974—Oakland	Amer.	PR	1	0	1	0	0	0	0	0	.000	0	0	0	.000
1980—Philadelphia	Nat.	2B	5	21	1	8	2	1	0	4	.381	18	25	1	.977
Championship Series Totals—2 Years			6	21	2	8	2	1	0	4	.381	18	25	1	.977

WORLD SERIES RECORD

Year	Club	League	Pos.	G.	AB.	R.	H.	2B.	3B.	HR.	RBI.	B.A.	PO.	A.	E.	F.A.
1980—Philadelphia	Nat.	2B	6	23	4	5	2	0	0	2	.217	14	25	1	.975

ALL-STAR GAME RECORD

Year	League	Pos.	AB.	R.	H.	2B.	3B.	HR.	RBI.	B.A.	PO.	A.	E.	F.A.
1977—National		2B	1	0	0	0	0	0	0	.000	0	1	0	1.000
1981—National		2B	2	0	0	0	0	0	0	.000	1	1	0	1.000
1982—National		2B	2	0	1	0	0	0	0	.500	0	1	0	1.000
1983—American		2B	3	1	1	0	0	0	0	.333	3	1	0	1.000
All-Star Game Totals—4 Years			8	1	2	0	0	0	0	.250	4	4	0	1.000

STEVEN RUSSELL TROUT
(Steve)

Born July 30, 1957, at Detroit, Mich.
Height, 6.04. Weight, 195.
Throws and bats lefthanded.
Son of Paul (Dizzy) Trout, pitcher with Detroit Tigers, Boston Red Sox and
Baltimore Orioles, 1939 through 1952 and 1957.

Major League saves: 1979 (4).

Led American League in hit batsmen with 9 in 1980.

Year	Club	League	G.	IP.	W.	L.	Pct.	H.	R.	ER.	SO.	BB.	ERA.
1976—Sarasota White Sox	Gulf Coast	9	38	1	3	.250	28	18	11	35	29	2.61
1977—Appleton	Midwest	21	111	6	8	.429	113	66	50	101	66	4.05
1977—Iowa	Am. Assoc.	5	24	0	4	.000	27	16	15	14	11	5.63
1978—Knoxville	Southern	12	71	8	3	.727	46	16	13	48	33	1.65
1978—Iowa	Am. Assoc.	9	55	3	4	.429	57	36	32	38	22	5.24
1978—Chicago	American	4	22	3	0	1.000	19	10	10	11	11	4.09
1979—Iowa	Am. Assoc.	4	27	3	1	.750	24	10	9	12	19	3.00
1979—Chicago	American	34	155	11	8	.579	165	77	67	76	59	3.89
1980—Chicago	American	32	200	9	16	.360	229	102	82	89	49	3.69
1981—Chicago	American	20	125	8	7	.533	122	53	48	54	38	3.46
1982—Chicago†	American	25	120⅓	6	9	.400	130	76	57	62	50	4.26
1983—Chicago	National	34	180	10	14	.417	217	105	93	80	59	4.65

Year Club	League	G.	IP.	W.	L.	Pct.	H.	R.	ER.	SO.	BB.	ERA.
1984—Chicago‡	National	32	190	13	7	.650	205	80	72	81	59	3.41
1985—Chicago§	National	24	140⅔	9	7	.563	142	57	53	44	63	3.39
American League Totals—5 Years		115	622⅓	37	40	.481	665	318	264	292	207	3.82
National League Totals—3 Years		90	510⅔	32	28	.533	564	242	218	205	181	3.84
Major League Totals—8 Years		205	1133	69	68	.504	1229	560	482	497	388	3.83

Selected by Chicago White Sox' organization in 1st round (eighth player selected) of free-agent draft, June 8, 1976.
†Traded with Pitcher Warren Brusstar to Chicago Cubs for Pitchers Dick Tidrow and Randy Martz and Infielders Scott Fletcher and Pat Tabler, January 25, 1983.
‡Granted free agency, November 8, 1984; re-signed by Cubs, December 7, 1984.
§On disabled list, July 23 to August 23, 1985.

CHAMPIONSHIP SERIES RECORD

Year Club	League	G.	IP.	W.	L.	Pct.	H.	R.	ER.	SO.	BB.	ERA.
1984—Chicago	National	2	9	1	0	1.000	5	2	2	3	3	2.00

MICHAEL ANDREW TRUJILLO

Name pronounced Tru-HEEY-O.

(Mike)

Born January 12, 1960, at Denver, Colo.
Height, 6.01. Weight, 180.
Throws and bats righthanded.
Attended University of Northern Colorado, Greeley, Colo.

Major League saves: 1985 (1).
Led Midwest League pitchers in games started with 29 and tied for lead in complete games with 11 in 1983.

Year Club	League	G.	IP.	W.	L.	Pct.	H.	R.	ER.	SO.	BB.	ERA.
1982—Sarasota White Sox	Gulf Coast	1	7⅓	0	0	.000	1	2	1	6	4	1.23
1982—Niagara Falls	NYP	12	79	5	4	.556	54	33	21	100	25	2.39
1983—Appleton	Midwest	29	★198⅔	15	8	.652	146	75	53	148	63	2.40
1984—Glens Falls	Eastern	20	121⅔	13	3	.813	107	47	32	69	25	2.37
1984—Denver†‡	Am. Assoc.	8	30	2	5	.286	38	27	26	9	20	7.80
1985—Boston	American	27	84	4	4	.500	112	55	45	19	23	4.82
Major League Totals—1 Year		27	84	4	4	.500	112	55	45	19	23	4.82

Selected by Chicago White Sox' organization in 7th round of free-agent draft, June 7, 1982.
†Traded with First Baseman Pat Adams to San Francisco Giants, September 7, 1984, completing deal in which San Francisco traded Infielder Tom O'Malley to Chicago White Sox for two players to be named later, September 1, 1984.
‡Drafted by Boston Red Sox, December 3, 1984.

JOHN THOMAS TUDOR

Born February 2, 1954, at Schenectady, N.Y.
Height, 6.00. Weight, 185.
Throws and bats lefthanded.
Attended North Shore Community College, Beverly, Mass. and received bachelor of science degree in criminal justice from Georgia Southern College, Statesboro, Ga.

Pitched seven-inning, 2-0 no-hit victory against Reading, June 28, 1977.
Major League saves: 1981 (1).
Led National League in shutouts with 10 in 1985.
Named lefthanded pitcher on THE SPORTING NEWS National League All-Star Team, 1985.

Year Club	League	G.	IP.	W.	L.	Pct.	H.	R.	ER.	SO.	BB.	ERA.
1976—Winston-Salem	Carolina	25	82	5	2	.714	77	26	25	76	28	2.74
1977—Bristol	Eastern	27	115	6	5	.545	113	57	45	78	35	3.52
1977—Pawtucket	Int'national	4	4	1	1	.500	5	1	1	1	3	2.25
1978—Pawtucket	Int'national	26	105	7	4	.636	100	46	36	83	56	3.09
1979—Pawtucket	Int'national	25	163	10	11	.476	145	73	53	103	52	2.93
1979—Boston	American	6	28	1	2	.333	39	23	20	11	9	6.43
1980—Pawtucket	Int'national	12	74	4	5	.444	67	36	30	51	33	3.65
1980—Boston	American	16	92	8	5	.615	81	35	31	45	31	3.03
1981—Boston	American	18	79	4	3	.571	74	44	40	44	28	4.56
1982—Boston	American	32	195⅔	13	10	.565	215	90	79	146	59	3.63
1983—Boston†	American	34	242	13	12	.520	236	122	110	136	81	4.09
1984—Pittsburgh‡	National	32	212	12	11	.522	200	81	77	117	56	3.27
1985—St. Louis	National	36	275	21	8	.724	209	68	59	169	49	1.93
American League Totals—5 Years		106	636⅔	39	32	.549	645	314	280	382	208	3.96
National League Totals—2 Years		68	487	33	19	.635	409	149	136	286	105	2.51
Major League Totals—7 Years		174	1123⅔	72	51	.585	1054	463	416	668	313	3.33

Selected by New York Mets' organization in 21st round of free-agent draft, June 4, 1975.
Selected by Boston Red Sox' organization in secondary phase of free-agent draft, January 7, 1976.
†Traded to Pittsburgh Pirates for Outfielder Mike Easler, December 6, 1983.
‡Traded with Outfielder Brian Harper to St. Louis Cardinals for Outfielder-First Baseman George Hendrick and Catcher Steve Barnard, December 12, 1984.

CHAMPIONSHIP SERIES RECORD

Year Club	League	G.	IP.	W.	L.	Pct.	H.	R.	ER.	SO.	BB.	ERA.
1985—St. Louis	National	2	12⅔	1	1	.500	10	5	4	8	3	2.84

Year	Club	League	G.	IP.	W.	L.	Pct.	H.	R.	ER.	SO.	BB.	ERA.
1985—St. Louis		National	3	18	2	1	.667	15	6	6	14	7	3.00

BYRON LEE TUNNELL

Name pronounced TUNN-ul.
(Known by middle name.)
Born October 30, 1960, at Tyler, Tex.
Height, 6.00. Weight, 180.
Throws and bats righthanded.
Attended Baylor University, Waco, Tex.

Major League saves: 1984 (1).

Year	Club	League	G.	IP.	W.	L.	Pct.	H.	R.	ER.	SO.	BB.	ERA.
1981—Bradenton Pirates		Gulf Coast	1	4	0	0	.000	0	0	0	6	1	0.00
1981—Buffalo		Eastern	12	71	5	5	.500	76	38	35	45	37	4.44
1982—Portland		P. Coast	28	189⅔	12	9	.571	182	93	73	112	91	3.46
1982—Pittsburgh		National	5	18⅓	1	1	.500	17	8	8	4	5	3.93
1983—Pittsburgh		National	35	177⅔	11	6	.647	167	81	72	95	58	3.65
1984—Pittsburgh†		National	26	68⅓	1	7	.125	81	44	40	51	40	5.27
1985—Pittsburgh		National	24	132⅓	4	10	.286	126	70	59	74	57	4.01
1985—Hawaii		P. Coast	7	46⅔	4	1	.800	32	12	12	29	24	2.31
Major League Totals—4 Years			90	396⅔	17	24	.415	391	203	179	224	160	4.06

Selected by Pittsburgh Pirates' organization in 2nd round of free-agent draft, June 8, 1981.
†On disabled list, July 2 to July 23, 1984.

SCOTT MATTHEW ULLGER

Name pronounced ULL-jer.

Born June 10, 1956, at New York, N.Y.
Height, 6.03. Weight, 196.
Throws and bats righthanded.
Attended St. John's University, Jamaica, N.Y.

Tied for Southern League lead in sacrifice flies with 9 in 1981.

Year	Club	League	Pos.	G.	AB.	R.	H.	2B.	3B.	HR.	RBI.	B.A.	PO.	A.	E.	F.A.
1977—Wisconsin Rapids	Midw.		3B	81	276	52	81	17	4	5	35	.293	54	101	13	.912
1978—Visalia	Calif.		3B-SS-2B	134	465	105	149	*36	2	20	108	.320	124	289	33	.926
1979—Orlando	South.		3B-SS-OF	126	412	66	111	21	4	8	50	.269	95	219	29	.915
1980—Orlando	South.		OF	135	460	55	121	25	0	8	51	.263	283	11	4	*.987
1981—Orlando	South.		OF-1B-3B	138	483	86	130	23	2	20	87	.269	268	27	6	.980
1982—Toledo	Int.		OF-3B-1B	115	352	77	102	16	4	14	60	.290	201	29	4	.983
1983—Minnesota	Amer.		1B-3B	35	79	8	15	4	0	0	5	.190	186	11	2	.990
1984—Toledo†	Int.		1-2-O-3	113	357	50	92	16	1	11	58	.258	746	74	6	.993
1985—Toledo	Int.		3-1-O-2	112	384	58	112	13	6	15	58	.292	378	144	9	.983
Major League Totals—1 Year				35	79	8	15	4	0	0	5	.190	186	11	2	.990

Selected by Minnesota Twins' organization in 18th round of free-agent draft, June 7, 1977.
†Granted free agency, October 15, 1984; re-signed by Twins' organization, October 23, 1984.

WILLIE CLAY UPSHAW

Born April 27, 1957, at Blanco, Tex.
Height, 6.00. Weight, 185.
Throws and bats lefthanded.
Cousin of Gene Upshaw, guard with Oakland Raiders, 1967 through 1981;
and currently executive director of NFL Players Association; and Marvin Upshaw,
lineman with Cleveland Browns, Kansas City Chiefs and St. Louis Cardinals, 1968 through 1976.

Major League stolen bases: 1978 (4), 1980 (1), 1981 (2), 1982 (8), 1983 (10), 1984 (10), 1985 (8). Total—43.
Led American League first basemen in total chances with 1,556 in 1982.

Year	Club	League	Pos.	G.	AB.	R.	H.	2B.	3B.	HR.	RBI.	B.A.	PO.	A.	E.	F.A.
1975—Oneonta	NYP		OF	29	91	8	8	1	0	0	4	.088	7	1	0	1.000
1976—Fort Lauderdale	Fla. St.		OF	84	263	20	60	6	0	3	22	.228	22	0	0	1.000
1977—Fort Lauderdale	Fla. St.		1B-OF	87	335	38	92	13	7	3	29	.275	358	31	14	.965
1977—West Haven†	East.		OF-1B	41	157	20	47	5	2	4	22	.299	40	0	4	.909
1978—Toronto	Amer.		OF-1B	95	224	26	53	8	2	1	17	.237	131	4	7	.951
1979—Syracuse	Int.		OF-1B	140	526	71	131	25	8	12	68	.249	544	24	14	.976
1980—Syracuse	Int.		OF-1B	100	358	55	91	13	7	9	52	.254	355	19	7	.982
1980—Toronto	Amer.		1B-OF	34	61	10	13	3	1	1	5	.213	51	7	1	.983
1981—Toronto	Amer.		1B-OF	61	111	15	19	3	1	4	10	.171	72	6	0	1.000
1982—Toronto	Amer.		1B	160	580	77	155	25	7	21	75	.267	*1438	101	*17	.989
1983—Toronto	Amer.		1B	160	579	99	177	26	7	27	104	.306	1294	117	*21	.985
1984—Toronto	Amer.		1B	152	569	79	158	31	9	19	84	.278	1246	103	14	.990
1985—Toronto	Amer.		1B	148	501	79	138	31	5	15	65	.275	1157	104	10	.992
Major League Totals—7 Years				810	2625	385	713	127	32	88	360	.272	5389	442	70	.988

Selected by New York Yankees' organization in 5th round of free-agent draft, June 4, 1975.
†Drafted by Toronto Blue Jays, December 5, 1977.

Year	Club	League	Pos.	G.	AB.	R.	H.	2B.	3B.	HR.	RBI.	B.A.	PO.	A.	E.	F.A.
1985—Toronto	Amer.		1B	7	26	2	6	2	0	0	1	.231	53	7	1	.984

JOSE ALTA URIBE

(Name pronounced Oo-REE-bay.)
(Formerly known as Jose Alta Gonzalez.)

Born January 21, 1959, at San Cristobal, D.R.
Height, 5.10. Weight, 156.
Throws right and bats left and righthanded.

Major League stolen bases: 1984 (1), 1985 (8). Total—9.
Led American Association in sacrifice hits with 14 in 1983.
Led American Association shortstops in total chances with 720 and double plays with 96 in 1984.
Led American Association shortstops in total chances with 664 and double plays with 90 in 1983.
Led Texas League shortstops in double plays with 88 in 1982.

Year	Club	League	Pos.	G.	AB.	R.	H.	2B.	3B.	HR.	RBI.	B.A.	PO.	A.	E.	F.A.
1981—St. Petersburg†	Fla. St.		SS	128	463	54	124	15	2	0	40	.268	171	*387	32	.946
1982—Arkansas	Texas		SS	123	465	73	115	17	7	0	41	.247	185	385	36	.941
1982—Louisville	A. A.		SS	8	28	5	10	2	0	0	4	.357	15	18	1	.971
1983—Louisville	A. A.		SS	122	423	64	120	19	6	3	44	.284	206	425	*33	.950
1984—Louisville	A. A.		SS	145	484	68	135	20	2	3	46	.279	*233	*455	*32	*.956
1984—St. Louis‡	Nat.		SS-2B	8	19	4	4	0	0	0	3	.211	7	15	1	.957
1985—San Francisco	Nat.		SS-2B	147	476	46	113	20	4	3	26	.237	209	438	26	.961
Major League Totals—2 Years				155	495	50	117	20	4	3	29	.236	216	453	27	.961

Signed as free agent by New York Yankees' organization, February 18, 1977.
†Released, July 5, 1977; signed by St. Louis Cardinals' organization, August 18, 1980.
‡Traded with First Basemen David Green and Gary Rajsich and Pitcher Dave LaPoint to San Francisco Giants for Outfielder-First Baseman Jack Clark, February 1, 1985.

ELLIS CLARENCE VALENTINE

Born July 30, 1954, at Helena, Ark.
Height, 6.04. Weight, 218.
Throws and bats righthanded.

Major League stolen bases: 1976 (14), 1977 (13), 1978 (13), 1979 (11), 1980 (5), 1982 (1), 1983 (2). Total—59.
Led International League in total bases with 226 in 1975.
Led Eastern League outfielders in double plays with 5 in 1974.
Named outfielder on THE SPORTING NEWS National League All-Star fielding team, 1978.

Year	Club	League	Pos.	G.	AB.	R.	H.	2B.	3B.	HR.	RBI.	B.A.	PO.	A.	E.	F.A.
1972—Cocoa Expos	Fl. E.C.		OF	53	177	24	47	8	0	1	18	.266	76	4	1	.988
1973—W. Palm Beach	Fla. St.		OF	119	403	59	124	18	4	8	61	.308	169	11	5	.973
1974—Quebec City	East.		OF	130	426	46	112	11	7	5	50	.263	204	*20	10	.957
1975—Memphis	Int.		OF-1B	*139	494	*87	*151	●30	3	13	66	.306	266	12	6	.979
1975—Montreal	Nat.		OF	12	33	2	12	4	0	1	3	.364	12	1	2	.867
1976—Denver	A. A.		OF	57	204	31	63	9	1	7	32	.309	122	8	2	.985
1976—Montreal	Nat.		OF	94	305	36	85	15	2	7	39	.279	162	12	5	.972
1977—Montreal	Nat.		OF	127	508	63	149	28	2	25	76	.293	232	9	7	.972
1978—Montreal†	Nat.		OF	151	570	75	165	35	2	25	76	.289	296	●24	10	.970
1979—Montreal	Nat.		OF	146	548	73	151	29	3	21	82	.276	281	10	5	.983
1980—Montreal‡	Nat.		OF	86	311	40	98	22	2	13	67	.315	154	6	5	.970
1981—Mont.§x-N.Y.	Nat.		OF	70	245	23	51	11	1	8	36	.208	115	8	4	.969
1982—New York y	Nat.		OF	111	337	33	97	14	1	8	48	.288	159	10	3	.983
1983—California z	Amer.		OF	86	271	30	65	10	2	13	43	.240	152	5	6	.963
1983—Edmonton	P. C.		OF	3	9	2	2	0	0	0	0	.222	3	0	0	1.000
1984—Edmonton ab	P. C.		DH	2	3	0	0	0	0	0	0	.000	0	0	0	.000
1985—Oklahoma City	A. A.		OF	46	169	26	53	18	0	10	33	.314	15	3	1	.947
1985—Texas c	Amer.		OF	11	38	5	8	1	0	2	4	.211	7	0	0	1.000
National League Totals—8 Years				797	2857	345	808	158	13	108	427	.283	1411	80	41	.973
American League Totals—2 Years				97	309	35	73	11	2	15	47	.236	159	5	6	.965
Major League Totals—10 Years				894	3166	380	881	169	15	123	474	.278	1570	85	47	.972

Selected by Montreal Expos' organization in 2nd round of free-agent draft, June 6, 1972.
†On suspended list, September 20 to September 22, 1978.
‡On disabled list, May 31 to July 6, 1980.
§On disabled list, May 20 to June 5, 1981.
xTraded to New York Mets for Pitcher Jeff Reardon and Outfielder Dan Norman, May 29, 1981.
yGranted free agency, November 10, 1982; signed by California Angels, January 21, 1983.
zOn disabled list, March 30 to May 6, 1983; included rehabilitation disability assignment to Edmonton, May 2 to May 6, 1983.
aOn California disabled list, April 1, 1984 through remainder of season; included rehabilitation disability assignment to Edmonton, August 23 to August 27, 1984.
bReleased, November 7, 1984; signed by Oklahoma City (Texas Rangers' organization), July 10, 1985.
cReleased, December 20, 1985; invited to Texas Rangers spring training.

ALL-STAR GAME RECORD

Year	League	Pos.	AB.	R.	H.	2B.	3B.	HR.	RBI.	B.A.	PO.	A.	E.	F.A.
1977—National		OF	1	0	0	0	0	0	0	.000	0	0	0	.000

FERNANDO VALENZUELA (ANGUAMEA)

Name pronounced Val-en-ZWAY-luh.

Born November 1, 1960, at Navajoa, Sonora, Mexico.
Height, 5.11. Weight, 180.
Throws and bats lefthanded.

— 516 —

Tied modern major league record for most shutout games won or tied, rookie year (8), 1981.
Major League saves: 1980 (1).
Led National League in complete games with 11 and shutouts with 8 in 1981.
Tied for National League lead in games started by pitchers with 25 in 1981.
Led Mexican Center League in wild pitches with 13 in 1978.
Named Major League Player of the Year by THE SPORTING NEWS, 1981.
Named National League Pitcher of the Year by THE SPORTING NEWS, 1981.
Won National League Cy Young Memorial Award, 1981.
Named National League Rookie Pitcher of the Year by THE SPORTING NEWS, 1981.
Named National League Rookie of the Year by Baseball Writers' Association of America, 1981.
Named lefthanded pitcher on THE SPORTING NEWS National League All-Star Team, 1981.
Named pitcher on THE SPORTING NEWS National League Silver Slugger team, 1981 and 1983.

Year Club	League	G.	IP.	W.	L.	Pct.	H.	R.	ER.	SO.	BB.	ERA.
1978—Guanajuato	Mex. Cent.	16	93	5	6	.455	88	46	23	★91	46	2.23
1979—Yucatan†	Mexican	26	181	10	12	.455	157	68	50	141	70	2.49
1979—Lodi	California	3	24	1	2	.333	21	10	3	18	3	1.13
1980—San Antonio	Texas	27	174	13	9	.591	156	70	60	★162	70	3.10
1980—Los Angeles	National	10	18	2	0	1.000	8	2	0	16	5	0.00
1981—Los Angeles	National	25	★192	13	7	.650	140	55	53	★180	61	2.48
1982—Los Angeles‡	National	37	285	19	13	.594	247	105	91	199	83	2.87
1983—Los Angeles	National	35	257	15	10	.600	245	★122	107	189	99	3.75
1984—Los Angeles	National	34	261	12	17	.414	218	109	88	240	★106	3.03
1985—Los Angeles	National	35	272⅓	17	10	.630	211	92	74	208	101	2.45
Major League Totals—6 Years		176	1285⅓	78	57	.578	1069	485	413	1032	455	2.89

†Sold to Los Angeles Dodgers' organization, July 6, 1979.
‡Appeared in one game as outfielder with no chances.

DIVISION SERIES RECORD

Year Club	League	G.	IP.	W.	L.	Pct.	H.	R.	ER.	SO.	BB.	ERA.
1981—Los Angeles	National	2	17	1	0	1.000	10	2	2	10	3	1.06

CHAMPIONSHIP SERIES RECORD

Established National League Championship Series records for most bases on balls (10) and most strikeouts (13), six-game Series, 1985; most bases on balls, game (8), October 14, 1985.

Year Club	League	G.	IP.	W.	L.	Pct.	H.	R.	ER.	SO.	BB.	ERA.
1981—Los Angeles	National	2	14⅔	1	1	.500	10	4	4	10	5	2.45
1983—Los Angeles	National	1	8	1	0	1.000	7	1	1	5	4	1.13
1985—Los Angeles	National	2	14⅓	1	0	1.000	11	3	3	13	10	1.88
Championship Series Totals—3 Years		5	37	3	1	.750	28	8	8	28	19	1.95

WORLD SERIES RECORD

Year Club	League	G.	IP.	W.	L.	Pct.	H.	R.	ER.	SO.	BB.	ERA.
1981—Los Angeles	National	1	9	1	0	1.000	9	4	4	6	7	4.00

ALL-STAR GAME RECORD

Year League	IP.	W.	L.	Pct.	H.	R.	ER.	SO.	BB.	ERA.
1981—National	1	0	0	.000	2	0	0	0	0	0.00
1982—National	⅔	0	0	.000	0	0	0	0	2	0.00
1984—National	2	0	0	.000	2	0	0	3	0	0.00
1985—National	1	0	0	.000	0	0	0	1	1	0.00
All-Star Game Totals—4 Years	4⅔	0	0	.000	4	0	0	4	3	0.00

Member of National League All-Star Team in 1983; did not play.

DAVID VALLE

Name pronounced Valley.

(Dave)

Born October 30, 1960, at Bayside, N. Y.
Height, 6.02. Weight, 200.
Throws and bats righthanded.
Brother of John Valle, minor league outfielder, 1972 through 1984.

Led Northwest League catchers in double plays with 6 and tied for lead in passed balls with 23 in 1978.

Year Club	League	Pos.	G.	AB.	R.	H.	2B.	3B.	HR.	RBI.	B.A.	PO.	A.	E.	F.A.
1978—Bellingham	N'west	C	57	167	12	34	2	0	2	21	.204	★338	65	10	.976
1979—Alexandria†	Carol.	C	58	169	17	36	5	0	6	25	.213	290	44	11	.968
1980—San Jose	Calif.	C	119	430	81	126	14	0	12	70	.293	570	★102	17	.975
1981—Lynn‡	East.	C	93	318	38	82	16	0	11	54	.258	445	56	6	.988
1982—Salt Lake City	P. C.	C-1B	75	234	28	49	11	1	4	28	.209	347	49	11	.973
1983—Chattanooga§	South.	C-1B	53	176	20	42	11	0	3	22	.239	239	24	4	.985
1984—Salt Lake City x	P. C.	C	86	284	54	79	13	1	12	54	.278	433	34	6	.987
1984—Seattle	Amer.	C	13	27	4	8	1	0	1	4	.296	56	5	0	1.000
1985—Seattle y	Amer.	C	31	70	2	11	1	0	0	4	.157	117	7	3	.976
1985—Calgary	P. C.	C	42	131	17	45	8	0	6	26	.344	202	11	1	.995
Major League Totals—2 Years			44	97	6	19	2	0	1	8	.196	173	12	3	.984

Selected by Seattle Mariners' organization in 2nd round of free-agent draft, June 6, 1978.
†On disabled list, July 26 to August 25, 1979.
‡On disabled list, June 24 to July 3, 1981.
§On disabled list, April 13 to June 20 and June 27 to July 7, 1983.

PITCHING RECORD

Year	Club	League	G.	IP.	W.	L.	Pct.	H.	R.	ER.	SO.	BB.	ERA.
1980—San Jose		California	1	1	0	0	.000	1	0	0	2	2	0.00

EDWARD JOHN VANDE BERG
(Ed)

Born October 26, 1958, at Redlands, Calif.
Height, 6.01. Weight, 170.
Throws left and bats righthanded.
Attended San Bernardino Valley, San Bernardino, Calif. and Arizona State University, Tempe, Ariz.
Established major league record for most games by pitcher, rookie season (78), 1982.
Major League saves: 1982 (5), 1983 (5), 1984 (7), 1985 (3). Total—20.
Named American League Rookie Pitcher of the Year by THE SPORTING NEWS, 1982.

Year	Club	League	G.	IP.	W.	L.	Pct.	H.	R.	ER.	SO.	BB.	ERA.
1980—Bellingham		Northwest	14	101	9	0	*1.000	82	40	32	78	46	2.85
1981—Spokane		P. Coast	49	62	4	3	.571	62	33	26	49	29	3.77
1982—Seattle		American	*78	76	9	4	.692	54	21	20	60	32	2.37
1983—Seattle		American	68	64½	2	4	.333	59	32	24	40	22	3.36
1984—Seattle†		American	50	130½	8	12	.400	165	76	69	71	50	4.76
1985—Seattle‡		American	76	67⅔	2	1	.667	71	30	28	34	31	3.72
Major League Totals—4 Years			272	338⅓	21	21	.500	349	159	141	214	135	3.75

Selected by San Diego Padres' organization in 3rd round of free-agent draft, January 10, 1978.
Selected by St. Louis Cardinals' organization in secondary phase of free-agent draft, June 6, 1978.
Selected by Seattle Mariners' organization in 13th round of free-agent draft, June 3, 1980.
†Appeared in one game as a pinch-runner.
‡Traded to Los Angeles Dodgers for Catcher Steve Yeager, December 11, 1985.

DAVID THOMAS VAN GORDER
(Dave)

Born March 27, 1957, at Los Angeles, Calif.
Height, 6.02. Weight, 205.
Throws and bats righthanded.
Attended University of Southern California, Los Angeles, Calif.
Major League stolen bases: 1982 (1).
Led American Association catchers in putouts with 666, total chances with 736 and double plays with 14 in 1983.
Led American Association catchers in putouts with 705, total chances with 785, and fielding percentage with .991 in 1981.
Named catcher on THE SPORTING NEWS College Baseball All-America Team, 1978.

Year	Club	League	Pos.	G.	AB.	R.	H.	2B.	3B.	HR.	RBI.	B.A.	PO.	A.	E.	F.A.
1978—Nashville		South.	C	73	217	23	57	10	0	1	25	.263	396	38	5	.989
1979—Nashville		South.	C	137	461	58	131	27	1	6	64	.284	*726	*74	6	*.993
1980—Indianapolis†		A. A.	*C-1B	71	253	11	57	12	1	3	26	.225	442	45	4	*.992
1981—Indianapolis		A. A.	C-1B	123	432	50	108	21	0	15	66	.250	712	75	8	.990
1982—Indianapolis		A. A.	C	54	174	21	46	7	0	4	29	.264	260	36	3	.990
1982—Cincinnati		Nat.	C	51	137	4	25	3	1	0	7	.182	273	18	4	.986
1983—Indianapolis		A. A.	*C-OF	117	380	38	86	17	0	5	48	.226	673	68	3	*.996
1984—Wichita		A. A.	C-1B	67	205	26	54	14	1	4	36	.263	350	26	4	.989
1984—Cincinnati		Nat.	C-1B	38	101	10	23	2	0	0	6	.228	194	11	0	1.000
1985—Cincinnati‡		Nat.	C	73	151	12	36	7	0	2	24	.238	255	11	3	.989
Major League Totals—3 Years				162	389	26	84	12	1	2	37	.216	722	40	7	.991

Selected by Philadelphia Phillies' organization in 9th round of free-agent draft, June 4, 1975.
Selected by Cincinnati Reds' organization in 2nd round of free-agent draft, June 6, 1978.
†On disabled list, July 10 to September 30, 1980.
‡On disabled list, July 6 to July 20, 1985.

ANDREW JAMES VAN SLYKE
(Andy)

Born December 21, 1960, at Utica, N.Y.
Height, 6.01. Weight, 190.
Throws right and bats lefthanded.
Tied Major League record for fewest double plays by outfielder, season, for leader in double plays (4), 1985.
Major League stolen bases: 1983 (21), 1984 (28), 1985 (34). Total—83.
Tied for National League lead in double plays by outfielders with 4 in 1985.
Received reported $50,000 bonus to sign with St. Louis Cardinals, 1979.

Year	Club	League	Pos.	G.	AB.	R.	H.	2B.	3B.	HR.	RBI.	B.A.	PO.	A.	E.	F.A.
1979—Johnson City†		Appal.					(Did not play)									
1980—Gastonia		S. Atl.	OF	126	426	62	115	15	4	8	59	.270	177	16	●16	.923
1981—St. Petersburg‡		Fla. St.	OF	94	282	42	62	11	3	1	25	.220	168	10	5	.973
1982—Arkansas		Texas	OF	123	416	83	116	13	*11	16	70	.279	266	17	7	.976
1983—Louisville		A. A.	3B-1B-OF	54	220	52	81	21	4	6	41	.368	201	78	16	.946
1983—St. Louis		Nat.	OF-3B-1B	101	309	51	81	15	5	8	38	.262	203	59	6	.978

Year Club	League	Pos.	G.	AB.	R.	H.	2B.	3B.	HR.	RBI.	B.A.	PO.	A.	E.	F.A.
1984—St. Louis.................. Nat.	OF-3B-1B	137	361	45	88	16	4	7	50	.244	357	82	8	.982
1985—St. Louis.................. Nat.	OF-1B	146	424	61	110	25	6	13	55	.259	237	13	1	.996
Major League Totals—3 Years................		384	1094	157	279	56	15	28	143	.255	797	154	15	.984

Selected by St. Louis Cardinals' organization in 1st round (sixth player selected) of free-agent draft, June 5, 1979.
†On disabled list, June 8, 1979 through remainder of season.
‡On disabled list, April 10 to May 14, 1981.

CHAMPIONSHIP SERIES RECORD

Year Club	League	Pos.	G.	AB.	R.	H.	2B.	3B.	HR.	RBI.	B.A.	PO.	A.	E.	F.A.
1985—St. Louis.................. Nat.	OF-PR	5	11	1	1	0	0	0	1	.091	6	0	0	1.000

WORLD SERIES RECORD

Year Club	League	Pos.	G.	AB.	R.	H.	2B.	3B.	HR.	RBI.	B.A.	PO.	A.	E.	F.A.
1985—St. Louis.................. Nat.	O-PH-PR	6	11	0	1	0	0	0	0	.091	8	0	0	1.000

JOSE ELIGIO VARGAS (HENRIQUEZ)

Born July 14, 1965, at Santo Domingo, Dominican Republic.
Height, 6.02. Weight, 160.
Throws and bats righthanded.
Tied for Gulf Coast League lead in balks with 3 in 1984.

Year Club	League	G.	IP.	W.	L.	Pct.	H.	R.	ER.	SO.	BB.	ERA.
1983—Sarasota Astros........................... Gulf Coast		3	13⅔	0	1	.000	10	2	0	6	1	0.00
1984—Sarasota Astros........................... Gulf Coast		14	75⅓	2	1	.667	80	46	34	46	25	4.06
1985—Asheville... S. Atlantic		24	161	13	7	.650	135	70	57	136	64	3.19

Signed as free agent by Houston Astros' organization, May 11, 1983.

WILLIAM McKINLEY VENABLE JR.
(Max)

Born June 6, 1957, at Phoenix, Ariz.
Height, 5.10. Weight, 185.
Throws right and bats lefthanded.
Major League stolen bases: 1979 (3), 1980 (8), 1981 (3), 1982 (9), 1983 (15), 1984 (1), 1985 (11). Total—50.

Year Club	League	Pos.	G.	AB.	R.	H.	2B.	3B.	HR.	RBI.	B.A.	PO.	A.	E.	F.A.
1976—Bellingham† .... N'west	OF	51	162	25	35	2	0	1	16	.216	58	4	8	.886
1977—Clinton.................... Midw.	OF-2B	125	425	72	115	19	4	9	63	.271	149	13	13	.926
1978—Lodi‡ .... Calif.	OF	●140	566	134	180	30	9	17	101	.318	220	8	8	.966
1979—San Francisco ...... Nat.	OF	55	85	12	14	1	1	0	3	.165	25	30	2	.914
1979—Shreveport .... Texas	OF	18	69	11	16	1	2	0	3	.232	28	2	1	.968
1979—Phoenix.................. P. C.	OF	38	150	27	46	5	4	0	11	.307	96	4	3	.971
1980—Phoenix.................. P. C.	OF	78	312	52	89	10	10	5	40	.285	179	7	4	.979
1980—San Francisco ...... Nat.	OF	64	138	13	37	5	0	0	10	.268	61	0	0	1.000
1981—Phoenix§.............. P. C.	OF	104	428	81	122	24	10	8	48	.285	263	6	3	.989
1981—San Francisco ...... Nat.	OF	18	32	2	6	0	2	0	1	.188	12	0	0	1.000
1982—San Francisco x... Nat.	OF	71	125	17	28	2	1	1	7	.224	66	6	1	.986
1982—Phoenix.................. P. C.	OF	8	32	5	8	1	2	0	3	.250	16	0	0	1.000
1983—San Francisco y... Nat.	OF	94	228	28	50	7	4	6	27	.219	141	5	1	.993
1984—Indianapolis.......... A. A.	OF	99	330	57	82	13	3	9	47	.248	183	4	4	.979
1984—Montreal................ Nat.	OF	38	71	7	17	2	0	2	7	.239	33	0	0	1.000
1985—Indy. z-Den. .... A. A.	OF	46	172	27	42	7	5	4	19	.244	93	2	1	.990
1985—Cincinnati.............. Nat.	OF	77	135	21	39	12	3	0	10	.289	60	3	0	1.000
Major League Totals—7 Years................		417	814	100	191	29	11	9	65	.235	398	44	4	.991

Selected by Los Angeles Dodgers' organization in 3rd round of free-agent draft, June 8, 1976.
†On disabled list, June 26 to July 10, 1976.
‡Drafted by San Francisco Giants, December 4, 1978.
§On disabled list, April 23 to May 16, 1981.
xOn disabled list, April 21 to June 1, 1982; included rehabilitation disability assignment to Phoenix, May 22 to June 1, 1982.
yTraded to Montreal Expos' organization, March 31, 1984, completing deal in which Montreal traded First Baseman Al Oliver to San Francisco Giants for Pitcher Fred Breining and a player to be named later, February 27, 1984. (San Francisco traded Pitcher Andy McGaffigan to Montreal, March 31, 1984, as compensation for the injury that Breining arrived with. Breining remained with Montreal.)
zTraded to Cincinnati Reds' organization for Infielder Skeeter Barnes, April 26, 1985.

FRANK JOHN VIOLA JR.

Name pronounced Vy-OH-luh.

Born April 19, 1960, at Hempstead, N.Y.
Height, 6.04. Weight, 209.
Throws and bats lefthanded.
Attended St. John's University, Jamaica, N.Y.

Year Club	League	G.	IP.	W.	L.	Pct.	H.	R.	ER.	SO.	BB.	ERA.
1981—Orlando .... Southern		17	97	5	4	.556	112	47	37	50	33	3.43
1982—Toledo .... Int'national		8	58	2	3	.400	61	27	25	34	18	3.88
1982—Minnesota.. American		22	126	4	10	.286	152	77	73	84	38	5.21
1983—Minnesota.. American		35	210	7	15	.318	242	*141	*128	127	92	5.49

Year—Club	League	G.	IP.	W.	L.	Pct.	H.	R.	ER.	SO.	BB.	ERA.
1984—Minnesota	American	35	257⅔	18	12	.600	225	101	92	149	73	3.21
1985—Minnesota	American	36	250⅔	18	14	.563	262	*136	114	135	68	4.09
Major League Totals—4 Years		128	844⅓	47	51	.480	881	455	407	495	271	4.34

Selected by Kansas City Royals' organization in 16th round of free-agent draft, June 6, 1978.
Selected by Minnesota Twins' organization in 2nd round of free-agent draft, June 8, 1981.

OSVALDO JOSE VIRGIL JR.
(Ozzie)

Born December 7, 1956, at Mayaguez, P. R.
Height, 6.01. Weight, 195.
Throws and bats righthanded.
Son of Ozzie Virgil, infielder-catcher with New York N.L., Detroit, Kansas City, Baltimore, Pittsburgh
and San Francisco, 1956 through 1958, 1960 through 1962, 1965, 1966 and 1969; coach,
San Francisco Giants, 1970 through 1972, 1974 and 1975; scout, San Francisco Giants, 1973;
coach, Montreal Expos, 1976 through 1981; and coach with San Diego Padres since 1982.

Major League stolen bases: 1984 (1).
Led Carolina League in total bases with 234 in 1978.
Named Carolina League Most Valuable Player, 1978.

Year—Club	League	Pos.	G.	AB.	R.	H.	2B.	3B.	HR.	RBI.	B.A.	PO.	A.	E.	F.A.
1976—Auburn	NYP	C	39	113	10	16	1	2	1	10	.142	153	14	5	.971
1977—Spartanburg	W. Car.	C	107	365	53	103	21	1	14	54	.282	502	*68	18	.969
1978—Peninsula	Carol.	C	126	409	79	124	21	1	*29	*98	.303	581	45	8	.987
1979—Reading	East.	C	128	429	57	99	17	1	8	66	.231	532	64	12	.980
1980—Reading	East.	C-1B	135	456	92	123	15	2	28	*104	.270	592	62	16	.976
1980—Philadelphia	Nat.	C	1	5	1	1	1	0	0	0	.200	4	0	0	1.000
1981—Oklahoma City†	A. A.	C	83	275	41	63	11	2	11	44	.229	201	28	4	.983
1981—Philadelphia	Nat.	C	6	6	0	0	0	0	0	0	.000	2	0	0	1.000
1982—Philadelphia	Nat.	C	49	101	11	24	6	0	3	8	.238	173	14	7	.964
1983—Philadelphia	Nat.	C	55	140	11	30	7	0	6	23	.214	228	24	9	.966
1984—Philadelphia	Nat.	C	141	456	61	119	21	2	18	68	.261	722	58	6	.992
1985—Philadelphia‡	Nat.	C	131	426	47	105	16	3	19	55	.246	667	52	4	*.994
Major League Totals—6 Years			383	1134	131	279	51	5	46	154	.246	1796	148	26	.987

Selected by Philadelphia Phillies' organization in 6th round of free-agent draft, June 8, 1976.
†On disabled list, April 14 to April 27 and June 2 to June 29, 1981.
‡Traded with Pitcher Pete Smith to Atlanta Braves for Pitcher Steve Bedrosian and Outfielder Milt Thompson, December 10, 1985.

CHAMPIONSHIP SERIES RECORD

Year—Club	League	Pos.	G.	AB.	R.	H.	2B.	3B.	HR.	RBI.	B.A.	PO.	A.	E.	F.A.
1983—Philadelphia	Nat.	PH	1	1	0	0	0	0	0	0	.000	0	0	0	.000

WORLD SERIES RECORD

Year—Club	League	Pos.	G.	AB.	R.	H.	2B.	3B.	HR.	RBI.	B.A.	PO.	A.	E.	F.A.
1983—Philadelphia	Nat.	PH-C	3	2	0	1	0	0	0	1	.500	1	0	0	1.000

ALL-STAR GAME RECORD

Year—League		Pos.	AB.	R.	H.	2B.	3B.	HR.	RBI.	B.A.	PO.	A.	E.	F.A.
1985—National		C	1	0	1	0	0	0	2	1.000	3	0	0	1.000

PAUL KENNETH VOIGT

Born December 8, 1958, at Bellerose, N.Y.
Height, 6.02. Weight, 190.
Throws and bats righthanded.
Received bachelor of science degree in electrical engineering from
University of Virginia, Charlottesville, Va.

Led Texas League pitchers in games started with 28 and shutouts with 3 in 1982.
Tied for American Association lead in hit batsmen with 10 in 1985.

Year—Club	League	G.	IP.	W.	L.	Pct.	H.	R.	ER.	SO.	BB.	ERA.
1979—Wisconsin Rapids	Midwest	14	84	4	7	.364	82	37	31	50	47	3.32
1980—Wisconsin Rapids†	Midwest	24	157	12	8	.600	153	81	61	106	70	3.50
1981—Visalia‡	California	27	184	*16	7	.696	195	91	66	143	62	3.23
1982—San Antonio	Texas	28	187⅔	12	13	.480	208	102	83	129	68	3.98
1983—Albuquerque	P. Coast	29	155	9	12	.429	183	107	89	70	69	5.17
1984—Albuquerque§	P. Coast	33	164	9	6	.600	183	100	88	66	87	4.83
1985—Nashville	Am. Assoc.	28	176	11	9	.550	155	75	62	95	85	3.17

Selected by Minnesota Twins' organization in 9th round of free-agent draft, June 5, 1979.
†On disabled list, May 16 to June 6, 1980.
‡Traded with Catcher Scotti Madison to Los Angeles Dodgers' organization for Pitcher Bobby Castillo and Outfielder Bobby Mitchell, January 6, 1982.
§Released, January 24, 1985; signed by Nashville (Detroit Tigers' organization), February 11, 1985.

—DID YOU KNOW—

That New York Yankee farm teams compiled the highest 1985 won-loss percentage in baseball with a .596 mark? All five of their teams made the playoffs.

DAVID VON OHLEN
(Dave)

Born October 25, 1958, at Flushing, N.Y.
Height, 6.02. Weight, 200.
Throws and bats lefthanded.

Major League saves: 1983 (2), 1984 (1). Total—3.

Year Club	League	G.	IP.	W.	L.	Pct.	H.	R.	ER.	SO.	BB.	ERA.
1976—Marion	Ap'lachian	5	20	1	0	1.000	11	5	3	12	6	1.35
1976—Wausau	Midwest	9	31	1	4	.200	42	27	16	18	21	4.65
1977—Lynchburg	Carolina	37	65	6	3	.667	75	39	34	49	28	4.71
1978—Lynchburg	Carolina	34	72	6	7	.462	62	28	23	54	22	2.88
1979—Jackson	Texas	37	34	4	1	.800	28	11	7	26	10	1.85
1980—Tidewater	Int'national	45	87	5	4	.556	88	40	31	44	27	3.21
1981—Jackson	Texas	11	29	4	0	1.000	20	3	3	24	4	0.93
1981—Tidewater†	Int'national	10	25	0	4	.000	30	22	16	18	11	5.76
1982—Tidewater‡	Int'national	36	64⅓	4	1	.800	64	22	20	44	25	2.80
1983—Louisville	Am. Assoc.	12	15⅓	1	0	1.000	16	8	8	13	5	4.70
1983—St. Louis	National	46	68⅓	3	2	.600	71	27	25	21	25	3.29
1984—Louisville	Am. Assoc.	22	43⅓	1	3	.250	30	11	11	22	18	2.28
1984—St. Louis§	National	27	34⅔	1	0	1.000	39	13	12	19	8	3.12
1985—Cleveland x	American	26	43⅓	3	2	.600	47	20	14	12	20	2.91
1985—Maine	Int'national	4	23⅔	2	1	.667	26	11	10	7	2	3.80
National League Totals—2 Years		73	103	4	2	.667	110	40	37	40	33	3.23
American League Totals—1 Year		26	43⅓	3	2	.600	47	20	14	12	20	2.91
Major League Totals—3 Years		99	146⅓	7	4	.636	157	60	51	52	53	3.14

Selected by New York Mets' organization in 17th round of free-agent draft, June 8, 1976.
†On disabled list, July 19 to September 1, 1981.
‡Granted free agency, October 22, 1982; signed by St. Louis Cardinals, December, 1982.
§Released, November 9, 1984; signed by Cleveland Indians' organization, January 9, 1985.
xOn disabled list, May 16 to September 1, 1985; included rehabilitation disability assignment to Maine, June 12 to July 2, 1985.

EDWARD JOHN VOSBERG
(Ed)

Born September 28, 1961, at Tucson, Ariz.
Height, 6.01. Weight, 190.
Throws and bats lefthanded.
Attended University of Arizona, Tucson, Ariz.

Tied for Texas League lead in games started by pitchers with 27 in 1984 and 1985.

Year Club	League	G.	IP.	W.	L.	Pct.	H.	R.	ER.	SO.	BB.	ERA.
1983—Reno	California	15	97⅔	6	6	.500	111	61	42	70	39	3.87
1983—Beaumont	Texas	1	7	1	0	1.000	2	0	0	1	2	0.00
1984—Beaumont	Texas	27	183⅔	13	●11	.542	196	87	70	100	74	3.43
1985—Beaumont	Texas	27	175	9	11	.450	178	92	76	124	69	3.91

Selected by St. Louis Cardinals' organization in 3rd round of free-agent draft, June 5, 1979.
Selected by Toronto Blue Jays' organization in 11th round of free-agent draft, June 7, 1982.
Selected by San Diego Padres' organization in 3rd round of free-agent draft, June 6, 1983.

PETER DENNIS VUCKOVICH

Name pronounced VOO-ko-vitch.

(Pete)

Born October 27, 1952, at Johnstown, Pa.
Height, 6.04. Weight, 220.
Throws and bats righthanded.
Attended Clarion State College, Clarion, Pa.

Major League saves: 1977 (8), 1978 (1), 1980 (1). Total—10.
Won American League Cy Young Memorial Award, 1982.

Year Club	League	G.	IP.	W.	L.	Pct.	H.	R.	ER.	SO.	BB.	ERA.
1974—Appleton	Midwest	5	15	1	0	1.000	10	2	2	22	3	1.20
1974—Knoxville	Southern	13	47	2	5	.286	50	32	22	42	29	4.21
1975—Denver	Am. Assoc.	19	116	11	4	●.733	103	63	56	86	54	4.34
1975—Chicago	American	4	10	0	1	.000	17	15	15	5	7	13.50
1976—Chicago†	American	33	110	7	4	.636	122	59	57	62	60	4.66
1977—Toronto‡	American	53	148	7	7	.500	143	64	57	123	59	3.47
1978—St. Louis	National	45	198	12	12	.500	187	65	56	149	59	2.55
1979—St. Louis	National	34	233	15	10	.600	229	108	93	145	64	3.59
1980—St. Louis§	National	32	222	12	9	.571	203	96	84	132	68	3.41
1981—Milwaukee	American	24	150	●14	4	★.778	137	61	59	84	57	3.54
1982—Milwaukee	American	30	223⅔	18	6	●.750	234	96	83	105	102	3.34
1983—Milwaukee x	American	3	14⅔	0	2	.000	15	9	8	10	10	4.91
1984—Milwaukee y	American					(Did not play)						
1985—Milwaukee za	American	22	112⅔	6	10	.375	134	74	69	55	48	5.51
American League Totals—7 Years		169	769	52	34	.605	802	378	348	444	343	4.07
National League Totals—3 Years		111	653	39	31	.557	619	269	233	426	191	3.21
Major League Totals—10 Years		280	1422	91	65	.583	1421	647	581	870	534	3.68

Selected by Chicago White Sox' organization in 3rd round of free-agent draft, June 5, 1974.
†Selected by Toronto Blue Jays in American League expansion draft, November 5, 1976.
‡Traded with a player to be named later to St. Louis Cardinals for Pitchers Tom Underwood and Victor Cruz, December 6, 1977. St. Louis organization acquired Outfielder John Scott to complete deal, December 16, 1977.
§Traded with Pitcher Rollie Fingers and Catcher Ted Simmons to Milwaukee Brewers for Outfielders Sixto Lezcano and David Green and Pitchers Lary Sorensen and Dave LaPoint, December 12, 1980.
xOn disabled list, March 24 to August 22, 1983.
yOn disabled list, March 27, 1984 through entire season.
zOn disabled list, May 11 to June 4, 1985.
aGranted free agency after refusing to report to minors, November 21, 1985.

DIVISION SERIES RECORD

Year Club	League	G.	IP.	W.	L.	Pct.	H.	R.	ER.	SO.	BB.	ERA.
1981—Milwaukee	American	2	5⅓	1	0	1.000	2	1	0	4	3	0.00

CHAMPIONSHIP SERIES RECORD

Year Club	League	G.	IP.	W.	L.	Pct.	H.	R.	ER.	SO.	BB.	ERA.
1982—Milwaukee	American	2	14⅓	0	1	.000	15	7	7	8	7	4.40

WORLD SERIES RECORD

Year Club	League	G.	IP.	W.	L.	Pct.	H.	R.	ER.	SO.	BB.	ERA.
1982—Milwaukee	American	2	14	0	1	.000	16	9	7	4	5	4.50

GEORGE STEPHEN VUKOVICH

Name pronounced VOO-ko-vitch.

Born June 24, 1956, at Chicago, Ill.
Height, 6.00. Weight, 198.
Throws right and bats lefthanded.
Attended Southern Illinois University, Carbondale, Ill.

Major League stolen bases: 1981 (1), 1982 (2), 1983 (3), 1984 (1), 1985 (2). Total—9.
Led Eastern League in sacrifice flies with 14 in 1979.
Tied for Eastern League lead in double plays by outfielders with 3 in 1979.
Named designated hitter on THE SPORTING NEWS College Baseball All-America Team, 1977.

Year Club	League	Pos.	G.	AB.	R.	H.	2B.	3B.	HR.	RBI.	B.A.	PO.	A.	E.	F.A.
1977—Auburn	NYP	OF	1	2	0	1	0	0	0	0	.500	0	0	0	.000
1978—Peninsula	Carol.	OF-1B	135	453	*94	141	26	●9	10	69	.311	208	14	10	.957
1979—Reading	East.	OF	138	501	80	147	14	10	13	88	.293	238	13	8	.969
1980—Philadelphia	Nat.	OF	78	58	6	13	1	1	0	8	.224	14	0	1	.933
1981—Oklahoma City	A. A.	OF-1B	62	232	40	70	15	2	8	48	.302	99	8	1	.991
1981—Philadelphia	Nat.	OF	20	26	5	10	0	0	1	4	.385	10	0	0	1.000
1982—Philadelphia†	Nat.	OF	123	335	41	91	18	2	6	42	.272	168	4	4	.977
1983—Cleveland	Amer.	OF	124	312	31	77	13	2	3	44	.247	203	3	3	.986
1984—Cleveland	Amer.	OF	134	437	38	133	22	5	9	60	.304	316	13	2	.994
1985—Cleveland‡	Amer.	OF	149	434	43	106	22	0	8	45	.244	250	4	3	.988
National League Totals—3 Years			221	419	52	114	19	3	7	54	.272	192	4	5	.975
American League Totals—3 Years			407	1183	112	316	57	7	20	149	.267	769	20	8	.990
Major League Totals—6 Years			628	1602	164	430	76	10	27	203	.268	961	24	13	.987

Selected by Philadelphia Phillies' organization in 4th round of free-agent draft, June 7, 1977.
†Traded with Second Baseman Manny Trillo, Infielder Julio Franco, Pitcher Jay Baller and Catcher Gerry Willard to Cleveland Indians for Outfielder Von Hayes, December 9, 1982.
‡Sold to Seibu Lions of Japanese baseball, December 10, 1985.

DIVISION SERIES RECORD

Year Club	League	Pos.	G.	AB.	R.	H.	2B.	3B.	HR.	RBI.	B.A.	PO.	A.	E.	F.A.
1981—Philadelphia	Nat.	PH-OF	5	9	1	4	0	0	1	2	.444	6	0	0	1.000

CHAMPIONSHIP SERIES RECORD

Year Club	League	Pos.	G.	AB.	R.	H.	2B.	3B.	HR.	RBI.	B.A.	PO.	A.	E.	F.A.
1980—Philadelphia	Nat.	OF-PH	4	3	0	0	0	0	0	0	.000	0	0	0	.000

THOMAS DAVID WADDELL

Name pronounced WADD-ell.

(Tom)

Born September 17, 1958, at Dundee, Scotland.
Height, 6.01. Weight, 185.
Throws and bats righthanded.
Received bachelor of science degree in education from Manhattan College, Bronx, N.Y. in 1980.
Cousin of Peter Lorimer, former Scottish/English soccer player.

Major League saves: 1984 (6), 1985 (9). Total—15.

Year Club	League	G.	IP.	W.	L.	Pct.	H.	R.	ER.	SO.	BB.	ERA.
1981—Bradenton Braves	Gulf Coast	2	10	0	1	.000	5	2	1	7	1	0.90
1981—Anderson	S. Atlantic	13	63	6	3	.667	57	24	20	51	12	2.86
1982—Anderson	S. Atlantic	4	9⅓	0	0	.000	9	5	5	13	6	4.82
1982—Durham	Carolina	42	74⅓	5	3	.625	44	20	12	102	26	1.45
1983—Savannah†	Southern	29	44⅓	8	2	.800	32	11	7	40	13	1.42

Year Club	League	G.	IP.	W.	L.	Pct.	H.	R.	ER.	SO.	BB.	ERA.
1983—Richmond‡	Int'national	13	24⅔	5	0	1.000	26	12	12	29	6	4.38
1984—Cleveland	American	58	97	7	4	.636	68	35	33	59	37	3.06
1985—Cleveland	American	49	112⅔	8	6	.571	104	61	61	53	39	4.87
Major League Totals—2 Years		107	209⅔	15	10	.600	172	96	94	112	76	4.03

Signed as free agent by Atlanta Braves' organization, April 1, 1981.
†On disabled list, May 17 to May 31, 1983.
‡Drafted by Cleveland Indians, December 5, 1983.

MICHAEL RICHARD WAITS
(Rick)

Born May 15, 1952, at Atlanta, Ga.
Height, 6.03. Weight, 195.
Throws left and bats left and righthanded.
Attended Clayton Junior College and Atlanta Baptist College, Chamblee, Ga.

Pitched 7-0 no-hit victory against Portland, June 20, 1985.
Major League saves: 1973 (1), 1975 (1), 1977 (2), 1984 (3), 1985 (1). Total—8.
Tied for Eastern League lead in balks with 2 in 1971.

Year Club	League	G.	IP.	W.	L.	Pct.	H.	R.	ER.	SO.	BB.	ERA.
1970—Anderson	W. Carol.	9	42	2	3	.400	27	25	22	37	33	4.71
1971—Pittsfield	Eastern	25	139	5	9	.357	123	65	50	98	82	3.24
1972—Pittsfield	Eastern	25	116	8	8	.500	104	66	40	84	82	3.10
1973—Spokane	P. Coast	28	154	14	7	.667	153	96	67	99	103	3.92
1973—Texas	American	1	1	0	0	.000	1	1	1	0	1	9.00
1974—Spokane	P. Coast	26	153	12	6	.667	152	98	75	90	95	4.41
1975—Spokane†	P. Coast	11	67	5	4	.556	76	46	36	38	37	4.84
1975—Oklahoma City	Am. Assoc.	9	53	1	5	.167	55	29	26	31	27	4.42
1975—Cleveland	American	16	70	6	2	.750	57	25	23	34	25	2.96
1976—Cleveland‡	American	26	124	7	9	.438	143	60	55	65	54	3.99
1977—Cleveland	American	37	135	9	7	.563	132	67	60	62	64	4.00
1978—Cleveland	American	34	230	13	15	.464	206	97	82	97	86	3.21
1979—Cleveland	American	34	231	16	13	.552	230	123	114	91	91	4.44
1980—Cleveland	American	33	224	13	14	.481	231	118	111	109	82	4.46
1981—Cleveland§	American	22	126	8	10	.444	173	74	69	51	44	4.93
1982—Cleveland	American	25	115	2	13	.133	128	74	69	44	57	5.40
1983—Cleveland x-Milwaukee y	American	18	49⅔	0	3	.000	62	33	27	33	20	4.89
1984—Milwaukee z	American	47	73	2	4	.333	84	32	29	49	24	3.58
1985—Vancouver	P. Coast	16	116	10	5	.667	108	43	37	64	22	2.87
1985—Milwaukee ab	American	24	47	3	2	.600	67	37	34	24	20	6.51
Major League Totals—12 Years		317	1425⅔	79	92	.462	1514	741	674	659	568	4.25

Selected by Washington Senators' organization in 5th round of free-agent draft, June 4, 1970.
†Traded with Pitchers Jim Bibby and Jackie Brown and an estimated $100,000 to Cleveland Indians for Pitcher Gaylord Perry, June 12, 1975.
‡On disabled list, April 30 to May 29, 1976.
§Granted free agency, November 13, 1981; re-signed by Indians, January 15, 1982.
xTraded with Outfielder Rick Manning to Milwaukee Brewers for Outfielder Gorman Thomas and Pitchers Jamie Easterly and Ernie Camacho, June 6, 1983.
yOn disabled list, July 11 to September 1, 1983.
zOn disabled list, April 2 to April 20, 1984.
aStruck out in only at-bat.
bReleased, November 14, 1985.

ROBERT VERNON WALK
(Bob)

Born November 26, 1956, at Van Nuys, Calif.
Height, 6.03. Weight, 200.
Throws and bats righthanded.
Attended College of the Canyons, Valencia, Calif.

Led Pacific Coast League in complete games with 12 in 1985.
Led International League in complete games with 11 and tied for lead in games started by pitchers with 28 and home runs allowed with 22 in 1983.
Led Carolina League in hit batsmen with 13 in 1978.

Year Club	League	G.	IP.	W.	L.	Pct.	H.	R.	ER.	SO.	BB.	ERA.
1977—Spartanburg	W. Carol.	15	99	6	9	.400	90	55	40	66	46	3.64
1977—Peninsula	Carolina	8	36	0	2	.000	44	31	17	23	20	4.25
1978—Peninsula	Carolina	26	187	13	8	.619	147	58	44	150	64	2.12
1979—Reading	Eastern	24	185	12	7	.632	156	62	46	★135	77	★2.24
1980—Oklahoma City	Am. Assoc.	8	49	5	1	.833	39	21	16	36	17	2.94
1980—Philadelphia†	National	27	152	11	7	.611	163	82	77	94	71	4.56
1981—Atlanta‡	National	12	43	1	4	.200	41	25	22	16	23	4.60
1981—Richmond	Int'national	4	22	2	1	.667	18	7	6	13	11	2.45
1982—Atlanta	National	32	164⅓	11	9	.550	179	101	89	84	59	4.87
1983—Richmond	Int'national	28	★185	11	12	.478	179	★119	★107	123	102	5.21
1983—Atlanta§	National	1	3⅔	0	0	.000	7	3	3	4	2	7.36
1984—Hawaii	P. Coast	18	127⅓	9	5	.643	100	39	32	85	42	★2.26
1984—Pittsburgh x	National	2	10⅓	1	1	.500	8	5	3	10	4	2.61

Year Club	League	G.	IP.	W.	L.	Pct.	H.	R.	ER.	SO.	BB.	ERA.
1985—Hawaii	P. Coast	24	173	*16	5	.762	143	57	51	124	61	*2.65
1985—Pittsburgh	National	9	58⅔	2	3	.400	60	27	24	40	18	3.68
Major League Totals—6 Years		83	432	26	24	.520	458	243	218	248	177	4.54

Selected by California Angels' organization in 5th round of free-agent draft, January 9, 1975.
Selected by Philadelphia Phillies' organization in 5th round of free-agent draft, January 7, 1976.
Selected by Philadelphia Phillies' organization in secondary phase of free-agent draft, June 8, 1976.
†Traded to Atlanta Braves for Outfielder Gary Matthews, March 25, 1981.
‡On disabled list, May 26 to August 9, 1981.
§Released, March 26, 1984; signed by Pittsburgh Pirates' organization, April 3, 1984.
xOn disabled list, July 23, 1984 through remainder of season.

CHAMPIONSHIP SERIES RECORD

Year Club	League	G.	IP.	W.	L.	Pct.	H.	R.	ER.	SO.	BB.	ERA.
1982—Atlanta	National	1	1	0	0	.000	2	1	1	1	1	9.00

WORLD SERIES RECORD

Year Club	League	G.	IP.	W.	L.	Pct.	H.	R.	ER.	SO.	BB.	ERA.
1980—Philadelphia	National	1	7	1	0	1.000	8	6	6	3	3	7.71

ANTHONY BRUCE WALKER
(Tony)

Born July 1, 1960, at San Diego, Calif.
Height, 6.02. Weight, 205.
Throws and bats righthanded.

Year Club	League	Pos.	G.	AB.	R.	H.	2B.	3B.	HR.	RBI.	B.A.	PO.	A.	E.	F.A.
1981—Waterbury	East.	OF	17	22	2	2	0	0	0	0	.091	9	0	1	.900
1981—Tampa	Fla. St.	OF	18	40	11	12	3	2	0	3	.300	21	0	0	1.000
1981—Eugene	N'west	OF	18	58	16	22	1	1	1	4	.379	22	1	1	.958
1982—Tampa†‡	Fla. St.	OF	128	499	73	136	9	5	2	28	.273	277	●23	*12	.962
1983—Daytona Beach‡	Fla. St.	OF	92	350	84	114	8	2	0	41	.326	196	4	3	.985
1983—Columbus‡	South.	OF	44	171	22	38	7	1	0	10	.222	83	4	0	1.000
1984—Columbus‡	South.	OF	132	408	65	101	18	4	3	35	.248	281	15	8	.974
1985—Columbus‡	South.	OF	135	530	88	156	23	5	12	65	.294	335	16	7	.980

Signed as free agent by Cincinnati Reds' organization, March 22, 1981.
†Traded with Pitcher Bill Dawley to Houston Astros for Catcher Alan Knicely, March 31, 1983.
‡Switch-hitter.

CLEOTHA WALKER
(Chico)

Born November 25, 1957, at Jackson, Miss.
Height, 5.09. Weight, 170.
Throws right and bats left and righthanded.

Major League stolen bases: 1980 (3), 1985 (1). Total—4.
Led International League in intentional bases on balls received with 9 in 1984.
Led Eastern League in caught stealing with 16 in 1979.
Tied for International League lead in double plays by second basemen with 74 in 1980.

Year Club	League	Pos.	G.	AB.	R.	H.	2B.	3B.	HR.	RBI.	B.A.	PO.	A.	E.	F.A.
1976—Elmira	NYP	2B	22	28	9	5	1	2	0	1	.179	9	18	3	.900
1977—Elmira	NYP	2B-SS	64	227	26	50	4	3	1	14	.220	122	196	15	.955
1978—Winter Haven	Fla. St.	SS-3B-2B	133	480	66	134	10	6	3	52	.279	172	380	42	.929
1979—Bristol†	East.	2B	123	498	75	132	19	*12	8	57	.265	252	357	23	.964
1980—Pawtucket	Int.	2B	139	536	59	146	18	7	8	52	.272	252	*394	*21	.969
1980—Boston	Amer.	2B	19	57	3	12	0	0	1	5	.211	15	31	2	.958
1981—Pawtucket	Int.	OF-2B-3B	138	535	50	148	21	5	17	68	.277	209	178	13	.968
1981—Boston	Amer.	2B	6	17	3	6	0	0	0	2	.353	4	10	0	1.000
1982—Pawtucket	Int.	O-2-3-S	133	494	71	124	22	2	15	66	.251	209	48	11	.959
1983—Pawtucket	Int.	3-O-S-2	125	442	78	119	18	1	18	56	.269	122	126	16	.939
1983—Boston	Amer.	OF	4	5	2	2	0	2	0	1	.400	4	1	0	1.000
1984—Pawtucket	Int.	2B-OF-3B	130	499	●91	131	26	5	18	51	.263	223	241	20	.959
1984—Boston‡	Amer.	2B	3	2	0	0	0	0	0	1	.000	0	1	0	1.000
1985—Iowa	A. A.	OF-3B	89	331	47	94	17	8	5	46	.284	177	6	5	.973
1985—Chicago	Nat.	OF-2B	21	12	3	1	0	0	0	0	.083	4	0	0	1.000
American League Totals—4 Years			32	81	8	20	0	2	1	9	.247	23	43	2	.971
National League Totals—1 Year			21	12	3	1	0	0	0	0	.083	4	0	0	1.000
Major League Totals—5 Years			53	93	11	21	0	2	1	9	.226	27	43	2	.972

Selected by Boston Red Sox' organization in 22nd round of free-agent draft, June 8, 1976.
†On disabled list, August 22 to September 19, 1979.
‡Granted free agency, October 15, 1984; signed by Iowa (Chicago Cubs' organization), November 9, 1984.

DUANE ALLEN WALKER

Born March 13, 1957, at Pasadena, Tex.
Height, 6.00. Weight, 180.
Throws and bats lefthanded.
Attended San Jacinto College, Pasadena, Tex.

Major League stolen bases: 1982 (9), 1983 (6), 1984 (7), 1985 (2). Total—24.

Year Club	League	Pos.	G.	AB.	R.	H.	2B.	3B.	HR.	RBI.	B.A.	PO.	A.	E.	F.A.
1976—Tampa	Fla. St.	OF	29	91	9	19	1	0	0	3	.209	36	5	2	.953
1976—Eugene	N'west.	OF	46	172	41	49	11	5	10	24	.285	51	5	3	.949
1977—Tampa	Fla. St.	OF	122	466	67	116	13	7	2	37	.249	180	12	3	.985
1978—Nashville	South.	OF	103	288	38	69	15	3	2	31	.240	133	7	5	.966
1979—Nashville	South.	OF	143	545	97	165	28	*15	9	57	.303	237	9	12	.953
1980—Indianapolis	A. A.	OF	109	351	41	87	16	4	6	30	.248	169	14	9	.953
1981—Indianapolis	A. A.	OF	130	450	80	127	22	1	19	80	.282	213	3	6	.973
1982—Indianapolis	A. A.	OF	36	115	21	33	6	1	4	19	.287	68	3	2	.973
1982—Cincinnati	Nat.	OF	86	239	26	52	10	0	5	22	.218	110	7	1	.992
1983—Cincinnati	Nat.	OF	109	225	14	53	12	1	2	29	.236	104	4	5	.956
1984—Cincinnati†	Nat.	OF	83	195	35	57	10	3	10	28	.292	110	3	6	.950
1985—Cincinnati‡	Nat.	OF	37	48	5	8	2	1	2	6	.167	15	0	2	.882
1985—Texas§	Amer.	OF	53	132	14	23	2	0	5	11	.174	51	6	0	1.000
National League Totals—4 Years			315	707	80	170	34	5	19	85	.240	339	14	14	.962
American League Totals—1 Year			53	132	14	23	2	0	5	11	.174	51	6	0	1.000
Major League Totals—4 Years			368	839	94	193	36	5	24	96	.230	390	20	14	.967

Selected by San Francisco Giants' organization in 34th round of free-agent draft, June 4, 1975.
Selected by Cincinnati Reds' organization in secondary phase of free-agent draft, January 7, 1976.
†On disabled list, May 18 to June 4 and August 5 to September 1, 1984.
‡Traded with a player to be named later to Texas Rangers for Third Baseman Buddy Bell, July 19, 1985; Texas organization acquired Pitcher Jeff Russell to complete deal, July 23, 1985.
§Released, December 20, 1985; re-signed by Rangers, January 17, 1986.

GREGORY LEE WALKER
(Greg)

Born October 6, 1959, at Douglas, Ga.
Height, 6.03. Weight, 210.
Throws right and bats lefthanded.

Major League stolen bases: 1983 (2), 1984 (8), 1985 (5). Total—15.
Led Midwest League first basemen in double plays with 108 in 1980.

Year Club	League	Pos.	G.	AB.	R.	H.	2B.	3B.	HR.	RBI.	B.A.	PO.	A.	E.	F.A.
1977—Auburn†	NYP	1B	33	98	12	25	1	2	2	8	.255	5	0	0	1.000
1978—Spartanburg	W. Car.	1B-3B-C	100	341	51	71	16	2	11	47	.208	538	50	13	.978
1979—Peninsula‡	Carol.	1B	122	446	59	125	*27	4	10	61	.280	973	53	19	.982
1980—Appleton	Midw.	1B	135	464	88	130	20	3	21	*98	.280	*1298	*88	10	*.993
1981—Glens Falls	East.	1B	135	508	*117	*163	*33	2	22	86	.321	*1215	77	11	.992
1982—Edmonton§	P. C.	1B	35	117	18	41	8	0	3	12	.350	94	11	0	1.000
1982—Chicago	Amer.	DH	11	17	3	7	2	1	2	7	.412	0	0	0	.000
1983—Chicago	Amer.	1B	118	307	32	83	16	3	10	55	.270	426	19	7	.985
1984—Chicago	Amer.	1B	136	442	62	130	29	2	24	75	.294	791	51	4	.995
1985—Chicago	Amer.	1B	*163	601	77	155	38	4	24	92	.258	1217	97	8	.994
Major League Totals—4 Years			428	1367	174	375	85	10	60	229	.274	2434	167	19	.993

Selected by Philadelphia Phillies' organization in 20th round of free-agent draft, June 7, 1977.
†On disabled list, June 21, 1977 through remainder of season.
‡Drafted by Iowa (Chicago White Sox' organization), December 4, 1979.
§On disabled list, April 23 to July 27, 1982.

CHAMPIONSHIP SERIES RECORD

Year Club	League	Pos.	G.	AB.	R.	H.	2B.	3B.	HR.	RBI.	B.A.	PO.	A.	E.	F.A.
1983—Chicago	Amer.	PH-1B	2	3	0	1	0	0	0	0	.333	7	1	0	1.000

TIMOTHY CHARLES WALLACH
(Tim)

Born September 14, 1957, at Huntington Park, Calif.
Height, 6.03. Weight, 220.
Throws and bats righthanded.
Attended Saddleback Junior College, Mission Viejo, Calif., and
California State University, Fullerton, Calif.

Tied major league record by hitting home run in first major league at-bat, September 6, 1980.
Major League stolen bases: 1982 (6), 1984 (3), 1985 (9). Total—18.
Led National League third basemen in total chances with 515 in 1984 and 549 in 1985.
Led National League third basemen in double plays with 29 in 1984 and 34 in 1985.
Led American Association in total bases with 295, game-winning RBIs with 16 and tied for lead in sacrifice flies with 9 in 1980.
Named third baseman on THE SPORTING NEWS National League All-Star Team, 1985.
Named third baseman on THE SPORTING NEWS National League All-Star fielding team, 1985.
Named third baseman on THE SPORTING NEWS National League Silver Slugger team, 1985.
Named College Player of the Year by THE SPORTING NEWS, 1979.
Received reported $90,000 bonus to sign with Montreal Expos, 1979.
Named first baseman on THE SPORTING NEWS College Baseball All-America Team, 1979.

Year Club	League	Pos.	G.	AB.	R.	H.	2B.	3B.	HR.	RBI.	B.A.	PO.	A.	E.	F.A.
1979—Memphis	South.	1B-3B	75	257	50	84	16	4	18	51	.327	290	35	4	.988
1980—Denver	A. A.	3B-OF-1B	134	512	103	144	29	7	36	124	.281	222	147	21	.946
1980—Montreal	Nat.	OF-1B	5	11	1	2	0	0	1	2	.182	12	0	0	1.000
1981—Montreal	Nat.	OF-1B-3B	71	212	19	50	9	1	4	13	.236	207	31	1	.996
1982—Montreal	Nat.	*3-O-1	158	596	89	160	31	3	28	97	.268	*132	287	23	.948

Year Club	League	Pos.	G.	AB.	R.	H.	2B.	3B.	HR.	RBI.	B.A.	PO.	A.	E.	F.A.
1983—Montreal	Nat.	3B	156	581	54	156	33	3	19	70	.269	*151	265	19	.956
1984—Montreal	Nat.	*3B-SS	160	582	55	143	25	4	18	72	.246	*162	*332	21	.959
1985—Montreal	Nat.	3B	155	569	70	148	36	3	22	81	.260	*148	*383	18	.967
Major League Totals—6 Years			705	2551	288	659	134	14	92	335	.258	812	1298	82	.963

Selected by California Angels' organization in 8th round of free-agent draft, June 6, 1978.
Selected by Montreal Expos' organization in 1st round (10th player selected) of free-agent draft, June 5, 1979.

DIVISION SERIES RECORD

Year Club	League	Pos.	G.	AB.	R.	H.	2B.	3B.	HR.	RBI.	B.A.	PO.	A.	E.	F.A.
1981—Montreal	Nat.	OF	4	4	1	1	1	0	0	0	.250	4	0	0	1.000

CHAMPIONSHIP SERIES RECORD

Year Club	League	Pos.	G.	AB.	R.	H.	2B.	3B.	HR.	RBI.	B.A.	PO.	A.	E.	F.A.
1981—Montreal	Nat.	PH	1	1	0	0	0	0	0	0	.000	0	0	0	.000

ALL-STAR GAME RECORD

Year League	Pos.	AB.	R.	H.	2B.	3B.	HR.	RBI.	B.A.	PO.	A.	E.	F.A.
1984—National	3B	1	0	0	0	0	0	0	.000	0	0	0	.000
1985—National	3B	2	1	1	1	0	0	0	.500	1	1	0	1.000
All-Star Game Totals—2 Years		3	1	1	1	0	0	0	.333	1	1	0	1.000

DENNIS MARTIN WALLING
(Denny)

Born April 17, 1954, at Neptune, N.J.
Height, 6.01. Weight, 185.
Throws right and bats lefthanded.
Attended Brookdale Community College, Lincroft, N.J., and
Clemson University, Clemson, S.C.
Brother of Gregory Walling, minor league outfielder, 1967.

Major League stolen bases: 1978 (9), 1979 (3), 1980 (4), 1981 (2), 1982 (4), 1983 (2), 1984 (7), 1985 (5). Total—36.
Named outfielder on THE SPORTING NEWS College Baseball All-America Team, 1975.

Year Club	League	Pos.	G.	AB.	R.	H.	2B.	3B.	HR.	RBI.	B.A.	PO.	A.	E.	F.A.
1975—Oakland	Amer.	OF	6	8	0	1	1	0	0	2	.125	3	0	0	1.000
1976—Chattanooga	South.	OF	115	369	48	95	15	5	9	42	.257	241	8	2	*.992
1976—Oakland	Amer.	OF	3	11	1	3	0	0	0	0	.273	8	0	1	.889
1977—San Jose†‡	P. C.	OF	3	10	1	3	0	0	0	4	.300	8	0	0	1.000
1977—Charleston	Int.	OF	29	89	17	31	4	1	4	14	.348	66	0	0	1.000
1977—Houston	Nat.	OF	6	21	1	6	0	1	0	6	.286	14	0	0	1.000
1978—Houston	Nat.	OF	120	247	30	62	11	3	3	36	.251	140	4	3	.980
1979—Houston	Nat.	OF	82	147	21	48	8	4	3	31	.327	65	2	1	.985
1980—Houston	Nat.	1B-OF	100	284	30	85	6	5	3	29	.299	525	31	6	.989
1981—Houston	Nat.	1B-OF	65	158	23	37	6	0	5	23	.234	226	9	2	.992
1982—Houston	Nat.	OF-1B	85	146	22	30	4	1	1	14	.205	167	11	1	.994
1983—Houston§	Nat.	1B-3B-OF	100	135	24	40	5	3	3	19	.296	134	29	6	.964
1984—Houston x	Nat.	3B-1B-OF	87	249	37	70	11	5	3	31	.281	116	102	7	.969
1985—Houston	Nat.	3B-1B-OF	119	345	44	93	20	1	7	45	.270	326	124	12	.974
American League Totals—2 Years			9	19	1	4	1	0	0	2	.210	11	0	1	.917
National League Totals—9 Years			764	1732	232	471	71	23	28	234	.272	1713	312	38	.982
Major League Totals—11 Years			773	1751	233	475	72	23	28	236	.271	1724	312	39	.981

Selected by San Francisco Giants' organization in 8th round of free-agent draft, June 5, 1974.
Selected by Oakland A's organization in secondary phase of free-agent draft, June 4, 1975.
†On disabled list, April 18 to June 15, 1977.
‡Traded with cash to Houston Astros' organization for Outfielder Willie Crawford, June 15, 1977.
§Granted free agency, November 7, 1983; re-signed by Astros, December 20, 1983.
xOn disabled list, May 2 to May 24, 1984.

DIVISION SERIES RECORD

Year Club	League	Pos.	G.	AB.	R.	H.	2B.	3B.	HR.	RBI.	B.A.	PO.	A.	E.	F.A.
1981—Houston	Nat.	PH-1B	3	6	0	2	0	0	0	1	.333	6	1	1	.875

CHAMPIONSHIP SERIES RECORD

Year Club	League	Pos.	G.	AB.	R.	H.	2B.	3B.	HR.	RBI.	B.A.	PO.	A.	E.	F.A.
1980—Houston	Nat.	1-O-PH	3	9	2	1	0	0	0	2	.111	6	0	0	1.000

GENE WINSTON WALTER

Born November 22, 1960, at Chicago, Ill.
Height, 6.04. Weight, 200.
Throws and bats lefthanded.
Received degree from Eastern Kentucky University, Richmond, Ky.

Major League saves: 1985 (3).

Year Club	League	G.	IP.	W.	L.	Pct.	H.	R.	ER.	SO.	BB.	ERA.
1982—Walla Walla	Northwest	17	72⅔	4	4	.500	73	55	39	61	46	4.83
1983—Miami	Florida St.	42	121⅓	6	13	.316	114	73	51	105	61	3.78
1984—Miami	Florida St.	9	59	3	5	.375	43	22	15	70	27	2.29
1984—Beaumont	Texas	34	76	7	3	.700	53	25	22	71	40	2.61

Year	Club	League	G.	IP.	W.	L.	Pct.	H.	R.	ER.	SO.	BB.	ERA.
1985—Las Vegas†		P. Coast	45	95	7	5	.583	75	34	29	107	35	2.75
1985—San Diego		National	15	22	0	2	.000	12	6	5	18	8	2.05
Major League Totals—1 Year			15	22	0	2	.000	12	6	5	18	8	2.05

Selected by Montreal Expos' organization in 25th round of free-agent draft, June 8, 1981.
Selected by San Diego Padres' organization in 29th round of free-agent draft, June 7, 1982.
†Appeared in one game as an outfielder with one putout.

COLIN NORVAL WARD

Born November 22, 1960, at Los Angeles, Calif.
Height, 6.03. Weight, 190.
Throws and bats lefthanded.
Attended Citrus College, Azusa, Calif., and
University of California, Los Angeles, Calif.

Year	Club	League	G.	IP.	W.	L.	Pct.	H.	R.	ER.	SO.	BB.	ERA.
1982—Lakeland		Florida St.	11	63	2	2	.500	55	29	24	37	44	3.43
1983—Birmingham†		Southern	26	150⅔	10	3	.769	139	81	69	71	★109	4.12
1984—Phoenix		P. Coast	46	126⅔	7	8	.467	143	85	74	95	71	5.26
1985—Phoenix‡		P. Coast	22	41⅓	3	0	1.000	45	27	27	31	30	5.88
1985—San Francisco§		National	6	12⅓	0	0	.000	10	6	6	8	7	4.38
Major League Totals—1 Year			6	12⅓	0	0	.000	10	6	6	8	7	4.38

Selected by San Francisco Giants' organization in 32nd round of free-agent draft, June 3, 1980.
Selected by Detroit Tigers' organization in 3rd round of free-agent draft, June 7, 1982.
†Traded to San Francisco Giants' organization for Pitcher Pat Larkin, February 8, 1984.
‡On disabled list, April 11 to June 24, 1985.
§Traded to Cincinnati Reds' organization for Pitcher Bob Buchanan, November 11, 1985.

GARY LAMELL WARD

Born December 6, 1953, at Los Angeles, Calif.
Height, 6.02. Weight, 207.
Throws and bats righthanded.

Major League stolen bases: 1981 (5), 1982 (13), 1983 (8), 1984 (7), 1985 (26). Total—59.
Hit for the cycle, September 18, 1980 (first game).
Led American League outfielders in double plays with 4 in 1981.
Led New York-Pennsylvania League first basemen in errors with 12 in 1973.
Tied for Midwest League lead in assists by outfielders with 18 in 1974.

Year	Club	League	Pos.	G.	AB.	R.	H.	2B.	3B.	HR.	RBI.	B.A.	PO.	A.	E.	F.A.
1973—Geneva		NYP	1B-OF-3B	61	211	36	57	13	1	10	38	.270	336	20	14	.962
1974—Wis. Rapids		Midw.	OF-1B	126	★467	★104	122	12	5	26	78	.261	184	19	11	.949
1975—Orlando		South.	OF-C	124	438	45	117	18	5	8	71	.267	204	10	4	.982
1976—Orlando		South.	OF	132	475	50	119	17	2	9	65	.251	235	●16	●10	.962
1977—Tacoma		P. C.	OF-3B	125	413	62	97	15	8	8	43	.235	212	34	10	.961
1978—Toledo		Int.	★O-1-3	139	511	82	150	20	12	14	79	.294	260	6	★13	.953
1979—Toledo		Int.	OF	134	506	75	133	16	9	13	67	.263	323	12	●11	.968
1979—Minnesota		Amer.	DH-PH	10	14	2	4	0	0	0	1	.286	0	0	0	.000
1980—Toledo†		Int.	OF-1B	128	496	82	140	22	8	13	66	.282	269	14	8	.973
1980—Minnesota		Amer.	OF	13	41	11	19	6	2	1	10	.463	14	0	0	1.000
1981—Minnesota		Amer.	OF	85	295	42	78	7	6	3	29	.264	185	8	5	.975
1982—Minnesota		Amer.	OF	152	570	85	165	33	7	28	91	.289	343	10	4	.989
1983—Minnesota‡		Amer.	OF	157	623	76	173	34	5	19	88	.278	374	★24	9	.978
1984—Texas		Amer.	OF	155	602	97	171	21	7	21	79	.284	376	11	5	.987
1985—Texas		Amer.	OF	154	593	77	170	28	7	15	70	.287	304	11	10	.969
Major League Totals—7 Years				726	2738	390	780	129	34	87	368	.285	1596	67	33	.981

Signed as free agent by Minnesota Twins' organization, August 29, 1972.
†On disabled list, April 16 to April 26, 1980.
‡Traded to Texas Rangers for Pitchers Mike Smithson and John Butcher and Catcher Sam Sorce, December 7, 1983.

ALL-STAR GAME RECORD

Year	League	Pos.	AB.	R.	H.	2B.	3B.	HR.	RBI.	B.A.	PO.	A.	E.	F.A.
1983—American		PH	1	0	0	0	0	0	0	.000	0	0	0	.000
1985—American		PH	1	0	0	0	0	0	0	.000	0	0	0	.000
All-Star Game Totals—2 Years			2	0	0	0	0	0	0	.000	0	0	0	.000

KEVIN MICHAEL WARD

Born September 28, 1961, at Lansdale, Pa.
Height, 6.01. Weight, 195.
Throws and bats righthanded.
Attended University of Arizona, Tucson, Ariz.

Year	Club	League	Pos.	G.	AB.	R.	H.	2B.	3B.	HR.	RBI.	B.A.	PO.	A.	E.	F.A.
1983—Bend		N'west	OF	55	199	33	61	12	2	2	29	.307	70	3	●9	.890
1984—Peninsula		Carol.	OF	130	456	84	119	18	5	13	69	.261	217	4	10	.957
1985—Reading		East.	OF	42	132	23	40	9	6	1	21	.303	84	1	0	1.000

Selected by St. Louis Cardinals' organization in 29th round of free-agent draft, June 7, 1982.
Selected by Philadelphia Phillies' organization in 6th round of free-agent draft, June 6, 1983.

ROY DUANE WARD

(Known by middle name.)

Born May 28, 1964, at Parkview, N.M.
Height, 6.04. Weight, 185.
Throws and bats righthanded.

Year Club	League	G.	IP.	W.	L.	Pct.	H.	R.	ER.	SO.	BB.	ERA.
1982—Bradenton Braves	Gulf Coast	8	45⅔	2	3	.400	45	25	23	31	24	4.53
1982—Anderson	S. Atlantic	5	23⅔	1	2	.333	24	16	14	18	15	5.32
1983—Durham	Carolina	28	178⅓	11	13	.458	165	103	85	115	49	4.29
1984—Greenville†	Southern	21	104⅔	4	9	.308	108	71	58	54	57	4.99
1985—Greenville	Southern	28	150	11	10	.524	141	83	70	100	★105	4.20
1985—Richmond	Int'national	5	5⅓	0	1	.000	8	9	7	3	8	11.81

Selected by Atlanta Braves' organization in 1st round (ninth player selected) of free-agent draft, June 7, 1982.
†On disabled list, May 7 to May 29 and July 14 to August 7, 1984.

CURTIS RAY WARDLE

(Curt)

Born November 16, 1960, at Downey, Calif.
Height, 6.05. Weight, 220.
Throws and bats lefthanded.
Attended San Bernardino Valley, San Bernardino, Calif., and
University of California, Riverside, Calif.

Major League saves: 1985 (1).
Tied for Southern League lead in saves with 17 in 1984.

Year Club	League	G.	IP.	W.	L.	Pct.	H.	R.	ER.	SO.	BB.	ERA.
1981—Wisconsin Rapids	Midwest	16	53	4	3	.571	49	27	19	41	32	3.23
1982—Visalia	California	28	79⅓	3	4	.429	114	66	59	42	56	6.69
1983—Visalia	California	49	146	8	6	.571	118	52	43	134	55	2.65
1984—Orlando	Southern	45	78	6	1	.857	41	10	6	75	30	0.69
1984—Minnesota	American	2	4	0	0	.000	3	2	2	5	0	4.50
1985—Minnesota†-Cleveland	American	50	115	8	9	.471	127	83	79	84	62	6.18
Major League Totals—2 Years		52	119	8	9	.471	130	85	81	89	62	6.13

Selected by St. Louis Cardinals' organization in 45th round of free-agent draft, June 6, 1978.
Selected by California Angels' organization in secondary phase of free-agent draft, January 9, 1979.
Selected by San Diego Padres' organization in 2nd round of free-agent draft, January 8, 1980.
Selected by Minnesota Twins' organization in 3rd round of free-agent draft, June 8, 1981.
†Traded with Outfielder Jim Weaver and Infielder Jay Bell to Cleveland Indians for Pitcher Bert Blyleven, August 1, 1985.

MICHAEL BRUCE WARREN

(Mike)

Born March 26, 1961, at Inglewood, Calif.
Height, 6.01. Weight, 175.
Throws and bats righthanded.

Pitched 3-0 no-hit victory against Chicago White Sox, September 29, 1983.

Year Club	League	G.	IP.	W.	L.	Pct.	H.	R.	ER.	SO.	BB.	ERA.
1979—Bristol	Ap'lachian	13	36	0	3	.000	32	27	16	43	40	4.00
1980—Bristol	Ap'lachian	12	68	2	7	.222	68	51	40	45	39	5.29
1980—Lakeland†	Florida St.	13	52	3	6	.333	60	45	41	33	48	7.10
1981—Modesto‡	California	22	123	9	6	.600	110	76	57	91	74	4.17
1982—Stockton§-Modesto	California	28	195	★19	4	★.826	160	76	65	154	83	3.00
1983—Albany	Eastern	10	72	6	2	.750	56	38	26	87	33	3.25
1983—Oakland	American	12	65⅔	5	3	.625	51	33	30	30	18	4.11
1983—Tacoma	P. Coast	11	79	6	3	.667	72	34	31	85	36	3.53
1984—Oakland	American	24	90	3	6	.333	104	52	49	61	44	4.90
1984—Tacoma	P. Coast	11	67⅓	4	3	.571	67	45	37	44	33	4.95
1985—Oakland	American	16	49	1	4	.200	52	42	36	48	38	6.61
1985—Tacoma x	P. Coast	12	23	1	2	.333	17	15	13	24	24	5.09
Major League Totals—3 Years		52	204⅔	9	13	.409	207	127	115	139	100	5.06

Selected by Detroit Tigers' organization in 12th round of free-agent draft, June 5, 1979.
†Released, April 2, 1981; signed by Modesto (Oakland A's organization), April 30, 1981.
‡Drafted by Vancouver (Milwaukee Brewers' organization) December 8, 1981.
§Traded with First Baseman John Evans to Oakland A's organization for Infielder Rob Picciolo, May 14, 1982.
xReleased, December 20, 1985.

CLAUDELL WASHINGTON

Born August 31, 1954, at Los Angeles, Calif.
Height, 6.00. Weight, 190.
Throws and bats lefthanded.
Brother of Don Washington, outfielder in Los Angeles Dodgers' and
Oakland A's organizations, 1975 through 1977.

Hit three home runs in a game, July 14, 1979 and June 22, 1980.
Major League stolen bases: 1974 (6), 1975 (40), 1976 (37), 1977 (21), 1978 (5), 1979 (19), 1980 (21), 1981 (12), 1982 (33), 1983 (31), 1984 (21), 1985 (14). Total—260.
Led Midwest League in total bases with 218 in 1973.

Year Club League	Pos.	G.	AB.	R.	H.	2B.	3B.	HR.	RBI.	B.A.	PO.	A.	E.	F.A.
1972—C's Bay-N. Bend....N'west.	OF	33	111	13	31	3	2	2	15	.279	37	1	6	.864
1973—Burlington .... Midw.	OF	108	447	*92	144	25	5	13	81	.322	149	10	*15	.914
1974—Birmingham .... South.	OF	74	294	64	106	23	3	11	55	.361	116	5	13	.903
1974—Oakland................ Amer.	OF	73	221	16	63	10	5	0	19	.285	63	2	1	.985
1975—Oakland................ Amer.	OF	148	590	86	182	24	7	10	77	.308	305	8	7	.978
1976—Oakland†‡............. Amer.	●OF	134	490	65	126	20	6	5	53	.257	276	10	●11	.963
1977—Texas§................ Amer.	OF	129	521	63	148	31	2	12	68	.284	255	11	6	.978
1978—Tex. x-Chi. y .... Amer.	OF	98	356	34	90	16	5	6	33	.253	170	6	8	.957
1979—Chicago .... Amer.	OF	131	471	79	132	33	5	13	66	.280	256	7	7	.974
1980—Chicago z.............. Amer.	OF	32	90	15	26	4	2	1	12	.289	41	1	3	.933
1980—New York a .... Nat.	OF	79	284	38	78	16	4	10	42	.275	123	12	3	.978
1981—Atlanta b............... Nat.	OF	85	320	37	93	22	3	5	37	.291	145	5	1	.993
1982—Atlanta .... Nat.	OF	150	563	94	150	24	6	16	80	.266	221	9	12	.950
1983—Atlanta .... Nat.	OF	134	496	75	138	24	8	9	44	.278	218	8	6	.974
1984—Atlanta c .... Nat.	OF	120	416	62	119	21	2	17	61	.286	170	4	6	.967
1985—Atlanta .... Nat.	OF	122	398	62	110	14	6	15	43	.276	122	3	5	.962
American League Totals—7 Years		745	2739	358	767	138	32	47	328	.280	1366	45	43	.970
National League Totals—6 Years		690	2477	368	688	121	29	72	307	.278	999	41	33	.969
Major League Totals—12 Years		1435	5216	726	1455	259	61	119	635	.279	2365	86	76	.970

Signed as free agent by Oakland A's organization, July 7, 1972.
†On disabled list, August 16 to September 1, 1976.
‡Traded to Texas Rangers for Pitcher Jim Umbarger, Infielder Rodney Scott and cash estimated at $100,000, March 26, 1977.
§On disabled list, May 27 to June 11, 1977.
xTraded with Outfielder Rusty Torres and cash to Chicago White Sox for Outfielder Bobby Bonds, May 16, 1978.
yOn disabled list, May 22 to June 16, 1978.
zTraded to New York Mets for Pitcher Jesse Anderson, June 7, 1980.
aGranted free agency, October 31, 1980; signed by Atlanta Braves, November 15, 1980.
bOn disabled list, June 5 to August 9, 1981.
cOn disabled list, May 30 to June 14, 1984.

CHAMPIONSHIP SERIES RECORD

Year Club League	Pos.	G.	AB.	R.	H.	2B.	3B.	HR.	RBI.	B.A.	PO.	A.	E.	F.A.
1974—Oakland................ Amer.	OF-PH	4	11	1	3	1	0	0	0	.273	11	0	0	1.000
1975—Oakland................ Amer.	OF-DH	3	12	1	3	1	0	1	1	.250	1	0	2	.333
1982—Atlanta .... Nat.	OF	3	9	0	3	0	0	0	0	.333	5	1	0	1.000
Championship Series Totals—3 Years		10	32	2	9	2	0	0	1	.281	17	1	2	.900

WORLD SERIES RECORD

Tied World Series record for most positions played, Series (3), 1974 (all three outfield positions).

Year Club League	Pos.	G.	AB.	R.	H.	2B.	3B.	HR.	RBI.	B.A.	PO.	A.	E.	F.A.
1974—Oakland................ Amer.	OF-PH	5	7	1	4	0	0	0	0	.571	3	0	0	1.000

ALL-STAR GAME RECORD

Year League	Pos.	AB.	R.	H.	2B.	3B.	HR.	RBI.	B.A.	PO.	A.	E.	F.A.
1975—American.............................	PR-OF	1	0	1	0	0	0	0	1.000	1	0	0	1.000
1984—National	OF	2	0	1	1	0	0	0	.500	1	0	0	1.000
All-Star Game Totals—2 Years....................		3	0	2	1	0	0	0	.667	2	0	0	1.000

RANDY LYNN WASHINGTON

Born August 17, 1963, at Stockton, Calif.
Height, 5.11. Weight, 190.
Throws and bats righthanded.

Year Club League	Pos.	G.	AB.	R.	H.	2B.	3B.	HR.	RBI.	B.A.	PO.	A.	E.	F.A.
1981—Batavia................... NYP	OF	66	226	41	74	11	*8	11	48	.327	107	6	8	.934
1982—Waterloo† .... Midw.	OF	18	41	6	7	2	0	0	8	.171	20	1	4	.840
1982—Batavia................... NYP	OF	65	225	31	65	12	0	10	46	.289	89	5	5	.949
1983—Waterloo............... Midw.	OF	127	413	66	120	24	3	19	89	.291	147	12	4	.975
1984—Buffalo .... East.	OF-1B	120	379	66	107	12	3	9	63	.282	198	9	5	.976
1985—Waterbury .... East.	OF	125	449	75	138	14	5	14	84	.307	179	16	4	.980

Selected by Cleveland Indians' organization in 4th round of free-agent draft, June 8, 1981.
†On disabled list, April 9 to May 3, 1982.

RONALD WASHINGTON
(Ron)

Born April 29, 1952, at New Orleans, La.
Height, 5.11. Weight, 160.
Throws and bats righthanded.
Attended Manatee Junior College, Bradenton, Fla.

Major League stolen bases: 1977 (1), 1981 (4), 1982 (3), 1983 (10), 1984 (1), 1985 (5). Total—24.

Year Club League	Pos.	G.	AB.	R.	H.	2B.	3B.	HR.	RBI.	B.A.	PO.	A.	E.	F.A.
1971—Sara. Royals† .... Gulf C.	C	38	127	29	37	2	●6	1	23	.291	*213	23	3	*.987
1972—Waterloo .... Midw.	C-OF-3B	76	241	37	55	3	1	1	30	.228	424	48	8	.983
1973—Waterloo .... Midw.	SS	85	289	35	80	13	5	6	34	.277	130	198	29	.919
1974—San Jose‡ .... Calif.	2B-SS-C	109	425	49	104	16	3	2	41	.245	233	266	33	.938

Year Club League	Pos.	G.	AB.	R.	H.	2B.	3B.	HR.	RBI.	B.A.	PO.	A.	E.	F.A.
1975—Jacksonville§ .... South.	2-3-S-1	96	267	22	61	7	1	0	20	.228	133	199	22	.938
1976—Waterbury x .... East.	3B-2B	115	436	61	128	9	10	4	32	.294	170	249	26	.942
1977—San Antonio y ...... Texas	SS	39	158	24	44	8	4	0	13	.278	78	92	12	.934
1977—Albuquerque .... P. C.	SS	85	359	71	116	17	8	8	59	.323	204	250	*33	.932
1977—Los Angeles .... Nat.	SS	10	19	4	7	0	0	0	1	.368	4	14	3	.857
1978—Albuquerque z ...... P. C.	3B	31	122	26	42	10	3	5	32	.344	23	58	8	.910
1979—Aguila .... Mex.	3B	42	165	22	43	3	3	0	14	.261	35	96	10	.929
1979—Tidewater a .... Int.	3B-SS	83	273	18	72	13	4	1	26	.264	77	157	13	.947
1980—Toledo .... Int.	3B-2B-SS	114	407	62	117	•31	5	3	36	.287	131	268	30	.930
1981—Toledo .... Int.	3B-OF-SS	138	*544	84	157	27	8	15	54	.289	130	287	26	.941
1981—Minnesota .... Amer.	SS-OF	28	84	8	19	3	1	0	5	.226	64	80	8	.947
1982—Minnesota .... Amer.	SS-2B-3B	119	451	48	122	17	6	5	39	.271	201	269	13	.973
1983—Minnesota .... Amer.	SS-2B-3B	99	317	28	78	7	3	4	26	.246	140	246	16	.960
1984—Minnesota .... Amer.	SS-2B-3B	88	197	25	58	11	5	3	23	.294	77	134	4	.981
1985—Minnesota .... Amer.	S-2-3-1	70	135	24	37	6	4	1	14	.274	55	100	7	.957
National League Totals—1 Year.............		10	19	4	7	0	0	0	1	.368	4	14	3	.857
American League Totals—5 Years		404	1184	133	314	44	19	13	107	.265	537	829	48	.966
Major League Totals—6 Years................		414	1203	137	321	44	19	13	108	.267	541	843	51	.964

Signed as free agent by Kansas City Royals' organization, July 17, 1970.
†On military list, September 30, 1971 through March 3, 1972.
‡On temporary inactive list, July 4 to July 25, 1974.
§On disabled list, June 19 to June 30, 1975.
xTraded to Los Angeles Dodgers' organization for Catcher Steve Patchin, November 2, 1976.
yOn temporary inactive list, April 12 to April 22, 1977.
zOn disabled list, May 12 to June 26 and July 17 to September 10, 1978.
aTraded to Minnesota Twins' organization for Infielder Wayne Caughey, March 26, 1980.

U. L. WASHINGTON

Born October 27, 1953, at Atoka, Okla.
Height, 5.11. Weight, 175.
Throws right and bats left and righthanded.
Attended Murray State College, Tishomingo, Okla.

Switch-hit home runs in one game, September 21, 1979.
Major League stolen bases: 1977 (1), 1978 (12), 1979 (10), 1980 (20), 1981 (10), 1982 (23), 1983 (40), 1984 (4), 1985 (6). Total—126.
Led American Association batters in strikeouts with 145 in 1975.
Led Appalachian League in sacrifice flies with 8 in 1973.
Led Appalachian League shortstops in double plays with 29 in 1973.

Year Club League	Pos.	G.	AB.	R.	H.	2B.	3B.	HR.	RBI.	B.A.	PO.	A.	E.	F.A.
1973—Kingsport .... Appal.	SS	68	244	47	69	14	4	5	51	.283	89	176	36	.880
1974—San Jose .... Calif.	SS-2B	68	245	38	61	9	2	6	21	.249	81	201	34	.892
1974—Jacksonville.......... South.	SS	47	167	29	43	11	1	2	20	.257	71	172	17	.935
1975—Omaha.................... A. A.	SS	128	475	60	113	11	8	5	37	.238	195	367	*46	.924
1976—Omaha†.................. A. A.	SS	30	120	20	30	3	2	4	16	.250	48	102	15	.909
1977—Omaha .... A. A.	*SS-2B	131	*514	82	131	13	10	2	37	.255	218	391	*48	.927
1977—Kansas City.......... Amer.	SS	10	20	0	4	1	1	0	1	.200	13	21	5	.872
1978—Kansas City.......... Amer.	SS-2B	69	129	10	34	2	1	0	9	.264	79	92	9	.950
1979—Kansas City.......... Amer.	SS-2B-3B	101	268	32	68	12	5	2	25	.254	174	243	18	.959
1980—Kansas City.......... Amer.	SS	153	549	79	150	16	11	6	53	.273	237	467	32	.957
1981—Kansas City.......... Amer.	SS	98	339	40	77	19	1	2	29	.227	135	297	12	.973
1982—Kansas City‡........ Amer.	SS	119	437	64	125	19	3	10	60	.286	173	371	22	.961
1983—Kansas City.......... Amer.	SS	144	547	76	129	19	6	5	41	.236	201	448	*36	.947
1984—Kansas City§x...... Amer.	SS	63	170	18	38	6	0	1	10	.224	81	166	10	.961
1985—Montreal yz.......... Nat.	2B-SS-3B	68	193	24	48	9	4	1	17	.249	76	130	7	.967
American League Totals—8 Years		757	2459	319	625	94	28	26	228	.254	1093	2105	144	.957
National League Totals—1 Year..............		68	193	24	48	9	4	1	17	.249	76	130	7	.967
Major League Totals—9 Years................		825	2652	343	673	103	32	27	245	.254	1169	2235	151	.958

Signed as free agent by Kansas City Royals' organization, August 4, 1972.
†On disabled list, May 21 to September 6, 1976.
‡On disabled list, May 3 to May 26, 1982.
§On disabled list, March 28 to April 12, July 18 to August 2 and August 16, 1984 through remainder of season.
xTraded to Montreal Expos for Outfielder Ken Baker and Pitcher Mike Kinnunen, January 7, 1985.
yOn disabled list, June 8 to June 24 and June 28, 1985 through remainder of season.
zGranted free agency, November 12, 1985.

DIVISION SERIES RECORD

Year Club League	Pos.	G.	AB.	R.	H.	2B.	3B.	HR.	RBI.	B.A.	PO.	A.	E.	F.A.
1981—Kansas City........... Amer.	SS	3	9	0	2	0	0	0	0	.222	7	11	1	.947

CHAMPIONSHIP SERIES RECORD

Year Club League	Pos.	G.	AB.	R.	H.	2B.	3B.	HR.	RBI.	B.A.	PO.	A.	E.	F.A.
1980—Kansas City........... Amer.	SS	3	11	1	4	1	0	0	1	.364	5	7	0	1.000
1984—Kansas City........... Amer.	PH-PR	2	1	0	0	0	0	0	0	.000	0	0	0	.000
Championship Series Totals—2 Years.....		5	12	1	4	1	0	0	1	.333	5	7	0	1.000

WORLD SERIES RECORD

Year Club League	Pos.	G.	AB.	R.	H.	2B.	3B.	HR.	RBI.	B.A.	PO.	A.	E.	F.A.
1980—Kansas City........... Amer.	SS	6	22	1	6	0	0	0	2	.273	8	20	1	.966

JOHN DAVID WATHAN

Born October 4, 1949, at Cedar Rapids, Ia.
Height, 6.02. Weight, 205.
Throws and bats righthanded.
Attended University of San Diego, San Diego, Calif., and
Mount Mercy College, Cedar Rapids, Ia.

Major League stolen bases: 1977 (2), 1978 (2), 1979 (2), 1980 (17), 1981 (11), 1982 (36), 1983 (28), 1984 (6), 1985 (1).
Total—105.

Year	Club	League	Pos.	G.	AB.	R.	H.	2B.	3B.	HR.	RBI.	B.A.	PO.	A.	E.	F.A.
1971—San Jose	Calif.	C-OF	64	215	37	56	11	2	1	29	.260	438	31	14	.971
1971—Waterloo	Midw.	C-OF-1B	43	147	31	41	4	4	3	21	.279	282	18	1	.997
1972—San Jose†	Calif.	C-1B-3B	48	148	25	40	8	0	4	15	.270	324	31	3	.992
1972—Omaha	A. A.	C	18	51	8	15	1	1	0	2	.294	94	5	1	.990
1972—Jacksonville	South.	C	16	54	6	17	3	1	0	3	.315	111	7	4	.967
1973—Jacksonville‡	South.	C-1B-3B	65	233	20	58	8	3	5	34	.249	294	28	4	.988
1974—Jacksonville	South.	1B-OF-C	120	428	63	105	14	2	7	47	.245	760	50	7	.991
1975—Omaha	A. A.	C-OF	104	360	42	109	14	4	8	46	.303	532	45	10	.983
1976—Omaha§	A. A.	C-OF	24	84	4	13	5	0	0	6	.155	128	14	4	.973
1976—Kansas City	Amer.	C-1B	27	42	5	12	1	0	0	5	.286	63	4	1	.985
1977—Kansas City	Amer.	C-1B	55	119	18	39	5	3	2	21	.328	156	9	2	.988
1978—Kansas City x	Amer.	1B-C	67	190	19	57	10	1	2	28	.300	385	28	2	.995
1979—Kansas City	Amer.	1B-C-OF	90	199	26	41	7	3	2	28	.206	336	24	3	.992
1980—Kansas City	Amer.	C-OF-1B	126	453	57	138	14	7	6	58	.305	472	33	8	.984
1981—Kansas City	Amer.	C-OF-1B	89	301	24	76	9	3	1	19	.252	316	28	7	.980
1982—Kansas City y	Amer.	C-1B	121	448	79	121	11	3	3	51	.270	482	40	10	.981
1983—Kansas City	Amer.	C-1B-OF	128	437	49	107	18	3	2	32	.245	615	58	9	.987
1984—Kansas City	Amer.	C-1B-OF	97	171	17	31	7	1	2	10	.181	304	31	6	.982
1985—Kansas City	Amer.	C-1B	60	145	11	34	8	1	1	9	.234	259	29	4	.986
Major League Totals—10 Years			860	2505	305	656	90	25	21	261	.262	3388	284	52	.986

Selected by Kansas City Royals' organization in 4th round of free-agent draft, January 13, 1971.
†On disabled list, May 5 to May 30, 1972.
‡On disabled list, May 25 to June 28, 1973.
§On disabled list, July 29 to September 1, 1976.
xOn disabled list, June 16 to July 7, 1978.
yOn disabled list, July 6 to August 10, 1982.

DIVISION SERIES RECORD

Year	Club	League	Pos.	G.	AB.	R.	H.	2B.	3B.	HR.	RBI.	B.A.	PO.	A.	E.	F.A.
1981—Kansas City	Amer.	C	3	10	1	3	0	0	0	0	.300	11	4	1	.938

CHAMPIONSHIP SERIES RECORD

Tied American League Championship Series records for most positions played, total Series (3); most times on losing club (4).

Year	Club	League	Pos.	G.	AB.	R.	H.	2B.	3B.	HR.	RBI.	B.A.	PO.	A.	E.	F.A.
1976—Kansas City	Amer.	C	1	0	0	0	0	0	0	0	.000	0	0	0	.000
1977—Kansas City	Amer.	C-1-D-PH	4	6	0	0	0	0	0	0	.000	19	0	0	1.000
1978—Kansas City	Amer.	1B	1	3	0	0	0	0	0	0	.000	7	0	0	1.000
1980—Kansas City	Amer.	OF-PH	3	6	1	0	0	0	0	0	.000	7	0	0	1.000
1984—Kansas City	Amer.	PR-DH	1	1	0	0	0	0	0	0	.000	0	0	0	.000
Championship Series Totals—5 Years			10	16	1	0	0	0	0	0	.000	33	0	0	1.000

WORLD SERIES RECORD

Year	Club	League	Pos.	G.	AB.	R.	H.	2B.	3B.	HR.	RBI.	B.A.	PO.	A.	E.	F.A.
1980—Kansas City	Amer.	PH-OF-C	3	7	1	2	0	0	0	1	.286	7	1	0	1.000
1985—Kansas City	Amer.	PH-PR	2	1	0	0	0	0	0	0	.000	0	0	0	.000
World Series Totals—2 Years			5	8	1	2	0	0	0	1	.250	7	1	0	1.000

JAMES FRANCIS WEAVER
(Jim)

Born October 10, 1959, at Kingston, N.Y.
Height, 6.04. Weight, 190.
Throws and bats lefthanded.
Attended Manatee Junior College, Bradenton, Fla., and
Florida State University, Tallahassee, Fla.

Led California League in intentional bases on balls received with 11 in 1982.
Named outfielder on THE SPORTING NEWS College Baseball All-America Team, 1980.
Tied for Southern League lead in double plays by outfielders with 4 in 1983.
Led International League outfielders in double plays with 6 in 1985.

Year	Club	League	Pos.	G.	AB.	R.	H.	2B.	3B.	HR.	RBI.	B.A.	PO.	A.	E.	F.A.
1980—Orlando	South.	OF	58	208	19	44	9	0	0	15	.212	121	3	3	.976
1981—Orlando	South.	OF	17	57	6	12	2	0	1	9	.211	21	1	2	.917
1981—Visalia	Calif.	OF	81	300	53	85	12	5	7	44	.283	110	7	4	.967
1982—Visalia	Calif.	OF	125	454	68	130	21	4	15	86	.286	261	6	9	.967
1983—Orlando	South.	OF	138	497	85	123	25	2	15	84	.247	259	20	9	.969
1984—Orlando†	South.	OF	24	81	13	21	3	2	3	16	.259	38	4	0	1.000
1984—Toledo†	Int.	OF	111	409	49	94	12	5	15	64	.230	114	3	10	.921

Year Club	League	Pos.	G.	AB.	R.	H.	2B.	3B.	HR.	RBI.	B.A.	PO.	A.	E.	F.A.
1985—Detroit	Amer.	OF	12	7	2	1	1	0	0	0	.143	1	0	0	1.000
1985—Toledo‡-Maine	Int.	OF	91	331	54	73	10	6	12	46	.221	135	●13	7	.955
Major League Totals—1 Year			12	7	2	1	1	0	0	0	.143	1	0	0	1.000

Selected by Montreal Expos' organization in 2nd round of free-agent draft, January 9, 1979.
Selected by Minnesota Twins' organization in 2nd round of free-agent draft, June 3, 1980.
†Drafted by Detroit Tigers, December 3, 1984; returned, May 22, 1985.
‡Traded with Pitcher Curt Wardle and Infielder Jay Bell to Cleveland Indians for Pitcher Bert Blyleven, August 1, 1985.

MITCHELL DEAN WEBSTER
(Mitch)

Born May 16, 1959, at Larned, Kan.
Height, 6.01. Weight, 170.
Throws left and bats left and righthanded.

Major League stolen bases: 1985 (15).
Led International League outfielders in double plays with 5 and total chances with 385 in 1982.

Year Club	League	Pos.	G.	AB.	R.	H.	2B.	3B.	HR.	RBI.	B.A.	PO.	A.	E.	F.A.
1977—Lethbridge	Pion.	OF	55	168	45	59	4	0	0	31	.351	81	3	8	.913
1978—Clinton	Midw.	OF	45	157	18	38	3	1	0	9	.242	92	6	7	.933
1978—Lethbridge	Pion.	OF	55	182	58	58	5	1	0	18	.319	77	3	0	★1.000
1979—Clinton†	Midw.	OF	123	473	95	★154	17	7	2	40	★.326	★272	10	10	.966
1980—Syracuse	Int.	OF	49	161	23	35	4	2	1	12	.217	112	3	5	.958
1980—Kinston	Carol.	OF	65	258	43	76	7	3	0	28	.295	129	8	5	.965
1981—Knoxville	South.	OF	140	554	89	163	26	6	1	42	.294	317	7	10	.970
1982—Syracuse	Int.	OF	137	513	95	144	21	7	13	68	.281	★367	16	2	★.995
1983—Syracuse	Int.	OF-1B	135	462	77	120	26	8	9	45	.260	266	16	10	.966
1983—Toronto	Amer.	OF	11	11	2	2	0	0	0	0	.182	5	0	0	1.000
1984—Toronto	Amer.	OF-1B	26	22	9	5	2	1	0	4	.227	16	0	2	.889
1984—Syracuse	Int.	OF	95	360	60	108	22	5	3	25	.300	239	7	7	.972
1985—Toronto‡	Amer.	OF	4	1	0	0	0	0	0	0	.000	0	0	0	.000
1985—Syracuse‡	Int.	OF	47	189	32	52	5	3	3	23	.275	83	10	1	.989
1985—Montreal	Nat.	OF	74	212	32	58	8	2	11	30	.274	133	3	1	.993
American League Totals—3 Years			41	34	11	7	2	1	0	4	.206	21	0	2	.913
National League Totals—1 Year			74	212	32	58	8	2	11	30	.274	133	3	1	.993
Major League Totals—3 Years			115	246	43	65	10	3	11	34	.264	154	3	3	.981

Selected by Los Angeles Dodgers' organization in 23rd round of free-agent draft, June 7, 1977.
†Drafted by Syracuse (Toronto Blue Jays' organization), December 4, 1979.
‡Sold to Montreal Expos, June 22, 1985.

WILLIAM EDWARD WEGMAN
(Bill)

Born December 19, 1962, at Cincinnati, O.
Height, 6.05. Weight, 200.
Throws and bats righthanded.

Led Pacific Coast League in home runs allowed with 21 in 1985.
Led California League in balks with 5 and tied for lead in complete games with 15 and shutouts with 4 in 1983.

Year Club	League	G.	IP.	W.	L.	Pct.	H.	R.	ER.	SO.	BB.	ERA.
1981—Butte	Pioneer	14	82	6	5	.545	94	51	38	47	44	4.17
1982—Beloit	Midwest	25	179⅔	12	6	.667	176	77	56	129	38	2.81
1983—Stockton	California	24	186⅔	★16	5	.762	149	33	27	135	45	★1.30
1984—El Paso	Texas	10	64	4	5	.444	62	25	19	42	15	2.67
1984—Vancouver†	P. Coast	6	27⅔	0	3	.000	30	11	6	16	8	1.95
1985—Vancouver	P. Coast	28	188	10	11	.476	187	93	84	113	52	4.02
1985—Milwaukee	American	3	17⅔	2	0	1.000	17	8	7	6	3	3.57
Major League Totals—1 Year		3	17⅔	2	0	1.000	17	8	7	6	3	3.57

Selected by Milwaukee Brewers' organization in 5th round of free-agent draft, June 8, 1981.
†On disabled list, June 18 to August 11, 1984.

DAVID THOMAS WEHRMEISTER

Name pronounced WAIR-my-stur.

(Dave)

Born November 9, 1952, at Berwyn, Ill.
Height, 6.04. Weight, 190.
Throws and bats righthanded.
Attended Northeast Missouri State College, Kirksville, Mo.

Major League saves: 1985 (2).

Year Club	League	G.	IP.	W.	L.	Pct.	H.	R.	ER.	SO.	BB.	ERA.
1973—Alexandria	Texas	23	137	8	12	.400	110	64	49	84	60	3.22
1974—Hawaii	P. Coast	4	12	0	3	.000	17	13	12	7	9	9.00
1974—Alexandria	Texas	18	130	5	10	.333	119	73	59	90	65	4.08
1975—Alexandria†	Texas	17	105	5	8	.385	103	54	40	58	36	3.43
1975—Hawaii	P. Coast	10	52	3	5	.375	63	37	37	31	24	6.40
1976—San Diego	National	7	19	0	4	.000	27	17	16	10	11	7.58

Year Club	League	G.	IP.	W.	L.	Pct.	H.	R.	ER.	SO.	BB.	ERA.
1976—Hawaii	P. Coast	23	112	6	11	.353	137	85	72	61	54	5.79
1977—Hawaii	P. Coast	5	39	2	2	.500	34	14	11	23	8	2.54
1977—San Diego	National	30	70	1	3	.250	81	53	47	32	44	6.04
1978—Hawaii	P. Coast	21	129	2	11	.154	140	89	81	61	64	5.65
1978—San Diego	National	4	7	1	0	1.000	8	5	5	2	5	6.43
1979—Hawaii‡	P. Coast	13	96	8	5	.615	70	24	20	56	24	1.88
1979—Columbus	Int'national	17	75	2	8	.200	84	43	41	54	28	4.92
1980—Columbus§	Int'national	39	86	3	4	.429	66	30	27	67	36	2.83
1981—Columbus	Int'national	24	136	11	3	*.786	117	53	47	83	48	3.11
1981—New York	American	5	7	0	0	.000	6	4	4	7	7	5.14
1982—Columbus	Int'national	36	151⅔	10	7	.588	162	85	77	96	74	4.57
1983—Columbus x	Int'national	13	75	4	5	.444	62	41	36	41	50	4.32
1983—Portland y	P. Coast	15	98⅔	8	2	.800	93	51	46	64	34	4.20
1984—Portland	P. Coast	28	114⅔	7	8	.467	120	79	73	98	49	5.73
1984—Philadelphia z	National	7	15	0	0	.000	18	12	12	13	7	7.20
1985—Buffalo	Am. Assoc.	30	126⅓	5	8	.385	134	88	81	89	55	5.77
1985—Chicago	American	23	39⅓	2	2	.500	35	15	15	32	10	3.43
National League Totals—4 Years		48	111	2	7	.222	134	87	80	57	67	6.49
American League Totals—2 Years		28	46⅓	2	2	.500	41	19	19	39	17	3.69
Major League Totals—6 Years		76	157⅓	4	9	.308	175	106	99	96	84	5.66

Selected by San Diego Padres' organization in 1st round (third player selected) of free-agent draft, January 10, 1973.

†On disabled list, May 2 to May 17, 1975.

‡Traded to New York Yankees' organization for Outfielder Jay Johnstone, June 15, 1979.

§Drafted by Kansas City Royals, December 8, 1980; returned, April 3, 1981.

xTraded to Philadelphia Phillies' organization for Pitchers Jim Rasmussen and Kelly Faulk, June 17, 1983.

yGranted free agency, October 20, 1983; re-signed by Phillies' organization, July 2, 1984.

zGranted free agency, October 15, 1984; signed by Buffalo (Chicago White Sox' organization), January 14, 1985.

ROBERT LYNN WELCH
(Bob)

Born November 3, 1956, at Detroit, Mich.
Height, 6.03. Weight, 190.
Throws and bats righthanded.
Attended Eastern Michigan University, Ypsilanti, Mich.

Major League saves: 1978 (3), 1979 (5). Total—8.

Year Club	League	G.	IP.	W.	L.	Pct.	H.	R.	ER.	SO.	BB.	ERA.
1977—San Antonio	Texas	14	71	4	5	.444	94	44	35	56	17	4.44
1978—Albuquerque	P. Coast	11	69	5	1	.833	72	33	29	53	19	3.78
1978—Los Angeles	National	23	111	7	4	.636	92	28	25	66	26	2.03
1979—Los Angeles	National	25	81	5	6	.455	82	42	36	64	32	4.00
1980—Los Angeles	National	32	214	14	9	.609	190	85	78	141	79	3.28
1981—Los Angeles	National	23	141	9	5	.643	141	56	54	88	41	3.45
1982—Los Angeles†	National	36	235⅔	16	11	.593	199	94	88	176	81	3.36
1983—Los Angeles	National	31	204	15	12	.556	164	73	60	156	72	2.65
1984—Los Angeles	National	31	178⅔	13	13	.500	191	86	75	126	58	3.78
1985—Los Angeles‡	National	23	167⅓	14	4	.778	141	49	43	96	35	2.31
1985—Vero Beach	Florida St.	3	17	0	0	.000	15	4	4	9	1	2.12
Major League Totals—8 Years		224	1332⅔	93	64	.592	1200	513	459	913	424	3.10

Selected by Chicago Cubs' organization in 14th round of free-agent draft, June 5, 1974.

Selected by Los Angeles Dodgers' organization in 1st round (20th player selected) of free-agent draft, June 7, 1977.

†Appeared in one game as outfielder with no chances.

‡On disabled list, April 29 to June 5, 1985; included rehabilitation disability assignment to Vero Beach, May 21 to June 5, 1985.

DIVISION SERIES RECORD

Year Club	League	G.	IP.	W.	L.	Pct.	H.	R.	ER.	SO.	BB.	ERA.
1981—Los Angeles	National	1	1	0	0	.000	0	0	0	1	1	0.00

CHAMPIONSHIP SERIES RECORD

Tied Championship Series record for most bases on balls, inning (4), October 12, 1985 (first inning).

Year Club	League	G.	IP.	W.	L.	Pct.	H.	R.	ER.	SO.	BB.	ERA.
1978—Los Angeles	National	1	4⅓	1	0	1.000	2	1	1	5	0	2.08
1981—Los Angeles	National	3	1⅔	0	0	.000	2	1	1	2	0	5.40
1983—Los Angeles	National	1	1⅓	0	1	.000	0	2	1	0	2	6.75
1985—Los Angeles	National	1	2⅔	0	1	.000	5	4	2	2	6	6.75
Championship Series Totals—4 Years		6	10	1	2	.333	9	8	5	9	8	4.50

WORLD SERIES RECORD

Year Club	League	G.	IP.	W.	L.	Pct.	H.	R.	ER.	SO.	BB.	ERA.
1978—Los Angeles	National	3	4⅓	0	1	.000	4	3	3	6	2	6.23
1981—Los Angeles	National	1	0	0	0	.000	3	2	2	0	1	....
World Series Totals—2 Years		4	4⅓	0	1	.000	7	5	5	6	3	10.38

ALL-STAR GAME RECORD

Year League		IP.	W.	L.	Pct.	H.	R.	ER.	SO.	BB.	ERA.
1980—National		3	0	0	.000	5	2	2	4	1	6.00

DONALD RAY WELCHEL

Name pronounced WELL-chul.

(Don)

Born February 3, 1957, at Atlanta, Tex.
Height, 6.04. Weight, 205.
Throws and bats righthanded.
Attended Sam Houston State University, Huntsville, Tex.

Tied for Southern League lead in complete games with 12 in 1980.

Year Club	League	G.	IP.	W.	L.	Pct.	H.	R.	ER.	SO.	BB.	ERA.
1978—Bluefield	Ap'lachian	12	89	4	5	.444	78	30	24	57	25	2.43
1978—Miami	Florida St.	2	15	2	0	1.000	13	5	3	10	5	1.80
1979—Miami	Florida St.	14	95	5	6	.455	86	34	31	53	34	2.94
1979—Charlotte	Southern	13	86	5	4	.556	95	47	37	40	39	3.87
1980—Charlotte	Southern	28	202	9	12	.429	*210	86	65	56	47	2.90
1981—Rochester	Int'national	8	12	1	1	.500	9	5	3	7	4	2.25
1981—Charlotte	Southern	22	161	13	7	.650	161	76	52	90	63	2.91
1982—Rochester	Int'national	30	163	12	7	.632	180	91	84	82	82	4.64
1982—Baltimore	American	2	4⅓	1	0	1.000	6	6	4	3	2	8.31
1983—Baltimore	American	11	26⅔	0	2	.000	33	18	16	16	10	5.40
1983—Rochester	Int'national	18	110⅔	4	12	.250	128	65	57	61	46	4.64
1984—Hagerstown	Carolina	4	26⅔	4	0	1.000	22	4	3	24	7	1.01
1984—Rochester†	Int'national	9	53	4	5	.444	53	29	26	29	32	4.42
1985—Rochester†	Int'national	26	117⅞	7	4	.636	123	56	49	63	49	3.75
Major League Totals—2 Years		13	31	1	2	.333	39	24	20	19	12	5.81

Selected by Cincinnati Reds' organization in 10th round of free-agent draft, June 4, 1975.
Selected by Baltimore Orioles' organization in 7th round of free-agent draft, June 6, 1978.
†On disabled list, April 10 to June 26, 1984.
‡Granted free agency, October 15, 1985; signed by Oklahoma City (Texas Rangers' organization), November 30, 1985.

BRAD EUGENE WELLMAN

Born August 17, 1959, at Lodi, Calif.
Height, 6.00. Weight, 165.
Throws and bats righthanded.
Attended Chabot College, Hayward, Calif.

Major League stolen bases: 1983 (5), 1984 (10), 1985 (5). Total—20.

Year Club	League	Pos.	G.	AB.	R.	H.	2B.	3B.	HR.	RBI.	B.A.	PO.	A.	E.	F.A.
1979—Sarasota Royals	Gulf C.	SS	48	170	24	44	6	0	2	24	.259	79	159	20	.922
1980—Fort Myers	Fla. St.	2B-SS	105	390	67	130	15	7	1	39	.333	175	301	27	.946
1981—Jacksonville	South	2B-SS	135	498	72	131	25	2	6	47	.263	286	368	25	.963
1982—Omaha†	A. A.	2B	6	24	5	7	3	0	1	3	.292	14	23	0	1.000
1982—Phoenix	P. C.	2B-3B	102	339	64	110	19	7	4	42	.324	201	257	14	.970
1982—San Francisco	Nat.	2B	6	4	1	1	0	0	0	0	.250	0	1	0	1.000
1983—Phoenix	P. C.	2B-SS	45	167	32	52	6	4	2	28	.311	79	123	4	.981
1983—San Francisco	Nat.	2B-SS	82	182	15	39	3	0	1	16	.214	94	167	9	.967
1984—Phoenix	P. C.	2B	43	159	26	47	8	1	0	11	.296	91	123	6	.973
1984—San Francisco	Nat.	2B-SS-3B	93	265	23	60	9	1	2	25	.226	151	258	11	.974
1985—San Francisco‡	Nat.	2B-3B-SS	71	174	16	41	11	1	0	16	.236	66	107	9	.951
Major League Totals—4 Years			252	625	55	141	23	2	3	57	.226	311	533	29	.967

Signed as free agent by Kansas City Royals' organization, August 27, 1978.
†Traded to San Francisco Giants' organization, April 19, 1982, completing deal in which San Francisco traded Pitchers Vida Blue and Bob Tufts to Kansas City Royals for Pitchers Atlee Hammaker, Craig Chamberlain and Renie Martin and a player to be named later, March 30, 1982.
‡On disabled list, May 30 to June 28, 1985.

CHRISTOPHER CHARLES WELSH

(Chris)

Born April 14, 1955, at Wilmington, Del.
Height, 6.02. Weight, 185.
Throws and bats lefthanded.
Received bachelor of arts degree in marketing from
University of South Florida, Tampa, Fla.

Led New York-Pennsylvania League in complete games with 12, shutouts with 4 and tied for lead in games started by pitchers with 14 in 1977.
Tied for Eastern League lead in wild pitches with 18 and balks with 2 in 1978.

Year Club	League	G.	IP.	W.	L.	Pct.	H.	R.	ER.	SO.	BB.	ERA.
1977—Oneonta	NYP	14	*112	8	5	.615	77	40	31	*125	54	2.49
1978—Fort Lauderdale	Florida St.	2	15	1	1	.500	5	5	1	13	10	0.60
1978—West Haven	Eastern	24	164	11	9	.550	159	88	63	115	68	3.46
1979—Columbus	Int'national	36	114	8	4	.667	120	67	59	79	48	4.70
1980—Columbus†	Int'national	29	158	9	12	.429	134	78	48	84	68	2.73
1981—San Diego	National	22	124	6	7	.462	122	55	52	51	41	3.77
1982—San Diego‡	National	28	139⅓	8	8	.500	146	88	76	48	63	4.91
1983—San Diego§-Montreal	National	23	59	0	2	.000	59	35	29	22	20	4.42
1983—Wichita	Am. Assoc.	11	56⅔	3	6	.333	72	47	44	27	29	6.99
1984—Indianapolis x	Am. Assoc.	29	167⅔	13	4	.765	165	63	56	87	80	*3.01

Year Club	League	G.	IP.	W.	L.	Pct.	H.	R.	ER.	SO.	BB.	ERA.
1985—Texas	American	25	76⅓	2	5	.286	101	40	35	31	25	4.13
1985—Oklahoma City y	Am. Assoc.	8	52	6	1	.857	49	26	26	22	27	4.50
National League Totals—3 Years		73	322⅓	14	17	.452	327	178	157	121	124	4.38
American League Totals—1 Year		25	76⅓	2	5	.286	101	40	35	31	25	4.13
Major League Totals—4 Years		98	398⅔	16	22	.421	428	218	192	152	149	4.33

Selected by New York Yankees' organization in 24th round of free-agent draft, June 8, 1976.
Selected by New York Yankees' organization in 21st round of free-agent draft, June 7, 1977.
†Traded with Outfielders Ruppert Jones and Joe Lefebvre and Pitcher Tim Lollar to San Diego Padres for Outfielder Jerry Mumphrey and Pitcher John Pacella, April 1, 1981.
‡On disabled list, March 23 to April 27, 1982.
§Sold to Montreal Expos, May 4, 1983.
xTraded to Texas Rangers' organization for First Baseman Dave Hostetler, November 7, 1984.
yReleased, November 9, 1985.

DONALD PAUL WERNER
(Don)

Born March 8, 1953, at Appleton, Wis.
Height, 6.01. Weight, 180.
Throws and bats righthanded.

Major League stolen bases: 1978 (1), 1980 (1). Total—2.
Led American Association catchers in double plays with 9 in 1979.

Year Club	League	Pos.	G.	AB.	R.	H.	2B.	3B.	HR.	RBI.	B.A.	PO.	A.	E.	F.A.
1971—Brad'ton Reds	Gulf C.	C-3B	10	21	7	7	1	1	0	5	.333	45	2	1	.979
1971—Tampa	Fla. St.	C	36	122	10	21	3	1	0	16	.172	186	22	1	.995
1972—Tampa	Fla. St.	C	116	377	42	97	8	1	1	31	.257	736	75	15	.982
1973—Three Rivers	East.	C-OF	110	284	31	57	9	1	5	34	.201	452	47	11	.978
1974—Tampa	Fla. St.	C	120	397	44	92	13	1	2	38	.232	580	71	3	*.995
1975—Indianapolis	A. A.	C	86	228	39	64	11	5	9	34	.281	423	51	7	*.985
1975—Cincinnati	Nat.	C	7	8	0	1	0	0	0	0	.125	10	2	1	.923
1976—Indianapolis	A. A.	C-1B	38	112	14	23	4	1	1	12	.205	208	28	6	.975
1976—Richmond	Int.	C-OF	49	151	19	40	1	1	2	21	.265	215	22	5	.979
1976—Cincinnati	Nat.	C	3	4	0	2	1	0	0	1	.500	7	2	0	1.000
1977—Indianapolis†	A. A.	C-1B	34	94	12	20	5	1	5	13	.213	182	23	4	.981
1977—Cincinnati	Nat.	C	10	23	3	4	0	0	2	4	.174	40	4	0	1.000
1978—Indianapolis	A. A.	C	40	125	14	30	6	1	3	22	.240	202	24	7	.970
1978—Cincinnati	Nat.	C	50	113	7	17	2	1	0	11	.150	214	21	3	.987
1979—Indianapolis	A. A.	C-1-0-3	99	260	35	66	18	3	7	36	.254	476	57	12	.978
1980—Cincinnati	Nat.	C	24	64	2	11	2	0	0	5	.172	119	6	5	.962
1980—Indianapolis‡	A. A.	C-1B-3B	65	219	32	60	10	2	6	35	.274	355	25	8	.979
1981—Wichita	A. A.	C-1B	83	246	23	67	13	1	4	26	.272	336	29	4	.989
1981—Texas	Amer.	DH	2	8	1	2	0	0	0	0	.250	0	0	0	.000
1982—Denver	A. A.	C	8	16	2	7	2	0	1	2	.438	41	4	1	.978
1982—Texas	Amer.	C	22	59	4	12	2	0	0	3	.203	91	5	2	.980
1983—Okla. City§xy	A. A.	C-OF-3B	76	232	39	67	14	1	6	38	.289	241	20	6	.978
1984—Iowa za	A. A.	O-C-1-3	131	427	64	121	22	3	25	77	.283	352	22	4	.989
1985—Birmingham	South.	C	10	32	6	6	1	1	1	4	.188	52	4	2	.966
1985—Nash. b-Okla. C. c	A. A.	C-OF-1B	20	61	10	12	2	0	1	5	.197	79	5	3	.966
National League Totals—5 Years		94	212	12	35	5	1	2	21	.165	390	35	9	.979
American League Totals—2 Years		24	67	5	14	2	0	0	3	.209	91	5	2	.980
Major League Totals—7 Years		118	279	17	49	7	1	2	24	.176	481	40	11	.979

Selected by Cincinnati Reds' organization in 5th round of free-agent draft, June 8, 1971.
†On disabled list, May 3 to July 27, 1977.
‡Traded to Texas Rangers' organization for Catcher Greg Mahlberg, December 16, 1980.
§On disabled list, April 15 to April 26, 1983.
xGranted free agency, October 20, 1983; signed by Kansas City Royals, December 9, 1983.
ySold to Chicago Cubs, March 30, 1984.
zGranted free agency, October 15, 1984; signed by Phoenix (San Francisco Giants' organization), January 4, 1985.
aReleased, April 1, 1985; signed by Birmingham (Detroit Tigers' organization), June 30, 1985.
bReleased, August 15, 1985; signed by Oklahoma City (Texas Rangers' organization), August 15, 1985.
cGranted free agency, October 15, 1985; re-signed by Rangers' organization, November 26, 1985.

DAVID LEE WEST

Born September 1, 1964, at Memphis, Tenn.
Height, 6.06. Weight, 205.
Throws and bats lefthanded.

Won 3-0 no-hit victory against Spartanburg, August 14, 1985.
Led New York-Pennsylvania League in wild pitches with 16 in 1984.

Year Club	League	G.	IP.	W.	L.	Pct.	H.	R.	ER.	SO.	BB.	ERA.
1983—Sarasota Mets	Gulf Coast	12	53⅔	2	4	.333	41	28	17	56	52	2.85
1984—Columbia	S. Atlantic	12	60⅔	3	5	.375	41	47	42	60	68	6.23
1984—Little Falls	NYP	13	62	6	4	.600	42	35	23	79	62	3.34
1985—Columbia	S. Atlantic	26	150	10	9	.526	105	97	76	194	*111	4.56

Selected by New York Mets' organization in 4th round of free-agent draft, June 6, 1983.

MATTHEW TERRY WEST
(Matt)

Born January 13, 1960, at Santa Monica, Calif.
Height, 6.04. Weight, 195.
Throws right and bats left and righthanded.
Attended Cabrillo College, Aptos, Calif. and received bachelor of arts degree
in political science from California State University, Long Beach, Calif. in 1981.

Pitched 1-0 no-hit loss against Jacksonville, May 21, 1982.
Tied for Southern League lead in balks with 3 in 1982.

Year Club	League	G.	IP.	W.	L.	Pct.	H.	R.	ER.	SO.	BB.	ERA.
1981—Bradenton Braves	Gulf Coast	9	44	3	4	.429	32	19	13	44	24	2.66
1982—Savannah†	Southern	22	115⅔	6	8	.429	97	70	59	91	91	4.59
1983—Durham‡	Carolina	12	65⅓	2	5	.286	66	51	31	42	48	4.27
1984—Greenville	Southern	26	145	10	7	.588	143	81	72	102	75	4.47
1985—Richmond§	Int'national	23	133⅓	8	9	.471	122	64	55	73	64	3.71

Signed as free agent by Atlanta Braves' organization, June 29, 1981.
†On disabled list, June 1 to July 1, 1982.
‡On disabled list, July 16, 1983 through remainder of season.
§On disabled list, June 8 to July 1, 1985.

LOUIS RODMAN WHITAKER
(Lou)

Born May 12, 1957, at Brooklyn, N.Y.
Height, 5.11. Weight, 160.
Throws right and bats lefthanded.

Major League stolen bases: 1977 (2), 1978 (7), 1979 (20), 1980 (8), 1981 (5), 1982 (11), 1983 (17), 1984 (6), 1985 (6).
Total—82.
Led American League second basemen in total chances with 811 and double plays with 120 in 1982.
Led Florida State League second basemen in double plays with 30 in 1976.
Named second baseman on THE SPORTING NEWS American League All-Star Team, 1983 and 1984.
Named second baseman on THE SPORTING NEWS American League All-Star fielding team, 1983 through 1985.
Named second baseman on THE SPORTING NEWS American League Silver Slugger team, 1983 through 1985.
Named American League Rookie of the Year by Baseball Writers' Association of America, 1978.
Named Florida State League Most Valuable Player, 1976.

Year Club	League	Pos.	G.	AB.	R.	H.	2B.	3B.	HR.	RBI.	B.A.	PO.	A.	E.	F.A.
1975—Bristol	Appal.	3B-SS	42	114	17	27	6	1	1	17	.237	38	82	16	.882
1976—Lakeland	Fla. St.	3B	124	343	★70	129	12	5	1	62	.297	★99	★267	★30	★.924
1977—Montgomery†	South.	2B	107	396	★81	111	13	4	3	48	.280	208	285	15	.970
1977—Detroit	Amer.	2B	11	32	5	8	1	0	0	2	.250	17	18	0	1.000
1978—Detroit	Amer.	2B	139	484	71	138	12	7	3	58	.285	301	458	17	.978
1979—Detroit‡	Amer.	2B	127	423	75	121	14	8	3	42	.286	280	369	9	.986
1980—Detroit	Amer.	2B	145	477	68	111	19	1	1	45	.233	340	428	12	.985
1981—Detroit	Amer.	2B	●109	335	48	88	14	4	5	36	.263	227	★354	9	.985
1982—Detroit	Amer.	2B	152	560	76	160	22	8	15	65	.286	331	★470	10	★.988
1983—Detroit	Amer.	2B	161	643	94	206	40	6	12	72	.320	299	447	13	.983
1984—Detroit	Amer.	2B	143	558	90	161	25	1	13	56	.289	290	405	15	.979
1985—Detroit	Amer.	2B	152	609	102	170	29	8	21	73	.279	314	414	11	.985
Major League Totals—9 Years			1139	4121	629	1163	176	43	73	449	.282	2199	3363	96	.983

Selected by Detroit Tigers' organization in 5th round of free-agent draft, June 4, 1975.
†On disabled list, May 3 to May 14, 1977.
‡On disabled list, June 13 to June 28, 1979.

CHAMPIONSHIP SERIES RECORD

Year Club	League	Pos.	G.	AB.	R.	H.	2B.	3B.	HR.	RBI.	B.A.	PO.	A.	E.	F.A.
1984—Detroit	Amer.	2B	3	14	3	2	0	0	0	0	.143	5	6	0	1.000

WORLD SERIES RECORD

Tied World Series record for most runs, five-game Series (6), 1984.

Year Club	League	Pos.	G.	AB.	R.	H.	2B.	3B.	HR.	RBI.	B.A.	PO.	A.	E.	F.A.
1984—Detroit	Amer.	2B	5	18	6	5	2	0	0	0	.278	15	18	0	1.000

ALL-STAR GAME RECORD

Year League	Pos.	AB.	R.	H.	2B.	3B.	HR.	RBI.	B.A.	PO.	A.	E.	F.A.
1983—American	PH-2B	1	1	1	0	1	0	2	1.000	1	0	0	1.000
1984—American	2B	3	0	2	1	0	0	0	.667	0	5	0	1.000
1985—American	2B	2	0	0	0	0	0	0	.000	1	1	0	1.000
All-Star Game Totals—3 Years		6	1	3	1	1	0	2	.500	2	6	0	1.000

DEVON MARKES WHITE

Born December 29, 1962, at Kingston, Jamaica.
Height, 6.01. Weight, 170.
Throws right and bats left and righthanded.

Major League stolen bases: 1985 (3).
Led California League outfielders in total chances with 351 in 1984.
Led Midwest League outfielders in total chances with 286 in 1983.

Year	Club	League	Pos.	G.	AB.	R.	H.	2B.	3B.	HR.	RBI.	B.A.	PO.	A.	E.	F.A.
1981—Idaho Falls	Pion.	OF-3B-1B	30	106	10	19	2	0	0	10	.179	33	10	3	.935
1982—Danville†	Midw.	OF	57	186	21	40	6	1	1	11	.215	89	3	8	.920
1983—Peoria	Midw.	OF	117	430	69	109	17	6	13	66	.253	267	8	11	.962
1983—Nashua	East.	OF	17	70	11	18	7	2	0	2	.257	37	0	3	.925
1984—Redwood	Calif.	OF	138	520	101	147	25	5	7	55	.283	★322	16	13	.963
1985—Midland	Texas	OF	70	260	52	77	10	4	4	35	.296	176	10	4	.979
1985—Edmonton	P. C.	OF	66	277	53	70	16	5	4	39	.253	205	6	2	.991
1985—California	Amer.	OF	21	7	7	1	0	0	0	0	.143	10	1	0	1.000
Major League Totals—1 Year			21	7	7	1	0	0	0	0	.143	10	1	0	1.000

Selected by California Angels' organization in 6th round of free-agent draft, June 8, 1981.

†On suspended list, June 11 to June 12 and July 19, 1982 through remainder of season.

FRANK WHITE JR.

Born September 4, 1950, at Greenville, Miss.
Height, 5.11. Weight, 170.
Throws and bats righthanded.
Attended Manatee Junior College, Bradenton, Fla., and
Longview Community College, Lee's Summit, Mo.

Hit for the cycle, September 26, 1979 and August 3, 1982.
Major League stolen bases: 1973 (3), 1974 (3), 1975 (11), 1976 (20), 1977 (23), 1978 (13), 1979 (28), 1980 (19), 1981 (4), 1982 (10), 1983 (13), 1984 (5), 1985 (10). Total—162.
Led American League second basemen in total chances with 849 in 1985.
Led Gulf Coast League in stolen bases with 18 in 1971.
Led Gulf Coast League shortstops in double plays with 27 in 1971.
Named second baseman on THE SPORTING NEWS American League All-Star Team, 1978.
Named second baseman on THE SPORTING NEWS American League All-Star fielding team, 1977 through 1982.

Year	Club	League	Pos.	G.	AB.	R.	H.	2B.	3B.	HR.	RBI.	B.A.	PO.	A.	E.	F.A.
1971—Sara. Royals	Gulf C.	SS	50	158	31	39	6	3	1	21	.247	70	★149	17	★.928
1972—San Jose	Calif.	SS	49	187	44	55	7	2	10	26	.294	77	138	14	.939
1972—Jacksonville	South.	SS	91	333	34	84	12	2	2	23	.252	124	306	31	.933
1973—Omaha	A. A.	2B-SS	86	348	49	92	19	2	4	32	.264	163	221	21	.948
1973—Kansas City	Amer.	SS-2B	51	139	20	31	6	1	0	5	.223	71	121	12	.941
1974—Kansas City	Amer.	2B-SS-3B	99	204	19	45	6	3	1	18	.221	119	189	12	.963
1975—Kansas City	Amer.	2-S-3-C	111	304	43	76	10	2	7	36	.250	182	275	12	.974
1976—Kansas City	Amer.	2B-SS	152	446	39	102	17	6	2	46	.229	296	479	23	.971
1977—Kansas City	Amer.	★2B-SS	152	474	59	116	21	5	5	20	.245	310	437	8	★.989
1978—Kansas City	Amer.	2B	143	461	66	127	24	6	7	50	.275	325	385	16	.978
1979—Kansas City†	Amer.	2B	127	467	73	124	26	4	10	48	.266	317	332	12	.982
1980—Kansas City	Amer.	2B	154	560	70	148	23	4	7	60	.264	395	448	10	.988
1981—Kansas City	Amer.	2B	94	364	35	91	17	1	9	38	.250	226	263	6	.988
1982—Kansas City	Amer.	2B	145	524	71	156	45	6	11	56	.298	★361	389	★17	.978
1983—Kansas City	Amer.	2B	146	549	52	143	35	6	11	77	.260	★390	442	8	★.990
1984—Kansas City‡	Amer.	2B	129	479	58	130	22	5	17	56	.271	299	425	11	.985
1985—Kansas City	Amer.	2B	149	563	62	140	25	1	22	69	.249	342	★490	★17	.980
Major League Totals—13 Years			1652	5534	667	1429	277	50	109	609	.258	3633	4675	164	.981

Signed as free agent by Kansas City Royals' organization, July 2, 1970.

†On disabled list, May 9 to June 11, 1979.

‡On disabled list, July 6 to July 21, 1984.

DIVISION SERIES RECORD

Year	Club	League	Pos.	G.	AB.	R.	H.	2B.	3B.	HR.	RBI.	B.A.	PO.	A.	E.	F.A.
1981—Kansas City	Amer.	2B	3	11	1	2	0	0	0	0	.182	5	6	1	.917

CHAMPIONSHIP SERIES RECORD

Year	Club	League	Pos.	G.	AB.	R.	H.	2B.	3B.	HR.	RBI.	B.A.	PO.	A.	E.	F.A.
1976—Kansas City	Amer.	2B-PR	4	8	2	1	0	0	0	0	.125	6	11	0	1.000
1977—Kansas City	Amer.	2B	5	18	1	5	1	0	0	2	.278	13	16	0	1.000
1978—Kansas City	Amer.	2B	4	13	1	3	0	0	0	2	.231	9	12	0	1.000
1980—Kansas City	Amer.	2B	3	11	3	6	1	0	1	3	.545	9	10	1	.950
1984—Kansas City	Amer.	2B	3	11	1	1	0	0	0	0	.091	7	3	0	1.000
1985—Kansas City	Amer.	2B	7	25	1	5	0	0	0	3	.200	9	28	0	1.000
Championship Series Totals—6 Years			26	86	9	21	2	0	1	10	.244	53	80	1	.993

WORLD SERIES RECORD

Tied World Series records for fewest runs, Series (0), 1980; most at-bats, nine-inning game, no hits (5), October 18, 1980; most unassisted double plays by second baseman, game (1), October 17, 1980; fewest chances accepted, second baseman, game (0), October 20, 1985.

Year	Club	League	Pos.	G.	AB.	R.	H.	2B.	3B.	HR.	RBI.	B.A.	PO.	A.	E.	F.A.
1980—Kansas City	Amer.	2B	6	25	0	2	0	0	0	0	.080	13	21	2	.944
1985—Kansas City	Amer.	2B	7	28	4	7	3	0	1	6	.250	10	20	0	1.000
World Series Totals—2 Years			13	53	4	9	3	0	1	6	.170	23	41	2	.970

ALL-STAR GAME RECORD

Year	League	Pos.	AB.	R.	H.	2B.	3B.	HR.	RBI.	B.A.	PO.	A.	E.	F.A.
1978—American		2B	1	0	0	0	0	0	0	.000	1	2	0	1.000
1979—American		2B	2	0	0	0	0	0	0	.000	2	2	0	1.000
1981—American		PR-2B	1	0	0	0	0	0	0	.000	1	0	0	1.000
1982—American		2B	1	0	0	0	0	0	0	.000	2	1	0	1.000
All-Star Game Totals—4 Years			5	0	0	0	0	0	0	.000	6	5	0	1.000

LARRY DAVID WHITE

Born September 25, 1958, at San Fernando, Calif.
Height, 6.04. Weight, 185.
Throws and bats righthanded.
Attended Los Angeles Pierce College, Woodland Hills, Calif., and
San Francisco State University, San Francisco, Calif.

Led Pacific Coast League in hit batsmen with 10 in 1983.
Led Southern League in balks with 5 in 1981.

Year	Club	League	G.	IP.	W.	L.	Pct.	H.	R.	ER.	SO.	BB.	ERA.
1979—Batavia	NYP	12	41	3	0	1.000	30	24	21	21	30	4.61
1979—Waterloo	Midwest	1	6	0	1	.000	4	4	1	8	2	1.50
1980—Waterloo	Midwest	26	179	15	7	.682	143	85	66	120	86	3.32
1981—Chattanooga†	Southern	27	172	10	12	.455	158	93	67	101	65	3.51
1982—Albuquerque	P. Coast	28	165	12	5	.706	168	93	81	114	81	4.42
1983—Albuquerque	P. Coast	29	184⅔	13	8	.619	201	96	77	135	93	3.75
1983—Los Angeles	National	4	7	0	0	.000	4	1	1	5	3	1.29
1984—Albuquerque	P. Coast	37	159⅔	7	12	.368	196	128	108	94	*89	6.09
1984—Los Angeles	National	7	12	0	1	.000	9	5	4	10	6	3.00
1985—Albuquerque‡	P. Coast	31	159⅔	8	12	.400	186	96	77	114	54	4.34
Major League Totals—2 Years		11	19	0	1	.000	13	6	5	15	9	2.37

Selected by Oakland A's organization in 10th round of free-agent draft, January 10, 1978.
Selected by Cleveland Indians' organization in 31st round of free-agent draft, June 5, 1979.
†Traded with Outfielder Jorge Orta and Catcher Jack Fimple to Los Angeles Dodgers for Pitcher Rick Sutcliffe and Second Baseman Jack Perconte, December 9, 1981.
‡Granted free agency, October 15, 1985.

LEONARD JOSEPH WHITEHOUSE JR.

(Len)

Born September 10, 1957, at Burlington, Vt.
Height, 5.09. Weight, 175.
Throws and bats lefthanded.

Pitched seven-inning, 2-0 no-hit victory against Shreveport, June 22, 1979 (second game).
Major League saves: 1983 (2), 1984 (1), 1985 (1). Total—4.

Year	Club	League	G.	IP.	W.	L.	Pct.	H.	R.	ER.	SO.	BB.	ERA.
1977—Asheville	W. Carol.	5	7	0	2	.000	15	15	7	3	6	9.00
1977—Sarasota Rangers	Gulf Coast	11	40	3	3	.500	45	30	20	27	21	4.50
1978—Asheville	W. Carol.	32	92	6	6	.500	89	60	44	79	57	4.30
1979—Tulsa	Texas	25	102	5	7	.417	126	75	64	79	45	5.65
1980—Tulsa	Texas	10	48	3	2	.600	52	35	29	38	22	5.44
1980—Charleston	Int'national	18	99	8	9	.471	110	62	47	64	37	4.27
1981—Wichita	Am. Assoc.	20	105	6	5	.545	106	51	45	59	39	3.86
1981—Texas	American	2	3	0	1	.000	8	7	6	2	2	18.00
1982—Denver†	Am. Assoc.	30	121⅓	4	8	.333	146	97	85	65	45	6.30
1983—Minnesota	American	60	73⅔	7	1	.875	70	34	34	44	44	4.15
1984—Toledo	Int'national	4	4⅓	0	0	.000	5	0	0	3	0	0.00
1984—Minnesota	American	30	31⅓	2	2	.500	29	11	11	18	17	3.16
1985—Toledo	Int'national	37	64	2	4	.333	69	48	40	30	34	5.63
1985—Minnesota‡	American	5	7⅓	0	0	.000	12	9	9	4	2	11.05
Major League Totals—4 Years		97	115⅓	9	4	.692	119	61	60	68	65	4.68

Signed as free agent by Texas Rangers' organization, December 25, 1976.
†Traded to Minnesota Twins for Pitcher John Pacella, November 1, 1982.
‡Granted free agency, October 15, 1985.

TERRY BERTLAND WHITFIELD

Born January 12, 1953, at Blythe, Calif.
Height, 6.01. Weight, 200.
Throws right and bats lefthanded.

Major League stolen bases: 1975 (1), 1977 (2), 1978 (5), 1979 (5), 1980 (4), 1984 (1). Total—18.
Led International League batters in strikeouts with 129 in 1974.
Led Carolina League in total bases with 234 in 1973.
Led Appalachian League in total bases with 125 in 1971.
Tied for International League lead in double plays by outfielders with 3 in 1976.
Named Carolina League Player of the Year, 1973.
Named Appalachian League co-Player of the Year, 1971.

Year	Club	League	Pos.	G.	AB.	R.	H.	2B.	3B.	HR.	RBI.	B.A.	PO.	A.	E.	F.A.
1971—Johnson City	Appal.	OF	67	252	42	73	14	4	*10	*43	.290	104	6	●9	.924
1972—Fort Lauderdale	Fla. St.	OF	49	153	21	25	3	5	1	15	.163	57	4	5	.924
1972—Oneonta	NYP	OF	●70	256	*65	70	6	●11	7	47	.273	120	7	3	.977
1973—Kinston	Carol.	OF	129	451	94	151	25	2	●18	81	*.335	197	9	11	.949
1974—Syracuse	Int.	OF	140	499	71	129	25	4	17	71	.259	*345	12	5	.986
1974—New York	Amer.	OF	2	5	0	1	0	0	0	0	.200	0	0	0	.000
1975—Syracuse	Int.	OF	111	390	47	106	24	4	11	69	.272	208	10	10	.956
1975—New York	Amer.	OF	28	81	9	22	1	1	0	7	.272	42	3	1	.978
1976—Syracuse	Int.	OF	●138	*525	81	152	25	6	16	89	.290	208	13	15	.936
1976—New York†	Amer.	OF	1	0	0	0	0	0	0	0	.000	0	0	0	.000
1977—San Francisco	Nat.	OF	114	326	41	93	21	3	7	36	.285	167	4	5	.972
1978—San Francisco	Nat.	OF	149	488	70	141	20	2	10	32	.289	249	7	3	.988

Year	Club	League	Pos.	G.	AB.	R.	H.	2B.	3B.	HR.	RBI.	B.A.	PO.	A.	E.	F.A.
1979—San Francisco	.....	Nat.	OF	133	394	52	113	20	4	5	44	.287	167	10	8	.957
1980—San Francisco‡	....	Nat.	OF	118	321	38	95	16	2	4	26	.296	140	11	2	.987
1981—Seibu	......	Pacific	OF	123	469	....	148	....	....	22	100	.316	Figures unavailable			
1982—Seibu	......	Pacific	OF	122	453	....	123	....	....	25	71	.272	Figures unavailable			
1983—Seibu§	......	Pacific	OF	129	485	....	135	....	....	38	109	.278	Figures unavailable			
1984—Los Angeles x	....	Nat.	OF	87	180	15	44	8	0	4	18	.244	76	4	1	.988
1985—Los Angeles	....	Nat.	OF	79	104	8	27	7	0	3	16	.260	23	2	2	.926
American League Totals—3 Years	....			31	86	9	23	1	1	0	7	.267	42	3	1	.978
National League Totals—6 Years				680	1813	224	513	92	11	33	172	.283	822	38	21	.976
Major League Totals—9 Years	....			711	1899	233	536	93	12	33	179	.282	864	41	22	.976

Selected by New York Yankees' organization in 1st round (19th player selected) of free-agent draft, June 8, 1971.

†Traded to San Francisco Giants for Second Baseman Marty Perez, March 14, 1977.

‡Sold to Seibu Lions of Japanese baseball, March 4, 1981.

§Signed as free agent by Los Angeles Dodgers, January 13, 1984.

xOn disabled list, August 21 to September 5, 1984.

CHAMPIONSHIP SERIES RECORD

Year	Club	League	Pos.	G.	AB.	R.	H.	2B.	3B.	HR.	RBI.	B.A.	PO.	A.	E.	F.A.
1985—Los Angeles	....	Nat.	PH	1	0	0	0	0	0	0	0	.000	0	0	0	.000

EDDIE LEE WHITSON
(Ed)

Born May 19, 1955, at Johnson City, Tenn.
Height, 6.03. Weight, 200.
Throws and bats righthanded.

Major League saves: 1978 (4), 1979 (1), 1982 (2), 1983 (1). Total—8.
Led Carolina League in complete games with 16 in 1976.
Led Western Carolinas League in hit batsmen with 15 in 1975.

Year	Club	League	G.	IP.	W.	L.	Pct.	H.	R.	ER.	SO.	BB.	ERA.
1974—Bradenton Pirates	....	Gulf Coast	8	44	1	4	.200	45	28	21	25	15	4.30
1975—Charleston	....	W. Carol.	24	142	8	★15	.348	140	★96	★80	120	99	5.07
1976—Salem	....	Carolina	26	★203	●15	9	.625	168	75	57	★186	65	2.53
1977—Columbus	....	Int'national	26	175	8	13	.381	175	74	65	120	68	3.34
1977—Pittsburgh	....	National	5	16	1	0	1.000	11	6	6	10	9	3.38
1978—Columbus	....	Int'national	7	51	2	2	.500	56	25	21	55	10	3.71
1978—Pittsburgh	....	National	43	74	5	6	.455	66	31	27	64	37	3.28
1979—Pittsburgh†-San Francisco	....	National	37	158	7	11	.389	151	83	72	93	75	4.10
1980—San Francisco	....	National	34	212	11	13	.458	222	88	73	90	56	3.10
1981—San Francisco‡	....	National	22	123	6	9	.400	130	61	55	65	47	4.02
1982—Cleveland§	....	American	40	107⅔	4	2	.667	91	43	39	61	58	3.26
1983—San Diego x	....	National	31	144⅓	5	7	.417	143	73	69	81	50	4.30
1983—Las Vegas	....	P. Coast	3	12	1	0	1.000	15	9	9	11	5	6.75
1984—San Diego y	....	National	31	189	14	8	.636	181	72	68	103	42	3.24
1985—New York	....	American	30	158⅔	10	8	.556	201	100	86	89	43	4.88
National League Totals—7 Years	....		203	916⅓	49	54	.476	904	414	370	506	316	3.63
American League Totals—2 Years	....		70	266⅓	14	10	.583	292	143	125	150	101	4.22
Major League Totals—9 Years	....		273	1182⅔	63	64	.496	1196	557	495	656	417	3.77

Selected by Pittsburgh Pirates' organization in 6th round of free-agent draft, June 5, 1974.

†Traded with Pitchers Fred Breining and Al Holland to San Francisco Giants for Infielders Bill Madlock and Lenny Randle and Pitcher Dave Roberts, June 28, 1979.

‡Traded to Cleveland Indians for Second Baseman Duane Kuiper, November 16, 1981.

§Traded to San Diego Padres for Pitcher Juan Eichelberger and First Baseman-Outfielder Broderick Perkins, November 18, 1982.

xOn disabled list, April 18 to May 28, 1983; included rehabilitation disability assignment to Las Vegas, May 10 to May 28, 1983.

yGranted free agency, November 8, 1984; signed by New York Yankees, December 27, 1984.

CHAMPIONSHIP SERIES RECORD

Year	Club	League	G.	IP.	W.	L.	Pct.	H.	R.	ER.	SO.	BB.	ERA.
1984—San Diego	....	National	1	8	1	0	1.000	5	1	1	6	2	1.13

WORLD SERIES RECORD

Year	Club	League	G.	IP.	W.	L.	Pct.	H.	R.	ER.	SO.	BB.	ERA.
1984—San Diego	....	National	1	⅔	0	0	.000	5	3	3	0	0	40.50

ALL-STAR GAME RECORD

Member of National League All-Star Team in 1980; did not play.

LEO ERNEST WHITT
(Ernie)

Born June 13, 1952, Detroit, Mich.
Height, 6.02. Weight, 200.
Throws right and bats lefthanded.
Attended Macomb County Community College, Warren, Mich.

Major League stolen bases: 1980 (1), 1981 (5), 1982 (3), 1983 (1), 1985 (3). Total—13.

Led International League in passed balls with 16 in 1978.
Led Eastern League catchers in fielding percentage with .992 in 1974.
Tied for Carolina League lead in double plays by catchers with 7 in 1973.

Year Club	League	Pos.	G.	AB.	R.	H.	2B.	3B.	HR.	RBI.	B.A.	PO.	A.	E.	F.A.
1972—Williamsport........	NYP	1B	1	4	1	2	1	0	0	0	.500	8	1	0	1.000
1972—Winter Haven.......	Fla. St.	C-1B-OF	31	82	3	15	1	1	0	7	.183	151	14	5	.971
1973—Winston-Salem	Carol.	C-OF-1B	130	424	63	123	23	3	1	50	.290	686	70	15	.980
1974—Bristol.................	East.	C-OF-1B	111	385	55	96	10	1	9	56	.249	557	50	6	.990
1975—Bristol†.................	East.	C-OF	82	252	29	64	9	1	2	19	.254	357	36	7	.982
1976—Bristol.................	East.	C	26	87	12	19	2	3	1	10	.218	127	25	1	.993
1976—Rhode Island	Int.	C-1-O-3	90	304	33	81	16	2	7	42	.266	487	59	9	.984
1976—Boston‡	Amer.	C	8	18	4	4	2	0	1	3	.222	24	0	0	1.000
1977—Charleston............	Int.	C-3B	29	94	12	24	6	0	0	7	.255	129	28	7	.957
1977—Toronto§	Amer.	C	23	41	4	7	3	0	0	6	.171	62	4	0	1.000
1978—Syracuse	Int.	C-1B-OF	121	399	50	98	16	3	12	53	.246	673	79	7	.991
1978—Toronto	Amer.	C	2	4	0	0	0	0	0	0	.000	7	1	0	1.000
1979—Syracuse	Int.	★C-OF-3B	114	382	32	95	18	4	7	43	.249	494	69	3	★.995
1980—Toronto	Amer.	C	106	295	23	70	12	2	6	34	.237	436	56	7	.986
1981—Toronto	Amer.	C	74	195	16	46	9	0	1	16	.236	297	46	3	.991
1982—Toronto	Amer.	C	105	284	28	74	14	2	11	42	.261	406	30	8	.982
1983—Toronto	Amer.	C	123	344	53	88	15	2	17	56	.256	554	50	5	.992
1984—Toronto x..............	Amer.	C	124	315	35	75	12	1	15	46	.238	583	40	4	.994
1985—Toronto	Amer.	C	139	412	55	101	21	2	19	64	.245	649	38	8	.988
Major League Totals—9 Years.................			704	1908	218	465	88	9	70	267	.244	3018	265	35	.989

Selected by Boston Red Sox' organization in 15th round of free-agent draft, June 6, 1972.
†On disabled list, April 11 to June 13, 1975.
‡Selected by Toronto Blue Jays in American League expansion draft, November 5, 1976.
§On disabled list, August 17 to September 27, 1977.
xOn disabled list, June 16 to July 1, 1984.

CHAMPIONSHIP SERIES RECORD

Year Club	League	Pos.	G.	AB.	R.	H.	2B.	3B.	HR.	RBI.	B.A.	PO.	A.	E.	F.A.
1985—Toronto	Amer.	C	7	21	1	4	1	0	0	2	.190	50	3	0	1.000

ALL-STAR GAME RECORD

Year League	Pos.	AB.	R.	H.	2B.	3B.	HR.	RBI.	B.A.	PO.	A.	E.	F.A.
1985—American	C	0	0	0	0	0	0	0	.000	2	0	0	1.000

ALAN ANTHONY WIGGINS

Born February 17, 1958, at Los Angeles, Calif.
Height, 6.02. Weight, 160.
Throws right and bats left and righthanded.
Attended Pasadena City College, Pasadena, Calif.

Tied modern National League record for most stolen bases, game (5), May 17, 1984.
Major League stolen bases: 1981 (2), 1982 (33), 1983 (66), 1984 (70), 1985 (30). Total—201.
Led National League in caught stealing with 21 in 1984.
Led California League in stolen bases with 120 in 1980.
Tied for Pioneer League lead in sacrifice hits with 5 in 1977.

Year Club	League	Pos.	G.	AB.	R.	H.	2B.	3B.	HR.	RBI.	B.A.	PO.	A.	E.	F.A.
1977—Idaho Falls...........	Pion.	2B	63	225	64	61	3	1	1	23	.271	137	163	28	.915
1978—Quad Cities†‡........	Midw.	2B	49	169	30	34	3	0	1	12	.201	96	130	12	.950
1979—Clinton...............	Midw.	S-O-1-2-3	95	296	57	76	3	1	0	27	.257	196	198	32	.925
1980—Lodi§	Calif.	O-2-1-S	135	513	108	148	10	5	0	35	.288	365	76	23	.950
1981—Hawaii..................	P. C.	OF-2B	133	513	97	155	17	8	0	33	.302	234	26	7	.974
1981—San Diego	Nat.	OF	15	14	4	5	0	0	0	0	.357	6	0	2	.750
1982—Hawaii..................	P. C.	OF	19	77	14	24	2	4	1	4	.312	33	4	0	1.000
1982—San Diego x...........	Nat.	OF2-2B	72	254	40	65	3	3	1	15	.256	140	8	5	.967
1983—San Diego	Nat.	OF-1B	144	503	83	139	20	2	0	22	.276	572	35	8	.987
1984—San Diego	Nat.	2B	158	596	106	154	19	7	3	34	.258	★391	410	32	.962
1985—San Diego y...........	Nat.	2B	10	37	3	2	1	0	0	0	.054	22	21	0	1.000
1985—Las Vegas	P. C.	2B	2	8	2	2	0	0	0	1	.250	2	6	0	1.000
1985—Rochester	Int.	2B	6	22	1	4	1	0	0	1	.182	18	15	2	.943
1985—Baltimore z...........	Amer.	2B	76	298	43	85	11	4	0	21	.285	148	186	14	.960
National League Totals—5 Years...........			399	1404	236	365	43	12	4	71	.260	1131	474	47	.972
American League Totals—1 Year			76	298	43	85	11	4	0	21	.285	148	186	14	.960
Major League Totals—5 Years.................			475	1702	279	450	54	16	4	92	.264	1279	660	61	.970

Selected by California Angels' organization in 1st round (seventh player selected) of free-agent draft, January 11, 1977.
†On suspended list, June 8 to June 10, 1978.
‡Released, June 10, 1978; signed by Los Angeles Dodgers' organization, January 26, 1979.
§Drafted by San Diego Padres, December 8, 1980.
xOn disabled list, July 21 to September 19, 1982.
yTraded to Baltimore Orioles' organization for Pitcher Roy Lee Jackson and a player to be named later, June 27, 1985; San Diego Padres acquired Pitcher Rich Caldwell to complete deal, September 16, 1985.
zOn disabled list, June 27 to July 5, 1985; included rehabilitation disability assignment to Rochester, June 27 to July 5, 1985.

CHAMPIONSHIP SERIES RECORD

Year Club	League	Pos.	G.	AB.	R.	H.	2B.	3B.	HR.	RBI.	B.A.	PO.	A.	E.	F.A.
1984—San Diego	Nat.	2B	5	19	4	6	0	0	0	1	.316	11	11	0	1.000

WORLD SERIES RECORD

Year Club	League	Pos.	G.	AB.	R.	H.	2B.	3B.	HR.	RBI.	B.A.	PO.	A.	E.	F.A.
1984—San Diego	Nat.	2B	5	22	2	8	1	0	0	1	.364	13	6	2	.905

MILTON EDWARD WILCOX
(Milt)

Born April 20, 1950, at Honolulu, Hawaii.
Height, 6.02. Weight, 215.
Throws and bats righthanded.

Pitched seven-inning, 2-0 no-hit victory against Evansville, July 4, 1970.
Major League saves: 1970 (1), 1971 (1), 1974 (4). Total—6.
Led American Association in shutouts with 5 in 1970 and tied for lead with 3 in 1971.
Named American Association Pitcher of the Year, 1970.

Year Club	League	G.	IP.	W.	L.	Pct.	H.	R.	ER.	SO.	BB.	ERA.
1968—Tampa	Florida St.	8	47	3	3	.500	28	11	7	48	18	1.34
1968—Sarasota Reds	Gulf Coast	6	33	3	2	.600	24	10	4	33	11	1.09
1969—Tampa†‡	Florida St.	15	46	4	1	.800	53	30	28	38	29	5.48
1970—Indianapolis	Am. Assoc.	28	168	12	10	.545	144	58	53	110	53	2.84
1970—Cincinnati	National	5	22	3	1	.750	19	6	6	13	7	2.45
1971—Indianapolis	Am. Assoc.	16	102	8	5	.615	84	29	25	62	22	2.20
1971—Cincinnati§	National	18	43	2	2	.500	43	22	16	21	17	3.35
1972—Cleveland	American	32	156	7	14	.333	145	67	59	90	72	3.40
1973—Cleveland xy	American	26	134	8	10	.444	143	90	87	82	68	5.84
1974—Cleveland za	American	41	71	2	2	.500	74	42	37	33	24	4.69
1975—Wichita	Am. Assoc.	8	48	4	3	.571	56	31	23	18	15	4.31
1975—Chicago	National	25	38	0	1	.000	50	27	24	21	17	5.68
1976—Wichita b-Evansville	Am. Assoc.	27	130	6	7	.462	141	72	55	94	63	3.81
1977—Evansville	Am. Assoc.	14	107	9	4	.692	89	38	29	69	40	2.44
1977—Detroit	American	20	106	6	2	.750	96	46	43	82	37	3.65
1978—Detroit	American	29	215	13	12	.520	208	94	90	132	68	3.77
1979—Detroit	American	33	196	12	10	.545	201	105	95	109	73	4.36
1980—Detroit	American	32	199	13	11	.542	201	112	99	97	68	4.48
1981—Detroit	American	24	166	12	9	.571	152	61	56	79	52	3.04
1982—Detroit c	American	29	193⅔	12	10	.545	187	91	78	112	85	3.62
1983—Detroit d	American	26	186	11	10	.524	164	89	82	101	74	3.97
1983—Evansville e	Am. Assoc.	2	8	0	1	.000	8	5	3	5	6	3.38
1984—Detroit	American	33	193⅔	17	8	.680	183	99	86	119	66	4.00
1985—Detroit fg	American	8	39	1	3	.250	51	24	21	20	14	4.85
National League Totals—3 Years		48	103	5	4	.556	112	55	46	55	41	4.02
American League Totals—12 Years		333	1855⅓	114	101	.530	1805	920	833	1056	701	4.04
Major League Totals—15 Years		381	1958⅓	119	105	.531	1917	975	879	1111	742	4.04

Selected by Cincinnati Reds' organization in 2nd round of free-agent draft, June 7, 1968.
†On military list, April 16 to May 9, 1969.
‡On temporary inactive list, June 11 to July 1, 1969.
§Traded to Cleveland Indians for Outfielder Ted Uhlaender, December 6, 1971.
xOn military list, June 16 to June 30, 1973.
yOn disabled list, July 24 to August 15, 1973.
zOn military list, July 20 to August 4, 1974.
aTraded to Chicago Cubs for Pitcher Dave LaRoche and Outfielder Brock Davis, February 28, 1975.
bSold to Detroit Tigers, June 10, 1976.
cOn disabled list, July 19 to August 9, 1982.
dOn disabled list, August 1 to September 1, 1983; included rehabilitation disability assignment to Evansville, August 12 to September 1, 1983.
eGranted free agency, November 7, 1983; re-signed by Tigers, December 29, 1983.
fOn disabled list, June 13, 1985 through remainder of season.
gReleased, December 20, 1985.

CHAMPIONSHIP SERIES RECORD

Year Club	League	G.	IP.	W.	L.	Pct.	H.	R.	ER.	SO.	BB.	ERA.
1970—Cincinnati	National	1	3	1	0	1.000	1	0	0	5	2	0.00
1984—Detroit	American	1	8	1	0	1.000	2	0	0	8	2	0.00
Championship Series Totals—2 Years		2	11	2	0	1.000	3	0	0	13	4	0.00

WORLD SERIES RECORD

Year Club	League	G.	IP.	W.	L.	Pct.	H.	R.	ER.	SO.	BB.	ERA.
1970—Cincinnati	National	2	2	0	1	.000	3	2	2	2	0	9.00
1984—Detroit	American	1	6	1	0	1.000	7	1	1	4	2	1.50
World Series Totals—2 Years		3	8	1	1	.500	10	3	3	6	2	3.38

—DID YOU KNOW—

That St. Louis rookie Vince Coleman's 110 stolen bases were equal to or more than the team totals for 13 clubs in the major leagues last season?

ROBERT DONALD WILFONG
(Rob)

Born September 1, 1953, at Pasadena, Calif.
Height, 6.01. Weight, 185.
Throws right and bats lefthanded.
Attended Mount San Antonio Junior College, Walnut, Calif.
Brother of James Wilfong, outfielder in Detroit Tigers' organization, 1978.

Major League stolen bases: 1977 (10), 1978 (8), 1979 (11), 1980 (10), 1981 (2), 1982 (4), 1984 (3), 1985 (4). Total—52.
Led American League in sacrifice hits with 25 in 1979.
Led American League second basemen in fielding percentage with .995 in 1980.

Year Club	League	Pos.	G.	AB.	R.	H.	2B.	3B.	HR.	RBI.	B.A.	PO.	A.	E.	F.A.
1972—Charlotte†	W. Car.	2B	102	363	64	107	18	2	2	35	.295	212	224	16	.965
1973—Lynchburg	Carol.	2B	131	520	94	143	13	9	7	37	.275	*323	326	18	.973
1974—Orlando	South.	2B	109	403	58	99	7	4	3	23	.246	249	303	8	*.986
1975—Orlando	South.	2B	125	403	54	99	14	1	4	37	.246	274	347	16	.975
1976—Tacoma	P. C.	2B	69	220	41	67	8	3	3	16	.305	163	191	6	.983
1977—Tacoma	P. C.	2B	34	123	26	40	8	1	2	17	.325	83	101	8	.958
1977—Minnesota	Amer.	2B	73	171	22	42	1	1	1	13	.246	114	164	12	.959
1978—Minnesota‡	Amer.	2B	92	199	23	53	8	0	1	11	.266	152	196	5	.986
1979—Minnesota	Amer.	2B-OF	140	419	71	131	22	6	9	59	.313	287	379	14	.979
1980—Minnesota	Amer.	2B-OF	131	416	55	103	16	5	8	45	.248	245	338	4	.993
1981—Minnesota	Amer.	2B	93	305	32	75	11	3	3	19	.246	183	268	9	.980
1982—Minn.§-Calif.	Amer.	2-3-O-S	90	192	24	38	5	2	1	16	.208	60	155	5	.978
1983—California	Amer.	2B-3B-SS	65	177	17	45	7	1	2	17	.254	107	144	2	.992
1984—California x	Amer.	2B-SS	108	307	31	76	13	2	6	33	.248	162	268	12	.973
1985—California	Amer.	2B	83	217	16	41	3	0	4	13	.189	124	216	5	.986
Major League Totals—9 Years			865	2394	291	604	86	20	35	226	.252	1443	2128	68	.981

Selected by Minnesota Twins' organization in 13th round of free-agent draft, June 8, 1971.
†On disabled list, May 22 to June 2, 1972.
‡On disabled list, March 22 to April 7, 1978.
§Traded with Pitcher Doug Corbett to California Angels for Outfielder Tom Brunansky, Pitcher Mike Walters and cash, May 12, 1982.
xGranted free agency, November 8, 1984; re-signed by Angels, January 10, 1985.

CHAMPIONSHIP SERIES RECORD

Year Club	League	Pos.	G.	AB.	R.	H.	2B.	3B.	HR.	RBI.	B.A.	PO.	A.	E.	F.A.
1982—California	Amer.	PH-PR	2	1	0	0	0	0	0	0	.000	0	0	0	.000

CURTIS VERNON WILKERSON
(Curt)

Born April 26, 1961, at Petersburg, Va.
Height, 5.09. Weight, 160.
Throws right and bats left and righthanded.

Major League stolen bases: 1983 (3), 1984 (12), 1985 (14). Total—29.
Tied for Texas League lead in sacrifice hits with 11 in 1982.

Year Club	League	Pos.	G.	AB.	R.	H.	2B.	3B.	HR.	RBI.	B.A.	PO.	A.	E.	F.A.
1980—Sarasota Rangers	Gulf C.	SS-2B	37	105	15	20	2	0	0	8	.190	38	86	17	.879
1981—Asheville	S. Atl.	SS-2B	106	333	45	68	7	3	0	19	.204	188	372	28	.952
1982—Burlington	Midw.	SS-2B	56	198	18	50	6	0	0	13	.253	78	159	16	.937
1982—Tulsa	Texas	SS	72	266	32	71	6	3	2	14	.267	102	225	18	.948
1983—Oklahoma City†	A. A.	SS	89	343	51	107	19	4	3	31	.312	135	272	19	.955
1983—Texas	Amer.	SS-2B-3B	16	35	7	6	0	1	0	1	.171	18	31	1	.980
1984—Texas	Amer.	SS-2B	153	484	47	120	12	0	1	26	.248	227	391	30	.954
1985—Texas	Amer.	SS-2B	129	360	35	88	11	6	0	22	.244	165	328	21	.959
Major League Totals—3 Years			298	879	89	214	23	7	1	49	.243	410	750	52	.957

Selected by Texas Rangers' organization in 4th round of free-agent draft, June 3, 1980.
†On disabled list, May 19 to June 21, 1983.

WILLIAM CARL WILKINSON
(Bill)

Born August 10, 1964, at Greybull, Wyo.
Height, 5.10. Weight, 160.
Throws left and bats righthanded.

Year Club	League	G.	IP.	W.	L.	Pct.	H.	R.	ER.	SO.	BB.	ERA.
1983—Bellingham	Northwest	13	63⅔	4	5	.444	54	41	24	87	54	3.39
1984—Wausau	Midwest	19	103⅓	6	4	.600	79	47	38	117	52	3.31
1985—Salinas	California	9	59⅔	6	1	.857	47	19	18	75	23	2.72
1985—Calgary†	P. Coast	9	57⅓	5	1	.833	44	21	17	42	25	2.67
1985—Seattle	American	2	6	0	2	.000	8	9	9	5	6	13.50
Major League Totals—1 Year		2	6	0	2	.000	8	9	9	5	6	13.50

Selected by Seattle Mariners' organization in 4th round of free-agent draft, June 6, 1983.
†On disabled list, July 18, 1985 through remainder of season.

GERALD DUANE WILLARD JR.
(Jerry)

Born March 14, 1960, at Oxnard, Calif.
Height, 6.02. Weight, 200.
Throws right and bats lefthanded.
Attended Oxnard College, Oxnard, Calif.

Major League stolen bases: 1984 (1).
Led International League catchers in assists with 78 in 1983.

Year	Club	League	Pos.	G.	AB.	R.	H.	2B.	3B.	HR.	RBI.	B.A.	PO.	A.	E.	F.A.
1980—Central Oregon	N'west		C	65	231	53	85	21	1	5	59	.368	283	37	•18	.947
1981—Peninsula	Carol.		C	107	334	43	87	17	1	12	60	.260	319	28	3	.991
1982—Reading	East.		C	81	281	43	82	10	1	12	51	.292	534	64	13	.979
1982—Oklahoma City†	A. A.		C	36	95	13	22	5	0	2	14	.232	169	35	8	.962
1983—Charleston	Int.	C-3B-OF	127	396	61	119	22	2	19	77	.301	613	79	12	.983
1984—Cleveland	Amer.		C	87	246	21	55	8	1	10	37	.224	335	35	7	.981
1985—Cleveland	Amer.		C	104	300	39	81	13	0	7	36	.270	427	52	5	.990
1985—Maine	Int.		C	11	40	5	9	3	0	1	4	.225	56	11	2	.971
Major League Totals—2 Years				191	546	60	136	21	1	17	73	.249	762	87	12	.986

Signed as free agent by Philadelphia Phillies' organization, December 20, 1979.
†Traded with Second Baseman Manny Trillo, Infielder Julio Franco, Outfielder George Vukovich and Pitcher Jay Baller to Cleveland Indians for Outfielder Von Hayes, December 9, 1982.

DANA LAMONT WILLIAMS

Born March 20, 1963, at Weirton, W. Va.
Height, 5.10. Weight, 170.
Throws and bats righthanded.
Attended Enterprise State Junior College, Enterprise, Ala.

Led Eastern League in caught stealing with 16 and tied for lead in grounding into double plays with 15 in 1985.

Year	Club	League	Pos.	G.	AB.	R.	H.	2B.	3B.	HR.	RBI.	B.A.	PO.	A.	E.	F.A.
1983—Elmira	NYP	2B-SS	29	99	24	38	6	1	0	2	.384	35	46	6	.931
1983—Winston-Salem	Carol.	SS-2B-OF	24	86	10	24	4	0	0	7	.279	22	48	8	.897
1984—Winter Haven	Fla. St.	OF	135	511	65	•167	27	8	1	54	★.327	226	12	8	.967
1985—New Britain	East.	OF	115	450	56	139	16	7	1	39	.309	198	6	3	.986

Selected by Cincinnati Reds' organization in 34th round of free-agent draft, June 8, 1981.
Selected by Detroit Tigers' organization in secondary phase of free-agent draft, January 12, 1982.
Signed as free agent by Boston Red Sox' organization, May 17, 1983.

EDWARD LAQUAN WILLIAMS
(Eddie)

Born November 1, 1964, at Shreveport, La.
Height, 6.00. Weight, 175.
Throws and bats righthanded.

Led Midwest League in being hit by pitch with 15 in 1985.
Named Midwest League Most Valuable Player, 1985.

Year	Club	League	Pos.	G.	AB.	R.	H.	2B.	3B.	HR.	RBI.	B.A.	PO.	A.	E.	F.A.
1983—Little Falls	NYP	3B	50	190	30	50	6	2	6	28	.263	50	53	13	.888
1984—Columbia†	S. Atl.	3B	43	152	17	28	4	2	3	24	.184	24	76	16	.862
1984—Tampa	Fla. St.	3B	50	138	20	35	8	0	2	16	.254	25	43	11	.861
1985—Cedar Rapids‡	Midw.	3B	119	406	71	106	13	3	20	83	.261	83	204	33	.897

Selected by New York Mets' organization in 1st round (fourth player selected) of free-agent draft, June 6, 1983.
†Traded with Pitchers Matt Bullinger and Jay Tibbs to Cincinnati Reds for Pitcher Bruce Berenyi, June 15, 1984.
‡Drafted by Cleveland Indians, December 10, 1985.

FRANK LEE WILLIAMS

Born February 13, 1958, at Seattle, Wash.
Height, 6.01. Weight, 180.
Throws and bats righthanded.
Attended Shoreline Community College, Seattle, Wash.,
and Lewis-Clark State College, Lewiston, Ida.

Major League saves: 1984 (3).
Led California League in hit batsmen with 18 in 1980 and 13 in 1981.
Led Pioneer League in hit batsmen with 9 in 1979.
Tied for Texas League lead in hit batsmen with 13 in 1982.
Tied for California League lead in complete games with 14 in 1981.

Year	Club	League	G.	IP.	W.	L.	Pct.	H.	R.	ER.	SO.	BB.	ERA.
1979—Great Falls	Pioneer	13	91	6	•7	.462	85	53	34	81	53	3.36
1980—Fresno	California	21	114	12	3	.800	105	53	42	80	70	3.32
1981—Fresno	California	27	187	14	9	.609	170	81	70	170	85	3.37
1982—Shreveport	Texas	27	169⅔	11	9	.550	143	96	74	145	99	3.93
1983—Shreveport	Texas	21	42	7	2	.778	22	14	8	54	25	1.71
1983—Phoenix	P. Coast	25	47⅔	5	3	.625	45	22	19	37	24	3.59
1984—San Francisco	National	61	106⅓	9	4	.692	88	42	42	91	51	3.55
1985—San Francisco	National	49	73	2	4	.333	65	39	34	54	35	4.19
1985—Phoenix	P. Coast	9	13⅔	1	1	.500	10	8	6	10	14	3.95
Major League Totals—2 Years		110	179⅓	11	8	.579	153	88	76	145	86	3.81

Selected by San Francisco Giants' organization in 11th round of free-agent draft, June 5, 1979.

JEFFREY LEON WILLIAMS
(Jeff)

Born September 10, 1962, at Lincoln Heights, O.
Height, 6.00. Weight, 170.
Throws and bats lefthanded.

Year Club	League	Pos.	G.	AB.	R.	H.	2B.	3B.	HR.	RBI.	B.A.	PO.	A.	E.	F.A.
1980—Bluefield................	Appal.	OF	58	214	34	74	10	2	1	28	.346	115	3	*10	.922
1981—Miami	Fla. St.	OF	113	382	38	82	15	5	0	36	.215	257	12	*16	.944
1982—Hagerstown	Carol.	OF	109	375	61	97	17	5	8	46	.259	205	15	10	.957
1983—Charlotte.............	South.	OF	124	425	56	106	10	8	7	34	.249	245	*26	13	.954
1984—Char.†-Nash.‡	South.	OF	90	271	28	62	10	2	3	26	.229	133	5	13	.914
1984—Hagerstown	Carol.	OF	23	46	7	9	1	0	0	3	.196	17	1	1	.947
1985—Hagerstown	Carol.	OF	95	339	57	91	10	10	3	41	.268	185	7	3	.985

Selected by Baltimore Orioles' organization in 1st round (26th player selected) of free-agent draft, June 3, 1980.
†Sold to Nashville (New York Yankees' organization), July 24, 1984.
‡Sold to Charlotte (Baltimore Orioles' organization), September 9, 1984.

KENNETH ROYAL WILLIAMS
(Ken)

Born April 6, 1964, at Berkeley, Calif.
Height, 6.02. Weight, 187.
Throws and bats righthanded.
Attended Stanford University, Stanford, Calif.
Received reported $165,000 bonus to sign with Chicago White Sox, 1982.

Year Club	League	Pos.	G.	AB.	R.	H.	2B.	3B.	HR.	RBI.	B.A.	PO.	A.	E.	F.A.
1982—Sarasota W. Sox...	Gulf C.	OF	31	104	19	31	2	1	1	11	.298	61	2	0	1.000
1983—Appleton	Midw.	OF	124	415	60	96	18	2	12	53	.231	218	10	10	.958
1984—Appleton	Midw.	OF	38	147	23	42	11	2	5	26	.286	58	5	2	.969
1984—Glens Falls...........	East.	OF	97	309	35	76	7	5	8	47	.246	173	10	5	.973
1985—Glens Falls...........	East.	OF	133	*520	*87	130	16	6	16	66	.250	296	*20	*14	.958

Selected by Chicago White Sox' organization in 3rd round of free-agent draft, June 7, 1982.

MATTHEW EVAN WILLIAMS
(Matt)

Born July 25, 1959, at Houston, Tex.
Height, 6.01. Weight, 195.
Throws right and bats left and righthanded.
Received bachelor of arts degree in managerial studies
from Rice University, Houston, Tex.
Brother of Mike Williams, pitcher in Kansas City Royals', Los Angeles Dodgers' and
San Francisco Giants' organizations, 1974 through 1981, and with
Nuevo Laredo of Mexican League, 1982; and Robert Williams,
pitcher in Cincinnati Reds' organization, 1975.
Led International League in intentional bases on balls issued with 7 in 1984.
Led Southern League in wild pitches with 31 in 1982.

Year Club	League	G.	IP.	W.	L.	Pct.	H.	R.	ER.	SO.	BB.	ERA.
1981—Florence	S. Atlantic	15	91	7	4	.636	81	33	22	76	27	2.18
1982—Knoxville	Southern	28	193⅓	11	13	.458	173	106	92	157	107	4.28
1983—Syracuse	Int'national	21	148	8	8	.500	106	61	56	116	64	3.41
1983—Toronto	American	4	8	1	1	.500	13	13	13	5	7	14.63
1984—Syracuse	Int'national	32	178	9	12	.429	172	81	66	118	63	3.34
1985—Syracuse†‡	Int'national	22	136	7	12	.368	124	73	67	100	51	4.43
1985—Oklahoma City	Am. Assoc.	1	4	0	0	.000	4	2	1	4	0	2.25
1985—Texas...	American	6	26	2	1	.667	20	7	7	22	10	2.42
Major League Totals—2 Years............................		10	34	3	2	.600	33	20	20	27	17	5.29

Selected by Milwaukee Brewers' organization in 4th round of free-agent draft, June 3, 1980.
Selected by Toronto Blue Jays' organization in 1st round (fifth player selected) of free-agent draft, June 8, 1981.
†On disabled list, July 26 to August 14, 1985.
‡Traded with Pitcher Jeff Mays to Texas Rangers' organization, August 29, 1985, as partial completion of deal in which Toronto Blue Jays acquired designated hitter Cliff Johnson for three players to be named later, August 28, 1985; Texas acquired Pitcher Greg Ferlenda to complete deal, November 14, 1985.

MITCHELL STEVEN WILLIAMS
(Mitch)

Born November 17, 1964, at Santa Ana, Calif.
Height, 6.03. Weight, 180.
Throws and bats lefthanded.
Brother of Bruce Williams, pitcher in Milwaukee Brewers' organization.
Led Northwest League pitchers in wild pitches with 14 and tied for lead in games started with 14 and balks with 2 in 1983.

Year Club	League	G.	IP.	W.	L.	Pct.	H.	R.	ER.	SO.	BB.	ERA.
1982—Walla Walla	Northwest	12	58⅓	3	4	.429	37	37	31	66	*72	4.78
1983—Reno	California	11	58	1	7	.125	58	56	46	44	60	7.14
1983—Spokane	Northwest	14	92⅓	7	6	.538	84	51	●46	87	55	4.48

Year Club	League	G.	IP.	W.	L.	Pct.	H.	R.	ER.	SO.	BB.	ERA.
1984—Reno†‡	California	26	164	9	8	.529	163	113	91	165	127	4.99
1985—Salem..................................	Carolina	22	99	6	9	.400	57	64	60	138	★117	5.45
1985—Tulsa	Texas	6	33	2	2	.500	17	24	17	37	48	4.64

Selected by San Diego Padres' organization in 8th round of free-agent draft, June 7, 1982.
†Drafted by Texas Rangers, December 3, 1984; returned, April 6, 1985.
‡Traded to Texas Rangers for Third Baseman Randy Asadoor, April 6, 1985.

REGINALD DEWAYNE WILLIAMS
(Reggie)

Born August 29, 1960, at Memphis, Tenn.
Height, 5.11. Weight, 185.
Throws and bats righthanded.
Received bachelor of science degree in business
from Southern University, New Orleans, La.

Major League stolen bases: 1985 (1).

Year Club	League	Pos.	G.	AB.	R.	H.	2B.	3B.	HR.	RBI.	B.A.	PO.	A.	E.	F.A.
1982—Lethbridge	Pion.	OF	67	253	40	76	8	2	3	33	.300	★141	12	7	.956
1983—Vero Beach†........	Fla. St.	OF	81	293	53	83	11	3	4	32	.283	142	3	8	.948
1984—Vero Beach‡........	Fla. St.	OF	60	222	31	53	5	2	0	19	.239	87	5	1	.989
1985—San Antonio...........	Texas	OF	120	436	73	127	17	4	10	53	.291	209	14	11	.953
1985—Los Angeles	Nat.	OF	22	9	4	3	0	0	0	0	.333	8	1	1	.900
Major League Totals—1 Year..................			22	9	4	3	0	0	0	0	.333	8	1	1	.900

Selected by St. Louis Cardinals' organization in 6th round of free-agent draft, June 8, 1981.
Selected by Los Angeles Dodgers' organization in 13th round of free-agent draft, June 7, 1982.
†On disabled list, June 22 to August 11, 1983.
‡On disabled list, April 6 to June 28, 1984.

CARL BLAKE WILLIS

Born December 28, 1960, at Danville, Va.
Height, 6.03. Weight, 210.
Throws right and bats lefthanded.
Attended University of North Carolina, Wilmington, N.C.

Major League saves: 1984 (1), 1985 (1). Total—2.

Year Club	League	G.	IP.	W.	L.	Pct.	H.	R.	ER.	SO.	BB.	ERA.
1983—Bristol.................	Ap'lachian	2	2⅔	0	1	.000	0	1	1	3	4	3.38
1983—Lakeland...............	Florida St.	4	9⅔	3	0	1.000	6	0	0	7	5	0.00
1983—Birmingham	Southern	14	20⅓	3	1	.750	16	9	9	13	7	3.98
1984—Evansville	Am. Assoc.	40	60⅓	5	3	.625	59	26	25	27	20	3.73
1984—Detroit†	American	10	16	0	2	.000	25	13	13	4	5	7.31
1984—Cincinnati	National	7	9⅔	0	1	.000	8	4	4	3	2	3.72
1985—Cincinnati	National	11	13⅔	1	0	1.000	21	18	14	6	5	9.22
1985—Denver‡	Am. Assoc.	37	78	4	4	.500	82	39	36	27	30	4.15
American League Totals—1 Year.......................		10	16	0	2	.000	25	13	13	4	5	7.31
National League Totals—2 Years......................		18	23⅓	1	1	.500	29	22	18	9	7	6.94
Major League Totals—2 Years............................		28	39⅓	1	3	.250	54	35	31	13	12	7.09

Selected by San Francisco Giants' organization in 31st round of free-agent draft, June 7, 1982.
Selected by Detroit Tigers' organization in 23rd round of free-agent draft, June 6, 1983.
†Traded to Cincinnati Reds, September 1, 1984, completing deal in which Cincinnati traded Pitcher Bill Scherrer to Detroit Tigers for cash and a player to be named later, August 27, 1984.
‡Drafted by California Angels, December 10, 1985.

FRANK LEE WILLS JR.

Born October 26, 1958, at New Orleans, La.
Height, 6.02. Weight, 200.
Throws and bats righthanded.
Attended Tulane University, New Orleans, La.

Major League saves: 1985 (1).
Pitched seven-inning, 1-0 no-hit victory against Tacoma, May 31, 1985 (first game).
Tied for Southern League lead in wild pitches with 15 in 1981.
Named righthanded pitcher on THE SPORTING NEWS College Baseball All-America Team, 1980.

Year Club	League	G.	IP.	W.	L.	Pct.	H.	R.	ER.	SO.	BB.	ERA.
1980—Sarasota Royals-Blue	Gulf Coast	4	23	2	0	1.000	18	7	5	20	8	1.96
1980—Charleston.......................	S. Atlantic	9	57	2	5	.286	59	33	23	48	32	3.63
1981—Jacksonville...................................	Southern	27	192	9	14	.391	199	104	85	174	91	3.98
1982—Omaha..................................	Am. Assoc.	41	107⅓	7	10	.412	110	71	62	77	★81	5.20
1983—Jacksonville................................	Southern	8	54⅓	5	2	.714	44	19	15	40	23	2.48
1983—Omaha............................	Am. Assoc.	16	95	4	11	.267	96	56	50	65	45	4.74
1983—Kansas City	American	6	34⅔	2	1	.667	35	17	16	23	15	4.15
1984—Omaha..........................	Am. Assoc.	15	89⅔	7	4	.636	75	32	28	69	49	2.81
1984—Kansas City†‡§............................	American	10	37	2	3	.400	39	21	21	21	13	5.11
1985—Calgary	P. Coast	9	46⅓	4	3	.571	44	27	25	31	25	4.86
1985—Seattle................................	American	24	123	5	11	.313	122	85	82	67	68	6.00
Major League Totals—3 Years............................		40	194⅔	9	15	.375	196	123	119	111	96	5.50

Selected by Kansas City Royals' organization in 1st round (16th player selected) of free-agent draft, June 3, 1980.

†On disabled list, August 1 to August 16, 1984.
‡Traded to New York Mets' organization as part of a six-player, four-team deal in which Kansas City Royals acquired Catcher Jim Sundberg from Milwaukee Brewers, Texas Rangers acquired Catcher Don Slaught from Kansas City, Milwaukee acquired Pitcher Danny Darwin and a player to be named later from Texas and Pitcher Tim Leary from New York, January 18, 1985; Milwaukee organization acquired Catcher Bill Hance from Texas to complete deal, January 30, 1985.
§Traded to Seattle Mariners' organization for Pitcher Wray Bergendahl, March 29, 1985.

GLENN DWIGHT WILSON

Born December 22, 1958, at Baytown, Tex.
Height, 6.01. Weight, 190.
Throws and bats righthanded.
Attended Sam Houston State University, Huntsville, Tex.

Tied major league record for fewest double plays by outfielder, season, for leader in double plays (4), 1985.
Major League stolen bases: 1982 (2), 1983 (1), 1984 (7), 1985 (7). Total—17.
Tied for National League lead in double plays by outfielders with 4 in 1985.
Received reported $60,000 bonus to sign with Detroit Tigers, 1980.
Named third baseman on THE SPORTING NEWS College Baseball All-America Team, 1980.

Year—Club	League	Pos.	G.	AB.	R.	H.	2B.	3B.	HR.	RBI.	B.A.	PO.	A.	E.	F.A.
1980—Montgomery	South.	3B	77	284	36	75	16	2	7	31	.264	56	189	*33	.881
1981—Birmingham	South.	OF	124	496	77	152	24	6	18	82	.306	292	18	5	.984
1981—Evansville	A. A.	OF-1B	10	37	5	9	2	0	2	7	.243	16	2	0	1.000
1982—Detroit	Amer.	OF	84	322	39	94	15	1	12	34	.292	215	8	3	.987
1982—Evansville†	A. A.	OF	42	105	24	40	7	2	10	33	.279	96	6	3	.971
1983—Detroit‡	Amer.	OF	144	503	55	135	25	6	11	65	.268	225	12	3	.988
1984—Philadelphia	Nat.	OF-3B	132	341	28	82	21	3	6	31	.240	153	7	7	.958
1985—Philadelphia	Nat.	OF	161	608	73	167	39	5	14	102	.275	343	*18	*12	.968
American League Totals—2 Years			228	825	94	229	40	7	23	99	.278	440	20	6	.987
National League Totals—2 Years			293	949	101	249	60	8	20	133	.262	496	25	19	.965
Major League Totals—4 Years			521	1774	195	478	100	15	43	232	.269	936	45	25	.975

Selected by Detroit Tigers' organization in 1st round (18th player selected) of free-agent draft, June 3, 1980.
†On disabled list, May 27 to June 9 and June 17 to June 27, 1982.
‡Traded with Catcher-First Baseman John Wockenfuss to Philadelphia Phillies for First Baseman Dave Bergman and Pitcher Willie Hernandez, March 24, 1984.

ALL-STAR GAME RECORD

Year—League	Pos.	AB.	R.	H.	2B.	3B.	HR.	RBI.	B.A.	PO.	A.	E.	F.A.
1985—National	PH	1	0	0	0	0	0	0	.000	0	0	0	.000

JAMES GEORGE WILSON
(Jim)

Born December 29, 1960, at Corvallis, Ore.
Height, 6.03. Weight, 230.
Throws and bats righthanded.
Attended Oregon State University, Corvallis, Ore.

Led International League in total bases with 251, game-winning RBIs with 16 and grounding into double plays with 20 in 1985.
Led International League batters in strikeouts with 113 in 1984.
Led Eastern League in being hit by pitch with 10 and tied for lead in grounding into double plays with 18 in 1983.
Led International League first basemen in total chances with 1,199 and double plays with 96 in 1985.

Year—Club	League	Pos.	G.	AB.	R.	H.	2B.	3B.	HR.	RBI.	B.A.	PO.	A.	E.	F.A.
1982—Chattanooga	South.	1B	11	40	3	7	1	0	0	5	.175	29	1	1	.968
1982—Waterloo	Midw.	3B-OF-1B	55	204	40	73	17	1	14	48	.358	17	32	8	.860
1983—Buffalo	East.	1B	136	496	84	144	25	0	26	*105	.290	701	57	13	.983
1984—Maine	Int.	1B	133	490	56	128	19	1	15	●84	.261	715	53	9	.988
1985—Maine	Int.	1B	*139	523	75	150	23	0	*26	*101	.287	*1104	*85	10	.992
1985—Cleveland	Amer.	1B	4	14	2	5	0	0	0	4	.357	23	0	0	1.000
Major League Totals—1 Year			4	14	2	5	0	0	0	4	.357	23	0	0	1.000

Selected by Cleveland Indians' organization in 2nd round of free-agent draft, June 7, 1982.

WILLIAM HAYWARD WILSON
(Mookie)

Born February 9, 1956, at Bamberg, S. C.
Height, 5.10. Weight, 170.
Throws right and bats right and lefthanded.
Attended Spartanburg Methodist College, Spartanburg, S. C.,
and University of South Carolina, Columbia, S. C.
Brother of John Wilson, outfielder in New York Mets' organization; and
Phil Wilson, outfielder in Minnesota Twins' organization.

Major League stolen bases: 1980 (7), 1981 (24), 1982 (58), 1983 (54), 1984 (46), 1985 (24). Total—213.
Led National League outfielders in double plays with 6 in 1984.

Year—Club	League	Pos.	G.	AB.	R.	H.	2B.	3B.	HR.	RBI.	B.A.	PO.	A.	E.	F.A.
1977—Wausau	Midw.	OF	68	245	50	71	10	2	6	32	.290	150	8	9	.946
1978—Jackson	Texas	OF	132	497	72	145	13	*15	7	72	.292	282	10	7	.977
1979—Tidewater	Int.	OF	*141	529	84	141	22	10	5	36	.267	317	11	7	.979

Year	Club	League	Pos.	G.	AB.	R.	H.	2B.	3B.	HR.	RBI.	B.A.	PO.	A.	E.	F.A.
1980—Tidewater	Int.		OF	132	515	*92	*152	11	*14	4	44	.295	*350	11	7	.981
1980—New York	Nat.		OF	27	105	16	26	5	3	0	4	.248	72	1	2	.973
1981—New York	Nat.		OF	92	328	49	89	8	8	3	14	.271	226	3	4	.983
1982—New York	Nat.		OF	159	639	90	178	25	9	5	55	.279	415	12	5	.988
1983—New York	Nat.		OF	152	*638	91	176	25	6	7	51	.276	422	5	7	.984
1984—New York	Nat.		OF	154	587	88	162	28	10	10	54	.276	396	8	4	.990
1985—New York†	Nat.		OF	93	337	56	93	16	8	6	26	.276	216	0	8	.964
Major League Totals—6 Years				677	2634	390	724	107	44	31	204	.275	1747	29	30	.983

Selected by Los Angeles Dodgers' organization in 4th round of free-agent draft, January 7, 1976.
Selected by New York Mets' organization in 2nd round of free-agent draft, June 7, 1977.
†On disabled list, July 2 to September 1, 1985.

WILLIE JAMES WILSON

Born July 9, 1955, at Montgomery, Ala.
Height, 6.03. Weight, 187.
Throws right and bats left and righthanded.

Established major league records for most at-bats season (705), 1980; most at-bats by switch-hitter, season (705), 1980.

Tied major league records by collecting 100 or more hits righthanded and lefthanded, season, 1980; for most hits by switch-hitter, season (230), 1980.

Established American League records for most triples by switch-hitter, season (21), 1985; highest stolen base percentage, lifetime, 300 or more attempts (.843); fewest times, grounded into double play, season (1), 1979.

Tied American League records for most consecutive stolen bases without caught stealing (32); fewest times caught stealing, season, 50 or more stolen bases (8), 1983.

Major League stolen bases: 1976 (2), 1977 (6), 1978 (46), 1979 (83), 1980 (79), 1981 (34), 1982 (37), 1983 (59), 1984 (47), 1985 (43). Total—436.

Switch-hit home runs in one game, June 15, 1979.
Led American League in stolen bases with 83 in 1979.
Led Gulf Coast League in stolen bases with 24 in 1974, Midwest League with 76 in 1975 and American Association with 74 in 1977.
Led Midwest League in being hit by pitch with 13 in 1975.
Named outfielder on THE SPORTING NEWS American League All-Star fielding team, 1980.
Named outfielder on THE SPORTING NEWS American League Silver Slugger team, 1980 and 1982.
Named Midwest League Most Valuable Player, 1975.
Received reported $90,000 bonus to sign with Kansas City Royals, 1974.

Year	Club	League	Pos.	G.	AB.	R.	H.	2B.	3B.	HR.	RBI.	B.A.	PO.	A.	E.	F.A.
1974—Sarasota Royals	Gulf C.		OF	47	155	30	39	3	5	1	14	.252	92	8	4	.962
1975—Waterloo	Midw.		OF	127	486	92	*132	18	4	8	73	.272	249	●17	*17	.940
1976—Jacksonville	South.		OF	107	388	54	98	13	6	1	35	.253	273	5	8	.972
1976—Kansas City	Amer.		OF	12	6	0	1	0	0	0	0	.167	6	1	1	.875
1977—Omaha	A. A.		OF	132	495	67	139	10	6	4	47	.281	*278	7	11	.963
1977—Kansas City	Amer.		OF	13	34	10	11	2	0	0	1	.324	24	0	1	.960
1978—Kansas City	Amer.		OF	127	198	43	43	8	2	0	16	.217	171	6	4	.978
1979—Kansas City	Amer.		OF	154	588	113	185	18	13	6	49	.315	384	12	6	.985
1980—Kansas City	Amer.		OF	161	*705	*133	*230	28	●15	3	49	.326	482	9	6	.988
1981—Kansas City	Amer.		OF	102	439	54	133	10	7	1	32	.303	299	*14	4	.987
1982—Kansas City	Amer.		OF	136	585	87	194	19	*15	3	46	*.332	215	8	3	.987
1983—Kansas City†‡	Amer.		OF	137	576	90	159	22	8	2	33	.276	354	3	9	.975
1984—Kansas City	Amer.		OF	128	541	81	163	24	9	2	44	.301	383	6	4	.990
1985—Kansas City	Amer.		OF	141	605	87	168	25	*21	4	43	.278	378	4	2	.995
Major League Totals—10 Years				1111	4277	698	1287	156	92	21	313	.301	2696	63	40	.986

Selected by Kansas City Royals' organization in 1st round (18th player selected) of free-agent draft, June 5, 1974.
†On disabled list, August 21 to September 6, 1983.
‡On suspended list, December 15, 1983 through May 15, 1984.

DIVISION SERIES RECORD

Year	Club	League	Pos.	G.	AB.	R.	H.	2B.	3B.	HR.	RBI.	B.A.	PO.	A.	E.	F.A.
1981—Kansas City	Amer.		OF	3	13	0	4	0	0	0	1	.308	6	0	0	1.000

CHAMPIONSHIP SERIES RECORD

Established American League Championship Series record for most singles, seven-game Series (8), 1985.
Tied American League Championship Series records for most times on losing club (4); most hits, seven-game Series (9), 1985.

Year	Club	League	Pos.	G.	AB.	R.	H.	2B.	3B.	HR.	RBI.	B.A.	PO.	A.	E.	F.A.
1978—Kansas City	Amer.		PR-OF	3	4	0	1	0	0	0	0	.250	2	0	0	1.000
1980—Kansas City	Amer.		OF	3	13	2	4	2	1	0	4	.308	6	1	0	1.000
1984—Kansas City	Amer.		OF	3	13	0	2	0	0	0	0	.154	10	0	0	1.000
1985—Kansas City	Amer.		OF	7	29	5	9	0	0	1	2	.310	12	0	0	1.000
Championship Series Totals—4 Years				16	59	7	16	2	1	1	6	.271	30	1	0	1.000

WORLD SERIES RECORD

Established World Series record for most strikeouts, six-game and any length Series (12), 1980.
Tied World Series record for most at bats, inning (2), October 18, 1980 (first inning).

Year	Club	League	Pos.	G.	AB.	R.	H.	2B.	3B.	HR.	RBI.	B.A.	PO.	A.	E.	F.A.
1980—Kansas City	Amer.		OF	6	26	3	4	1	0	0	0	.154	15	1	0	1.000
1985—Kansas City	Amer.		OF	7	30	2	11	0	1	0	3	.367	19	1	0	1.000
World Series Totals—2 Years				13	56	5	15	1	1	0	3	.268	34	2	0	1.000

Year League	Pos.	AB.	R.	H.	2B.	3B.	HR.	RBI.	B.A.	PO.	A.	E.	F.A.
1982—American	OF	2	0	0	0	0	0	0	.000	1	0	0	1.000
1983—American	OF	1	0	1	1	0	0	1	1.000	2	0	0	1.000
All-Star Game Totals—2 Years		3	0	1	1	0	0	1	.333	3	0	0	1.000

ROBERT PAUL WINE JR.
(Robbie)

Born July 13, 1962, at Norristown, Pa.
Height, 6.02. Weight, 190.
Throws and bats righthanded.
Attended Oklahoma State University, Stillwater, Okla.
Son of Bobby Wine Sr., shortstop with Philadelphia Phillies and Montreal Expos, 1960 and 1962 through 1972;
coach, Philadelphia Phillies, 1972 through 1983; coach with Atlanta Braves, 1985;
interim manager, Atlanta Braves, August 26, 1985 through remainder of season;
and scout, Atlanta Braves, 1984 and 1986.

Led Southern League catchers in putouts with 502 and passed balls with 18 in 1985.
Led Florida State League catchers in assists with 124, double plays with 14, passed balls with 25 and total chances with 743 in 1984.
Named College Player of the Year by THE SPORTING NEWS, 1983.
Named catcher on THE SPORTING NEWS College Baseball All-America Team, 1983.

Year Club	League	Pos.	G.	AB.	R.	H.	2B.	3B.	HR.	RBI.	B.A.	PO.	A.	E.	F.A.
1983 Auburn	NYP	C	53	108	33	48	15	3	5	22	.343	327	35	6	.984
1984—Daytona Beach	Fla. St.	C-3B	124	430	66	105	*36	2	13	79	.244	601	126	18	.976
1985—Columbus	South.	C-OF	109	384	53	73	13	2	21	55	.190	503	63	8	.986

Selected by Houston Astros' organization in 1st round (eighth player selected) of free-agent draft, June 6, 1983.

DAVID MARK WINFIELD
(Dave)

Born October 3, 1951, at St. Paul, Minn.
Height, 6.06. Weight, 220.
Throws and bats righthanded.
Attended University of Minnesota, Minneapolis, Minn.

Major League stolen bases: 1974 (9), 1975 (23), 1976 (26), 1977 (16), 1978 (21), 1979 (15), 1980 (23), 1981 (11), 1982 (5), 1983 (15), 1984 (6), 1985 (19). Total—189.
Led National League in total bases with 333 and intentional bases on balls received with 24 in 1979.
Named outfielder on THE SPORTING NEWS American League All-Star Team, 1982 through 1984.
Named outfielder on THE SPORTING NEWS National League All-Star Team, 1979.
Named outfielder on THE SPORTING NEWS American League All-Star fielding team, 1982 through 1985.
Named outfielder on THE SPORTING NEWS National League All-Star fielding team, 1979 and 1980.
Named outfielder on THE SPORTING NEWS American League Silver Slugger team, 1981 through 1985.
Received reported $100,000 bonus to sign with San Diego Padres, 1973.
Selected by Atlanta Hawks in 5th round of 1973 NBA draft.
Selected by Utah Stars in 6th round of 1973 ABA draft.
Selected by Minnesota Vikings in 17th round of 1973 NFL draft.
Named outfielder on THE SPORTING NEWS College Baseball All-America Team, 1973.

Year Club	League	Pos.	G.	AB.	R.	H.	2B.	3B.	HR.	RBI.	B.A.	PO.	A.	E.	F.A.
1973—San Diego	Nat.	OF-1B	56	141	9	39	4	1	3	12	.277	65	1	3	.957
1974—San Diego	Nat.	OF	145	498	57	132	18	4	20	75	.265	276	11	●12	.960
1975—San Diego	Nat.	OF	143	509	74	136	20	2	15	76	.267	302	9	9	.972
1976—San Diego	Nat.	OF	137	492	81	139	26	4	13	69	.283	304	*15	6	.982
1977—San Diego	Nat.	OF	157	615	104	169	29	7	25	92	.275	368	15	11	.972
1978—San Diego	Nat.	OF-1B	158	587	88	181	30	5	24	97	.308	328	8	7	.980
1979—San Diego	Nat.	OF	159	597	97	184	27	10	34	*118	.308	344	14	5	.986
1980—San Diego†	Nat.	OF	162	558	89	154	25	6	20	87	.276	273	20	4	.987
1981—New York	Amer.	OF	105	388	52	114	25	1	13	68	.294	196	1	3	.985
1982—New York‡	Amer.	OF	140	539	84	151	24	8	37	106	.280	279	*17	8	.974
1983—New York	Amer.	OF	152	598	99	169	26	8	32	116	.283	313	5	7	.978
1984—New York§	Amer.	OF	141	567	106	193	34	4	19	100	.340	306	3	2	.994
1985—New York	Amer.	OF	155	633	105	174	34	6	26	114	.275	316	13	3	.991
National League Totals—8 Years			1117	3997	599	1134	179	39	154	626	.284	2260	93	57	.976
American League Totals—5 Years			693	2725	446	801	143	27	127	504	.294	1410	39	23	.984
Major League Totals—13 Years			1810	6722	1045	1935	322	66	281	1130	.288	3670	132	80	.979

Selected by Baltimore Orioles' organization in 40th round of free-agent draft, June 5, 1969.
Selected by San Diego Padres' organization in 1st round (fourth player selected) of free-agent draft, June 5, 1973.
†Granted free agency, October 22, 1980; signed by New York Yankees, December 15, 1980.
‡On disabled list, May 20 to June 4, 1982.
§On disabled list, April 16 to May 1, 1984.

DIVISION SERIES RECORD

Year Club	League	Pos.	G.	AB.	R.	H.	2B.	3B.	HR.	RBI.	B.A.	PO.	A.	E.	F.A.
1981—New York	Amer.	OF	5	20	2	7	3	0	0	0	.350	10	1	0	1.000

CHAMPIONSHIP SERIES RECORD

Year Club	League	Pos.	G.	AB.	R.	H.	2B.	3B.	HR.	RBI.	B.A.	PO.	A.	E.	F.A.
1981—New York	Amer.	OF	3	13	2	2	1	0	0	2	.154	6	0	0	1.000

WORLD SERIES RECORD

Tied World Series record for fewest runs, Series (0), 1981.

Year Club	League	Pos.	G.	AB.	R.	H.	2B.	3B.	HR.	RBI.	B.A.	PO.	A.	E.	F.A.
1981—New York	Amer.	OF	6	22	0	1	0	0	0	1	.045	13	1	0	1.000

ALL-STAR GAME RECORD

Tied All-Star Game record for most at bats, game (5), July 17, 1979.

Year League	Pos.	AB.	R.	H.	2B.	3B.	HR.	RBI.	B.A.	PO.	A.	E.	F.A.
1977—National	OF	2	0	2	1	0	0	2	1.000	1	0	0	1.000
1978—National	OF	2	1	1	0	0	0	0	.500	1	0	0	1.000
1979—National	OF	5	1	1	1	0	0	1	.200	3	0	0	1.000
1980—National	OF	2	0	0	0	0	0	1	.000	2	0	0	1.000
1981—American	OF	4	0	0	0	0	0	0	.000	0	1	0	1.000
1982—American	OF	2	0	1	0	0	0	0	.500	0	0	0	.000
1983—American	OF	3	2	3	1	0	0	1	1.000	3	0	0	1.000
1984—American	OF	4	0	1	1	0	0	0	.250	2	1	0	1.000
1985—American	OF	3	0	1	0	0	0	0	.333	0	0	0	.000
All-Star Game Totals—9 Years		27	4	10	4	0	0	5	.370	12	2	0	1.000

JAMES FRANCIS WINN
(Jim)

Born September 23, 1959, at Stockton, Calif.
Height, 6.03. Weight, 190.
Throws and bats righthanded.
Attended John Brown University, Siloam Springs, Ark.

Major League saves: 1984 (1).

Year Club	League	G.	IP.	W.	L.	Pct.	H.	R.	ER.	SO.	BB.	ERA.
1981—Bradenton Pirates	Gulf Coast	1	4	0	0	.000	1	0	0	6	0	0.00
1981—Buffalo	Eastern	12	65	2	5	.286	60	40	33	44	23	4.57
1982—Buffalo†	Eastern	3	6⅔	0	2	.000	6	7	4	7	5	5.40
1982—Alexandria	Carolina	7	28	1	2	.333	31	17	12	20	11	3.86
1983—Pittsburgh	National	7	11	0	0	.000	12	9	9	3	6	7.36
1983—Hawaii	P. Coast	31	38⅔	0	1	.000	49	23	17	22	22	3.96
1984—Hawaii	P. Coast	21	44⅔	6	1	.857	44	19	17	28	28	3.43
1984—Pittsburgh	National	9	18⅔	1	0	1.000	19	8	8	11	9	3.86
1985—Hawaii	P. Coast	7	42⅔	5	2	.714	31	19	16	33	20	3.38
1985—Pittsburgh	National	30	75⅔	3	6	.333	77	45	44	22	31	5.23
Major League Totals—3 Years		46	105⅓	4	6	.400	108	62	61	36	46	5.21

Selected by Pittsburgh Pirates' organization in 1st round (14th player selected) of free-agent draft, June 8, 1981.
†On disabled list, April 12 to May 24 and June 8 to July 16, 1982.

HERMAN S. WINNINGHAM
(Herm)

Born December 1, 1961, at Orangeburg, S.C.
Height, 6.00. Weight, 165.
Throws right and bats lefthanded.
Attended DeKalb Community College South, Decatur, Ga.

Major League stolen bases: 1984 (2), 1985 (20). Total—22.

Year Club	League	Pos.	G.	AB.	R.	H.	2B.	3B.	HR.	RBI.	B.A.	PO.	A.	E.	F.A.
1981—Kingsport	Appal.	OF	58	204	44	52	7	4	2	14	.255	128	3	2	*.985
1982—Lynchburg	Carol.	OF	120	430	65	127	20	5	6	61	.295	235	6	5	.980
1983—Jackson	Texas	OF	78	288	54	102	13	6	4	41	.354	157	5	6	.964
1983—Tidewater†	Int.	OF	29	113	18	30	5	2	1	11	.265	70	1	3	.959
1984—Tidewater	Int.	OF	115	406	50	114	20	3	3	47	.281	228	8	4	.983
1984—New York‡	Nat.	OF	14	27	5	11	1	1	0	5	.407	7	0	0	1.000
1985—Montreal§	Nat.	OF	125	312	30	74	6	5	3	21	.237	229	6	4	.983
1985—Indianapolis	A. A.	OF	11	35	3	6	0	0	0	2	.171	22	0	1	.957
Major League Totals—2 Years		139	339	35	85	7	6	3	26	.251	236	6	4	.984

Selected by Pittsburgh Pirates' organization in 38th round of free-agent draft, June 5, 1979.
Selected by Milwaukee Brewers' organization in secondary phase of free-agent draft, January 8, 1980.
Selected by Montreal Expos' organization in secondary phase of free-agent draft, June 3, 1980.
Selected by New York Mets' organization in secondary phase of free-agent draft, January 13, 1981.
†On disabled list, August 9 to September 20, 1983.
‡Traded with Infielder Hubie Brooks, Catcher Mike Fitzgerald and Pitcher Floyd Youmans to Montreal Expos for Catcher Gary Carter, December 10, 1984.
§On disabled list, June 24 to July 13, 1985; included rehabilitation disability assignment to Indianapolis, July 4 to July 13, 1985.

MATTHEW LIITTLETON WINTERS
(Matt)

Born March 18, 1960, at Buffalo, N.Y.
Height, 6.03. Weight, 200.
Throws right and bats lefthanded.

Led South Atlantic League in bases on balls received with 118 in 1982.
Led South Atlantic League in game-winning RBIs with 12 in 1980 and tied for lead with 12 in 1982.

Named South Atlantic League Most Valuable Player, 1982.

Year Club	League	Pos.	G.	AB.	R.	H.	2B.	3B.	HR.	RBI.	B.A.	PO.	A.	E.	F.A.
1978—Oneonta	NYP	OF	60	203	38	53	7	*11	2	36	.261	79	6	4	.955
1979—Fort Lauderdale	Fla. St.	OF	34	89	8	14	2	1	1	10	.157	28	1	2	.935
1979—Oneonta	NYP	OF-1B	62	188	40	53	6	2	●10	38	.282	79	2	4	.953
1980—Greensboro	S. Atl.	OF-1B	112	363	72	116	15	2	20	92	.320	165	10	7	.962
1981—Greensboro	S. Atl.	OF-1B	125	404	85	121	23	2	16	76	.300	109	10	5	.960
1982—Greensboro	S. Atl.	OF-1B	104	326	76	106	20	2	20	93	.325	163	3	3	.982
1982—Nashville	South.	OF	29	99	22	30	5	2	4	17	.303	40	3	0	1.000
1983—Columbus	Int.	OF	133	431	89	126	24	3	29	99	.292	150	2	2	.987
1984—Columbus	Int.	OF-1B	130	407	57	101	17	4	10	54	.248	206	14	3	.987
1985—Columbus†	Int.	OF	45	130	19	40	14	1	3	19	.308	45	1	1	.979
1985—Albany‡	East.	OF	14	47	7	13	2	0	2	6	.277	19	0	0	1.000

Selected by New York Yankees' organization in 1st round (24th player selected) of free-agent draft, June 6, 1978.
†On disabled list, April 22 to July 7, 1985.
‡Released, November 12, 1985; signed by Chicago White Sox' organization, December 22, 1985.

MICHAEL ALLEN WISHNEVSKI
(Mike)

Born March 29, 1961, at Johnstown, Pa.
Height, 6.00. Weight, 207.
Throws and bats lefthanded.
Attended Indiana Central University, Indianapolis, Ind.

Year Club	League	Pos.	G.	AB.	R.	H.	2B.	3B.	HR.	RBI.	B.A.	PO.	A.	E.	F.A.
1982—Wausau	Midw.	OF	59	176	25	51	7	2	4	14	.290	38	2	3	.930
1983—Wausau	Midw.					(Did not play)									
1984—Wausau	Midw.	OF	110	361	52	96	18	0	11	57	.266	127	13	8	.946
1985—Salinas	Calif.	OF	119	414	70	125	26	6	13	91	.302	189	8	6	.970

Selected by Seattle Mariners' organization in 2nd round of free-agent draft, June 7, 1982.

MICHAEL ATWATER WITT
(Mike)

Born July 20, 1960, at Fullerton, Calif.
Height, 6.07. Weight, 185.
Throws and bats righthanded.
Attending Cypress Junior College, Cypress, Calif.
Pitched 1-0 perfect game against Texas Rangers, September 30, 1984.
Major League saves: 1983 (5).
Tied for American League lead in hit batsmen with 11 in 1981.

Year Club	League	G.	IP.	W.	L.	Pct.	H.	R.	ER.	SO.	BB.	ERA.
1978—Idaho Falls	Pioneer	13	86	7	1	.875	88	45	34	79	26	3.56
1979—Salinas	California	30	141	8	10	.444	156	96	80	94	70	5.11
1980—Salinas	California	13	90	7	3	.700	85	30	21	76	35	2.10
1980—El Paso	Texas	12	70	5	5	.500	72	53	45	64	39	5.79
1981—California	American	22	129	8	9	.471	123	60	47	75	47	3.28
1982—California	American	33	179⅔	8	6	.571	177	77	70	85	47	3.51
1983—California	American	43	154	7	14	.333	173	90	84	77	75	4.91
1984—California	American	34	246⅔	15	11	.577	227	103	95	196	84	3.47
1985—California	American	35	250	15	9	.625	228	115	99	180	98	3.56
Major League Totals—5 Years		167	959⅓	53	49	.520	928	445	395	613	351	3.71

Selected by California Angels' organization in 4th round of free-agent draft, June 6, 1978.

CHAMPIONSHIP SERIES RECORD

Year Club	League	G.	IP.	W.	L.	Pct.	H.	R.	ER.	SO.	BB.	ERA.
1982—California	American	1	3	0	0	.000	2	2	2	3	2	6.00

ROBERT ANDREW WITT
(Bobby)

Born May 11, 1964, at Canton, Mass.
Height, 6.02. Weight, 190.
Throws and bats righthanded.
Attended University of Oklahoma, Norman, Okla.
Named as righthanded pitcher on THE SPORTING NEWS College Baseball All-America Team, 1985.
Member of 1984 U.S. Olympic baseball team.

Year Club	League	G.	IP.	W.	L.	Pct.	H.	R.	ER.	SO.	BB.	ERA.
1985—Tulsa	Texas	11	35	0	6	.000	26	26	25	39	44	6.43

Selected by Cincinnati Reds' organization in 7th round of free-agent draft, June 7, 1982.
Selected by Texas Rangers' organization in 1st round (third player selected) of free-agent draft, June 3, 1985.

—DID YOU KNOW—

That Joe DiMaggio holds the record for playing the most consecutive complete All-Star Games? He played the entire game from 1936 through 1942, a period of seven years. Those also were his first seven years in the major leagues.

JOHNNY BILTON WOCKENFUSS

Name pronounced WAHK-en-fuss.

(John)

Born February 27, 1949, at Welch, W. Va.
Height, 6.00. Weight, 180.
Throws and bats righthanded.

Tied major league record for most unassisted double plays by catcher, game (1), June 21, 1975.
Major League stolen bases: 1979 (2), 1980 (1), 1983 (1), 1984 (1). Total—5.
Led American Association in passed balls with 10 in 1974.
Led Eastern League catchers in putouts with 770 and tied for lead in passed balls with 24 in 1972.
Led Eastern League outfielders in fielding percentage with .987 in 1970.

Year	Club	League	Pos.	G.	AB.	R.	H.	2B.	3B.	HR.	RBI.	B.A.	PO.	A.	E.	F.A.
1967—Geneva	NYP	OF	3	7	0	1	0	0	0	1	.143	0	0	1	.000
1968—Geneva	NYP	OF-3B	39	132	13	26	1	1	4	17	.197	50	5	7	.887
1969—Burlington	Carol.	OF	62	197	23	33	7	1	4	15	.168	110	4	4	.966
1969—Shelby	W. Car.	OF	39	157	26	51	12	0	7	29	.325	77	7	4	.955
1970—Pittsfield	East.	OF-3B-2B	123	429	65	106	11	6	15	47	.247	219	11	4	.983
1971—Pittsfield	East.	OF-C	103	331	37	77	11	1	9	41	.233	182	5	3	.984
1972—Pittsfield	East.	★C-OF	125	410	57	118	20	2	9	60	.288	772	★68	7	★.992
1973—Spokane†	P. C.	C-OF	20	54	6	11	2	0	1	6	.204	64	4	3	.953
1973—Tulsa‡	A. A.	C-OF	60	184	22	49	12	1	2	22	.266	298	32	5	.985
1974—Evansville	A. A.	C	84	233	40	64	11	2	10	43	.275	412	41	10	.978
1974—Detroit	Amer.	C	13	29	1	4	1	0	0	2	.138	45	10	4	.932
1975—Evansville	A. A.	C-OF	43	142	20	41	11	0	6	28	.289	174	26	3	.985
1975—Detroit	Amer.	C	35	118	15	27	6	3	4	13	.229	195	23	4	.982
1976—Detroit	Amer.	C	60	144	18	32	7	2	3	10	.222	221	19	15	.941
1977—Detroit	Amer.	C-OF	53	164	26	45	8	1	9	25	.274	181	20	3	.985
1978—Detroit	Amer.	OF	71	187	23	53	5	0	7	22	.283	89	2	2	.978
1979—Detroit	Amer.	1B-C-OF	87	231	27	61	9	1	15	46	.264	318	26	3	.991
1980—Detroit	Amer.	1B-OF-C	126	372	56	102	13	2	16	65	.274	575	47	11	.983
1981—Detroit	Amer.	1B-C-OF	70	172	20	37	4	0	9	25	.215	197	6	3	.985
1982—Detroit	Amer.	C-1-O-3	70	193	28	58	9	0	8	32	.301	228	14	2	.992
1983—Detroit§	Amer.	C-1-3-O	92	245	32	66	8	1	9	44	.269	225	21	2	.992
1984—Philadelphia	Nat.	1B-C-3B	86	180	20	52	3	1	6	24	.289	323	20	7	.980
1985—Philadelphia x	Nat.	1B-C	32	37	1	6	0	0	0	2	.162	44	1	0	1.000
American League Totals—10 Years			677	1855	246	485	70	10	80	284	.261	2274	188	51	.980
National League Totals—2 Years			118	217	21	58	3	1	6	26	.267	367	21	7	.982
Major League Totals—12 Years			795	2072	267	543	73	11	86	310	.262	2641	209	58	.980

Selected by Washington Senators' organization in 42nd round of free-agent draft, June 6, 1967.
†Traded with Pitcher Mike Nagy to St. Louis Cardinals for Pitcher Jim Bibby, June 6, 1973.
‡Traded to Detroit Tigers for Infielder Larry Elliott, December 3, 1973.
§Traded with Outfielder Glenn Wilson to Philadelphia Phillies for First Baseman Dave Bergman and Pitcher Willie Hernandez, March 24, 1984.
xReleased, August 19, 1985.

JAMES EUGENE WOHLFORD

(Jim)

Born February 28, 1951, at Visalia, Calif.
Height, 5.11. Weight, 175.
Throws and bats righthanded.
Attended College of the Sequoias, Visalia, Calif.

Major League stolen bases: 1973 (1), 1974 (16), 1975 (12), 1976 (22), 1977 (17), 1978 (3), 1979 (6), 1980 (1), 1982 (8), 1984 (3). Total—89.
Led Pioneer League in stolen bases with 32 in 1970.
Led American Association second basemen in errors with 27 in 1972.
Led Pioneer League shortstops in errors with 33 in 1970.

Year	Club	League	Pos.	G.	AB.	R.	H.	2B.	3B.	HR.	RBI.	B.A.	PO.	A.	E.	F.A.
1970—Billings	Pion.	SS-2B-3B	62	221	42	68	7	2	3	37	.308	72	158	36	.865
1971—San Jose	Calif.	2B-SS	120	491	82	149	27	6	11	41	.303	193	327	30	.945
1972—Omaha	A. A.	2B-3B-OF	132	475	75	138	13	10	7	47	.291	247	292	32	.944
1972—Kansas City	Amer.	2B	15	25	3	6	1	0	0	0	.240	7	12	1	.950
1973—Omaha	A. A.	OF	65	246	30	76	9	4	3	30	.309	91	5	2	.980
1973—Kansas City	Amer.	OF	45	109	21	29	1	3	2	10	.266	31	2	0	1.000
1974—Kansas City	Amer.	OF	143	501	55	136	16	7	2	44	.271	273	7	5	.982
1975—Kansas City	Amer.	OF	116	353	45	90	10	5	0	30	.255	175	9	9	.953
1976—Kansas City†	Amer.	OF-2B	107	293	47	73	10	2	1	24	.249	190	8	5	.975
1977—Milwaukee	Amer.	OF-2B	129	391	41	97	16	3	2	36	.248	246	7	5	.981
1978—Milwaukee	Amer.	OF	46	118	16	35	7	2	1	19	.297	52	2	1	.982
1979—Milwaukee‡	Amer.	OF	63	175	19	46	13	1	1	17	.263	126	0	4	.969
1980—San Francisco	Nat.	OF-3B	91	193	17	54	6	4	1	24	.280	89	3	2	.979
1981—San Francisco	Nat.	OF	50	68	4	11	3	0	1	7	.162	3	1	0	1.000
1982—San Francisco§	Nat.	OF	97	250	37	64	12	1	2	25	.256	122	4	1	.992
1983—Montreal	Nat.	OF	83	141	7	39	8	0	1	14	.277	80	2	1	.988
1984—Montreal x	Nat.	OF-3B	95	213	20	64	13	2	5	29	.300	85	4	1	.989
1985—Montreal	Nat.	OF	70	125	7	24	5	1	1	15	.192	58	1	0	1.000
American League Totals—8 Years			664	1965	247	512	74	23	9	190	.261	1100	47	30	.975
National League Totals—6 Years			486	990	92	256	47	8	11	114	.259	437	15	5	.989
Major League Totals—14 Years			1150	2955	339	768	121	31	20	304	.260	1537	62	35	.979

Selected by California Angels' organization in 11th round of free-agent draft, June 5, 1969.
Selected by Kansas City Royals' organization in secondary phase of free-agent draft, January 17, 1970.
†Traded with Infielder Jamie Quirk and a player to be named later to Milwaukee Brewers for Pitcher Jim Colborn and Catcher Darrell Porter, December 6, 1976; Milwaukee acquired Pitcher Bob McClure to complete deal, March 15, 1977.
‡Granted free agency, November 1, 1979; signed by San Francisco Giants, November 28, 1979.
§Traded to Montreal Expos for Infielder Chris Smith, February 2, 1983.
xGranted free agency, November 8, 1984; re-signed by Expos, January 11, 1985.

CHAMPIONSHIP SERIES RECORD

Year	Club	League	Pos.	G.	AB.	R.	H.	2B.	3B.	HR.	RBI.	B.A.	PO.	A.	E.	F.A.
1976—Kansas City		Amer.	OF-PH	5	11	3	2	0	0	0	0	.182	7	0	0	1.000

EDWARD DAVID WOJNA

Name pronounced WOHJ-nuh.

(Ed)

Born August 20, 1960, at Bridgeport, Conn.
Height, 6.01. Weight, 195.
Throws and bats righthanded.
Attended Indian River Community College, Ft. Pierce, Fla.

Led Eastern League in hit batsmen with 9 in 1983.
Tied for Pacific Coast League lead in wild pitches with 16 in 1984.

Year	Club	League	G.	IP.	W.	L.	Pct.	H.	R.	ER.	SO.	BB.	ERA.
1981—Spartanburg		S. Atlantic	27	178	11	13	.458	181	●107	●82	130	69	4.15
1982—Peninsula		Carolina	27	176⅔	12	8	.600	156	79	57	116	49	2.90
1983—Reading†		Eastern	28	161⅔	13	7	.650	147	80	66	83	78	3.67
1984—Las Vegas		P. Coast	29	159⅓	14	8	.636	182	99	90	95	81	5.08
1985—Las Vegas		P. Coast	18	111⅓	5	8	.385	121	63	55	66	43	4.45
1985—San Diego		National	15	42	2	4	.333	53	35	27	18	19	5.79
Major League Totals—1 Year			15	42	2	4	.333	53	35	27	18	19	5.79

Selected by Baltimore Orioles' organization in 6th round of free-agent draft, January 8, 1980.
Selected by Philadelphia Phillies' organization in secondary phase of free-agent draft, June 3, 1980.
†Traded with Pitchers Marty Decker, Darren Burroughs and Lance McCullers to San Diego Padres, September 20, 1983, as partial completion of deal in which San Diego traded Outfielder Sixto Lezcano and a player to be named later to Philadelphia Phillies for four players to be named later, August 31, 1983; Philadelphia organization acquired Pitcher Steve Fireovid to complete deal, October 11, 1983.

MICHAEL CARY WOODARD

(Mike)

Born March 2, 1960, at Melrose Park, Ill.
Height, 5.09. Weight, 155.
Throws right and bats lefthanded.

Major League stolen bases: 1985 (6).
Led Eastern League in stolen bases with 54 in 1982.
Led Eastern League in caught stealing with 23 in 1981.
Led Pacific Coast League second basemen in total chances with 702 and double plays with 89 in 1985.
Led Northwest League second basemen in double plays with 34 in 1978.

Year	Club	League	Pos.	G.	AB.	R.	H.	2B.	3B.	HR.	RBI.	B.A.	PO.	A.	E.	F.A.
1978—Bend		N'west	2B	62	231	45	79	8	1	0	12	.342	141	136	●20	.933
1979—Modesto		Calif.	2B	118	431	90	124	8	3	2	31	.288	230	253	★30	.942
1980—Modesto		Calif.	2B-OF	73	289	52	86	8	1	0	32	.298	177	165	19	.947
1980—West Haven†		East.	2B	6	13	2	0	0	0	0	0	.000	8	9	2	.895
1981—West Haven		East.	2B	133	427	59	96	9	3	1	25	.225	249	299	19	.967
1982—West Haven‡		East.	2B-3B	104	348	55	95	13	1	1	43	.273	198	208	13	.969
1983—Tacoma		P. C.	2B-SS-3B	122	323	45	78	7	1	0	27	.241	120	236	12	.967
1984—Albany		East.	2B	23	96	19	34	2	0	0	9	.354	62	72	6	.957
1984—Tacoma§		P. C.	2B-OF-SS	95	325	47	89	8	2	1	17	.274	191	229	6	.986
1985—Phoenix		P. C.	2B	140	★573	85	★181	16	9	3	63	.316	★283	★404	15	.979
1985—San Francisco		Nat.	2B	24	82	12	20	1	0	0	9	.244	49	46	1	.990
Major League Totals—1 Year			24	82	12	20	1	0	0	9	.244	49	46	1	.990

Selected by Oakland A's organization in 4th round of free-agent draft, June 6, 1978.
†On disabled list, July 8, 1980 through remainder of season.
‡On disabled list, July 4 to July 14 and July 20 to July 31, 1982.
§Granted free agency, October 15, 1984; signed by Phoenix (San Francisco Giants' organization), November 20, 1984.

GARY LEE WOODS

Born July 20, 1954, at Santa Barbara, Calif.
Height, 6.02. Weight, 190.
Throws and bats righthanded.
Attended Santa Barbara City Junior College, Santa Barbara, Calif.

Major League stolen bases: 1977 (5), 1978 (1), 1980 (1), 1981 (2), 1982 (3), 1983 (5), 1984 (2). Total—19.
Led Pacific Coast League outfielders in putouts with 354 in 1976.

Year Club League	Pos.	G.	AB.	R.	H.	2B.	3B.	HR.	RBI.	B.A.	PO.	A.	E.	F.A.
1973—Lewiston .... N'west.	OF	63	220	23	45	7	3	2	15	.205	87	2	7	.927
1974—Burlington .... Midw.	OF	117	405	68	115	*30	3	11	59	.284	228	4	8	.967
1975—Birmingham .... South.	OF	134	484	76	126	15	6	1	43	.260	355	*20	7	.982
1976—Tucson .... P. C.	OF-3B	137	526	79	162	22	6	8	67	.308	355	14	13	.966
1976—Oakland† .... Amer.	OF	6	8	0	1	0	0	0	0	.125	7	0	0	1.000
1977—Toronto .... Amer.	OF	60	227	21	49	9	1	0	17	.216	154	4	1	.994
1977—Toledo .... Int.	OF	89	313	46	85	17	4	4	33	.272	231	5	6	.975
1978—Syracuse .... Int.	OF	133	504	74	136	*33	6	13	45	.270	*316	8	11	.967
1978—Toronto‡ .... Amer.	OF	8	19	1	3	1	0	0	0	.158	12	0	0	1.000
1979—Charleston§ .... Int.	OF	97	338	46	90	25	1	6	49	.266	253	7	9	.967
1980—Tucson .... P. C.	OF	140	517	102	162	*42	6	8	86	.313	264	13	5	.982
1980—Houston .... Nat.	OF	19	53	8	20	5	0	2	15	.377	19	1	0	1.000
1981—Houston x.............. Nat.	OF	54	110	10	23	4	1	0	12	.209	61	1	1	.984
1982—Chicago .... Nat.	OF	117	245	28	66	15	1	4	30	.269	161	6	0	1.000
1983—Chicago y.............. Nat.	OF-2B	93	190	25	46	9	0	4	22	.242	97	4	3	.971
1984—Chicago .... Nat.	OF-2B	87	98	13	23	4	1	3	10	.235	54	3	0	1.000
1985—Chicago z............. Nat.	OF	81	82	11	20	3	0	0	4	.244	42	1	0	1.000
American League Totals—3 Years		74	254	22	53	10	1	0	17	.209	173	4	1	.994
National League Totals—6 Years		451	778	95	198	40	3	13	93	.254	434	16	4	.991
Major League Totals—9 Years		525	1032	117	251	50	4	13	110	.243	607	20	5	.992

Signed as free agent by Oakland A's organization, May 12, 1973.
†Selected by Toronto Blue Jays in American League expansion draft, November 5, 1976.
‡Traded to Houston Astros for Outfielder Don Pisker, December 5, 1978.
§On disabled list, July 14 to August 13, 1979.
xTraded to Chicago Cubs' organization for Outfielder Jim Tracy, December 9, 1981.
yOn disabled list, July 15 to July 30, 1983.
zOn disabled list, April 11 to April 26, 1985.

DIVISION SERIES RECORD

Year Club League	Pos.	G.	AB.	R.	H.	2B.	3B.	HR.	RBI.	B.A.	PO.	A.	E.	F.A.
1981—Houston .... Nat.	PH	2	2	0	0	0	0	0	0	.000	0	0	0	.000

CHAMPIONSHIP SERIES RECORD

Year Club League	Pos.	G.	AB.	R.	H.	2B.	3B.	HR.	RBI.	B.A.	PO.	A.	E.	F.A.
1980—Houston .... Nat.	OF-PH	4	8	0	2	0	0	0	1	.250	1	0	0	1.000
1984—Chicago .... Nat.	PH-OF	1	1	0	0	0	0	0	0	.000	1	0	0	1.000
Championship Series Totals—2 Years		5	9	0	2	0	0	0	1	.222	2	0	0	1.000

TONY VERDELLE WOODS

Born January 6, 1962, at Merced, Calif.
Height, 6.02. Weight, 185.
Throws and bats righthanded.
Attended Whittier College, Whittier, Calif.

Led New York-Pennsylvania League shortstops in total chances with 339 in 1982.
Tied for Midwest League lead in errors by third basemen with 29 in 1983.

Year Club League	Pos.	G.	AB.	R.	H.	2B.	3B.	HR.	RBI.	B.A.	PO.	A.	E.	F.A.
1982—Geneva................... NYP	SS	73	282	45	74	11	2	9	45	.262	112	197	30	.912
1983—Quad Cities† .... Midw.	3B-SS	122	425	59	118	20	7	5	63	.278	88	252	31	.916
1984—Midland‡ .... Texas	3B	73	242	26	68	7	2	7	29	.281	50	98	11	.931
1985—Iowa .... A. A.	3B	22	74	11	17	5	1	1	4	.230	18	30	4	.923
1985—Pittsfield .... East.	3B	78	242	27	60	11	0	2	29	.248	56	105	20	.890

Selected by Chicago Cubs' organization in 1st round (17th player selected) of free-agent draft, June 7, 1982.
†On disabled list, May 18 to May 28, 1983.
‡On disabled list, April 20 to June 7, 1984.

ROBERT JOHN WOODWARD
(Rob)

Born September 28, 1962, at Hanover, N.H.
Height, 6.03. Weight, 185.
Throws and bats righthanded.

Led Eastern League pitchers in hit batsmen with 12 and tied for lead in games started with 27 in 1984.
Tied for Carolina League lead in games started by pitchers with 29 in 1983.

Year Club	League	G.	IP.	W.	L.	Pct.	H.	R.	ER.	SO.	BB.	ERA.
1981—Elmira..............................	NYP	12	77	4	3	.571	77	38	29	47	23	3.39
1982—Winter Haven..............................	Florida St.	27	126⅔	7	9	.438	140	85	72	50	62	5.12
1983—Winston-Salem	Carolina	30	197⅔	13	11	.542	177	103	91	157	100	4.14
1984—New Britain	Eastern	28	166	10	•12	.455	167	87	73	100	65	3.96
1985—New Britain	Eastern	12	86⅓	7	5	.583	71	42	34	54	36	3.54
1985—Pawtucket	Int'national	15	82⅔	3	8	.273	79	46	41	70	41	4.46
1985—Boston	American	5	26⅔	1	0	1.000	17	8	5	16	9	1.69
Major League Totals—1 Year.............................		5	26⅔	1	0	1.000	17	8	5	16	9	1.69

Selected by Boston Red Sox' organization in 3rd round of free-agent draft, June 8, 1981.

TODD ROLAND WORRELL

Name pronounced Wor-RELL.

Born September 28, 1959, at Arcadia, Calif.
Height, 6.05. Weight, 215.
Throws and bats righthanded.
Received bachelor of science degree in Christian education from
Biola College, La Mirada, Calif.

Major League saves: 1985 (5).
Named righthanded pitcher on THE SPORTING NEWS College Baseball All-America Team, 1982.

Year Club	League	G.	IP.	W.	L.	Pct.	H.	R.	ER.	SO.	BB.	ERA.
1982—Erie	NYP	9	51⅔	4	1	.800	52	23	19	57	15	3.31
1983—Louisville	Am. Assoc.	15	79⅔	4	2	.667	76	49	42	46	42	4.74
1983—Arkansas	Texas	10	70⅓	5	2	.714	57	33	24	74	37	3.07
1984—Arkansas	Texas	18	100⅓	3	10	.231	109	72	50	88	67	4.49
1984—St. Petersburg	Florida St.	8	47⅓	3	2	.600	41	22	11	33	24	2.09
1985—Louisville	Am. Assoc.	34	127⅔	8	6	.571	114	59	51	★126	47	3.60
1985—St. Louis	National	17	21⅔	3	0	1.000	17	7	7	17	7	2.91
Major League Totals—1 Year		17	21⅔	3	0	1.000	17	7	7	17	7	2.91

Selected by St. Louis Cardinals' organization in 1st round (21st player selected) of free-agent draft, June 7, 1982.

CHAMPIONSHIP SERIES RECORD

Year Club	League	G.	IP.	W.	L.	Pct.	H.	R.	ER.	SO.	BB.	ERA.
1985—St. Louis	National	4	6⅓	1	0	1.000	4	1	1	3	2	1.42

WORLD SERIES RECORD

Tied World Series record for most consecutive strikeouts, game (6), October 24, 1985.

Year Club	League	G.	IP.	W.	L.	Pct.	H.	R.	ER.	SO.	BB.	ERA.
1985—St. Louis	National	3	4⅔	0	1	.000	4	2	2	6	2	3.86

RONALD ALLAN WOTUS
(Ron)

Born March 3, 1961, at Colchester, Conn.
Height, 6.01. Weight, 180.
Throws and bats righthanded.

Year Club	League	Pos.	G.	AB.	R.	H.	2B.	3B.	HR.	RBI.	B.A.	PO.	A.	E.	F.A.
1979—Bradenton Pir.	Gulf C.	SS-1B-3B	40	147	16	40	6	2	1	14	.272	148	93	8	.968
1979—Salem	Carol.	3B-1B	8	26	4	8	0	0	0	2	.308	17	22	2	.951
1980—Shelby†	S. Atl.	SS-3B	45	158	19	36	7	1	0	19	.228	61	105	8	.954
1981—Hagers.-Alex.	Carol.	S-3-2-1	134	487	72	138	20	4	4	63	.283	178	306	27	.947
1982—Buffalo	East.	2-O-S-1-3	86	321	50	96	13	4	8	39	.299	171	174	17	.953
1982—Portland	P. C.	2B-SS	42	145	27	42	6	5	3	23	.290	65	88	4	.975
1983—Hawaii	P. C.	2B-SS-1B	125	465	94	140	28	6	10	62	.301	286	324	19	.970
1983—Pittsburgh	Nat.	SS-2B	5	3	0	0	0	0	0	0	.000	2	2	0	1.000
1984—Hawaii	P. C.	2B-1B-SS	61	224	32	57	15	4	5	23	.254	165	148	7	.978
1984—Pittsburgh	Nat.	SS-2B	27	55	4	12	6	0	0	2	.218	28	72	2	.980
1985—Nashua‡§	East.	DH	37	102	9	19	3	2	0	14	.186	0	0	0	.000
Major League Totals—2 Years			32	58	4	12	6	0	0	2	.207	30	74	2	.981

Selected by Pittsburgh Pirates' organization in 16th round of free-agent draft, June 5, 1979.
†On disabled list, June 28, 1980 through remainder of season.
‡On Pittsburgh disabled list, March 25 to July 12, 1985.
§Granted free agency, October 15, 1985.

GEORGE DEWITT WRIGHT

Born December 22, 1958, at Oklahoma City, Okla.
Height, 5.11. Weight, 185.
Throws right and bats right and lefthanded.

Major League stolen bases: 1982 (3), 1983 (8), 1985 (4). Total—15.
Led Western Carolinas League outfielders in double plays with 6 in 1979.
Tied for Texas League lead in double plays by outfielders with 4 in 1980.

Year Club	League	Pos.	G.	AB.	R.	H.	2B.	3B.	HR.	RBI.	B.A.	PO.	A.	E.	F.A.
1977—Sarasota Rangers	Gulf C.	OF	31	87	11	16	0	2	0	8	.184	44	4	1	.980
1978—Asheville	W. Car.	OF	110	335	66	83	16	1	1	27	.248	203	15	7	.969
1979—Asheville	W. Car.	OF	115	379	53	97	17	4	4	40	.256	★245	★22	7	.974
1980—Tulsa	Texas	OF	●136	458	60	126	22	5	5	65	.275	★319	22	11	.969
1981—Tulsa	Texas	OF	●133	489	58	127	29	8	11	58	.260	286	8	7	.977
1982—Texas	Amer.	OF	150	557	69	147	20	5	11	50	.264	398	14	8	.981
1983—Texas	Amer.	OF	●162	634	79	175	28	6	18	80	.276	460	6	7	.985
1984—Texas†	Amer.	OF	101	383	40	93	19	4	9	48	.243	175	3	3	.983
1984—Oklahoma City	A. A.	DH	8	30	7	10	2	1	1	8	.333	0	0	0	.000
1985—Texas	Amer.	OF	109	363	21	69	13	0	2	18	.190	213	8	2	.991
1985—Oklahoma City	A. A.	OF	39	142	22	36	4	2	8	27	.254	108	2	1	.991
Major League Totals—4 Years			522	1937	209	484	80	15	40	196	.250	1246	31	20	.985

Selected by Texas Rangers' organization in 4th round of free-agent draft, June 7, 1977.
†On disabled list, June 12 to July 12, 1984; included rehabilitation disability assignment to Oklahoma City, June 14 to July 12, 1984.

JAMES RICHARD WRIGHT
(Ricky)

Born November 22, 1958, at Paris, Tex.
Height, 6.03. Weight, 190.
Throws and bats lefthanded.
Attended Paris Junior College, Paris, Tex.,
and University of Texas, Austin, Tex.
Nephew of Larry Click, minor league outfielder, 1957 through 1962.

Pitched 4-2 no-hit victory against Portland, May 4, 1983.
Led Texas League in wild pitches with 17 and tied for lead in balks with 4 in 1980.

Year Club	League	G.	IP.	W.	L.	Pct.	H.	R.	ER.	SO.	BB.	ERA.
1980—San Antonio†	Texas	23	152	8	10	.444	144	85	71	127	85	4.20
1981—Albuquerque	P. Coast	27	155	14	6	.700	141	81	73	112	90	4.24
1982—Albuquerque‡	P. Coast	15	60⅓	4	3	.571	63	45	38	57	36	5.67
1982—Los Angeles	National	14	32⅔	2	1	.667	28	12	11	24	20	3.03
1983—Albuquerque	P. Coast	33	83⅓	7	6	.538	75	60	45	68	58	4.86
1983—Los Angeles§	National	6	6⅓	0	0	.000	5	2	2	5	2	2.84
1983—Texas	American	1	2	0	0	.000	0	0	0	2	1	0.00
1984—Oklahoma City x	Am. Assoc.	31	48⅔	2	1	.667	37	14	13	38	24	2.40
1984—Texas	American	8	14⅔	0	2	.000	20	10	10	6	11	6.14
1985—Oklahoma City y	Am. Assoc.	17	82⅔	5	4	.556	67	30	25	55	37	2.72
1985—Texas	American	5	7⅔	0	0	.000	5	4	4	7	5	4.70
National League Totals—2 Years		20	39	2	1	.667	33	14	13	29	22	3.00
American League Totals—3 Years		14	24⅓	0	2	.000	25	14	14	15	17	5.18
Major League Totals—4 Years		34	63⅓	2	3	.400	58	28	27	44	39	3.84

Selected by St. Louis Cardinals' organization in 2nd round of free-agent draft, June 7, 1977.
Selected by Los Angeles Dodgers' organization in secondary phase of free-agent draft, January 8, 1980.
†On temporary inactive list, July 26 to August 14, 1980.
‡On disabled list, April 5 to May 10, 1982.
§Traded to Texas Rangers, September 16, 1983, completing deal in which Los Angeles Dodgers traded Pitcher Dave Stewart and a player to be named later to Texas for Pitcher Rick Honeycutt, August 19, 1983.
xOn disabled list, July 28 to August 13, 1984.
yOn disabled list, May 6 to June 18, 1985.

DAVID BRUCE WYATT

Born December 5, 1961, at Montgomery, Ala.
Height, 6.00. Weight, 175.
Throws left and bats righthanded.
Attended Alabama Christian Junior College, Montgomery, Ala.;
and Auburn University, Auburn, Ala.

Year Club	League	G.	IP.	W.	L.	Pct.	H.	R.	ER.	SO.	BB.	ERA.
1982—Little Falls	NYP	1	2	0	0	.000	0	0	0	2	2	0.00
1982—Shelby	S. Atlantic	11	23	1	0	1.000	28	6	4	13	11	1.57
1983—Lynchburg	Carolina	24	77⅓	4	2	.667	78	40	30	49	36	3.49
1984—Columbia†	S. Atlantic	13	74⅓	6	4	.600	69	45	30	55	25	3.63
1985—Lynchburg	Carolina	9	67⅓	8	1	.889	51	12	11	51	13	1.47
1985—Jackson‡	Texas	10	59⅔	6	1	.857	64	32	26	40	24	3.92

Selected by New York Mets' organization in 16th round of free-agent draft, January 12, 1982.
†On disabled list, July 16 to August 6 and August 20, 1984 through remainder of season.
‡On suspended list, April 9 to May 22, 1985.

HAROLD DELANO WYNEGAR JR.

Name pronounced WY-nuh-ger.

(Butch)

Born March 14, 1956, at York, Pa.
Height, 6.00. Weight, 194.
Throws right and bats left and righthanded.

Major League stolen bases: 1977 (2), 1978 (1), 1979 (2), 1980 (3), 1983 (1), 1984 (1). Total—10.
Led American League catchers in double plays with 13 in 1980.
Led California League in bases on balls received with 142 in 1975.
Led Appalachian League catchers in double plays with 9 in 1974.
Named American League Rookie Player of the Year by THE SPORTING NEWS, 1976.

Year Club	League	Pos.	G.	AB.	R.	H.	2B.	3B.	HR.	RBI.	B.A.	PO.	A.	E.	F.A.
1974—Elizabethton	Appal.	C	60	191	32	66	10	0	8	51	★.346	344	39	5	★.987
1975—Reno	Calif.	C	●139	468	106	147	18	6	19	★112	.314	★734	★99	9	★.989
1976—Minnesota	Amer.	C	149	534	58	139	21	2	10	69	.260	650	78	★16	.978
1977—Minnesota	Amer.	C-3B	144	532	76	139	22	3	10	79	.261	676	84	5	.993
1978—Minnesota	Amer.	C-3B	135	454	36	104	22	1	4	45	.229	582	70	8	.988
1979—Minnesota	Amer.	C	149	504	74	136	20	0	7	57	.270	653	65	6	.992
1980—Minnesota	Amer.	C	146	486	61	124	18	3	5	57	.255	670	72	9	.988
1981—Minnesota	Amer.	C	47	150	11	37	5	0	0	10	.247	162	24	1	.995
1982—Minn.‡-N.Y. §	Amer.	C	87	277	36	74	12	1	4	28	.267	523	26	5	.991
1983—New York x	Amer.	C	94	301	40	89	18	2	6	42	.296	480	29	8	.985
1984—New York	Amer.	C	129	442	48	118	13	1	6	45	.267	757	59	6	.993
1985—New York yz	Amer.	C	102	309	27	69	15	0	5	32	.223	547	34	6	.990
Major League Totals—10 Years			1282	3989	467	1029	166	13	57	464	.258	5700	541	70	.989

Selected by Minnesota Twins' organization in 2nd round of free-agent draft, June 5, 1974.
†On disabled list, April 6 to May 16 and August 26 to September 11, 1981.
‡Traded with Pitcher Roger Erickson to New York Yankees for Infielder Larry Milbourne and Pitchers John Pacella and Pete Filson, May 12, 1982.
§On disabled list, July 25 to September 1, 1982.
xOn disabled list, May 12 to May 27, 1983.
yOn disabled list, June 18 to July 18 and July 22 to August 2, 1985.
zGranted free agency, November 12, 1985; re-signed by Yankees, January 8, 1986.

ALL-STAR GAME RECORD

Year League	Pos.	AB.	R.	H.	2B.	3B.	HR.	RBI.	B.A.	PO.	A.	E.	F.A.
1976—American	PH	0	0	0	0	0	0	0	.000	0	0	0	.000
1977—American	C	2	1	1	0	0	0	0	.500	3	0	0	1.000
All-Star Game Totals—2 Years		2	1	1	0	0	0	0	.500	3	0	0	1.000

MARVELL WYNNE

Name pronounced Win.

Born December 17, 1959, at Chicago, Ill.
Height, 5.11. Weight, 176.
Throws and bats lefthanded.

Major League stolen bases: 1983 (12), 1984 (24), 1985 (10). Total—46.
Led South Atlantic League in total bases with 256 in 1980.
Led South Atlantic League outfielders in assists with 17 in 1980.
Tied for International League lead in game-winning RBIs with 14 in 1982.
Tied for Gulf Coast League lead in being hit by pitch with 5 in 1979.

Year Club	League	Pos.	G.	AB.	R.	H.	2B.	3B.	HR.	RBI.	B.A.	PO.	A.	E.	F.A.
1979—Sarasota Royals	Gulf C.	OF	50	190	21	54	6	4	4	28	.284	108	9	4	.967
1980—Charleston†	S. Atl.	OF-2B-3B	137	*547	106	152	20	*15	18	98	.278	281	19	13	.958
1981—Jackson	Texas	OF	127	497	69	142	29	2	4	50	.286	267	21	6	.980
1982—Tidewater	Int.	OF	130	512	76	118	15	7	10	65	.230	283	13	12	.961
1983—Tidewater‡	Int.	OF	51	175	32	50	13	1	3	29	.286	114	5	2	.983
1983—Pittsburgh	Nat.	OF	103	366	66	89	16	2	7	26	.243	223	3	4	.983
1984—Pittsburgh	Nat.	OF	154	653	77	174	24	11	0	39	.266	373	8	4	.990
1985—Pittsburgh§	Nat.	OF	103	337	21	69	6	3	2	18	.205	229	7	3	.987
Major League Totals—3 Years			360	1356	164	332	46	16	9	83	.245	825	18	11	.987

Signed as free agent by Kansas City Royals' organization, September 3, 1978.
†Traded with Pitcher John Skinner to New York Mets' organization for Pitcher Juan Berenguer, March 31, 1981.
‡Traded with Pitcher Steve Senteney to Pittsburgh Pirates for Catcher Junior Ortiz and Pitcher Arthur Ray, June 14, 1983.
§On disabled list, April 20 to May 5 and June 3 to June 18, 1985.

STEPHEN WAYNE YEAGER

Name pronounced YAY-gur.

(Steve)

Born November 24, 1948, at Huntington, W. Va.
Height, 6.00. Weight, 200.
Throws and bats righthanded.

Nephew of retired Air Force Brigadier General Chuck Yeager, first man to break sound barrier.

Tied major league record for most putouts, extra-inning game, catcher (22), August 8, 1972 (19 innings).
Established National League record for most chances accepted, extra-inning game, catcher (24), August 8, 1972 (19 innings).
Major League stolen bases: 1973 (1), 1974 (2), 1975 (2), 1976 (3), 1977 (1), 1979 (1), 1980 (2), 1983 (1), 1984 (1). Total—14.

Year Club	League	Pos.	G.	AB.	R.	H.	2B.	3B.	HR.	RBI.	B.A.	PO.	A.	E.	F.A.
1967—Ogden	Pion.	C	1	0	0	0	0	0	0	0	.000	0	0	0	.000
1967—Dubuque	Midw.	C-1B	14	35	0	6	0	0	0	2	.171	67	3	3	.959
1968—Daytona Beach	Fla. St.	C	59	144	17	22	3	1	1	6	.153	314	23	9	.974
1969—Bakersfield	Calif.	C	22	65	8	10	1	0	0	2	.154	145	26	4	.977
1969—Albuquerque	Texas	PH	1	1	0	0	0	0	0	0	.000	0	0	0	.000
1970—Albuquerque	Texas	C-OF-3B	55	151	23	42	5	1	3	24	.278	224	29	5	.981
1971—Albuquerque	Texas	C	107	339	49	93	16	5	8	53	.274	678	84	*14	.982
1972—Albuquerque	P. C.	C	82	257	46	72	6	6	13	45	.280	494	26	9	.983
1972—Los Angeles	Nat.	C	35	106	18	29	0	1	4	15	.274	220	19	4	.984
1973—Los Angeles	Nat.	C	54	134	18	34	5	0	2	10	.254	230	24	5	.981
1974—Los Angeles	Nat.	C	94	316	41	84	16	1	12	41	.266	552	58	5	.992
1975—Los Angeles	Nat.	C	135	452	34	103	16	1	12	54	.228	*806	62	7	.992
1976—Los Angeles	Nat.	C	117	359	42	77	11	3	11	35	.214	522	*77	9	.985
1977—Los Angeles	Nat.	C	125	387	53	99	21	2	16	55	.256	690	89	*18	.977
1978—Los Angeles†	Nat.	C	94	228	19	44	7	0	4	23	.193	373	55	5	.988
1979—Los Angeles	Nat.	C	105	310	33	67	9	2	13	41	.216	513	56	9	.984
1980—Los Angeles	Nat.	C	96	227	20	48	8	0	2	20	.211	382	36	7	.984
1981—Los Angeles	Nat.	C	42	86	5	18	2	0	3	7	.209	142	13	1	.994
1982—Los Angeles‡	Nat.	C	82	196	13	48	5	2	2	18	.245	338	42	4	.990
1983—Los Angeles§	Nat.	C	113	335	31	68	8	3	15	41	.203	579	63	10	.985
1984—Los Angeles	Nat.	C	74	197	16	45	4	0	4	29	.228	317	30	2	.994
1985—Los Angeles xy	Nat.	C	53	121	4	25	4	1	0	9	.207	212	28	2	.992
Major League Totals—14 Years			1219	3454	347	789	116	16	100	398	.228	5876	652	88	.987

Selected by Los Angeles Dodgers' organization in 4th round of free-agent draft, June 6, 1967.
†On disabled list, August 8 to August 25, 1978.
‡On disabled list, July 12 to August 9, 1982.
§On disabled list, August 1 to August 23, 1983.
xGranted free agency, November 12, 1985; re-signed by Dodgers, November 26, 1985.
yTraded to Seattle Mariners for Pitcher Ed Vande Berg, December 11, 1985.

DIVISION SERIES RECORD

Year	Club	League	Pos.	G.	AB.	R.	H.	2B.	3B.	HR.	RBI.	B.A.	PO.	A.	E.	F.A.
1981—Los Angeles		Nat.	PH-C	2	5	1	2	1	0	0	0	.400	6	0	0	1.000

CHAMPIONSHIP SERIES RECORD

Tied National League Championship Series record for most Series played, one club (6).

Year	Club	League	Pos.	G.	AB.	R.	H.	2B.	3B.	HR.	RBI.	B.A.	PO.	A.	E.	F.A.
1974—Los Angeles		Nat.	C	3	9	1	0	0	0	0	0	.000	14	1	0	1.000
1977—Los Angeles		Nat.	C	4	13	1	3	0	0	0	2	.231	22	1	0	1.000
1978—Los Angeles		Nat.	C	4	13	2	3	0	0	1	2	.231	21	2	0	1.000
1981—Los Angeles		Nat.	PH-C	1	2	1	1	0	0	0	0	.500	2	0	0	1.000
1983—Los Angeles		Nat.	C	2	6	0	1	1	0	0	0	.167	7	1	0	1.000
1985—Los Angeles		Nat.	PH-C	1	2	0	0	0	0	0	0	.000	4	0	0	1.000
Championship Series Totals—6 Years				15	45	5	8	1	0	1	4	.178	70	5	0	1.000

WORLD SERIES RECORD

Tied World Series record for most at-bats, inning (2), October 28, 1981 (sixth inning).

Year	Club	League	Pos.	G.	AB.	R.	H.	2B.	3B.	HR.	RBI.	B.A.	PO.	A.	E.	F.A.
1974—Los Angeles		Nat.	C	4	11	0	4	1	0	0	1	.364	32	4	1	.973
1977—Los Angeles		Nat.	C	6	19	2	6	1	0	2	5	.316	32	6	0	1.000
1978—Los Angeles		Nat.	C	5	13	2	3	1	0	0	0	.231	23	2	0	1.000
1981—Los Angeles		Nat.	PH-C	6	14	2	4	1	0	2	4	.286	20	0	0	1.000
World Series Totals—4 Years				21	57	6	17	4	0	4	10	.298	107	12	1	.992

RICHARD MARTIN YETT
(Rich)

Born October 6, 1962, at Pomona, Calif.
Height, 6.02. Weight, 187.
Throws and bats righthanded.

Led International League in wild pitches with 16 in 1985.

Year	Club	League	G.	IP.	W.	L.	Pct.	H.	R.	ER.	SO.	BB.	ERA.
1980—Elizabethton		Ap'lachian	10	52	3	4	.429	46	30	25	35	19	4.33
1981—Wisconsin Rapids		Midwest	25	164	12	6	.667	147	87	67	121	77	3.68
1982—Visalia		California	27	196⅔	16	9	.640	183	98	80	121	97	3.66
1983—Orlando†		Southern	24	162	8	10	.444	153	82	68	93	78	3.78
1984—Toledo		Int'national	26	174⅔	12	9	.571	159	71	63	129	66	3.25
1985—Minnesota		American	1	⅓	0	0	.000	1	1	1	0	2	27.00
1985—Toledo‡-Maine		Int'national	25	165	9	11	.450	162	82	76	99	★101	4.15
Major League Totals—1 Year			1	⅓	0	0	.000	1	1	1	0	2	27.00

Selected by Minnesota Twins' organization in 26th round of free-agent draft, June 3, 1980.
†On disabled list, April 8 to April 25, 1983.
‡Sold to Maine (Cleveland Indians' organization), September 17, 1985.

DAVID LOUIS YOBS
Name pronounced Yabs.
(Dave)

Born January 17, 1959, at Encino, Calif.
Height, 6.00. Weight, 196.
Throws and bats lefthanded.
Attended Los Angeles Valley College, Van Nuys, Calif.,
and Oral Roberts University, Tulsa, Okla.

Tied for American Association lead in sacrifice flies with 7 in 1985.

Year	Club	League	Pos.	G.	AB.	R.	H.	2B.	3B.	HR.	RBI.	B.A.	PO.	A.	E.	F.A.
1981—Appleton		Midw.	OF-1B	65	221	30	67	15	6	2	23	.303	81	5	5	.945
1982—Glens Falls†		East.	OF	119	441	72	131	26	1	25	93	.297	158	6	5	.970
1983—Denver		A. A.	OF	60	219	28	55	12	0	6	20	.251	50	4	4	.931
1983—Glens Falls		East.	OF	54	184	31	58	16	0	8	28	.315	81	3	2	.977
1984—Denver‡		A. A.	DH	93	309	43	77	10	3	10	47	.249	0	0	0	.000
1985—Buffalo§		A. A.	OF	95	280	34	84	11	1	5	37	.300	2	0	0	1.000

Selected by California Angels' organization in 10th round of free-agent draft, January 10, 1978.
Selected by New York Yankees' organization in 8th round of free-agent draft, June 3, 1980.
Selected by Chicago White Sox' organization in 14th round of free-agent draft, June 8, 1981.
†On disabled list, July 29 to August 12, 1982.
‡On disabled list, August 1 to September 16, 1984.
§On disabled list, June 24 to July 4, 1985.

EDGAR FREDERICK YOST
(Ned)

Born August 19, 1955, at Eureka, Calif.
Height, 6.01. Weight, 185.
Throws and bats righthanded.
Attended Chabot Junior College, Hayward, Calif.

Major League stolen bases: 1982 (3), 1983 (1), 1984 (1). Total—5.
Led Texas League in passed balls with 16 in 1976.

Year Club	League	Pos.	G.	AB.	R.	H.	2B.	3B.	HR.	RBI.	B.A.	PO.	A.	E.	F.A.
1974—Batavia	NYP	C	44	123	14	31	2	2	2	11	.252	199	21	*11	.952
1975—Wausau	Midwest	C	79	265	26	51	7	0	6	27	.192	450	42	●19	.963
1976—Jackson	Texas	C	83	266	25	53	5	0	3	25	.199	390	42	7	.984
1977—Jackson	Texas	C	30	94	7	29	9	0	1	8	.309	145	21	4	.976
1977—Tidewater†	Int.	C	60	165	27	48	8	1	12	31	.291	171	29	3	.985
1978—Spokane‡	P. C.	C	89	267	38	70	16	1	7	42	.262	367	49	15	.965
1979—Vancouver	P. C.	C	130	419	43	110	12	2	3	53	.263	604	64	10	.985
1980—Vancouver	P. C.	C-1B	80	259	32	80	20	4	2	41	.309	312	34	8	.977
1980—Milwaukee	Amer.	C	15	31	0	5	0	0	0	0	.161	41	5	0	1.000
1981—Milwaukee	Amer.	C	18	27	4	6	0	0	3	3	.222	37	6	2	.956
1982—Milwaukee	Amer.	C	40	98	13	27	6	3	1	8	.276	121	6	3	.977
1983—Milwaukee§x	Amer.	C	61	196	21	44	5	1	6	28	.224	252	16	8	.971
1984—Texas y	Amer.	C	80	242	15	44	4	0	6	25	.182	368	20	2	.995
1985—Indianapolis	A. A.	C-1B	95	267	17	70	15	0	2	24	.262	375	48	12	.972
1985 Montreal z	Nat.	C	5	11	1	2	0	0	0	0	.182	24	1	1	.962
American League Totals—5 Years			214	594	53	126	15	4	16	64	.212	819	53	15	.983
National League Totals—1 Year			5	11	1	2	0	0	0	0	.182	24	1	1	.962
Major League Totals—6 Years			219	605	54	128	15	4	16	64	.212	843	54	16	.982

Signed as free agent by New York Mets' organization, June 11, 1974.
†Drafted by Milwaukee Brewers, December 5, 1977.
‡On disabled list, July 10 to July 28, 1978.
§On disabled list, July 11 to August 15, 1983.
xTraded with Pitcher Dan Scarpetta to Texas Rangers for Catcher Jim Sundberg, December 8, 1983.
yReleased, April 1, 1985; signed by Montreal Expos, April 28, 1985.
zReleased, December 19, 1985.

WORLD SERIES RECORD

Year Club	League	Pos.	G.	AB.	R.	H.	2B.	3B.	HR.	RBI.	B.A.	PO.	A.	E.	F.A.
1982—Milwaukee	Amer.	C	1	0	0	0	0	0	0	0	.000	1	0	0	1.000

FLOYD EVERETT YOUMANS

Name pronounced YOO-muns.

Born May 11, 1964, at Tampa, Fla.
Height, 6.02. Weight, 180.
Throws and bats righthanded.

Year Club	League	G.	IP.	W.	L.	Pct.	H.	R.	ER.	SO.	BB.	ERA.
1982—Kingsport	Ap'lachian	10	39⅓	2	4	.333	35	39	27	31	39	6.18
1983—Columbia	S. Atlantic	23	134⅓	12	3	.800	112	77	51	117	73	3.42
1984—Lynchburg	Carolina	7	39⅔	5	2	.714	31	19	16	45	27	3.63
1984—Jackson†‡	Texas	16	86	6	7	.462	75	47	44	87	74	4.60
1985—Jacksonville	Southern	14	85⅔	7	3	.700	65	35	32	86	57	3.36
1985—Montreal	National	14	77	4	3	.571	57	27	21	54	49	2.45
1985—Indianapolis	Am. Assoc.	6	37⅔	3	2	.600	19	14	13	38	26	3.11
Major League Totals—1 Year		14	77	4	3	.571	57	27	21	54	49	2.45

Selected by New York Mets' organization in 2nd round of free-agent draft, June 7, 1982.
†On disabled list, June 11 to June 21, 1984.
‡Traded with Infielder Hubie Brooks, Catcher Mike Fitzgerald and Outfielder Herm Winningham to Montreal Expos for Catcher Gary Carter, December 10, 1984.

CURTIS ALLEN YOUNG
(Curt)

Born April 16, 1960, at Saginaw, Mich.
Height, 6.01. Weight, 175.
Throws left and bats righthanded.
Attended Central Michigan University, Mt. Pleasant, Mich.

Led California League pitchers in games started with 28 in 1982.

Year Club	League	G.	IP.	W.	L.	Pct.	H.	R.	ER.	SO.	BB.	ERA.
1981—Medford	Northwest	8	53	2	2	.500	45	27	25	49	32	4.25
1981—Modesto	California	5	31	2	1	.667	28	15	12	22	16	3.48
1982—Modesto	California	28	205	15	8	.652	189	90	79	162	81	3.47
1983—Tacoma	P. Coast	27	158⅔	12	9	.571	175	94	89	109	52	5.05
1983—Oakland	American.	8	9	0	1	.000	17	17	16	5	5	16.00
1984—Tacoma	P. Coast	14	95⅓	6	4	.600	88	45	40	61	28	3.78
1984—Oakland	American	20	108⅔	9	4	.692	118	53	49	41	31	4.06
1985—Oakland†	American	19	46	0	4	.000	57	38	37	19	22	7.24

Year	Club	League	G.	IP.	W.	L.	Pct.	H.	R.	ER.	SO.	BB.	ERA.
1985—Modesto	California	2	5⅔	0	0	.000	7	4	3	3	6	4.76
1985—Tacoma	P. Coast	3	15	2	0	1.000	10	7	6	8	7	3.60
Major League Totals—3 Years		47	163⅔	9	9	.500	192	108	102	65	58	5.61

Selected by Oakland A's organization in 4th round of free-agent draft, June 8, 1981.

†On disabled list, April 30 to July 5, 1985; included rehabilitation disability assignment to Modesto, June 29 to July 5, 1985.

JOHN ANTHONY YOUNG

Born December 14, 1960, at Meridian, Miss.
Height, 6.02. Weight, 175.
Throws left and bats righthanded.
Attended Black Hawk College, Moline, Ill., and
Bradley University, Peoria, Ill.

Led Texas League in wild pitches with 16 in 1984.

Year	Club	League	G.	IP.	W.	L.	Pct.	H.	R.	ER.	SO.	BB.	ERA.
1982—Erie	NYP	9	34	4	3	.571	35	20	18	41	21	4.76
1983—Springfield	Midwest	23	133⅓	15	4	.789	87	56	40	162	★104	2.70
1984—Arkansas†	Texas	26	151⅔	9	7	.563	132	84	60	★136	★122	3.56
1985—Jackson‡	Texas	21	112	6	3	.667	96	54	47	91	76	3.78

Selected by St. Louis Cardinals' organization in 3rd round of free-agent draft, June 7, 1982.

†Traded with Shortstop Argenis Salazar to New York Mets' organization for Shortstop Jose Oquendo and Pitcher Mark Jason Davis, April 2, 1985.

‡On disabled list, May 14 to June 2, 1985.

MATTHEW JOHN YOUNG
(Matt)

Born August 9, 1958, at Pasadena, Calif.
Height, 6.03. Weight, 200.
Throws and bats lefthanded.
Attended Pasadena City College, Pasadena, Calif., and
University of California, Los Angeles, Calif.

Major League saves: 1985 (1).

Year	Club	League	G.	IP.	W.	L.	Pct.	H.	R.	ER.	SO.	BB.	ERA.
1980—Bellingham	Northwest	12	73	4	5	.444	73	46	40	53	62	4.93
1981—Lynn	Eastern	14	81	3	9	.250	80	47	36	57	38	4.00
1982—Salt Lake City	P. Coast	29	176	12	10	.545	192	113	91	118	75	4.65
1983—Seattle	American	33	203⅔	11	15	.423	178	86	74	130	79	3.27
1984—Seattle†	American	22	113⅓	6	8	.429	141	81	72	73	57	5.72
1984—Salt Lake City	P. Coast	6	41⅔	6	0	1.000	32	9	7	37	20	1.51
1985—Seattle	American	37	218⅓	12	★19	.387	242	135	119	136	76	4.91
Major League Totals—3 Years		92	535⅓	29	42	.408	561	302	265	339	212	4.46

Selected by Boston Red Sox' organization in 2nd round of free-agent draft, January 10, 1978.

Selected by Seattle Mariners' organization in 2nd round of free-agent draft, June 3, 1980.

†On disabled list, July 4 to July 29, 1984.

ALL-STAR GAME RECORD

Year	League	IP.	W.	L.	Pct.	H.	R.	ER.	SO.	BB.	ERA.
1983—American		1	0	0	.000	0	0	0	1	0	0.00

MICHAEL DARREN YOUNG
(Mike)

Born March 20, 1960, at Hayward, Calif.
Height, 6.02. Weight, 195.
Throws right and bats left and righthanded.
Attended St. Mary's College, Moraga, Calif.; and Chabot College, Hayward, Calif.

Switch-hit home runs in one game, August 13, 1985.
Major League stolen bases: 1983 (1), 1984 (6), 1985 (1). Total—8.
Led International League batters in strikeouts with 140 in 1982.
Tied for Florida State League lead in double plays by outfielders with 4 in 1980.

Year	Club	League	Pos.	G.	AB.	R.	H.	2B.	3B.	HR.	RBI.	B.A.	PO.	A.	E.	F.A.
1980—Miami	Fla. St.	OF	115	393	72	105	13	8	5	52	.267	212	★17	7	.970
1981—Miami	Fla. St.	OF	63	235	32	81	19	6	3	34	.345	135	7	1	.993
1981—Charlotte	South.	OF	75	275	58	88	16	3	12	45	.320	190	5	5	.975
1981—Rochester	Int.	OF	1	3	0	1	0	0	0	0	.000	1	0	0	1.000
1982—Rochester	Int.	OF	137	502	86	133	22	11	16	62	.265	291	7	11	.964
1982—Baltimore	Amer.	OF	6	2	2	0	0	0	0	0	.000	1	0	0	1.000
1983—Rochester	Int.	OF	102	373	62	106	14	8	14	66	.284	198	4	6	.971
1983—Baltimore	Amer.	OF	25	36	5	6	2	1	0	2	.167	25	1	2	.929
1984—Rochester	Int.	OF	20	72	17	24	6	1	4	15	.333	39	0	3	.929
1984—Baltimore	Amer.	OF	123	401	59	101	17	2	17	52	.252	216	4	4	.982
1985—Baltimore	Amer.	OF	139	450	72	123	22	1	28	81	.273	190	6	5	.975
Major League Totals—4 Years			293	889	138	230	41	4	45	135	.259	432	11	11	.976

Selected by Cleveland Indians' organization in 7th round of free-agent draft, June 6, 1978.

Selected by Baltimore Orioles' organization in secondary phase of free-agent draft, January 8, 1980.

JOEL RANDOLPH YOUNGBLOOD III

Born August 28, 1951, at Houston, Tex.
Height, 5.11. Weight, 175.
Throws and bats righthanded.

Established major league record for most clubs, one or more hits for, one day (2), August 4, 1982.
Tied major league record for most clubs played, one day (2), August 4, 1982.
Major League stolen bases: 1976 (1), 1977 (1), 1978 (4), 1979 (18), 1980 (14), 1981 (2), 1982 (2), 1983 (7), 1984 (5), 1985
(3). Total—57.
Led National League third basemen in errors with 36 in 1984.
Led National League outfielders in double plays with 6 in 1980.
Led Northern League second basemen in errors with 19 in 1970.
Tied for Northern League lead in being hit by pitch with 5 in 1970.

Year Club	League	Pos.	G.	AB.	R.	H.	2B.	3B.	HR.	RBI.	B.A.	PO.	A.	E.	F.A.
1970—Tampa	Fla. St.	SS	17	54	7	12	0	0	0	3	.222	22	40	9	.873
1970—Sioux Falls	North.	2B-3B-SS	65	236	27	53	11	1	0	17	.225	110	134	26	.904
1971—Tampa	Fla. St.	3B-SS-OF	136	443	75	113	25	4	5	44	.255	159	207	26	.934
1972—Three Rivers	East.	OF-3B	104	366	57	106	15	5	12	60	.290	118	80	30	.868
1973—Indianapolis	A. A.	OF-SS-3B	124	451	88	143	24	9	11	50	.317	136	112	28	.899
1974—Indianapolis†	A. A.	OF	103	316	55	90	17	4	13	49	.285	115	6	4	.968
1975—Indianapolis‡	A. A.	OF-2B	123	418	65	110	21	●9	6	51	.263	201	13	7	.968
1976—Cincinnati‡	Nat.	1-O-C-2	55	57	8	11	1	1	0	1	.193	15	3	1	.947
1977—St.L.§-N.Y	Nat.	2B-OF-3B	95	209	17	51	13	1	0	12	.244	107	94	8	.962
1978—New York	Nat.	O-2-3-S	113	266	40	67	12	8	7	30	.252	160	96	13	.952
1979—New York	Nat.	OF-2B-3B	158	500	80	162	37	5	10	80	.275	307	57	9	.978
1980—New York	Nat.	OF-3B-2B	146	514	58	142	26	2	8	69	.276	318	65	13	.967
1981—New York x	Nat.	OF	43	143	16	50	10	2	4	25	.350	70	6	3	.962
1982—N.Y. y-Mont. z	Nat.	O-2-S-3	120	292	37	70	14	0	3	29	.240	149	23	7	.961
1983—San Francisco	Nat.	2B-3B-OF	124	373	59	109	20	3	17	53	.292	147	182	19	.945
1984—San Francisco	Nat.	3B-OF-2B	134	469	50	119	17	1	10	51	.254	102	206	37	.893
1985—San Francisco a	Nat.	OF-3B	95	230	24	62	6	0	4	24	.270	103	6	6	.948
Major League Totals—10 Years			1083	3143	399	843	156	23	69	354	.268	1508	738	116	.951

Selected by Cincinnati Reds' organization in 2nd round of free-agent draft, January 17, 1970.
†On disabled list, June 7 to June 19, 1974.
‡Traded to St. Louis Cardinals for Pitcher Bill Caudill, March 28, 1977.
§Traded to New York Mets for Shortstop Mike Phillips, June 15, 1977.
xOn disabled list, June 6 to August 1 and August 15 to September 15, 1981.
yTraded to Montreal Expos for a player to be named later, August 4, 1982; New York Mets' organization acquired Pitcher Tom Gorman to complete deal, August 14, 1982.
zGranted free agency, November 10, 1982; signed by San Francisco Giants, February 7, 1983.
aReleased, December 20, 1985.

ALL-STAR GAME RECORD

Year League	Pos.	AB.	R.	H.	2B.	3B.	HR.	RBI.	B.A.	PO.	A.	E.	F.A.
1981—National	PH	1	0	0	0	0	0	0	.000	0	0	0	.000

ROBIN R. YOUNT

Born September 16, 1955, at Danville, Ill.
Height, 6.00. Weight, 170.
Throws and bats righthanded.
Brother of Larry Yount, pitcher with Houston Astros, 1971.

Major League stolen bases: 1974 (7), 1975 (12), 1976 (16), 1977 (16), 1978 (16), 1979 (11), 1980 (20), 1981 (4), 1982 (14), 1983 (12), 1984 (14), 1985 (10). Total—152.
Led American League in total bases with 367 and slugging percentage with .578 in 1982.
Led American League shortstops in double plays with 104 and total chances with 831 in 1976.
Named Major League Player of the Year by THE SPORTING NEWS, 1982.
Named American League Player of the Year by THE SPORTING NEWS, 1982.
Named American League Most Valuable Player by Baseball Writers' Association of America, 1982.
Named shortstop on THE SPORTING NEWS American League All-Star Team, 1978, 1980 and 1982.
Named shortstop on THE SPORTING NEWS American League All-Star fielding team, 1982.
Named shortstop on THE SPORTING NEWS American League Silver Slugger team, 1980 and 1982.

Year Club	League	Pos.	G.	AB.	R.	H.	2B.	3B.	HR.	RBI.	B.A.	PO.	A.	E.	F.A.
1973—Newark	NYP	SS	64	242	29	69	15	3	3	25	.285	43	85	18	.877
1974—Milwaukee	Amer.	SS	107	344	48	86	14	5	3	26	.250	148	327	19	.962
1975—Milwaukee	Amer.	SS	147	558	67	149	28	2	8	52	.267	273	402	★44	.939
1976—Milwaukee	Amer.	●SS-OF	●161	638	59	161	19	3	2	54	.252	●290	510	31	.963
1977—Milwaukee	Amer.	SS	154	605	66	174	34	4	4	49	.288	256	449	29	.964
1978—Milwaukee†	Amer.	SS	127	502	66	147	23	9	9	71	.293	246	453	30	.959
1979—Milwaukee	Amer.	SS	149	577	72	154	26	5	8	51	.267	267	517	25	.969
1980—Milwaukee	Amer.	SS	143	611	121	179	★49	10	23	87	.293	239	455	28	.961
1981—Milwaukee	Amer.	SS	96	377	50	103	15	5	10	49	.273	161	370	8	★.985
1982—Milwaukee	Amer.	SS	156	635	129	★210	●46	12	29	114	.331	253	★489	24	.969
1983—Milwaukee	Amer.	SS	149	578	102	178	42	★10	17	80	.308	256	420	19	.973
1984—Milwaukee	Amer.	SS	160	624	105	186	27	7	16	80	.298	199	402	18	.971
1985—Milwaukee	Amer.	OF-1B	122	466	76	129	26	3	15	68	.277	267	5	8	.971
Major League Totals—12 Years			1671	6515	961	1856	349	75	144	781	.285	2855	4799	280	.965

Selected by Milwaukee Brewers' organization in 1st round (third player selected) of free-agent draft, June 5, 1973.
†On disabled list, March 28 to May 3, 1978.

DIVISION SERIES RECORD

Year	Club	League	Pos.	G.	AB.	R.	H.	2B.	3B.	HR.	RBI.	B.A.	PO.	A.	E.	F.A.
1981—Milwaukee		Amer.	SS	5	19	4	6	0	1	0	1	.316	6	16	1	.957

CHAMPIONSHIP SERIES RECORD

Year	Club	League	Pos.	G.	AB.	R.	H.	2B.	3B.	HR.	RBI.	B.A.	PO.	A.	E.	F.A.
1982—Milwaukee		Amer.	SS	5	16	1	4	0	0	0	0	.250	11	12	1	.958

WORLD SERIES RECORD

Established World Series record for most games, Series, four or more hits (2), 1982.
Tied World Series record for most at-bats, nine-inning game, (6), October 12, 1982.

Year	Club	League	Pos.	G.	AB.	R.	H.	2B.	3B.	HR.	RBI.	B.A.	PO.	A.	E.	F.A.
1982—Milwaukee		Amer.	SS	7	29	6	12	3	0	1	6	.414	20	19	3	.929

ALL-STAR GAME RECORD

Year	League	Pos.	AB.	R.	H.	2B.	3B.	HR.	RBI.	B.A.	PO.	A.	E.	F.A.
1980—American		SS	2	0	0	0	0	0	0	.000	3	2	0	1.000
1982—American		SS	3	0	0	0	0	0	0	.000	0	2	0	1.000
1983—American		SS	2	1	0	0	0	0	1	.000	0	1	0	1.000
All-Star Game Totals—3 Years			7	1	0	0	0	0	1	.000	3	5	0	1.000

PATRICK PAUL ZACHRY
(Pat)

Born April 24, 1952, at Richmond, Tex.
Height, 6.05. Weight, 175.
Throws and bats righthanded.

Major League saves: 1982 (1), 1984 (2). Total—3.
Tied for National League lead in home runs allowed with 13 in 1981.
Led Eastern League in intentional bases on balls issued with 15 in 1973.
Named National League co-Rookie of the Year by Baseball Writers' Association of America, 1976.

Year	Club	League	G.	IP.	W.	L.	Pct.	H.	R.	ER.	SO.	BB.	ERA.
1970—Bradenton Reds		Gulf Coast	9	54	1	4	.200	53	29	15	55	24	2.50
1970—Sioux Falls		Northern	3	21	2	1	.677	20	9	8	19	5	3.43
1971—Tampa†		Florida St.	22	143	12	4	.750	125	58	51	115	72	3.21
1972—Three Rivers		Eastern	25	133	7	7	.500	110	55	39	102	79	2.64
1973—Three Rivers		Eastern	42	178	●12	12	.500	158	81	65	130	★127	3.29
1974—Indianapolis		Am. Assoc.	33	151	10	7	.588	129	69	59	98	71	3.52
1975—Indianapolis		Am. Assoc.	27	159	10	7	.588	120	52	43	100	70	★2.44
1976—Cincinnati		National	38	204	14	7	.667	170	70	62	143	83	2.74
1977—Cincinnati‡-New York		National	31	195	10	13	.435	207	104	92	99	77	4.25
1978—New York§		National	21	138	10	6	.625	120	57	51	78	60	3.33
1979—New York x		National	7	43	5	1	.833	44	19	17	17	21	3.56
1980—New York y		National	28	165	6	10	.375	145	65	55	88	58	3.00
1981—New York		National	24	139	7	●14	.333	151	78	64	76	56	4.14
1982—New York z		National	36	137⅓	6	9	.400	149	69	62	69	57	4.05
1983—Los Angeles		National	40	61⅓	6	1	.857	63	22	17	36	21	2.49
1984—Los Angeles a		National	58	82⅔	5	6	.455	84	38	35	55	51	3.81
1985—Philadelphia b		National	10	12⅔	0	0	.000	14	7	6	8	11	4.26
Major League Totals—10 Years			293	1178⅓	69	67	.507	1147	529	461	669	495	3.52

Selected by Cincinnati Reds' organization in 19th round of free-agent draft, June 4, 1970.
†Appeared in one game as a second baseman with two assists.
‡Traded with Infielder Doug Flynn and Outfielders Dan Norman and Steve Henderson to New York Mets for Pitcher Tom Seaver, June 15, 1977.
§On disabled list, August 1 to September 7, 1978.
xOn disabled list, April 24 to May 23 and June 10 to September 27, 1979.
yOn disabled list, April 27 to May 3, 1980.
zTraded to Los Angeles Dodgers for Outfielder Jorge Orta, December 28, 1982.
aTraded to Philadelphia Phillies for First Baseman Al Oliver, February 4, 1985.
bReleased, June 8, 1985.

CHAMPIONSHIP SERIES RECORD

Year	Club	League	G.	IP.	W.	L.	Pct.	H.	R.	ER.	SO.	BB.	ERA.
1976—Cincinnati		National	1	5	1	0	1.000	6	2	2	3	3	3.60
1983—Los Angeles		National	2	4	0	0	.000	4	1	1	2	2	2.25
Championship Series Totals—2 Years			3	9	1	0	1.000	10	3	3	5	5	3.00

WORLD SERIES RECORD

Year	Club	League	G.	IP.	W.	L.	Pct.	H.	R.	ER.	SO.	BB.	ERA.
1976—Cincinnati		National	1	6⅔	1	0	1.000	6	2	2	6	5	2.70

ALL-STAR GAME RECORD

Member of National League All-Star Team for 1978 game; did not play.

—DID YOU KNOW—

That the 1985 Rangers led the majors with a combined pinch-hitting average of .288?

GEOFFREY CLAYTON ZAHN
(Geoff)

Born December 19, 1946, at Baltimore, Md.
Height, 6.01. Weight, 185.
Throws and bats lefthanded.
Received bachelor of science degree in education from
University of Michigan, Ann Arbor, Mich., in 1968.

Pitched 1-0 no-hit loss against St. Petersburg, June 30, 1968.
Major League saves: 1975 (1).
Tied for American League lead in shutouts with 5 in 1984.
Tied for American League lead in home runs allowed with 18 in 1981.
Led Texas League in hit batsmen with 9 in 1971.
Named lefthanded pitcher on THE SPORTING NEWS American League All-Star Team, 1982.

Year	Club	League	G.	IP.	W.	L.	Pct.	H.	R.	ER.	SO.	BB.	ERA.
1968—Daytona Beach†	Florida St.	21	138	8	9	.471	97	44	32	108	38	2.09
1969—Albuquerque‡§	Texas	15	98	9	3	.750	103	42	38	44	29	3.49
1970—Spokane x	P. Coast	27	53	1	1	.500	67	41	32	22	32	5.43
1971—Albuquerque y	Texas	29	164	8	12	.400	155	77	39	126	50	2.14
1972—El Paso	Texas	9	73	7	2	.778	54	21	15	77	17	1.85
1972—Albuquerque	P. Coast	18	109	10	1	.909	126	66	57	80	30	4.71
1973—Albuquerque z	P. Coast	25	177	13	8	.619	185	81	60	103	66	3.05
1973—Los Angeles	National	6	13	1	0	1.000	5	2	2	9	2	1.38
1974—Los Angeles	National	21	80	3	5	.375	78	28	18	33	16	2.03
1975—Los Angeles a-Chicago b	National	18	66	2	8	.200	69	40	34	22	31	4.64
1976—Wichita	Am. Assoc.	21	137	8	8	.500	142	81	65	66	61	4.27
1976—Chicago c	National	3	8	0	1	.000	16	10	10	4	2	11.25
1977—Minnesota	American	34	198	12	14	.462	234	116	103	88	66	4.68
1978—Minnesota	American	35	252	14	14	.500	260	101	85	106	81	3.04
1979—Minnesota d	American	26	169	13	7	.650	181	74	67	58	41	3.57
1980—Minnesota e	American	38	233	14	18	.438	273	★138	114	96	66	4.40
1981—California	American	25	161	10	11	.476	181	★93	★79	52	43	4.42
1982—California	American	34	229⅓	18	8	.692	225	100	95	81	65	3.73
1983—California f	American	29	203	9	11	.450	212	90	75	81	51	3.33
1984—California g	American	28	199⅓	13	10	.565	200	78	69	61	48	3.12
1985—California hi	American	7	37	2	2	.500	44	19	18	14	14	4.38
American League Totals—9 Years		256	1681⅔	105	95	.525	1810	809	705	637	475	3.77
National League Totals—4 Years		48	167	6	14	.300	168	80	64	68	51	3.45
Major League Totals—13 Years		304	1848⅔	111	109	.505	1978	889	769	705	526	3.74

Selected by Chicago White Sox' organization in 28th round of free-agent draft, June, 1966.
Selected by Boston Red Sox' organization in secondary phase of free-agent draft, January 28, 1967.
Selected by Detroit Tigers' organization in secondary phase of free-agent draft, June 7, 1967.
Selected by Los Angeles Dodgers' organization in secondary phase of free-agent draft, January 27, 1968.
†On restricted list, April 11 to May 2, 1968.
‡On temporary inactive list, April 22 to June 16, 1969.
§On disabled list, June 16 to July 7, 1969.
xAppeared as a first baseman with no chances.
yAppeared as an outfielder with no chances.
zOn disabled list, June 18 to June 30, 1973.
aTraded with Pitcher Eddie Solomon to Chicago Cubs for Pitcher Burt Hooton, May 2, 1975.
bOn disabled list, July 21 to September 2, 1975.
cReleased, January 17, 1977; signed by Minnesota Twins, March 18, 1977.
dOn disabled list, May 2 to June 2, 1979.
eGranted free agency, October 23, 1980; signed by California Angels, December 2, 1980.
fOn disabled list, June 10 to July 11, 1983.
gOn disabled list, March 27 to April 11 and August 10 to September 1, 1984.
hOn disabled list, April 27 to August 3 and August 19, 1985 through remainder of season.
iReleased, December 20, 1985.

CHAMPIONSHIP SERIES RECORD

Year	Club	League	G.	IP.	W.	L.	Pct.	H.	R.	ER.	SO.	BB.	ERA.
1982—California	American	1	3⅔	0	1	.000	4	3	3	2	1	7.36

LLOYD JEFFREY ZASKE

Name pronounced ZASS-kee.

(Jeff)

Born October 6, 1960, at Seattle, Wash.
Height, 6.05. Weight, 193.
Throws and bats righthanded.
Attended Edmonds Community College, Lynnwood, Wash.

Led Eastern League in saves with 24 and games finished in relief with 44 in 1983.

Year	Club	League	G.	IP.	W.	L.	Pct.	H.	R.	ER.	SO.	BB.	ERA.
1979—Shelby	W. Carol.	25	100	5	10	.333	91	80	58	88	96	5.22
1980—Salem	Carolina	26	132	8	10	.444	101	68	62	103	★116	4.23
1981—Buffalo	Eastern	4	10	0	1	.000	10	6	4	4	8	3.60
1981—Alexandria	Carolina	21	110	5	9	.357	105	64	54	75	72	4.42
1982—Alexandria	Carolina	48	74⅔	7	4	.636	63	30	24	84	29	2.89
1983—Lynn	Eastern	48	70⅓	5	3	.625	54	20	17	72	38	2.18

Year Club	League	G.	IP.	W.	L.	Pct.	H.	R.	ER.	SO.	BB.	ERA.
1983—Hawaii	P. Coast	6	6	1	0	1.000	6	4	4	4	6	6.00
1984—Hawaii	P. Coast	37	60⅓	2	4	.333	51	28	24	60	40	3.58
1984—Pittsburgh	National	3	5	0	0	.000	4	0	0	2	1	0.00
1985—Hawaii	P. Coast	46	68⅔	2	7	.222	51	28	26	75	57	3.41
Major League Totals—1 Year		3	5	0	0	.000	4	0	0	2	1	0.00

Selected by Pittsburgh Pirates' organization in 27th round of free-agent draft, June 6, 1978.

PAUL ZUVELLA

Born October 31, 1958, at San Mateo, Calif.
Height, 6.00. Weight, 170.
Throws and bats righthanded.
Received bachelor of arts degree in communications
from Stanford University, Stanford, Calif.

Major League stolen bases: 1985 (2).
Led International League in being hit by pitch with 8 in 1984.
Led International League shortstops in total chances with 644 and double plays with 85 in 1984.
Led Southern League shortstops in total chances with 661 in 1981.

Year Club	League	Pos.	G.	AB.	R.	H.	2B.	3B.	HR.	RBI.	B.A.	PO.	A.	E.	F.A.
1980—Bradenton Brav...	Gulf C.	SS	2	8	0	1	0	0	0	1	.125	4	9	1	.929
1980—Durham†	Carol.	SS	48	149	21	47	7	0	2	19	.315	58	140	12	.943
1981—Savannah	South.	SS	138	485	61	145	17	2	11	68	.299	220	*406	35	.947
1982—Richmond	Int.	SS	133	455	63	128	15	2	9	54	.281	245	335	22	.963
1982—Atlanta	Nat.	SS	2	1	0	0	0	0	0	0	.000	0	4	1	.800
1983—Richmond	Int.	SS	117	415	53	119	13	2	6	64	.287	169	324	18	*.965
1983—Atlanta	Nat.	SS	3	5	0	0	0	0	0	0	.000	1	2	1	.750
1984—Richmond	Int.	SS	127	462	77	140	18	●6	6	55	.303	*219	*409	16	*.975
1984—Atlanta	Nat.	2B-SS	11	25	2	5	1	0	0	1	.200	13	21	0	1.000
1985—Richmond	Int.	SS	8	32	3	7	0	0	1	3	.219	10	30	3	.930
1985—Atlanta	Nat.	2B-SS-3B	81	190	16	48	8	1	0	4	.253	112	173	8	.973
Major League Totals—4 Years		97	221	18	53	9	1	0	5	.240	126	200	10	.970

Selected by Milwaukee Brewers' organization in 11th round of free-agent draft, June 5, 1979.
Selected by Atlanta Braves' organization in 15th round of free-agent draft, June 3, 1980.
†On disabled list, August 27, 1980 through remainder of season.

MITCHELL PAUL ZWOLENSKY
(Mitch)

Born December 29, 1959, at Owosso, Mich.
Height, 6.02. Weight, 200.
Throws and bats righthanded.
Attended Eastern Michigan University, Ypsilanti, Mich.

Led Texas League in complete games with 10 in 1983.

Year Club	League	G.	IP.	W.	L.	Pct.	H.	R.	ER.	SO.	BB.	ERA.
1981—Sarasota Rangers	Gulf Coast	6	19	2	0	1.000	18	5	3	16	9	1.42
1981—Asheville	S. Atlantic	9	27	1	4	.200	42	20	20	21	14	6.67
1982—Wausau-Burlington	Midwest	26	52	2	3	.400	40	23	14	38	25	2.42
1982—Sarasota Rangers	Gulf Coast	9	20⅓	3	1	.750	20	9	4	26	3	1.77
1983—Tulsa	Texas	26	162⅓	12	10	.545	158	81	60	101	61	3.33
1983—Oklahoma City	Am. Assoc.	2	2⅔	0	0	.000	2	0	0	2	0	0.00
1984—Oklahoma City†	Am. Assoc.	32	138⅓	7	8	.467	149	70	67	74	52	4.36
1985—Oklahoma City	Am. Assoc.	18	87	7	5	.583	94	51	43	50	32	4.45

Selected by Texas Rangers' organization in 4th round of free-agent draft, June 6, 1978.
Selected by Texas Rangers' organization in 11th round of free-agent draft, June 8, 1981.
†Appeared as an outfielder with no chances.

PLAYER MOVES

The following player deals involve players in the Register with the transactions occurring after January 22, 1986 and including January 31.

BAIR, DOUG: Invited to Chicago White Sox' spring training.
BENIQUEZ, JUAN: Signed by Baltimore Orioles, January 28, 1986.
CAMPBELL, BILL: Signed by Detroit Tigers, January 31, 1986.
FORD, DAN: Released by Baltimore Orioles, January 23, 1986.
IORG, DANE: Signed by San Diego Padres, January 28, 1986.
KEOUGH, MATT: Invited to Chicago Cubs' spring training.
KUIPER, DUANE: Named special minor league instructor with Cleveland Indians, January 31, 1986.
PERLMAN, JON: Signed by Phoenix (San Francisco Giants' organization), January 27, 1986.
PORTER, DARRELL: Signed by Texas Rangers, January 28, 1986.
SAMBITO, JOE: Signed by Boston Red Sox' organization, January 31, 1986.
SORENSEN, LARY: Re-signed by Chicago Cubs, January 26, 1986.
STODDARD, BOB: Signed by Tacoma (Oakland A's organization), January 29, 1986.

Major League Managers

GEORGE LEE ANDERSON
(Sparky)
Detroit Tigers

Born February 22, 1934, at Bridgewater, S. D.
Height, 5.09. Weight, 168.
Threw and batted righthanded.

Major League stolen bases: 1959 (6).
Led Western League in sacrifice hits with 20 in 1954 and International League with 15 in 1960.
Led Texas League second basemen in double plays with 117 in 1955, Pacific Coast League with 135 in 1957 and International League with 104 in 1958 and 89 in 1960.
Led California League shortstops in double plays with 83 in 1953.
Tied for Texas League lead in sacrifice hits with 22 in 1955 and International League lead with 15 in 1960.

Year	Club	League	Pos.	G.	AB.	R.	H.	2B.	3B.	HR.	RBI.	B.A.	PO.	A.	E.	F.A.
1953—Santa Barbara	Calif.		SS	●141	*598	98	157	21	4	5	55	.263	*277	395	32	.955
1954—Pueblo	West.		2B	147	497	72	147	13	5	0	62	.296	*397	432	20	●.976
1955—Fort Worth	Texas		2B	158	594	86	158	24	1	0	42	.266	*456	*469	18	*.981
1956—Montreal	Int.		2B	140	453	65	135	17	5	0	47	.298	372	391	15	.981
1957 Los Angeles	P. C.		*●2B-SS	●168	619	74	161	15	0	2	35	.260	*524	*488	●15	*.985
1958—Montreal†	Int.		2B	●155	580	78	156	35	5	2	56	.269	*387	*464	10	*.983
1959—Philadelphia	Nat.		2B	152	477	42	104	9	3	0	34	.218	343	403	12	.984
1960—Toronto	Int.		2B	148	543	67	123	11	5	5	21	.227	319	*416	12	.984
1961—Toronto	Int.		2B	97	275	30	66	17	0	0	22	.240	189	203	6	.985
1962—Toronto	Int.		2B	124	432	56	111	18	2	2	38	.257	282	327	8	*.987
1963—Toronto	Int.		2B	116	358	56	89	12	5	3	25	.249	226	256	6	*.988
Major League Totals—1 Year				152	477	42	104	9	3	0	34	.218	343	403	12	.984

†Recalled by Los Angeles Dodgers; traded to Philadelphia Phillies for Pitchers Jim Golden and Gene Snyder and Outfielder Eldon (Rip) Repulski, December 23, 1958.

RECORD AS MANAGER

Year	Club	League	Position	W.	L.
1964—Toronto	Int.		Fifth	80	72
1965—Rock Hill	W. Carol.		Eighth	24	40
(Second Half)			†First	35	23
1966—St. Petersburg	Fla. St.		Second	42	24
(Second Half)			‡First	49	21
1967—Modesto	Calif.		§Second	38	32
(Second Half)			xFirst	41	29
1968—Asheville	South.		First	86	54
1970—Cincinnati	Nat.		First(W)	102	60
1971—Cincinnati	Nat.		yFourth(W)	79	83
1972—Cincinnati	Nat.		First(W)	95	59
1973—Cincinnati	Nat.		First(W)	99	63
1974—Cincinnati	Nat.		Second(W)	98	64
1975—Cincinnati	Nat.		First(W)	108	54

Year	Club	League	Position	W.	L.
1976—Cincinnati	Nat.		First(W)	102	60
1977—Cincinnati	Nat.		Second(W)	88	74
1978—Cincinnati	Nat.		Second(W)	92	69
1979—Detroit z	Amer.		Fifth(E)	56	50
1980—Detroit	Amer.		Fifth(E)	84	78
1981—Detroit a	Amer.			60	49
1982—Detroit	Amer.		Fourth(E)	83	79
1983—Detroit	Amer.		Second(E)	92	70
1984—Detroit	Amer.		First(E)	104	58
1985—Detroit	Amer.		Third (E)	84	77
American League Totals—7 Years				563	461
National League Totals—9 Years				863	586
Major League Totals—16 Years				1426	1047

†Won playoff against Salisbury (First Half winner), two games to none.
‡Lost playoff against Leesburg (First Half winner), three games to two.
§Tied for position with Santa Barbara.
xLost playoff against San Jose (First Half winner), two games to none.
yTied for position with Houston Astros.
zReplaced Les Moss (and interim manager Dick Tracewski) with club in fifth place (record of 29-26), June 14, 1979.
aFirst Half. . . . Fourth (E) (record of 31-26); Second Half. . . . Third (E) (record of 29-23).
Coach, San Diego Padres, 1969.
Manager, American League All-Star Team, 1985.
Manager, National League All-Star Team, 1971, 1973, 1976 and 1977.
Coach, National League All-Star Team, 1974.
Coach, American League All-Star Team, 1982 and 1984.

CHAMPIONSHIP SERIES RECORD

Year	Club	League	W.	L.
1970—Cincinnati	National		3	0
1972—Cincinnati	National		3	2
1973—Cincinnati	National		2	3
1975—Cincinnati	National		3	0
1976—Cincinnati	National		3	0
1984—Detroit	American		3	0
Championship Series Totals—6 Years			17	5

WORLD SERIES RECORD

Year	Club	League	W.	L.
1970—Cincinnati	National		1	4
1972—Cincinnati	National		3	4
1975—Cincinnati	National		4	3
1976—Cincinnati	National		4	0
1984—Detroit	American		4	1
World Series Totals—5 Years			16	12

—DID YOU KNOW—

That when Jimmy Key received credit for a victory on May 1, 1985, it marked the first win for a starting Toronto lefthander since October 4, 1980, when Paul Mirabella recorded a victory?

GEORGE IRVIN BAMBERGER
Milwaukee Brewers

Born August 1, 1925, at Staten Island, N.Y.
Height, 5.11. Weight, 190.
Threw right and batted left and righthanded.

Pitched 1-0 no-hit victory against Toronto, June 17, 1951.
Led Pacific Coast League in wild pitches with 13 in 1950.
Led International League in wild pitches with 11 in 1949.
Tied for International League lead in shutouts with 5 in 1949 and tied for Pacific Coast League lead with 5 in 1958.

Year Club	League	G.	IP.	W.	L.	Pct.	H.	R.	ER.	SO.	BB.	ERA.
1946—Erie	Mid. Atl.	26	160	13	3	.813	121	52	24	107	87	*1.35
1947—Manchester	N. England	33	165	12	11	.522	135	87	64	134	99	3.49
1948—Jersey City	Int'national	25	65	2	2	.500	83	52	46	28	4	6.37
1949—Jersey City	Int'national	32	194	14	11	.560	193	119	97	98	87	4.50
1950—Oakland	P. Coast	39	236	17	13	.567	226	120	111	133	112	4.23
1951—New York	National	2	2	0	0	.000	4	4	4	1	2	18.00
1951—Ottawa	Int'national	26	174	11	11	.500	158	75	65	68	57	3.36
1952—New York	National	5	4	0	0	.000	6	4	4	0	6	9.00
1952—Oakland	P. Coast	27	150	14	6	.700	129	59	48	67	36	2.88
1953—Oakland	P. Coast	47	245	15	16	.484	289	*146	*136	111	100	5.00
1954—Oakland	P. Coast	40	179	11	8	.579	170	75	70	61	81	3.53
1955—Oakland	P. Coast	35	180	12	14	.462	182	87	83	70	61	4.15
1956—Vancouver	P. Coast	30	186	9	14	.391	215	101	84	69	45	4.07
1957—Vancouver	P. Coast	34	200	14	12	.538	*244	98	89	73	46	4.01
1958—Vancouver	P. Coast	31	184	15	11	.577	183	58	50	71	26	*2.45
1959—Baltimore	American	3	8	0	0	.000	15	7	7	2	2	7.88
1959—Vancouver	P. Coast	25	160	11	7	.611	167	60	53	75	27	2.98
1960—Vancouver	P. Coast	35	206	12	12	.500	238	111	87	89	34	3.80
1961—Vancouver	P. Coast	31	196	12	6	.667	195	97	82	105	42	3.77
1962—Vancouver	P. Coast	34	228	12	12	.500	227	98	80	135	37	3.16
1963—Dallas-Fort Worth	P. Coast	35	169	7	15	.318	205	101	85	86	29	4.53
National League Totals—2 Years		7	6	0	0	.000	10	8	8	1	8	12.00
American League Totals—1 Year		3	8	0	0	.000	15	7	7	2	2	7.88
Major League Totals—3 Years		10	14	0	0	.000	25	15	15	3	10	9.64

Player-Coach, Vancouver, Pacific Coast League, 1960 through 1962; Dallas-Ft. Worth, Pacific Coast League, 1963; Minor League Pitching Instructor, Baltimore Orioles, 1964 through 1967; Coach, Baltimore Orioles, 1968 through 1977.

RECORD AS MANAGER

Named Major League Manager of the Year by THE SPORTING NEWS, 1978.

Year Club	League	Position	W.	L.
1978—Milwaukee	Amer.	Third(E)	93	69
1979—Milwaukee	Amer.	Second(E)	95	66
1980—Milwaukee†‡	Amer.	Fourth(E)	47	45
1982—New York	Nat.	Sixth(E)	65	97
1983—New York§	Nat.	Sixth(E)	16	30
1985—Milwaukee	Amer.	Sixth(E)	71	90
American League Totals—4 Years			306	270
National League Totals—2 Years			81	127
Major League Totals—6 Years			387	397

†Replaced interim manager Buck Rodgers with club in second place with 26-21 record after recouperating from a heart attack suffered in spring training, June 6, 1980.
‡Retired and replaced by Buck Rodgers, September 7, 1980 with club tied for fourth place (record of 73-66 since start of season).
§Retired and replaced by interim manager Frank Howard, June 3, 1983.
Special Assistant to the General Manager, Milwaukee Brewers, 1981.
Minor league coach, New York Mets, 1984.

PATRICK CORRALES

Name pronounced Corr-AL-ees.

(Pat)

Cleveland Indians

Born March 20, 1941, at Los Angeles, Calif.
Height, 6.00. Weight, 195.
Threw and batted righthanded.
Attended Fresno City College, Fresno, Calif.

Tied major league record for most times awarded first base on catcher's interference, game (2), September 29, 1965.
Major League stolen bases: 1966 (1).
Led Florida State League catchers in double plays with 18 in 1960 and tied for Sally League lead with 10 in 1963.

Year Club	League	Pos.	G.	AB.	R.	H.	2B.	3B.	HR.	RBI.	B.A.	PO.	A.	E.	F.A.
1959—Bakersfield	Calif.	C	5	5	0	0	0	0	0	0	.000	4	2	1	.857
1959—Johnson City	Appal.	C	23	74	10	18	4	0	2	13	.243	124	5	3	.977
1960—Tampa	Fla. St.	C	128	386	73	95	18	5	1	60	.246	*1011	83	23	*.979
1961—Des Moines	I.I.I.	C	104	333	33	103	18	0	3	36	.309	707	42	*19	.975
1962—Dallas-Ft. W.	A. A.	C	42	121	10	27	6	1	2	14	.223	180	16	3	.985

Year Club	League	Pos.	G.	AB.	R.	H.	2B.	3B.	HR.	RBI.	B.A.	PO.	A.	E.	F.A.
1962—Williamsport........	East.	C-OF	42	136	9	26	1	0	1	10	.191	237	24	7	.974
1963—Chattanooga	Sally	C	127	415	42	108	15	1	3	51	.260	715	59	17	.979
1964—Arkansas...............	P. C.	C	101	335	36	102	19	1	9	48	.304	682	51	7	.991
1964—Philadelphia	Nat.	PH	2	1	1	0	0	0	0	0	.000	0	0	0	.000
1965—Philadelphia†	Nat.	C	63	174	16	39	8	1	2	15	.224	358	24	7	.982
1965—Arkansas...............	P. C.	C	28	85	6	16	4	0	0	4	.188	181	14	2	.990
1966—St. Louis..............	Nat.	C	28	72	5	13	2	0	0	3	.181	133	23	4	.975
1967—Tulsa‡...................	P. C.	C-1B	130	435	55	119	18	1	10	54	.274	714	69	8	.990
1968—Indianapolis	P. C.	C-1B	77	242	26	66	11	3	6	34	.273	461	42	5	.990
1968—Cincinnati	Nat.	C	20	56	3	15	4	0	0	6	.268	101	8	1	.991
1969—Cincinnati..........	Nat.	C	29	72	10	19	5	0	1	5	.264	133	7	2	.986
1970—Cincinnati..........	Nat.	C	43	106	9	25	5	1	1	10	.236	167	11	3	.983
1971—Cincinnati..........	Nat.	C	40	94	6	17	2	0	0	6	.181	145	4	3	.980
1972—Indianapolis	A. A.	C	30	98	9	31	4	0	1	12	.316	193	10	0	1.000
1972—Cinn.§-S. Diego	Nat.	C	46	120	6	23	0	0	0	6	.192	251	23	2	.993
1973—San Diego	Nat.	C	29	72	7	15	2	1	0	3	.208	130	6	2	.986
1974—Hawaii x..............	P. C.	C	53	169	21	42	6	0	5	24	.249	324	17	3	.991
1975—Alexandria	Texas	C-1B	1	0	0	0	0	0	0	0	.000	4	0	0	1.000
Major League Totals—9 Years............			300	767	63	166	28	3	4	54	.216	1418	106	24	.984

†Traded with Pitcher Art Mahaffey and Outfielder Alex Johnson to St. Louis Cardinals for First Baseman Bill White, Shortstop Dick Groat and Catcher Bob Uecker, October 27, 1965.

‡Recalled by St. Louis Cardinals; traded to Cincinnati Reds' organization with Infielder Jim Williams for Catcher John Edwards, February 8, 1968.

§Traded to San Diego Padres for Catcher Bob Barton, June 11, 1972.

xReleased, September 27, 1974.

WORLD SERIES RECORD

Year Club	League	Pos.	G.	AB.	R.	H.	2B.	3B.	HR.	RBI.	B.A.	PO.	A.	E.	F.A.
1970—Cincinnati.............	Nat.	PH	1	1	0	0	0	0	0	0	.000	0	0	0	.000

RECORD AS MANAGER

Year Club	League	Position	W.	L.
1975—Alexandria	Texas	Fourth(E)	58	72
1978—Texas†......................	Amer.	‡Second(W)	1	0
1979—Texas........................	Amer.	Third(W)	83	79
1980—Texas........................	Amer.	Fourth(W)	76	85
1982—Philadelphia	Nat.	Second(E)	89	73
1983—Philadelphia§.......	Nat.	First(E)	43	42
1983—Cleveland x	Amer.	Seventh(E)	30	32
1984—Cleveland................	Amer.	Sixth(E)	75	87
1985—Cleveland................	Amer.	Seventh(E)	60	102
American League Totals—5 Years			325	385
National League Totals—2 Years.................			132	115
Major League Totals—6 Years......................			457	500

†Replaced Billy Hunter with club tied for second place (record of 86-75), October 1, 1978.

‡Tied for position with California Angels.

§Replaced by Paul Owens, July 18, 1983.

xReplaced Mike Ferraro with club in seventh place (record of 40-60), July 31, 1983.

Coach, Texas Rangers, part of 1975 through September 30, 1978.

Coach, American League All-Star Team, 1979.

Coach, National League All-Star Team, 1983.

CHARLES KEITH COTTIER

Name pronounced Cot-TEE-er.

(Chuck)
Seattle Mariners

Born January 8, 1936, at Delta, Colo.
Height, 5.11. Weight, 178.
Threw and batted righthanded.

Major League stolen bases: 1960 (1), 1961 (9), 1962 (14), 1963 (2), 1964 (2). Total—28.

Led Western League second basemen in double plays with 130 in 1957.

Led Evangeline League second basemen in double plays with 106 in 1955.

Led Georgia-Florida League second basemen in double plays with 76 in 1954.

Tied for Pacific Coast League lead in sacrifice hits with 11 in 1967.

Year Club	League	Pos.	G.	AB.	R.	H.	2B.	3B.	HR.	RBI.	B.A.	PO.	A.	E.	F.A.
1954—Ameri's-Cordele...	Ga.-Fla.	2B	138	507	71	127	22	9	2	49	.250	★370	★398	★46	.943
1955—New Iberia.............	Evang.	2B	139	521	63	132	20	1	3	52	.253	361	★401	38	.953
1956—Jacksonville†........	Sally	2B	4	11	0	2	1	0	0	0	.182	5	0	0	1.000
1956—Topeka	West.	2B	29	102	13	22	2	1	3	14	.216	71	77	5	.967
1956—Baton Rouge.........	Evang.	2B	42	155	32	40	8	3	5	14	.258	125	109	4	.983
1957—Topeka	West.	2B	151	603	95	158	29	4	20	79	.262	389	★479	●30	.967
1958—Atlanta‡	South.	2B	153	583	32	157	29	8	8	62	.269	★414	★455	31	.966
1959—Milwaukee.............	Nat.	2B	10	24	1	3	1	0	0	1	.125	18	22	1	.976
1959—Louisville	A. A.	2B	122	425	54	96	22	6	4	40	.226	290	339	21	.968
1960—Louisville	A. A.	2B	46	181	24	56	11	3	4	19	.309	132	108	11	.956
1960—Milwaukee§...........	Nat.	2B	95	229	29	52	8	0	3	19	.227	180	214	13	.968

Year Club	League	Pos.	G.	AB.	R.	H.	2B.	3B.	HR.	RBI.	B.A.	PO.	A.	E.	F.A.
1961—Det. x-Wash..........	Amer.	2B-SS	111	344	39	81	14	4	2	35	.235	242	323	11	.981
1962—Washington	Amer.	2B	136	443	50	107	14	6	6	40	.242	368	354	14	.981
1963—Washington	Amer.	2B-SS-3B	113	337	30	69	16	4	5	21	.205	233	286	25	.954
1964—Washington	Amer.	2B-3B-SS	73	137	16	23	6	2	3	10	.168	110	115	5	.978
1965—Hawaii y	P. C.	2B-SS	93	309	38	64	11	1	3	27	.207	201	270	9	.981
1965—Washington	Amer.	PH-PR	7	1	1	0	0	0	0	0	.000	0	0	0	.000
1966—Hawaii z	P. C.	2B	97	321	39	82	20	1	4	39	.255	199	266	16	.967
1967—Seattle..................	P. C.	2B	140	482	50	119	29	2	5	61	.247	313	400	15	.979
1968—Sea.-Portland a.....	P. C.	2B	88	294	33	65	7	4	7	31	.221	216	241	14	.970
1968—California.............	Amer.	3B-2B	33	67	2	13	4	1	0	1	.194	15	45	2	.968
1969—California b...........	Amer.	2B	2	2	0	0	0	0	0	0	.000	1	1	0	1.000
1969—Hawaii cd...........	P. C.					(Did not play)									
American League Totals—7 Years			475	1331	138	293	54	17	16	107	.220	969	1124	57	.973
National League Totals—2 Years............			105	253	30	55	9	0	3	20	.217	198	236	14	.969
Major League Totals—9 Years................			580	1584	168	348	63	17	19	127	.220	1167	1360	71	.973

†On disabled list, May 21 to May 31, 1956.
‡On military list, September 24, 1958 through April 2, 1959.
§Traded with Pitcher Terry Fox, Catcher Dick Brown and Outfielder Billy Bruton to Detroit Tigers for Second Baseman Frank Bolling and Outfielder Neil Chrisley, December 7, 1960.
xTraded to Washington Senators for Pitcher Hal Woodeshick, June 5, 1961.
yOn disabled list, August 17 to August 30, 1965.
zSold to California Angels' organization, February 16, 1967.
aOn disabled list, June 15 to June 25, 1968.
bOn disabled list, April 8 to April 30, 1969.
cOn disabled list, May 13, 1969 through remainder of season.
dReleased, April 6, 1970.

RECORD AS MANAGER

Named New York-Pennsylvania League Manager of the Year, 1972.

Year Club	League	Position	W.	L.
1971—Niagara Falls†	NYP	Second	8	3
1972—Niagara Falls	NYP	First	48	22
1973—Charleston..............	W. Carol.	Second	35	25
(Second Half)		Second	37	27
1977—Quad Cities..............	Midw.	Third(S)	41	29
(Second Half)		Third(S)	34	35
1978—Salinas	Calif.	Second(S)	42	28
(Second Half)		Second(S)	42	28
1984—Seattle‡....................	Amer.	§Fifth(W)	15	12
1985—Seattle......................	Amer.	Sixth(W)	74	88
Major League Totals—2 Years.....................			89	100

†Replaced due to injury by Dick Cole, July 3, 1971.
‡Replaced Del Crandall with club in seventh place (record of 59-76), September 1, 1984.
§Tied for position with Chicago White Sox.
Coach, New York Mets, 1979 through 1981.
Coach, Seattle Mariners, 1982 through August 31, 1984.

ROGER LEE CRAIG
San Francisco Giants

Born February 17, 1931, at Durham, N. C.
Height, 6.04. Weight, 196.
Threw and batted righthanded.
Attended North Carolina State College, Raleigh, N. C.

Tied major league record for most 1-0 games lost, season (5), 1963.
Tied National League record for most consecutive losses, season (18), May 4 through August 4, 1963, inclusive.
Tied for National League lead in shutouts with 4 in 1959.

Year Club	League	G.	IP.	W.	L.	Pct.	H.	R.	ER.	SO.	BB.	ERA.
1950—Newport News	Piedmont	6	19	0	1	.000	22	17	15	7	23	7.11
1950—Valdosta	Ga.-Fla.	23	167	14	7	.667	136	86	58	152	150	3.13
1951—Newport News	Piedmont	38	21	14	11	.560	175	109	90	119	★175	3.67
1952-53—Elmira	Eastern					(In Military Service)						
1954—Elmira	Eastern	3	2	0	0	.000	4	6	2	1	2	9.00
1954—Pueblo	Western	6	14	1	1	.500	14	17	15	8	19	9.64
1954—Newport News	Piedmont	20	125	8	3	.727	107	44	35	108	56	2.50
1955—Montreal	Int'national	22	117	10	2	.833	105	48	46	68	64	3.54
1955—Brooklyn	National	21	91	5	3	.625	81	37	28	48	43	2.77
1956—Brooklyn	National	35	199	12	11	.522	169	90	82	109	87	3.71
1957—Brooklyn	National	32	111	6	9	.400	102	58	57	69	47	4.62
1958—Los Angeles................................	National	9	32	2	1	.667	30	20	16	16	12	4.50
1958—St. Paul	Am. Assoc.	28	182	5	●17	.227	180	100	79	119	77	3.91
1959—Spokane..	P. Coast	14	96	6	7	.462	86	39	34	46	26	3.19
1959—Los Angeles................................	National	29	153	11	5	.688	122	49	35	76	45	2.06
1960—Los Angeles................................	National	21	116	8	3	.727	99	48	42	69	43	3.26
1961—Los Angeles†	National	40	113	5	6	.455	130	87	77	63	52	6.13
1962—New York......................................	National	42	233	10	★24	.294	261	133	117	118	70	4.52
1963—New York‡....................................	National	46	236	5	★22	.185	249	117	99	108	58	3.78
1964—St. Louis§....................................	National	39	166	7	9	.438	180	76	60	84	35	3.25

Year Club	League	G.	IP.	W.	L.	Pct.	H.	R.	ER.	SO.	BB.	ERA.
1965—Cincinnati x	National	40	64	1	4	.200	74	33	26	30	25	3.66
1966—Philadelphia	National	14	23	2	1	.667	31	15	14	13	5	5.48
1966—Seattle	P. Coast	6	22	0	1	.000	15	11	6	11	9	2.45
1968—Albuquerque	Texas	1	4	0	0	.000	3	0	0	2	2	0.00
Major League Totals—12 Years		368	1537	74	98	.430	1528	763	653	803	522	3.82

†Selected by New York Mets in National League expansion draft, October 10, 1961.
‡Traded to St. Louis Cardinals for Pitcher Bill Wakefield and Outfielder George Altman, November 4, 1963.
§Traded to Cincinnati Reds with Outfielder Charlie James for Pitcher Bob Purkey and a player to be named later, December 14, 1964.
xReleased by Cincinnati Reds and signed by Philadelphia Phillies, April 11, 1966.

WORLD SERIES RECORD

Year Club	League	G.	IP.	W.	L.	Pct.	H.	R.	ER.	SO.	BB.	ERA.
1955—Brooklyn	National	1	6	1	0	1.000	4	2	2	4	5	3.00
1956—Brooklyn	National	2	6	0	1	.000	10	8	8	4	3	12.00
1959—Los Angeles	National	2	9⅓	0	1	.000	15	9	9	8	5	8.68
1964—St. Louis	National	2	5	1	0	1.000	2	0	0	9	3	0.00
World Series Totals—3 Years		7	26⅓	2	2	.500	31	19	19	25	16	6.49

RECORD AS MANAGER

Year Club	League	Position	W.	L.
1968—Albuquerque	Texas	Second(W)	70	69
1978—San Diego	Nat.	Fourth(W)	84	78
1979—San Diego	Nat.	Fifth(W)	68	93
1985—San Francisco†	Nat.	Sixth(W)	6	12
Major League Totals—3 Years			158	183

†Replaced Jim Davenport with club in sixth place (record of 56-88), September 18, 1985.
Scout, Los Angeles Dodgers, 1967; coach, San Diego Padres, 1969 through 1972; minor league pitching instructor, Los Angeles Dodgers, 1973; coach, Houston Astros, 1974 and 1975; coach, San Diego Padres, 1976 and 1977; named manager of Padres (replacing Alvin Dark), March 21, 1978; coach, Detroit Tigers, 1980 through 1983; scout, Detroit Tigers, March 2, 1985 through September 18, 1985.

JOHN FREDERICK FELSKE

Name pronounced FELL-skee.

Philadelphia Phillies

Born May 30, 1942, at Chicago, Ill.
Height, 6.04. Weight, 225.
Threw and batted righthanded.
Attended University of Illinois, Urbana, Ill.

Led American Association catchers in double plays with 12 in 1971.
Led Texas League catchers in double plays with 14 in 1964 and tied for lead with 8 in 1966.
Led Northern League in passed balls with 19 in 1963.
Led Florida State League catchers in double plays with 9 in 1962.

Year Club	League	Pos.	G.	AB.	R.	H.	2B.	3B.	HR.	RBI.	B.A.	PO.	A.	E.	F.A.
1962—Palatka	Fla. St.	C	94	269	29	50	12	1	5	32	.186	546	60	11	∗.982
1962—St. Cloud	North.	C	5	9	0	0	0	0	1	.000	22	2	0	1.000
1963—St. Cloud	North.	C	117	396	52	99	22	2	12	58	.250	656	∗86	8	.989
1964—Fort Worth	Texas	C	108	319	28	58	15	1	6	28	.182	528	∗86	11	.982
1965—Salt Lake City	P. C.	C	41	124	10	23	4	0	3	11	.185	226	21	0	1.000
1965—Dallas-Ft.Worth	Texas	C	74	231	21	51	8	1	2	18	.221	383	41	7	.984
1966—Tacoma	P. C.	C	2	5	1	0	0	0	0	0	.000	0	0	0	.000
1966—Dallas-Ft. Worth	Texas	C	73	220	18	44	10	0	6	24	.200	456	49	7	.986
1967—Dallas-Ft. W.†	Texas	C-OF	68	203	18	53	3	1	3	20	.261	352	31	7	.982
1968—Tacoma	P. C.	C-OF	84	249	19	53	9	1	7	29	.213	388	41	7	.984
1968—Chicago	Nat.	C	4	2	0	0	0	0	0	0	.000	5	0	1	.833
1969—San Antonio	Texas	C-1B-OF	91	265	25	72	14	1	9	44	.272	438	48	7	.986
1970—Portland	P. C.	∗C-1B	131	432	70	136	25	2	18	75	.315	∗778	60	●10	.988
1971—Evansville	A. A.	1-C-O-3	119	402	54	118	20	4	14	68	.294	802	92	9	.990
1972—Evansville	A. A.	C-1B	33	113	14	27	5	2	1	16	.239	211	20	1	.996
1972—Milwaukee	Amer.	C-1B	37	80	6	11	3	0	1	5	.138	124	9	3	.978
1973—Milwaukee‡	Amer.	C-1B	13	22	1	3	0	1	0	4	.136	41	4	0	1.000
National League Totals—1 Year			4	2	0	0	0	0	0	0	.000	5	0	1	.833
American League Totals—2 Years			50	102	7	14	3	1	1	9	.137	165	13	3	.983
Major League Totals—3 Years			54	104	7	14	3	1	1	9	.135	170	13	4	.979

†On disabled list, August 22 to September 4, 1967.
‡Released, October 23, 1973.

—DID YOU KNOW—

That two players for Modesto (California League) hit for the cycle in the same game last May? Bob Loscalzo and Kevin Stock accomplished their feats in a 23-4 win over Visalia. Stock, son of Wes Stock, former major league pitcher and A's pitching coach, hit a grand slam and drove in seven runs in five at-bats.

RECORD AS MANAGER

Named Pacific Coast League Manager of the Year, 1983.

Year Club	League	Position	W.	L.
1974—Newark	NYP	†Fifth	30	36
1975—Thetford Mines	East.	Fifth	28	35
(Second Half)		Eighth	31	45
1976—Berkshire	East.	Third(N)	68	68
1977—Spokane	P. C.	Second(W)	75	69
1978—Spokane	P. C.	Fourth(W)	64	75
1979—Vancouver	P. C.	Third(N)	39	36
(Second Half)		‡First(N)	40	32
1982—Reading	East	Third(S)	33	31
(Second Half)		Third(S)	30	44
1983—Portland	P. C.	Third(N)	34	38
(Second Half)		§First(N)	41	29
1985—Philadelphia	Nat.	Fifth (E)	75	87
Major League Totals—1 Year			75	87

†One tie.

‡Lost playoff to Hawaii, two games to one.

§Won Northern Division Championship from Edmonton, three games to one; won league championship from Albuquerque, three games to none; lost in Triple A World Series playoff.

Coach, Toronto Blue Jays, 1980 and 1981.

Coach, Philadelphia Phillies, 1984.

JAMES GOTTFRIED FREY
(Jim)
Chicago Cubs

Born May 26, 1931, at Cleveland, O.
Height, 5.09. Weight, 170.
Threw and batted lefthanded.
Attended Ohio State University, Columbus, O.

Led Texas League in total bases with 294 and tied for lead in stolen bases with 21 in 1957.
Named Most Valuable Player in Texas League, 1957.

Year Club	League	Pos.	G.	AB.	R.	H.	2B.	3B.	HR.	RBI.	B.A.	PO.	A.	E.	F.A.
1950—Evansville	I.I.I.			(appeared in less than 10 games; no record available)											
1950—Paducah	M.O.V.	OF	106	412	73	134	21	11	1	58	.325	180	17	6	.970
1951—Evansville	I.I.I.	OF	119	447	69	145	24	9	1	58	.324	197	18	10	.956
1952—Hartford	East.	OF	20	80	12	21	8	0	0	7	.263	23	2	0	1.000
1952—Evansville	I.I.I.	OF	90	307	66	103	25	3	2	54	.336	145	15	6	.964
1953—Jacksonville	So. Atl.	OF	117	429	64	136	25	4	2	37	.317	241	18	2	*.992
1954—Jacksonville	So. Atl.	OF	139	529	89	167	*40	4	11	65	.316	314	18	5	.985
1955—Toledo	A. A.	OF	142	486	88	137	36	0	4	54	.282	209	17	11	.954
1956—Atlanta	S. A.	OF	25	87	14	22	4	0	1	11	.253	39	5	2	.957
1956—Austin†-Ft. W.‡	Texas	OF	126	447	63	125	20	2	6	39	.280	224	7	10	.959
1957—Tulsa§	Texas	OF	*155	589	*102	*198	*50	*11	8	74	*.336	310	16	12	.964
1958—Omaha	A. A.	OF	117	420	63	119	19	7	4	45	.283	211	8	6	.973
1959—Rochester	Int.	OF	114	338	56	100	17	2	11	42	.296	157	7	4	.976
1960—Rochester x	Int.	OF	125	441	78	140	21	4	16	66	*.317	199	12	8	.963
1961—Buffalo	Int.	OF	115	354	49	93	17	1	10	47	.263	180	8	4	.979
1962—Buffalo y	Int.	OF	134	448	67	121	18	1	16	59	.270	196	17	5	.977
1963—Col.z-Atl.ab	Int.	OF	62	108	11	28	3	0	2	12	.259	29	2	3	.912

†Traded by Milwaukee Braves' organization to Brooklyn Dodgers' organization for Outfielder Ray Shearer, July 4, 1956.

‡Sold by Brooklyn Dodgers' organization to Tulsa, April 12, 1957.

§Sold to St. Louis Cardinals' organization, July 31, 1957, to be announced after the season was over.

xReleased by St. Louis Cardinals' organization to Buffalo, October 5, 1960.

yReleased to Pittsburgh Pirates' organization, December 3, 1962.

zReleased, May 7, 1963; signed as free agent by St. Louis Cardinals' organization, May 18, 1963.

aOn disabled list, July 8 to July 29, 1963.

bReleased, October 15, 1963.

PITCHING RECORD

Year Club	League	G.	IP.	W.	L.	Pct.	H.	R.	ER.	SO.	BB.	ERA.
1956—Austin	Texas	1	....	0	0	.000	....	....	....	....	....	....
1957—Tulsa	Texas	4	....	0	0	.000	....	....	....	....	....	....
1960—Rochester	Int'national	1	....	0	0	.000	....	....	....	....	....	....
1961—Buffalo	Int'national	2	....	0	0	.000	....	....	....	....	....	....

RECORD AS MANAGER

Named Major League Manager of the Year by THE SPORTING NEWS, 1984.

Year Club	League	Position	W.	L.
1964—Bluefield	Appal.	Fourth	27	44
1965—Bluefield	Appal.	Fifth	31	38
1980—Kansas City	Amer.	First(W)	97	65
1981—Kansas City††‡	Amer.		30	40
1984—Chicago	Nat.	First(E)	96	65
1985—Chicago	Nat.	Fourth(E)	77	84
American League Totals—2 Years			127	105
National League Totals—2 Years			173	149
Major League Totals—4 Years			300	254

Year Club	League	W.	L.
1980—Kansas City	American	3	0
1984—Chicago	National	2	3
Championship Series Totals—2 Years		5	3

Year Club	League	W.	L.
1980—Kansas City	American	2	4

†Replaced by Dick Howser, August 31, 1981.
‡First Half....Fifth(W) (record of 20-30); Second Half....Third(W) (record of 10-10).
Scout, Baltimore Orioles, 1966 through 1969; coach, Baltimore Orioles, 1970 through 1979; coach, New York Mets, 1982 and 1983.
Manager, American League All-Star Team, 1981.
Coach, National League All-Star Team, 1985.
Coach, American League All-Star Team, 1980.

DORREL NORMAN ELVERT HERZOG
(Relly or Whitey)
(Named "Relly" by mother from his first name; "Whitey" by Bill Speith, McAlester sportscaster, because of light hair.)
St. Louis Cardinals
Born November 9, 1931, at New Athens, Ill.
Height, 5.11. Weight, 187.
Threw and batted lefthanded.

Major League stolen bases: 1956 (8), 1957 (1), 1959 (1), 1961 (1), 1962 (2). Total—13.

Year Club	League	Pos.	G.	AB.	R.	H.	2B.	3B.	HR.	RBI.	B.A.	PO.	A.	E.	F.A.
1949—McAlester	Soo. St.	OF	96	398	53	111	19	7	0	31	.279	222	14	0	*1.000
1950—McAlester	Soo. St.	OF	132	467	107	164	36	10	4	85	.351	272	15	7	*.976
1951—Norfolk	Pied.	OF	5	17	5	1	0	0	0	2	.059	13	0	1	.926
1951—Joplin	W. A.	OF-1B	113	418	99	119	14	8	7	48	.285	454	19	9	.981
1952—Beaumont	Texas	OF	35	121	11	24	4	1	0	9	.198	83	3	5	.945
1952—Quincy	I. I. I.	OF	68	225	53	65	9	6	7	44	.289	131	9	5	.966
1952—Kansas City	A. A.	OF-1B	14	27	5	8	1	0	1	5	.296	21	1	1	.957
1953-54—					(In Military Service.)										
1955—Denver†	A. A.	OF-1B	149	515	101	149	24	7	21	98	.289	324	10	4	.988
1956—Washington	Amer.	OF-1B	117	421	49	103	13	7	4	35	.245	274	10	7	.976
1957—Washington	Amer.	OF	36	78	7	13	3	0	0	4	.167	53	0	1	.981
1957—Miami	Int.	OF	77	257	48	70	14	5	2	25	.272	114	5	4	.967
1958—Wash.‡-K.C.	Amer.	OF-1B	96	101	11	23	1	2	0	9	.228	146	6	3	.981
1959—Kansas City	Amer.	OF-1B	38	123	25	36	7	1	1	9	.293	87	2	3	.967
1960—Kansas City§	Amer.	OF-1B	83	252	43	67	10	2	8	38	.266	137	6	4	.973
1961—Baltimore	Amer.	OF	113	323	39	94	11	6	5	35	.291	143	2	0	1.000
1962—Baltimore x	Amer.	OF	99	263	34	70	13	1	7	35	.266	132	4	3	.978
1963—Detroit	Amer.	1B-OF	52	53	5	8	2	1	0	7	.151	44	1	1	.978
Major League Totals—8 Years			634	1614	213	414	60	20	25	172	.257	1016	31	22	.979

†Traded to Washington Senators with Pitcher Bob Wiesler, Catcher Lou Berberet, Second Baseman Herb Plews and Outfielder Dick Tettelbach for pitcher Maury McDermott and Shortstop Bob Kline (assigned to the Yankees' American Association farm club—Denver). Other players in deal assigned February 8, 1956; Herzog, April 2, 1956.
‡Sold to Kansas City Athletics, May 14, 1958.
§Traded to Baltimore Orioles with Outfielder Russ Snyder and a player to be named at later date, for Pitcher Jim Archer, Catcher Clint Courtney, First Baseman Bob Boyd, Infielder Wayne Causey and Outfielder Al Pilarcik, January 24, 1961; Courtney returned to the Orioles, April 15, 1961, to complete deal.
xTraded to Detroit Tigers with Catcher Gus Triandos for Catcher Dick Brown, November 26, 1962.

RECORD AS MANAGER
Named Man of the Year by THE SPORTING NEWS, 1982.
Named Major League Manager of the Year by THE SPORTING NEWS, 1982.

Year Club	League	Position	W.	L.
1973—Texas†	Amer.	Sixth(W)	47	91
1974—California‡	Amer.	Sixth(W)	2	2
1975—Kansas City§	Amer.	Second(W)	41	25
1976—Kansas City	Amer.	First(W)	90	72
1977—Kansas City	Amer.	First(W)	102	60
1978—Kansas City	Amer.	First(W)	92	70
1979—Kansas City	Amer.	Second(W)	85	77
1980—St. Louis xy	Nat.	Fourth(E)	38	35

Year Club	League	Position	W.	L.
1981—St. Louis z	Nat.		59	43
1982—St. Louis	Nat.	First(E)	92	70
1983—St. Louis	Nat.	Fourth(E)	79	83
1984—St. Louis	Nat.	Third(E)	84	78
1985—St. Louis	Nat.	First(E)	101	61
National League Totals—6 Years			453	370
American League Totals—7 Years			459	397
Major League Totals—13 Years			912	767

†Replaced by Billy Martin, September 8, 1973 (Del Wilber served as interim manager, September 7).
‡Served as interim manager, June 27 to June 30, 1974 after Dick Williams replaced Bobby Winkles, June 26.
§Replaced Jack McKeon with club in second place (record of 50-46), July 24, 1975.
xReplaced Ken Boyer (and interim manager Jack Krol) with club in sixth place (record of 18-33), June 9, 1980.
yNamed General Manager, August 29, 1980, with Red Schoendienst serving as manager remainder of season.
zFirst Half.... Second(E) (record of 30-20); Second Half.... Second(E) (record of 29-23).
Scout, Kansas City Athletics, 1964.; coach, Kansas City Athletics, 1965; New York Mets, 1966; California Angels, 1974 and part of 1975.
Director of Player Development, New York Mets, 1967 through 1972.
Manager, National League All-Star Team, 1983.
Coach, American League All-Star Team, 1973, 1974 and 1978.

Year Club	League	W.	L.		Year Club	League	W.	L.
1976—Kansas City	American	2	3		1982—St. Louis	National	4	3
1977—Kansas City	American	2	3		1985—St. Louis	National	3	4
1978—Kansas City	American	1	3		World Series Totals—2 Years		7	7
1982—St. Louis	National	3	0					
1985—St. Louis	National	4	2					
Championship Series Totals—5 Years		12	11					

RICHARD DALTON HOWSER
(Dick)
Kansas City Royals

Born May 14, 1937, at Miami, Fla.
Height, 5.09. Weight, 155.
Threw and batted righthanded.
Received bachelor of science degree in education from
Florida State University, Tallahassee, Fla.

Tied American League record for most games played by shortstop, season (162), 1964.
Major League stolen bases: 1961 (37), 1962 (19), 1963 (9), 1964 (20), 1965 (17), 1966 (2), 1967 (1). Total—105.
Tied for American League lead in sacrifice hits with 6 in 1964.
Led Three-I League in stolen bases with 31 in 1959.
Named American League Rookie of the Year by THE SPORTING NEWS, 1961.
Received reported $21,000 bonus to sign with Kansas City Athletics, 1958.

Year Club	League	Pos.	G.	AB.	R.	H.	2B.	3B.	HR.	RBI.	B.A.	PO.	A.	E.	F.A.
1958—Winona	I.I.I.	SS	83	333	80	96	16	1	6	30	.288	152	233	28	.932
1959—Sioux City	I.I.I.	2B-SS	111	392	●107	109	17	5	4	39	.278	240	289	33	.941
1960—Sioux City	I.I.I.	SS	44	149	59	52	15	1	5	21	.349	63	130	20	.906
1960—Shreveport	South.	SS	88	331	78	112	20	6	4	38	.338	189	270	31	.937
1961—Kansas City	Amer.	SS	158	611	108	171	29	6	3	45	.280	★299	427	★38	.950
1962—Kansas City†	Amer.	SS	83	286	53	68	8	3	6	34	.238	138	191	13	.962
1963—K.C.‡-Cleve.	Amer.	SS	64	203	29	48	5	0	1	11	.236	101	113	11	.951
1964—Cleveland	Amer.	SS	162	637	101	163	23	4	3	52	.256	291	463	20	.974
1965—Cleveland	Amer.	SS-2B	107	307	47	72	8	2	1	6	.235	144	211	7	.981
1966—Cleveland§	Amer.	SS-2B	67	140	18	32	9	1	2	4	.229	53	95	5	.967
1967—New York x	Amer.	2B-3B-SS	63	149	18	40	6	0	0	10	.268	64	76	3	.979
1968—New York	Amer.	2B-3B-SS	85	150	24	23	2	1	0	3	.153	61	106	3	.982
Major League Totals—8 Years			789	2483	398	617	90	17	16	165	.248	1151	1682	100	.966

†On disabled list, June 26 to August 10, 1962.
‡Traded to Cleveland Indians with Catcher Jose Azcue for Catcher Howard Edwards and reported $100,000, May 25, 1963.
§Traded to New York Yankees for Pitcher Gil Downs and cash, December 20, 1966.
xOn disabled list, July 17 to September 1, 1967.

ALL-STAR GAME RECORD

Year League	Pos.	AB.	R.	H.	2B.	3B.	HR.	RBI.	B.A.	PO.	A.	E.	F.A.
1961—American (first game)	3B	1	0	0	0	0	0	0	.000	0	1	0	1.000

Member of American League All-Star Team in 1961 (second game); did not play.

RECORD AS MANAGER

Year Club	League	Position	W.	L.
1980—New York	Amer.	First(E)	103	59
1981—Kansas City†‡	Amer.		20	13
1982—Kansas City	Amer.	Second(W)	90	72
1983—Kansas City	Amer.	Second(W)	79	83
1984—Kansas City	Amer.	First(W)	84	78
1985—Kansas City	Amer.	First(W)	91	71
Major League Totals—6 Years			467	376

†Replaced Jim Frey with club in third place during second half (record of 10-10), August 31, 1981.
‡Second Half. . . . First(W) (record of 20-13).
Coach, New York Yankees, 1969 through 1978, scout, New York Yankees, November 21, 1980 through August 30, 1981.
Baseball coach at Florida State University, 1979. Record: 43 wins, 17 losses, 1 tie.
Coach, American League All-Star Team, 1982 and 1985.

Year Club	League	W.	L.		Year Club	League	W.	L.
1981—Kansas City	American	0	3		1980—New York	American	0	3
					1984—Kansas City	American	0	3
					1985—Kansas City	American	4	3
					Championship Series Totals—3 Years		4	9

WORLD SERIES RECORD

Year Club	League	W.	L.
1985—Kansas City	American	4	3

DAVID ALLEN JOHNSON
(Dave)
New York Mets

Born January 30, 1943, at Orlando, Fla.
Height, 6.01. Weight, 182.
Threw and batted righthanded.
Attended Texas A&M University, College Station, Tex., received bachelor of
science degree in mathematics from Trinity University, San Antonio, Tex.,
and attended Johns Hopkins University, Baltimore, Md.

Established major league record for most home runs by second baseman, season, (42), 1973.
Tied major league records for fewest triples, season (150 or more games), (0), 1973; most home runs, bases filled, season, pinch-hitter (2), 1978.
Major League stolen bases: 1965 (3), 1966 (3), 1967 (4), 1968 (7), 1969 (3), 1970 (2), 1971 (3), 1972 (1), 1973 (5), 1974 (1), 1977 (1). Total—33.
Tied for American League lead in sacrifice flies with 8 in 1967.
Led National League second basemen in total chances with 877 and tied for lead in double plays with 106 in 1973.
Led American League second basemen in double plays with 103 in 1971.
Led California League shortstops in double plays with 63 in 1962.
Named National League Comeback Player of the Year by THE SPORTING NEWS, 1973.
Named second baseman on THE SPORTING NEWS National League All-Star Team, 1973.
Named second baseman on THE SPORTING NEWS American League All-Star Team, 1970.
Named second baseman on THE SPORTING NEWS American League All-Star fielding team, 1969 through 1971.

Year Club	League	Pos.	G.	AB.	R.	H.	2B.	3B.	HR.	RBI.	B.A.	PO.	A.	E.	F.A.
1962—Stockton	Calif.	SS	97	343	58	106	18	●12	10	63	.309	135	307	40	★.917
1963—Elmira	East.	SS-2B	63	233	47	76	11	6	13	42	.326	115	155	12	.957
1963—Rochester	Int.	2B-OF	63	211	31	52	9	3	6	22	.246	141	138	11	.962
1964—Rochester	Int.	2B-SS	●155	590	87	156	29	14	19	73	.264	326	445	39	.952
1965—Baltimore	Amer.	3B-2B-SS	20	47	5	8	3	0	0	1	.170	11	37	3	.941
1965—Rochester	Int.	SS	52	193	29	58	9	3	4	22	.301	96	161	10	.963
1966—Baltimore	Amer.	★2B-SS	131	501	47	129	20	3	7	56	.257	294	357	★20	.970
1967—Baltimore	Amer.	2B-3B	148	510	62	126	30	3	10	64	.247	344	351	14	.980
1968—Baltimore	Amer.	2B-SS	145	504	50	122	24	4	9	56	.242	294	370	15	.978
1969—Baltimore	Amer.	2B-SS	142	511	52	143	34	1	7	57	.280	358	370	12	.984
1970—Baltimore	Amer.	●2B-SS	149	530	68	149	27	1	10	53	.281	●382	391	8	.990
1971—Baltimore	Amer.	2B	142	510	67	144	26	1	18	72	.282	361	367	12	.984
1972—Baltimore†	Amer.	2B	118	376	31	83	22	3	5	32	.221	286	307	6	★.990
1973—Atlanta	Nat.	2B	157	559	84	151	25	0	43	99	.270	383	464	★30	.966
1974—Atlanta	Nat.	1B-2B	136	454	56	114	18	0	15	62	.251	789	231	11	.989
1975—Atlanta‡	Nat.	PH	1	1	0	1	1	0	0	1	1.000	0	0	0	.000
1975—Yomiuri	Central	3B-SS	91	289	29	57	7	0	13	38	.197	85	157	11	.957
1976—Yomiuri§	Central	2B-3B-1B	108	371	48	102	16	2	26	74	.275	226	28	11	.979
1977—Philadelphia x	Nat.	1B-2B-3B	78	156	23	50	9	1	8	36	.321	299	31	0	1.000
1978—Phil. y-Chi. z	Nat.	3B-2B-1B	68	138	19	32	3	1	4	20	.232	61	63	11	.919
1979—Miami	Int.-Am.	1B	10	25	7	6	2	0	1	2	.240	Figures Unavailable			
American League Totals—8 Years			995	3489	382	904	186	16	66	391	.259	2330	2550	90	.982
National League Totals—5 Years			440	1308	182	348	56	2	70	218	.266	1532	789	52	.978
Major League Totals—13 Years			1435	4797	564	1252	242	18	136	609	.261	3862	3339	142	.981

†Traded with Pitchers Pat Dobson and Roric Harrison and Catcher Johnny Oates to Atlanta Braves for Catcher Earl Williams and Infielder Taylor Duncan, November 30, 1972.
‡Released, April 11, 1975; signed by Yomiuri Giants of Japanese baseball.
§Released, January 21, 1977; signed as free agent with Philadelphia Phillies, February 3, 1977.
xOn supplemental disabled list, June 15 to July 1, 1977.
yTraded to Chicago Cubs for Pitcher Larry Anderson, August 6, 1978.
zReleased, October 17, 1978.

CHAMPIONSHIP SERIES RECORD

Tied American League Championship Series record for most home runs, three-game Series (2), 1970.

Year Club	League	Pos.	G.	AB.	R.	H.	2B.	3B.	HR.	RBI.	B.A.	PO.	A.	E.	F.A.
1969—Baltimore	Amer.	2B	3	13	2	3	0	0	0	0	.231	5	11	0	1.000
1970—Baltimore	Amer.	2B	3	11	4	4	0	0	2	4	.364	11	4	0	1.000
1971—Baltimore	Amer.	2B	3	10	2	3	2	0	0	0	.300	5	6	1	.917
1977—Philadelphia	Nat.	1B	1	4	0	1	0	0	0	2	.250	8	0	0	1.000
Championship Series Totals—4 Years			10	38	8	11	2	0	2	6	.289	29	21	1	.980

WORLD SERIES RECORD

Established World Series record for highest fielding average by second baseman, four-game Series (1.000 with 24 chances), 1966.

Year Club	League	Pos.	G.	AB.	R.	H.	2B.	3B.	HR.	RBI.	B.A.	PO.	A.	E.	F.A.
1966—Baltimore	Amer.	2B	4	14	1	4	1	0	0	1	.286	12	12	0	1.000
1969—Baltimore	Amer.	2B	5	16	1	1	0	0	0	0	.063	8	15	0	1.000
1970—Baltimore	Amer.	2B	5	16	2	5	2	0	0	2	.313	15	9	0	1.000
1971—Baltimore	Amer.	2B	7	27	1	4	0	0	0	3	.148	18	12	0	1.000
World Series Totals—4 Years			21	73	5	14	3	0	0	6	.192	53	48	0	1.000

ALL-STAR GAME RECORD

Year League	Pos.	AB.	R.	H.	2B.	3B.	HR.	RBI.	B.A.	PO.	A.	E.	F.A.
1968—American	2B	1	0	0	0	0	0	0	.000	1	1	0	1.000

Year League	Pos.	AB.	R.	H.	2B.	3B.	HR.	RBI.	B.A.	PO.	A.	E.	F.A.
1970—American	2B	5	0	1	0	0	0	0	.200	5	1	0	1.000
1973—National	2B	1	0	0	0	0	0	0	.000	1	1	0	1.000
All-Star Game Totals—3 Years		7	0	1	0	0	0	0	.143	7	3	0	1.000

Named to American League All-Star Team for 1969 game; replaced due to injury.

RECORD AS MANAGER

Year Club	League	Position	W.	L.
1979—Miami	Inter-Amer.	First	43	17
(Second Half)		First	8	4
1981—Jackson	Texas	†First(E)	39	27
(Second Half)		Third(E)	29	39
1983—Tidewater	Int.	‡Fourth	71	68
1984—New York	Nat.	Second(E)	90	72
1985—New York	Nat.	Second(E)	98	64
Major League Totals—2 Years			188	136

†Defeated Tulsa, two games to one, and San Antonio (finals), three games to none, for championship.
‡Defeated Columbus, three games to two, and Richmond (finals), three games to one, for championship.
Instructor, New York Mets' organization, 1982.

HAROLD CLIFTON LANIER
(Hal)
Houston Astros

Born July 4, 1942, at Denton, N.C.
Height, 6.02. Weight, 186.
Threw and batted righthanded.
Son of Max Lanier, pitcher with St. Louis Cardinals, New York Giants
and St. Louis Browns, 1938 through 1953.

Major League stolen bases: 1964 (2), 1965 (2), 1966 (1), 1967 (2), 1968 (2), 1970 (1), 1972 (1). Total—11.
Led Eastern League second basemen in double plays with 85 in 1963.
Received reported $50,000 bonus to sign with San Francisco Giants, 1961.

Year Club	League	Pos.	G.	AB.	R.	H.	2B.	3B.	HR.	RBI.	B.A.	PO.	A.	E.	F.A.
1961—Quincy	Midw.	SS	73	295	61	93	7	5	1	25	.315	112	204	18	.946
1962—Fresno	Calif.	2B	133	555	89	173	20	4	5	49	.312	★358	★321	23	★.967
1963—Springfield	East.	2B	138	★577	77	★163	27	9	6	49	.282	★359	★379	18	★.976
1964—Tacoma	P. C.	2B-SS	61	254	33	83	17	1	4	28	.327	140	152	9	.970
1964—San Francisco	Nat.	2B-SS	98	383	40	105	16	3	2	28	.274	226	298	11	.979
1965—San Francisco	Nat.	2B-SS	159	522	41	118	15	9	0	39	.226	294	445	18	.976
1966—San Francisco	Nat.	2B-SS	149	459	37	106	14	2	3	37	.231	303	423	13	.982
1967—San Francisco	Nat.	2B-SS	151	525	37	112	16	3	0	42	.213	253	519	20	.975
1968—San Francisco	Nat.	SS	151	486	37	100	14	1	0	27	.206	★282	496	17	★.979
1969—San Francisco	Nat.	SS	150	495	37	113	9	1	0	35	.228	252	530	25	.969
1970—San Francisco	Nat.	SS-2-1	134	438	33	101	13	1	2	41	.231	263	399	22	.968
1971—San Francisco†	Nat.	3-2-S-1	109	206	21	48	8	0	1	13	.233	91	130	6	.974
1972—New York	Amer.	3-S-2	60	103	5	22	3	0	0	6	.214	32	87	4	.967
1973—New York‡	Amer.	S-2-3	35	86	9	18	3	0	0	5	.209	45	81	4	.969
1974—Tulsa	A. A.	2-3-S	103	357	45	96	15	0	1	32	.269	158	203	10	.973
1975—Tulsa§x	A. A.	3B-2B	21	74	11	15	1	1	1	7	.203	26	50	0	1.000
1979—Springfield	A. A.	SS	1	2	0	1	0	0	0	0	.500	3	1	0	1.000
National League Totals—8 Years			1101	3514	283	803	105	20	8	262	.229	1964	3240	132	.975
American League Totals—2 Years			95	189	14	40	6	0	0	11	.212	77	168	8	.968
Major League Totals—10 Years			1196	3703	297	843	111	20	8	273	.228	2041	3408	140	.975

†Sold to New York Yankees, February 2, 1972.
‡Released, December 10, 1973; signed by St. Louis Cardinals' organization, April 8, 1974.
§On disabled list, June 7 to August 13, 1975.
xReleased, September 19, 1975.

CHAMPIONSHIP SERIES RECORD

Year Club	League	Pos.	G.	AB.	R.	H.	2B.	3B.	HR.	RBI.	B.A.	PO.	A.	E.	F.A.
1971—San Francisco	Nat.	3B	1	1	0	0	0	0	0	0	.000	1	0	0	1.000

RECORD AS MANAGER

Named Minor League Manager of the Year by THE SPORTING NEWS, 1980.
Named Western Carolinas League Manager of the Year, 1977.

Year Club	League	Position	W.	L.
1976—St. Petersburg	Fla. St.	Third(N)	70	71
1977—Gastonia†	W.Car.	‡Second	37	32
(Second Half)		First	45	25
1978—St. Petersburg§	Fla. St.	First(N)	41	25
(Second Half)		Second(N)	x43	31
1979—Springfield	A. A.	Second(E)	73	63
1980—Springfield y	A. A.	First(E)	75	61

†Won championship playoff from Greenwood, three games to one.
‡Tied for postion.
§Lost playoff to Lakeland, one game to none.
xOne tie game.
yLost championship playoff to Denver, four games to one.
Coach, St. Louis Cardinals, 1981 through 1985.

ANTHONY LaRUSSA JR.
(Tony)
Chicago White Sox

Born October 4, 1944, at Tampa, Fla.
Height, 6.00. Weight, 185.
Threw and batted righthanded.
Attended University of Tampa, Tampa, Fla., and received degree in industrial management from University of Southern Florida, Tampa, Fla.; and received law degree from Florida State University, Tallahassee, Fla. in 1980.
Led International League in being hit by pitch with 11 in 1972.
Received reported $50,000 bonus to sign with Kansas City A's, 1962.

Year Club League	Pos.	G.	AB.	R.	H.	2B.	3B.	HR.	RBI.	B.A.	PO.	A.	E.	F.A.
1962—Daytona Beach .... Fla. St.	SS	64	225	37	58	7	0	1	32	.258	135	173	38	.890
1962—Binghamton .... East.	SS-2B	12	43	3	8	0	0	0	4	.186	20	27	8	.855
1963—Kansas City .... Amer.	SS-2B	34	44	4	11	1	1	0	1	.250	29	25	2	.964
1964—Lewiston† .... N'west	2B-SS	90	329	50	77	22	1	1	25	.234	188	218	18	.958
1965—Birmingham‡ .... South.	2B	75	259	24	50	11	2	1	18	.193	202	161	21	.945
1966—Modesto................ Calif.	2B	81	316	67	92	20	1	7	54	.291	201	212	20	.954
1966—Mobile.................. South.	2B	51	170	20	50	9	4	4	26	.294	117	133	10	.962
1967—Birmingham§ .... South.	2B	41	139	12	32	6	1	5	22	.230	88	120	5	.977
1968—Oakland................ Amer.	PH	5	3	0	1	0	0	0	0	.333	0	0	0	.000
1968—Vancouver............ P. C.	2B	122	455	55	109	16	8	5	29	.240	249	321	14	*.976
1969—Iowa .... A. A.	2B	67	235	37	72	11	1	4	27	.306	177	222	15	.964
1909—Oakland................ Amer.	PH	8	8	0	0	0	0	0	0	.000	0	0	0	.000
1970—Iowa.................... A. A.	2B	22	88	13	22	5	0	2	5	.250	52	59	3	.974
1970—Oakland................ Amer.	2B	52	106	6	21	4	1	0	6	.198	67	89	5	.969
1971—Iowa .... A. A.	2-3-S-O	28	107	21	31	5	1	2	11	.290	70	85	2	.987
1971—Oakland x .... Amer.	2B-SS-3B	23	8	3	0	0	0	0	0	.000	8	7	2	.882
1971—Atlanta .... Nat.	2B	9	7	1	2	0	0	0	0	.286	8	6	1	.933
1972—Richmond y .... Int.	2B	122	389	68	120	13	2	10	42	.308	305	289	20	.967
1973—Wichita.................. A. A.	2B-1B-3B	106	392	82	123	16	0	5	75	.314	423	213	26	.961
1973—Chicago z .... Nat.	PR	1	0	1	0	0	0	0	0	.000	0	0	0	.000
1974—Charleston a .... Int.	2B	139	457	50	119	17	1	8	35	.260	262	*378	17	.974
1975—Denver .... A. A.	3-O-S-2	118	354	87	99	23	2	7	46	.280	95	91	10	.949
1976—Iowa bc .... A. A.	INF-O-P	107	332	53	86	11	0	4	34	.259	132	160	22	.930
1977—New Orleans de ... A. A.	2B-3B	50	128	17	24	2	2	3	6	.188	66	87	7	.956
American League Totals—5 Years		122	169	13	33	5	2	0	7	.195	104	121	9	.962
National League Totals—2 Years		10	7	2	2	0	0	0	0	.286	8	6	1	.933
Major League Totals—6 Years		132	176	15	35	5	2	0	7	.199	112	127	10	.960

†On disabled list, May 9 to September 8, 1964.
‡On disabled list, June 3 to July 15, 1965.
§On disabled list, April 12 to May 6 and July 3 to September 5, 1967.
xSold to Atlanta Braves, August 14, 1971.
yTraded to Chicago Cubs for Pitcher Tom Phoebus, October 20, 1972.
zSold to Pittsburgh Pirates' organization.
aReleased, April 4, 1975; signed by Chicago White Sox' organization, April 7, 1975.
bOn disabled list, August 8 to August 18, 1976.
cSold to St. Louis Cardinals' organization, December 13, 1976.
dNamed coach, June 20, 1977.
eReleased, September 29, 1977.

PITCHING RECORD

Year Club	League	G.	IP.	W.	L.	Pct.	H.	R.	ER.	SO.	BB.	ERA.
1976—Iowa	Am. Assoc.	3	3	0	0	.000	3	1	1	0	0	3.00

RECORD AS MANAGER

Named Major League Manager of the Year by THE SPORTING NEWS, 1983.

Year Club	League	Position	W.	L.	Year Club	League	Position	W.	L.
1978—Knoxville .... South.	First(W)	49	21		1982—Chicago .... Amer.	Third(W)	87	75	
(Second Half)†	Third(W)	4	4		1983—Chicago .... Amer.	First(W)	99	63	
1979—Iowa‡ .... A. A.	Second(E)	54	52		1984—Chicago .... Amer.	yFifth(W)	74	88	
1979—Chicago§ .... Amer.	Fifth(W)	27	27		1985—Chicago .... Amer.	Third(W)	85	77	
1980—Chicago .... Amer.	Fifth(W)	70	90		Major League Totals—7 Years			496	472
1981—Chicago x................. Amer.		54	52						

†Replaced by Joe Jones, July 3, 1978.
‡Replaced by Joe Sparks, August 3, 1979.
§Replaced Don Kessinger with club in fifth place (record of 46-60), August 3, 1979.
xFirst Half.... Third (W) (record 31-22); Second Half.... Sixth (W) (record of 23-30).
yTied for position with Seattle Mariners.
Coach, Chicago White Sox, July 3 through remainder of 1978 season.
Coach, American League All-Star Team, 1984.

CHAMPIONSHIP SERIES RECORD

Year Club	League	W.	L.
1983—Chicago .... American		1	3

THOMAS CHARLES LASORDA
Name pronounced Luh-SORR-duh.

(Tom)
Los Angeles Dodgers

Born September 22, 1927, at Norristown, Pa.
Height, 5.09. Weight, 195.
Threw and batted lefthanded.

Tied National League record by making three wild pitches in an inning, first inning, May 5, 1955.
Led International League in complete games with 16 and tied for lead in shutouts with 5 in 1958.
Led Canadian-American League in wild pitches with 20 in 1948 and led International League with 14 in 1953.
Named International League Pitcher of the Year, 1958.

Year	Club	League	G.	IP.	W.	L.	Pct.	H.	R.	ER.	SO.	BB.	ERA.
1945—Concord		N. C. St.	27	121	3	12	.200	115	84	55	91	100	4.09
1946-47—†		E. Shore					(In Military Service)						
1948—Schenectady‡§		Can.-Am.	32	192	9	12	.429	180	122	99	195	153	4.64
1949—Greenville		Sally	45	178	7	7	.500	141	81	58	151	138	2.93
1950—Montreal		Int'national	31	146	9	4	.692	136	73	60	85	82	3.70
1951—Montreal		Int'national	31	165	12	8	.600	145	75	64	80	87	3.49
1952—Montreal		Int'national	33	182	14	5	.737	156	90	74	77	93	3.66
1953—Montreal		Int'national	36	208	17	8	.680	171	77	65	122	94	2.81
1954—Montreal		Int'national	23	154	14	5	.737	142	66	60	75	79	3.51
1954—Brooklyn		National	4	9	0	0	.000	8	5	5	5	5	5.00
1955—Brooklyn		National	4	4	0	0	.000	5	6	6	4	6	13.50
1955—Montreal x		Int'national	22	143	9	8	.529	125	58	52	92	62	3.27
1956—Kansas City y		American	18	45	0	4	.000	40	38	31	28	45	6.20
1956—Denver		Am. Assoc.	16	83	3	4	.429	94	54	46	54	34	4.99
1957—Denver z		Am. Assoc.	6	17	0	2	.000	29	25	23	8	6	12.18
1957—Los Angeles		P. Coast	29	132	7	10	.412	134	73	57	72	59	3.90
1958—Montreal		Int'national	34	*230	*18	6	.750	191	77	64	126	76	2.50
1959—Montreal		Int'national	29	188	12	8	.600	192	93	80	64	77	3.83
1960—Montreal a		Int'national	12	45	2	5	.286	79	48	41	17	24	8.20
American League Totals—1 Year			18	45	0	4	.000	40	38	31	28	45	6.20
National League Totals—2 Years			8	13	0	0	.000	13	11	11	9	11	7.62
Major League Totals—3 Years			26	58	0	4	.000	53	49	42	37	56	6.52

†On National Defense list, May 14, 1946 through February 2, 1948.
‡On disabled list, July 9 to July 19, 1948.
§Drafted by Nashua (Brooklyn Dodgers' organization) from Philadelphia Phillies' organization, November 24, 1948.
xSold by Brooklyn Dodgers' organization to Kansas City Athletics for an estimated $35,000, March 2, 1956.
yTraded to New York Yankees for Pitcher Wally Burnette and cash, July 11, 1956.
zSold by New York Yankees' organization to Brooklyn Dodgers' organization, May 26, 1957.
aReleased, July 9, 1960.

RECORD AS MANAGER

Named Minor League Manager of the Year by THE SPORTING NEWS, 1970.
Named Pacific Coast League co-Manager of the Year, 1970.
Named Pioneer League Manager of the Year, 1967.

Year	Club	League	Position	W.	L.	Year	Club	League	Position	W.	L.
1965—Pocatello	Pion.	†Second	33	33		1978—Los Angeles	Nat.	First(W)	95	67	
1966—Ogden	Pion.	First	39	27		1979—Los Angeles	Nat.	Third(W)	79	83	
1967—Ogden	Pion.	First	41	25		1980—Los Angeles	Nat.	Second(W)	92	71	
1968—Ogden	Pion.	First	39	25		1981—Los Angeles y	Nat.		63	47	
1969—Spokane	P. C.	Second(N)	71	73		1982—Los Angeles	Nat.	Second(W)	88	74	
1970—Spokane	P. C.	‡First(N)	94	52		1983—Los Angeles	Nat.	First(W)	91	71	
1971—Spokane	P. C.	Third(N)	69	76		1984—Los Angeles	Nat.	Fourth(W)	79	83	
1972—Albuquerque	P. C.	§First(E)	92	56		1985—Los Angeles	Nat.	First(W)	95	67	
1976—Los Angeles x	Nat.	Second(W)	2	2		Major League Totals—10 Years				782	629
1977—Los Angeles	Nat.	First(W)	98	64							

†Tied for position with Magic Valley.
‡Won championship playoff against Hawaii, four games to none.
§Won championship playoff against Eugene, three games to one.
xReplaced retiring Walter Alston with club in second place (record of 90-68), September 29, 1976.
yFirst Half.... First(W) (record of 36-21); Second Half.... Fourth(W) (record of 27-26).
Scout, Los Angeles Dodgers, 1961 through 1965; manager Los Angeles farm team in Arizona Instructional League, 1969; coach, Los Angeles Dodgers, 1973 through 1976.
Manager, National League All-Star Team, 1978, 1979 and 1982.
Coach, National League All-Star Team, 1977, 1983 and 1984.

DIVISION SERIES RECORD

Year	Club	League	W.	L.
1981—Los Angeles	National	3	2

CHAMPIONSHIP SERIES RECORD

Year	Club	League	W.	L.
1977—Los Angeles	National	3	1
1978—Los Angeles	National	3	1
1981—Los Angeles	National	3	2
1983—Los Angeles	National	1	3
1985—Los Angeles	National	2	4
Championship Series Totals—5 Years		12	11

Year	Club	League	W.	L.
1977—Los Angeles		National	2	4
1978—Los Angeles		National	2	4
1981—Los Angeles		National	4	2
World Series Totals—3 Years			8	10

JAMES RICHARD LEYLAND

Named pronounced LEE-land.

(Jim)
Pittsburgh Pirates

Born December 15, 1944, at Toledo, O.
Height, 5.11. Weight, 170.
Threw and batted righthanded.

Year	Club	League	Pos.	G.	AB.	R.	H.	2B.	3B.	HR.	RBI.	B.A.	PO.	A.	E.	F.A.
1964—Lakeland†		Fla. St.	C	52	129	8	25	0	1	0	8	.194	268	17	6	.979
1964—Cocoa Tigers		Rookie	C	24	52	2	12	1	1	0	4	.231	122	15	3	.979
1965—Jamestown		NYP	C-3B-P	82	211	18	50	7	2	1	21	.237	318	36	6	.983
1966—Rocky Mount		Carol.	C	67	173	24	42	6	0	0	16	.243	369	23	1	.997
1967—Montgomery		South.	C	62	171	11	40	3	0	1	16	.234	350	25	6	.984
1968—Montgomery		South.	C-3B-SS	81	204	19	51	0	0	0	20	.103	511	42	7	.988
1969—Montgomery		South.	C	16	39	1	8	0	0	0	1	.205	64	6	3	.959
1969—Lakeland		Fla. St.	C-P	60	179	20	43	8	0	1	16	.240	321	28	4	.989
1970—Montgomery‡		South.	C	2	3	0	0	0	0	0	0	.000	6	0	1	.857

Signed as free agent by Detroit Tigers' organization, September 21, 1963.
†On disabled list, June 15 to June 27, 1964.
‡Player-coach.

PITCHING RECORD

Year	Club	League	G.	IP.	W.	L.	Pct.	H.	R.	ER.	SO.	BB.	ERA.
1965—Jamestown		NYP	1	2	0	0	.000	2	0	0	1	0	0.00
1969—Lakeland		Florida St.	1	2	0	0	.000	4	2	2	1	0	9.00

RECORD AS MANAGER

Named American Association Manager of the Year, 1979.
Named Florida State League Manager of the Year, 1977 and 1978.

Year	Club	League	Position	W.	L.	Year	Club	League	Position	W.	L.
1971—Bristol		Appal.	Third(S)	31	35	1976—Lakeland		Fla. St.	‡Second(N)	74	64
1972—Clinton		Midw.	Fifth(N)	22	41	1977—Lakeland		Fla. St.	§First(N)	85	53
(Second Half)			Fourth(N)	27	36	1978—Lakeland		Fla. St.	Fourth(N)	31	38
1973—Clinton		Midw.	Second(N)	36	26	(Second Half)			xFirst(N)	47	22
(Second Half)			†First(N)	37	25	1979—Evansville		A. A.	yFirst(E)	78	58
1974—Montgomery		South.	Third(W)	61	76	1980—Evansville		A. A.	Second(E)	61	74
1975—Clinton		Midw.	Fourth(N)	29	31	1981—Evansville		A. A.	zFirst(E)	73	63
(Second Half)			Second(S)	38	30						

†Lost playoff to Wisconsin Rapids, two games to none.
‡Defeated Miami, two games to none in semifinals, and defeated Tampa, two games to none for championship.
§Defeated Miami, two games to none in semifinals, and defeated St. Petersburg, three games to one for championship.
xDefeated St. Petersburg, one game to none for Northern Division championship, and lost to Miami, two games to one for championship.
yDefeated Oklahoma City, four games to two for championship.
zLost to Denver, three games to one in semifinals.
Coach, Detroit Tigers' organization, 1970 through June 5, 1971; Coach, Chicago White Sox, 1982 through 1985.

GENE WILLIAM MAUCH
California Angels

Born November 18, 1925, at Salina, Kan.
Height, 5.10. Weight, 173.
Threw and batted righthanded.
Brother-in-law of Roy Smalley, Jr., infielder with Chicago Cubs, Milwaukee Braves and
Philadelphia Phillies, 1948 through 1958; Uncle of Roy Smalley III, infielder with
Minnesota Twins; and Harry Mauch, minor league outfielder, 1978 and 1980.
Major League stolen bases: 1948 (1), 1949 (3), 1950 (1), 1957 (1). Total—6.

Year	Club	League	Pos.	G.	AB.	R.	H.	2B.	3B.	HR.	RBI.	B.A.	PO.	A.	E.	F.A.
1943—Durham		Pied.	SS	32	115	19	37	5	1	0	14	.322	77	81	19	.893
1943—Montreal		Int.	2B-SS	31	77	5	13	1	0	0	4	.169	36	41	12	.865
1944—Brooklyn		Nat.	SS	5	15	2	2	1	0	0	2	.133	7	9	0	1.000
1944—Montreal†		Int.	SS	14	53	12	15	0	0	0	2	.283	25	39	8	.889
1945—Brooklyn		Nat.						(In Military Service)								
1946—St. Paul‡		A. A.	SS	149	536	74	133	19	3	6	55	.248	296	*417	*64	.918
1947—Pittsburgh		Nat.	2B-SS	16	30	8	9	0	0	0	1	.300	18	20	3	.927
1947—Indianapolis§		A. A.	2B	58	217	37	65	13	4	0	16	.300	176	174	12	.967
1948—Brook.x-Chicago		Nat.	2B-SS	65	151	19	30	3	2	1	7	.199	90	105	12	.942

Year	Club	League	Pos.	G.	AB.	R.	H.	2B.	3B.	HR.	RBI.	B.A.	PO.	A.	E.	F.A.
1949—Chicago y	Nat.		2B-SS-3B	72	150	15	37	6	2	1	7	.247	98	125	9	.961
1950—Boston	Nat.		2B-3B-SS	48	121	17	28	5	0	1	15	.231	83	85	7	.960
1951—Boston	Nat.		SS-3B-2B	19	20	5	2	0	0	0	1	.100	16	16	1	.970
1951—Milwaukee za	A. A.		INF	37	109	30	33	2	0	1	16	.303	76	89	7	.959
1952—St. Louis b	Nat.		SS	7	3	0	0	0	0	0	0	.000	1	0	1	.500
1952—Milwaukee	A. A.		SS-2B	102	327	58	106	24	3	4	60	.324	202	258	12	.975
1953—Atlanta c	South.		2B	111	340	65	91	23	3	9	51	.268	200	239	18	.961
1954—Los Angeles	P. C.		2B	153	565	81	162	26	2	11	58	.287	354	380	19	.975
1955—Los Angeles	P. C.		★2B-3B	155	584	93	173	37	4	8	49	.296	★436	375	18	.978
1956—Los Angeles d	P. C.		2B-3B	146	566	123	197	29	3	20	84	.348	348	403	24	.969
1956—Boston	Amer.		2B	7	25	4	8	0	0	0	1	.320	12	17	2	.935
1957—Boston	Amer.		2B	65	222	23	60	10	3	2	28	.270	127	153	11	.962
1958—Minneapolis	A. A.		2B-3B	65	210	25	51	12	2	3	29	.243	108	136	16	.938
1959—Minneapolis	A. A.		PH	8	8	1	4	0	0	0	0	.500	0	0	0	.000
American League Totals—2 Years				72	247	27	68	10	3	2	29	.275	139	170	13	.960
National League Totals—7 Years				232	490	66	108	15	4	2	33	.220	313	360	33	.953
Major League Totals—9 Years				304	737	93	176	25	7	5	62	.239	452	530	46	.955

†Entered Military Service in May, 1944.

‡Recalled by Brooklyn Dodgers and traded to Pittsburgh Pirates with Pitchers Kirby Higbe and Cal McLish and Catcher Homer (Dixie) Howell for Outfielder Al Gionfriddo and reported $100,000, May 3, 1947.

§Recalled by Pittsburgh Pirates and traded to Brooklyn Dodgers with Pitcher Elwin (Preacher) Roe and Shortstop Billy Cox for Pitchers Hal Gregg and Vic Lombardi and Outfielder Fred (Dixie) Walker, December 7, 1947.

xSold to Chicago Cubs, June 17, 1948.

yTraded to Boston Braves with cash for Pitcher Bill Voiselle, December 14, 1949.

zDrafted by New York Yankees from Milwaukee (Boston Braves' organization), November 19, 1951.

aSold via waivers by New York Yankees to St. Louis Cardinals, March 26, 1952.

bReturned by Cardinals to Milwaukee (Boston Braves' organization), May 21, 1952.

cReleased to Los Angeles (Chicago Cubs' organization), September 28, 1953.

dReleased to Boston Red Sox, September 10, 1956.

RECORD AS MANAGER

Established major league record for most consecutive years, no championships won as manager (24), 1960 through 1982 and 1985.

Established National League record for most years, no championships won as manager (16), 1960 through 1975.

Named American Association Manager of the Year, 1958 and 1959.

Named Major League Manager of the Year by THE SPORTING NEWS, 1973.

Year	Club	League	Position	W.	L.	Year	Club	League	Position	W.	L.
1953—Atlanta	South.		Third	84	70	1972—Montreal	Nat.		Fifth(E)	70	86
1958—Minneapolis	A. A.		†Third	82	71	1973—Montreal	Nat.		Fourth(E)	79	83
1959—Minneapolis	A. A.		‡Second(E)	95	67	1974—Montreal	Nat.		Fourth(E)	79	82
1960—Philadelphia §	Nat.		Eighth	58	94	1975—Montreal	Nat.		zFifth(E)	75	87
1961—Philadelphia	Nat.		Eighth	47	107	1976—Minnesota	Amer.		Third(W)	85	77
1962—Philadelphia	Nat.		Seventh	81	80	1977—Minnesota	Amer.		Fourth(W)	84	77
1963—Philadelphia	Nat.		Fourth	87	75	1978—Minnesota	Amer.		Fourth(W)	73	89
1964—Philadelphia	Nat.		xSecond	92	70	1979—Minnesota	Amer.		Fourth(W)	82	80
1965—Philadelphia	Nat.		Sixth	85	76	1980—Minnesota a	Amer.		Fourth(W)	54	71
1966—Philadelphia	Nat.		Fourth	87	75	1981—California bc	Amer.			29	34
1967—Philadelphia	Nat.		Fifth	82	80	1982—California	Amer.		First(W)	93	69
1968—Philadelphia y	Nat.		Fifth	28	27	1985—California	Amer.		Second(W)	90	72
1969—Montreal	Nat.		Sixth(E)	52	110	American League Totals—8 Years				590	569
1970—Montreal	Nat.		Sixth(E)	73	89	National League Totals—16 Years				1146	1311
1971—Montreal	Nat.		Fifth(E)	71	90	Major League Totals—24 Years				1736	1880

†Won playoffs by defeating Wichita, four games to two and Denver, four games to none; won Junior World Series by defeating Montreal (International League), four games to none.

‡Won playoffs by defeating Omaha, four games to two and Fort Worth, four games to three; lost Junior World Series to Havana (International League), four games to three.

§Replaced Eddie Sawyer, who resigned after managing Phils in season opener (Coach Andy Cohen served as acting manager for second game), April 15, 1960.

xTied for position with Cincinnati Reds.

yReplaced by Bob Skinner, June 16, 1968.

zTied for position with Chicago Cubs.

aReplaced by John Goryl, August 24, 1980.

bFirst Half. . . . Fourth(W) (record of 9-4); Second Half. . . . Seventh(W) (record of 20-30).

cReplaced Jim Fregosi with club in fourth place (record of 22-25), May 28, 1981.

Manager, National League All-Star Team, 1965.

Coach, National League All-Star Team, 1961 (first game), 1963 and 1973; American League All-Star Team, 1976; Director of Player Personnel, California Angels, 1983 and 1984.

CHAMPIONSHIP SERIES RECORD

Year	Club	League	W.	L.
1982—California		American	2	3

—DID YOU KNOW—

That in the Phillies' 10-4 triumph over the Cubs on August 17, Juan Samuel, Glenn Wilson, Mike Schmidt and Darren Daulton all homered during the seventh inning? The first three homers were consecutive.

JOHN FRANCIS McNAMARA
Boston Red Sox

Born June 4, 1932, at Sacramento, Calif.
Height, 5.10. Weight, 175.
Threw and batted righthanded.
Attended Sacramento State College, Sacramento, Calif.

Led Northwest League in sacrifice hits with 18 in 1959.
Led Northwest League catchers in double plays with 15 in 1958, 10 in 1959 and 14 in 1962.

Year Club	League	Pos.	G.	AB.	R.	H.	2B.	3B.	HR.	RBI.	B.A.	PO.	A.	E.	F.A.
1951—Fresno	Calif.	C	60	182	20	38	2	0	0	12	.209	284	46	11	.968
1952—Houston	Texas	....	6	13	0	1	0	0	0	0	.077	....	....	....	....
1952—Lynchburg	Pied.	C	102	303	25	54	8	0	0	19	.178	489	57	8	★.986
1953—Winston-Salem	Carol.					(In Military Service)									
1954—Omaha†	West.					(In Military Service)									
1955—Lewiston	N'west	C	129	427	49	102	24	4	1	54	.239	544	★93	●15	.977
1956—Sacramento	P. C.	C	76	181	22	31	5	1	1	18	.171	256	25	0	1.000
1956—Albuquerque	West.	C	29	83	11	23	2	2	1	9	.277	191	23	1	.995
1957—Tulsa	Texas	C	19	47	5	7	2	0	0	5	.149	92	9	2	.981
1957—Amarillo	West.	C	43	93	17	26	8	0	0	21	.280	177	13	3	.984
1958—Lewiston	N'west	C	133	439	62	117	20	2	2	63	.276	★892	★76	9	★.991
1959—Lewiston	N'west	C	141	491	74	122	25	4	1	44	.248	714	★84	8	.990
1960—Lewiston	N'west	C	120	387	62	98	19	2	0	42	.253	★726	48	7	★.991
1961—Lewiston	N'west	C	77	204	28	54	6	0	0	27	.265	368	37	4	.990
1962—Lewiston	N'west	C	93	281	41	77	11	2	1	33	.274	670	74	8	★.989
1963—Binghamton	East.	C	69	199	19	45	10	1	0	24	.226	483	34	2	.996
1964—Dallas	P. C.	C-3B	13	13	1	6	0	0	1	1	.194	58	7	0	1.000
1965—Birmingham	South.					(Did Not Play)									
1966—Mobile	South.	C	8	17	3	4	0	0	0	0	.235	44	1	0	1.000
1967—Birmingham	South.	C	2	6	1	0	0	0	0	1	.000	10	1	0	1.000

†Released by St. Louis Cardinals' organization, April 16, 1955.

PITCHING RECORD

Year Club	League	G.	IP.	W.	L.	Pct.	H.	R.	ER.	SO.	BB.	ERA.
1960—Lewiston	Northwest	5	....	0	0	.000	....	....	....	....	....	....
1961—Lewiston	Northwest	4	....	0	0	.000	....	....	....	....	....	....
1962—Lewiston	Northwest	4	9	0	0	.000	13	6	6	3	2	6.00
1963—Binghamton	Eastern	1	1	0	0	.000	0	0	0	0	0	0.00

RECORD AS MANAGER

Year Club	League	Position	W.	L.	Year Club	League	Position	W.	L.
1959—Lewiston	N'west	Second	36	34	1974—San Diego	Nat.	Sixth(W)	60	102
(Second Half)		Third	39	32	1975—San Diego	Nat.	Fourth(W)	71	91
1960—Lewiston	N'west	Third	38	29	1976—San Diego	Nat.	Fifth(W)	73	89
(Second Half)		Third	40	34	1977—San Diego§	Nat.	Fifth(W)	20	28
1961—Lewiston	N'west	†First	41	25	1979—Cincinnati	Nat.	First(W)	90	71
(Second Half)		Second	43	31	1980—Cincinnati	Nat.	Third(W)	89	73
1962—Lewiston	N'west	Fifth	31	38	1981—Cincinnati x	Nat.		66	42
(Second Half)		Fourth	35	37	1982—Cincinnati y	Nat.	Sixth(W)	34	58
1963—Binghamton	East.	Fourth	65	75	1983—California	Amer.	zFifth	70	92
1964—Dallas	P. C.	Sixth(E)	53	104	1984—California	Amer.	zSecond(W)	81	81
1965—Birmingham	South.	Eighth	54	85	1985—Boston	Amer.	Fifth(E)	81	81
1966—Mobile	South.	First	88	52	American League Totals—5 Years			329	332
1967—Birmingham	South.	First	84	55	National League Totals—8 Years			503	554
1969—Oakland‡	Amer.	Second(W)	8	5	Major League Totals—13 Years			832	886
1970—Oakland	Amer.	Second(W)	89	73					

†Won playoff by defeating Yakima (Second Half winner), four games to one.
‡Replaced Hank Bauer with club in second place (record of 80-69), September 19, 1969.
§Replaced by Alvin Dark, May 30, 1977 (Bob Skinner served as interim manager, May 29).
xFirst Half....Second (W) (record of 35-21); Second Half....Second (W) (record of 31-21).
yReplaced by Russ Nixon, July 21, 1982.
zTied for position with Minnesota Twins.
Coach, Oakland Athletics, 1968 and 1969; San Francisco Giants, 1971 through 1973; California Angels, 1978.
Coach, National League All-Star Team, 1976, 1980 and 1982.

CHAMPIONSHIP SERIES RECORD

Year Club	League	W.	L.
1979—Cincinnati	National	0	3

RAYMOND ROGER MILLER
(Ray)
Minnesota Twins

Born April 30, 1945, at Takoma Park, Md.
Height, 6.03. Weight, 215.
Threw and batted righthanded.

Pitched eight-inning 0-0 tie (rain) no-hit game against Statesville, August 3, 1964.
Led Midwest League in hit batsmen with 16 in 1965 and led California League with 12 in 1966 and 13 in 1968.
Led Western Carolinas League in shutouts with 5 in 1964.

Year Club	League	G.	IP.	W.	L.	Pct.	H.	R.	ER.	SO.	BB.	ERA.
1964—Lexington†	W. Carol.	36	159	9	*11	.450	97	64	33	195	*109	1.87
1965—Salinas	California	3	6	0	1	.000	3	4	4	5	8	6.00
1965—Dubuque‡	Midwest	30	122	7	9	.438	97	66	51	147	78	3.76
1966—Pawtucket	Eastern	1	2	0	0	.000	3	2	2	2	1	9.00
1966—Reno§	California	24	93	5	7	.417	87	75	66	94	55	6.39
1967—Reno x	California	34	60	1	3	.250	50	40	33	49	41	4.95
1968—Reno y	California	29	193	16	8	.667	170	86	69	206	81	3.22
1969—Portland	P. Coast	45	112	5	11	.313	107	51	42	73	56	3.38
1970—Wichita z	Am. Assoc.	B56	98	6	6	.500	94	49	40	87	46	3.67
1971—Wichita	Am. Assoc.	8	11	0	1	.000	12	3	3	10	5	2.45
1971—Rochester	Int'national	44	57	3	2	.600	49	26	20	48	28	3.16
1972—Rochester	Int'national	47	73	7	5	.583	66	31	26	61	38	3.21
1973—Rochester a	Int'national	14	26	1	1	.500	13	8	4	15	4	1.38

Signed as free agent by San Francisco Giants' organization, August 15, 1963.
†Drafted by Cleveland Indians, November 30, 1964.
‡On disabled list, June 24 through July 8, 1965.
§On disabled list, June 28 through July 24, 1966.
xOn temporary inactive list, June 17 through July 4, 1967.
yOn temporary inactive list, June 13 through July 1, 1968; appeared in one game as outfielder.
zOn temporary inactive list, May 15 through May 18, 1970.
aPlayer-coach.

RECORD AS MANAGER

Year Club	League	Position	W.	L.
1985—Minnesota†	Amer.	‡Fourth (W)	50	50

†Replaced Billy Gardner with club in sixth place (record of 27-35), June 21, 1985.
‡Tied for position with Oakland A's.
Minor league pitching instructor, Baltimore Orioles, 1974 through 1977; named pitching coach of Texas Rangers, November 21, 1977; Released from contract to become pitching coach of Baltimore Orioles, 1978 through June 20, 1985.

JACKIE SPENCER MOORE
Oakland A's

Born February 19, 1939, at Jay, Fla.
Height, 6.00. Weight, 181.
Threw and batted righthanded.

Year Club	League	Pos.	G.	AB.	R.	H.	2B.	3B.	HR.	RBI.	B.A.	PO.	A.	E.	F.A.
1957—Montgomery	Al.-Fla.	O-C	71	263	36	62	6	1	7	35	.236	237	18	10	.962
1958—Valdosta	Ga.-Fla.	C-3B	87	333	61	100	20	3	9	78	.300	445	75	11	.979
1958—Augusta	Sally	C-OF	13	35	4	8	1	1	1	12	.229	31	3	0	1.000
1959—Durham	Carol.	C-OF	94	305	43	79	18	2	8	55	.259	407	33	8	.982
1960—Knoxville	Sally	C	97	314	40	85	15	3	10	40	.271	541	46	10	.983
1961—Knoxville	Sally	C-2B-3B	43	151	14	45	6	3	0	30	.298	248	22	2	.993
1961—Denver	A. A.	C	43	134	8	32	3	0	0	8	.239	218	26	3	.988
1962—Denver†	A. A.	C-OF	32	98	10	25	3	0	0	14	.255	164	10	3	.983
1962—Toronto	Int.	C	12	29	3	4	0	0	0	2	.138	56	6	1	.984
1963—Syracuse‡	Int.	C	73	213	23	63	5	1	7	37	.296	371	30	4	.990
1964—Syracuse	Int.	C	99	286	34	68	8	1	1	31	.238	449	35	6	.988
1965—Detroit	Amer.	C	21	53	2	5	0	0	0	2	.094	128	6	2	.985
1965—Syracuse§	Int.	C	17	50	3	9	2	0	0	4	.100	80	4	1	.988
1966—Syracuse x	Int.	C	89	290	24	60	11	2	2	17	.207	429	37	4	*.991
1967—Toronto y	Int.	C	100	307	21	61	4	0	3	30	.199	*643	40	4	*.994
Major League Totals—1 Year			21	53	2	5	0	0	0	2	.094	128	6	2	.985

†On disabled list, June 19 to August 2, 1962.
‡Conditionally released by Detroit Tigers' organization to Los Angeles Angels, October 11, 1963; returned by Angels to Tigers, March 27, 1964.
§On disabled list, July 31 to August 14, 1965.
xAssigned by Detroit Tigers to Boston Red Sox, October 13, 1966, to complete deal in which Tigers obtained Pitcher Bill Monbouquette from Red Sox for Outfielder George Thomas and Infielder George Smith, October 4, 1965.
yReleased, February 21, 1968.

RECORD AS MANAGER

Year Club	League	Position	W.	L.
1968—Jamestown	NYP	Seventh	31	44
1969—Jamestown	NYP	Sixth	33	41
1975—Pittsfield	East.	Fourth	27	32
(Second Half)†			13	8
1984—Oakland‡	Amer.	Fourth(W)	57	61
1985—Oakland	Amer.	§Fourth(W)	77	85
Major League Totals—2 Years			134	146

†Replaced by Orlando Martinez, July 24, 1975.
‡Replaced Steve Boros with club tied for fourth place (record of 20-24), May 24, 1984.
§Tied for position with Minnesota Twins.
Coach, Milwaukee Brewers, 1970 through 1972; coach, Texas Rangers, 1973 and 1974, part of 1975, 1976 and 1980; coach, Toronto Blue Jays, 1977 through 1979; coach, Oakland A's, 1981 through May 24, 1984.

LOUIS VICTOR PINIELLA
Name pronounced Pin-ELLA.
(Lou)
New York Yankees

Born August 28, 1943, at Tampa, Fla.
Height, 6.02. Weight, 199.
Throws and bats righthanded.
Attended University of Tampa, Tampa, Fla.
Cousin of Dave Magadan, first baseman in New York Mets' organization.

Tied major league record for most assists by outfielder, inning (2), May 27, 1974 (third inning).
Major League stolen bases: 1969 (2), 1970 (3), 1971 (5), 1972 (7), 1973 (5), 1974 (1), 1977 (2), 1978 (3), 1979 (3), 1983 (1). Total—32.
Led American League in grounding into double plays with 25 in 1972.
Named American League Rookie of the Year by Baseball Writers' Association of America, 1969.

Year Club	League	Pos.	G.	AB.	R.	H.	2B.	3B.	HR.	RBI.	B.A.	PO.	A.	E.	F.A.
1962—Selma†	Ala.-Fl.	OF	70	278	40	75	10	5	8	44	.270	94	6	9	.917
1963—Peninsula	Carol.	OF	143	548	71	170	29	4	16	77	.310	271	*23	8	.974
1964—Aberdeen‡§	North.	OF	20	74	8	20	8	3	0	12	.270	37	1	1	.974
1964—Baltimore	Amer.	PH	4	1	0	0	0	0	0	0	.000	0	0	0	.000
1965—Elmira x	East.	OF	126	490	64	122	29	6	11	64	.249	176	5	7	.963
1966—Portland	P. C.	OF	133	457	47	132	22	3	7	52	.289	177	11	11	.945
1967—Portland	P. C.	OF	113	396	49	122	20	1	8	56	.308	199	7	6	.972
1968—Portland	P. C.	OF	88	331	49	105	15	3	13	62	.317	167	6	7	.961
1968—Cleveland yz	Amer.	OF	6	5	1	0	0	0	0	1	.000	1	0	0	1.000
1969—Kansas City	Amer.	OF	135	493	43	139	21	6	11	68	.282	278	13	7	.977
1970—Kansas City	Amer.	OF-1B	144	542	54	163	24	5	11	88	.301	250	6	4	.985
1971—Kansas City a	Amer.	OF	126	448	43	125	21	5	3	51	.279	201	6	3	.986
1972—Kansas City	Amer.	OF	151	574	65	179	*33	4	11	72	.312	275	8	7	.976
1973—Kansas City b	Amer.	OF	144	513	53	128	28	1	9	69	.250	196	9	3	.986
1974—New York	Amer.	OF-1B	140	518	71	158	26	0	9	70	.305	270	16	3	.990
1975—New York c	Amer.	OF	74	199	7	39	4	1	0	22	.196	65	5	1	.986
1976—New York	Amer.	OF	100	327	36	92	16	6	3	38	.281	199	10	4	.981
1977—New York	Amer.	OF-1B	103	339	47	112	19	3	12	45	.330	86	3	2	.978
1978—New York	Amer.	OF	130	472	67	148	34	5	6	69	.314	213	4	7	.969
1979—New York	Amer.	OF	130	461	49	137	22	2	11	69	.297	204	13	4	.982
1980—New York	Amer.	OF	116	321	39	92	18	0	2	27	.287	157	8	5	.971
1981—New York d	Amer.	OF	60	159	16	44	9	0	5	18	.277	69	2	1	.986
1982—New York	Amer.	OF	102	261	33	80	17	1	6	37	.307	68	2	0	1.000
1983—New York e	Amer.	OF	53	148	19	43	9	1	2	16	.291	67	4	3	.959
1984—New York fg	Amer.	OF	29	86	8	26	4	1	1	6	.302	40	3	0	1.000
Major League Totals—18 Years			1747	5867	651	1705	305	41	102	766	.291	2639	112	54	.981

Signed as free agent by Cleveland Indians' organization, June 9, 1962.
†Drafted by Washington Senators, November 26, 1962.
‡On military list, March 9 to July 20, 1964.
§Traded to Baltimore Orioles' organization, August 4, 1964, completing deal in which Baltimore traded Pitcher Lester (Buster) Narum to Washington Senators for cash and a player to be named later, March 31, 1964.
xTraded to Cleveland Indians' organization for Catcher Cam Carreon, March 10, 1966.
ySelected by Seattle Pilots in expansion draft, October 15, 1968.
zTraded by Seattle Pilots to Kansas City Royals for Outfielder Steve Whitaker and Pitcher John Gelnar, April 1, 1969.
aOn disabled list, May 5 to June 8, 1971.
bTraded with Pitcher Ken Wright to New York Yankees for Pitcher Lindy McDaniel, December 7, 1973.
cOn disabled list, June 17 to July 6, 1975.
dOn disabled list, August 23 to September 7, 1981.
eOn disabled list, March 30 to April 22, 1983.
fOn voluntarily retired list, June 17, 1984.
gNamed New York Yankees coach, June 25, 1984 through 1985.

DIVISION SERIES RECORD

Year Club	League	Pos.	G.	AB.	R.	H.	2B.	3B.	HR.	RBI.	B.A.	PO.	A.	E.	F.A.
1981—New York	Amer.	DH-PH	4	10	1	2	1	0	1	3	.200	0	0	0	.000

CHAMPIONSHIP SERIES RECORD

Year Club	League	Pos.	G.	AB.	R.	H.	2B.	3B.	HR.	RBI.	B.A.	PO.	A.	E.	F.A.
1976—New York	Amer.	DH-PH	4	11	1	3	1	0	0	0	.273	0	0	0	.000
1977—New York	Amer.	OF-DH	5	21	1	7	3	0	0	2	.333	9	1	0	1.000
1978—New York	Amer.	OF	4	17	2	4	0	0	0	0	.235	13	0	0	1.000
1980—New York	Amer.	OF	2	5	1	1	0	0	1	1	.200	5	0	0	1.000
1981—New York	Amer.	PH-D-O	3	5	2	3	0	0	1	3	.600	0	0	0	.000
Championship Series Totals—5 Years			18	59	7	18	4	0	2	6	.305	27	1	0	1.000

WORLD SERIES RECORD

Tied World Series record for one or more hits, each game, six-game Series, 1978.

Year Club	League	Pos.	G.	AB.	R.	H.	2B.	3B.	HR.	RBI.	B.A.	PO.	A.	E.	F.A.
1976—New York	Amer.	D-O-PH	4	9	1	3	1	0	0	0	.333	1	0	0	1.000
1977—New York	Amer.	OF	6	22	1	6	0	0	0	3	.273	16	1	1	.944
1978—New York	Amer.	OF	6	25	3	7	0	0	0	4	.280	14	1	0	1.000
1981—New York	Amer.	OF-PH	6	16	2	7	1	0	0	3	.438	7	0	0	1.000
World Series Totals—4 Years			22	72	7	23	2	0	0	10	.319	38	2	1	.976

Year League	Pos.	AB.	R.	H.	2B.	3B.	HR.	RBI.	B.A.	PO.	A.	E.	F.A.
1972—American	PH	1	0	0	0	0	0	0	.000	0	0	0	.000

ROBERT LEROY RODGERS
(Bob or Buck)
Montreal Expos

Born August 16, 1938, at Delaware, O.
Height, 6.01. Weight, 190.
Threw right and batted left and righthanded.
Attended Ohio Wesleyan University, Delaware, O., and Ohio Northern
University, Ada, O.

Established American League record for most games, by catcher, rookie season (150), 1962.
Tied American League record for fewest assists by catcher, season, 150 or more games (73), 1962.
Major League stolen bases: 1962 (1), 1963 (2), 1964 (4), 1965 (4), 1966 (3), 1967 (1), 1968 (2). Total—17.
Led American League catchers in double plays with 14 in 1962 and 14 in 1964.

Year Club	League	Pos.	G.	AB.	R.	H.	2B.	3B.	HR.	RBI.	B.A.	PO.	A.	E.	F.A.
1956—Jamestown	Pony	OF	48	153	28	36	8	1	6	26	.235	43	6	3	.942
1957—Erie	NYP	*C-OF	114	430	79	127	26	4	12	80	.295	568	*77	*25	.963
1958—Lancaster	East.	C	19	63	8	16	3	0	3	8	.254	111	11	2	.984
1958—Idaho Falls	Pion.	*C-OF	99	378	73	115	15	6	12	74	.304	524	45	*20	.966
1959—Birmingham	South.	C	3	13	1	1	0	1	0	2	.077	28	0	1	.966
1959—Knoxville	Sally	*C-OF	105	355	53	102	18	6	7	55	.287	565	60	*13	.980
1960—Denver	A. A.	C	23	84	12	20	7	1	3	12	.238	127	15	4	.973
1960—Birmingham	South.	C	93	313	36	77	14	1	5	38	.246	456	*68	7	.987
1961—Dallas-Ft. W.†	A. A.	C	124	427	55	122	22	3	3	62	.286	*595	*70	11	.984
1961—Los Angeles	Amer.	C	16	56	8	18	2	0	2	13	.321	71	11	3	.965
1962—Los Angeles	Amer.	C	155	565	65	146	34	6	6	61	.258	826	73	●10	.989
1963—Los Angeles	Amer.	C	100	300	24	70	6	0	4	23	.233	416	48	*10	.979
1964—Los Angeles	Amer.	C	148	514	38	125	18	3	4	54	.243	884	*87	*13	.987
1965—California	Amer.	C	132	411	33	86	14	3	1	32	.209	682	52	7	.991
1966—California	Amer.	C	133	454	45	107	20	3	7	48	.236	662	*69	6	.992
1967—California	Amer.	*C-OF	139	429	29	94	13	3	6	41	.219	728	*73	7	.991
1968—California	Amer.	C	91	258	13	49	6	0	1	14	.190	407	50	7	.985
1969—Hawaii	P. C.	C-3B	44	145	15	37	5	0	0	12	.255	215	26	4	.984
1969—California	Amer.	C	18	49	4	9	1	0	0	2	.196	74	9	0	1.000
1975—Salinas‡	Calif.	PH	4	3	1	1	0	0	0	0	.333	0	0	0	.000
1977—El Paso§	Texas	PH	1	0	0	0	0	0	0	0	.000	0	0	0	.000
Major League Totals—9 Years			932	3033	259	704	114	18	31	288	.232	4750	472	63	.988

†Selected by Los Angeles Angels from Detroit Tigers in American League expansion draft, December 14, 1960.
‡Player-manager, August 24 through September 15, 1975.
§Player-manager, July 15 through August 14, 1977.

RECORD AS MANAGER

Named Minor League Manager of the Year by THE SPORTING NEWS, 1984.
Named American Association Manager of the Year, 1984.
Named Texas League Manager of the Year, 1977.

Year Club	League	Position	W.	L.	Year Club	League	Position	W.	L.
1975—Salinas	Calif.	Fifth	35	35	1982—Milwaukee x	Amer.	yFifth(E)	23	24
(Second Half)		Sixth	32	38	1984—Indianapolis	A. A.	zFirst	91	63
1977—El Paso	Texas	First(W)	38	24	1985—Montreal	Nat.	Third(E)	84	77
(Second Half)		†First(W)	40	28	American League Totals—3 Years			124	102
1980—Milwaukee‡	Amer.	Third(E)	39	31	National League Totals—1 Year			84	77
1981—Milwaukee§	Amer.		62	47	Major League Totals—4 Years			208	179

†Lost league championship to Arkansas, two games to none.
‡Began season as interim manager for ill George Bamberger who returned June 6, 1980, with club in second place (record of 26-21); named manager when Bamberger retired with club tied for fourth place (record of 73-66), September 7, 1980.
§First Half . . . Third (E) (record of 31-25); Second Half . . . First (E) (record of 31-22).
xReplaced by Harvey Kuenn, June 2, 1982.
yTied for position with Baltimore Orioles.
zLost semifinal playoff series to Louisville, four games to two.
Coach, Minnesota Twins, 1970 through 1974; San Francisco Giants, 1976; Milwaukee Brewers, 1978 through 1980.

DIVISION SERIES RECORD

Year Club	League	W.	L.
1981—Milwaukee	American	2	3

Pete Rose's managerial record is listed under his playing record beginning on page 429

CHARLES WILLIAM TANNER JR.
(Chuck)
Atlanta Braves

Born July 4, 1929, at New Castle, Pa.
Height, 6.00. Weight, 185.
Threw and batted lefthanded.
Father of Mark Tanner, pitcher in Chicago Cubs', Chicago White Sox' and Texas Rangers' organizations, 1972 through 1975; and Bruce Tanner, pitcher in Chicago White Sox' organization.

Tied major league record by hitting home run in first time at bat in major leagues, eighth inning, April 12, 1955.
Major League stolen bases: 1958 (1), 1960 (1). Total—2.

Year Club	League	Pos.	G.	AB.	R.	H.	2B.	3B.	HR.	RBI.	B.A.	PO.	A.	E.	F.A.
1946—Evansville	I.I.I.	OF	2	1	0	0	0	0	0	0	.000	0	0	1	.000
1946—Owensboro	Kitty	OF	23	80	15	20	3	1	0	7	.250	50	3	4	.930
1947—Owensboro	Kitty	OF	25	104	32	35	9	3	0	20	.337	47	3	2	.962
1947—Eau Claire	North.	OF	40	151	29	49	6	3	7	27	.325	76	3	9	.898
1948—Eau Claire	North.	OF	67	263	60	95	22	5	7	52	.361	89	4	9	.912
1948—Pawtucket	N. Eng.	OF	46	171	26	47	1	6	2	20	.275	60	6	5	.930
1949—Denver	West.	OF	124	467	92	146	32	5	5	53	.313	206	13	12	.948
1950—Denver	West.	OF	154	619	111	*195	34	9	7	86	.315	248	16	14	.950
1951—Atlanta	South.	OF	134	506	84	161	28	6	4	44	.318	286	6	4	.986
1952—Milwaukee	A. A.	OF	11	27	2	4	1	1	0	4	.148	11	1	0	1.000
1952—Atlanta	South.	OF	117	440	64	152	18	11	2	65	.345	212	9	6	.974
1953—Toledo	A. A.	OF	17	52	5	10	3	0	2	5	.192	29	2	0	1.000
1953—Atlanta	South.	OF	126	465	71	148	29	11	6	57	.318	220	8	3	.987
1954—Atlanta	South.	OF	●155	594	109	192	35	12	20	101	.323	290	21	7	.978
1955—Milwaukee	Nat.	OF	97	243	27	60	9	3	6	27	.247	101	4	2	.981
1956—Milwaukee	Nat.	OF	60	63	6	15	2	0	1	4	.238	4	0	1	.800
1957—Mil.†-Chi.	Nat.	OF	117	387	47	108	19	2	9	48	.279	191	5	2	.990
1958—Chicago‡	Nat.	OF	73	103	10	27	6	0	4	17	.262	21	0	1	.955
1959—Minneapolis§	A. A.	OF	152	549	79	175	*41	10	12	78	.319	194	5	4	.980
1959—Cleveland	Amer.	OF	14	48	6	12	2	0	1	5	.250	18	0	0	1.000
1960—Cleveland	Amer.	OF	21	25	2	7	1	0	0	4	.280	5	0	0	1.000
1960—Toronto	Int.	OF	28	92	13	27	5	2	4	14	.293	40	1	0	1.000
1961—Toronto x	Int.	OF	70	218	19	49	5	3	6	22	.225	84	7	3	.968
1961—Dallas-Ft. Worth	A. A.	OF	48	170	28	51	12	5	1	18	.300	74	5	5	.940
1961—Los Angeles	Amer.	OF	7	8	0	1	0	0	0	0	.125	0	0	0	.000
1962—Los Angeles	Amer.	OF	7	8	0	1	0	0	0	0	.125	0	0	0	.000
1962—Dallas-Ft. Worth	A. A.	OF	114	359	43	113	28	2	5	41	.315	181	16	8	.961
1968—El Paso	Texas	PH	1	1	0	0	0	0	0	0	.000	0	0	0	.000
American League Totals—4 Years			49	89	8	21	3	0	1	9	.236	23	0	0	1.000
National League Totals—4 Years			347	796	90	210	36	5	20	96	.264	317	9	6	.982
Major League Totals—8 Years			396	885	98	231	39	5	21	105	.261	340	9	6	.983

†Sold on waivers to Chicago Cubs, June 8, 1957.
‡Traded to Boston Red Sox for Pitcher Robert W. Smith, March 9, 1959.
§Purchased from Boston Red Sox by Cleveland Indians, September 9, 1959.
xSold by Cleveland Indians to Los Angeles Angels, September 8, 1961.

RECORD AS MANAGER

Named Major League Manager of the Year by THE SPORTING NEWS 1972.
Named Pacific Coast League co-Manager of the Year, 1970.

Year Club	League	Position	W.	L.
1963—Quad Cities	Midw.	Fourth	29	32
(Second Half)		Second	37	25
1964—Quad Cities	Midw.	Eighth	24	31
(Second Half)		Second	38	25
1965—El Paso	Texas	Third(W)	53	87
1966—El Paso	Texas	Fifth	62	78
1967—Seattle	P. C.	Fifth(W)	69	79
1968—El Paso	Texas	†First(W)	77	60
1969—Hawaii	P. C.	Third(S)	74	72
1970—Hawaii	P. C.	‡First(S)	98	48
1970—Chicago§	Amer.	Sixth(W)	3	13
1971—Chicago	Amer.	Third(W)	79	83
1972—Chicago	Amer.	Second(W)	87	67
1973—Chicago	Amer.	Fifth(W)	77	85
1974—Chicago	Amer.	Fourth(W)	80	80
1975—Chicago	Amer.	Fifth(W)	75	86
1976—Oakland x	Amer.	Second(W)	87	74
1977—Pittsburgh	Nat.	Second(E)	96	66
1978—Pittsburgh	Nat.	Second(E)	88	73
1979—Pittsburgh	Nat.	First(E)	98	64
1980—Pittsburgh	Nat.	Third(E)	83	79
1981—Pittsburgh y	Nat.		46	56
1982—Pittsburgh	Nat.	Fourth(E)	84	78
1983—Pittsburgh	Nat.	Second(E)	84	78
1984—Pittsburgh	Nat.	Sixth(E)	75	87
1985—Pittsburgh	Nat.	Sixth(E)	57	104
National League Totals—9 Years			711	685
American League Totals—7 Years			488	488
Major League Totals—16 Years			1199	1173

†Won playoff by defeating Arkansas, three games to one.
‡Lost playoff to Spokane, four games to none.
§Replaced Don Gutteridge (and interim manager Billy Adair) with club in sixth place (record of 53-93), September 14, 1970.
xTraded to Pittsburgh Pirates for Catcher Manny Sanguillen and $100,000 cash, November 5, 1976.
yFirst Half. . . . Fourth(E) (record of 25-23); Second Half. . . . Sixth(E) (record of 21-33).
Manager, National League All-Star Team, 1980.
Coach, American League All-Star Team, 1973.
Coach, National League All-Star Team, 1978, 1982 and 1984.

CHAMPIONSHIP SERIES RECORD					WORLD SERIES RECORD				
Year Club	League		W.	L.	Year Club	League		W.	L.
1979—Pittsburgh	National		3	0	1979—Pittsburgh	National		4	3

ROBERT JOHN VALENTINE
(Bobby)
Texas Rangers

Born May 13, 1950, at Stamford, Conn.
Height, 5.10. Weight, 185.
Threw and batted righthanded.
Attended Arizona State University, Tempe, Ariz.
and University of Southern California, Los Angeles, Calif.
Son-in-law of Ralph Branca, pitcher with Brooklyn Dodgers, Detroit Tigers
and New York Yankees, 1944 through 1954 and 1956.

Major League stolen bases: 1971 (5), 1972 (5), 1973 (6), 1974 (8), 1975 (1), 1978 (1), 1979 (1). Total—27.
Led Pioneer League in stolen bases with 20 in 1968.
Led Pacific Coast League in total bases with 324, sacrifice flies with 10 and double plays by shortstops with 106 in 1970.
Named Pacific Coast League Player of the Year in 1970.

Year Club	League	Pos.	G.	AB.	R.	H.	2B.	3B.	HR.	RBI.	B.A.	PO.	A.	E.	F.A.
1968—Odgen	Pion.	*OF-SS	62	224	*62	63	14	4	6	26	.281	*111	●10	6	.953
1969—Spokane	P. C.	*SS-OF	111	402	61	104	19	5	3	35	.259	166	254	*38	.917
1969—Los Angeles	Nat.	PR	5	0	3	0	0	0	0	0	.000	0	0	0	.000
1970—Spokane	P. C.	*SS-2B	●146	*621	*122	*211	*39	*16	14	80	*.340	*217	474	*54	.928
1971—Spokane	P. C.	SS	7	30	7	10	2	0	1	2	.333	13	18	3	.912
1971—Los Angeles	Nat.	S-3-2-O	101	281	32	70	10	2	1	25	.249	123	176	16	.949
1972—Los Angeles†	Nat.	2-3-O-S	119	391	42	107	11	2	3	32	.274	178	245	23	.948
1973—California‡	Amer.	SS-OF	32	126	12	38	5	2	1	13	.302	63	75	6	.958
1974—California§x	Amer.	OF-SS-3B	117	371	39	97	10	3	3	39	.261	160	116	17	.942
1975—Charleston	Int.	3B	56	175	27	41	4	0	1	17	.234	44	74	6	.952
1975—Salt Lake City	P. C.	1-O-3-2	46	147	29	45	6	1	0	17	.306	92	14	3	.972
1975—California y	Amer.	1B-3B-OF	26	57	5	16	2	0	0	5	.281	27	1	2	.933
1975—San Diego	Nat.	OF	7	15	1	2	0	0	1	1	.133	4	0	0	1.000
1976—Hawaii	P. C.	1-O-3-S	120	395	67	120	23	2	13	89	.304	578	47	4	.994
1976—San Diego	Nat.	OF-1B	15	49	3	18	4	0	0	4	.367	55	6	0	1.000
1977—S.D.z-N.Y.	Nat.	SS-1B-3B	86	150	13	23	4	0	2	13	.153	119	64	3	.984
1978—New York a	Nat.	2B-3B	69	160	17	43	7	0	1	18	.269	78	109	6	.969
1979—Seattle b	Amer.	S-O-2-3-C	62	98	9	27	6	0	0	7	.276	32	38	2	.972
National League Totals—7 Years			402	1046	111	263	36	4	8	93	.251	557	600	48	.960
American League Totals—4 Years			237	652	65	178	23	5	4	64	.273	282	230	27	.950
Major League Totals—10 Years			639	1698	176	441	59	9	12	157	.260	839	830	75	.957

Selected by Los Angeles Dodgers' organization in 1st round (fifth player selected) of free-agent draft, June 7, 1968.
†Traded with Infielder Billy Grabarkewitz, Outfielder Frank Robinson and Pitchers Bill Singer and Mike Strahler to California Angels for Pitcher Andy Messersmith and Third Baseman Ken McMullen, November 28, 1972.
‡On disabled list, May 17, 1973 through remainder of season.
§On disabled list, May 29 to June 13, 1974.
xLoaned to Charleston (Pittsburgh Pirates' organization), April 4, 1975; returned, June 20, 1975.
yTraded with a player to be named later to San Diego Padres for Pitcher Gary Ross, September 17, 1975; San Diego acquired Infielder Rudy Meoli to complete deal, November 4, 1975.
zTraded with Pitcher Paul Siebert to New York Mets for Infielder-Outfielder Dave Kingman, June 15, 1977.
aReleased, March 26, 1979; signed by Seattle Mariners, April 10, 1979.
bGranted free agency, November 1, 1979.

RECORD AS MANAGER

Year Club	League	Position	W.	L.
1985—Texas†	Amer.	Seventh(W)	53	76

†Replaced Doug Rader with club in seventh place (record of 9-23), May 16, 1985.
Scout and minor league instructor, San Diego Padres, 1981; minor league instructor, New York Mets, 1982; coach, New York Mets, 1983 through May 15, 1985.

EARL SIDNEY WEAVER
Baltimore Orioles

Born August 14, 1930, at St. Louis, Mo.
Height, 5.07. Weight, 180.
Threw and batted righthanded.

Led Western League second basemen in double plays with 112 in 1953 and Southern League with 110 in 1955.
Led Western League in being hit by pitch with 13 in 1954.
Named Most Valuable Player in Illinois State League, 1948.

Year Club	League	Pos.	G.	AB.	R.	H.	2B.	3B.	HR.	RBI.	B.A.	PO.	A.	E.	F.A.
1948—West Frankfort	Ill. St.	2B	*120	447	96	120	20	4	2	49	.268	*302	323	21	*.967
1949—St. Joseph	W. Assn	2B	138	500	80	141	22	4	2	101	.282	307	369	26	.963
1950—Winston-Salem	Carol.	2B	127	439	57	121	20	0	3	60	.276	352	345	16	*.978
1951—Houston	Texas	2B	13	43	9	10	4	0	0	2	.233	43	40	2	.976
1951—Omaha	West.	2B	142	506	81	141	35	2	0	52	.279	330	393	25	.967
1952—Houston	Texas	2B	57	201	24	44	7	1	2	21	.219	148	128	11	.962
1952—Omaha	West.	2B	97	353	63	98	15	0	0	34	.278	239	267	16	.969
1953—Omaha†	West.	2B	141	478	57	116	16	0	3	47	.243	344	389	17	*.977
1954—Denver	West.	2B	143	541	124	153	30	2	6	59	.283	325	409	18	.976
1955—New Orleans	South.	2B	119	392	77	109	19	2	6	69	.278	294	342	10	*.985
1956—New Orleans	South.	2B	26	101	11	23	4	0	0	8	.228	60	69	5	.963

Year Club League	Pos.	G.	AB.	R.	H.	2B.	3B.	HR.	RBI.	B.A.	PO.	A.	E.	F.A.
1956—Mont.-Knox. .... Sally	2B	113	417	47	99	10	3	4	22	.237	300	309	11	*.982
1957—Fitzgerald.............. Ga.-Fla.	2B	112	354	70	102	15	3	6	38	.288	321	289	19	.970
1958—Dublin.................... Ga.-Fla.	2B	37	85	27	25	6	0	4	21	.294	54	41	3	.969
1959—Aberdeen.............. North.	2B	13	35	8	7	2	0	0	3	.200	40	25	2	.970
1960—Fox Cities .... I.I.I.	2B-OF	28	30	3	7	1	0	0	4	.233	10	20	1	.968
1965—Elmira.................... East.	2B	1	0	0	0	0	0	0	0	.000	0	0	0	.000

†Released by St. Louis Cardinals' organization to Pittsburgh Pirates' organization, September 23, 1953.

PITCHING RECORD

Year Club League	G.	IP.	W.	L.	Pct.	H.	R.	ER.	SO.	BB.	ERA.
1957—Fitzgerald................. Ga.-Fla.	5	....	1	0	1.000	....	....	....	....	....	....
1958—Dublin .... Ga.-Fla.	2	....	0	0	.000	....	....	....	....	....	....
1959—Aberdeen .... Northern	1	....	0	0	.000	....	....	....	....	....	....

RECORD AS MANAGER

Named Major League Manager of the Year by THE SPORTING NEWS, 1977 and 1979.

Year Club League	Position	W.	L.	Year Club League	Position	W.	L.
1956—Knoxville†.............. Sally	Eighth	10	24	1970—Baltimore............... Amer.	First(E)	108	54
1957—Fitzgerald............. Ga.-Fla.	Fourth	37	33	1971—Baltimore............... Amer.	First(E)	101	57
(Second Half)	Sixth	28	41	1972—Baltimore............... Amer.	Third(E)	80	74
1958—Dublin................. Ga.-Fla.	Third	37	28	1973—Baltimore............... Amer.	First(E)	97	65
(Second Half)	Third	35	28	1974—Baltimore............... Amer.	First (E)	91	71
1959—Aberdeen................ North.	Second	69	55	1975—Baltimore............... Amer.	Second(E)	90	69
1960—Fox Cities............. I.I.I.	First	82	56	1976—Baltimore............... Amer.	Second(E)	88	74
1961—Fox Cities .... I.I.I.	Fourth	67	62	1977—Baltimore............... Amer.	ySecond(E)	97	64
1962—Elmira................ East.	‡Second	72	68	1978—Baltimore............... Amer.	Fourth(E)	90	71
1963—Elmira................ East.	Second	76	64	1979—Baltimore............... Amer.	First(E)	102	57
1964—Elmira................ East.	First	82	58	1980—Baltimore............... Amer.	Second(E)	100	62
1965—Elmira................ East.	Second	83	55	1981—Baltimore z............ Amer.		59	46
1966—Rochester.............. Int.	§First	83	64	1982—Baltimore............... Amer.	Second(E)	94	68
1967—Rochester.............. Int.	Second	80	61	1985—Baltimore a............ Amer.	Fourth(E)	53	52
1968—Baltimore x............ Amer.	Second	48	34	Major League Totals—16 Years...............		1407	971
1969—Baltimore .... Amer.	First(E)	109	53				

†Replaced Dick Bartell, August 8, 1956.
‡Won playoffs by defeating York, two games to one and Williamsport, three games to one.
§Lost in playoffs to Richmond, three games to one.
xReplaced Hank Bauer with club in third place (record of 43-37), July 11, 1968.
yTied for position with Boston Red Sox.
zFirst Half.... Second (E) (record of 31-23); Second Half.... Fourth (E) (record of 28-23).
aReplaced Joe Altobelli (and interim manager Cal Ripken Sr.) with club in fourth place (30-26), June 14, 1985.
Coach, Baltimore Orioles, 1968 (through July 10).
Manager, American League All-Star Team, 1970 through 1972 and 1980.
Coach, American League All-Star Team, 1969 and 1974.

CHAMPIONSHIP SERIES RECORD				WORLD SERIES RECORD			
Year Club League		W.	L.	Year Club League		W.	L.
1969—Baltimore .... American		3	0	1969—Baltimore .... American		1	4
1970—Baltimore .... American		3	0	1970—Baltimore .... American		4	1
1971—Baltimore .... American		3	0	1971—Baltimore .... American		3	4
1973—Baltimore .... American		2	3	1979—Baltimore .... American		3	4
1974—Baltimore .... American		1	3	World Series Totals—4 Years		11	13
1979—Baltimore .... American		3	1				
Championship Series Totals—6 Years.....		15	7				

JAMES FRANCIS WILLIAMS
(Jimy)
Toronto Blue Jays

Born October 4, 1943, at Santa Maria, Calif.
Height, 5.11. Weight, 170.
Threw and batted righthanded.
Received bachelor of science degree in agribusiness from
Fresno State College, Fresno, Calif.

Year Club League	Pos.	G.	AB.	R.	H.	2B.	3B.	HR.	RBI.	B.A.	PO.	A.	E.	F.A.
1965—Waterloo†............. Midw.	SS	115	435	64	125	19	3	2	31	.287	173	*312	26	*.949
1966—St. Louis‡.............. Nat.	SS-2B	13	11	1	3	0	0	0	1	.273	2	5	0	1.000
1967—Arkansas............... Texas	SS	28	101	8	21	1	1	0	8	.208	49	80	2	.985
1967—Tulsa .... P. C.	SS	61	164	18	37	2	0	1	21	.226	87	156	26	.903
1967—St. Louis§.............. Nat.	SS	1	2	0	0	0	0	0	0	.000	6	1	0	1.000
1968—Indianapolis x......... P. C.	SS-2B	120	403	38	91	19	5	2	34	.226	198	323	27	.951
1969—Vancouver y .... P. C.	3B-OF-SS	35	66	7	17	1	1	0	9	.258	17	23	2	.952
1970—Buf. z-Winn. .... Int.	SS-2B-3B	109	361	49	83	15	0	3	18	.230	178	244	30	.934
1971—Winn. ab-Tide. c.... Int.	SS-3B-2B	105	327	40	84	7	4	5	31	.257	120	219	22	.939
1975—El Paso de .... Texas	DH	6	17	3	2	0	0	0	2	.118	0	0	0	.000
Major League Totals—2 Years................		14	13	1	3	0	0	0	1	.231	8	6	0	1.000

†Drafted by St. Louis Cardinals from Toronto (Boston Red Sox' organization), November 29, 1965.
‡In military service, July 24, 1966 through remainder of season.

§Traded with Catcher Pat Corrales to Cincinnati Reds for Catcher John Edwards, February 8, 1968.
xRecalled by Cincinnati Reds; selected by Montreal Expos from Cincinnati in expansion draft, October 14, 1968.
yOn disabled list, May 13 to May 30 and June 24 to September 2, 1969.
zFranchise transferred from Buffalo to Winnipeg, June 4, 1970.
aOn suspended list, June 7 to June 16, 1971.
bSold to New York Mets' organization, June 16, 1971.
cOn temporary inactive list, August 12 to August 16, 1971.
dPlayer-manager.
eOn disabled list, May 15 to July 17 and July 29 to August 20, 1975.

RECORD AS MANAGER

Named Pacific Coast League Manager of the Year, 1976 and 1979.

Year Club	League	Position	W.	L.
1974—Quad Cities	Midw.	First(S)	33	26
(Second Half)		†Third(S)	32	32
1975—El Paso	Texas	Third(W)	62	71
1976—Salt Lake City	P. C.	‡First(E)	90	54
1977—Salt Lake City	P. C.	Second(E)	74	65
1978—Springfield	A. A.	Third(E)	70	66
1979—Salt Lake City	P. C.	Fourth(S)	34	40
(Second Half)		§First(S)	46	28

†Lost playoff to Danville, two games to one.
‡Lost championship playoff to Hawaii, three games to two.
§Won playoff from Albuquerque, two games to none; won championship playoff from Hawaii, three games to none.

Coach, Toronto Blue Jays, 1980 through 1985.

RICHARD HIRSHFELD WILLIAMS
(Dick)
San Diego Padres

Born May 7, 1929, at St. Louis, Mo.
Height, 6.00. Weight, 190.
Threw and batted righthanded.
Attended Pasadena City College, Pasadena, Calif.
Father of Ricky Williams, pitcher in Montreal Expos' organization, 1977 through 1980;
and minor league instructor and coach in Montreal Expos' organization since 1981.

Major League stolen bases: 1956 (5), 1957 (3), 1959 (4). Total—12.

Year Club	League	Pos.	G.	AB.	R.	H.	2B.	3B.	HR.	RBI.	B.A.	PO.	A.	E.	F.A.
1947—Santa Barbara	Calif.	OF-3B	79	313	47	77	20	2	4	50	.246	165	36	5	.976
1948—Santa Barbara	Calif.	OF	97	385	82	129	29	2	16	90	.335	245	19	9	.967
1948—Fort Worth	Texas	OF-3B	41	140	16	29	1	0	4	16	.207	60	2	1	.984
1949—Fort Worth	Texas	*O-2-3	154	562	109	174	30	6	23	114	.310	*446	18	8	.983
1950—Fort Worth	Texas	OF	144	510	69	153	30	1	11	72	.300	401	20	6	.986
1951—Brooklyn†	Nat.	OF	23	60	5	12	3	1	1	5	.200	21	1	0	1.000
1952—Brooklyn	Nat.	OF-1B-3B	36	68	13	21	4	1	0	11	.309	51	3	0	1.000
1953—Brooklyn	Nat.	OF	30	55	4	12	2	0	2	5	.218	24	0	2	.923
1953—Montreal	Int.	OF	66	230	28	64	12	1	2	33	.278	111	3	2	.983
1954—Brooklyn	Nat.	OF	16	34	5	5	0	0	1	2	.147	12	0	0	1.000
1954—St. Paul	A. A.	OF-1B	49	162	23	40	8	0	6	18	.247	212	15	3	.987
1955—Fort Worth	Texas	OF-1B	153	596	82	189	29	4	24	91	.317	580	22	7	.989
1956—Brooklyn	Nat.	PH	7	7	0	2	0	0	0	0	.286	0	0	0	.000
1956—Montreal‡	Int.	1B	13	50	3	13	3	0	0	6	.260	106	17	4	.969
1956—Baltimore	Amer.	O-1-2-3	87	353	45	101	18	4	11	37	.286	249	17	4	.985
1957—Balt.§-Cleve.x	Amer.	OF-3B-1B	114	372	49	97	17	2	7	34	.261	244	72	8	.975
1958—Baltimore y	Amer.	O-3-1-2	128	409	36	113	17	0	4	32	.276	359	61	8	.981
1959—Kansas City	Amer.	3-1-O-2	130	488	72	130	33	1	16	75	.266	349	181	13	.976
1960—Kansas City z	Amer.	3B-1B-OF	127	420	47	121	31	0	12	65	.288	376	131	11	.979
1961—Baltimore	Amer.	OF-1B-3B	103	310	37	64	15	2	8	24	.206	209	16	3	.987
1962—Baltimore ab	Amer.	OF-1B-3B	82	178	20	44	7	1	1	18	.247	180	13	0	1.000
1963—Boston	Amer.	3B-1B-OF	79	136	15	35	8	0	2	12	.257	64	28	1	.989
1964—Boston	Amer.	1B-3B-OF	61	69	10	11	2	0	5	11	.159	50	21	1	.986
American League Totals—9 Years			911	2735	331	716	148	10	66	308	.262	2080	540	49	.982
National League Totals—5 Years			112	224	27	52	9	2	4	23	.232	108	4	2	.982
Major League Totals—13 Years			1023	2959	358	768	157	12	70	331	.260	2188	544	51	.982

†On National Defense Service List, February 7 to May 29, 1951.
‡Recalled by Brooklyn Dodgers and sold to Baltimore Orioles, June 25, 1956.
§Traded to Cleveland Indians for Outfielder Jim Busby, June 13, 1957.
xTraded with Pitcher Bud Daley and Outfielder Gene Woodling to Baltimore Orioles for Pitcher Don Ferrarese and Outfielder Larry Doby, April 1, 1958.
yTraded to Kansas City Athletics for Shortstop Chico Carrasquel, October 2, 1958.
zTraded with Pitcher Dick Hall to Baltimore Orioles for Pitcher Jerry Walker and Outfielder Chuck Essegian, April 13, 1961.
aSold to Houston Colts, October 12, 1962.
bTraded by Houston Colts to Boston Red Sox for Outfielder Carroll Hardy, December 10, 1962.

WORLD SERIES RECORD

Year Club	League	Pos.	G.	AB.	R.	H.	2B.	3B.	HR.	RBI.	B.A.	PO.	A.	E.	F.A.
1953—Brooklyn	Nat.	PH	3	2	0	1	0	0	0	0	.500	0	0	0	.000

RECORD AS MANAGER

Named Major League Manager of the Year by THE SPORTING NEWS, 1967.

Year Club	League	Position	W.	L.	Year Club	League	Position	W.	L.
1965—Toronto	Int.	†Third	81	64	1978—Montreal	Nat.	Fourth(E)	76	86
1966—Toronto	Int.	‡Second	82	65	1979—Montreal	Nat.	Second(E)	95	65
1967—Boston	Amer.	First	92	70	1980—Montreal	Nat.	Second(E)	90	72
1968—Boston	Amer.	Fourth	86	76	1981—Montreal ab	Nat.		44	37
1969—Boston§	Amer.	Third(E)	82	71	1982—San Diego	Nat.	Fourth(W)	81	81
1971—Oakland	Amer.	First(W)	101	60	1983—San Diego	Nat.	Fourth(W)	81	81
1972—Oakland	Amer.	First(W)	93	62	1984—San Diego	Nat.	First(W)	92	70
1973—Oakland x	Amer.	First(W)	94	68	1985—San Diego	Nat.	cThird(W)	83	79
1974—California y	Amer.	Sixth(W)	36	48					
1975—California	Amer.	Sixth(W)	72	89	National League Totals—9 Years			717	658
1976—California z	Amer.	Fourth(W)	39	57	American League Totals—9 Years			695	601
1977—Montreal	Nat.	Fifth(E)	75	87	Major League Totals—18 Years			1412	1259

†Won playoffs by defeating Atlanta, four games to none and Columbus, four games to one.

‡Tied for position during regular season. Won playoffs by defeating Columbus, three games to two and Richmond, four games to one.

§Replaced by interim manager Eddie Popowski, September 23, 1969.

xQuit as manager of the Oakland Athletics following 1973 World Series. Signed contract to manage New York Yankees but American League President Joe Cronin ruled that Williams must honor the two years remaining on his Oakland contract.

yReplaced Bobby Winkles (and interim manager Whitey Herzog) with club in sixth place (record of 32-46), July 1, 1974.

zReplaced by Norm Sherry, July 23, 1976.

aFirst Half . . . . Third (E) (record of 30-25); Second Half . . . . Second (E) (record of 14-12).

bReplaced by Jim Fanning, September 8, 1981.

cTied for position with Houston Astros.

Coach, Montreal Expos, 1970.

Manager, National League All-Star Team, 1985.

Manager, American League All-Star Team, 1968, 1973 and 1974.

Coach, American League All-Star Team, 1972.

Coach, National League All-Star Team, 1981.

CHAMPIONSHIP SERIES RECORD

Year Club	League	W.	L.
1971—Oakland	American	0	3
1972—Oakland	American	3	2
1973—Oakland	American	3	2
1984—San Diego	National	3	2
Championships Series Totals—4 Years		9	9

WORLD SERIES RECORD

Year Club	League	W.	L.
1967—Boston	American	3	4
1972—Oakland	American	4	3
1973—Oakland	American	4	3
1984—San Diego	National	1	4
World Series Totals—4 Years		12	14

1986 Hall of Fame Inductee

WILLIE LEE McCOVEY

Born January 10, 1938, at Mobile, Ala.
Height, 6.04. Weight, 225.
Threw and batted lefthanded.

Established major league records for most intentional bases on balls, season (45), 1969; most seasons by first baseman (22).

Tied major league records for most home runs, inning (2) and most total bases, inning (8), April 12, 1973 (fourth inning) and June 27, 1977 (sixth inning); most grand slams by pinch-hitter, lifetime (3); most triples, first major league game (2), July 30, 1959; most seasons leading league in intentional bases on balls (4); most years leading league in errors by first baseman (5).

Tied modern major league record for most long hits, inning (2), April 12, 1973 (fourth inning) and June 27, 1977 (sixth inning).

Established National League records for most home runs by lefthanded hitter, lifetime (521); most home runs by first baseman, lifetime (439); most grand slams, lifetime (18).

Tied National League record for fewest errors by first baseman for leader in errors, season (13), 1977.

Major League stolen bases: 1959 (2), 1960 (1), 1961 (1), 1962 (3), 1963 (1), 1964 (2), 1966 (2), 1967 (3), 1968 (4), 1973 (1), 1974 (1), 1975 (1), 1977 (3), 1978 (1). Total—26.

Hit three consecutive home runs in a game, on two occasions—September 22, 1963, and April 22, 1964. Hit three home runs in a game, September 17, 1966.

Hit home runs in all 12 National League parks, 1970.

Led National League in slugging percentage with .545 in 1968, .656 in 1969 and .612 in 1970.

Led National League in bases on balls received with 137 in 1970.

Led Georgia State League first basemen in double plays with 73 in 1955.

Led Pacific Coast League first basemen in double plays with 119 in 1958.

Named Major League Player of the Year by THE SPORTING NEWS, 1969.

Named National League Most Valuable Player by Baseball Writers' Association of America, 1969.

Named THE SPORTING NEWS National League Comeback Player of the Year, 1977.

Named National League Rookie of the Year by THE SPORTING NEWS and National League Rookie of the Year by Baseball Writers' Association of America, 1959.

Named first baseman on THE SPORTING NEWS National League All-Star Team, 1965 and 1968 through 1970.

Named to Hall of Fame, 1986.

Year	Club	League	Pos.	G.	AB.	R.	H.	2B.	3B.	HR.	RBI.	B.A.	PO.	A.	E.	F.A.
1955—Sandersville	Ga. St.		1B	107	410	82	125	24	1	19	★113	.305	★897	51	23	.976
1956—Danville	Carol.		1B	152	519	119	161	★38	8	29	89	.310	1273	87	★34	.976
1957—Dallas	Texas		1B	115	395	63	111	21	9	11	65	.281	960	80	10	.990
1958—Phoenix	P. C.		1B	146	527	91	168	37	10	14	89	.319	★1171	69	★18	.986
1959—Phoenix	P. C.		1B	95	349	84	130	26	11	★29	●92	.372	896	43	16	.983
1959—San Francisco	Nat.		1B	52	192	32	68	9	5	13	38	.354	424	29	5	.989
1960—San Francisco	Nat.		1B	101	260	37	62	15	3	13	51	.238	557	39	9	.985
1960—Tacoma	P. C.		1B	17	63	14	18	1	2	3	16	.286	149	4	3	.980
1961—San Francisco	Nat.		1B	106	328	59	89	12	3	18	50	.271	669	55	11	.985
1962—San Francisco	Nat.		OF-1B	91	229	41	67	6	1	20	54	.293	186	9	3	.985
1963—San Francisco	Nat.		★OF-1B	152	564	103	158	19	5	●44	102	.280	363	21	★15	.962
1964—San Francisco	Nat.		OF-1B	130	364	55	80	14	1	18	54	.220	273	19	14	.954
1965—San Francisco	Nat.		1B	160	540	93	149	17	4	39	92	.276	1310	87	13	.991
1966—San Francisco	Nat.		1B	150	502	85	148	26	6	36	96	.295	1287	81	22	.984
1967—San Francisco	Nat.		1B	135	456	73	126	17	4	31	91	.276	1221	81	●15	.989
1968—San Francisco	Nat.		1B	148	523	81	153	16	4	★36	★105	.293	1305	103	★21	.985
1969—San Francisco	Nat.		1B	149	491	101	157	26	2	★45	★126	.320	1392	79	12	.992
1970—San Francisco	Nat.		1B	152	495	98	143	39	2	39	126	.289	1217	★134	★15	.989
1971—San Francisco	Nat.		1B	105	329	45	91	13	0	18	70	.277	828	63	★15	.983
1972—San Francisco†	Nat.		1B	81	263	30	56	8	0	14	35	.213	617	32	9	.986
1973—San Francisco‡	Nat.		1B	130	383	52	102	14	3	29	75	.266	930	76	12	.988
1974—San Diego	Nat.		1B	128	344	53	87	19	1	22	63	.253	815	47	11	.987
1975—San Diego	Nat.		1B	122	413	43	104	17	0	23	68	.252	979	73	15	.986
1976—San Diego§	Nat.		1B	71	202	20	41	9	0	7	36	.203	420	44	4	.991
1976—Oakland x	Amer.		DH	11	24	0	5	0	0	0	0	.208	0	0	0	.000
1977—San Francisco	Nat.		1B	141	478	54	134	21	0	28	86	.280	1072	60	★13	.989
1978—San Francisco	Nat.		1B	108	351	32	80	19	2	12	64	.228	721	44	10	.987
1979—San Francisco	Nat.		1B	117	353	34	88	9	0	15	57	.249	740	48	10	.987
1980—San Francisco y	Nat.		1B	48	113	8	23	8	0	1	16	.204	241	12	2	.992
National League Totals—22 Years				2577	8173	1229	2206	353	46	521	1555	.270	17567	1236	256	.987
American League Totals—1 Year				11	24	0	5	0	0	0	0	.208	0	0	0	.000
Major League Totals—22 Years				2588	8197	1229	2211	353	46	521	1555	.270	17567	1236	256	.987

Signed as free agent by San Francisco Giants' organization, March 12, 1955.

†On disabled list, April 19 through June 2, 1972.

‡Traded with Outfielder Bernie Williams to San Diego Padres for Pitcher Mike Caldwell, October 25, 1973.

§Sold to Oakland A's, August 30, 1976.

xPlayed out option year and granted free agency; signed as free agent with San Francisco Giants, January 6, 1977.

yOn voluntarily retired list, July 10, 1980.

CHAMPIONSHIP SERIES RECORD

Year	Club	League	Pos.	G.	AB.	R.	H.	2B.	3B.	HR.	RBI.	B.A.	PO.	A.	E.	F.A.
1971—San Francisco	Nat.		1B	4	14	2	6	0	0	2	6	.429	34	3	1	.974

WILLIE McCOVEY

WORLD SERIES RECORD

Tied World Series record for most positions played, Series (3), 1962 (first base, right field and left field).

Year	Club	League	Pos.	G.	AB.	R.	H.	2B.	3B.	HR.	RBI.	B.A.	PO.	A.	E.	F.A.
1962—San Francisco		Nat.	1B-OF	4	15	2	3	0	1	1	1	.200	23	4	2	.931

ALL-STAR GAME RECORD

Tied All-Star Game records for most home runs, game (2), July 23, 1969; most strikeouts, nine-inning game (3), July 9, 1968.

Year	League	Pos.	AB.	R.	H.	2B.	3B.	HR.	RBI.	B.A.	PO.	A.	E.	F.A.
1963—National		PH	1	0	0	0	0	0	0	.000	0	0	0	.000
1966—National		1B	3	0	0	0	0	0	0	.000	10	1	0	1.000
1968—National		1B	4	0	0	0	0	0	0	.000	10	0	0	1.000
1969—National		1B	4	2	2	0	0	2	3	.500	2	0	0	1.000
1970—National		1B	2	0	1	0	0	0	1	.500	1	0	0	1.000
1971—National		1B	2	0	0	0	0	0	0	.000	4	0	0	1.000
All-Star Game Totals—6 Years			16	2	3	0	0	2	4	.188	27	1	0	1.000

NOTES

NOTES

NOTES